INFORMATION
PLEASE
ALMANAC

Atlas and Yearbook

1977

Thirty-First Edition

•

Editor

ANN GOLENPAUL

SIMON AND SCHUSTER · New York City

A Profile of the United States

GEOGRAPHY

Number of states: 50.

Land area (1970): 3,615,122. Share of world land area (1969): 6.9%.

Northernmost point: Point Barrow, Alaska.

Easternmost point: West Quoddy Head, Maine.

Southernmost point: Ka Lae (South Cape), Hawaii.

Westernmost point: Cape Wrangell, Alaska.

Geographic center: In Butte County, S. D. (44°58′ N. lat., 103°46′ W. long.).

POPULATION

Total (est. July 1, 1977): 216,814,000.

Center of population (1970): 5 miles east-southeast of Mascoutah, Illinois.

Males (est. 1977): 105,684,000.

Females (est. 1977): 111,130,000.

White persons (1977): 187,888,000.

Black persons (1977): 25,243,000.

Breakdown by age groups (est. 1977):
Under 5 years: 15,589,000.
5–14 years: 36,394,000.
15–24 years: 41,428,000.
25–64 years: 100,377,000.
65 and over: 23,203,000.

Median age (est. 1977): 29.3.

Rural population (est.): 65,750,000.

Metropolitan population (est.): 144,000,000.

Families (est. 1977): 58,130,000.

Average family size (1976): 3.39.

Married persons (est.): 125,000,000.

Unmarried persons (14 years and over) (est.): 45,000,000.

Widowers (est.): 2,000,000.

Widows (est.): 10,000,000.

Divorced persons (est.): 6,250,000.

VITAL STATISTICS

Births (1975): 3,149,000.

Deaths (1975): 1,910,000.

Marriages (1975): 2,126,000.

Divorces (1975): 1,026,000.

CIVILIAN LABOR FORCE

Males (July 1976): 51,694,000 (93.9% employed).

Females (July 1976): 34,583,000 (92.4% employed).

Teenagers 16–19 (July 1976): 9,056,000 (81.9% employed).

INCOME

Gross national product (est. 1976): $1,710,000,000,000.

Personal income per capita (1975): $5,902.

Family income, median (1975): $13,719 (white: $14,268; black, $8,779).

Personal savings accounts (est.): $70,000,000,000.

Individual shareholders (est.): 33,000,000.

Home ownership (est.): 42,000,000.

Number of millionaires (net worth): 121,000.

Poverty (1975): 17,770,000, white; 8,106,000, black and other minorities.

EDUCATION

Elementary and secondary schools (1975): 86,334.

Elementary and secondary pupils (1975): 86,334,000.

Elementary and secondary teachers (1975): 2,168,000.

High school graduates (est. 1976): 3,150,000.

Money spent on elementary and secondary education (1976): $67,100,000.

Institutions of higher learning (est. 1976): 2,660.

College graduates (1975): 979,000.

CONVENIENCES

TV sets (1975): 125,300,000.

Radios (1975): 413,000,000.

TV stations (1976): 961.

Radio stations (standard and FM, 1976): 8,131.

Automobiles (est. 1976): 106,000,000.

Telephones (1975): 143,427,000.

Newspaper circulation (morning and evening 1975): 60,655,400.

TRAVEL

Road mileage (all vehicles) (1976): 1,390,000,000,000.

Railroad passenger-miles: 5,743,650,000.

Airline passenger-miles: 120,000,000,000.

These figures are based on calculations from various sources. In many cases, they are approximate. In some cases, they are specific. Since we are merely trying to profile the face of America, we ask our readers to accept these figures with indulgence and understanding.

INFORMATION PLEASE ALMANAC

Atlas and Yearbook

1977

Editor
Ann Golenpaul

Associate Editors
Albert Bronson   Arthur Reed

Production Editor
Ruth T. Graham

American Economy ■ Will Lissner, Editor, Journal of Economics & Sociology

Space, Science ■ Nicholas Panagakos, NASA

Sports ■ Bill Braddock

World History ■ Don Shannon, United Nations Correspondent, L.A. Times

Researchers
Natalie M. Aust, Arthur Neuhauser, Muriel Hecht Silberner

Maps
Vaughn Gray, Dyno Lowenstein

Cover Design
Frank Pagnato

Information Please Almanac, 502 Park Avenue, New York, N.Y., 10022

Planned and Supervised by

DAN GOLENPAUL ASSOCIATES

TABLE OF CONTENTS

Library of Congress Catalog Card No. 47-845

Printed in the U. S. A.

0-671-22397-6 Casebound
0-671-22398-4 Paperback

Analysis of the Presidential Sweepstakes

By R. W. Apple, Jr.
National Political Correspondent, The New York Times

The election of 1976 was the child of Watergate, that tormenting episode in American history that ended the career of Richard M. Nixon and forever altered so many others. Child of Watergate in that the scandal: Propelled Gerald R. Ford, a journeyman Congressman from Grand Rapids, Mich. into the Presidency—made possible the rise of Jimmy Carter from the obscurity of the piney woods of South Georgia—prompted the creation of a new election financing system, a "reform" that reshaped both primary and general election campaigns—and evoked a mood of suspicion and distrust in the voters that neither candidate ever managed wholly to deal with.

It is too soon, perhaps, for us to understand the ultimate place of 1976 in the story of American politics. Was it truly a pivotal election like that of 1932, changing the course of policy and party? Or was it an aberration, like 1968? All that is clear now is, first, that it was one of those relatively rare Presidential contests where both men had a chance to win until the last moment, or at least where both thought they did, and that, despite that fact, it was a race strikingly devoid of drama, because millions upon millions of voters found themselves dissatisfied with both nominees. There was a sense in the land, somehow, that neither measured up to the Presidential past, a sense that may or may not be confirmed in the years to come.

The whole, long, convoluted process began early in 1975 as the Democrats scurried for position. It would be months before it was clear that Jimmy Carter was the right general for this war at this time in this place. He understood the terrain, correctly calculated the intentions and weaknesses of his Democratic enemies, exploited his own strength to the fullest, cannily devised a strategy and tactics, and chose the correct weapons. He had the good sense, moreover, to ignore the derision from the politically learned quarters of Georgetown, Manhattan and Cambridge, Mass., that greeted him when he joined the fray.

The Political Miracle of Our Time

So the 51-year-old Georgian was able to bring off the political miracle of our time, winning his party's Presidential nomination in an accomplishment even more stunning than the 1940 coup of Wendell Willkie in that, unlike Mr. Willkie, he brought it off without the help of those experienced in national affairs. But there was no alchemy in the triumph of the peanut farmer with the big grin and the cool eyes.

Begin with Jimmy Carter's region. Ironically, he was written off as a candidate in part because he was a Southerner, yet he succeeded in large part because he *was* a Southerner. Carter understood things about the South that had escaped those inured to old stereotypes. He understood the region's economic boom, which brought with it an infusion of Yankee blood and the willingness to soften old racial animosities. And he understood that Gov. George C. Wallace of Alabama, partially paralyzed and thrice defeated in bids for the Presidency, had become a Wizard of Oz awaiting only someone brave enough to lift the curtain. He understood, too, the South's fierce pride and he calculated correctly that, if he could show that he had a real chance to be elected President, Southerners of both races and many viewpoints would rally to him.

Carter's grand strategy was made possible by his God-given energy; by his self-discipline, a legacy from his years as a submarine officer; by the income from his farm, which made him financially independent; and by his departure from public office, which gave him free time. He decided to run everywhere—in states where his opponents were active and in states where they were not. He would win enough victories to establish his credibility (or, in the vogue word of 1976, to generate "momentum.") But he would also pick up some delegates even in states where someone else got the majority.

And so it came to be. Carter gained delegates in California despite a trouncing by Gov. Edmund G. Brown, Jr.; in Alabama, Mr. Wallace's home territory; in Illinois, where his opponents feared to tread; in New York and Massachusetts, where he finished well back in the pack. Like many candidates who win, Carter was lucky in his adversaries. The two most logical nominees,

Senators Edward M. Kennedy of Massachusetts and Hubert H. Humphrey of Minnesota, remained on the sidelines—Mr. Kennedy because of family difficulties and the miasma of Chappaquiddick, Mr. Humphrey because of indecision and a final unwillingness to risk another defeat.

Mr. Carter was lucky again when, in the crucial tests in Iowa and New Hampshire, where early defeats would probably have eliminated him, he was the only candidate who was something other than a liberal. Bayh, Shriver, Harris and Udall were there, splintering the liberal vote, but Senator Henry M. Jackson of Washington, who might have competed with Mr. Carter for the centrists and the conservatives, stayed away. He was lucky in Florida when the liberals stayed away, leaving Carter only Wallace and Jackson to dispose of. And he was lucky yet again in Pennsylvania, perhaps his most perilous moment following embarrassments in New York and Wisconsin, when Humphrey meddled so visibly that Jackson came to be viewed as a "weak Humphrey stand-in."

Saw the Issue as Loss of Trust

Almost from the start, it was argued by his critics that Jimmy Carter was "fuzzy" on the issues and it was true that on a number of questions—Vietnam, for example, and abortion—he seemed to say different things at different times. More to the point, he often formulated his responses in a way that perturbed ideologues because he seemed to be trying to give something to those on both sides of particularly vexing questions. The issue—the only real issue, he believed—was the loss of trust by the American people in their institutions and their leaders in the wake of Vietnam and Watergate. He seldom talked about those issues in overt terms; instead he talked about trust, honesty, anti-elitism, the family, and his own background as a non-Washington, non-lawyer. When the moment came, on the night of June 8 following the final primaries, the pieces fell suddenly into place. George Wallace rallied around, his face saved, in a gesture of Southern solidarity. Richard J. Daley, the Mayor of Chicago, eager to return to his role as a kingmaker after his exclusion from Miami Beach in 1972, added his voice to the chorus. Henry Jackson, irked by Mr. Humphrey's tactics and vaguely respectful of what Carter had wrought, saw no reason to resist. For all intents and purposes, the nomination was decided then, although the Democrats did not meet in convention until July 12.

When they gathered in New York City, for the first time since 1924, they were in high spirits, sensing that they had a winner. It might have been a dull affair, since the outcome had been known to everyone for weeks, but it was not. There was the excitement of the Vice-Presidential choice, with Carter methodically eliminating possibilities until he settled on Walter F. Mondale of Minnesota, and telling not even his wife until the last moment. There was the emotion of the appearance by two eloquent blacks, Representative Barbara Jordan of Texas and the Rev. Dr. Martin Luther King, Sr. Above all, there was a sense of history in the decision of the Democratic Party to choose as its nominee the first major party standard-bearer from the Deep South since Zachary Taylor in 1848. Brown of California held out the longest, but after the first and only roll-call he switched his delegates to Carter and then the delegates declared Carter the choice by acclamation. His speech on the final night, delivered in his sing-song cadence and his peculiarly reedy voice, restated his populist themes and set the agenda for the campaign that later followed.

The Plight of the President

Not since Chester A. Arthur was denied renomination in 1884 had an incumbent President come as close to repudiation by his party as Gerald Ford did in Kansas City a month later. Ford had demonstrated during the primary season startling political weaknesses—weaknesses far greater than those exhibited by Harry S. Truman in 1952 or Lyndon B. Johnson in 1968 when they decided not to seek re-election.

How did the President get into such a mess? William R. Keech of the University of North Carolina offered two basic explanations: Ford's tenuous hold on the Presidency and Ronald Reagan's potency as a rival. "Ford had never been selected by a national party convention as a candidate for either President or Vice President," Keech said in a study for the American Political Science Association. "Nor had he ever campaigned for such an office and, of course, the fact that he had been chosen by a President who resigned in disgrace was another liability. Ronald Reagan was truly the most threatening figure who might have challenged President Ford. The remarkably close contest for the 1976 Republican nomination can best be understood, then, in the context of the strongest challenger to an incumbent President since former President [Theodore] Roosevelt ran against President [William Howard] Taft in 1912, and in the context of an incumbent with the weakest electoral claim on the office ever."

That was the strategic picture when the primary campaign began in New Hampshire in January and that was the strategic picture when the delegates arrived in Kansas City. All the jet flights, all the flights of oratory, all the sudden surges and near collapses and comebacks, all the victories and defeats, served only to confirm the initial reality. The President won the first three tests—in New Hampshire, Florida and Illinois—and it seemed that Reagan would have to withdraw. But the Californian then arrived on the more hospitable ground of North Carolina, where he made two important changes in his campaign style, turning to the heavy use of television to capitalize on his experience as an actor and savaging Ford's record, particularly in foreign policy. The result was a victory that kept his campaign alive. There followed a series of important Reagan victories—in Texas, where he stunned the Ford camp by sweeping all one hundred delegates, in Indiana and in Nebraska.

But the President hung grimly on and Reagan never quite scored the knockout blow that he needed to win. The decisive victories eluded him in Michigan, Ford's home state; in Ohio, where he made only a token campaign in the last few days, and elsewhere. His sweeps in Texas and California kept him close to the President in the delegate count, and he ended up by winning more total primary votes than Ford. Reagan dominated the convention delegations from the South and the West, Ford those from the East and Midwest—a different alignment from that along which the Republicans have historically split, with Midwest opposing East. The explosive growth of the sunbelt states, the dramatic improvement of Republican fortunes in the South and a Republican apportionment system that favored the smaller states combined to alter the political arithmetic in favor of the Californian. In the South and West, the conservative gospel preached by Reagan had a far broader appeal than Ford's almost equally conservative but far less fervent message. Reagan made skillful use in those states of trigger issues—that is, relatively narrow topics that suggest far broader ones. Perhaps the best example was the Panama Canal, which seemed to summon up for many conservative voters a whole series of images, not least the American humiliation in Vietnam.

The Many Faces of Gerald Ford

One of the President's most serious problems was finding the proper way to use the powers of incumbency. All year long, his advisors debated the question and, during the campaign, the nation was shown several Gerald Fords: Ford the sugar daddy handing out Federal projects in New Hampshire and Florida like a ward boss distributing Christmas turkeys; Ford the frantic campaigner, dashing from state to state to implore his party not to reject him; Ford the statesman, avoiding campaigning in an effort to appear more "Presidential"; and, finally, Ford the armtwister, inviting individual delegates to the White House to try to persuade them, sometimes giving one obscure delegate more of his time in one day than he gave in an entire year to the Ambassador from a middle-sized country. In the end, only the decision of most elected Republican officials to observe party regularity saved him.

John Sears, the consummate tactician who ran the Reagan campaign, had two final cards to play. First, he persuaded the Californian to name his Vice-Presidential choice in advance— Senator Richard Schweiker of Pennsylvania. Then he tried to persuade the convention to force Ford to do the same, reasoning that no matter whom the President chose, some of his delegates would be offended and would bolt. It almost worked, failing in the climactic roll-call at Kansas City on Tuesday night by only a few votes, chiefly because of the Mississippi delegation's decision, in its anger over the choice of the liberal Schweiker, to side with Ford.

The nomination Wednesday was an anti-climax, after so many weeks of exhausting maneuvering, even though Ford's margin was excruciatingly thin: 1,187 to 1,070. He bowed to Reagan's pressure and chose Senator Robert Dole of Kansas as a running mate, hoping to promote party unity, and he shattered tradition in his acceptance speech by challenging Carter to debate him—something no sitting President had ever done. The debates would be the first since 1960.

After a brief pause, the general election campaigns began on Labor Day—Carter's a succession of dashes about the country, Ford's a series of declarations from the White House Rose Garden, broken only occasionally by a barn-storming trip. The President's strategists had returned to the thought that it would be wisest for him to act "Presidential" in the hope of eroding Carter's 15-point lead in the polls.

Carter had an apparently unbreakable hold on most of the South, which seemed to guarantee him at least 125 of the 270 electoral votes he needed. That meant that Ford would have to win most of the big states—California, Texas and the belt bordering the Great Lakes from Wisconsin to New York—if he was going to stop the Georgian short. It was there that he spent most of his time, and there that he concentrated a blitz of television advertising and furious stumping in the final ten days.

Debates Televised Nationally

The campaign was given structure by the four debates—three between the Presidential rivals and one between Dole and Mondale—which were televised nationally to huge audiences, and each produced endless exegeses. Polls showed Ford the winner of the first, a dull affair marked by a blizzard of statistics and little warmth, with Carter obviously tense and fearful of showing disrespect for the Presidency. A majority of the electorate considered Carter the winner of the second, which was notable for Carter's aggressive tactics and for Ford's flub on a question about Eastern Europe, and of the third as well, according to the poll-takers. (Nobody took a poll after the Dole/Mondale confrontation, in which Dole behaved so belligerently that he reminded many viewers of Nixon.) It was never clear exactly how many votes the debates actually changed, but the second one clearly helped to slow a Carter slide that had begun immediately after Labor Day.

The reasons for Carter's decline—or, if you prefer, Ford's gain—were numerous. Neither man was well known to the voters, in the sense that Eisenhower and Nixon and Humphrey were when they ran, both having emerged on center stage only within the last three months. In that situation, incumbency finally counted for something. Then, too, Carter had trouble shaking the "wishy-washy" image that had begun to develop during the primaries. And he no longer seemed the fresh-faced, fresh-thinking political outsider, especially when he started comparing himself to Franklin D. Roosevelt and Harry S. Truman.

A Democratic Sweep That Fizzled

It should have been a Democratic sweep, given Watergate, high inflation and higher unemployment, Ford's reputation as a bumbler who could not seem to stop hitting his head on helicopter doors, and the feebleness of the Republican Party. That it was not was a measure of Carter's failure, as one of his own advisors said, "to dominate the campaign by shaping the campaign."

The result was a campaign almost completely barren of serious discussion of issues, a campaign dominated by a succession of small controversies that loomed large, a campaign with bewildering changes of momentum that demonstrated the shaky hold each candidate had on his supporters. As many as one-fifth of the voters—having lived through Carter's problems with a *Playboy* interview in which he used coarse language and Ford's problems with Agriculture Secretary Earl Butz, who used coarser language to describe blacks—apparently remained undecided with only a week to go.

The End of a Long Campaign

But, in the end, Jimmy Carter became the President-elect. He narrowly defeated President Ford by sweeping his native South and adding enough Northern industrial states to give him a bare electoral vote majority.

Carter won three closely contested battleground states in returns just after midnight on election night—New York, Pennsylvania and Texas. Carter lost New Jersey and Michigan, Ford's home state.

Thus, Carter became the first man from the Deep South to be elected President in a century and a quarter. Mr. Ford, the first appointed President, was also the first incumbent since Herbert Hoover to lose a Presidential election.

Several states that Mr. Ford had counted on went to Carter, among them Louisiana, Mississippi and Wisconsin. Carter carried Pennsylvania with the help of Mayor Rizzo of Philadelphia and Texas where Robert S. Strauss, Democratic National Chairman, had worked intensively. Carter took every border state and every Southern state except Virginia.

Carter won enormous margins among black and Hispanic voters. Labor unions had supported the Carter campaign with a computer-designed operation which helped bring out the voters in numbers that surprised pre-election analysts. Good weather in most of the nation provided a traditional stimulus for a heavy turnout. The turnout also made certain that Congress will remain overwhelmingly Democratic.

Thus a tough and idealistic candidate fought his way to victory from almost total obscurity. With Ford's departure from the White House, the Watergate chapter in our history will now be finally closed.

The President: Is He the People's Choice?
Selecting the Presidential Nominees in 1976

By Stephen Hess*

At a point in May of 1976, an astute columnist for The Washington Post, David S. Broder, surveyed the confusing prophecies of the national press corps and offered a special award to any reporter who, at the beginning of the Presidential election year, had correctly predicted the eventual winners of the Democratic and Republican nominations. Broder's prize was not claimed.

Indeed, the previous July, a New York Times writer gave the odds on the Democratic contest as Edward Kennedy—2 to 5; Hubert Humphrey—4 to 1; Edmund Muskie—5 to 1; Jimmy Carter, Birch Bayh and Morris Udall—8 to 1.

That Carter became the Democratic nominee, although his most notable experience in government had been as a one-term Governor of Georgia, and that an incumbent President, Gerald Ford, was so sorely pressed by Ronald Reagan before winning the Republican nomination, combined to make 1976 one of the more interesting and unpredictable political years.

In retrospect, what was distinctive about the candidate selection process in 1976 and how well did it work? Many ask whether the President is the people's choice.

The Candidates—A Larger Choice

A persistent criticism of the process that produces the two major Presidential nominees is that "the best people" do not choose to enter the field. Given that there are over 200 million people in the United States—and only a handful of names is placed in nomination at the conventions—there is a certain surface logic to the argument.

But, of course, the Presidency is the highest *political* office in the country. The White House is not the place for on-the-job training and the real question should be whether the system attracts the best people who follow a political calling.

In 1976 there were 14 announced candidates for the Democratic nomination—Birch Bayh, Lloyd Bentsen, Edmund G. (Jerry) Brown, Jr., Robert C. Byrd, Jimmy Carter, Frank Church, Fred Harris, Henry M. Jackson, Ellen McCormack, Terry Sanford, Milton J. Shapp, Sargent Shriver, Morris K. Udall and George C. Wallace. Half were serving or had served in Congress (six in the Senate and one in the House of Representatives); five were Governors or former Governors. Of the other two, Shriver had been Ambassador to France, Peace Corps Director and the party's 1972 Vice-Presidential nominee; McCormack, an anti-abortion leader, was the only non-politician in the running. (Another former Democratic Senator, Eugene J. McCarthy, opted to run for President as an Independent.)

It would be difficult to conclude that this was not a representative list of prominent Democratic leaders, covering the ideological spectrum within the party from Harris on the left to Wallace on the right. Political or personal considerations—rather than something inherent in the system—kept out of the race a number of others, such as Senators Kennedy, Humphrey, McGovern, Mondale and Muskie. In fact, the choice was somewhat larger in 1976 than in the past—perhaps as a result of Federal financial support for candidates and the expansion of state primary elections.

A New "Population Democracy"

The system clearly did not discriminate in favor of candidates from the larger states as was once the case. California, the most populous state, had its candidate and so did Idaho, one of the least populated states. The eventual Democratic winner came from Georgia, ranked 14th in number of residents. Undoubtedly, this relatively new "population democracy" can be attributed to the expanded role of television. Although TV has a built-in bias in favor of coverage in Washington, where most network crews are based, once the candidates take to the hustings they receive attention on the basis of "news worthiness," not place of domicile.

---

* Mr. Hess is a Senior Fellow at the Brookings Institution in Washington and the author of "Organizing the Presidency."

Yet two changes in the backgrounds of candidates deserve special note:

• For 20 years, neither party had chosen a Presidential nominee with gubernatorial experience. (Adlai Stevenson in 1956 was the last such candidate until Jimmy Carter.) One reason in favor of Washington-based candidates has been the importance of foreign policy in the Presidential job description. But as the country seemed to turn its attention inward in 1976, the liability of picking someone from a statehouse was removed and, apparently, we may now see more Governors seeking the Presidency.

• The second change is that two of the most serious contenders—Carter and Reagan—were politically unemployed, i.e. they did not hold public office in 1975 and 1976. While Senators and incumbent Governors were tied down by legislative sessions and other duties, the ex-Governors were making a full-time job of running for President. And more and more, running for President—building a multimillion dollar organization, campaigning in 30 state primaries and the caucus states, preparing media presentations, raising money and lining up support—has become a full-time job. The implications of this fact of political life may well shape the behavior of future Presidential hopefuls. It certainly expands the pool of talent available.

A related factor that might also affect later races has to do with the pluses and minuses of Presidential incumbency. It has been generally assumed that a President who wishes to run for a second term will have no trouble getting his party's endorsement. This has been the case with every 20th-century Chief Executive. The advantages of incumbency—jobs and contracts to distribute, visibility, logistical support, even giving invitations to White House dinners—are considerable. To some degree, this did work for Gerald Ford.

As R. W. Apple, Jr., of The New York Times, wrote after the nation's great July 4th celebration: "At the encampment of the wagon trains at Valley Forge, at the convocation outside Independence Hall in Philadelphia, at Operation Sail in New York and at the naturalization ceremonies at Monticello, it was the President—not Ronald Reagan or Jimmy Carter—who stood in the spotlight, visible and audible to tens of thousands in person and to uncounted millions on television."

Still, President Ford was hard-pressed to narrowly defeat Reagan. Incumbency has become a two-edged sword. A President takes credit for everything that goes well during his years in office, whether he deserves credit or not, and he also will be blamed for what goes wrong, again whether he is at fault or not. Moreover, the challenger can make proposals that are outside the constraints of what would be feasible if he were in office. Because Ford was the first appointed President and had served for a fairly short period, 1976 may not be a true test. But the experience of 1976 should be encouraging to those who may consider running against a President of their own party.

Selecting the Delegates

Every fourth year, a greater percentage of delegates to the two national conventions are picked in primary elections, rather than by the caucus method that favors party activists over rank-and-file voters. Using figures for the Democratic Party (the Republican Party reflects the same trend), in 1964 and 1968, roughly half the convention delegates were chosen in primaries; in 1972, two-thirds of the delegates came from primary states; and, in 1976, the 30 primary elections accounted for more than three-fourths of the delegates. Voters may choose not to exercise their franchise, but they are given greater opportunity to participate than in the past.

The delegate selection system is drawn out and confusing. Yet in 1976, as in other recent Presidential election years, it did produce clear-cut decisions in both parties. The large field of Democratic contenders gradually narrowed as each early primary election seemed to come up with a decisive loser. (It was sometimes more difficult to spot the winner.) Thus, as the candidates fought it out in New Hampshire (Feb. 24), Massachusetts (March 2), Florida (March 9), Illinois (March 16), North Carolina (March 23), New York and Wisconsin (April 6), one by one such losers as Bayh, Bentsen, Harris, Sanford, Shapp and Shriver dropped out of the race. The Pennsylvania primary of April 27 was the key victory for Carter, although two late-blooming candidates, Brown and Church, kept the outcome unsettled through the final primaries on June 8.

The situation was somewhat different on the Republican side, where Ford had a string of early victories, followed by a string of defeats, and ultimately gained the nomination by winning over a small but crucial number of uncommitted delegates during the weeks before the August convention in Kansas City.

If the basic outline of the system works well, it is still not without troubling elements. In both 1972 and 1976, a factor that might have denied party members their preferred nominee was the "crossover" provisions of certain state primaries, which permit Democrats to vote in Republican primaries and vice versa. In the 1972 Wisconsin primary, many Republicans (seeing no real contest in their party) chose to vote for Democrat George Wallace. And in 1976, after Wallace no longer appeared to be a serious possibility, many of his Democratic supporters in such states as Texas and Indiana voted in Republican primaries for Reagan. Since the parties' nominees should be the choice of party members, this is a situation that demands reform.

Delegate selection also becomes excessively chaotic when states in different parts of the country hold primaries on the same day, as happened on June 8, in California, New Jersey and Ohio. Candidates and reporters frantically try to cover all bases.

Mondale's Regional Primary Plan

To make the process more orderly and rational in 1980, Walter Mondale has a highly useful proposal: He suggests six regional primary dates. Under the Mondale plan, no state has to choose delegates by primary election, but any state holding a primary would have to conduct it on the same day as the other states in the same region.

The six regional primary dates would fall between late March and mid-June, with the order of the regions determined by lot. No state would be allowed by unilateral decision to have the advantage of being first or last. There would be a two-week interval between each regional primary date. This would allow a fortnight in which the candidates and the news media would be expected to focus on the particular concerns of each region.

Within these ground rules, each state could do its own thing with only three sensible exceptions: • (1) No state could use the "crossover" system. • (2) The names of all those who run for convention delegate must appear on the state ballot bracketed with the name of their preference for President. • (3) All Presidential candidates who receive Federal campaign funds must be entered in at least one primary in each region.

(Ironically, Mondale's regional primary proposal was favored in the Republican Platform, and was not mentioned in the Democratic Platform.)

The Campaign for the Nomination

Clearly one of the major changes in the campaign was that declared candidates were entitled to Federal money for the first time. Any candidate who could raise $100,000—$5,000 in each of 20 states in amounts of $250 or less—was eligible to receive matching funds from the U.S. Treasury for all contributions under $250. A ceiling of $1,000 was placed on individual gifts.

There was some confusion when the Supreme Court in December 1975 declared unconstitutional parts of the Campaign Financing Act, and Congress spent all winter rewriting the statute. Candidates had serious cash flow problems until the new law went into effect. However, this situation is not likely to be repeated in 1980.

The end result of partial public financing during the preconvention period was probably not a lowering of the total amount spent on all campaigns. But it did have the desired effect of limiting the influence of "fat cats" and broadening the base of candidates' financial support—an important objective of this post-Watergate reform.

The other major change since 1972 was the elimination of the winner-take-all primary in the Democratic Party. Where once a candidate received the entire state delegation if he even narrowly won a primary, in 1976 he earned convention delegates that roughly reflected his percentage of the vote in each primary.

Carter was the only candidate who seemed to understand that the rules had changed since the last election and to take full advantage of the new rules. By getting started early, he was able to build local organizations that could gather the necessary small contributions to entitle him to Federal money. The late-starters, on the other hand, were unable to match his fundraising effort. Also, by entering all state primaries under the new proportional representation system, Carter was able to win some delegates even in states where he lost the election. The other candidates who chose to follow the traditional strategy of entering only primaries whose outcomes were thought favorable misread the arithmetic of the convention.

Carter's message to the voters was equally resourceful. The nation had been staggered by the back-to-back events of Vietnam and Watergate. And here was Carter telling the American people, in effect: "This wasn't your fault. It was the politicians' fault. I want government to be as good as you are." The genius of Jimmy Carter was that he offered absolution. He remained deliberately vague on most issues. Given the broad range of conflicting ideology within the Democratic Party, this had the effect of minimizing strife—which had been so harmful in the McGovern campaign—while adding an intriguing sense of mystery that seems to have had a certain voter appeal.

And he did all this—strategy and message—with hardly a footfault. In nearly two years of campaigning for the nomination, Carter made only one error, an unfortunate remark about "ethnic purity," for which he quickly apologized and the incident was forgotten.

The unique aspect of Reagan's challenge was that it centered on foreign policy. At first, in the New Hampshire primary, he did offer a plan for drastically reducing the Federal domestic budget—popularly known as his "$90-billion misunderstanding." But he rebounded after unfavorable comment by directing his subsequent attacks against the President to such matters as détente with the Soviet Union, which he viewed as one-sided, and a tough stand on maintaining United States rights over the Panama Canal.

Reagan's stance may have struck such a responsive chord—allowing him to maintain his position as a serious contender following a shaky start—because of some pent-up emotion within the American people. Strangely, there had been no overwhelming backlash in the United States in the wake of failure in Vietnam as there had been after the Korean war and the Communist victory on the China mainland. Reagan's "hard" line may have substituted for the usual reaction to traumatic world events. The result of Reagan's campaign was that it moved Ford further to the right. It also forced the President to sharpen his election organization, which would not have been the case if he had been given the nomination without real opposition.

There was only one notable innovation in the preconvention Republican struggle—Reagan's highly effective use of a half-hour televised speech in early April. The conventional wisdom in recent years has been that audiences will not pay attention to lengthy TV talks, and most candidates have featured short presentations, not exceeding five minutes. Of course, this may not start a new trend since Reagan, as a former actor, had a special advantage that few other candidates will be able to match.

The campaign was remarkable for the clean behavior of the candidates in both parties. There was nothing comparable to the "dirty tricks" that figured so prominently in the Ervin Committee's investigation of Nixon's 1972 activities. Only one radio spot, used by the Ford organization in California, was thought by some to be in questionable taste.

The news media did the best job to date of covering the preconvention activities. The New York Times and CBS were particularly imaginative in their use of public-opinion polling data. Although the press still tended to play up the "horse race" aspects of the campaign—who's ahead and who's behind—the failure to shed light on issues was primarily caused by the candidates, not the reporters. One distortion, as in the past, was the media's overemphasis on the New Hampshire primary. Paul Weaver noted one scholarly survey that showed more than 53 percent of the TV networks' presidential campaign stories between Nov. 24, 1975 and Feb. 27, 1976 dealt with New Hampshire. He concluded, "By contrast, the 11 states holding caucuses or conventions in the pre-New Hampshire period received less than 10 percent of the networks' stories, though they accounted for a total of 587 delegates as against New Hampshire's 38. Delegate for delegate, that is, New Hampshire received more than 80 times as much coverage as these early non-primary states. That seems a bit excessive."

At the Conventions

The last national convention to take more than one ballot to nominate a Presidential candidate was in 1952. Increasingly, the conventions merely ratify the choices made by the voters in state primaries. This hardly means, however, that the conventions have no important work to conduct. There are matters of rules, platform and Vice-Presidential selection that must be attended to.

The two platforms were the product of far more democratic processes than in previous conventions. It has been usual, for example, for a President who is to be nominated to bring his own draft of the platform to the convention where the platform committee simply gives its seal of approval. But at the 1976 Republican convention, the platform was totally written by delegates in sessions that were open to the press and the public.

Yet such a system does not necessarily result in a coherent and consistent document. The delegates on the platform committee have very little time, work under great pressure and are rarely experts in key areas of national policy. Doing the job properly will require much more detailed staff work in advance. The national parties should give serious consideration to presenting each platform committee member with a briefing book that would contain information on all issues that might be raised, including careful cost estimates and summaries of the positions taken by past platforms, the candidates, the majority of the party's representatives in Congress and the opposition party.

As it turned out, the 1976 Democratic Platform was probably somewhat to the left of the mainstream of the party and the Republican Platform about the same distance to the right of its elected officials. Nevertheless, the two platforms presented very clear differences and should have been useful to those voters who read them. In addition, and perhaps most important, the platform deliberations defined the outer boundaries of what the parties stand for, thus allowing each voter to determine for himself whether he is able to continue to remain within his party.

The solitary rules fight in 1976 came at the Republican convention over a proposal to force Presidential candidates to announce their choices for running-mate before the balloting for President. This was a gambit by the Reagan forces, which they lost, to counter the adverse effects of Reagan's selection of Senator Richard S. Schweiker, a liberal from Pennsylvania.

While the Reagan move cannot be considered primarily as an effort to reform the system, the system of choosing Vice-Presidential nominees is very much in need of reform. The problems associated with picking Thomas Eagleton and Spiro Agnew in 1972 remain, even though the selection went smoothly in 1976. In the Democratic Party, this was because Carter sewed up his nomination well in advance and therefore had ample time to devote to sifting the qualifications of potential Vice Presidents. Yet this need not always happen in the future.

There are at least three ways that the system could be changed to assure adequate time for consideration.

• First, the Presidential nomination could come before the approval of the platform, thereby adding an extra day for the Presidential nominee to make up his mind.

• Second, an extra day could be added to the normal convention calendar.

• And third, the Presidential nominee could be given the option of asking the national committee to convene a month after the convention for the purpose of choosing a Vice-Presidential candidate.

The third alternative—which was used by the Democrats after the Eagleton affair—has the advantage of giving potential Vice-Presidential candidates a chance to wage mini-campaigns for the office.

The choices of Republican Senator Robert J. Dole and Democratic Senator Walter F. Mondale fitted the traditional patterns of "ticket-balancing." Mondale's selection was designed to appeal to the more liberal wing of his party and Dole was chosen for his appeal to conservative Republicans. Although both men were experienced legislators, they were selected more for electoral reasons than for how well they might do if called upon to assume the Presidency.

The final usefulness of party conventions is the sense of unity that they are able to produce. In this regard, both conventions in 1976 were successful and all elements in the parties were able to leave New York and Kansas City feeling that they could support their parties' nominees— even when the nominees were not their first choices.

Conclusions

H. L. Mencken once wrote: "There is something about a national convention that makes it as fascinating as a revival or a hanging. It is vulgar, it is ugly, it is stupid, it is tedious, it is hard upon both the higher cerebral centers and the *gluteus maximus*, and yet it is somehow charming. One sits through long sessions wishing heartily that all the delegates and alternates were dead and in hell—and then suddenly there comes a show so gaudy and hilarious, so melodramatic and obscene, so unimaginably exhilarating and preposterous that one lives a gorgeous year in an hour."

One need not agree with the Sage of Baltimore that our way of selecting Presidential candidates is either charming or obscene in order to conclude that we could do better. I have already made a number of proposals to this end.

A regional primary system would require Congressional enactment.

Eliminating "crossover" voting in primaries would require rewriting state laws.

Changes in the Vice-Presidential selection would require action by the national parties.

Changes in preparation for drafting party platforms would require no amending of laws or party rules, merely the will to function in a more useful fashion.

The Campaign Financing Act, hastily written in 1976, should have a critical assessment now that it has been in operation for an election. Are there loopholes that need to be plugged? Does the law infuse enough money or too much money into the campaigns?

Doing something, however, boils down to whether there is an urge to reform in the body politic. With Watergate fading into history, will politicians choose to stick with the status quo?

The system of nominating Presidential and Vice-Presidential candidates does not call for a complete overhaul, but some fine-tuning is definitely in order.

Presidential Campaign Highlights

1975

NOV. 2 Vice President Nelson A. Rockefeller says "party squabbles" force him to withdraw from Vice-Presidential race.

1976

JAN. 1 President Ford, confident of nomination and election, suggests campaign themes—peace, improved economy, more political freedom.

FEB. 11 Sen. Lloyd M. Bentsen of Texas withdraws from the race.

24 Ford defeats Reagan in New Hampshire; Jimmy Carter leads in Democratic primary.

MAR. 2 Sen. Henry M. Jackson wins in Massachusetts primary; Ford defeats Reagan. Carter takes Vermont primary, while Ford defeats Reagan.

4 Reagan attacks Ford's foreign policy and defense programs; claims Soviet is stronger and says that Ford and Henry A. Kissinger "must be held accountable to history."

9 Ford wins in Florida primary; Carter defeats Gov. George C. Wallace; Gov. Milton J. Shapp withdraws from race.

16 Howard H. Callaway is suspended as Ford's campaign manager pending investigation of charges of improper influence to promote ski resort.

23 Reagan scores surprise upset over Ford in North Carolina Republican primary. First victory after five losses gives new life to his campaign.

25 Sen. Jackson pledges increased U.S. school aid to hard-pressed systems such as New York City's.

26 President Ford says he will not "play Russian roulette" with national security by allowing Congressional Democrats to cut his military spending requests.

30 President Ford names Rogers C. B. Morton to replace Howard H. Callaway as chairman of campaign organization.

31 Jimmy Carter, as Georgia Governor, revealed to have taken free rides on executive jets of Lockheed Aircraft and Coca-Cola, even though state provides planes and travel funds.

APR. 1 Humphrey, in New York, urges a Marshall plan to rebuild nation's cities.

3 Advertising agency for Jimmy Carter got lucrative Georgia contracts while Carter was Governor.

6 Jimmy Carter says U.S. should not try to change "ethnic purity" of some neighborhoods. He later apologizes for use of "ethnic purity" phrase, but is firm in opposing use of Federal force to change a neighborhood's ethnic character.

15 Udall backs Carter views on open housing, but is "disturbed" by talk of "ethnic purity."

16 Carter calls for nationwide mandatory health insurance plan financed through employer and payroll taxes as well as general tax revenues.

19 Ford, in answer to Reagan, says it would be "absolutely irresponsible" to terminate Panama Canal negotiations, which would turn all Latin America against U.S.

21 Ford accuses Reagan of "preposterous" and "demagogic" statements that U.S. is slipping behind Soviet Union in military preparedness.

21 Justice Dept. rules 513 political jurisdictions in 30 states must hold elections in more than one language to comply with 1965 Voting Rights Act.

23 Ford, replying to an attack by Reagan on foreign policy, denies U.S. plans to establish diplomatic relations with North Vietnam.

27 Carter wins Pennsylvania Democratic primary, his seventh Presidential primary victory of year. Jackson suffers critical blow to campaign.

MAY 1 Sen. Jackson ends "active pursuit" of Democratic Presidential nomination. Concedes long lead by Carter.

1 Reagan captures all 96 Republican delegates in Texas primary, with aid of massive Democratic crossover vote. Carter in sweeping victory over Sen. Bentsen, Texas' favorite son.

11 President signs revised Federal Election Campaign Act, meeting Supreme Court requirements, with commission members appointed by President. Measure limits campaign spending and role of wealthy contributors. Each major-party candidate has $21.8 million in Federal funds for general election campaign, coming from income tax checkoffs. National committees can spend $3.2 million each on Presidential candidates. Individuals and committees can spend unlimited amounts for advertising, but completely independent of campaign. Primary contributions are limited to $1,000 for an individual, $5,000 for a committee. Spending by primary candidates limited to $10.9 million each. Enactment clears way to release matching Federal funds for primary candidates.

13 Carter, at U.N. conference, calls for voluntary moratorium by all nations on purchase or sale of nuclear fuel enrichment and reprocessing plants as means of curbing spread of nuclear weapons.

15 Analysis of Reagan income and taxes shows he almost certainly paid no Federal income tax in 1970 despite an income in excess of $73,000. In two other years, he paid less than people with fraction of income. Investments apparently within the law. Spokesman says later report is wrong, but declines to say how much tax Reagan did pay.

25 Ford is winner in Kentucky, Tennessee and Oregon primaries; Reagan captures Arkansas, Idaho and Nevada. Carter takes Arkansas, Kentucky and Tennessee but loses Idaho and Oregon to Church and Nevada to Brown.

JUNE 1 Carter and Reagan win in South Dakota; Carter captures majority of Rhode Island delegates; Ford wins all 19 Rhode Island delegates. Reagan and Church win in Montana.

2 Ford and Reagan vie for conservative vote in attack on court-ordered busing to correct racial imbalance; Reagan pledges that Federal agencies will be told to "get off the backs of local boards."

20 Ford ties anti-busing stance to his fight on Big Government. Compares court-ordered busing to the violation of civil liberties by C.I.A. and F.B.I. and to the intrusion of the Federal bureaucracy in state and local government activities.

24 Ford backers get important convention posts— Sen. Howard H. Baker as keynote speaker and Sen. Robert Dole as temporary chairman.

30 Sen. Goldwater gives formal but restrained endorsement to President Ford, urging that GOP nominate him to continue "turning this country back in the right direction."

JULY 6 Twenty-nine of nation's 36 Democratic governors endorse Carter for nomination, setting aside old antagonisms for sake of party unity.

12 Thirty-seventh Democratic National Convention opens at New York City's Madison Square Garden, with 3,000 delegates. National Chairman Robert S. Strauss calls for end of "eight years of Nixon-Ford, eight long years of Kissinger, Simon, Morton and Butz." Gov. Hugh L. Carey and Mayor Abraham D. Beame attack Republican Government. Keynote speeches are given by Sen. Glenn of Ohio and Barbara Jordan, black Representative from Texas.

12 Carter and leading feminists reach compromise on future role of women in party and a Carter Administration. The next day, women's caucus, after often angry debate, agrees to compromise, which would commit party to "promote" rather than "require" equal representation for women in 1978 and thereafter. Vote is setback for militant feminists.

13 Democrats adopt platform bearing Carter imprint after defeating proposal for discussion of three unspecified issues.

14 Jimmy Carter is nominated on first roll-call vote to be Democratic Presidential nominee.

15 Carter picks Sen. Mondale as Vice-Presidential candidate and convention enthusiastically endorses Minnesotan.

15 In address to convention, Carter says nation needs "time for healing" after living through "time of torment." Mondale, in acceptance speech, is cheered as he denounces Ford for pardoning Nixon.

15 Carter is defeated in convention vote to abolish winner-take-all primaries in Congressional districts.

16 Carter warns party, at National Committee meeting, against overconfidence, saying, "Our goal is not to lose a single state." Praises Robert S. Strauss, whom he is keeping as party chairman.

19 A.F.L.-C.I.O. Executive Council abandons neutrality and endorses Carter-Mondale ticket. George Meany says he is "very happy with Carter."

26 Reagan picks Sen. Richard S. Schweiker of Pennsylvania as running mate, breaking with tradition. Schweiker is one of most liberal and pro-labor GOP voices in Senate.

AUG. 3 Carter, in first major speech since nomination, in New Hampshire, pledges as President to act in ways to restore faith in the family system. Accuses Ford of using "rhetoric and not reason."

16 Republicans open 31st National Convention at Kansas City, Mo. Keynote speaker, Sen. Howard H. Baker, Jr., of Tennessee warns Democrats against "rattling the dusty old skeletons of Watergate." He joins Vice President Rockefeller, Sen. Robert J. Dole of Kansas and Sen. Goldwater of Arizona in denouncing Jimmy Carter.

17 With Ford's delegates steadily mounting, President wins key test as convention, 1,180 to 1,069, rejects Reagan move to force Ford to name Vice-Presidential choice before nomination roll call.

17 Convention adopts conservative platform generally advocating less government by Washington.

18 Ford nominated for Presidency, winning 1,187 votes, 57 more than a majority, to 1,070 for Reagan. His name placed in nomination by Gov. William G. Milliken of Michigan as "the present and future President." Ronald Reagan nominated by his campaign chairman, Sen. Paul Laxalt of Nevada.

19 Ford picks Sen. Dole as running mate. Selection conforms to wishes of Reagan.

19 Convention ratifies selection of 53-year-old Dole, placed in nomination by Vice President Rockefeller.

25 Ford names James A. Baker 3rd to replace Rogers C.B. Morton as campaign chairman.

30 U.S. Election Commission rules League of Women Voters can finance debates between national candidates of major parties, without violating new ban on private campaign contributions.

31 Roman Catholic bishops disappointed at Carter's stand in continuing to withhold support for an anti-abortion amendment.

SEPT. 1 Ford and Carter to meet on Sept. 23 to debate domestic and economic issues, under agreement by representatives. Will have three debates, under agreement announced by League of Women Voters.

5 Gulf Oil lobbyist reported to have told Federal grand jury that in 1973 he made an illegal corporate contribution to Sen. Dole, GOP Vice-Presidential nominee. Dole aide says Senator finds no indication in his records of receiving money. On Sept. 8, lobbyist says he is "confident" he was in error about 1970 gift of $2,000 to Dole.

7 Carter says he would have dismissed F.B.I. Director Clarence M. Kelley for accepting gifts and personal services, but declines to say he would oust Kelley if he becomes President.

8 Ford calls Carter callous and indecisive in making "contradictory" public appraisals of Clarence Kelley.

10 Roman Catholic bishops say they are "encouraged" but not "satisfied" by President Ford's support of proposed Constitutional amendment that would permit states to regulate abortions.

12 Sen. Dole, under continued questioning, repeats denials that he took unreported campaign contributions from the Gulf Oil Co. in 1970 and 1973.

15 President Ford, at Ann Arbor, Mich., formally opens campaign, pledging "specifics, not smiles," and a plan to spur home ownership. In address to University of Michigan students, he attacks Carter, saying "it is not enough for anyone to say 'Trust me.' "

17 Carter accepts help of two of the most prominent segregationists—Sens. James O. Eastland and John C. Stennis of Mississippi.

20 Carter says, in *Playboy* magazine interview, that he has "looked on a lot of women with lust" and that he has "committed adultery in my heart many times," but that "God forgives me for it." He asserts own moral standards would not lead him to try to impose stricter laws on private behavior. Spot interviews later in week show wide concern over remarks.

23 U.S. Steel reports it gave President Ford five golfing holidays during his last 10 years in House of Representatives. White House declines comment.

23 President Ford and Jimmy Carter meet in first TV campaign debate. Program, 90 minutes long, is broadcast nationwide from Philadelphia and viewed at least in part by approximately 94 million persons. A technical failure interrupts debate for 27 minutes. Both candidates focus largely on jobs and taxes, in response to questions from a panel of three reporters. Watergate is mentioned only indirectly. On following Monday, a poll by *New York Times* and CBS shows that of 1,167 respondents, 37 percent thought President did better, 24 percent thought Carter had won, 35 percent called it a draw, and 4 percent expressed no opinion.

28 White House concedes that President Ford was golfing guest of several major corporations while in the House of Representatives. Says activities in no way violated House's code of ethics.

29 President Ford, vetoing $56-billion appropriation bill for manpower, health, education and welfare programs, says Democratic Congress passed bill with deliberate intention of embarrassing him politically.

30 President Ford denies ever diverting campaign funds for personal use. On Oct. 1, F.B.I. is reported to have found no evidence to substantiate criminal charges of campaign financing irregularities.

On. Oct. 14, Charles F. Ruff, Watergate special prosecutor, reports no evidence for allegation that Ford misused political contributions from maritime unions or a "reason to believe that any other violations of law had occurred." Findings based on examination of records of unions and political committees, and review of records of Ford's personal finances and I.R.S. audit of tax returns from 1967 to 1972.

OCT. 1 Records of a major Georgia company show that Carter and his family spent several days at a forest resort as company guests while he was Governor. Spokesman says visits had been publicized at the time. Earlier, Carter had said that while Governor he had accepted transportation on private aircraft owned by major corporations but travel was all business.

5 Sen. Mondale in speech charges Ford Administration with "fundamental failure to heed the lessons of Watergate," starting with Nixon pardon and continuing since.

6 President Ford and Jimmy Carter hold second debate, on foreign policy. Both stress support for Israel and strong defense. Ford's denial of Soviet domination of Eastern Europe stirs protest from ethnic Americans. Ford later says he meant only to show his refusal to accept such domination. President also says Commerce Department would name companies that had taken part in Arab boycott. Next day, however, President orders only "future" reports be made public. Aides indicate he had misspoken in original statement.

Polls, impartial analysts and even some Republicans give Carter clear edge over Ford, after debate. Viewing audience estimated at 85 million.

7 Lester Maddox, segregationist former Governor of Georgia, campaigns as Presidential candidate of American Independent Party. His platform pledges income tax repeal, isolationism and virtual elimination of Federal bureaucracy.

8 Eugene J. McCarthy pushes his independent campaign for the Presidency with the announcement of five men for his Cabinet, representing wide range of population. Former Wisconsin Democratic Senator is fighting new campaign spending law as unfair to minor candidates. Also urges tax reform, defense spending cuts and energy conservation.

15 Senators Dole and Mondale stage first-ever televised debate between Vice-Presidential candidates.

17 Carter lists $57,000 in corporate and business contributions while running for Governor of Georgia in 1970. Included were donations from concerns dealing with state and an organization later under Federal investigation. A later analysis shows small group of powerful Georgians, including bankers, business executives, contractors, gave Carter half of $690,000 contribution total.

22 Ford and Carter stage third and final debate. Outcome viewed as indecisive. Candidates, in low-key performance, express concern for the country and avoid personal attacks. TV broadcast viewed by about 85 million.

28 The President promises to make another Federal income tax reduction "The number one NO priority in the next Ford administration."

28 Jimmy Carter says that he will consider a tax cut if elected President but that he cannot make this consideration a firm promise.

28 National Poll indicates that Mr. Carter's standing in the polls has dropped 27 percentage points to a slender six-point lead since his nomination in July.

NOV. 1 Fifty-state survey of probable electoral balloting indicates a very close Presidential race with final efforts playing a decisive role.

1 Deacons of Plains, Ga., Baptist Church, Mr. Carter's home congregation, recommend dismissal of their pastor because of his remarks in connection with the turning away of black minister at the church. The President Ford Committee condemns Carter for failure to "influence decision of his own church on racial matters." Campaign Committee later disavows criticism.

2 Carter wins Bicentennial Presidential election with a bare electoral majority, 272 to 235, with Oregon and Ohio still undecided twenty-four hours after the election.

James Earl Carter, Jr.

Jimmy Carter, the 51-year-old peanut farmer from the Deep South, became the Democrats' choice for President after waging a hard-fought, four-year campaign. With single-minded pragmatic purpose, he ranged across the country in the bid for support, ignoring skepticism and ridicule. His passion for planning reflected the background of rural Georgia where, as a farmboy, James Earl Carter, Jr., kept pace with the needs of farm routine. And he became the first major party nominee from the South since Zachary Taylor in 1848.

Carter was born in the tiny village of Plains, Ga., Oct. 1, 1924, and grew up on the family farm at nearby Archery. Although his father, James Earl Carter, was a segregationist, he treated his black and white workers equally and was noted for his lenient credit policies. Carter's mother was Lillian Gordy, now 78 years old, a matriarchal woman who broke racial rules in her home and in her work as a registered nurse. Indeed, the mother worked for integration in Plains in the 1950s and 1960s.

Jimmy Carter was baptized in the Southern Baptist Church in 1935, and speaks openly of his faith in the conservative and evangelical denomination, and of having been "born again" as a Christian. But he has repeatedly stated his commitment to separation of church and state.

In 1942, Carter realized his ambition of entering the U.S. Naval Academy at Annapolis. After graduation, he entered the nuclear submarine program, working for Adm. Hyman G. Rickover. He studied nuclear physics and traveled extensively.

Took Over Family Business

In 1946, Carter married Rosalynn Smith of a neighboring family. John William, their first child, was born a year later in Portsmouth, Va. Their other children are James Earl, 3rd, born in Honolulu in 1950; Donnel Jeffrey, born in New London, Conn., in 1952, and Amy Lynn, born in Plains in 1967.

In 1954, after his father's death, Carter resigned from the Navy and returned to Plains to take over the family business. He built up the enterprise, combining a warehouse, cotton gin and several thousand acres for growing seed peanuts. He became a church deacon and was active in the community. In 1962, he was elected to the Georgia Senate. In 1966, he ran for Governor and lost; in 1970, he ran again and was elected.

During his term as Governor, a state government reorganization sharply reduced the number of agencies, boards and commissions, promoting economy and efficiency. Carter cited unprecedented industrial development, a comprehensive program of judicial reform, upgraded programs in family planning, mental health and the treatment of mental retardation, improved law enforcement and highway improvement. There was no general state-wide tax increase.

In 1972, deciding to run for President, Carter embarked on a strenuous schedule of speeches and strategy sessions, flashing the toothy smile that has become his trademark. In 1974, he became chairman of the Democratic Campaign Committee, traveling across the country to support candidates, while building a base for himself.

Backed By Civil Rights Coalition

He won the support of most of the old Southern civil rights coalition when his candidacy was endorsed in 1975 by Representative Andrew Young, black Democrat from Atlanta, closest aide of the late Rev. Dr. Martin Luther King, Jr. This helped erase the typical-Southern-white-man image that had bothered Carter even though, at his inauguration as Governor in 1971, he had called for an end to all forms of discrimination in Georgia and had hung a portrait of Dr. King in the state Capitol.

In the spring of 1976, he won 19 of the 31 primaries with a broad appeal to conservatives and liberals, black and white, poor and well-to-do. His defeat of Gov. George C. Wallace of Alabama in Florida's primary, March 9, cemented his position as the South's outstanding politician.

During the primary campaign, Carter was criticized for his use of the phrase "ethnic purity" in opposing Federal action to change a neighborhood's ethnic character. Then, after his nomination, he also stirred widespread criticism over his remark in a Playboy magazine interview that he had "looked on a lot of women with lust," in saying that his own moral standards would not lead him to try to impose stricter laws on private behavior.

He is viewed as following a centrist course—to the right of the most liberal Democrats, slightly left of the conservative wing. In accepting the nomination, he stressed the nation's need for a "time of healing," and appealed for "great national deeds."

Carter indicated during the convention that he could bring to Washington what he says it has not had under the Republicans—efficiency and honesty.

Gerald Rudolph Ford

Despite his promise not to seek a full term as an elected President, Gerald Ford announced his intention to be a candidate on July 8, 1975. It was widely believed that this early declaration was aimed at pre-empting right-wing opposition in his own party. This opposition had fought an increasingly bitter campaign to nominate Ronald Reagan.

President Ford moved on many fronts to secure his nomination and election. He frequently referred with pride to his record of 63 vetoes, many of them for budgetary reasons. He repeatedly called for a "new realism" in spending and taxes and attacked the "empty promises" and "give-away proposals" of the Democratic majority in Congress. Thus, he bolstered his conservative economic image. He appealed for business support by vetoing such measures as expanded picketing rights for construction unions. He sought Catholic support by opposing liberal abortion laws and expressing concern over "the increased irreverance for life." He took a strong stand against busing for school integration. In an effort to appease his right-wing critics, he dumped Nelson Rockefeller in the Vice-Presidential nomination contest.

On the other hand, he appealed to the liberal wing of the Republican Party by dismissing hard-liner James R. Schlesinger as Secretary of Defense, appointing Elliot L. Richardson as Secretary of Commerce, supporting moderate reforms in the Central Intelligence Agency, supporting détente negotiations with the Soviet Union, normalizing relations with the People's Republic of China and achieving some modifications in the Panama Canal Treaty.

A Peace and Prosperity Program

At the beginning of 1976, President Ford optimistically predicted his nomination and election on a program of peace and prosperity. He accused Ronald Reagan of ultra-conservatism in domestic and foreign policy.

The early state primaries suggested an easy victory for the President. Despite Reagan's bitter attacks on the Administration's foreign policies and defense programs, President Ford defeated his rival in the New Hampshire, Vermont, Massachusetts and Florida primaries. The President's appeal for Republican unity helped him to win a victory in Illinois.

But on March 24, Reagan's surprise victory in North Carolina gave new life to the campaign. On May 2, in a stunning victory, the former California Governor captured all 96 delegates in the Texas primary. By the end of the state primaries on June 9, the delegate count was 957 to 860, with President Ford in the lead and 1,130 required for the nomination.

In the struggle for state convention delegates, the issue was not resolved. Some Republican leaders were calling for a Ford-Reagan ticket to prevent a disastrous party split at the Kansas City national convention in August.

Complications in a Strange Conflict

Reagan's pre-convention selection of liberal Republican Senator Richard S. Schweiker of Pennsylvania as his prospective running mate and John B. Connally's early endorsement of President Ford were complicating factors.

All the power and prestige of an incumbent President were used to influence uncommitted delegates—media events, invitations to White House galas, appointments of Federal judges, receptions and interviews in the Oval Office and promises to meet specific needs of local groups. Charges of undue influence and unfair campaign methods were aired by both sides.

As late as Aug. 1, both candidates were claiming a first-ballot victory at Kansas City, but delegate sentiment in many crucial states seemed to be wavering. The Reagan forces, by their brilliant and unconventional strategy, succeeded in preventing a pre-convention Ford victory.

In one of the most divided conventions in political history, Ford won a narrow victory, 1,187 to 1,070. In his acceptance speech, he castigated the Democratic Congress and offered to debate the issues over television with Jimmy Carter.

He took credit for restoring the nation to "peace, prosperity and trust in the White House." He claimed that the major accomplishment of his Administration had been a turnaround in the economy with the end of double-digit inflation and a reduction in unemployment. The President also called attention to the new spirit of national unity as marked by the dramatic July 4th Bicentennial celebrations.

His Record Under Attack

But, despite his convention defeat, Reagan had moved the Republican Party further to the right and away from the mainstream by pressuring for the nomination of Senator Robert J. Dole and for the adoption of platform planks criticizing détente and the Helsinki Agreements.

More important was the fact that Mr. Ford was widely regarded as a caretaker President lacking the vision and the background for strong leadership in a critical period of our history. His critics regarded him as a "veto President," a "negative President," not only Richard Nixon's hand-picked successor but a loyal follower of the disgraced ex-President's programs and policies.

Walter Frederick Mondale

Democratic Vice-Presidential Candidate

A Senator with a passion for compassion was Jimmy Carter's choice for Vice President—Walter Frederick Mondale of Minnesota, who himself had long before given up his own race for the No. 1 spot.

As Minnesota Attorney General in the early 1960s, he fought for the right of poor defendants to have public counsel. In a dozen years in the Senate, he has led the fight for such issues as open housing, Indian education, migrant workers and child nutrition.

Described by Mr. Carter and himself as "compatible," Mr. Mondale is like Carter in his devotion to detail.

Senator Mondale was born January 5, 1928, in Ceylon, Minn., one of seven children of a minister devoted to the social gospel. "Fritz" Mondale attended Macalester College in St. Paul and as a 20-year-old student campaigned for Hubert H. Humphrey for the Senate and became a protégé of Mr. Humphrey. They have remained close since.

After two years as an Army corporal in Korea, Mondale entered the University of Minnesota Law School. After four years' law practice in the firm headed by Gov. Orville L. Freeman, the Governor appointed him State Attorney General in 1960, and that year he was elected in his own right and later re-elected.

In 1964, after Mr. Humphrey was elected Vice President, Mondale was named by then Gov. Karl F. Rolvaag to Humphrey's Senate seat. In the Senate, he became known as fighter for civil rights legislation and other liberal issues. In the Finance Committee, however, he disappointed some by willingness to yield to the conservative chairman, Russell B. Long, Democrat of Louisiana. In that committee, Mr. Mondale admittedly has used his position to get tax concessions for Minnesota companies.

Some of his Senate colleagues and other observers believe he often seeks a compromise instead of giving battle on an issue. He himself says: "I don't like buttonholing and arm-twisting. That's not my style. I'm uncomfortable asking people for things."

The Senator and his wife, Joan, have three children, Theodore, Eleanor Jane and William.

Robert Joseph Dole

Republican Vice-Presidential Candidate

Although President Ford had been expected to select a running mate who would broaden the regional and ideological appeal of the Republican Party, the nomination of 53-year-old Senator Robert J. Dole of Kansas conformed to the wishes of Ronald Reagan, thus pacifying and reuniting a divided party.

Robert Joseph Dole was born on July 22, 1923 in a two-room house in Russell, Kansas, a farm town with a population of 3,000. His father operated a cream and egg station and the son worked odd jobs after school. He played basketball in high school and began a pre-medical course at the University of Kansas. World War II interrupted his education. He served in the Army as a captain, was wounded in Italy in 1945 and returned home with many decorations and a useless left arm.

Mr. Dole served in the Kansas state legislature and then, for eight years, in the United States House of Representatives. In the process, he became an expert in farm-state politics. From his first days in the Senate in 1969, he was a political protégé and a strong supporter of Richard M. Nixon on such major issues as Supreme Court appointments, Vietnam and Watergate. His support was rewarded when Nixon made him chairman of the Republican National Committee in 1972.

President Ford has stated that "Bob Dole's philosophy and mine coincide almost identically."

Regarded as a tough campaigner, Senator Dole has friends in all wings of the Republican Party. He has liberal views on racial issues and the food stamp program. He supported all the major civil rights bills of the 1960s, including open housing. He feels that Republicans should broaden their appeal and reach out to minorities and to the disadvantaged by presenting a more compassionate image. But his primary interest is in his farm constituency. In his own words, "If I bring anything to the ticket, it's a close identification with agriculture, small towns, rural America."

Senators Dole and Mondale agreed to debate the issues in the first nationally televised confrontation between Vice-Presidential candidates.

Senator Dole is a Methodist. After a divorce in 1975, he married Elizabeth Hanford, a Federal Trade Commissioner.

(For brief resumés of the platforms of Eugene McCarthy and Lester Maddox, *see* Presidential Campaign Highlights.)

GLOSSARY OF POLITICAL AND GOVERNMENTAL TERMS

Balanced ticket—A party ticket listing candidates chosen to win support from regional, ethnic, minority and other elements of the population.

Beauty Contest—The preferential primary in which voters indicate their preference for a candidate in a nonbinding ballot. *See* "Presidential Primary."

Bloc—Group of legislators, usually of both major parties, who vote together for some particular interest.

Brokered Convention—Decisions on candidates and major issues made by party leaders rather than by rank-and-file delegates.

Bullet Vote—Balloting in which the electorate concentrates on single candidates or issues to the neglect of the rest of the slate.

Cloture—Mechanism for closing debate or ending obstructive tactics so that a vote can be expedited on an issue. Specifically, the procedure by which the Senate limits otherwise unrestricted debate by vote of 60 Senators. *See* "Filibuster."

Confirmation—Senate action to validate an appointment, treaty or other action by the President.

Dark Horse—An entrant into a political contest not previously mentioned. A person unexpectedly nominated, especially at a party convention.

Direct Primary—A party primary in which its members nominate the candidates by direct vote. Also used to choose convention delegates and party leaders. Primaries can be open to members of all parties, making a "crossover" vote possible, or restricted to members of the one party.

Electoral College—A body of electors chosen by the voters in each state to elect the President and Vice President. The electors meet and ballot in the capitals of their respective states. Each state is entitled to a number of electors equal to the total of its Senators and Representatives. Today the college is largely symbolic, the electors being pledged to nominees of parties on the ballot. If no candidate has a majority of electors, the choice of President and Vice President falls to the House of Representatives from among the three highest candidates. A candidate can win a majority of the popular vote, but less than a majority of electors.

Equal Time—The legal right to equivalent time on radio or television to reply to charges in a political campaign made on the same media.

Favorite Son—A state political leader to whom the party organization pledges its Presidential nominating delegates to avoid early pressure from declared candidates and to increase the state delegation's bargaining power at the nominating convention.

Federal Election Commission—Body originally set up under the Federal Election Campaign Act of 1975 to oversee and police the requirements of that act, its decisions to have the force of law unless disapproved by Congress within 30 days of submission. Commission reconstituted by Congress in bill signed by President May 12, 1976, with modifications to meet Supreme Court objections, and with other changes.

Filibuster—A parliamentary device—protracted debate or the use of obstructive tactics, usually in the Senate—to prevent a vote on a measure generally favored. An exceptionally long speech, often lasting more than a day, to accomplish this purpose. Custom and Senate rules provide for unlimited debate before a motion can be put to a vote, unless cloture is invoked. *See* "Cloture."

Gerrymander—The division of a state, county or other political unit into election districts so as to give one political party a majority in many districts and to concentrate the other party's voting strength into as few districts as possible. In brief, boundary manipulation for political advantage.

Impeachment and Conviction—Impeachment is the presentation of formal charges against a public official by the House of Representatives or the like house of other bicameral legislature. A verdict for or against conviction follows trial in the Senate or other upper house, with a two-thirds vote required.

Junket—Travel abroad at public expense.

Machine Politics—The control of party decisions by the organized group of persons who conduct or direct the activities of a political party or similar organization.

Nominating Convention—Quadrennial assembly of a political party to nominate Presidential and Vice-Presidential candidates and adopt platforms and party rules, and to choose the national committee.

Open Convention—A nominating convention in which major nominations and decisions are made on the floor without previous commitments.

Plurality and Majority—Plurality is the excess of votes for the leading candidate, in an election in which there are three or more candidates, over those received by the next candidate. A majority is the number of voters in agreement who number more than half the total.

Presidential Primary—Primary elections in which the sentiment of the voters is tested and delegates to the parties' national convention are chosen. The "preferential primary" in some states, known as "beauty contest," allows the voters to indicate their preference for candidates in a nonbinding ballot. In the delegate-selection primary, the party members vote for delegates to a party convention that in turn selects the nominees. The delegates are usually pledged to one or another candidate. In a few states, delegates are selected by the party organization but are bound to support the candidate designated by the voters in the preferential ballot.

Protest Vote—A vote expressing broad disapproval of an official or party policy, stressing negative reaction.

Slush fund—A Congressman's office account—contributions are unlimited—the money is used to help run his office, mailings, etc.

Stalking Horse—A candidate used to conceal the candidacy of a more important candidate or to draw votes from a rival.

Veto—Action by which a President, Governor or other chief executive rejects legislation passed by both houses of Congress or legislature. Veto power is the legislative power vested in such an executive to return a bill unsigned with the reason for his objections. A "pocket veto" is a veto in which the executive fails to sign a bill presented to him within 10 days of the adjournment of Congress, or similar body. The bill is then dead, the pocket veto power being absolute. A bill becomes law without the President's signature if he holds the bill for 10 days without signing or vetoing while Congress is still in session. The "overriding" of a veto is the passage of vetoed legislation by the two-thirds vote of both houses of Congress or other legislatures.

Platform of the Democratic Party

Excerpts

Full Employment, Price Stability and Balanced Growth—The Democratic Party is committed to the right of all adult Americans willing, able and seeking work to have opportunities for useful jobs at living wages . . . we pledge ourselves to the support of legislation that will make every responsible effort to reduce adult employment to 3 percent within four years.

To meet our goals we must set annual targets for employment, production and price stability. Tax, spending and credit policies must be carefully coordinated with our economic goals. . . .

Consistent and coherent economic policy requires Federal anti-recession grant programs to state and local governments. . . .

We must be absolutely certain that no person is excluded from the fullest opportunity for economic and social participation in our society on the basis of sex, age, color, religion or national origin.

A comprehensive anti-inflation policy must be established to assure relative price stability. Such a program should emphasize increased production and productivity. . . .

We pledge the Democratic Party to a complete overhaul of the present tax system. . . . A responsible Democratic tax reform program could save over $5 billion in the first year, with larger savings in the future.

We will reduce the use of unjustified tax shelters. . . .

Labor Standards and Rights—We will support the full right of construction workers to picket a job site peacefully.

We will seek repeal of Section 14(b) of the Taft-Hartley Act, which allows states to legislate an anti-union open shop.

Government Reform—The Democratic Party is committed to the adoption of reforms such as zero-based budgeting, mandatory reorganization timetables and sunset laws which do not jeopardize the implementation of basic human and political rights.

The Democratic Party is committed to openness throughout the Government. . . .

Health Care—We need a comprehensive national health insurance system with universal and mandatory coverage. Such a national health insurance system should be financed by a combination of employer-employee-shared payroll taxes and general tax revenues.

Welfare Reform—We should move toward replacement of our existing inadequate and wasteful system with a simplified system of income maintenance, substantially financed by the Federal Government. . . .

Civil and Political Rights—We seek ratification of the Equal Rights Amendment.

We support vigorous enforcement of voting rights legislation. . . .

We fully recognize the religious and ethical nature of the concerns which many Americans have on the subject of abortion. We feel, however, that it is undesirable to attempt to amend the U.S. Constitution to overturn the Supreme Court decision in this area.

Education—With increased Federal funds, it is possible to enhance educational opportunity by eliminating spending disparities within state borders.

Mandatory transportation of students beyond their neighborhoods for the purpose of desegregation remains a judicial tool of last resort for the purpose of achieving school desegregation.

States, Counties and Cities—The Democratic Party recognizes that a number of major, older cities—including the nation's largest city—have been forced to undertake even greater social responsibilities, which have resulted in unprecedented fiscal crises. There is a national interest in helping such cities in their present travail. . . .

Energy—We should narrow the gap between oil and natural gas prices. . . .

. . . the United States' coal production can and must be increased.

U.S. dependence on nuclear power should be kept to the minimum necessary to meet our needs.

Agriculture—We must continue and intensify efforts to expand agriculture and long-term markets abroad but, at the same time, we must prevent irresponsible and inflationary sales from the American granary to foreign purchasers.

Environmental Quality—A vigorous program with national minimum environmental standards fully implemented, recognizing basic regional differences, will insure that states and workers are not penalized by pursuing environmental programs.

International Relations—Defense policy and spending for military forces must be consistent with meeting the real security needs of the American people.

. . . pursuit of détente will require maintenance of a strong American military deterrent. . . .

The International Economy—We will support reform of the international monetary system to strengthen institutional means of coordinating national economic policies.

Defense Policy—Our strategic nuclear forces must provide a strong and credible deterrent to nuclear attack and nuclear blackmail. Our conventional forces must be strong enough to deter aggression in areas whose security is vital to our own.

. . . we believe we can reduce present defense spending by about $5 billion to $7 billion.

Middle East—We shall continue to seek a just and lasting peace in the Middle East. The cornerstone of our policy is a firm commitment to the independence and security of the State of Israel.

We will avoid efforts to impose on the region an externally devised formula for settlement. . . .

Asia—The Vietnam War has taught us the folly of becoming militarily involved where our vital interests were not at stake.

The Americas—We pledge support for a new Panama Canal treaty, which insures the interest of the United States in that waterway.

Africa—Our policy must be reformulated toward unequivocal and concrete support of majority rule in southern Africa.

Platform of the Republican Party

Excerpts

The Role of Government—We prefer local and state government to national government and decentralized national government wherever possible.

All steps must be taken to insure that unnecessary Federal agencies and programs are eliminated.

The Economy—We are proposing only actions that the nation can afford and are opposing excessive tinkering with an economic system that works better than any other in the world.

The No. 1 destroyer of jobs is inflation. It is, above all else, deficit spending by the Federal Government which erodes the purchasing power of the dollar.

Sound job creation can only be accomplished in the private sector of the economy. Americans must not be fooled into accepting government as the employer of last resort.

The Republican Party advocates a legislative policy to obtain a balanced Federal budget and reduced tax rates. We support economic and tax policies to insure the necessary job-producing expansion of our economy.

Social Programs—Fighting crime is—and should be—primarily a local responsibility.

We support the right of citizens to keep and bear arms. We oppose Federal registration of firearms.

We oppose forced busing to achieve a racial balance in our schools. Local communities wishing to conduct nonsectarian prayers in their public schools should be able to do so. We favor a Constitutional amendment to achieve this end.

Responsibility for education, particularly on the elementary and secondary levels, belongs to local communities and parents. Intrusion by the Federal Government must be avoided.

The Republican Party opposes compulsory national health insurance.

The way to end discrimination is not by resurrecting the much-discredited quota system.

The Republican Party reaffirms its support for the ratification of the Equal Rights Amendment.

The Republican Party favors a continuance of the public dialogue on abortion and supports the efforts of those who seek enactment of a Constitutional amendment to restore protection of the right to life of unborn children.

Union membership as a condition of employment [Section H(b) of the Taft-Hartley Act] should continue to be determined by the states.

We oppose federalizing the welfare system; local levels of government are most aware of the needs of their communities.

Federal, state and local government resources combined are not enough to solve our urban problems. The private sector must be the major participant.

Energy Policy—The Democrats propose to dismember the American oil industry. We oppose such divestiture of oil companies.

We totally oppose this [creating a national oil company] expensive, inefficient and wasteful intrusion into an area which is best handled by private enterprise.

Environment and Natural Resources—Public lands should not be closed to exploration for minerals or to mining without an overriding national interest.

The emphasis on environmental concerns must be brought into balance with the needs for industrial and economic growth so that we can continue to provide jobs for an ever-growing work force.

National Defense—Growing Soviet military power requires a period of sustained growth in our defense effort.

As a necessary component of our long-range strategy, we will produce and deploy the B-1 bomber.

The composition of the fleet must assure that no adversary will gain naval superiority.

The United States must have the best intelligence system in the world. We favor the creation of an independent oversight function by Congress.

Asia and the Pacific—The refusal of the Democrat-controlled Congress to give support to Presidential requests for military aid to Indochina brought about the collapse of South Vietnam, Cambodia and Laos.

American troops will never again be committed . . . without the clear purpose of achieving our stated diplomatic and military objectives.

While engaged in a normalization of relations with the People's Republic of China, we will continue to support the freedom and independence of our friend and ally, the Republic of Taiwan.

The Americas—In any talks with Panama, the United States negotiators on no way cede, dilute, forfeit, negotiate or transfer any rights, power, authority, jurisdiction, territory or property that are necessary for the protection and security of the United States and the Western Hemisphere.

The Middle East—Our policy must remain one of decisive support for the security and integrity of Israel.

We must continue our efforts to secure a just and durable peace for all nations in that complex region.

Africa—We support all forces which promote negotiated settlements and racial peace.

Our policy is to strengthen the forces of moderation, recognizing that solutions to African problems will not come quickly.

United States-Soviet Relations—[We favor] trade in nonstrategic areas [but] we shall not permit the Soviet Union or others to determine our agricultural policies by irregular and unpredictable purchases.

[We] will work on the basis of strict reciprocity toward new agreements which will help achieve peace and stability.

International Cooperation—We favor an extension of the territorial sea from 3 to 12 miles and a 200-mile economic zone in which coastal states would have exclusive exploratory rights.

We condemn illegal corporate payments made at home and abroad.

The Republican Party will cooperate fully in strengthening the international trade and monetary system.

Presidential Election of 1976

Source: The Associated Press.

PRINCIPAL CANDIDATES FOR PRESIDENT AND VICE PRESIDENT

Democratic—Jimmy Carter; Walter F. Mondale.

Republican—Gerald R. Ford; Robert J. Dole.

State	Total	Carter Dem.	Ford Rep.	Plurality	Electoral vote R	Electoral vote D	Votes at 1976 Natl. Convs. Dem.	Rep.
Alabama	1,140,119	644,375	495,744	148,631 D		9	35	37
Alaska	62,002	22,994	39,008	16,014 R	3		10	19
Arizona	712,081	294,668	417,413	122,745 R	6		25	29
Arkansas	762,622	495,909	266,713	229,196 D		6	26	27
California	7,540,017	3,709,815	3,837,202	127,387 R	45		280	167
Colorado	1,013,370	447,006	566,364	119,358 R	7		35	31
Connecticut	1,353,424	641,010	712,414	71,404 R	8		51	35
Delaware	232,536	122,610	109,926	12,684 D		3	12	17
D.C.	152,746	127,562	25,184	102,378 D		3	17	14
Florida	2,936,679	1,561,383	1,375,296	186,087 D		17	81	66
Georgia	1,420,765	951,636	469,129	482,507 D		12	50	48
Hawaii	287,378	147,375	140,003	7,372 D		4	17	19
Idaho	330,049	126,175	203,874	77,699 R	4		16	21
Illinois	4,537,229	2,218,056	2,319,173	101,117 R	26		169	101
Indiana	2,169,606	1,002,936	1,166,670	163,734 R	13		75	54
Iowa	1,250,565	618,898	631,667	12,769 R	8		47	36
Kansas	930,762	429,003	501,759	72,756 R	7		34	34
Kentucky	1,133,581	609,410	524,171	85,239 D		9	46	37
Louisiana	1,289,716	683,512	606,204	77,380 D		10	41	41
Maine	465,717	231,283	234,434	3,151 R	4		20	20
Maryland	1,384,598	735,618	648,980	86,638 D		10	53	43
Massachusetts	2,395,799	1,391,201	1,004,598	386,603 D		14	104	43
Michigan	3,522,924	1,667,000	1,855,924	188,924 R	21		133	84
Minnesota	1,844,885	1,067,536	817,349	250,187 D		10	65	42
Mississippi	733,359	372,448	360,911	11,537 D		7	24	30
Missouri	1,901,316	984,413	916,903	67,510 D		12	71	49
Montana	315,599	146,291	169,308	23,017 R	4		17	20
Nebraska	579,888	230,152	349,736	119,584 R	5		23	25
Nevada	192,809	92,023	100,786	8.763 R	3		11	18
New Hampshire	333,090	147,618	185,472	37,854 R	4		17	21
New Jersey	2,898,526	1,420,668	1,477,858	57,190 R	17		108	67
New Mexico	406,943	199,225	207,718	8,493 R	4		18	21
New York	6,397,360	3,336,665	3,060,695	275,970 D		41	274	154
North Carolina	1,657,712	921,110	736,602	184,508 D		13	61	54
North Dakota	276,884	130,325	146,559	16,234 R	3		13	18
Ohio	3,992,416	2,000,001	1,992,415	7,585 D		25	152	97
Oklahoma	1,068,709	528,761	539,948	11,187 R	8		37	36
Oregon[1]	963,974	481,881	482,093	212 R	6		34	30
Pennsylvania	4,502,522	2,315,494	2,187,038	128,456 D		27	178	103
Rhode Island	389,129	216,991	172,138	44,853 D		4	22	19
South Carolina	786,310	443,901	342,409	101,492 D		8	31	36
South Dakota	297,772	146,153	151,619	5,466 R	4		17	20
Tennessee	1,464,325	821,594	632,731	188,863 D		10	46	43
Texas	3,907,878	2,031,562	1,876,316	155,246 D		26	130	100
Utah	516,118	180,974	335,144	154,170 R	4		18	20
Vermont	176,728	77,746	98,982	21,236 R	3		12	18
Virginia	1,645,178	810,636	834,542	23,906 R	12		54	51
Washington	1,322,964	643,333	679,631	36,298 R	9		53	38
West Virginia	741,416	430,404	311,012	118,988 D		6	33	28
Wisconsin	2,040,095	1,037,056	1,003,039	34,017 D		11	68	45
Wyoming	155,098	62,267	92,831	30,564 R	3		10	17
TOTAL	78,603,842	40,173,854	38,429,988	1,743,866 D	241	297	3,008[2]	2,259[3]

[1] Final results subject to canvass.   [2] Includes 34 votes allocated to U.S. territories and Democrats abroad.   [3] Includes 16 votes allocated to U.S. territories. NOTE: Figures are 99% complete.

OTHER CANDIDATES FOR PRESIDENT: Eugene J. McCarthy, Independent, 644,634; Lester G. Maddox, American Independent Party, 166,959; Tom Anderson, American Party; Gus Hall, Communist Party; Peter Camejo, Socialist Workers Party; Lyndon H. LaRouche, Jr., United States Labor Party; Roger L. MacBride, Free Libertarian Party; Julius Levin, Socialist Labor Party; Benjamin Bubar, Prohibitionist Party; Margaret Wright, People's Party.

Presidential Election Results, 1964-1972

	1964		1968			1972		
	Johnson	Goldwater	Nixon	Humphrey	Wallace	Nixon	McGovern	Schmitz
Popular vote . .	43,129,484	27,178,188	31,785,480	31,275,166	9,906,473	47,169,911	29,170,383	1,099,482
% of vote . . .	61.1	38.5	43.4	42.7	13.5	60.7	37.5	1.4
Electoral vote . .	486	52	301	191	46	520	17	0

Electoral Vote and Popular Vote Since 1920

Year	President Elected	Popular Vote	Electoral Vote	Losing Candidate	Popular Vote	Electoral Vote
1920[1]	Harding (R)	16,152,200	404	Cox (D)	9,147,353	127
1924	Coolidge (R)	15,725,016	382	Davis (D)	8,385,586	136
				LaFollette (PR)	4,822,856	13
1928	Hoover (R)	21,392,190	444	Smith (D)	15,016,443	87
1932	Roosevelt (D)	22,821,857	472	Hoover (R)	15,761,841	59
				Thomas (Soc.)	884,781	0
1936	Roosevelt (D)	27,751,597	523	Landon (R)	16,679,583	8
1940	Roosevelt (D)	27,243,466	449	Willkie (R)	22,304,755	82
1944[2]	Roosevelt (D)	25,602,505	432	Dewey (R)	22,006,278	99
1948	Truman (D)	24,105,812	303	Dewey (R)	21,970,065	189
				Thurmond (SR)	1,169,021	39
				Wallace (PR)	1,157,172	0
1952	Eisenhower (R)	33,936,252	442	Stevenson (D)	27,314,992	89
1956[3]	Eisenhower (R)	35,585,316	457	Stevenson (D)	26,031,322	73
1960[4]	Kennedy (D)	34,227,096	303	Nixon (R)	34,108,546	219
1964	Johnson (D)	43,126,506	486	Goldwater (R)	27,176,799	52
1968	Nixon (R)	31,783,783	301	Humphrey (D)	31,271,839	191
				Wallace (AI)	9,899,557	46
1972[5]	Nixon (R)	47,169,911	520	McGovern (D)	29,170,383	17
				Schmitz (Am)	1,099,482	0

[1] President Harding died at San Francisco, Calif., Aug. 2, 1923, and was succeeded by Vice President Coolidge. [2] President Roosevelt died at Warm Springs, Ga., on April 12, 1945, and was succeeded by Vice President Truman. [3] Democrats elected 74 electors, but one from Alabama who refused to vote for Stevenson voted for Walter B. Jones. [4] Sen. Harry F. Byrd received 15 electoral votes. President Kennedy was shot and fatally wounded by an assassin Nov. 22, 1963, in Dallas, Texas; he was succeeded by Lyndon B. Johnson. [5] Nixon resigned Aug. 9, 1974, and was succeeded by Gerald R. Ford.

Voting by Groups in Presidential Elections, 1956-1972
(by percentages)

Group	1956		1960		1964		1968			1972	
	Stevenson	Eisenhower	Kennedy	Nixon	Johnson	Goldwater	Humphrey	Nixon	Wallace	McGovern	Nixon
Men	45	55	52	48	60	40	41	43	16	37	63
Women	39	61	49	51	62	38	45	43	12	38	62
White	41	59	49	51	59	41	38	47	15	32	68
Non-white	61	39	68	32	94	6	85	12	3	87	13
College	31	69	39	61	52	48	37	54	9	37	63
High School	42	58	52	48	62	38	42	43	15	34	66
Grade School	50	50	55	45	66	34	52	33	15	49	51
Prof. & Bus.	32	68	42	58	54	46	34	56	10	31	69
White Collar	37	63	48	52	57	43	41	47	12	36	64
Manual	50	50	60	40	71	29	50	35	15	43	57
Under 30	43	57	54	46	64	36	47	38	15	48	52
30-49 years	45	55	54	46	63	37	44	41	15	33	67
50 years & older	39	61	46	54	59	41	41	47	12	36	64
Protestant	37	63	38	62	55	45	35	49	16	30	70
Catholic	51	49	78	22	76	24	59	33	8	48	52
Republicans	4	96	5	95	20	80	9	86	5	5	95
Democrats	85	15	84	16	87	13	74	12	14	67	33
Independents	30	70	43	57	56	44	31	44	25	31	69
East	40	60	53	47	68	32	50	43	7	42	58
Midwest	41	59	48	52	61	39	44	47	9	40	60
South	49	51	51	49	52	48	31	36	33	29	71
West	43	57	49	51	60	40	44	49	7	41	59
NATIONAL	42.2	57.8	50.1	49.9	61.3	38.7	43.0	43.4	13.6	38	62

Percentage of Population Voting in Presidential Elections from 1920 to 1972

Election Year	Percent	Election Year	Percent
1920	44	1948	52
1924	44	1952	63
1928	52	1956	60
1932	53	1960	64
1936	57	1964	62
1940	59	1968	61
1944	54	1972	56

What Percentage of Women Voted the First Time and What Percentage of the Women Voted Since 1920

Election Year	Percentage	Election Year	Percentage
1920	26	1960	64
(no data available)		1964	61
1952	60	1968	61
1956	58		

Vote for Minority Parties in Presidential Elections from 1920 to 1972

Year	Candidate and (Party)	Votes
1920	Robert M. LaFollette (Pr.)	4,822,856
1932	Norman Thomas (Socialist)	884,781
1948	J. Strom Thurmond (Sr.)	1,169,021
	Henry A. Wallace (Pr.)	1,157,172
1968	George C. Wallace (Am. Ind.)	9,899,557
1972	John G. Schmitz (American)	1,099,482

Union Labor Vote in Presidential Elections
(in percent)

Election Year	Democrat	Republican
1936	80	20
1940	72	28
1944	72	28
1948	74[1]	26
1952	61	39
1956	57	43
1960	65	35
1964	73	27
1968[2]	56	29
1972	46	54

[1] Includes vote for Democratic, Progressive and States' Rights tickets. [2] 15 per cent cast votes for American Independent Party candidate George Wallace in 1968.

How Voters Classified Themselves Politically from 1940 to 1976
(in percent)

Date of Survey	Republican	Democrat	Independent
1976	22	45	33
1975	21	44	35
1974	23	47	30
1973	24	43	33
1972	28	43	29
1968	27	46	27
1967	27	42	31
1966	27	48	25
1964	25	53	22
1960	30	47	23
1950	33	45	22
1940	38	42	20

NOTE: The proportion who do not classify themselves in one of the three categories—ranging from 2 to 4 percent—has been excluded in each set of figures.

How Independents Voted from 1940 to 1972
(in percent)

Election Year	Republican	Democrat
1940	61	39
1944	62	38
1948	57[1]	43
1952	35	65
1956	30	70
1960	43	57
1964	56	44
1968[2]	31	44
1972	69	31

[1] Includes votes cast for States' Rights and Progressive parties. [2] Vote for George Wallace: 25 percent.

How Males and Females Voted
(in percent)
Males

Election Year	Democrat	Republican
1956	45	55
1960	52	48
1964	60	40
1968	41 16[1]	43
1972	37	63

Females

Election Year	Democrat	Republican
1956	39	61
1960	49	51
1964	62	38
1968	45 12[1]	43
1972	38	62

[1] Vote for Wallace.

How the Young and Old Voted
(in percent)
21-29 years

Election Year	Republican	Democrat
1936	32	68
1940	40	60
1944	42	58
1948	38	62[1]
1952	49	51
1956	43	57
1960	46	54
1964	46	54
1968	47	38 (15)[2]
1972	52	48

30-49 years

Election Year	Republican	Democrat
1936	35	65
1940	44	56
1944	47	53
1948	43	57[1]
1952	47	53
1956	45	55
1960	54	46
1964	63	37
1968	44	41 (15)[2]
1972	67	33

50 and older

Election Year	Republican	Democrat
1936	44	56
1940	49	51
1944	49	51
1948	50	50[1]
1952	39	61
1956	39	61
1960	46	54
1964	59	41
1968	41	47 (12)[2]
1972	64	36

[1] Includes Democratic, Progressive, and States' Rights votes.   [2] Wallace third party vote.

(Tables on pages 25-27 were compiled by the *American Institute of Public Opinion*.)

How 13 Southern States Voted in Presidential Elections, 1940-1972
(in percent)

	Democrat	Republican	States' Rights	Wallace
1940	73	27	. . .	. . .
1944	69	31	. . .	. . .
1948	53	30	17	. . .
1952	51	49	. . .	. . .
1956	49	51	. . .	. . .
1960	51	49	. . .	. . .
1964	52	48	. . .	. . .
1968	31	36	. . .	33
1972	29	71	. . .	. . .

The Vote of Public School, High School and College Graduates
(in percent)
College

Election Year	Republican	Democrat	Third Party
1952	66	34	–
1956	69	31	–
1960	61	39	–
1964	48	52	–
1968	54	37	9
1972	63	37	–

NOTE: College includes persons who have not graduated as well as graduates.

High School

1952	55	45	–
1956	58	42	–
1960	48	52	–
1964	38	62	–
1968	43	43	15
1972	66	34	–

Grade School

1952	48	52	–
1956	50	50	–
1960	45	55	–
1964	34	66	–
1968	33	52	15
1972	51	49	–

Some Minority Political Parties

American Party: P.O. Box 1098, Pigeon Forge, Tenn. 37863. Chairman: Thomas J. Anderson.

Conservative Party of the State of New York: 468 Park Ave. South, New York, N.Y. 10016. Chairman: J. Daniel Mahoney; Executive Director: Serphin R. Maltese; Secretary: Barbara A. Keating; Treasurer: James E. Doherty.

Liberal Party of New York State: 1560 Broadway, New York, N.Y. 10036. Chairman: Donald S. Harrington; First Vice Chairman: David Dubinsky; Secretary and Executive Director: Ben Davidson; Treasurer: Bernice Benedick.

National States' Rights Party: P.O. Box 1211, Marietta, Ga. 30061. Chairman: J. B. Stoner; Secretary: Edward R. Fields; Treasurer: Peter Xavier.

Prohibition Party: P.O. Box 2635, Denver, Colo. 80201. National Chairman: Charles Wesley Ewing; Executive Secretary: Earl F. Dodge; National Secretary: Roger C. Storm.

Socialist Labor Party (in Minnesota, Industrial Government Party): 914 Industrial Ave., Palo Alto, Calif. 94303. National Secretary: Nathan Karp.

Characteristics of Voters in 1972 Presidential Election

(in millions)

Source: Bureau of the Census.

Characteristic	Persons of voting age	Persons reporting they voted		% reporting they did not vote	Characteristic	Persons of voting age	Persons reporting they voted		% reporting they did not vote
		Total	%				Total	%	
Male	63.8	40.9	64.1	35.9	Residence:				
Female	72.4	44.9	62.0	38.0	Metropolitan . . .	99.2	63.8	64.3	35.7
White	121.2	78.2	64.5	35.5	Nonmetropolitan .	37.0	22.0	59.4	40.6
Black	13.5	7.0	52.1	47.9	North and West . .	93.7	62.2	66.4	33.6
Age:					South	42.6	23.6	55.4	44.6
18–20 years . . .	11.0	5.3	48.3	51.7	Education:				
21–24 years . . .	13.6	6.9	50.7	49.3	8 years or less . .	28.1	13.3	47.4	52.6
25–34 years . . .	26.9	16.1	59.7	40.3	9–11 years	22.3	11.6	52.0	48.0
35–44 years . . .	22.2	14.7	66.3	33.7	12 years	50.7	33.2	65.4	34.6
45–64 years . . .	42.3	30.0	70.8	29.2	More than 12 years	35.1	27.7	78.8	21.2
65 years and over .	20.1	12.7	63.5	36.5	Employed	80.2	52.9	66.0	34.0
Median years . . .	42.4	44.9	(x)	(x)	Unemployed	3.7	1.9	49.9	50.1
					Not in labor force . .	52.3	31.0	59.3	40.7

Third Parties in U.S. Elections Since 1900

Party	Year and Candidate	Vote	Political Philosophy
Socialist	1900—Eugene V. Debs . . . . 1904 1908 1912 1920 1916—A.L. Benson . . . . . . 1928—Norman Thomas 1932 1936 1940 1944 1948	94,768 402,400 420,820 897,011 917,799 585,113 267,420 884,781 187,720 99,557 80,518 139,572	Public ownership of means of production; women suffrage; public works to relieve unemployment; social insurance programs; abolition of war.
Progressive[1] (Bull Moose)	1912—Theodore Roosevelt . . .	4,126,020	Direct primary, popular election of Senators; social insurance programs; wage and hours laws, recall of judicial decisions; federal supervision of business; government retention of all natural resources except agriculture.
Progressive[1]	1924—Robert M. LaFollette . .	4,822,856	Break-up of monopolies; return of naval oil reserves; public ownership of railroads and water power, abolition of power of Supreme Court to declare acts of Congress unconstitutional; right of labor to organize and bargain collectively; abolition of conscription and outlawing of war.
Progressive[1]	1948—Henry A. Wallace	1,157,326	Opposed to Truman's foreign policy; favored efforts to improve relations with Soviet Union and continuation of New Deal programs of social and economic reforms.
States' Rights (Dixiecrats)	1948—J. Strom Thurmond . . .	1,176,125	Opposed to federal civil rights program and to concentration of power in Washington.
American Independent	1968—George C. Wallace . . .	9,906,473	Anti-civil right program; opposed to federal intervention in racial matters and to growing power of federal bureaucracy.
American	1972—John G. Schmitz	1,099,482	(Same as for American Independent)

[1] Same name but totally different parties.

VOTE CAST FOR PRESIDENT, 1920 TO 1972, BY POLITICAL PARTIES

Prior to 1958, excludes Alaska and Hawaii. Includes vote cast for major party candidates endorsed by minor parties.

	CANDIDATES FOR PRESIDENT			VOTE CAST FOR PRESIDENT					
				Democratic			Republican		
YEAR	Democratic	Republican	Total popular vote [1]	Popular vote		Electoral vote	Popular vote		Electoral vote
				Number	Percent		Number	Percent	
1920	Cox	Harding	26,748	9,130	34.1	127	16,143	60.4	404
1924	Davis	Coolidge	29,086	8,385	28.8	136	15,718	54.0	382
1928	Smith	Hoover	36,812	15,016	40.8	87	21,392	58.1	444
1932	F. D. Roosevelt	Hoover	39,732	22,810	57.4	472	15,759	39.7	59
1936	F. D. Roosevelt	Landon	45,643	27,753	60.8	523	16,675	36.5	8
1940	F. D. Roosevelt	Willkie	49,900	27,313	54.7	449	22,348	44.8	82
1944	F. D. Roosevelt	Dewey	47,977	25,613	53.4	432	22,018	45.9	99
1948	Truman	Dewey	48,794	24,179	49.6	303	21,991	45.1	189
1952	Stevenson	Eisenhower	61,551	27,315	44.4	89	33,936	55.1	442
1956	Stevenson	Eisenhower	62,027	26,023	42.0	73	35,590	57.4	457
1960	Kennedy	Nixon	68,838	34,227	49.7	303	34,108	49.5	219
1964 [2]	Johnson	Goldwater	70,645	43,130	61.1	486	27,178	38.5	52
1968 [2]	Humphrey	Nixon	73,212	31,275	42.7	191	31,785	43.4	301
1972 [2]	McGovern	Nixon	77,719	29,170	37.5	17	47,170	60.7	520

[1] Includes votes for minor party candidates, independents, unpledged electors, and scattered write-in votes.
[2] Includes District of Columbia.

BLACK ELECTED OFFICIALS, BY OFFICE, 1969 TO 1975, AND BY REGION AND STATES, 1975

As of April, except as indicated. Five States had no Black elected officials in 1975; Hawaii, North Dakota, South Dakota, Utah, and Vermont.

YEAR, REGION, AND STATE	Total	U.S. and State legislatures [1]	City and county offices [1]	Law enforcement [2]	Education [3]	STATE	Total	U.S. and State legislatures	City and county offices [1]	Law enforcement [2]	Education [3]
1969	1,185	(NA)	(NA)	(NA)	(NA)	Kans	35	6	16	1	12
1970 (Feb.)	1,472	182	715	213	362	Ky	59	3	39	7	10
1971 (Mar.)	1,860	216	905	274	465	La	237	9	114	34	80
1972 (Mar.)	2,264	224	1,108	263	669	Maine	4	1	2	–	1
1973	2,621	256	1,264	334	767	Md	83	[5] 20	50	8	5
1974	2,991	256	1,602	340	793	Mass	24	[7] 9	9	–	6
						Mich	223	[6] 18	99	25	81
1975	3,503	299	1,878	387	939	Minn	8	2	1	3	2
						Miss	192	1	111	41	39
Northeast	503	56	179	74	194	Mo	113	[5] 16	65	15	17
North Central	869	87	476	85	221	Mont	1	1	–	–	–
South	1,913	129	1,142	198	444	Nebr	4	1	1	–	2
West	218	27	81	30	80	Nev	7	3	1	1	2
						N.H	1	1	–	–	–
Ala	161	15	75	51	20	N.J	142	7	67	–	68
Alaska	5	1	1	–	3	N. Mex	3	1	2	–	–
Ariz	17	2	5	1	9	N.Y	159	[6] 16	28	27	88
Ark	171	4	101	1	65	N.C	194	6	137	5	46
Calif	147	[4] 12	57	18	60	Ohio	146	[5] 12	94	13	27
						Okla	68	4	43	1	20
Colo	15	4	6	4	1	Oreg	6	1	1	2	2
Conn	48	6	29	4	9	Pa	122	[5] 15	42	43	22
Del	14	3	9	–	2	R.I	3	1	2	–	–
D.C	20	[5] 1	12	–	7	S.C	132	13	78	15	26
Fla	87	3	70	6	8	Tenn	96	[5] 12	70	6	8
						Tex	150	[5] 10	61	9	70
Ga	168	[5] 22	101	8	37	Va	64	2	59	3	–
Idaho	1	–	1	–	–						
Ill	246	[6] 21	145	16	64	Wash	15	2	7	4	2
Ind	66	6	44	10	6	W. Va	17	1	12	3	1
Iowa	13	2	4	1	6	Wis	15	3	7	1	4
						Wyo	1	1	–	–	1

NA Not available. — Represents zero. [1] County commissioners and councilmen, mayors, vice mayors, aldermen, and other. [2] Judges, magistrates, constables, marshals, sheriffs, justices of the peace, other. [3] College boards, school boards, other. [4] Includes 3 U.S. Representatives. [5] Includes 1 U.S. Representative. [6] Includes 2 U.S. Representatives. [7] Includes 1 U.S. Senator. Source: Joint Center for Political Studies, Washington, D.C., *National Roster of Black Elected Officials*, annual.

Election Campaign Costs for National Offices: 1972

Covers some prenomination expenditures. Data are provided by the U.S. General Accounting Office, Office of Federal Elections (O.F.E.), newly created to administer the Federal Elections Campaign Act of 1971, effective as of April 7, 1972. Previously, only committees operating in two or more States were required to report receipts and expenditures. In 1968 there were 222 such committees, not all of which contributed to a presidential campaign. The new requirement of comprehensive disclosure resulted in 1,785 committees filing reports with the O.F.E. in 1972, all of which contributed in some way, but not exclusively to a presidential candidate. Except for Congressional spending, all other figures are from the O.F.E.

ITEM	1972	ITEM	1972
Campaign costs .... mil. dol..	225. 2	Republican committees: [1]	
		Number reporting	418
National spending (includes Presidential and		Spending .... mil. dol..	69.3
Party) .... mil. dol..	137. 3	Percent of national spending	50. 3
Congressional spending .... mil. dol..	87. 9	Third party committees: [1]	
		Number reporting	57
Democratic committees: [1]		Spending .... mil. dol..	1. 2
Number reporting	1, 048	Percent of national spending	0. 9
Spending .... mil. dol..	66. 8	Miscellaneous committees: [2]	
Percent of national spending	48. 6	Number reporting	262
		Spending (direct disbursements) ...mil. dol..	8. 0
		Percent of national spending	5. 7

[1] Excluding Congressional.   [2] Includes labor, business, and professional, and ideological committees.
Source: Citizens' Research Foundation, Princeton, N.J., unpublished data.

Expenditures for Political Broadcasts for Elections, by Medium and Party: 1960 to 1972

In thousands of dollars. Represents media charges before commissions and after discounts, except 1970 represents charges after both commissions and discounts.

MEDIUM AND PARTY	GENERAL ELECTION		ELECTIONS, 1968		ELECTIONS, 1970		ELECTIONS, 1972 [1]	
	1960	1964	General	Primary	General	Primary	General	Primary
Total..........	14,195	24,604	40,403	18,485	33,051	17,558	38,127	21,513
Republican..........	7,559	13,033	22,505	5,355	16,716	5,135	17,521	3,238
Democratic..........	6,205	11,013	15,448	12,418	14,385	11,709	17,506	16,908
Other..........	431	559	2,451	712	1,951	714	3,100	1,367
Television..........	10,052	17,496	27,087	10,891	21,633	10,254	24,567	12,641
Republican..........	5,431	9,431	15,183	3,521	11,143	3,219	11,619	1,824
Democratic..........	4,415	7,715	10,424	6,960	9,335	6,780	11,433	10,145
Other..........	206	350	1,480	409	1,154	255	1,515	672
Radio..........	4,143	7,108	13,316	7,594	11,419	7,304	13,510	8,849
Republican..........	2,128	3,601	7,322	1,834	5,573	1,916	5,879	1,411
Democratic..........	1,790	3,298	5,024	5,457	5,049	4,929	6,054	6,750
Other..........	225	209	970	303	797	459	1,577	688

[1] Includes cable television. Source: U.S. Federal Communications Commission, *Report of Political Broadcasting*, April 1961, July 1965, August 1969, June 1971, and March 1973.

Nonnetwork Expenditures for Political Broadcasts for Elections— States: 1968, 1970, and 1972

In thousands of dollars. See headnote, in table above.

STATE	1968	1970	1972	STATE	1968	1970	1972	STATE	1968	1970	1972
U.S...	49,315	50,292	51,437	Kans.....	589	544	880	N.C......	1,125	672	2,686
				Ky.......	412	77	541	N. Dak...	305	228	196
Ala.......	453	1,728	1,147	La.......	884	474	2,369	Ohio......	2,731	2,653	1,719
Alaska....	356	624	387	Maine.....	170	165	193	Okla......	670	726	747
Ariz....	448	448	439	Md........	467	962	366	Oreg......	1,190	414	592
Ark.......	986	1,191	684					Pa........	2,120	2,314	1,298
Calif......	5,031	5,405	3,339	Mass.....	600	1,552	886	R.I.......	414	385	491
Colo......	351	333	387	Mich.....	1,144	1,463	1,770	S.C.......	601	653	751
Conn.....	334	936	272	Minn.....	447	1,095	670	S. Dak....	223	222	322
Del.......	97	101	177	Miss......	63	62	601	Tenn.....	1,747	1,605	1,089
D.C......	427	99	100	Mo.......	2,420	937	2,005				
Fla.......	2,335	2,291	3,200	Mont.....	317	225	305	Tex.......	3,576	2,546	5,560
Ga.......	867	1,472	1,448	Nebr.....	315	318	321	Utah......	253	348	300
Hawaii....	555	675	356	Nev......	361	867	211	Vt........	69	272	86
Idaho.....	142	190	232	N.H......	161	80	265	Va........	299	410	544
Ill.......	2,765	2,066	3,563	N.J......	238	803	306	Wash.....	675	350	829
Ind.......	1,608	1,241	1,214	N. Mex...	313	346	406	W. Va.....	661	150	833
Iowa.....	772	382	638	N.Y......	3,874	5,974	2,529	Wis.......	2,281	990	1,099
								Wyo......	73	229	83

Source: U.S. Federal Communications Commission, *Report of Political Broadcasting, Primary and General Election Campaigns of 1968; Survey of Political Broadcasting, Primary and General Election Campaigns, 1970*; and *Report on Political Broadcasting and Cablecasting, Primary and General Election Campaigns of 1972.*

THE NINETY-FIFTH CONGRESS

Source: Congressional Directory

MEMBERS OF 94TH AND 95TH CONGRESSES

	94th Congress						95th Congress					
	Dem.	Rep.	Male	Female	White	Black & Other	Dem.	Rep.	Male	Female	White	Black & Other
Senate...........	68[1]	32[2]	100	0	97	3	62[1]	38	100	0	97	3
House	286[3]	145	412	19	415	16	289[4]	143[4]	417	18	419	16

[1] Includes one Independent (Byrd of Virginia). [2] Includes one Conservative-Republican (Buckley of New York). [3] Four vacancies caused by death. [4] Three seats undecided (Illinois, Texas and Washington).

THE SENATE

Senior Senator is listed first. Year of birth is in first column, period of service in the second. All terms are for six years and expire in January. Asterisk (*) denotes election or re-election in 1976.

ALABAMA
| 1899 | 1946–79 | John J. Sparkman, D |
| 1912 | 1969–81 | James B. Allen, D |

ALASKA
| 1923 | 1968–79 | Ted Stevens, R |
| 1930 | 1969–81 | Mike Gravel, D |

ARIZONA
| 1909 | 1969–81 | Barry Goldwater, R |
| 1937 | 1977–83* | Dennis DeConcini, D |

ARKANSAS
| 1896 | 1943–79 | John L. McClellan, D |
| 1925 | 1975–81 | Dale Bumpers, D |

CALIFORNIA
| 1914 | 1969–81 | Alan Cranston, D |
| 1906 | 1977–83* | S. I. Hayakawa, R |

COLORADO
| 1916 | 1973–79 | Floyd K. Haskell, D |
| 1937 | 1975–81 | Gary W. Hart, D |

CONNECTICUT
| 1910 | 1963–81 | Abraham A. Ribicoff, D |
| 1931 | 1971–83* | Lowell P. Weicker, Jr., R |

DELAWARE
| 1921 | 1971–83* | William V. Roth, Jr., R |
| 1942 | 1973–79 | Joseph R. Biden, Jr., D |

FLORIDA
| 1930 | 1971–83* | Lawton Chiles, D |
| 1928 | 1975–81 | Richard Stone, D |

GEORGIA
| 1913 | 1957–81 | Herman E. Talmadge, D |
| 1938 | 1973–79 | Sam Nunn, D |

HAWAII
| 1924 | 1963–81 | Daniel K. Inouye, D |
| 1916 | 1977–83* | Spark M. Matsunaga, D |

IDAHO
| 1924 | 1957–81 | Frank Church, D |
| 1924 | 1973–79 | James A. McClure, R |

ILLINOIS
| 1919 | 1967–79 | Charles H. Percy, R |
| 1930 | 1971–81 | Adlai E. Stevenson, D |

INDIANA
| 1928 | 1963–81 | Birch Bayh, D |
| 1932 | 1977–83* | Richard G. Lugar, R |

IOWA
| 1929 | 1973–79 | Richard G. Clark, D |
| 1932 | 1975–81 | John C. Culver, D |

KANSAS
| 1920 | 1962–79 | James B. Pearson, R |
| 1923 | 1969–81 | Robert Dole, R |

KENTUCKY
| 1926 | 1973–79 | Walter Huddleston, D |
| 1924 | 1975–81 | Wendell H. Ford, D |

LOUISIANA
| 1918 | 1948–81 | Russell B. Long, D |
| 1932 | 1973–79 | J. Bennett Johnston, Jr., D |

MAINE
| 1914 | 1959–83* | Edmund S. Muskie, D |
| 1924 | 1973–79 | William D. Hathaway, D |

MARYLAND
| 1922 | 1969–81 | Charles McC. Mathias, Jr., R |
| 1933 | 1977–83* | Paul S. Sarbanes, D |

MASSACHUSETTS
| 1932 | 1962–83* | Edward M. Kennedy, D |
| 1919 | 1967–79 | Edward W. Brooke, R |

MICHIGAN
| 1923 | 1966–79 | Robert P. Griffin, R[1] |
| 1938 | 1977–83* | Donald W. Riegle, Jr., D |

MINNESOTA
| 1911 | 1971–83* | Hubert H. Humphrey, D |
| | | (Vacant) |

MISSISSIPPI
| 1904 | 1943–79 | James O. Eastland, D |
| 1901 | 1947–83* | John C. Stennis, D |

MISSOURI
| 1929 | 1968–81 | Thomas F. Eagleton, D |
| 1936 | 1977–83 | John C. Danforth, R |

MONTANA
| 1911 | 1961–79 | Lee Metcalf, D |
| 1924 | 1977–83* | John Melcher, D |

NEBRASKA
| 1905 | 1955–79 | Carl T. Curtis, R |
| 1929 | 1977–83* | Edward Zorinsky, D |

NEVADA
| 1912 | 1959–83* | Howard W. Cannon, D |
| 1922 | 1975–81* | Paul D. Laxalt, R |

NEW HAMPSHIRE
| 1915 | 1962–79 | Thomas J. McIntyre, R |
| 1936 | 1975–81 | John A. Durkin, D |

[1] Assistant minority leader (whip).

		NEW JERSEY			**SOUTH DAKOTA**
1904	1955–79	Clifford P. Case, R	1922	1963–81	George McGovern, D
1919	1959–83*	Harrison A. Williams, Jr., D	1931	1973–79	James G. Abourezk, D

NEW MEXICO

					TENNESSEE
1932	1973–79	Pete V. Domenici, R	1925	1967–79	Howard H. Baker, Jr., R
1935	1977–83*	Harrison H. Schmitt, R	1931	1977–83*	James R. Sasser, D

NEW YORK

					TEXAS
1904	1957–81	Jacob K. Javits, R	1925	1961–79	John G. Tower, R
1927	1977–83*	Daniel P. Moynihan, D	1921	1971–83*	Lloyd M. Bentsen, D

NORTH CAROLINA

					UTAH
1921	1973–79	Jesse A. Helms, R	1932	1975–81	E. J. (Jake) Garn, R
1925	1975–81	Robert B. Morgan, D	1934	1977–83*	Orrin G. Hatch, R

NORTH DAKOTA

					VERMONT
1897	1945–81	Milton R. Young, R	1913	1971–83*	Robert T. Stafford, R
1921	1960–83*	Quentin N. Burdick, D	1940	1975–81*	Patrick J. Leahy, D

OHIO

					VIRGINIA
1921	1975–81	John H. Glenn, Jr., D	1914	1965–83*	Harry F. Byrd, Jr., I
1917	1977–83*	Howard M. Metzenbaum, D	1915	1973–79	William L. Scott, R

OKLAHOMA

					WASHINGTON
1921	1969–81	Henry L. Bellmon, R	1905	1944–81	Warren G. Magnuson, D
1919	1973–79	Dewey F. Bartlett, R	1912	1953–83*	Henry M. Jackson, D

OREGON

					WEST VIRGINIA
1922	1967–79	Mark O. Hatfield, R	1902	1958–79	Jennings Randolph, D
1932	1969–81	Bob Packwood, R	1918	1959–83*	Robert C. Byrd, D[1]

PENNSYLVANIA

					WISCONSIN
1926	1969–81	Richard S. Schweiker, R	1915	1957–83*	William Proxmire, D
1938	1977–83*	H. John Heinz III, R	1916	1963–81*	Gaylord Nelson, D

RHODE ISLAND

					WYOMING
1918	1961–79	Claiborne Pell, D	1912	1967–79	Clifford P. Hansen, R
1922	1977–83*	John H. Chafee, R	1933	1977–83*	Malcolm Wallop, R

SOUTH CAROLINA

1902	1956–79	Strom Thurmond, R
1922	1966–81	Ernest F. Hollings, D

[1] Assistant majority leader (whip).

THE HOUSE OF REPRESENTATIVES

The numerals indicate the Congressional Districts of the states; the designation AL means At-Large. An asterisk (*) indicates that the Representative was returned to office in the 1976 elections. The terms of all members of the House end January 1979.

ALABAMA
(7 Representatives)

1. Jack Edwards, R*
2. William L. Dickerson, R*
3. William Nichols, D*
4. Tom Bevill, D*
5. Ronnie G. Flippo, D
6. John H. Buchanan, Jr., R*
7. Walter Flowers, D*

(1 Representative)
AL Donald E. Young, R*

ARIZONA
(4 Representatives)

1. John J. Rhodes, R*[1]
2. Morris K. Udall, D*
3. Robert Stump, D
4. Tony Mason, D

ARKANSAS
(4 Representatives)

1. Bill Alexander, D*
2. Jim Guy Tucker, D

[1] Minority leader.

3. John P. Hammerschmidt, R*
4. Ray Thornton, D*

CALIFORNIA
(43 Representatives)

1. Harold T. Johnson, D*
2. Don H. Clausen, R*
3. John E. Moss, D*
4. Robert L. Leggett, D*
5. John L. Burton, D*
6. Phillip Burton, D*
7. George Miller, D*
8. Ronald V. Dellums, D*
9. Fortney H. Stark, Jr., D*
10. Don Edwards, D*
11. Leo J. Ryan, D*
12. Paul N. McCloskey, Jr., R*
13. Norman Y. Mineta, D*
14. John J. McFall, D*
15. B. F. Sisk, D*
16. Leon E. Panetta, D
17. John H. Krebs, D*
18. William M. Ketchum, R*
19. Robert J. Lagomarsino, R*
20. Barry M. Goldwater, Jr., R*
21. James C. Corman, D*

22. Carlos J. Moorhead, R*
23. Anthony C. Beilenson, D
24. Henry A. Waxman, D*
25. Edward R. Roybal, D*
26. John H. Rousselot, R*
27. Robert K. Dornan, R
28. Yvonne B. Burke, D*
29. Augustus F. Hawkins, D*
30. George E. Danielson, D*
31. Charles H. Wilson, D*
32. Glenn M. Anderson, D*
33. Del Clawson, R*
34. Mark W. Hannaford, D*
35. James F. Lloyd, D*
36. George E. Brown, Jr., D*
37. Shirley N. Pettis, R*
38. Jerry M. Patterson, D*
39. Charles E. Wiggins, R*
40. Robert E. Badham, R
41. Bob Wilson, R*
42. Lionel Van Deerlin, D*
43. Clair W. Burgener, R*

COLORADO
(5 Representatives)

1. Patricia Schroeder, D*

2. Timothy E. Wirth, D*
3. Frank E. Evans, D*
4. James P. Johnson, R*
5. William L. Armstrong, R*

CONNECTICUT
(6 Representatives)

1. William R. Cotter, D*
2. Christopher J. Dodd, D*
3. Robert N. Giaimo, D*
4. Stewart B. McKinney, R*
5. Ronald A. Sarasin, R*
6. Toby Moffett, D*

DELAWARE
(1 Representative)

AL Thomas B. Evans, Jr., R

FLORIDA
(15 Representatives)

1. Robert L. F. Sikes, D*
2. Don Fuqua, D*
3. Charles E. Bennett, D*
4. William V. Chappell, Jr., D*
5. Richard Kelly, R*
6. C. W. Bill Young, R*
7. Sam M. Gibbons, D*
8. Andrew P. Ireland, D
9. Louis Frey, Jr., R*
10. L. A. Bafalis, R*
11. Paul G. Rogers, D*
12. J. Herbert Burke, R*
13. William Lehman, D*
14. Claude D. Pepper, D*
15. Dante B. Fascell, D*

GEORGIA
(10 Representatives)

1. Ronald B. Ginn, D*
2. Dawson Mathis, D*
3. Jack T. Brinkley, D*
4. Elliott H. Levitas, D*
5. Andrew Young, D*
6. John J. Flynt, Jr., D*
7. Lawrence P. McDonald, D*
8. Billy Lee Evans, D
9. Edgar L. Jenkins, D
10. Douglas Barnard, D

HAWAII
(2 Representatives)

1. Cecil Heftel, D
2. Daniel Akaka, D

IDAHO
(2 Representatives)

1. Steven D. Symms, R*
2. George V. Hansen, R*

ILLINOIS
(24 Representatives)

1. Ralph H. Metcalfe, D*
2. Morgan F. Murphy, D*
3. Martin A. Russo, D*
4. Edward J. Derwinski, R*
5. John G. Fary, D*
6. Henry J. Hyde, R*

7. Cardiss Collins, D*
8. Dan Rostenkowski, D*
9. Sidney R. Yates, D*
10. Abner J. Mikva, D*[1]
10. Samuel H. Young, R[1]
11. Frank Annunzio, D*
12. Philip M. Crane, R*
13. Robert McClory, R*
14. John N. Erlenborn, R*
15. Tom Corcoran, R
16. John B. Anderson, R*
17. George M. O'Brien, R*
18. Robert H. Michel, R*
19. Tom Railsback, R*
20. Paul Findley, R*
21. Edward R. Madigan, R*
22. George E. Shipley, D*
23. Melvin Price, D*
24. Paul Simon, D*

INDIANA
(11 Representatives)

1. Adam Benjamin, Jr., D
2. Floyd J. Fithian, D*
3. John Brademas, D*
4. J. Danforth Quayle, R
5. Elwood H. Hillis, R*
6. David W. Evans, D*
7. John T. Myers, R*
8. David L. Cornwell, D
9. Lee H. Hamilton, D*
10. Philip R. Sharp, D*
11. Andrew Jacobs, Jr., D*

IOWA
(6 Representatives)

1. James A. S. Leach, R
2. Michael T. Blouin, D*
3. Charles E. Grassley, R*
4. Neal Smith, D*
5. Thomas R. Harkins, D*
6. Berkley W. Bedell, D*

KANSAS
(5 Representatives)

1. Keith G. Sebelius, R*
2. Martha E. Keys, D*
3. Larry Winn, Jr., R*
4. Dan Glickman, D
5. Joe Skubitz, R*

KENTUCKY
(7 Representatives)

1. Carroll Hubbard, Jr., D*
2. William H. Natcher, D*
3. Romano L. Mazzoli, D*
4. M. G. (Gene) Snyder, R*
5. Tim Lee Carter, R*
6. John B. Breckinridge, D*
7. Carl D. Perkins, D*

LOUISIANA
(8 Representatives)

1. Richard E. Tonry, D
2. Corinne (Lindy) Boggs, D*
3. David C. Treen, R*
4. Joe D. Waggonner, Jr., D*
5. Jerry Huckaby, D
6. W. Henson Moore, D*
7. John B. Breaux, D*
8. Gillis W. Long, D*

MAINE
(2 Representatives)

1. David F. Emery, R*
2. William S. Cohen, R*

MARYLAND
(8 Representatives)

1. Robert E. Bauman, R*
2. Clarence D. Long, D*
3. Barbara A. Mikulski, D
4. Marjorie S. Holt, R*
5. Gladys N. Spellman, D*
6. Goodloe E. Byron, D*
7. Parren J. Mitchell, D*
8. Newton Steers, R

MASSACHUSETTS
(12 Representatives)

1. Silvio O. Conte, R*
2. Edward P. Boland, D*
3. Joseph D. Early, D*
4. Robert F. Drinan, D*
5. Paul E. Tsongas, D*
6. Michael J. Harrington, D*
7. Edward J. Markey, D
8. Thomas P. O'Neill, Jr., D*[2]
9. John J. Moakley, D*
10. Margaret M. Heckler, R*
11. James A. Burke, D*
12. Gerry E. Studds, D*

MICHIGAN
(19 Representatives)

1. John Conyers, Jr., D*
2. Edward C. Pierce, D
3. Garry Brown, R
4. David A. Stockman, R
5. Richard F. Vander Veen, D*
6. M. Robert Carr, D*
7. Dale E. Kildee, D
8. Bob Traxler, D*
9. Guy Vander Jagt, R*
10. Elford A. Cederberg, R*
11. Philip E. Ruppe, R*
12. David E. Bonior, D
13. Charles C. Diggs, Jr., D*
14. Lucien N. Nedzi, D*
15. William D. Ford, D*
16. John D. Dingell, D*
17. William M. Brodhead, D*
18. James J. Blanchard, D*
19. William S. Broomfield, R*

MINNESOTA
(8 Representatives)

1. Albert H. Quie, R*
2. Thomas M. Hagedorn, R*
3. Bill Frenzel, R*
4. Bruce F. Vento, D
5. Donald M. Fraser, D*
6. Richard M. Nolan, D*
7. Bob S. Bergland, D*
8. James L. Oberstar, D*

MISSISSIPPI
(5 Representatives)

1. Jamie L. Whitten, D*
2. David R. Bowen, D*
3. G. V. (Sonny) Montgomery, D*

[2] Majority leader.

4. Thad Cochran, R*
5. Trent Lott, R*

MISSOURI
(10 Representatives)
1. William L. Clay, D*
2. Robert A. Young, D
3. Richard A. Gephardt, D
4. Ike Skelton, D
5. Richard Bolling, D*
6. E. Thomas Coleman, R
7. Gene Taylor, R*
8. Richard H. Ichord, D*
9. Harold L. Volkmer, D
10. Bill D. Burlison, D*

MONTANA
(2 Representatives)
1. Max Baucus, D*
2. Thomas E. Towe, D

NEBRASKA
(3 Representatives)
1. Charles Thone, R*
2. John J. Cavanaugh, D
3. Virginia Smith, R*

NEVADA
(1 Representative)
AL James D. Santini, D*

NEW HAMPSHIRE
(2 Representatives)
1. Norman E. D'Amours, D*
2. James C. Cleveland, R*

NEW JERSEY
(15 Representatives)
1. James J. Florio, D*
2. William J. Hughes, D*
3. James J. Howard, D*
4. Frank Thompson, Jr., D*
5. Millicent Fenwick, R*
6. Edwin B. Forsythe, R*
7. Andrew Maguire, D*
8. Robert A. Roe, D*
9. Harold C. Hollenbeck, R
10. Peter W. Rodino, Jr., D*
11. Joseph G. Minish, D*
12. Matthew J. Rinaldo, R*
13. Helen S. Meyner, D*
14. Joseph A. LeFante, D
15. Edward J. Patten, D*

NEW MEXICO
(2 Representatives)
1. Manuel Lujan, Jr., R*
2. Harold Runnels, D*

NEW YORK
(39 Representatives)
1. Otis G. Pike, D*
2. Thomas J. Downey, D*
3. Jerome A. Ambro, D*
4. Norman F. Lent, R*
5. John W. Wydler, R*
6. Lester L. Wolff, D*
7. Joseph P. Addabbo, D*
8. Benjamin S. Rosenthal, D*
9. James J. Delaney, D*

10. Mario Biaggi, D*
11. James H. Scheuer, D*
12. Shirley Chisholm, D*
13. Stephen J. Solarz, D*
14. Frederick W. Richmond, D*
15. Leo C. Zeferetti, D*
16. Elizabeth Holtzman, D*
17. John M. Murphy, D*
18. Edward I. Koch, D*
19. Charles B. Rangel, D*
20. Theodore S. Weiss, D
21. Herman Badillo, D*
22. Jonathan B. Bingham, D*
23. Bruce F. Caputo, R
24. Richard L. Ottinger, D*
25. Hamilton Fish, Jr., R*
26. Benjamin A. Gilman, R*
27. Matthew F. McHugh, D*
28. Samuel S. Stratton, D*
29. Edward W. Pattison, D*
30. Robert C. McEwen, R*
31. Donald J. Mitchell, R*
32. James M. Hanley, D*
33. William F. Walsh, R*
34. Frank Horton, R*
35. Barber B. Conable, Jr., R*
36. John J. LaFalce, D*
37. Henry J. Nowak, D*
38. Jack F. Kemp, R*
39. Stanley N. Lundine, D*

NORTH CAROLINA
(11 Representatives)
1. Walter B. Jones, D*
2. L. H. Fountain, D*
3. Charles Whitley, D
4. Ike F. Andrews, D*
5. Stephen L. Neal, D*
6. Richardson Preyer, D*
7. Charles G. Rose III, D*
8. W. G. Hefner, D*
9. James G. Martin, R*
10. James T. Broyhill, R*
11. Lamar Gudger, D

NORTH DAKOTA
(1 Representative)
AL Mark Andrews, R*

OHIO
(23 Representatives)
1. Willis D. Gradison, Jr., R*
2. Thomas A. Luken, R
3. Charles W. Whalen, Jr., R*
4. Tennyson Guyer, R*
5. Delbert L. Latta, R*
6. William H. Harsha, R*
7. Clarence J. Brown, R*
8. Thomas N. Kindness, R*
9. Thomas L. Ashley, D*
10. Clarence E. Miller, R*
11. J. William Stanton, R*
12. Samuel L. Devine, R*
13. Donald J. Pease, D
14. John F. Seiberling, D*
15. Chalmers P. Wylie, R*
16. Ralph S. Regula, R*
17. John M. Ashbrook, R*
18. Douglas Applegate, D
19. Charles J. Carney, D
20. Mary Rose Oakar, D
21. Louis Stokes, D*

22. Charles A. Vanik, D*
23. Ronald M. Mottl, D*

OKLAHOMA
(6 Representatives)
1. James R. Jones, D*
2. Theodore M. Risenhoover, D*
3. Wes Watkins, D
4. Tom Steed, D*
5. Mickey Edwards, R
6. Glenn English, D*

OREGON
(4 Representatives)
1. Les AuCoin, D*
2. Al Ullman, D*
3. Robert B. Duncan, D*
4. James H. Weaver, D*

PENNSYLVANIA
(25 Representatives)
1. Michael (Ozzie) Myers, D
2. Robert N. C. Nix, D*
3. Raymond F. Lederer, D
4. Joshua Eilberg, D*
5. Richard T. Schulze, R*
6. Gus Yatron, D*
7. Robert W. Edgar, D*
8. Peter H. Kostmayer, D
9. E. G. (Bud) Shuster, R*
10. Joseph M. McDade, R*
11. Daniel J. Flood, D*
12. John P. Murtha, D*
13. R. Lawrence Coughlin, R*
14. William S. Moorhead, D*
15. Fred B. Rooney, D*
16. Robert S. Walker, R
17. Allen E. Ertel, D
18. Douglas Walgren, D
19. William F. Goodling, R*
20. Joseph M. Gaydos, D*
21. John H. Dent, D*
22. Austin J. Murphy, D
23. Joseph S. Ammerman, D
24. Marc Marks, R
25. Gary A. Myers, R*

RHODE ISLAND
(2 Representatives)
1. Fernand J. St. Germain, D*
2. Edward P. Beard, D*

SOUTH CAROLINA
(6 Representatives)
1. Mendel J. Davis, D*
2. Floyd Spence, R*
3. Butler C. Derrick, Jr., D*
4. James R. Mann, D*
5. Kenneth L. Holland, D*
6. John W. Jenrette, Jr., D*

SOUTH DAKOTA
(2 Representatives)
1. Larry L. Pressler, R*
2. James Abdnor, R*

TENNESSEE
(8 Representatives)
1. James H. Quillen, R*
2. John J. Duncan, R*

3. Marilyn L. Lloyd, D*
4. Albert Gore, Jr., D*
5. Clifford Allen, D*
6. Robin L. Beard, Jr., R*
7. Ed Jones, D*
8. Harold E. Ford, D*

TEXAS
(24 Representatives)

1. Sam B. Hall, D*
2. Charles Wilson, D*
3. James M. Collins, R*
4. Ray Roberts, D*
5. Jim Mattox, D
6. Olin E. Teague, D*
7. Bill Archer, R*
8. Bob Eckhardt, D*
9. Jack Brooks, D*
10. J. J. (Jake) Pickle, D*
11. W. R. Poage, D*
12. James C. Wright, Jr., D*
13. Jack E. Hightower, D*
14. John Young, D*
15. Eligio de la Garza, D*
16. Richard C. White, D*
17. Omar Burleson, D*
18. Barbara C. Jordan, D*
19. George H. Mahon, D*
20. Henry B. Gonzalez, D*
21. Robert C. Krueger, D*
22. Ron Paul, R*[1]
22. Robert Gammage, D[1]

23. Abraham Kazen, Jr., D*
24. Dale Milford, D*

UTAH
(2 Representatives)

1. K. Gunn McKay, D*
2. Dan Marriott, R

VERMONT
(1 Representative)

AL James M. Jeffords, R*

VIRGINIA
(10 Representatives)

1. Paul S. Trible, Jr., R
2. G. William Whitehurst, R*
3. David E. Satterfield III, D*
4. Robert W. Daniel, Jr., R*
5. W. C. (Dan) Daniel, D*
6. M. Caldwell Butler, R*
7. J. Kenneth Robinson, R*
8. Herbert E. Harris II, D*
9. William C. Wampler, R*
10. Joseph L. Fisher, D*

WASHINGTON
(7 Representatives)

1. Joel Pritchard, R*

2. Lloyd Meeds, D*[1]
2. John Nance Garner, R[1]
3. Don Bonker, D*
4. Mike McCormack, D*
5. Thomas S. Foley, D*
6. Norman D. Dicks, D
7. Brock Adams, D*

WEST VIRGINIA
(4 Representatives)

1. Robert H. Mollohan, D*
2. Harley O. Staggers, D*
3. John M. Slack, D*
4. Nick Joe Rahall, D

WISCONSIN
(9 Representatives)

1. Les Aspin, D*
2. Robert W. Kastenmeier, D*
3. Alvin J. Baldus, D*
4. Clement J. Zablocki, D*
5. Henry S. Reuss, D*
6. William A. Steiger, R*
7. David R. Obey, D*
8. Robert J. Cornell, D
9. Robert W. Kasten, Jr., R*

WYOMING
(1 Representative)

AL Teno Roncalio, D*

[1] Undecided at press time. NOTE: The District of Columbia is represented by a nonvoting delegate (Walter E. Fauntroy, D). Puerto Rico has a resident commissioner in the House.

The Governors of the Fifty States

Except where indicated, all terms begin in January. Asterisk (*) denotes winner in 1976 election.

State	Governor	Year of birth	Current term	State	Governor	Year of birth	Current term
Ala.	George C. Wallace, D.	1919	1975–79	Mont.	Thomas L. Judge, D	1934	1977–81*
Alaska	Jay S. Hammond, R	1922	1974–78[1]	Neb.	J. James Exon, D	1921	1975–79
Ariz.	Raul H. Castro, D	1916	1975–79	Nev.	Mike O'Callaghan, D	1930	1975–79
Ark.	David Pryor, D	1934	1977–79*	N.H.	Meldrim Thomson, Jr., R	1912	1977–79*
Calif.	Edmund G. Brown, Jr., D	1938	1975–79	N.J.	Brendan T. Byrne, D	1924	1974–78
Colo.	Richard D. Lamm, D	1935	1975–79	N.M.	Jerry Apodaca, D	1934	1975–79
Conn.	Ella T. Grasso, D	1919	1975–79	N.Y.	Hugh L. Carey, D	1919	1975–79
Del.	Pierre S. du Pont, IV, R	1935	1977–81*	N.C.	James B. Hunt, Jr., D	1937	1977–81*
Fla.	Reubin Askew, D	1928	1975–79	N.D.	Arthur A. Link, D	1914	1977–81*
Ga.	George Busbee, D	1927	1975–79	Ohio	James A. Rhodes, R	1909	1975–79
Hawaii	George R. Ariyoshi, D	1926	1974–78[1]	Okla.	David L. Boren, D	1941	1975–79
Idaho	Cecil D. Andrus, D	1932	1975–79	Ore.	Robert W. Straub, D	1920	1975–79
Ill.	James R. Thompson, R	1936	1977–81*	Pa.	Milton J. Shapp, D	1912	1975–79
Ind.	Otis R. Bowen, R	1918	1977–81*	R.I.	J. Joseph Garrahy, D	1931	1977–79*
Iowa	Robert D. Ray, R	1928	1975–79	S.C.	James B. Edwards, R	1927	1975–79
Kan.	Robert F. Bennett, R	1927	1975–79	S.D.	Richard F. Kneip, D	1933	1975–79
Ky.	Julian M. Carroll, D	1931	1975–79[1]	Tenn.	Ray Blanton, D	1930	1975–79
La.	Edwin W. Edwards, D	1927	1976–80[2]	Tex.	Dolph Briscoe, D	1923	1975–79
Me.	James B. Longley, I	1924	1975–79	Utah	Scott M. Matheson, D	1929	1977–81*
Md.	Marvin Mandel, D	1920	1975–79	Vt.	Stella B. Hackel, D	1927	1977–79*
Mass.	Michael S. Dukakis, D	1934	1975–79	Va.	Mills E. Godwin, R	1914	1974–78
Mich.	William G. Milliken, R	1922	1975–79	Wash.	Dixy Lee Ray, D	1914	1977–81*
Minn.	Wendell R. Anderson, D	1933	1975–79	W.Va.	John D. Rockefeller IV	1927	1977–81*
Miss.	Cliff Finch, D	1927	1976–80	Wis.	Patrick J. Lucey, D	1918	1975–79
Mo.	Joseph P. Teasdale, D	1936	1977–81*	Wyo.	Ed C. Herschler, D	1918	1975–79

[1] December.   [2] May.

CONGRESSIONAL STANDING COMMITTEES

Source: Congressional Directory.

(Based on organization of 94th Congress. Subject to changes when 95th Congress convenes in January 1977.)

Committees of the Senate

Aeronautical and Space Sciences (10 members):
Chairman: Frank E. Moss (Utah)[1]
Ranking Repub.: Barry Goldwater (Ariz.)

Agriculture and Forestry (14 members):
Chairman: Herman E. Talmadge (Ga.)
Ranking Repub.: Robert Dole (Kan.)

Appropriations (26 members):
Chairman: John L. McClellan (Ark.)
Ranking Repub.: Milton R. Young (N.D.)

Armed Services (16 members):
Chairman: John C. Stennis (Miss.)
Ranking Repub.: Strom Thurmond (S.C.)

Banking, Housing, and Urban Affairs (13 members):
Chairman: William Proxmire (Wis.)
Ranking Repub.: John G. Tower (Tex.)

Budget (16 members):
Chairman: Edmund S. Muskie (Me.)
Ranking Repub.: Henry Bellmon (Okla.)

Commerce (18 members):
Chairman: Warren G. Magnuson (Wash.)
Ranking Repub.: James B. Pearson (Kan.)

District of Columbia (7 members):
Chairman: Thomas F. Eagleton (Mo.)
Ranking Repub.: Charles McC. Mathias, Jr. (Md.)

Finance (18 members):
Chairman: Russell B. Long (La.)
Ranking Repub.: Carl T. Curtis (Neb.)

Foreign Relations (16 members):
Chairman: John Sparkman (Ala.)
Ranking Repub.: Clifford P. Case (N.J.)

Government Operations (14 members):
Chairman: Abraham A. Ribicoff (Conn.)
Ranking Repub.: Charles H. Percy (Ill.)

Interior and Insular Affairs (14 members):
Chairman: Henry M. Jackson (Wash.)
Ranking Repub.: Paul J. Fannin (Ariz.)[2]

Judiciary (15 members):
Chairman: James O. Eastland (Miss.)
Ranking Repub.: Roman L. Hruska (Neb.)[2]

Labor and Public Welfare (16 members):
Chairman: Harrison A. Williams, Jr. (N.J.)
Ranking Repub.: Jacob K. Javits (N.Y.)

Post Office and Civil Service (9 members):
Chairman: Gale W. McGee (Wyo.)[1]
Ranking Repub.: Hiram L. Fong (Hawaii)[2]

Public Works (14 members):
Chairman: Jennings Randolph (W. Va.)
Ranking Repub.: Howard H. Baker, Jr. (Tenn.)

Rules and Administration (9 members):
Chairman: Howard W. Cannon (Nev.)
Ranking Repub.: Mark O. Hatfield (Ore.)

Select Small Business (17 members):
Chairman: Gaylord Nelson (Wis.)
Ranking Repub.: Jacob K. Javits (N.Y.)

Veterans' Affairs (9 members):
Chairman: Vance Hartke (Ind.)[1]
Ranking Repub.: Clifford P. Hansen (Wyo.)

Committees of the House

Agriculture (43 members):
Chairman: Thomas S. Foley (Wash.)
Ranking Repub.: William C. Wampler (Va.)

Appropriations (55 members):
Chairman: George H. Mahon (Tex.)
Ranking Repub.: Elford A. Cederberg (Mich.)

Armed Services (40 members):
Chairman: Melvin Price (Ill.)
Ranking Repub.: Bob Wilson (Calif.)

Banking, Currency and Housing (43 members):
Chairman: Henry S. Reuss (Wis.)
Ranking Repub.: Albert W. Johnson (Pa.)[1]

Budget (25 members):
Chairman: Brock Adams (Wash.)
Ranking Repub.: Delbert L. Latta (Ohio)

District of Columbia (25 members):
Chairman: Charles C. Diggs, Jr. (Mich.)
Ranking Repub.: Gilbert Gude (Md.)[2]

Education and Labor (40 members):
Chairman: Carl D. Perkins (Ky.)
Ranking Repub.: Albert H. Quie (Minn.)

Government Operations (43 members):
Chairman: Jack Brooks (Tex.)
Ranking Repub.: Frank Horton (N.Y.)

House Administration (25 members):
Chairman: Frank Thompson, Jr. (N.J.)
Ranking Repub.: William L. Dickinson (Ala.)

Interior and Insular Affairs (43 members):
Chairman: James A. Haley (Fla.)[2]
Ranking Repub.: Joe Skubitz (Kan.)

International Relations (37 members):
Chairman: Thomas E. Morgan (Pa.)[2]
Ranking Repub.: William S. Broomfield (Mich.)

Interstate and Foreign Commerce (43 members):
Chairman: Harley O. Staggers (W.Va.)
Ranking Repub.: Samuel L. Devine (Ohio)

Judiciary (34 members):
Chairman: Peter W. Rodino, Jr. (N.J.)
Ranking Repub.: Edward Hutchinson (Mich.)[2]

Merchant Marine and Fisheries (40 members):
Chairman: Leonor K. Sullivan (Mo.)[2]
Ranking Repub.: Philip E. Ruppe (Mich.)

Post Office and Civil Service (28 members):
Chairman: David N. Henderson (N.C.)[2]
Ranking Repub.: Edward J. Derwinski (Ill.)

Public Works and Transportation (40 members):
Chairman: Robert E. Jones (Ala.)[2]
Ranking Repub.: William H. Harsha (Ohio)

Rules (16 members):
Chairman: Ray J. Madden (Ind.)[3]
Ranking Repub.: James H. Quillen (Tenn.)

Science and Technology (37 members):
Chairman: Olin E. Teague (Tex.)
Ranking Repub.: Charles A. Mosher (Ohio)[2]

Small Business (37 members):
Chairman: Joe L. Evins (Tenn.)[2]
Ranking Repub.: Silvio O. Conte (Mass.)

Standards of Official Conduct (12 members):
Chairman: John J. Flynt, Jr. (Ga.)
Ranking Repub.: Floyd D. Spence (S.C.)

Veterans' Affairs (28 members):
Chairman: Ray Roberts (Tex.)
Ranking Repub.: John Paul Hammerschmidt (Ark.)

Ways and Means (37 members):
Chairman: Al Ullman (Ore.)
Ranking Repub.: Herman T. Schneebeli (Pa.)[2]

[1] Defeated for re-election.   [2] Retired.   [3] Defeated in primary.

SPEAKERS OF THE HOUSE OF REPRESENTATIVES

Source: Congressional Directory.

Name and state	Congress	Dates served	Name and state	Congress	Dates served
Frederick A. C. Muhlenberg (Pa.)	1	1789–1791	Schuyler Colfax (Ind.)	38–40	1863–1869
Jonathan Trumbull (Conn.)	2	1791–1793	Theodore M. Pomeroy (N. Y.)[5]	40	1869–1869
Frederick A. C. Muhlenberg (Pa.)	3	1793–1795	James G. Blaine (Me.)	41–43	1869–1875
Jonathan Dayton (N. J.)[1]	4–5	1795–1799	Michael C. Kerr (Ind.)[6]	44	1875–1876
Theodore Sedgwick (Mass.)	6	1799–1801	Samuel J. Randall (Pa.)	44–46	1876–1881
Nathaniel Macon (N. C.)	7–9	1801–1807	J. Warren Keifer (Ohio)	47	1881–1883
Joseph B. Varnum (Mass.)	10–11	1807–1811	John G. Carlisle (Ky.)	48–50	1883–1889
Henry Clay (Ky.)[2]	12–13	1811–1814	Thomas B. Reed (Me.)	51	1889–1891
Langdon Cheves (S. C.)	13	1814–1815	Charles F. Crisp (Ga.)	52–53	1891–1895
Henry Clay (Ky.)[3]	14–16	1815–1820	Thomas B. Reed (Me.)	54–55	1895–1899
John W. Taylor (N. Y.)	16	1820–1821	David B. Henderson (Iowa)	56–57	1899–1903
Philip P. Barbour (Va.)	17	1821–1823	Joseph G. Cannon (Ill.)	58–61	1903–1911
Henry Clay (Ky.)	18	1823–1825	Champ Clark (Mo.)	62–65	1911–1919
John W. Taylor (N. Y.)	19	1825–1827	Frederick H. Gillett (Mass.)	66–68	1919–1925
Andrew Stevenson (Va.)[4]	20–23	1827–1834	Nicholas Longworth (Ohio)	69–71	1925–1931
John Bell (Tenn.)	23	1834–1835	John N. Garner (Tex.)	72	1931–1933
James K. Polk (Tenn.)	24–25	1835–1839	Henry T. Rainey (Ill.)[7]	73	1933–1934
Robert M. T. Hunter (Va.)	26	1839–1841	Joseph W. Byrns (Tenn.)[8]	74	1935–1936
John White (Ky.)	27	1841–1843	William B. Bankhead (Ala.)[9]	74–76	1936–1940
John W. Jones (Va.)	28	1843–1845	Sam Rayburn (Tex.)	76–79	1940–1947
John W. Davis (Ind.)	29	1845–1847	Joseph W. Martin, Jr. (Mass.)	80	1947–1949
Robert C. Winthrop (Mass.)	30	1847–1849	Sam Rayburn (Tex.)	81–82	1949–1953
Howell Cobb (Ga.)	31	1849–1851	Joseph W. Martin, Jr. (Mass.)	83	1953–1955
Linn Boyd (Ky.)	32–33	1851–1855	Sam Rayburn (Tex.)[10]	84–87	1955–1961
Nathaniel P. Banks (Mass.)	34	1855–1857	John W. McCormack (Mass.)[11]	87–91	1962–1971
James L. Orr (S. C.)	35	1857–1859	Carl Albert (Okla.)[12]	92–94	1971–1977
Wm. Pennington (N. J.)	36	1859–1861			
Galusha A. Grow (Pa.)	37	1861–1863			

[1] George Dent (Md.) was elected Speaker pro tempore for Apr. 20 and May 28, 1798. [2] Resigned during 2d session of 13th Congress. [3] Resigned between 1st and 2d sessions of 16th Congress. [4] Resigned during 1st session of 23d Congress. [5] Elected Speaker and served the day of adjournment. [6] Died between 1st and 2d sessions of 44th Congress. During 1st session, there were two Speakers pro tempore: Samuel S. Cox (N.Y.), appointed for Feb. 17, May 12 and June 19, 1876, and Milton Sayler (Ohio), appointed for June 4, 1876. [7] Died 1934 after adjournment of 2d session of 73rd Congress. [8] Died during 2d session of 74th Congress. [9] Died during 3d session of 76th Congress. [10] Died between 1st and 2d sessions of 87th Congress. [11] Not a candidate in 1970 election. [12] Not a candidate in 1976 election.

FLOOR LEADERS OF THE SENATE

Source: United States Senate, Secretary for the Majority.

Democratic

Thomas S. Martin (Va.): Maj. 1917–19.
Gilbert M. Hitchcock (Neb.): Min. 1919–20.
Oscar W. Underwood (Ala.): Min. 1920–23.
Joseph T. Robinson (Ark.): Min. 1923–33, Maj. 1933–37.
Alben W. Barkley (Ky.): Maj. 1937–46, Min. 1947–48.
Scott W. Lucas (Ill.): Maj. 1949–50.
Ernest W. McFarland (Ariz.): Maj. 1951–52.
Lyndon B. Johnson (Tex.): Min. 1953–54, Maj. 1955–60.
Mike Mansfield (Mont.): Maj. 1961–1977.

Republican

Henry Cabot Lodge (Mass.): Maj. 1919–24.
Charles Curtis (Kan.): Maj. 1925–29.
James E. Watson (Ind.): Maj. 1929–33.
Charles L. McNary (Ore.): Min. 1933–44.
Wallace H. White, Jr. (Me.): Min. 1944–47, Maj. 1947–48.
Kenneth S. Wherry (Neb.): Min. 1949–51.
Styles Bridges (N. H.): Min. 1951–52.
Robert A. Taft (Ohio): Maj. 1953.
William F. Knowland (Calif.): Maj. 1953–54, Min. 1955–58.
Everett M. Dirksen (Ill.): Min. 1959–69.
Hugh Scott (Pa.): Min. 1969–1977.

NOTE: Maj. stands for Majority Leader; Min. for Minority Leader.

National Committee Chairmen Since 1928

Chairman and (state)	Term	Chairman and (state)	Term
Republican		Robert Dole (Kan.)	1971–73
Hubert Work (Colo.)	1928–29	George H. Bush (Tex.)	1973–74
Claudius H. Houston (Tenn.)	1929–30	Mary Louise Smith (Iowa)	1974–
Simeon D. Fess (Ohio)	1930–32		
Everett Sanders (Ind.)	1932–34	**Democratic**	
Henry P. Fletcher (Pa.)	1934–36	John J. Raskob (N. Y.)	1928–32
John Hamilton (Kan.)	1936–40	James A. Farley (N. Y.)	1932–40
Joseph W. Martin, Jr. (Mass.)	1940–42	Edward J. Flynn (N. Y.)	1940–43
Harrison E. Spangler (Iowa)	1942–44	Frank C. Walker (Mont.)	1943–44
Herbert Brownell, Jr. (N. Y.)	1944–46	Robert E. Hannegan (Mo.)	1944–47
Carroll Reece (Tenn.)	1946–48	J. Howard McGrath (R. I.)	1947–49
Hugh D. Scott, Jr. (Pa.)	1948–49	William M. Boyle, Jr. (Mo.)	1949–51
Guy G. Gabrielson (N. J.)	1949–52	Frank E. McKinney (Ind.)	1951–52
Arthur E. Summerfield (Mich.)	1952–53	Stephen A. Mitchell (Ill.)	1952–54
Wesley Roberts (Kan.)	1953–53	Paul M. Butler (Ind.)	1955–60
Leonard W. Hall (N. Y.)	1953–57	Henry M. Jackson (Wash.)	1960–61
Meade Alcorn (Conn.)	1957–59	John M. Bailey (Conn.)	1961–68
Thruston B. Morton (Ky.)	1959–61	Lawrence F. O'Brien (Mass.)	1968–69
William E. Miller (N. Y.)	1961–64	Fred R. Harris (Okla.)	1969–70
Dean Burch (Ariz.)	1964–65	Lawrence F. O'Brien (Mass.)	1970–72
Ray C. Bliss (Ohio)	1965–69	Jean Westwood (Utah)	1972
Rogers C. B. Morton (Md.)	1969–71	Robert S. Strauss (Tex.)	1972–

Republican National Committee: 310 First St., SE., Washington, D. C. 20003.
Democratic National Committee: 2600 Virginia Ave., NW., Washington, D. C. 20037.

Voter Registration in the South

Source: Voter Education Project.

State	1975 White	1975 Black	1975 % Black	1969 White	1969 Black	1969 % Black	1960 White	1960 Black	1960 % Black
Alabama	1,485,574	307,112[1]	17.1	1,280,000	295,000	18.7	860,073	66,009	7.1
Arkansas	796,987	199,998[1]	20.0	694,000	150,000	17.8	517,897	72,604	12.3
Florida	3,118,535	355,555	9.8	2,465,000	315,000	11.3	1,819,342	183,197	9.1
Georgia	1,534,268	555,999[1]	26.5	1,590,000	370,000	18.9	1,020,000	180,000	15.0
Louisiana	1,338,368	392,628	22.6	1,123,000	313,000	21.8	993,118	159,033	14.0
Mississippi	865,670	285,879[1]	24.8	672,000	281,000	29.5	478,000	22,000	4.4
North Carolina	1,918,906	354,609	15.4	1,572,000	296,000	15.8	1,861,430	210,450	10.1
South Carolina	660,416	221,903	25.1	640,000	203,000	24.0	480,973	58,122	10.8
Tennessee	1,696,717	261,998[1]	13.3	1,637,000	289,000	15.0	1,300,000	185,000	12.5
Texas	4,251,708	609,998[1]	11.4	3,020,000	475,000	13.6	2,078,500	226,818	9.8
Virginia	1,761,811	288,998[1]	14.0	1,476,000	261,000	15.0	866,794	100,100	10.4
TOTALS	19,428,960	3,834,677	16.0	16,169,000	3,248,000	16.7	12,276,127	1,463,333	10.7

[1] Estimated.

Registration in the South, 1974

Group	All persons	Reported Registered	%	Reported voted	%[1]	Registered, didn't vote	%
White male: 18–34 years	6,948,000	3,356,000	48.3	1,794,000	25.8	1,562,000	47.0
35–64 years	8,188,000	5,870,000	71.7	3,998,000	48.8	1,872,000	32.0
65 and over	2,335,000	1,793,000	76.8	1,235,000	52.9	558,000	24.0
White female: 18–34 years	7,423,000	3,530,000	47.6	1,790,000	24.1	1,740,000	49.3
35–64 years	8,886,000	6,012,000	67.7	3,812,000	43.0	2,200,000	36.6
65 and over	3,295,000	2,050,000	62.2	1,221,000	37.1	829,000	40.4
Black male: 18–34 years	1,438,000	607,000	42.2	285,000	19.8	322,000	55.0
35–64 years	1,460,000	901,000	61.7	559,000	33.8	342,000	34.0
65 and over	432,000	285,000	66.0	145,000	33.6	140,000	49.1
Black female: 18–34 years	1,717,000	800,000	47.0	368,000	21.4	432,000	54.0
35–64 years	1,723,000	1,135,000	66.0	657,000	38.1	478,000	42.1
65 and over	630,000	381,000	60.3	204,000	32.4	177,000	46.6
TOTAL	44,475,000	26,720,000	60.0	16,068,000	36.0	10,652,000	39.0

[1] Percent of all persons.

U. S. National Conventions Since 1856

Opening date	Party	Where held	Presidential nominee	Vote
June 17, 1856	Republican	Philadelphia	John C. Frémont	520
June 2, 1856	Democratic	Cincinnati	James Buchanan	296
May 16, 1860	Republican	Chicago	Abraham Lincoln	364
April 23, 1860	Democratic	Charleston & Baltimore	S. A. Douglas	181
June 7, 1864	Republican [1]	Baltimore	Abraham Lincoln	Unanimous
Aug. 29, 1864	Democratic	Chicago	Geo. B. McClellan	202½
May 20, 1868	Republican	Chicago	U. S. Grant	Unanimous
July 4, 1868	Democratic	New York City	Horatio Seymour	Unanimous
June 5, 1872	Republican	Philadelphia	U. S. Grant	Unanimous
June 9, 1872	Democratic	Baltimore	Horace Greeley	688
June 14, 1876	Republican	Cincinnati	R. B. Hayes	384
June 28, 1876	Democratic	St. Louis	S. J. Tilden	508
June 2, 1880	Republican	Chicago	J. A. Garfield	399
June 23, 1880	Democratic	Cincinnati	W. S. Hancock	705
June 3, 1884	Republican	Chicago	J. G. Blaine	541
July 11, 1884	Democratic	Chicago	Grover Cleveland	683
June 19, 1888	Republican	Chicago	Benjamin Harrison	544
June 6, 1888	Democratic	St. Louis	Grover Cleveland	By acclamation
June 7, 1892	Republican	Minneapolis	Benjamin Harrison	535⅙
June 21, 1892	Democratic	Chicago	Grover Cleveland	617½
June 16, 1896	Republican	St. Louis	William McKinley	661½
July 7, 1896	Democratic	Chicago	William J. Bryan	500
June 19, 1900	Republican	Philadelphia	William McKinley	Unanimous
July 4, 1900	Democratic	Kansas City	William J. Bryan	By acclamation
June 21, 1904	Republican	Chicago	Theodore Roosevelt	Unanimous
July 6, 1904	Democratic	St. Louis	Alton B. Parker	678
June 16, 1908	Republican	Chicago	William H. Taft	702
July 7, 1908	Democratic	Denver	William J. Bryan	892½
June 18, 1912	Republican	Chicago	William H. Taft	561
June 25, 1912	Democratic	Baltimore	Woodrow Wilson	990
June 7, 1916	Republican	Chicago	Charles E. Hughes	949½
June 14, 1916	Democratic	St. Louis	Woodrow Wilson	By acclamation
June 8, 1920	Republican	Chicago	Warren G. Harding	692⅕
June 28, 1920	Democratic	San Francisco	James M. Cox	732½
June 10, 1924	Republican	Cleveland	Calvin Coolidge	1,065
June 24, 1924 [2]	Democratic	New York City	John W. Davis	839 [3]
June 12, 1928	Republican	Kansas City	Herbert Hoover	837
June 26, 1928	Democratic	Houston	Alfred E. Smith	849½
June 14, 1932	Republican	Chicago	Herbert Hoover	1,126½
June 27, 1932	Democratic	Chicago	F. D. Roosevelt	945
June 9, 1936	Republican	Cleveland	Alfred M. Landon	984
June 23, 1936	Democratic	Philadelphia	F. D. Roosevelt	By acclamation
June 24, 1940	Republican	Philadelphia	Wendell L. Willkie	Unanimous
July 15, 1940	Democratic	Chicago	F. D. Roosevelt	Unanimous
June 26, 1944	Republican	Chicago	Thomas E. Dewey	1,056
July 19, 1944	Democratic	Chicago	F. D. Roosevelt	1,086–90
June 21, 1948	Republican	Philadelphia	Thomas E. Dewey	1,094–0
July 12, 1948	Democratic	Philadelphia	Harry S. Truman	947½–263½
July 17, 1948	(4)	Birmingham	J. Strom Thurmond	By acclamation
July 22, 1948	Progressive	Philadelphia	Henry A. Wallace	By acclamation
July 7, 1952	Republican	Chicago	Dwight D. Eisenhower	845–361
July 21, 1952	Democratic	Chicago	Adlai E. Stevenson	By acclamation
Aug. 20, 1956	Republican	San Francisco	Dwight D. Eisenhower	Unanimous
Aug. 13, 1956	Democratic	Chicago	Adlai E. Stevenson	By acclamation
July 25, 1960	Republican	Chicago	Richard M. Nixon	Unanimous
July 11, 1960	Democratic	Los Angeles	John F. Kennedy	Unanimous
July 13, 1964	Republican	San Francisco	Barry M. Goldwater	Unanimous
Aug. 24, 1964	Democratic	Atlantic City	Lyndon B. Johnson	By acclamation
Aug. 5, 1968	Republican	Miami Beach	Richard M. Nixon	Unanimous
Aug. 26, 1968	Democratic	Chicago	Hubert H. Humphrey	Unanimous
July 10, 1972	Democratic	Miami Beach	George McGovern	1,618
Aug. 21, 1972	Republican	Miami Beach	Richard M. Nixon	1,347–1
July 12, 1976	Democratic	New York City	Jimmy Carter	2,238½–769½
Aug. 16, 1976	Republican	Kansas City, Mo.	Gerald R. Ford	1,187–1,070

[1] The Convention adopted name Union party to attract War Democrats and others favoring prosecution of war.   [2] In session until July 10, 1924.   [3] 103d ballot.   [4] States' Rights delegates from 13 Southern states. NOTE: For allocation of convention votes to states, 1960–72, see pages 556–59.

News Chronology of 1975–76

This News Chronology is topically arranged from November 1975 through mid-October 1976. Below is an alphabetical listing of the headings and the pages where they will be found.

Major Events—October 1976

1976 Nobel Prize Winners

For the first time, all winners have been citizens of the same country—the United States. The Peace Prize was not awarded in 1976.

Medicine—Baruch S. Blumberg, University of Pennsylvania Medical School, and D. Carleton Gajdusek, of the National Institute for Neurological Diseases, for discoveries about origin and spread of infectious diseases.

Economics—Milton Friedman, University of Chicago, for work on consumption analysis.

Physics—Burton Richter, of Stanford, and Samuel C.C. Ting, of M.I.T., for separate discoveries of subatomic particle.

Chemistry—William N. Liscomb, of Harvard, for work on the structure and bonding mechanisms of boranes.

Literature—Saul Bellow for "the human understanding and subtle analysis of contemporary culture that are combined in his work."

1 Federal judge issues temporary restraining order blocking restrictions on use of Medicaid funds for abortions. Restrictions later declared unconstitutional.

1 California law gives terminally ill persons the right to authorize the withdrawal of life-sustaining procedures.

1 Catholic bishop in Rhodesia sentenced to 10 years in prison for aid to guerrillas.

3 West German Social Democrats retain power with narrow margin in national election.

3 Secretary of Agriculture Earl L. Butz criticized for racial remarks; many leaders call for his resignation or dismissal. Butz resigns the next day.

3 International Monetary Fund and World Bank meet in Manila; wealthier nations asked to help solve world's poverty problems.

3 Antitrust Division of Justice Dept. calls for stiffer penalties, including jail sentences for criminal violators of the antitrust laws.

4 Supreme Court lifts stay on death penalties as it decides not to reconsider recent decision upholding the death penalty for murder.

5 Federal judge fines Allied Chemical $13,375,000 for dumping toxic insecticide Kepone into Virginia's James River.

5 Nuclear test in China ten days before results in radioactive fallout on East Coast of United States.

5 Ford Motor Co. reaches tentative accord with striking U.A.W.

5 Fear of renewed economic downturn leads to sharp drop in Dow-Jones industrial average to 966, a decline of 42 points in one week.

6 Military seizes power in Thailand after bloody battles with university students in which hundreds are killed and wounded; democratic rights are abolished.

6 Cuban jet plunges into sea near Barbados; all 78 persons aboard are killed.

7 Swedish research institute issues alarming report on the inevitability of nuclear war.

7 Hospital interns strike and police engage in illegal and disorderly demonstrations in labor dispute stemming from New York City's fiscal crisis.

8 Commerce Dept. announces that all demands for participation in the Arab boycott made on or after Oct. 7 will have to be made available for public scrutiny.

8 Prime Minister John Vorster rejects demand by black leaders for a multiracial convention to discuss South Africa's racial problems.

9 Peking wall posters state that Prime Minister Hua Kuo-feng has been chosen chairman of the Chinese Communist Party.

11 Guerrilla war continues in Spanish Sahara between Moroccan forces and Polisario independence movement backed by Algeria. Moroccan leaders say they are fighting an undeclared war with Algeria.

13 United Nations issues report of economists indicating that, by the year 2000, global resources could support growing populations and higher living standards without environmental damage.

13 New "independent" state of Transkei reveals its political complexion by arresting two well-known black actors for criticism of apartheid.

14 Peking embassies report rumors of the arrest of Chinese leftist officials, including Chiang Ch'ing, widow of Mao Tse-tung.

14 Swine flu immunizations are resumed after temporary suspension in many states because of the death of about 40 elderly persons who received the vaccine.

14 Martha Graham, American dancer and choreographer, receives Medal of Freedom, nation's highest civilian honor, from President Ford.

15 Prime Minister Fidel Castro of Cuba will renounce the anti-hijacking treaty with the United States in retaliation for alleged American complicity in the crash of a sabotaged Cuban airliner in the Caribbean the week before.

16 Saudi Arabia arranges cease-fire in Lebanon; sends plane to take P.L.O. leader Yasir Arafat to Arab meeting in Riyadh, Saudi Arabian capital.

16 Economists attribute slowdown in economic recovery to continued recession in most Western nations but predicts U.S. economic expansion in 1978.

18 New Lebanese peace plan signed by six Arab leaders in Saudi Arabia calls for cease-fire and supervision by large Arab force.

18 Experts predict substantial price increase in price of oil by O.P.E.C. in December.

19 Britain, United States and France veto U.N. resolution embargoing arms shipments to South Africa because of failure to give up control of Namibia.

19 Growth rate of U.S. economy down to 4% but housing starts reach highest level since Feb. 1974.

20 U.S. Information Agency poll in Western Europe indicates that American image is at lowest level in more than two decades.

22 Federal Home Loan Bank Board reports that average price for a new home is now $50,500 as compared with less than $30,000 a decade ago.

28 Geneva conference on Rhodesia opens with conflicting positions on the control of the transitional government outlined in Kissinger proposals.

31 At this late date, pollsters cannot forecast outcome of Presidential elections.

Chronology, 1975–76

Abroad

For detailed analyses of recent events in specific countries, *see* World History Section.

1975

NOV. 25 Surinam becomes independent of the Netherlands.

1976

JAN. 1 India accuses U.S. agents of "destabilization tactics" similar to those which led to the fall of the Allende government in Chile.

9 Death of Chou En-lai leads to speculation on a struggle for political power in China.

13 Japanese Prime Minister Takeo Miki ignores Soviet warnings; announces readiness to sign treaty with China, including provision opposing efforts of any third nation to achieve hegemony in Asia.

14 British government announces plans to grant some form of home rule to Scotland and Wales; Scottish Nationalist Party, stressing importance of offshore oil, demands greater economic autonomy.

29 European Socialists, meeting in Denmark, split on advisability of political links with Communists.

Lebanon

THROUGHOUT THE YEAR, there were desperate efforts to find a political common denominator acceptable to the clashing Lebanese religious, political and economic groups in order to end the long civil war with its frightful toll of 30,000 deaths. The war threatened to destroy the fragile fabric of the Moslem-Christian state, to exacerbate bitter inter-Arab rivalries and to create new areas of Arab-Israeli tension.

The basic issue was the disproportionate share of political power and wealth held by the minority Maronite Christian community. Moslem and leftist groups allied with Palestinian guerrillas in the country demanded a reorganization of the political structure which would reflect their majority status.

In January 1976, Syrian troops entered Lebanon to force the conflicting groups into a negotiated peace, while hoping to achieve a more significant role in the Arab world by controlling developments in the embattled country. Despite the election of a new compromise president, Elias Sarkis, the civil war continued unabated. The interventionists had not counted on the Palestine Liberation Organization and rivals in the rest of the Arab world. These rivalries account for the fact that, by mid-summer, Syria unexpectedly found itself the protector of Lebanon's Christian minority.

Yasir Arafat feared Syrian hegemony in Lebanon which might restrict the P.L.O.'s use of the country as a major base. This fear was supported by some Arab leaders who preferred a more radical Moslem state on Israel's borders.

The Syrians warned against the possibility of a secessionist Christian state which could become the focus of Israeli influence on their western flank and might even plunge Syria into an ill-timed war with Israel. Thus, in trying to stem the ascendancy of Moslem-Palestinian-leftist groups, the Syrians found themselves the protectors of the conservative minority.

Israel warned that their security and Middle East stability would be endangered if the war ended with Palestinian or Syrian control of Lebanon. But this potential danger was reduced by the fact that Syria seemed to have abandoned the goal of a Moslem-P.L.O. state ruled from Damascus.

Nineteen Arab League countries, in an effort to soften the bitterness created by the Syrian incursion, met in Cairo on June 10 and agreed to put a token peace-keeping force in Lebanon, consisting of troops from the Sudan, Saudi Arabia, Libya, Syria, Algeria and the P.L.O. The first units of the symbolic Arab force arrived in embattled Beirut on June 11 and the 39th cease-fire went into effect on June 22.

Both the United States and the Soviet Union, concerned with the possibility of a wider Middle East conflict, urged a negotiated settlement but, despite the cease-fire and Arab efforts to resolve the crisis, the war continued with heavy fighting taking place in Beirut. The assassination of U.S. Ambassador Francis E. Meloy, Jr., in Beirut on June 17 led to the evacuation of hundreds of American citizens by sea. On July 16, the American Embassy advised Americans that it would eliminate its consular service and urged all Americans to leave the country.

On July 28, the P.L.O. made a major concession by signing an agreement which accepted the continued presence of Syrian troops in Lebanon. But an anti-Egyptian clause condemning the Sinai disengagement agreement was a new source of Syrian-Egyptian-Libyan hostility and made an effective cease-fire and a political settlement of the civil war more distant than ever.

FEB. 8 Hua Kuo-feng succeeds Chou En-lai as Acting Prime Minister of China; observers see top-level dissension.

28 Soviet Party Congress hears calls for greater diversity in world communist movement. French leaders praise national or Euro- Communism, "socialism in the colors of France"; Italian leaders insist that, even with communists in the government, "Italy will remain in NATO."

28 Canadian Eskimos claim one-fifth of Canada as a province to be called Nunavut.

MAR. 7 South Vietnam's Foreign Minister reports severe economic problems necessitating some measure of private enterprise even after unification.

15 Egypt abrogates Soviet-Egyptian Treaty of Friendship and Cooperation; seeks support from the U.S.; Anwar el-Sadat's action denounced by Moscow.

Portugal

P ORTUGAL, one of Europe's underdeveloped countries, has been struggling to overcome economic and political stagnation, the heritage of 50 years of fascism. In 1975, the Portuguese Revolution seemed to be moving in the direction of a left-wing dictatorship, with agrarian reform and public ownership as the major items on the agenda.

In 1976, the political wheel turned to the right. The left-wing members of the Armed Forces Movement were ousted and more moderate and conservative forces came to the fore. Exiled António de Spinola, former President, confirmed the fact that he headed the clandestine Democratic Movement for the Liberation of Portugal.

By mid-February, rallies in Lisbon and Oporto were drawing many thousands of rightists. The Armed Forces Movement now indicated a willingness to surrender political power held since the beginning of the revolution. In April, parliamentary elections were held for the first time in 50 years.

The parliamentary elections indicated that the Portuguese people were deeply divided without a clear governing majority, although most voters approved parties favoring West European democracy. The voters seemed to confirm political democracy, land reform, substantial nationalization and a mixed economy. Although the moderate Socialists under Mario Soares won a plurality of 35% of the vote, the strong minority position of the Communist Party was consolidated and there was a moderate shift to the right.

Since Soares, with a minority of 106 out of 263 seats in the new National Assembly, rejected an alliance with Communist or centrist groups, the presidential election in June assumed considerable significance. According to the new constitution which went into effect on April 25, the president has broad powers including the naming of the prime minister and the chief of the armed forces.

On June 27, the conservative law-and-order Presidential candidate, General António Ramalho Eanes was elected with over 61% of the vote. Mario Soares, the new Socialist Prime Minister, was immediately challenged by the far right. Clandestine groups supporting the old regime were held responsible for a series of violent incidents and, at the end of July, the rightists held a mass for the sixth anniversary of the death of former dictator Salazar.

But although Portugal faces major political and economic problems—settling the colonial refugees or "ritornados," reviving industrial activity, preserving labor and agrarian reforms—there has been a relative stabilization in recent months with general order restored in the country and in the armed forces. The new Prime Minister's program seeks a consensus to restore the authority of the government, revive the paralyzed economy and improve the quality of life. Portugal's survival as a democracy depends on the achievement of this program.

21 After breaking off negotiations with black nationalists, Rhodesian Prime Minister Ian D. Smith declares readiness to revoke declaration of independence from Britain in effort to resolve constitutional crisis with black majority.

24 Sec. of State Henry A. Kissinger says U.S. does not rule out invasion of Cuba over any new intervention in Africa.

25 Argentine military junta proclaims martial law after bloodless coup; Isabel Martínez de Perón under arrest.

26 South Africa announces plan to withdraw all forces from Angola.

28 Prime Minister Indira Gandhi's Congress Party regains two-thirds majority in India's Upper house.

30 U.S. Senate votes extension of fisheries to 200 miles offshore.

Spain

W ITH THE DEATH of Generalissimo Francisco Franco after 36 years of dictatorial rule and the coronation of King Juan Carlos I, all the hidden political conflicts of Fascist Spain surfaced. Prime Minister Carlos Arias Navarro suggested moderate political reforms, but opposition groups attacked his proposals as undemocratic.

Underground political parties, labor unions and student groups organized protest meetings, strikes and demonstrations calling for civil and political liberties and the end of government wage controls. More than 200,000 workers were on strike in January. In Catalonia and the Basque country, there were demonstrations demanding regional autonomy.

After a brief period of relative toleration, the police attacked students and workers, arrested labor lawyers meeting to promote basic freedoms and labor reforms, conscripted rail workers and striking mailmen in an effort to stem labor agitation.

Rebellious sentiments reached into the army. On March 10, nine officers were court-martialed on a charge of inciting to rebellion. They were convicted and sentenced to long prison terms.

In Franco's last message, he warned his countrymen that "the enemies of Spain and Christian civilization are on the alert" and the ultras are now including all reformers among these enemies. The conservatives are not willing to see 40 years of Fascist controls disappear without a struggle. But the reform-minded are making some headway. On May 8, the government proposed a two-house parliament, with all of the lower house and most of the senate directly elected. The right of workers to form independent unions was also recognized.

King Juan Carlos, in an address to the U.S. Congress, stated that the monarchy was committed to "authentic liberty" for the Spanish people. He favors an open Spain in which every citizen has full scope for full participation of any kind and without undue sectarian or extremist pressures.

But the application of these democratic reforms reflected the continuing conflict between reformers and the adherents of the old regime. On June 10, the government legalized political parties but it retained the power to reject communist, anarchist and separatist groups, a power broad enough to discourage any serious opposition to government policies. On June 11, the government banned a meeting of amnesty supporters despite a recent law that indoor meetings of more than 20 persons no longer require official authorization. It appears that the law gives the authorities the power to ban meetings "with criminal aims."

On July 1, Spain's Prime Minister Carlos Arias Navarro, a holdover from the Franco regime, resigned. Program for democratic change thrown into confusion. On July 3, Adolfo Suárez González, a personal friend of King Juan Carlos I, was named Prime Minister. The choice of Mr. Suárez, who was Minister in charge of the National Movement, Spain's only legal party, did not herald substantial change in the program of democratic development. Mr. Suárez is viewed as a reformist.

On July 30, King Juan Carlos granted amnesty for all political prisoners except terrorists. Those freed included some conscientious objectors and army officers who had supported political liberalization. Furthermore, some university professors were reinstated.

Despite this trend toward the rule of justice and the full exercise of civil liberties, it appears that the transition from dictatorship to democracy in Spain will be a long and tortuous one.

APR. 2 Former Philippines President Diosdado Macapagal denounces martial-law government in the Philippines as lawless dictatorship.

5 Thousands riot in Peking square; observers interpret demonstration as support for the late Chou En-lai's moderate political and economic policies.

5 James Callaghan, Foreign Secretary, succeeds Harold Wilson as Britain's Prime Minister.

6 Prince Norodom Sihanouk resigns as Cambodia's figurehead chief of state.

7 Sec. of State Kissinger warns that NATO will be destroyed if communist governments are elected in western Europe.

8 Hua Kuo-feng, named Prime Minister and Deputy First Chairman of Chinese Communist Party, becomes leading potential successor to Chairman Mao Tse-tung.

14 Palestinian nationalists and Arab radicals win West Bank municipal elections in Israel; victors claim that results demonstrate desire of area for an independent Palestinian state.

16 India will send an ambassador to China for first time in 15 years.

17 Indian government raises minimum marriage age and offers payments for voluntary sterilization as part of broad birth control policy.

Angola

AFTER 400 YEARS of Portuguese rule, Angola was in danger of becoming the scene of a new Vietnam as civil war involved the major powers and the countries of southern Africa.

The rival factions were Agosthino Neto's Popular Movement for the Liberation of Angola (M.P.L.A.) reinforced by Soviet arms and thousands of Cuban troops, Holden Roberto's Front for the National Liberation of Angola (F.L.N.A.) and Jonas Savimbi's National Union for the Total Independence of Angola (U.N.I.T.A.) supported by Zaire, Zambia, South African troops, American funds and British mercenaries.

Angola offered rich rewards to the victor. The area is rich in farmland and mineral deposits—oil, gold, coffee, copper, iron ore, diamonds, manganese. Angola is strategically vital to the African continent and to the sea lanes of the Atlantic, and serves as an outlet for the products of Zaire and landlocked Zambia. Events in Angola affect the future of all of southern Africa—Rhodesia, South Africa and Namibia, as well as the more conservative African states in the area.

By February 13, M.P.L.A. announced victory in the civil war. The opposing factions abandoned all major towns and prepared for guerrilla tactics. The Luanda regime was recognized by countries throughout the world as the legitimate government, the People's Republic of Angola. The U.S., although withholding recognition, permitted Gulf Oil to resume oil operations in the Angolan enclave of Cabinda. South Africa withdrew its armed forces from the country, while Rhodesia prepared for guerrilla warfare by nationalists based in Angola and Mozambique.

On May 20, Angolan leaders stated that their foreign policy was based on preferential relations with Socialist countries, particularly Cuba. On May 31, the Soviet Union promised military and developmental aid after a state visit by Prime Minister Lopo do Nacimento. Similar aid was promised to Mozambique after a visit by Samora Michel, leader of the Frelimo nationalist movement in that country. These are signs of a growing Soviet involvement in the countries of southern Africa.

On June 28, ignoring British and American appeals for clemency, an American and three British mercenaries were executed by an Angolan firing squad.

MAY 1 Portugal moves to grant some autonomy to Atlantic islands of Azores and Madeira to counter separatist campaigns.

6 Delegates from 150 countries open U.N. Conference on Trade and Development (U.N.C.T.A.D.) in Nairobi, Kenya; Sec. of State Kissinger warns Third World countries against using bloc economic power at conference.

11 Despite criticism at home and abroad, Israel plans new settlements in occupied Arab territory, ranging from agricultural villages to industrial towns.

15 Pakistan and India resume diplomatic relations, including resumption of airline and rail links.

16 Seventh annual Islamic Conference supports Palestinians, Turkish Cypriots and a variety of insurgents from the Philippines to southern Africa.

22 NATO accuses the Soviet Union of endangering détente by arms build-up in Central Europe.

28 Syria agrees to extend U.N.-observed force on Golan Heights for 60 days.

28 U.S. and U.S.S.R. sign treaty limiting size of underground nuclear explosions and providing for some on-site inspection of compliance.

JUNE 1 Portuguese Timor becomes a province of Indonesia by unilateral resolution of Timor's legislature.

2 State visit of Philippine President Ferdinand E. Marcos to U.S.S.R. leads to establishment of diplomatic relations.

5 Canada and Mexico extend fishing limits to 200 miles.

16 Many killed and wounded when South African police fire on student demonstration in Soweto, black township near Johannesburg and largest black urban center in the country; students were demonstrating against the use of Afrikaans as language of school instruction.

19 176 dead and thousands injured as riots spread in black townships of South Africa; Organization of African Unity threatens violent reprisals against regime; observers refer to riots as the worst upheaval South Africa has ever known.

19 Thailand and Cambodia agree on border demarcation and establishment of embassies. Thailand is the first non-Communist government to establish official ties with new Cambodian government.

22 Christian Democrats remain Italy's dominant party, but the Communist Party is not far behind with substantial increases in the Chamber of Deputies. In that body, the C.D.s win 38%, the C.P. 36%, of the seats. Most observers claim that the political crisis is unresolved. The C.D. captures popular vote but C.P. gain of 49 seats in the Chamber narrows gap between the two major parties and suggests further parliamentary deadlock.

India

SINCE INDEPENDENCE, India has been regarded as one of the major democracies in the Third World. One of the most startling reversals in postwar history occurred on January 3 when Prime Minister Indira Gandhi called upon the Congress Party to support the postponement of parliamentary elections and to extend the state of emergency indefinitely.

Since then, democratic rights have been eroded in India. The press has been gagged, political dissidents have been jailed and silenced and local governments have been placed under Federal control.

On April 29, the Supreme Court of India upheld the right of the government to imprison political opponents without court hearings.

Abroad, India's antidemocratic policies have been severely criticized.

23 West German Foreign Minister, speaking on behalf of the nine governments of the European community, criticizes South African apartheid and calls for the independence of South-West Africa or Namibia; stresses South African responsibility to end minority regime in Rhodesia.

25 National Assembly of reunified Vietnam opens in Hanoi, symbolizing the end of a divided country.

25 Polish Government cancels food price increases as striking workers protest the rise in the cost of living.

30 Leaders of 29 Communist parties from Eastern and Western Europe end East Berlin conference with document endorsing independence of each party to find its own path to Socialism.

JULY 1 Western European farmers forced to slaughter cattle as region suffers effects of weeks of serious drought. Experts blame persistent changes in Atlantic weather patterns.

3 Israeli airborne commandos attack Uganda's Entebbe Airport and free 103 hostages held by pro-Palestinian hijackers of Air France jetliner. Uganda threatens retaliation.

7 Blacks in South Africa win agreement by government to end compulsory use of Afrikaans as teaching medium in black schools, issue that had touched off rioting in which 176 people died.

8 Spain's Prime Minister Adolfo Suárez González announces formation of Cabinet of relatively young reform-minded officials of old Franco regime committed to prepare for legislative elections and party democracy.

Northern Ireland

THERE WAS NO END in sight for the Protestant-Catholic civil strife in Northern Ireland. The New Year opened with dramatic violence when ten Protestant workmen were shot dead in retaliation for the killing of five Catholics in an earlier incident.

It was clear that terrorist bombs were stirring a militant response in both factions. On January 13, the British government suggested a constitutional convention to seek a formula for a new political settlement. But on March 9, Britain dissolved the North Ireland Convention, thus abandoning all efforts to reconcile the contending groups.

Britain will continue to run Ulster as in the past.

On July 22, one of the most dramatic murders of the civil war occurred in Dublin when Britain's Ambassador to Ireland, Christopher T. E. Ewart Biggs, was killed by a bomb.

Thus, this bitter Catholic-Protestant conflict continues with more than 200 killed in 1976, more than 1,500 dead and 14,000 injured since 1969.

12 Chief U.S. Delegate William W. Scranton tells U.N. Security Council Israel's raid on Uganda to rescue victims of pro-Palestinian hijackers was a "combination of guts and brains that has seldom if ever been surpassed." Scranton concedes Israeli action "involved a temporary breach of the territorial integrity of Uganda," but gives this justification: ". . . there is a well-established right to use limited force for the protection of one's own nationals from an imminent threat of injury or death in a situation where the state in whose territory they are located either is unwilling or unable to protect them."

15 African members of U.N. Security Council, faced with defeat, withdraw resolution to condemn, as "flagrant violation" of Uganda's sovereignty, the Israeli raid to rescue hijacking victims. British-American resolution calling for punishment of all airline hijackers fails to get necessary votes.

16 Taiwan withdraws from Olympic Games when denied right to compete as the Republic of China.

19 Seventeen nations, including Kenya, Nigeria and Guyana, withdraw from Olympic Games in protest against New Zealand rugby team tour of South Africa.

23 Britain to cut government spending next year by £1 billion in move to protect pound, reduce budget deficit and sustain economic recovery.

27 Communists win four chairmanships in Italian Parliament, reflecting growing strength of party.

Action does not block expected aid from other nations.

27 British Government breaks diplomatic relations with Uganda; first break with Commonwealth country.

30 Brezhnev attacks agreement of Western nations not to grant loans to Italy if Communists are allowed into the new government as a violation of the democratic right of Italians to choose their own government.

AUG. 2 Forty-nine U.S. citizens and dependents leave Vietnam for Thailand, virtually ending American presence in the country.

2 Soweto blacks demand racial reforms in South Africa, including recognition of black trade unions and an end to job discrimination.

3 Israel, seeking to create anti-Palestinian sentiment among southern Lebanese, expands "open fence" policy permitting Lebanese to take temporary jobs in Israeli factories.

9 Police kill two black youths as unrest in South Africa spreads from Soweto to 11 other areas; 188 lives lost since disturbances erupted eight weeks ago.

11 Grenade-hurling terrorists attack passengers waiting to board Israeli El Al jetliner at Istanbul; four killed, 20 wounded; two Palestinians captured.

12 Right-wing Christians in Lebanon take Palestinian camp of Tell Zaatar after siege since mid-June. Thousands of civilians surrender to rightists.

14 Syria virtually closes border with Lebanon. Damascus reported to be sending more troops to war-torn country.

16 Former Prime Minister Kakuei Tanaka indicted for accepting $1.6 million in bribes to arrange purchase of Lockheed aircraft by Japan's largest airline.

18 Constitutional committee in South-West Africa announces, under U.N. ultimatum, plans for multiracial government to lead territory to independence from South Africa by the end of 1978. Plan is rejected by the outlawed Southwest Africa Peoples Organization.

18 Two Americans are killed and nine Americans and South Koreans wounded in attack by North Koreans in demilitarized zone in dispute over pruning of tree that blocked view. North Korea calls incident "regretful" and both sides consider partition of truce village.

20 Colombo, Sri Lanka, conference of nonaligned nations ends with stinging warning to rich nations that they must yield more of their wealth to a new international economic order.

20 South Africa, in new concession to urban blacks, gives unrestricted title to land in home purchases.

23 Egyptian airliner with 100 aboard seized by Arab guerrillas and recaptured by government troops; three Arabs captured.

25 Gaullist Prime Minister Jacques Chirac replaced by Raymond Barre. Chirac charges that he was not given sufficient authority by President d'Estaing to deal with France's problems.

26 Prince Bernhard of the Netherlands resigns all military and business posts after Government commission criticizes "unacceptable" relationship with Lockheed Aircraft. Future of Queen Wilhelmina put into question.

26 U.N. Sec.-Gen. Kurt Waldheim rejects South African independence proposals for South-West Africa.

27 U.S. agrees to sell Iran 160 F-16 fighter planes at a cost of about $3.4 billion.

31 Irish government plans longer jail sentences for I.R.A. members and seeks emergency legislation to quell suspected terrorists. On Sept. 1, Parliament declares a state of emergency.

SEPT. 6 Sec. Kissinger says three days of talks at Zurich with South African Prime Minister John Vorster have opened the way for blacks and whites to settle the key problems of Rhodesia and South-West Africa.

8 Crises mount in southern Africa as blacks riot in Cape Town and Kimberley while Prime Minister Vorster tells Nationalist Party rally that he will never consent to sharing power with blacks in South Africa. The killing of many people of mixed ancestry, the "colored," shocks whites. Rumored U.S.-British plan will provide financial guarantees for Rhodesian whites in the event of a transfer to black rule in that country.

9 Death of Mao Tse-tung at age of 82 makes China's political situation uncertain. Some observers predict collective leadership headed by the new Prime Minister, Hua Kuo-feng.

13 President Ford prepares to veto Vietnam's bid for U.N. membership because failure to make a full accounting of MIAs (Missing In Action) showed a lack of commitment to peace and humanitarianism required for membership. U.N. later postpones vote on Vietnam admission until November.

15 After talks with Sec. Kissinger, Tanzania's President Julius K. Nyerere does not see possibility of negotiated settlements for South-West Africa or Rhodesia. President Kenneth D. Kaunda of Namibia warns of wår if Kissinger shuttle talks fail. A few days later, Kissinger meets Vorster and Smith in Pretoria for further talks.

22 South African government sanctions multiracial sports teams in national and international competition as black anti-apartheid protests spread to center of white Johannesburg.

22 Elias Sarkis is inaugurated as President of Lebanon under protection of Syrian army. Yasir Arafat orders cease-fire by guerrilla forces of Palestine Liberation Organization.

24 Prime Minister Ian D. Smith accepts plan for black rule in Rhodesia based on temporary biracial government, majority rule in two years, an end to economic sanctions and guerrilla warfare and aid to the economy and for whites who wish to leave the country.

26 Five "front line" African Presidents charge that Kissinger plan for interim government "if accepted, would be tantamount to legalizing the colonialist and racist structures of power in Rhodesia."

27 African diplomats say U.N. will not lift economic sanctions against Rhodesia until full agreement is reached on transition government.

28 Syrian and left-wing Lebanese armed forces open major offensive against Palestinian units; Syrian groups challenge Arafat leadership of Palestine Liberation Organization.

29 Britain, in message to Ian D. Smith, proposes bi-racial conference in southern Africa to discuss interim government for transition to black majority rule.

U.S. and World Economy

THE RECESSION that began in 1973 finally came to an end two years later. By mid-1976, business expansion was in full swing and the leading economic indicators suggested that the country was in the early recovery phase of the business cycle, with more than 87 million Americans employed in the process. But a few dour forecasters, noting excessive unemployment, inflation and interest rates, insisted that the recession would be over when all of America was back to work. One could hardly speak of recovery when more than seven million Americans were unemployed by official count. These clashing interpretations are reminiscent of the story about the glass that is half full and therefore half empty. The optimists point to the full half, while the pessimists stress the empty half. In 1976, the economic scene provided ample material for both the Panglosses and Cassandras.

In the first half of the year, the leading economic indicators seemed to confirm the optimistic analysis. The stock market, traditional barometer of the state of the economy, was bullish, with the Dow-Jones Index passing the 1000 mark in the biggest rally since World War II. Double-digit inflation came to an end and increasing consumer confidence was reflected in soaring automobile and retail sales. There was a drop in the unemployment rate, a record trade surplus, new confidence in the American dollar in foreign exchange markets, record corporate profits, a rise in industrial production and even a slight improvement in the lagging construction industry. Furthermore, American recovery was accompanied by similar trends in some of the Western industrial nations and Japan. The near collapse of these economies as a result of the oil and energy crisis of the early 1970s had been averted and a moderate recovery was under way.

The pessimists acknowledged what they termed the modest improvements of 1976 but they viewed the recovery as a fragile one. In terms of unemployment, 1976 was the second worst year since the Great Depression of the 1930s, with more than 7% of the labor force out of work. Despite recovery, the economy is still marked by unused labor and industry capacity. The nation's banks were still troubled by loan losses, especially the billions of dollars lost as a result of the collapse of the real estate holding companies. The economy was weakened by some of the biggest bank failures in American history and the F.D.I.C. listed some of the giant banks as "problem banks." The building construction industry was still depressed with housing starts 40% below the peaks of the early 1970s. There were empty office buildings in the North and unsold condominiums in the South. There were increasing signs of urban crisis and decay. The largest city in the country, and the financial capital of the world, was in virtual bankruptcy—closing hospitals, libraries, firing thousands of policemen, firemen, tenured teachers, and other civil servants with years of experience. Cities and states throughout the country reported similar fiscal problems, with budget-cutting austerity programs the order of the day. There were spectacular business failures headed by the bankruptcy of the giant W. T. Grant retail chain. Giant airline companies such as Pan Am were in trouble and there was an unusual slump in the life insurance industry. There were retrenchments and rising tuition costs in the colleges, declining living standards among the aged, the poor and the minorities, uncertainty about energy supplies and energy costs.

Furthermore, the world economy was still depressed. In the Western industrial countries, especially England and Italy, continued unemployment and inflation still posed dangerous threats. The dramatic fall of the pound and the lira provided convincing evidence that the economic crisis was still a fact of life.

The economists seemed to be as confused as the rest of us about the nature of the recovery. Was it a temporary surface phenomenon which failed to cope with underlying causes? Would the economy benefit by balanced budgets, austerity programs, belt-tightening or increased spending for massive works programs to create new jobs.

1975

NOV. 6 The economic picture in October brought little comfort—wholesale price index up by 1.8%, unemployment rate up to 8.6%, or over 8 million unemployed.

15 The six-nation economic summit meeting in Paris reaches agreement on guidelines for world trade and currency exchange.

DEC. 24 U.S. reports record-high trade surplus for 1975.

1976

JAN. 1 Gallup poll in 12 nations reveals that public opinion is pessimistic about prospects for a prosperous global economy in 1976.

1 Social Security taxes increase 8.5% for workers earning $15,300 a year or more.

1 Builders report drop in housing construction to lowest levels since 1959.

2 Sikorsky Aircraft, helicopter manufacturer, lays off 700 workers.

2 Bureau of Labor Statistics reports that New York City area is hit harder by the effects of recession than the rest of the nation.

8 Argentina reports 1975 witnessed a 335% rise in the cost of living.

9 International Monetary Fund approves new system of floating exchange rates for currencies and liberalization of lending terms for non-oil-producing, less developed countries.

15 Two-year slump in auto industry ends with 50% increase in January sales.

15 Nation's banks plan to write off $3 billion in bad loans for 1975; some concern expressed for safety of billions of dollars that banks have loaned to developing countries.

JAN. 14–FEB. 6 Comptroller of the Currency denies *Washington Post* report on unsound financial condition of First National and Chase Manhattan Banks but lists 28 national banks in critical condition; F.D.I.C. has 350 banks on "problem" list, many in serious state.

30 Wall Street finishes month with the biggest point advance on record—122 points and some of busiest days in trading history.

FEB. 8 Labor Dept. reports January decline in the jobless rate to 7.8% of labor force, biggest monthly decline since 1959.

13 Federal judge orders total liquidation of W. T. Grant Co. within 60 days; largest retail bankruptcy in history.

17 European Common Market approves $1 billion loan to Italy to bolster foreign currency reserves.

MAR. 2 Prime Minister Alexei N. Kosygin reports that Soviet economic growth rate averages 7.4% as compared with 1.2% in U.S. and Western Europe; Soviet Union leads the world in production of steel, oil, cement, tractors, coal, cotton and wool.

9 National unemployment rate drops to 7.6% in February, a total of 7,136,000. A.F.L.-C.I.O. leaders claim that "official figures seriously underestimate unemployment."

10 Common Market Commission predicts gross national product (G.N.P.) rise of 3% in 1976—recovery still fragile—unemployment will remain high—inflation dangers remain in the nine-nation group.

11 Dow-Jones Index passes 1000 for the first time in three years; brightens economic picture.

16 European currencies in turmoil as France withdraws from European currency float; pound, franc, lira fall.

18 Sharp drop in raw sugar prices hurts foreign-exchange earnings of Third World countries.

APR. 3 March employment rose 375,000 to a record 86.7 million.

16 Industrial production up .6% in March. Personal income rising at $7.6 billion annual rate.

20 Commerce Dept. reports 7.5% "real" rise in G.N.P. from January to March as economic recovery picks up speed after pause in final quarter of 1975. Inflation rate is 3.7%, lowest since third quarter of 1972. Consumer spending booming.

21 United Rubber Workers strike Big Four companies—Goodyear, Firestone, Goodrich and Uniroyal—seeking wage increase, cost-of-living clause, and pension, health and fringe benefits.

23 Volkswagen reported to have decided to invest $250 million in automobile assembly plant in U.S.

29 General Motors, recovering from depressed earnings, reports sharp rise in first-quarter earnings to $800 million, or $2.78 a share.

MAY 3 Building service workers strike at many New York City apartment houses for higher pay and improved benefits.

5 American new-car sales up 55% in last 10 days of April.

6 British Treasury and union leaders agree to tough new policy restricting wage increases to 4.5% in year beginning Aug. 1. Ceiling for rises set at $7.32 a week for those earning more than $150.

6 I.R.S. figures show third-year increase for 1974 to 244 persons in number with incomes over $200,000 who paid no income taxes.

7 Wholesale Price Index up .8% in April after months of decline. Increase led by upturn in farm and food prices.

8 Nation's employment soars to a 87,399,000 record in April. Unemployment totals 7,040,000, seasonally unchanged from March. Jobless rate of 7.5% unchanged from March.

18 British pound falls below $1.80 for first time before staging slight recovery. Drop laid to strength of dollar.

22 Consumer Price Index rises .4% in April due to upswing in food prices.

JUNE 4 Federal Reserve reports continued upward trend in interest rates as business loans expand at New York City banks. New car sales up 17% in May for eighth monthly gain.

8 U.S. and other industrialized countries provide $5.3 billion standby short-term credit to bolster declining British pound.

17 Economic reports for May show a rise in industrial output, personal income and new housing starts.

19 G.N.P. growth of less than 5% is indicated for second quarter as compared with 8.5% in the first quarter.

23 May rise of 6/10ths of 1% in Consumer Price Index indicates "underlying" 6% inflation rate in 1976.

28 Summit meeting of seven major industrial nations opens in Puerto Rico to discuss the problems of world economic recovery and expansion. Joint statement at end of conference announces go-slow approach, agreeing to pursue objective of sustained economic growth with policies that seek to avoid reviving worldwide inflation.

29 I.R.S. revokes tax-exempt status of Teamsters Union's pension fund, citing mismanagement and questionable loan practices.

JULY 3 U.S. unemployment rate in June rose to 7.5% from 7.3% in May, Labor Dept. reports. Economists and officials disagree on significance.

10 Wholesale Price Index rose a moderate .4% in June. Less inflation in agriculture, more in industrial prices.

14 Kansas-based long-haul trucking company buys block of land in lower Manhattan for $1.5 million to establish new terminal to ease traffic congestion.

17 Ford officials assert economic gains are outstripping predictions. President claims credit for his policies. Industrial output reported higher in June, but at a slower pace.

21 Gold tumbles nearly 12% in five business days, from $122 an ounce to $107.75, in London. Political and economic consequences likely for South Africa and Russia, major gold producers.

21 G.N.P. growth slowed to 4.4% in second quarter, from first quarter's 9.2%.

22 Consumer Price Index up moderately for June, with energy replacing food as main factor.

23 Three of New York City's largest retailers—Macy's, Korvettes and Alexander's—plan first large-scale Sunday openings of department stores in metropolitan area as the result of court rejection of state's blue laws.

27 U.S. ends 1976 fiscal year with $65.6 billion budget deficit, $10.4 billion below estimates.

28 General Motors earns $909 million in second quarter, second highest quarterly earnings in American business history.

AUG. 3 Federal judge disagrees with Federal Communications Commission trial staff recommendation that the commission ask Congress to divest A.T.&T. of the Western Electric Co., its manufacturing and supply subsidiary.

3 The Federal Trade Commission and the Justice Dept. announce an antitrust investigation of the nation's automobile manufacturers.

13 U.S. Steel raises prices second time in three months, citing increased labor costs.

16 Nearly all striking coal miners back at work after month-long wildcat tie-up in Eastern coal fields.

20 Consumer prices up 0.5% in July. Inflation running at annual rate of 5 to 6%.

25 G.M. raising retail price of average car to $6,000.

26 Commerce Dept. reports July trade deficit of U.S. biggest in almost two years, reflecting rising petroleum imports. Imports are $827.1 million above exports.

30 U.S. Steel rescinds, under competitive and customer pressure, 4.5% price increase scheduled for Oct. 1. Inland and Bethlehem follow suit.

SEPT. 2 Wholesale prices down in August, reflecting sharpest drop in farm prices in 18 months. Industrial prices higher.

3 Jobless rate for August up to 7.9%, third consecutive monthly rise.

9 House-Senate conferees agree on tax bill which will provide $1.6 billion in new revenue to Treasury as result of estate tax reforms and new taxes for those who use tax shelters.

14 British pound continues to fall, indicating pessimism on prospects for recovery based on threats of major strikes and more inflation.

15 United Auto Workers calls strike at Ford Motor Co. Economists fear damaging effects on economic recovery.

21 Dow Jones Index closes at 1,014, highest in 44 months.

24 Failure of American Bank & Trust Co. laid to corruption and bad management.

27 British pound falls to new all-time low of $1.63.

28 August drop of 1.5% in leading economic indicators reported by Dept. of Commerce; some economists pessimistic about pace of economic recovery.

U.S. Foreign Policy

As HUMPTY DUMPTY said, "When I use a word, it means just what I choose it to mean, neither more nor less." To which Alice replied, "The question is whether you can make words mean so many different things."

The State Department, the politicians and the media have not taken Humpty Dumpty seriously in the use of the word "détente," one of the more controversial terms of 1976.

President Ford wanted to abolish the word and substitute something called "peace through strength." The Russians once called it "peaceful coexistence." Academics use the expression "relaxation of tensions." To the man in the street, it means Olga Korbut, Bolshoi Ballet, Soviet hockey teams and pianists. To the liberal, it means Helsinki Agreements, interim SALT Agreements, the end of the arms race and the end of the specter of nuclear war, for he is certain that nuclear war between armed superpowers has become suicidal and therefore outside the bounds of rational policy. And he is also sanguine about the possibility of gradually opening up the Soviet system by expanding East-West trade and cultural exchanges.

To the conservative, it means strengthening Russia through grain sales and the sale of American technology. It means a one-way street ending with Soviet military superiority. Conservative support for détente is further eroded by evidence that the

Soviets continue to insist on the right to support their own kind of social change and national liberation in the Third World.

Détente became an issue in the Presidential primary campaigns. But whatever it is and wherever it will lead, Sec. of State Henry A. Kissinger assured us in his Boston speech that "no policy will soon, if ever, eliminate the competition and irreconcilable ideological differences between the U.S.A. and the U.S.S.R."

In the meantime, military budgets continue to rise, the destructive arms race continues and the political rhetoric thrives with little attention paid to the wise words of Humpty Dumpty.

1975

NOV. 5 Egyptian President Anwar el-Sadat tells joint session of Congress that Palestinian question is core of Mideast troubles.

DEC. 1 U.S. will participate in Security Council debate on Middle East but continues diplomatic boycott of P.L.O.

4 President Ford and Chinese leaders end four-day Peking meeting; apparent understanding of mutual interests in countering an expansion of Soviet interests; no substantive change in Chinese-American relations.

1976

JAN. 3 President Ford insists that policy of détente will continue despite Soviet involvement in Angola.

9 Sec. of State Kissinger begins policy of withholding American aid for those nations who have opposed the U.S. in U.N. votes; food and humanitarian relief included in cutbacks.

15 Sec. Kissinger announces Moscow trip for SALT talks which he considers "more important than day-to-day issues like Angola."

25 U.S. and Spain sign five-year Treaty of Friendship and Cooperation; U.S. gets air and naval bases for $1.2 billion in credits and grants; critics claim that treaty bolsters anti-democratic Spanish regime.

25 House of Representatives cuts off aid for two pro-Western factions in Angolan civil war.

28 In letter to Sec. of State and all American embassies, U.N. Ambassador Daniel P. Moynihan accuses State Dept. of not supporting his efforts to break up the anti-American voting blocs in U.N.

30 House Select Committee on Intelligence reveals payment of $800,000 by American embassy to rightist Italian general who headed Italy's military intelligence agency.

FEB. 18 Talks with India on resumption of economic aid are broken off; State Dept. alleges anti-American attitudes.

18 William W. Scranton replaces Daniel P. Moynihan as U.S. Ambassador to the U.N.

22 U.S. sale of planes to Morocco suggests support of King Hassan II in conflict with Algeria for control of phosphate-rich Spanish Sahara.

22 State Dept. approves Gulf Oil and Boeing business relationships with Luanda regime in Angola.

23 Private Citizen Nixon criticizes State Dept. implicitly for naiveté in signing Helsinki Agreement with Soviet Union; Nixon and President Ford deny this interpretation.

24 Senate votes to give northern Mariana Islands commonwealth status, first territorial expansion of U.S.A. since 1925.

MAR. 1 In Florida campaign speech, Ford labels Cuba "international outlaw"; asserts continued U.S. policy of nonrecognition.

3 Sadat reveals secret agreements with U.S. in 1975 Sinai accord—Israel would not attack Syria and U.S. would make every effort to insure Palestinian participation in Middle East settlement.

8 Sec. of Treasury William E. Simon announces $1.85 billion aid to Egypt; praises Sadat for breaking with Soviet Union and liberalizing economy.

APR. 10 U.S. and Soviet agree on treaty for limiting size of underground nuclear tests for peaceful purposes.

23 Sec. Kissinger leaving on African tour committed to policy of promoting black majority rule in Rhodesia and furthering African political unity and economic development.

23 Vice President Nelson A. Rockefeller, reporting on seven-nation trip, says U.S. friends are gravely concerned about the reliability and consistency of U.S. foreign policy.

MAY 2 Kissinger, in Senegal speech, appeals to industrial nations to join $7.5-billion rescue operation to "roll back the desert" in a drought-devastated region of West Africa.

5 Former Defense Sec. James R. Schlesinger says Administration undermines "moral support" for Israel by undue pressure to make concessions to Arabs.

7 President Ford vetoes $4.4-billion foreign aid bill, his 49th veto. Says "unprecedented restrictions" in authorization measure would "seriously inhibit my ability to implement a coherent and consistent foreign policy."

JUNE 4 Kissinger to meet South Africa's Prime Minister Balthazar Johannes Vorster in Europe to discuss Rhodesian problem and methods of averting "race war" in southern Africa.

12 U.S. will discuss plans for military aid programs to Kenya and Zaire. Sec. of Defense Donald Rumsfeld to visit both countries for discussions.

12 Kissinger in Mexico City holds personal discussions with President Luis Echeverría Alvarez to ease recent tensions between the two countries.

17 U.S. will sell Kenya F-5 planes as Sec. of Defense Rumsfeld tells Kenyans "it is not for the Soviet Union or Cuba or any nation to dictate to African nations."

23 Sec. Kissinger states that indecisive Italian vote suggests necessity for coalition between Christian Democrats and Socialists to keep Communist party out of a coalition government.

23 Kissinger claims U.S. is attempting to resolve the problems of southern Africa by negotiations rather than by force and violence; denies that exploratory talks with Prime Minister Vorster suggests American endorsement of South African policies.

23 U.S. vetoes entry of Angola in U.N., citing presence of Cuban forces.

27 President Ford warns Cuba against meddling in relations between the U.S. and Puerto Rico.

JULY 17 U.S. and West Germany agree to end agreement by which Bonn had helped defray costs of U.S. troops.

17 U.S., West Germany, France and Britain reach informal understanding to bar further loans to Italy if Communists get cabinet posts.

AUG. 3 Sec. Kissinger admits "past omissions" in U.S. policy toward Africa; tells Urban League conference that the U.S. "will pursue our new Africa policy with conviction and dedication."

United Nations

1975

NOV. 10 U.N. General Assembly approves resolution classifying Zionism as a form of racism and racial discrimination.

1976

JAN. 1 U.N. Sec.-Gen. Kurt Waldheim refers to 1975 General Assembly session as one of the most difficult in U.N. history; urges 144 member nations to view present shortcomings and failures from long-range perspective that governments must learn to cooperate.

3 In year-end review, U.N. cites Cyprus and Middle East as most time-consuming issues in Security Council; membership of 144 now includes new admissions: Cape Verde, São Tomé e Príncipe, Mozambique, Papua New Guinea, the Comoros and Surinam.

13 Middle East debate opens in Security Council with P.L.O. seated by 11-1 vote; Arabs stress "national rights" of Palestinians.

13 Bombs found and defused in areas of U.N. and Iraqui Mission on eve of Middle East debate.

19 Sec.-Gen. Waldheim warns that civil war in Lebanon could lead to disastrous war in entire Middle East because of danger of Syrian and Israeli intervention.

27 U.S. vetoes Security Council resolution for an independent Palestinian state and the total withdrawal by Israel from post-1967 Arab lands.

FEB. 3 Ambassador Daniel P. Moynihan resigns post at U.N.; denies interest in New York Democratic Senatorial nomination.

14 U.N. Commission on Human Rights approves resolution accusing Israel of committing war crimes in occupied Arab areas.

25 U.S. vote in U.N. Security Council blocks resolution deploring Israeli policies in Jerusalem and occupied areas on West Bank.

APR. 2 U.S. member of Human Rights Commission attacks third-world bloc over handling of rights issues in U.N.

7 U.N. Security Council unanimously broadens sanctions against white Rhodesian government barring insurance and other benefits.

MAY 8 Eight weeks of negotiations in U.N. Law of the Sea Conference end without settling basic disputes on uses of oceans and mining of deep seabed minerals.

12 Black African nations stop Algerian move to link Zionism with racism in two resolutions in Economic and Social Council.

JUNE 12 U.N. Conference on Human Settlements (Habitat) calls for restrictions on: the private ownership of land, redistribution of land in poor countries, management of land as a public resource rather than a profit-generating commodity, more equitable distribution of wealth.

SEPT. 21 U.N. General Assembly convenes to discuss such crucial issues as southern Africa, Middle East and disarmament.

National Government and Politics

1975

NOV. 2 President Ford dismisses Secretary of Defense James R. Schlesinger and C.I.A. Director William E. Colby. Sec. of State Henry A. Kissinger is asked to relinquish post as White House National Security Adviser. Donald Rumsfeld is named Sec. of Defense, Elliot L. Richardson is new Sec. of Commerce and George Bush is C.I.A. Director.

DEC. 12 President Ford signs into legislation bill repealing the "Fair Trade" laws.

19 Congress passes tax-cut extension bill with nonbinding commitment to control government spending acceptable to the President.

23 Federal Election Commission authorizes Treasury Dept. to make initial payments of $2.6 million to both parties and 11 Presidential contenders.

1976

JAN. 2 President Ford vetoes bill expanding picketing rights for construction unions. John T. Dunlop resigns as Sec. of Labor.

20 In State of the Union message, President Ford urges "new realism" in taxes and spending.

29 Congress overrides President's veto of $45 billion appropriation for health, welfare and manpower programs.

FEB. 5 W. J. Usery, Jr., confirmed as Sec. of Labor.

14 President Ford vetoes $6.2-billion bill for job-creating works programs, his 46th veto. Senate sustains the veto on Feb. 20.

MAR. 5 Majority Leader Mike Mansfield, Senator from Montana, will not seek re-election in 1976.

31 Representative F. Edward Hébert of Louisiana will retire after 36 years in the House.

APR. 3 House of Representatives votes bill to reform scandal-ridden grain inspection system.

14 Collectors line up across nation to buy first-day issues of new $2 bill.

29 House of Representatives sustains President Ford's veto of bill revising the Hatch Act to let 2.8 million Federal Civil Service employees take part in politics.

MAY 5 Continental Grain Co. fined $500,000 by Federal judge on charges of false declarations of weights of foreign shipments while scales were rigged.

5 Senate fails to override President Ford's veto of $125-million bill on child day care. Federally supported child care centers in danger of closing.

7 Cook Industries and Mississippi River Grain Elevator fined in New Orleans on charges of conspiracy in systematic thefts of grain from foreign commerce.

18 U.S. Appeals Court unanimously affirms conviction of John D. Ehrlichman and G. Gordon Liddy for roles in 1971 Ellsberg's psychiatrists' office break-in.

22 Reconstituted Federal Election Commission, with Vernon W. Thomson as new chairman, begins to distribute more than $3 million in matching funds to nine Presidential candidates.

28 House of Representatives begins drive to divest Rep. Wayne L. Hays of three committee chairmanships as result of disclosures of his relationship with Elizabeth Ray, self-styled mistress on government payroll.

JUNE 10 Hays wins nomination for 15th consecutive term in office. He is ousted from chairmanship of Democratic National Congressional Committee.

19 Rep. Hays resigns under pressure as chairman of powerful House Administration Committee.

25 President Ford proposes legislation to restrict the power of the courts to order busing as a remedy for segregated schools.

JULY 7 Ford vetoes $3.95-billion public works jobs bill, saying it epitomizes "empty promises and giveaway programs" of the Democratic majority in Congress.

20 President Ford, at news conference, calls for creation of special prosecutor's office to investigate wrongdoing by Government officials. Defends pardon of Nixon.

22 Senate, 73–24, overrides Ford veto of scaled-down $3.95-billion public works measure to stimulate construction employment. Next day House also overrides veto, 310 to 96, enacting bill into law. Of 53 Ford vetoes, nine have been overridden. Congress sustains veto of legislation to delay closing of military bases. Both matters loom as important campaign issues.

30 House votes reprimand for Rep. Robert L. F. Sikes, Florida Democrat, on complaints he used office for personal gain.

AUG. 18 U.S. inquiry clears Rep. John Young, Dem. of Texas, of charge he paid secretary in part to be his mistress.

25 Senate rejects House bill to forbid use of Federal money for abortions.

29 President Ford, in policy reversal, will ask $1.5 billion in next decade to expand national parks.

31 Senate, 63–26, breaks filibuster by Alabama Sen. James B. Allen against major antitrust bill.

SEPT. 1 Ohio Rep. Wayne L. Hays resigns after 28 years in House as result of sex scandal involving Elizabeth L. Ray.

13 President Ford signs "Sunshine Act" which opens meetings and records of many Federal agencies to the public.

22 U.S. Steel reports payment for five golfing holidays for Mr. Ford while he was a member of the House of Representatives.

29 President Ford vetoes $56-billion appropriation bill for HEW programs; accuses Congress of "partisan political purpose." Two days later, Congress overrides veto; House Majority Leader Thomas P. O'Neill charges Ford with "negativism which has kept Americans out of work."

30 Nixon spokesman denies report that former President, in his memoirs, disclaims personal responsibility for Watergate and regards the episode as a partisan political scandal used by his political enemies.

Supreme Court

1975

NOV. 12 William O. Douglas retires from the Supreme Court after 36 years.

DEC. 17 Senate confirms nomination of John Paul Stevens to Supreme Court.

1976

JAN. 3 Chief Justice Warren E. Burger calls upon Congress to increase the number of judges in the Federal courts.

15 Supreme Court overrules 105-year-old decision that had limited the power of states and cities to tax imported goods.

20 Court upholds winner-take-all rule for California Republican Presidential primary.

30 Court upholds the principle of public financing for Presidential contests but orders changes in the Federal campaign law.

MAR. 2 Court refuses to hear a challenge to Church Amendment which permits federally aided private hospitals to decline to perform abortions or sterilizations.

24 Court, in landmark civil rights ruling, decides, 5–3, that blacks and other minorities are entitled to retroactive job seniority.

29 Justices, 6–3, uphold state curbs on homosexual acts in private.

APR. 6 Justices refuse to review courtmartial conviction of former Army Lieut. William L. Calley, Jr., major figure in the Vietnam My Lai murders in 1968.

20 Justices, 8–0, rule that Federal courts can order creation of low-cost public housing for minorities in a city's white suburbs to relieve racial segregation in housing within the city.

27 Court upholds constitutionality of drug sale convictions, even if police agents or informers have supplied seller and other agents were the buyers.

MAY 20 Lower court reversed on ruling that suspects have rights of silence and a lawyer when called to testify before grand jury.

24 Supreme Court rules that advertising is entitled to protection under free speech guarantees of the First Amendment.

JUNE 2 Court rules, 5–4, that the Civil Service Commission may not bar resident aliens from Federal Civil Service jobs.

8 Court rules that a statute or official act must have a "racially discriminatory purpose" to be deemed unconstitutional.

15 Court refuses to review court-ordered plan for desegregating Boston's public schools.

17 Court unanimously upholds the President's authority to impose fees on imported oil when it is decided that oil imports must be limited for national security.

25 In a 5–4 vote, the Court voids an act of Congress extending Federal minimum wage and maximum hours provisions to state and municipal employees.

24 Court rules, 5–4, that cities can use zoning ordinances to limit sexually oriented adult-film movie theaters.

26 Court rules, 7–2, that Civil Rights Act protects whites against racial discrimination to the same extent it protects blacks.

JULY 1 Court rules unanimously that judges generally may not forbid press to publish information about criminal cases even if judge thinks gag order will help assure defendant fair trial by preventing prejudicial publicity.

1 Court rules, 6–3, that states may not require women to get husband's consent before having abortion, and forbids "blanket" state restrictions on rights of girls under 18 to have abortions.

3 Court, 7–2, rules that death penalty is not inherently cruel or unusual and is constitutionally acceptable form of punishment, at least for murder, so long as judges and juries have been given adequate information and guidance.

23 Justice Lewis F. Powell, Jr., stays executions in three states until Court can reconsider decision upholding capital punishment.

State and Local Governments

1975

NOV. 5 Democrats win most of major contests in state and local elections.

26 President Ford in policy reversal proposes legislation to aid New York City in its financial crisis.

1976

JAN. 4 Government studies reveal that many states lose millions of dollars because of the failure of military personnel to pay state income taxes.

28 New York's Governor Hugh L. Carey authorizes State Prosecutor Maurice H. Nadjari to investigate alleged political corruption. The case involves Democratic Party leaders and has implications for the Presidential campaign.

MAR. 3 New York City's unemployment rate at 12.2%, highest since World War II.

22 Exporters claim that New York law making Arab boycott of Israel a misdemeanor is diverting cargo to other ports.

23 New York's Mayor Abraham D. Beame notifies the Federal government that the city plans to withdraw from the Social Security System in two years.

MAY 27 Accused of payoffs, conspiracy and tampering with evidence, Patrick J. Cunningham, New York State Democratic Party Chairman, is indicted in growing political scandal.

JUNE 16 Treasury Department asks New York City to submit new financial plan and obtain new labor agreements as a condition for further Federal loans.

18 Parts of Sabbath closing laws, known as "blue laws," ruled unconstitutional by New York City's Court of Appeals; court refers to "gallimaufry of exceptions" created over the years.

JULY 9 New Jersey gets state income tax, clearing way for reopening of 2,500 public schools, closed by court order.

SEPT. 13 New York City Comptroller audit reveals six close-knit syndicates sharing leases of day-care centers and dealing in such leases for profit and tax advantage.

14 Daniel P. Moynihan edges out Bella S. Abzug in New York primary election for Democratic nomination for U.S. Senate. Moynihan will face James L. Buckley in November.

16 Recall petition against Mayor Frank L. Rizzo of Philadelphia is upheld by local judge.

28 New York City off-duty police defy court order, create disorders at Yankee Stadium boxing match; police later reject agreement reached by leaders in contract dispute.

31 Pennsylvania Supreme Court rules that Mayor Rizzo of Philadelphia does not have to face special recall election.

Defense

1975

NOV. 18 Senate approves $90.7-billion defense appropriation bill.

1976

JAN. 24 Pentagon officials admonished for accepting Northrup invitations to company hunting lodge.

APR. 9 House of Representatives approves funds for Air Force B-1 strategic bomber that will ultimately cost $21 billion for 244 aircraft.

10 House of Representatives approves $33.4-billion military authorization bill adding $2 billion to Administration defense program primarily for nuclear ships. Curbs on new weapons are rejected.

27 President Ford calls for increase in defense budget to continue production of Minutemen missiles. Cites lag in strategic arms talks with the Soviet Union.

MAY 3 Secret Pentagon data show that the United States has built twice as many large combat ships as the Soviet Union in past 15 years.

27 Dept. of Defense will become contracting agent for Lockheed Aircraft to help overcome the effect of bribe disclosures in Japan.

JULY 29 Ford appoints Gen. Bernard W. Rogers as Army Chief of Staff.

SEPT. 15 Pentagon will ask the White House to approve a $130-billion military budget for fiscal 1978, a sharp increase over fiscal 1977 budget.

Civil Rights

1975

DEC. 9 Federal judge, charging Boston School Committee with stalling on desegregation, places South Boston High School under jurisdiction of court-appointed trustee.

1976

JAN. 1 Demonstration for amnesty at Madrid prison smashed by police; repressive policies of Franco regime continue.

11 International Covenant on Economic, Social and Cultural Rights, adopted in 1966, comes into force without ratification by the United States.

30 India's Parliament approves legislation granting the government permanent censorship over the nation's press.

FEB. 21 House of Representatives moves to revoke press credentials of CBS correspondent Daniel Schorr for leaking intelligence report to New York newspaper. CBS relieves Schorr of all duties; bars him from covering news events as a CBS employee pending results of inquiry. Newsmen regard treatment of Schorr as a violation of the First Amendment.

MAY 1 United Airlines agrees to pay $1,050,000 to minority group members and women to settle discrimination complaints brought by the Equal Employment Opportunity Commission. Rejected black pilots and mechanics are also awarded retroactive seniority.

19 President Ford asks Attorney-General Edward H. Levi to seek "appropriate and proper case" to ask Supreme Court for review of school busing for integration.

29 International Commission of Jurists charges Shah of Iran's secret police with psychological and physical torture of political suspects.

JUNE 8 Inter-American Human Rights Commission accuses Chilean military dictatorship of torture of political prisoners and false statements to mislead world public opinion.

12 Inter-American Human Rights Commission appeals to Cuban Government to end "cruel, inhuman and degrading" treatment of political prisoners.

JULY 5 N.A.A.C.P. ends 67th annual convention in Memphis with power placed in board of directors, ending one-man rule of Roy Wilkins, executive director.

11 Seneca Nation of Indians concludes historic pact with New York State, permitting construction of new road through reservation in western New York.

24 Yugoslavia frees Yugoslav-born American accused of economic espionage. Laszlo Toth, 44-year-old Colorado engineer, is flown to U.S. after nearly a year in prison.

AUG. 20 American Federation of Teachers convention votes moderate resolution favoring school busing for integration.

SEPT. 1 Louisville, Kentucky, school busing program resumes without incident.

3 Four Fresno, Calif., newsmen start serving jail sentences for refusing to reveal a source.

8 Civil Service Commission orders deletion of all political loyalty questions on applications for Federal jobs.

15 CBS news correspondent Daniel Schorr cites First Amendment rights in refusing to tell House Ethics Committee how he obtained Pike Committee report on intelligence agencies.

Women

FEMINISTS DID NOT REGARD the bicentennial year as an occasion for celebration. The year of the conservative backlash witnessed a number of factional disputes and schisms as well as a number of setbacks.

There were a few encouraging signs. President Ford appointed an assistant for Women's Affairs. The British Parliament passed laws against sex discrimination: the Equal Pay Act and the Sex Discrimination Act. There was a new international interest in the feminist movement as suggested by the World Plan of Action adopted at the International Women's Year Conference in Mexico City and the proceedings of the International Tribunal on Crimes against Women held in Brussels on March 8. Finally, the new ERAmerica organization indicated that a major campaign was in the making to assure the adoption of the Equal Rights Amendment.

The setbacks were highlighted by the rejection of the Equal Rights Amendment in New York and New Jersey and the threats of rescission by other states. This was a major blow. The political campaigns by the Right-to-Life antiabortionists threatened one of the major achievements of the movement. President Ford's attack on the Supreme Court's abortion decision suggested that women's liberation was now on the defensive.

1975

NOV. 4 Equal Rights Amendment in New York and New Jersey is defeated in elections.

DEC. 6 World Council of Churches elects, for the first time, two women, an American and a Russian, as Presidents.

29 British law bars sex discrimination, giving women more freedom to chart their own lives.

1976

JAN. 11 WHO attacks cult of male dominance over and victimization of women and recommends broad programs of sex education free from sexual taboos and myths.

14 Air Force announces new program for training women as undergraduate pilots.

22 Feminists invade Milan cathedral in protest against Vatican's views on abortion, as expressed in papal document on sexual ethics.

28 In giving up her Iranian public relations job, Marion Javits expresses sadness that American public will not extend women's new rights to wife of a public official; feminists criticize her stand, alleging a simple case of conflict of interest.

29 Senate confirms Anne L. Armstrong as first woman ambassador to the Court of St. James's.

FEB. 4 President Ford criticizes 1973 Supreme Court abortion decision; favors constitutional amendment giving states more authority to restrict abortions.

MAR. 4 Yale women's varsity crew, protesting the lack of shower facilities as a violation of Title IX (equal facilities for women's athletic teams), strip in the office of the director of physical education who later announces that new facilities would be built.

8 President Ford appoints Jeanne M. Holm as Special Assistant for Women's Affairs.

10 New York State Legislature kills bill which would have eliminated the concept of alimony by providing maintenance payments to either party depending on economic need and would have divided all assets and property of a marriage equitably regardless of which party had legal title to them.

19 Another feminist first: Naval Academy announces that seven women will become plebes on July 6.

MAY 2 Maine Maritime Academy's top-ranking graduate is Deborah B. Doane of Essex, Conn., school's first female student. First woman in U.S. to graduate from a four-year maritime school.

JUNE 3 New York State Senate kills bill requiring equitable distribution of the property of a marriage and giving financial value to a woman's contribution as homemaker and child rearer.

12 Jimmy Carter reaffirms his support of the E.R.A.

23 Women's Tennis Association threatens to boycott next year's Wimbledon unless prize money for men and women is equalized.

JULY 30 Labor Minister Tina Anselmi, former school teacher, is first woman minister in Italy's history.

SEPT. 13 Second International Festival of Women's Films opens in New York City.

Food

JAN. 10 Food and Drug Administration proposes ban on DES (diethylsilbestrol) used as growth stimulant in cattle as possible cancer-causing substance.

11 Carnegie Endowment for International Peace alleges starvation of 500,000 in Ethiopian drought of 1973–74 as result of the silence of relief agencies, diplomats and embassies.

20 Red No. 2, nation's most widely used dye, is banned by the Food and Drug Administration as cancer-causing agent. U.S. Appeals Court upholds ruling.

29 Poor harvest leads to soaring potato prices in Europe.

FEB. 1 Soviet Union confirms poor harvest in 1975, lowest in a decade.

APR. 29 Soviet Union purchases American corn and wheat valued at more than $400 million.

MAY 12 Food and Drug Administration refuses to lift ban on cyclamate, the artificial sweetener.

JUNE 19 Federal judge stays Agriculture Dept. order to cut back $1 billion in food stamp benefits.

26 India harvests a food surplus; two bumper crops enable the country to retain a buffer stock large enough to last for two scarcity years.

SEPT. 9 Agriculture Dept. predicts smaller sales of American wheat to Soviet Union because of larger anticipated Russian grain harvest.

22 F.D.A. bans use of Red No. 4 dye and carbon black in food items.

Health and Medicine

1975

NOV. 13 World Health Organization announces that Asia is free of smallpox for the first time in history.

DEC. 10 Diabetes is reported to be the third ranking cause of death in nation.

1976

JAN. 1 Medicare premiums jump from $6.70 to $7.20 a month; officials urge further increase for actuarial soundness.

1 West Coast doctors stage slowdown to protest soaring malpractice rates.

FEB. 15 Population Council report states that women over forty who take oral contraceptives face risk of death greater than that created by any other method of birth control.

18 A three-drug treatment after breast cancer surgery has reduced its recurrence among patients who face high risk of relapse.

20 Center for Disease Control in Atlanta alerts World Health Organization on possibility of influenza pandemic comparable to that of 1917–18.

26 Indian state prepares compulsory sterilization law limiting the number of children in a family. Delhi residents and government employees who do not limit their families to two children will be denied all government assistance.

MAR. 1 Doctors discover that nitrous oxide (laughing gas) relieves pain from heart attacks.

24 President Ford calls for government-supported campaign to inoculate whole U.S. population against new influenza virus, to forestall epidemic next winter.

MAY 5 Nationwide study finds sterilization is fastest-growing contraceptive technique among married Americans.

16 Survey reveals that only a minority of American men now smoke cigarettes, indicating an increasing awareness of the health hazards involved.

JULY 21 General Accounting Office inquiry finds F.D.A., drug makers, doctors and research scientists expose humans to unnecessary risks in testing new drugs.

23 F.D.A. warns doctors popular tranquilizers—Valium, Librium, Miltown and others—may cause birth defects if taken early in pregnancy.

AUG. 3 Internal Army report tells of Government effort to conceal Army sponsorship of experiments with hallucinogenic drugs that resulted in death of civilian subject in New York 23 years ago.

4 27 die, 115 ill from mysterious "American Legion" disease after Legion convention in Philadelphia.

7 Indian state of Maharashtra first political entity in world to legislate population control by enforced sterilization.

20 Federal Government moving to tighten controls on Darvon, mild pain-killer. Overuse by addicts linked to many deaths.

25 National Cancer Institute and National Cancer Society advise curbs on breast X-rays for women under 50.

29 Senate inquiry finds fraud and waste cause loss of over fourth of $15 billion spent yearly in Medicaid program in eight cities.

SEPT. 2 Health authorities on worldwide alert for new strain of gonorrhea resistant to penicillin.

17 Senate bans most abortions paid by Medicaid.

Consumers

JAN. 2 Federal Trade Commission orders used-car dealers to disclose all relevant information to prospective purchasers.

MAR. 23 Government antitrust action charges General Motors with monopoly of crash replacement parts.

23 President Ford signs bill prohibiting discrimination in giving credit.

MAY 15 Federal Trade Commission issues new rules to protect consumers in the purchase of defective merchandise. Lenders in an installment contract are now liable for claims made by the debtor.

25 Supreme Court decision permitting pharmacists to advertise prescription drug prices is hailed as a victory for consumers.

SEPT. 10 Federal judge bars Dept. of Agriculture regulations permitting bits of bone to be included in ground meats.

22 Eight consumer groups charge President Ford with anti-consumer behavior resulting in lower living standards and endangered public health and safety.

Energy

THERE WAS NOT MUCH EVIDENCE of an energy crisis during the past year.

Furthermore, economic recovery meant a growing demand for energy, while production of natural gas and crude oil was falling off and expansion of coal and nuclear power was slowed by environmental debates, increased capital costs and concern about nuclear safety. The conservation record of the United States is best described by the report of the International Energy Agency that this country has the poorest conservation record among the 18 member nations.

The Presidential campaign offered little enlightenment to the electorate on energy problems and issues. Although the Democratic platform offered such radical proposals as the break-up of vertical and horizontal energy monopolies, forcing the major oil companies out of producing, refining or marketing and

preventing them from investing in coal, such proposals made little impression as conservative personalities supplanted issues as major considerations in the campaign. And so the oil companies continued to respond to the crisis by increasing their advertising budgets and their support of cultural programs on the media.

Thus, "Project Independence" seems as remote as ever.

1975

DEC. 22 President Ford signs most comprehensive energy legislation in nation's history, the Energy Policy and Conservation Act of 1975. Some provisions:

● Allows moderate rise in oil prices

● Auto makers must comply with gasoline mileage standards

● Establishes strategic petroleum reserves

● Authorizes the President to develop contingency plans for energy emergencies, including possible fuel rationing.

● Authorizes loans to coal operators investing in new underground mines.

1976

JAN. 1 Dept. of Interior announces sale of leases to oil companies; more than a million acres on New England continental shelf leased for oil exploration.

1 Federal Power Commission authorizes interstate natural gas pipelines to lend money to oil companies to finance exploration.

30 International Energy Agency, an organization of the 18 leading oil-consuming nations, agrees on long-term program of energy development to lessen dependence on foreign oil.

FEB. 5 President Ford's natural gas deregulation bill defeated in the House.

27 In annual energy message to Congress, President Ford asks for $1 billion to help states cope with problems arising from development of energy resources on Federal lands.

MAR. 5 Congress authorizes full-scale oil production at naval petroleum reserves, including Teapot Dome in Wyoming.

APR. 10 Claiming that benefits outweigh environmental effects, Nuclear Regulatory Commission backs construction permits for world's first floating nuclear plant off New Jersey coast; state demands that Federal government analyze all risks.

MAY 11 Federal report says safe management of radioactive wastes from increased nuclear energy production is feasible.

JUNE 19 Energy shortages revive interest in the use of Bay of Fundy tides to generate electric power.

JULY 26 Ford signs bill for $1.6 billion to aid coastal communities to deal with problems resulting from development of offshore gas and oil.

AUG. 13 Federal judge in Brooklyn enjoins U.S. from carrying out first sale of oil and natural-gas leases in Atlantic Ocean, citing deficiency in environmental-impact statement.

SEPT. 22 British royal commission on environmental pollution urges postponement of nuclear energy expansion. Defeat of Swedish Social Democrats attributed to same issue.

Environment and Pollution

IT WAS A BAD YEAR for reform movements. The environmentalist movement was no exception. Despite the moderate recovery, officials in industry and government were demanding a relaxation of controls in the name of helping the economy. As New York's Governor Hugh L. Carey put it: "It will be little good if we rescue our environment at the expense of the economy."

Although environmentalists pointed to the tangible economic benefits of environmental improvement in the form of capital investments for sewage-treatment programs and pollution control, industry was not convinced. The campaign to slow down the introduction of environmental controls continued.

There were decreased appropriations for the enforcement of environmental statutes. Electric utilities asked for permission to burn higher sulfur fuel. There was a slackening in the rate of pollution abatement. More frequently, one heard recommendations that would have been unacceptable a few years ago. For example, one official recommended that General Electric be given more time to reduce its discharges of toxic compounds into the Hudson River to avert the possible closing of plants with 1,200 workers.

Governor James A. Rhodes of Ohio summed it all up when he called environmental concerns a luxury that can be ill afforded at this time. And the Governor made certain that he would not be misunderstood when he denounced the state's Environmental Protection Agency as a harasser of local governments and private industry.

JAN. 1 Environmental Protection Agency orders United States Steel to close Gary, Ind., coke plants in violation of Federal clean air standards.

1 100,000 gallons of home heating oil spill into Hudson River when barge hits bridge abutment; officials fear effects may last for years.

6 California fines American Motors Corp. $4.2 million for violating state's automotive pollution control standards.

FEB. 3 Three General Electric engineers specializing in nuclear reactors quit jobs for volunteer work in movement to halt spread of nuclear power.

10 New York State's Dept. of Environmental Conservation finds General Electric guilty of discharging toxic polychlorinated biphenyls (PCBs) into Hudson River.

12 Governor Brendan T. Byrne says New Jersey will relax emission standards permitting industries and power companies to burn fuel with higher sulfur content; Governor Carey of New York suggests stress on economic recovery even at expense of some environmental gains.

17 Mediterranean nations sign pact to halt further pollution of the inland sea.

18 New York State's Environmental Conservation Commission orders closing of Hudson River as commercial fishery because of PCB contamination.

MAR. 11 Canadian-American agency reports that it will take more than a decade to clean up the polluted waters of the Great Lakes.

25 Environmentalists name "dirty dozen" members of the House of Representatives with poor voting records on ecological issues.

APR. 15 Power companies cancel plans for power plant project in scenic area of Utah; conservationists claim a victory while others see a setback to national energy development program.

29 Ogden R. Reid, ardent conservationist, resigns as New York State's Commissioner of Environmental Conservation, citing disagreements on basic policies.

MAY 8 U.S. jury indicts Allied Chemical Corp. on criminal charge of discharging Kepone into Virginia's James River, forcing a shutdown of a multimillion-dollar fishing industry. Kepone has caused tremors and sight impairment to those exposed.

JUNE 1 U.N. Conference on Human Settlements (Habitat) opens in Vancouver to explore the reasons for the failure of human settlements in both rich and poor countries to meet people's needs.

15 Proposition 15, limiting construction of nuclear power plants in California, defeated by a 2–1 vote.

16 International Society for Protection of Animals organizes Operation Noah II in Panama to rescue animals of all species from rising waters of new dam.

19 U.S. Fish and Wildlife Service will publish a list of endangered plants for the first time.

22 Long Island beaches are closed when sewage and debris floats ashore.

JULY 30 Scientists state that dumping site near New Jersey shore operated by Army Corps of Engineers is a threat to the waters south of New York City.

AUG. 6 Senate approves omnibus bill broadening Clean Air Act of 1970 and giving the automobile industry more time to meet exhaust emission standards.

SEPT. 7 New York State's Dept. of Environmental Conservation and the General Electric Co. agree on terms to finance the cleansing of the Hudson River of toxic PCBs dumped there by the company.

13 National Academy of Sciences report calls for two-year delay before action is taken to limit use of fluorocarbon gases in spray cans, which results in damage to the atmosphere's ozone layer. Later Dr. Russell W. Peterson, chairman of Council on Environmental Quality, urges industry to phase out its use of fluorocarbons, particularly as spray-can propellants.

Intelligence Agencies

1975

NOV. 20 Senate panel reports that government officials instigated assassination plots against foreign leaders.

DEC. 4 Senate panel clears C.I.A. of direct role in 1973 Chile coup, but finds that the U.S. encouraged the overthrow of Salvador Allende Gossens.

23 Richard S. Welch, station chief in Athens for the C.I.A., is killed by gunmen.

1976

JAN. 2 Federal Bureau of Investigation files indicate that confidential talks between Julius and Ethel Rosenberg and their attorney were reported to the F.B.I. by an informant.

15 House of Representatives Intelligence Committee report charges that:

● Intelligence agencies operate in such secret ways that they are beyond Congressional scrutiny.

- The C.I.A. violated a Presidential directive prohibiting secret assistance to educational institutions.

- Secret budget figures given to Congress were inaccurate ($10 billion spent, rather than $3 billion).

- C.I.A. is guilty of wastefulness, questionable expenditures and inadequate auditing.

30 President Ford and the C.I.A. are victorious when the House of Representatives withholds final report of the Select Committee on Intelligence until it has been approved by the executive branch. Chairman Otis G. Pike declares the move "a complete travesty of the whole doctrine of separation of powers."

FEB. 6 Senator Frank Church of Idaho, citing evidence of criminal activity, calls for a special prosecutor to investigate the C.I.A. and the F.B.I.

18 Reorganization of U.S. intelligence agencies by President Ford includes a three-man oversight board and centralization in the National Security Council. Critics charge the plan with more secrecy, greater executive power and less Congressional oversight.

MAR. 2 Former Mobil Oil engineer commits suicide when exposed as double agent for Soviet Union and F.B.I. by Dallas newspaper.

3 House of Representatives Ethics Committee prepares for major investigation into the leaking of the House Intelligence Committee Report to newspapers by newsman Daniel Schorr.

10 Rep. Pike accuses C.I.A. of seeking to discredit him and Congress in an effort to gloss over the findings of the House Select Committee on Intelligence.

APR. 1 Att. Gen. Edward H. Levi names panel of lawyers to review F.B.I. domestic counterintelligence program and orders F.B.I. to notify victimized citizens that they were targets of harassment and disruption.

23 Senate documents show F.B.I. has maintained network of confidential informers inside major news organizations, universities and charitable foundations.

28 Senate Select Intelligence Committee, ending 15-month investigation, finds:

- F.B.I. and other domestic intelligence agencies illegally investigated political activities of hundreds of thousands of citizens.

- Government officials knowingly took part in illegal activities. Presidents from Franklin D. Roosevelt onward and their aides requested or accepted politically useful information from the F.B.I. about their opponents and critics.

- The F.B.I., C.I.A., Army Intelligence and other intelligence agencies created files on more than 500,000 U.S. citizens, opened 500,000 pieces of first-class mail, monitored telegrams and overseas calls, listed 26,000 citizens for detention in a national emergency and subjected many to harassment designed to destroy their reputations.

- The targets were such varied organizations and individuals as the N.A.A.C.P., Ku Klux Klan, the anti-Vietnam war groups, John Birch Society, the feminist movement, Martin Luther King, Jr., congressmen and senators.

- Failure at all levels to control covert activities. The Senate Committee made the following recommendations:

- Congress should adopt an omnibus law creating charters for agencies in foreign and military intelligence and sharply limit covert action in foreign policy.

- Attempts to assassinate foreign leaders and subvert democratic governments should be banned.

- Congress and the Executive should be partners in overseeing intelligence operations.

- No intelligence agency should be permitted to undertake activities not expressly authorized by law.

- Court approval should be required for wiretapping and unauthorized break-ins.

- All domestic non-criminal intelligence activity should be vested in the F.B.I. and monitored by Congress.

MAY 6 Senate Committee staff reports that the F.B.I. tried to smear Martin Luther King, Jr., even after his death, treating him much like a Soviet agent and even had plans to harass his widow.

19 Senate votes permanent watchdog committee with broad powers to monitor intelligence agencies, including exclusive oversight over the C.I.A.

JUNE 24 Dept. of Justice conducts nationwide investigation of alleged illegal burglaries since 1971 by the F.B.I. against New Left organizations.

JULY 1 Clarence M. Kelley, F.B.I. director, concedes that bureau carried out in 1972 and 1973 "a limited number" of break-ins directed at radical domestic and terrorist groups. Had previously insisted burglaries halted in 1966.

AUG. 11 In response to criticism of F.B.I.'s domestic intelligence operations, Director Kelley announces extensive internal reorganization of bureau.

17 W. Mark Felt, former F.B.I. associate director, says he approved two F.B.I. burglaries in 1972. Next day, a former F.B.I. official says L. Patrick Gray 3rd, former director, authorized burglary by agents.

21 Justice Dept. investigators find evidence that F.B.I. stole mail as part of drive on war foes.

31 F.B.I. Chief Kelley acknowledges questioning about his possible misuse of Government services and property in his home. On Sept. 4, President Ford decides to let Kelley stay on in office despite gifts from aides and use of U.S. property.

Multinational

JAN. 1 Reports to SEC describe Gulf Oil's contributions to politicians and candidates here and abroad as "shot through with illegality."

FEB. 15 Tenneco, a multinational conglomerate, tells S.E.C. of foreign and domestic payments to military groups, politicians, public utility regulators and judges.

MAR. 5 Gulf Oil will try to recover the $12.3 million given to politicians here and abroad for more than a decade.

APR. 1 President Ford, denouncing "corrupt business practices," names 10 to panel to review issue of overseas bribes by American corporations.

14 S.E.C. and Lockheed Aircraft agree on settlement of charges that company illegally made secret payments of $25 million to foreign officials, thus clearing the way for company's recapitalization plan.

MAY 7 Senators offer legislation calling for major reforms to end bribery by American companies doing business abroad.

11 General Tire and Rubber agrees to settle S.E.C. suit charging illegal campaign contributions and illegal payments abroad.

27 Twenty-four O.E.C.D. countries (Organization for Economic Cooperation and Development) agree on voluntary guidelines for multinational corporations after disclosures of widespread bribery.

JUNE 10 Loews Corp. admits $1.5 million payments abroad to promote sale of tobacco products.

JULY 9 Tokuji Wakasa, president of All Nippon Airways, Japan's largest airline, is seventh arrested in investigation into Lockheed payoff scandal.

28 Japan's former prime minister, Kakuei Tanaka, arrested on charges of accepting Lockheed money.

SEPT. 10 Three U.S. corporations—Reynolds Industries, Gulf Oil and Gulf and Western—report questionable payments to promote business and political interests.

Religion

1975

DEC. 23 Pope Paul VI ends 1975 Holy Year of the Roman Catholic Church by sealing the Holy Door of St. Peter's Basilica in Rome.

1976

JAN. 4 University of Delaware is appealing a state court decision denying the right of the university to prohibit religious services on campus.

16 Vatican calls for sexual morality condemning premarital sex, homosexual acts and masturbation.

MAR. 24 Survey finds Papal stand on birth control has harmed Roman Catholic Church in the U.S.

JUNE 22 Supreme Court rules that states may provide funds to church-affiliated colleges.

SEPT. 11 Presiding Bishop of Episcopal Church proposes that women he ordained to the priesthood in areas where they would be accepted.

Space

JAN. 2 National Aeronautics and Space Administration (NASA) announces 18 major satellite launchings beginning with a communications technology satellite from Cape Canaveral on Jan. 13.

MAR. 25 Huge magnetic tail reported on Jupiter in data from Pioneer 10 spacecraft.

APR. 2 Scientists find evidence that planet Pluto is partly covered with methane ice.

MAY 7 New observations indicate that fluorocarbons, used in spray cans and air-conditioning systems, may be depleting protective layer of ozone in stratosphere at slower rate than supposed.

JULY 7 Two-man Soviet spacecraft launched, apparently destined for rendezvous with orbiting research station.

7 Two Soviet astronauts pilot Soyuz 21 spacecraft to a safe docking with orbiting Salyut 5 space station, then board station for what may be stay up to three months.

21 Viking 1 Robot lands safely on Mars after voyage of 11 months and nearly half a billion miles. Transmits photos of rocky, wind-scoured desert plain, in first direct search for life on another world. Billion dollar project eight years in preparation. First analysis data sent back to earth provide clues to planet's history, including possibility of water hidden beneath surface. More photos reveal pink skies above reddish soil, and rocks of varied chemistry. Data indicate 3% of Martian air is nitrogen and 1.5% argon. Discovery of nitrogen rekindles hopes that planet may once have harbored life. Viking's robot arm balks in test but finally releases a metal pin. Arm scoops up soil and pours it into automated biological laboratories to test for evidence of life. Scoop apparently fails in attempt to drop sample for testing for organic material. First soil analysis results sent back show soil is made up of iron, sand and other elements reddened or rusted by thin coating of iron oxides.

AUG. 24 Two Soviet astronauts home safely after two months aboard orbiting Salyut 5.

SEPT. 3 Viking 2 lander settles on Mars and sends signal. On Sept. 4, Viking 2 photos show boulder-strewn landscape.

9 American astronomers obtain radar images of Venus which reveal a huge lava flow, impact basin similar to those on moon and earth-like mountain-building processes.

Transportation

JAN. 4 One of the longest strikes in domestic aviation history ends with acceptance of new contract by National Airlines flight attendants.

FEB. 5 Transportation Sec. William T. Coleman, Jr., rules that supersonic Concorde airliner can land in New York and Washington on 16-month trial basis; decision protested by motorcade at John F. Kennedy Airport in New York. New York State Legislature bars SST at New York airports on basis of high noise levels. Port Authority of New York and New Jersey votes to ban flights at Kennedy Airport until noise levels can be studied.

APR. 2 New York transit strike averted by two-year pact calling for cost-of-living wage adjustment tied to productivity savings.

4 Teamsters Union and major truckers reach agreement to end nationwide strike.

MAY 9 Strike by municipal craft workers ends in San Francisco after 39 days when city and union leaders agree on back-to-work settlement.

24 Concorde jets arrive in Washington after four-hour flight from London and Paris.

JUNE 29 Canadian pilots end nine-day walkout following Government announcement that extension of use of French language at Quebec airports will be re-examined and submitted to Parliament.

JULY 26 Passengers debark from Queen Elizabeth 2 liner in London after fire halts cruise to New York.

SEPT. 2 C.A.B. approves new category of charter flights expanding opportunity for low-cost travel.

Bicentennial

JAN. 1 Liberty Bell moved from historic Independence Hall to nearby pavilion for easier viewing by tourists.

MAY 7 Britain presents a visiting Congressional delegation with a gold-embossed reproduction of the Declaration of Independence.

JUNE 27 The phrase is now "A Slow Boat to Newport" as belated fleet of square-riggers, becalmed in the ocean for two days, finally enters Newport in Bicentennial sailing race.

JULY 2 First 20 of tall ships, international flotillas of warships and sailing ships, moved toward New York for international naval review and Operation Sail.

3 International warships from 22 nations sail into New York Harbor and more than 200 high-masted sailing ships occupy temporary berths in preparation for Bicentennial observance. Crowds flock to see the ships. In Washington, 500,000 see parade. In series of speeches, President Ford praises "American adventurers."

4 On Independence Day, the nation celebrates its 200th anniversary with pageantry and prayer, games, parades, picnics, bell-ringing and protests. The celebrations begin with a flag-raising atop Mars Hill Mountain in Maine, where dawn reaches the continent, and move on to Fort McHenry in Baltimore Harbor. The activities end nearly a day later with an indigenous festival in American Samoa in the Pacific.

At least a million people celebrate in Philadelphia, where bells ring, bands blare, choirs sing and fireworks explode. President Ford recalls the first Fourth of July as the "beginning of a continuing adventure." In the nation's keynote address at Independence Hall, he declares: "Liberty is a living flame to be fed, not dead ashes to be revered." The main protests are staged in Philadelphia by various leftist, minority and women's groups.

In New York, millions of New Yorkers and visitors observe the anniversary with panoramic spectacles that include an armada of tall-masted ships, a massive fireworks display and numerous festivals, many of ethnic character.

6 Queen Elizabeth II greeted enthusiastically in Philadelphia as she starts East Coast tour celebrating Bicentennial. Says Independence Day should be celebrated as much in Britain as in America "in sincere gratitude to the Founding Fathers of the great Republic for having taught Britain a very valuable lesson."

10 Queen Elizabeth entertains Fords and Sec. of State Henry A. Kissinger aboard royal yacht Britannia at U.S. naval base at Newport, R.I.

12 Queen applauded by crowds as she spends last day of her U.S. visit in Boston. Security is heavy. Queen gives no evidence of seeing demonstrators protesting British actions in Ireland.

Disasters

1975

DEC. 27 Mine blast and cave-in in India traps 372 miners.

1976

JAN. 2 Crash of Lebanese jet in Saudi Arabia results in death of 82 passengers and crewmen.

FEB. 5 Major earthquake hits Guatemala, leaving 22,000 dead and 40,000 injured.

MAR. 10 Fall of cable car leads to death of 42 skiers at Italian ski resort.

APR. 10 Two earth tremors in Ecuador kill 7 and injure 50.

28 American Airlines jet crashes on landing at Charlotte Amalie in the Virgin Islands; 37 dead.

MAY 5 Collision in Netherlands between the Rhine Express and a Dutch commuter train kills 23 passengers.

7 Strong earthquake strikes northeast Italy, resulting in 1,000 deaths.

22 School bus carrying California high school choir crashes through barrier and overturns; 20 killed and 20 seriously injured.

JUNE 7 Collapse of Teton Dam in Idaho leads to flooding of 35 miles of farmland; 6 dead.

JULY 9 Indonesia puts death toll above 9,000 in earthquake and landslides on New Guinea June 26.

16 Earthquake on Island of Bali kills at least 440 people and injures almost 3,000.

28-29 Second powerful earthquake, at 7.9 on Richter scale, strikes northeast China 16 hours after major tremor of force 8.2 on Richter scale hits same area. Diplomats believe at least 10,000 people were killed of two million estimated to live within 25 miles of epicenter.

AUG. 1 Sudden downpour starts cascade down heavily traveled route 34, Big Thompson Canyon, near Loveland, Colo. Three days later, death toll eventually reaches 138 with scores missing.

18 Earthquake on Philippines island of Mindanao leaves more than 3,000 dead.

28 Two giant Air Force transport jet planes crash in separate accidents in Britain and Greenland. At least 38 killed.

SEPT. 4 68 killed in Azores crash of Venezuelan plane carrying choir to Spain.

10 Mid-air collision of British and Yugoslavian planes near Zagreb results in death of all 176 persons aboard; worst collision in aviation history.

Crime and Violence

1975

NOV. 17 F.B.I. reports that criminals struck 19 times every minute to claim 20,000 lives and $2.6 billion in loot as crime in U.S. rose 18% last year.

DEC. 17 Lynette Fromme is sentenced to life imprisonment for attempting to kill President Ford.

21 Terrorists raid O.P.E.C. meeting in Vienna, killing two; oil ministers flown to Algeria and released.

29 Powerful bomb explosion in baggage claim area of New York City's La Guardia Airport leaves 11 dead and 70 injured.

1976

JAN. 7 Ralph G. Newman, literary appraiser, fined $10,000 for helping Nixon get a $450,000 tax deduction by back-dating Vice-Presidential papers.

11 New York City prosecutor reports widespread abuses in nursing home business and Medicaid overcharges of at least $70 million.

16 Sara Jane Moore sentenced to life imprisonment for attempted assassination of President Ford.

FEB. 3 Eugene Hollander, major nursing home owner, admits fraud on Medicaid; agrees to pay more than $1 million to government.

MAR. 7 Rabbi Bernard Bergman, key figure in New York City's nursing home scandal, pleads guilty to $1.2 million Medicare fraud and to the bribery of Albert H. Blumenthal, Assembly majority leader. Blumenthal indictment for bribes and misconduct is later dismissed.

21 Patricia Hearst convicted of armed robbery and the use of a gun to commit a felony.

APR. 8 W. A. Boyle, former United Mine Workers president, begins serving three consecutive life sentences in Yablonski murders.

MAY 6 Governor Arch A. Moore of West Virginia acquitted by Federal jury of plotting to extort $25,000 from businessman seeking a state bank charter.

17 El Salvador's chief of staff is charged with a plot to sell 10,000 submachine guns to underworld groups in the U.S.

20 Dr. Mario E. Jascalevich is indicted in New Jersey on a charge of killing five patients at Oradell hospital by administering curare, a muscle relaxant.

25 $800,000 theft at Kennedy International Airport in New York City is the largest in U.S. Postal Service history.

JUNE 12 Don Bolles, newspaper reporter, dies after bomb explosion in his car; was investigating corruption in Arizona involving the Mafia.

JUNE 17 Two nurses are charged with first-degree murder for introducing poison into intravenous medicine at Michigan Veterans' Hospital.

JULY 8 I.R.S. inspectors investigating allegations that service employees who reviewed tax matters for Gulf Oil Corp. regularly accepted gratuities from corporation representatives.

17 Twenty-six school children and bus driver disappear in rural central California community. Next day children and driver escape from an underground cell. Three men later held as abductors.

21 Thieves get $10 million to $15 million from vault of bank in Nice, France, after digging 30-foot tunnel from sewer.

AUG. 9 William and Emily Harris, members of self-styled Symbionese Liberation Army, convicted of kidnaping, robbery and motor vehicle charges stemming from flight with Patricia Hearst from near arrest at a sporting goods store.

20 Former lobbyist Jake Jacobsen gets two years' probation for part in milk price scandal in Nixon Administration.

24 Rep. Allan T. Howe of Utah guilty in second trial for soliciting sex acts from police decoys. Gets suspended 30-day jail sentence.

28 Three Americans convicted in Moscow court and sentenced to total of 20 years in labor camps on charges of having attempted to smuggle heroin through Soviet Union.

SEPT. 3 Two get life terms in Yablonski killings. Testimony had helped to convict W. A. Boyle and other U.M.W. leaders.

10 TWA plane en route from New York to Chicago hijacked by Croatian nationalists; one policeman killed by explosion of bomb left in New York City locker by hijackers. Hostages later released in Paris and hijackers flown to U.S.

14 Rabbi Bernard Bergman sentenced to one-year prison term for bribery of public official in nursing home scandal; court castigates Bergman as "corrupt individual warped by greed."

21 Bomb kills former Foreign Minister of Chile, Orlando Letelier, in Washington, D.C. Many attribute the murder to Chilean military junta whose secret police have harassed enemies of regime in other world capitals.

Arts

JAN. 1 Metropolitan Opera signs two-year agreement with orchestra, guaranteeing 44 weeks of employment with supplementary unemployment insurance benefits.

1 Dorothy Kirsten, soprano, retires from Metropolitan Opera after a 30-year career.

3 Rembrandt painting titled "Elsbeth van Rij," stolen in April, is returned to Boston's Museum of Fine Arts.

13 Sarah Caldwell sets precedent as first woman to conduct Metropolitan Opera orchestra; leads orchestra in Verdi's "La Traviata" with Beverly Sills as Violetta.

17 Painter Mark Rothko's daughter is appointed sole administrator of her father's estate consisting principally of 798 paintings.

FEB. 2 $4.5-million art theft in Avignon, France, includes 119 Picasso paintings.

26 Zubin Mehta is named new Music Director of the New York Philharmonic, succeeding Pierre Boulez.

MAR. 16 Pianist Artur Rubinstein, at 89, gives concert in Carnegie Hall, the 70th anniversary of his debut in the same hall.

30 "Cuckoo's Nest" wins Oscars for best film, best actor and actress of 1975.

MAY 4 Saul Bellow wins Pulitzer prize in fiction for novel, "Humboldt's Gift."

5 "1600 Pennsylvania Avenue," musical by Leonard Bernstein and Alan Jay Lerner, opens to critical reviews and closes after six performances.

17 Avery Fisher Hall in New York City's Lincoln Center, the home of the Philharmonic Orchestra, undergoes another acoustical renovation at cost of $5 million.

JUNE 4 Picasso estate valued at more than $1 billion, of which $250 million consists of Picasso paintings and sculptures.

JULY 26 Vladimir Horowitz, 71-year-old piano virtuoso, to teach at Mannes College of Music in New York City.

31 Strange "Ring" cycle ends at Bayreuth, Germany, with "Götterdämmerung". Four operas produced in Victorian and modern dress.

AUG. 23 John Philip Sousa inducted into Hall of Fame for Great Americans.

SEPT. 7 Milan's La Scala Opera makes historic U.S. debut before élite audience in Washington's Kennedy Center.

8 In a Bicentennial tribute, Paris Opera opens with Mozart's *Le Nozze de Figaro* at New York's Metropolitan Opera House.

29 Rembrandt's painting "Juno" purchased by Armand Hammer for $3,250,000.

Education and Science

JAN. 1 Physicists discover indestructible subatomic particles of matter known as "charmed" quarks.

FEB. 5 UNESCO reports failure of 10-year drive to end world illiteracy; estimate 800 million illiterates on planet.

21 Two-year community colleges throughout the country are endangered by financial pressures and critical attitudes toward nonselective admissions and low tuition policies.

25 Scientists find more clues to "master switch" of genetic control system in cells.

APR. 8 National Cancer Institute links pesticide Kepone to liver cancer in animals.

MAY 7 Officers on West Point legal staff ask Army inquiry into academy's handling of cadet cheating scandal.

11 President Ford signs bill to re-establish White House Office of Science and Technology, giving scientists first access to Oval Office since Nixon ended the agency three years ago.

29 Chancellor closes City University of New York, one of the largest in the world, because of fiscal crisis; tuition will be charged for the first time in 129 years.

JUNE 18 Physicists believe mica specimens from Africa contain some superheavy elements, including Number 126 in the Periodic Table of Elements.

22 Senate Armed Services subcommittee examines all academic procedures at West Point in the wake of mass cheating scandal and violations of honor system by cadets.

24 National Institutes of Health issue guidelines to curb hazards in genetic research.

JULY 9 Use of glass fiber, thin as human hair, begins in television transmission. New technology reported to be finding use in computer, aircraft and telephone industries.

AUG. 23 West Point cadets ousted in cheating scandal offered opportunity to reapply after year in service.

23 U.S. Appeals Court upholds busing desegregation plan for Louisville and suburbs that set off violence a year previously.

28 M.I.T. scientists for first time synthesize a functioning gene, complete with regulatory mechanisms. Process called major step in procedure for learning how genes are controlled.

29 U.S. Appeals Court, in Cleveland suburb case, rules school officials cannot arbitrarily remove books from school library.

SEPT. 11 Report indicates continued decline in scores of high school seniors on their college board examinations.

21 Report by National Assessment of Educational Progress indicates that children's reading ability held steady in 1970s with 9-year-olds showing marked improvement.

21 Scientists propose quasi-judicial "science court" to weigh evidence behind such controversial issues as nuclear reactor safety, food additives and effects of pesticides and fluorocarbons.

People and Things

1975

NOV. 17 Eldridge Cleaver, former leader of Black Panther Party and fugitive from justice, returns to the United States after seven years of voluntary exile.

1976

JAN. 1 Doc, a lion at St. Paul zoo, dies after attack by two lionesses who had been his mates in recent years.

8 Census Bureau reports that American adults are slower to marry and quicker to divorce than in the past.

15 Marion B. Javits registers as foreign agent of Iran; denies conflict of interest although her husband is a member of the Senate Foreign Relations Committee.

FEB. 12 Private Citizen Richard M. Nixon to visit China as guest of the Chinese government.

20 Marlon Brando turns down award from N.A.A.C.P. on the ground that "a white man cannot know what the black experience is."

26 Gen. Bernard W. Rogers pays government over $900 because his golf shoes were flown to him in an otherwise empty military plane.

MAR. 18 Twenty-five congressmen get a free trip to England to receive a copy of Magna Carta for bicentennial display in the U.S.

25 Tax-fraud charges against Ingmar Bergman are dropped; world-famous film director leaves Sweden to work abroad.

APR. 1 New Jersey Supreme Court rules father can let Karen Anne Quinlan die by stopping respirator if doctors see no hope of recovery for 22-year-old girl in coma almost a year.

2 President Ford gives Artur Rubinstein, 89-year-old pianist, Medal of Freedom, nation's highest civilian award.

8 Associates of late Howard H. Hughes believe eccentric billionaire left no will. Legal battle shapes up over division of $1.5-billion fortune.

22 Last American-built convertible, a white-on-white Cadillac with white leather and vinyl interior rolls off assembly line.

MAY 5 Australia adopts "Waltzing Matilda" as national anthem. Keeps "God Save the Queen" for royal occasions.

15 Cyril E. LaBrecque, captain of shipwrecked schooner, is found not guilty of manslaughter when his dog remained in lifeboat while two crewmen perished in the Atlantic.

27 Dorothy Schiff, New York Post editor and publisher, reveals "personal relationship" with Franklin D. Roosevelt from 1936 to 1943.

JUNE 18 American-born novelist Henry James who became a British subject is admitted to Westminster Abbey to join the great names of Britain's literary past.

JULY 2 Russian freighter rescues Karl Thomas, bobbing about in Atlantic in jettisoned gondola of "Spirit of '76" balloon after failure of attempted flight across ocean.

8 New York State Appellate Division disbars Richard Nixon on charges relating to Watergate.

24 Nixons sell second residence in Key Biscayne, Fla., compound for reported price of $390,000.

29 Spiro T. Agnew heads nonprofit foundation Education for Democracy, which expresses sympathy for Palestinian refugees in Middle East and is critical of détente with Soviet.

SEPT. 9 Expedition reports the finding of the Bonhomme Richard, the flagship of John Paul Jones, off the English coast.

15 Canada's Metric Commission announces timetables for metric conversion affecting autos, schools and real estate.

DEATHS IN 1975–1976

Day	Name	Age	Day	Name	Age

NOVEMBER

1   PASOLINI, Pier Paolo (film director; *The Decameron, Oedipus Rex, A Thousand and One Nights*) 53

5   SULLIVAN, Annette Kellerman (swimmer, originator of one-piece bathing suit) 87

5   TRILLING, Lionel (literary critic, Columbia U. professor) 70

10   SCHAEFFER, Jake (world champion billiard player) 81

11   ANDERSON, Clinton P. (ex-Secretary of Agriculture, ex-Senator from New Mexico) 80

13   SHERRIFF, Robert C. (playwright; *Journey's End*) 79

16   MORGAN, Arthur E. (first T.V.A. chairman, ex-president of Antioch College) 97

17   BRONK, Detlev W. (biophysicist, ex-president of Rockefeller U., Johns Hopkins U., National Academy of (Sciences) 78

20   FRANCO, Generalissimo Francisco (ruler of Spain 36 years) 82

23   HEALD, Henry T. (ex-head of Ford Foundation, ex-president of N.Y.U. and Illinois Institute of Technology) 71

26   PORTER, Paul A. (Washington lawyer, ex-head of O.P.A.) 71

29   HILL, Graham (British world champion racing driver) 46

DECEMBER

1   HALSTED, Anna Roosevelt (only daughter of F.D.R.) 69

1   FOX, Nellie (White Sox second baseman, American League MVP in 1959) 47

1   KENNY, Nick (newspaper columnist, writer of songs and verse) 80

2   MEYER, John C. (World War II ace, ex-commander of S.A.C.) 56

4   PHILLIPS, Wendell (millionaire oilman) . .54

4   ARENDT, Hannah (political scientist; *The Origins of Totalitarianism, Eichmann in Jerusalem*) 69

7   WILDER, Thornton (won three Pulitzer Prizes for writing; *The Bridge of San Luis Rey, Our Town, The Skin of Our Teeth*) 78

9   WELLMAN, William (film director; *Wings, A Star Is Born, Public Enemy*) . .79

14   TREACHER, Arthur (actor famed for portrayal of butlers) 81

17   SISSLE, Noble (band leader, song writer) 86

18   WHEELER, Earle G. (ex-chairman of Joint Chiefs of Staff) 67

24   LOSCH, Tilly (exotic dancer of 1920s and 1930s) 71

24   HERRMANN, Bernard (composer and Oscar winner) 64

29   GIBBONS, Euell (proponent of natural foods) 64

JANUARY

3   KIRCHWEY, Freda (editor and publisher of The Nation) 82

---

5   COSTELLO, John A. (ex-Prime Minister of Ireland) 84

8   CHOU En-lai (Premier of Red China since 1949) 78

9   GRANGER, Lester B. (ex-head of National Urban League) 79

12   CHRISTIE, Dame Agatha (writer of mysteries; *The Murder of Roger Ackroyd, Ten Little Indians, Murder on the Orient Express, The Mousetrap*) 85

13   LEIGHTON, Margaret (actress; *Night of the Iguana, Separate Tables*) 53

17   AUGUST, Jan (pianist; "Malaguena," "Misirlou," "Babalu") 71

18   THORNTON, Dan (ex-Governor of Colorado) 64

22   LESLIE, Edgar (lyricist; "Moon Over Miami," "For Me and My Gal," "Oh What a Pal Was Mary," "By the River Saint Marie") 90

23   ROBESON, Paul (all-America Rutgers end, concert singer, rights activist, actor: *Emperor Jones, Othello*) 77

24   LAVON, Pinhas (ex-Defense Minister of Israel) 71

FEBRUARY

5   SHUTTA, Ethel (singer in Broadway musicals; *Whoopie, Ziegfeld Follies*) . . .79

9   FAITH, Percy (orchestra conductor, arranger) 67

11   COBB, Lee J. (actor; *Death of a Salesman, On the Waterfront, King Lear*) 64

12   MINEO, Sal (actor; *Rebel Without a Cause, Exodus, The Longest Day*) 37

12   HERZBERG, Joseph G. (veteran newspaperman with *New York Herald Tribune, New York Times, Information Please Almanac*) 69

13   PONS, Lily (coloratura with Metropolitan Opera 25 years) 71

18   DOWLING, Eddie (song-and-dance man, playwright, producer, song writer; *Ziegfeld Follies*) 86

19   SULLIVAN, Frank (humorist; wrote for the *New Yorker*) 83

22   BADDELEY, Angela (actress; *Upstairs, Downstairs*) 71

24   SMITH, H. Allen (newspaperman, humorist; *Low Man on the Totem Pole, Rhubarb, Lost in the Horse Latitudes*) 68

MARCH

1   MARTINON, Jean (orchestra conductor; led Chicago Symphony in 1960s) 66

3   GILBERT, Ray (song writer; won 1947 Oscar for "Zip-a-Dee-Doo-Dah") 63

5   LEDERER, Charles (stage and screen writer; *Kismet, The Front Page, Mutiny on the Bounty*) 65

6   ROSENBLOOM, Maxie (ex-light heavyweight boxing champion; actor) 71

7   PATMAN, Wright (dean of House of Representatives; ex-chairman of Committee on Banking, Currency and Housing) 82

Day	Name	Age
14	BERKELEY, Busby (dance director in films; *Gold Diggers, 42d Street, Footlight Parade*)	.80
14	MIELZINER, Jo (theatrical set designer; *Guys and Dolls, South Pacific, Death of a Salesman*)	.74
17	VISCONTI, Luchino (film director; *Death in Venice, The Leopard, Rocco and His Brothers*)	.69
24	MONTGOMERY, Viscount of Alamein (top British commander in World War II)	.88
26	LIN Yutang (poet; historian; philosopher; *The Importance of Living*)	.80
28	ARLEN, Richard (actor; *Wings*)	.75
30	BLOOM, Rube (song writer; *"Give Me the Simple Life," "Penthouse Serenade," "Don't Worry 'Bout Me," "Fools Rush In"*)	.73
31	STREETER, Edward (humorist; *Father of the Bride, Dere Mable*)	.84

APRIL

Day	Name	Age
1	ERNST, Max (surrealist painter and sculptor)	.85
5	DAVIS, Meyer (society orchestra leader)	.81
5	HUGHES, Howard (reclusive billionaire industrialist)	.70
7	McBRIDE, Mary Margaret (pioneer in radio talk shows)	.76
9	OCHS, Phil (folk singer, guitarist)	.35
12	FORD, Paul (actor); *The Teahouse of the August Moon*, "Sgt. Bilko" show on TV)	.74
15	SMITH, Gerald L.K. (right-wing crusader)	.78
18	BELKIN, Samuel (chancellor of Yeshiva University; Talmudic scholar)	.64
22	BROWN, Joe David (novelist; *Addie Pray, Kings Go Forth*)	.60
25	REED, Sir Carol (film director; *The Third man, Odd Man Out*)	.69
28	HUGHES, Richard (British novelist; *A High Wind in Jamaica*)	.76

MAY

Day	Name	Age
3	NEVERS, Ernie (star fullback at Stanford in 1920s)	.73
9	KOERNER, Otto (ex-Governor of Illinois and a U.S. judge; headed commission on civil disorders; served jail term in race-track scandal)	.67
15	MORISON, Samuel Eliot (admiral; Pulitzer Prize-winning biographer; *John Paul Jones, Admiral of the Ocean Sea: A life of Christopher Columbus*)	.88
20	INGERSOLL, Royal E. (commanded Atlantic Fleet in World War II)	.92
21	ERNST, Morris L. (lawyer; won 1933 case that found James Joyce's *Ulysses* not obscene)	.87
31	MITCHELL, Martha (outspoken wife of ex-Attorney General)	.57
31	MONOD, Jacques (biologist; director of Pasteur Institute in Paris; co-winner of 1965 Nobel Prize)	.66

JUNE

Day	Name	Age
3	McBRIDE, Katharine E. (president of Bryn Mawr College 1942–70)	.72
6	GETTY, J. Paul (billionaire oilman)	.83

Day	Name	Age
7	HACKETT, Bobby (jazz cornetist)	.61
9	FARLEY, James A. (ex-Postmaster General; managed F.D.R.'s election campaigns)	.88
9	THORNDIKE, Dame Sybil (leading British actress for 70 years)	.93
10	ZUKOR, Adolph (producer of first U.S. feature film; founder of Paramount Pictures)	103
15	DYKES, Jimmy (third baseman on Philadelphia Athletics; managed four American League clubs)	.79
17	ODLUM, Floyd B. (millionaire industrialist; founded Atlas Corp.)	.84
21	GORDON, Kermit (Brookings Institution president; economic adviser to Kennedy and Johnson)	.59
25	MERCER, Johnny (song writer; winner of four Oscars; "Atchison, Topeka and the Santa Fe," "Cool, Cool of the Evening," "Moon River, "Days of Wine and Roses')	.66

JULY

Day	Name	Age
7	HEINEMANN, Gustav (ex-President of West Germany)	.76
9	YAWKEY, Tom (owner of Boston Red Sox)	.73
12	MACK, Ted (host of TV's Original Amateur Hour)	.72
12	HOWE, James Wong (cameraman; *The Rose Tattoo, Hud, Funny Lady*)	.76
15	GALLICO, Paul (sportswriter and author; *The Snow Goose, The Poseidon Adventure*)	.78
17	HORNBLOW, Arthur (stage and screen producer; *Witness for the Prosecution, Asphalt Jungle, Ruggles of Red Gap*)	.83

AUGUST

Day	Name	Age
2	LANG, Fritz (film director; *M, Clash by Night*)	.85
4	THOMSON, Lord (British newspaper publisher)	.82
5	CLOONEY, Betty (popular singer)	.45
6	PIATIGORSKY, Gregor (cello virtuoso)	.73
19	SIM, Alastair (British actor; *Lavender Hill Mob*)	.75
22	KUBITSCHEK, Juscelino (ex-President of Brazil)	.73
22	BACHAUER, Gina (concert pianist)	.63
26	LEHMANN, Lottie (Wagnerian soprano, lieder singer)	.88

SEPTEMBER

Day	Name	Age
9	MAO Tse-Tung (leader of Chinese Communist revolution; nation's head since 1949)	.82
10	TRUMBO, Dalton (blacklisted film writer; *Kitty Foyle, Johnny Got His Gun, The Brave One*)	70
20	BLOOMGARDEN, Kermit (stage producer; *Death of a Salesman, Look Homeward, Angel, The Music Man*)	.71
28	FOLSOM, Marion B. (chief drafter of Social Security laws; Secretary of H.E.W. in Eisenhower Administration)	82

OCTOBER

Day	Name	Age
7	LYONS, Leonard (Broadway columnist)	70
11	BOSWELL, Connee (singer, actress)	68
14	EVANS, Dame Edith (first lady of British stage)	88

AMERICAN ECONOMY

The American Economy: Underpinning Growth in 1977

By Will Lissner

Editor, American Journal of Economics & Sociology

Most forecasters and policy makers were in agreement on the need for an improvement in the pace of business expansion to assure a sustained period of prosperity in 1977. Shortages of capital and jobs emerged as greater public concerns as the American economy sought to consolidate the slow but steady recovery of 1976 and to avoid a setback that might wipe out all the gains of the past two years.

The total output of goods and services in the United States was expected to be rising at a rate of some 6.6% annually by midyear 1977.

This was indicated in detailed numerical forecasts made by 48 leading business, government and academic economists who participate in the quarterly Business Outlook Surveys of the American Statistical Association and the National Bureau of Economic Research.

These forecasts would put the economy's total output for 1977—its Gross National Product—at between $1,800 and $1,900 billion, compared with a total around $1,685 billion for 1976.

This total, if realized throughout 1977, would be a substantial gain, attaining even more significance if the small abatement in the rate of inflation persisted.

Measuring in dollars of constant value like 1972 dollars, this would mean an advance from a gross product for 1976 estimated and projected at something in the neighborhood of $1,160 billion, to one for 1977 of $1,340 billion. That is, that the recovery thus far in the actual physical volume of goods and services produced has proceeded somewhat faster than the economy's normal real growth rate during the past half century.

On this basis, economists expected a small degree of acceleration in the rate of recovery in 1977 from the most severe recession the United States has suffered since the second world war, that of 1973-75.

The recovery that began in 1975 differs markedly from previous recoveries.

For one thing, prosperity in agriculture continues, based on a record 1976 corn crop of some 6.2 billion bushels—the U.S. produces 50% of the world's corn—and on a wheat crop of some 2.1 billion bushels, the U.S. normally accounting for 12% of the world's wheat along with 68% of its soybeans and large shares of other important foodstuffs. Record and heavy crops commanded satisfactory, if slightly lower, prices because demand for food products in general continued strong and demand for agricultural products grown for industry improved.

Factories, like the labor force, remained underemployed during the first year of the recovery. Only by the end of 1976 was the physical volume of production expected to equal the quarterly rate achieved at the peak of the last expansion in the last quarter of 1973. By midyear 1977, the rate was expected to be 4.7% above the peak level, a fast rate of advance for the second year of recovery but a slow rate of expansion for the two-year period. But these enterprises—those in manufacturing, mining and the production of energy and water, the utilities—are the ones that were hardest hit in 1974 and 1975.

Alongside sluggish improvement in the rate of business investment in general, and almost none in the expansion of plant capacity in general—the 28% improvement in business profits in 1976 and the indicated 16% in 1977 arose from better utilization of plant as well as labor—there is developing a "mini-boom" in investment in certain industries.

The industries establishing new plants are those for coal-fired electricity production, nuclear-fueled power plants, experimental applications of solar energy, industries exploiting other new technological developments and enterprises engaged in exploration for new fuel and other mineral resources in the oceans, on the mainland and in the laboratory.

Business expenditures for plant and equipment were on the order of $112.8 billion in 1975, $123 billion in 1976, and were considered likely to be at the rate of $138 billion by midyear 1977. The rate of real increase was rising from 9 to 14% a year. Housing starts are recovering from a 1.5 million level in midyear 1976 to an indicated level of 1.76 million for midyear 1977, still below the 2 million a year, year after year, needed to overcome the housing shortage.

National economic policy has failed to end inflation despite efforts to manage the money supply for the purpose of bridling the demand for goods even though such policies might result in idle machines and idle men.

As is common in the early stage of business expansion, the inflation dropped below an annual rate of 6%. But this was produced by cost reductions usually achieved in the recovery phase of the business cycle, chiefly by improved productivity.

Thus the basic problem of inflation, too many dollars chasing too few goods, remained to be solved. Obviously the only fundamental solution was to increase the output of goods from present inputs of labor and capital, relying on taxation and debt reduction to combat inflation.

Also remaining to be solved was the problem of persistent high unemployment. During the last business cycle peak, in 1973, unemployment remained at the high level of 4.7%. The minimum rate in the recession's trough was 10% practically everywhere. In the first phase of the recovery, it dropped below 8% and was headed below 6%. But the goal of moderates for 1977 was 5%.

In urban areas and in central cities, inhabited to a considerable extent by members of minority groups and the poor, the jobless rate—30% in the trough—persisted far above the national average.

Thus American society, in the throes of a technological revolution promising a higher quality of life for all, was confronted with the challenge of overcoming inflation while generating additional employment for people and machines, without halting the economy's advance toward prosperity.

The effects of the recovery in America contributed toward greater stability in the world economy. For the United States economy still dominates that of the world.

Gross National Product or Expenditure
(in millions of dollars)
Source: Department of Commerce, Office of Economic Analysis.

Item	1976[1]	1975	1970	1951	1945	1938	1933	1929
Gross national product..............	1,674,100	1,516,338	977,080	328,404	211,945	84,670	55,601	103,095
GNP in constant (1972) dollars	1,259,400	1,191,700	722,500[2]	383,400[2]	355,200[2]	192,900[2]	141,500[2]	203,600[2]
Personal consumption expenditures..	1,064,700	973,216	617,644	206,266	119,701	63,920	45,795	77,222
Durable goods...................	155,000	131,726	91,298	29,648	8,044	5,686	3,469	9,212
Nondurable goods................	434,800	409,124	263,779	108,753	71,903	33,953	22,257	37,686
Services.......................	474,900	432,366	262,567	67,865	39,754	24,281	20,069	30,324
Gross private domestic investment...	239,200	183,698	136,275	59,340	10,576	6,475	1,401	16,228
Residential structures............	65,300	51,172	31,179	17,234	1,523	2,024	563	3,954
Nonresidential structures........	54,900	52,029	36,145	11,159	2,802	1,897	931	4,959
Producers' durable equipment.....	103,000	95,113	64,423	20,651	7,285	3,468	1,471	5,601
Change in business inventories....	16,000	−14,616	4,528	10,296	−1,034	−914	−1,564	1,714
Net exports of goods and services....	8,100	20,471	3,630	3,671	−613	1,291	358	1,148
Government purchases.............	362,000	338,953	219,531	59,127	82,281	12,984	8,047	8,497
Federal........................	131,200	124,417	96,182	37,652	74,179	5,409	2,000	1,261
National defense..............	86,900	84,282	74,588	33,584	73,507	n.a.	n.a.	n.a.
Other......................	44,300	40,135	21,594	4,068	672	n.a.	n.a.	n.a.
State and local..................	230,900	214,536	123,349	21,475	8,102	7,575	6,047	7,236

[1] Second quarter annual rate. [2] In constant (1958) dollars.

Per Capita Personal Income in the U.S., 1951-1975
Source: Bureau of Labor Statistics.

Year	Amount	Year	Amount	Year	Amount	Year	Amount	Year	Amount
1951	$1,652	1956	$1,975	1961	$2,274	1966	$3,001	1971	$4,195
1952	1,733	1957	2,045	1962	2,381	1967	3,188	1972	4,537
1953	1,804	1958	2,067	1963	2,469	1968	3,457	1973	5,049
1954	1,785	1959	2,167	1964	2,603	1969	3,733	1974	5,486
1955	1,876	1960	2,222	1965	2,785	1970	3,966	1975	5.902

Per Capita Personal Income by States, 1974-1975
Source: Bureau of Labor Statistics.

State and region	Income 1975	Income 1974	State and region	Income 1975	Income 1974	State and region	Income 1975	Income 1974
New England	$6,098	$5,668	Plains	$5,785	$5,364	Southwest	$5,487	$5,019
Connecticut	6,973	6,487	Iowa	6,077	5,561	Arizona	5,355	5,152
Maine	4,786	4,536	Kansas	6,023	5,615	New Mexico	4,775	4,299
Massachusetts	6,114	5,667	Minnesota	5,807	5,469	Oklahoma	5,250	4,823
New Hampshire	5,315	4,986	Missouri	5,510	5,065	Texas	5,631	5,106
Rhode Island	5,841	5,355	Nebraska	6,087	5,379			
Vermont	4,960	4,602	North Dakota	5,737	5,698	Rocky Mountains	5,576	5,222
			South Dakota	4,924	4,860	Colorado	5,985	5,549
Mideast	6,433	5,968				Idaho	5,159	5,140
Delaware	6,748	6,284	Southeast	5,055	4,740	Montana	5,422	5,079
District of Columbia	7,742	7,043	Alabama	4,643	4,284	Utah	4,923	4,539
Maryland	6,474	5,973	Arkansas	4,620	4,379	Wyoming	6,131	5,644
New Jersey	6,722	6,242	Florida	5,638	5,406			
New York	6,564	6,120	Georgia	5,086	4,798	Far West	6,481	5,976
Pennsylvania	5,943	5,485	Kentucky	4,871	4,565	California	6,593	6,089
			Louisiana	4,904	4,456	Nevada	6,647	6,161
Great Lakes	6,121	5,731	Mississippi	4,052	3,837	Oregon	5,769	5,398
Illinois	6,789	6,268	North Carolina	4,952	4,649	Washington	6,247	5,646
Indiana	5,653	5,295	South Carolina	4,618	4,390			
Michigan	6,173	5,846	Tennessee	4,895	4,567	Alaska	9,448	7,037
Ohio	5,810	5,481	Virginia	5,785	5,377	Hawaii	6,658	6,010
Wisconsin	5,669	5,281	West Virginia	4,918	4,480	United States	5,902	5,486

Median Family Income, 1970-1975

Source: Bureau of the Census.

Year	Median family income	Annual per cent gain	Annual % gain or loss in real family income	Year	Median family income	Annual per cent gain	Annual % gain or loss in real family income
1975.....	$13,719	....	....	1972	11,116	$8.1	4.6
1974.....	12,836	7.0	−4.0	1971	10,285	4.2	0.0
1973	12,051	8.4	2.2	1970	9,867	4.6	−1.2

What Americans Pay[1] in Personal Taxes and What They Save

(in millions of current dollars)

Source: Department of Commerce, Office of Economic Analysis.

	1976[3]	1975	1972	1970
Gross personal income.................................	1,362,000	1,249,673	942,536	808,290
Social insurance contributions..........................	54,300	49,999	34,170	27,991
Tax and non-tax payments to governments...............	189,500	168,816	141,237	116,591
Income available for spending, saving[2]..................	1,172,500	1,080,857	801,299	691,699
Income available per capita (dollars).....................	5,455	5,062	3,837	3,376
Personal saving.......................................	82,900	83,964	49,370	56,200
Rate of personal saving................................	7.1%	7.8%	6.2%	8.1%

[1] Personal income basis: direct taxes and payments only; corporate taxes and payments, paid by shareholders or customers, and hidden and consumption taxes not included. [2] Personal disposable income, [3] Second quarter annual rate (preliminary).

Consumer Price Index for Cities and Selected Areas (1967 = 100)

Source: Bureau of Labor Statistics.

	1976[1]		1975			1976[1]		1975	
City or area	Food	All items	Food	All items	City or area	Food	All items	Food	All items
Atlanta, Ga.	184.4	168.5	181.8	161.7	Milwaukee, Wis.	180.1	165.9[3]	171.9	157.0
Baltimore, Md.	185.2	173.7	178.2	165.2	Minneapolis–St. Paul,				
Boston, Mass.	183.4	172.5[2]	175.2	162.1	Minn.	186.3	168.7[2]	178.9	160.9
Buffalo, N.Y.	178.9	169.1[3]	173.6	161.8	New York, N.Y.-NE N.J. .	185.7	176.0	179.6	166.6
Chicago, Ill.–NW Ind. . .	180.3	164.9	175.1	157.6	Philadelphia, Pa.-N.J. . .	186.3	171.9	179.6	164.2
Cincinnati, Ohio–Ky. . .	184.1	169.9	177.4	160.4	Pittsburgh, Pa.	181.4	166.7[2]	177.4	160.0
Cleveland, Ohio	186.9	166.9[3]	175.8	160.9	Portland, Ore.-Wash. . .	175.5[2]	164.4[2]	168.4	156.5
Dallas, Tex.	177.4	166.2[3]	172.5	158.2	St. Louis, Mo.-Ill.	180.5	165.2	174.3	156.1
Detroit, Mich.	175.7	168.1	171.6	160.3	San Diego, Calif.	179.6	169.3[3]	173.9	160.8
Honolulu, Hawaii	182.9	162.3	176.7	154.4	San Francisco–Oakland,				
Houston, Tex.	187.5	174.1[2]	181.2	164.9	Calif.	172.8	166.9	171.2	159.1
Kansas City, Mo.-Kan. .	178.9	165.9	177.8	157.9	Seattle, Wash.	173.4	162.6[3]	169.6	155.8
Los Angeles–Long Beach,					Washington, D.C.-Md.-Va. .	186.9	170.0[3]	180.7	161.6
Calif.	173.1	167.0	170.1	157.6	U.S. CITY AVERAGE	180.9	170.1	175.4	161.2

[1] June unless otherwise indicated. [2] April. [3] May.

Consumer Price Indexes, 1951-1975 (1967 = 100)

Source: Bureau of Labor Statistics.

Year	Commodities	Services	All items	% change[1]	Year	Commodities	Services	All items	% change[1]
1951	85.9	61.8	77.8	5.3	1971	117.4	128.4	121.3	4.3
1955	85.1	70.9	80.2	−0.4	1972	120.9	133.3	125.3	3.3
1960	91.5	83.5	88.7	1.6	1973	129.9	139.1	133.1	6.2
1965	95.7	92.2	94.5	1.7	1974	145.5	152.0	147.7	11.0
1970	113.5	121.6	116.3	5.9	1975	158.4	166.6	161.2	9.1

[1] Over previous year.

Consumer Price Index by Groups (1967 = 100)
Source: Bureau of Labor Statistics.

Items	1976[1]	1975	1974	1970	1959	1945	1941
All items........................	170.1	161.2	147.7	116.3	87.3	53.9	44.1
Food total......................	180.9	175.4	161.7	114.9	87.1	50.7	38.4
Apparel and upkeep	146.9	142.3	136.2	116.1	88.2	61.5	44.8
Housing total...................	176.5	166.8	150.6	118.9	88.6	59.1	53.7
Rent	144.4	137.3	130.6	110.1	90.4	58.8	57.2
Gas and electricity............	188.5	169.6	145.8	107.3	94.7	79.6	81.4
Fuel oil and coal..............	247.3	235.3	214.6	110.1	89.8	48.0	40.5
House operation[2].............	168.5	158.1	140.5	113.4	93.1	....	....
House furnishings	150.9	144.4	130.8	111.4	99.0	73.3	54.0
Transportation.................	165.9	150.6	137.7	112.7	89.6	47.8	44.2
Medical care...................	183.7	168.6	150.5	120.6	76.4	42.1	37.0
Personal care	159.8	150.7	137.3	113.2	88.7	55.1	41.2
Reading and recreation..........	150.9	144.4	133.8	113.4	85.3	62.4	47.7

[1] June. [2] Combines house furnishings and operation.

Wholesale Price Indexes by Major Commodity Groups (1967 = 100)
Source: Bureau of Labor Statistics.

Commodity	1976[1]	1975	1974	1970	1959	1955
All commodities...................................	183.1	174.9	160.1	110.4	94.8	87.8
Farm products.....................................	196.5	186.7	187.7	111.0	97.5	98.2
Processed foods...................................	181.8	182.6	170.9	112.1	89.4	85.0
Textile products and apparel......................	148.1	137.9	139.1	107.1	98.4	98.7
Hides, skins, and leather products................	167.4	148.5	145.1	110.3	94.2	77.3
Fuels and related products and power..............	260.3	245.1	208.3	106.2	95.3	91.2
Chemicals and allied products.....................	187.1	181.3	146.8	102.2	101.6	98.5
Rubber and plastic products......................	157.2	150.2	136.2	108.3	102.9	102.4
Lumber and wood products.........................	199.8	176.9	183.6	113.6	98.8	97.1
Pulp, paper, and allied products..................	179.5	170.4	151.7	108.2	97.3	87.8
Metals and metal products........................	196.4	185.6	171.9	116.6	92.3	82.1
Machinery and equipment	170.2	161.4	139.4	111.4	91.3	75.7
Furniture and household durables..................	145.3	139.7	127.9	107.5	99.3	93.3
Nonmetallic mineral products.....................	186.0	174.0	153.2	112.9	97.0	87.5
Transportation equipment (Dec. 1968=100)	149.1	141.5	125.5	104.6	....	....
Miscellaneous products	154.4	147.7	133.1	109.9	92.2	86.5

Industrial Production Indexes, by Industry Groups (1967 = 100)
Source: Federal Reserve Board.

Industry	1976[1]	1975	1970	1950	Industry	1976[1]	1975	1970	1950
Total industrial production ..	130.4	117.8	106.7	44.9	Rubber and plastics				
Total manufactures	130.4	116.3	105.2	45.0	products	190.6	166.7	115.7	30.5
Durable manufactures ..	123.1	109.3	101.5	43.7	Paper and products ..	135.5[2]	116.3	113.3	46.3
Primary metals	117.3	96.4	106.9	71.4	Printing and publishing	119.3	113.4	104.1	48.5
Fabricated metal products	122.9	109.9	109.4	56.5	Chemicals and products	170.1[2]	147.3	120.3	24.6
Machinery	135.0	125.1	100.3	n.a.	Petroleum products ..	133.7	124.1	112.6	48.2
Transportation equipment	111.5	97.4	90.4	40.7	Foods...........	130.6	123.4	111.7	57.7
Instruments and products	151.0	132.3	110.8	26.1	Tobacco products ...	114.5[2]	111.8	100.0	68.7
Clay, glass, stone products	133.7[2]	117.9	106.4	58.3	Mining............	112.8[3]	112.8	109.7	65.7
Lumber and products ..	122.6[2]	107.6	106.3	65.3	Coal...........	104.8	113.4	105.7	106.4
Furniture and fixtures .	129.9[2]	118.2	99.4	52.4	Oil and gas extraction .	111.7	113.3	109.7	58.8
Nondurable manufactures ..	140.8	126.4	110.6	46.2	Metal mining	121.2[2]	115.8	131.3	75.3
Textile mill products	138.4[2]	122.3	106.3	61.4	Stone and earth minerals	116.2[2]	107.0	98.8	50.9
Apparel products ...	131.0[3]	107.6	97.8	64.4	Utilities	153.0	146.0	128.3	26.5
Leather products ...	87.4[2]	76.5	90.8	91.9					

[1] July estimate. [2] June preliminary figure. [3] May. NOTE: n.a. means not available.

Industrial Production Indexes for Western Europe and U.S.S.R. (1970 = 100)

Source: Monthly Bulletin of Statistics, United Nations, 1976

Country	1975	1974	1973	1969	1967	Country	1975	1974	1973	1969	1967
Austria...........	118	126	120	92	77	Italy...........	108	120	114	94	85
Belgium..........	108	120	116	97	83	Luxembourg....	93	119	114	100	83
Denmark.........	n.a.	n.a.	115	97	85	Netherlands....	115	121	118	91	73
France...........	112	123	120	94	81	Norway........	128	120	116	96	89
Germany (West)...	105	111	113	94	76	Sweden........	115	118	111	94	83
Greece...........	151	144	147	91	75	Un. Kingdom....	101	106	110	100	92
Ireland...........	116	125	121	96	80	U.S.S.R.........	143	133	123	93	79

NOTE: n.a. means not available.

Increases in Worldwide Consumer Prices, 1974-1975
(in percent)
Source: International Monetary Fund.

Country	1975	1974	Country	1975	1974	Country	1975	1974
North America			China, Republic of .	5.6	48.1	Luxembourg . . .	10.8	9.5
Canada	10.8	10.9	India	6.6	28.5	Malta	8.9	7.3
Costa Rica	21.0	22.0	Indonesia	19.1	41.1	Netherlands . . .	10.2	9.6
Dominican Republic	14.5	13.2	Iran	13.1	14.1	Norway	11.7	9.4
El Salvador	19.3	16.8	Iraq	9.5	8.3	Portugal	15.4	25.1
Guatemala	14.0	16.4	Israel	40.0	39.4	Spain	17.0	15.6
Haiti	16.8	14.9	Japan	12.2	22.7	Sweden	9.9	9.8
Honduras	6.2	13.3	Jordan	12.1	20.2	Switzerland . . .	6.8	9.8
Jamaica	16.6	27.4	Korea, Rep. of . .	26.2	23.6	Turkey	. . . .	15.8
Mexico	17.0	22.4	Malaysia	4.6	17.5	United Kingdom . .	24.2	15.9
Panama	6.1	16.2	Pakistan	21.3	27.2	Yugoslavia . . .	23.5	22.1
Trinidad & Tobago .	17.1	22.1	Philippines	8.4	34.5	Africa		
United States . . .	9.2	11.0	Saudi Arabia . . .	34.6	21.4	Congo	17.4	5.4
South America			Sri Lanka	6.8	12.4	Ghana	40.8	24.2
Argentina	171.2	23.4	Syria	15.9	15.6	Ivory Coast . . .	11.6	17.4
Bolivia	8.1	64.0	Thailand	4.3	23.3	Kenya	19.2	18.0
Brazil	29.0	27.5	Europe			Morocco	. . . .	17.7
Chile	380.2	585.9	Austria	8.4	9.5	Nigeria	34.0	12.5
Colombia	26.1	24.5	Belgium	12.8	12.6	Senegal	21.8	15.0
Ecuador	15.7	23.4	Denmark	9.8	15.3	South Africa . . .	13.5	11.6
Paraguay	6.8	25.3	Finland	17.7	17.0	Sudan	24.1	26.7
Peru	23.6	16.9	France	11.8	13.6	Tunisia	9.6	4.3
Uruguay	83.1	76.9	Germany (West) . .	5.9	7.0	Zaire	28.5	29.5
Venezuela . . .	10.4	8.3	Greece	13.4	27.5	Oceania		
Asia			Iceland	50.0	42.1	Australia	15.2	15.1
Burma	31.4	26.4	Ireland	21.0	16.9	New Zealand . . .	14.6	11.1
			Italy	17.2	19.1			

Business Population
(in thousands of concerns)

Sources: Departments of Commerce and the Treasury; Dun & Bradstreet.

Item	1973[1]	1972[1]	1971[1]	1970[1]	1965[1]	1953	1949	1941	1933	1929
Total operating businesses[2]	13,579	12,978	12,437	12,001	11,417	4,188	3,984	3,276	2,782	3,029
Manufacturing...........	448	436	414	410	408	331	322	230	167	257
Wholesale trade..........	548	559	515	470	444	283	260	190	142	148
Retail trade..............	2,327	2,331	2,297	2,210	2,044	1,846	1,783	1,561	1,291	1,327
Service industries........	3,364	3,181	3,053	2,964	2,565	750	739	615	575	591
Contract construction.....	1,097	1,020	932	875	876	405	339	194	185	234
All other[3]	5,795	5,451	5,225	5,072	5,080	573	541	486	422	472
New Incorporations[4]	330	317	288	264	204	352	331	290	(5)	(5)
Commercial and industrial failures[6]	9.3	9.6	10.7	10.7	13.5	8.9	9.2	11.8	19.9	22.9

[1] Data for total operating businesses are now based on tax returns; not comparable with earlier figures. [2] 1929–33, annual average; 1941–53, as of Jan. 1. [3] Includes agriculture, forestry and fishing; mining; transportation, communication, electric, gas and sanitary services; finance, insurance and real estate; wholesale and retail trade not allocable; and nature of business not allocable. [4] Annual total. [5] Not available. [6] Closures resulting in a known loss to creditors. NOTE: Data are latest available.

National Income by Distributive Shares
(in millions of dollars)
Source: Department of Commerce. Office of Economic Analysis.

Type of share	1976[2]	1976 % of Total	1975	1970	1951	1945	1938	1933
National income	1,336,300	100.0	1,207,584	800,462	277,978	181,485	67,372	40,312
Compensation of employees	1,017,200	76.1	928,781	603,869	180,687	123,097	44,996	29,547
Wages and salaries	881,100	65.9	806,663	541,976	171,093	117,493	42,978	29,005
Supplements to wages and salaries	136,200	10.2	122,118	61,893	9,594	5,604	2,018	542
Proprietors' income	100,300	7.7	90,168	66,919	41,963	31,422	11,297	5,915
Business and professional	72,800	5.4	65,304	50,017	26,125	19,199	6,926	3,331
Farm	27,500	2.1	24,864	16,902	15,838	12,223	4,371	2,584
Rental income of persons	39,500	3.0	36,961	23,938	10,321	5,634	2,560	1,971
Corporate profits[1]	115,300	8.6	91,604	69,420	42,731	19,158	4,932	−1,187
Net interest	80,300	6.0	74,628	36,396	2,276	2,174	3,587	4,066

[1] Includes inventory valuation adjustment.   [2] Second quarter annual rate.

How Consumers Spend Their Dollar
Source: Department of Commerce.

	1975	1975 % of total	(in millions of dollars)							
			1974	1970	1958	1949	1945	1939	1932	1929
Food and tobacco	224,286	23.0	203,840	141,181	82,363	56,593	43,520	20,916	12,687	21,239
Clothing, accessories, and jewelry	81,742	8.4	76,148	62,834	29,868	23,333	19,645	8,406	6,042	11,193
Personal care	14,271	1.5	13,434	10,420	4,604	2,306	1,982	1,004	817	1,116
Housing	150,219	15.4	136,363	90,926	41,127	19,252	12,479	9,139	9,011	11,530
Household operation	142,190	14.6	130,358	87,360	42,274	25,938	15,530	9,624	6,779	10,735
Medical care	86,425	8.9	76,142	47,401	16,472	8,110	5,042	2,848	2,127	2,937
Personal business	50,287	5.2	44,751	35,314	12,768	6,210	4,656	3,313	2,875	4,158
Transportation	126,037	13.0	115,257	77,776	35,634	20,793	6,845	6,365	3,981	7,612
Recreation	65,999	6.8	60,765	40,653	15,817	10,010	6,139	3,452	2,442	4,331
Private education and research	14,653	1.5	13,607	10,363	3,140	1,507	936	620	570	664
Religious and welfare activities	12,113	1.2	11,578	8,601	4,178	2,150	1,735	938	973	1,196
Foreign travel and other—net	4,994	0.5	5,251	4,815	1,824	601	1,192	209	285	511
Total personal consumption expenditures	973,216	100.0	887,494	617,644	290,069	176,803	119,701	66,834	48,589	77,222

Consumer Credit
(in millions of dollars)
Source: Federal Reserve Board.

End of year	Total	Installment credit	Non-installment credit[1]	Charge accounts
1929	7,116	3,524	1,596	1,996
1933	3,885	1,723	876	1,286
1939	7,222	4,503	1,305	1,414
1943	4,901	2,136	1,325	1,440
1949	17,364	11,590	2,920	2,854
1953	31,393	23,005	4,114	4,274
1958	45,129	33,642	6,427	5,060
1960[2]	56,141	42,968	7,844	5,329
1964	80,268	62,692	11,381	6,195
1968	110,770	87,745	15,832	7,193
1970	127,163	102,064	17,131	7,968
1972	157,939	127,448	21,610	8,881
1973	180,803	148,273	23,332	9,198
1974	191,457	158,101	23,850	9,506
1975	196,745	161,819	24,536	10,390

[1] Single payment loans and service credit.   [2] Beginning with 1960, data include Alaska and Hawaii.

U. S. Consumption of Principal Foods[1]
(in pounds per capita)
Source: Department of Agriculture.

Foods	1975[6]	1957–59 avg.	1935–39 avg.
Red meats	181.1	156.6	127.0
Poultry	49.3	33.5	15.6
Eggs[2]	278.0	356	300
Fluid milk and cream	248.0	337	330
Cheese	14.5	7.9	5.6
Butter	4.8	8.2	17.0
Margarine	11.2	8.9	2.9
Fats and oils[3]	40.5	31.5	29.3
Fresh fruits	83.1	95.5	135.5
Processed fruits[4]	48.9	47.8	25.5
Fresh vegetables	97.9	104.1	113.2
Processed vegetables	65.0	49.9	29.5
Potatoes, sweet potatoes	127.5	115.2	151.6
Sugar	88.7	96.1	97.5
Corn products[5]	73.0	40.1	51.9
Wheat flour	107.0	120	160
Coffee	12.3	15.7	14.0
Cocoa	3.3	3.5	4.4

[1] Civilian consumption only. [2] Number, not pounds. [3] Excludes butter and margarine. [4] Pack year. Excludes chilled fruits and juices. [5] Corn used in food products. [6] Preliminary.

Annual Budgets for 4-Person Urban Families, Autumn 1975

Source: Bureau of Labor Statistics.

	Lower Budget		Intermediate Budget		Higher Budget	
	Amount	% increase 1974–75	Amount	% increase 1974–75	Amount	% increase 1974–75
Food	$2,952	6.8	$3,827	7.9	$4,819	8.2
Housing	1,857	5.6	3,533	9.2	5,353	9.2
Transportation	702	9.2	1,279	9.2	1,658	9.0
Clothing	771	1.6	1,102	1.6	1,613	1.5
Personal care	248	7.4	331	6.8	470	7.1
Medical care	818	10.8	822	10.8	857	10.7
Other family consumption	447	5.7	831	5.7	1,371	5.7
Total family consumption	7,795	6.5	11,725	7.8	16,141	7.8
Other items	436	5.1	701	5.9	1,182	6.2
Personal income taxes	781	−14.2	2,057	2.3	4,130	5.9
Social security and disability	577	4.3	834	6.9	841	6.9
Total budget	9,588	4.2	15,318	6.9	22,294	7.3

NOTE: Above budgets illustrate three levels of living based on estimates of costs for goods and services rather than actual expenditures.

Total Household Income, 1968–1975

(figures in per cent)

Source: Bureau of the Census.

Household income	1975	1974	1973	1972	1971	1970	1969	1968
Total households	72,867	71,120	69,859	68,251	66,676	64,778	63,401	62,214
Under $3,000	9.5	10.9	12.0	13.7	15.0	15.8	16.2	17.4
$3,000 to $4,999	10.4	10.2	10.9	11.2	11.7	11.6	11.9	13.1
$5,000 to $6,999	9.3	9.7	10.0	10.6	11.3	11.8	12.4	13.9
$7,000 to $9,999	13.2	13.9	14.6	16.0	17.4	18.5	19.7	21.1
$10,000 to $11,999	8.5	9.5	9.7	10.3	11.0	11.0	11.3	11.0
$12,000 to $14,999	12.0	12.5	12.9	12.7	12.4	12.2	11.8	10.8
$15,000 to $24,999	25.5	23.7	22.1	19.3	16.5	15.1	13.4	10.5
$25,000 and over	11.7	9.5	7.8	6.2	4.5	4.0	3.2	2.3
Median income	$11,800	$11,101	$10,512	$9,698	$9,027	$8,734	$8,389	$7,743

Wood Pulp, Paper, and Lumber

Sources: Department of Commerce, Bureau of the Census and National Forest Products Assn.

Year	Wood pulp (in thousands of short tons)	Paper and paperboard (in thousands of short tons)	Lumber (in millions of board feet)
1929	4,863	11,140	36,886
1939	6,993	13,510	25,148
1941[1]	10,011	17,036	33,613
1945	10,167	17,371	28,122
1950	14,849	24,375	38,902
1958	21,614	30,229	33,275
1965	30,120	43,746	36,895
1970	43,663	52,210	34,462
1972	46,767	59,445	38,867
1973	48,327	61,304	38,658
1974	48,417	59,934	34,463
1975	40,997[2]	52,297	31,851

[1] Coverage for paper and paperboard increased in 1941.
[2] Data not comparable to earlier periods.

Expenditures for New Plant and Equipment[1]

(in millions of dollars)

Source: Department of Commerce.

Year	Manufacturing and mining	Transportation	All other[2]	Total[3]
1939	2,269	645	2,598	5,512
1945	4,366	1,122	3,204	8,692
1948	9,940	2,540	8,700	21,300
1950	8,230	2,370	9,600	20,210
1952	12,660	2,970	10,800	26,430
1960	16,390	3,120	17,230	36,750
1965	24,900	4,890	24,620	54,420
1970	33,840	6,040	39,830	79,710
1972	33,770	5,720	48,960	88,440
1973	40,750	6,030	52,960	99,740
1974	49,190	6,660	56,560	112,400
1975	51,740	7,570	53,470	112,780
1976[4]	56,330	6,510	57,190	120,030

[1] Data exclude agriculture. [2] Includes electric and gas utilities, trade, service, communications, construction, and finance. [3] Details may not add up to totals because of rounding. [4] Estimates.

Terms on Conventional First Mortgages: All Major Types of Lenders
Source: Federal Home Loan Bank Board.

Type of homes & year	Contract rate (%)	Fees and charges (%)	Maturity (years)	Loan-to-price ratio (%)	Purchase price ($000)	Loan amount ($000)
New homes: 1976[1] . . .	8.69	1.27	26.5	75.1	48.9	36.2
1975	8.75	1.54	26.8	76.1	44.6	33.3
1974	8.72	1.30	26.3	75.8	40.1	29.8
1973 . . . . •	7.78	1.11	26.3	77.3	37.1	28.1
1972	7.45	0.88	27.2	76.8	37.3	28.1
Existing homes: 1976[1] . . .	9.01	1.19	24.0	73.4	38.2	27.4
1975	8.84	1.09	23.0	72.4	34.7	24.5
1974	8.84	1.09	23.0	72.4	34.7	24.5
1973	7.86	0.94	23.2	75.2	31.2	22.8
1972	7.38	0.81	25.7	76.0	33.4	24.9

[1] June.

Strikes and Lockouts
Source: Bureau of Labor Statistics.

Year	Strikes and lockouts Number	Workers involved Number (thousands)	Man-days idle Number (thousands)	Year	Strikes and lockouts Number	Workers involved Number (thousands)	Man-days idle Number (thousands)
1895.	1,255	407	n.a.	1939.	2,613	1,171	17,812
1900.	1,839	568	n.a.	1945.	4,750	3,470	38,025
1915.	1,593	n.a.	n.a.	1949.	3,606	3,030	50,500
1917.	4,450	1,227	n.a.	1952.	5,117	3,540	59,100
1920.	3,411	1,463	n.a.	1964.	3,655	1,640	22,900
1925.	1,301	428	n.a.	1970.	5,716	3,305	66,414
1932.	841	324	10,502	1972.	5,010	1,714	27,066
1933.	1,695	1,168	16,872	1974.	6,074	2,778	47,991
1935.	2,014	1,117	15,456	1975.	5,031	1,746	31,237

NOTE: n.a. means not available.

Why Strikes in 1975?
Source: Bureau of Labor Statistics.

Major issues	% of stoppages	% of workers involved	Major issues	% of stoppages	% of workers involved
All issues.	100.0	100.0	Union organization and security	5.3	5.3
General wage changes.	52.1	46.4	Job security.	5.1	11.8
Supplementary benefits.	1.1	1.3	Plant administration.	22.7	24.7
Wage adjustments.	2.5	2.2	Other working conditions.	2.7	2.3
Hours of work.	0.1	(1)	Interunion or intraunion matters	6.3	4.5
Other contractual matters.	1.5	1.4	Not reported.	0.6	0.1

[1] Less than 0.5%.

Gross Weekly Average Earnings and Hours of Production of Nonsupervisory Workers in Nonmanufacturing Industries
Source: Bureau of Labor Statistics.

Industry	1976 (June) Earnings	Hours worked	1975 Earnings	Hours worked	1970 Earnings	Hours worked	1958 Earnings	Hours worked	1949 Earnings	Hours worked
Bituminous coal and lignite mining. . . .	$305.75	39.3	$284.53	39.2[1]	$186.41	40.8	$97.57	33.3	$60.63	32.3
Metal mining.	287.00	42.9	250.72	42.3	165.68	42.7	94.96	38.6	61.05	41.0
Nonmetallic minerals	239.59	44.7	213.09	43.4	155.11	44.7	88.33	43.3	55.04	43.1
Telephone communications	239.09	38.5	221.18	38.4	131.60	39.4	78.72	38.4	51.78	38.5
Telegraph communications	n.a.	n.a.	240.44	41.1	154.45	42.2	90.06	41.5	62.85	44.7
Electric, gas and sanitary services.	269.45	41.2	246.79	41.2	172.64	41.5	98.57	40.9	n.a.	n.a.
Local and suburban transportation.	215.34	40.1	196.89	40.1	142.30	42.1	87.29	43.0	n.a.	n.a.
Wholesale trade.	199.95	38.9	188.75	38.6	137.60	40.0	84.02	40.2	55.49	40.8
Retail trade	114.37	32.4	108.22	32.4	82.47	33.8	54.10	38.1	38.42	40.4
Hotels, tourist courts, motels · · · · · · · ·	96.64	32.0	89.64	31.9	68.16	34.6	40.89	39.7	n.a.	n.a.
Laundries and dry cleaning plants.	114.43	35.1	106.05	35.0	77.47	35.7	45.28	38.7	n.a.	n.a.
General building contracting.	274.91	36.9	254.88	36.0	184.40	36.3	96.92	35.5	64.17	36.4

[1] 11-month average. NOTE: n.a. = not available.

Gross Average Weekly Earnings and Hours of Production Workers in Manufacturing Industries

Source: Bureau of Labor Statistics.

Industry	1976 (July) Earnings	Hours worked	1975 Earnings	Hours worked	1970 Earnings	Hours worked	1958 Earnings	Hours worked	1953 Earnings	Hours worked	1949 Earnings	Hours worked
All manufacturing[1]	$206.28	39.9	$189.51	39.4	$133.73	39.8	$82.71	39.2	$70.47	40.5	$53.88	39.1
Durable goods	222.46	40.3	205.09	39.9	143.07	40.3	89.27	39.5	76.63	41.2	57.25	39.4
Primary metal industries	278.92	41.2	246.80	40.0	159.17	40.5	101.11	38.3	84.46	41.0	60.94	38.4
Iron and steel foundries	257.92[2]	41.6[2]	220.99	40.4	151.03	40.6	86.86	37.6	77.64	41.3	55.98	37.8
Nonferrous foundries	212.22[2]	40.5[2]	190.03	39.1	138.16	39.7	90.85	39.5	79.73	41.1	59.87	39.0
Fabricated metal products	218.16	40.4	201.60	40.0	143.67	40.7	89.78	39.9	76.49	41.8	57.45	39.7
Hardware, cutlery, hand tools	206.96	39.8	187.07	39.3	132.33	40.1	82.92	39.3	71.80	41.5	53.16	39.2
Other hardware	221.68[2]	40.6[2]	195.42	39.4	133.46	40.2	84.32	39.4	72.63	41.5	53.96	39.1
Structural metal products	211.87	39.9	202.61	40.2	142.61	40.4	92.63	40.1	79.71	42.4	59.51	40.4
Electrical equipment, supplies	192.27	39.4	180.91	39.5	130.54	39.8	83.95	39.6	70.99	40.8	55.77	39.5
Machinery, except electrical	234.19	40.8	219.22	40.9	154.95	41.1	94.33	39.8	82.68	42.4	60.31	39.6
Transportation equipment	265.92	41.1	242.61	40.3	163.22	40.3	100.40	40.0	85.28	41.6	65.10	39.6
Motor vehicles and equipment	320.40[2]	45.0[2]	262.68	40.6	170.07	40.3	101.24	39.7	89.88	42.0	67.33	39.7
Lumber and wood products	185.10	39.3	167.35	39.1	117.51	39.7	69.09	38.6	60.76	39.2	48.02	39.2
Furniture and fixtures	152.08	38.5	142.13	37.9	108.58	39.2	69.95	39.3	62.99	40.9	49.36	40.0
Nondurable goods	183.92	39.3	168.78	38.8	120.43	39.1	74.11	38.8	62.57	39.6	50.38	38.9
Textile mill products	148.34	40.2	133.28	39.2	97.76	39.9	57.51	38.6	53.18	39.1	44.41	37.6
Apparel and other textile products	119.28	35.5	111.97	35.1	84.37	35.3	54.05	35.1	48.74	36.1	42.80	35.4
Leather and leather products	127.88	37.5	120.80	37.4	92.63	37.2	57.25	36.7	50.90	37.7	41.07	36.6
Food and kindred products	201.38	40.6	184.17	40.3	127.98	40.5	79.15	40.8	63.50	41.5	50.53	41.9
Tobacco manufactures	172.89	34.1	171.38	38.0	110.00	37.8	62.17	39.1	47.63	38.1	37.26	37.3
Paper and allied products	231.80	42.3	207.58	41.6	144.14	41.9	87.99	41.9	71.81	43.0	55.42	41.7
Printing and publishing	213.19	37.6	198.32	37.0	147.78	37.7	94.62	38.0	82.29	39.0	68.64	38.8
Chemicals and allied products	245.27	41.5	219.63	40.9	153.50	41.6	93.20	40.7	74.21	41.0	57.67	40.7
Petroleum and coal products	304.59	42.6	267.07	41.6	182.76	42.7	111.66	40.9	90.35	40.7	72.46	40.3

[1] Average weekly earnings in 1919 = $21.84, 1929 = $24.76, 1932 = $16.89, 1939 = $23.64. Average hours worked per week in 1914 = 49.4, 1919 = 46.3, 1929 = 44.2, 1932 = 38.3, 1939 = 37.7. [2] June.

Employment and Unemployment, 1929-1976

(in millions of persons)

Source: Bureau of Labor Statistics.

Employment Status[1]	1976[2]	1975	1970	1959	1950	1945	1941	1932	1929
Total noninstitutional population	155.9	153.4	140.2	117.9	106.6	105.5	101.5	....	....
Total labor force	96.8	94.8	85.9	70.9	63.9	65.3	57.5	51.3	49.4
Per cent of population	62.1	61.8	61.3	60.2	59.9	61.9	56.7	....	....
Civilian labor force	94.6	92.6	82.7	68.4	62.2	53.9	55.9	51.0	49.2
Employed	87.5	84.8	78.6	64.6	58.9	52.8	50.4	38.9	47.6
Agriculture	3.3	3.4	3.5	5.6	7.2	8.6	9.1	10.2	10.5
Nonagricultural industries	84.2	81.4	75.2	59.1	51.8	44.2	41.3	28.8	37.2
Unemployed	7.1	7.8	4.1	3.7	3.3	1.0	5.6	12.1	1.6
Per cent of labor force	7.5	8.5	4.9	5.5	5.3	1.9	9.9	23.6	3.2
Not in labor force	59.1	58.7	54.3	47.0	42.8	40.2	44.0	....	....
Industry									
Total nonagricultural employment	79.9	77.0	70.9	53.3	45.2	40.4	36.6	23.6	31.3
Goods-producing industries	23.5	22.6	23.5	20.4	18.5	17.5	15.9	8.6	13.3
Mining	0.8	0.7	0.6	0.7	0.9	0.8	1.0	0.7	1.1
Contract construction	3.6	3.5	3.5	3.0	2.3	1.1	1.8	1.0	1.5
Manufacturing: Durable goods	11.2	10.7	11.2	9.4	8.1	9.1	7.0	....	....
Nondurable goods	7.9	7.7	8.2	7.3	7.1	6.5	6.2	....	....
Services-producing industries	56.4	54.4	47.7	32.9	26.7	22.9	20.6	15.0	18.1
Transportation and public utilities	4.6	4.5	4.5	4.0	4.0	3.9	3.3	2.8	3.9
Trade: Wholesale	4.3	4.2	3.8	2.9	2.5	1.9	1.9	....	....
Retail	13.3	12.8	11.2	8.2	6.9	5.5	5.4	....	....
Finance, insurance, real estate	4.3	4.2	3.7	2.6	1.9	1.5	1.5	1.3	1.5
Services	14.8	14.0	11.6	7.1	5.4	4.2	3.9	2.9	3.4
Federal government	2.8	2.7	2.7	2.2	1.9	2.8	1.3	0.6	0.5
State and local government	12.4	12.0	9.8	5.9	4.1	3.1	3.3	2.7	2.5

[1] For 1929-45, figures on labor force status relate to persons 14 years and over; beginning 1950, 16 years and over. [2] June. NOTE: Figures may not add to totals due to rounding.

Number of Employed Persons by Major Occupations, 1975
(in thousands)
Source: Bureau of Labor Statistics.

Professional and technical workers	12,748
Accountants	782
Computer specialists	363
Dietitians and therapists	191
Draftsmen	301
Editors and reporters	177
Electrical, electronic engineering technicians	177
Engineers, technical	1,150
Health technologists and technicians	397
Lawyers and judges	392
Librarians, archivists, curators	190
Life and physical scientists	277
Nurses, registered	935
Physicians and dentists	647
Social and recreation workers	402
Teachers, college	543
Teachers, elementary and secondary	3,022
Writers, artists, entertainers	1,055
Managers and administrators, except farm	8,891
Bank officials, financial managers	518
Buyers and purchasing agents	370
Officials and administrators	361
Restaurant, cafeteria, bar managers	501
Sales managers, retail trade	315
School administrators	366
Clerical workers	15,128
Bank tellers	350
Bookkeepers	1,689
Cashiers	1,180
Office machine operators	714
Secretaries	3,245
Stock clerks and storekeepers	473
Telephone operators	344
Typists and stenographers	1,125

Sales workers	5,460
Insurance agents, brokers, underwriters	504
Real estate agents and brokers	414
Sales persons and sales clerks	4,002
Craft and kindred workers	10,972
Automobile mechanics, body repairers	1,102
Carpenters	988
Brickmasons and stonemasons	160
Electricians	534
Machinists	461
Mechanics, except automobile	1,795
Painters, construction, maintenance	420
Plumbers and pipe fitters	386
Printing craft workers	375
Foremen	1,393
Telephone installers and repairers	314
Operatives and kindred workers	12,856
Delivery and route workers	583
Garage workers, gas station attendants	450
Meat cutters and butchers	307
Truckdrivers	1,694
Private household workers	1,171
Service workers except private household	10,486
Bartenders	247
Child-care workers except private household	422
Cooks except private household	1,001
Guards	492
Nursing aides, orderlies, attendants	1,001
Police	473
Practical nurses	370
Waiters and busboys	1,347
Farm workers	2,936
Nonfarm laborers	4,134
TOTAL	84,783

Where the Jobs Will Be Through the Mid-'80's
(Anticipated annual job openings for selected occupations, 1974-85)
Source: Bureau of Labor Statistics.

Occupation	Estimated employment 1974	Average annual openings[1]	
		Number	Per cent of 1974 employment
Stenographers and secretaries	3,300,000	439,000	13.3
Retail trade salesworkers	2,800,000	190,000	6.8
Building custodians	1,900,000	146,000	7.7
Bookkeeping workers	1,700,000	121,000	7.1
Kindergarten and elementary school teachers	1,276,000	94,000	7.4
Secondary school teachers	1,086,000	37,500	3.5
Nurses aides, orderlies and attendants	970,000	123,000	12.7
Cashiers	1,111,000	97,000	8.7
Waiters and waitresses	1,180,000	105,000	8.9
Foremen	1,460,000	61,000	4.2
Receptionists	460,000	57,500	12.5
Cooks and chefs	955,000	78,600	8.2
Cosmetologists	500,000	50,800	10.2
Private household workers	1,200,000	52,000	4.3
Local truck drivers	1,600,000	38,500	2.4
Inspectors (manufacturing)	790,000	51,000	6.5
Industrial machinery repairers	500,000	42,500	8.5
Bank clerks	517,000	54,000	10.4
Accountants	805,000	45,500	5.6
Assemblers	1,140,000	63,000	5.5
Engineering and science technicians	560,000	32,000	5.7

[1] Annual openings include jobs resulting from growth and deaths and retirements. Transfers to other fields of work are not reflected. Annual openings as a per cent of occupational employment provide a measure of relative job opportunities by occupation.

Employed Persons 16 Years and Over,
by Race and Occupational Groups, 1974–75

Source: Department of Labor, Bureau of Labor Statistics.

	1975		1974		Per cent change, 1974–75
Color and occupational group	Number	Per cent distri-bution	Number	Per cent distri-bution	
WHITE					
White-collar workers	39,126,000	51.7	38,761,000	50.6	0.9
Professional and technical workers	11,711,000	15.5	11,368,000	14.8	3.0
Managers and administrators, except farm	8,493,000	11.2	8,562,000	11.2	−0.8
Sales workers	5,218,000	6.9	5,203,000	6.8	0.3
Clerical workers	13,705,000	18.1	13,629,000	17.8	0.6
Blue-collar workers	24,568,000	32.4	26,029,000	34.0	−5.6
Craft and kindred workers	10,177,000	13.4	10,603,000	13.8	−4.0
Operatives, except transport	8,274,000	10.9	9,075,000	11.8	−8.8
Transport equipment operatives	2,768,000	3.7	2,805,000	3.7	−1.3
Nonfarm laborers	3,349,000	4.4	3,547,000	4.6	−5.6
Private household workers	728,000	1.0	755,000	1.0	−3.6
Service workers, except private household	8,590,000	11.3	8,282,000	10.8	3.7
Farm workers	2,700,000	3.6	2,793,000	3.6	−3.3
TOTAL	75,713,000	100.0	76,620,000	100.0	−1.2
BLACK AND OTHER					
White-collar workers	3,101,000	34.2	2,977,000	32.0	4.2
Professional and technical workers	1,037,000	11.4	970,000	10.4	6.9
Managers and administrators, except farm	398,000	4.4	379,000	4.1	5.0
Sales workers	242,000	2.7	214,000	2.3	13.1
Clerical workers	1,423,000	15.7	1,414,000	15.2	0.6
Blue-collar workers	3,394,000	37.4	3,747,000	40.2	−9.4
Craft and kindred workers	795,000	8.8	874,000	9.4	−9.0
Operatives, except transport	1,363,000	15.0	1,553,000	16.7	−12.2
Transport equipment operatives	451,000	5.0	488,000	5.2	−7.6
Nonfarm laborers	785,000	8.7	833,000	8.9	−5.8
Private household workers	443,000	4.9	474,000	5.1	−6.5
Service workers, except private household	1,896,000	20.9	1,863,000	20.0	1.8
Farm workers	237,000	2.6	254,000	2.7	6.7
TOTAL	9,070,000	100.0	9,315,000	100.0	−2.6

Women in the Working Population of the U.S., 1880–1975

Sources: Bureau of the Census and Bureau of Labor Statistics.

	Working women[1]		
Year	Number (thousands)	Per cent of female population ages 10 and over[1]	Per cent of total working population ages 10 and over[1]
1880	2,647	14.7	15.2
1890	4,006	17.4	17.2
1900	5,319	18.8	18.3
1910	7,445	21.5	19.9
1920	8,637	21.4	20.4
1930	10,752	22.0	22.0
1940	12,845	25.4	24.3
1950	18,412	33.9	17.3
1960[2]	23,272	37.8	19.4
1970	31,560	43.4	22.5
1975	37,087	46.4	24.2

[1] For 1880–1930; data relate to population and gainful workers at ages 10 and over; for 1940, to ages 14 and over; for 1950–75, to population at ages 16 and over. [2] Beginning in 1960, figures include Alaska and Hawaii.

Per Cent Unemployed in the Civilian Labor Force, 1930–1976

Source: Bureau of Labor Statistics.

Year	Per cent unemployed	Year	Per cent unemployed
1930	8.7	1961	6.7
1932	23.6	1962	5.5
1934	21.7	1963	5.7
1936	16.9	1964	5.2
1938	19.0	1965	4.5
1940	14.6	1966	3.8
1942	4.7	1967	3.8
1944	1.2	1968	3.6
1946	3.9	1969	3.5
1948	3.8	1970	4.9
1950	5.3	1971	5.9
1952	3.0	1972	5.6
1953	2.9	1973	4.9
1954	5.5	1974	5.6
1955	4.4	1975	8.5
1956	4.1	1976, Jan.	7.8
1957	4.3	May	7.3
1958	6.8	Aug.	7.9
1960	5.5	Sept.	7.8

NOTE: Estimates prior to 1940 are based on sources other than direct enumeration.

Persons in the Labor Force of the U.S., 1820–1970

Source: Bureau of the Census.

Year	Working population Number (thou-sands)	% total population aged 10 and over[1]	Per cent of working population in Farm occupation	Nonfarm occupation	Year	Working population Number (thou-sands)	% total population aged 10 and over[1]	Per cent of working population in Farm occupation	Nonfarm occupation
1820	2,881	44.4	71.8	28.2	1900	29,073	50.2	37.5	62.5
1830	3,932	45.5	70.5	29.5	1910	37,371	52.2	31.0	69.0
1840	5,420	46.6	68.6	31.4	1920	42,434	51.3	27.0	73.0
1850	7,697	46.8	63.7	36.3	1930	48,830	49.5	21.4	78.6
1860	10,533	47.0	58.9	41.1	1940	52,966	52.4	17.0	83.0
1870	12,925	44.4	53.0	47.0	1950	59,671	53.4	11.5	88.5
1880	17,392	47.3	49.4	50.6	1960	69,877	55.3	5.9	94.1
1890	23,318	49.2	42.6	57.4	1970	82,897	55.5	2.9	97.1

[1] For 1820 to 1930, the data relate to the population and gainful workers at ages 10 and over. For 1940 to 1970, the data relate to the population and labor force at ages 14 and over; the farm and nonfarm percentages relate only to the experienced labor force.

Composition of the Civilian Labor Force and Unemployment, 1975–1976
(in thousands)
Source: Bureau of Labor Statistics.

Race, sex, and age	1976[1] Civilian labor force Number	Per cent distribution	Unemployed Number	Per cent distribution	Rate	1975 Civilian labor force Number	Per cent distribution	Unemployed Number	Per cent distribution	Rate
Men, 20 years and older	51,454	54.4	3,063	42.3	6.0	50,855	54.9	3,428	43.8	6.7
Women, 20 years and older	34.290	36.2	2,445	34.2	7.1	32,959	35.6	2,649	33.8	8.0
Teenagers, 16 to 19 years	8,899	9.4	1,635	22.9	18.4	8,799	9.5	1,752	22.4	19.9
WHITE	83,805	88.5	5,685	79.6	6.8	82,084	88.6	6,371	81.4	7.8
BLACK AND OTHER	10,826	11.4	1,444	20.2	13.3	10,529	11.4	1,459	18.6	13.9
TOTAL	94,643	100.0	7,143	100.0	7.5	92,613	100.0	7,830	100.0	8.5

[1] June. NOTE: Totals may not add due to rounding.

Employed College Graduates in Professional and Managerial Occupations, by Sex and Race, 1964–1975
(In thousands)
Source: Department of Labor, Bureau of Labor Statistics.

Year and color	Men Number	Per cent in professional and managerial occupations Total	Professional	Managerial	Women Number	Per cent in professional and managerial occupations
1975						
White	8,669,000	78.1	54.1	24.1	4,183,000	76.6
Black and other	576,000	74.1	58.0	16.1	485,000	77.7
1964						
White	5,158,000	81.8	60.0	21.8	2,107,000	82.7
Black and other	266,000	69.2	63.9	5.3	166,000	72.9

Government Employment and Payrolls

Source: Bureau of the Census.

Year and function	Employees (in thousands)				Payrolls (in millions)			
	Total	Federal[1]	State	Local	Total	Federal[1]	State	Local
1950	6,402	2,117	1,057	3,228	$1,528	$ 613	$ 218	$ 696
1960	8,808	2,421	1,527	4,860	3,333	1,118	524	1,691
1965	10,589	2,588	2,028	5,973	4,884	1,484	849	2,551
1968	12,342	2,984	2,495	6,864	6,889	2,137	1,257	3,495
1969	12,685	2,969	2,614	7,102	7,588	2,335	1,431	3,882
1970	13,028	2,881	2,755	7,392	8,334	2,428	1,612	4,294
1972	13,759	2,795	2,957	8,007	9,950	2,710	1,937	5,303
1973	14,139	2,786	3,013	8,339	11,027	3,012	2,158	5,857
1974	14,628	2,874	3,155	8,599	12,086	3,294	2,410	6,382
1975, total	14,986	2,890	3,268	8,828	13,243	3,584	2,651	7,008
National defense and international relations....	1,051	1,051	....	....	1,295	1,295	....	....
Postal service	692	692	....	....	846	846	....	....
Education	6,294	22	1,400	4,872	4,985	24	1,022	3,939
Teachers	3,523	....	406	3,117	3,560	....	482	3,078
Highways	609	5	275	329	497	8	251	238
Health and hospitals	1,448	247	592	609	1,188	281	471	436
Police protection	664	55	69	540	668	83	75	510
Local fire protection	291	....	....	291	250	....	....	250
Sewerage and sanitation....	213	....	....	213	172	....	....	172
Local parks and recreation..	218	....	....	218	121	....	....	121
Natural resources	454	253	165	36	473	313	137	23
Financial administration.....	390	105	113	172	348	130	100	118
All other	2,663	460	654	1,548	2,401	604	595	1,201

[1] Civilians only.

Value of New Construction Put in Place, 1929–1975

(in millions of dollars)

Source: Bureau of the Census.

Activity	1975	1974	1970	1960	1950	1940	1933	1929
Total new construction activity	132,043	138,526	94,855	54,738	33,575	8,682	2,879	10,793
New private construction activity	93,034	100,179	66,759	38,875	26,709	5,504	1,231	8,307
Residential	46,476	50,378	31,864	22,975	18,126	2,985	470	3,625
New dwelling units	34,412	40,645	24,272	17,279	15,551	2,560	290	3,040
Additions and alterations	10,924	8,046	6,234	4,831	2,400	335	145	340
Nonhousekeeping	1,140	1,687	1,358	865	175	90	35	245
Nonresidential building, except farm and public utility	26,406	29,644	21,417	10,149	3,904	1,025	406	2,694
Industrial	8,017	7,902	6,538	2,851	1,062	442	176	949
Commercial[1]	12,804	15,945	9,754	4,180	1,415	348	130	1,135
Other	5,585	5,797	5,125	3,118	1,427	235	100	610
Public utility	16,759	16,625	11,020	4,621	3,045	771	261	1,578
Railroads	443	575	306	....	167	94	510
Telephone and telegraph	3,689	4,279	2,968	1,088	440	122	45	354
Farm construction	2,326	2,533	1,512	849	1,522	240	49	307
New public construction activity	39,009	38,347	28,096	15,863	6,866	3,628	1,648	2,486
Residential	649	1,007	1,107	716	345	200	...	...
Nonresidential building	13,967	13,986	9,550	4,395	2,387	615	230	659
Industrial	919	766	499	407	224	164	2	...
Educational	7,393	7,311	5,619	2,818	1,133	156	52	389
Hospital and institutional	1,663	1,240	837	401	499	54	49	101
Other	3,992	4,669	2,595	1,169	531	241	127	169
Military facilities	1,391	1,188	718	1,366	177	385	36	19
Highway	10,345	12,069	9,981	5,437	2,134	1,302	847	1,266
Sewer and water	6,253	4,066	2,638	1,487	659	338	95	253
Conservation and development	3,227	2,741	1,908	1,175	942	528	359	115

[1] Warehouses, office and loft buildings; stores, restaurants and garages.

Membership of Representative American Labor Unions, 1974

Source: Bureau of Labor Statistics.

Name of Union	Affiliation	No. of Members
Amalgamated Clothing Workers	AFL–CIO	350,000
Amalgamated Meat Cutters and Butcher Workmen	AFL–CIO	525,000
Amalgamated Transit Union	AFL–CIO	140,000
American Federation of Government Employees	AFL–CIO	300,000
American Federation of Musicians	AFL–CIO	330,000
Bricklayers, Masons and Plasterers	AFL–CIO	147,715
Brotherhood of Maintenance of Way Employees	AFL–CIO	119,184
Brotherhood of Painters and Allied Trades	AFL–CIO	211,373
Brotherhood of Railway and Steamship Clerks	AFL–CIO	235,000
Communications Workers of America	AFL–CIO	498,743
Hotel & Restaurant Employees and Bartenders International Union	AFL–CIO	451,989
International Association of Bridge, Structural and Ornamental Iron Workers	AFL–CIO	181,647
International Association of Fire Fighters	AFL–CIO	171,674
International Association of Machinists and Aerospace Workers	AFL–CIO	943,280
International Brotherhood of Boilermakers	AFL–CIO	138,000
International Brotherhood of Electrical Workers	AFL–CIO	991,228
International Brotherhood of Teamsters	Ind.	1,973,272
International Ladies' Garment Workers' Union	AFL–CIO	404,737
International Typographical Union	AFL–CIO	111,362
International Union of Electrical, Radio and Machine Workers	AFL–CIO	298,231
Laborers' International Union of North America	AFL–CIO	650,000
National Association of Letter Carriers	AFL–CIO	232,000
Oil, Chemical and Atomic Workers	AFL–CIO	177,433
Retail Clerks International Association	AFL–CIO	650,876
Retail, Wholesale and Department Store Union	AFL–CIO	180,000
Service Employees' International Union	AFL–CIO	550,000
Sheet Metal Workers' International Association	AFL–CIO	160,860
State, County and Municipal Employees	AFL–CIO	648,160
Textile Workers Union	AFL–CIO	167,000
Transport Workers Union	AFL–CIO	150,000
United Association of Plumbers and Pipe Fitters	AFL–CIO	228,000
United Automobile, Aerospace and Agricultural Implement Workers of America	Ind.	1,544,859
United Brotherhood of Carpenters and Joiners	AFL–CIO	820,000
United Electrical, Radio and Machine Workers of America	Ind.	163,000
American Postal Workers[1]	AFL–CIO	249,000
United Mine Workers	Ind.	220,000
United Paperworkers International Union	AFL–CIO	300,684
United Rubber, Cork, Linoleum and Plastic Workers of America	AFL–CIO	190,523
United Steelworkers of America	AFL–CIO	1,300,000
United Transportation Union[2]	AFL–CIO	238,000

[1] In February 1971 the United Federation of Postal Clerks merged with four other postal unions to form the American Postal Workers Union (AFL-CIO). [2] United Transportation Union was formed Jan. 1, 1969 by merger of four unions: Brotherhood of Locomotive Firemen and Enginemen (AFL-CIO); Brotherhood of Railroad Trainmen (AFL-CIO); Switchmen's Union of North America (AFL-CIO); and Order of Railway Conductors and Brakemen (Ind.).

New Housing Starts,[1] Mobile Homes
(in thousands)

Source: Housing Construction Statistics, 1900–1965, and Construction Reports, Housing Starts, 1966–1975, Dept. of Commerce; Manufactured Housing Institute.

Year	No. of units started	Year	No. of units started	Year	Mobile homes shipped
1900	189	1960[1]	1,274	1965	216
1910	387	1964	1,561	1967	240
1920	247	1966	1,196	1968	318
1929	509	1968	1,545	1969	413
1933	93	1970	1,469	1970	401
1937	336	1971	2,085	1971	497
1939	515	1972	2,379	1972	576
1943	191	1973	2,057	1973	567
1949	1,466	1974	1,352	1974	329
1950	1,952	1975	1,171	1975	214

[1] Prior to 1960, starts limited to nonfarm housing; from 1960 on, figures include farm housing.

Monthly Average Railroad Carloadings
(in thousands of cars)

Source: Association of American Railroads.

Year	Total	Year	Total
1920	3,760	1960	2,537
1929	4,402	1962	2,394
1932	2,348	1964	2,419
1939	2,826	1965	2,437
1940	3,030	1967	2,340
1943	3,537	1968	2,354
1947	3,709	1969	2,383
1949	2,993	1970	2,263
1950	3,242	1971	2,105
1951	3,375	1972	2,175
1953	3,185	1973	2,278
1957	2,958	1974	2,182
1959	2,585	1975	1,936

Largest U.S. and Foreign Corporations, 1975

(millions of dollars)

Source: Fortune Magazine.

20 Largest Industrial Corporations

	Sales	Assets
Exxon	$44,865	$32,839
General Motors	35,725	21,665
Texaco	24,507	17,262
Ford Motor	24,009	14,020
Mobil Oil	20,620	15,050
Standard Oil of California	16,822	12,898
International Business Machines	14,437	15,530
Gulf Oil	14,268	12,425
General Electric	13,399	9,764
Chrysler	11,699	6,267
International Telephone & Telegraph	11,368	10,408
Standard Oil (Indiana)	9,955	9,854
U.S. Steel	8,167	8,148
Shell Oil	8,143	7,011
Atlantic Richfield	7,308	7,365
Continental Oil	7,254	5,185
E. I. du Pont de Nemours	7,222	6,425
Western Electric	6,590	5,000
Proctor & Gamble	6,082	3,653
Westinghouse Electric	5,863	4,866

10 Largest Commercial Banks

	Assets	Deposits
BankAmerica Corp.	$66,763	$56,545
Citicorp	57,850	44,681
Chase Manhattan	41,414	33,928
Manufacturers Hanover	28,291	23,471
J. P. Morgan & Co.	25,832	19,938
Chemical New York	23,771	19,392
Bankers Trust New York	20,611	16,945
Continental Illinois	20,226	15,300
First Chicago	19,012	14,193
Western Bancorp	18,713	15,119

10 Largest Life Insurance Companies

	Assets	Premium and annuity income
Prudential	$39,309	$5,590
Metropolitan	35,138	4,967
Equitable Life Assurance	19,819	3,428
New York Life	13,862	1,801
John Hancock Mutual	12,801	1,935
Aetna	10,415	2,731
Northwestern Mutual	7,918	817

Connecticut General Life	7,682	1,583
Travelers	7,169	2,160
Massachusetts Mutual	5,848	827

10 Largest Foreign Industrial Corporations

	Sales	Assets
Royal Dutch/Shell Group (Netherlands–Britain)	$32,105	$28,349
National Iranian Oil (Iran)	18,855	5,415
British Petroleum (Britain)	17,286	14,615
Unilever (Britain–Netherlands)	15,016	6,971
Philips' Glöeilampenfabrieken (Netherlands)	10,746	11,187
Cie Française des Pétroles (France)	9,146	8,037
Nippon Steel (Japan)	8,797	9,480
August Thyssen-Hütte (Germany)	8,765	4,903
Hoechst (Germany)	8,462	7,758
ENI (Italy)	8,334	12,475

10 Largest Transportation Companies

	Operating revenues	Assets
Trans World Airlines	$2,640	$1,929
United Airlines	2,410	2,686
Penn Central Transportation	2,173	4,392
Union Pacific	1,755	3,418
American Airlines	1,710	1,605
Southern Pacific	1,647	3,724
Eastern Air Lines	1,624	1,290
United Parcel Service	1,615	696
Pan American World Airways	1,606	1,470
Burlington Northern	1,595	3,279

10 Largest Utilities

	Assets	Operating revenues
American Telephone & Telegraph	$80,156	$28,957
General Telephone & Electronics	12,714	5,948
Southern Company	7,237	1,999
Pacific Gas & Electric	6,621	2,233
American Electric Power	6,408	1,644
Consolidated Edison	6,315	2,668
Commonwealth Edison	5,180	1,722
Southern California Edison	4,650	1,668
Public Service Electric & Gas	4,473	1,631
Philadelphia Electric	3,961	1,135

Financial Condition of U. S. Life Insurance Companies

(in millions of dollars)

Source: Institute of Life Insurance.

Year	Assets (admitted) Dec. 31	Total income	Premium receipts	Benefit payments[1]
1910	3,876	781	593	387
1920	7,320	1,764	1,381	745
1929	17,482	4,337	3,343	1,962
1939	29,243	5,453	3,776	2,642
1945	44,797	7,674	5,159	2,667
1955	90,432	16,544	12,546	5,383
1960	119,576	23,007	17,365	8,119
1965	158,884	33,167	24,604	11,417
1970	207,254	49,054	33,996	16,449
1973	252,436	64,753	48,668	20,313
1975	289,304	78,022	58,575	22,536

[1] Life Insurance Benefit Payments in the U.S.

Life Insurance in Force in U. S.

(in millions of dollars)

Source: Institute of Life Insurance.

Dec. 31	Ordinary	Group	Industrial	Credit	Total
1910	11,783	. . . .	3,125	. . . .	14,908
1915	16,650	100	4,279	. . . .	21,029
1925	52,892	4,247	12,318	18	69,475
1930	78,576	9,801	17,963	73	106,413
1933	70,872	8,681	16,630	63	96,246
1940	79,346	14,938	20,866	380	115,530
1948	131,158	37,068	31,253	1,729	201,208
1955	216,812	101,345	39,682	14,493	373,332
1960	341,881	175,903	39,563	29,101	586,448
1965	499,638	308,078	39,818	53,020	900,554
1970	734,730	551,357	38,644	77,392	1,402,123
1972	853,911	640,689	39,975	93,410	1,627,985
1973	928,192	708,322	40,632	101,154	1,778,300
1974	1,009,038	827,018	39,441	109,623	1,985,120
1975	1,083,421	904,695	39,423	112,032	2,139,571

Sales of Leading Retail Outlets

Source: Fortune Magazine

	1975 Sales (in thousands)
DEPARTMENT STORES	
J. C. Penney	$7,678,600
Federated Department Stores	3,712,864
May Department Stores	2,017,366
Allied Stores	1,770,635
Dayton Hudson	1,692,528
Associated Dry Goods	1,390,966
R. H. Macy	1,297,672
Carter Hawley Hale Stores	1,252,082
Zayre	1,084,011
Gimbel Bros.	890,191
VARIETY STORES	
S. S. Kresge	$6,883,613
F. W. Woolworth	4,650,290
G. C. Murphy	553,700
GROCERY STORES	
Safeway Stores	$9,716,889
Great Atlantic & Pacific Tea	6,537,897
Kroger	5,339,225
American Stores	3,207,248
Lucky Stores	3,109,406
Winn-Dixie Stores	2,962,165
Jewel Companies	2,817,754
Food Fair Stores	2,482,539

	1975 Sales (in thousands)
Grand Union	1,611,195
Supermarkets General	1,550,408
National Tea	1,472,341
Fisher Foods	1,379,994
DRUG STORES	
Dart Industries	$1,280,400
Walgreen	1,079,144
Sterling Drug	957,146
MAIL ORDER HOUSES	
Sears, Roebuck	$13,639,887
Montgomery Ward	3,775,032
Gamble-Skogmo	1,559,043
MIXED STORES	
City Products	$2,224,968
Southland	1,787,928
Stop & Shop	1,359,776
Vornado	1,017,525
SHOE STORES	
Melville	$908,321
U.S. Shoe	473,420
FURNITURE STORES	
Wickes	$1,136,769

Estimated Volume of Retail Sales by Kind of Business, 1974-1975
(in millions of dollars)

Source: Bureau of the Census.

Kind of business	Annual sales 1975	1974	Kind of business	Annual sales 1975	1974
Retail stores, total	584,423	537,782	Hardware, plumbing, heating equipment	17,196	17,997
Food group	131,723	119,763	Lumber, construction materials	15,921	17,821
Eating and drinking places	47,514	41,840	Machinery, equipment, supplies	51,819	50,666
General merchandise group with nonstores	95,402	89,286	Metals, metalwork (except scrap)	25,075	32,027
Apparel and accessory stores	26,749	24,864	Scrap, waste materials	8,559	14,421
Furniture, home furnishings and equipment stores	26,123	25,544	Nondurable goods (excluding farm products and raw materials), total	208,729	199,769
Automotive dealers	102,105	93,089	Groceries and related products	89,758	80,513
Gasoline service stations	43,895	39,910	Beer, wine, distilled alcoholic beverages	20,161	18,296
Building materials, hardware, farm equipment dealers	34,204	32,547	Drugs, chemicals, allied products	15,117	15,343
Drug and proprietary stores	18,098	16,785	Tobacco, tobacco products	8,467	7,882
Liquor stores	10,974	10,285	Dry goods, apparel	15,466	15,017
Merchant wholesale trade, total	439,000	448,127	Paper, paper products, excluding wallpaper	11,528	12,622
Farm products and raw materials	44,349	46,015	Other nondurable goods	49,086	50,007
Merchant wholesalers, total	394,651	402,112	Hotel services	10,668	10,236
Durable goods, total	185,922	202,341	Personal services	15,090	13,785
Motor vehicles, automotive equipment	33,610	32,928	Business services	46,114	42,364
Electrical goods	24,246	26,347	Automotive services	17,313	15,187
Furniture, home furnishings	6,691	7,012	Miscellaneous repair services	9,255	8,465
			Motion pictures, amusement and recreation services	15,583	14,161

50 Leading Stocks in Market Value (December 31, 1975)

Source: New York Stock Exchange.

The 50 leading stocks with the largest market value at the end of 1975 accounted for $312 billion or 47% of the total value of the 1,531 stocks listed on the New York Stock Exchange. The largest five issues were valued at $117 and represented 18% of the total.

Six corporations joined the list in 1975—Monsanto Company, Hewlett Packard Company, International Paper, Georgia Pacific Corporation, Federated Department Stores and McDonald's Corporation.

Stock	Listed shares (millions)	Market value (millions)	Stock	Listed shares (millions)	Market value (millions)
International Business Machines	149.5	$33,533	Caterpillar Tractor	57.3	$3,994
American Telephone & Telegraph	582.0	29,610	Union Carbide	61.8	3,780
Exxon Corporation	226.6	20,111	Citicorp	126.9	3,745
Eastman Kodak	161.6	17,146	Ford Motor	82.0	3,607
General Motors	287.6	16,574	Eli Lilly & Co.	69.5	3,598
Sears Roebuck	158.6	10,230	U.S. Steel	54.3	3,527
Dow Chemical	98.4	9,018	Shell Oil	68.9	3,376
General Electric	186.8	8,614	Burroughs Corporation	39.9	3,341
Procter & Gamble	82.5	7,342	Getty Oil	20.2	3,296
Texaco Inc.	274.3	6,412	Continental Oil	53.7	3,270
Standard Oil (Indiana)	150.0	6,396	General Telephone & Electronics	126.8	3,218
Minnesota Mining & Mfg.	114.9	6,375	J.C. Penney	62.9	3,150
E.I. du Pont de Nemours	48.3	6,113	Philip Morris	59.4	3,146
American Home Products	166.8	5,565	Warner-Lambert	78.7	2,864
Merck & Co.	75.8	5,247	Halliburton Company	19.5	2,847
Johnson & Johnson	58.1	5,218	Schering-Plough	54.0	2,842
Standard Oil of California	169.9	4,989	Reynolds Industries	45.4	2,794
Coca-Cola Company	60.1	4,944	Monsanto Company	35.1	2,681
Mobil Oil	103.3	4,883	Hewlett Packard Company	27.6	2,607
Weyerhaeuser Company	128.6	4,775	International Paper	45.0	2,598
Schlumberger Ltd.	58.9	4,474	Georgia Pacific Corporation	60.3	2,541
Gulf Oil	211.9	4,344	Federated Department Stores	46.2	2,439
Atlantic Richfield	47.5	4,289	McDonald's Corporation	40.2	2,346
Phillips Petroleum	76.3	4,137	Pacific Telephone & Telegraph	168.6	2,318
S.S. Kresge	120.6	4,041	TOTAL	5,381.9	$312,316
Xerox Corporation	78.8	4,011			

25 Companies with Largest Number of Stockholders, 1976

Source: New York Stock Exchange.

Company	Stockholders	Company	Stockholders
American Telephone & Telegraph	2,934,000	Sears, Roebuck	271,000
General Motors	1,311,000	Southern Company	265,000
Exxon Corp.	707,000	Eastman Kodak	239,000
International Business Machines	589,000	Tenneco Inc.	238,000
General Electric	530,000	International Telephone & Telegraph	235,000
General Telephone & Electronics	500,000	Chrysler Corporation	234,000
Gulf Oil	372,000	Mobil Oil	226,000
Texaco Inc.	362,000	E.I. du Pont de Nemours	213,000
Ford Motor	352,000	Westinghouse Electric	202,000
Consolidated Edison	303,000	American Electric Power	201,000
RCA Corporation	299,000	Detroit Edison	194,000
U.S. Steel	291,000	Philadelphia Electric	193,000
Standard Oil of California	276,000	TOTAL	11,537,000

Bonds of Corporations and Governments (Listed Dec. 31, 1975)

Source: New York Stock Exchange.

Major group	Number of issuers	Number of issues	Par value (millions)	Market value (millions)
Total U.S. companies	984	2,337	$146,268	$123,056
Foreign companies	24	31	986	838
U.S. Govt. & N.Y. City	2	83	186,532	183,102
International banks	4	54	6,522	5,862
Foreign governments	52	127	2,926	2,545
TOTAL	1,066	2,632	$343,233	$315,405

Stocks Favored by Institutional Investors

Source: New York Stock Exchange.

Company	Instit'l holdings No. Inst.	Shs. (000)	Company	Instit'l holdings No. Inst.	Shs. (000)	Company	Instit'l holdings No. Inst.	Shs. (000)
Int'l Business Mach.	1,210	15,602	Caterpillar Tractor	303	6,176	Deere & Co.	217	5,375
Exxon Corporation	781	18,484	Texas Utilities	301	9,795	McDonald's Corp.	213	8,359
Eastman Kodak	732	11,918	Procter & Gamble	293	3,186	Bristol-Myers	211	4,901
American Tel. & Tel.	718	22,681	Standard Oil of Calif.	293	12,087	Houston Ltg. & Power	211	4,668
General Motors	682	14,448	Monsanto Company	286	5,547	J.P. Morgan & Co.	211	4,573
General Electric	667	17,016	Philip Morris	283	10,795	Reynolds Industries	209	5,289
Xerox Corporation	570	8,821	Pfizer Inc.	279	9,177	Florida Pwr. & Light	207	6,390
Texaco Inc.	514	21,062	Goodyear Tire & Rub.	270	10,717	Sperry Rand	201	7,493
Sears, Roebuck & Co.	443	6,441	Warner-Lambert	269	10,990	Honeywell Inc.	199	2,776
Citicorp	439	17,601	Halliburton Company	264	8,427	Westinghouse Electric	199	6,728
Minn. Mining & Mfg.	422	8,086	International Paper	264	7,111	So. Calif. Edison	198	5,528
Dow Chemical	406	9,028	Johnson & Johnson	262	4,291	Tenneco Inc.	190	7,722
Merck & Co.	403	7,876	Continental Oil	259	5,762	Kerr-McGee	186	5,540
Standard Oil (Ind.)	393	12,491	J.C. Penney	251	3,657	Texas Instruments	186	4,877
Atlantic Richfield	389	6,244	Schlumberger Ltd.	249	6,042	U.S. Steel	186	5,176
Ford Motor	381	9,549	Weyerhaeuser Co.	243	10,325	Central & So. Western	184	8,239
Mobil Oil	365	9,184	Southern Company	239	5,839	General Foods	179	3,224
E.I. du Pont de Nem.	355	17,076	Inco Ltd.	231	8,508	Amer. Elec. Power	177	2,479
General Tel. & Elec.	351	12,935	Schering-Plough	231	6,494	Gillette Company	176	4,427
Amer. Home Products	344	10,424	Int'l Tel. & Tel.	230	7,607	Sterling Drug	175	6,088
Burroughs Corp.	342	7,359	Com'w'lth Edison	224	6,222	Chase Manhattan	172	2,628
Phillips Petroleum	342	6,884	Coca-Cola Company	223	3,207	Alcan Aluminum Ltd.	171	5,562
Union Carbide	338	8,464	Fed. Dept. Stores	223	4,565	Aluminum Co. of Amer.	171	6,193
S.S. Kresge	325	12,090	Eli Lilly & Co.	220	3,224	Middle So. Utilities	170	6,954
Gulf Oil	307	9,141	Avon Products	218	7,038	Virginia Elec. & Pwr.	170	5,852

Stocks Increasing Dividend in Each of Last 10 Years

Source: New York Stock Exchange.

Company	Paid 1975 $	Company	Paid 1975 $	Company	Paid 1975 $
Air Products & Chemical	0.19s	Dun & Bradstreet	0.99	Nicor Inc.	1.98
Alcon Laboratories	0.23	Echlin Manufacturing	0.41	Oklahoma Gas & Electric	1.40
Allied Maintenance	0.57	General American Oil of Texas	0.77s	Papercraft Corporation	0.58
American Home Products	0.90	Genuine Parts	0.62	Pargas Inc.	0.98
American Hospital Supply	0.31	Georgia-Pacific Corporation	0.76s	Pittston Company	0.58b
AMP Inc.	0.37	H.J. Heinz	1.24	Portland General Electric	1.56
ARA Services	1.01	Heublein Inc.	1.10	Riviana Foods	0.90
Atlantic City Electric	1.51	Holiday Inns	0.34	Rochester Gas & Electric	1.21s
Avon Products	1.51	Int'l Business Machines	6.50	Rollins Inc.	0.28
Baxter Laboratories	0.19	Int'l Flavors & Fragrances	0.29s	Sabine Royalty	0.57s
Central & South Western	1.16	Iowa Public Service	1.54	Schering-Plough	0.84
Central Telephone & Util.	1.16	Johnson & Johnson	0.85e	Southern Indiana Gas & Elec.	2.28
Cleveland Electric Illum.	2.48	S.S. Kresge	0.23	Standards Brands Paint	0.31
Coca-Cola Company	2.30	Longs Drug Stores	0.77	Sun Company Inc.	0.94s
Colgate-Palmolive	0.70	Louisville Gas & Electric	1.85	Texas Industries	0.94s
Columbia Gas System	2.06	Lucky Stores	0.47s	Texas Utilities	1.22
Continental Illinois	2.23	Oscar Mayer & Co.	0.94	Toledo Edison	2.03
Dart Industries	0.58s	Melville Corporation	0.48	Tootsie Roll Industries	0.38s
Diebold Inc.	0.39s	Minnesota Mining & Mfg.	1.35	Trans Union	1.58
Dillon Companies	0.84	Missouri Public Service	0.81s	United Telecommunications	1.10
Walt Disney Productions	0.11s	National Presto Industries	1.80e	Utah International	1.00e
Dr. Pepper	0.31	Nevada Power	1.47	Winn-Dixie Stores	1.38

NOTE: Table covers only companies showing the more significant increases. s = also stock. e = includes extra. b = both stock and extra.

Agricultural Output by States, 1975 Crops

Source: Department of Agriculture.

State	Corn (1,000 bu.)	Wheat (1,000 bu.)	Cotton (1,000 ba.)[1]	Potatoes (1,000 cwt.)	Tobacco (1,000 lbs.)	Cattle[2] (1,000 head)	Swine[3] (1,000 head)
Alabama	34,980	3,240	312	3,336	1,190	2,850	820
Alaska	......	......	......	......	......	9	1
Arizona	396	22,720	611	2,236	......	1,280	97
Arkansas	1,900	15,600	687	......	......	2,385	302
California	27,686	62,227	1,954	24,716	......	5,000	138
Colorado	49,290	50,950	......	10,655	......	3,250	290
Connecticut	......	......	......	598	6,387	110	7
Delaware	17,290	1,156	......	1,530	......	33	55
Florida	17,730	520	3	5,533	29,595	2,920	240
Georgia	103,400	3,645	148	......	150,978	2,370	1,300
Hawaii	......	......	......	......	......	245	58
Idaho	2,075	60,050	......	81,195	......	1,875	90
Illinois	1,242,360	67,470	......	248	......	3,400	5,600
Indiana	551,740	64,500	......	1,375	16,950	2,225	3,900
Iowa	1,091,700	2,550	......	660	......	7,500	12,600
Kansas	137,760	350,900	......	......	......	6,450	1,650
Kentucky	87,780	11,968	......	......	456,654	3,450	1,000
Louisiana	3,120	400	346	252	60	1,880	170
Maine	......	......	......	36,400	......	141	7
Maryland	50,050	5,304	......	294	24,150	460	235
Massachusetts	......	......	......	800	1,950	107	55
Michigan	152,800	38,760	......	9,926	......	1,650	700
Minnesota	407,400	87,839	......	17,425	......	4,430	3,000
Mississippi	5,945	4,440	1,040	190	......	2,723	351
Missouri	170,100	48,510	196	......	6,129	6,600	3,200
Montana	730	155,925	......	1,750	......	3,150	145
Nebraska	503,200	98,240	......	1,542	......	6,550	2,700
Nevada	......	1,175	2	3,188	......	651	9
New Hampshire	......	......	......	144	......	72	9
New Jersey	6,723	1,944	......	2,430	......	110	98
New Mexico	7,000	10,062	73	840	......	1,650	53
New York	39,610	7,410	......	13,718	......	1,915	90
North Carolina	103,180	9,300	46	2,753	956,995	1,130	1,900
North Dakota	6,732	264,392	......	22,950	......	2,380	350
Ohio	321,080	74,340	......	2,641	23,860	2,305	1,675
Oklahoma	6,800	160,800	170	......	......	6,400	300
Oregon	935	56,370	......	17,482	......	1,440	90
Pennsylvania	88,560	11,385	......	7,360	19,800	1,960	660
Rhode Island	......	......	......	1,034	......	12	9
South Carolina	34,650	4,185	98	......	189,000	725	540
South Dakota	83,250	63,294	222	371	......	4,500	1,400
Tennessee	36,900	9,610	2,393	540	134,569	3,100	920
Texas	113,300	131,100	......	3,206	......	15,600	780
Utah	1,650	7,164	......	1,481	......	927	43
Vermont	......	......	1	220	......	346	5
Virginia	48,590	9,052	......	4,030	142,054	1,650	660
Washington	3,264	145,140	......	41,160	......	1,375	71
West Virginia	5,525	544	......	323	3,115	555	50
Wisconsin	198,370	2,820	......	14,000	20,801	4,550	1,150
Wyoming	1,440	6,802	......	1,528	......	1,580	30
TOTAL	5,766,991	2,133,803	8,301,600	342,060	2,184,237	127,976	49,602

[1] 480-lb. net-weight bales. [2] Number on farms as of Jan. 1, 1976. [3] Number on farms as of Dec. 1, 1975.

Livestock on Farms: Number and Value

Source: Department of Agriculture.

January 1:	Number (thousands)						Value (millions of dollars)
	Cattle	Dairy cows[1]	Sheep	Swine[2]	Chickens[2]	Turkeys[2]	
1945	85,573	27,770	46,520	59,373	516,497	7,082	8,012
1960	96,236	19,527	33,170	59,026	369,484	5,633	15,206
1970	112,369	12,091	20,423	57,046	424,295	6,715	23,480
1973	121,534	11,409	17,724	59,180	406,241	3,303[3]	34,076
1974	127,670	11,219	16,394	61,106	412,503	3,553[3]	45,925
1975	131,826	11,151	14,512	55,062	383,579	2,943	24,585

[1] Beginning in 1970, dairy cows and heifers that have calved. [2] Beginning in 1972, figures are for Dec. 1 of preceding year. [3] Breeder hens only, 26 leading states.

Farm Income—Estimated Receipts from Major Farm Marketings
(in millions of dollars)
Source: Department of Agriculture.

Year	Cotton and cotton-seed	Tobacco	Food grains	Oil-bearing crops	Feed grains and hay	Vege-tables[1]	Fruits and nuts[2]	Meat animals	Dairy products	Poultry & eggs
1919.........	2,282	500	1,743	92	1,166	593	632	4,045	1,522	1,106
1929.........	1,511	279	788	85	694	711	631	3,016	1,839	1,184
1932.........	461	115	220	30	245	347	321	1,158	986	559
1939.........	627	271	465	111	507	527	439	2,271	1,346	770
1944.........	1,548	690	1,375	590	1,271	1,484	1,528	5,705	2,915	2,468
1951.........	2,858	1,190	2,004	986	2,091	1,728	1,157	11,360	4,254	3,605
1957.........	1,756	971	1,868	1,181	2,395	1,710	1,292	9.336	4,628	3,076
1965.........	2,330	1,186	2,042	2,173	3,693	2,618	1,650	12,878	5,038	3,583
1970..........	1,254	1,388	2,542	3,590	5,109	2,814	2,070	18,475	6,525	4,250
1971..........	1,487	1,328	2,485	3,789	5,525	3,011	2,311	19,515	6,811	3,963
1972..........	1,842	1,442	3,498	4,393	5,854	3,286	2,557	23,974	7,135	4,202
1973..........	2,798	1,570	7,194	7,580	10,605	4,351	3,444	30,403	8,080	6,935
1974..........	2,893	2,097	8,762	9,817	13,958	5,308	3,424	25,192	9,445	6,253
1975[3]	2,372	2,155	8.347	7,920	12,513	5,370	3,548	25,810	9,866	6,739

[1] Includes melons 1949 to date.   [2] Includes melons 1910–48.   [3] Preliminary.

Farm Income (in millions of dollars)
Source: Department of Agriculture.

Year	Crops	Livestock and livestock products	Government payments	Total cash income
1919......	7,603	6,935	....	14,538
1929......	5,130	6,182	....	11,312
1931......	2,540	3,841	....	6,381
1935......	2,977	4,143	573	7,693
1941......	4,619	6,492	544	11,655
1946......	11,016	13,786	772	25,574
1950......	12,356	16,105	283	28,744
1960......	15,259	18,989	702	34,950
1962......	16,310	20,158	1,747	38,215
1964......	17,378	19,948	2,181	39,507
1966......	18,409	25,026	3,277	46,712
1968......	18,696	25,487	3,462	47,645
1969......	19,606	28,573	3,794	51,973
1970......	20,976	29,563	3,717	54,256
1971......	22,276	30,583	3,145	56,004
1972......	25,520	35,670	3,961	65,151
1973......	41,132	45,936	2,607	89,675
1974	51,271	41,377	530	93,178
1975[1]	46,661	42,902	807	90,370

[1] Preliminary.

U.S. Farm Index (1967 = 100)
Source: Department of Agriculture.

Year	Prices paid by farmers[1]	Prices rec'd by farmers[2]	Parity ratio
1935–39 average .	36	43	119
1945............	56	83	148
1950............	75	103	136
1963............	91	97	105
1969............	108	107	100
1972............	125	125	100
1973	144	179	124
1974	166	192	116
1975	181	185	102

[1] Commodities, interest and taxes, and wage rates.
[2] All crops and livestock.

Farm to Market Basket Retail Food Price Spreads
Source: Department of Agriculture.

Year	Retail cost[1]	Farm value[2]	Farmer's share (%)
Average:			
1913–19.......	$ 487	$228	47
1925–29.......	592	245	41
1933............	373	120	32
1937............	489	202	41
1939............	428	163	38
1945............	618	329	53
1950............	878	415	47
1957............	960	388	40
1960............	996	393	39
1965............	1,037	416	40
1970...........	1,228	478	39
1973............	1,537	701	46
1974............	1,750	748	43
1975	1,876	784	42

[1] Retail cost of average quantities purchased annually per household in 1960–61 by urban wage-earner and clerical-worker families and single workers.   [2] Farm value of equivalent quantities sold by producers adjusted for value of by-products.

Farms—Population and Property
Source: Department of Agriculture.

Item	1976[1]	1954	1930
Farm population (thousands) ..	8,864[2]	19,019	30.529
Number of farms (thousands)..	2,786	4,782	6,295
Tenancy as % of total.........	n.a.	24.0	42.4
All land in farms (million acres)	1,085	1,158	990
Average acreage per farm.....	389.3	242.2	157.3
Value of farm (millions of dol-lars) land and buildings	420,000	97,583	47,994

[1] Preliminary.   [2] 1975 figure. NOTE: n.a. means not available.

Domestic Passenger Traffic by Major Carriers
(in millions of passenger-miles)
Sources: Interstate Commerce Commission; Civil Aeronautics Board; Association of American Railroads.

Year	Railroads		Buses		Air carriers		Electric Interurban railways		Inland waterways[1]	
	Passenger-miles	% of total	Passenger-miles	% of total	Passenger-miles	% of total	Passenger-miles	% of total	Passenger-miles	% of total
1939	23,669	67.7	9,100	26.0	683	2.0	956	2.7	1,486	4.3
1941	29,406	62.7	13,100	27.9	1,385	3.0	1,777	2.5	1,821	3.9
1944	95,663	74.2	26,920	20.8	2,178	1.7	2,042	1.6	2,187	1.7
1953	31,679	41.2	28,397	36.9	14,974	19.2	582	0.8	1,487-	1.9
1960	21,574	28.6	19,327	25.7	31,730	42.1	290	0.4	2,688	3.6
1970	10,903	7.3	25,300	16.9	109,499	73.1	(2)	(2)	4,000	2.7
1973	9,450	5.5	25,400	14.8	132,456	77.3	(2)	(2)	4,000	2.4
1974	10,500	5.9	26,700	15.1	135,474	76.7	(2)	(2)	4,000	2.3
1975[3]	10,000	5.7	25,000	14.3	136,880	77.7	(2)	(2)	4,000	2.3
1974[3]	10,300	5.8	27,600	15.6	135,468	76.4	(2)	(2)	4,000	2.2

[1] Rivers, canals, and Great Lakes. [2] Now included in railroads. [3] Estimated. NOTE: Beginning in 1970, data are for 50 states.

Domestic Freight Traffic by Major Carriers
(in millions of ton-miles)[1]
Sources: Interstate Commerce Commission; Corps of Engineers, USA; Civil Aeronautics Board; Association of American Railroads.

Year	Railroads		Inland waterways[2]		Motor trucks		Oil pipelines		Air carriers	
	Ton-miles	% of total	Ton-miles	% of total	Ton-miles	% of total	Ton-miles	% of total	Ton-miles	% of total
1940	379,201	61.3	118,057	19.1	62,043	10.0	59,277	9.6	14	...
1945	690,809	67.3	142,737	13.9	66,948	6.5	126,530	12.3	91	...
1950	596,940	56.2	163,344	15.4	172,860	16.3	129,175	12.1	318	...
1955	631,385	49.5	216,508	17.0	223,254	17.5	203,244	16.0	481	...
1960	579,130	44.1	220,253	16.8	285,483	21.7	228,626	17.4	778	...
1965	708,700	43.3	262,421	16.0	359,218	21.9	306,393	18.7	1,910	0.1
1970	771,168	39.8	318,560	16.4	412,000	21.3	431,000	22.3	3,295	0.2
1973	858,114	38.4	358,222	16.1	505,000	22.6	507,000	22.7	3,943	0.2
1974	855,700	38.6	354,882	16.1	495,000	22.3	506,000	22.8	3,910	0.2
1975[3]	761,000	36.8	354,000	17.1	441,000	21.3	510,000	24.6	3,731	0.2

[1] Mail and express included, except railroads for 1970. [2] Rivers, canals, and domestic traffic on Great Lakes. [3] Preliminary.

Commerce at Leading Great Lakes Ports
Source: Bureau of the Census.
(in thousands of tons)

Port or Harbor	Foreign				Domestic			Total
	Imports		Exports		Lakewise & Coastwise		Internal & Local	
	Canadian	Overseas	Canadian	Overseas	Receipts	Shipments		
Chicago, Ill.	1,376	1,235	1,554	1,076	11,067	50,522	24,526	45,886
Cleveland, Ohio	3,344	586	110	67	16,881	90	43	21,934
Conneaut, Ohio	1,182	....	4,700	....	8,639	2,046	....	16,566
Detroit, Mich.	1,781	1,441	166	483	22,601	571	498	27,541
Duluth-Superior, Minn.-Wis.	163	109	2,748	2,051	2,602	32,672	926	40,345
Indiana, Ind.	2,244	156	....	....	9,774	3,343	1,648	17,165
Toledo, Ohio	766	327	3,900	542	5,273	10,520	227	21,557

Waterborne Commerce at Selected U.S. Ports, 1974

Source: Bureau of the Census.
(in thousands of tons)

| | Foreign | | Domestic | | | | | |
| | | | Coastwise | | Internal | | | |
Port or Harbor	Imports	Exports	Receipts	Ship-ments	Receipts	Ship-ments	Local	Total
Baton Rouge, La. . . .	12,427	7,660	1,721	5,965	11,237	19,306	811	59,126
Baltimore, Md. . . .	25,231	12,876	6,266	2,238	5,030	2,597	5,653	59,891
Beaumont, Tex. . . .	6,205	4,232	819	11,978	5,391	4,573	307	33,504
Boston, Mass.	8,397	881	12,216	3,059	362	....	1,175	25,729
Corpus Christi, Tex. . .	11,143	4,598	577	9,915	1,599	4,446	566	32,844
Houston, Tex.	18,763	15,908	5,234	19,706	13,663	11,951	3,881	89,106
Lake Charles, La. . . .	2,255	1,074	406	2,179	7,101	3,853	697	16,565
Long Beach, Calif. . .	11,943	6,125	6,221	1,669	523	254	159	26,894
Los Angeles, Calif. . .	10,463	3,348	4,986	5,273	454	522	874	25,919
Marcus Hook, Pa. . .	9,515	146	6,000	2,238	2,442	2,692	414	23,446
Mobile, Ala.	9,416	3,963	448	3,771	7,149	7,017	1,392	33,154
Newport News, Va. . .	1,063	10,482	87	234	2,799	3,018	15	17,682
New Orleans, La. . . .	13,537	37,188	2,398	14,707	48,680	23,429	4,251	144,189
New York, N.Y.	58,666	7,862	33,810	22,669	6,270	17,234	48,494	195,096
Norfolk, Va.	8,913	33,345	2,469	548	3,039	5,950	1,042	55,304
Paulsboro, N.J. . . .	13,191	63	4,480	1,732	3,425	6,434	269	29,593
Philadelphia, Pa. . . .	33,112	6,025	2,440	3,272	10,208	2,914	1,950	59,920
Portland, Me.	22,791	17	3,739	894	5	1	159	27,606
Portland, Ore.	2,245	6,821	3,209	246	4,259	1,994	1,997	20,771
Port Arthur, Tex. . . .	7,779	3,021	3,467	8,334	1,056	4,110	22	27,800
St. Louis, Mo.	....	....	4	13	6,640	13,754	1,251	21,662
Tampa, Fla.	5,803	12,883	14,321	7,240	9	422	240	40,919
Texas City, Tex. . . .	2,804	457	580	5,160	6,194	4,943	14	20,152

Homes With Selected Electrical Appliances, 1952–1975

Sources: Billboard Publications, Inc. and *Merchandising Week.*

| Item | 1975 | | 1965 | | 1960 | | 1952 | |
	No.[1]	Pct.	No.[1]	Pct.	No.[1]	Pct.	No.[1]	Pct.
Air-conditioners, room . . .	38.4	52.8	13.9	24.2	7.8	15.1	0.6	1.3
Clothes dryers (incl. gas) .	42.0	57.7	15.2	26.4	10.1	19.6	1.5	3.6
Clothes washers	50.8	69.9	50.3	87.4	44.1	85.4	32.2	76.2
Coffeemakers	71.0	97.7	41.3	71.7	30.2	58.3	21.6	51.0
Dishwashers	27.9	38.3	7.8	13.5	3.7	7.1	1.3	3.0
Electric blankets	41.4	57.0	20.0	34.7	12.2	23.6	3.6	8.6
Food waste disposers . . .	28.2	38.8	7.9	13.6	5.4	10.5	1.4	3.3
Freezers, home.	31.6	43.5	15.7	27.2	12.1	23.4	4.9	11.5
Mixers	65.6	90.2	41.9	72.8	29.0	56.0	12.6	29.7
Radios[2]	72.6	99.9	58.2	99.3	50.3	94.3	43.7	96.2
Ranges, electrical	49.8	68.5	24.4	42.3	19.3	37.3	10.2	24.1
Refrigerators	72.6	99.9	57.3	99.5	50.8	98.2	37.8	89.2
Television: Black and white .	72.6	99.9	55.9	97.1	46.2	89.4	19.8	46.7
Color.	54.1	74.4	5.5	9.5	n.a.	n.a.	....	....
Toasters	71.7	98.6	48.1	83.6	37.2	72.0	30.0	70.9
Vacuum cleaners	72.1	99.2	48.1	83.5	38.4	74.3	25.1	59.4
Total number of wired homes	72.7	100.0	57.6	100.0	51.7	100.0	42.3	100.0

NOTES: Percentages based on total number of homes wired for electricity. n.a. indicates not available. [1] In millions. [2] Radio data based on 53,300,000 homes in 1960 and 58,566,000 in 1965.

State Motor Vehicle Registration, 1975

(in thousands)

Source: Federal Highway Administration.

	Autos[1]	Buses[2]	Trucks	Total	State	Autos[1]	Buses[2]	Trucks	Total
Alabama	1,900	8.4	584	2,493	Montana	370	1.2	230	602
Alaska[3]	143	1.0	82	226	Nebraska	824	3.1	350	1,178
Arizona	1,064	3.1	392	1,459	Nevada	346	1.0	117	464
Arkansas	865	7.4	411	1,283	New Hampshire	405	1.3	795	485
California	11,226	20.9	2,643	13,891	New Jersey	3,736	11.2	409	4,155
Colorado	1,440	5.1	480	1,925	New Mexico	554	3.6*	268	827
Connecticut	1,793	7.5	149	1,949	New York[3]	6,735	31.3	825	7,591
Delaware	289	1.4	60	351	North Carolina	2,860	22.3	807	3,690
D.C.	236	2.5	17.0	255	North Dakota	331	1.8	218	551
Florida	4,499	17.8	878	5,395	Ohio	6,288	22.0	869	7,179
Georgia	2,510	13.1	688	3,213	Oklahoma	1,432	8.3	672	2,113
Hawaii	395	2.3	65	462	Oregon	1,320	6.5	301	1,628
Idaho	407	2.7	238	647	Pennsylvania	6,589	24.5	1,043	7,659
Illinois	5,350	24.5	969	6,344	Rhode Island[3]	499	0.9	63	563
Indiana	2,565	14.3	736	3,315	South Carolina	1,400	9.3	363	1,772
Iowa	1,543	9.2	547	2,099	South Dakota	336	2.1	183	521
Kansas	1,241	4.8	559	1,805	Tennessee	2,093	8.3	624	2,726
Kentucky	1,675	6.5	563	2,245	Texas	6,217	29.4	2,150	8,396
Louisiana	1,661	15.7	510	2,188	Utah	587	1.1	257	845
Maine	499	2.1	147	648	Vermont	233	1.1	53	287
Maryland	2,072	11.1	339	2,423	Virginia	2,710	11.1	530	3,251
Massachusetts	2,776	9.6	322	3,108	Washington	1,883	11.1	645	2,540
Michigan	4,628	14.5	903	5,545	West Virginia[3]	735	2.4	229	966
Minnesota	1,952	12.4	560	2,525	Wisconsin	2,126	9.5	455	2,591
Mississippi	990	8.3	378	1,377	Wyoming	202	2.0	133	337
Missouri	2,177	9.2	680	2,866	TOTAL	106,713	462.1	25,776	132,950

[1] Including taxicabs. [2] Estimates by Federal Highway Administration of number in operation, rather than registration counts of the states. [3] Estimate by Federal Highway Administration.

Saga of the U. S. Passenger Car

Source: Environmental Protection Agency and Motor Vehicle Manufacturers Association.

	1974	1960	1950	1940
U. S. passenger cars and taxis registered (thousands)	104,901	61,671	40,339	27,466
Total mileage of U. S. passenger cars (millions)	995,500	588,083	363,613	249,600
Total fuel consumption of U. S. passenger cars (millions of gallons)	73,797	41,169	24,305	16,323
Pollutants emitted by U.S. passenger cars (10^3 tons):				
Carbon monoxide	51,200	43,100	26,900	14,500
Hydrocarbons	7,450	8,700	5,400	3,700
Nitrogen oxides	4,760	2,600	1,600	1,100
World registration of cars, trucks, and buses (thousands)	314,335	126,908	70,424	n.a.
U. S. registration of cars, trucks, and buses (thousands)	129,938	73,858	49,162	32,453
U. S. share of world registration of cars, trucks, and buses	41.3%	58.2%	69.8%	n.a.

NOTE: n.a. means not available.

Advertising Expenditures by Medium

Sources: McCann-Erickson, Inc.; *Advertising Age.*

	1975		1974		1968		1958		1948	
Medium	Amount (million dollars)	% of total	Amount (million dollars)	% of total	Amount (million dollars)	% of total	Amount (million dollars)	% of total	Amount (million dollars)	% of total
Newspapers	8,442	29.9	8,001	29.9	5,232	28.9	3,176	30.8	1,745	35.8
Magazines	1,465	5.2	1,504	5.6	1,283	7.1	734	7.1	477	9.8
Business papers	919	3.2	900	3.4	714	4.0	525	5.1	251	5.2
Farm papers[1]	74	0.3	72	0.3	68	0.4	67	0.7	56	1.2
Radio	2,025	7.2	1,837	6.9	1,190	6.6	620	6.0	562	11.5
Television	5,272	18.6	4,851	18.1	3,231	17.9	1,387	13.4	--	--
Direct mail	4,155	14.7	3,986	14.9	2,612	14.4	1,589	15.4	689	14.1
Outdoor	335	1.2	309	1.2	208	1.1	192	1.9	132	2.7
Miscellaneous	5,583	19.7	5,270	19.7	3,552	19.6	2,020	19.6	958	19.7
TOTAL	28,270	100.0	26,730	100.0	18,090	100.0	10,310	100.0	4,870	100.0

[1] Regional farm papers.

U.S. Passenger Car Production by Makes, 1967–1975

Source: Motor Vehicle Manufacturers Association of the U.S.

	1975	1974	1973	1972	1967
American Motors Corporation	323,796	352,088	355,855	279,132	229,057
Chrysler Corporation					
Plymouth	443,550	602,606	742,957	613,486	610,098
Dodge	354,482	463,993	592,863	533,594	497,380
Chrysler	102,940	96,630	205,601	204,881	240,712
Imperial	1,930	13,433	14,956	15,393	15,506
Total	902,902	1,176,662	1,556,377	1,367,354	1,363,696
Ford Motor Company					
Ford	1,301,414	1,716,975	1,909,209	1,868,010	1,377,388
Mercury	405,104	400,701	453,250	427,843	284,503
Lincoln	101,520	87,569	133,394	105,018	34,333
Total	1,808,038	2,205,245	2,495,853	2,400,871	1,696,224
General Motors Corporation					
Chevrolet	1,687,077	1,903,861	2,334,113	2,299,771	1,920,665
Pontiac	523,468	502,083	866,598	702,571	857,171
Oldsmobile	654,491	548,658	918,119	807,194	552,997
Buick	535,820	400,262	826,206	688,557	573,866
Cadillac	278,404	230,649	307,698	277,251	213,161
Total	3,679,260	3,585,513	5,252,734	4,775,344	4,117,860
Checker Motors Corporation	3,181	4,996	6,333	5,504	5,822
Total Passenger Cars	6,717,177	7,324,504	9,667,152	8,828,205	7,412,659

Domestic and Export Factory Sales of Motor Vehicles

Source: Motor Vehicle Manufacturers Association of the U.S.

	From plants located in United States[1] (in thousands)								
	Passenger cars			Motor trucks and buses			Total motor vehicles		
	Total	Domestic	Exports	Total	Domestic	Exports	Total	Domestic	Exports
1965	9,297	9,092	205[2]	1,700	1,564	136[2]	10,997	10,656	341[2]
1970	6,531	6,171	359	1,642	1,515	127	8,173	7,686	486
1972	8,811	8,340	471	2,413	2,260	153	11,224	10,600	624
1973	9,644	9,065	579	2,953	2,760	193	12,597	11,825	772
1974	7,322	6,712	609	2,678	2,420	258	10,000	9,133	868
1975	6,708	6,068	640	2,235	1,966	269	8,943	8,034	909

[1] Excludes factory sales to all Federal government agencies.   [2] Starting with 1965 data not comparable with previous years.

Metals Production (in short tons)

Sources: American Iron & Steel Institute; Department of Commerce.

Year	Pig iron and ferroalloys	Steel ingots and castings (raw steel)	Rolled iron and steel products (tons)		Aluminum (primary)	Copper (smelter output from domestic ore)	Zinc (slab smelter output, all grades)[1]	Mine production of recoverable lead in the U. S.
			Total	Plates and sheets				
1953	77,250,168	111,609,719	85,943,724	35,699,732	1,252,013	926,448	971,191	328,012
1954	59,806,242	88,311,652	68,464,640	28,406,447	1,460,565	835,472	868,242	322,271
1961	66,565,063	98,014,492	73,411.563	35,302,092	1,903 200	1,180,800	843.600	260,400
1970	87,933,000	131,514,000	90,798,000	43,166,000	3 976,100	1,521,200	955,000	571,800
1972	89,400,000	133,241,000	91,805,000	47,415,000	4.122.000	1,680,400	706,900	618,900
1973	101,208,000	150,799,000	111,430,000	46,941,000	4,530,000	1,698,300	628,800	603,000
1974	95,909,000	145,720,000	109,472,000	44,968,000	4,903,000	1,420,900	633,600	663,900
1975	79,922,000	116,642,000	79,957,000	32,804,000	3,879,000	1,299,000	496,000	620,700

[1] From 1941 includes both foreign and domestic ores.

Money and Interest Rates
(per cent per annum)
Source: Federal Reserve Board.

Year	Open market rate in New York City[1]			Commercial loan rates					
	Prime commercial paper, 4–6 months	Prime bankers' acceptances, 90 days	Call loans, renewal rate[2]	New York City	7 other Northeast centers	8 North Central centers	7 Southeast centers	8 Southwest centers	4 West Coast centers
1935	.75	.13	.56	1.76	3.39			3.76	
1941	.53	.44	1.00	1.97	2.55			3.19	
1945	.75	.44	1.00	1.99	2.51			2.73	
1949	1.49	1.13	1.63	2.37	2.71			3.10	
1957	3.81	3.45	4.38	4.47	4.63			4.83	
1960	3.85	3.51	4.99	4.67	5.15			5.45	
1965	4.38	4.22	4.69	4.82	5.09			5.34	
1970[3]	7.72	7.31	7.95	8.22	8.86	8.46	8.44	8.52	8.49
1972[3]	4.69	4.47	5.16	5.57	6.07	5.74	6.07	6.02	5.80
1973[3]	8.15	8.08	8.27	8.06	8.65	8.29	6.07	6.02	8.26
1974[3]	9.84	9.89	11.08	11.12	11.83	11.25	11.01	11.07	11.15
1975[3]	6.33	6.30	8.02	8.37	8.91	8.54	9.01	8.75	8.86
1976[3,4]	5.54	5.53	6.88	6.99	7.79	7.44	7.66	7.51	7.75

[1] Average of daily quotations. [2] Separate figures for new and renewal rates were discontinued beginning March 1957, and only the going rate is available. [3] The Quarterly Survey of Interest Rates on Business Loans was revised in Feb. 1967 and Feb. 1971. [4] May.

U. S. Money in Circulation by Denomination[1]
(in millions of dollars)
Source: Department of the Treasury.

Denomination	1976[4]	1975[4]	1974	1973	1970	1968	1961	1950	1945	1939
Coin............	9,244	8,496	8,331	7,759	6,281	5,691	2,582	1,554	1,274	590
$1[2]...............	2,706	2,616	2,720	2,639	2,310	2,049	1,588	1,113	1,039	559
$2...............	619	135	135	135	136	136	92	64	73	36
$5...............	3,689	3,571	3,718	3,614	3,161	2,993	2,313	2,049	2,313	1,019
$10.............	10,363	10,239	10,503	10,226	9,170	8,786	6,878	5,998	6,782	1,772
$20.............	28,701	26,798	26,197	23,915	18,581	16,508	10,935	8,529	9,201	1,576
$50.............	8,447	7,671	7,444	6,514	4,896	4,186	2,869	2,422	2,327	460
$100............	24,726	21,280	20,298	17,288	12,084	10,068	6,106	5,043	4,220	919
$500............	174	177	179	185	215	244	242	368	454	191
$1,000..........	202	206	209	216	252	292	300	588	801	425
$5,000..........	2	2	2	2	3	3	3	4	7	20
$10,000.........	4	4	4	4	4	4	10	12	24	32
TOTAL[3].........	88,878	81,196	79,723	72,497	57,093	50,961	33,918	27,741	28,515	7,598

[1] End of year. [2] Paper currency only. $1 coins reported under coin. [3] Includes unassorted currency. [4] June 30.

Public Debt of the United States
Source: Department of the Treasury.

Year[1]	Gross debt		Year[1]	Gross debt	
	Amount (in millions of dollars)	Per capita (dollars)		Amount (in millions of dollars)	Per capita (dollars)
1800 (Jan. 1)..........	83	15.87	1945.................	258,682	1,848.60
1860.................	65	2.06	1955.................	272,807[2]	1,650.63
1865.................	2,678	75.01	1962.................	295,364[2]	1,582.40
1900.................	1,263	16.60	1965.................	313,819[2]	1,612.70
1915.................	1,191	11.85	1970.................	370,094	1,807.09
1920.................	24,299	228.23	1971.................	397,305	1,918.80
1929	16,931	139.04	1972.................	426,435	2,041.91
1932.................	19,487	156.10	1973.................	457,317	2,173.60
1935.................	28,701	225.55	1974	474,235	2,238.07
1939.................	40,440	308.98	1975[2]................	533,189	2,496.90
1943.................	136,696	999.83	1976[3]................	620,433	2,884.29

[1] For years ending June 30. [2] Adjusted to exclude issues to International Monetary Fund and other international institutions to conform to the budget presentation. [3] Preliminary.

Receipts and Outlays of the Federal Government (in millions of dollars)

Source: Department of the Treasury.

Yearly average for year ended June 30	Customs (including tonnage tax)[1]	Income and profits tax	Other	Miscellaneous taxes and receipts	Total receipts	Net receipts[2]	Department of Defense (Army, 1789–1950)	Department of the Navy	Interest on public debt	All other	Net outlays[3]	Surplus (+) or deficit (−)
1789–1800	6	....	....	....	7	7	2	....	3	1	6	+1
1801–1810	12	....	....	....	13	13	2	1	4	2	9	+4
1811–1820	16	....	2	3	21	21	11	5	5	3	24	−3
1821–1830	20	....	....	2	22	22	4	3	4	5	16	+6
1831–1840	20	....	....	10	30	30	8	5	....	11	24	+6
1841–1850	24	....	....	3	27	27	13	7	1	11	32	−5
1851–1860	54	....	....	6	60	60	16	12	....	29	60	
1861–1865	69	17	55	20	161	161	548	65	3	36	684	−523
1866–1870	179	51	171	46	447	447	128	28	135	86	377	+70
1871–1880	166	4	115	28	313	313	39	20	106	107	271	+42
1881–1890	418	....	259	65	742	742	83	34	108	312	537	+205
1891–1900	362	....	357	69	788	788	161	77	68	515	821	−33
1901–1905	260	....	255	44	559	559	133	86	28	288	535	+24
1906–1910	311	4	257	56	628	628	169	113	23	334	639	−11
1915	210	80	335	72	698	683	202	142	23	379	746	−63
1918	180	2,314	872	299	3,665	3,645	4,870	1,279	190	6,339	12,677	−9,032
1929	602	2,331	607	493	4,033	3,862	426	365	678	1,658	3,127	+734
1933	251	746	858	225	2,080	1,997	435	349	689	3,125	4,598	−2,602
1939	319	2,189	2,972	188	5,668	4,979	695	673	941	6,533	8,841	−3,862
1943	324	16,094	6,050	934	23,402	21,947	42,526	20,888	1,808	14,146	79,368	−57,420
1944	431	34,655	7,030	3,325	45,441	43,563	49,438	26,538	2,609	16,401	94,986	−51,423
1945	355	35,173	8,729	3,494	47,750	44,362	50,490	30,047	3,617	14,149	98,303	−53,941
1947	494	29,306	10,074	4,635	44,508	39,677	9,172	5,597	4,958	19,196	38,923	+754
1950	423	28,263	11,186	1,439	41,311	36,422	5,789	4,130	5,750	23,875	39,544	−3,122
1956[4]	705	56,639	20,564	389	78,297	74,547	35,693	....	6,787	27,981	70,460	+4,087
1960	1,123	67,151	28,266	1,190	97,730	92,492	43,969	....	9,180	39,075	92,223	+269
1965	1,478	79,792	39,996	1,598	122,863	116,833	47,179	....	11,346	59,904	118,430	−1,596
1969	2,387	135,778	59,602	2,909	200,676	187,784	79,137	....	16,588	88,823	184,548r	+3,236
1970	2,494	138,689	65,276	3,424	209,883	193,743	78,360	....	19,304	98,924	196,588	−2,845
1971	2,657	131,072	69,760	3,858	207,348	188,392	75,922	....	20,959	114,544	211,425	−23,033
1972	3,394	143,805	76,713	3,633	227,544	208,649	76,679	....	21,849	133,348	231,876	−23,227
1973	3,308	164,157	86,589	3,921	257,975	232,225	75,000	....	24,167	147,359	246,526	−14,301
1974	3,444	184,648	99,553	5,369	293,014	264,932	79,307	....	29,319	159,766	268,392	−3,460
1975	3,782	202,146	108,371	6,711	321,010	280,997	87,471	....	32,665	204,465	324,601	−43,604
1976p	4,209	205,752	115,719	8,028	333,708	300,005	90,160	....	37,063	238,387	365,610	−65,605

[1] Beginning 1933, tonnage tax incl. in "Other receipts." [2] Net receipts equal total receipts less (a) appropriations to Federal old-age and survivors' insurance trust fund beginning fiscal year 1939 and (b) refunds of receipts beginning fiscal year 1933. [3] Includes Air Force 1950–65 (in millions): 1950—$3,521; 1953—$15,085; 1956—$16,750; 1960—$19,065; 1965—$18,471. [4] Beginning 1956, computed on unified budget concepts; not strictly comparable with preceding figures. NOTE: p = preliminary.

FEDERAL BUDGET—RECEIPTS, BY SOURCE, AND OUTLAYS, BY DETAILED FUNCTION: 1972 TO 1975

In billions of dollars. For years ending June 30. Receipts reflect collections; outlays stated in terms of checks issued or cash payments. Covers all Federal agencies and programs and both Federal funds and trust funds. Excludes government-sponsored but privately-owned corporations, Federal Reserve System, District of Columbia government, and money held in suspense as deposit funds.

SOURCE OR FUNCTION	1972	1973	1974	1975 est.
Total surplus or deficit (−)	−23.2	−14.3	−3.5	−34.7
BY SOURCE				
Total receipts [1]	208.6	232.2	264.9	278.8
Individual income taxes	94.7	103.2	119.0	117.7
Corporation income taxes	32.2	36.2	38.6	38.5
Social insurance taxes and contributions	53.9	64.5	76.8	86.2
Employment taxes and contributions	46.1	54.9	65.9	74.6
Unemployment insurance	4.4	6.1	6.8	7.2
Contributions for other insur. and retirement	3.4	3.6	4.1	4.4
Excise taxes	15.5	16.3	16.8	19.9
Estate and gift taxes	5.4	4.9	5.0	4.8
Customs duties	3.3	3.2	3.3	3.9
Miscellaneous receipts	3.6	3.9	5.4	7.7
BY FUNCTION				
Total outlays	231.9	246.5	268.4	313.4
National defense [1]	77.4	75.1	78.6	85.3
Dept. of Defense military	75.2	73.3	77.6	83.0
Military assistance	.8	.5	.8	1.8
Atomic energy defense activities	1.4	1.4	1.5	1.6
Defense related activ.	(z)	−.2	−1.3	−1.1
International affairs and finance [1]	3.7	3.0	3.6	4.9
Foreign economic and financial assistance	3.3	2.8	2.8	4.1
Conduct of foreign affairs	.5	.5	.6	.7
Foreign information and exchange activities	.3	.3	.3	.4
General science, space res. and technology [1]	4.3	4.2	4.2	4.2
General science and basic research [2]	1.1	1.1	1.2	1.2
Manned space flight	1.7	1.5	1.5	1.5
Space science, applications and technology	1.1	1.2	1.2	1.0
Natural resources, environment, energy [1]	5.0	5.5	6.4	9.4
Water resources, power	2.3	2.5	2.5	3.3
Conservation and land management	.8	.7	.8	1.3
Recreational resources	.5	.6	.7	.8
Pollution control and abatement	.8	1.1	2.0	2.9
Energy	.6	.7	.6	1.5
Agriculture	5.3	4.9	2.2	1.8
Farm income stabilization	4.6	4.1	1.5	.9
Research and services	.7	.8	.8	.9
Commerce and transportation [1]	10.6	9.9	13.1	11.8
Mortgage credit and thrift insurance	(−z)	−1.2	1.5	−1.0
Payment to Postal Serv.	1.8	1.6	1.7	1.8
Other advancement and regulation of commerce	.5	.6	.7	.7
Ground transportation	−5.4	5.6	5.6	6.4
Air transportation	1.9	2.2	2.2	2.5
Water transportation	1.1	1.2	1.4	1.5

FUNCTION	1972	1973	1974	1975 est.
Total outlays [1]—Con.				
Community and regional development [1]	4.7	5.9	4.9	4.9
Community development	3.1	3.1	3.0	3.3
Area and regional dev.	1.4	1.4	1.1	1.1
Disaster relief and insurance	.4	1.6	.8	.5
Education, manpower, and social services [1]	11.7	11.9	11.6	14.7
Elementary, secondary, and vocational educ.	4.0	3.7	3.8	4.2
Higher education	1.4	1.5	1.3	2.1
Research and general educ. tion aids	.5	.7	.9	.8
Manpower training [3]	2.9	3.5	3.1	4.4
Social services	2.7	2.5	2.5	3.1
Health [1]	17.5	18.8	22.1	26.5
Health care services	14.5	15.5	18.5	22.3
Health research and ed.	2.0	2.3	2.3	2.7
Prevention and control of health problems	.5	.6	.8	.9
Health planning and construction	.4	.4	.5	.6
Income security [1]	63.9	73.0	84.4	106.7
General retirement and disability insurance	42.0	51.7	58.6	67.5
Federal employee retirement and disability	3.8	4.5	5.6	7.1
Unemployment insurance	7.1	5.4	6.1	14.7
Public assist. and other income supplements	11.1	11.4	14.1	17.4
Veterans benefits and service [1]	10.7	12.0	13.4	15.5
Income security	6.3	6.5	6.8	7.7
Education, training, and rehabilitation	2.0	2.8	3.2	4.0
Hospital and med. care	2.4	2.7	3.0	3.6
Housing	−.3	−.4	(−z)	−.3
Law enforce. and justice [1]	1.6	2.1	2.5	3.0
Federal law enforcement and prosecution	1.0	1.2	1.3	1.6
Fed. judicial activities	.2	.2	.2	.3
Federal correctional and rehab. activities	.1	.2	.2	.2
Law enforcement assist.	.4	.6	.8	.9
General government [1]	2.5	2.7	3.3	2.6
Legislative functions	.4	.4	.5	.6
Management, direction	.9	1.0	1.2	.4
Central fiscal operations	1.2	1.2	1.3	1.7
General revenue sharing	–	6.6	6.1	6.2
Other general purpose assistance	1.0	7.8	7.4	7.9
Interest	20.6	22.8	28.1	31.3
On the public debt	21.8	24.2	29.3	32.9
Other	−1.3	−1.4	−1.2	−1.6
Undistributed offsetting receipts	−8.1	−12.3	−16.7	−16.8
Employer share, employee retirement	−2.8	−2.9	−3.3	−4.1
Interest received by trust funds	−5.1	−5.4	−6.6	−7.8
Rents and royalties on Outer Continental Shelf	−.3	−4.0	−6.7	−5.0

— Represents zero. Z Less than $500,000. [1] Totals reflect interfund and intragovernmental transactions and applicable receipts, and other functions, not shown separately. [2] Includes earth sciences. [3] Includes other manpower services. Source: U.S. Office of Management and Budget, *The Budget of the United States Government,* annual.

INDIVIDUAL INCOME TAX RETURNS—SOURCES OF INCOME, BY ADJUSTED GROSS INCOME CLASSES: 1973

In millions of dollars, except percent.

YEAR AND SOURCE OF INCOME	Total income[1]	ADJUSTED GROSS INCOME CLASSES FOR TAXABLE RETURNS							
		Total	Under $5,000	$5,000–$9,999	$10,000–$14,999	$15,000–$49,999	$50,000–$499,999	$500,000–$999,999	1,000,000 and over
Adjusted gross income [2]	827,148	799,709	40,724	146,570	194,507	354,745	59,622	1,750	1,790
Salaries, gross	687,179	663,512	35,144	128,453	176,987	296,235	26,324	239	130
Percent of gross income	83.1	83.0	86.3	87.6	91.0	83.5	44.2	13.7	7.3
Dividends [3]	18,734	17,764	548	1,612	1,632	6,367	6,588	489	529
Interest	32,174	29,207	2,425	5,921	5,129	11,867	3,621	130	113
Rents and royalties:									
Net income	7,811	7,557	486	1,135	1,070	3,253	1,537	43	33
Net loss	3,451	2,779	99	357	552	1,320	425	14	12
Business or profession: [4]									
Net profit	42,164	39,759	999	4,674	5,690	20,165	8,071	85	73
Net loss	4,062	2,155	236	435	440	694	295	30	25
Farm: [4] Net profit	11,303	10,054	215	1,177	1,563	5,583	1,508	7	1
Net loss	4,075	2,323	144	517	499	732	400	19	12
Partnership: Net profit	18,081	12,132	−185	844	1,068	5,527	4,839	10	29
Net loss	6,921	4,041	298	175	251	1,408	1,741	100	68
Sales of capital assets:									
Net gain	18,201	16,828	537	1,245	1,664	6,179	5,706	674	822
Net loss	1,529	1,388	54	167	247	778	143	(Z)	(Z)
Sales of property other than capital assets:									
Net gain	981	807	20	65	108	363	218	17	15
Net loss	603	309	7	55	54	122	65	5	1
Annuities and pensions, taxable portion [1]	13,244	11,831	1,320	3,894	2,711	3,473	426	5	3
Other sources [5]	−2,083	−787	−245	−919	−1,323	−621	2,112	119	92

Z Less than $500,000. [1] Excludes returns with no adjusted gross income. [2] Income from sources subject to tax, less certain exclusions. [3] Dividends in adjusted gross income. [4] Business profit and loss without deduction for net operating loss. [5] Comprises all income subject to income tax not elsewhere listed, less adjustments. Source: U.S. Internal Revenue Service, Preliminary Report, *Statistics·of Income, 1973, Individual Income Tax Returns.*

INTERNAL REVENUE COLLECTIONS, BY SELECTED SOURCES: 1965 TO 1974

For years ending June 30. Includes collections outside United States.

SOURCE OF REVENUE	COLLECTIONS (bil. dol.)						PERCENT DISTRIBUTION					
	1965	1970	1971	1972	1973	1974	1965	1970	1971	1972	1973	1974
All taxes	114.4	195.7	191.6	209.9	237.8	269.0	100.0	100.0	100.0	100.0	100.0	100.0
Corporation income taxes	26.1	35.0	30.3	34.9	39.0	41.7	22.8	17.9	15.8	16.6	16.4	15.5
Individual income and employment taxes [1]	70.8	141.1	140.7	152.6	177.2	205.0	61.8	72.1	73.4	72.7	74.5	76.2
Not withheld and self employment	17.9	28.2	26.2	27.7	29.4	33.8	15.6	14.4	13.7	13.2	12.4	12.6
Withheld and old-age disability insurance	51.7	111.2	112.4	122.8	145.2	171.2	45.1	56.8	58.7	58.5	61.1	63.7
Estate and gift taxes	2.7	3.7	3.7	3.8	5.0	5.1	2.4	1.9	2.0	2.6	2.1	1.9
Excise taxes, total	14.8	15.9	16.9	16.8	16.6	17.1	12.9	8.1	8.8	8.0	7.0	6.4
Alcohol taxes [2]	3.8	4.7	4.8	5.1	5.1	5.4	3.3	2.4	2.5	2.4	2.1	2.0
Tobacco taxes [2]	2.1	2.1	2.2	2.2	2.3	2.4	1.9	1.1	1.2	1.1	1.0	0.9
Manufacturers' excise [1]	6.4	6.7	6.7	5.7	5.4	5.7	5.6	3.4	3.2	2.7	2.3	2.1
Gasoline	2.7	3.4	3.5	3.7	3.9	4.1	2.3	1.8	1.9	1.8	1.6	1.5
Motor vehicles, bodies, parts, etc.	2.6	2.5	2.4	1.2	.5	.6	2.2	1.3	1.3	0.5	0.2	0.2
All other excise taxes	2.5	2.4	3.2	3.8	3.8	3.6	2.1	1.2	1.5	1.8	1.6	1.3

[1] Includes taxes not shown separately. [2] Includes taxes collected in Puerto Rico on manufactures coming into the United States. Source: U.S. Internal Revenue Service, *Annual Report of the Commissioner.*

Social Welfare Expenditures Under Public Programs: 1950 to 1974

In millions of dollars, except percent. For Federal Government, most States, and some localities, years ending June 30. Represents expenditures under public law and from trust accounts. Includes administrative expenditures and capital outlay; also includes some expenditures and payments outside U.S.

YEAR AND SOURCE OF FUNDS	Total social welfare [1]	Social insurance [1]	Public aid	Health and medical programs	Veterans programs	Education	Housing	Other social welfare	All health and medical care [2]	TOTAL SOCIAL WELFARE AS— Percent of gross national product	Percent of total government outlays [1]
TOTAL											
1950	23,508	4,947	2,496	2,064	6,866	6,674	15	448	3,065	8.9	37.6
1955	32,640	9,835	3,003	3,103	4,834	11,157	89	619	4,421	8.6	32.7
1960	52,293	19,307	4,101	4,464	5,479	17,626	177	1,139	6,395	10.6	38.0
1965	77,175	28,123	6,283	6,246	6,031	28,108	318	2,066	9,535	11.8	42.4
1968	113,840	42,740	11,092	8,459	7,247	40,590	428	3,285	20,039	13.8	43.2
1969	127,149	48,772	13,439	9,006	7,934	43,673	532	3,792	22,936	14.1	44.7
1970	145,962	54,691	16,488	9,753	9,018	50,905	701	4,406	25,237	15.3	47.8
1971	171,983	66,369	21,262	10,916	10,396	56,950	1,047	5,043	28,603	17.0	51.8
1972	192,350	74,799	26,077	12,423	11,456	60,580	1,332	5,684	33,025	17.5	53.4
1973	214,179	86,118	28,697	12,640	12,952	65,258	2,180	6,335	35,819	17.5	55.2
1974 (prel.)	242,386	98,502	33,628	14,054	13,923	72,763	2,582	6,934	41,311	18.0	55.8
FEDERAL											
1950	10,541	2,103	1,103	604	6,386	157	15	174	1,362	4.0	26.2
1955	14,623	6,385	1,504	1,150	4,772	485	75	252	1,948	3.9	22.3
1960	24,957	14,307	2,117	1,737	5,367	868	144	417	2,918	5.0	28.1
1965	37,712	21,807	3,594	2,781	6,011	2,470	238	812	4,625	5.8	32.6
1968	60,314	35,390	6,455	4,233	7,214	5,000	325	1,697	13,069	7.3	35.1
1969	68,355	40,847	7,829	4,543	7,883	4,923	426	1,905	15,229	7.6	37.5
1970	77,334	45,245	9,649	4,775	8,952	5,873	582	2,259	16,600	8.1	40.1
1971	92,570	53,903	12,991	5,148	10,331	6,580	872	2,746	18,766	9.1	44.9
1972	106,310	61,246	16,290	6,322	11,405	6,709	1,183	3,155	22,082	9.7	47.4
1973	122,534	72,232	18,067	6,698	12,903	7,389	1,750	3,494	24,280	10.0	50.4
1974 (prel.)	139,580	82,508	21,237	8,005	13,878	8,046	2,132	3,774	28,343	10.3	52.1
STATE AND LOCAL											
1950	12,967	2,844	1,393	1,460	480	6,518	(X)	274	1,704	4.9	60.1
1955	18,017	3,450	1,499	1,953	62	10,672	15	367	2,473	4.7	55.3
1960	27,337	4,999	1,984	2,727	112	16,758	33	723	3,477	5.5	58.3
1965	39,464	6,316	2,690	3,466	20	25,638	80	1,254	4,911	6.0	61.7
1968	53,526	7,350	4,636	4,226	33	35,589	103	1,589	6,970	6.5	60.0
1969	58,794	7,925	5,610	4,464	51	38,750	107	1,888	7,707	6.5	59.8
1970	68,628	9,446	6,839	4,978	67	45,032	120	2,147	8,637	7.2	62.4
1971	79,412	12,466	8,272	5,768	65	50,371	175	2,296	9,837	7.8	64.0
1972	86,040	13,553	9,787	6,101	51	53,871	149	2,528	10,943	7.8	64.3
1973	91,645	13,885	10,630	5,942	48	57,868	430	2,841	11,540	7.5	64.0
1974 (prel.)	102,806	15,994	12,391	6,049	45	64,717	450	3,160	12,968	7.6	62.6
PERCENT OF TOTAL EXPENDITURES, BY TYPE											
1950	100.0	21.0	10.6	8.8	29.2	28.4	0.1	1.9	13.0	(X)	(X)
1955	100.0	30.1	9.2	9.5	14.8	34.2	0.3	1.9	13.5	(X)	(X)
1960	100.0	36.9	7.8	8.5	10.5	33.7	0.3	2.2	12.2	(X)	(X)
1965	100.0	36.4	8.1	8.1	7.8	36.4	0.4	2.7	12.4	(X)	(X)
1970	100.0	37.5	11.3	6.7	6.2	34.9	0.5	3.0	17.2	(X)	(X)
1974	100.0	40.6	13.9	5.8	5.7	30.0	1.1	2.9	17.0	(X)	(X)
PERCENT FEDERAL OF TOTAL											
1950	44.8	42.5	44.2	29.2	93.0	2.3	100.0	38.9	44.4	(X)	(X)
1955	44.8	64.9	50.1	37.1	98.7	4.3	83.7	40.7	44.1	(X)	(X)
1960	47.7	74.1	51.6	38.9	98.0	4.9	81.2	36.6	45.6	(X)	(X)
1965	48.9	77.5	57.2	44.5	99.7	8.8	74.9	39.3	48.5	(X)	(X)
1970	53.0	82.7	58.5	49.0	99.3	11.5	82.9	51.3	65.8	(X)	(X)
1974	57.6	83.8	63.2	57.0	99.7	11.1	82.6	54.4	68.6	(X)	(X)

X Not applicable.   [1] Although total welfare and insurance expenditures include workmen's compensation and temporary disability insurance payments made through private insurance carriers and self-insurers, such private payments have been omitted in computing percentages relating to all government expenditures.
[2] Combines "Health and medical programs" with medical services provided in connection with social insurance, public aid, veterans, and other social welfare programs.

Source: U.S. Social Security Administration, *Social Security Bulletin*, January 1975.

Economic Growth in Latin America
(in percentages[1])
Source: U. N. Economic Commission for Latin America.

Countries	1974[2]	1973	1970–72	1965–70	1960–65	Countries	1974[2]	1973	1970–72	1965–70	1960–65
Argentina......	7.2	3.8	3.5	4.1	3.5	Haiti...........	3.0	4.5	5.0	1.8	1.1
Bolivia.........	5.7	5.4	4.5	6.3	4.1	Honduras......	−0.5	5.0	3.8	4.7	5.3
Brazil..........	9.6	11.4	10.8	7.5	4.5	Mexico.........	5.9	7.6	5.3	6.9	7.1
Colombia.......	6.1	7.5	6.4	5.8	4.6	Nicaragua.....	7.7	2.2	4.9	4.2	8.1
Costa Rica......	4.1	6.2	6.6	6.9	6.3	Panama........	4.0	6.5	7.3	7.4	8.3
Chile...........	5.0	−4.0	4.8	3.8	5.0	Paraguay......	8.0	7.2	4.9	4.1	4.8
Dom. Rep.......	8.9	11.2	11.5	7.8	1.0	Peru...........	6.6	6.0	6.3	3.6	6.6
Ecuador........	9.2	9.3	6.2	5.6	4.0	Uruguay.......	1.9	1.0	−1.2	2.3	0.8
El Salvador.....	6.0	5.1	5.2	4.4	6.9	Venezuela.....	5.1	5.9	3.3	4.1	5.0
Guatemala......	4.7	7.6	6.4	5.7	5.3	Total	7.0	7.2	6.4	5.8	5.1

[1] Percentage increases in the total output of goods and services valued at the cost of the factors of production.   [2] Preliminary.

U.S. Government Foreign Assistance, Calendar Years 1945-1975
(in millions of dollars)
Source: Department of Commerce, Bureau of Economic Analysis.

Calendar years	Economic assistance (net)				Military grants (net)	Net assistance[1]
	Net new grants	Net new credits	Net other assistance	Total		
July 1945–1955	28,869	8,642	541	38,052	16,445	54,497
1956–1965	17,675	7,025	2,802	27,503	19,158	46,661
1966–1970	8,808	9,430	−564	17,674	12,028	29,702
1971	2,043	1,845	−246	3,642	3,580	7,221
1972	2,173	1,484	−213	3,444	4,527	7,971
1973	1,938	1,690	−49	3,580	2,852	6,432
1974	4,538	−348	−247	3,943	2,842	6,785
1975	2,246	2,848	29	5,122	2,916	8,039
Total postwar period[2] . .	68,290	32,618	2,052	102,960	64,347	167,308

[1] Excludes investment in international nonmonetary financial institutions of $4,010 million.   [2] Includes transactions after V-J Day (Sept. 2, 1945).   NOTE: Detail may not add to total due to rounding.

U.S. Contributions to International Organizations
(for fiscal year 1975[1] in millions of dollars)
Source: Department of State.

Organization	Amount	Organization	Amount
United Nations and Specialized Agencies:		Regional organizations:	
United Nations	$63.47	NATO Civilian Headquarters	$9.60
Food and Agricultural Organization	13.53	Organization for Economic Cooperation and	
International Atomic Energy Agency	7.38	Development	8.26
International Civil Aviation Organization . .	2.81	Others	1.02
Joint Financing Program	2.43	Total	18.88
International Labor Organization	11.28	Other international organizations:	
UNESCO	18.54	International Institute for Cotton	1.81
World Health Organization	31.73	General Agreement on Tariffs and Trade . . .	1.51
Others	3.12	Others	3.36
Total	154.29	Total	6.68
Peacekeeping forces:		Special voluntary programs:	
U.N. Emergency Force	28.84	U.N. Fund for Population Activities	20.00
U.N. Force in Cyprus	9.60	United Nations Development Program . . .	77.90
Total	38.44	United Nations Children's Fund	17.00
Inter-American organizations:		U.N. Relief and Works Agency	39.20
Organization of American States	22.71	U.N./FAO World Food Program	70.00[2]
Pan American Health Organization	13.90	International Commission of Control and	23.00
Inter-American Institute of Agricultural		Supervision (Vietnam)	
Sciences	3.94	Others	74.51
Others	1.03	Total	321.61
Total	41.58	Total contribution to all agencies	581.48

[1] Estimated. [2] Includes cash, commodities, and services.

U.S. Exports of Leading Commodities
(value in millions of dollars)

U.S. Imports of Leading Commodities
(value in millions of dollars)

Source: Department of Commerce, Domestic and
International Business Administration.

Commodity	1975	1974
Food and live animals	$15,487	$13,986
Meat and preparations	528	381
Dairy products and eggs	134	67
Grains and preparations	11,643	10,331
Wheat, including wheat flour	5,292	4,589
Rice	858	852
Fruits and nuts	871	757
Vegetables	406	391
Feed for animals	987	1,287
Beverages and tobacco	1,310	1,247
Tobacco and manufactures	1,221	1,133
Beverages and other tobacco	89	114
Crude materials, inedible, except fuels	9,784	10,934
Hides and skins, except fur skins	296	339
Soybeans, other oilseeds, peanuts	3,134	3,819
Synthetic rubber	261	290
Wood: rough, shaped	751	744
Wood pulp	876	820
Textile fibers and wastes	1,345	1,782
Ores and metal scrap	1,355	1,475
Mineral fuels and related materials	4,465	3,444
Coal	3,259	2,437
Petroleum and products	907	792
Animal and vegetable oils and fats	944	1,423
Soy bean oil	266	519
Chemicals	8,705	8,819
Chemical elements and compounds	3,315	3,398
Medicines and pharmaceuticals	866	800
Fertilizers, manufactured	1,083	815
Plastic materials and resins	1,173	1,618
Machinery and transport equipment	45,710	38,189
Machinery	29,215	24,318
Machinery, nonelectrical	21,628	17,298
Power generating machinery	3,380	2,733
Agricultural machinery	706	544
Tractors and parts	752	483
Office machines	2,639	2,699
Metalworking machinery	920	639
Textile and leather machinery	486	528
Electrical apparatus	7,587	7,019
Transport equipment	16,495	13,871
Railway vehicles	462	282
Road motor vehicles and parts	9,298	7,248
Aircraft, parts, and accessories	6,171	5,766
Other manufactured goods	16,590	16,515
Rubber manufactures	544	544
Paper and manufactures	1,448	1,522
Nonmetallic mineral manufactures	964	994
Metals and manufactures	5,363	5,465
Iron and steel-mill products	2,382	2,500
Nonferrous base metals	1,090	1,300
Other manufactures of metals	1,891	1,665
Textiles, other than clothing	1,625	1,795
Furniture	176	152
Clothing	382	372
Scientific instruments	804	699
Photographic equipment, supplies	664	1,113
Printed matter	548	486
Other transactions	3,162	2,587
TOTAL EXPORTS	**$106,157**	**$97,144**

Commodity	1975	1974
Food and live animals	$8,509	$9,386
Cattle, except for breeding	77	108
Meat and preparations	1,141	1,353
Cheese	165	235
Fish	1,356	1,500
Grains and feed for animals	259	247
Fruits and nuts	637	628
Vegetables	355	388
Sugar	1,870	2,247
Coffee, green	1,561	1,505
Cocoa or cacao beans	321	317
Tea	88	79
Spices	99	110
Beverages and tobacco	1,419	1,322
Alcoholic beverages	1,033	1,029
Tobacco, unmanufactured	343	254
Crude materials, inedible, except fuels	5,564	6,066
Hides and skins, except fur skins	78	78
Fur skins, undressed	79	79
Rubber, including latex	353	507
Lumber	866	1,141
Wood pulp	1,032	1,126
Textile fibers and wastes	174	225
Industrial diamonds	42	48
Asbestos, unmanufactured	117	131
Ores and metal scrap	1,977	1,848
Iron ores and concentrates	864	700
Ores and concentrates, nonferrous metals	1,113	1,148
Mineral fuels and related products	26,476	25,454
Petroleum and products	24,814	24,270
Natural gas	1,081	505
Animal and vegetable oils and fats	554	544
Chemicals	3,696	4,018
Organic chemicals	1,028	1,363
Inorganic chemicals	835	740
Medicinal and pharmaceutical products	235	211
Fertilizers, manufactured	626	631
Machinery and transport equipment	23,465	24,060
Machinery	11,970	11,811
Machinery, nonelectrical	7,059	6,472
Electrical apparatus	4,911	5,339
Transport equipment	11,495	12,251
Automobiles and parts	9,921	10,264
Aircraft and parts	519	508
Other manufactured goods	23,929	27,145
Wood manufactures, excluding furniture	573	685
Paper and manufactures	1,673	1,852
Glass, glassware, and pottery	531	534
Diamonds, excluding industrial	730	775
Metals and manufactures	8,944	11,109
Pig iron and ferroalloys	558	393
Iron and steel-mill products	4,037	4,756
Platinum group metals	244	451
Nonferrous base metals	2,063	3,038
Textiles, other than clothing	1,219	1,615
Clothing	2,562	2,331
Footwear	1,275	1,134
Furniture	407	451
Scientific and photographic apparatus	368	404
Clocks and watches	426	389
Printed matter	284	270
Toys, games, and sporting goods	633	724
Artworks and antiques	681	948
Other transactions	2,529	2,256
TOTAL GENERAL IMPORTS	**$96,140**	**100,251**

U. S. Exports and General Imports by Countries and Areas
(value in millions of dollars)

Source: Department of Commerce, Domestic and International Business Administration.

Area and country	Exports, including re-exports				General imports			
	1975	1970	1960	1949	1975	1970	1960	1949
Total	107,652	43,224	20,558	12,051	96,140	39,952	12,018	6,592
NORTH AND SOUTH AMERICA	(1970 and 1975 figures include special categories)							
Canada	21,759	9,079	3,709	1,925	21,747	11,092	3,153	1,550
19 American Republics	15,670	5,695	3,477	2,632	11,840	4,779	3,528	2,301
Argentina	628	441	350	123	215	172	99	97
Bolivia	138	46	25	34	89	25	9	48
Brazil	3,056	840	430	365	1,464	670	570	551
Chile	533	300	195	138	138	157	193	152
Colombia	643	395	246	167	590	269	299	241
Costa Rica	212	94	44	26	195	117	180	22
Cuba	n.a.	n.a.	223	347	n.a.	n.a.	357	387
Dominican Republic	453	143	41	35	634	184	111	24
Ecuador	414	127	55	31	461	109	65	17
El Salvador	194	64	42	25	180	48	32	40
Guatemala	255	100	63	43	173	87	59	43
Haiti	144	34	25	23	106	32	18	19
Honduras	151	89	34	32	145	102	34	15
Mexico	5,144	1,704	820	454	3,059	1,218	443	243
Nicaragua	156	77	30	14	131	61	21	6
Panama	317	208	89	114	194	76	24	11
Paraguay	33	18	9	7	19	11	9	5
Peru	904	214	143	81	399	340	183	40
Uruguay	51	41	62	33	24	19	21	54
Venezuela	2,243	759	551	503	3,624	1,082	948	278
Bahamas	208	173	49	n.a.	880	82	8	n.a.
Jamaica	381	218	48	n.a.	308	187	54	n.a.
Netherlands Antilles	228	126	63	75	1,558	416	263	111
Trinidad and Tobago	256	84	35	n.a.	1,170	232	55	n.a.
EUROPE								
Western Europe	29,939	14,463	6,318	3,973	20,735	11,169	4,185	909
Austria	181	74	80	149	238	120	49	9
Belgium and Luxembourg	2,427	1,195	439	300	1,190	696	364	94
Denmark	445	227	110	91	461	248	98	6
Finland	261	99	56	26	148	114	52	27
France	3,031	1,483	582	465	2,137	924	396	61
Germany, West	5,194	2,741	1,071	817	5,382	3,127	897	45
Greece	450	203	64	7	111	52	34	15
Iceland	32	13	12	7	85	47	11	2
Ireland	190	112	40	n.a.	176	135	28	n.a.
Italy	2,867	1,353	654	461	2,397	1,316	393	70
Netherlands	4,183	1,651	715	268	1,083	528	213	59
Norway	510	196	90	87	403	142	66	30
Spain	2,161	712	190	49	831	353	60	24
Sweden	925	543	301	81	877	399	170	54
Switzerland	1,153	700	253	137	867	459	198	93
Turkey	608	315	126	82	145	70	60	55
United Kingdom	4,525	2,536	1,411	662	3,784	2,194	993	227
Yugoslavia	328	168	86	19	260	96	41	14
Soviet Bloc	2,787	354	193	61	731	226	80	67
ASIA AND OCEANIA								
Total Asia and Oceania	31,281	1,294	4,121	2,159	28,591	10,515	2,987	1,309
Western Asia:	8,977	1,423	n.a.	n.a.	5,432	371	n.a.	n.a.
Egypt	683	77	137	50	28	23	47	9
Iran	3,242	326	117	77	1,400	67	51	16
Iraq	310	22	n.a.	n.a.	19	3	n.a.	n.a.
Israel	1,551	592	126	76	313	150	27	6
Jordan	195	63	n.a.	n.a.	1	(1)	n.a.	n.a.
Kuwait	366	62	41	22	111	25	124	38
Lebanon	402	64	44	39	33	13	4	2
Saudi Arabia	1,502	141	43	81	2,625	20	65	19
Syrian Arab Republic	128	11	38	n.a.	7	2	7	n.a.

Area and country	Exports, including re-exports				General imports			
	1975	1970	1960	1949	1975	1970	1960	1949
Far East:	19,660	8,682	n.a.	n.a.	21,492	9,272	n.a.	n.a.
China (Taiwan)	1,660	527	111	23	1,938	549	21	2
Hong Kong	808	406	123	113	1,575	944	139	4
India	1,290	572	641	240	548	298	228	238
Indonesia	810	266	86	119	2,221	182	216	120
Japan	9,565	4,652	1,341	466	11,268	5,875	1,149	82
Korea, South	1,761	643	153	49	1,416	370	5	1
Malaysia[2]	395	67	18	36	766	270	156	195
Pakistan	372	325	170	41	49	80	36	27
Philippines	832	373	297	424	754	472	307	204
Singapore	994	240	41	n.a.	532	81	19	n.a.
Thailand	357	150	65	29	217	100	56	48
Vietnam, South[3]	213	352	53	16	6	1	4	1
Australia	1,816	986	387	124	1,147	611	142	98
New Zealand and Samoa	414	135	75	40	246	222	119	24
AFRICA								
Total Africa	4,267	1,502	766	591	8,277	1,090	627	337
Algeria	632	62	24	22	1,359	10	1	4
Ghana	100	59	17	n.a.	150	91	53	n.a.
Liberia	90	46	36	51	97	51	39	11
Libya	232	108	42	n.a.	1,046	39	(¹)	n.a.
Morocco	200	89	34	28	10	10	11	6
Nigeria	536	129	26	n.a.	3,282	71	40	n.a.
South Africa[4]	1,302	563	277	257	841	290	200	116

[1] Less than $500,000. [2] Excluding Sarawak and Sabah through 1970. [3] Figures for 1949 include Cambodia and Laos. [4] South-West Africa, Bechuanaland and Swaziland included for 1949 and 1960; South-West Africa (Namibia) included for 1970 and 1975. NOTE: n.a. = not available.

Balance of Payments of the U.S., 1949-1975 (in millions of dollars)

(— denotes debits; sum of credits equals sum of debits)

Source: Department of Commerce, Bureau of Economic Analysis.

Item	1975	1974	1970	1965	1960	1955	1949
Exports of goods and services (excl. transfers under military grants)	148,410	144,773	62,483	39,548	27,595	19,948	15,834
Merchandise adjusted, excl. military	107,133	98,310	42,469	26,461	19,650	14,424	12,213
Transfers under U. S. military agency sales contracts	3,897	2,952	1,501	830	335	200	n.s.s.
Receipts of income on U. S. investments abroad	18,219	26,233	8,575	5,719	3,350	2,602	1,495
Other services	19,162	17,278	9,938	6,538	4,260	2,722	2,126
Imports of goods and services	−132,141	−141,187	−59,545	−32,443	−23,555	−17,795	−9,616
Merchandise, adjusted, excl. military	−98,150	−103,679	−39,866	−21,510	−14,758	−11,527	−6,874
Direct defense expenditures	−4,780	−5,035	−4,855	−2,952	−3,087	−2,901	−621
Payments of income on foreign investments in the U. S.	−12,212	−16,006	−5,056	−1,730	−1,063	−520	−342
Other services	−16,999	−16,466	−9,768	−6,251	−4,647	−2,847	−1,779
Unilateral transfers, excl. military grants, net	−4,620	−7,184	−3,294	−2,854	−2,308	−2,498	−5,638
U. S. Government capital flows, net	−3,463	−365	−1,589	−1,605	−1,100	−310	−652
U. S. private capital flows, net	−27,061	−32,323	−6,920	−3,793	−3,878	−1,255	−553
Foreign capital flows, net	14,879	32,433	5,923	382	2,120	1,357	174
Transactions in U. S. official reserve assets, net	−607	−1,434	2,477	1,222	2,145	182	−266
Allocation of special drawing rights (SDR)	....	....	867	....	....	....	....
Statistical discrepancy	4,602	4,557	−402	−457	−1,019	371	717
Balance on goods and services	16,269	3,586	2,938	7,105	4,040	2,153	6,218
Balance on goods, services, and remittances	14,542	1,877	1,380	6,059	3,404	1,556	5,577
Balance on current account	11,650	−3,598	−356	4,251	1,732	−345	580

NOTE: Details may not add to totals because of rounding. n.s.s. = not shown separately. n.a. = not available.

Glossary of Wall Street and Economic Terms

Agency for International Development (AID)—Carries out the United States' overseas programs of economic and technical assistance designed to assist underdeveloped countries toward the goal of self-sufficiency.

Bulls and Bears—A bull believes the market will rise; a bull market is an advancing market. A bear believes the market will decline; a bear market is a declining market.

Capital Gain and Loss—Profit or loss from the sale of a capital asset. A short-term capital gain (up to 6 months) is taxed at full income tax rate.

Cartel—An association of independent financial or industrial companies in the same business formed to influence the market price by regulating competition.

Consumer Price Index—A monthly figure prepared by the Bureau of Labor Statistics which indicates the percentage price changes in 400 commodities as compared with a base period which is an average of the years 1957–59. Thus if the price index stands at 110, it means that consumer prices have risen 10% above the 1957–59 base.

Consumerism—A term describing the consumer revolution of recent years which protests against shoddy materials, poor quality, weak warranties and environmental abuse.

Cost-push—Inflation occurs not because of demand but because the cost of making the item has risen due to increased costs of labor, raw materials, energy, et al.

Deficit Financing—During periods of depression, governments frequently borrow the money required to pay for goods and services for which no cash is available in the Treasury.

Demand-pull—Inflation occurs when the amount of money available for spending increases without a similar rise in the production of goods available for purchase. There is a greater demand for goods which are in short supply.

Dow Jones Industrial Average—An average compiled by adding the prices of 30 leading industrial stocks. It is used to gauge the trend of prices in the stock market over a period of time.

Economic Indicators—Measures of economic activity indicating trends in the nation's production of goods and services, inventories, activity in the housing market, expenditures for new plants and equipment, the monthly unemployment rate and other economic factors.

Escalator Clause—Some wage agreements provide for adjustments in wage rates on the basis of increases or decreases in consumer prices. This is one example of the theory of *indexation*, proposed by some economists, which would tie wages, rents and other economic factors to the rate of inflation.

Eurodollars—Credits expressed in dollars owned by non-American nationals deposited in European banks and used in European money markets.

Fiscal Policy—The size of the Government's budget surplus or deficit determined by government spending, tax rates, etc.

Growth Stock—Stock of a company with a record of growth in earnings at a relatively rapid rate.

Inflation—A rise in the general level of prices. The demand-pull theory attributes the rise in prices to an increase in the amount of money available for spending increases without a similar rise in the production of goods available for purchase. There is a greater demand for goods which are in short supply. The cost-push theory attributes price rises, not to increased demand, but to increased production costs in labor, raw materials, energy, etc.

Keynesian Economics—During the Great Depression of the 1930s, John Maynard Keynes declared that the lack of mass purchasing power was delaying economic recovery. He recommended heavy government spending to bring back prosperity. His proposals were used in the New Deal economic programs.

Monetary Policy—The power of the Federal Reserve System to change the supply and the cost of money (interest rates).

Multinational Corporation—A company with manufacturing plants and other types of investment throughout the world. Fundamental decisions are made in terms of global alternatives available to the company.

Over-The-Counter—Companies not listed on the major exchanges are traded by dealers and brokers via telephone.

Par—The par value of a stock is the dollar amount assigned to the share by the company's charter. Par value has little significance as far as market value of common stock is concerned. In the case of preferred stock, par signifies the dollar value upon which dividends are figured.

Price-Earnings Ratio—The price of a share of stock divided by earnings per share for a 12-month period. A stock selling for $50 a share and earning $5 a share is said to be selling at a price-earnings ratio of 10 to 1.

Option—A contract to buy 100 shares of a stock at a set price within a specified time. The total price of the contract is the premium, and the price at which the shares may be bought is the exercise or striking part.

Organization of Petroleum Exporting Countries (OPEC)—An international oil cartel formed in 1959 after the old cartel of multinational oil companies unilaterally cut the price of oil. The new cartel is composed of the 13 leading oil-producing countries of the Middle East, Africa, Asia and Latin America but the cartel is dominated by the oil-rich Arab nations of the Middle East. Their control of production and the world price of oil is illustrated by the fact that, between 1970 and 1974, the price of oil rose from $1.50 to $10 a barrel.

Stabilization Policy—The efforts of the Federal Government to use fiscal and monetary policy to combat unemployment, inflation or both.

Stagflation (or Inflump)—New terms suggested by economists to describe the current phenomenon of a stagnant economy marked by both rising unemployment and a rising price level.

Short Sale—A speculator who anticipates a price drop places himself in a short position in the market by selling shares at one price expecting to be able to buy them later at a lower price.

Stock Certificate—Evidence of part ownership of a corporation. *Common stock* normally carries the right to share in the management of the corporation. *Preferred stock* is entitled to a specific dividend ahead of the common stock and to a prior claim to the assets of the corporation in case of liquidation.

ENERGY

What Ever Happened to the Energy Crisis?

By Nicholas Panagakos

Is the energy crisis a thing of the past? According to a recent poll, most Americans think the crisis vanished, along with the long gasoline queues of 1973-74—and many of them are not too sure that it wasn't a big company-engineered hoax in the first place. The evidence seems to be all around. Gasoline price wars flaring. Big car sales up. Sub-compact sales down. And the ultimate: A lot of gasoline stations are back to cleaning customer's windshields while pouring the gas—without being asked.

Actually, the shortage grows more serious daily. The supply of available oil must run out by the turn of the century, posing staggering problems of transition to other sources. The one thing that must be done for the short term is to take all prudent energy-saving conservation measures—and quickly.

As the shortage becomes more acute, natural gas supplies are shrinking while prices soar. Oil imports are rising; the nation is now dependent on overseas suppliers for nearly half the oil it consumes. Most of it comes from the Arab countries that imposed the 1973 embargo.

Imported petroleum will be largely responsible for an anticipated trade deficit this year of $3.2 billion. And the situation is growing worse. Unless something changes, we will be increasingly at the mercy of foreign imports in ensuing years. Production of the U.S.'s own crude oil has dropped 16% since the Arab embargo, and production of natural gas has fallen 11% in the past two years.

Conservation Drive was Short-Lived

Against this backdrop, the actual rate of growth of our energy consumption, which since 1975 has been 4.5% annually, is soaring. During the 1973 shortage, the nation for the first time gave serious attention to energy conservation with these actions:

● Gasoline distribution was curtailed at the retail level.

● The maximum speed limit was reduced on the nation's highways.

● Consumption of aircraft jet fuel was cut back.

● Outdoor lighting was reduced.

● Thermostats were lowered. But the apparent abundance of petroleum in mid-1974 significantly dampened the ardor of government, industry and the general public for energy conservation. "We seem to be forgetting last year's lessons and gradually returning to the 'good old days' that existed prior to the Arab embargo," says a Congressional report on energy conservation.

The expert consensus that oil and gas reserves will be exhausted by the end of the century is based on the assumption that demand will rise at a modest 2.5% annual rate between now and then,

and that imports will average only about 35% of consumption.

The Problems with Substitute Fuels

What about other sources besides oil? The United States has many, and would not have to depend on oil if substitute energy forms—nuclear, geo-thermal, solar—could be developed on a large scale. However, each of the substitute fuels has drawbacks, in some cases almost insurmountable. Twenty years ago, for example, nuclear energy looked like the answer to our problems. But more recently, increasingly high construction costs and more and more questions about the safety of nuclear-power plants have decreased the popularity of this method. Almost 70% of the nuclear power plants planned or scheduled to be built in the U.S. by 1985 have been canceled or postponed.

Solar energy has immense popular appeal, but the costs of solar heating cannot yet be proved to be competitive with conventional heating plants. For one thing, the methods for storing energy when the sun isn't shining are unreliable at best, and so today most solar systems are designed for supplementary energy only. In all probability, the end result will be a mix of new energy sources, with perhaps coal supplying the bulk of power. It is cheap and it is available.

Conservation is Needed—Now

This, then, seems to be the situation: with the supply of available oil running out, the United States will be increasingly dependent on supplies from imports, with the possibility that the spigot could be turned off at any time.

Thus, quick action is needed on energy-saving conservation measurements. Fifty percent of all energy generated in the United States is wasted, according to the Federal Energy Administration. For instance, most of the nation's 50 million single family homes are poorly insulated. Better insulation could save as much as 10 million barrels of oil a day.

The states as well as Congress can act to encourage conservation. In addition to reinstituting some of the measures that were begun during the "crisis," Congress could offer tax incentives, say, to homeowners who installed insulation. It is clear that conservation measures create hardships for some and unfair profits for others, and the nation's lawmakers are reluctant to impose hardships and condone profiteering. This is especially true in an election year. But it is equally clear that there will be no solutions unless the Federal government—in concert with individuals, industry and state governments—sets the basic policy.

(For new developments, see "Energy" in the 1976 News Chronology.)

World's Ten Largest Electric Energy Producers, 1974[1]
(in million kilowatt-hours)

Country	PRODUCTION				Country	PRODUCTION			
	Hydro	Nuclear	Thermal	Total		Hydro	Nuclear	Thermal	Total
United States ..	306,405[2]	112,696	1,548,188	1,967,289	Italy	41,328[2]	3,410	102,382	147,120
U.S.S.R.	132,030	8,000[3]	835,724[3]	975,754	China	35,000[3]	. . .	83,000[3]	118,000[3]
Japan	82,599[2]	10,000[3]	368,106[3]	460,705	Poland	2,459	. . .	89,145	91,604
West Germany . .	17,877	12,136	281,642	311,655	Subtotal	889,483	207,655	3,707,661	4,804,799
Canada	210,159	13,864	54,931	278,954	All Others	543,639	25,900	871,064	1,440,603
United Kingdom .	4,796	33,617	234,903	273,316	World Total .	1,433,122	233,555	4,578,275	6,245,402
France	56,830	13,932	109,640	180,402					

[1] *Source:* United Nations *World Energy Supplies* (Statistical Papers, Series J, No. 19), New York, 1976. [2] Production from geothermal sources included. [3] Estimate.

World's Per Capita Electric Energy Consumption, 1974[1]
(Selected Countries)

Country	KWh Per Capita[2]	Population (000)	Production plus Net Imports[3]	Country	KWh Per Capita[2]	Population (000)	Production plus Net Imports[3]
Norway	17,829	3,988	71,103	Neth. Antilles	6,723	238	1,600
Panama, Canal Zone . .	17,348	46	798	Finland	6,222	4,682	29,132
New Caledonia	13,561	132	1,790	New Zealand	6,063	3,027	1,8352
Luxembourg	13,219	360	4,759	Bermuda	5,436	55	299
Guam	12,887	97	1,250	Switzerland	5,342	6,462	34,520
U.S. Virgin Islands . . .	11,538	65	750	Australia	5,229	13,339	69,743
Canada	11,833	22,479	265,997	West Germany	5,119	62,041	317,566
Iceland	10,916	215	2,347	United Kingdom . . .	4,873	56,094	273,366
Sweden	9,566	8,161	78,067	Kuwait	4,764	934	4,450
United States	9,344	211,890	1,979,983	WORLD	1,613	. . .	. . .
Christmas Islands . . .	9,000	3	27				

Source: [1] United Nations *World Energy Supplies* (Statistical Paper, Series J, No. 19), New York, 1976. [2] Production plus Net Imports divided by total population. [3] In million kilowatt-hours. NOTE: Data on consumption refer to "apparent inland" consumption, and are derived from the formula "production plus imports minus exports minus bunkers plus or minus additions to stocks." Accordingly, the series on apparent consumption may occasionally represent only an indication of the magnitude of actual (i.e., "measured") gross inland availability: this statement is particularly apposite either when stock data are unavailable or unreliable, or when apparent consumption is a small residual element derived from calculations between large aggregate series and thus is sensitive to small variations in these series. This latter point is also appropriate with respect to the *per capita* consumption calculations presented in some tables: where the quantities involved are small, the series tend to exaggerate the effects of such elements as stock additions or withdrawals; also, *where relatively small populations are involved, large fluctuations in per capita consumption series may accrue, in fact, to only small quantitative variations.*

ENERGY CONSUMPTION—TOTAL AND PER CAPITA; 1940 TO 1974
Total in trillions, per capita in millions, of British thermal units.

YEAR	ALL ENERGY		NATURAL GAS [1]		COAL [2]		CRUDE PETROLEUM [3]	
	Total	Per capita	Total	Per capita	Total	Per capita	Total	Per capita
1940_____	23,908	181	2,726	21	12,535	95	7,487	57
1945_____	31,541	238	3,973	30	15,972	121	9,619	73
1950_____	34,153	226	6,140	41	12,913	85	12,706	84
1955_____	39,956	243	9,232	56	11,703	71	16,328	99
1960_____	44,816	249	12,736	71	10,414	58	18,608	103
1965_____	53,969	278	16,097	83	12,358	64	21,566	111
1970_____	67,143	330	22,029	108	12,698	62	29,537	145
1971_____	68,698	338	22,819	111	12,043	58	30,570	148
1972_____	71,946	346	23,025	111	12,426	60	32,966	158
1973_____	74,743	356	22,712	108	13,294	63	34,851	166
1974_____	73,121	346	22,237	105	13,169	62	33,490	158

[1] Dry gas only. Marketed production minus shrinkage caused by liquids extraction (34 cubic feet per gallon produced). [2] Includes bituminous coal and lignite and anthracite coal. [3] Includes petroleum products. Source: 1920–1972, Library of Congress, *Energy Facts*, November 1973.

Electric Energy Output of Utilities[1]
(in millions of kilowatt hours)
Source: Federal Power Commission.

Year	Total	Ownership						Source of energy	
		Privately owned	Publicly owned	Municipal	Federal	Co-operatives, power districts, state projects	% public to total	Fuels	Fuels as % of total
1920.........	39,405	37,716	1,689	1,373	58	94	4.3	23,644	60.0
1929.........	92,180	87,514	4,667	3,498	300	451	5.1	59,533	64.6
1933.........	81,740	76,668	5,072	3,583	458	654	6.2	48,283	59.1
1939.........	127,642	115,078	12,564	5,688	5,476	944	9.8	84,078	65.9
1943.........	217,759	180,247	37,511	9,223	24,485	3,156	17.2	144,127	66.2
1951.........	370,673	301,845	68,828	17,617	44,120	6,204	18.6	270,922	73.1
1956.........	753,350	578,600	174,750	36,924	112,321	25,505	23.2	607,834	80.7
1960.........	1,144,350	880,837	263,513	52,627	153,068	57,819	23.0	949,594	83.0
1970.........	1,531,609	1,183,190	348,419	71,394	185.753	91,273	22.7	1.284.153	83.8
1973.........	1,856,216	1,448,860	407,356	80,872	211,715	144,769	21.9	1,584,582	85.4
1974[2].........	1,866,616	1,442,120	424,497	78,713	219,959	125,825	22.7	1,565,553	83.9
1975[2].........	1,915,883	1,486,090	429,793	81,486	221,167	127,140	22.4	1,616,027	84.3

[1] Data for 1920 through 1960 do not include Alaska and Hawaii; data since 1970 include those states. Output by industrial establishments was as follows (in millions of kilowatt hours): 1939—33,667; 1943—49,781; 1951—62,685; 1956—84,136; 1960—88,266; 1970—108,429; 1973—102,529; 1974—102,688.   [2] Preliminary. NOTE: Detail may not add up to totals because of rounding.

Largest Nuclear Power Plants in the United States
Source: Nuclear Regulatory Commission.

Location	Operating Utility	Capacity (kilowatts)	Year operative
Columbia County, Ore.	Portland General Electric Co.	1,130,000	1975
Decatur, Ala. (Unit 1)	Tennessee Valley Authority	1,065,000	1974
Decatur, Ala. (Unit 2)	Tennessee Valley Authority	1,065,000	1974
Peach Bottom, Pa. (Unit 2) . . .	Philadelphia Electric Co.	1,065,000	1974
Peach Bottom, Pa. (Unit 3)	Philadelphia Electric Co.	1,065,000	1974
Zion, Ill. (Unit 1)	Commonwealth Edison Co.	1,050,000	1973
Zion, Ill. (Unit 2)	Commonwealth Edison Co.	1,050,000	1974
Bridgman, Mich. (Unit 1)	Indiana & Michigan Power Electric Co.	1,050,000	1975
Clay Station, Calif.	Sacramento Municipal Utility District	913,000	1975
Seneca, S.C. (Unit 1)	Duke Power Co.	886,000	1973
Seneca, S.C. (Unit 2)	Duke Power Co.	886,000	1974
Seneca, S.C. (Unit 3)	Duke Power Co.	886,000	1974
Indian Point, N.Y. (Unit 2) . . .	Consolidated Edison Co.	873,000	1973
Buchanan, N.Y. (Unit 3)	New York State Power Authority	873,000	1976
Beaver County, Pa. (Unit 1) . . .	Duquesne Light Co.	852,000	1976
Russellville, Ark.	Arkansas Power & Light Co.	850,000	1974
Richland, Wash.	Energy Research and Development Administration . .	850,000	1966
Lusby, Md. (Unit 1)	Baltimore Gas & Electric Co.	845,000	1975
Waterford, Conn. (Unit 2)	Northeast Nuclear Energy Co.	828,000	1975
Scriba, N.Y.	New York State Power Authority	821,000	1975
Southport, N.C.	Carolina Power & Light Co.	821,000	1975
Goldsboro, Pa. (Unit 1)	Metropolitan Edison Co.	819,000	1974
Ft. Pierce, Fla. (Unit 1)	Florida Power & Light Co.	810,000	1976
Morris, Ill. (Unit 2)	Commonwealth Edison Co.	809,000	1970
Morris, Ill. (Unit 3)	Commonwealth Edison Co.	809,000	1971
TOTAL ALL PLANTS	. . . .	22,971,000	....

NOTE: 74 plants with a total capacity of 77,000,000 kilowatts are under construction; 83 plants, totaling 93,000,000 kilowatts, are in the planning stage, with reactors already ordered. Another 21 plants, totaling 26,000,000 kilowatts, have been publicly announced.

Leading Exporters of Crude Oil to U.S., 1960–1974
(in millions of 42-gallon barrels)
Source: Bureau of Mines.

Country	1960	1970	1973	1974	Country	1960	1970	1973	1974
Canada	41	245	365	289	Ecuador	0	0	17	15
Nigeria	0	17	164	254	Gabon	0	0	0	9
Iran	13	12	79	169	Qatar	2	0	3	6
Saudi Arabia	28	15	169	160	Tunisia	0	0	7	5
Venezuela	173	98	126	116	Egypt	1	8	5	3
Indonesia	27	26	73	103	Bolivia	0	1	0.9	2
Algeria	(¹)	2	44	66	Kuwait	48	12	15	2
United Arab Emirates	0	23	26	25	Libya	0	17	49	1
Trinidad	0	(¹)	22	23	Total all countries	372	483	1,184	1,269
Angola	0	0	18	18					

¹ Less than 500,000 barrels.

Oil Production by States
Source: Bureau of Mines.

State	1974¹ Barrels (thousands)	1974¹ % total U.S.	1970 Barrels (thousands)	1970 % total U.S.	1966 Barrels (thousands)	1966 % total U.S.
Texas	1,262,126	39.4	1,249,697	35.5	1,057,706	34.9
Louisiana	737,324	23.0	906,907	25.8	674,318	22.3
California	323,003	10.1	372,191	10.6	345,295	11.4
Oklahoma	177,785	5.5	223,574	6.4	224,839	7.4
Wyoming	139,997	4.4	160,345	4.6	134,470	4.4
New Mexico	98,695	3.1	128,184	3.6	124,154	4.1
Alaska	70,603	2.2	83,616	2.4	14,358	0.5
Kansas	61,691	1.9	84,853	2.4	103,738	3.4
Mississippi	50,779	1.6	65,119	1.9	55,227	1.8
Utah	39,363	1.2	23,370	0.7	24,112	0.8
Colorado	37,508	1.2	24,723	0.7	33,492	1.1
Montana	34,554	1.1	37,879	1.1	35,380	1.2
Illinois	27,553	0.9	43,747	1.2	61,661	2.0
North Dakota	19,697	0.6	21,998	0.6	27,126	0.9
Michigan	18,021	0.6	11,693	0.3	14,273	0.5
Arkansas	16,527	0.5	18,035	0.5	23,824	0.8
Kentucky	7,837	0.2	11,575	0.3	18,066	0.6
Nebraska	6,611	0.2	11,451	0.3	13,850	0.5
Others	72,911	2.3	38,493	1.1	41,874	1.4
Total U.S.	3,202,585	100.0	3,517,450	100.0	3,027,763	100.0

¹ Preliminary.

Fuel Production
Sources: Department of Interior; Department of Commerce; American Gas Association.

Year	Coke, in thousands of short tons	Anthracite coal, in thousands of short tons	Bituminous coal, in thousands of short tons	Natural gas, in millions of therms	Manufactured gas, in millions of therms¹	Crude petroleum, in thousands of 42-gal. barrels
1929	59,884	73,828	534,989	20,490²	2,070²	1,007,323
1933	27,589	49,541	333,631	16,640²	1,820	905,656
1939	44,327	51,487	394,855	26,220	1,830	1,264,962
1949	63,637	42,702	437,868	55,770	2,680	1,841,940
1959	55,864	20,649	412,028	120,461	952	2,574,590
1965	66,854	14,866	512,088	160,398	230	2,848,500
1970	66,525	9,729	602,932	219,206	n.a.	3,517,450
1972	60,507	7,106	595,386	225,317	n.a.	3,455,368
1973	64,325	6,830	591,738	226,476	n.a.	3,360,903
1974	61,581	6,617	603,406	216,005	n.a.	3,202,585

¹ Includes all manufactured gas products produced by gas utilities.   ² Estimated.   NOTE: n.a. = not available.

1976 Environmental Quality Index

Source: Copyright 1976 by the National Wildlife Federation. Reprinted from the February-March issue of the *National Wildlife Magazine.*

In 1969, the first EQ Index was conceived by the National Wildlife Federation. It was an independent, pioneering attempt to evaluate the Environmental Quality of the United States. In the 7th Annual EQ Index, the survey has come up with the following conclusions.

WILDLIFE: Cause for Alarm—EQ Index for wildlife is down again. Last year, the list grew to 126 U.S. Endangered Species with the addition of six animals, including the American crocodile. Because about 1.2 million acres were converted from rural to urban use last year and only 86,000 acres added to our national refuges, nearly 24,000 plants and animals lost their habitat and are under consideration for inclusion on the EQ Index.

Last year, the National Wildlife Federation initiated a computerized data bank to help the endangered bald eagle and other birds. Controlled alligator harvests were permitted in three Louisiana parishes. The International Whaling Commission cut the allowable whale harvest by almost one-fourth for 1976, but populations are already so low that this action might well be too late.

AIR: Turning the Corner—EQ Index for air was up slightly. The air is cleaner, but rural air pollution is still high. The program is still behind schedule, and air pollution killed 4,000 Americans last year. EPA reports it will cost $14 billion per year to control air pollution. This cost will be largely offset by the potential savings of $12 billion per year by eliminating the damages caused by air pollution. Four out of five major stationary sources of pollution in this country are complying with laws, or are on abatement schedules to comply, to reduce pollution emissions.

Smog—which damages health, crops and materials—has recently been measured in high concentrations 50 miles or more from urban areas in the eastern third of the U.S. Sulfur dioxide levels have dropped about 25% nationally since 1970, but still exceed standards in 14% of the air quality control regions in this country.

MINERALS: A State of Complacency—EQ Index for minerals is down again. Research is still lagging on alternative energy sources.

The most recent U.S. Geological Survey estimates of undiscovered, recoverable petroleum reserves in the U.S. have plummeted from between 320–160 billion barrels in the mid-1960s to 50 billion barrels today. Canada, Mexico and the U.S. own almost half of all the world's energy reserves.

The U.S. is more than 90% dependent on imports of five important metals: manganese, cobalt, chromium, titanium, niobium, etc.; 75% dependent on imports for six others: aluminum, platinum, tin, tantalum, bismuth and mercury. By the year 2000, the U.S. may be 100% dependent on imports for at least 12 minerals.

Recycling of vital minerals, mostly talk, has lagged badly. Only about 7% of consumer and commercial waste is recycled, even though it not only saves minerals, but saves energy supplies as well.

SOIL: Pressure to Produce—EQ Index for soil is down again. But U.S. soil is still the bright spot in a hungry world. Big villains: soil erosion and continued urban sprawl. One-half of all U.S. cropland is adequately protected against soil erosion, compared to only about one-third just 10 years ago. But to meet booming food demands, millions of erosion-prone acres are being converted to needed crops—nine million in 1974 alone—so that we are using more. Last year, another 212 million acres of valuable farmland were lost to other uses.

TIMBER: Who Owns the Forest—EQ Index for timber remains unchanged. Timber yields held steady and the goals of multiple-use remained elusive. The 1976 timber sales goal for all national forest reflects big, harvestable reserves. Multiple use is the keystone of national forest management. But 50-year projections tend to give timber production top priority. A West Virginia judge, citing an 1897 law, says only "mature or dead trees" can be cut. Due to the decision, operations were restricted in nine eastern national forests.

WATER: A Long, Long Way to Go—EQ Index for water is down again. Some progress in clean-up in 1975, but new research reveals nation's water problem is much worse than expected. Federal allocations to cities to build sewage treatment facilities have risen sharply. The EPA has issued 26,000 industrial permits for dumping wastes into the nation's waterways. But spot checks showed two out of three were in violation.

New pollutants that were never before treated or detected in the nation's drinking water supplies pose potential dangers. Nutrients that speed deterioration of water bodies are increasing. Bacteria, organic waste levels are decreasing. Continuing problems with trace metals and pesticides. Annual cost of clean-up is about $13.2 billion, but, deducting credit for $11.5 billion in water pollution damages, the net cost is $1.7 billion, and that is not so high.

LIVING SPACE: The Big Squeeze—EQ Index for living space is down again. More people, more haphazard growth. Americans must decide soon the lifestyle they want for their children. About 1.2 million acres of rural land is converted to urban uses annually in the U.S., giving us less land. World population reached four billion in 1975, giving us more people. If growth rate continues at present rate, it will double in less than 45 years.

SOME ENDANGERED SPECIES OF THE WORLD

Source: Fish and Wildlife Service, Department of Interior

Amphibians & Reptiles

Species	Habitat	Species	Habitat
Boa, Jamaican	Jamaica	Tortoise (various)	Austl., Galapagos I., Madagascar
Crocodile (various)	Afr., Cuba., Mex., S. Amer.		
Frog (various)	Israel, New Zealand	Turtle (various)	Amaz. Riv. Bas., Mex., Orinoco Riv. Bas.
Iguana (various)	Anegada I., Galapagos I.		

Birds

Species	Habitat	Species	Habitat
Albatross, Short-tailed	Japan	Malkoha, Red faced	Sri Lanka
Bristlebird, Western	Australia	Megapode (various)	W Pacific
Bulbul, Mauritius	Mauritius	Ostrich (various)	Jordan, Sau. Arabia
Bullfinch, São Miguel	Azores, E Atlantic	Owl (various)	Indian Ocean, W Pacific
Bustard, Great Indian	India, Pakistan	Owlet, Mrs. Morden's	Kenya
Cahow (Bermuda Petrel)	Bermuda, W Atlantic	Parakeet (various)	Austl., Braz., N.Z.
Condor	S America	Parrot (various)	Austl., Braz., Mex., N.Z.
Crane (various)	Asia, Japan, USSR	Pelican, Brown	C & S Amer., West Indies
Cuckoo-shrike (various)	Mauritius, Réunion I.	Penguin, Galapagos	Galapagos I.
Curassow (various)	Brazil, Trinidad	Pheasant (various)	Asia, India
Curlew, Eskimo	Can. to Arg.	Pigeon (various)	Azores, N.Z., Portugal
Dove (various)	Grenada, N. Cal., Palau I.	Plover, Shore	New Zealand
Duck, White-winged Wood	Asia, India, Indonesia	Rhea, Darwin's	Arg., Bol., Peru, Urug.
Eagle (various)	Afr., Phil. I, Spain	Roller, Long-tailed Ground	Madagascar
Egret, Chinese	China, Korea	Scrub-bird, Noisy	Australia
Flycatcher (various)	Austl., N.Z., S & W Pacific	Starling (various)	Bali, Caroline I.
Fody, Weaver-finch	Seychelles	Stork, White Oriental	China, Jap., Kor., USSR
Goshawk	Christmas I.	Thrasher, White-breasted	Martinique, St. Lucia
Grackle, Slender-billed	Mexico	Thrush (various)	Philippines, Seychelles
Grebe, Atitlan	Guatemala	Trembler, Martinique Brown	Martinique
Guan, Horned	Guatemala, Mex.	Wanderer, Plain	Australia
Gull, Audouin's	Mediterranean Sea	Warbler (various)	Cuba, W Indies, W Pacific
Hawk (various)	Comoro & Galapagos I.	Wattlebird (various)	N.Z., Réunion I., Seychelles
Honeyeater, Helmeted	Australia	Whipbird	Australia
Ibis, Japanese crested	China, Japan, Korea, USSR	White-eye (various)	Caroline I., Seychelles
Kakapo (Owl Parrot)	New Zealand	Woodpecker, Imperial	Mexico
Kestrel (various)	Mauritius, Seychelles	Wren (various)	Guadeloupe, St. Lucia, N.Z.
Kite (various)	Cuba, Grenada		

Fishes

Species	Habitat	Species	Habitat
Ala Balik	Turkey	Cicek	Turkey
Ayumodoki	Japan	Nekogigi	Japan
Blindcat, Mexican	Mexico	Tango, Miyako	Japan
Catfish	Thailand		

Mammals

Species	Habitat	Species	Habitat
Anoa	Indonesia	Gazelle (various)	N & S Africa
Armadillo, Pink fairy	Argentina	Gibbon (various)	SE Asia
Ass, Wild (various)	Afr., SW & C Asia	Gorilla	C & W Africa
Avahis	Madagascar	Hartebeest, Swayne's	Ethiopia
Aye-aye	Madagascar	Hog, Pygmy	Nepal, Bhutan
Bandicoot (various)	Australia	Hyaena (various)	Morocco, S Africa
Banteng	SE Asia	Ibex (various)	Ethiopia, Spain
Bison, Wood	Canada	Impala, Black-faced	Angola, SW Africa
Cat, Tiger	Costa Rica to S Amer.	Indris	Madagascar, Comoro I.
Cheetah	Africa to India	Jaguar	C & S America
Colobus, Red	Kenya, Tanzania	Kangaroo (various)[1]	Australia
Deer (various)[1]	India, Indonesia SE Asia, Mex.	Kouprey	Cambodia
		Langur (various)	China, Indonesia
Dibbler	Australia	Lechwe, Black	Zambia
Dog, Asiatic Wild (Dhole)	India, USSR	Lemur (various)	Comoro I., Madagascar
Dugong	E Afr. to Ryukyu I.	Leopard (various)	Africa, Asia & C Asia
Fox, Northern Kit	Canada	Lion, Asiatic	India

Species	Habitat	Species	Habitat
Lynx, Spanish	Spain	Quokka	Australia
Macaque, Lion-tailed	India	Rabbit, Volcano	Mexico
Manatee, Amazonian	Amazon Riv. Bas.	Rat (various)	Australia
Mangabey, Tana River	Kenya	Rhinoceros (various)	Africa, Asia
Margay	C & S America	Saki, White-nosed	Brazil
Marmoset (various)	Braz., Col., Ecuador, Peru	Seal, Mediterranean Monk	NW Afr., Black Sea, Med.
Marsupial (various)	Australia	Seledang (Gaur)	Asia, SE Asia
Marten, Yellow-throated	Taiwan	Serval (Barbary)	Algeria
Monkey, Spider	Costa Rica, Nic., Panama	Shou	Bhutan, Tibet
Mouse (various)	Australia	Sifakas	Madagascar
Native-cat, Eastern	Australia	Sloth, Brazilian Three-toed	Brazil
Numbat	Australia	Solenodon (various)	Cuba, Dom. Rep., Haiti
Ocelot	C & S America	Stag (various)	Algeria, Kashmir, Tunisia
Orangutan	Brunei, Malaysia, Indonesia	Tapir (various)	Mex., S. America
		Tiger (various)	Asia, Australia
Oryx, Arabian	Arabian Peninsula	Vicuna	Arg., Bol., Peru
Otter (various)	Cameroons, S America	Wallaby (various)	Australia
Planigale	Australia	Whale (various)	Oceania
Porcupine, Thin-spined	Brazil	Wolf, Maned	S America
Possum (various)	Australia	Wombat (various)	Australia
Prairie Dog, Mexican	Mexico	Yak, Wild	India, Tibet

SOME ENDANGERED SPECIES IN THE U.S.

Source: Fish and Wildlife Service, Department of Interior

Amphibians & Reptiles

Species	Habitat	Species	Habitat
Alligator, American[1]	Atl. coast to Tex.	Salamander (various)	Calif., Tex.
Boa, Puerto Rican	Puerto Rico	Snake, San Francisco Garter	California
Crocodile, American	S. Fla., Fla. Keys	Toad, Houston	Tex.
Lizard, Blunt-nosed leopard	California		

Birds

Species	Habitat	Species	Habitat
Bald Eagle, Southern	Atl. & Gulf Coasts	Kite, Florida Everglade (snail kite)	Florida
Bobwhite, Masked	Ariz., N.M.[2]	Parrot, P.R.[1]	Puerto Rico
Clapper rail, Light-footed	Ariz., Calif.[2]	Thick-billed[2]	Ariz., N.M.
California	California	Pelican, Brown	East & West
Yuma	Ariz., Calif.[2]	Petrel, Dark-rumped	Hawaii
Condor, California	California	Pheasant (various)	([3])
Coot, Hawaiian	Hawaii	Pigeon, Puerto Rican Plain	Puerto Rico
Crane, Sandhill	Miss.	Po'o, Uli	Hawaii
Whooping	Canada, U.S.	Prairie chicken, Attwater's	Texas
Crow, Hawaiian	Hawaii	Shearwater, Newell's Manx[1]	Hawaii
Duck, Hawaiian[1]	Hawaii	Sparrow, Cape Sable	Florida
Laysan	Hawaii	Dusky Seaside	Florida
Mexican	Ariz., Tex.[2]	Santa Barbara	California
Falcon (various)	Western states[2]	Stilt, Hawaiian	Hawaii
Finch (various)	Hawaii, U.S.	Teal, Laysan	([3])
Gallinule	Hawaii	Thrush (various)	Hawaii
Goose, Aleutian	Western states	Warbler (various)	SE, Hawaii
Hawaiian	Hawaii	Whip-poor-will	Puerto Rico
Hawk (various)	Hawaii, P.R.	Woodpecker (various)	S. Central & SE[2]
Honeycreeper (various)	Hawaii		

Fishes

Species	Habitat	Species	Habitat
Bonytail, Pharnagat	Nevada	Pike, Blue	Lakes Erie, Ontario
Chub (various)	Ariz., Calif., Utah, Wyo.	Pupfish (various)	Calif., Nev., Tex.
Cisco, Longjaw	Great Lakes	Squawfish, Colorado River	Colorado Riv. Sys.
Dace (various)	Nevada, Wyoming	Stickleback, Unarmored Threespine	California
Darter (various)	Ala., Fla., Md., Miss., Tex.	Sturgeon, Shortnose/Lake	Atl. Coast, Grt. Lakes
Gambusia (various)	Tex.	Topminnow, Gila	Ariz.[2]
Killifish, Pahrump	Nevada	Trout (various)[1]	Ariz.,Calif.,Col., Nev., N.M.
Madtom, Scioto	Ohio	Woundfin	Utah

Mammals

Species	Habitat	Species	Habitat
Bat (various)	Hawaii. East & Midwest	Lemur, Black[1]	[3]
Bear, Grizzly[1,2]	Ida., Mont., Wyo.	Ring-tailed[1]	[3]
Glacier	Alaska	Leopard[1]	[3]
Beaver, Mexican[2]	N.M., Tex.	Mouse, Salt Marsh harvest	California
Cougar, Eastern	Eastern U.S.	Panther, Florida	Florida
Deer, Columbian white-tailed	Ore., Wash.	Prairie dog, Utah	Utah
Key	Fla.	Pronghorn (various)	Arizona[2]
Ferret, Black-footed	Ariz., Tex., Rockies	Sea Cow (Manatee)	Florida
Fox, San Joaquin kit	California	Tiger[1]	[3]
Fox Squirrel	Md.	Wolf, Eastern Timber	Northeast
Jaguar[1]	[3]	Northern Rocky Mountain	Montana, Wyoming
Kangaroo rat, Morro Bay	California	Red	La., Texas

[1] Threatened species. [2] Also endangered in Mexico. [3] In captivity in U.S.

Speed of Animals

Source: Natural History Magazine, March 1974. Copyright © The American Museum of Natural History, 1974.

Most of the following measurements are for maximum speeds over approximate quarter-mile distances. Exceptions—which are included to give a wide range of animals—are the lion and elephant, whose speeds were clocked in the act of charging; the whippet, which was timed over a 200-yard course; the cheetah over a 100-yard distance; man for a 15-yard segment of a 100-yard run; and the black mamba, six-lined race runner, spider, giant tortoise, three-toed sloth, and garden snail, which were measured over various small distances.

Animal	Speed mph	Animal	Speed mph	Animal	Speed mph
Cheetah	70	Mongolian wild ass	40	Man	27.89
Pronghorn antelope	61	Greyhound	39.35	Elephant	25
Wildebeest	50	Whippet	35.5	Black mamba snake	20
Lion	50	Rabbit (domestic)	35	Six-line race runner	18
Thomson's gazelle	50	Mule deer	35	Squirrel	12
Quarter horse	47.5	Jackal	35	Pig (domestic)	11
Elk	45	Reindeer	32	Chicken	9
Cape hunting dog	45	Giraffe	32	Spider (Tegenearia atrica)	1.17
Coyote	43	White-tailed deer	30	Giant Tortoise	0.17
Gray fox	42	Wart hog	30	Three-toed sloth	0.15
Hyena	40	Grizzly bear	30	Garden snail	0.03
Zebra	40	Cat (domestic)	30		

Gestation, Incubation, and Longevity of Certain Animals

Animal	Gestation or incubation, in days & (average)	Longevity, in years & (record exceptions)	Animal	Gestation or incubation, in days & (average)	Longevity, in years & (record exceptions)
Ass	365	18–20 (63)	Horse	264–420 (336)†	20–25 (50+)
Bear	180–240*	15–20 (36)	Kangaroo	32–39*	4–6 (23)
Cat	52–69 (63)	10–12 (26+)	Lion	105–113 (108)	10 (29)
Chicken	22	7–8 (14)	Man	253–303	††
Cow	c. 280	9–12 (25)	Monkey	139–270*	12–15* (29)
Deer	197–222	10–15 (26)	Mouse	19–31*	1–3 (4)
Dog	53–71 (63)	10–12 (24)	Parakeet (Budgerigar)	17–20 (18)	8 (12+)
Duck	21–35* (28)	10 (15)	Pig	101–130 (115)	10 (22)
Elephant	510–730 (624)*	30–40 (71)	Pigeon	11–19	10–12 (39)
Fox	51–63*	8–10 (14)	Rabbit	30–35 (31)	6–8 (15)
Goat	136–160 (151)	12 (17)	Rat	21	3 (5)
Groundhog	31–32	4–9	Sheep	144–152 (151)*	12 (16)
Guinea pig	58–75 (68)	3 (6)	Squirrel	44	8–9 (15)
Hamster, golden	15–17	2 (8)	Whale	365–547*	
Hippopotamus	220–255 (240)	30 (49+)	Wolf	60–63	10–12 (16)

* Depending on kind. † Horse has the greatest variation of gestation period of any species. This is caused by seasonal or feed factors. ‡ For life expectancy charts, *see* Index.

Animal Group Terminology

Ants—**colony**
Bears—**sleuth**
Bees—**grist, hive, swarm**
Birds—**flight, volery**
Cattle—**drove**
Cats—**clutter**
Chicks—**brood, clutch**
Clams—**bed**
Cranes—**sedge, seige**
Crows—**murder**

Ducks—**brace, team**
Elephants—**herd**
Elks—**gang**
Fish—**school, shoal, draught**
Foxes—**leash, skulk**
Geese—**flock, gaggle, skein**
Gnats—**cloud, horde**
Goldfinches—**charm**
Gorillas—**band**
Hares—**down, husk**

Hawks—**cast**
Horses—**pair, team**
Hounds—**cry, mute, pack**
Larks—**exhaltation**
Leopards—**leap**
Lions—**pride**
Mules—**span**
Nightingales—**watch**
Oxen—**yoke**
Oysters—**bed**

Partridge—**covey**
Peacocks—**muster**
Pheasant—**nest**
Pigs—**litter**
Quail—**bevy, covey**
Sheep—**drove, flock**
Swans—**bevy**
Vipers—**nest**
Whales—**gam, pod**
Wolves—**pack**

Animal Names: Male, Female, and Young

Source: Grace Davall, N.Y. Zoological Society.

Animal	Male	Female	Young	Animal	Male	Female	Young
Ass	Jack	Jenny	Foal	Goose	Gander	Goose	Gosling
Bear	He-bear	She-bear	Cub	Horse	Stallion	Mare	Foal
Cat	Tom	Queen	Kitten	Lion	Lion	Lioness	Cub
Cattle	Bull	Cow	Calf	Rabbit	Buck	Doe	Bunny
Chicken	Rooster	Hen	Chick	Sheep	Ram	Ewe	Lamb
Deer	Buck	Doe	Fawn	Swan	Cob	Pen	Cygnet
Dog	Dog	Bitch	Pup	Swine	Boar	Sow	Piglet
Duck	Drake	Duck	Duckling	Tiger	Tiger	Tigress	Cub
Elephant	Bull	Cow	Calf	Whale	Bull	Cow	Calf
Fox	Dog	Vixen	Cub	Wolf	Dog	Bitch	Pup

Water Supply of the World[1]

Source: Department of the Interior, Geological Survey.

The Antarctic Icecap is the largest supply of fresh water, nearly 2 per cent of the world's total of fresh and salt water. As can be seen from the table below, the amount of water in our atmosphere is over ten times as large as the water in all the rivers taken together. The fresh water actually available for human use in lakes and rivers and the accessible ground water amounts to only about one third of one per cent of the total.

	Surface area (square miles)	Volume (cubic miles)	Percentage of total
SALT WATER			
The oceans	139,500,000	317,000,000	97.2
Inland seas and saline lakes	270,000	25,000	0.008
FRESH WATER			
Freshwater lakes	330,000	30,000	0.009
All rivers (average level)	......	300	0.0001
Antarctic Icecap	6,000,000	6,300,000	1.9
Arctic Icecap and glaciers	900,000	680,000	0.15
Water in the atmosphere	197,000,000	3,100	0.001
Ground water within half			
a mile from surface	......	1,000,000	0.31
Deep lying ground water	......	1,000,000	0.31
TOTAL (rounded)	......	326,000,000	100.00

[1] All figures are estimated.

AIR POLLUTANT EMISSIONS: 1970 AND 1974

Quantity in millions of tons per year. Estimates.

ITEM	Total quantity	CONTROLLABLE						Miscellaneous, uncontrollable
		Transportation		Fuel combustion [1]		Industrial processes	Solid waste disposal	
		Total	Road vehicles	Total	Electric utilities			
1970								
Carbon monoxide	107.3	82.3	71.6	1.1	0.2	11.8	5.5	6.6
Sulfur oxides	34.3	.7	0.3	27.0	20.0	6.4	.1	.1
Hydrocarbons	32.1	14.7	12.9	1.6	0.1	2.9	1.4	11.5
Particulates [2]	27.5	1.2	0.8	8.3	4.7	15.7	1.1	1.2
Nitrogen oxides	20.4	9.3	6.9	10.1	5.5	.6	.3	.1
Percent of total, by source:								
Carbon monoxide	100.0	76.7	87.0	1.0	18.2	11.0	5.1	6.2
Sulfur oxides	100.0	2.0	42.9	78.7	74.1	18.7	0.3	0.3
Hydrocarbons	100.0	45.8	87.8	5.0	6.3	9.0	4.4	35.8
Particulates [2]	100.0	4.4	66.7	30.2	56.6	57.1	4.0	4.4
Nitrogen oxides	100.0	45.6	74.2	49.5	54.5	2.9	1.5	.5
1974								
Carbon monoxide	94.6	73.5	63.6	.9	0.3	12.7	2.4	5.1
Sulfur oxides	31.4	.8	0.4	24.3	18.7	6.2	–	.1
Hydrocarbons	30.4	12.8	11.0	1.7	0.1	3.1	.6	12.2
Particulates [2]	19.5	1.3	0.9	5.9	3.3	11.0	.5	.8
Nitrogen oxides	22.5	10.7	8.1	11.0	7.0	.6	.1	.1
Percent of total, by source:								
Carbon monoxide	100.0	77.7	86.5	1.0	33.3	13.4	2.5	5.4
Sulfur oxides	100.0	2.5	50.0	77.4	77.0	19.7	–	0.3
Hydrocarbons	100.0	42.1	85.9	5.6	5.9	10.2	2.0	40.1
Particulates [2]	100.0	6.7	69.2	30.3	55.9	56.4	2.6	4.1
Nitrogen oxides	100.0	47.6	75.7	48.9	63.6	2.7	0.4	0.4

— Represents zero.   [1] Stationary. Source: U.S. Environmental Protection Agency, unpublished data.

POLLUTING DISCHARGES REPORTED IN U.S. WATERS: 1970 TO 1973

ITEM	Number	VOLUME		ITEM	Number	VOLUME	
		Gallons (1,000)	Liters (1,000)			Gallons (1,000)	Liters (1,000)
1970, total discharges	3,711	15,253	57,961	1973—Con.			
1971, total discharges	8,736	8,840	33,592	Type of pollutant:			
1972, total discharges	9,931	18,806	71,180	Light oil	2,467	3,409	12,954
1973, total discharges	13,328	24,315	92,397	Heavy oil	5,580	8,862	33,676
				Other oil	2,956	2,577	9,793
Vessel	3,550	7,919	30,092	Other and unknown	2,325	9,467	35,975
Tanker	825	4,495	17,081				
Tank barge	718	1,572	5,974	Location:			
Other	2,007	1,853	7,037	Atlantic Coast	3,505	4,231	16,078
Onshore facilities	2,163	5,774	21,940	Gulf Coast	4,422	3,789	14,398
Offshore facilities	1,955	874	3,320	Pacific Coast	3,173	8,541	32,456
Pipelines	559	1,847	7,018	Great Lakes	506	637	2,421
Other and unknown	5,101	7,902	30,027	Inland, U.S.	1,722	7,117	27,045

Source: U.S. Coast Guard, *Polluting Incidents In and Around U.S. Waters,* 1973.

OCEAN DUMPING OF WASTE MATERIALS: 1968 AND 1973

In approximate tons. Excludes dredged material.

TYPE OF WASTE	SHORT TONS (1,000)								METRIC TONS (1,000)							
	Total		Atlantic		Gulf		Pacific		Total		Atlantic		Gulf		Pacific	
	1968	1973	1968	1973	1968	1973	1968	1973	1968	1973	1968	1973	1968	1973	1968	1973
Total	9,783	11,996	8,079	10,588	696	1,408	1,007	(Z)	8,873	10,880	7,328	9,603	631	1,277	913	(Z)
Industrial	4,691	5,405	3,013	3,997	696	1,408	981	–	4,255	4,902	2,733	3,625	631	1,277	890	–
Sewage sludge	4,477	5,429	4,477	5,429	–	–	–	–	4,061	4,924	4,061	4,924	–	–	–	–
Const. and demolition debris	574	1,161	574	1,161	–	–	–	–	521	1,053	521	1,053	–	–	–	–
Solid waste	26	(Z)	–	–	–	–	26	(Z)	24	(Z)	–	–	–	–	24	(Z)
Explosives	15	–	15	–	–	–	–	–	14	–	14	–	–	–	–	–

— Represents zero.   Z Less than 500 tons. Source: 1968, U.S. Council on Environmental Quality; 1973, U.S. Environmental Protection Agency, unpublished data.

LEADING NATIONS IN RICHES AND RESOURCES

Source: Statistical Yearbook of the United Nations, 1975.
(All figures are provisional.)

Agriculture

BARLEY (thousands of metric tons, 1974):

1. U.S.S.R. 54,208
2. China 20,501
3. France 9,972
4. United Kingdom . . 9,126
5. Canada 8,802
6. West Germany . . . 7,048
7. United States . . . 6,708
8. Denmark 5,967
9. Spain 5,404
10. Poland 3,914

BUTTER (thousands of metric tons, 1974):

1. U.S.S.R. 1,360
2. France 585
3. West Germany . . . 510
4. India 450
5. United States 436
6. East Germany . . . 262
7. Poland 259
8. New Zealand 219
9. Pakistan 200
10. Australia 178

CATTLE (number in million head, 1974):

1. India 179.9
2. United States 127.7
3. U.S.S.R. 106.3
4. Brazil 88.1
5. China 63.4
6. Argentina 58.0
7. Australia 30.9
8. Mexico 27.5
9. Bangladesh 26.7
10. Ethiopia 24.7

CHEESE (thousands of metric tons, 1974):

1. United States 1,699
2. India 1,503
3. U.S.S.R. 1,330
4. France 870
5. West Germany . . . 593
6. Italy 505
7. Netherlands 376
8. Poland 330
9. Argentina 223
10. United Kingdom . . . 218

COFFEE (thousands of metric tons, 1974):

1. Brazil 1,620
2. Colombia 468
3. Ivory Coast 268
4. Angola 220

5. Uganda 215
6. Mexico 208
7. Indonesia 182
8. Ethiopia 180
9. El Salvador 140
10. Guatemala 138

COTTON LINT (thousands of metric tons, 1974):

1. U.S.S.R. 2,661
2. United States 2,513
3. China 2,147
4. India 1,214
5. Pakistan 613
6. Turkey 598
7. Brazil 564
8. Mexico 477
9. Egypt 441
10. Sudan 229

MEAT (thousands of metric tons, 1974):

1. United States 17,189
2. U.S.S.R. 12,950
3. China 12,171
4. West Germany . . . 3,629
5. France 3,473
6. Brazil 2,902
7. Argentina 2,609
8. Poland 2,535
9. United Kingdom . . 2,348
10. Australia 1,977

MILK, COW'S (thousands of metric tons, 1974):

1. U.S.S.R. 91,800
2. United States 52,352
3. France 28,710
4. West Germany . . . 21,554
5. Poland 16,667
6. United Kingdom . . 14,076
7. Italy 10,200
8. Netherlands 9,900
9. India 8,492
10. East Germany . . . 8,076

OATS (thousands of metric tons, 1974):

1. U.S.S.R. 15,302
2. United States 9,007
3. Canada 3,929
4. West Germany . . . 3,482
5. Poland 3,244
6. China 2,789
7. France 2,059
8. Sweden 1,686
9. Finland 1,113
10. United Kingdom . . 961

PIGS (number in million head, 1974):

1. China 239.0
2. U.S.S.R. 70.0
3. United States 61.1
4. Brazil 34.0
5. Poland 21.5
6. West Germany . . . 20.5
7. Mexico 11.7
8. France 11.4
9. East Germany 10.9
10. Romania 9.0

POTATOES (thousands of metric tons, 1974):

1. U.S.S.R. 81,022
2. Poland 48,635
3. China 38,027
4. United States 15,431
5. West Germany . . . 14,549
6. East Germany . . . 13,404
7. France 7,483
8. United Kingdom . . 6,791
9. Spain 5,693
10. Netherlands 5,595

RICE (thousands of metric tons, 1974):

1. China 115,213
2. India 60,000
3. Indonesia 22,732
4. Bangladesh 17,679
5. Japan 15,618
6. Thailand 13,386
7. Burma 8,582
8. South Vietnam . . . 7,200
9. Brazil 6,483
10. South Korea 6,178

RUBBER, NATURAL (thousands of metric tons, 1974):

1. Malaysia, West . . . 1,485.1
2. Indonesia 855.0
3. Thailand 379.2
4. Sri Lanka 132.0
5. India 128.4
6. Liberia 87.6
7. Malaysia, East . . . 64.2
8. Nigeria 60.0
9. Philippines 28.6
10. Zaire 26.6

RUBBER, SYNTHETIC (thousands of metric tons, 1974):

1. United States 2,516.5
2. Japan 857.9
3. France 462.7
4. United Kingdom . . 327.4

5. West Germany	324.3
6. Italy	250.0
7. Netherlands	245.3
8. Canada	208.8
9. Brazil	155.2
10. East Germany	139.4

SHEEP (number in thousand head, 1974):

1. Australia	145,304
2. U.S.S.R.	142,634
3. China	72,633
4. New Zealand	55,883
5. Argentina	41,500
6. Turkey	40,093
7. India	40,000
8. Iran	36,500
9. South Africa	31,000
10. United Kingdom	28,498

SUGAR (thousands of metric tons, 1974):[1]

1. U.S.S.R.	8,526
2. Brazil	6,931
3. Cuba	5,926
4. United States	5,136
5. India	4,489

[1] Figures are based on beet and cane raw sugar.

6. China	3,900
7. Australia	2,938
8. Mexico	2,838
9. France	2,709
10. Philippines	2,525

TEA (thousands of metric tons, 1974):

1. India	492.1
2. China	318.0
3. Sri Lanka	204.0
4. Kenya	53.4
5. Burma	46.0
6. Turkey	44.9
7. Bangladesh	31.8
8. Malawi	23.3
9. Uganda	21.7
10. Mozambique	17.6

TOBACCO (thousands of metric tons, 1974):

1. China	968.0
2. United States	902.6
3. India	441.4
4. Brazil	304.1
5. Turkey	178.9
6. Japan	139.0
7. Indonesia	121.5

8. Bulgaria	120.6
9. Canada	117.2
10. Argentina	97.6

WHEAT (thousands of metric tons, 1974):

1. U.S.S.R.	83,913
2. United States	48,807
3. China	37,002
4. India	22,073
5. France	19,100
6. Canada	13,295
7. Australia	11,249
8. Turkey	11,080
9. West Germany	7,761
10. Pakistan	7,629

WOOL (thousands of metric tons, 1974):

1. Australia	790
2. U.S.S.R.	461
3. New Zealand	294
4. Argentina	184
5. South Africa	105
6. United States	65
7. Uruguay	62
8. United Kingdom	49
9. Turkey	48
10. India	35

Mineral and Metal Production

ANTIMONY ORE (thousands of metric tons, 1974):[1]

1. South Africa	15.1
2. Bolivia	12.3
3. China	12.0
4. U.S.S.R.	7.3
5. Turkey	5.9
6. Thailand	4.4
7. Mexico	2.4
8. Yugoslavia	2.0
9. Morocco	1.9
10. Australia	1.5

[1] Antimony content.

BAUXITE (thousands of metric tons, 1974):

1. Australia	18.5
2. Jamaica	15.2
3. Surinam	6.9
4. Guinea	6.6
5. U.S.S.R.	4.3
6. Guyana	3.0
7. France	2.9
8. Greece	2.8
9. Hungary	2.7
10. United States	2.4

CHROMIUM ORE (thousands of metric tons, 1974):[1]

1. South Africa	825.9
2. U.S.S.R.	820.0
3. Southern Rhodesia	292.0

[1] Chromium content.

4. Albania	286.0
5. Turkey	270.1
6. India	194.9
7. Philippines	191.7
8. Iran	98.0
9. Finland	69.5
10. Madagascar	64.7

COAL (millions of metric tons, 1974):

1. United States	530.1
2. U.S.S.R.	473.4
3. China	430.0
4. Poland	162.0
5. United Kingdom	110.2
6. West Germany	100.9
7. India	83.9
8. South Africa	65.0
9. Australia	59.8
10. North Korea	33.9

COPPER ORE (thousands of metric tons, 1974):[1]

1. United States	1,448.8
2. U.S.S.R.	1,200.0
3. Chile	904.8
4. Canada	842.4
5. Zambia	829.5
6. Zaire	493.9
7. Australia	246.7
8. Philippines	225.5
9. Peru	213.2
10. Poland	198.0

[1] Copper content.

GOLD (thousands of kilograms, 1974):[1]

1. South Africa	759.5
2. Canada	52.2
3. United States	34.9
4. Japan	32.1
5. Papua-New Guinea	21.1
6. Ghana	19.1
7. Philippines	16.7
8. Australia	16.4
9. Southern Rhodesia	15.0
10. West Germany	9.7

[1] Excludes U.S.S.R. and China, for which no figures are available.

IRON ORE (millions of metric tons, 1974):[1]

1. U.S.S.R.	123.2
2. Australia	57.8
3. United States	51.1
4. Brazil	41.2
5. China	34.5
6. Canada	29.1
7. Liberia	24.5
8. Sweden	22.9
9. India	22.1
10. France/Venezuela	16.7

[1] Iron content.

LEAD (thousands of metric tons, 1974):[1]

1. United States	619.5

[1] Recovered directly from ores, concentrates or scrap.

2. U.S.S.R. 475.0
3. Japan 218.3
4. Australia 201.0
5. Mexico 182.7
6. United Kingdom . . . 137.0
7. Canada 126.5
8. France 124.3
9. West Germany 116.1
10. Yugoslavia 113.9

LEAD ORE (thousands of metric tons, 1974):[1]

1. United States 602.3
2. U.S.S.R. 475.0
3. Australia 370.4
4. Canada 304.8
5. Mexico 218.0
6. Peru 193.0
7. Yugoslavia 119.8
8. Bulgaria 110.0
9. North Korea 101.0
10. China 100.0
    [1] Lead content.

MANGANESE ORE (thousands of metric tons, 1974)[1]

1. U.S.S.R. 2,847.5
2. South Africa 1,895.0
3. Brazil[2] 1,141.5
4. Gabon 1,091.0
5. Australia 770.6
6. India 549.7
7. Ghana[2] 313.0
8. China 300.0
9. Mexico 145.1
10. Morocco 140.9
    [1] Manganese content. [2] 1973 figures.

MERCURY (metric tons, 1974):

1. Spain 2,075
2. U.S.S.R. 1,860
3. China 900
4. Italy 896
5. Mexico 894
6. Yugoslavia 546
7. Canada 532
8. Algeria 465
9. Turkey 306
10. Czechoslovakia . . . 191

NATURAL GAS (million cubic meters, 1974):

1. United States 586,531
2. U.S.S.R. 260,553
3. Netherlands 83,703
4. Canada 73,367
5. United Kingdom . . . 34,718
6. Romania 28,643
7. Indonesia 22,126
8. West Germany 19,826
9. Italy 15,273
10. Mexico 13,950

NICKEL ORE (thousands of metric tons, 1974):[1]

1. Canada 271.8
2. New Caledonia 136.8
3. U.S.S.R. 122.0
4. Australia 42.2
5. Cuba 32.0
6. Dominican Republic . 31.2
7. South Africa 21.4
8. Indonesia 21.0
9. United States 15.9
10. Greece 15.1
    [1] Nickel content.

PETROLEUM CRUDE (millions of metric tons, 1974):

1. U.S.S.R. 458.9
2. United States 432.8
3. Saudi Arabia 421.4
4. Iran 300.9
5. Venezuela 155.8
6. Kuwait 128.1
7. Nigeria 111.6
8. Iraq 96.9
9. United Arab Emirates . 81.1
10. Canada 80.3

PHOSPHATE ROCK (thousands of metric tons, 1974):

1. United States 41,446
2. U.S.S.R. 22,500
3. Morocco 19,749
4. Tunisia 3,826
5. China 3,000
6. Togo 2,552
7. Nauru 2,288
8. Sahara 2,168
9. Christmas Isle 1,764
10. Jordan 1,676

SALT (millions of metric tons, 1974):

1. United States 42.2
2. China 18.0
3. U.S.S.R. 13.4
4. West Germany 11.5
5. France 6.0
6. India 5.9
7. Mexico 5.5
8. Canada 5.2
9. Australia 4.7
10. Italy 4.0

SILVER (metric tons, 1974):

1. Canada 1,361
2. U.S.S.R. 1,310
3. Peru 1,275
4. Mexico 1,168
5. United States 1,050
6. Australia 674
7. Japan 306
8. Bolivia 148
9. Yugoslavia 146
10. Sweden 141

TIN (metric tons, 1974):

1. Malaysia 84,394
2. Thailand 19,827
3. Indonesia 15,065
4. United Kingdom . . . 11,998
5. Bolivia 6,907
6. Australia 6,714
7. Spain 6,222
8. United States 6,100
9. Nigeria 5,574
10. Brazil 4,848

TIN CONCENTRATES (thousands of metric tons, 1974):[1,2]

1. Malaysia 68.1
2. Bolivia 29.2
3. Indonesia 25.6
4. Thailand 20.3
5. Australia 10.1
6. Nigeria 5.5
7. Zaire 4.8
8. Brazil 3.6
9. United Kingdom . . . 3.2
10. South Africa 2.5
    [1] Excludes Albania, China, Czechoslovakia, North Korea, Vietnam, East Germany, Mongolia and U.S.S.R. [2] Tin content.

URANIUM (metric tons, 1974):[1]

1. United States 8,800
2. Canada 3,420
3. South Africa 2,711
4. France 1,610
5. Niger 1,250
6. Gabon 436
7. Portugal 89
8. Spain 60
9. Argentina 50
10. West Germany 26
    [1] Uranium content.

ZINC (thousands of metric tons, 1974):

1. Japan 836.5
2. U.S.S.R. 680.0
3. United States 503.7
4. Canada 426.3
5. Belgium 293.6
6. Australia 281.6
7. France 276.5
8. West Germany 249.7
9. Poland 233.1
10. Italy 200.0

ZINC ORE (thousands of metric tons, 1974):[1]

1. Canada 1,159.5
2. U.S.S.R. 680.0
3. United States 453.5
4. Australia 441.3
5. Peru 398.8
6. Mexico 262.7
7. Japan 240.8
8. Poland 200.0
9. North Korea 161.0
10. West Germany 116.0
    [1] Zinc content.

Manufacturing, Trade, Communications

AIRLINES (millions of passenger-kilometers, 1974):[1]

1. United States 45,248
2. United Kingdom . . . 25,229
3. France 16,457
4. Canada 11,193
5. West Germany . . . 11,005
6. Japan 10,970
7. Australia 9,546
8. Netherlands 9,341
9. Italy 9,180
10. Spain 7,260

[1] Excludes China and U.S.S.R., for which no figures are available.

ALUMINUM (thousands of metric tons, 1974):

1. United States 4,448.7
2. U.S.S.R. 1,430.0
3. Japan 1,124.0
4. Canada 1,006.9
5. West Germany . . . 688.9
6. Norway 649.3
7. France 393.3
8. United Kingdom . . 293.1
9. Netherlands 251.7
10. Australia 209.9

CEMENT (thousands of metric tons, 1974):

1. U.S.S.R. 115,145
2. United States . . . 73,407
3. Japan 73,108
4. Italy 36,309
5. West Germany . . . 35,977
6. France 32,469
7. Spain 23,660
8. China[1] 23,000
9. United Kingdom . . 17,781
10. Poland 16,765

[1] 1973 figure.

ELECTRIC ENERGY (production, millions of KWH, 1974):[1,2]

1. United States . . . 1,967,289
2. U.S.S.R. 975,754
3. Japan 460,705
4. West Germany . . . 311,655
5. Canada 278,954
6. United Kingdom . . 273,316
7. France 180,402
8. Italy 147,120
9. Poland 91,604
10. Spain 81,110

[1] Total gross generation of electricity. [2] Excludes China, for which no figures are available.

EMPLOYMENT INDEX (excl. agriculture, 1974; 1970 = 100):

1. Mauritius 156
2. Malawi 139
3. Singapore/Swaziland/Thailand[1] 138

[1] 1973 figures. [2] Socialized sector.

4. Turkey 137
5. Tunisia 129
6. South Korea/Malaysia . 124
7. Fiji[1] 121
8. Spain 120
9. Yugoslavia/Romania[2] . 119
10. Canada 118

MERCHANT FLEETS (shipping, million gross registered tons, 1975):

1. Liberia 65.8
2. Japan 39.7
3. United Kingdom . . . 33.2
4. Norway 26.2
5. Greece 22.5
6. U.S.S.R. 19.2
7. United States[1] . . . 14.6
8. Panama 13.7
9. France 10.7
10. Italy 10.1

[1] Incl. Great Lakes shipping.

MOTOR VEHICLES (production in thousands, 1974):[1]

1. United States . . . 7,331.0
2. Japan 3,931.8
3. France 3,045.7
4. West Germany . . . 2,840.0
5. Italy 1,631.0
6. United Kingdom . . 1,534.0
7. Canada 1,166.0
8. U.S.S.R. 1,119.0
9. Spain 722.4
10. Brazil 561.7

[1] Excludes China.

PIG IRON AND FERRO-ALLOYS (thousands of metric tons, 1974):

1. U.S.S.R. 99,868
2. Japan 92,704
3. United States . . . 89,281
4. West Germany . . . 40,504
5. China 35,000
6. France 22,404
7. United Kingdom . . 14,115
8. Belgium 13,020
9. Italy 11,935
10. Canada 9,761

RAILWAYS FREIGHT (billions of net-ton kilometers, 1974):[1]

1. U.S.S.R. 3,097.7
2. United States . . . 1,246.7
3. Canada 202.4
4. India[2] 135.8
5. Poland 125.2
6. France 77.0
7. West Germany . . . 69.1
8. Czechoslovakia . . . 68.0
9. South Africa . . . 61.9
10. Japan 54.5

[1] Excludes China. [2] 1973 figures.

RETAIL TRADE INDEX (1974; 1970 = 100):

1. Colombia 472
2. Argentina 420
3. Israel 347
4. Yugoslavia 274
5. Finland 182
6. Japan 178
7. Italy 171
8. New Zealand/S. Africa 169
9. Southern Rhodesia . 168
10. Greece/Ireland . . . 166

STEEL, CRUDE (thousands of metric tons, 1974):

1. U.S.S.R. 136,229
2. United States . . . 132,196
3. Japan 117,131
4. West Germany . . . 53,231
5. France 27,023
6. China 27,000
7. Italy 23,083
8. United Kingdom . . 22,426
9. Belgium 16,230
10. Poland 14,220

TELEPHONES (number in use in thousand units and per 100 inhabitants, 1974):

1. Monaco 82.4
2. United States . . . 67.7
3. Sweden 63.3
4. Liechtenstein . . . 61.4
5. Channel Islands . . 51.2
6. New Zealand . . . 48.1
7. Denmark 42.8
8. Guam 41.1
9. Iceland 40.4
10. Australia 37.7

NEWSPRINT (thousands of metric tons, 1974):

1. Canada 8,661
2. United States . . . 2,924
3. Japan 2,233
4. U.S.S.R. 1,334
5. Finland 1,219
6. Sweden 1,210
7. China 720
8. West Germany . . . 522
9. Norway 519
10. United Kingdom . . 383

MAGNESIUM (metric tons, 1974):

1. United States[1] . . . 111,068
2. U.S.S.R. 60,000
3. Norway 38,245
4. Italy 9,180
5. Japan 8,923
6. France 6,531
7. Canada 5,928
8. United Kingdom . . 3,786
9. West Germany . . . 1,714
10. China 1,000

[1] 1973 figures.

Major Nutrients and Where to Find Them

Source: Department of Agriculture

For Recommended Daily Dietary Allowances and Nutritional Values, see page 115.

Nutrient[1,2]	What They Do	Where Found
Protein	Keeps body processes working. Carries oxygen into system. Produces antibodies in blood stream that fight off disease and infection. Builds muscle tissue.	Meat, poultry, fish, milk, cheese, eggs, bread, cereal and vegetables (soybeans, dry beans and peanuts).
Fats	Provide energy. Some contain vitamins A,D,E and K. Protect vital organs by providing a cushion around them.	Butter, margarine, shortening, salad oils and dressings, cream, most cheeses, mayonnaise, nuts and bacon.
Carbohydrates	Major source of energy. Help body make best use of other nutrients.	Wheat, oats, corn and rice and foods made from them, such as bread and pasta. Potatoes, sweet potatoes, peas, dry beans, peanuts and soybeans. Dried fruits.
MINERALS: Calcium	Builds bones and teeth. Aids blood clotting and heart function. Aids nervous system.	Milk and cheese. Dark green leafy vegetables (collards, mustard or turnip greens). Salmon and sardine bones.
Iron	Combines with protein to make hemoglobin. Needed to prevent iron deficiency anemia.	Liver, heart, kidney, shellfish (especially oysters). Enriched bread and cereals. Dark leafy green vegetables.
Iodine	Assists thyroid gland function. Prevents goiter.	Iodized salt and seafood.
VITAMINS: Vitamin A (retinol)	Needed for normal vision. Protects against night blindness. Keeps skin and mucous membranes resistant to infection.	Spinach, beet and turnip greens, carrots, squash, sweet potatoes. Yellow peaches, apricots, cantaloupe and papayas also help. Liver and whole milk.
Vitamin B₁ (thiamin)	Promotes normal appetite and digestion. Necessary for a healthy nervous system.	Lean pork, dry beans, peas, some of the organ meats, some nuts.
Vitamin B₂ (riboflavin)	Helps cells use oxygen. Helps maintain good vision. Needed for good skin.	Meats, milk, whole grain or enriched breads and cereals. Green leafy vegetables.
Vitamin B₆ and B₁₂, Folacin	Maintain normal hemoglobin (carry oxygen to tissues).	Occur in foods of animal origin, brown rice, bananas, pears.
Vitamin C (ascorbic acid)	Maintains cementing material that holds body cells together. Needed for healthy gums. Aids body to resist infection.	Citrus fruits and juices, potatoes, sweet potatoes, tomatoes, peppers, green vegetables (broccoli, turnip greens, raw cabbage and collards).
Vitamin D	Builds strong bones and teeth. Aids calcium absorption.	Milk fortified with vitamin D, egg yolk, fish liver, liver, oils. Sunlight.
Vitamin E	Not fully understood.	Abundant in vegetable oils and margarines. Wheat germ and lettuce.
Vitamin K	Aids blood clotting.	Green and leafy vegetables, tomatoes, cauliflower, egg yolks, soybean oil and liver.

[1] Other essential elements include calcium, iron and iodine. The body also requires zinc, copper, sodium, potassium, magnesium and phosphorus. These show up in most foods of the above. Magnesium abounds in nuts, whole grain products, dry beans and dark green vegetables. Phosphorus is in the same foods that supply you with protein and calcium. [2] The B-Vitamins should be taken together because an inadequate intake of one may impair the utilization of the other.

Calories, Minerals, and Vitamins of Selected Foods

Source: U. S. Department of Agriculture.

Food and amount	Energy (Calories)	Protein (Gm.)	Fat (Gm.)	Minerals Calcium (Mg.)	Iron (Mg.)	Vitamin A (I.U.)	Vitamins Vitamin B₁ (thiamine) (Mg.)	Vitamin B₂ (riboflavin) (Mg.)	Niacin (Mg.)	Vitamin C (ascorbic acid) (Mg.)
Apple, 1 medium, raw	70			8	.4	50	.04	.02	.1	3
Applesauce, 1 cup, canned, unsweetened	100	1		10	1.2	100	.05	.02	.1	2
Bacon, 2 slices, crisp	90	5	8	2	.5		.08	.05	.8	
Bananas, 1 medium	100	1		10	.8	230	.06	.07	.8	12
Beans, snap green, 1 cup cooked	30	2		63	.8	680	.09	.11	.6	15
Beans, red kidney, 1 cup cooked	230	15	1	74	4.6	10	.13	.10	1.5	
Beans, baked, pork and molasses	385	16	12	161	5.9		.15	.10	1.3	
Beef cuts, cooked: Chuck, boned, 3 ounces	245	23	16	10	2.9	30	.04	.18	3.5	
Hamburger, 3 ounces	245	21	17	9	2.7	30	.07	.18	4.6	
Rib roast, 3 ounces boned	375	17	34	8	2.2	70	.05	.13	3.1	
Round, 3 ounces boned	220	24	13	10	3.0	20	.07	.13	4.8	
Sirloin, 3 ounces boned	330	20	27	9	2.5	50	.05	.19	4.0	
Beef stew with vegetables, 1 cup	210	15	10	28	2.8	2,310	.13	.16	4.4	15
Beets, 1 cup cooked	55	2		24	.9	30	.05	.07	.7	10
Breads: Cracked wheat, ½-inch slice	65	2	1	22	.3		.03	.02	.3	
Italian, 1 pound unenriched	1,250	41	4	77	3.2		.41	.27	3.6	
Raisin, ½-inch slice unenriched	65	2	1	18	.3		.01	.02	.2	
Rye (American), ½-inch slice	60	2		19	.4		.05	.02	.4	
White, ½-inch slice toasted, untoasted	70	2	1	21	.6		.06	.05	.6	
Whole wheat, ½-inch slice	65	3	1	24	.8		.09	.03	.8	
Butter, 1 tbs.	100		12	3		470				
Cabbage, 1 cup, raw, coarsely shredded	15	1		34	.3	90	.04	.04	.2	33
Cake: Sponge, average slice	195	5	4	20	.8	300	.03	.09	.1	
Pound, average slice	140	2	9	6	.2	80	.01	.03	.1	
Candies: Caramels, 1 ounce	115	1	3	42	.4		.01	.05	.1	
Chocolate, milk, 1 ounce	145	2	9	65	.3	80	.02	.10	.1	
Cantaloups, ½ melon	60	1		27	.8	6,540	.08	.06	1.2	63
Carrots, raw, 1 average size	20	1		18	.4	5,500	.03	.03	.3	4
Catsup, 1 tbs.	15			3	.1	210	.01	.01	.2	2
Cheese: Cheddar, 1 ounce	115	7	9	213	.3	370	.01	.13		
Cottage, creamed, 1 cup	170	34	7	180	.8	20	.06	.56	.2	
Cottage, uncreamed, 1 cup	170	34	1	180	.8	20	.06	.56	.2	
Cream cheese, 1 ounce	106	3	11	18	.1	435		.06		
Swiss, natural, 1 ounce	105	8	8	262	.3	320		.11		
Swiss, processed, 1 ounce	100	8	8	251	.3	310	.11	.11		
Chicken, broiled, 3 ounces	115	20	3	8	1.4	80	.05	.16	7.4	

Food	Calories	Protein (gm.)	Fat (gm.)	Calcium (mg.)	Iron (mg.)	Vitamin A (I.U.)	Thiamine (mg.)	Riboflavin (mg.)	Niacin (mg.)	Vitamin C (mg.)
Chicken, fried, ½ breast, 3.3 ounces	155	25	5	9	1.3	70	.04	.17	11.2	
Chicken, canned, boned, 3 ounces	170	18	10	18	1.3	200	.03	.11	3.7	
Clams, raw, 3 ounces	65	11	1	59	5.2	90	.08	.15	1.1	
Cocoa, 1 cup, homemade	245	10	12	295	1.0	400	.10	.45	.5	3
Coffee: black, 1 cup										
Cola, carbonated, 12 ounces	145									
Corn, average ear	70	3	1	2	.5	310	.09	.08	1.0	7
Corn flakes, 1 cup	100	2		4	.4		.11	.02	.5	
Crabmeat, canned, 3 ounces	85	15	2	38	.7		.07	.07	1.6	
Crackers, Graham, 4	110	2	1	11	.4		.01	.06		
Saltines, 4	50	1	1	2	.1				.1	
Cream: Light, table, 1 cup	505	7	49	245	.1	2,020	.07	.36	.1	
Heavy, whipping, 1 cup	840	5	90	179	.1	3,670	.05	.26	.1	
Sour, 1 cup	485	7	47	235	.1	1,930	.07	.35	.1	
Whipped topping (pressurized), 1 cup	155	2	14	67		570		.02		
Doughnuts, 1 plain	125	1	6	13	.4	30	.05	.05	.4	
Eggs: Raw or cooked in shell, 1	80	6	6	27	1.1	590	.05	.15		
Omelet, scrambled, 1	110	7	8	51	1.1	690	.08	.18		
Frankfurters, 1	170	7	15	3	.8		.08	.11	1.4	
Fruit cocktail, 1 cup canned	195	1		23	1.0	360	.05	.03	1.3	5
Grapefruit: Raw, ½	45	1		19	.5	10	.05	.02	.2	44
Canned, syrup, 1 cup	180	2		33	.8	30	.08	.05	.2	76
Juice, fresh, 1 cup	95	1		22	.5	20	.09	.04	.4	92
Haddock, breaded, fried, 3 ounces	140	17	5	34	1.0		.03	.06	2.7	2
Honey, strained, 1 tbs.	65			1	.1			.01		
Ice cream, 1 cup	255	6	14	194	.1	590	.05	.28	.1	1
Jellies, 1 tbs.	50			4	.3			.01		1
Lamb: Rib chop, boned, 4 ounces	400	25	33	10	1.5		.14	.25	5.6	
Leg roast, 3 ounces, boned	235	22	16	9	1.4		.13	.23	4.7	
Lemon, 1 medium	20	1		19	.4	10	.03	.01	.1	39
Liver: Beef, fried, 2 ounces	130	15	6	6	5.0	30,280	.15	2.37	9.4	15
Luncheon meat: Boiled ham, 2 ounces	135	11	10	6	1.6		.25	.09	1.5	
Canned, spiced or unspiced, 2 ounces	165	8	14	5	1.2		.18	.12	1.6	
Macaroni, enriched, 1 cup	155	5	1	8	1.3		.20	.11	1.5	
Macaroni and cheese, 1 cup	430	17	22	362	1.8	860	.20	.40	1.8	
Margarine, 1 tbs.	100		12	3		470		.01		
Mayonnaise, 1 tbs.	100		11		.1	40				
Milk: Whole, 1 cup	160	9	9	288	.1	350	.07	.41	.2	2
Skim (non-fat), 1 cup	90	9		296	.1	10	.09	.44	.2	2
Buttermilk, 1 cup	90	9		296	.1	10	.10	.44	.2	2
Mushrooms, canned, 1 cup	40	5		15	1.2		.04	.60	4.8	4
Nuts: Almonds, 1 cup shelled	850	26	77	332	6.7		.34	1.31	5.0	
Peanuts, roasted, 1 cup	840	37	72	107	3.0		.46	.19	24.7	
Oatmeal, 1 cup cooked	130	5	2	22	1.4		.19	.05	.2	
Oils: salad, cooking, 1 tbs.	125		14							
Oranges, 1 medium	65	1		54	.5	260	.13	.05	.5	66

Food and amount	Energy (Calories)	Protein (Gm.)	Fat (Gm.)	Calcium (Mg.)	Iron (Mg.)	Vitamin A (I.U.)	Vitamin B₁ (thiamine) (Mg.)	Vitamin B₂ (riboflavin) (Mg.)	Niacin (Mg.)	Vitamin C (ascorbic acid) (Mg.)
Orange juice, fresh, 1 cup	110	2	1	27	.5	500	.22	.07	1.0	124
Frozen, diluted with 3 parts water, 1 cup	100	1	...	25	.2	20	.10	.04	.5	96
Oysters, raw, 1 cup	160	20	4	226	13.2	740	.33	.43	6.0	...
Pancakes, wheat, 1 average	60	2	2	27	.4	30	.05	.06	.4	...
Peaches, raw, 1 medium	35	1	...	9	.5	1,320	.02	.05	1.0	7
Peanut butter, 1 tbs.	95	4	8	9	.3	...	.02	.02	2.4	...
Peas, green, 1 cup	115	9	1	37	2.9	860	.44	.17	3.7	33
Pie: Apple, 4-inch wedge	350	3	15	11	.4	40	.03	.03	.5	1
Cherry, 4-inch wedge	350	4	15	19	.4	590	.03	.03	.7	...
Lemon meringue, 4-inch wedge	305	4	12	17	.6	200	.04	.10	.2	4
Pineapple, raw, 1 cup diced	75	1	...	24	.7	100	.12	.04	.3	24
Pineapple juice, canned, 1 cup	135	1	...	37	.7	120	.12	.04	.5	22
Pizza (cheese), 5½-inch wedge	185	7	6	107	.7	290	.04	.12	.7	4
Pork: Roast, 3 ounces	310	21	24	9	2.7	...	.78	.72	4.7	...
Chop, with bone, 3.5 ounces	260	16	21	8	2.2	...	.63	.18	3.8	...
Potatoes: Baked, 1 medium	90	3	...	9	.7	...	.10	.04	1.7	20
French fried, deep fat, 10 pieces	155	2	7	9	.7	...	.07	.04	1.8	12
Mashed with milk, 1 cup	125	4	1	47	.8	50	.16	.10	2.0	19
Potato chips, 10	115	1	8	8	.4	...	.04	.01	1.0	3
Prune juice, 1 cup canned	200	1	...	36	10.5	...	.03	.03	1.0	5
Rice: White, enriched, 1 cup cooked	204	4.2	.2	14	.5	...	.10	.02	1.9	...
White, 1 cup cooked	225	4	...	21	1.8	...	.23	.02	2.1	...
Puffed, nutriments added, 1 cup	60	1	...	3	.3	30	.07	.01	.7	...
Salad dressings: Mayonnaise type, 1 tbs.	65	...	6	2	.1	...	...	...	...	...
French, 1 tbs.	65	...	6	2	.1	...	...	...	...	...
French, low calory, 1 tbs.	...	...	...	2	.1	...	...	...	...	...
Salmon: Canned, 3 ounces	120	17	5	167	.7	60	.03	.16	6.8	111
Sardines, canned, 3 ounces	175	20	9	372	2.5	190	.02	.17	4.6	...
Spaghetti, 1 cup cooked	155	5	1	11	1.3	...	.20	1.11	1.5	...
Spinach, 1 cup cooked	40	5	1	167	4.0	14,580	.13	.25	1.0	50
Sugar, 1 teaspoon	40	...	...	...	...	...	...	...	...	...
Tomato juice, canned, 1 cup	45	2	...	17	2.2	1,940	.12	.07	1.9	39
Tuna fish, 3 ounces	170	24	7	7	1.6	70	.04	.10	10.1	...
Veal, 3-ounce cutlet	185	23	9	9	2.7	...	.06	.21	4.6	111
Yogurt, from whole milk, 1 cup	150	7	8	272	.1	340	.07	.39	.2	2

NOTE: Gm.—gram; Mg.—milligram; I.U.—International Unit. Leaders (...) indicate little or no basis for assigning value.

Recommended Daily Dietary Allowances[1]

Designed for the maintenance of good nutrition of practically all healthy persons in the U.S.

Source: Food and Nutrition Board, National Academy of Sciences.

Persons	Age (years)	Wgt. Lbs.	Hgt. (in.)	Fat-Soluble Vitamins Vitamin A Activity (IU)	Vitamin D (IU)	Vitamin E Activity[2] (IU)	Water-Soluble Vitamins Ascorbic Acid (mg)	Folacin[3] (µg)	Niacin[4] (mg)	Riboflavin (mg)	Thiamin (mg)	Vitamin B_6 (mg)	Vitamin B_{12} (µg)	Minerals Calcium (mg)	Phosphorus (mg)	Iodine (µg)	Iron (mg)	Magnesium (mg)	Zinc (mg)
Infants	0.0–0.5	14	24	1,400	400	4	35	50	5	0.4	0.3	0.3	0.3	360	240	35	10	60	3
	0.5–1.0	20	28	2,000	400	5	35	50	8	0.6	0.5	0.4	0.3	540	400	45	15	70	5
Children	1–3	28	34	2,000	400	7	40	100	9	0.8	0.7	0.6	0.1	800	800	60	15	150	10
	4–6	44	44	2,500	400	9	40	200	12	1.1	0.9	0.9	1.5	800	800	80	10	200	10
	7–10	66	54	3,300	400	10	40	300	16	1.2	1.2	1.2	2.0	800	800	110	10	250	10
Males	11–14	97	63	5,000	400	12	45	400	18	1.5	1.4	1.6	3.0	1,200	1,200	130	18	350	15
	15–18	134	69	5,000	400	15	45	400	20	1.8	1.5	2.0	3.0	1,200	1,200	150	18	400	15
	19–22	147	69	5,000	400	15	45	400	20	1.8	1.5	2.0	3.0	800	800	140	10	350	15
	23–50	154	69	5,000	…	15	45	400	18	1.6	1.4	2.0	3.0	800	800	130	10	350	15
	51+	154	69	5,000	…	15	45	400	16	1.5	1.2	2.0	3.0	800	800	110	10	350	15
Females	11–14	97	62	4,000	400	12	45	400	16	1.3	1.2	1.6	3.0	1,200	1,200	115	18	300	15
	15–18	119	65	4,000	400	12	45	400	14	1.4	1.1	2.0	3.0	1,200	1,200	115	18	300	15
	19–22	128	65	4,000	400	12	45	400	14	1.4	1.1	2.0	3.0	800	800	100	18	300	15
	23–50	128	65	4,000	…	12	45	400	13	1.2	1.0	2.0	3.0	800	800	100	18	300	15
	51+	128	65	4,000	…	12	45	400	12	1.1	1.0	2.0	3.0	800	800	80	10	300	15
Pregnant				5,000	400	15	60	800	+2	+0.3	+0.3	2.5	4.0	1,200	1,200	125	18+[5]	450	20
Lactating				6,000	400	15	80	600	+4	+0.5	+0.3	2.5	4.0	1,200	1,200	150	18	450	25

[1] Allowances provide for individual variances among most normal persons living in the United States under usual environmental stresses. [2] Retinol equivalents. [3] Pure forms of folacin may be effective in doses of less than one-fourth. [4] Although expressed as niacin, the average 1 mg. of niacin is derived from each 60 mg. of dietary tryptophan. [5] Cannot be met by ordinary diets; use of supplemental iron is recommended. NOTE: mg—milligram; µg—microgram; IU—International Unit; Lbs.—Pounds; Wgt.—Weight; Hgt.—Height.

WORLD HISTORY
★
A GUIDE TO MAIN HISTORICAL, POLITICAL, ECONOMIC, GEOGRAPHIC, AND SOCIAL FACTS

WORLD'S TROUBLE SPOTS

After years of dire predictions, Southern Africa in 1976 appeared to be at the point of explosion at last. Soviet intervention in Angola, with Cuban troops on the ground, added the menacing ingredient of superpower conflict to the basic confrontation between blacks and whites.

The eventual victory of the Soviet-backed Popular Movement for the Liberation of Angola (MPLA), led by Agostinho Neto, was somewhat of an anti-climax. U.S. Secretary of State Henry A. Kissinger had invoked the image of a Marxist bastion for the military subjugation of the remaining white-ruled territories of South-West Africa (Namibia), Rhodesia and South Africa itself. Angola in the aftermath of war, however, looked much more like a severely damaged colonial economy preoccupied with recovery and the attainment of political unity it never had.

Whether Dr. Kissinger's assessment was an overreaction or not, the Angolan war had two important effects. There was an unquestionable psychological impact in the defeat of the UNITA faction backed by U.S. aid and South African troops, encouraging nationalist guerrillas to increase their efforts in Rhodesia and against the South African occupation of Namibia. More disturbing, demonstrations that began against the teaching of Afrikaans—the language of the Boers—in the schools of Soweto near Johannesburg grew into riots spreading throughout South Africa.

For the first time, voices within the Nationalist Party of Prime Minister Johannes Vorster called for a softening of government policy. In addition to dropping the study of Afrikaans, the government moved to permit Africans to buy land in the segregated areas to which they are confined. Some of the restrictions of "petty apartheid" also fell and by the end of the year interracial sports were being permitted.

Rhodesia

Meanwhile, Dr. Kissinger's new interest in Southern Africa produced other developments. His persuasion was credited with securing the withdrawal of South African troops and helicopters from Rhodesia, the most telling blow to the beleaguered government of Prime Minister Ian Smith. In a series of historic meetings with Vorster and subsequently Smith in September, Dr. Kissinger was able to secure the agreement of whites and blacks to a conference in Geneva which would negotiate the establishment of an interim government for Rhodesia. Although there was immediate disagreement on conditions, the U.S. and British governments insisted that the only advance commitment was to majority rule within two years.

At the same time, Kissinger sought to accelerate the 1978 independence date for Namibia, but militant Africans asserted that the U.S. Secretary of State had concentrated his efforts on Rhodesia and allowed Mr. Vorster to buy time in Namibia and at home. While U.S. and British diplomats exuded confidence in peaceful solutions, militant Africans insisted that they must win their fight with armed force.

Lebanon

Lebanon remained the open wound of the long-standing Middle East problem in 1976. After 18 months of fighting and dozens of ineffective cease-fires, 40,000 Lebanese were believed to have died in a struggle which by the end of the year had partitioned the country into three zones occupied by invading Syrian forces, rightist Christians and leftist Moslems led by the Palestine Liberation Organization. Meanwhile, there was no further progress toward an over-all settlement between Israel and the Arab states. Negotiations remained stalled where they had been a year earlier, with Israel refusing to attend a Geneva peace conference with the P.L.O. represented and Arab states refusing to come without the P.L.O.

The Mediterranean

Stalemate also marked the dispute in Cyprus, where Turkish troops continued to occupy 40% of the island to protect the Turkish minority. Turkey and Greece also found a new source of contention in conflicting claims to oil deposits beneath the Aegean sea. Here, however, they were able to agree on settling the problem by negotiation.

Although the possible instability of Spain, Portugal and Italy in the western Mediterranean worried NATO planners in 1975, post-Franco Spain appeared to be achieving its goal of democracy by degrees. A moderate Socialist government in Portugal was gaining credentials and Italy had survived Communist election gains without admitting the party to the cabinet.

Southeast Asia

A general leftward movement in the area in the wake of the Indo-China war was countered by a rightist coup in Thailand in October. Observers feared, however, that the new regime faced immediate and probably insurmountable difficulties.

East Asia

The succession of Hua Kuo-feng to Mao Tse-tung, holding even greater power as Communist Party chairman, Premier and head of the armed forces, dominated events in the area. Internal dissension despite the position accorded to Hua was indicated by the reported purge of leftist radicals, including Mao's widow. In Japan, the conservative party which has governed with only a brief interlude since World War II was threatened by the Lockheed scandal.

South Asia

The dictatorial rule imposed by Premier Indira Gandhi in India the year before tightened during 1976. Despite protests by opposition politicians, public support for Mrs. Gandhi appeared strong.

Latin America

Political ferment following the ouster of President Isabel Perón, with accompanying economic disorder, subsided at the year's end. Argentina and neighboring Chile, however, remained the continent's most anxiously watched states.

Don Shannon

(For later events, see News Chronology of 1976, pages 40–60.)

COUNTRIES OF THE WORLD BY GROUPINGS

NORTH AMERICA

Canada
Mexico*
United States*

SOUTH AMERICA

Argentina*
Bolivia*
Brazil *
Chile*
Colombia*
Ecuador*
Guyana
Paraguay*
Peru*
Surinam
Uruguay*
Venezuela*

CENTRAL AMERICA

Costa Rica*
El Salvador*
Guatemala*
Honduras*
Nicaragua*
Panama*

CARIBBEAN REGION

Bahamas
Barbados*
Cuba
Dominican Republic*
Grenada
Haiti*
Jamaica*
Trinidad and Tobago*

EUROPE

Albania
Andorra
Austria
Belgium
Bulgaria
Cyprus
Czechoslovakia

Denmark
Estonia
Finland
France
Germany (East)
Germany (West)
Greece
Hungary
Iceland
Ireland
Italy
Latvia
Liechtenstein
Lithuania
Luxembourg
Malta
Monaco
Netherlands
Norway
Poland
Portugal
Romania
San Marino
Spain
Sweden
Switzerland
U.S.S.R.
United Kingdom
Vatican City State
Yugoslavia

MIDDLE EAST

Bahrain
Egypt
Iran
Iraq
Israel
Jordan
Kuwait
Lebanon
Oman
Qatar
Saudi Arabia
Syrian Arab Republic
Turkey
United Arab Emirates

Yemen, People's Dem. Rep. of
Yemen

FAR EAST

China (mainland)
China (Taiwan)
Japan
Korea (North)
Korea (South)
Mongolian People's Rep.
Philippines

SOUTHEAST ASIA

Cambodia
Indonesia
Laos
Malaysia
Singapore
Thailand
Vietnam (North)
Vietnam (South)

SOUTH ASIA

Afghanistan
Bangladesh
Bhutan
Burma
India
Maldives
Nepal
Pakistan
Sri Lanka (Ceylon)

OCEANIA

Australia
Fiji
Nauru
New Zealand
Papua New Guinea
Tonga
Western Samoa

AFRICA

Algeria
Angola
Benin (Dahomey)
Botswana
Burundi

Cameroon
Cape Verde
Central African Rep.
Chad
Comoro Islands
Congo
Egypt
Equatorial Guinea
Ethiopia
Gabon
Gambia
Ghana
Guinea
Guinea-Bissau
Ivory Coast
Kenya
Lesotho
Liberia
Libya
Madagascar (Malagasy Rep.)
Malawi
Mali
Mauritania
Mauritius
Morocco
Mozambique
Niger
Nigeria
Rhodesia
Rwanda
São Tomé and Príncipe
Senegal
Seychelles
Sierra Leone
Somalia
South Africa, Rep. of
Sudan
Swaziland
Tanzania
Togo
Transkei
Tunisia
Uganda
Upper Volta
Zaire
Zambia

* Member of the Organization of American States (OAS).

WORLD HISTORY
Countries, Territories, Dependencies

For later developments, see News Chronology and Addenda in Table of Contents. A listing of countries by geographical division is on page 117.

AFGHANISTAN (Republic)

(Jamhouriat Afghánistán)

President: Mohammed Daud (1973).
Area: 249,999 sq mi. (647,497 sq km).
Population (est. 1976): 19,730,000 (Pushtu, 60.5%; Tajik, 30.7%; Uzbek, 5%; Mongolian and others, 3.8%).
Density per square mile: 78.9.
Capital: Kabul.
Largest cities (est. 1974): Kabul, 352,700; (est. 1973): Kandahar, 140,000; Baghlan, 110,900; Herat, 108,750.
Monetary unit: Afghani.
Languages: Pushtu and Dari Persian (both official).
Religion: Moslem (Sunni, 90%; Shiah, 10%).

Mohammed Daud, a former Prime Minister and brother-in-law of the King, ousted King Mohammad Zahir Shah in a coup July 17, 1973, while the King was out of the country. Daud, a retired general, proclaimed the country a republic, abolished all royal titles (including his own: Sardar, meaning prince) and promised reforms and to establish a democracy.

However, he ended a 10-year experiment with parliamentary democracy, suspending the 1964 Constitution, abolishing the Shura (parliament) and bringing the courts under the executive branch. He took for himself the titles of Prime Minister, Foreign Minister and Defense Minister, as well as President.

The country is ruled through a Central Committee. A Cabinet has been formed in which two of its 12 members are military men. Daud has promised a new Constitution in the future. The former King was born in 1914 and rose to the throne in 1933 when his father, Mohammed Nadir Shah, was assassinated. Prince Ahmad Shah, born in 1934, was heir apparent to the ousted King.

History. Wedged between the Soviet Union, China, Pakistan and Iran without an outlet to the sea, Afghanistan occupies the land route to India trod by many conquerors, among them Darius I and Alexander the Great. The Moslems conquered the country from the west, beginning in the 7th century A.D. Genghis Khan in the 13th century and Tamerlane in the 14th century were later conquerors. Tamerlane's descendant, Baber, used the Afghanistan town of Kabul from 1504 to achieve the Mogul conquest of India. The country was torn by tribal and family warfare until Nadir Shah of Persia conquered the area in the 18th century. His commander, Ahmad Shah, established an emirate in 1747 and unified the country.

A later ruler, Dost Mohammed, and his son, Sher Ali, reigned as Great Britain and Czarist Russia struggled for Central Asia and waged the Afghan Wars (1838–42 and 1878–81) against Britain, conflicts remembered for the massacre of the British at Kabul in 1842 and for the subsequent assaults on the Khyber Pass.

Afghanistan regained independence, though still under British influence, by the Anglo-Russian agreement of 1907, and full sovereignty by the Treaty of Rawalpindi in 1919. Emir Amanullah founded the kingdom in 1926.

Economic Conditions. Only a fifth of the soil is under cultivation, the greater part of the country being mountainous and rocky. Farming is confined to the fertile valleys and plains, sometimes with the aid of irrigation. Two crops a year are usually grown. Important ones include fruits and nuts, castor beans, cereals, madder, tobacco, cotton and vegetables. Wheat is the staple food in Afghanistan. The fat-tailed indigenous sheep is a principal source of meat and wearing apparel.

Industry is still in a primary stage of development in Afghanistan. Manufactures include cotton and woolen textiles and clothing, soap, leather, matches, beet sugar and furniture.

The country's mineral and forest resources are largely unexploited.

Chief exports in 1974–75 were fruits and nuts (40%), cotton (15%), natural gas (12%), carpets (9%) and karakul (persian lamb) skins (6%). Leading customers in 1972–73 were U.S.S.R. (29%), India (24%), United Kingdom (16%), West Germany (6%). Leading suppliers were U.S.S.R. (25%), Japan (15%), U.S. (11%), West Germany (9%), India (7%).

Afghanistan has no railways or navigable streams. Camels and pack horses are still used.

Natural Features. Afghanistan, approximately the size of Texas, is split east to west by the Hindu Kush mountain range, rising in the east to heights of 24,000 feet. With the exception of the southwest, most of the country is covered by high snow-capped mountains and deep valleys.

ALBANIA (People's Republic)

(Republíka Popullóre e Shqipërísë)

President of Presidium: Haxhi Lleshi (1953).
Premier: Mehmet Shehu (1953).
Area: 11,100 sq mi. (28,748 sq km).
Population (est. 1976): 2,545,000.
Density per square mile: 229.3.
Capital and largest city (est. 1975): Tirana, 180,000.
Monetary unit: Lek.
Language: Albanian.
Religions: Moslem, 70%; Greek Orthodox, 20%; Roman Catholic, 10%.

Under its Constitution, adopted in 1946, Albania has a People's Democracy government. Supreme power is vested in the popularly elected National Assembly, to which the Cabinet, headed by the Premier, is responsible. The 240 members of the National Assembly all belong to the Labor Party and Democratic Front.

Political Party. Labor (Communist) Party, led by First Secretary Enver Hoxha.

History. Albania proclaimed its independence on Nov. 28, 1912, after a history of Roman, Byzantine, and Turkish dominion.

A battlefield in World War I, Albania reasserted its independence in 1920. A chief, Ahmet Zogu, proclaimed himself President in 1925 and monarch (King Zog) in 1928. Italy under Benito Mussolini drove him into exile in 1939 and annexed the country. The Communists under Enver Hoxha established a government in 1944, issuing a Constitution in 1946, amended in 1950, declaring the country a people's republic. Close relations with Yugoslavia ended in 1948 with the Soviet-Yugoslav break, and with the U.S.S.R. in 1961 with the Soviet-Chinese rupture. Thereafter, Albania functioned as a Peking satellite, receiving massive Chinese aid to offset the Soviet boycott.

In 1967, the regime closed all of the nation's 2,169 churches and mosques in a move to make the country "the first atheist state in the world."

But in 1970, the country began re-emerging from its isolation from the West, setting up trade ties with Greece and exchanging diplomatic representatives with several West European nations.

Economic Conditions. Albania is still a primitive country where each family tries to provide most of its own needs. Nearly the whole population is engaged in combined farming and stock raising. Only a small portion of the central part is fit for tilling. Corn is the chief crop. Others are grains, tobacco, olives and citrus fruit.

Factories produce food products, cement and textiles; a large dam and power station was completed near Tirana in 1950.

Mineral wealth, thought to be considerable, is relatively unexploited.

Albania's postwar trade has shifted from the U.S.S.R. because of political and ideological differences that resulted from the Tirana Government's siding with Communist China.

Chief exports in 1964 were fuels, minerals, and metals (incl. bitumen, crude oil, iron ore, chrome ore, and copper) (54%), foodstuffs (incl. vegetables, wine and fruit) (23%) and raw materials (incl. tobacco and wool) (17%). Leading customers were China (40%), Czechoslovakia (19%), East Germany (10%). Leading suppliers were China (63%), Czechoslovakia (10%), Poland (8%).

Natural Features. Albania is a mountainous state, largely over 3,000 feet above sea level with a narrow, marshy coastal plain crossed by several rivers.

The interior mountain plateaus and basins contain the centers of population.

ALGERIA (Republic)

(République Algérienne Démocratique et Populaire)

President: Houari Boumediène (1965).
Area: 919,595 sq mi. (2,381,741 sq km).
Population (est. 1976): 17,290,000.
Density per square mile: 18.8.
Capital: Algiers.
Largest cities (est. 1970): Algiers, 1,839,000; (1966 census): Oran, 327,493; Constantine, 243,558; Annaba (Bône), 152,006.
Monetary unit: Algerian dinar.
Languages: Arabic and French.
Religion: Moslem.

Algeria is governed by its National Revolutionary Council of 24 members presided over by President Houari Boumediène, who also heads the Cabinet and is the Minister of Defense. In September 1974 Boumediène was named the nation's President for life.

Political Party. The National Liberation Front, which led the struggle for independence from France, is the only legal party.

History. As ancient Numidia, Algeria became a Roman colony at the close of the Punic Wars (145 B.C.). Conquered by the Vandals about A.D. 440, it fell from a high state of civilization to virtual barbarism, from which it partially recovered after invasion by the Moslems about A.D. 650.

In 1492 the Moors and Jews, who had been expelled from Spain, settled in Algeria. Falling under Turkish control in 1518, Algiers became for three centuries the headquarters of the Barbary pirates. The French took Algiers in 1830 and made it a part of France in 1848.

The fight by Algerian nationalists for independence had widespread political, diplomatic, military and financial repercussions in France. Politically, it brought General de Gaulle to power when the Army and extremist French colonists virtually seceded, set up a "Committee of Public Safety" and demanded that de Gaulle be given power. Ironically, it was General de Gaulle who determined to put an end to the fighting by granting Algeria self-determination and independence, while his former Army and French colonial supporters in Algeria joined to create a Secret Army Organization (OAS), a terrorist group which tried to block independence. But metropolitan France, weary of continued warfare, voted by some 15,-000,000 to 5,000,000 in January 1961, to approve de Gaulle's proposals.

On July 5, 1962, Algeria was proclaimed independent. A constituent assembly, elected in September 1962, adopted a Constitution, which was ratified by referendum in September 1963. In October 1963, Ahmed Ben Bella was elected President. He began to nationalize foreign holdings and aroused opposition. He was overthrown in a military coup on June 19, 1965, by Col. Houari Boumediène, who suspended the Constitution and sought to restore financial stability. While retaining close economic and financial relations with France and the United States, Algeria entered the Arab bloc and joined the war against Israel in 1967. Thereafter, the Soviet Union stepped up development aid.

Friction with Morocco continued in 1976 as Algeria opposed the annexation of the Spanish Sahara by Morocco and Mauritania following a mass invasion of the former Spanish colony by Moroccan civilians. Algeria formally recognized a Saharan Arab Democratic Republic—composed of Polisario front leaders who fought unsuccessfully for an independent Sahara—on Feb. 27, 1976. The move was accompanied by a break in diplomatic relations with Morocco.

Economic Conditions. The principal crops are wheat, barley and oats. Algeria is a leading wine producer.

European industries include those dependent on crops, such as distilling and oil and flour milling, as well as the making of leather, tobacco and matches. There are also small native industries.

Algeria is a leading producer of phosphates. Iron ore, zinc, lead, crude petroleum and salt are also important minerals.

Chief exports in 1974 were crude oil (88%) and petroleum products (5%). Leading customers in 1973 were France (22%), West Germany (22%), Italy (10%), Spain (9%), U.S. (6%), United Kingdom (6%). Leading suppliers were France (32%), West Germany (14%), U.S. (8%), Italy (8%), Spain (5%), Belgium-Luxembourg (5%).

Natural Features. Low plains cover small areas near the coast, but 68% of Algeria is a plateau between 2,625 and 5,250 feet above sea level. The region between the Sahara and the Mediterranean reaches a high point of 7,641 feet.

ANDORRA (Principality)

(Les Vallées d'Andorre—Valls d'Andorra)

Episcopal Co-Prince: Bishop of Urgel.
French Co-Prince: Valéry Giscard d'Estaing, President of France.
First Syndic: Julià Reig-Ribó (1974).
Area: 175 sq mi. (453 sq km).
Population (est. 1976): 30,000.
Density per square mile: 171.4.
Capital (est. 1975): Andorra la Vella, 10,900.
Monetary units: French franc and Spanish peseta.
Languages: Catalán (official); French, Spanish.
Religion: Roman Catholic.

A Council General of 24 members, elected for four years, chooses the First Syndic and Second Syndic.

Political Parties. There are no political parties.

History. An autonomous and semi-independent principality on the French-Spanish border, Andorra, high in the Pyrenees, has been under the joint suzerainty of the French state and the Spanish bishops of Urgel since 1278.

Economic Conditions. With animal husbandry the principal occupation, the country survives as an example of medieval agrarian communal organization. There are no income taxes or customs duties (smuggling imports abroad is an important activity). The inhabitants enjoy the cheapest electricity, gasoline, tobacco, and alcoholic beverages in Europe. They also have no social services.

ANGOLA (People's Republic of)

President: Agostinho Neto (1976).
Prime Minister: Lopo do Nascimento (1976).
Area: 481,350 sq mi. (1,246,700 sq km).
Population (est. 1975): 6,000,000.
Density per square mile: 12.5
Capital and largest city (est. 1970): Luanda, 480,600.
Monetary unit: Angola escudo.
Languages: Bantu and Portuguese.
Religion: Animist, Roman Catholic, Protestant.

Last of Portugal's African colonies to gain independence, Angola was born amid civil war Nov. 11, 1975. Four months later, the Popular Movement for the Liberation of Angola (MPLA) conquered two rival factions with the aid of Soviet weapons and Cuban troops. As the United States, its allies and China backed the losers, the struggle in the depths of Africa built international tensions that were only partly abated by Cuban Premier Fidel Castro's April pledge that he would withdraw all troops by the end of 1976.

The U.S. nevertheless vetoed Angolan membership in the United Nations June 23, and the subsequent trial and execution of four Western mercenaries—three Britons and one American, Daniel F. Gearhart—was expected to delay Angola's acceptance further.

History. Discovered by Portuguese navigator Diego Cao in 1482, Angola became a link in trade with India and the Far East. Later it was a major source of slaves for Portugal's New World colony of Brazil. Development of the interior began after the treaty of Berlin in 1885 fixed the colony's borders and British and Portuguese investment pushed mining, railways and agriculture.

Following World War II, independence movements began but were sternly suppressed by military force. Lisbon insisted that its African possessions were not colonies, but overseas provinces of the motherland. Despite rising world opinion, Portugal maintained its rigid policy until the April revolution of 1974 brought a total reversal and President Francisco da Costa Gomes, on Jan. 15, 1975, signed an agreement to liberate Angola. The plan called for election of a constituent assembly and a settlement of differences by the MPLA and the National Front for the Liberation of Angola (FNLA) and the National Union for the Total Independence of Angola (UNITA).

Despite covert aid to FNLA by the United States and open support by neighboring Zaire for the Front's leader, Holden Roberto, the MPLA had the initial advantage of strength in the capital region. Cuban troops were introduced in October and soon routed the poorly trained and equipped FNLA and UNITA forces. U.S. Secretary of State Henry A. Kissinger warned against outside intervention and asked for increased aid funds for FNLA and UNITA but Congress refused.

The Organization of African Unity, split over the issue earlier, recognized the MPLA government led by Agostinho Neto on Feb. 11, 1976, and the People's Republic of Angola became the 47th member of the organization.

The new government nationalized 19 major industries May 19, mostly Portuguese-owned. This, together with Lisbon's objection to the refueling of Cuban troop transports in the Azores, led to a break between the former mother country and Angola on May 19.

Although militarily victorious, Neto's regime had yet to consolidate its power in opposition strongholds in the east and south. Less militantly Marxist than their colleagues in the former East African colony of Mozambique, the new leaders sought help from both the Western and Eastern worlds. Yet the regime conducted a dramatic trial of 13 British and U.S. mercenaries and executed four, ignoring pleas from their governments and using the trial to attack Washington.

Economic Conditions. Angola is agriculturally rich among African nations, exporting coffee, cotton, corn, rice, sisal, sugar and timber before independence. Light industrial products included cigarettes, textiles, processed foods and fish meal. Diamonds, gold, iron and other minerals are traditional exports, and in recent years oil produced by the Gulf Oil Corporation in the enclave of Cabinda has become an important source of revenue. Dislocation by the war was reported to have reduced the Angolan economy to 20% of its pre-independence volume.

Chief exports in 1973 were crude oil (29%), coffee (26%), diamonds (10%), and iron ore (6%). Leading customers were U.S. (28%), Portugal (25%), Canada (10%), Japan (9%), West Germany (5%). Leading suppliers were Portugal (26%), West Germany (13%), U.S. (10%), United Kingdom (8%), France (7%), South Africa (6%), Japan (6%).

ARGENTINA (Republic)

(República Argentina)

President: Gen. Jorge Rafael Videla (1976).
Area: 1,072,157 sq mi. (2,776,889 sq km).
Population (est. 1976): 25,715,000 (approximately 97% of European descent, chiefly Spanish and Italian; 3% Indian and others).
Density per square mile: 24.0.
Capital: Buenos Aires.
Largest cities (est. 1975): Buenos Aires, 2,977,000; (1970 census): Rosario, 810,840*; Córdoba, 798,663*; La Plata, 506,287*; Mendoza, 470,896.*
Monetary unit: Peso.
Language: Spanish.
Religions: Roman Catholic, 93.6%; Protestant, 1.9%; Jewish, 1.6%; others and unknown, 2.9%.

Argentina is a federal union of 22 provinces and the federal district. Under the Constitution of 1853 (restored by a Constituent National Convention in 1957 and amended in 1972), the President and Vice President are elected every four years by direct vote. The President appoints his Cabinet. The Vice President presides over the Senate but has no other powers. The Congress consists of two houses: a 69-member Senate and a 243-member Chamber of Deputies. All legislators are elected by direct vote for four-year terms.

Major Political Parties. Justicialista Liberation Party, with 45 of the 69 Senate seats and 146 of the 243 Chamber seats. Major opposition is the Radical Civic Union (15 Senators, 51 Deputies).

History. Discovered in 1516 by Juan Díaz de Solís, Argentina developed slowly under Spanish colonial rule. Buenos Aires was settled in 1580; the cattle industry was thriving as early as 1600.

Invading British forces were expelled in 1806–07, and when Napoleon conquered Spain, the Argentinians set up their own government in the name of

*For urban agglomeration.

the Spanish King in 1810. On July 9, 1816, independence was formally declared.

The Rosas dictatorship (1835–52) only temporarily ended strife between Buenos Aires and the rest of the country and between adherents of a strong central government and states' rights. Despite these internal differences, the country prospered, and electoral reforms were enacted in 1912.

As in World War I, Argentina proclaimed neutrality at the outbreak of World War II, but in general cooperated in hemispheric defense programs. In the closing months of the war, the nation declared war on the Axis (Mar. 27, 1945) and signed the Act of Chapultepec the following Apr. 4. Diplomatic recognition and admission to the U.N. followed. Juan D. Perón, an army colonel, emerged as strongman and won the 1946 presidential elections. He was reelected in 1951.

Long-smoldering opposition, fanned by worsening relations with the Catholic Church, finally resulted in Perón's overthrow on Sept. 19, 1955, in a coup led by the armed forces. Perón fled to exile and his party and Congress were dissolved.

Constitutional government was restored with the election of Arturo Frondizi to the presidency with Peronista support in 1958. Peronista electoral victories led the armed forces to remove Frondizi on Mar. 29, 1962, replacing him with José María Guido. Political turmoil continued until the election to the presidency in 1964 of Arturo Illía. Although he annulled oil contracts with U.S. firms and inflated the currency to win popular support, he failed, and a military coup in 1966 installed as President Lieut. Gen. Juan Carlos Onganía.

But Onganía, whose rule became increasingly personal, was himself ousted in June, 1970, by the junta (the three service chiefs) and replaced by Brig. Gen. Roberto Marcelo Levingston, a former army intelligence chief. The junta held "guiding power" intended to preclude one-man rule.

Levingston was in turn dismissed in 1971 by Gen. Alejandro Agustín Lanusse, army chief of staff and long-time power behind the throne. But continued economic crises (inflation doubling every three years), urban guerrilla terrorism and political kidnappings led to the restoration of constitutional government by Lanusse, (who had spent four years in jail under Perón).

Turned down by the junta as a presidential candidate, Perón endorsed Hector Cámpora from his exile in Spain. As the candidate of a 15-party coalition led by the Justicialista Liberation Party, Cámpora narrowly won the first free election since 1952. He resigned July 13, 1973, seven weeks after his inauguration, in a move to restore power to Perón, who returned from exile to run for President with his third wife, Maria Estela (Isabel) Martínez de Perón as his running mate. They were swept in with 61% of the vote in an election held Sept. 23, 1973.

Perón launched a three-year plan to double the economic growth rate and boost family incomes by a third; it involved price freezes, wage boosts and increased government spending. He persuaded subsidiaries of two U.S. auto firms to sell vehicles to Cuba under a $1.2-billion export grant. It was an early break in the hemispheric boycott of Cuba.

Perón died of a heart attack at the age of 78 on July 1, 1974. His widow became the hemisphere's first woman chief of state, but she took over a nation racked by acute economic and political polarization reflected in mounting civil disorders.

A two-day general strike called by the 3.5 million-member General Confederation of Labor—the historic bedrock of Peronism—persuaded the government on July 8, 1975, to rescind a plan to clamp a 50% ceiling on pay raises.

Mrs. Perón was re-elected head of the Peronist movement Aug. 24, 1975 at a tumultuous party Congress at which 118 of 238 delegates walked out before the vote. In mid-September she announced she would take a month-long leave of absence to recover from nervous strain and turned the presidential duties over to Italo A. Luder, president of the Senate.

Returning to take up her duties again Oct. 16, Mrs. Perón was greeted with demands for her resignation as both the economic recession and terrorism increased. The inflation rate for 1975 was 334.8%, compared with 40% for 1974, and labor protest mounted despite massive wage boosts.

The long-anticipated military revolt came March 24, 1976, with a junta composed of Army Lt. Gen. Jorge Rafael Videla, Adm. Emilio Massera and Air Force Brig. Orlando Agosti taking power. Mrs. Perón and her closest advisers were arrested and subsequently charged with misuse of government funds, while thousands of Peronist government officials and labor leaders were placed under detention.

Videla took office as President March 29 and formed a government of two civilians—including José Martínez de Hoz as Finance Minister—and six military officers. The new regime set a harsh economic policy aimed at restoring the peso. It suspended the Justicialista (Peronist) Party as well as the Communist Party and also decreed new security laws and censorship.

Economic Conditions. A farming and stock-raising nation, Argentina devotes some 40% of its area to pasture and 10% to cultivation. Cotton, sugar cane and fruits are important, and Argentina is the world's largest producer of yerba maté (Paraguay tea).

Cattle raising predominates on the pampas, especially in Buenos Aires Province. Sheep raising is more important in Patagonia.

The principal industry is meat packing, followed by flour milling, textiles, sugar refining and dairy products.

Argentina must import most of nearly every mineral it uses. Oil is produced in Patagonia. The government announced discovery of uranium deposits in Argentina in February, 1947.

Chief exports in 1973 were meat (24%), corn (11%), wheat (8%), wool (6%) and animal feedstuffs (5%). Leading customers were Italy (12%), Brazil (10%), West Germany (8%), U.S. (8%), Chile (7%), Kuwait (6%), The Netherlands (6%), United Kingdom (6%). Leading suppliers were U.S. (22%), Japan (11%), West Germany (11%), Brazil (9%), Italy (8%), U.K. (5%).

Natural Features. Second in South America to Brazil in size and population, Argentina is a plain, rising from the Atlantic to the Chilean border and the towering Andes peaks, including Aconcagua (23,034 ft), the highest peak in the world outside Asia. The northern area is the swampy and partly wooded Gran Chaco. South of that are the rolling, fertile pampas, rich for agriculture and grazing and supporting most of

Argentina's population. Next southward is Patagonia, a region of cool, arid steppes with some wooded and fertile sections. The eastern part of Tierra del Fuego, the island southern tip of South America, belongs to Argentina.

The three great rivers which make up the Plata system—the Paraná, Paraguay and Uruguay—are important commercial arteries in northern Argentina. Rosario and Santa Fé, 260 and 360 miles, respectively, above Buenos Aires on the Paraná, are accessible to ocean vessels.

AUSTRALIA, Commonwealth of

(Member of Commonwealth of Nations)

Sovereign: Queen Elizabeth II.
Governor-General: Sir John Robert Kerr (1974).
Prime Minister: Malcolm Fraser (1975).
Area: 2,967,892 sq mi. (7,686,848 sq km).
Population (est. 1976): 13,685,000 (including aborigines).
Density per square mile: 4.6.
Capital (est. 1974): Canberra, 197,900.
Largest cities (est 1974): Sydney, 2,898,330; Melbourne, 2,620,400; Brisbane, 940,800; Adelaide, 885,400; Perth, 760,000; Hobart, 161,320.
Monetary unit: Australian dollar.
Language: English.
Religions (1971 census): Anglican, 31.3%; Roman Catholic, 27.0%; Presbyterian, 8.3%; Methodist, 8.6%; other Christians, 11.2%; others, 13.6%.

The Federal Parliament consists of a bicameral legislature. The House of Representatives has 127 members elected for three years by adult (male and female) suffrage. The Senate has 64 members elected by popular vote for six years. One-half of the Senate is elected every three years. Voting is compulsory at 18. Federal judicial power is vested in a Federal Supreme Court of seven justices, appointed by the Governor-General in Council. Each of the states has its own judicial system.

Major Political Parties. Liberal Party (68 of 127 seats in House of Representatives), led by Prime Minister Malcolm Fraser; Labor Party (36 seats), led by Gough Whitlam; National Country Party (23 seats), led by J. Douglas Anthony.

History. Australia was the last continent to be discovered. Dutch, Portuguese and Spanish ships sighted it in the 17th century; the Dutch landed at the Gulf of Carpentaria in March 1606. In 1642, Abel Tasman (for whom Tasmania was named) proved that Australia was not part of the Antarctic Continent. Australia was called New Holland, Botany Bay and New South Wales until about 1820.

Captain James Cook, in 1770, claimed possession for Great Britain. A British penal colony was set up at what is now Sydney, then Port Jackson, in 1788, and about 161,000 transported English convicts were settled there until the system was suspended in 1839.

Free settlers established six colonies: New South Wales (1786), Tasmania (then Van Diemen's Land) (1825), Western Australia (1829), South Australia (1834), Victoria (1851) and Queensland (1859).

Sheep raising and wheat growing built the economy, and the white population, which had dwindled to 34,000 in 1820, grew to 400,000 by 1850. Discovery of gold in Victoria in 1851 led immigrants to pour in. The six colonies became states and in 1901 federated into the Commonwealth of Australia with a constitution merging British parliamentary tradition and U. S. federal experience. Australia became known for liberal legislation: free compulsory education, protected trade unionism with industrial conciliation and arbitration, the "Australian" ballot facilitating selection, the secret ballot, woman suffrage, maternity allowances, and sickness and old age pensions. During World War II child subsidies and unemployment and health insurance were added. Suffrage is universal, voting compulsory. New South Wales ceded territory for a new capital at Canberra in 1911. The seat of Parliament was established there in 1927.

The Labor Government of Prime Minister Gough Whitlam, elected in 1972, was itself a victim of the twin economic troubles which hit Australia along with most of the world—inflation and recession. Opposition parties blocked passage of government budget requests to force Whitlam to resign and, in what he called an unconstitutional action, Gov. Gen. Sir John Kerr dissolved both houses of Parliament on Nov. 11, 1975. Kerr asked Malcolm Fraser, the Liberal Party chief, to form a caretaker government until a new general election on Dec. 13.

Reversing Whitlam's policies of cutting ties with Britain and the United States and moving closer to the Third World countries, Fraser early in 1976 reinstated the traditional national anthem, "God Save the Queen," and in July made a state visit to the United States to reaffirm the U.S.-Australian alliance.

Economic Conditions. About 55% of Australia's total area is suitable (mining excepted) only for pastoral pursuits.

Sugar and cotton are grown in Queensland and New South Wales, tobacco in Northeast Victoria and vines chiefly in South Australia and Victoria.

New South Wales is the leading industrial state. Power for industry comes mainly from coal.

Australia possesses considerable mineral resources. Most important is gold, followed by coal, mined near Sydney and Brisbane, and in eastern Tasmania. The Broken Hill mines in New South Wales are one of the most valuable silver-led-zinc areas in the world. Other important minerals include tin, copper, iron ore, bauxite and uranium. Petroleum was discovered in Western Australia in 1953, at Moonie, Queensland. A 190-mile pipeline has been built to Brisbane.

Forest products of Australia include timber (rough sawn), eucalyptus oil, sandalwood oil, tan bark and yacca gum. Sea products include bêche-de-mer, oysters, pearls, pearl shell, tortoise shell and agar-agar.

Chief exports in 1973-74 were wool (17%), meat (12%), wheat (7%), iron ore (7%) and coal (5%). Leading customers in 1974 were Japan (29%), U.S. (9%), New Zealand (7%), United Kingdom (6%). Leading suppliers were U.S. (21%), Japan (18%), U.K. (14%), West Germany (7%).

Natural Features. Australia is approximately equal in area to the United States (excluding Alaska and Hawaii) and is more than three-fourths the size of Europe.

Along the east coast, ranges of mountains run from north to south, reaching their highest point in Mt. Kosciusko (7,352 ft.). The western half of the continent is occupied by a desert plateau which rises into barren, rolling hills near the west coast. It includes the Great Victoria Desert, to the south, and the Great Sandy Desert, to the north. The island of Tasmania (26,215 sq. mi.) lies off the southeastern coast.

Australian Dependencies

Norfolk Island (14 sq. mi.) was placed under Australian administration in 1914. Population in 1973 was about 1,800.

The Ashmore and Cartier Islands (.8 sq. mi.) were placed under Australian administration in 1931. In 1938 the islands, which are uninhabited, were annexed to the Northern Territory.

The Australian Antarctic Territory (2,472,000 sq. mi.), comprising all the islands and territories, other than Adélie Land, situated south of 60° south latitude and lying between 160° and 45° east longitude, was placed under Australian administration in 1936.

Heard Island and the McDonald Islands (158 sq. mi.) were placed under Australian administration in 1947.

The Cocos (Keeling) Islands (5.5 sq. mi.) were placed under Australian administration in 1955. Population in 1974 was about 640.

Christmas Island (52 sq. mi.) was placed under Australian administration in 1958. Population in 1974 was about 3,000.

Coral Sea Islands (400,000 sq. mi., but only a few sq. mi. of land) became a territory of Australia in 1969. There is no permanent population on the islands.

AUSTRIA (Republic)

(Republik Österreich)

President: Rudolf Kirschläger (1974).
Chancellor: Bruno Kreisky (1970).
Area: 32,375 sq mi. (83,849 sq km).
Population (est. 1975 by U.N.): 7,520,000.
Density per square mile: 232.3.
Capital: Vienna.
Largest cities (1971 census): Vienna, 1,614,841; Graz, 248,500; Linz, 202,874; Salzburg, 128,845; Innsbruck, 115,197; Klagenfurt, 74,326.
Monetary unit: Schilling.
Language: German.
Religions (1970): Roman Catholic, 89%; Protestant, 6%; others, 5%.

The federal republic of Austria is composed of nine provinces (Länder), including Vienna. The President is elected by the people directly for a term of six years. The bicameral legislature consists of the Bundesrat, with 58 members chosen by the provincial assemblies, and the Nationalrat, with 183 members popularly elected for four years. Presidency of the Bundesrat revolves each six months, going to the provinces in alphabetical order.

Major Political Parties. Socialist Party (93 of 183

seats in Nationalrat), led by Chancellor Bruno Kreisky; People's Party (80 seats); Freiheitliche Partei (10 seats).

History. Settled in prehistoric times, the Central European land that is now Austria was overrun in pre-Roman times by various tribes, including the Celts. Upon the fall of the Roman empire the country became a margravate of Charlemagne's empire. In 1252, Ottokar, King of Bohemia, gained possession, only to lose the territories to Rudolf of Hapsburg in 1278. Thereafter, until World War I, Austria's history was largely that of its ruling house, the Hapsburgs.

Hapsburg power grew over three centuries until Charles V (1519–56) ruled a vast area of Europe. In 1806, during the Napoleonic Wars, Emperor Francis I relinquished the Holy Roman Empire's crown.

Austria emerged from the Congress of Vienna in 1815 as the Continent's dominant power. The *Ausgleich* of 1867 provided for a dual sovereignty, the empire of Austria and the kingdom of Hungary, under Francis Joseph I, who ruled until his death on Nov. 21, 1916. He was succeeded by his grandnephew, Charles I.

During World War I, Austria-Hungary was one of the Central Powers with Germany, Bulgaria, and Turkey; and the war left the country in political chaos and economic ruin. Austria, shorn of Hungary, was proclaimed a republic in 1918 and the monarchy was dissolved in 1919.

A parliamentary democracy was set up by the Constitution of Nov. 10, 1920. To check the power of Nazis advocating union with Germany, Chancellor Engelbert Dollfuss in 1933 established a dictatorship but was assassinated by the Nazis on July 25, 1934. Kurt von Schuschnigg, his successor, struggled to keep Austria independent, but on Mar. 12, 1938, German troops occupied the country and Hitler proclaimed its *Anschluss* (union) with Germany, annexing it to the Third Reich.

After World War II the United States and Great Britain declared the Austrians a "liberated" people. But the Russians prolonged the occupation. Finally Austria concluded a state treaty with the U.S.S.R. and the other occupying powers and regained her independence on May 15, 1955. The second Austrian republic, established Dec. 19, 1945, on the basis of the 1920 Constitution amended in 1929, was declared by the federal parliament to be permanently neutral. Austria became a member of the Council of Europe in 1956.

Vienna has become a headquarters for international organizations, such as the International Atomic Energy Agency and the United Nations Industrial Development Organization. In 1974 the Organization of Petroleum Exporting Countries (O.P.E.C.) established headquarters there and in December 1975 was the target of a sensational attack by Palestinian guerrillas. Three persons were killed and 11 O.P.E.C. ministers and 70 other hostages were taken to Algeria by the guerrillas in a hijacked Austrian airliner.

Economic Conditions. Agriculture employs approximately one-third of the population but the country is heavily dependent on imported foodstuffs. Mixed farming predominates. Rye and wheat are the leading cereals. Stock raising and dairy farming are of importance.

Austria is primarily an industrial country, with 41% of the population engaged in industry. Most important are the metallurgical, engineering, textile and food-processing industries. Nationalized plants employ one fifth of the industrial labor force. Major steel and aluminum plants are in Upper Austria.

Austria possesses valuable mineral resources. In Styria lies one of the largest European deposits of iron ore. Copper is mined in Salzburg, Tyrol and Lower Austria, and lead and zinc in Carinthia. Large supplies of coal and coke must be imported, but extensive water power resources are available for exploitation. Petroleum fields are in the Zistersdorf and Mühlberg areas.

Chief exports in 1974 were machinery (19%), iron and steel (13%), textile yarns and fabrics (11%), timber (7%), chemicals (10%) and paper and board (6%). Leading customers were EEC (44%; incl. West Germany 20%, Italy 10%, United Kingdom 6%), Switzerland (10%), Yugoslavia (5%). Leading suppliers were EEC (62%; incl. West Germany 40% and Italy 7%) and Switzerland (7%).

Austria's tourist trade annually covers almost completely the country's balance-of-trade deficit.

Natural Features. Austria covers an area about equal to that of Scotland and includes much of the mountainous territory of the eastern Alps (about 92% of the country). The country contains many snowfields, glaciers, and snow-capped peaks. The principal river, is the Danube. Forests and woodlands cover about 40%.

BAHAMAS (Independent Commonwealth)

(Member of Commonwealth of Nations)

Governor-General: Sir Milo Butler, Sr. (1973).
Prime Minister: Lynden O. Pindling (1967).
Area: 5,382 sq mi. (13,935 sq km).
Population (est. 1976): 215,000.
Density per square mile: 41.8.
Capital (est. 1975 for urban agglomeration): Nassau, 120,000.
Monetary unit: Bahaman dollar.
Language: English.
Religions: Baptist, 28.8%; Anglican, 22.7%; Roman Catholic, 22.5%; Methodist, 7.3%.

The Bahamas are an archipelago of about 3,000 islands, islets (cays) and rocks, east of Florida and north of Cuba, extending from northwest to southeast for about 800 miles. Only about 20 of the islands are inhabited; the most important is New Providence (83 sq. mi.) on which Nassau is located. Other islands include Grand Bahama, Abaco, Eleuthera, Andros, Cat Island, San Salvador (or Watling's Island), Exuma, Long Island, Crooked Island, Acklins Island, Mayaguana, and Inagua. The islands were reached by Columbus in October, 1492, and were a favorite pirate resort in the early 18th century. They have been a crown colony since 1717. The colony was granted internal self-government on Jan. 7, 1964.

The Bahamas moved toward greater autonomy in 1968 after the overwhelming victory in general elections of the Progressive Liberal Party, led by Prime Minister Pindling. The black leader's party won 29 seats in the House of Assembly to only 7 for the predominantly white United Bahamians, who had controlled the islands for decades before Pindling became Prime Minister in 1967.

With its new mandate from the 85%-black population, Pindling's government negotiated a new Constitution with Britain under which the colony became the Commonwealth of the Bahama Islands in 1969. On July 10, 1973, the Bahamas became an independent nation. The Bahamas established diplomatic relations with Cuba in 1974.

Major Political Parties. Progressive Liberal Party (30 of 38 seats in Parliament), led by Prime Minister Pindling, and the Free National Movement (8 seats).

Economic Conditions: The principal agriculture products are tomatos, citrus fruit and sisal. From the sea come sponges, lobsters and crayfish. Chief exports are cement, rum and pulpwood.

Tourism is the main source of foreign exchange. In 1972, more than 1.5 million visitors spent over $285 million in the islands.

Chief exports in 1974 were petroleum products (91%). Leading customers were U.S. (83%) and Puerto Rico (8%). Leading suppliers were Saudi Arabia (26%), Nigeria (17%), Iran (15%), U.S. (12%), Libya (8%), Gabon (5%), Canada (5%).

BAHRAIN (State of)

Amir: Sheik Isa bin Sulman al Khalifa.
Area: 240 sq mi. (622 sq km).
Population (est. 1976): 275,000.
Density per square mile: 1,145.8.
Capital (est. 1974): Manama, 98,300.
Monetary unit: Bahrain dinar.
Languages: Arabic (official), Persian, English.
Religion: Moslem.

A sheikdom which passed from the Persians to the Al Khalifa family from Arabia in 1782, this island group in the Persian Gulf has been, by treaty, a British protectorate since 1820. It has become a major Middle Eastern oil center and, through use of oil revenues, is one of the most developed of the Persian Gulf sheikdoms. The Amir, Sheik Isa bin Sulman al Khalifa, who succeeded to the post in 1961, is a member of the Al Khalifa family that has governed Bahrain since 1782, originating in Arabia. The refinery on Bahrain Island is the Middle East's second largest. Bahrain announced its independence as a sovereign state on Aug. 14, 1971.

A new Constitution was approved in 1973. It created the first elected parliament in the country's history. Called the National Council, it consisted of 30 members elected by male citizens for four-year terms, plus up to 14 cabinet ministers as ex-officio members. In August 1975, the Amir dissolved the National Council and suspended a constitutional provision that called for new elections in two months.

Economic Conditions: Chief exports in 1974 were crude oil and petroleum products and aluminum (44% of nonoil exports). Leading customers were Japan (35%), Saudi Arabia (31%), Dubai (5%). Leading suppliers were U.S. (18%), United Kingdom (15%), Japan (13%), China (6%), West Germany (5%).

BANGLADESH (People's Republic of)

(Member of Commonwealth of Nations)

President: Abu Sadat Mohammed Sayem (1975).
Area: 55,598 sq mi. (143,998 sq km).
Population (est. 1976): 78,700,000.
Density per square mile: 1,415.5.
Capital and largest city (est. 1974): Dacca, 1,311,000.
Monetary unit: Taka.
Principal languages: Bengali (official), English.
Religion: Moslem predominantly, Hindu (est. 13%), also small Buddhist and Christian minorities.

Bangladesh, formerly East Pakistan, proclaimed itself independent of West Pakistan in March 1971, but came into being only after India had sided with it and defeated West Pakistan's army in a two-week war in December 1971. Sheik Mujibur Rahman, leader of the Awami League Party, which dominated East Pakistan and led the rebellion, became its first Prime Minister after being released from jail in West Pakistan at the end of the war.

Mujibur was assassinated Aug. 15, 1975, in a military coup that installed Khondakar Mushtaque Ahmed as President.

Bangladesh was established as a parliamentary democracy. A Constitution, approved in December, 1972, provided for a 315-seat National Assembly. By a 294–0 vote on Jan. 25, 1975, the parliament amended the Constitution to make Mujibur President (he was then Prime Minister) and to give him total executive powers. Ahmed assumed the same powers after the coup.

Ahmed himself was forced out by a second coup Nov. 6, 1975, which installed former Supreme Court Chief Justice Abu Sadat Mohammed Sayem as President and "chief martial law administrator."

Political Parties. In January, 1975, the National Assembly authorized establishment of the Awami League as the sole political party. Ahmed ordered dissolution of the League on Aug. 30, 1975, and banned formation of any new parties.

History. The former East Pakistan, like West Pakistan and India, was part of imperial British India until Britain withdrew in 1947. The two Pakistans were united by religion (Moslem) but their peoples were separated by culture, physical features and 1,000 miles of Indian territory. Bangladesh is on the Bay of Bengal and is totally surrounded by India except for a small common border with Burma. It consists primarily of East Bengal (West Bengal is part of India and its people are primarily Hindu) plus the Sylhet district of Assam. For almost 25 years after independence from Britain, its history was as part of Pakistan (*see* Pakistan).

The East Pakistanis unsuccessfully sought greater autonomy from West Pakistan. The first general elections in Pakistani history, in December 1970, saw virtually all 171 seats of the region (out of 300 for both East and West Pakistan) go to Sheik Mujibur Rahman's Awami League, with the rest to other similarly independence-minded minor parties. Attempts to write an all-Pakistan Constitution to replace the military regime of Gen. Yahya Khan failed. General strikes in East Pakistan followed at Mujibur's direction; he also told his followers to stop paying taxes. Yahya bloodily put down his revolt in March 1971. An estimated one million Bengalis were killed in the fighting or later slaughtered. Ten million more took refuge in India. In December 1971,

India invaded East Pakistan, routed the West Pakistani occupation forces and created Bangladesh. The United States opposed its violent creation but recognized Bangladesh in April, 1972, and provided several hundred million dollars in relief aid.

Reconstruction was complicated by inflation, which doubled the price of rice within a few months, and by roving bands of armed former freedom fighters. India supplied aid for millions of returning refugees. Most industry was nationalized, along with banks and insurance and shipping firms. In March, 1972, Bangladesh signed a friendship treaty with the Soviet Union, and Soviet-oriented Communists backed the government and clashed with those that leaned to Peking.

In February, 1974, Pakistan agreed to recognize the independence of Bangladesh. India, Pakistan and Bangladesh signed an agreement April 19, 1974, that provided for release of all Pakistani prisoners, improved conditions for the Bihari minority seeking to emigrate from Bangladesh to Pakistan and negotiations to restore normal communication among the three states.

The charismatic Mujibur had a following of millions and near-dictatorial powers, but he failed to cope with poverty, starvation, sporadic political violence and widespread government corruption. In June, after press criticism, his government nationalized the press, closing down all but four daily newspapers.

Before dawn on Aug. 15, 1975, Mujibur, his wife and several relatives were assassinated in a coup led by young Army officers. As the new President, they installed Khondakar Mushtaque Ahmed, a founder of the Awami League who was then serving as Minister of Foreign Trade and Commerce. After sporadic fighting in which a reported 200 persons died, borders were sealed, martial law was imposed and Ahmed was established at the head of a government run mostly by ministers inherited from Mujibur.

The new government's greatest challenge was to forestall wholesale famine in a nation whose population has been growing at the rate of 3% a year, while food production has been increasing 1%.

Civilian rule under Sayem has been tempered by a three-man military advisory council which he named to assist him. Sayem personally took over the major Cabinet posts such as Foreign Relations and Defense, however.

Economic Conditions. Predominantly a rural economy, with principal crops of rice, tea and jute. Chief exports are raw jute and jute products (about 90%); also leather, textile yarn and thread, cotton fabrics and shrimp.

Chief exports in 1973–74 were jute products (55%) and jute (33%). Leading customers in 1973 were U.S. (c. 29%), United Kingdom (c. 15%), Italy (c. 7%), West Germany (c. 6%), Belgium-Luxembourg (c. 6%), Argentina (c. 5%), France (c. 5%). Leading suppliers were India (c. 25%), U.S. (c. 18%), Japan (c. 10%), West Germany (c. 10%), Canada (c. 8%), U.K. (7%).

Natural Features. Low-lying, riverine land, largely formed by the many branches and tributaries of the Ganges and Brahmaputra rivers, with elevation averaging less than 600 feet above sea level. Tropical monsoon climate, with frequent floods and cyclones inflicting serious damage in delta region.

BARBADOS (Parliamentary Democracy)

(Member of Commonwealth of Nations)

Governor General: Sir William Douglas (acting).
Prime Minister: J. M. G. Adams (1976).
Area: 166 sq mi. (431 sq km).
Population (est. 1976): 252,000.
Density per square mile: 1,518.1.
Capital and largest city (1970 census): Bridgetown, 8,789.
Monetary unit: Barbados dollar.
Language: English.
Religions: Anglican, 53%; Methodist, 9%; Roman Catholic, 4%.

The Barbados legislature dates from 1627. It is bicameral, with a Senate of 21 appointed members and an Assembly of 24 elected members.

Major Political Parties. Barbados Labour Party (17 of 24 seats in Assembly), led by Prime Minister J. M. G. Adams; Democratic Labour Party (7 seats), led by Errol W. Barrow.

History. Barbados, an island east of St. Vincent in the West Indies' Windward Islands, with a population 90% black, was settled by the British in 1627. It became a crown colony in 1885. It was a member of the Federation of the West Indies from 1958 to 1962. Britain granted the colony independence on Nov. 30, 1966, and it became a parliamentary democracy, retaining the 24-member legislature established in 1639.

While retaining membership in the Commonwealth of Nations and economic ties with Great Britain, the new nation seeks broader economic and political relations with Western Hemisphere countries. Diplomatic ties with Cuba were established in 1972.

In a surprise victory in the September 1976 elections, J. M. G. Adams became Prime Minister, defeating Errol W. Barrow, who had been leader of Barbados since independence.

Economic Conditions. Agricultural products include sugar, cotton, maize, and cassava. Manufactures include rum and molasses.

Chief export in 1974 was sugar (30%); in 1973, chemicals (7%), clothing (6%) and rum (5%). Leading customers in 1974 were United Kingdom (26%), U.S. (16%), Windward Islands (7%), Trinidad and Tobago (6%), Canada (6%). Leading suppliers were U.K. (21%), U.S. (19%), Trinidad and Tobago (12%), Venezuela (10%), Canada (9%).

BELGIUM (Kingdom)

(Royaume de Belgique—Koninkrijk België)

Sovereign: King Baudouin I (1951).
Premier: Léo Tindemans (1974).
Area: 11,781 sq mi. (30,513 sq km).
Population (est. 1976): 9,580,000.
Density per square mile: 832.1.
Capital: Brussels.

Largest cities (est. 1975): Brussels, 1,055,000; (est. 1974): Antwerp, 673,000; Liège, 444,000; Charleroi, 316,000; Ghent, 235,000.
Monetary unit: Belgian franc.
Languages: Dutch, 59%; French, 40%; German, 1%.
Religion: Predominantly Roman Catholic.

Belgium is a constitutional monarchy consisting of nine provinces. Its bicameral legislature has a Senate, with its 181 members elected for four years, 106 by general election, 50 by provincial councillors and 25 by the Senate itself. The 212-member Chamber of Representatives is directly elected for four years by proportional representation. There is universal suffrage, and those who do not vote are fined. Belgium joined the North Atlantic Alliance in April 1949 and is a member of the European Community. NATO and the Council and the Commission of the European Communities have their headquarters in Brussels. The present Cabinet is a coalition of the Social Christian Party, the Party for Liberty and Progress and the Walloon Party.

The sovereign, Baudouin I, was born Sept. 7, 1930, the son of King Leopold III and Queen Astrid. He became King on July 17, 1951, after the abdication on July 16 of his father. He married Doña Fabiola de Mora y Aragón on Dec. 15, 1960. Since he has no children, his brother, Prince Albert, is heir to the throne.

Major Political Parties. Social Christian Party (72 seats in Chamber of Representatives and 66 seats in Senate), led by Wilfried Martens and Charles-Ferdinand Nothomb; Socialist Party (59 seats in lower house and 50 in Senate), led by André Cools and Willy Claes; Liberty and Progress Party (30 seats in lower house and 27 in Senate), led by Frans Grootjans and André Damseaux; Rassemblement Wallon/Front des Francophones (25 seats in lower house and 21 in Senate), led by P. Gendebien and Léon Defosset; Flemish Volksunie (22 seats in lower house and 16 in Senate), led by Frans Van der Elst.

History. A constitutional monarchy on the North Sea in Northwest Europe, Belgium occupies part of the Roman province of Belgica, named after the Belgae, a people of ancient Gaul. The area was conquered by Julius Caesar in 57–50 B.C., then was overrun by the Franks in the 5th century. It was part of Charlemagne's empire in the 8th century, then in the next century was absorbed into Lotharingia and later into the Duchy of Lower Lorraine. In the 12th century it divided into the Duchies of Brabant and Luxembourg, the Bishopric of Liège, and the domain of the Count of Hainaut, which included Flanders. The rise of the wool industry brought prosperity and power to the country, particularly to the semi-independent cities—Ghent, Burges and Ypres. In the 16th century, Belgium, with most of the area of the Low Countries, passed to the Duchy of Burgundy and was the marriage portion of Archduke Maximilian of Hapsburg and the inheritance of his grandson, Charles V, who incorporated it into his empire. Then, in 1555, they were united with Spain.

By the treaty of Utrecht in 1713, the country's sovereignty passed to Austria. During the wars that followed the French Revolution, Belgium was

occupied and later annexed to France. But with the downfall of Napoleon, the Congress of Vienna in 1815 gave the country to the Netherlands. The Belgians revolted in 1830 and declared their independence.

Germany's invasion of Belgium in 1914 set off World War I. The Treaty of Versailles (1919) gave the areas of Eupen, Malmédy and Moresnet to Belgium. Leopold III succeeded Albert, King during World War I, in 1934. In World War II, Belgium was overwhelmed by Nazi Germany, and Leopold III was made prisoner. When he attempted to return in 1950, Socialists and Liberals revolted. He abdicated July 16, 1951, and his son, Baudouin, became King the next day.

The country has long been torn by language disputes between the Dutch-speaking Flemish people and the French-speaking Walloons. Political parties have two leaders, one from each community. Constant compromises must be struck within the government to allow the country to remain unified. In 1972, a major clash occurred over transferring six small hamlets from Flemish to Walloon administrative jurisdiction. When a balancing change was not implemented, the government fell. A new one under Edmond Leburton was formed; this, in turn, was replaced in April, 1974, by one under Léo Tindemans of the moderate Social Christian Party.

Parliament voted in June, 1975, to buy 102 U.S.-made jet fighters, thus clearing the way for a $2-billion purchase of 306 of the planes by a four-nation consortium. With her partners, Denmark, Norway and the Netherlands, Belgium turned down a competing bid from France, which called the decision a blow to European unity.

Economic Conditions. About 60% of the total area of Belgium is under cultivation, and one half the farmed area is devoted to forage crops. Other crops are fodder beets, flax and fruit. The pastoral industry, especially dairy farming, flourishes.

Industry chiefly processes imported raw materials for re-export in semifinished or finished form. Of primary importance are iron and steel, nonferrous metals, fabricated metal products and textiles. Associated with iron and steel are a considerable engineering industry, ship-building in Antwerp, and machinery and railway stock in Brussels. The centuries-old textile industry produces linen (Courtrai); cotton (the southeast); and synthetic fibers. Antwerp rivals Amsterdam in diamond cutting. The principal mineral is coal.

Chief exports in 1974 were iron and steel (18%), chemicals (13%), machinery (10%), textile yarns and fabrics (8%), food (8%), motor vehicles (8%) and nonferrous metals (6%). Leading customers were EEC (70%; incl. West Germany 21%, France 20%, Netherlands 17%, United Kingdom 5%) and U.S. (6%). Leading suppliers were EEC (66%; incl. West Germany 22%, France 17%, Netherlands 16%, U.K. 6%) and U.S. (6%).

Natural Features. The northern third of Belgium is a plain extending eastward from the coast of the North Sea. North of the Sambre-Meuse rivers is a low plateau, varying from 250 to more than 600 feet in height, and to the south lies the Ardennes plateau, rising to a maximum of about 2,300 feet.

BENIN (People's Republic)

(formerly Dahomey)

(République Populaire du Benin)

President: Lieut. Col. Mathieu Kerekou (1972).
Area: 43,483 sq mi. (112,622 sq km).
Population (est. 1976): 3,190,000.
Density per square mile: 73.4.
Capital: Porto-Novo.
Largest cities (est. 1972): Cotonou, 200,000; Porto-Novo, 100,000; Abomey, 50,000; Ouidah, 30,000.
Monetary unit: Franc CFA.
Ethnic groups: Fons and Adjas, Boribas, Yorubas, Mahis.
Languages: French, African languages.
Religions: Animist, Christian, Moslem.

The change in name from Dahomey to Benin for this West African country was announced by President Mathieu Kerekou Nov. 30, 1975. Benin commemorates an African kingdom on the Gulf of Guinea which flourished in the 17th century. At the same time, Kerekou announced the formation of a political organization, the Party of the People's Revolution of Benin, to mark the first anniversary of his declaration of a "new society" guided by Marxist-Leninist principles.

One of the smallest and most densely populated states in Africa, Benin was annexed by the French in 1893. The area was incorporated into French West Africa in 1904. After World War II it became in 1958 an autonomous republic within the French Community, and on Aug. 1, 1960, was granted its independence within the Community. General Christophe Soglo who deposed the first President, Hubert Maga, in an army coup in 1963, dismissed the civilian government in 1965, proclaiming himself chief of state. A group of young army officers seized power in December, 1967, deposing Soglo. They promulgated a new Constitution in 1968.

On Dec. 10, 1969, Benin had its fifth coup of the decade, with the Army again taking power. A military triumvirate held elections in March 1970, in which three ex-Presidents and President Emile D. Zinsou stood as candidates, but suspended them just before completion (elections take a full month), allegedly because of violence in two northern provinces where former President Maga was winning a great majority. The military instead created in May 1970 a three-man presidential commission to take over the government. The commission has a six-year term; each member serves as President for two years. Maga turned over power as scheduled to Justin Ahomadegbe in May 1972, but six months later, yet another Army coup ousted the triumvirate and installed Lieut. Col. Mathieu Kerekou as President.

With Mali, Mauritania, Ivory Coast, Senegal, Niger and Upper Volta, Benin formed the Economic Community for West Africa in a treaty aimed at promoting economic development of the seven states.

Economic Conditions. The most important economic activity is the production of palm oil. Other agricultural products include cassava, peanuts, cottonseed, sweet potatoes, corn and coffee.

Chief exports in 1971 were palm products (34%), cocoa (24%) and cotton (19%). Leading customers in 1972 were France (37%), West Germany (16%), The Netherlands (14%). Leading suppliers were France (40%), U.S. (7%), West Germany (6%), The Netherlands (6%), United Kingdom (6%).

BHUTAN (Constitutional monarchy)

(Druk-yul)

Ruler: King Jigme Singye Wangchuk (1972).
Area: 18,147 sq mi. (47,000 sq km).
Population (est. 1974): 1,146,000.
Density per square mile: 63.2.
Capital (est. 1974): Thimphu, 15,000.
Monetary unit: Ngultrum and Indian rupee.
Language: Dzongkha.
Religion: Buddhist, 75%; Hindu, 25%.

Bhutan is a constitutional monarchy. The King rules with a Council of Ministers and a nine-member Advisory Council, of whom five are elected by the people; two represent the monastic order and two are named by the King. There is a National Assembly (Parliament), which meets semiannually.

Political Parties. There are no political parties in Bhutan.

History. Bhutan is situated on the southeast slope of the Himalayas, bordered on the north and east by Tibet and on the south and west by India. After almost a century of conflict, British troops invaded the country in 1865 and negotiated an agreement under which Britain undertook to pay an annual allowance to Bhutan on condition of good behavior. A treaty with India in 1949 increased this subsidy and placed Bhutan's foreign affairs under Indian control.

In the 1960s, Bhutan undertook modernization, abolishing slavery and the caste system, emancipating women, breaking up estates and limiting farms to 30 acres.

Economic Conditions. The chief crops are rice, corn and millet; the fields, laid out on hillside terraces, are watered by an ingenious system of irrigation. Bhutan is famous for its small though sturdy mountain ponies.

The chief industries are metal work, cloth weaving and the fine basket and mat work. Trade is insignificant, much of it by barter. About 95% of external trade is with India. The main exports are timber, coal, fruit and fruit products.

Natural Features. The whole of Bhutan presents a succession of lofty and rugged mountains running generally from north to south and separated by deep valleys. Mountains in the north reach a height of 24,000 feet.

BOLIVIA (Republic)

(República de Bolivia)

President: Gen. Hugo Banzer Suárez (1971).
Area: 424,162 sq mi. (1,098,581 sq km).
Population (est. 1976): 5,790,000 (1972: Indian, 52.9%; mestizo, 32%; white, 14.8%; others, .3%).
Density per square mile: 13.7.
Capital (est. 1973 by U.N.): Sucre, 106,590.*
Largest cities (est. 1973 by U.N.): La Paz, 605,200; Cochabamba, 169,930; Oruro, 135,010.
Monetary unit: Peso Boliviano.
Languages: Spanish, Quéchua, Aymará.
Religion: Roman Catholic.

* Sucre is the legal capital; the seat of government is actually at La Paz.

Bolivia is a republic, electing by popular vote a President every four years, a 27-member Senate every six years and a 102-member Chamber of Deputies every four years. The President appoints the members of his Cabinet. Congress was dissolved in September, 1969, and has not been reconvened.

In 1967, a new Constitution replaced the Constitution of 1947.

A succession of coups d'etat in recent years has produced an average of one new President a year, ending with the seizure of power by Col. Hugo Banzer Suárez in August 1971. Banzer's tenure has set a record for continuous leadership in Bolivia.

Major Political Parties. Falange Socialista Boliviana (FSB) and Movimiento Nacionalista Revolucionario (MNR). No election has been held since 1966. Party activity was banned in November, 1974.

History. Famous since Spanish colonial days for its mineral wealth, modern Bolivia was once a part of the ancient Incan Empire. After the Spaniards had defeated the Incas in the 16th century, Bolivia's predominantly Indian population was reduced to slavery. The country won its independence in 1825; the new republic was named after Simón Bolívar, the famed liberator.

Since 1825 Bolivia has had more than sixty revolutions, seventy Presidents, and eleven Constitutions.

Harassed by internal strife, Bolivia lost great slices of territory to three neighbor nations. Several thousand square miles and its outlet to the Pacific were taken by Chile after a disastrous war in 1879-83. In 1903 a piece of Bolivia's Acre province, rich in rubber, was ceded to Brazil. And in 1938, after a war with Paraguay, Bolivia gave up claim to nearly 100,000 square miles of the Gran Chaco.

Great prosperity came with World War II and its demand for two important Bolivian products, tin and wolframite. But rising prices provoked strikes which were ruthlessly broken and promoted growth of the Leftist National Revolutionary Movement. The movement seized power in 1943 but was ousted by a moderate government in 1947. The government in 1951 nationalized the Patiño, Hochschild and Aramayo tin mines and began an agrarian land reform. But technological development and new mines reduced demand for Bolivian tin, and the miners suffered serious unemployment.

In 1965 a guerrilla movement mounted from Cuba and headed by Maj. Ernesto (Ché) Guevara began a revolutionary war. With the aid of U.S. military advisers, the Bolivian Army, helped by the peasants, smashed the guerrilla movement, wounding and capturing Guevara on Oct. 8, 1967, and shooting him to death the next day.

Banzer, on accession in 1971, promised that general elections would be held, but this was rescinded in November, 1974, when the armed forces took control following suppression of a revolt by disaffected troops. Banzer remained President, but the military assumed political and administrative powers through 1980. Claiming to have uncovered left-wing plots, the regime outlawed all political activity.

In January 1976, Banzer appointed a commission to study a proposal by Chile to grant Bolivia a corridor to the Pacific. Peruvian agreement would be required, because the coastal area under consideration was ceded to Chile by Peru after the War of the Pacific in 1879-86.

Economic Conditions. Production of such basic foodstuffs as wheat and rice is insufficient for domestic needs, and considerable quantities must be imported. Cattle are raised in the more temperate regions of the east and south, sheep in the departments of La Paz and Cochabamba, and llamas, alpacas and vicuñas, important sources of hides, wool and meat, are raised on the plateaus.

The fur-bearing chinchilla, a native of the colder plateau regions, is also raised.

Mining is the backbone of the economy. Tin is by far the most important mineral.

Because Bolivia has no access to the sea, foreign trade must pass through free ports in Chile and river ports on the Amazon.

Chief exports in 1974 were tin (42%), crude oil (29%), zinc (7%), antimony (5%) and silver (5%). Leading customers in 1972 were United Kingdom (22%), Argentina (15%), U.S. (15%), Japan (10%), West Germany (7%), Brazil (6%). Leading suppliers were U.S. (26%), Japan (16%), Brazil (13%), Argentina (13%), West Germany (8%).

Natural Features. Landlocked Bolivia is a low alluvial plain throughout 60% of its area toward the east, drained by the Amazon and Plata river systems. The western part, enclosed by two chains of the Andes, is a great plateau—the Altiplano, with an average altitude of 12,000 feet. More than 80% of the population lives on the plateau, which also contains La Paz, the highest capital city in the world. Lake Titicaca, half the size of Lake Ontario, is one of the highest large lakes in the world, at an altitude of 12,507 feet. Islands in the lake hold ruins of the ancient Incas.

BOTSWANA (Republic)

(Member of Commonwealth of Nations)

President: Sir Seretse Khama (1966).
Area: 231,804 sq mi. (600,372 sq km).
Population (est. 1976): 720,000.
Density per square mile: 3.1.
Capital (est. 1976): Gaborone, 31,000.
Largest city (est. 1969): Serowe, 34,186.
Monetary unit: Pula.
Languages: English and Setswana.
Religions: Christian (60%), animist.

The Botswana Constitution provides, in addition to the unicameral National Assembly, for a House of Chiefs which has a voice on bills affecting tribal affairs. There is universal adult suffrage.

Major Political Parties. Botswana Democratic Party (28 of 33 elective seats in 36-man Legislative Assembly), led by Sir Seretse Khama; Botswana People's Party (2 seats), led by Philip Matante; Botswana National Front (2 seats), led by Bathoen Gaseitsiwe; Botswana Independence Party (1 seat), led by Motsamai Mpho. The assembly also has four specially elected members. The 36th member is the Attorney General, who has no vote.

History. A republic in south central Africa, between South Africa and Rhodesia, Botswana is the land of the Batawana tribes, who, when threatened by the Boers in Transvaal got Britain, in 1885, to establish a protectorate over the country, then known as Bechuanaland. In 1961, Britain granted a Constitution to the country. Self-government began in 1965. On Sept. 30, 1966, the country became an independent member of the Commonwealth of Nations. In 1971, it was offered associate membership in the European Common Market. The association was ratified in 1975.

Economic Conditions. The country is essentially pastoral, chiefly cattle raising and dairy farming.

Chief exports in 1972–73 were mineral products (44%) and meat and products (42%).

BRAZIL (Republic)

(Brasil)

President: Gen. Ernesto Geisel (1974).
Area: 3,286,487 sq mi. (8,511,965 sq km).
Population (est. 1976): 107,985,000 (approx.: white, 60%; Mestizo, 26%; black, 11%; other, 3%).
Density per square mile: 32.8.
Capital (est. 1975): Brasília, 763,300.
Largest cities (1970 census): São Paulo, 5,901,333; Rio de Janeiro, 4,296,782; Belo Horizonte, 1,232,708; Recife, 1,078,819; Salvador, 1,000,647.
Monetary unit: Cruzeiro.
Language: Portuguese.
Religion: Roman Catholic, 93%.

Under the Constitution, Brazil is a union of 21 states, 5 territories and 1 federal district. The President is elected by the vote of an electoral college for a term of five years. The National Congress is composed of two houses—the Senate, whose members serve for eight-year terms, and the Chamber of Deputies, elected for four-year terms. Members of Congress are elected by equal, direct, compulsory and secret suffrage under proportional representation.

The military took control in 1963, ousting the last elected civilian President and installing a military man (with the Congress ratifying the junta's choice). Gen. Arthur Costa e Silva became President in 1966, but when he died suddenly three years later, the junta (composed of three service ministers) brushed aside the legitimate successor, Vice President Pedro Aleixo, a civilian, and named Gen. Emilio Garrastazu Médici as President. Congress then elected him to the post. In 1970, Médici announced that the military would rule indefinitely (until "economic, social, racial and political democracy" is attained).

Médici and the military chose Gen. Ernesto Geisel to become his successor in 1974.

Major Political Parties. Alianca Renovadora Nacional (ARENA), led by Senator Petronio Portela; Movimento Democratico Brasileiro (MDB), led by Congressman Ulysses Guimarães.

History. The only Latin American nation deriving its language and culture from Portugal, Brazil is the largest country in South America, covering nearly half the continent. In size Brazil ranks after the Soviet Union, China, Canada and the United States.

Admiral Pedro Alvares Cabral claimed the territory for the Portuguese in 1500. He brought to Portugal a cargo of wood, pau-brasil, from which the land received its name. Portugal began colonization in 1532 and made the area a royal colony in 1549.

During the Napoleonic wars, King John VI, then Prince Regent, fled the country in 1807 in advance of the French armies and in 1808 set up his court in Rio de Janeiro. John was drawn home in 1820 by a revolution, leaving his son as Regent. When Portugal sought to reduce Brazil again to colonial status, the prince declared Brazil's independence on Sept. 7, 1822, and became Pedro I, Emperor of Brazil.

Harassed by his parliament, Pedro I abdicated in 1831 in favor of his five-year-old son, who became Emperor in 1840 as Pedro II. The son was a popular monarch but discontent built up, and in 1889, following a military revolt, he had to abdicate. A republic was set up, but until 1893, Brazil was under two military dictatorships. A revolt permitted a gradual return to stability under civilian Presidents. Slavery was abolished in 1888.

The President during World War I, Wenceslau Braz, cooperated with the Allies and declared war on Germany. The President from 1926 to 1930, Washington Luiz Pereira da Souza, was overthrown by a revolutionary group under Getulio Vargas, who took over as provisional President.

Vargas' 1934 Constitution curtailed states' rights and established a nationalistic policy. In 1937, Vargas seized absolute power and adopted another Constitution, extending his term indefinitely. In World War II, Brazil cooperated with the Western Allies, welcoming Allied air bases, patrolling the South Atlantic and joining the invasion of Italy after declaring war on the Axis.

Vargas was overthrown on Oct. 29, 1945. Succeeding presidents were Gen. Eurico Gaspar Dutra (1945–50); Getulio Vargas (1950–54); João Cafe Filho (1954–55); Juscelino Kubitschek de Oliveira (1955–60); Janio Quadros (1960); João Goulart (1960–63); Gen. Humberto de Alencar Castelo Branco (1963–66); Gen. Arthur Costa e Silva (1966–69); Gen. Emilio Garrastazu Médici (1970–74).

In the 1960's, urban guerrillas, in an effort to embarrass the military dictatorship, embarked on a widespread campaign of bombings, bank robberies, take-overs of radio stations and kidnaping of foreign diplomats. The first kidnaping victim, in September, 1969, was the U.S. Ambassador, C. Burke Elbrick, who was ransomed for 15 political prisoners.

Elections in November, 1974, brought sharp gains for the Brazilian Democratic Movement (MDB) party. These were interpreted as a rebuke to Geisel and the ruling ARENA party for violations of human rights and an inflation rate estimated at 33%. The election was the freest in a decade and the least violent in many years. Press censorship was relaxed under a policy of "decompression."

Harsh repression of political opposition, coupled with reports of torture and mistreatment of political prisoners, has continued to draw international criticism of the military regime, however. The Catholic clergy has spoken out increasingly for social reform.

Economic Conditions. Agriculture is a mainstay of Brazil's economy, but only 4% of its area is under cultivation, the rest being grazing, forest or non-productive land. Brazil leads the world in production of coffee and castor beans, and ranks third in cacao. Export of both coffee and cacao is government controlled.

Livestock is raised nearly everywhere, with the great centers in the central and northern states.

Industry is now an important segment of the economy. The principal fields are automobile manufacturing, electric-power production, cement production, shipbuilding and oil refining.

Brazil's vast mineral resources are among her least developed assets. Important minerals are coal, iron ore, gold, manganese ore, crude petroleum, bauxite, diamonds, silver, quartz crystals and uranium.

The nation's first nuclear power plant, under construction near Rio de Janeiro, was expected to become the first producing unit in South America on its completion in late 1976 or early 1977.

The largest single forest commodities are timber, chiefly pine from the southern states, and the wax of the carnauba palm, used for insulation and phonograph records and produced commercially only in Brazil.

Chief exports in 1974 were sugar (12%), coffee (11%) and iron ore (7%). Leading customers in 1973 were U.S. (18%), Netherlands (10%), West Germany (9%), Japan (7%), Italy (6%), United Kingdom (5%). Leading suppliers were U.S. (28%), West Germany (13%), Japan (8%), Saudi Arabia (5%), Argentina (5%).

Natural Features. Brazil covers about three sevenths of South America, extends 2,965 miles north-south, 2,691 miles east-west, and borders every South American state except Chile and Ecuador.

More than a third of Brazil is drained by the Amazon and its more than 200 tributaries. The Amazon is navigable for ocean steamers to Iquitos, Peru, 2,300 miles upstream. Southern Brazil is drained by the Plata system—the Paraguay, Uruguay and Paraná rivers. The most important stream entirely within Brazil is the São Francisco, navigable for a thousand miles but broken near its mouth by the 260-foot Paulo Affonso Falls.

BULGARIA (People's Republic)

(Narodna Republika Bulgariya)

President of the State Council: Todor Zhivkov (1971).
Prime Minister (Chairman of Council of Ministers): Stanko Todorov (1971).
Area: 42,823 sq mi. (110,912 sq km).
Population (est. 1976): 8,765,000. (Bulgarian, 90%; some Turkish, Gypsy).
Density per square mile: 204.7.
Capital: Sofia.
Largest cities (est. 1975): Sofia, 979,300; (est. 1973 by U.N.): Plovdiv, 274,700; Varna, 255,850; Roussé, 165,000; Bourgas, 143,000; Stara Zagora, 118,400; Pleven, 110,500.
Monetary unit: Lev.
Languages: Bulgarian.
Religions: Orthodox, 84.4%; Mohammedan, 13.5%; Jewish, .8%; Roman Catholic, .8%.

The present Constitution has been in effect since May 18, 1971. The National Assembly, consisting of 400 members elected for five-year terms, is the governing body. It elects the State Council and the Council of Ministers.

Major Political Parties. Communist Party, led by the president of the State Council, Todor Zhivkov; National Agrarian Union, led by Peter Tanchev.

History. The first Bulgarians, a tribe of wild horsemen akin to the Huns, crossed the Danube from the north in A.D. 679 and subjugated the Slavonic population of Moesia. They adopted a Slav dialect and Slavic customs and twice conquered most of the Balkan peninsula between 893 and 1280. After the Serbs subjected their kingdom in 1330, the Bulgars gradually fell prey to the Turks, and from 1396 to 1878 Bulgaria was a Turkish province. In 1878, Russia forced Turkey to give the country its independence; but the European powers, fearing that Bulgaria might become a Russian dependency, intervened. By the Treaty of Berlin (July 1878), Bulgaria became autonomous under Turkish sovereignty.

In 1887, Prince Ferdinand of Saxe-Coburg-Gotha was elected ruler of Bulgaria; on Oct. 5, 1908, he declared the country independent.

Bulgaria joined Germany in World War I and lost. On Oct. 3, 1918, Tsar Ferdinand abdicated in favor of his son, Tsar Boris III. Boris assumed dictatorial powers in 1934–35. When Hitler awarded Bulgaria Southern Dobruja, taken from Romania in 1940, the weak but land-hungry Boris joined the Nazis in war the next year and occupied parts of Yugoslavia and Greece. Later the Germans tried to force Boris to send his troops against the Russians. Boris resisted and died under mysterious circumstances on Aug. 28, 1943.

Simeon II, infant son of Boris, became nominal ruler under a regency. Three days after Russia declared war on Bulgaria on Sept. 5, 1944, Bulgaria declared war on Germany. Russian troops streamed in the next day, and under an informal armistice a coalition "Fatherland Front" Cabinet was set up under Kimon Georgiev.

A peace treaty negotiated in 1947 permitted Bulgaria to keep southern Dobrudja. A Constitution was adopted in 1947 establishing a Soviet-type people's republic.

Bulgaria joined the Council for Economic Mutual Assistance in 1949 and the Warsaw Treaty Organization and the United Nations in 1955.

In 1974, Bulgaria signed consular and trade pacts with the U.S. and agreed to stop jamming Voice of America broadcasts.

Economic Conditions. Bulgaria is still predominantly agrarian, with most of the population engaged in agriculture. Because of the mountainous character of the country, however, less than half of the land is tilled or used for pasture. Collectivization is well advanced. More than half the cultivated area is devoted to cereals, including wheat, corn, barley, oats and rye. Other crops are tobacco, alfalfa, cotton, flax, potatoes and sugar. There are extensive vineyards in the southern valleys.

Industries are of minor importance and with few exceptions—tobacco, wines and liquors, fertilizers, and flour—confined to domestic markets.

Soft coal is Bulgaria's principal mineral; others include chromite, gypsum, iron ore, manganese ore, rock salt and silver.

Chief exports in 1970 were machinery (19%), tobacco and cigarettes (13%), transport equipment (7%), wines and spirits (6%), fruits and vegetables (6%), clothing (6%) and iron and steel (5%). Leading customers in 1973 were U.S.S.R. (55%), East Germany (8%), Poland (5%). Leading suppliers were U.S.S.R. (52%), East Germany (9%), Czechoslovakia (6%), Poland (5%).

Natural Features. Two mountain ranges and two great valleys mark Bulgaria's topography. The Balkan belt crosses the center of the country, almost due east-west, rising to a height of 7,800 feet. The Rhodope range breaks off from the Balkans in the west, curves, and then straightens out to run nearly parallel along the southern border. Between the two ranges is the valley of the Maritsa, Bulgaria's principal river. Between the Balkan range and the Danube, which forms most of the northern boundary with Rumania, is the Danubian tableland.

Southern Dobruja, a fertile region of 2,900 square miles below the Danube delta, is an area of low hills, fens and sandy steppes.

BURMA (Socialist Republic of the Union of)

(Pyi-Daung-Su Socialist Thamada Myanma-Nainggan)

President: U Ne Win (1974).
Prime Minister: U Sein Win (1975).
Area: 261,789 sq mi. (678,033 sq km).
Population (est. 1976): 32,000,000.
Density per square mile: 122.2.
Capital: Rangoon.
Largest cities (est. 1973 for urban agglomeration): Rangoon, 2,056,100; Mandalay, 417,300; Moulmein, 171,800; Bassein, 126,150.
Monetary unit: Kyat.
Languages: Burmese, English.
Religions: Buddhist, 85%; Christian, Mohammedan, Hindu.

On Mar. 2, 1962, the Government of U Nu was overthrown and replaced by a Revolutionary Council, which assumed all power in the state. Gen. U Ne Win, as chairman of the Revolutionary Council, became the chief executive.

A new Constitution was approved in 1973 and took effect Jan. 4, 1974. Under it, Burma is a Socialist Democratic Republic with a 451-seat unicameral legislature called the People's Congress. In 1972, Ne Win and his colleagues resigned their military titles and thereafter ruled as "civilians." In March 1974, Ne Win dissolved the Revolutionary Council and became President under the new Constitution; he is also chairman of the Council of State.

Major Political Party. Burmese Socialist Program Party (the only legal party), led by Ne Win.

History. In 1612, the British East India Company sent agents to Burma, but the Burmese long resisted efforts of British traders, and Dutch and Portuguese as well, to establish posts on the Bay of Bengal. By the Anglo-Burmese War in 1824–26 and two following wars, the British East India Company expanded to the whole of Burma by 1886. Burma was annexed to India. It became a separate colony in 1937.

During World War II, Burma was a key battleground; the 800-mile Burma Road was the Allies' vital supply line to China. The Japanese invaded the country in December, 1941, and by May 1942, had occupied most of it, cutting the Burma Road. After one of the most difficult campaigns of the war, Allied forces liberated most of Burma prior to the Japanese surrender in August 1945. Burma became independent on Jan. 4, 1948. The new government was soon faced by armed uprisings of Communists and of Karen tribesmen. In 1949 the Karen rebels won a large degree of autonomy.

In 1951 and 1952 the Socialists achieved power, and Burma became the first Asian country to introduce social legislation.

In 1968, after the government had made headway against the Communist rebels, the military regime adopted a policy of strict nonalignment and followed "the Burmese Way" to socialism. But the insurgents, reportedly numbering several thousand and armed by China, continued active.

Economic Conditions. The natives in general are Mongolian; the Burmese are the most advanced. Indians, settled in the Irrawaddy delta region, supply most of the coolie labor, while the Chinese constitute the artisan and merchant class. Buddhism, the national religion, profoundly affects the national character.

Burma is essentially agricultural, with crop growing concentrated in the delta and river valleys. It is a leading producer of rice, the staple food, which occupies two thirds of the cultivated area. Crops grown in the dry zone in upper Burma include millet, cotton, peanuts and sesame. Other crops include tobacco, fruit, vegetables and cereals. The number of rubber plantations has increased.

The principal domestic animals are water buffalo, which are used as beasts of burden in the delta, and small humped oxen, which predominate in other areas.

Under the Socialist regime, all industry and rice production were nationalized and made monopolies of the state. All banks were also nationalized.

Leading industries include silk weaving and dyeing, rice husking, oil refining, and wood carving. The Baluchaung hydroelectric plant, one of the largest in Southeast Asia, was completed in 1960.

Mineral resources include lead, silver, zinc, nickel, cobalt, copper, gold, iron ore, molybdenum, coal, rubies, sapphires and jade.

More than half of Burma is forested. Teak, valuable for naval construction, is the main timber product. Its cutting is strictly controlled.

Chief exports in 1974 were rice (39%), teak (22%) and oilcakes (6%). Leading customers in 1972 were Sri Lanka (14%), Japan (12%), United Kingdom (9%), Singapore (9%), West Germany (5%), Mauritius (5%). Leading suppliers were Japan (27%), China (10%), West Germany (9%), India (7%), U.K. (7%), U.S. (5%).

Natural Features. Slightly smaller than Texas, Burma is divided into three natural regions: the Arakan Yoma, a long, narrow mountain range forming the barrier between Burma and India; the Shan Plateau in the east, extending southward into Tenasserim; and the Central Basin, running down to the flat fertile delta of the Irrawaddy in the south. This delta contains a network of intercommunicating canals and nine principal mouths.

BURUNDI (Republic)

(Republika Y'Uburundi)

President: Lieut. Gen. Michel Micombero (1966).
Area: 10,747 sq mi. (27,843 sq km).
Population (est. 1976): 3,845,000.
Density per square mile: 357.8.
Capital and largest city (est. 1970 for urban agglomeration); Bujumbura, 110,000.
Monetary unit: Burundi franc.
Languages: Kirundi (official); French, Swahili.
Religions: Roman Catholic, 51%; animist, 45%; Protestant, 4%.

Legislative power is vested in the President and the Political Bureau of the National Political Party, which is composed of 40 nominated members.

Burundi's first Constitution was approved July 11, 1974. It placed UPRONA in control of national policy and automatically made Lieut. Gen. Michel Micombero President. He was installed for a second seven-year term in November, 1974.

Political Party. UPRONA (Unity and National Progress) is the Party of the Union.

History. A republic in East Central Africa, Burundi was once part of German East Africa. An integrated society developed among the Watusi, a tall, warlike people and nomad cattle raisers, and the Bahutu, a Bantu people, who were subject farmers. Belgium won a League of Nations mandate in 1923, and subsequently it was transferred to the status of a U.N. trust territory.

In 1962, Burundi gained independence and became a kingdom under Mwami Mwambutsa IV, with his son, Louis Rwangasore, as Premier. Shortly after, the son was assassinated. The second man to succeed him, Pierre Ngendandumwe, who took office in 1963, was assassinated in 1965 when an unsuccessful coup against the Watusi led to the massacre of many Bahutus. Crown Prince Charles, returning from Europe, rallied Watusi extremists, ousted the Premier, suspended the Constitution, and renewed relations with Communist China. He deposed his father in 1966, reigned as Ntare V, with Michel Micombero as Premier. Three months later, Micombero, in a military coup, overthrew the Mwami and established a republic, installing himself as President.

One of Africa's worst tribal wars, which became genocide, occurred in Burundi in April 1972, following the return of Ntare. He was given a safe-conduct promise in writing by Micombero but "judged and immediately executed" by the Burundi leader. His return was apparently attended by an invasion of exiles of Burundi's Hutu tribe. Although Hutus make up 85% of the population, they have been dominated for centuries by the minority Tutsi tribe of Micombero. Whether Hutus living in Burundi joined the invasion is unclear, but after it failed, the victorious Tutsis proceeded to massacre many of them. By official count some 100,000 persons were killed in six weeks, with possibly 100,000 more slain by summer.

Economic Conditions. Because of overpopulation, poor soil and irregular rainfall, Burundi, principally an agricultural and cattle-raising country, is just able to feed itself.

Agricultural products include sweet potatoes, dry beans, coffee and cotton. Livestock include cattle and sheep.

Chief export in 1974 was coffee (84%). Leading customers in 1973 were U.S. (55%), Italy (11%), West Germany (10%), United Kingdom (9%), Spain (5%). Leading suppliers were Belgium-Luxembourg (24%), France (12%), West Germany (9%), Iran (6%), Kenya (5%).

CAMBODIA

Area: 69,898 sq mi. (181,035 sq km).
Population (est. 1976): 8,335,000.
Density per square mile: 119.2.
Capital and largest city (est. 1971): Phnom Penh, 479,300.
Monetary unit: Riel.
Languages: Khmer (official), French, Vietnamese, Chinese, Cham, English.
Religion: Theravada Buddhist.

A bloodless coup toppled Prince Sihanouk in March 1970. It was led by Lon Nol and Prince Sisowath Sirik Matak (Sihanouk's cousin). The National Assembly approved the coup and gave "full power" to Lon Nol. Sihanouk moved to Peking to head a government-in-exile. On Oct. 9, 1970, Cambodia became the Khmer Republic and Lon Nol proclaimed himself President.

In April 1973, in a de facto coalition government, Lon Nol agreed to share power with three others as part of a High Political Council. Other members were Sirik Matak (who headed the Republican Party), In Tam (who headed the Democratic Party) and Cheng Heng. A parliament totally made up of Lon Nol's Social Republican Party approved formation of the Council and dissolved itself for six months, giving legislative power to the Council.

The Lon Nol regime was overthrown in April, 1975, and replaced by xenophobic leaders of the Communist-Khmer Rouge forces, who rule through revolutionary cadres.

History. Cambodia, an independent state in Southeast Asia surrounded by South Vietnam, Laos and Thailand, came under Khmer rule about 600 A.D. Under the Khmers, magnificent temples were built at Angkor. The Khmer kingdom once ruled over most of Southeast Æsia, but attacks by the Thai and the Vietnamese almost annihilated the empire until the French joined Cambodia, Laos and Vietnam into French Indochina.

Under King Norodom Sihanouk, enthroned in 1941, and particularly under Japanese occupation during World War II, nationalism revived. After the ouster of the Japanese, the Cambodians sought independence, but the French returned in 1946, granting the country a Constitution in 1947 and independence within the French Union in 1949. Sihanouk won full military control during the French-Indochinese War in 1953. He abdicated in 1955 in favor of his parents, remaining head of the government, and when his father died in 1960, became chief of state without returning to the throne. In 1963, Prince Sihanouk sought a guarantee of Cambodia's neutrality from all parties to the Vietnam War.

Sihanouk first favored the Communist-backed Vietcong in Vietnam, but in 1967 he accused the Communists of planning a revolt and veered away from them. In 1968 he announced that under certain conditions he would not oppose "hot pursuit" by American troops of Communist forces across the Cambodian border.

On March 18, 1970, while Sihanouk was abroad trying to get 'North Vietnamese and the Vietcong out of border sanctuaries near Vietnam, anti-Vietnamese riots occurred, and Sihanouk was overthrown in a bloodless coup by Lon Nol and Sirik Matak, a move legalized by the legislature. The historically anti-Vietnamese (north and south) Cambodians largely stayed with the government.

North Vietnamese and Vietcong units in border sanctuaries began moving deeper into Cambodia, threatening rapid overthrow of Lon Nol. A hostile Cambodia would threaten eventual U.S. withdrawal from Vietnam, President Nixon said in sending South Vietnamese and U.S. troops across the border April 30. U.S. ground forces, limited to 30-kilometer penetration, withdrew by June 30, after which Nixon promised no American ground troops and only American bombing to stop Communist movements toward Vietnam.

The Vietnam peace agreement of 1973 stipulated withdrawal of foreign forces from Cambodia, but fighting continued between Hanoi-backed insurgents and U.S.-supplied government troops. U.S. air support for the government forces was ended by Congress on Aug. 15, 1973. Lon Nol made overtures for a negotiated settlement, but neither Sihanouk nor leaders of the Khmer Rouge rebels would deal with him.

Fighting continued through 1974, then reached a quick climax early in 1975. In January, the rebels cut off the Mekong River as a supply route to Phnom Penh and fought their way to the outskirts of the capital and began shelling it. In February, the U.S. Congress ignored a request from President Ford for $222 million to supplement Phnom Penh's dwindling arms stores, but a U.S. food airlift to the besieged capital went forward.

As government troops fell back in bitter fighting, there were student protests in Phnom Penh and foreigners began leaving the country. Lon Nol fled by air April 1, leaving the government under the interim control of Premier Long Boret. On April 16, the government's capitulation ended the five-year war, but not the travails of war-ravaged Cambodia.

The new regime embarked immediately on a sweeping, inward-looking agrarian revolution. Cambodian borders were closed, but 6,000 refugees escaped to Thailand. They reported that all cities had been evacuated, with inhabitants marched off to found new farm settlements in the jungle. They said policy was enforced by Communist troops and teen-aged revolutionaries who summarily shot dissidents and former government soldiers.

The leadership of the new regime was obscure, although Khieu Samphan, wartime leader of the Khmer Rouge and Deputy Premier when the new government was established, appeared to be the strong man of the egalitarian regime. Sihanouk, the nominal chief of state, who had been in exile in Peking, returned to Phnom Penh in September, 1975, ending a five-and-a-half-year absence.

A new Constitution was proclaimed in December, establishing a 250-member People's Assembly, a State Presidium with a President and two Vice Presidents and a Supreme Judicial Tribunal. The Assembly was elected as of March 20, 1976, and Sihanouk, until then described as Chief of State, resigned April 7. Samphan was reported to have replaced him as Chief of State.

Economic Conditions. About 85% of the population is Cambodian, 5% Annamese, and 6% Chinese. The forested regions of the northeast are inhabited by various primitive peoples.

Agriculture is the basis of the economy. The chief crop is rice, grown principally in the Battambang area. Second in importance is rubber. Other crops include tobacco, kapok, cotton, pepper, and maize. Cattle breeding is of major importance. Native industries include silk and cotton weaving, rice milling, and the salting of fish obtained from Lake Tonle Sap during the low-water season.

Forests cover 75% of the land but most are unexploited. Deposits of iron ore, limestone, and phosphate are undeveloped.

Chief export in 1973 was rubber (93%). Leading customers were Hong Kong (c. 23%), Japan (c. 22%), Malaysia (c. 18%), France (c. 12%), Spain (c. 10%). Leading suppliers were U.S. (c. 69%), Thailand (c. 11%), Singapore (c. 5%), Japan (c. 5%).

Natural Features. Cambodia consists chiefly of a large alluvial plain that is ringed in by mountains and on the east by the Mekong river. The plain is centered on Lake Tonle Sap, which is a natural storage basin of the Mekong.

CAMEROON (United Republic of)

(République Unie du Cameroun)

President: Ahmadou Ahidjo (1960).
Prime Minister: Paul Biya (1975).
Area: 183,569 sq mi. (475,442 sq km).
Population (est. 1976): 6,525,000.
Density per square mile: 35.5.
Capital: Yaoundé.
Largest cities (est. 1973): Douala, 340,000; Yaoundé, 230,000.
Monetary unit: Franc CFA.
Languages: French and English (both official); Foulbé, Bamiléké, Ewondo, Donala, Mungaka, Bassa.
Religions: Animist, Christian, Moslem.

After a 1972 plebiscite, a unitary nation was formed out of East and West Cameroon to replace the former Federal Republic. A Constitution was adopted, providing for election of a President every five years and of a 120-seat National Assembly, whose nominal five-year term can be extended or shortened by the President.

Political Parties. The Cameroon National Union is the only political party.

History. An independent state in West Africa on the Gulf of Guinea, the Federal Republic of Cameroon lies in the midst of Nigeria, Chad, Central African Republic, Congo (Brazzaville) and Gabon. It is inhabited by Hamitic and Semitic peoples in the north, where Islam is the principal religion, and by Bantu peoples in the central and southern regions, where native animism prevails. The tribes were conquered by many invaders.

The land escaped colonial rule until 1884, when treaties with tribal chiefs brought the area under

German domination. After World War I, the League of Nations gave the French a mandate over 80% of the area, and the British 20% adjacent to Nigeria. After World War II, when the country came under a U.N. trusteeship in 1946, self-government was granted and the Cameroun People's Union emerged as the dominant party by campaigning for reunification of French and British Cameroon and for independence. Accused of being under Communist control, it waged a campaign of revolutionary terror from 1955 to 1958, when it was crushed. In British Cameroon, unification was pressed also by the leading party, the Kamerun National Democratic Party led by John Foncha.

France set up Cameroun as an autonomous state in 1957, and in 1958, its legislative assembly voted for independence by 1960. In 1959 a fully autonomous government of Cameroun was formed under Ahmadou Ahidjo, who immediately began consultations on unification with Foncha. Cameroun became an independent republic on Jan. 1, 1960, adopted a Constitution in a referendum in February, and chose a National Assembly in April. The Assembly elected Ahidjo President. A federal Constitution was approved in 1961, and the Federal Republic of Cameroon came into being in October, 1961, headed by Ahidjo and Foncha.

Ahidjo was re-elected in 1975 for a fourth five-year term. Paul Biya was named Prime Minister.

Economic Conditions. Agricultural products include sweet potatoes, cassava, coffee, cocoa, bananas, peanuts, rubber, cotton, corn, dry beans, millet and sorghum, palm kernels and oil, and timber. Mineral resources include titanium, tin and gold.

Chief exports in 1974 were cocoa (27%), coffee (25%), timber (10%) and aluminum (3%). Leading customers in 1973 were France (29%), Netherlands (24%), West Germany (10%), U.S. (7%), Japan (5%). Leading suppliers were France (48%), West Germany (10%), U.S. (9%), Gabon (4%), Italy (4%).

CANADA

(Member of Commonwealth of Nations)

Sovereign: Queen Elizabeth II.
Governor General: Jules Léger (1974).
Prime Minister: Pierre Elliott Trudeau (1968).
Area: 3,851,809 sq mi. (9,976,139 sq km).
Population (est. 1976): 23,200,000 (British, 44.6%; French, 28.7%; other European, 15.5%; Indian and Eskimo, 1.4%).
Density per square mile: 6.2.
Capital: Ottawa, Ont.
Largest cities (est. 1973): Montreal, Que., 1,214,355; Toronto, Ont., 712,785; Edmonton, Alta., 438,150; Vancouver, B.C., 426,260; Calgary, Alta., 403,320; Hamilton, Ont., 309,175; Ottawa, Ont., 302,345; Winnipeg, Man., 246,245; London, Ont., 223,225; Windsor, Ont., 203,300; Quebec, Que., 186,090; Regina, Sask., 139,470.
Monetary Unit: Canadian dollar.
Languages: English and French.
Religions: Roman Catholic, 46.2%; United Church, 17.5%; Anglican, 11.8%; Presbyterian, 4%; Baptist, 3.1%; others, 17.4%.

Canada, a self-governing member of the Commonwealth of Nations, is a federal union of ten provinces whose powers are laid down in the British North America Act of 1867. The executive powers nominally rest in the hands of the Governor General, who represents the Queen and is appointed by her upon the recommendation of the Canadian government.

Actually the Governor General acts only with the advice of the Canadian Prime Minister and the members of the Cabinet who at the same time sit in the federal Parliament. The Parliament has two houses: a Senate numbering 102 members appointed for life, and a House of Commons numbering 264 members apportioned according to provincial population. Elections are held at least every five years or whenever the party in power is voted down in the House of Commons or considers it expedient to appeal to the people. The Prime Minister is the leader of the majority party in the House of Commons—or, if no single party holds a majority, the leader of the party able to command the support of a majority of members of the House. Laws must be passed by both houses of Parliament and signed by the Governor General in the Queen's name.

The ten provincial governments are nominally headed by Lieutenant Governors appointed by the federal government, but the executive power in each actually is vested in a Cabinet headed by a Premier, who is leader of the majority party. In nine of the ten provinces the legislature is composed of a one-house assembly elected by the people for four years. In Quebec there is a second chamber, the Legislative Council, composed of nominees of the Provincial Government.

The judicial system consists of a Supreme Court in Ottawa (established in 1875), with appellate jurisdiction, and a Supreme Court in each province, as well as country courts with limited jurisdiction in most of the provinces. The Governor General in Council appoints these judges.

Political Parties. Liberal Party (139 of 264 seats in House of Commons), led by Prime Minister Pierre Elliott Trudeau; Progressive Conservatives (95 seats), led by Joseph C. Clark; New Democratic Party (16 seats), led by John Edward Broadbent; Social Credit (11 seats), led by Real Caouette; independent (1 seat).

History. The Norse explorer Leif Ericson probably reached the shores of Canada (Labrador or Nova Scotia) in A.D. 1000, but the history of the white man in the country actually began in 1497, when John Cabot, an Italian in the Service of Henry VII of England, reached the shore of Newfoundland or Nova Scotia. Canada was taken for France in 1534 by Jacques Cartier. The actual settlement of New France, as it was then called, began in 1604 at Port Royal in what is now Nova Scotia; in 1608 Quebec was founded. France's colonization efforts were not very successful, but French explorers by the end of the 17th century had penetrated beyond the Great Lakes to the western prairies and south along the Mississippi to the Gulf of Mexico. Meanwhile, the English Hudson's Bay Company had been established in 1670. Because of the valuable fisheries and fur trade, a conflict developed between the French and English; in 1713, Newfoundland, Hudson Bay and Nova Scotia (Acadia) were lost to England.

During the Seven Years' War (1756–63), Eng-

Canadian Governors General and Prime Ministers Since 1867

Term of office	Governor General	Term	Prime Minister	Party
		1867–1873	Sir John A. Macdonald	Conservative
1867–1868	Viscount Monck*	1873–1878	Alexander Mackenzie	Liberal
1869–1872	Baron Lisgar	1878–1891	Sir John A. Macdonald	Conservative
1872–1878	Earl of Dufferin	1891–1892	Sir John J. C. Abbott	Conservative
1878–1883	Marquess of Lorne	1892–1894	Sir John S. D. Thompson	Conservative
1883–1888	Marquess of Lansdowne	1894–1896	Sir Mackenzie Bowell	Conservative
1888–1893	Baron Stanley of Preston	1896	Sir Charles Tupper	Conservative
1893–1898	Earl of Aberdeen	1896–1911	Sir Wilfrid Laurier	Liberal
1898–1904	Earl of Minto	1911–1917	Sir Robert L. Borden	Conservative
1904–1911	Earl Grey	1917–1920	Sir Robert L. Borden	Unionist
1911–1916	Duke of Connaught	1920–1921	Arthur Meighen	Unionist
1916–1921	Duke of Devonshire	1921–1926	W. L. Mackenzie King	Liberal
1921–1926	Baron Byng of Vimy	1926	Arthur Meighen	Conservative
1926–1931	Viscount Willingdon	1926–1930	W. L. Mackenzie King	Liberal
1931–1935	Earl of Bessborough	1930–1935	Richard B. Bennett	Conservative
1935–1940	Baron Tweedsmuir	1935–1948	W. L. Mackenzie King	Liberal
1940–1946	Earl of Athlone	1948–1957	Louis S. St. Laurent	Liberal
1946–1952	Viscount Alexander	1957–1963	John G. Diefenbaker	Progressive-
1952–1959	Vincent Massey			Conservative
1959–1967	George P. Vanier			
1967–1973	Roland Michener	1963–1968	Lester B. Pearson	Liberal
1974–	Jules Léger	1968–	Pierre Elliott Trudeau	Liberal

* Became Governor General of British North America in 1861.

land extended its conquest, and the British general Wolfe won his famous victory over Montcalm outside Quebec (Sept. 13, 1759). The Treaty of Paris (1763) gave England control.

At that time the population of Canada was almost entirely French, but in the next few decades, thousands of British colonists emigrated to Canada from the British Isles and from the American colonies. In 1849 the right of Canada to self-government was recognized. By the British North America Act of 1867, the Dominion of Canada was created through the confederation of Upper and Lower Canada, Nova Scotia, and New Brunswick. Prince Edward Island joined the Dominion in 1873. In 1869 Canada had purchased from the Hudson's Bay Company the vast middle west (Rupert's Land) from which the provinces of Manitoba (1870), Alberta and Saskatchewan (1905) were later formed. In 1871, British Columbia joined the Dominion. The country was linked from coast to coast in 1885 by the Canadian Pacific Railway.

During the formative years between 1866 and 1896, the Conservative Party, led by Sir John A. Macdonald, governed the country, except during the years 1873–78. In 1896 the Liberal Party took over and under Sir Wilfrid Laurier, an eminent French Canadian, ruled until 1911. In World War I, more than 500,000 Canadian soldiers fought for the Allied cause. After the Treaty of Versailles, Canada, a full-fledged nation, was admitted to the League of Nations and appointed its own representatives in foreign countries. By the Statute of Westminster (1931) the British Dominions, including Canada, were formally declared to be partner nations with Britain, "equal in status, in no way subordinate to each other," and bound together only by allegiance to a common crown.

Newfoundland became Canada's 10th province on Mar. 31, 1949, following a plebiscite. Besides the provinces, Canada includes two territories—the Yukon Territory, the area north of British Columbia and east of Alaska, and the Northwest Territories, including all of Canada north of 60°

North latitude except Yukon and the northernmost sections of Quebec and Newfoundland. This area includes all of the Arctic north of the mainland, Norway having recognized Canadian sovereignty over the Svendrup Islands in the Arctic in 1931.

The Liberal Party of Sir Wilfrid Laurier and William Lyon Mackenzie King, Prime Minister in 1935–48, remained in power until 1957, when it was succeeded by the Progressive Conservatives. The Liberals, under the leadership of Lester B. Pearson, returned to power in 1963. Pearson remained Prime Minister until 1968, when he retired at 71, and was replaced as party leader and Prime Minister by a former law professor, Pierre Elliott Trudeau. Trudeau maintained Canada's defensive alliance with the United States but began moving toward a more independent policy in world affairs.

Trudeau set about creating what he termed a "just society," stressing domestic reforms. Trudeau's election was considered in part a response to the most serious problem confronting the country, the division between French- and English-speaking Canadians, which had led to a separatist movement in the predominantly French province of Quebec. Trudeau, himself a French Canadian, supported programs for bilingualism and an increased measure of provincial autonomy, although he would not tolerate the idea of separatism. In July 1974 the provincial government voted to make French the official language of Quebec.

A serious challenge to the bilingualism policy came in June 1976, when airline pilots and air controllers struck against the use of French in Quebec airports for flight control. Amid opposition from supporters of French, the government put an end to the strike by imposing an "English only" policy pending the outcome of a study by a three-member commission.

Trudeau sought to improve relations between the federal and provincial governments. In answer to demands from Quebec that Canada be reorganized as a republic, Trudeau, although he had omitted the traditional statement of loyalty to Elizabeth II of the United Kingdom as Queen of

Provinces and Territories

Provinces	Land area. sq. ml.	Population (est. 1975)
Alberta	255,285	1,788,000
British Columbia	366,255	2,471,000
Manitoba	251,000	1,021,000
New Brunswick	28,354	681,000
Newfoundland	156,185	553,000
Nova Scotia	21,425	827,000
Ontario	412,582	8,270,000
Prince Edward Island	2,184	120,000
Quebec	594,860	6,208,000
Saskatchewan	251,700	925,000
Territories		
Northwest Territories	1,304,903	38,000
Yukon Territory	207,076	19,000

Provinces	Capital	Premier 1976
Alberta	Edmonton	E. Peter Lougheed[1]
British Columbia	Victoria	William R. Bennett[2]
Manitoba	Winnipeg	Edward Schreyer[3]
New Brunswick	Fredericton	Richard Hatfield[1]
Newfoundland	St. John's	Frank Moores[1]
Nova Scotia	Halifax	Gerald Regan[4]
Ontario	Toronto	William G. Davis[1]
Prince Edward Island	Charlottetown	Alexander B. Campbell[4]
Quebec	Quebec	Robert Bourassa[4]
Saskatchewan	Regina	A. E. Blakeney[3]
Territories		
Northwest Territories	Yellowknife	Stuart M. Hodgson[5]
Yukon	Whitehorse	James Smith[5]

[1] Progressive-Conservative. [2] Social Credit. [3] New Democratic Party. [4] Liberal. [5] Commissioner.

Canada, declared that the monarchy would stay until "the people of Canada demanded a change."

Canada · established diplomatic relations with China in late 1970, opening the way for other Western nations, notably the United States, to begin dialogues with the Communist state.

Trudeau was very nearly turned out of office in the 1972 elections, the closest in Canada's history. No party received an absolute majority, but Trudeau remained in power as head of a minority government until 1974, when, in new elections, he and his party regained virtually all of the ground lost two years earlier.

Global economic conditions affected U.S.-Canadian relations in 1974-75. Pressures of the energy crisis led Canada to boost the price of natural gas exports to the U.S. by 67% and to increase its export tax on crude oil. Although U.S. Ambassador William J. Porter denounced "unnecessary nationalism," Canada embarked in January, 1975, on a plan for an eight-year phase-out of oil exports to the United States. The oil export tax was raised again.

To combat continuing inflation, the Trudeau government in October 1975 imposed wage and price controls, expanding them in March 1976 to cover all major industries.

Canada was host to the 1976 Olympic Games in Montreal. Trudeau aroused widespread criticism when he refused to permit a team from Taiwan to compete as representatives of the Republic of China. The Games were also marred by a boycott of African states protesting the presence of New Zealand, which had allowed a rugby team to tour South Africa.

Economic Conditions. Agriculture, including horticulture, fruit growing and the raising of stock and poultry, is the largest single industry. Canada is one of the world's greatest wheat-exporting countries; production is concentrated in Manitoba, Saskatchewan and Alberta.

Stock raising and dairy farming have grown greatly since 1920. Ontario and Quebec are the most important dairying provinces.

Canadian manufactures rely mainly on domestic raw materials; growing industries which depend largely on material imported in a raw or semifinished state include the manufacture of automobiles, sugar, and rubber goods, as well as the iron and steel industry in Nova Scotia, Quebec and Ontario. The latter two provinces account for more than 80% of all manufactures. The abundance of cheap water power is one of the chief factors in the growth of Canadian industry.

The most important industries in terms of output are pulp and paper, nonferrous-metals smelting and refining, petroleum products, meatpacking, motor vehicles, and sawmill products.

Canada's mineral resources are both rich and varied. Metals come mainly from two widely separated regions, the mountain ranges of the Pacific coast and the province of Ontario. Copper ore also exists in Quebec, Manitoba and Newfoundland. Production of petroleum centers in Alberta. There are deposits of uranium in the Northwest Territories.

The total area of land covered by forests is estimated at 1,300,000 square miles, of which only 435,000 are commercially productive and accessible. The manufacture of pulp and paper is one of the leading industries.

Fishing, Canada's oldest industry, is carried on along the Atlantic and Pacific coasts and on the inland lakes.

Chief exports in 1974 were motor vehicles (17%), crude oil (11%), metal ores (8%), wheat (6%), nonferrous metals (6%), timber (6%), wood pulp (6%), newsprint (6%). Leading customers were U.S. (66%), EEC (13%; incl. United Kingdom 6%), Japan (7%). Leading suppliers U.S. (66%) and EEC (10%).

Natural Features. Covering most of the northern part of the North American continent and with an area larger than that of the United States, Canada's topography is extremely diversified. The northeastern region, including most of Quebec, northern Ontario and Manitoba, and the Northwest Territories, with Hudson Bay in the center, is an important source of minerals, wood pulp and water power. In the east the mountainous maritime provinces have an irregular coast line on the Gulf of St. Lawrence and the Atlantic. The St. Lawrence plain, covering most of southern

Quebec and Ontario, and the interior continental plain, covering southern Manitoba and Saskatchewan and most of Alberta, are the principal cultivable areas. They are separated by a forested plateau rising from lakes Superior and Huron. Westward toward the Pacific, most of British Columbia, Yukon and part of western Alberta are covered by parallel mountain ranges including the Rockies. The Pacific border of the coast range is ragged with fiords and channels. The highest point in Canada is Mt. Logan (19,850 ft.), which is located in the Yukon.

Canada has an abundance of large and small lakes. In addition to the Great Lakes on the U.S. border, there are 9 others which are more than 100 miles long and 35 which are more than 50 miles long.

The two principal river systems are the Mackenzie and the St. Lawrence. The St. Lawrence, with its tributaries, is navigable for over 1,900 miles.

CAPE VERDE (Republic)

President: Aristides Pereira (1975).
Premier: Pedro Pires (1975).
Area: 1,557 sq mi. (4,033 sq km).
Population (est. 1976): 300,000.
Density per square mile: 192.7.
Capital (1970 census): Praia, 21,494.
Largest city: Mindelo (est. 1970): 28,800.
Monetary unit: Cape Verde escudo.
Language: Portuguese.
Religions: Roman Catholic and animist.

The islands became Africa's 44th independent nation July 5, 1975, under an agreement negotiated with Portugal in 1974. A 56-member National Assembly elected June 30 chose Aristides Pereira as President and Pedro Pires as Premier. All members of the Assembly belong to the African Party for the Independence of Portuguese Guinea and Cape Verde (P.A.I.C.G.), then the only party that entered candidates in the election. P.A.I.C.G. is committed to union with Guinea-Bissau, another former Portuguese colony.

History. Uninhabited upon its discovery in 1456, the Cape Verde archipelago, in the Atlantic 270 miles west of Dakar, Senegal, became part of the Portuguese empire in 1495. There are 10 principal islands. A majority of their modern inhabitants are of mixed Portuguese and African ancestry. A coaling station developed during the 19th century on the island of São Vicente has grown in recent years to an oil and gasoline storage depot for ships and aircraft. Portugal's desire to retain the depot complicated the joint P.A.I.C.G. negotiations on independence. Lisbon agreed to independence for the Cape Verdes on Dec. 18, 1974, and accepted the P.A.I.C.G. as the only ruling party during the transitional period.

Economic Conditions. The main occupations are livestock breeding and fishing. Because of a drought that has lasted since 1968 and antiquated agricultural methods, there is little farming. The main crops are bananas, sugar cane, maize, sweet potatoes and beans.

Chief exports in 1973 were fish (33%) (shellfish 12%), fish products (20%), salt (8%), bananas (6%) and metals (6%). Leading customers were Portugal (61%), U.S. (25%), ships' stores (6%). Leading suppliers were Portugal (53%), United Kingdom (13%), Angola (11%).

Natural Features. The islands that make up Cape Verde are mostly mountainous, with the land deeply scarred by erosion. There is an active volcano on Fogo.

The islands are divided into two groups: Barlavento in the north, comprising Santo Antão (291 sq mi.), Boavista (240 sq mi.), São Nicolau (132 sq mi.), São Vicente (88 sq mi.), Sal (83 sq mi.) and Santa Luzia (13 sq mi.); Sotavento in the south, consisting of São Tiago (383 sq mi.), Fogo (184 sq mi.), Maio (103 sq mi.), and Brava (25 sq mi.).

CENTRAL AFRICAN REPUBLIC

(République Centrafricaine)

(Member of French Community)
President of the Government: Marshal Jean-Bédel Bokassa (1966).
Area: 240,535 sq mi. (622,984 sq km).
Population (est. 1974 by U.N.): 2,610,000.
Density per square mile: 10.9.
Capital and largest city (est. 1971): Bangui, 187,000.
Monetary unit: Franc CFA.
Ethnic groups: Mandja-Baya, Banda, Mbaka, Azande.
Languages: French (official) and Sango.
Religions: Christian, 50%; animist and Catholic.

Since Dec. 31, 1965, the country has been ruled by a military government headed by Marshal Bokassa and a Cabinet of his own choosing. The Constitution was suspended and the National Assembly dissolved in 1966.

Political Party. MESAN (Mouvement d'Evolution Sociale de l'Afrique Noire), led by Marshal Bokassa.

History. As the colony of Ubangi-Shari, what is now the Central African Republic was united with Chad in 1905 and joined with Gabon and Middle Congo in French Equatorial Africa in 1910. After World War II a rebellion in 1946 forced the French to grant self-government. In 1958 the territory voted to become an autonomous republic within the French Community, but on Aug. 13, 1960, President David Dacko proclaimed the republic's independence from France.

Dacko undertook to move the country into Peking's orbit, but was overthrown in 1966 in a coup led by Army chief of staff, Col. Jean-Bédel Bokassa, who installed himself as chief of state. In 1972, MESAN named Bokassa president for life. In January, 1975, he appointed Elisabeth Domitien to be Premier, the first woman chief of government in Africa. Bokassa abolished the post of Premier April 7, 1976, and Mrs. Domitien lost her unique distinction.

Economic Conditions. Coffee, cotton, sesame, diamonds and lumber are the leading products.

Chief exports in 1973 were diamonds (32%), cotton (31%) and coffee (30%). Leading customers were France (41%), U.S. (15%), Israel (11%), Italy (6%). Leading suppliers were France (57%), U.S. (9%), West Germany (7%).

CHAD (Republic)

(République du Tchad)

(Member of French Community)
Chief of State: Brig. Gen. Félix Malloum (1975).
Area: 495,752 sq mi. (1,284,000 sq km).
Population (est. 1976): 4,110,000.
Density per square mile: 8.9.
Capital and largest city (est. 1973): Ndjamena (formerly Fort-Lamy), 193,000.
Monetary unit: Franc CFA.
Ethnic groups: Baguirmiens, Kanembous, Saras, Massas, Arabs, Toubous, Goranes.
Languages: French (official), Sara, Kenembou, Ouddai, Massa, Arabic, Gorane.
Religions: Moslem, Christian and animist.

After a coup on April 13, 1975, a nine-member military council took over all governmental functions, including those of the 75-member Legislative Assembly. Political parties were banned.

History. A landlocked country in North Central Africa, Chad was absorbed into the colony of French Equatorial Africa, as part of Ubangi-Shari, in 1910. France began the country's development after 1920, when it became a separate colony. In 1946, French Equatorial Africa was admitted to the French Union. The Chad territory by referendum in 1958 became an autonomous republic within the French Union. An independence movement led by the first Premier and President, François (later Ngarta) Tombalbaye, achieved complete independence on Aug. 11, 1960. After a coup failed in 1963, Tombalbaye as President and chief of state promulgated a new Constitution and organized a new government dominated by the south.

A six-year sub-Sahara drought caused mass migrations, thousands of deaths and famine conditions for some 2 million Chadians in 1974. International relief efforts were disrupted Oct. 25, when President Tombalbaye ordered rejection of U.S. grain shipments (45% of the total). He charged that U.S. officials had barred Chadians from policy roles.

Tombalbaye was killed in the April 13 coup and the government is now headed by Brig. Gen. Félix Malloum, whom Tombalbaye had once imprisoned for plotting.

Economic Conditions. The principal agricultural product of Chad is cotton. Rice and peanuts are also cultivated. Livestock include camels, cattle and sheep.

Chief exports in 1973 were cotton (63%), beef and veal (7%) and cattle (5%). Leading customers not separately distinguished (62%), Nigeria (6%), Congo (5%). Leading suppliers were France (42%) and Nigeria (12%).

CHILE (Republic)

(República de Chile)

President: Gen. Augusto Pinochet Ugarte (1973).
Area: 292,257 sq mi. (756,945 sq km).
Population (est. 1976): 10,420,000.
Density per square mile: 35.7.
Capital: Santiago.
Largest cities (est. 1975 for urban agglomeration): Santiago, 3,263,000; (est. 1971 by U.N.): Valparaiso, 250,400; Viña del Mar, 179,600; Concepción, 161,000; Talcahuano, 148,000; Antofagasta, 125,100.
Monetary Unit: Peso.
Language: Spanish.
Religion: Roman Catholic.

Under the pre-coup constitution, the nation elected a President every six years, a Senate of 50 members every eight years (one-half renewable every four years), and a Chamber of Deputies of 150 members every four years.

Major Political Parties. Christian Democratic Party National Party, Communist Party and Socialist Party (which had been led by President Salvador Allende). Until the 1973 coup, two large coalitions opposed each other in Congress—the Democratic Confederation (CODE), consisting of the Christian Democratic, National, Radical Left, Radical Democratic and National Democratic Parties; and the Allende-backed Popular Unity (UP), composed of the Socialist, Communist, Radical, Independent Action and Christian Left Parties and the United Popular Action Movement. In the 1973 Congressional elections, CODE retained control of both houses: 87 to 63 in the Chamber of Deputies, 30 to 20 in the Senate.

History. This republic in South America south of Peru and west of Bolivia and Argentina fills a narrow 1,800-mile strip between the Andes and the Pacific. It was originally under the control of the Incas in the north and the fierce Araucanian people in the south. In 1541, a Spaniard, Pedro de Valdiva, founded Santiago. Chile won its independence from Spain in 1818 under Bernardo O'Higgins and an Argentinian, José de San Martin. O'Higgins, dictator until 1823, laid the foundations of the modern state with a two-party system and a centralized government.

The dictator from 1830 to 1837, Diego Portales, fought a war with Peru in 1836-39 which expanded Chilean territory. The Conservatives were in power from 1831 to 1861. Then the Liberals, winning a share of power for the next 30 years, disestablished the church and limited presidential power. Chile fought the war of the Pacific with Peru and Bolivia from 1879 to 1883, winning Antofagasta, Bolivia's only outlet to the sea, and extensive areas from Peru. A revolt in 1890 led by Jorge Montt overthrew, in 1891, José Balmaceda and established a parliamentary dictatorship that persisted until a new Constitution was adopted in 1925. Industrialization began before World War I and led to the formation of Marxist groups.

Juan Antonio Ríos, President during World War II, was originally pro-Nazi but in 1944 led his country into the war on the side of the United States. After the war Gabriel González Videla, elected by a coalition including the Communists, turned on them. The Communist Party was outlawed until 1958.

A small abortive army uprising in 1969 raised fear of military intervention to prevent a Marxist, Salvador Allende Gossens, from taking office after his election to the presidency on Sept. 4, 1970, with 36.3% of the vote in a three-way battle. Dr. Allende was the first President in a non-Communist country freely elected on a Marxist-Leninist program.

Allende quickly established relations with Cuba and the People's Republic of China and nationalized several American companies. He promised compensation but imposed retroactive taxes to cancel out most claims, leading to cool but proper relations with the United States. By 1972, inflation was running over 100% annually.

A middle-class general strike led to a military coup Sept. 11, 1973, then to Allende's overthrow and mysterious death in an army assault on the presidential palace. More than 2,700 deaths were reported in the coup and many thousands were arrested. The coup ended a 46-year era of constitutional government in Chile, which had boasted the longest such record in Latin America.

The takeover was run by a four-man junta headed by Army chief of staff Augusto Pinochet Ugarte, who assumed the office of President and governed under a state of siege that was kept in force by extensions every six months.

Committed to "exterminate Marxism," the junta embarked on a right-wing dictatorship. It suspended parliament, banned political activity and broke relations with Cuba. Mexico, which recognized the Havana regime, severed relations with Chile in 1974.

Faced with widespread charges of mass arrests, torture and executions of its foes, the junta admitted in April, 1975, that 41,259 persons had been arrested since the coup, but said it had freed 36,605 of the prisoners, of whom 9,167 were exiled. Roman Catholic sources estimated the arrest total at 95,000.

The Human Rights Commission of the Organization of American States charged the junta with "most grave violations" of basic liberties, but the O.A.S. voted in May, 1975, not to hear the report until further evidence was supplied. In July, Chile denied entry to a U.N. investigatory panel.

In September, 1974, it was disclosed that the U.S. Central Intelligence Agency had secretly aided Allende's opponents before his election and had later worked covertly to "destabilize" his government. President Ford admitted that there had been a clandestine U.S. effort under the Nixon Administration to "assist the preservation" of opposition news media and political parties, but said the United States had "no involvement in any way with the coup itself."

The junta honored claims of corporations nationalized under Allende, among them the International Telephone & Telegraph Corporation, which was promised $125.2 million, and the Kennecott Copper Corporation, which agreed to a $68-million settlement.

With an economy depressed by a slump in world copper prices, the military regime in October 1975 designated a new currency, the peso, equivalent to 1,000 escudos, the much-devalued former monetary unit. Under the impact of an austerity program launched earlier, the rate of inflation—375% for 1975—slowed to 10% a month for the first half of 1976.

Economic Conditions. Chilean agriculture is mostly confined to the temperate central valley, similar to that of California. Productive land is extremely limited, and most of it must be irrigated. Wheat is the leading crop. Grapes are next to wheat in acreage. Feudal-type estates averaging 2,500 acres predominate.

The basis of the country's economy is its mineral resources in the northern desert provinces of Atacama, Antofagasta, and Tarapacá, where the only natural nitrate in the world is found. Some 60% of the world's iodine is obtained as a by-product of nitrate processing. Chile's world monopoly in nitrate, however, declined with the development of the synthetic product.

The world's largest copper reserve, estimated at 134 billion pounds, is in Chile, and also more than 900 million tons of high-grade iron ore. The reserve of Chilean coal, noted for quantity rather than quality, exceeds two billion tons.

Chief exports in 1973 were copper and copper ore (86%); in 1972, iron ore (7%). Leading customers in 1972 were Japan (17%), West Germany (14%), United Kingdom (11%), U.S. (10%), Netherlands (8%), Italy (7%), Argentina (6%). Leading suppliers were U.S. (17%), Argentina (15%), West Germany (9%), U.K. (6%).

Natural Features. A narrow, mountainous land, Chile has one third of its area covered by the towering ranges of the Andes. In the north is the mineral-rich Atacama Desert, between the coast mountains and the Andes. In the center is a 700-mile-long valley, thickly populated, between the Andes and the coastal plateau. In the south, the Andes border on the ocean.

At the southern tip of Chile's mainland is Punta Arenas, the southernmost city in the world, and beyond that lies the Strait of Magellan and Tierra del Fuego, an island divided between Chile and Argentina. The southernmost point of South America is Cape Horn, a 1,390-foot rock on Horn Island in the Wollaston group, which belongs to Chile.

The Juan Fernández Islands, in the South Pacific about 400 miles west of the mainland, and Easter Island, about 2,000 miles west, are Chilean possessions.

CHINA, People's Republic of

(Chung-Hua Jen-Min Kung-Ho Kuo)

Head of State: (Vacant).
Premier: Hua Kuo-feng (1976).
Area: 3,705,406 sq mi. (9,596,961 sq km).*
Population (est. 1976): 852,500,000.
Density per square mile: 230.0*
Capital: Peking.
Largest cities (est. 1970): Shanghai, 10,820,000; Peking, 7,570,000; Tientsin, 4,280,000; Wuhan, 4,250,000; Lüta (Port Arthur and Dairen), 4,000,000; Mukden, 3,750,000; Chungking, 3,500,000; Harbin, 2,750,000; Taiyüan, 2,725,000; Canton, 2,300,000; Nanking, 2,000,000.
Monetary unit: Chinese dollar (yuan).
Language: Chinese, (Mandarin, Cantonese and local dialects).
Religions: Principally Confucianist, Buddhist, and Taoist.

With 3,040 deputies, elected for four-year terms by universal suffrage, the National People's Congress is the chief legislative organ. A State Council has the executive authority. The Congress elects the Chairman and Vice Chairman of the country. The State Council, headed by the Premier, Hua Kuo-feng, has under it all ministries.

Political Party. The Communist Party controls the government.

History. By 2000 B.C., the Chinese were living in the Hwang Ho basin, and they had achieved an advanced stage of civilization by 1200 B.C. The great philosophers Lao-tse, Confucius, Mo Ti, and

* Including Manchuria and Tibet.

Mencius lived during the Chou dynasty (1122–249 B.C.). The warring feudal states were first united under Emperor Ch'in Shih Huang Ti, during whose reign (246–210 B.C.) work was begun on the Great Wall. Under the Han dynasty (206 B.C.–A.D. 220) China prospered and traded with the West.

The T'ang dynasty (618–907) has often been called the golden age of Chinese history. Painting, sculpture, and poetry flourished, and printing made its earliest known appearance.

The Mings, last of the native rulers (1368–1644), overthrew the Mongol, or Yuan, dynasty (1280–1368) established by Kublai Khan. The Mings in turn were overthrown in 1644 by invaders from the north, the Manchus.

The Chinese closely restricted foreign activities, and by the end of the 18th century only Canton and the Portuguese port of Macao were open to European merchants. Following the Anglo-Chinese War of 1839–42, however, several treaty ports were opened, and Hong Kong was ceded to Britain. Treaties signed after further hostilities (1856–60) weakened Chinese sovereignty and removed foreigners from Chinese jurisdiction. The disastrous Chinese-Japanese War of 1894–95 was followed by a scramble for Chinese concessions by European powers, leading to the Boxer Rebellion (1900), suppressed by an international force.

The death of the Empress Dowager Tzu Hsi in 1908 and the accession of the infant Emperor Hsüan T'ung (Pu-Yi) were followed by a nationwide rebellion led by Dr. Sun Yat-sen, who became first President of the Provisional Chinese Republic in 1911. The Manchus abdicated on Feb. 12, 1912. Dr. Sun resigned in favor of Yuan Shih-k'ai, who suppressed the republicans but was forced by a serious rising in 1915–16 to abandon his intention of declaring himself Emperor. Yuan's death in June, 1916, was followed by years of civil war between rival militarists and Dr. Sun's republicans. The death in 1925 of Dr. Sun, who had controlled only the Canton area in opposition to the recognized regime, was followed by a revival of the Kuomintang Party, which practically deified him. Nationalist forces, led by Gen. Chiang Kai-shek and with the advice of Communist experts, soon occupied most of China, setting up a Kuomintang regime in 1928. Internal strife continued, however, and Chiang broke with the Communists.

An alleged explosion on the South Manchurian Railway on Sept. 18, 1931, brought invasion of Manchuria by Japanese forces, who installed the last Manchu Emperor, Henry Pu-Yi, as nominal ruler of the puppet state of "Manchukuo." Japanese efforts to take China's northern provinces in July, 1937, were resisted by Chiang Kai-shek, who meanwhile had succeeded in uniting most of China behind him. Within two years, however, Japan seized most of the ports and railways. The Kuomintang government retreated first to Hankow and then to Chungking, while the Japanese set up a puppet government at Nanking headed by Wang Ching-wei.

When the Japanese surrendered in 1945, China signed a treaty with the Soviet Union providing for Soviet withdrawal from Manchuria, joint Chinese-Soviet control of Manchurian railways for 30 years, a joint Chinese-Soviet naval base at Port Arthur, and a free port at Dairen.

Japan's surrender touched off civil war between Nationalist forces under Chiang Kai-shek and Communist forces led by Mao Tse-tung, the party chairman. Despite U. S. aid, the Chiang forces were overcome by the Maoists, backed by the Soviet bloc, and were expelled from the mainland. The Mao regime, established in Peking as the new capital, proclaimed the People's Republic of China on Oct. 1, 1949, with Chou En-lai as Premier. The soviet-type government, after prolonged negotiations, signed a 30-year treaty of friendship and mutual aid with the Soviet Union on Feb. 14, 1950. Its published terms provided for return of the Changchun railroad to China and the eventual return of Port Arthur and Dairen, occupied by Soviet troops. Later in the year, Chinese troops invaded Tibet and began its subjugation, a campaign which brought China into conflict with India. After the Korean War began in June, 1950, China led the Communist bloc in supporting North Korea, and on Nov. 26, 1950, the Mao regime intervened openly.

A deterioration of relations between Peking and Moscow was indicated in 1958 when Peking emerged as an independent center of Communist power, challenging the leadership role of the U.S.S.R. in the Soviet bloc.

In 1958, Mao undertook the "Great Leap Forward" campaign which combined the establishment of rural communes with a crash program of village industrialization. These efforts also failed, causing Mao to lose influence to Liu Shao-chi, who became President in 1959, to Premier Chou and to Party Secretary Teng Hsiao-ping. Meanwhile China's backing of subversive movements in Asia soured relations with India and Burma, although it very nearly achieved the conquest of Indonesia, and culminated in war on the borders of India late in 1962. By 1963 the break with the Soviet Union was complete.

Mao, with the backing of supporters—his wife, Chiang Ching; the Defense Minister, Marshal Lin Piao; his former secretary, Chen Po-ta; and Premier Chou—began a struggle to regain power. Chou proposed the movement that became known as the Cultural Revolution at the party congress in 1964, the same year China exploded its first atomic (fission) bomb (it achieved the fusion bomb in 1967).

Mao moved to Shanghai, and from that base he and his supporters waged their own Cultural Revolution. President Liu and the party secretary, Teng, took over, and their followers denounced hundreds of party and government officials at rallies and in wall posters. Then, in 1966, Chen became director of the Cultural Revolution, the army chief of staff, Lo Jui-ching, was purged, and Lin replaced Liu as No. 2 in the hierarchy. In the spring of 1966 the Mao group formed Red Guard units dominated by youths and students, closing the schools to free the students for agitation. On Aug. 18, 1966, a few days after a Central Committee session at which Liu and Teng retained membership, a rally was held in Peking at which hundreds of thousands of Red Guards took part. During the fall more than 11 million Red Guards went to Peking to take part in rallies, demonstrations, and purges.

The Red Guards campaigned against "old ideas, old culture, old habits and old customs." Often they were no more than uncontrolled mobs, and brutality was frequent. Early in 1967 efforts were made to restore control. The Red Guards were urged to return home. Schools started opening. But the height of violence was only reached in September, 1967, when in Canton the opposing factions used tanks and artillery against each other.

Persistent overtures by the Nixon Administration (relaxed trade and travel restrictions) abruptly climaxed in an invitation to a U.S. table tennis team to visit Peking in April 1971. This was followed by the dramatic announcement in July that Henry Kissinger, Mr. Nixon's national security adviser, had secretly visited Peking and reached agreement on a visit by the President to Red China.

The movement toward reconciliation, which signaled the end of the U.S. containment policy toward China, provided irresistible momentum for Chinese admission to the U.N. Despite U.S. opposition to expelling Taiwan (Nationalist China), the world body overwhelmingly ousted Chiang Kai-shek in seating Peking.

Mr. Nixon went to Peking for a week early in 1972, meeting Mao as well as Chou. The summit ended with a historic communiqué on Feb. 28, in which both nations promised to work toward improved relations. They differed over Vietnam as well as Taiwan, although the U.S. noted it was withdrawing from Vietnam and said its ultimate goal was withdrawal from Taiwan as well, with interim reductions of those forces as tension in the area diminished. The U.S. also did not challenge Peking's view that Taiwan is part of China and its status should be settled by the Chinese themselves.

In 1973, the U.S. and China agreed to set up "liaison offices" in each other's capitals, which constituted de facto diplomatic relations. Full diplomatic relations were barred by China as long as the U.S. continued to recognize Nationalist China (Taiwan).

The quarrel with the Soviet Union did not ease, however, and massive military concentrations on both sides of the common border were not reduced despite Sino-Soviet talks about the frontier problem. The dispute initially focused on Damansky and other islands in the Ussuri River, but China broadly claimed that much of its territory was illegally annexed by Tsars, and Red Russia would not return it.

The National People's Congress held its first meeting in a decade in Peking, Jan. 13–17, 1975. With Mao absent, it re-elected Chou as Premier. It approved a government realignment which placed Marshal Yeh Chien-ying, 77, in the post of Defense Minister vacant since Lin's death. It revised the 1954 Constitution to reassert the primacy of the Communist Party and to specify limited rights of citizens to strike and demonstrate, to hold private farm plots and to work for themselves.

Chou predicted in a keynote address that "fierce contention" between the United States and the Soviet Union "is bound to lead to world war some day." He said there is "no détente, let alone lasting peace in the world today."

The same warnings against détente were made during President Ford's visit to China, Dec. 8–12, 1975, by Vice Premier Teng Hsiao-Ping. Teng served as chief host because Chou was now seriously ill with cancer and Mao, visibly failing, saw the visitor only briefly.

Jan. 8, 1976, amid a national outpouring of grief, Chou died. Demonstrations in the capital turned into near riots when mourners suspected the government of trying to suppress the display of emotion. Teng, who had been rehabilitated by Chou and designated as his successor, was supplanted within a month by Hua Kuo-feng, 54, former Minister of Public Security. Hua, believed to be a compromise between radicals and the moderates represented by the ousted

Teng, became permanent Premier in April. In October he was named successor to Mao as Chairman of the Communist Party.

Mao died Sept. 10, apparently of Parkinson's disease, and China for the second time in a year went into a period of national mourning. Although there was speculation about new political turmoil after the death of the architect of the revolution, there was no immediate change. Party leaders, possibly in anticipation of Mao's death, had already issued a call for unity in late August, signaling an end to a six-month campaign against the "capitalist roader," Teng.

For the moment, at least, foreign policy continued to be strongly anti-Soviet, with frequent warnings to the Western world against détente. Internally, China faced the task of rebuilding the cities damaged by the August earthquake and the political reconstruction indicated by 16 vacancies in the 22-member Politburo.

On July 28, an earthquake measuring 8.6 on the Richter scale struck northern China, inflicting heavy damage and casualties in Peking, Tientsin and Tangshan. There were 100,000 dead reported in Tangshan alone.

Economic Conditions. In China, nearly 80% of the population depends on the land for livelihood. Subsistence crops are necessarily emphasized, but China is still not self-sufficient in food.

In northern China, wheat, barley, corn, sorghum, millet and other cereals, and beans and peas predominate, whereas in the south, rice, sugar, and indigo are most important.

The Yangtze basin, one of the most favored agricultural regions in the world, is China's premier granary. Tea is grown mainly in the central uplands, coastal ranges, and Szechwan.

Silkworm culture is practiced widely, especially in the lower Yangtze valley. Soybeans and cotton are of ever-increasing importance. Other crops include fibers, tobacco, vegetable oils, cane sugar, and many medicinal plants and spices.

Industrially, China is still in its infancy. Development has been mainly in the erection of textile mills, silk and flour mills, match factories, tanneries, and a few steel and cement mills. The production of consumer's goods far exceeds that of producer's goods, which must still be imported.

Mineral resources are considerable. Iron ore, far less plentiful than coal, is mined principally in the lower Yangtze valley and in north China. Tin, mined in Yunnan and southwest Szechwan, has been a major mineral export. Of some rarer minerals, notably antimony and tungsten, China is sometimes the world's leading producer. Lead, zinc, silver, mercury and gold are also mined. The discovery of uranium has been reported.

China urgently needs reforestation. Most remaining forests are on inaccessible mountain slopes. Bamboo is cultivated in groves throughout the country south of the Tsinling mountains.

Chief exports in 1974 were foodstuffs (c. 40%; meat and products, cereals, fruits and vegetables), crude oil (c. 20%) and textiles and clothing (c. 20%). Leading customers were Japan (c. 22%), Hong Kong (c. 20%). Leading suppliers were Japan (c. 29%), U.S. (c. 12%), Canada (c. 6%), West Germany (c. 6%), Australia (c. 5%).

Natural Features. China has about one and a quarter times the area of the continental United States. Its coast line is roughly a semicircle, about

2,150 miles long. The greater part of the country is mountainous, and only in the lower reaches of the Yellow and Yangtze rivers are there extensive low plains.

The principal mountain ranges are the Tien Shan, to the northwest; the Kunlun chain, running south of the Takla Makan and Gobi deserts; and the Trans-Himalaya, connecting the Kunlun with the borders of China and Tibet. Manchuria is largely an undulating plain connected with the north China plain by a narrow lowland corridor. Inner Mongolia contains the relatively fertile southern and eastern portions of the Gobi. The large island of Hainan (13,500 sq. mi.) lies off the southern coast.

Hydrographically, China proper consists of three great river systems. The northern part of the country is drained by the Yellow River (Hwang Ho), 2,900 miles long and mostly unnavigable. The central part is drained by the Yangtze Kiang, the fourth longest river in the world (3,602 mi.). The Si Kiang in the south is about 1,236 miles long and navigable for a considerable distance. In addition, the Amur (2,704 mi.) forms part of the northeastern boundary.

TIBET

Status: Autonomous Region of China.
Area: 471,660 sq mi. (1,221,599 sq km).
Population (est. 1968): 1,300,000.
Capital: Lhasa (est. 1970): 175,000.
Monetary unit: Sang.
Exports: wool, live animals, salt, hides, borax, tea, musk.
Agricultural products: barley, fruits, pulse, vegetables.
Minerals: borax, salt, coal, gold.

History. Tibet, inhabited by people of Mongolian stock, is the highest country in the world, averaging 16,000 feet in elevation and having many peaks ranging up to more than 25,000 feet.

Buddhism entered the country around the 7th century, merging with local cults, and was transformed into Lamaism, a developed monastic form, in the 8th century. Missionaries visited the land in the 17th and 18th centuries, but thereafter the Living Buddha (Dalai Lama) isolated his country from the world. In the 20th century the British in India achieved some influence and encouraged the Dalai Lama in 1913 to declare his independence from China. Thereafter, the British and subsequently the Indians maintained influence with the Dalai Lama's government but the No. 2 ruler, the Panchen Lama, continued amenable to Chinese influence.

Chinese Communist troops invaded the area in October 1950. An agreement signed by Communist China and Tibet in May 1951 recognized the Dalai Lama as spiritual and temporal ruler but constituted Tibet a national autonomous region of the People's Republic of China. In the 1950's the Chinese Communist Control Commission introduced land reforms which despoiled the monastic orders and also drove the monks from the lamaseries. The peasantry in various localities staged rebellions beginning in 1956, and in March 1959 a nationwide revolt broke out. The Dalai Lama fled to India on Mar. 31. The revolt was crushed, and the Panchen Lama was installed by Peking as a puppet ruler. He was ousted in December 1964.

On Sept. 1, 1965, the Chinese made Tibet an autonomous region like Sinkiang and exploited it as if it were an overseas colony. As the 1960's closed, repeated revolts were reported by refugees, and the Dalai Lama charged the Chinese with genocide on a mass scale. Chinese settlers were being shipped into the country.

Social Conditions. The religion and predominant factor in Tibet's social system is Lamaism, a late form of Buddhism modified by animism and primitive magic. Education is in the control of the many monasteries, some of which have more than a thousand monks. A large number of the population are lamas, mostly celibates. Both polyandry and polygyny are practiced in Tibet.

CHINA, Republic of

President: C. K. Yen (1975).
Premier: Chiang Ching-kuo (1972).
Area: 13,893 sq mi.* (35,566 sq km).
Population (est. 1976): 16,200,000.
Density per square mile: 1,166.1.
Capital: Taipei.
Largest cities (est. 1976): Taipei, 2,046,900; Kaohsiung, 1,000,700; Taichung, 548,500; Tainan, 524,000; Keelung, 341,200.
Monetary unit: New Taiwan dollar.
Language: Chinese (Mandarin).
Religions: Principally Confucianist, Buddhist, Christian and Taoist.

The President and the Vice President are elected by the National Assembly for a term of six years. There are five major governing bodies called Yuans: Executive, Legislative, Judicial, Control and Examination. Taiwan's internal affairs are administered by the Taiwan Provincial Government under the supervision of the Provincial Assembly, which is popularly elected.

Political Parties. The majority and ruling party is the Kuomintang (Nationalist Party) led by Chiang Ching-kuo. There are also two minority parties: the China Democratic Socialist Party and the Young China Party.

History. The remnant of the Republic of China founded by Sun Yat-sen in the Canton area and extended by Chiang Kai-shek to all the Chinese mainland consists of the former Taiwan province, including Taiwan, an island 100 miles off the mainland in the Pacific Ocean, two offshore islands, Quemoy and Matsu, and nearby islets of the Pescadores chain. Taiwan was inhabited by aborigines of Malayan descent when Chinese from the areas now designated as Fukien and Kwangtung began settling it beginning in the seventh century, becoming the majority.

The Portuguese explored the area in 1590, naming it The Beautiful (Formosa). In 1624 the Dutch set up forts in the South, the Spanish in the North. The Dutch threw out the Spanish in 1641 and controlled the island until 1661, when the Chinese General Koxinga took it over, established an independent kingdom and expelled the Dutch. The Manchus seized the island in 1683 and held it until 1895 when it passed to Japan after the first Sino-Japanese War. Japan developed and exploited

* Excluding Quemoy and Matsu.

it and it was heavily bombed by American planes during World War II, after which it was restored to China. After the defeat of its armies on the mainland, the Nationalist Government of Generalissimo Chiang retreated to Taiwan on Dec. 8, 1949, and proceeded to make it a showcase of democracy in Asia, with land reform and democratically planned development. With only 15% of the population consisting of the 1949 immigrants, Chiang dominated the island, maintaining a 600,000-man army in the hope of eventually recovering the mainland. Japan renounced its claim to the island by the San Francisco Peace Treaty of 1951. By a fleet in the Strait of Formosa the United States prevented a mainland invasion in 1953, and in 1955 the U.S. signed a mutual defense treaty by which it is committed to defend Taiwan and the neighboring islands. In 1968 free public education was extended from six to nine years. All through the 1960's Taiwan enjoyed the highest level of prosperity in Asia except for Japan.

The "China seat" in the U.N., which the Nationalists held with U.S. help for over two decades, was lost in October 1971, when the People's Republic of China was admitted and Taiwan ousted by the world body. The move followed news that President Nixon would visit Peking, which profoundly shocked the Nationalists and unintentionally led to their expulsion from the U.N. Mr. Nixon's summit meeting with Chinese leaders and the February 1972 Sino-American communiqué further eroded Taiwan's position. In it, the U.S. said its eventual goal was complete withdrawal of its forces from Taiwan and progressive cutbacks as tensions in the area eased. With the end of U.S. participation in the war in Vietnam, withdrawal of U.S. air-support forces on the island began in 1973.

The U.S. on March 11, 1976 announced that it would reduce by an indefinite number its forces on Taiwan, estimated in 1972 to be about 2,500.

Chiang Kai-shek died at 87 of a heart attack on April 5, 1975. His son, Chiang Ching-kuo, continued as Premier and dominant power in the Taipei regime. His position was solidified April 26, when a conference of the Kuomintang leadership named him head of the governing party. Vice President Yen Chiakan succeeded Chiang as President.

Economic Conditions. Taiwan is essentially agricultural, with the greater part of the population dependent on farming. It is self-sufficient in most basic foodstuffs and produces surpluses of a number of others, notably rice and sugar. Farms are generally small. Cattle and water buffalo are the chief livestock.

Food processing is the major industry in Taiwan.

Chief exports in 1974 were electrical machinery and equipment (17%), clothing (16%), textile yarns and fabrics (11%), sugar (6%), wood manufactures (5%), fruit and vegetables (5%) and footwear (5%). Leading customers were U.S. (37%), Japan (15%), Hong Kong (6%), West Germany (6%). Leading suppliers were Japan (32%), U.S. (24%), West Germany (7%), Kuwait (6%), Saudi Arabia (5%).

Natural Features. Taiwan is divided by a central mountain range running from north to south, which rises sharply on the east coast of the island and declines gradually to the broad western plain, where cultivation is concentrated.

COLOMBIA (Republic)

(República de Colombia)

President: Alfonso López Michelson (1974).
Area: 439,735 sq mi. (1,138,914 sq km).
Population (est. 1976): 24,190,000 (mestizo, 68%; white, 20%; Indian, 7%; black, 5%).
Density per square mile: 55.0.
Capital: Bogotá.
Largest cities (1973 census): Bogotá, 2,850,000; Medellín, 1,064,741; Cali, 898,253; Barranquilla, 664,533; Cartagena, 356,424; Bucaramanga, 328,328.
Monetary unit: Peso.
Language: Spanish.
Religion: Roman Catholic.

Colombia's President, who appoints his own Cabinet serves for a four-year term. The Senate, the upper house of Congress, has 113 members elected for four years by direct vote. The Chamber of Deputies of 199 members is directly elected for four years.

Major Political Parties. From 1958 until 1974, the Conservative and Liberal parties cooperated in a National Front, dividing offices equally and rotating the national presidency. Under a new arrangement, the majority party in an election assumes the presidency and, until 1978, the minority gets representation in the Cabinet.

History. Colombia is the only South American country bordering both the Atlantic and Pacific Oceans. Spaniards in 1510 founded Darien, the first permanent European settlement on the American mainland. In 1538 the Spaniards established the colony of New Granada, the area's name until 1861. Independence was won in a 14-year struggle in 1824 after Simón Bolívar's Venezuelan troops won the Battle of Boyacá in Colombia on Aug. 7, 1819. Bolívar united Colombia, Venezuela, Panama, and Ecuador in the Republic of Greater Colombia (1819–30) but lost Venezuela and Ecuador to separatists. Bolívar's Vice President, Francisco de Paula Santander, founded the Liberal Party as the Federalists while Bolívar established the Conservatives as the Centralists.

Santander's presidency (1832–36) re-established order, but later periods of Liberal dominance (1849–57 and 1861–80), when the Liberals sought to disestablish the Roman Catholic Church, were marked by insurrection and even civil war. Rafael Nuñez, in a 15-year-presidency, restored the power of the central government and the church, which led in 1899 to a bloody civil war and the loss in 1903 of Panama over ratification of a lease to the United States of the Canal Zone. For 21 years until 1930, the Conservatives held power as revolutionary pressures built up.

The Liberal administrations of Enrique Olaya Herrera and Alfonso López (1930–38) were marked by social reforms which failed to solve the country's problems and in 1946, after World War II, insurrection and banditry broke out which claimed hundreds of thousands of lives by 1958. Laureano Gómez (1950–53), the army chief of staff, General Gustavo Rojas Pinilla (1953–56), and a military junta (1956–57) sought to curb disorder by repression.

Subsequent presidents were Alberto Lleras Camargo (1957–62); Guillermo León Valencia (1962–66);

Carlos Lleras Restrepo (1966-70); Misael Pastrana Borrero (1970-74).

The Liberal Party's Alfonso López Michelson was elected President April 21, 1974 by a landslide (over 500,000 votes) over the Conservative Alvaro Gómez Murtado and three opposition candidates. The Liberals also won control of both houses of Congress.

Inaugurated Aug. 7, 1974, López Michelson formed a coalition Cabinet. Early in 1975, his government was faced with growing unrest, including guerrilla uprisings and a threat of a general strike by a combination of 100 unions, representing 100,000 workers demanding steep pay boosts. The government blamed the disaffection on a leftist conspiracy.

Economic Conditions. Most of the people live by farming and cattle herding, but only a small part of the land is cultivated, and that by primitive means. Colombia's coffee, the nation's principal crop, is a mild variety that does not compete with Brazilian types.

The leading manufacturing industries are foodstuff processing, textiles and beverages.

Rich in minerals, Colombia has the third largest oil industry in Latin America (70% controlled by U.S. interests). The country is also rich in platinum and has world-famous emerald mines at Muzo in the eastern Andes.

Forest products include vanilla, quinine, ipecac, sarsaparilla, gums and balsams, tanning agents, and dyewoods.

Chief export in 1974 was coffee (47%); in 1973, emeralds (7%) and cotton (6%). Leading customers in 1974 were U.S. (37%), West Germany (12%), Spain (5%). Leading suppliers in 1973 were U.S. (40%), West Germany (9%), Japan (8%), France (5%).

Natural Features. Through the western half of the country, three Andean ranges run north and south, merging into one at the Ecuadorean border. The eastern half is a low, jungle-covered plain, drained by spurs of the Amazon and Orinoco, inhabited mostly by uncivilized Indians. The fertile plateau and valley of the eastern range is the most densely populated part of the country.

COMORO ISLANDS

Head of State: Ali Soilih (1975).
Prime Minister: Abdallah Mohammed (1976).
Area: 838 sq mi. (2,171 sq km).
Population (est. 1976): 315,000.
Density per square mile: 375.9.
Capital and largest city (est. 1974 by U.N.): Moroni (on Grand Comoro), 12,000.
Monetary unit: Franc CFA.
Language: French.
Religions: Moslem and Christian.

A chain of four volcanic islands in the Indian Ocean between Africa and Madagascar, under French rule since 1886, the Comoros declared themselves independent July 6, 1975. Mayotte, the most populous and advanced island, with a Christian majority, voted against joining the other, predominantly Moslem, islands in a 1974 referendum. Another vote, in February 1976 at the request of the French government,

resulted in a 99.41% vote by Mayotte affirming its desire to remain French.

In the United Nations Security Council on Feb. 8, 1976, France vetoed a resolution sponsored by African members calling for the cession of Mayotte to the new republic. The three Moslem islands have asserted that the separatist votes in Mayotte are invalid and have associated the republic with the Conference of Islamic States as of May 1976. The French government has insisted that it will respect the wishes of the inhabitants of Mayotte.

The National Council of the Revolution and the National Executive Council of the republican government on Jan. 2, 1976 elected Ali Soilih, Minister of Justice and Defense, as head of state, succeeding Prince Said Mohamed Jaffar. Mohammed Hassanaly, Production Minister, was named Vice President. Soilih on Jan. 6 appointed Abdallah Mohammed as Premier.

Economic Conditions. Agriculture is the principal industry of the Comoro Islands, which consist of Mayotte, Grand Comoro, Moheli and Anjouan. The chief crop is aromatic plants, whose essences are important to the perfume industry. The islands also produce cassava, yams, rice and maize. The chief exports are vanilla, copra and cloves.

CONGO, People's Republic of

(République du Congo)

(Member of French Community)

Head of State: Maj. Marien Ngouabi (1969).
Prime Minister: Louis Sylvain Goma (1975).
Area: 132,046 sq mi. (342,000 sq km).
Population (est. 1976): 1,380,000.
Density per square mile: 10.5.
Capital and largest city (est. 1974): Brazzaville, 310,500.
Monetary unit: Franc CFA.
Ethnic groups: Bavilis, Balalis, Batékés, M'Bochis.
Languages: French, Lingala, Kikongo.
Religions: Animist, 50%; Christian, Moslem.

Since the coup d'etat of September 1968 the country has been governed by a National Council of the Revolution. On Jan. 1, 1969, Major Ngouabi, head of the council, became Head of State.

Political Party. The Congolese Labor Party (PCT) is the only party.

History. Formerly the French Congo, the Republic of the Congo is in West Africa. The inhabitants, mainly Bantu peoples with Pygmies in the north, were subjects of several kingdoms in earlier times.

The Frenchman Pierre Savorgnan de Brazza signed a treaty with Makoko, ruler of the Bateke people, in 1880, which established French control. The area, with Gabon and Ubangi-Shari, was constituted the colony of French Équatorial Africa in 1910. It joined Chad in supporting the Free French cause in World War II. It proclaimed its independence without leaving the French Community in 1960. The republic was a target of Chinese Communist subversion, and in 1965 the United States broke off relations with it.

Ngouabi was sworn in to a second five-year term in January, 1975, and Henri Lopes began his second term as Prime Minister. A visit to Moscow by Ngouabi in March ended with the signing of a Soviet-Congolese economic and technical aid pact.

Following a general strike in which the government was attacked for economic failures, Lopes was removed as Prime Minister Dec. 18, 1975 and replaced by Louis Sylvain Goma.

Economic Conditions. The chief agricultural products of the Republic of the Congo are cocoa, coffee and tobacco. Okoume and limba woods are important forest products. Oil, lead and cassiterite (tin) are the principal minerals.

Chief export in 1973 was crude oil (53%); in 1972, timber (33%), potassic fertilizer (21%), veneers and plywood (14%) and sugar (7%). Leading customers were France (16%), West Germany (14%), South Africa (8%), Netherlands (5%). Leading suppliers were France (54%), West Germany (8%), U.S. (6%), China (5%).

COSTA RICA (Republic)

(República de Costa Rica)

President: Daniel Oduber Quirós (1974).
Area: 19,575 sq mi. (50,700 sq km)
Population (est. 1976): 2,000,000 (approx.: white and Mestizo, 97.6%; black, 1.9%; Indian, .4%; Asiatic, .1%).
Density per square mile: 102.2.
Capital and largest city (est. 1974): San José, 220,700.
Monetary unit: Colón.
Language: Spanish.
Religion: Roman Catholic (state).

Under the 1949 Constitution, the President and the one-house Legislative Assembly of 57 members are elected for terms of four years.

The army was abolished in 1949. There is a police force of 3,000 and a rural guard of 2,500.

Major Political Parties. National Liberation Party (27 of 57 seats in Legislative Assembly), led by President Daniel Oduber Quirós; National Unification Party (16 seats), led by Fernando Trejos-Escalante; National Independent Party (6 seats), led by Jorge González-Martén.

History. This Central American country between Nicaragua and Panama was inhabited by 25,000 Indians when Columbus discovered it and probably named it in 1502. Few of the Indians survived the Spanish conquest, which began in 1563. The region was administered as a Spanish province. It achieved independence in 1821 but was absorbed for two years by Agustín de Iturbide in his Mexican Empire. It was established as a republic in 1848.

Except for the military dictatorship of Tomás Guardia from 1870 to 1882, Costa Rica has enjoyed one of the most democratic governments in Latin America.

Presidents in the post-World War II era were: Ottilio Ulate (1948–53); José Figueres (1953–66, 1970–74); José Joachín Trejos Fernández (1966–70); and Daniel Oduber Quirós, the present incumbent.

Costa Rica revised its extradition laws in March, 1974, to provide a refuge for fugitive U.S. financier Robert Vesco, owner of property there valued at $25 million. Despite anti-Vesco protests, Oduber announced Dec. 8 that Vesco would be allowed to remain.

In November, 1974, Costa Rica joined seven other coffee-producing states in creation of a multinational corporation formed to halt a decline in high world coffee prices.

Economic Conditions. Coffee, bananas, abaca, fiber, cacao and sugar are the basic agricultural products. The mountain slopes yield such forest products as balsa, cedar, dyewood, mahogany and rosewood.

Chief exports in 1974 were coffee (29%) and bananas (22%); in 1973, meat (9%), chemicals (7%) and sugar (6%). Leading customers in 1973 were U.S. (33%), West Germany (13%), Nicaragua (8%), Guatemala (6%), El Salvador (5%), Italy (5%). Leading suppliers were U.S. (35%), Japan (9%), Guatemala (7%), West Germany (7%), El Salvador (5%), Nicaragua (5%), Venezuela (5%).

Natural Features. Most of Costa Rica is tableland, from 3,000 to 6,000 feet above sea level. Cocos Island (10 sq mi.), about 300 miles off the Pacific Coast, is under Costa Rican sovereignty; although it is mostly tropical jungle, it is of potential strategic importance in defense of the Panama Canal.

CUBA (Republic)

(República de Cuba)

President: Osvaldo Dorticós Torrado (1959).
Premier: Fidel Castro Ruz (1959).
Area: 44,218 sq mi. (114,524 sq km).
Population (est. 1975): 9,265,000 (white, 72.8%; mulatto, 14.5%; black, 12.4%; Asiatic, .3%).
Density per square mile: 209.5.
Capital: Havana.
Largest cities (est. 1974): Havana, 1,838,000; (1970 census): Santiago de Cuba, 277,600; Camagüey, 197,720; Holguín, 131,6656; Santa Clara, 130,241; Guantánamo, 129,005.
Monetary unit: Peso.
Language: Spanish.
Religion: Roman Catholic.

There have been no national elections since 1958. Fidel Castro heads the Council of Ministers, the chief governing body.

Political Party. Cuban Communist Party, with a 100-member Central Committee; the power rests with a Politbureau of 8 and a Secretariat of 6.

History. The largest island of the West Indies group, Cuba is also the westernmost, just west of Hispaniola (Haiti and Dominican Republic) and 90 miles south of Key West, Florida, at the entrance to the Gulf of Mexico. It was occupied by the Arawak Indians when Columbus discovered the island in 1492; they died off from diseases brought by sailors and settlers. Spaniards under Diego Velásquez by 1511 founded settlements which served as bases for Spanish exploration. Cuba soon after served as an assembly point for treasure looted by the conquistadores, attracting French and English pirates. Black slaves and free laborers were imported to work the sugar and tobacco plantations; their revolts helped to shape Cuba's evolution from a colony to an independent republic.

Repeated waves of immigration, chiefly from Spain, have helped to preserve the European element in the island's culture.

Open warfare raged between Cuban rebels and Spanish troops from 1867 to 1878. New revolts followed and in 1895 the poet José Martí led the final one.

Pro-rebel sentiment in the United States and the sinking of the battleship *Maine* resulted in a U.S. invasion of Cuba. The Spanish were defeated and ratified in 1899 a treaty which made Cuba an independent republic under U.S. protection. U.S. occupation ended in 1902 after suppressing yellow fever and improving economic conditions. U.S. investment in Cuban enterprises built the economy but also exposed the United States to charges of imperialism. The United States resumed occupation, invoking the Platt Amendment, which gave it the right to intervene, in 1906–09, to suppress a revolt by José Miguel Gómez. U.S. troops returned in 1912 to establish order during the black insurrection, and in 1917 after an uprising.

Gerardo Machado, President during the depression, planned vast social reforms but abandoned them. The United States, under President Franklin D. Roosevelt, scrapped the Platt Amendment in 1934. Fulgencio Batista, an army sergeant, led a revolt in 1934 which overthrew the Machado regime and developed into a Batista dictatorship. A succession of constitutionally elected Presidents—Ramón Grau San Martín, Carlos Mendieta, Miguel Mariano Gómez, Carlos Prío Socarrás—pushed through social reforms, hampered by overwhelming corruption manipulated by Batista. Batista seized power in 1952.

Fidel Castro staged a hopeless revolt in 1953. Captured and paroled he went to Oriente Province and, aided by an Argentinian adventurer, Ernesto (Ché) Guevara, rebuilt his forces and waged a guerrilla war. The United States withdrew support from Batista in 1958. With funds from Soviet sources, Castro bought off the leaders of Batista's army. This and popular support from the intellectual and laboring classes demoralized the army, and Castro's forces grew as he marched on Havana. Batista fled to the Dominican Republic on Jan. 1, 1959.

Executions and torture by the new Castro regime caused a world outcry. Castro antagonized the United States in 1959 by confiscating U.S. investments in banks and industries and by seizing large U.S. landholdings, turning them at first into collective farms, then into Soviet-type state farms.

The United States broke off relations on Jan. 3, 1961, and Castro disclosed his alliance with the Soviet Union and the Soviet bloc. Thousands of Cubans fled to the United States. From their ranks an invasion force was recruited by an all-party coalition financed and guided by the U.S. Central Intelligence Agency and trained in Florida and Guatemala. It landed in the Bay of Pigs, Cuba, on Apr. 17, 1961, but when John F. Kennedy, then President, refused it air support under Soviet and Latin American pressure, the effort collapsed.

In 1962 the Soviet Union built missile sites in Cuba and provided Castro's army with troops, planes and submarines. Alarmed, President Kennedy on Oct. 22, 1962, served notice that the United States was willing to risk war to enforce a demand that the Soviets remove weapons and troops considered to threaten U.S. security. The United States confronted Soviet vessels with U.S. warships. Nikita Khrushchev, then Soviet Premier, agreed to remove the missiles, and the blockade was lifted on Nov. 20. Shortly before Christmas, Castro released 1,113 Bay of Pigs prisoners.

Castro's exorbitant demands for economic help led to a rupture in relations with China, and he returned to the Soviet bloc. Castro's attempts to wage guerrilla warfare in Latin America aided U.S. efforts to build an economic blockade and by 1964 only Mexico and Canada were not ranged against him. In 1970, the new Marxist government of Chile broke the trade and diplomatic boycott of the Organization of American States against Cuba.

Trying to break free from Soviet economic debts, Castro pledged the "honor" of the revolution to an unprecedented goal of a 10-million-ton sugar harvest for 1970. When it failed by 1.5 million tons, he fired the sugar industry minister but admitted his own inefficiency as leader and indicated Cubans were worse off than at any time since he took over.

Russia, spending over $1 million a day (about $400 million a year) to keep Cuba afloat, had to increase its contribution by over $100 million in 1971, but gained greater control over Cuba's economy by setting up a joint Soviet-Cuban economic commission on management and efficiency.

In September 1970, a mini-missile crisis erupted when Russia began using Cuban ports to refuel its growing navy, including vessels that could carry short-range, nuclear missiles. When evidence appeared that the Soviets were building facilities at Cienfuegos for servicing nuclear submarines that carry long-range nuclear missiles, an American warning was issued. Resultant negotiations ended in an "understanding" that the Soviet Union would not build a military base in Cuba and the United States had no intention of invading Cuba.

Neither nation formally admitted it, but U.S.-Cuban relations began to thaw with negotiation of a 1973 agreement to end air hijacking. Except for political refugees, criminal hijackers will be extradited to their home country or tried for the crime where they land; also, both nations pledged to forbid attacks on the other to be mounted from their territory.

In 1975, both sides signaled readiness to improve relations. U.S. curbs on travel by Cuba's United Nations delegation were eased in February. On July 29, the United States joined 15 Latin American republics in voting to scrap economic and diplomatic sanctions the O.A.S. imposed against Cuba in 1964. Only Chile, Paraguay and Uruguay opposed the resolution. Eight Latin states had resumed relations with Havana, and Mexico had maintained its ties throughout the boycott.

The improving U.S.-Cuban climate cooled in late 1975 with the disclosure that Cuban troops were being used to bolster the Popular Movement for the Liberation of Angola in the former Portuguese African colony. President Ford warned on Dec. 20 that the Angolan intervention as well as continued Cuban support for a Puerto Rican independence faction "erodes any chance for improvement of relations."

Despite a May 1976 commitment by Cuba to begin withdrawal from Angola, there were reports of Cuban troops in the Congo, Somalia and the Mideast continuing to "export revolution."

Economic Conditions. Half of the employed are engaged in agriculture, which normally accounts for more than 90% of the exports. About two thirds of the cultivated area is devoted to sugar cane. Other important crops are tobacco, coffee, cacao, fruits, vegetables, henequen, corn, pineapples and rice.

Manufactured products include sugar, molasses, syrup, brandy, rum, alcohol, cigars, cigarettes, cigar boxes, sponges, cement, cordage, salt, dressed hides, dairy products and canned goods.

Rich mineral beds, mostly in the eastern province of Oriente, include iron, copper, manganese, chromium and nickel.

Chief exports in 1971 were sugar (74%) and nonferrous metal ores (16%). Leading customers were U.S.S.R. (35%), Japan (12%), East Germany (6%), Czechoslovakia (5%). Leading suppliers were U.S.S.R. (53%) and East Germany (5%).

Natural Features. Cuba has mountainous areas in the southeast, the central area, and the west, but the rest of the country is flat or rolling.

CYPRUS (Republic)

(Kypriaki Dimokratia)

(Member of Commonwealth of Nations)

President: Archbishop Makarios III (1974).
Area: 3,572 sq mi. (9,251 sq km).
Population (est. 1976): 650,000 (Greek, 82%, Turkish 18%).
Density per square mile: 182.0.
Capital and largest city (est. 1974): Nicosia, 117,100.
Monetary unit: Cyprus pound.
Languages: Greek, Turkish, English.
Religions: Greek Orthodox, 77%; Moslem, 18%.

Under the republic's Constitution, for the protection of the Turkish minority the Vice President as well as three of the ten Cabinet ministers must be from the Turkish community, while the House of Representatives shall be elected by each community separately, 70% Greek Cypriote and 30% Turkish Cypriote representatives.

Under the Constitution, the Greek and Turkish communities are self-governing in questions of religion, education, and culture. Other governmental matters are under the jurisdiction of the central government. Each community is entitled to a Communal Chamber.

The Greek Communal Chamber, which had 23 members, was abolished in March 1965 and its function was absorbed by the Ministry of Education. The Turkish Communal Chamber, however, has continued to function.

Political Parties. The members of the Parliament were elected Sept. 5, 1976. Thirty-five seats are held by Greeks and 15 by Turks. The following is a breakdown of the 35 seats held by Greeks: Democratic Front of Spyros Kyprianon (21); AKEL (Progressive Party of the Working People) (9); EDEK Socialist Party of Dr. Vassos Lyssarides (4); Independents (1). The 15 Turkish members have not attended sessions of the House since January 1964.

History. The third largest island in the Mediterranean, Cyprus was the site of early Phoenician and Greek colonies. For centuries its rule passed through many hands. It fell to the Turks in 1571, and a large Turkish colony settled on the island.

In World War I on the outbreak of hostilities with Turkey, Britain annexed the island. It was declared a crown colony in 1925.

For centuries the Greek population of the island, regarding Greece as their mother country, have sought self-determination and reunion with it (enosis). The resulting quarrel with Turkey threatened the North Atlantic Alliance. Cyprus became an independent nation on Aug. 16, 1960, with Britain, Greece, and Turkey as guarantor powers. After troubled years, a dangerous crisis was averted in 1968 when an American mediator, Cyrus Vance, induced Turkey, Greece, and Cyprus to accept a solution proposed by U.N. Secretary General Thant for withdrawal of the Greek troops and the dismantling of Turkish invasion forces. The ethnic blocs began long direct negotiations for a new Constitution.

Archbishop Makarios, who had been president since 1959, was overthrown July 15, 1974 by a military coup led by the Cypriot National Guard. The new regime named Nikos Giorgiades Sampson as president and Bishop Gennadios as head of the Cypriot Church to replace Makarios. The rebels were led by rightist Greek officers who supported enosis.

Diplomacy failed to resolve the crisis. Turkey invaded Cyprus by sea and air July 20, 1974, asserting its right to protect the Turkish Cypriote minority. Greece rejected a Turkish demand for withdrawal of the 650 Greek officers who had engineered the coup. The crisis forced resignation of the military junta that had ruled Greece for seven years.

Geneva talks involving Greece, Turkey, Great Britain and the two Cypriote factions failed in mid-August, and the Turks kept control of 40% of the island. Greece made no armed response to the superior Turkish force, but bitterly suspended military participation in the NATO alliance.

On Cyprus, U.S. Ambassador Rodger P. Davies was shot to death in August during Greek Cypriote riots. The tension continued after Makarios returned to replace Sampson in the presidency on Dec. 7, 1974. He offered self-government to the Turkish minority, but rejected any solution "involving transfer of populations and amounting to partition of Cyprus."

Turkish Cypriots proclaimed a separate state in the northern 40% of the island and proposed a "bi-regional federation." Some 200,000 Greek Cypriots demanded return to homes in the Turkish zone and an estimated three fourths of the 45,000 ethnic Turks in the Greek zone crossed into the Turkish area.

Negotiations between the two communities resumed in Vienna on April 28, 1975. Despite U.S. Secretary of State Henry A. Kissinger's parallel efforts to win support for agreement from Greek and Turkish leaders, the two sides remained deadlocked at the end of the summer of 1976.

Economic Conditions. Agriculture is the principal industry of the island. Products include barley, wheat, potatoes, wine and fruit. Mining is also important.

Chief exports in 1974 were citrus fruit (21%), copper (11%), potatoes (9%) and wine (9%). Leading customers were United Kingdom (38%), U.S.S.R. (7%), West Germany (6%), Libya (5%). Leading suppliers were U.K. (21%), West Germany (9%), Italy (8%), Greece (7%), France (7%), U.S. (6%).

CZECHOSLOVAKIA (Republic)

(Československá Socialistická Republika)

President: Gustav Husak (1975).
Premier: Lubomir Strougal (1970).
Area: 49,373 sq mi. (127,869 sq km).
Population (est. 1976): 14,910,000 (1974: Czech, 65%; Slovak, 29%).
Density per square mile: 302.0.
Capital: Prague.
Largest cities (est. 1974 by U.N.): Prague, 1,095,615; Brno, 343,860; Bratislava, 328,765; Ostrava, 292,404; Kosice, 166,240; Plzen (Pilsen), 154,126.
Monetary unit: Koruna.
Languages: Czech (65%), Slovak (29%), Hungarian (4%), German, Ukrainian, Polish.
Religions: Roman Catholic, 70%; Czechoslovak Church, 8%; Protestant, 7%; Greek Orthodox, 5%; Jewish, .5%; others and no confession, 14%.

Since 1969 the supreme organ of the state has been the Federal Assembly with two equal chambers: the Chamber of People with 200 deputies and the Chamber of Nations with 150 deputies (75 from the Czech Socialist Republic and 75 from the Slovak Socialist Republic). The chief executive is the President, who is elected by the Federal Assembly for a five-year term. The Premier and his Cabinet are appointed by the President but are responsible to the Federal Assembly.

Political Parties. Communist Party, led by First Secretary Gustav Husak in both republics; Socialist Party; People's Party in the Czech Socialist Republic; Slovak Freedom Party and Slovak Reconstruction Party in the Slovak Socialist Republic. Together with trade unions, youth organizations, and other organizations, they form the National Front.

History. Probably about the fifth century A.D., Slavic tribes from the Vistula basin settled in the region of modern Czechoslovakia. Slovakia came under Magyar domination. The Czechs founded the kingdom of Bohemia, the Premyslide dynasty, which ruled Bohemia and Moravia from the 10th to the 16th century. One of the Bohemian kings, Charles IV, Holy Roman Emperor, made Prague an imperial capital and a center of Latin scholarship. The Hussite movement founded by Jan Hus (1369?–1415), linked the Slavs to the Reformation and revived Czech nationalism, previously under German domination. A Hapsburg, Ferdinand I, ascended the throne in 1526. The Czechs rebelled in 1618. Defeated in 1620, they were ruled for the next 300 years as part of the Austrian Empire.

In World War I, Czech and Slovak patriots, notably Thomas G. Masaryk and Milan Stefanik, promoted Czech-Slovak independence from abroad while their followers fought against the Central Powers. On Oct. 28, 1918, Czechoslovakia proclaimed itself a republic. Shortly thereafter Masaryk was unanimously elected first President.

Hitler, dictator of Nazi Germany, provoked the country's German minority in the Sudetenland, led by Konrad Henlein, to agitate for autonomy. At the Munich Conference on Sept. 30, 1938, France and Britain, seeking to avoid World War II, agreed that the Nazis could take the Czech Sudetenland. Dr. Eduard Beneš, who had succeeded Masaryk, resigned on Oct. 5, 1938, and fled to London. Czechoslovakia became a federal union in the German orbit. In March 1939, the Nazis occupied the country. Benes organized a government-in-exile in London in 1940.

Soon after Czechoslovakia was liberated in World War II and the government returned in April 1945, it was obliged to cede Ruthenia to the Soviet Union. On July 3, 1946, a Communist, Klement Gottwald, formed a six-party coalition Cabinet. Pressure from Moscow increased until Feb. 23–25, 1948, when the Communists seized complete control in a coup d'état. Following constituent assembly elections in which the Communists and their allies were unopposed, a new Constitution was adopted. Benes refused to sign it and resigned on June 7, 1948; he died mysteriously on Sept. 3, 1948. The Constitution was promulgated June 9, 1948. Thereafter agriculture was collectivized, industry almost completely socialized, and foreign trade conducted chiefly with the Soviet bloc. Industrialization was intensified and concentrated upon heavy industry. The "people's democracy" was converted into a "socialist" state by a new Constitution adopted June 11, 1960.

After the death of the Soviet dictator Joseph Stalin and the relaxing of Soviet controls, Czechoslovakia witnessed a nationalist awakening. In 1968 conservative Stalinists were driven from power and replaced by more liberal, reform-minded Communists.

In more orthodox circles of the Soviet Union and her East European satellites, fears arose that the trend was undermining Communist rule. Soviet military maneuvers on Czechoslovak soil in May 1968 were followed in July by a meeting of the Soviet Union and Poland, Bulgaria, East Germany and Hungary in Warsaw that demanded an accounting, which Prague refused. Czechoslovak-Soviet talks on Czechoslovak territory, at Cierna, in late July 1968 led to an accord. But the Russians charged that the Czechoslovaks reneged on pledges to modify their policies, and on Aug. 20–21, 1968, troops of the five powers, estimated at 600,000, executed a lightning invasion and occupation.

Soviet secret police seized the Czechoslovak top leadership and detained it for several days in Moscow. But Soviet efforts to establish a puppet regime failed. President Ludvik Svoboda negotiated an accord providing for a gradual troop withdrawal in return for "normalization" of political policy.

Then began a slow troop pullback, rigid press censorship, removal of key liberals, and the election of a new party presidium. In October 1968, a treaty gave the Soviet Union the right to station troops in Czechoslovakia.

The purge of liberals was virtually completed in 1970. Only Svoboda remained from 1968. Husak, who became Secretary General of the Communist Party in 1969, promised no show trials, but most liberals were punished. Czechoslovakia signed a new friendship treaty with the Soviet Union that codified the "Brezhnev doctrine," under which Russia can invade any Eastern European socialist nation that threatens to leave the satellite camp.

Continuing ferment surfaced early in 1975 with publication in the West of a long letter of protest against repression written by Alexander Dubček, First Secretary of the Czechoslovak Communist Party during the 1968 "Prague Spring." The letter, addressed to the Presidium of Czechoslovakia's Federal Assembly, charged that the regime had purged thousands of creative workers. Dubček was later reported transferred to a menial forester's job.

President Svoboda was reported incapacitated by illness in mid-1974, and Parliament elected Husak his successor. When Husak assumed the presidency May 29, 1975, he retained the no. 1 post of Communist Party General Secretary. Husak, who had once been a Stalinist prisoner, was viewed as a realistic moderate whose goal is to achieve a middle ground between unpopular hard-line Communism and the permissiveness that Moscow crushed in 1968.

Economic Conditions. Nationalization of all enterprises with more than 50 employees as well as concerns of any size operating in key industries was completed between 1945 and 1948. Distribution of large estates had already been accomplished by the 1919 Land Reform Law. Total collectivization of agriculture was the professed aim of the Communist regime.

Sugar beets, wheat, corn and high-grade barley and hops for beer brewing are cultivated in the low-lying areas. In more elevated regions, the cultivation of potatoes, rye and oats predominates. Higher lands are also used for growing fodder crops or for grazing.

Abundance of coal and presence of iron ore give the country a big metallurgical industry. The Skoda steel works at Pilsen are among the largest in Europe.

Other industries are glass, porcelain and pottery making, while large forest areas provide raw material for the timber, paper and cellulose industries. Also highly developed are the textile industries, including cotton, wool flax and jute production, and the shoe industry. The famous Bat'a shoe factories, now nationalized, are at Gottwaldov, formerly Zlin.

Most important of Czechoslovakia's varied minerals are pit coal and lignite, with the principal coal fields in the Ostrava-Karvinná area, connected with the Polish fields of Upper Silesia.

Iron ore is produced in Czechoslovakia, but much ore is imported to meet the demands of the flourishing iron and steel industry. Excellent porcelain raw materials, particularly kaolin, are obtained in western Bohemia and southern Moravia. Other minerals are antimony, gold, magnesite, oil, uranium, silver and zinc.

Chief exports in 1973 were machinery (37%), iron and steel (10%), motor vehicles (9%), chemicals (7%) and metal ores (5%). Leading customers were U.S.S.R. (32%), East Germany (11%), Poland (10%), West Germany (6%), Hungary (5%). Leading suppliers were U.S.S.R. (30%), East Germany (13%), Poland (8%), Hungary (6%), West Germany (6%).

Natural Features. Czechoslovakia lies athwart the great central-European watershed between the Baltic, Black, and North seas. Mountains form several of its boundaries. Many of the valleys are made fertile by the Danube, Elbe and Vltava (Moldau) rivers and their tributaries.

DAHOMEY
See Benin

DENMARK (Constitutional monarchy)
(Kongeriget Danmark)

Sovereign: Queen Margrethe II (1972).
Premier: Anker Jorgensen (1975).
Area: 16,629 sq mi. (43,069 sq km).*
Population (est. 1976): 5,080,000.*
Density per square mile: 305.5.
Capital: Copenhagen.
Largest cities (est. 1974): Copenhagen (including Frederiksberg) 1,380,000; (est. 1973 by U.N.): Aarhus, 245,200; Alborg, 154,850; (1970 census): Odense, 167,793.
Monetary unit: Krone.
Language: Danish.
Religion: Evangelical Lutheran (state).

Denmark has been a constitutional monarchy since 1849. Legislative power is held jointly by the Sovereign and parliament. The Constitution of 1953 provides for a unicameral parliament called the Folketing consisting of 179 popularly elected members serving for four years. The Cabinet is presided over by the Sovereign, who appoints the Prime Minister.

The Sovereign, Queen Margrethe II, was born April 16, 1940, and became Queen—the first in Denmark's history—Jan. 15, 1972, the day after her father, King Frederik IX, died at 72 in the 25th year of his reign. Margrethe was the eldest of his three daughters (by Princess Ingrid of Sweden). The nation's Constitution was amended in 1953 to permit her to succeed her father in the absence of a male heir to the throne. (Denmark was ruled five centuries ago by Margrethe I but she was never crowned queen since there was no female right of succession.) Margrethe's sisters are Benedikte (born 1944) and Anne Marie (born 1946), now the former Queen of Greece.

Major Political Parties. Social Democratic Party (53 of 179 seats in Folketing), led by Premier Jorgensen; Liberal Democrats (42 seats), led by Poul Hartling; Progress Party (24 seats), led by Mogens Glistrup; Radical Liberals (13 seats), led by Hilmar Baunsgaard; Conservative Party (10 seats), led by Poul Schlüter; Christian People's Party (9 seats), led by Jens Moller; Socialist People's Party (9 seats), led by Gert Petersen; Communist Party (7 seats), led by Knud Jespersen; others, 8 seats.

History. Smallest of the three Scandinavian countries, Denmark emerged with establishment of the Norwegian dynasty of the Ynglinger in Jutland at the end of the eighth century. Danish mariners played a major role in the raids of the Vikings or Norsemen on Western Europe and particularly England. It was Christianized by St. Ansgar and Harald Blaatand (Bluetooth)—the first Christian king—in the tenth century. Harald's son, Sweyn,

---

* Excluding Faeroe Islands and Greenland.

conquered England in 1013. His son, Canute the Great, who reigned from 1014 to 1035, united Denmark, England, and Norway under his rule; the southern part of Sweden was part of Denmark until the 17th century. On Canute's death, civil war tore the country until Waldemar I (1157–82) re-established Danish hegemony over the north. In 1282 the nobles won the Great Charter, and Eric V was forced to share power with parliament and a Council of Nobles. Waldemar IV (1340–75) restored Danish power, checked only by the Hanseatic League of North German cities allied with ports from Holland to Poland. His daughter, Margaret, in 1397 united under her rule Denmark, Norway, and Sweden. But Sweden achieved autonomy and in 1523, under Gustavus I, independence.

Denmark supported Napoleon, for which she was punished at the Congress of Vienna in 1815 by the loss of Norway to Sweden. In 1864 Bismarck, together with the Austrians, made war on the little country as an initial step in the unification of Germany. Denmark was neutral in World War I. In 1939 Denmark signed a 10-year pact with Hitler, but less than a year later she was invaded by the Nazis. King Christian X cautioned his fellow countrymen to accept the occupation, but there was widespread resistance against the Nazi occupation. In 1944, Iceland declared its independence from Denmark, thus putting an end to a union that had existed since 1380.

Liberated by British troops in May 1945, Denmark joined the United Nations in 1945 and the North Atlantic Treaty Organization in 1949. The country staged a fast recovery after World War II in both agriculture and manufacturing and was a leader in liberalizing trade.

The Social Democrats largely ran Denmark after the war but were ousted in 1973 when, in a December election dominated by protests against high taxes, all established parties lost heavily. The big winner was the new Progress Party. A minority government was formed by the Liberal Democrats, with their leader, Poul Hartling, as Premier.

Hartling called general elections for Jan. 9, 1975, after a majority of the parties in Parliament opposed an austerity program he proposed to combat Denmark's 16% inflation rate. Although his moderate Liberals increased their representation, Hartling resigned Jan. 29 after losing a confidence vote. Returned to power were the Social Democrats, headed by Anker Jorgensen, who had been Premier in 1972–73.

In 1969, Denmark became the first Western nation to legalize the sale of written and pictorial pornography; police reported sex crimes down 30% to 50% in the following year.

Denmark's application to join the European Economic Community (Common Market) was approved in 1972 along with those of Britain, Norway and Ireland.

In 1975, the Jorgensen government granted initial concessions for oil and natural gas exploration off the west coast of Greenland. Leases for 15,000 square miles of ocean bottom were awarded to six groups involving 20 companies from nine nations.

Economic Conditions. Denmark's principal agricultural products are wheat, barley, oats, rye, potatoes and sugar beets.

The largest industries are food processing and iron and metal. Others include chemicals and pharmaceuticals, wood and paper, clothing, textiles, machinery, beverages, and leather.

The fishing industry, centered at Copenhagen but carried on also in the shallow fiords and in the deeper waters of the Baltic, North Sea and Skagerrak, is a basic part of the Danish economy.

Chief exports in 1974 were machinery (16%), meat and meat products (13%), chemicals (8%) and dairy products (5%). Leading customers were EEC (40%; incl. United Kingdom 16%, West Germany 12%), Sweden 15%, Norway 6%, U.S. 5%. Leading suppliers were EEC (46%; incl. West Germany 18%, U.K. 10%, Netherlands 6%), Sweden 13%, U.S. 6%.

Natural Features. Denmark, only three miles from Sweden at the closest point, consists of the Jutland peninsula and islands in the Baltic. The largest islands are Zealand, the site of Copenhagen; Funen; and, far to the east, Bornholm. The narrow waters to the north are called Skagerrak; to the east, Kattegat.

Outlying Territories of Denmark

FAEROE ISLANDS

Status: Autonomous part of Denmark.
Commissioner: L. Groth (1972).
Area: 540 sq mi. (1,399 sq km).
Population (est. 1976): 43,000.
Capital (est. 1974): Thorshavn, 11,200.
Chief exports: fish and products.

This group of 21 islands, lying in the North Atlantic about 200 miles northwest of the Shetland Islands, joined Denmark in 1386 and has since been part of the Danish kingdom. The islands were occupied by British troops during World War II, after the German occupation of Denmark. The principal pursuits are fishing and sheep grazing. The Faeroes have home rule under a bill enacted in 1948; they also have two representatives in the Danish Folketing.

Economic Conditions. Chief exports in 1973 were fish and products (90%) (incl. fish meal 15%). Leading customers were Denmark (22%), U.S. (13%), United Kingdom (13%), Spain (9%), Italy (8%), Iceland (5%), Poland (5%). Leading suppliers in 1972 were Denmark (73%), Norway (7%), U.K. (6%).

GREENLAND

Status: Integral part of Kingdom of Denmark.
Governor: H. J. Lassen (1973).
Area: 839,999 sq mi. (incl. 708,069 sq mi. covered by icecap) (2,175,600 sq km).
Population (est. 1976): 56,000.
Capital (est. 1974): Godthaab, 8,300.
Chief exports: fish, fur skins, cryolite.

Greenland, the world's largest island, was colonized in 985–86 by Eric the Red. Danish sovereignty, which covered only the west coast, was extended over the whole island in 1917. In 1941 the United States signed an agreement with the Danish minister in Washington, placing it under U.S. protection during World War II but maintaining Danish sovereignty. A definitive agreement for the joint defense of Greenland within the framework of NATO was signed on Apr. 27, 1951. A large U.S. air base at Thule in the far north was completed in 1953.

Under 1953 amendments to the Danish Constitution, Greenland is part of Denmark and has two representatives in the Danish Folketing. There is a popularly elected council.

Greenland is the world's only source of natural cryolite, important in making aluminum.

DOMINICAN REPUBLIC

(República Dominicana)

President: Dr. Joaquín Balaguer (1966).
Area: 18,816 sq mi. (48,734 sq km).
Population (est. 1976): 4,840,000 (approx.: mestizo and mulatto, 73%; white, 16%; black, 11%).
Density per square mile: 257.2.
Capital: Santo Domingo.*
Largest cities (est. 1973): Santo Domingo,* 817,300; (1970 census): Santiago de los Caballeros, 155,151.
Monetary unit: peso.
Language: Spanish.
Religion: Roman Catholic.

The President is elected by direct vote every four years. Legislative powers rest with a Senate and a Chamber of Deputies, both elected by direct vote, also for four years. All citizens must vote when 18 years old or even before that age if they are married.

Major Political Parties. Reformist Party, led by President Joaquín Balaguer; Dominican Liberation Party, led by Juan Bosch; PQD (Partido Quisquellano Demócrata), led by Elías Wessin y Wessin); MIDA (Movimiento de Integración Democrática Anti-Reeleccionista), led by Augusto Lora.

History. A republic in the West Indies on the eastern two thirds of the island of Hispaniola, which it shares with Haiti, the Dominican Republic was discovered by Columbus in 1492. He named it La Española, and his son, Diego, was its first viceroy. The capital, Santo Domingo, founded in 1496, is the oldest white settlement in the Western Hemisphere. Spain ceded the colony to France in 1795, and Haitian blacks under Toussaint L'Ouverture conquered it in 1801.

In 1808 the people revolted and in 1809 captured Santo Domingo, setting up the first republic. Spain regained title to the colony in 1814. In 1821 the people overthrew Spanish rule, but in 1822 they were reconquered by the Haitians. They revolted again in 1844, threw out the Haitians, and established the Dominican Republic headed by Pedro Santana. Uprisings and Haitian attacks led Santana to make the country a province of Spain from 1861 to 1865. The U.S. Senate refused to ratify a treaty of annexation. Disorder continued until Ulíses Heureaux established a ruthless dictatorship from 1882 to 1899. With further disorder, U.S. Marines occupied the country from 1916 to 1934.

A sergeant in the Dominican Army trained by the marines, Rafaél Leonides Trujillo Molina, overthrew Horacio Vásquez in 1930 and established a dictatorship that lasted until his assassination in 1961. To end border clashes, Trujillo mounted an invasion of Haiti in 1937, killing more than 10,000 Haitians. Trujillo established a ruthless dictatorship, developing the country but running it for his own benefit and that of his followers; he wound up owning much of the economy.

* Called Ciudad Trujillo from 1936 to 1961.

After Trujillo's assassination on May 30, 1961, disorders forced out the President, Joaquín Balaguer, but a governing council, in spite of an abortive military coup, steered the country to a return to constitutional government.

In September 1962, a new Constitution was adopted under which the first free election since 1924 was held in the following December. Juan Bosch, a leader of the democratic Left, was elected by a large plurality. He planned a program of reforms with U.S. support, but a right-wing military coup in September 1963 deposed Bosch and installed a civilian triumvirate.

The Left, in which Communists were achieving a dominant role, staged a revolution on April 24, 1965. President Johnson sent in 400 U.S. marines to aid the evacuation of U.S. citizens. The OAS called for a cease-fire, which was signed on May 6. The United States became more conciliatory toward the rebels and a compromise was reached in September, installing Hector García-Godoy as Provisional President.

Elections were held in June 1966, in which Balaguer triumphed over Bosch. An OAS force of 9,000 U.S. troops and 2,000 from other republics was withdrawn. Balaguer led the country to political and economic stability, launched a 15-year development program, and arranged free and open campaigning for the presidency. Bosch returned from self-imposed exile to take part.

Economic Conditions. Primarily agricultural, the country produces sugar, coffee, cacao, tobacco, bananas, rice, corn, cassava, beans, and sweet potatoes. Cattle raising is of growing importance. Sugar refining is the only important industry, although several new industries have been established in recent years.

Chief exports in 1974 were sugar (53%), cocoa (8%), coffee (7%) and tobacco (6%). Leading customers in 1973 were U.S. (66%) and Netherlands (8%). Leading suppliers were U.S. (c. 61%), Japan (c. 9%), West Germany (c. 7%).

Natural Features. Crossed from northwest to southeast by a mountain range with maximum elevations exceeding 10,000 feet, the country has fertile, well-watered land on the northeast side, where nearly two thirds of the population lives. The southwest part of the country is arid and with poor soil except around Santo Domingo.

ECUADOR (Republic)

(República del Ecuador)

President of Supreme Council: Vice. Adm. Alfredo Poveda (1976).
Area: 109,483 sq mi. (283,561 sq km).
Population (est. 1975 by U.N.): 6,730,000.
Density per square mile: 61.5.
Capital: Quito.
Largest cities (1974 census): Guayaquil, 814,100; Quito, 597,100.
Monetary unit: Sucre.
Languages: Spanish, Quéchua, Jibaro.
Religion: Roman Catholic.

A bloodless military coup on Jan. 11, 1976 brought to power a three-man military junta headed by Vice Adm. Alfredo Poveda, deposing Brig. Gen. Guillermo

Rodríguez Lara. Lara led a three-man junta in a similar coup Feb. 15, 1972, and had subsequently assumed the Presidency.

Poveda did not immediately take the title, but as of August 1976 styled himself only President of the Supreme Council. The other members of the junta also constituting the Supreme Council were Army Brig. Guillermo Durán Arcentales and Air Force Brig. Gen. Luís Leoro Franco.

In discussions with political, labor and business leaders, the junta promised that it would return Ecuador to constitutional rule by 1978.

History. Ecuador was inhabited in early times by many peoples. The tribes in the northern highlands formed the Kingdom of Quito around 1000 A.D. It was absorbed, by conquest and marriage, into the Inca Empire. Pizarro conquered the land in 1532 and through the 17th century a thriving colony was built by exploitation of the Indians. The first revolt against Spain occurred in 1809. Ecuador then joined Venezuela, Colombia and Panama in a confederacy founded by Simón Bolívar and known as Greater Colombia. On the collapse of this union in 1830, Ecuador became independent. Subsequent history was one of revolts and dictatorships; it had 48 Presidents during the first 131 years of the republic. Conservatives ruled until the Revolution of 1895 ushered in nearly a half century of Radical Liberal rule, when the church was disestablished and freedom of worship, speech and press was introduced. Over the years Ecuador lost territory to its neighbors, Peru particularly, which by invasion won most of the Amazon Basin territory. Army juntas ruled until 1948, when Galo Plaza Lasso became President and restored political freedom. His successor in 1952, Dr. José María Velasco Ibarra, sought to expand the economy by inflation, causing a crisis that led Congress to depose him. The next President, Carlos Julio Arosemena Monroy, was overthrown by the military in 1963, and a junta held power until 1966, when it was overthrown by the military high command.

On June 23, 1970, following six months of strife between university students and police, Velasco, elected in 1968 for the fifth time, took supreme powers to "avoid social and economic chaos." He closed universities, jailed some professors and businessmen, and demanded "reform" of the Supreme Court. Opposition political leaders were arrested and a military shake-up ensued.

Following Velasco's ouster by the junta in 1972, the new government sharply increased exploration fees charged to foreign oil companies. In July, 1974, Rodríguez Lara ordered that elections and political activity be suspended for five years.

U.S.-Ecuadorian relations took a bad turn in 1971 when more than a score of U.S. tuna fishing boats were seized for operating within the 200-mile limit claimed by Ecuador. Total fines for fishing without licenses exceeded $1 million, which the U.S. government appears committed to repaying to the fishermen. The seizures continued into 1974. The U.S. does not recognize the 200-mile claim (which eight Latin American nations make) and has cut off military sales to Ecuador.

Economic Conditions. Although agriculture is the basis of Ecuador's economy, less than 12,000,000 acres are devoted to it. Cacao, the chief crop, is grown in coastal regions and lower river valleys. The plateaus and mountain valleys are used for grazing and dairying, and raising cereals and potatoes. After textiles, one of Ecuador's main industries is the manufacture of Panama hats, which are made of toquilla straw.

Ecuador produces gold, silver, copper, lead and petroleum. It is the world's chief source of light, strong balsa wood.

Chief exports in 1974 were crude oil (58%), bananas (12%), cocoa (10%) and coffee (6%). Leading customers in 1973 were U.S. (32%), Trinidad and Tobago (12%), Panama (9%), Peru (6%), Netherlands Antilles (6%), West Germany (5%). Leading suppliers were U.S. (34%), Japan (14%), West Germany (12%), Colombia (6%), United Kingdom (6%).

Natural Features. Two high and parallel ranges of the Andes, traversing Ecuador from north to south, are topped by tall volcanic peaks.

The Galápagos Islands (or Colón Archipelago) (3,029 sq. mi.), located in the Pacific Ocean about 600 miles west of the South American mainland, became part of Ecuador in 1832.

EGYPT (Arab Republic of)

President: Anwar el-Sadat (1970).
Premier: Mamdouh Salem (1975).
Area: 386,661 sq mi. (1,001,449 sq km).
Population (est. 1976): 38,000,000.
Density per square mile: 98.3.
Capital: Cairo.
Largest cities (est. 1975): Cairo, 5,859,000; (est. 1970 by U.N.): Alexandria, 2,032,000; Giza, 711,900; Suez, 315,000; Port Said, 313,000; El Mahalla el Kúbra, 255,800.
Monetary unit: Egyptian pound.
Language: Arabic.
Religions: Moslem, 93%; Christian (mostly Copt), 7%.

Executive power is held by the President, who appoints the Premier and one or more Vice Presidents.

Political Party. There is only one political party: the Arab Socialist Union.

History. Egyptian history dates back to about 4000 B.C., when the kingdoms of upper and lower Egypt, already highly civilized, were united. Egypt's "Golden Age" coincided with the 18th and 19th dynasties (16th to 13th centuries B.C.), during which the empire was established. Persia conquered Egypt in 525 B.C.; Alexander the Great subdued it in 332 B.C.; and then the dynasty of the Ptolemies ruled the land until 30 B.C., when Cleopatra, last of the line, committed suicide and Egypt became a Roman province. From 641 to 1517 the Arab caliphs ruled Egypt, and then the Turks took it for their Ottoman Empire.

Napoleon's armies occupied the country from 1798 to 1801. In 1805, Mohammed Ali, leader of a band of Albanian soldiers, became Pasha of Egypt. After completion of the Suez Canal in 1869, both the French and British took increasing interest in Egypt.

British troops occupied Egypt in 1882, and British resident agents became its actual administrators, though it remained under nominal Turkish sovereignty. On Dec. 18, 1914, this fiction was ended, and Egypt became a protectorate of Britain.

Pressure by Egyptian nationalists forced Britain to declare Egypt an independent, sovereign state on Feb. 28, 1922, although the British reserved rights for the protection of the Suez Canal and the defense of Egypt. On Aug. 26, 1936, by an Anglo-Egyptian treaty of alliance, all British troops and officials were to be withdrawn, except from the Suez Canal zone. When World War II started, Egypt remained neutral. British imperial troops finally ended the Nazi threat to Suez in 1942 in the battle of El Alamein, which took place west of Alexandria.

In October 1951, Egypt abrogated the 1936 treaty and the 1899 Anglo-Egyptian condominium of the Sudan (*See* Sudan.) Rioting and attacks on British troops in the Suez Canal zone followed, reaching a climax in January 1952. The army, led by Gen. Mohammed Naguib, seized power on July 23, 1952. On July 26, King Farouk abdicated in favor of his infant son. Naguib took over the premiership on Sept. 7, 1952, and promised far-reaching reforms. The monarchy was abolished and a republic proclaimed on June 18, 1953, with Naguib holding the posts of both Provisional President and Premier. He relinquished the latter post on Apr. 18, 1954, to Gamal Abdel Nasser, leader of the ruling military junta. Naguib was deposed on Nov. 14, 1954. Nasser was confirmed as President in a popular referendum on June 23, 1956.

Nasser's policies embroiled his country in continual conflict. In July 1956, the United States and Britain withdrew their pledges of financial aid for the building of the Aswan High Dam. In reply, Nasser nationalized the Suez Canal and expelled British oil and embassy officials. Israel, barred from the canal and exasperated by terrorist raids, invaded the Gaza Strip and the Sinai peninsula. Britain and France, after demanding Egyptian evacuation of the canal zone, attacked Egypt on Oct. 31, 1956. Worldwide pressure forced Britain, France, and Israel to halt the hostilities. A U.N. emergency force occupied the canal zone, and all troops were evacuated in the spring of 1957.

On Feb. 1, 1958, Egypt and Syria formed the United Arab Republic, which was joined by Yemen on Mar. 8 in an association known as the United Arab States. However, Syria withdrew from the United Arab Republic on Sept. 29, 1961, and on Dec. 26, Egypt dissolved its ties with Yemen in the United Arab States. On Sept. 2, 1971, Egypt finally shed the name United Arab Republic.

On June 5, 1967, Israel invaded the Sinai Peninsula, the east bank of the Jordan River and the zone around the Gulf of Aqaba. Only a U.N. cease-fire on June 10 saved the Arabs from complete rout. The war left the U.A.R. army, its prestige and its economy in ruins. The Suez Canal was blocked by wrecks and closed to all traffic. Nasser at first resigned as President, then withdrew the resignation, getting increased power to rebuild the stricken nation. He obtained economic and financial help from the Soviet Union, Communist China, Kuwait, and former King Saud.

Nasser declared the 1967 cease-fire void along the canal on Apr. 23, 1969, and began a war of attrition. Egyptian artillery fire across the canal sparked Israeli "deep penetration" raids that attempted to topple Nasser. He went to Moscow in January 1970, and by March, Russians were flying planes with Egyptian markings to defend the Nile delta and were manning some antiaircraft missiles. An estimated 10,000 to 12,000 Russians were in Egypt in 1970. Missiles were moved into the canal zone, challenging Israeli air superiority. The U.S. peace plan of June 19, 1970 resulted in Egypt's agreement to reinstate the cease-fire for at least three months (from Aug. 7) and, to accept Israel's existence within "recognized and secure" frontiers that might emerge from U.N.-mediated talks. In return, Israel accepted the principle of withdrawing from occupied territories.

Then, on Sept. 28, 1970, Nasser died, at 52, of a heart attack in the midst of Jordan-Palestinian guerrilla hostilities and the hijacking by these guerrillas of four Western jet planes. The new President was Anwar Sadat.

With Nasser's death, the pan-Arabism he advocated disintegrated. Sadat seemed more willing to reach a peace settlement with Israel. While receiving more arms from the Soviet Union (matched by U.S. sales to Israel), he responded to U.S. peace initiatives by promising to sign a peace agreement if Israel withdrew to its pre-war 1967 borders. The Israelis refused, however.

In 1971, Sadat signed a 15-year treaty of friendship and cooperation with Moscow that legitimized Soviet penetration of Egypt.

The Aswan High Dam, whose financing by the Soviet Union was its first step into Egypt, was completed and dedicated in January 1971.

In July 1972, Sadat ordered the expulsion of Soviet "advisors and experts" from Egypt because the Russians had not provided the sophisticated weapons he felt were needed to retake territory lost to Israel in 1967. Moscow pulled out virtually all of its 18,000 men.

The fourth major Arab-Israeli war broke out Oct. 6, 1973, while Israelis were commemorating Yom Kippur, the Jewish high holy day. Egypt swept deep into the Sinai, while Syria strove to throw Israel off the Golan Heights. Arab oil-producing countries cut off shipments to the U.S. and other Western nations, helping to precipitate a worldwide energy crisis.

A United Nations-sponsored truce was called Oct. 22, with Egyptian forces in the Sinai split by an Israeli invasion into Egypt itself. In January 1974, the two nations agreed to a six-point settlement, negotiated by U.S. Secretary of State Henry A. Kissinger, which left Egypt in possession of a narrow strip along the entire Sinai bank of the Suez Canal.

President Nixon, in June 1974, made the first visit by a U.S. President to Egypt following a Kissinger-mediated settlement between Israel and Syria. A joint Egyptian-American economic commission was set up which promised U.S. aid to Egypt, and relatively large U.S. atomic reactors were to be provided Egypt for making electricity. Full diplomatic relations between the countries were resumed.

In October, 1974, Kissinger renewed efforts to bring Egypt and Israel to a second-stage agreement on disengagement in the Sinai, but the negotiations collapsed March 22, 1975. On June 5, Egypt reopened the Suez Canal to traffic after basic repairs of damage caused by the 1967 war. Quiet, three-cornered disengagement negotiations resumed, with the U.S.

acting as middle man between Cairo and Jerusalem. The principal sticking-point was Egypt's insistence on return of the strategic Mitla and Giddi passes and captured oil fields at Abu Rudeis.

Kissinger resumed his "shuttle diplomacy" Aug. 21, and midwifed an agreement that was formally initialed in Alexandria the night of Sept. 1. It was not a peace accord, but it was a concrete step toward a possible Mideastern settlement. It called for Israeli withdrawal from the Mitla and Giddi passes and the Abu Rudeis oil fields. It committed both governments to resolve disputes by peaceful means and required annual renewal of the mandate of the U.N. peace-keeping force. It also committed Egypt to permit nonmilitary cargoes bound to and from Israel to move through the Suez Canal.

A key section called for a U.S. force of about 200 civilian technicians to man early-warning systems in the Sinai to alert both sides and the U.N. if infractions occurred. Both Egypt and Israel insisted on this provision, which came under intensive scrutiny by the U.S. Congress, as did Ford Administration commitment to earmark about $600 million in military and economic aid for Egypt.

The agreement drew the United States directly into the Middle Eastern diplomatic picture. It also undercut Egypt's relations with the Soviet Union, which criticized the U.S. presence in the Sinai. Sadat was denounced by Syria and the Palestine Liberation Organization for selling out the Arab cause. The accord gave the Sadat government leeway for fulfillment of programs to strengthen the economy of Egypt, which was beset by 30% inflation and serious unemployment.

In a referendum on Sept. 16, 1976, Sadat, running unopposed, was nominated for a second six-year term, winning a 99.9% vote of approval.

Economic Conditions. Agriculture is the chief industry, engaging more than half the population. Only about 3.5% of the total area is arable, and only about 6,000,000 acres are actually under cultivation, almost entirely in the Nile valley and delta. More than half the cultivated area comprises farms of less than 20 acres. Irrigation is indispensable to agriculture; the Aswan reservoir above the first cataract of the Nile holds up to 5,500,000,000 cubic meters of water and the reservoir of Gebel Aulia, in the Sudan, 2,000,000,000 cubic meters. In the delta and in middle Egypt, where perennial or canal irrigation is possible, two or three crops a year can be grown. The chief cash crop is cotton.

Industry includes sugar refining, cotton ginning, cement manufacture, milling and pottery, soap and perfume making.

The most important mineral deposits in Egypt are manganese ore, phosphate, and petroleum. Gold, iron ochres, nickel, sodium carbonate, sulfate talc, and tungsten also are mined.

Chief exports in 1974 were cotton (46%), fruit and vegetables (9%) and rice (7%); in 1973, cotton yarn (10%) and crude oil (8%). Leading customers in 1973 were U.S.S.R. (33%), Czechoslovakia (6%), Japan (5%). Leading suppliers were U.S. (13%), France (8%), West Germany (8%), U.S.S.R. (7%), Australia (5%), East Germany (5%), Italy (5%), Romania (5%).

Natural Features. Egypt, at the northeast corner of Africa, is a very rough square, with the historic Nile flowing northward through its eastern third. On either side of the Nile valley are desert plateaus, spotted with oases. In the north, toward the Mediterranean, plateaus are low, while south of Cairo they rise to a maximum of 1,015 feet above sea level. At the head of the Red Sea, at the northeast corner of Egypt, is the Sinai peninsula, between the Suez Canal and Israel.

Navigable throughout its course in Egypt, the Nile is used largely as a means of cheap transport for heavy goods. The principal port is Alexandria.

The Nile delta starts 100 miles south of the Mediterranean and fans out to a sea front of 155 miles between the cities of Alexandria and Port Said. From Cairo north, the Nile branches into many streams, the principal ones being the Damietta and the Rosetta.

Except for a narrow belt located along the Mediterranean, Egypt lies in an almost rainless area, in which high daytime temperatures fall quickly at night.

Suez Canal. The Suez Canal, in Egyptian territory between the Arabian Desert and the Sinai Peninsula, is an artificial waterway about 100 miles long between Port Said on the Mediterranean and Suez on the Red Sea. Construction work, directed by the French engineer Ferdinand de Lesseps, was begun Apr. 25, 1859, and the canal was opened Nov. 17, 1869. The cost was 432,807,882 francs. The concession was held by an Egyptian joint stock company, *Compagnie Universelle du Canal Maritime de Suez,* in which the British government held 353,504 out of a total of 800,000 shares. The concession was to expire Nov. 17, 1968, but the company was nationalized July 26, 1956, by unilateral action of the Egyptian government.

The canal was closed in June, 1967, after the Arab-Israeli conflict. With the help of the U.S. Navy, work was begun on clearing the canal in 1974, after the cease-fire ending the Arab-Israeli war. It was reopened to traffic June 5, 1975.

EL SALVADOR (Republic)

(República de El Salvador)

President: Col. Arturo Armanda Molina (1972).
Area: 8,260 sq mi. (21,393 sq km).
Population (est. 1976): 4,130,000.
Density per square mile: 500.0.
Capital: San Salvador.
Largest cities (est. 1974): San Salvador, 416,900; (est. 1969): Santa Ana, 168,000.
Monetary unit: Colón.
Language: Spanish.
Religion: Roman Catholic.

The Constitution provides for a President, popularly elected for five years and ineligible to succeed himself, and a unicameral legislature, the National Assembly, consisting of 52 members elected by universal popular vote for two years.

Major Political Parties: National Conciliation Party (32 of 52 seats) led by President Arturo Armanda Molina; Christian Democrat Party (14 seats); and two minor parties holding the remaining seats.

History. Pedro de Alvarado, a ·lieutenant of Cortés, conquered El Salvador in 1525. El Salvador, with the other countries of Central America, declared its independence· from Spain on Sept. 15, 1821, and was part of a federation of Central American states until that union was dissolved in 1838. Its independent career for several decades thereafter was marked by numerous revolutions and wars against other Central American republics. In January 1931, the first free election in 20 years was held, but Gen. Maximiliano Hernández Martínez took power in December of that year and maintained a dictatorship until ousted in May 1944. For nearly two decades, politics remained turbulent and unstable, until the 1962 elections.

The new President, Julio Adalberto Rivera, restored free elections. In the next few years, El Salvador assumed a leading role in the Central American Common Market. But in 1968, a drop in exports of coffee and cotton produced a slump. Widespread unemployment in El Salvador and land hunger in Honduras resulted in a conflict between El Salvador and Honduras in July 1969. Deportation from Honduras of several thousand Salvadorans led to an invasion by El Salvador. Under threats of economic sanctions and military intervention El Salvador withdrew its troops. The clash left 1,000 dead, tens of thousands homeless.

By June 1970, with land trade to the south hurt by Honduran roadblocks to its goods on the Pan American Highway, El Salvador and Honduras agreed to a demilitarized zone of 1.8 miles on each side of their poorly defined border. They also agreed to restore diplomatic relations and work toward a peace agreement as well as toward reviving the common market, but the peace talks broke down in 1973.

Presidential elections on Feb. 20, 1972, gave none of four candidates a clear majority, so the National Assembly, where the National Conciliation Party had an overwhelming majority, proclaimed its candidate, Col. Arturo Armanda Molina, as President. Molina was re-elected in the 1974 elections.

Economic Conditions. El Salvador is one of the most intensively cultivated countries in Latin America. Important agricultural products are coffee, cotton lint, sugar, rice and corn. There has been considerable recent development in industry. Products include cement, steel and electricity.

Gold, silver, coal, copper, iron, zinc, mercury and sulfur are the nation's chief minerals. Forest resources include dyewood, mahogany, cedar and walnut. El Salvador is a leading source of balsam.

Chief exports in 1973 were coffee (45%) and cotton (10%). Leading customers were U.S. (33%), Guatemala (18%), West Germany (13%), Japan (10%), Nicaragua (7%), Costa Rica (6%). Leading suppliers were U.S. (29%), Guatemala (16%), Japan (10%), West Germany (8%), Costa Rica (5%), Netherlands (5%).

Natural Features. Most of El Salvador is a fertile volcanic plateau about 2,000 feet high. There are several volcanoes, some still active, and many lovely crater lakes. It is the only Central American country without an Atlantic coastline.

EQUATORIAL GUINEA (Republic)

President: Francisco Macías Nguema Biyogo (1968).
Area: 10,830 sq mi. (28,051 sq km).
Population (est. 1976): 320,000.
Density per square mile: 29.5.
Capital and largest city (est. 1970): Malabo (formerly Santa Isabel), 19,300.
Monetary unit: Equatorial Guinea peseta (ekuele).
Languages: Spanish, Fang, Bubi.
Religions: Roman Catholic, Protestant, animist.

Executive power is vested in a Council of Ministers appointed by and responsible to the President. Legislative power is vested in a 60-member People's National Assembly.

A new Constitution was approved in 1973 and the capital's name was changed from Santa Isabel to Malabo.

Political Party. The Partido Unico Nacional de Trabajadores (PUNT), headed by President Francisco Macías Nguema Biyogo.

History. Equatorial Guinea, formerly Spanish Guinea, consists of Río Muni (10,045 sq mi.), on the western coast of Africa, and several islands, the largest of which is Macías Nguema Biyogo (formerly Fernando Po) (785 sq mi.). The other islands are Pagalu (formerly Annobón), Corisco, Elobey Grande, and Elobey Chico.

Fernando Po and Annobón came under Spanish control in 1778. From 1827 to 1844, with Spanish consent, Britain administered Fernando Po, but in the latter year Spain reclaimed the island. Río Muni was given to Spain in 1885 by the Treaty of Berlin.

Negotiations with Spain led to independence on Oct. 12, 1968.

In February 1969, anti-Spanish incidents in Río Muni, including the tearing down of a Spanish flag by national troops, caused 5,000 Spanish residents to flee for their safety, and diplomatic relations between the two nations became strained. The United Nations sent a Bolivian official as mediator. A month later Macías claimed a coup had been attempted against him. He seized dictatorial powers and arrested 80 opposition politicians and even several of his Cabinet ministers and the secretary of the National Assembly.

Economic Conditions. Agricultural products include cocoa, coffee, palm kernels and oil, and timber.

Chief exports in 1970 were cocoa (66%), coffee (24%) and timber (9%).

ESTONIA

Area: 17,413 sq mi. (45,100 sq km).
Population (est. 1975): 1,429,000 (est: Estonians, 68.2%; Russians, 24.7%; others, 7.1%).
Density per square mile: 82.1.
Capital and largest city (est. 1973): Tallinn, 386,000.
Language: Estonian (Finno-Ugrian).
Religions: Lutheran, 78%; Greek Orthodox, 19%; others, 3%.

History. Born out of World War I, this small Baltic state enjoyed two short decades of independence before it was absorbed again by its powerful neighbor, Russia. In the 13th century, the Estonians had been conquered by the Teutonic Knights of Germany, who reduced them to serfdom. In 1521, the Swedes took over, and the power of the German (Balt) landowning class was curbed somewhat. But after 1721, when Russia succeeded Sweden as the ruling power, the Estonians were subjected to a double bondage—the Balts and the tsarist officials. The oppression lasted until the closing months of World War I, when Estonia finally achieved independence.

Shortly after the start of World War II, the nation was occupied by Russian troops and was incorporated as the 16th republic of the U.S.S.R. in 1940. Germany occupied the nation from 1941 to 1944, when it was retaken by the Russians. Most of the nations of the world, including the United States and Great Britain, have not recognized the Soviet incorporation of Estonia.

ETHIOPIA (Socialist State)

Chairman of the Provisional Military Council: Brig. Gen. Teferi Benti (1974).
Area: 471,778 sq mi. (1,221,900 sq km).
Population (est. 1976): 28,685,000 (Amhara, 20%; Gala, 40%, others 40%).
Density per square mile: 60.8.
Capital: Addis Ababa.
Largest cities (1974 census): Addis Ababa, 1,083,420; Asmara, 296,044.
Monetary unit: Ethiopian dollar.
Languages: Amharic (official), Galligna and Tigrigna.
Religions: Copt (Christian), Moslem.

A provisional military government headed by a 120-member officers' committee (the Dirgue) deposed Ethiopia's traditional monarchy in 1974, suspended parliament and ruled by decree. It proclaimed Ethiopia a socialist state.

History. Black Africa's oldest state, Ethiopia can trace 2,000 years of recorded history. Its now-deposed royal line claimed descent from King Menelik I, by tradition the son of the Queen of Sheba and King Solomon. The present nation is a consolidation of smaller kingdoms that owed feudal allegiance to the Ethiopian Emperor.

Hamitic peoples migrated to Ethiopia from Asia Minor in prehistoric times. Semitic traders from Arabia penetrated the region in the 7th Century B.C. Its Red Sea ports were important to the Roman and Byzantine Empires. Coptic Christianity came to the country in A.D. 341 and a variant of that communion became Ethiopia's state religion.

Ancient Ethiopia reached its peak in the 5th Century, then was isolated by the rise of Islam and weakened by feudal wars. Modern Ethiopia emerged under Emperor Menelik II, who established its independence by routing an Italian invasion in 1896. He expanded Ethiopia by conquest.

Disorders that followed Menelik's death brought his daughter to the throne in 1917, with his cousin, Tafari Makonnen, as regent, heir presumptive and strong man. When the Empress died in 1930, Tafari was crowned Emperor Haile Selassie I.

As regent, Haile Selassie outlawed slavery. As Emperor, he worked for centralization of his diffuse realm, in which 70 languages are spoken, and for

moderate reform. In 1931, he granted a Constitution, revised in 1955, that created a parliament with an appointed Senate and an elected Chamber of Deputies, and a system of courts. But basic power remained with the Emperor.

Bent on colonial empire, fascist Italy invaded Ethiopia Oct. 3, 1935, forcing Haile Selassie into exile in May, 1936. Ethiopia was annexed to Eritrea, then an Italian colony, and Italian Somaliland to form Italian East Africa, losing its independence for the first time in recorded history. In 1941, British troops routed the Italians, and Haile Selassie returned to Addis Ababa.

The Emperor's gradual reforms failed to make headway against key problems. Although 85% of Ethiopians were subsistence farmers, feudal laws vested ownership of 55% of its land in the crown, the church and the nobility; there was strong pressure for land reform. There was also mounting insurgency in Eritrea, a culturally distinct province where Christians and Moslems have long vied for control, which the United Nations placed under Ethiopian rule in 1952. Violent agitation for Eritrean independence was begun in 1969 by the Moslem-led Eritrean Liberation Front (ELF), which used Arab-supplied arms to field a 4,000-man guerrilla force.

Deep discontent erupted in the fall of 1973. A long drought had caused famine that killed 100,000 peasants and drove thousands of others to cities, where food was scarce and inflation was rampant. Charges of mismanagement of drought relief sparked riots in Addis Ababa in February, 1974, and unpaid troops in Asmara, capital of Eritrea, mutinied to protest conditions. The Cabinet headed by Premier Aklilou Habte-wold resigned.

The Emperor named Endalkachew Makonnen, a moderate, to succeed as Prime Minister and agreed to call a constitutional convention. But there was a general strike, students rioted and mutiny spread to the Air Force. In mid-April, with disorders growing, Army and police units arrested over 200 high-placed individuals. Late in June, the Army took virtual control of Addis Ababa and made more arrests.

Endalkachew was ousted as Prime Minister on July 24, arrested and later executed. Under his successor, Michael Imru, a draft constitution proposing a constitutional monarchy was put forward, but power shifted relentlessly to a new Armed Forces Committee (AFC).

In August, the AFC nationalized Haile Selassie's palace and estates and directed him not to leave Addis Ababa. On Sept. 12, 1974, Haile Selassie was peacefully deposed after nearly 58 years as regent and emperor. The 82-year-old "Lion of Judah" was placed under guard. Parliament was dissolved, the Constitution suspended and a provisional military government took over pending elections for which no date was set.

To head the new government, the AFC chose Lieut. Gen. Aman Michael Andom, Army chief of staff. A power struggle within the AFC led on Nov. 23 to the killing of Aman while resisting arrest. The AFC also executed 59 other former high officials.

On Dec. 20, the AFC announced that Ethiopia would become a socialist state directed by one political organization called the Supreme Progressive Council. All financial concerns were nationalized in January, 1975. In March, the regime proclaimed nationalization of all rural land, ending 2,000 years of feudal tenure.

On Aug. 27, 1975, Haile Selassie died in a small apartment in his former Addis Ababa palace where he had been treated as a state prisoner. He was 83.

After the coup, revolt in Eritrea escalated from guerrilla conflict to open war. The ELF, armed by Libya and other Arab states, demanded full independence. The regime tried and failed to negotiate with the ELF, then began vigorous military action. Some 22,000 government troops were in combat in Eritrea by February, 1975, and 6,000 deaths, mostly of civilians, were said to have resulted in March. There were reports of atrocities by government troops against Eritrean villages, but rigid censorship blocked verification.

U.S. military aid, which had been going to Ethiopia for 20 years, was suspended after the 1974 coup but resumed in April 1976. Arms deliveries were also reported from Israel, Turkey, Czechoslovakia and Yugoslavia.

In April, 1975, a $15-million agricultural loan and $7.8 million in drought rehabilitation loans were extended to Ethiopia by the U.S.

Economic Conditions. Ethiopia is generally fertile, predominantly agricultural and pastoral, with many regions yielding two crops a year. The chief crops are maize, wheat, barley, rye, cotton, sugar cane, millet, hemp, vegetables, coffee and teff (the common bread grain). The country's inadequate transport system, however, makes crop growing largely a local industry.

A number of industries have been established under consecutive five-year plans, such as sugar, beverages, cement and iron. Hydroelectric power has been developed.

Gold, produced from placer mines worked by natives in the south and west, is Ethiopia's main mineral. Platinum also is mined in fair commercial quantities. Other minerals are rock salt, cinnabar, copper, iron, mercury, mica, potash and sulfur. Oil deposits are believed to exist, and all drilling rights have been sold to the Sinclair Refining Company of the United States.

Chief exports in 1974 were coffee (27%), pulses (19%), oilseeds (17%) and hides and skins (8%). Leading customers in 1973 were U.S. (30%), West Germany (9%), Italy (8%), Afars and Issas (7%), Saudi Arabia (6%), Japan (6%). Leading suppliers were Italy (15%), Japan (12%), West Germany (12%), United Kingdom (9%), U.S. (9%), Iran (7%).

Natural Features. Over its main plateau land, Ethiopia has several high mountains. The Blue Nile, or Abbai, rises in the northwest and flows in a great semicircle east, south, and northwest before entering Sudan. Its chief reservoir, Lake Tana, lies in the northwestern part of the plateau.

FIJI

(Member of Commonwealth of Nations)

Governor General: Sir George Cakobau.
Prime Minister: Sir Kamisese Mara (1970).
Area: 7,055 sq mi. (18,272 sq km).
Population (est. 1976): 580,000.
Density per square mile: 85.0.
Capital (est. 1974): Suva (on Viti Levu), 71,600.
Monetary unit: Fijian dollar.

Languages: Fijian, Hindustani, English, Chinese.
Religions: Christian, Hindu, Moslem.

Executive authority is vested in the Cabinet. Legislative authority is vested in the Parliament.

Political Parties. Alliance Party, led by Sir Kamisese Mara; National Federation Party, led by S. M. Koya, and Fijian Nationalist Party, led by Mr. Butadroka.

History. Fiji consists of more than 500 islands situated in the southwestern Pacific Ocean about 1,960 miles from Sydney, Australia. The two largest islands are Viti Levu (4,109 sq mi.) and Vanua Levu (2,242 sq mi.). The island of Rotuma (18 sq mi.), about 400 miles to the north, is a dependency of Fiji.

In 1874, an offer of cession by the Fijian chiefs was accepted, and Fiji was proclaimed a possession and dependency of the British Crown.

During World War II, the archipelago was an important air and naval station on the route from the United States and Hawaii to Australia and New Zealand.

Fiji became an independent nation on Oct. 10, 1970. The next year it joined the five-island South Pacific Forum, which intends to become a permanent regional group to promote collective diplomacy of the newly independent members. Besides Fiji, the Forum includes Western Samoa, Tonga, Nauru and the self-governing segments of the Cook Islands.

Economic Conditions. Agricultural products include sugar, coconut oil, copra, bananas and pineapples.

Chief exports in 1973 were sugar (67%), coconut products (12%) and gold (12%). Leading customers were United Kingdom (29%), U.S. (17%), Australia (12%), Canada (8%), New Zealand (6%). Leading suppliers were Australia (31%), Japan (16%), U.K. (14%), New Zealand (13%), U.S. (5%).

FINLAND (Republic)

(Suomen Tasavalta Republiken Finland)

President: Urho K. Kekkonen (1956).
Premier: Martti Miettunen (1975).
Area: 130,119 sq mi. (337,009 sq km).
Population (est. 1976): 4,740,000 (Finnish, 90%; Swedish, 10%).
Density per square mile: 36.4.
Capital: Helsinki.
Largest cities (est. 1973 by U.N.): Helsinki, 509,700; Tampere, 164,100; Turku, 160,830.
Monetary unit: Markka.
Languages: Finnish, 93%, Swedish, 7%.
Religions: Evangelical Lutheran, 91.7%; Greek Orthodox.

The President of the Republic of Finland, chosen for six years by the Electoral College of 300 members who are elected by the people, appoints the Cabinet. The one-chamber Diet, the Eduskunta, consists of 200 members elected for four-year terms by proportional representation.

Major Political Parties. Social Democratic Party (54 of 200 seats in Eduskunta); People's Democratic League (Communist) (40 seats); Center Party (39 seats), led by Premier Martti Miettunen; Conservative Party (35 seats); Swedish People's Party (10 seats); Liberal Party (9 seats); Christian League (9 seats). Premier Miettunen heads a minority government composed of the Center Party, Liberal Party and Swedish People's Party.

History.

At the end of the seventh century, the Finns came to Finland from their Volga settlements, taking the country from the Lapps, who retreated northward. The Finns' repeated raids on the Scandinavian coast impelled Eric IX, the Swedish King, to conquer the country in 1157 and bring it into contact with Western Christendom. By 1809 the whole of Finland was conquered by Alexander I of Russia, who set up Finland as a Grand Duchy.

The first period of Russification (1899–1905) resulted in a lessening of the powers of the Finnish Diet. The Russian language was made official, and the Finnish military system was superseded by the Russian. The pace of Russification was intensified from 1908 to 1914. When Russian control was weakened as a consequence of the March Revolution of 1917, the Finnish Diet on July 20, 1917, proclaimed Finland's independence, which became complete on Dec. 6, 1917.

When its territorial demands on Finland were rejected, the Soviet Union attacked Finland on Nov. 30, 1939. The Finns made an amazing stand of three months. Finland finally capitulated, ceding 16,000 square miles to the U.S.S.R. Under German pressure the Finns joined the Nazis against Russia in 1941, but were defeated again, and ceded the Petsamo area to Soviet Russia. In 1948, a 20-year treaty of friendship and mutual assistance was signed by the two nations and renewed for another 20 years in 1970.

In 1970 Finland entered into a trade agreement with the enlarged European Economic Community (Common Market), which includes Norway and Denmark, and also with Comecom, the Communist East European Economic Group.

The world oil crisis added a practical new reason for maintenance of an unimpaired relationship with Moscow, for Finland imports two thirds of its oil from the Soviet Union. In October, 1974, the two nations signed a 10-year energy cooperation pact providing for delivery to Finland of two 440-megawatt nuclear power stations to go into operation in 1981-82.

Helsinki was the site in late July, 1975, of a summit conference of 35 heads of government convened for the signing of a European security agreement. It was the most inclusive gathering of European leaders since the Congress of Vienna in 1815.

A coalition Cabinet headed by Martti Miettunen of the Center Party took office Nov. 30, 1975, after six months of government by a caretaker Cabinet. Miettunen sought to resign May 13, 1976 after a series of major strikes, and did resign on Sept. 17, 1976, when his five-party coalition collapsed. However, he returned to office 12 days later, heading a minority three-party coalition.

Economic Conditions.

The chief crops are oats, barley, rye and potatoes. Other food must be imported, such as wheat, rye, sugar, fruits and vegetables, to supplement local production. Grazing lands are extensive.

Leading industrial products include wood and paper, cement, cellulose, food, luxury items, machinery and textiles. With the cession of the Karelian Isthmus and the city of Viipuri to the Soviet Union, Finland lost valuable manufacturing areas. Helsinki is the principal industrial center.

Finland has no coal or oil, and many of its ore deposits are remote from transportation. Hydroelectricity supplies 70% or more of the total power supply. Finland's sulfide ore is 4% copper, 26% sulfur and 27% iron, with some zinc, cobalt, gold, and silver. Limestone, soapstone and red granite deposits are extensive, and uranium deposits are believed to exist. Wood and peat are the only natural fuels.

Chief exports in 1974 were paper (31%), timber (11%), machinery (10%), wood pulp (6%), ships (6%) and clothing (5%). Leading customers were United Kingdom (19%), Sweden (16%), U.S.S.R. (14%), West Germany (9%). Leading suppliers were Sweden (18%), U.S.S.R. (18%), West Germany (15%), U.K. (9%), U.S. (7%).

Natural Features.

Finland stretches 700 miles from the Gulf of Finland on the south to Soviet Petsamo, north of the Arctic Circle. Off the southwest coast are the Aland Islands, controlling the entrance to the Gulf of Bothnia. Finland has more than 60,000 lakes. Of the few rivers, only the Oulu (Ulea) is navigable to any important extent.

The Swedish-populated Aland Islands (581 sq. mi.) have an autonomous status under a law passed in 1951.

FRANCE (Republic)

(République Française)

President: Valéry Giscard d'Estaing (1974).
Premier: Raymond Barre (1976).
Area: 211,208 sq mi. (547,026 sq km).
Population (est. 1976): 53,250,000.
Capital: Paris.
Largest cities (1975 census): Paris, 2,290,900; Marseilles, 907,900; Lyons, 457,000; Toulouse, 383,200; Nice, 344,500; Strasbourg, 257,300; Nantes, 257,300; Bordeaux, 221,100.
Monetary unit: Franc.
Religion (est.): Roman Catholic, 90%; Protestant, Jewish, Moslem and others, 10%.

The President is elected for seven years by universal suffrage. He appoints the Premier, and the Cabinet is responsible to Parliament. The President has the right to dissolve the National Assembly or to ask Parliament for reconsideration of a law. The Parliament consists of two Houses: the National Assembly and the Senate.

Major Political Parties.*

Union of Democrats for the Republic (171 of 489 seats in National Assembly), led by Claude Labbé; Radical and Socialist Party (107 seats), led by Gaston Defferre; Communist Party (74 seats), led by Robert Ballanger; Independent Republicans (70 seats), led by Roger Chinaud; Reformists, Centrists and Social Democrats (51 seats), led by Max LeJeune.

History.

France, the Gaul of ancient times, began its history as France, a separate nation, with the Treaty of Verdun (843), by which the territories

* Figures include both members enrolled and members affiliated with party. In addition, there are 15 unaffiliated members in the National Assembly.

The French Republic

roughly comprising what are today France, Germany and Italy were divided among Charlemagne's three grandsons.

Caesar conquered part of Gaul in 57–52 B.C. and the Franks overran it in the fifth century A.D. The first of the Capetians, Hugh Capet (987–96), ruled over the principality of the Ile-de-France, from which the Capetian domain was gradually expanded by conquest, purchase, marriage, inheritance, and forfeiture. The task of breaking English power in France was begun by Philip II Augustus (1180–1223) and continued in a long series of conflicts called the Hundred Years' War (1338–1453). Beginning as a feudal conflict between French kings and the English Angevin house, this strife ended as a national war, with France emerging as a modern centralized national state. The English had won at Crécy in 1346 and at Agincourt in 1415 but were defeated at Orléans in 1429 by the French under Joan of Arc.

Relics of half-overthrown medievalism still survived in 18th-century France. Louis XVI (1774–93) was unable to solve the accumulated crises. The Old Regime, with its autocratic monarch and its privileged nobility, was an outworn society ready to collapse under the impact of revolution. The French Revolution, beginning in 1789, resulted from lack of intelligent government, lack of political liberty, an arbitrary system of taxation, survival of medieval abuses, economic evils, and the ideas of the intellectual reformers of the Age of Reason. It was a bloody affair which kept France in turmoil for years. The First Republic was proclaimed on Sept. 21, 1792.

Napoleon Bonaparte gave France a short period of glory and then the humiliation of a stunning defeat. Napoleon hardened the changes that had been brought about by the French Revolution and made some of them permanent before the forces of reaction set in. He spread revolutionary reforms to conquered German and Italian territories, nourished the growth of nationalism, and consolidated the Industrial Revolution in France.

The Congress of Vienna (1815), called to remake the map of Europe after the downfall of Napoleon, restored the Bourbons to the throne. Louis Philippe abdicated and fled to England at the start of the Revolution of 1848, and the Second French Republic was established.

Taking advantage of a factional split, Prince Louis Napoleon assumed control of France in the coup d'état of 1851. A year later, on Dec. 2, 1852, he proclaimed himself Napoleon III, Emperor of the French. His opposition to the national unification of Germany collided with Bismarck's plans. The result was the Franco-Prussian War (1870–71). Napoleon III was captured at Sedan, and the Second Empire collapsed.

Reconstruction after the Franco-Prussian War was rapid, with reorganization of the army and economic and social reforms, and a new France emerged from World War I as the dominant power on the Continent. But after four years of hostile occupation, the fires of war had reduced the once-thriving area of Northeast France to ruins. The Third French Republic was plagued by political instability and economic chaos.

From 1919 on, the aim of French foreign policy was to maintain German weakness by a system of military alliances isolating Germany. The rise of Hitler and the establishment of the Nazi dictatorship meant the failure of France's foreign policy. On June 5, 1940, the mechanized Nazi troops attacked the French. As the German armies drew close to Paris, Italy declared war on France and England. The Germans marched into undefended Paris, and three days later Marshal Henri Philippe Pétain, head of the French government then at Bordeaux, asked for an armistice. It was granted on June 22, 1940, and the French armies surrendered. France was split into occupied and unoccupied zones. The unoccupied portion, Vichy France, became a totalitarian state with Marshal Pétain as Chief of State.

France was liberated by the Allied armies in August 1944. The French Committee of National Liberation, formed in Algiers in 1943, established a provisional government with General Charles de Gaulle as President of Council. With the adoption of a new Constitution on Dec. 24, 1946, the Fourth French Republic was born.

In the Fourth Republic the empire was transformed into the French Union, the national assembly was strengthened and the presidency weakened, and France adhered to the North Atlantic Treaty Organization. Uprisings involved France in a war in Indo-China against local Communists backed by the Soviet bloc, a war from which France withdrew after the defeat at Dienbienphu. The independence of Tunisia and Morocco and the War for Algeria brought the threat of a right wing military coup in Algeria by the

Secret Army Organization. This sounded the knell of the Fourth Republic. General de Gaulle, returned to power, reorganized it along lines he had cherished, giving the President equal power with the legislature. A popular referendum approved the plan on Sept. 28, 1958, and the Fifth Republic was inaugurated on Oct. 5, 1958. De Gaulle took office as President of France on Jan. 8, 1959. He suppressed the Secret Army Organization and negotiated the independence of Algeria. On Feb. 13, 1960, France exploded its first atom bomb, in the Sahara.

De Gaulle introduced the direct election of the President in 1962 and won broad majorities. Thereupon he sought to restore the position of France in international affairs by building the French Community as the successor of the French Union and the French Empire and by launching upon an independent course as leader of the "third world" of countries aligned neither with the Western Allies nor the Soviet bloc. He negotiated close relations with West Germany in 1963 and recognition of Communist China in 1964, while improving relations with the Soviet Union at the expense of relations with the United States.

De Gaulle took France out of NATO in 1967, expelling all foreign-controlled troops from the country, and in a visit to Canada aroused a storm by speaking out for a "free Quebec." Although he had been re-elected to a seven-year term in 1965, the end of his reign was foreshadowed in 1968 by a rebellion of students. The disorders spread to the workers, who seized plants across the country, resulting in a general strike supported by half the labor force. Obtaining assurances of support from his army commanders, de Gaulle offered, then canceled a referendum, and held elections on the promise of reforms which gave his supporters an overwhelming victory.

In September and October 1968, de Gaulle reformed the universities to give students and faculty a voice in choosing presidents and in controlling most major policy areas. De Gaulle went on to attempt to achieve a long cherished plan of regional reform. This, however, aroused wide opposition. He decided to stake his fate on a referendum. At the voting on Apr. 27, 1969 the electorate defeated the plan, 53% to 47%. His successor Georges Pompidou, de Gaulle's Premier for six years, reversed the de Gaulle policy of opposing the unification of Europe, which had led de Gaulle to oppose the entrance of Britain into the Common Market in 1963.

Pompidou continued the de Gaulle policies of seeking to expand France's influence in the Mideast and Africa, selling arms to South Africa (despite the U.N. embargo), to Libya, and to Greece. He also continued de Gaulle's efforts to improve relations between France and individual members of the Communist bloc, notably the Soviet Union and China, and in 1971 he endorsed British entry into the Common Market.

Pompidou died of cancer in April 1974 and was succeeded by Valéry Giscard d'Estaing, the first non-Gaullist President in 15 years. He narrowly defeated the Socialist leader, Francois Mitterand, who had Communist backing, by less than 1% of 26 million votes cast.

Giscard was no Gaullist, but depended on Gaullist votes for parliamentary support. He adhered to basic foreign policies set by de Gaulle and Pompidou, but was more cordial and flexible in relations with the United States. He took no part in the NATO heads of state meeting in Brussels May 28-29, 1965, but attended a state dinner and thereafter met privately with President Ford. He maintained French aloofness from military participation in NATO, asserting that he did not wish to encourage Soviet fears of military pressure from the West. He cultivated good relations with China. Domestically, he successfully supported liberalized abortion and divorce laws and lowering of the voting age to 18.

Under Giscard's leadership, the French National Planning Council in January, 1975, adopted a 10-year program to reduce dependence on foreign fuel to below 60% from the 76% level that prevailed in 1973. Giscard announced May 9, 1975 that France would rejoin the European joint currency float because of disruptions caused by the energy crisis.

Giscard's uneasy alliance with the Gaullists ended Aug. 25, 1976 with the resignation of his Premier, Jacques Chirac, who protested that he needed greater powers to tackle rising political and economic problems. The President, saying he could brook no challenge to his own authority, appointed as Chirac's successor a technician without party affiliation, Raymond Barre.

France continued her independent nuclear arms program and emerged as a supplier of peacefully intended nuclear equipment to other nations. In March 1974, France agreed to sell five 1,000-megawatt reactors to Iran.

On May 29, 1976, South Africa announced a $1-billion contract with a French consortium to build a nuclear power plant at Koeberg, the first on the African continent.

Religion. The predominant faith is Roman Catholicism, but church and state were separated in 1905. Diplomatic relations with the Vatican were resumed in 1921, and lesser church property was returned to diocesan associations in 1924.

Economic Conditions. Silk culture once thrived in the lower Rhône valley, but production fell sharply between wars.

Principal industrial areas are Paris, Artois, lower Seine and Lyons; the textile industry is concentrated in the north. Leading manufactures are iron, steel, chemicals, textiles, automobiles, machinery and beet sugar.

French coalfields, most extensive in the northeast, ordinarily supply about 70% of domestic needs. Lorraine, Anjou and Normandy have valuable iron ore deposits. Provence has bauxite. Alsace has potash and oil. Limousin has kaolin, zinc, lead and tar.

France produces forest products, including resin, turpentine, timber and nuts. The annual fish catch is among the largest in Europe.

Chief exports in 1974 were machinery (18%), chemicals (12%), motor vehicles (9%) and iron and steel (9%). Leading customers were EEC (53%; incl. West Germany 17%, Italy 12%, Belgium-Luxembourg 11%, United Kingdom 7%, Netherlands 5%), Switzerland (6%), U.S. (5%). Leading suppliers were EEC (48%; incl. West Germany 19%, Belgium-Luxembourg 10%, Italy 7%, Netherlands 6%), U.S. (8%) and Saudi Arabia (6%).

Natural Features. France is second in size to Russia among Europe's nations. In the Alps near the

Italian and Swiss borders is France's highest point —Mont Blanc (15,781 ft.). The forest-covered Vosges Mountains are in the northeast, and the Pyrenees are along the Spanish border. Except for extreme northern France, which is part of the Flanders plain, the country may be described as four river basins and a plateau. Three of the streams flow west—the Seine into the English Channel, the Loire into the Atlantic, and the Garonne into the Bay of Biscay. The Rhône flows south into the Mediterranean. For about a hundred miles, the Rhine is France's eastern border. West of the Rhône and northeast of the Garonne lies the Central Plateau, covering about 15% of France's area, and rising to a maximum elevation of 6,188 feet. In the Mediterranean, about 115 miles east-southeast of Nice, is Corsica (3,367 sq. mi.).

Overseas Departments and Territories of France

FRENCH GUIANA (including ININI)

Status: Overseas Department.
Prefect: Hervé Bourseiller (1974).
Area: 35,135 sq mi. (91,000 sq km).
Population (1975 census): 55,125.
Capital (1967 census): Cayenne, 19,700.
Chief exports: shrimps, timber.
Agricultural products: bananas, cacao, corn, manioc, rice, sugar cane.
Mineral: gold.

French Guiana, lying north of Brazil and east of Surinam (Dutch Guiana) on the northeast coast of South America, was first settled in 1626. Penal settlements, embracing the area around the mouth of the Maroni River and the Iles du Salut (including Devil's Island), were founded in 1852; they have since been abolished.

During World War II, French Guiana at first adhered to the Vichy government, but the Free French took over in March 1943. French Guiana accepted in September 1958 the new Constitution of the French Fifth Republic and remained an Overseas Department of the French Republic.

Economic Conditions. Chief exports in 1973 were shrimps (76%) and ships and boats (6%). Leading customers were U.S. (81%) and Surinam (9%). Leading suppliers were France (67%), U.S. (10%), Trinidad and Tobago (5%).

FRENCH POLYNESIA

Status: Overseas Territory.
Governor: Charles Schmitt (1975).
Area: 1,544 sq mi. (4,000 sq km).
Population (est. 1976): 132,000.
Capital (1971): Papeete (on Tahiti), 25,300.
Chief exports: copra, vanilla.
Agricultural products: copra, vanilla, coffee.
Mineral: phosphates.

The term French Polynesia is applied to the scattered French possessions in the eastern Pacific —Mangareva (Gambier), Makatea, Marquesas Islands, Rapa, Rurutu, Rimatara, Society Islands, Tuamotu Archipelago, Tubuai, and Raivavae— which were organized into a single colony in 1903. The appointed Governor is assisted by a Privy Council and a popularly elected Representative Assembly. The principal and most populous island —Tahiti, in the Society group—was claimed as French in 1768. In September, 1958, French Polynesia voted in favor of the new Constitution of the French Fifth Republic and remained an Overseas Territory of the French Republic. The natives are mostly Polynesians.

Economic Conditions. Chief exports in 1973 were copra, vanilla, coffee and citrus fruit. Leading customer was France (82%). Leading suppliers were France (59%) and U.S. (15%).

FRENCH TERRITORY OF THE AFARS AND THE ISSAS (formerly French Somaliland)

Status: Overseas Territory.
High Commissioner: Camille d'Ornano (1976).
Prime Minister: Abdallah Mohamed Kamil (1976).
Area: 8,494 sq mi. (22,000 sq km).
Population (est. 1974): 150,000.
Capital (est. 1973): 120,000.
Chief exports: manufactures, hides.
Mineral: salt.

This territory, at the southern entrance to the Red Sea, was acquired by France between 1843 and 1886 by treaties with the Somali sultans, although posts on the coast had been acquired in 1856. The small, largely arid, and sparsely populated region is important chiefly because of the port of Djibouti, the main artery of Ethiopia's trade via the Djibouti-Addis Ababa railway.

In October 1958, French Somaliland voted in favor of the new Constitution establishing the French Fifth Republic. In December 1958, and again in 1967, it voted to remain an Overseas Territory of the French Republic.

The name was changed to the French Territory of the Afars and the Issas in 1967.

A referendum has been set for January 1977 to determine whether the people of the territory wish to remain under French rule.

Economic Conditions. Chief exports in 1973 were ships and boats (16%) and leather and shoes (7%). Leading customer was France (84%). Leading suppliers were France (49%), Ethiopia (12%), Japan (6%), United Kingdom (6%).

GUADELOUPE

Status: Overseas Department.
Prefect: Jean-Claude Aurousseau.
Area: 687 sq mi. (1,779 sq km).
Population (1975 census): 324,530.
Capital (est. 1974): Basse-Terre, 15,500.
Largest city (est. 1970): Pointe-à-Pitre, 82,530.
Chief exports: sugar, bananas, rum.
Agricultural products: sugar, bananas, coffee, cacao, vanilla, tobacco.
Manufactures: rum, sugar.

Guadeloupe, lying in the West Indies about 300 miles southeast of Puerto Rico, was discovered by Columbus in 1493. French colonization began in 1635. In September 1958, Guadeloupe voted in favor of the new Constitution of the French Fifth Republic and remained an Overseas Department of the French Republic.

Economic Conditions. Chief exports in 1973 were sugar (43%), bananas (36%) and rum (8%). Leading customers were France (82%) and Martinique (7%). Leading supplier was France (75%).

MARTINIQUE

Status: Overseas Department.
Prefect: Paul Noirot-Cosson.
Area: 425 sq mi. (1,102 sq km).
Population (1975 census): 324,832.
Capital (est. 1971): Fort-de-France, 100,000.
Chief exports: bananas, sugar, rum, canned fruit.
Agricultural products: sugar, bananas, pineapples, cacao, coffee.
Manufactures: rum, sugar.

Martinique, lying in the Lesser Antilles about 300 miles northeast of Venezuela, was probably discovered by Columbus in 1502 and was taken for France in 1635. Following the Franco-German armistice of 1940 it had a semiautonomous status under the High Commissioner, Admiral Georges Robert, until 1943, when he relinquished his authority to the Free French. The area, administered by a Prefect assisted by an elected council, is represented in the French Parliament. In September 1958, Martinique voted in favor of the new Constitution of the French Fifth Republic and remained an Overseas Department of the French Republic.

NEW CALEDONIA AND DEPENDENCIES

Status: Overseas Territory.
High Commissioner: Gabriel Eriau.
Area: 7,358 sq mi. (19,058 sq km).*
Population (est. 1976): 140,000.
Capital (est. 1973): Nouméa, 57,000.
Chief exports: nickel castings, nickel.
Agricultural products: coffee, copra, corn, cotton, manioc, rice, tobacco.
Minerals: nickel, chromite, iron ore.
Sea product: mother-of-pearl.

New Caledonia (6,466 sq mi.), lying about 1,070 miles northeast of Sydney, Australia. was discovered by Captain James Cook in 1774 and annexed by France in 1853. The government also administers the Isle of Pines, the Loyalty Islands (Uvéa, Lifu and Maré) and the Belep Islands.

New Caledonia chose in 1958 to remain an Overseas Territory of the French Republic. The natives are Melanesians; about one-third of the population is white and one fifth Indo-chinese and Javanese.

Economic Conditions. Chief exports in 1973 were ferronickel (45%), nickel (26%) and nickel castings (24%). Leading customers were France (45%), Japan (33%), U.S. (11%). Leading suppliers were France (49%) and Australia (12%).

NEW HEBRIDES

Status: Anglo-French condominium.
British Resident Commissioner: Colin Hamilton Allan.
French Resident Commissioner: Robert Gauger (1974).
Area: 5,700 sq mi. (14,763 sq km).
Population (est. 1976): 105,000.
Capital (est. 1972): Vila (on Efate), 8,500.
Chief exports: copra, fish, manganese ore.
Agricultural products: copra, cocoa, coffee.
Sea products: trochus and burghaus shell.

* Including dependencies.

The New Hebrides, under joint Anglo-French administration since October 1906, lie northeast of New Caledonia. The islands, about 40 in number, joined the Free French movement after a plebiscite in July 1940. Most of the natives are Melanesians of mixed blood. The largest island is Espiritu Santo (875 sq. mi.). The French and British high commissioners in the Pacific are represented by resident commissioners.

Economic Conditions. Chief exports in 1973 were fish (59%), copra (24%), timber (5%) and beef and veal (5%). Leading customers were U.S. (55%), France (27%), Japan (10%), New Caledonia (6%). Leading suppliers were Australia (37%), France (17%), Japan (11%), New Zealand (8%), New Caledonia (5%).

RÉUNION (Bourbon)

Status: Overseas Department.
Prefect: Robert Lamy (1975).
Area: 970 sq mi. (2,510 sq km).
Population (1975 census): 476,675.
Capital (est. 1973): Saint-Denis, 98,000.
Chief exports: sugar, essential oils, rum, vanilla.
Agricultural products: sugar, vanilla, tea, tobacco.

Discovered by Portuguese navigators in the 16th century, the island of Réunion, then uninhabited, was taken as a French possession in 1643. It is located about 450 miles east of Madagascar, in the Indian Ocean. In September 1958, Réunion approved the Constitution of the Fifth French Republic and remained an Overseas Department of the French Republic.

Economic Conditions. Chief exports in 1973 were sugar (85%) and essences (7%). Leading customers were France (75%) and Italy (22%). Leading suppliers were France (64%) and Madagascar (6%).

ST. PIERRE AND MIQUELON

Status: Overseas Territory.
Administrator: Jean Massendes (1975).
Area: 93 sq mi. (242 sq km).
Population (est. 1974): 5,450.
Capital (1967 census): St. Pierre, 4,565.
Chief exports: fresh and frozen fish, livestock, dried fish, fish meal.

The sole remnant of the French colonial empire in North America, these islands were first occupied by the French in 1664. Their only importance arises from proximity to the Grand Banks, located 10 miles south of Newfoundland, making them the center of the French Atlantic cod fisheries. In September, 1958, St. Pierre and Miquelon voted in favor of the new Constitution of the French Fifth Republic and remained an Overseas Territory of the French Republic.

Economic Conditions. Chief exports in 1974 were petroleum products (as ship's stores) (53%); cattle (30%) and fish (12%). Leading customers (excl. ship's stores) were Canada (70%) and U.S. (25%). Leading suppliers were Canada (54%) and France (38%).

SOUTHERN AND ANTARCTIC LANDS

Status: Overseas Territory.
Administrator: Roger Barberot.

Area: 169,614 sq mi. (439,300 sq km).
Population (1972): 189.
Capital (1972): Port-au-Français: 93.

This territory is uninhabited except for the personnel of scientific bases. It consists of Adélie Land (166,752 sq mi.) on the Antarctic mainland and the following islands in the southern Indian Ocean: the Kerguelen and Crozet archipelagos, and the islands of Saint-Paul and New Amsterdam.

WALLIS and FUTUNA ISLANDS

Status: Overseas Territory.
Administrator Superior: Yves Arbellot-Repaire (1975).
Area: 77 sq mi. (200 sq km).
Population (est. 1972): 7,500.
Capital: Mata-Utu (on Uvea), (1969): 600.
Agricultural products: copra, taro, yams, cassava, bananas.

The two island groups in the South Pacific between Fiji and Samoa were settled by French missionaries at the beginning of the 19th century. A protectorate was established in the 1880's. Following a referendum by the Polynesian inhabitants, the status was changed to that of an Overseas Territory in July 1961.

GABON (Republic)

(République Gabonaise)

(Member of French Community)

President: Omar Bongo (1967).
Premier: Léon Mebiame (1975).
Area: 103,346 sq mi. (267,667 sq km).
Population (est. 1976): 535,000.
Density per square mile: 5.2.
Capital and largest city (est. 1975 for urban agglomeration): Libreville, 169,200.
Monetary unit: Franc CFA.
Ethnic groups: Bateke, Obamba, Bakota, Shake, Pongwés, Adounas, Chiras, Punu, and Lumbu.
Languages: French and Bantu dialects.
Religions: Animist, Christian, Moslem.

The President is elected for a seven-year term. Legislative powers are exercised by a 49-member National Assembly, which is elected for a seven-year term. After his conversion to Islam in 1973, President Bongo changed his given names Albert Bernard to Omar.

Major Political Party. Parti Démocratique Gabonais (all 49 seats in National Assembly), led by President Bongo.

History. This West African land with the Atlantic Ocean as its western border is surrounded by Equatorial Guinea, Cameroon, and Congo (Brazzaville). Little is known of its history, even in oral tradition, but Pygmies are believed to be the original inhabitants. Now there are many tribal groups in the country, the largest being the Fang people who account for a third of the population.

Gabon was first visited by the Portuguese navigator Diego Cam in the 15th century. In 1839, the French founded their first settlement on the left bank of the Gabon River and gradually occupied the hinterland during the second half of the 19th

century. It was organized as a French territory in 1888, and became an autonomous republic within the French Union after World War II and an independent republic on Aug. 17, 1960.

Immense resources in oil, uranium, manganese and iron help give Gabon's inhabitants a per capita annual income of $225 to $250, the highest in Black Africa. To speed exploitation of a billion-ton iron ore reserve in the Belinga Mekambo region, the government began work in 1969 on a 350-mile railroad leading from the coast into the area. The project was initiated by President León Mba, who died in 1967, and has been continued by his hand-picked successor, President Omar Bongo.

In 1974, Bongo negotiated 60% control of an iron-ore venture half-owned by the Bethlehem Steel Corp. In October, 1974, he visited Peking and concluded an economic and technical agreement with China.

Bongo was re-elected without opposition in 1973. In April, 1975, he announced constitutional changes that created the post of Premier and did away with the office of Vice President, then installed former Vice President Léon Mebiame as Premier.

Economic Conditions. Agricultural products include corn, coffee, cocoa, bananas, and timber.

Chief exports in 1973 were crude oil (87%), timber (c. 8%) and manganese (c. 5%). Leading customers were France (37%), West Germany (10%), Netherlands (7%), U.S. (7%), United Kingdom (6%). Leading suppliers were France (59%), West Germany (9%), U.S. (9%).

GAMBIA (Republic)

(Member of Commonwealth of Nations)

President: Sir Dawda K. Jawara (1970).
Area: 4,361 sq mi. (11,295 sq km).
Population (est. 1976): 530,000.
Density per square mile: 121.5.
Capital and largest city (est. 1975): Banjul, 42,400.
Monetary unit: Dalasi.
Languages: Native tongues, English.
Religions: Moslem, Christian, Animist.

In addition to 32 elective seats in the House of Representatives, tribal chiefs elect 4 members, 2 are appointed, and the speaker, called the Attorney-General, is elected. Executive power is vested in the President and the Cabinet.

Gambia became a republic within the Commonwealth of Nations on Apr. 24, 1970.

Political Parties. People's Progressive Party (28 of 32 seats in House of Representatives), led by President Jawara; United Party, led by Pierre N'Jie (3 seats); one independent.

History. During the 17th century, Gambia was settled by various companies of English merchants. Slavery was the chief source of revenue until it was abolished in 1807. Gambia became a crown colony in 1843 and achieved its independence on Feb. 18, 1965.

After approval in an April 1970 referendum, Africa's smallest state proclaimed itself a republic.

Prime Minister Jawara moved up to become President. The election was held in 1972.

Economic Conditions. The principal economic activity of Gambia is the cultivation of peanuts.

Chief exports in 1973–74 were peanuts and products (94%). Leading customers were United Kingdom (37%), France (23%), Netherlands (17%), Portugal (8%), West Germany (7%), Italy (6%). Leading suppliers were U.K. (24%), China (10%), Netherlands (6%), France (5%), Poland (5%), U.S. (5%), Senegal (5%).

GERMAN DEMOCRATIC REPUBLIC (East)

(Deutsche Demokratische Republik)

Chairman of Council of State: Willi Stoph (1973).
Chairman of Council of Ministers: Horst Sindermann (1973).
Area: 41,923 sq mi. (108,178 sq km).*
Population (est. 1975 by U.N.): 16,850,000.*
Density per square mile: 401.9.
Capital: East Berlin.
Largest cities (est. 1975): East Berlin, 1,094,100; (1974 census): Leipzig, 574,432; Dresden, 506,067; Karl-Marx Stadt, 302,409; Magdeburg, 274,146; Halle/Saale, 245,681; Rostock, 207,285; Erfurt, 201,826.
Monetary unit: Mark der Deutschen Demokratischen Republik.
Religions: Protestant, 80%; Roman Catholic, 10%.

The People's Chamber, composed of 500 deputies elected for four-year terms, chooses the chairman and Council of State and the chairman and Council of Ministers, which carries on executive functions.

Political Parties. Socialist Unity (Communist) Party, led by Secretary General Erich Honecker; Christian Democratic Union, Liberal Democratic Party, Democratic Farmers' Party, National Democratic Party.

History. The area now occupied by East Germany, as well as adjacent areas in Eastern Europe, consists of Mecklenburg, Brandenburg, Lusatia, Saxony and Thuringia. Soviet armies conquered the five territories by 1945. In the division of 1945 they were allotted to the Soviet Union. Soviet forces created a State controlled by the secret police with a single party, the Socialist Unity (Communist) party. The Russians appropriated East German plants to restore their war-ravaged industry.

When the Federal Republic of Germany was established in West Germany, the East German states adopted a more centralized constitution for the Democratic Republic of Germany and it was put into effect on Oct. 7, 1949. The Soviet Union thereupon dissolved its occupation zone but Soviet troops remained. The Western Allies declared that the East German Republic was a Soviet creation undertaken without self-determination and refused to recognize it. It was recognized only within the Soviet bloc.

In June 1953, the Soviet Union transferred control of East Germany from the military commander to a civilian commissioner and announced a more liberal policy. Continued austerity and political repression led to workers' riots in East Berlin and other cities,

*Including East Berlin (156 square miles, with population of 1,094,100, which has been incorporated into the German Democratic Republic.

allegedly instigated by the Soviet secret police as part of a power struggle within the Kremlin. Soviet troops ruthlessly reestablished order. But the Soviet authorities made efforts to revive the East German economy.

In 1955, Walter Ulbricht, hard-line dictator, won Soviet recognition of the East German republic and joined the Warsaw Treaty Organization, organizing troops under the guide of police forces. In the middle and late 1960's East Germany also came to enjoy economic prosperity. Trade, formerly limited largely to the Soviet bloc, expanded to West Germany and developing nations. But trade agreements obliging the East Germans to sell to Russia at low fixed prices and to buy from the Soviets at prices higher than the world market held per capita income well below that of West Germany.

East German troops took part in the Soviet-bloc occupation of Czechoslovakia in August, 1968, but reportedly were withdrawn after the Soviet Union questioned whether the 1945 Potsdam agreements permitted German troops on foreign soil. A new Constitution adopted in April 1968 reaffirmed one-party rule and narrowed civil rights. Ulbricht continued pressure on West Berlin; opposed liberalization in Czechoslovakia and other parts of the Soviet bloc; impeded Bonn's establishment of ties with East Europe, and pressured Bonn to acknowledge the existence of the two German states.

Talks between the two German states on normalization began in 1970, with the East seeking recognition of its existence and the West wanting easing of pressure on Berlin. West Germany's nonaggression treaty with the Soviet Union was cooly received by Ulbricht. In 1971 he resigned and rapprochement between the two Germanys accelerated with agreement on a variety of issues (for details, *see* West Germany). By 1973, normal relations were established, and the two states entered the United Nations.

An agreement announced Dec. 12, 1974, made $340 million a year in interest-free West German credits available to East Germany until 1981 to increase trade. However, a new Constitution unanimously approved by the East German parliament on Sept. 27, 1974, pointedly deleted any reference to eventual reunification of the two Germanys, a principle maintained in the West German constitution.

A 25-year diplomatic hiatus between East Germany and the United States ended Sept. 4, 1974, with the establishment of formal relations.

At the ninth party congress in East Berlin on May 22, 1976, Erich Honecker was elected Secretary-General of the party. Prime Minister Sindermann announced a five-year plan for 1976–80 aimed primarily at reducing energy consumption and cutting industrial costs.

Economic Conditions. About 22% of the population is engaged in agricultural pursuits and the area is almost self-sufficient in foodstuffs. Postwar yields have, however, suffered from droughts and shortages of fertilizers.

Most of the industrial establishments, particularly in heavy industry, have been nationalized. The area accounted for 26% of prewar Germany's industrial production, ranking first in textiles, paper and pulp, and ceramics and glass (especially optical glass produced by the famous Jena works). In the first quarter of 1974, trade with the West increased 8%.

The area is not rich in minerals. It has only minor deposits of coal, but it does have important deposits of lignite and crude potash.

Chief exports in 1970 were machinery (38%), transport equipment (11%) (ships and boats, 5%), and chemicals, lignite, textiles and furniture. Leading customers in 1973 were U.S.S.R. (38%), Czechoslovakia (10%), Poland (9%), West Germany (7%). Leading suppliers were U.S.S.R. (32%), Czechoslovakia (9%), West Germany (8%), Poland (8%), Hungary (6%).

GERMANY, FEDERAL REPUBLIC OF (WEST)

(Bundesrepublik Deutschland)

President: Walter Scheel (1974).
Chancellor: Helmut Schmidt (1974).
Area: 95,791 sq mi. (248,577 sq km).*
Population (est. 1975 by U.N.): 61,830,000.*
Density per square mile: 645.4.
Capital (est. 1974 by U.N.): Bonn, 283,260.
Largest cities (1974 by U.N.): Hamburg, 1,751,620; Munich, 1,336,575; Cologne, 832,400; Essen, 674,000; Frankfurt, 663,400; Dortmund, 632,300; Düsseldorf, 628,500; Stuttgart, 624,800; Bremen, 584,265; Hannover, 505,100.
Monetary unit: Deutsche Mark.
Language: German.
Religions: Protestant, 49%; Roman Catholic, 44.6%; Jewish, 0.1%; others, 6.3%.

The Constitution of the Federal Republic of Germany embodies the best features of the French Declaration of the Rights of Man, the first ten amendments to the American Constitution, the British Bill of Rights, and the Weimar Constitution. It was adopted by the Parliamentary Council on May 8, 1949, and approved by the High Commissioners on May 12, 1949. It provides for a Federal President, chosen for a term of five years by a Federal Convention. The Parliament consists of two legislative houses. The upper house, the Bundesrat, represents and is appointed by the governments of the Länder, or states. The lower house, the Bundestag, is elected for a period of four years by universal suffrage. The Chancellor, or Prime Minister, is elected by a majority of the Bundestag on proposal of the President. Each of the 11 constituent Länder (including West Berlin) is required to have a republican form of government with an assembly chosen by the people.

Major Political Parties. Social Democratic Party (213 of 496 seats in the Bundestag), led by Chancellor Helmut Schmidt; Christian Democratic Union-Christian Social Union (244 seats), led by Helmut Kohl; and the Free Democratic Party (39 seats), led by Hans-Dietrich Genscher. Schmidt's government is a coalition with the Free Democrats.

History. In Caesar's time, the territory that is now Germany was inhabited by barbarous tribes that came originally perhaps from Central Asia. One of these Germanic tribes, the Franks, attained supremacy in western Europe under Charlemagne, who was crowned Holy Roman Emperor in A.D.

* Excluding West Berlin (184 square miles, with population of 2,024,000.

800. By the Treaty of Verdun (843), Charlemagne's lands east of the Rhine were ceded to the German Prince Louis. Additional territory acquired by the Treaty of Mersen (870) gave Germany approximately the area she maintained throughout the Middle Ages. For several centuries after Otto the Great was crowned King in 936, the German rulers were also usually heads of the Holy Roman Empire.

Relations between state and church were changed by the Reformation, which began with Martin Luther's 95 theses, and came to a head in 1547, when Charles V scattered the forces of the Protestant League at Mühlberg. Freedom of worship was obtained by the Peace of Augsburg (1555), but a Counter Reformation took place later, and a dispute over the succession to the Bohemian throne brought on the Thirty Years' War (1618–48) which devastated Germany and left the empire divided into hundreds of small principalities virtually independent of the Emperor. Meanwhile, Prussia was developing into a province of considerable strength. Frederick the Great (1740–86) reorganized the Prussian army and defeated Maria Theresa of Austria in a struggle over Silesia. The conflict with revolutionary France hastened the disintegration of the empire, and in 1806, Francis II of Austria laid down the Imperial German crown. After the defeat of Napoleon at Waterloo (1815), the struggle between Austria and Prussia for supremacy in Germany continued, reaching its climax in the defeat of Austria in the Seven Weeks' War (1866) and the formation of the Prussian-dominated North German Confederation (1867).

The architect of German unity was Otto von Bismarck, a conservative, monarchist, and militaristic Prussian Junker who had no use for "empty phrase-making and constitutions." From 1862 until his retirement in 1890 he dominated not only the German but also the entire European scene. He unified all Germany in a series of three wars against Denmark (1864), Austria (1866), and France (1870–71). Historians differ on the responsibility for these wars, but many believe they were instigated and promoted by Bismarck in his zeal to obtain national unity through "blood and iron."

On Jan. 18, 1871, King William I of Prussia was proclaimed William I, German Emperor, at the Hall of Mirrors, Versailles. The North German Confederation, created in 1867, was abolished, and the new Second German Reich, consisting of both North and South German states, was born. As King of Prussia, the German Emperor exercised what amounted to dictatorial control over all Germany. With a powerful army, an efficient bureaucracy, and a loyal bourgeoisie, Chancellor Bismarck consolidated a powerful centralized state.

William II dismissed Bismarck in 1890 and embarked upon a "New Course" stressing an intensified colonialism and a powerful navy. His chaotic foreign policy gradually culminated in the diplomatic isolation of Germany and the nearly fatal outcome of World War I (1914–18).

The Second German Empire collapsed following the defeat of the German armies in 1918, the naval mutiny at Kiel, and the flight of William II to the Netherlands on Nov. 10. The Social Democrats, led by Friedrich Ebert and Philipp Scheidemann, crushed the Communists and established a moderate republic with Ebert as President.

The Weimar Constitution of 1919 provided for a President to be elected for seven years by direct universal suffrage; a bicameral legislature, consisting of the Reichsrat, representing the states, and the Reichstag, representing the people. It contained a model Bill of Rights. It was weakened by including a provision (Article 48) enabling the President to rule by decree.

President Ebert died Feb. 28, 1925, and on Apr. 26, Field Marshal Paul von Hindenburg was elected President of Germany.

The mass of Germans regarded the Weimar Republic as a child of defeat, imposed upon a Germany whose legitimate aspirations to world leadership had been thwarted by a world conspiracy. Added to this were a crippling currency debacle, a tremendous burden of reparations and acute economic distress.

Capital of Germany's misery was made by Adolf Hitler, a former Austrian war veteran, a fanatical nationalist. He fanned discontent by promising a Greater Germany, the abrogation of the Treaty of Versailles, the restoration of Germany's lost colonies, and the destruction of the Jews. When the Social Democrats and the Communists refused to combine against the Nazi threat, President Hindenburg made Hitler Chancellor on Jan. 30, 1933.

With the death of President Hindenburg on Aug. 2, 1934, Hitler became complete master of Germany. He repudiated the Treaty of Versailles and began full-scale rearmament. In 1935 he withdrew from the League of Nations, and in 1936 he reoccupied the Rhineland and signed the anti-Comintern pact with Japan, at the same time strengthening relations with Italy. Austria was annexed in March 1938. By the Munich agreement (September 1938) he gained the Czech Sudetenland, and in violation of this agreement he completed the dismemberment of Czechoslovakia in March 1939. But his invasion of Poland on Sept. 1, 1939, precipitated World War II.

On May 8, 1945, Germany surrendered unconditionally to Allied and Soviet military commanders, and on June 5 the four-nation Allied Control Council became the *de facto* government of Germany.

At the Berlin (or Potsdam) Conference (July 17–Aug. 2, 1945) Truman, Stalin, and Attlee set forth the principles by which the Allied Control Council was to be guided. They were: Germany's complete disarmament and demilitarization; destruction of its war potential; rigid control of industry; decentralization of the political and economic structure. Pending final determination of territorial questions at a peace conference, the three victors agreed in principle to the ultimate transfer of the city of Königsberg (now Kaliningrad) and its adjacent area to the Soviet Union, and to the administration by Poland of former German territories lying generally east of the Oder-Neisse line.

For purposes of control Germany was divided in 1945 into four national occupation zones, each headed by a Military Governor, assisted by appropriate supervisory and operating staffs.

Efforts to unify Germany were totally unsuccessful, and the Western powers were unable to agree with the Soviet Union on any fundamental issue. Work of the Allied Control Council was hamstrung by repeated Soviet vetoes; and finally, on Mar. 20, 1948, Russia walked out of the Council. Meanwhile, the United States and Britain had taken steps to merge their zones economically (Bizone); and on May 31, 1948, the United States, Britain, France, and the Benelux countries agreed to set up a German state comprising the three western zones. At the same time the Western powers introduced a new German currency.

The Soviet Union reacted by clamping a blockade on all ground communications between the Western Zones and Berlin, an enclave in the Soviet Zone. The Western Allies countered by organizing a gigantic airlift to fly supplies into the beleaguered city, assigning 60,000 men to it. The Soviet Union was finally forced to lift the blockade on May 12, 1949.

The Federal Republic of Germany (West Germany), comprising those portions of Germany and Greater Berlin which had been assigned to the American, British, and French zones, was proclaimed on May 23, 1949, with its capital at Bonn. In free elections West German voters gave a majority in the Constituent Assembly to the Christian Democrats, with the Social Democrats largely comprising the opposition. Konrad Adenauer became Chancellor and Theodor Heuss of the Free Democrats was elected first President.

With admission into the European Coal and Steel Community and later into the Common Market, German prosperity was strengthened. In 1950 a Constitution was given West Berlin which provided for autonomous municipal government and representation in the Bundestag. A peace contract was given West Germany on May 26, 1952, which created within the North Atlantic Treaty Organization a European Defense Community but it was later vetoed by France. A conference at Paris reached agreements signed on Oct. 23, 1954, giving the Federal Republic full independence and complete sovereignty; it came into force on May 5, 1955. Under it, Germany and Italy became members of the Brussels treaty organization created in 1948 and renamed the Western European Union. Germany also became a member of NATO. In 1955 the Soviet Union recognized the Federal Republic. The Saar territory, under an agreement between France and West Germany, held a plebiscite and despite economic links to France voted to rejoin West Germany. It became a province of West Germany on Jan. 1, 1957.

On Jan. 22, 1963, Chancellor Adenauer concluded a treaty of mutual cooperation and friendship with France and then retired. He was succeeded by his chief inner-party critic, Ludwig Erhard, who was followed in 1966 by Kurt Georg Kiesinger. He, in turn, was succeeded in 1969 by Willy Brandt, former Mayor of West Berlin.

The division between West Germany and East Germany was signalized when the Communists erected the Berlin Wall in 1961. In June, 1968, the East German Communist leader, Walter Ulbricht, imposed restrictions on West German movements into West Berlin. The Soviet-bloc invasion of Czechoslovakia in August, 1968, added to the tension.

Willy Brandt's Socialist government, pushed through an "Ostpolitik" policy that led to the first official meetings of leaders of East and West Germany on Mar. 19, 1970. A treaty with the Soviet Union was signed in Moscow in August 1970, in which force was renounced and respect for the "territorial integrity" of present European states declared.

Three months later, Germany signed a similar treaty with Poland, renouncing force and setting Poland's western border as the Oder-Neisse line (which acknowledged Poland's post-war annexation of 40,000 square miles of former German territory); and subsequently resumed formal relations with Czechoslovakia in a pact that declared "void" the Munich treaty that gave Nazi Germany the Sudetenland.

Both German states were admitted to the United Nations in 1973.

Brandt, winner of a Nobel Peace Prize for his foreign policies, was forced to quit in .May 1974 when an East German Communist spy was discovered as one of .his top staff members. Succeeding him was a moderate Social Democrat, Helmut Schmidt.

Schmidt's government was plagued with recurring violence by anarchist urban guerrillas. Peter Lorenz, leader of the Christian Democratic Union in West Berlin, was kidnaped Feb. 27, 1975, and held until five imprisoned anarchists were freed and given a plane to fly to South Yemen. The government refused to release 26 other anarchists after armed men seized Bonn's embassy in Stockholm on April 24, and the building was dynamited, causing three deaths. Schmidt called it "the most serious incident in the 26-year history of our democracy."

Economic Conditions. Agriculture is characterized by mixed farming, the climate and the soil permitting cultivation of a variety of crops and most types of livestock. Rye and potatoes are staple crops in the north; grains and sugar beets in the central regions.

The northwestern and southern areas are noted for dairying, while the west is the chief fruit- and wine-producing region. The soil is generally poor, and high crop yields are dependent upon large-scale use of fertilizers.

West Germany's industry is well developed and diversified. It accounted for about two thirds of Germany's prewar industrial production and for a large part of iron and steel production. Shipbuilding has regained its former prominence.

West Germany is a member of the European Coal and Steel Community, which commenced activities on Aug. 10, 1952. It has jurisdiction over the production and allocation of coal and steel by its member nations.

Aside from rich deposits of coal and potash, West Germany's mineral wealth is not considerable. The Ruhr, Krefeld and Aachen districts constitute one of the world's greatest coal-mining regions.

About 23% of the total area of West Germany is covered by commercial forests, which yield timber as well as material for paper, wood fiber, cellulose and other products.

Chief exports in 1974 were machinery (28%), motor vehicles (12%), iron and steel (12%), chemicals (10%) and textile yarns and fabrics (6%). Leading customers were EEC (45%; incl. France 12%, Netherlands 10%, Italy 8%, Belgium-Luxembourg 8%, United Kingdom 5%), U.S. (8%), Switzerland (6%). Leading suppliers were EEC (48%; incl. Netherlands 14%, France 12%, Belgium-Luxembourg 9%, Italy 8%) and U.S. (8%).

Shipping on the Rhine is controlled by the Central Commission of the Rhine—an international body composed provisionally of U.S., British,

French, Swiss, Dutch, and Belgian representatives —which was reconvened in October 1945.

Natural Features. The northern plain, the central hill country, and the southern mountain district constitute the main physical divisions of West Germany. The Bavarian plateau in the southwest averages 1,600 feet above sea level, but it reaches 9,721 feet in the Zugspitze, which is the highest point in Germany.

There are several important navigable rivers. In the south the Danube, rising in the Black Forest, flows east across Bavaria into Austria. The other important rivers flow north. The Rhine, which rises in Switzerland and flows across the Netherlands in two channels to the North Sea, is navigable by smaller vessels as far as Cologne. The Rhine and the Elbe, which also empties into the North Sea, are navigable within Germany for ships of 400 tons. The Weser, flowing into the North Sea, and the Main and Mosel (Moselle), both tributaries of the Rhine, are also important.

BERLIN

Status: West Berlin: State of West Germany; East Berlin: capital of East Germany.
Governing Mayor, West Berlin: Klaus Schütz (1967).
Mayor, East Berlin: Herbert Fechner (1967).
Area: 340 square miles (West Berlin, 184; East Berlin, 156).
Population (est. 1975): 3,118,100 (West Berlin, 2,024,000, East Berlin, 1,094,000.

Berlin, the capital of prewar Germany, is surrounded by East Germany. After the war, Berlin was occupied by the forces of the United States, the United Kingdom, France, and the Soviet Union. The three western sectors, now known as West Berlin, contain 55% of the area and two thirds of the population.

West Berlin is a state of the Federal Republic of Germany, but supreme authority remains in the hands of the three Western powers in accordance with postwar agreements. The government is composed of the Governing Mayor, the 11-member Senate (his Cabinet), and House of Representatives, a popularly elected legislative body that elects the Governing Mayor and the Senate.

East Berlin is governed by a City Assembly elected by Communist Party voters; and a Magistrat (city council) chosen by the Assembly and headed by the Mayor. In violation of the Four-Power Agreements, the Soviet Sector has been incorporated into the German Democratic Republic and is now the capital of that country.

Major anti-Communist riots broke out in East Berlin in June 1953 and, since Aug. 13, 1961, the Soviet Sector has been virtually sealed off by a Communist-built wall, 26½ miles long, running through the city. It was built to stem the flood of refugees seeking freedom in the West, 200,000 having fled in 1961, before the wall was erected.

GHANA (Republic)

(Member of Commonwealth of Nations)

Head of State and Government: Gen. Ignatius Kutu Acheampong (1972).
Area: 92,100 sq mi. (238,537 sq km).
Population (est. 1976): 10,140,000.

Density per square mile: 110.1.
Capital: Accra.
Largest cities (est. 1972): Accra, 633,880; Kumasi, 342,982; Sekondi-Takoradi, 161,071.
Monetary unit: Cedi.
Languages: Native tongues (Twi, Fanti, Ga, Ewe, Dagbani); English.
Religions: Christian (43%), Moslem (12%), animist (38%).

On Jan. 13, 1972, a military coup led by Gen. Ignatius Kutu Acheampong seized power bloodlessly and deposed Kofi A. Busia, who had been Premier since 1969. The Constitution was suspended, Parliament dissolved and a National Redemption Council was set up. It consists of nine members, seven of whom are military men, the Inspector-General of Police and a civilian Attorney General. The activities of political parties were banned.

History. Created an independent country on Mar. 6, 1957, Ghana is the former British colony of the Gold Coast. The area was first seen by Portuguese traders in 1470. They were followed by the English (1553), the Dutch (1595) and the Swedes (1640). British rule over the Gold Coast began in 1820, but it was not until after quelling the severe resistance of the Ashanti in 1901 that it was firmly established. British Togoland, formerly a colony of Germany, was incorporated into Ghana by referendum in 1956. As the result of a plebiscite, Ghana became a republic on July 1, 1960.

Premier Kwame Nkrumah attempted to take leadership of the Pan-African Movement, holding the All-African People's Congress in his capital, Accra, in 1958 and organizing the Union of African States with Guinea and Mali in 1961. But he oriented his country toward the Soviet Union and China and built an autocratic rule over all aspects of Ghanaian life.

In February 1966, while Nkrumah was visiting Peking and Hanoi, he was deposed by a military coup led by Emmanuel K. Kotoka. The United States recognized it and gave it financial aid. In April, 1967, a military junta was crushed, but General Kotoka was killed. The military leaders took steps to restore civilian rule and a new Constitution was approved in May, 1969.

But a new military group, charging the previous government with "general mismanagement," took over in January, 1972, survived a counter-coup, and promised to turn the government back to civilian rule "as soon as circumstances permit." Its leader, Gen. Acheampong, proclaimed himself both Head of State and chairman of the National Redemption Council, and promised continuation of the nation's foreign policies.

Economic Conditions. The mainstay of the economy is the cultivation of cacao, in the production of which Ghana leads the rest of the world. Secondary export crops include palm kernels, copra, kola nuts, coffee, rubber and timber.

Chief exports in 1974 were cocoa (63%), timber (21%) and aluminum (7%). Leading customers in 1973 were United Kingdom (19%), U.S. (15%), Netherlands (9%), Japan (9%), West Germany (9%), Italy (7%), U.S.S.R. (6%). Leading suppliers were U.K. (16%), U.S. (16%), West Germany (12%), Japan (7%), France (6%).

Mineral resources are abundant. Most important is gold, mined at Tarkwa, Bibiani and Obuasi. Others include diamonds, manganese ore and bauxite. Forest resources are extensive and large amounts of hardwoods, notably mahogany, are exported from the forests in the interior.

The coastal belt, extending about 270 miles along the Gulf of Guinea, is sandy, marshy, and generally exposed. Behind it is a gradually widening grass strip. The forested plateau region to the north is broken by ridges and hills.

GREECE (Parliamentary Republic)

(Hellas)

President: Constantine Tsatsos (1975).
Premier: Constantine Caramanlis (1974).
Area: 50,944 sq mi. (131,944 sq km).
Population (est. 1976): 9,120,000.
Density per square mile: 179.0.
Capital: Athens.
Largest cities (1971 census): Athens, 867,023; Salonika, 345,799; Piraeus, 187,458.
Monetary unit: Drachma.
Language: Greek.
Religions: Greek Orthodox, 96%; Moslem, 2%; Jewish, 1.1%.

Greece became a "presidential parliamentary republic" in 1973 after George Papadopoulos decreed an end to the "crowned democracy" under which King Constantine II, in exile, had remained sovereign under the 1968 Constitution. Papadopoulos, a former army intelligence colonel, was himself ousted later that year by military leaders who installed Lieut. Gen. Phaidon Gizikis as President. Civilian government was restored in 1974.

Political Parties. New Democracy Party (216 of 300 seats in the unicameral parliament reconstituted in 1974), led by Premier Constantine Caramanlis; Center Union (61 seats), led by George Mavros; Panhellenic Socialist Movement (15 seats), led by Andreas Papandreou; United Left Party (8 seats), a Communist coalition.

History. Greece, with a recorded history going back to 766 B.C., reached the peak of its glory in the fifth century B.C., and by the middle of the second century B.C., it had declined to the status of a Roman province. It remained within the Eastern Roman Empire until Constantinople fell to the Crusaders in 1204.

In 1453, the Turks took Constantinople, and by 1460, Greece was a Turkish province. The insurrection made famous by the poet Lord Byron broke out in 1821, and in 1827, Greece was set up as an independent nation, with sovereignty guaranteed by Britain, France, and Russia.

King George encouraged the adoption of a Constitution which made possible the development of a democratic parliamentary system. Greek territory was considerably extended as a result of the Balkan Wars, but an expedition into Turkish Asia Minor after World War I was unsuccessful, and claims to Greek-inhabited areas were finally settled by an exchange of populations. A republic was proclaimed in 1924, following the departure of King George II and a plebiscite which showed a republican majority. The monarchy was restored in 1935, however, following a coup d'état. Greece resisted an Italian invasion so successfully in 1940 that Nazi Germany had to come to the aid of her Axis partner the following year. British and Greek troops liberated Greece in October 1944. For some time after that, guerrilla warfare was conducted by Communist sympathizers.

King Constantine II, failing in an attempt to overthrow the military junta that had seized power in April 1967, left the country on Dec. 14, 1967.

In 1968, George Papadopoulos emerged as the strong man of the junta. He took the title of Premier. A new Constitution was adopted in a referendum on Sept. 29, 1968. It stripped the King of virtually all powers.

The military regime tortured political prisoners as a matter of policy and denied fundamental human rights to citizens.

In 1973, the "crowned democracy" of 1968 was abolished and the country proclaimed a "presidential parliamentary republic" (the third republic in Greek history). Papadopoulos took the title of President (he had been Premier). His first act upon being installed as President in August 1973 was to decree an end to martial law and a general amnesty for all political prisoners.

But Papadopoulos was thrown out in a bloodless military coup in November 1973, allegedly for moving too fast toward parliamentary elections. The ouster followed a week of clashes between thousands of students in Athens and Greek troops. Installed as figurehead President was Phaedon Gizikis, a former general. He resigned Dec. 11, 1974. His interim replacement was Michael Stassinopoulos.

The military regime in Athens resigned July 23, 1974 following the failure of its attempt to manipulate the Cyprus coup and take political control of the island. The Junta turned power over to a civilian government after it became clear the Cyprus coup had brought the establishment of Turkish military forces on the island and war with Turkey might result.

Former Premier Caramanlis returned to Athens and was sworn in as Premier of Greece's first civilian government since 1967. The new government declared amnesty for all political prisoners and recognized Archbishop Makarios as the legal head of Cyprus.

In October 1974, Papadopoulos and four junta members were exiled to an Aegean island. They were jailed in January, 1975, on charges of insurrection and high treason. In February, the government announced that a coup by junta supporters had been foiled; it retired 22 generals and purged 48 Army officers.

As he dealt with the junta, Caramanlis advanced restoration of democratic government. The new regime set Nov. 17, 1974, for elections to choose a newly constituted 300-seat unicameral parliament. The balloting gave Caramanlis's New Democracy Party 54.37% of the vote and 220 seats. In a Dec. 8 referendum, Greek voters rejected by better than 2-to-1 former King Constantine's proposal that he return to the throne as a "democratic monarch." Caramanlis supporters held 216 parliamentary seats after by-elections in April, 1975. A new republican Constitution was adopted June 7, 1975, at a parliamentary session boycotted by all 84 opposition members.

Following the Turkish military offensive on Cyprus, in mid-August, 1974, Greece cut its military ties with the North Atlantic Treaty Organization. The new government expressed its bitterness at the failure of the U.S. and other NATO allies to restrain Turkey, also a NATO member. Greece bowed to Turkey's superior military position and did not send troops to Cyprus.

Diplomatic efforts to effect a Greek-Turkish agreement on Cyprus continued through 1976 with no success and a growing anti-American sentiment, reflecting both the official and popular view that Washington has leaned toward Turkey in the controversy.

On Feb. 9, 1976, Foreign Ministers of the European Community unanimously endorsed a Greek application for full membership. The negotiations for accession could take two years or more to complete.

Economic Conditions. About three quarters of the population engages in agricultural pursuits, although only one fifth of the land is arable. Most of the cultivated area is devoted to cereals: wheat, barley and maize. There are also olive trees, vines, tobacco and currants. The principal fruits are oranges, lemons, figs, mandarins, apples and pears.

Development of large-scale Greek manufacturing is blocked by lack of coal resources and of capital. The most valuable products are textiles, chemicals and food items. Among other processed or manufactured products are olive oil, wine, spirits, flour, carpets, leather, cigarettes and building materials.

Greek minerals are varied but are exploited only moderately. Principal ones are lignite, iron ore, iron pyrites, magnesite, chromite, lead, bauxite, molybdenum, emery, marine salt and marble.

A fifth of the country is forested, largely with pine, fir and oak. Resin and turpentine are main forest products. The major sea product is sponges.

Chief exports in 1974 were textile yarns and fabrics (10%), petroleum products (10%), iron and steel (9%), tobacco (8%), dried fruit (5%), fresh fruit (5%), aluminum (5%) and chemicals (5%). Leading customers were EEC (50%; incl. West Germany 21%, Italy 9%, France 6%, United Kingdom 6%, Netherlands 5%), U.S. (6%), Libya (5%). Leading suppliers were EEC (43%; incl. West Germany 16%, Italy 9%, France 7%, U.K. 5%), U.S. (9%), Japan (6%).

Natural Features. North central Greece, Epirus and western Macedonia all are mountainous. The main chain of the Pindus Mountains rises to 9,000 feet in places, separating Epirus from the plains of Thessaly. Greek Thrace is mostly a lowland region separated from European Turkey by the lower Maritsa River.

Among the many islands are the Ionian group off the west coast; the Cyclades group to the southeast; other islands in the eastern Aegean, including Lesbos, Samos, and Chios; and Crete, the fourth largest Mediterranean island.

The Dodecanese, a group of islands in the Aegean Sea near the coast of Asia Minor, were ceded to Greece by the 1947 Italian peace treaty and were formally transferred on Mar. 7, 1948.

GRENADA (Parliamentary State)

(Member of Commonwealth of Nations)

Prime Minister: Eric M. Gairy (1974).
Governor General: Sir Leo de Gale.
Area: 133 sq mi. (344 sq km).
Population (est. 1976): 110,000 (Black, 53%; mixed, 42%).
Density per square mile: 827.1.
Capital and largest city (est. 1973): St. George's, 12,000.
Monetary unit: Eastern Caribbean dollar.
Ethnic groups: Caribs and Indians.
Language: English.
Religions: Roman Catholic, Anglican, Baptist.

The most southerly of the Windward Islands in the Caribbean Sea, Grenada (the first 'a' is pronounced as in "gray") was discovered by Columbus in 1498. After more than 200 years of British rule, most recently as part of the West Indies Associated States, Grenada became independent Feb. 7, 1974.

The country began its independence in chaos, as opponents of Prime Minister Eric M. Gairy's curbs on civil liberties—notably the professionals and educated class, as well as some union leaders and businessmen—paralyzed Grenada with a general strike that ended after two weeks when Gairy promised to disband his secret police force.

In September, 1974, Grenada became a member of the United Nations.

Political Parties. The United Labor Party, led by Prime Minister Gairy, holds 14 of 15 seats in the House of Assembly, the island's parliament.

Economic Conditions. The principal sources of revenue are derived from tourism, bananas, nutmeg and cocoa.

Chief exports in 1968 were cocoa (c. 37%), nutmegs (c. 28%), bananas (c. 22%) and mace (6%). Leading customers were United Kingdom (54%), Canada (22%), U.S. (10%). Leading suppliers were U.K. (33%), U.S. (10%), Canada (10%).

GUATEMALA (Republic)

(República de Guatemala)

President: Gen. Kjell Eugenio Laugerud (1974).
Area: 42,042 sq mi. (108,889 sq km).
Population (est. 1976): 6,000,000 (Indian, 53.5%; mixed and other, 46.5%).
Density per square mile: 142.7.
Capital and largest city (est. 1973): Guatemala City, 717,300.
Monetary unit: Quetzal.
Languages: Spanish and some Indian dialects.
Religion: Roman Catholic.

Executive power is vested in the President, who is elected for a term of four years, and his Cabinet of 10 members. Legislative power is vested in the 61 member National Congress.

Major Political Parties. Coalition of the National Liberation Movement and Institutional Democratic Party (36 of 61 seats in National Congress), led by Mario Sandoval; Revolutionary Party, former governing party (10 seats); Christian Democratic Party (15 seats); contested (3 seats).

History. Once the site of the ancient Mayan civilization, Guatemala, conquered by Spain in 1524, set itself up as a republic in 1839. From 1898 to 1920, the dictator Manuel Estrada Cabrera ran the country, and from 1931 to 1944, General Jorge Ubico Castaneda was the "strong man." In July 1944 the National Assembly elected General Federico Ponce President, but he was overthrown in October. In December Dr. Juan José Arévalo was elected as the head of a leftist regime which continued to press its reform program. Jacobo Arbenz Guzmán, administration candidate with pro-Communist leanings, won the 1950 elections.

Arbenz expropriated the large estates, including plantations of the United Fruit Company, and exterminated his political enemies. With covert U.S. backing, a revolt was led by Col. Carlos Castillas Armas and Arbenz took refuge in Havana. Castillo Armas became President but was assassinated in 1957. Constitutional government was restored in 1958, and General Miguel Ydigoras Fuentes was elected President. He was host to the Cuban force which trained for the disastrous landing at the Bay of Pigs in April 1961. In 1963 the Ydigoras government was overthrown by Enrique Peralta Azurdia, who ruled until 1966, when elections, under a new Constitution, led to Congress's choice of Dr. Julio César Méndez Montenegro. In 1967, terrorists of the Left and Right began plaguing the country. The U.S. military and naval attachés were assassinated in Guatemala City in January, 1968, and the U.S. Ambassador, John Gordon Mein, was slain in August 1968, when he resisted kidnapping. In a little over two years at least 1,000 people—some estimates make it 4,000—were murdered by extremists.

The left-wing terrorists, abetted by counterterrorists of the right, created wide-spread fear of anarchy which led to the election of the Coalition's conservative, business-backed Carlos Arana Osorio on Mar. 1, 1970. Arana had won fame as an army chief who bloodily put down one rural guerrilla movement (1,500-3,000 peasants killed). On taking office, Arana surprisingly pledged social reform.

Gen. Kjell Laugerud won the March 1974 elections for President. Political violence attended his inauguration in July and continued after he took office.

A devastating earthquake struck Guatemala on Feb. 4, 1976, killing an estimated 22,000 and injuring 74,000. Despite the heavy casualties, little damage was done to the nation's small, but growing, industrial base.

Economic Conditions. Agricultural products include corn, cotton, cane sugar, coffee and bananas. The country's vast forests, mostly in the Petén region, yield chicle for chewing gum, cinchona bark, some rubber, and dyewoods and cabinet woods.

Chief exports in 1974 were coffee (28%), cotton (11%), sugar (11%) and bananas (6%). Leading customers were U.S. (33%), El Salvador (11%), West Germany (11%), Nicaragua (7%), Costa Rica (6%), Japan (5%). Leading suppliers were U.S. (32%), Venezuela (12%), El Salvador (10%), Japan (9%), West Germany (8%).

Natural Features. Most of Guatemala is mountainous, with many volcanic peaks. The northern part is the great plain of Petén, largely uncultivated and sparsely populated. The narrow Pacific slope, well watered and fertile, is the most populated.

GUINEA (Republic)

(République de Guinée)

President: Ahmed Sékou Touré (1958).
Premier: Louis Lansana Beavogui.
Area: 94,964 sq mi. (245,957 sq km).
Population (est. 1976): 4,530,000 (chiefly Fulani, Malinké, and Susu).
Density per square mile: 47.8.
Capital and largest city (est. 1974): Conakry, 412,000.
Monetary unit: Syli.
Languages: French (official), native tongues (Malinké, Soussou, Fulani).
Religions: Mostly Moslem, animist.

The National Assembly has 150 members elected by universal suffrage from a list prepared and presented by the Parti Démocratique de Guinée.

Political Party. Parti Démocratique de Guinée, led by President Touré, who is Secretary General of the party.

History. Previously part of French West Africa, Guinea achieved independence by rejecting the new French Constitution, and on Oct. 2, 1958, became an independent State with Sékou Touré as President. Touré led the country into being the first avowedly Marxist state in Africa. Diplomatic relations with France were suspended in 1965, with the Soviet Union replacing France as the country's chief source of economic and technical assistance. In 1966, when a Ghanian military coup deposed Kwame Nkrumah as President, Touré welcomed him to Guinea and declared him joint President and party leader. The titles proved to be only honorary. Touré accused Ghana of being an American imperialist puppet, and the U.S. embassy in his capital, Conakry, was sacked. In retaliation the United States ended financial aid. An exchange of letters between the Guinea and U.S. Presidents restored relations.

In 1968, President Touré sought to establish more normal relations with his neighbors. Prosperity came in 1969 after the start of exploitation of bauxite deposits. Touré was re-elected to a seven-year term in December, 1974.

Economic Conditions. Guinea is well equipped economically to be independent. It is the second richest country in French Africa. It is rich in bauxite and has great reserves of hydraulic power.

Chief exports in 1970 were alumina and bauxite (65%), coffee (11%), pineapples (9%) and palm products (6%). Leading customers in 1972 were Spain (c. 16%), Norway (c. 15%), West Germany (c. 14%), Cameroon (c. 10%), Switzerland (c. 5%), Yugoslavia (5%). Leading suppliers were France (c. 31%), U.S. (c. 13%), Belgium-Luxembourg (c. 12%), U.S.S.R. (c. 12%), Italy (c. 5%), West Germany (c. 5%).

GUINEA-BISSAU (Republic)

President: Luis Cabral (1974).
Premier: Francisco Mendès (1975).
Area: 13,948 sq mi. (36,125 sq km).
Population (est. 1976): 540,000.
Density per square mile: 38.7.
Capital: Madina do Boé.
Largest city (est. 1970 for urban agglomeration): Bissau, 71,200.

Monetary Unit: Guinea escudo.
Religions: Animist, Moslem, Roman Catholic.

History. A former Portuguese overseas province, Guinea-Bissau lies on the west African coast. It was discovered in 1446 by the Portuguese Nuno Tristão, and colonists in the Cape Verde Islands obtained trading rights in the territory. In 1879 the connection with the Cape Verde Islands was broken. Early in the 1900's the Portuguese managed to pacify some tribesmen, although resistance to colonial rule remained.

The African Party for the Independence of Guinea-Bissau was founded in 1956 and several years later began guerrilla warfare that grew increasingly effective. By 1974 the rebels controlled most of the countryside, where they formed a government that was soon recognized by scores of countries. The military coup in Portugal in April 1974 brightened the prospects for freedom, and in August the Lisbon government signed an agreement granting independence to the province effective Sept. 10. The new republic took the name of Guinea-Bissau. Its government was immediately recognized by the United States.

Economic Conditions. Agriculture is the principal industry, the leading exports being peanuts and oil-palm kernels. Cattle-breeding provides hides for export.

Deposits of bauxite, oil and minerals have been found, but the years of guerrilla war prevented any development.

Chief exports in 1973 were peanuts (46%), transport equipment (transit) (21%), coconuts (7%) and timber (5%). Leading customer was Portugal (90%). Leading suppliers were Portugal (56%), Spain (7%), United Kingdom (5%), Japan (5%).

Natural Features. Guinea-Bissau consists of a low-lying coastal region consisting mainly of swamps, rain forests and mangrove-covered wetlands, and about 60 islands off the coast. The Bissagos archipelago extends 30 miles out to sea. Internal communications depend mainly on deep estuaries and meandering rivers, since there are no railroads. Bissau, the capital, is the main port.

GUYANA (Republic)

(Member of Commonwealth of Nations)

President: Arthur Chung (1970).
Prime Minister: Forbes Burnham (1964).
Area: 83,000 sq mi. (214,969 sq km).
Population (est. 1976): 810,000. (East Indian, 51%; African, 30.7%; mixed, 11.4%; Amerindian, 4.4%).
Density per square mile: 9.6.
Capital and largest city (est. 1972): Georgetown, 101,008.
Monetary unit: Guyana dollar.
Languages: English (official), Hindi, Arabic.
Religions: Protestant, Moslem, Roman Catholic.

Guyana, on the northern coast of South America east of Venezuela, proclaimed itself a republic on Feb. 23, 1970, ending its tie with Britain while remaining in the Commonwealth.

Guyana has a unicameral legislature, the National Assembly, with 53 members elected for five-year terms. A 24-member Cabinet is headed by the Prime Minister.

Major Political Parties. People's National Congress (37 of 53 seats in National Assembly), led by Prime Minister Burnham; People's Progressive Party (14 seats), led by Dr. Cheddi B. Jagan.

History. Formerly British Guiana, this independent nation, a member of the Commonwealth of Nations, won internal self-government in 1952. The next year the Leftist People's Progressive Party, headed by Cheddi Jagan, an East Indian dentist, won the elections and Jagan became Prime Minister. British authorities deposed him for alleged Communist connections. In 1962, Conservatives rioted over his first effort at fiscal reform. A coalition ousted Jagan in 1964, installing a moderate Socialist, Forbes Burnham, a black, as Prime Minister. On May 26, 1966, the country became an independent member of the Commonwealth and resumed its traditional name, Guyana.

In 1970, after a clash between Guyanan soldiers and cattle rancher rebels who allegedly were supported by Venezuela, Guyana and Venezuela called a 12-year moratorium on their border dispute (in which Venezuela claims 50,000 of Guyana's 83,000 square miles).

The government nationalized mining operations of the U.S.-owned Reynolds Metals Co. on Jan. 1, 1975.

Economic Conditions. Agricultural products include cane sugar and rice. Minerals include bauxite, manganese and diamonds.

Chief exports in 1973 were bauxite (48%), sugar (31%), alumina (9%), rice (9%) and fish (5%). Leading customers were United Kingdom (30%), U.S. (17%), Trinidad and Tobago (10%), U.S.S.R. (6%), Jamaica (6%). Leading suppliers were U.K. (27%), U.S. (26%), Trinidad and Tobago (13%), Canada (6%).

HAITI (Republic)

(République d'Haïti)

Life President: Jean-Claude Duvalier (1971).
Area: 10,714 sq mi. (27,750 sq km).
Population (est. 1976): 4,650,000. (black, 95%; mulatto, 5%).
Density per square mile: 434.0.
Capital and largest city (est. 1975): Port-au-Prince, 625,000.
Monetary unit: Gourde.
Languages: French, Creole.
Religion: Roman Catholic.

In 1964, the late President, François Duvalier, known as "Papa Doc," made himself President for life, a tenure that his son, Jean-Claude, 19, known as "Baby Doc," inherited on his father's death, April 21, 1971. Under a Constitution revised in 1964, the President in periods of crisis may dismiss the National Assembly and Cabinet and govern by decree.

Political Party. Parti d'Unité Nationale (all 58 seats in National Assembly), led by President Duvalier. This is the only legal party in the country.

History. Haiti started its struggle for independence under Toussaint L'Ouverture at the time of the French Revolution in the 1790's. Although this first attempt was suppressed by Napoleon Bona-parte, a successful uprising led by Jean Jacques Dessalines in 1804 finally established Haiti as an independent nation.

A long period of struggle between Mulattoes and Blacks reduced the economy to one of primitive agriculture. The United States established a customs receivership from 1905 to 1941. In 1915 the Haitian Congress was forced to accept U.S. control. In 1930 the Forbes Commission recommended U.S. withdrawal, effected by 1934. Export crops were developed. The measure of prosperity under the occupation led to overpopulation and Haiti was plagued with a population density twice that of any other Latin American country. Frequent border clashes embittered relations with the Dominican Republic and in 1937 Dominican troops, invading Haiti, slaughtered more than 10,000 Haitians.

In December 1945, a revolution put President Dumarsais Estimé in power. His regime was one of the few democratic episodes the country has experienced.

However, President Estimé's attempt to perpetuate himself in power after his term had expired in December, 1949, brought another revolution, the victor of which was General Paul Magloire, who ruled until December 1956. His regime, a dictatorship, continued many of the social and economic policies of its predecessor. President Magloire, in turn, attempted to stay in office after his term had ended and was overthrown. From December 1956 until September 1957, when President François Duvalier was installed, there was a period of chaos.

Duvalier established a dictatorship based on a secret police known as the "Ton-ton Macoutes," which gunned down opponents of the regime. In 1964 he amended the Constitution, making himself President for life.

Frequent assassinations and the famine in the interior led to the loss of the tourist trade, and the country's modern hotels were largely empty as terror and stagnation ravaged the country, the poorest nation in the Western Hemisphere.

Three months before he died in 1971 of natural causes at age 64, Duvalier named Jean-Claude, then 19 years old, his successor.

An economic comeback of sorts attended Jean-Claude Duvalier's regime. With urban unemployment at 60% and the minimum wage at $1.30 a day, some 150 foreign firms established Haitian branches to take advantage of cheap labor and the order enforced by a still-authoritarian government. The rate of new investment was estimated at $100 million yearly, but per capita income for the masses was about $70 in 1975.

Economic Conditions. Haiti is predominantly agricultural. Coffee is the principal crop, followed by sisal, sugar cane, cotton, bananas and cacao. Manufacturing is almost entirely for local consumption.

Mineral resources in Haiti include gold, silver, tin and copper.

Chief exports in 1973 were coffee (33%), sugar (9%) and bauxite (8%). Leading customers in 1972-73 were U.S. (60%), France (9%), Belgium-Luxembourg (9%), Italy (7%), Netherlands (5%). Leading suppliers were U.S. (41%), Japan (9%), Canada (8%), France (6%), West Germany (6%), United Kingdom (5%).

Natural Features. Haiti, about the size of Maryland, is two thirds mountainous, with the rest marked by great valleys, extensive plateaus and small plains. The most densely populated region is the Cul de Sac plain, near Port-au-Prince.

HONDURAS (Republic)

(República de Honduras)

Chief of State: Gen. Juan Alberto Melgar (1975).
Area: 43,277 sq mi. (112,088 sq km).
Population (est. 1976): 3,150,000 (mestizo, 60%).
Density per square mile: 72.8.
Capital and largest city (est. 1975): Tegucigalpa, 350,000.
Monetary unit: Lempira.
Languages: Spanish, some Indian dialects.
Religion: Roman Catholic.

The 1965 Constitution provides for a President elected by popular vote for six years. He may not serve two consecutive terms. The unicameral Congress has 64 members elected by popular vote for six years.

Under a unique unity scheme proposed by the outgoing President, Gen. Oswaldo López Arellano, the two parties, following the 1971 elections, split equally the seats in the National Assembly, with leadership going to the winner in the presidential contest (National Party); the cabinet was equally divided between the parties, as was the Supreme Court, although the Chief Justice was chosen by the losing (Liberal) party. However, the plan did not work, and in December 1973, López again seized power, proclaiming himself President.

Major Political Parties. National Party; Liberal Party.

History. Columbus discovered Honduras on his last voyage in 1502. Honduras, with four other countries of Central America, declared its independence from Spain in 1821, and was part of a federation of Central American states until 1838. In that year it seceded from the federation and became a completely independent country.

It has been troubled by revolution and war ever since. American Marines intervened in 1903 and 1923. In 1931, 1932 and 1937, major revolutions were crushed by force.

In July 1969, El Salvador invaded Honduras after Honduran landowners had deported several thousand Salvadorans. The fighting left 1,000 dead and tens of thousands homeless. By threatening economic sanctions and military intervention, the OAS induced El Salvador to withdraw.

In June 1970, Honduras and El Salvador agreed to a demilitarized zone of 1.8 miles on each side of their ill-defined border and accepted an OAS police force. A year later they agreed, despite two more border flare-ups, to negotiate a peace settlement. Honduras remained largely out of the five-nation Central America Common Market, however, until the Pan-American Highway link with El Salvador was reopened in 1972.

In 1971, Ramon Ernesto Cruz, a lawyer, diplomat, and teacher, became Honduras's first freely elected President since 1949. But strongman Oswaldo López Arellano citing "chaos and weakness" under the coalition, again seized control (for the third time in two decades).

López was ousted by the armed forces April 22, 1975, after he refused to cooperate with an investigation of reports that he was the unnamed Honduran official to whom United Brands Company, a multinational banana exporter, had admitted paying a $1,250,000 bribe. He was replaced by Gen. Juan Alberto Melgar.

The bribe scandal came to light at a time of severe adversity for Honduras, which had sustained about $500 million in damage from a hurricane that destroyed 70% of the banana plantations operated by United Brands. Concern that the bribe charge would discourage foreign-financed reconstruction efforts contributed to the pressure that forced the ouster of López.

Economic Conditions. Agricultural products include corn, rice, coffee, sugar and bananas. Gold and silver are the most important mineral products.

Chief exports in 1974 were bananas (27%), coffee (16%), timber (16%) and, in 1973, meat (9%). Leading customers in 1973 were U.S. (57%), West Germany (12%), Canada (7%). Leading suppliers were U.S. (41%), Japan (10%), Venezuela (8%), Guatemala (6%).

Natural Features. Honduras, in the north central part of Central America, has a 400-mile Caribbean coastline and a 40-mile Pacific frontage. Generally mountainous, it has fertile plateaus, river valleys and narrow coastal plains.

HUNGARY (People's Republic)

(Magyar Népköztarsaság)

President: Pál Losonczi (1967).
Premier: Gyorgy Lazar (1975).
Area: 35,919 sq mi. (93,030 sq km).
Population (est. 1976): 10,600,000 (Magyar, German, Slovak).
Density per square mile: 295.1.
Capital: Budapest.
Largest cities (est. 1975): Budapest, 2,058,000; (est. 1973 by U.N.): Miskolc, 192,300; Debrecen, 175,000; Szeged, 163,350; Pécs, 158,150; Györ, 111,800.
Monetary unit: Forint.
Languages: Hungarian, 98.2%; German, 0.5%; others, 1.3%.
Religions (1970): Roman Catholic (60%), Protestant, atheist.

According to the 1949 Constitution, Hungary is a People's Republic. Legislative power is vested in the unicameral National Assembly, whose 352 members are elected by the people for four-year terms. The supreme body of state power is the 21 member Presidential Council elected by the National Assembly. The supreme body of state administration is the Council of Ministers, headed by the Premier.

Major Political Party. Hungarian Socialist Workers (Communist) Party, led by János Kádár.

History. About 2,000 years ago, Hungary was part of the Roman provinces of Pannonia and Dacia. In A.D. 896 it was invaded by the Magyars, who founded a kingdom. Christianity was accepted during the reign of Stephen I (St. Stephen) (997–1038).

The peak of Hungary's great period of medieval power came during the reign of Louis I the Great

(1342–82), whose dominions touched the Baltic, Black and Mediterranean seas.

War with the Turks broke out in 1389, and when the Turks smashed a Hungarian army in 1526, western and northern Hungary accepted Hapsburg rule to escape Turkish occupation. Transylvania became independent under Hungarian princes. Intermittent war with the Turks was waged until a peace treaty was signed in 1699.

After the suppression of the 1848 revolt against Hapsburg rule led by Louis Kossuth, the dual monarchy of Austria-Hungary was set up in 1867.

The dual monarchy was defeated with the other Central Powers in World War I, and the new Hungary underwent hard times. First there was a short-lived republic in 1918. The chaotic Communist rule of 1919 under Béla Kun ended with the Romanians occupying Budapest on Aug. 4, 1919. When the Romanians left, Admiral Nicholas Horthy entered the capital with a national army. The Treaty of Trianon of June 4, 1920, cost Hungary 67.8% of its land and 58% of its population. Meanwhile, the National Assembly had restored the legal continuity of the old monarchy; and, on Mar. 1, 1920, Horthy was elected Regent.

Following the German invasion of Russia on June 22, 1941, Hungary joined the attack against the Soviet Union, but the war was not popular and Hungarian troops were almost entirely withdrawn from the eastern front by May 1943. German occupation troops set up a puppet government after Admiral Horthy's appeal for an armistice with advancing Soviet troops on Oct. 15, 1944, had resulted in his overthrow. The German regime soon fled the capital, however, and on Dec. 23 a provisional government was formed in Soviet-occupied eastern Hungary. On Jan. 20, 1945, it signed an armistice in Moscow. On Feb. 1, 1946, the National Assembly approved a constitutional law abolishing the thousand-year-old monarchy and establishing a republic.

By the Treaty of Paris (1947) Hungary had to give up all territory it had acquired since 1937 and to pay $300 million reparations to the Soviet Union, Czechoslovakia, and Yugoslavia. A coalition government instituted land reform. In 1948 the Communist Party, with the support of Soviet bayonets, seized control. Hungary was proclaimed a People's Republic and one-party state in 1949. Industry was nationalized, the land collectivized into State farms, and the opposition terrorized by the secret police.

The terror, modeled after that of the Soviet Union, reached its height with the trial of Jozsef Cardinal Mindszenty, Roman Catholic primate. He confessed to fantastic charges under duress of drugs or brainwashing and was sentenced to life imprisonment on Feb. 8, 1949. Protests were voiced in all parts of the world.

On Oct. 23, 1956, anti-Communist revolution broke out in Budapest. To cope with it the Communists set up a coalition government and called former Premier Imre Nagy back to head it. But he and most of his ministers were swept by the logic of events into the anti-Communist opposition, and he declared Hungary a neutral power, withdrawing from the Warsaw Treaty and appealing to the United Nations for help. One of his ministers, János Kádár, established a counter-regime and asked the Soviet Union to send in military power. Soviet troops and tanks suppressed the revolution in bloody fighting after 190,000 people had fled the country and Mindszenty, freed from jail on Oct. 30, had taken refuge in the U.S. Embassy. By treachery, Nagy and some of his ministers were abducted by the Soviet occupation troops and executed.

Kádár was succeeded as Premier, but not party secretary, by Cyula Kallai in 1965. In 1966 the party announced drastic economic reforms to raise living standards and improve productive efficiency. Continuing his program of national reconciliation, Kádár emptied prisons, reformed the secret police, and eased travel restrictions. But 60,000 Soviet troops remained in Hungary. Further sweeping reforms liberalized the economy in 1968.

Hungary developed the reputation of being the freest East European state, with Kádár's new motto —"If you're not against us, you're with us"—replacing previous police state suspicions. Significant Western capitalist investment was welcomed and some capitalistic methods embraced.

In 1968, Hungary initiated a "New Economic Model" (NEM) designed to reduce central planning and to increase productivity and trade with the West. But NEM fell on hard times as inflation drove the cost of Western imports up. Hungary recorded a $700-million deficit from trade with the non-Communist world in 1974, as against a $100-million surplus for 1973.

At the 11th Congress of the Hungarian Socialist Workers (Communist) Party held in Budapest in March, 1975, economic setbacks were acknowledged. Kádár was retained as party First Secretary, but six weeks later Premier Jeno Fock resigned after eight years in office. Fock was replaced by Gyorgy Lazar, an economic planner recently promoted by the Hungarian Politburo.

After 15 years' asylum in the U.S. Embassy, Mindszenty, under an agreement between the Vatican and the Hungarian regime, was allowed to travel into exile to Rome in September 1971. In a move applauded by Kádár, Pope Paul VI removed Mindszenty from his honorary post as Primate of Hungary in February, 1974. The Cardinal died in Vienna in 1975.

Relations with the United States improved in 1972 when World War II debt claims between the two nations were settled.

Economic Conditions. Agriculture is the basis of Hungarian economic life, engaging about a third of the population. The Land Reform Act issued in March 1945 provided for the confiscation of all estates over 284 acres; about 8,000,000 acres were divided among some 500,000 families. Cereals grown in the fertile Danubian plains are the chief crops. Leading crops are corn, sugar beets, wheat, potatoes, barley, rye and oats.

In addition, cultivation of vines, fruit and garden produce is important. The famous Tokay wine is produced on the southern slopes of the Hegyalja in the northeast part of the country.

The dominant industries are all based on agriculture, with flour milling in first place, followed by sugar refining, brewing and canning. The second group of industries make hardware and machinery. Most of the machine industry is concentrated in Budapest and Györ. Cotton leads the textile industry, especially in Budapest, which is also a center of woolen manufactures.

While Hungary generally is mineral-poor, it has

about 20% of the world's known reserves of bauxite.

Chief exports in 1973 were machinery (22%), transport equipment (11%), chemicals (7%), fruit and vegetables (6%), iron and steel (5%), cereals (5%), clothing (5%) and livestock (5%). Leading customers in 1974 were U.S.S.R. (32%), East Germany (10%), Czechoslovakia (9%), West Germany (6%), Poland (6%). Leading suppliers were U.S.S.R. (28%), West Germany (10%), East Germany (9%), Czechoslovakia (8%), Austria (5%), Poland (5%).

Natural Features. Most of Hungary is a fertile, rolling plain lying east of the Danube and drained by the Danube and the Tisza rivers.

In the extreme northwest is the Little Hungarian Plain. South of that area is Lake Balaton (250 sq. mi.).

ICELAND (Republic)

(Island)

President: Kristjan Eldjarn (1968).
Prime Minister: Geir Hallgrimsson (1974).
Area: 39,768 sq mi. (103,000 sq km).†
Population (est. 1976): 227,000.
Density per square mile: 5.7.†
Capital and largest city (est. 1974): Reykjavik, 84,800.
Monetary unit: Króna.
Language: Icelandic.
Religion: Evangelical Lutheran.

Constitutionally, the President of Iceland is elected for four years by popular vote. Executive power of the state resides in the Prime Minister and his Cabinet. The Althing (Parliament) is composed of 60 members in two houses. At an election the 60 members elect 20 of themselves to constitute the Upper House, the remaining 40 members representing henceforth the Lower House. The Althing can dismiss the Cabinet and the latter can dissolve the former.

Major Political Parties. Independence Party (25 of 60 seats in Althing), led by Geir Hallgrimsson; Social Democratic Party (5 seats); Progressive Party (17 seats), led by Olafur Jóhannesson; People's Alliance (10 seats).

History. Iceland was first settled shortly before 900, mainly by Norse. A Constitution drawn up about 930 created a form of democracy and provided for an Althing, or General Assembly, now the oldest legislative body in the world.

In 1262–64, Iceland came under Norwegian rule and passed to ultimate Danish control through the formation of the Union of Kalmar in 1483. In 1874, Icelanders obtained their own Constitution. In 1918, Denmark recognized Iceland as a separate state with unlimited sovereignty but still nominally under the Danish king.

On June 17, 1944, after a popular referendum, the Althing proclaimed Iceland a completely independent republic.

The British occupied Iceland in 1940, immediately after the German invasion of Denmark. In 1942, the United States took over the burden of protection. Iceland refused to abandon its neutrality in World War II, and thus forfeited charter

† Including several off-shore islands.

membership in the United Nations, but it was cooperative with the Allies throughout. Iceland joined the North Atlantic Treaty Organization in 1949.

Iceland unilaterally extended her territorial waters from 12 to 50 nautical miles in 1972, precipitating a running dispute with Great Britain known as the "cod war." Icelandic warships harassed British trawlers, which then received aid from British gunboats; some trawlers were shelled, and Icelandic and British warships collided in 1973. The World Court ruled in July, 1974, that the 50-mile limit could not be applied unilaterally, but Iceland rejected the ruling.

Another "cod war" broke out in late 1975 at the expiration of a two-year agreement reached in 1973 and Britain sent warships to guard its fishing boats. Iceland closed its airspace and ports to British military aircraft and ships and on Feb. 19 broke diplomatic relations with Britain.

A June 2 agreement calling for registration of all British trawlers fishing within 200 miles of Iceland and a 24-hour time limit on incursions brought a resumption of relations on June 3.

Economic Conditions. Approximately six sevenths of Iceland is unproductive, and only about 1% is under cultivation. With about 20% of the population engaged in farming, sheep raising is the most important branch of this industry. Hay, potatoes and turnips are the principal crops.

Vegetation is of the Arctic type, mostly stunted. Except for peat and fisheries, Iceland has no natural resources.

About one tenth of the people are engaged in fishing. Many European fishing craft visit Iceland's fisheries, which lead the world in cod and are important for herring, plaice, and halibut.

Chief exports in 1974 were fish (65%), aluminum (15%) and fish meal (10%). Leading customers were U.S. (22%), Portugal (10%), West Germany (9%), United Kingdom (9%), U.S.S.R. (8%), Denmark (6%), Switzerland (6%), Spain (5%). Leading suppliers were West Germany (12%), U.K. (11%), U.S.S.R. (10%), Denmark (9%), Norway (8%), U.S. (8%), Sweden (7%), Netherlands (7%), Australia (5%).

Natural Features. Iceland, a bleak island about the size of Kentucky, has maximum dimensions of 298 by 194 miles. It is one of the most volcanic regions in the world.

Small fresh-water lakes are to be found throughout the island, and there are many natural oddities, including hot springs, geysers, sulfur beds, canyons, waterfalls and swift rivers. More than 13% of the area is covered by snowfields and glaciers, and most of the people live in the 7% of the island comprising fertile coastlands.

INDIA (Republic)

(Bharat)

(Member of Commonwealth of Nations)

President: Fakhruddin Ali Ahmed (1974).
Prime Minister: Mrs. Indira Gandhi (1966).
Area: 1,266,594 sq mi. (3,280,483 sq km).
Population (est. 1976): 610,000,000 (Hindu, 82.7%; Moslem, 11.2%; Christian, 2.6%; Sikh, 1.9%).
Density per square mile: 481.6.

Capital (1971 census): New Delhi, 301,801.
Largest cities (1971 census): Greater Bombay, 5,970,575; Delhi, 3,287,883; Calcutta, 3,148,746; Madras, 2,469,449; Bangalore, 1,540,741; Ahmedabad, 1,585,544; Kanpur, 1,154,388.
Monetary unit: Rupee.
Principal languages: Hindi (official), Bengali, Sindhi, Gujarati, Kannarese, Kashmiri, Malayalam, Marathi, Oriya, Punjabi, Sanskrit, Tamil, Telugu, Urdu, English.
Religions: Hindu, 83%; Moslem, 11%; Christian, 3%; Sikh, 2%; Buddhist, 0.7%.

India is a sovereign democratic republic. It is also a member of the Commonwealth of Nations, a status defined at the London Conference of Prime Ministers on Apr. 27, 1949, by which India recognizes the Queen as head of the Commonwealth. Under the Constitution passed by the Constituent Assembly on Nov. 26, 1949, and effective Jan. 26, 1950, India has a parliamentary type of government. The constitutional head of the state is the President, who is elected every five years. He is advised by the Prime Minister and a Cabinet based on a majority of the bicameral Parliament, which consists of a Council of States (Rajya Sabha) representing the constituent units of the republic, and a House of the People (Lok Sabha) elected every five years by universal adult (21 years) suffrage.

Major Political Parties.
Congress Party (355 of 523 seats in the Lok Sabha), led by Mrs. Gandhi. Opposition (largely conservative) are the Bharatiya Lok Dal (People's Party of India), a 12-party coalition); Jan Sangh Party (militant Hindus), Socialist Party, the Dravida Munnetra Kazhagam, Communist Party of India, and independents.

History.
The Aryans or Hindus who invaded India between 2400 and 1500 B.C. from the northwest found a land already well civilized. Buddhism was founded in the sixth century B.C. and spread through northern India. The first exact date in Indian history is 327 B.C., when Alexander the Great invaded India.

In 1526, Mohammedan invaders founded the great Mogul empire, centered on Delhi, which lasted at least in name until 1857. Akbar the Great (1542–1605) strengthened this empire and became the ruler of a greater portion of India than had ever before acknowledged the suzerainty of one man. The long reign of his great-grandson, Aurangzeb (1658–1707), represents both the culmination of Mogul power and the beginning of its decay.

Vasco da Gama, the Portuguese explorer, visited India first in 1498, and for the next hundred years the Portuguese had a virtual monopoly on trade with the subcontinent. Meanwhile, the English founded the East India Company, which set up its first factory at Surat in 1612 and began expanding its influence, fighting against the Indian rulers and the French, Dutch and Portuguese traders simultaneously.

Bombay, taken from the Portuguese, became the seat of English rule in 1687. The defeat of French and Moslem armies by Lord Clive in the decade ending in 1760 laid the foundation of the British Empire in India. From then until 1858, when the administration of India was formally transferred to the British crown following the great mutiny of native troops in 1857, the East India Company suppressed native uprisings and extended British rule.

After World War I, in which the Indian states sent more than 6 million troops to fight beside the Allies, Indian nationalist unrest rose to new heights under the leadership of a little Hindu lawyer, Mohandas K. Gandhi, called Mahatma Gandhi. His tactics called for nonviolent revolts against British authority. He soon became the leading spirit of the All-India Congress Party, which was the spearhead of Indian revolt. In 1919 the British gave added responsibility to Indian officials, and in 1935 India was given a federal form of government and a measure of self-rule.

In 1942, with the Japanese pressing hard on the eastern borders of India, the British war Cabinet tried and failed to reach a political settlement with nationalist leaders. The Congress Party took the position that the British must quit India. In August 1942, fearing mass civil disobedience, the government of India carried out widespread arrests of Congress leaders, including Gandhi.

Gandhi was released in May 1944, and other leaders later. Negotiations for a settlement were resumed, but they proved fruitless. Finally, in February 1947, the Labour government announced its determination to transfer power to "responsible Indian hands" by June 1948, even if a Constitution had not been worked out.

With the appointment at the same time of Lord Mountbatten as Governor-General, events moved swiftly. By early June 1947, agreement was reached on the partitioning of India along religious lines (a plan previously opposed by the predominant Hindus and by Britain) and on the splitting of the provinces of Bengal and the Punjab, which the Moslems had claimed.

The Indian Independence Act, passed quickly by both houses of the British Parliament, received royal assent on July 18, 1947, and on Aug. 15 the Indian Empire passed into history.

Jawaharlal Nehru, leader of the Congress Party, was made Prime Minister of India. Before an exchange of populations could be arranged, terrible riots occurred among the communal groups, and armed conflict broke out over rival claims to the princely state of Jammu and Kashmir. Peace was restored only with the greatest difficulty. In 1949 a Constitution, along the lines of the U.S. Constitution, was adopted making India a sovereign republic, an independent member of the Commonwealth of Nations. Under a federal structure the states were organized on linguistic lines. For a considerable period the dominance of the Congress Party contributed stability. In 1956 the republic absorbed the former French settlements. Five years later it forcibly annexed the Portuguese enclaves of Goa, Damão and Diu. After a decade of independence India was once again the target of invasion. Communist China provoked a border dispute in 1957 which proceeded by local skirmishes until Oct. 20, 1962, when the Chinese mounted a massive offensive against Ladakh in Kashmir and against the North East Frontier Agency. After gaining much territory claimed by India, the Chinese announced a cease-fire on Nov. 20, 1962. An uneasy truce has since prevailed, maintained by limited U.S. military aid and extensive Soviet weapons, including delivery, beginning in 1968, of 100 Soviet fighter planes.

Nehru died in 1964. His successor, Lal Bahadur Shastri, died on Jan. 10, 1966, a few hours after concluding talks with President Ayub Khan of

POLITICAL SUBDIVISIONS OF REPUBLIC OF INDIA

Subdivisions	Area sq. mi.	Population 1971 census	Subdivisions	Area sq. mi.	Population 1971 census
States			Uttar Pradesh	113,452	88,341,144
Andhra Pradesh	106,052	43,502,708	West Bengal	33,928	44,312,011
Assam	30,400[1]	14,625,152[1]	**Union Territories**		
Bihar	67,198	56,353,369	Andaman and Nicobar		
Gujarat	72,154	26,697,475	Islands	3,215	115,133
Haryana	16,670	10,036,808	Arunachal Pradesh	31,400	467,511
Himachal Pradesh	10,880	3,460,434	Chandigarh	44	257,251
Jammu and Kashmir[2]	85,861	4,616,632	Dadra and Nagar-		
Karnataka[3]	74,122	29,299,014	Haveli	189	74,170
Kerala	15,003	21,347,375	Delhi	573	4,065,698
Madhya Pradesh	171,210	41,654,119	Goa, Daman and		
Maharashtra	118,530	50,412,235	Diu	1,619	857,771
Manipur	8,628	1,072,753	Lakshadweep[6]	11	31,810
Meghalaya	8,700[1]	1,011,699[1]	Mizoram	8,100	332,390
Nagaland	6,236	516,449	Pondicherry	196	471,707
Orissa	60,182	21,944,615			
Punjab	21,630	13,551,060			
Rajasthan	132,151	25,765,806			
Sikkim[4]	2,744	215,000			
Tamil Nadu[5]	50,132	41,199,168			
Tripura	4,022	1,556,342			

[1] After reorganization of North East Frontier Agency in December, 1971. [2] Status in dispute with Pakistan. [3] Formerly Mysore. [4] Sikkim became an Indian state in May, 1975. Population figure is 1974 estimate. [5] Formerly Madras. [6] Formerly Laccadive, Minicoy and Amindivi Islands.

Pakistan arranging for an interim settlement of their differences. Nehru's daughter, Mrs. Indira Gandhi, became Prime Minister on Jan. 19, 1966. She continued the policy of nonalignment and made it clear that India's only concern with Communist China was its threat to India's borders.

In the national elections of February, 1967, the Congress Party suffered a startling setback. A drought which caused serious food shortages was a factor. In the May presidential election, however, the Congress candidate, Dr. Zakir Husain, won easily and became India's first Moslem President.

The long-standing controversy with Pakistan erupted in war in December 1971, after the Pakistan army had moved into East Pakistan to crush its independence movement earlier in the year. Some 10 million Bengali refugees poured across the border into India, creating social, economic and health problems. Clandestine aid was given the Bengali rebels early in the year, and after the new rapport between China and the United States began emerging in July, India signed a friendship treaty with the Soviet Union in August 1971. Thereafter, huge quantities of Soviet arms entered India. After numerous border incidents, India invaded East Pakistan (renamed Bangladesh) and in two weeks crushed the Pakistani Army, taking 93,000 prisoners. Bangladesh was established as an independent state.

India moved further toward the Soviet Union in 1973 with a 15-year economic, technological and trade cooperation agreement under which the U.S.S.R. is to build up to 90 heavy-industry projects for the Indians.

India startled the world on May 18, 1974 by exploding an atomic device made of plutonium it had surreptitiously removed from a peaceful reactor given by Canada. It became the sixth nation of the world to set off a nuclear blast, and while India disclaimed any intention to make nuclear weapons, there were widespread misgivings about its aims.

In the summer of 1975, an unprecedented constitutional crisis wrought basic changes in the world's largest democracy and led to reconsideration of plans

for President Ford to visit India in 1976. It began June 12 when a judge in Allahabad, Mrs. Gandhi's home constituency, found her landslide victory in the 1971 Parliamentary elections invalid because public employees had illegally aided her campaign. Faced with possible disqualification from office until 1981, Mrs. Gandhi asked for and got a unanimous confidence vote from the Congress Party majority in Parliament and appealed to the Supreme Court. An interim order by one justice said she could continue as Prime Minister, but not vote in Parliament, pending the full court's decision. There was a round of anti-Gandhi demonstrations and opposition demands for her resignation.

At dawn, June 26, the government decreed a state of emergency to deal with an unspecified "threat of internal disturbances." There were mass arrests of government critics—including leaders of all major opposition parties except the Communists. (Two months later, the government admitted to 4,400 arrests, while opponents put the figure at 54,000; all those detained could be held as long as a year, and a decree barred court review of the arrests.) Rigid censorship was clamped on the Indian press, long the freest in Asia, and five British and American correspondents were expelled for writing stories displeasing to the regime.

Legislation extending the emergency indefinitely passed Parliament July 23. Opposition members walked out after the vote. Their boycott was still in force during the next fortnight, when unhampered Congress Party majorities successively enacted: a bill forbidding courts to invalidate the government's emergency decrees; a constitutional amendment retroactively barring lawsuits challenging the elections of high government officers, including the Prime Minister; and a bill retroactively wiping out Mrs. Gandhi's conviction in the 1971 election case.

As she effectively suspended India's equivalent of the U.S. Bill of Rights and took apparent steps toward one-party government, Mrs. Gandhi also initiated actions which she said would improve the lot of India's largely apolitical masses. On July 1, she announced a 21-point program of social and economic reforms that could make up the Congress

Party platform in the next general elections, which should have been held by March 1976 under India's Constitution but were delayed indefinitely.

Even before the reform program was announced, there were signs of improvement in India's long-troubled economy. A year of conservative fiscal policy had reduced the inflation rate from 30% in 1974 to 10% in 1975, and good rains appeared to have ensured a better-than-average 1975 harvest of basic food crops.

On July 24, 1976, India and Pakistan formally renewed diplomatic relations, which had been broken off in 1971. Air and land transportation between the two nations was also restored.

Native States. Most of the 560-odd native states and subdivisions of pre-1947 India acceded to the new nation, and the central government pursued a vigorous policy of integration. This took three forms: (1) merger into adjacent provinces, (2) conversion into centrally administered areas, and (3) grouping into unions of states. Finally, under a controversial reorganization plan effective Nov. 1, 1956, the unions of states were abolished and merged into adjacent states, and India became a union of 15 states and 8 centrally administered areas. A 16th state was added in 1962, and in 1966, Punjab was partitioned into two states.

The status of the large princely state of Jammu and Kashmir on the northwest frontier is in dispute with Pakistan. It is 85% Moslem, but its Hindu ruling prince acceded to India, which took over administration following invasion by Moslem troops in late 1947. The U.N. Security Council voted on Apr. 21, 1948, to hold a plebiscite in the area, but it was never held. The part occupied by India was incorporated into India in 1957.

The controversy over Jammu and Kashmir was waged in the halls of the United Nations until 1965, when India announced that its civil servants would assume administration of the state. Pakistan sent guerrillas into the territory, and India, in response, invaded in August 1965. In September the United Nations sponsored a cease-fire and stationed observers to make sure it was honored, but there were violations. The Soviet Union intervened and arranged a meeting in Tashkent between Prime Minister Shastri of India and President Ayub Khan of Pakistan. With the Soviet Union as mediator, they reached an interim settlement, the Declaration of Tashkent, in January 1966. It provided for the withdrawal of troops, observance of the U.N. cease-fire, and continued attempts to resolve their disputes by diplomatic means.

Resolution of the territorial dispute over Kashmir grew out of peace negotiations following the two-week India-Pakistan war of 1971. After sporadic skirmishing, an accord reached July 3, 1972, committed both powers to withdraw troops from a temporary cease-fire line after the border was fixed. Agreement on the border was reached Dec. 7, 1972.

In April, 1975, the Indian Parliament voted to make the 300-year-old kingdom of Sikkim a full-fledged Indian state, and the annexation took effect May 16. Although the merger had won 50-to-1 approval by more than a third of Sikkim's 215,000 inhabitants, it was vehemently protested by Palden Thondup Namgyal, the ousted monarch, and by Pakistan and China, both of which accused India of expansionist policies.

Situated in the Himalayas, Sikkim was a virtual dependency of Tibet until the early 19th century. Under an 1890 treaty between China and Great Britain, it became a British protectorate, and was made an Indian protectorate after Britain quit the subcontinent.

Economic Conditions. Agricultural products include wheat, rice, barley, corn, potatoes, cassava, tea, sugar, millet, sorghum and peanuts. Industrial products include pig iron, crude steel, aluminum, cement, yarn and fabrics and jute manufactures.

Chief exports in 1974–75 were sugar (10%), jute fabrics (9%), tea (7%), cotton fabrics (7%) and iron ore (5%). Leading customers were U.S. (11%), U.S.S.R. (13%), United Kingdom (9%), Japan (9%), Iran (6%). Leading suppliers in 1973–74 were U.S. (17%), Iran (9%), U.S.S.R. (9%), West Germany (7%).

The republic has rich mineral resources, including coal, iron ore, monazite, diamonds, magnesite, uranium, zircon, silver, graphite, gypsum, tungsten, and sapphires. Assam and Punjab produce oil.

Natural Features. The Indian republic contains a large part of the great Indo-Gangetic plain, which extends from the Bay of Bengal on the east to the Afghan frontier and the Arabian Sea on the west. This plain is the richest and most densely settled part of the subcontinent. Another distinct natural region is the Deccan, a plateau of 2,000 to 3,000 feet in elevation, occupying the southern portion of the subcontinent.

Forming a part of the republic are several groups of islands—the Laccadives (14 islands) in the Arabian Sea, and the Andamans (204 islands) and the Nicobars (19 islands) in the Bay of Bengal.

India's three great river systems, all rising in the Himalayas, have extensive deltas. The Ganges flows south and then east for 1,540 miles across the northern plain to the Bay of Bengal; part of its delta, which begins 220 miles from the sea, is within the republic. The Indus, starting in Tibet, flows northwest for several hundred miles in Kashmir before turning southwest toward the Arabian Sea; it is important for irrigation in Pakistan. The Brahmaputra, also rising in Tibet, flows eastward first through India and then south into Pakistan and the Bay of Bengal.

INDONESIA (Republic)

(Republik Indonesia)

President and Prime Minister: General Suharto (1968).*
Area: 581,655 sq mi. (1,506,486 sq km).
Population (est. 1976): 133,680,000 (mostly Indonesians).
Density per square mile: 229.8.
Capital: Jakarta.
Largest cities (est. 1975): Jakarta, 5,490,000; (1971 census): Surabaja, 1,556,255; Bandung, 1,201,730; Semarang, 646,590; Medan, 635,562; Palembang, 582,961.
Monetary unit: Rupiah.

* General Suharto served as Acting President of Indonesia from 1967 to 1968. † Excluding West Irian (former Netherlands New Guinea), renamed Irian Jaya in March, 1973 (159,375 sq. mi.). Includes East Timor (5,762 sq mi.), annexed in 1976.

Languages: Bahasa Indonesia (Malay) (official), Dutch, Javanese, Sudanese, Madurese.
Religions: Moslem, 89%; Christian, 7%; Hindu, Buddhist.

The President is elected by the People's Consultative Assembly, whose 920 members include the functioning legislative arm, the 460-member House of Representatives. Meeting at least once every five years, the Assembly has broad policy functions. The House, 100 of whose members are appointed by the President, meets at least once annually. The first national election in 16 years was held July 5, 1971, for the House. Another election is scheduled for 1977.

Major Political Parties. Sekber Golkar, the government coalition, with 236 of 360 contested seats in the House; Moslem scholars, 58 seats; Parmusi (Moslem-based), 24 seats; Indonesian National Party founded by late President Sukarno), 20 seats.

History. Indonesia is a Malay archipelago in Southeast Asia inhabited by Malayan and Papuan peoples ranging from the more advanced Javanese and Balinese to the more primitive Dyaks of Borneo. Invasions from South China and India contributed Chinese and Indian admixtures.

The sovereign state of Indonesia, a group of islands with a total area more than twice that of Texas, constitutes one of the world's richest natural areas. These islands—Sumatra, Java, Madura, central and southern Borneo, Celebes, and the Moluccas—have great wealth in tin, rubber, spices, oil, quinine and copra.

During the first few centuries of the Christian era, most of the islands came under the influence of Hindu priests and traders, who spread their culture and religion. Moslem invasions began in the 13th century, and most of the area was Moslem by the 15th century. Portuguese traders arrived early in the 16th century but were ousted by the Dutch about 1595. After Napoleon subjugated the Netherlands homeland in 1811, the British seized the islands but returned them to the Dutch in 1816. In 1922 the islands were made an integral part of the Netherlands kingdom.

In World War II, the Japanese military occupation with nominal native self-government continued until August, 1945. About the time of the Japanese surrender, a self-styled Indonesian Republic headed by Achmed Sukarno took over effective control of parts of Sumatra and Java. Allied forces, mostly British Indian troops, moved in, and fought the nationalists until Nov. 15, 1946, when Dutch-Indonesian parleys resulted in a draft agreement that contemplated the formation by Jan. 1, 1949, of a Netherlands-Indonesian Union, consisting on the one hand of the Netherlands, the Netherlands Antilles and Surinam and on the other of the United States of Indonesia, which was to be a sovereign nation composed of three equal states—the Republic of Indonesia, East Indonesia, and Borneo. Differences of interpretation ensued, and the Dutch resorted to force on July 20, 1947. Both sides issued cease-fire orders on Aug. 4, 1947, in response to a call from the U.N. Security Council.

On Nov. 2, 1949, Dutch and Indonesian leaders agreed upon the terms of union. Dr. Sukarno was elected President of the federation on Dec. 16 and the first all-Indonesian Cabinet was formed with Mohammed Hatta as Premier. The transfer of sovereignty took place at Amsterdam on December 27, 1949.

In 1963, Netherlands New Guinea was transferred to Indonesia, and it was renamed West Irian. In 1973 it became Irian Jaya.

Sukarno, who had himself declared "President for Life," launched a series of guerrilla raids in September, 1963, to scuttle formation of the new Federation of Malaysia. A treaty between Indonesia and Malaysia in August, 1966, ended the open conflict. Meanwhile, with Sukarno's encouragement, Communist influence increased.

Early in 1966, led by Moslem students, the masses undertook an anti-Communist campaign which is believed to have assassinated more than 300,000 Indonesians suspected of Communist ties. Sukarno was forced in March 1966 to yield power to General Suharto, whom Sukarno had made army chief of staff, who began a series of trials of Sukarno's associates. The Communist Party was outlawed. Sukarno was forced to give up all power on Feb. 22, 1967 and Suharto became acting President in March, 1967. He ended hostilities against Malaysia and established close ties with the Western democracies, including the United States. Suharto introduced a "New Order" emphasizing austerity and fiscal responsibility and with Western aid of $200 million—a third provided by the United States—began rebuilding the country. In March, 1968, the Consultative Assembly elected Suharto President for a five-year term.

Suharto also permitted national elections, which moved the nation back toward representative government. The Consultative Assembly elected him unanimously for a second five-year term in 1973. He was unopposed.

The economic and political stability achieved by the Suharto regime was tested by external events in 1975. Tightening of world money markets put serious pressures on ambitious industrial development plans underwritten by Pertamina, the state-owned oil company. Communist triumphs in Vietnam and Cambodia encouraged Jakarta toward a policy of non-alignment with any great power and toward closer relationships with other members of the Association of Southeast Asian Nations, a regional grouping of five non-Communist states.

Indonesia annexed the former Portuguese half of the island of Timor after the provisional government of the area requested annexation May 31, 1976. Earlier, Indonesian "volunteers" and regulars had entered the area to fight leftist Fretelin forces who sought independence.

Economic Conditions. Agriculture engages about 70% of the adult males. Rich in a variety of crops, the islands prior to World War II produced about 31% of the world's copra, 37% of its rubber, 83% of its pepper and nearly all of its quinine. The big-estate agriculture on Java and Sumatra is devoted mainly to export. The rest is subsistence agriculture. Rice is the staple food and chief crop. Major plantation crops are rubber, tea, coffee, cinchona bark, palm kernels and sugar. Others are copra, cacao, spices, agava fiber and Kapok. In addition to rice, the chief food crops are maize, cassava, sweet potatoes, peanuts and soybeans.

Industry, especially in Java, developed rapidly after 1930. In addition to industries connected with the processing of the rich natural products, there were established chemical works, textile and paper mills, soap factories, breweries, shipyards, a Goodyear tire and rubber plant, and a General Motors assembly plant.

Petroleum is the principal mineral product of modern Indonesia. The tin industry attained pre-war levels more rapidly than others after World War II. Other important minerals include bauxite, coal, salt, nickel and manganese.

Most valuable timber is teak. Ebony, sandal-wood and ironwood also are cut.

Chief exports in 1974 were crude oil (68%) and rubber (7%). Leading customers were Japan (53%), U.S. (20%), Singapore (7%). Leading suppliers were Japan (30%), U.S. (16%), West Germany (8%), Singapore (7%).

Natural Features. A backbone of mountain ranges extends throughout the main islands of the archi-pelago. Earthquakes are frequent, and there are many active volcanoes.

IRAN (Constitutional monarchy)

(Keshvaré Shahanshahiyé Irân)

Monarch: Shah Mohammad Reza Pahlavi (1941).
Premier: Amir Abbas Hoveida (1965).
Area: 636,296 sq mi. (1,648,000 sq km).
Population (est. 1976): 33,900,000 (Iranian, Kurdish, Azerbaijani).
Density per square mile: 53.3.
Capital: Teheran.
Largest cities (est. 1975): Teheran, 4,000,000; Isfahan, 700,000; Mashed, 600,000; Tabriz, 510,000.
Monetary unit: Rial.
Languages: Farsi (Persian), Kurdish, Azerbaijani.
Religions: Shi'ite Moslem, 93%; Sunni Moslem, 5%.

Iran is a constitutional monarchy, and the Shah has the usual powers of the head of a parliamen-tary state. Executive power is exercised by a Cabinet headed by the Premier, who is appointed by the Shah and who is responsible to Parliament, the lower house of which (Majlis) has 268 popu-larly elected members and the upper house of which (senate) has 60 members, half of whom are appointed by the Shah.

Major Political Parties. One-party rule was imposed March 2, 1975, when the Shah proclaimed the Na-tional Resurgence Party, headed by Premier Hoveida, as the state's only political organization for "at least the next two years." The decree dissolved two existing parties. Iran Novin (New Iran) Party, led by Manouchehr Kalali, and the Mardom Party, led by Yahya Adi.

History. Oil-rich Iran was called Persia before 1935. Its key location blocks the lower land gate to Asia and also stands in the way of traditional Russian ambitions for access to the Indian Ocean. After periods of Assyrian, Median and Achae-menidian rule, Persia became a powerful empire under Cyrus the Great, reaching from the Indus to the Nile at its zenith in 525 B.C. It fell to Alex-ander in 331–30 B.C. and to the Selucidae in 312–02 B.C., and a native Persian regime arose about 130 B.C. Another Persian regime arose about A.D. 224, but it fell to the Arabs in 637. In the 12th century, the Mongols took their turn ruling Per-sia, and in the early part of the 18th century, the Turks occupied it.

An Anglo-Russian convention of 1907 divided Iran into two spheres of influence. British attempts to impose a protectorate over all of Iran were defeated in 1919. On Feb. 26, 1921, General Reza Pahlavi seized the government and was elected hereditary Shah in 1925. Subsequently he did much to modernize the country and abolished all foreign extraterritorial rights.

Increased pro-Axis activity led to Anglo-Russian occupation of Iran in August, 1941, and deposition of the Shah in favor of his son, Mohammad Reza Pahlavi.

Ali Razmara became Premier on June 26, 1950, and pledged to restore efficient and honest govern-ment, but he was assassinated Mar. 7, 1951. Mo-hammed Mossadegh took over April 29. Parlia-ment completed action on a bill nationalizing the oil industry over strong British protests.

Mossadegh was ousted Aug. 19, 1953, by Fazol-lah Zahedi, whom the Shah had named Premier. The oil dispute was settled in August 1954.

Iran established closer relations with the United States and the West, and the United States began a vast program of economic and military aid. In 1955 the country joined the Central Treaty Organi-zation (then called the Baghdad Pact). At the Shah's insistence the government undertook a broad program of reform, especially agrarian land reform, distributing crown lands and estates to the landless peasants.

The Shah maintained continuing cordial relations with the West, despite Iran's role as a founding member of the Organization of Petroleum Export-ing Countries. Iran did not participate in OPEC's 1973 embargo on oil shipments to the West, and it continued to supply Israel with oil during the 1973 Arab-Israeli war. But it benefited hugely from the fivefold boost in world oil prices forced by OPEC, realizing $18 billion in oil revenues in 1974. The oil profits have financed an extraordinary mod-ernization program of education, industrialization and construction, which is expected to cost over $400 billion in the next 13 years.

Iran also embarked on an enormous military buildup, contracting for over $2 billion in U.S. military equipment, including modern aircraft, naval vessels and sophisticated electronic devices. As he has built Iran's forces, the Shah has worked to exclude the superpowers from the Persian Gulf area and to ease disputes in the region. A March, 1975, agreement ended long-standing border fric-tions with Iraq, and Iranian relations with Saudi Arabia and Egypt warmed noticeably in 1975. At the same time, the Shah visited Washington in May, 1975, to discuss Arab-Israeli peace negotiations with President Ford.

A non-Arab Moslem nation, Iran has never shared Arab antipathy toward Israel and its military buildup was not welcomed by Arab Socialist states, which accused the Shah of subservience to the U.S. Iranian radicals have taken to guerrilla operations; they killed one U.S. adviser in 1973 and two in 1975. Several bombs were exploded during President Nixon's visit to Teheran in 1972.

In June 1974 Iran and France signed a 10-year, $4-billion development agreement that included sale of five 1,000-megawatt nuclear reactors to Iran.

Economic Conditions. Iran is predominantly agri-cultural, and irrigation is common, especially on the central plateau. The principal crops are wheat and barley. Other important crops include rice, grapes, dates, apricots, tobacco, tea, cotton, sugar beets and corn. There are extensive grazing lands.

Although Iran was famous for centuries for her handicrafts and carpets, her Western-style industrialization began only in the 1920's and took momentum in the postwar era. The main industrial products are textiles, sugar, cement, copper, refractory material, chemicals and pharmaceuticals, plastics, rubber and tires, automobile assemblies, etc.

Considerable mineral wealth exists, but only oil is exploited commercially. The principal field, near Shushtar in the southwest, was worked until 1951 by the Anglo-Iranian Oil Company. The latter's concession began in 1901 and was to run until 1993, but its properties were nationalized by the Iranian government in April 1951. Production under Iranian control was negligible. Under an agreement signed Sept. 19, 1954, Iran's oil is being produced, refined, and marketed by a consortium of eight Western oil companies, with 50% of the profits going to Iran.

Chief export in 1974 was crude oil (96%). Leading customers in 1973 were Japan (c. 28%), West Germany (c. 9%), United Kingdom (c. 9%), Netherlands (c. 8%), Italy (c. 7%), U.S. (c. 6%), France (c. 5%). Leading suppliers were West Germany (19%), Japan (14%), U.S. (14%), U.K. (10%), U.S.S.R. (5%), France (5%).

Natural Features. Iran is, in general, a plateau averaging 4,000 feet elevation. In addition, there are maritime lowlands along the Persian Gulf and the Caspian Sea. The Elburz Mountains in the north rise to 18,603 feet at Mt. Demavend. From northwest to southeast, the country is crossed by a desert 800 miles long.

IRAQ (Republic)

(Al Jumhouriya al 'Iraqia)

President: Marshal Ahmed Hassan al-Bakr (1968).
Area: 167,925 sq mi. (434,926 sq km).
Population (est. 1976): 11,470,000 (Arab, 75%; Kurdish, 15%; Iranian, 3.75%; others, 6.25%).
Density per square mile: 68.3.
Capital: Baghdad.
Largest cities (est. 1974): Baghdad, 2,800,000; (1965 census): Basra, 310,950; Mosul, 264,146; Kirkuk, 175,303; Najaf, 134,027.
Monetary unit: Dinar.
Languages: Arabic, Kurdish, Persian and Turkish.
Religions: Moslem, 95.5%; Christian, 3.3%; others, 1.2%.

Since the coup d'etat of July 1968, Iraq has been governed by the Arab Ba'ath Socialist Party through a Council of Command of the Revolution headed by the President of Iraq. There is also a Council of Ministers headed by the President.

History. Iraq, a triangle of mountains, desert and fertile river valley, is bounded east by Iran, north by Turkey, west by Syria and Jordan, and south by Saudi Arabia. From earliest times it has been known as Mesopotamia—the land between the rivers—for it embraces a large part of the alluvial plains of the Tigris and Euphrates.

An advanced civilization existed in Mesopotamia by 4000 B.C. Sometime after 2000 B.C. it became

the center of the ancient Babylonian and Assyrian empires. It was conquered by Cyrus the Great of Persia in 538 B.C., and by Alexander in 331 B.C. After an Arab conquest in A.D. 637-40, Baghdad became capital of the ruling caliphate. The country was cruelly pillaged by the Mongols in 1258, and during the 16th, 17th, and 18th centuries was the object of repeated Turkish-Persian competition.

Nominal Turkish suzerainty imposed in 1638 was replaced by direct Turkish rule in 1831. In World War I an Anglo-Indian force occupied most of the country, and Britain was given a mandate over the area in 1920. The British recognized Iraq as a kingdom in 1922 and terminated the mandate in 1932, when Iraq was admitted to the League of Nations. In World War II, Iraq generally adhered to its 1930 treaty of alliance with Britain, but in 1941, British troops were compelled to put down a pro-Axis revolt led by Premier Rashid Ali. Iraq became a charter member of the Arab League in March 1945 and Iraqi troops took part in the Arab invasion of Palestine in 1948. The 1930 treaty of alliance with Britain was terminated in April, 1955, and replaced by a defense cooperation agreement.

King Faisal II, born on May 2, 1935, succeeded his father, Ghazi I, who was killed in an automobile accident on Apr. 4, 1939. King Faisal and his uncle, Crown Prince Abdul-Ilah, were assassinated in August 1958 in a swift revolutionary coup which brought to power a military junta headed by Abdul Karem Kassim. The short-lived "Arab Union," formed by the federation of Iraq and Jordan in February, 1958, came abruptly to an end with recognition by the U.A.R. of the rebel government of Iraq. Kassim, in turn, was overthrown and killed in a coup d'état staged Mar. 8, 1963, by the Ba'ath Socialist Party.

President Abdel Salam Arif, a leader in the March coup, staged another coup in November 1963, driving the Ba'ath members of the revolutionary council from power. He adopted a new Constitution in 1964. In 1966, he, two Cabinet members, and other supporters died in a helicopter crash. His brother, General Abdel Rahman Arif, assumed the presidency, crushed the opposition and won an indefinite extension of his term in April 1967. In May he took over the premiership, but his regime was ousted in July 1968 by a junta led by Maj. Gen. Ahmed Hassan al-Bakr.

In March 1970, the Baghdad government announced a settlement of the 8½-year sporadic war with the Kurds, an ethnic people in northeastern Iraq (who spread over the border into Turkey and Iran), accepting two nationalities in Iraq (Arabs and Kurds) and promising a Kurdish Vice President of Iraq and proportional Kurdish representation in a new parliament. The Kurds ultimately refused the government's terms. Bakr fired five Kurdish ministers from his Cabinet, and, after 11 prominent members of the Kurdish Democratic Party were executed by the government, the Kurd-Iraqi war resumed.

The Kurdish rebellion flared anew in April, 1974, following collapse of an Iraqi plan for Kurdish self-rule. The rebels, armed and reinforced from Iran, withstood Soviet-supplied Iraqi forces until Iran ended its aid under an agreement with Iraq reached March 5, 1975. Some 200,000 Kurds fled to Iran and the revolt was liquidated within a month. The March 5 agreement also provided for resolution of old border disputes with Iran.

Iraq's Revolutionary Command Council relaxed its militant support of socialist revolution sufficiently in the spring of 1975 to reach a border agreement with Saudi Arabia and to propose a plan for settlement of a long-standing boundary dispute with Kuwait.

In April 1972, Iraq signed a 15-year treaty of friendship and cooperation with the Soviet Union (akin to the Soviet-Egyptian pact), and took the first Communist into the Cabinet since 1963. With Moscow approving, the Baghdad government in 1972 also nationalized the Iraq Petroleum Co. (U.S., French, British and Dutch firms in a consortium) over a dispute about production quantities and pricing policy, and paid compensation.

Economic Conditions. The chief economic activity is agriculture, dependent upon irrigation and confined to the valleys of the Tigris and Euphrates. Iraq supplies about 80% of the world's dates. Chief among the cereal products of Iraq are barley, wheat, rice, sorghum, maize and millet. Many fruits and some tobacco and cotton are grown. Herding is the principal occupation of the many nomadic and seminomadic tribes.

Industry is still embryonic. Of some 100 firms, the most important are those making brick, tile, woolen textiles, vegetable oils, soap, glass and cigarettes.

Oil production is concentrated at the Baba Gurgur fields near Kirkuk, which are operated on behalf of an international group by the British-managed Iraq Petroleum Company. Associated companies operate fields at Zubair and Rumaila near Basra and at Ain Zalah and Butmah. The Khanaqin Oil Company, a British Petroleum subsidiary, operates another field which produces only for local consumption.

Oil is piped to Tripoli in Lebanon, Baniyas in Syria and Fao on the Persian Gulf.

Chief export in 1974 was crude oil (96%). Leading customers in 1973 were Italy (c. 25%), France (c. 23%), Brazil (c. 10%), U.S.S.R. (c. 6%). Leading suppliers were U.S.S.R. (9%), United Kingdom (9%), France (8%), Japan (7%), Brazil (6%), U.S. (6%), Czechoslovakia (6%).

The only port for seagoing vessels is Basra, which is located on the Shatt-al-Arab River near the head of the Persian Gulf.

Natural Features. Iraq has arid desertland west of the Euphrates, a broad central valley between the Euphrates and Tigris, and mountains in the northeast. The fertile lower valley is formed by the delta of the two rivers, which join about 120 miles from the head of the Persian Gulf. The gulf coastline is 26 miles.

IRELAND (Republic)

(Éire)

President: Cearbhail Ó Dalaigh (resigned in 1976).
Taoiseach (Prime Minister): Liam Cosgrave (1973).
Area: 27,136 sq mi. (70,283 sq km).
Population (est. 1976): 3,175,000.
Density per square mile: 117.0.

Capital: Dublin.
Largest cities (1971 census): Dublin, 566,034; Cork, 128,235.
Monetary unit: Irish pound.
Languages: Irish, English.
Religions: Roman Catholic, 95%; Protestant, 5%.

Ireland is a sovereign, independent, democratic state. The President is elected by direct vote for a term of seven years. The Oireachtas (National Parliament) consists of the President and two Houses, Dáil Éireann (House of Representatives), and Seanad Éireann (Senate), which have a maximum term of five years. The House of Representatives has 144 members elected by proportional representation, while the Senate has 60 members, of whom 11 are nominated directly by the Prime Minister, 6 are elected by the universities, and the remaining 43 are elected from five vocational panels. The Taoiseach (Prime Minister) is appointed by the President on the nomination of the Dáil.

Major Political Parties. Fine Gael (55 of 144 seats in the Dáil), led by Prime Minister Liam Cosgrave, and Labour Party (19 seats), led by Brendan Corish, form a coalition government; Fianna Fáil (66 seats), led by John Lynch.

History. In pre-Christian times Ireland, occupying the island in the Atlantic Ocean which is the second largest of the British Isles, was inhabited by Picts in the north and a people called the Erainn in the south, the same stock, apparently, as in all the isles before the Anglo-Saxon invasion of Britain. They were in the stone and bronze ages. About the fourth century B.C. tall, red-haired Celts arrived from Gaul or Galicia. They subdued and assimilated the inhabitants and established a Gaelic civilization.

By the beginning of the Christian Era, Ireland was divided into five kingdoms—Ulster, Connacht, Leinster, Meath and Munster. St. Patrick introduced Christianity in 432 and the country developed into a center of Gaelic and Latin learning. Irish monasteries, the equivalent of universities, attracted the intellectuals as well as the pious, and sent out missionaries to many parts of Europe and, some believe, to North America.

Norse depredations along the coasts, starting in 795, ended in 1014 with Norse defeat at the Battle of Clontarf by forces under Brian. In the middle of the 12th century, the Pope gave all Ireland to the English Crown as a papal fief. In 1171, Henry II of England was acknowledged "Lord of Ireland," but local sectional rule continued for centuries, and English control over the whole island was not reasonably absolute until the 17th century. By the Act of Union (1800), England and Ireland became the "United Kingdom of Great Britain and Ireland."

A steady decline in the Irish economy followed in the next decades. The population had reached 8¼ million when the great potato famine of 1846–48 took many lives and drove millions to emigrate to America. By 1921 it was down to 4.3 million.

In the meantime, anti-British agitation continued along with demands for Irish home rule. The advent of World War I delayed the institution of home rule and resulted in the Easter Rebellion in Dublin (Apr. 24–29, 1916), in which Irish nationalists unsuccessfully attempted to throw off British rule. Guerrilla warfare against British forces followed proclamation of a republic by the rebels in 1919.

The Irish Free State was established as a dominion on Dec. 6, 1921 with the six northern counties as part of the United Kingdom. Ireland was neutral in World War II.

In 1948, Éamon de Valera, leader of the Sinn Fein, who had won establishment of the Free State in 1921 in negotiations with Britain's David Lloyd George, was defeated by John A. Costello, who demanded final independence from Britain. The Republic of Ireland was proclaimed on Apr. 18, 1949. It withdrew from the Commonwealth but in 1955 entered the United Nations, where it played a role that far outweighed its resources. Since 1949 the prime concern of successive governments has been the development of Ireland.

De Valera, who retired in 1973 after two terms in the largely ceremonial presidency, died Aug. 29, 1975, at the age of 92.

Through the 1960's two antagonistic currents dominated Irish politics. One sought to bind the wounds of the rebellion and civil war, symbolized in 1967 by the merger of Protestant Trinity College and Catholic University College into the University of Dublin. The other was the effort of the outlawed extremist Irish Republican Army to bring Northern Ireland into the republic. Despite public sympathy for unification of Ireland, the Dublin government dealt rigorously with I.R.A. guerrillas caught inside the republic's borders.

In what appeared to be another I.R.A. guerrilla action, the new British Ambassador to Ireland, Christopher Ewart-Biggs, was killed when a land mine blew his car apart July 21, 1976. Prime Minister Cosgrave denounced the assassination and declared a national day of mourning.

In the February 1973 elections, a less conservative coalition toppled the Fianna Fáil, which had held power for the previous 16 years (and 35 of the previous 41 years of the Republic), largely on economic issues involving taxes, inflation and housing.

Ireland's fourth President, Erskine H. Childers, died Nov. 17, 1974. The three major parties agreed unanimously on the choice of Cearbhail O. Dalaigh, former Chief Justice, to fill the balance of the Presidential term, which expires in 1980.

Economic Conditions. Agriculture is still the principal occupation in Ireland. The main crops are wheat, oats, potatoes and sugar beets. Other staple crops are rye, flax, turnips, cabbage, hay.

Ireland supplies most of its own consumer goods and is now producing a wide variety of goods for world markets. Leading manufactures are ordinarily beverages, tobacco, wood, paper, clothing, textiles and metals.

Chief exports in 1974 were meat (16%), chemicals (9%), machinery (9%), textiles (8%), dairy products (8%) and livestock (6%). Leading customers were United Kingdom (56%), U.S. (9%), West Germany (6%). Leading suppliers were U.K. (46%), West Germany (8%), U.S. (6%), France (5%).

Natural Features. Occupying the entire island except for the six northern counties of Ulster, Ireland resembles a basin—a central plain rimmed with mountains, except in the Dublin region. The mountains are low, with the highest peak, Carrantuohill, in County Kerry, rising to 3,415 feet.

The principal river is the Shannon, which begins in the north central area, flows south and southwest for about 240 miles, and empties into the Atlantic.

ISRAEL (Republic)

(Medinat Israel)

President: Dr. Ephraim Katzir (1973).
Prime Minister: Yitzhak Rabin (1974).
Area: 7,992 sq. mi. (20,700 sq km).*
Population (est. 1976): 3,445,000.
Density per square mile: 431.1.
Capital: Jerusalem.
Largest cities (est. 1974): Tel Aviv-Jaffa, 357,600; Jerusalem, 344,200; Haifa, 225,000; Ramat-Gan, 120,200.
Monetary unit: Israeli lira.
Languages: Hebrew, Arabic.
Religions: Jewish, 84.8%; Moslem and Christian.

Israel, which does not have a written Constitution, has a republican form of government headed by a President elected for a five-year term by the Knesset, a one-chamber legislature. He may be elected twice. The Knesset has 120 members who are elected by universal suffrage under proportional representation for four years. The government is administered by the Cabinet, which is headed by the Prime Minister.

The Knesset decided in June 1950 that Israel would acquire a Constitution gradually through the years by the enactment of fundamental laws. Israel grants automatic citizenship to every Jew who desires to settle within its borders, subject to control of the Knesset.

Major Political Parties. Israel Labor Party, consisting of the merged Mapai, Mapam, Rafi, and Ahdut-Avodah (51 of 120 seats in Knesset) Likud coalition, including Gahal (39 seats); National Religious Party (10 seats).

History. The history of Palestine, cradle of two great religions and homeland of the modern state of Israel, is mostly a chronicle of invasion, conquest, and confusing divisions. Known to the ancient Hebrews as the "Land of Canaan" Palestine derives its name from the Philistines of Biblical times. About 1,000 B.C. the Hebrews succeeded in establishing a single monarchy, which later split up into two kingdoms—Judah and Israel. The country was subsequently invaded and overcome by many peoples, including the Assyrians, Babylonians, Egyptians, Persians, Macedonians, Romans, and Byzantines. In A.D. 645-36, Palestine was wrested from the Byzantine Empire by the Arabs. Frankish Crusaders captured Jerusalem in 1099 and set up a feudal kingdom which endured until Saladin (1187) restored Moslem rule. In 1516 suzerainty over the area was transferred from the Mamelukes of Egypt to the Turks. It remained part of the Ottoman Empire until World War I, when British forces under General Allenby defeated the Turks and captured Jerusalem (Dec. 9, 1917). A League of Nations mandate awarding Palestine to Great Britain was put in force in 1923.

Meanwhile, a movement had been founded in 1897 by Theodor Herzl to create a Jewish homeland in Palestine, and a considerable number of Jewish immigrants had entered the country prior

---

* Excluding 26,473 sq mi. occupied in 1967 war. † Includes East Jerusalem.

to World War I. On Nov. 2, 1917, British recognition was given both to the growing Arab nationalist movement and to Zionist aspirations by the Balfour Declaration.

A British royal commission report (July 7, 1937) recommended partition of Palestine into an Arab and a Jewish state separated by a mandated area in the vicinity of Jerusalem and at Nazareth. The Arabs opposed the proposal, advocating instead the establishment of an independent Palestine with full minority rights for the Jews. In May 1939, a British White Paper called the establishment of a Jewish state contrary to British obligations to the Arabs. It promised after a 10-year transition, establishment of an independent Palestine in which Arabs and Jews would share authority in government. During the next five years, 75,000 Jews were to be allowed to enter Palestine. These proposals did not satisfy either party, but the outbreak of World War II overshadowed all other issues.

The end of European hostilities in 1945 brought a renewal of friction and the formation of the Arab League. Attempts to bring Jewish immigrants into Palestine illegally were intensified thereafter, and terrorism grew apace.

Termination of the British mandate May 14, 1948 and withdrawal of British forces brought new violence. An independent state of Israel was immediately proclaimed by the Jewish National Council, and Arab forces converged on Palestine from the south, north, and east, spearheaded by the crack British-trained Arab Legion of King Abdullah of Jordan. Within a few hours Arab-Jewish hostilities erupted. On June 11, however, there went into effect a four-week truce supervised by Count Folke Bernadotte, Swedish U.N. mediator in Palestine. Fighting resumed on July 9, with Israeli forces gaining on all fronts except in Jerusalem, part of which had been taken by Jordanian troops prior to the truce. On July 17 a second U.N. truce took effect. Bernadotte was assassinated on Sept. 17 by unidentified Jewish terrorists, and his duties were taken over by Dr. Ralph Bunche of the United States. After a cease-fire beginning Jan. 7, 1949, an armistice agreement was concluded with Egypt on Feb. 24 and with Jordan on Apr. 3.

During the hostilities Israel increased the territory allotted to it under the partition plan about 50% by gaining western Galilee, a broad corridor to Jerusalem through central Palestine and part of modern Jerusalem. In April 1950, Jordan incorporated eastern and central Palestine, including the Old City of Jerusalem.

Israel's governmental structure took shape rapidly. The provisional leaders, Chaim Weizmann and David Ben-Gurion, were confirmed as President and Prime Minister, respectively. Recognized by most non-Arab countries, the new nation was admitted to the U.N. on May 11, 1949.

In 1956 Egypt nationalized the Suez Canal and barred Israel from it. Israel dispatched troops to invade Egypt on Oct. 29, 1956, and quickly took the Gaza Strip and almost all the Sinai peninsula up to the canal. Following U.N. intervention the Israeli troops were withdrawn. During the next nine years Egypt sought to organize the Arab states to carry through a holy war against Israel, while Tunisia sought to get them to recognize Israel. Egypt made a mutual defense pact with Syria in 1966. Border clashes from terrorist raids mounted from Syria and

Jordan accelerated in 1966, and in November 1966 Israel subjected Jordan to a limited retaliatory offense. The United Nations censured Israel.

In 1967, Syria continued sporadic bombardment and terrorist raids against Israeli border settlements. Israel warned of retaliation. Syria asked for Egyptian aid. Egypt moved up troops to the Israeli border and demanded removal of the U.N. Peacekeeping Force. The United Nations acceded to the demand. Egypt effected a total mobilization and closed the Gulf of Aqaba to Israeli shipping. Israel also mobilized but sought to end the dispute by diplomatic means. Maj. Gen. Moshe Dayan, who commanded the Sinai campaign in 1956, was made Defense Minister.

In June 1967, Israel defeated the Arab nations in a brilliant six-day war. Israeli air attacks on air fields and installations in Egypt, Syria and Jordan, paralyzed Arab air power. A three-front ground and air battle against Egyptian forces in the Sinai, Jordanian troops on the eastern frontier, and Syrian troops massed in the north achieved an Israeli victory humiliating to the Arab coalition. Israel held the Gaza Strip, the Sinai, the east bank of the Suez, the fortifications at Sharm el Sheikh, the old city of Jerusalem, the west bank of the Jordan River, and the Golan Heights commanding the Sea of Galilee. The conquest expanded Israeli-controlled territory by 200%, and brought a population half as large as Israel's under its dominion. Israel permitted Arab refugees to return.

Israel celebrated the 20th anniversary of nationhood in 1968 amidst constant small-scale violence. Shelling and raiding continued into 1969. The Israelis settled down for a long stay, making clear that any peace settlement would have to guarantee that the occupied territories would never again constitute a threat to Israel's existence. They also rejected all proposals that involved changing Jerusalem's status as a unified city and that did not include direct Arab-Israel negotiations. The Soviet Union rearmed the Leftist Arab states. The United States provided arms to Jordan, which was seeking peace with Israel, and to Israel.

Egypt's President Nasser, reportedly under the pressure of Arab fedayeen (terrorist) competition, declared a 1967 cease-fire along the canal void on Apr. 23, 1969, and began a "war of attrition" in which larger numbers of Russian-provided artillery took an increasing toll of Israeli forces across the water. Israel embarked on "deep penetration" raids of Egypt's industrial and population centers with American-provided planes. Nasser went to Moscow in January 1970, and by March, Russian-made and -piloted aircraft and Russian-made and sometimes -manned antiaircraft missiles were defending Egypt's Nile delta.

In June 1970, the U.S. announced a peace initiative to "stop shooting and start talking." A standstill cease-fire along the canal was immediately violated by Egyptian (and Russian) forward movement of anti-aircraft missiles, but continued despite incidents. The U.S. sold Israel more planes and equipment to compensate for the effects of the violations. Talks via a United Nations intermediary did not go well, however. Egypt (under its new President, Anwar Sadat) promised to sign a peace agreement with Israel if Israel withdrew from all the occupied territories, but Israel flatly refused to return to the borders of prewar 1967.

The fourth major Arab-Israeli war in 25 years

erupted Oct. 6, 1973 with a surprise Egyptian and Syrian assault on the Israeli high holy day, Yom Kippur. Israel invaded Egypt proper (in Africa), trapping about 20,000 Egyptian troops on a deep thrust into the Sinai. Syria advanced on the Golan Heights but was turned back, with Israel gaining more territory before a cease-fire was called two weeks later. Through the negotiating skills of U.S. Secretary of State Henry A. Kissinger, the two Arab states and Israel disengaged their forces over the following months, with Egypt and Syria recovering small amounts of the land they had lost in the 1967 war.

The United States gave over $2 billion in arms to Israel, and when the Soviet Union at one point threatened to intervene with its forces against Israel, the United States put its nuclear forces on world alert to deter the move. All parties in the Mideast conflict, except the Palestinian refugees, began negotiations at Geneva to reach a lasting peace in the region. The unreconciled Palestinians continued their terrorist raids inside and outside of Israel, however, massacring Christian pilgrims, Olympic athletes and Israeli school children on indiscriminate suicide missions.

Lack of preparedness for the Yom Kippur war became a major issue in Israel. Elections late in 1973 cost the ruling Labor coalition of Premier Golda Meir five seats; former hero and Defense Minister Moshe Dayan was widely criticized, and the Army's chief of staff quit after an inquiry found he should be dismissed for negligence. Mrs. Meir put together a minority government briefly but quit April 10, 1974. Former General Yitzhak Rabin eventually formed a successor government, leaving out Dayan and long-time Foreign Minister Abba Eban. Rabin's three-party coalition was approved by the Knesset by 61 votes, the minimum necessary and the closest vote for a new government in Israel's history. Party realignments in October 1974 gave Rabin's coalition a 65-vote base.

In October 1974, the activist Palestine Liberation Organization (P.L.O.) was recognized as "the representative of the Palestinian people" in resolutions passed by the U.N. General Assembly and by an Arab summit meeting at Rabat, Morocco, which approved $2.3 billion in arms aid to Israel's Arab neighbors. There were continuing guerrilla attacks on Israel and counterattacks by Israeli forces against Palestinian bases in Lebanon. Rabin refused to negotiate with the P.L.O., holding that the Palestinian question should be resolved in negotiations between Israel and Jordan, which sought a troop disengagement along the Israeli-occupied west bank of the Jordan and rejected any deal that would turn the territory over to the P.L.O.

Kissinger began a round of negotiations in January 1975 to achieve a second-stage agreement between Israel and Egypt for disengagement in the Sinai. The talks with Egypt stalled March 22, 1975, partly because Israel insisted on a formal Egyptian pledge of nonbelligerency. U.S. criticism of Israel's rigid position strained relations between Jerusalem and Washington. The disengagement talks resumed in June, and a three-year agreement was formally signed in Geneva Sept. 4.

The accord committed Israel to yield control of the strategic Mitla and Gidi Passes and to return captured oil fields at Abu Rudeis. Egypt agreed to permit Israeli cargoes through the newly reopened Suez Canal. Both sides pledged not to resort to

force to settle disputes and agreed that 200 U.S. civilian technicians should monitor early-warning systems to alert either side to any violation of a widened U.N. buffer zone that paralleled Egypt's narrow holding on the west bank of the canal. The accord was approved by the Knesset on Sept. 3.

After the agreement was signed, extensive U.S. commitments in support of Israel were disclosed in Ford Administration submissions to Congress. Politically, there was an assurance of a coordinated U.S.-Israeli position at any reconvened session of the Geneva conference on the Middle East. Economically, the Administration agreed to ask Congress for $400 million in extra aid to assure Israel's fuel supplies after cession of the Abu Rudeis oil fields. Militarily, the way was clear for Israel to acquire about $1 billion worth of U.S. weapons in the short run and substantially more in years ahead. On Israel's shopping list was the Pershing missile, which has a 460-mile range and was designed for a nuclear warhead.

Although progress toward a permanent peace settlement remained stalled through 1976, Israel scored a stunning blow against Arab terrorism when on July 4 an airborne commando unit raided Entebbe airport in Uganda to rescue 103 hostages in a hijacked Air France plane. The first Palestinian hijacking in a year and a half was carried out by a group which claimed membership in the Popular Front for the Liberation of Palestine.

At the insistence of relatives of passengers, Prime Minister Rabin agreed to negotiate with the terrorists for the exchange of prisoners in Israel and in other countries, despite the government's policy never to negotiate in such cases. After learning that the Israeli hostages might face death in any event, the government launched a surprise attack that killed the terrorists and a score of Ugandan soldiers, rescued all but two of the hostages and lost only one of the rescuers.

Uganda charged bad faith and called on the United Nations Security Council to condemn Israel for aggression. The United States and Britain proposed an alternate resolution condemning terrorism. Neither measure won the necessary nine votes, and Israeli Ambassador Chaim Herzog triumphantly claimed vindication of his assertion that international law sanctioned his government's action,

Economic Conditions. Agriculture is the chief economic activity, but industrialization has been the most important feature of Israel's economic development recently. The maritime plain, the plain of Esdraelon and the northern Jordan valley are the principal agricultural areas. Citrus growing, confined largely to the maritime plain, normally furnishes the major export crop. Others include olives, rice, fruits and vegetables, figs, tobacco, wheat, barley, corn, sesame and potatoes.

Industry is developing rapidly, especially the food-processing, textile, metalworking and chemical groups. Diamond cutting, although dependent on rough diamond imports, is of major importance; and there are oil refineries and storage tanks at Haifa, a terminus of the pipeline from the Iraqi oil fields, which have been suspended since 1948.

Mineral resources are limited. They include gypsum, sulfur, limestone and rock salt, together with potash, phosphates and bromine from the Dead Sea.

Chief exports in 1974 were diamonds (35%),

chemicals (15%), citrus fruit and products (10%), machinery (7%), clothing (5%) and textiles (5%). Leading customers were U.S. (17%), United Kingdom (9%), Belgium-Luxembourg (5%), France (5%). Leading suppliers were U.S. (18%), West Germany (16%), U.K. (13%), Italy (5%), Netherlands (5%).

Natural Features. Northern Israel is largely a plateau traversed from north to south by mountains and broken by great depressions, also running from north to south.

The maritime plain of Israel is remarkably fertile. The southern Negev region, which comprises almost half the total area, is largely a wide desert steppe area. The National Water Project irrigation scheme is now transforming it into fertile land. The Jordan, the only important river, flows from the north through Lake Hule (Waters of Merom) and Lake Kinneret (Sea of Galilee or Sea of Tiberias), finally entering the Dead Sea (1,290 ft below sea level). This "sea," which is actually a salt lake (394 sq mi.), has no outlet, its water balance being maintained by evaporation.

ITALY (Republic)

(Repubblica Italiana)

President: Giovanni Leone (1971).
Premier: Giulio Andreotti (1976).
Area: 116,304 sq mi. (301,225 sq km).
Population (est. 1976): 56,250,000.
Density per square mile: 483.6.
Capital: Rome.
Largest cities (est. 1974): Rome, 2,833,100; (est. 1976): Milan, 1,700,000; Palermo, 700,000; (est. 1975): Naples, 1,300,000; Turin, 1,200,000; Genoa, 806,400; Bologna, 493,000; Venice, 364,900; (1971 census): Florence, 457,803; Catania, 400,886.
Monetary unit: Lira.
Language: Italian.
Religions: Roman Catholic, 99.6%.

The President is elected for a term of seven years by Parliament in joint session with regional representatives. The President nominates the Premier and, upon the Premier's recommendations, the members of the Cabinet. Parliament is composed of two houses: a Senate with 315 elective members and a Chamber of Deputies of 630 members elected by the people for a five-year term.

Major Political Parties. Christian Democratic Party (263 seats in Chamber of Deputies), led by Benigno Zaccagnini; Italian Community Party (227 seats), led by Enrico Berlinguer; Socialist Party (57 seats), led by Francesco De Martino; Socialist Movement Party (35 seats), led by Giorgio Almirante; Social Democratic Party (15 seats), led by Giuseppe Saragat; Republican Party (14 seats), led by Oddo Biasini; Proletariat's Democratic Party (6 seats); Liberal Party (5 seats), led by Valerio Zanone.

History. Until A.D. 476, when the German Odoacer became head of the Roman Empire in the west, the history of Italy was largely the history of Rome. From A.D. 800 on, the Holy Roman Emperors, Popes, Normans, and Saracens all vied for control over various segments of the Italian peninsula. Numerous city states, such as Venice and Genoa, and many small principalities flourished in the late Middle Ages.

In 1713, after the War of the Spanish Succession, Milan, Naples, and Sardinia were handed over to Austria, which lost some of its Italian territories in 1735. After 1800, Italy was unified by Napoleon, who crowned himself King of Italy on May 26, 1805; but after the Congress of Vienna in 1815, Austria once again became the dominant power in Italy.

Recent Italian experience seems to be an extension of a troubled history. In 1815 the Congress of Vienna restored the Italies to their former position of confused disunity, like the Germanies a "geographical expression." The tyranny of the Restoration met with opposition by the Carbonari (charcoal burners), a secret society which demanded constitutional government and national unification. But Austrian armies crushed Italian uprisings in 1820, 1821 and 1831. In the 1830's Joseph Mazzini, brilliant liberal nationalist, organized the Risorgimento (Resurrection), which laid the foundation for Italian unity.

Disappointed Italian patriots looked to Sardinia for leadership. Count Camille di Cavour (1810–1861), Prime Minister of Sardinia in 1852 and the architect of United Italy, joined England and France in the Crimean War (1853–56), and in 1859 helped France in a war against Austria, thereby obtaining Lombardy. By plebiscite in 1860, Modena, Parma, Tuscany, and the Romagna voted to join Sardinia. In 1860, Giuseppe Garibaldi conquered Sicily and Naples and turned them over to Sardinia. Victor Emmanuel II, King of Sardinia, was proclaimed King of Italy on Mar. 17, 1861.

Allied with Germany and Austria-Hungary in the Triple Alliance of 1882, Italy declared her neutrality upon the outbreak of World War I on the ground that Germany had embarked upon an offensive war. In 1915, Italy entered the war on the side of the Allies.

Benito Mussolini, a former Socialist, organized discontented Italians in 1919 into the Fascist Party to "rescue Italy from Bolshevism." He led his Black Shirts in a march on Rome and, on Oct. 28, 1922, became Premier. He transformed Italy into a dictatorship, embarking on an expansionist foreign policy with the invasion and annexation of Ethiopia in 1935 and allying himself with Adolf Hitler in the Rome-Berlin Axis in 1936. Defeated in World War II, Il Duce was executed by Partisans at Dongo on Lake Como, April 28, 1945.

Following the overthrow of Mussolini's dictatorship and the armistice with the Allies (Sept. 3, 1943), Italy joined the war against Germany as a co-belligerent. King Victor Emmanuel III abdicated May 9, 1946, and left the country after installing his son as King Humbert II. However, a provisional government held a popular plebiscite on June 2, and the Italians voted to establish a republic. On June 13, King Humbert followed his father into exile.

The peace treaty which took effect Sept. 15, 1947, required Italian renunciation of all claims in Ethiopia and Greece, and the cession of the Dodecanese to Greece and of five small Alpine areas to France. In addition, the major part of the Istrian Peninsula, including Fiume and Pola, went to Yugoslavia.

The Trieste area west of the new Yugoslav territory was made a free territory (until 1954, when the city and a 90-square-mile zone were transferred to Italy and the rest to Yugoslavia). Italy was required to pay nearly $400 million in reparations, chiefly to the Soviet Union, Yugoslavia, Greece, Ethiopia, and Albania.

Economic problems continue to vie with political discord as Italy's greatest impediment to stability in the first half of the 1970s.

The Rumor government fell Oct. 3, 1974, following setbacks that included failure by the Christian Democrats to persuade voters in a May referendum to repeal the 1970 divorce law. After a 51-day crisis, Italy's 37th postwar government was formed under Aldo Moro, a left-centrist Christian Democrat who had been Premier three times before. The reconstituted coalition government faced cumulative problems: Tripled outlays for the Middle Eastern oil that fuels 85% of Italy's industry and a resultant doubling of Italy's foreign trade deficit; 25% inflation; 6% unemployment; massive industrial strikes, and endemic corruption, crime and civil disorders.

The economy appeared to stabilize in the summer of 1975. Provincial and regional elections in June resulted in Communist gains and in left-wing administrators being seated in all major cities north of Rome. Fanfani was ousted after 25 years as party leader of the Christian Democrats.

Withdrawal of Socialist backing forced the resignation of Premier Aldo Moro's coalition government—the 32nd since the end of World War II—on Jan. 7, 1976. Moro asked to form a new minority government but resigned April 30, and elections were called for June 20.

Expected Communist gains still left the Christian Democrats in first place; they opted to continue their efforts to rule as a minority under the leadership of Giulio Andreotti, a recognition of U.S. and West German warnings against a Communist coalition. Communist Deputy Pietro Ingrao was named President of the Chamber of Deputies, however, and Communists won 7 of 26 parliamentary chairmanships.

Religion. Although the country is predominantly Roman Catholic, religious freedom is permitted. Catholic religious teaching is given in all elementary and intermediate schools. Relations with the Church are regulated by the treaty with the Holy See of Feb. 11, 1929, which established the temporal power of the Pope over Vatican City.

Economic Conditions. Agriculture engages more than a third of the population. It is extremely diversified; differences of altitude, soil and climate allow the production of all European crops from rye to rice, from apples to oranges, and from hemp to cotton. Italy ranks next to France in wine production, and next to Spain in olive-oil production.

Livestock and dairy farming are important in Italy. Of the 50-odd varieties of Italian cheese, the best known are the hard parmesan and pecorino (the latter made from ewe's milk) and the soft bel paese and gorgonzola.

Industrial production is centered in the north. The nature of the Fascist corporate state had a tendency to foster industrial concentration prior to World War II. The textile industry is the largest and most important and supplies the home market as well as furnishing a large proportion of Italy's exports. The metal industries are handicapped by lack of coal, which must be imported in large quantities, and by insufficient iron-ore reserves. The chemical, clothing and food industries are also important.

Italy is a member of the European Coal and Steel Community.

Production includes cotton yarn, woven cotton fabrics, rayon yarn, pig iron and ferroalloys, raw steel, cement, automobiles, and trucks.

Italy is ordinarily the world's largest producer of mercury; it is also an important producer of sulfur. The nation must import coal, oil and iron.

In Alto Adige and in the central Apennines, there are abundant hydroelectric power resources and deposits of natural gas.

Chief exports in 1974 were machinery (18%), chemicals (10%), motor vehicles (10%), textile yarns and fabrics (9%), petroleum products (8%), food (7%) and clothing and footwear (7%). Leading customers were EEC (45%; incl. West Germany 18%, France 13%, United Kingdom 5%) and U.S. (8%). Leading suppliers were EEC (42%; incl. West Germany 18%, France 13%), U.S. (8%), Saudi Arabia (7%), Libya (6%).

Natural Features. Approximately 600 of boot-shaped Italy's 708 miles of length are in the long peninsula that projects into the Mediterranean from the fertile basin of the Po River. The Apennines, branching off from the Alps between Nice and Genoa, form the peninsula's backbone, and rise to a maximum height of 9,560 feet at the Gran Sasso d'Italia (Corno). The Alps are Italy's northern boundary.

Several islands form part of Italy. Sicily (9,926 sq mi.) lies off the toe of the boot, across the Strait of Messina, with a steep and rock-bound northern coast and gentler slopes to the sea in the west and south. Mt. Etna, an active volcano, rises to 10,741 feet, and most of Sicily is more than 500 feet in elevation. Sixty-two miles southwest of Sicily lies Pantelleria (45 sq mi.), and south of that are Lampedusa and Linosa. Sardinia (9,301 sq mi.), which is located just south of Corsica and about 125 miles west of the mainland, is mountainous, stony, and unproductive.

Italy has many northern lakes, lying below the snow-covered peaks of the Alps. The largest are Garda (143 sq mi.), Maggiore (83 sq mi.) and Como (55 sq mi.).

The Po, the principal river, flows from the Alps on Italy's western border and crosses the Lombard plain to the Adriatic.

IVORY COAST (Republic)

(République de Côte d'Ivoire)

President and Premier: Félix Houphouet-Boigny (1960).
Area: 124,504 sq mi. (322,463 sq km).
Population (est. 1976): 5,000,000.
Density per square mile: 40.2.
Capital and largest city (est. 1972): Abidjan, 500,000.
Monetary unit: Franc CFA.
Ethnic groups, Agnis, Baoulés, Senoufos, Kroumen, Mandes, Dan-Gouros, and other groups.
Languages: French and African languages.
Religions: Animist, 65%; Moslem, 23%; Christian, 12%.

The government is headed by a President who is elected every five years by universal direct suffrage, together with a National Assembly of 100 members.

Political Party. Parti Démocratique de la Côte d'Ivoire, member of Rassemblement Démocratique Africain (P.D.C.I./R.D.A.).

History. The Ivory Coast attracted both French and Portuguese merchants in the 15th century. French traders set up establishments early in the 19th century, and in 1842, the French obtained territorial concessions from local tribes, gradually extending their influence along the coast and inland. The area was organized as a territory in 1893, became an autonomous republic in the French Union after World War II, and achieved independence on Aug. 7, 1960.

Ivory Coast formed, with Dahomey, Niger, and Upper Volta, a customs union in 1959. The country is one of the most prosperous and stable in West Africa. Ivory Coast succeeded in getting a $10-million loan from European and U.S. private capital in April 1960 for low-cost housing and other development work. It also obtained a $30-million U.S. loan to assist in construction of a $96.5-million hydroelectric project.

Houphouet-Boigny was re-elected in 1970 with a claimed 99.97% of votes cast, and all the 100-member National Assembly, also unopposed, was elected with a claimed 99.89% of the vote.

Ivory Coast joined a seven-nation Economic Community for West Africa Jan. 1, 1973, to promote regional economic development.

Economic Conditions. Agricultural products include corn, sweet potatoes, cassava, coffee, cocoa, bananas and peanuts.

Chief exports in 1974 were coffee (22%), cocoa (21%) and timber (18%). Leading customers were France (26%), Netherlands (15%), Italy (9%), West Germany (9%), Dahomey (8%), U.S. (7%), Taiwan (6%). Leading suppliers were France (39%), U.S. (7%), West Germany (6%), Iraq (6%), Nigeria (5%).

JAMAICA (Parliamentary state)

(Member of Commonwealth of Nations)

Governor-General: Florizel Glasspole (1973).
Prime Minister: Michael Manley (1972).
Area: 4,232 sq mi. (10,962 sq km).
Population (est. 1976): 2,065,000.
Density per square mile: 487.9.
Capital and largest city (est. 1974): Kingston, 169,800.
Monetary unit: Jamaican dollar.
Language: English.
Religions: Anglican, Baptist, Roman Catholic.

The island legislature is a 53-member House of Representatives elected by universal suffrage, and an appointed Senate of 21 members. The Prime Minister is appointed by the Governor-General and must in the Governor-General's opinion be the person best able to command the confidence of a majority of the members of the House of Representatives.

Major Political Parties. People's National Party (35 seats in the House of Representatives), led by Prime Minister Michael Manley; and Jamaica Labour Party (16 seats), led by Edward P. G. Seaga; Independent (2 seats).

History. A republic on the island of Jamaica in the West Indies, Jamaica was inhabited by Arawak Indians when Columbus discovered it in 1494 and named it St. Jago. It remained under Spanish rule until 1655, then became a British possession. Jamaica prospered from wealth brought by buccaneers, to their base, Port Royal, the capital, until the city disappeared in the sea in 1692 after an earthquake. The Arawaks died off from disease and exploitation and slaves, mostly black, were imported to work sugar plantations. Abolition of the slave trade (1807), emancipation of the slaves (1833), and a gradual drop in sugar prices led to depressed economic conditions which resulted in an uprising in 1865. The following year the government was changed to that of a colony, and conditions improved considerably. Introduction of banana cultivation made the island less dependent on the sugar crop for its well-being. Overpopulation and problems inherited from the colonial era, such as illiteracy, produced chronic substantial unemployment, leading to much emigration to the Caribbean countries and to the United States.

On May 5, 1953, the island of Jamaica attained internal autonomy, and in 1958 it led in organizing the West Indies Federation. This effort at Caribbean unification failed. A nationalist labor leader, Sir Alexander Bustamente, led a campaign for withdrawal from the federation. As the result of a popular referendum in 1961, Jamaica became an independent nation on Aug. 6, 1962.

Manley became Prime Minister in 1972 and initiated a Jamaican-style socialist program to achieve what he has called "the most peaceful and constitutional revolution in history." There have been sharp boosts in taxes on land and luxuries and on the extraction of bauxite. The government has acquired 51% control of the Jamaican operations of five U.S.- and Canadian-owned bauxite companies and of the island's sugar industry. It has moved to combat illiteracy and it has set up farm cooperatives and youth work programs. Continuing pressure from black radical groups for faster land reform and full nationalization of foreign holdings has caused concern in the propertied class.

Economic Conditions. Jamaica is the world's largest producer of bauxite. Its most important agricultural products are sugar, bananas, tobacco and citrus fruits.

Chief exports in 1974 were alumina (52%), bauxite (20%) and sugar (12%). Leading customers were U.S. (46%), United Kingdom (15%), Norway (12%), Canada (5%). Leading suppliers were U.S. (35%), Venezuela (15%), Canada (5%), Trinidad and Tobago (5%).

JAPAN (Constitutional monarchy)

(Nippon)

Emperor: Hirohito (1926).
Prime Minister: Takeo Miki (1974).
Area: 143,750 sq mi. (372,313 sq km).
Population (est. 1976): 112,200,000.
Density per square mile: 780.5.
Capital: Tokyo.

Largest cities (est. 1974)*: Tokyo, 8,708,300; (est. 1973 by U.N.): Osaka, 2,841,950; Yokohama, 2,494,-785; Nagoya, 2,075,250; Kyoto, 1,435,250; Kobe, 1,338,700; Sapporo, 1,130,800; Kitakyushu, 1,051,000.
Monetary unit: Yen.
Language: Japanese.
Religions: Shintoist, Buddhist, Christian.

Japan's Constitution, promulgated on Nov. 3, 1946, replaced the Meiji Constitution of 1889. The 1946 Constitution, sponsored by the United States during its occupation of Japan, brought fundamental changes to the Japanese political system, including the abandonment of the Emperor's divine rights. The Diet (Parliament) consists of a House of Representatives of 491 members, elected for four years, and a House of Councilors of 252 members, half of whom are elected every three years for six-year terms. Executive power is vested in the Cabinet, which is headed by a Prime Minister, nominated by the Diet from its members.

Emperor Hirohito, who was born Apr. 29, 1901, succeeded his father, Yoshihito, on Dec. 25, 1926. He was married on Jan. 26, 1974 to Princess Nagako, born in 1903. They have two sons—Crown Prince Akihito (born Dec. 23, 1933) and Prince Hitachi (born Nov. 28, 1935)—and four daughters. Succession to the Japanese throne is in the male line only.

Major Political Parties. Liberal Democratic Party (280 of 491 seats in House of Representatives), led by Prime Minister Takeo Miki; Socialist Party (118 seats), led by Tomomi Narita; Japan Communist Party (40 seats), led by Sanzo Nosaka; Komeito (Clean Government) Party (30 seats), led by Yoshikatsu Takeiri; Democratic Socialist Party (20 seats), led by Ikko Kasuga.

History. A series of legends attributes creation of Japan to the sun goddess, from whom the later emperors were allegedly descended. The first of them was Jimmu Tennō, supposed to have ascended the throne on Feb. 11, 660 B.C.

Recorded Japanese history begins with the first contact with China in the fifth century A.D. Japan was then divided into strong feudal states, all nominally under the Emperor, but with real power often held by a court minister or clan. In 1185, Yoritomo, chief of the Minamoto clan, was designated Shogun (Generalissimo) with the administration of the islands under his control. A dual government system—Shogun and Emperor—persisted till 1867.

First contact with the West came about 1542, when a Portuguese ship off course arrived in Japanese waters. Portuguese traders, Jesuit missionaries, and Spanish, Dutch, and English traders followed. Suspicious of Christianity and of Portuguese support of a local Japanese revolt, the shoguns restricted all foreigners in 1636–38 except the Dutch, who were confined to Nagasaki. Western attempts to renew trading relations failed until 1853, when Commodore Matthew Perry sailed an American fleet into Tokyo Bay.

Japan now quickly made the transition from a medieval to a modern power. Feudalism was abolished and industrialization was speeded. An imperial army was established with conscription. The shogun system was abolished in 1868 by Emperor

* Except for Tokyo, figures refer to *shi*, a minor division that may include some scattered or rural population as well as an urban center.

Meiji, and parliamentary government was established in 1889. After a brief war with China in 1894–95, Japan acquired Formosa (Taiwan), the Pescadores islands, and part of southern Manchuria. China also recognized the independence of Korea (Chosen), which Japan later annexed (1910).

In 1904–05, Japan defeated Russia in the Russo-Japanese War, gaining the territory of southern Sakhalin (Karafuto) and Russia's port and rail rights in Manchuria. In World War I, Japan, which took a negligible part in military operations, seized Germany's Pacific islands and leased areas in China. The Treaty of Versailles then awarded her a mandate over the islands.

At the Washington Conference of 1921–22, Japan agreed to respect Chinese national integrity. The series of Japanese aggressions which was to lead to the nation's downfall began in 1931 with the invasion of Manchuria. The following year, Japan set up this area as a puppet state, "Manchukuo," under Emperor Henry Pu-Yi, last of China's Manchu dynasty. On Nov. 25, 1936, Japan joined the Axis by signing the anti-Comintern pact. The invasion of China came the next year, and the Pearl Harbor attack on Dec. 7, 1941.

For many months after Pearl Harbor, the Japanese army and navy enjoyed spectacular success, but by the end of 1942 the tide had begun to turn. Three years later the dropping of atomic bombs on Hiroshima and Nagasaki knocked Japan swiftly into surrender.

Japan surrendered formally on Sept. 2, 1945, aboard the battleship *Missouri* in Tokyo Bay. Southern Sakhalin and the Kurile Islands reverted to Russia, and Formosa (Taiwan) and Manchuria to China. The Pacific islands remained under U.S. occupation. General of the Army Douglas MacArthur was appointed Supreme Commander for the Allied Powers (SCAP) on Aug. 14, 1945.

A new Japanese Constitution was approved in 1946 and went into effect in 1947. In 1949, many of the responsibilities of government were returned to the Japanese. Full sovereignty was granted to Japan by the Japanese Peace Treaty in 1951.

The treaty took effect on Apr. 28, 1952, when Japan returned to full status as a nation. It was admitted into the United Nations in 1958. Japan regained its former economic position in Asia, becoming a leading producer of cotton textiles and ships. Much agitation led the United States to withdraw its troops in 1958.

Following the visit of Prime Minister Eisaku Sato to Washington in November, 1969, the United States agreed to return Okinawa and other Ryukyu Islands to Japan in 1972, and both nations renewed the security treaty in June 1970.

Events of the 1970s tested Japan's special relationship with the United States. Trade ties were strained in 1972 by Washington's inconclusive effort to curb textile imports from Japan. The focus of Japanese diplomacy was altered when President Nixon opened a dialogue with Peking in 1972. Prime Minister Kakuei Tanaka, who succeeded Sato in July, 1972, quickly established diplomatic relations with the mainland Chinese and severed ties with Formosa.

The jump in world oil prices that followed the 1973 Arab boycott squeezed Japan, which imports

85% of its oil from the Middle East. Japan greatly expanded its exports to the oil states and accepted some Arab investments.

Following Communist triumphs in Southeast Asia in the spring of 1975, Japan began moving into the diplomatic and commercial vacuum that followed U.S. withdrawal from the area.

Spending on defense in 1975 was less than 1% of the gross national product, and Japan's all-volunteer Self-Defense Forces numbered only 232,000—12% below authorized strength.

President Ford visited Japan Nov. 18-24, 1974, the first U.S. President to do so. Substantive results were minimized by Tanaka's domestic political troubles. They stemmed partly from a 24% inflation rate and an economic slowdown, but primarily from charges that Tanaka had enriched himself from political contributions. Tanaka resigned Nov. 26, 1974, and was succeeded Dec. 2 by Takeo Miki, a compromise choice from the progressive wing of the Liberal Democrats.

In July 1975, Japan's inflation rate was down to 14% and there were signs of an upturn in the sharpest Japanese recession since World War II.

While economic recovery continued in 1976, the Lockheed scandal pursued the ruling Liberal Democrats. With the disclosure by the U.S. Senate in February that $6.3 million in "promotion" money had been paid by the aircraft company to Yoshio Kodama, a rightwing political "fixer," Miki was placed under strong pressure to investigate the ultimate recipients.

After the arrest of several lesser figures, former Prime Minister Tanaka himself was jailed in August, charged with having received $1.7 million of the Lockheed money as a bribe in violation of exchange controls. Outraged Tanaka supporters in the party demanded Miki's resignation for having failed to protect the former Prime Minister from arrest. Miki, however, declared his intention to complete the investigations and lead the Liberal Democrats in the House elections scheduled to come before the end of the year.

Economic Conditions. Japan is traditionally a land of small farms and, except in Hokkaido, the northernmost island, there is almost no large-scale farming and animal husbandry. The average holding is less than three acres. Double cropping makes self-sufficiency possible, but on a low level of subsistence.

Prewar Japan was one of the world's leading industrial nations and the only country in the Far East with highly developed textile, steel, machinery, chemical and electrical industries. The textile industry was dominant but, after 1931, considerable expansion took place in the heavy industries —metal, machinery-building and chemical—which were adaptable to war purposes.

Postwar industrial rehabilitation proceeded slowly at first but, by the end of 1956, average industrial output was more than twice the 1934-36 level. Since the end of World War II, Japan's shipbuilding industry has consistently ranked among the world leaders.

The huge interlocking monopolies *(Zaibatsu),* controlling prewar business and finance, were dissolved in 1945, and reconcentration was prohibited by postwar legislation. However, there has been a growing tendency toward "bigness" in the last few years.

Japan is relatively poor in minerals, and large imports of coal, petroleum and iron ore are necessary. Other minerals include lead, silver, gold and copper.

Chief exports in 1974 were machinery (21%) (telecommunications apparatus 6%), iron and steel (19%), motor vehicles (13%), ships (10%), chemicals (7%) and textile yarns and fabrics (6%). Leading customers were U.S. (23%) and South Korea (5%). Leading suppliers were U.S. (20%), Saudi Arabia (8%), Iran (8%), Indonesia (7%), Australia (6%).

Before World War II the merchant marine carried almost 80% of the foreign trade and was surpassed only by those of the United States and Britain. Wartime losses were enormous, but recovery was fairly steady.

Natural Features. Japan's four main islands are Honshu, Hokkaido, Kyushu and Shikoku. The Ryukyu chain to the southwest was U.S.-occupied and the Kuriles to the northeast are Russian-occupied. The surface of the main islands consists largely of mountains separated by narrow valleys. There are about 50 more or less active volcanoes.

JORDAN, The Hashemite Kingdom of

(Al Mamlaka al Urduniya al Hashemiyah)

Ruler: King Hussein (1952).
Prime Minister: Zaid al-Rifai (1973).
Area: 37,738 sq mi. (97,740 sq km)*.
Population (est. 1976): 2,780,000.
Density per square mile: 73.7.
Capital: Amman.
Largest cities (est. 1975): Amman, 615,000; (est. 1973 by U.N.): Zarka, 220,000; Irbid, 116,000.
Monetary unit: Jordanian dinar.
Language: Arabic.
Religions: Moslems, 94%; Christian, 6%.

Jordan is a constitutional monarchy with a bicameral parliament. Its Chamber of Deputies of 60 members is elected for four years by the people, and the 30 members of the Senate are appointed by the King.

Political Parties. All political parties were banned in 1957.

History. Jordan was known in the time of Moses as Edom and Moab. In A.D. 106 it became part of the Roman province of Arabia and in 633-36 was conquered by the Arabs.

Taken from the Turks by the British in World War I, Jordan was separated from the Palestine mandate in 1920, and in 1921, placed under the rule of Abdullah ibn Hussein.

In 1923, Britain recognized Jordan's independence, subject to the mandate. In 1946, Britain abolished the mandate and recognized the independence of Jordan. That part of Palestine occupied by Jordanian troops was formally incorporated by action of the Jordanian Parliament on Apr. 24, 1950. Jordan's rejection of the Baghdad Pact in December 1955 set off a period of instability.

* Includes territory occupied by Israel in 1967 war.

Abdullah was assassinated June 20, 1951. His son Talal was deposed as mentally ill on Aug. 11, 1952. Talal's son Hussein, born May 2, 1935, succeeded him.

King Hussein, formally enthroned May 2, 1953, sought close association with the United States and the United Kingdom to get aid against nationalists seeking union with the United Arab Republic. The government's decision to join the Central Treaty Organization (then the Baghdad Pact) in 1955 caused riots. Israel's invasion of the U.A.R. and the intervention by Britain and France at the Suez strengthened the nationalists. An agreement on Oct. 25, 1956, put the Jordanian Army under the nominal command of an Egyptian, supreme commander of the armies of Syria and the U.A.R.

The break-up of the U.A.R. in September 1961 reduced the threat to Hussein, who was the first to recognize Syria when it withdrew from the U.A.R. Hussein established diplomatic relations with the Soviet Union in 1966. In that year Israel charged Jordan was sheltering terrorists who raided Israel. In the six-day Israeli-Arab war of June 1967, Jordan lost the old city of Jerusalem and territory west of the Jordan River.

The power of the Palestinian guerrillas grew until they mocked the throne and the army. Clashes occurred and after the guerrillas hijacked four Western airliners in September 1970 a full-scale civil war ensued. Thousands of casualties were reported.

Syria intervened with tanks on the side of the guerrillas. Apparently the Jordanians defeated the Syrians alone, but the U.S. implicitly threatened to intervene on Hussein's side unless the Syrians withdrew. About 20,000 U.S. troops in Europe were alerted, and the U.S. Seventh Fleet in the Eastern Mediterranean was reinforced before the Soviet Union urged the Syrians to pull back. Not least a factor was Israeli armor massing on the Golan Heights to strike into Syria if she did not leave Jordan. The 12,000 Iraqi troops in Jordan since the 1967 war were asked to leave by a Hussein now clearly in control of his country. He ignored calls, demands and warnings from other Arab countries to go easy on the guerrillas and by mid-1971 had crushed the Palestinians to the point where some fled to Israeli jails in preference to those of fellow Arabs.

The United States supplied an average of $30 million annually in military arms to keep Jordan secure. In the Arab-Israeli war of 1973, Jordan remained virtually aloof from the fighting.

At an Arab summit conference in Rabat, Morocco, in October 1974, Hussein concurred in resolutions calling for creation of an independent Palestinian state on any land liberated from Israel and recognizing the Palestinian Liberation Organization as "the sole legitimate representative of the Palestinian people." Under these circumstances, Hussein said, Jordan had no place in further negotiations on the future of the West Bank. He offered Palestinians living in Jordan a choice of Palestinian or Jordanian citizenship and initiated revisions in Jordan's Constitution to exclude representation for residents of Israeli-occupied territory.

Hussein agreed at talks with President Ford in Washington in August 1974 to work for disengagement of Jordanian and Israeli troops along the Jordan River, but he also sought to rebuild Jordan's military strength. In January 1975 he received a

$175 million first installment of military aid from Arab oil countries but his plan to buy $350 million worth of Hawk air defense missiles from the U.S. was blocked by Congressional opposition.

In the summer of 1976, with Congressional obstacles removed, the price of the missiles had risen to $500 million and Hussein was negotiating for additional aid from Saudi Arabia to finance the purchase. Before visiting Moscow (June 17–28), he had hinted at buying Soviet missiles, but U.S. officials were reported to have threatened to cut aid if he did.

Economic Conditions. Agriculture and tourism constitute Jordan's main source of national income. The area of cultivable land is estimated at 4,000 square miles. Agricultural products include grains, cereals, vegetables, and fruits such as bananas, citrus fruits, grapes, quinces, pears, apples, peaches, almonds, figs and olives. The Ghor area, which is situated on both banks of the Jordan River, comprises the most fertile land. Limited but growing mineral exploitation also contributes to Jordan's national income. Minerals include phosphates, marble and potash.

Industry is expanding in Jordan. There are now industries producing canned vegetables, cement, cigarettes, aluminum products and other light consumer goods.

Chief exports in 1974 were phosphates (21%), vegetables (13%), aircraft (re-exports) (12%), cement (7%), oranges (7%) and tobacco (5%). Leading customers were India (13%), Saudi Arabia (11%), Lebanon (8%), Japan (8%), Syria (6%), Kuwait (6%), Iran (5%). Leading suppliers were U.S. (11%), West Germany (9%), United Kingdom (8%), Lebanon (5%), Egypt (5%).

KENYA (Republic)

(Member of Commonwealth of Nations)

President: Jomo Kenyatta (1964).
Area: 224,960 sq mi. (582,646 sq km).
Population (est. 1976): 13,500,000.
Density per square mile: 60.0.
Capital: Nairobi.
Largest cities (est. 1975): Nairobi, 700,000; (est. 1973 by U.N.): Mombasa, 301,000.
Monetary unit: Kenyan shilling.
Languages: Swahili (official), Bantu, Kikuyu, English.
Religions: Protestant, 36%; Roman Catholic, 22%; Moslem, 6%; Animist.

Under its Constitution of 1963, amended in 1964, Kenya has a one-house National Assembly of 171 members, elected for five years by universal adult suffrage. Since 1969, the President has been chosen by the public through a general election.

Political Party. Kenya African National Union, led by President Jomo Kenyatta.

History. A republic in East Africa, Kenya, formerly a British colony and protectorate, was made a crown colony in 1920. The whites' alienation of the rich plateau area, the White Highlands, long regarded by the Kikiyu people as their territory, was a factor leading to native terrorism, called the Mau Mau movement, in 1952. In 1954 the British began preparing the territory for African rule and independence. In 1961 Jomo Kenyatta was freed from banishment to become leader of the Kenya African National Union. Internal self-government was granted in 1963; Kenya became an independent republic on Dec. 12, 1963 with Kenyatta the first President. Kenya obtained economic and technical assistance from Communist China beginning in 1964 and later a World Bank loan. In 1967 Kenya, Uganda, and Tanzania agreed to establish an East African trading community and a development bank. Kenya also sought to end dominance of retail trade by the Indian community of 188,000. In 1968 it began a drive against the Asians, and 20,000 left the country. In 1972, Kenyatta ordered all Asians with Kenyan passports to leave, allegedly for foreign-currency manipulations.

In July 1969, Tom Mboya, a member of the Luo tribe and Secretary General of Kenyatta's KANU party, was assassinated by a rival Kikuyu tribesman (Kenyatta is a Kikuyu). Anti-government riots followed. Opposition leader Odinga was arrested and his KPU party banned, returning Kenya to one-party rule.

Kenyatta was re-elected Oct. 14, 1974, unopposed in an election from which all former KPU candidates, including Odinga, were barred. He faced bitter accusations following the discovery March 11, 1975 of the mutilated body of Josiah M. Kariuki, who was emerging as an opposition leader within KANU. After a National Assembly report implicated Kenyatta aides, the President dismissed three ministers who voted for the report and warned that dissidents would not be tolerated.

During 1976, border skirmishes and a "gasoline war" marred Kenya's relations with neighboring Uganda. President Idi Amin accused Kenya of aiding the July 4 Israeli raid on Entebbe airport. Earlier, Amin made territorial claims against Kenya, and tensions increased when Kenya halted gasoline deliveries to Uganda because of nonpayment.

Economic Conditions. The country is predominantly agricultural, and a large area is cultivated by Europeans. The altitude ranges from sea level to more than 9,000 feet, allowing for tropical, subtropical and temperate climate crops.

The principal agricultural products are coffee, tea and sisal. Minerals include gold, silver, salt and sodium carbonate.

Chief exports in 1974 were petroleum products (19%), coffee (18%), tea (9%), sisal (8%) and chemicals (7%). Leading customers were Uganda (13%), Tanzania (9%), United Kingdom (9%), West Germany (8%), Netherlands (5%). Leading suppliers were U.K. (17%), Japan (11%), Iran (10%), West Germany (10%), Saudi Arabia (7%), U.S. (6%).

KOREA, DEMOCRATIC PEOPLE'S REPUBLIC OF (North)

(Chosun Minchu-chui Inmin Konghwa-guk)

President: Kim II Sung (1948).
Premier: Pak Sung Chol (1976).
Area: 46,540 sq mi. (120,538 sq km).
Population (est. 1976): 16,275,000.
Density per square mile: 349.7.
Capital and largest city (1974): Pyongyang, 1,500,000.
Monetary unit: Won.

Languages: Korean, Chinese, Japanese.
Religions: Buddhist, Confucianist, Taoist.

The elected Supreme People's Assembly, as the chief organ of government, chooses a Presidium and a Cabinet. The Cabinet, which exercises executive authority, is subject to approval by the Assembly and the Presidium.

Political Party. Korean Workers (Communist) Party, led by President Kim II Sung.

History. Korea, a 600-mile peninsula jutting from Manchuria, China (and a small portion of the Soviet Union) into the Sea of Japan and the Yellow Sea, is occupied by a country which, according to myth was founded in 2333 B.C. by Tangun. In the 17th century, Korea became a vassal of China and was isolated from all but Chinese influence and contact until 1876 when Japan forced Korea to negotiate a commercial treaty, opening the land to the U. S. and Europe. Japan achieved control as the result of its war with China (1894–95) and with Russia (1904–05) and annexed Korea in 1910. Japan developed the country but never won over the Korean nationalists.

After the Japanese surrender in 1945, the country was divided into two occupation zones, the Soviet Union north of and the United States south of the 38th parallel. When the cold war developed between the U.S. and U.S.S.R., trade between the zones was cut off. In 1948, the division between the zones was made permanent with the establishment of separate regimes in the north and south. By mid-1949, the U.S. and Soviet Union withdrew all troops. The Democratic People's Republic of Korea (North Korea) was established on May 1, 1948. The Communist Party, headed by Kim Il Sung, was established in power.

On June 25, 1950, the North Korean Army launched a surprise attack on South Korea. On June 26, the U.N. Security Council condemned the invasion as aggression and ordered withdrawal of the invading forces. On June 27, U.S. President Truman ordered air and naval units into action to enforce the U.N. order. The British government did the same and soon a multinational U.N. command was set up to aid the South Koreans. The North Korean invaders took Seoul and pushed the South Koreans into the southeast corner of their country. With U.N. aid the South Korean lines held firm. Gen. Douglas MacArthur, U.N. commander, made an amphibious landing at Inchon on Sept. 15 behind the North Korean lines which resulted in the complete rout of the North Korean Army. The U.N. forces drove north across the 38th parallel, approaching the Yalu River. Then Communist China entered the war, forcing the U.N. forces into headlong retreat. Seoul was lost again, then regained; ultimately the war stabilized near the 38th parallel but dragged on for two years while the belligerents negotiated. An armistice was achieved July 27, 1953.

In 1966, North Korea proclaimed its ideological independence from both Moscow and Peking, a move which in effect aligned North Korea with the Soviet Union. North Korea became embroiled with the United States again on Jan. 23, 1968, when it seized the American intelligence ship *Pueblo* and its crew of 83. After more than a year, the crew was released.

On July 4, 1972, North and South Korea announced an agreement to work for peaceful reunification. A series of talks failed to produce concrete results and, on April 19, 1975, President Kim Il Sung declared during a Peking visit that Korean peace would depend on withdrawal of U.S. troops from the South.

While border incidents have been common, an extraordinarily violent clash between North Korean and U.S. guards over the Americans' attempt to cut back a tree in the Panmunjom Joint Security Area on Aug. 18, 1976 left two American officers dead. U.S. forces in the Far East went on alert, Kim himself sent an apology and the two sides agreed on Sept. 6 to divide the truce site to minimize contact between North Korean and U.S. military personnel.

Although Kim appears to be revered, economic troubles have beset his rigidly collectivist country. World bankers say a record of unpaid accounts due the Soviet Union, as well as non-Communist states, has demolished North Korea's international credit standing. Its armed forces, numbering 467,000, are about three-fourths of the South's military establishment, but the North's 600-plane air force holds a 3-to-1 edge over its potential foes, who have relied on U.S. air support in the event of war.

Economic Conditions. North Korea, which has 57% of the peninsula's area and less than one third of its population, has by far the larger part of the peninsula's industry, including abundant hydroelectric resources.

The chief agricultural products of North Korea are rice, corn and other grains. The chief industrial products are pig iron, steel, rolled metals, cement, fertilizers and electricity. The chief mineral products are coal and iron ore.

Chief exports in 1964 were metals (50%), minerals (12%) and farm products (11%). Leading customers in 1973 were China (65%), U.S.S.R. (18%), Japan (7%). Leading suppliers were China (50%), U.S.S.R. (30%), Japan (10%), France (6%).

KOREA, REPUBLIC OF (South)

(Han Kook)

President: Park Chung Hee (1963).
Premier: Choi Kyu Ha (acting) (1975).
Area: 38,022 sq mi. (98,484 sq km).
Population (est. 1976): 34,400,000.
Density per square mile: 904.7.
Capital: Seoul.
Largest cities (est. 1973): Seoul, 6,289,600; (1970 census): Pusan, 1,842,259; Taegu, 1,063,553; Inchon, 634,046; Kwangchu, 493,634; Taejon, 406,910; Chonchu, 257,530.
Monetary unit: Won.
Language: Korean.
Religions: Buddhist, Confucianist, Taoist, Christian.

The Constitution, modified by President Park in 1972, provides for a one-house legislature. The National Assembly is comprised of 219 members, two-thirds of whom are elected by direct popular vote for six-year terms and the rest appointed by the President for three-year terms.

The Constitution was also amended to allow Park to run for re-election indefinitely (initially there was a two-term limit) and extended the presidential terms

from four to six years each. Park was re-elected to his fourth term in 1972. Instead of popular vote, the President is now chosen by between 2,500 and 5,000 electors, who are elected by popular vote. Park now may also reduce parliament's powers and curb civil liberties by decree.

Major Political Parties. Democratic Republican Party (68 of 219 seats in the National Assembly), led by President Park; New Democratic Party (57 seats); Democratic Unification Party (3 seats); and 14 independents. Beyond this election result (1973), Park appointed 73 supporters to the Assembly, of whom at least 25 were aligned with his Democratic Republican Party.

History. South Korea came into being in the aftermath of World War II as the result of a 1945 agreement making the 38th parallel the boundary between a northern zone occupied by the Soviet Union and a southern zone occupied by U.S. forces. (For details, *see* North Korea.)

Elections were held in the U.S. zone on May 10, 1948 for a national assembly, which on July 12 adopted a republican Constitution and on July 20 elected Syngman Rhee President. The new republic was proclaimed on Aug. 15 and was recognized as the legal government of Korea by the U.N. General Assembly on Dec. 12, 1948.

On June 25, 1950, South Korea was attacked by North Korean Communist forces. U.S. armed intervention was ordered on June 27 by U.S. President Truman, and on the same day the United Nations invoked military sanctions against North Korea. Gen. Douglas MacArthur was named commander of the U.N. forces on July 7. U.S. and South Korean troops fought a heroic holding action but, by the first week of August, they had been forced back to a 4,000-square-mile beachhead in southeast Korea. There they stood off superior North Korean forces until Sept. 15, when a major U.N. amphibious attack was launched far behind the Communist lines at Inchon, port of Seoul. By Sept. 30, U.N. forces were in complete control of South Korea. They then invaded North Korea and were nearing the Manchurian and Siberian borders when several hundred thousand Chinese Communist troops entered the conflict in late October. U.N. forces were then forced to retreat below the 38th parallel.

On May 24, 1951, U.N. forces recrossed the parallel and had made important new inroads into North Korea when truce negotiations began on July 10. An armistice was finally signed at Panmunjom on July 27, 1953, leaving a devastated Korea in need of large-scale rehabilitation. The armistice contemplated an international political conference on the status of Korea, but negotiations for arranging it broke down. The question was discussed without result at the Geneva conference on Far Eastern problems, which was held Apr. 26–June 19, 1954.

The United States and South Korea signed a mutual-defense treaty on Oct. 1, 1953.

Syngman Rhee, President since his election in 1948, resigned on Apr. 27, 1960, in the face of rising disorders.

Posun Yun was elected to succeed Rhee as President, but political instability continued. In 1961, Gen. Park Chung Hee took power in a coup and, in 1962, Posun Yun resigned in protest over continuance of military rule. Park maintained a policy of close cooperation with the United States. He built up the country, maintaining an average growth rate in the economy of 8.5%. The United States stepped up military aid, building up South Korea's armed forces to 600,000 men. The South Koreans sent 50,000 troops to Vietnam, most of their cost paid by the United States.

In mid-1972, following President Nixon's summit meetings in Moscow and Peking, the two Koreas issued a mutual declaration setting a goal of peaceful reunification. (For details, *see* North Korea).

The prospective détente with North Korea failed to materialize, and agitation against Park's repressive regime was on the rise when President Ford visited the country Nov. 22-23, 1974. In talks with Park, Mr. Ford affirmed that U.S. forces would remain in South Korea and supported negotiations for unification of the country.

The fall of Cambodia and South Vietnam and the U.S. withdrawal from Southeast Asia in April, 1975, escalated Korean tensions. Park warned that 1975 would be "the year of aggression against the South," tightened internal security a few more notches and readied the ROK armed forces, which numbered 625,000, about 150,000 more than the North had under arms. Washington reaffirmed its commitments to Seoul and moved to bring the U.S. force to its full authorized strength of 42,000.

The U.N. General Assembly on Nov. 18, 1975 adopted conflicting resolutions on Korea. One, advanced by the United States, called for an end to vestigial U.N. command in Korea if negotiations by the United States, South Korea, China and North Korea could agree on an alternative plan for keeping the 1953 armistice. A Communist-supported resolution demanded dissolution of the command, withdrawal of U.S. troops from the South and a settlement to be negotiated between the U.S. and North Korea alone. No action was taken to implement either resolution.

On Dec. 19, 1975, Premier Kim Jong Pil and his entire Cabinet resigned. He was replaced by former Foreign Minister Choi Kyu Ha.

Economic Conditions. South Korea, with 43% of the peninsula's area and over two-thirds of its population, is predominantly agricultural. The major agricultural products are rice, barley, sweet potatoes and yams. Although industrial development was speeded in the peninsula during the last years of Japanese rule, by far the smaller part of the industry is located in South Korea.

Mineral products include iron ore, copper ore, tungsten, graphite, kaolin, talc, fluorite, limestone, coal, gold and silver.

Chief exports in 1974 were clothing (21%), textile yarns and fabrics (11%), electrical machinery and equipment (11%), iron and steel (10%) and food (7%). Leading customers were U.S. (33%), Japan (31%), West Germany (5%). Leading suppliers were Japan (38%), U.S. (25%), Saudi Arabia (10%).

KUWAIT (Emirate)

(Dowlat al Kuwait)

Emir: Sheik Sabah al-Salem al-Sabah (1965).
Prime Minister: Sheik Jaber al-Ahmed al-Sabah (1965).

Area: 6,880 sq mi. (17,818 sq km).
Population (est. 1976): 1,050,000.
Density per square mile: 152.6.
Capital (est. 1975): Kuwait, 78,000.
Largest city (est. 1975): Hawalli, 130,300.
Monetary unit: Dinar.
Languages: Arabic and English.
Religions: Moslem, 94.7%; Christian, 4.6%.

Sheik Sabah al-Salem al-Sabah rules as Emir of Kuwait and appoints the Prime Minister, who in turn appoints his Cabinet (Council of Ministers. A National Assembly has 50 members elected by adult males. Servicemen and policemen are not eligible to vote.

Political Parties. There are no political parties in Kuwait.

History. A sheikdom in northeastern Arabia at the head of the Persian Gulf, Kuwait obtained British protection in 1897 when the Sheik feared that the Turks would take over the area. In 1961, Britain ended the protectorate, giving Kuwait independence, but agreed to give military aid on request. Iraq immediately threatened to occupy the area and Sheik Sabah al-Salem al-Sabah called in British troops in July 1961. Soon afterward the Arab League sent in troops replacing the British. The prize was oil.

Oil was discovered in the 1930's. Kuwait proved to have 20% of the world's known oil resources. It has been a major producer since 1946, the world's second largest oil exporter, with the main concession held by a British-American concern. The Sheik, who gets half the profits, devotes most of them for the education, welfare, and modernization of his kingdom. In 1966, Sheik Sabah designated a relative, Jaber al-Ahmed al-Sabah, as his successor. By 1968 the sheikdom had established a model welfare state, and it sought to establish dominance among the sheikdoms and emirates of the Persian Gulf.

Kuwait contributed handsomely to Egypt and Jordan after the 1967 war with Israel and supported the 1973 war against Israel with funds and by joining the Arab oil boycott of Western nations.

Quadrupling of prices following the embargo sent Kuwait's oil profits rocketing from $2 billion in 1973 to almost $9 billion in 1974, with $7 billion estimated for 1975, when the oil output was reduced somewhat. With per capita income at about $10,000—nearly twice that of the United States—little Kuwait became an overnight financial power. It financed domestic improvements on a lavish scale, sponsored a foreign-aid program for favored Arab and African states and ploughed over $10 billion into profitable corporate investments overseas.

In March, 1975, the government nationalized Kuwaiti operations of Gulf Oil and British Petroleum. The acquisition, which cost about $180 million, gave Kuwait full control of an estimated 60 billion barrels of petroleum reserves.

Economic Conditions. Chief exports in 1974 were crude oil (81%) and petroleum products (15%). Leading customers were Japan (26%), United Kingdom (16%), France (10%), Singapore (5%), Italy (5%). Leading suppliers were Japan (17%), U.S. (14%), West Germany (11%), U.K. (8%).

LAOS (People's Democratic Republic of)

President: Prince Souphanouvong (1975).
Prime Minister: Kaysone Phomvihane (1975).
Area: 91,429 sq mi. (236,800 sq km).
Population (est. 1976): 3,350,000.
Density per square mile: 36.6.
Capital and largest city (est. 1973): Vientiane,* 176,600.
Monetary unit: Kip.
Languages: Lao (official) and French.
Religion: Buddhist.

Laos is a People's Democratic Republic with executive power in the hands of the Premier. The monarchy was abolished Dec. 3, 1975, when the Pathet Lao ousted a coalition government and King Savang Vathana abdicated. The King was appointed "Supreme Adviser" to the President, the former Prince Souphanouvong. Prince Souvanna Phouma. Premier since 1962, was made an "adviser" to the government.

Political Party: The Lao People's Revolutionary Party (the Pathet Lao), led by President Souphanouvong and Premier Kaysone Phomvihane, is the only political party.

History. A landlocked kingdom in Southeast Asia surrounded by China, Vietnam, Cambodia, Thailand, and Burma, Laos occupies the northwestern portion of Indo-China. It became a French protectorate in 1893, and the territory was incorporated into the union of Indo-China. A strong nationalist movement developed during World War II, but France re-established control in 1946 and made the King of Luang Prabang constitutional monarch of all Laos. France granted semiautonomy in 1949 and then, spurred by the Viet Minh rebellion in Vietnam, full independence within the French Union, in 1950. In 1951, Prince Souphanouvong organized the Pathet Lao, a Communist independence movement, in North Vietnam. The Viet Minh in 1953 established the Pathet Lao in power at Samneua. Viet Minh and Pathet Lao forces invaded central Laos, and civil war resulted.

By the Geneva Agreements of 1954 and an armistice of 1955, two northern provinces were given the Pathet Lao, the royal regime the rest. Full sovereignty was given the kingdom by the Paris agreements of Dec. 29, 1954. In 1957, Prince Souvanna Phouma, the royal Premier, and the Pathet Lao leader, Prince Souphanouvong, the Premier's half-brother, agreed to re-establishment of a unified government with Pathet Lao participation, and integration of Pathet Lao forces into the royal army. The agreement broke down in 1959, and armed conflict broke out again.

In 1960, the struggle became three-way as Gen. Phoumi Nosavan, controlling the bulk of the royal army, set up in the south a pro-Western revolutionary government headed by Prince Boun Gum. General Phoumi took Vientiane in December 1960, driving Souvanna Phouma into exile in Cambodia. The Soviet bloc supported Souvanna Phouma. In May 1961, a cease-fire was arranged and, in October, the three princes agreed to a coalition government headed by Souvanna Phouma.

But North Vietnam, the U.S. (in the form of Central Intelligence Agency personnel) and China remained active in Laos after the settlement. North

* Vientiane is the administrative capital; the royal capital is Luang Prabang.

Vietnam used a supply line (Ho Chi Minh trail) running down the mountain valleys of eastern Laos into Cambodia and South Vietnam, particularly after the U.S.-South Vietnamese incursion into Cambodia in 1970 stopped supplies via Cambodian seaports.

An agreement, reached in September 1973 and implemented the following April, revived coalition government. Royal Laotian rule continued in populous areas, the Pathet Lao controlled the mountainous east and the two groups exercised joint rule over Vientiane Province. With Souvanna Phouma as Premier and Souphanouvong as President of a 42-member National Political Council representing both factions, joint operation of the government began.

A series of anti-American demonstrations in April and May 1975 focused on installations of the Agency for International Development, which had spent over $1 billion in Laos over 20 years, much of it to combat the Pathet Lao. The U.S. economic and military aid programs, which totaled $60 million in 1975, were ended June 30. The number of U.S. officials in Laos was reduced from 800 on April 1 to 22 on July 1.

With the collapse of U.S.-supported regimes in Saigon and Phnom Penh in April 1975, the Pathet Lao moved to seize power in Laos. They were in effective control within a month and the December change in government was actually only a formality.

Economic Conditions. About 95% of the Laotians are farmers. The chief food crop is rice; other crops are maize, vegetables, cotton, cardamom and tobacco.

Chief exports in 1973 were tin (57%) and timber (36%). Leading customers were Thailand (65%) and Malaysia (29%). Leading suppliers were Thailand (47%), Japan (13%), France (10%), U.S. (7%), Switzerland (5%), Singapore (5%).

LATVIA

Area: 24,595 sq mi. (63,701 sq km).
Population (est. 1975): 2,478,000 (approx.: Latvian, 56.8%; Russian, 29.8%; others, 13.4%.
Density per square mile: 100.7.
Capital and largest city (est. 1973): Riga, 765,000.
Language: Latvian.
Religions (approx.): Lutheran, 56.6%; Roman Catholic, 23.7%; Greek Orthodox, 8.9%; others, 10.8%.

History. Descended from Aryan stock, the Latvians were early tribesmen who settled along the Baltic Sea and, lacking a central government, fell an easy prey to more powerful peoples. The German Teutonic knights first conquered them in the 13th century and ruled the area, consisting of Livonia and Courland, until 1562.

Poland conquered the territory in 1562 and ruled until 1795 in Courland; control of Livonia was disputed between Sweden and Poland from 1562 to 1629. Sweden controlled Livonia from 1629 to 1721. Russia took over Livonia in the latter year and Courland after the third partition of Poland in 1795.

From that time until 1918, the Latvians remained Russian subjects, although they preserved their language, customs, and folklore. The Russian Revolution of 1917 gave them their opportunity for freedom, and the Latvian republic was proclaimed on Nov. 18, 1918.

The republic lasted little more than 20 years. It was occupied by Russian troops in 1939 and incorporated into the Soviet Union in 1940. German armies occupied the nation from 1941 to 1943-44, when they were driven out by the Russians. Most countries, including the United States, have refused to recognize the Soviet annexation of Latvia.

LEBANON (Republic)

(Al-Joumhouriya Al-Lubnaniya)

President: Elias Sarkis (1976).
Premier: Rashid Karami (1975).
Area: 4,015 sq mi. (10,400 sq km).
Population (est. 1976): 2,965,000 (Arabian, Armenian, Circassian, Turkish).
Density per square mile: 738.5.
Capital: Beirut.
Largest cities (est. 1975): Beirut, 1,172,000; (est. 1964): Tripoli, 127,611.
Monetary unit: Lebanese pound.
Languages: Arabic (official); French, English.
Religions: Christian, 50%; Moslem, 40%; others, 10%.

Lebanon is governed by a President elected by Parliament for a six-year term, and a Cabinet of Ministers appointed by the President but responsible to Parliament.

Parliament has 99 members elected for a four-year term by universal suffrage and chosen by proportional division of religious groups.

Major Political Parties. Party breakdown of the Chamber of Deputies is difficult because of the religious groupings required by law, and because of the fact that many deputies join in major parliamentary blocs—Democratic Front, Tri-Partite Coalition, and National Struggle Front. The parties represented in Parliament are: Al-Kataib, led by Pierre Al-Jumayeh; Al-Wataniyin Al-Ahrar, led by Camille Chamoun; Al-Takadumi Al-Ishteraki, led by Kamal Jumblatt; Al-Kutla Al-Wataniya, led by Raymond Edde; Al-Dimocrati Al-Eshteraki, led by Kamel El-Assad.

History. In ancient times Lebanon was the mountainous hinterland of the Phoenician coast towns. From the 7th to the 11th centuries there infiltrated into southern Lebanon the heretics of Islam, who finally coalesced into the Druse community.

In the 19th century the Turkish Sultanate encouraged the Druses to wage civil war against the Christian Maronites. After a massacre of 2,500 Christians in 1860, Lebanon was occupied by the French for a year. From 1864 to 1914, a Christian military government ruled the area under nominal Turkish sovereignty. After World War I, France received a League of Nations mandate over Syria and Lebanon. The French drew a Lebanese border in 1920 to offset predominantly Moslem Syria and proclaimed the area a republic under French control on May 23, 1926. Complete independence came on Nov. 26, 1941. Lebanon joined the Arab League and took part in the invasion of Palestine on May 15, 1948.

In May 1958, a civil war broke out, with the Moslems Kamal Jumblatt and Saeb Salam leading the opposition to the Maronite Christian government. Threatened with defeat, President Camille Chamoun obtained the intervention of the U.S. military forces. In September 1958, a Maronite Christian military man, Gen. Fouad Chehab, took over the presidency. After a U.N. resolution demanded it, the U.S. forces withdrew.

Palestinian guerrillas using Lebanese territory drew Lebanon into conflict with Israel. Terrorist attacks on Israeli airliners led to an Israeli raid on Arab airlines at Beirut, and terrorist assaults on Israel's northern settlements drew punitive raids against guerrillas in Lebanon by Israeli army and air units. Lebanon appeared powerless to resist the guerrillas or the Israelis. In 1973, after an unsuccessful attack by Palestinian terrorists on the Israeli ambassador in Cyprus, Israeli forces struck again, including a unit that entered Beirut and assassinated three high guerrilla leaders. And in 1974, terrorist massacres of school children in Maalot drew further Israeli retaliation.

In May and June, 1975, repeated clashes between guerrilla sympathizers and conservative Christian Phalangist militiamen left more than 400 dead in street fighting in Beirut. On July 1, after two changes of governments, a "rescue cabinet" was installed under Premier Rashid Karami that included all major Christian and Moslem groups and order was restored.

On June 29, extremist guerrillas kidnaped U.S. Col. Ernest R. Morgan at Beirut Airport and held him for 13 days until free food was distributed in a poor Moslem section of the city devastated in the fighting.

Intensifying civil war through 1976 led to the ousting of President Suleiman Franjieh by Parliament in May after the virtual destruction of Beirut. Franjieh refused to step down until the end of his six-year term in October when his successor, Elias Sarkis, took office.

At the time of Sarkis' inauguration, Lebanon was divided into three sections: a northern region occupied by Syrians, a central area held by Christians and a southern enclave held by the Palestine Liberation Organization and leftist Moslems. After 40,000 dead in 18 months of war, it was feared that the partition would become permanent. The Arab world was as divided as Lebanon over the matter, the majority supporting the Syrians and Christians, with Libya and Egypt backing the P.L.O.

Economic Conditions. Lebanon produces tobacco, olives, grapes and other fruits, wheat and silk. Manufacturing is confined mainly to local consumers' goods. The silk industry is important in Beirut and Tripoli. Tobacco manufacturing is a government monopoly.

Chief exports in 1973 were machinery (14%), fruit and vegetables (12%), chemicals (8%), aircraft (6%), clothing (6%), textile yarns and fabrics (6%) and motor vehicles (5%). Leading customers were Saudi Arabia (15%), France (9%), United Kingdom (8%), Libya (7%), Kuwait (6%), Syria (5%). Leading suppliers were U.S. (12%), West Germany (11%), France (10%), Italy (10%), U.K. (8%).

LESOTHO (Constitutional monarchy)

(Member of Commonwealth of Nations)

Sovereign: King Moshoeshoe II (1966).
Prime Minister: Chief Leabua Jonathan (1966).
Area: 11,720 sq mi. (30,355 sq km).
Population (est. 1976): 1,065,000.
Density per square mile: 90.9.
Capital and largest city (est. 1972): Maseru, 18,800.
Monetary unit: South African rand.
Languages: English and Sesotho (both official).
Religions: Roman Catholic (38.7%), Lesotho Evangelical Church (24.3%), Anglican (10.4%), non-Christian (18.2%).

There is a 93-member interim National Assembly made up of 60 representatives of various political parties, 22 leading chiefs and 11 appointees.

Major Political Parties. Basotho National Party, led by Prime Minister Jonathan; Basutoland Congress Party led by G. P. Ramoreboli.

History. Lesotho (formerly Basutoland) is a mountainous enclave surrounded by the Republic of South Africa and bounded by the Orange Free State, Cape Province and Natal. Basutoland was constituted a native state under British protection by a treaty signed with the native chief Moshesh in 1843. It was annexed to Cape Colony in 1871, but in 1884 it was restored to direct control by the crown.

The colony of Basutoland became the independent nation of Lesotho on Oct. 4, 1966.

In the January 1970, elections, Mokhehle claimed a victory, but Jonathan declared a state of emergency, suspended the Constitution, and arrested Mokhehle. The major issue in the election was relations with South Africa, with Jonathan for close ties to the surrounding white nation, while Mokhehle was for more independent policy. Jonathan jailed 45 opposition politicians, declared the King had "technically abdicated" by siding with the opposition party, exiled him to the Netherlands in April, and named his Queen and her seven-year-old son as regent.

The King returned after a compromise with Jonathan in which the new Constitution would name him head of state but forbid his participation in politics.

Economic Conditions. Agricultural products include corn, wheat, and sorghum. Sheep raising is highly developed.

Chief exports in 1973 were wool (36%), cattle (18%), mohair (17%) and sheep (5%). Leading customer and supplier is South Africa.

LIBERIA (Republic)

President: William R. Tolbert (1971).
Area: 43,000 sq mi. (111,369 sq km).
Population (est. 1976): 1,750,000.
Density per square mile: 40.7.
Capital and largest city (est. 1974): Monrovia, 180,000.
Monetary unit: Liberian dollar.
Languages: English (official), native tongues.
Religions: Protestant Christian (official); Moslem, Catholic, tribal religions.

The government is republican in form and closely resembles that of the United States. The President and the Vice President are popularly elected for one eight-year term. The members of the House of Representatives are elected for four years and the members of the Senate for six years.

Political Party. True Whig Party.

History. Liberia was founded in 1822 as a result of the efforts of the American Colonization Society to settle freed American slaves in West Africa. In 1847, it became the Free and Independent Republic of Liberia.

The government of Africa's first republic was modeled after that of the United States, and Joseph J. Roberts of Virginia was elected the first President. He laid the foundations of a modern state and initiated efforts, never too successful but pursued for more than a century, to bring the aboriginal inhabitants of the territory to the level of the emigrants. The English-speaking descendants of U.S. blacks, known as Americo-Liberians, are the intellectual and ruling class. The indigenous inhabitants, divided, constitute 99% of the population. The Americo-Liberians amount to only 0.8% of the population. The country's only big enterprises are the million-acre concession granted in 1925 to the Firestone Plantations Co. for rubber cultivation, and a large iron ore concession developed by Republic Steel Corp., beginning in 1951. After 1920, considerable progress was made toward opening up the interior, a process which was spurred in 1951 by the establishment of a 43-mile railroad to the Bomi Hills from Monrovia.

In July 1971, while serving his sixth term as President of Africa's oldest independent republic, William V. S. Tubman died following surgery and was succeeded by his long-time associate, Vice President Tolbert.

Economic Conditions. Agricultural products include rice, cassava, rubber, cocoa and coffee.

Chief exports in 1974 were iron ore (65%), rubber (16%) and diamonds (7%). Leading customers in 1973 were U.S. (20%), Belgium-Luxembourg (18%), West Germany (17%), Netherlands (13%), Italy (12%), France (6%), Japan (5%). Leading suppliers were U.S. (28%), West Germany (12%), U.K. (10%), Japan (6%), Sweden (5%).

LIBYA (Arab Republic of)

(Aljumhuria Al-Arabia Allibya)

Chairman of the Revolutionary Council and President: Col. Muammar el-Qaddafi (1969).
Premier: Maj. Abdul Salam Jallud (1972).
Area: 679,362 sq mi. (1,759,540 sq km).
Population (est. 1976): 2,530,000.
Density per square mile: 3.7.
Capital: Tripoli.
Largest cities (1973 census): Tripoli, 551,477; Bengasi, 282,192.
Monetary unit: Libyan dinar.
Languages: Arabic.
Religion: Moslem.

In a bloodless coup d'état on Sept. 1, 1969, the

military seized power in Libya. King Idris I, who had ruled the country since 1951, was deposed, and Libya was proclaimed a republic with the new name of Libyan Arab Republic.

Since the coup, power has been in the hands of a Revolutionary Council.

Political Party. The Arab Socialist Union Organization is the only political party.

History. Libya, stretching along the northern coast of Africa between Tunisia and Egypt, was a part of the Turkish dominions from the 16th century until 1911. Following the outbreak of hostilities between Italy and Turkey in that year, Italian troops occupied Tripoli; Italian sovereignty was recognized in 1912.

Libya was the scene of much desert fighting during World War II. After the fall of Tripoli on Jan. 23, 1943, it came under Allied administration. The United Nations General Assembly voted on Nov. 21, 1949, that Libya should become independent by 1952.

Following the adoption by the constituent assembly of a Constitution, the independence of the country was proclaimed by King Idris I on Dec. 24, 1951.

Discovery of oil in the Libyan Desert promised financial stability and funds for economic development. Although maintaining cordial relations with the United States, the government asked for evacuation of the U.S. Wheelus air base by 1971. The first crude oil moved in January 1967 through the 320-mile pipeline from the Sarir oil field to Tobruk, where it was loaded on British tankers. The flow was halted in June 1967, when Libya joined the Arab oil boycott of Britain and the United States as a result of the Middle Eastern war but was soon resumed thereafter.

Libya provided about $158 million a year, from its reported $1.3-billion annual oil revenues, for the anti-Israel forces. The new regime ordered 110 Mirage jets from France (which in 1973 were using Egyptian as well as Libyan airfields) and received its first arms shipments from Russia in July 1970, including over 100 tanks and armored troop carriers. It also expelled in July all Italians (tens of thousands) and Jews (a few hundred) and expropriated their property.

Qadaffi bitterly attacked Egypt's conduct of the 1973 war with Israel, and Egypt accused Qadaffi, a very volatile person, of financing an attempted coup against President Anwar el-Sadat in 1974. Qadaffi, in April, 1974, gave up his domestic political powers to Premier Abdul Salam Jallud, but remained Libya's leader in foreign affairs.

Qadaffi and Sadat met in August 1974 to resolve their differences but matters worsened. In May 1976, Egypt accused Libyan agents of planting bombs in Alexandria and elsewhere, and Qadaffi described relations with his neighbor as "tenuous."

A more serious rift developed between Libya and Sudan, stemming from an attempted coup against Sudanese President Gaafar el-Nimeiri July 2-3. Libya was accused by Nimeiri before a summit meeting of the Organization of African Unity and before the United Nations Security Council of having instigated the plot, but Libyan officials denied responsibility.

Libya's relations with the Soviet Union, meanwhile, improved steadily. In May, 1975, following a visit by Soviet Premier Alexei N. Kosygin, a major deal for Soviet arms sales to Libya, reported to involve $1 billion to $4 billion in modern military equipment, was concluded. It was followed by a Soviet agreement to supply Libya with a nuclear research reactor in the 2–10 megawatt range.

Economic Conditions. Animal husbandry, which was the basic economic activity of Libya, has been superseded by petroleum and natural gas.

Agriculture is possible only in the Mediterranean coastal region, where dates, olives, citrus fruit, wheat and barley are grown, and in oases in the Fezzan and elsewhere; here the principal product is dates.

Sponge and tuna fisheries are carried on off the Libyan coast.

Chief export in 1974 was crude oil (99.6%). Leading customers in 1973 were Italy (28%), West Germany (21%), United Kingdom (12%), U.S. (8%), France (5%). Leading suppliers in 1973 were Italy (26%), West Germany (10%), France (8%), U.K. (7%), Japan (6%), U.S. (5%).

LIECHTENSTEIN (Principality)

Ruler: Prince Franz Josef II (1938).
Prime Minister: Walter Keiber (1974).
Area: 61 sq mi. (157 sq km).
Population (est. 1976): 22,850.
Density per square mile: 374.6.
Capital and largest city (est. 1974): Vaduz, 4,400.
Monetary unit: Swiss franc.
Language: German (Alemannish dialect).
Religion: Roman Catholic.

The Constitution of 1921, amended in 1972, provides for a legislature, the Landtag, of 15 members elected by direct suffrage. All males over 21 may vote.

The ruler, Prince Franz Josef II, was born in 1906, and succeeded his great uncle, Franz I, in 1938. In 1943 he married Countess Gina Wilczek of Austria.

Major Political Parties. Progressive Citizens 'Party (8 of 15 seats in the Landtag) and Homeland Union (7 seats).

History. Tiny Liechtenstein lies on the east bank of the Rhine, just south of Lake Constance, between Austria and Switzerland. It abolished its army in 1868 and has managed to stay neutral and undamaged in all European wars since that date.

Founded in 1719, Liechtenstein became independent in 1866.

A member of the German Confederation from 1815 to 1866, it managed to remain free of ties through World War I. Since then it has been oriented toward Switzerland.

Economic Conditions. Liechtenstein adopted Swiss currency in 1921 and has been part of the Swiss Customs Union since 1924. Switzerland administers Liechtenstein's telegraph and postal service and its foreign affairs.

Wheat, wine and fruit are the chief agricultural products. There are small manufactures of cotton products, leather and pottery. The chief mineral is marble.

Chief exports in 1972 were metal manufactures, furniture and pottery. Leading customers were Switzerland (44%) and EEC (26%).

Natural Features. Liechtenstein's area includes low valley land and upland peaks—Falknis (8,401 ft) and Naafkopf (8,432 ft).

LITHUANIA

Area: 25,174 sq mi. (64,445 sq km).
Population (est. 1975): 3,290,000 (1970: Lithuanian, 80.1%; Russian, 8.6%; Poles, 7.7%; others, 3.6%).
Density per square mile: 130.7.
Capital: Vilnius.
Largest cities (est. 1975): Vilnius, 433,200; Kaunas, 344,400.
Language: Lithuanian.

History. Southernmost of the three Baltic states, Lithuania in the Middle Ages was a grand duchy joined to Poland through royal marriage. Poles and Lithuanians merged forces to defeat the Teutonic knights of Germany at Tannenberg in 1410 and extended their power far into Russian territory. In 1795, however, following the third partition of Poland, Lithuania fell into Russian hands and did not gain its independence until 1918, toward the end of the first World War.

The republic was occupied by the Soviet Union in 1939 and annexed outright the following year. From 1940 to 1944 it was occupied by German troops and then was retaken by Russia. Western countries, including the United States, have not recognized the Russian annexation of Lithuania.

LUXEMBOURG (Grand Duchy)

(Grand-Duché de Luxembourg)

Ruler: Grand Duke Jean (1964).
Premier: Gaston Thorn (1974).
Area: 999 sq mi. (2,586 sq km).
Population (est. 1976): 370,000 (Luxembourgian, French, German).
Density per square mile: 373.7.
Capital and largest city (est. 1975): Luxembourg, 78,300.
Monetary unit: Luxembourg franc.
Languages: Luxembourgian, French, German.
Religion: Mainly Roman Catholic.

Luxembourg's unicameral legislature, the Chamber of Deputies, consists of 59 members elected for five years.

Major Political Parties. Christian Social Party (18 of 59 seats in Chamber of Deputies), led by Pierre Werner; Socialist-Labor (17 seats), led by A. Wehenkel; Democratic Party (14 seats), led by Gaston Thorn; Social Democratic Party (5 seats), led by Henry Cravatte; Communist Party (5 seats), led by D. Urbany.

History. Sigefroi, Count of Ardennes, an offspring of Charlemagne, was Luxembourg's first sovereign ruler. In 1060, the country came under the rule of the House of Luxembourg. From the 15th to the 18th centuries, Spain, France, and Austria held it in turn. The Congress of Vienna in 1815 made it a Grand Duchy and gave it to William I, King of the Netherlands. In 1839 the Treaty of London ceded the western part of Luxembourg to Belgium.

The eastern part, continuing in personal union with the Netherlands and a member of the German Confederation, became autonomous in 1848 and a neutral territory by decision of the London Conference of 1867, governed by its grand duke. Germany occupied the duchy in World Wars I and II. Allied troops liberated the enclave in 1944.

In 1961, Prince Jean, son and heir of Grand Duchess Charlotte, was made head of the state, acting for his mother. She abdicated in 1964, and Prince Jean became Grand Duke.

Economic Conditions. As the soil is not very fertile, agriculture is not prosperous. Principal crops are potatoes, oats, wheat, rye and grapes.

The mining and metallurgical industries, based on iron ore found in the south, are the most important.

By a customs union between Belgium and Luxembourg, which came into force on May 1, 1922, to last for 50 years, customs frontiers between the two countries were abolished. On Jan. 1, 1948, an economic union with Belgium and the Netherlands (Benelux) came into existence. Luxembourg's foreign-trade figures are included in those of Belgium, and no separate statistics are available. Exports consist chiefly of iron and steel products.

Luxembourg's prosperity depends largely on its steel mills.

MADAGASCAR (Democratic Republic of Madagascar)

(Repoblika Demokratika Malagasy)

President and Head of State: Lt. Comdr. Didier Ratsiraka (1975).
Prime Minister: Justin Rakotoniaina (1976).
Area: 226,658 sq mi. (587,041 sq km).
Population (est. 1975): 8,020,000.
Density per square mile: 35.4.
Capital and largest city (est. 1972): Tananarive, 336,530.
Monetary unit: Malagasy franc.
Ethnic groups: Merina (or Hova), Betsimisaraka, Betsileo, Tsimihety, Antaisaka, Sakalava, Antandroy.
Languages: Malagasy, French.
Religions: Christian (50%) and Animist.

The legislature has two houses—a Senate with 18 appointed members and 36 elected, and a lower chamber with 107 members, all elected. Both houses were closed in 1972 by General Ramanantsoa.

The assassination of President Richard Ratsimandrava in 1975 led to the take-over of the government by a 19-member military directorate, which ruled by modified martial law and suspended political party activities. Lt. Comdr. Didier Ratsiraka, a former Foreign Minister, was named President.

History. On the fourth largest island in the world, the Democratic Republic of Madagascar (Malagasy

Republic) is an independent state. The present population is of black and Malay stock, with perhaps some Polynesian, called Malagasy. The French took over a protectorate in 1885, and then in 1894–95 ended the monarchy, exiling Queen. Rànavàlona III to Algiers. A colonial administration was set up to which the Comoro Islands were attached in 1908, and other territories later. In World War II, the British occupied Madagascar, which adhered to Vichy France.

An autonomous republic within the French Community since October 1958, Madagascar became an independent member of the Community on June 25, 1960. In May 1973, an army coup led by Maj. Gen. Gabriel Ramanantsoa ousted Philibert Tsiranana, who had been President since 1959, and promised economic and social reforms, including help for the poor. A cabinet of four army officers and six civilians ruled. A referendum under police-state conditions approved military rule for the next five years.

With unemployment and inflation both high, Ramanantsoa resigned Feb. 5, 1975, five weeks after an abortive military coup. His leftist-leaning successor, Interior Minister Richard Ratsimandrava, an Army lieutenant colonel, was killed Feb. 11 by a machine-gun ambush in Tananarive, the capital. Control passed to a military directorate headed by Gen. Gilles Andriamahazo, which imposed martial law and press.censorship.

On June 15, 1975, Lt. Comdr. Didier Ratsiraka was named President and lifted the martial law in effect since February. Ratsiraka announced that he would follow a socialist course and, after nationalizing banks and insurance companies, declared all mineral resources nationalized. Following approval of his continued rule by a national referendum, Ratsiraka was sworn in Jan. 4, 1976 as President of the second Malagasy Republic.

Economic Conditions. Leading agricultural products are rice, cassava, corn, peanuts, sugar cane, coffee, sisal, vanilla, rubber and tobacco. Livestock include sheep, cattle, goats, pigs and poultry.

Chief exports in 1973 were coffee (30%), cloves (9%) and vanilla (5%). Leading customers were France (37%), U.S. (17%), Réunion (9%), Japan (6%), Malaysia (6%). Leading suppliers were France (49%), West Germany (8%), U.S. (7%), Japan (5%).

MALAWI (Republic)

(Member of Commonwealth of Nations)

Life President: H. Kamuzu Banda (1966).
Area: 45,747 sq mi. (118,484 sq km).
Population (est. 1976): 5,160,000.
Density per square mile: 112.8.
Capital (est. 1974): Lilongwe, 86,900.
Largest city (est. 1972): Blantyre, 160,100.
Monetary unit: Kwacha.
Languages: English (official), Chichewa.
Religion: Animist.

Under a new Constitution, which came into effect on July 6, 1966, the President is the sole head of state; there is neither a Prime Minister nor a Vice President. The National Assembly has 87 members.

Political Party. Under the 1966 Constitution, there is only one national party—the Malawi Congress Party (all 87 seats in the National Assembly), led by President H. Kamuzu Banda.

History. Formerly a British protectorate called Nyasaland in East Africa, Malawi is a republic within the Commonwealth of Nations. The first European to make extensive explorations in the area was David Livingstone in the 1850's and 1860's. In 1884, Cecil Rhodes's British South African Company received a charter to develop the country. The company came into conflict with the Arab slavers in 1887–89 and after Britain annexed the territory in 1891, making it a protectorate in 1892, Sir Harry Johnstone, the first high commissioner, using Royal Navy gunboats, wiped out the slavers.

Nyasaland became the independent nation of Malawi on July 6, 1964. Two years later, on July 6, 1966, it became a republic within the Commonwealth of Nations.

Dr. Hastings K. Banda, its first Prime Minister, became its first President. He pledged to follow a policy of "discretionary nonalignment." Britain and other Western governments gave economic and financial assistance to the new republic. Banda alienated much of Black Africa by maintaining good relations with such white-ruled nations as South Africa and Rhodesia. He argued that his landlocked country had to rely on white-ruled countries for access to the sea and trade.

Economic Conditions. Malawi's principal export is labor—men who work in the copper mines in Zambia (Northern Rhodesia). The country is usually self-supporting in agricultural products, except for sugar and wheat flour.

Chief exports in 1974 were tobacco (39%), tea (17%) and peanuts (5%). Leading customers were United Kingdom (31%), U.S. (9%), Rhodesia (7%), Netherlands (7%). Leading suppliers were South Africa (23%), U.K. (23%), Rhodesia (13%), Japan (5%), West Germany (5%).

MALAYSIA

(Member of Commonwealth of Nations)

Paramount Ruler: Yahya Petra, Sultan of Kelantan (1975).
Prime Minister: Hussein bin Onn (1976).
Area: 127,316 sq mi. (329,749 sq km).
Population (est. 1975 by U.N.): 11,900,000.
Density per square mile: 93.5.
Capital: Kuala Lumpur.
Largest cities (1970 census): Kuala Lumpur, 451,728; George Town, 270,019; Ipoh, 247,689.
Monetary unit: Ringgit (Malaysian dollar).
Languages: Malay (official), Chinese, Tamil, English.
Religions: Moslem, Christian, Buddhist, Hindu.

Malaysia is a sovereign constitutional monarchy within the Commonwealth of Nations, recognizing the Queen as head of the Commonwealth. The Paramount Ruler is elected by the hereditary rulers of the states from among themselves, for a five-year term. He is advised by the Prime Minister and his Cabinet. There is a bicameral legislature. The Federal Senate, whose role is comparable more to that of the British House of Lords than to the U.S. Senate, has 58 members, partly appointed by the Paramount Ruler to represent minority and special interests, and partly elected by the legislative assemblies of the various states.

The House of Representatives, or lower house, is made up of 154 members who are elected for five-year terms.

Major Political Parties. The Alliance Party, a coalition of former Prime Minister Tunku Abdul Rahman's United Malay National Organization, the Malaysian Indian Congress and the Malaysian Chinese Association. Six additional parties are also part of the 120-seat National Front Coalition. Opposition parties include Democratic Action Party, Social Justice Party and People's Socialist Party of Malaya. The Sarawak National Party joined the government coalition in March 1976.

History. Malaysia came into existence on Sept. 16, 1963, as a federation of Malaya, Singapore, Sabah (North Borneo), and Sarawak. On Aug. 9, 1965, Singapore withdrew from the federation. Since 1966, the 11 states of former Malaya have been known as West Malaysia, and Sabah and Sarawak have been known as East Malaysia.

The Union of Malaya was established Apr. 1, 1946, being formed from the Federated Malay States of Negri Sembilan, Pahang, Perak, and Selangor; the Unfederated Malay States of Johore, Kedah, Kelantan, Perlis and Trengganu; and two of the Straits Settlements—Malacca and Penang. The Malay states had been brought under British administration during the late 19th and early 20th centuries.

The Union became the Federation of Malaya on Feb. 1, 1948, and the Federation attained full independence within the Commonwealth of Nations on Aug. 31, 1957.

Sabah (formerly North Borneo), constituting the extreme northern portion of the island of Borneo, was a British protectorate administered under charter by the British North Borneo Company from 1881 to July 15, 1946, when it assumed the status of a colony. It was occupied by Japanese troops from 1942 to 1945.

Sarawak extends along the northwestern coast of Borneo for about 500 miles. In 1841, part of the present territory was granted by the Sultan of Brunei to Sir James Brooke. Sarawak continued to be ruled by members of the Brooke family until the Japanese occupation.

From 1963, when Malaysia became independent, it was the target of guerrilla infiltration from Indonesia, but beat off invasion attempts. In 1966, when Sukarno fell and the Communist Party was liquidated in Indonesia, hostilities ended.

In the late 1960's, the country was torn by communal rioting directed against Chinese and Indians, who controlled a disproportionate share of the country's wealth. Beginning in 1968, the government moved to achieve greater economic balance through a rural development program.

In September 1970, Prime Minister Tunku Abdul Rahman stepped down in favor of his deputy, Tun Abdul Razak, whose ruling National Front Coalition was returned to power by the August, 1974, elections. The Coalition won 135 of 154 seats in the House of Representatives.

Prime Minister Abdul Razak died Jan. 14, 1976. He was replaced by Datuk Hussein bin Onn, who had served as Deputy Premier for two years.

Economic Conditions. Agricultural products include timber, rubber, palm oil, copra, rice, tea and bananas.

Malaysia is the largest tin producer in the world, and it also produces iron ore, bauxite, crude oil and gold.

Chief exports in 1974 were rubber (28%), timber (15%), tin (15%), palm oil (11%) and crude oil (7%). Leading customers were Singapore (22%), Japan (17%), U.S. (14%), United Kingdom (7%), Netherlands (5%). Leading suppliers were Japan (22%), U.S. (10%), U.K. (9%), Singapore (8%), Australia (7%), West Germany (6%), China (5%).

MALDIVES (Republic)

President: Ibrahim Nasir (1972).
Prime Minister: Ahmed Zaki (1973).
Area: 115 sq mi. (298 sq km).
Population (est. 1976): 125,000.
Density per square mile: 1,087.0.
Capital and largest city (est. 1974): Malé, 16,250.
Monetary unit: Maldivian rupee.
Languages: Sinhalese, Arabic.
Religion: Moslem.

The 8-member Cabinet is headed by the President of the republic. The Majlis (People's Council) is a unicameral legislature consisting of 54 members. Eight of these are appointed by the President. The other 46 are elected for five-year terms—8 from the capital island of Malé and 2 from each of the 19 administrative atolls.

Political Parties. There are no political parties.

History. A republic on a group of atolls in the Indian Ocean, southwest of Ceylon, Maldives (formerly called the Maldive Islands) is inhabited by a Moslem seafaring people.

Originally the islands were under the suzerainty of Ceylon. They came under British protection in 1887 and were a dependency of the then colony of Ceylon until 1948.

The independence agreement with Britain was signed July 26, 1965.

For centuries a sultanate, the islands adopted a republican form of government in 1952, but the sultanate was restored in 1954. On Nov. 11, 1968, however, as the result of a March referendum, a republic was again established in the islands.

Economic Conditions. The people are great traders and fishermen. Besides fishing, coir making is the chief local industry. Exports include fish, fish meal, coir yarn, and copra.

Chief exports in 1973 (in metric tons) were fish (7,760), shells (65) and copra (20). Leading customers were mainly Sri Lanka and Japan.

MALI (Republic)

(République du Mali)

Chief of State and Head of Government: Col. Moussa Traoré (1968).
Area: 478,766 sq mi. (1,240,000 sq km).
Population (est. 1976): 5,840,000.
Density per square mile: 12.2.

Capital and largest city (est. 1972 for urban agglomeration): Bamako, 196,800.
Monetary unit: Mali franc.
Ethnic groups: Bambara, Peuls, Markas, Songhais, Malinkes, Touareg and others.
Languages: French (official), African languages.
Religions: Moslem, 65%; Animist, 30%; Christian and others, 5%.

The army overthrew the government on Nov. 19, 1968, and formed a provisional government. The Military Committee of National Liberation (CMLN) consists of 14 members and forms the decision-making body.

In late 1969 an attempted coup was foiled, and Lieut. Moussa Traoré, president of the Military Committee of National Liberation, assumed the powers of chief of state and head of government, ousting Capt. Yoro Diakité as Premier.

History. Subjugated by France by the end of the 19th century, this area became a colony in 1904 (named French Sudan in 1920) and in 1946 became part of the French Union. On June 20, 1960, it became independent and, under the name of Sudanese Republic, was federated with the Republic of Senegal in the Mali Federation. However, Senegal seceded from the Federation on Aug. 20, 1960, and the Sudanese Republic then changed its name to the Republic of Mali on Sept. 22.

In the 1960's, Mali concentrated on economic development, continuing to accept aid from both Soviet bloc and Western nations, as well as international agencies. In the late 1960's, it began retreating from close ties with Communist China. But a purge of conservative opponents brought greater power to President Modibo Keita, and in 1968 the influence of the Communist Chinese and their Malian sympathizers increased. By a treaty signed in Peking in May 1968, China agreed to help build a railroad from Mali to Guinea, providing Mali with vital access to the sea.

The Chinese are also building a number of factories in Mali, and it is hoped that this will raise the level of living from subsistence.

Mali, with Mauritania, Ivory Coast, Senegal, Dahomey, Niger and Upper Volta signed a treaty establishing the Economic Community for West Africa to promote economic development among the seven nations. It came into force on Jan. 1, 1973.

A six-year sub-Sahara drought devastated Mali before disastrously heavy rains began in August, 1974. Emergency shipments from a dozen nations and international organizations helped alleviate a famine that affected 1.8 million Malians and killed thousands.

A new Constitution authorizing the CMLN to run Mali's government for five more years was ratified June 2, 1974, by 99% of the voters.

In December, 1974, a four-nation commission was named to seek a settlement of a 13-year dispute between Mali and Upper Volta over a 100-mile strip of mineral-rich border land. After some skirmishing, the two states agreed in February, 1975, to disengage troops in the border area.

Economic Conditions. Mali's agricultural products include rice, cotton and peanuts. Only about one fifth of the land is suitable for cultivation. The raising of livestock is an important industry.

Chief exports in 1973–74 were cotton (36%) and peanuts (10%). Leading customers in 1973 were France (c. 34%), Ivory Coast (c. 28%), Upper Volta (c. 8%), Japan (c. 6%), West Germany (c. 5%), United Kingdom (c. 5%). Leading suppliers were France (c. 57%), Ivory Coast (c. 15%), U.S. (c. 7%), West Germany (c. 6%), Belgium-Luxembourg (c. 5%).

MALTA (Republic of)

(Member of Commonwealth of Nations)

President: Sir Anthony Mamo (1974).
Prime Minister: Dom Mintoff (1971).
Area: 122 sq mi. (316 sq km).
Population (est. 1976): 333,000.
Density per square mile: 2,729.5.
Capital (est. 1974): Valetta, 14,000.
Largest city (est. 1973): Sliema, 20,120.
Monetary unit: Maltese pound.
Languages: Maltese, English.
Religion: Roman Catholic.

The government is headed by a Prime Minister, responsible to a 65-member House of Representatives elected by universal suffrage.

Major Political Parties. Malta Labor Party (34 of 65 seats in House of Representatives), led by Prime Minister Dom Mintoff; Nationalist Party (31 seats), led by Giorgio Borg Oliver.

History. An independent state within the Commonwealth of Nations, occupying the Maltese islands in the Mediterranean, the strategic importance of Malta was recognized by the Phoenicians, who occupied it, as did in their turn the Greeks, Carthaginians, and Romans. The apostle Paul was shipwrecked there in A.D. 58.

The Knights of St. John (Malta), who obtained the Maltese islands of Malta, Gozo, and Comino from Charles V in 1530, reached their highest fame when they withstood an attack by superior Turkish forces in 1565.

Napoleon seized Malta in 1798, but the French forces were ousted by British troops in 1799, and British rule was confirmed by the Treaty of Paris in 1814.

Malta was heavily attacked by German and Italian aircraft during World War II but was never invaded by the Axis.

Malta became an independent nation on Sept. 21, 1964.

By vote of its parliament, Malta became a republic Dec. 13, 1974, but retained its formal ties with the British Commonwealth. Governor-General Mamo was sworn in as first President and Mintoff remained Prime Minister. The new government proposed to Parliament a seven-year plan to end economic dependence on foreign military bases by 1980. It called for a $568-million investment program to create 20,000 new jobs. Britain announced its intention to withdraw from Malta in 1979, thus ending its annual subsidy of $33 million for use of the island's port facilities.

Mintoff was narrowly elected to a second five-year term in the September 1976 elections. His Labor party increased its margin over the Nationalists in the House of Representatives from one to three seats.

Economic Conditions. Much of Malta's economy has depended on expenditures at the large British naval installations, but with the gradual withdrawal of some of the military forces, Britain agreed to provide economic assistance valued at $140 million during the first 10 years of independence. Some local industrialization has been started. The principal agricultural products are potatoes, cereals, onions and fruit.

There are also some livestock raising and a fishing industry.

Chief exports in 1974 were clothing (38%), petroleum products (11%), Textile yarns and fabrics (10%), machinery (7%), rubber products (6%) and food (6%). Leading customers were United Kingdom (28%), West Germany (10%), Belgium-Luxembourg (9%), Italy (7%), Sweden (6%), Libya (5%). Leading suppliers were U.K. (25%), Italy (17%), West Germany (8%), Netherlands (6%) U.S. (6%), France (5%).

MAURITANIA (Islamic Republic of)

(République Islamique de Mauritanie)

President: Moktar Ould Daddah (1960).
Area: 397,955 sq mi. (1,030,700 sq km).
Population (est. 1976): 1,350,000.
Density per square mile: 3.4.
Capital and largest city (est. 1975): Nouakchott, 70,000.
Monetary unit: Ouguyia.
Ethnic groups: Moors; a black minority (Toucouleurs, Soninkes and Wolofs).
Languages: Arabic, French.
Religion: Moslem.

The President is elected by direct vote for a term of five years. The 50-member Assembly is also elected for a five-year term.

Political Party. Parti du Peuple Mauritanien, led by President Daddah.

History. Mauritania, in Northwest Africa, was first explored by the Portuguese. The French organized the area as a territory in 1904.

Mauritania became an independent nation on Nov. 28, 1960, and was admitted to the United Nations in 1961 over the strenuous opposition of Morocco, which claims the territory. With Moors, Arabs, Berbers and Blacks frequently in conflict, the government in the late 1960s sought to make Arab culture dominant to unify the land. Iron ore was discovered at Feyreck in the north, and commercial exploitation was begun in 1968.

Sizable deposits of copper also have been found and an Atlantic fishing industry is being developed. But the dispersed, largely nomadic population is a handicap to modernization.

On Jan. 1, 1973, Mauritania became part of a seven-nation Economic Community for West Africa, which is intended to promote economic development among members. Other members are Mali, Ivory Coast, Senegal, Dahomey, Niger and Upper Volta.

By a secret agreement reported in the French press in November 1975, Mauritania and Morocco planned to divide the territory of the former Spanish Sahara after the departure of the colonial administration. Mauritanian troops moved into the territory but encountered resistance from the Polisario Front, a Saharan independence movement backed by Algeria. Mauritania broke diplomatic relations with Algeria in March 1976, after Algerian recognition of the area as an independent state.

Economic Conditions. Livestock raising is the principal economic activity in Mauritania. Some crops are produced. Minerals include iron and copper.

Chief export in 1974 was iron ore (73%); in 1972, fish (11%) and copper concentrates (10%). Leading customers in 1972 were France (20%), United Kingdom (18%), Italy (14%), Belgium-Luxembourg (12%), Spain (11%), Japan (9%), West Germany (8%). Leading suppliers were France (41%), U.S. (11%), U.K. (7%), Senegal (7%), West Germany (5%).

MAURITIUS

(Member of Commonwealth of Nations)

Governor-General: Sir Abdool Raman Osman (1973).
Prime Minister: Sir Seewoosagur Ramgoolam (1961).
Area: 790 sq mi. (2,045 sq km).
Population (est. 1976): 875,000 (Indian, 50%; Creole, 31%; Pakistani, 16%).
Density per square mile: 1,107.6.
Capital and largest city (est. 1973): Port Louis, 136,600.
Monetary unit: Mauritius rupee.
Languages: English (official), French, Creole, Indian and Chinese dialects.
Religions: Hindu, 50%; Christian (mainly Roman Catholic), 33%; Moslem, 16%.

Mauritius is a member of the British Commonwealth, with Queen Elizabeth II as Head of State. She is represented by a Governor-General, who chooses the Prime Minister from the unicameral Legislative Assembly. The Legislative Assembly has 70 members, 62 of whom are elected by direct suffrage. The remaining 8 are chosen from the best unsuccessful candidates.

Major Political Parties. The Labour Party, Social Democratic Party and Comité d'Action Musulman form the governing coalition. Opposition parties are the Independent Forward Bloc, l'Union Democratique Mauricienne and Mouvement Militant Mauricien.

History. Mauritius, a mountainous island in the Indian Ocean east of Madagascar, was seized from France by British troops in 1810 and ceded to Britain by the Treaty of Paris in 1814. Until 1903, Mauritius and the Seychelles were administered as a single colony. The colony of Mauritius became an independent nation on Mar. 12, 1968.

The nation has an Indian majority, descendants of laborers imported from India to work the sugar plantations after the abolition of slavery in 1834. The native blacks speak French and are Roman Catholics.

Over-population and unemployment continue to be major problems.

Economic Conditions. Agricultural products include

cane sugar, tea and tobacco; and industrial products include alcohol and molasses.

Chief export in 1974 was sugar (89%). Leading customers were Canada (36%), United Kingdom (35%), U.S. (8%). Leading suppliers were U.K. (14%), South Africa (9%), Taiwan (8%), Iran (8%), France (8%), West Germany (6%), Japan (6%), U.S. (5%), Australia (5%).

MEXICO (Republic)

(Estados Unidos Mexicanos)

President: José López Portillo (1976).
Area: 761,600 sq mi. (1,972,547 sq km).
Population (est. 1976): 63,150,000 (55% mestizo; 29% Indian).
Density per square mile: 82.9.
Capital: Mexico City.
Largest cities (est. 1975): Mexico City, 8,591,800; (est. 1974 by U.N.): Guadalajara, 1,478,400; Monterrey, 1,006,200.
Languages: Spanish, Indian languages.
Religion: Mainly Roman Catholic.

The President, who is popularly elected for six years and is ineligible to succeed himself, governs with a Cabinet of ministers. Congress has two houses—a 211-member Chamber of Deputies (one member for each 250,000 of population), elected for three years, and a 64-member Senate, elected for six years.

Each of the 31 states has considerable autonomy, with a popularly elected governor, a legislature, and a local judiciary. The President of Mexico appoints the governor of the Federal District.

Major Political Parties. Partido Revolucionario Institucional (197 of 198 elected seats in Chamber of Deputies), led by Porfirio Muñoz Ledo; National Action and Authentic Party (1 seat).

History. Mexico's early history is shrouded in mystery. At least two civilized races—the Mayas and later the Toltecs—preceded the wealthy Aztec empire, conquered in 1519–21 by the Spanish under Hernando Cortés. Spain ruled for the next 300 years until 1810 (the date was Sept. 16 and is now celebrated as Independence Day), when the Mexicans first revolted. They continued the struggle and finally won independence in 1821.

Turbulent years followed. From 1821 to 1877, there were two emperors, several dictators, and enough presidents and provisional executives to make a new government on the average of every nine months. Mexico lost Texas (1836), and after defeat in the war with the United States (1846–48) it lost the area comprising the present states of California, Nevada, and Utah, most of Arizona and New Mexico, and parts of Wyoming and Colorado.

In 1855, the Indian patriot Benito Juárez began a series of liberal reforms, including the disestablishment of the Catholic Church, which had acquired vast property. A subsequent civil war was interrupted by the French invasion of Mexico (1861), the crowning of Maximilian of Austria as Emperor (1864), and then his overthrow and execution by forces under Juárez, who again became President in 1867.

The years after the fall of the dictator Porfirio Diaz (1877–80 and 1884–1911) were marked by bloody political-military strife and trouble with the United States culminating in the punitive expedition into northern Mexico (1916–17) in unsuccessful pursuit of the revolutionary Pancho Villa. There was a continuous succession of various presidents and of internal strife until 1917, when a new Congress was elected and a liberal Constitution adopted. Since a brief period of civil war in 1920, Mexico has enjoyed a period of gradual agricultural, political, and social reforms. Relations with the United States were again disturbed in 1938 when all foreign oil wells were expropriated. Agreement on compensation was finally reached in 1941.

Lázaro Cardenas (1934–40), President during the oil seizures, also began a program of distributing land to the peasants and of broad labor reforms. Manuel Avila Camacho, President during World War II, followed Cardenas' policy at home but cooperated closely with the United Nations, and established cordial relations with the United States. His policy was followed by his immediate successors, Miguel Alemán, Adolfo Ruíz Cortines, and Adolfo López Mateos. López Mateos redefined Mexican foreign policy as "independent" rather than neutral or partial, a course followed by Gustavo Díaz Ordaz, who became President in 1964.

Mexico maintained ties with Cuba after the Organization of American States approved a U.S.-sponsored boycott of Fidel Castro's regime in 1962. Mexico opposed the boycott until the OAS repealed it July 29, 1975.

The PRI Presidential candidate, Luis Echeverría Alvarez, easily won the 1970 election. He took over a burgeoning economy, but there were signs of softening in late 1974 as recession struck the U.S., the market for two-thirds of Mexico's exports. A 23.3% rise in the cost-price index in 1974 bore hardest on peasants, who had shared few of the fruits of prosperity. A population growth rate of 3.5% (one of the hemisphere's highest) ate into economic gains. The government launched a birth-control information program in 1974.

Echeverría worked vigorously in Latin America and elsewhere in the underdeveloped world to promote more benefits for developing nations from the raw materials they export. In December 1974, Mexico sponsored a nonbinding resolution that passed the U.N. General Assembly 120–6 asserting the right of every nation to control its own wealth, resources and economic activities.

Mexico and Venezuela proposed formation of a Latin American economic system (SELA) to promote regional economic development, and the organization held its first meeting in Caracas in January 1976.

Economic Conditions. Primitive agricultural methods are steadily giving way to modern practices. The Yucatán peninsula, at the southern end of the Gulf of Mexico, raises more than half of the world supply of sisal hemp. Stockraising is important on nonarable land.

The leading industrial products are cotton cloth and thread, beer, sugar, iron and steel.

Important minerals are silver, gold, lead, copper, zinc, antimony, tin, coal and iron ore.

Most of the Mexican mining properties are foreign-owned, and the industry is declining in relative importance. The oilfields, lying along the east coast, were seized in 1938, but later the foreign owners were indemnified.

Mexico's forests are of considerable importance; they include pine, oak, fir, mahogany, red and white cedar, and primavera. Resins, turpentine and vegetable wax are also produced. Yucatán produces nearly all of the world's chicle, used as the base of chewing gum.

Chief exports in 1974 were nonferrous metals (13%), textile yarns and fabrics (9%), chemicals (9%), sugar (7%), cotton (6%), machinery (6%), coffee (5%), fish (4%), and petroleum and petroleum products (4%). Leading customers were U.S. (53%) and Japan (4%). Leading suppliers were U.S. (62%), West Germany (8%), Japan (4%).

Natural Features. Mexico is a great, high plateau, open to the north, with mountain chains on east and west and with ocean-front lowlands lying outside of them. It has two big spears—the peninsula of Lower California, which is mountainous, and the Yucatán peninsula, which is mostly a low plain.

MONACO (Principality)

Ruler: Prince Rainier III (1949).
Area: 0.73 square mile (465 acres).
Population (est. 1976): 25,000, of whom 4,500 are Monagesque citizens.
Density per square mile: 38,461.5.
Largest city (1968 census): Monte Carlo, 9,948.
Monetary unit: French franc.
Languages: French and Monégasque.
Religion: Roman Catholic.

Prince Albert of Monaco gave the principality a Constitution in 1911, creating a National Council of 18 members popularly elected for five years. The government is under a ministry, acting on the Prince's authority.

Prince Rainier III, born May 31, 1923, succeeded his grandfather, Louis II, on the latter's death, May 9, 1949. Rainier was married Apr. 18, 1956, to Grace Kelly, U.S. actress. A daughter, Princess Caroline Louise Marguerite, was born on Jan. 23, 1957; a son, Prince Albert Louis Pierre, on Mar. 14, 1958; and another daughter, Princess Stéphanie Marie Elisabeth, on Feb. 1, 1965.

The special significance attached to the birth of descendants to Prince Rainier stems from a clause in the Treaty of July 17, 1919, between France and Monaco stipulating that in the event of vacancy of the Crown, the Monégasque territory would become an autonomous state under a French protectorate.

Major Political Party. National and Democratic Union (all 18 seats in National Council), led by Auguste Medecin.

History. A tiny, hilly wedge driven into the French Mediterranean coast nine miles east of Nice, Monaco is a little land of pleasure with a tourist business that runs as high as 1,500,000 visitors a year. Monaco had popular gaming tables as early as 1856. Five years later, a 50-year concession to operate the games was granted to François Blanc, of Bad Homburg. This concession passed into the hand of a private company in 1898.

The Phoenicians, and after them the Greeks, had a temple on the Monacan headland honoring

Hercules. From *Monoikos*, the Greek surname for this mythological strong man, the principality took its name. After being independent for 800 years, Monaco was annexed to France in 1793 by the French Revolutionists and was placed under Sardinia's protection in 1815. In 1861, it went under French guardianship but continued to be independent.

By a treaty in 1918, France stipulated that the French government be given a veto over the succession to the throne.

Monaco's practice of providing a tax shelter for French businessmen resulted in a dispute between the countries. When Rainier refused to end the practice, France retaliated with a customs tax. In 1967, Rainier took control of the Société des Bains de Mer, operator of the famous Monte Carlo gambling casino, in a program to increase hotel and convention space, paying $8 million to Greek shipping magnate Aristotle Onassis for his shares.

MONGOLIAN PEOPLE'S REPUBLIC
(Outer Mongolia)

(Bügd Nayramdakh Mongol Ard Uls)

Chairman of Presidium of Great People's Khural (President): Yumjaagiin Tsedenbal (1973).
Chairman of Council of Ministers (Premier): Jambyn Batmunkh (1973).
Area: 604,250 sq mi. (1,565,000 sq km).
Population (est. 1976): 1,480,000 (Mongol, except for about 100,000 Russians and 50,000 Chinese).
Density per square mile: 2.4.
Capital and largest city (est. 1974): Ulan Bator, 320,000.
Monetary unit: Tugrik.
Languages: Mongolian, Russian.
Religion: Lama-Buddhist.

The Mongolian People's Republic is a socialist state in the form of a People's democracy. The highest organ of state power is the Great People's Khural (Parliament), which is elected for a term of three years and is convened once a year. The Great People's Khural elects the Presidium, which consists of a chairman, vice-chairman, secretary and six members. The Council of Ministers is set up by the Great People's Khural and consists of a chairman, vice-chairman and ministers.

Political Party. Mongolian People's Revolutionary Party, led by President Tsedenbal.

History. The Mongolian People's Republic, known as Outer Mongolia, is a Russian satellite that measures more than twice the area of Texas. It contains the original homeland of the historic Mongols, whose power reached its zenith during the 13th century under Kublai Khan. The area accepted Manchu rule in 1689, but after the Chinese Revolution of 1911 and the fall of the Manchus in 1912, the northern Mongol princes expelled the Chinese officials and declared independence under the Khutukhtu or "Living Buddha."

In 1921, Soviet troops entered the country and facilitated the establishment of a republic by Mongolian revolutionaries in 1924 after the death of the last Living Buddha. China, meanwhile, continued to claim Outer Mongolia but was unable to back the claim with any strength. Under the 1945

Chinese-Russian Treaty, China agreed to give up Outer Mongolia, which, after a plebiscite, became a nominally independent country.

The country allied itself with the Soviet Union in the dispute between the U.S.S.R. and China. It has mobilized troops along its borders since 1968 when the two powers became involved in border clashes on the Kazakh-Sinkiang frontier to the west and on the Amur and Ussuri rivers. Under a 20-year treaty of friendship and cooperation signed in 1966, it was entitled to call upon the U.S.S.R. for military aid in the event of invasion.

Economic Conditions. The country is largely pastoral. There are few areas suitable for crop growing, but some millet, rye and wheat are produced. Most of the people are essentially nomadic or seminomadic; flocks and herds remain the chief source of wealth.

Reserves of 500,000,000 tons of coal are said to exist in the Nalaikha field, located near Ulan Bator. Some gold is mined. Deposits of antimony, copper, iron ore, lead, graphite, mercury, sulfur, and silver exist.

Chief exports in 1970 were agricultural raw materials (58%), raw materials for food (20%) and foodstuffs (10%). Leading customers were U.S.S.R. (70%) and Czechoslovakia (9%). Leading suppliers were U.S.S.R. (c. 80%) and Czechoslovakia (c. 5%).

Natural Features. The productive regions of Outer Mongolia—a tableland ranging from 3,000 to 5,000 feet in elevation—are in the north, which is well drained by numerous rivers, including the Kerulen, Tola, Orkhon and Selenga.

MOROCCO (Constitutional Monarchy)

(Al-Mamlaka al-Maghrebia)

Ruler: King Hassan II (1961).
Premier: Ahmed Osman (1972).
Area: 172,414 sq mi. (446,550 sq km).
Population (est. 1976): 17,760,000.
Density per square mile: 102.1.
Capital: Rabat-Salé.
Largest cities (1971 census): Casablanca, 1,371,330; Rabat-Salé, 435,510; Marrakech, 330,400; Fez, 321,460.
Monetary unit: Dirham.
Languages: Arabic, French, Spanish.
Religions: Chiefly Moslem.

The King in 1965 suspended the 1962 Constitution, dissolved Parliament, and assumed all legislative and executive powers. In 1970 he promulgated a new Constitution but reformed it two years later after an unsuccessful coup and assassination attempt. Although it is more democratic, no elections for the new parliament were held immediately and the old legislature was dissolved. The King continued to hold power and to appoint the government and rule by decree in emergencies.

The new unicameral legislature, called the Chamber of Deputies, is to consist of 240 members, two-thirds elected by direct vote and the rest named by local political and economic entities (such as rural government councils and chambers of commerce, peasants, etc.). The proportion of elected to appointed members was essentially reversed from that in the 1970 Constitution.

Major Political Parties. Istiqlal Party; National Union of Popular Forces; and the Popular Movement.

History. Morocco, about the size of California, is just south of Spain across the Strait of Gibraltar and looks out on the Atlantic from the northwest shoulder of Africa. It was once the home of the Berbers, who helped the Arabs invade Spain in A.D. 711 and then revolted against them and gradually won control of large areas of Spain for a time after 739.

The country was ruled successively by various native dynasties and maintained regular commercial relations with Europe, even during the 17th and 18th centuries when it was the headquarters of the famous Salé pirates. In the 19th century clashes with the French and Spanish became frequent. Finally, in 1904, France and Spain divided Morocco into zones of French and Spanish influence, and these were established as protectorates in 1912.

Meanwhile, Morocco had become the object of big-power rivalry, which almost led to a European war in 1905 when Germany attempted to gain a foothold in the rich mineral country. By terms of the Algeciras Conference (1906), Morocco was internationalized economically, and France's privileges were limited.

The Tangier Statute, concluded by Britain, France, and Spain in 1923, created an international zone at the port of Tangier, permanently neutralized and demilitarized. In World War II, Spain occupied the zone, ostensibly to ensure order, but was forced to withdraw in 1945.

Sultan Mohammed V was deposed by the French in August 1953, and replaced by his uncle, but nationalist agitation forced his return in November 1955. On his death on Feb. 26, 1961, his son, Hassan, became King.

France recognized the independence and sovereignty of Morocco on Mar. 2, 1956. Spain followed on Apr. 7, 1956. The Tangier international zone was abolished by a declaration signed Oct. 29, 1956. Morocco was admitted to the United Nations on Nov. 12, 1956.

In the Middle East War of 1967, Morocco joined the Arab States in their attack on Israel. In 1968 the country embarked on a $1-billion 5-year plan designed to make it self-sufficient in agricultural products and the granary of Europe through multiplying irrigated lands six times.

On Nov. 6, 1975, tens of thousands of Moroccans crossed the border into Spanish Sahara in a "green march," the climax to years of Moroccan contention that the northern half of the territory was historically part of Morocco. Hassan was reported to have reached a secret agreement to divide the Sahara with Mauritania, which claimed the southern half.

Despite Spanish threats to resist a takeover, the march went off without incident and Spain withdrew from the territory. Algeria refused to acquiesce in the Moroccan-Mauritainian action, however, and formally recognized a Saharan republic in March 1976, leading to a break in relations among the three states. Algerian-backed guerrillas of the Polisario Front have continued to fight in the

Moroccan sector, preventing the exploitation of the region's only known resource, a rich deposit of phosphorus.

Economic Conditions. Morocco is essentially agricultural. Corn, beans, peas, hemp, wheat, barley, sorghum, citrus fruits, olives and dates are raised.

Since independence, large-scale efforts to industrialize the country have been undertaken. Manufacturing industries produce chemicals, flour, leather, beverages and textiles. Native industries include carpet weaving and making Turkish slippers.

Major minerals are phosphates, antimony, coal, cobalt, iron ore, manganese ore, molybdenum, tin, zinc and lead.

Chief exports in 1974 were phosphates (55%) and citrus fruit (5%). Leading customers in 1973 were France (34%), West Germany (10%), Italy (7%), Spain (5%), United Kingdom (5%). Leading suppliers were France (32%), U.S. (11%), West Germany (8%), Spain (5%), Italy (5%).

Casablanca has perhaps the world's largest artificial port.

Natural Features. On the Atlantic coast there is a fertile plain. The Mediterranean coast is mountainous, making most of the former Spanish zone a rugged area. The Atlas Mountains, running northeastward from the south to the Algerian frontier, average 11,000 feet in elevation.

After a brief period of cooperation with neighboring white-ruled Rhodesia, Mozambique closed its border on March 3, 1976, cutting off Rhodesia's most direct link to the sea. A series of border clashes between Rhodesian forces and guerrillas based in Mozambique continued, escalating to an air strike by Rhodesian planes on June 10 against a Mozambican army post.

Economic Conditions. Ninety per cent of the population is engaged in agriculture, with the principal crops being cotton, cashew nuts, tea, copra and sugar. Livestock production is limited because of the widespread presence of the tsé-tsé fly.

The country's mineral resources include gold, coal, graphite and mica. The forests produce large quantities of timber.

Chief exports in 1973 were cashew nuts (22%), cotton (20%), sugar (10%), minerals (6%) and vegetable oils (5%). Leading customers were Portugal (36%), U.S. (14%), South Africa (9%), United Kingdom (6%). Leading suppliers were South Africa (20%), Portugal (19%), West Germany (13%), France (8%), U.K. (8%), Japan (5%), U.S. (5%).

Natural Features. Mozambique is generally a lowlying plateau broken up by 25 sizable rivers that flow into the Indian Ocean. The largest is the Zambezi, which provides access to central Africa.

The chief ports are Maputo (Lourenço Marques) and Beira, which is also the port for Rhodesia.

MOZAMBIQUE

President: Samor Moises Machel (1975).
Premier: Joaquin Chissano (1975).
Area: 302,328 sq mi. (783,030 sq km).
Population (est. 1976): 9,450,000.
Density per square mile: 31.3.
Capital and largest city (est. 1970 by U.N.): Maputo (Lourenço Marques), 383,775.
Monetary unit: Mozambique escudo.
Languages: Bantu and Portuguese.
Religions: Animist, Christian, Moslem.

After being under Portuguese colonial rule for 470 years, Mozambique became independent on June 25, 1975. It is a Marxist state. The first President, Samora Moises Machel, is a militant Maoist and a former nurse who headed the National Front for the Liberation of Mozambique (FRELIMO) in its 10-year guerrilla war for independence.

History. Mozambique, stretching for 1,535 miles along Africa's southeast coast, was discovered by Vasco da Gama in 1498, although the Arabs had penetrated into the area as early as the 10th century. It was first colonized in 1505, and by 1510, the Portuguese were masters of all the former Arab sultanates on the east African coast.

An independence movement, FRELIMO, was organized in 1963. By the early 1970s, guerrilla activity had become so extensive that by 1973 Portugal had dispatched 40,000 troops to fight the rebels. A cease-fire was signed in September, 1974, and at the same time Portugal agreed to grant Mozambique independence.

NAURU (Republic)

President and Premier: Hammer de Roburt (1971).
Area: 8.2 sq mi. (21 sq km).
Population (est. 1974 by U.N.): 7,000.
Density per square mile: 853.7.
Capital: Yaren.
Seat of government: Domaneab.
Monetary unit: Australian dollar.
Languages: Nauruan, English.
Religions: Nauruan Protestant, Roman Catholic.

Legislative power is invested in a popularly elected 18-member Parliament, which elects the President from among its members. Executive power is invested in the President, who is assisted by a five-member Cabinet. The first Parliament was elected Jan. 26, 1968.

History. Nauru, an island 2,215 miles northeast of Sydney, Australia, was annexed by Germany in 1888. It was placed under joint Australian, New Zealand, and British mandate after World War I, and in 1947 it became a U.N. trusteeship administered by the same three powers.

On Jan. 31, 1968, Nauru became an independent republic. Later that year, on Nov. 30, it became a member of the (British) Commonwealth of Nations in a special relationship. Although the island will not be represented at meetings of Commonwealth heads, it will participate at other levels and will be eligible for Commonwealth technical aid.

The tiny republic is one of the world's chief phosphate producers. The 7,000 islanders earn $4,000 per capita in royalties from production of

1.6 million tons out of a reserve of 61.4 million tons.

Economic Conditions. Chief export in 1973 was phosphate. Leading customers were Australia (c. 67%), New Zealand (c. 22%), Japan (11%). Leading suppliers were Japan (c. 54%), Australia (c. 46%).

NEPAL (Constitutional Monarchy)

Ruler: King Birendra Bír Bikram Shah Deva (1972).
Prime Minister: Nagendra Prashad Rijal (1973).
Area: 54,362 sq mi. (140,797 sq km).
Population (est. 1976): 12,820,000 (Magar, Gurung, Bhotia, Newar).
Density per square mile: 235.8.
Capital and largest city (1971 census): Katmandu, 150,402.
Monetary unit: Nepalese rupee.
Language: Nepali (official), Newari, Bhutia.
Religions: Hindu (89.4%), Buddhist (7.5%).

A new Constitution promulgated by King Mahendra in December 1962 provided for a unicameral legislature called the National Panchayat.

Political Parties. All political parties were banned in 1960.

History. A landlocked country about the size of Iowa, lying between the Republic of India and Tibet, Nepal contains Mt. Everest, the tallest measured mountain in the world.

The Kingdom of Nepal was unified in 1768 by King Prithwi Narayan Shah. A commercial treaty was signed with Britain in 1792, and in 1816, after more than a year's hostilities, the Nepalese agreed to allow British residents to live in Katmandu, the capital. In 1923, Britain recognized the absolute independence of Nepal. Between 1846 and 1951, the country was ruled by the Rana family, which always held the office of Premier. In 1951, however, the King took over all power and proclaimed a constitutional monarchy. Nepal was admitted to the United Nations in 1955.

Mahendra Bir Bikram Shah became King in 1955. Tension developed between India and Nepal in the 1950's. Nepal and Communist China settled their differences in 1956, and thereafter Nepal accepted economic aid from the Chinese. The United States and the Soviet Union also provide aid.

After Mahendra, who had ruled since 1955, died of a heart attack in 1972, Prince Birendra, at 26, succeeded to the throne.

Economic Conditions. Cultivated and irrigated where possible, the main valley of Nepal grows rice, wheat, pulse, fruits, vegetables, spices, sugar cane and potatoes. A few sheep and cattle are grazed. Manufacturing is limited to native handicraft, but jute and textile mills are being established.

Mineral resources, nearly all unexploited, include lignite, copper, zinc, lead, sulfur, marble and iron. Southern Nepal has valuable forests which yield gum, timber, resin and dye. Hemp plants grow wild.

Chief exports in 1974 were rice (36%), jute (9%), jute products (6%) and butter (5%). Leading customers were India (c. 60%), Belgium-Luxembourg (c. 10%), Japan (c. 5%). Leading suppliers were India (c. 75%) and Japan (c. 10%).

Natural Features. Along its southern border, Nepal has a strip of level land which is partly forested, partly cultivated. North of that is the slope of the Himalayan Range, including Mt. Everest and many other peaks higher than 20,000 feet.

THE NETHERLANDS (Kingdom)

(Koninkrijk der Nederlanden)

Sovereign: Queen Juliana (1948).
Premier: Joop M. den Uyl (1973).
Area: 15,770 sq mi. (40,844 sq km).
Population (est. 1976): 13,765,000.
Density per square mile: 872.9.
Capital: Amsterdam.
Largest cities (est. 1976): Amsterdam, 751,200; Rotterdam, 614,800; The Hague, 479,400; Utrecht, 250,900.
Monetary unit: Guilder.
Language: Dutch.
Religions: Roman Catholic, 40%; Protestant, 33.7%; unaffiliated, 23.6%.

The Netherlands and its former colony of the Netherlands Antilles form the Kingdom of the Netherlands.

The Netherlands is a constitutional monarchy with a bicameral Parliament. The Upper Chamber has 75 members elected for six years by representative bodies of the provinces, half of the members retiring every three years. The Lower Chamber has 150 members elected by universal suffrage for four years. The two Chambers have the right of investigation and interpellation; the Lower Chamber can initiate legislation and amend bills.

The sovereign, Queen Juliana, born Apr. 30, 1909, was married on Jan. 7, 1937 to Prince Bernhard of Lippe-Biesterfeld (born 1911). They have four daughters: Beatrix (born 1938); Irene (born 1939); Margriet Francisca (born 1943); and Maria Christina (born 1947). Crown Princess Beatrix in 1966 married a commoner, a former West German diplomat, Claus von Amsberg, who served in the German army in World War II. In 1967, she gave birth to a son, Willem Alexander, a male heir to the throne, the first since 1884.

Major Political Parties: Premier Joop M. den Uyl leads a five-party, center-left coalition government with 97 of the 150 seats in the lower house of the States-General. The coalition consists of his Labor Party (43 seats), the Catholic People's Party (27 seats), the Anti-Revolutionary (Calvinist Protestant) Party (14 seats), the Radical Political Party (Catholic) (7 seats), and Democracy '66 (6 seats). Major opposition parties include the Liberal Party (22 seats), the Christian Historical Union (Protestant) (7 seats) and the Communist Party (7 seats).

History. Julius Caesar found the low-lying Netherlands inhabited by Germanic tribes—the Nervii, Frisii, and Batavi. The Batavi on the Roman frontier did not submit to Rome's rule until 13 B.C., and then only as allies.

A part of Charlemagne's empire in the 8th and 9th centuries A.D., the area later passed into the hands of Burgundy and the Austrian Hapsburgs, and finally in the 16th century came under Spanish rule.

When Philip II of Spain suppressed political liberties and the growing Protestant movement in the Netherlands, a revolt led by William of Orange broke out in 1568. Under the Union of Utrecht (1579), the seven northern provinces became the Republic of the United Netherlands.

The Dutch East India Company was established in 1602, and by the end of the 17th century Holland was one of the great sea and colonial powers of Europe.

The nation's independence was not completely established until after the Thirty Years' War (1618–48), after which the country's rise as a commercial and maritime power began. In 1814, all the provinces of Holland and Belgium were merged into one kingdom, but in 1830 the southern provinces broke away to form the Kingdom of Belgium. A liberal Constitution was adopted by the Netherlands in 1848.

In spite of its neutrality in World War II, the Netherlands was invaded by the Nazis in May 1940, and the East Indies were later taken by the Japanese. The nation was liberated in May 1945. In 1948, after a reign of 50 years, Queen Wilhelmina resigned and was succeeded by her daughter Juliana.

In 1949, after a four-year war, the Netherlands granted independence to the East Indies, which became the Republic of Indonesia. In 1963, it turned over the western half of New Guinea to the new nation, ending 300 years of Dutch presence in Asia. Attainment of independence by Surinam on Nov. 25, 1975, left the Dutch Antilles as the Netherlands' only overseas territory.

The Lockheed bribery scandals, which caused a major scandal in Japan, also brushed the House of Orange in 1976. Prince Bernhard, reported to have been the high official whom a Lockheed Aircraft Corporation executive said was paid more than $1 million to influence the choice of a fighter plane by the Dutch air force, was cleared of the bribe charge by a government panel. Because he was criticized for his business connections by the group, however, Bernhard resigned all his business and military posts.

Economic Conditions. Dutch farms are characteristically small, with only a few larger than 250 acres. Dairying is more important than crop growing; production of cheese, milk, butter and eggs is under state control.

An important industry is the raising of tulip, hyacinth and other flower bulbs in the area around Haarlem.

The Netherlands is a highly industrialized nation, utilizing both overseas raw materials and domestic agricultural products. Leading industries are textiles, clothing, shipbuilding, shoes, food and building materials.

Netherlands minerals are few. The only important ones are coal, crude petroleum and salt. There also are peat swamps and about 600,000 acres of forest.

Chief exports in 1974 were chemicals (17%), food (17%), petroleum products (12%), electrical machinery and equipment (7%), nonelectrical machinery (6%), textile yarns and fabrics (5%) and iron and steel (5%). Leading customer was EEC (70%; incl. West Germany 30%, Belgium-Luxembourg 13%, France 10%, United Kingdom 9%, Italy 5%). Leading suppliers were EEC (57%; incl. West Germany 26%, Belgium-Luxembourg 14%, France 7%, U.K. 5%), Iran (9%), U.S. (9%).

Natural Features. Part of the great plain of north and west Europe, the Netherlands has maximum dimensions of 190 by 160 miles, and is low and flat except in Limburg in the southeast, where some hills rise to 300 feet. About half the country's area is below sea level, making the famous Dutch dikes a requisite to the use of much land. Reclamation of land from the sea through dikes has continued through recent times.

All drainage reaches the North Sea, and the principal rivers—Rhine, Maas (Meuse) and Schelde —have their sources outside the country. The Rhine is the most heavily used waterway in Europe.

Netherlands Autonomous Country

NETHERLANDS ANTILLES

Status: Part of the Kingdom of the Netherlands.
Governor: B. M. Leito (1970).
Premier: J. M. G. Evertsz (1973).
Area: 371 sq mi. (961 sq km).
Population (est. 1976): 250,000.
Capital (est. 1970): Willemstad, 50,000.
Chief export: refined petroleum products (from crude oil imported from Venezuela).
Agricultural products: aloes, beans, corn.
Manufactures: refined petroleum, straw hats.
Mineral products: lime phosphate, salt.

The Netherlands Antilles comprise two groups of Caribbean islands 500 miles apart: one, about 40 miles off the Venezuelan coast, consists of Curaçao (173 sq mi.), Bonaire (95 sq mi.), and Aruba (69 sq mi.); the other, lying to the northeast, consists of three small islands with a total area of 34 square miles. The Dutch acquired the island of Curaçao from Spain in 1634.

There is a constitutional government formed by the Governor and Cabinet and an elected Legislative Council. The area has complete autonomy in domestic affairs.

Economic Conditions. Chief export in 1972 was petroleum products (91%). Leading customers were U.S. (64%) and Canada (5%). Leading suppliers were Venezuela (61%), U.S. (12%), Nigeria (6%), Netherlands (6%).

NEW ZEALAND (Parliamentary State)

(Member of Commonwealth of Nations)

Sovereign: Queen Elizabeth II.
Governor-General: Sir Dennis Blundell (1972).
Prime Minister: Robert D. Muldoon (1975).
Area: 103,736 sq mi. (268,676 sq km) (excluding dependencies).
Population (est. 1976): 3,150,000 (European, 89.5%; Maori and other Polynesian, 9.5%).
Density per square mile: 30.4.
Capital: Wellington.
Largest cities (est. 1975): Auckland, 796,660; Wellington, 354,660; Christchurch, 326,410.
Monetary unit: New Zealand dollar.
Language: English (official) and Maori.
Religions (1971): Church of England (31%); Presbyterian (20%); Roman Catholic (16%).

New Zealand was granted self-government in 1852, a full parliamentary system and ministries in 1856, and dominion status on Sept. 26, 1907. Meanwhile, from 1861 to 1871 there was fierce intermittent fighting with the native Maoris. The Queen is represented by a Governor-General, and the Cabinet is responsible to a unicameral Parliament of 83 European and 4 Maori members who are elected by popular vote for three years.

Major Political Parties. National Party (55 of 87 seats in House of Representatives), led by Prime Minister Robert D. Muldoon; and Labor Party (32 seats) led by Wallace E. Rowling.

History. New Zealand, about 1,250 miles east of Australia, consists of two main islands and a number of smaller outlying islands so scattered that they range from the tropical to the antarctic. The islands, which have approximately the area of Italy, were discovered and named New Zealand in 1642 by Abel Tasman, a Dutch navigator. Captain James Cook explored them in 1769. On Jan. 22, 1840, Britain formally annexed them.

From the first, the country has been in the forefront in adopting social welfare legislation. It adopted old age pensions (1898); a national child welfare program (1907); social security for the aged, widows, and orphans along with family benefit payments; minimum wages; a 40-hour week and unemployment and health insurance (1938); and socialized medicine (1941). The currency was converted to the decimal system based on the dollar in 1967.

The country supported U.S. policy in Vietnam and supplied military aid to South Vietnam. Britain's entry into the European Common Market and its large-scale pullout from the Far East caused New Zealand to orient its policies more toward its Asian neighbors and the United States, but in 1971 it signed, with Britain, Australia, Malaysia and Singapore, an agreement creating a joint defense consultative group for the region.

A Labour Party caucus picked Rowling as Prime Minister in September 1974, after Norman E. Kirk, his predecessor, died of a heart attack.

The Labour Government was ousted in elections on Nov. 29, in which Muldoon charged Rowling with permitting a rise in the rate of inflation from 6.6% to 14.8% in the preceding year. Muldoon also promised to cut immigration.

Economic Conditions. New Zealand is primarily a grazing country. The chief crops are grass, wheat, oats, barley, potatoes, onions, tobacco, fruits and vegetables.

Principal minerals are coal and gold. Other minerals of importance include tungsten, pumice, silica sand, asbestos, scheelite, iron ore and phosphate. About 30% of the total area is forested.

Numerous rushing streams give New Zealand a great volume of hydroelectric power.

Chief exports in 1973 were meat and meat products (30%), wool (23%), lamb and mutton (15%), beef and veal (14%), butter (7%), milk (6%), and hides and skins (5%). Leading customers in 1974 were United Kingdom (20%), U.S. (14%), Japan (13%), Australia (11%). Leading suppliers were Australia (20%), U.K. (18%), Japan (15%), U.S. (13%).

Natural Features. New Zealand's two main components are North Island and South Island, separated by Cook Strait, which varies from 16 to 190 miles in width. North Island (44,281 sq mi.) is 515 miles long and volcanic in its south-central part. It contains many hot springs and beautiful geysers. South Island (58,093 sq mi.) has the Southern Alps along its west coast, with Mt. Cook (12,349 ft) the highest point.

Steward Island (670 sq mi.) and Chatham Islands (44 sq. mi.) are counties of South Island. There are also various outlying islands that are included within the geographical boundaries of New Zealand. The largest of these are the Auckland Islands (234 sq mi.), Campbell Island (44 sq mi.), the Antipodes Islands (24 sq mi.), and the Kermadec Islands (13 sq mi.).

Cook Islands and Overseas Territories

The Cook Islands (93 sq mi.; 241 sq km) were placed under New Zealand administration in 1901. They achieved self-governing status in association with New Zealand in 1965. Population in 1975 was 25,000. The seat of government is on Rarotonga Island.

Niue (100 sq mi.; 259 sq km) was formerly administered as part of the Cook Islands. It was placed under separate New Zealand administration in 1922 and achieved self-government status in association with New Zealand in 1974. The capital is Alofi.

The Ross Dependency (160,000 sq mi.; 414,400 sq km), an Antarctic region, was placed under New Zealand administration in 1923.

The Tokelau (Union) Islands (4 sq mi.) were formerly administered as part of the Gilbert and Ellice Islands colony. It was placed under New Zealand administration in 1926. Its population in 1974 was 1,600.

NICARAGUA (Republic)

(República de Nicaragua)

President: Anastasio Somoza Debayle (1974).
Area: 50,193 sq mi. (130,000 sq km).
Population (est. 1976): 2,250,000 (mestizo, 70%; white 17%; black, 9%; Indian, 4%).
Density per square mile: 44.8.
Capital and largest city (est. 1974): Managua, 313,400.
Monetary unit: Córdoba.
Language: Spanish.
Religion: Roman Catholic.

Anastasio Somoza Debayle, whose family has ruled Nicaragua since 1934, was elected President in 1974 after a two-year constitutional crisis in which Congress and the Constitution were suspended. A new Constituent Assembly, elected in 1972, rewrote the Constitution to permit Somoza to run for a second term. During the interim, Nicaragua was ruled by a triumvirate friendly to him.

Major Political Parties. National Liberal party (60 seats in Assembly), led by Anastasio Somoza Debayle; Conservative Party, led by Edmundo Paguaga-Irias.

History. Nicaragua, which established independence

in 1838, was first visited by the Spaniards in 1522. The chief of the country's leading Indian tribe at that time was called Nicaragua, from whom the nation derived its name. A U.S. naval force intervened in 1909 after two American citizens had been executed, and a few U.S. Marines were kept in the country from 1912 to 1925. The Bryan-Chamorro Treaty of 1916 (terminated 1970) gave the United States an option on a canal route through Nicaragua, and naval bases. Disorder after the 1924 elections brought in U.S. Marines again, but they were withdrawn after the U.S.-supervised elections of 1928.

A guerrilla leader, General César Augusto Sandino, began fighting the Marine occupation force in 1927. He fought the U.S. troops successfully until their withdrawal in 1933. They trained General Anastasio (Tacho) Somoza García to head a National Guard. In 1934, Somoza assassinated Sandino and overthrew the Liberal President Juan Batista Sacassa, establishing a military dictatorship which he headed as President. He spurred the economic development of the country, meanwhile enriching his family through estates in the countryside and investments in air and shipping lines, pursuing a pro-U.S. policy. On his assassination in 1956, he was succeeded by his son Luis, who alternated with trusted family friends in the Presidency until his death in 1967. Another son, Maj. Gen. Anastasio Somoza Debayle, became President for a five-year term on May 1, 1967. He sought to spur development while curbing government spending.

Somoza resigned the presidency in May, 1972, but remained commander-in-chief and national strongman while the Constitution was rewritten to permit him to run for a second term. The civilian triumvirate exercised nominal rule until Sept. 3, 1974, when Somoza was declared the winner of a runaway election. Critics called his 20-1 victory margin farcical because special laws disqualified most opponents.

Following his inauguration Dec. 1, 1974, Somoza obtained loans from the United States and international banks totaling $127 million for the reconstruction of Managua. Shortly afterward, he declared martial law after leftist guerrillas kidnapped 14 prominent officials, and Nicaragua remained under martial law in 1976.

One of the worst earthquakes in Nicaragua's history struck Managua on Dec. 23, 1972, destroying an estimated 90% of its commercial establishments and 70% of its housing. Over 6,000 were killed, 20,000 injured, 300,000 made homeless and 60,000 were jobless as a result. Rebuilding costs were put at $772 million.

Economic Conditions. More than half of Nicaragua is jungle-covered. Agriculture, the leading industry, utilizes only 10% of the total land.

Since 1961, the economic situation has constantly improved. Production of cotton, coffee, and meat products has increased substantially.

Gold and silver are the most important minerals. One-third wooded, Nicaragua produces mahogany, rosewood, cedar, rubber and ipecac root.

Chief exports in 1974 were cotton (36%), coffee (12%) and meat (6%). Leading customers in 1973 were U.S. (33%), Japan (12%), West Germany (9%), Costa Rica (8%), El Salvador (5%). Leading suppliers were (U.S. (34%), Guatemala (9%), Costa Rica (8%), El Salvador (8%), West Germany (7%), Japan (7%), Venezuela (5%).

Natural Features. Largest but most sparsely populated of the Central American nations, Nicaragua is mountainous in the west, with fertile valleys. A plateau slopes eastward toward the Caribbean.

Two big lakes—Nicaragua, about 100 miles long, and Managua, about 38 miles long—are connected by the Tipitapa River. The Pacific coast is bald and rocky. The Caribbean coast, swampy and indented, is aptly called the "Mosquito Coast."

NIGER (Republic)

(République du Niger)

Chief of State: Lieut. Col. Séyni Kountche (1974).
Area: 489,191 sq mi. (1,267,000 sq km).
Population (est. 1976): 4,725,000.
Density per square mile: 9.7.
Capital and largest city (est. 1973): Niamey, 121,900.
Monetary unit: Franc CFA.
Ethnic groups: Hausas, 53.7%; Djermas and Songhais, 23.6%; Fulanis, 10.6%; Beriberi-Mangas, 9.1%.
Languages: French, Sudanic dialects.
Religions: Moslem, Animist, Christian.

After a military coup on April 15, 1974, Lieut. Col. Séyni Kountche suspended the Constitution and instituted rule by decree. Previously, the President was elected by direct universal suffrage for a five-year term and a National House of Assembly of 50 members was elected for the same term.

Political Party. Parti Progressiste Nigerien, the only political party, was dissolved by the military government in 1974.

History. A republic in West Africa's Sahara region, Niger was incorporated into French West Africa in 1896. Rebellions were constant, but when order was restored in 1922, the French made the area a colony. In 1958 the voters approved the French Constitution and voted to make the territory an autonomous republic within the French Community. The republic adopted a Constitution in 1959 and in 1960 withdrew from the Community, proclaiming its independence.

On Jan. 1, 1973, Niger joined the seven-nation Economic Community for West Africa, whose purpose is to promote regional economic development.

The 1974 army coup ousted President Hamani Diori, who had held office since 1960, claiming Diori had mishandled relief for the terrible drought that has devastated Niger and five neighboring sub-Saharan nations for several years. An estimated 2 million people were starving in Niger, but 200,000 tons of imported food, half U.S.-supplied, substantially ended famine conditions by the year's end. The new President, Lieut. Col. Séyni Kountche, chief of staff of the army, installed a 12-man military government.

Economic Conditions. Agricultural products include peanuts, rice and dates. Livestock raising is an important activity.

Chief exports in 1973 were uranium (39%) and peanuts (14%). Leading customers were France (51%), Nigeria (26%), Italy (6%), West Germany (5%). Leading suppliers were France (43%), West Germany (8%), U.S. (7%), Nigeria (6%).

NIGERIA (Republic)

(Member of Commonwealth of Nations)

Head of State: Lieut. Gen. Olusegun Obasanjo (1976).
Area: 356,669 sq mi. (923,768 sq km).
Population (est. 1976): 64,630,000.
Density per square mile: 181.2.
Capital: Lagos.
Largest cities (est. 1973): Lagos, 970,262; (est. 1971): Ibadan, 758,332; Ogbomosho, 386,650; Kano, 357,098.
Monetary unit: Naira.
Languages: English (official), native tongues.
Religions: Moslem, Animist, Christian.

Since January 1966, a Supreme Military Council has been running the government. The Council has promised a return to civilian government when reconstruction and rehabilitation programs have been completed.

Political Parties. Political parties were banned by the military government in 1966.

History. Nigeria, with an area twice that of California, is situated on the Gulf of Guinea in West Africa. Between 1879 and 1914, private colonial developments by the British, with reorganizations of the crown's interest in the region, resulted in the formation of Nigeria as it exists today. During World War I, native troops of the West African frontier force joined with French forces to defeat the German garrison in the Cameroons.

Nigeria became independent on Oct. 1, 1960. It is black Africa's wealthiest and most populous nation.

Organized as a loose federation of self-governing states, the independent nation faced an overwhelming task of unifying a country with 250 ethnic and linguistic groups. The largest were the Hausa and Fulani in the north and the Ibo and Yoruba in the south, each of which had kingdoms in the late Middle Ages.

The people of the northern section of the British Cameroons voted to join the federation in 1961. In 1963, the people of Benin and Delta provinces, mainly of the Edo tribe, voted to form a new region, the Midwest. Full independence within the Commonwealth was achieved in 1963.

Rioting broke out again in 1966, the military commander was seized, and Col. Yakubu Gowon took power. Also in that year, the Moslem Hausas in the north massacred the predominantly Christian Ibos in the east, many of whom had been driven from the north. Thousands of Ibos took refuge in the Eastern Region. The military government there asked Ibos to return to the region and, in May 1967, the assembly voted to secede from the federation and set up the Republic of Biafra. Civil war broke out.

In January 1970, after 31 months of civil war, Biafra surrendered to the federal government. An estimated one million persons, mostly Ibos of the defeated state, were homeless and hungry, but a massive international relief operation kept the death toll down. The overall cost of the civil war was estimated at $840 million.

Gowon's nine-year rule was ended July 29, 1975 by a bloodless coup that made Army Brigadier Muritala Rufai Mohammed the new chief of state. Gowon was attending a summit meeting of the Organization of African Unity in Uganda at the time of the coup and accepted its results.

Deep-seated problems had brought on Gowon's ouster. Although Nigeria was the world's sixth largest oil producer (its 1974 oil revenues totaled $8 billion), the country's per capita income was $120 per year. Known for personal honesty, Gowon seemed unable to control institutionalized graft within the government. Students had demonstrated after Gowon withdrew a promise to return the government to civilian rule in 1976 because he feared the move would spark renewal of tribal warfare. Inflation was rampant and a wave of civil service strikes had caused widespread discontent.

Mohammed was assassinated Feb. 13, 1976, by a group of seven young officers, who failed to seize control of the government. The 20-member Supreme Military Council chose Lieut. Gen. Olusegun Obasanjo, chief of staff of the armed forces, as the new head of the Council and President. The assassins were publicly executed by firing squads on March 11.

In August 1976 the government announced plans for elections of local government councils, designed to return Nigeria to democratic rule by 1979. The elections were scheduled for November and December.

Economic Conditions. Aside from small industry, there is little manufacturing in Nigeria.

Chief export in 1974 was crude oil (91%). Leading customers in 1973 were U.S. (24%), United Kingdom (19%), Netherlands (13%), France (13%), Japan (5%). Leading suppliers were U.K. (27%), West Germany (15%), U.S. (10%), Japan (9%), France (7%).

Nigeria is a leading tin producer from mines on the Bauchi plateau. Other minerals are coal, gold, lead, silver, tungsten and petroleum. Over half the area is forested.

NORWAY (Constitutional Monarchy)

(Kongeriket Norge)

Sovereign: King Olav V (1957).
Prime Minister: Oddvar Nordli (1976).
Area: 125,182 sq mi. (324,219 sq km).
Population (est. 1976): 4,035,000.
Density per square mile: 32.2.
Capital: Oslo.
Largest cities (est. 1974): Oslo, 465,300; (est. 1972): Bergen, 213,700; Trondheim, 131,500.
Monetary unit: Krone.
Language: Norwegian.
Religions: Evangelical Lutheran (state), 96.2%; others, 3.8%.

Norway is a constitutional hereditary monarchy. Executive power is vested in the King together with a Cabinet, or Council of State, consisting of a Prime Minister and at least seven other members. The Storting, or Parliament, is composed of 155 members elected by the people under proportional representation. The Storting discusses and votes on political and financial questions, but divides itself into two sections (Lagting and Odelsting) to discuss and pass on legislative matters. The King cannot dissolve the Storting before the expiration of its term.

The sovereign is Olav V, born July 2, 1903, only son of Haakon VII and Princess Maud (1869–1938), third daughter of Edward VII of England. He succeeded to the throne on the death of his father Sept. 20, 1957. He married Princess Märtha of Sweden (1901–1954) on March 21, 1929. Their children are Princess Ragnhild Alexandra (born 1930), Princess Astrid (born 1932), and Crown Prince Harald (born 1937). In 1968, the Crown Prince married Sonja Haraldsen, a commoner.

Major Political Parties: Labor Party (62 of 155 seats in the Storting or parliament), led by Prime Minister Nordli, supported by a leftist coalition (16 seats) led by Reidar Larsen; Christian Democratic Party (20 seats), led by Lars Korvald; Conservative Party (29 seats); and Center Party (21 seats).

History. Norwegians, like the Danes and Swedes, are of Teutonic origin. The Norsemen, also known as Vikings, ravaged the coasts of northwestern Europe from the 8th to the 11th centuries.

In 1815, Norway, contrary to her wishes, fell under the control of Sweden. The union of Norway, inhabited by fishermen, sailors, merchants and peasants, and Sweden, an aristocratic country of large estates and tenant farmers, was not a happy one, but it lasted for nearly a century. In 1905, the Norwegian Parliament arranged a peaceful separation and invited a Danish prince to the Norwegian throne—King Haakon VII. A treaty with Sweden provided that all disputes be settled by arbitration and that no fortifications be erected on the common frontier. Since the separation the two countries have lived amicably as neighbors.

When World War I broke out, Norway joined with Sweden and Denmark in a decision to remain neutral and to co-operate in the joint interest of the three countries. In World War II, Norway was invaded by the Germans on Apr. 9, 1940. She resisted for two months before the Nazis took over complete control. King Haakon and his government fled to London, where they established a government-in-exile. Major Vidkun Quisling, who collaborated with the Nazis, was executed by the Norwegians on Oct. 24, 1945.

Despite severe war losses, Norway recovered quickly. The country led the world in social experimentation. A neighbor of the Soviet Union, Norway sought to retain good relations with it without losing its identity with the West. It entered the North Atlantic Treaty Organization in 1949.

In 1971, the Labor Party returned to power after a six-year hiatus (it had ruled for 30 years before 1965) and Prime Minister Trygve Bratteli promised a real effort to enter the EEC. But in a referendum on Sept. 25, EEC membership was rejected, 54% to 46%. Bratteli resigned, but returned to power after the 1973 elections. He resigned Jan. 9, 1976, and was succeeded by Oddvar Nordli.

Verification of U.S. and Soviet oil strikes in separated areas of Norway's sector of the North Sea bottom led the Storting in May 1975 to impose stiff tax and royalty rates on concession holders. Following discovery of a new North Sea field expected to produce 900,000 barrels a day by 1984, Parliament on Jan. 7, 1976 approved establishment of a national refining and distributing company to market petroleum products at home and abroad.

Economic Conditions. Land suitable for cultivation, estimated at less than 5% of the total area, consists of strips in the deep narrow valleys and around fiords and lakes. Foodstuff production is insufficient to meet domestic needs. Leading crops are potatoes, barley, oats, wheat and rye. The country is more adapted to stock raising than to crop growing.

Raw materials produced in Norway form the basis of most of the manufactures. The most important industries are food, machinery, metals, wood, paper and electro-chemicals.

Mineral resources are extensive, but coal deposits are entirely lacking except in Spitsbergen. Important minerals are iron ore, aluminum, pyrite ore, zinc, copper ore, molybdenum ore, tungsten, antimony ore, tin and silver.

Cheap electric power, produced mainly by hydroelectric plants, makes possible the extraction of nitrogen from the air and manufacture of potassium nitrate, an important fertilizer. The forests, largely in the south and southeast, are one of the chief natural resources. Fishing is one of the principal industries.

Chief exports in 1974 were ships (18%), machinery (10%), chemicals (8%), iron and steel (7%), aluminum (7%), paper (7%), fish (6%) and petroleum and products (5%). Leading customers were Sweden (18%), United Kingdom (17%), West Germany (10%), Denmark (8%), U.S. (5%). Leading suppliers were Sweden (19%), West Germany (14%), U.K. (10%), U.S. (8%), Japan (6%), Denmark (6%).

Natural Features. Nearly 70% of Norway is uninhabitable and covered by mountains, glaciers, moors and rivers. The hundreds of deep fiords that cut into Norway's coastline give it an overall ocean front of more than 12,000 miles. Islands off the coast, almost 150,000, form a breakwater and make a safe coastal shipping channel.

Dependencies of Norway

Svalbard (23,957 sq mi.; 62,049 sq km), located in the Arctic Ocean about 360 miles north of Norway, consists of the Spitsbergen group and several smaller islands, including Bear Island, Hope Island, King Charles Land and White Island (or Gillis Land). It came under Norwegian administration in 1925. The population in 1974 was 2,900.

Bouvet Island (23 sq mi.; 60 sq km), located in the South Atlantic about 1,600 miles south-southwest of the Cape of Good Hope, came under Norwegian administration in 1928.

Jan Mayen Island (144 sq mi.; 273 sq km), located in the Arctic Ocean between Norway and Greenland, came under Norwegian administration in 1929. Its population in 1973 was 37.

Peter I Island (96 sq mi.; 249 sq km), lying off Antarctica in the Bellinghausen Sea, came under Norwegian administration in 1931.

Queen Maud Land, a section of Antarctica, came under Norwegian administration in 1939.

OMAN (Sultanate)

Sultan: Qaboos Bin Said (1970).
Area: 82,030 sq mi. (212,457 sq km).
Population (est. 1976): 800,000.*

Density per square mile: 9.8.
Capital (est. 1973): Muscat, 15,000.
Largest city (est. 1973): Matrah, 30,000.
Monetary unit: Riyal Omani.
Language: Arabic.
Religion: Moslem.

The Sultan of Oman (formerly called Muscat and Oman), an absolute monarch, is assisted by several Personal Advisers, 17 Ministers and other government officials.

Political Parties. There are no political parties.

History. Although Oman is an independent state under the rule of the Sultan, it has been under British protection since the early 19th century.

Muscat, the capital of the geographical area known as Oman, was occupied by the Portuguese from 1508 to 1648. Then it fell to Persian princes and later was regained by the Sultan.

The Kuria Muria Islands, formerly part of Aden, were given to Oman by the British on Dec. 2, 1967.

In a palace coup on July 23, 1970, the Sultan, Sa'id bin Taimur, who had ruled since 1932, was overthrown by his son, who promised to establish a modern government and use new-found wealth to aid the people of this very isolated state.

With the shrinkage of British power, oil-rich little Oman has moved into the Iranian military orbit. Iranian troops were detailed in 1973–74 to help the Omani army put down Marxist rebels in Dhofar Province.

Economic Conditions. Chief export in 1973 was crude oil (99%). Leading customers were Japan (c. 35%), Spain (c. 18%), France (c. 12%), United Kingdom (c. 9%), Norway (c. 7%). Leading suppliers were United Arab Emirates (23%), U.K. (19%), Japan (9%), Netherlands (9%), West Germany (5%), Australia (5%), India (5%).

* Excluding the Kuria Muria Islands.

PAKISTAN (Islamic Republic of)

President: Fazal Elahi Chaudhry (1973).
Prime Minister: Zulfikar Ali Bhutto (1973).
Area: 310,404 sq mi. (803,943 sq km).*
Population (est. 1976): 72,350,000 (Moslem, 97%).
Density per square mile: 233.1.
Capital (1972 census): Islamabad, 77,000.
Largest cities (est. 1972): Karachi, 3,469,000; Lahore, 2,148,000; Lyalpur, 820,000; Hyderabad, 624,000; Rawalpindi, 615,000.
Monetary Unit: Pakistan rupee.
Principal languages: Urdu (national), English (official), Punjabi, Sindhi, Pashtu and Baluchi.
Religions: Islam (97%), Hindu, Christian, Buddhist.

Zulfikar Ali Bhutto succeeded Gen. Yahya Khan in 1971, following Pakistan's crushing defeat at the hands of India in their two-week war over East Pakistan (now Bangladesh). Under terms of a new Constitution approved on April 12, 1973, Bhutto became Prime Minister in August and Fazal Elahi Chaudhry, former speaker of the National Assembly, was named President by the legislature.

* Excluding Kashmir and Jammu.

The new Constitution sets up a federal parliamentary government with the President as head of state and the Prime Minister, elected by the National Assembly, as chief executive officer.

A bicameral legislature is composed of the National Assembly, with 210 members, including 10 women, who are elected by direct vote, and the Senate, with 63 members, 14 from each of the four provinces, five from the federally administered tribal areas and two from the Federal capital area of Islamabad. The Senate is elected by members of provincial assemblies. The Prime Minister can be voted out by the Assembly but his successor must be named in the ouster motion. Islam for the first time was declared the state religion.

Major Political Parties: Pakistan People's Party, led by Prime Minister Bhutto (91 of 146 seats in the old National Assembly, won in the 1970 elections). The National Awami Party, once the major opposition, was banned in 1975, following the assassination of a government minister. Other parties include the Democratic Party, the Jamati Islami, the Tehrik Istiqlal, the Muslim League and the Jamati Ulema-e-Islam.

History. Pakistan, a self-governing member of the Commonwealth of Nations, was one of the two original successor states to British India. For almost 25 years following independence in 1947, it consisted of two separate regions, East and West Pakistan, but now comprises only the western sector. It is washed by the Arabian Sea and is bordered by Iran, Afghanistan, China and India. Internally, it consists of Sind, Baluchistan, the former North-West Frontier Province, western Punjab, the princely state of Bahawalpur and several other smaller native states.

The British became the dominant power in the region in 1797 following Lord Clive's military victory, but rebellious tribes have kept the northwest in turmoil. In the northeast, the formation of the Moslem League in 1906 estranged the Moslems from the Hindus. In 1930, the league, led by Mohammed Ali Jinnah, demanded creation of a Moslem state wherever Moslems were in the majority. He supported Britain during the war. Afterward, the league received almost a unanimous Moslem vote in 1946 and Britain agreed to the formation of Pakistan as a separate dominion.

Pakistan was proclaimed a republic Mar. 23, 1956 and Iskander Mirza, then Governor General, was elected Provisional President. H. S. Suhrawardy, the first non-Moslem League Prime Minister, took office Sept. 12, 1956.

On Oct. 27, 1958, President Iskander Mirza surrendered his power to General Yahya Khan, who purged corrupt and inefficient officeholders, broke up the feudal land system, eliminated much of the black market, tax evasion, and hoarding and revolutionized education. A vote of confidence in February 1960 extended Yahya's dictatorial rule for five years and gave him power to write a new Constitution. It went into effect in June 1962.

The election of Dec. 7, 1970—the first direct general elections in Pakistani history—set the stage for bloody civil war. The Awami League, led by Sheik Mujibur Rahman, swept all Assembly seats allotted the more populous East Pakistan, while the major West Pakistani party, the People's Party, led by Zulfikar Ali Bhutto, won only 82 seats. Gen. Yahya directed the newly elected Assembly to meet March

1, 1971 and in 120 days write a Constitution. The Assembly never convened. Sheik Mujibur called general strikes, which turned bloody, and told East Pakistanis to stop paying taxes to the central government. West Pakistan troops moved in and fighting began. The independent state of Bangladesh, or Bengali nation, was proclaimed March 26, 1971.

The intervention of Indian troops permitted the new state to emerge and brought Yahya down. Bhutto took over and accepted Bangladesh as an independent entity, and met with Indian Premier Indira Gandhi in July 1972 and reached a first-step peace agreement that calls for disputes to be negotiated. India appeared to have also gained a permanent partition of Kashmir along cease-fire lines of 1971. The over-all effect was to leave Pakistan a much smaller and weaker nation, no longer able to seriously challenge India. Pakistan withdrew in 1972 from the Southeast Asia Treaty Organization (SEATO), through which it had been nominally allied with the United States.

India's explosion of a nuclear device on May 18, 1974 caused alarm in Karachi, eased somewhat by the February 1975 lifting of the 10-year U.S. embargo on arms shipments to Pakistan. The U.S. opposed Pakistan's purchase of a French nuclear reprocessing plant in February 1976, fearing that it could be used to make a nuclear bomb as India had done. Sale of the plant was approved by the International Atomic Energy Agency, however, because safeguards were judged adequate.

Diplomatically, 1976 saw the resumption of formal relations between India and Pakistan on July 21. At the same time, civilian air traffic between the two nations was restored after an 11-year interruption.

Economic Conditions. Pakistan, poor in industry and natural resources, is mainly an agricultural nation. The Punjab contains important wheat-growing areas.

Mineral resources are limited to petroleum, coal, lignite, chromite and gypsum. Vast quantities of natural gas were discovered at Sui, Baluchistan, in 1952.

Chief exports in 1974 were rice (21%), cotton fabrics (20%), cotton yarn (18%) and leather (7%). Leading customers were Indonesia (6%), Iran (6%), United Kingdom (6%), Hong Kong (6%), Japan (6%), Saudi Arabia (6%), Sri Lanka (5%), U.S. (5%). Leading suppliers were U.S. (23%), Japan (10%), West Germany (8%), U.K. (7%), Saudi Arabia (6%), Kuwait (6%).

Natural Features. Almost all of Sind and the west Punjab are a continuation of north-central plains leading up to rugged mountains in the north and west which traverse Baluchistan and the North-West Frontier Province.

PANAMA (Republic)

(República de Panamá)

President: Demetrio Basilio Lakas (1972).
Head of Government: Gen. Omar Torrijos (1972).
Area: 29,208 sq mi. (75,650 sq km).
Population (est. 1976): 1,720,000; (mestizo, 65.34%; black, 13.31%; white, 11.07%; Indian, 9.53%; others, .75%).
Density per square mile: 58.9.

Capital and largest city (est. 1975): Panama City, 404,190.
Monetary unit: Balboa.
Language: Spanish (official).
Religion: Roman Catholic, 90%, Protestant.

Following a military coup in 1968, a two-man junta ruled briefly but was in turn overthrown by Gen. Omar Torrijos, head of the National Guard (which is Panama's army). The Constitution was suspended.

In 1972, a new Constitution was approved by a new 505-seat National Assembly of Community Representatives (corregidores), which was created in the first election in five years. The Charter provides for indirect election of the President by the Assembly. The Assembly elected Demetrio Basilio Lakas President but named General Torrijos as Head of Government with all civil and military powers for six years. Otherwise the Assembly will be more a consultative than legislative body. Torrijos named a legislative committee to assist him in drafting laws.

Political Parties: All political parties were suspended in 1968 but a pro-Torrijos New Panama movement operated before the 1972 elections.

History. Visited by Columbus in 1502 on his fourth voyage and explored by Balboa in 1513, Panama was the principal transshipment point for Spanish treasure and supplies to and from South and Central America in colonial days. In 1821, when Central America revolted against Spain, Panama joined Colombia, which already had declared its independence. For the next 82 years, Panama attempted unsuccessfully to break away from Colombia. After U. S. proposals for canal rights over the narrow isthmus had been rejected by Colombia, Panama proclaimed its independence with U.S. backing in 1903.

For canal rights in perpetuity, the United States paid Panama $10,000,000, and agreed to pay $250,000 each year, increased to $430,000 after devaluation of the U.S. dollar in 1933 and to $1,930,000 under a revised treaty signed Jan. 25, 1955. In exchange, the United States got the Canal Zone—a ten-mile-wide strip across the isthmus—and a considerable degree of influence in Panama's affairs.

In 1968, Dr. Arnulfo Arias was elected President for the third time in three decades. And for the third time, he was thrown out of office by the military. A two-man junta, Col. José M. Pinilla and Col. Bolívar Urrutia, took control. They were ousted by Gen. Omar Torrijos, who named a new junta, with Lakas as President and Albert Surce as deputy.

A U.S.-Panamanian agreement signed Feb. 7, 1974 set principles for negotiation of a new treaty under which the Canal Zone would eventually revert to Panama. On March 4, 1975, with negotiations still under way, 37 U.S. Senators—three more than the minimum required to vote down a treaty—united in a statement opposing any agreement to yield U.S. sovereignty over the canal. On March 24, the Presidents of Venezuela, Colombia and Costa Rica joined Torrijos in a declaration of Panama's claim to full sovereignty over the Canal Zone.

On Jan. 17, 1976, the U.S. and Panama announced that talks would continue, but it was understood that neither side would press for a conclusion in a U.S. Presidential election year. Ex-Gov. Ronald Reagan of California, campaigning for the Republican nomination later in the year, insisted that the U.S. should retain the Canal Zone "as is." The Republican platform asserted that negotiators of a new treaty should "in no way cede" power or property necessary for U.S. security. Democrats called for a new treaty insuring U.S. interests but capable of "hemispheric support."

Economic Conditions. About five-eighths of the nation is unoccupied. A fourth of the population is in Colón and in Panama City, the oldest white settlement on the Pacific coast of the Americas. In the cities, the lower classes are descendants of British West Indian laborers on the canal.

Chief exports in 1974 were petroleum products (42%), bananas (25%) and shrimps (7%). Leading customers were U.S. (52%), Canal Zone (17%), West Germany (6%), Italy (6%), Netherlands (5%). Leading suppliers were U.S. (27%), Ecuador (17%), Venezuela (11%), Saudi Arabia (8%), Japan (6%).

The Panama Canal is the country's biggest economic asset. The main railway is the U.S. government-owned Panama Railroad (47.64 mi.) bridging the isthmus from Panama City to Colón. In recent years many foreign ships have been registered in Panama to escape high labor costs and governmental regulations in other nations.

Revenues from canal tolls are of decreasing importance, and the country is beginning to exploit natural resources which have not been touched since independence was achieved. A steel mill has been built, a manganese mine has been opened, and farm land is being extended.

Natural Features. Panama is roughly the size of South Carolina. At the narrowest and lowest point, the canal bisects the country. Outlying islands number about 630 in the Caribbean and 116 in the Pacific.

PAPUA NEW GUINEA (Parliamentary state)

(Member of Commonwealth of Nations)

Sovereign: Queen Elizabeth II.
Prime Minister: Michael Somare (1975).
Governor General: Sir John Guise.
Area: 178,259 sq mi. (461,691 sq km).
Population (est. 1976): 2,860,000.
Density per square mile: 160.4.
Capital and largest city (est. 1975): Port Moresby, 104,500.
Monetary unit: Kina.
Languages: English (official), Papuan, Melanesian.
Religions: Roman Catholic, Lutheran.

Papua New Guinea attained independence Sept. 16, 1975, ending a United Nations trusteeship under the administration of Australia. Chief Minister Michael Somare became the first Prime Minister, heading a coalition Cabinet. Parliamentary democracy was established by a Constitution that invests power in a single-chamber national legislature.

Just before independence, dissidents on the island of Bougainville, whose copper resources provide the chief foreign earnings for the central government, declared their intention to secede. The central government responded by taking direct control on Oct. 16, 1975, amid warnings from Australia that it would oppose secession. Somare met with pro-secessionists early in 1976 and, after conceding extra powers for a restored provincial government, appeared to have resolved the dispute.

Although members of the coalition Cabinet resigned and called for the election of a new national assembly, Somare declared his intention to hold off a general election until 1977.

History. The eastern half of New Guinea was first visited by Spanish and Portuguese explorers in the 16th century, but a permanent European presence was not established until 1884, when Germany declared a protectorate over the northern coast and Britain took similar action in the south. Both nations formally annexed their protectorates and, in 1901, Britain transferred its rights to a newly independent Australia. Australian troops invaded German New Guinea in World War I and retained control under a League of Nations mandate that eventually became a United Nations trusteeship, incorporating a territorial government in the southern region, known as Papua.

Australia granted limited home rule in 1951 and, in 1964, organized elections for the first House of Assembly. Autonomy in internal affairs came nine years later.

Economic Conditions. Papua New Guinea is heavily dependent on foreign aid, 90% of which comes from Australia. It is basically an agricultural country, its biggest export having traditionally been copra, but cocoa, coffee and tea are rising in value.

Copper leads the mineral production, with gold an important export, and extensive exploration for oil in progress.

Chief exports in 1972–73 were copper ores (55%), coffee (10%) and cocoa (5%). Leading customers were Japan (35%), West Germany (23%), Australia (20%), U.S. (5%). Leading suppliers were Australia (54%), Japan (16%), U.S. (9%).

Natural Features. Papua New Guinea shares the island of New Guinea with the Indonesian province of Irian Jaya. Offshore to the north and east are the islands of Manus, New Britain, New Ireland and Bougainville.

The mountainous interior of the main island territory has only recently been explored. The high plateau climate is temperate in contrast with the tropical climate of the coastal plains. Two major rivers, the Sepik and the Fly, are navigable for shallow-draft vessels.

PARAGUAY (Republic)

(República del Paraguay)

President: Gen. Alfredo Stroessner (1954).
Area: 157,047 sq mi. (406,752 sq km).
Population (est. 1976): 2,730,000 (mestizo, 94.9%; white, 3.0%; Indian, 2.1%).
Density per square mile: 17.4.
Capital and largest city (est. 1972): Asunción, 387,700.
Monetary unit: Guaraní.
Languages: Spanish (official), Guaraní.
Religion: Roman Catholic (official).

The President is elected by popular vote for five years. The legislature is bicameral, consisting of a Senate of 30 members and a Chamber of Representatives of 60 members. There is also a Council of State, whose members are nominated by the government.

Major Political Parties. Colorado Party (40 of 60 seats in House of Representatives), led by Juan Ramón Chávez; Liberal Radical Party (16 seats), led by Domingo Laino; Liberal Party; Febrerista Party.

History. In 1526 and again in 1529, Sebastian Cabot explored the first years when he sailed up the Paraná and Paraguay rivers. From 1608 until their expulsion from the Spanish dominions in 1767, the Jesuits maintained an extensive establishment in the south and east of Paraguay. In 1811, Paraguay revolted against Spanish rule and became a nominal republic under two Consuls.

Actually, Paraguay was governed by three dictators during the first 60 years of independence. The third, Francisco López, declared war on both Brazil and Argentina in 1864–65, a conflict in which the male population was almost wiped out. A new Constitution in 1870, designed to prevent dictatorships and internal strife, failed to do so, and not until 1912 did a period of comparative economic and political stability begin. The dispute between Paraguay and Bolivia over the Chaco region led to war in 1932 and was finally settled by the 1935 Buenos Aires peace conference, which gave most of the Chaco to Paraguay.

After World War II, politics became particularly unstable. Juan Natalicio González was elected President in the February 1948 elections, and took office on Aug. 15, 1948. Successive revolts on Jan. 30 and Feb. 26, 1949 ousted him and his successor. The leader of the second revolt, Felipe Molas López, was elected President on April 17 but gave way to Federico Chaves.

Chaves was re-elected in 1953, but he was ousted by the army, and Gen. Alfredo Stroessner was elected to complete his term.

Stroessner ruled under a state of siege until 1965, when the dictatorship was relaxed and exiles returned. The Constitution was revised in 1967 to permit Stroessner to be re-elected, and press freedom was briefly restored before the regime again moved to repress opposition.

Charges of a bomb plot against President Stroessner in November, 1974, led to "more than 1,000 arrests," the Interior Ministry reported in February 1975. Many of those arrested were said to be members of Stroessner's Colorado Party who urged his replacement on the expiration of his term in 1978.

U.S. companies began exploration for oil in 1974 in the desolate Chaco Boreal section of northwest Paraguay under 40-year contracts that the regime's critics denounced as over-generous. No oil has been found.

Economic Conditions. A well-favored land, Paraguay is predominantly a cattle country, keeping about four million head. The chief cash crop is cotton.

Forest resources are considerable, especially in the Chaco. Quebracho—the "axe-breaker," a wood so heavy that it will not float—is the principal commercial tree. The wood has many uses, from paving blocks to ox-cart wheels. Quebracho tannic extract is the chief product.

Chief exports in 1974 were meat (21%), timber (15%), cotton (10%), oilseeds (8%) and tobacco (7%). Leading customers were Argentina (23%), West Germany (13%), U.S. (11%), Netherlands (9%), Switzerland (9%), United Kingdom (9%). Leading suppliers were Argentina (28%), Brazil (18%), U.S. (10%), West Germany (9%), U.K. (7%).

Natural Features. Eastern Paraguay, between the Paraná and Paraguay rivers, is upland country with the thickest population settled on the grassy slope that inclines toward the Paraguay River. The greater part of the Chaco region which is located to the west, is covered with marshes, lagoons, dense forests and jungles.

PERU (Republic)

(República del Perú)

President: Gen. Francisco Morales Bermúdez (1975).
Premier: Gen. Guillermo Arbulu Galliani (1976).
Area: 496,222 sq mi. (1,285,216 sq km).
Population (est. 1976): 16,380,000 (white and mestizo, 52%; Indian, 46%; Asiatic, black, and other, 2%).
Density per square mile: 33.0.
Capital: Lima.
Largest cities (est. 1973 by U.N. for metropolitan area): Lima, 3,158,400; Arequipa, 304,600; Callao, 296,200; Trujillo, 241,900.
Monetary unit: Sol.
Languages: Spanish, Quéchuan.
Religion: Roman Catholic.

Since the bloodless coup d'état of Oct. 3, 1968, the Constitution has remained suspended, and the country has been governed by a military junta. Its leader, Gen. Francisco Morales Bermúdez, is President.

Political Parties. Acción Popular, led by Fernando Belaunde Terry; Partido Aprista Peruano, led by Victor R. Haya de la Torre; Partido Democrático Cristiano, led by Héctor Cornejo Chávez; Partido Popular Cristiano, led by Luis Bedoya Reyes; Movimiento Democrático Peruano.

History. Peru, once part of the great Incan empire and later the major vice-royalty of Spanish South America, is more than three times the size of California. It was conquered in 1531–33 by Francisco Pizarro. On July 28, 1821, Peru proclaimed its independence, but the Spanish were not finally defeated until 1824.

For a hundred years thereafter, the Peruvian course was rough. Revolutions were frequent, and a new war was fought with Spain in 1864–66. A dispute with Chile over Tacna and Arica was not finally settled until 1929.

Peru emerged from 20 years of dictatorship in 1945 with the inauguration of President José Luis Bustamente y Rivero after the first free election in many decades. But he served for only three years and was succeeded in turn by Gen. Manuel A. Odria, Manuel Prado y Ugarteche and Fernando Belaunde Terry. On Oct. 3, 1968, Belaunde was overthrown in a bloodless coup by Gen. Juan Velasco Alvarado.

Velasco nationalized the nation's second biggest bank and turned two large newspapers over to

Marxists in 1970, but he also allowed a new agreement with a copper-mining consortium of four American firms.

The World Bank granted Peru $470 million in credits in 1973, which appeared to end a boycott by international financial institutions in which the U.S. has a strong influence. American copper and fishing firms were seized in 1974 but compensation was paid. Peru also became in 1974 the first nation in the Western Hemisphere to receive Soviet military advisers.

A strike by Lima police in February 1975 touched off bloody riots that were put down with troops. Officials said they resulted in over 100 deaths, 1,000 arrests and destruction estimated at $22 million, but unofficial estimates doubled these figures. The government declared a state of emergency and suspended constitutional guarantees for two months after the outbreak. Later that month, the regime named a committee to study formation of a political movement to strengthen public support for the government and later issued a declaration stating its goals for a "nationalist and independent" movement based on "revolutionary humanism."

On Aug. 29, President Velasco was replaced in a bloodless coup by his Premier, Gen. Francisco Morales Bermúdez. Morales eased censorship, which had caused public unrest, and in the summer of 1976 was enlisting aid from foreign banks to overcome severe economic problems.

On May 31, 1970, the country suffered the hemisphere's worst natural disaster, an earthquake which, together with a mud slide it caused, took an estimated 50,000 lives.

Economic Conditions. Land under cultivation is estimated at only slightly more than 10% of the total area, with more than 50% of the population being dependent on agriculture. Cotton is an important crop. Stock raising supplies domestic needs and valuable exports. Llamas, used as beasts of burden, and vicuñas and alpacas, noted for their wool, are native to Peru.

Peru has vast mineral resources. Important products are petroleum, coal, iron ore, lead, zinc, copper, tungsten, silver and gold.

An important industry on the outlying islands is the gathering of guano (bird excrement), a valuable fertilizer.

Chief exports in 1974 were copper (23%), fish meal (13%), silver (11%), zinc (11%), sugar (10%) and cotton (6%). Leading customers were U.S. (36%), Japan (13%), West Germany (8%), China (5%). Leading suppliers were U.S. (31%), Japan (12%), West Germany (10%), Ecuador (5%).

Natural Features. The Andes Mountains divide Peru into three sharply differentiated zones. To the west is the coastline, much of it arid, extending for 50 to 100 miles inland.

The mountain area, with peaks over 20,000 feet high, lofty plateaus and deep valleys, lies centrally. Beyond the mountains to the east is the heavily forested slope leading to the Amazonian plains.

THE PHILIPPINES (Republic)

(Republika ng Pilipinas)

President and Prime Minister: Ferdinand E. Marcos (1965).
Area: 115,831 sq mi. (300,000 sq km).
Population (est. 1976): 43,750,000.
Density per square mile: 377.7.
Capital: Quezon City.
Largest cities (est. 1976 for urban agglomeration): Manila, 7,800,000; (est. 1974): Quezon City, 946,390; (est. 1973): Davao, 463,700; Cebu, 384,800.
Monetary unit: Peso.
Languages: English, Tagalog, Visayan, Spanish, Ilocano, Bicol.
Religions: Roman Catholic, 84%; Aglipayan (Independent Philippine Christian, 5%; Moslem, 5%; Protestant, 3%; others, 3%.

President Ferdinand E. Marcos proclaimed ratification of the Constitution in 1973, which he said was approved by a referendum, replacing the U.S.-style democracy with a British-like parliamentary system. Under it he can rule indefinitely. The President remains but only as symbolic head of state; the Prime Minister is head of the government and a National Assembly is the law-making body. Marcos assumed both the presidential and prime ministerial jobs. Since Sept. 21, 1972, the nation has been under martial law, however, with Marcos ruling by decree. His new system, he said, amounts to "constitutional authoritarianism."

Major Political Parties. The Nacionalista and Liberal Parties ceased to exist with the adoption of the 1973 Constitution, which dissolved the legislature.

History. Fernando Magellan, the Portuguese navigator in the service of Spain, discovered the Philippines on Mar. 16, 1521. Twenty-one years later, a Spanish exploration party named the group of islands in honor of Prince Philip, later Philip II of Spain. Spain retained possession of the islands for the next 350 years.

The Philippines were ceded to the United States in 1899 by the Treaty of Paris after the Spanish-American War. Meanwhile, the Filipinos, led by Emilio Aguinaldo, had declared their independence. They continued guerrilla warfare against U.S. troops until the capture of Aguinaldo in March 1901. By July 1902, peace was established except among the Moros.

The first U.S. civilian Governor-General was William Howard Taft (1901–04). The Jones Law (1916) provided for the establishment of a Philippine Legislature composed of an elective Senate and House of Representatives. The Tydings-McDuffie Act (1934) provided for a transitional period until 1946, at which time the Philippines would become completely independent.

Under a Constitution approved by the people of the Philippines on May 14, 1935, the Commonwealth of the Philippines was inaugurated on Nov. 15, 1935. Manuel Quezon y Molina was elected President on Sept. 17, 1935.

On Dec. 8, 1941, the Philippines were invaded by Japanese troops. Following the fall of Bataan and Corregidor, President Quezon established a government-in-exile, which he headed until his death in 1944. He was succeeded by Vice President Sergio Osmeña.

U.S. forces led by Gen. Douglas MacArthur reinvaded the Philippines in October 1944 and, after the liberation of Manila in February 1945, Osmena re-established the government.

The Philippines achieved full independence on July 4, 1946. Manuel A. Roxas y Acuña was elected President on Apr. 23, 1946. Subsequent Presidents have been Elpidio Quirino (1948–53). Ramón Magsaysay (1953–57). Carlos P. García (1957–61), Diosdado Macapagal (1961–65), and Ferdinand E. Marcos (from Dec. 30, 1965).

The Philippines joined Indonesia, Thailand, Singapore and Malaysia in founding the Association of Southeast Asia Nations in August 1967. However, the Philippines and Malaysia almost came to hostilities over Sabah, a Malaysian State on the island of Borneo. But the Philippines, while reiterating its claim to the territory, renounced the use of force to press its claim.

Marcos became the first President in Philippine history to win re-election, Nov. 11, 1969, when he overwhelmingly defeated Sergio Osmena, Jr., with campaign promises to become less dependent on the United States and to establish ties with Communist countries. The campaign violence led to 59 deaths. After inauguration, the worst peacetime riots in Philippine history occurred when a student-led demonstration tried to storm the presidential palace, with 5 dead and 157 injured, to protest government corruption.

Economically, the nation went through a difficult time and, in mid-1970, the government decreed that the peso would "float" on international currency markets, rather than be pegged at a guaranteed exchange rate. The move cut the value of the peso by about 75%.

Political, civil and religious unrest was responsible for the deaths of almost 500 persons in 1971, and disastrous month-long rains that caused enormous flooding added to the toll in 1972. In September 1972, Marcos declared martial law and arrested hundreds of political opponents, journalists and leftists.

The legality of martial rule was affirmed Feb. 1, 1975 by a 10–1 vote of the Philippine Supreme Court. After a referendum four weeks later, the government said its continuance was approved by 90% of the voters.

The Philippines notified the United States April 12, 1975 that it was reviewing mutual defense arrangements in the light of the shifting power balance caused by the Communist takeover in Indochina. Talks on revision of agreements permitting maintenance of U.S. bases began in May.

Diplomatic relations between the Philippines and China were established June 9. Taiwan broke its ties with Manila immediately thereafter.

On Aug. 16, 1976, an earthquake measuring 8 on the Richter scale hit Mindanao, causing heavy damage, increased by 24-foot tidal waves. Nearly 5,000 persons were believed to have died in Mindanao and other southern islands, with as many as 150,000 made homeless. The disaster brought a respite in a rebellion by dissidents in Mindanao's Moslem majority, which had won concessions from the government in 1975 although Manila refused to consider demands for Moslem autonomy.

Economic Conditions. Agriculture is the chief industry. Average size of the farms is ten acres, but there are many large plantations. Rice (palay) is the staple native food cereal, but production is insufficient to meet home consumption. The Philippines normally produce about half the world's copra supply and a large proportion of the abacá (Manila hemp) supply. They are also a leading source of sugar and sugar products. Other crops include sisal, kapok, cotton, corn, tobacco, coffee, rubber, cacao, citrus fruits and bananas.

There are no large industrial establishments, and activity is limited primarily to the processing of agricultural and forest products, such as sugar cane, coconuts, tobacco, abacá and timber. The preparation of fine embroideries is important.

The Philippines possess large but relatively undeveloped mineral resources. Most important are gold, silver, iron ore, copper ore, chromite, manganese ore, lead and zinc.

Chief exports in 1974 were sugar (27%), coconut products (22%), copper (15%) and timber (9%). Leading customers were U.S. (42%), Japan (35%), Netherlands (6%). Leading suppliers were Japan (27%), U.S. (24%), Saudi Arabia (11%), Kuwait (5%).

Natural Features. The Philippines are an archipelago of approximately 7,083 islands lying about 500 miles off the southeast coast of Asia. The northernmost island, Y'Ami, is 65 miles from Taiwan, while the southernmost, Saluag, is 30 miles east of Borneo. Only 466 of the islands have an area of more than one square mile, and only 2,441 have names. The largest islands are Luzon in the north (40,420 sq mi.), Mindanao in the south (36,537 sq mi.), Samar (5,124 sq mi.), Negros (4,903 sq mi.), and Palawan (4,550 sq mi.).

POLAND (People's Republic)

(Polska Rzeczpospolita Ludowa)

President of the Council of State: Henryk Jablonski (1972).
Prime Minister: Piotr Jaroszewicz (1972).
Area: 120,725 sq mi. (312,677 sq km).
Population (est. 1976): 34,350,000.
Density per square mile: 284.5.
Capital: Warsaw.
Largest cities (est. 1975): Warsaw, 1,427,400; (est. 1973 by U.N.): Lodz, 777,800; Krakow, 651,300; Wroclaw (Breslau), 557,200; Poznan, 495,200; Gdansk (Danzig), 394,000; Szczecin, 355,600.
Monetary unit: Zloty.
Language: Polish (more than 90%).
Religions: Roman Catholic, Greek Orthodox, Protestant, Jewish.

The 1952 Constitution describes Poland as a People's Republic. The supreme organ of state authority is the Sejm (Parliament), which is composed of 460 members elected for four years.

Major Political Parties. Polish United Workers' (Communist) Party (255 of 460 seats in Sejm), led by First Secretary Edward Gierek; United Peasant Party (117 seats), led by Stanislaw Gucwa; Democratic Party (39 seats), led by Tadeusz W. Mlynczak, and non-party Catholic organizations (49 seats).

History. Little of certainty is known about Polish history before the 11th century, when King Boleslaus I (the Brave) ruled over Bohemia, Saxony and Moravia. Mongol invasions in 1241 and 1259 were repelled. Meanwhile, the Teutonic knights were erecting in Prussia a state which included part of Poland and barred the latter's access to the Baltic. The knights were defeated by Wladislaus II at Tannenberg in 1410 and became Polish vassals, and Poland regained a Baltic shoreline. Poland reached the peak of power between the 14th and 16th centuries. Poles scored military successes against the Russians and Turks. In 1683, King John Sobieski turned back the Turkish tide near Vienna.

These successes did not halt the process of decline which resulted from the lack of strong central authority, and Prussia, Russia and Austria were able to carry out a first partition of the country in 1772, a second in 1792 and a third in 1795–96. For more than a century thereafter, there was no Polish state, but the Poles never ceased their efforts to regain their independence.

The independence of Poland was formally proclaimed in November 1918 and Marshal Josef Pilsudski was made Chief of State. In 1919, Ignace Paderewski, the famous pianist and patriot, became the first Premier.

On Apr. 25, 1920, in an attempt to wrest the Ukraine from the Bolsheviks, Poland attacked Russia. The Poles reached Kiev in May, but in June the Russians launched a counterattack, driving the Poles back to Warsaw by August. The Poles, under Pilsudski and aided by the French, then drove back the Russians, forcing them to abandon their conquests in Poland.

On May 12, 1926, Marshal Pilsudski seized complete power in a coup d'état and ruled the country dictatorially until his death on May 12, 1935, when he was succeeded as commander of the army by Marshal Edward Smigly-Rydz.

Despite a 10-year nonaggression pact signed with Germany in 1934, Hitler attacked Poland on Sept. 1, 1939. Russian troops invaded from the east on Sept. 17, and on Sept. 28 a German-Russian agreement was signed dividing Poland between Russia and Germany. W. Raczkiewicz formed a government-in-exile in France with Gen. Wladyslaw Sikorski as Premier. This government moved to London after France's defeat in 1940.

All of Poland was occupied by Germany after the Nazi attack on the Soviet Union in June 1941. On July 30, 1941, Poland concluded an agreement with the Soviet Union voiding all German-Soviet agreements effected after Sept. 1, 1939.

The legal Polish government soon fell out with the Russians, however, and, in July 1944, a Communist-dominated Polish Committee of National Liberation received Soviet recognition. Moving to Lublin after that city's liberation, it proclaimed itself the Provisional Government of Poland on Dec. 31, 1944. Some former members of the Polish government in London joined with the Lublin government to form the Polish Government of National Unity on June 28, 1945. Britain and the U.S. recognized this government in 1945.

On Aug. 2, 1945, in Berlin, President Truman, Marshal Stalin and Prime Minister Attlee established a new *de facto* western frontier for Poland along the rivers Oder and Lausitzer Neisse. (The border was finally agreed to by West Germany in a nonaggression pact signed Dec. 7, 1970.) On Aug. 16, 1945, the Soviet Union and Poland signed a treaty delimiting the Soviet-Polish frontier. Under these agreements, Poland was shifted westward. In the east it lost 69,860 square miles with 10,772,000 inhabitants; in the west it gained (subject to final peace-conference approval) 38,986 square miles with a prewar population of 8,621,000.

In 1946, a unicameral Parliament was established by referendum. A limited legal opposition was countenanced at first. Then, in 1947, the government bloc won a huge majority in government-controlled elections and after much fighting the underground opposition was suppressed and the Sovietization of Poland begun, with Soviet Marshal Konstantin Rokossovsky as Defense Minister and army commander.

In 1952, a Constitution was promulgated making Poland a "people's democracy" of the Soviet type. In 1955, Poland, which had joined the Council for Economic Mutual Assistance in 1949, became a member of the Warsaw Treaty Organization, and its foreign policy became identical with the Soviet Union's. The government undertook persecution of the Roman Catholic Church as one of the remaining foci of opposition and in 1953 arrested the primate, Stefan Cardinal Wyszynski. But in 1956, worker and student riots in Poznan (June 28–30) forced reconsideration of the repression.

Wladyslaw Gomulka was elected leader of the United Workers (Communist) Party in October 1956. He denounced the Stalinist terror, ousted many Stalinists, relieved Rokossovsky, freed Wyszynski, and improved relations with the church. Most collective farms were dissolved, and the press became freer. Gomulka retained his position despite opposition from the Stalinist and liberal wings of his party.

Much as the Poznan bread riots of 1956 brought Gomulka to power, so pre-Christmas rioting in 1970 in Gdansk and other Baltic coastal towns caused Gomulka to fall and elevated Gierek to the key post of party boss. Cause of the worker riots, in which at least 45 and probably over 200 died when police and army troops crushed the protest, was steep price rises on meat and other foods. Significantly, no students or intellectuals were involved.

Serious resistance to increased food prices again brought rioting in Polish cities in the summer of 1976 after the government announced on June 24 a new schedule of prices. Railroad tracks were torn up in Warsaw, workers staged illegal strikes and looting took place before the government, on July 13, modified some of the advances.

Economic Conditions. Industrial facilities, although severely damanged during World War II, were not greatly affected by territorial concessions to the Soviet Union, with the exception of the Lwów area. On the other hand, important German industrial areas, especially Silesia and the city of Stettin, are located in the territories under *de facto* Polish administration.

The acquisition of large coal deposits in German Silesia, combined with much larger reserves in the southwestern region, makes Poland one of the world's leading coal producers. Iron ore deposits are located in the Kielce and Radom districts and in German Silesia (metal content 34%). Zinc and lead ores are located chiefly in Upper Silesia and the voivodships of Kielce and Kraków. Pre-war Poland's principal oil-producing areas, Boryslaw-Drohobycz, are in the territory ceded to the Soviet

Union. Among other deposits, Poland possesses copper, sulfur, chalk, clay, kaolin, marble and granite.

Chief exports in 1974 were machinery (29%), coal (13%), chemicals (11%), food (10%), textiles and clothing (9%), metals (8%) and ships and boats (5%). Leading customers were U.S.S.R. (29%), East Germany (9%), Czechoslovakia (7%), West Germany (6%). Leading suppliers were U.S.S.R. (22%), West Germany (12%), East Germany (7%), Czechoslovakia (6%), United Kingdom (5%), U.S. (5%).

Natural Features. Most of Poland is a plain with no natural boundaries except the Carpathian Mountains on the south and the Oder and Neisse rivers on the west.

PORTUGAL (Republic)

(República Portuguesa)

President: Gen. António Ramalho Eanes (1976).
Premier: Mário Soares (1976).
Area: 35,553 sq mi. (92,082 sq km).
Population (est. 1976): 8,750,000.
Density per square mile: 246.1.
Largest cities (est. 1973): Lisbon, 757,700; (est. 1972): Oporto (Porto), 304,700.
Monetary unit: Escudo.
Language: Portuguese.
Religion: Roman Catholic.

The new Portuguese Constitution, adopted in April 1976, provides for a President elected by universal suffrage for a term of five years and for a legislature, the Assembly of the Republic, of 265 members elected for four-year terms.

A military coup on April 25, 1974 dissolved the former bicameral legislature and also dissolved what had been for 40 years the only authorized political party, the National Popular Action Party.

Political Parties. Socialist Party (107 of 265 seats in Assembly), led by Premier Mario Soares; Popular Democratic Party (73 seats), led by Dr. Francisco Sa Carneiro; Democratic Social Center Party (42 seats), led by Prof. Diogo Freitas do Amaral; and Communist Party (40 seats), led by Dr. Alvaro Cunhal.

History. Portugal was a part of Spain until it won its independence in the middle of the 12th century. King John I (1385–1433) unified his country at the expense of the Castilians and the Moors of Morocco. The expansion of Portugal was brilliantly coordinated by John's son, Prince Henry the Navigator. In 1488, Bartholomew Diaz reached the Cape of Good Hope, proving that the Far East was accessible by sea. In 1498, Vasco da Gama reached the west coast of India. By the middle of the 16th century, the Portuguese Empire included West and East Africa, Brazil, Persia, Indo-China and Malaya.

In 1581, Philip II of Spain invaded Portugal and held her captive for 60 years. There followed a catastrophic decline of Portuguese commerce. Courageous and shrewd explorers, the Portuguese proved to be inefficient and corrupt colonizers. By the time the Portuguese dynasty was restored in 1640, Dutch, English and French competitors began to seize the lion's share of the world's colonies and commerce. Portugal retained Angola and Mozambique in Africa, and Brazil (until 1822), but her place as an imperial power was lost forever.

In the first half of the 19th century, Portugal's political history was distinguished by dynasty quarrels and factional strife. The corrupt King Carlos, who ascended the throne in 1889, made João Franco the Premier with dictatorial power in 1906. In 1908, Carlos and his heir were shot dead on the streets of Lisbon. The new King, Manuel II, was driven from the throne in the Revolution of 1910. Portugal was proclaimed a republic with a system modeled upon that of France.

Traditionally friendly to Great Britain, Portugal entered World War I on the Allies' side, and Portuguese troops fought on the Western Front and in Africa. In 1926, a revolution drove out the President, and six years later the dictatorship of Antonio Oliveira Salazar began. He kept Portugal neutral in World War II but gave the Allied powers naval and air bases in 1943.

Refused admission to the United Nations in 1946, Portugal was granted membership in 1955.

In 1961, Indian forces took Goa, Daman and Diu, but Portugal crushed an insurrection in Angola and thereafter fought a disastrous war against guerrillas. Through the 1960s, the country opposed nationalists also in its other African possessions. U.N. resolutions calling for self-determination in these territories were ignored.

In September 1968, Premier Salazar suffered a cerebral hemorrhage and lapsed into a coma. (He died in 1970.) Marcello Caetano was named to succeed him. He continued to support military suppression of independence movements in various overseas territories. In 1971, however, Portugal granted greater autonomy for her overseas territories, particularly Angola and Mozambique.

The military coup of April 25, 1974 installed Gen. António de Spínola as Provisional President and promised sweeping domestic reforms and peace to the African colonies. The coup leaders were younger officers, notably Col. Vasco dos Santos Gonçalves, who later became Premier. The Communist Party leader was included in the Cabinet, and Socialist leader Mario Soares became Foreign Minister. Caetano and former President Américo Tomás were sent into exile. Relatively little blood was shed in the coup. Amnesty was declared for all political prisoners, and press curbs were removed.

The primary cause of the revolt was the refusal of the Caetano government to give up the nation's overseas colonies despite the continued high cost in men and money to fight the independence movements.

Called the "happy revolution" because it easily unseated a detested rightist dictatorship, the coup headed by the Armed Forces Movement (M.F.A.) had a strong leftward thrust. António de Spínola, a popular general installed by the M.F.A. as provisional President, appointed a moderate-left Cabinet that failed to deal with the political ferment that followed the coup. On July 14, 1974, the M.F.A. named Gonçalves Premier. Spinola resigned as President Sept. 30 after having failed to organize moderate sentiment, and was replaced by Gen. Francisco da Costa Gomes, Chief of Staff of the armed forces. Communist influences accelerated under Gonçalves.

While the far left was strong in Lisbon, resistance elsewhere in conservative Portugal surfaced when elections were held April 25, 1975 for delegates to a Constituent Assembly empowered to draft a democratic Constitution. The Socialists won 38% of the vote, the Popular Democrats 26% and the Communists trailed badly with 12.5%. But the message was blunted by a pre-election deal between the parties and the Supreme Revolutionary Council of the M.F.A. which specified that changes in government could be made solely by the President on the advice of the Premier and the Revolutionary Council.

Portugal's deepening political crisis was compounded in mid-July 1975, when the Socialists and the Popular Democrats withdrew from the Cabinet in a protest sparked by Communist seizure of a Socialist newspaper. The resignations left the Communists in control of the Cabinet and, despite many hostile demonstrations, the government pressed ahead with the M.F.A.'s program of "direct democracy," which included expropriation of large landholdings, nationalization of large industries and repression of opposition.

Anti-Communist violence in rural areas and intense pressure from non-Communists in the government and the M.F.A. led to Goncalves' ouster on Aug. 29, 1975. His replacement was Vice Adm. José Pinheiro de Azevedo, Vice President of the provisional government. On Sept. 19, a new government—Portugal's fifth since the "happy revolution"—was sworn in amid hopes that it could survive until the Constituent Assembly finished drafting the Constitution. The new Cabinet included five military officers, four Socialists, two Popular Democrats and only one Communist. Its first instruction from da Costa Gomes was to give priority to problems of the economy, which was beset by 10% unemployment, a 30% inflation rate and a serious balance of payments deficit.

The rise of Communist influence in Portugal with the approval and reputed support of the Soviet Union caused concern within the North Atlantic Treaty Organization because of Portugal's strategic location at the western approaches to the Mediterranean.

The United States and Western European countries granted emergency aid of $272 million in early October. A revolt by leftist air force and other military units was put down in November and the state of siege was lifted Dec. 1. In January 1976, the government modified the land reform program, which had aroused strong opposition in the north.

Despite pre-election violence, the first elections under the new Constitution were carried out on June 27, 1976 with Gen. António Ramalho Eanes, army Chief of Staff, winning a landslide victory. Eanes promised austerity measures to restore an economy that showed signs of recovery, measures expected to meet resistance from the left.

Economic Conditions. Portugal's corporate state has a planned economy in which each producing unit regulates itself in the interest of the nation. Corporate units have been established in agriculture, industry, and finance.

One of the world's leading wine-makers, Portugal produces two famous kinds—Port in the vicinity of Oporto, and Madeira in the islands of the same name.

Leading crops include wheat, barley, oats, rye, maize, rice and potatoes. Portugal is a leading producer of olive oil.

Mineral resources have not been fully developed, but wolfram, coal, iron ore, copper, manganese, iron pyrites, lead, tin and other ores are found.

Portugal is one of the world's leading producers of cork.

The fishing industry is a basic part of the national economy. Of special importance is the sardine industry centered at Setúbal.

Chief exports in 1974 were textile yarns and fabrics (17%), machinery (11%), clothing (11%), chemicals (8%), wine (7%), electrical equipment (7%), cork and manufactures (6%) and fruit and vegetables (5%). Leading customers were United Kingdom (23%), U.S. (10%), West Germany (8%), Sweden (6%), Angola (6%), France (6%). Leading suppliers were West Germany (14%), U.K. (9%), U.S. (9%), Angola (8%), France (8%), Italy (5%), Spain (5%).

Natural Features. Portugal is crossed by many small rivers, and also by three large ones which rise in Spain, flow into the Atlantic, and divide the country into three geographic areas. The Minho (Miño in Spain) River, part of the northern boundary, cuts through a mountainous area that extends south to the vicinity of the Douro (Duero) River. South of the Douro, the mountains slope to the plains about the Tagus (Tejo) River. The remaining division is the southern one of Alentejo.

The Azores, stretching over a distance of 340 miles in the Atlantic, consist of nine islands divided into three groups, with a total area of 924 square miles. The nearest continental land is Cape da Roca, Portugal, which lies 875 miles to the east. The Azores are an important station on Atlantic air routes, and both Britain and the United States established air bases there during World War II. Madeira, consisting of two inhabited islands, Madeira and Porto Santo, and two groups of uninhabited islands, lies in the Atlantic about 535 miles southwest of Lisbon.

Portuguese Overseas Province

Under the 1971 Constitution, Portugal's overseas provinces were governed by Lisbon. In 1972, limited autonomy was granted and, in 1973, for the first time, elections took place for local assemblies. After the April 1974 revolution, the military junta moved to grant independence to the territories, beginning with Portuguese Guinea in September 1974, which became the republic of Guinea-Bissau.

Mozambique and Angola followed, leaving only Portuguese Timor and Macao of the former Empire. Despite Lisbon's objections, Indonesia annexed Timor. The last of the provinces in 1976, with no immediate plans for change, was Macao.

MACAO

Status: Overseas province.
Governor: Major José Garcia Leandro.
Area: 6 sq mi. (15.5 sq km).
Population (est. 1976): 280,000.
Capital (1970 census): Macao, 241,413.
Chief exports: textiles, chemicals.
Manufactures: textiles, firecrackers, footwear, porcelain.

Macao comprises the peninsula of Macao and the two small islands of Taipa and Colôane on the South China coast, about 35 miles from Hong Kong. Established by the Portuguese in 1557, it is the oldest European outpost in the China trade, but Portugal's sovereign rights to the port were not recognized by China until 1887, and its boundaries are still not delimited. The port has been eclipsed in importance by Hong Kong, but it is still a busy distribution center and also has an important fishing industry. It is notorious for its opium trade and gambling houses. Most of the population is Chinese.

Macao's future is under negotiation between Portugal and China, which asserted a claim to the enclave in 1972.

Economic Conditions. Chief exports in 1973 were textiles (75%) and fish (5%). Leading customers were France (16%), U.S. (16%), West Germany (12%), Portugal (11%), Hong Kong (10%), Angola (6%), Belgium-Luxembourg (5%), Italy (5%). Leading suppliers were Hong Kong (67%) and China (26%).

QATAR

Ruler: Sheik Khalifa bin Hamad al-Thani (1972).
Area: 4,247 sq mi. (11,000 sq km).
Population (est. 1975): 200,000.
Density per square mile: 33.9.
Capital (est. 1975): Doha, 140,000.
Monetary unit: Qatar riyal.
Language: Arabic.
Religion: Moslem.

Qatar is one of the Persian Gulf sheikdoms, between Bahrain and Trucial Oman. For a long time, it was under Turkish protection, but in 1916, the sultan took British protection. After the discovery of oil in the 1940's and its exploitation in the 1950's and 1960's, political unrest spread to the sheikdoms. Qatar declared its independence in 1971. The next year the current Sheik, Khalifa bin Hamad al-Thani, ousted his cousin, then ruler, in a bloodless coup.

Economic Conditions. Chief exports in 1974 were crude oil and products (98%). Leading customers in 1973 were United Kingdom (c. 24%), Netherlands (c. 22%), France (c. 20%), Italy (c. 12%), West Germany (c. 5%). Leading suppliers in 1974 were Japan (18%), U.K. (14%), U.S. (10%), Lebanon (6%), West Germany (6%).

RHODESIA (Republic)

President: John J. Wraithall (1976).
Prime Minister: Ian Smith (1964).
Area: 150,803 sq mi. (390,580 sq km).
Population (est. 1976): 6,520,000 (black, 95%; white, 5%).
Density per square mile: 43.2.
Capital: Salisbury.
Largest cities (1975 est. for urban agglomeration): Salisbury, 555,000; (est. 1973 by U.N.): Bulawayo, 307,000.
Monetary unit: Rhodesian dollar.

Languages: English (official), Bantu languages, Sindebele, Shona.
Religions: Christian, 20%; Animist.

Executive authority is vested in a 14-minister Cabinet, which is headed by the Prime Minister, and legislative authority is vested in a Legislative Assembly of 65 members.

Major Political Parties. Rhodesian Front (all 50 white seats of 65-seat Legislative Assembly), led by Prime Minister Ian Smith; Rhodesia Party (7 black elective seats). Eight other black seats are elected by black tribes.

History. Rhodesia, formerly called Southern Rhodesia, was part of the Federation of Rhodesia and Nyasaland, which came to an end on Dec. 31, 1963. In 1964, both Northern Rhodesia and Nyasaland became independent states, but Rhodesia, because of its white-supremacy policies, became the target of attacks by other African states and the site of considerable dissension.

Rhodesia was opened by Cecil Rhodes's British South Africa Company, which administered the area until 1923. At that time, in a referendum, the Europeans voted to become a self-governing colony rather than merge with what was then the Union of South Africa.

On Nov. 11, 1965, the white-minority government of Rhodesia unilaterally declared its independence from Great Britain.

Britain's first reaction was to vest constitutional authority in the Governor, making the independent government illegal. Then it applied sanctions. In 1967, Rhodesia became the first country against which the United Nations ever imposed mandatory sanctions. The United States stopped virtually all trade with Rhodesia. The country refused to cave in, but began a slow movement toward meeting the demands of the Black Africans. The white minority regime of Prime Minister Ian Smith in 1968 withstood British pressure, economic sanctions, guerrilla attacks and a Right-wing assault.

On Mar. 1, 1970, Rhodesia formally proclaimed herself a republic, and within the month nine nations, including the United States, closed their consulates there. On Mar. 17, the United States used its veto in the U.N. Security Council for the first time to defeat a resolution censuring the British for failing to use force against the Rhodesian rebels.

In 1972 the international economic boycott of Rhodesia began to break down. The U.S. was one country that resumed trade by buying Rhodesian chrome ore, but restored the ban one year later.

Black terrorism, which began late in 1972, resulted in the death of several hundred black rebels and several dozen white citizens and soldiers. The army draft size was doubled and other steps were taken to counter the security threat, including uprooting 8,000 black Africans from the area bordering Mozambique in an attempt to create a 200-mile-long buffer zone.

Smith's Rhodesian Front won its third successive sweep of all 50 white Parliamentary seats in the July, 1974, elections. In December, Smith announced achievement of a cease-fire in fighting with black nationalist guerrillas. He released imprisoned black nationalist leaders, including the Rev. Ndabaningi

Sithole, a militant, and said a constitutional conference would be held on the entry of blacks into the government. After negotiations on terms for the conference stalled, Sithole was rearrested in March, 1975, then released a month later. There was renewed guerrilla activity.

British Commonwealth leaders, meeting in Jamaica, agreed May 6 to tighten economic sanctions to pressure the Smith regime into an accommodation with the blacks. The International Olympic Committee voted May 22 to exclude Rhodesia from the 1976 Olympic Games because of its racist policies.

Heightened guerrilla war and a withdrawal of South African military aid—particularly helicopters—marked the beginning of the collapse of Smith's 11 years of resistance in the spring of 1976. Under pressure from South African Prime Minister Johannes Vorster, Smith agreed with U.S. Secretary of State Henry A. Kissinger on Sept. 19 that majority rule should come within two years.

As a first step, the white government and black nationalist leaders were scheduled to assemble in Geneva Oct. 21 under the chairmanship of Ivor Richard of Britain to work out an interim government which would preside over the transition to majority rule.

Economic Conditions. Agricultural products include tobacco, corn, tea, sugar and peanuts. Minerals include coal, chrome ore, asbestos, iron ore, gold.

Chief exports in 1965 were tobacco (51%), asbestos (12%), machinery (9%), meat (7%), copper (7%), clothing (6%) and chemicals (5%). Leading customers were Zambia (29%), United Kingdom (20%), South Africa (11%), West Germany (8%), Malawi (6%), Japan (5%). Leading suppliers were U.K. (30%), South Africa (23%), U.S. (7%), Japan (6%).

ROMANIA (Socialist Republic)

(Republica Socialista Romania)

President: Nicolae Ceausescu (1967).
Premier: Manea Manescu (1974).
Area: 91,700 sq mi. (237,500 sq km).
Population (est. 1976): 21,480,000 (approx.: Romanian, 88%; Hungarian, 9%).
Density per square mile: 234.2.
Capital: Bucharest.
Largest cities (est. 1973): Bucharest, 1,528,600; (est. 1973 by U.N.): Cluj, 212,690; Timisoara, 204,700; Jassy, 202,000; Brasov, 193,100; Galati, 191,100; Crajova, 188,300.
Monetary unit: Lei.
Languages: Romanian, Hungarian, German, Turkish.
Religions: Romanian Orthodox, 70%; Greek Orthodox, 10%.

The supreme body of state power and the sole legislative body is the Grand National Assembly, with 465 members elected for five-year terms. It elects a State Council to provide continuity of state power and to settle problems between sessions of the Assembly. The supreme executive and administrative body is the Council of Ministers elected by the Assembly.

Political Party. Communist Party, led by Secretary General Nicolae Ceausescu.

History. Most of Romania was the Roman province of Dacia from about A.D. 100 to 275. From the 6th to the 12th centuries, wave after wave of barbarian conquerers—Vlachs, Bulgars and others—passed over the area. It became a kingdom in 1881 after the Congress of Berlin.

King Ferdinand acceded to the throne in 1914. At the start of World War I Romania proclaimed its neutrality, but later joined the Allied side and in 1916 declared war on the Central Powers. Most of the country was overrun by German and Austrian forces, which enforced a harsh peace. By November 1918, the Allies had driven the enemy forces out, and Romania was back in the war on the Allied side. The armistice of Nov. 11, 1918 annulled the Treaty of Bucharest. Romania took vast territories from Russia, Austria and Hungary.

The gains of World War I, making Romania the largest Balkan state, included Bessarabia, Transylvania and Bukovina. The Banat, a Hungarian area, was divided with Yugoslavia.

In 1925, Crown Prince Carol renounced his rights to the throne, and when King Ferdinand died on July 20, 1927, Carol's son, Michael (Mihai) became King under a regency. However, Carol returned from exile in 1930, was crowned King Carol II, and gradually became a powerful political force in the country. On Feb. 10, 1938, he abolished the democratic Constitution of 1923. On June 21, 1940, the country was reorganized along Fascist lines, and the Fascist Iron Guard became the nucleus of the new totalitarian party. On June 27, the Soviet Union occupied Bessarabia and northern Bukovina. By the Axis-dictated Vienna Award of 1940, two fifths of Transylvania went to Hungary, after which the King dissolved Parliament and granted the new Premier, Ion Antonescu, full power. Carol abdicated and again went into exile.

Romania subsequently signed the Axis Pact on Nov. 23, 1940, and the following June joined in Germany's attack on the Soviet Union, reoccupying Bessarabia. Following the invasion of Romania by the Red Army in August 1944, King Michael led a coup d'état which ousted the Antonescu government. An armistice with the Soviet Union was signed Sept. 12, 1944 in Moscow.

Elections held Nov. 19, 1946 resulted in a victory for the Communist-dominated government bloc. Michael abdicated on Dec. 30, 1947, and thereafter the nation was declared a "people's republic."

A new Constitution in 1952 made Romania a "people's democracy" of the Soviet type. It dissolved joint companies with the Soviet set up by a law of 1948 which had nationalized industry and collectivized agriculture. In 1955, Romania joined the Warsaw Treaty Organization and the United Nations. In 1961, Gheorghe Gheorghiu-Dej, leading Communist, was elected President of a newly created State council, and foreign and domestic policy was closely aligned with that of the Soviet Union. But beginning in 1963, and particularly after Gheorghiu-Dej's death in 1965, Romania became increasingly independent of Soviet influence, while remaining firmly in the Soviet bloc. A new Constitution was adopted in 1965, which, while proclaiming Romania a socialist republic, emphasized national autonomy.

Through the decade, Romania under Nicolae Ceausescu grew more independent of Moscow, exchanging trade and military delegations with Red China and Albania and, on Aug. 2–3, 1969, hosting the visit of President Richard M. Nixon. Ceausescu continued his rapport with Peking, and visited Red China in 1971. In contrast to his flexibility in foreign affairs, he clamped down on liberal tendencies at home and took increasing personal power, becoming chief of the armed forces.

Ceausescu's power base was reaffirmed Nov. 26, 1974, when the 11th Romanian Communist Party Congress re-elected him to a new five-year term as the party's general secretary. Although he pledged "resolute steps" to cement relations with Moscow, there were signs of a continuing independent course. In its first postwar accord with Washington, Romania exchanged cultural and scientific agreements with the United States in December, 1974. In May, 1975, the Romanian Communist Party organ proposed that both the Warsaw Pact and NATO scrap their military organizations.

For the first time in 29 years, Romanians were offered some choice of candidates when they voted, on March 9, 1975, in parliamentary and local elections. There were contests for 39% of the parliamentary seats, but all candidates were Communist Party members. Officials said 99.9% of the voters turned out.

Economic Conditions. Romania is predominantly agricultural, with about 65% of the population engaged on the soil. In wheat, rye, and other grains, it is one of the richest countries of southeastern Europe. The largest acreage is usually devoted to corn and wheat. Other crops are flax, hemp, fruit, vegetables, potatoes, sugar beets, sunflower seeds, tobacco and grapes. Stock raising is important.

Probably the most important industries are food processing, textiles, metals, chemicals, wood and paper. All but small business enterprises are nationalized.

The Romanians have proclaimed their economic independence from the Soviet Union.

By far the most valuable of Romanian minerals is oil, produced chiefly in the Ploesti region about 35 miles north of Bucharest.

Natural gas from Transylvania is the second most important mineral. Other important minerals are iron ore, lignite, copper, gold and silver. Uranium deposits have been reported.

Chief exports in 1974 were machinery and transport equipment (21%), food (20%), chemicals (11%), petroleum products (11%) and industrial raw materials (7%). Leading customers were U.S.S.R. (17%), West Germany (10%), East Germany (6%), Italy (5%), United Kingdom (5%), Czechoslovakia (5%). Leading suppliers were West Germany (15%), U.S.S.R. (15%), U.K. (6%), East Germany (5%), U.S. (5%).

Natural Features. The Carpathian Mountains divide Romania's upper half from north to south and connect near the center of the country with the Transylvanian Alps, running east and west.

North and west of these ranges lies the Transylvanian plateau, and to the south and east are the plains of Moldavia and Walachia. In its last 190 miles, the Danube River flows through Romania only. It enters the Black Sea in northern Dobruja, just south of the border of the Soviet Union.

RWANDA (Republic)

President: Maj. Gen. Juvénal Habyalimana (1973).
Area: 10,169 sq mi. (26,338 sq km).
Population (est. 1976): 4,285,000.
Density per square mile: 421.4.
Capital and largest city (est. 1971): Kigali, 60,000.
Monetary unit: Rwandan franc.
Languages: Kinyarwanda and French.
Religions: Roman Catholic (46%), Animist (43%), Protestant (7%), Moslem (1%).

History. Rwanda, which was part of German East Africa, was first visited by European explorers in 1854. During World War I it was occupied in 1916 by Belgian troops. After the war it became a Belgian League of Nations mandate, along with Burundi, under the name of Ruanda-Urundi. The mandate was made a U.N. trust territory in 1946. Until the Belgian Congo achieved independence on June 30, 1960, Ruanda-Urundi was administered as part of that colony.

Ruanda became the independent nation of Rwanda on July 1, 1962.

Grégoire Kayibanda was President from 1962 until he was overthrown in a bloodless coup July 5, 1973 by the military led by Gen. Juvénal Habyalimana. The legislative Assembly was dissolved and all activities of Kayibanda's Parmenhutu Party, the only one permitted at the time, were suspended.

Economic Conditions. Rwanda is primarily an agricultural and cattle-raising country. Among its natural resources are tin, tungsten, beryllium, methane and hydroelectric potential. It also produces pyrethrum, coffee, tea, cotton, tobacco and food crops. There is little industry because of the lack of cheap power.

Chief exports in 1974 were coffee (64%), tin (12%), tea (6%) and pyrethrum extract (5%). Leading customers in 1973 were U.S. (c. 36%), Kenya (c. 19%), Belgium-Luxembourg (c. 18%). Leading suppliers in 1974 were Belgium-Luxembourg (16%), Kenya (10%), Japan (9%), West Germany (9%), France (7%), Italy (7%), Iran (7%), U.S. (5%).

SAN MARINO (Republic)

(Repubblica di San Marino)

Regents: Two selected every six months by Grand Council.
Area: 23.6 sq mi. (61 sq km).
Population (est. 1976): 20,500 (mostly Italian).
Density per square mile: 868.6.
Capital and largest city (est. 1974 for metropolitan area): San Marino, 4,400.
Monetary unit: Italian lira.
Language: Italian.
Religion: Roman Catholic.

Executive power is exercised by Regents, two of whom are appointed every six months from the popularly elected Grand Council. In April 1959, the Grand Council granted women the vote.

Major Political Parties. Christian Democratic Party (27 of 60 seats in Grand and General Council); Communist Party (14 seats), Democratic Socialist Party (11 seats), Socialist Party (7 seats).

History. San Marino, the oldest republic in the world, is one-tenth the size of New York City. It is entirely surrounded by Italy, in the Apennines near Rimini. According to tradition, San Marino was founded about A.D. 350 and had good luck for centuries in staying out of the interminable wars and feuds on the Italian peninsula.

In elections on Sept. 7, 1969, slight changes occurred in the Council, but a coalition of the Christian Democratic and Democratic Socialist parties stayed in power. The Christian Democrats flew about 400 former countrymen from the United States to vote in the elections, and Communists brought in about the same number from Europe. These moves were legal, since a person born in San Marino remains a citizen wherever he lives.

Economic Conditions. San Marino derives much revenue from the exporting of its postage stamps, which are changed often to keep philatelists buying. Other exports are barley, wine and cattle, as well as building stone from Mount Titano.

SÃO TOMÉ AND PRÍNCIPE
(Democratic Republic of)

President: Manuel Pinto da Costa (1975).
Premier: Miguel Trovoada (1975).
Area: 372 sq mi. (964 sq km).
Population (est. 1976): 85,500.
Density per square mile: 229.8.
Capital (est. 1970): São Tomé, 17,400.
Monetary unit: Guinea-Bissau escudo.
Language: Portuguese.
Religion: Roman Catholic.

History. The tiny volcanic islands of São Tomé and Príncipe, lying in the Gulf of Guinea about 150 miles off the west coast of Africa, became independent of Portugal on July 12, 1975. They were discovered by the Portuguese in 1471. The majority of the early inhabitants were convicts, Jews from Portugal and slaves from Brazil and the mainland.

Manuel Pinto da Costa, who headed the Movement for the Liberation of São Tomé and Príncipe, was named first President of the new nation, which took the name Democratic Republic of São Tomé and Principe.

Economic Conditions. The principal industry is commercial agriculture. There are about 110 coffee and cocoa plantations on São Tomé, nearly all owned by Portuguese companies. Fishing is being developed slowly.

Chief exports in 1973 were cocoa (87%) and copra (8%). Leading customers were Portugal (36%), Netherlands (32%), West Germany (12%), U.S. (8%). Leading suppliers were Portugal (47%), Angola (23%), Netherlands (6%), France (5%).

Natural Features. São Tomé is covered by a dense mountainous jungle out of which have been carved large plantations. Príncipe's topography consists of jagged mountains.

SAUDI ARABIA (Kingdom)
(Al-Mamlaka al-'Arabiya as-Sa'udiya)

Ruler and Prime Minister: King Khalid Bin Abdul-Aziz (1975).
Area: 829,995 sq mi. (2,149,690 sq km).
Population (est. 1976): 9,100,000.
Density per square mile: 11.0.
Capital: Riyadh.
Largest cities (est. 1965): Riyadh, 225,000; Jidda, 194,000; Mecca, 185,000.
Monetary unit: Riyal.
Language: Arabic.
Religion: Moslem.

Saudi Arabia is an independent monarchy whose legitimacy rests on *Shariah* (the Law of Islam) and custom. A Council of Ministers was formed in November, 1953. It acts as a Cabinet under the leadership of the King and is composed of 21 ministries.

Royal and ministerial decrees account for most of the promulgated legislation, treaties, and conventions.

Political Parties. There are no political parties in Saudi Arabia.

History. Mohammed united the Arabs in the seventh century, and his followers, led by the caliphs, founded a great empire with its capital at Medina. Later, the caliphate capital was transferred to Damascus and then Baghdad, but Arabia retained its importance because of the holy cities of Mecca and Medina. In the 16th and 17th centuries, the Turks established at least nominal rule over much of Arabia, and in the middle of the 18th century, it was divided into separate principalities.

The kingdom of Saudi Arabia, which occupies most of the Arabian peninsula, is almost entirely the creation of King Ibn Saud (1882–1953). A descendant of earlier Wahabi rulers, he seized Riyadh, the capital of Nejd, in 1901 and set himself up as leader of the Arab nationalist movement. By 1906 he had established Wahabi dominance in Nejd. He conquered Hejaz in 1924–25, consolidating it and Nejd into a dual kingdom in 1926. In 1932, Hejaz and Nejd became a single kingdom, which was officially named Saudi Arabia. A year later the region of Asir was incorporated into the kingdom.

Oil was discovered in 1936 and commercial production began during World War II. Saudi Arabia was neutral until nearly the end of the war, but it was permitted to be a charter member of the United Nations. The country joined the Arab League in 1945, and took part in the 1948–49 war against Israel, but has followed a less extremist policy as opposed to the line of the United Arab Republic. In 1951, the United States was allowed to build an air base at Dhahran.

On Ibn Saud's death in 1953, the eldest son, Saud, succeeded to the throne. Saud at first supported the Nasser regime in Egypt, but in 1956 he entered an alliance with the Hashemite rulers of Jordan and Iraq. In 1958 he opposed the union of Egypt and Syria in the United Arab Republic, and he became a bitter foe of U.A.R. policy.

In 1964, Saud was deposed, and the Premier, Crown Prince Faisal, succeeded to the throne. In the Middle Eastern War in 1967 Faisal gave vocal support to Egypt but no military help. He joined the 5-month Arab oil boycott of the West, including the U.S., in the wake of the 1973 Arab-Israeli war, and sent a token force, 1,000 strong, to help Syria in the war.

Faisal's assassination by a deranged kinsman March 25, 1975, shook the Middle East, but failed to alter his kingdom's course. His successor was his brother, Prince Khalid, chosen within hours by five senior princes of the House of Saud. King Khalid gave influential support to Egypt during negotiations on Israeli withdrawal from the Sinai desert. His government made it clear to the industrial West that Saudi Arabia's relatively moderate oil pricing policies could change if consumer nations flouted Saudi views.

The Saudi Council of Ministers approved in May, 1975, a $140-billion, five-year plan to develop industry, transportation and education to service the welfare state created under Faisal and to modernize the armed forces. With oil revenues exceeding $25 billion yearly, financing seemed feasible, but foreign experts questioned whether Saudi Arabia could muster the equipment, supplies and trained manpower required to carry out the ambitious plan by 1980.

Economic Conditions. The majority of the inhabitants are Bedouin—nomads following their flocks over the desert. The population is predominantly Sunni Moslem, and the religious law of Islam is the common law of the land. Mecca and Medina are the leading religious centers of Islam, and the annual influx of pilgrims to those cities is the most important commercial activity outside the oil industry.

Saudi Arabia's desert climate restricts agriculture to the highlands of Asir and scattered oases. Dates are the staple crop; grain, fruits and vegetables are also grown.

Oil, discovered in 1936 in the province of al-Hasa along the Persian Gulf, is produced by the Arabian American Oil Co. (Aramco), owned 60% by the Saudi government and 40% by four U.S. companies that operate it. The main production centers are in Ghawar, Abqaiq, Safaniya, Dammam, Qatif and Khursaniya. Production has skyrocketed since World War II. The company's expenditures and payroll are important invisible exports, and oil revenues have greatly strengthened the financial position of the kingdom, which receives one half the company's profits. The oil fields are connected by pipeline with the port of Sidon, Lebanon.

Chief exports in 1974 were crude oil (94%) and petroleum products (6%). Leading customers in 1972 were Japan (15%), Netherlands (12%), Italy (11%), France (9%), United Kingdom (8%), U.S. (5%). Leading suppliers were U.S. (19%), Japan (14%), Lebanon (12%), U.K. (7%), West Germany (6%).

SENEGAL (Republic)

(République du Sénégal)

President: Léopold Sédar Senghor (1960).
Premier: Abdou Diouf (1970).
Area: 75,750 sq mi. (196,192 sq km).
Population (est. 1976): 4,300,000.
Density per square mile: 56.8.

Capital and largest city (est. 1974): Dakar, 714,100.
Monetary unit: Franc CFA.
Ethnic groups: Wolofs, Sereres, Peuls, Tukulers, and others.
Languages: French (official), Wolof, Peular (Fulani), other tribal dialects.
Religions: Moslem, 90%; Christian, 6%.

There is a National Assembly of 100 members, elected every five years. There is universal suffrage and a constitutional guarantee of equality before the law.

Major Political Parties. Union Progressive Senegalaise, led by President Senghor. Legal opposition was reconstituted in 1974 with formation of the Senegalese Democratic Party, headed by Abdoulaye Wade, which urged reduction in French and Western influences. The National Democratic Rally, led by Sheik Anta Diop, was formed in 1976.

History. The Portuguese had some stations on the banks of the Senegal River in the 15th century, and the first French settlement was made at Saint-Louis about 1650. The British took parts of Senegal at various times, but the French gained possession in 1840 and organized Sudan as a territory in 1904. In 1946, together with other parts of French West Africa, Senegal became part of the French Union. On June 20, 1960, it became an independent republic federated with the Sudanese Republic in the Mali Federation, from which it withdrew on Aug. 20.

In 1970, a referendum overwhelmingly approved the draft of a new Constitution, which provided again for a Premier, and Senghor immediately named Abdou Diouf.

On Jan. 1, 1973, Senegal joined with six other states to create the West African Economic Community to promote economic development within the region. The 1973–74 sub-Sahara drought killed thousands of cattle and seriously damaged the peanut crop that accounts for nearly half of Senegal's earnings. Iran extended an $8.5-million development loan in 1974.

U.S. Secretary of State Henry A. Kissinger, speaking in Dakar on May 1, 1976, proposed a $7.5 billion international aid plan to "roll back the desert," inviting the Soviet Union to take part.

Economic Conditions. Agricultural products include peanuts, millet, cassava, cotton, tobacco and sisal.

Chief exports in 1973 were peanut oil (19%), peanut oil cake (15%), phosphates (11%) and fish and products (9%). Leading customers were France (49%), Ivory Coast (8%), Mauritania (7%). Leading suppliers were France (46%), U.S. (7%), China (5%), West Germany (5%).

SEYCHELLES (Republic)

(Member of Commonwealth of Nations)

President: James Mancham (1976).
Prime Minister: Albert Rene (1976).
Area: 145 sq mi. (376 sq km).
Population (est. 1976): 65,000.
Density per square mile: 448.3.
Capital (est. 1973): Victoria, 14,000.
Monetary unit: Seychelles rupee.

Languages: English, French, Creole.
Religions: Roman Catholic, 90%, Anglican, 7.5%.

Seized from France by Britain in 1810, this archipelago in the Indian Ocean northeast of Madagascar remained a colony until June 28, 1974. The new state is an independent republic within the Commonwealth.

The principal islands are Mahé (55 sq mi.), Praslin (15 sq mi.) and La Digue (4 sq mi.) but there are a total of 85 islands in the archipelago. The Aldabra, Farquhar and Desroches groups, once optioned for lease by the United States for use as an Indian Ocean defense base, were included in the territory of the new republic.

The chief industry is tourism. The Seychelles export copra and cinnamon bark.

SIERRA LEONE (Republic)·

(Member of Commonwealth of Nations)

President: Dr. Siaka P. Stevens (1971).
Prime Minister: Christian A. Kamara-Taylor (1975).
Area: 27,699 sq mi. (71,740 sq km).
Population (est. 1976): 2,790,000.
Density per square mile: ⸱ ˆ9.7.
Capital and largest city (est. 1972): Freetown, 195,800.
Monetary unit: Leone.
Languages: English (official), Mende, Temne, Creole.
Religions: Animist, 66%; Moslem, 28%; Christian, 10%.

Sierra Leone became an independent nation on Apr. 27, 1961.

Political Parties. All Peoples Congress (APC), led by Dr. Siaka P. Stevens, with 84 of 97 seats in Parliament. Twelve of the remaining 13 seats are held by tribal chiefs.

History. The coastal area of Sierra Leone was ceded to English settlers in 1788 as a home for blacks discharged from the British armed forces and also for runaway slaves who had found asylum in London. The British protectorate over the hinterland was proclaimed in 1896.

After elections in 1967, the British Governor-General replaced Sir Albert Margai, head of the Peoples Party, which had held power since independence, with Dr. Stevens, head of the All Peoples Congress Party, as Prime Minister. The Army took over the government. Then another coup in April 1968 restored civilian rule and put the military men in jail.

Following some curious events in early 1971, the nation became a republic but remained in the British Commonwealth. A coup attempt by the army commander was apparently foiled by loyal army officers, but the then Prime Minister Stevens called in troops of neighboring Guinea's army, under a 1970 mutual defense pact, to guard his residence. After perfunctorily blaming the U. S. for the coup attempt, Stevens switched Governors-General, changed the Constitution, and ended up with a Republic, of which he was first President. He was accused of taking "sweeping dictatorial powers."

Economic Conditions. Agricultural products include palm kernels and coffee. Sierra Leone is one of seven nations that produce 63% of the world's bauxite.

Chief exports in 1974 were diamonds (60%), iron ore (10%) and palm kernels (6%). Leading customers were United Kingdom (61%), Netherlands (15%), U.S. (6%), Japan (5%). Leading suppliers were U.K. (21%), Japan (10%), Nigeria (8%), West Germany (7%), Pakistan (5%), France (5%), China (5%).

SINGAPORE (Republic)

(Member of Commonwealth of Nations)

President: Benjamin Sheares (1970).
Prime Minister: Lee Kuan Yew (1959).
Area: 226 sq mi. (581 sq km).
Population (est. 1976): 2,280,000 (Chinese, 76%; Malay, 15%; Indian, 7%).
Density per square mile: 10,088.5.
Capital (1970 census): Singapore, 2,074,507.
Monetary unit: Singapore dollar.
Languages: Malay, Chinese (Mandarin), Tamil, English.
Religions: Moslem, Christian, Buddhist, Hindu, Confucianist, Taoist.

The head of state is the President. There is a Cabinet, headed by the Prime Minister, and a Parliament of 65 members elected by universal suffrage.

Major Political Party. People's Action Party (all 65 seats in Parliament), led by Prime Minister Lee.

History. Singapore, founded in 1819 by Sir Stamford Raffles, comprises the island of Singapore, off the southern tip of the Malay peninsula, and adjacent islets. It became a separate crown colony of Great Britain on Apr. 1, 1946, when the former colony of the Straits Settlements was dissolved. The other two settlements—Penang and Malacca—were transferred to the Union of Malaya, and the small island of Labuan was transferred to North Borneo. The Cocos (or Keeling) Islands were transferred to Australia in 1951 and Christmas Island in 1958.

Singapore attained full internal self-government in 1959. On Sept. 16, 1963, it joined Malaya, Sabah (North Borneo) and Sarawak in the federation of Malaysia. It withdrew from the federation on Aug. 9, 1965, and proclaimed itself a republic in September of that year.

Economic Conditions. The basis of Singapore's prosperity is its entrepôt trade. It handled a large part of the export trade of the Federation of Malaysia, and it conducts a large volume of trade with Indonesia.

Fruits and vegetables are the chief agricultural products of Singapore. Industries include shipbuilding and oil refining. Offshore fishing is also an important economic activity.

Chief exports in 1974 were petroleum products (26%), machinery (17%), rubber (14%), chemicals (6%) and food (6%). Leading customers were Malaysia (17%), U.S. (15%), Japan (11%), Hong Kong (6%), Australia (5%). Leading suppliers were Japan (18%), U.S. (14%), Malaysia (13%), Kuwait (6%), Saudi Arabia (6%), Iran (6%), United Kingdom (5%).

SOMALIA (Democratic Republic)

(Jamhuuriyadda Dimuqradiga Soomaaliya)

President of Supreme Revolutionary Council: Maj. Gen. Mohamed Siad Barre.
Area: 246,201 sq mi. (637,657 sq km).
Population (est. 1976): 3,250,000.
Density per square mile: 13.2.
Capital and largest city (est. 1972): Mogadishu, 230,000.
Monetary unit: Somali shilling.
Language: Somali.
Religion: Moslem.

Since the bloodless coup d'état of Oct. 21, 1969, Somalia has been governed by a Supreme Revolutionary Council, which immediately dissolved the National Assembly and arrested all members of the former government. Maj. Gen. Mohamed Siad Barre is president of the Council and the country's chief executive. He is assisted by three vice presidents.

The Revolutionary Council, which is composed of 21 members of the armed forces, rules by decree according to Socialist principles, with a foreign policy based on nonalignment. Return to civilian authority and resumption of political activities were promised when "conditions permit."

The business of government is administered by the 18-member Cabinet Secretaries of State, a predominantly civilian body.

Political Parties. All political parties were banned by the military government.

History. British troops first came to Somaliland in 1884 to protect British interests there, and gradually a number of protectorates were established. From 1901 to 1920, much of the interior was inaccessible because of a holy war, which did not end until the fanatic Somali mullah who led it died.

The Italian protectorate was established in 1889 and was under British military administration from 1941 to 1949. Italy took over the U.N. trusteeship in 1950.

British Somaliland and Italian Somaliland united and became the independent Republic of Somalia on July 1, 1960.

Somalia broke off diplomatic relations with Britain in 1963 when the former colonial ruler announced that the largely Somali-populated Northern Frontier District of Kenya would be given a large measure of autonomy. Hostilities broke out with Ethiopia in 1964 over migrations of nomadic Somalis into that country, but a cease-fire was arranged.

On Oct. 15, 1969, the President, Abdi Rashid Ali Shermarke, was assassinated by a national policeman, and the army seized power in a bloodless coup, dissolving the legislature and arresting all government leaders. The nation was renamed the Somali Democratic Republic. The 9,000-man army has 500 Russian advisers and is entirely equipped and trained by the Soviets. The 6,000-man police force is advised and trained by the United States, West Germany and Italy.

Famine caused by the long sub-Sahara drought led to declaration of a state of emergency in November, 1974, by the government, which said that 140,000 drought victims had fled from stricken areas to refugee camps.

Economic Conditions. Somalia is primarily a pastoral and agricultural country; about 80% of the population are engaged in livestock raising. Agricultural products include sugar cane, bananas and maize.

In 1968, Somalia reported discovery of major reserves of uranium and other rare minerals.

Chief exports in 1972 were livestock (54%), bananas (26%), meat and products (8%) and hides and skins (6%). Leading customers were Saudi Arabia (53%), Italy (18%), U.S.S.R. (6%), Kuwait (6%), Yemen (5%). Leading suppliers were Italy (29%), U.S.S.R. (10%), U.S. (6%), United Kingdom (6%), China (6%), Japan (6%), Kenya (5%), West Germany (5%).

SOUTH AFRICA (Republic)

(Republiek van Suid-Afrika)

State President: Nicolaas Diederichs (1975).
Prime Minister: Balthazar Johannes Vorster (1966).
Area: 471,445 sq mi. (1,221,037 sq km).*
Population (est. 1976): 26,000,000.* (Bantu, 71.2%; white, 16.7%; colored (mixed), 9.3%; Asian, 2.8%).
Density per square mile: 55.1.*
Administrative capital: Pretoria.
Legislative capital: Cape Town.
Judicial capital: Bloemfontein.
Largest cities (est. 1974): Johannesburg, 1,319,900; Cape Town, 790,900; Pretoria, 604,700; (1970 census): Durban, 729,857; Port Elizabeth, 386,577.
Monetary unit: Rand.
Languages: English, Afrikaans, Bantu languages.
Religions (1960): Dutch Reformed, 12.8%; Methodist, 8.5%; Anglican, 7.7%; Roman Catholic, 4.3%; Lutheran, 3.1%; Presbyterian, 1.7%; other Christian churches and sects, 61.9%.

At the head of the country is the Republic Government, and within each of the four provinces (Cape, Transvaal, Orange Free State, and Natal) there are Provincial Councils. The Republic has three capitals (Cape Town, legislative; Bloemfontein, judicial; and Pretoria, administrative), and two official languages (English and Afrikaans). The Parliament is made up of a Senate consisting of 54 members and a House of Assembly consisting of 171 members. Members of both Houses hold their seats for five years unless Parliament is dissolved before the end of their term.

To handle the routine business of South Africa's racial enclaves, there are nine black state governments with unicameral legislatures elected by black voters; a Colored (mulatto) Representative Council, with 40 of 60 members elected, and an Indian Council, with 15 of 30 members elected.

Major Political Parties. National Party (122 of 171 seats in House of Assembly), led by Prime Minister Vorster; United Party (35 seats), led by Sir de Villiers Graaff; Progressive-Reform Party (12 seats), led by Colin Eglin.

History. Dutch settlers first came to South Africa in 1652. By the beginning of the 18th century, nearly 2,000 settlers were established. Although the

* Excluding South-West Africa (Namibia).

colony was made up of Europeans from various countries, it assumed a Dutch character.

In consequence of the Napoleonic wars, Britain gained control over the Cape Colony in 1814, and within seven years, 5,000 British settlers had taken up residence. The British administration freed the slaves upon whom many Boer farmers depended for labor and sought to establish equality of rights for the colored population, who worked in the main for Boer landowners. By the mid-19th century the final form of the Union was emerging; settlers were scattered on the northern side of the Vaal and Orange rivers. In 1877, the British annexed the Transvaal territory and, although it was relinquished again in 1881, the act created bitter resentment among the Dutch settlers. The conflict between the imperialism of England and the republicanism of the Boer colonies culminated in the Jameson Raid, which was the opening gun of the bitter Boer War (1899–1902).

The two years of war paved the way for the Union of South Africa, which was established in 1910.

The first Prime Minister, Louis Botha, a Boer, allied South Africa to Great Britain during World War I. Two political parties developed, the Unionists, headed by Jan Christiaan Smuts, who favored alignment with Britain, and the Nationalists, who urged secession from the British Commonwealth. In World War II, the Nationalists opposed without success South Africa's entry into the war on the Allied side. South Africa was a charter member of the United Nations in 1945 but because of its separatist racial policy and discrimination against the Bantu-speaking black peoples refused to sign the Universal Declaration of Human Rights. Apartheid—racial separation—became the dominant political issue and the Nationalists won increasing dominance by promising greater restriction of the Negro and mulatto populations.

The Republic of South Africa was established on May 31, 1961. Personal freedom was restricted in 1963, and the government became increasingly totalitarian. In 1966, Prime Minister H. F. Verwoerd was assassinated. Balthazar J. Vorster, a Nationalist, succeeded him. The United Nations took direct responsibility for South-West Africa. Vorster began taking steps to improve its relations with black Africa, setting up a development loan fund. He announced five-year plans for the development of the reserve Bantu areas, Bantustans, with limited self-government. The economy boomed, bringing rising incomes to all classes and making the nonwhites better off than most blacks in Africa. But the whites, a fifth of the population, continued to receive two thirds of the national income.

General elections in April, 1974, increased the National Party's big majority in the House of Assembly and were construed as a vote of confidence in Vorster's "separate development" policies. South Africa continued to deal harshly with nonwhite offenders (police used dogs, gas and guns to break up recurrent mine disorders, and hanging remained the ultimate punishment; there were 24 executions in the first six months of 1974). At the same time, there were signs of moderation.

Vorster negotiated quietly for détente with black nationalists even as he assigned South African police to help Rhodesia fight black guerrillas in the winter of 1974–75. In December, 1974, the South African army accepted black enlisted men for the first time, but assigned them to segregated units. In May, 1975, blacks were permitted to buy 30-year leases in segregated sections adjoining white areas; they had previously been denied permanent occupancy of premises outside the Bantustans.

A Third World resolution to expel South Africa from the United Nations because of its apartheid policy was blocked by United States, British and French vetoes in the Security Council in October 1974, but the General Assembly then barred South Africa from its seat anyway. Vorster moved toward granting independence to South-West Africa (Namibia) by 1978, but black Africans demanded inclusion in the negotiations and an earlier target date.

In the 1975–76 Angolan civil war, Vorster engaged 4,000 troops on the side of UNITA, which lost to the Soviet-backed Popular Movement for the Liberation of Angola (MPLA). Defeat in Angola was followed by a wave of riots in black townships in South Africa, originating in protests against the use of the Afrikaans language in schools. More than 300 died as the movement widened to ask more freedoms, the strongest challenge to the white regime in a generation.

At the same time, outside pressure forced Vorster to withdraw military aid to Rhodesia in mid-1976. He met with U.S. Secretary of State Henry A. Kissinger in Zurich in September. As a result, Premier Ian Smith of Rhodesia's white government agreed to negotiate with nationalists in Rhodesia for majority rule. Kissinger incurred criticism, however, because of his failure to obtain quicker liberation of Namibia and increased rights for blacks inside South Africa.

Economic Conditions. South Africa is predominantly a pastoral country, with less than 15% of its area considered arable. Sheep and cattle raising are the principal occupations.

Climate and differences in terrain combine to give South Africa a great variety of agricultural products. The staple crop is maize, which is grown widely. In southwest Cape Province, products of the Mediterranean type predominate, while in the coastal belt of Natal and in northern Transvaal, subtropical crops, especially sugar, are grown.

Food, beverages and tobacco and metal products are leading products.

As a result of the need for armaments, a wartime iron and steel industry was established, and cement, chemical, textile and auto assembly plants were expanded.

Extensive mineral resources account for the economic prosperity. South Africa is the world's leading gold producer. Diamond production is now surpassed in importance by coal. Uranium, gypsum, tin and tungsten also are mined.

The whaling industry, centered at Durban on the east coast, produces considerable amounts of whale oil. South Africa has extensive fishery resources.

Chief exports in 1974 were diamonds (10%), gold coins (10%), cereals (8%), sugar (7%), iron and steel (7%), copper (6%), metal ores (5%) and textiles (5%). Leading customers were United Kingdom (29%), Japan (11%), West Germany (9%), U.S. (7%). Leading suppliers were West Germany (19%), U.K. (17%), U.S. (16%), Japan (12%).

Natural Features. South Africa has a high interior plateau, or veldt, nearly half of which averages 4,000 feet in elevation.

There are no important mountain ranges, although the Great Escarpment, separating the veldt from the coastal plain, rises to over 10,000 feet. The principal river is the Orange, rising in Lesotho and flowing westward for 1,300 miles to the Atlantic.

The southernmost point of Africa is Cape Agulhas, located in Cape Province about 100 miles east-southeast of the Cape of Good Hope.

SOUTH-WEST AFRICA (Namibia)

Status: Mandate.
Area: 318,261 sq mi. (824,292 sq km).
Population (est. 1976): 920,000.
Density per square mile: 2.9.
Administrator, B. J. van der Walt.
Capital (est. 1972): Windhoek, 65,000.
Chief exports: diamonds, other minerals, karakul pelts.
Agricultural products: hides and skins, butter, corn, wheat.
Minerals: diamonds, vanadium concentrates, tungsten, lead, tin, iron ore, copper, zinc.

The mandate, bounded on the north by Angola, and on the east by Bechuanaland and South Africa, was discovered by the Portuguese explorer Diaz in the late 15th century. It is for the most part a portion of the high plateau of southern Africa with a general elevation of from 3,000 to 4,000 feet. It became a German colony in 1884 but was conquered by South African forces in 1915, becoming a South African mandate by the terms of the Treaty of Versailles. South Africa's application for incorporation of the territory was rejected by the U.N. General Assembly on Dec. 14, 1946, and South Africa was invited to prepare a trusteeship agreement instead. By a law passed in April 1949, however, the territory was brought into much closer association with South Africa—including representation in the South African Parliament.

In 1969, South Africa extended her laws to the mandate over the objection of the United Nations, particularly its black African members. When South Africa refused to withdraw them, the U.N. Security Council condemned it in December.

After the United Nations Security Council endorsed independence for the territory in 1972, South Africa's Prime Minister Vorster offered to form an advisory council composed of representatives of the "Bantu homelands" to run the state under his personal direction. Blacks objected to the idea, however.

Under a 1974 Security Council resolution, South Africa was required to begin the transfer of power to the Namibians by May 30, 1975, or face U.N. action, but 10 days before the deadline Vorster rejected U.N. supervision. He said, however, that his government was prepared to negotiate Namibian independence, but not with the Southwest African People's Organization, the principal black separatist group. Meanwhile, the all-white legislature of South-West Africa eased several laws on apartheid in public places.

SPAIN (Kingdom)

(Estado España)

Ruler: King Juan Carlos I (1975).
Premier: Adolfo Suárez González (1976).
Area: 194,897 sq mi. (504,782 sq km).*
Population (est. 1976): 35,815,000 (Spanish, Basque, Catalan).
Density per square mile: 183.8.
Capital: Madrid.
Largest cities (est. 1976): Madrid, 3,750,850; Barcelona, 1,846,250; Valencia, 748,730; Seville, 612,900; Zaragoza, 589,600; Bilbao, 486,600.
Monetary unit: Peseta.
Languages: Spanish, Basque, Catalan, Galician.
Religion: Roman Catholic.

King Juan Carlos I (b. Jan. 5, 1938) succeeded Generalissimo Francisco Franco Bahamonde as Chief of State Nov. 22, 1975. The King appoints the Premier from a list of three candidates submitted by the Council of the Realm.

The Cortes, or Parliament, previously consisted of 563 members—366 elected and the remainder appointed or chosen by special constituencies. Reform of the Cortes was under study in 1976 to create a more democratic body; election of a new Cortes has been postponed until June 1977.

Political Parties. During the Franco regime, only one party, the National Movement, was permitted. All parties except the Communists were authorized under Juan Carlos' declared intention to restore democracy. Dozens were organized in 1976, with the Christian Democrats, the Spanish Democratic Union (UDE), and the Spanish Socialist Workers Party (PSOE) among the leaders.

History. Spain, originally inhabited by Celts, Iberians, and Basques, became a part of the Roman Empire in 201 B.C., when it was conquered by Scipio Africanus. In A.D. 412, the barbarian Visigothic leader Ataulf crossed the Pyrenees and ruled Spain, first in the name of the Roman emperor and then independently. In 711, the Moslems under Tariq entered Spain from Africa and within a few years completed the subjugation of the country. In 732, the Franks, led by Charles Martel, defeated the Moslems near Poitiers, thus preventing the further expansion of Islam in southern Europe. Internal dissension of Spanish Islam invited a steady Christian conquest from the north.

Aragon and Castile became the most important Spanish states from the 13th to the 15th centuries, in time absorbing all the other peoples of Spain. Aragon and Castile were consolidated by the marriage of Ferdinand II and Isabella I. The last Moslem stronghold, Granada, was captured in January 1492, the same year in which Columbus, under the sponsorship of Isabella, discovered America. With Moslem control ended, Roman Catholicism was established as the official state religion. The Jews (1492) and the Moslems (1502) were expelled from Spain at the cost of incalculable suffering and loss of life.

In the era of exploration, discovery and colonization, Spain won tremendous wealth and a vast colonial empire. The conquest of Peru by Pizarro (1532–33) and of Mexico by Cortés (1519–21) brought great prosperity to the motherland. The

---

* Including the Balearic and Canary Islands.

Spanish Hapsburg monarchy, through wars, diplomatic negotiations and marriages, became for a time one of the most powerful in the world.

In 1588, Philip II sent his Invincible Armada to invade England, but its destruction cost Spain her supremacy on the seas and paved the way for England's colonization of America. Spain then sank rapidly to the status of a second-rate power and never again played a major role in European politics. Its colonial empire in the Americas and the Philippines vanished in wars and revolutions during the 18th and 19th centuries.

In World War I, Spain maintained a position of neutrality. In 1923, General Miguel Primo de Rivera became dictator. In 1930, Alfonso XIII revoked the dictatorship, but a strong antimonarchist and republican movement led to his leaving Spain in 1931.* The new Constitution declared Spain a workers' republic, broke up the large estates, separated church and state, and secularized the schools. The elections held in 1936 returned a strong Popular Front majority, with Manuel Azaña as President.

But political chaos persisted. On July 18, 1936, a conservative army officer in Morocco, Francisco Franco Bahamonde, led a mutiny against the government. The terrible civil war that followed lasted for three years and cost the lives of nearly a million people. It was, in effect, a dress rehearsal for World War II. Franco was aided by Fascist Italy and Nazi Germany, while Soviet Russia helped the Loyalist side. Several hundred leftist Americans served in the Abraham Lincoln brigade on the side of the republic. The war ended when Franco took Madrid on Mar. 28, 1939.

Franco became head of the state, national chief of the Falange Party (the governing party) and Premier and Caudillo (leader) of the empire. The country was ruled by Franco's Cabinet, the National Council of the Falange Party, and the Cortes, which formulated laws subject to Franco's veto. At first the jails were filled with Franco opponents. But after the dictator consolidated his power, he undertook a policy of reconciliation under which the wounds of civil war slowly healed.

In a referendum held July 6, 1947, the Spanish people approved a Franco-drafted succession law declaring Spain a monarchy again. Franco, however, continued as Chief of State.

In 1969, Franco and the Cortes designated Prince Juan Carlos Alfonso Victor María de Borbón (who married Princess Sophia of Greece on May 14, 1962) to become King of Spain when the provisional government headed by Franco comes to an end. Prince Juan Carlos is the grandson of Alfonso XIII and the son of Don Juan, pretender to the throne.

Spain concluded in 1967 its first economic-social development plan, which had raised levels of living dramatically within a decade and, combined with Spanish migration to higher-wage countries in Western Europe, had virtually extinguished unemployment. A new Constitution, adopted in 1966, allowed for the direct election of a fourth of the Cortes.

Basque nationalists, who have long agitated for a separate state, increased their agitation in the last years of Franco's reign. After worldwide pro-

* However, he did not abdicate. In 1941, shortly before his death, he renounced his claim to the throne in favor of his third son, Don Juan.

test, Franco commuted death sentences for six nationalists convicted of murder in December 1970. On Sept. 27, 1975, despite similar protests, Franco permitted the execution of five Basque terrorists.

Franco relinquished the post of Premier in June 1973 to his old and close friend, Adm. Luis Carrero Blanco, but six months later, Carrero Blanco was assassinated by Basque nationalists. In July 1974 Franco, 81 years old, took seriously ill and delegated his powers as ruler of Spain to his designated successor, Prince Juan Carlos. But in September, after his doctors had pronounced him fully recovered, Franco reassumed power.

Franco's health failed again and Prince Juan Carlos assumed the powers of chief of state Oct. 30, 1975, when the Generalissimo suffered a heart attack. He died Nov. 20 and Juan Carlos was proclaimed King on Nov. 22.

A new Cabinet was sworn in on Dec. 13, headed by Franco's last Prime Minister, Carlos Arias Navarro. Juan Carlos dismissed Arias on July 1, 1976 and replaced him with Adolfo Suárez González, charging the new Cabinet to prepare for parliamentary elections in June 1977.

Economic Conditions. Leading agricultural products include wheat, barley, corn, and potatoes.

The textile industry, concentrated in Catalonia, leads all others. The paper and chemical industries are also important, as well as pig iron and steel.

Spain's mineral wealth, second to agriculture in the national economy, yields millions of tons of ore, including coal, lignite, iron ore (metal content 50%), potash ore, lead ore, zinc ore and mercury. Spain also produces copper, gold, magnesite, sulfur, tungsten, phosphates, silver and, reportedly, uranium. Spanish forests yield lumber, pine resins, cork and esparto.

Chief exports in 1974 were food (17%), machinery (12%), chemicals (8%), petroleum products (7%), ships and boats (6%), footwear (5%) and motor vehicles (5%). Leading customers were EEC (47%; incl. France 12%, West Germany 11%, United Kingdom 9%, Italy 5%, Netherlands 5%) and U.S. (11%). Leading suppliers were EEC (36%; incl. West Germany 11%, France 8%, Italy 5%, U.K. 5%), U.S. (15%), Saudi Arabia (12%).

Natural Features. Spain, less than 10 miles from Africa at the closest point, and separated from France by the Pyrenees, is generally a broad plateau sloping to south and east and crossed by a series of mountain ranges and river valleys.

Outlying Islands. Off Spain's east coast in the Mediterranean are the Balearic Islands (1,936 sq. mi.), the largest of which is Majorca. Sixty miles west of Africa are the Canary Islands (2,808 sq. mi.).

Spanish Colonial Territory

SPANISH PLAZAS IN NORTH AFRICA

Area: 19.6 sq mi. (50.8 sq km).
Population (est. 1969): 164,000.

These plazas, or presidios, consist of Alhucemas, Ceuta, Chafarinas, Melilla and Peñon de Vélez de la Gomera.

The chief export in 1973 was phosphate ore.

SRI LANKA (Republic)
(formerly Ceylon)

(Member of Commonwealth of Nations)

President: William Gopallawa (1972).
Prime Minister: Mrs. Sirimavo Ratwatte Dias Bandaranaike (1972).
Area: 25,332 sq mi. (65,610 sq km).
Population (est. 1976): 14,300,000 (Sinhalese, 72%; Tamil, 21%; Moors, 7%).
Density per square mile: 564.5.
Capital: Colombo.
Largest cities (est. 1973 by U.N.): Colombo, 618,000; Dahiwala-Mount Lavinia. 136,000: Jaffna. 112,000.
Monetary unit: Sri Lanka rupee.
Languages: Sinhalese, Tamil, English.
Religions: Buddhist, 67%; Hindu, 18%; Christian, 7%; Moslem, 7%.

After 24 years as a British Dominion, Ceylon became an independent Republic and reverted to the traditional name Sri Lanka (resplendent island) on May 22, 1972. A new Constitution was adopted, replacing the 1948 one. The island remains a part of the Commonwealth. William Gopallawa, the former Governor-General, was named President and Mrs. Sirimavo R. D. Bandaranaike remained Prime Minister.

The new Constitution set up the National State Assembly, which consists of such number of elected representatives of the people as a Delimitation Commission may determine. The Assembly is a unicameral legislature and serves for six years unless dissolved earlier. There are presently 157 members.

Major Political Parties. Sri Lanka Freedom Party (87 seats), led by Prime Minister Bandaranaike, in coalition with the Moscow-oriented Communist Party (6 seats); United National Party (18 seats), led by J. R. Jayawardene; the Trotskyite Lanka Sama Samaj Party (17 seats), led by N. M. Perera; Federal Party (12 seats), led by S.J.V. Chelvanayakam.

History. Following Portuguese and Dutch rule, Ceylon became an English crown colony in 1798. The British developed coffee, tea and, rubber plantations and granted four Constitutions between 1798 and 1910. A fifth in 1920 granted partial self-government, a sixth in 1924 enlarging the powers of a legislative council. The Constitution of 1931 gave a large measure of self-government. Ceylon became a self-governing dominion of the Commonwealth of Nations in 1948. Rioting by the Tamils seeking a separate state within a federal system occurred in 1958 and 1961, resulting in the outlawing of their party. In 1962, the Prime Minister, Mrs. Sirimavo Bandaranaike, a radical, nationalized Western oil and other business facilities and became embroiled with the United States and Britain over compensation. She was ousted in the 1965 elections by a multiparty coalition.

Following considerable pre-election violence, Mrs. Bandaranaike was returned to power in a landslide victory on May 27, 1970, with her three-party leftist coalition capturing over two-thirds of parliament. An important factor was the 800,000 youths 18-to-21 years old given the vote for the first time; they proved largely left-leaning.

Mrs. Bandaranaike nationalized three Western oil companies, but apparently moved too slowly for far leftists who, reportedly 20,000 strong, began a rebellion in early 1971 that was put down speedily but with difficulty.

Sixteen newspapers were closed in April 1974 following criticism of the government for food shortages and high prices. Because steep boosts in prices for imported oil drained funds needed for food imports, Sri Lanka was permitted to draw on an emergency account set up by the International Monetary Fund to cushion the effects of the oil crisis.

Economic Conditions. Sri Lanka is heavily dependent on food imports, particularly rice, the staple food. A large part of the cultivated land (25% of the total area) is devoted to the chief export crops—tea, rubber, and coconut products, all of which are grown for the most part on plantations. Other crops include rice, fruits, cinnamon, citronella.

Mineral resources include graphite (plumbago), gem stones, mica, magnesite and vanadium.

Chief exports in 1974 were tea (39%), rubber (21%) and coconut products (11%). Leading customers in 1973 were United Kingdom (11%), China (9%), Pakistan (8%), U.S. (7%), Japan (5%). Leading suppliers were U.S. (9%), Japan (9%), France (8%), China (8%), U.K. (7%).

Natural Features. Most of the island is flat, but mountains in the south rise to 8,000 feet. The island extends to a maximum of 270 miles north and south, and 140 miles east and west.

SUDAN, THE (Democratic Republic)

(Jamhuryat es-Sudan Al Democratia)

President: Maj. Gen. Gaafar Mohamed Nimeiri (1969).
Area: 967,494 sq mi. (2,505,813 sq km).
Population (est. 1976): 18,215,000.
Density per square mile: 18.8.
Capital: Khartoum.
Largest cities (est. 1973): Khartoum, 400,000; Omdurman, 350,000; Port Sudan, 130,000.
Monetary unit: Sudanese pound.
Languages: Arabic, English, tribal dialects.
Religions: Moslem (Sunni), Christian, Animist.

Since the revolution of May 25, 1969, the Sudan has been governed by a 10-member Council for the Revolution. The provisional Constitution was abrogated.

Political Parties. All political parties were dissolved by the Council for the Revolution.

History. The early history of the Sudan (known as the Anglo-Egyptian Sudan between 1898 and 1955) is connected with that of Nubia, where a powerful local kingdom was formed in Roman times with its capital at Dongola. After conversion to Christianity in the 6th century A.D., it joined with Ethiopia and resisted Mohammedanization until the 14th century. Thereafter the area was broken up into many small states until 1820–22, when it was conquered by Mohammed Ali, Pasha of Egypt. Egyptian forces were evacuated during the Mahdist revolt (1881–98), but the Sudan was reconquered by the Anglo-Egyptian expeditions of 1896–98, and in 1899 became an Anglo-Egyptian condominium, which was reaffirmed by the Anglo-Egyptian treaty of 1936.

Egypt and Britain agreed in February 1953 to grant self-government to the Sudan under an appointed Governor-General. Under the self-government statute of Mar. 31, 1953, an all-Sudanese Parliament was elected in November-December 1953. and an all-Sudanese government was formed. In December 1955, the Parliament declared the independence of the Sudan, which, with the approval of Britain and Egypt, was proclaimed on Jan. 1, 1956.

In October 1969, Maj. Gen. Gaafar Mohamed Nimeiri, the President of the Council for the Revolution, took over the office of Prime Minister. He was elected the nation's first President in October 1971 by a reported 98.6% of the vote in a national referendum. His term runs for six years. In July 1972, Sudan and the U.S. resumed diplomatic relations that were broken as a result of the Arab-Israeli War of 1967.

On Mar. 2, 1973, eight terrorists of the Black September Palestinian group invaded the Saudi Arabian embassy in Khartoum and killed two American diplomats—the ambassador and the chargé d'affaires—and one Belgian diplomat after their demands for the release of Arab terrorist prisoners in different countries were refused. The terrorists surrendered after three days and were captured, but Nimeiri postponed bringing them to trial in the face of Arab calls for their release.

The terrorists were convicted of murder June 24, 1974, but Nimeiri freed them the next day and turned them over to the Palestine Liberation Army, which flew them to Cairo. The U.S. withdrew its Ambassador in protest, but he returned in October 1974 after the men were imprisoned in Egypt. All new U.S. aid programs and military sales to the Sudan were suspended indefinitely.

On July 2 and 3, 1976, a third attempted coup against Nimeiri left 1,000 rebels and loyal troops dead after a fierce battle in Khartoum. Nimeiri accused President Muammar Qadaffi of Libya of having instigated the attempt and broke relations with Libya. On Aug. 4, firing squads executed 81 convicted rebels.

Economic Conditions. The northern part of the country is peopled by Arabic-speaking Moslems, while in the backward south, pagan tribes predominate.

Long-staple cotton, the chief export crop, is grown under irrigation in the Kassala and Tokar areas of the north and in narrow strips along the main Nile; durra, peanuts, corn and oilseeds are grown elsewhere.

Livestock raising is the occupation of most of the population of the Sudan.

Salt is produced at Port Sudan, and gold deposits are worked at Gebeit, near the Red Sea. Most of the world's gum arabic comes from the semiarid Kordofan area of the west.

Chief exports in 1974 were cotton (35%), peanuts (15%) and gum arabic (12%). Leading customers in 1973 were China (14%), Italy (11%), Japan (11%), West Germany (9%), France (6%), India (6%), Netherlands (5%). Leading suppliers were United Kingdom (17%), China (8%), U.S. (7%), India (7%), Brazil (7%), West Germany (6%), U.S.S.R. (5%), Japan (5%).

Natural Features. About one-fourth the size of Europe, the Sudan extends from north to south about 1,200 miles and west to east about 1,000 miles. The northern region is a continuation of the Libyan Desert. The southern region is fertile, abundantly watered, and, in places, heavily forested. It is traversed from north to south by the Nile, all of whose great tributaries are partly or entirely within its borders.

The highest elevation is a mountain range parallel to the Red Sea, with heights of 4,000 to over 7,000 feet.

SURINAM (Republic)

President: Johan H. E. Ferrier (1975).
Prime Minister: Henk Arron (1975).
Area: 63,037 sq mi. (163,265 sq km).
Population (est. 1976): 450,000 (approx.: Hindustani, 33%; Creole, 31%; Indonesian, 15%; Bush Negro, 9%).
Density per square mile: 7.1.
Capital and largest city (est. 1973): Paramaribo, 150,000.
Monetary unit: Surinam guilder.
Language: Dutch, Taki-taki (lingua franca).
Religions: Roman Catholic, Dutch Reformed, Hindu.

Surinam became an independent republic on Nov. 25, 1975, after 308 years of British, French and Dutch rule, the last continuous from 1815. Known as Dutch Guiana before independence, it lies on the northeast coast of South America, surrounded by Guyana, Brazil and French Guiana.

After gradual progress toward internal autonomy, Surinam was granted a federal status with the Dutch Antilles and the Netherlands in a kingdom whose common interests were to be administered by the Council of the Realm in The Hague and whose internal affairs would be directed by an elected Legislative Council.

Race riots over unemployment and high inflation in 1973 prompted the Netherlands to offer complete independence to both Surinam and the Antilles. Henk Arron, leader of a coalition of Creole parties (Surinamese of African descent), backed independence as Jaggernath Lachmon, leader of the Vatan Hitkaric (Progressive Reform Party), fought for a delay.

Lachmon represented largely the 150,000 Surinamese of East Indian descent, known as Hindustanis, who before independence were outnumbered by 165,000 Creoles. An exodus of Creoles to the Netherlands after independence is believed to have reduced their number to less than 150,000. The remainder of the population is comprised of 67,000 persons of Indonesian descent; 40,000 "bush negroes," descendants of escaped slaves; 40,000 American Indians and a few thousand Chinese, Europeans and others.

Economic Conditions. Surinam is third among the world's bauxite producers, exporting 7 million metric tons annually. Bauxite earnings accounted for 92% of the nation's 1975 income of $156 million. Other exports include rice, gold and timber.

Chief exports in 1973 were alumina (45%), bauxite (27%) and aluminum (14%). Leading customers were U.S. (35%), West Germany (14%), Netherlands (12%), Norway and Sweden (10%). Leading suppliers were U.S. (34%), Netherlands (24%), Trinidad and Tobago (11%), United Kingdom (5%).

SWAZILAND (Constitutional Monarchy)

(Member of Commonwealth of Nations)

Ruler: King Sobhuza II (1967).
Prime Minister: Prince Makhosini Dlamini (1967).
Area: 6,704 sq mi. (17,363 sq km).
Population (est. 1976): 550,000.
Density per square mile: 82.0.
Capital (est. 1973): Mbabane, 20,755.
Monetary unit: Lilangeni.
Languages: English (official), Siswati.
Religions: Christian, 60%; Animist.

In April 1967, a new Constitution established King Sobhuza II as head of state and provided for an Assembly of 24 elected members by universal adult suffrage and six nominated members. There is also a Senate of 12 members, of whom six are appointed by the King on the advice of his Cabinet, and six are elected by the Assembly. But on Apr. 12, 1973, the King renounced the Constitution because of its "destructive elements" and took total power for himself.

Major Political Parties. Imbokodvo National Movement (21 elected seats in House of Assembly), led by Prince Makhosini; Ngwane National Liberatory Congress (3 seats), led by Dr. Ambrose Zwane. All political parties were suspended in 1973 by the King, however.

History. Swaziland is surrounded by the Republic of South Africa and Mozambique.

Bantu peoples migrated southwest to the area of Mozambique in the 16th century. A number of clans broke away from the main body in the 18th century and settled in Swaziland. In the 19th century they organized as a tribe, partly because they were in constant conflict with the Zulu. Their ruler, Mswazi, applied to the British in the 1840's for help against the Zulu. The British and the Transvaal governments guaranteed the independence of Swaziland in 1881. In 1890 a provisional government, representing the Swazi, the British, and the Transvaal, was established.

South Africa held Swaziland as a protectorate from 1894 to 1899, but after the close of the Boer War, in 1902, Swaziland was transferred to British administration. An elected European advisory council was established in 1921. The Paramount Chief was recognized as the native authority in 1941.

In 1963 the territory was constituted a protectorate, and on Sept. 6, 1968, it became the independent nation of Swaziland.

Economic Conditions. Herding is the principal native occupation. Tropical and subtropical crops are raised in the lower areas.

Important agricultural products are sugar, sorghums, corn, rice, cotton lint, peanuts and tobacco. Mineral products include iron ore, coal, asbestos and gold. There are timber and paper pulp industries.

Chief exports in 1973 were wood pulp (20%), sugar (18%), iron ore (11%), asbestos (9%), timber (8%), citrus fruit (5%) and meat and products (5%). Leading customers in 1970 were United Kingdom (25%), Japan (24%), South Africa (21%).

SWEDEN (Constitutional Monarchy)

(Konungariket Sverige)

Sovereign: King Carl XVI Gustaf (1973).
Prime Minister: Thorbjörn Fälldin (1976).
Area: 173,732 sq mi. (449,964 sq km).
Population (est. 1976): 8,230,000.
Density per square mile: 47.4.
Capital: Stockholm.
Largest cities (1975): Stockholm, 681,300; (est. 1973 by U.N.): Göteborg, 449,470; Malmö, 251,431; Uppsala, 136,067.
Monetary unit: Krona.
Language: Swedish.
Religion: Swedish Lutheran, 95%.

Sweden is a constitutional monarchy. Under the new Constitution, which became effective Jan. 1, 1975, the Riksdag is the sole governing body. The Prime Minister is the political chief executive.

In 1967, agreement was reached on part of a new Constitution after 13 years of work. It provides for a single-house Riksdag of 350 members (later amended to 349 seats) to replace the 104-year old bicameral Riksdag. The members are popularly elected for a term of three years. The first Riksdag under the new Constitution was installed in January 1971. Seventy-seven present members of the Riksdag are women.

Sovereign: The King, Carl XVI Gustaf, was born Apr. 30, 1946, and became the world's youngest reigning monarch when he succeeded to the throne Sept. 19, 1973, on the death of his grandfather, Gustaf VI Adolf at 90. The King's father, Prince Gustaf Adolf, born in 1906, was killed in a plane crash in 1947. Carl Gustaf was married June 19, 1976, to Silvia Sommerlath, a West German commoner.

Major Political Parties. Center Party (86 of 349 seats), led by Prime Minister Thorbjörn Fälldin; Moderate Party (55 seats), led by Gösta Bohman; Liberal Party (39 seats), led by Per Ahlmark; Social Democratic Party (152 seats), led by former Prime Minister Olof Palme; Leftist (Communist) Party, 17 seats. The first three parties constitute the governing coalition with a total of 180 seats.

History. The earliest historical mention of Sweden is found in Tacitus' *Germania,* where reference is made to the powerful king and strong fleet of the Suiones. Toward the end of the 10th century, Olaf Sköttkonung established a Christian stronghold in Sweden. Around 1400, an attempt was made to unite the northern nations into one kingdom, but this led to bitter strife between the Danes and the Swedes.

In 1520, the Danish King, Christian II, conquered Sweden and in the "Stockholm Blood-Bath" put leading Swedish personalities to death. Gustavus Vasa (1523–60) broke away from Denmark and fashioned the modern Swedish state.

Sweden played a leading role in the second phase (1630–35) of the Thirty Years' War (1618–48). By the Treaty of Westphalia (1648), Sweden obtained western Pomerania and some neighboring territory on the Baltic. In 1700, a coalition of Russia, Poland and Denmark united against Sweden and by the Peace of Nystad (1721) forced her to relinquish Livonia, Ingria, Estonia and parts of Finland.

From the Napoleonic wars, Sweden emerged with the gain of Norway from Denmark and with a new royal dynasty stemming from Marshal Bernadotte of France, who became King Charles XIV (1818-44). The artificial union between Sweden and Norway led to an unhappy feud. It was finally dissolved in 1905.

Sweden maintained a position of neutrality in both World Wars.

An elaborate structure of welfare legislation, imitated by many larger nations, began with the establishment of old-age pensions in 1911. Economic prosperity based on its neutralist policy enabled Sweden, together with Norway, to pioneer in public health, housing and job security programs.

Forty-four years of Socialist government was ended Sept. 19, 1976 by a conservative coalition headed by Thorbjörn Fälldin, a 50-year-old sheep farmer. The surprise conservative victory was credited to public opposition to a nuclear power program backed by the Socialists and to a program which would have given control of all businesses to labor unions within 20 years.

Economic Conditions. Milk, butter, meat, grain, potatoes and sugar beets are products of the broad fertile plains of the south; the north is limited to cattle raising and dairy farming.

The highly specialized machine industry produces separators, motors, electrical machines and apparatus, agricultural machinery, ball bearings, telephone equipment and harbor works.

There are also large woolen, glass and porcelain industries. Shipyards build for Swedish and foreign fleets. Timber and woodworking industries are extensive.

Sweden's iron ore deposits (metal content 60%) are among the world's richest. Those in central Sweden produce principally for domestic use, while the ones in Lapland to the north are worked largely for export, with much of the output being shipped through the Norwegian port of Narvik. Other minerals are copper, gold, lead, arsenic ore, manganese ore and silver. Coal production is insignificant; imports of several million tons a year are therefore necessary.

About 60% of Sweden is forested, mostly conifers, and there are vast forest products industries in the north. Sweden supplies a large percentage of the world's mechanical and chemical pulp.

Chief exports in 1974 were machinery (24%), paper (10%), motor vehicles (9%), iron and steel (8%), wood pulp (8%), timber (6%), chemicals (5%) and ships and boats (5%). Leading customers were United Kingdom (13%), Norway (10%), West Germany (10%), Denmark (8%), Finland (7%), U.S. (5%), France (5%). Leading suppliers were West Germany (19%), U.K. (11%), Denmark (7%), Norway (7%), U.S. (7%), Finland (6%), Netherlands (5%).

Natural Features. Sweden slopes eastward and southward from its peak elevation in the Kjölen Mountains along the Norwegian border. In the north are mountains and many lakes. To the south and east are central lowlands, and south of them are fertile areas of forest, valley, and plain. Along Sweden's rocky coast, chopped up by bays and inlets, are many islands, the largest of which are Gotland and Öland.

SWITZERLAND (Confederation)

(Schweiz-Suisse-Svizzera)

President: Rudolf Gnägi (1976).
Vice President: Kurt Furgler.
Area: 15,941 sq mi. (41,288 sq km).
Population (est. 1975 by U.N.): 6,400,000 (Swiss, 85%; Italian, 8.3%; German, 1.8%; Spanish, 1.6%; French, 0.8%; others 2.5%—figures by place of birth).
Density per square mile: 401.5.
Capital: Bern.
Largest cities (est. 1974 by U.N.): Zurich, 401,600; Basel, 199,600; Geneva, 163,100; Berne, 154,700; Lausanne, 136,100.
Monetary unit: Swiss franc.
Languages: German, 65%; French, 18%; Italian, 12%; Romansch, 1%.
Religions: Roman Catholic, 49%; Protestant, 48%.

The Swiss Confederation consists of 22 sovereign cantons. Federal authority is vested in a bicameral legislature. The Ständerat, or State Council, consists of 44 members, two from each canton. The lower house, the Nationalrat, or National Council, has 200 deputies, elected for four-year terms.

Executive authority is lodged in a board called the Bundesrat, or Federal Council, of seven members chosen by parliament. The parliament elects the President, who serves for a term of one year and is ordinarily succeeded by the Vice President. The Federal Government regulates matters of foreign policy, railroads, postal service and the national mint. Each canton reserves for itself important local powers.

A constitutional amendment adopted in February 1971 by referendum gave women the vote in federal elections and right to hold federal office for the first time. Women previously had the rights in some cantons and were expected to get total suffrage in all elections soon.

Major Political Parties. Social Democratic Party (55 of 200 seats in National Council), led by Helmut Hubacher; Radical Democratic Party (47 seats), led by Fritz Honegger; Conservative Christian-Social Party (46 seats), led by Hans Wyer; People's Party (21 seats), led by Hans Conzett; Independent Party (11 seats), led by Claudius Alder.

History. Called Helvetia in ancient times, Switzerland in the Middle Ages was a federation of fiefs of the Holy Roman Empire. Fashioned around the nucleus of three German forest districts of Schwyz, Uri, and Nidwalden, the Swiss Confederation slowly added new cantons. In 1648 the Treaty of Westphalia gave Switzerland her independence from the Holy Roman Empire.

French revolutionary troops occupied Switzerland in 1798 and named it the Helvetic Republic, but Napoleon in 1803 restored its federal government. At this time, and again in 1815, the French- and Italian-speaking peoples of Switzerland were raised to political equality.

In 1815, the Congress of Vienna neutralized and recognized the independence of Switzerland. In the revolutionary period of 1847 the Catholic cantons seceded and organized a separate union called the *Sonderbund.* In 1848 the new Swiss Constitution established a union modeled upon that of the United States. The Federal Constitution of 1874 established a strong central government while maintaining large powers of control in each canton.

National unity and political conservatism grew as the country prospered from its neutrality. Its banking system became the world's leading repository for international accounts. Armed neutrality was its policy through World Wars I and II. Geneva was the seat of the League of Nations, and Geneva and The Hague became the headquarters of a number of international organizations.

Through the 1960's, prosperity reached such levels that the 1968 census showed 970,000 foreigners resident in Switzerland, and laws were passed to cut the number.

Faced with signs of recession in 1974, Switzerland halted all recruitment of foreign labor. In 1975, with consumer prices up 9% in a year and economic growth stalled, parliament enacted emergency measures to stimulate private construction, encourage exports and broaden unemployment insurance coverage.

In 1971, the Swiss Supreme Court ruled that Swiss banks must show U.S. tax officials records of U.S. citizens suspected of tax fraud, thus significantly modifying a 1934 law that had seemed to forbid any bank disclosures.

A government-sponsored move to liberalize a law prohibiting abortions except for medical reasons was rejected by the National Council in March 1975. A national referendum on an even more liberal law was pending.

Economic Conditions. Leading agricultural products include wheat, barley, oats, rye, potatoes and fruit.

Chief exports in 1974 were machinery (29%), chemicals (23%), watches and clocks (10%), textile yarns and fabrics (5%), precious metals (5%) and instruments (5%). Leading customers were EEC (44%; incl. West Germany 14%, France 9%, Italy 8%, United Kingdom 7%), U.S. (7%), Austria (7%). Leading suppliers were EEC (67%; incl. West Germany 29%, France 14%, Italy 9%, U.K. 7%), U.S. (7%), Austria (5%).

Natural Features. Most of Switzerland comprises a mountainous plateau bordered by the great bulk of the Alps on the south and by the Jura Mountains on the northwest. About a fourth of the total area is covered by mountains and glaciers.

The country's largest lakes—Geneva, Constance (Boden See), and Maggiore—straddle the French, German-Austrian and Italian borders, respectively.

The Rhine, navigable from Basel to the North Sea, is the principal inland waterway.

SYRIAN ARAB REPUBLIC

(Al-Jamhouriya al Arabia as-Souriya)

President: Hafez el-Assad (1971).
Premier: Mahmoud Ayoubi (1972).
Area: 71,586 sq mi. (185,180 sq km).
Population (est. 1976): 7,580,000 (Arab, Armenian, Kurdish, Turkish, French).
Density per square mile: 105.9.
Capital: Damascus.
Largest cities (est. 1975): Damascus, 974,900; (est. 1972): Aleppo, 750,000; Homs, 231,900; Hama, 196,200.
Monetary unit: Syrian pound.

Languages: Arabic (official), Kurdish, Armenian, Turkish, Circassian.
Religions: Moslem, 86.3%; Christian, 12.6%; Jewish, 1%.

Following a coup by the military wing of the Ba'ath Arab Socialist Party against its political wing in November 1970, the new leadership appointed a People's Council (parliament) but retained all effective powers.

Syria's first permanent Constitution was approved in 1973, replacing a provisional charter that had been in force for 10 years. It provides for a 186-member People's Council as the legislature. No national religion is specified, although Moslem law is the basis of the state law.

Political Parties: In the first election in 10 years, in 1973, the Ba'ath Arab Socialist Party of President Hafez el-Assad, running on a unified National Progressive ticket with the Communists and Socialist parties, won 70% of the vote and a commensurate proportion of the seats in the People's Council.

History. Ancient Syria was conquered by Egypt about 1500 B.C., and after that by Hebrews, Phoenicians, Assyrians, Chaldeans, Persians, and Greeks. From 64 B.C. until the Arab conquest in A.D. 636, it was part of the Roman Empire except during brief periods. The Arabs made it a trade center for their whole empire, but it suffered severely from the Mongol invasion in 1260 and fell to the Ottoman Turks in 1516. Syria remained a Turkish province until World War I.

A secret Anglo-French pact of 1916 put Syria in the French zone of influence. The League of Nations gave France a mandate over Syria after World War I, but the French were forced to put down several nationalist uprisings. In 1930, France recognized Syria as an independent republic, but still subject to the mandate. After nationalist demonstrations in 1939, the French High Commissioner suspended the Syrian Constitution. In 1941, British and Free French forces invaded Syria to eliminate Vichy control. During the rest of World War II, Syria was an Allied base. Again in 1945, nationalist demonstrations broke into actual fighting, and British troops had to restore order. Syrian forces met a series of reverses while participating in the Arab invasion of Palestine in 1948. On Feb. 1, 1958, with the formation of the United Arab Republic through the union of Egypt and Syria, Gamal Abdel Nasser became President of the new republic. However, Syria became independent again on Sept. 29, 1961, following a revolution.

In the Middle Eastern War of 1967, Israel quickly vanquished the Syrian army. Before acceding to the U.N. cease-fire, the Israeli forces secured the fortified heights commanding the Sea of Galilee.

Syria joined Egypt in attacking Israel in October 1973 in the fourth Arab-Israeli war, but was pushed back from initial successes on the Golan Heights to end up losing more land. However, in the settlement worked out by Secretary of State Henry A. Kissinger in May 1974, the Syrians recovered all the territory lost in 1973 and a token amount of territory, including the deserted town of Quneitra, lost in 1967. Syria agreed to negotiate a permanent settlement with Israel, its first de facto recognition of Israel.

Relations between the United States and Syria, severed since the 1967 war, were renewed June 16, 1974 and Syria somewhat moderated the tone, but not the goals, of its policies toward Israel. Syria joined with Egypt in September 1974 in a statement declaring the Palestine Liberation Army to be "the sole representative of the Palestinian people" and initiated a resolution asserting this principle, which passed the United Nations General Assembly the following month.

Syria's often-strained relations with neighboring Jordan seemed improved in June, 1975, when the two nations agreed to form a permanent Joint High Commission to coordinate military, political, economic and cultural policies. In a joint declaration, they said Middle Eastern peace depended on Israeli withdrawal from all captured Arab lands and Israeli recognition of "the rights of the Palestinian people in their homeland."

Syria became involved in the Christian-Moslem civil war in neighboring Lebanon after warning in January 1976 against any attempt at partition. A Syrian-led truce effort succeeded in briefly restoring peace, but with the renewal of fighting Syria began moving troops into Lebanon in April. Despite cautions from Israel and the United States, Damascus increased its forces to 20,000 near the year's end and took over the brunt of the fighting against the Palestine Liberation Organization and leftist Moslem forces. In the process, Syria had turned from traditional enmity toward the Christians to a quasi-alliance with them and a one-third share in the three-way partitioning of Lebanon.

Economic Conditions. Agriculture and animal breeding are the main industries. Only half the land is arable, and only a third is actually cultivated. Most crops require irrigation. Leading crops include sorghum, olives, cotton, wheat, barley, grapes, lentils and tobacco. Stock raising is important among the nomads.

Chief exports in 1974 were crude oil (55%) and cotton (26%). Leading customers were Greece (18%), West Germany (15%), U.S.S.R. (14%), United Kingdom (10%), Lebanon (7%), China (5%). Leading suppliers were West Germany (12%), Italy (9%), France (9%), Lebanon (8%).

Natural Features. Coastal Syria is a narrow plain. Back of that is a range of coastal mountains, and still farther inland is a steppe area. In the east is the Syrian Desert, and in the southeast next to Jordan is the Jebel Druze Range.

TANZANIA (United Republic of)

(Member of Commonwealth of Nations)

President: Julius K. Nyerere (1964).
Area: 364,900 sq mi. (945,087 sq km).*
Population (est. 1976): 15,575,000.
Density per square mile: 42.7.
Capital and largest city (est. 1972): Dar es Salaam, 396,700.
Monetary unit: Tanzanian shilling.
Languages: Swahili, Bantu, Arabic, English.
Religions: Animist, Christian, Moslem.

Under the republican form of government, Tanzania has a President elected by universal suffrage who appoints the Cabinet ministers. The 218-member National Assembly is composed of 96 elected members from the mainland, 10 members ap-

* Including Zanzibar.

pointed by the President (from both Tanganyika and Zanzibar), 35 National members (elected by the National Assembly after nomination by various national institutions), 32 members of the Zanzibar Revolutionary Council, 20 other Zanzibar members appointed by the President in agreement with the President of Zanzibar, and 25 ex-officio members.

Political Party. Tanganyika African National Union (TANU) (mainland) and Afro-Shirazi Party in Zanzibar and Pemba.

History. Arab traders first began to colonize the area in A.D. 700. Portuguese explorers reached the coastal regions in 1500 and held some control until the 17th century, when the Sultan of Oman took power. With what are now Burundi and Rwanda, Tanganyika became the colony of German East Africa in 1885. After World War I, it was administered by Britain under a League of Nations mandate and later as a U.N. trust territory.

Although not mentioned in old histories until the 12th century, Zanzibar was believed always to have had connections with southern Arabia. The Portuguese made it one of their tributaries in 1503 and later established a trading post, but they were driven out by Arabs from Oman in 1698. Zanzibar was declared independent of Oman in 1861 and, in 1890, it became a British protectorate.

Tanganyika became an independent nation on Dec. 9, 1961; Zanzibar, on Dec. 10, 1963. On Apr. 26, 1964, the two nations merged into a single nation—the United Republic of Tanganyika and Zanzibar. The name was changed to Tanzania on Oct. 29, 1964.

Tanzania joined with Kenya and Uganda in 1967 to form a customs union, the East African Community.

In February 1969, Tanzania evicted the Peace Corps; it had been the first country to get volunteers.

In March, 1974, Nyerere returned from a trip to Peking (his third) with a pledge from Chairman Mao Tse-tung of a $75-million interest-free loan for development of coal and iron areas in the south. In June, Great Britain announced resumption of capital aid to Tanzania after a nine-year break and agreed to a $24-million interest-free rural development loan in return for a Tanzanian commitment to pay compensation for nationalized British properties.

On Oct. 23, 1975, the 1,163-mile Tanzam railway linking the Tanzanian port of Dar es Salaam with Zambia was officially opened. Built and financed by China, the railway provided a direct route for Zambian copper exports to the sea, replacing a longer route through white-ruled Rhodesia to Mozambique.

Economic Conditions. The mainland portion of Tanzania is sparsely populated, and two-thirds of it is uninhabited. It is the world's largest producer of sisal hemp. Production of cloves is the chief industry of the island of Zanzibar.

Chief exports in 1974 were cotton (17%), sisal (15%), coffee (13%), petroleum products (10%), cashew nuts (7%) and sisal fabrics (5%). Leading customers were United Kingdom (13%), U.S. (7%), Kenya (6%), Hong Kong (6%), India (5%), West Germany (5%), Belgium-Luxembourg (5%). Leading suppliers were China (11%), U.K. (10%), Japan (9%), West Germany (8%), Saudi Arabia (7%), Iran (7%), U.S. (7%), Kenya (7%).

THAILAND (Constitutional Monarchy)

(Muang Thai)

Ruler: King Bhumibol Adulyadej (1946).
Prime Minister: Tanin Kraivixien (1976).
Area: 198,500 sq mi. (514,000 sq km).
Population (est. 1975 by U.N.): 41,870,000 (1960: Thai, 98.2%;* Chinese, 1.6%; others, 0.2%).
Density per square mile: 210.9.
Capital: Bangkok.
Capital and largest city (est. 1975 for urban agglomeration): Bangkok, 4,129,600.
Monetary unit: Baht.
Languages: Thai (Siamese), Chinese, English.
Religions: Buddhist, 95%; Moslem, 4%.

King Bhumibol Adulyadej, who was born Dec. 5, 1927, second son of Prince Mahidol of Songkhla, succeeded to the throne on June 9, 1946, when his brother, King Ananda Mahidol, died of a gunshot wound. He was married on Apr. 28, 1950, to Queen Sirikit; their son, Vajiralongkorn, born July 28, 1952, is the Crown Prince.

Legislative power had been vested in the National Assembly, and the executive was run by a Council of Ministers led by the Prime Minister. However, in November 1971, Field Marshal Thanom Kittikachorn led a five-man Revolutionary Council that seized all government powers, abolished the constitution, dissolved Parliament, disbanded the Cabinet and established martial law. He later formed a 16-man ruling junta, again with himself as head. Communist insurgents in the north as well as obstructionism by politicians and labor groups were cited for the move.

In December 1972, Kittikachorn proclaimed (through the King) a new Constitution, ending 13 months of rule by decree, under which a new 299-member National Assembly was created as the legislature. Kittikachorn resigned Oct. 14, 1973 in the wake of student demonstrations, and Thailand got its first civilian government in 20 years. The first general elections were held in January 1975, and the new government was formed two months later.

Major Political Parties. Democratic Party (115 seats of 279 in National Assembly); Thai Nation Party (54 seats); Social Action Party (45 seats); Social Justice Party (28 seats); Social Agrarian (8 seats); Social Nationalists (8 seats); minor parties (19 seats).

History. The Thais first began moving down into their present homeland from the Asiatic continent in the 6th century A.D., and by the end of the 13th century ruled most of the western portion. During the next 400 years, the Thais fought sporadically with the Cambodians to the east and the Burmese to the west. The British obtained recognition of paramount interest in Thailand in 1824, and in 1896 an Anglo-French accord guaranteed the independence of Thailand.

A coup on June 24, 1932, changed the absolute monarchy into a representative government with universal suffrage. After five hours of token resistance on Dec. 8, 1941, Thailand yielded to Japanese occupation and became one of the springboards in World War II for the Japanese campaign against Malaya. After the fall of its pro-Japanese puppet government in July, 1944, Thailand pursued a pol-

*Including about 2,500,000 of Chinese descent born in Thailand.

icy of passive resistance against the Japanese, and on Aug. 16, 1945, after the Japanese surrender, Thailand repudiated the declaration of war it had been forced to make against Britain and the United States in 1942. By a treaty signed with Britain and India on Jan. 1, 1946, Thailand renounced all wartime acquisitions of Malayan territory.

Thailand's major problem in the late 1960s was suppressing Communist guerrilla action by invaders in the north. The prospect of a U.S. withdrawal from Southeast Asia alarmed the Thais, who sought and obtained reassurance from the United States that they would not be abandoned.

Although Thailand had received $2 billion in U.S. economic and military aid since 1950 and had sent troops (paid by the U.S.) to Vietnam while permitting U.S. bomber bases on its territory, the collapse of South Vietnam and Cambodia in the spring of 1975 brought rapid changes in the country's diplomatic posture.

At the Thai government's insistence, the U.S. agreed in June 1975 to withdraw all 23,000 U.S. military personnel remaining in Thailand by March 1976. Diplomatic relations with China were established July 1, 1975. Meanwhile, overtures toward an accommodation with the new regime in South Vietnam were initiated.

Thailand protested vigorously when 1,100 U.S. Marines were airlifted to Thai bases May 14 for use in the rescue of the crew of the cargo ship Mayaguez after its seizure by a Cambodian gunboat. (*See* Cambodia for details.) The marines were withdrawn May 15 and Thailand later accepted a U.S. apology for unauthorized use of its territory.

On Oct. 7, 1976, a military coup ousted the government of Premier Seni Pramoj after rioting by left-wing students at Thannasat University in Bangkok left 39 dead. Two days later, the head of the ruling junta, Adm. Sa-ngad Chaloryu, announced that Thanin Kraivixien, a Supreme Court justice, would become Premier when the situation had stabilized but did not say whether the junta would step aside at that time. He also announced the formation of a commission to begin drafting a new Constitution.

Economic Conditions. Almost 80% of the population work at agriculture. Rice is the principal crop, the staple food and the leading export. It is the basis of Thailand's whole economy and the key to its prosperity. Next most important is rubber. Other products include teak, tin, cassava, coconuts, corn, tobacco, sesame, sugar cane and soybeans. Livestock is fair in quality.

Industry is of growing importance. Industrial products include cement and tin, tungsten and lead concentrates.

There are small deposits of many important minerals and some precious stones. Only tin, gold, tungsten and salt are in commercial production.

Almost 70% of Thailand's total land area is forested. Teak, the principal forest product, covers over one third of this area, chiefly in the northern hill country.

Chief exports in 1974 were rice (19%), corn (12%), rubber (10%), sugar (7%), tapioca (7%) and tin (6%). Leading customers were Japan (26%), The Netherlands (9%), Singapore (8%), U.S. (8%), Hong Kong (7%), Taiwan (7%), Malaysia (5%). Leading suppliers were Japan (31%), U.S. (13%), West Germany (7%), Qatar (6%), Kuwait (5%), Saudi Arabia (5%), United Kingdom (5%).

Natural Features. Thailand, about three fourths the size of Texas, supports most of its population in the central alluvial plain, which is drained by the Chao Phaya River and tributaries.

TOGO, Republic of

President: Gnassingbé Eyadema (1967).
Area: 21,622 sq mi. (56,000 sq km).
Population (est. 1976): 2,265,000.
Density per square mile: 104.8.
Capital and largest city (est. 1975): Lomé, 214,200.
Monetary unit: Franc CFA.
Languages: Ewé, Mina (south), Kabyé, Cotocoli (north), French (official), and many dialects.
Religions: Animist, Christian, Moslem.

The government of Nicolas Grunitzky was overthrown in a bloodless coup on Jan. 13, 1967, led by Lieut. Col. Etienne Eyadema (now Gen. Gnassingbé Eyadema). A National Reconciliation Committee was set up to rule the country. In April, however, Eyadema dissolved the Committee and took over as President.

Political Party. The Assembly of the Togolese People is the only political party.

History. Brazilians were the first traders to settle in Togo. Established as a German colony (Togoland) in 1884, the area was split between the British and the French as League of Nations mandates after World War I and subsequently administered as U. N. trusteeships. The British portion voted for incorporation with Ghana.

Togo became an independent nation on Apr. 27, 1960.

Sylvanus Olympio, who became first President of the African republic in 1961, was assassinated in 1963 and was succeeded by Nicolas Grunitzky.

Economic Conditions. Agriculture and herding are the chief industries, with coffee, cacao, palm kernels and oil, cotton and copra the principal exports. Togo also produces dyewoods and oil palms and some iron ore.

Chief exports in 1973 were phosphates (46%), cocoa (26%) and coffee (14%). Leading customers were Netherlands (36%), France (31%), West Germany (12%), Belgium-Luxembourg (5%). Leading suppliers were France (38%), West Germany (10%), United Kingdom (7%), Netherlands (7%).

Natural Features. The coastline, only 32 miles long, is low, sandy, and without harbors. The Togo hills traverse the central section.

TONGA (Kingdom)

(Member of Commonwealth of Nations)
Sovereign: King Taufa'ahau Tupou IV (1965).
Prime Minister: Prince Tu'ipelehake (1965).
Area: 270 sq mi. (699 sq km).
Population (est. 1976): 106,000.

Density per square mile: 392.6.
Capital (est. 1975): Nuku'alofa, 25,000.
Monetary unit: Pa'anga.
Languages: Tongan, English.
Religion: Christian.

Executive authority is vested in the Sovereign, a Privy Council, and a Cabinet headed by the Prime Minister. Legislative authority is vested in the Legislative Assembly.

History. Located east of the Fiji Islands in the South Pacific, Tonga (also called the Friendly Islands) consists of 150 islands. Of these, 36 are inhabited.

The present dynasty of Tonga was founded in 1831 by Taufa'ahau Tupou, who took the name of George I. He consolidated the kingdom by conquest, and in 1875 he granted a Constitution.

In 1900, his great-grandson, George II, signed a treaty of friendship with Great Britain, and the country became a British protected state. The treaty was revised in 1959.

Queen Salote Tupou reigned from 1918 to 1964 and was succeeded by her son, who became King Taufa'ahau Tupou IV.

Tonga became an independent nation on June 4, 1970.

Economic Conditions. Tonga is primarily an agricultural country.

Chief exports in 1974 were copra (70%), desiccated coconut (9%) and bananas (8%). Leading customers were Netherlands (40%), Australia (29%), New Zealand (22%), Fiji (6%). Leading suppliers were New Zealand (39%), Fiji (24%), Australia (22%).

TRANSKEI (Republic)

Prime Minister: Chief Kaiser Matanzima.
Area: 17,000 sq mi. (44,330 sq km).
Population: 1.7 million (1970 census)
Density per square mile: 100.0.
Capital: Umtata.
Monetary unit: South African rand.
Languages: English, Xhosa.
Religions: Christian, tribal.

Transkei was granted independence by South Africa as of Oct. 26, 1976. A new Constitution called for organization of a parliament composed of 75 representative chiefs and 75 elected members, with a ceremonial President and executive power in the hands of a Prime Minister.

The Organization of African States and the chairman of the United Nations Special Committee against Apartheid denounced the new state as a sham and urged governments not to recognize it, because South Africa has declared 1.3 million Xhosas living there to be Transkei citizens, depriving them of South African citizenship.

History. British rule was established over the Transkei region between 1866 and 1894 and the Transkeian Territories were formed in 1903. Under the Native Land Act of 1913, the Territories were reserved for black occupation. In 1963, Transkei was given internal self-government and a legislature which elected Paramount Chief Kaiser Matanzima as Chief Minister, a post he retained in subsequent elections in 1968 and 1973.

Economic Conditions. Some 60% of Transkei is cultivated, producing corn, wheat, beans and sorghum. Grazing is important. Some light industry has been established. Transkei has a 270-mile coastline along the Indian Ocean but no port. Umtata is connected by rail to the South African port of East London, 100 miles to the southwest.

Pitch Lake, is another important natural resource. Sugar, cacao, and coconuts are grown in the rich soil, which yields many tropical crops. The principal products of Tobago are copra and cocoa.

Chief exports in 1974 were petroleum products (61%) and crude oil (29%). Leading customers were U.S. (61%), Puerto Rico and U.S. Virgin Islands (7%), ship and aircraft bunker stores (6%). Leading suppliers were Saudi Arabia (36%), Indonesia (18%), U.S. (11%), Iran (9%), Ecuador (7%), United Kingdom (5%).

TRINIDAD AND TOBAGO (Republic)

(Member of Commonwealth of Nations)

President: Sir Ellis Clarke (1976).
Prime Minister: Dr. Eric E. Williams (1962).
Area: 1,980 sq mi. (5,128 sq km).
Population (est. 1976): 1,085,000 (black, 43%; East Indian, 40%; mixed, 14%).
Density per square mile: 548.0.
Capital and largest city (est. 1973): Port-of-Spain, 60,400.
Monetary unit: Trinidad and Tobago dollar.
Languages: English, Indian and Chinese dialects.
Religions: Christian, 66%; Hindu, 23%; Moslem, 6%.

The legislature consists of a 24-member Senate and a 36-member House of Representatives.

Major Political Parties. Popular National Movement, led by Prime Minister Eric Williams, 24 seats (of 36 seats in the House of Representatives); United Labor Front (10 seats), led by George Weekes and Panday Shah; Congress of Democratic Action, (2 seats).

History. Trinidad, the larger of the two islands comprising the nation, was discovered by Columbus in 1498 and remained in Spanish possession, despite raids by other European nations, until it capitulated to the British in 1797 during a war between Great Britain and Spain.

Trinidad was ceded to Britain in 1802, and in 1899, it was united with Tobago as a colony. From 1958 to 1962, Trinidad and Tobago was a part of the West Indies Federation, and on Aug. 31, 1962, it became an independent nation.

Serious unemployment among the non-white majority contributed to two months of black power demonstrations that exploded in April, 1970, in rioting and an unsuccessful Army mutiny that caused four deaths and led to 149 arrests.

Although the sharp increase in world oil prices improved the economy of the oil-producing island state in 1974–75, strikes in the oil and sugar industries tied up the economy in March and April, 1975, at an estimated cost of $150 million.

On Aug. 1, 1976, Trinidad and Tobago cut its ties with Britain and became a republic, remaining within the Commonwealth and recognizing Queen Elizabeth II only as head of that organization.

Economic Conditions. Petroleum and petroleum products are the most important part of the nation's economy. Although wells were drilled as early as 1867, no oil was exported until 1910. Now much of it is refined on the island, whose refineries also handle Venezuelan, Colombian, and Saudi Arabian crude oil. Asphalt, which is taken from the apparently inexhaustible supplies of

TUNISIA (Republic)

(Al-Djoumhouria Attunusia)

President: Habib Bourguiba (1957).
Premier: Hédi Nouira (1970).
Area: 63,170 sq mi. (163,610 sq km).
Population (est. 1976): 5,924,000.
Density per square mile: 93.8.
Capital and largest city (est. 1976): Tunis, 960,000.
Monetary unit: Tunisian dinar.
Languages: Arabic, French, Italian.
Religions: Predominantly Moslem; Roman Catholic, Jewish, Greek Orthodox.

The executive power is vested by the Constitution in the President, who is elected for five years and may be re-elected for two additional terms. Legislative power is vested in a National Assembly elected by universal suffrage.

In March, 1975, the National Assembly amended Tunisia's Constitution to make Habib Bourguiba President for life. At 71, Bourguiba was re-elected to a fourth five-year term when he ran unopposed in November, 1974.

Political Party. Socialist Destourian Party, led by President Bourguiba.

History. Tunisia was settled by the Phoenicians and Carthaginians in ancient times. Except for an interval of Vandal conquest in A.D. 439–533, it was part of the Roman Empire until the Arab conquest of 648–69. It was ruled by various Arab and Berber dynasties until the Turks took it in 1570–74.

Throughout much of its history, Tunisia was essentially a pirate state, preying on Mediterranean shipping. In modern times, Italy became the foremost economic power in the area, but after French troops occupied the country in 1881, the Bey signed a treaty acknowledging a French protectorate.

Following the Allied landings in North Africa in 1942, Tunisia became a battleground, with the Axis forces pinched between the British 8th Army advancing from Libya and the U.S. British and French forces from Algeria.

Nationalist agitation forced France to grant internal autonomy to Tunisia in June 1955, and to recognize Tunisian independence and sovereignty in March 1956. Tunisia was admitted to the United Nations on Nov. 12, 1956. The Constituent Assembly deposed the Bey on July 25, 1957, declared Tunisia a republic and elected Habib Bourguiba as the first President.

Bourguiba maintained a pro-Western foreign policy that earned him enemies. Tunisia refused to break relations with the United States during the Israeli-Arab war in June 1967, and it cracked down on anti-U.S. demonstrators.

Economic Conditions. Agriculture is the chief industry. Over a quarter of the arable land is in wheat. Other important crops are barley, oats, corn, sorghum, beans and peas. The Cape Bon region is largely devoted to citrus fruits, the southern oases to dates.

Leading industries include flour milling, oil refining, lead smelting and distilling. Native industries include the spinning and weaving of wool, and the making of pottery and leather goods.

Tunisia's extremely rich deposits of phosphates are mined principally in the Gafsa and Kef regions. The iron ore is of good quality (55% metal content). Other minerals are lead, zinc, mercury, manganese, copper and salt.

Chief exports in 1974 were crude oil (34%), olive oil (18%), phosphates (12%) and fertilizers (9%). Leading customers were Italy (25%), France (22%), Greece (10%), Brazil (6%), U.S. (5%), West Germany (5%). Leading suppliers were France (31%), Italy (11%), U.S. (8%), West Germany (8%).

Natural Features. Tunisia, at the northernmost bulge of Africa, thrusts out toward Sicily to mark the division between the eastern and western Mediterranean. The country is mountainous in the north, is covered by plains in the east, and projects southward to the Sahara area.

TURKEY (Republic)

(Türkiye Cumhuriyeti)

President: Fahri Korutürk (1973).
Premier: Suleyman Demirel (1975).
Area: 301,380 sq mi. (incl. 9,121 in Europe) (780,576 sq km).
Population (est. 1976): 40,000,000.
Density per square mile: 132.7.
Capital: Ankara.
Largest cities (1975 census): Istanbul, 2,500,000; Ankara, 1,700,000; Izmir (Smyrna), 640,000; Adana, 470,000; Bursa, 350,000; Gaziantep, 300,000.
Monetary unit: Turkish lira.
Languages: Turkish, 90.7%; Kurdish, 6.7%; Arabic, 1.3%; others, 1.3%.
Religion: Moslem.

Turkey's President is elected by the Grand National Assembly for a seven-year term and is not eligible for re-election. The government operates under a revised Constitution approved in 1961. The bicameral Grand National Assembly has a Senate of 150 members and a National Assembly of 450 members.

Major Political Parties. Justice Party (159 of 450 seats in National Assembly), led by Premier Suleyman Demirel; and Republican People's Party (190 seats), led by Bulent Ecevit (resigned as Premier Sept. 18, 1974 to head a caretaker government); National Salvation Party (49 seats); Democratic Party (23 seats); Confidina Party (13 seats); Republican Reliance Party (10 seats).

History. The Ottoman Turks first appeared in the early 13th century. Under the leadership of their Sultans, they gradually spread their hegemony over most of the Near East and the Balkans, capturing Constantinople in 1453 and storming the gates of Vienna in the 17th century. At the height of its power, the empire stretched from the Persian Gulf to the frontiers of Poland and from the shores of the Caspian Sea to Oran in Algeria.

The defeat of the Turkish navy at Lepanto in 1571 by the Holy League and of Turkish forces besieging Vienna in 1683 portended the decline of Ottoman power. Russia moved into the Balkans in the 18th century and made herself official protector of the Balkan Christians. Fear of a Russian drive on Constantinople prompted England and France to declare war on Russia, and the Crimean War (1853–56) followed. As a result of the Russo-Turkish war (1877–78), Bulgaria became practically independent, and Romania and Serbia threw off their nominal allegiance to the sultan. Further defeats were suffered by Turkey in a war with Italy (1911–12) and in the Balkan Wars (1912–13). Meanwhile, a revolt led by the Young Turks, an organization of youthful liberals, had forced the abdication of Sultan Abdul-Hamid in 1909 and established a constitutional regime.

On Aug. 2, 1914, at the outbreak of World War I, a secret alliance was signed between Germany and Turkey, whose army was advised by a German military mission, and in September the Allies declared war on Turkey. Turkish forces successfully defended the strategic Dardanelles, but British forces seized Palestine, Mesopotamia, and Syria; and the Hejaz revolted. By 1918, Allied forces held the territory along the Dardanelles and the Bosporus, and later Greek forces occupied Smyrna.

In 1919, the new Nationalist movement, headed by Mustafa Kemal, was organized to resist the Allied occupation and, in 1920, a National Assembly elected him President of both the Assembly and the government. Under his leadership, the Nationalist government was recognized by foreign powers, the Greeks were driven out of Smyrna and other Allied forces were withdrawn. The present Turkish boundaries (with the exception of Alexandretta, ceded to Turkey by France in 1939) were fixed by the Treaty of Lausanne (1923) and later negotiations. The caliphate and sultanate were separated, and the sultanate was abolished Oct. 1, 1922. On Oct. 29, 1923, Turkey formally became a republic with Mustafa Kemal, who took the name of Kemal Atatürk, as its first President. The caliphate was abolished Mar. 3, 1924, and Atatürk proceeded to carry out an extensive program of reform, modernization and industrialization.

The Montreux Convention (1936) gave Turkey sole responsibility for the defense of the Dardanelles.

General Ismet Inönü was elected to succeed Kemal Atatürk on the latter's death in 1938 and was re-elected in 1939, 1943 and 1946. However, he was defeated in 1950 and was succeeded by Celâl Bayar. On Oct. 19, 1939, a mutual assistance pact was concluded with Britain and France. Turkey followed a neutral course during most of

World War II. However, on Feb. 23, 1945, it declared war on Germany and Japan, but took no active part in the conflict.

Turkey became a full member of NATO in 1952.

In March 1971, the Turkish military demanded the ouster of Ismet Inonu, Premier since 1961, who was replaced by Nihat Erim. He pushed through a law that forbade growing of opium poppies after 1972. The move was taken under strong U.S. requests because about two thirds of illicit heroin reaching U.S. markets is grown in Turkey.

The poppy-growing ban was shelved after Bulent Ecivit, a liberal, became Premier in January 1974. Instead, the government required bulk-harvesting of all poppies and consignment of dried "poppy hay" to legal refineries abroad, maintaining that the method would prevent farmers from diverting raw opium to illicit channels. The system was continued after conservative Premier Suleyman Demirel took over the government March 31, 1975.

Turkey invaded Cyprus by sea and air July 20, 1974, following the failure of diplomatic efforts to resolve the crisis caused by Archbishop Makarios' ouster. Turkey, asserting its right to protect the minority Turkish Cypriot community, demanded the withdrawal of the 650 Greek officers who had led the coup. Greece refused the demand.

Talks in Geneva between Greece, Turkey, Great Britain, Greek Cypriot and Turkish Cypriot leaders broke down in mid-August. Turkey was apparently determined to achieve through military means what it had failed to achieve in negotiations: the establishment of an autonomous Turkish Cypriot region encompassing the northern third of Cyprus. Turkey unilaterally announced a cease-fire August 16, after gaining control of 40% of Cyprus.

More than a year of diplomatic negotiations failed to produce a settlement on Cyprus, where tensions were compounded after Turkish Cypriots established their own state on the northern 40% of the island Feb. 13, 1975.

U.S.-Turkish relations, excellent for a generation, were seriously damaged when Congress voted to end arms sales to Turkey on Feb. 5, 1975, because arms the U.S. had supplied for mutual defense had been used in the invasion of Cyprus. Congress maintained the ban despite warnings from President Ford that it would imperil the future of 20 U.S. air and ntelligence bases in Turkey and could affect Turkey's ole as NATO's anchor in the Eastern Mediterranean.

On July 25, 1975, after a 30-day warning, Turkey ook over control of all the installations except the big joint defense base at Incirlik, which it reserved or "NATO tasks alone." Some 7,000 U.S. military men remained on duty under Turkish orders, but relations between Ankara and Washington hit a 30-year low.

As Turkey and Greece remained deadlocked over Cyprus, a new issue arose between the two neighbors when Greece in August 1976 complained to the International Court of Justice that Turkish oil exploration was violating Greece's continental shelf in the Aegean. Greece asked the court to enjoin further exploration until it could determine the limits of Greek undersea rights.

Economic Conditions. Agriculture is the principal economic activity, engaging about 41% of the population. Only about 30% of the land is under cultivation, but the government has made great efforts to modernize and improve farming. The most important cash crops are tobacco, cotton, fruits and nuts. Cotton is grown in the south of Asia Minor, while figs come exclusively from the Smyrna region. Grain crops include wheat and barley. Turkey is a leading producer of olive oil; the, Bursa region and the Ionian coast are the principal areas of cultivation. Opium poppies are grown in the Smyrna, Malatia and Tokat regions.

Staple industries have been established in iron, steel, textiles, paper, glass, sugar and cement. A large proportion of the factories are government-operated. Istanbul is the major industrial area.

Turkey's rich mineral resources are still comparatively unexploited. Deposits of copper are found in the large field at Arghana, near the Iraqi-Syrian frontier. Turkey is also relatively rich in coal, with large deposits in the Eregli region on the Pontic coast some 150 miles from Istanbul. A virtual world monopoly is enjoyed in meerschaum, found in the Eskisehir district. Other important minerals include chromite, petroleum, manganese ore, iron ore (metal content 65%), emery and antimony.

Chief exports in 1974 were cotton (16%), tobacco (13%) and hazelnuts (11%). Leading customers were West Germany (22%), U.S. (9%), Lebanon (7%), Switzerland (6%), Italy (6%), United Kingdom (5%), U.S.S.R. (5%). Leading suppliers were West Germany (18%), U.S. (9%), Iraq (9%), Italy (7%), U.K. (7%), Saudi Arabia (7%), France (6%), Switzerland (6%), Japan (5%).

Natural Features. Turkey is divided into two natural areas by the historic waterway formed by the Dardanelles, the Sea of Marmara and the Bosporus.

Turkey in Europe comprises an area about equal to the state of Massachusetts. It is hilly country drained by the Maritsa River and its tributaries. Almost all the population is concentrated in and near the three important towns, Istanbul (Constantinople), Ankara, and Edirne (Adrianople). Turkey in Asia, or Anatolia, about the size of Texas, is roughly a rectangle in shape with its short sides on the east and west. Its center is a treeless plateau rimmed by mountains.

UGANDA (Republic)

(Member of Commonwealth of Nations)

President for Life: Gen. Idi Amin (1971).
Area: 91,134 sq mi. (236,036 sq km).
Population (est. 1976): 11,915,000.
Density per square mile: 130.7.
Capital and largest city (1969 census for urban agglomeration): Kampala, 330,700.
Monetary unit: Uganda shilling.
Languages: English (official), Swahili, Luganda, Ateso, Luo.
Religions: Christian, Moslem.

Following the military coup against President Milton Obote, who had been in office since 1962, Gen. Idi Amin assumed all legislative and executive powers and appointed a council of ministers to help him run the country. He banned all political activity (Obote's People's Congress had been the only legal party).

History. Uganda was first visited by European explorers as well as Arab traders in 1844. An Anglo-

German agreement of 1890 declared it to be in the British sphere of influence in Africa, and the Imperial British East Africa Company was chartered to develop the area. The company did not prosper financially, and in 1894 a British protectorate was proclaimed.

Uganda became an independent nation on Oct. 9, 1962.

As first President, the country chose Mutesa II, King of the ancient kingdom of Buganda. Dr. Milton Obote had been Prime Minister. In 1965, he suspended the Constitution and assumed the powers of the government, later abolishing the offices of President and Vice President.

Obote in 1970 passed laws declaring that 40,000 British Asians—Asian-born persons, mostly Indian, who live in Uganda but chose British citizenship in 1962 rather than Ugandian—needed a variety of passes and permits to remain in the country and keep business there; and, further, that all non-citizens would lose their jobs. President Amin, an unpredictable former Army sergeant, began expelling the Asians in 1972. He also expelled Israeli advisors rather than pay Israel's military aid bill and applauded Hitler's treatment of Jews.

Amin's flamboyant ruthlessness drew world attention. In June 1974, the International Commission of Jurists reported that a "reign of terror" had brought "a total breakdown of law" in Uganda. In November 1974, Amin charged public immorality when he fired the former fashion model he had appointed as Foreign Minister. In January 1975, Finance Minister Emmanuel Wakhweya quit, saying Amin had brought Uganda to the brink of economic catastrophe.

With his country's potentially rich agricultural economy in turmoil, partly because of large purchases of weapons for its 20,000-man army, Amin nationalized all its land in June 1975, without compensation to former owners. A loan from Saudi Arabia helped defray the cost of a lavish Organization of African Unity meeting held in Kampala in August. Only 19 of the 46 OAU heads of state attended.

On June 25, 1976, Amin had himself proclaimed President for Life by the Defense Council, which replaced the Council of Ministers as Uganda's ruling body.

An Israeli commando raid against Entebbe airport on July 4 freed 103 hostages in a hijacked French airliner which had been held at the airport for a week by Palestinian guerrillas. Hostages, and the government of Israel, charged that Amin had collaborated with the hijackers. Amin denied the charge, but gave military funerals to the Palestinians who were killed, along with a score of Ugandan soldiers who were guarding the plane. Amin demanded U.N. Security Council condemnation of Israel but was unable to muster sufficient support.

Economic Conditions. Agriculture, including livestock, is the basis of the economy.

Chief exports in 1974 were coffee (71%), cotton (12%), copper (5%) and tea (5%). Leading customers were U.S. (23%), United Kingdom (18%), Japan (9%), West Germany (5%). Leading suppliers were Kenya (36%), U.K. (17%), West Germany (9%), Japan (5%), Italy (5%).

UNION OF SOVIET SOCIALIST REPUBLICS

(Soyuz Sovyetskikh Sotsialisticheskikh Respublik)

Chairman of Presidium (President): Nikolai V. Podgorny (1965).
Chairman of Council of Ministers (Premier): Aleksei N. Kosygin (1964).
Area: 8,649,489 sq mi. (22,402,200 sq km).
Population (est. 1976): 256,700,000 (Russian, 55%; Ukrainian, 18%; Byelorussian, 4%; Uzbek, 3%; Tatar, 2%, others, 18%).
Density per square mile: 29.7.
Capital: Moscow.
Largest cities (est. 1975): Moscow, 7,635,000; Leningrad, 4,311,000; Kiev, 1,947,000; Tashkent, 1,595,000; Baku, 1,383,000; Kharkov, 1,357,000; Gorki, 1,283,000; Novosibirsk, 1,265,000; Kuibyshev, 1,164,000; Sverdlovsk, 1,147,000; Minsk, 1,147,000; Tblisi, 1,006,000; Odessa, 1,002,000; Chelyabinsk, 969,000; Dnepropetrovsk, 958,000; Donetsk, 950,000.
Monetary unit: Ruble.
Languages: See Population, above.
Religions: Russian Orthodox (predominant), Moslem, Roman Catholic, Jewish, Lutheran.

Legislative authority is vested in the Supreme Soviet of the U.S.S.R., which consists of two chambers—the Soviet of the Union, with 767 members, and the Soviet of Nationalities, with 750 members. All members of the Supreme Soviet are elected for four years by the people of the Soviet Union.

A Presidium is elected by the Supreme Soviet to deal with state matters when the latter is not in session. It consists of a chairman, 15 vice chairmen (one for each Union Republik), 20 members and a secretary. The chairman of the Presidium is sometimes referred to as the President of the Soviet Union.

Executive authority is vested in the Council of Ministers. It is appointed by the Supreme Soviet and includes a chairman, a first vice chairman, and various vice chairmen, chairmen of committees, ministers, etc. The chairman of the Council of Ministers is often referred to as the Premier of the Soviet Union.

Judicial authority is vested in the Supreme Court of the U.S.S.R. It consists of a chairman and 15 other members, who are elected by the Supreme Soviet for five years.

Each of the 15 Union Republics and the 20 Autonomous Republics has a Supreme Soviet (with a Presidium), a Council of Ministers, and a Supreme Court. Each of the eight Autonomous Regions has a Soviet of Workers' Deputies.

Political Party. The Communist Party of the Soviet Union (CPSU) is the only party. It is the basic power in the country and today has a membership of over 14,000,000.

The supreme organ of the party is the Party Congress, which meets at least once in four years. It elects a Central Committee, consisting of 241 members and 155 candidate members, to carry on party work between sessions of the Congress.

Within the Central Committee is a Political Bureau (Politburo), which was called the Presidium from 1952 to 1966. It functions between sessions of the Central Committee. Also within the Central Committee is the Secretariat. The present General Secretary of the Secretariat, Leonid I. Brezhnev, has served since Oct. 15, 1964. Earlier First Secretaries were Nikita S. Khrushchev (1953–64), Georgi M. Malenkov (briefly in 1953) and Joseph Stalin (1922–53).

History. Tradition says the Viking Rurik came to Russia in A.D. 862 and founded the first Russian dynasty in Novgorod. The various tribes were united by the spread of Christianity in the 10th and 11th centuries; Vladimir "the Saint" was converted in 988. During the 11th century, the grand dukes of Kiev held such centralizing power as existed. In 1240, Kiev was destroyed by the Mongols, and the Russian territory was split into numerous smaller dukedoms, out of which three large centers emerged—Galicia, Moscow and Novgorod. The early dukes of Moscow extended their dominions through their office of tribute collector for the Mongols.

In the late 15th century, Duke Ivan III acquired Novgorod and Tver and threw off the Mongol yoke. Ivan IV, the Terrible (1533–84), first Muscovite Tsar, is considered to have founded the Russian State. He crushed the power of rival princes and boyars (great landowners), but Russia remained largely medieval until the reign of Peter the Great (1682–1725), grandson of the first Romanov Tsar, Michael (1613–45). Peter made extensive reforms aimed at westernization and, through his defeat of Charles XII of Sweden at the Battle of Poltava (1709), he extended Russia's boundaries to the west. Catherine the Great (1762–96) continued Peter's westernization program and also expanded Russian territory, acquiring the Crimea and part of Poland. During the reign of Alexander I (1801–25), Napoleon's attempt to subdue Russia was defeated (1812–13), and new territory was gained, including Finland (1809) and Bessarabia (1812). Alexander originated the Holy Alliance which for a time crushed Europe's rising liberal movement.

Alexander II (1855–81), pushed Russia's borders to the Pacific and into central Asia. Serfdom was abolished in 1861, but heavy restrictions were imposed on the emancipated class. Revolutionary strikes following Russia's defeat in the war with Japan forced Nicholas II (1894–1917) to grant a representative national body (Duma), elected by narrowly limited suffrage. It met for the first time in 1906. Nicholas continued in his reactionary course, however, and the overwhelmingly liberal Duma had little or no influence.

World War I demonstrated tsarist corruptness and the inefficiency of the tsarist regime, although the call of patriotism held the poorly equipped army together for a time. Disorders broke out in Petrograd (now Leningrad) in March 1917, and defection of the Petrograd garrison launched the revolution. Nicholas II was forced to abdicate on Mar. 15, 1917, and he and his family were killed by revolutionists on July 16, 1918.

A provisional government composed of conservative and radical elements under the successive premierships of Prince Lvov and moderate Alexander Kerensky lost ground to the radical, or Bolshevik, wing of the Socialist Democratic Labor Party. On Nov. 7, 1917, came the Bolshevik revolution, engi-

REPUBLICS OF THE U.S.S.R.

Republic and capital	Area sq. mi.	Population est. 1975 (thousands)
Russian S.F.S.R. (Moscow)	6,593,391*	133,728
Ukraine (Kiev)	233,089	48,830
Kazakhstan (Alma-Ata)	1,064,092	14,170
Byelorussia (Minsk)	80,154	9,340
Uzbekistan (Tashkent)	158,069	13,695
Georgia (Tbilisi)	26,872	4,923
Azerbaijan (Baku)	33,475	5,606
Lithuania† (Vilnius)	25,174	3,290
Moldavia (Kishinev)	13,012	3,806
Latvia† (Riga)	24,595	2,478
Kirghizia (Frunze)	76,641	3,294
Tadzhikistan (Duschambe)	55,019	3,385
Armenia (Erevan)	11,506	2,790
Turkmenistan (Ashkhabad)	188,417	2,495
Estonia† (Tallinn)	17,413	7,429

* Including the Karelo-Finnish S.S.R., incorporated into the R.S.F.S.R. in July 1956. † Discussed under World History in alphabetical position.

neered by N. Lenin* and Leon Trotsky. The Kerensky government was overthrown, and authority was vested in a Council of People's Commissars, with Lenin as Premier.

The humiliating Treaty of Brest-Litovsk (Mar. 3, 1918) concluded the war with Germany, but civil war and foreign intervention delayed Communist control of all Russia until 1920. A brief war with Poland in 1920 resulted in Russian defeat.

The Union of Soviet Socialist Republics was established as a federation on Dec. 30, 1922.

The death of Lenin on Jan. 21, 1924 precipitated an intraparty struggle between Joseph Stalin, General Secretary of the party, and Trotsky, who favored swifter socialization at home and fomentation of revolution abroad. Stalin won. Trotsky was dismissed as Commissar of War in 1925 and banished from the Soviet Union in 1929. He was murdered in Mexico City on Aug. 21, 1940 by a political agent.

Stalin further consolidated his power by a series of purges in the mid and late 1930s. Among the many victims were prominent party leaders and military officers. Stalin assumed the premiership May 6, 1941.

Soviet foreign policy—first featured by friendship with Germany and antagonism toward England and France and then, after Hitler's rise to power in 1933, by participation in the League of Nations and an anti-Fascist program—took another abrupt turn on Aug. 24, 1939 with the signing of a Soviet-German nonaggression pact. Territory seized from Poland (September 1939) became part of the Ukrainian and Byelorussian S.S.R.'s; that secured from Finland at the conclusion of the Finnish war of 1939–40, part of the Karelian S.S.R. set up Mar. 31, 1940; that secured from Romania (Bessarabia and northern Bukovina), part of the Moldavian S.S.R. set up Aug. 2, 1940; and finally the formerly independent states of Estonia, Latvia and Lithuania, occupied in June 1940, were absorbed into the U.S.S.R. as the 14th, 15th and 16th Soviet Republics. The latter annexations have not been recognized by the United States, Britain and the majority of other nations.

* N. Lenin was the pseudonym taken by Vladimir Ilich Ulyanov. It is sometimes given as Nikolai Lenin or V. I. Lenin.

Immediately following their attack (June 22, 1941), the Germans seized approximately 500,000 square miles of Soviet territory, but Soviet forces resisted stubbornly, aided by increasing amounts of matériel from the United States and Britain. The great Soviet counteroffensive in the Stalingrad area (November 1942-February 1943) marked the turning point. Soviet troops gradually pushed the Nazis back and unleashed their final great offensive on Jan. 12, 1945. The nonaggression pact with Japan (1941) was denounced in April 1945 and, following the declaration of war on Japan (Aug. 8, 1945), Soviet Far Eastern forces quickly occupied Manchuria, Karafuto and the Kuriles.

Postwar territorial acquisitions include the Carpatho-Ukraine (12,617 sq mi.) obtained from Czechoslovakia June 29, 1945, incorporated into the Ukrainian S.S.R.; the Republic of Tannu Tuva in central Asia (64,000 sq mi.), incorporated early in 1945 into the Russian Soviet Federal Socialist Republic (R.S.F.S.R.); Karafuto or southern Sakhalin (13,935 sq mi.) and the Kurile Islands (3,944 sq. mi.), occupied by Soviet troops in August 1945 and incorporated into the R.S.F.S.R.; the northern part of eastern Prussia (about 7,000 sq mi.), placed under *de facto* Soviet administration at the Potsdam Conference and incorporated into the R.S.F.S.R.; the Petsamo district of Finland, obtained *de jure* under the 1947 treaty and incorporated into the R.S.F.S.R.; and Poland east of the Curzon Line (69,860 sq mi.), under terms of the Soviet-Polish treaty of Aug. 16, 1945, incorporated into the Ukrainian and Byelorussian S.S.R.'s.

In all the Eastern European countries where Soviet troops were in occupation at the war's end, the Soviet Union achieved a cordon of satellite Communist states running from Poland in the north to Albania and Bulgaria and including East Germany, Czechoslovakia, Hungary, Romania and Yugoslavia. An effort by the Soviet bloc to take over Greece by an invasion through Yugoslavia was checkmated by the intervention of the United States and the Western democracies.

With its Eastern European satellites drawn together into a solid bloc, the Soviet Union launched a full-scale political offensive against the non-Communist world. At Berlin, Soviet troops blockaded communication through East Germany. The Western powers countered with an airlift, completed unification of West Germany and united Western Europe into opposition to Communist aggression through the North Atlantic Treaty Organization Pact.

Stalin died Mar. 6, 1953. The next day Georgi M. Malenkov succeeded him as Premier. Malenkov's chief rivals for power—L. P. Beria, chief of the Secret Police, N. A. Bulganin and L. M. Kaganovich—were named First Deputy Premiers. The expected intraparty struggle for power was revealed by the announcement of July 10, 1953 of the purging of Beria. He was executed Dec. 23, 1953.

There followed a rise in importance of N. S. Khrushchev, First Secretary of the Communist Party. On Feb. 8, 1955, Malenkov was replaced as Premier by Bulganin. In July 1957, Khrushchev removed Molotov, Malenkov, Kaganovich and several others from the governing group. At the 20th Party Congress in 1956, Khrushchev denounced the rule and "personality cult" of Stalin. He replaced Bulganin as Premier on Mar. 27, 1958, heading the state as well as the party.

A seven-year plan begun in 1959 was integrated in 1961 with a longer range plan for economic development. The Soviet Union formalized its East European system' with a Council for Mutual Economic Assistance and a Warsaw Pact Treaty Organization. Yugoslavia was the first of the satellites to get out from under the Soviet yoke. Later, Poland, Romania and Czechoslovakia gained a measure of independence, and Albania joined China, which became Communist in 1950, in a struggle against Soviet hegemony in the Communist world.

The 1956 uprising in Hungary was ruthlessly quelled, as was the 1968 political struggle for liberalization in Czechoslovakia, when, in August, Soviet troops led invasion forces of four other satellites in an invasion that penetrated to Prague. But elsewhere the Soviet iron fist was gloved.

In its technological race with the United States, the Soviet Union exploded a hydrogen bomb in 1953, developed the intercontinental ballistic missile by 1957, sent the first artificial satellite into space (Sputnik I) in 1957, put Yuri Gagarin in the first orbital flight around the earth in 1961 and later put astronauts into space who "walked" between space vehicles. On July 24, 1975, the 44-hour link-up of a Soviet Soyuz bearing two cosmonauts and a U.S. Apollo with a three-man crew ended successfully. After this well-publicized first step toward space cooperation, Moscow tightened up again on news about its space program.

Although the Soviets emphasized collective leadership after the death of Stalin, Khrushchev achieved great personal power. But he was blamed for two fiascos of Soviet strategy. One was the arming of Cuba with missiles and the provoking of a confrontation with the United States in 1962, when the willingness of the U.S. to face the threat of nuclear war forced the U.S.S.R. to back down and remove the missiles. Khrushchev was blamed for the ideological dispute and break with Communist China beginning in 1963. He also was accused of establishing a personality cult of his own. On Oct. 15, 1964, he was retired. Leonid I. Brezhnev became First Secretary, and Alexei N. Kosygin became Premier.

President Nixon visited the Soviet Union for a week of summit talks in May 1972 and concluded agreements on a wide variety of issues, notably strategic arms limitations and a declaration of principles that were to guide mutual relations in the future. The fact that the Soviets received Nixon while the U.S. was bombing and blockading North Vietnam indicated a search for détente after 25 years of the Cold War. There were parallel Soviet moves in Europe. The Soviet Union and Poland signed nonaggression treaties with West Germany that were tantamount to a World War II settlement.

The Soviet economy experienced some difficulty in the early years of the new decade, but internal pressures for more and better consumer products, plus a greater need for faster economic growth, were thought responsible for a Soviet agreement with the U.S. to set up a joint economic trade commission.

The first deal involved over $1 billion in U.S. grain sales, spread over several years. Trading tripled by the end of 1972 (to over $600 million) and doubled again in 1973 (to over $1.5 billion), with the U.S. selling about seven times more than it bought from the U.S.S.R.

The agreements on the limitations of strategic arms were the first of the nuclear age. In the 1972 treaty, both nations were prohibited from building more than 200 antiballistic missiles (ABMs). And in 1974, the number of ABMs allowed each side was halved, to 100 each. Some offensive weapons were also brought under quantitative, but not qualitative, control for five years. The Soviets were frozen at 1,618 land-based intercontinental ballistic missiles (ICBMs) while the U.S. was limited to 1,054. Submarine-based missiles were also limited under a complicated formula, under which the Soviets had a numerical advantage of launchers, but the U.S. compensated in its superiority of warheads per missile and the better reliability and accuracy of its weapons. Negotiations were undertaken for a treaty to limit indefinitely all offensive strategic weapons in number and kind; if no agreement is reached, the interim offensive treaty will lapse in 1977.

Of potentially greater significance is the "Declaration of Principles," a kind of political nonaggression pact between the two sides, in which both undertake to refrain from seeking marginal advantages in areas of competition that might escalate into a nuclear confrontation.

Brezhnev, who emerged as the top leader of the Soviet Union, visited the U.S. June 16–25, 1973 for a return summit and, with Mr. Nixon, concluded six agreements that essentially extended those made at their 1972 meeting. On strategic arms, the two nations promised to reach a permanent agreement on offensive weapon systems in 1974 that would replace the 1972 five-year agreement.

But at Summit III, held in Moscow from June 27 to July 3, 1974, the two nations failed to agree on curbing offensive arms and reduced their goal— aiming at a 10-year pact (instead of a permanent one) and giving themselves until 1977 (instead of 1974) to reach it. They further limited anti-missile systems and agreed to a partial underground nuclear test ban (air, sea and space tests were already prohibited), but neither could mask the larger failure to stop the proliferation of multi-warhead missiles (called MIRVs).

Tentative agreement on a formula for a 10-year strategic arms limitation treaty was reached Nov. 23–24, 1974, when President Ford, during a Far Eastern tour, met Brezhnev at the Soviet Pacific port of Vladivostok. They endorsed a treaty based on the principle of equivalency in strategic forces and voiced hope that it could be negotiated during 1975 at the Strategic Arms Limitation (SALT) talks in Geneva. They agreed to a ceiling of 2,400 ICBMs for each side, of which no more than 1,320 would be MIRVs. The SALT talks were slowed by tough bargaining on two issues: verification of compliance, and determination whether new U.S. subsonic missiles and new Soviet supersonic bombers should be covered by the ceiling. President Ford said he would seek $2.8 billion more for nuclear arms if the year ended without an agreement.

Ford and Brezhnev renewed the discussions when they met at Helsinki, Finland, where the 35-nation Conference on Security and Cooperation in Europe convened July 30 for the signing of a document asserting principles for assuring European peace. One provision recognized the permanence of Europe's postwar boundaries unless they are changed "by peaceful means and by agreement." This commitment, long a goal of Russian policy, was criticized as tacit recognition of Soviet territorial seizures after World War II.

A long Soviet campaign to end U.S. tariff discrimination was derailed in January 1975, after President Ford reluctantly signed a new trade act which conditioned such concessions on relaxation of Soviet curbs on Jewish emigration. Moscow then announced that its 1972 trade agreement with the U.S. would not be put in force because the new law interfered in Soviet domestic affairs.

The Kremlin claimed that 98.5% of all applications from Jews seeking to emigrate to Israel had been granted during the preceding decade. But Jewish refugee groups reported that emigration had risen from 13,500 in 1971 to a peak of 31,000 in 1973, then fallen back to 20,600 in 1974 and was down to about 1,100 a month in the first half of 1975, when Moscow's policy toward Jewish dissidents appeared to harden.

Drought-caused crop shortages led Moscow in the summer of 1975 to negotiate for purchase abroad of over 20 million tons of grain. Fulfillment of orders for 9.8 million tons of U.S. grain was suspended by the U.S. government pending an appraisal of the U.S. crop after completion of the harvest in October.

Despite recurrent friction, desire for détente appeared to moderate the Kremlin's policies toward the United States after the 1972 summit. There was a near-confrontation during the Arab-Israeli war of October 1973, when a Soviet threat to intervene to aid trapped Egyptian forces led Washington to call a world-wide nuclear alert, but the crisis was eased when the United Nations approved a truce plan developed by the U.S. and the U.S.S.R. After the war, Moscow provided arms and encouragement to militant Arab states, but did not actively resist the Israeli-Egyptian interim accord of 1975. The Kremlin made no overt move to capitalize on the fall of U.S.-backed governments in Indochina in the spring of 1975, but hailed the war's end as an incentive to improvement in relations with the U.S.

The 25th Congress of the Communist Party, meeting in the Kremlin Feb. 24–Mar. 5, 1976, was told by Brezhnev that "détente does not in the slightest abolish and cannot abolish or alter the laws of class struggle," but he praised the "positive development of Soviet-U.S. relations and the considerable progress achieved in relations with capitalist states in general."

Economic Conditions. Formerly an agricultural country, the Soviet Union has grown since about 1920 into an industrial-agricultural power.

Almost all industry in the Soviet Union is carried on by organizations owned or controlled by the state. Industrialization of the country has been a major objective of its leaders. Completion of the first two five-year plans (1928–32, 1933–37) and of most of the third (1938–42) saw a great increase in the volume and versatility of Soviet industry.

The large-scale evacuation of plants to the East and the construction of new plants there during World War II, coupled with the eastward orientation of industry prior to the war, has shifted the balance to newly developed regions in Central Asia and Siberia from the Moscow-Leningrad area and the Ukraine. The new regions are now the center of Soviet industrial power, accounting for almost all magnesium and aluminum production, and more than 60% of the pig iron and steel production. The production of consumers' goods continues to be subordinate to the production of heavy capital equipment.

The Soviet Union is probably the richest country in the world in mineral resources, containing deposits of almost every known mineral. It ranks among the top producing nations in coal, chromite, iron ore, petroleum, gold, copper, manganese and other products. The richest mineral region is that of the Ural Mountains, which lacks only good coking coal.

With a forested area of about 2,500,000,000 acres, the Soviet Union possesses a large proportion of the world's timber reserves. Most of the forested area is in Siberia, but there are also valuable stands in the Caucasus. Plans were made late in 1948 for the planting of huge forest belts 60 to 90 miles wide in the southern steppes to protect fertile food-producing areas from the dry winds.

The rivers, lakes and surrounding seas (except the Black Sea) are rich in fish. The acquisition of former Japanese fisheries in Sakhalin and the Kuriles greatly increased output of the Far Eastern fish industry. Trapping is an important secondary industry, especially in eastern Siberia.

Soviet foreign trade is a state monopoly, and foreign goods are purchased in accordance with an over-all plan conducted under the supervision of the Foreign Trade Ministry.

Chief exports in 1974 were machinery and transport equipment (19%), crude oil (11%), petroleum products (10%), timber (7%), iron and steel (7%) and nonferrous metals (5%). Leading customers were Sino-Soviet area (58%; incl. East Germany 10%, Poland 9%, Czechoslovakia 7%, Bulgaria 7%, Hungary 5%) and Finland (5%). Leading suppliers were Sino-Soviet area (59%; incl. East Germany 11%, Poland 9%, Czechoslovakia 8%, Bulgaria 8%, Hungary 6%) and West Germany (7%).

Natural Features. The Soviet Union is the largest unbroken political unit in the world, occupying more than one seventh of the land surface of the globe. The greater part of its territory is a vast plain stretching from eastern Europe to the Pacific Ocean. This plain, relieved only occasionally by low mountain ranges (notably the Urals), consists of three zones running east and west: (1) the frozen marshy tundra of the Arctic; (2) the more temperate forest belt; and (3) the steppes or prairies to the south, which in southern Soviet Asia become sandy deserts. The topography is more varied in the South, particularly in the Caucasus between the Caspian and Black seas, and in the Tien-Pamir mountain system bordering Afghanistan, Sinkiang, and Mongolia. Mountains (Stanovoi and Kolyma) and great rivers (Amur, Yenisei, Lena) also break up the sweep of the plain in Siberia.

UNITED ARAB EMIRATES
(Formerly Trucial States)

Head of State: Sheik Zayed Bin Sultan Al-Nihayan (1971).
Prime Minister: Sheik Maktoum Bin Rashid (1972).
Area: 32,278 sq mi. (83,600 sq km).
Population (est. 1974): 340,000.
Density per square mile: 7.1.
Capital and largest city (est. 1974): Abu Dhabi, 125,500.
Monetary unit: Dirham.
Language: Arabic.
Religion: Moslem.

The United Arab Emirates was formed in 1971 by the seven Trucial States—Abu Dhabi (the largest), Dubai, Sharjah, Ajman, Fujairah, Ras al Khaimah and Um al-Quwain—that extend along part of the Gulf of Oman and the southern coast of the Persian Gulf.

The loose federation, spurred by the British pullout from the area, allows joint policies in foreign relations, defense and development, with each member state keeping its internal local system of government headed by its own ruler. A 40-member legislature consists of eight seats each for Abu Dhabi and Dubai, six seats each for Ras al Khaimah and Sharjah, and four each for the others. It is a member of the Arab League. The United Arab Emirates was admitted to the U.N. and signed a treaty of friendship with Great Britain.

Originally the area was inhabited by a seafaring people who were converted to Islam in the seventh century. Later, a dissident sect, the Carmathians established a powerful sheikdom, and its army conquered Mecca. After the sheikdom disintegrated, its people became pirates.

Threatening the sultanate of Muscat and Oman in the early 19th century, the pirates provoked the intervention of the British, who in 1820 enforced a partial truce, and in 1853 a permanent truce. Thus what had been called the Pirate Coast was renamed the Trucial Coast.

Economic Conditions. Chief export in 1974 was crude oil (c. 98%). Leading customers in 1973 were Japan (c. 33%), France (c. 21%), West Germany (c. 15%), United Kingdom (c. 10%), Netherlands (c. 5%). Leading suppliers were Japan (c. 18%), U.K. (16%), U.S. (c. 13%), West Germany (5%).

UNITED KINGDOM OF GREAT BRITAIN AND NORTHERN IRELAND
(Constitutional monarchy)

Sovereign: Queen Elizabeth II (1952).
Prime Minister: James Callaghan (1976).
Area: 94,529 sq mi. (244,046 sq km).*
Population (est. 1976): 56,100,000.* (English, Scottish, Welsh, Northern Irish).
Density per square mile: 593.5.
Capital: London, England.
Largest cities (est. 1974): London (Greater), England, 7,168,000; Birmingham, England, 1,086,000; Glasgow, Scotland, 816,000; Leeds, England, 748,000; Liverpool, England, 561,000; Sheffield, England, 561,000; Manchester, England, 516,000; Edinburgh, Scotland, 450,000; Bristol, England, 419,000.
Monetary unit: Pound sterling (£).
Languages: English, Welsh, Gaelic.
Religions: Church of England (established church); Church of Wales (disestablished); Church of Scotland (established church—Presbyterian); Church of Ireland (disestablished); Roman Catholic; Methodist; Congregational; Baptist; Jewish.

The United Kingdom is a constitutional monarchy, with a Queen and a Parliament which has two houses: the House of Lords with about 830 hereditary peers, 26 spiritual peers, about 270 life peers and peeresses, and 9 law-lords, who are hereditary or life peers, and the House of Commons, which has numbered, since 1974, 635 members

* Including the Channel Islands and the Isle of Man.

elected by practically universal suffrage. Supreme legislative power is vested in Parliament, which remains in being for five years unless sooner dissolved. The executive power of the Crown is exercised by the Cabinet, headed by the Prime Minister. The latter, normally the head of the party commanding a majority in the House of Commons, is appointed by the sovereign, with whose consent he in turn appoints the rest of the Cabinet. All ministers must be members of one or the other house of Parliament; they are individually and collectively responsible to the Crown and Parliament. The Cabinet proposes bills and arranges the business of Parliament, but it depends entirely on the votes in the House of Commons. The Lords cannot hold up "money" bills, but they can delay other bills for a period of at most one year.

By the Act of Union (1707), the Scottish Parliament was assimilated with that of England, and Scotland is now represented in Commons by seventy-one members. The Secretary of State for Scotland, a member of the Cabinet, is responsible for the administration of Scottish affairs.

Legislation was to be introduced in November 1976, granting local assemblies for home rule of both Scotland and Wales. The veto power of the Secretary of State for Scotland was to be eliminated and only limited veto powers were to remain with the Parliament at Westminster.

Ruler: Queen Elizabeth II, born April 21, 1926, elder daughter of King George VI and Queen Elizabeth, succeeded to the throne on the death of her father, Feb. 6, 1952; married Nov. 20, 1947 to Prince Philip, Duke of Edinburgh, born June 10, 1921; their children are Prince Charles† (heir presumptive), born Nov. 14, 1948; Princess Anne, born Aug. 15, 1950; Prince Andrew, born Feb. 19, 1960; and Prince Edward, born Mar. 10, 1964. The Queen's sister is Princess Margaret, born Aug. 21, 1930.

Major Political Parties. Labor Party (313 of 635 seats in House of Commons), led by Prime Minister James Callaghan; Conservative Party (277 seats), led by Mrs. Margaret Thatcher; Liberal Party (13 seats), led by David Steel; Scottish National Party (11 seats); United Ulster Unionists (10 seats).

History. Roman invasions of the first century B.C. brought Britain into contact with the continent. When the Roman legions withdrew in the fifth century A.D., Britain fell easy prey to the invading hordes of Angles, Saxons and Jutes from Scandinavia and the Low Countries. Seven large kingdoms were established, and the original Britons were forced into Wales and Scotland. It was not until the 11th century that the country finally became united under the Danish King Canute. Following the death of Edward the Confessor (1066), a dispute about the succession arose, and William Duke of Normandy invaded England, defeating the Saxon king, Harold II, at the Battle of Hastings (1066). The Norman conquest was accompanied by the introduction of Norman law and feudalism, changing the customs of England.

The reign of Henry II (1154–89), first of the Plantagenets, saw an increasing centralization of royal power at the expense of the nobles, but in

† The title Prince of Wales, which is not inherited, was conferred on Prince Charles by his mother on July 26, 1958. The investiture ceremony took place on July 1, 1969. The previous Prince of Wales was Prince Edward Albert, who held the title from 1911 to 1936 before he became Edward VIII.

Area and Population of United Kingdom

Subdivision	Area sq. mi.	Population (est. 1974)
England and Wales	58,350	49,175,000
Scotland	30,414	5,226,000
Northern Ireland	5,463	1,547,000
Channel Islands	75	125,000
Isle of Man	227	56,000
Total	94,529	56,129,000

1215 John (1199–1216) was forced to sign the Magna Carta, which awarded the people, especially the nobles, certain basic rights. Edward I (1272–1307) continued the conquest of Ireland, reduced Wales to subjection and made some gains in Scotland. In 1314, however, English forces led by Edward II were ousted from Scotland after the battle of Bannockburn. The late 13th and early 14th centuries saw the development of a separate House of Commons with tax-raising powers.

Edward III's claim to the throne of France led to the Hundred Years' War (1338–1453), which ended with the loss of almost all the large English territory in France. In England the great poverty and discontent caused by the war were intensified by the Black Death, a plague which reduced the population by about one-third. The War of the Roses (1455–85), a struggle for the throne between the House of York and the House of Lancaster, were ended by the victory of Henry Tudor (Henry VII) at Bosworth Field (1485).

During the reign of Henry VIII (1509–47), the Church in England asserted its independence from the Roman Catholic Church. Under Edward VI and Mary, the two extremes of religious fanaticism were reached and it remained for Henry's daughter, Elizabeth I (1558–1603), to set up the Church of England on a moderate basis. In 1588, the Spanish Armada, a fleet sent out by Catholic King Philip II of Spain, was defeated by the English and destroyed during a storm. During Elizabeth's reign, England became a world power.

Elizabeth's heir was of the house of Stuart—James VI of Scotland—who joined the two crowns as James I (1603–25). The Stuart kings incurred large debts and were forced either to depend on Parliament for taxes or to raise money by illegal means. In 1642, war broke out between Charles I and a large portion of the Parliament; Charles was defeated and executed in 1649, and the monarchy was then abolished. The Puritan Commonwealth endured for ten years but, after the death (1658) of Oliver Cromwell, the Lord Protector, the government fell to pieces and Charles II was restored to the throne in 1660. The struggle between the King and Parliament continued, but Charles II knew when to compromise. His brother James II (1685–88) possessed none of his ability and was ousted by the Revolution of 1688, which confirmed the predominant position of Parliament. James' daughter, Mary, and her husband, William of Orange, were now the rulers.

The reign of Queen Anne (1702–14) was marked by the Duke of Marlborough's victories over France at Blenheim, Oudenarde and Malplaquet in the War of the Spanish Succession. England and Scotland meanwhile were joined together by the Act of Union (1707). Upon the death of Anne, the distant claims of the elector of Hanover were recognized, and he became King of England as George I.

The Commonwealth

The Commonwealth is an association of sovereign, independent states, together with certain dependencies, protected states and protectorates, as listed in the following table. For further information about these countries and dependencies, *see* the pages indicated.

EUROPE

Political subdivision	Population[1]	Page
United Kingdom[2]	56,100,000	249
Cyprus	650,000	148
Gibraltar	30,000	256
Malta	333,000	203

AFRICA

Botswana	720,000	129
British Indian Ocean Territory	[3]	255
Gambia	530,000	164
Ghana	10,140,000	168
Kenya	13,500,000	192
Lesotho	1,065,000	198
Malawi	5,160,000	201
Mauritius	875,000	204
Nigeria	64,630,000	213
St. Helena	5,000[4]	257
Seychelles	65,000	228
Sierra Leone	2,280,000	229
Swaziland	550,000	236
Tanzania	15,575,000	239
Uganda	11,915,000	244
Zambia	5,100,000	266

WESTERN HEMISPHERE

Bahamas	215,000	124
Barbados	252,000	126
Belize	150,000	254
Bermuda	65,000	254
British Virgin Islands	11,000[5]	255
Canada	23,200,000	135
Cayman Islands	11,400[5]	256
Falkland Islands	2,000[5]	256
Grenada	110,000	171
Guyana	810,000	172
Jamaica	2,065,000	189
Montserrat	13,500	257
Trinidad and Tobago	1,085,000	242

WESTERN HEMISPHERE (Cont'd.)

Political subdivision	Population[1]	Page
Turks and Caicos Islands	6,000[6]	257
Anguilla	6,500	258
West Indies Associated States:		
Antigua	77,000	258
Dominica	80,000	258
St. Kitts-Nevis-Anguilla	70,000	258
St. Lucia	113,000	258
St. Vincent	112,000	258

ASIA

Bangladesh	78,700,000	125
Brunei	160,000	255
Hong Kong	4,450,000	256
India	610,000,000	176
Malaysia	11,900,000	201
Singapore	2,280,000	229
Sri Lanka (Ceylon)	14,300,000	234

OCEANIA

Australia	13,685,000	122
Fiji	600,000	158
Nauru[7]	7,000	208
New Zealand	3,150,000	210
Papua New Guinea	2,860,000	217
Pitcairn Island	70[5]	257
Tonga	106,000	241
Pacific Islands (British):		
Gilbert Islands	47,000	256
New Hebrides[8]	105,000	163
Solomon Islands	192,000	257
Tuvalu (formerly Ellice Islands)	5,900[4]	258
Western Samoa	165,000	262

ANTARCTICA

British Antarctic Territory	79[6]	255

[1] Figures are for 1976 unless otherwise indicated. [2] Consists of England, Scotland, Wales, Northern Ireland, Channel Islands and Isle of Man. [3] No permanent civilian population. [4] 1974 figure. [5] 1975 figure. [6] 1972 figure. [7] Special member of the Commonwealth. [8] Anglo-French condominium.

The 18th century was a period of gradual growth and change. At home, the unwillingness of the Hanoverian kings to rule resulted in the formation by the King's ministers of a Cabinet, headed by a Prime Minister, which directed all public business. Abroad, the constant wars with France resulted in expansion of the British Empire all over the globe, particularly in North America and India. This imperial growth was checked by the revolt of the American colonies (1775–81).

The age-long struggle with France broke out again in 1793 and, during the lengthy Napoleonic Wars, which ended at Waterloo (1815), England was pitted at one time against almost all of Europe.

The Victorian era, named after Queen Victoria (1837–1901), saw the growth of a democratic system of government which had begun with the Reform Bill of 1832. The two important wars in Victoria's reign were the Crimean War against Russia (1853–56) and the Boer War (1899–1902).

The latter was accompanied by enormous extension of Britain's sway in Africa.

The reign of Edward VII (1901–10) was marked by increasing uneasiness at home and abroad. Within four years after the accession of George V (1910), Britain entered World War I when Germany invaded Belgium. The nation was led by coalition Cabinets, headed first by Herbert Asquith and then (December 1916) by the Welsh statesman, David Lloyd George. The years after the war were marked by labor unrest which culminated in the general strike of 1926.

King Edward VIII succeeded to the throne on Jan. 20, 1936 at his father's death but abdicated on Dec. 11, 1936 (in order to marry an American, Wallis Warfield Simpson, whose second divorce was then pending) in favor of his brother, who became King George VI.

The efforts of Prime Minister Neville Chamberlain to meet by peaceful means the rising threat of Nazism in Germany failed with the German invasion of Poland (Sept. 1, 1939), which was followed by Britain's entry into World War II (Sept. 3). Serious Allied reverses in the spring of 1940 led to Chamberlain's resignation and the formation of another coalition war Cabinet by Conservative leader Winston Churchill, who led Britain through most of World War II. Churchill resigned as the coalition leader shortly after V-E Day, but then formed a "caretaker" government which remained in office until after the parliamentary elections of July 5, 1945, in which the Labour party won an overwhelming victory. The government formed by Clement R. Attlee on July 26 began a moderate socialistic program.

In 1951, Winston Churchill again became Prime Minister at the head of a Conservative government. George VI died Feb. 6, 1952, and was succeeded by his daughter, Elizabeth II.

Churchill voluntarily stepped down on Apr. 5, 1955 in favor of Sir Anthony Eden, who led the Conservatives to another victory in elections held May 26, 1955. He resigned on grounds of ill health (Jan. 9, 1957), and was succeeded in turn by Harold Macmillan and Sir Alec Douglas-Home (Oct. 18, 1963). In 1964, Harold Wilson led the Labour Party to victory and became Prime Minister on Oct. 16.

Wilson, the first Labour Prime Minister in 13 years, pursued policies not too different from those of the Conservatives, but managed to get popular support which widened his majority in the House of Commons in 1966. But continuing sterling crises, unemployment and a lagging rate of economic growth forced the adoption of an austerity program. He maintained loose relations with the United States, continued the liquidation of the empire and sought to expand Britain's influence in international affairs. In this he was aided by a wide acceptance of British culture abroad in popular music, films and drama, and fashions. In 1967, Britain renewed its effort to gain entry into the customs union, the Common Market. Balked by Charles de Gaulle, Wilson limited the conditions Britian had set for entry.

A Conservative victory in the 1970 elections made Edward Heath Prime Minister. Heath found a new mood in post-de Gaulle France and, after intensive negotiations, steered Britain into membership in the European Economic Community on Jan. 1, 1973. On June 5, 1975, the question of entry into the EEC was put to a referendum, Britain's first, and the decision was affirmed by 67.2% of the voters. Campaigners for the EEC included Margaret Thatcher, who became Britain's first woman party leader in February 1975, when she replaced Heath as the head of the Conservative Party.

Heath was unseated by the February 1974 elections in which the principal issue was a floundering economy worsened by a crippling coal strike. The returns gave neither party a majority, and Wilson returned as Prime Minister to head the first minority government since 1929. A second election, in October 1974, gave Labour a three-seat majority.

Rampant inflation fed by waves of pay boosts led the Labour-controlled Parliament on Aug. 4, 1975 to pass an emergency bill (cleared with trades union leaders) that limited wage increases.

With the pound sterling sinking to record lows, the House of Commons on Aug. 2, 1976 adopted a £2 billion ($3.56 billion) package of spending cuts and tax increases designed to stabilize the currency. Labor unions, with unemployment at a post-World War II high of 6.3%, reluctantly accepted the deflationary program.

Economic Conditions. Agriculture remains one of Britain's chief industries, employing about 800,000 persons. Cattle occupy a predominant position in British agriculture, accounting for about 40% of the total farm output.

The most important British manufacture is heavy goods such as machinery, tools, bridges and locomotives; industry is concentrated in the north and Midlands of England. South Wales produces 26% of the total crude-steel output, and Sheffield produces 11% of it. The china industry is concentrated in the Midlands. The cotton industry is centered in Lancashire; Liverpool, Manchester, Oldham, Preston and Bolton are the main manufacturing towns. The wool industry, England's oldest large trade, is located just east of the cotton towns, at Leeds, Bradford, and Hull in Yorkshire. An important industrial region is the central Lowlands of Scotland, where woolens and other fabrics, lace, glass, paper, steel and pig iron are produced. Important shipyards are located along the coast.

Historically, coal has been Britain's most important mineral resource, the base for her industrial supremacy in the 18th and 19th centuries. Nationalized in 1946, the mines recorded a decline in production and profit during the last decade until oil price increases raised coal demand and prices for 1974-75, reversing the deficits of recent years.

Discovery of oil beneath the North Sea in 1969 raised hopes for a valuable new energy resource in addition to natural gas already discovered offshore. The first oil was pumped June 11, 1975, but thus far has furnished only a negligible part of English oil consumption in 1975. Oil supplied 42% of the nation's energy needs in that year; coal 30% and natural gas 17%, with the remainder coming from nuclear and hydroelectricity.

Petroleum production is expected to meet consumption by 1980. Continental shelf reserves were estimated in 1976 at 2.3 billion tons.

The country produces small quantities of iron, tin, copper, lead and zinc. The entire supply of china clay (kaolin)—important to the ceramic, paper-making, bleaching and chemical industries—comes from Cornwall.

Britain is among the world's leaders in sea fishing. Salted herring normally represents about 70% of the exports.

Chief exports in 1974 were nonelectric machinery (19%), chemicals (13%), motor vehicles (8%), electrical machinery and equipment (7%), diamonds (5%) and textile yarns and fabrics (5%). Leading customers were EEC (33%; incl. West Germany 6%, Netherlands 6%, France 6%, Belgium-Luxembourg 5%, Ireland 5%) and U.S. (11%). Leading suppliers were EEC (33%; incl. West Germany 8%, Netherlands 7%, France 6%), U.S. (10%), Saudi Arabia (5%).

Natural Features. The United Kingdom, consisting of England, Wales, Scotland and Northern Ireland, is a third the size of Texas. England, in the southeast part of the British Isles, is separated from Scotland on the north by the granite Cheviot

Hills; from them the Pennine chain of uplands extends south through the center of England, reaching its highest point in the Lake District in the northwest. To the west along the border of Wales—a land of steep hills and valleys—are the Cambrian Mountains, while the Cotswolds, a range of hills in Gloucestershire, extend into the surrounding shires. The remainder of England is plain land, though not necessarily flat, with the rocky sand-topped moors in the southwest, the rolling downs in the south and southeast and the reclaimed marshes of the low-lying Fens in the east central districts. Scotland is divided into three physical regions—the Highlands, the Central Lowlands, containing two-thirds of the population, and the Southern Uplands. The western Highland coast is intersected throughout by long, narrow sea-lochs, or fiords. Scotland also includes the Outer and Inner Hebrides and other islands off the west coast and the Orkney and Shetland islands off the north coast.

Wales is generally hilly; the Snowdon range in the northern part culminates in Mt. Snowdon (3,560 ft.), highest in both England and Wales.

Important rivers flowing into the North Sea are the Thames, Humber, Tees and Tyne. In the west are the Severn and the Wye, which empty into the Bristol Channel and are navigable, as are the Mersey and Ribble.

NORTHERN IRELAND

Status: Part of United Kingdom.
Secretary of State: Merlyn Rees (1974).
Area: 5,463 sq mi. (14,148 sq km).
Population (est. 1974): 1,547,000.
Density per square mile: 283.2.
Capital and largest city (est. 1974): Belfast, 374,000.
Monetary unit: Pound sterling.
Languages: English, Gaelic.
Religions: Roman Catholic, 34.9%; Presbyterian, 29%; Church of Ireland, 24.2%; Methodist, 5%.

Northern Ireland is an integral part of the United Kingdom (it has 12 representatives in the British House of Commons), but under the terms of the Government of Ireland Act (1920), it had a semiautonomous government. But on Mar. 28, 1972, after three years of internal strife resulted in over 400 dead and thousands injured, Britain suspended the Ulster parliament and the province became governed directly from London after an attempt to return certain powers to an elected Assembly in Belfast.

The Northern Ireland Assembly was dissolved Mar. 28, 1975, and a Constitutional Convention was elected on May 1 to write a Constitution acceptable to Protestants and Catholics. The convention failed to reach agreement and was dissolved Mar. 5, 1976.

Major Political Parties. United Ulster Unionist Coalition (Protestant) (46 of 78 delegates to Constitutional Convention); Social Democratic Labour Party (Catholic) (17 delegates); Alliance Party (8 delegates); New Unionist Party of Northern Ireland (Protestant) (5 delegates).

History. Northern Ireland comprises the six predominantly Protestant counties of Antrim, Armagh, Down, Fermanagh, Londonderry and Tyrone, collectively known as Ulster, which form the northern part of the Island of Ireland, the westernmost of the Atlantic Ocean's British Isles.

Ulster was part of Catholic Ireland until the reign of Elizabeth I (1558–1603), when, after crushing three Irish rebellions, the crown confiscated lands in Ireland and settled in Ulster Scot Presbyterians who became rooted there. Another rebellion in 1641–51, crushed as brutally by Oliver Cromwell, resulted in the settlement of Anglican Englishmen in Ulster. Subsequent political policy favoring Protestants and disadvantaging Catholics encouraged further settlement in Northern Ireland.

But the North did not separate from the South until William Gladstone presented in 1886 his proposal for home rule in Ireland as a means of settling the Irish Question. The Protestants in the north, although they had grievances like the Catholics in the south, feared domination by the Catholic majority. Industry, moreover, was concentrated in the north and depended on the British market. When World War I began, civil war threatened between the regions. Northern Ireland, however, did not become a political entity until the six counties accepted the Home Rule Bill of 1920. This set up a semiautonomous Parliament in Belfast and a crown-appointed Governor advised by a Cabinet of the Prime Minister and eight ministers, as well as a 12-member representation in the House of Commons at London.

As the Republic of Ireland gained its sovereignty, relations improved between North and South, although the Irish Republican Army, outlawed in recent years, continued the struggle to end the partition of Ireland. In 1966–69, communal rioting and street fighting between Protestants and Catholics occurred in Londonderry, fomented by extremist nationalist Protestants, who feared the Catholics might attain a local majority, and by Catholics demonstrating for civil rights.

Rioting, terrorism and sniping killed more than 1,600 persons from 1969 through 1976, and the religious communities, Catholic and Protestant, became hostile armed camps. British troops were brought in to separate them but themselves became a target of Catholics.

The bloodshed intensified in 1972, forcing Britain to impose direct rule from London after dissolving the Ulster parliament, which was unable to end the strife.

Catholics boycotted a March 8, 1973 referendum that produced a 591,820-to-6,463 vote for Ulster's continuance in the United Kingdom.

Two weeks later, a new British charter created a 78-member Assembly elected by proportional representation that gave more weight to Catholic strength. It created a Province Executive with committee chairmen of the Assembly heading all government departments except law enforcement, which remained under London's control. Assembly elections June 28, 1973 produced a majority for the new Constitution that included Catholic assemblymen. Dublin urged Ulster Catholics to work with the new system.

Ulster's leaders agreed in November 1973 to create an 11-member Executive Body with six seats assigned to Unionists (Protestants) and four to members of Catholic parties. Unionist leader Brian Faulkner headed the Executive. Also agreed to was a Council of Ireland with 14 seats evenly divided between Dublin and Belfast which could act only by unanimous vote.

Although the Council lacked real authority, its creation sparked a general strike by Protestant extremists in May, 1974. The two-week strike caused Faulkner's resignation from the Executive and resumption of direct rule from London.

Return of a Labour government in Britain in February 1974 led promptly to the assignment of Merlyn Rees to replace the less conciliatory William Whitelaw as Secretary of State for Northern Ireland. In April 1974, London instituted a new program that responded to some Catholic grievances, but assigned more British troops to cut off movement of arms and munitions to Ulster's violence-racked cities.

In addition to pledging recruitment of more Catholics in the overwhelmingly Protestant Royal Ulster Constabulary, the London government proposed phased release of suspected terrorists whose imprisonment without trial had caused Catholic protests. The releases were made contingent on an end to the violence.

Violence continued unabated, with new heights reached early in 1976 when the British government announced the end of special privileges for political prisoners in Northern Ireland. British Prime Minister James Callaghan visited Belfast in July and pledged that Ulster would remain part of the United Kingdom unless a clear majority wished to separate.

Economic Conditions. Agriculture is the largest single industry; about two-thirds of the country is devoted to crops and pasture under a system of mixed farming. The leading crops include potatoes, oats, and flax.

The two principal manufacturing industries are linen and shipbuilding, both centered in Belfast. The linen industry was established by Huguenot weavers who fled France after the revocation of the Edict of Nantes in 1685.

ISLE OF MAN

Status: Dependency.
Lieutenant Governor: Sir John Paul (1973).
Area: 227 sq mi. (588 sq km).
Population (est. 1973): 56,000.
Capital (1971 census): Douglas, 20,389.

Located in the Irish Sea, equidistant from Scotland, Ireland and England, the Isle of Man is administered according to its own laws by a government composed of the Lieutenant Governor, a Legislative Council, and a House of Keys, one of the most ancient legislative assemblies in the world.

CHANNEL ISLANDS

Status: Dependency.
Lieutenant Governor of Jersey: Gen. Sir Desmond Fitzpatrick.
Lieutenant Governor of Guernsey: Vice Adm. Sir John Martin (1974).
Area: 75 sq mi. (194 sq km).
Population (est. 1973): 124,000.
Capital of Jersey: St. Helier.
Capital of Guernsey: St. Peter Port.

This group of islands, lying in the English Channel off the northwest coast of France, is the only portion of the Duchy of Normandy belonging

to the English Crown, to which it has been attached since the conquest of 1066. It was the only British possession occupied by Germany during World War II.

For purposes of government, the islands are divided into Jersey (45 sq mi.) and the Bailiwick of Guernsey (30 sq mi.), including Alderney (3 sq mi.), Sark (2 sq mi.), Herm, Jethou, etc. The islands are administered according to their own laws and customs by local governments. Acts of Parliament in London are not binding on the islands unless they are specifically mentioned. The Queen is represented in each Bailiwick by a Lieutenant Governor.

English is now the language in daily use, although the French patois is still spoken by some people. New legislation is drafted in English, but French has been retained for ceremonial purposes in the legislative bodies.

Dependencies of the United Kingdom

ANGUILLA. }   See WEST INDIES
ANTIGUA. }   ASSOCIATED STATES.

BELIZE

Status: Self governing dependency.
Governor: Peter McEntee (1976).
Prime Minister: George C. Price (1961).
Area: 8,867 sq mi. (2,474 sq km).
Population (est. 1976): 150,000.
Capital: (est. 1973): Belmopan, 5,000.
Chief exports: sugar, citrus fruit and products, mahogany, lobsters, clothing.
Agricultural products: bananas, sugar cane, citrus fruits.
Forest products: cedar lumber and logs, mahogany lumber and logs, pine lumber.

Formerly known as British Honduras, Belize became a British Crown Colony in 1884. It is situated in Central America south of Mexico and east and north of Guatemala on the Caribbean sea. Belize was probably overrun by Hernando Cortés in 1524. British buccaneers settled the former capital, Belize, in the 17th century.

In the first popular election in 1954, the People's United Party, nationalistic and anti-British, came to power. Eventually the nationalists won a Constitution, which, effective in 1964, established self-government under a British-appointed Governor.

Economic Conditions. Chief exports in 1970 were sugar (48%), orange juice (7%), grapefruit segments (5%), timber (8%), lobster (5%) and clothing (5%). Leading customers were U.S. (30%), United Kingdom (24%), Mexico (22%), Canada (13%). Leading suppliers were U.S. (34%), U.K. (25%), Jamaica (7%), Netherlands (7%).

BERMUDA

Status: Self-governing dependency.
Governor: Sir Edwin Leather (1973).
Government Leader: Sir Edward Richards (1973).
Area: 20 sq mi. (52 sq km).
Population (est. 1976): 65,000.
Capital (est. 1970): Hamilton, 2,060.

Chief exports: drugs and medicines.
Agricultural products: lily bulbs, potatoes, vegetables, arrowroot.

Bermuda is an archipelago of about 360 small islands, 580 miles east of North Carolina. The largest is (Great) Bermuda, or Main Island. Discovered by Juan de Bermúdez, a shipwrecked Spaniard, early in the 16th century, the islands were settled in 1612 by an offshoot of the Virginia Company and became a crown colony in 1684.

In 1940, sites on the islands were leased for 99 years to the United States for air and navy bases. Bermuda is also the headquarters of the West Indies and Atlantic squadron of the Royal Navy.

Bermuda got a new Constitution, its first Prime Minister and almost full autonomy in 1968. Still a British colony, the lovely tourist haven is in full charge of its affairs, except for foreign relations, defense and internal security, under the Constitution that went into effect in May. Sir Henry Tucker, a member of one of the island's oldest white families, became Prime Minister in the same month after his predominantly white United Bermuda Party won 30 of 40 seats in the Assembly. The voting was the first without restrictions based on property ownership, but the "establishment" United Bermuda Party defeated the Progressive Laborites, a largely black party. Almost two-thirds of Bermuda's people are blacks. The elections came against a background of rioting and looting in Hamilton in April, the result in large part of racial tensions.

Economic Conditions. Chief exports in 1973 (domestic only) were drugs and medicines (59%) and liquor (5%). Leading customers in 1972 (domestic only) were U.S. (89%) and Canada (6%). Leading suppliers were U.S. (45%), United Kingdom (20%), Canada (10%).

BRITISH ANTARCTIC TERRITORY

Status: Dependency.
High Commissioner: Neville A. I. French.
Area: 500,000 sq mi. (1,395,000 sq km).
Population (1972): 79.

The British Antarctic Territory consists of the South Shetland Islands and the South Orkney Islands and nearby Graham Land on the Antarctic continent, largely uninhabited. They were dependencies of the British crown colony of the Falkland Islands but received a separate administration in 1962, being governed by a British-appointed high commissioner who is governor of the Falklands.

BRITISH INDIAN OCEAN TERRITORY

Status: Dependency.
Commissioner: Colin H. Allan.
Administrator: D. K. H. Dale.
Area: 85 sq mi. (220 sq km).

This dependency, consisting of the Chagos Archipelago, was formed in November 1965 by agreement with Maurtius and the Seychelles. There is no permanent civilian population in the territory.

BRITISH VIRGIN ISLANDS

Status: Dependency.
Governor: Walter W. Wallace.

Area: 59 sq mi. (153 sq km).
Population (est. 1975): 11,000.
Capital (est. 1975): Road Town (on Tortola): 3,500.
Chief exports: fish, livestock, bananas.

Some 36 islands in the Caribbean Sea northeast of Puerto Rico and west of the Leeward Islands, the British Virgin Islands are economically interdependent with the U.S. Virgin Islands to the south. They were formerly part of the administration of the Leeward Islands. They received a separate administration in 1956 as a crown colony. In 1967 a new Constitution was promulgated which provided for a ministerial system of government headed by the Governor. The principal islands are Tortola, Virgin Gorda, Anegada and Jost Van Dyke.

Economic Conditions. Chief exports in 1973 were motor vehicles (re-exports) (15%); nonelectric machines (re-exports) (14%), gravel and sand (10%), fish (9%), timber (re-exports) (6%), beverages (re-exports) (5%). Leading customers were U.S. Virgin Islands (59%), Netherlands Antilles (12%), St. Martin (8%), United Kingdom (7%). Leading suppliers were U.S. (24%), Puerto Rico (19%), U.K. (16%), U.S. Virgin Islands (15%), Trinidad and Tobago (8%).

BRUNEI

Status: Protected state.
Sultan: Hassanel Bolkiah (1968).
High Commissioner: J. A. Davidson.
Area: 2,226 sq mi. (5,765 sq km).
Population (est. 1976): 160,000.
Capital (1971 census): Bandar Seri Begawan, 36,574.
Chief export: crude oil.
Agricultural products: rice, rubber.
Mineral: Petroleum.

A sultanate on the northwest coast of the island of Borneo on the South China Sea, Brunei consists of two prongs into the territory of Sarawak, East Malaysia. It was a powerful state from the 16th to the 19th century, ruling over the northern part of Borneo and adjacent island chains. But it fell into decay and lost Sarawak in 1841, becoming a British protectorate in 1888 and a British dependency in 1905. The Sultan regained control over internal affairs by a Constitution he instituted in 1959, along with an agreement with the Crown delegating responsibilty for defense and foreign affairs. Britain, which is responsible for foreign affairs, is represented by a High Commissioner; government is by a Privy Council and Council of Ministers, both presided over by the Sultan, and a Legislative Council.

Sultan Bolkiah was crowned in August 1968 at the age of 22. He succeeded his father, Sir Omar Ali Saifuddin, who abdicated.

Most of the inhabitants are Malays and Borneans; in the 1971 census, 23.4% were Chinese and only 1.5% European. The bulk of the population lives in and around the capital, situated on the Brunei River nine miles from its mouth. The interior is largely forested and contains rich timber. All petroleum is exported to Sarawak for refining.

Economic - Conditions. Chief export in 1972 was crude oil (99%). Leading customers were Japan (52%), Malaysia (11%), Singapore (8%), U.S. (8%), Thailand (6%). Leading suppliers were Japan (20%),

U.S. (19%), Singapore (15%), United Kingdom (14%), Malaysia (6%), Netherlands (6%).

CAYMAN ISLANDS

Status: Dependency.
Governor: T. Russell (1974).
Area: 100 sq mi. (259 sq km).
Population (est. 1975): 11,400.
Capital (1970 census): Georgetown (on Grand Cayman), 4,106.

This dependency consists of three islands—Grand Cayman (76 sq mi.), Cayman Brac (14 sq mi.) and Little Cayman (10 sq mi.)—situated about 180 miles northwest of Jamaica. They were dependencies of Jamaica until 1959, when they became a unit territory within the Federation of the West Indies. In 1962, upon the dissolution of the Federation, the Cayman Islands became a British dependency.

DOMINICA. See WEST INDIES ASSOCIATED STATES.

FALKLAND ISLANDS AND DEPENDENCIES

Status: Dependency.
Governor: Neville A. I. French.
Area: 6,150 sq mi. (11,961 sq km).
Population (est. 1975): 2,000.
Capital (est. 1972): Stanley (on East Falkland), 1,100.
Chief exports: wool, hides, skins.

This sparsely inhabited dependency consists of a group of islands in the south Atlantic, about 250 miles east of the South American mainland. The largest islands are East Falkland and West Falkland. Dependencies are South Georgia Island (1,450 sq mi.) and the South Sandwich Islands. Three former dependencies—the Graham Coast, the South Shetland Islands and the South Orkney Islands—were established as a new British dependency, the British Antarctic Territory, in 1962.

The chief industry is sheep raising and, apart from the production of wool, hides and skins, and tallow, there are no known resources. The whaling industry is carried on from South Georgia Island.

GIBRALTAR

Status: Non-self-governing territory, with Gibraltar officials responsible for domestic affairs, under Constitution of May, 1969.
Governor: Sir John Grandy.
Chief Minister: Sir Joshua Hassan.
Area: 2.25 sq mi. (5.8 sq km).
Population (est. 1976): 30,000.

Gibraltar, at the south end of the Iberian Peninsula, is a rocky promontory commanding the western entrance to the Mediterranean. Aside from its strategic importance, it is also a free port, naval base and coaling station. It was captured by the Arabs crossing from Africa into Spain in A.D. 711. In the 15th century, it passed to the Moorish ruler of Granada and later became Spanish. It was captured by an Anglo-Dutch force in 1704 during the War of the Spanish Succession and passed to Britain by the Treaty of Utrecht in 1713. Most of

the inhabitants of Gibraltar are of Spanish, Italian and Maltese descent.

Spanish efforts to recover Gibraltar culminated in a referendum in September 1967 in which the residents voted overwhelmingly to retain their link with Britain. This vote followed months of discussions, marked by Spanish restrictions on travel from the mainland or by air to Gibraltar.

GILBERT ISLANDS

Status: Dependency.
Governor: J. H. Smith (1973).
Area: 102 sq mi. (264 sq km).
Population (est. 1976): 47,000.
Capital (1968 census): Tarawa, 12,642.
Chief exports: phosphates, copra.

Formerly the Gilbert and Ellice Islands, the islands in these groups (including the Gilbert group; the Ellice group; Ocean Island, Fanning, Washington and Christmas islands; and the Phoenix group) were proclaimed a British protectorate in 1892 and annexed as a colony in 1915. The most important product is high-grade phosphate.

Ownership of Canton and Enderbury islands in the Phoenix group was long in dispute between Great Britain and the United States until 1939, when an agreement for "use in common" was reached by the two governments. Several of the Gilbert islands were occupied by Japanese forces in World War II, and Tarawa was the scene of one of the fiercest battles in U.S. Marine Corps history in November 1943.

In 1975, the Gilbert and Ellice Islands were divided into two colonies, the Gilberts retaining the name and the Ellice group becoming Tuvalu.

HONG KONG

Status: Dependency.
Governor: Sir Murray MacLehose (1971).
Area: 403 sq mi. (1,040 sq km).
Population (est. 1976): 4,450,000.
Capital (est. 1971): Victoria, 520,900.
Chief export: clothing, textiles, electrical equipment.
Agricultural products: vegetables, poultry, pigs.
Major industries: shipbuilding, rope making, cement, textiles, electrical products.

The dependency of Hong Kong comprises the island of Hong Kong (32 sq mi.), Stonecutters' Island, and the Kowloon peninsula and the New Territories on the adjoining mainland. The island of Hong Kong, located at the mouth of the Canton River about 90 miles southeast of Canton, was ceded to Britain in 1841.

Stonecutters' Island and Kowloon were annexed in 1860, and the New Territories, which are mainly agricultural lands, were leased from China in 1898 for 99 years. Hong Kong was attacked by Japanese troops Dec. 7, 1941, and surrendered the following Christmas. It remained under Japanese occupation until August 1945.

Possessing an excellent natural harbor, the only safe deep-sea anchorage between Shanghai and Indo-China, Hong Kong is the entrepôt for trade throughout southern China and the western Pacific.

The cities of Victoria and Kowloon contain the greater part of the population, which is overwhelmingly Chinese. Besides those Chinese engaged in agriculture or industry, many live in sampans or junks either in Victoria harbor or neighboring bays, supporting themselves by fishing or by performing labor on the wharves.

In November 1974, Hong Kong rescinded a policy of accepting illegal immigrants from China that had, since 1968, made the crowded city a sanctuary for thousands of Chinese refugees. Increased unemployment in Hong Kong caused the change.

Economic Conditions. Chief exports in 1974 were clothing (30%), chemicals (21%), machines (15%), textile yarns and fabrics (13%) and instruments (5%). Leading customers were U.S. (26%), United Kingdom (10%), West Germany (8%), Japan (7%), Singapore (5%), Australia (5%). Leading suppliers were Japan (21%), China (17%), U.S. (13%), U.K. (6%), Singapore (5%), Taiwan (5%).

LEEWARD ISLANDS. See BRITISH VIRGIN ISLANDS; MONTSERRAT; WEST INDIES ASSOCIATED STATES.

MONTSERRAT

Status: Dependency.
Governor: N. D. Matthews (1974).
Area: 40 sq mi. (104 sq km).
Population (est. 1976): 13,500.
Capital (est. 1974): Plymouth, 3,000.
Chief exports: fruit, vegetables, cotton, tires.

The island of Montserrat is located in the Lesser Antilles of the West Indies. Until 1956, it was a division of the Leeward Islands. It did not join the West Indies Associated States established in 1967.

PACIFIC ISLANDS (British)

High Commissioner in Western Pacific: D. C. C. Luddington.
Population (est. 1975): 112,000.

Island groups in the Pacific administered by the British High Commissioner in the Western Pacific include: the British Solomon Islands and the New Hebrides Condominium (*see* French Overseas Territories). The High Commissioner has headquarters at Honiara, Solomon Islands.

PITCAIRN ISLAND

Status: Dependency.
Governor: H. Smedley.
Island Magistrate: Pervis Young.
Area: 1.75 square miles.
Population (1975): 70.
Capital: Adamstown.

Pitcairn Island, located in the South Pacific about midway between Australia and South America, consists of the island of Pitcairn and the three uninhabited islands of Henderson, Ducie and Oeno. The island of Pitcairn was settled in 1790 by British mutineers from the ship *Bounty*, commanded by Captain William Bligh. It was annexed as a British colony in 1838. Overpopulation forced removal of the settlement to Norfolk Island in 1856, but about 40 persons soon returned.

The island is governed by a 10-member Council presided over by the Island Magistrate, who is elected for a three-year term.

ST. HELENA

Status: Dependency.
Governor: G. C. Guy (1976).
Area: 47 sq mi. (122 sq km).
Population (est. 1974): 5,000.
Capital (est. 1974): Jamestown, 1,600.
Agricultural products: vegetables.

St. Helena is a volcanic island in the South Atlantic about 1,100 miles from the west coast of Africa. It is famous as the place of exile of Napoleon (1815–21).

It was taken for Britain in 1659 by the East India Company and was brought under the direct government of the Crown in 1834.

St. Helena has two dependencies: Ascension (34 sq mi.), an island about 700 miles northwest of St. Helena; and Tristan da Cunha (40 sq mi.), a group of six islands about 1,500 miles south-southwest of St. Helena.

ST. KITTS-NEVIS.
ST. LUCIA. } See WEST INDIES ASSOCIATED STATES.
ST. VINCENT.

SOLOMON ISLANDS

Status: Protectorate.
High Commissioner: Colin H. Allan.
Area: 10,983 sq mi. (28,446 sq km).
Population (est. 1976): 192,000.
Capital (est. 1971): Honiara (on Guadalcanal), 13,350.
Chief exports: copra, timber, fish.

This protectorate, lying east of New Guinea, consists of the southern islands of the Solomon group: Guadalcanal, Malaita, San Cristobal, New Georgia, Santa Isabel, Choiseul and numerous smaller islands. The protectorate does not include the northern islands of Bougainville and Buka, which are part of the U.N. trust territory of New Guinea, administered by Australia.

The islands, which came under British protection late in the 19th century, were the scene of several important U.S. naval and military victories during World War II.

Britain has promised to grant the islands independence by mid-1977 if Parliament approves.

Economic Conditions. Chief exports in 1973 were timber (40%), copra (29%) and fish (17%). Leading customers were Japan (53%), American Samoa (13%), West Germany (7%), Australia (7%), Norway (5%). Leading suppliers were Australia (45%), United Kingdom (13%), Japan (12%), Singapore (7%).

TURKS AND CAICOS ISLANDS

Status: Dependency.
Governor: A. C. Watson.
Area: 166 square miles.
Population (est. 1972): 6,000.
Capital (1970 census): Grand Turk, 2,287.
Chief exports: crayfish, salt.

These two groups of islands are situated at the southeast end of the Bahamas. The principal islands in the Turks group are Grand Turk and Salt Cay; the principal ones in the Caicos group are South Caicos, East Caicos, Middle (or Grand) Caicos, North Caicos, Providenciales and West Caicos.

The Turks and Caicos Islands were dependencies of Jamaica until 1959, when they became a unit territory within the Federation of the West Indies. In 1962, when Jamaica became independent, the Turks and Caicos became a British Crown Colony. The present Constitution has been in force since June 18, 1969.

TUVALU

(formerly Ellice Islands)

Status: Dependency.
Commissioner: T. H. Layng.
Area: 10 sq mi. (26 sq km).
Population (est. 1974): 5,900.
Seat of government: Funafuti, 900.
Chief exports: copra and phosphates.

Formerly the Ellice Islands, Tuvalu was separated from the Gilbert and Ellice Islands in 1975 and became a separate colony. The group consists of nine main islands just south of the equator in the western Pacific.

VIRGIN ISLANDS. See BRITISH VIRGIN ISLANDS.

WEST INDIES ASSOCIATED STATES

Status: Self-governing territories in free association with the United Kingdom, which is responsible for defense and external affairs. The British Government conducts its affairs with the West Indies Associated States through an official representative, whose office is in Castries, St. Lucia.
Governors: Antigua, David F. B. le Breton; Dominica, Sir Louis Cools-Lartigue; St. Kitts-Nevis-Anguilla, Sir Mitton S. Allen; St. Lucia, Ira Simmonds (acting); St. Vincent, Sir Rupert John; Anguilla, D.F.B. Le Bolton (commissioner).
Area: Antigua, 171 square miles; Dominica, 290; St. Kitts-Nevis-Anguilla, 118; St. Lucia, 238; St. Vincent, 150; Anguilla, 35.
Population (est. 1976): Antigua, 77,000; Dominica, 80,000; St. Kitts-Nevis-Anguilla, 70,000; St. Lucia, 113,000; St. Vincent, 112,000; Anguilla, 6,500.
Capitals (1960 census): Antigua: St. Johns, 21,595; Dominica: Roseau, 10,417; St. Kitts-Nevis-Anguilla: Basseterre, 15,726; St. Lucia: Castries, 4,353; St. Vincent: Kingstown, 4,308.

The West Indies Associated States were established in February–March 1967 and consisted of Antigua and St. Kitts-Nevis-Anguilla of the Leeward Islands, and Dominica, Grenada (which became independent in 1974), St. Lucia and St. Vincent of the Windward Islands. Statehood for St. Vincent was held up until October 1969 because of local political uncertainties.

Two dependencies of the Leeward group—the British Virgin Islands and Montserrat—did not become Associated States.

Each of the Associated States is fully self-governing in its internal affairs.

The association between Britain and each state is to be free and voluntary. As a guarantee of its voluntary nature, association will be terminable by either party. On termination of association,

the state would become independent of Britain.

An interval of 90 days must elapse between introduction in a state legislature of an intent to terminate association and any consideration of it.

In July 1967, Anguilla declared its independence from the St. Kitts-Nevis-Anguilla federation. Britain, however, did not recognize this action. In February 1969, Anguilla voted to cut all ties with Britain and become an independent republic. In March, Britain landed troops on the island and, on Mar. 30, a truce was signed. In July 1971, Anguilla became a dependency of Britain and two months later Britain ordered the withdrawal of all her troops.

A new Constitution for Anguilla, effective in February 1976, provides for separate administration and a government of elected representatives. The Associated State of St. Kitts-Nevis-Anguilla remains in being, but Anguilla has a separate relationship with Britain.

Economic Conditions: Chief exports of Antigua are petroleum products; of Dominica, bananas, essential oils and fruit juices; of St. Kitts-Nevis, sugar and preparations; of St. Vincent, bananas and arrowroot.

Chief exports of St. Lucia in 1972 were bananas (55%), coconut oil (14%), machinery (re-exports) (6%). Leading customers were United Kingdom (58%), Leeward and Windward islands (18%), Jamaica (7%), Trinidad and Tobago (6%). Leading suppliers were U.K. (31%), U.S. (15%), Trinidad and Tobago (10%), Netherlands and possessions (6%).

WINDWARD ISLANDS. See WEST INDIES ASSOCIATED STATES.

UPPER VOLTA (Republic)

(République de Haute-Volta)

President and Premier: Gen. Sangoulé Lamizana (1966).
Area: 105,870 sq mi. (274,200 sq km).
Population (est. 1976): 6,150,000.
Density per square mile: 58.1.
Capital and largest city (est. 1974): Ouagadougou, 150,000.
Monetary unit: Franc CFA.
Ethnic groups: Mossis, Bobos.
Languages: French, African languages.
Religions: Animist, 75%; Moslem, 20%; Christian, 5%.

On Jan. 3, 1966, the President was deposed and the then Col. Sangoulé Lamizana dissolved the National Assembly, suspended the Constitution and became President. In that same year, a new Constitution was adopted, providing for a National Assembly of 57 members, to be elected every four years.

Dissension within the African Democratic Union, the major political party, led to a take-over by the military on Feb. 8, 1974. The Constitution was suspended, the National Assembly was dissolved and all political activity banned. Lamizana remained President and formed a mostly military Cabinet. In July, 1974, he installed a new National Council for Renewal. The 65-member body purportedly replaces the National Assembly, but has only consultive power.

Political Party: The Mouvement pour le Renouveau, formed by Lamizana, is the only political party.

History. Upper Volta consists chiefly of the lands of the Mossi Empire, where France established a protectorate over the Kingdom of Ouagadougou in 1897. Upper Volta became a separate colony in 1919, was partitioned among the Niger, Sudan and Ivory Coast in 1933, and was reconstituted in 1947. An autonomous republic within the French Community, it became independent on Aug. 5, 1960. On Jan. 4, 1966, Colonel Sangoulé Lamizana became chief of state.

On Jan. 1, 1973, Upper Volta formed, with six other nations, the Economic Community for West Africa to promote economic development in the region.

Economic Conditions. Agricultural products include millet, sorghum, peanuts, beans and maize.

Chief exports in 1972 were livestock (41%), cotton (20%), peanuts (7%) and sesame seed (5%). Leading customers were Ivory Coast (46%), France (19%), Italy (7%), Ghana (5%), Mali (5%). Leading suppliers were France (46%), Ivory Coast (17%), West Germany (5%).

URUGUAY (Republic)

(República Oriental del Uruguay)

President: Aparicio Mendez (1976).
Area: 68,536 sq mi. (177,508 sq km).
Population (est. 1976): 3,090,000.
Density per square mile: 45.1.
Capital and largest city (est. 1975): Montevideo, 1,229,700.
Monetary unit: New peso.
Language: Spanish.
Religion: Roman Catholic.

The President serves for a term of five years. He appoints a Council of 11 ministers to assist him. Congress consisted of two houses—a Senate and a House of Deputies. Members remained in office for five years.

In June 1973, President Juan María Bordaberry yielded to military pressure and dissolved Congress, thus ending 40 years of constitutional rule. The June decree announced creation of a Council of State to perform Congressional functions, oversee presidential activities and formulate constitutional reforms for a national plebiscite.

Political Parties. Colorado Party (41 of 99 seats in House of Deputies), led by Bordaberry; National Party (40 seats), and Broad Front (18 seats). Political activity has been banned since Congress was dissolved in 1973.

History. Juan Díaz de Solis, a Spaniard, discovered Uruguay in 1516, but the Portuguese were first to settle it when they founded Colonia in 1680. After a long struggle, Spain wrested the country from Portugal in 1778. Uruguay revolted against Spain in 1811, only to be conquered in 1816–20 by the Portuguese from Brazil. Independence was reasserted with Argentine help in 1825, and the republic was set up in 1830.

Independence, however, did not restore order, and a revolt in 1836 touched off nearly fifty years of factional strife with occasional armed interven-

tion from Argentina and Brazil. Since 1900, there has been social and economic progress.

In 1951, the Constitution of 1934 was amended to place executive power in a National Council of nine members rather than in an individual President. The chairmanship of the council was rotated each year.

In 1966, Uruguayans voted to replace the National Council with a one-man chief executive.

Alberto Heber, who became President in 1966, vigorously championed reform, and a referendum authorized revision of the Constitution to vest executive powers in a President and a Cabinet of Ministers. Oscar Diego Gestido, elected President in 1966, devoted much effort to improving the ailing economy. But he died in November 1967, and was succeeded by Jorge Pacheco Areco.

Siege-state regulations continued as the "Tupamaros," first urban guerrilla organization, kept up spectacular kidnappings, bank and casino robberies (one gold haul netted over $250,000), and arms raids on military arsenals to embarrass what was then the most democratic government in South America. In 1970, the Tupamaros kidnapped a U.S. aid adviser, Dan Mitrione, and killed him when their ransom demands were not met.

The continuing economic, political and guerrilla problems precipitated impeachment proceedings against Pacheco in 1971. A bitterly fought election followed, with Juan María Bordaberry, Pacheco's hand-picked choice, the winner.

Disputes between the government and the military, coupled with worsening economic problems (the peso was devalued 32 times during Bordaberry's first three years in office), led to a military revolt in February 1973 that ended in an agreement with Bordaberry in which the military promised to maintain the constitutional system but virtually took over control of the government.

Despite the military takeover, inflation soared at a 100% yearly rate and the Tupamaros continued to be active. Their assassinations and bombings were matched by government repression; an estimated 3,500 persons were arrested on political charges in the year after Congress was dissolved and the press was kept tightly in line.

Bordaberry said in September 1974 that the ban on political activity imposed when Congress was dissolved would continue indefinitely. Elections scheduled for November 1976 will not take place, he said, under the "system which died 27 June, 1973."

All Marxist parties were permanently outlawed by Bordaberry on Jan. 1, 1975. Three days later, the Communist Party leader, Rodney Arismendi, was released from prison and deported to Europe.

Military leaders, citing Bordaberry's opposition to the return of constitutional government, removed him from Office June 12, 1976. The National Council of 25 military officers and 21 civilians designated Aparicio Mendez to take over the Presidency on Sept. 1 for a five-year term. Elections scheduled for November and canceled by Bordaberry would not take place, the new regime announced, but political parties other than the Communists were expected to return and the legislature to be reconvened in 1979.

Economic Conditions. Cattle, sheep, meat, and wool dominate the Uruguayan economy. The chief crop is wheat.

Chief exports in 1974 were meat (38%), wool (23%) and hides and skins (6%). Leading customers in 1973 were West Germany (14%), Spain (12%), Italy (8%), Netherlands (7%), France (7%), United Kingdom (6%), Brazil (5%). Leading suppliers were Argentina (21%), Brazil (16%), U.S. (9%), Nigeria (7%), West Germany (7%), Kuwait (6%), U.K. (5%).

Natural Features. Uruguay, a low, rolling plain in the south and a low plateau in the north, has a 120-mile Atlantic shore line, a 235-mile frontage on the Rio de la Plata and 270 miles on the Uruguay River, its western boundary.

VATICAN CITY STATE

(Stato della Città del Vaticano)

Ruler: Pope Paul VI (1963).
Area: 0.17 square mile.
Population (est. 1976): 1,000 (Italian, 85%; Swiss and others, 15%).
Density per square mile: 5,882.4.
Monetary unit: Lira.
Languages: Latin, Italian.
Religion: Roman Catholic.

The Pope has full legal, executive and judicial powers. Executive power over the area is in the hands of a Governor appointed by the Pope. The College of Cardinals is the Pope's chief advisory body, and upon his death the cardinals elect his successor for life. The cardinals themselves are created for life by the Pope.

The central administration of the Roman Catholic Church throughout the world is carried on in the Vatican by twelve congregations, three tribunals, three main secretariats and numerous councils, committees and commissions. In its diplomatic relations, the Holy See is represented by the Papal Secretary of State.

The present Pope is Paul VI, who was elected June 21, 1963, to succeed John XXIII, who had died June 3. Pope Paul was born Giovanni Battista Montini in Concesio, Italy, on Sept. 26, 1897. He was created a cardinal in 1958.

History. The Vatican City State, sovereign and independent, is situated on the Vatican hill on the right bank of the Tiber in northwest Rome. The area has been intimately associated with the history of the Roman Catholic Church since the time of the martyrdom of St. Peter. From it the Pope exercised temporal sway for many centuries over a large part of central Italy; in 1859, the Papal States comprised an area of some 17,000 square miles. During the struggle for Italian unification, from 1860 to 1870, most of this area became part of Italy.

By an Italian law of May 13, 1871, the temporal power of the Pope was abrogated, and the territory of the Papacy was confined to the Vatican and Lateran palaces and the Villa of Castel Gandolfo. The Popes consistently refused to recognize this arrangement and, by the Lateran Treaty of Feb. 11, 1929 between the Vatican and the Kingdom of Italy, the exclusive dominion and sovereign jurisdiction of the Holy See over the city of the Vatican was again recognized, thus restoring the Pope's temporal authority over the area.

The first session of Ecumenical Council Vatican II was opened by John XXIII on Oct. 11, 1962 to plan and set policies for the modernization of the Roman Catholic Church. Paul VI continued the Council, opening the second session on Sept. 29, 963.

Pope Paul has stood implacably against relaxing the church's traditional stand against birth control, on the Latin rite's insistence upon clerical celibacy, and on conservatism in theological speculation. He has paid much attention, however, to improving its ecumenical relations with other denominations, visiting the Ecumenical Patriarch of the Greek Orthodox Church in Istanbul and the World Council of Churches in Geneva, and with other faiths, Jewish, Moslem and Buddhist.

(For a listing of all the Popes, *see* the Index.)

VENEZUELA (Republic)

(República de Venezuela)

President: Carlos Andrés Pérez (1974).
Area: 352,143 sq mi. (912,050 sq km).
Population (est. 1976): 12,375,000 (mestizo, 69%; white, 20%; black, 9%; Indian, 2%).
Density per square mile: 35.1.
Capital: Caracas.
Largest cities (est. 1975): Caracas (metropolitan area), 2,487,000; (1971 census): Maracaibo, 651,574; Barquisimeto, 330,815; San Cristóbal, 151,717.
Monetary unit: Bolívar.
Language: Spanish.
Religion: Roman Catholic.

Venezuela has a bicameral Congress, the 52 members of the Senate and the 213 members of the Chamber of Deputies being elected by direct popular vote to five-year terms. The President is also elected for five years. He must be a Venezuelan by birth and over 30 years old. He is not eligible for re-election until 10 years after the end of his term.

Major Political Parties. Democratic Action Party, with 28 of 52 Senate seats and 102 of 213 seats in the Chamber of Deputies; Social Christian Party, People's Electoral Movement, Democratic Republican Union.

History. Venezuela, a third larger than Texas, is the world's second greatest producer of oil, outranked only by the United States. Simón Bolívar, who led the liberation of much of the continent from Spain, was born in Caracas in 1783.

Columbus discovered Venezuela on his third voyage in 1498. A subsequent Spanish explorer gave the country its name, meaning "Little Venice." There were no important settlements until Caracas was founded in 1567. With Bolívar taking part, Venezuela was one of the first South American colonies to revolt against Spain in 1810, but it was not until 1821 that independence was won. Federated at first with Colombia and Ecuador, the country set up a republic in 1830, and then sank for many decades into a condition of revolt, dictatorship and corruption.

From 1908 to 1935, General Juan Vicente Gómez ruled tyrannically over the nation, picking satellites to alternate with him in the presidential palace. Thereafter, there was a struggle between democratic forces and those backing a return to strong-man rule. Dr. Rómulo Betancourt and the liberal Acción Democrática Party won a majority of seats in a constituent assembly to draft a new Constitution in 1946. A well-known writer, Rómulo Gallegos, candidate of Betancourt's party, easily won the presidential election of 1947. But in 1948, the army ousted Gallegos and instituted a military junta.

Following elections in 1952, the junta presented its resignations to the army, which named Col. Marcos Pérez Jiménez as Provisional President. He re-established strong-man rule. But the country overthrew the dictatorship in 1958 and thereafter enjoyed democratic government. Rafael Caldera Rodríguez, President from 1969 to 1974, legalized the Communist Party and established diplomatic relations with Moscow.

Venezuela and neighboring Guyana in 1970 called a 12-year moratorium on their border dispute (Venezuela claims 50,000 square miles of Guyana's 83,000).

As a charter member of the Organization of Petroleum Exporting Countries (O.P.E.C.), Venezuela shared the benefits of the tripled oil prices engineered by O.P.E.C., but did not join the 1973 Arab oil boycott. President Carlos Andrés Pérez took office in March, 1974, committed to give all Venezuelans a stake in the oil bonanza that made his country the richest in South America.

On Jan. 1, 1976, Venezuela nationalized 21 oil companies, mostly subsidiaries of U.S. firms, offering compensation of $1.28 billion. Pérez declared it "neither convenient nor acceptable" that the nation's basic industry remain in foreign hands. Venezuela's oil income for 1975 was $7.6 billion, nearly $1 billion less than in 1974, and 1976 income was expected to be less because of heavy cutbacks in production.

Venezuela invested a third of its 1974–75 oil revenues abroad in a series of hemispheric foreign aid programs, and it helped other states organize cartels on the O.P.E.C. pattern to increase and support prices of raw products. It restored full relations with Cuba in December 1974 and promptly became Cuba's prime oil supplier.

Domestically, Venezuela continued to invest oil funds in irrigation, road construction and farm loans, but declining revenues forced a reduction in these projects. An ambitious plan to educate 10,000 young Venezuelans at home and abroad through government scholarships, initiated in 1974, was unable to take new applicants in 1976.

Economic Conditions. Agricultural production has failed to keep pace with the food needs of the rapidly increasing population. The principal crop is coffee, grown on 60,000 plantations on the slopes of the coastal mountains. Stock raising, which is centered east of Lake Maracaibo, and on the llanos, is important.

There are few industries, the most important being woodworking, cotton textiles, and tobacco products. Electric power is plentiful.

Oil, most of which is found on the shore of Lake Maracaibo, gives the country a big foreign trade balance and a treasury surplus.

Chief exports in 1974 were crude oil (64%) and petroleum products (32%). Leading customers in 1973 were U.S. (c. 57%), Canada (c. 17%). Leading suppliers were U.S. (42%), West Germany (13%), Japan (8%).

Natural Features. Mountain systems break Venezuela into four distinct areas: (1) the Maracaibo lowlands; (2) the mountainous region in the north and northwest; (3) the Orinoco basin, with the llanos (vast grass-covered plains) on its northern border and great forest areas in the south and southeast; (4) the Guiana Highlands, south of the Orinoco, accounting for nearly half the national territory. About 80% of Venezuela is drained by the Orinoco and its tributaries.

VIETNAM, Socialist Republic of

President: Ton Duc Thang (1976).
Premier: Pham Van Dong (1976).
Area: 128,302 sq mi. (332,559 sq km).
Population (est. 1973 for former South Vietnam, est. 1975 for former North): 43,155,000.
Density per square mile: 336.3.
Capital: Hanoi.
Largest cities: (est. 1973) Saigon,* 1,825,300; (est. 1974) Hanoi, 1,378,000; (est. 1973) Da Nang, 492,200; Na Trang, 216,200; Qui Non, 213,750; Hue, 209,000; (1960 census) Haiphong, 182,490.
Monetary unit: Dong.
Languages: Vietnamese, French, Chinese.
Religions: Buddhist, Roman Catholic, Cao-Dai, Hoa-Hao, Taoist, Confucian.

Unification of North and South Vietnam was put at least five years away after a May 1975 North-South meeting following the capitulation of the former Republic of Vietnam on April 30, 1975.

Less than a year later, however, a joint National Assembly convened with 249 deputies representing the North and 243 representing the South. At a session beginning June 24, the Assembly set July 2, 1976 as the official reunification date. Hanoi became the capital and Ton Duc Thang, President of the Northern regime since 1969, became President of the new republic.

Pham Van Dong, Premier in Hanoi since 1955, took over the new administration, and the Northern flag, anthem and crest became the symbols of the new Vietnam. The only concession to the former Provisional Revolutionary Government of South Vietnam, which nominally administered the South in the interim period, was the installation of its President Nguyen Huu Tho, as one of two Vice Presidents.

Political Party. Lao Dong (Communist) Party, led by First Secretary Le Duan.

History. The Vietnamese are descendants of Mongoloid nomads from China and migrants from Indonesia. The Vietnamese recognized Chinese suzerainty until the 15th century, an era of nationalistic expansion when Cambodians were pushed out of the southern area of what is now Vietnam.

A century later, the Portuguese were the first Europeans to enter the area. France established its influence early in the 19th century and within 80 years conquered the three regions into which the country was then divided—Cochin-China in the south, Annam in the center and Tongking in the north.

France first unified Vietnam in 1887 when a single governor-generalship was created, followed by the first physical links between north and south—

* Includes suburb of Cholon.

a rail and road system. Even at the beginning of World War II, however, there were internal differences among the three regions.

Japan took over military bases in Vietnam in 1940 and a pro-Vichy French administration remained until 1945. A veteran Communist leader, Ho Chi Minh, organized an independence movement known as the Vietminh to exploit a confused situation. At the end of the war, Ho's followers seized Hanoi and declared a short-lived republic, which ended with the arrival of French forces in 1946.

Paris proposed a unified government within the French Union under the former Annamite emperor, Bao Dai. Cochin-China and Annam accepted the proposal and Bao Dai was proclaimed emperor of all Vietnam in 1949. Ho and the Vietminh withheld support, and the revolution in China gave them the outside help needed for a war of resistance against French and Vietnamese troops largely armed by the United States.

A bitter defeat at Dien Bien Phu in northwest Vietnam on May 5, 1954 broke the French military campaign and brought the division of Vietnam at the conference of Geneva that year. More than 1 million North Vietnamese, mainly Christians, fled south across the 17th parallel dividing line.

In the new South, Ngo Dinh Diem, Premier under Bao Dai, deposed the monarch in 1955 and established a republic with himself as President. Diem used strong U.S. backing to create an authoritarian regime which suppressed all opposition but could not eradicate the Northern-supplied Communist Viet Cong.

Skirmishing grew into a full-scale war, with escalating U.S. involvement. A military coup, U.S.-inspired in the view of many, ousted Diem Nov. 1, 1963 and a kaleidoscope of military governments followed. The most savage fighting of the war occurred in early 1968, during the Tet holidays.

Although the Viet Cong failed to overthrow the Saigon government, U.S. public reaction to the apparently endless war forced a limitation of U.S. troops to 550,000 and a new emphasis on shifting the burden of further combat to the South Vietnamese. Ho Chi Minh's death on Sept. 3, 1969 brought a quadrumvirate to replace him but no flagging in Northern will to fight.

U.S. bombing and invasion of Cambodia in the summer of 1970—an effort to destroy Viet Cong bases in the neighboring state—marked the end of major U.S. participation in the fighting. Most American ground troops were withdrawn from combat by mid-1971 as heavy bombing of the Ho Chi Minh trail from North Vietnam appeared to cut the supply of men and matériel to the South.

Secret negotiations for peace by Secretary of State Henry A. Kissinger with North Vietnamese officials during 1972 after heavy bombing of Hanoi and Haiphong brought the two sides near agreement in October. When the Northerners demanded the removal of the South's President Nguyen Van Thieu as their price, President Nixon ordered the "Christmas bombing" of the North. The conference resumed and a peace settlement was signed in Paris on Jan. 27, 1973. It called for release of all U.S. prisoners, withdrawal of U.S. forces and limitation of both sides' forces inside South Vietnam and a commitment to peaceful reunification.

Despite Chinese and Soviet endorsement, the agreement foundered in a welter of charges and countercharges—the North asserting that the United States was violating the limitation on arms supplies, Washington and Saigon accusing Hanoi of infiltrating troops to the south. U.S. bombing of Communist-held areas in Cambodia was halted by Congress in August 1973, and in the following year Communist action in South Vietnam increased.

An armored attack across the 17th parallel in January 1975 panicked the South Vietnamese army and brought the invasion within 40 miles of Saigon by April 9. Thieu resigned on April 21 and fled, to be replaced by Vice President Tran Van Huong, who quit a week later, turning over the office to Gen. Duong Van Minh. "Big Minh" surrendered Saigon on April 30, ending a war which took 1.3 million Vietnamese and 56,000 American lives, at the cost of $141 billion in U.S. aid.

U.S. helicopters evacuated 1,373 Americans and 5,595 Vietnamese from Saigon in the final days and 135,000 other South Vietnamese escaped in small boats to seek refuge in the United States. Congress appropriated $405 million to resettle 130,000 Indochinese refugees—mostly Vietnamese—in the United States.

Although the new regime in the South at first appeared to be taking a moderate line, "re-education" of former South Vietnamese government and army personnel began immediately. By mid-1976, virtually all foreigners were expelled, even those married to Vietnamese. There were reports of pressure on city residents to return to the countryside, although there was no forced exodus as in Cambodia. There were also reports that Northern carpetbaggers were moving into government posts in the South.

A U.S. pledge under the 1973 Paris agreement was to aid in the reconstruction of Vietnam, something Hanoi has cited as evidence of Washington's failure to keep its commitments. On July 22, 1976, Kissinger in a speech in Seattle warned that any aid must await an accounting of 2,505 U.S. servicemen missing in action during the war. "There can be no progress toward improved relations with Hanoi without a wholly satisfactory accounting for these men," he said.

By September 1976, the remains of only five Americans had been returned.

Economic Conditions. Vietnam is basically an agricultural economy, the Mekong delta being one of the leading rice-exporting regions of the world. High-quality coal is found in the North, but there is no heavy industry in either North or South. Aside from Rice, Vietnam also produces tea, coffee, tobacco, rubber and spices.

WESTERN SAMOA

(Member of Commonwealth of Nations)

Head of State: Malietoa Tanumafili II (1962).
Prime Minister: Taisi Tupuola Efi (1976).
Area: 1,097 sq mi. (2,842 sq km).
Population (est. 1976): 165,000.
Density per square mile: 150.4.
Capital and largest city (est. 1973): Apia, 30,000.
Monetary unit: Tala.
Languages: Samoan and English.
Religion: Christian.

Western Samoa has a 46-member Legislature, consisting mainly of the titleholders (chiefs) of family or tribal groups, with two members elected by universal suffrage to represent those not belonging to such groups. When the present Chiefs of State die, successors will be elected by the Legislature.

History. The Samoan islands were discovered in the 18th century and visited by Dutch and French traders. Toward the end of the 19th century, conflicting interests of the United States, Great Britain and Germany resulted in a treaty signed in 1899. It recognized the paramount interests of the United States in those islands east of 171° west longitude (American Samoa), and Germany's interests in the other islands (Western Samoa); the British withdrew in return for recognition of her rights in Tonga and the Solomons.

New Zealand occupied Western Samoa in August 1914, and was granted a League of Nations mandate. In 1947, the islands became a U.N. trust territory administered by New Zealand.

Western Samoa became an independent nation on Jan. 1, 1962.

Economic Conditions. Agriculture is the basis of Western Samoa's economy, but there is little level land except in the coastal areas.

Chief exports in 1972 were copra (45%), cocoa (28%) and bananas (12%). Leading customers were New Zealand (33%), West Germany (25%), Netherlands (20%), U.S. (9%). Leading suppliers were New Zealand (31%), Australia (20%), Japan (12%), United Kingdom (10%), U.S. (8%).

YEMEN (People's Democratic Republic of)

Chairman of Presidential Council: Salim Robea Ali (1969).
Premier: Ali Nasser Mohammed Hasani (1972).
Area: 111,074 sq mi. (287,683 sq km).*
Population (est. 1976): 1,700,000.
Density per square mile: 15.3.*
Capital: Medina al-Eshaab.
Largest city (est. 1973 by U.N.): Aden, 264,300.
Monetary unit: Yemen dinar.
Language: Arabic.
Religion: Moslem.

On June 23, 1969, President Qahtan Mohammed al Shaabi resigned and was replaced by a five-man Presidential Council. Legislative power is vested in the General Command of the National Liberation Front.

A Constitution published in 1970 changed the state's name from Southern Yemen and provided for free and direct elections by October 1971 of a 101-seat legislature, the People's Supreme Council, to take over from the Front's general command.

The two Yemens agreed on Oct. 28, 1972 to become a unified Yemen Republic, ending five years of border fighting. A new Constitution was to be drafted, but meanwhile the three branches of government plus the ruling Presidential Councils were merged. However, renewed clashes between the two were reported in 1973 and one presidential counselor was assassinated.

* Excluding Perim and Kamaran islands.

Political Party. The only legal political party is the National Liberation Front.

History. The People's Republic of Southern Yemen was established Nov. 30, 1967, when Great Britain granted independence to the Federation of South Arabia. This Federation consisted of the state (once the colony) of Aden and 16 of the 20 states of the Protectorate of South Arabia (once the Aden Protectorate). The four states of the Protectorate that did not join the Federation have since become part of Southern Yemen.

The islands of Kamaran, Perim and Socotra are part of Southern Yemen. The Kuria Muria Islands, formerly part of Aden, were given to Oman by the British in 1967.

The Federation of South Arabia had its beginning in 1959, when six states of the Aden Protectorate set up a Federation of Arab Amirates of the South. One additional state joined the Federation in 1959, three in 1960, one in 1962, three (including the state of Aden) in 1963 and three in 1965. The name Federation of South Arabia was adopted in May 1962.

Economic Conditions. The city of Aden is essentially a transshipment point and bunkering station, and is also the commercial center for Yemen and the African coast opposite. The chief industry is petroleum refining.

YEMEN (Republic)

(al Jamhuriya al Arabiya al Yamaniya)

Chief of State: Col. Ibrahim al-Hamidi (1974).
Premier: Abdul Ghani (1975).
Area: 75,290 sq mi. (195,000 sq km).
Population (est. 1976): 6,860,000.
Density per square mile: 91.1.
Capital and largest city (est. 1975): Sana, 134,600.
Monetary unit: Riyal.
Language: Arabic.
Religion: Moslem.

The country's first permanent Constitution was submitted to the National Assembly in 1971. It provides for a 179-member legislature, the Consultative Council, 20 of whose members would be chosen by the President and the rest elected by the people every four years. A five-man executive Presidential Council is to be chosen by the Consultative Council.

A merger agreement between Yemen and the People's Democratic Republic of Yemen (Southern Yemen) was signed by the two states Oct. 28, 1972, after bitter border clashes between them over a five-year period. A new Constitution was to be drafted, but meanwhile the joint government was to be "republican, nationalist and democratic," ruled by a single, merged Presidential Council, and unified legislative, executive and judicial branches. However, renewed fighting was reported in 1973, with one Yemeni leader assassinated, allegedly by Southern Yemeni forces.

In June 1974, the army ousted the government in a bloodless coup and suspended the Constitution and its various legislative bodies. No political organizations are permitted.

History. The history of Yemen dates back to the Minaean kingdom (1200–650 B.C.). It accepted Islam in A.D. 628, and in the 10th century came under the control of the Rassite dynasty of the Zaidi sect, which still rules. The Turks occupied the area from 1538 to 1630 and from 1849 to 1918. The sovereign status of Yemen was confirmed by treaties signed with Saudi Arabia and Britain in 1934.

Yemen joined the Arab League in 1945, established diplomatic relations with the United States in 1946 and joined the United Nations in 1947.

In 1962, a military revolt of elements favoring President Gamal Abdel Nasser of Egypt broke out. A ruling junta proclaimed a republic, and Yemen became an international battleground, with Egypt and the Soviet Union supporting the revolutionaries, and King Saud of Saudi Arabia and King Hussein of Jordan the royalists. The civil war continued until the Middle Eastern War between the Arab States and Israel broke out in June 1967. Nasser had to pull out many of his troops and agree at a conference in Khartoum to a cease-fire and withdrawal of foreign forces.

But the war resumed in 1967 and continued sporadically through 1968, although a stalemate seemed to have been reached. By mid-1969, republican forces had captured the major rebel stronghold near the Southern Arabian frontier, and its leaders declared the civil war ended.

Economic Conditions. Unlike most of Arabia, the Yemen highlands are well adapted to agriculture; they produce grain, fruit, vegetables and Mocha coffee. Stock-raising flourishes.

Chief exports in 1972 were cotton (36%), coffee (27%), hides and skins (16%) and kat (5%). Leading customers were China (38%), Yemen (Aden; 21%), Saudi Arabia (11%), U.S.S.R. (9%), Italy (5%). Leading suppliers were Australia (13%), Yemen (Aden; 11%), Japan (10%), West Germany (7%), France (7%), Saudi Arabia (6%), United Kingdom (5%).

YUGOSLAVIA (Socialist Republic)

(Socijalisticka Federativna Republika Jugoslavija)

President: Marshal Tito (Josip Broz) (1953).
President of Federal Executive Council (Premier): Dzemal Bijedic (1971).
Area: 98,766 sq mi. (255,804 sq km).
Population (est. 1976): 21,550,000 (Serbian, 41.7%; Croat, 23.5%; Slovene, 8.8%; Macedonian, 5.3%; Albanian, 4.4%; Others, 16.3%).
Density per square mile: 218.1.
Capital: Belgrade.
Largest cities (1971 census): Belgrade, 746,105; Zagreb, 566,224; Skopije, 312,980; Sarajevo, 243,980; Ljubljana, 173,853; Split, 152,905.
Monetary unit: Dinar.
Languages: Serbo-Croat, Slovene, Macedonian (all official).
Religions: Greek Orthodox, 41.4%; Roman Catholic, 31.8%; Moslem, 12.3%; others, 14.5%.

Yugoslavia is a federal republic composed of six socialist republics—Serbia (which includes provinces of Vojvodina and Kosovo), Croatia, Slovenia, Bosnia-Herzegovina, Macedonia and Montenegro. Actual administration is carried on by the Federal Executive Council and its secretaries.

Political Parties. League of Communists, led by President Tito, and Socialist Alliance of the Working People.

History. Yugoslavia, fronting on the Adriatic Sea opposite Italy, was formed in 1919 out of some of Europe's oldest trouble spots in the Balkans. After a brief and unstable history of 25 years, it emerged from World War II as a Russian satellite.

The 1919 components of Yugoslavia were the old kingdoms of Serbia and Montenegro, and the following: Bosnia-Herzegovina, formerly administered jointly by Austria and Hungary; Croatia-Slavonia, which had had limited autonomy under Hungary; and Slovena and Dalmatia, formerly administered by Austria.

Alexander I, son of King Peter of Serbia, became the first King of the new country on Aug. 16, 1921. His reign was a rocky one because the Croats, under Dr. Stephen Radić, unceasingly sought autonomy. Finally, a Croat assassinated Alexander in 1934 and, since his son Peter was a minor, a regency was set up under Prince Paul, the new King's uncle.

After pursuing an increasingly pro-Axis policy under the regent, Yugoslavia signed the Axis Pact on Mar. 25, 1941; this caused the overthrow of the government two days later. On Apr. 6, the country was invaded by the Nazis and occupied. While the King and government fled to the Near East and later to London, Yugoslavia was divided into German, Italian, Hungarian and Bulgarian occupation zones.

Inside Yugoslavia, the Axis occupation was fought by two guerrilla armies—the Chetniks under Draža Mihajlović, who supported the monarchy; and the Partisans under Marshal Tito (Josip Broz), who leaned toward Russia. These two groups fought not only the Germans, but also each other. In November 1943, Tito established an Executive National Committee of Liberation, which was to function as a provisional government, thus repudiating King Peter.

In the elections of Nov. 11, 1945, Tito's forces won overwhelmingly, partly because the monarchist factions boycotted the balloting. Convening on Nov. 29, the new Assembly abolished the monarchy and set up the Federal People's Republic of Yugoslavia. Tito was Prime Minister, and his government won recognition from Britain and the United States.

The Tito government embarked upon an internal policy of ruthless oppression and elimination of opposition factions, including the summary trial and execution of Mihajlović in 1946.

Soviet support enabled the nation to secure the greater part of Italian Istria under the 1947 peace treaty, but efforts to secure sovereignty over the key port of Trieste were unsuccessful. Zone B of the former free territory of Trieste was, however, transferred to Yugoslavia in 1954.

Tito was elected President under the new Constitution on Jan. 14, 1953. He was named President for life in a revised Constitution adopted Apr. 7, 1963.

Yugoslavia's relations with the Soviet Union and other Communist states in the Soviet bloc improved after 1963. In the Soviet row with Communist China, Tito supported the Soviets. But in the invasion of Czechoslovakia in 1968, he supported the forces fighting to maintain Czechoslovak sovereignty. Tito also continued to show independence from the Soviet Union by improving ties to Red China and Albania.

On July 29, 1971, the 79-year-old President was unanimously re-elected to a five-year term by Parliament. Under a new Constitution approved Feb. 21, 1974, Tito remains President for life but will be succeeded by a body of nine persons, each of whom would be President for one year on a rotating basis.

Economic Conditions. The principal crops are corn, wheat, sugar beets, hemp, hops, opium (in Macedonia) and tobacco (chiefly in Macedonia and Herzegovina).

Yugoslavia is the principal mineral producer of the Balkans. Important minerals are iron, bauxite, antimony, chrome, manganese, copper, lead, zinc and aluminum.

Chief exports in 1974 were machinery (13%), transport equipment (12%), nonferrous metals (12%), chemicals (10%), food (9%), steel (8%), ships and boats (7%) and timber (5%). Leading customers were U.S.S.R. (18%), West Germany (10%), U.S. (8%), Czechoslovakia (5%). Leading suppliers were West Germany (18%), Italy (12%), U.S.S.R. (10%), Austria (5%), U.S. (5%).

Natural Features. About half of Yugoslavia is mountainous. In the north, the Dinaric Alps rise abruptly from the sea and progress eastward as a barren limestone plateau called the Karst. Montenegro is a jumbled mass of mountains, containing also some grassy slopes and fertile river valleys. Southern Serbia, too, is mountainous. A rich plain in the north and northeast, drained by the Danube, is the most fertile area of the country.

ZAIRE (Republic)

(République de Zaire)

President: Mobutu Sese Seko (1965).
Area: 905,562 sq mi. (2,345,409 sq km).
Population (est. 1976): 25,700,000.
Density per square mile: 28.4.
Capital: Kinshasa.
Largest cities (1974 by U.N.): Kinshasa, 2,008,250; Kananga, 601,250; Lubumbashi, 403,600; (est. 1972 by U.N.): Luluabourg, 506,000.
Monetary unit: Zaire.
Languages: French; Bantu dialects, mainly Swahili, Lingala, Tshiluba and Kikongo.
Religions: Animism, 50%; Roman Catholic, Protestant, Moslem.
Ethnic groups: Bantu, Sudanese, Nilotics, Pygmies, Hamites.

Under the Constitution approved by referendum in June 1967 and amended in 1974, the third Constitution since 1960, the President and a unicameral Legislature are elected by universal suffrage for five-year terms.

In 1971, the government proclaimed that the Democratic Republic of the Congo would be known as the Republic of Zaire, since the Congo River's name had been changed to the Zaire. In addition, President Joseph D. Mobutu took the name Mobutu Sese Seko and Katanga province became Shaba.

Political Party. There is only one political party: the Popular Movement of the Revolution, led by President Mobutu.

History. Formerly the Belgian Congo, this territory in Central Africa was inhabited by ancient Negrito peoples (Pygmies), pushed into the mountains by Bantu and Nilotic invaders. Interest in the interior was aroused by the American correspondent Henry M. Stanley, who went down the river in 1877. King Leopold II of Belgium commissioned Stanley to make development treaties with tribal chiefs. Portugal and other countries advanced claims, but the Berlin Conference of 1885 recognized Leopold's sovereignty. Forced labor was used to establish mines and plantations. Criticism of this exploitation led to transfer of the territory to the status of a colony of Belgium.

Belgium retained the colony after World War II, but in 1959, Communist and non-Communist advocates of independence staged bloody riots which were repressed. Under pressure, Belgium agreed to grant independence, and on June 30, 1960, the Republic of the Congo was proclaimed.

Moise Tshombe, head of Shaba (Katanga Province), announced its secession on July 11, 1960, followed on Aug. 8, 1960 by another rich mining province, South Kasai. Many Belgian administrators fled the country; others were the victims of riotous troops. Belgium sent paratroopers. The government, torn by a conflict between Patrice Lumumba, Premier, and Joseph Kasavubu, President, appealed to the United Nations. It sent in a peacekeeping force.

In September 1960, Kasavubu staged an army coup, seizing Lumumba and handing him over to Shaba, which in February 1961 announced that he and his two aides had been killed by tribesmen. A U.N. investigating commission found that Lumumba had been killed by a Belgian mercenary in the presence of Tshombe and other Shaba leaders. U.N. troops protected Parliament in 1961 when it elected a new Premier, Cyrille Adoula.

Dag Hammarskjöld, U.N. Secretary General, was killed when a plane in which he was flying to Northern Rhodesia for a conference with Tshombe crashed. His successor, U Thant, submitted a plan for national reconciliation in a federal government in August 1962. Tshombe rejected it, and in December his troops fired on the U.N. force. The U.N. troops overcame the Shaba troops and ended the secession with the capitulation of Tshombe on Jan. 14, 1963. Peasant rebellions followed in half the country. The U.N. troops withdrew on June 30, 1964; Tshombe, designated Premier, organized mercenaries to fight the rebels. By diplomatic arrangement, the United States airlifted Belgian paratroopers who disarmed the rebels.

Kasavubu dismissed Tshombe in October 1965. After a parliamentary deadlock, General Joseph Mobutu, army chief, staged a coup, nationalized the Union Minière, the Belgian copper mining cartel, and suppressed a revolt by white mercenaries. Tshombe, flying abroad for medical treatment was captured in June 1967, when his plane was hijacked and forced to land in Algeria. His death of a heart attack on June 29, 1969 was announced by the Algerian government.

Mobutu was reelected after barring opposition parties in 1970. He traveled to the U.S., where he sought (reportedly with success) American investment capital. He subsequently awarded mining concessions to American and South African firms and nationalized a Belgian company.

In January 1975, the government proclaimed nationalization of industries, building trades and distribution services. Foreign branch banking was forbidden outside Kinshasa, and religious instruction in schools was prohibited.

In the Angolan civil war of 1975–76, Mobutu continued to back the National Front for the Liberation of Angola (FNLA), whose leader, Holden Roberto, is related by marriage. Mobutu also furnished the chief channel for U.S. military aid to FNLA and the National Union for the Total Independence of Angola (UNITA). Zaire was the leader of the opposition within Africa to the recognition of the Soviet-backed Popular Movement for the Liberation of Angola (MPLA), which eventually triumphed and became the government of the neighboring state. Mobutu belatedly and reluctantly accepted the outcome.

Economic Conditions. Mineral-rich Zaire is one of the world's most important sources of uranium. It also is a source of copper, tin, diamonds (mainly industrial), gold, cobalt and zinc.

Agricultural products include palm oil and kernels, cottonseed, rubber, cotton lint, coffee, peanuts, sweet potatoes and yams and cassava.

Chief exports in 1973 were copper (62%), coffee (7%), and diamonds (6%). Leading customers were Belgium-Luxembourg (c. 48%), Italy (c. 13%), Japan (c. 7%), France (7%), U.S. (6%), West Germany (c. 6%), United Kingdom (5%). Leading suppliers were Belgium-Luxembourg (c. 20%), U.S. (c. 17%), West Germany (c. 14%), France (c. 11%), Italy (c. 8%), Japan (c. 7%), Netherlands (c. 5%).

ZAMBIA (Republic)

(Member of Commonwealth of Nations)

President: Kenneth D. Kaunda (1964).
Prime Minister: Elijah Mudenda (1975).
Area: 290,586 sq mi. (752,614 sq km).
Population (est. 1976): 5,100,000.
Density per square mile: 17.6.
Capital: Lusaka.
Largest cities (est. 1974 for urban agglomeration): Lusaka, 415,000; (est. 1972 by U.N.): Kitwe, 290,100; Ndola, 201,300; Chingola, 181,500.
Monetary unit: Kwacha.
Languages: Bamba, Nyanja, Lozi, Tonga, English.
Religion: Animist.

Zambia (formerly Northern Rhodesia) is governed by a President, elected by universal suffrage, and a Legislative Assembly, consisting of 105 members elected by universal suffrage and up to 5 additional members nominated by the President.

Major Political Parties. The Assembly, in December 1972, passed a law making the ruling United National Independence Party, led by President Kaunda, the only legal political party. Until then, it had held 78 of the 105 seats in the Assembly. Major opposition is the African National Congress Party, with 17 seats. All the opposition walked out of the Assembly before the vote was taken, and the count was 78 to 0 for the measure.

History. Empire builder Cecil Rhodes obtained mining concessions in 1889 from King Lewanika of the Barotse and sent settlers to the area soon thereafter. It was ruled by the British South Africa Company, which he established, until 1924, when the British government took over the administration.

From 1953 to 1964, Northern Rhodesia was federated with Southern Rhodesia and Nyasaland in the Federation of Rhodesia and Nyasaland. On Oct. 24, 1964, Northern Rhodesia became the independent nation of Zambia.

Kenneth Kaunda, the first President, kept Zambia within the Commonwealth of Nations. The country's economy, dependent on copper exports, was threatened when Rhodesia declared its independence from British rule in 1965 and defied U.N. sanctions, which Zambia supported, an action that deprived Zambia of its trade route through Rhodesia. The United States, Britain and Canada organized an airlift in 1966 to ship gasoline into Zambia. In 1967, Britain agreed to finance new trade routes for Zambia. Kaunda visited Communist China in 1967, and China later agreed to finance a 1,000-mile railroad from the copper fields to Dar es Salaam in Tanzania. A pipeline was opened in 1968 from Ndola in Zambia's copper belt to the Indian Ocean at Dar es Salaam, ending the three-year oil drought.

In August 1969, Kaunda announced the nationalization of the foreign copper-mining industry, with Zambia to take 51% (over $1 billion, estimated), and by October an agreement was reached with the companies on payment. He then announced a similar take-over of foreign oil producers.

Falling world copper prices halved Zambia's 1974–75 receipts from its principal source of foreign exchange. In a move to aid the ailing economy, Kaunda announced sweeping new nationalization moves. To halt land speculation by a growing capitalist class, the government nationalized all land holdings, as well as private hospitals, movie theaters and the country's two major newspapers (British-owned, like most of the theaters). One result was to put all mass communications under state control.

Despite the opening of the Tanzam railroad in 1975, congestion at the port of Dar es-Salaam, eastern terminal of the line, reduced the value of Zambia's new link to the Indian Ocean. Fighting in Angola during the latter part of 1975 and early 1976 brought the Benguela railway to a halt, forcing Zambia to stockpile a third of its copper production. Shipping problems, together with continuing low prices, brought a government prediction that there would be no revenues from the nation's chief industry in 1976.

Economic Conditions. In addition to copper, Zambia supplies zinc, lead, cobalt and manganese. Its principal agricultural crops are tobacco, corn and peanuts.

Chief export in 1974 was copper (93%). Leading customers in 1973 were Japan (24%), United Kingdom (20%), Italy (12%), West Germany (10%), France (8%), Brazil (5%). Leading suppliers were U.K. (22%), South Africa (12%), U.S. (9%), Japan (9%), West Germany (7%), Iran (5%), Italy (5%).

For late reports, see News Chronology of 1976 in Table of Contents.

Value of Exports and Imports
(in millions of U. S. dollars)
Source: Monthly Bulletin of Statistics, United Nations, 1976.

Country	Exports[1]	Imports[1]	Country	Exports[1]	Imports[1]
Algeria	4,377	4,035[2]	Kuwait	8,991	2,263
Angola	1,218[2]	624[2]	Lebanon	589[3]	1,333[3]
Argentina	3,931	3,656	Liberia	406	331
Australia	11,575	9,811	Libya	6,454	2,762[2]
Austria	7,518	9,391	Madagascar	244[2]	286[2]
Bahamas	1,444[2]	1,908[2]	Malawi	136	248
Bangladesh	311	710	Malaysia	4,126	3,888
Belgium-Luxembourg	28,807	30,691	Mauritius	312[2]	170[2]
Bolivia	548[2]	196[3]	Mexico	2,909	6,631
Brazil	8,656	13,558	Morocco	1,542	2,560
Bulgaria	4,691	5,408	Netherlands	35,075	34,573
Burma	158	125	New Zealand	2,152	3,152
Cameroon	447	599	Nicaragua	376	517
Canada	31,881	34,306	Nigeria	8,078	6,103
Central African Republic	48[2]	46[2]	Norway	7,207	9,718
Chad	37[2]	92[2]	Pakistan	1,005	2,125
Chile	2,480[2]	1,911[2]	Panama	272	795[2]
Colombia	1,358	1,558	Papua New Guinea	476	516
Congo	294[2]	125[3]	Paraguay	187	186
Costa Rica	454	637	Peru	1,514[2]	1,531[2]
Cyprus	151	306	Philippines	2,241	3,375
Czechoslovakia	8,358	9,081	Poland	10,283	12,536
Denmark	8,716	10,366	Portugal	1,939	3,840
Dominican Republic	895	773	Rhodesia	652[3]	541[3]
Ecuador	844	943	Romania	4,874[2]	5,144[2]
Egypt	1,402	3,951	Saudi Arabia	27,113	3,473[2]
El Salvador	463[2]	562[2]	Senegal	451	559
Ethiopia	238	310	Sierra Leone	131	187
Finland	5,487	7,602	Singapore	5,376	8,133
France	52,214	54,247	Somalia	65[2]	129[2]
Gabon	942	469	Spain	7,691	16,097
Germany (East)	10,088	11,290	Sri Lanka	519	691[2]
Germany (West)	91,620	3,768	Sudan	443	887
Ghana	720	805	Sweden	17,439	17,874
Greece	2,288	5,457	Switzerland	3,317	13,305
Guatemala	586[2]	700[2]	Syrian Arab Republic	930	1,669
Guyana	359	342	Tanzania	349	714
Honduras	283	400	Thailand	2,485	3,143[2]
Hungary	6,091	7,176	Togo	189[2]	109[2]
Iceland	308	487	Trinidad and Tobago	1,754	1,470
India	4,365	6,094	Tunisia	855	1,422
Indonesia	7,103	4,708	Turkey	1,401	4,640
Iran	20,249	10,343	Uganda	263	133
Iraq	8,756	2,365[2]	U.S.S.R.	33,310	36,969
Ireland	3,177	3,768	United Kingdom	43,760	53,262
Israel	1,835	4,140	United States	106,157	102,984
Italy	34,821	38,366	Uruguay	382[2]	487[2]
Ivory Coast	1,181	1,127	Venezuela	10,214	5,359
Jamaica	707	1,113	Yemen, People's Dem. Rep.	203[2]	187[2]
Jordan	158	731	Yugoslavia	4,061	7,697
Kenya	496	938	Zaire	1,359[2]	780[2]
Korea (South)	4,948	7,275	Zambia	1,401[2]	783[2]

[1] 1975 unless otherwise indicated.   [2] 1974.   [3] 1973.

U.S. Industry Spending $7.3 Billion to Curb Pollution

American industry will spend an estimated $7.3 billion in new plants and equipment to abate air and water pollution and to dispose of solid waste. This represents a 12% rise over the $6.5 billion spent in the previous year. Nearly half of this increase is expected to be accounted for by the electric utility industry. Of the total amount to be spent, 44% is for the abatement of water pollution, compared with 38% in 1975. Five industries accounted for 70% of the 1975 expenditures: electric utilities, $1.7 billion; petroleum, $1.2 billion; chemicals, $700 million; and nonferrous metals and paper, $500 million each.

Minimum Voting Age by Country

Country	Age	Country	Age	Country	Age	Country	Age
Afghanistan	18	Dominican Republic	18	Kuwait	21[1]	Poland	18
Albania	18	Ecuador	18	Laos	18	Portugal	18
Algeria	18	Egypt	18	Lebanon	21	Romania	18
Andorra	25	El Salvador	18	Lesotho	21	Rwanda	18
Argentina	18	Equatorial Guinea	18	Liberia	18	San Marino	21
Australia	18	Estonia	18	Libyan Arab Republic	18	Senegal	21
Austria	19	Ethiopia	21	Liechtenstein	20[1]	Sierra Leone	21
Bahamas	18	Fiji	21	Lithuania	18	Singapore	21
Bahrain	18	Finland	18	Luxembourg	18	South Africa	18[5]
Bangladesh	18	France	18	Madagascar	20	Spain	21[4]
Barbados	18	Gabon	21	Malawi	21	Sri Lanka (Ceylon)	18
Belgium	18	Germany (East)	18	Malaysia	21	Sudan	18
Benin	21	Germany (West)	18	Maldives	21	Swaziland	21
Bhutan	([3])	Ghana	21	Mali	21	Sweden	18
Bolivia	21	Greece	21	Malta	18	Switzerland	20
Botswana	21	Guatemala	18	Mauritania	21	Syrian Arab Republic	18
Brazil	18	Guinea	21	Mauritius	21	Tanzania	18
Bulgaria	18	Guyana	18	Mexico	18	Thailand	20
Burma	18	Haiti	18	Monaco	18	Togo	21
Burundi	18	Honduras	18	Mongolian People's		Tonga	21
Cambodia	18	Hungary	18	Republic	18	Trinidad and Tobago	21
Cameroon	21	Iceland	20	Morocco	18	Tunisian Republic	20
Canada	18	India	21	Nepal	18	Turkey	21
Chad	18	Indonesia	18	Netherlands	18	Uganda	21
Chile	18	Iran	18	New Zealand	18	U.S.S.R.	18
China, People's Rep. of	18	Ireland	18	Nicaragua	18	United Kingdom	18
China, Nationalist	20	Israel	18	Niger	21	United States	18
Colombia	18	Italy	18[2]	Nigeria	21	Upper Volta	21
Congo	18	Ivory Coast	21	Norway	20	Uruguay	18
Costa Rica	18	Jamaica	18	Pakistan	18	Venezuela	18
Cuba	21	Japan	20	Panama	18	Yemen	18
Cyprus	21	Jordan	21	Paraguay	18	Yugoslavia	18
Czechoslovakia	18	Kenya	21	Peru	21	Zaire	18
Denmark	20	Korea (South)	20	Philippines	15	Zambia	18

[1] Males only. [2] For Senate elections, 25. [3] Each family has one vote. [4] Heads of families and self-supporting men and women. [5] For whites. For Colored and Xhosa, 21. NOTE: Voting ages shown are for national elections. In some countries, persons may vote at a younger age if married.

Estimates of World Population by Regions, 1650–1974

Source: W. F. Willcox, 1650–1900; United Nations, 1930–1974.

Year	Estimated population in millions							
	North America[1]	Latin America[2]	Europe[3]	Russia (U.S.S.R.)	Asia[4]	Africa	Oceania	World total
1650	1	7	103	([5])	257	100	2	470
1750	1	10	144	([5])	437	100	2	694
1850	26	33	274	([5])	656	100	2	1,091
1900	81	63	423	([5])	857	141	6	1,571
1930	134	108	355[6]	179	1,120[7]	164	10	2,070
1960	199	216	425[6]	214	1,644[7]	273	16	2,986
1970	226	283	459[6]	243	2,027[7]	352	19	3,610
1974	235	315	470[6]	252	2,206[7]	391	21	3,890

[1] U.S. (including Alaska and Hawaii), Bermuda, Canada, Greenland, and St. Pierre and Miquelon. [2] Mexico, Central and South America, and Caribbean Islands. [3] Includes Russia 1650–1900. [4] Excludes Russia (U.S.S.R.). [5] Included in Europe. [6] Excludes European Turkey, which is included in Asia. [7] Includes both Asian and European Turkey.

Area and Population by Country

Country	Area[1]	Population	Year[2]	Country	Area[1]	Population	Year[2]
Afghanistan	249,999	19,730,000	1976E	Italy	116,304	56,250,000	1976E
Albania	11,100	2,545,000	1976E	Ivory Coast	124,504	5,000,000	1976E
Algeria	919,595	17,290,000	1976E	Jamaica	4,232	2,065,000	1976E
Andorra	175	30,000	1976E	Japan	143,750	112,200,000	1976E
Angola	481,350	6,000,000	1975E	Jordan	37,738	2,780,000	1976E
Argentina	1,072,157	25,715,000	1976E	Kenya	224,960	13,500,000	1976E
Australia[4]	2,967,892	13,685,000	1976E	Korea (North)	46,540	16,275,000	1976E
Austria	32,375	7,520,000	1975E[3]	Korea (South)	38,022	34,400,000	1976E
Bahamas	5,382	215,000	1976E	Kuwait	6,880	1,050,000	1976E
Bahrain	240	275,000	1976E	Laos	91,429	3,350,000	1976E
Bangladesh	55,598	78,700,000	1976E	Latvia	24,595	2,278,000	1975E
Barbados	166	252,000	1976E	Lebanon	4,015	2,965,000	1976E
Belgium	11,781	9,830,000	1976E	Lesotho	11,720	1,065,000	1976E
Benin (Dahomey)	43,483	3,190,000	1976E	Liberia	43,000	1,750,000	1976E
Bhutan	18,147	1,146,000	1976E	Libya	679,362	2,530,000	1976E
Bolivia	424,162	5,790,000	1976E	Liechtenstein	61	22,850	1976E
Botswana	231,804	720,000	1976E	Lithuania	25,174	3,290,000	1975E
Brazil	3,286,487	107,985,000	1976E	Luxembourg	999	370,000	1976E
Bulgaria	42,823	8,765,000	1976E	Madagascar	226,658	8,020,000	1975E
Burma	261,789	32,000,000	1976E	Malawi	45,747	5,160,000	1976E
Burundi	10,747	3,845,000	1976E	Malaysia	127,316	11,900,000	1975E[3]
Cambodia	69,898	8,335,000	1976E	Maldives	115	125,000	1976E
Cameroon	183,569	6,525,000	1976E	Mali	478,766	5,840,000	1976E
Canada	3,851,809	23,200,000	1976E	Malta	122	333,000	1976E
Cape Verde	1,557	300,000	1976E	Mauritania	397,955	1,350,000	1976E
Central African Republic	240,535	2,610,000	1974E[3]	Mauritius	790	875,000	1976E
Chad	495,752	4,110,000	1976E	Mexico	761,600	63,150,000	1976E
Chile	292,257	10,420,000	1976E	Monaco	([13])	25,000	1976E
China, People's Rep. of[5]	3,705,406	852,500,000	1976E	Mongolian People's Rep.	604,250	1,480,000	1976E
China, Republic of[6]	13,893	16,200,000	1976E	Morocco	172,414	17,760,000	1976E
Colombia	439,735	24,190,000	1976E	Mozambique	302,328	9,450,000	1976E
Comoro Islands	838	315,000	1976E	Nauru	8.2	7,000	1974E[3]
Congo	132,046	1,380,000	1976E	Nepal	54,362	12,820,000	1976E
Costa Rica	19,575	2,000,000	1976E	Netherlands	15,770	13,765,000	1976E
Cuba	44,218	9,265,000	1975E	New Zealand[14]	103,736	3,150,000	1976E
Cyprus	3,572	650,000	1976E	Nicaragua	50,193	2,250,000	1976E
Czechoslovakia	49,373	14,910,000	1976E	Niger	489,191	4,725,000	1976E
Denmark[7]	16,629	5,080,000	1976E	Nigeria	356,669	64,630,000	1976E
Dominican Republic	18,816	4,840,000	1976E	Norway	125,182	4,035,000	1976E
Ecuador	109,483	6,730,000	1975E[3]	Oman[15]	82,030	800,000	1976E
Egypt	386,661	38,000,000	1976E	Pakistan[16]	310,404	72,350,000	1976E
El Salvador	8,260	4,130,000	1976E	Panama	29,208	1,720,000	1976E
Equatorial Guinea	10,830	320,000	1976E	Papua New Guinea	178,259	2,860,000	1976E
Estonia	17,413	1,429,999	1975E	Paraguay	157,047	2,730,000	1976E
Ethiopia	471,778	28,685,000	1976E	Peru	496,222	16,380,000	1976E
Fiji	7,055	580,000	1976E	Philippines	115,831	43,750,000	1976E
Finland	130,119	4,740,000	1976E	Poland	120,725	34,350,000	1976E
France	211,208	53,250,000	1976E	Portugal	35,553	8,750,000	1976E
Gabon	103,346	535,000	1976E	Qatar	4,247	144,000	1975E
Gambia	4,361	530,000	1976E	Rhodesia	150,803	6,520,000	1976E
Germany (East)[8]	41,923	16,850,000	1975E[3]	Romania	91,700	21,480,000	1976E
Germany (West)[9]	95,791	61,830,000	1975E[3]	Rwanda	10,169	4,285,000	1976E
Ghana	92,100	10,140,000	1976E	San Marino	23.6	20,500	1976E
Greece	50,944	9,120,000	1976E	São Tomé and Príncipe	372	85,500	1976E
Grenada	133	110,000	1976E	Saudi Arabia	829,995	9,100,000	1976E
Guatemala	42,042	6,000,000	1976E	Senegal	75,750	4,300,000	1976E
Guinea	94,964	4,530,000	1976E	Seychelles	145	65,000	1976E
Guinea-Bissau	13,948	540,000	1976E	Sierra Leone	27,699	2,790,000	1976E
Guyana	83,000	810,000	1976E	Singapore	226	2,280,000	1976E
Haiti	10,714	4,650,000	1976E	Somalia	246,201	3,250,000	1976E
Honduras	43,277	3,150,000	1976E	South Africa[17]	471,445	26,000,000	1976E
Hungary	35,919	10,600,000	1976E	Spain[18]	194,897	35,815,000	1976E
Iceland	39,768	227,000	1976E	Sri Lanka (Ceylon)	25,332	14,300,000	1976E
India[10]	1,266,594	610,000,000	1976E	Sudan	967,494	18,215,000	1976E
Indonesia[11]	581,655	133,680,000	1976E	Surinam	63,037	450,000	1976E
Iran	636,296	33,900,000	1976E	Swaziland	6,704	550,000	1976E
Iraq	167,925	11,470,000	1976E	Sweden	173,732	8,230,000	1976E
Ireland	27,136	3,175,000	1976E	Switzerland	15,941	6,400,000	1976E[3]
Israel	7,992[12]	3,445,000	1976E	Syrian Arab Republic	71,586	7,580,000	1976E

Country	Area[1]	Population	Year[2]	Country	Area[1]	Population	Year[2]
Tanzania[19]	364,900	15,575,000	1976E	Upper Volta	105,870	6,150,000	1976E
Thailand	198,500	41,870,000	1976E[3]	Uruguay	68,536	3,090,000	1976E
Togo	21,622	2,265,000	1976E	Vatican City State	([21])	1,000	1976E
Tonga	270	106,000	1976E	Venezuela	352,143	12,375,000	1976E
Trinidad and Tobago	1,980	1,085,000	1976E	Vietnam	128,302	43,155,000	([22])
Tunisia	63,170	5,924,000	1976E	Western Samoa	1,097	165,000	1976E
Turkey	301,380	40,000,000	1976E	Yemen	75,290	6,860,000	1976E
Uganda	91,134	11,915,000	1976E	Yemen, Democratic	111,074	1,700,000	1976E
U.S.S.R.	8,649,489	256,700,000	1976E	Yugoslavia	98,766	21,550,000	1976E
United Arab Emirates	32,278	340,000	1974E	Zaire	905,562	25,700,000	1976E
United Kingdom[20]	94,529	56,100,000	1976E	Zambia	290,586	5,100,000	1976E
United States	3,540,939	215,115,000	1976E				

[1] In square miles. [2] E—estimated; C—census. [3] U.N. estimate. [4] Population figure excludes aborigines. [5] Including Manchuria and Tibet. [6] Excluding Quemoy and Matsu. [7] Excluding Faeroe Islands and Greenland. [8] Including East Berlin. [9] Excluding West Berlin. [10] Including Jammu and Kashmir and Sikkim. [11] Including Portuguese East Timor, annexed in 1976; excluding Irian Jaya (former Netherlands New Guinea and later West Irian). [12] Excluding territory occupied in 1967 war. [13] 0.65 square mile. [14] Excluding dependencies. [15] Excluding Kuria Muria Islands. [16] Excluding Jammu and Kashmir. [17] Excluding South-West Africa (Namibia). [18] Including Baleric and Canary Islands. [19] Including Zanzibar. [20] Including Channel Islands and Isle of Man. [21] 0.17 square mile. [22] Estimated 1973 for former South Vietnam; estimated 1975 for former North. [23] Excluding Perim and Kamaran Islands.

Largest Cities of the World

Source: United Nations *Demographic Yearbook, 1974*, and official estimates.

(An exact rating of cities is impossible because of the diversity of the years for which census or estimated population figures have been issued. Therefore, the rating shown in this listing must be considered only approximate.)

City and country	Population	Year[1]	City and country	Population	Year[1]
1. Shanghai, China	10,820,000	1970E	11. São Paulo, Brazil	5,901,300	1970C
2. Tokyo, Japan	8,708,000	1974E	12. Cairo, Egypt	5,859,000	1975E
3. Mexico City, Mexico	8,591,800	1975E	13. Jakarta, Indonesia	5,490,000	1975E
4. Manila, Philippines	7,800,000	1976E	14. Rio de Janeiro, Brazil	4,296,000	1970C
5. Moscow, U.S.S.R.	7,635,000	1975E	15. Tientsin, China	4,280,000	1970E
6. Peking, China	7,570,000	1970E	16. Leningrad, U.S.S.R.	4,243,000[2]	1975E
7. New York, N.Y., U.S.A.	7,567,900	1975E	17. Bangkok, Thailand	4,129,600[2]	1975E
8. London (Greater) England	7,168,000	1974E	18. Teheran, Iran	4,000,000	1975E
9. Seoul, South Korea	6,289,000	1973E	19. Madrid, Spain	3,750,850	1976E
10. Bombay, India	5,970,575	1971C	20. Mukden, China	3,750,000	1970E

Some Other Large Foreign Cities

City and country	Population	Year[1]	City and country	Population	Year[1]
Addis Ababa, Ethiopia	1,083,420	1974C	Bucharest, Romania	1,528,600	1973E
Ahmedabad, India	1,585,544	1971C	Budapest, Hungary	2,058,000	1975E
Alexandria, Egypt	2,032,000	1970E	Buenos Aires, Argentina	2,977,000	1975E
Algiers, Algeria	1,839,000	1970E	Calcutta, India	3,148,746	1971C
Alma Ata, U.S.S.R.	794,000	1972E	Cali, Colombia	898,253	1973C
Amsterdam, the Netherlands	751,200	1976E	Canton, China	2,300,000	1970E
Ankara, Turkey	1,700,000	1975C	Cape Town, South Africa	790,900	1974E
Antwerp, Belgium	673,000	1974E	Caracas, Venezuela	2,487,000[2]	1975E
Athens, Greece	867,023	1971C	Casablanca, Morocco	1,371,330	1971C
Auckland, New Zealand	796,660	1975E	Chungking, China	3,500,000	1970E
Baghdad, Iraq	2,800,000	1974E	Cologne, West Germany	832,400	1974E
Baku, U.S.S.R.	1,383,000	1975E	Copenhagen, Denmark	1,380,000[2]	1974E
Bandung, Indonesia	1,201,730	1971C	Córdoba, Argentina	798,663[2]	1970C
Bangalore, India	1,540,741	1971C	Dacca, Bangladesh	1,311,000	1974E
Barcelona, Spain	1,846,250	1976E	Damascus, Syrian Arab Rep.	836,179	1972E
Barranquilla, Colombia	664,533	1973C	Delhi, India	3,287,883	1971C
Belfast, Northern Ireland	374,000	1974E	Donetsk, U.S.S.R.	950,000	1975E
Belgrade, Yugoslavia	746,105	1971C	Dnepropetrovsk, U.S.S.R.	958,000	1975E
Belo Horizonte, Brazil	1,232,708[2]	1970C	Dublin, Ireland	562,866	1971C
Berlin, Germany[3]	3,118,100	1975E	Edinburgh, Scotland	450,000	1974E
Bern, Switzerland	154,700	1974E	Florence, Italy	457,803	1971C
Birmingham, England	1,086,000	1974E	Frankfurt, West Germany	663,400	1974E
Bogotá, Colombia	2,850,000	1973C	Fukuoka, Japan	914,877[2]	1973E
Bonn, West Germany	283,260	1974E	Geneva, Switzerland	163,100	1974E
Brisbane, Australia	940,800[2]	1974E	Genoa, Italy	806,400	1975E
Brussels, Belgium	1,055,000[2]	1975E	Glasgow, Scotland	816,000	1974E

Some Other Large Foreign Cities (continued)

City and country	Population	Year[1]	City and country	Population	Year[1]
Gorki, U.S.S.R.	1,283,000	1975E	Nanking, China	2,000,000	1970E
Guadalajara, Mexico	1,478,400	1974E	Nantes, France	257,300	1975C
Guyaquil, Ecuador	814,100	1974C	Naples, Italy	1,232,877[2]	1971C
Haifa, Israel	225,000	1974E	Nice, France	344,500	1975C
Hamburg, West Germany	1,751,620	1974E	Novosibirsk, U.S.S.R.	1,265,000	1975E
Harbin, China	2,750,000	1970E	Odessa, U.S.S.R.	1,002,000	1975E
Havana, Cuba	1,838,000	1974E	Osaka, Japan	2,841,950[2]	1973E
Helsinki, Finland	509,700	1973E	Oslo, Norway	465,300	1974E
Hyderabad, India	1,607,396	1971C	Paris, France	2,290,900	1975C
Hyderabad, Pakistan	624,000	1972E	Poona, India	856,105	1971C
Ibadan, Nigeria	758,332	1971E	Porto Alegre, Brazil	869,795[2]	1973E
Istanbul, Turkey	2,500,000	1975C	Prague, Czechoslovakia	1,095,615	1974E
Jerusalem, Israel	344,200	1974E	Pusan, South Korea	1,842,259	1970C
Johannesburg, South Africa	1,316,900	1974E	Quezon City, Philippines	946,390	1974E
Kanpur, India	1,154,388	1971E	Rangoon, Burma	2,056,100[2]	1973E
Karachi, Pakistan	3,469,000[2]	1972E	Recife, Brazil	1,078,819[2]	1970C
Kharkov, U.S.S.R.	1,357,000	1975E	Rome, Italy	2,833,100	1974E
Kiev, U.S.S.R.	1,947,000	1975E	Rosario, Argentina	810,840[2]	1970C
Kinshasa, Zaire	1,798,576	1973E	Rotterdam, the Netherlands	614,800	1976E
Kitakyushu, Japan	1,051,000[2]	1973E	Rostov-on-Don, U.S.S.R.	867,000	1974E
Kobe, Japan	1,338,700[2]	1973E	Saigon, South Vietnam	2,000,000[2]	1972E
Kuibyshev, U.S.S.R.	1,164,000	1975E	Salvador, Brazil	1,000,647[2]	1970C
Kunming, China	1,700,000	1970E	Santiago, Chile	3,263,000[2]	1975E
Kyoto, Japan	1,435,250[2]	1973E	Sapporo, Japan	1,130,800[2]	1973E
Lahore, Pakistan	2,148,000	1972E	Seville, Spain	612,900	1976E
La Paz, Bolivia	605,000	1973E	Singapore, Singapore	2,074,507	1970C
Lausanne, Switzerland	136,100	1974E	Sofia, Bulgaria	979,300	1975E
Liège, Belgium	444,000	1974E	Stockholm, Sweden	681,300	1975E
Lima, Peru	3,158,400[2]	1973E	Surabaja, Indonesia	1,556,255	1971C
Lisbon, Portugal	757,700	1973E	Sverdlovsk, U.S.S.R.	1,147,000	1975E
Liverpool, England	561,000	1974E	Sydney, Australia	2,898,330[2]	1974E
Lódz, Poland	777,800	1974E	Taipei, Taiwan	2,046,900	1976E
Lucknow, India	749,239	1971C	Tashkent, U.S.S.R.	1,595,000	1975E
Lyalpur, Pakistan	820,000	1972E	Tbilisi, U.S.S.R.	1,006,000	1975E
Lyons, France	457,000	1975C	Tel Aviv-Jaffa, Israel	357,600	1974E
Madras, India	2,469,449	1971C	Toronto, Canada	712,785	1973E
Marseilles, France	907,900	1975C	Tunis, Tunisia	960,000	1976E
Medellín, Colombia	1,064,741	1973C	Turin, Italy	1,200,000	1975E
Melbourne, Australia	2,620,400[2]	1974E	Valencia, Spain	748,730	1976E
Milan, Italy	1,700,000	1976E	Venice, Italy	364,900	1975E
Minsk, U.S.S.R.	1,147,000	1975E	Vienna, Austria	1,614,841	1971C
Monterrey, Mexico	1,006,200	1974E	Volgograd, U.S.S.R.	869,000	1973E
Montevideo, Uruguay	1,229,700	1975E	Warsaw, Poland	1,427,400	1975E
Montreal, Canada	1,214,355	1973E	Wellington, New Zealand	354,660	1975E
Munich, West Germany	1,336,575	1974E	Wuhan, China	3,000,000	1970E
Nagoya, Japan	2,075,250[2]	1973E	Yokohama, Japan	2,494,975[2]	1973E
Nagpur, India	866,076	1971C	Zurich, Switzerland	401,600	1974E

[1] E—estimated; C—census. [2] Figure is for urban agglomeration and may include suburbs, metropolitan areas or some rural population. [3] West Berlin, 2,024,000, East Berlin, 1,094,100. [4] Includes suburb of Cholon. NOTE: The population of many other cities will be found throughout the World History section under individual countries. *See* Table of Contents.

MAP SECTION
Prepared by Vaughn Gray

EUROPE

⭐ Countries in which West has bases
● Capitals

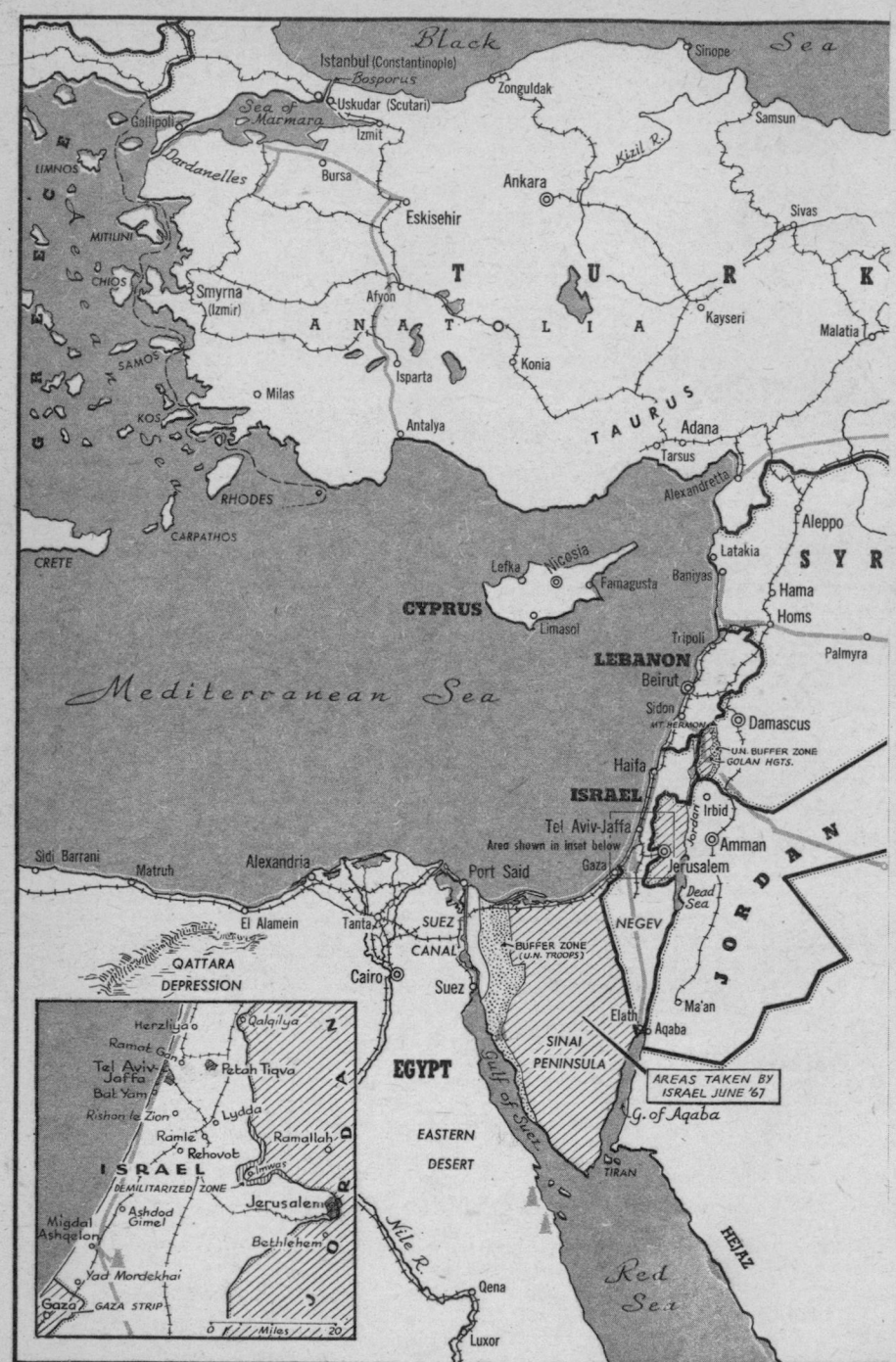

Black Sea

Istanbul (Constantinople)
Bosporus
Uskudar (Scutari)
Sinope
Zonguldak
Samsun
Gallipoli
Sea of Marmara
Izmit
Bursa
Ankara
Kizil R.
Sivas
Eskisehir
T   U   R   K
LIMNOS
MITILINI
CHIOS
SAMOS
KOS
RHODES
CARPATHOS
CRETE
Smyrna (Izmir)
Afyon
A   N   A   T   O   L   I   A
Kayseri
Malatia
Konia
Isparta
Milas
Antalya
T A U R U S
Adana
Tarsus
Alexandretta
Aleppo
SYR
Latakia
Baniyas
Hama
Homs
Palmyra
Tripoli
Lefka
Nicosia
Famagusta
CYPRUS
Limasol
LEBANON
Beirut
Sidon
MT. HERMON
Damascus
U.N. BUFFER ZONE
GOLAN HGTS.
Mediterranean Sea
Haifa
ISRAEL
Tel Aviv-Jaffa
Area shown in inset below
Irbid
Amman
JORDAN
Sidi Barrani
Matruh
Alexandria
Port Said
Gaza
Jerusalem
Dead Sea
El Alamein
Tanta
SUEZ CANAL
NEGEV
Ma'an
QATTARA DEPRESSION
Cairo
Suez
BUFFER ZONE
(U.N. TROOPS)
EGYPT
EASTERN DESERT
Gulf of Suez
SINAI PENINSULA
Elath
Aqaba
AREAS TAKEN BY
ISRAEL JUNE '67
G. of Aqaba
Nile R.
TIRAN
HEJAZ
Qena
Luxor
Red Sea

Herzliya
Qalqilya
Ramat Gan
Petah Tiqva
Tel Aviv-Jaffa
Bat Yam
Rishon le Zion
Lydda
Ramle
Rehovot
Ramallah
ISRAEL
DEMILITARIZED ZONE
Imwas
JORDAN
Jerusalem
Ashdod Gimel
Migdal Ashqelon
Bethlehem
Yad Mordekhai
Gaza
GAZA STRIP
Miles 20

274

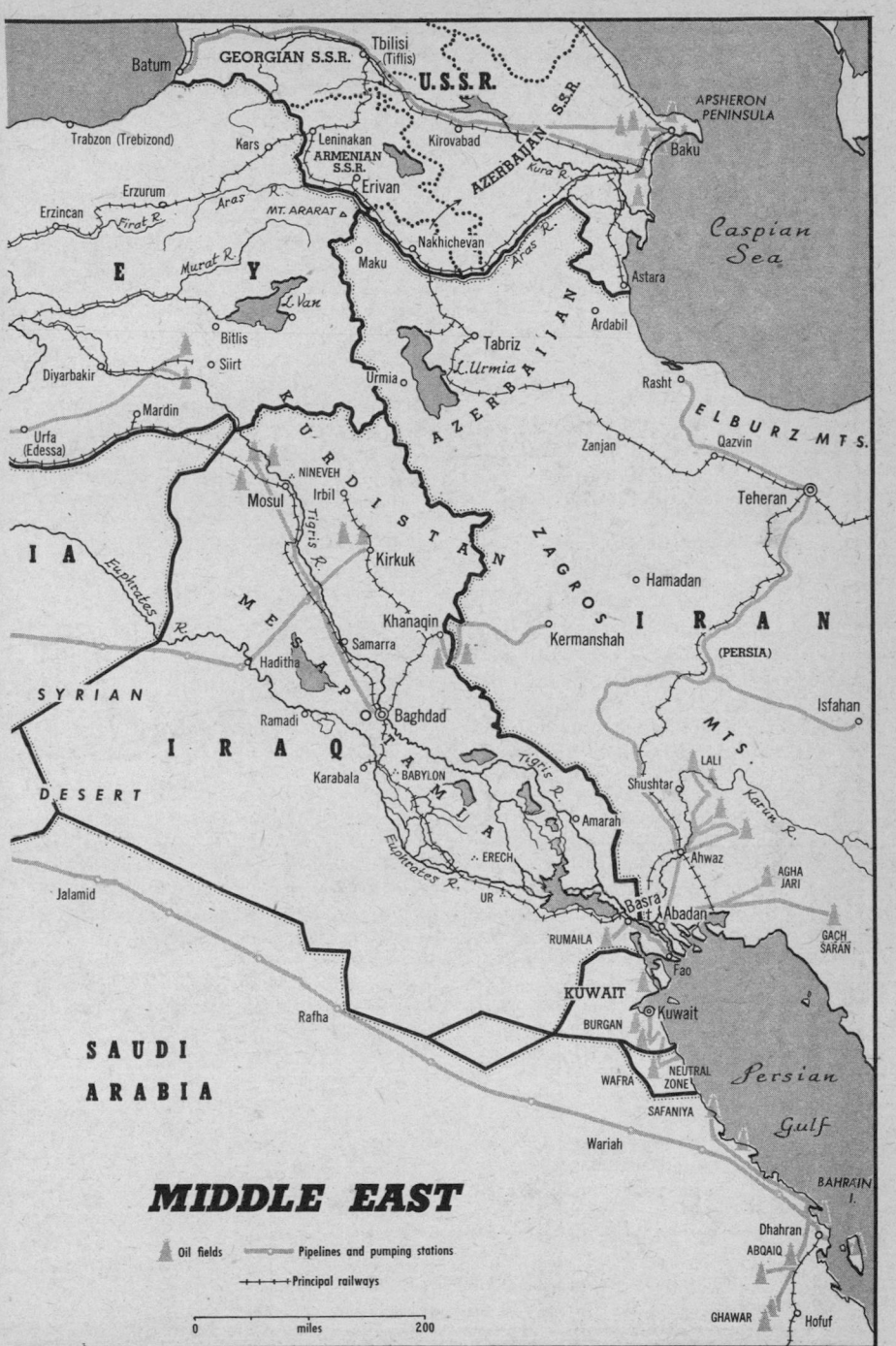

MIDDLE EAST

Batum

Trabzon (Trebizond)

GEORGIAN S.S.R.

Tbilisi (Tiflis)

U.S.S.R.

APSHERON PENINSULA

Kars

Leninakan

Kirovabad

Baku

ARMENIAN S.S.R.

AZERBAIJAN S.S.R.

Erzurum

Erivan

MT. ARARAT

Caspian Sea

Erzincan

Firat R.

Aras

Nakhichevan

Aras R.

E   Y

Murat R.

Maku

Astara

L. Van

Ardabil

Bitlis

Tabriz

AZERBAIJAN

Rasht

Diyarbakir

Siirt

Urmia

L. Urmia

ELBURZ MTS.

Mardin

Zanjan

Qazvin

Urfa (Edessa)

K U R D I S T A N

Teheran

Mosul

NINEVEH

Irbil

ZAGROS

Hamadan

Tigris R.

Kirkuk

I R A N

I A

Khanaqin

Kermanshah

(PERSIA)

Euphrates

M E

Samarra

R.

Haditha

Isfahan

S Y R I A N

Ramadi

Baghdad

MTS.

LALI

D E S E R T

I R A Q

Karabala

BABYLON

Tigris R.

Shushtar

Amarah

Ahwaz

AGHA JARI

Jalamid

ERECH

Euphrates R.

UR

Basra

Abadan

GACH SARAN

RUMAILA

Fao

KUWAIT

Persian

Rafha

BURGAN

Kuwait

SAUDI

WAFRA

NEUTRAL ZONE

Gulf

ARABIA

SAFANIYA

Wariah

BAHRAIN I.

Dhahran

ABQAIQ

miles

GHAWAR

Hofuf

△ Oil fields   ▭ Pipelines and pumping stations

┼┼┼ Principal railways

0   miles   200

275

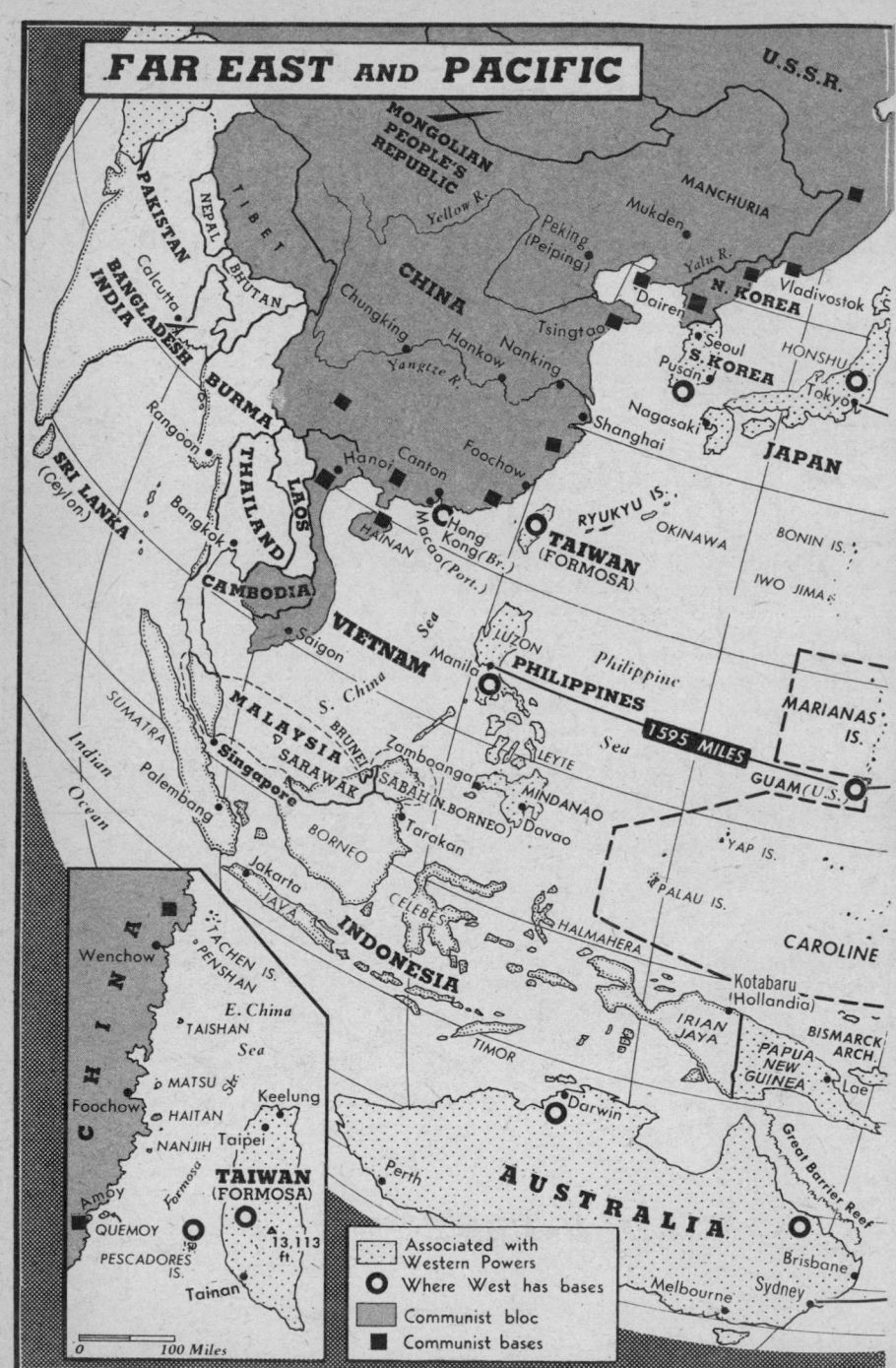

FAR EAST AND PACIFIC

U.S.S.R.

MONGOLIAN PEOPLE'S REPUBLIC

MANCHURIA

Mukden

Vladivostok

PAKISTAN

NEPAL

BHUTAN

TIBET

Yellow R.

Peking (Peiping)

Yalu R.

N. KOREA

BANGLADESH

INDIA

Calcutta

CHINA

Chungking

Hankow

Nanking

Tsingtao

Dairen

Seoul

S. KOREA

Pusan

HONSHU

Tokyo

BURMA

Rangoon

Yangtze R.

Nagasaki

Shanghai

JAPAN

SRI LANKA (Ceylon)

THAILAND

Bangkok

LAOS

Hanoi

Canton

Foochow

HAINAN

Macao (Port.)

Hong Kong (Br.)

TAIWAN (FORMOSA)

RYUKYU IS.

OKINAWA

BONIN IS.

IWO JIMA

CAMBODIA

VIETNAM

Saigon

S. China Sea

LUZON

Manila

PHILIPPINES

Philippine Sea

1595 MILES

MARIANAS IS.

SUMATRA

MALAYSIA

SARAWAK

Singapore

Palembang

BRUNEI

SABAH

N. BORNEO

Zamboanga

LEYTE

MINDANAO

Davao

Tarakan

GUAM (U.S.)

YAP IS.

PALAU IS.

Indian Ocean

Jakarta

JAVA

BORNEO

CELEBES

INDONESIA

HALMAHERA

CAROLINE

Kotabaru (Hollandia)

IRIAN JAYA

PAPUA NEW GUINEA

BISMARCK ARCH.

Lae

TIMOR

Darwin

AUSTRALIA

Perth

Great Barrier Reef

Brisbane

Melbourne

Sydney

Inset map

CHINA

Wenchow

TACHEN IS.

PENSHAN

E. China Sea

TAISHAN

MATSU

Foochow

HAITAN

NANJIH

Keelung

Taipei

Formosa

Amoy

QUEMOY

PESCADORES IS.

Tainan

TAIWAN (FORMOSA)

13,113 ft.

0   100 Miles

Legend

- Associated with Western Powers
- ○ Where West has bases
- Communist bloc
- ■ Communist bases

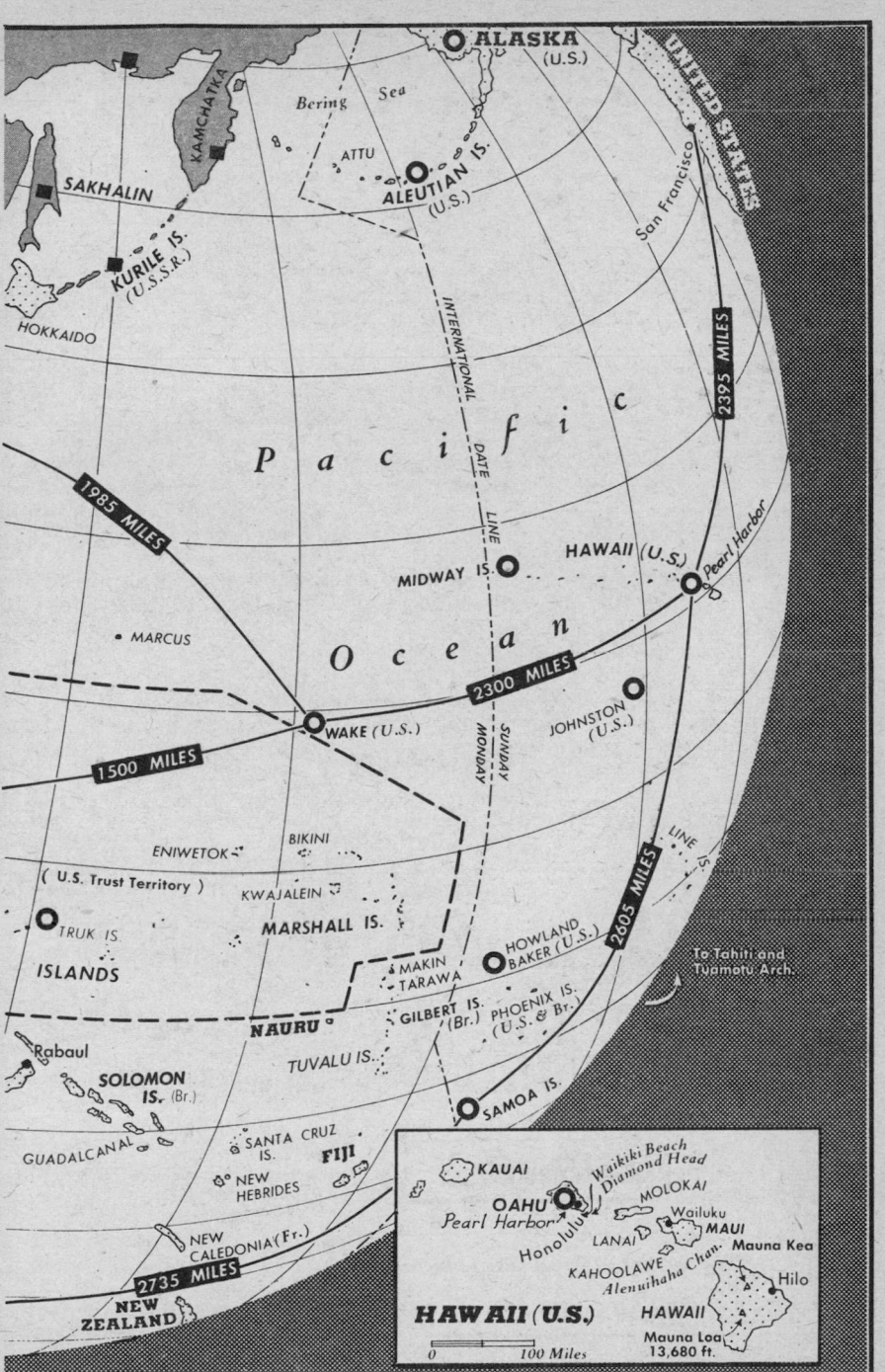

ALASKA (U.S.)

Bering Sea

KAMCHATKA

ATTU

ALEUTIAN IS. (U.S.)

SAKHALIN

KURILE IS. (U.S.S.R.)

HOKKAIDO

San Francisco

UNITED STATES

2395 MILES

1985 MILES

Pacific

INTERNATIONAL DATE LINE

MIDWAY IS.

HAWAII (U.S.)

Pearl Harbor

• MARCUS

Ocean

2300 MILES

WAKE (U.S.)

JOHNSTON (U.S.)

SUNDAY MONDAY

1500 MILES

ENIWETOK

BIKINI

(U.S. Trust Territory)

KWAJALEIN

MARSHALL IS.

LINE IS.

2605 MILES

TRUK IS.

ISLANDS

MAKIN TARAWA

HOWLAND BAKER (U.S.)

To Tahiti and Tuamotu Arch.

NAURU

GILBERT IS. (Br.)

PHOENIX IS. (U.S. & Br.)

Rabaul

SOLOMON IS. (Br.)

TUVALU IS.

GUADALCANAL

SANTA CRUZ IS.

FIJI

SAMOA IS.

NEW HEBRIDES

NEW CALEDONIA (Fr.)

2735 MILES

NEW ZEALAND

KAUAI

Waikiki Beach
Diamond Head

OAHU

Pearl Harbor

Honolulu

MOLOKAI

LANAI

Wailuku

MAUI

Mauna Kea

KAHOOLAWE

Alenuihaha Chan.

Hilo

HAWAII (U.S.)

HAWAII

Mauna Loa
13,680 ft.

0   100 Miles

EURASIA

C CENTO (Central Treaty Organization, formerly Baghdad Pact)

U.S.S.R. and satellites

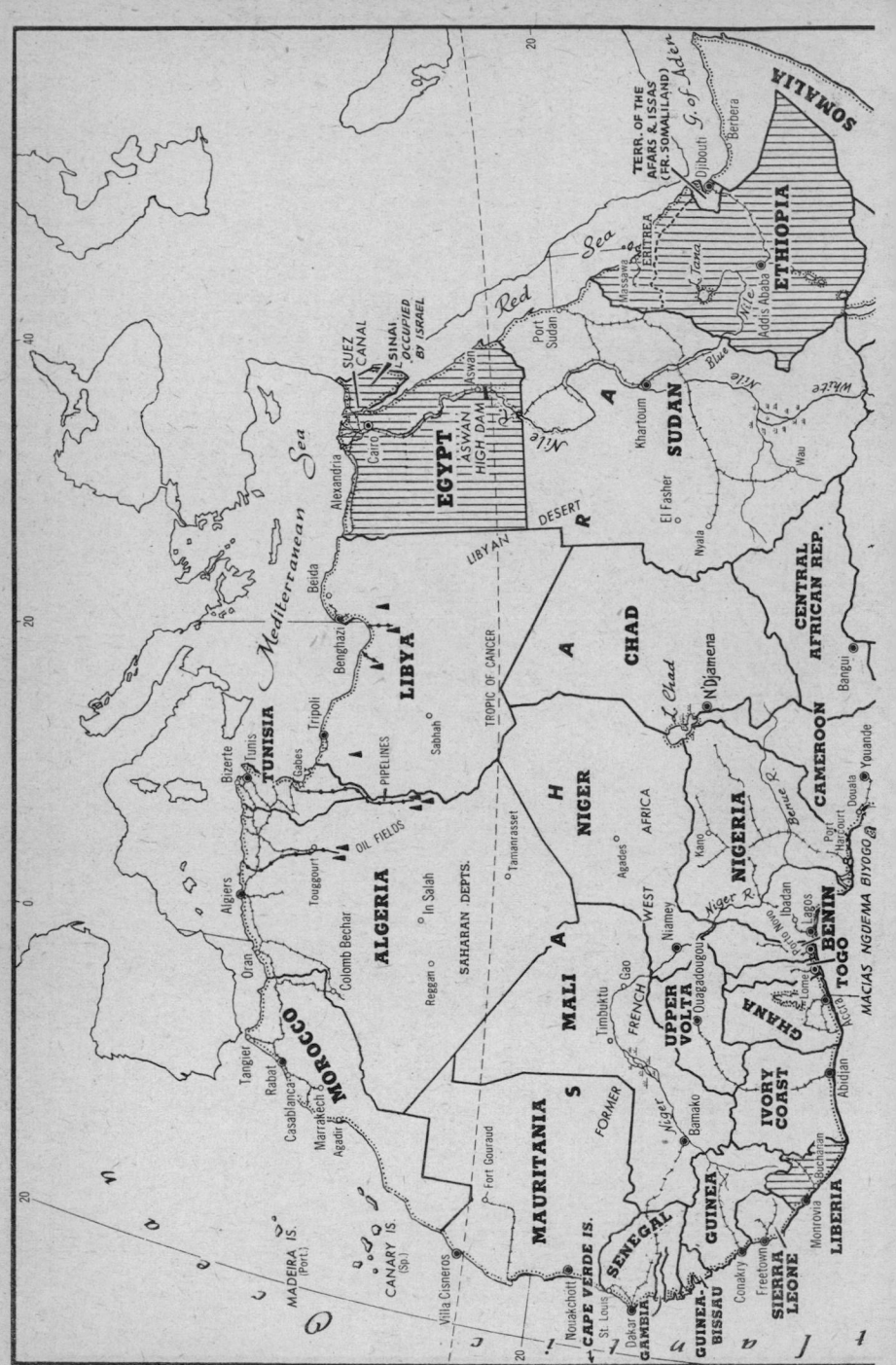

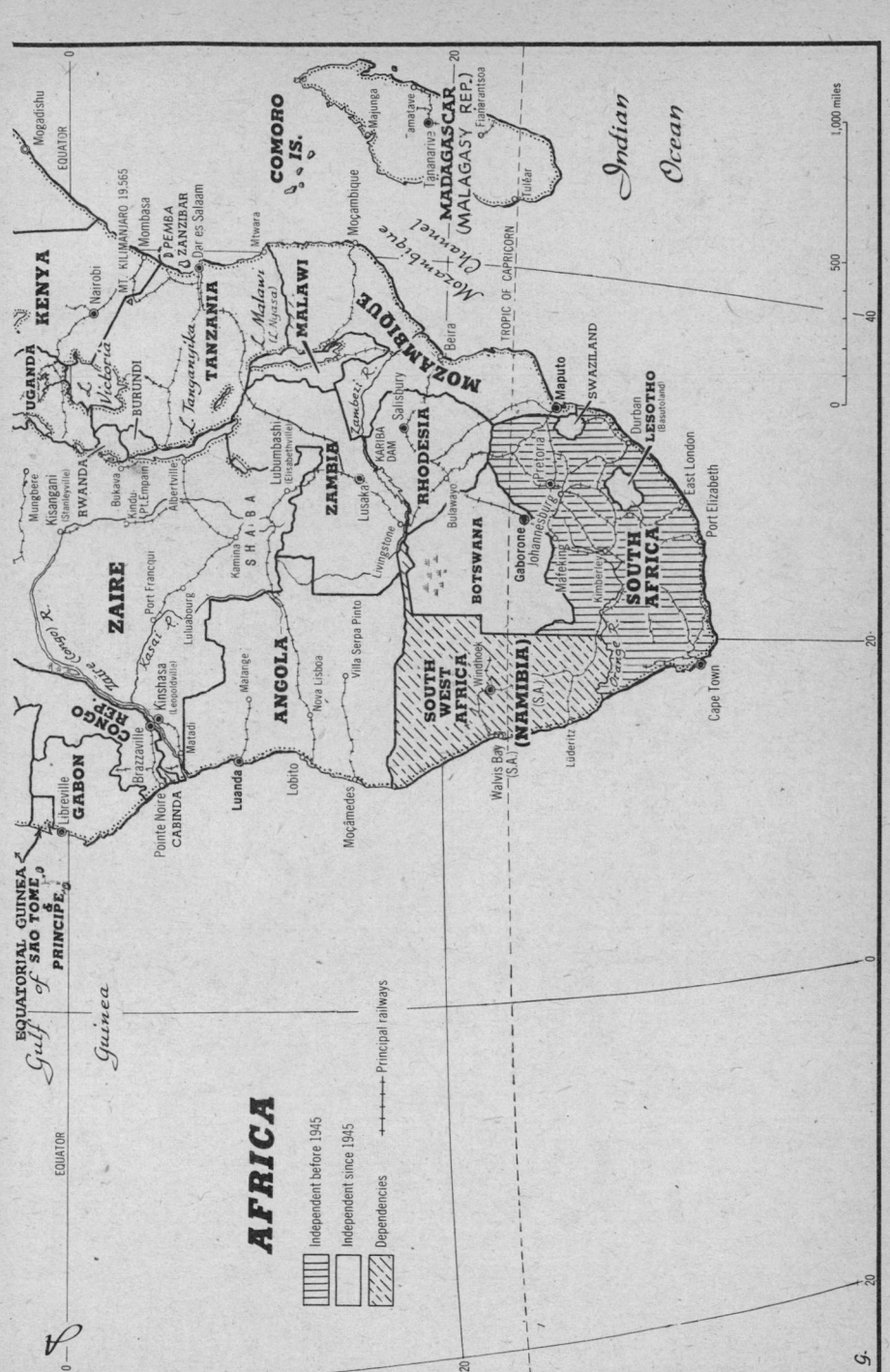

AFRICA

Independent before 1945

Independent since 1945

Dependencies

←←←←← Principal railways

1,000 miles

EQUATOR

Gulf of Guinea

Guinea

EQUATORIAL GUINEA
SAO TOME &
PRINCIPE

GABON

CONGO REP.

Libreville

Brazzaville

Pointe Noire

CABINDA

Matadi

Kinshasa (Leopoldville)

ZAIRE

Zaire (Congo) R.

Mungbere

Kisangani (Stanleyville)

RWANDA

BURUNDI

Bukavu

Kindu (Pt.Empain)

Albertville

Kasai R.

Port Francqui

Luluaburg

Kamina

SHABA

Lubumbashi (Elisabethville)

UGANDA

KENYA

Mogadishu

EQUATOR

Nairobi

L. Victoria

MT. KILIMANJARO 19,565

Mombasa

PEMBA

ZANZIBAR

Dar es Salaam

TANZANIA

L. Tanganyika

L. Nyasa (L. Nyassa)

Mtwara

COMORO IS.

Majunga

Tananarive (Tananarive)

Tamatave

MADAGASCAR (MALAGASY REP.)

Fianarantsoa

Tulear

MALAWI

Mozambique Channel

Moçambique

Indian Ocean

500

40

ZAMBIA

Lusaka

Zambezi R.

KARIBA DAM

Livingstone

Villa Serpa Pinto

ANGOLA

Malange

Luanda

Lobito

Nova Lisboa

Moçâmedes

RHODESIA

Bulawayo

Salisbury

Beira

TROPIC OF CAPRICORN

MOZAMBIQUE

BOTSWANA

SOUTH WEST AFRICA (NAMIBIA) (S.A.)

Walvis Bay (S.A.)

Windhoek

Lüderitz

Gaborone

Mafeking

Kimberley

Pretoria

Johannesburg

SOUTH AFRICA

SWAZILAND

Maputo

Durban

LESOTHO (Basutoland)

East London

Port Elizabeth

Cape Town

20

0

20

0

20

20

0

281

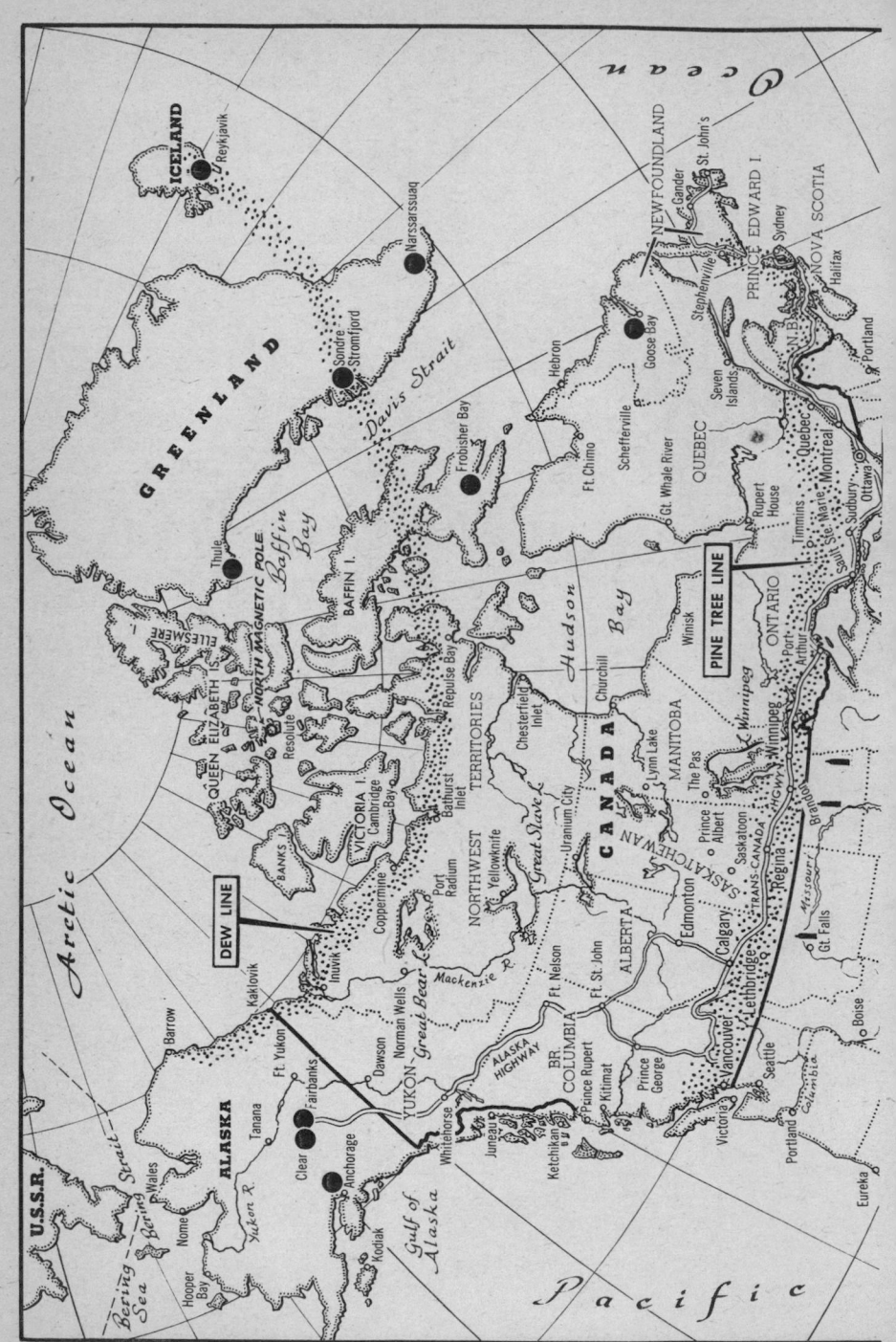

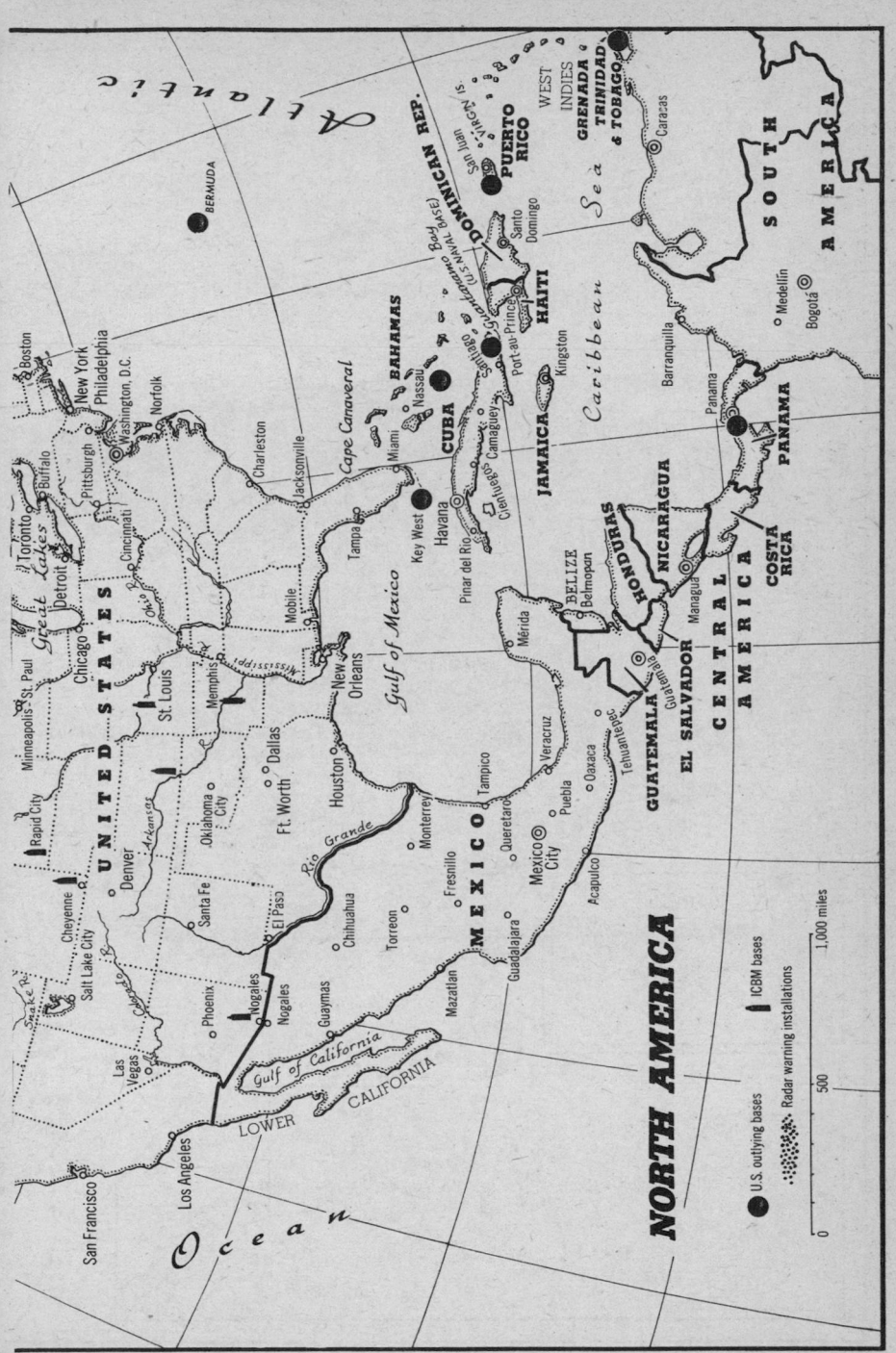

NORTH AMERICA

Legend:
- U.S. outlying bases
- ICBM bases
- Radar warning installations

Scale: 0 — 500 — 1,000 miles

Labels on map:

Atlantic Ocean

BERMUDA

WEST INDIES
GRENADA
TRINIDAD & TOBAGO
PUERTO RICO
San Juan Is.
DOMINICAN REP.
Santo Domingo
HAITI
Port-au-Prince
Guantánamo Bay (U.S. NAVAL BASE)
Santiago
Caracas
Caribbean Sea
Kingston
JAMAICA
BAHAMAS
Nassau
CUBA
Camagüey
Cienfuegos
Havana
Pinar del Río
Key West
Miami
Cape Canaveral
Jacksonville
Charleston
Norfolk
Washington, D.C.
Philadelphia
New York
Boston
Buffalo
Toronto
Detroit
Pittsburgh
Cincinnati
Great Lakes
Chicago
Minneapolis · St. Paul
Rapid City
Denver
Cheyenne
Salt Lake City
Santa Fe
El Paso
Nogales
Phoenix
Las Vegas
Los Angeles
San Francisco
Snake R.
UNITED STATES
St. Louis
Memphis
Oklahoma City
Ft. Worth
Dallas
Houston
New Orleans
Mobile
Tampa
Gulf of Mexico
Arkansas
Mississippi
Ohio
Rio Grande
Monterrey
Tampico
Veracruz
Mérida
BELIZE
Belmopan
HONDURAS
GUATEMALA
Guatemala
EL SALVADOR
NICARAGUA
Managua
COSTA RICA
PANAMA
Panama
CENTRAL AMERICA
Barranquilla
Medellín
Bogotá
SOUTH AMERICA
MEXICO
Mexico City
Querétaro
Puebla
Oaxaca
Acapulco
Tehuantepec
Fresnillo
Torreón
Chihuahua
Guadalajara
Mazatlán
Guaymas
Nogales
LOWER CALIFORNIA
Gulf of California
Ocean

283

PACIFIC TIME
9 A.M.

MOUNTAIN TIME
10 A.M.

CANADA

Ocean

Port Angeles
Bellingham
Everett
Seattle
Tacoma
Hoquiam
OLYMPIA
WASHINGTON
Spokane
Astoria
Vancouver
Yakima
Portland
The Dalles
Oregon City
Walla Walla
Lewiston
Pendleton
SALEM
Corvallis
Albany
Eugene
Bend
OREGON
Baker
Caldwell
Grants Pass
Medford
Klamath Falls
Yreka

Columbia River

Kalispell
Coeur d'Alene
Missoula
Havre
Great Falls
Missouri R.
Williston
Minot
Grand Forks
NORTH DAKOTA
Dickinson
Mandan
BISMARCK
Fargo
Wahpeton
Anaconda
HELENA
Butte
Bozeman
MONTANA
Billings
Miles City
Salmon
IDAHO
BOISE
Idaho Falls
YELLOWSTONE NAT'L PARK
Sheridan
Lead
Rapid City
Aberdeen
SOUTH DAKOTA
Watertown
PIERRE
Snake R.
Twin Falls
Pocatello
WYOMING
Lander
Sioux Falls
Yankton

Eureka
Redding
Santa Rosa
Marysville
Sacramento
Stockton
San Francisco
Oakland
San Jose
Fresno
Monterey
Visalia
CALIFORNIA
Bakersfield
San Luis Obispo
Santa Barbara
Glendale
Pomona
Riverside
Los Angeles
Long Beach
Santa Ana
Palm Springs
San Diego
Brawley

Winnemucca
Elko
NEVADA
Reno
Sparks
Carson City
Austin
Tonopah
Goldfield
Las Vegas
Needles

Great Salt Lake
Brigham
Logan
Ogden
Tooele
SALT LAKE CITY
Provo
UTAH
Price
Cedar City
St. George
River
Durango

Rock Springs
Green River
Casper
Rawlins
Laramie
CHEYENNE
Fort Collins
Longmont
Greeley
Grand Junction
Leadville
DENVER
Colorado Springs
COLORADO
Pueblo
Trinidad
Raton

Norfolk
North Platte
NEBRASKA
Kearney
LINCOLN
Beatrice

Platte R.

Salina
Garden City
KANSAS
Wichita
Arkansas City
Ponca City
Enid
OKLAHOMA CITY
OKLAHOMA

Colorado
Flagstaff
Grand Canyon
Prescott
ARIZONA
PHOENIX
Mesa
Globe
Yuma
Tucson
Nogales Bisbee Douglas
Silver City

SANTA FE
Gallup
Albuquerque
Socorro
NEW MEXICO
Tucumcari
Clovis
Roswell
Hobbs
Las Cruces
Carlsbad
El Paso

Amarillo
Borger
Red R.
Lawton
Wichita Falls
Ardmore
Denison
Denton
Lubbock
Abilene
Fort Worth
Sweetwater
Big Spring
San Angelo
TEXAS
Waco
Temple
AUSTIN
Del Rio
San Antonio
Victoria
Corpus Christi
Laredo

Pacific

HAWAII

KAUAI
OAHU
Pearl Harbor
Honolulu
MOLOKAI
LANAI
MAUI
7 A.M.
HAWAII
Hilo
100 mi.

ST. LAWRENCE I.
Bering Sea
SHEMYA
PRIBILOF IS.
6 A.M.
ALEUTIAN IS.
ATKA
Unalaska
400 miles

Barrow
Kaktovik
Wales
Nome
Tanana
Ft. Yukon
Fairbanks
ALASKA
Hooper Bay
Summit
Tanacross
Anchorage
7 A.M.
Seward
Kodiak
8 A.M.
Gulf of Alaska
Juneau
9 A.M.

MEXICO
Rio Grande

CENTRAL TIME

11 A.M.

EASTERN TIME

12 N.

ST. LAWRENCE SEAWAY

UNITED STATES

Gulf of Mexico

C U B A

Atlantic Ocean

0   Miles   500

285

SOUTH AMERICA

Miles
0 — 1000

CLIMATE
Tropical Rainforest
Savanna
Highland
Subtropical
Marine
Desert and Steppe

Symbol	Legend
OIL	
IRON	
STEEL	
TUNGSTEN	
MANGANESE	
TIN	
COPPER	
NITRATES	
BAUXITE	
COAL	
DIAMONDS	
RUBBER	
COFFEE	
COCOA	
CATTLE	
SHEEP	

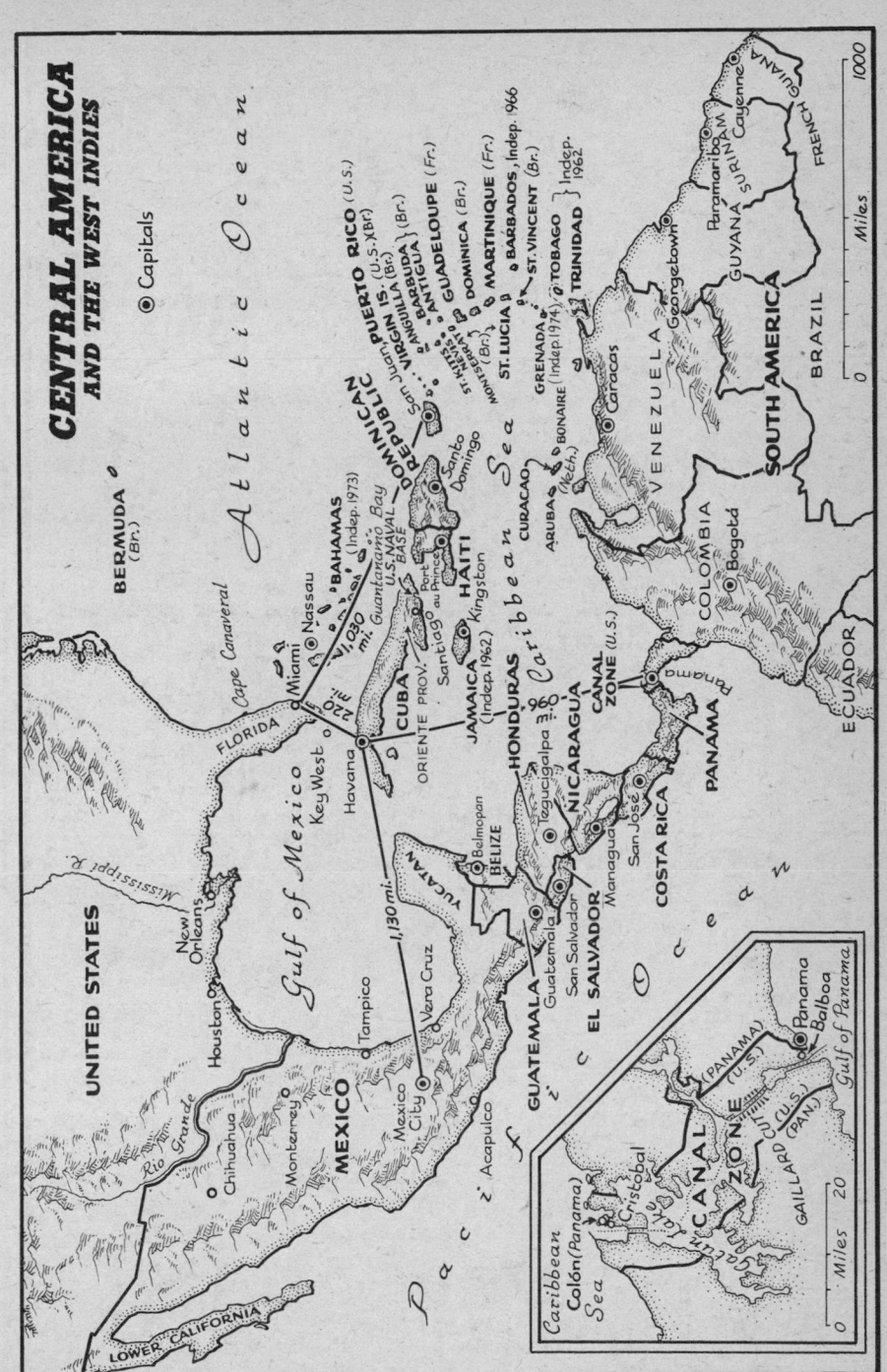

CENTRAL AMERICA
AND THE WEST INDIES

⊙ Capitals

UNITED STATES

Mississippi R.

New Orleans

Houston

Rio Grande

Chihuahua

Monterrey

MEXICO

Tampico

Vera Cruz

Mexico City

Acapulco

LOWER CALIFORNIA

Gulf of Mexico

Key West

Havana

CUBA

ORIENTE PROV.

YUCATAN

BELIZE
Belmopan

GUATEMALA
Guatemala

San Salvador

EL SALVADOR

HONDURAS
Tegucigalpa

NICARAGUA
Managua

San José

COSTA RICA

960 mi.

Caribbean Sea

1,130 mi.

Pacific Ocean

Cape Canaveral

FLORIDA

Miami

Nassau

BAHAMAS
(Indep. 1973)

BERMUDA
(Br.)

Atlantic Ocean

1,030 mi.

U.S. NAVAL BASE
Guantanamo Bay

220 mi.

JAMAICA
(Indep. 1962)
Kingston

Santiago

Port au Prince

HAITI

DOMINICAN REPUBLIC
Santo Domingo

PUERTO RICO (U.S.)
San Juan

VIRGIN IS. (U.S.-Br.)

ANGUILLA (Br.)

ST. KITTS-NEVIS (Br.)
MONTSERRAT (Br.)

ANTIGUA

GUADELOUPE (Fr.)

DOMINICA (Br.)

MARTINIQUE (Fr.)

ST. LUCIA

BARBADOS, Indep. 1966

ST. VINCENT (Br.)

GRENADA (Indep. 1974)

TOBAGO
TRINIDAD } Indep. 1962

CURAÇAO

ARUBA
(Neth.)

BONAIRE
(Neth.)

Caracas

VENEZUELA

Georgetown

GUYANA

SURINAM
Paramaribo

FRENCH GUIANA
Cayenne

BRAZIL

SOUTH AMERICA

COLOMBIA
Bogotá

ECUADOR

PANAMA
Panama

CANAL ZONE (U.S.)

Miles

0 1000

Inset map

Caribbean (Panama) Sea

Colón (Panama)

Cristóbal (U.S.)

CANAL ZONE

GAILLARD CUT

(PANAMA)
(U.S.)
(PAN.)

Panama
Balboa

Gulf of Panama

Miles
0 20

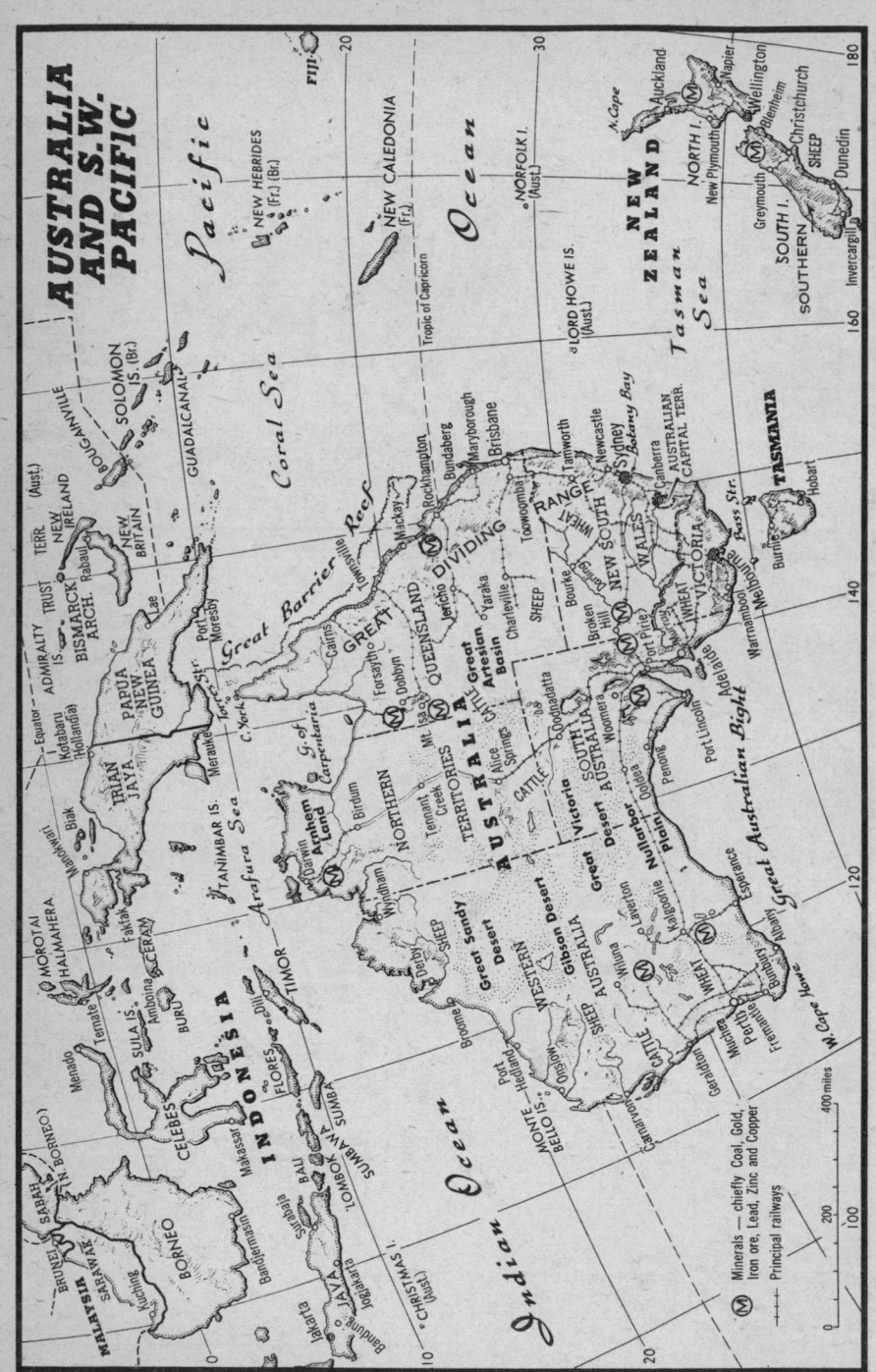

Longitude and Latitude of Foreign Cities
and Time Corresponding to 12:00 Noon, Eastern Standard Time

City	Long.	Lat.	Time	City	Long.	Lat.	Time
Aberdeen, Scotland	2 9 w	57 9 n	5:00 p.m.‡	Lima, Peru	77 2 w	12 0 s	12:00 noon
Adelaide, Australia	138 36 e	34 55 s	2:30 a.m.*	Lisbon, Portugal	9 9 w	38 44 n	5:00 p.m.
Algiers, Algeria	3 0 e	36 50 n	6:00 p.m.	Liverpool, England	3 0 w	53 25 n	5:00 p.m.‡
Amsterdam, Netherlands	4 53 e	52 22 n	6:00 p.m.	London, England	0 5 w	51 32 n	5:00 p.m.‡
Ankara, Turkey	32 55 e	39 55 n	7:00 p.m.	Lyons, France	4 50 e	45 45 n	6:00 p.m.
Asunción, Paraguay	57 40 w	25 15 s	1:00 p.m.	Madrid, Spain	3 42 w	40 26 n	6:00 p.m.
Athens, Greece	23 43 e	37 58 n	7:00 p.m.	Makassar, Indonesia	119 30 e	5 9 s	1:00 a.m.*
Auckland, New Zealand	174 45 e	36 52 s	5:00 a.m.*	Manchester, England	2 15 w	53 30 n	5:00 p.m.‡
Bangkok, Thailand	100 30 e	13 45 n	0:00 a.m.*	Manila, Philippines	120 57 e	14 35 n	1:00 a.m.*
Barcelona, Spain	2 9 e	41 23 n	6:00 p.m.	Marseilles, France	5 20 e	43 20 n	6:00 p.m.
Belém, Brazil	48 29 w	1 28 s	2:00 p.m.	Mazatlán, Mexico	106 25 w	23 12 n	10:00 a.m.
Belfast, Northern Ireland	5 56 w	54 37 n	5:00 p.m.‡	Mecca, Saudi Arabia	39 45 e	21 29 n	8:00 p.m.
Belgrade, Yugoslavia	20 32 e	44 52 n	6:00 p.m.	Melbourne, Australia	144 58 e	37 47 s	3:00 a.m.*
Berlin, Germany	13 25 e	52 30 n	6:00 p.m.	Mexico City, Mexico	99 7 w	19 26 n	11:00 a.m.
Birmingham, England	1 55 w	52 25 n	5:00 p.m.‡	Milan, Italy	9 10 e	45 27 n	6:00 p.m.
Bogotá, Colombia	74 15 w	4 32 n	12:00 noon	Montevideo, Uruguay	56 10 w	34 53 s	2:00 p.m.
Bombay, India	72 48 e	19 0 n	10:30 p.m.	Moscow, U.S.S.R.	37 36 e	55 45 n	8:00 p.m.
Bordeaux, France	0 31 w	44 50 n	6:00 p.m.	Munich, Germany	11 35 e	48 8 n	6:00 p.m.
Bremen, Germany	8 49 e	53 5 n	6:00 p.m.	Nagasaki, Japan	129 57 e	32 48 n	2:00 a.m.*
Brisbane, Australia	153 8 e	27 29 s	3:00 a.m.*	Nagoya, Japan	136 56 e	35 7 n	2:00 a.m.*
Bristol, England	2 35 w	51 28 n	5:00 p.m.‡	Nairobi, Kenya	36 55 s	1 25 s	8:00 p.m.
Brussels, Belgium	4 22 e	50 52 n	6:00 p.m.	Nanking, China	118 53 e	32 3 n	1:00 a.m.*
Bucharest, Romania	26 7 e	44 25 n	7:00 p.m.	Naples, Italy	14 15 e	40 50 n	6:00 p.m.
Budapest, Hungary	19 5 e	47 30 n	6:00 p.m.	Newcastle-on-Tyne, Eng.	1 37 w	54 58 n	5:00 p.m.‡
Buenos Aires, Argentina	58 22 w	34 35 s	2:00 p.m.	Odessa, U.S.S.R.	30 48 e	46 27 n	8:00 p.m.
Cairo, Egypt	31 21 e	30 2 n	7:00 p.m.	Osaka, Japan	135 30 e	34 32 n	2:00 a.m.*
Calcutta, India	88 24 e	22 34 n	10:30 p.m.	Oslo, Norway	10 42 e	59 57 n	6:00 p.m.
Canton, China	113 15 e	23 7 n	1:00 a.m.*	Panama City, Panama	79 32 w	8 58 n	12:00 noon
Cape Town, South Africa	18 22 e	33 55 s	7:00 p.m.	Paramaribo, Surinam	55 15 w	5 45 n	1:30 p.m.
Caracas, Venezuela	67 2 w	10 28 n	12:30 p.m.	Paris, France	2 20 e	48 48 n	6:00 p.m.
Cayenne, French Guiana	52 18 w	4 49 n	1:00 p.m.	Peking, China	116 25 e	39 55 n	1:00 a.m.*
Chihuahua, Mexico	106 5 w	28 37 n	11:00 a.m.	Perth, Australia	115 52 e	31 57 s	1:00 a.m.*
Chungking, China	106 34 e	29 46 n	1:00 a.m.*	Plymouth, England	4 5 w	50 25 n	5:00 p.m.‡
Copenhagen, Denmark	12 34 e	55 40 n	6:00 p.m.	Port Moresby, Papua New Guinea	147 8 e	9 25 s	3:00 a.m.*
Córdoba, Argentina	64 10 w	31 28 s	2:00 p.m.	Prague, Czechoslovakia	14 26 e	50 5 n	6:00 p.m.
Dakar, Senegal	17 28 w	14 40 n	5:00 p.m.	Rangoon, Burma	96 0 e	16 50 n	11:30 p.m.
Darwin, Australia	130 51 e	12 28 s	2:30 a.m.*	Reykjavik, Iceland	21 58 w	64 4 n	4:00 p.m.
Djibouti, Afars-Issas	43 3 e	11 30 n	8:00 p.m.	Rio de Janeiro, Brazil	43 12 w	22 57 s	2:00 p.m.
Dublin, Ireland	6 15 w	53 20 n	5:00 p.m.	Rome, Italy	12 27 e	41 54 n	6:00 p.m.
Durban, South Africa	30 53 e	29 53 s	7:00 p.m.	Salvador, Brazil	38 27 w	12 56 s	2:00 p.m.
Edinburgh, Scotland	3 10 w	55 55 n	5:00 p.m.‡	Santiago, Chile	70 45 w	33 28 s	1:00 p.m.
Frankfurt am Main, Ger	8 41 e	50 7 n	6:00 p.m.	São Paulo, Brazil	46 31 w	23 31 s	2:00 p.m.
Georgetown, Guyana	58 15 w	6 45 n	1:15 p.m.	Shanghai, China	121 28 e	31 10 n	1:00 a.m.*
Glasgow, Scotland	4 15 w	55 50 n	5:00 p.m.‡	Singapore, Singapore	103 55 e	1 14 n	0:30 a.m.*
Guatemala City, Guatemala	90 31 w	14 37 n	11:00 a.m.	Sofia, Bulgaria	23 20 e	42 40 n	7:00 p.m.
Guayaquil, Ecuador	79 56 w	2 10 s	12:00 noon	Stockholm, Sweden	18 3 e	59 17 n	6:00 p.m.
Hamburg, Germany	10 2 e	53 33 n	6:00 p.m.	Sydney, Australia	151 0 e	34 0 s	3:00 a.m.*
Hammerfest, Norway	23 38 e	70 38 n	6:00 p.m.	Tananarive, Madagascar	47 33 e	18 50 s	8:00 p.m.
Havana, Cuba	82 23 w	23 8 n	12:00 noon	Teheran, Iran	51 45 e	35 45 n	8:30 p.m.
Helsinki, Finland	25 0 e	60 10 n	7:00 p.m.	Tokyo, Japan	139 45 e	35 40 n	2:00 a.m.*
Hobart, Tasmania	147 19 e	42 52 s	3:00 a.m.*	Tripoli, Libya	13 12 e	32 57 n	7:00 p.m.
Iquique, Chile	70 7 w	20 10 s	1:00 p.m.	Venice, Italy	12 20 e	45 26 n	6:00 p.m.
Irkutsk, U.S.S.R.	104 20 e	52 30 n	1:00 a.m.*	Veracruz, Mexico	96 10 w	19 10 n	11:00 a.m.
Jakarta, Indonesia	106 48 e	6 16 s	0:30 a.m.*	Vienna, Austria	16 20 e	48 14 n	6:00 p.m.
Johannesburg, South Africa	28 4 e	26 12 s	7:00 p.m.	Vladivostok, U.S.S.R.	132 0 e	43 10 n	3:00 a.m.*
Kingston, Jamaica	76 49 w	17 59 n	12:00 noon	Warsaw, Poland	21 0 e	52 14 n	6:00 p.m.
Kinshasa, Zaire	15 17 e	4 18 s	6:00 p.m.	Wellington, New Zealand	174 47 e	41 17 s	5:00 a.m.*
La Paz, Bolivia	68 22 w	16 27 s	1:00 p.m.	Zürich, Switzerland	8 31 e	47 21 n	6:00 p.m.
Leeds, England	1 30 w	53 45 n	5:00 p.m.‡				
Leningrad, U.S.S.R.	30 18 e	59 56 n	8:00 p.m.				

* On the following day. ‡ In 1968, the United Kingdom began the use of British Standard Time for a three-year test period. This time, equivalent to Central European Time, was an hour ahead of Greenwich Mean Time and six hours ahead of Eastern Standard Time. In November, 1971, the U.K. returned to Greenwich Mean Time, which is five hours ahead of Eastern Standard Time.

Longitude and Latitude of U. S. and Canadian Cities
and Time Corresponding to 12:00 Noon, Eastern Standard Time

City	Long. w.	Lat. n.	Time*	City	Long. w.	Lat. n.	Time*
	° ′	° ′			° ′	° ′	
Albany, N. Y.	73 45	42 40	12:00 noon	Memphis, Tenn.	90 3	35 9	11:00 a.m.
Amarillo, Tex.	101 50	35 11	11:00 a.m.	Miami, Fla.	80 12	25 46	12:00 noon
Anchorage, Alaska	149 54	61 13	7:00 a.m.	Milwaukee, Wis.	87 55	43 2	11:00 a.m.
Atlanta, Ga.	84 23	33 45	12:00 noon	Minneapolis, Minn.	93 14	44 59	11:00 a.m.
Atlantic City, N. J.	74 25	39 22	12:00 noon	Mobile, Ala.	88 3	30 42	11:00 a.m.
Austin, Nev.	117 4	39 29	9:00 a.m.	Montgomery, Ala.	86 18	32 21	11:00 a.m.
Baker, Ore.	117 50	44 47	9:00 a.m.	Montpelier, Vt.	72 32	44 15	12:00 noon
Baltimore, Md.	76 38	39 18	12:00 noon	Montreal, Que.	73 35	45 30	12:00 noon
Bangor, Me.	68 47	44 48	12:00 noon	Moose Jaw, Sask.	105 31	50 37	10:00 a.m.
Birmingham, Ala.	86 50	33 30	11:00 a.m.	Nashville, Tenn.	86 47	36 10	11:00 a.m.
Bismarck, N. D.	100 47	46 48	11:00 a.m.	Needles, Calif.	114 36	34 50	9:00 a.m.
Boise, Idaho	116 13	43 36	10:00 a.m.	Nelson, B. C.	117 17	49 30	9:00 a.m.
Boston, Mass.	71 5	42 21	12:00 noon	New Haven, Conn.	72 55	41 19	12:00 noon
Buffalo, N. Y.	78 50	42 55	12:00 noon	New Orleans, La.	90 4	29 57	11:00 a.m.
Calgary, Alberta	114 1	51 1	10:00 a.m.	New York, N. Y.	73 58	40 47	12:00 noon
Carlsbad, N. M.	104 15	32 26	10:00 a.m.	Nogales, Ariz.	110 56	31 21	10:00 a.m.
Charleston, S. C.	79 56	32 47	12:00 noon	Nome, Alaska	165 30	64 25	6:00 a.m.
Charleston, W. Va.	81 38	38 21	12:00 noon	North Platte, Neb.	100 46	41 8	11:00 a.m.
Charlotte, N. C.	80 50	35 14	12:00 noon	Oklahoma City, Okla.	97 28	35 26	11:00 a.m.
Cheyenne, Wyo.	104 52	41 9	10:00 a.m.	Ottawa, Ont.	75 43	45 24	12:00 noon
Chicago, Ill.	87 37	41 50	11:00 a.m.	Philadelphia, Pa.	75 10	39 57	12:00 noon
Cincinnati, Ohio	84 30	39 8	12:00 noon	Phoenix, Ariz.	112 4	33 29	10:00 a.m.
Cleveland, Ohio	81 37	41 28	12:00 noon	Pierre, S. D.	100 21	44 22	11:00 a.m.
Columbia, S. C.	81 2	34 0	12:00 noon	Pittsburgh, Pa.	79 57	40 27	12:00 noon
Columbus, Ohio	83 1	40 0	12:00 noon	Port Arthur, Ont.	89 17	48 30	12:00 noon
Dallas, Tex.	96 46	32 46	11:00 a.m.	Portland, Me.	70 15	43 40	12:00 noon
Denver, Colo.	105 0	39 45	10:00 a.m.	Portland, Ore.	122 41	45 31	9:00 a.m.
Des Moines, Iowa	93 37	41 35	11:00 a.m.	Providence, R. I.	71 24	41 50	12:00 noon
Detroit, Mich.	83 3	42 20	12:00 noon	Quebec, Que.	71 11	46 49	12:00 noon
Dubuque, Iowa	90 40	42 31	11:00 a.m.	Raleigh, N. C.	78 39	35 46	12:00 noon
Duluth, Minn.	92 5	46 49	11:00 a.m.	Reno, Nev.	119 49	39 30	9:00 a.m.
Eastport, Me.	67 0	44 54	12:00 noon	Richfield, Utah	112 5	38 46	10:00 a.m.
El Centro, Calif.	115 33	32 38	9:00 a.m.	Richmond, Va.	77 29	37 33	12:00 noon
El Paso, Tex.	106 29	31 46	11:00 a.m.	Roanoke, Va.	79 57	37 17	12:00 noon
Eugene, Ore.	123 5	44 3	9:00 a.m.	Sacramento, Calif.	121 30	38 35	9:00 a.m.
Fargo, N. D.	96 48	46 52	11:00 a.m.	St. John, N. B.	66 10	45 18	1:00 p.m.
Flagstaff, Ariz.	111 41	35 13	10:00 a.m.	St. Louis, Mo.	90 12	38 35	11:00 a.m.
Fresno, Calif.	119 48	36 44	9:00 a.m.	Salmon, Idaho	113 54	45 11	10:00 a.m.
Garden City, Kan.	100 53	37 58	10:00 a.m.	Salt Lake City, Utah	111 54	40 46	10:00 a.m.
Grand Junction, Colo.	108 33	39 5	10:00 a.m.	San Antonio, Tex.	98 33	29 23	11:00 a.m.
Grand Rapids, Mich.	85 40	42 58	12:00 noon	San Diego, Calif.	117 10	32 42	9:00 a.m.
Havre, Mont.	109 43	48 33	10:00 a.m.	San Francisco, Calif.	122 26	37 47	9:00 a.m.
Helena, Mont.	112 2	46 35	10:00 a.m.	San Juan, P. R.	66 10	18 30	1:00 p m.
Honolulu, Hawaii	157 50	21 18	7:00 a.m.	Santa Fe, N. M.	105 57	35 41	10:00 a.m.
Hoquiam, Wash.	123 54	46 59	9:00 a.m.	Sault Ste. Marie, Mich.	84 21	46 30	11:00 a.m.
Hot Springs, Ark.	93 3	34 31	11:00 a.m.	Savannah, Ga.	81 5	32 5	12:00 noon
Idaho Falls, Idaho	112 1	43 30	10:00 a.m.	Scranton, Pa.	75 39	41 24	12:00 noon
Indianapolis, Ind.	86 10	39 46	12:00 noon	Seattle, Wash.	122 20	47 37	9:00 a.m.
Jackson, Miss.	90 12	32 20	11:00 a.m.	Shreveport, La.	93 42	32 28	11:00 a.m.
Jacksonville, Fla.	81 40	30 22	12:00 noon	Sioux Falls, S. D.	96 44	43 33	11:00 a.m.
Juneau, Alaska	134 24	58 18	9:00 a.m.	Sitka, Alaska	135 15	57 10	9:00 a.m.
Kansas City, Mo.	94 35	39 6	11:00 a.m.	Spokane, Wash.	117 26	47 40	9:00 a.m.
Key West, Fla.	81 48	24 33	12:00 noon	Springfield, Ill.	89 38	39 48	11:00 a.m.
Kingston, Ont.	76 30	44 15	12:00 noon	Springfield, Mass.	72 34	42 6	12:00 noon
Klamath Falls, Ore.	121 44	42 10	9:00 a.m.	Springfield, Mo.	93 17	37 13	11:00 a.m.
Knoxville, Tenn.	83 56	35 57	12:00 noon	Syracuse, N. Y.	76 8	43 2	12:00 noon
Lander, Wyo.	108 40	42 50	10:00 a.m.	Tampa, Fla.	82 27	27 57	12:00 noon
Las Vegas, Nev.	115 12	36 10	9:00 a.m.	Toronto, Ont.	79 24	43 40	12:00 noon
Lewiston, Idaho	117 2	46 24	9:00 a.m.	Trinidad, Colo.	104 30	37 10	10:00 a.m.
Lincoln, Neb.	96 40	40 50	11:00 a.m.	Victoria, B. C.	123 21	48 25	9:00 a.m.
London, Ont.	81 34	43 2	12:00 noon	Watertown, N. Y.	75 55	43 58	12:00 noon
Los Angeles, Calif.	118 15	34 3	9:00 a.m.	Wichita, Kan.	97 17	37 43	11:00 a.m.
Louisville, Ky.	85 46	38 15	12:00 noon	Wilmington, N. C.	77 57	34 14	12:00 noon
Manchester, N. H.	71 30	43 0	12:00 noon	Winnipeg, Man.	97 7	49 54	11:00 a.m.

WORLD GEOGRAPHY AND MISCELLANEOUS

Explorations and Discoveries

(All years are A.D. unless B.C. is specified.)

Africa

Country or place	Event	Explorer or discoverer	Date
Sierra Leone	Visited	Hanno, Carthaginian seaman	c. 520 B.C.
Congo River	Mouth discovered	Diogo Cão, Portuguese	c. 1484
Cape of Good Hope	Doubled	Bartholomeu Diaz, Portuguese	1488
Gambia River	Explored	Mungo Park, Scottish explorer	1795
Sahara Desert	Crossed	Dixon Denham and Hugh Clapperton, English explorers	1822–23
Zambezi River	Discovered	David Livingstone, Scottish explorer	1851
Sudan	Explored	Heinrich Barth, German explorer	1852–55
Victoria Falls	Discovered	Livingstone	1855
Lake Tanganyika	Discovered	Richard Burton and John Speke, British explorers	1858
Congo River	Traced	Sir Henry M. Stanley, British explorer	1877

Asia

Country or place	Event	Explorer or discoverer	Date
Punjab (India)	Visited	Alexander the Great	327 B.C
China	Visited	Marco Polo, Italian traveler	c. 1272
Tibet	Visited	Odoric of Pordenone, Italian monk	c. 1325
Southern China	Explored	Niccolò dei Conti, Venetian traveler	c. 1440
India	Visited (Cape route)	Vasco da Gama, Portuguese navigator	1498
Japan	Visited	St. Francis Xavier of Spain	1549
Arabia	Explored	Carsten Niebuhr, German explorer	1762
China	Explored	Ferdinand Richthofen, German scientist	1868
Mongolia	Explored	Nikolai M. Przhevalsky, Russian explorer	1870–73
Central Asia	Explored	Sven Hedin, Swedish scientist	1890–1908

Europe

Country or place	Event	Explorer or discoverer	Date
Shetland Islands	Visited	Pytheas of Massilia (Marseille)	c. 325 B.C.
North Cape	Rounded	Ottar, Norwegian explorer	c. 870
Iceland	Colonized	Norwegian noblemen	c. 890–900

North America

Country or place	Event	Explorer or discoverer	Date
Greenland	Colonized	Eric the Red, Norwegian	c. 985
Labrador; Nova Scotia (?)	Discovered	Leif Ericson, Norse explorer	1000
West Indies	Discovered	Christopher Columbus, Italian	1492
North America	Coast discovered	Giovanni Caboto (John Cabot), for British	1497
Pacific Ocean	Discovered	Vasco Núñez de Balboa, Spanish explorer	1513
Florida	Explored	Ponce de León, Spanish explorer	1513
Mexico	Conquered	Hernando Cortés, Spanish adventurer	1519–21
St. Lawrence River	Discovered	Jacques Cartier, French navigator	1534
Southwest U. S.	Explored	Francisco Coronado, Spanish explorer	1540–42
Colorado River	Discovered	Hernando de Alarcón, Spanish explorer	1540
Mississippi River	Discovered	Hernando de Soto, Spanish explorer	1541
Frobisher Bay	Discovered	Martin Frobisher, English seaman	1576
Maine Coast	Explored	Samuel de Champlain, French explorer	1604
Jamestown, Va.	Settled	John Smith, English colonist	1607
Hudson River	Explored	Henry Hudson, English navigator	1609
Hudson Bay (Canada)	Discovered	Hudson	1610

Country or place	Event	Explorer or discoverer	Date
Baffin Bay	Discovered	William Baffin, English navigator	1616
Lake Michigan	Navigated	Jean Nicolet, French explorer	1634
Arkansas River	Discovered	Jacques Marquette and Louis Jolliet, French explorers	1673
Mississippi River	Explored	Sieur de La Salle, French explorer	1682
Bering Strait	Discovered	Vitus Bering, Danish explorer	1728
Alaska	Discovered	Bering	1741
Mackenzie River (Canada)	Discovered	Sir Alexander Mackenzie, Scottish-Canadian explorer	1789
Northwest U. S.	Explored	Meriwether Lewis and William Clark	1804–06
Northeast Passage (Arctic Ocean)	Navigated	Nils Nordenskjöld, Swedish explorer	1879
Greenland	Explored	Robert Peary, American explorer	1892
Northwest Passage	Navigated	Roald Amundsen, Norwegian explorer	1906

South America

Continent	Visited	Columbus, Italian	1498
Brazil	Discovered	Pedro Alvarez Cabral, Portuguese	1500
Peru	Conquered	Francisco Pizarro, Spanish explorer	1532–33
Amazon River	Explored	Francisco Orellana, Spanish explorer	1541
Cape Horn	Discovered	Willem C. Schouten, Dutch navigator	1615

Oceania

New Guinea	Visited	Jorge de Menezes, Portuguese explorer	1526
Australia	Visited	Abel Janszoon Tasman, Dutch navigator	1642
Tasmania	Discovered		
Australia	Explored	John M. Sturt, English explorer	1828
Australia	Explored	Robert Burke and William Wills, Australian explorers	1861
New Zealand	Sighted (and named)	Tasman	1642
New Zealand	Visited	James Cook, English navigator	1769

Arctic, Antarctic, and Miscellaneous

Ocean exploration	Expedition	Magellan's ships circled globe	1519–22
Galápagos Islands	Visited	Diego de Rivadeneira, Spanish captain	1535
Spitsbergen	Visited	Willem Barents, Dutch navigator	1596
Antarctic Circle	Crossed	James Cook, English navigator	1773
Antarctica	Discovered	Nathaniel Palmer, U. S. whaler (archipelago) and Fabian Gottlieb von Bellingshausen, Russian admiral (mainland)	1820–21
Antarctica	Explored	Charles Wilkes, American explorer	1840
North Pole	Reached	Peary, American explorer	1909
South Pole	Reached	Amundsen, Norwegian explorer	1911

Ancient Empires

The *Egyptian* and *Babylonian* empires, Near Eastern civilizations whose cultures mark the beginning of written history, had their origins in the nebulous period of ancient history prior to the year 4000 B.C. They developed rapidly in the fertile river valleys of the Nile in Egypt and the Tigris-Euphrates in Mesopotamia after the discovery of metals and the invention of writing. Their governments were all-powerful, with the people subjugated and without political rights. The Egyptians regarded their king as a god. In Babylon, the ruler

was a priest-king, earthly representative of the gods. Nevertheless, these Near East cultures made great contributions to the eternal march of man; they advanced the ways of making and doing things, produced the earliest literature, developed the principles of law (the code of Hammurabi, Babylonian king of the 18th [or possibly 17th] century B.C., the oldest code of law) and science.

The influence of Babylon and Egypt was felt in the rise of the Semitic tribes of Syria, the Hittites in Asia Minor, and the people of the Aegean region. Between the years 1200 and 800 B.C., the small Syrian states grew to great power and then were overwhelmed by the great empire of the *Assyrians,* the warlike peasants of the Tigris valley, who took the lessons learned from the Babylonians and spread that culture over their domains. The Assyrians, like the Egyptians and the Babylonians, in turn fell under the power of the *Persian* kings in the century between 600 and 500 B.C. By 525 B.C., the Persian Empire extended from India to Egypt.

The lessons learned by these early Near Eastern civilizations were transmitted to *Greece,* which developed its illustrious empire in the Aegean region, after the inhabitants of the island of Crete had absorbed the Egyptian culture. The mainland Greeks overthrew the Cretans and in turn were succeeded by the Doric Greeks, who spread their culture across the Aegean, the Asia Minor coast, and into the Mediterranean and Black Sea regions. The characteristic Greek political institution was the city-state, first ruled by kings and often temporary monarchical tyrannies, and finally by the participation of free citizens. Literature and the arts flourished, and by the 5th century B.C., when Athens became the great city of the Greeks, drama had risen to full maturity with the great tragedies of Sophocles and Euripides and the comedies of Aristophanes. Architecture and art advanced apace. The Greeks, learning much from their Egyptian teachers, produced such superb buildings as the Parthenon and created amazingly beautiful statues through the use of living models. Religion, which was closely linked with art, also flourished, as did the development of philosophy, under Socrates, Plato and Aristotle. Wars weakened the city-states, and they fell to Alexander the Great in the 4th century B.C.

Last among the great ancient empires was the *Roman,* which developed in Italy and gained control over the Mediterranean region after absorbing the culture of Greece and combining with it new principles of law and art and teaching this new learning to the West. The development of the Roman civilization began in 510 or 509 B.C., when the peoples on the peninsula of Italy freed themselves from the rule of the Etruscans. The Romans, with a republican form of government, speedily conquered Italy and the Mediterranean region, and the Roman governors became men of great wealth, corrupting the city-state system and making it a graft-ridden machine of exploitation. The failure of the government to check this self-seeking influence brought on a revolt which resulted eventually in the rise of Julius Caesar to dictatorship in 46–44 B.C. Caesar's murder in the Senate at Rome was followed in 27 B.C. by the establishment of the one-man rule of Augustus over the Roman Empire. Legal practices were developed and became the foundations of modern law. This great ancient civilization began to crumble in the third century.

Universities—Medieval and Modern

Universities, in the modern sense of the term, sprang up in the 12th and 13th centuries in response to the resurgence of learning that preceded the Renaissance in Europe. Procedure at the early universities was informal, with students gathering at some place in a city to listen to a preeminent teacher. There were no campuses, buildings or endowments. Actually, the term "university" once meant a guild or corporation; there were, in the medieval period, "universities" of bootmakers, weavers, etc. Thus the university of learning was similar in organization to the guilds. The students filled the role of apprentices and the teachers were the masters.

The first European university was that of *Salerno* in the 9th century, when it was known as a school of medicine. By the 11th century, it had become one of the most famous medical schools of Europe.

University of Bologna. Originated in the 12th century as student guilds for protection against the merchants and citizens of Bologna who had raised prices of food and lodging. It was famous for its legal scholars. The students were organized into two guilds and exercised a great deal of authority over the administration.

Other Italian universities famed in the Middle Ages included those at *Arezzo, Ferrara, Florence, Modena, Naples, Padua, Pavia, Perugia, Siena* and *Vicenza.*

University of Paris. Originated between 1150 and 1170 in a cathedral school on the Ile de la Cité, it was later moved to the left (south) bank of the Seine, although it remained under the authority of the chancellor of Notre Dame. It developed into the most famous continental center of learning of its day. Its four principal schools were theology, medicine, law and arts. By the 14th century, the university had some 40 colleges, of which the *Sorbonne* became the most celebrated.

The universities of Paris and Bologna had a marked influence in the subsequent creation of other university centers. About 1167–68 there was a migration of students from Paris to *Oxford* (founded in the 12th century) and about 1210, from Oxford to *Cambridge* (also founded in the 12th century).

Other famous universities of the Middle Ages include the *University of Toulouse*

(1233), *Salamanca* (1243), *Seville* (1254), *Orléans* (1305), *Valladolid* (1346), *Prague* (1347), *Kraków* (1364), *Vienna* (1364), *Erfurt* (1379), *Heidelberg* (1385), *Cologne* (1388), *Leipzig* (1409), *Rostock* (1419) and *Louvain* (1426).

The Renaissance

The Renaissance gave fresh impetus to the universities of Europe. In France three of importance arose in the 15th century —the *University of Aix* (1409, Provence), the *University of Poitiers* (1431) and the *University of Caen* (1437).

Other French institutions of note that arose in this era were at *Bordeaux* (1441), *Valence* (1452), *Nantes* (1463) and *Bourges* (1465). New European universities were also founded at *Trier* (1450), *Freiburg* (1455), *Ingolstadt* (1459), *Basel* (1460), *Budapest* (1475), *Mainz* (1476), *Uppsala* (1477), *Tübingen* (1477), *Copenhagen* (1479), *Wittenberg* (1502), *Frankfurt an der Oder* (1506) and *Coimbra* (1537).

St. Andrews, founded in 1411, was the first university in Scotland. Others were the *University of Glasgow* (1453) and the *University of Aberdeen* (1494). The *University of Edinburgh* was established as a college in the post-Reformation period (1582). In Ireland, *Trinity College* was founded in Dublin in 1591. The earliest Dutch university, *Leyden,* was founded in 1575.

Reformation and Post-Reformation

Until the Reformation, most of the institutions of higher learning in Europe were under the tutelage of the Catholic Church. After 1520, however, many established universities declared their independence of the Church. Cromwell's rule brought about new scholastic methods at both Oxford and Cambridge and the establishment of new colleges thoroughly imbued with Protestantism.

But the first Protestant university was that of *Marburg,* Germany, founded in 1527. Other Protestant universities were: *Königsberg* (1544); *Jena* (1558); *Helmstedt* (1575); *Altdorf* (1575); *Giessen* (1607); *Strasbourg* (1621); *Halle* (1693).

18th, 19th, and 20th Centuries

Among the more famous institutions in this era was *Göttingen* (1736), whose school of history became celebrated

throughout Europe. Others were: *Erlangen* (1743); *Berlin* (1809); *Lemberg* (Lwów) (1816); *Bonn* (1818); *Helsingfors* (1828); the *National University* at Athens (1837); *Bucharest* (1864); *Tokyo* (1877); *Sofia* (1888) and *Kyoto* (1897).

Among the more famous British universities established in the 19th and 20th centuries were the *University of London* (1828); *Manchester* (1851); the *Mason University College* in Birmingham, later *Birmingham University* (1900); *Liverpool* (1903); *Leeds* (1904); and the *University of Sheffield* (1905). The *University of Wales* (1893) is composed of the colleges of Aberystwyth, Bangor, Cardiff and Swansea.

There are many large and important universities in the British Commonwealth. In Canada, the famous *McGill University* in Montreal was founded in 1821. Others are the *University of Toronto* (1827); *Queens University* at Kingston, Ont. (1841); *Laval University,* Quebec (1852); *Dalhousie,* Halifax (1818), and *Montreal University* (1878).

The early universities in India were patterned after London University rather than on the Oxford-Cambridge style, and were purely examining institutions. *Calcutta, Bombay* and *Madras* universities were founded in 1857 as examining bodies.

In Australia, the state plays an important role in the development of universities. The *University of Melbourne* (1853) has the largest enrollment. Among the others are *Adelaide* (1874); *Tasmania* (1890); *Queensland* (1909); *Sydney* (1850), and *Western Australia* (1911).

There are also many well-endowed universities in New Zealand and other parts of the Commonwealth.

By 1800, Russia had only three universities—*Vilna* (1578), *Dorpat* (1632) and *Moscow* (1755). Other institutions developed later were the *University of Kharkov* (1804); *Kazan* (1804); *Warsaw,* now Polish (originally established 1816, but closed 1832–69); *St. Petersburg* (1819); *St. Vladimir* in Kiev (1835); *Odessa* (1865) and *Tomsk,* in Siberia (1888). The building of universities after the Revolution of 1917 was spurred by the Soviet government.

In China, the growth of universities was hampered by the chaotic state of the government in the 1900's, the recurring civil wars and the conflict with Japan.

The United States

Universities in the United States marched in step with the progress of the nation. The early settlers brought a heritage of European culture which they planted in New England soil. The first university in the country was started as *Harvard College* in 1636, with an endowment totaling 800 pounds. Harvard was to become probably the most famous of the

American universities.

The *College of William and Mary* (1693) was the second institution of higher learning established in the colonies. Others started during the colonial period (current names only) are: *Yale* (1701); *University of Pennsylvania* (1740); *Princeton* (1746); *Washington and Lee* (1749); *Columbia* (1754); *Brown* (1764); *Rutgers*

(1766) and *Dartmouth* (1769).

After the Revolution of 1776, the state tax-supported university was established. The *University of Virginia* (1819) was a notable early example of this type.

Colleges for women grew up in the second quarter of the 19th century. Among these are: *Mt. Holyoke* (1837); *Elmira* (1855); *Vassar* (1861); *Wells* (1868);

Hunter (1870); *Wellesley* (1870); *Smith* (1871) and *Bryn Mawr* (1885).

In the latter part of the 19th century, universities established by private endowments arose. Typical of these are: *Cornell* (1865), which is also a land-grant institution; *Johns Hopkins* (1876); *Stanford* (1885) and the *University of Chicago* (1891).

Libraries of the World

Europe and Asia

Among the great libraries of the world, the *British Museum* remains in the first rank with more than 6,000,000 printed volumes and 60,000 manuscripts. It contains such outstanding treasures as the *Codex Alexandrinus* and the *Codex Sinaiticus* of the Bible, the best collection of Greek papyri from Egypt, and vast collections of original historical manuscripts of incalculable value. Some 150,000 volumes were destroyed in air raids during World War II, but many were replaced later.

One of the finest libraries in the world is the *Bibliothèque Nationale* in Paris, which has approximately 6,000,000 printed works.

The *State Library* in Berlin, founded in 1659–61, was amalgamated in 1947 with the library of the University of Berlin. Prior to World War II, the State Library had 2,850,000 volumes; the new combined library has 1,500,000. Other large libraries in West Germany are those of the Universities of Bonn (950,000 volumes); Erlangen (1,200,000); Freiburg (920,000); Göttingen (1,615,000); Hamburg (1,000,000); Heidelberg (1,600,000); Cologne (1,200,000); Munich (915,000); and Tübingen (1,350,000).

The *Nationalbibliothek* in Vienna has about 1,500,000 volumes, a large collection of papyri, and a notable theater and motion picture collection.

While not as large as some of the European state libraries, the *Biblioteca Apostolica Vaticana* in Rome has many priceless old manuscripts bequeathed to the Vatican over the centuries, including the *Codex Vaticanus* of the 4th century.

Three of the more important Italian libraries are *Biblioteca Nazionale* in Naples, with 1,515,000 volumes; the *Biblioteca Nazionale Centrale* in Florence, with 3,600,000 volumes; and the *Biblioteca Nazionale Centrale* in Rome, with 2,000,000 volumes.

Other large European libraries are *Bibliothèque Royale* in Brussels (2,000,000 volumes); the *Biblioteca Nacional* in Madrid (1,500,000); the *University Library* in Am-

sterdam (2,000,000); and the *Royal Library* in Stockholm (900,000). The *Lenin State Library* in Moscow is said to contain 15,000,000 volumes (a figure that probably includes periodicals), besides many collections of valuable historical documents. The library of Moscow State University has 6,000,000 volumes. In Leningrad, the *Public Library* claims 10,000,000 volumes, and the *Library of the Academy of Sciences* some 8,000,000. The *Leningrad State University Library* contains 3,360,180 volumes. There are said to be 382,000 libraries in the U.S.S.R. with a total of 1,890,000,000 volumes.

In the Far East, the most extensive libraries are found in Japan, although war damage in 1944–45 was severe. In Tokyo, the *National Diet Library* (formerly the *Imperial Library*) was organized in 1948. With its 30 branches, it contains more than 4,100,000 volumes. The *University Library* in Kyoto has 2,291,600 volumes.

The oldest national libraries in South America are those of Argentina and Brazil, each founded in 1810; the former has about 600,000 volumes, the latter 1,000,000.

The United States and Canada

The earliest libraries in the colonial era were privately owned, although in 1731 Benjamin Franklin projected the first subscription library in Philadelphia. Endowments helped to set up many of the large libraries, although many of these institutions are now receiving state or municipal support.

The largest library in the United States is the *Library of Congress*, established in 1800 by Congress. Its extensive collections, totaling 72,466,926 volumes in 1973, are universal in scope. They include more than 16,466,899 books and pamphlets in a multitude of languages and manuscript collections of more than 30,000,000 items relating to American history. The Library extends services to members of Congress and other government departments, and also offers excellent facilities for persons engaged in scholarly research.

The *New York Public Library*, with more

than 8,426,600 volumes, 9,000,000 manuscripts and 310,000 maps in 1974, is the largest public library in the United States.

The growth of libraries attached to colleges and universities in the United States has been phenomenal, and some of the university libraries rank with the largest in the country. Among these, as listed by the Association of Research Libraries for 1974–75 are Harvard, 9,206,670 volumes; Yale, 6,618,848; Illinois, 5,509,926; Michigan, 4,668,188; Columbia, 4,661,913; California, Berkeley, 4,649,533; Cornell, 4,272,959; Stanford, 4,092,362; Indiana, 3,891,379; Texas, 3,726,134; Chicago, 3,622,285; Minnesota, 3,559,511.

Others are California, Los Angeles, 3,519,424; Ohio State, 3,033,132; Wisconsin, 2,793,300; Princeton, 2,715,458; Pennsylvania, 2,640,013; Duke, 2,622,167; Northwestern, 2,474,852; New York University, 2,456,226; Washington (St. Louis), 2,187,917; North Carolina, 2,125,640; Michigan State, 2,102,452; Johns Hopkins, 2,049,722; Virginia, 2,006,454.

The *American Library Directory* for 1976-77 will list approximately 26,000 libraries in the United States and Canada, including some 10,000 public libraries, 4,000 college and university libraries and 12,000 special and other type of libraries.

In Canada, the largest public libraries are those of Montreal, with 1,086,252 volumes and Toronto, 864,232, as listed in the *American Library Directory* for 1974–75. Major Canadian university libraries include Toronto, 4,056,585; McGill, 2,985,242; Queens, 1,037,694, and Laval, 672,788. There are about 2,000 libraries in Canada.

Museums of the World

(For Museums of the U. S., see Index)

The modern museum originated during the Renaissance, when the revival of interest in the arts and classical antiquity led princes, nobles and humanists to amass specimens of historical value and to house their collections in special buildings or galleries.

Art Museums

The British Museum, London, contains some of the most famous historical objects of the world, including the Elgin Marbles and the Rosetta Stone.

Victoria and Albert Museum, London, whose primary object is to furnish examples to illustrate the history of art, emphasizes architecture and sculpture, ceramics, engraving, book production, paintings, textiles, etc. The library is devoted principally to fine and applied arts of all countries.

National Gallery, London, contains a great number of old Masters, including paintings by Da Vinci, Michelangelo, Tintoretto, Mantegna, Titian, Bellini, Jan van Eyck, Rubens, Rembrandt, Holbein, Constable, and Turner.

Tate Gallery, London, established as part of the National Gallery, was badly damaged during air raids of World War II, but was completely restored by 1949.

Wallace Collection, London, has many *objets d'art* and curios of French origin, and first-rank canvases and etchings of Italian, Spanish, Flemish, Dutch, and English artists.

In France, the most famous gallery is the *Louvre* in Paris, noted for the magnificence of its architecture as well as for its art collection, which is the largest in the world. Other Parisian museums of importance are *Cluny, Rodin, Guimet,* and *Carnavalet.*

Among the magnificent Italian museums, the *National Museum* at Naples contains one of the best arranged and classified collections. The *Uffizi Gallery* in Florence, founded by the Medicis, has one of the world's largest and best collections of Italian art. Other galleries in Florence are the *Gallery of Modern Art (Pitti Palace)* and the *National Museum (Bargello).* Rome has numerous museums, including several in the Vatican.

In Berlin, the paintings of the former *National Gallery* are on exhibit at Charlottenburg Castle.

The *Royal Museum of Fine Arts* in Brussels has a fine collection of French, Flemish, and Dutch masters, and houses many canvases by Rubens, Van Dyck, Jordaens, Rembrandt, Frans Hals, and Jan Steen.

The *State Museum* in Amsterdam contains superb works by Rembrandt, Vermeer, and others.

Among the notable art museums in other countries are the world-famous *Museo del Prado* in Madrid; the *Tretyakov Gallery* and the *Pushkin State Museum of Fine Arts* in Moscow; the *Hermitage State Museum* in Leningrad; and the *National Museum* in Tokyo, famed for its many oriental paintings and objects of art.

Science Museums

The *Ashmolean Museum*, oldest in Great Britain, was founded in 1683 by Oxford University and houses a collection of archeological and classical rarities.

Science Museum of London has exhibits of scientific instruments and appliances which review the progress of science and the history of invention. Other London museums of science are the *Natural History (British Museum)*, the *Imperial War Museum* (exhibits of both World Wars) and the *Geological Museum*.

The *Liverpool Museums* contain valuable collections of natural history and antiquities and are divided into departments of zoology, botany, geology, archeology, and ethnology. The buildings were almost completely destroyed during World War II, although most of the exhibits were saved.

The *Manchester Museum* serves as both a municipal and a university museum. The *Bristol Museum* contains departments of geology, zoology, botany, archeology, and Bristol antiquities. The *National Museum of Wales* at Cardiff has departments of art, archeology, botany, geology, and zoology.

In Edinburgh, Scotland, are the famed *Royal Scottish Museum*, which has collections in art, ethnography, natural history, technology, and archeology; and the *National Museum of Antiquities of Scotland*, noted for its coin and manuscript collections.

The *National Museum* in Dublin and the *Municipal Museum* in Belfast have important science collections.

Notable institutions of continental Europe include the *Natural History Museum* in Paris, the *Museum of Oceanography* in Monaco, the *Natural History Museum* in Lisbon, the *State Museum of Geology*

and Mineralogy in Leyden (Netherlands), the *Museum of Natural History* in Stockholm, the *Natural History Museum* in Vienna, the *Hungarian National Museum* in Budapest, the *National Museum* in Prague, and the various science museums in Bern, Geneva, Zürich, and Neuchâtel, Switzerland. Most larger cities of the U.S.S.R. have science museums of varying sizes, some specializing in local exhibits of natural history.

Famous science museums in Germany are the Deutsches Museum in Munich (mainly history of technology), the Völkerkunde-Museum (ethnology) in Berlin-Dahlem, and the museum of the same name in Hamburg.

In Calcutta is the *Indian Museum*, outstanding for its marine fauna and vertebrate fossils, and in Bombay the *Victoria and Albert Museum*.

In Australia are the *Queensland Museum* and the *Botanic Museum* in Brisbane, the *South Australian Museum* in Adelaide, and the *Australian Museum* in Sydney.

New Zealand contains the *Canterbury Museum*, Christchurch, rich in local fauna, flora and geological items, and a Maori and Polynesian ethnological collection

In Africa, the *South African Museum*, Capetown, holds general and local history collections and others illustrating anthropology, ethnology, and archeology. The *Durban Museum* contains much anthropological material. In Cairo are the notable collections of the *Egyptian Museum*.

Other museums of note include the *Archeological Museums* at Istanbul, the *Tokyo Science Museum*, the *National Museum of Natural History* in Santiago (Chile), the *National Museum* at Rio de Janeiro, and the *Argentine National Museum of Natural Sciences* at Buenos Aires.

The Seven Wonders of the World

(Not all classical writers list the same items as the Seven Wonders, but most of them agree on the following.)

THE PYRAMIDS OF EGYPT

A group of three pyramids, *Khufu, Khafra*, and *Menkaura* at Giza, outside modern Cairo, is often called the first wonder of the world; it is also the oldest and only surviving "wonder." The largest pyramid, built by Khufu (Cheops), had an original estimated height of 482 ft. (now approximately 450 ft.). The exact date of its construction is unknown and has been estimated as early as 4700 B.C. but is probably closer to 2900 B.C.

HANGING GARDENS OF BABYLON

Often listed as the second wonder, these gardens were supposedly built by Nebuchadnezzar about 600 B.C. to please his queen,

Amuhia. They are also associated with the mythical Assyrian Queen, Semiramis. Archeologists surmise that the gardens were laid out atop a vaulted building, with provisions for raising water. The terraces were said to rise from 75 to 300 ft.

The Walls of Babylon, also built by Nebuchadnezzar, are sometimes referred to as the second (or the seventh) wonder instead of the Hanging Gardens.

STATUE OF ZEUS (JUPITER)
AT OLYMPIA

The work of Phidias (5th century B.C.), this colossal figure in gold and ivory was reputedly 40 ft. high. All trace of it is lost, except for reproductions on coins.

TEMPLE OF ARTEMIS (DIANA) AT EPHESUS

A beautiful structure, begun about 350 B.C. in honor of a non-Hellenic goddess who later became identified with the Greek goddess of the same name. The temple, with Ionic columns 60 ft. high, was destroyed by invading Goths in A.D. 262.

MAUSOLEUM AT HALICARNASSUS

This famous monument was erected by Queen Artemisia in memory of her husband, King Mausolus of Caria in Asia Minor, who died in 353 B.C. Some remains of the structure are in the British Museum. This shrine is the source of the modern word "mausoleum."

COLOSSUS AT RHODES

This bronze statue of Helios (Apollo), about 105 ft. high, was the work of the sculptor Chares, who reputedly labored for 12 years before completing it in 280 B.C. It was destroyed during an earthquake in 224 B.C.

PHAROS OF ALEXANDRIA

The seventh wonder was the Pharos (lighthouse) of Alexandria, built by Sostratus of Cnidus during the 3rd century B.C. on the island of Pharos off the coast of Egypt. It was destroyed by an earthquake in the 13th century.

Famous Structures

Ancient

The Great Sphinx of Egypt, one of the wonders of ancient Egyptian architecture, adjoins the pyramids of Giza and has a length of 240 ft. It was built in the 4th dynasty.

Other Egyptian buildings of note include the *Temples of Karnak* and *Edfu* and the *Tombs at Beni Hassan.*

The Parthenon of Greece, built on the Acropolis in Athens, was the chief temple to the goddess Athena. It was believed to have been completed by 438 B.C. The present temple remained intact until the 5th century A.D. Today, though the Parthenon is in ruins, its majestic proportions are still discernible.

Other great structures of ancient Greece were the *Temples at Paestum* (about 540 and 420 B.C.); the *Temple of Poseidon* (about 460 B.C.); the *Temple of Apollo* at Corinth (about 540 B.C.); the *Temple of Apollo* at Bassae (about 450–420 B.C.); the famous *Erechtheum* atop the Acropolis (about 421–405 B.C.); the *Temple of Athena Niké* at Athens (about 426 B.C.); the *Olympieum* at Athens (174 B.C.–A.D. 131); the *Athenian Treasury* at Delphi (about 515 B.C.); the *Propylaea* of the Acropolis at Athens (437–432 B.C.); the *Theater of Dionysus* at Athens (about 350–325 B.C.); the *"House of Cleopatra"* at Delos (138 B.C.) and the *Theater* at Epidaurus (about 325 B.C.).

The Colosseum (Flavian Amphitheater) of Rome, the largest and most famous of the Roman amphitheaters, was opened for use A.D. 80. Elliptical in shape, it consisted of three stories and an upper gallery, rebuilt in stone in its present form in the third century A.D. Its seats rise in tiers, which in turn are buttressed by concrete vaults and stone piers. It could seat between 40,000 and 50,000 spectators. It was principally used for gladiatorial combat.

The Pantheon at Rome, begun by Agrippa in 27 B.C. as a temple, was rebuilt in its present circular form by Hadrian (A.D. 110–25). Literally the Pantheon was intended as a temple of "all the gods." It is remarkable for its perfect preservation today, and it has served continuously for 20 centuries as a place of worship.

Famous Roman arches include the *Arch of Constantine* (about A.D. 315) and the *Arch of Titus* (about A.D. 80).

Later European

St. Mark's Cathedral in Venice (1063–67), one of the great examples of Byzantine architecture, was begun in the 9th century. Partly destroyed by fire in 976, it was later rebuilt as a Byzantine edifice.

Other famous Byzantine examples of architecture are *St. Sophia* in Istanbul (A.D. 532–37); *San Vitale* in Ravenna (542); *St. Paul's Outside the Walls,* Rome (5th century); the *Kremlin* baptism and marriage church, Moscow (begun in 1397); and *St. Lorenzo Outside the Walls,* Rome, begun in 588.

The Cathedral Group at Pisa (1067–1173), one of the most celebrated groups of structures built in Romanesque style, consists of the cathedral, the cathedral's baptistery, and the *Leaning Tower.* This trio forms a group by itself in the northwest corner of the city. The cathedral and baptistery are built in varicolored marble. The campanile (Leaning Tower) is 179 ft. high and leans more than 16 feet out of the perpendicular. There is little reason to believe that the architects intended to have the tower lean.

Other examples of Romanesque architecture include the *Vézelay Abbey* in France (1130); the *Church of Notre-Dame-du-Port* at Clermont-Ferrand in France (1100); the *Church of San Zeno* (begun in 1138) at Verona, and *Durham Cathedral* in England.

The Alhambra (1248–1354), located in Granada, Spain, is universally esteemed as one of the greatest masterpieces of Moslem architecture. Designed as a palace and fortress for the Moorish monarchs of Granada, it is surrounded by a heavily fortified wall more than a mile in perimeter. The location of the Alhambra in the Sierra Nevada provides a magnificent setting for this jewel of Moorish Spain.

The *Tower of London* is a group of buildings and towers covering 13 acres along the north bank of the Thames. The central *White Tower*, begun in 1078 during the reign of William the Conqueror, was originally a fortress and royal residence, but was later used as a prison. The *Bloody Tower* is associated with Anne Boleyn and other notables.

Westminster Abbey, in London, was begun in 1045 and completed in 1065. It was rebuilt and enlarged in 1245-50.

Notre-Dame de Paris (begun in 1163), one of the great examples of Gothic architecture, is a twin-towered church with a steeple over the crossing and immense flying buttresses supporting the masonry at the rear of the church.

Other famous Gothic structures are *Chartres Cathedral* (12th century); *Sainte Chapelle*, Paris (1246-48); *Laon Cathedral*, France (1160-1205); *Reims Cathedral* (about 1210-50; rebuilt after its almost complete destruction in World War I); *Rouen Cathedral* (13th-16th centuries); *Amiens Cathedral* (1218-69); *Beauvais Cathedral* (begun 1247); *Salisbury Cathedral* (1220-60); *York Minster* or the *Cathedral of St. Peter* (begun in the 7th century); *Milan Cathedral* (begun 1386); and *Cologne Cathedral* (13th-19th centuries; badly damaged in World War II).

The Duomo (cathedral) in Florence was founded in 1298, completed by Brunelleschi and consecrated in 1436. The oval-shaped dome dominates the entire structure.

The *Vatican* is a group of buildings in Rome comprising the official residence of the Pope. The *Basilica of St. Peter*, the largest church in the Christian world, was begun in 1450. The *Sistine Chapel*, begun in 1473, is noted for the art masterpieces of Michelangelo, Botticelli, and others. The *Basilica of the Savior* (known as *St. John Lateran*) is the first-ranking Catholic Church in the world, for it is the cathedral of the Pope.

Other examples of Renaissance architecture are the *Palazzo Riccardi*, the *Palazzo Pitti* and the *Palazzo Strozzi* in Florence; the *Farnese Palace* in Rome; *Palazzo Grimani* (completed about 1550) in Venice; the *Escorial* (1563-93) near Madrid; the *Town Hall* of Seville (1527-32); the *Louvre*, Paris; the *Château* at Blois, France; *St. Paul's Cathedral*, London (1675-1710; badly damaged in World War II); the *Ecole Militaire*, Paris (1752); the *Pazzi Chapel*,

Florence, designed by Brunelleschi (1429); the Palace of *Fontainebleau* and the *Château de Chambord* in France.

The *Palace of Versailles*, containing the famous Hall of Mirrors, was built during the reign of Louis XIV and served as the royal palace until 1793.

Outstanding European buildings of the 18th and 19th centuries are the *Superga* at Turin, the *Hôtel-Dieu* in Lyons, the *Belvedere Palace* at Vienna, the *Royal Palace* of Stockholm, the *Opera House* of Paris (1863-75); the *Bank of England*, the *British Museum*, the *University of London*, and the *Houses of Parliament*, all in London; the *Panthéon*, the *Church of the Madeleine*, the *Bourse* and the *Palais de Justice* in Paris.

The *Eiffel Tower*, in Paris, was built for the Exposition of 1889 by Alexandre Eiffel. It is 984 ft. high.*

Asiatic and African

The *Taj Mahal* (1632-50), at Agra, India, built by Shah Jahan as a tomb for his wife, is considered by some as the most perfect example of the Mogul style and by others as the most beautiful building in the world. Four slim white minarets flank the building, which is topped by a white dome; the entire structure is of marble.

Other examples of Indian architecture are the temples at Benares and Tanjore.

Among famed Moslem edifices are the *Dome of the Rock* or *Mosque of Omar*, Jerusalem (A.D. 691); the *Citadel* (1166), and the *Tombs of the Mamelukes* (15th century), in Cairo;; the *Tomb of Humayun* in Delhi; the *Blue Mosque* (1468) at Tabriz and the *Tamerlane Mausoleum* at Samarkand.

Angkor Vat, outside the city of Angkor Thom, Cambodia, is one of the most beautiful examples of Cambodian or Khmer architecture. The sanctuary was built during the 12th century.

Great Wall of China (228 B.C.?), designed specifically as a defense against nomadic tribes, has numerous large watch towers which could be called buildings. It was erected by Emperor Ch'in Shih Huang Ti and is 1,400 miles long. Built mainly of earth and stone, it varies in height between 18 and 30 feet.

Typical of Chinese architecture are the pagodas or temple towers. Among some of the better-known pagodas are the *Great Pagoda of the Wild Geese* at Sian (founded in 652); *Nan t'a* (11th century) at Fang Shan; the *Pagoda of Sung Yueh Ssu* (A.D. 523) at Sung Shan, Honan.

Other well-known Chinese buildings are the *Drum Tower* (1273), the *Three Great Halls* in the Purple Forbidden City (1627), *Buddha's Perfume Tower* (19th century), the *Porcelain Pagoda* and the *Summer Palace*, all at Peking.

*1,056 ft., including the television tower.

United States

Rockefeller Center, in New York City, extends from 5th Ave. to the Avenue of the Americas between 48th and 52nd Sts. (and halfway to 7th Ave. between 47th and 51st Sts.). It occupies more than 25 acres and has 21 buildings.

Grant's Tomb, at Riverside Dr. near 122nd St. in New York City, contains the bodies of Ulysses S. Grant and his wife. It was completed in 1897.

The Cathedral Church of St. John the Divine, at 112th St. and Amsterdam Ave. in New York City, was begun in 1892 and is now in the final stages of completion. When completed, it will be the largest Gothic cathedral in the world: 601 ft. long 146 ft. wide at the nave, 320 ft. wide at the transept.

St. Patrick's Cathedral, at 5th Ave. and 50th St. in New York City, has a seating capacity of 4,500. The nave was opened in 1877, and the cathedral was dedicated in 1879.

Lincoln Memorial, in Washington, D. C., was dedicated in 1922. It has 36 columns (the number of states in 1865), each 44 ft. high. The main chamber contains a statue of Lincoln.

Independence Hall, in Philadelphia, was the scene of the signing of the Declaration of Independence and the drawing up of the U. S. Constitution. It was built between 1732 and 1756 as the State House. The Liberty Bell is on the first floor.

Volcanoes of the World

There are approximately 430 volcanoes (275 in the Northern Hemisphere and 155 in the Southern) with recorded eruptions in historical times. Of the 2,500 recorded eruptions, more than 2,000 have taken place in the Pacific area. Of known active volcanoes, about 80 are of the submarine type.

ATLANTIC-INDIAN AREA

Mediterranean Region

Italy: Mt. Vesuvius, southeast of Naples (3,858 ft; 1,176 m). Only active volcano on mainland of Europe. Pompeii buried by an eruption, A.D. 79. Latest eruption in 1944.

Sicily: Mt. Etna, eastern Sicily (10,902 ft; 3,323 m). Two new craters formed in eruptions of Feb.–Mar. 1947. Worst eruption in 50 years occurred Nov. 1950–Jan. 1951. Erupted again in Jan.–Mar. 1974 and Nov. 1975.

Lipari Islands (north of Sicily): Stromboli (about 3,000 ft; 914 m). Called "Lighthouse of the Mediterranean." Reported active in 1971.

Atlantic Area

Canary Islands: Pico de Teide (Teneriffe), on island of Teneriffe (12,192 ft; 3,716 m).

Cape Verde Islands: Fogo (over 8,000 ft; 2,438 m). Severe eruption in 1857; lasted until 1951.

Iceland: At least 25 volcanoes active in historic times. These volcanoes very similar to those in Hawaii. Askja (4,600 ft; 1,402 m) is the largest.

Lesser Antilles (*West Indian Islands*): Mt. Pelée, in northwestern Martinique (about 4,400 ft; 1,341 m). Eruption in 1902 destroyed town of St. Pierre and killed approximately 40,000.

Indian Ocean Region

Comoro Islands (east of northern Mozambique): One volcano, Kartala (over 8,500 ft; 2,591 m) is visible for over 100 miles. Last erupted in 1904.

Réunion Island (east of Madagascar): Piton de la Fournaise (Le Volcan) (8,610 ft; 2,624 m). Large lava flows. Last erupted in 1972.

THE PACIFIC AREA

Northwest Portion

Kamchatka: 14–18 active volcanoes. Klyuchevskaya (Kluchev) (15,912 ft; 4,850 m). Reported active in 1974.

Kurile Islands: At least 13 active volcanoes and several submarine outbreaks.

Japan: At least 33 active vents.

Fujiyama (Fujisan), southwest of Tokyo (12,385 ft; 3,775 m). Symmetrical in outline, snow-covered. Regarded as a sacred mountain.

Adzumayama (7,733 ft; 2,359 m).

Asamayama (8,182 ft; 2,488 m). Continuously active; violent eruption in 1783.

Chokai. Erupted in 1974 after having been inactive since 1821.

Sakurazima. (3,667.9 ft; 1,118 m). Strong smoke emissions and explosions began Nov. 1973 and continued through next year.

Volcano Islands: Mt. Suribachi, on Iwo Jima (546 ft; 166 m). A sulfurous steaming volcano. Raising of U. S. flag over Mt. Suribachi was one of the dramatic episodes of World War II.

Samoan archipelago: Savaii. An eruption in 1905 did considerable damage. Niuafoou (Tin Can) between Samoa and Fiji Islands has a crater 6,000 feet below and 600 feet above water.

Philippine Islands: About 100 eruptive centers; Hibok Hibok on Camiguin island erupted in Sept. 1950, and again in Dec. 1951, when about 750 were reported killed or missing; eruptions continued during 1952–53.

Taal (4,752 ft; 1,448 m) on Luzon. Major eruption in 1965 killed 190.

Hawaiian group: Mauna Loa (13,680 ft; 4,170 m). Also called "Long Mountain." Discharges more lava than any other volcano. Largest volcanic mountain in the world in cubic content, with crater of 3.7 sq. mi. Violent eruption in June, 1950, with lava pouring 25 mi. into the ocean. Last major eruption in July 1975.

Mauna Kea (13,796 ft; 4,205 m). Highest mountain in group.

Kilauea (4,090 ft; 1,247 m). A vent in side of Mauna Loa but apparently erupts independently of it. One of the most spectacular and active craters. Crater has an area of 4.14 sq mi. Earthquake in July 1975 caused major eruption.

Southwest Portion

Sumatra: Ninety volcanoes have been discovered; 12 are now active. The most famous, Krakatoa, is a small volcanic island in the Sunda Strait. Numerous volcanic discharges occurred in 1883. One explosion caused the disappearance of the highest peak and the northern part of the island. Fine dust was carried around the world in the upper atmosphere. Over 36,000 persons lost their lives in resultant tidal waves, which were felt as far away as Cape Horn. Active in 1972.

New Zealand: Tarawera, on North Island. Severe eruption in 1886 destroyed the famous pink and white sinter terraces of Rotomahana, a hot lake.

Ngauruhoe (7,515 ft; 2,291 m). Emits steam and vapor incessantly. Erupted 1974.

Papua and New Guinea: Karkar Island (4,921 ft; 1,500 m). Mild eruptions 1974.

Northeast Portion

Aleutian area: There are 32 active vents known, and numerous inactive cones.

Alaska: Wrangell (14,163 ft; 4,317 m) and Katmai (about 7,500 ft; 2,286 m).

On June 6, 1912, a violent eruption of the volcano Nova Rupta occurred, during which the "Valley of Ten Thousand Smokes" was formed.

Great Sitkin (5,741 ft; 1,750 m). Explosive activity Feb.–Sept. 1974, accompanied by earthquake originating at volcano that registered 2.3 on Richter scale.

Akutan Island (2,080 ft; 634 m). Erupted 1974, with ash and debris rising over 300 feet.

California, Oregon, Washington: Lassen Peak (10,453 ft; 3,186 m) in California is the only observed active volcano in the U. S. outside Alaska and Hawaii. The last period of activity was 1914–17. Other mountains of volcanic origin include Mt. Shasta (California), Mt. Hood and the

mountain containing Crater Lake (Oregon), Mt. Rainier (Washington) and Mt. Baker (Washington), which showed signs of excessive steaming in Oct. 1975.

Mexico: Popocatepetl (17,887 ft; 5,452 m). Crater 673 ft. deep and 2½ mi. in circumference. Not entirely extinct; steam still escapes.

Colima (14,239 ft; 4,340 m) in group that has had frequent eruptions.

Orizaba (Citlaltepetl) (18,701 ft; 5,700 m).

Paricutín. First appeared in Feb., 1943. In less than a week over 140 ft high developed with a crater one quarter mile in circumference. Cone grew over 1,500 ft (457 m) in 1943. Erupted 1952.

Boquerón ("Big Mouth"). Newest volcano in Western Hemisphere, discovered Sept., 1952 on San Benedicto island, about 250 mi. south of Lower California.

Guatemala: Santa María Quezaltenango (12,361 ft; 3,768 m). Frequent activity between 1902–08 and 1922–28 after centuries of quiescence. Most dangerously active vent of Central America. Other volcanoes include Tajumulco (13,814 ft; 4,211 m) and Atitlán (11,633 ft; 3,546 m).

Caribbean: On Guadeloupe, La Soufriere (4,869 ft; 1,484 m). Violent activity in July-Aug. 1976 caused evacuation of 73,-000 people.

El Salvador: Izalco, "beacon of Central America," which first appeared in 1770 and is still growing (erupted in 1950, 1956; last erupted in Oct.–Nov. 1966); San Salvador, which had a violent eruption in 1923, and Conchagua, which erupted with considerable damage early in 1947.

Nicaragua: Volcanoes include Telica, Coseguina and Momotombo. Between Momotombo on the west shore of Lake Managua and Coseguina overlooking the Gulf of Fonseca, there is a string of more than 20 cones, many still active. One of these, Cerro Negro, erupted in July, 1947, with considerable damage and loss of life, and again in 1971.

Concepción (5,282 ft; 1,610 m). Ash eruptions 1973–74.

Southeast Portion

Colombia: Huila (18,700 ft; 5,700 m). A vapor-emitting volcano, and Tolima (17,-109 ft; 5,213 m).

Eruption of Puracé (15,420 ft; 4,700 m), 1949, killed 17.

Ecuador: Cotopaxi (19,344 ft; 5,896 m). Perhaps highest active volcano in the world. Possesses a beautifully formed cone.

Cayambe (19,170 ft; 5,843 m). Almost on equator.

Reventador (11,434 ft; 3,485 m). Observed in active state late 1973.

Chile and Argentina: About 25 active or potentially active.

Zoological Gardens

North America has more than 30 major zoos, in the United States, Canada, and Mexico. The *Quebec Zoological Society*'s collection is made up of Canadian species; Toronto has many exotic species.

The first zoological garden in the United States was established in Philadelphia in 1874. Since that time nearly every large city in the country has acquired a zoo. Among the largest are the celebrated *Bronx Zoo* and the *Central Park Zoo* in New York, the *Lincoln Park Zoo* and the *Brookfield Zoo* in Chicago, and those in St. Louis, Cincinnati, Detroit, Kansas City, and San Diego. The *National Zoological Park* in Washington, D. C., in a beautiful setting of hills, woods, and streams, was established in 1890 by an act of Congress. Some of the U. S. zoos exhibit their collections in open-air, barless pits; the Brookfield Zoo is an example.

In Europe, zoological gardens have long been popular public institutions. The *Jardin d'Acclimatation*, in the Bois de Boulogne, Paris, is the oldest and largest. Others are located at Clères, Ermenonville, Lyons, Marseilles, Maubeuge, Mulhouse, and Nancy.

Germany had about 20 zoological gardens, many of which were developed in the peacetime years between World Wars I and II. Large zoos were located in Berlin and Frankfurt am Main. In Munich, the animals were grouped according to the continent of their origin. At Stellingen near Hamburg, the *Hagenback Garden* became an outstanding show place and distributing center for animals. At present, there are only four zoological gardens in West Germany, at Stellingen, Berlin, Munich, and Frankfurt.

The *Schönbrunn* at Vienna is one of the oldest zoos in Europe. The Budapest zoological gardens house a fine collection of European birds. At Antwerp, the *Royal Zoological Society* founded a large menagerie in 1843. It was seriously damaged by German bombs during World War II.

In the British Isles, the outstanding collection is in the garden of the *London Zoological Society* in Regent's Park. Although this zoo received a number of direct bomb hits in 1940–41 and again in 1944, it remained open throughout World War II; visitors during this period numbered 6,500,000. Manchester and Clifton have smaller gardens, and the one at Edinburgh is famous for its collection of penguins. The *Dublin Zoo* is noted for its lions, many of which were born there.

The Amsterdam zoo, with its East Indian collection and its aquarium, and the Rotterdam gardens are the two best known in the Netherlands. Built on a high elevation, the *Skansen Zoo* in Stockholm exhibits north European specimens. The most important gardens in the U.S.S.R. are found in Moscow, where northern as well as exotic species are collected. The zoo at Rome has part of its collection confined in barless pits. At Lisbon there is a small zoological garden, and in Madrid a part of the original royal menagerie.

Geysers

Geysers exist in many volcanic regions of the world such as Japan and South America, but their greatest development is in Iceland, New Zealand, and Yellowstone National Park.

Iceland. The principal geyser area is about 30 miles northwest of Mt. Hekla, where there are more than 100 geysers and hot springs in about two square miles. Much of the hot water is utilized for heating the city of Reykjavik. The main ones are the following:

Great Geyser (Geysir). Sends up a column 160 to 180 ft. high intermittently from an opening more than 9 ft. across and about 70 ft. deep.

Strokkr (Churn). Constant bubbling and occasional eruptions.

New Zealand. There is a great profusion of boiling springs, steam jets and mud volcanoes northeast of Lake Taupo on North Island. Main geysers are *Waikite*, with a 30–35 ft. column, *Pohutu* and *Waimauku*. Utilization of steam jets for power generation is under active study.

United States. There are 120 named geysers in Yellowstone National Park, Wyoming, and perhaps half that number unnamed. Most of the geysers and the 4,000 or more hot springs are located in the western portion of the park. The most important are the following:

Norris Geyser Basin has 24 or more active geysers; the number varies. There are scores of steam vents and hot springs. *Valentine* is highest, erupting 50–75 ft. at intervals varying from 18 hr. to 3 days or more. *Minuté*, 15–20 ft. high, several hours apart. Others include *Steamboat, Fearless, Veteran, Vixen, Corporal, Whirligig, Little Whirligig* and *Pinwheel*.

Lower Geyser Basin has at least 18 active geysers. *Fountain* throws water 50–75 ft. in all directions at unpredictable intervals. *Clepsydra* erupts violently from four vents up to 30 ft. *Great Fountain* plays every 8 to 15 hr. in spurts from 30 to 90 ft. high.

Midway Geyser Basin has vast steaming terraces of red, orange, pink and other colors; there are pools and springs, including the beautiful *Grand Prismatic Spring*. *Excelsior* crater discharges boiling water into Firehole River at the rate of 6 cu. ft. per second.

Giant erupts up to 200 ft. at intervals of 2½ days to 3 mo.; eruptions last about 1½ hr. *Daisy* sends water up to 75 ft. but is irregular and frequently inactive.

Old Faithful sends up a column varying from 116 to 175 ft. at intervals of about 65 min., varying from 33 to 90 min. Eruptions last about 4 min., during which time about 12,000 gal. are discharged.

Giantess seldom erupts, but during its active periods sends up streams 150–200 ft.

Lion Group: *Lion* plays up to 60 ft. every 2–4 days when active; *Little Cub* up to 10 ft. every 1–2 hr. *Big Cub* and *Lioness* seldom erupt.

Castle usually erupts twice daily to a height of 75 ft.

Mammoth Hot Springs: There are no geysers in this area. The formation is travertine. Sides of a hill are steps and terraces over which flow the steaming waters of hot springs laden with minerals. Each step is tinted by algae to many shades of orange, pink, yellow, brown, green, and blue. Terraces are white where no water flows.

World Extremes of Climate

Highest recorded shade temperature:
World: 136.4° F. at Azizia, Libya, North Africa, Sept. 13, 1922.
United States: 134° F. at Death Valley, Calif., July 10, 1913.
Lowest recorded temperature:
World: −126.9° F. at Vostok, near south geomagnetic pole, Antarctica, Aug. 24, 1960.
In Siberia: −89.9° F. at Oimekon,* Feb. 6, 1933, and −89.7° F. at Verkhoyansk, Feb. 5 and 7, 1892.
United States: −79.8° F. at Prospect Creek, Alaska, Jan. 23, 1971.

Highest mean annual temperature:
World: 94° F. at Dallol, Ethiopia (1960–66).
United States: 78.2° F. at Key West, Fla., 30-year normal.

Lowest mean annual temperature:
World: −70° F. at Plateau Station, Antarctica (1966–68).
United States: 9.3° at Barrow, Alaska, 30-year normal.

Maximum rainfall for 24-hour period:
World: 73.62 inches at Cilaos, Réunion Island, Indian Ocean, Mar. 16, 1952.
Contiguous United States: 38.7 inches at Yankeetown, Fla., Sept. 5–6, 1950. From a recording gauge: 26.12 inches at Hoegees Camp, Calif., Jan. 22–23, 1943.
Maximum rainfall in one month:
World: 366.14 inches at Cherrapunji, India, July, 1861 (over 150 inches fell in five consecutive days in August, 1841).
United States: 107.00 inches at Kukui, Maui, Hawaii, March, 1942.
Maximum average annual precipitation (calendar year):
World: 460 inches at Mt. Waialeale, Island of Kauai, Hawaiian Islands, 1912–1958; 450.0 inches at Cherrapunji, India, 74-year average.
United States: Same as World above.
Minimum average annual precipitation (calendar year):
World: 0.03 inch at Arica, Chile, 59-year average.
United States: 1.63 inches at Greenland Ranch, Calif., 49-year average. (Bagdad, Calif., holds the U. S. record for the longest period with no measurable rain, 767 days, Oct. 3, 1912, to Nov. 8, 1914.)
Other U. S. precipitation extremes:
Wettest area: West Olympia Coast Division of Washington, 30-year normal of 94.82 inches.
Driest area: Southwest division of Arizona, 30-year normal of 4.13 inches.
Heavy U. S. snowfall records:
Greatest average annual: 587.4 in. at Paradise Ranger Station, Rainier Park, Wash.
Greatest amount in one season: (1,121.4) inches at Paradise Ranger Station, Rainier Park, Wash., 1971–72.
Greatest amount in a calendar month: 390 inches at Tamarack, Calif., January, 1911.
Greatest in 24 hours: 76 inches at Silver Lake, Colo., Apr. 14–15, 1921. (This storm, Apr. 12–15, produced highest known rates in U. S. for durations up to 3 days—95 inches in 48 hours; 98 inches in 72 hours; 100 inches in 85 hours.)
In the New York City blizzard of Dec. 26, 1947, 25.8 inches of snow fell in about 24 hours, almost 5 inches more than fell in the blizzard of March, 1888.
Largest hailstone definitely recorded in United States: 1.67 pounds by weight, at Coffeyville, Kan., Sept. 3, 1970.

* The minimum at Oimekon is listed at −71°C. (−95.8°F.) in various publications, but this is unacceptable at present because of insufficient information.

The Continents

A continent is defined as a large unbroken land mass completely surrounded by water, although in some cases continents are (or were in the past) connected by land bridges.

A hypothesis first suggested late in the 19th century is that the continents consist of lighter rocks that rest on heavier crustal material, in about the same manner that icebergs float on water. That the rocks forming the continents are lighter than the material below them and under the ocean bottoms is now established. As a consequence of this fact, Alfred Wegener (for the first time in 1912) suggested that the continents are slowly moving, at a rate of about one yard per century, so that their relative positions are not rigidly fixed. Many geologists that were originally skeptical have come to accept this theory of Continental Drift.

When describing a continent, it is important to remember that there is a fundamental difference between a deep ocean, like the Atlantic, and shallow seas, like the Baltic and most of the North Sea, which are merely flooded portions of a continent. Another and entirely different point to remember is that political considerations have often overridden geographical facts when it came to naming continents.

Geographically speaking, Europe, including the British Isles, is a large western peninsula of the continent of Asia; and many geographers, when referring to Europe and Asia, speak of the Eurasian Continent. But traditionally, Europe is counted as a separate continent, with the Ural and the Caucasus mountains forming the line of demarcation between Europe and Asia.

To the south of Europe, Asia has an odd-shaped peninsula jutting westward, which has a large number of political subdivisions. The northern section is taken up by Turkey; to the south of Turkey there are Syria, Iraq, Israel, Jordan, Saudi Arabia, and a number of smaller Arab countries. All this is part of Asia. Traditionally, the island of Cyprus in the Mediterranean is also considered to be part of Asia, while the island of Crete is counted as European.

The large islands of Java, Borneo, and Sumatra and the smaller islands near them are counted as part of "tropical Asia," while New Guinea is counted as related to Australia. In the case of the Americas, the problem arises as to whether they should be considered one or two continents. There are good arguments on both sides, but since there is now a land bridge between North and South America (in the past it was often flooded) and since no part of the sea east of the land bridge is deep ocean, it is more logical to consider the Americas as one continent.

Politically, based mainly on history, the Americas are divided into North America (from the Arctic to the Mexican border), Central America (from Mexico to Panamá, with the Carribbean islands), and South America. Greenland is considered a section of North America, while Iceland is traditionally counted as a European island because of its political ties with the Scandinavian countries.

The island groups in the Pacific are often called "Oceania," but this name does *not* imply that scientists consider them the remains of a continent.

Oceans and Seas

Name	Area, sq. mi.	Average depth, feet	Greatest known depth, ft.	Place of greatest known depth
Pacific Ocean	64,000,000	13,215	37,782	Mindanao Deep
Atlantic Ocean	31,815,000	12,880	30,246	Puerto Rico Trough
Indian Ocean	25,300,000	13,002	24,460	Sunda Trench
Arctic Ocean	5,440,200	3,953	18,456	77° 45′ N.; 175° W.
Mediterranean Sea*	1,145,100	4,688	15,197	Off Cape Matapan, Greece
Caribbean Sea	1,049,500	8,685	22,788	Off Cayman Islands
South China Sea	895,400	5,419	16,456	West of Luzon
Bering Sea	884,900	5,075	15,659	Off Buldir Island
Gulf of Mexico	615,000	4,874	12,425	Sigsbee Deep
Okhotsk Sea	613,800	2,749	12,001	146° 10′ E.; 46° 50′ N.
East China Sea	482,300	617	9,126	25° 16′ N.; 125° E.
Hudson Bay	475,800	420	600	Near entrance
Japan Sea	389,100	4,429	12,276	Central Basin
Andaman Sea	308,000	2,854	12,392	Off Car Nicobar Island
North Sea	222,100	308	2,165	Skagerrak
Red Sea	169,100	1,611	7,254	Off Port Sudan
Baltic Sea	163,000	180	1,380	Off Gotland

* Includes Black Sea and Sea of Azov. NOTE: For Caspian Sea, see Large Lakes of World elsewhere in this section.

Table of Geological Periods

It is now generally assumed that planets are formed by the accretion of gas and dust in a cosmic cloud, but there is no way of estimating the length of this process. Our earth acquired its present size, more or less, between 4,000 and 5,000 million years ago. Life on earth originated about 2,000 million years ago, but there are no good fossil remains from periods earlier than the Cambrian, which began about 550 million years ago. The largely unknown past before the Cambrian Period is referred to as the Pre-Cambrian and is subdivided into the Lower (or older) and Upper (or younger) Pre-Cambrian—also called the Archaeozoic and Proterozoic Eras.

The known geological history of the earth since the beginning of the Cambrian Period is subdivided into three "eras," each of which comprises a number of "periods." They, in turn, are subdivided into "subperiods." In a subperiod, a certain section may be especially well known because of rich fossil finds. Such a section is called a "formation," and it is usually identified by a place name.

PALEOZOIC ERA

This era began 550 million years ago and lasted for 355 million years. The name was compounded from Greek *palaios* (old) and *zoön* (animal).

Period	Duration[1]	Subperiods	Events
Cambrian (from *Cambria,* Latin name for Wales)	70	Lower Cambrian Middle Cambrian Upper Cambrian	Invertebrate sea life of many types, proliferating during this and the following period.
Ordovician (from Latin *Ordovices,* people of early Britain)	85	Lower Ordovician Upper Ordovician	
Silurian (from Latin *Silures,* people of early Wales)	40	Lower Silurian Upper Silurian	First known fishes; gigantic sea scorpions.
Devonian (from Devonshire in England)	50	Lower Devonian Upper Devonian	Proliferation of fishes and other forms of sea life; land still largely lifeless.
Carboniferous (from Latin *carbo* = coal + *fero* = to bear)	85	Lower or Mississippian Upper or Pennsylvanian	Period of maximum coal formation in swampy forests; early insects and first known amphibians.
Permian (from district of Perm in Russia)	25	Lower Permian Upper Permian	Early reptiles and mammals; earliest form of turtles.

MESOZOIC ERA

This era began 195 million years ago and lasted for 135 million years. The name was compounded from Greek *mesos* (middle) and *zoön* (animal). Popular name: Age of Reptiles.

Period	Duration[1]	Subperiods	Events
Triassic (from *trias* = triad)	35	Lower or Buntsandstein (from German *bunt* = colorful + *Sandstein* = sandstone) Middle or Muschelkalk (from German *Muschel* = clam + *Kalk* = limestone) Upper or Keuper (old miners' term)	Early saurians.
Jurassic (from Jura Mountains)	35	Lower or Black Jurassic, or Lias (from French *liais* = hard stone) Middle or Brown Jurassic, or Dogger (old provincial English for round stones) Upper or White Jurassic, or Malm (Middle English for sand)	Many sea-going reptiles; early large dinosaurs; somewhat later, flying reptiles (pterosaurs), earliest known birds.
Cretaceous (from Latin *creta* = chalk)	65	Lower Cretaceous Upper Cretaceous	Maximum development of dinosaurs; birds proliferating; opossum-like mammals.

CENOZOIC ERA

This era began 60 million years ago and includes the geological present. The name was compounded from Greek *kainos* (new) and *zoön* (animal). Popular name: Age of Mammals.

Period	Duration[1]	Subperiods	Events
Tertiary (originally thought to be the third of only three periods)	ca. 60	Paleocene (from Greek *palaios* = old + *kainos* = new)	First mammals other than marsupials.
		Eocene (from Greek *eos* = dawn + *kainos* = new)	Formation of amber; rich insect fauna; early bats.
		Oligocene (from Greek *oligos* = few + *kainos* = new)	Steady increase of large mammals.
		Miocene (from Greek *meios* = less + *kainos* = new)	
		Pliocene (from Greek *pleios* = more + *kainos* = new)	Mammals closely resembling present types; protohumans.
Pleistocene (from Greek *pleistos* = most + *kainos* = new) (popular name: Ice Age)	1	Four major glaciations, named Günz, Mindel, Riss, and Würm, originally the names of rivers. Last glaciation ended 10,000 to 15,000 years ago	Various forms of early man.
Holocene (from Greek *holos* = entire + *kainos* = new)		The present	The last 3,000 years are called "history."

[1] In millions of years.

Interesting Caves and Caverns of the World

Aggtelek. In village of same name, northern Hungary. Large stalactitic cavern about 5 miles long.

Altamira Cave. Near Santander, Spain. Contains animal paintings (Old Stone Age art) on roof and walls.

Antiparos. On island of same name in the Grecian Archipelago. Some stalactites are 20 ft. long. Brilliant colors and fantastic shapes.

Blue Grotto. On island of Capri, Italy. Cavern hollowed out in limestone by constant wave action. Now half filled with water because of sinking coast. Name derived from unusual blue light permeating the cave. Source of light is a submerged opening, light passing through the water.

Carlsbad Caverns. Southeast New Mexico. Largest underground labyrinth yet discovered. Three levels: 754, 900, and 1,320 feet below the surface.

Fingal's Cave. On island of Staffa off coast of western Scotland. Penetrates about 200 ft. inland. Contains basaltic columns almost 40 ft. high.

Ice Cave. Near Dobsina, Czechoslovakia. Noted for its beautiful crystal effects.

Jenolan Caves. In Blue Mountain plateau, New South Wales, Australia. Beautiful stalactitic formations.

Kent's Cavern. Near Torquay, England. Source of much information on Paleolithic man.

Luray Cavern. Near Luray, Va. Has large stalactitic and stalagmitic columns of many colors.

Mammoth Cave. Limestone cavern in central Kentucky. Cave area is about 10 miles in diameter but has at least 150 miles of irregular subterranean passageways at various levels. Temperature remains fairly constant at 54°F.

Peak Cavern or **Devil's Hole.** Derbyshire, England. About 2,250 ft. into a mountain. Lowest part is about 600 ft. below the surface.

Postojna (Postumia) Grotto. Near Postumia in Julian Alps, about 25 miles N.E. of Trieste. Stalactitic cavern, largest in Europe. Piuca (Pivka) River flows through part of it. Caves have numerous beautiful stalactites.

Singing Cave. Iceland. A lava cave; name derived from echoes of people singing in it.

Wind Cave. In Black Hills of South Dakota. Limestone caverns with stalactites and stalagmites almost entirely missing. Variety of crystal formations called "boxwork."

Wyandotte Cave. In Crawford County, southern Indiana. A limestone cavern with five levels of passages; one of the largest in North America. "Monumental Mountain," approximately 135 ft. high, is believed to be one of the world's largest underground "mountains."

Principal Rivers of the World

(For other U. S. Rivers, see Index)

River	Source	Outflow	Approx. length miles	km
Nile	Rwanda and Ethiopia	Mediterranean Sea	4,157	6,690
Amazon	Glacier-fed lakes, Peru	Atlantic Ocean	3,912	6,296
Mississippi–Missouri–Red Rock	Source of Red Rock River, Montana	Gulf of Mexico (mouth of Southwest Pass)	3,741	6,020
Yangtze Kiang	Tibetan plateau	China Sea	3,602	5,797
Ob	Altai Mts., U.S.S.R.	Gulf of Ob	3,459	5,567
Yellow River (Hwang Ho)	East part of Kunlun Mts., west China	Gulf of Chihli	2,900	4,667
Yenisei	Tannu Ola Mts., western Mongolia	Arctic Ocean	2,800	4,506
Paraná	Confluence of Paranaiba and Grande rivers, southeast Brazil	Rio de la Plata Atlantic Ocean)	2,795	4,498
Irtish	Altai Mts., U.S.S.R.	Ob River	2,758	4,438
Congo	Between Lakes Nyasa and Tanganyika	Atlantic Ocean	2,716	4,371
Amur	Confluence of Shika (U.S.S.R.) and Argun (Manchuria) rivers	Tartary Strait	2,704	4,352
Lena	Tannu Ola Mts., western Mongolia	Arctic Ocean	2,652	4,268
Mackenzie	Head of Finlay River, British Columbia	Beaufort Sea (Arctic)	2,635	4,241
Niger	Border of Sierra Leone	Gulf of Guinea	2,600	4,184
Mékong	Tibetan highlands	South China Sea	2,500	4,023
Mississippi	Lake Itasca, Minnesota	Gulf of Mexico	2,348	3,779
Missouri	Confluence of Jefferson, Gallatin, and Madison rivers, Montana	Mississippi River	2,315	3,726
Volga	Valdai plateau, U.S.S.R.	Caspian Sea	2,291	3,687
Madeira	Confluence of Gauporé and Maumoré rivers, Bolivia-Brazil border	Amazon River	2,012	3,238
Purús	Southwest Amazonas, Brazil	Amazon River	1,993	3,207
São Francisco	Southwest Minas Geraes, Brazil	Atlantic Ocean	1,987	3,198
St. Lawrence	St. Louis River, Minnesota	Gulf of St. Lawrence	1,900	3,058
Rio Grande	San Juan Mts., Colorado	Gulf of Mexico	1,885	3,034
Brahmaputra	Himalayas	Ganges River (Bay of Bengal)	1,800	2,897
Yukon	Junction of Lewes and Pelly rivers, Yukon Territory, Canada	Bering Sea	1,800	2,897
Indus	Himalayas	Arabian Sea	1,800	2,897
Danube	Black Forest, Germany	Black Sea	1,766	2,842
Euphrates	Dumlu Dagh (mts.), Turkey	Persian Gulf	1,739	2,799
Darling	Central part of Eastern Highlands, Australia	Murray River	1,702	2,739
Zambezi	11° 21′ S., 24° 22′ E., Zambia	Indian Ocean	1,700	2,736
Tocantins	Near Pyrenopolis, southeast Brazil	Pará River (Atlantic Ocean)	1,677	2,699
Murray	Australian Alps, New South Wales	Indian (Southern) Ocean	1,609	2,589
Nelson	Head of Bow River, west Alberta, Canada	Hudson Bay	1,600	2,575
Paraguay	Mato Grosso, Brazil	Paraná River	1,584	2,549
Ural	Southern Ural Mts., U.S.S.R.	Caspian Sea	1,574	2,533
Ganges	Himalayas	Bay of Bengal	1,557	2,506
Amu Darya (Oxus)	Nicholas Range, Pamir Mts., U.S.S.R.	Lake Aral	1,500	2,414
Japurá	Andes, Colombia	Amazon River	1,500	2,414
Salween	Tibet, south of Kunlun Mts.	Gulf of Martaban	1,500	2,414
Arkansas	Central Colorado	Mississippi River	1,450	2,333

River	Source	Outflow	Approx. length miles	km
Colorado	Grand County, Colorado	Gulf of California	1,450	2,333
Dnieper	Valdai Hills, U.S.S.R.	Black Sea	1,419	2,284
Ohio-Allegheny	Potter County, Pennsylvania	Mississippi River	1,306	2 102
Irrawaddy	Confluence of N'mai and Mali rivers, northeast Burma	Bay of Bengal	1,300	2,092
Orange	Lesotho	Atlantic Ocean	1,300	2,092
Orinoco	Sierra Parima on Venezuela-Brazil border	Atlantic Ocean	1,281	2,062
Pilcomayo	Cordillera Central, Bolivia	Paraguay River	1,242	1,999
Si Kiang	Eastern Yünnan Province, China	China Sea	1,236	1,989
Columbia	Columbia Lake, British Columbia, Canada	Pacific Ocean	1,232	1,983
Don	Lake Ivan, U.S.S.R.	Sea of Azov	1,223	1,968
Sungari	Sungari Reservoir, Manchuria, China	Amur River	1,215	1,955
Saskatchewan	Western Alberta, Canada	Lake Winnipeg	1,205	1,939
Peace	Stikine Mts., British Columbia	Great Slave River	1,195	1,923
Tigris	Taurus Mts., Turkey	Euphrates River (Persian Gulf)	1,180	1,899

Large Lakes of the World

Name and location	Area sq mi	sq km	Length mi	km	Maximum depth feet	meters
Caspian Sea, U.S.S.R.-Iran*	152,239	394,299	745	1,199	3,104	946
Superior, U.S.A.-Canada	31,820	82,414	383	616	1,333	406
Victoria, East Central Africa	26,828	69,485	200	322	270	82
Aral, U.S.S.R.	25,659	66,457	266	428	223	68
Huron, U.S.A.-Canada	23,010	59,596	247	397	750	229
Michigan, U.S.A.	22,400	58,016	321	517	923	281
Tanganyika, East Central Africa	12,700	32,893	420	676	4,708	1,435
Baikal, U.S.S.R.	12,162	31,500	395	636	5,712	1,741
Great Bear, Canada	12,000	31,080	232	373	270	82
Nyasa, Southeast Africa	11,600	30,044	360	579	2,316	706
Great Slave, Canada	11,170	28,930	298	480	2,015	614
Chad,‡ Central Africa	9,946	25,760	...	...	23	7
Erie, U.S.A.-Canada	9,930	25,719	241	388	210	64
Winnipeg, Canada	9,094	23,553	264	425	204	62
Ontario, U.S.A.-Canada	7,520	19,477	193	311	778	237
Balkash, U.S.S.R.	7,115	18,428	376	605	87	27
Ladoga, U.S.S.R.	7,000	18,130	124	200	738	225
Onega, U.S.S.R.	3,819	9,891	154	248	361	110
Titicaca, Bolivia-Peru	3,141	8,135	110	177	1,214	370
Nicaragua, Nicaragua	3,089	8,001	110	177	230	70
Athabaska, Canada	3,058	7,920	208	335	407	124
Rudolf, Eastern Africa	2,473	6,405	154	248	...	...
Reindeer, Canada	2,444	6,330	152	245	...	...
Eyre, South Australia	ca.2,400†	6,216	130	209	varies	varies
Issyk-Kul, U.S.S.R.	2,394	6,200	113	182	2,297	700
Urmia,‡ Iran	2,317	6,001	81	130	49	15
Torrens, South Australia	2,200	5,698	130	209	...	...
Vänern, Sweden	2,141	5,545	87	140	322	98
Winnipegosis, Canada	2,086	5,403	152	245	59	18
Mobutu Sese Seko, Uganda	2,046	5,299	100	161	180	55
Nettiling, Baffin Island, Canada	1,950	5,051	70	113	...	...
Nipigon, Canada	1,870	4,843	72	116	...	...
Manitoba, Canada	1,817	4,706	140	225	22	7
Great Salt, U.S.A.	1,800	4,662	75	121	15/25	5/8
Kioga, Uganda	1,700	4,403	50	80	ca.30	9
Koko-Nor, China	1,630	4,222	66	106	...	...
Mweru, Zambia-Zaire	1,620	4,196	75	121	...	...
Dubawnt, Canada	1,600	4,144	69	111	...	...

* The Caspian Sea is called "sea" because the Romans, finding it salty, named it *Mare Caspium*. Many geographers, however, consider it a lake because it is land-locked.   † Varies with the rainfall of the wet season. It has been reported to dry up almost completely on occasion.   ‡ Figures represent high-water data.

World's Greatest Man-Made Lakes[1]

Source: Bureau of Reclamation, Department of the Interior.

Name of dam	Location	Millions of cubic meters	Thousands of acre-feet	Year completed
Owen Falls	Uganda	204,800	166,000	1954
Bratsk	U.S.S.R.	169,270	137,220	1964
High Aswan (Saad-El-Aali)	Egypt	169,000	137,000	1970
Kariba	Rhodesia-Zambia	160,368	130,000	1959
Akosombo	Ghana	148,000	120,000	1965
Daniel Johnson	Canada	141,852	115,000	1968
Krasnoyarsk	U.S.S.R.	73,300	59,425	1972
W. A. C. Bennett	Canada	70,309	57,006	1967
Zeya	U.S.S.R.	68,400	55,452	1975
Cabora Bassa	Mozambique	64,000	51,900	1974
Ust-Ilimsk	U.S.S.R.	59,300	48,100	UC
Volga-V. I. Lenin	U.S.S.R.	58,000	47,020	1955
LaGrande	Canada	55,000	44,589	UC
Bukhtarma	U.S.S.R.	53,000	42,970	1960
Irkutsk	U.S.S.R.	46,000	37,290	1956
Hoover	Nevada-Arizona	36,703	29,755	1936
Vilyui	U.S.S.R.	35,900	29,104	1967
Sobradinho	Brazil	34,200	27,700	UC
Volgograd-22nd Congress	U.S.S.R.	33,500	27,160	1958
Glen Canyon	Utah-Arizona	33,305	27,000	1964
Sayanskaya	U.S.S.R.	31,300	25,353	UC
Keban	Turkey	31,000	25,110	1974
Garrison	North Dakota	30,000	24,321	1956
Iroquois	U.S.A.-Canada	29,960	24,288	1958
Oahe	South Dakota	29,100	23,591	1963

[1] Formed by construction of dams. NOTE: UC means under construction in 1975.

Highest Waterfalls of the World

			Height	
Waterfall	Location	River	feet	meters
Angel	Venezuela	Tributary of Caroni	3,281	1,000
Tugela	Natal, South Africa	Tugela	3,000	914
Kukenaam	Guyana	Kukenaam	2,000	610
Sutherland	South Island, N.Z.	Arthur	1,904	580
Ribbon (Yosemite)	California	Creek, flowing into Yosemite	1,612	491
Upper Yosemite	California	Yosemite Creek, tributary of Merced	1,430	436
Gavarnie	Southwest France	Gave de Pau	1,384	422
Takkakaw	British Columbia	Tributary of Yoho	1,248	380
Silverstrand (Widow's Tears) (Yosemite)	California	Tributary of Merced	1,170	357
Staubbach	Switzerland	Staubbach (Lauterbrunnen Valley)	984	300
Vettis	Norway	Mörkedola	853	260
King Edward VIII	Guyana	Courantyne	850	259
Gersoppa	India	Sharavati	829	253
Kaieteur	Guyana	Pataro	822	251
Skykjefos	Norway	In Skykjedal (valley of Inner Hardanger Fjord)	820	250
Kalambo	Tanzania-Zambia		704	215
Fairy (Mt. Rainier Park)	Washington	Stevens Creek	700	213
Trummelbach	Switzerland	Trummelbach (Lauterbrunnen Valley)	700	213
Teverone	Italy	Tevere (Tiber)	680	207
Middle Cascade (Yosemite)	California	Yosemite Creek, tributary of Merced	675	206
Maradalsfos	Norway	Stream flowing into Ejkisdals-vand (lake)	643	196
Feather Falls	California	Fall River	640	195
Maletsunyane	Lesotho	Upper Congo	630	192
Bridal Veil (Yosemite)	California	Yosemite Creek	620	189

Waterfall	Location	River	Height feet	Height meters
Multnomah	Oregon	Multnomah Creek, tributary of Columbia	620	189
Vöringsfos	Norway	Bjoreia	597	182
Nevada (Yosemite)	California	Merced	594	181
Skjaeggedalsfos	Norway	Tysso	525	160
Terni	Italy	Velino, tributary of Nera	525	160
Tequendama	Colombia	Funza, tributary of Magdalena	515	157
Marina	Guyana	Tributary of Kuribrong, a tributary of the Pataro	500	152
Handol	Sweden	Handolsa	427	130
King George's	Cape of Good Hope, South Africa	Orange	400	122
Guayra	Paraguay–Brazil	Paraná	374	114
Illilouette (Yosemite)	California	Illilouette Creek, tributary of Merced	370	113
Victoria	Rhodesia	Zambezi	355	108
Lower Yosemite	California	Yosemite	320	98
Comet (Mt. Rainier Park)	Washington	Van Trump Creek	320	98
Lower Yellowstone	Wyoming	Yellowstone	319	97
Vernal (Yosemite)	California	Merced	317	97
Virginia	Canada, Northwest Territories	South Nahanni, tributary of Mackenzie	315	96

NOTE: Niagara Falls (New York–Ontario), though of great volume, has a drop of only 167 feet.

World's Largest Hydroelectric Plants

Source: Bureau of Reclamation, Department of the Interior.

Name of dam	Location	Rated Capacity (MW) Present	Rated Capacity (MW) Ultimate	Year of initial operation
Itaipu	Brazil-Paraguay	....	12,600	UC
Grand Coulee	Washington	2,161	9,780	1941
Paulo Afonso	Brazil	1,299	6,774	1955
Guri	Venezuela	524	6,500	1967
Tucurui	Brazil	....	6,480	UC
Sayansk	U.S.S.R.	....	6,400	UC
Krasnoyarsk	U.S.S.R.	6,096	6,096	1968
LaGrande	Canada	....	5,416	UC
Churchill Falls	Canada	5,225	5,225	1971
Bratsk	U.S.S.R.	4,100	4,600	1964
Sukhovo	U.S.S.R.	....	4,500	UC
Ust-Ilimsk	U.S.S.R.	720	4,320	1974
Ilha Solteira	Brazil	3,200	4,100	1973
Cabora Bassa	Mozambique	2,000	4,000	1975
John Day	Oregon, Washington	2,160	2,700	1968
Volgograd-22nd Congress	U.S.S.R.	2,560	2,560	1958
Volga-V.I. Lenin	U.S.S.R.	2,300	2,300	1955
W.A.C. Bennett	Canada	1,816	2,270	1969
High Aswan (Saad-El-Aali)	Egypt	2,100	2,100	1967
Iron Gate	Romania-Yugoslavia	2,100	2,100	1970
Chief Joseph	Washington	1,024	2,069	1956
Robert Moses-Niagara	New York	1,950	1,950	1961
St. Lawrence Power Dam	Canada-U.S.	1,824	1,824	1958
The Dalles	Washington	1,807	1,807	1957
Beauharnois	Canada	1,021	1,670	1950
Kemano	Canada	813	1,670	1954
Kariba	Rhodesia-Zambia	600	1,500	1959
Tumut-3	Australia	750	1,500	1972
Marimbondo	Brazil	1,440	1,440	1975
Jupia	Brazil	1,411	1,411	1966
McNary	Oregon	980	1,406	1953
Cheboksary	U.S.S.R.	1,404	1,404	1972

NOTE: UC means under construction in 1975.

World's Highest Dams

Source: Bureau of Reclamation, Department of the Interior.

Maximum height				Reservoir capacity	Year
feet	meters	Name	River	in acre-feet	completed
1,066	325	Rogunsky	Vakhsh, U.S.S.R.	9,485,000	UC
1,040	317	Nurek	Vakhsh, U.S.S.R.	8,424,000	UC
935	285	Grand Dixence	Dixence, Switzerland	324,000	1962
892	272	Inguri	Inguri, U.S.S.R.	801,000	UC
858	262	Vaiont	Vaiont, Italy	137,000	1961
794	242	Mica	Columbia, Canada	20,000,000	1974
794	242	Sayansk	Yenesei, U.S.S.R.	25,353,000	UC
787	240	Chicoasen	Grijalva, Mexico	1,346,000	UC
787	240	Patia	Patia, Colombia	15,322,000	UC
778	237	Chivor	Bata, Colombia	661,000	1975
777	237	Mauvoisin	Drance de Bagnes, Switzerland	146,000	1957
770	235	Oroville	Feather R., Calif.	3,538,000	1968
764	233	Chirkey	Sulak, U.S.S.R.	2,252,000	1975
742	226	Bhakra	Sutlej, India	8,000,000	1963
726	221	Hoover	Colorado R., Ariz.-Nev.	29,755,000	1936
722	220	Contra	Verzasca, Switzerland	70,000	1965
722	220	Mratinje	Piva, Yugoslavia	713,000	1975
717	219	Dworshak	North Fork, Clearwater, Idaho	3,453,000	1974
710	216	Glen Canyon	Colorado R., Ariz.	27,000,000	1964
703	214	Daniel Johnson	Manicougan, Canada	115,000,000	1968
699	213	Toktogul	Naryn, U.S.S.R.	15,800,000	UC
685	209	Auburn	North Fork, American, Calif.	2,300,000	UC
682	208	Luzzone	Brenno di Luzzone, Switzerland	70,000	1963
679	207	Keban	Firat, Turkey	25,110,000	1974
666	203	Mohamed Reza Shah Pahlavi	Dez, Iran	2,707,000	1963
662	202	Almendra	Tormes, Spain	2,148,000	1970
656	200	Reza Shah Kabir	Karoun, Iran	2,351,000	1975
650	198	Kölnbrein	Malta, Austria	162,000	UC
637	194	New Bullard's Bar.	North Yuba, Calif.	960,000	1970
625	191	New Melones	Stanislaus, Calif.	2,400,000	1975
610	186	Kurobe No. 4	Kurobe, Japan	162,000	1964
610	186	Swift	Lewis, Wash.	756,000	1958
607	185	Oymapinar	Manavgat, Turkey	243,000	UC
605	184	Mossyrock	Cowlitz, Wash.	1,300,000	1968
602	183	Shasta	Sacramento R., Calif.	4,552,000	1945
600	183	W.A.C. Bennett	Peace, Canada	57,006,000	1967
591	180	Tignes	Isere, France	186,000	1952
591	180	Amir Kabir	Karadj, Iran	166,000	1962
591	180	Tachien	Tachia, Taiwan	207,000	1974
591	180	Itaipu	Parana, Brazil-Paraguay	23,510,000	UC
591	180	Dartmouth	Mitta-Mitta, Australia	5,232,000	1975
591	180	Kara Kaya	Euphrates, Turkey	7,767,000	UC
590	180	Emosson	Barberine, Switzerland	182,000	1974
585	178	Don Pedro (New)	Tuolume, Calif.	2,030,000	1971
584	178	Alpe Gera	Comor, Italy	53,000	1965
580	177	Kopperston Tailings No. 2	Jones Branch, W.Va.	....	1963
577	176	Takase	Takase, Japan	62,000	UC
574	175	Hasan Ugurlu	Yesilirmak, Turkey	874,000	UC
564	172	Hungry Horse	South Fork, Flathead, Mont.	3,468,000	1953
561	171	Idikki	Periyar, India	1,182,000	1974
561	171	Cabora Bassa	Zambezi, Mozambique	51,900,000	1974
551	168	Charvak	Chirchik, U.S.S.R.	1,620,000	1970
550	168	Grand Coulee	Columbia, Wash.	9,724,000	1942
549	167	Vidraru	Arges, Romania	377,000	1965
541	165	King Paul (Kremasta)	Acheloos, Greece	3,850,000	1965
540	165	Ross	Skagit, Wash.	1,435,000	1949
537	164	Trinity	Trinity, Calif.	2,448,000	1962
530	162	Talbingo	Tumut, Australia	747,000	1971
525	160	Yellowtail	Bighorn, Mont.	1,375,000	1966
525	160	Gokcekaya	Sakarya, Turkey	737,000	1973
519	158	Cougar	South Fork, McKenzie, Ore.	219,000	1964
518	158	Curnera	Rein de Curnera, Switzerland	33,000	1966
515	157	Okutadami	Tadami, Japan	487,000	1961
514	157	Speccheri	Leno di Vallarsa, Italy	8,000	1957
512	156	Zeuzier	Lienne, Switzerland	41,000	1957

Maximum height feet	meters	Name	River	Reservoir capacity, in acre-feet	Year completed
510	155	Sakuma	Tenryu, Japan	265,000	1956
509	155	Monteynard	Drac, France	195,000	1962
509	155	Nagawado	Nan and Azusa, Japan	99,000	1969
508	155	Goescheneralp	Goeschenerreous, Switzerland	61,000	1960
505	154	Bhumiphol (Yanhee)	Pinz, Thailand	10,914,000	1964
502	153	Flaming Gorge	Green, Utah	3,789,000	1964
502	153	Place Moulin	Buthier, Italy	81,000	1965
500	152	Gepatsch	Faggenbach, Austria	113,000	1965
500	152	Santa Giustina	Noce, Italy	148,000	1950
495	151	Zervreila	Valserrhein, Switzerland	81,000	1957
492	150	Roseland	Doron-de-Beaufort, France	152,000	1961
492	150	Canelles	Noguera Ribagorzana, Spain	549,000	1960
486	148	Tarbela	Indus, Pakistan	11,100,000	1975
480	146	Fontana	Little Tennessee, N.C.	1,444,300	1944
463	141	Akosombo-Main	Volta, Ghana	120,000,000	1965
456	139	Anderson Ranch	South Fork, Boise, Idaho	493,200	1950
454	138	Detroit	North Santiam, Ore.	455,000	1953
450	137	Chambon	Romanche, France	43,780	1934
450	137	Warragamba	Warragamba, Australia	1,649,000	1960
435	133	Beas	Beas, India	6,600,000	1975
430	131	Pine Flat	Kings, Calif.	1,000,000	1954
430	131	O'Shaughnessy	Toulumne, Calif.	360,360	1938
426	130	Sautet	Drac, France	106,000	1934
425	130	Mud Mountain	White, Wash.	106,000	1949
420	128	Kariba	Zambezi, Rhodesia	130,000,000	1959
417	127	Owyhee	Owyhee, Ore.	1,120,000	1932
410	125	Bratsk	Angara, U.S.S.R.	137,220,000	1964
407	124	Krasnoyarsk	Yenesei, U.S.S.R.	59,425,000	1972
407	124	Navajo	San Juan, N.M.	1,709,000	1963

NOTE: UC means under construction in 1975.

World's Largest Dams

Source: Bureau of Reclamation, Department of the Interior.

Dam	Location	Volume (thousands) Cubic meters	Cubic yards	Year completed
New Cornelia Tailings	Arizona	209,500	274,026	1973
Tarbela	Pakistan	142,000	186,000	1975
Fort Peck	Montana	96,034	125,612	1940
Oahe	South Dakota	70,343	92,008	1963
Oosterschelde	Netherlands	70,000	91,560	UC
Rogunsky	U.S.S.R.	70,000	91,560	UC
Yacyreta-Apipe	Argentina-Paraguay	70,000	91,560	UC
Mangla	Pakistan	65,651	85,872	1967
Gardiner	Canada	65,553	85,743	1968
Afsluitdijk	Netherlands	63,400	82,927	1932
Oroville	California	59,639	78,008	1968
San Luis	California	59,378	77,666	1967
Nurek	U.S.S.R.	58,000	75,864	UC
Garrison	North Dakota	50,846	66,506	1956
Cochiti	New Mexico	49,417	64,631	1975
Tabka	Syria	46,000	60,168	1975
Kiev	U.S.S.R.	44,000	57,552	1964
W. A. C. Bennett	Canada	43,733	57,203	1967
High Aswan (Saad-El-Aili)	Egypt	43,733	57,203	1970
Saratov	U.S.S.R.	40,400	52,843	1967
Mission Tailings #2	Arizona	40,088	52,435	1973
Fort Randall	South Dakota	38,383	50,205	1956
Kanev	U.S.S.R.	37,860	49,520	1974
Kakhova	U.S.S.R.	35,640	46,617	1955
Tsimlyanska	U.S.S.R.	33,891	44,323	1952

NOTE: Based on total volume of dam structure. All dams listed are predominantly earth or rockfill and may contain masonry sections. UC means under construction in 1975.

Highest Mountain Peaks of the World

(For other U. S. Mountain Peaks, see Index)

Mountain peak	Range	Location	Height feet	meters
Everest*	Himalayas	Nepal-Tibet	29,028	8,848
Godwin Austen (K-2)	Karakoram	India	28,250	8,611
Kanchenjunga	Himalayas	Nepal-Sikkim	28,168	8,586
Makalu	Himalayas	Tibet-Nepal	27,790	8,470
Dhaulagiri	Himalayas	Nepal	26,790	8,166
Nanga Parbat	Himalayas	India	26,660	8,126
Annapurna	Himalayas	Nepal	26,496	8,076
Gosainthan	Himalayas	Tibet	26,289	8,013
Nanda Devi	Himalayas	India	25,645	7,817
Chomolonzo	Himalayas	Nepal-Tibet	25,640	7,815
Rakaposhi	Himalayas	India	25,550	7,788
Kamet	Himalayas	India-Tibet	25,447	7,756
Namcha Barwa	Himalayas	Tibet	25,445	7,756
Gurla Mandhata	Himalayas	Tibet	25,355	7,728
Ulurgh Muztagh	Kunlun	Tibet	25,341	7,724
Turich Mir	Hindukush	Pakistan	25,236	7,692
Kula Gangri	Himalayas	Tibet	24,783	7,554
Muztagh Ata	Muztagh Ata	China	24,757	7,546
Skyang Kangri	Himalayas	Kashmir	24,750	7,544
Communism Peak	Pamir	U.S.S.R.	24,547	7,482
Victory Peak	Pamir	U.S.S.R.	24,406	7,439
Sia Kangri	Himalayas	Kashmir	24,340	7,419
Chamlang	Himalayas	Nepal	24,012	7,319
Alung Gangri	Himalayas	Tibet	23,999	7,315
Chomo Lhari	Himalayas	Tibet-Bhutan	23,996	7,314
Muztagh (K-5)	Kunlun	China	23,891	7,282
Amne Machin	Kunlun	China	23,490	7,160
Gaurisankar	Himalayas	Nepal-Tibet	23,440	7,145
Lenin Peak	Pamir	U.S.S.R.	23,405	7,134
Korzhenevski Peak	Pamir	U.S.S.R.	23,310	7,105
Kangto	Himalayas	Tibet	23,260	7,090
Dunagiri	Himalayas	India	23,184	7,066
Pauhunri	Himalayas	India-Tibet	23,180	7,065
Aconcagua	Andes	Argentina-Chile	23,034	7,021
Revolution Peak	Pamir	U.S.S.R.	22,880	6,974
Kangchenjhan	Himalayas	India	22,700	6,919
Siniolchu	Himalayas	India	22,620	6,895
Ojos des Salado	Andes	Argentina-Chile	22,588	6,885
Bonete	Andes	Argentina-Chile	22,546	6,872
Simvoo	Himalayas	India	22,346	6,811
Tup	Andes	Argentina	22,309	6,800
Kungpu	Himalayas	Bhutan	22,300	6,797
Falso-Azufre	Andes	Argentina-Chile	22,277	6,790
Moscow Peak	Pamir	U.S.S.R.	22,260	6,785
Veladero	Andes	Argentina	22,244	6,780
Pissis	Andes	Argentina	22,241	6,779
Mercedario	Andes	Argentina-Chile	22,211	6,770
Huascarán	Andes	Peru	22,198	6,766
Tocorpuri	Andes	Bolivia-Chile	22,162	6,755
Karl Marx Peak	Pamir	U.S.S.R.	22,067	6,726
Llullaillaco	Andes	Argentina-Chile	22,057	6,723
Libertador	Andes	Argentina	22,047	6,720
Kailas	Himalayas	Tibet	22,027	6,714
Lingtren	Himalayas	Nepal-Tibet	21,972	6,697
Incahuasi	Andes	Argentina-Chile	21,719	6,620
Carnicero	Andes	Peru	21,689	6,611
Kurumda	Pamir	U.S.S.R.	21,686	6,610
Garmo Peak	Pamir	U.S.S.R.	21,637	6,595
Sajama	Andes	Bolivia	21,555	6,570
Ancohuma	Andes	Bolivia	21,490	6,550
El Muerto	Andes	Argentina-Chile	21,456	6,540
Nacimiento	Andes	Argentina	21,302	6,493
Illimani	Andes	Bolivia	21,184	6,457
Antofalla	Andes	Argentina-Chile	21,129	6,440
Coropuña	Andes	Peru	21,079	6,425
Cuzco (Ausangate)	Andes	Peru	20,995	6,399
Toro	Andes	Argentina-Chile	20,932	6,380
Parinacota	Andes	Bolivia-Chile	20,768	6,330

Mountain peak	Range	Location	Height (feet)	meters
Chimboraso	Andes	Ecuador	20,702	6,310
Salcantay	Andes	Peru	20,575	6,271
General Manuel Belgrano	Andes	Argentina	20,505	6,250
Chañi	Andes	Argentina	20,341	6,200
Caca Aca	Andes	Bolivia	20,328	6,196
McKinley	Alaska	Alaska	20,320	6,194
Vudor Peak	Pamir	U.S.S.R.	20,118	6,132
Condoriri	Andes	Bolivia	20,095	6,125
Solimana	Andes	Peru	20,069	6,117
Nevada	Andes	Argentina	20,023	6,103
Logan	St. Elias	Canada	19,850	6,050
North Peak	Alaska	Alaska	19,470	5,934
Kilimanjaro	(solitary)	Tanzania	19,340	5,895
Potro	Andes	Chile-Argentina	19,127	5,830
Orizaba (Citlaltepetl)	Sierra Madre Oriental	Mexico	18,701	5,700
Demavend (Damavand)	Elburz	Iran	18,603	5,670
Elbrus	Caucasus	U.S.S.R.	18,431	5,618
St. Elias	St. Elias	Alaska-Canada	18,008	5,489
Popocatepetl	Altiplano de Mexico	Mexico	17,887	5,452
Maipo	Andes	Argentina	17,464	5,323
Foraker	Alaska	Alaska	17,400	5,304
Ixtacihuatl	Altiplano de Mexico	Mexico	17,342	5,286
Lucania	St. Elias	Canada	17,150	5,227
King	St. Elias	Canada	17,130	5,221
Sosneado	Andes	Argentina	17,020	5,188
Ararat	Ararat Range	Turkey	16,946	5,165

* The U. S. Air Force Planning Charts list the height of Mt. Everest as 29,141 ft. There are a number of secondary peaks in this general area which, of course, have local names and are sometimes listed individually. Actually they are all a part of the Everest massif.

Principal Deserts of the World

Desert	Location	Approximate size	Appx. elevation, ft.
Atacama	North Chile	400 mi. long	7,000–13,500
Black Rock	Northwest Nevada	About 1,000 sq. mi.	2,000–5,000
Colorado	Southeast California from San Gorgonio Pass to Gulf of California	200 mi. long and a maximum width of 50 mi.	Few feet above to 250 below sea level
Dasht-i-Kavir	Southeast of Caspian Sea in Iran		2,000
Dasht-i-Lut	Northeast of Kerman in Iran		1,000
Gobi (Shamo)	Covers most of Mongolia	300,000 sq. mi.	3,000–5,000
Great Arabian	Most of Arabia	1,500 mi. long	
Syrian (El Hamad)	North of 30° N. Latitude		1,850
Nefud (Red Desert)	South of Jauf	400 mi. by average of 200 mi.	3,000
Dahna	Southeast of Nefud	400 by 30 mi.	
Rub' al Khali	South portion of Nejd		
Great Australian	Western portion of Australia	About one-half the continent	600–1,000
Great Salt Lake	West of Great Salt Lake to Nevada-Utah line.	80 by 50 mi.	4,500
Kalahari	South Africa between the Orange and Zambezi Rivers	400 by 600 mi., or about 120,000 sq. mi.	Over 3,000
Kara Kum (Desert of Khiva)	Southwest Turkestan south of Lake Aral	110,000 sq. mi.	
Kizil Kum	Central Turkestan southeast of Lake Aral	370 by 220 mi., or about 70,000 sq. mi.	160 near Lake Aral to 2,000 in southeast
Libyan	Eastern Sahara west of Nile	More than 500,000 sq. mi.	
Mohave	North of Colorado Desert and south of Death Valley in SE California	15,000 sq. mi.	2,000
Nubian	From Red Sea to great west bend of the Nile		2,500
Painted Desert	Northeast Arizona	75 mi. wide	High plateau 5,000
Sahara	Northern states of Africa to about 15° N. Lat. and from Red Sea to the Atlantic Ocean	3,200 mi. greatest length along 20° N. Lat.; area over 3,500,000 sq. mi.	440 below sea level to 11,000 above; av. elevation, 1,400–1,600
Takla Makan	S. Central Sinkiang in Tarim Basin	700 mi. long	
Thar (Indian)	Chiefly Rajputana, India	About 300 mi. by 380 mi.	About 500

Large Islands of the World

Island	Location and Status	Area sq mi.	sq km
Greenland	North Atlantic (Danish)	839,999	2,175,597
New Guinea	Southwest Pacific (Irian Jaya, Indonesian, west part; Papua New Guinea, east part)	316,615	820,033
Borneo	West mid-Pacific (Indonesian, south part; British protectorate, and Malaysian, north part)	286,914	743,107
Madagascar	Indian Ocean (Malagasy Republic)	226,657	587,042
Baffin	North Atlantic (Canadian)	183,810	476,068
Sumatra	Northeast Indian Ocean (Indonesian)	182,859	473,605
Honshu	Sea of Japan-Pacific (Japanese)	88,925	230,316
Great Britain	Off coast of NW Europe (England, Scotland and Wales)	88,758	229,883
Ellesmere	Arctic Ocean (Canadian)	82,119	212,688
Victoria	Arctic Ocean (Canadian)	81,930	212,199
Celebes	West mid-Pacific (Indonesian)	72,986	189,034
South Island	South Pacific (New Zealand)	58,093	150,461
Java	Indian Ocean (Indonesian)	48,990	126,884
North Island	South Pacific (New Zealand)	44,281	114,688
Cuba	Caribbean Sea (republic)	44,218	114,525
Newfoundland	North Atlantic (Canadian)	42,734	110,681
Luzon	West mid-Pacific (Philippines)	40,420	104,688
Iceland	North Atlantic (republic)	39,768	102,999
Mindanao	West mid-Pacific (Philippines)	36,537	94,631
Ireland	West of Great Britain (republic, south part; United Kingdom, north part))	32,597	84,426
Hokkaido	Sea of Japan—Pacific (Japanese)	30,372	78,663
Hispaniola	Caribbean Sea (Dominican Republic, east part; Haiti, west part)	29,355	76,029
Tasmania	South of Australia (Australian)	26,215	67,897
Sri Lanka (Ceylon)	Indian Ocean (republic)	25,332	65,610
Sakhalin (Karafuto)	North of Japan (U.S.S.R.)	24,560	63,610
Banks	Arctic Ocean (Canadian)	23,230	60,166
Devon	Arctic Ocean (Canadian)	20,861	54,030
Tierra del Fuego	Southern tip of South America (Argentinian, east part; Chilean, west part)	18,605	48,187
Kyushu	Sea of Japan—Pacific (Japanese)	16,223	42,018
Melville	Arctic Ocean (Canadian)	16,141	41,805
Axel Heiberg	Arctic Ocean (Canadian)	15,779	40,868
Southampton	Hudson Bay (Canadian)	15,700	40,663

Famous Ship Canals of the World

Name	Location	Year opened	Length (mi.)*	Width (ft.)	Depth (ft.)	Locks
Albert	Belgium	1939	80.0	53.0	16.5	6
Amsterdam-Rhine	Netherlands	1952	45.0	164.0	41.0	3
Beaumont-Port Arthur	United States	1916	40.0	200.0	34.0	..
Chesapeake and Delaware	United States	1927	19.0	250.0	27.0	..
Houston	United States	1914	43.0	300.0	34.0	..
Kiel (Nord-Ostsee Kanal)	Germany	1895	61.3	144.0	36.0	4
Panama	Canal Zone	1914	50.7	110.0	41.0	12
St. Lawrence Seaway	U.S. & Canada	1959	2,400.0†	‡	..	..
Montreal to Prescott	U.S. & Canada	1959	11.5	80.0	30.0	7
Welland	Canada	1931	27.5	80.0	27.0	8
Sault Ste. Marie	Canada	1895	1.2	60.0	16.8	1
Sault Ste. Marie	United States	1915	1.6	80.0	25.0	4
Suez	U.A.R. (Egypt)	1869	100.6§	197.0	36.0	..

* In statute miles.   † From Montreal to Duluth.   ‡ 442 ft.–550 ft.; there are 11½ miles of locks, 80 ft. wide and 30 ft. deep.   § From Port Said lighthouse to entrance channel in Suez roads.

Notable Modern Bridges

Sources: Encyclopaedia Britannica and American Society of Civil Engineers.

Suspension

Length of main span, feet	Name	Location	Year completed
4,626	Humber	Hull, Britain	UC[1]
4,260	Verrazano-Narrows	Lower New York Bay	1964
4,200	Golden Gate	San Francisco Bay	1937
3,800	Mackinac Straits	Michigan	1957
3,524	Bosporus	Istanbul, Turkey	1973
3,500	George Washington	Hudson River at New York City	1931
3,323	"Ponte 25 de Abril"	Tagus River at Lisbon, Portugal	1966
3,300	Forth Road	Queensferry, Scotland, U.K.	1964
3,240	Severn	Severn River at Beachley, Britain	1966
2,800	Tacoma Narrows	Puget Sound at Tacoma, Washington	1950
2,336	Kanmon Straits	Kyushu-Honshu, Japan	1973
2,336	Angostura	Orinoco River at Ciudad Bolívar, Venezuela	1967
2,310	Transbay (twin spans)	San Francisco Bay	1936
2,300	Bronx-Whitestone	East River, New York City	1939
2,190	Pierre Laporte	St. Lawrence River at Quebec, Canada	1970
2,150	Delaware Memorial (twin bridges)	Delaware River near Wilmington, Del.	1951 & 1968
2,150	Seaway Skyway	St. Lawrence R. at Ogdensburg, N.Y.	1960
2,000	Gas Pipe Line	Atchafalaya River, La.	1951
2,000	Walt Whitman	Delaware River at Philadelphia, Pa.	1957
1,995	Tancarville	Seine River at Tancarville, France	1959
1,969	Lillebaelt	Lillebaelt Strait, Denmark	1970
1,850	Ambassador International	Detroit River at Detroit, Michigan	1929
1,800	Throgs Neck	East River, New York City	1961
1,750	Benjamin Franklin	Delaware River at Philadelphia, Pa.	1926
1,722	Skjomen	Narvik, Norway	1972
1,722	Kvalsund	Hammerfest, Norway	UC[1]
1,640	Emmerich	Rhein River at Emmerich, Germany	1965
1,632	Bear Mountain	Hudson River at Peekskill, New York	1924
1,600	Wm. Preston Lane, Jr., Memorial (twin bridges)	Near Annapolis, Maryland	1952 & 1973
1,600	Williamsburg	East River, New York City	1903
1,600	Newport	Narragansett Bay at Newport, Rhode Island	1969
1,595	Brooklyn	East River, New York City	1883

Cantilever

1,800	Quebec Railway	St. Lawrence River at Quebec, Canada	1917
1,710	Forth Railway (twin spans)	Queensferry, Britain	1890
1,673	Minato Ohashi	Osaka, Japan	1974
1,644	Commodore John Barry	Chester, Pennsylvania	1974
1,576	Greater New Orleans	Mississippi River, La.	1958
1,500	Howrah	Hooghly River at Calcutta, India	1943
1,235	Baton Rouge	Mississippi River, La.	1968
1,212	Tappan Zee	Hudson River at Tarrytown, New York	1955
1,200	Longview	Columbia River at Longview, Washington	1930
1,200	Patapsco River	Baltimore Harbor Outer Crossing, Md.	1976
1,182	Queensboro	East River, New York City	1909

Steel Arch

1,700	New River Gorge	Fayetteville, W. Va.	1977
1,652	Bayonne	Kill Van Kull at Bayonne, New Jersey	1931
1,650	Sydney Harbour	Sydney, Australia	1932
1,255	Fremont	Portland, Ore.	1973
1,200	Port Mann	Fraser River at Vancouver, British Columbia	1964
1,128	Thatcher Ferry	Panama Canal, Panama	1962
1,100	Laviolette	St. Lawrence River, Trois Rivieres, Que., Can.	1967
1,083	Zdákov	Vltava River, Czechoslovakia	1967
1,082	Runcorn-Widnes	Mersey River, Britain	1961
1,080	Birchenough	Sabi River at Ft. Victoria, Rhodesia	1935

Cable-Stayed

1,500	Second Hooghly	Calcutta, India	UC[1]
1,325	Saint-Nazaire	Loire River, France	1975
1,235	Mississippi River	Luling, La.	UC[1]
1,205	Dusseldorf-Flehe	Rhine River, W. Germany	UC[1]
1,148	Duisburg-Neuenkamp	Duisburg, Germany	1970
1,116	Mesopotamia	Corrientes, Argentina	1972
1,102	West Gate	Lower Yarra River at Melbourne, Australia	1970
1,083	Zárate	Paraná River, Argentina	1975

Length of main span, feet	Name	Location	Year completed
1,083	Brazo Largo	.Paraná River, Argentina	1976
1,066	Köhlbrand	.Hamburg, Germany	1974
1,050	Kniebrücke	.Rhein River at Düsseldorf, Germany	1969
1,050	Brotonne[2]	.Seine River, France	1976
1,000	Erskine	.Clyde River at Glasgow, Britain	1971

Continuous Truss

1,232	Astoria	.Columbia River at Astoria, Oregon	1966
1,066	Oshima	.Oshima Island, Japan	1976
1,052	Croton Reservoir	.Croton, New York	1970
984	Tenmon	.Kumamoto, Japan	1966
984	Kuronoseto	.Nagashima-Kyushu, Japan	1974
902	Ravenswood	.Ohio Riv., Ravenswood, W. Va.	UC[1]
845	Dubuque	.Mississippi River at Dubuque, Iowa	1943
840	Braga Memorial	.Taunton River at Somerset, Massachusetts	1966
839	Graf Spee	.Germany	1936

Concrete Arch

1,000	Gladesville	.Parramatta River at Sydney, Australia	1964
951	Amizade	.Paraná River at Foz do Iguassu, Brazil	1964
886	Arrábida	.Porto, Portugal	1963
866	Sandö	.Angerman River at Kramfors, Sweden	1943
808	Shibenik	.Krka River, Yugoslavia	1966
758	Fiumarella	.Catanzaro, Italy	1961
748	Zaporozhe	.Old Dnepr River, U.S.S.R.	1952
692	Novi Sad	.Danube River, Yugoslavia	1961

[1]Under construction. [2]Concrete bridge.

Notable Tunnels of the World
Railroad, excluding subways

Length, miles	Name	Location	Year completed
33.1	Seikan	Tsugara Straits, Japan	UC[3]
12.3	Simplon (I and II)	Alps, Switzerland–Italy	1906 & 1922
11.6	Kammon Straits	Honshu to Kyoshu Islands, Japan	UC[3]
11.5	Apennine	Genoa, Italy	1934
9.3	St. Gotthard	Swiss Alps	1881
9.1	Lötschberg	Swiss Alps	1911
8.5[1]	Mont Cénis	French Alps	1871
7.8	New Cascade	Cascade Mts., Washington	1929
7.0	Vosges	Vosges, France	1940
6.3	Arlberg	Austrian Alps	1884
6.2	Moffat	Rocky Mts., Colorado	1928
6.1	Shimuzu	Shimuzu, Japan	1931
5.5	Rimutaka	Wairarapa, New Zealand	1955
5.5	Kaimai	Bay of Plenty, New Zealand	UC[3]
5.3	Ricken	Swiss Alps	1910
5.3	Grenchenberg	Swiss Alps	1915
5.3	Arthurs Pass	Otira, New Zealand	1923

Vehicular

10.2	St. Gotthard	Alps, Switzerland	UC[3]
7.5	Mt. Blanc	Alps, France–Italy	1965
3.4	Great St. Bernard	Alps, Switzerland–Italy	1964
3.2	Mount Royal	Montreal, Canada	1918
2.5	Lincoln	Hudson River, New York–New Jersey	1937
2.2	Queensway Road	Mersey River, Liverpool, England	1934
2.1	Brooklyn-Battery	East River, New York City	1950
1.7	Holland	Hudson River, New York–New Jersey	1927
1.4	Hampton Roads	Norfolk, Virginia	1957
1.3	Queens-Midtown	East River, New York City	1940
1.2	Liberty Tubes	Pittsburgh, Pennsylvania	1923
1.2	Baltimore Harbor	Baltimore, Maryland	1957
1.2	Allegheny Tunnels	Pennsylvania Turnpike	1940[2]
1.1	Sumner	Boston, Massachusetts	1934
1.0	Detroit International	Detroit, Mich.–Windsor, Ont.	1930
1.0	Tuscarora Tunnels	Pennsylvania Turnpike	1968

[1] Lengthened to its present 8.5 miles in 1881. [2] New Parallel tunnel built in 1965, twin tunnel in 1966. [3] Under construction.

Population, Land Areas of the World, and World Elevations

Area	Estimated population, in thousands, 1974	Approximate land area, in thousands of sq. mi.	Per cent of total land area	Population density per sq. ml.	Elevation, feet Highest	Elevation, feet Lowest	Dimensions, miles East-West	Dimensions, miles North-South
WORLD	3,890,000	58,473	100.0	74.1[1]	Mt. Everest, Asia, 29,028	Dead Sea, Asia, 1,290 below sea level	24,902	24,860
ASIA, incl. Philippines, Indonesia, and European and Asiatic Turkey; excl. Asiatic U.S.S.R.	2,206,000	10,678	18.2	206.6	Mt. Everest, Tibet-Nepal, 29,028	Dead Sea, Israel-Jordan, 1,290 below sea level	5,400[2]	5,300[2]
AFRICA	391,000	11,707	20.0	33.4	Mt. Kilimanjaro, Tanzania, 19,340	Qattara Depression, Egypt, 440 below sea level	4,600	5,000
NORTH AMERICA, including Hawaii, Central America, and Caribbean region	338,000	9,362	16.0	36.1	Mt. McKinley, Alaska, 20,320	Death Valley, Calif., 282 below sea level	3,200[5]	4,000[5]
SOUTH AMERICA	212,000	6,885	11.8	30.8	Mt. Aconcagua, Arg.-Chile, 23,034	Sea level	3,200	4,600
ANTARCTICA	....	6,000	10.3	....	Vinson Massif, Sentinel Range, 16,863	Sea level	....	....
EUROPE, incl. Iceland; excl. European U.S.S.R. and European Turkey	470,000	1,906	3.3	246.6	Mont Blanc, France, 15,781	Sea level	3,300[3]	2,400[3]
OCEANIA, incl. Australia, New Zealand, Micronesia, Melanesia, and Polynesia[4]	20,900	3,286	5.6	6.4	Mauna Kea, Hawaii, 13,796	Lake Eyre, Australia, 38 below sea level	....	....
U.S.S.R., both European and Asiatic	252,000	8,649	14.8	29.1	Mt. Elbrus, Caucasus, 18,431	Caspian Sea, 96 below sea level	5,000	2,500

[1] In computing density per square mile, the area of Antarctica is omitted. [2] Including Asiatic U.S.S.R. [3] Including European U.S.S.R. [4] Although Hawaii is geographically part of Oceania, its population is included in the population figure for North America. [5] Excludes Hawaii.

Some Countries With High Population Densities (per square mile)

Monaco 38,461.5	South Korea 904.7	Lebanon 738.5	El Salvador 500.0
Singapore 10,088.5	Netherlands 872.9	West Germany 645.4	Italy 483.6
Bangladesh 1,415.5	Belgium 832.7	United Kingdom ... 593.5	India 481.6
China, Rep. of 1,166.1	Japan 780.5	Sri Lanka 564.5	Israel 431.1

HISTORICAL AND NEWS EVENTS
FROM ANCIENT TO MODERN TIMES
(See also *Headline History of Our Times,* page 323)

Actium, Battle of (31 B.C.). Octavius defeats Mark Anthony.

Alexander the Great conquers Greece, Persia, Egypt, and part of India (334–323 B.C.). Major battles: Granicus (334 B.C.), Issus (333), Arbela (331).

American Revolution (1775–83). Outstanding events: 1775—Battle of Lexington-Concord (Apr. 19). Battle of Bunker Hill (June 17). 1776—Battle of Long Island (Aug. 27). 1777—Burgoyne surrenders at Saratoga (Oct. 17). 1781—Battle of Cowpens (Jan. 17). Battle of Yorktown (Sept. 28–Oct. 19), and British surrender by Cornwallis. 1783—Treaty of Paris (Sept. 3).

"Babylonian Captivity" of Papacy with seat at Avignon (1309–77).

Bacon's Rebellion (May 10–Oct. 18, 1676). Nathaniel Bacon leads unsuccessful insurrection in Virginia because of abuses in government administration and taxation.

Balkan Wars (1912–13). Bulgaria, Serbia, Greece, and Montenegro defeat Turkey; later, Bulgaria attacks Serbia and Greece and is defeated. Treaty of Bucharest (Aug. 10, 1913).

Bastille destroyed (July 14, 1789).

Benedictine Order founded at Monte Cassino (c. A.D. 529).

Bible translated by Wycliffe into English (1382–84); Douay Version published (1582 & 1609–10); King James Version published (1611).

Black Death (beginning c. 1347). Plague wipes out at least one-quarter of population of Europe.

Black Friday (Sept. 24, 1869). Financial panic results from gold corner in U. S.

Boer War (1899–1902). Boers (descendants of Dutch settlers in South Africa) defeated by British; sign peace treaty at Pretoria (May 31, 1902).

Boston Massacre (Mar. 5, 1770). British soldiers fire on Boston mob, killing 3.

Boston Tea Party (Dec. 16, 1773). Colonials dump tea in Boston Harbor because of tea tax.

Boxer Rebellion (1900). Uprising by secret society in northern China against foreigners.

Brown, John, and 18 followers raid Harpers Ferry (Oct. 16, 1859) and seize arsenal; taken prisoners by U. S. Marines (Oct. 18); Brown hanged (Dec. 2).

Burr-Hamilton duel. *See* Hamilton.

Carthage founded by Phoenicians (c. 900 B.C.); destroyed by Romans (146 B.C.).

Châlons, Battle of (A.D. 451). Attila the Hun defeated by Romans.

Charlemagne crowned Emperor of the West (A.D. 800).

Charles I beheaded (Jan. 30, 1649). *See also* Great Rebellion.

Children's Crusade (1212). About 50,000 unarmed children set out to recover Holy Sepulchre; all are lost or die on the way.

Chinese-Japanese War (1894–95). Japan wins Formosa, Pescadores, and part of southern Manchuria; Korea becomes independent (annexed by Japan, 1910); Treaty of Shimonoseki (Apr. 17, 1895).

Christianity made official religion of Roman Empire (A.D. 330).

Civil War, American (1861–65). Outstanding events: 1861—First Battle of Bull Run (July 21). 1862—*Monitor* defeats *Merrimack* (Mar. 9). Battle of Antietam (Sept. 15–17). 1863—Lincoln's Emancipation Proclamation (Jan. 1). Battle of Gettysburg (July 1–3). Grant captures Vicksburg (July 4). Battle of Lookout Mountain (Nov. 23–25). 1864—Battle of the Wilderness (May 5–6). Sherman's March through Georgia (Nov. 14–Dec. 22). 1865—Lee surrenders at Appomattox (Apr. 9).

Code Napoléon, unified codification of French law, adopted (1804).

Code of Hammurabi (c. 2300 B.C.). Oldest existing written code of laws.

Columbus, Christopher, on first voyage 1492–93) reaches Bahamas (Oct. 12, 1492). Ships: *Santa María, Pinta,* and *Niña.* Other voyages: second (1493–96); third (1498–1500); fourth (1502–04).

Communist Manifesto issued by Karl Marx and Friedrich Engels (1848).

Compromise of 1850 admits California as free state; organizes Utah and New Mexico as territories without mention of slavery; prohibits slave trade in D. C.; returns fugitive slaves to masters; pays Texas $10 million for her claim to New Mexico.

Confederate States of America (Confederacy) proclaimed (Feb. 9, 1861); Jefferson Davis becomes provisional President (Feb. 18, 1861), President (Feb. 22, 1862); last Confederate Cabinet meeting (Apr. 24, 1865); last Confederate army surrenders (May 26, 1865).

Congress of Berlin (1878) meets to revise Treaty of San Stefano, which ended Russo-Turkish War; makes extensive redivision of southeastern Europe.

Congress of Paris (1856) meets to settle problems in Eastern Europe following Crimean War; Treaty of Paris signed (Mar. 30).

Congress of Vienna (1814–15). European powers, under leadership of Metternich, meet to settle problems of territory and government resulting from Napoleonic Wars.

Constantinople founded (as Byzantium) by Greeks (c. 660 B.C.); made capital of Eastern Roman Empire by Constantine the Great (A.D. 330); captured by Turks (1453); renamed Istanbul (1930).

Council of Nicaea (A.D. 325). Called by Constantine the Great; establishes official creed of Christianity (Nicene Creed).

Council of Trent (1545–64). Called by Pope Paul III, at suggestion of Emperor Charles V, to establish Catholic Counter Reformation.

"Coxey's Army" (Mar. 25–May 1, 1894). Jacob S. Coxey leads 20,000 unemployed on Washington, D. C.

Crimean War (1853–56). Russia loses claim to Greek Christians under Turkish flag. *See also* Congress of Berlin.

Crucifixion of Christ (c. A.D. 29). According to New Testament, Christ rose from the dead two days later.

Crusades (1096–1291). European Christians, in seven periods of conflict, attempt to recover Holy Land from Moslems. *See also* Children's Crusade.

Custer massacre (June 25, 1876). Gen. George A. Custer and his forces are killed at Battle of the Little Big Horn by Sioux.

Divine Comedy by Dante begun (1307); probably finished in last year of his life (1321).

Dominican Order founded (1215).

Dorr Rebellion (1841–42). Thomas W. Dorr leads unsuccessful attempt to extend franchise in Rhode Island; franchise extended 1843.

Dred Scott case (1846). Dred Scott, black slave, sues for freedom on claim he has lived for a time on free soil; U. S. Supreme Court rules (Mar. 6, 1857) that Scott is not a citizen and has no standing in court.

Dreyfus case (1894). Capt. Alfred Dreyfus found guilty of treason in France and sentenced to Devil's Island. Finally acquitted (1906).

Edict of Nantes (1598). Extends tolera-

tion to Huguenots (French Protestants); its revocation (1685) causes widespread persecution of Huguenots.

Evolution trial. *See* Scopes.

Fawkes, Guy. *See* Gunpowder Plot.

Feudalism, lord-vassal social system, established throughout Europe (9th century); begins to break up (14th–15th centuries).

Franciscan Order founded (1210).

Franco-Prussian War (1870–71). France defeated by German states; loses Alsace-Lorraine; Treaty of Frankfurt (May 10, 1871).

Freedom of press established in America as John Peter Zenger, New York editor, is acquitted in libel case against Gov. Cosby (1735).

French and Indian War. *See* Seven Years' War.

French Revolution (1789–99). Outstanding events: 1789—Bastille destroyed (July 14). Feudal rights abolished (Aug. 4). 1792—September Massacres (Sept. 2–6). France becomes republic (Sept. 21). 1793—Louis XVI beheaded (Jan. 21); Marie Antoinette beheaded (Oct. 16). Reign of Terror (spring 1793–summer 1794). 1795—Napoleon heads army. Directory established (Oct. 27). (Revolution merges into Napoleonic Wars.)

Gold Rush develops as gold is discovered at Sutter's Mill, near Sacramento, Calif. (Jan. 24, 1848).

Great Rebellion (1642–49). Civil wars in England. Charles I beheaded (Jan. 30, 1649); Cromwell establishes Commonwealth (1649).

Gunpowder Plot (1605). Guy Fawkes, agent of conspirators against King and Parliament, seized as he is about to blow up House of Lords (Nov. 5).

Hamilton-Burr duel (July 11, 1804) results in Hamilton's death next day.

Hastings, Battle of (1066). Normans led by William the Conqueror invade England.

Hegira (A.D. 622). Mohammed flees from Mecca to Medina. Year I of Moslem calendar.

Holy Alliance formed by Russia, Austria, and Prussia (Sept. 26, 1815); intended to regulate government according to Christianity but actually used for repressing political liberty.

Holy Roman Empire founded by Otto the Great (962); dissolved by Napoleon (1806).

Huguenots. *See* Edict of Nantes; St. Bartholomew Massacre.

Hundred Years' War (1338–1453). England loses lands in France. Major battles: Crécy (1346), Poitiers (1356), Agincourt (1415).

Industrial Revolution begins in England (c. 1760). Machines gradually replace hand tools, bringing about vast industrial and social changes.

Inquisition established (c. 1233) to combat heresy; put under state control in Spain (1480); abolished in France (1772), in Spain (1834).

International, First (1864). Founded in London to further world socialism; dissolved in Philadelphia (1876).

International, Second (1889). Founded in Paris to celebrate 100th anniversary of French Revolution.

International, Third (1919). Founded in Moscow as protest against inactivity of Second International; dissolved (1943). Also called *Communist International* or *Comintern*.

Jamestown, Va., settled by British under Capt. John Smith (1607).

Jerusalem destroyed by Nebuchadnezzar (586 B.C.); returned to Jews by Cyrus (538 B.C.); captured by Titus (A.D. 70); captured by Crusaders (1099); captured by Saladin (1187).

Jesuits (Society of Jesus) founded by Ignatius of Loyola (1534).

Joan of Arc burned at stake (1431).

Justinian Code (A.D. 533). Codification of Roman law by Byzantine Emperor Justinian.

Kansas-Nebraska Act (1854) abrogates Missouri Compromise; permits territories of Kansas and Nebraska local option on slavery question; results in rioting and bloodshed.

Korean War. *See* index.

Leopold-Loeb case (1924). Nathan Leopold and Richard Loeb kidnap and kill Bobby Franks in Chicago (May 22); defended by Clarence Darrow; sentenced to life imprisonment (July 21); Loeb killed by fellow convict (Jan. 28, 1936); Leopold receives parole (1958), released from parole (1963). Died in 1971.

Lindbergh kidnapping case (1932). Charles A. Lindbergh's baby son kidnapped (Mar. 1); found slain (May 12); Bruno Richard Hauptmann arrested (Sept. 20, 1934) and accused of crime; convicted (Feb. 13, 1935); electrocuted (Apr. 3, 1936).

Locarno Conferences (Oct. 1925) seek to insure peace and preserve boundaries in Europe by mutual guarantees.

Louis XVI beheaded (Jan. 21, 1793). *See also* French Revolution.

Magna Carta, charter listing rights and privileges of English barons, proclaimed at Runnymede (June 15, 1215); King John forced by barons to accept it.

Manhattan Island purchased by Peter Minuit from Indians (1626) for trinkets worth 60 guilders (about $24).

Mary, Queen of Scots, convicted in England (1586) of being accomplice in plot to murder Queen Elizabeth; beheaded (Feb. 8, 1587).

Maximilian, Emperor of Mexico, executed by Benito Juárez (June 19, 1867) after Napoleon III of France withdraws support of Mexican empire.

Merrimack. *See* Monitor.

Mexican War (1846–1848) ends in American victory; Treaty of Guadalupe Hidalgo (Feb. 2, 1848).

Ming Dynasty (1368–1644). Noted for great development of culture and art in China.

Missouri Compromise (1820) admits Maine as free state, Missouri as slave state; slavery prohibited in Louisiana Territory north of 36° 30'. *See also* Kansas-Nebraska Act.

Monitor, Union ship, defeats *Merrimack,* Confederate ship (Mar. 9, 1862).

Mooney, Tom, sentenced to death for bomb explosion in San Francisco during Preparedness Day Parade (July 22, 1916); sentence commuted to life (1918); freed (1939).

Mormonism (Church of Jesus Christ of Latter-day Saints) founded by Joseph Smith at Fayette, N. Y. (Apr. 6, 1830).

Moses leads Jews out of Egypt (c. 1300 B.C.).

Napoleonic Wars (1796–1815). Outstanding events: 1798—Campaign in Egypt. 1805 —Nelson defeats French at Battle of Trafalgar (Oct. 21). French defeat Russians and Austrians at Battle of Austerlitz (Dec. 2). 1813—French defeated in Battle of Leipzig (Oct. 16–19). 1814— Napoleon abdicates (Apr. 11); sent to Elba. 1815—Napoleon flees Elba (Feb. 26); defeated in Battle of Waterloo (June 18); again abdicates (June 22); exiled by British government to St. Helena (arrival Oct. 16). *See also* Congress of Vienna.

Northwest Ordinance (1787). Adopted for territory north of Ohio River. Establishes method for admitting new states; prohibits slavery in territory.

Orthodox Eastern Church excommunicated by Pope Leo IX (1054); schism final between Western and Eastern Churches.

Parliament established in England (1295).

Peloponnesian War (431–404 B.C.). Sparta under Lysander defeats Athens.

Persian Wars (499–478 B.C.). Greece defeats Persia. Major battles: Marathon (490 B.C.), Thermopylae (480), Salamis (480), Plataea (479), Mycale (479).

Pilgrims land at Plymouth Rock (Dec. 21, 1620).

Plague in London ("Great Plague") causes 68,596 deaths (1665).

Plymouth Rock. *See* Pilgrims.

Poland partitioned out of existence among Prussia, Russia, and Austria (1772, 1793, 1795).

Pony Express (1860–61). Between St. Joseph, Mo., and Sacramento, Calif.

Pullman strike (June–July 1894). Strike smashed by Federal troops; Eugene V. Debs jailed for contempt.

Punic Wars (264–146 B.C.). Romans defeat Carthaginians and destroy Carthage (146 B.C.). Major battles: Cannae (216 B.C.), Zama (202).

Reformation (beginning 16th century). Outstanding events: Luther nails his 95 theses to church door at Wittenberg, Germany (1517). Zwingli begins Reformation in Switzerland (1519). Luther burns papal bull and canon law (1520). Calvin publishes *Institutes of the Christian Religion* (1536). Act of Supremacy makes King head of Church of England (1534). Calvin organizes Geneva as theocratic state (1541). Knox establishes Presbyterian Church in Scotland (1560).

Renaissance (14th–16th centuries). Revival of classical learning in Europe stimulates vigorous activity in arts, literature, humanities, etc.

Roman Empire established under Augustus (27 B.C.); divided into Western and Eastern Empires (A.D. 395); Western Empire falls (476); Eastern Empire falls with capture of Constantinople (1453).

Rome founded, according to legend, by Romulus (753 B.C.); burned, perhaps by Nero (A.D. 64); sacked by Visigoths under Alaric (410); sacked by Vandals under Genseric (455).

Russian Revolution (1917). Revolution begins in Petrograd (Mar. 8). New provisional government headed by Prince Lvov (Mar. 12). Tsar Nicholas II abdicates (Mar. 15). Kerensky replaces Lvov (July 20). Bolsheviks seize power (Nov. 6–7) and Lenin becomes ruler of Russia.

Russo-Japanese War (1904–05). Port Arthur surrenders to Japanese (Jan. 2, 1905); Treaty of Portsmouth, N. H. (Sept. 5).

Russo-Turkish War (1877–78). Power of Turkey in Europe broken; Treaty of San Stefano (Mar. 3, 1878). *See also* Congress of Berlin.

Sacco-Vanzetti case (1920–27). Paymaster and guard are killed in holdup of shoe factory in South Braintree, Mass. (Apr. 15, 1920); anarchists Nicola Sacco and Bartolomeo Vanzetti are arrested (May 5) and accused of crime; convicted (July 14, 1921); executed (Aug. 23, 1927).

St. Bartholomew, massacre of (Aug. 24–Oct. 3, 1572). Some 50,000 Huguenots (French Protestants) killed in Paris and provinces at instigation of Catherine de Médicis.

Savonarola, Florentine priest and dictator, tried for sedition and heresy (1498); hanged and burned (May 23).

Seven Years' War (1756–63). France, Austria, Sweden, Russia vs. England and Prussia. Clive defeats French at Battle of Plassey (1757), giving British supremacy in India; England wins Canada; Prussia retains Silesia. (American phases of war known as French and Indian War, 1754–63.)

Shays' Rebellion (1786). Capt. Daniel Shays leads unsuccessful insurrection against Massachusetts government because of economic crisis.

Slavery in British Empire abolished by Parliament (1833).

Slavery introduced into American Colonies at Jamestown, Va. (1619); abolished in U. S. by 13th Amendment (1865).

Snyder-Gray case (1927). Ruth Snyder and Judd Gray murder her husband, Albert Snyder (Mar. 20); both executed at Sing Sing (Jan. 12, 1928).

Spanish-American War (1898). Outstanding events: U. S. battleship *Maine* blown up in Havana harbor (Feb. 15). Dewey destroys Spanish fleet at Manila (May 1). Charge of San Juan Hill (July 1). Cervera's fleet destroyed off Santiago, Cuba, by U. S. ships (July 3). Treaty of Paris (Dec. 10).

Spanish Armada destroyed by British (1588).

Spanish Civil War (1936–39). Troops led by Gen. Franco revolt in Spanish Morocco (July 17, 1936), and uprisings follow in Spain. Franco named Chief of State by rebels (Oct. 1). War in Spain continues until Madrid falls to rebels (Mar. 28 1939).

Spartacus, Roman slave and gladiator, leads unsuccessful slave insurrection (73–71 B.C.).

Stamp Act (effective Nov. 1, 1765). First direct tax placed on America by Britain; protested by Stamp Act Congress in New York (Oct. 7–25); repealed by Britain (Mar. 18, 1766).

Texan war of independence from Mexico (1836). Major battles: Alamo (Mar. 6), San Jacinto (Apr. 21).

Thaw-White case (1906). Harry K. Thaw, millionaire, murders Stanford White, noted architect, in Madison Square Garden, New York City (June 25).

Thirty Years' War (1618–1648). England, Holland, France, Sweden, and German Protestants against Spain, Italy, and German Catholics; Peace of Westphalia ends conflict, Alsace going to France, Swiss independence recognized, and German secularized states given religious freedom.

Tours, Battle of (A.D. 732). Charles Martel defeats Moslems, checking their advance in western Europe. Also called Battle of Poitiers.

Trojan War (c. 1200 B.C.). Greeks defeat Trojans in 10-year war; destroy city of Troy.

Tweed Ring, corrupt New York political group headed by William Marcy Tweed, Tammany Boss, broken up (1872); Tweed convicted (Nov. 5).

Vietnam War. *See* index.

War of 1812 (1812–1815). Outstanding events: 1813—Battle of Lake Erie (Sept. 10). 1814—British burn White House at Washington (Aug. 24–25). Battle of Lake Champlain (Sept. 11). U. S. signs treaty with Britain at Gent (Dec. 24). 1815—Battle of New Orleans (Jan. 8). (Slowness of communications was responsible for continuation of hostilities after treaty.)

Wars of the Roses (1455–85). House of York (white rose) against House of Lancaster (red rose). Richard III slain at Battle of Bosworth Field (1485); Tudor line started by Henry VII.

Whisky Insurrection (July–Nov. 1794). Farmers in western Pennsylvania revolt unsuccessfully against excise tax of 1791.

Witch trials in Salem, Mass., result in death sentences for 19 women by Judge Samuel Sewall (1692).

World War I (1914–18). Central Powers (Austria-Hungary, Germany, Bulgaria, Turkey) vs. Allies (U. S., Britain, France, Russia, Belgium, Serbia, Greece, Rumania, Montenegro, Portugal, Italy, Japan). Outstanding events: 1914—Austria declares war on Serbia (July 28). Germany declares war on Russia (Aug. 1) and on France (Aug. 3). Germany invades Belgium (Aug. 4). Britain declares war on Germany (Aug. 4). Germans defeat Russians at Tannenberg, East Prussia (Aug. 31). First Battle of the Marne (Sept. 5–12). 1915 Dardanelles campaign against Turkey fails. 1916—Battle of Jutland (May 31). Battles of the Somme (July–Nov.). Germans turned back at Verdun (Sept. 3). Rumania overrun by Central Powers; fall of Bucharest (Dec. 6). 1917—Germany begins unrestricted submarine warfare. U. S. declares war (Apr. 6). Battle of Caporetto (Oct. 24–Dec. 26). 1918—Russia signs Treaty of Brest-Litovsk with Germany (Mar. 3). Second Battle of the Somme (Aug. 21–Sept. 3). Third Battle of the Aisne (May 27–June 6). Second Battle of the Marne (July 15–Aug. 7). U. S. troops take St. Mihiel (Sept. 13). Battle of the Meuse-Argonne (Sept. 20–Nov. 11). Allies break Hindenburg line (Oct. 5). Armistice signed (Nov. 11).

World War II (1939–45). Axis powers (Germany, Italy, Japan, Hungary, Romania, Bulgaria) vs. United Nations (U. S., Britain, France, U.S.S.R., Australia, Belgium, Brazil, Canada, China, Denmark, Greece, Netherlands, New Zealand, Norway, Poland, South Africa, Yugoslavia). For major events of war, see years 1939–1945 in Headline History of Our Times, which follows.

Zenger case. *See* Freedom of press.

HEADLINE HISTORY OF OUR TIMES

Based on Newspaper Accounts of Important Events through 1975

For Conferences and Treaties, see pages 572–77. For Vietnam War summary, see page 334.

1914

July 28—Austria declares war on Serbia; World War I begins.

Aug. 15—Panama Canal opens.

Aug. 20—Pope Pius X dies. He is succeeded Sept. 3 by Cardinal Della Chiesa, who becomes Benedict XV.

1915

May 7—British steamer *Lusitania* sunk off Irish coast by German submarine; 1,198 dead, including 124 Americans.

1916

Dec. 16—"Mad Monk" Grigori Rasputin killed by group of Russian noblemen.

1917

Mar. 8—Russian Revolution begins.

Mar. 15—Tsar Nicholas II abdicates.

Apr. 6—U.S. enters World War I.

Nov. 2—Balfour Declaration promises Jewish homeland in Palestine.

Nov. 6–7—Bolsheviks seize power in Russia.

1918

Jan. 8—President Wilson makes 14-point address to Congress outlining program for peace.

July 16—Tsar Nicholas II and his family shot in Russia.

Nov. 10—Kaiser William II flees from Germany to Netherlands.

Nov. 11—World War I ends.

Nov. 11—Emperor Charles I of Austria abdicates; Austria becomes republic on Nov. 12.

1919

Feb. 11—Friedrich Ebert becomes President of new German republic.

June 28—Treaty of Versailles signed.

Aug. 11—Weimar Constitution promulgated in Germany.

1920

Jan. 10—League of Nations inaugurated.

Jan. 16—Prohibition begins in U.S.

1921

Mar. 4—Warren G. Harding inaugurated President of United States.

Dec. 6—Britain grants southern Ireland dominion status as Irish Free State.

1922

Jan. 22—Pope Benedict XV dies. He is succeeded Feb. 6 by Cardinal Ratti, who becomes Pius XI.

Oct. 28—Mussolini marches on Rome; forms Cabinet on Oct. 31.

Nov. 4—Tutankhamen's tomb discovered in Egypt by Lord Carnarvon and Howard Carter.

Dec. 30—Union of Soviet Socialist Republics (U.S.S.R.) organized as federation.

1923

Aug. 2—Harding dies; Calvin Coolidge becomes President on Aug. 3.

Nov. 8-9—Munich beer hall putsch led by Hitler put down; Hitler sentenced to five years. (He serves less than one year, writing *Mein Kampf* in jail.)

1924

Jan. 21—Lenin dies; struggle for power begins between Stalin and Trotsky.

1925

Feb. 28—President Friedrich Ebert of Germany dies; Paul von Hindenburg elected Apr. 26.

July 10-21—Scopes evolution trial in Dayton, Tenn. John T. Scopes is prosecuted by William Jennings Bryan for teaching evolution in Tennessee school; is defended by Clarence Darrow. (Scopes is convicted, but decision is later set aside.)

1927

May 20-21—Lindbergh flies solo across Atlantic.

Aug. 23—Sacco and Vanzetti executed (*see* Index).

1929

Jan.—Trotsky expelled from Soviet Union.

Feb. 14—St. Valentine's Day massacre in Chicago; six members of Moran gang shot by rival gang.

Mar. 4—Herbert Hoover inaugurated President of United States.

Oct.-Nov.—Depression begins.

1931

Apr. 14—Alfonso XIII leaves Spain.

Sept. 18-19—Explosion on Manchurian railway serves as pretext for Japan to begin occupation of Manchuria.

Oct. 24—Gangster Al Capone sentenced to 11 years for income-tax evasion. (Released in 1939; died in 1947.)

1932

Jan. 7—Stimson Doctrine: U.S. will not recognize gains achieved by armed force; recognition of Manchukuo (Manchuria) withheld.

Jan. 28—Japan begins invasion of international settlement of Shanghai.

Mar. 1—Charles A. Lindbergh's baby son kidnapped.

June 7—Bonus March on Washington, D.C.

1933

Jan. 30—Hitler made Chancellor of Germany by President Hindenburg.

Feb. 27—German Reichstag burns; Communists accused.

Mar. 4—Franklin Delano Roosevelt inaugurated President of United States.

Mar. 5—Reichstag elections give Nazis and nationalist allies 52% of vote.

Mar. 6—Roosevelt proclaims bank holiday; embargoes gold.

Mar. 12—FDR's first "Fireside Chat."

Mar. 23—Reichstag gives Hitler blanket powers for four years.

Mar. 28—Nazis begin systematic boycott of Jewish businessmen, doctors, lawyers.

May 27-Nov. 12—Century of Progress Exposition in Chicago. (Also open May 26-Oct. 31, 1934.)

Oct. 14—Germany withdraws from League of Nations (effective two years later).

Nov. 17—U.S. recognizes Soviet Union.

Dec. 5—Prohibition ends in U.S.

1934

May 28—Birth of Dionne quintuplets—Annette, Cecile, Emilie (died Aug. 6, 1954), Marie (died Feb. 27, 1970), and Yvonne—in Callender, Ontario, Canada.

July 22—Bank robber John Dillinger shot to death by FBI in Chicago.

July 25—Chancellor Engelbert Dollfuss of Austria assassinated by Nazi conspirators.

Aug. 2—Hindenburg dies; Hitler becomes absolute dictator of Germany.

1935

Mar. 16—Hitler defies Versailles Treaty by reestablishing universal military training in Germany.

Aug. 15—Will Rogers and Wiley Post killed in plane crash near Point Barrow, Alaska.

Aug. 20—Third International decides Soviet Union will side with democracies against Fascist states.

Sept. 15—Nuremberg laws deprive Jews in Germany of citizenship, bar intermarriage.

Oct. 3—Italy invades Ethiopia.

Oct. 7—League of Nations condemns Italy.

1936

Jan. 20—George V dies; Prince of Wales becomes Edward VIII.

Mar. 7—Hitler sends German troops into Rhineland, defying Versailles Treaty; denounces Locarno Pact.

July 17—Spanish civil war begins.

Aug. 19-23—Zinoviev and Kamenev executed in Russia as collaborators with Trotsky and Nazi secret police.

Oct. 27—Rome-Berlin Axis formed. (Japan joins Axis on Sept. 27, 1940.)

Nov. 25—Japan signs anti-Comintern treaty with Germany; Italy adheres Nov. 6, 1937.

Dec. 1-23—Buenos Aires conference: 21 American republics pledge to consult if peace is imperiled; no nation to interfere with another's domestic affairs.

Dec. 11—Edward VIII abdicates; his brother becomes George VI.

1937

Feb. 5—FDR asks power to enlarge Supreme Court to 15 Justices.

July 2—Amelia Earhart Putnam missing in Pacific in round-the-world flight. (No trace of her ever found.)

July 22—Senate defeats FDR's plan for increasing Supreme Court membership.

Dec. 13—U.S. gunboat *Panay* sunk by Japanese planes; 2 killed, 30 wounded.

1938

Mar. 12-13—German army occupies Austria; Hitler proclaims Austrian-German union (*Anschluss*).

Sept. 29-30—Britain, France, Italy, Germany in parley at Munich agree to dismemberment of Czechoslovakia; Chamberlain returns to London with "peace in our time."

Oct. 30—"Attack from Mars" radio program by Orson Welles causes widespread panic in U.S.

1939

Feb. 10—Pope Pius XI dies. He is succeeded Mar. 2 by Cardinal Pacelli, who becomes Pius XII.

Mar. 15—Germany seizes Czechoslovakia.

Apr. 30-Oct. 31—New York World's Fair. (Also open May 11-Oct. 21, 1940.)

Aug. 24—Germany and Soviet Union sign 10-year nonaggression pact.

Sept. 1—Germany invades Poland and annexes Danzig; Britain and France give Hitler ultimatum.

Sept. 3—Britain and France declare war.

Sept. 28—Poland partitioned by Germany and Soviet Union.

Dec. 17—Disabled German pocket battleship *Admiral Graf Spee* blown up off Montevideo, Uruguay, by order of Hitler.

1940

May 10—Nazis invade Netherlands, Belgium, and Luxembourg.

May 10—Chamberlain resigns as Prime Minister; Churchill takes over.

May 12—Germans cross French frontier.

May 26-June 3—Dunkerque evacuation: about 335,000 out of 400,000 Allied soldiers rescued from Belgium by civilian and naval craft from Britain.

June 10—Italy declares war on France and Britain; invades France.

June 14—Germans enter Paris; city undefended.

June 22—France and Germany sign armistice at Compiègne.

Aug. 21—Leon Trotsky dies in Mexico City of wounds inflicted by political agent.

Sept. 3—U.S. trades 50 over-age destroyers to Britain in return for right to lease sites for eight naval bases in British possessions.

Nov. 14—Nazis bomb Coventry.

1941

Apr. 17—Yugoslavia surrenders; Gen. Mihajlović continues guerrilla warfare; Tito leads left-wing guerrillas.

Apr. 27—Nazi tanks enter Athens; remnants of British army quit Greece.

June 22—Hitler attacks Russia.

Aug. 14—Atlantic Charter: FDR and Churchill agree on war aims.

Dec. 7—Japan attacks Pearl Harbor, Philippines, Guam, forcing U.S. into war Dec. 8; Pacific Fleet crippled.

Dec. 8—U.S. and Britain declare war on Japan.

Dec. 11—Germany and Italy declare war on U.S.; Congress declares war on those countries.

1942

Feb. 15—British surrender Singapore.

Apr. 9—U.S. forces on Bataan surrender.

May 6—U.S. and Filipino troops on Corregidor surrender to Japanese.

June 10—Village of Lidice in Czechoslovakia razed by Nazis in reprisal for assassination of Reinhard Heydrich.

Nov. 8—U.S. and Britain land great army in French North Africa.

1943

Jan. 14-24—Casablanca Conference: Churchill and FDR agree on unconditional-surrender goal.

Feb. 1-2—German 6th Army surrenders at Stalingrad; turning point of war in Russia.

May 12—Remnants of Nazis trapped on Cape Bon, ending war in Africa.

June 10—FDR signs withholding tax.

June 19-20—Race riots in Detroit; 25 Negroes and 9 whites killed.

July 25—Mussolini deposed; Badoglio is Premier.

Sept. 3—Allied troops land on Italian mainland.

Sept. 8—Italy surrenders.

Sept. 10—Nazis seize Rome.

Nov. 22-26—Cairo Conference: FDR, Churchill, Chiang Kai-shek pledge defeat of Japan, free Korea.

Nov. 28-Dec. 1—Teheran Conference: FDR, Churchill, Stalin agree on invasion plans.

1944

Jan. 22—U.S. and British troops land at Anzio on west Italian coast and hold beachhead.

June 4—U.S. and British troops enter Rome.

June 6—D-Day: Allies launch Normandy invasion.

July 20—Hitler wounded in bomb plot.

Aug. 25—Paris liberated.

Oct. 13—Athens liberated by Allied forces.

Oct. 20—Americans invade Philippines.

Dec. 16—Germans launch counteroffensive in Belgium (Battle of Bulge).

1945

Feb. 11—Yalta Agreement signed by FDR, Churchill, and Stalin.

Apr. 12—FDR dies; Harry S. Truman becomes President same day.

Apr. 28—Mussolini and mistress, Clara Petacci, killed at Lake Como.

May 1—Adm. Doenitz takes command in Germany; death of Hitler announced.

May 2—Berlin falls.

May 7—V-E Day: Germany signs unconditional surrender terms at Reims.

July 17-Aug. 2—Potsdam Conference: Truman, Churchill (Attlee after July 28), Stalin establish council of foreign ministers to prepare peace treaties; plan German postwar government and reparations.

Aug. 6—A-bomb blasts Hiroshima.

Aug. 8—U.S.S.R. declares war on Japan.

Aug. 9—Nagasaki hit by A-bomb.

Aug. 14—Japan surrenders.

Sept. 2—Japanese sign surrender terms aboard battleship *Missouri* (V-J Day).

Oct. 24—U.N. officially established.

1946

Jan. 10—First meeting of U.N. General Assembly opens in London. Trygve Lie becomes Secretary-General on Feb. 1.

Apr. 8-18—Final Assembly session at Geneva dissolves League of Nations.

May 9—King Victor Emmanuel III abdicates in favor of his son, Humbert; Italy abolishes monarchy June 2.

Oct. 1—Verdict in Nuremberg war trial: 12 Nazi leaders (including 1 tried in absentia) sentenced to hang; 7 imprisoned; 3 acquitted.

Oct. 15—Goering commits suicide a few hours before 10 other Nazis are executed Oct. 16.

1947

Jan. 1—Britain nationalizes coal mines.

Feb. 10—Peace treaties for Italy, Rumania, Bulgaria, Hungary, Finland signed in Paris.

Mar. 4—Soviet Union rejects U.S. plan for U.N.

atomic-energy control.

Mar. 12—Truman Doctrine proposed (*see* Index).

June 5—Marshall Plan proposed (*see* Index).

Aug. 15—India freed by Britain.

Nov. 20—Princess Elizabeth of England is married to Lt. Philip Mountbatten.

1948

Jan. 17—U.N. Good Offices Commission effects truce in Indonesia.

Jan. 30—Gandhi assassinated in New Delhi by Hindu fanatic.

Feb. 23-25—Communists seize power in Czechoslovakia.

May 14—Nation of Israel proclaimed; British end mandate at midnight; Arab armies attack.

June 21—Berlin airlift begins; ends May 12, 1949.

June 28—Stalin and Tito break.

Aug. 15—Independent Republic of Korea is proclaimed, following election supervised by U.N.

Sept. 17—Count Folke Bernadotte, U.N. mediator, assassinated in Jerusalem.

Nov. 4—General Assembly approves U.S.-sponsored atomic control plan.

Nov. 12—Verdict in Japanese war trial: Tojo and six others sentenced to hang (hanged Dec. 23); 18 imprisoned.

1949

Jan. 7—Cease-fire in Palestine.

Jan. 20—Truman proposes Point Four program to help world's backward areas.

Feb. 24—Israel signs armistice with Egypt.

Apr. 4—Start of North Atlantic Treaty Organization (NATO); treaty signed by 12 nations.

Sept. 21—German Federal Republic (West Germany) established.

Sept. 23—Truman discloses Soviet Union has set off atomic explosion.

Oct. 1—Communist People's Republic of China formally proclaimed.

1950

Jan. 31—Truman orders development of hydrogen bomb.

June 25—North Koreans cross 38th parallel to invade South Korea. Start of Korean War.

June 27—Truman orders U.S. air and sea aid to South Koreans.

Oct. 7—U.S. 1st Cavalry makes first U.S. crossing of 38th parallel in Korea.

Nov. 20—U.S. 7th Division unit reaches Manchurian border.

Nov. 24—U.S. forces launch general offensive in hope of ending Korean War.

Nov. 26—Red Chinese enter Korean War and throw back U.S. forces.

1951

Feb. 1—General Assembly condemns (44-7) Red China as an aggressor.

Mar. 19—Six nations initial Schuman Plan to pool European coal and steel market. (In effect Feb. 10, 1953.)

Apr. 11—Truman removes MacArthur from all commands in Korea.

July 10—Truce talks begin in Korea.

Sept. 8—Japanese peace treaty signed in San Francisco by 49 nations.

1952

Feb. 6—George VI dies; his daughter becomes Elizabeth II.

Feb. 20-25—NATO conference approves European Army; sets goal of 50 divisions and 4,000 planes by end of 1952.

May 26—Western Allies and West Germany sign peace contract at Bonn.

Nov. 16—AEC announces "satisfactory" experiments in hydrogen-weapons research; eyewitnesses tell of blasts near Eniwetok.

1953

Jan. 20—Gen. Dwight D. Eisenhower inaugurated President of United States.

Mar. 5—Stalin dies.

Mar. 6—Malenkov becomes Soviet Premier; Beria is Minister of Interior; Molotov is Foreign Minister.

Apr. 10—Dag Hammarskjöld begins term as U.N. Secretary-General.

May 29—Edmund Hillary, of New Zealand, and Tenzing Norkay, of Nepal, reach top of Mt. Everest.

June 17—East Berliners rise against Communist rule; quelled by tanks.

June 19—Julius and Ethel Rosenberg, convicted of espionage in 1951 for passing atomic secrets to the Russians, are executed in New York's Sing Sing Prison.

July 27—Korean armistice signed.

Aug. 20—Moscow announces explosion of hydrogen bomb.

1954

Jan. 21—First atomic-powered submarine, *Nautilus,* launched at Groton, Conn.

Mar. 1—Five U.S. Congressmen shot on floor of House as Puerto Rican nationalists fire from spectators' gallery. All five recover from wounds.

Apr. 22-June 17—Army vs. McCarthy inquiry; Senate subcommittee report Aug. 31 blames both sides.

May 7—Dienbienphu falls to Indochina Red rebels.

May 17—U.S. Supreme Court unanimously bans racial segregation in public schools.

July 21—Indochina truce signed at Geneva conference; Reds get half of Vietnam.

Sept. 6—Eisenhower launches world atomic pool without Soviet Union.

Sept. 8—Eight-nation Southeast Asia defense treaty (SEATO) signed at Manila.

Oct. 23—West Germany is granted sovereignty and is admitted to NATO and Western European Union.

1955

Jan. 17—Submarine *Nautilus* goes to sea under atomic power.

Feb. 8—Nikolai A. Bulganin becomes Soviet Premier, replacing Malenkov.

Apr. 5—Churchill resigns; Anthony Eden succeeds him Apr. 6.

Sept. 19—Argentina ousts Peron.

Sept. 24—President Eisenhower suffers coronary thrombosis in Denver.

Dec. 5—AFL and CIO become one organization named American Federation of Labor and Congress of Industrial Organizations (AFL-CIO).

1956

Feb. 24—Nikita Khrushchev, First Secretary of Communist Party in U.S.S.R., denounces Stalin's methods of ruling.

May 21—First aerial H-bomb tested over Namu islet, Bikini Atoll (10 million tons TNT equivalent).

June 28-30—Workers' uprising against Communist rule in Poznan, Poland, is crushed by tanks.

July 26—Egypt announces seizure of Suez Canal control.

Oct. 23-24—Revolt starts in Hungary. Soviet troops and tanks in Hungary fight anti-Communist rebellion, Imre Nagy is new Premier. Revolt crushed in November, and Nagy executed.

Oct. 29—Israel launches attack on Egypt's Sinai Peninsula and drives toward Suez Canal.

Nov. 5—British and French invade Egypt at Port Said.

Nov. 6—British and French cease fire at Port Said and halt Suez advance.

1957

Jan. 5—Eisenhower Doctrine proposed (*see* Index).

Jan. 10—Harold Macmillan becomes British Prime Minister, replacing Eden.

Sept. 24—Eisenhower sends Army troops to Little Rock, Ark., to quell mob and protect school integration.

1958

Jan. 31—Army's Jupiter-C rocket fires first U.S. earth satellite, Explorer I, into orbit.

Feb. 1—Egypt and Syria merge into one nation—United Arab Republic.

Mar. 27—Khrushchev becomes Premier of Soviet Union as Bulganin resigns.

July 15—Eisenhower orders U.S. Marines into Lebanon at request of President Chamoun, who fears overthrow.

Oct. 9—Pope Pius XII dies. He is succeeded Oct. 28 by Cardinal Roncalli, who becomes John XXIII.

1959

Jan. 1—President Batista resigns and flees Cuba. Castro's revolt wins.

Jan. 8—De Gaulle takes office as President of France for seven years.

Mar. 31—Tibet's Dalai Lama escapes into India.

Apr. 25—St. Lawrence Seaway opens, allowing ocean ships to go into Midwest.

1960

Feb. 13—France explodes its first atomic device, in Sahara.

May 16—Khrushchev kills Paris summit conference because of U-2 incident; tells Eisenhower not to visit Soviet Union.

Aug. 7—Cuba begins confiscation of $770 million of U.S. property.

Aug. 19—Soviet Union sentences U-2 American spy flier, Francis Gary Powers, to 10 years. Powers returned Feb. 10, 1962, in exchange for Soviet spy Rudolf Abel.

1961

Jan. 3—U.S. breaks diplomatic relations with Cuba.

Jan. 20—John F. Kennedy inaugurated President of United States.

Mar. 13—Kennedy proposes 10-year plan to raise Latin American living standards (Alliance for Progress) (*see* Index).

Apr. 12—Moscow announces putting first man into space in orbit around earth—Maj. Yuri A. Gagarin.

Apr. 17—Cuba invaded at Bay of Pigs by an estimated 1,200 anti-Castro exiles aided by U.S.; invasion crushed.

May 5—First U.S. spaceman, Navy Cmdr. Alan B. Shepard, Jr., rockets 116.5 miles up in 302-mile trip.

May 30—Generalissimo Rafael Trujillo, dictator of Dominican Republic for 31 years, assassinated.

July 21—Virgil Grissom becomes second American astronaut, making 118-mile-high, 303-mile-long rocket flight over Atlantic.

Aug. 6—Gherman Stepanovich Titov is launched in Soviet spaceship *Vostok II;* makes 17½ orbits in 25 hours, covering 434,960 miles before landing safely.

Aug. 13—East German Wall blocks all crossings between East and West Berlin to halt flood of refugees.

Oct. 29—U.S.S.R. fires 50-megaton hydrogen bomb, biggest explosion in history.

1962

Feb. 20—Lt. Col. John H. Glenn, Jr., is first American to orbit earth—3 times in 4 hr., 55 min.

May 31—Adolf Eichmann hanged in Israel for his part in Nazi extermination of six million Jews.

July 3—France transfers sovereignty to new republic of Algeria.

Oct. 1—James H. Meredith, escorted by Federal marshals, registers in University of Mississippi.

Oct. 11—Pope John XXIII opens Second Vatican Council; council holds four sessions, finally closing Dec. 8, 1965.

Oct. 22—Kennedy announces U.S. air-sea blockade of Cuba to halt inflow of offensive weapons; reveals Soviet has missiles in Cuba. Lifts blockade Nov. 20.

Dec. 24—Cuba releases 1,113 prisoners of 1961 invasion attempt.

1963

Jan. 22—France and West Germany sign treaty of cooperation to end four centuries of conflict.

June 3—Pope John XXIII dies. He is succeeded June 21 by Cardinal Montini, who becomes Paul VI.

June 17—U.S. Supreme Court rules no locality may require recitation of Lord's Prayer or Bible verses in public schools.

Aug. 28—200,000 blacks and whites hold civil-rights rally in Washington, D.C.

Aug. 30—Washington-to-Moscow "hot line" communications link opened; designed to reduce risk of accidental war.

Nov. 22—President Kennedy shot and killed by sniper in Dallas, Tex. Lyndon B. Johnson becomes President same day.

Nov. 24—Lee Harvey Oswald, accused assassin of President Kennedy, is shot and killed by Jack Ruby, Dallas nightclub owner.

1964

Feb. 17—U.S. Supreme Court rules, 6–3, that Congressional districts should be roughly equal in population.

Mar. 14—Jack Ruby convicted of murder in slaying of Lee Harvey Oswald; sentenced to death by Dallas jury. (Conviction reversed Oct. 5, 1966. Ruby dies Jan. 3, 1967, before second trial can be held.)

Aug. 10—Pope Paul VI issues encyclical, *Ecclesiam Suam* (His Church), in which he proclaims his readiness to intervene for peace between nations.

Sept. 27—President's Commission on the Assassination of President John F. Kennedy issues report (Warren Report); concludes that Lee Harvey Oswald acted alone in assassination of President.

1965

Feb. 1—Rev. Dr. Martin Luther King, Jr., and more than 2,600 other blacks arrested in Selma, Ala., during three-day demonstrations against vote-registration rules.

Feb. 21—Malcolm X, black-nationalist leader, shot to death at Harlem rally in New York City.

Apr. 28—U.S. Marines land in Dominican Republic as fighting persists between rebels and Dominican army.

June 9—White House confirms that U.S. ground forces in South Vietnam have been authorized to enter into combat in support of South Vietnamese forces, but insists primary mission—to protect important bases—is unchanged.

Nov. 9—Power failure in Ontario plant blacks out parts of eight northeastern states of U.S. and two provinces of southeastern Canada.

1966

Mar. 15—Black teen-agers riot in Watts, Los Angeles; two men killed and at least 25 injured.

Apr. 21—Surgeons implant artificial heart in human for first time at Houston hospital. Plastic device functions, and patient lives.

June 13—U.S. Supreme Court gives police strict new guidelines to protect suspects from self-incrimination, including rule that prisoner may not be questioned when alone if he raises any objection.

1967

Jan. 27—Three Apollo astronauts—Col. Virgil I. Grissom, Col. Edward White II, and Lt. Comdr. Roger B. Chaffee—killed in fire in spacecraft during simulation launch.

May 5—*World Journal Tribune* ceases publication, leaving New York City with only one evening newspaper.

June 5—Israeli and Arab forces battle. Six-day war ends with Israel occupying Sinai Peninsula, Golan Heights, Gaza Strip and east bank of Suez Canal.

June 17—Red China announces explosion of its first hydrogen bomb.

June 20—All-white jury finds Cassius Clay, former world's heavyweight boxing champion, guilty for refusing induction into military service; judge sentences him to serve five years in prison and to pay $10,000 fine.

July 23—Racial violence brings terror to Detroit, where 7,000 National Guardsmen aid police after night of rioting. Similar outbreaks occur in New York City's Spanish Harlem, Rochester, N.Y., Birmingham, Ala., and New Britain, Conn.

Dec. 3—Dr. Christiaan N. Barnard and team of South African surgeons perform world's first successful human heart transplant on Louis Washkansky, 55-year-old grocer. Washkansky dies of pneumonia 18 days later.

1968

Jan. 23—North Korea seizes U.S. Navy ship *Pueblo;* holds 83 on board as spies.

Mar. 31—President Johnson announces, "I shall not seek and I will not accept the nomination of my party as President."

Apr. 4—Martin Luther King, Jr., civil rights leader, is slain in Memphis. James Earl Ray, indicted in murder, is captured in London on June 8.

June 5—Sen. Robert F. Kennedy is shot and critically wounded in Los Angeles hotel after winning California primary; dies June 6. Sirhan Bishara Sirhan is seized and held by police.

Aug. 20—Czechoslovakia is invaded by Russians and four other Warsaw Pact forces; Prague urges people not to resist.

Aug. 28—Chicago police drive back 3,000 demonstrators attempting to storm Conrad Hilton Hotel, Democratic Convention headquarters.

1969

Jan. 20—Richard M. Nixon is inaugurated 37th President of the United States.

Mar 10—James Earl Ray pleads guilty in Memphis to 1968 assassination of Rev. Martin Luther King, Jr.; sentenced to jail for 99 years.

Apr. 17—Sirhan Bishara Sirhan is convicted in slaying of Sen. Robert F. Kennedy and is sentenced to death.

July 20—Apollo 11 astronauts—Neil A. Armstrong, Edwin E. Aldrin, Jr., and Michael Collins—take man's first walk on moon.

July 25—Sen. Edward M. Kennedy pleads guilty to leaving scene of fatal accident at Chappaquiddick, Mass., on July 18, in which Mary Jo Kopechne was drowned; gets two-month suspended sentence.

Dec. 18—House of Lords permanently abolishes death penalty for murder in Britain.

1970

Jan. 12—Biafra surrenders after 32-month fight for independence from Nigeria.

Mar. 1—Rhodesia severs last tie with British Crown and declares itself a racially segregated republic.

Mar. 18—New York mailmen strike, crippling nation's business center. Action spreads across nation, and on Mar. 23 President Nixon activates Reserve Army units to sort piled-up mail in New York. Workers return Mar. 25 as talks begin on pay increases.

May 4—Four students at Kent State University in Ohio slain by National Guardsmen at demonstration protesting April 30 incursion into Cambodia.

May 15—Two black students at Jackson State College in Mississippi are killed by police gunfire.

June 22—President Nixon signs bill lowering voting age in national elections from 21 to 18.

June 24—Senate repeals Gulf of Tonkin resolution.

Dec. 15—Nation's gross national product reaches $1-trillion mark.

1971

Apr. 20—Supreme Court rules unanimously that busing of students may be ordered to achieve racial desegregation.

May 3—Anti-war militants attempt to disrupt government business in Washington. Police and military units arrest as many as 12,000; most are later released.

June 28—Supreme Court overturns draft evasion conviction of former heavyweight champion Muhammad Ali (Cassius Clay), who objected to military service on religious grounds.

Sept. 9—More than 1,000 prisoners seize cell block in state prison at Attica, N.Y., and hold 32 guards as hostages. After three days of negotiations, state troopers and National Guardsmen storm prison on Sept. 13, killing 32 prisoners and 9 hostages.

Oct. 25—U.N. seats Communist China and expels Nationalist China.

Nov. 22—India launches incursion into East Pakistan.

1972

Mar. 24—Britain takes over direct rule of Northern Ireland in bid for peace.

May 14—Okinawa reverts to Japan after 27 years of U.S. rule.

May 15—Gov. George C. Wallace of Alabama is shot by Arthur H. Bremer at Laurel, Md., political rally. Wallace is paralyzed for life from the waist down. Bremer is sentenced to 63 years in prison on Aug. 4.

June 17—Five men are apprehended by police in attempt to bug Democratic National Committee headquarters in Washington's Watergate complex.

June 29—Supreme Court rules that death penalty is unconstitutional "cruel and unusual" punishment.

Sept. 1—Bobby Fischer becomes first American world chess champion, defeating Boris Spassky of U.S.S.R., 12½–8½, in Reykjavik, Iceland.

Sept. 5—Eleven Israeli athletes at Olympic Games in Munich are killed after eight members of the extremist Black September Arab terrorist group invade Olympic Village and 20 hours later engage in shootout with police at a nearby airbase. Five guerrillas and one policeman are also killed.

1973

Feb. 21—Israeli fighter planes down civilian Libyan airliner that strayed over Sinai desert; 108 of 111 aboard die in crash.

Feb. 28—Some 400 Indians hold 10 hostages after seizing settlement of Wounded Knee, S.D., and demand Government discuss their grievances. Siege ends on May 9 when Indians surrender.

Apr. 30—Nixon, on national TV, accepts responsibility, but not blame, for Watergate; accepts resignations of advisers H. R. Haldeman and John D. Ehrlichman, fires John W. Dean III as counsel. He pledges "no whitewash" at White House.

May 11—Case against Daniel Ellsberg and Anthony Russo in Pentagon Papers trial is dismissed by Judge W. Matthew Byrne, Jr., because of "improper government conduct."

Aug. 15—U.S. bombing of Cambodia ends, marking official halt to 12 years of combat activity in Southeast Asia.

Sept. 11—Violent military coup in Chile deposes President Salvador Allende Gossens, who reportedly commits suicide.

Oct. 6—Egyptian and Syrian forces attack Israel as Jews mark Yom Kippur, holiest day in their calendar. Fierce tank battles rage on Sinai Peninsula and Golan Heights.

Oct. 10—Spiro T. Agnew resigns as Vice President and then, in Federal Court in Baltimore, pleads no contest to charges of evasion of income taxes on $29,500 he received in 1967 while Governor of Maryland. He is fined $10,000 and put on three years' probation.

Oct. 20—In what has become known as "the Saturday night massacre," Nixon fires special Watergate prosecutor Archibald Cox and Deputy Attorney General William D. Ruckelshaus; Attorney General Elliot L. Richardson resigns.

Nov. 11—Egypt and Israel sign U.S.-sponsored cease-fire agreement and begin talks to carry out pact.

1974

Feb. 5—Patricia Hearst, 19-year-old daughter of publisher Randolph Hearst, kidnapped by Symbionese Liberation Army, which demands $2-million ransom. Later, $230 million in free food for California's poor is also sought.

Mar. 3—Turkish jumbo jet crashes near Paris, killing all 346 passengers and crew in aviation's worst disaster.

Apr. 11—W. A. (Tony) Boyle, ex-president of United Mine Workers, is convicted of 1969 murders of Joseph A. Yablonski, his wife and daughter.

Apr. 15—Gang believed to be Symbionese Liberation Army, holds up San Francisco bank and escapes with $10,960. Photos taken by automatic cameras show kidnapped Patricia Hearst carrying weapon.

May 15—Twenty-one high school students are killed in Maalot, Israel, when soldiers storm school in which three Arab guerrillas were holding about 90 youths hostage. Earlier, terrorists shot three members of a Jewish family.

May 17—Six members of Symbionese Liberation Army are killed in gun battle with Los Angeles police. Leader of group, Donald DeFreeze, known as "General Field Marshal Cinque," among those slain.

July 24—Supreme Court rules, 8–0, that President Nixon must turn over 64 White House tapes to special prosecutor.

July 30—House Judiciary Committee adopts three articles of impeachment charging President with obstruction of justice, failure to uphold laws and refusal to produce material subpoenaed by the committee.

Aug. 2—John W. Dean III, ex-Nixon counsel, sentenced to one to four years' imprisonment in conspiracy to obstruct justice in Watergate cover-up.

Aug. 8—Richard M. Nixon announces he will resign the next day, the first President to do so.

Aug. 9—Vice President Gerald R. Ford of Michigan is sworn in as 38th President of the United States. He asks members of Nixon Cabinet and heads of agencies to stay on.

Aug. 26—Charles A. Lindbergh, first to fly Atlantic nonstop from New York to Paris, dies of cancer in Hawaii at 72.

Sept. 8—Ford grants "full, free and absolute pardon" to ex-President Nixon; his press secretary, J. F. terHorst, resigns in protest.

Sept. 12—Emperor Haile Selassie of Ethiopia deposed by military.

Sept. 20—Hurricane Fifi strikes northern Honduras, leaving 8,000 dead and 100,000 homeless.

Sept. 8—Franklin National Bank, country's 20th largest, is declared insolvent in biggest bank failure in U.S. history.

Oct. 29—Ex-President Nixon goes into vascular shock after surgery to combat a blood clot. Condition is critical for several days.

Nov. 8—U.S. judge orders acquittal of one member and seven former members of Ohio National Guard in 1970 killing of four students at Kent State U.

Nov. 8—Army grants parole to Lt. William L. Calley, Jr., who is serving 10-year term for Mylai massacre. Parole effective Nov. 19.

Nov. 25—Dr. Christiaan N. Barnard implants second heart in body of 58-year-old South African man to ease burden on patient's own diseased heart.

Nov. 27—Louis B. Russell, the teacher who lived for six years with a transplanted heart, the longest on record, dies at 49 as a result of uncontrolled irregularities in the second organ.

Dec. 19—Nelson A. Rockefeller sworn in as 41st Vice President after House votes final confirmation.

1975

Jan. 1—John N. Mitchell, H. R. Haldeman, John D. Ehrlichman and Robert C. Mardian found guilty of Watergate cover-up. Mitchell, Haldeman and Ehrlichman are sentenced on Feb. 21 to 30 months to 8 years in jail and Mardian to 10 months to 3 years.

Jan. 3—President Ford signs Trade Reform Act, providing benefits for many nations, but leaves uncertain part that would give trade benefits to Soviet Union in return for assurances of freer emigration policies.

Jan. 5—President names commission to investigate charges of domestic spying by C.I.A. Vice President Rockefeller heads it.

Jan. 13—In "179-degree" turn from his economic policies, President Ford proposes $16-billion income tax cut and $12-billion rebate on 1974 taxes but calls for imposts on imported crude oil.

Jan. 14—Soviet Union nullifies 1972 trade agreement with U.S. on grounds that Congressional proviso on its emigration policies interfered with its internal affairs.

Jan. 15—C.I.A. Director William E. Colby admits that files were kept on 10,000 Americans, starting 1967.

Jan. 16—American Civil Liberties Union, in behalf of 1,200 clients, wins $12-million damage suit over violation of rights of those arrested in antiwar demonstration in Washington in 1971.

Jan. 20—Chemical Bank takes over Security National Bank of Long Island, third large institution to go under in a year.

Feb. 3—President presents $349.4-billion budget for fiscal 1976, with estimated deficit of $51.9 billion, a peacetime record.

Feb. 3—General Motors, its 1974 earnings off 60%, loses first place to Exxon as world's biggest industrial corporation.

Feb. 11—Col. Richard Ratsimandrava is assassinated a week after becoming head of Madagascar (Malagasy Republic).

Feb. 13—Turkish Cypriotes set up separate state covering two-fifths of Cyprus.

Feb. 14—A record 35.16 million shares are traded on New York Stock Exchange.

Feb. 15—Dr. Kenneth C. Edelin is convicted in Boston on charge he permitted death of a fetus after an abortion. He is given one-year probation.

Feb. 18—Supreme Court rules unanimously that ex-President Nixon did not have right to impound $9 billion Congress appropriated to fight water pollution.

Feb. 25—Elijah Muhammad, Black Muslim leader, dies at 77.

Feb. 27—Fire cuts 170,000 phones in downtown New York. Nine smaller fires follow in other offices.

Feb. 28—London subway train smashes into end of tunnel, killing 41 people and injuring more than 90.

Mar. 2—Rubber factory in Shelton, Conn., is destroyed by bombs, leaving 900 jobless. On Apr. 24, charges of arson and conspiracy are brought against 10 men, including head of corporation owning the plant.

Mar. 4—U.S. and Iran sign five-year economic agreement by which Iran will buy $15 billion in American goods and services and will also invest $7 billion in nuclear power plants.

Mar. 12—Maurice H. Stans, former Commerce Secretary, pleads guilty to five misdemeanor charges. Third member of Nixon Cabinet to be convicted, he is fined $5,000 on May 14.

Mar. 13—A.&P. supermarket chain to close 1,250 of its 3,500 stores to improve profits.

Mar. 17—Some 3,000 interns and residents at 21 New York City hospitals, protesting working hours, stage nation's first doctors' strike. They return three days later.

Mar. 17—Supreme Court rules that Federal Government, not states, has rights to oil and gas resources beyond three-mile limit.

Mar. 18—C.I.A., using Howard Hughes-built salvage ship, recovered part of Soviet submarine sunk in Pacific in 1968. Called Project Jennifer, it cost a reported $350 million.

Mar. 19—Supreme court rules that Social Security provision denying widowers survivors' benefits is unconstitutional.

Mar. 22—Secretary of State Henry A. Kissinger suspends efforts for peace between Israel and Egypt after two weeks of step-by-step diplomacy.

Mar. 25—King Faisal of Saudi Arabia is assassinated by a nephew, who is beheaded June 18.

Mar. 27—Congress passes $22.8-billion tax cut bill, calling for 1974 rebates, 1975 credits and higher Social Security benefits. Bill cuts oil depletion allowance by $2 billion.

Apr. 1—Mayor Richard L. Daley of Chicago is elected to unprecedented sixth four-year term.

Apr. 3—Bobby Fischer's world chess title goes to Anatoly Karpov by default after American fails to agree to rules of World Chess Federation.

Apr. 4—American transport bringing 243 Vietnamese orphans to U.S. crashes after take-off from Saigon; 100 children and 25 escorts are killed.

Apr. 5—Chiang Kai-shek, President of Nationalist China, dies at 87.

Apr. 15—Supreme Court strikes down as "unequal treatment" Utah law making girl an adult at 18 and a boy at 21.

Apr. 15—Communist units move into Phnom Penh. Cambodia.

Apr. 17—John B. Connally, former Secretary of the Treasury, is acquitted of charges of accepting gratuities after dairy interests got increased prices.

Apr. 24—Terrorists, rebuffed in demand for release of 26 anarchists jailed in West Germany, blow up West German embassy in Stockholm. Two hostages are killed and six terrorists captured; one dies.

Apr. 27—Duong Van Minh (Big Minh) becomes South Vietnam's third President in a week. Two days later he announces unconditional surrender to Viet Cong, and on Apr. 30 Communist troops take over Saigon.

May 6—Jozsef Cardinal Mindszenty, former Catholic Prelate of Hungary and a symbol of anti-Communism, dies in Vienna at 83.

May 14—President Ford turns down New York City plea for $1.5 billion aid.

May 15—American merchant ship Mayaguez, seized by Cambodian forces, is rescued in operation by U.S. Navy and Marines. Thirty-eight servicemen are killed.

May 19—Zaire leftists kidnap three U.S. students —Barbara Smuts, Carrie Jane Hunter and Kenneth Smith—and one Dutch student from wildlife research station in Tanzania. All are subsequently released, Smith on July 27 after Stanford University, his employer, pays a ransom.

May 24—Two Soviet cosmonauts are launched in Soyuz spacecraft for link-up two days later with Salyut 4, in orbit since December.

May 25—U.S. fertility rate drops to 1.86, a record low, below level of 2.10 at which births and deaths balance.

May 29—President Ford vetoes $5.3-billion fund for 900,000 new jobs; House sustains veto.

May 29—Gen. Edward G. Lansdale, former C.I.A. officer, says he was ordered by Attorney General Robert F. Kennedy, with President Kennedy's approval, to "depose" Premier Fidel Castro of Cuba.

May 29—President Ford, in Brussels for NATO conference, assures allies of U.S. steadfastness. Continuing trip, he discusses U.S. bases in Spain with Generalissimo Francisco Franco and Mideast situation with President Anwar el-Sadat of Egypt in Vienna and is received by Pope Paul VI.

June 5—Suez Canal reopens eight years after it was closed during Arab-Israeli war of June 1967.

June 6—May unemployment rate rises to 9.2%, highest since 1941.

June 7—Belgium, the Netherlands, Norway and Denmark choose General Dynamics' F-16 jet fighter over French Mirage in $2-billion contract.

June 7—Jacqueline Kennedy Onassis to get $250,000 a year from Aristotle Onassis' estate; half of estate goes to Onassis' daughter, Christina, half to charitable foundation.

June 9—Philippines establish diplomatic relations with China, breaking ties with Nationalists on Taiwan.

June 9—Daniel P. Moynihan, outspoken critic of third world countries in U.N., confirmed as representative to world body.

June 9—Joseph Remiro and Russel Little of Symbionese Liberation Army convicted in slaying of Dr. Marcus Foster, Oakland, Calif., school superintendent. They get life sentences.

June 12—India's Supreme Court convicts Prime Minister Indira Gandhi of using illegal means to win re-election in 1971. She is allowed to remain in office but is deprived of vote in Parliament.

June 17—Northern Mariana Islands vote to join U.S. as commonwealth; area is now a U.N. trust territory.

June 24—President Ford vetoes $1.2-billion housing bill as damaging to economy; House sustains veto.

June 24—Mozambique becomes independent after 470 years of Portuguese rule.

June 26—Supreme Court rules that mental patients cannot be confined against their will if they threaten no one.

June 27—Ex-President Nixon gives 11 hours of testimony to lawyers for Watergate grand jury; first such questioning of a President or former President.

June 30—New York City to cut 40,000 municipal employees from payroll as budget crisis mounts.

July 1—Lieut. Gen. Daniel James, Jr., named chief of Air Defense Command; first black to attain four-star rank.

July 3—New Cabinet of Rashid Karami takes control of Lebanon as fighting between Nationalist Christians and Moslems, who include Palestinian guerrillas, lessens. At least 800 have been killed in four months of street fighting.

July 6—Mauna Loa on Hawaii erupts for first time in 25 years.

July 8—President Ford announces candidacy for 1976 Republican presidential nomination.

July 8—Argentine unions end two-day strike as entire Cabinet resigns and President Isabel Perón accepts pay demands.

July 14—Trial of Joan Little, accused of killing jailer she says tried to rape her, opens in Raleigh, N.C. She is acquitted July 15.

July 15—Seven months after Christmas truce of provisional wing of Irish Republican Army began, 130 have been killed in Northern Ireland, three-fourths of them sectarian murders.

July 15—Apollo and Soyuz spacecraft take off for first U.S.-Soviet link-up in space. On July 17, Brig. Gen. Thomas P. Stafford, Donald K. Slayton and Vance D. Brand exchange visits with Col. Aleksei A. Leonov and Valery N. Kubasov 140 miles above earth.

July 21—Secretary of State Kissinger cautions third world majority in U.N. against "arbitrary tactics." Later warns that U.S. will take "clear action" if U.N. ousts Israel.

July 21—Bunge Corporation, one of world's largest grain companies, and 13 others are indicted by federal grand jury in export thefts. Bunge is convicted Oct. 8.

July 21—Soyuz spacecraft lands safely in Soviet; Apollo astronauts splash down in Pacific three days later. They are hospitalized for respiratory irritation from gas that filled cabin during descent.

July 22—Soviet Union buys 381 million bushels of grain from U.S. and 137 million from Canada.

July 23—Government sources disclose that ex-President Nixon ordered C.I.A. "all-out effort" to prevent election of Salvador Allende Gossens as President of Chile.

July 24—House defeats Ford effort to lift arms embargo against Turkey; Turkey says it will halt operations at most U.S. bases, except for defense activities of NATO.

July 25—In 35th veto, President Ford turns down $7.9-billion education bill. Congress overrides veto Sept. 15.

July 25—President leaves for 35-nation Conference on European Security and Cooperation in Helsinki, where he signs charter for peace and progress in Europe. On 10-day trip, he visits

Poland, Romania, Bonn and President Tito of Yugoslavia.

July 28—Voting Rights Act of 1965 extended for seven years and broadened to include Spanish-speaking Americans and other "language minorities."

July 29—Organization of American States abolishes 1964 embargo on Cuba for fostering Communist guerrilla activities in hemisphere.

July 29—Gen. Yakubu Gowon of Nigeria ousted in military coup.

July 29—For first time in 1975, Congress overrides a Presidential veto when it votes $2-billion health bill.

July 30—James R. Hoffa, former head of Teamsters Union, disappears. By year's end his fate remains a mystery.

Aug. 2—F.B.I. said to have begun in 1950s secret "Security Index" of Americans "targeted for detention" in national emergency.

Aug. 6—Ex-Senator Edward J. Gurney of Florida acquitted of five counts concerning election fund-raising.

Aug. 9—Samuel Bronfman 2d, 21-year-old heir to Seagram liquor fortune, kidnaped in Westchester County, N.Y. He is found in a Brooklyn apartment nine days later and $2.3-million ransom is recovered. Mel Patrick Lynch, a New York fireman, and Dominic Byrne, a limousine operator, are held.

Aug. 15—Sheik Mujibur Rahman, President of Bangladesh, killed in military coup.

Aug. 23—Ex-President George Papadopoulos of Greece and two aides sentenced to death for treason. Cabinet commutes sentences to life imprisonment.

Aug. 27—Haile Selassie, deposed ruler of Ethiopia, dies at 83.

Aug. 27—Federal jury clears Gov. James A. Rhodes of Ohio, Robert J. White, former Kent State University president, and 27 Ohio National Guardsmen in $46-million damage suit brought by nine wounded students and parents of four slain on campus in 1970.

Aug. 29—Gen. Vasco Concalves ousted as Premier of Portugal's leftist military regime. He loses post as Army Chief of Staff a week later.

Aug. 29—Eamon de Valera, ex-President of Ireland, dies at 92.

Aug. 31—Price controls on oil end.

Sept. 3—Chicago teachers' strike keeps 900,000 pupils from returning to school.

Sept. 5—President Ford escapes assassination attempt in Sacramento, Calif., when woman points .45-caliber pistol at him and is subdued by Secret Service agents. She is Lynette Alice Fromme, 26, a member of the Charles Manson "family." On Nov. 26 she is convicted of attempted assassination of a President and is later sentenced to life imprisonment.

Sept. 6—Kentucky National Guard called out to quell riots in Louisville over court-ordered school busing to integrate schools.

Sept. 8—Boston police arrest more than 100 as federal marshals backed by National Guardsmen protect students riding buses on orders of court to achieve racial balance in schools.

Sept. 9—Teachers' strike in New York closes 260 schools and keeps 1.1 million pupils out of classes for six days.

Sept. 10—U.S. Appeals Court reinstates conviction of ex-Lieut. William L. Calley, Jr., in My Lai killings.

Sept. 11—W. A. (Tony) Boyle, ex-head of United Mine Workers, sentenced to three life terms for 1969 murder of Joseph A. Yablonsky, his wife and daughter.

Sept. 14—Pope Paul VI beatifies Mother Elizabeth Ann Bayley Seton, first American-born saint.

Sept. 14—Knife-wielding man slashes Rembrandt's masterpiece "The Night Watch" in Amsterdam museum. Officials say painting can be restored.

Sept. 18—Musicians' strike shuts down 12 Broadway musicals. Ends after 25 days.

Sept. 18—Patricia Hearst, kidnaped Feb. 7, 1974, apprehended by F.B.I. in San Francisco with William and Emily Harris, remnants of Symbionese Liberation Army. She faces bank-robbery charges.

Sept. 22—President Ford escapes second assassination attempt in 17 days when a woman fires .38-caliber pistol at him in San Francisco. Deflected bullet lands on pavement. Police seize Sara Jane Moore, 45, said to be former F.B.I. informant. On Dec. 12 she pleads guilty and is sentenced to life imprisonment on Jan. 15.

Sept. 25—Congress passes bill to reinstate price controls on oil until Nov. 15.

Sept. 27—Organization of Petroleum Exporting Countries raises oil prices 10% as of Oct. 1 and freezes that price for nine months.

Sept. 27—Five Basque separatists executed in Spain for killing police; protests spread across Europe.

Sept. 29—Casey Stengel, ex-manager of Yankees and Mets, dies at 85.

Sept. 30—Emperor Hirohito of Japan begins two-week U.S. visit with his wife.

Oct. 2—W. T. Grant chain, billion dollars in debt, files voluntary bankruptcy.

Oct. 3—President Ford, in 39th veto, rejects $2.7-billion school lunch bill; Congress overrides veto, the seventh in Ford term.

Oct. 4—Canada opens $500-million Mirabel Airport at Montreal, called world's largest.

Oct. 6—Court-appointed panel of firearms experts finds no evidence that more than one gun was used in 1968 slaying of Senator Robert F. Kennedy.

Oct. 10—Israel signs Sinai accord with Egypt, calling for withdrawal from about 1,900 square miles of territory within five months.

Oct. 17—New York City avoids last-minute default on $450 million in notes when teachers' union agrees to buy $150 million in bonds with pension fund money.

Oct. 30—Prince Juan Carlos de Borbón, designated successor to critically ill Generalissimo Francisco Franco, assumes powers of Spain's Chief of State.

(For later events, see News Chronology of 1976 in Table of Contents.)

VIETNAM, 1954 TO 1976

American involvement in Vietnam began in 1950 when President Truman sent a 35-man military advisory group to aid the French. After the defeat of the French at Dienbienphu, the Geneva Agreements of July 1954 provided for withdrawal of French and Vietminh forces to either side of a demarcation zone (DMZ) pending a reunification election in 1956. Elections were never held.

From 1954 onward, Presidents Eisenhower and Kennedy sent civilian advisers to South Vietnam but then replaced them with military personnel to train the South Vietnamese. In 1960, the communists announced formation of the National Liberation Front (Viet Cong) in South Vietnam. The U.S. called on North Vietnam to end subversion in South Vietnam but Ho Chi Minh, North Vietnam's President, replied that U.S. must withdraw all troops. On November 1, 1963, a military coup led to the murder of Ngo Dinh Diem, South Vietnam's Premier. The number of U.S. military advisers in South Vietnam rose from 2,000 in 1961 to 15,000 in 1963.

On August 2, 1964, North Vietnamese torpedo boats reportedly attacked U.S. destroyers in the Gulf of Tonkin. President Johnson ordered retaliatory air strikes and, on August 7, Congress approved the Gulf of Tonkin resolution authorizing the President to take necessary steps to maintain peace. On February 7, 1965, Viet Cong forces attacked U.S. installations at Pleiku. U.S. planes began combat missions over South Vietnam. In June 1965, 23,000 American advisers were committed to combat and, by the end of the year, there were over 184,000 U.S. armed forces personnel in the area. On April 7, 1965, President Johnson stated that U.S. was prepared to begin unconditional discussions. Hanoi again insisted that U.S. must withdraw from Vietnam.

On July 31, 1966, U.S. B-52s bombed demilitarized zone, claiming North Vietnam was using DMZ as entry into the south. In March 1967, North Vietnam rejected President Johnson's offer of direct talks. On October 2, 1967, South Vietnam's National Assembly approved election of Nguyen Van Thieu as President. By mid-1968, U.S. had almost 525,000 men in Vietnam.

In the Tet offensive of January-February 1968, Viet Cong guerrillas attacked Saigon, Hue and many provincial capitals. On May 18, at peace talks in Paris, North Vietnam demanded full bombing halt. U.S. demanded that Hanoi acknowledge presence of its troops in South Vietnam. On October 31, 1968, President Johnson ordered halt to all U.S. bombardment of North Vietnam. Saigon and National Liberation Front (Viet Cong) were brought into Paris Peace talks.

On May 14, 1969, President Nixon announced Vietnam peace offer and in June U.S. began troop withdrawals. On June 10, Viet Cong announced formation of Provisional Revolutionary Government (PRG). On June 25, U.S. Senate adopted resolution calling for curb on commitments, urging the President not to send soldiers or funds abroad unless Congress agreed. On September 3, 1969, Ho Chi Minh, 79-year-old President of North Vietnam, died in Hanoi. North Vietnam announced that a collective leadership would govern the country. On September 18, 1969, Nixon told U.N. General Assembly members he hoped to end war in Vietnam by end of 1970. He rejected move to set deadline for withdrawal of all U.S. troops. On September 30, the withdrawal of U.S. troops from Southeast Asia gained momentum with announced pullback of 6,000 men from Thailand and 1,000 marines from Vietnam. On October 15, there were massive demonstrations in the U.S. to protest or support Vietnam War policies. On April 30, 1970, President Nixon told nation he had sent troops into Cambodia. Student protests at Kent State University in Ohio led to killing of four students by National Guardsmen. By June 29, last U.S. troops were removed from Cambodia.

On January 1, 1971, Congress set limits on U.S. role in Southeast Asia, barring use of combat troops in Laos and Cambodia but not air power. On June 13, the *New York Times* published "Pentagon Papers," consisting of classified material detailing expansion of U.S. involvement in Vietnam.

President Nixon responded to North Vietnamese drive across DMZ by ordering mining of North Vietnam's ports. President Nixon ordered heavy bombing of Hanoi-Haiphong area.

On January 15, President Nixon ordered halt to offensive military operations in North Vietnam. On January 27, representatives of North and South Vietnam, the U.S. and the Viet Cong signed peace pacts in Paris, ending the longest war in U.S. history (about 12 years).

Throughout 1974, there were frequent violations of the cease-fire agreement with both sides accusing each other of ignoring the promises made in the peace agreement.

These violations ended with the resumption of full-scale warfare ending with a Communist victory on April 30, 1975. South Vietnam's Premier Nguyen Van Thieu resigned on April 21 claiming that President Nixon had broken his promise to intervene in the event that the Communists broke the Paris Agreement of 1973.

American troops were evacuated from Saigon on April 30. More than 140,000 Vietnamese refugees left by air and sea, many of whom settled in the United States.

The Provisional Revolutionary Government took control on June 6. Confronted with serious problems of reconstruction, the new regime instituted a rural resettlement program to reduce the swollen population of the major cities and a re-education program to indoctrinate the officials of the old regime with the new orthodoxy.

The election of a National Assembly paved the way for reunification of North and South Vietnam on April 30, 1976, ending a two-year division along the 17th parallel which had never been recognized by the Communists. Hanoi became the new capital of a unified Vietnam with Saigon as a regional and cultural center to be known as Ho Chi Minh City.

Thus ended a turbulent and violent era in the country's history. An intensified national pride suggested that the new Vietnam with a population of 45 million was destined to play an important role in the affairs of the Asian continent.

For more current developments, *see* News Chronology, pages 40–60.

MILITARY STRENGTH OF WORLD NATIONS

Source: Institute for Strategic Studies, London.

Country	Regular armed forces (thousands)	Defense expenditures			
		Spent 1975 (millions, U. S. dollars)	Spent 1975 per capita	Spent 1975 as % of total output	Planned 1976 (millions, U. S. dollars)
United States	2,087	88,983	417	5.9	102,961
U.S.S.R.	3,650	124,000	490	n.a.	n.a.
China (Peking)	3,525	n.a.	n.a.	n.a.	n.a.
Warsaw Pact					
Bulgaria	165	457	52	2.7	438
Czechoslovakia	180	1,706	116	3.8	1,805
Germany, East	157	2,550	148	5.5	2,729
Hungary	100	506	48	2.4	551
Poland	290	2,011	59	3.1	2,252
Rumania	181	707	33	1.7	759
North Atlantic Treaty					
Belgium	88	1,971	200	3.0	2,013
Britain	344	11,118	198	4.9	10,734
Canada	78	2,965	130	2.2	3,231
Denmark	35	939	185	2.2	861
France	513	13,984	264	3.9	12,857
Germany, West	495	16,142	259	3.7	15,220
Greece	200	1,435	159	6.9	1,249
Italy	352	4,700	84	2.6	3,821
Luxembourg	.6	22	65	1.1	23
Netherlands	112	2,978	218	3.6	2,825
Norway	39	929	232	3.1	902
Portugal	60	1,088	124	6.0	748
Turkey	480	2,200	55	9.0	2,800
Other European countries					
Austria	37	410	54	1.0	433
Eire	14	128	41	1.6	134
Finland	36	388	83	1.4	364
Spain	302	1,701	48	1.8	1,766
Sweden	65	2,483	303	3.4	2,418
Switzerland	47	1,047	160	1.8	1,221
Yugoslavia	250	1,705	80	5.6	1,798
Middle East, Mediterranean					
Algeria	69	285	17	n.a.	312
Egypt	343	6,103	163	n.a.	4,859
Iran	300	8,800	268	17.4	9,500
Iraq	158	1,191	107	n.a.	n.a.
Israel	159	3,552	1,045	35.9	4,214
Jordan	68	155	57	12.2	155
Libya	30	203	83	1.7	n.a.
Morocco	73	224	13	2.8	258
Saudi Arabia	52	6,771	1,153	n.a.	6,771
Sudan	53	120	7	n.a.	n.a.
Syria	227	706	96	15.1	1,003
Africa					
Ethiopia	51	84	3	2.9	n.a.
Nigeria	230	1,786	28	n.a.	2,434
Rhodesia	9	102	16	3.0	130
South Africa	52	1,332	53	5.3	1,494
Asia and Australasia					
Australia	69	2,492	184	3.2	2,733
China (Taiwan)	63	1,000[1]	63[1]	7.2[1]	n.a.
India	1,056	2,660	4	3.0	2,812
Indonesia	246	1,108	9	3.8	n.a.
Japan	235	4,620	42	0.9	5,058
Korea, South	595	943	28	5.1	1,500
Malaysia	62	385	31	4.0	353
New Zealand	13	243	79	1.8	n.a.
Pakistan	428	725	10	7.2	807
Philippines	78	407	10	2.6	410
Singapore	31	344	152	5.3	340

| Country | Defense expenditures | | | | |
	Regular armed forces (thousands)	Spent 1975 (millions, U.S. dollars)	Spent 1975 per capita	Spent 1975 as % of total output	Planned 1976 (millions, U.S. dollars)
Thailand	210	542	13	3.7	n.a.
Latin America					
Argentina	133	1,031	41	n.a.	n.a.
Brazil	257	1,283	12	1.3	1,780
Colombia	80	102[1]	4[1]	8.0[1]	n.a.
Mexico	90	586	10	0.7	n.a.
Peru	63	383	24	3.1	n.a.
Uruguay	23	68[2]	23[2]	3.1[2]	n.a.
Venezuela	42	494	41	1.7	n.a.

[1] 1974.   [2] 1973.

APPROXIMATE STRENGTH OF MILITARY FORMATIONS, 1976-77

Source: Institute for Strategic Studies, London.

| Country | Division | | | | | Brigade | | | | Squadron |
| | Armored | | Mechanized | | Airborne | Armored | | Mechanized | | Fighter/FGA |
	Men	Tanks	Men	Tanks	Men	Men	Tanks	Men	Tanks	aircraft
United States	16,500	324	16,000	216	15,000	4,200	108	4,500	54	18-24
U.S.S.R.	11,000	316	14,000	266	7,000	3,000[1]	95[1]	2,500[1]	40[1]	10-14
China	10,000	270	12,000[2]	30[2]	9,000[2]	1,200[1]	90[1]	2,000[1]	...	9-10
Britain[3]	12,500	300	12,000	300	....	4-5,000	100	4-5,000	50	8-15
Germany	14,000	300	15,000	250	8-9,000	3,550[4]	108[4]	3,900[4]	54[4]	15-21
India	15,000	200	17,500[2]	...	....	6,000	150	4,500	...	12-20
Israel	....	...	....	...	....	3,500	80-100	3,500	36-40	15-20
Egypt	11,000	300	12,000	190	....	3,500	96	3,500	36	10-12

[1] Strength of regiment, which is the equivalent formation in the U.S.S.R. and Chinese command structure.   [2] Infantry division.   [3] Britain is proposing to eliminate the brigade as a formation and have armored divisions smaller than above and a new infantry formation of about brigade size, to be known as a Field Force.   [4] Proposed new armored brigades will have 3,026 men and 99 tanks, mechanized brigades 3,730 men and 66 tanks. NOTE: Divisional strengths exclude support units or services outside the divisional structure. Warsaw Pact forces strength is similar to the Soviet Union. NATO forces have strength similar to Germany. Iran, Pakistan, the Philippines, Thailand, Japan, South Korea and Taiwan tend to adopt American military organization. Australia, New Zealand, Malaysia and Singapore follow British practice.

U.S. AND SOVIET STRATEGIC FORCE LEVELS

Source: U. S. Department of Defense.

| Offensive and Defense forces | Mid-1976 | | Mid-1975 | |
	U.S.A.	U.S.S.R.	U.S.A.	U.S.S.R.
Intercontinental ballistic missile launchers[1,2]	1,054	1,500	1,054	1,600
Submarine-launched ballistic missile launchers[1,3]	656	850	656	730
Long range bombers[4,5]	421	180	497	160
Force loadings weapons[6]	8,900	3,500	8,500	2,800
Air defense surveillance radars[7]	61	5,500	59	4,500
Air defense interceptors[7,8]	315	2,600	412	2,600
Surface-to-air launchers[7,9]	0	10,000	0	10,000
Antiballistic missile launchers	100	64	36	64

[1] Includes on-line missile launchers as well as those in the final stages of construction, in overhaul, repair, conversion and modernization. [2] Does not include test and training launchers, but, for the U.S.S.R., does include launchers at test ranges which are probably part of the operational force. [3] Includes launchers on all nuclear-powered submarines, and, for the U.S.S.R., operational launchers for modern SLBms on G-class diesel submarines. [4] The following long-range bombers are placed in this category: for the U.S.: B-52s, FB-111, B-1; for the U.S.S.R.: Bear, Bison, Backfire. [5] Includes deployed, strike-configured aircraft only. [6] Total force loadings reflect only those independently-targetable weapons associated with on-line ICBMs/SLBMs and UE aircraft. Weapons reserved for restrike and weapons on inactive status are not included. [7] Excludes radars and launchers at test sites or outside CONUS. [8] These numbers represent Total Active Inventory (TAI). [9] These 10,000 launchers accommodate about 12,000 SAM interceptors. Some of the launchers have multiple rails.

NATO AND WARSAW PACT MILITARY BALANCE, 1976-77[1]

Source: Institute for Strategic Studies, London.

Category	Northern and Central Europe			Southern Europe		
	NATO	WARSAW PACT	(of which) USSR	NATO	WARSAW PACT	(of which) USSR
Ground forces available in peacetime (division equivalents):						
Armored	11	31	19	6	6	3
Infantry, mechanized and airborne	18	36	21	35	27	7
Combat and direct support troops available (thousands)	635	910	620	540	395	155
Main battle tanks available in peacetime	7,000	19,000	11,000	4,000	7,500	2,750
Tactical aircraft in operational service:						
Light bombers	185	225	200	...	50	50
Fighter/ground attack	1,250	1,375	950	450	250	100
Interceptors	375	2,050	950	275	700	200
Reconnaissance	275	550	400	150	100	50

Missile strength (all theaters)	Intercontinental ballistic missiles	Submarine launched ballistic missiles	Long-range bombers
USA[2]	1,054	656	387
USSR[2]	1,527	845	135

[1] On NATO side, the commands for which AFCENT and AFNORTH commanders have responsibility. France (not part of NATO's integrated commands) is not included. On Warsaw Pact side, armed forces of Bulgaria, Hungary, and Romania are not included. [2] 1976.

SOVIET EXPANSION 1940-1948

Source: North Atlantic Treaty Organization.

Annexed or under Soviet administration

Year	Countries	Population (millions)	Area (sq. mi.)
1940	Part of Finland	0.5	17,600
1940	Estonia	1.4	17,413
1940	Latvia	2.4	24,595
1940	Lithuania	3.2	25,174
1945	Part of German East Prussia	1.2	5,400
1945	Part of Poland	11.8	69,900
1945	Part of Czechoslovakia	0.7	4,900
1945	Part of Rumania	3.7	19,400
	Total	24.0	182,400

Controlled by USSR

Year	Countries	Population (millions)	Area (sq. mi.)
1945	Soviet Zone of Germany	18.8	42,900
1945	Poland	33.1	120,725
1948	Czechoslovakia	14.4	49,373
1947	Hungary	10.4	35,902
1948	Rumania	16.1	91,584
1946	Bulgaria	8.6	42,823
1946	Albania	2.3	11,100
	Total	91.9	393,547

Coast Guard Personnel on Active Duty: 1950 to 1974

[As of June 30]

YEAR	Total	Officers	Cadets	Enlisted	YEAR	Total	Officers	Cadets	Enlisted
1950	23,190	2,906	296	19,988	1971	38,057	5,754	684	31,619
1955	28,607	3,520	533	24,554	1972	38,039	5,702	1,956	31,281
1960	30,616	4,020	405	26,191	1973	36,645	5,798	1,119	29,728
1965	31,776	4,476	440	26,860	1974	36,742	5,731	1,099	29,912
1970	37,689	5,512	653	31,524					

Source: 1950-1965, U.S. Dept. of the Treasury

Military Personnel on Active Duty, by Location: 1960 to 1974

In thousands. As of Dec. 31. Shore-based includes Navy personnel temporarily on shore.

YEAR	TOTAL			UNITED STATES [2]			FOREIGN COUNTRIES		
	Total	Shore-based	Naval afloat [1]	Total	Shore-based	Naval afloat [1]	Total	Shore-based	Naval afloat [1]
1960	2,494	2,209	285	1,861	1,661	200	633	548	85
1965	2,857	2,517	340	2,004	1,789	215	853	728	125
1966	3,334	2,894	440	2,223	1,929	294	1,111	965	146
1967	3,398	2,984	414	2,218	1,950	268	1,180	1,034	146
1968	3,408	3,105	303	2,237	2,037	200	1,171	1,068	103
1969	3,298	3,008	290	2,209	2,012	197	1,088	996	92
1970	2,874	2,627	247	1,987	1,807	180	888	820	67
1971	2,519	2,290	229	1,846	1,677	169	673	613	60
1972	2,348	2,109	239	1,752	1,618	134	596	491	105
1973	2,202	1,982	220	1,709	1,544	165	493	438	55
1974	2,140	1,929	211	1,660	1,508	152	480	421	59

[1] Navy and Marine Corps.   [2] Includes outlying areas. Source: U.S. Dept. of Defense, Office of the Secretary, *Selected Manpower Statistics,* annual.

U.S. Military Personnel in Asia, by Country: 1950 to 1974
In thousands.

COUNTRY	U.S. TROOP LEVELS							MILITARY DEPENDENTS			
	1950	1958	1971 (Feb.)	1971 (June)	1972 (Sept.)	1973 (June)	1974 (Sept.)	1970	1972	1973 (Sept.)	1974 (Sept.)
Total	147	163	545	459	208	166	141	101.0	83.9	79.6	85.4
China (Taiwan)	(z)	12	9	9	8	9	5	6.0	6.0	5.5	3.6
Japan	115	58	38	27	21	} 57	} 52	41.0	29.6	} 43.8	} 43.2
Ryukyu Islands	21	29	50	45	41			25.0	23.8		
Philippines	10	12	24	18	16	16	18	21.2	17.6	20.6	20.5
South Korea	1	52	52	43	42	42	40	3.6	2.2	5.6	11.3
South Vietnam	–	(1)	336	284	35	(z)	(z)	–	–	(z)	(z)
Thailand	–	–	36	32	45	42	26	4.2	4.7	4.1	6.8

— Represents zero.   Z Less than 500.   [1] U.S. military advisory presence between 1954 and 1960 averaged 650 men; the first ground combat forces (about 1,000–1,200 men) arrived in March 1965. Source: 1950 to 1971, Congressional Quarterly Inc., Washington, D.C., *Congressional Quarterly Weekly Report,* No. 7, Feb. 12, 1971 (copyright); thereafter, U.S. Dept. of Defense, Office of the Secretary, release.

Military Personnel on Active Duty, Civilian Employees of Military Agencies, and Payroll: 1950 to 1974

In thousands, except as indicated. Personnel as of December 31; payroll for years ending June 30. Excludes "indirect hire" civilians, i.e., foreign nationals rendering personal services to the military departments.

ITEM	1950	1955	1960	1965	1968	1969	1970	1971	1972	1973	1974
Total personnel	3,345	4,054	3,526	3,915	4,681	4,561	4,026	3,642	3,428	3,228	3,183
Military	2,357	2,887	2,494	2,857	3,408	3,298	2,874	2,519	2,348	2,202	2,140
Civilian [1]	988	1,167	1,032	1,057	1,273	1,263	[2]1,152	[2]1,123	[2]1,082	[2]1,026	[2]1,043
Army	1,510	1,521	1,257	1,448	1,931	1,901	1,664	1,386	1,261	1,148	1,145
Military	[3]1,077	[3]1,084	877	1,075	1,463	1,432	1,234	966	862	782	773
Civilian	434	437	381	373	468	469	430	420	399	366	372
Air Force	746	1,262	1,117	1,134	1,198	1,164	1,056	1,047	981	942	898
Military	[3]559	[3]937	811	842	887	843	759	754	707	674	625
Civilian	186	326	307	292	311	322	297	293	274	268	273
Navy and Marine Corps	1,087	1,269	1,150	1,275	1,480	1,426	1,242	1,149	1,117	1,065	1,066
Military	721	867	806	940	1,058	1,024	882	799	777	746	742
Civilian	366	402	343	335	422	402	360	350	340	319	324
Total payroll..bil. dol.	7.5	14.0	15.2	18.1	25.3	27.5	30.2	30.2	31.4	32.0	32.7
Military.....bil. dol.	4.6	9.2	9.4	11.0	15.9	17.3	18.9	18.6	19.2	19.7	19.9
Civilian.....bil. dol.	2.9	4.8	5.8	7.1	9.4	10.2	11.3	11.6	12.2	12.3	12.8
Cost per soldier:											
Avg. active force..1,000.	1,539	3,178	2,489	2,668	3,436	3,467	3,294	2,891	2,512	2,324	2,207
Manpower cost, DOD budget.....bil. dol.	5.3	12.3	12.1	15.2	22.7	24.0	25.6	25.3	26.1	27.0	(NA)
Cost per soldier...$1,000.	3.4	3.9	4.9	5.7	6.6	6.9	7.8	8.8	10.4	11.6	(NA)

NA Not available.   [1] Includes personnel assigned to Office of Secretary of Defense, Organization of Joint Chiefs of Staff, Army Corps of Engineers Civil Functions, and other defense activities, not shown separately.   [2] Excludes students and disadvantaged youth in special employment categories.   [3] Represents "Command Strength." Source: U.S. Dept. of Defense, Office of the Secretary, *Selected Manpower Statistics,* annual, and *Selected Defense Department Economic Indicators,* monthly.

Budget Outlays for National Defense Functions: 1960 to 1975

In billions of dollars, except as indicated. For years ending June 30.

ITEM	1960	1965	1967	1968	1969	1970	1971	1972	1973	1974	1975 est.
Total	45.9	49.6	70.1	80.5	81.2	80.3	77.7	78.3	76.0	78.6	85.3
Dept. of Defense, military	41.5	46.0	67.5	77.4	77.9	77.2	74.5	75.2	73.3	77.6	83.0
Military personnel	11.0	13.4	18.0	19.9	21.4	23.0	22.6	23.0	23.2	23.7	25.0
Percent of total military	26.6	29.1	26.6	25.7	27.4	29.9	30.4	30.7	31.7	30.0	27.4
Active forces	10.4	12.7	17.1	19.0	20.5	22.0	21.4	21.6	21.7	22.9	24.1
Reserve forces	.7	.7	.9	.9	.9	1.1	1.2	1.4	1.5	.8	.9
Retired military personnel	.7	1.4	1.8	2.1	2.4	2.8	3.4	3.9	4.4	5.1	6.3
Operation [1]	10.2	12.3	19.0	20.6	22.2	21.6	20.9	21.7	21.1	22.5	25.7
Procurement	13.3	11.8	19.0	23.3	24.0	21.6	18.9	17.1	15.7	15.2	14.8
Army	(NA)	1.8	4.4	5.8	6.1	5.2	4.4	3.9	2.8	2.6	2.1
Navy (incl. Marine Corps)	(NA)	4.9	6.5	8.0	8.5	7.9	7.3	7.1	7.0	7.3	7.3
Air Force	(NA)	5.1	8.1	9.4	9.3	8.4	7.1	6.0	5.8	5.4	5.3
Defense agencies	(NA)	(Z)	(Z)	(Z)	.1	.1	.1	.1	(Z)	.1	.1
Research and development	4.7	6.2	7.2	7.7	7.5	7.2	7.3	7.9	8.2	8.6	8.7
Military construction	1.6	1.0	1.5	1.3	1.4	1.2	1.1	1.1	1.1	1.4	1.5
Family housing	(X)	.6	.5	.5	.6	.6	.6	.7	.7	.9	1.1
Civil defense	(X)	.1	.1	.1	.1	.1	.1	.1	.1	.1	.1
Other [2]	−.2	−.9	.4	1.9	−1.7	−1.0	−.3	−.3	−1.1	−.2	−.3
Military assistance	1.6	1.1	.9	.7	.8	.7	1.0	.8	.5	.8	1.8
Atomic energy program	2.6	2.6	2.3	2.5	2.5	2.5	2.3	2.4	2.4	1.5	1.6
Defense-related activities	.2	.1	(Z)	.1	.3	.1	−.1	.1	.2	−1.3	−1.1
Offsetting receipts, deduct	−.1	−.3	−.5	−.1	−.1	−.1	−.1	−.1	−.4	–	–

- Represents zero. NA Not available. X Not applicable. Z Less than $50 million. [1] Includes maintenance. [2] Revolving and management funds, trust funds, special foreign currency program, allowances, and offsetting receipts.

Department of Defense—Funds Available and Outlays: 1960 to 1975

In billions of dollars, except as indicated. For years ending June 30.

ITEM	1960[1]	1965	1967	1968	1969	1970	1971	1972	1973	1974	1975[2] est.
Funds available	52.5	64.2	89.0	92.9	93.5	90.5	85.8	88.8	92.7	95.9	101.9
New oblig. authority	41.3	50.5	73.6	77.8	78.3	75.4	72.6	76.8	79.6	82.9	86.6
Military	40.4	49.2	72.3	76.4	77.0	74.2	71.2	75.1	77.6	81.1	84.8
Civil	.9	1.3	1.4	1.4	1.3	1.2	1.3	1.6	2.0	1.8	1.8
Unobligated balance	11.2	13.8	15.4	15.1	15.2	15.1	13.2	12.1	13.1	13.0	15.3
Military	11.1	13.6	15.1	14.8	14.9	14.8	13.0	11.9	12.7	12.6	15.1
Civil	.1	.1	.2	.2	.3	.3	.2	.2	.4	.4	.2
Outlays	41.8	47.2	68.8	78.7	79.1	78.4	75.9	76.7	75.0	79.3	84.4
Military	40.9	46.0	67.5	77.4	77.9	77.2	74.5	75.2	73.3	77.6	82.5
Civil	.9	1.2	1.3	1.3	1.3	1.2	1.4	1.5	1.7	1.7	1.9
Ratio of outlays to—											
Funds available	0.8	0.7	0.8	0.8	0.8	0.9	0.9	0.9	0.8	0.8	0.8
Unobligated balance	3.7	3.4	4.5	5.2	5.2	5.2	5.8	6.3	5.7	6.1	5.5

[1] Excludes military assistance funds which were included in Dept. of Defense budget in 1960 but in funds appropriated to the President in later years shown. [2] Excludes military assistance to South Vietnamese forces. Source: U.S. Office of Management and Budget, *The Budget of the United States Government,* annual.

Department of Defense Outlays, by Branch of Service: 1965 to 1974

For years ending June 30. Excludes civil functions. Includes military assistance.

YEAR	OUTLAYS (mil. dol.)					PERCENT DISTRIBUTION			
	Total Defense Dept.	Army	Navy	Air Force	Other	Army	Navy	Air Force	Other
1965	47,098	11,552	13,339	18,146	4,061	24.5	28.3	38.5	8.6
1967	68,315	20,952	19,246	22,918	5,199	30.7	28.2	33.5	7.6
1968	78,027	25,223	22,071	25,734	4,999	32.3	28.3	33.0	6.4
1969	78,660	25,610	22,691	26,114	4,245	32.6	28.8	33.2	5.4
1970	78,349	25,147	22,656	25,233	5,313	32.1	28.9	32.2	6.8
1971	76,005	23,909	22,374	24,749	4,973	31.5	29.4	32.6	6.5
1972	76,674	23,473	22,736	24,845	5,620	30.6	29.7	32.4	7.3
1973	74,473	21,140	22,985	24,538	5,811	28.4	30.9	32.9	7.8
1974	77,651	22,371	24,616	25,736	4,927	28.8	31.7	33.1	6.4

Source: U.S. Dept. of the Treasury, Office of the Secretary, *Combined Statement of Receipts, Expenditures, and Balances of the United States Government,* annual.

STATUS OF SELECTIVE SERVICE INDUCTEES EXAMINED FOR MILITARY SERVICE—PERCENT DISTRIBUTION: 1955 TO 1973

Includes Puerto Rico, Guam, Mariana Islands, and Virgin Islands. Based on preinduction examinations. Inductions were were effective July 1, 1973.

STATUS	1955	1960	1965	1968	1969	1970	1971	1972	1973 [1]
Total examined	206	259	1,229	1,165	1,326	1,017	596	471	21
PERCENT DISTRIBUTION									
Found acceptable	61.6	55.1	56.0	57.9	55.1	54.0	50.5	52.5	46.1
Disqualified	38.4	44.9	44.0	42.1	44.9	46.0	49.5	47.5	53.9
Medically disqualified only	17.5	22.1	21.8	29.9	32.8	37.4	40.4	35.4	43.0
Failed mental requirements only	15.4	18.8	18.6	9.5	9.2	6.2	5.4	7.4	2.4
Failed mental test only [2]	15.4	18.8	10.7	8.0	7.8	5.3	4.3	4.1	1.3
Trainability limited [3]	(X)	(X)	7.9	1.5	1.4	0.9	1.1	3.3	1.1
Failed mental test and medically disqualified	2.8	2.9	2.3	1.8	2.2	1.4	2.2	3.4	1.7
Administratively disqualified	2.7	1.1	1.3	0.9	0.7	1.0	1.5	1.3	6.8

X Not applicable. [1] 1973 data are for January through June. [2] Examinees who failed minimum requirement (10 percentile) on Armed Forces Qualification Test (AFQT) or minimum requirement (below raw score of 60) on its equivalent (ECFA) administered to Spanish-speaking examinees in Puerto Rico. [3] Examinees classified as mental group IV on basis of AFQT but who failed to meet additional aptitude area requirements effective in August 1958 and called Army Classification Battery (ACB) tests until mid-September 1961 and Army Qualification Battery (AQB) thereafter. The AQB requirements were raised in May 1963 and lowered in November 1965, April 1966, October 1966, and December 1966. Source: U.S. Dept. of the Army, Office of the Surgeon General, unpublished data.

SELECTIVE SERVICE INDUCTEES FOUND ACCEPTABLE FOR MILITARY SERVICE—PERCENT DISTRIBUTION, BY MENTAL GROUP: 1960 TO 1973

Includes Puerto Rico, Guam, Mariana Islands, and Virgin Islands. Inductions were halted effectively July 1, 1973.

MENTAL GROUP AND PERCENTILE SCORE	1960	1965	1967	1968	1969	1970	1971	1972	1973 [1]
Group I (93–100)	14.3	7.5	8.7	9.0	7.8	9.5	7.9	6.8	9.5
Group II (65–92)	31.9	34.9	33.0	33.6	34.1	38.3	37.2	39.2	44.9
Group III (31–64)	34.5	43.2	34.3	36.7	38.0	36.5	38.1	42.9	38.3
Group IV (10–30) [2]	19.0	13.2	22.9	19.7	19.4	15.2	16.2	10.5	6.9
Administrative acceptees [3]	0.3	1.2	1.1	1.0	0.7	0.5	0.6	0.6	0.4

[1] January through June. [2] See footnotes 2 and 3, table above. [3] Draftees who failed mental test or additional aptitude tests, but who were administratively declared acceptable on basis of their education and findings of a personal interview. Source: U.S. Dept. of the Army, Office of the Surgeon General, unpublished data.

SELECTIVE SERVICE ACT VIOLATIONS—DISPOSITION OF DEFENDANTS: 1950 TO 1974

For years ending June 30. Covers defendants charged in U.S. District Courts with violations of Selective Training and Service Act of 1940 and Universal Military Training and Service Act of 1948. Excludes District of Columbia, Canal Zone, Guam, and Virgin Islands.

ITEM	1950	1955	1960	1965	1967	1968	1969	1970	1971	1972	1973	1974
Total defendants	449	719	239	341	996	1,192	1,744	2,833	2,973	4,906	3,495	2,094
Not convicted, total	274	430	73	99	248	408	844	1,806	1,937	3,264	2,518	1,295
Dismissed	272	367	65	88	224	353	747	1,570	1,701	2,937	2,338	1,196
Acquitted	2	63	8	11	24	55	97	236	236	327	180	99
Convicted, total	175	289	166	242	748	784	900	1,027	1,036	1,642	977	799
Percent of total	39.0	40.2	69.5	71.0	75.1	65.8	51.6	36.3	34.8	33.5	28.0	38.2
By plea of guilty or nolo	156	157	131	197	538	520	511	570	590	934	631	643
By court or jury	19	132	35	45	210	264	389	457	446	708	346	156
Imprisonment, total	109	217	126	189	666	580	544	450	377	458	260	155
Average sentence...mo.	13.4	24.8	21.5	21.0	32.1	37.3	36.3	33.5	29.1	22.0	17.5	14.5
Probation	65	70	37	52	78	202	350	572	650	1,178	707	637
Fine and other	1	2	3	1	4	2	6	5	9	6	10	7

Source: Administrative Office of the U.S. Courts, *Annual Report of the Director.*

THE UNITED NATIONS

The U.N. in Action; A Year of Crises

By William B. Buffum
United Nations Under-Secretary-General

The United Nations demonstrated again in 1976 that it is far more than a debating society.

In 1976, as in previous years, crises around the globe found their echo in the United Nations. As a result, the Security Council had one of its busiest years in history, with some successes and some failures. But, as on many previous occasions, the United Nations helped prevent some potential threats to world peace from growing into armed confrontation.

While national interests and priorities often conflict, the United Nations has helped moderate these conflicts. That is shown by its record of achievement despite what is often a scene of controversy, frustration and political maneuvering. There have recently been increasing allegations that the U.N. is just a huge meeting hall in New York filled with rhetoric and political theatrics. But when people criticize the U.N. for what it does or does not do, they often forget that it is not a world government; instead it is an association of 145 sovereign states, each with its own interests and priorities.

Since it has no independent capacity to settle conflicts, the U.N. can make a contribution only if these governments are ready to use it. Yet in its 30-year history, the United Nations has helped to keep over 70 crises from developing into open warfare.

As we enter the last quarter of the twentieth century, mankind faces new problems. Energy resources, environment, population growth and the use of the seas and outer space now rank with more traditional questions of military and political security. And a new pattern of relationships must be fashioned out of the old political and economic order that has been transformed since the end of World War II by the creation of nearly 100 new states. These new nations rely heavily on the United Nations in seeking a more equitable share in the world's prosperity.

To help strengthen world peace and improve the human condition, the United Nations provides a network of institutions that carry out active programs in such fields as health, food, economic development and the environment. With a constant increase in the scale and complexity of the problems of global interdependence, there is an obvious and growing need for institutions to manage them.

Actions for Peace and Security

As the only organization with virtually universal membership, the United Nations reflects the world's tensions and conflicts. For the Security Council, of particular importance in 1976 were decisions to ex-

tend the mandate of the United Nations Emergency Force between Egypt and Israel, the United Nations Disengagement Observer Force between Israel and Syria, and the United Nations Force in Cyprus separating the Greek and Turk Cypriot communities.

The contribution of the United Nations peacekeeping force in helping prevent the Middle East conflict from spreading remained one of the organization's most important contributions to world peace.

On the negative side, the United Nations was unable to help end the tragic fighting in Lebanon. Although the Secretary-General repeatedly appealed for a cease-fire and formally drew the attention of the Security Council to the seriousness of the conflict, no member saw fit to seek United Nations action on Lebanon. The organization's contribution was thus concentrated on coordinating an international relief effort to alleviate the suffering of the Lebanese people.

African problems engaged the Security Council on several occasions in 1976. It reviewed the progress of the application of sanctions against Rhodesia, condemned the practice of apartheid in South Africa and pressed for an end to South Africa's occupation of Namibia (previously called South-West Africa). Substantial United Nations assistance programs were established to help the people and countries most directly affected.

The Menace of International Terrorism

The Council also confronted the critical issue of international terrorism following Israel's raid in July on Entebbe Airport in Uganda to retrieve hijacked hostages. The Council failed to adopt a resolution on the subject but nearly every member condemned international terrorism. The General Assembly also reopened its consideration of the subject during its fall session. An item on this subject has been on its agenda each year since 1972, when Secretary-General Kurt Waldheim requested its inscription.

On the Greek-Turkish dispute over the Aegean shelf, the Security Council adopted a resolution urging negotiations for a peaceful settlement, which served as a basis for a new dialogue between the two parties.

In addition, Secretary-General Waldheim was called upon to continue his good offices in the search for a solution to the conflict in Cyprus, as well as the dispute over the Western Sahara and East Timor.

These and other conflict situations represented potential threats to international peace.

The World's Arms Bill—The Nuclear Threat

While great power rivalry was less intense in 1976, the global arms race continued its upward spiral. United Nations expressions of concern in this area remained largely hortatory as individual members exercised their sovereign right to assess their own defense needs. Yet the annual global arms bill, which has grown to over $300 billion with no end in sight, aroused increasing concern and growing demands that a greater share of the world's precious resources be devoted to economic development for an ever-expanding world population.

Pressure of world public opinion expressed in earlier General Assemblies was largely responsible for the Non-Proliferation Treaty of 1970 and the Limited Test Ban Treaty of 1973. Although the Assembly achieved only limited success with appeals for a complete halt to all nuclear testing, it continued to press for other disarmament measures that would reduce the risk of war, including the establishment of nuclear-free zones.

A special session of the General Assembly and/or World Disarmament Conference is expected to be convened in a year or so, devoted exclusively to disarmament problems.

Gains in Improving Human Welfare

During 1976, the specialized agencies of the United Nations made further headway in their labors to create a better world:

● One of mankind's most ancient enemies—smallpox—was virtually eliminated, thanks to an eradication program of the World Health Organization.

● The Food and Agriculture Organization intensified its struggle against world hunger, and a billion-dollar fund for agricultural development was established to increase food production.

● The United Nations Children's Fund improved the basic health and nutrition care for over 100 million underprivileged children.

● The United Nations High Commissioner for Refugees cared for millions of displaced persons, with major new programs in Southeast Asia.

● The United Nations Environment Program continued to develop a world-wide system of environmental monitoring and information exchange, including an international register of potentially toxic chemicals.

● And the United Nations-related Atomic Energy Agency strengthened the safeguard system which can help limit the dangers inherent in the further spread of nuclear energy.

Among many other activities, the United Nations system fostered the development of high-yield and enriched grains; drug control, research and rehabilitation; international regulation of radio and television frequencies; training for thousands of teachers; emergency disaster relief; world cancer research and much more.

Human Rights

The United Nations Human Rights Commission continued its efforts to promote respect for individual human rights and devoted particular attention to the situation in Chile. Again, the Commission's efforts were limited by the fact that human rights practices involve a sensitive area of national sovereignty, and the United Nations Charter prohibits the Organization from intervening in matters which are essentially within the domestic jurisdiction of any state.

The Economy

The international community also intensified its efforts on several fronts during 1976 to implement the elements of a "new international economic order" adopted at the highly successful seventh special session of the United Nations General Assembly in the fall of 1975. The Fourth Session of the United Nations Conference on Trade and Development met in Kenya in May 1976 and launched a program to restructure global commodity trade in order to stabilize and increase earnings of developing countries. Yet much remains to be done to assure that the 70% of the world's population receiving only 30% of its income have a better chance to achieve a decent standard of living.

The year also saw a continuation of the largest and longest conference in United Nations history as thousands of delegates sought to hammer out the complex provisions that would give the world its first agreed regime of Law of the Sea. However, disagreement on exploitation of the mineral riches of the deep-sea bed continued to stall progress.

Increasing concern about activities of the world's transnational corporations gave new impetus to the United Nations Commission on Transnational Corporations, recently established (1974) under the Economic and Social Council, and an information and research center.

[7]Following its earlier sponsorship of successful global conferences on population, environment, food and the status of women, the United Nations convened a world conference on human settlements in Vancouver during June 1976.

The Problems and Threats Ahead

In dealing with the imperatives of the last quarter of the twentieth century, mankind must moderate and resolve regional conflicts lest they develop into a global threat. The proliferation of nuclear weapons and the possibility of diverting fissionable materials for aggressive purposes increase the risk of a nuclear holocaust.

The United Nations has the machinery and facilities to deal with the new imperatives in many ways:

● It can help reduce today's intolerable situation where millions periodically die of starvation or cannot realize their human potential because of malnutrition.

● It can apply modern science to combat contagious disease on a global scale.

● It can promote a peaceful search for more equitable economic relationships between rich and poor societies.

● It can provide a forum where massive violations of human rights can be brought before the conscience of the world.

● It can help reduce the dangers in the spread of nuclear power.

● It can help prevent or stop conflicts that bear the seeds of a world war which could mark the end of the human race.

The world might well ponder whether the potential of the United Nations to help cope with such problems is being adequately utilized by the national governments which comprise its membership.

Major Cases and Actions

IRAN

Iran presented first case before Security Council on Jan. 19, 1946, demanding an end to Russian "interference" in Azerbaijan province and withdrawal of troops. U.S.S.R. withdrew troops May 6.

GREECE

On Dec. 3, 1946, Greece complained to Security Council that Albania, Bulgaria and Yugoslavia were aiding Communist-led rebels in Northern Greece. However, Greek rebellion faded out after Marshal Tito's Yugoslavia broke with Moscow on June 28, 1948.

ATOMIC ENERGY CONTROL

Eleven-nation U.N. commission on Dec. 31, 1946, recommended U.S. "Baruch plan" for international control and inspection. Russia dissented and submitted plan limiting international inspection so that secret making of atomic bombs could not be detected. Soviet Union vetoed U.S. plan in Security Council. General Assembly approved U.S. plan but Soviet-bloc opposition prevented carrying it out.

PALESTINE

In November 1947, General Assembly approved plan for partitioning Palestine into an Arab and Jewish state but this plan proved impossible to enforce. On May 14, 1948, Israel proclaimed her independence and was then attacked by five neighboring Arab states. After truce and intermittent fighting, Israel signed armistices with Egypt and Jordan. On May 11, 1949, the U.N. accepted Israel as 59th member.

INDONESIA

The Security Council sent a Good Offices Commission to Indonesia in 1947 to end fighting between Netherlands and Indonesian Republic. It effected a truce Jan. 17, 1948. Indonesia peacefully achieved independence from the Netherlands.

SOVIET BOYCOTT

Soviet Union boycotted Security Council from January to August 1950 over Council's refusal of U.S.S.R. demand that Communist China replace Nationalist China in U.N.

KOREA

Russia occupied northern half of Korea after World War II and U.S. the southern half. Russia refused to follow agreement for independent republic to govern whole country. U.S. referred question to U.N., and General Assembly voted Nov. 5, 1947, to send commission to set up free government. Russia boycotted the commission, which helped set up Republic of Korea in south with capital at Seoul.

HUNGARY

Communist Government asked Soviet help in October 1956 to quell uprisings, and Russians sent tanks. Communists sought to appease populace by installing as Premier Imre Nagy, who had been ousted from party as "Titoist."

Nagy promised to get Russians out and, by Nov. 1, Soviet tanks and troops had withdrawn from Budapest. On Nov. 4 tanks returned in force, shooting freely and killing civilians. Russians set up puppet regime headed by Janos Kadar.

On Nov. 4 and subsequently, General Assembly demanded that Russia withdraw troops, and a resolution was voted, 55-8, Dec. 12 condemning "violation of the Charter by the U.S.S.R." Thousands fled Hungary.

SUEZ

Oct. 29, 1956, Israel attacked Gaza Strip and Egypt's Sinai territory, and Britain and France became involved in fighting. U.N. General Assembly, in an emergency session, voted U.S. resolution for cease-fire. On Nov. 3, Britain and France heeded the call. By General Assembly direction, U.N. Emergency Force landed at a midway point on Suez Canal Nov. 11, 1956. On Feb. 21, Israel pulled out last troops on condition that U.N. Force station peace-keeping troops on Aqaba Gulf and in Gaza Strip. The troops became the first U.N. uniformed peace-preserving unit.

LEBANON

In July 1956, the United States sent Marines to Lebanon, torn by insurrection allegedly aided from neighboring Syria, which had just affiliated with Egypt in the new United Arab Republic. Nearby Jordan requested and received British troops to safeguard pro-West regime. In Security Council, the Soviet Union voted resolutions to strengthen U.N. forces in Mideast. Emergency session of General Assembly directed Secretary-General Dag Hammarskjöld to go to Middle East to seek to restore stability and facilitate withdrawal of U.S. and British troops.

THE CONGO

Belgian Congo was in chaos after becoming independent on June 30, 1960. On appeal from the Congo, U.N. rushed police force with troops from 18 nations. Katanga province, which had own army officered by foreigners, mostly Belgian, wanted to secede. Security Council ordered Katanga to expel the foreigners. U.N. troops used force to carry out order, with casualties on both sides. Secession ended and Katanga was split into three provinces after defeat of provincial forces in January 1963.

Principal Organs of the United Nations

SECRETARIAT

This is the directorate on U.N. operations, apart from political decisions. All members contribute to its upkeep. Its staff of over 4,000 specialists is recruited from member nations in proportion to their budget contributions. The staff works under the Secretary-General, whom it assists and advises.

Secretaries-General

Trygve Lie, of Norway, Feb. 1, 1946, to Apr. 10, 1953.

Dag Hammarskjöld, of Sweden, Apr. 11, 1953, to Sept. 17, 1961.

U Thant, of Burma, Nov. 3, 1961, to Dec. 31, 1971.

Kurt Waldheim, of Austria, Jan. 1, 1972.

GENERAL ASSEMBLY

The General Assembly is the world's forum for discussing matters affecting world peace and security, and for making recommendations concerning them. It has no power of its own to enforce decisions.

The Assembly is composed of the 51 original member nations and those admitted since, a total of 145. Each nation is allowed five representatives, but only one vote. On major questions involving international peace and security, a two-thirds majority of those present and voting is required. The Charter sets precise rules for eligibility.

The Assembly's agenda can be as broad as the Charter. It can make recommendations to member nations, the Security Council or both. Emphasis is given questions relating to international peace and security brought before it by any member, the Security Council or nonmembers.

The Assembly also maintains a broad program of international cooperation in economic, social, cultural, educational and health fields, and for assisting in human rights and freedoms.

Among other duties, the Assembly has functions relating to the trusteeship system, and considers and approves the U.N. Budget. Every member contributes to operating expenses according to its means.

Main Committees

First Committee (Political and Security, including the regulation of armaments).

Special Political Committee (to share work of First Committee).

Second Committee (Economic and Financial).

Third Committee (Social, Humanitarian and Cultural).

Fourth Committee (Trusteeship, including Non-Self-Governing Territories).

Fifth Committee (Administrative and Budgetary).

Sixth Committee (Legal).

Presidents of the General Assembly

Paul-Henri Spaak, of Belgium, 1946, First Session.

Oswaldo Aranha, of Brazil, 1947, First Special Session and Second Regular Session.

Dr. José Arce, of Argentina, 1948, Second Special Session.

Herbert V. Evatt, of Australia, 1948–49, Third Session.

Carlos P. Romulo, of the Philippines, 1949, Fourth Session.

Nasrollah Entezam, of Iran, 1950–51, Fifth Session.

Luis Padilla Nervo, of Mexico, 1951–52, Sixth Session.

Lester B. Pearson, of Canada, 1952–53, Seventh Session.

Mrs. Vijaya Lakshmi Pandit, of India, 1953–54, Eighth Session.

Eelco N. van Kleffens, of the Netherlands, 1954, Ninth Session.

José Maza, of Chile, 1955, Tenth Session.

Rudecindo Ortega, of Chile, Nov., 1956, First and Second Emergency Special Sessions.

Prince Wan Waithayakon, of Thailand, 1956–57, Eleventh Session.

Sir Leslie Munro, of New Zealand, 1957–58, Twelfth Session and Third Emergency Special Session.

Charles Malik, of Lebanon, 1958–1959, Thirteenth Session.

Víctor Andrés Belaúnde, of Peru, 1959–60, Fourteenth Session and Fourth Emergency Special Session.

Frederick Henry Boland, of Ireland, 1960–61, 15th Session and 3d Special Session.

Mongi Slim, of Tunisia, 1961–62, Sixteenth Session.

Muhammad Zafrulla Khan, of Pakistan, 1962–63, Seventeenth Session and Fourth Special Session.

Carlos Sosa Rodriguez, of Venezuela, 1963, Eighteenth Session.

Alex Quaison-Sackey, of Ghana, 1964–65, Nineteenth Session.

Amintore Fanfani, of Italy, 1965, Twentieth Session.

Abdul Rahman Pazhwak, of Afghanistan, 1966–67, 21st Session, Fifth Special Session, Fifth Emergency Special Session.

Corneliu Manescu, of Romania, 1967–68, 22nd Session.

Emilio Arenales Catalán, of Guatemala, 1968, 23rd Session.

Miss Angie E. Brooks, of Liberia, 1969, 24th Session.

Edvard Hambro, of Norway, 1970, 25th Session.

Adam Malik, of Indonesia, 1971, 26th Session.

Stanislaw Trepczynski, of Poland, 1972, 27th Session.

Leopoldo Benites, of Ecuador, 1973-74, 28th Session, 6th Special Session.

Abdelaziz Bouteflika, of Algeria, 1974-75, 29th Session, 7th Special Session.

Gaston Thorn, of Luxembourg, 1975, 30th Session.

Hamilton Shirley Amerasinghe, 1976, 31st Session.

SECURITY COUNCIL

The Security Council is the primary instrument for implementing the United Nations' purposes and principles. Its main purpose is to prevent war by settling disputes between nations and by limiting armaments.

Under the Charter, the Council is permitted to dispatch a U.N. force to stop aggression and restore law and order. All member nations undertake to make available armed forces, assistance and facilities to maintain international peace and security. The Council has a Military Staff Committee to advise on questions relating to the Council's military requirements for maintaining international peace and security.

Any member may bring a dispute before the Security Council or the General Assembly. Any nonmember may do so if it accepts the charter obligations of pacific settlement.

The Security Council has five permanent members: the United States, the Soviet Union, Britain, France and China. There are also 10 temporary members elected by the General Assembly for two-year terms, with different regions of the world rotating.

Voting on procedural matters requires a nine-vote majority to carry. But on questions of substance, the vote of each of the five permanent members is required. Thus, any one of the five possesses a veto. A vetoed motion can be passed on to the General Assembly by a vote of any seven members.

ECONOMIC AND SOCIAL COUNCIL

This agency is composed of 54 members elected by the General Assembly to 2-year terms. It works closely with the General Assembly as a link with groups formed within the U.N. to help peoples in such fields as education, health and human rights. It insures that there is no overlapping, and sets up commissions to deal with economic conditions and collect facts and figures on conditions over the world. It issues studies and reports and may make recommendations to the Assembly and specialized agencies.

Functional Commissions
Statistical Commission; Population Commission; Commission for Social Development; Commission on Human Rights; Commission on the Status of Women;

Commission on Narcotic Drugs; Commission on Transnational Corporations.

Regional Economic Commissions
Economic Commission for Europe; Economic and Social Commission for Asia and the Pacific; Economic Commission for Latin America; Economic Commission for Africa; Economic Commission for Western Asia.

TRUSTEESHIP COUNCIL

This council supervises territories that had been ruled as colonies by another nation. It appoints a member nation to administer each territory. Such nation is charged with developing the self-government of the territory and preserving and advancing the cultural, political, economic and other forms of welfare of the people.

The Trusteeship Council is currently composed of 5 members: 1 member—the United States—which administers trust territories, and 4 members—China, France, the Soviet Union, and the United Kingdom—which are permanent members of the Security Council but do not administer trust territories.

The following countries ceased to be administering members because of the independence of territories they had administered: Italy and France in 1960, Belgium in 1962, New Zealand and the United Kingdom in 1968 and Australia in 1975. France and the U. K. became nonadministering members.

As of July, 1976, there was only one trust territory: the Trust Territory of the Pacific Islands (administered by the United States).

The following areas ceased to be trust territories in the year shown:

British Togoland (1957): joined the Gold Coast to become the nation of Ghana.

French Cameroöns (1960): became the nation of Cameroon.

Italian Somaliland (1960): joined British Somaliland to become the nation of Somalia.

French Togoland (1960): became the nation of Togo.

Northern British Cameroons (1961): joined Nigeria.

Southern British Cameroons (1961): joined Cameroon.

Tanganyika (1961): became the nation of Tanganyika (later, with Zanzibar: Tanzania).

Western Samoa (1962): became the nation of Western Samoa.

Ruanda-Urundi (1962): became the nations of Rwanda and Burundi.

Nauru (1968): became nation of Nauru.

New Guinea (1975): became nation of Papua New Guinea.

INTL. COURT OF JUSTICE

The International Court of Justice sits at The Hague, the Netherlands. Its 15-judge bench was established to hear disputes among U.N. members, who must agree to accept its verdicts. Its judges, charged with administering justice under international law, deal mainly with territorial and transportation disputes

President: Eduardo Jiménez de Aréchaga, Uruguay (1979)
Vice President: Nagendra Singh, India (1982)
Isaac Forster, Senegal (1982)
André Gros, France (1982)
Hardy C. Dillard, U.S. (1979)
Louis Ignacio-Pinto, Dahomey (1979)
Federico de Castro, Spain (1979)
Platon D. Morozov, USSR (1979)
Sir Humphrey Waldock, U.K. (1982)
José Maria Ruda, Argentina (1982)
Taslim Olawale Elias, Nigeria (1985)
Manfred Lachs, Poland (1985)
Hermann Mösler, W. Germany (1985)
Shigeru Oda, Japan (1985)
Salah El Dine Tarazi, Syria (1985)

Agencies of the United Nations

International Atomic Energy Agency (IAEA)

Established: Statute for IAEA, approved on October 26, 1956 at a conference held at U. N. Headquarters, New York, came into force on July 29, 1957. The Agency, while not a specialized agency, is under the aegis of the U. N.

Purposes: To promote the peaceful uses of atomic energy, and to ensure that assistance provided by it or at its request or under its supervision or control is not used in such a way as to further any military purpose.

Headquarters: Kaerntnerring 11, A-1010, Vienna, Austria.

Specialized Agencies

Food and Agriculture Organization of the United Nations (FAO)

Established: Oct. 16, 1945, when constitution became effective.

Purposes: To raise nutrition levels and living standards; to secure improvements in production and distribution of food and agricultural products.

Headquarters: Via delle Terme di Caracalla 00100, Rome, Italy.

General Agreement on Tariffs and Trade (GATT). *Established:* January 1, 1948.

Purposes: An International Trade Organization (ITO) was planned when the U. N. Agencies were first set up. Although this agency has not materialized, some of its objectives have been embodied in an international commercial treaty, the General Agreement on Tariffs and Trade. It sponsors trade negotiations.

Headquarters: Villa La Fenetre, Palais des Nations, 1211 Geneva 10, Switzerland.

Inter-Governmental Maritime Consultative Organization (IMCO)

Established: January 13, 1959.

Purposes: To give advisory and consultative help to promote international cooperation in maritime navigation, and to encourage the highest standards of safety and navigation. It has started efforts to bring about a uniform system of measuring ship tonnage; systems now vary widely in different parts of the world. Other activities include cooperation with other U. N. agencies in relation to matters affecting the maritime field.

Headquarters: 101-104 Piccadilly, London, WIV-OAE, England.

International Bank for Reconstruction and Development (IBRD) (World Bank)

Established: Dec. 27, 1945, when Articles of Agreement drawn up at Bretton Woods Conference in July, 1944, came into force. Began operations June 25, 1946.

Purposes: To assist in reconstruction and development of economies of members by making loans to governments and by furnishing technical advice.

Headquarters: 1818 H St., NW, Washington, D. C. 20433.

International Civil Aviation Organization (ICAO)

Established: Apr. 4, 1947, after working as a provisional organization since June, 1945.

Purposes: To study problems of international civil aviation and the establishment of international standards and regulations. It promotes safety measures, uniform regulations for operation, and simpler procedures at international borders, and the use of new technical methods and equipment. It has evolved a pattern for meteorological services, traffic control, communications, radio beacons and ranges, search and rescue organization, and other facilities. It has brought about much simplification of customs, immigration, and public health regulations as they apply to international air transport. It drafts international air law conventions, and is concerned with economic aspects of air travel.

Headquarters: Succursale: Place de l'Aviation Internationale, 1000 Sherbrooke St. West, Montreal, Quebec, Canada H3A2R2.

International Development Association (IDA)

Established: Sept. 24, 1960. An affiliate of the World Bank, IDA has the same officers and staff as the Bank.

Purposes: To further economic development of its members by providing finance on terms which bear less heavily on balance of payments of members than those of conventional loans.

Headquarters: 1818 H St., NW, Washington, D. C. 20433.

International Finance Corporation (IFC)

Established: Charter of IFC came into force on July 20, 1956. Although IFC is affiliated with the World Bank, it is a separate legal entity and its funds are entirely separate from those of the Bank. However, membership in the Corporation is open only to Bank members.

Purposes: Its objective is to further economic development by encouraging the growth of productive private enterprise in its member countries, particularly in the less developed areas. It is empowered to invest in productive private enterprises in association with private investors, and without government guarantee of repayment in cases where sufficient private capital is not available on reasonable terms; and to serve as a clearing house to bring together investment opportunities, private capital, both foreign and domestic, and experienced management.

Headquarters: 1818 H St., NW, Washington, D. C. 20433.

International Labour Organisation (ILO)

Established: Apr. 11, 1919, when constitution was adopted as Part XIII of Treaty of Versailles. Became specialized agency of U. N. in 1946.

Purposes: To contribute to establishment of lasting peace by promoting social justice; to improve, through international action, labor conditions and living standards; to promote economic and social stability.

Headquarters: 4, route des Morillons, 1211 Geneva 22, Switzerland.

International Monetary Fund (IMF)

Established: Dec. 27, 1945, when Articles of Agreement drawn up at Bretton Woods Conference in July 1944 came into force. Fund began operations on March 1, 1947.

Purposes: To promote international monetary co-operation and expansion of international trade; to promote exchange stability; to assist in establishment of multilateral system of payments in respect of current transactions between members.

Headquarters: 700 19th St., N.W., Washington, D. C. 20431.

International Telecommunication Union (ITU)

Established: 1865. Became specialized agency of U. N. in 1947.

Purposes: To extend technical assistance to help members keep up with present day telecommunication needs, to standardize communications equipment and procedures, and to lower costs. It also works for orderly sharing of radio frequencies, and makes studies and recommendations to benefit its members.

Headquarters: Place des Nations, 1211 Geneva 20, Switzerland.

United Nations Educational, Scientific and Cultural Organization (UNESCO)

Established: Nov. 4, 1946, when 20th signatory to constitution deposited instrument of acceptance with government of United Kingdom.

Purposes: To promote collaboration among nations through education, science and culture in order to further justice, rule of law and human rights and freedoms without distinction of race, sex, language or religion.

Headquarters: UNESCO House, 7, Place de Fontenoy, 75700 Paris, France.

Universal Postal Union (UPU)

Established: Oct. 9, 1874. Became specialized agency of U. N. in 1947.

Purposes: Reciprocal exchange of correspondence by uniform procedures by all UPU members. Helps governments modernize and speed up mailing procedures.

Headquarters: Weltpoststrasse 4, Berne 1, Switzerland.

World Health Organization (WHO)

Established: Apr. 7, 1948, when 26 members of the U. N. had accepted its constitution, adopted July 22, 1946, by International Health Conference in New York City.

Purposes: To aid attainment by all peoples of highest possible level of health.

Headquarters: 20 Avenue Appia, 1211 Geneva, Switzerland.

World Meteorological Organization (WMO)

Established: Mar. 23, 1950, succeeding the International Meteorological Organization, a non-governmental organization founded in 1878.

Purposes: The international exchange of weather reports and maximum standardization of observations. It also helps underdeveloped countries set up weather services for their own economic needs; seeks to fill gaps in observing stations; promotes meteorological investigations affecting jet aircraft, satellites, energy resources, etc.

Headquarters: 41 Avenue Giuseppe-Motta, Geneva, Switzerland.

World Intellectual Property Organization (WIPO)

Established: April 26, 1970, when its Convention came into force. Originated as International Bureau of Paris Union (1883) and of Berne Union (1886), later succeeded by United International Bureaux for the Protection of Intellectual Property (BIRPI). Became a U.N. specialized agency in December 1974.

Purposes: Promotes legal protection of intellectual property, including artistic and scientific works, artistic performances, sound recordings, broadcasts, inventions, trademarks, industrial designs and commercial names.

Headquarters: 32 Chemin des Colombettes, CH-1211 Geneva 20, Switzerland.

Elected Member States Serving Terms on U. N. Councils

Security Council

Jan. 1946–Dec. 1946: Egypt; México; Netherlands.

Jan. 1946–Dec. 1947: Australia; Brazil; Poland.

Jan. 1947–Dec. 1948: Belgium; Colombia; Syria.

Jan. 1948–Dec. 1949: Argentina; Canada; Ukrainian S.S.R.

Jan. 1949–Dec. 1950: Cuba; Egypt; Norway.

Jan. 1950–Dec. 1951: Ecuador; India; Yugoslavia.

Jan. 1951–Dec. 1952: Brazil; Netherlands; Turkey.

Jan. 1952–Dec. 1953: Chile; Greece; Pakistan.

Jan. 1953–Dec. 1954: Colombia; Denmark; Lebanon.

Jan. 1954–Dec. 1955: Brazil; N. Z.; Turkey.

Jan. 1955–Dec. 1956: Belgium, Iran, Peru.

Jan. 1956–Dec. 1957: Australia; Cuba; Yugoslavia. Yugoslavia resigned at the end of 1956 and was replaced by the Philippines.

Jan. 1957–Dec. 1958: Colombia; Iraq; Sweden.

Jan. 1958–Dec. 1959: Canada; Japan; Panama.

Jan. 1959–Dec. 1960: Argentina; Italy; Tunisia.

Jan. 1960–Dec. 1961: Ceylon; Ecuador; Poland. Poland resigned at the end of 1960 and was replaced by Turkey.

Jan. 1961–Dec. 1962: Chile; Liberia; U.A.R. Ireland replaced Liberia in 1962.

Jan. 1962–Dec. 1963: Ghana; Romania; Venezuela. Philippines replaced Romania in January, 1963.

Jan. 1963–Dec. 1964: Brazil; Morocco; Norway.

Jan. 1964–Dec. 1965: Bolivia; Czechoslovakia; Ivory Coast. Malaysia replaced Czechoslovakia in January, 1965.

Jan. 1965–Dec. 1966: Jordan; Netherlands; Uruguay. Mali replaced Jordan in January, 1966.

Jan. 1966–Dec. 1966: New Zealand; Uganda.

Jan. 1966–Dec. 1967: Argentina; Bulgaria; Japan; Mali; Nigeria.

Jan. 1967–Dec. 1968: Brazil; Canada; Denmark; Ethiopia; India.

Jan. 1968–Dec. 1969: Algeria; Hungary; Pakistan; Paraguay; Senegal.

Jan. 1969–Dec. 1970: Colombia; Finland; Nepal; Spain; Zambia.

Jan. 1970–Dec. 1971: Burundi; Nicaragua; Poland; Sierra Leone; Syria.

Jan. 1971–Dec. 1972: Argentina; Belgium; Italy; Japan; Somalia.

Jan. 1972–Dec. 1973: Guinea; India; Panama; Sudan; Yugoslavia.

Jan. 1973–Dec. 1974: Australia; Austria; Indonesia; Kenya; Peru.

Jan. 1974–Dec. 1975: Byelorussia; Cameroon; Costa Rica; Iraq; Mauritania.

Jan. 1975–Dec. 1976: Guyana, Italy, Japan, Sweden, Tanzania.

Jan. 1976–Dec. 1977: Benin (Dahomey), Libya, Pakistan, Panama, Romania.

Economic and Social Council

Jan. 1946–Dec. 1946: Colombia; Greece; Lebanon; Ukrainian S.S.R.; U. S.; Yugoslavia.

Jan. 1946–Dec. 1947: Cuba; Czechoslovakia; India; Norway; United Kingdom; U.S.S.R.

Jan. 1946–Dec. 1948: Belgium (resigned in 1947 and was replaced by Netherlands); Canada; Chile; China; France; Peru.

Jan. 1947–Dec. 1949: Byelorussian S.S.R.; Lebanon; New Zealand; Turkey; U. S.; Venezuela.

Jan. 1948–Dec. 1950: Australia; Brazil; Denmark; Poland; United Kingdom; U.S.S.R.

Jan. 1949–Dec. 1951: Belgium; Chile; China; France; India; Peru.

Jan. 1950–Dec. 1952: Canada; Czechoslovakia; Iran; Mexico; Pakistan; U. S.

Jan. 1951–Dec. 1953: Philippines; Poland; Sweden; U. K.; Uruguay; U.S.S.R.

Jan. 1952–Dec. 1954: Argentina; Belgium; China; Cuba; Egypt; France.

Jan. 1953–Dec. 1955: Australia; India; Turkey; U. S.; Venezuela; Yugoslavia.

Jan. 1954–Dec. 1956: Czechoslovakia; Ecuador; Norway; Pakistan; U. K.; U.S.S.R.

Jan. 1955–Dec. 1957: Argentina; China; Dominican Rep.; Egypt; France; Netherlands.

Jan. 1956–Dec. 1958: Brazil; Canada; Greece; Indonesia; U. S.; Yugoslavia.

Jan. 1957–Dec. 1959: Finland; Mexico; Pakistan; Poland; U.S.S.R.; United Kingdom.

Jan. 1958–Dec. 1960: Chile; China; Costa Rica; France; Netherlands; Sudan.

Jan. 1959–Dec. 1961: Afghanistan; Bulgaria; New Zealand; Spain; U. S.; Venezuela.

Jan. 1960–Dec. 1962: Brazil; Denmark; Japan; Poland; U.S.S.R.; United Kingdom.

Jan. 1961–Dec. 1963: El Salvador; Ethiopia; France; Jordan; Uruguay.

Apr. 1961–Dec. 1963: Italy.

Jan. 1962–Dec. 1964: Australia; Colombia; India; Senegal; United States; Yugoslavia.

Jan. 1963–Dec. 1965: Argentina; Austria; Czechoslovakia; Japan; U.S.S.R.; U. K.

Jan. 1964–Dec. 1966: Algeria; Chile; Ecuador; France; Iraq; Luxembourg.

Jan. 1965–Dec. 1967: Canada; Gabon; Pakistan; Peru; Romania; U. S.

Jan. 1966–Dec. 1966: Greece; Sierra Leone; Tanzania.

Jan. 1966–Dec. 1967: Cameroon; Dahomey; India.

Jan. 1966–Dec. 1968: Czechoslovakia; Iran; Morocco; Panama; Philippines; Sweden; U.S.S.R.; United Kingdom; Venezuela.

Jan. 1967–Dec. 1969: Belgium; France; Guatemala; Kuwait; Libya; Mexico; Sierra Leone; Tanzania; Turkey.

Jan. 1968–Dec. 1970: Argentina; Bulgaria; Chad; Congo (Brazzaville); India; Ireland; Japan; U. S.; Upper Volta.

Jan. 1969–Dec. 1971: Indonesia; Jamaica; Norway; Pakistan; Sudan; U.S.S.R.; United Kingdom; Uruguay; Yugoslavia.

Jan. 1970–Dec. 1972: Brazil; Ceylon; France; Ghana; Greece; Italy; Kenya; Peru; Tunisia.

Jan. 1971–Dec. 1973: Haiti; Hungary; Lebanon; Madagascar, Malaysia; New Zealand; Niger; U. S.; Zaire.

Jan. 1972–Dec. 1974: Bolivia; Burundi; Chile[1] China; Finland; Japan; Poland; U.S.S.R., United Kingdom.[1]

Jan. 1973–Dec. 1975: Algeria; Brazil[1]; Fiji;

France[1]; German Federal Republic; Guatemala; Guinea; Indonesia; Mali; Mongolia; Netherlands; Senegal; Spain; Trinidad and Tobago; Turkey; Uganda; Venezuela; Yugoslavia.

Jan. 1974–Dec. 1976: Australia, Belgium, Colombia, Congo, Egypt, German Democratic Republic, Iran, Italy, Ivory Coast, Jamaica, Jordan, Liberia, Mexico, Romania, Thailand, U.S., Democratic Yemen, Zambia.

Jan. 1975–Dec. 1977: Argentina; Bulgaria;

Canada; China[1]; Czechoslovakia; Denmark; Ecuador; Ethiopia; Gabon; Japan[1]; Kenya; Norway; Pakistan; Peru; U.S.S.R.[1]; United Kingdom[1]; Yemen; Zaire.

Jan. 1976:–Dec. 1978: Afghanistan; Algeria[1]; Argentina; Austria; Bangladesh; Bolivia; Brazil[1]; Cuba; France[1]; German Federal Republic[1]; Greece; Malaysia; Nigeria; Portugal; Togo; Tunisia; Uganda[1]; Venezuela[1]; Yugoslavia.[1]

[1] Re-elected.

Principal Officers of the Secretariat as of July, 1976

Secretary-General
Kurt Waldheim (Austria).

Under-Secretaries-General[1]

William B. Buffum (U.S.): Under-Secretary-General for Political and General Assembly Affairs.

Gamani Corea (Sri Lanka): Secretary-General, Conference on Trade and Development (Geneva, Switzerland).

George F. Davidson (Canada): Under-Secretary-General for Administration and Management.

Issoufou S. Djermakoye (Niger): Under-Secretary-General, Commissioner for Technical Cooperation.

Roberto E. Guyer (Argentina): Under-Secretary-General for Special Political Affairs.

Sir Robert Jackson (Australia): Under-Secretary-General, Coordinator of U.N. Assistance to Indochina, Zambia and Cape Verde.

Abd-El Rahman Khane (Algeria): Executive Director, Industrial Development Organization (Vienna, Austria).

Bohdan Lewandowski (Poland): Under-Secretary-General for Conference Services and Special Assignments.

C. V. Narasimhan (India): Under-Secretary-General for Inter-Agency Affairs and Coordination.

Enrique Peñalosa (Colombia): Secretary-General of Habitat, U.N. Conference on Human Settlements.

Arkady Nikolaevich Shevchenko (U.S.S.R.): Under-Secretary-General for Political and Security Council Affairs.

Eric Suy (Belgium): Under-Secretary-General for Legal Affairs, the Legal Counsel.

Tang Ming-chao (China): Under-Secretary-General for Political Affairs and Decolonization.

Brian E. Urquhart (U.K.): Under-Secretary-General for Special Political Affairs.

Gabriel Van Laethem (France): Under-Secretary-General for Economic and Social Affairs.

Vittorio Winspeare Guicciardi (Italy): Director-General, U.N. Office at Geneva, Switzerland.

Bernardo Zuleta (Colombia): Under-Secretary-General, Special Representative of the Secretary-General to third U.N. Conference on Law of the Sea.

[1] Including officials of equivalent rank.

Other Senior Officials

Adebayo Adedeji (Nigeria): Executive Secretary, Economic Commission for Africa (Addis Ababa, Ethiopia).

Prince Sadruddin Aga Khan (Iran): U.N. High Commissioner for Refugees (Geneva, Switzerland).

Rafeeuddin Ahmed (Pakistan): Executive Assistant to the Secretary-General.

Genichi Akatani (Japan): Assistant Secretary-General for Public Information.

Mohamed Said Al-Attar (Yemen): Executive Secretary, Economic Commission for Western Asia (Beirut, Lebanon).

Stanislas Aquarone (Australia): Registrar, International Court of Justice (The Hague).

Faruk N. Berkol (Turkey): U.N. Disaster Relief Coordinator (Geneva, Switzerland).

Helmut Debatin (West Germany): Controller; Assistant Secretary-General for Financial Services.

Jacobus De Beus (Netherlands): Executive Director, U.N. Fund for Drug Abuse Control (Geneva, Switzerland).

Abdulrahim Abby Farah (Somalia): Assistant Secretary-General for Special Political Questions.

Mohamed Habib Gherab (Tunisia): Assistant Secretary-General for Personnel Services.

John A. Hannah (U.S.): Executive Director, World Food Council (Rome, Italy).

James M. Hester (U.S.): Rector, U.N. University (Tokyo, Japan).

Enrique V. Iglesias (Uruguay): Executive Secretary, Economic Commission for Latin America (Santiago, Chile).

Henry R. Labouisse (U.S.): Executive Director, U.N. Children's Fund.

Sean MacBride (Ireland): U.N. Commissioner for Namibia.

J. B. P. Maramis (Indonesia): Executive Secretary, Economic and Social Commission for Asia and the Pacific (Bangkok, Thailand).

Bradford Morse (U.S.): Administrator, U.N. Developmental Program.

Davidson Nicol (Sierra Leone): Executive Director, U.N. Institute for Training and Research.

Sir John Rennie (U.K.): Commissioner-General, U.N. Relief and Works Agency for Palestine Refugees in Near East (Beirut, Lebanon).

Robert J. Ryan (U.S.): Assistant Secretary-General for General Services.

Klaus A. Sahlgren (Finland): Executive Director, U.N. Center on Transnational Corporations.

Rafael Salas (Philippines): Executive Director, U.N. Fund for Population Activities.

Mrs. Helvi Sipilä (Finland): Assistant Secretary-General for Social Development and Humanitarian Affairs.

Janez I. Stanovnik (Yugoslavia): Executive Secretary, Economic Commission for Europe (Geneva, Switzerland).

Mostafa Kamal Tolba (Egypt): Executive Director, U.N. Environment Program (Nairobi, Kenya).

The 145 Members of the United Nations

Country	Joined U.N.[1]	Country	Joined U.N.[1]	Country	Joined U.N.[1]
Afghanistan	1946	Ghana	1957	Oman	1971
Albania	1955	Greece	1945	Pakistan	1947
Algeria	1962	Grenada	1974	Panama	1945
Argentina	1945	Guatemala	1945	Papua New Guinea	1975
Australia	1945	Guinea	1958	Paraguay	1945
Austria	1955	Guinea-Bissau	1974	Peru	1945
Bahamas	1973	Guyana	1966	Philippines	1945
Bahrain	1971	Haiti	1945	Poland	1945
Bangladesh	1974	Honduras	1945	Portugal	1955
Barbados	1966	Hungary	1955	Qatar	1971
Belgium	1945	Iceland	1946	Romania	1955
Benin (Dahomey)	1960	India	1945	Rwanda	1962
Bhutan	1971	Indonesia	1950	São Tomé and Principe	1975
Bolivia	1945	Iran	1945	Saudi Arabia	1945
Botswana	1966	Iraq	1945	Senegal	1960
Brazil	1945	Ireland	1955	Seychelles	1976
Bulgaria	1955	Israel	1949	Sierra Leone	1961
Burma	1948	Italy	1955	Singapore	1965
Burundi	1962	Ivory Coast	1960	Somalia	1960
Byelorussian S.S.R.	1945	Jamaica	1962	South Africa	1945
Cambodia	1955	Japan	1956	Spain	1955
Cameroon, United Rep. of	1960	Jordan	1955	Sri Lanka (Ceylon)	1955
Canada	1945	Kenya	1963	Sudan	1956
Cape Verde	1975	Kuwait	1963	Surinam	1975
Central African Republic	1960	Laos	1955	Swaziland	1968
Chad	1960	Lebanon	1945	Sweden	1946
Chile	1945	Lesotho	1966	Syrian Arab Republic	1945
China, People's Rep. of[2]	1945	Liberia	1945	Tanzania, United Rep. of	1961
Colombia	1945	Libyan Arab Republic	1955	Thailand	1946
Comoro Islands	1975	Luxembourg	1945	Togo	1960
Congo	1960	Madagascar	1960	Trinidad and Tobago	1962
Costa Rica	1945	Malawi	1964	Tunisia	1956
Cuba	1945	Malaysia	1957	Turkey	1945
Cyprus	1960	Maldives	1965	Uganda	1962
Czechoslovakia	1945	Mali	1960	Ukrainian S.S.R.	1945
Denmark	1945	Malta	1964	U.S.S.R.	1945
Dominican Republic	1945	Mauritania	1961	United Arab Emirates	1971
Ecuador	1945	Mauritius	1968	United Kingdom	1945
Egypt	1945	Mexico	1945	United States	1945
El Salvador	1945	Mongolia	1961	Upper Volta	1960
Equatorial Guinea	1968	Morocco	1956	Uruguay	1945
Ethiopia	1945	Mozambique	1975	Venezuela	1945
Fiji	1970	Nepal	1955	Yemen	1947
Finland	1955	Netherlands	1945	Yemen, Democratic	1967
France	1945	New Zealand	1945	Yugoslavia	1945
Gabon	1960	Nicaragua	1945	Zaire	1960
Gambia	1965	Niger	1960	Zambia	1964
German Democratic Rep.	1973	Nigeria	1960		
Germany, Federal Rep. of	1973	Norway	1945		

[1] The U.N. officially came into existence on Oct. 24, 1945. [2] On Oct. 25, 1971, the U.N. voted membership to the People's Republic of China, which replaced Nationalist China (Taiwan) in the world body.

Member Countries' Assessments to U.N. Budget, 1976

Country	Total	Country	Total	Country	Total
Afghanistan	$ 73,801	Germany, Federal Rep. of	$26,199,216	Niger	$ 73,801
Albania	73,801	Ghana	147,601	Nigeria	369,003
Algeria	295,202	Greece	1,180,809	Norway	1,586,713
Argentina	3,062,725	Grenada	73,801[1]	Oman	73,801
Australia	5,313,643	Guatemala	110,700	Pakistan	516,604
Austria	2,066,417	Guinea	73,801	Panama	73,801
Bahamas	73,801	Guinea-Bissau	73,801[1]	Paraguay	73,801
Bahrain	73,801	Guyana	73,801	Peru	258,302
Bangladesh	295,202[1]	Haiti	73,801	Philippines	664,205
Barbados	73,801	Honduras	73,801	Poland	4,649,438
Belgium	3,874,532	Hungary	1,217,710	Portugal	553,504
Benin (Dahomey)	73,801[1]	Iceland	73,801	Qatar	73,801
Bhutan	73,801	India	4,428,036	Romania	1,107,009
Bolivia	73,801	Indonesia	701,105	Rwanda	73,801
Botswana	73,801	Iran	738,006	Saudi Arabia	221,401
Brazil	2,841,323	Iraq	184,501	Senegal	73,801
Bulgaria	516,604	Ireland	553,504	Sierra Leone	73,801
Burma	110,700	Israel	774,906	Singapore	147,601
Burundi	73,801	Italy	13,284,109	Somalia	73,801
Byelorussian, S.S.R.	1,697,414	Ivory Coast	73,801	South Africa	1,845,015
Cambodia	73,801[1]	Jamaica	73,801	Spain	3,653,130
Cameroon, United Rep. of	73,801	Japan	23,383,717	Sri Lanka	110,700
Canada	11,734,296	Jordan	73,801	Sudan	73,801
Central African Rep.	73,801	Kenya	73,801	Swaziland	73,801
Chad	73,801	Kuwait	332,102	Sweden	4,797,039
Chile	516,604	Laos	73,801	Syrian Arab Republic	73,801
China, People's Rep. of	20,295,167	Lebanon	110,700	Tanzania, United Rep. of	73,801
Colombia	590,405	Lesotho	73,801	Thailand	405,903
Congo	73,801	Liberia	73,801	Togo	73,801
Costa Rica	73,801	Libyan Arab Republic	405,903	Trinidad and Tobago	73,801
Cuba	405,903	Luxembourg	147,601	Tunisia	73,801
Cyprus	73,801	Madagascar	73,801	Turkey	1,070,108
Czechoslovakia	3,284,127	Malawi	73,801	Uganda	73,801
Denmark	2,324,719	Malaysia	258,302	Ukrainian S.S.R.	6,309,952
Dominican Rep.	73,801	Maldives	73,801	U.S.S.R.	47,859,694
Ecuador	73,801	Mali	73,801	United Arab Emirates	73,801
Egypt	442,803	Malta	73,801	United Kingdom	19,594,061
El Salvador	73,801	Mauritania	73,801	United States	92,250,761
Equatorial Guinea	73,801	Mauritius	73,801	Upper Volta	73,801
Ethiopia	73,801	Mexico	3,173,426	Uruguay	221,401
Fiji	73,801	Mongolia	73,801	Venezuela	1,180,809
Finland	1,549,812	Morocco	221,401	Yemen(People's Dem.Rep. of)	73,801[1]
France	21,623,578	Nepal	73,801	Yemen (Republic)	73,801
Gabon	73,801	Netherlands	4,575,637	Yugoslavia	1,254,610
Gambia	73,801	New Zealand	1,033,208	Zaire	73,801
German Democratic Rep.	4,501,827	Nicaragua	73,801	Zambia	73,801

[1] Assessments have not yet been fixed for the six countries admitted to membership in 1975.

Council Members in 1976

Security Council: Benin (Dahomey),[3] China,[1] France,[1] Guyana,[2] Italy,[2] Japan,[2] Libya,[3] Pakistan,[3] Panama,[3] Romania,[3] Sweden,[2] U.S.S.R.,[1] United Kingdom,[1] United Republic of Tanzania,[2] United States.[1]

Economic and Social Council: Afghanistan,[4] Algeria,[4] Argentina,[3] Australia,[2] Austria,[4] Bangladesh,[4] Belgium,[2] Bolivia,[4] Brazil,[4] Bulgaria,[3] Canada,[3] China,[3] Colombia,[2] Cuba,[4] Czechoslovakia,[3] Democratic Yemen,[2] Denmark,[3] Ecuador,[3] Egypt,[2] Ethiopia,[3] France,[4] Gabon,[3] German Democratic Republic,[2] Federal Republic of Germany,[4] Greece,[4] Iran,[2] Italy,[2] Ivory Coast,[2] Jamaica,[2] Japan,[3] Jordan,[2] Kenya,[3] Liberia,[2] Malaysia,[4] Mexico,[2] Nigeria,[4] Norway,[3] Pakistan,[3] Peru,[3] Portugal,[4] Romania,[2] Thailand,[2] Togo,[4] Tunisia,[4] Uganda,[4] United Kingdom,[3] United States,[2] U.S.S.R.,[3] Venezuela,[4] Yemen,[3] Yugoslavia,[4] Zaire[3] and Zambia.[2]

Trusteeship Council: China, France, U.S.S.R., United Kingdom, United States.

[1] Permanent members. [2] Term expires Dec. 31, 1976. [3] Term expires Dec. 31, 1977. [4] Term expires Dec. 31, 1978.

United Nations Costs

In December 1975, the General Assembly adopted a budget of $745,813,800 for the two-year period 1976-77.

Delegation Heads to the United Nations[1]

Afghanistan: (Vacant).
Albania: (Vacant).
Algeria: Abdellatif Rahal.
Argentina: Dr. Carlos Ortiz de Rozas.
Australia: Ralph L. Harry.
Austria: Peter Jankowitsch.
Bahamas: Livingston Basil Johnson.
Bahrain: Dr. Salman Mohamed Al Saffar.
Bangladesh: Khwaja Mohammed Kaiser.
Barbados: J. Cameron Tudor.
Belgium: Edouard Longerstaey.
Benin: Thomas S. Boya.
Bhutan: Dago Tshering.
Bolivia: Dr. Mario R. Gutierrez.
Botswana: Thebe David Mogami.
Brazil: Sérgio Corrêa da Costa.
Bulgaria: Alexander Yankov.
Burma: U Myint Maung.
Burundi: Patrice A. H. Mikanagu.
Byelorussian S.S.R.: Guerodot Gavrilovich Tchernouchtchenko.
Cameroon: Ferdinand Léopold Oyono.
Canada: (Vacant).
Central African Republic: Jean-Arthur Bandio.
Chad: Beadengar Dessande.
Chile: Vice Adm. Ismael Huerta.
China: Huang Hua.
Colombia: Dr. Germán Zea.
Congo: Nicolas Mondjo.
Costa Rica: Fernando Salazar.
Cuba: Dr. Ricardo Alarcon de Quesada.
Cyprus: Zenon Rossides.
Czechoslovakia: Dr. Ladislav Šmíd.
Denmark: Henning Hjorth-Nielsen.
Dominican Republic: Dr. Alfonso Moreno-Martinez.
Ecuador: (Vacant).
Egypt: Dr. Ahmed Esmat Abdel Meguid.
El Salvador: Dr. Reynaldo Galindo Pohl.
Equatorial Guinea: Benjamin Ecua Miko.
Ethiopia: Mohamed Hamid Ibrahim.
Fiji: Semesa K. Sikivou.
Finland: Aarno Karhilo.
France: Louis de Guiringaud.
Gabon: Jean-Baptiste Essonghe.
German Democratic Republic: Peter Florin.
Germany, Federal Republic of: Baron Rüdiger von Wechmar.

Ghana: Frank Edmund Boaten.
Greece: George Papoulias.
Grenada: Mrs. Marie-Jo McIntyre.
Guatemala: Julio Asensio-Wunderlich.
Guinea: (Vacant).
Guinea-Bissau: Gil Fernandes.
Guyana: Rashleigh Esmond Jackson.
Haiti: Raoul Siclait.
Honduras: Roberto Martinez Ordoñez.
Hungary: Imre Hollai.
Iceland: Ingvi S. Ingvarsson.
India: Rikhi Jaipal.
Indonesia: Chaidir Anwar Sani.
Iran: Fereydoun Hoveyda.
Iraq: Dr. Abdul Karim Al-Shaikhly.
Ireland: Dr. Eamonn Kennedy.
Israel: Chaim Herzog.
Italy: Piero Vinci.
Ivory Coast: Siméon Ake.
Jamaica: Donald O. Mills.
Japan: Isao Abe.
Jordan: Sherif Abdul Hamid Sharaf.
Kenya: Charles Gatere Maina.
Kuwait: Abdalla Yaccoub Bishara.
Laos: (Vacant).
Lebanon: Edouard Ghorra.
Lesotho: David Ketso 'Noto.
Liberia: Mrs. Angie Brooks-Randolph.
Libyan Arab Republic: Mansur Rashid Kikhia.
Luxembourg: Jean Rettel.
Madagascar: Blaise Rabetafika.
Malawi: T.J.X. Muwamba.
Malaysia: Tan Sri Zaiton Ibrahim.
Mali: Mamadou Boubacar Kante.
Malta: Joseph Attard Kingswell.
Mauritania: Moulaye el Hassen.
Mauritius: Radha Krishna Ramphul.
Mexico: Roberto de Rosenzweig-Díaz.
Mongolia: Tsevegzhavyn Puntsagnorov.
Morocco: (Vacant).
Mozambique: José Carlos Lobo.
Nepal: Shailendra Kumar Upadhyay.
Netherlands: Dr. Johan Kaufmann.
New Zealand: Malcolm J. C. Templeton.
Nicaragua: Dr. Guillermo Sevilla-Sacasa.
Niger: André Joseph Wright.
Nigeria: Leslie O. Harriman.
Norway: Ole Ålgård.

Oman: Dr. Kamal M. Hagras.
Pakistan: Iqbal A. Akhund.
Panama: Dr. Jorge Enrique Illueca.
Papua and New Guinea: Paulias Nguna Matane.
Paraguay: Dr. Francisco M. Barreiro.
Peru: Carlos T. Alzamora.
Philippines: Narciso G. Reyes.
Poland: Henryk Jaroszek.
Portugal: José Manuel Galvão Teles.
Qatar: Jasim Yousif Jamal.
Romania: Ion Datcu.
Rwanda: Ignace Karuhije.
Saudi Arabia: (Vacant).
Senegal: Médoune Fall.
Sierra Leone: Dr. Edward Wilmot Blyden III.
Singapore: T. T. B. Koh.
Somalia: Abdirizak Haji Hussen.
South Africa: Roelof F. Botha.
Spain: Don Jaime de Piniés.
Sri Lanka: Hamilton Shirley Amerasinghe.
Sudan: Mustafa Medani.
Surinam: Henricus A.F. Heidweiller.
Swaziland: N. M. Malinga.
Sweden: Olof Rydbeck.
Syrian Arab Republic: Mowaffak Allaf.
Tanzania: Salim Ahmed Salim.
Thailand: Dr. Pracha Guna-Kasem.
Togo: (Vacant).
Trinidad and Tobago: Frank Owen Abdulah.
Tunisia: Rachid Driss.
Turkey: Ilter Türkmen.
Uganda: Khalid Younis Kinene.
Ukrainian S.S.R.: Vladimir Nikiphorovich Martynenko.
U.S.S.R.: Yakov A. Malik.
United Arab Emirates: Dr. Ali Humaidan.
United Kingdom: Ivor Richard.
United States: William W. Scranton.
Upper Volta: Télesphore Yaguibou.
Uruguay: Dr. Carlos Giambruno.
Venezuela: Dr. Simón A. Consalvi.
Yemen: Mohamed A. Sallam.
Yemen, Democratic: Abdalla Saleh Ashtal.
Yugoslavia: Jakša Petrić.
Zaire: Umba di Lutete.
Zambia: Dunstan Weston Kamana.

[1] Permanent representatives as of September 1976. Not all nations maintain permanent missions at the United Nations.

United States Permanent Mission to U. N.

William W. Scranton: Permanent Representative to U. N.

W. Tapley Bennett: Deputy Permanent Representative to U. N.

Albert W. Sherer, Jr.: Deputy Permanent Representative on Security Council.

Nancy V. Rawls: Alternate Representative for Special Political Affairs.

Jacob M. Myerson: Representative on Economic and Social Council.

Robert W. Kitchen, Jr.: Minister Counselor and Deputy Permanent Representative on Economic and Security Council.

Leonard Garment: Special Advisor to Delegation and Representative on Human Rights Commission of Economic and Social Council.

Mrs. Jean Picker: Representative on Social Development Commission of Economic and Social Council.

John N. Faigle: Secretary of Mission.

U.N. CHARTER: Preamble, Purposes and Principles, Membership

The Charter of the United Nations was adopted at the San Francisco Conference of 1945. The complete text may be found in previous editions of the *Information Please Almanac* or may be obtained by writing directly to the United Nations.

WE the peoples of the United Nations determined to save succeeding generations from the scourge of war, which twice in our lifetime has brought untold sorrow to mankind, and

To reaffirm faith in fundamental human rights, in the dignity and worth of the human person, in the equal rights of men and women and of nations large and small, and

To establish conditions under which justice and respect for the obligations arising from treaties and other sources of international law can be maintained, and

To promote social progress and better standards of life in larger freedom, and for these ends

To practice tolerance and live together in peace with one another as good neighbors, and

To unite our strength to maintain international peace and security, and

To insure, by the acceptance of principles and the institution of methods, that armed force shall not be used, save in the common interest, and

To employ international machinery for the promotion of the economic and social advancement of all peoples, have resolved to combine our efforts to accomplish these aims.

Accordingly, our respective Governments, through representatives assembled in the city of San Francisco, who have exhibited their full powers found to be in good and due form, have agreed to the present Charter of the United Nations and do hereby establish an international organization to be known as the United Nations.

CHAPTER I

PURPOSES AND PRINCIPLES

Article 1

The purposes of the United Nations are:

1. To maintain international peace and security, and to that end: to take effective collective measures for the prevention and removal of threats to the peace, and for the suppression of acts of aggression or other breaches of the peace, and to bring about by peaceful means, and in conformity with the principles of justice and international law, adjustment or settlement of international disputes or situations which might lead to a breach of the peace;

2. To develop friendly relations among nations based on respect for the principle of equal rights and self-determination of peoples, and to take other appropriate measures to strengthen universal peace;

3. To achieve international cooperation in solving international problems of an economic, social, cultural, or humanitarian character, and in promoting and encouraging respect for human rights and for fundamental freedoms for all without distinction as to race, sex, language, or religion; and

4. To be a center for harmonizing the actions of nations in the attainment of these common ends.

Article 2

The Organization and its Members, in pursuit of the Purposes stated in Article 1, shall act in accordance with the following Principles:

1. The Organization is based on the principle of the sovereign equality of all its Members.

2. All Members, in order to ensure to all of them the rights and benefits resulting from membership, shall fulfill in good faith the obligations assumed by them in accordance with the present Charter.

3. All Members shall settle their international disputes by peaceful means in such a manner that international peace and security, and justice, are not endangered.

4. All Members shall refrain in their international relations from the threat or use of force against the territorial integrity or political independence of any state, or in any other manner inconsistent with the Purposes of the United Nations.

5. All Members shall give the United Nations every assistance in any action it takes in accordance with the present Charter, and shall refrain from giving assistance to any state against which the United Nations is taking preventive or enforcement action.

6. The Organization shall ensure that states which are not Members of the United Nations act in accordance with these Principles so far as may be necessary for the maintenance of international peace and security.

7. Nothing contained in the present Charter shall authorize the United Nations to intervene in matters which are essentially within the domestic jurisdiction of any state or shall require the Members to submit such matters to settlement under the present Charter; but this principle shall not prejudice the application of enforcement measures under Chapter VII.

CHAPTER II

MEMBERSHIP

Article 3

The original Members of the United Nations shall be the states which, having participated in the United Nations Conference on International Organization at San Francisco, or having previously signed the Declaration by United Nations of January 1, 1942, sign the present Charter and ratify it in accordance with Article 110.

Article 4

1. Membership in the United Nations is open to all other peace-loving states which accept the obligations contained in the present Charter and, in the judgment of the Organization, are able and willing to carry out these obligations.

2. The admission of any such state to membership in the United Nations will be effected by a decision of the General Assembly upon the recommendation of the Security Council.

Article 5

A Member of the United Nations against which preventive or enforcement action has been taken by the Security Council may be suspended from the exercise of the rights and privileges of membership by the General Assembly upon the recommendation of the Security Council. The exercise of these rights and privileges may be restored by the Security Council.

Article 6

A Member of the United Nations which has persistently violated the Principles contained in the present Charter may be expelled from the Organization by the General Assembly upon the recommendation of the Security Council.

United Nations Headquarters

The first regular session of the General Assembly held at Central Hall, Westminster, London, voted that interim headquarters of the Organization should be located in New York. From London the U. N. moved to Hunter College in the Bronx. In August, 1946, an interim headquarters was set up at Lake Success on Long Island, in a part of the Sperry Gyroscope Co.'s plant. The New York City building at Flushing Meadows, site of the 1939 World's Fair, was converted for the use of the General Assembly. The search for a permanent home ended in December, 1946, when the General Assembly accepted an offer from John D. Rockefeller, Jr., of $8,500,000 * for the purchase of the present

* This amount paid for two-thirds of the land; New York City gave one-third.

Headquarters site—an 18-acre tract in Manhattan alongside the East River. The U. S. Government loaned the U. N. $65,-000,000 interest free, which is being repaid in annual installments.

Architectural plans drawn up by an international Board of Design were approved by the Assembly, and construction began in September, 1948. By mid-1950, the 39-story Secretariat Building was ready for occupancy, and in the spring of 1951 "United Nations, New York" became the Organization's permanent address.

Tours of the building are available to the public seven days a week, from 9:15 A.M. to 4:45 P.M., except Christmas Day and New Year's Day. The price is $2 for adults; $1.50 for students on presentation of ID card; and $1 for children over 5.

COMMONLY USED ABBREVIATIONS AND ACRONYMS

Source: United States Government Organization Manual.

AEC—Atomic Energy Commission.
AID—Agency for International Development.
CAB—Civil Aeronautics Board.
CAP—Civil Air Patrol.
CIA—Central Intelligence Agency.
DEA—Drug Enforcement Administration.
DNA—Defense Nuclear Agency.
DOD—Department of Defense.
EEC—European Economic Community.
EEO—Equal Employment Opportunity.
FAA—Federal Aviation Administration.
FAS—Foreign Agricultural Service.
FBI—Federal Bureau of Investigation.
FCA—Farm Credit Administration.
FCC—Federal Communications Commission.
FDA—Food and Drug Administration.
FDIC—Federal Deposit Insurance Corporation.
FEO—Federal Energy Office.
FNA—Food and Nutrition Service.
FPC—Federal Power Commission.
FRS—Federal Reserve System.
FTC—Federal Trade Commission.
GNP—Gross National Product.

HEW—Department of Health, Education, and Welfare.
HUD—Department of Housing and Urban Development.
INTERPOL—International Criminal Police Organization.
IRS—Internal Revenue Service.
NASA—National Aeronautics and Space Adm.
NATO—North Atlantic Treaty Organization.
NRC—National Research Council.
NSA—National Security Agency.
NSC—National Security Council.
OAS—Organization of American States.
OJT—On-the-Job Training.
OMB—Office of Management and Budget.
PHS—Public Health Service.
SBA—Small Business Administration.
SEC—Securities and Exchange Commission.
SSA—Social Security Administration.
SSS—Selective Service System.
TVA—Tennessee Valley Authority.
USDA—United States Department of Agriculture.
USES—United States Employment Service.

Diplomatic Personnel To and From the U. S.

Source: U. S. Department of State.

Country	U.S. Representative to[1]	Rank	Representative from[1]	Rank
Afghanistan	Theodore L. Eliot, Jr.	Amb.	Abdullah Malikyar	Amb.
Algeria	Richard B. Parker	Amb.	Abdelkader Maadini	Cd'A.
Argentina	Robert C. Hill	Amb.	Rafael M. Vazquez	Amb.
Australia	James W. Hargrove	Amb.	Nicholas F. Parkinson	Amb.
Austria	Wiley T. Buchanan, Jr.	Amb.	Arno Halusa	Amb.
Bahamas	Seymous Weiss	Amb.	Livingston B. Johnson	Amb.
Bahrain	Joseph W. Twinam	Amb.		
Bangladesh	Davis E. Boster	Amb.	Mustafizur R. Siddiqi	Amb.
Barbados	Theodore R. Britton	Amb.	Maurice A. King	Amb.
Belgium	Leonard K. Firestone	Amb.	Willy Van Cauwenberg	Amb.
Benin	(Vacant)		Thomas S. Boya	Amb.
Bolivia	William P. Stedman, Jr.	Amb.	Alberto Crespo	Amb.
Botswana	David B. Bolen	Amb.	Amos M. Dambe	Amb.
Brazil	John H. Crimmins	Amb.	João Baptista Pinheiro	Amb.
Bulgaria	Martin F. Herz	Amb.	Lubomir D. Popov	Amb.
Burma	David L. Osborn	Amb.	U Tin Lat	Amb.
Burundi	David E. Mark	Amb.	Clement Sambira	Cd'A.
Cameroon	Herbert Spiro	Amb.	Eric Dikoko Quan	Cd'A.
Canada	Thomas O. Enders	Amb.	Jack H. Warren	Amb.
Central Afr. Rep.	Anthony C.E. Quainton	Amb.	Christophe Maidou	Amb.
Chad	(Vacant)		Bawoyeu Alingue	Amb.
Chile	David H. Popper	Amb.	Manuel Trucco	Amb.
China (Taiwan)	Leonard Unger	Amb.	James C. H. Shen	Amb.
Colombia	Philip V. Sanchez	Amb.	Julio C. Turbay-Ayala	Amb.
Costa Rica	Terance A. Todman	Amb.	Rodolfo Silva	Amb.
Cyprus	William R. Crawford, Jr.	Amb.	Nicos G. Dimitriou	Amb.
Czechoslovakia	Thomas R. Byrne	Amb.	Dr. Jaromir Johanes	Amb.
Denmark	John Gunther Dean	Amb.	Otto R. Borch	Amb.
Dominican Republic	Robert A. Hurwitch	Amb.	Dr. Horacio Vicioso-Soto	Amb.
Ecuador	Richard J. Bloomfield	Amb.	José C. Cardenas	Amb.
Egypt, Arab Rep. of	Hermann F. Eilts, Jr.	Amb.	Ashraf A. Ghorbal	Amb.
El Salvador	Igmacio E. Lozano, Jr.	Amb.	Dr. Francisco Bertrand Galindo	Amb.
Equatorial Guinea	Herbert Spiro[2]	Amb.	(No Embassy)	
Ethiopia	Arthur W. Hummel	Amb.	Ghebeyehou Mekbib	Cd'A.
Fiji	Armistead I. Selden, Jr.[6]	Amb.	S. K. Sikivou	Amb.
Finland	Mark Evans Austad	Amb.	Leo Tuominen	Amb.
France	Kenneth Rush	Amb.	Jacques Kosciusko-Morizet	Amb.
Gabon	Andrew L. Steigman	Amb.	Vincent Movoungou	Amb.
Gambia	O. Rudolph Aggrey[3]	Amb.	(No Embassy)	
Germany (East)	John Sherman Cooper	Amb.	Dr. Rolf Sieber	Amb.
Germany (West)	Martin J. Hillenbrand	Amb.	Berndt Von Staden	Amb.
Ghana	(Vacant)	Amb.	Samuel E. Quarm	Amb.
Great Britain	Anne L. Armstrong	Amb.	Sir Peter Ramsbotham	Amb.
Greece	Jack B. Kubisch	Amb.	Menelas Alexandrakis	Amb.
Grenada, State of	Theodore R. Britton, Jr.	Amb.	Marie J. McIntyre	Amb.
Guatemala	(Vacant)	Amb.	F. A. Maldonado Gularte	Amb.
Guinea	William C. Harrop	Amb.	Habib Bah	Amb.
Guinea-Bissau	(Vacant)	Amb.	G. V. Vas Fernandes	Amb.
Guyana	William W. McGuire	Amb.	Laurence A. Mann	Amb.
Haiti	Heyward Isham	Amb.	George Salomon	Amb.
Honduras	Philip V. Sanchez	Amb.	Dr. Roberto Lazarus	Amb.
Hungary	Eugene W. McAuliffe	Amb.	Ferenc Esztergalyos	Amb.
Iceland	James J. Blake	Amb.	Haraldur Kroüyer	Amb.
India	William B. Saxbe	Amb.	Triloki Nath Kaul	Amb.
Indonesia	David D. Newson	Amb.	Roesmin Nurjadin	Amb.
Iran	Richard Helms	Amb.	Ardeshir Zahedi	Amb.
Ireland	Walter J. P. Curley, Jr.	Amb.	John Gerald Molloy	Amb.
Israel	Malcolm Toon	Amb.	Simcha Dinitz	Amb.
Italy	John A. Volpe	Amb.	Roberto Gaja	Amb.
Ivory Coast	Robert S. Smith	Amb.	Timothée N'Guetta Ahoua	Amb.
Jamaica	Sumner Gerard	Amb.	Alfred A. Rattray	Amb.
Japan	James D. Hodgson	Amb.	Fumihiko Togo	Amb.
Jordan	Thomas R. Pickering	Amb.	Abdullah Salah	Amb.
Kenya	Anthony D. Marshall	Amb.	Ernest M. Mungai	Cd'A.
Korea (South)	Richard L. Sneider	Amb.	Dr. Pyong-choon Hahm	Amb.

Country	U. S. representative to[1]	Rank	Representative from[1]	Rank
Kuwait	Frank E. Maestrone	Amb.	Khalid M. Jaffar	Amb.
Laos	Christian A. Chapman	Amb.	Somphong Vanitsaveth	Cd'A.
Lebanon	(Vacant)	Amb.	Najati Kabbani	Amb.
Lesotho	David B. Bolen[7]	Amb.	Teboho J. Mashologu	Amb.
Liberia	W. Beverly Carter, Jr.	Amb.	S. Edward Peal	Amb.
Libya	(Vacant)	Amb.	Shaban F. Gashut	Cd'A.
Luxembourg	Rosemary L. Ginn	Amb.	Adrien Meisch	Amb.
Madagascar	(Vacant)	Amb.	Charles Randrianasolo	Cd'A.
Malawi	Robert A. Stevenson	Amb.	Jacob T. X. Muwamba	Amb.
Malaysia	Francis T. Underhill, Jr.	Amb.	Zain Azraai	Amb.
Mali	(Vacant)	Amb.	Mamadou B. Kante	Amb.
Malta	Robert P. Smith	Amb.	Joseph Attard-Kingswell	Amb.
Mauritania	Holsey G. Handyside	Amb.	Mohamed Said Hamody	Cd'A.
Mauritius	Robert V. Keeley	Amb.	Pierre Guy Girald Balancy	Amb.
Mexico	Joseph J. Jova	Amb.	Dr. José Juan de Olloqui	Amb.
Morocco	Robert Anderson	Amb.	Abdelhadi Boutaleb	Amb.
Mozambique	Willard R. De Pree	Amb.		
Nepal	Marquita M. Maytag	Amb.	Padma Bahadur Khatri	Amb.
Netherlands	Kingdon Gould, Jr.	Amb.	Age R. T. Bakker	Amb.
New Zealand	Armistead I. Selden, Jr.	Amb.	Lloyd White	Amb.
Nicaragua	Thomas D. Theberge	Amb.	Dr. Guillermo Sevilla-Sacassa	Amb.
Niger	L. Douglas Heck	Amb.	Illa Salifou	Amb.
Nigeria	Donald B. Easum	Amb.	Edward Olusola Sanu	Amb.
Norway	William A. Anders	Amb.	Soren C. Sommerfelt	Amb.
Oman	William Wolle	Amb.	Ahmed Macki	Amb.
Pakistan	Henry A. Byroade	Amb.	Sahabzada Yaqub-Khan	Amb.
Panama	William J. Jorden	Amb.	Nicolas Gonzalez-Revilla	Amb.
Papua New Guinea	Mary S. Olmsted	Amb.	Paulias Nguna Matane	Amb.
Paraguay	George W. Landau	Amb.	Miguel Solano-Lopez	Amb.
Peru	Robert W. Dean	Amb.	Carlos Garcia-Bedoya	Amb.
Philippines	William H. Sullivan	Amb.	Eduardo Z. Romualdez	Amb.
Poland	Richard T. Davies	Amb.	Witold Trampczynski	Amb.
Portugal	Frank C. Carlucci	Amb.	João Hall Themido	Amb.
Qatar	Robert P. Paganelli	Amb.	Abdullah Saleh Al-Mana	Amb.
Romania	Harry G. Barnes, Jr.	Amb.	Corneliu Bogdan	Amb.
Rwanda	(Vacant)	Amb.	Joseph Nizeyimana	Amb.
Saudi Arabia	William A. Porter	Amb.	Ali Abdallah Alireza	Amb.
Senegal	O. Rudolph Aggrey	Amb.	André Coulbary	Amb.
Sierra Leone	Michael Samuels	Amb.	Philip J. Palmer	Amb.
Singapore	John H. Holdridge	Amb.	Dr. Ernest Steven Monteiro	Amb.
Somalia	John Loughran	Amb.	Dr. Abdullahi Ahmed Addou	Amb.
South Africa	William G. Bowdler	Amb.	R. F. Botha	Amb.
Spain	Wells Stabler	Amb.	Jaime Alba	Amb.
Sri Lanka[5]	John H. Reed	Amb.	Neville Kanakaratne	Amb.
Sudan	William D. Brewer	Amb.	Dr. Francis M. Deng	Amb.
Surinam	J. Owen Zurhellen	Amb.		
Swaziland	David B. Bolen[7]	Amb.	J. L. F. Simelane	
Sweden	David S. Smith	Amb.	Count Wilhelm Wachtmeister	Amb.
Switzerland	Nathaniel Davis	Amb.	Raymond Probst	Amb.
Syrian Arab Republic	Richard W. Murphy	Amb.	Dr. Sabah Kabbani	Amb.
Tanzania	James W. Spain	Amb.	Paul Bomani	Amb.
Thailand	Charles S. Whitehouse	Amb.	Upadit Pachariyangkun	Amb.
Togo	Nancy V. Rawls	Amb.	Messanvi K. Kekeh	Amb.
Trinidad & Togabo	Albert B. Fay	Amb.	Victor McIntyre	Amb.
Tunisia	Edward W. Mulcahy	Amb.	Ali Hedda	Amb.
Turkey	William B. Macomber, Jr.	Amb.	Melih Esenbel	Amb.
United Arab Emirates	Michael Sterner	Amb.	Saeed A. Ghobash	Amb.
U.S.S.R.	Walter J. Stoessel, Jr.	Amb.	Anatoliy F. Dobrynin	Amb.
Upper Volta	Pierre Graham	Amb.	Telesphore Yaguibou	Amb.
Uruguay	Ernest V. Siracusa	Amb.	Jose Perez Caldas	Amb.
Venezuela	Viron P. Vaky	Amb.	Miguel A. Burelli	Amb.
Yemen Arab Republic	Thomas I. Scotes	Amb.	Yahya M. Al-Mutawekel	Amb.
Yugoslavia	Laurence H. Silberman	Amb.	Dimce Belovski	Amb.
Zaire	Walter L. Cutler	Amb.	Ndagano Bulumba	Cd'A.
Zambia	Stephen Low	Amb.	Siteke G. Mwale	Amb.

[1] As of August. [2] Resident in Yaounde, Cameroon. [3] Resident in Dakar, Senegal. [4] Cambodia. [5] Formerly Ceylon. [6] Resident in Wallington, N.Z. [7] Resident in Gabarone, Botswana.

NOTE: Diplomatic relations between the U.S. and Cuba were severed on Jan. 3, 1961. On Aug. 13, 1965, the U.S. withdrew all personnel from its Embassy in Congo (Brazzaville).

(Amb.—Ambassador; Min.—Minister; CG—Consul General; Cd'A—Chargé d'Affaires; F'Sy.—First Secretary)

ASTRONOMY AND CALENDAR

By

NICHOLAS PANAGAKOS

Astronomical Terms

Planet is the term used for a body in orbit around the sun. Its origin is Greek; even in antiquity it was known that a number of "stars" did not stay in the same relative positions to the other stars, as did the majority of all stars. There were five such restless "stars" known—Mercury, Venus, Mars, Jupiter, and Saturn—and the Greeks referred to them as *planetes,* a word which means "wanderers." That the earth is one of the planets was realized later and, of course, additional planets were discovered after the invention of the telescope.

Satellite (or "moon") is the term for a body in orbit around a planet. As long as our own Moon was the only moon known, there was no need for a general term for the moons of planets. But when Galileo Galilei discovered the four main moons of the planet Jupiter, Johannes Kepler (in a letter to Galileo) suggested "satellite" (from the Latin *satelles,* which means attendant) as a general term for such bodies. It is used interchangeably with "moons"; astronomers speak and write about the moons of Neptune, Saturn, etc. The size does not matter; a satellite is a body in orbit around a planet.

Orbit is the term for the path traveled by a body in space. It comes from the Latin *orbis,* which means circle, circuit, etc., and *orbita,* which means a rut or a wheel track. Theoretically, four mathematical figures are possible orbits: two are open (hyperbola and parabola) and two are closed (ellipse and circle), but in reality all closed orbits are ellipses. These ellipses can be nearly circular, as are the orbits of most planets, or very elongated, as are the orbits of most comets. In each case the sun is in one focal point of the ellipse, and the other focal point is empty. For satellite orbits, the planet stands in one focal point of the orbit. When discussing orbits generally, the term "primary" is often used; it means the body in the focal point. For planets, the point of the orbit closest to the Sun is called the *perihelion,* and the point farthest from the Sun is called the *aphelion.* For orbits around the Earth, the corresponding terms are *perigee* and *apogee;* for orbits around other planets, corresponding terms are coined when necessary.

Two heavenly bodies are in *conjunction* when they have the same Right Ascension, or are in the same meridian; that is, when one is due north or south of the other. If the bodies are near each other as seen from the Earth, they will rise and set at the same time. They are in *opposition* when they are in opposite quarters of the heavens, or when one rises as the other is setting. *Greatest elongation* is the greatest apparent angular distance from the Sun, when a planet is most favorably suited for observation. Mercury can be seen with the naked eye only at this time. An *occultation* of a planet or star is an eclipse of it by some other body, usually the Moon.

Stars are the basic units of population in the universe. Our Sun is the nearest star. Stars are very large (our Sun has a diameter of 865,400 miles—a comparatively small star), and are intensely hot, deriving their energy from nuclear reactions going on in their interiors.

Stars are clustered in groups called *galaxies.* Each galaxy is separated from other galaxies by almost completely empty space, containing no stars and no more than a few atoms of hydrogen. All the stars you can see in the sky (with a very few exceptions) are part of our galaxy—a system of, roughly, 100 billion stars. The few exceptions are other galaxies. Our own galaxy, the rim of which we see as the "Milky Way," is about 100,000 light-years in diameter and about 10,000 light-years in thickness. Its shape is generally that of a thick lens; more precisely it is a "spiral nebula," a term first used for other galaxies when they were discovered and before it was realized that these were separate and distant galaxies. The nearest other galaxy (visible to the naked eye) is the one in the constellation Andromeda; it is somewhat larger than our own galaxy.

Origin of the Universe

Evidence uncovered in recent years tends to confirm that the universe began its existence about 15 billion years ago as a dense, hot globule of gas expanding rapidly outward. At that time, the universe contained nothing but hydrogen and a small amount of helium. There were no stars and no planets. The first stars probably began to condense out of the primordial hydrogen when the universe was about 100 million years old and continued to form as the universe aged. The Sun arose in this way 4.5 billion years ago, when the universe was about 5 billion years old. Many stars came into being before the Sun was formed; many others formed after the Sun appeared. This process continues, and through telescopes we can now see stars forming out of compressed pockets of hydrogen in outer space.

Birth and Death of A Star

When a star begins to form as a dense cloud of gas, the individual hydrogen atoms fall toward the center of the cloud under the force of the star's gravity; as they fall, they pick up speed, and their energy increases. The increase in energy heats the gas and raises its temperature. When this process has continued for some millions of years, the temperature reaches about 20 million degrees Fahrenheit. At this temperature, the hydrogen within the star ignites and burns in a continuing series of

Astronomical Constants

light-year (distance traveled by light in one year)	5,880,000,000,000 mi.
parsec (parallax of one second, for stellar distances)	3.259 light-yrs.
velocity of light	186,281.7 mi./sec.
astronomical unit (A.U.) or mean distance earth-to-sun	ca. 93,000,000 mi.*
mean distance, earth to moon	238,860 mi.
general precession	50".26
obliquity of the ecliptic	23° 27' 8".26−0".4684(t−1900) †
equatorial radius of the earth	3963.34 statute mi.
polar radius of the earth	3949.99 statute mi.
earth's mean radius	3958.89 statute mi.
oblateness of the earth	$\frac{1}{297}$
equatorial horizontal parallax of the moon	57' 2".70
earth's mean velocity in orbit	18.5 mi./sec.
sidereal year	365^d.2564
tropical year	365^d.2422
sidereal month	27^d.3217
synodic month	29^d.5306
sidereal day	23^h 56^m 4^s.091 of mean solar time
mean solar day	24^h 3m 56^s.555 of sidereal time

* Actual mean distance derived from radar bounces: 92,935,700 mi. The value of 92,897,400 mi. (based on parallax of 8".80) is used in calculations. † *t* refers to the year in question, for example, 1958.

---

nuclear reactions in which all the elements in the universe are manufactured from hydrogen and helium. The onset of these reactions marks the birth of a star. When a star begins to exhaust its hydrogen supply, its life nears an end. The first sign of old age is a swelling and reddening of its outer regions. Such an aging, swollen star is called a red giant. The Sun, a middle-aged star, will probably swell to a red giant in 5 billion years, vaporizing the earth and any creatures that may be left on its surface. When all its fuel has been exhausted, a star cannot generate sufficient pressure at its center to balance the crushing force of gravity. The star collapses under the force of its own weight; if it is a small star, it collapses gently and remains collapsed. Such a collapsed star, at its life's end, is called a white dwarf. The Sun will probably end its days in this way. A different fate awaits a large star. Its final collapse generates a violent explosion, blowing the innards of the star out into space. There the materials of the exploded star mix with the primeval hydrogen of the universe. Later in the history of the galaxy, other stars are formed out of this mixture. The Sun is one of these stars. It contains the debris of countless other stars that exploded before the Sun was born.

Formation of the Solar System

The Sun, like other stars, seems to have been formed 4.5 billion years ago from a cloud of hydrogen mixed with small amounts of other substances that had been manufactured in the bodies of other stars before the Sun was born. This was the parent cloud of the solar system. The dense hot gas at the center of the cloud gave rise to the Sun; the outer regions of the cloud—cooler and less dense—gave birth to the planets.

Our solar system consists of one star (the Sun), nine planets and all their moons, several thousand minor planets called asteroids or planetoids, and an equally large number of comets.

The Sun

All the stars, including our Sun, are gigantic balls of superheated gas, kept hot by atomic reactions in their centers. In our Sun, this atomic reaction is hydrogen fusion; four hydrogen atoms are combined to form one helium atom. The temperature at the core of our Sun must be 20 million degrees centigrade, the surface temperature is around 6,000 degrees centigrade, or about 11,000 degrees Fahrenheit. The diameter of the sun is 865,400 miles so that its surface area is approximately 12,000 times that of the Earth. Compared with other stars our Sun is just a bit below average in size and temperature. Its fuel supply (hydrogen) is estimated to last for another 5 billion years.

Our Sun is not motionless in space; in fact it has two proper motions. One is a straight-line motion (as far as is known) in the direction of the constellation Hercules at the rate of about 12 miles per second. But since the Sun is a part of the Milky Way system and since the whole system rotates slowly around its own center, the Sun also moves at the rate of 175 miles per second as part of the rotating Milky Way system.

In addition to this the Sun rotates on its axis. Observing the motion of the sun spots (darkish areas which look like enormous whirling storms) and the exceptionally bright spots called "solar flares" which are usually associated with sun spots has shown that the rotational period of our Sun is just short of 25 days. But this figure is valid for the Sun's equator only; the sections near the Sun's poles seem to have a rotational period of 34 days. Naturally, since the Sun generates its own heat and light, there is no temperature difference between poles and equator.

What we call the Sun's "surface" is technically known as the photosphere. Since the whole Sun is a ball of very hot gas, there is really no such thing as a surface; it is a question of visual impression. Outside the photosphere we have another layer called the "chromosphere," which extends several thousand miles beyond the photosphere. It is in steady motion and often enormous "prominences" can be seen to burst from it, extending as much as 100,000 miles into space. Outside the chromosphere there is the so-called "corona." The corona consists of very tenuous gases (essentially hydrogen), but it makes a magnificent sight when the Sun is eclipsed.

The Moon

The Earth is the planet nearest to the Sun of all the planets which have moons. The two planets nearer the Sun, Mercury and Venus, do not have any moons. The next planet farther out, Mars, has two very small moons. Jupiter has four major moons and eight minor ones. Saturn, the ringed planet, has ten known moons, of which one (Titan) is larger than the planet Mercury. Uranus has five known moons (four of them large), while Neptune has one large and one small moon. Pluto is moonless and is considered by some a "runaway moon" of Neptune.

Our own Moon, with a diameter of 2,160 miles, is one of the large moons in our solar system and is especially large when compared with the planet around which it goes. In fact the common center of gravity of the Earth-Moon system is only about 1,000 miles below the Earth's surface. The closest our Moon can come to us (perigee) is 221,463 miles; the farthest it can go away (apogee) is 252,710 miles. Like all the other moons in our solar system the period of rotation of our Moon is equal to its period of revolution around the Earth. Hence from Earth we can see only one hemisphere of the Moon. Both periods are 27 days, 7 hours, 43 minutes and 11.47 seconds. But while the rotation of the Moon is regular, its velocity in its orbit is not, since it moves more slowly in apogee than in perigee. Consequently some portions near the rim which are not normally visible will appear briefly. This phenomenon is called "libration," and by taking advantage of the librations astrono-mers have succeeded in mapping approximately 59% of the lunar surface. The other 41% can never be seen from the earth but has been mapped by American and Russian Moon-orbiting spacecraft.

Though the Moon goes around the Earth in the time mentioned, the interval from new Moon to new Moon is 29 days, 12 hours, 44 minutes and 2.78 seconds. This delay of nearly two days is due to the fact that the Earth is moving around the Sun, so that the Moon needs two extra days to reach a spot in its orbit where no part is illuminated by the Sun, as seen from Earth.

If the plane of the Earth's orbit around the Sun (the ecliptic) and the plane of the Moon's orbit around the Earth were the same, the Moon would be eclipsed by the Earth every time it is full, and the Sun would be eclipsed by the Moon every time the Moon is "new" (it would be better to call it the "black Moon" when it is in this position). But because the two orbits do not coincide, the Moon's shadow normally misses the Earth and the Earth's shadow misses the Moon. The inclination of the two orbital planes to each other is 5 degrees. The tides are, of course, caused by the Moon, but in the open ocean they are surprisingly low, amounting to about one yard. The very high tides which can be observed near the shore in some places are due to funnelling effects of the shorelines. At new Moon and at full Moon the tides raised by the Moon are reinforced by the Sun; these are the "spring tides." If the Sun's tidal raising power does not reinforce that of the Moon we get the low "neap tides."

The Brightest Stars

Star	Constellation	Position, 1950 R.A.	Dec.	Mag.	Dist.	On meridian 9 p.m.
		h m	° ′		l.-y.	
Sirius	Canis Major	6 42.9	−16 39	−1.6	8	Feb. 16
Canopus	Carina	6 22.8	−52 40	−0.9	650	Feb. 11
Alpha Centauri	Centaurus	14 36.2	−60 38	+0.1	4	June 16
Vega	Lyra	18 35.2	+38 44	0.1	23	Aug. 15
Capella	Auriga	5 13.0	+45 57	0.2	42	Jan. 24
Arcturus	Boötes	14 13.4	+19 27	0.2	32	June 10
Rigel	Orion	5 12.1	− 8 15	0.3	545	Jan. 24
Procyon	Canis Minor	7 36.7	+ 5 21	0.5	10	Mar. 2
Achernar	Eridanus	1 35.9	−57 29	0.6	70	Nov. 30
Beta Centauri	Centaurus	14 0.3	−60 8	0.9	130	June 7
Altair	Aquila	19 48.3	+ 8 44	0.9	18	Sept. 3
Betelgeuse	Orion	5 52.5	+ 7 24	0.9	300	Feb. 3
Aldebaran	Taurus	4 33.0	+16 25	1.1	54	Jan. 14
Spica	Virgo	13 22.6	−10 54	1.2	190	May 28
Pollux	Gemini	7 42.3	+28 9	1.2	31	Mar. 3
Antares	Scorpius	16 26.3	−26 19	1.2	170	July 14
Fomalhaut	Piscis Austrinus	22 54.9	−29 53	1.3	27	Oct. 20
Deneb	Cygnus	20 39.7	+45 6	1.3	465	Sept. 16
Regulus	Leo	10 5.7	+12 13	1.3	70	Apr. 9
Beta Crucis	Crux	12 44.8	−59 25	1.5	465	May 18
Eta Carinae	Carina	10 43.1	−59 25	1—7	...	Apr. 17
Alpha-one Crucis	Crux	12 23.8	−62 49	1.6	150	May 13
Castor	Gemini	7 31.4	+32 0	1.6	44	Feb. 28
Gamma Crucis	Crux	12 28.4	−56 50	1.6	...	May 15
Epsilon Canis Majoris	Canis Major	6 56.7	−28 54	1.6	325	Feb. 19
Epsilon Ursae Majoris	Ursa Major	12 51.8	+56 14	1.7	50	May 20
Bellatrix	Orion	5 22.4	+ 6 18	1.7	215	Jan. 27
Lambda Scorpii	Scorpius	17 30.2	−37 4	1.7	205	July 30
Epsilon Carinae	Carina	8 21.5	−59 21	1.7	325	Mar. 13
Mira	Cetus	2 16.8	− 3 12	2—9	250	Dec. 11

Data for Sun, Moon, and Planets

	Mean distance from sun in millions of miles	Period of revolution around the sun	Eccentricity of orbit	Inclination to ecliptic		Diameter	Period of rotation on axis	Inclination of equator to orbit plane	Surface gravity (earth =1)	Density $H_2O = 1$	Number of Satellites	Mean velocity in orbit	Max. stellar mag.
				°	′	miles		°				mi./sec.	
Sun......	......	....	.....	......		865,400	24d.64†	7.2	28	1.4	0	......	−26.7
Moon....	......	(27d.322)*	0.05	5	8	2,160	27d.322	6.7	0.16	3.3	0	0.63	−12.6
Mercury..	36.00	87d.969	0.21	7	0	3,100	58.66d	7	0.28	3.8	0	30	−1.2
Venus....	67.27	224d.701	0.01	3	24	7,700	243.2d	?	0.85	5.1	0	22	−4.4
Earth....	93.00	365d.256	0.02	0	0	7,927‡	23h 56m	23.4	1.00	5.5	1	18.5	.....
Mars.....	141.71	1y.881	0.09	1	51	4,200	24h 37m	25.2	0.38	4.0	2	15	−2.8
Jupiter...	483.88	11y.862	0.05	1	18	88,700‡	9h 50m†	3.1	2.6	1.3	12	8	−2.5
Saturn...	887.14	29y.458	0.06	2	29	75,100‡	10h 14m†	26.8	1.2	0.7	10	6	−0.4
Uranus...	1783.98	84y.013	0.05	0	46	32,000	10 ¾ h	98	1.1	1.3	5	4	+5.7
Neptune .	2795.46	164y.794	0.01	1	46	27,700	15h.8	29	1.4	2.2	2	3	+7.8
Pluto....	3675.27	248y.430	0.25	17	9	3,600	??	??	??	?	0	<3	+14

* Period of revolution around the earth. † This is the rotation at the equator. ‡ The equatorial diameters of the earth, Jupiter, and Saturn are given; polar diameters are: earth, 7,900.0 mi., Jupiter 82,789 mi., Saturn 67,170 mi.

OTHER DATA ON THE EARTH: Equatorial circumference, 24,902.4 mi.; total area, 196,949,970 sq. mi.; mass, 6.6 sextillion tons; mean diameter, 7,917.8 mi.

Planets of the Solar System

OUR PLANET EARTH

The Earth, circling the Sun at an average distance of 93 million miles, is the fifth largest planet, and the third from the Sun. It orbits the Sun at a speed of 67,000 miles an hour, making one revolution in 365 days, 5 hours, 48 minutes and 45.51 seconds. The Earth completes one rotation on its axis every 23 hours, 56 minutes and 4.09 seconds. Actually a bit pear-shaped rather than a true sphere, the Earth has a diameter of 7,908 miles at the Equator and a few miles less at the poles. It has an estimated mass of about 6½ sextillion tons, with an average density of 5.52 grams per cubic centimeter. The Earth's surface area encompasses 197,272,000 square miles, of which three-fourths is water.

Origin of the Earth

The Earth, along with the other planets, is believed to have been born 4.6 billion years ago as a solidified cloud of dust and gases left over from the creation of the Sun. For perhaps 500 million years, the interior of the Earth stayed solid and relatively cool, perhaps 2000° F. The main ingredients, according to the best available evidence, were iron and silicates, with small amounts of other elements, some of them radioactive. As millions of years passed, energy released by radioactive decay—mostly of uranium, thorium and potassium—gradually heated the Earth, melting some of its constituents. The iron melted before the silicates, and, being heavier, sank toward the center. This forced upward the silicates that it found there. After many years, the iron reached the center, almost 4,000 miles deep, and began to accumulate. No eyes were around at that time to view the turmoil which must have taken place on the face of the Earth—

gigantic heaves and bubbling of the surface, exploding volcanoes and flowing lava covering everything in sight. Finally, the iron in the center accumulated as the core. Around it, a thin but fairly stable crust of solid rock formed as the Earth cooled. Depressions in the crust formed natural basins in which water, rising from the interior of the planet through volcanoes and fissures, collected to form the oceans. Slowly the Earth acquired its present appearance.

The Earth Today

As a result of radioactive heating over millions of years, the Earth's molten core is probably fairly hot today, around 11,000° F. By comparison, lead melts at around 800° F. Most of the Earth's 2,100-mile-thick *core* is liquid, but there is evidence that the center of the core is solid. The liquid outer portion, about 1,300 miles thick, is constantly in motion, causing the Earth to have a magnetic field that makes compass needles point north and south. The details are not known, but the latest evidence suggests that planets which have a magnetic field have a liquid core; those without a magnetic field probably have a solid core or a partially liquid one.

Outside the core is the Earth's *mantle*, 1,800 miles thick, and extending nearly to the surface. The mantle is composed of heavy silicate rock, similar to that brought up by volcanic eruptions. It is somewhere between liquid and solid, slightly yielding, and therefore contributing to an active moving Earth. Most of the Earth's radioactive material is in the thin *crust* which covers the mantle, but some is in the mantle and continues to give off heat. The crust's thickness ranges from 5 to 25 miles.

Continental Drift

A great deal of recent evidence confirms the long-disputed theory that the continents of the Earth, made mostly of light granite, float like icebergs in the slightly yielding mantle, like logs in a pond. For many years it had been noticed that, if North and South America could·be pushed toward western and southern Europe and western Africa, they would fit like pieces in a jigsaw puzzle. Today, there is little question—the continents have drifted widely, and continue to do so.

In 10 million years, the world as we know it may be unrecognizable, with California drifting out to sea, Florida joining South America, and Africa moving farther away from Europe and Asia.

The Earth's Atmosphere

The thin blanket of atmosphere which envelops the Earth extends several hundred miles into space. From sea level—the very bottom of the ocean of air—to a height of about 60 miles, the air in the atmosphere is made up of the same gases in the same ratio: about 78% nitrogen, 21% oxygen and the remaining 1% being a mixture of argon, carbon dioxide and tiny amounts of neon, helium, krypton, xenon and other gases. The atmosphere becomes less dense with increasing altitude, and more than three-fourths of the Earth's huge envelope is concentrated in the first 5 to 10 miles above the surface. At sea level, a cubic foot of the atmosphere weighs about an ounce and a quarter. The entire atmosphere weighs 5,700,000,000,000,000 tons, and the force with which gravity holds it in place causes it to exert a pressure of nearly 15 pounds per square inch. Going out from the Earth's surface, the atmosphere is divided into five regions. The regions, and the heights to which they extend, are: *Troposphere,* 0 to 7 miles; *stratosphere,* 7 to 30 miles; *mesosphere,* 30 to 50 miles, *thermosphere,* 50 to 400 miles, and *exosphere,* above 400 miles. The boundaries between each of the regions are known respectively as the *tropopause, stratopause, mesopause* and *thermopause.*

The Seasons

Seasons are caused by the tilt of the Earth's axis, which alternately turns the North and South Poles toward the Sun. Points where the Sun crosses the Equator are known as *equinoxes.* Points where the Sun is at the greatest distance from the Equator are known as *solstices.* That is when the lengths of the days are most unequal. If the Earth's axis were perpendicular to the plane of the Earth's orbit around the Sun, there would be no seasons, and the days always would be equal in length. However, the axis is at slight angles to the Sun only in March (vernal equinox) and September (autumnal equinox). In the Northern Hemisphere, spring begins at the vernal equinox, summer at the summer solstice, fall at the autumnal equinox and winter at the winter solstice. The situation is reversed in the Southern Hemisphere.

MERCURY

Mercury is the smallest planet in the solar system, and the one nearest the Sun. Appropriately named for the wing-footed Roman messenger of the gods, Mercury whizzes around the Sun at a speed of 30 miles a second, completing one circuit

in 88 days. The planet rotates on its axis over a period of nearly 59 days. Daytime on cratered Mercury is hot, about 800 degrees F., although at night the temperature may fall to room temperature. Mercury has no moons, but it does have a trace of atmosphere and a weak magnetic field, according to findings of Mariner 10. Until this spacecraft flew by Mercury in 1974 and 1975, very little was known about the planet. This is primarily because of its short angular distance from the Sun as seen from Earth, putting it too much in line with Sun to be easily observed against the sky.

● Mercury is a naked eye object at morning or evening twilight.

VENUS

Although Venus is Earth's nearest neighbor, little is known about this planet because it is permanently covered by thick clouds. Beginning in 1962, Soviet and American space probes, coupled with Earth-based radar and infrared spectroscopy, slowly began unraveling some of the mystery surrounding Venus. According to these results, Venus' atmosphere is nearly 100% carbon dioxide, exerting a pressure at the surface 100 times greater than Earth's. Walking on Venus would be as difficult as walking a half-mile beneath the ocean. Because of the thick blanket of carbon dioxide, a "greenhouse effect" exists on Venus: Venus intercepts twice as much of the Sun's light as does the Earth. The light enters freely through carbon dioxide gas and is changed to heat radiation in molecular collisions. But carbon dioxide prevents the heat from escaping. Consequently, the temperature of the surface of Venus is nearly 800 degrees F., hot enough to melt lead. Radar bounced off the planet recently revealed what appear to be large craters. In 1978, NASA plans to launch a multi-probe spacecraft toward Venus to conduct a detailed scientific examination of this enigmatic planet. Unlike other planets, Venus rotates in retrograde (clockwise) motion. Reason is not known.

● Venus can readily be seen with the naked eye. It is the opposite of Mercury, hanging in the sky like a distant searchlight trained at us. As late as 100 years ago, a French warship tried to shoot it down because it was thought to be an enemy balloon, and in recent years Venus has often been reported as a "flying saucer."

MARS

Mars, on the other side of the Earth from Venus, is the direct opposite in terms of physical properties. Its atmosphere is cold, thin and transparent, and readily permits observation of the planet's features. We know more about Mars than any other planet except Earth. Mars is a forbidding, rugged planet with huge volcanoes and deep chasms. The largest volcano, Nix Olympia, rises 78,000 feet above the surface, higher than Mount Everest. The plains of Mars are pockmarked by the hits of thousands of meteorites over the years. Most of our information about Mars comes from the Mariner 9 spacecraft, which orbited the planet in 1971. Mariner 9, photographing 100 per cent of the planet, uncovered spectacular geological formations, including a Martian Grand Canyon which dwarfs the one on Earth. The spacecraft's cameras also recorded what appeared to be dried riverbeds, suggesting the onetime presence of water on the planet. The latter idea provides encouragement to scientists looking for life on Mars, for where there is water, there may be life. Temperatures near the equator range from −17 degrees F. in the daytime to −130 degrees F. at night. Mars rotates upon its axis in nearly the same period as Earth—24 hours, 37 minutes—so that a Mars day is almost identical to an Earth day. Mars takes 687 days to make one trip around the Sun. Because of its eccentric orbit, Mars' distance from the Sun can vary by about 36 million miles, and its distance from Earth can vary by as much as 200 million miles. The atmosphere of Mars is much thinner than Earth's; atmospheric pressure is about 1/100th that of our planet. Its gravity is one-third of Earth's. Major constituents are carbon dioxide and nitrogen. Water and oxygen are minor constituents. Mars' polar caps, composed mostly of carbon dioxide, recede and advance according to the Martian seasons. Mars was named for the Roman god of war because when seen from Earth its distinct red color reminded the ancient people of blood. We know now that the reddish hue reflects the oxidized (rusted) iron in the surface material. The landing of two robot Viking spacecraft on the surface of Mars in 1976 promises to provide more information about Mars in a few months than in all the time that has gone before.

● Mars becomes especially bright when nearest to us because we then see its daylight side fully illuminated by the Sun. This happens roughly every two years and two months. The last time was in December 1975.

JUPITER

Jupiter, with an equatorial diameter of 88,000 miles, is the largest of a group of planets which differ markedly from the terrestrial planets. The others in the group are Saturn, Uranus and Neptune. All are large, with very dense atmospheres and indeed may be giant balls of gas without any perceptible surfaces. They all whirl rapidly around their axes, but more slowly around the Sun, resulting in short days and long years. They have many moons. Majestic Jupiter, named for the Roman king of the gods, rotates so fast that it is flattened at the poles. According to Pioneers 10 and 11, which flew past Jupiter in 1974 and 1975, this planet is a whirling ball of liquid hydrogen with perhaps an Earth-sized iron core. Other atmospheric constituents are helium, methane and ammonia. Its clouds are probably ammonia ice crystals, becoming ammonia droplets deeper towards the "surface." Temperatures range from perhaps minus 300 degrees F. at the tops of the cloud decks to 100,000 degrees F. or more deep down at the center. The pressure at the center of the planet is estimated to be a crushing 10 million pounds per square inch. The most prominent feature on Jupiter is the Great Red Spot, the size of four Earths. According to Pioneer scientists, the Red Spot is the vortex of a huge 25,000-mile-wide hurricane which has been raging for at least 700 years. Jupiter has 13 satellites, more than any other planet. The four largest moons, called Galilean moons, are Europa, Ganymede, Io and Callisto.

● Even when nearest the Earth, Jupiter is still almost 400 million miles away. But because of its size, it may rival Venus in brilliance when near. Jupiter's four large moons may be seen through field glasses, moving rapidly around Jupiter and changing their position from night to night.

SATURN

Saturn, one of the giant planets in the solar system, is also the least dense. It would float in an ocean, if there were one big enough to hold it. Aside from its rings, Saturn is very similar to Jupiter except that it is probably colder, being twice as far from the Sun. Recent radar observations of Saturn's rings indicate that they are no more than 10 miles thick, and probably composed of chunks of rock and ice averaging a meter in size. There are four rings. The system begins about 7000 miles from the planet's disk, and extends out to about 35,000 miles. Saturn has 10 satellites. The United States will launch a Mariner-type spacecraft to Jupiter in August 1977. After flying past Jupiter in 1981, taking pictures and making measurements, the spacecraft will go on to Saturn and possibly Uranus.

● Saturn is the last of the planets visible to the naked eye. Saturn is never an object of overwhelming brilliance, but will look like a bright star. The rings cannot be seen except with a professional telescope.

URANUS AND NEPTUNE

Little is known about the distant giant planets Uranus and Neptune, but they are believed to be similar to Saturn and Jupiter. Being twice as far from the Sun as Saturn, Uranus must be a grim frozen world, and Neptune, 11 A.U. beyond Uranus, must be even colder and darker. The axis of Uranus is tilted at 98 degrees, so it goes around the Sun nearly lying on its side. Uranus has five known moons; Neptune, two. Neptune's larger moon, Triton, Jupiter's Ganymede and Callisto, and Saturn's Titan are the four largest moons of the solar system.

● Uranus and Neptune can—on rare occasion—become bright enough to be seen with the naked eye, if one knows exactly where to look; normally, they are objects for good field glasses or small portable telescopes.

PLUTO

Pluto, the outermost planet in the solar system, looks more like a terrestrial planet than a giant planet. But so little is known about it, that it is difficult to classify. Appropriately named for the Roman god of the underworld, it must be frozen, dark and dead. Most of what we know about Pluto is deduced from its gravitational effect on the motion of Neptune. This tells us that Pluto's mass is less than 1/5 that of Earth, and its density is about 1½ times greater.

Pluto was predicted by calculation when Percival Lowell noticed irregularities in the orbits of Uranus and Neptune. Clyde Tombaugh discovered the planet in 1930, precisely where Lowell predicted it would be. The name Pluto was chosen because the first two letters represent the initials of Percival Lowell.

● Pluto has the most eccentric orbit in the solar system, bringing it at times closer to the Sun than Neptune. Pluto is now approaching the perihelion of its orbit, and for the rest of this century will be closer to the Sun than Neptune. Even then, it can be seen only with a large telescope.

The First Ten Minor Planets (Asteroids)

Name	Year of discovery	Mean distance from sun (millions of miles)	Orbital period (years)	Diameter (miles)	Magnitude
1. Ceres.	1801	257.0	4.60	485	7.4
2. Pallas.	1802	257.4	4.61	304	8.0
3. Juno.	1804	247.8	4.36	118	8.7
4. Vesta.	1807	219.3	3.63	243	6.5
5. Astraea.	1845	239.3	4.14	50	9.9
6. Hebe.	1847	225.2	3.78	121	8.5
7. Iris.	1847	221.4	3.68	121	8.4
8. Flora.	1847	204.4	3.27	56	8.9
9. Metis.	1848	221.7	3.69	78	8.9
10. Hygeia.	1849	292.6	5.59	40 (?)	9.5

The Asteroids

Between the orbits of Mars and Jupiter are an estimated 30,000 pieces of rocky debris, known collectively as the asteroids, or planetoids. The first and, incidentally, the largest was discovered during the New Year's night of 1801 by the Italian astronomer Father Piazzi, and its orbit was calculated by the German mathematician Karl Friedrich Gauss. (Gauss invented a new method of calculating orbits on that occasion.) A German amateur astronomer, the physician Olbers, discovered the second asteroid. The number now known, catalogued, and named is around 1,600; the estimated total is about 20 times that figure. A few asteroids do not move in orbits beyond the orbit of Mars, but in orbits which cross the orbit of Mars. The first of them was named Eros because of this peculiar orbit. It had become the rule to bestow female names on the asteroids, but when it was found that Eros crossed the orbit of a major planet, it received a male name. Since then around two dozen orbit-crossers have been discovered, and they are often referred to as the "male asteroids." A few of them—Albert, Adonis, Apollo, Amor, and Icarus—cross the orbit of the Earth, and two of them may come closer than our Moon; but the crossing is like a bridge crossing a highway, not like two highways intersecting. Hence there is no danger of collision from these bodies. They are all small, three to five miles in diameter, and therefore very difficult objects to identify, even when quite close. Some scientists believe the asteroids represent the remains of an exploded planet.

Beyond the "asteroid belt" is the largest planet of our solar system, Jupiter. Even when nearest the Earth, Jupiter is still almost 400 million miles away. But because of its size it may rival Venus in brilliance when near. The next planet beyond Jupiter is Saturn, famous for its rings. It is never an object of overwhelming brilliance but will look like a bright star. Uranus, the next planet, can occasionally become bright enough to be seen with the naked eye if you know just where to look; normally it is an object for good fieldglasses or small portable telescopes. The same goes for Neptune. Pluto, the planet "beyond Neptune," as it is usually called, is now approaching the perihelion of its orbit and for the rest of this century will be closer to the Sun than Neptune. Even then it can be seen only with a large telescope.

Comets

The appearance of a large and brilliant comet in the skies cannot be predicted any earlier than 1986, when Halley's comet will approach perihelion (the point of its orbit closest to the Sun) again. But a large and brilliant comet is possible at any time. More than 1,000 comets are on the lists now, with several new ones being discovered every year. But while you have a comet visible to the unaided eye almost every year, none of them since the last appearance of Halley's comet in 1910-11 has been conspicuous to a casual watcher.

Since comets appeared in the sky without any warning, people in classical times and especially during the Middle Ages believed that they had a special "meaning," which, of course, was bad. Since a natural catastrophe of some sort or a military conflict occurs every year, it was quite simple to blame the comet which happened to be visible. But even in the past there were some people who used logical reasoning. When, in Roman times, a comet was blamed for the loss of a battle and hence was called a "bad omen," a Roman writer observed that the victors in the battle probably did not think so.

Up until the middle of the sixteenth century comets were believed to be phenomena of the upper atmosphere; they were usually "explained" as "burning vapors" which had risen from "distant swamps." That nobody had ever actually seen burning vapors rise from a swamp did not matter.

21 Famous Comets

Year and no.	Name of comet	Period, years
1744	De Chéseaux's Comet.	.....
1806	Biela's Comet.	6.7
1811 I	Great Comet of 1811.	3000
1812	Di Vico's Comet.	70.7
1815	Olbers' Comet.	74.0
1819 I	Encke's Comet.	3.3
1819	Pons-Winnecke Comet.	6.0
1835 III	Halley's Comet.	76.3
1843 I	Great Comet of 1843.	512.4
1844 II	Great Comet of 1844.	102,050
1858 VI	Donati's Comet.	2,040 (?)
1864 II	Great Comet of 1864.	2,800,000
1871 III	Tuttle's Comet.	13.8
1874 III	Coggia's Comet.	6,000 (?)
1879	Brorsen's Comet.	5.6
1881 II	Tebbutt's Comet.	.....
1889 IV	Swift's 2nd Comet.	7.0
1892 III	Holmes' Comet.	6.9
1923	d'Arrest's Comet.	6.6
1925 II	Comet Schwassmann-Wachmann.	16.2
1973 f	Comet Kohoutek	75,000 (?)

But a large comet which appeared in 1577 was carefully observed by Tycho Brahe, a Danish astronomer who is often, and with the best of reasons, called "eccentric" but who insisted on precise measurements for everything. It was Tycho Brahe's accumulation of literally thousands of precise measurements which later enabled his younger collaborator, Johannes Kepler, to discover the laws of planetary motion. Measuring the motion of the comet of 1577, Tycho Brahe could show that it had been far beyond the atmosphere, even though he could not give figures for the distance. Tycho Brahe's work proved that comets were astronomical and not meteorological phenomena.

In 1682 the second Astronomer Royal of Great Britain, Dr. Edmond Halley, checked the orbit of a bright comet that was in the sky then and compared it with earlier comet orbits which were known in part. Halley found that the comet of 1682 was the third to move through what appeared to be the same orbit. And the three appearances were roughly 76 years apart. Halley concluded that this was the same comet, moving around the Sun in a closed orbit, like the planets. He predicted that it would reappear in 1758 or 1759. Halley himself died in 1742, but a large comet appeared sixteen years after his death as predicted and was immediately referred to as "Halley's comet."

In the Spring of 1974, the discovery of comet Kohoutek, apparently headed for a close Christmastime rendezvous with the Sun, created worldwide excitement. The comet was a visual disappointment, but turned out to be a treasure trove of information on these little-understood celestial objects. Given an unprecedented advance notice of nine months on the advent of the fiery object, scientists were able to study the comet in visible, ultraviolet and infrared light; with optical telescopes, radio telescopes and radar. They observed it from the ground, from high-flying aircraft, with instruments aboard unmanned satellites, with sounding rockets, and telescopes and cameras on the Earth-orbiting Skylab space station. Kohoutek may well have been the most-scrutinized object in the history of astronomy. Scientists learned more about the nature of comets from this single event than from all the cometary observations that had gone before.

Astronomers refer to comets as "periodic" or as "non-periodic" comets, but the latter term does not mean that these comets have no period; it merely means that their period is not known. The actual periods of comets run from 3.3 years (the shortest known) to several thousand years. Their orbits are elliptical, like those of the planets, but they are very eccentric, long and narrow ellipses. Only comet Schwassmann-Wachmann has an orbit which has such a low eccentricity (for a cometary orbit) that it could be the orbit of a minor planet.

When a comet, coming from deep space, approaches the Sun, it is at first indistinguishable from a minor planet. Somewhere between the orbits of Mars and Jupiter its outline becomes fuzzy; it is said to develop a "coma" (the word used here is the Latin word *coma,* which means "hair," not the phonetically identical Greek word which means "deep sleep"). Then, near the orbit of Mars, the comet develops its tail, which at first trails behind. This grows steadily as the comet comes closer and closer to the Sun. As it rounds the Sun (as first noticed by Girolamo Fracastoro) the tail always points away from the Sun so that the comet, when moving away from the Sun, points its tail ahead like the landing lights of an airplane.

The reason for this behavior is that the tail is pushed in these directions by the radiation pressure of the Sun. It sometimes happens that a comet loses its tail at perihelion; it then grows another one. Although the tail is clearly visible against the black of the sky, it is very tenuous. It has been said that if the tail of Halley's comet could be compressed to the density of iron, it would fit into a small suitcase.

The chemical make-up of comets has been explained by Fred L. Whipple. Comets are enormous "snowballs" of frozen gases (mostly carbon dioxide, methane or marsh gas, water vapor, etc.) containing very little solid material. The whole behavior of a comet, therefore, is explainable as the behavior of a ball of frozen gas being heated by the Sun. The Kohoutek observations seem to confirm the "dirty snowball" theory of Whipple.

Meteors and Meteorites

The term "meteor" for what is usually called a "shooting star" bears an unfortunate resemblance to the term "meteorology," the science of weather and weather forecasting. This resemblance is due to an ancient misunderstanding which wrongly considered meteors an atmospheric phenomenon. Actually the streak of light in the sky which scientists call a meteor is essentially an astronomical phenomenon: the entry of a small piece of cosmic matter into our atmosphere.

The distinction between "meteors" and "fireballs" (formerly also called "bolides") is merely one of convenience; a fireball is an unusually bright meteor. Incidentally, it also means that a fireball is larger than a faint meteor. A bright fireball produces enough light to see by and may light up the night landscape like the full Moon.

Bodies which enter our atmosphere become visible when they are about 60 miles above the ground. The fact that they grow hot enough to emit light is not due to the "friction" of the atmosphere, as one can often read. The phenomenon responsible for the heating is one of compression. Since unconfined air cannot move faster than the speed of sound but the entering meteorite moves with 30 to 60 times the speed of sound, the air simply cannot get out of the way. Therefore it is compressed like the air in the cylinder of a Diesel engine and is heated by compression. This heat—

Important Meteor Showers

Approx. date	Name of meteor stream	Radiant in constellation
Jan. 1–4	Quadrantids	Boötes
Feb. 5–10	Alpha Aurigids	Auriga
Mar. 10–12	Zeta Boötids	Boötes
Apr. 19–23	Lyrids	Hercules
May 1–6	May Aquarids	Aquarius
May 30	Eta Pegasids	Pegasus
June 27-30	Pons-Winnecke meteors	Draco
July 14	Alpha Cygnids	Cygnus
July 26–31	Delta Aquarids	Aquarius
Aug. 10–14	Perseids	Cassiopeia
Aug. 10–20	Kappa Cygnids	Cygnus
Aug. 21–31	Zeta Draconids	Draco
Sept. 22	Alpha Aurigids	Auriga
Oct. 2	Quadrantids	Boötes
Oct. 9	Giacobinids	Draco
Oct. 18–23	Orionids	Orion
Nov. 14–18	Leonids	Leo
Dec. 10–13	Geminids	Gemini

or part of it—is transferred to the moving body. The details of this process are now fairly well understood as a result of re-entry tests with ballistic-missile nose cones.

The average weight of a body producing a faint "shooting star" is only a small fraction of an ounce. Even a bright fireball may not weigh more than 2 or 3 pounds. Naturally the smaller bodies are worn to dust by the passage through the atmosphere; only rather large ones reach the ground. Those that are found are called meteorites. (The "meteor," to repeat, is the term for the light streak in the sky.)

The largest meteorite known is still imbedded in the ground near Grootfontein in SW Africa and is estimated to weigh 70 tons. The second largest known is the 34-ton Anighito (on exhibit in the Hayden Planetarium, New York), which was found by Admiral Peary at Cape York in Greenland. The largest meteorite found in the United States is the Willamette meteorite (found in Oregon, weight ca. 15 tons), but large portions of this meteorite weathered away before it was found and its weight as it struck the ground may have been 20 tons.

All these are iron meteorites (an iron meteorite normally contains about 7 per cent nickel), which form one class of meteorites. The other class are the stony meteorites and between them there are the so-called "stony irons." The so-called "Tektites" consist of glass similar to our volcanic glass obsidian, and because of the similarity there is doubt in a number of cases whether the glass is of terrestrial or of extra-terrestrial origin.

Though no meteorite larger than the Grootfontein is actually known, we do know that the Earth has, on occasion, been struck by much larger bodies. Evidence for such hits are the meteorite craters, of which an especially good example is located near the Cañon Diablo in Arizona. Another meteor crater in the United States is a rather old crater near Odessa, Texas. A large number of others are known, especially in eastern Canada; and for many "probables," meteoric origin has now been proved.

The meteor showers are caused by multitudes of very small bodies travelling in swarms; these showers, though looking most spetacular on occasion, do not seem to contain large pieces.

The 88 Recognized Constellations

In astronomical works the Latin names of the constellations are used. The letter N or S following the Latin name indicates whether the constellation is located to the north or to the south of the Zodiac. The letter Z indicates that the constellation is within the Zodiac.

Latin name	Letter	English version	Latin name	Letter	English version	Latin name	Letter	English version
Andromeda.....	N	Andromeda	Delphinus....	N	Dolphin	Pavo.........	S	Peacock
Antlia.........	S	Airpump	Dorado.......	S	Swordfish	Pegasus......	N	Pegasus
Apus..........	S	Bird of Paradise			(Goldfish)	Perseus......	N	Perseus
Aquarius......	Z	Water Bearer	Draco........	N	Dragon	Phoenix......	S	Phoenix
Aquila........	N	Eagle	Equuleus....	N	Filly	Pictor........	S	Painter (or his
Ara...........	S	Altar	Eridanus.....	S	Eridanus (river)			Easel)
Aries..........	Z	Ram	Fornax.......	S	Furnace	Pisces.......	Z	Fishes
Auriga........	N	Charioteer	Gemini.......	Z	Twins	Piscis		
Boötes........	N	Herdsmen	Grus........	S	Crane	Austrinus ..	S	Southern Fish
Caelum........	S	Sculptor's Tool	Hercules.....	N	Hercules	Puppis.......	S	Poop (of Argo)*
Camelopardalis.	N	Giraffe	Horologium...	S	Clock	Pyxis........	S	Mariner's
Cancer.........	Z	Crab	Hydra........	N	Sea Serpent			Compass
Canes Venatici .	N	Hunting Dogs	Hydrus........	S	Water Snake	Reticulum....	S	Net
Canis Major....	S	Great Dog	Indus........	S	Indian	Sagitta.......	N	Arrow
Canis Minor....	S	Little Dog	Lacerta.......	N	Lizard	Sagittarius....	Z	Archer
Capricornus....	Z	Goat (or Sea-	Leo..........	Z	Lion	Scorpius.....	Z	Scorpion
		Goat)	Leo Minor....	N	Little Lion	Sculptor......	S	Sculptor
Carina.........	S	Keel (of Argo)*	Lepus........	S	Hare	Scutum......	N	Shield
Cassiopeia.....	N	Cassiopeia	Libra........	Z	Scales	Serpens......	N	Serpent
Centaurus.....	S	Centaur	Lupus........	S	Wolf	Sextans......	S	Sextant
Cepheus.......	N	Cepheus	Lynx........	N	Lynx	Taurus.......	Z	Bull
Cetus.........	S	Whale	Lyra.........	N	Lyre (Harp)	Telescopium..	S	Telescope
Chamaeleon....	S	Chameleon	Mensa.......	S	Table	Triangulum...	N	Triangle
Circinus.......	S	Compasses			(mountain)	Triangulum		Southern
Columba.......	S	Dove	Microscopium.	S	Microscope	Australe.....	S	Triangle
Coma Berenices	N	Berenice's Hair	Monoceros....	S	Unicorn	Tucana.......	S	Toucan
Corona Australis	S	Southern Crown	Musca.......	S	Southern Fly	Ursa Major...	N	Big Dipper
Corona Borealis	N	Northern Crown	Norma.......	S	Rule	Ursa Minor...	N	Little Dipper
Corvus........	S	Crow (Raven)			(straightedge)	Vela.........	S	Sail (of Argo)*
Crater.........	S	Cup	Octans.......	S	Octant	Virgo........	Z	Virgin
Crux..........	S	Southern Cross	Ophiuchus ...	N	Serpent-Bearer	Volans.......	S	Flying Fish
Cygnus........	N	Swan	Orion........	N	Orion	Vulpecula....	N	Fox

* The original constellation Argo Navis (the Ship Argo) has been divided into Carina, Puppis, and Vela. Normally the brightest star in each constellation is designated by alpha, the first letter of the Greek alphabet, the second brightest by beta, the second letter of the Greek alphabet, and so forth. But the Greek letters run through Carina, Puppis, and Vela as if it were still one constellation.

The Constellations

Constellations are groupings of stars which form patterns that can be easily recognized and remembered, for example, Orion and the Big Dipper. Actually the stars of the majority of all constellations do not "belong together." Usually they are at greatly varying distances from the Earth and just happen to lie more or less in the same line of sight as seen from our solar system. But in a few cases the stars of a constellation are actually associated; most of the bright stars of the Big Dipper travel together and form what astronomers call an open cluster.

If you observe a planet, say Mars, for one complete revolution, you will see that it passes successively through twelve constellations. All planets can be observed only in these twelve constellations, which form the so-called Zodiac, and the Sun also moves through the signs of the Zodiac, though the Sun's apparent movement is actually caused by the movement of the Earth. The twelve signs of the Zodiac are listed elsewhere in this section.

Although the constellations are mainly due to the optical accident of line of sight and have no real significance, astronomers have retained them as reference areas. It is much easier to speak of a star in Orion than to give its geometrical position in the sky. During the Astronomical Congress of 1928 it was decided to have 88 recognized constellations. A description of their agreed-upon boundaries was published at Cambridge, England, in 1930, under the title *Atlas Céleste*.

The Auroras

The "northern lights" *(Aurora borealis)* as well as the "southern lights" *(Aurora australis)* are upper-atmosphere phenomena but of astronomical origin. The auroras center around the magnetic (not the geographical) poles of the Earth, which explains why, in the Western Hemisphere, they have been seen as far to the south as New Orleans or Florida while the equivalent latitude in the eastern hemisphere never sees an aurora. The northern magnetic pole happens to be in the Western Hemisphere.

The lower limit of an aurora is at about 50 miles. Upper limits have been estimated to be as high as 400 miles, but this figure is an estimate, not a measurement. Since about 1880 a connection between the auroras on Earth and the sun spots has been suspected and has gradually come to be accepted. It was said that the sun spots probably eject "particles" (later the word electrons was substituted) which on striking the Earth's atmosphere, cause the auroras. But this explanation suffered from certain difficulties. Sometimes a very large sun spot group on the Sun, with individual spots bigger than the Earth itself, would not cause an aurora. Moreover, even if a sun spot caused an aurora, the time that passed between the appearance of the one and the occurrence of the other was highly unpredictable.

In addition to these two theoretical difficulties there was a practical one. If an aurora was the result of Earth being hit by a stream of electrons from the Sun, the aurora should, of course, be "bipolar," meaning that it should appear near both the North and South Poles simultaneously. The practical difficulty here was that when the North Pole has winter and darkness, the South Pole has summer and bright daylight, so that an *aurora australis,* if there were one, would simply be invisible with the Sun shining in the southern sky at the same time.

This practical problem has been solved by means of an instrument especially developed for the International Geophysical Year. The answer was affirmative; auroras *are* bipolar. The other problem of the time lag is, in all probability, answered by the discovery of the Van Allen layer by artificial satellite *Explorer I*. The Van Allen layer is a double layer of charged sub-atomic particles around the Earth. The inner layer, with its center some 1,500 miles from the ground, reaches from about 40°N. to about 40°S. and does not touch the atmosphere. The outer layer, much larger and with its center several thousand miles from the ground, does touch the atmosphere in the vicinity of the magnetic poles.

It seems probable that the "leakage" of electrons from the Outer Van Allen layer causes the auroras. A new burst of electrons from the Sun seems to be caught in the outer layer first. Under the assumption that all electrons are first caught in the outer layer, the time lag can be understood. There has to be an "overflow" from the outer layer to produce an aurora.

The Atmosphere

Astronomically speaking, the presence of our atmosphere is deplorable. Though reasonably transparent to visible light, the atmosphere may absorb as much as 60 per cent of the visible and near-visible light. It is opaque to most other wavelengths, except certain fairly short radio waves. In addition to absorbing much light, our atmosphere bends light rays entering slantwise (for a given observer) so that the true position of a star not too high above the horizon is not what it seems to be. One effect is that we see the Sun above the horizon before it actually is. And the steady movement of the atmosphere causes the "twinkling" of the stars, which may be romantic but is a nuisance when it comes to observing. On "bad" nights the image of a star may jump out of the narrow field of vision of a telescope.

The composition of our atmosphere near the ground is 78 per cent nitrogen and 21 per cent oxygen, the remaining 1 per cent consisting of other gases, most of it argon. The composition stays the same to an altitude of at least 70 miles (except that higher up two impurities, carbon dioxide and water vapor, are missing) but the pressure drops very fast. At 18,000 feet half of the total mass of the atmosphere is below, and at 100,000 feet, 99 per cent of the mass of the atmosphere is below. The upper limit of the atmosphere is usually given as 120 miles; no definitive figure is possible, since there is no boundary line between the incredibly attenuated gases 120 miles up and space.

Astronomical Telescopes

Optical telescopes used in astronomy are of two basic kinds: refracting and reflecting. In the *refractor telescope,* a lens is used to collect light from a distant object and bring it to a focus. A second lens, the eyepiece, then magnifies the image which may be examined visually or photographed directly. The *reflector telescope* uses a concave mirror instead of a lens, which reflects the light rays back toward the upper end of the telescope where they are magnified and observed or photographed. Most large telescopes now being built are reflectors.

Radio telescopes are used to study radio waves coming from outside the Earth's atmosphere. The waves are gathered by an antenna or "dish," which is a parabolic reflecting surface made of metal or finely meshed wire. radio signals have been received from the Sun, Moon and planets, and from the center of our galaxy and other galaxies, and are the instruments by which the strange quasars and pulsars were recently discovered.

Notable Reflector Telescopes

Source: American Astronomical Society.

Size in inches	Observatory	Location	Size in inches	Observatory	Location
236*	USSR Academy of Sciences	Zelenchukskaya, USSR	120	Lick	Mount Hamilton, Calif.
200	Hale	Mount Palomar, Calif.	107	McDonald	Mount Locke, Tex.
158	Kitt Peak National	Tucson, Ariz.	102	Crimean Astrophysical	Nauchny, USSR
158*	Inter-American	Cerro Tololo, Chile	101*	Carnegie Southern	Cerro Las Campanas, Chile
150*	Australian National	Siding Spring Mt., Australia	100	Hale	Mount Wilson, Calif.
142*	European Southern	Cerro La Silla, Chile	98	Royal Greenwich	Herstmonceux, England
140*	French, Canadian, Hawaiian	Mauna Loa, Hawaii	90	Steward	Tucson, Ariz.

* Under construction.

Some Radio Telescopes

Diameter in feet	Observatory	Location	Diameter in feet	Observatory	Location
	National Radio Astronomy Observatory[1]	Socorro, New Mexico	210	Australian National Radio Astronomy	New South Wales, Australia
9842[2]	Solar Physics	Culgoora, Australia	210	NASA/JPL Goldstone Deep Space Communications Complex	Goldstone, Calif.
5249[3]	Westerbork Radio	Hooghalen, Netherlands			
1900[4]	U.S.S.R. Academy of Sciences	Caucasus, U.S.S.R.	341/70	Ohio State-Ohio Wesleyan Radio	Delaware, Ohio
1001	Arecibo	Arecibo, Puerto Rico	150	Stanford Center for Radar Astronomy	Stanford, Calif.
3000/397	Mullard Radio Astronomy	Cambridge, England	150	Sagamore Hill Radio	Hamilton, Mass.
328	Effelsberg Radiotelescope	Bonn, West Germany	150	Algonquin Radio	Lake Traverse, Canada
			140	National Radio Astronomy	Green Bank, W. Va.
300	National Radio Astronomy	Green Bank, W. Va.			
656/131	Paris-Meudon	Nancy, France	130	Owens Valley Radio	Big Pine, Calif.
249	Nuffield Radio Astronomy	Jodrell Bank, Macclesfield, England	118	Haystack	Tyngsboro, Mass.

[1] Symmetrical Y, each arm 7 miles long and consisting of nine 25-meter telescopes. [2] Diameter of 96-telescope circular array. [3] Length of 12-telescope array. [4] Under construction.

The Calendar

History of the Calendar

The purpose of a calendar is to reckon time in advance, to show how many days have to elapse until a certain event takes place—the harvest, a religious festival, or whatever. The earliest calendars, naturally, were crude, and they must have been strongly influenced by the geographical location of the people who made them. In the Scandinavian countries, for example, where the seasons are pronounced, the concept of the year was determined by the seasons, specifically by the end of winter. The Norsemen, before becoming Christians, are said to have had a calendar consisting of ten months of 30 days each; for the remainder of the year they stayed indoors.

But in warmer countries, where the seasons are less pronounced, the Moon became the basic unit for time reckoning; an old Jewish book actually makes the statement that "the Moon was created for the counting of the days." All the oldest calendars of which we have actual information were lunar calendars, based on the time interval from one new moon to the next—a so-called "lunation." But even in a warm climate there are annual events

which pay no attention to the phases of the Moon. In some areas it was a rainy season; in Egypt it was the annual flooding of the Nile. It was, therefore, necessary to regulate daily life and religious festivals by lunations, but to take care of the annual event in some manner.

The calendar of the Assyrians was based on the phases of the Moon. The month began with the first appearance of the lunar crescent, and since this can best be observed in the evening, the day began with sunset. They knew that a lunation was 29½ days long, so their lunar year had a duration of 354 days, falling eleven days short of the solar year.[1] After three years such a lunar calendar would be off by 33 days, or more than one lunation. We know that the Assyrians added an extra month from time to time, but we do not know whether they had developed a special rule for doing so or whether the priests proclaimed the necessity for

[1] The correct figures are: lunation: 29 d., 12 h., 44 m., 2.8 sec. (29.530585 days); solar year: 365 d., 5 h., 48 m., 46 sec. (365.242216 days); 12 lunations: 354 d., 8 h., 48 m., 34 sec. (354.3671 days).

Drift of the Vernal Equinox in the Julian Calendar

Date	Julian year	Date	Julian year	Date	Julian year
March 21	325 A.D.	March 17	837 A.D.	March 13	1349 A.D.
March 20	453 A.D.	March 16	965 A.D.	March 12	1477 A.D.
March 19	581 A.D.	March 15	1093 A.D.	March 11	1605 A.D.
March 18	709 A.D.	March 14	1221 A.D.		

an extra month from observation. If they made every third year a year of 13 lunations, their three-year period would cover 1,091½ days (using their value of 29½ days for one lunation), or just about four days too short. In one century this mistake would add up to 133 days by their reckoning (in reality closer to 134 days), requiring four extra lunations per century.

We now know that an eight-year period, consisting of five years with 12 months and three years with 13 months would lead to a difference of only 20 days per century, but we do not know whether such a calendar was actually used.

The best approximation that was possible in antiquity was a 19-year period, with seven of these 19 years having 13 months. This means that the period contained 235 months. This, still using the old value for a lunation, made a total of 6,932½ days, while 19 solar years added up to 6,939.7 days, a difference of just one week per period and about five weeks per century. Even the 19-year period required constant adjustment, but it was the period which became the basis of the religious calendar of the Jews. The Arabs used the same calendar at first, but Mohammed forbade shifting from 12 months to 13 months, so that the Mohammedan religious calendar, even today, has a lunar year of 354 days. As a result the Mohammedan religious festivals run through all the seasons of the year three times per century.

The Egyptians had a traditional calendar with 12 months of 30 days each. At one time they added five extra days at the end of every year. These turned into a five-day festival because it was thought to be unlucky to work during that time.

When Rome emerged as a world power, the difficulties of making a calendar were well known, but the Romans complicated their lives because of their superstition that even numbers were unlucky. Hence their months were 29 or 31 days long, with the exception of February, which had 28 days. However, four months of 31 days, seven months of 29 days, and one month of 28 days added up to only 355 days. Therefore, the Romans invented an extra month called Mercedonius of 22 or 23 days. It was added every second year.

Even with Mercedonius, the Roman calendar was so far off that Caesar, advised by the astronomer Sosigenes, ordered a sweeping reform in 45 B.C. One year, made 445 days long by imperial decree, brought the calendar back in step with the seasons. Then the solar year (with the value of 365 days and 6 hours) was made the basis of the calendar. The months were 30 or 31 days in length, and to take care of the six hours, every fourth year was made a 366-day year. Moreover, Caesar decreed, the year began with the first of January, not with the vernal equinox in late March.

This was the Julian calendar, named after Julius Caesar. It is still the calendar of the Eastern Orthodox churches.

However, the year is 11½ minutes shorter than the figure written into Caesar's calendar by Sosigenes, and after a number of centuries, even 11½ minutes add up, as the table above shows.

While Caesar could decree that the vernal equinox should not be used as the first day of the new year, the vernal equinox is still a fact of Nature which could not be disregarded. One of the first (as far as we know) to become alarmed about this was Roger Bacon. He sent a memorandum to Pope Clement IV, who apparently was not impressed. But Pope Sixtus IV (reigned 1471 to 1484) decided that another reform was needed and called the German astronomer Regiomontanus to Rome to advise him. Regiomontanus arrived in 1475, but one year later he died in an epidemic, one of the recurrent outbreaks of the plague. The Pope himself survived, but his reform plans died with Regiomontanus.

Less than a hundred years later, in 1545, the Council of Trent authorized the then Pope, Gregory XIII, to reform the calendar once more. Most of the mathematical and astronomical work was done by Father Christopher Clavius, S.J. The immediate correction, advised by Father Clavius and ordered by Pope Gregory XIII, was that Thursday, October 4, 1582, was to be the last day of the Julian calendar. The next day was Friday, with the date of October 15. For long-range accuracy, a formula suggested by the Vatican librarian Aloysius Giglio (latinized into Lilius) was adopted: every fourth year is a leap year *unless* it is a century year like 1700 or 1800. Century years can be leap years *only* when they are divisible by 400 (e.g., 1600). This rule eliminates three leap years in four centuries, making the calendar sufficiently correct for all ordinary purposes.

Unfortunately, all the Protestant princes in 1582 chose to ignore the papal bull; they continued with the Julian calendar. It was not until 1698 that the German professor Erhard Weigel persuaded the Protestant rulers of Germany and of the Netherlands to change to the new calendar. In England the shift took place in 1752, and in Russia it needed the revolution to introduce the Gregorian calendar in 1918.

The average year of the Gregorian calendar, in spite of the leap year rule, is about 26 seconds longer than the earth's orbital period. But this discrepancy will need 3,323 years to build up to a single day.

Modern proposals for calendar reform do not aim at a "better" calendar, but at one which is more convenient to use, especially for commercial purposes. A 365-day year cannot be divided into equal halves or quarters; the number of days per month is haphazard; the months begin or end in the middle of a week; a holiday fixed by date (e.g., the Fourth of July) will wander through a week; a holiday fixed in another manner (e.g., Easter) can fall on thirty-five possible dates. The Gregorian calendar, admittedly, keeps the calendar dates in

The 13-Month Calendar of Auguste Comte

Monday	Tuesday	Wednesday	Thursday	Friday	Saturday	Sunday
1	2	3	4	5	6	7
8	9	10	11	12	13	14
15	16	17	18	19	20	21
22	23	24	25	26	27	28

reasonable unison with astronomical events, but it still is full of minor annoyances. Moreover, you need a calendar every year to look up dates; an ideal calendar should be one that you can memorize for one year and that is valid for all other years, too

In 1834 an Italian priest, Marco Mastrofini, suggested taking one day out of every year. It would be made a holiday and *not* be given the name of a weekday. That would make every year begin with January 1 as a Sunday. The leap-year day would be treated the same way, so that in leap years there would be two unnamed holidays at the end of the year.

About a decade later the philosopher Auguste Comte also suggested a 364-day calendar with an extra day, which he called Year Day. He intended to do away with the uneven months and suggested 13 months of 28 days each. This would result in a scheme valid for every one of the 13 months, as shown in the table at the top of this page.

No matter what could be said in favor of such a scheme, and Comte said it very well, it was doomed to failure. Not only did it offend tradition and the practices of *all* religions, it also ran into the stubborn wall of superstitious fear of the number thirteen.

In 1900 Professor L. A. Grosclaude offered a new scheme for a calendar. It later became known as the World Calendar, tirelessly advocated by Miss Elisabeth Achelis. It also contains the nameless extra holiday, but it does produce a very simple calendar. constructed with a quarter year as the basic unit. In each quarter the first month begins with a Sunday and has 31 days; the second and third months have 30 days each and the last day of the third month is a Saturday, so that the next quarter begins with a Sunday again. The first month of the quarter therefore has five Sundays and the other two months have four each, so that every month, all the year round, has 26 weekdays. The total number of days per quarter is 91, and the total number of weeks per quarter is 13.

In such a calendar each date in the year could be compared (say for sales volume) with the corresponding date in every other year. And the calendar could be memorized.

But in spite of much publicity and favorable reactions from many groups and even whole countries, the World Calendar has not been adopted.

Time and Calendar

The two natural cycles on which time measurements are based are the year and the day. The year is defined as the time required for the Earth to complete one revolution around the Sun, while the day is the time required for the Earth to complete one turn upon its axis. Unfortunately the Earth needs 365 days plus about six hours to go around the Sun once, so that the year does not consist of so and so many days; the fractional day has to be taken care of by an extra day every fourth year.

But because the Earth, while turning upon its axis, also moves around the Sun there are two kinds of days. A day may be defined as the interval between the highest point of the Sun in the sky on two successive days. This, averaged out over the year, produces the customary 24-hour day. But one might also define a day as the time interval between the moments when a certain point in the sky, say a conveniently located star, is directly overhead. This is called

Sidereal time. Astronomers use a point which they call the "vernal equinox" for the actual determination. Such a sidereal day is somewhat shorter than the "solar day," namely by about 3 minutes and 56 seconds of so-called "mean solar time."

Apparent solar time is the time based directly on the Sun's position in the sky. In ordinary life the day runs from midnight to midnight. It begins when the Sun is invisible by being 12 hours from its zenith. Astronomers use the so-called "Julian Day," which runs from noon to noon; the concept was invented by the astronomer, Joseph Scaliger, who named it after his father Julius. To avoid the problems caused by leap-year days and so forth, Scaliger picked a conveniently remote date in the past and suggested just counting days without regard to weeks, months and years. The Julian Day 2,440,225.5 is January 1, 1969. The reason for having the Julian Day run from noon to noon is the practical one that astronomical observations usually extend across the midnight hour, which would require a change in date (or in the Julian Day number) if the astronomical day, like the civil day, ran from midnight to midnight.

Mean solar time, rather than apparent solar time, is what is actually used most of the time. The mean solar time is based on the position of a

(Continued on page 374.)

The Basic Unit of the World Calendar

Days	First month					Second month					Third month				
Sunday	1	8	15	22	29	—	5	12	19	26	—	3	10	17	24
Monday	2	9	16	23	30	—	6	13	20	27	—	4	11	18	25
Tuesday	3	10	17	24	31	—	7	14	21	28	—	5	12	19	26
Wednesday	4	11	18	25	—	1	8	15	22	29	—	6	13	20	27
Thursday	5	12	19	26	—	2	9	16	23	30	—	7	14	21	28
Friday	6	13	20	27	—	3	10	17	24	—	1	8	15	22	29
Saturday	7	14	21	28	—	4	11	18	25	—	2	9	16	23	30

PERPETUAL CALENDAR

1800	4	1844	9	1888	8	1932	13	1976	12	2020	11
1801	5	1845	4	1889	3	1933	1	1977	7	2021	6
1802	6	1846	5	1890	4	1934	2	1978	1	2022	7
1803	7	1847	6	1891	5	1935	3	1979	2	2023	1
1804	8	1848	14	1892	13	1936	11	1980	10	2024	9
1805	3	1849	2	1893	1	1937	6	1981	5	2025	4
1806	4	1850	3	1894	2	1938	7	1982	6	2026	5
1807	5	1851	4	1895	3	1939	1	1983	7	2027	6
1808	13	1852	12	1896	11	1940	9	1984	8	2028	14
1809	1	1853	7	1897	6	1941	4	1985	3	2029	2
1810	2	1854	1	1898	7	1942	5	1986	4	2030	3
1811	3	1855	2	1899	1	1943	6	1987	5	2031	4
1812	11	1856	10	1900	2	1944	14	1988	13	2032	12
1813	6	1857	5	1901	3	1945	2	1989	1	2033	7
1814	7	1858	6	1902	4	1946	3	1990	2	2034	1
1815	1	1859	7	1903	5	1947	4	1991	3	2035	2
1816	9	1860	8	1904	13	1948	12	1992	11	2036	10
1817	4	1861	3	1905	1	1949	7	1993	6	2037	5
1818	5	1862	4	1906	2	1950	1	1994	7	2038	6
1819	6	1863	5	1907	3	1951	2	1995	1	2039	7
1820	14	1864	13	1908	11	1952	10	1996	9	2040	8
1821	2	1865	1	1909	6	1953	5	1997	4	2041	3
1822	3	1866	2	1910	7	1954	6	1998	5	2042	4
1823	4	1867	3	1911	1	1955	7	1999	6	2043	5
1824	12	1868	11	1912	9	1956	8	2000	14	2044	13
1825	7	1869	6	1913	4	1957	3	2001	2	2045	1
1826	1	1870	7	1914	5	1958	4	2002	3	2046	2
1827	2	1871	1	1915	6	1959	5	2003	4	2047	3
1828	10	1872	9	1916	14	1960	13	2004	12	2048	11
1829	5	1873	4	1917	2	1961	1	2005	7	2049	6
1830	6	1874	5	1918	3	1962	2	2006	1	2050	7
1831	7	1875	6	1919	4	1963	3	2007	2	2051	1
1832	8	1876	14	1920	12	1964	11	2008	10	2052	9
1833	3	1877	2	1921	7	1965	6	2009	5	2053	4
1834	4	1878	3	1922	1	1966	7	2010	6	2054	5
1835	5	1879	4	1923	2	1967	1	2011	7	2055	6
1836	13	1880	12	1924	10	1968	9	2012	8	2056	14
1837	1	1881	7	1925	5	1969	4	2013	3	2057	2
1838	2	1882	1	1926	6	1970	5	2014	4	2058	3
1839	3	1883	2	1927	7	1971	6	2015	5	2059	4
1840	11	1884	10	1928	8	1972	14	2016	13	2060	12
1841	6	1885	5	1929	3	1973	2	2017	1	2061	7
1842	7	1886	6	1930	4	1974	3	2018	2	2062	1
1843	1	1887	7	1931	5	1975	4	2019	3	2063	2

DIRECTIONS: The number given with each year in the key above is number of calendar to use for that year

7

```
      JANUARY              FEBRUARY               MARCH                 APRIL
S  M  T  W  T  F  S    S  M  T  W  T  F  S    S  M  T  W  T  F  S    S  M  T  W  T  F  S
            1                1  2  3  4  5          1  2  3  4  5                      1  2
2-3 4  5  6  7  8     6  7  8  9 10 11 12     6  7  8  9 10 11 12     3  4  5  6  7  8  9
9 10 11 12 13 14 15   13 14 15 16 17 18 19   13 14 15 16 17 18 19   10 11 12 13 14 15 16
16 17 18 19 20 21 22  20 21 22 23 24 25 26   20 21 22 23 24 25 26   17 18 19 20 21 22 23
23 24 25 26 27 28 29  27 28                  27 28 29 30 31         24 25 26 27 28 29 30
30 31

        MAY                  JUNE                  JULY                 AUGUST
S  M  T  W  T  F  S    S  M  T  W  T  F  S    S  M  T  W  T  F  S    S  M  T  W  T  F  S
1  2  3  4  5  6  7             1  2  3  4                   1  2       1  2  3  4  5  6
8  9 10 11 12 13 14   5  6  7  8  9 10 11    3  4  5  6  7  8  9     7  8  9 10 11 12 13
15 16 17 18 19 20 21  12 13 14 15 16 17 18   10 11 12 13 14 15 16   14 15 16 17 18 19 20
22 23 24 25 26 27 28  19 20 21 22 23 24 25   17 18 19 20 21 22 23   21 22 23 24 25 26 27
29 30 31              26 27 28 29 30         24 25 26 27 28 29 30   28 29 30 31
                                             31

      SEPTEMBER              OCTOBER              NOVEMBER              DECEMBER
S  M  T  W  T  F  S    S  M  T  W  T  F  S    S  M  T  W  T  F  S    S  M  T  W  T  F  S
            1  2  3                   1                1  2  3  4  5                1  2  3
4  5  6  7  8  9 10   2  3  4  5  6  7  8    6  7  8  9 10 11 12     4  5  6  7  8  9 10
11 12 13 14 15 16 17  9 10 11 12 13 14 15   13 14 15 16 17 18 19   11 12 13 14 15 16 17
18 19 20 21 22 23 24  16 17 18 19 20 21 22  20 21 22 23 24 25 26   18 19 20 21 22 23 24
25 26 27 28 29 30     23 24 25 26 27 28 29  27 28 29 30            25 26 27 28 29 30 31
                      30 31
```

8

```
      JANUARY              FEBRUARY               MARCH                 APRIL
S  M  T  W  T  F  S    S  M  T  W  T  F  S    S  M  T  W  T  F  S    S  M  T  W  T  F  S
1  2  3  4  5  6  7          1  2  3  4                1  2  3  4                1  2  3
8  9 10 11 12 13 14   5  6  7  8  9 10 11    4  5  6  7  8  9 10    4  5  6  7  8  9 10
15 16 17 18 19 20 21  12 13 14 15 16 17 18   11 12 13 14 15 16 17   11 12 13 14 15 16 17
22 23 24 25 26 27 28  19 20 21 22 23 24 25   18 19 20 21 22 23 24   18 19 20 21 22 23 24
29 30 31              26 27 28 29            25 26 27 28 29 30 31   25 26 27 28 29 30

        MAY                  JUNE                  JULY                 AUGUST
S  M  T  W  T  F  S    S  M  T  W  T  F  S    S  M  T  W  T  F  S    S  M  T  W  T  F  S
      1  2  3  4  5                   1  2   1  2  3  4  5  6  7             1  2  3  4
6  7  8  9 10 11 12   3  4  5  6  7  8  9    8  9 10 11 12 13 14    5  6  7  8  9 10 11
13 14 15 16 17 18 19  10 11 12 13 14 15 16   15 16 17 18 19 20 21   12 13 14 15 16 17 18
20 21 22 23 24 25 26  17 18 19 20 21 22 23   22 23 24 25 26 27 28   19 20 21 22 23 24 25
27 28 29 30 31        24 25 26 27 28 29 30   29 30 31               26 27 28 29 30 31

      SEPTEMBER              OCTOBER              NOVEMBER              DECEMBER
S  M  T  W  T  F  S    S  M  T  W  T  F  S    S  M  T  W  T  F  S    S  M  T  W  T  F  S
                  1          1  2  3  4  5                1  2  3                      1
2  3  4  5  6  7  8   7  8  9 10 11 12 13    4  5  6  7  8  9 10    2  3  4  5  6  7  8
9 10 11 12 13 14 15   14 15 16 17 18 19 20   11 12 13 14 15 16 17   9 10 11 12 13 14 15
16 17 18 19 20 21 22  21 22 23 24 25 26 27   18 19 20 21 22 23 24   16 17 18 19 20 21 22
23 24 25 26 27 28 29  28 29 30 31            25 26 27 28 29 30      23 24 25 26 27 28 29
30                                                                  30 31
```

9

```
      JANUARY              FEBRUARY               MARCH                 APRIL
S  M  T  W  T  F  S    S  M  T  W  T  F  S    S  M  T  W  T  F  S    S  M  T  W  T  F  S
1  2  3  4  5  6                1  2  3                   1  2  3    1  2  3  4  5  6
7  8  9 10 11 12 13   4  5  6  7  8  9 10    4  5  6  7  8  9 10    7  8  9 10 11 12 13
14 15 16 17 18 19 20  11 12 13 14 15 16 17   11 12 13 14 15 16 17   14 15 16 17 18 19 20
21 22 23 24 25 26 27  18 19 20 21 22 23 24   18 19 20 21 22 23 24   21 22 23 24 25 26 27
28 29 30 31           25 26 27 28            25 26 27 28 29 30 31   28 29 30

        MAY                  JUNE                  JULY                 AUGUST
S  M  T  W  T  F  S    S  M  T  W  T  F  S    S  M  T  W  T  F  S    S  M  T  W  T  F  S
         1  2  3  4                      1   1  2  3  4  5  6                   1  2  3
5  6  7  8  9 10 11   2  3  4  5  6  7  8    7  8  9 10 11 12 13    4  5  6  7  8  9 10
12 13 14 15 16 17 18  9 10 11 12 13 14 15   14 15 16 17 18 19 20   11 12 13 14 15 16 17
19 20 21 22 23 24 25  16 17 18 19 20 21 22   21 22 23 24 25 26 27   18 19 20 21 22 23 24
26 27 28 29 30 31     23 24 25 26 27 28 29   28 29 30 31           25 26 27 28 29 30 31
                      30

      SEPTEMBER              OCTOBER              NOVEMBER              DECEMBER
S  M  T  W  T  F  S    S  M  T  W  T  F  S    S  M  T  W  T  F  S    S  M  T  W  T  F  S
1  2  3  4  5  6  7             1  2  3  4                1  2      1  2  3  4  5  6  7
8  9 10 11 12 13 14   6  7  8  9 10 11 12    3  4  5  6  7  8  9    8  9 10 11 12 13 14
15 16 17 18 19 20 21  13 14 15 16 17 18 19   10 11 12 13 14 15 16   15 16 17 18 19 20 21
22 23 24 25 26 27 28  20 21 22 23 24 25 26   17 18 19 20 21 22 23   22 23 24 25 26 27 28
29 30                 27 28 29 30 31         24 25 26 27 28 29 30   29 30 31
```

10

```
      JANUARY              FEBRUARY               MARCH                 APRIL
S  M  T  W  T  F  S    S  M  T  W  T  F  S    S  M  T  W  T  F  S    S  M  T  W  T  F  S
         1  2  3  4                1  2                   1  2  3                1  2  3
6  7  8  9 10 11 12   3  4  5  6  7  8  9    2  3  4  5  6  7  8    4  5  6  7  8  9 10
13 14 15 16 17 18 19  10 11 12 13 14 15 16   9 10 11 12 13 14 15   11 12 13 14 15 16 17
20 21 22 23 24 25 26  17 18 19 20 21 22 23   16 17 18 19 20 21 22   18 19 20 21 22 23 24
27 28 29 30 31        24 25 26 27 28         23 24 25 26 27 28 29   25 26 27 28 29 30
                                             30 31

        MAY                  JUNE                  JULY                 AUGUST
S  M  T  W  T  F  S    S  M  T  W  T  F  S    S  M  T  W  T  F  S    S  M  T  W  T  F  S
            1  2  3   1  2  3  4  5  6  7             1  2  3  4                   1  2
4  5  6  7  8  9 10   8  9 10 11 12 13 14    6  7  8  9 10 11 12    3  4  5  6  7  8  9
11 12 13 14 15 16 17  15 16 17 18 19 20 21   13 14 15 16 17 18 19   10 11 12 13 14 15 16
18 19 20 21 22 23 24  22 23 24 25 26 27 28   20 21 22 23 24 25 26   17 18 19 20 21 22 23
25 26 27 28 29 30 31  29 30                  27 28 29 30 31         24 25 26 27 28 29 30
                                                                    31

      SEPTEMBER              OCTOBER              NOVEMBER              DECEMBER
S  M  T  W  T  F  S    S  M  T  W  T  F  S    S  M  T  W  T  F  S    S  M  T  W  T  F  S
      1  2  3  4  5             1  2  3  4                      1    1  2  3  4  5  6
7  8  9 10 11 12 13   5  6  7  8  9 10 11    2  3  4  5  6  7  8    7  8  9 10 11 12 13
14 15 16 17 18 19 20  12 13 14 15 16 17 18   9 10 11 12 13 14 15   14 15 16 17 18 19 20
21 22 23 24 25 26 27  19 20 21 22 23 24 25   16 17 18 19 20 21 22   21 22 23 24 25 26 27
28 29 30              26 27 28 29 30 31       23 24 25 26 27 28 29   28 29 30 31
                                             30
```

11

```
      JANUARY              FEBRUARY               MARCH                 APRIL
S  M  T  W  T  F  S    S  M  T  W  T  F  S    S  M  T  W  T  F  S    S  M  T  W  T  F  S
         1  2  3  4                      1   1  2  3  4  5  6  7                1  2  3  4
5  6  7  8  9 10 11   2  3  4  5  6  7  8    8  9 10 11 12 13 14    5  6  7  8  9 10 11
12 13 14 15 16 17 18  9 10 11 12 13 14 15   15 16 17 18 19 20 21   12 13 14 15 16 17 18
19 20 21 22 23 24 25  16 17 18 19 20 21 22   22 23 24 25 26 27 28   19 20 21 22 23 24 25
26 27 28 29 30 31     23 24 25 26 27 28 29   29 30 31               26 27 28 29 30

        MAY                  JUNE                  JULY                 AUGUST
S  M  T  W  T  F  S    S  M  T  W  T  F  S    S  M  T  W  T  F  S    S  M  T  W  T  F  S
                  1  2 1  2  3  4  5  6                1  2  3  4             1
3  4  5  6  7  8  9   7  8  9 10 11 12 13    5  6  7  8  9 10 11    2  3  4  5  6  7  8
10 11 12 13 14 15 16  14 15 16 17 18 19 20   12 13 14 15 16 17 18   9 10 11 12 13 14 15
17 18 19 20 21 22 23  21 22 23 24 25 26 27   19 20 21 22 23 24 25   16 17 18 19 20 21 22
24 25 26 27 28 29 30  28 29 30               26 27 28 29 30 31      23 24 25 26 27 28 29
31                                                                  30 31

      SEPTEMBER              OCTOBER              NOVEMBER              DECEMBER
S  M  T  W  T  F  S    S  M  T  W  T  F  S    S  M  T  W  T  F  S    S  M  T  W  T  F  S
      1  2  3  4  5                1  2  3   1  2  3  4  5  6  7                1  2  3  4  5
6  7  8  9 10 11 12   4  5  6  7  8  9 10    8  9 10 11 12 13 14    6  7  8  9 10 11 12
13 14 15 16 17 18 19  11 12 13 14 15 16 17   15 16 17 18 19 20 21   13 14 15 16 17 18 19
20 21 22 23 24 25 26  18 19 20 21 22 23 24   22 23 24 25 26 27 28   20 21 22 23 24 25 26
27 28 29 30           25 26 27 28 29 30 31   29 30                  27 28 29 30 31
```

12

```
      JANUARY              FEBRUARY               MARCH                 APRIL
S  M  T  W  T  F  S    S  M  T  W  T  F  S    S  M  T  W  T  F  S    S  M  T  W  T  F  S
               1  2  3 1  2  3  4  5  6  7   1  2  3  4  5  6  7                1  2  3
4  5  6  7  8  9 10   8  9 10 11 12 13 14    8  9 10 11 12 13 14    4  5  6  7  8  9 10
11 12 13 14 15 16 17  15 16 17 18 19 20 21   15 16 17 18 19 20 21   11 12 13 14 15 16 17
18 19 20 21 22 23 24  22 23 24 25 26 27 28   22 23 24 25 26 27 28   18 19 20 21 22 23 24
25 26 27 28 29 30 31  29                     29 30 31               25 26 27 28 29 30

        MAY                  JUNE                  JULY                 AUGUST
S  M  T  W  T  F  S    S  M  T  W  T  F  S    S  M  T  W  T  F  S    S  M  T  W  T  F  S
                  1             1  2  3  4  5          1  2  3    1  2  3  4  5  6  7
2  3  4  5  6  7  8   6  7  8  9 10 11 12    4  5  6  7  8  9 10    8  9 10 11 12 13 14
9 10 11 12 13 14 15   13 14 15 16 17 18 19   11 12 13 14 15 16 17   15 16 17 18 19 20 21
16 17 18 19 20 21 22  20 21 22 23 24 25 26   18 19 20 21 22 23 24   22 23 24 25 26 27 28
23 24 25 26 27 28 29  27 28 29 30            25 26 27 28 29 30 31   29 30 31
30 31

      SEPTEMBER              OCTOBER              NOVEMBER              DECEMBER
S  M  T  W  T  F  S    S  M  T  W  T  F  S    S  M  T  W  T  F  S    S  M  T  W  T  F  S
         1  2  3  4                1  2      1  2  3  4  5  6                1  2  3  4
5  6  7  8  9 10 11   3  4  5  6  7  8  9    7  8  9 10 11 12 13    5  6  7  8  9 10 11
12 13 14 15 16 17 18  10 11 12 13 14 15 16   14 15 16 17 18 19 20   12 13 14 15 16 17 18
19 20 21 22 23 24 25  17 18 19 20 21 22 23   21 22 23 24 25 26 27   19 20 21 22 23 24 25
26 27 28 29 30        24 25 26 27 28 29 30   28 29 30               26 27 28 29 30 31
                      31
```

13

```
      JANUARY              FEBRUARY               MARCH                 APRIL
S  M  T  W  T  F  S    S  M  T  W  T  F  S    S  M  T  W  T  F  S    S  M  T  W  T  F  S
                  1  2 1  2  3  4  5  6      1  2  3  4  5  6                      1  2
3  4  5  6  7  8  9   7  8  9 10 11 12 13    7  8  9 10 11 12 13    3  4  5  6  7  8  9
10 11 12 13 14 15 16  14 15 16 17 18 19 20   14 15 16 17 18 19 20   10 11 12 13 14 15 16
17 18 19 20 21 22 23  21 22 23 24 25 26 27   21 22 23 24 25 26 27   17 18 19 20 21 22 23
24 25 26 27 28 29 30  28 29                  28 29 30 31            24 25 26 27 28 29 30
31

        MAY                  JUNE                  JULY                 AUGUST
S  M  T  W  T  F  S    S  M  T  W  T  F  S    S  M  T  W  T  F  S    S  M  T  W  T  F  S
1  2  3  4  5  6  7             1  2  3  4                   1  2   1  2  3  4  5  6
8  9 10 11 12 13 14   5  6  7  8  9 10 11    3  4  5  6  7  8  9    7  8  9 10 11 12 13
15 16 17 18 19 20 21  12 13 14 15 16 17 18   10 11 12 13 14 15 16   14 15 16 17 18 19 20
22 23 24 25 26 27 28  19 20 21 22 23 24 25   17 18 19 20 21 22 23   21 22 23 24 25 26 27
29 30 31              26 27 28 29 30         24 25 26 27 28 29 30   28 29 30 31
                                             31

      SEPTEMBER              OCTOBER              NOVEMBER              DECEMBER
S  M  T  W  T  F  S    S  M  T  W  T  F  S    S  M  T  W  T  F  S    S  M  T  W  T  F  S
            1  2  3                   1                1  2  3  4  5                1  2  3
4  5  6  7  8  9 10   2  3  4  5  6  7  8    6  7  8  9 10 11 12    4  5  6  7  8  9 10
11 12 13 14 15 16 17  9 10 11 12 13 14 15   13 14 15 16 17 18 19   11 12 13 14 15 16 17
18 19 20 21 22 23 24  16 17 18 19 20 21 22  20 21 22 23 24 25 26   18 19 20 21 22 23 24
25 26 27 28 29 30     23 24 25 26 27 28 29  27 28 29 30            25 26 27 28 29 30 31
                      30 31
```

14

```
      JANUARY              FEBRUARY               MARCH                 APRIL
S  M  T  W  T  F  S    S  M  T  W  T  F  S    S  M  T  W  T  F  S    S  M  T  W  T  F  S
1                           1  2  3  4  5          1  2  3  4  5                      1
2  3  4  5  6  7  8   6  7  8  9 10 11 12     6  7  8  9 10 11 12    2  3  4  5  6  7  8
9 10 11 12 13 14 15   13 14 15 16 17 18 19   13 14 15 16 17 18 19   9 10 11 12 13 14 15
16 17 18 19 20 21 22  20 21 22 23 24 25 26   20 21 22 23 24 25 26   16 17 18 19 20 21 22
23 24 25 26 27 28 29  27 28                  27 28 29 30 31         23 24 25 26 27 28 29
30 31                                                               30

        MAY                  JUNE                  JULY                 AUGUST
S  M  T  W  T  F  S    S  M  T  W  T  F  S    S  M  T  W  T  F  S    S  M  T  W  T  F  S
      1  2  3  4  5                1  2  3                   1  2       1  2  3  4  5  6
7  8  9 10 11 12 13   4  5  6  7  8  9 10    3  4  5  6  7  8  9    7  8  9 10 11 12 13
14 15 16 17 18 19 20  11 12 13 14 15 16 17   10 11 12 13 14 15 16   14 15 16 17 18 19 20
21 22 23 24 25 26 27  18 19 20 21 22 23 24   17 18 19 20 21 22 23   21 22 23 24 25 26 27
28 29 30 31           25 26 27 28 29 30      24 25 26 27 28 29 30   28 29 30 31
                                             31

      SEPTEMBER              OCTOBER              NOVEMBER              DECEMBER
S  M  T  W  T  F  S    S  M  T  W  T  F  S    S  M  T  W  T  F  S    S  M  T  W  T  F  S
               1  2                   1                1  2  3  4                1  2
3  4  5  6  7  8  9   2  3  4  5  6  7  8    5  6  7  8  9 10 11    3  4  5  6  7  8  9
10 11 12 13 14 15 16  9 10 11 12 13 14 15   12 13 14 15 16 17 18   10 11 12 13 14 15 16
17 18 19 20 21 22 23  16 17 18 19 20 21 22  19 20 21 22 23 24 25   17 18 19 20 21 22 23
24 25 26 27 28 29 30  23 24 25 26 27 28 29  26 27 28 29 30         24 25 26 27 28 29 30
                      30 31                                         31
```

1977

JANUARY

SUN.	MON.	TUE.	WED.	THU.	FRI.	SAT.
						1
2	3	4	5	6	7	8
9	10	11	12	13	14	15
16	17	18	19	20	21	22
23	24	25	26	27	28	29
30	31					

FEBRUARY

SUN.	MON.	TUE.	WED.	THU.	FRI.	SAT.
		1	2	3	4	5
6	7	8	9	10	11	12
13	14	15	16	17	18	19
20	21	22	23	24	25	26
27	28					

MARCH

SUN.	MON.	TUE.	WED.	THU.	FRI.	SAT.
		1	2	3	4	5
6	7	8	9	10	11	12
13	14	15	16	17	18	19
20	21	22	23	24	25	26
27	28	29	30	31		

APRIL

SUN.	MON.	TUE.	WED.	THU.	FRI.	SAT.
					1	2
3	4	5	6	7	8	9
10	11	12	13	14	15	16
17	18	19	20	21	22	23
24	25	26	27	28	29	30

1—New Year's Day
6—Epiphany

2—Groundhog Day
12—Lincoln's Birthday
14—St. Valentine's Day
21—Washington's Birthday
23—Ash Wednesday

4—Purim
17—St. Patrick's Day

3—Palm Sunday
3—1st Day of Passover
8—Good Friday
10—Easter

MAY

SUN.	MON.	TUE.	WED.	THU.	FRI.	SAT.
1	2	3	4	5	6	7
8	9	10	11	12	13	14
15	16	17	18	19	20	21
22	23	24	25	26	27	28
29	30	31				

JUNE

SUN.	MON.	TUE.	WED.	THU.	FRI.	SAT.
			1	2	3	4
5	6	7	8	9	10	11
12	13	14	15	16	17	18
19	20	21	22	23	24	25
26	27	28	29	30		

JULY

SUN.	MON.	TUE.	WED.	THU.	FRI.	SAT.
					1	2
3	4	5	6	7	8	9
10	11	12	13	14	15	16
17	18	19	20	21	22	23
24	25	26	27	28	29	30
31						

AUGUST

SUN.	MON.	TUE.	WED.	THU.	FRI.	SAT.
	1	2	3	4	5	6
7	8	9	10	11	12	13
14	15	16	17	18	19	20
21	22	23	24	25	26	27
28	29	30	31			

8—Mother's Day
19—Ascension Day
23—1st Day of Shabuoth
29—Pentecost
30—Memorial Day

5—Trinity Sunday
14—Flag Day
19—Father's Day

4—Independence Day

SEPTEMBER

SUN.	MON.	TUE.	WED.	THU.	FRI.	SAT.
				1	2	3
4	5	6	7	8	9	10
11	12	13	14	15	16	17
18	19	20	21	22	23	24
25	26	27	28	29	30	

OCTOBER

SUN.	MON.	TUE.	WED.	THU.	FRI.	SAT.
						1
2	3	4	5	6	7	8
9	10	11	12	13	14	15
16	17	18	19	20	21	22
23	24	25	26	27	28	29
30	31					

NOVEMBER

SUN.	MON.	TUE.	WED.	THU.	FRI.	SAT.
		1	2	3	4	5
6	7	8	9	10	11	12
13	14	15	16	17	18	19
20	21	22	23	24	25	26
27	28	29	30			

DECEMBER

SUN.	MON.	TUE.	WED.	THU.	FRI.	SAT.
				1	2	3
4	5	6	7	8	9	10
11	12	13	14	15	16	17
18	19	20	21	22	23	24
25	26	27	28	29	30	31

5—Labor Day
13—1st Day of Rosh Hashana
22—Yom Kippur
27—1st Day of Sukkoth

10—Columbus Day
24—Veterans Day
31—Halloween

1—All Saints' Day
8—Election Day
24—Thanksgiving Day
27—1st Sunday of Advent

5—1st Day of Hanukkah
25—Christmas

On June 24, 1968, a law was passed, effective in 1971, approving four Monday holidays for Federal employees—Washington's Birthday, Memorial Day, Columbus Day and Veterans' Day—to create 3-day weekends. Most states have since adopted the same days of observance as legal holidays. For exceptions, see detailed listing of legal holidays on pp. 436-37.

Seasons for the Northern Hemisphere, 1977
Eastern Standard Time

March 20, 12:43 P.M., sun enters sign of Aries; spring begins

June 21, 7:14 A.M., sun enters sign of Cancer; summer begins

Sept. 22, 10:30 P.M., sun enters sign of Libra; fall begins

Dec. 21, 6:24 P.M., sun enters sign of Capricorn; winter begins

For additional information
SEE INDEX UNDER:

CALENDAR, for 1976 and 1978 Calendars

HOLIDAYS, for Religious Holidays

ASTRONOMY, for General Information

1976

JANUARY	FEBRUARY	MARCH	APRIL
S M T W T F S - - - - 1 2 3 4 5 6 7 8 9 10 11 12 13 14 15 16 17 18 19 20 21 22 23 24 25 26 27 28 29 30 31	S M T W T F S 1 2 3 4 5 6 7 8 9 10 11 12 13 14 15 16 17 18 19 20 21 22 23 24 25 26 27 28 29	S M T W T F S - 1 2 3 4 5 6 7 8 9 10 11 12 13 14 15 16 17 18 19 20 21 22 23 24 25 26 27 28 29 30 31	S M T W T F S - - - - 1 2 3 4 5 6 7 8 9 10 11 12 13 14 15 16 17 18 19 20 21 22 23 24 25 26 27 28 29 30

MAY	JUNE	JULY	AUGUST
S M T W T F S - - - - - - 1 2 3 4 5 6 7 8 9 10 11 12 13 14 15 16 17 18 19 20 21 22 23 24 25 26 27 28 29 30 31	S M T W T F S - - 1 2 3 4 5 6 7 8 9 10 11 12 13 14 15 16 17 18 19 20 21 22 23 24 25 26 27 28 29 30	S M T W T F S - - - - 1 2 3 4 5 6 7 8 9 10 11 12 13 14 15 16 17 18 19 20 21 22 23 24 25 26 27 28 29 30 31	S M T W T F S 1 2 3 4 5 6 7 8 9 10 11 12 13 14 15 16 17 18 19 20 21 22 23 24 25 26 27 28 29 30 31

SEPTEMBER	OCTOBER	NOVEMBER	DECEMBER
S M T W T F S - - - 1 2 3 4 5 6 7 8 9 10 11 12 13 14 15 16 17 18 19 20 21 22 23 24 25 26 27 28 29 30	S M T W T F S - - - - - 1 2 3 4 5 6 7 8 9 10 11 12 13 14 15 16 17 18 19 20 21 22 23 24 25 26 27 28 29 30 31	S M T W T F S - 1 2 3 4 5 6 7 8 9 10 11 12 13 14 15 16 17 18 19 20 21 22 23 24 25 26 27 28 29 30	S M T W T F S - - - 1 2 3 4 5 6 7 8 9 10 11 12 13 14 15 16 17 18 19 20 21 22 23 24 25 26 27 28 29 30 31

1978

JANUARY	FEBRUARY	MARCH	APRIL
S M T W T F S 1 2 3 4 5 6 7 8 9 10 11 12 13 14 15 16 17 18 19 20 21 22 23 24 25 26 27 28 29 30 31	S M T W T F S - - - 1 2 3 4 5 6 7 8 9 10 11 12 13 14 15 16 17 18 19 20 21 22 23 24 25 26 27 28	S M T W T F S - - - 1 2 3 4 5 6 7 8 9 10 11 12 13 14 15 16 17 18 19 20 21 22 23 24 25 26 27 28 29 30 31	S M T W T F S - - - - - - 1 2 3 4 5 6 7 8 9 10 11 12 13 14 15 16 17 18 19 20 21 22 23 24 25 26 27 28 29 30

MAY	JUNE	JULY	AUGUST
S M T W T F S - 1 2 3 4 5 6 7 8 9 10 11 12 13 14 15 16 17 18 19 20 21 22 23 24 25 26 27 28 29 30 31	S M T W T F S - - - 1 2 3 4 5 6 7 8 9 10 11 12 13 14 15 16 17 18 19 20 21 22 23 24 25 26 27 28 29 30	S M T W T F S - - - - - - 1 2 3 4 5 6 7 8 9 10 11 12 13 14 15 16 17 18 19 20 21 22 23 24 25 26 27 28 29 30 31	S M T W T F S - - 1 2 3 4 5 6 7 8 9 10 11 12 13 14 15 16 17 18 19 20 21 22 23 24 25 26 27 28 29 30 31

SEPTEMBER	OCTOBER	NOVEMBER	DECEMBER
S M T W T F S - - - - 1 2 3 4 5 6 7 8 9 10 11 12 13 14 15 16 17 18 19 20 21 22 23 24 25 26 27 28 29 30	S M T W T F S 1 2 3 4 5 6 7 8 9 10 11 12 13 14 15 16 17 18 19 20 21 22 23 24 25 26 27 28 29 30 31	S M T W T F S - - - 1 2 3 4 5 6 7 8 9 10 11 12 13 14 15 16 17 18 19 20 21 22 23 24 25 26 27 28 29 30	S M T W T F S - - - - - 1 2 3 4 5 6 7 8 9 10 11 12 13 14 15 16 17 18 19 20 21 22 23 24 25 26 27 28 29 30 31

The Names of the Days

Latin	Saxon	English	Spanish	German
Dies Solis	Sun's Day	Sunday	domingo	Sonntag
Dies Lunae	Moon's Day	Monday	lunes	Montag
Dies Martis	Tiw's Day	Tuesday	martes	Dienstag
Dies Mercurii	Woden's Day	Wednesday	miércoles	Mittwoch
Dies Jovis	Thor's Day	Thursday	jueves	Donnerstag
Dies Veneris	Frigg's Day	Friday	viernes	Freitag
Dies Saturni	Seterne's Day	Saturday	sábado	Sonnabend

Note: The Romans gave one day of the week to each planet known, the Sun and Moon being considered planets in this connection. The Saxon names are a kind of translation of the Roman names: Tiw was substituted for Mars, Woden (Wotan) for Mercury, Thor for Jupiter (Jove), Frigg for Venus, and Seterne for Saturn. The English names are adapted Saxon. The Spanish names, which are normally not capitalized, are adapted Latin. The German names follow the Saxon pattern with two exceptions: Wednesday is Mittwoch (Middle of the Week), and Saturday is Sonnabend (Sunday's Eve).

fictitious "mean sun." The reason why this fictitious sun has to be introduced is the following: the Earth turns on its axis regularly; it needs the same number of seconds regardless of the season. But the movement of the Earth around the Sun is not regular because the Earth's orbit is an ellipse. This has the result (as explained in the section The Seasons) that the Earth moves faster in January and slower in July. Though it is the Earth which changes velocity it looks to us as if the Sun did. In January, when the Earth moves faster, the *apparent* movement of the Sun looks faster. The "mean sun" of time measurements, then, is a sun which moves regularly all year round; the real Sun will be either ahead or behind the "mean sun." The difference between the real Sun and the fictitious mean sun is called the *equation of time.*

When the real Sun is west of the mean sun we have the "sun fast" condition, with the real Sun crossing the meridian ahead of the mean sun. The opposite is the "sun slow" situation when the real Sun crosses the meridian after the mean sun. Of course what is observed is the real Sun. The equation of time is needed to establish mean solar time, kept by the reference clocks.

But if all clocks were actually set by mean solar time we would be plagued by a welter of time differences which would be "correct" but a major nuisance. A clock on Long Island, correctly showing mean solar time for its location (this would be *local civil time*) would be slightly ahead of a clock in Newark, New Jersey. The Newark clock would be slightly ahead of a clock in Trenton, New Jersey which, in turn, would be ahead of a clock in Philadelphia. This condition actually prevailed in the past until 1883, when *standard time* was introduced. Standard time is the correct mean solar time for a designated meridian, and this time is used for a certain area to the east and west of this meridian. In the United States four meridians have been designated to supply standard times; they are 75°, 90°, 105°, and 120° west of Greenwich. The 75° meridian determines Eastern Standard Time. It happens to run through Camden, New Jersey, where standard time, therefore, is also mean solar time and local civil time. The 90° meridian (which happens to pass through the western part of Memphis, Tenn.) determines Central Standard Time, the 105° meridian (passing through Denver) determines Mountain Standard Time and the 120° meridian (which runs through Lake Tahoe) determines Pacific Standard Time.

Canada, extending over more territory from west to east, adds one time zone on either side: Atlantic Standard Time (based on 60° west of Greenwich) for New Brunswick, Nova Scotia, and Quebec, and Yukon Standard Time (determined by the 135° meridian) for its extreme West. Alaska, extending still farther to the west, adds two more time zones, Alaska Standard Time (determined by the 150° meridian which passes through Anchorage) and Nome Standard Time, based on the 165° meridian just east of Nome.

In general the Earth is divided into 24 such time zones, which run one hour apart. For practical purposes the time zones sometimes show indentations, and there are a few "subzones" which differ from the neighboring zone by only half an hour, e.g., Newfoundland.

The Date-line. While the time zones are based on the natural event of the Sun crossing the meridian, the date must be an arbitrary decision. The meridians are traditionally counted from the meridian of the observatory of Greenwich in En-

The Names of the Months

January: named after Janus, protector of the gateway to heaven.

February: named after Februalia, a time period when sacrifices were made to atone for sins.

March: named after Mars, the god of war, presumably signifying that the campaigns interrupted by the winter could be resumed.

April: from *aperire,* Latin for "to open" (buds).

May: named after Maia, the goddess of growth of plants.

June: from *juvenis,* Latin for "youth."

July: named after Julius Caesar.

August: named after Augustus, the first Roman Emperor.

September: from *septem,* Latin for "seven."

October, from *octo,* Latin for "eight."

November: from *novem,* Latin for "nine."

December: from *decem,* Latin for "ten."

NOTE: The earliest Latin calendar was a 10-month one; thus September was the seventh month, October, the eighth, etc. July was originally called Quintilis, as the fifth month; August was originally called Sextilis, as the sixth month.

gland, which is called the zero meridian. The logical place for changing the date is 12 hours, or 180°, from Greenwich. Fortunately the 180th meridian runs mostly through the open Pacific. The date line makes a zig-zag in the north to incorporate the eastern tip of Siberia into the Siberian time system and then another one to incorporate a number of islands into the Alaska time system. In the south there is a similar zig-zag for the purpose of tying a number of British-owned islands to the New Zealand time system. Otherwise the date line is the same as 180° from Greenwich. At points to the east of the date-line the calendar is one day earlier than at points to the west of it. A traveller going eastward across the date-line from one island to another would not have to re-set his watch because he would stay inside the time zone (provided he does so where the date-line does *not* coincide with the 180° meridian), but it would be the same time of the previous day.

The Seasons

The seasons are caused by the tilt of the Earth's axis (23½°) and not by the fact that the Earth's orbit around the Sun is an ellipse. The average distance of the Earth from the Sun is 93 million miles; the difference between aphelion (farthest away) and perihelion (closest to the Sun) is 3 million miles, so that perihelion is about 91½ million miles from the Sun. The Earth goes through the perihelion point a few days after New Year, just when the northern hemisphere has winter. Aphelion is passed during the first days in July. This by itself shows that the distance from the Sun is not important within these limits. What is im-

portant is that when the Earth passes through perihelion, the northern end of the Earth's axis happens to tilt away from the Sun, so that the places beyond the Tropic of Cancer receive only slanting rays from a Sun low in the sky.

The tilt of the Earth's axis is responsible for four lines you find on every globe. When, say, the North Pole is tilted away from the Sun as much as possible, the farthest points in the North which can still be reached by the Sun's rays are 23½° from the pole. This is the Arctic Circle. The Antarctic Circle is the corresponding limit 23½° from the South Pole; the Sun's rays cannot reach beyond this point when we have mid-summer in the North.

When the Sun is vertically above the equator, the day is of equal length all over the Earth. This happens twice a year, and these are the "equinoxes" in March and in September. After having been over the equator in March, the Sun will seem to move northward. The northernmost point where the Sun can be straight overhead is 23½° north of the equator. This is the Tropic of Cancer; the Sun can never be vertically overhead to the north of this line. Similarly the Sun cannot be vertically overhead to the south of a line 23½° south of the equator—the Tropic of Capricorn.

This explains the climatic zones. In the belt (the Greek word *zone* means "belt") between the Tropic of Cancer and the Tropic of Capricorn, the Sun can be straight overhead; this is the tropical zone. The two zones where the Sun cannot be overhead but will be above the horizon every day of the year are the two temperate zones; the two areas where the Sun will not rise at all for varying lengths of time are the two polar areas, Arctic and Antarctic.

PHENOMENA, 1977
Configurations of Sun, Moon and Planets

d	h	JANUARY
1	02	Jupiter 0 deg .8 N. of Moon
3	10	Earth at perihelion
8	00	Saturn 6 deg N. of Moon
9	02	Vesta at opposition
12	12	Mercury 4 deg N. of Moon
14	04	Uranus 0 deg .6 S. of Mars
15	20	Jupiter stationary
16	12	Neptune 2 deg S. of Moon
17	07	Mercury stationary
18	01	Mercury 2 deg S. of Moon
18	12	Mars 6 deg S. of Moon
23	09	Pluto stationary
23	11	Venus 3 deg S. of Moon
24	12	Venus greatest elong. E. (47 deg)
28	10	Jupiter 1 deg N. of Moon
29	00	Mercury greatest elong. W. (25 deg)

d	h	FEBRUARY
2	10	Saturn in opposition
4	04	Saturn 6 deg N. of Moon
10	10	Uranus 0 deg .9 S. of Moon
10	12	Pallas in opposition
11	19	Ceres stationary
12	19	Mercury 0 deg .1 S. of Mars
12	20	Neptune 2 deg S. of Moon
14	22	Uranus stationary
16	12	Mars 6 deg S. of Moon
16	17	Mercury 7 deg S. of Moon
21	17	Venus 3 deg N. of Moon
24	22	Jupiter 2 deg N. of Moon
26	09	Vesta stationary

d	h	MARCH
1	02	Venus greatest brilliancy
3	09	Saturn 6 deg N. of Moon
9	15	Uranus 1 deg S. of Moon
11	07	Pallas stationary
12	02	Neptune 3 deg S. of Moon
14	19	Venus stationary
17	12	Mars 6 deg S. of Moon
18	11	Neptune stationary
20	18	Equinox
21	07	Juno stationary
21	13	Venus 8 deg N. of Moon
24	15	Jupiter 2 deg N. of Moon
24	20	Ceres at opposition
27	19	Mercury 8 deg S. of Venus
30	17	Saturn 6 deg N. of Moon

d	h	APRIL
2	16	Pluto at opposition
5	22	Uranus 1 deg S. of Moon
6	06	Venus in inferior conjunction
8	08	Neptune 3 deg S. of Moon
10	16	Mercury greatest elong. E. (19 deg)
11	07	Saturn stationary
15	12	Mars 4 deg S. of Moon
16	20	Venus 5 deg N. of Moon
19	16	Mercury 5 deg N. of Moon
20	10	Mercury stationary
21	09	Jupiter 3 deg N. of Moon
24	21	Venus stationary
27	01	Saturn 6 deg N. of Moon
30	06	Uranus in opposition

d	h	MAY
3	07	Uranus 1 deg S. of Moon
5	16	Neptune 3 deg S. of Moon
11	23	Venus greatest brilliancy
13	00	Mercury stationary
13	04	Juno at opposition
13	18	Venus 1 deg .3 N. of Mars
14	11	Venus 1 deg S. of Moon
14	12	Mars 2 deg S. of Moon
16	07	Mercury 2 deg S. of Moon
17	06	Ceres stationary
20	13	Jupiter 5 deg N. of Aldebaran
24	11	Saturn 6 deg N. of Moon
27	23	Mercury greatest elong. W. (25 deg)
30	16	Uranus 0 deg .9 S. of Moon

d	h	JUNE
2	02	Neptune 2 deg S. of Moon
3	13	Venus 1 deg .2 S. of Moon
4	10	Jupiter in conjunction with Sun
5	14	Neptune at opposition
12	11	Mars 0 deg .1 N. of Moon
12	15	Venus 2 deg S. of Moon
15	05	Mercury 2 deg N. of Moon
15	07	Venus greatest elong. W. (46 deg)
16	15	Mercury 5 deg N. of Aldebaran
20	07	Mercury 0 deg .1 N. of Jupiter
20	21	Saturn 6 deg N. of Moon
21	12	Solstice
27	00	Uranus 1 deg S. of Moon
28	21	Pluto stationary
29	11	Neptune 2 deg S. of Moon

d	h	JULY
5	20	Earth at aphelion
11	11	Mars 2 deg N. of Moon
12	09	Venus 1 deg N. of Moon
12	20	Juno stationary
13	19	Jupiter 4 deg N. of Moon
15	19	Venus 3 deg N. of Aldebaran
16	14	Uranus stationary
18	03	Mercury 6 deg N. of Moon
18	09	Saturn 6 deg N. of Moon
20	01	Mercury 0 deg .4 N. of Saturn
24	07	Uranus 1 deg S. of Moon
26	19	Neptune 3 deg S. of Moon
28	03	Mercury 0 deg .1 S. of Regulus
30	06	Venus 1 deg .5 S. of Jupiter

d	h	AUGUST
1	12	Mars 5 deg N. of Aldebaran
8	20	Mercury greatest elong. E. (27 deg)
9	11	Mars 4 deg N. of Moon
10	13	Jupiter 4 deg N. of Moon
11	14	Venus 4 deg N. of Moon
13	06	Saturn in conjunction with Sun
16	23	Mercury 0 deg .9 S. of Moon
20	13	Uranus 2 deg S. of Moon
21	23	Mercury stationary
23	01	Neptune 3 deg S. of Moon
23	17	Venus 7 deg S. of Pollux
25	17	Neptune stationary

d	h	SEPTEMBER
4	22	Mars 0 deg .5 N. of Jupiter
7	07	Jupiter 5 deg N. of Moon
7	09	Mars 5 deg N. of Moon
10	21	Venus 5 deg N. of Moon
11	13	Saturn 5 deg N. of Moon
13	19	Mercury stationary
15	08	Vesta in conjunction with Sun
16	21	Uranus 2 deg S. of Moon
18	13	Venus 0 deg .4 S. of Saturn
19	07	Neptune 3 deg S. of Moon
21	08	Mercury greatest elong. W. (18 deg)
22	03	Venus 0 deg .4 N. of Regulus
23	04	Equinox
27	08	Penumbral eclipse

d	h	OCTOBER
4	21	Jupiter 5 deg N. of Moon
6	03	Mars 6 deg N. of Moon
7	12	Pluto in conjunction with Sun
9	04	Saturn 5 deg N. of Moon
11	01	Venus 4 deg N. of Moon
12	21	Solar eclipse
13	14	Mars 6 deg S. of Pollux
14	07	Uranus 2 deg S. of Moon
16	14	Neptune 3 deg S. of Moon
19	01	Pallas in conjunction with Sun
24	11	Jupiter stationary

d	h	NOVEMBER
1	05	Jupiter 5 deg N. of Moon
3	12	Saturn 0 deg .8 N. of Regulus
3	14	Mars 7 deg N. of Moon
3	20	Venus 4 deg N. of Spica
4	16	Uranus in conjunction with Sun
5	18	Saturn 5 deg N. of Moon
10	00	Venus 0 deg .1 N. of Moon
13	00	Neptune 3 deg S. of Moon
15	19	Mercury 3 deg N. of Antares
20	08	Mercury 4 deg S. of Neptune
20	10	Venus 0 deg .9 N. of Uranus
23	05	Ceres in conjunction with Sun
28	08	Jupiter 5 deg N. of Moon

d	h	DECEMBER
1	13	Mars 7 deg N. of Moon
3	03	Saturn 5 deg N. of Moon
3	08	Mercury greatest elong. E. (21 deg)
8	02	Neptune in conjunction with Sun
8	10	Uranus 2 deg S. of Moon
10	23	Venus 5 deg N. of Antares
12	00	Mercury stationary
12	00	Mercury 6 deg S. of Moon
12	07	Saturn stationary
13	19	Mars stationary
15	17	Juno in conjunction with Sun
21	23	Solstice
23	01	Jupiter at opposition
25	07	Jupiter 5 deg N. of Moon
28	18	Mars 8 deg N. of Moon
30	09	Saturn 5 deg N. of Moon
31	23	Mercury stationary

NOTE: The hour listings are in Universal Time. For conversion into U.S. time zones, see conversion table in this section. For lunar phases and positions, for perihelion and aphelion passages of the planets, and for conjunctions of Mercury, see separate tables.

Symbols

☉ the sun	♃ Jupiter	• occultation
☾ the moon	♄ Saturn	☍ opposition
☿ Mercury	♅ Uranus	● new moon
♀ Venus	♆ Neptune	☽ first quarter
⊕ the earth	♇ Pluto	○ full moon
♂ Mars	☌ conjunction	☾ last quarter

The Zodiac and Average Date of Sun Entering

	Sign	Constel- lation			Sign	Constel- lation
Aries	♈ Mar. 21	Apr. 18		Libra	♎ Sept. 23	Oct. 31
Taurus	♉ Apr. 20	May 14		Scorpius	♏ Oct. 23	Nov. 23
Gemini	♊ May 21	June 21		Sagittarius	♐ Nov. 22	Dec. 17
Cancer	♋ June 21	July 20		Capricornus	♑ Dec. 22	Jan. 19
Leo	♌ July 23	Aug. 10		Aquarius	♒ Jan. 20	Feb. 16
Virgo	♍ Aug. 23	Sept. 16		Pisces	♓ Feb. 19	Mar. 11

Phases of the Moon for 1977

Phase	Date	U.T.	E.S.T.	C.S.T.	M.S.T.	P.S.T.
Full Moon JANUARY	5	12	07 A	06 A	05 A	04 A
Last Quarter	12	20	03 P	02 P	01 P	12 N
New Moon	19	14	09 A	08 A	07 A	06 A
First Quarter	27	05	*12 M	*11 P	*10 P	*09 P
Full Moon FEBRUARY	4	04	*11 P	*10 P	*09 P	*08 P
Last Quarter.	11	04	*11 P	*10 P	*09 P	*08 P
New Moon	18	04	*11 P	*10 P	*09 P	*08 P
First Quarter.	26	03	*10 P	*09 P	*08 P	*07 P
Full Moon MARCH	5	17	12 N	11 A	10 A	09 A
Last Quarter.	12	12	07 A	06 A	05 A	04 A
New Moon	19	19	02 P	01 P	12 N	11 A
First Quarter	27	22	05 P	04 P	03 P	02 P
Full Moon APRIL	4	04	*11 P	*10 P	*09 P	*08 P
Last Quarter	10	19	02 P	01 P	12 N	11 A
New Moon	18	11	06 A	05 A	04 A	03 A
First Quarter	26	15	10 A	09 A	08 A	07 A
Full Moon MAY	3	13	08 A	07 A	06 A	05 A
Last Quarter.	10	04	*11 P	*10 P	*09 P	*08 P
New Moon	18	02	*09 P	*08 P	*07 P	*06 P
First Quarter	26	03	*10 P	*09 P	*08 P	*07 P
Full Moon JUNE	1	21	04 P	03 P	02 P	01 P
Last Quarter.	8	15	10 A	09 A	08 A	07 A
New Moon	16	18	01 P	12 N	11 A	10 A
First Quarter.	24	13	08 A	07 A	06 A	05 A
Full Moon JULY	1	03	*10 P	*09 P	*08 P	*07 P
Last Quarter	8	05	*12 M	*11 P	*10 P	*09 P
New Moon	16	09	04 A	03 A	02 A	01 A
First Quarter	23	20	03 P	02 P	01 P	12 N
Full Moon	30	11	06 A	05 A	04 A	03 A
Last Quarter AUGUST	6	21	04 P	03 P	02 P	01 P
New Moon	14	22	05 P	04 P	03 P	02 P
First Quarter	22	01	*08 P	*07 P	*06 P	*05 P
Full Moon	28	20	03 P	02 P	01 P	12 N
Last Quarter SEPTEMBER . . .	5	15	10 A	09 A	08 A	07 A
New Moon	13	09	04 A	03 A	02 A	01 A
First Quarter	20	06	01 A	*12 M	*11 P	*10 P
Full Moon	27	08	03 A	02 A	01 A	*12 M
Last Quarter OCTOBER	5	09	04 A	03 A	02 A	01 A
New Moon	12	21	04 P	03 P	02 P	01 P
First Quarter.	19	13	08 A	07 A	06 A	05 A
Full Moon	26	23	06 P	05 P	04 P	03 P
Last Quarter NOVEMBER . . .	4	04	*11 P	*10 P	*09 P	*08 P
New Moon	11	07	02 A	01 A	*12 M	*11 P
First Quarter	17	22	05 P	04 P	03 P	02 P
Full Moon	25	18	01 P	12 N	11 A	10 A
Last Quarter DECEMBER . . .	3	21	04 P	03 P	02 P	01 P
New Moon	10	18	01 P	12 N	11 A	10 A
First Quarter	17	11	06 A	05 A	04 A	03 A
Full Moon	25	13	08 A	07 A	06 A	05 A

* Denotes the previous day; dates are given in Universal Time, in which 05 corresponds to midnight E.S.T.

Conversion of Universal Time (U. T.) to Civil Time
(M—Midnight; N—Noon)

U. T.	E. D. T.[1]	E. S. T.[2]	C. S. T.[3]	M. S. T.[4]	P. S. T.[5]	U. T.	E. D. T.[1]	E. S. T.[2]	C. S. T.[3]	M. S. T.[4]	P. S. T.[5]
.00	*8 P	*7 P	*6 P	*5 P	*4 P	12	8 A	7 A	6 A	5 A	4 A
.01	*9 P	*8 P	*7 P	*6 P	*5 P	13	9 A	8 A	7 A	6 A	5 A
.02	*10 P	*9 P	*8 P	*7 P	*6 P	14	10 A	9 A	8 A	7 A	6 A
.03	*11 P	*10 P	*9 P	*8 P	*7 P	15	11 A	10 A	9 A	8 A	7 A
.04	M	*11 P	*10 P	*9 P	*8 P	16	N	11 A	10 A	9 A	8 A
.05	1 A	M	*11 P	*10 P	*9 P	17	1 P	N	11 A	10 A	9 A
.06	2 A	1 A	M	*11 P	*10 P	18	2 P	1 P	N	11 A	10 A
.07	3 A	2 A	1 A	M	*11 P	19	3 P	2 P	1 P	N	11 A
.08	4 A	3 A	2 A	1 A	M	20	4 P	3 P	2 P	1 P	N
.09	5 A	4 A	3 A	2 A	1 A	21	5 P	4 P	3 P	2 P	1 P
.10	6 A	5 A	4 A	3 A	2 A	22	6 P	5 P	4 P	3 P	2 P
.11	7 A	6 A	5 A	4 A	3 A	23	7 P	6 P	5 P	4 P	3 P

* Denotes the previous day. [1] Eastern Daylight Time. [2] Eastern Standard Time, same as Central Daylight Time. [3] Central Standard Time, same as Mountain Daylight Time. [4] Mountain Standard Time, same as Pacific Daylight Time. [5] Pacific Standard Time.

Morning and Evening Stars, 1977

Planet	Morning	Evening
Mercury . . .	Jan. 10–Mar. 4; May 7–Jun. 22; Sept. 11–Oct. 5; Dec. 26–Dec. 31	Mar. 26–Apr. 24; July 9–Sept. 1; Nov. 4–Dec. 17
Venus	Apr. 15–Dec. 1	Jan. 1–Mar. 31
Mars	Jan. 15–Dec. 31	
Jupiter	June 15–Dec. 22	Jan. 1–May 15 Dec. 23–Dec. 31
Saturn	Jan. 1–Feb. 1 Sept. 1–Dec. 31	Feb. 2–July 31

Dates approximate. An *evening star* is any planet that is above the horizon at sunset, and a *morning star* is any planet that is above the horizon at sunrise. Periods of best visibility for the five "naked eye" planets are given above. *Evening stars* appear in the western sky; *morning stars* appear in the eastern sky.

Perigee and Apogee Positions of the Moon, 1977

Perigee	U.T.	E.S.T.	Apogee	U.T.	E.S.T.
Dec. 19, '76	12	07 A	Dec. 31, '76	09	04 A
Jan. 16, '77	10	05 A	Jan. 28, '77	06	01 A
Feb. 11 .	04	*11 P	Feb. 25 .	03	*10 P
Mar. 8 .	23	06 P	Mar. 24 .	22	05 P
Apr. 5 . .	21	04 P	Apr. 21 .	12	07 A
May 4 . .	05	*12 M	May 18 .	18	01 P
June 1 . .	15	10 A	June 14 .	21	04 P
June 30 .	00	*07 P	July 12 .	08	03 A
July 28 .	02	*09 P	Aug. 9 . .	00	*07 P
Aug. 24 .	09	04 A	Sept. 5 .	18	01 P
Sept. 18 .	09	04 A	Oct. 3 . .	14	09 A
Oct. 15 .	09	04 A	Oct. 31 . .	08	03 A
Nov. 12 .	12	07 A	Nov. 27 .	21	04 P
Dec. 10 .	23	06 P	Dec. 24 .	21	04 P
Jan. 8, '78	12	07 A			

* Denotes previous day. N for noon.

Eclipses of the Sun and the Moon, 1977

April 4: Partial eclipse of the Moon. Visible in western Europe, West Africa and the Americas except the extreme Northwest.

April 18: Annular eclipse of the Sun. Visible in the northeast of South America, Africa except the northwest, Antarctica, and Southern Asia.

Sept. 27: Penumbral eclipse of the Moon. Visible in western Africa, North America, South America, the Atlantic Ocean, Arctic, most of Pacific Ocean and part of Antarctica.

Oct. 12: Total eclipse of the Sun. Visible in northeast Asia, Hawaiian Islands, North America except the Northeast, West Indies and the northwest of South America.

Conjunctions of Mercury, 1977

Inferior conjunction	U.T.	E.S.T.	Superior conjunction	U.T.	E.S.T.
Jan. 6 . . .	08	03 A	Mar. 16 . .	05	*12 M
Apr. 30 . .	17	12 N	June 30 . .	00	*07 P
Sept. 5 . .	06	01 A	Oct. 18 . .	23	06 P
Dec. 21 . .	14	09 A			

* Denotes previous day.

Perihelion and Aphelion Passages, 1977

Planet	Passes through its:	
	Perihelion	Aphelion
Mercury	Jan. 1	Feb. 14
	Mar. 30	May 13
	June 26	Aug. 9
	Sept. 22	Nov. 5
	Dec. 19	. . . .
Venus	Feb. 25	June 17
	Oct. 7	. . . .
Mars	Apr. 30	. . . .

NOTE: There are no perihelion or aphelion passages by Jupiter, Saturn, Uranus, Neptune or Pluto in 1977.

THE SPACE AGE

By

NICHOLAS PANAGAKOS

★

SPACE HIGHLIGHTS OF 1976

Viking: Searching For Life Beyond Earth

Just Seventeen Seconds Late

An aspiration nearly as old as human history was fulfilled in 1976 with the landing of a robot spacecraft on the planet Mars to begin the search for life beyond Earth. America's Viking 1 made its historic touchdown on a rocky, boulder-strewn Martian plain on July 20 at 7:53:17 a.m. EDT, just 17 seconds later than flight engineers had predicted. The landing, culminating a half-billion-mile voyage, represented a feat as spectacular for the mechanical precision of the machine as it was for the ingenuity and determination of the humans who sent it there. Within minutes after landing, two specially designed cameras on the bug-shaped craft began nodding—up, down, left, right—taking the world's first closeup pictures of the alien land. A miniature weather station aboard Viking monitored the thin Martian air. Other instruments noted magnetism, radiation—all the data scientists sought. Viking sent its reports Earthward, taking 19 minutes to transmit the data over the 200-million-mile void between Mars and Earth.

Razor-Sharp Pictures

At the Viking control center at NASA's Jet Propulsion Laboratory in Pasadena, Calif., scientists watched as thousands of signals poured in, unscrambled, and, line by line, formed a picture on a television monitor. Outside, a special van picked up the signals, feeding them to the television networks. Within hours, the photos were being viewed by the public on TV screens across the country. What they saw was a sweeping panoramic view of Viking's surroundings. The craft had landed in an area called Chryse, land of gold, at the mouth of the Martian Grand Canyon, 20,000 feet deep and 150 miles across —from end to end as long as the Mississippi River. Far beyond the western horizon rested the Great Volcano, its frigid vent towering 78,000 feet above the surface—higher than Mount Everest. Directly in front of the cameras, the landscape was filled with boulders and rocks, and the surface seemed roiled. Gently sloping sand dunes and hills completed the scene.

To Viking investigators, the steady flow of razor-sharp, closeup pictures, two or three a day for more than three months, was a scientific feast. The ultimate, of course, would have been to photograph a herd of cattle, peacefully grazing among grass and flowers in a Martian field. But since no scientist expected such a lively scene, Viking was prepared to search for the form of life most common on Earth—microbes—on the assumption that these would be most common on Mars too.

Searching for Life

The task of detecting these tiny traces of life fell to the biology laboratory carried inside the Viking. It is probably the most complicated piece of miniaturized machinery ever created. Imagine a device that is only a cubic foot in size—the size of a hat box—weighing only 35 pounds, yet containing 40,000 electronic parts and amounting to the equivalent of three fully equipped laboratories. On Earth, 40 technicians would be required to operate them. It cost $55 million to develop and seven years to build.

This "life machine" was activated eight days after landing. A scrawny ten-foot arm unrolled from the 1300-pound spacecraft and its clawlike hand ripped into the Martian dirt. Small amounts of soil were dropped into three devices within the biology laboratory. These instruments are designed to recognize anything similar to the hundreds of thousands of microorganisms on Earth. The Viking unit automatically pulverizes, illuminates, heats and adds nutrients to the soil samples. Then it monitors any biological reactions.

At publication time, data coming back from the biology experiments were both delighting and puzzling the Viking scientists. The data indicated the presence of compounds which were conceivably of biological origin—although the biological explanation was only one of a number of alternative explanations. It could be, for example, that there was no life on Mars, but that the planet's chemistry was unlike anything experienced before.

The Red Planet

If Viking fails to find life, that won't be the final word. It's possible scientists have been looking in the wrong place or for the wrong thing. A chance to sample a different area of Mars came on September 3, when a sister ship, Viking 2, touched down on the Red Planet at Utopia, an area about 1000 miles nearer to Mars' polar cap than Chryse. There's more moisture there, a fact that could increase significantly the chances for finding life.

CHRONOLOGY OF UNMANNED LUNAR AND PLANETARY PROBES

SPACECRAFT	LAUNCH DATE	DESTINATION	REMARKS
Pioneer 1 (U.S.)	Oct. 11, 1958	Moon	Reached maximum altitude of 71,300 miles. Re-entered atmosphere over South Pacific 43 hours and 17.5 minutes after take-off.
Pioneer 2 (U.S.)	Nov. 8, 1958	Moon	Third stage failed to ignite, re-entered 42.4 minutes after take-off. Peak altitude not announced; must have been over 1,000 miles.
Pioneer 3 (U.S.)	Dec. 6, 1958	Moon	Reached maximum altitude of 66,654 miles. Discovered outer Van Allen layer. Burn-up over French Equatorial Africa 88 hours and 6 minutes after take-off.
Metchta (U.S.S.R.)	Jan. 2, 1959	Moon	Missed moon by 4,600 miles. Radio transmission stopped soon after passing moon.
Pioneer 4 (U.S.)	Mar. 3, 1959	Moon	Passed moon on March 4 at a distance of 37,300 miles. Weight 13.4 lbs.
Lunik 1 (U.S.S.R.)	Sept. 12, 1959	Moon	Impact on moon in the area of **Mare serenitatis** 35 hours after take-off.
Pioneer 5 (U.S.)	Mar. 11, 1960	Interplanetary	Fired into orbit around sun between orbits of earth and of Venus. Radio transmission over record distance of more than 20 million miles.
Venus probe (U.S.S.R.)	Feb. 12, 1961	Venus	Fired from orbiting Sputnik VIII. Must have passed Venus about May 20, 1961, but no signals received.
Ranger 3 (U.S.)	Jan. 26, 1962	Moon	Ranger III, 727-lb. instrument capsule designed to impact on moon. Missed moon.
Ranger 4 (U.S.)	April 23, 1962	Moon	Lunar probe weighing 730 lbs. Failed to transmit soon after take-off; capsule impacted on moon's far side, April 26, 1962.
Mariner 1 (U.S.)	July 22, 1962	Venus	Atlas Agena rocket deviated from course and was destroyed.
Mariner 2 (U.S.)	Aug. 27, 1962	Venus	Planetary probe bound for Venus. Mid-course correction of orbit made on Sept. 4 was successful; Mariner II passed Venus on Dec. 14, 1962, at distance of 21,648 miles. Reported surface temperature of planet to be 800°F. No magnetic field discovered. Radio contact with Mariner II was lost Jan. 3, 1963, when distance had grown to 54 million miles.
Ranger 5 (U.S.)	Oct. 18, 1962	Moon	Was to take TV pictures of moon prior to landing on moon. Electrical power gave out 2 hours after take-off. The 755-lb. vehicle passed moon at distance of 450 miles on Oct. 20.
Mars 1 (U.S.S.R.)	Nov. 1, 1962	Mars	Aimed for Mars, fired from parking orbit. Was intended to pass Mars at distance of 600 miles in June, 1963, but radio contact was lost Mar. 31, 1963.
Luna 4 (U.S.S.R.)	April 2, 1963	Moon	Fired from parking orbit, possibly intended for soft landing. Passed moon at distance of 5,300 mi.
Ranger 6 (U.S.)	Jan. 30, 1964	Moon	Made perfect flight and impacted near crater Arago, but TV cameras did not work.
Zond 1 (U.S.S.R.)	April 2, 1964	Venus	No data.
Ranger 7 (U.S.)	July 28, 1964	Moon	Impacted moon near crater Guericke 68½ hours after take-off. Took and transmitted 4,316 pictures during last 15 minutes of flight; last transmitted picture taken 1,000 feet above lunar surface.
Mariner 3 (U.S.)	Nov. 5, 1964	Mars	Malfunction of a fairing which had not been jettisoned prevented power-producing solar panels from unfolding.

SPACECRAFT	LAUNCH DATE	DESTINATION	REMARKS
Mariner 4 (U.S.)	Nov. 28, 1964	Mars	Made perfect flight to planet Mars after successful midcourse correction on Dec. 5, 1964. Passed behind (as seen from earth) planet on July 14, 1965, taking 22 pictures from distance of about 6,000 miles.
Zond 2 (U.S.S.R.)	Nov. 30, 1964	Mars	Power supply failed completely.
Ranger 8 (U.S.)	Feb. 17, 1965	Moon	Weighing 809 lbs., reached moon 64.9 hrs. after take-off, crashing into **Mare tranquillitatis** 2.59° north of lunar equator. Transmitted 7,137 photographs.
Ranger 9 (U.S.)	Mar. 21, 1965	Moon	Crashed in crater Alphonsus 64.5 hours after take-off. Transmitted 5,814 pictures.
Luna 5 (U.S.S.R.)	May 9, 1965	Moon	Malfunctioned and crashed on lunar surface instead of intended soft landing (May 12). Was followed by Luna VI on June 8, which because of malfunction of the mid-course correction motor missed moon by about 100,000 miles and is now in orbit around the sun.
Zond 3 (U.S.S.R.)	July 18, 1965	Moon	Zond III took and transmitted a number of good close-ups of the moon, covering about 3 million square miles. Now in orbit around sun.
Luna 7 (U.S.S.R.)	Oct. 4, 1965	Moon	Designed for soft landing. Crashed on moon Oct. 7.
Venera 2 (U.S.S.R.)	Nov. 12, 1965	Venus	Venera II, followed on Nov. 16 by Venera III. Each weighed 2,112 lbs. Venera II passed Venus on Feb. 27, 1966, at distance of 14,912 miles, while Venera III entered planet's atmosphere on Mar. 1, 1966, and presumably crashed. In both cases, no data were transmitted.
Luna 8 (U.S.S.R.)	Dec. 3, 1965	Moon	Took off for soft landing on moon, but crashed into lunar surface on Dec. 6, 1965.
Pioneer 6 (U.S.)	Dec. 16, 1965	Interplanetary	Fired into orbit around sun to check on conditions in space between orbits of earth and of Venus. Successful, orbiting sun with perihelion at 75.6 million miles and aphelion at 90.7 million miles. Orbital period is 311 days.
Luna 9 (U.S.S.R.)	Jan. 31, 1966	Moon	Russian moon probe weighing 3,428 lbs., was fired for soft landing. Instrument capsule that came to rest on moon weighed 220 lbs. Landing took place on Feb. 3, 1966. Spacecraft transmitted about 30 pictures.
Luna 10 (U.S.S.R.)	Mar. 31, 1966	Moon	Orbit was achieved Apr. 2, 1966. Weight of spacecraft was 540 lbs. It was not equipped to take and transmit pictures.
Surveyor 1 (U.S.)	May 30, 1966	Moon	Made perfect landing on June 2, 1966, and transmitted close to 10,400 pictures—a number of them after it had survived 14-day lunar night.
Lunar Orbiter 1 (U.S.)	Aug. 10, 1966	Moon	Orbit around moon achieved Aug. 14. Total of 21 pictures obtained.
Pioneer 7 (U.S.)	Aug. 17, 1966	Sun Orbit	In orbit around sun. Perihelion at 92 million mi., aphelion at 102 million mi., orbital period 400 days.
Luna II (U.S.S.R.)	Aug. 24, 1966	Moon	Orbit around moon achieved Aug. 27. Apolune 745 mi., perilune 99 mi.
Surveyor 2 (U.S.)	Sept. 20, 1966	Moon	Tumbled in flight, crashed on moon Sept. 23.
Luna 12 (U.S.S.R.)	Oct. 22, 1966	Moon	Fired for orbit around moon. Orbit achieved Oct. 25; orbital period 3½ hours. Had transmission difficulties; generally unsuccessful.
Lunar Orbiter 2 (U.S.)	Nov. 7, 1966	Moon	Orbit achieved Nov. 10. Transmitted hundreds of excellent pictures.

SPACECRAFT	LAUNCH DATE	DESTINATION	REMARKS
Luna 13 (U.S.S.R.)	Dec. 21, 1966	Moon	Soft-landed ca. 80 hrs. after take-off. Picture transmission was good. Drove spike into moon's surface to test its strength.
Lunar Orbiter 3 (U.S.)	Feb. 4, 1967	Moon	Achieved orbit around moon on Feb. 8. Lifetime terminated Oct. 9, 1967. Excellent pictures.
Surveyor 3 (U.S.)	April 17, 1967	Moon	Soft-landed on dark area called **Oceanus procellarum** after 65 hrs. of flight. Equipped with scoop that dug small trenches to test lunar soil.
Lunar Orbiter 4 (U.S.)	May 4, 1967	Moon	Achieved orbit around moon May 7; orbit was later changed. Final orbit: apolune 2,450 mi., perilune 48 mi., orbital period 5 hrs. 44 mins.
Venera 4 (U.S.S.R.)	June 12, 1967	Venus	Reached planet on Oct. 17. Successful; instrument capsule entered atmosphere and transmitted temperature measurements and partial chemical analysis.
Mariner 5 (U.S.)	June 14, 1967	Venus	Made successful flyby on Oct. 19 and confirmed findings of Mariner II; measurements in fair agreement with Russian results from Venera IV.
Surveyor 4 (U.S.)	July 14, 1967	Moon	Fired for landing in **Sinus medii,** small black area in center of visible hemisphere. Contact lost at 9:06 P.M. EST on July 16, about 2½ minutes before landing. Apparently retrorocket exploded on ignition.
Explorer 35 (U.S.)	July 19, 1967	Moon	Orbit achieved July 22. Perilune 500 mi., apolune 4,000 mi.
Lunar Orbiter 5 (U.S.)	Aug. 2, 1967	Moon	Achieved orbit Aug. 5. Perilune 125 mi., apolune 3,760 mi., orbital period 3 hrs. 50 mins. After it had used up its film it was crashed on moon.
Surveyor 5 (U.S.)	Sept. 8, 1967	Moon	Made successful landing in spite of leaking helium tank on Sept. 10. Near lunar equator in **Mare tranquillitatis.** Made radiological analysis of lunar soil. Mechanical claw dug small trenches.
Surveyor 6 (U.S.)	Nov. 7, 1967	Moon	Made successful landing in **Sinus medii** on Nov. 10. On Nov. 17 performed 8-foot jump in order to photograph position where it had been. Transmitted 11,524 pictures.
Pioneer 8 (U.S.)	Dec. 12, 1967	Sun Orbit	Launched into solar orbit. Ceased functioning Apr. 28, 1968.
Surveyor 7 (U.S.)	Jan. 6, 1968	Moon	Landed successfully near crater Tycho on Jan. 10. Equipped with mechanical claw for soil analysis. Transmitted 3,343 pictures.
Zond 4 (U.S.S.R.)	Mar. 2, 1968	Unknown	Achieved parking orbit but stayed in orbit. Re-entered Mar. 3.
Luna 14 (U.S.S.R.)	April 7, 1968	Moon	Achieved orbit around moon on Apr. 10. Perilune 100 mi., apolune 540.6 mi., period 2 hrs. 40 mins.
Zond 5 (U.S.S.R.)	Sept. 14, 1968	Moon	Circumlunar flight.
Pioneer 9 (U.S.)	Nov. 8, 1968	Sun Orbit	Launched into solar orbit; six experiments returned data on solar radiation.
Zond 6 (U.S.S.R.)	Nov. 10, 1968	Moon	Circumlunar flight.
Venera 5 (U.S.S.R.)	Jan. 5, 1969	Venus	Venera V landed on Venus on May 16, 1969; returned data on composition and temperature of Venus atmosphere.
Venera 6 (U.S.S.R.)	Jan. 10, 1969	Venus	Venera VI landed on Venus on May 17, 1969; returned data similar to type provided by Venera V.
Mariner 6 (U.S.)	Feb. 24, 1969	Mars	Mariner VI made its nearest approach to Mars, 2,000 miles, on July 31, 1969; returned data and TV pictures.
Mariner 7 (U.S.)	Mar. 27, 1969	Mars	Flew past Mars at distance of about 2,000 miles on Aug. 5, 1969; returned data and TV pictures.
Luna 15 (U.S.S.R.)	July 13, 1969	Moon	Lunar orbiter Luna XV landed on moon on July 21, 1969, after completing several lunar orbits at varying altitudes.

SPACECRAFT	LAUNCH DATE	DESTINATION	REMARKS
Zond 7 (U.S.S.R.)	Aug. 8, 1969	Moon	Zond 7, circumlunar, was recovered Aug. 14, 1969.
Pioneer E (U.S.)	Aug. 27, 1969	Interplanetary	Designed to obtain information on particles and magnetic fields, failed to achieve orbit.
Venera 7 (U.S.S.R.)	Aug. 17, 1970	Venus	Reached planet about Dec. 15, 1970, transmitting data for 58 minutes, apparently from the surface.
Luna 16 (U.S.S.R.)	Sept. 12, 1970	Moon	Luna 16 soft-landed on moon on Sept. 24, scooped up samples of rock, and returned to earth on Sept. 24, 1970.
Zond 8 (U.S.S.R.)	Oct. 20, 1970	Moon	Zond 8, on circumlunar flight, photographed lunar and earth surface. Landed in Indian Ocean Oct. 27, 1970.
Luna 17 (U.S.S.R.)	Nov. 10, 1970	Moon	Luna 17 soft-landed on moon's Sea of Rains on Nov. 17. Used first propelled vehicle, Lunokhod 1, for moon exploration. Made analyses of lunar soil, sent TV photos to earth, and performed various research activities.
Mariner 8 (U.S.)	May 8, 1971	Mars	Mariner 8 designed to orbit Mars for about 90 days was lost due to vehicle failure.
Mars 2 (U.S.S.R.)	May 19, 1971	Mars	Reached Mars on Nov. 27 and dropped a landing capsule on the planet's surface.
Mars 3 (U.S.S.R.)	May 28, 1971	Mars	Companion to Mars 2, Mars 3 capsule landed on Dec. 2, 1971, but television transmission was cut short due to antenna failure in parent craft.
Mariner 9 (U.S.)	May 30, 1971	Mars	Reached planet on Nov. 13, becoming first craft to orbit Mars. Obtained 7300 pictures including first closeup photos of Mars' moon. Transmission-ended on Oct. 27, 1972.
Luna 18 (U.S.S.R.)	Sept. 2, 1971	Moon	Luna 18 crashed into moon after 54 lunar orbits. Third successive Soviet space failure.
Luna 19 (U.S.S.R.)	Sept. 28, 1971	Moon	In orbit around the moon for an indefinite time, making measurements and taking photographs.
Luna 20 (U.S.S.R.)	Feb. 14, 1972	Moon	Soft-landed on the moon on Feb. 21 in Sea of Fertility. Returned to earth on Feb. 25 with lunar rock samples.
Pioneer 10 (U.S.)	March 3, 1972	Jupiter	Pioneer 10, launched towards Jupiter to take man's first close look at the giant planet. Its 620-million mile flight path took the unmanned craft through the asteroid belt and past Jupiter on Dec. 3, 1973. After crossing the orbits of Saturn, Uranus, Neptune and Pluto, it would become, in 1986, the first manmade object to escape the solar system.
Venera 8 (U.S.S.R.)	March 27, 1972	Venus	Venera 8 landed on planet Venus on July 22, and sent signals for 50 minutes before going silent. Capsule was apparently incinerated or crushed by intense heat and pressure on surface of Venus. Information returned on atmosphere and nature of rocks on the surface.
Luna 21 (U.S.S.R.)	Jan. 8, 1973	Moon	Luna 21 soft-landed on moon, Jan. 16, 1973. Lunokhod-2 (moon car) scooped up lunar samples which were returned to earth; recovered by U.S.S.R., Jan. 24, 1973.
Pioneer 11 (U.S.)	Apr. 6, 1973	Jupiter	Pioneer 11 launched toward Jupiter, along flight path similar to Pioneer 10. Flew by Jupiter in Dec. 1974 at a distance of about 25,000 miles, three times closer than its predecessor, Pioneer 10.
Mars 4 (U.S.S.R.)	July 21, 1973	Mars	Mars 4 launched by U.S.S.R. toward Mars, arriving in February 1974, and briefly transmitting photographs of the planet back to Earth.
Mars 5 (U.S.S.R.)	July 25, 1973	Mars	Sister craft to Mars 4.
Mars 6 (U.S.S.R.)	Aug. 5, 1973	Mars	Mars 6 launched toward Mars by U.S.S.R. for arrival in early Mar. 1974, but missed its target.

SPACECRAFT	LAUNCH DATE	DESTINATION	REMARKS
Mars 7 (U.S.S.R.)	Aug. 9, 1973	Mars	Mars 7 launched toward Mars by U.S.S.R. for arrival in early Mar. 1974, but missed its target.
Mariner 10 (U.S.)	Nov. 3, 1973	Venus Mercury	Mariner 10 flew by Venus on Feb. 5, 1974, arriving at Mercury for man's first closeup look at that planet on Mar. 29, 1974. First time in which gravity of one planet (Venus) was used to whip spacecraft toward another (Mercury). Mariner 10 had a second encounter with Mercury on Sept. 21, 1974, and a third on March 16, 1975.
Luna 22 (U.S.S.R.)	May 29, 1974	Moon	Luna 22 went into orbit around Moon on June 2, 1974.
Luna 23 (U.S.S.R.)	Oct. 28, 1974	Moon	Crashed into Moon on Nov. 6, 1974.
Venera 9 (U.S.S.R.)	June 8, 1975	Venus	Double-barreled Soviet probe designed to land capsules on Venus. Soft-landed on planet on Oct. 25, 1976.
Venera 10 (U.S.S.R.)	June 14, 1975	Venus	
Viking 1 (U.S.)	Aug. 20, 1975	Mars	Unmanned spacecraft, carrying life-detection laboratories, landed on surface of Mars on July 20 and Sept. 3, 1976, for detailed scientific examination of planet, including pictures.
Viking 2 (U.S.)	Sept. 9, 1975	Mars	
Luna 24 (U.S.S.R.)	Aug. 9, 1976	Moon	Soft-landed on Moon on Aug. 18, 1976, scooped up lunar soil sample and returned to Earth on Aug. 22, 1976.

MAJOR U.S. SPACE PROJECTS
Scientific Satellites

Applications Technology Satellite (ATS)—Series of spacecraft designed to test techniques and equipment in space for future communications, weather and navigational systems. Weight: Approximately 700 lbs. Scientific equipment: 100 to 300 lbs. Orbit: 6,500 miles or 22,200 miles. *ATS-1* was launched Dec. 6, 1966. *ATS-6*, the most powerful and versatile communications satellite ever developed, was launched on May 30, 1974. It is transmitting educational TV programs and health services to scores of isolated communities in Appalachia, the Rocky Mountains and Alaska, as well as to school children and adults in 5,000 isolated villages and cities in India.

Biosatellite—Earth-orbiting biological laboratory, carrying a variety of plants and animals into space to determine effects of weightlessness (zero gravity). *Biosatellite 1,* launched Dec. 14, 1966, was unrecovered. *Biosatellite 2,* launched Sept. 7, 1967, was highly successful. The last in the series, *Biosatellite 3,* launched June 29, 1969, was returned to Earth because of deteriorating condition of its primate passenger.

Explorer—Largest group of satellites in U.S. space program. Used for a variety of scientific purposes in atmosphere, ionosphere and interplanetary space. *Explorer 1,* launched July 1, 1958, was America's first successful satellite. It confirmed the existence of the Van Allen radiation belts which girdle the Earth. *Explorer 52 (Hawkeye)* was launched June 3, 1974. First Explorer weighed about 18 lbs; current spacecraft average about 100 lbs, but some weigh as much as 500 lbs. Orbits and design vary.

Geodynamic Experimental Ocean Satellite (GEOS)—A series of geodetic satellites designed to test new instrumentation for NASA's Earth and Ocean Physics Applications program. Measures ocean topography, the state of the seas, and other features of Earth. *GEOS-3*

was launched April 9, 1975, into a nearly circular 840-mile Earth orbit. Weight: 750 lbs.

Helios—A joint U.S.-German program to obtain new information on interplanetary space in the region close to the Sun. *Helios 1,* launched Dec. 10, 1974, flew within 28 million miles of the Sun—closer than any previous spacecraft—at times encountering temperatures hot enough to melt lead (700 degrees F.). *Helios 2* was launched on Jan. 15, 1976.

High Energy Astronomy Observatory (HEAO)—Series of space platforms designed for research in high-energy astrophysics—the domain of peculiar astronomical objects such as quasars, pulsars and black holes in space. Weighing 2,200 lbs, *HEAO-1* is scheduled to be launched into a 225-mile Earth orbit in 1977 to perform a detailed X-ray survey of the celestial sphere. *HEAO-2,* 1978; *HEAO-3,* 1979. After that, HEAO scientific instruments will be carried into space by NASA's Space Shuttle.

Intelsat—Series of communications satellites launched by NASA on a reimbursable basis for the Communications Satellite Corporation (Comsat) to form a commercial, worldwide communications satellite system. Comsat is the U.S. member of the 50-nation consortium that owns the Intelsat network. *Early Bird,* launched April 6, 1965, was the world's first operational commercial communications satellite. The network now is composed of more than nine satellites, furnishing communications service including telecasts for North America, Europe and Asia. The satellites are positioned about 22,000 miles above the Equator and, moving at the same speed as Earth, appear to hover permanently over one spot. *Intelsat 4A* was launched on Jan. 29, 1976.

Landsat—Series of NASA satellites conducting a variety of earth resources observations (minerology, geography, mapping, land use) from space. *ERTS-1* (now called *Landsat 1*) was launched July 23, 1972, into a 570-mile circular polar-orbit around Earth. Weight: 1,800 lbs. *Landsat 2* (formerly called *ERTS-2*) was launched April 9, 1975. Orbiting Earth 14 times a day, Landsats scan a swath 115 miles wide in four bands of the spectrum that reveal much about Earth's natural resources that can be used to help manage them more wisely. The satellites pass over almost the entire globe every 18 days. More than 100,000 pictures have been radioed back since the first launch, showing all the U.S. repeatedly and three fourths of the world's land masses and coastal areas. Research investigators in 43 states and 48 countries use the Landsat data.

Laser Geodynamic Satellite (LAGEOS)—Laser-carrying satellite designed to make detailed measurements of plate tectonic (continental drift) motions, regional fault motions, and the rotation and wobble of Earth. Weighing about 900 lbs. each LAGEOS is a solid sphere fitted with 600 laser retroreflectors. Laser beams from ground stations are bounced off it and returned to Earth, permitting very accurate positioning of both ground station and satellite. The first *LAGEOS*, launched on May 4, 1976, is in a circular Earth orbit at 3,440 miles.

Large Space Telescope (LST)—The LST program calls for the construction of a 10-ton telescope orbiting the Earth at a distance of 380 miles. This national facility, with a 3-meter (10-foot) aperture, would make possible astronomical observations 10 times deeper and with more detail than has ever been possible. It would be placed in orbit via the United States' Space Shuttle in 1981 or 1982.

Marisat—Series of three satellites that will make up the first Maritime Communications Satellite systems, owned by the Communications Satellite Corp. (Comsat). *Marisat 1* was launched on Feb. 19, 1976, into a geosynchronous (appearing to hover over one spot on Earth) orbit.

Nimbus—Advanced meteorological satellites for detailed global weather and atmosphere soundings. Equipped with advanced television cameras and a high resolution infrared camera system, Nimbus can provide both day and night pictures of Earth's cloud cover. *Nimbus 1* was launched Aug. 28, 1964. *Nimbus 6* was launched June 11, 1975.

Orbiting Astronomical Observatory (OAO)—Earth-orbiting observatory, operating above the obscuring effects of Earth's atmosphere, is able to study entire celestial sphere in electromagnetic wavelengths not easily accessible from the ground. *OAO-3* carrying 11 telescopes, is heaviest U.S. unmanned satellite (4,900 lbs). It was launched Aug. 21, 1972, into a nearly circular 740-mile Earth orbit.

Orbiting Geophysical Observatory (OGO)—Large (1000 lbs) multipurpose space platforms designed to study Earth, Sun and the interplanetary space in between. Carrying many scientific instruments, OGO has the advantage over smaller satellites of being able to observe numerous phenomena simultaneously over prolonged periods of time. *OGO 1* was launched Sept. 5, 1964, into a 13,910–92,845-mile orbit around Earth. The last *OGO* in the series was launched June 5, 1969.

Orbiting Solar Observatory (OSO)—Series of one-ton space platforms designed to study the Sun and phenomena such as solar flares above the obscuring effects of Earth's atmosphere. Most sophisticated version, *OSO-1*, was launched June 20, 1975. Carrying such instruments as X-ray and gamma-ray monitors, the OSO's have provided scientists with invaluable basic details about the functioning of the

Sun. They orbit Earth at a distance of about 300 miles.

Pegasus—Among the heaviest (3,000 lbs) of U.S. scientific satellites, with a wing-like structure spanning 96 feet. Designed to determine the frequency and depth of punctures by micrometeoroids (tiny particles of matter speeding through space faster than a bullet). Data from Pegasus helped prepare man for the Apollo lunar landing mission. *Pegasus 1,* was launched Feb. 16, 1965; *Pegasus 2,* May 25, 1965; *Pegasus 3,* July 30, 1965.

Relay—Communications satellite system designed to demonstrate feasibility of intercontinental and transoceanic transmission of television and radio signals with a medium-altitude (up to 12,000 miles) radio-equipped satellite. *Relay 1* was launched Dec. 13, 1962. *SAS-3* was launched in May 1976.

Small Astronomy Satellite (SAS)—X-ray satellites designed to monitor the intensity of X-ray sources in our Galaxy and beyond. *SAS-1,* weighing about 400 lbs, was launched Dec. 12, 1970.

Seasat—Series of satellites which would be the first to study ocean data exclusively. It will circle the globe 14 times a day. First launch scheduled for 1978.

Synchronous Meteorological Satellite (SMS)—Series of geostationary (hovering over same spot above Earth) satellites designed to keep continuous watch on fast-changing storms, such as hurricanes and tornadoes, sending back high resolution pictures every 30 minutes. *SMS-1* was launched May 17, 1974. With the launch of a second *SMS*, on Feb. 6, 1975, day-and-night surveillance is provided over the U.S. and adjacent ocean areas.

Syncom—First communications satellite to be placed in a synchronous Earth orbit for global communication. Three Syncom satellites were launched between Feb. 14, 1963, and Aug. 19, 1964.

Telstar—Early experimental communications satellite system operated by American Telephone and Telegraph Co. *Telstar 1* was launched July 1, 1962 by NASA for AT&T on a reimbursable basis.

Tiros—Spectacularly successful early weather satellite system developed by NASA. *Tiros 1,* launched April 1, 1960, took more than 22,000 cloud-cover pictures in 78 days and transmitted them to ground stations. Operational system, called ITOS (Improved Tiros), is now handled by the National Oceanic and Atmospheric Administration (NOAA) of the Department of Commerce. Tiros stands for Television and Infrared Observation Satellite. Contributes significantly to early detection of hurricanes and other destructive storms. Provides weathermen with daily pictures of weather over the entire globe. Weight: Approximately 750 lbs. Orbits Earth at distance of about 450 miles. *ITOS-I (TIROS-M)* was launched Jan. 23, 1970, and was deactivated by NOAA on June 17, 1971. *ITOS-H (NOAA-5)* was launched on July 29, 1976. *TIROS-N,* scheduled for launch in mid-1977, will use new and advanced instruments and will be the prototype of the next generation of polar-orbiting operational weather satellites.

Transit—Department of Defense navigational satellite system for military vessels. Consisting of four satellites, system is designed to allow ships to determine their precise position regardless of weather or time of day.

Vanguard—Earth-orbiting geodetic survey satellites. *Vanguard 1,* launched March 17, 1958, determined that Earth is slightly pear-shaped.

Westar—Domestic communications system developed by Western Union. Spacecraft are launched into a 200-by-19,500-mile Earth orbit. Program was begun in 1974, with the launch of *Westar 1* on April 13. *Westar 2* was launched Oct. 10, 1974.

Unmanned Planetary and Lunar Programs

Lunar Orbiter—Series of spacecraft designed to orbit the Moon, taking pictures and obtaining data in support of the subsequent manned Apollo landings. The U.S. launched five *Lunar Orbiters* between Aug. 10, 1966 and Aug. 2, 1967.

Mariner—Designation for a series of unmanned spacecraft designed to fly past or orbit the planets, particularly Mercury, Venus and Mars. Mariners provided the early information on Venus and Mars. *Mariner 9*, orbiting Mars in 1971, returned the most startling photographs of that planet to date, and helped pave the way for a Viking landing in 1976. Mariners are being prepared for flights to Jupiter and Saturn in 1977, and to Uranus at a later date.

Pioneer—Designation for the United States' first series of sophisticated planetary spacecraft. Two Pioneers have flown past Jupiter, and are headed for Saturn and the outer reaches of the solar system. They are providing us with the first information on the giant outer planets—Jupiter, Saturn, Uranus,

Neptune and Pluto. *Pioneer Venus,* slated for launching in 1978, is expected to provide the most detailed look yet at that cloud-shrouded planet.

Ranger—NASA's earliest moon exploration program. Spacecraft were designed for a crash landing on the Moon, taking pictures and returning scientific data up to the moment of impact. Provided mankind with the first closeup views of the lunar surface. The Rangers provided more than 17,000 closeup pictures, giving us more information about the Moon in a few years than in all the time that had gone before.

Surveyor—Series of unmanned spacecraft designed to land gently on the Moon and provide information on the surface in preparation for the manned lunar landings. Their legs were instrumented to return data on the surface hardness of the Moon. Surveyor dispelled once and for all the fear that Apollo spacecraft might sink several feet or more into the lunar dust.

Manned Space Flight Projects

Mercury—Project Mercury, America's first manned space program, was designed to accumulate knowledge about man's capabilities in space. Mercury 7, with astronaut Gordon L. Cooper, was the longest flight. It proved conclusively that man can live and work in space for at least 34 hours, despite the high-gravity forces of launch and re-entry, and weightlessness.

Gemini—Gemini was an extension of Project Mercury, to determine the effects of prolonged space flight on man—two weeks or longer. "Walks in space" provided invaluable information for astronauts' later walks on the Moon. The Gemini spacecraft, twice as large as the Mercury capsule, accommodated two men.

Apollo—Apollo was the designation for the United States' effort to land a man on the Moon and return him safely to Earth. The goal was successfully accomplished with Apollo 11 on July 20, 1969, culminating eight years of rehearsal and centuries of dreaming. Astronauts Neil A. Armstrong and Col. Edwin E. Aldrin, Jr., scooped up and brought back the first lunar rocks ever seen on Earth—about 47 pounds. Six Apollo flights followed, ending with Apollo 17 in December, 1972. The last three Apollos carried mechanized vehicles called lunar rovers for wide-ranging surface exploration of the Moon by astronauts. The rendezvous and docking of an Apollo spacecraft with a Russian Soyuz craft in Earth orbit on July 18, 1975 closed out the Apollo program.

Skylab—America's first Earth-orbiting space station. Project Skylab was designed to demonstrate that men can work and live in space for prolonged periods without ill effects. Actually the spent third stage of a Saturn 5 moon rocket, Skylab measured 118 feet from stem to stern, and carried the most varied as-

sortment of experimental equipment ever assembled in a single spacecraft. Three three-man crews visited the space stations spending more than 740 hours observing the Sun and bringing home more than 175,000 solar pictures. These were the first recordings of solar activity above Earth's obscuring atmosphere. Skylab also evaluated systems designed to gather information on Earth's resources and environmental conditions. Skylab biomedical findings indicated that man adapts well to space for at least a period of three months, provided he has a proper diet and adequately programmed exercise, sleep, work and recreation periods. Skylab orbited Earth at a distance of about 300 miles.

Space Shuttle—The Space Shuttle is a new manned space transportation system being developed by NASA to reduce the cost of using space for commercial, scientific and defense needs. In effect, the Shuttle is a manned rocket which, after depositing its payload in space, can be flown back to Earth like a conventional airplane and be available for re-use. Because of its versatility and large cargo-carrying capacity, the Space Shuttle can combine missions. For example, on one trip to space the Shuttle might place a weather satellite and a scientific satellite into different orbits, and then retrieve a communications satellite and return it to Earth for servicing. Or, if the repairs required by the communications satellite were relatively simple, the Shuttle might carry technicians who would repair it in orbit. Although most of its cargoes will be unmanned, the Shuttle can serve as an inhabited Earth-orbiting laboratory for up to 30 days. The system is scheduled to become operational in late 1979.

MAJOR SOVIET SPACE PROJECTS
Scientific Satellites

Cosmos—Cosmos appeared as a designator in 1962 to be used for explaining many different Soviet activities in space without giving specific details each time. *Cosmos 786* was launched Dec. 16, 1975.

Elektron—Satellites launched in pairs to map radiation belts. Apogee: 4,000 miles; perigee: 40,000 miles. Four Elektron satellites were launched in 1964.

Intercosmos—Russian scientific satellites carrying experiments from other countries. The announced countries participating are from the Soviet bloc. *Intercosmos 1* was launched October 14, 1969. *Intercosmos 14* was launched Dec. 11, 1975.

Oreol—Scientific satellites designed to study the upper atmosphere. Launched jointly with France.

Oreol 1 was launched in 1971; *Oreol 2*, 1973.

Meteor—Earth-orbiting weather satellites. Twenty-one have been launched over the past eight years, beginning with *Meteor 1* in 1967. *Meteor 23* was launched Dec. 25, 1975.

Molniya—A communications satellite appearing in a highly elliptical orbit over the same portion of Earth each day on each of its climbs to apogee (the highest point), giving good coverage to the Soviet Union. *Molniya 1* and *2* were launched October 14, 1965. *Molniya 34* was launched Dec. 27, 1975.

Prognoz—A solar irradiation and magnetosphere satellite for the study of the solar wind. The last *Prognoz* was launched Dec. 22, 1975.

Polyot—Earth satellites incorporating on-board propulsion systems which enable them to change their orbits. Only two have been launched to date, in 1963 and 1964.

Sputnik—An early designation for Soviet unmanned spacecraft. *Sputnik 1,* launched October 4, 1957, was the world's first Earth-orbiting satellite, and is considered to have ushered in the Space Age.

Unmanned Planetary and Lunar Programs

Luna—Unmanned spacecraft launched to the Moon. These include lunar orbiters, lunar landers, and lunar lander return missions.

Mars—Unmanned spacecraft launched to explore the planet Mars. Three spacecraft, each weighing about 1,940 lbs, were launched in 1962, but failed to reach their target. *Mars 4* was launched July 21, 1973, arriving at Mars in February, 1974, and briefly transmitting photographs of the planet back to Earth. *Mars 5, 6,* and *7* were launched between July 25 and August 9, 1974, but missed the planet.

Venus (Venera)—Unmanned spacecraft launched to explore the planet Venus. The program was begun in 1961 but, out of 10 known tries, only four can be termed successful. *Venera 9* and *10* were launched June 8 and June 14, 1975, respectively. They reached Venus on Oct. 25, 1976.

Zond—Soviet lunar and planetary probes not otherwise designated. Zond spacecraft have been launched to Venus, Mars and the Moon.

Manned Space Flight Programs

Vostok—The Soviets' first manned capsule, roughly spherical, used to place the first six cosmonauts in Earth orbit (1961–65).

Voskhod—Adaptation of the Vostok capsule to accommodate two and three cosmonauts. *Voskhod 1* orbited three persons, and *Voskhod 2* orbited two persons performing the world's first manned extravehicular activity.

Soyuz—Late-model manned spacecraft with provisions for three cosmonauts and a "working compartment" accessible through a hatch. Soyuz is the Russian word for "union". *Soyuz 21,* carrying two cosmonauts, was launched July 6, 1976, and linked up with *Salyut 5* for a 50-day study.

Salyut—Earth-orbiting space station intended for prolonged occupancy and re-visitation by cosmonauts. They are usually launched by Soviet Proton rockets. *Salyut 1* was launched April 19, 1971, and decayed on October 11, 1971. *Salyut 2,* launched April 3, 1973, malfunctioned in orbit and was never occupied. It decayed May 28, 1973. *Salyut 3,* visited by the *Soyuz 14* and *16* cosmonauts, was launched June 25, 1974, and decayed Jan. 24, 1975. *Salyut 4* was launched Dec. 26, 1974, and is still in orbit. *Soyuz 18* docked with the space station on May 24, 1975, and its two-man crew spent 1511 hours, 20 minutes, in space—a Soviet space record. *Salyut 5* was launched June 22, 1976.

FEDERAL OBLIGATIONS FOR RESEARCH AND DEVELOPMENT: 1960 TO 1975

[In millions of dollars. For years ending June 30. Excludes research and development plant. For any given year obligations differ from expenditures because not all funds are expended during year obligated.

ITEM	1960	1965	1968	1969	1970	1971	1972	1973	1974	1975 [1]
Total R and D.....	7,552	14,614	15,921	15,641	15,340	15,564	16,512	16,821	17,408	18,780
Basic research............	610	1,690	2,056	2,077	2,042	2,132	2,411	2,420	} 7,163	7,545
Applied research..........	1,331	3,164	3,304	3,151	3,555	3,942	4,146	4,080		
Development..............	5,611	9,760	10,561	10,413	9,743	9,490	9,955	10,321	10,245	11,235
Total research.....	1,941	4,854	5,361	5,228	5,597	6,074	6,557	6,500	7,163	7,545
Life sciences...............	511	1,167	1,538	1,499	1,533	1,673	1,982	2,059	(NA)	(NA)
Psychological sciences....	38	103	98	104	114	116	126	116	(NA)	(NA)
Physical sciences..........	} 608	{ 1,029	1,132	1,169	1,012	1,042	1,139	1,126	(NA)	(NA)
Environmental sciences..		{ 676	656	538	575	677	783	791	(NA)	(NA)
Mathematical sciences....	25	105	119	115	102	120	136	126	(NA)	(NA)
Engineering sciences.....	690	1,576	1,572	1,509	1,980	2,040	1,965	1,760	(NA)	(NA)
Social sciences...........	35	127	195	215	209	304	310	296	(NA)	(NA)
Other sciences...........	33	70	52	80	72	103	116	226	(NA)	(NA)

[1] Estimated.

CHRONOLOGY OF MANNED FLIGHTS

Designation & Country	Date	Astronauts	Orbit: perigee/apogee (mi.)	Orbital period (min.)	Number of orbits	Flight time (hr./min.)	Remarks
Vostok 1 (USSR)	Apr. 12, 1961	Yuri A. Gagarin	(¹)/188	....	1	1/48	First manned orbital flight.
MR III (US)	May 5, 1961	Alan B. Shepard, Jr.	....	....	(²)	0/15	Range 302 mi., peak 116.5 mi.; capsule recovered.
MR IV (US)	July 21, 1961	Virgil I. Grissom	....	....	(²)	0/16	Range 303 mi., peak 118 mi.; capsule lost.
Vostok 2 (USSR)	Aug. 6–7, 1961	Gherman S. Titov	110.3/159.3	88.6	17.5	25/18	First long-duration flight.
MA VI (US)	Feb. 20, 1962	John H. Glenn, Jr.	100.3/162.7	88.5	3	4/55	First American in orbit.
MA VII (US)	May 24, 1962	M. Scott Carpenter	100/166.8	88.5	3	4/56	Overshot landing area; otherwise fine.
Vostok 3 (USSR)	Aug. 11–15, 1962	Andrian G. Nikolayev	112.3/145.8	90³	64	94/22	Vostoks 3 and 4 approached within 3 mi.
Vostok 4 (USSR)	Aug. 12–15, 1962	Pavel R. Popovich	111.7/147.1	90³	48	70/57	
MA VIII (US)	Oct. 3, 1962	Walter M. Schirra, Jr.	100/176	88.55	6	9/13	First splashdown close to aiming point.
MA IX (US)	May 15–16, 1963	L. Gordon Cooper, Jr.	100.2/166.1	88.40	22	34/20	Longest Mercury flight.
Vostok 5 (USSR)	June 14–19, 1963	Valery F. Bykovsky	99/146	90³	81	119/6	Longest Russian orbital flight to date.
Vostok 6 (USSR)	June 16–19, 1963	Valentina V. Tereshkova	108/143	90³	48	70/50	First orbital flight by female cosmonaut.
Voskhod 1 (USSR)	Oct. 12, 1964	Vladimir M. Komarov, Konstantin P. Feoktistov; Boris G. Yegorov	111/254	88	16	24/17	First 3-man orbital flight; also first flight without space suits.
Voskhod 2 (USSR)	Mar. 18, 1965	Alexei A. Leonov; Pavel I. Belyayev	108/307.5	91.4	17	26/2	First "space walk" (by Leonov), 10 min.
GT III (US)	Mar. 23, 1965	Virgil I. Grissom; John W. Young	100/140	90³	3	4/53	First manned test of Gemini spacecraft.
GT IV (US)	June 3–7, 1965	James A. McDivitt; Edward H. White 2d	100/175	90³	62	97/48	First American "space walk" (by White), lasting slightly over 20 min.
GT V (US)	Aug. 21–29, 1965	L. Gordon Cooper, Jr.; Charles Conrad, Jr.	100.6/217.3	90³	120	190/56	Longest flight to date.
GT VII (US)	Dec. 4–18, 1965	Frank Borman; James A. Lovell, Jr.	144/190	90³	206	330/35	Longest space flight to date.
GT VI (US)	Dec. 15–16, 1965	Walter M. Schirra, Jr.; Thomas P. Stafford	100/167	90³	16	25/52	Orbit was extended to 185 mi. to make rendezvous with orbiting GT VII.
GT VIII (US)	Mar. 16–17, 1966	Neil A. Armstrong; David R. Scott	100/168	88.8	6.5	10/42	Only Gemini flight cut short by malfunction: one thruster kept firing after rendezvous and docking with an orbiting Agena rocket had been accomplished.
GT IX (US)	June 3–6, 1966	Thomas P. Stafford; Eugene A. Cernan	167/169	95³	44	72/21	Rendezvous (but no docking).
GT X (US)	July 18–21, 1966	John W. Young; Michael Collins	183/190	95.2	43	70/47	Docking with orbiting Agena rocket.
GT XI (US)	Sept. 12–15, 1966	Charles Conrad, Jr.; Richard F. Gordon, Jr.	185/185	95³	44	71/17	Docking with orbiting Agena on first orbit; apogee of orbit then extended to 850 miles.

Mission	Crew	Date					Remarks
GT XII (US)	James A. Lovell, Jr.; Edwin E. Aldrin, Jr.	Nov. 11–15, 1966	155/180	90.0	59	94/33	Docking with Agena visually, without computer; co-pilot outside spacecraft for total of 5½ hours.
Soyuz 1 (USSR)	Vladimir M. Komarov	Apr. 23, 1967	122/223	88.7	17	26/40	First test of Soyuz spacecraft; crashed after re-entry, killing Komarov.
Apollo 7 (US)	Walter M. Schirra, Jr.; Donn F. Eisele; R. Walter Cunningham	Oct. 11–22, 1968	142.3/190	89.9	163	260/9	First manned test of Apollo command module; first live TV transmissions from orbit.
Soyuz 3 (USSR)	Georgi T. Beregovoi	Oct. 26–30, 1968	113.6/127.4	88.3	64	94/51	First manned rendezvous and possible docking by Soviet cosmonaut.
Apollo 8 (US)	Frank Borman; James A. Lovell, Jr.; William A. Anders	Dec. 21–27, 1968	....	....	10⁴	147/	First spacecraft in circumlunar orbit; TV transmissions from this orbit.
Soyuz 4 (USSR)	Vladamir A. Shatalov	Jan. 14–17, 1969	107/140	88.25	48	71/14	Rendezvoused and docked with Soyuz 5.
Soyuz 5 (USSR)	Boris V. Volynov; Alexei S. Yeliseyev; Yevgeny V. Khrunov	Jan. 15–18, 1969	124/143	88.7	49	72/46	Rendezvoused and docked with Soyuz 4; Khrunov and Yeliseyev perform EVA and transfer to Soyuz 4.
Apollo 9 (US)	James A. McDivitt; David R. Scott; Russell L. Schweikart	Mar. 3–13, 1969	118/120	....	151	241/1	First manned flight of Lunar Module.
Apollo 10 (US)	Thomas P. Stafford; Eugene A. Cernan; John W. Young	May 18–26, 1969	....	....	....	192/3	First descent to within 9 miles of moon's surface by manned craft.
Apollo 11 (US)	Neil A. Armstrong; Edwin E. Aldrin, Jr.; Michael Collins	July 16–24, 1969	....	....	....	195/18	First manned landing and EVA on moon; soil and rock samples collected; experiments left on lunar surface.
Apollo 12 (US)	Charles Conrad, Jr.; Richard F. Gordon, Jr.; Alan Bean	Nov. 14–24, 1969	....	....	....	244/36	Manned lunar landing mission; investigated Surveyor 3 spacecraft; collected lunar samples. EVA time: 15 hr. 30 min.
Apollo 13 (US)	James A. Lovell, Jr.; Fred W. Haise, Jr.; John L. Swigert, Jr.	Apr. 11–17, 1970	....	....	....	142/54	Third manned lunar landing attempt aborted due to loss of pressure in liquid oxygen in Service Module and failure of fuel cells.
Soyuz 6 (USSR)	Gorgiy Shonin; Valriy Kubasov	Oct. 11–16, 1969	115.6/138.6	88.6	80	118/42	Three spacecraft and seven men put into earth orbit simultaneously for first time.
Soyuz 7 (USSR)	Anatoley Filipchenko; Viktor Gorbakov; Vladislav Volkov	Oct. 12–17, 1969	128.6/140.4	88.4	80	118/42	
Soyuz 8 (USSR)	Vladimir Shatalov; Aleksey Yeliseyev	Oct. 13–18, 1969	127.4/138.6	88.6	80	118/42	
Soyuz 9 (USSR)	Andreyan Nikolayev; Vitaly Sevastianov	June 1–7, 1970	....	....	287	17 d. 16 hr. 59 m.	Longest manned flight in history; designed to test man's ability to withstand long periods of weightlessness.
Apollo 14 (US)	Alan B. Shepard; Stuart A. Roosa; Edgar D. Mitchell	Jan. 31–Feb. 9, 1971	....	....	....	216/42	Third manned lunar landing; returned largest amount of lunar material.
Soyuz 10 (USSR)	Vladimir A. Shatalov; Alexei S. Yeliseyev; Nikolai Rukavishnikov	Apr. 22–24, 1971	....	....	....	47/46	Linked up for 5½ hours with orbiting space station, Salyut¹.

Designation & Country	Date	Astronauts	Orbit: perigee/apogee (mi.)	Orbital period (min.)	Number of orbits	Flight time (hr./min.)	Remarks
Soyuz 11 (USSR)	June 6-30, 1971	Georgiy Tomofeyevich Dobrovolskiy; Vladislav Nikolayevich Volkov; Viktor Ivanovich Patsyev	.....	.....	.....	569/40	Linked up with first space station, Salyut 1. Astronauts died just before re-entry due to loss of pressurization in spacecraft.
Apollo 15 (US)	July 26–Aug. 7, 1971	David R. Scott; James B. Irwin; Alfred M. Worden	.....	.....	.....	295/12	Fourth manned lunar landing; first use of Lunar Rover propelled by Scott and Worden; first live pictures of LM lift-off from moon; longest exploration time on moon surface (18 hours).
Apollo 16 (U.S.)	Apr. 16-27, 1972	John W. Young, Thomas K. Mattingly, Charles M. Duke, Jr.	.....	.....	.....	265/51	Fifth manned lunar landing; second use of Lunar Rover Vehicle, propelled by Young and Duke. Total exploration time on the moon was 20 hrs. 14 mins., setting new record. Mattingly's in-flight "walk in space" was 1 hr. 23 mins. Approximately 213 lbs. of lunar rock returned.
Apollo 17 (US)	Dec. 7, 1972–Dec. 19, 1972	Eugene A. Cernan, Ronald E. Evans, Harrison H. Schmitt	.....	.....	.....	301/51	Sixth and last manned lunar landing; third to carry lunar rover. Cernan and Schmitt, during three EVA's, completed total of 22 hrs. 05 mins, 3 secs. USS Ticonderoga recovered crew and about 250 lbs of lunar samples.
SKYLAB SL-1 (U.S.)	May 14, 1973	.....	265/273	93.4	.....	.....	Unmanned portion of Skylab, comprised of Orbital Workshop (OWS), Airlock Module (AM), Multiple Docking Adapter (MDA), Apollo Telescope Mount (ATM), Instrument Unit (IU), and Payload Shroud (PS).
SKYLAB SL-2 (US)	May 25, 1973	Charles Conrad, Jr.; Joseph P. Kerwin; Paul J. Weitz	264/249	93.2	.....	672/50	First, manned Skylab launch. Objectives: Establish the Skylab Orbital Assembly in earth orbit, occupy it and conduct a series of scientific experiments and medical experiments associated with long-duration manned space flight.
SKYLAB SL-3 (US)	July 28, 1973	Alan L. Bean, Jr.; Jack R. Lousma; Owen K. Garriott	264/249	93.2	.....	1427/9	Second manned Skylab launch. New crew remained in space for 59 days, continuing scientific and medical experiments and earth observations from orbit.
SKYLAB SL-4 (US)	Nov. 16, 1973	Gerald Carr, Edward Gibson, William Pogue	264/249	93.2	.....	2017/16	Third manned Skylab launch; obtained medical data on crew for use in extending the duration of manned space; flight crews "walked in space" 4 times, totaling 44 hrs. 40 mins. Longest space mission yet–84 days, 1 hour, 16 minutes. Splashdown in Pacific, Feb. 9, 1974.

Spacecraft	Date	Crew				Remarks
Soyuz 12 (USSR)	Sept. 27, 1973	Vasily G. Lazarev, Oleg K. Makarov	116/152 (estimated)	.....	50/12	Two-day test flight. First Soviet manned flight since ill-fated Soyuz 11.
Soyuz 13 (USSR)	Dec. 18, 1973	Piotr Klimuk, Valentin Lebedev	.....	.....	188/55	Modified spacecraft to be used for rendezvous with U.S. spacemen in 1975.
Soyuz 14 (USSR)	July 3, 1974	Pavel Popovich, Yuri Artyukhin	.....	.....	377/29	Crewmen spent two weeks on board Soviet space station Salyut 3.
Soyuz 15 (USSR)	Aug. 26, 1974	Lt. Col. Sarafanov, Lev Demin	.....	.....	48/12	Overshot Salyut 4 space station and failed to dock. Cosmonauts returned to earth.
Soyuz 16 (USSR)	Dec. 2, 1974	Col. Filipchenck, Nikolay Rukavishnikov	.....	.....	142/24	Docked with Salyut 4.
Soyuz 17 (USSR)	Jan. 11, 1975	Col. Aleksey Gubarev, Gregory Grechko	.....	.....	709/20	Crew spent 30 days in Salyut 4 space station, which was launched Dec. 26, 1974 and placed in Earth orbit.
Soyuz 18 (USSR)	May 24, 1975	Lt. Col. Pyotr Klimuk, Vitaly Sevastyanov	.....	.....	.....	Second Soviet crew to visit orbiting space station Salyut 4.
Apollo/Soyuz Test Project (U.S.)	July 15, 1975	U.S.: Brig. Gen. Thomas P. Stafford, Vance D. Brand, Donald K. Slayton	140/140	89 (docked)	138 (docked)	U.S.: 216/05	World's first international manned rendezvous and docking in space; aimed at developing a space rescue capability. Apollo and Soyuz docked and crewmen exchanged visits on July 17, 1975. Mission duration for Soyuz: 142 hours, 31 min. For Apollo: 217 hours, 28 min.
(US and USSR)	July 16, 1975	USSR: Col. A. A. Leonov, V. N. Kubasov	360/360	89 (docked)	138 (docked)	USSR: 223/35	
Soyuz 21 (USSR)	July 6, 1976	Col. Boris Volynow, Lt. Col. Vitali Zholobov	.....	138 (docked)	1218/24	Crew spent 50 days aboard Salyut 5 space station, which was launched June 22, 1976.

1 Ground level. 2 Suborbital flight. 3 Approximate time. 4 Number of orbits.
NOTE: The letters MR stand for Mercury (capsule) and Redstone (rocket); MA, for Mercury and Atlas (rocket); GT, for Gemini (capsule) and Titan-II (rocket). The first astronaut listed in the Gemini and Apollo flights is the command pilot. The Mercury capsules had names: MR-III was *Freedom 7*, MR-IV was *Liberty Bell 7*, MR-VI was *Friendship 7*; MA-VII was *Aurora 7*, MA-VIII was *Sigma 7*, and MA-IX was *Faith 7*. The figure 7 referred to the fact that the first group of U.S. astronauts numbered seven men. Only one Gemini capsule had a name: GT-III was called *Molly Brown* (after the Broadway musical *The Unsinkable Molly Brown*); thereafter the practice of naming the capsules was discontinued.

NASA, Outlays for Research and Development: 1970-75

(in millions of dollars)

Source: Office of Management and Budget.

Performance	1970	1971	1972	1973	1974	1975
Manned space flight	2,195	1,877	1,727	1,532	1,448	1,486
Space science, applications, technology	963	926	1,111	1,220	1,156	1,033
Aircraft technology	183	206	221	235	283	296
Supporting activities	358	329	314	284	294	292

Facilities	1970	1971	1972	1973	1974	1975
Manned space flight	14	8	13	5	25	52
Space science, applications, technology	21	6	7	11	12	7
Aircraft technology	5	4	6	7	9	8
Supporting activities	14	26	24	22	29	33

NASA Launch Vehicles

	Scout	Thor-Agena D	Delta	Atlas-Agena D	Atlas-Centaur
Overall height (ft.).......	68	76.3	90	91	100
Overall weight (lbs.)......	38,500		114,200		300,000
Payload capacity (lbs.)....	240	1,600	880/150*	5,950	8,500/2,300*
First stage..............	Algol IIB	DM-21	DM-21	Atlas D	Atlas D
Length (ft.)............	30.8	55.9	55.9	67.4	75
Diameter (ft.)...........	4	8	8	10	10
Thrust (lbs.)...........	88,000	170,000	170,000	388,000	388,000
Second stage............	Castor	Agena D	....	Agena D	Centaur
Length (ft.)............	20.7	20.9	20.6	20.9	32
Diameter (ft.)...........	31 in.	5	4.3	5	10
Thrust (lbs.)...........	61,000	16,000	7,500	16,000	30,000
Third stage..............	Antares X-259	....	Altair	....	....
Length (ft.)............	11.5	....	59 in.	....	....
Diameter (in.).........	30	....	18	....	....
Thrust (lbs.)...........	23,000	....	5,800	....	....
Fourth stage............	Altair	....	....	....	....
Length (in.)...........	59	....	....	....	....
Diameter (in.).........	18	....	....	....	....
Thrust (lbs.)...........	5,800	....	....	....	....
Programs..............	Explorer, San Marco, re-entry, probes, ISIS, ESRO	Alouette, OGO, Nimbus, Sert II, PAGEOS	Biosatellite, OSO, Explorer, Tiros, Syncom, Relay, ESSA, Telstar, TOS, Ariel, Pioneer, Early Bird	Lunar Orbiter, OAO, Mariner, Ranger, OGO, ATS	Mariner, Surveyor

	Titan 3E/Centaur	Saturn I	Uprated Saturn I	Saturn V
Overall height (ft.).......	109†	190†	225†	365†
Overall weight (lbs.)......	300,000	1,165,000	1,300,000	6,200,000
Payload capacity (lbs.)....	7,000	22,500	40,000	285,000/100,000*
First stage..............	....	S-I	S-IB	S-IC
Length (ft.)............	71	82	80	138
Diameter (ft.)...........	10	21.6	21.6	33
Thrust (lbs.)...........	430,000	1,504,000	1,600,000	7,500,000
Second stage............	....	S-IV	S-IVB	S-II
Length (ft.)............	19	40	59	80
Diameter (ft.)...........	10	18	21.7	33
Thrust (lbs.)...........	100,000	90,000	200,000	1,000,000
Third stage.............	....	....	....	S-IVB
Length (ft.)............	....	....	....	59
Diameter (ft.).........	....	....	....	21.7
Thrust (lbs.)...........	....	....	....	200,000
Programs..............	Gemini	Apollo (unmanned tests), Pegasus	Apollo (Earth orbit tests, including manned Apollo 7)	Apollo (moon flights)

* Payload capacity for escape of earth's gravity; unstarred part is earth orbit capacity.   † Height includes payload.

Lunar Geology

From the Apollo moon flight data, geologists divided the Moon's interior into five concentric layers: (1) An outer crust of plagioclase-rich rock extending to a depth of 60 km (37 mi.); (2) An upper mantle of olivine- and pyroxene-rich rock extending from 60 to 300 km (185 mi.); (3) A middle mantle from 300 to 800 km (500 mi.), possibly composed of primitive lunar rock from which the outer layers formed during an earlier period of melting; (4) A lower mantle lying at a depth of 800 to 1,400 km (865 mi.) that may be partially molten; and (5) Below 1,400 km a core, perhaps of molten iron sulfide.

Russian Missiles

Name (nickname)	Length (ft.)	Take-off weight, lb.	Range (miles)	Take-off thrust, lb.[1]	Remarks
GROUND–TO–GROUND:					
Scud-A................	32	c. 9,000	100	15,000	Liquid fuel; operational
Scud-B................	37	10,000	135	17,000	Liquid fuel; status unknown
Shaddock..............	36	c. 14,000	245	20,000	Probably solid fuel
Sandal................	66.5	c. 50,000	350	80,000	Liquid fuel; obsolescent
SS-2..................	52	c. 32,000	300	50,000	Liquid fuel; production stopped
Shyster...............	75	c. 45,000	900+	75,000	Liquid fuel; larger version known to exist
SS-5..................	85	c. 90,000	1,900	125,000	Liquid fuel; obsolescent
Iron Maiden...........	c. 40	c. 70,000	1,200+	100,000	Solid fuel
SS-6..................	110	c. 200,000	6,000	350,000	Liquid fuel; ICBM
SS-7..................	80	c. 150,000	7,500	250,000	Storable liquid; ICBM
Snark[2]..............	47.5	??	1,500	??	Solid fuel
SURFACE–TO–AIR:					
Guideline (SA-2).......	35	c. 5,000	12–18	9,500	First stage solid, second stage liquid
Guild.................	38	c. 6,000	18–20	11,000	Liquid fuel; deployed
Griffon...............	52	c. 5,000	up to 100	9,000	First stage solid, second stage liquid
Goa...................	20	c. 1,000	10–12	2,000	Truck-launched, solid fuel
Little Sister...........	55	c. 30,000	??	??	Solid fuel
TACTICAL, UNGUIDED:					
Frog II...............	30	c. 4,800	17	9,000	Solid fuel; operational
Frog III..............	35	c. 4,400	up to 28	9,000	Solid fuel; operational
Frog IV...............	35	c. 4,200	31	8,000	Solid fuel; probably operational
Gannef[3].............	28	c. 4,200	??	8,000	See notes

[1] Estimated. [2] *Snark* (NATO designation) is a submarine-launched Polaris-type missile. It is uncertain whether underwater launch is possible or whether submarine has to surface for launch. Said to have a land-based version. [3] *Gannef* may be a solid-fuel missile, but the solid-fuel units are believed to be take-off help only, with ramjet propulsion acting as a sustainer engine. Could be a dual-purpose weapon, both for antiaircraft use and for tactical support. The rocket nicknamed *Big Brother* is a three-stage solid-fuel missile of a length of about 120 feet. Its take-off thrust is believed to exceed one million pounds. Claims that *Big Brother* was the rocket that launched the *Vostok* and *Voskhod* manned spacecraft turned out to be wrong. The *Vostok* rocket, shown in Paris in 1967, was a special design.

U. S. Ballistic Missiles of Operational and Near-operational Status

Name	Length (ft.)	Take-off weight, lb.	Range (miles)	Fuel	Take-off thrust, lb.	Prime Contractor
GROUND–TO–GROUND:						
Atlas..................	82	265,000	6,000+	Liquid	360,000	Convair
Titan.................	90	222,000	7,000+	Liquid	340,000	Martin
Thor..................	62	110,000	1,500	Liquid	160,000	Douglas
Jupiter...............	59	110,000	1,500	Liquid	160,000	Chrysler
Pershing..............	34	10,000	c. 350	Solid	......	Martin
Redstone..............	63	61,000	200	Liquid	110,000	Chrysler
Corporal..............	46	12,000	50	Liquid	20,000	Firestone
Sergeant..............	30	......	50+	Solid	......	JPL/Sperry
Honest John[1]........	27	6,000	15	Solid	......	Emerson–
Little John[1].........	15	......	15?	Solid	......	Douglas
Lacrosse..............	19	2,300	20	Solid	......	Martin
Polaris A-1...........	28	28,000	1,200	Solid	c. 100,000	Lockheed
Polaris A-2...........	30.5	30,000	1,500	Solid	c. 100,000	Lockheed
Polaris A-3...........	30.5	30,000	2,500	Solid	c. 100,000	Lockheed
Minuteman............	54	65,000+	6,000	Solid	100,000+	Boeing
SURFACE–TO–AIR:						
Nike Hercules.........	27	......	75+	Solid	......	Western El.
Terrier...............	15	3,000	10	Solid	......	Convair
AIR–TO–SURFACE:						
Bullpup...............	11	571	3	Solid	......	Martin
Hound Dog (GAM-77)...	42.5	9,600	c. 660	Liquid	7,500	No. America
ANTI–SUBMARINE:						
Able..................	8.5	500	......	......	......	Avco
AIR–TO–AIR:						
Falcon................	6.5	100	......	Solid	......	Hughes
Genie[2]..............	8	......	1.5	Solid	......	Douglas
Sidewinder 1-A........	9	155	2	Solid	......	Philco
Sparrow I[3]..........	12	300	5+	Solid	......	Sperry
Sparrow III[3]........	12	350	......	Solid	......	Raytheon

[1] Honest John and Little John are unguided artillery rockets. [2] Genie is an unguided rocket. [3] Sparrow I is being replaced by Sparrow III.

SCIENCE

By
NICHOLAS PANAGAKOS

SCIENCE HIGHLIGHTS OF 1976

A Chilling Possibility: Another Ice Age

The world's climate is changing.

Scientists have been convinced of that for years, but the magnitude and the meaning of the change were subjects of deepening debate and concern in 1976.

The majority of climatologists are convinced that the Earth is cooling, and that the weather aberrations experienced in recent years may be the harbinger of another Ice Age.

This view is supported by a recent report produced by the National Academy of Sciences. Says the panel of experts who participated in the study:

"There seems little doubt that the present period of unusual warmth will eventually give way to a time of colder climate, but there is no consensus with regard to either the magnitude or rapidity of the transition."

Maybe Later, Maybe Sooner

An Ice Age could be a thousand years in the offing, or it could be upon us in the next few hundred years—nobody knows, but everybody worries.

There is little quarrel with the notion that the Earth's atmosphere is cooling. The clues are all around us, from the thickening and more persistent ice packs in the Arctic to the ever-southward migration of armadillos from the Midwest. Most ominously, it was recently discovered that the average surface temperature in the Northern Hemisphere had dropped nearly 3 degrees Fahrenheit between 1958 and 1963. Before that, the Earth's mean temperature had been increasing steadily since the 1880s.

Cooling Temporary, or Really on the Way?

But the central question around which debate and concern are swirling is this: Is the present slow cooling temporary, or is it a trend which presages the coming of another Ice Age?

A major problem in seeking to assess the trend is to distinguish among year-to-year fluctuations, those spread over decades, and those spread over centuries and thousands of years. In 1974, for example, climatologists predicted that the winter would be unusually severe. But Boston had its warmest winter in decades, and in Moscow it was the second warmest in more than two centuries.

What are we to make of all this? It is difficult to assess current trends because there is lack of agreement among experts as to the factors that control climate change. Although people have talked about the weather since the beginning of time, climatology is a relatively new science. Serious attempts to understand global climate have been possible only since the advent of the computer and the Earth-orbiting satellite which can monitor weather, atmospheric and oceanic conditions. But even with these sophisticated Space Age tools, the answers are elusive.

Adding to the problem of understanding climate are the effects of man's presence on Earth. It is still unclear whether the increased levels of carbon dioxide and other pollutants in the atmosphere will raise or lower the global temperature. Indeed, some scientists suggest that man may inadvertently ward off another Ice Age by balancing off the temperature drop with his production of waste heat. But others say just the opposite will happen—man-made pollution will trigger a new Ice Age before its time by blocking sunlight and preventing it from warming the surface of the Earth.

Scientists Seek Large-Scale Research

Most theories on the causes of climate change have to do with small variations in the amount of solar energy reaching the Earth at a particular time in a particular place. One theory—recurrent since it was first proposed in the early 1920s—is that changes in the Earth's tilt and distance from the Sun significantly increase or decrease the amount of solar radiation falling on either hemisphere, thus altering the climate. Other theories, less satisfactory, try to tie climatic change to the Sun's 11-year sunspot cycle.

It is clear that vastly more information is needed about the major influences on Earth's climate. The National Academy of Sciences is urging a large-scale research program beginning with about $18 million in funding and growing to about $67 million a year by the end of this decade.

The consequences of failing to understand the changing climate could be serious. Even a slight change in temperature and rainfall patterns could seriously reduce global food stores.

In the past three quarters of a million years, there have been at least seven Ice Ages on Earth. The last 10,000 years have been a period of relative warmth, interlaced with cold "ups and downs." But history tells us that the warm periods have rarely lasted more than 8,000 to 12,000 years—and they tend to end abruptly. It is this last fact that has made climatological Cassandras more than a little apprehensive in recent years.

Thinking Metric

The United States is slowly but inexorably inching toward adoption of the metric system of weights and measures.

A number of American institutions have recognized the inevitable—that the metric system is coming. Most federal agencies have joined the metric parade. Many rules and services now come in metric measurements. The giants of U.S. industry—General Motors, Ford, IBM, General Electric—have embraced the metric method, and the list is growing as more and more companies market the same products at home and abroad.

In schools several states already require that pupils learn metrics as a primary language of measurement. Many more states are slated to follow in 1977. Many highway signs now post distances in both miles and kilometers, and more and more food products are coming with measurements in the two systems.

The creeping conversion to the metric system is still unofficial. The United States still remains the last industrialized country in the world to adopt the system. The Senate passed a bill in 1972 which would force metric conversion over a ten-year period. But the measure failed in the House when labor, and some businesses, insisted they be compensated for the cost of the switch. Passage of a bill in the immediate future—probably next year—seems inevitable, however.

Estimates of the economic impact of conversion run over $10 billion for a 10-year process. A typical machinist might spend several thousand dollars just for a new set of tools with metric measurements. And to the consumer, it will mean practically learning his basic arithmetic all over again.

Why bother, then? The answer is simple: Times have changed. Until relatively recent times, the undeveloped nations of the world had more need for American (and British) products than we did for theirs. They had to take these goods according to British and American measurements. With the industrialization of the rest of the world, however, the majority took a look at various systems and adopted metric. The industrialized world is now telling the United States (the British went metric in 1965): "If you want us to buy your goods, they had better come in metric measurements."

There is little question that the initial conversion cost will be expensive. But once conversion is complete, the global standard will allow a freer flow of U.S. goods abroad. Some see as much as a $2-billion improvement in the balance of payments.

What is so great about the metric system? Proponents say it is much simpler and less awkward than the U.S. Customary System because it relates to multiples of ten, just as our monetary system works in tens. (Ten pennies equal one dime; ten dimes equal one dollar). In the U.S. system, all units are odd. Ten inches don't make a foot, ten feet don't make a yard and 1000 yards don't make a mile. Because the U.S. system deals in odd units, we are forced to multiply and divide to get the answer. In the metric, one simply adds or subtracts zeroes.

No one expects the transition to be easy. The old system has been ingrained in the English language since the Romans brought the *pondus* (pound) and *uncia* (inch) to Britain some 2000 years ago. The main task, as some highway signs are already exhorting, is to THINK METRIC.

MEASURES AND WEIGHTS

Source: National Bureau of Standards, Department of Commerce.

The International System (Metric)

The International System of Units is a modernized version of the metric system, established by international agreement, i.e. provides a logical and interconnected framework for all measurements in science, industry, and commerce. The system is built on a foundation of seven basic units, and all other units are derived from them. (Use of metric weights and measures was legalized in the United States in 1866, and our customary units of weights and measures are defined in terms of the meter and kilogram.)

Length—Meter. The meter is defined as 1,650,763.73 wavelengths in vacuum of the orange-red line of the spectrum of krypton-86.

Time—Second. The second is defined as the duration of 9,192,631,770 cycles of the radiation associated with a specified transition of the cesium 133 atom.

Mass—Kilogram. The standard for the kilogram is a cylinder of platinum-iridium alloy kept by the International Bureau of Weights and Measures at Paris. A duplicate at the National Bureau of Standards serves as the mass standard for the United States. The kilogram is the only base unit still defined by an artifact.

Temperature—Kelvin. The kelvin is defined as the fraction $1/273.16$ of the thermodynamic temperature of the triple point of water; that is, the point at which water forms an interface of solid, liquid and vapor. This is defined as $0.01°C$ on the Centigrade or Celsius scale and $32.02°F$ on the Fahrenheit scale. The temperature $0°K$ is called "absolute zero."

Electric Current—Ampere. The ampere is defined as that current that, if maintained in each of two long parallel wires separated by one meter in free space, would produce a force between the two wires (due to their magnetic fields) of 2×10^{-7} newton for each meter of length. (A newton is the unit of force which when applied to one kilogram mass would experience an acceleration of one meter per second per second.)

Luminous Intensity—Candela. The candela is defined as the luminous intensity of $1/600,000$ of a square meter of a cavity at the temperature of freezing platinum ($2,042K$).

Amount of Substance—Mole. The mole is the amount of substance of a system that contains as many elementary entities as there are atoms in 0.012 kilograms of carbon-12.

Prefixes and Multiples

Prefix	Symbol	Equivalent	Multiple/Submultiple	Prefix	Symbol	Equivalent	Multiple/Submultiple
atto	a	quintillionth part	10^{-18}	deci	d	tenth part	10^{-1}
femto	f	quadrillionth part	10^{-15}	deka	da	tenfold	10
pico	p	trillionth part	10^{-12}	hecto	h	hundredfold	10^2
nano	n	billionth part	10^{-9}	kilo	k	thousandfold	10^3
micro	μ	millionth part	10^{-6}	mega	M	millionfold	10^6
milli	m	thousandth part	10^{-3}	giga	G	billionfold	10^9
centi	c	hundredth part	10^{-2}	tera	T	trillionfold	10^{12}

Tables of Metric Weights and Measures

LINEAR MEASURE

10 millimeters (mm)	= 1 centimeter (cm)
10 centimeters	= 1 decimeter (dm) = 100 millimeters
10 decimeters	= 1 meter (m) = 1,000 millimeters
10 meters	= 1 dekameter (dam)
10 dekameters	= 1 hectometer (hm) = 100 meters
10 hectometers	= 1 kilometer (km) = 1,000 meters

AREA MEASURE

100 square millimeters (mm²)	= 1 sq centimeter (cm²)
10,000 square centimeters	= 1 sq meter (m²) = 1,000,000 sq millimeters
100 square meters	= 1 are (a)
100 ares	= 1 hectare (ha) = 10,000 sq meters
100 hectares	= 1 sq kilometer (km²) = 1,000,000 sq meters

VOLUME MEASURE

10 milliliters (ml)	= 1 centiliter (cl)
10 centiliters	= 1 deciliter (dl) = 100 milliliters

Volume Measure (Cont'd.)

10 deciliters	= 1 liter (l) = 1,000 milliliters
10 liters	= 1 dekaliter (dal)
10 dekaliters	= 1 hectoliter (hl) = 100 liters
10 hectoliters	= 1 kiloliter (kl) = 1,000 liters

CUBIC MEASURE

1,000 cubic millimeters (mm³)	= 1 cu centimeter (cm³)
1,000 cubic centimeters	= 1 cu decimeter (dm³) = 1,000,000 cu millimeters
1,000 cubic decimeters	= 1 cu meter (m³) = 1 stere = 1,000,000 cu centimeters = 1,000,000,000 cu millimeters

WEIGHT

10 milligrams (mg)	= 1 centigram (cg)
10 centigrams	= 1 decigram (dg) = 100 milligrams
10 decigrams	= 1 gram (g) = 1,000 milligrams
10 grams	= 1 dekagram (dag)
10 dekagrams	= 1 hectogram (hg) = 100 grams
10 hectograms	= 1 kilogram (kg) = 1,000 grams
1,000 kilograms	= 1 metric ton (t)

Tables of U.S. Customary Weights and Measures

LINEAR MEASURE

12 inches (in.)	= 1 foot (ft)
3 feet	= 1 yard (yd)
5½ yards	= 1 rod (rd), pole, or perch (16½ ft)
40 rods	= 1 furlong (fur) = 220 yds = 660 ft
8 furlongs	= 1 statute mile (mi) = 1,760 yds = 5,280 ft
3 land miles	= 1 league
5,280 feet	= 1 statute or land mile
6,076.11549 feet	= 1 international nautical mile

AREA MEASURE

144 square inches	= 1 sq ft
9 square feet	= 1 sq yd = 1,296 sq in.
30¼ square yards	= 1 sq rd = 272¼ sq ft
160 square rods	= 1 acre = 4,840 sq yds = 43,560 sq ft
640 acres	= 1 sq mi
1 mile square	= 1 section (of land)
6 miles square	= 1 township = 36 sections = 36 sq mi

CUBIC MEASURE

1,728 cubic inches	= 1 cu ft
27 cubic feet	= 1 cu yd

LIQUID MEASURE

When necessary to distinguish the liquid pint or quart from the dry pint or quart, the word "liquid" or the abbreviation "liq" should be used in combination with the name or abbreviation of the liquid unit.

4 gills (gi)	= 1 pint (pt) (=28.875 cu in.)
2 pints	= 1 quart (qt) (=57.75 cu in.)
4 quarts	= 1 gallon (gal) (=231 cu in.) = 8 pts = 32 gills

APOTHECARIES FLUID MEASURE

60 minims (min.)	= 1 fluid dram (fl dr) (= 0.2256 cu in.)
8 fluid drams	= 1 fluid ounce (fl oz) (= 1.8047 cu in.)
16 fluid ounces	= 1 pt (= 28.875 cu in.) = 128 fl drs
2 pints	= 1 qt (= 57.75 cu in.) = 32 fl oz = 256 fl drs
4 quarts	= 1 gal (= 231 cu in.) = 128 fl oz = 1,024 fl drs

DRY MEASURE

When necessary to distinguish the dry pint or quart from the liquid pint or quart, the word "dry" should be used in combination with the name or abbreviation of the dry unit.

2 pints	= 1 qt (=67.2006 cu in.)
8 quarts	= 1 peck (pk) (=537.605 cu in.) = 16 pts
4 pecks	= 1 bushel (bu) (= 2,150.42 cu in.) = 32 qts

AVOIRDUPOIS WEIGHT

When necessary to distinguish the avoirdupois dram from the apothecaries dram, or to distinguish the avoirdupois dram or ounce from the fluid dram or ounce, or to distinguish the avoirdupois ounce or pound from the troy or apothecaries ounce or pound, the word "avoirdupois" or the abbreviation "avdp." should be used in combination with the name or abbreviation of the avoirdupois unit.

(The "grain" is the same in avoirdupois, troy, and apothecaries weights.)

27 11/32 grains	= 1 dram (dr)
16 drams	= 1 oz = 437½ grains

16 ounces	= 1 lb = 256 drams = 7,000 grains
100 pounds	= 1 hundredweight (cwt)*
20 hundredweights	= 1 ton (tn) = 2,000 lbs*

In "gross" or "long" measure, the following values are recognized:

| 112 pounds | = 1 gross or long cwt* |
| 20 gross or long hundredweights | = 1 gross or long ton = 2,240 lbs* |

* When the terms "hundredweight" and "ton" are used unmodified, they are commonly understood to mean the 100-pound hundredweight and the 2,000-pound ton, respectively; these units may be designated "net" or "short" when necessary to distinguish them from the corresponding units in gross or long measure.

UNITS OF CIRCULAR MEASURE

Unit	Comparison
Second (″)	
Minute (′)	60 seconds
Degree (°)	60 minutes
Right angle	90 degrees
Straight angle	180 degrees
Circle	360 degrees

TROY WEIGHT

24 grains	= 1 pennyweight (dwt)
20 pennyweights	= 1 ounce troy (oz t) = 480 grains
12 ounces troy	= 1 pound troy (lb t) = 240 pennyweights = 5,760 grains

APOTHECARIES WEIGHT

20 grains	= 1 scruple (s ap)
3 scruples	= 1 dram apothecaries (dr ap) = 60 grains
8 drams apothecaries	= 1 ounce apothecaries (oz ap) = 24 scruples = 480 grains
12 ounces apothecaries	= 1 pound apothecaries (lb ap) = 96 drams apothecaries = 288 scruples = 5,760 grains

GUNTER'S OR SURVEYOR'S CHAIN MEASURE

7.92 inches	= 1 link (li)
100 links	= 1 chain (ch) = 4 rods = 66 ft
80 chains	= 1 statute mile = 320 rods = 5,280 ft

Metric and U.S. Tables of Equivalents

1 angstrom[1] (light wave measurement)	0.1 millimicron 0.000 1 micron 0.000 000 1 millimeter 0.000 000 004 inch
1 cable's length	120 fathoms 720 ft 219.456 meters
1 centimeter	0.393 7 in.
1 chain (Gunter's or surveyor's)	66 ft 20.1168 meters
1 decimeter	3.937 in.
1 dekameter	32.808 ft
1 fathom	6 ft 1.8288 meters
1 foot	0.3048 meter
1 furlong	10 chains (surveyor's) 660 ft 220 yds 1/8 statute mile 201.168 meters
1 inch	2.54 centimeters
1 kilometer	0.621 mile
1 league (land)	3 statute miles 4.828 kilometers
1 link (Gunter's or surveyor's)	7.92 in. 0.201 168 meter
1 meter	39.37 in. 1.094 yds
1 micron	0.001 millimeter 0.000 039 37 in.
1 mil	0.001 in. 0.025 4 millimeter
1 mile (statute or land)	5,280 ft 1.609 kilometers
1 mile (nautical international)	1.852 kilometers 1.151 statute miles 0.999 U.S. nautical miles
1 millimeter	0.039.37 in.
1 millimicron (mμ)	0.001 micron 0.000 000 039 37 in.
1 nanometer	0.001 micrometer or 0.000 000 039 37 in.
1 point (typography)	0.013 837 in. 1/72 inch (approximately) 0.351 millimeter

| 1 rod, pole, or perch | 16½ ft 5.0292 meters |
| 1 yard | 0.9144 meter |

AREAS OR SURFACES

1 acre	43,560 sq ft 4,840 sq yds 0.405 hectare
1 are	119.599 sq yds 0.025 acre
1 hectare	2.471 acres
1 square centimeter	0.155 sq in.
1 square decimeter	15.500 sq in.
1 square foot	929,030 sq centimeters
1 square inch	6.4516 sq centimeters
1 square kilometer	0.386 sq mile 247.105 acres
1 square meter	1.196 sq yds 10.764 sq ft
1 square mile	258.999 hectares
1 square millimeter	0.002 sq in.
1 square rod, sq. pole, or sq. perch	25.293 sq meters
1 square yard	0.836 sq meter

CAPACITIES OR VOLUMES

1 barrel, liquid	31 to 42 gal[2]
1 barrel, standard for fruits, vegetables, and other dry commodities except cranberries	7,056 cu in. 105 dry qts 3.281 bushels, struck measure
1 barrel, standard, cranberry	5.286 cu in. 86 45/64 dry qts 2.709 bushels, struck measure
1 bushel (U.S.) struck measure	2,150.42 cu in. 35.238 liters
1 bushel, heaped (U.S.)	2 747.715 cu in. 1.278 bushels, struck measure[3]
1 cord (firewood)	128 cu ft
1 cubic centimeter	0.061 cu in.
1 cubic decimeter	61.024 cu in.
1 cubic foot	7.481 gals 28.316 cu decimeters

1 cubic inch	0.554 fl oz
	4.433 fl drs
	16.387 cu centimeters
1 cubic meter	1.308 cu yds
1 cubic yard	0.765 cu meter
1 cup, measuring	8 fl oz
	½ liquid pt
1 dram, fluid or liquid	¼ fl oz
(U.S.)	0.226 cu in.
	3.697 milliliters
	1.041 British fluid drachms
1 dekaliter	2.642 gals
	1.135 pecks
1 gallon (U.S.)	231 cu in.
	3.785 liters
	0.833 British gal
	128 U.S. fl oz
1 gallon (British	277.42 cu in.
Imperial)	1.201 U.S. gals
	4.546 liters
	160 British fl oz
1 gill	7.219 cu in.
	4 fl oz
	0.118 liter
1 hectoliter	26.418 gals
	2.838 bushels
1 liter	1.057 liquid qts
	0.908 dry qt
	61.024 cu in
1 milliliter	0.271 fl dr
	16.231 minims
	0.061 cu in.
1 ounce, fluid or	1.805 cu in.
liquid (U.S.)	29.574 milliliters
	1.041 British fl oz
1 peck	8.810 liters
1 pint, dry	33.600 cu in.
	0.551 liter
1 pint, liquid	28.875 cu in.
	0.473 liter
1 quart, dry (U.S.)	67.201 cu in.
	1.101 liters
	0.969 British qt
1 quart, liquid (U.S.)	57.75 cu in.
	0.946 liter
	0.833 British qt
1 quart (British)	69.354 cu in.
	1.032 U.S. dry qts
	1.201 U.S. liquid qts

1 tablespoon,	3 teaspoons
measuring	4 fluid drs
	½ fl oz
1 teaspoon, measuring	⅓ tablespoon
	1⅓ fl drs
1 assay ton[4]	29,167 grams
1 carat	200 milligrams
	3.086 grains
1 dram, apothecaries	60 grains
	3.888 grams
1 dram, avoirdupois	27 11/32 (=27.344) grains
	1.772 grams
1 grain	64.798 91 milligrams
1 gram	15.432 grains
	0.035 oz, avoirdupois
1 hundredweight,	112 lbs
gross or long[5]	50.802 kilograms
1 hundredweight,	100 lbs
net or short	45.359 kilograms
1 kilogram	2.205 lbs
1 microgram [μg (the	
Greek letter mu in	
combination with the	
letter g)]	0.000 001 gram
1 milligram	0.015 grain
1 ounce, avoirdupois	437.5 grains
	0.911 troy or apothecaries oz
	28.350 grams
1 ounce, troy or	480 grains
apothecaries	1.097 avoirdupois oz
	31.103 grams
1 pennyweight	1.555 grams
1 point	0.01 carat
	2 milligrams
1 pound, avoirdupois	7 000 grains
	1.215 troy or apothecaries lbs
	453.592 37 grams
1 pound, troy or	5 760 grains
apothecaries	0.823 avoirdupois lb
	373.242 grams
1 ton, gross on long[5]	2,204 lbs
	1.12 net tons
	1.016 metric tons
1 ton, metric	2,204.623 lbs
	0.984 gross ton
	1.102 net tons
1 ton, net or short	2,000 lbs
	0.893 gross ton
	0.907 metric ton

[1] The angstrom is basically defined as 10⁻¹⁰ meter.
[2] There are a variety of "barrels" established by law or usage. For example, federal taxes on fermented liquors are based on a barrel of 31 gallons; many state laws fix the "barrel for liquids" at 31½ gals; one state fixes a 36-gal barrel for cistern measurement; federal law recognizes a 40-gal barrel for "proof spirits"; by custom, 42 gals comprise a barrel of crude oil or petroleum products for statistical purposes, and this equivalent is recognized "for liquids" by four states.   [3] Frequently recognized as 1¼ bushels, struck measure.   [4] Used in assaying. The assay ton bears the same relation to the milligram that a ton of 2,000 lbs avoirdupois bears to the ounce troy; hence the weight in milligrams of precious metal obtained from one assay ton of ore gives directly the number of troy ounces to the net ton.   [5] The gross or long ton and hundredweight are used commercially in the United States to only a limited extent, usually in restricted industrial fields. These units are the same as the British "ton" and "hundredweight."

KELVIN SCALE

Absolute zero, −273.16° on the Celsius (Centigrade) scale, is 0° Kelvin. Thus, degrees Kelvin are equivalent to degrees Celsius plus 273.16. The freezing point of water, 0°C. and 32°F., is 273.16°K. The conversion formula is $K° = C° + 273.16$.

FAHRENHEIT AND CELSIUS (CENTIGRADE) SCALES

Zero on the Fahrenheit scale represents the temperature produced by the mixing of equal weights of snow and common salt.

	F	C
Boiling point of water	212°	100°
Freezing point of water	32°	0°
Absolute zero	−459.6°	−273.1°

Absolute zero is theoretically the lowest possible temperature, the point at which all molecular motion would cease.

To convert Fahrenheit to Celsius (Centigrade), subtract 32 and multiply by 5/9.

To convert Celsius (Centigrade) to Fahrenheit, multiply by 9/5 and add 32.

HANDY CONVERSION TABLES FOR CONSUMERS

For Travelers: Conversion of Miles to Kilometers and Kilometers to Miles

Miles	Kilometers	Miles	Kilometers	Kilometers	Miles	Kilometers	Miles
1	1.6	20	32.1	1	0.6	20	12.4
2	3.2	30	48.2	2	1.2	30	18.6
3	4.8	40	64.3	3	1.8	40	24.8
4	6.4	50	80.4	4	2.4	50	31.0
5	8.0	60	96.5	5	3.1	60	37.2
6	9.6	70	112.6	6	3.7	70	43.4
7	11.2	80	128.7	7	4.3	80	49.7
8	12.8	90	144.8	8	4.9	90	55.9
9	14.4	100	160.9	9	5.5	100	62.1
10	16.0	1000	1609	10	6.2	1000	621

For the Person in the Kitchen

U.S. Customary System				Metric			
Capacity		Weight		Capacity		Weight	
1/5 teaspoon	1 milliliter	1 fluid oz	30 milliliters	1 milliliter	1/5 teaspoon	1 gram	.035 ounce
1 teaspoon	5 ml		28 grams	5 ml	1 teaspoon	100 grams	3.5 ounces
1 tablespoon	15 ml	1 pound	454 grams	15 ml	1 tablespoon	500 grams	1.10 pounds
1/5 cup	50 ml			34 ml	1 fluid oz.	1 kilogram	2.205 pounds
1 cup	240 ml			100 ml	3.4 fluid oz.		35 oz.
2 cups (1 pint)	470 ml			240 ml	1 cup		
4 cups (1 quart)	.95 liter			1 liter	34 fluid oz.		
4 quarts (1 gal.)	3.8 liters				4.2 cups		
					2.1 pints		
					1.06 quarts		
					0.26 gallon		

Bolts and Screws: Conversion from Fractions of an Inch to Millimeters

Inch	Mm	Inch	Mm	Inch	Mm	Inch	Mm
1/64	0.40	17/64	6.75	33/64	13.10	49/64	19.45
1/32	0/79	9/32	7.14	17/32	13.50	25/32	19.84
3/64	1.19	19/64	7.54	35/64	13.90	51/64	20.24
1/16	1.59	5/16	7.94	9/16	14.29	13/16	20.64
5/64	1.98	21/64	8.33	37/64	14.69	53/64	21.03
3/32	2.38	11/32	8.73	19/32	15.08	27/32	21.43
7/64	2.78	23/64	9.13	39/64	15.48	55/64	21.83
1/8	3.18	3/8	9.53	5/8	15.88	7/8	22.23
9/64	3.57	25/64	9.92	41/64	16.27	57/64	22.62
5/32	3.97	13/32	10.32	21/32	16.67	29/32	23.02
11/64	4.37	27/64	10.72	43/64	17.06	59/64	23.42
3/16	4.76	7/16	11.11	11/64	17.46	15/16	23.81
13/64	5.16	29/64	11.51	45/64	17.86	61/64	24.21
7/32	5.56	15/32	11.91	23/32	18.26	31/32	24.61
15/64	5.95	31/64	12.30	47/64	18.65	63/64	25.00
1/4	6.35	1/2	12.70	3/4	19.05	1	25.40

Handy Conversion Factors

To change	To	Multiply by	To change	To	Multiply by
acres	hectares	.4047	centimeters	feet	.03281
acres	square feet	43,560	circumference	radians	6.283
acres	square miles	.001562	cubic feet	cubic meters	.0283
atmospheres	cms. of mercury	76	cubic meters	cubic feet	35.3145
BTU	horsepower-hrs.	.0003931	cubic meters	cubic yards	1.3079
BTU	kilowatt-hrs.	.0002928	cubic yards	cubic meters	.7646
BTU/hr.	watts	.2931	degrees	radians	.01745
bushels	cubic inches	2150.4	dynes	grams	.00102
bushels (U. S.)	hectoliters	.3524	fathoms	feet	6.0
centimeters	inches	.3937	feet	meters	.3048

Handy Conversion Factors (Contd.)

To change	To	Multi-ply by	To change	To	Multi-ply by
feet	miles (nautical)	.0001645	miles	feet	5280
feet	miles (statute)	.0001894	miles (nautical)	miles (statute)	1.1516
feet/sec.	miles/hr.	.6818	miles (statute)	miles (nautical)	.8684
furlongs	feet	660.0	miles/hr.	feet/min.	88
furlongs	miles	.125	millimeters	inches	.0394
gallons (U. S.)	liters	3.7853	ounces avdp.	grams	28.3495
grains	grams	.0648	ounces	pounds	.0625
grams	grains	15.4324	ounces (troy)	ounces (avdp)	1.09714
grams	ounces avdp.	.0353	pecks	liters	8.8096
grams	pounds	.002205	pints (dry)	liters	.5506
hectares	acres	2.4710	pints (liquid)	liters	.4732
hectoliters	bushels (U. S.)	2.8378	pounds ap or t	kilograms	.3782
horsepower	watts	745.7	pounds avdp.	kilograms	.4536
hours	days	.04167	pounds	ounces	16
inches	millimeters	25.4000	quarts (dry)	liters	1.1012
inches	centimeters	2.5400	quarts (liquid)	liters	.9463
kilograms	pounds avdp or t	2.2046	radians	degrees	57.30
kilometers	miles	.6214	rods	meters	5.029
kilowatts	horsepower	1.341	rods	feet	16.5
knots	nautical miles/hr.	1.0	square feet	square meters	.0929
knots	statute miles/hr.	1.151	square kilometers	square miles	.3861
liters	gallons (U. S.)	.2642	square meters	square feet	10.7639
liters	pecks	.1135	square meters	square yards	1.1960
liters	pints (dry)	1.8162	square miles	square kilometers	2.5900
liters	pints (liquid)	2.1134	square yards	square meters	.8361
liters	quarts (dry)	.9081	tons (long)	metric tons	1.1060
liters	quarts (liquid)	1.0567	tons (short)	metric tons	.9072
meters	feet	3.2808	tons (long)	pounds	2240
meters	miles	.0006214	tons (short)	pounds	2000
meters	yards	1.0936	watts	BTU/hr.	3.4129
metric tons	tons (long)	.9842	watts	horsepower	.001341
metric tons	tons (short)	1.1023	yards	meters	.9144
miles	kilometers	1.6093	yards	miles	.0005682

COMMON FORMULAS

Circumference

Circle: $C=\pi d$, in which π is 3.1416 and d the diameter.

Area

Triangle: $A=\dfrac{ab}{2}$, in which a is the base and b the height.

Square: $A=a^2$, in which a is one of the sides.

Rectangle: $A=ab$, in which a is the base and b the height.

Trapezoid: $A=\dfrac{h(a+b)}{2}$, in which h is the height, a the longer parallel side, and b the shorter.

Regular pentagon: $A=1.720a^2$, in which a is one of the sides.

Regular hexagon: $A=2.598a^2$, in which a is one of the sides.

Regular octagon: $A=4.828a^2$, in which a is one of the sides.

Circle: $A=\pi r^2$, in which π is 3.1416 and r the radius.

Volume

Cube: $V=a^3$, in which a is one of the edges.

Rectangular prism: $V=abc$, in which a is the length, b the width, and c the depth.

Pyramid: $V=\dfrac{Ah}{3}$, in which A is the area of the base and h the height.

Cylinder: $V=\pi r^2 h$, in which π is 3.1416, r the radius of the base, and h the height.

Cone: $V=\dfrac{\pi r^2 h}{3}$, in which π is 3.1416, r the radius of the base, and h the height.

Sphere: $V=\dfrac{4\pi r^3}{3}$, in which π is 3.1416 and r the radius.

Miscellaneous

Speed per second acquired by falling body: $v=32t$, in which t is the time in seconds.

Distance in feet traveled by falling body: $d=16t^2$, in which t is the time in seconds.

Speed of sound in feet per second through any given temperature of air:

$V=\dfrac{1087\sqrt{273+t}}{16.52}$, in which t is the temperature Centigrade.

Cost in cents of operation of electrical device: $C=\dfrac{Wtc}{1000}$, in which W is the number of watts, t the time in hours, and c

the cost in cents per kilowatt-hour.

Conversion of matter into energy (Einstein's Theorem): $E=mc^2$, in which E is the energy in ergs, m the mass of the matter in grams, and c the speed of light in centimeters per second. ($c^2=9\cdot10^{20}$).

DECIMAL EQUIVALENTS OF COMMON FRACTIONS

$\frac{1}{2}$	.5000	$\frac{1}{32}$	.0313	$\frac{3}{11}$	.2727	$\frac{6}{11}$	.5455
$\frac{1}{3}$	.3333	$\frac{1}{64}$	.0156	$\frac{4}{5}$	.8000	$\frac{7}{8}$	.8750
$\frac{1}{4}$	.2500	$\frac{2}{3}$	.6667	$\frac{4}{7}$	.5714	$\frac{7}{9}$	.7778
$\frac{1}{5}$	.2000	$\frac{2}{5}$	.4000	$\frac{4}{9}$	.4444	$\frac{7}{10}$	.7000
$\frac{1}{6}$	.1667	$\frac{2}{7}$	.2857	$\frac{4}{11}$	.3636	$\frac{7}{11}$	.6364
$\frac{1}{7}$	.1429	$\frac{2}{9}$	.2222	$\frac{5}{6}$	.8333	$\frac{7}{12}$	.5833
$\frac{1}{8}$	.1250	$\frac{2}{11}$	.1818	$\frac{5}{7}$	.7143	$\frac{8}{9}$	.8889
$\frac{1}{9}$	.1111	$\frac{3}{4}$	.7500	$\frac{5}{8}$	.6250	$\frac{8}{11}$	.7273
$\frac{1}{10}$	.1000	$\frac{3}{5}$	.6000	$\frac{5}{9}$	.5556	$\frac{9}{10}$	.9000
$\frac{1}{11}$	.0909	$\frac{3}{7}$	.4286	$\frac{5}{11}$	.4545	$\frac{9}{11}$	.8182
$\frac{1}{12}$	.0833	$\frac{3}{8}$	.3750	$\frac{5}{12}$	.4167	$\frac{10}{11}$	.9091
$\frac{1}{16}$	.0625	$\frac{3}{10}$	.3000	$\frac{6}{7}$	.8571	$\frac{11}{12}$	.9167

ROMAN NUMERALS

Roman numerals are expressed by letters of the alphabet and are rarely used today except for formality or variety.

There are three basic principles for reading Roman numerals:

1. A letter repeated once or twice repeats its value that many times. (XXX= 30, CC=200, etc.)

2. One or more letters placed after another letter of greater value increases the greater value by the amount of the smaller. (VI=6, LXX=70, MCC=1200, etc.).

3. A letter placed before another letter of greater value decreases the greater value by the amount of the smaller. (IV=4, XC= 90, CM=900, etc.).

Letter	Value	Letter	Value
I	1	LX	60
II	2	LXX	70
III	3	LXXX	80
IV	4	XC	90
V	5	C	100
VI	6	D	500
VII	7	M	1,000
VIII	8	$\overline{\text{V}}$	5,000
IX	9	$\overline{\text{X}}$	10,000
X	10	$\overline{\text{L}}$	50,000
XX	20	$\overline{\text{C}}$	100,000
XXX	30	$\overline{\text{D}}$	500,000
XL	40	$\overline{\text{M}}$	1,000,000
L	50		

Prime Numbers Between 1 and 1,000

1	2	3	5	7	11	13	17	19	23
29	31	37	41	43	47	53	59	61	67
71	73	79	83	89	97	101	103	107	109
113	127	131	137	139	149	151	157	163	167
173	179	181	191	193	197	199	211	223	227
229	233	239	241	251	257	263	269	271	277
281	283	293	307	311	313	317	331	337	347
349	353	359	367	373	379	383	389	397	401
409	419	421	431	433	439	443	449	457	461
463	467	479	487	491	499	503	509	521	523
541	547	557	563	569	571	577	587	593	599
601	607	613	617	619	631	641	643	647	653
659	661	673	677	683	691	701	709	719	727
733	739	743	751	757	761	769	773	787	797
809	811	821	823	827	829	839	853	857	859
863	877	881	883	887	907	911	919	929	937
941	947	953	967	971	977	983	991	997	(1009)

Mean and Median

The mean, also called the average, of a series of quantities is obtained by finding the sum of the quantities and dividing it by the number of quantities. In the series 1,3,5,18,19,20,25, the mean or average is 13 —i.e., 91 divided by 7.

The median of a series is that point which so divides it that half the quantities are on one side, half on the other. In the above series, the median is 18.

The median often better expresses the common-run, since it is not, as is the mean, affected by an excessively high or low figure. In the series 1,3,4,7,55, the median of 4 is a truer expression of the common-run than is the mean of 14.

SIMPLE INTEREST FOR $100

To find the interest for any amount of money, move the decimal point of that amount two places to the left and multiply by the figure obtained from the table. For figuring simple interest, the year is considered to have 360 days.

	1 Day	7 Days	1 Month	3 Months	6 Months	1 Year
2%	$.00556	$.03889	$.16667	$.50000	$1.00000	$2.00000
2½%	.00694	.04861	.20833	.62500	1.25000	2.50000
3%	.00833	.05833	.25000	.75000	1.50000	3.00000
3½%	.00972	.06806	.29167	.87500	1.75000	3.50000
4%	.01111	.07778	.33333	1.00000	2.00000	4.00000
4½%	.01250	.08750	.37500	1.12500	2.25000	4.50000
5%	.01389	.09722	.41667	1.25000	2.50000	5.00000
5½%	.01528	.10694	.45833	1.37500	2.75000	5.50000
6%	.01667	.11667	.50000	1.50000	3.00000	6.00000
6½%	.01806	.12639	.54167	1.62500	3.25000	6.50000
7%	.01944	.13611	.58333	1.75000	3.50000	7.00000
8%	.02222	.15556	.66667	2.00000	4.00000	8.00000
9%	.02500	.17500	.75000	2.25000	4.50000	9.00000
10%	.02778	.19444	.83333	2.50000	5.00000	10.00000

Square Roots and Cube Roots of Whole Integers from 1 to 100

	Square root	Cube root		Square root	Cube root		Square root	Cube root
1	1.000 000	1.000 000	35	5,916 080	3.271 066	69	8.306 624	4.101 566
2	1.414 214	1.259 921	36	6.000 000	3.301 927	70	8.366 600	4.121 285
3	1.732 051	1.442 250	37	6.082 763	3.332 222	71	8.426 150	4.140 818
4	2.000 000	1.587 401	38	6.164 414	3.364 975	72	8.485 281	4.160 168
5	2.236 068	1.709 976	39	6.244 998	3.391 211	73	8.544 004	4.179 339
6	2.449 490	1.817 121	40	6.324 555	3.419 952	74	8.602 325	4.198 336
7	2.645 751	1.912 931	41	6.403 124	3.448 217	75	8.660 254	4.217 163
8	2.828 427	2.000 000	42	6.480 741	3.476 027	76	8.717 798	4.235 824
9	3.000 000	2.080 084	43	6.557 439	3.503 398	77	8.774 964	4.254 321
10	3.162 278	2.154 435	44	6.633 250	3.530 348	78	8.831 761	4.272 659
11	3.316 625	2.223 980	45	6.708 204	3.556 893	79	8.888 194	4.290 840
12	3.464 102	2.289 428	46	6.782 330	3.583 048	80	8.944 272	4.308 869
13	3.605 551	2.351 335	47	6.855 655	3.608 826	81	9.000 000	4.326 749
14	3.741 657	2.410 142	48	6.928 203	3.634 241	82	9.055 385	4.344 481
15	3.872 983	2.466 212	49	7.000 000	3.659 306	83	9.110 434	4.362 071
16	4.000 000	2.519 842	50	7.071 068	3.684 031	84	9.165 151	4.379 519
17	4.123 106	2.571 282	51	7.141 428	3.708 430	85	9.219 544	4.396 830
18	4.242 641	2.620 741	52	7.211 103	3.732 511	86	9.273 618	4.414 005
19	4.358 899	2.668 402	53	7.280 110	3.756 286	87	9.327 379	4.431 048
20	4.472 136	2.714 418	54	7.348 469	3.779 763	88	9.380 832	4.447 960
21	4.582 576	2.758 924	55	7.416 198	3.802 952	89	9.433 981	4.464 745
22	4.690 416	2.802 039	56	7.483 315	3.825 862	90	9.486 833	4.481 405
23	4.795 832	2.843 867	57	7.549 834	3.848 501	91	9.539 392	4.497 941
24	4.898 979	2.884 499	58	7.615 773	3.870 877	92	9.591 663	4.514 357
25	5.000 000	2.924 018	59	7.681 146	3.892 996	93	9.643 651	4.530 655
26	5.099 020	2.962 496	60	7.745 967	3.914 868	94	9.695 360	4.546 836
27	5.196 152	3.000 000	61	7.810 250	3.936 497	95	9.746 794	4.562 903
28	5.291 503	3.036 589	62	7.874 008	3.957 892	96	9.797 959	4.578 857
29	5.385 165	3.072 317	63	7.937 254	3.979 057	97	9.848 858	4.594 701
30	5.477 226	3.107 233	64	8.000 000	4.000 000	98	9.899 495	4.610 436
31	5.567 764	3.141 381	65	8.062 258	4.020 726	99	9.949 874	4.626 065
32	5.656 854	3.174 802	66	8.124 038	4.041 240	100	10.000 000	4.641 589
33	5.744 563	3.207 534	67	8.185 353	4.061 548			
34	5.830 952	3.239 612	68	8.246 211	4.081 655			

Squares and Cubes of Whole Integers from 1 to 100

	Square	Cube		Square	Cube		Square	Cube		Square	Cube
1	1	1	26	676	17,576	51	2,601	132,651	76	5,776	438,976
2	4	8	27	729	19,683	52	2,704	140,608	77	5,929	456,533
3	9	27	28	784	21,952	53	2,809	148,877	78	6,084	474,552
4	16	64	29	841	24,389	54	2,916	157,464	79	6,241	493,039
5	25	125	30	900	27,000	55	3,025	166,375	80	6,400	512,000
6	36	216	31	961	29,791	56	3,136	175,616	81	6,561	531,441
7	49	343	32	1,024	32,768	57	3,249	185,193	82	6,724	551,368
8	64	512	33	1,089	35,937	58	3,364	195,112	83	6,889	571,787
9	81	729	34	1,156	39,304	59	3,481	205,379	84	7,056	592,704
10	100	1,000	35	1,225	42,875	60	3,600	216,000	85	7,225	614,125
11	121	1,331	36	1,296	46,656	61	3,721	226,981	86	7,396	636,056
12	144	1,728	37	1,369	50,653	62	3,844	238,328	87	7,569	658,503
13	169	2,197	38	1,444	54,872	63	3,969	250,047	88	7,744	681,472
14	196	2,744	39	1,521	59,319	64	4,096	262,144	89	7,921	704,969
15	225	3,375	40	1,600	64,000	65	4,225	274,625	90	8,100	729,000
16	256	4,096	41	1,681	68,921	66	4,356	287,496	91	8,281	753,571
17	289	4,913	42	1,764	74,088	67	4,489	300,763	92	8,464	778,688
18	324	5,832	43	1,849	79,507	68	4,624	314,432	93	8,649	804,357
19	361	6,859	44	1,936	85,184	69	4,761	328,509	94	8,836	830,584
20	400	8,000	45	2,025	91,125	70	4,900	343,000	95	9,025	857,375
21	441	9,261	46	2,116	97,336	71	5,041	357,911	96	9,216	884,736
22	484	10,648	47	2,209	103,823	72	5,184	373,248	97	9,409	912,673
23	529	12,167	48	2,304	110,592	73	5,329	389,017	98	9,604	941,192
24	576	13,824	49	2,401	117,649	74	5,476	405,224	99	9,801	970,299
25	625	15,625	50	2,500	125,000	75	5,625	421,875	100	10,000	1,000,000

Atomic Weights of the Elements Based on Carbon-12 as Standard*

Atomic number	Element	Atomic weight	Atomic number	Element	Atomic weight	Atomic number	Element	Atomic weight
1	Hydrogen	1.0080	36	Krypton	83.80	70	Ytterbium	173.04
2	Helium	4.00260	37	Rubidium	85.4678	71	Lutetium	174.97
3	Lithium	6.941	38	Strontium	87.62	72	Hafnium	178.49
4	Beryllium	9.01218	39	Yttrium	88.9059	73	Tantalum	180.9479
5	Boron	10.81	40	Zirconium	91.22	74	Tungsten	183.85
6	Carbon	12.011	41	Niobium		75	Rhenium	186.2
7	Nitrogen	14.0067		(Columbium)	92.9064	76	Osmium	190.2
8	Oxygen	15.9994	42	Molybdenum	95.94	77	Iridium	192.22
9	Fluorine	18.9984	43	Technetium	98.9062†	78	Platinum	195.09
10	Neon	20.179	44	Ruthenium	101.07	79	Gold	196.9665
11	Sodium	22.9898	45	Rhodium	102.9055	80	Mercury	200.59
12	Magnesium	24.305	46	Palladium	106.4	81	Thallium	204.37
13	Aluminum	26.9815	47	Silver	107.868	82	Lead	207.2
14	Silicon	28.08	48	Cadmium	112.40	83	Bismuth	208.9806
15	Phosphorus	30.9738	49	Indium	114.82	84	Polonium	210†
16	Sulfur	32.06	50	Tin	118.69	85	Astatine	210†
17	Chlorine	35.453	51	Antimony	121.75	86	Radon	222†
18	Argon	39.94	52	Tellurium	127.60	87	Francium	223†
19	Potassium	39.102	53	Iodine	126.9045	88	Radium	226.0254
20	Calcium	40.08	54	Xenon	131.30	89	Actinium	227†
21	Scandium	44.9559	55	Cesium	132.9055	90	Thorium	232.0381
22	Titanium	47.90	56	Barium	137.34	91	Protactinium	231.0359
23	Vanadium	50.9414	57	Lanthanum	138.9055	92	Uranium	238.029
24	Chromium	51.996	58	Cerium	140.12	93	Neptunium	237.0482
25	Manganese	54.9380	59	Praseodymium	140.9077	94	Plutonium	244†
26	Iron	55.847	60	Neodymium	144.24	95	Americium	243†
27	Cobalt	58.9332	61	Promethium	145†	96	Curium	247†
28	Nickel	58.71	62	Samarium	150.4	97	Berkelium	247†
29	Copper	63.546	63	Europium	151.96	98	Californium	251†
30	Zinc	65.38	64	Gadolinium	157.25	99	Einsteinium	254†
31	Gallium	69.72	65	Terbium	158.9254	100	Fermium	257†
32	Germanium	72.59	66	Dysprosium	162.50	101	Mendelevium	256†
33	Arsenic	74.9216	67	Holmium	164.9303	102	Nobelium	254†
34	Selenium	78.96	68	Erbium	167.26	103	Lawrencium	257†
35	Bromine	79.904	69	Thulium	168.9342			

* Instead of oxygen = 16.0000.   † Mass of the heaviest known isotope.

Chemical Elements

Element	Symbol	Atomic no.	Atomic weight	Specific gravity	Melting point °C.	Boiling point °C.	Valence	Number of isotopes†	Discoverer	Year
Actinium	Ac	89	227†	10.07†	1050	3200 ± 300	3	11	Debierne	1899
Aluminum	Al	13	26.9815	2.6989	660.37	2467	3	8	Wöhler	1827
Americium	Am	95	243¶	13.67	994 ± 4	2607	2, 3, 4, 5 or 6	13‡	Seaborg et al.	1944
Antimony	Sb	51	121.75	6.691	630.74	1750	3 or 5	29	Early historic times	....
Argon	Ar	18	39.948	1.7837§	−189.2	−185.7	0	8	Rayleigh and Ramsay	1894
Arsenic (gray)	As	33	74.9216	5.73	817 (28 atm.)	613|	3 or 5	14	Albertus Magnus	1250?
Astatine	At	85	~210	....	302	337	1, 3, 5, or 7	21	Corson et al.	1940
Barium	Ba	56	137.34	3.5	725	1640	2	25	Davy	1808
Berkelium	Bk	97	247¶	14.00**	....	....	3 or 4	8‡	Seaborg et al.	1949
Beryllium	Be	4	9.01218	1.848	1278 ± 5	2970 (5 mm.)	2	6	Vauquelin	1798
Bismuth	Bi	83	208.9806	9.747	271.3	1560 ± 5	3 or 5	19	Geoffroy	1753
Boron	B	5	10.81	2.37††	2300	2550|	3	6	Gay-Lussac and Thénard; Davy	1808
Bromine	Br	35	79.904	3.12§	−7.2	58.78	1, 3, 5 or 7	19	Balard	1826
Cadmium	Cd	48	112.40	8.65	320.9	765	2	22	Stromeyer	1817
Calcium	Ca	20	40.08	1.55	839 ± 2	1484	2	14	Davy	1808
Californium	Cf	98	251¶	....	....	....	3	12‡	Seaborg et al.	1950
Carbon	C	6	12.011	1.8–3.5‡‡	~3550	4827	2, 3 or 4	7	Prehistoric	....
Cerium	Ce	58	140.12	6.771	798 ± 3	3257	3 or 4	19	Berzelius and Hisinger; Klaproth	1803
Cesium	Cs	55	132.9055	1.873	28.40	678.4	1	22	Bunsen and Kirchhoff	1860
Chlorine	Cl	17	35.453	1.56§	−100.98	−34.6	1, 3, 5 or 7	11	Scheele	1774
Chromium	Cr	24	51.996	7.18–7.20	1857 ± 20	2672	2, 3 or 6	9	Vauquelin	1797
Cobalt	Co	27	58.9332	8.9	1495	2870	2 or 3	14	Brandt	c.1735
Copper	Cu	29	63.546	8.96	1083.4 ± 0.2	2567	1 or 2	11	Prehistoric	....
Curium	Cm	96	247¶	13.51†	1340 ± 40	....	3 or 4	13‡	Seaborg et al.	1944
Dysprosium	Dy	66	162.50	8.540	1409	2335	3	21	Boisbaudran	1886
Einsteinium	Es	99	254¶	....	....	....	3	12‡	Ghiorso et al	1952
Erbium	Er	68	167.26	9.045	1522	2510	3	16	Mosander	1843
Europium	Eu	63	151.96	5.283	822 ± 5	1597	2 or 3	21	Demarcay	1896
Fermium	Fm	100	257¶	....	....	....	3	10‡	Ghiorso et al	1953
Fluorine	F	9	18.9984	1.108§	−219.62	−188.14	1	6	Moissan	1886
Francium	Fr	87	223¶	....	27†	677†	1	21	Perey	1939
Gadolinium	Gd	64	157.25	7.898	1311 ± 1	3233	3	17	Marignac	1880
Gallium	Ga	31	69.72	5.904	29.78	2403	2 or 3	14	Boisbaudran	1875
Germanium	Ge	32	72.59	5.323	937.4	2830	2 or 4	17	Winkler	1886
Gold	Au	79	196.9665	19.32	1064.43	2807	1 or 3	21	Prehistoric	....
Hafnium	Hf	72	178.49	13.31	2227 ± 20	4602	4	17	Coster and von Hevesy	1923
Helium	He	2	4.00260	0.1785§	−272.2 (26 atm.)	−268.934	0	5	Janssen	1868
Holmium	Ho	67	164.9303	8.781	1470	2720	3	29	Delafontaine and Soret	1878
Hydrogen	H	1	1.0080	0.070§	−259.14	−252.87	1	3	Cavendish	1766
Indium	In	49	114.82	7.31	156.61	2080	1, 2 or 3	34	Reich and Richter	1863
Iodine	I	53	126.9045	4.93	113.5	184.35	1, 3, 5 or 7	24	Courtois	1811
Iridium	Ir	77	192.22	22.42	2410	4130	3 or 4	25	Tennant	1803
Iron	Fe	26	55.847	7.894	1535	2750	2, 3, 4 or 6	10	Prehistoric	....
Krypton	Kr	36	83.80	3.733§	−156.6	−152.30 ± 0.10	0	23	Ramsay and Travers	1898
Lanthanum	La	57	138.9055	6.166	920 ± 5	3454	3	19	Mosander	1839
Lawrencium	Lr	103	257¶	....	....	....	3?	20‡	Ghiorso et al.	1961
Lead	Pb	82	207.2	11.35	327.502	1740	2 or 4	29	Prehistoric	....
Lithium	Li	3	6.941	0.534	180.54	1347	1	5	Arfvedson	1817
Lutetium	Lu	71	174.97	9.835	1656 ± 5	3315	3	22	Urbain	1907
Magnesium	Mg	12	24.305	1.738	648.8 ± 0.5	1090	2	8	Black	1755
Manganese	Mn	25	54.9380	7.21–7.44§§	1244 ± 3	1962	1, 2, 3, 4, 6 or 7	11	Gahn, Scheele and Bergman	1774
Mendelevium	Md	101	256¶	....	....	....	2 or 3	3‡	Ghiorso et al.	1955
Mercury	Hg	80	200.59	13.546	−38.87	356.58	1 or 2	26	Prehistoric	....

Element	Symbol	Atomic no.	Atomic weight	Specific gravity	Melting point °C.	Boiling point °C.	Valence	Number of isotopes†	Discoverer	Year
Molybdenum	Mo	42	95.94	10.22	2617	4612	2, 3, 4?, 5? or 6	20	Scheele	1778
Neodymium	Nd	60	144.24	6.80 & 7.004§§	1010	3127	3	16	von Welsbach	1885
Neon	Ne	10	20.179	0.89990 (g/l 0°C/1 atm)	−248.67	−246.048	0	8	Ramsay and Travers	1898
Neptunium	Np	93	237.0482	20.25	640 ± 1	3902	3, 4, 5, or 6	15‡	McMillan and Abelson	1940
Nickel	Ni	28	58.71	8.902	1453	2732	1, 2, or 3	11	Cronstedt	1751
Niobium (Columbium)	Nb	41	92.9064	8.57	2468 ± 10	4742	2, 3, 4? or 5	24	Hatchett	1801
Nitrogen	N	7	14.0067	0.808§	−209.86	−195.8	3 or 5	8	Rutherford	1772
Nobelium	No	102	254¶	....	....	....	3	7‡	Ghiorso et al.	1957
Osmium	Os	76	190.2	22.57	3045 ± 30	5027 ± 100	3, 4, 6 or 8	19	Tennant	1803
Oxygen	O	8	15.9994	1.14§	−218.4	−182.962	2	8	Priestley	1774
Palladium	Pd	46	106.4	12.02	1552	3140	2, 3 or 4	21	Wollaston	1803
Phosphorus	P	15	30.9738	1.82 (white)	44.1	280	3 or 5	7	Brand	1669
Platinum	Pt	78	195.09	21.45	1772	3827 ± 100	1?, 2, 3 or 4	32	Ulloa	1735
Plutonium	Pu	94	244¶	19.84	641	3232	3, 4, 5 or 6	16‡	Seaborg et al.	1940
Polonium	Po	84	~210¶	9.32	254	962	2, 3?, 4 or 6	34	Curie	1898
Potassium	K	19	39.102	0.862	63.65	774	1	10	Davy	1807
Praseodymium	Pr	59	140.9077	6.772	931 ± 4	3212	3 or 4	15	von Welsbach	1885
Promethium	Pm	61	145¶	....	~1080	2460?	3	14	Marinsky et al.	1945
Protactinium	Pa	91	231.0359	15.37†	<1600	....	4 or 5	14	Hahn and Meitner	1917
Radium	Ra	88	226.0254	5.0?	700	1140	2	15	P. and M. Curie	1898
Radon	Rn	86	222¶	4.4§	−71	−61.8	0	20	Dorn	1900
Rhenium	Re	75	186.2	21.02	3180	5627**	2, 3, 4, 5 6 or 7	21	Noddack, Berg and Tacke	1925
Rhodium	Rh	45	102.9055	12.41	1966 ± 3	3727 ± 100	2, 3, 4, 5 or 5	20	Wollaston	1803
Rubidium	Rb	37	85.4678	1.532	38.89	688	1, 2, 3 or 4	20	Bunsen and Kirchoff	1861
Ruthenium	Ru	44	101.07	12.44	2310	3900	1, 2, 3, 4, 5, 6, 7 or 8	16	Klaus	1844
Samarium	Sm	62	150.4	7.536	1072 ± 5	1778	2 or 3	17	Boisbaudran	1879
Scandium	Sc	21	44.9559	2.989	1539	2832	3	15	Nilson	1879
Selenium	Se	34	78.96	4.79 (gray)	217	684.9 ± 1	4 or 6	20	Berzelius	1817
Silicon	Si	14	28.086	2.33	1410	2355	4	8	Berzelius	1824
Silver	Ag	47	107.868	10.50	961.93	2212	1 or 2	27	Prehistoric	....
Sodium	Na	11	22.9898	0.971	97.81 ± 0.03	882.9	1	7	Davy	1807
Strontium	Sr	38	87.62	2.54	769	1384	2	18	Davy	1808
Sulfur	S	16	32.06	2.07‖	112.8	444.674	2, 4, or 6	10	Prehistoric	....
Tantalum	Ta	73	180.9479	16.654	2996	5425 ± 100	2?, 3, 4? or 5	19	Ekeberg	1802
Technetium	Tc	43	98.9062	11.50†	2172	4877	2, 4, 5, 6 or 7	23	Perrier and Segré	1937
Tellurium	Te	52	127.60	6.24	449.5 ± 0.3	989.8 ± 3.8	2, 4 or 6	29	von Reichenstein	1782
Terbium	Tb	65	158.9254	8.234	1360 ± 4	3041	3 or 4	24	Mosander	1843
Thallium	Tl	81	204.37	11.85	303.5	1457 ± 10	1 or 3	28	Crookes	1861
Thorium	Th	90	232.0381	11.72	1750	~4790	2?, 3?, or 4	12	Berzelius	1828
Thulium	Tm	69	168.9342	9.314	1545 ± 15	1727	2 or 3	18	Cleve	1879
Tin	Sn	50	118.69	7.31 (white)	231.9681	2270	2 or 4	28	Prehistoric	....
Titanium	Ti	22	47.90	4.55	1660 ± 10	3287	2, 3 or 4	9	Gregor	1791
Tungsten (Wolfram)	W	74	183.85	19.3	3410 ± 20	5660	2, 3, 4, 5 or 6	22	J. and F. d'Elhuyar	1783
Uranium	U	92	238.029	~18.95	1132.3 ± 0.8	3818	2, 3, 4, 5 or 6	15	Peligot	1841
Vanadium	V	23	50.9414	6.11	1890 ± 10	3380	2, 3, 4 or 5	9	del Rio	1801
Xenon	Xe	54	131.30	3.52§	−111.9	−107.1 ± 3	0	31	Ramsay and Travers	1898
Ytterbium	Yb	70	173.04	6.972	824 ± 5	1193	2 or 3	16	Marignac	1878
Yttrium	Y	39	88.9059	4.457	1523 ± 8	3337	3	21	Gadolin	1794

| Zinc | Zn | 30 | 65.38 | 7.133 | 419.58 | 907 | 2 | 15 | Prehistoric | .... |
| Zirconium | Zr | 40 | 91.22 | 6.506† | 1852 ± 2 | 4377 | 2, 3 or 4 | 20 | Klaproth | 1789 |

* Isotopes are different forms of the same element having the same atomic number but different atomic weights. † Calculated figure. ‡ Artificially produced. § Liquid. | Sublimation point. ¶ Mass number of the isotope of longest known life. ** Estimated. †† Amorphous. ‡‡ Depending on whether amorphous, graphite or diamond. §§ Depending on allotropic form. || Rhombic. ¶¶ Rediscovered by Marggraf in 1746. ~ Is approximately. '< Is less than.

NOTE: Elements 104 (proposed name Rutherfordium) and 105 (proposed name Hahnium) were discovered by Ghiorso et al in 1969 and 1970, respectively. Neither name will be official until approved by the International Union for Pure and Applied Science.

MISCELLANEOUS UNITS

ACRE: An area of 43,000 square feet. Originally, the area a yoke of oxen could plow in one day.

AGATE: Originally a measurement of type size (5½ points). Now equal to 1/14 inch. Used in printing for measuring column length.

AMPERE: Unit of electric current. A potential difference of one volt across a resistance of one rhm produces a current of one ampere.

ASTRONOMICAL UNIT (A.U.): 93,000,000 miles, the average distance of the earth from the sun. Used in astronomy.

BALE: A large bundle of goods. In the U. S., the approximate weight of a bale of cotton is 500 pounds. The weight varies in other countries.

BOARD FOOT (fbm): 144 cubic inches (12 in. x 12 in. x 1 in.). Used for lumber.

BOLT: 40 yards. Used for measuring cloth.

BTU: British thermal unit. Amount of heat needed to increase the temperature of one pound of water by one degree Fahrenheit (252 calories).

CARAT (c): 200 milligrams or 3.086 grains troy. Originally the weight of a seed of the carob tree in the Mediterranean region. Used for weighing precious stones. *See also* Karat.

CHAIN (ch): a chain 66 feet or one-tenth of a furlong in length, divided into 100 parts called links. One mile is equal to 80 chains. Used in surveying and sometimes called Gunter's or surveyor's chain.

CUBIT: 18 inches or 45.72 cm. Derived from distance between elbow and tip of middle finger.

DECIBEL: Unit of relative loudness. One decibel is the smallest amount of change detectable by the human ear.

ELL, ENGLISH: 1¼ yards or 1/32 bolt. Used for measuring cloth.

FREIGHT TON (also called MEASUREMENT TON): 40 cubic feet of merchandise. Used for cargo freight.

GREAT GROSS: 12 gross or 1728.

GROSS: 12 dozen or 144.

HAND: 4 inches or 10.16 cm. Derived from the width of the hand. Used for measuring the height of horses at withers.

HERTZ: Modern unit for measurement of electromagnetic wave frequencies (equivalent to "cycles per second").

HOGSHEAD (hhd): 2 liquid barrels or 14,653 cubic inches.

HORSEPOWER: The power needed to lift 33,000 pounds a distance of one foot in length in one minute (about 1½ times the power an average horse can exert). Used for measuring power of steam engines, etc.

KARAT (kt): A measure of the purity of gold, indicating how many parts out of 24 are pure. For example, 18 karat gold is ¾ pure. Sometimes spelled *carat*.

KNOT: Not a distance, but the rate of speed of one nautical mile per hour. Used for measuring speed of ships.

LEAGUE: Rather indefinite and varying measure, but usually estimated at 3 miles in English-speaking countries.

LIGHT-YEAR: 5,880,000,000,000 miles, the distance light travels in a year at the rate of 186,281.7 miles per second. (If an astronomical unit were represented by one inch, a light-year would be represented by about one mile.) Used for measurements in interstellar space.

MAGNUM: Two-quart bottle. Used for measuring wine, etc.

OHM: Unit of electrical resistance. A circuit in which a potential difference of one volt produces a current of one ampere has a resistance of one ohm.

PARSEC: Approximately 3.26 light-years or 19.2 trillion miles. Term is combination of first syllables of *par*allax and *sec*ond, and distance is that of imaginary star when lines drawn from it to both earth and sun form a maximum angle or parallax of one second (1/3600 degree). Used for measuring interstellar distances.

PI (π): 3.14159265+. The ratio of the circumference of a circle to its diameter. For practical purpose, the value is used to four decimal places: 3.1416.

PICA: ⅙ inch or 12 points. Used in printing for measuring column width, etc.

PIPE: 2 hogsheads. Used for measuring wine and other liquids.

POINT: .013837 (approximately 1/72) inch or 1/12 pica. Used in printing for measuring type size.

QUINTAL: 100,000 grams or 220.46 pounds avoirdupois.

QUIRE: Used for measuring paper. Sometimes 24 sheets but more often 25. There are 20 quires in a ream.

REAM: Used for measuring paper. Sometimes 480 sheets, but more often 500 sheets.

ROENTGEN: Dosage unit of radiation exposure produced by X-rays.

SCORE: 20 units.

SPAN: 9 inches or 22.86 cm. Derived from the distance between the end of the thumb and the end of the little finger when both are outstretched.

SQUARE: 100 square feet. Used in building.

STONE: Legally 14 pounds avoirdupois in Great Britain.

TOWNSHIP: U. S. land measurement of almost 36 square miles. The south border is 6 miles long. The east and west borders, also 6 miles long, follow the meridians, making the north border slightly less than 6 miles long. Used in surveying.

TUN: 252 gallons, but often larger. Used for measuring wine and other liquids.

WATT: Unit of power. The power used by a current of one ampere across a potential difference of one volt equals one watt.

Communicable Diseases

Source: *Control of Communicable Diseases in Man*, an official report of the American Public Health Assn.

(This list is incomplete but we have tried to include those diseases that are most common and worldwide.)

Disease	Incubation period*	Period of communicability
Chickenpox (varicella)	2 to 3 weeks	From 5 days before appearance of vesicles to 6 days after.
Common Cold	12 to 72 hours; usually 24 hrs	From 1 day before onset to 5 days after.
Conjunctivitis	1 to 3 days	During course of active infection.
Diphtheria.	2 to 5 days	Usually 2 weeks or less; seldom more than 4 weeks.
Dysentery, amebic	2 to 4 weeks (varies widely)	During intestinal infection; possibly for years if untreated.
Enterobiasis (pinworm) . . .	3 to 6 weeks	Not directly transmitted.
Food poisoning: Botulism . . .	12 to 36 hours	Not applicable.
Salmonella infection	6 to 72 hours; usually 36	3 days to 3 weeks (extremely variable).
Staphylococcus intoxication .	2 to 4 hours	Not applicable.
German measles (rubella) . . .	8 to 10 days; usually 14	1 week before and at least 4 days after onset of rash.
Gonorrhea	2 to 5 days; sometimes longer	Indefinite unless treated.
Hepatitis (serum)	45 to 160 days; usually 80 to 100	Many weeks before onset of symptoms.
Herpes Simplex	Up to 2 weeks	As long as 7 weeks after recovery.
Impetigo contagiosa	4 to 10 days; sometimes longer	Until lesions are healed.
Infectious mononucleosis . . .	Varies 2 to 6 weeks	Unknown.
Influenza	Usually 1 to 3 days	Probably limited to 3 days from clinical onset.
Measles (rubeola)	10 days (to onset) 14 days (to rash)	From beginning of prodromal period to 4 days after onset of rash.
Meningitis, meningococcal . . .	2 to 10 days	Usually 1 day after appropriate medication.
Mumps	12 to 26 days; commonly 18	From 6 days before distinctive symptoms up to 9 days after.
Pediculosis	Apprx. 2 weeks	While lice remain alive.
Pneumonia: Bacterial	Usually 1 to 3 days	Unknown.
Viral	Believed to be 1 to 3 days	Unknown.
Poliomyelitis	3 to 21 days; commonly 7 to 12	7 to 10 days before and after onset of symptoms.
Rabies	2 to 8 weeks or longer	From animals, 3 to 5 days before onset and during course of the disease.
Respiratory (acute viral) . . .	Few days to 1 week or more	Duration of active disease.
Ringworm (of body)	4 to 10 days	As long as lesions are present.
(Athlete's foot)	Unknown	As long as lesions are present.
Scarlet fever and streptococcal sore throat	1 to 3 days	Uncomplicated cases apprx. 10 to 21 days; in untreated cases, weeks or months.
Smallpox	7 to 17 days; commonly 10 to 12	During first week.
Syphilis	10 days to 10 weeks; usually 3 weeks	Variable and indefinite.
Tetanus	4 days to 3 weeks	Not applicable.
Trichinosis	2 to 28 days after ingestion of infected meat; usually 9 days	Not directly transmitted.
Tuberculosis	4 to 12 weeks (to primary phase)	As long as tubercle bacilli are discharged by patient.
Typhoid fever	1 to 3 weeks; average 2 weeks	As long as typhoid bacilli appear in excreta; 2 to 5% of patients become permanent carriers.
Whooping cough (pertussis) . .	Commonly 7 days, almost uniformly within 10 days, and not exceeding 21 days	From 7 days after exposure to 3 weeks after onset of typical paroxysms.

* Usual limits.

Scientific Inventions, Discoveries, and Theories

Source: Encyclopaedia Britannica.

Inventions

Adding machine, recording: William S. Burroughs, 1888.

Airplane: Wilbur and Orville Wright, 1903.

Air brake, railroad: George Westinghouse, 1868.

Air pump: Otto von Guericke, 1650.

Automobile: (Product of inventions of many men. Gottlieb Daimler is frequently given credit, c.1887.)

Bakelite: Leo H. Baekeland, 1908.

Balloon, hot-air: Joseph and Jacques Montgolfier, 1783.

Barometer: Evangelista Torricelli, 1643.

Camera, Kodak: George Eastman, 1888.

Carburetor, spray: Charles E. Duryea, 1892.

Cellophane: J. E. Brandenberger, 1911.

Celluloid: John W. and I. S. Hyatt, 1870.

Clock, pendulum: Christiaan Huygens, 1656.

Converter, Bessemer: William Kelly, 1851. (Patent bought by Sir Henry Bessemer, who made a similar invention in 1856.)

Cotton gin: Eli Whitney, 1793.

Cyanide: Nikodem Caro and Adolf Frank, 1905.

Cyclotron: Ernest O. Lawrence, 1931.

Daguerreotype process: Louis J. M. Daguerre, 1839.

Diesel engine: Rudolf Diesel, 1897.

Dynamite: Alfred B. Nobel, 1862.

Dynamo: Michael Faraday, 1831.

Dynamo, industrial: Zénobe Gramme, 1872.

Electromagnet: William Sturgeon, 1823.

Electroplating: Luigi Brugnatelli, 1805.

Elevator, passenger: Elisha G. Otis, 1857.

Elevator safety device: Elisha G. Otis, 1852.

Engine, high-speed internal-combustion: Gottlieb Daimler, 1885.

Filament, tungsten: Irving Langmuir, 1915.

Flying shuttle: John Kay, 1733.

Food preservation, hermetically sealed (meat): François (Nicolas) Appert, 1810, with little success.

Fountain pen: Lewis E. Waterman, 1884. (First successful one.)

Frequency modulation (FM): Edwin H. Armstrong, 1933.

Guncotton: Christian Schönbein, 1845.

Gyrocompass: Elmer A. Sperry, 1905.

Gyroscope: Léon Foucault, 1852.

Helicopter: Igor I. Sikorsky, 1909.

Hydroplane: Charles M. Ramus propounded idea around 1870; Glenn H. Curtiss, 1911.

Jet propulsion (aircraft): Sir Frank Whittle, 1930.

Lamp, electric incandescent: (Inventor uncertain; Thomas A. Edison, who made a lamp in 1879, is sometimes credited.)

Lens, bifocal: Benjamin Franklin, c.1760.

Lightning rod: Benjamin Franklin, 1752.

Linotype machine: Ottmar Mergenthaler, 1885 (patent); first used, 1886.

Lithography: Aloys Senefelder, 1796.

Machine gun: Richard J. Gatling, 1861.

Match, friction: John Walker, 1827.

Mercury-vapor lamp: Peter C. Hewitt, 1912.

Microscope, compound: Zacharias Janssen, 1590.

Microscope, electron: Vladimir Zworykin et al., 1939.

Miner's safety lamp: Sir Humphry Davy, 1815.

Monotype machine: Tolbert Lanston, 1887.

Motion pictures: Thomas A. Edison, 1893.

Motion pictures, sound: (Product of various inventions. First picture with synchronized musical score: *Don Juan*, 1926; with spoken dialogue: *The Jazz Singer*, 1927; both Warner Bros.)

Motor, A-C: Nikola Tesla, 1892.

Ophthalmoscope: Hermann von Helmholtz, 1851.

Phonograph: Thomas A. Edison, 1877.

Photography, color: Gabriel Lippmann, 1891.

Power loom: Edmund Cartwright, 1785.

Printing, movable-type: Johann Gutenberg (?), c.1440.

Printing press, rotary: Richard Hoe, 1847.

Radar: Gregory Breit & Merle A. Tuve, 1925.

Radio: (Product of various inventions. First practical system of wireless telegraphy: Guglielmo Marconi, 1895.)

Radio telephone: Lee De Forest, 1906.

Radio tube, diode: Sir John Ambrose Fleming, 1904.

Radio tube, triode: Lee De Forest, 1906.

Rayon: George Andemars (first known patent), 1855; perfected by Sir Joseph W. Swan, 1883.

Reaper: Cyrus McCormick, 1834.

Revolver: Samuel Colt, 1835.

Rifle, automatic: John M. Browning, 1918.

Rubber, vulcanized: Ch. Goodyear, 1839.

Screw propeller: John Ericsson, 1837.

Self-starter, automobile: Charles F. Kettering, 1911.

Sewing machine: Elias Howe, 1846 (patented). Idea of lockstitch machine conceived independently by Walter Hunt, 1832–4.

Spinning frame: Sir Richard Arkwright, 1769.

Spinning jenny: James Hargreaves, 1764.

Spinning mule: Samuel Crompton, 1779.

Steam engine: James Watt, 1765. (First practical one.)

Steamboat: Robert Fulton, 1807. (First commercially successful one in U. S.)

Tank, military: Sir Ernest Swinton, 1914.

Telegraph, electromagnetic recording: Samuel F. B. Morse, 1837.

Telephone: Alexander Graham Bell, 1876.

Telescope: Hans Lippershey (?), c.1608.

Television: Successful demonstration by J. L. Baird in England and C. F. Jenkins in U. S., in early 1920's. (First commercial TV: July 1, 1941, over WNBT, N. Y.)

Thermometer: Galileo Galilei, 1593; improved version: G. D. Fahrenheit, 1717.

Tire, pneumatic: John B. Dunlop, 1888.

Tractor, (T) tracked type: Benj. Holt, 1900.

Transformer, electric: Wm. Stanley, 1885.

Transistor: John Bardeen, William Shockley and Walter Brattain, 1948.

Typewriter: First practical one invented by Christopher Sholes, Carlos Glidden and Samuel W. Soule in 1867; patented by Sholes in 1868.

Zeppelin: Ferdinand von Zeppelin, 1900.

Discoveries and Theories

Adrenaline, isolation of: Jokichi Takamine, 1901.

Aluminum manufacture by electrolytic action: Charles M. Hall, 1886.

Antitoxin, diphtheria: Emil von Behring, 1890.

Atom smashing with slow neutrons: Enrico Fermi, 1934.

Atomic numbers: Henry Moseley, 1913.

Atomic theory: John Dalton, 1803.

Aureomycin: Benjamin M. Duggar, 1948.

Bacteria: Anton van Leeuwenhoek, 1683.

Blood, circulation of: William Harvey, 1628.

Classification of plants and animals: Carolus Linnaeus, 1737–53.

Combustion, nature of: Antoine Lavoisier, 1777.

Conditioned reflex: Ivan Pavlov, c.1910.

Deuterium (heavy hydrogen): Harold C. Urey, 1931.

Displacement of water, principle of: Archimedes, 3rd century B.C.

Electromagnetic waves: Heinrich Hertz, 1886.

Electron: Sir Joseph J. Thomson, 1897.

Electron, wave nature of: Louis Victor de Broglie, 1924.

Ether, first used as anesthetic: Crawford W. Long, 1842.

Evolution by natural selection: Charles Darwin, 1859.

Falling bodies, law of: Galileo Galilei, 1590.

Gases, laws governing: Joseph Gay-Lussac, 1809.

Gravitation, law of: Sir Isaac Newton, 1687.

Helium on sun: Sir Joseph Lockyer, 1868.

Heredity, laws of: Gregor Mendel, 1865.

Induction, electric: Joseph Henry, 1828.

Insulin: Sir Frederick G. Banting and J. J. R. MacLeod, 1922.

Intelligence testing, modern: Alfred Binet and Theodore Simon, 1905.

Isotopes, mass spectra of: Francis W. Aston, 1919.

Isotopes, theory of: Frederick Soddy, 1912.

Laser (Light amplification by stimulated emission of radiation): C. H. Townes and Arthur L. Schawlow, 1958; first working model, 1960, by T. H. Maiman.

Light, electromagnetic theory of: James Clerk Maxwell, 1873.

Light, velocity of: Olaus Römer, 1675.

Measles vaccine: Based on work of John F. Enders, who isolated measles virus; vaccine reported successful, 1963.

Molecular hypothesis: Amadeo Avogadro, 1811.

Neutron: James Chadwick, 1932.

Ohm's Law: Georg S. Ohm, 1827.

Ozone: Christian Schönbein, 1839.

Penicillin: Sir Alexander Fleming, 1929.

Periodic table: Dmitri Mendeleev, 1869.

Positron: Carl D. Anderson, 1932.

Proton: Ernest Rutherford, 1919.

Psychoanalysis: Sigmund Freud, c.1904.

Quantum mechanics: Werner Heisenberg, 1925.

Quantum theory: Max von Planck, 1901.

Rabies preventive: Louis Pasteur, 1885.

Radioactivity: Antoine Becquerel, 1896.

Radioactivity, artificial: Frédéric and Irène Joliot-Curie, 1934.

Relativity, theories of: Albert Einstein, 1905–53.

Sabin oral antipolio vaccine: Accepted as suitable for licensing, 1960.

Salk antipolio vaccine: Jonas E. Salk, announced successful Apr. 12, 1955.

Schick test of susceptibility to diphtheria: Béla Schick, 1913.

Secretin, isolation of: Sir William Bayliss and Ernest Starling, 1902.

Soda manufacture from salt: Ernest Solvay, 1861.

Solar system, heliocentricity of: Nicolaus Copernicus, 1530. (Also Aristarchus of Samos, 3rd century B.C.)

Spectrum analysis: Robert Bunsen and Gustav Kirchhoff, 1859.

Sulfa drugs as bactericides: Gerhard Domagk, 1932.

Surgery, antiseptic: Sir Joseph Lister, 1867.

Tuberculosis bacillus: Robert Koch, 1882.

Vaccination against smallpox; Edward Jenner, 1796.

Van Allen Belt: James A. Van Allen, 1958.

Virus, crystallized: Wendell M. Stanley, 1935.

Vitamin A: Elmer V. McCollum and M. Davis, 1912–14.

Vitamin B: Elmer V. McCollum, 1915–16.

Vitamin C: A. Holst and T. Froehlich, 1912.

Vitamin D: Elmer V. McCollum, 1922.

Vitamin D, irradiated: Harry Steenbock, 1924.

Wassermann test for syphilis: August von Wassermann, 1906.

Wilson Cloud Chamber: Charles T. R. Wilson, 1911.

X-rays: Wilhelm Konrad Roentgen, 1895.

Atomic Energy

Just as the Space Age is said to have started with the orbiting of Sputnik I, the Atomic Age is said to have started with the explosion of a test bomb on July 16, 1945, near Alamogordo, N. M., at 5:30 A.M. local time. The bomb was placed on top of a steel tower, and observers were stationed in bunkers 10,000 yards away. The explosion vaporized the steel tower, produced a mushroom cloud rising to 40,000 feet, and melted the desert sand into glass for distances up to 800 yards from the tower.

The first operational use of an atom bomb took place only three weeks later, when a uranium bomb was exploded over Hiroshima, Japan, on Aug. 6, 1945. The bomb, cylindrical in shape, 10 feet long with a diameter of 2 feet 4 inches, weighed about 9,000 pounds. Its explosive force was equal to 20,000 tons of TNT, hence the term "20-kiloton bomb." Three days later another atomic bomb, this time of plutonium, was exploded over Nagasaki.

Of course, the Atomic Age did not begin with the explosion of the test bomb at Alamogordo, just as the Space Age did not begin with the orbiting of the first artificial satellite. In both cases these visible feats were just experiments which proved the theory that had been built up patiently over decades.

At the turn of the century, scientists began to wonder whether the atoms of the chemical elements might not be composed of smaller particles. This was actually a contradiction in terms, because the Greek word *atomos*, from which the word *atom* was derived, meant "indivisible." But there were some indications of particles smaller than an atom—the electrons. In 1905, Albert Einstein suggested that matter might just be "condensed energy" and gave the conversion formula $E = mc^2$, in which E represents the energy, m the mass, and c the velocity of light. If this formula was correct, a small piece of matter should represent enormous amounts of energy.

FISSION AND FUSION

As is now generally known, atomic energy can be released in two ways. One is the *fission* of elements with very heavy atoms, such as uranium and plutonium, which will split when struck by a neutron, a subatomic particle. The splitting of the heavy atom releases more neutrons, which are then available to split other atoms—the so-called chain reaction. The other way of obtaining atomic energy is *fusion;* four light atoms (hydrogen) are fused together into the next heavier element (helium). The fusion reaction requires enormous heat and very high pressures. These pressures, coupled with very high temperatures, can most easily be produced by exploding a fission bomb, which is the reason why it is often said that a fission bomb is the trigger for a fusion (hydrogen) bomb.

Interestingly enough, the fusion reaction was discovered first, though only on paper. For the period from, say, 1910 to 1930, most physicists believed that the release of atomic energy, if it could be done, would be of no practical value. They asserted that causing the release would require more energy than could be obtained. Most astronomers, on the other hand, were convinced that atomic energy is released in the sun and the other stars because there was no other way to account for the energy the stars radiated into space. Trying to account for the energy radiated by the stars led to theoretical papers predicting what we now call the fusion reaction. At the time (1930), atomic fission was still unknown; it was discovered first by Fermi in 1934, and the process was repeated by Hahn and Strassmann in 1938. But nobody yet knew that the sudden bursts of energy observed in the experiments were due to the fission of the uranium-235 atom. This was established (by way of calculation) by Dr. Lise Meitner. Once it was known what happened, the way to a premeditated release of atomic energy was clear.

But nobody could be quite certain whether the release would take the form of an explosion or whether it would be slow enough to be used to generate power. American scientists proceeded under the assumption that the release would be sudden and violent (and the Alamogordo test proved them right), while Professor Heisenberg in Germany thought the slow release to be more likely, which is the reason why the Germans did not start a large-scale atomic energy project.

INTERNATIONAL SCOREBOARD

The beneficial aspects of atomic energy lie in the field of research (physical, chemical, and medical); it provides both new materials and new techniques. Practical applications of the slow release of fission energy are the power reactors, including the power plants for seagoing vessels. On May 18, 1974, India exploded an underground nuclear device of 10 to 15 kilotons, becoming the world's sixth nuclear power. The international scoreboard is now as follows:

Fission bomb explosions: U. S., Britain, France, U.S.S.R., Communist China, India.

Fusion bomb explosions: U. S., Britain, France, U.S.S.R., Communist China.

Power reactors: U. S., Britain, France, U.S.S.R., Norway, Sweden, Israel, Belgium, West Germany. (Egypt is rumored to have power reactors, but reports are unconfirmed.)

Atomic rocket propulsion: Under development in U. S. and probably in U.S.S.R.

RELIGION

Estimated Membership of the Principal Religions of the World

Source: Britannica Book of the Year, 1976.

Statistics of the world's religions are only very rough approximations. Aside from Christianity, few religions, if any, attempt to keep statistical records; and even Protestants and Catholics employ different methods of counting members. All persons of whatever age who have received baptism in the Catholic Church are counted as members, while in most Protestant Churches only those who "join" the church are numbered. The compiling of statistics is further complicated by the fact that in China one may be at the same time a Confucian, a Taoist, and a Buddhist. In Japan, one may be both a Buddhist and a Shintoist.

Religion	North America[1]	South America	Europe	Asia	Africa	Oceania[2]	Total
Total Christian........	229,006,000	164,884,000	354,894,600	87,683,000	101,144,100	17,155,000	954,766,700
Roman Catholic......	131,596,500	154,067,000	174,141,000	42,285,000	32,314,500	3,200,000	540,704,000
Eastern Orthodox....	4,120,000	55,000	63,900,600	1,781,000	16,442,000	355,000	86,653,600
Protestant..........	93,289,500	10,762,000	116,833,000	40,617,000	52,367,000	13,600,000	327,509,100
Jewish[3]...............	6,653,725	686,700	3,489,750	3,089,150	359,465	75,000	14,353,790
Muslim...............	242,100	195,300	8,370,000	430,267,000	99,073,500	66,000	538,213,900
Zoroastrian	250	–	–	229,650	480	–	230,380
Shinto...............	60,000	92,000	–	60,004,000	–	–	60,156,000
Taoist................	16,000	12,000	–	30,375,700	–	–	30,403,700
Confucian............	96,000	85,000	30,000	185,850,700	500	42,000	186,104,300
Buddhist.............	150,500	190,300	222,000	249,296,500	2,000	16,000	249,877,300
Hindu...............	75,000	533,000	350,000	522,184,500	490,550	640,000	524,273,050
TOTAL............	236,299,675	166,678,300	367,356,350	1,568,980,200	201,070,595	17,994,000	2,558,379,120

[1] Includes Central America and West Indies. [2] Includes Australia and New Zealand, as well as islands of the South Pacific. [3] Includes total Jewish population, whether or not related to the synagogue. NOTE: Because of war and persecution, there are about 18,000,000 refugees throughout the world who are not integrated into religious statistics of the land of their temporary residence.

Major Religions of the World

Judaism

The determining factors of Judaism are: descendance from Israel, the *Torah,* and Tradition.

The name Israel (Jacob, a patriarch) also signifies his descendants as a people. During the 15th–13th centuries B.C., Israelite tribes, coming from South and East, gradually settled in Palestine, then inhabited by Canaanites. They were held together by Moses, who gave them religious unity in the worship of *Jahweh,* the God who had chosen Israel to be his people.

Under Judges, the 12 tribes at first formed an amphictyonic covenant. Saul established kingship (circa 1050 B.C.), and under David, his successor (1000–960 B.C.), the State of Israel comprised all of Palestine with Jerusalem as religio-political center. A golden era followed under Solomon (965–926 B.C.), who built *Jahweh* a temple.

After Solomon's death, the kingdom separated into Israel in the North, and Juda in the South. A period of conflicts ensued, which ended with the conquest of Israel by Assyria in 722 B.C. The Babylonians defeated Juda in 586 B.C., destroying Jerusalem and its temple, and deporting many to Babylon.

The era of the kings is significant also in that the great prophets worked in that time, emphasizing faith in *Jahweh* as both God of Israel and God of the universe, and stressing social justice.

When the Persians permitted the Jews to return from exile (836 B.C.), temple and cult were restored in Jerusalem. The Persian rulers were succeeded by the Seleucides. The Maccabaean revolt against these Hellenistic kings gave independence to the Jews in 128 B.C., which lasted till the Romans occupied the country.

Important groups that exerted influence during these times were the Sadducees, priests in the temple in Jerusalem; the Pharisees, teachers of the Law in the synagogues; Essenes, a religious order (from whom Dead Sea Scrolls, discovered in 1947, came); Apocalyptists, who were expecting the heavenly Messiah; and Zealots, who were prepared to fight for national independence.

When the latter turned against Rome in A.D. 66, Roman armies under Titus suppressed the revolt, destroying Jerusalem and its temple in A.D. 70. The Jews were scattered in the *diaspora* (Dispersion), subject to oppressions until the Age of the Enlightenment (18th century) brought their emancipation, although persecutions did not end entirely.

The fall of the Jerusalem temple was an important event in the religious life of the Jews, which now developed around *Torah* (Law) and synagogue. Around A.D. 100 the Sacred Scriptures were codified. Synagogue worship became central, with readings from *Torah* and prophets. Most important prayers are the *Shema* (Hear) and the Prayer of the 18 Benedictions.

411

Religious life is guided by the commandments contained in the *Torah:* circumcision and *Sabbath,* as well as other ethical and ceremonial commandments.

The *Talmud,* based on the *Mishnah* and its interpretations, took shape over many centuries in the Babylonian and Palestinian Schools. It was a strong binding force of Judaism in the Dispersion.

In the 12th century, Maimonides formulated his "13 Articles of Faith," which carried great authority. Fundamental in this creed are: belief in God and his oneness (*Shema*), belief in the changeless *Torah,* in the words of Moses and the prophets, belief in reward and punishment, the coming of the Messiah, and the resurrection of the dead.

Judaism is divided into theological schools, the main divisions of which are Orthodox and Reform.

Christianity

Christianity is founded upon Jesus Christ, to whose life the New Testament writings testify. Jesus, a Jew, was born in about 7 B.C., and assumed his public life, after his 30th year, in Galilee. The Gospels tell of many extraordinary deeds which accompanied his ministry. He proclaimed the Kingdom of God, a future reality which is at the same time already present. Nationalistic-Jewish expectations of the Messiah he rejected. Rather, he referred to himself as the "Son of Man," the Christ, who has power to forgive sins now, and who shall also come as Judge at the end of time. Jesus set forth the religio-ethical demands for participation in the Kingdom of God as change of heart and love of God and neighbor.

At the Last Supper, he signified his death as a sacrifice, which would inaugurate the New Covenant, by whom many would be saved. Circa A.D. 30 he died on a cross in Jerusalem. The early Church carried on Jesus' proclamation, the apostle Paul emphasizing his death and resurrection.

The person of Jesus is fundamental to the Christian faith since it is believed that in his life, death, and resurrection, God's revelation became historically tangible. He is seen as the turning point in history, and man's relationship to God as determined by his attitude to Jesus.

Historically Christianity thus arose out of Judaism, claiming fulfillment of the promises of the Old Testament in Jesus. The early Church designated itself as "the true Israel," which expected the speedy return of Jesus. The mother church was at Jerusalem, but churches were soon founded in many other places. The apostle Paul was instrumental in founding and extending a Gentile Christianity that was free from Jewish legalism.

The new religion spread rapidly throughout the eastern and western parts of the Roman Empire. In coming to terms with other religious movements within the Empire, Christianity began to take definite shape as an organization in its doctrine, liturgy, and ministry circa A.D. 200. In the 4th century the Catholic Church had taken root in countries stretching from Spain in the West to Persia and India in the East. Christians had been repeatedly subject to persecution by the Roman state, but finally gained tolerance under Constantine the Great (A.D. 313). Since that time, the Church became favored under his successors and

in 380 the Emperor Theodosius proclaimed Christianity the State religion. Paganism was suppressed and public life was gradually molded in accordance with Christian ethical demands.

It was in these years also, that the Church was able to achieve a certain unity of doctrine. Due to differences of interpretation of basic doctrines concerning Christ, which threatened to divide the Catholic Church, a standard Christian Creed was formulated by bishops at successive Ecumenical Councils, the first of which was held in A.D. 325 (Nicaea). The chief doctrines formulated concerned the doctrine of the Trinity, i.e., that there is one God in three persons: Father, Son, and Holy Spirit (Constantinople, A.D. 381); and the nature of Christ as both divine and human (Chalcedon, A.D. 541).

Through differences and rivalry between East and West the unity of the Church was broken by schism in 1054. In 1517 a separation occurred in the Western Church with the Reformation. From the major Protestant denominations [Lutheran, Presbyterian, Anglican (Episcopalian)], many Free Churches separated themselves in an age of individualism.

In the 20th century, however, the direction is toward unity. The Ecumenical Movement led to the formation of the World Council of Churches in 1948 (Amsterdam), which has since been joined by many Protestant and Orthodox Churches.

Through its missionary activity Christianity has spread to most parts of the globe.

Eastern Orthodoxy

Eastern Orthodoxy comprises the faith and practice of Churches stemming from ancient Churches in the Eastern part of the Roman Empire. The term covers: Orthodox Churches in communion with the See of Constantinople, Uniate Churches in communion with Rome, and Nestorian and Monophysite Churches.

The Orthodox, Catholic, Apostolic Church is the direct descendant of the Byzantine State Church and consists of a series of independent national churches which are united by Doctrine, Liturgy and Hierarchical organization (deacons and priests, who may either be married or be a monk before ordination, and bishops, who must be celebates). The heads of these Churches are patriarchs or metropolitans; the Patriarch of Constantinople is only "first among equals." Rivalry between the Pope of Rome and the Patriarch of Constantinople, aided by differences and misunderstandings that existed for centuries between the Eastern and Western parts of the Empire, led to a schism in 1054. Repeated attempts at reunion have failed in past centuries. The mutual excommunication pronounced in that year have been lifted in 1965, however, and because of greater interaction in theology between Orthodox Churches and those in the WNt, a climate of better understanding has been created in the 20th century. First contacts were with Anglicans and Old Catholics. Orthodox Churches belong to the World Council of Churches.

The Eastern Orthodox Churches recognize only the canons of the seven Ecumenical Councils (325–787) as binding for faith, and they reject doctrines that have been added in the West.

The central worship service is called the Liturgy, which is understood as representation of God's acts of salvation. Its center is the celebration of the Eucharist, or Lord's Supper.

In their worship *icons* (sacred pictures) are used which have a sacramental meaning as representation. The Mother of Christ, angels, and Saints are highly venerated.

The number of sacraments in the Orthodox Church is the same as in the Western Catholic Church.

Orthodox Churches are found in the Balkans and the Soviet Union; since the 20th century also in Western Europe and other parts of the world, particularly in America.

Eastern Orthodoxy also includes the Uniate Churches that recognize the authority of the Pope, but keep their own traditional liturgies; and those Churches, dating back to the 5th century, which emancipated themselves from the Byzantine State Church: the Nestorian Church in the Near East and India, with approximately half a million members, and the Monophysite Churches with some 17 million members. (Coptic, Ethiopian, Syrian, Armenian and the Mar Thoma Church in India).

Roman Catholicism

Roman Catholicism comprises the belief and practice of the Roman Catholic Church. The Church stands under the authority of the Bishop of Rome, the Pope, and is ruled by him and bishops who are held to be, through ordination, successors of Peter and the Apostles, respectively. Fundamental to the structure of the Church is the juridical aspect: doctrine and sacraments are bound to the power of jurisdiction and consecration of the hierarchy. The Pope, as the head of the hierarchy of archbishops, bishops, priests, and deacons, has full ecclesiastical power, granted him by Christ, through Peter. As successor to Peter, he is the Vicar of Christ. The powers that others in the hierarchy possess are delegated.

Roman Catholics believe their Church to be the one, holy, catholic, and apostolic Church, possessing all the properties of the one, true Church of Christ.

The faith of the Church is understood to be identical with that taught by Christ and his Apostles and contained in Bible and Tradition, i.e. the original deposit of faith, to which nothing new may be added. New definitions of doctrines, such as the Immaculate Conception of Mary (1854) and the bodily Assumption of Mary (1950), have been declared by Popes, however, in accordance with the principle of development (implicit-explicit doctrine).

At Vatican Council I (1870) the Pope was proclaimed "endowed with infallibilty, *ex cathedra*, i.e., when exercising the office of Pastor and Teacher of all Christians."

The center of Roman Catholic worship is the Sacrament of the Mass, which is the commemoration of Christ's sacrificial death and of his resurrection. Other sacraments are: Baptism, Confirmation, Confession, Matrimony, Ordination, and Extreme Unction, seven in total. The Virgin Mary and Saints, and their relics, are highly venerated, and prayers are made to them to intercede with God, in whose presence they are believed to dwell.

The Roman Catholic Church is the largest Christian organization in the world, found in most countries. Some eight million belong to the Uniate rites; the vast majority to the Latin rite.

Since Vatican Council II (1962–65), and the effort to "update" the Church, many interesting changes and developments have been taking place.

Protestantism

Protestantism comprises the Christian Churches that separated from Rome during the Reformation in the 16th century, initiated by an Augustinian monk, Martin Luther. "Protestant" was originally applied to followers of Luther, who protested at the Diet of Spires (1529) against the decree which prohibited all further ecclesiastical reforms. Subsequently, Protestantism came to mean rejection of attempts to tie God's revelation to earthly institutions, and a return to the Gospel and the Word of God, as sole authority in matters of faith and practice. Central in the biblical message is the justification of the sinner by faith alone. The Church is understood as a fellowship, and the priesthood of all believers stressed.

The Augsburg Confession (1530) was the principle statement of Lutheran faith and practice. It became a model for other Confessions of Faith, which in their turn had decisive influence on Church polity. Major Protestant denominations are the Lutheran, Reformed (Calvinist), Presbyterian, and Anglican (Episcopal). Smaller ones are the Mennonite, Schwenkfeldians, and Unitarians. In Britain and America there are the Congregationalists, Baptists, Quakers, Methodists, and other free church types of communities.*

Since the latter part of the 19th century, national councils of Churches have been established in many countries, e.g. the Federal Council of Churches of Christ in America in 1908. Denominations across countries joined in federations and world alliances, beginning with the Anglican Lambeth Conference in 1867.

Protestant missionary activity, particularly strong in the last century, resulted in the founding of many Younger Churches in Asia and Africa. The Ecumenical Movement which originated with Protestant missions, aims at the unity among Christians and Churches.

Islam

Islam is the religion founded in Arabia by Mohammed between 610 and 632. Its 400 million adherents are found in countries stretching from Morocco in the West to Indonesia in the East.

Mohammed was born in A.D. 570 at Mecca and belonged to the Quraysh tribe, which was active in caravan trade. At the age of 25 he joined the caravan trade from Mecca to Syria in the employment of a rich widow, Khadiji, whom he married. Critical of the idolatry of the inhabitants of Mecca, he began to lead a contemplative life in the deserts. There he received a series of revelations. Encouraged by Khadiji, he gradually became convinced that he was given a God-appointed task to devote himself to the reform of religion and society. Idolatry was to be abandoned.

The *Hijra* (migration) of Mohammed from Mecca, where he was not honored, to Medina, where he was well received, occurred in 622 and marks the beginning of the Muslim era. In 630 he marched on Mecca and conquered it. He died at Medina in 632. His grave there has since been a place of pilgrimage.

Mohammed's followers, called Muslims, revered him as the prophet of *Allah* (God), beside whom

* In regarding themselves as being faithful to original biblical Christianity, these Churches differ from such religious bodies as Unitarians, Mormons, Jehovah's Witnesses, and Christian Scientists, who either teach new doctrines or reject old ones.

there is no other God. Although he had no close knowledge of Judaism and Christianity, he considered himself succeeding and completing them as the seal of the Prophets. Sources of the Islamic faith are the *Qur'an,* regarded as the uncreated, eternal Word of God, and Tradition (*hadith*), regarding sayings and deeds of the prophet.

Islam means surrender to the will of *Allah.* He is the all-powerful, whose will is supreme and determines man's fate. Good and evil deeds will be rewarded at the Last Judgment in paradise or in hell.

The Five Pillars, primary duties, of Islam are: witness; confessing the oneness of God and of Mohammed, his prophet; prayer, to be performed five times a day; almsgiving to the poor and the mosque (house of worship); fasting during daylight hours in the month of Ramadan; pilgrimage to Mecca, at least once in the Muslim's lifetime.

The practice of Holy War (*jihad*), at first responsible for the rapid growth of the new religion, could not be maintained. Mohammed curtailed the practice of polygamy by limiting it to four wives. In modern times the position of women has improved, due to Western influence. The eating of pork and drinking of intoxicants is forbidden.

Islam, upholding the law of brotherhood, succeeded in uniting an Arab world that had disintegrated into tribes and castes. Disagreements concerning the succession of the prophet caused a great division in Islam between *Sunnis* and *Shias.* Among these, other sects arose (*Wahhabi*). Doctrinal issues also led to the rise of different schools of thought in theology. Nevertheless, since Arab armies turned against Syria and Palestine in 635, Islam has expanded successfully under Mohammed's successors. Its rapid victorious conquests in Asia and Africa are unsurpassed in history. Turning against Europe, Muslims conquered Spain in 713. In 1453, Constantinople fell into their hands, and in 1529, Muslim armies besieged Vienna. Since then, Islam has lost its foothold in Europe.

In modern times it has made great gains in Africa.

Hinduism

In India alone there are more than 300 million adherents of Hinduism. In contrast to other religions, it has no founder. Considered the oldest religion in the world, it dates back, perhaps, to prehistoric times.

Hinduism is hard to define, there being no common creed, no one doctrine to bind Hindus together. Intellectually there is complete freedom of belief, and one can be monotheist, polytheist, or atheist. What matters is the social system: a Hindu is one born into a caste.

As a religion, Hinduism is founded on the sacred scriptures, written in Sanskrit and called the *Vedas* (*Veda*-knowledge). There are four Vedic books, among which the *Rig Veda* is the most important. It speaks of many gods and also deals with questions concerning the universe and creation. The dates of these works are unknown (1000 B.C.?).

The *Upanishads* (dated 1000–300 B.C.), commentaries on the Vedic texts, have philosophical speculations on the origin of the universe, the nature of deity, of *atman* (the human soul), and its relationship to *Brahman* (the universal soul).

Brahman is the principal and source of the universe who can be indicated only by negatives. As the divine intelligence, he is the ground of the visible world, a presence that pervades all beings. Thus the many Hindu deities came to be understood as manifestations of the one *Brahman* from whom everything proceeds and to whom everything ultimately returns. The religio-social system of Hinduism is based on the concept of reincarnation and transmigration in which all living beings, from plants below to gods above, are caught in a cosmic system that is an everlasting cycle of becoming and perishing.

Life is determined by the law of *karma,* according to which rebirth is dependent on moral behavior in a previous phase of existence. The doctrine of transmigration thus provides a rationale for the caste system. In this view, life on earth is regarded as transient (*maya*), and a burden. The goal of existence is liberation from the cycle of rebirth and redeath and entrance into the indescribable state of what in Buddhism is called *nirvana* (extinction of passion).

Further important sacred writings are the Epics (*puranas*), which contain legendary stories about gods and men. They are the *Mahabharata* (composed between 200 B.C. and A.D. 200) and the *Ramayana.* The former includes the *Bhagavad-Gita* (Song of the Lord), its most famous part, that tells of devotion to *Krishna* (Lord), who appears as an *avatar* (incarnation) of the god *Vishnu,* and of the duty of obeying caste rules. The work begins with a praise of the *yoga* (discipline) system.

The practice of Hinduism consists of rites and ceremonies, performed within the framework of the caste system, and centering on the main socio-religious occasions of birth, marriage, and death. There are many Hindu temples, which are dwelling places of the deities and to which people bring offerings. There are also places of pilgrimages, the chief one being Benares on the Ganges, most sacred among the rivers in India. .

In modern times work has been done to reform and revive Hinduism. One of the outstanding reformers was Ramakrishna (1836–86), who inspired many followers, one of whom founded the Ramakrishna mission, which seeks to convert others to its religion. The mission is active both in India and in other countries.

Buddhism

Founded in the sixth century B.C. in northern India by Gautama Buddha, who was born in southern Nepal, as son to a king. His birth is surrounded by many legends, but Western scholars agree that he lived from 563–483 B.C. Warned by a sage that his son would become an ascetic or a universal monarch, the king confined him to his home. He was able to escape and began the life of a homeless wanderer in search of peace, passing through many disappointments until he finally came to the Tree of Enlightenment, under which he lived in meditation till enlightenment came to him and he became a Buddha (enlightened one).

Now he understood the origin of suffering, summarized in the *Four Noble Truths,* which constitutes the foundation of Buddhism. The Four are the truth of suffering, which all living beings must endure; of the origin of suffering, which is craving and which leads to re-birth; that it can be destroyed; of the way that leads to cessation of pain, i.e., the *Noble Eightfold Way*, which is the rule of practical Buddhism: right views, right intention, right speech, right action, right livelihood, right effort, right concentration, and right ecstasy.

Nirvana is the goal of all existence, the state of complete redemption, into which the redeemed enters. Buddha's insight can free every man from the law of reincarnation through complete emptying of the self.

The nucleus of Buddha's church or association was originally formed by monks and lay-brothers, whose houses gradually became monasteries used as places for religious instruction. The worship service consisted of a sermon, expounding of Scripture, meditation, and confession. At a later stage pilgrimages to the holy places associated with the Buddha came into being, as well as veneration of relics.

In the third century B.C., King Ashoka made Buddhism the State religion of India, but as centuries passed, it gradually fell into decay through splits, persecutions, and the hostile Brahmans. Buddhism spread to countries outside India, however.

At the beginning of the Christian era, there occurred a split which gave rise to two main types: *Hinayana* (Little Vehicle), or southern Buddhism, and *Mahayana* (Great Vehicle), or northern Buddhism. The former type, more individualistic, survived in Ceylon and southern Asia. Hinayana retained more closely the original teachings of the Buddha, which did not know of a personal god or soul. *Mahayana*, more social, polytheistic, and developing a pluralistic pompous cult, was strong in the Himalayas, Tibet, Mongolia, China, Korea, and Japan.

In the present century, Buddhism has found believers also in the West, and Buddhist associations have been established in Europe and the U. S.

Confucianism

Confucius (K'ung Fu-tzu), born in the state of Lu (northern China), lived from 551–479 B.C. Tradition, exaggerating the importance of Confucius in life, has depicted him as a great statesman, but, in fact, he seems to have been a private teacher. Anthologies of ancient Chinese classics, along with his own Analects (*Lun Yu*) became the basis of Confucianism. These Analects were transmitted as a collection of his sayings as recorded by his students, with whom he discussed ethical and social problems. They developed into men of high moral standing, who served the State as administrators.

In his teachings, Confucius emphasized the importance of an old Chinese concept (*li*) which has the connotation of proper conduct. There is some disagreement as to the religious ideas of Confucius but he held high the concepts handed down from centuries before him. Thus he believed in Heaven (*T'ien*), and sacrificed to his ancestors. Ancestor worship he indeed encouraged as an expression of filial piety, which he considered the loftiest of virtues.

Piety to Confucius was the foundation of the family as well as the State. The family is the nucleus of the State and the "five relations," between king and subject, father and son, man and wife, older and younger brother, friend and friend, are determined by the virtues of love of fellow men, righteousness, and respect.

An extension of ancestor worship may be seen in the worship of Confucius, which became official in the second century B.C. when the emperor, in recognition of Confucius' teachings, as supporting the imperial rule, offered sacrifices at his tomb.

Mencius (Meng Tse), who lived around 400 B.C., did much to propagate and elaborate Confucianism in its concern with ordering society. Thus, for two millennia, Confucius' doctrine of State, with its emphasis on ethics and social morality, rooted in ancient Chinese tradition and developed and continued by his disciples, has been standard in China and the Far East.

With the revolution of 1911 in China, however, students, burning Confucius in effigy, called for the removal of "the old curiosity shop."

Shintoism

Shinto, the Chinese term for the Japanese *Kami no Michi*, i.e., the Way of the Gods, comprises the religious ideas and cult indigenous to Japan. *Kami*, or gods, considered divine forces of nature that are worshipped, may reside in rivers, trees, rocks, mountains, certain animals, or, particularly, in the sun and moon. The worship of ancestors, heroes, and deceased emperors was incorporated later.

After Buddhism had come from Korea, Japan's native religion at first resisted it. Then there followed a period of compromise and amalgamation with Buddhist beliefs and ceremonies, resulting, since the ninth century A.D., in a syncretistic religion, a Twofold Shinto. Buddhist deities came to be regarded as manifestations of Japanese deities, and Buddhist priests took over most of the Shinto shrines.

In modern times Shinto regained independence from Buddhism. Under the reign of the Emperor Meiji (1868–1912) it was elevated to official State religion, in which loyalty to the emperor was emphasized. The line of succession of emperors is traced back to the first Emperor Jimmu (660 B.C.) and beyond him to the Sun-goddess *Amaterasu-omi-kami*.

The centers of worship are the shrines and temples in which the deities are believed to dwell, and believers approach them through *torii* (gateways). Most important among the shrines is the imperial shrine of the Sun-goddess at Ise, where state ceremonies were once held in June and December. The *Yasukuni* shrine of the war dead in Tokyo is also well known.

Acts of worship consist of prayers, clapping of hands, acts of purification, and offerings. On feast days processions and performances of music and dancing take place, and priests read prayers before the gods in the shrines, asking for good harvest, the well-being of people and emperor, etc. In Japanese homes there is a god-shelf, a small wooden shrine which contains the tablets bearing the names of ancestors. Offerings are made and candles lit before it.

After World War II the Allied Command ordered the disestablishment of State Shinto. To be distinguished from State Shinto is Sect Shinto, consisting of 13 recognized sects. These have arisen in modern times, gaining large followings. Most important among them is *Tenrikyo* in Tenri City (Nara), in which healing by faith plays a central role.

Taoism

Taoism, a religion of China, was, according to tradition, founded by Lao Tse, a Chinese philosopher, long considered one of the prominent religious leaders from the sixth century B.C.

Data about him are for the most part legendary, however, and the *Tao Te Ching* (the classic of the Way and of its Power), traditionally ascribed to him, is now believed by many scholars to have originated in the third century B.C. The book is composed in short chapters, written in aphoristic rhymes. Central are the word *Tao,* which means way or path, and, in a deeper sense, signifies the principle which underlies the reality of this world and which manifests itself in nature and in the lives of men; and the word *Te* (power).

The virtuous man draws power from being absorbed in *Tao,* the ultimate reality within an everchanging world. By non-action and keeping away from human striving is it possible for man to live in harmony with the principles that underlie and govern the universe. *Tao* cannot be comprehended by reason and knowledge, but only by inward quiet.

Beside the *Tao Te Ching,* dating from approximately the same period, are two Taoist works, written by Chuang Tse and Lieh Tse.

Theoretical Taoism of this classical philosophical movement of the fourth and third centuries B.C. in China differed from popular Taoism, into which it gradually degenerated. The standard of theoretical Taoism was maintained in the classics, of course, and among the upper classes it continued to be alive until modern times.

Religious Taoism is a form of religion dealing with deities and spirits, magic and soothsaying. In the second century A.D. it was organized with temples, cult, priests, and monasteries, and was able to hold its own in the competition with Buddhism that came up at the same time.

After the seventh century A.D., however, Taoist religion further declined. Split into numerous sects which often operate like secret societies, it has become a syncretistic folk religion in which some of the old deities and saints live on.

History of Leading Religious Groups in the United States

(50,000 members or over)

Source: Yearbook of American Churches, 1976.

Baptist

American Baptist Association.—A group of independent Missionary Baptist Churches, mainly in the South, Southeast, and Southwest, organized in 1905. Members (1975): 1,071,000.

American Baptist Churches in the U.S.A. —Formerly known as the Northern Baptist Convention and the American Baptist Convention, this body changed its name in 1973. Although national missionary organizational developments began in 1814 with the establishment of the American Baptist Foreign Mission Society, the Convention was not formed until 1907. Members (1974): 1,579,029.

Baptist General Conference.—Formerly known as the Swedish Baptist General Conference of America. It has operated as a general conference since 1879. Members (1974): 111,093.

Baptist Missionary Association of America.—Formerly called the North American Baptist Association. It was organized in 1950 in Little Rock, Ark. Members (1974): 211,000.

Conservative Baptist Association of America.—Organized in 1947. Adherents regard the Bible as infallible. Local churches are independent, autonomous, and free from ecclesiastical or political authority. Members (1974): 300,000.

Free Will Baptists.—A body of evangelical Baptists, organized in 1727 in the South and 1780 in the North. Members (1974): 215,000.

The General Association of Regular Baptist Churches.—Founded in 1932 in Chicago by a group of churches which had withdrawn from the Northern Baptist Convention (now the American Baptist Convention) because of doctrinal differences. Members (1975): 250,000.

General Baptists (General Association of). An Arminian group of Baptists, organized in England in 1607 and transplanted to the colonies in 1714. It died out along the Seaboard, but revived in the Midwest in 1823. Members (1974): 70,000.

National Baptist Convention, U. S. A., Inc.—The older and parent convention of Black Baptists. This body is to be distinguished from the National Baptist Convention of America, usually referred to as the "unincorporated" body. Members (1958): 5,500,000.

U. S. Church Membership

Source: Yearbook of American Churches, 1976.

Religious group	Members
Protestant bodies and others	72,485,146
Roman Catholics	48,881,872
Jewish congregations[1]	6,115,000
Eastern churches	3,695,860
Old Catholic, Polish National Catholic, Armenian churches	849,052
Buddhist Churches of America	60,000
Miscellaneous	380,557
TOTAL[2]	132,467,487

[1] Includes Orthodox, Conservative, and Reform. [2] As reported in the *1976 Yearbook* from statistics furnished by 223 religious bodies in the United States.

National Baptist Convention of America. —This is a body usually referred to as the "unincorporated" convention, not to be confused with the "incorporated" National Baptist Convention, U. S. A., Inc., from which this body withdrew. Organized in 1880. Members (1956) : 2,668,799.

National Baptist Evangelical Life and Soul Saving Assembly of U. S. A.—Organized in 1921 as a charitable, educational, and evangelical organization. Members (1951) : 57,674.

National Primitive Baptist Convention, Inc.—A group of Baptists having local associations and a National Convention. Organized in 1907. Members (1971) : 1,645,000.

North American Baptist Association.— See Baptist Missionary Association of America.

Primitive Baptists.—A large group of Baptists, largely through the South, who are opposed to all centralization and to modern missionary societies. Members (1950) : 72,000.

Progressive National Baptist Convention, Inc.—A body that held its organizational meeting in Cincinnati in 1961 and its first annual session in Philadelphia in 1962. Members (1967) : 521,692.

Southern Baptist Convention.—In 1845, Southern Baptists withdrew from the General Missionary Convention over the question of slavery and other matters and formed the Southern Baptist Convention. Members (1974) : 12,513,378.

The United Free Will Baptist Church.— A body which set up its organization in 1870. Members (1952) : 100,000.

Catholic and Orthodox

The American Carpatho-Russian Orthodox Greek Catholic Church.—This church is a self-governing diocese in communion with the Ecumenical Patriarchate of Constantinople. On Sept. 19, 1938, the late Patriarch Benjamin I canonized the diocese in the name of the Orthodox Church of Christ. Members (1974): 100,000.

Antiochian Orthodox Christian Archdiocese of North America, The—Formed in 1975 by merger of the Antiochian Orthodox Christian Archdiocese of New York and All North America (formerly the Syrian Antiochian Orthodox Archdiocese of New York and North America) and the Antiochian Orthodox Archdiocese of Toledo, Ohio, and Dependencies in North America. The new Archdiocese is under the jurisdiction of the Patriarch of Antioch. Members (1975): 130,000.

Armenian Apostolic Church of America. —The Armenian Church divided into two separate dioceses in 1933 because of a dispute regarding the political activities of the prelate at that time, and because of the status of the church in Soviet Armenia. Since 1956, this diocese has been under the jurisdiction of the Holy See of Cilicia, Beirut, Lebanon. Members (1972): 125,000.

Armenian Church of America, Diocese of the (including Diocese of California).—The American branch of the Ancient Church of Armenia. Established in the U. S. in 1889. Diocesan organization is under the jurisdiction of the Holy See of Etchmiadzin, Armenia, U.S.S.R. Members (1972): 372,000.

Bulgarian Eastern Orthodox Church. (Diocese of North and South America and Australia).—A Synod of the Bulgarian Eastern Orthodox Church, established as the Bulgarian Orthodox Mission in 1909. Became a canonical metropolitan archdiocese in 1947. Members (1971): 86,000.

Greek Orthodox Archdiocese of North and South America.—Greek-speaking Orthodox Christians have parishes in the U. S., Canada, and South America. These are under the Ecumenical Patriarchate of Constantinople. Members (1975): 1,950,000.

North American Old Roman Catholic Church.—A body with the doctrine of the Old Catholics; identical with the Roman Catholic Church in most worship and discipline. It is not under Papal jurisdiction. Members (1974): 60,098.

The Orthodox Church in America (The Russian Orthodox Greek Catholic Church of America).—This body entered Alaska in 1792. In 1872, its headquarters were moved from Sitka to San Francisco and, in 1905, to New York. Members (1975): 1,000,000.

Polish National Catholic Church of America.—After long dissatisfaction with Roman Catholic administration and ideology, this group was organized in 1897. Members (1960) : 282,411.

The Roman Catholic Church.—The largest single group of Christians in the U. S., the Roman Catholic Church is under the spiritual leadership of Pope Paul VI. This group dates back to the priests who accompanied Columbus on his second voyage to the New World. A settlement, later discontinued, was made at St. Augustine, Fla. The continuous history of this Church in the colonies began at St. Mary's in 1634, in Maryland. Members (1976) : 48,881,872.

Russian Orthodox Church in the U.S.A., Patriarchal Parishes of the—This autonomous body is the direct canonical successor of the Orthodox Catholic mission established in Alaska by the Russian Orthodox Church in 1793. It is under the spiritual jurisdiction of the Patriarch of

Moscow and all Russia, His Holiness Pimen. In 1962 an administration was established for the Orthodox Mission in Puerto Rico and the Spanish-speaking people in the United States. Members (1974): 51,500.

The Russian Orthodox Church Outside Russia—The governing body was set up in Constantinople. In 1950, it came to the U. S. Members (1955) : 55,000.

Serbian Eastern Orthodox Church for the U.S.A. and Canada.—This body of the Eastern Orthodox Church is autonomous. Members (1967) : 65,000.

Syrian Antiochian Orthodox Archdiocese of New York and North America.—See Antiochian Orthodox Christian Archdiocese of New York and All North America.

Syrian Orthodox Church of Antioch (Archdiocese of the U.S.A. and Canada).— This group is in a direct ecclesiastical line of the Syrian Orthodox Church established in Antioch. There are 10 parishes in the U.S. and two in the Province of Quebec. Members (1972): 50,000.

Ukrainian Orthodox Church in the U.S.A.—This church was organized in the U. S. in 1919. Members (1966): 87,745.

Lutheran

The American Lutheran Church.—This church is the result of the merger in 1960 of the American Lutheran Church, the Evangelical Lutheran Church, and the United Evangelical Lutheran Church. In 1963, the Lutheran Free Church merged with The American Lutheran Church. Members (1975): 2,415,687.

Lutheran Church—Missouri Synod.—This body, the largest constituent part of the Evangelical Lutheran Synodical Conference of North America, was organized in 1847. It is the leader in the conservative group among the Lutherans. Members (1975): 2,762,966.

Lutheran Church in America.—This body was organized in 1962 by the consolidation of the American Evangelical Lutheran Church (1874), the Augustana Evangelical Lutheran Church (1860), the Finnish Evangelical Lutheran Church (1890), and the United Lutheran Church in America (1918). Members (1975): 2,987,647.

Wisconsin Evangelical Lutheran Synod. —This body was organized in Wisconsin in 1850. Members (1975): 395,440.

Methodist

African Methodist Episcopal Church.— This church began in 1787 in Philadelphia when persons in a Methodist Episcopal

Church withdrew. In 1816, the denomination was started. Members (1951): 1,166,-301.

African Methodist Episcopal Zion Church.—This group was organized in 1796, having withdrawn from the John Street Methodist Church, New York. Members (1973): 1,024,974.

Christian Methodist Episcopal Church.— In 1870, the General Conference of the M.E. Church, South, approved the request of its black membership for the formation of their conferences into a separate body. Members (1965): 466,718.

Free Methodist Church of North America. —This body, organized in 1860, grew out of a movement in the Genesee Conference of the Methodist Episcopal Church about 1850 towards a more original Methodism. Members (1974): 65,210.

United Methodist Church.—The United Methodist Church was formed in April, 1968, by the union of the Methodist Church and the Evangelical United Brethren Church. The two churches shared a common historical and spiritual heritage. The Methodist Church resulted in 1939 from the unification of three branches of Methodism—the Methodist Episcopal Church; the Methodist Episcopal Church, South; and the Methodist Protestant Church. The Methodist movement began in 18th-century England under the preaching of John Wesley, but the so-called Christmas Conference of 1784 in Baltimore is regarded as the date on which the organized Methodist Church was founded as an ecclesiastical organization. The Evangelical United Brethren Church was formed in 1946 with the merger of the Evangelical Church and the Church of the United Brethren in Christ, both of which had their beginnings in Pennsylvania in the evangelistic movement of the 18th and early 19th centuries. Members (1974): 10,-063,046.

Presbyterian

Cumberland Presbyterian Church.—An outgrowth of the Great Revival of 1800, the Cumberland Presbytery was organized in 1810 in Tennessee. A union with the Presbyterian Church, U.S.A., in 1906, was only partially successful, and the Cumberland Presbyterian Church continued as a separate denomination. Members (1974): 93,948.

Presbyterian Church in the United States.—This body is a branch of the Presbyterian Church established in separate existence in 1861. Members (1974) : 896,203.

The United Presbyterian Church in the United States of America.—This group was formed in 1958 by a merger of the Presbyterian Church in the U.S.A. (dating from

1706) and the United Presbyterian Church of North America (established in 1858). Members (1974): 2,723,565.

Other Religious Bodies

Apostolic Overcoming Holy Church of God.—A black body incorporated in Alabama in 1919. It is evangelistic in purpose and emphasizes sanctification, holiness, and divine healing. Members (1956): 75,-000.

Assemblies of God.—A pentecostal, evangelical, missionary denomination which grew out of the spiritual revivals of the early 1900's. The organization is composed of self-governing churches. Founded in Arkansas in 1914. Members (1975): 1,239,-197.

Bahá'í Faith.—Bahá'ís are followers of Bahá'u'lláh (1817–1892), whose religion upholds the basic principle of progressive revelation, religious unity and a new world order. There is a spiritual and administrative world center in Haifa, Israel.

Buddhist Churches of America.—Organized in 1914 as the Buddhist Mission of North America, this body was incorporated in 1942 under the present name and represents the Jodo Shinshu Sect of Buddhism in this country. Members (1974): 60,000.

The Christian and Missionary Alliance.—An evangelical, evangelistic, and missionary movement organized in 1887. It stresses "the deeper Christian life and consecration to the Lord's service." Members (1974): 144,245.

The Christian Congregation, Inc.—Incorporated in 1887, denomination provides ministerial affiliation for independent clergymen. Members (1974): 59,600.

Christian Church (Disciples of Christ).—In the revival period of the early nineteenth century, a movement resulted in the establishment of a fellowship called "Christians" or "Disciples." This movement calls for the reunion of the church on the basis of a return to New Testament faith and order. It is congregational in government. Members (1974): 1,312,326.

Christian Churches and Churches of Christ.—This fellowship, congregational in polity, has its origin in the movement to "restore the New Testament church in doctrine, ordinances and life." Members (1974): 1,034,047.

Christian Reformed Church.—A group of Dutch Calvinists which dissented from the Reformed Church in America in 1857 and which was strengthened by later accessions from the same source and by immigration. Members (1974): 206,000.

Church of Christ, Scientist.—Founded by Mary Baker Eddy in 1879 to reinstate the healing power of original Christianity. As defined by Mrs. Eddy, her religion is the scientific system of divine healing.*

The Church of God.—Inaugurated by Bishop A. J. Tomlinson, who served as General Overseer 1903–43. Episcopal in administration. Members (1973): 75,890.

Church of God (Anderson, Ind.).—This group is one of the largest of the groups which have taken the name "Church of God." It originated about 1880 and emphasizes Christian unity. Members (1974): 161,401.

Church of God (Cleveland, Tenn.).—This church is one of the large groups which use the name "Church of God." Organized in 1886 in Tennessee as the Christian Union, it was reorganized in 1902 as the Holiness Church, and in 1907 under its present name. Members (1974): 328,892.

The Church of God in Christ.—Organized in Arkansas in 1895, by C. P. Jones and C. H. Mason, who believed there was no salvation without holiness; incorporated 1897. Members (1965): 425,000.

The Church of God in Christ, International.—Organized in 1969 in Kansas City, Mo., by 14 bishops of the Church of God in Christ of Memphis, Tenn., after disagreement over polity and governmental authority. Church is Wesleyan in theology. Members (1971): 501,000.

The Church of God of Prophecy—Organized in 1903 at Murphy, N. C. Doctrine stresses justification by faith and the second coming of Christ. Members (1974): 62,743.

Church of the Brethren.—German pietists from Krefeld, Germany, under the leadership of Peter Becker, entered the colonies in 1719, and settled at Germantown, Philadelphia, Pa. They hold to the principles of nonviolence, temperance, and the expression of religion through the good life. Members (1974): 179,387.

Church of the Nazarene.—One of the larger holiness bodies, organized in Pilot Point, Tex., in 1908. It is in general accord with the early doctrines of Methodism and emphasizes entire sanctification. Members (1974): 430,128.

Churches of Christ.—This body is made up of a large group of churches, formerly reported with the Disciples of Christ but, since the religious census of 1906, reported separately. They are strictly congregational and have no organization larger than the local congregation. Members (1968): 2,400,000.

---

* Membership figure not available. The manual of the church forbids "the numbering of people and the reporting of such statistics for publication."

Congregational Christian Churches.— See United Church of Christ.

Congregational Christian Churches, National Association of.—Organized in Detroit, Mich., in 1955 to continue the Congregational way of faith and order in church life. It has no doctrinal requirements, and participation by member churches is voluntary. Members (1975): 90,000.

Disciples of Christ.—See Christian Church.

Episcopal Church.—See Protestant Episcopal Church.

Evangelical and Reformed Church.—See United Church of Christ.

The Evangelical Covenant Church of America.—This church has its roots in historical Christianity as it emerged in the Protestant Reformation in the biblical instruction of the Lutheran State Church of Sweden. Organized in 1885 in Chicago. Prior to 1957, it was known as the Evangelical Mission Covenant Church of America. Members (1974): 69,960.

Evangelical Free Church of America.— Organized in the 1880's in Boone, Iowa, as the Swedish Evangelical Free Mission. Later the name was changed to the Evangelical Free Church of America. In 1950, the Evangelical Free Church Association merged with this group. Members (1971): 70,490.

The Evangelical United Brethren Church. —See United Methodist Church under Methodist Churches.

Friends United Meeting.—The Five Years Meeting of Friends was formed in 1902 by 11 Yearly Meetings entering into a loose confederation. Since then, two of the original Yearly Meetings have withdrawn (Kansas and Oregon) and two American and three Yearly Meetings outside the U. S. have joined. In 1965, the name was changed to Friends United Meeting. Members (1975): 67,431.

Independent Fundamental Churches of America.—Organized in 1930 by representatives of various independent churches. Members (1975): 87,582.

International Church of the Foursquare Gospel.—An evangelistic missionary body organized by Aimee Semple McPherson in 1927. The parent church is Angelus Temple, which is located in Los Angeles. Members (1963): 89,215.

Jehovah's Witnesses.—A group calling themselves primitive Christians. They believe that the Kingdom under Christ will replace all earthly governments. Members (1974): 539,262.

Jewish Congregations.—Jews arrived in the colonies before 1650. The first congregation is recorded in 1654, in New York City, the Shearith Israel (Remnant of Israel). Members (1972): 6,115,000.

Latter-day Saints, Church of Jesus Christ of.—Organized in 1830. A group in which the Bible, the Book of Mormon, the Doctrine and Covenants, and the Pearl of Great Price are regarded as the word of God. Their belief is summed up in 13 Articles of Faith written by Joseph Smith. Members (1974): 2,683,573.

Latter-day Saints, Reorganized Church of Jesus Christ of.—A division among the Latter-day Saints (non-Mormon) occurred on the death of Joseph Smith in 1844. His son, Joseph Smith, became presiding officer of this group, which has headquarters at Independence, Mo. Members (1974): 156,-687.

Mennonite Church.—The largest group of the Mennonites who began arriving in the U. S. in 1683, settling in Germantown, Pa. They derive their name from Menno Simons, born 1496. Members (1974): 92,390.

Moravian Church in America (Unitas Fratrum).—In 1735, Moravian missionaries of the pre-Reformation faith of John Hus came to Georgia, in 1740 to Pennsylvania, and in 1753 to North Carolina. Members (Northern Province, 1974): 33,343; (Southern Province, 1974): 21,549.

Pentecostal Church of God of America, Inc.—Organized in 1919 at Chicago, Ill. The first convention was held in October, 1933. Members (1975): 135,000.

Pentecostal Holiness Church, Inc.—This body grew out of the holiness movement in the South and Middle West from 1895 to 1900. Members (1972): 74,108.

The Protestant Episcopal Church.—This group entered the colonies with the earliest settlers as the Church of England. It became autonomous, adopted its present name in 1789. It is an integral part of the Anglican Communion. In 1967, the General Convention adopted "The Episcopal Church" as an alternate name. Members (1974): 2,907,293.

Reformed Church in America.—This group was established by the earliest Dutch settlers of New York as the Reformed Protestant Dutch Church in 1628. Members (1974): 354,004.

The Salvation Army.—An evangelistic organization, with a military government, first set up by General William Booth in England in 1865 and introduced into the U.S. in 1880. Members (1974): 366,471.

Seventh-day Adventists.—This body developed out of an interdenominational movement in the early decades of the 19th century, but was not formally organized until 1863. Their two cardinal points of faith are belief in the personal, imminent, premillennial return of Christ and observance of the seventh day as the Sabbath. Members (1974): 479,799.

Spiritualists, International General Assembly of.—Organized in Buffalo, N. Y., in 1936. Members (1956): 164,072.

Triumph the Church and Kingdom of God in Christ (International).—Organized by Elder E. D. Smith in Georgia in 1902. This group emphasizes the sanctification and the Second Coming of Christ. Members (1972): 54,307.

Unitarian Universalist Association.—This association is the result of a merger in 1961 of the American Unitarian Association, formed in 1825, and the Universalist Church of America, organized in the 1770's. Members (1974): 192,510.

United Church of Christ.—A merger in 1961 of the Evangelical and Reformed Church and the Congregational Christian Churches. Members (1974): 1,841,312.

United Pentecostal Church International.—Pentecostal Church, Inc., and Pentecostal Assemblies of Jesus Christ merged in 1945 at St. Louis. Members (1973): 270,000.

The Wesleyan Church.—Originated through the uniting of the Pilgrim Holiness Church (1897) and the Wesleyan Methodist Church of America (1843) in 1968. Members (1974): 94,215.

Other Religious Groups
(Under 50,000 members)
Source: Yearbook of American Churches, 1976.

Advent Christian Church (1973: 31,057).
African Orthodox Church (1957: 6,000).
Albanian Orthodox Archdiocese in America (1974: 40,000).
Albanian Orthodox Diocese of America (1975: 5,240).
Amana Church Society (1970: 735).
American Catholic Church, Archdiocese of New York (1975: 700).
American Catholic Church (Syro-Antiochean) (1975: 495).
American Rescue Workers (1974: 2,700).
Anglican Orthodox Church (1972: 2,630).
Apostolic Christian Church (Nazarene) (1974: 4,000).
Apostolic Christian Churches of America (1973: 9,500).
Apostolic Faith (1974: 4,100).
Apostolic Lutheran Church of America (1974: 9,384).
Associate Reformed Presbyterian Church (General Synod) (1974: 31,154).
Beachy Amish Mennonite Church (1974: 4,297).
Berean Fundamental Church (1972: 2,530).
Bethel Ministerial Association (1971: 4,000).
Bible Protestant Church (1968: 2,254).
Bible Way Church of Our Lord Jesus Christ World Wide, Inc. (1970: 30,000).
Brethren Church (Ashland, Ohio) (1974: 16,279).
Brethren Churches, National Fellowship of (1972: 33,514).
Brethren in Christ Church (1974: 10,255).
Christ Catholic Church (Diocese of Boston) (1975: 983).
Christadelphians (1964: 15,800).
Christian Catholic Church (1975: 2,000).
Christian Church of North America, General Council (1974: 8,500).
Christian Nation Church U.S.A. (1971: 2,000).
Christian Union (1973: 5,301).
Christian Unity Baptist Association (1970: 345).
Christ's Sanctified Holy Church (1957: 600).
Church of Christ (1972: 2,400).
Church of Christ (Holiness) U.S.A. (1965: 9,289).
Church of Daniel's Band (1951: 200).
Church of God General Conference (Oregon, Ill.) (1974: 7,455).
Church of God (Seventh Day) (1960: 2,000).
Church of God (Seventh Day), Denver, Colo. (1974: 5,600).
Church of God and Saints of Christ (1959: 38,127).
Church of God by Faith (1973: 4,500).
Church of God in Christ (Mennonite) (1971: 6,204).
Church of God of the Mountain Assembly (1973: 3,500).
Church of Illumination (1963: 9,000).
Church of Jesus Christ (Bickertonites) (1974: 2,463).
Church of Our Lord Jesus Christ of the Apostolic Faith, Inc. (1954: 45,000).
Church of Revelation, Inc. (1975: 750).
Church of the Living God (1964: 45,320).
Church of the Lutheran Brethren of America (1973: 9,000).
Church of the Lutheran Confession (1974: 9,667).

Churches of Christ in Christian Union (1974: 9,786).
Churches of God, General Conference (1974: 37,040).
Congregational Holiness Church (1966: 4,859).
Conservative Congregational Christian Conference (1974: 21,975).
Duck River (and Kindred) Association of Baptists (1972: 8,909).
Eastern Orthodox Catholic Church in America (1974: 315).
Elim Fellowship (1973: 5,000).
Ethical Culture Movement (1974: 5,000).
Evangelical Church of North America (1974: 10,714).
Evangelical Congregational Church (1975: 29,636).
Evangelical Friends Alliance (1974: 27,206).
Evangelical Lutheran Church in America (Eielsen Synod) (1957: 2,500).
Evangelical Lutheran Synod (1974: 17,804).
Evangelical Mennonite Brethren Conference (1972: 3,784).
Evangelical Mennonite Church, Inc. (1974: 3,123).
Evangelical Methodist Church (1974: 10,502).
Fire Baptized Holiness Church (Wesleyan) (1958: 988).
Free Christian Zion Church of Christ (1956: 22,260).
Friends General Conference (1974: 26,184).
Fundamental Methodist Church, Inc. (1974: 692).
General Church of the New Jerusalem (1971: 2,143).
General Council of the Evangelical Baptist Churches, Inc. (1952: 2,200).
General Conference of Mennonite Brethren Churches (1974: 15,528).
General Convention the Swedenborgian Church (1974: 2,329).
General Six Principal Baptists (1970: 308).
Gospel Mission Corps, The (1972: 175).
Grace Gospel Fellowship (1974: 3,000).
Holiness Church of God, Inc. (1968: 927).
Holy Orthodox Church in America (Eastern Catholic and Apostolic) (1965: 260).
Holy Ukrainian Autocephalic Orthodox Church in Exile (1965: 4,800).
House of God, Which Is the Church of the Living God, the Pillar and Ground of the Truth, Inc. (1956: 2,350).
Hungarian Reformed Church in America (1974: 11,679).
Hutterian Brethren (1968: 3,405).
Independent Assemblies of God, International (membership not available).
International Pentecostal Assemblies (1971: 10,000).
Liberal Catholic Church (California) (1956: 4,000).
Liberal Catholic Church—Province of the United States of America (1973: 2,393).
Mennonite Church, The General Conference (1974: 35,534).
Metropolitan Church Association, Inc. (1958: 443).
Missionary Church, The (1972: 20,078).
National Spiritual Alliance of the U.S.A., The (1971: 3,230).
National Spiritualist Association of Churches (1974: 5,000).
Netherlands Reformed Congregations (1973: 7,447).

New Apostolic Church of North America (1974: 22,563).
North American Baptist General Conference (1974: 41,437).
North American Old Roman Catholic Church (1973: 972).
Old German Baptist Brethren (1965: 4,225).
Old Order Amish Church (1972: 14,720).
Old Order (Wisler) Mennonite (1972: 8,000).
Open Bible Standard Churches, Inc. (1974: 25,000).
(Original) Church of God, Inc., The (1971: 20,000).
Orthodox Presbyterian Church, The (1972: 14,871).
Pentecostal Assemblies of the World, Inc. (1960: 4,500).
Pentecostal Church of Christ (1974: 1,435).
Pentecostal Fire-Baptized Holiness Church (1967: 545).
Pentecostal Free-Will Baptist Church (1974: 10,000).
Pillar of Fire (1949: 5,100).
Plymouth Brethren (1973: 40,000).
Presbyterian Church in America (1973: 41,232).
Primitive Advent Christian Church (1974: 530).
Primitive Methodist Church, U.S.A. (1975: 11,024).
Protestant Conference (Lutheran), The (1974: 2,675).
Reformed Church in the United States (1974: 3,940).
Reformed Episcopal Church (1972: 6,532).
Reformed Mennonite Church (1970: 500).
Reformed Methodist Union Episcopal Church (1974: 2,192).
Reformed Presbyterian Church, Evangelical Synod (1974: 22,452).

Reformed Presbyterian Church of North America (1974: 5,445).
Reformed Zion Union Apostolic Church (1965: 16,000).
Religious Society of Friends (Conservative) (1974: 1,840).
Religious Society of Friends (Unaffiliated Meetings) (1974: 2,771).
Romanian Orthodox Episcopate of America, The (1974: 40,000).
Schwenkfelder Church, The (1974: 2,520).
Second Cumberland Presbyterian Church in U.S. (1959: 30,000).
Separate Baptists in Christ (1962: 7,496).
Seventh-Day Baptist General Conference (1974: 5,230).
Social Brethren (1974: 1,722).
Southern Methodist Church (1975: 11,000).
Ukrainian Orthodox Church in America (Ecumenical Patriarchate) (1973: 30,000).
United Brethren in Christ (1974: 26,335).
United Christian Church (1973: 422).
United Holy Church of America (1960: 28,980).
United Seventh Day Brethren (membership not available).
United Wesleyan Methodist Church of America (1972: 400).
United Zion Church (1973: 877).
Unity of the Brethren (1964: 6,142).
Vedanta Society of New York (1974: 1,000).
Volunteers of America (1974: 30,740).

Active Bishops of the Protestant Episcopal Church

Source: Executive Officer, Scott F. Bailey, 520 San Jacinto, Houston, Tex. 77002.

(Note: M—Missionary Bishop; C—Coadjutor; S—Suffragan)

Presiding Bishop: John M. Allin, 815 Second Ave., New York City 10017.

Alabama: Furman C. Stough, Birmingham.
Alaska: David R. Cochran, Fairbanks.
Albany (N. Y.): Wilbur E. Hogg, Jr., Charles B. Persell, Jr. (S).
American Churches in Europe, Convocation of: A. Ervine Swift.
Arizona: Joseph M. Harte, Phoenix. Joseph T. Heistand (C).
Arkansas: Christoph Keller, Jr., Little Rock.
Atlanta (Ga.): Bennet J. Sims.
Bethlehem (Pa.): Lloyd E. Gressle.
California: C. Kilmer Myers, G. Richard Millard (S), San Francisco.
Central Florida: William H. Folwell, Winter Park.
Central Gulf Coast: George M. Murray, Mobile, Ala.
Central New York: Ned Cole, Jr., Syracuse.
Central Pennsylvania: Dean T. Stevenson, Harrisburg.
Chicago: James W. Montgomery, Quintin E. Primo, Jr. (S).
Colombia: William A. Franklin (M), Bogota.
Colorado: William O. Frey, Denver.
Connecticut: Joseph Warren Hutchens, Hartford. Morgan Porteus (C).
Costa Rica: José Antonio Ramos (M), San José.
Dallas (Tex.): A. Donald Davies, Robert E. Terwilliger (S).
Delaware: William H. Clark, Wilmington.
Dominican Republic: Telesforo A. Isaac (M), Santo Domingo.
East Carolina: Hunley A. Elebash, Wilmington, N. C.
Eastern Oregon: William B. Spofford, Redmond.
Easton (Md.): W. Moultrie Moore.
Eau Claire (Wis.): Stanley Atkins.
Ecuador: Adrian D. Caceres, Quito.
Erie (Pa.): Donald J. Davis.

Executive Council: Milton L. Wood (Executive for Administration), Richard B. Martin (Executive for Ministries), Clarence E. Hobgood (Suffragan Bishop to Armed Forces), David E. Richards (National Coordinator for House of Bishops Committee on Pastoral Development).
Florida: Frank S. Cerveny, Jacksonville.
Fond du Lac (Wis.): William H. Brady.
Georgia: George R. Reeves, Savannah.
Guatemala: Anselmo Carral-Solar (M), Guatemala City, Honduras.
Haiti: Luc Anatole Jacques Garnier (M), Port-au-Prince.
Hawaii: Edmond L. Browning, Honolulu.
Idaho: Hanford L. King, Jr., Boise.
Indianapolis: John P. Craine.
Iowa: Walter C. Righter, Des Moines.
Kansas: Edward C. Turner, Topeka.
Kentucky: David B. Reed (D), Louisville.
Lexington (Ky.): Addison Hosea.
Liberia: George D. Browne (M), Monrovia.
Long Island: Jonathan G. Sherman, Robert C. Witcher (C).
Los Angeles: Robert C. Rusack.
Louisiana: James B. Brown, New Orleans.
Maine: Frederick B. Wolf, Portland.
Maryland: David K. Leighton, William J. Cox (S), Baltimore.
Massachusetts: John B. Coburn, Morris F. Arnold (S), Boston.
Mexico, Central and South: Jose G. Saucedo; Mexico City.
Mexico, Northern: Leonardo Romero, Monterrey.
Mexico, Western: Melchor Saucedo, Guadalajara.
Michigan: H. Coleman McGehee, Jr., Detroit.
Milwaukee: Charles T. Gaskell.
Minnesota: Philip F. McNairy, Minneapolis.
Mississippi: Duncan M. Gray, Jr., Jackson.

Missouri: William A. Jones, Jr., St. Louis.
Montana: Jackson E. Gilliam, Helena.
Nebraska: Vacant.
Nevada: Wesley Frensdorff, Reno.
New Hampshire: Phillip A. Smith, Concord.
New Jersey: Albert W. Van Duzer, Stockton, George P. M. Belshaw (S).
New York: Paul Moore, Jr., J. Stuart Wetmore (S), Harold L. Wright (S), New York City.
Newark: (N.J.): George E. Rath, John S. Spong (C).
Nicaragua: G. Edward Haynsworth (M), Managua.
North Carolina: Thomas A. Fraser, Jr.
North Dakota: George T. Masuda, Fargo.
Northern California: Clarence R. Haden, Jr., Sacramento.
Northern Indiana: William C. R. Sheridan, South Bend.
Northern Michigan: William Dimmick, Menominee.
Northwest Texas: Willis R. Henton, Lubbock.
Ohio: John H. Burt, Cleveland.
Oklahoma: Chilton Powell, Frederick W. Putnam, Jr. (S), Oklahoma City.
Olympia (Wash.): Robert H. Cochrane, Seattle.
Oregon: Matthew P. Bigliardi, Lake Oswego; Hal R. Gross (S), Portland.
Panama and the Canal Zone: Lemuel B. Shirley (M), Balboa.
Pennsylvania: Lyman C. Ogilby, Philadelphia.
Philippines, Central: Benito C. Cabanban (M), Manila.
Philippines, Northern: Richard A. Abellon (M), Bontoc.
Philippines, Southern: Constancio B. Manguramas (M), Cotabato City.
Pittsburgh: Robert B. Appleyard.
Puerto Rico: Francisco Reus-Froylán (M), St. Just.
Quincy (Ill.): Donald J. Parsons, Peoria.
Rhode Island: Frederick H. Belden, Providence.
Rio Grande: Richard M. Trelease, Jr., Albuquerque, N. Mex.
Rochester (N. Y.): Robert R. Spears, Jr.

San Diego (Calif.): Robert M. Wolterstoff.
San Joaquin (Calif.): Victor M. Rivera, Fresno.
South Carolina: Gray Temple, Charleston.
South Dakota: Walter H. Jones.
Southeast Florida: James L. Duncan, Miami.
Southwest Florida: E. Paul Haynes, St. Petersburg.
Southern Ohio: John M. Krumm, Cincinnati.
Southern Virginia: David S. Rose, Norfolk, C. Charles Vache (C).
Southwestern Virginia: William H. Marmion, Roanoke.
Spokane (Wash.): John R. Wyatt.
Springfield (Ill.): Albert W. Hillestad.
Taiwan: James Te Ming Pong, Taipei.
Tennessee: John Vander Horst, Nashville; William F. Gates, Jr. (S), Memphis; William E. Sanders (C), Knoxville.
Texas: J. Milton Richardson, Roger H. Cilley (S), Houston.
Upper South Carolina: George M. Alexander, Columbia.
Utah: E. Otis Charles, Salt Lake City.
Vermont: Robert S. Kerr, Burlington.
Virgin Islands: E. Mason Turner (M), St. Thomas.
Virginia: Robert B. Hall, John A. Baden (S), Alexandria.
Washington, D. C.: William F. Creighton, John T. Walker (S).
West Missouri: Arthur A. Vogel, Kansas City.
West Texas: Scott Field Bailey, San Antonio.
West Virginia: Robert P. Atkinson, Charleston.
Western Kansas: William Davidson (D), Salina.
Western Massachusetts: Alexander D. Stewart, Springfield.
Western Michigan: Charles E. Bennison, Kalamazoo.
Western New York: Harold B. Robinson, Buffalo.
Western North Carolina: William C. Weinhauer, Black Mountain.
Wyoming: David R. Thornberry, Laramie.

Bishops of the United Methodist Church

Source: United Methodist Communications, 475 Riverside Drive, New York, N.Y. 10027.

President: Bishop W. Kenneth Goodson, Richmond, Va.; President-designate, Bishop Paul W. Milhouse, Oklahoma City, Okla.; Secretary, Bishop James K. Mathews, 100 Maryland Avenue, N.E., Washington, D.C. 20002.

L. Scott Allen; Charlotte, N. C.
Ralph T. Alton; Indianapolis, Ind.
Edsel A. Ammons; Detroit, Mich.
A. James Armstrong; Aberdeen, S. D.
James M. Ault; Valley Forge, Pa.
Robert M. Blackburn; Raleigh, N. C.
Ole E. Borgen; Stockholm, Sweden
Monk Bryan; Lincoln, Neb.
William R. Cannon; Atlanta, Ga.
Alsie H. Carleton; Albuquerque, N. M.
Edward G. Carroll; Boston, Mass.
Emilio de Carvalho; Luanda, Angola
Wilbur W. Y. Choy; Seattle, Wash.
Wayne K. Clymer; Minneapolis, Minn.
Finis A. Crutchfield; Houston, Tex.
Jesse R. DeWitt; Sun Prairie; Wis.
Ernest T. Dixon; Topeka, Kan.

H. Ellis Finger, Jr.; Knoxville, Tenn.
Charles F. Golden; Los Angeles, Calif.
Robert E. Goodrich, Jr.; St. Louis, Mo.
W. Kenneth Goodson; Richmond, Va.
Paul L. A. Granadosin; Baguio City, Philippines
Armin Haertel; Dresden, Germany
Kenneth W. Hicks; Little Rock, Ark.
Leroy C. Hodapp; Springfield, Ill.
Earl G. Hunt, Jr.; Nashville, Tenn.
Ram Dutt Joshi; Bombay, India
Joseph R. Lance; Lucknow, India
Dwight E. Loder; Columbus, Ohio
J. Chess Lovern; San Antonio, Tex.
James K. Mathews; Washington, D. C.
Joel D. McDavid; Lakeland, Fla.
Paul W. Milhouse; Oklahoma City, Okla.

Eric A. Mitchell; Delhi, India
Abel T. Muzorewa; Salisbury, Rhodesia
Roy C. Nichols; Pittsburgh, Pa.
Fama J. Onema; Kananga, Zaire
M. Elia Peter; Hyderabad, India
Frank L. Robertson; Louisville, Ky.
Carl J. Sanders; Birmingham, Ala.
Franz W. Schaefer; Zurich, Switzerland
J. Kenneth Shamblin; New Orleans, La.
C. Ernst Sommer; Frankfurt, Germany
Mack B. Stokes; Jackson, Miss.
W. McFerrin Stowe; Dallas, Tex.
R. Marvin Stuart; San Francisco, Calif.
James S. Thomas; Canton, Ohio

Jack M. Tuell; Portland, Ore.
Edward L. Tullis; Columbia, S. C.
W. Ralph Ward; Rye, N. Y.
John B. Warman; Harrisburg, Pa.
Bennie D. Warner; Monrovia, Liberia
Paul A. Washburn; Chicago, Ill.
Lance Webb; Springfield, Ill.
D. Frederick Wertz; Charleston, W. Va.
Melvin E. Wheatley, Jr.; Denver, Colo.
C. Dale White; Princeton, N. J.
Joseph H. Yeakel; Syracuse, N. Y.
Escrivao A. Zunguze; Lourenco Marques, Mozambique

Roman Catholic Pontiffs

Source: National Catholic Almanac, from Annuario Pontificio.

St. Peter, of Bethsaida in Galilee, Prince of the Apostles, was the first Pope. He resided first in Antioch and then for twenty-five years in Rome, where he suffered martyrdom in 64 or 67 of the modern era. He was followed by St. Linus.

Name	Birthplace	Acces.	End of reign	Name	Birthplace	Acces.	End of reign
St. Linus	Tuscia	67	76	St. Sixtus III	Rome	432	440
St. Anacletus (Cletus)	Rome	76	88	St. Leo I (the Great)	Tuscany	440	461
St. Clement	Rome	88	97	St. Hilary	Sardinia	461	468
St. Evaristus	Greece	97	105	St. Simplicius	Tivoli	468	483
St. Alexander I	Rome	105	115	St. Felix III (II)[2]	Rome	483	492
St. Sixtus I	Rome	115	125	St. Gelasius I	Africa	492	496
St. Telesphorus	Greece	125	136	Anastasius II	Rome	496	498
St. Hyginus	Greece	136	140	St. Symmachus	Sardinia	498	514
St. Pius I	Aquileia	140	155	St. Hormisdas	Frosinone	514	523
St. Anicetus	Syria	155	166	St. John I	Tuscany	523	526
St. Soter	Campania	166	175	St. Felix IV (III)	Samnium	526	530
St. Eleutherius	Epirus	175	189	Boniface II	Rome	530	532
St. Victor I	Africa	189	199	John II	Rome	533	535
St. Zephyrinus	Rome	199	217	St. Agapitus I	Rome	535	536
St. Callistus I	Rome	217	222	St. Silverius	Campania	536	537
St. Urban I	Rome	222	230	Vigilius	Rome	537	555
St. Pontian	Rome	230	235	Pelagius I	Rome	556	561
St. Anterus	Greece	235	236	John III	Rome	561	574
St. Fabian	Rome	236	250	Benedict I	Rome	575	579
St. Cornelius	Rome	251	253	Pelagius II	Rome	579	590
St. Lucius I	Rome	253	254	St. Gregory I (the Great)	Rome	590	604
St. Stephen I	Rome	254	257	Sabinianus	Tuscany	604	606
St. Sixtus II	Greece	257	258	Boniface III	Rome	607	607
St. Dionysius	Unknown	259	268	St. Boniface IV	Marsi	608	615
St. Felix I	Rome	269	274	St. Deusdedit (Adeodatus I)	Rome	615	618
St. Eutychian	Luni	275	283	Boniface V	Naples	619	625
St. Caius	Dalmatia	283	296	Honorius I	Campania	625	638
St. Marcellinus	Rome	296	304	Severinus	Rome	640	640
St. Marcellus I	Rome	308	309	John IV	Dalmatia	640	642
St. Eusebius	Greece	309[1]	309[1]	Theodore I	Greece	642	649
St. Meltiades	Africa	311	314	St. Martin I	Todi	649	655
St. Sylvester I	Rome	314	335	St. Eugene I[3]	Rome	654	657
St. Marcus	Rome	336	336	St. Vitalian	Segni	657	672
St. Julius I	Rome	337	352	Adeodatus II	Rome	672	676
Liberius	Rome	352	366	Donus	Rome	676	678
St. Damasus I	Spain	366	384	St. Agatho	Sicily	678	681
St. Siricius	Rome	384	399	St. Leo II	Sicily	682	683
St. Anastasius I	Rome	399	401	St. Benedict II	Rome	684	685
St. Innocent I	Albano	401	417	John V	Syria	685	686
St. Zozimus	Greece	417	418	Conon	Unknown	686	687
St. Boniface I	Rome	418	422				
St. Celestine I	Campania	422	432				

Name	Birthplace	Acces.	End of reign	Name	Birthplace	Acces.	End of reign
St. Sergius I	Syria	687	701	Benedict IX (3rd time)	....	1047	1048
John VI	Greece	701	705	Damasus II	Bavaria	1048	1048
John VII	Greece	705	707	St. Leo IX	Alsace	1049	1054
Sisinnius	Syria	708	708	Victor II	Germany	1055	1057
Constantine	Syria	708	715	Stephen IX (X)	Lorraine	1057	1058
St. Gregory II	Rome	715	731	Nicholas II	Burgundy	1059	1061
St. Gregory III	Syria	731	741	Alexander II	Milan	1061	1073
St. Zachary	Greece	741	752	St. Gregory VII	Tuscany	1073	1085
Stephen II (III)[4]	Rome	752	757	Bl. Victor III	Benevento	1086	1087
St. Paul I	Rome	757	767	Bl. Urban II	France	1088	1099
Stephen III (IV)	Sicily	768	772	Paschal II	Ravenna	1099	1118
Adrian I	Rome	772	795	Gelasius II	Gaeta	1118	1119
St. Leo III	Rome	795	816	Callistus II	Burgundy	1119	1124
Stephen IV (V)	Rome	816	817	Honorius II	Fiagnano	1124	1130
St. Paschal I	Rome	817	824	Innocent II	Rome	1130	1143
Eugene II	Rome	824	827	Celestine II	Città di Castello	1143	1144
Valentine	Rome	827	827				
Gregory IV	Rome	827	844	Lucius II	Bologna	1144	1145
Sergius II	Rome	844	847	Bl. Eugene III	Pisa	1145	1153
St. Leo IV	Rome	847	855	Anastasius IV	Rome	1153	1154
Benedict III	Rome	855	858	Adrian IV	England	1154	1159
St. Nicholas I (the Great)	Rome	858	867	Alexander III	Siena	1159	1181
Adrian II	Rome	867	872	Lucius III	Lucca	1181	1185
John VIII	Rome	872	882	Urban III	Milan	1185	1187
Marinus I	Gallese	882	884	Gregory VIII	Benevento	1187	1187
St. Adrian III	Rome	884	885	Clement III	Rome	1187	1191
Stephen V (VI)	Rome	885	891	Celestine III	Rome	1191	1198
Formosus	Portus	891	896	Innocent III	Anagni	1198	1216
Boniface VI	Rome	896	896	Honorius III	Rome	1216	1227
Stephen VI (VII)	Rome	896	897	Gregory IX	Anagni	1227	1241
Romanus	Gallese	897	897	Celestine IV	Milan	1241	1241
Theodore II	Rome	897	897	Innocent IV	Genoa	1243	1254
John IX	Tivoli	898	900	Alexander IV	Anagni	1254	1261
Benedict IV	Rome	900	903	Urban IV	Troyes	1261	1264
Leo V	Ardea	903	903	Clement IV	France	1265	1268
Sergius III	Rome	904	911	Bl. Gregory X	Piacenza	1271	1276
Anastasius III	Rome	911	913	Bl. Innocent V	Savoy	1276	1276
Landus	Sabina	913	914	Adrian V	Genoa	1276	1276
John X	Tossignano	914	928	John XXI[7]	Portugal	1276	1277
Leo VI	Rome	928	928	Nicholas III	Rome	1277	1280
Stephen VII (VIII)	Rome	928	931	Martin IV[8]	France	1281	1285
John XI	Rome	931	935	Honorius IV	Rome	1285	1287
Leo VII	Rome	936	939	Nicholas IV	Ascoli	1288	1292
Stephen VIII (IX)	Rome	939	942	St. Celestine V	Isernia	1294	1294
Marinus II	Rome	942	946	Boniface VIII	Anagni	1294	1303
Agapitus II	Rome	946	955	Bl. Benedict XI	Treviso	1303	1304
John XII	Tusculum	955	964	Clement V	France	1305	1314
Leo VIII[5]	Rome	963	965	John XXII	Cahors	1316	1334
Benedict V[5]	Rome	964	966	Benedict XII	France	1334	1342
John XIII	Rome	965	972	Clement VI	France	1342	1352
Benedict VI	Rome	973	974	Innocent VI	France	1352	1362
Benedict VII	Rome	974	983	Bl. Urban V	France	1362	1370
John XIV	Pavia	983	984	Gregory XI	France	1370	1378
John XV	Rome	985	996	Urban VI	Naples	1378	1389
Gregory V	Saxony	996	999	Boniface IX	Naples	1389	1404
Sylvester II	Auvergne	999	1003	Innocent VII	Sulmona	1404	1406
John XVII	Rome	1003	1003	Gregory XII	Venice	1406	1415
John XVIII	Rome	1004	1009	Martin V	Rome	1417	1431
Sergius IV	Rome	1009	1012	Eugene IV	Venice	1431	1447
Benedict VIII	Tusculum	1012	1024	Nicholas V	Sarzana	1447	1455
John XIX	Tusculum	1024	1032	Callistus III	Jativa	1455	1458
Benedict IX[6]	Tusculum	1032	1044	Pius II	Siena	1458	1464
Sylvester III	Rome	1045	1045	Paul II	Venice	1464	1471
Benedict IX (2nd time)	....	1045	1045	Sixtus IV	Savona	1471	1484
				Innocent VIII	Genoa	1484	1492
Gregory VI	Rome	1045	1046	Alexander VI	Jativa	1492	1503
Clement II	Saxony	1046	1047	Pius III	Siena	1503	1503

Name	Birthplace	Acces.	End of reign	Name	Birthplace	Acces.	End of reign
Julius II	Savona	1503	1513	Bl. Innocent XI	Como	1676	1689
Leo X	Florence	1513	1521	Alexander VIII	Venice	1689	1691
Adrian VI	Utrecht	1522	1523	Innocent XII	Spinazzola	1691	1700
Clement VII	Florence	1523	1534	Clement XI	Urbino	1700	1721
Paul III	Rome	1534	1549	Innocent XIII	Rome	1721	1724
Julius III	Rome	1550	1555	Benedict XIII	Gravina	1724	1730
Marcellus II	Montepulciano	1555	1555	Clement XII	Florence	1730	1740
Paul IV	Naples	1555	1559	Benedict XIV	Bologna	1740	1758
Pius IV	Milan	1559	1565	Clement XIII	Venice	1758	1769
St. Pius V	Bosco	1566	1572	Clement XIV	Rimini	1769	1774
Gregory XIII	Bologna	1572	1585				
Sixtus V	Grottammare	1585	1590	Pius VI	Cesena	1775	1799
Urban VII	Rome	1590	1590	Pius VII	Cesena	1800	1823
Gregory XIV	Cremona	1590	1591	Leo XII	Genga	1823	1829
Innocent IX	Bologna	1591	1591	Pius VIII	Cingoli	1829	1830
Clement VIII	Florence	1592	1605	Gregory XVI	Belluno	1831	1846
Leo XI	Florence	1605	1605	Pius IX	Senegallia	1846	1878
Paul V	Rome	1605	1621	Leo XIII	Carpineto	1878	1903
Gregory XV	Bologna	1621	1623	St. Pius X	Riese	1903	1914
Urban VIII	Florence	1623	1644	Benedict XV	Genoa	1914	1922
Innocent X	Rome	1644	1655	Pius XI	Desio	1922	1939
Alexander VII	Siena	1655	1667	Pius XII	Rome	1939	1958
Clement IX	Pistoia	1667	1669	John XXIII	Sotto il Monte	1958	1963
Clement X	Rome	1670	1676	Paul VI	Concesio	1963	

[1] Or 310. [2] He should be called Felix II, and his successors of the same name should be numbered accordingly The discrepancy was caused by the erroneous insertion in some lists of the name of St. Felix of Rome, Martyr. [3] He was elected during the exile of St. Martin I, who endorsed him as Pope. [4] After St. Zachary died, a Roman priest named Stephen was elected but died before his consecration as Bishop of Rome. His name is not included in all lists for this reason. In view of this historical confusion, the *National Catholic Almanac* lists the true Stephen II as Stephen II (III), the true Stephen III as Stephen III (IV), etc. [5] Confusion exists concerning the legitimacy of claims. If the deposition of John was invalid, Leo was an antipope until after the end of Benedict's reign. If the deposition of John was valid, Leo was the legitimate Pope and Benedict an antipope. [6] If the triple removal of Benedict IX was not valid, Sylvester III, Gregory VI, and Clement II were antipopes. [7] Elimination was made of the name of John XX in an effort to rectify the numerical designation of Popes named John. The error dates back to the time of John XV. [8] The names of Marinus I and Marinus II were construed as Martin. In view of these two pontificates and the earlier reign of St. Martin I, this pontiff was called Martin IV.

The College of Cardinals
Cardinal Bishops (Cardinals of Suburban Sees)

Year of creation	Name	Office or dignity	Nationality
1958	Carlo Confalonieri	Titular Bishop of Palestrina	Italian
1959	Paolo Marella	Archpriest of the Basilica of St. Peter; Titular Bishop of Porto and Santa Rufina	Italian
1960	Luigi Traglia	Dean of the Sacred College; Titular Bishop of Albano	Italian
1965	Jean Villot	Secretary of State and Prefect of the Council for the Public Affairs of the Church; President of the Administration of the Patrimony of the Holy See; Camerlengo of the Holy Roman Church	French
1967	Antonio Samore	Prefect of the Sacred Congregation for the Discipline of the Sacraments	Italian
1969	Sebastiano Baggio	Prefect of the Sacred Congregation for Bishops; President of the Pontifical Commission for Latin America	Italian

Year of creation	Name	Office or dignity	Nationality

Cardinal Bishops (Eastern Rite Patriarchs)

1965	Stephanos I Sidarouss, C.M.	Patriarch of Alexandria for the Copts	Egyptian

Cardinal Priests

1929	Emanuel Goncalves Cerejeira	Patriarch of Lisbon (resigned)	Portuguese
1946	Carlo Carmelo de Vasconcellos Motta	Archbishop of Aparecida	Brazilian
1946	Norman Thomas Gilroy	Archbishop of Sydney (retired)	Australian
1946	Joseph Frings	Archbishop of Cologne (retired)	German
1946	Antonio Caggiano	Archbishop of Buenos Aires; Military Vicar for Argentina	Argentine
1953	Giuseppe Siri	Archbishop of Genoa (retired)	Italian
1953	James Francis McIntyre	Archbishop of Los Angeles (retired)	American
1953	Giacomo Lercaro	Archbishop of Bologna (resigned)	Italian
1953	Stefan Wyszynski	Archbishop of Gniezno and Warsaw; Primate of Poland (retired)	Polish
1953	Paul Émile Leger, S.S.	Archbishop of Montreal (resigned)	Canadian
1953	Valerian Gracias	Archbishop of Bombay	Indian
1953	Alfredo Ottaviani	Deacon of St. Mary (in Dominica) (retired)	Italian
1958	Antonio Maria Barbieri, O.F.M.	Archbishop of Montevideo	Uruguayan
1958	José María Bueno y Monreal	Archbishop of Seville	Spanish
1958	Franziskus König	Archbishop of Vienna; Military Vicar for Austria; President of the Secretariat for Non-Believers	Austrian
1958	Alberto di Jorio	Deacon of St. Pudentiana (retired)	Italian
1958	Francesco Roberti	Deacon of St. Mary (in Cosmedin); Prefect of the Supreme Tribunal of the Apostolic Signatura (retired)	Italian
1960	Bernard Jan Alfrink	Archbishop of Utrecht; Military Vicar for the Netherlands (retired)	Dutch
1960	Laurean Rugambwa	Archbishop of Dar-es-Salaam	Tanzanian
1961	José Humberto Quintero	Archbishop of Caracas	Venezuelan
1962	José da Costa Nunes	Member of Roman Curia (retired)	Portuguese
1962	Juan Landazuri Ricketts, O.F.M.	Archbishop of Lima	Peruvian
1962	Raul Silva Henriquez, S.D.B.	Archbishop of Santiago	Chilean
1962	Leo Josef Suenens	Archbishop of Malines-Brussels; Military Vicar for Belgium	Belgian
1965	Josyf Slipyj	Major-Archbishop of Lvov	Ukrainian
1965	Thomas B. Cooray, O.M.I.	Archbishop of Colombo	Singhalese
1965	Maurice Roy	Archbishop of Quebec; Military Vicar for Canada; President of the Council for the Laity and the Pontifical Commission of Studies	Canadian
1965	Owen McCann	Archbishop of Cape Town	South African
1965	Léon Etienne Duval	Archbishop of Algiers	French
1965	Ermenegildo Florit	Archbishop of Florence	Italian
1965	Franjo Seper	Prefect of the Sacred Congregation for the Doctrine of the Faith; President of the Pontifical Commission for Biblical Studies	Yugoslavian

Year of creation	Name	Office or dignity	Nationality
1965	Paul Zoungrana	Archbishop of Ougadougou	Upper Voltan
1965	Lawrence J. Shehan	Archbishop of Baltimore (retired)	American
1965	Agnelo Rossi	Prefect of the Sacred Congregation for the Evangelization of Peoples or for the Propagation of the Faith	Brazilian
1965	Giovanni Colombo	Archbishop of Milan	Italian
1965	William Conway	Archbishop of Armagh; Primate of All Ireland	Irish
1967	Gabriel Marie Garonne	Prefect of the Sacred Congregation for Catholic Education	French
1967	Patrick A. O'Boyle	Archbishop of Washington, D. C. (resigned)	American
1967	Egidio Vagnozzi	President of the Prefecture for the Holy See's Economic Affairs	Italian
1967	Maximilian de Fürstenberg	Prefect of the Sacred Congregation for the Oriental Churches (retired)	Dutch
1967	Francesco Carpino	Referendario of the Sacred Congregation for Bishops	Italian
1967	José Clemente Maurer	Archbishop of Sucre	Bolivian
1967	Pietro Parente	Member of the Sacred Congregation for the Discipline of the Sacraments; member of the Sacred Congregation for the Clergy (retired)	Italian
1967	Dino Staffa	Prefect of the Supreme Tribunal of the Apostolic Signatura	Italian
1967	John Joseph Krol	Archbishop of Philadelphia	American
1967	John Patrick Cody	Archbishop of Chicago	American
1967	Corrado Ursi	Archbishop of Naples	Italian
1967	Alfred Bengsch	Archbishop-Bishop of Berlin	German
1967	Justin Darmojuwono	Archbishop of Semarang	Indonesian
1967	Karol Wojtyla	Archbishop of Kraków	Polish
1967	Michele Pellegrino	Archbishop of Turin	Italian
1967	Alexandre C. Renard	Archbishop of Lyons	French
1969	Paul Yu Pin	Archbishop of Nanking (lives in Taiwan)	Chinese
1969	Alfredo Vicente Scherer	Archbishop of Pôrto Alegre	Brazilian
1969	Julio Rosales	Archbishop of Cebu	Filipino
1969	Gordon J. Gray	Archbishop of St. Andrews and Edinburgh	Scottish
1969	Paolo Bertoli	Prefect of the Sacred Congregation for the Causes of Saints (resigned)	Italian
1969	Miguel Dario Miranda y Gómez	Archbishop of Mexico City	Mexican
1969	Joseph Parecattil	Archbishop of Ernakulam, Chaldean Rite; President of the Pontifical Commission for Preparation of the Code of Oriental Canon Law	Indian
1969	John F. Dearden	Archbishop of Detroit	American
1969	François Marty	Archbishop of Paris	French
1969	George Flahiff	Archbishop of Winnipeg	Canadian
1969	Paul Gouyon	Archbishop of Rennes	French
1969	Mario Casariego	Archbishop of Guatemala	Guatemalan
1969	Vicente Enrique y Tarancón	Archbishop of Madrid-Alcala	Spanish
1969	Joseph Malula	Archbishop of Kinshasa	Congolese
1969	Paolo Munoz Vega, S.J.	Archbishop of Quito	Ecuadorian
1969	Antonio Poma	Archbishop of Bologna	Italian
1969	John J. Carberry	Archbishop of St. Louis	American
1969	Terence J. Cooke	Archbishop of New York	American
1969	Stephen Kim Sou Hwan	Archbishop of Seoul	Korean
1969	Eugenio de Araujo Sales	Archbishop of Rio de Janeiro	Brazilian

Year of creation	Name	Office or dignity	Nationality
1969	Joseph Hoeffner	Archbishop of Cologne	German
1969	John J. Wright	Prefect of the Sacred Congregation for the Clergy	American
1973	Albino Luciani	Patriarch of Venice	Italian
1973	Antonio Ribeiro	Patriarch of Lisbon	Portuguese
1973	James Robert Knox	Archbishop of Melbourne; Prefect of the Sacred Congregations for the Sacraments and Divine Worship	Australian
1973	Avelar Brandão Vilela	Archbishop of São Salvador de Bahia	Brazilian
1973	Joseph Cordeiro	Archbishop of Karachi	Pakistani
1973	Anibal Muñoz Duque	Archbishop of Bogotá	Colombian
1973	Luis Aponte Martínez	Archbishop of San Juan	Puerto Rican
1973	Raúl Francisco Primatesta	Archbishop of Córdoba	Argentinian
1973	Salvatore Pappalardo	Archbishop of Palermo	Italian
1973	Marcelo González Martín	Archbishop of Toledo	Spanish
1973	Louis Jean Guyot	Archbishop of Toulouse	French
1973	Ugo Poletti	Vicar General of His Holiness for the City of Rome	Italian
1973	Timothy Manning	Archbishop of Los Angeles	American
1973	Paul Yoshigoro Taguchi	Archbishop of Osaka	Japanese
1973	Maurice Otunga	Archbishop of Nairobi	Kenyan
1973	José Salazar Lopez	Archbishop of Guadalajara	Mexican
1973	Emile Biayenda	Archbishop of Brazzaville	Congolese
1973	Humberto S. Medeiros	Archbishop of Boston	American
1973	Paulo Evaristo Arns, O.F.M.	Archbishop of São Paulo	Brazilian
1973	James Darcy Freeman	Archbishop of Sydney	Australian
1973	Narcisco Jubany Arnau	Archbishop of Barcelona	Spanish
1973	Hermann Volk	Bishop of Mainz	German
1973	Pio Taofiñu'u	Bishop of Apia	W. Samoan
1976	Juan Carlos Aramburu	Archbishop of Buenos Aires	Argentinian
1976	William Wakefield Baum	Archbishop of Washington	American
1976	Octavio António Beras Rojas	Archbishop of Santo Domingo	Dominican
1976	Reginald John Delargey	Archbishop of Wellington	New Zealander
1976	Dominic Ekandem	Bishop of Ikot Ekpene	Nigerian
1976	Basil Hume	Archbishop of Westminster	British
1976	Joseph Marie Trin Nhu Khue	Archbishop of Hanoi	Vietnamese
1976	Laszlo Lekai	Archbishop of Esztergom	Hungarian
1976	Aloisio Lorscheider, O.F.M.	Archbishop of Fortaleza	Brazilian
1976	Emmanuel Nsubuga	Archbishop of Kampala	Ugandan
1976	Lawrence Trevor Picachy, S.J.	Archbishop of Calcutta	Indian
1976	Victor Razafimahatratra, S.J.	Archbishop of Tananarive	Madagascan
1976	Jaime L. Sin	Archbishop of Manila	Filipino
1976	Hyacinthe Thiandoum	Archbishop of Dakar	Senegalese

Cardinal Deacons

1967	Pericle Felici	President of the Pontifical Commission for the Revision of the Code of Canon Law	Italian
		Archbishop of Utrecht; President of the Secretariat for Promoting Christian Unity	Dutch
1969	Silvio Oddi	Apostolic nuncio to Belgium and Luxembourg (retired)	Italian
1969	Giuseppe Paupini	Major Penitentiary of the Sacred Apostolic Penitentiary	Italian
1969	Giacomo Violardo	Secretary of the Sacred Congregation for the Sacraments (retired)	Italian
1969	Mario Nasalli Rocca di Corneliano	Prefect of the Prefecture for the Apostolic Palace (retired)	Italian
1969	Sergio Guerri	Pro-president of the Pontifical Commission for the State of Vatican City	Italian

Year of creation	Name	Office or dignity	Nationality
1973	Sergio Pignedoli	President of the Secretariat for Non-Christians	Italian
1973	Umberto Mozzoni	Apostolic Nuncio to Brazil (retired)	Italian
1973	Paul Philippe	Prefect of the Sacred Congregation for the Oriental Churches	French
1973	Pietro Palazzini	Former Secretary of the Sacred Congregation for the Clergy	Italian
1973	Ferdinando Giuseppe Antonelli	Secretary of the Sacred Congregation for the Causes of the Saints (retired)	Italian
1976	Corrado Bafile	Pro-Prefect of the Congregation for the Causes of Saints	Italian
1976	Boleslaw Filipiak	Dean of the Tribunal of the Sacred Roman Rota	Polish
1976	Eduardo Pironio	Pro-Prefect of the Congregation for the Religious and the Secular Institutes	Argentinian
1976	Opilio Rossi	Apostolic Nuncio to Austria	Italian
1976	Joseph Schröffer	Secretary of the Congregation for Catholic Education	German
1976	Giuseppe Maria Sensi	Apostolic Nuncio to Portugal	Italian

Roman Catholic Hierarchy of the U. S.

Source: United States Catholic Conference, 1312 Massachusetts Ave., NW, Washington, D. C. 20005.

(Note: A—Auxiliary; C—Coadjutor; T—Titular. Archbishops are shown in boldface type, Bishops in lightface.

Archdioceses

Anchorage, Alaska: **Francis T. Hurley.**

Atlanta, Ga.: **Thomas A. Donnellan.**

Baltimore, Md.: **William D. Borders;** T. Austin Murphy (A); J. Francis Stafford (A); P. Francis Murphy (A).

Boston, Mass.: **Humberto Cardinal Medeiros;** Lawrence J. Riley (A); Daniel A. Hart (A); Thomas V. Dailey (A); John M. D'Arcy (A); John J. Mulcahy (A); Joseph J. Ruocco (A).

Chicago, Ill.: **John Cardinal Cody;** Alfred L. Abramowicz (A); Nevin W. Hayes (A).

Cincinnati, Ohio: **Joseph L. Bernardin;** Nicholas T. Elko (A); Daniel E. Pilarczyk (A).

Denver, Colo.: **James V. Casey;** George R. Evans (A); Richard Hanifen (A).

Detroit, Michigan: **John Cardinal Dearden;** Walter J. Schoenherr (A); Thomas J. Gumbleton (A); Joseph L. Imesch (A); Arthur H. Krawczak (A).

Dubuque, Iowa: **James J. Byrne;** Francis J. Dunn (A).

Hartford, Conn.: **John F. Whealon;** John F. Hackett (A); Joseph F. Donnelly (A).

Indianapolis, Ind.: **George J. Biskup.**

Kansas City, Kan.: **Ignatius J. Strecker.**

Los Angeles, Calif.: **Timothy Cardinal** Manning; John J. Ward (A); Juan A. Arzube (A).

Louisville, Ky.: **Thomas J. McDonough;** Charles G. Maloney (A).

Melchite: **Joseph Tawil.**

Miami, Fla.: **Coleman F. Carroll;** Edward A. McCarthy (C).

Milwaukee, Wis.: **William E. Cousins;** Leo J. Brust (A).

Munhall, Pa. (Byzantine Rite); **Stephen J. Kocisko;** John Bilock (A).

Newark, N. J.: **Peter L. Gerety;** John J. Dougherty (A); Joseph A. Costello (A); Jerome Pechillo (A); Joseph A. Francis (A); Robert F. Garner (A); Dominic A. Marconi (A).

New Orleans, La.: **Philip M. Hannan;** Harold R. Perry (A); Stanley J. Ott (A).

New York, N. Y.: **Terence Cardinal Cooke;** John J. Maguire (C); Joseph M. Pernicone (A); Edward E. Swanstrom (A); Patrick V. Ahern (A); James P. Mahoney (A); Anthony F. Mestice (A).

Oklahoma City, Okla.: **John R. Quinn.**

Omaha, Neb.: **Daniel E. Sheehan.**

Philadelphia, Pa.: **John Cardinal Krol;** Gerald V. McDevitt (A); John J. Graham (A); Martin N. Lohmuller (A); Edward T. Hughes (A).

Philadelphia, Pa. (Ukrainian Rite): Ambrose Senyshyn, O.S.B.M.; Basil H. Losten (A).

Portland, Ore.: **Cornelius M. Power.**

St. Louis, Mo.: **John Cardinal Carberry;** George J. Gottwald (A); Charles R. Koester (A); Edward T. O'Meara (A); John Wurm (A).

St. Paul-Minneapolis, Minn.: **John R. Roach.**

San Antonio, Tex.: **Francis J. Furey;** Patrick F. Flores (A); Hugo M. Gerbermann (A).

San Francisco, Calif.: **Joseph T. McGucken;** William J. McDonald (A).

Santa Fe, N. M.: **Robert F. Sanchez.**

Seattle, Wash.: **Raymond G. Hunthausen.**

Washington. D. C.: **William Cardinal Baum;** Thomas W. Lyons (A); Eugene A. Marino (A).

Dioceses

Agana, Guam; Felixberto C. Flores.
Albany, N. Y.: Vacant.
Alexandria, La.: Lawrence P. Graves.
Allentown, Pa.: Joseph McShea
Altoona-Johnstown, Pa.: James J. Hogan.
Amarillo, Tex.: Lawrence M. DeFalco.
Arlington, Va.: Thomas J. Welsh.
Austin, Tex.: Vincent M. Harris.

Baker, Ore.: Thomas J. Connolly.
Baton Rouge, La.: Joseph V. Sullivan.
Beaumont, Tex.: Warren L. Boudreaux.
Belleville, Ill.: William M. Cosgrove.
Belmont Abbey, N. C.: Jude G. Cleary.
Birmingham, Ala.: Joseph G. Vath.
Bismarck, N. D.: Hilary B. Hacker.
Boise, Idaho: Sylvester W. Treinen.
Bridgeport, Conn.: Walter W. Curtis.
Brooklyn, N. Y.: Francis J. Mugavero; John J. Boardman (A); Joseph P. Denning (A); Charles R. Mulrooney (A); John J. Snyder (A).
Brownsville, Tex.: John J. Fitzpatrick.
Buffalo, N. Y.: Edward D. Head; Bernard J. McLaughlin (A); Pius A. Benincasa (A).
Burlington, Vt.: John A. Marshall.
Camden, N. J.: George H. Guilfoyle; James L. Schad (A).
Caroline–Marshall Islands: Martin J. Neylon.
Charleston, S. C.: Ernest L. Unterkoefler.
Charlotte, N. C.: Michael J. Begley.
Cheyenne, Wyo.: Hubert M. Newell; Joseph H. Hart (A).
Chicago, Ill. (Ukrainian Rite): Jaroslav Gabro.
Cleveland, Ohio: James A. Hickey; Michael J. Murphy (A); Gilbert I. Sheldon (A).
Columbus, Ohio: Edward J. Herrmann; Edward G. Hettinger (A); George A. Fulcher (A).
Corpus Christi, Tex.: Thomas J. Drury.
Covington, Ky.: Richard H. Ackerman.
Crookston, Minn.: Victor H. Balke.

Dallas, Tex.: Thomas Tschoepe.
Davenport, Iowa: Gerald F. O'Keefe.
Des Moines, Iowa: Maurice J. Dingman.
Detroit, Mich. (Maronite): Francis M. Zayek.
Dodge City, Kan.: Marion F. Forst.
Duluth, Minn.: Paul F. Anderson.
El Paso, Tex.: Sidney M. Metzger.
Erie, Pa.: Alfred M. Watson.
Evansville, Ind.: Francis R. Shea.
Fairbanks, Alaska: Robert Whelan.
Fall River, Mass.: Daniel Cronin; James J. Gerrard (A).
Fargo, N. D.: Justin A. Driscoll.
Fort Wayne-South Bend, Ind.: William E. McManus; Joseph R. Crowley (A).
Fort Worth, Tex.: John J. Cassata.
Fresno, Calif.: Hugh A. Donohoe; Roger M. Mahony (A).
Gallup, N. M.: Jerome J. Hastrich.
Galveston-Houston, Tex.: John L. Morkovsky.
Gary, Ind.: Andrew Gregory Grutka.
Gaylord, Mich.; Edmund C. Szoka.
Grand Island, Neb.: John J. Sullivan.
Grand Rapids, Mich.: Joseph M. Breitenbeck; Joseph C. McKinney (A).
Great Falls, Mont.: Eldon Bernard Schuster.
Green Bay, Wis.: Aloysius J. Wycislo; John B. Grellinger (A); Mark F. Schmitt (A).
Greensburg, Pa.: William G. Connare; Norbert F. Gaughan (A).
Harrisburg, Pa.: Joseph T. Daley.
Helena, Mont.: Elden F. Curtiss.
Honolulu, Hawaii: John J. Scanlan.
Jefferson City, Mo.: Michael F. McAuliffe.
Joliet, Ill.: Romeo R. Blanchette; Raymond J. Vonesh (A).
Juneau, Alaska: Vacant.
Kalamazoo, Mich.: Paul V. Donovan.
Kansas City-St. Joseph, Mo.: Charles H. Helmsing; George K. Fitzsimmons (A).
La Crosse, Wis.: Frederick W. Freking.
Lafayette, Ind.: Raymond J. Gallagher.
Lafayette, La.: Gerard L. Frey.
Lansing, Mich.: Kenneth J. Povish; James S. Sullivan (A).
Lincoln, Neb.: Glennon P. Flavin.
Little Rock, Ark.: Andrew J. McDonald.
Madison, Wis.: Cletus F. O'Donnell.
Manchester, N. H.: Odore J. Gendron.
Marquette, Mich.: Charles A. Salatka.
Memphis, Tenn.: Carroll T. Dozier.
Mobile, Ala.: John L. May.
Monterey, Calif.: Harry Anselm Clinch.
Nashville, Tenn.: James D. Niedergeses.
Natchez-Jackson, Miss.: Joseph B. Brunini; Joseph L. Howze (A).
New Ulm, Minn.: Raymond A. Lucker.
Norwich, Conn.: Daniel P. Reilly.
Oakland, Calif.: Floyd L. Begin.
Ogdensburg, N. Y.: Stanislaus J. Brzana.
Orange, Calif.: William R. Johnson.
Orlando, Fla.: Thomas J. Grady.
Owensboro, Ky.: Henry J. Soenneker.

Parma, Ohio (Byzantine Rite): Emil J. Mihalik.

Passaic, N. J. (Byzantine Rite): Michael J. Dudick; Thomas Dolinay (A).

Paterson, N. J.: Lawrence B. Casey.

Pensacola-Tallahassee, Fla.: Rene H. Gracida.

Peoria, Ill.: Edward W. O'Rourke.

Phoenix, Ariz.: Vacant.

Pittsburgh, Pa.: Vincent M. Leonard; John B. McDowell (A); Anthony G. Bosco (A).

Portland, Me.: Edward C. O'Leary; Amedee W. Proulx (A).

Providence, R. I.: Louis E. Gelineau; Kenneth Angell (A).

Pueblo, Colo.: Charles A. Buswell.

Raleigh, N. C.: F. Joseph Gossman; George E. Lynch (A).

Rapid City, S. D.: Harold J. Dimmerling.

Reno, Nev.: Norman F. McFarland.

Richmond, Va.: Walter F. Sullivan.

Rochester, N. Y.: Joseph L. Hogan; Dennis W. Hickey (A); John E. McCafferty (A).

Rockford, Ill.: Arthur J. O'Neill.

Rockville Center, N. Y.: John R. McGann; Vincent J. Baldwin (A).

Sacramento, Calif.: Alden J. Bell; John S. Cummings (A).

Saginaw, Mich.: Francis F. Reh.

St. Augustine, Fla.: Paul F. Tanner.

St. Cloud, Minn.: George H. Speltz; James S. Rausch (A).

St. Petersburg, Fla.: Charles B. McLaughlin.

Salina, Kan.: Cyril J. Vogel.

Salt Lake City, Utah: J. Lennox Federal.

San Angelo, Tex.: Stephen A. Leven.

San Diego, Calif.: Leo T. Maher; Gilbert E. Chavez (A).

Santa Rosa, Calif.: Mark J. Hurley.

Savannah, Ga.: Raymond W. Lessard.

Scranton, Pa.: J. Carroll McCormick; James C. Timlin (A).

Sioux City, Iowa: Frank H. Greteman.

Sioux Falls, S. D.: Lambert A. Hoch.

Spokane, Wash.: Bernard J. Topel.

Springfield, Ill.: Joseph A. McNicholas.

Springfield, Mass.: Christopher J. Weldon; Joseph F. Maguire (C).

Springfield-Cape Girardeau, Mo.: Bernard F. Law.

Stamford, Conn. (Ukrainian Rite): Joseph M. Schmondiuk.

Steubenville, Ohio: John Mussio.

Stockton, Calif.: Merlin J. Guilfoyle.

Superior, Wis.: George A. Hammes.

Syracuse, N. Y.: David F. Cunningham; Francis J. Harrison (A).

Toledo, Ohio: John A. Donovan; Albert H. Ottenweller (A).

Trenton, N. J.: George W. Ahr; John C. Reiss (A).

Tucson, Ariz.: Francis J. Green.

Tulsa, Okla.: Bernard J. Ganter.

Virgin Islands: Edward J. Harper.

Wheeling-Charleston, W. Va.: Joseph H. Hodges; James E. Michaels (A).

Wichita, Kan.: David M. Maloney.

Wilmington, Del.: Thomas J. Mardaga.

Winona, Minn.: Loras J. Watters.

Worcester, Mass.: Bernard J. Flanagan; Timothy J. Harrington (A).

Yakima, Wash.: Vacant.

Youngstown, Ohio: James W. Malone; William Hughes (A).

Military Ordinariate: Terence Cardinal Cooke, Military Vicar; Joseph T. Ryan (C); William J. Moran (A); James J. Killeen (A).

Archbishops of Canterbury

Name	Created
Augustine (consecrated Bishop 597)	601
Laurentius	604
Mellitus	619
Justus	624
Honorius	627
Deusdedit	655
Theodorus	668
Beorhtweald	692
Tatwine	731
Nothelm	735
Cuthbeorht	740
Breguwine	761
Jaenbeorht	765
Æthelheard	793
Wulfred	805
Feologild	832
Ceolnoth	833
Æthelred	870
Plegmund	890
Æthelhelm	914
Wulfhelm	923
Oda	942
Ælfsige	959

Name	Created
Beorhthelm	959
Dunstan	959
Æthelgar	988
Sigeric Serio	990
Ælfric	995
Ælfheah	1005
Lyfing	1013
Æthelnoth	1020
Eadsige	1038
Robert (Champart) of Jumièges	1051
Stigand	1052
Lanfranc	1070
Anselm	1093
Ralph d'Escures	1114
William de Corbeil	1123
Theobald	1138
Thomas à Becket	1162
Richard (of Dover)	1174
Baldwin	1185
Hubert Walter	1193
Stephen Langton	1207
Richard le Grant (of Wetharshed)	1229
Edmund Rich	1234

Name	Created	Name	Created
Robert Kilwardby	1273	George Abbot	1611
John Pecham (Peckham)	1279	William Laud	1633
Robert Winchelsea	1294	William Juxon	1660
Walter Reynolds	1313	Gilbert Sheldon	1663
Simon Mepeham	1328	William Sancroft	1678
John de Stratford	1333	John Tillotson	1691
Thomas Bradwardine	1349	Thomas Tenison	1695
Simon Islip	1349	William Wake	1716
Simon Langham	1366	John Potter	1737
William Whittlesey	1368	Thomas Herring	1747
Simon of Sudbury	1375	Matthew Hutton	1757
William Courtenay	1381	Thomas Secker	1758
Thomas Arundel	1396	Frederick Cornwallis	1768
Roger Walden	1398	John Moore	1783
Thomas Arundel (restored)	1399	Charles Manners-Sutton	1805
Henry Chicheley	1414	William Howley	1828
John Stafford	1443	John Bird Sumner	1848
John Kemp	1452	Charles Thomas Longley	1862
Thomas Bourchier	1454	Archibald Campbell Tait	1868
John Morton	1486	Edward White Benson	1883
Henry Dean	1501	Frederick Temple	1896
William Warham	1503	Randall Thomas Davidson	1903
Thomas Cranmer	1533	Cosmo Gordon Lang	1928
Reginald Pole	1556	William Temple	1942
Matthew Parker	1559	Geoffrey Francis Fisher	1945
Edmund Grindal	1576	Arthur Michael Ramsey	1961
John Whitgift	1583	Frederick Donald Coggan	1974
Richard Bancroft	1604		

(NOTE: Anglicans consider the line of Archbishops unbroken from Augustine to the present day. Roman Catholics consider the office vacant since 1558, the death of Pole.)

Antipopes

Antipopes were those who falsely claimed Papal Sovereignty. The dates and, in some cases, Roman numerals after the names account for occasional discrepancies in the succession of the Popes.

Name	Alleged reign	Name	Alleged reign	Name	Alleged reign
St. Hippolytus	217–235	Christopher ..	903–904	Victor IV	1138
Novatian	251	Boniface VII .	974; 984–985	Victor IV [1] ...	1159–1164
Felix II	355–365	John XVI	997–998	Paschal III ...	1164–1168
Ursinus	366–367	Gregory	ended 1012	Callistus III ..	1168–1178
Eulalius	418–419	Benedict X ..	1058–1059	Innocent III ..	1179–1180
Lawrence	498; 501–505	Honorius II ..	1061–1072	Nicholas V ...	1328–1330
Dioscorus	530	Clement III ..	1080–1100	Clement VII ..	1378–1394
Theodore	ended 687	Theodoric	ended 1100	Benedict XIII	1394–1423
Paschal	ended 687	Albert	ended 1102	Alexander V ..	1409–1410
Constantine ..	767–769	Sylvester IV ..	1105–1111	John XXIII ..	1410–1415
Philip	768	Gregory VIII .	1118–1121	Felix V	1439–1449
John	ended 844	Celestine II ..	ended 1124		
Anastasius ...	855	Anacletus II ..	1130–1138		

[1] Did not recognize his predecessor of 1138, who, only two months after claiming the Papacy, submitted to the rightful Pope, Innocent II.

History of the Christian Church in England

5th century Arrival in England of Angles, Saxons, and Jutes. Church isolated from Rome.

597 Augustine sent to convert Saxons.

1534 Act of Supremacy makes king head of Church of England.

1554 Church again united with Rome under reign of Mary.

1558 Church restored to Crown at accession of Elizabeth I.

1611 King James version of Bible.

1646 Puritan rebellion. Presbyterianism becomes state religion.

1660 Restoration. Power of Church of England restored under Charles II.

1739 John Wesley founds Methodism.

1829 Roman Catholic emancipation.

1833–45 Oxford Movement attempts to bring Church of England closer to ideals of ancient Church. This movement continues as important influence.

Religious and Secular Holidays, 1977

On June 24, 1968, a law was passed effective in 1971, approving 4 Monday holidays for Federal employees—Washington's Birthday, Memorial Day, Veterans' Day and Columbus Day. Many states have since adopted the same days of observance as legal holidays. (See pp. 436–37 for specific information.)

NEW YEAR'S DAY—Saturday, Jan. 1—A legal holiday in all states and the District of Columbia, New Year's Day has its origin in Roman times, when sacrifices were offered to Janus, the two-faced Roman deity who looked back on the past and forward to the future.

EPIPHANY—Thursday, Jan. 6—Falls the twelfth day after Christmas and commemorates the manifestation of Jesus as the Son of God, as represented by the adoration of the Magi, the baptism of Jesus, and the miracle of the wine at the marriage feast at Cana. Epiphany originally marked the beginning of the carnival season preceding Lent, and the evening (sometimes the eve) is known as Twelfth Night.

LINCOLN'S BIRTHDAY—Saturday, Feb. 12—A legal holiday in many states, this day was first formally observed in Washington, D.C., in 1866, when both houses of Congress gathered for a memorial address in honor of the late President.

ST. VALENTINE'S DAY—Monday, Feb. 14—This day is the festival of two third-century martyrs, both named St. Valentine. It is not known why this day is associated with lovers. It may derive from an old pagan festival about this time of year, or it may have been inspired by the belief that birds mate on this day.

WASHINGTON'S BIRTHDAY—Tuesday, Feb. 22—The birthday of George Washington is celebrated as a legal holiday in almost every state of the Union, the District of Columbia, and all territories. The observance began in 1796.

SHROVE TUESDAY—Feb. 22—Falls the day before Ash Wednesday and marks the end of the carnival season, which once began on Epiphany but is now usually celebrated the last three days before Lent. In France, the day is known as Mardi Gras (Fat Tuesday), and Mardi Gras celebrations are also held in several American cities, particularly in New Orleans. The day is sometimes called Pancake Tuesday by the English because fats, which were prohibited during Lent, had to be used up.

ASH WEDNESDAY—Feb. 23—The first day of the Lenten season, which lasts forty days. Having its origin sometime before A.D. 1000, it is a day of public penance and is marked in the Roman Catholic Church by the burning of the palms blessed on the previous Palm Sunday. With his thumb, the priest then marks a cross upon the forehead of each worshipper. The Anglican Church and a few Protestant groups in the United States also observe the day, but generally without the use of ashes.

PURIM (Feast of Lots)—Friday, Mar. 4 (14 Adar)—A day of joy and feasting celebrating deliverance of the Jews from a massacre planned by the Persian Minister Haman. The Jewish Queen Esther interceded with her husband, King Ahasuerus, to spare the life of her uncle, Mordecai, and Haman was hanged on the same gallows he had built for Mordecai. The holiday is marked by the reading of the Book of Esther (megillah), and by the exchange of gifts, donations to the poor and the presentation of Purim plays.

ST. PATRICK'S DAY—Thursday, Mar. 17—St. Patrick, patron saint of Ireland, has been honored in America since the first days of the nation. There are many dinners and meetings but perhaps the most notable part of the observance is the annual St. Patrick's Day parade on Fifth Avenue in New York City.

PALM SUNDAY—Apr. 3—Is observed the Sunday before Easter to commemorate the entry of Jesus into Jerusalem. The procession and the ceremonies introducing the benediction of palms probably had their origin in Jerusalem.

FIRST DAY OF PASSOVER (Pesach)—Sunday, Apr. 3 (15 Nisan)—The Feast of the Passover, also called the Feast of Unleavened Bread, commemorates the escape of the Jews from Egypt. As the Jews fled they ate unleavened bread, and from that time the Jews have allowed no leavening in the houses during Passover, bread being replaced by matzoth.

GOOD FRIDAY—Apr. 8—This day commemorates the Crucifixion, which is retold during services from the Gospel according to St. John. A feature in Roman Catholic churches is the Liturgy of the Passion; there is no Consecration, the Host having been consecrated the previous day. The eating of hot cross buns on this day is said to have started in England.

EASTER SUNDAY—Apr. 10—Observed in all Christian churches, Easter commemorates the Resurrection of Jesus. It is celebrated on the first Sunday after the full moon which occurs on or next after March 21 and is therefore celebrated between March 22 and April 25 inclusive This date was fixed by the Council of Nicaea in 325. The Orthodox Church celebrates Easter on Apr. 25.

ASCENSION DAY—Thursday, May 19—Took place in the presence of His apostles 40 days after the Resurrection of Jesus. It is traditionally held to have occurred on Mount Olivet in Bethany.

FIRST DAY OF SHABUOTH (Hebrew Pentecost)—Monday, May 23—(6 Sivan)—This festival, sometimes called the Feast of Weeks, or of Harvest, or of the First Fruits, falls fifty days after Passover and originally celebrated the end of the seven-week grain harvesting season. In later tradition, it also celebrated the giving of the Law to Moses on Mt. Sinai.

PENTECOST (Whitsunday)—May 29 This day commemorates the descent of the Holy Ghost upon the apostles fifty days after the Resurrection. The sermon by the Apostle Peter, which led to the baptism of 3,000 who professed belief, originated the ceremonies that have since been followed. "Whitsunday" is believed to have come from "white Sunday" when, among the English, white robes were worn by those baptized on the day.

MEMORIAL DAY—Monday, May 30—Also known as Decoration Day, Memorial Day is a legal holiday in most of the states and in the territories, and is also observed by the armed forces. In 1868, General John A. Logan, Commander in Chief of the Grand Army of the Republic, issued an order designating the day as one in which the graves of soldiers would be decorated. The holiday was originally devoted to honoring the memory of those who fell in the Civil War, but is now also dedicated to the memory of all war dead.

FLAG DAY—Tuesday, June 14—This day commemorates the adoption by the Continental Congress on June 14, 1777, of the Stars and Stripes as the U. S. flag. Although it is a legal holiday only in Pennsylvania, President Truman, on Aug. 3, 1949, signed a bill requesting the President to call for its observance each year by proclamation.

INDEPENDENCE DAY—Monday, July 4—The day of the adoption of the Declaration of Independence in 1776, celebrated in all states and territories. The observance began the next year in Philadelphia.

LABOR DAY—Monday, Sept. 5—Observed the first Monday in September in all states and territories, Labor Day was first celebrated in New York in 1882 under the sponsorship of the Central Labor Union, following the suggestion of Peter J. McGuire, of the Knights of Labor, that the day be set aside in honor of labor.

FIRST DAY OF ROSH HASHANA (Jewish New Year)—Tuesday, Sept. 13 (1 Tishri)—This day marks the beginning of the Jewish year 5736 and opens the Ten Days of Penitence closing with Yom Kippur.

YOM KIPPUR (Day of Atonement)—Thursday, Sept. 22 (10 Tishri)—This day marks the end of the Ten Days of Penitence that began with Rosh Hashana. It is described in *Leviticus* as a "Sabbath of rest," and synagogue services begin the preceding sundown, resume the following morning, and continue to sundown.

FIRST DAY OF SUKKOTH (Feast of Tabernacles)—Tuesday, Sept. 27 (15 Tishri)—This festival, also known as the Feast of the Ingathering, originally celebrated the fruit harvest, and the name comes from the booths or tabernacles in which the Jews lived during the harvest, although one tradition traces it to the shelters used by the Jews in their wandering through the wilderness. During the festival many Jews build small huts in their back yards or on the roofs of their houses.

SIMHATH TORAH (Rejoicing of the Law) Wednesday, Oct. 5 (23 Tishri)—This joyous holiday falls on the eighth day of Sukkoth. It marks the end of the year's reading of the Torah (Five Books of Moses) in the synagogue every Saturday and the beginning of the new cycle of reading.

COLUMBUS DAY—Wednesday, Oct. 12—A legal holiday in many states, commemorating the discovery of America by Columbus in 1492. Quite likely the first celebration of Columbus Day was that organized in 1792 by the Society of St. Tammany, or Columbian Order, more widely known as Tammany Hall.

HALLOWEEN—Monday, Oct. 31—Eve of All Saints' Day, formerly called All Hallows and Hallowmass. Halloween is traditionally associated in some countries with old customs such as bonfires, masquerading, and the telling of ghost stories. These are old Celtic practices that marked the beginning of winter.

ALL SAINTS' DAY—Tuesday, Nov. 1—A Roman Catholic and Anglican holiday celebrating all saints, known and unknown.

ELECTION DAY (legal holiday in certain states)—Tuesday, Nov. 8—Since 1845, by Act of Congress, the first Tuesday after the first Monday in November is the date for choosing Presidential electors. State elections are also generally held on this day.

VETERANS DAY—Friday, Nov. 11—Armistice Day was established in 1926 to commemorate the signing in 1918 of the Armistice ending World War I. On June 1, 1954, the name was changed to Veterans Day to honor all men and women who have served America in its armed forces.

THANKSGIVING—Thursday, Nov. 24— Observed nationally on the fourth Thursday in November by Act of Congress (1941), the first such national proclamation having been issued by President Lincoln in 1863, on the urging of Mrs. Sarah J. Hale, editor of *Godey's Lady's Book.* Most Americans believe that the holiday dates back to the day of thanks ordered by Governor Bradford of Plymouth Colony in New England in 1621 but scholars point out that days of thanks stem from ancient times.

FIRST SUNDAY OF ADVENT—Nov. 27— Advent is the season in which the faithful must prepare themselves for the advent of the Saviour on Christmas. The four Sundays before Christmas are marked by special church services.

FIRST DAY OF HANUKKAH (Festival of Lights)—Monday, Dec. 5 (25 Kislev)— This festival was instituted by Judas Maccabaeus in 165 B.C. to celebrate the purification of the Temple of Jerusalem, which had been desecrated three years earlier by Antiochus Epiphanes, who set up a pagan altar and offered sacrifices to Zeus Olympius. In Jewish homes, a light is lighted on each night of the eight-day festival.

CHRISTMAS (Feast of the Nativity)— Sunday, Dec. 25—The most widely celebrated holiday of the Christian year, Christmas is observed as the anniversary of the birth of Jesus. Christmas customs are centuries old. The mistletoe, for example, comes from the Druids, who, in hanging the mistletoe, hoped for peace and good fortune. Use of such plants as holly comes from the ancient belief that such plants blossomed at Christmas. Comparatively recent is the Christmas tree, first set up in Germany in the 17th century, and the use of candles on trees developed from the belief that candles appeared by miracle on the trees at Christmas. Colonial Manhattan Islanders introduced the name Santa Claus, a corruption of the Dutch name for the 4th-century Asia Minor St. Nicholas.

Legal Holidays in the 50 States, D. C., and Puerto Rico

On June 24, 1968, a law was passed effective in 1971, approving 4 Monday holidays for Federal employees— Washington's Birthday, Memorial Day, Veterans' Day and Columbus Day. Many states have since adopted the same days of observance as legal holidays.

Holidays Widely Observed

January 1, New Year's Day: All states, D.C., Puerto Rico.

February 12, Lincoln's Birthday: Alaska, Arizona, California, Colorado, Connecticut, Illinois, Indiana, Iowa, Kansas, Kentucky, Maryland, Michigan, Missouri, Montana, Nebraska, New Jersey, New Mexico, New York, Pennsylvania, Utah, Vermont, Washington, West Virginia.

February (first Monday), Lincoln's Birthday: Delaware, Oregon.

February (third Monday), Washington's Birthday: All states, D.C. and Puerto Rico. Called **President's Day** in Hawaii. Called **Washington-Lincoln Day** in Minnesota, Ohio, South Dakota, Wisconsin and Wyoming.

May 30, Memorial Day: Illinois, Maryland, New Hampshire, New Mexico, Washington, and West Virginia.

May (last Monday), Memorial Day: All states, D.C. and Puerto Rico except those listed above, and Alabama, Mississippi and South Carolina.

July 4, Independence Day: All states, D.C., Puerto Rico.

September (1st Monday), Labor Day: All states, D.C., Puerto Rico.

October 12, Columbus Day: Maryland.

October (2nd Monday), Columbus Day: All states, D.C. and Puerto Rico except Alaska, Iowa, Maryland, Mississippi, Nevada, Oregon and South Carolina and Washington. Also called **Fraternal Day** in Alabama. Called **Discovers' Day** in Hawaii, **Farmers' Day** in Florida and **Pioneers' Day** in South Dakota.

October (fourth Monday) Veterans' Day: Arkansas, Colorado, D.C., Hawaii, Idaho, Montana, Ohio, Rhode Island, and Utah.

November (4th Thursday), Thanksgiving Day: All states, Puerto Rico.

November (first Tuesday after the first Monday), Election Day: Arizona, Arkansas, California, Colorado, D.C., Delaware, Florida, Hawaii, Idaho, Illinois, Indiana, Louisiana, Maryland, Michigan, Missouri, Montana, New Hampshire, New Jersey, New York, Oklahoma, Pennsylvania, Rhode Island, South Carolina, Tennessee, Texas, Vermont, Virginia, Washington, West Virginia, Wisconsin, Wyoming, Puerto Rico.

November 11, Veterans' Day: All states and Puerto Rico except those listed above for October (fourth Monday). Called **Armistice Day** and **Veterans' Day** in New Mexico.

December 25, Christmas: All states, D.C., Puerto Rico.

Other Holidays

January 6, Three Kings' Day: Puerto Rico.

January 8, Battle of New Orleans Day: Louisiana.

January 11, De Hostos' Birthday: Puerto Rico.

January 15, Martin Luther King Day: D.C., Illinois, Kentucky, Maryland and Massachusetts.

January 19, Robert E. Lee's Birthday: Arkansas, Florida, Georgia, Kentucky, Louisiana, South Carolina. Called **Confederate Heroes Day** in Texas, also in honor of Jefferson Davis and other Confederate heroes.

January (second Sunday), Martin Luther King Day: Connecticut.

January (third Monday), Martin Luther King Day: Ohio.

January (third Monday), Robert E. Lee's Birthday: Alabama, Mississippi. **Lee-Jackson Day** in Virginia.

January 30, F. D. Roosevelt's Birthday: Kentucky.

February or March (1 day before Ash Wednesday), Mardi Gras (Shrove Tuesday): Alabama, Florida (in some counties), Louisiana (in some parishes).

February 14, Admission Day: Arizona.

March (first Tuesday), Town Meeting Day: Vermont.

March 2, Texas Independence Day: Texas.

March 17, Evacuation Day: Massachusetts (in Suffolk Co. only).

March or April (2 days before Easter), Good Friday: Connecticut, Delaware, Florida, Hawaii, Indiana, Louisiana, Maryland, North Dakota, Pennsylvania, Tennessee, Wisconsin (11 A.M.–3 P.M.), Puerto Rico.

March or April (1 day after Easter), Easter Monday: North Carolina.

March 22, Abolition Day: Puerto Rico.

March 25, Maryland Day: Maryland.

March 26, Kuhio Day: Hawaii.

March (last Monday), Seward's Day: Alaska.

April 13, Thomas Jefferson's Birthday: Alabama, Oklahoma.

April 16, De Diego's Birthday: Puerto Rico.

April (third Monday), Patriot's Day: Maine, Mass.

April 21, San Jacinto Day: Texas.

April 22, Arbor Day: Nebraska.

April 22, Oklahoma Day: Oklahoma.

April 26, Confederate Memorial Day: Florida, Georgia.

April (4th Monday), Fast Day: New Hampshire.

April (last Monday), Confederate Memorial Day: Alabama, Mississippi.

April (last Monday), Arbor Day: Wyoming.

April (last Friday), Arbor Day: Utah.

May (1st Tuesday after first Monday), Primary Election Day: Indiana.

May (2nd Sunday), Mother's Day: Oklahoma.

May 4, Rhode Island Independence Day: Rhode Island.

May 8, Truman Day: Missouri.

May 10, Confederate Memorial Day: S.C.

May 20, Mecklenburg Independence Day: N.C.

June (first Monday), Jefferson Davis' Birthday: Alabama, Mississippi.

June 3, Jefferson Davis' Birthday: Florida, Georgia, South Carolina, also called **Confederate Memorial Day** in Kentucky and Louisiana.

June 9, Senior Citizens Day: Oklahoma.

June 11, Kamehameha Day: Hawaii.

June 14, Flag Day: Pennsylvania.

June 17, Bunker Hill Day: Massachusetts (in Suffolk Co. only).

June 20, West Virginia Day: West Virginia.

July 17, Muñoz Rivera's Birthday: Puerto Rico.

July 24, Pioneer Day: Utah.

July 25, Constitution Day: Puerto Rico.

July 27, Barbosa's Birthday: Puerto Rico.

August (first Monday), Colorado Day: Colorado.

August (second Monday), Victory Day: R.I.

August 16, Bennington Battle Day: Vermont.

August (third Friday), Admission Day: Hawaii.

August 27, Lyndon B. Johnson's Birthday: Texas.

August 30, Huey P. Long Day: Louisiana.

September 9, Admission Day: California.

September 12, Defenders' Day: Maryland.

September 16, Cherokee Strip Day: Oklahoma.

September (1st Saturday after full moon), Indian Day: Oklahoma.

October 10, Oklahoma Historical Day: Oklahoma.

October 18, Alaska Day: Alaska.

October 31, Nevada Day: Nevada.

November 4, Will Rogers Day Oklahoma.

November 19, Discovery Day: Puerto Rico.

Value of New Construction of Religious Buildings

Estimates of the annual value of new construction of religious buildings, 1925–1974 inclusive, indicate a downward trend, beginning in 1966, from the all-time high reported in 1965. Revised statistics for previous years indicate that both in current and constant dollars the downward trend in church building was reversed in 1974.

Stated in 1967 dollars, the value of new construction would be as follows: 1971 ($589,000,000); 1972 ($560,000,000); 1973 ($488,000,000); 1974 ($536,000,000). The 1974 building, although higher in constant dollars than in 1973, was only 51 percent of the total spent in 1967 for new religious buildings.

Year	Value	Year	Value	Year	Value
1925	$165,000,000	1955	$736,000,000	1970	$931,000,000
1930	135,000,000	1960	1,013,000	1971	813,000,000
1935	28,000,000	1965	1,207,000,000	1972	844,000,000
1940	59,000,000	1967	1,093,000,000	1973	814,000,000
1945	26,000,000	1968	1,079,000,000	1974	947,000,000
1950	409,000,000	1969	988,000,000		

Movable Holidays, 1977–1985

CHRISTIAN AND SECULAR

Year	Ash Wed.	Easter	Pentecost	Labor Day	Election Day	Thanksgiving	1st Sun. Advent
1977	Feb. 23	Apr. 10	May 29	Sept. 5	Nov. 8	Nov. 24	Nov. 27
1978	Feb. 8	Mar. 26	May 14	Sept. 4	Nov. 7	Nov. 23	Dec. 3
1979	Feb. 28	Apr. 15	June 3	Sept. 3	Nov. 6	Nov. 22	Dec. 2
1980	Feb. 19	Apr. 6	May 25	Sept. 1	Nov. 4	Nov. 27	Nov. 30
1981	Mar. 4	Apr. 19	June 7	Sept. 7	Nov. 3	Nov. 26	Nov. 29
1982	Feb. 24	Apr. 11	May 30	Sept. 6	Nov. 2	Nov. 25	Nov. 28
1983	Feb. 16	Apr. 3	May 22	Sept. 5	Nov. 8	Nov. 24	Nov. 27
1984	Mar. 7	Apr. 22	June 10	Sept. 3	Nov. 6	Nov. 22	Dec. 2
1985	Feb. 20	Apr. 7	May 26	Sept. 2	Nov. 5	Nov. 28	Dec. 1

Shrove Tuesday: 1 day before Ash Wednesday.
Palm Sunday: 7 days before Easter.
Maundy Thursday: 3 days before Easter.
Good Friday: 2 days before Easter.

Holy Saturday: 1 day before Easter.
Ascension Day: 10 days before Pentecost.
Trinity Sunday: 7 days after Pentecost.
Corpus Christi: 11 days after Pentecost.

NOTE: Easter is celebrated on April 10, 1977, by the Orthodox Church.

JEWISH

Year	Purim[1]	1st day Passover[2]	1st day Shabuoth[3]	1st day Rosh Hashana[4]	Yom Kippur[5]	1st day Sukkoth[6]	Simhath Torah[7]	1st day Hanukkah[8]
1977	Mar. 4	Apr. 3	May 23	Sept. 13	Sept. 22	Sept. 27	Oct. 5	Dec. 5
1978	Mar. 23	Apr. 22	June 11	Oct. 2	Oct. 11	Oct. 16	Oct. 24	Dec. 25
1979	Mar. 13	Apr. 12	June 1	Sept. 22	Oct. 1	Oct. 6	Oct. 14	Dec. 15
1980	Mar. 2	Apr. 1	May 21	Sept. 11	Sept. 20	Sept. 25	Oct. 3	Dec. 3
1981	Mar. 20	Apr. 19	June 8	Sept. 29	Oct. 8	Oct. 13	Oct. 21	Dec. 21
1982	Mar. 9	Apr. 8	May 28	Sept. 18	Sept. 27	Oct. 2	Oct. 10	Dec. 11
1983	Feb. 27	Mar. 29	May 18	Sept. 8	Sept. 17	Sept. 22	Sept. 30	Dec. 1
1984	Mar. 18	Apr. 17	June 6	Sept. 27	Oct. 6	Oct. 11	Oct. 19	Dec. 19
1985	Mar. 7	Apr. 6	May 26	Sept. 16	Sept. 25	Sept. 30	Oct. 8	Dec. 8

[1] Feast of Lots. [2] Feast of Unleavened Bread. [3] Hebrew Pentecost; or Feast of Weeks, or of Harvest, or of First Fruits. [4] Jewish New Year. [5] Day of Atonement. [6] Feast of Tabernacles, or of the Ingathering. [7] Rejoicing of the Law. [8] Festival of Lights.

Length of Jewish holidays (O = Orthodox, C = Conservative, R = Reform):

Passover: O & C, 8 days (holy days: first 2 and last 2); R, 7 days (holy days: first and last).
Shabuoth: O & C, 2 days; R, 1 day.
Rosh Hashana: O & C, 2 days; R, 1 day.
Yom Kippur: All groups, 1 day.
Sukkoth: All groups, 7 days (holy days: O & C, first 2; R, first only) O & C observe two additional days: Shemini

Atsereth (Eighth Day of the Feast) and Simhath Torah. R observes Shemini Atsereth but not Simhath Torah.
Hanukkah: All groups, 8 days.

NOTE: All holidays begin at sundown on the evening before the date given.

Jewish Congregational and Rabbinical Organizations

Central Conference of American Rabbis: 790 Madison Ave., New York, N. Y. 10021.

New York Board of Rabbis: 10 E. 73rd St., New York, N. Y. 10021.

Rabbinical Alliance of America: 156 Fifth Ave., New York, N. Y. 10010.

Rabbinical Assembly: 3080 Broadway, New York, N. Y. 10027.

Rabbinical Council of America, Inc.: 220 Park Ave. South, New York, N. Y. 10003.

Synagogue Council of America: 432 Park Ave. South, New York, N. Y. 10016.

Union of American Hebrew Congregations: 838 Fifth Ave., New York, N. Y. 10021.

Union of Orthodox Jewish Congregations of America: 116 E. 27th St., New York, N. Y. 10016.

Union of Orthodox Rabbis of the U. S. and Canada: 235 East Broadway, New York, N. Y. 10002.

Union of Sephardic Congregations: 8 W. 70th St., New York, N. Y. 10023.

United Synagogue of America: 3080 Broadway, New York, N. Y. 10027.

GREAT DISASTERS

(For later disasters, see News Chronology of 1976.)

Earthquakes and Volcanic Eruptions

A.D. 79 **Aug. 24, ITALY**: eruption of Mt. Vesuvius buried cities of Pompeii and Herculaneum, killing thousands.

1755 **Nov. 1, PORTUGAL**: one of the most severe of recorded earthquakes leveled Lisbon and was felt as far away as southern France and North Africa; 10,000–20,000 killed in Lisbon.

1883 **Aug. 26–28, NETHERLANDS INDIES**: eruption of Krakatoa; violent explosions destroyed two-thirds of island. Sea waves occurred as far away as Cape Horn, and possibly England. Estimated 36,000 dead.

1902 **May 8, MARTINIQUE, WEST INDIES**: Mt. Pelée erupted and wiped out city of St. Pierre; 40,000 dead.

1906 **April 18, SAN FRANCISCO, CALIF.**: earthquake accompanied by fire razed more than 4 sq. mi.; more than 500 dead or missing; property damage about 250–300 millions.

1908 **Dec. 28, MESSINA, SICILY**: about 85,000 killed and city totally destroyed.

1923 **Sept. 1, JAPAN**: earthquake destroyed third of Tokyo and most of Yokohama; more than 90,000 killed.

1935 **May 31, INDIA**: earthquake at Quetta killed an estimated 50,000.

1939 **Jan. 24, CHILE**: earthquake razed 50,000 sq. mi.; about 30,000 killed.

1939 **Dec. 27, NORTHERN TURKEY**: severe quakes destroyed city of Erzingan; about 100,000 casualties.

1949 **Aug. 5, ECUADOR**: earthquake killed about 6,000 and razed 50 towns.

1950 **Aug. 15, INDIA**: earthquake affected 30,000 sq. mi. in Assam; 20,000–30,000 believed killed.

1960 **May 21–22, 27–29, CHILE**: 5,700 dead in earthquakes.

1962 **Sept. 1, NORTHWEST IRAN**: more than 10,000 killed in earthquakes.

1963 **Mar. 20, BALI**: 1,100 killed in eruption of Mt. Agung.

1963 **July 26, SKOPLJE, YUGOSLAVIA**: four-fifths of city destroyed; 1,011 dead, 3,350 injured.

1964 **Mar. 27, ALASKA**: strongest earthquake ever to strike North America hits 80 miles east of Anchorage; followed by seismic wave 50 feet high that traveled 8,445 miles at 450 miles per hour; 131 killed and damage in Alaska and West Coast $500–$750 million.

1966 **Aug. 19–23, EASTERN TURKEY**: earthquake killed 2,477 persons.

1970 **Mar. 27, WESTERN TURKEY**: earthquake at Gediz killed 1,087.

1970 **May 31, PERU**: earthquake left 50,000 dead, 17,000 missing.

1971 **Feb. 9, LOS ANGELES, CALIF.**: Earthquake rocked San Fernando Valley. Death toll 64. damage $1-billion.

1972 **Apr. 10, IRAN**: 5,000 killed in earthquake 600 miles south of Teheran.

1972 **Dec. 22, MANAGUA, NICARAGUA**: earthquake devastated city, leaving up to 12,000 dead.

1974 **Dec. 28, PATTAN, PAKISTAN**: earthquake affecting 1,000 square miles in northern section killed over 5,000.

Floods, Avalanches, and Tidal Waves
WORLD

1228 **HOLLAND**: 100,000 persons reputedly drowned by sea flood in Friesland.

1642 **CHINA**: Rebels destroyed Kaifeng seawall; 300,000 drowned.

1887 **CHINA**: hundreds of thousands of lives were lost in Honan province in overflow of Hwang Ho River.

1896 **JAPAN**: earthquake and tidal wave at Sanriku killed 27,000.

1939 **CHINA**: floods in north; casualties estimated at 10,000,000 homeless, starved or drowned.

1947 **JAPAN**: floods in wake of typhoon killed 2,000 persons on Honshu Is.

1950 **CHINA**: floods in eastern and southern China left 1,000,000 homeless and killed 500.

1953 **NORTHWEST EUROPE**: storm followed by floods devastated North Sea coastal areas. Netherlands was hardest hit, with 1,794 dead.

1954 **IRAN**: flash flood reportedly killed 2,000 religious pilgrims.

1959 **Dec. 2, FRÉJUS, FRANCE**: flood caused by collapse of Malpasset Dam left 412 dead.

1960 **AGADIR, MOROCCO**: 10,000–12,000 dead as earthquake set off tidal wave and fire, destroying most of city.

1962 **Jan. 10, PERU**: avalanche down Huascarán, extinct Andean volcano, killed more than 3,000 persons.

1963 **Oct. 9, ITALY**: landslide collapsed Vaiont Dam; flood killed about 2,000.

1966 **Oct. 21, ABERFAN, WALES**: avalanche of coal, waste, mud, and rocks killed 144 persons, including 116 children in school.

1970 **Nov. 13, EAST PAKISTAN**: 200,000 killed by cyclone-driven tidal wave from Bay of Bengal. Over 100,000 missing.

1971 **Sept. 29, ORISSA STATE, INDIA**: cyclone

439

and tidal wave off Bay of Bengal killed as many as 10,000.

UNITED STATES

1889 PENNSYLVANIA: more than 2,000 died in Johnstown flood.

1913 OHIO AND INDIANA: floods of Ohio and Indiana rivers took 730 lives.

1927 MISSISSIPPI VALLEY: floods inundated 20,000 sq. mi.; 700,000 left homeless.

1955 NORTHERN CALIFORNIA AND OREGON: Rains caused $150,000,000 damage, 74 deaths.

1969 Jan. 18–26, SOUTHERN CALIFORNIA: floods and mudslides from heavy rains caused widespread property damage; at least 100 dead. Another downpour (Feb. 23–26) caused further floods and mudslides; at least 18 dead.

1972 Feb. 26, MAN, W. VA.: more than 118 died when slag-pile dam collapsed under pressure of torrential rains and flooded 17-mile valley.

1972 June 9–10, RAPID CITY, S.D.: flash flood caused 226 deaths and $120 million in damage.

1972 June 20, EASTERN SEABOARD: Tropical storm Agnes, in 10-day rampage, caused widespread flash floods. Death toll was 129, damage estimated at $3.5 billion and 115,000 were left homeless.

Storms and Weather
(For U. S. tornadoes and hurricanes, see Index)
WORLD

1864 Oct. 5, INDIA: most of Calcutta denuded by cyclone; 70,000 killed.

1876 Oct. 31, INDIA: cyclone, tidal wave swept 3,000 sq. mi.; 215,000 killed.

1882 June 6, INDIA: cyclone and tidal wave killed 100,000 in Bombay.

1906 CHINA: typhoon at Hong Kong killed about 10,000.

1930 Sept. 3, SANTO DOMINGO (now Ciudad Trujillo): hurricane killed about 2,000 and injured 6,000.

1934 Sept. 21, JAPAN: hurricane killed more than 4,000 on Honshu.

1935 Oct. 25, HAITI: hurricane, flood killed 2,000 in Jérémie and Jacmel.

1942 Oct. 16, INDIA: cyclone devastated Bengal; about 40,000 lives lost.

1954 Sept. 26, JAPAN: typhoon off Hakodate killed 1,200–1,600.

1963 May 28–29, EAST PAKISTAN: cyclone killed about 22,000 along coast.

1963 Oct. 2–7, CARIBBEAN: Hurricane Flora killed up to 7,000 in Haiti and Cuba.

1964 Aug. 22–24, GUADELOUPE and HAITI: 214 killed in Hurricane Cleo.

1965 May 11-12 and June 1-2, EAST PAKISTAN, cyclones killed about 47,000.

1965 Dec. 15, KARACHI, PAKISTAN: cyclone killed about 10,000.

1974 Sept. 20, HONDURAS: Hurricane Fifi strikes northern section of country, leaving 8,000 dead, 100,000 homeless.

1974 Dec. 25, DARWIN, AUSTRALIA: cyclone destroys nearly the entire city, causing mass evacuation.

Fires and Explosions
WORLD

1666 Sept. 2, ENGLAND: "Great Fire of London" destroyed St. Paul's Church, etc. Damage 10 million pounds.

1812 Sept. 14, RUSSIA: fire started by Russians in Moscow after French occupation destroyed 30,800 houses.

1906 Mar. 10, FRANCE: explosion in coal mine in Courrières killed 1,060.

1917 Dec. 6, CANADA: explosion and fire at Halifax when ammunition ship collided with a vessel; 1,500 dead.

1942 Apr. 26, MANCHURIA: explosion in Honkeiko Colliery killed 1,549.

1949 Sept. 2, CHINA: fire on Chungking waterfront killed 1,700.

1955 June 11, FRANCE: crash and explosion of racing car into crowd during Grand Prix race, Le Mans, killed 82.

1956 Aug. 7, COLOMBIA: about 1,100 reported killed when 7 army ammunition trucks exploded at Cali.

1956 Aug. 8, BELGIUM: 262 died in coal mine fire at Marcinelle.

1960 Jan. 21, COALBROOK, SOUTH AFRICA: coal mine explosion killed 437.

1960 Nov. 13, SYRIA: 152 children killed in movie-house fire.

1962 Feb. 7, SAARLAND, WEST GERMANY: coal mine gas explosion killed 298.

1963 Nov. 9, JAPAN: explosion in coal mine at Omuta killed 447.

1965 May 28, INDIA: coal mine fire in state of Bihar killed 375.

1965 June 1, near FUKUOKA, JAPAN: coal mine explosion killed 236.

1967 May 22, BRUSSELS, BELGIUM: fire in L'Innovation, major department store, left 322 dead.

1970 Nov. 1, SAINT-LAURENT-DU-PONT, FRANCE: fire in dance hall killed 146 young people.

1972 May 13, OSAKA, JAPAN: 118 people died in fire in nightclub on top floor of Sennichi department store.

1972 June 6, WANKIE, RHODESIA: explosion in coal mine killed 427.

1973 Nov. 29, KUMAMOTO, JAPAN: fire in Taiyo department store killed 101.

1974 Feb. 1, SAO PAULO, BRAZIL: fire in upper stories of bank building killed 189 persons, many of whom leaped to death.

1975   Dec. 27, DHANBAD, INDIA: explosion in coal mine followed by flooding from nearby reservoir left 372 dead.

UNITED STATES

1835   Dec. 16, NEW YORK CITY: 530 buildings destroyed by fire.

1871   Oct. 8, CHICAGO, ILL.: the "Chicago Fire" burned 17,450 buildings, killed 250 persons; $196 million damage.

1871   Oct. 8, PESHTIGO, WIS.: over 1,200 lives lost; 2 billion trees burned.

1872   Nov. 9, BOSTON, MASS.: fire destroyed 800 buildings; $75 million damage.

1876   Dec. 5, NEW YORK CITY: fire in Brooklyn Theater killed more than 300.

1900   May 1, SCOFIELD, UTAH: explosion of blasting powder in coal mine killed 1,200.

1903   Dec. 30, CHICAGO, ILL.: Iroquois Theatre fire killed 602.

1904   Feb. 7, BALTIMORE, MD.: Business section burned; estimated $125 million damage.

1909   Nov. 13, CHERRY, ILL.: explosion in coal mine killed 259.

1913   Oct. 22, DAWSON, N.M.: coal mine explosion left 263 dead.

1937   March 18, NEW LONDON, TEX.: explosion destroyed schoolhouse; 294 killed.

1942   Nov. 28, BOSTON, MASS.: Cocoanut GROVE night club fire killed 498.

1944   July 6, HARTFORD, CONN.: fire and ensuing stampede in main tent of Ringling Brothers Circus killed 168, injured 487.

1944   July 17, PORT CHICAGO, CALIF.: 300 killed as ammunition ships explode.

1946   Dec. 7, ATLANTA, GA.: fire in Winecoff Hotel killed 119.

1947   April 16–18, TEXAS CITY, TEX.: most of city destroyed, 516 dead following explosion on ship.

1953   Oct. 16, BOSTON, MASS.: explosion and fire aboard U.S.S. *Leyte* killed 37.

1954   May 26, off QUONSET POINT, R.I.: explosion and fire aboard aircraft *Bennington* killed 103 crewmen.

1958   Dec. 1, CHICAGO, ILL.: fire at Our Lady of the Angels school killed 96.

1960   Dec. 19, BROOKLYN, N. Y.: blaze on aircraft carrier *Constellation* killed 49 workmen.

1966   Oct. 17, NEW YORK CITY: 12 firemen were killed in sudden collapse of burning building.

1966   Oct. 26, off SOUTH VIETNAM: fire on U. S. carrier *Oriskany* killed 43.

1967   July 29, off NORTH VIETNAM: fire on U. S. carrier *Forrestal* killed 134.

1969   Jan. 14, PEARL HARBOR, HAWAII: nuclear aircraft carrier *Enterprise* ripped by explosions; 27 dead, 82 injured.

1969   Apr. 6, NEW ORLEANS, LA.: Taiwanese freighter and string of oil-loaded barges collided in fiery explosion on Mississippi River; 25 dead.

1970   Dec. 30, WOOTON, KY.: coal-dust explosion in coal mine killed 38.

1972   May 2, KELLOGG, IDAHO: fire in Sunshine silver mine killed 91 miners; two men survived.

1974   June 30, PORT CHESTER, N.Y.: fire attributed to arson killed 24 young people in discothèque.

Shipwrecks*
WORLD

1833   May 11, LADY OF THE LAKE: bound from England to Quebec, struck iceberg; 215 perished.

1853   Sept. 29, ANNIE JANE: emigrant vessel off coast of Scotland; 348 died.

1912   March 5, PRINCIPE DE ASTURIAS: Spanish steamer struck rock off Sebastien Point; 500 drowned.

1912   April 15, TITANIC: sank after colliding with iceberg; 1,513 died.

1914   May 29, EMPRESS OF IRELAND: sank after collision in St. Lawrence River; 1,024 perished.

1928   Nov. 12, VESTRIS: British steamer sank in gale off Virginia; 110 died.

1931   June 14. French excursion steamer overturned in gale off St. Nazaire; approximately 450 died.

1939   June 1, Submarine THETIS: sank in Liverpool Bay, England; 99 perished.

1942   Oct. 2, QUEEN MARY: rammed and sank a British cruiser; 338 aboard the cruiser died.

1948   Dec. 3, KIANGYA: Chinese refugee ship wrecked in explosion; about 1,000 believed dead.

1949   Jan. 27, TAIPING: Chinese liner collided with collier and both sank; at least 600 died.

1949   Sept. 17, NORONIC: Canadian Great Lakes cruise ship burned at Toronto dock; about 130 died.

1951   April 16, AFFRAY: British submarine sank in English Channel; 75 dead.

1953   Jan. 9, CHANG TYONG-HO: South Korean ferry foundered off Pusan; 249 reported dead.

1953   Jan. 31, PRINCESS VICTORIA: British ferry sank in Irish Sea; 133 lost.

1956   July 25, ANDREA DORIA: Italian liner

* Not including military or naval action.

collided with Swedish liner *Stockholm* off Nantucket Island, Mass., sinking next day; 52, mostly passengers on Italian ship, dead or unaccounted for; over 1,600 rescued.

1962 Apr. 8, DARA, British liner, exploded and sank in Persian Gulf: 236 persons dead. Caused by time bomb.

1963 May 4, U.A.R. ferry capsized and sank in upper Nile; over 200 died.

1964 Nov. 26, SHALOM: Israeli liner collided with Norwegian tanker *Stolt Dagali* off New Jersey coast; 19 of tanker's crew dead.

1965 Nov. 13, YARMOUTH CASTLE: cruise ship burned and sank 60 miles northeast of Nassau en route from Miami to Bahamas; 90 dead.

1970 Aug. 1, ferry between Basseterre, St. Kitts, and Charlestown, Nevis, capsized in Caribbean; 125 believed lost.

1970 Dec. 15, ferry in Korean Strait capsized; 261 lost.

U. S. AND U. S. LINES

1865 April 27, SULTANA: boiler explosion on Mississippi River steamboat near Memphis; 1,450 killed.

1898 Nov. 26, CITY OF PORTLAND: Loss of 157 off Cape Cod.

1904 June 15, GENERAL SLOCUM: excursion steamer burned in New York Harbor; 1,021 perished.

1915 July 24, EASTLAND: Great Lakes excursion steamer overturned in Chicago River; 812 died.

1934 Sept. 8, MORRO CASTLE: about 130 killed in fire off Asbury Park, N. J.

1939 May 23, SQUALUS: submarine with 59 men sank off Hampton Beach, N. H.; 33 saved.

1945 April 9: U. S. ship, loaded with aerial bombs, exploded at Bari, Italy; at least 360 killed.

1952 April 26, HOBSON: minesweeper collided with aircraft carrier *Wasp* and sank during night maneuvers in mid-Atlantic; 176 persons lost.

1963 Apr. 10, THRESHER: atomic-powered submarine sank in North Atlantic; 129 dead.

1968 Late May, SCORPION: nuclear submarine sank in Atlantic 400 miles SW of Azores; 99 dead. (Located Oct. 31.)

Aircraft Accidents*
WORLD

1921 Aug. 24, ENGLAND: ZR-2, British dirigible, broke in two on trial trip near Hull; 62 died.

* Not including military or naval action.

1957 March 17, near CEBU CITY, PHILIPPINES: President Ramón Magsaysay and 24 others killed in crash.

1960 Feb. 25, RIO DE JANEIRO, BRAZIL: U.S. Navy plane, flying Navy musicians to perform at dinner given by visiting President Eisenhower, collided with Brazilian airliner, killing 61.

1961 Feb. 15, near BRUSSELS, BELGIUM: 72 on board and farmer killed in crash of Sabena plane; U. S. figure skating team wiped out.

1962 June 3, PARIS, FRANCE: chartered Air France Boeing Jet 707 crashed at Orly Airport; 130 dead.

1962 June 22, GRANDE-TERRE in GUADELOUPE: Air France Boeing 707 crashed, killing all 113 aboard.

1966 Jan. 24, MONT BLANC: Indian airliner crashed into mountain in fog; 117 dead.

1966 Feb. 4, JAPAN: Japanese airliner crashed into Tokyo Bay; 133 dead.

1966 Mar. 5, JAPAN: British airliner caught fire and crashed into Mt. Fuji; 124 dead.

1967 Apr. 20, NICOSIA, CYPRUS: crash of chartered Swiss Turboprop killed 126.

1968 Apr. 20, WINDHOEK, SW AFRICA: South African airliner crashed; 122 dead.

1969 Mar. 16, MARACAIBO, VENEZUELA: Venezuelan jetliner crashed and exploded; 84 crew members and passengers died and 71 were killed on ground.

1969 Dec. 8, KERATEA, GREECE: rain and hurricane winds caused Greek airliner to crash into 2,000-foot mountain while approaching Athens; 90 dead.

1970 Feb. 15, SANTO DOMINGO, DOMINICAN REPUBLIC: Dominican Republic jetliner plunged into Caribbean on takeoff; 102 dead.

1970 July 4, ARBUCIAS, SPAIN: British Comet crashed into mountains while coming in for landing at Barcelona; 112 dead.

1970 July 5, TORONTO, CANADA: Canadian jetliner crashed on landing approach; 109 dead.

1970 Aug. 9, CUZCO, PERU: Peruvian turboprop with 51 teen-age U. S. students among passengers, crashed shortly after takeoff; 99 dead.

1971 July 30, MORIOKA, JAPAN: Japanese Boeing 727 and F-86 fighter collided in mid-air; toll was 162.

1972 May 5, PALERMO, SICILY: Alitalia DC-8 hit mountain, killing 115.

1972 June 18, LONDON, ENGLAND: B.E.A. Trident jetliner plunged into field minutes after take-off from Heathrow Airport; all 118 aboard dead.

1972 Aug. 14, EAST BERLIN, EAST GERMANY: Soviet-built East German Ilyushin plane crashed, killing 156.

1972 Oct. 13, Moscow, U.S.S.R.; 176 died when Soviet Ilyushin airliner crashed.

1972 Dec. 3, SANTA CRUZ TENERIFE, CANARY ISLANDS: Spanish charter jet carrying West German tourists crashed on take-off; all 155 aboard killed.

1973 Jan. 22, KANO, NIGERIA: 171 Nigerian Moslems returning from Mecca and five crewmen died in crash.

1973 Apr. 10, HOCHWALD, SWITZERLAND: British airliner carrying tourists to Swiss fair crashed in blizzard; 106 dead.

1973 July 11, PARIS: Boeing 707 of Varig Airlines, en route to Rio de Janeiro, crashed near airport, killing 122 of 134 passengers.

1974 Mar. 3, PARIS, FRANCE: Turkish DC-10 jumbo jet crashed in forest shortly after take-off; all 346 passengers and crew killed in worst aviation disaster to date.

1974 Dec. 4, COLOMBO, SRI LANKA: Dutch DC-8 carrying Moslems to Mecca crashed on landing approach, killing all 191 persons aboard.

1975 Aug. 3, AGADIR, MOROCCO: Chartered Boeing 707, returning Moroccan workers home after vacation in France, plunged into mountainside; all 188 aboard killed.

1975 Aug. 20, DAMASCUS, SYRIA: Czech airliner crashed while landing, killing 126 of 128 persons aboard.

U. S. AND U. S. LINES

1925 Sept. 3, CALDWELL, OHIO: U. S. dirigible *Shenandoah* broke apart; 14 dead.

1933 April 4, NEW JERSEY COAST: U. S. dirigible *Akron* crashed; 73 died.

1937 May 6, LAKEHURST, N. J.: German zeppelin *Hindenburg* destroyed by fire at tower mooring; 36 killed.

1945 July 28, NEW YORK CITY: U. S. Army bomber crashed into Empire State Building; 13 dead.

1946 May 20, NEW YORK CITY: U. S. Army plane crashed into Manhattan Co. building; 5 dead.

1949 Nov. 1, WASHINGTON, D. C.: fighter plane rammed airliner, killing 55.

1951 Dec. 16, ELIZABETH, N. J.: nonscheduled airliner crash killed 56.

1952 Jan. 22, ELIZABETH, N. J.: 29 killed, incl. former Secy. of War Robert P. Patterson, when airliner hit apartments; 7 of dead were on ground.

1952 Feb. 11, ELIZABETH, N. J.: third major air disaster in Elizabeth within two months fatally injured 33.

1953 June 18, near TOKYO JAPAN: crash of U. S. Air Force "Globemaster" killed 129 servicemen.

1955 Nov. 1, near LONGMONT, COLO.: time bomb hidden in luggage destroyed airliner in flight, killing 44.

1956 June 30, GRAND CANYON, ARIZ.: 128 died in collision of two airliners.

1957 Feb. 1, NEW YORK CITY: airliner crash on Rikers Island killed 20 of 101 aboard.

1959 Feb. 3, NEW YORK CITY: American Airlines Lockheed Electra turboprop plane crashed in East River; 65 dead.

1960 Jan. 6, en route from NYC to Miami: National Airlines plane disintegrated; 34 died. Bomb suspected.

1960 Mar. 17, over TELL CITY, IND.: Northwest Airlines turboprop Electra exploded in midair, killing 63.

1960 Sept. 19, near GUAM: crash shortly after take-off of World Airways plane took 78 lives.

1960 Oct. 4, BOSTON HARBOR: Eastern Airlines plane sank; 61 dead.

1960 Dec. 16, NEW YORK CITY: United and Trans World planes collided in fog, crashed in two boroughs, killing 134 in air and on ground.

1962 Mar. 1, NEW YORK CITY: American Airlines jetliner crashed into Jamaica Bay, near Idlewild Airport, killing all 95 on board.

1965 Feb. 8, NEW YORK CITY: Eastern Airlines DC-7B went down in Atlantic shortly after take-off from Kennedy International Airport; 84 dead.

1966 Dec. 24, BINH THAI, SOUTH VIETNAM: crash of military-chartered plane into village killed 129.

1967 July 19, near HENDERSONVILLE, N. C.: Piedmont Airlines Boeing 727 collided with private plane; 82 dead.

1968 May 3, near DAWSON, TEX.: Braniff airliner crashed; 85 dead.

1969 Sept. 9, SHELBYVILLE, IND.: Allegheny Airlines jetliner and single-engine plane flown by student pilot collided in air and crashed; 83 dead.

1970 Nov. 13, HUNTINGTON, W. VA.: chartered plane carrying 43 players and coaches of Marshall University football team crashed; 75 dead.

1971 June 6, near LOS ANGELES, CALIF.: Air West DC-9 and Navy F-4 fighter collided over San Gabriel Canyon; 49 killed; one Navy crewman parachuted to safety.

1971 Sept. 4, near JUNEAU, ALASKA: Alaska Airlines Boeing 727 crashed into Chilkoot Mountains; 109 killed.

1972 Dec. 30, MIAMI, FLA.: Eastern Airlines Lockheed 1011 TriStar Jumbo jet crashed into Everglades; 101 killed, 75 survived.

1973 July 31, BOSTON: Delta Airlines jet crashed in heavy fog in landing at Logan International Airport killing 88 of 89 aboard.

1974 Jan. 31, PAGO PAGO, SAMOA: Pan American 707 crashed while landing; 97 of 101 persons aboard killed.

1974 Dec. 1, UPPERVILLE, VA.: all 92 aboard killed in crash of TWA 727 into wooded area.

1975 June 24, NEW YORK CITY: Eastern Airlines Boeing 747, arriving from New Orleans, crashed at Kennedy International Airport, killing 133 in highest single-aircraft toll in U.S. to date.

Railroad Accidents
WORLD

1864 June 29, near BELOEIL, CANADA: about 90 killed when train ran through open switch.

1879 Dec. 28, DUNDEE, SCOTLAND: train blown off Tay bridge; 73 drowned.

1881 June 24, near CUARTLA, MEXICO: about 200 died when train fell into river.

1882 July 13, near TCHERNY, RUSSIA: more than 150 killed in derailment.

1889 June 12, near ARMAGH, IRELAND: about 80 killed in collision.

1891 June 14, near BASEL, SWITZERLAND: about 100 killed in collision.

1915 May 22, GRETNA, SCOTLAND: two passenger trains and troop train collided; 227 killed.

1917 Dec. 12, MODANE, FRANCE: almost 550 killed in derailment of troop train near mouth of Mt. Cenis tunnel.

1939 Dec. 22, near MAGDEBURG, GERMANY: more than 125 killed in collision; 99 killed in another wreck near Friedrichshafen.

1944 March 2, near SALERNO, ITALY: 521 suffocated when Italian train stalled in tunnel.

1949 Oct. 22, near NOWY DWOR, POLAND: more than 200 reported killed in derailment of Danzig-Warsaw express.

1952 Oct. 8, HARROW-WEALDSTONE, ENGLAND: two express trains crashed into commuter train; 112 dead.

1953 Dec. 24, near SAKVICE, CZECHOSLOVAKIA: two trains crashed; over 100 dead.

1956 Sept. 2, near MAHBUBNAGAR, INDIA: at least 120 killed when bridge collapsed under train.

1957 Sept. 1, near KENDAL, JAMAICA: about 175 killed when train plunged into ravine.

1957 Sept. 29, near MONTGOMERY, WEST PAKISTAN: express train crashed into standing oil train; nearly 300 killed.

1957 Dec. 4, ST. JOHN'S, ENGLAND: 92 killed, 187 injured as one commuter train crashed into another in fog.

1960 Nov. 14, PARDUBICE, CZECHOSLOVAKIA: two trains collided; 110 dead, 106 injured.

1962 May 3, near TOKYO, JAPAN: 163 killed and 400 injured when train crashed into wreckage of collision between inbound freight train and outbound commuter train.

1963 Nov. 9, near YOKOHAMA, JAPAN: two passenger trains crashed into derailed freight, killing 162.

1964 July 26, CUSTOIAS, PORTUGAL: passenger train derailed; 94 dead.

1970 Feb. 4, near BUENOS AIRES, ARGENTINA: 236 killed when express train crashed into standing commuter train.

1972 Oct. 6, near SALTILLO, MEXICO: train carrying religious pilgrims derailed and caught fire, killing 204 and injuring over 1,000.

1972 July 21, SEVILLE, SPAIN: head-on crash of two passenger trains killed 76.

1974 Aug. 30, ZAGREB, YUGOSLAVIA: train entering station derailed, killing 153 and injuring over 60.

UNITED STATES

1943 Dec. 16, near RENNERT, N. C.: 72 killed in derailment and collision.

1944 Dec. 31, near OGDEN, UTAH: 48 killed in collision.

1946 April 25, NAPERVILLE, ILL.: at least 47 killed in collision.

1950 Feb. 17, ROCKVILLE CENTRE, N. Y.: head-on crash of two commuter trains killed 30.

1950 Nov. 22, RICHMOND HILL, N. Y.: 79 died when one commuter train crashed into rear of another.

1951 Feb. 6, WOODBRIDGE, N. J.: 85 died when commuter train plunged through temporary overpass.

1958 Sept. 15, near BAYONNE, N. J.: over 40 killed when train went through open drawbridge.

1972 Oct. 30, CHICAGO, ILL.: two commuter trains collided during morning rush hour; 44 dead and over 200 injured.

AVIATION

Famous Firsts in Aviation

1782—First balloon flight. Jacques and Joseph Montgolfier of Annonay, Fr., sent up a small smoke-filled balloon about mid-November.

1783—First hydrogen-filled balloon flight. Jacques A. C. Charles, Paris physicist, supervised construction by A. J. and M. N. Robert of a 13-ft. diameter balloon which was filled with hydrogen. It got up to about 3,000 ft. and traveled about 16 mi. in a 45-min. flight (Aug. 27).

1783—First human balloon flights. A Frenchman, Jean Pilâtre de Rozier, made the first captive-balloon ascension (Oct. 15). With the Marquis d'Arlandes, Pilâtre de Rozier made the first free flight, reaching a peak altitude of about 500 ft., and traveling about 5½ mi. in 20 min. (Nov. 21).

1784—First powered balloon. Gen. Jean Baptiste Marie Meusnier developed the first propeller-driven and elliptically-shaped balloon—the crew cranking three propellers on a common shaft to give the craft a speed of about 3 mi. per hr.

1784—First woman to fly. Mme. Thible, a French opera singer (June 4).

1793—First balloon flight in America. Jean Pierre Blanchard, a French pilot, made it from Philadelphia to near Woodbury, Gloucester Co., N. J., in a little over 45 min. (Jan. 9).

1794—First military use of the balloon. Jean Marie Coutelle, using a balloon built for the French Army, made two 4-hr. observation ascents. The military value of the ascents seems to have been in damage to the enemy's morale.

1797—First parachute jump. André-Jacques Garnerin dropped from about 6,500 ft. over Monceau Park in Paris in a 23-ft. diameter 'chute made of white canvas with a basket attached (Oct. 22).

1843—First air transport company. In London, William S. Henson and John Stringfellow filed articles of incorporation for the Aerial Transit Company (Mar. 24). It failed.

1852—First dirigible. Henri Giffard, a French engineer, flew in a controllable (more or less) steam-engine-powered balloon, 144 ft. long and 39 ft. in diameter, inflated with 88,000 cu. ft. of coal gas. It reached 6.7 mi. per hr. on a flight from Paris to Trappe (Sept. 24).

1860—First aerial photographers. Samuel Archer King and William Black made two photos of Boston, still in existence.

1872—First gas-engine powered dirigible. Paul Haenlein, a German engineer, flew in a semi-rigid-frame dirigible, powered by a 4-cylinder internal-combustion engine running on coal gas drawn from the supporting bag.

1873—First transatlantic attempt. *The New York Daily Graphic* sponsored the attempt with a 400,000 cu. ft. balloon carrying a lifeboat. A rip in the bag during inflation brought collapse of the balloon and the project.

1897—First successful metal dirigible. An all-metal dirigible, designed by David Schwarz, a Hungarian, took off from Berlin's Tempelhof Field and, powered by a 16-hp. Daimler engine, got several miles before leaking gas caused it to crash (Nov. 13).

1900—First Zeppelin flight. Germany's Count Ferdinand von Zeppelin flew the first of his long series of rigid-frame airships. It attained a speed of 18 mi. per hr. and got 3½ mi. before its steering gear failed (July 2).

1903—First successful heavier-than-air machine flight. Aviation was really born on the sand dunes at Kitty Hawk, N.C., when Orville Wright crawled to his prone position between the wings of the biplane he and his brother Wilbur had built, opened the throttle of their homemade 12-hp. engine and took to the air. He covered 120 ft. in 12 sec. Later that day, in one of four flights, Wilbur stayed up 59 sec. and covered 852 ft. (Dec. 17).

1904—First airplane maneuvers. Orville Wright made the first turn with an airplane (Sept. 15); 5 days later his brother Wilbur made the first complete circle.

1905—First airplane flight over half an hour. Orville Wright kept his craft up 33 min. 17 sec. (Oct. 4).

1906—First European airplane flight. Alberto Santos-Dumont, a Brazilian, flew a heavier-than-air machine at Bagatelle Field, Paris (Sept. 13).

1908—First airplane fatality. Lt. Thomas E. Selfridge, U.S. Army Signal Corps, was in a group of officers evaluating the Wright plane at Fort Myer, Va. He was up about 75 ft. with Orville Wright when the propeller hit a bracing wire and was broken, throwing the plane out of control, killing Selfridge and seriously injuring Wright (Sept. 17).

1910—First licensed woman pilot. Baroness Raymonde de la Roche of France, who learned to fly in 1909, received ticket No. 36 on March 8.

1910—First flight from shipboard. Lt. Eugene Ely, USN, took a Curtiss plane off from the deck of cruiser *Birmingham* at Hampton Roads, Va., and flew to Norfolk (Nov. 14). The following January he reversed the process, flying from Camp Selfridge to the deck of the armored cruiser *Pennsylvania* in San Francisco Bay (Jan. 18).

1911—First U.S. woman pilot. Harriet Quimby, a magazine writer, who got ticket No. 37.

1913—First multi-engined aircraft. Built and flown by Igor Ivan Sikorsky while still in his native Russia.

1914—First aerial combat. In August, Allied and German pilots and observers started shooting at each other with pistols and rifles—with negligible results.

1915—First air raids on England. German Zeppelins started dropping bombs on four English communities (Jan. 19).

1918—First U.S. air squadron. The U.S. Army Air Corps made its first independent raids over enemy lines, in DH-4 planes (British-designed) powered with 400-hp. American-designed Liberty engines (Apr. 8).

1918—First regular airmail service. Operated for the Post Office Department by the Army, the first regular service was inaugurated with one round trip a day (except Sunday) between Washington, D.C., and New York City (May 15).

1919—First transatlantic flight. The NC-4, one of four Curtiss flying boats commanded by Lt. Comdr. Albert C. Read, reached Lisbon, Port. (May 27) after hops from Trepassy Bay, Nfld., to Horta, Azores (May 16–17), to Ponta Delgada (May 20). The Liberty-powered craft was piloted by Walter Hinton.

1919—First nonstop transatlantic flight. Capt. John Alcock and Lt. Arthur Whitten Brown, British World War I flyers, made the 1,900 mi. from St. John's, Nfld., to Clifden, Ire., in 16 hr. 12 min. in a Vickers-Vimy bomber with two 350-hp. Rolls-Royce engines (June 15–16).

1919—First lighter-than-air transatlantic flight. The British dirigible R-34, commanded by Maj. George H. Scott, left Firth of Forth, Scot. (July 2) and touched down at Mineola, L. I., 108 hr. later. The eastbound trip was made in 75 hr. (completed July 13).

1919—First scheduled passenger service (using airplanes). Aircraft Travel and Transport inaugurated London-Paris service (Aug. 25). Later the company started the first trans-channel mail service on the same route (Nov. 10).

1921—First naval vessel sunk by aircraft. Two battleships being scrapped by treaty

were sunk by bombs dropped from Army planes in demonstration put on by Brig. Gen. William S. Mitchell (July 21).

1921—First helium balloon. The C-7, non-rigid Navy dirigible was first to use non-inflammable helium as lifting gas, making a flight from Hampton Roads, Va., to Washington, D.C. (Dec. 1).

1922—First member of Caterpillar Club. Lt. (later Maj. Gen.) Harold Harris bailed out of a crippled plane he was testing at McCook Field, Dayton, Ohio (Oct. 20), and became the first man to join the Caterpillar Club—those whose lives have been saved by parachute.

1923—First nonstop transcontinental flight. Lts. John A. Macready and Oakley Kelly flew a single-engine Fokker T-2 nonstop from New York to San Diego, a distance of just over 2,500 mi. in 26 hr. 50 min. (May 2–3).

1923—First autogyro flight. Juan de la Cierva, brilliant Spanish mathematician, made the first successful flight in a rotary wing aircraft in Madrid (June 9).

1924—First round-the-world flight. Four Douglas Cruiser biplanes of the U.S. Army Air Corps took off from Seattle under command of Maj. Frederick Martin (Apr. 6). 175 days later two of the planes (Lt. Lowell Smith's and Lt. Erik Nelson's) landed in Seattle after a circuitous route—one source saying 26,345 mi., another saying 27,553 mi.

1926—First polar flight. Then-Lt. Cmdr. Richard E. Byrd, acting as navigator, and Floyd Bennett as pilot, flew a trimotor Fokker from Kings Bay, Spitsbergen, over the North Pole and back in 15½-hr. flight (May 8–9).

1927—First solo transatlantic flight. Charles Augustus Lindbergh lifted his Wright-powered Ryan monoplane, *Spirit of St. Louis,* from Roosevelt Field, L. I., to stay aloft 33 hr. 39 min. and cover 3,600 mi. to Le Bourget Field outside Paris (May 20–21).

1927—First transatlantic passenger. Charles A. Levine was piloted by Clarence D. Chamberlin from Roosevelt Field, L.I., to Eisleben, Ger., in a Wright-powered Bellanca (June 4–5).

1928—First east-west transatlantic crossing. Baron Guenther von Huenefeld, piloted by German Capt. Hermann Koehl and Irish Capt. James Fitzmaurice, left Dublin for New York City (Apr. 12) in a single-engine all-metal Junkers monoplane. Some 37 hr. later they cracked up on Greely Island, Labrador. Rescued.

1928—First U.S.–Australia flight. Sir Charles Kingsford-Smith and Capt. Charles T. P. Ulm, Australians, and two American navigators, Harry W. Lyon and James Warner, crossed the Pacific from Oakland to Brisbane. They went via

Hawaii and the Fiji Islands in a trimotor Fokker (May 31–June 8).

1928—First transarctic flight. Sir Hubert Wilkins, Australian explorer, piloted by Carl Ben Eielson, flew from Point Barrow, Alaska, to Spitsbergen (mid-April).

1929—First of the endurance records. With Air Corps Maj. Carl Spaatz in command and Capt. Ira Eaker as chief pilot, an Army Fokker, aided by refueling in the air, remained aloft 150 hr. 40 min. at Los Angeles (Jan. 1–7).

1929—First blind flight. James H. Doolittle proved the feasibility of instrument flying when he took off and landed entirely on instruments (Sept. 24).

1929—First rocket engine flight. Fritz von Opel, German auto maker, stayed aloft in his small rocket-powered craft for 75 sec., covering nearly 2 mi. (Sept. 30).

1929—First South Pole flight. Comdr. Richard E. Byrd, with Bernt Balchen as pilot, Harold I. June, radio operator, and Capt. A. C. McKinley, photographer, flew a trimotor Fokker from the Bay of Whales, Little America, over the South Pole and back (Nov. 28–29).

1930—First Paris–New York nonstop flight. Dieudonné Coste and Maurice Bellonte, French pilots, flew a Hispano-powered Breguet biplane from Le Bourget Field to Valley Stream, L. I., in 37 hr. 18 min. (Sept. 2–3).

1931—First flight into the stratosphere. Prof. Auguste Piccard, Swiss physicist, and Charles Knipfer, ascended in a balloon from Augsburg, Ger., and reached a height of 51,793 ft. in a 17-hr. flight that terminated on a glacier near Innsbruck, Austria (May 27).

1931—First nonstop transpacific flight. Hugh Herndon and Clyde Pangborn took off from Sabishiro Beach, Japan, dropped their landing gear and flew 4,860 mi. to near Wenatchee, Wash., in 41 hr. 13 min. (Oct. 4–5).

1932—First woman's transatlantic solo. Amelia Earhart, flying a Pratt & Whitney Wasp-powered Lockheed Vega, flew alone from Harbor Grace, Nfld., to Ireland in approximately 15 hr. (May 20–21).

1932—First westbound transatlantic solo. James A. Mollison, British pilot, took a de Havilland Puss Moth from Portmarnock, Ireland, to Pennfield, N. B. (Aug. 18).

1932—First woman airline pilot. Ruth Rowland Nichols, first woman to hold three international records at the same time—speed, distance, altitude—was employed by N.Y.-New England Airways.

1933—First round-the-world solo. Wiley Post took a Lockheed Vega, *Winnie Mae*, 15,596 mi. around the world in 7 days 18 hr. 49½ min. (July 15–22).

1937—First successful helicopter. Hanna Reitsch, German woman pilot, flew Dr. Heinrich Focke's FW-61 in free, fully controlled flight at Bremen (July 4).

1939—First turbojet flight. Just before their invasion of Poland, the Germans flew a Heinkel He-178 plane powered by a Heinkel S3B turbojet (Aug. 27).

1942—First American jet plane flight. Robert Stanley, chief pilot for Bell Aircraft Corp., flew the Bell XP-59 *Airacomet* at Muroc Army Base, Calif. (Oct. 1).

1947—First piloted supersonic flight in an airplane. Capt. Charles E. Yeager, U.S. Air Force, flew the X-1, rocket-powered research plane built by Bell Aircraft Corp., faster than the speed of sound at Muroc Air Force Base, California (Oct. 14).

1949—First round-the-world nonstop flight. Capt. James Gallagher and USAF crew of 13 flew a Boeing B-50A Superfortress around the world nonstop from Ft. Worth, Tex., returning to same point; 23,452 mi. in 94 hr. 1 min., with 4 aerial refuelings enroute (Feb. 27–Mar. 2).

1950—First nonstop transatlantic jet flight. Col. David C. Schilling (USAF) flew 3,300 mi. from England to Limestone, Me., in 10 hr. 1 min. (Sept. 22).

1951—First solo across North Pole. Charles F. Blair, Jr., flew a converted P-51 (May 29).

1952—First jetliner service. De Havilland Comet flight inaugurated by BOAC between London and Rome (Apr. 21). The round trip was 4 hr. 46 min. flying time.

1952—First transatlantic helicopter flight. Capt. Vincent H. McGovern and 1st Lt. Harold W. Moore piloted 2 Sikorsky H-19s from Westover, Mass., to Prestwick, Scot. (3,410 mi.). Trip was made in 5 steps; with flying time of 42 hr. 25 min. (July 15–31).

1952—First transatlantic round trip in same day. British Canberra twin-jet bomber flew from Aldergrove, N. Ire., to Gander, Nfld., and back in 7 hr. 59 min. flying time (Aug. 26).

1955—First transcontinental round trip in same day. Lt. John M. Conroy piloted F-86 Sabrejet across U.S. (Los Angeles–New York) and back—5,085 mi.—in 11 hr. 33 min. 27 sec. (May 21).

1957—First round-the-world, nonstop jet plane flight. Maj. Gen. Archie J. Old, Jr., USAF, led a flight of 3 Boeing B-52 bombers, powered with 8 10,000-lb.-thrust Pratt & Whitney Aircraft J57 engines around the world in 45 hr. 19 min.; distance 24,325 mi.; average speed 525 miles per hour. (Completed Jan. 18.)

1958—First transatlantic jet passenger service. BOAC, New York to London (Oct. 4). Pan American started daily service, N.Y. to Paris (Oct. 26).

1958—First domestic jet passenger service. National Airlines inaugurated service between New York and Miami (Dec. 10).

U.S. Scheduled Airlines, 1975[1]
Source: Civil Aeronautics Board.

Airline	Certificated route mileage	Revenue passenger-miles, 1975[1]
Domestic[2]		
Airlift[3]	8,453	...
Air New England	797	54,726
Alaska[2]	4,901[4]	610,779
Alleghany	7,743[5]	3,272,212
Aloha	494	276,136
American	42,885[5]	18,378,968
Aspen	112	12,899
Braniff	20,261	5,003,070
Continental	25,104	6,270,257
Delta	47,332[5]	16,056,402
Eastern	42,456[5]	14,500,517
Flying Tiger[3]	11,456	....
Frontier	19,564[5]	1,455,299
Hawaiian	400	372,081
Helicopter (Chicago)	42[6]	48
Helicopter (New York)	139[6]	4,754
Helicopter (San Francisco)	208[6]	3,568
Hughes	7,649[5]	1,496,984
National	8,425	3,568,988
North Central	6,616[5]	1,029,154
Northwest	30,090[5]	6,934,394
Ozark	5,765	936,042
Pan American	23,309	1,691,610
Piedmont	3,909	1,061,021
Southern	9,089	852,547
Texas International	6,966[5]	580,269
Trans World	28,099	14,388,406
United	47,805[5]	26,225,950
Western	23,949[5]	6,427,394
Wright Airlines	92	4,988
TOTAL	434,110	131,469,463
Foreign or Overseas		
Airlift[3]	2,203	....
Air Micronesia	14,602	....
American	15,484[5]	2,491,630
Braniff	32,333	1,287,350
Continental	14,602	86,062
Delta	8,885	404,061
Eastern	19,519	3,668,917
Flying Tiger[3]	13,884	....
National	4,541	296,206
Northwest	23,680	2,536,886
Pan American	219,784*	113,171,140
Seaboard World[3]	13,521	....
Trans World	70,317*	6,568,501
Western	3,938	570,915
TOTAL	457,263	131,081,668

*Multi-Entity International

Carriers	Atl.	Latin Am.	Pac.	Total
Pan American	92,667	41,006	86,111	219,784
Trans World	56,186	....	14,131	70,317

[1] Scheduled service. [2] Excluding intra-Alaska carrier. [3] All-cargo carriers. [4] Includes Alaska-Washington State mileage. [5] Includes small amounts of transborder mileage. [6] Flight pattern.

Active Pilot Certificates Held, January 1, 1964–1976
Source: Federal Aviation Administration.

Year	Total*	Airline transport	Commercial	Private
1964	378,700	20,269	96,341	152,209
1965	431,041	21,572	108,428	175,574
1966	479,770	22,440	116,665	196,393
1967	548,757	23,917	131,539	222,427
1968	617,931	25,817	150,135	254,069
1969	691,695	28,607	164,458	281,728
1970	720,028	31,442	176,585	299,491
1971	732,729	34,430	186,821	303,779
1972	741,009	35,949	192,409	312,656
1973	750,869	37,714	196,228	321,413
1974	714,607	38,139	182,444	298,921
1975	733,728	41,002	192,425	305,848
1976	728,187	42,592	189,342	305,863

* Includes other pilot categories—helicopter, glider, and lighter-than-air (1974: 13,658); and students (1974: 180,795).

Helicopter Records
Source: National Aeronautic Association.

DISTANCE IN STRAIGHT LINE
International: 2,213.04 mi.
Robert G. Ferry (U. S.) in Hughes YOH-6A helicopter powered by Allison T-63-A-5 engine; from Culver City, Calif., to Daytona Beach, Fla., Apr. 6–7, 1966.

DISTANCE, CLOSED CIRCUIT
International: 1,739.96 mi.
Jack Schweibold (U. S.) in Hughes YOH-6A helicopter powered by Allison T-63-A-5 engine; Edwards Air Force Base, Calif., Mar. 26, 1966.

ALTITUDE
International: 40,820 ft.
Jean Boulet (France) in Alouette SA 315–001 "Lama" powered by Artouste IIIB 735–KW engine; Istres, France, June 21, 1972.

MAXIMUM SPEED
International: 220.89 mph.
Kurt F. Cannon (U.S.) in Sikorsky S-67 helicopter powered by 2 G.E. T-58 turbine engines; Stratford, Conn., Dec. 19, 1970.

SPEED FOR 100 KM. (CLOSED CIRCUIT)
International: 211.35 mph.
Boris Galitsky (U.S.S.R.) in MI-6 helicopter; Podmoskovnoe, Aug. 26, 1964.

SPEED FOR 500 KM. (CLOSED CIRCUIT)
International: 205.688 mph.
Galina Galitsky (U.S.S.R.) in A-10 helicopter powered by 2 TV2 engines; Ramenskoye, U.S.S.R., Jan. 8, 1975.

SPEED FOR 1,000 KM. (CLOSED CIRCUIT)
International: 186.64 mph.
Boris Galitsky (U.S.S.R.) in MI-6 helicopter powered by 2 TB-2BM turboprop engines; Touchino, U.S.S.R., Sept. 15, 1962.

SPEED FOR 2,000 KM. (CLOSED CIRCUIT)
International: 141.523 mph.
CWO Richard D. Szczepanski (U. S. Army) in Hughes YOH-6A helicopter powered by Allison T-63-A-5 engine; Edwards Air Force Base, Calif., Mar. 20, 1966.

Official World Airplane Records

Source: National Aeronautic Association.

Speed Over Measured Straightaway Course

Speed (mph)	Date	Type plane	Pilot	Place
314.32	Dec. 25, '34	Caudron	Raymond Delmotte (France)	Istres, France
352.39	Sept. 13, '35	Hughes Special	Howard Hughes (U.S.A.)	Santa Ana, Calif.
379.63	Nov. 11, '37	BF-113R	Herman Wurster (Germany)	Augsburg, Germany
469.22	Apr. 26, '39	ME-109R	Fritz Wendel (Germany)	Augsburg, Germany
606.25	Nov. 7, '45	Gloster Meteor IV	Gp. Capt. H. Wilson (Gr. Britain)	Herne Bay, England
615.78	Sept. 7, '46	Gloster Meteor	Gp. Capt. E. M. Donalson (Gr. Britain)	Littlehampton, Eng.
650.80	Aug. 25, '47	Douglas D-558	Maj. Marion Carl, USMC (U.S.A.)	Muroc AFB, Calif.
670.98	Sept. 15, '48	North American F-86A	Maj. R. L. Johnson (USAF)	Muroc AFB, Calif.
698.51	Nov. 19, '52	North American F-86D	Capt. James S. Nash (USAF)	Salton Sea, Calif.
755.14	Oct. 29, '53	North American YF	Lt. Col. F. K. Everest, Jr. (USAF)	Salton Sea, Calif.
822.27	Aug. 20, '55	North American F-100C	Col. Horace A. Hanes (U.S.A.)	Palmdale, Calif.
1,132.14	Mar. 10, '56	Fairey Delta 2	L. Peter Twiss, D.S.C. (Gr. Britain)	Ford-Chichester, Eng.
1,207.60	Dec. 12, '57	McDonnell F-101A	Maj. Adrian E. Drew (USAF)	Edwards, Calif.
1,404.09	May 16, '58	Lockheed F104	Capt. Walter W. Irwin (USAF)	Edwards, Calif.
1,483.85	Oct. 31, '50	Sukhoi S-66	G. Mossolov (U.S.S.R.)	U.S.S.R.
1,525.96	Dec. 15, '59	F-106A Delta Wing Monoplane	Maj. Joseph W. Rogers (USAF)	Edwards, Calif.
1,606.32	Nov. 22, '61	McDonnell F4H	Lt. Col. R. B. Robinson (USMC)	Edwards, Calif.
1,665.89	July 7, '62	E-166 Jet	G. Mossolov (U.S.S.R.)	U.S.S.R.
2,070.101	May 1, '65	Lockheed YF-12A Jet	Col. R. L. Stephens (USAF)	Edwards, Calif.

Fastest U.S. continental: Capt. Robert G. Sowers (USAF)—Convair B-58 "Hustler"—from Long Beach, Calif., to Kennedy International Airport, N.Y.—2,458.58 statute miles—2 hr., 0 min., 58.71 sec.—average speed, 1,214.65 mph—Mar. 5, 1962.

Distance, Straight Line

Distance (mi.)	Date	Crew	From	To
4,911.93	Sept. 27–29, '29	Costes & Bellonte (France)	Le Bourget, Fr.	Manchuria
5,011.35	July 28–30, '31	Russel N. Boardman, John Polando (U.S.A.)	New York	Istanbul, Turkey
5,656.93	Aug. 5–7, '33	Maurice Rossi, Paul Codos (France)	New York	Ryack, Syria
6,305.66	July 12–14, '37	Col. M. Gromov, Youmachev, Daniline (U.S.S.R.)	Moscow, U.S.S.R.	San Jacinto, Calif.
7,158.44	Nov. 5–7, '38	Sqd. Ldr. R. Kellett (Gr. Britain)	Ismailia, Egypt	Darwin, Australia
7,916.00	Nov. 19–20, '45	Col. C. S. Irvine & Lt. Col. G. R. Stanley (U.S.A.)	Guam	Washington, D. C.
11,235.60	Sept. 29–Oct. 1, '46	Comdr. Thomas D. Davies, Comdrs. Eugene P. Rankin, Walter S. Reid, Lt. Comdr. Ray A. Tabeling (USN)	Perth, Australia	Columbus, Ohio
12,532.28	Jan. 10–11, '62	Maj. Clyde Evely (USAF)	Kadena, Okinawa	Madrid, Spain

Longest light airplane distance: Maximillian A. Conrad—U. S. Piper Comanche 250, Lycoming 0-540-AIA5 (250 hp.), from Casablanca, Morocco, to Los Angeles, Calif., 7,668.48 mi.—June 2-4, 1959.

Distance, Closed Course

Distance (mi.)	Date	Crew	Place
6,587.441	Mar. 23–26, '32	Bossoutrot & Rossi (France)	Oran
7,239.588	May 13–15, '38	Comm. Fujita & Sgt. Maj. Takahashi (Japan)	Kisarasu, Japan
8,037.899	July 30–Aug. 1 '39	Angelo Tondi, Roberto Dagasso, Ferrucio Vignoli (Italy)	Rome, Italy
8,854.308	Aug. 1–2, '47	Lt. Col. O. F. Lassiter (U.S.A.) Capt. W. J. Valentine (U.S.A.)	Tampa, Fla.
10,078.84	Dec. 13–14, '60	Lt. Col. J. R. Grissom (USAF)	Edwards, Calif.
11,336.92	June 6–7, '62	Capt. William Stevenson (USAF)	Seymour-Johnson, N.C.

Altitude

Height (ft.)	Date	Crew	Place
44,819	Sept. 28, '33	G. Lemoine (France)	Villacoublay, France
47,352	April 11, '34	Comdr. Renato Donati (Italy)	Rome, Italy
49,944	Sept. 28, '36	Sqd. Ldr. F. R. D. Swain (Gr. Britain)	South Farnborough, England
53,937	June 30, '37	Fl. Lt. M. J. Adam (Gr. Britain)	Farnborough, Eng.
56,046	Oct. 22, '38	Col. Mario Pezzi (Italy)	Montecelio
59,445*	Mar. 23, '48	John Cunningham (Gr. Britain)	Hatfield, England
63,668*	May 4, '53	Walter F. Gibb (Gr. Britain)	Bristol, England
65,889*	Aug. 29, '55	Walter F. Gibb (Gr. Britain)	Bristol, England
70,308*	Aug. 28, '57	Michael Randrup (Gr. Britain)	Luton, England
91,243*	May 7, '58	Maj. H. C. Johnson (USAF)	Palmdale, Calif.

(Table continued on next page)

Altitude (continued)

Height (ft.)	Date	Crew	Place
103,389*	Nov. 14, '59	Capt. Joe B. Jordan (USAF)	Edwards, Calif.
314,750†	July 17, '62	Maj. Robert M. White (USAF)	Edwards, Calif.
118,898	July 25, 1973	Alexander Fedotov (U.S.S.R.)	U.S.S.R.

* Jet-propelled aircraft. † X-15-1 rocket plane.

U. S. Airlines Transport Planes

Source: Aviation Week & Space Technology.

Manufacturer	Type	Number of passengers	Maximum speed, mph	Maximum weight, lbs.	Wingspan	Overall length
4-engine						
Boeing	707-120	100–181	600	258,000	130′9″	145′1″
Boeing	707-120B	100–181	600+	258,000	130′9″	145′1″
Boeing	707-320/Intercontinental	108–189	600+	316,000	142′4″	152′9″
Boeing	707-320B/Intercontinental	189	600+	336,000	145′8″	152′9″
Boeing	707-320C/Intercontinental	189	600+	336,000	145′8″	152′9″
Boeing	707-420/Intercontinental	108–189	600+	316,000	142′4″	152′9″
Boeing	720	88–167	600	230,000	130′9″	136′7″
Boeing	720B	167	600+	235,000	130′9″	136′7″
Boeing	747-100/Superjet	374–500	640	713,000	195′7″	231′3″
Boeing	747-200B/Superjet	374–500	640	778,000	195′7″	231′3″
Boeing	747-200C/Superjet	374–500	640	778,000	195′7″	231′3″
Boeing	747-SR	500	640	523,000	195′7″	231′3″
Boeing	747-SP	321	640	663,000	195′7″	176′7″
McDonnell Douglas	DC-8/Series 10	116–176	580	273,000	142′3″	150′5″
McDonnell Douglas	DC-8/Series 20	116–176	600	276,000	142′3″	150′5″
McDonnell Douglas	DC-8/Series 30	116–176	600	315,000	142′3″	150′5″
McDonnell Douglas	DC-8/Series 40	116–176	600	315,000	142′3″	150′5″
McDonnell Douglas	DC-8/Series 50	116–189	600	325,000	142′3″	150′5″
McDonnell Douglas	DC-8/Super 61	259	600	325,000	142′3″	187′4″
McDonnell Douglas	DC-8/Super 62	189	600	335,000	148′4″	157′4″
McDonnell Douglas	DC-8/Super 63	259	600	350,000	148′4″	187′4″
General Dynamics	880	88	615	185,000	120′0″	129′4″
General Dynamics	880M	88	615	193,500	120′0″	129′4″
General Dynamics	990/Coronado	96–146	621	255,000	120′0″	139′2″
Lockheed	188A/Electra	66–98	450	113,000	99′0″	104′5″
3-engine						
Boeing	727-100	70–131	600+	170,000	108′0″	133′1″
Boeing	727-200/Advanced	120–189	600+	191,500	108′0″	153′1″
McDonnell Douglas	DC-10/Series 10	250–380	600+	440,000	155′3″	182′3″
McDonnell Douglas	DC-10/Series 30	250–380	600+	565,000	165′3″	181′6″
McDonnell Douglas	DC-10/Series 40	250–380	600+	555,000	165′3″	182′3″
Lockheed	L-1011-I/TriStar	250–400	620	430,000	155′3″	177′7″
Lockheed	L-1011-100/TriStar	250–400	620	466,000	155′3″	177′7″
Lockheed	L-1011-200/TriStar	250–400	620	466,000	155′3″	177′7″
Lockheed	L-1011-250/TriStar	250–400	620	490,000	155′3″	177′7″
Lockheed	L-1011-500/TriStar	230–300	620	496,000	155′3″	164′2″
2-engine						
Beech	B-99	15	285	10,900	45′8″	44′6″
Boeing	737-100	112	586	111,000	93′0″	94′0″
Boeing	737-200/Advanced	115–130	586	117,500	93′0″	100′0″
Fairchild	F-27/Friendship	40–48	275	40,500	95′2″	77′2″
Fairchild	F-27A/Friendship	40–48	300	42,000	95′2″	77′2″
Fairchild	F-27B/Friendship	40–48	275	40,500	95′2″	77′2″
Fairchild	F-27J/Friendship	40–48	300	42,000	95′2″	77′2″
Fairchild	FH-227	44–52	300	43,500	95′2″	83′1″
Fairchild	FH-227B	44–52	300	45,500	95′2″	83′1″
Fairchild	FH-227C	44–52	300	43,500	95′2″	83′1″
Fairchild	FH-227D	44–52	300	45,500	95′2″	83′1″
Fairchild	FH-227E	44–52	300	43,500	95′2″	83′1″
General Dynamics	600	40–46	317	46,200	91′8″	74′8″
General Dynamics	640/S. Metropolitan	44–59	312	55,000	105′3″	81′5″
General Dynamics	580	53	. . .	54,600	105′3″	81′5″
McDonnell Douglas	DC-9/Series 10	90	586	90,700	89′4″	104′4″
McDonnell Douglas	DC-9/Series 20	56–90	586	98,000	93′3″	104′4″
McDonnell Douglas	DC-9/Series 30	115	586	121,000	93′3″	119′3″
McDonnell Douglas	DC-9/Series 40	125	586	121,000	93′3″	125′6″
McDonnell Douglas	DC-9/Series 50	139	586	121,000	93′3″	133′5″

Important American Aircraft Types (U.S. Air Force)

Source: U. S. Air Force.

Abbreviations: AiR—Garrett AiResearch; All—Detroit Diesel Allison Div. of General Motors; Con—Continental; GD—General Dynamics; GE—General Electric; Lyc—Lycoming; RI—Rockwell International; P&W—Pratt & Whitney; PWACL—Pratt & Whitney Aircraft of Canada, Ltd; Wr—Curtiss Wright; kt—knots.

Type	Manufacturer	Popular Name	Power Plant	Crew	Wing-span, ft/in.	Length ft/in.	Height ft/in.	Gross weight, lbs	Speed, mph
ATTACK									
A-7D	Vought Corp.	Corsair 2	1 All TF41-A-1	1	38.7	46.1	16.0	42,000	620
A-10	Fairchild Rep.	....	2 GE TF34-GE-100	1	57.5	53.3	14.6	46,038	400 kt
A-37B	Cessna	Dragonfly	2 GE J85-GE-17A	1	35.8	29.3	8.9	14,000	425 kt
BOMBERS									
B-1	RI/B-1 Division	....	4 GE F101-GE-F100	4	137.0[3]	150.0	34.0	388,000	Mach 2+
B-52G	Boeing	Stratofortress	8 P&W J57-P-43W	6	185.0	157.6	40.8	488,000	650
B-52H	Boeing	Stratofortress	8 P&W TF33-P-3	6	185.0	156.0	40.8	488,000	650
FB-111A	GD/Ft. Worth	....	2 P&W TF30-P-7	2	70.0[4]	73.6	17.0	114,000	Mach 2+
FIGHTERS									
F-4E	McDonnell Douglas	Phantom 2	2 GE J79-GE-17	2	38.6	63.0	16.5	58,000	Mach 2.2
F-15A	McDonnell Douglas	Eagle	2 P&W F100-PW-100	1	42.8	63.8	18.6	40,000	Mach 2.5
F-16	GD/Ft. Worth	....	1 P&W F100-PW-100	1	31.0	47.6	16.4	21,200	Mach 2
F-106A	GD/Convair	Delta Dart	1 P&W J75-P-17	1	38.3	70.8	20.3	36,000	Mach 2
F-111F	GD/Ft. Worth	....	2 P&W TF30-P-100	2	63.0[5]	73.6	17.0	100,000	Mach 2.5
YF-17	Northrop	....	2 GE YJ101-GE-100	1	35.0	56.0	14.6	23,000	Mach 2
RECONNAISSANCE									
RF-4C	McDonnell Douglas	Phantom 2	2 GE J79-GE-15	2	38.4	62.9	16.5	58,000	Mach 2.2
RWB-57F	GD/Ft. Worth	Canberra	2 P&W TF33-P-11	2	122.0	69.0	19.0	50,000	...
SR-71	Lockheed/Calif.	....	2 P&W J58	1	55.6	107.4	18.5	...	Mach 3+
U/WU-2	Lockheed/Calif.	....	1 P&W J75	1-2	80.0	49.6	13.0	17,000	...
OBSERVATION									
O-2A	Cessna	....	2 Con IO-360-D	1	38.0	29.9	9.4	4,850	157 kt
OV-10A[1]	RI/Columbus	Bronco	2 A&R T76-G-416/417	2	40.0	41.7	15.1	14,466	281
EARLY WARNING									
E-3A	Boeing	AWACS	4 P&W TF33-P-100A	17	145.9	153.0	42.0	325,000	...
E-4A/B	Boeing	....	4 P&W JT9D	3	195.7	231.3	63.5	775,000	...
CARGO/TRANSPORT									
C-5A	Lockheed/Georgia	Galaxy	4 GE TF39	6	222.8	247.8	65.1	769,000	550
C-7A	DH/Canada	Caribou	2 P&W R2000-7M2	3	95.7	72.6	31.8	28,500	STOL
C-9A	McDonnell Douglas	Nightingale	2 P&W JT8D-9	2-7	93.3	119.3	27.5	108,000	570
C-12A[2]	Beech	....	2 PWACL PT6A-38	2	54.5	43.8	15.4	12,500	260 kt
C-130E	Lockheed/Georgia	Hercules	4 All T56-A-7	4	132.6	99.5	38.4	155,000	360
C-131E	GD/Convair	....	2 P&W R2800-103W	2	105.3	81.5	28.2	52,000	310
C-140A	Lockheed/Georgia	Jetstar	4 P&W J60-P-5	5	54.4	60.4	20.4	40,921	525
C-141A	Lockheed/Georgia	Starlifter	4 P&W TF33-P-7	3-8	160.7	145.0	39.3	325,000	505
HC-130H	Lockheed/Georgia	Hercules	4 All T56-A-15	10	132.6	100.5	38.4	155,000	...
KC-135A	Boeing	Stratotanker	4 P&W J57-P-59W	4	130.9	136.3	38.4	297,000	530
VC-6B	Beech	....	2 PWACL PT6A-20	1-2	50.2	35.5	14.7	9,650	280
VC-137C	Boeing	....	4 P&W JT3D-3B	4	145.9	152.9	42.5	328,000	Mach 0.84
TC-14	Boeing	....	2 GE CF6-50	2	129.0	131.0	48.0	....	460
YC-15	McDonnell Douglas	....	4 P&W JT8D-17	2	110.3	124.3	43.3	216,680	460
TRAINERS									
T-28D	RI/Columbus	Trojan	1 Wr R1820-86A	2	40.6	32.9	12.7	12,104	350
T-29D	GD/Convair	....	2 P&W R2800-97	2	91.8	74.7	27.3	44,000	230
T-33A	Lockheed/Calif.	T-Bird	1 All J33-A-35	2	40.5	37.7	11.7	9,600	580
T-37B	Cessna	Tweet	2 CAE J69-T-25	2	33.8	29.3	9.2	6,618	425
T-38A	Northrop	Talon	2 GE J85-5	2	25.3	46.4	12.1	12,054	Mach 1.2
T-39A	RI/General Aviation	Sabreliner	2 P&W J60-P-3	2	44.5	43.8	15.9	18,650	Mach 0.75
T-41A/D	Cessna	....	1 Con IO-360H-1	2	36.2	26.5	8.9	2,550	142
T-43A	Boeing	....	2 P&W JT8D-9	2	93.0	100.0	37.0	109,000	...
UTILITY									
AU-23A	Fairchild	Peacemaker	1 AiR TPE 331-1-101F	1-3	49.7	36.8	12.3	6,100	174
AU-24A	Helio/Gen. Aircraft	Stallion	1 PWACL PT6A-27	1-3	41.0	39.9	9.3	6,300	216
U-4B	RI/Gen. Aviation	Aero Commander	2 Lyc GSO-480-A1A6	1	44.0	34.2	14.5	7,000	244
U-5A	Helio/Gen. Aircraft	H-500 Twin	2 Lyc O-540	1	41.0	32.0	8.8	5,400	185
U-10A/D	Helio/Gen. Aircraft	Courier	1 Lyc GO-480-G1D6	1	39.0	31.0	8.8	3,850	167

[1] Air Force/Marines. [2] Air Force/Army. [3] Wing extended. [4] Wing extended; 34 ft fully swept. [5] Wing extended; 31.11 ft fully swept.

Passenger Traffic of Leading U.S. Airports, 1975

Source: Airport Operators Council International.

Airport	Passengers[1]	Airport	Passengers[1]
O'Hare; Chicago, Ill.	37.3	Hopkins; Cleveland, Ohio	5.6
Hartsfield International; Atlanta, Ga.	25.3	International; Tampa, Fla.	5.2
International; Los Angeles, Calif.	19.5	P.R. International; San Juan, P.R.	5.0
Kennedy; New York City	19.5	International; San Diego, Calif.	4.5
International; San Francisco, Calif.	16.4	International; New Orleans, La.	4.4
LaGuardia; New York City	13.2	Memphis, Tenn.	4.4
International; Miami, Fla.	12.1	International; Kansas City, Mo.	4.3
Stapleton International; Denver, Colo.	12.0	Sky Harbor International; Phoenix, Ariz.	4.0
National; Washington, D.C.	11.2	Hollywood International; Ft. Lauderdale, Fla.	3.7
Logan; Boston, Mass.	10.5	Jetport at McCoy; Orlando, Fla.	3.3
International; Honolulu	10.0	International; Portland, Ore.	3.1
Love; Dallas, Tex.	8.3	International; Greater Buffalo, N.Y.[2]	2.8
International; Philadelphia, Pa.	7.5	Baltimore–Washington	2.8
Metro Wayne; Detroit, Mich.	7.4	Cincinnati, Ohio	2.6
International; St. Louis, Mo.	6.4	Weir Cook Municipal; Indianapolis, Ind.	2.6
International; Newark, N.J.	6.3	Dulles; Washington, D.C.	2.4
Intercontinental; Houston, Tex.	6.1	San Jose, Calif.	2.3
Seattle-Tacoma; Seattle, Wash.	6.1	Milwaukee, Wis.	2.2

[1] Arrivals and departures, in millions.　[2] Charter/supplemental carriers not included.

Airline Hijackings

World Airplane Hijackings and Attempts, 1930–75[1]

Source: Federal Aviation Administration.

Years	Place of flight origin		Total
	U.S.	Foreign	
1930–67	12	67	79
1968	22	13	35
1969	40	47	87
1970	27	56	83
1971	27	31	58
1972	31	31	62
1973	2	20	22
1974	7	19	26
1975	12	13	25
Total	180	297	477

[1] Through December 31, 1975.

Disposition of Hijackers of Aircraft in U.S. Commerce, 1930–75[1]

Source: Federal Aviation Administration.

Disposition of Case	Number
Convictions[2]	79
United States	[71]
Foreign	[8]
Acquittals	3
Committed to mental institution	20
Cases dismissed	3
No prosecution	2
Killed or Suicide	16
Cases pending	20
Fugitives[3]	101
Total	244

[1] Through December 31, 1975. [2] Foreign convictions include 1 in Mexico, 1 in Lebanon, 1 in Italy, 2 in Argentina and 3 in Cuba. [3] Includes a number of passive companions indicted along with hijackers.

Ransom Demands and Airline Hijackings[1]

Twenty-six commercial airline hijacking ransoms averaging over $500,000 each have been made since the first such hijacking on June 4, 1970. In most cases the airline paid the ransom but later recovered the money when the hijacker was captured, killed, or surrendered. In only one case was the ransom never recovered.

[1] As of December 31, 1975.

Average Hours and Earnings in Aircraft Industries

Source: Federal Aviation Administration.

Hours and Earnings	1950	1955	1960	1965	1970	1972	1973	1974
Average weekly hours								
Aircraft industries	41.4	41.4	40.6	41.2	41.0	41.7	41.1	39.4
Engines and parts industries	41.7	40.6	41.1	42.1	40.5	41.1	41.8	41.2
Average weekly earnings						$198		
Aircraft industries	$67	$90	$110	$130	$171	$193	$211	$219
Engines and parts industries	$69	$86	$112	$133	$166	$193	$211	$224
Average hourly earnings								
Aircraft industries	$1.62	$2.17	$2.71	$3.16	$4.17	$4.74	$5.13	$5.57
Engines and parts industries	$1.66	$2.13	$2.73	$3.17	$4.10	$4.70	$5.05	$5.43

NOTE: Figures are latest available.

TRAVEL DIRECTORY

This Directory presents a comprehensive listing of hundreds of sources which offer information to travelers and vacationists. Following the articles on New York City and Washington, D. C., there is a guide to where you may obtain travel information.

SIGHTSEEING IN NEW YORK CITY

The visitor coming to New York City for the first time should write in advance to the New York Convention and Visitors Bureau,* 90 East 42nd Street, New York City 10017, for the following five booklets:

"**Hotels in New York City.**" Lists hotels and motels in and near the city, with addresses and telephone numbers, and minimum and maximum room prices.

"**Visitors Guide and Map of New York.**" Includes a detailed map of Manhattan. Lists principal landmarks; sightseeing attractions with days and hours open to the public and admission fees where applicable for all boroughs; sightseeing boat excursions (Circle Line tours around Manhattan); and bus excursions, parks and beaches.

"**Quarterly Calendar of Events.**" A compendium of events ranging from sports events and concerts to activities for children.

"**Restaurant Guide.**" Lists restaurants according to geographical areas with their minimum prices for lunch and dinner, specialties of the house, and those with music for listening, dancing or entertainment.

"**Visitors Shopping Guide to New York City.**" Lists department stores, specialty shops, and special services including limousines, theater brokers, sightseeing, etc. These are listed according to types of merchandise or category of service.

The above booklets are also available at the city-run Hospitality and Information Center in Times Square at 43rd Street.

Transportation. Subways and buses offer the fastest and least expensive service. Most subway lines run north and south. The bus lines run north and south along the principal avenues as well as east and west on the main crosstown streets (check out nighttime, weekend and shopping bus ticket rates). Taxicabs are plentiful in the midtown area.

SIGHTSEEING

Manhattan can arbitrarily be divided into three areas: **downtown,** the section below 23rd Street; **midtown,** between 23rd and 59th Streets; and **uptown,** everything north of 59th Street.

DOWNTOWN. This is the city's financial center with Wall Street and the stock exchanges. Both have visitors' galleries and are well worth a visit. Located in this area are the newest skyscraper, the 1,350-ft twin-tower World Trade Center, and many historic landmarks, such as the Fraunces Tavern where Washington bade farewell to his

officers, Federal Hall National Memorial, where he took the oath of office as first President; Trinity Church; and Theodore Roosevelt's birthplace, the Theodore Roosevelt House.

Museums. These include the Fire Department Museum, South Street Seaport Museum and the Old Merchant's House.

An integral part of downtown Manhattan are the many famous neighborhoods: Gramercy Park, Chinatown, Little Italy, the Lower East Side, the Bowery, and Greenwich Village, the site of Washington Square and New York University.

MIDTOWN. This is the part of the city that is best known to most visitors. Here are the famous department stores and specialty shops, the theaters, leading hotels, Grand Central Terminal, Madison Square Garden, Pennsylvania Station, the New York Public Library and the New York Coliseum, the city's largest exhibition hall, and skyscrapers such as the Empire State, Rockefeller Center, Chrysler, R.C.A., and the Pan American building. Also, many restaurants offering every conceivable type of cooking—from American through French and Japanese to Scandinavian and Turkish.

Museums. These include the Museum of Modern Art, Museum of Primitive Art, New York Cultural Center, Museum of American Folk Arts, National Art Museum of Sport, N.Y. Jazz Museum and the Pierpont Morgan Library.

Important places of worship in the midtown area are St. Patrick's Roman Catholic Cathedral, St. Thomas Protestant Episcopal Church and the Little Church Around the Corner (the Protestant Episcopal Church of the Transfiguration). On the East River is the United Nations headquarters, with its towering glass Secretariat Building and domed General Assembly Building. Tours are offered daily.

UPTOWN. Uptown Manhattan is truly the place for the museum devotee. Located in this area are the Metropolitan Museum of Art, the spiral-shaped Guggenheim Museum designed by the late Frank Lloyd Wright, the Frick Collection, the Whitney Museum of American Art, the New York Historical Society, the Jewish Museum, the Hispanic Society of America, the Cloisters, the Museum of the American Indian, the Museum of the City of New York, and the American Museum of Natural History with its Hayden Planetarium.

Also in the uptown Manhattan area is the Lincoln Center for the Performing Arts, which includes the Metropolitan Opera House, Avery Fisher Hall, Alice Tully Hall, the Vivian Beaumont theater and the New York State Theater. Important places of worship in the uptown area

*The Bureau, a civic, nonprofit organization, also issues "20 Free Things to Do," "18 Only-in-New York Sights" and separate folders on each of the other boroughs: Brooklyn, Queens, Staten Island and The Bronx.

are the Protestant Episcopal Cathedral of St. John the Divine, Riverside Church, and Temple Emanu-El. Historic landmarks are the Jumel Mansion (1765), Hamilton Grange (1802), and the Dyckman House (1783).

Here also are the Lincoln Center campus of Fordham University, Columbia University, Barnard College, Hunter College, and City College of New York.

Central Park is located right in the center of this busy island-city.

Getting tickets to Broadway hit shows is a problem that plagues New York residents as much as it does visitors from out of town. The best procedure for the latter group is to write well in advance for tickets, giving alternate choices for both dates and locations of seats. The names and addresses of the various theaters at which the plays or musicals are being presented can be obtained from one of New York's daily newspapers or *The New Yorker* or *Cue* magazine. If tickets are not purchased in advance, they may in many cases be obtained for most productions (except smash hits) at the box office or at a ticket agency, which charges a fee for its services. A boon to the budget theater goer is the new *Times Square Ticket Center* at Broadway and 47th Street. Beginning at 3 p.m. for evening performances and 12 noon for matinees, half-price tickets to Broadway and off-Broadway shows (including ballet and opera) are sold (first-come, first-served) on the day of performance.

A municipal ferry connects Manhattan with Staten Island. The fare is twenty-five cents. During the hot summer months, it offers a pleasant, cool ride and a view of the mid- and downtown Manhattan skyline. These ferries leave from South Ferry at the southern tip of Manhattan. The departure point for the Statue of Liberty ferries is Battery Park. Circle Line Sightseeing Yachts that make trips around the island of Manhattan sail from Pier 83 at the foot of West 43rd St., and the Hudson River Day Line offers excursions to Bear Mountain, West Point and Poughkeepsie from Pier 81 at West 41st St. There are many sightseeing bus and helicopter trips around the island.

Manhattan is only one of New York City's five boroughs for sightseeing. In *Brooklyn* are Coney Island, one of the world's famous playgrounds, and the popular Aquarium, with its penguins, walruses, and other types of aquatic life; the Prospect Park Zoo and Children's Farmyard; Brooklyn Botanic Garden, and the Brooklyn Museum. In the *Bronx* are the Hall of Fame for Great Americans; the Bronx Zoo, where many animals are separated from the public only by moats; Yankee Stadium; and the famous New York Botanical Gardens. Historic landmarks located here are Poe Cottage, Bartow Mansion and Van Cortlandt Mansion. In *Queens* are Shea Stadium, Aqueduct Racetrack, New York City Science Museum and the Queens Zoo. Historic landmarks are the Bowne House (1661), Old Quaker Meeting House (1694) and King Mansion (1752). *Staten Island* boasts of a Tibetan temple and museum and of the country's oldest elementary school building—Voorlezers House at the Richmondtown Restoration.

SIGHTSEEING IN WASHINGTON, D. C.

The visitor to the nation's capital should write to the Washington Area Convention and Visitors Bureau, 1129 20th Street, N.W., Washington, D.C. 20036 for a copy of the tourist guide. This booklet includes a detailed map of downtown Washington with a list of what to see and when to see it and many hints on how to plan a trip to Washington and how to enjoy it while you're there. In addition there are pamphlets on tours and limousine service. Washington has excellent commercial sightseeing companies. They offer the best opportunity to see the major attractions in a short period of time. There are many boat excursions on the Potomac River. Rates and hours of admission are given, and all federal properties are free.

SIGHTSEEING

Washington was planned with the Capitol itself as the centerpiece. The Capitol is situated at the intersection of East Capitol Street, South Capitol Street, North Capitol Street and the Mall (in lieu of a "west" Capitol). The three streets and the Mall split the city into quadrants: Northeast, Northwest, Southeast, Southwest.

All numbered streets run north and south. Lettered streets run east and west. Streets with state names, such as Rhode Island and Connecticut, run diagonally throughout the city (don't be confused if you see "I" Street written "Eye" Street).

The actual geographic center of Washington's original 10-mile square area is the White House at 1600 Pennsylvania Avenue, N.W. The famed Mall traverses from the Capitol to the Potomac River, where you will find the Constitution Gardens, a new 42-acre park featuring a 6-acre lake and the Reflecting Pool. Dominating the skyline is the 555-foot-high Washington Monument, and to the south the Lincoln Memorial.

To the south of this are the Tidal Basin, the Japanese cherry trees which are the focal point of an annual spring festival and the Jefferson Memorial.

To the southwest of the White House and overlooking the Potomac River is the John F. Kennedy Center for the Performing Arts, and to the northwest is Explorers Hall of the National Geographic Society, and the U.S. Naval Observatory.

Another area of interest will be found roughly midway between the White House and the Capitol. This includes Ford's Theatre and Lincoln Museum, where Abraham Lincoln was shot, and the Peterson House across the street where he died; the Federal Bureau of Investigation; the Smithsonian Institution, which consists of the National Air and Space Museum, the Arts and Industries

Building, the Freer Gallery of Art, the Hirshhorn Museum and Sculpture Garden, the Museum of History and Technology, the Museum of Natural History, the National Collection of Fine Arts, the National Portrait Gallery and the Renwick Gallery; and the National Archives with its historical documents, including the original copy of the Declaration of Independence. Nearby toward the Capitol is the National Gallery of Art.

One of the most popular areas of interest centers on the Capitol, 751 feet long, 382 feet wide and containing 533 rooms. The central part of the building contains the Rotunda, the Statuary Hall and the old Supreme Court chamber. The two wings, constructed of marble, house the Senate and the House of Representatives. During sessions, the galleries in the Senate and House chambers are open to visitors.

In the Capitol area are the various Senate and House office buildings, and across the Capitol's east plaza, where Presidential inaugurations are held, are the Library of Congress and the Supreme Court. Just in back of these is the Folger Shakespeare Library.

Attractions in the nation's capital are not confined to historic sites. There are the National Zoological Park, situated in a setting of the 1,700-acre Rock Creek Park; the suburb of Georgetown, west of Rock Creek Park; the National Arboretum and the Decatur House. Close by in Vienna, Va., is the Wolf Trap Farm Park for the Performing Arts. Most embassies and legations are located in the District of Columbia.

Transportation. Bus lines crisscross the city and extend into the nearby Maryland and Virginia suburbs. Service is available to many points of interest. Taxicabs are available at moderate rates, especially for group riding. On March 28, 1976, a 4.6-mile segment of the projected 100-mile Metro subway system opened to the public, with other segments to be opened in 1977.

Churches. There are approximately 1,400 churches and synagogues serving 63 denominations. The most notable are the Washington Cathedral, the National Shrine of the Immaculate Conception; and the Greek Orthodox Church of St. Sophia. It has the nation's only mosque, the Islamic Center. The Mormon Temple is the largest temple of its kind in the world. Tourists are welcome to tour the grounds, but cannot enter the sanctuary.

Shopping. Major department stores and smaller specialty shops are located in the downtown area. Three of the largest are Garfinkel's, the Hecht Co., and Woodward & Lathrop. Nearby Georgetown is a charming, historic section jammed with specialty shops, boutiques and private art galleries.

Many historic landmarks and other points of interest lie outside Washington, principally in nearby Virginia. Just across the Potomac is the Arlington National Cemetery; Tomb of the Unknowns; Custis-Lee Mansion (now known as Arlington House); the Iwo Jima memorial for the Marine Corps valor in the Pacific during World War II. Also on the Virginia side is the Pentagon, housing the country's chief defense offices. Mount Vernon and the tombs of George and Martha Washington can be reached by an easy 16-mile drive on the George Washington Parkway through historic Alexandria.

(For additional information on Washington, D.C. *see* page 660.)

OFFICIAL STATE TOURIST AGENCIES

Virtually every state or territory of the United States has an official agency for the distribution of travel and vacation information which will be sent on request.

ALABAMA: Bureau of Publicity and Information, State Capitol, Montgomery 36130.

ALASKA: Alaska Division of Tourism, Department of Commerce and Economic Development, Pouch E, Juneau 99811.

ARIZONA: Arizona State Office of Economic Planning and Development, 1700 W. Washington, Suite No. 505, Phoenix 85007.

ARKANSAS: Department of Parks and Tourism, Suite 149, State Capitol, Little Rock 72201.

COLORADO: Travel Marketing Section, Division of Commerce and Development, 602 State Capitol Annex, Denver 80203.

CONNECTICUT: Connecticut Department of Commerce, 210 Washington St., Hartford 06106.

DELAWARE: Delaware State Visitors Service, Division of Economic Development, 630 State College Road, Dover 19901.

DISTRICT OF COLUMBIA: Washington Area Convention and Visitors Bureau, 1129 20th St., NW, Washington 20036.

FLORIDA: Florida News Bureau, Florida Department of Commerce, 107 W. Gaines St., Tallahassee 32304.

GEORGIA: Tourist Division, Georgia Bureau of Industry & Trade, P.O. Box 38097, Atlanta 30334.

HAWAII: Hawaii Visitors Bureau, 609 Fifth Ave., New York City 10017; Hawaii Visitors Bureau, 2270 Kalakaua Ave., Honolulu 96815.

IDAHO: Division of Tourism and Industrial Development, Room 108, State House, Boise 83720.

ILLINOIS: Office of Tourism, Dept. of Business and Economic Development, 222 South College, Springfield 62706.

INDIANA: Department of Natural Resources, Room 612, State Office Building, Indianapolis 46204.

IOWA: Iowa Development Commission, Travel Development Division, 250 Jewett Building, Des Moines 50309.

KANSAS: Travel Division, Kansas Department of Economic Development, 503 Kansas Ave., 6th Floor, Topeka 66603.

KENTUCKY: Department of Public Information, Advertising and Travel Promotion, Capitol Annex Building, Frankfort 40601.

LOUISIANA: Louisiana Tourist Development Commission, P.O. Box 44291, Capitol Station, Baton Rouge 70804.

MAINE: Maine Publicity Bureau, Gateway Circle, Portland 04102.

MARYLAND: Division of Tourist Development, Md. Department of Economic and Community Development, 1748 Forest Dr., Annapolis 21401.

MASSACHUSETTS: Division of Tourism, Bureau of Vacation Travel, Massachusetts Dept. of Commerce and Development, 100 Cambridge St., Boston 02202.

MICHIGAN: Michigan Travel Commission, 300 S. Capitol Ave., Suite 102, Lansing 48913.

MINNESOTA: Research Division, Minnesota Department of Economic Development, 480 Cedar St., St. Paul 55101.

MISSISSIPPI: Travel & Tourism, Mississippi A&I Board, P.O. Box 849, 1504 Walter Sillers Building, Jackson 39201.

MISSOURI: Missouri Division of Commerce and Industrial Development, Box 118, Jefferson City 65101.

MONTANA: Travel Promotion Unit, Department of Highways, Helena 59601.

NEBRASKA: Nebraskaland Magazine, 2200 North 33rd St., P.O. Box 30370, Lincoln 68503.

NEVADA: Department of Economic Development, State Capitol Building, Carson City 89710.

NEW HAMPSHIRE: New Hampshire Division of Economic Development, P.O. Box 856, Concord 03301.

NEW JERSEY: New Jersey Office of Tourism and Promotion, Department of Labor and Industry, P.O. Box 400, Trenton 08625.

NEW MEXICO: Tourist Division, New Mexico Department of Development, 113 Washington Ave., Santa Fe 87503.

NEW YORK: Travel Bureau, New York State Department of Commerce, 99 Washington Ave., Albany 12245.

NORTH CAROLINA: Travel Development Section, Department of Natural and Economic Resources, Raleigh 27611.

NORTH DAKOTA: Travel Department, State Highway Bldg., Bismarck 58505.

OHIO: Ohio Department of Economic and Community Development, Box 1001, Columbus 43216.

OKLAHOMA: Department of Tourism and Recreation, 500 Will Rogers Memorial Building, Oklahoma City 73105.

OREGON: Travel Information Section, Oregon State Highway Division, 101 Highway Building, Salem 97310.

PENNSYLVANIA: Travel Development Bureau, Pennsylvania Dept. of Commerce, 431 South Office Bldg., Harrisburg 17120.

PUERTO RICO: Tourism Development Company, G.P.O. Box BN, San Juan 00936; Commonwealth of Puerto Rico, Tourism Development Company, 1290 Ave. of the Americas, New York City 10019.

RHODE ISLAND: Rhode Island Department of Economic Development, 1 Weybosset Hill, Providence 02903.

SOUTH CAROLINA: Department of Parks, Recreation and Tourism, P.O. Box 71, Inquiry Section, Columbia 29201.

SOUTH DAKOTA: Division of Tourism Development, Joe Foss Building, Pierre 57501.

TENNESSEE: Department of Tourist Development, 505 Fessler's Lane, Nashville 37210.

TEXAS: State Department of Highways & Public Transportation, Travel and Information Division, P.O. Box 5064, Austin 78763.

UTAH: Utah Travel Council, Council Hall, Capitol Hill, Salt Lake City 84114,

VERMONT: Information/Travel Division, Agency of Development and Community Affairs, 61 Elm Street, Montpelier 05602.

VIRGIN ISLANDS OF U. S.: Visitors Bureau, Department of Commerce, P.O. Box 1692, St. Thomas 00801; and U.S. Virgin Islands Division of Tourism, 10 Rockefeller Plaza, NYC 10020; 1150 17th St., NW, Washington, D.C. 20036; 100 Biscayne Blvd., Miami, Fla. 33132; 307 N. Michigan Ave., Chicago 60601.

VIRGINIA: Virginia State Travel Service, 6 North Sixth St., Richmond 23219.

WASHINGTON: Travel Development Division, Department of Commerce and Economic Development, General Administration Building, Olympia 98504.

WEST VIRGINIA: Travel Development Division, West Virginia Department of Commerce, Building No. 6, 1900 Washington St., Charleston 25305.

WISCONSIN: Division of Tourism, 123 W. Washington Ave., Madison 53702.

WYOMING: Wyoming Travel Commission, I-25 at Etchepare Circle, Cheyenne 82002.

REGIONAL INFORMATION CENTERS

In most cities which have a large tourist or vacation trade, information can frequently be obtained from the local Chamber of Commerce. In addition, there are also regional information centers, among which are the following:

East and South

Berkshire Hills Conference, 107 South St., Pittsfield, Mass. 01201.

Cape Cod Chamber of Commerce, Hyannis, Mass. 02601.

Connecticut Department of Commerce, 210 Washington St., Hartford, Conn. 06106.

Finger Lakes Association, 309 Lake St., Penn Yan, N.Y. 14527.

Lakes Region Association, Box 300-A, Wolfeboro, New Hampshire 03894.

Merrimack Valley Region Association, P.O. Box 634, Manchester, N.H. 03105.

Monadnock Region Association, Box 269, Peterborough, N. H. 03458.

New England Vacation Center, 1268 Ave. of the Americas, New York City 10020.

New Hampshire Seacoast Regional Development Association, P.O. Box 476, 14 Front St., Exeter, N. H. 03833.

Ocean County Bureau of Public Relations, C.N. 2191, County Administration Building, Toms River, N. J. 08753.

Pioneer Valley Association, Inc., 333 Prospect St., Northampton, Mass. 01060.

Shenandoah Valley Travel Association, Box 488, New Market, Va. 22844.

Tennessee Valley Authority, Director of Information, 400 Commerce Ave., Knoxville, Tenn. 37902.

Thousand Islands International Council, Box 428, Dept. No. IP, Alexandria Bay, N.Y. 13607.

Ulster County, Chamber of Commerce of, 17 Albany Ave., Kingston, N.Y. 12401.

Vermont State Chamber of Commerce, Box 37, Montpelier, Vt. 05602.

Virginia State Chamber of Commerce, 611 East Franklin St., Richmond, Va. 23219.

Warren County Public Information and Tourism, Municipal Center, Lake George, N.Y. 12845.

White Mountains Region Association, 5 Middle St., Lancaster, N.H. 03584.

West and Midwest

Black Hills, Badlands and Lake Association, Box 539, Sturgis, S.D. 57785.

California Chamber of Commerce, P.O. Box 1736, Sacramento, Calif. 95808.

East Michigan Tourist Association, 1 Wenonah Park, Bay City, Mich. 48706.

Lake of the Ozarks Association, Lake Ozark, Mo. 65049.

Minnesota Arrowhead Association, Hotel Duluth, Duluth, Minn. 55802.

Ozark Playgrounds Association, 212 West Fourth St., Joplin, Mo. 64801.

Redwood Empire Association, 476 Post St., San Francisco, Calif. 94102.

Southeast Michigan Travel and Tourist Association, Plaza Building, 1200 Sixth Ave., Detroit, Mich. 48226.

Southern California Visitors Council, 705 W. Seventh St., Los Angeles, Calif. 90017.

Upper Peninsula Travel and Recreation Association, P.O. Box 400, Iron Mountain, Mich. 49801.

West Michigan Tourist Association, 136 Fulton East, Grand Rapids, Mich. 49502.

FOREIGN GOVERNMENT TOURIST OFFICES

(The number shown in parentheses is the zip code)

A number of foreign governments maintain offices in the United States for the distribution of information, pamphlets, maps, hotel lists, etc., to prospective tourists. Among them are the following:

Atlanta, Ga.

Israel Government Tourist Office, 795 Peachtree St., N.E. (30308).

Beverly Hills, Calif.

French Government Tourist Office, 9401 Wilshire Blvd. (90212).

Chicago, Ill.

Bahamas Tourist Office, 875 North Michigan Ave. (60611).

British Tourist Authority, Suite 2450, John Hancock Center (60611).

Canadian Government Office of Tourism, Suite 410, 332 South Michigan Ave. (60604).

German National Tourist Office, 104 South Michigan Ave. (60603).

Irish Tourist Board, 224 North Michigan Ave. (60601).

Israel Government Tourist Office, 5 South Wabash Ave. (60603).

Italian Government Travel Office, 500 North Michigan Ave. (60611).

Jamaica Tourist Board, 36 South Wabash Ave. (60603).

Mexican Government Ministry of Tourism, 625 North Michigan Ave. (60611).
Spanish National Tourist Office, 180 North Michigan Ave. (60601).

Dallas, Tex.

Bahamas Tourist Office, 211 North Ervay St. (75201).

Houston, Tex.

Mexican Ministry of Tourism, 805 Walker St. (77002).

Los Angeles, Calif.

Australian Tourist Commission, 3550 Wilshire Blvd. (90010).
Austrian National Tourist Office, 3440 Wilshire Blvd. (90010).
Bahamas Tourist Office, 510 West Sixth St. (90014).
British Tourist Authority, 612 South Flower St. (90017).
India Tourist Office, Government of, 3550 Wilshire Blvd., Suite No. 204 (90010).
Israel Government Tourist Office, 6380 Wilshire Blvd. Suite 1700 (90048).
Mexican Ministry of Tourism, 3106 Wilshire Blvd. (90010).
New Zealand Government Tourist Office, 10960 Wilshire Blvd. (90024).

Miami, Fla.

Bahamas Tourist Office, 255 Alhambra Circle, Suite 425 (33134).
Mexican Ministry of Tourism, 100 Biscayne Blvd. (33132).

New Orleans, La.

Mexican Ministry of Tourism, One Shell Square Building (70139).

New York City

Antigua/Barbuda Information Office, 101 Park Ave. (10017).
Arab Information Center, 747 Third Ave., (10017).
Australian Tourist Commission, 1270 Avenue of the Americas (10020).
Austrian National Tourist Office, 545 Fifth Ave. (10017).
Bahamas Tourist Office, 30 Rockefeller Plaza, Room 52, Mezzanine (10020).
Barbados Board of Tourism, 800 Second Ave. (10017).
Belgian National Tourist Office, 720 Fifth Ave. (10019).
Bermuda Department of Tourism, 630 Fifth Ave. (10020).
Brazilian Government Trade Bureau, 551 Fifth Ave. (10017).
British Tourist Authority, 680 Fifth Ave. (10019).
Canadian Government Office of Tourism 1251 Avenue of the Americas, (10020).
Caribbean Tourism Association, 20 East 46th St. (10017).
Colombian Government Tourist Office, 140 East 57th St. (10022).

Curaçao Tourist Board, 30 Rockefeller Plaza, Mezzanine, Room 50 (10020).
Danish National Tourist Office, 75 Rockefeller Plaza (10019).
Egyptian Government Tourist Office, 630 Fifth Ave. (10020).
European Travel Commission, 630 Fifth Ave. (10020).
Finland National Tourist Office, 75 Rockefeller Plaza (10019).
French Government Tourist Office, 610 Fifth Ave. (10020).
German National Tourist Office, 630 Fifth Ave. (10020).
Greek National Tourist Organization, 645 Fifth Ave., Olympic Tower-5th floor (10022).
Guatemalan Government Tourist Office, 501 Fifth Ave. (10017).
Haiti Government Tourist Bureau, 30 Rockefeller Plaza (10020).
India Tourist Office, Government of, 30 Rockefeller Plaza (10020).
Indonesian Consulate General, Tourist Desk, 5 East 68th St. (10021).
Iran Information and Tourism Center, 10 West 49th St. (10020).
Irish Tourist Board, 590 Fifth Ave. (10036).
Israel Government Tourist Office, 488 Madison Ave. (10022).
Italian Government Travel Office-ENIT, 630 Fifth Ave. (10020).
Jamaica Tourist Board, 866 Second Avenue (10017).
Japan National Tourist Organization, 45 Rockefeller Plaza (10020).
Permanent Mission of the Hashemite Kingdom of Jordan to the U.N., 866 U.N. Plaza (10017).
Kenya Tourist Office, 15 E. 51st St. (10022)
Luxembourg Tourist Office, One Dag Hammarskjold Plaza (10017).
Mexican Government Ministry of Tourism, 630 Fifth Ave., Room 351 (10020).
Monaco Government Tourist Office, 115 East 64th St. (10021).
Moroccan National Tourist Office, 597 Fifth Ave. (10017).
Netherlands National Tourist Office, 576 Fifth Ave. (10036).
New South Wales Centre, 5 World Trade Center (10048).
New Zealand Government Tourist Office, 630 Fifth Ave. (10020).
Norwegian National Tourist Office, 75 Rockefeller Plaza (10019).
Nova Scotia Government Tourist Information Office, 630 Fifth Ave. (10020).
Panama Government Tourist Bureau, 630 Fifth Ave. (10020).
Philippine Commercial Office, 556 Fifth Ave. (10036).
Portuguese National Tourist Office, 570 Fifth Ave. (10036).
Romanian National Tourist Office, 500 Fifth Ave. (10036).
Scandinavian National Tourist Offices, 75 Rockefeller Plaza (10019).

South African Tourist Corporation, 610 Fifth Ave. (10020).

Spanish National Tourist Office, 122 East 42nd St. (10017).

Surinam Tourist Bureau, 1 Rockefeller Plaza (10020).

Swedish National Tourist Office, 75 Rockefeller Plaza (10019).

Swiss National Tourist Office, The Swiss Center, 608 Fifth Ave. (10020).

Trinidad and Tobago Tourist Board, 400 Madison Ave. (10017).

Turkish Tourism and Information Office, 500 Fifth Ave. (10036).

Yugoslav State Tourist Office, 630 Fifth Ave. (10020).

Portland, Ore.

Austrian National Tourist Office, 1007 N.W. 24th Ave. (97210).

St. Augustine, Fla.

Spanish National Tourist Office, Hypolita and George Sts. (32084).

San Antonio, Tex.

Mexican Ministry of Tourism, 304 N. St. Mary's (78205).

San Francisco, Calif.

Egyptian Government Tourist Office, 3001 Pacific Ave. (94115).

German National Tourist Office, 323 Geary St. (94102).

Italian Government Travel Office (ENIT), 360 Post St., Suite 801 (94108).

Japan National Tourist Organization, 1737 Post St. (94115).

New Zealand Government Tourist Office, Alcoa Building, One Maritime Plaza (94111).

Pacific Area Travel Association, 228 Grant Ave. (94108).

Philippine Consulate General, Office of the Commercial Attaché, 447 Sutter St. (94108).

Spanish National Tourist Office, 209 Post St. (94108).

Swiss National Tourist Office, 661 Market St. (94105).

TOLL ROADS

Source: International Bridge, Tunnel and Turnpike Association.

Varying tolls, depending on mileage, are charged for using different sections of toll roads. Listed below are the agency or facility administering the road, the name of the road, the total mileage, and the toll charged for driving a passenger car the entire length of the road.

Connecticut Dept. of Transportation: *Connecticut Turnpike*[1], 129 miles, $2.00 (with 1-axle trailer, $2.70; with 2-axle trailer, $4.05). *Merritt Parkway*,[2] 20 cents. *Wilbur Cross Parkway*,[2] 35 cents.

Delaware Dept. of Highways and Transportation: *John F. Kennedy Memorial Highway*, 11.2 miles, 40 cents.

East Hudson Parkway Authority: *Hutchinson River Parkway*,[1] 15 miles, 25 cents. *Saw Mill River Parkway*,[1] 30.4 miles, 25 cents.

Florida Dept. of Transportation: *Airport Expressway*, 4.4 miles, 10 cents (with trailer, 15 cents). *Beeline Expressway*, 17.4 miles, 35 cents (with trailer, 70 cents). *Buccaneer Trail*, 15.9 miles, 50 cents (with trailer 75 cents). *East-West Expressway*, 2 miles, 10 cents (with trailer, 15 cents). *Everglades Parkway*, 78 miles, 75 cents (with trailer, $1.50). *Florida's Turnpike*, 265 miles, $4.80. *Holland East-West Expressway*, 13.8 miles (10 cents per axle). *South Dade Expressway*, 8 miles, 15 cents for 2-axle vehicles. *West Dade Expressway* (ext. of Florida's Turnpike), 50 miles, (2-axle, 4-tire vehicles, 80 cents; 2-axle, 6-tire vehicles, $1.10).

Illinois State Toll Highway Authority: *Tri-State Tollway*, 77 miles, $1.80 (with 1-axle trailer, $2.70; with 2-axle trailer $3.60). *Northwest Tollway*, 78 miles, $1.50 (with 1-axle trailer, $2.25; with 2-axle trailer, $3.00). *East-*

West Tollway, 96 miles, $1.90 (with 1-axle trailer, $2.85; with 2-axle trailer, $3.80).

Indiana Toll Road Commission: *East-West Toll Road*, 156 miles, $3.50 (with trailer, $4.00).

Jones Beach State Parkway Authority: *Southern State Parkway*,[1] 31.6 miles, 25 cents.

Kansas Turnpike Authority: *Kansas Turnpike*, 236 miles, $5.25 (with trailer, $6.75).

Kentucky, Turnpike Authority of: *Audubon Parkway*, 24 miles, 50 cents (with 1-axle trailer 80 cents; with 2-axle trailer $1.10). *Blue Grass Parkway*, 72 miles, $1.30 (with 1-axle trailer, $2.10; with 2-axle trailer, $2.90). *Cumberland Parkway*, 89 miles, $2.00 (with 1-axle trailer, $3.00, with 2-axle trailer, $4.00). *Daniel Boone Parkway*, 63 miles, $1.40 (with 1-axle trailer, $2.10; with 2-axle trailer, $2.80). *Green River Parkway*, 70 miles, $1.60 (with 1-axle trailer, $2.40; with 2-axle trailer, $3.20). *Jackson Purchase Parkway*, 53 miles, 90 cents (with 1-axle trailer, $1.45; with 2-axle trailer, $2.00). *Mountain Parkway* and *Mountain Parkway Extension*, 71 miles, $1.60 (with 1-axle trailer, $2.60; with 2-axle trailer, $3.60). *Pennyrile Parkway*, 59 miles, $1.00 (with 1-axle trailer, $1.60; with 2-axle trailer $2.20). *Western Kentucky Parkway* and *Western Kentucky Parkway Extension*, 133 miles, $2.20 (with 1-axle trailer, $3.55; with 2-axle trailer, $4.90).

Maine Turnpike Authority: *Maine Turnpike*, 100 miles, $2.15 (with trailer not exceeding 56.5 feet, $3.25).

Maryland Transportation Authority: *John F. Kennedy Memorial Highway*, 43 miles, $1.00.

Massachusetts Turnpike Authority: *Massachusetts Turnpike*, 123 miles, $2.75 (with trailer,

---

[1] Only passenger cars are allowed.   [2] Merritt Parkway and Wilbur Cross Parkway are 64 miles in length together.

$3.20). *Boston Extension,* 12 miles, 55 cents (with trailer, $1.15).

State of New Hampshire—Dept. of Public Works & Highways, Division of Turnpikes: *Everett Turnpike,* 40 miles, 25 cents (with 1-axle trailer, 40 cents; with 2-axle trailer, 55 cents). *New Hampshire Turnpike,* 15 miles, 40 cents (with 1-axle trailer, 60 cents; with 2-axle trailer, 80 cents). *Spaulding Turnpike,* 25 miles, 25 cents (with 1-axle trailer, 45 cents; with 2-axle trailer, 65 cents).

New Jersey Expressway Authority: *Atlantic City Expressway,* 44 miles, $1.25 (Buses and dual-tire trucks, $2.50; 3-axle vehicles, $3.75; 4 or more axles, $5.00).

New Jersey Highway Authority: *Garden State Parkway,* 173 miles, $2.75 (with semi-trailer, $3.85; with full trailer, $5.50).

New Jersey Turnpike Authority: *New Jersey Turnpike,* 118 miles, $2.25.

New York State Thruway Authority: *New York State Thruway (Main Line Section),* 465 miles, $7.75 (with 1-axle trailer, $10.60; with 2-axle trailer, $13.00; with 3-axle trailer, $21.85). *Yonkers Barrier,* 25 cents, (with 1-axle trailer, 30 cents; 2-axle trailer, 45 cents; 3-axle trailer, 65 cents). *Tappan Zee Bridge,* toll collected eastbound only, $1.50 (with trailer, $2.25–$2.70). *Controlled Section,* $6.40, (with 1-axle trailer, $8.10; 2-axle trailer, $12.55; 3-axle trailer, $21.20). *Erie Section,* 70 miles, $1.30 (with 1-axle trailer, $1.75; 2-axle trailer, $2.85; 3-axle trailer, $3.55). *Berkshire Section* (surcharge added when Castleton Bridge used for travel to and from Mainline Stations), 24 miles, 45 cents (with 1-axle trailer, 55 cents; 2-axle trailer, 65 cents; 3-axle trailer, 95 cents). *Niagara Section,* 21 miles, 55 cents (with 1-axle trailer, 75 cents; 2-axle trailer, $1.05; 3-axle trailer, $1.45). *New England Section,* 15 miles, 25 cents (with 1-axle trailer, 30 cents; 2-axle trailer, 45 cents; 3-axle trailer, 65 cents).

Ohio Turnpike Commission: *Ohio Turnpike,* 241 miles, $3.50.

Oklahoma Turnpike Authority: *Cimarron Turnpike,* 67.7 miles, $1.20 (with 1-axle trailer, $1.80; with 2-axle trailer, $2.40). *H.E. Bailey Turnpike,* 86.4 miles, $1.80 (with 1-axle trailer, $2.70; 2-axle trailer, $3.60). *Indian Nation Turnpike,* 105.2 miles, $2.30 (with 1-axle trailer, $3.45; 2-axle trailer, $4.60). *Muskogee Turnpike,* 53.1 miles, $1.10 (with 1-axle trailer, $1.65; 2-axle trailer, $2.20). *Turner Turnpike,* 86 miles, $1.80 (with 1-axle trailer, $2.70; 2-axle trailer, $3.60). *Will Rogers Turnpike,* 88.5 miles, $1.80 (with 1-axle trailer, $2.70; 2-axle trailer, $3.60).

Pennsylvania Turnpike Commission: *Pennsylvania Turnpike,* 470 miles, $8.45.

Richmond Metropolitan Authority: *Powhite Parkway,* 3.3 miles, 20 cents (with 1-axle trailer, 30 cents; with 2-axle trailer, 40 cents).

Texas Turnpike Authority: *Dallas-Fort Worth Turnpike,* 29 miles, 60 cents (with 1-axle trailer, $1.10; with 2-axle trailer, $1.35). *Dallas North Tollway,* 10 miles, 25 cents (with 1-axle trailer, 40 cents; with 2-axle trailer, 50 cents).

Virginia Department of Highways and Transportation: *Richmond-Petersburg Turnpike,* 34.7 miles, 95 cents. *Virginia Beach-Norfolk Expressway,* 12.1 miles, 25 cents.

West Virginia Turnpike Commission: *West Virginia Turnpike,* 88 miles, $3.00 (with 1-axle trailer, $4.50; 2-axle trailer, $6.00).

MAPS FROM OIL COMPANIES

Motorists who wish to obtain maps showing routes for vacation trips based on the latest highway information may write to the following oil companies:

California

Atlantic Richfield Company, 515 South Flower St., Los Angeles 90071.[1]

Georgia

ARCOtravel Club, P.O. Box 1017, Atlanta, 30348.[2]

Illinois

Texaco Travel Service, 312 South Michigan Ave., Chicago 60604.

Kentucky

Union Oil Company of California, Touring Service Department, P.O. Box 93, Versailles, 40383.[2]

New Jersey

Exxon Touring Service, P.O. Box 307, Florham Park 07932.[2]

New York

Getty Oil Company, (Eastern Operations) Inc., Advertising Department, 660 Madison Ave., New York City 10021.

Mobil Touring Service, 150 East 42nd St., New York City 10017. Attn.: Mr. A. J. Fury.

Texaco Travel Service, 135 East 42nd St., New York City 10017.

Ohio

Standard Oil Company, (Ohio), Midland Building, Cleveland 44115.

Oklahoma

Phillips Petroleum Company, Marketing Division, Adams Bldg., Bartlesville 74004.

Skelly Oil Company, Box 1650, Tulsa 74102.[2]

Texas

Exxon Touring Service, P.O. Box 2180, Exxon Bldg., Houston 77001.

Mobil Oil Corp., P.O. Box 900, Dallas 75221.

Sunoco Touring Service, P.O. Box 538, Comfort 78013.

[1] Does not provide free maps.   [2] Maps provided in limited editions and quantities.

ACCOMMODATIONS

There are so many different types of accommodations and groups or associations to which individual owners belong that it would be impossible to list them all. Most hotels, however, are listed in the Hotel Red Book, which is available at many libraries and local hotels. In addition, many hotels belong to state hotel associations whose membership lists are sometimes distributed by state information centers. The following list of motel associations and chains which send lists free or for postage fees is only a partial one.

Best Western Motels, Hotels, Resorts, 2910 Sky Harbor Blvd., Phoenix, Ariz. 85034. Over 1,700 members in U.S., Canada, Caribbean, Australia, New Zealand.

Canadian Trails, P.O. Box 63, Metis Beach, Quebec, Canada. Members coast to coast in Canada and Eastern U. S.

Dominion Automobile Assn., 201 King St., London, Ontario, Canada N6A 4T3.

Holiday Inns, Inc., 3742 Lamar Ave., Memphis, Tenn. 38118. Inns. World's largest hotel chain.

Howard Johnson's, Motor Lodges, 222 Forbes Rd., Braintree, Mass. 02184. Operates coast to coast in 42 states, Canada and Puerto Rico.

Quality Inns International Offices, 10750 Columbia Pike, Silver Spring, Md. 20901. Motels in over 350 locations throughout U. S. and Canada.

Ramada Inns, Inc., 3838 East Van Buren St., Phoenix, Ariz. 85008. Nearly 700 hotels worldwide.

Sheraton Hotels & Motor Inns, 470 Atlantic Ave., Boston, Mass. 02210. Over 375 establishments throughout U.S. and the world.

Superior Motels, Inc., P.O. Drawer "S," Hollywood, Fla. 33022. Motels throughout U. S. and in eastern Canada.

TraveLodge International, Inc., El Cajon, Calif. 92090. Motels in 45 states, D.C. and in Canada and Mexico.

STEAMSHIP PASSENGER LINES

Transatlantic—Northern Route from U. S.

Cunard Line Ltd., 555 Fifth Ave., New York City 10017.[1]

Holland-America Cruises, 2 Pennsylvania Plaza, New York City 10001.[1]

Transatlantic—Southern Route

American Export Lines, Inc., 17 Battery Place, New York City 10004.

Chandris Inc., 666 Fifth Ave., New York City 10019.

Italian Line, 17 Battery Place North, New York City 10004.[1]

Transatlantic—from Canada

Polish Ocean Lines, Gdynia America Line, 410 St. Nicholas St., Montreal 125, Quebec, H2Y-2P5.

Bermuda, Nassau, and Caribbean

Clipper Line, 277 Park Ave., 24th Floor, New York City 10017.

Flagship Cruises, Inc., 522 Fifth Ave., New York City 10036.

Home Lines Agency Inc., One World Trade Center, Suite 3969, New York City 10048.

Incres Line Agency, Inc., 277 Park Ave., New York City 10017.

Prudential Lines, Inc., One World Trade Center, New York City 10048.

South America

Costa Line Inc., 245 Park Ave., New York City 10017.

[1] During the off-season winter months many large transatlantic liners make cruises to Bermuda, the Caribbean and Nassau.

Cunard Line Ltd., 555 Fifth Ave., New York City 10017.

Flagship Cruises, Inc., 522 Fifth Ave., New York City 10036.

Moore-McCormack Lines, Incorporated, 2 Broadway, New York City 10004.

Prudential Lines, Inc., One World Trade Center, New York City 10048.

Transpacific

American President Lines, Ltd., 1950 Franklin St., Oakland, Calif. 94612.

Matson Navigation Co., 100 Mission St., San Francisco, Calif. 94105.

Princess Cruises, 2020 Avenue of the Stars, Los Angeles, Calif. 90067.

Mississippi-Ohio River Cruises

The Delta Queen Steamboat Co., 322 East Fourth St., Cincinnati, Ohio 45202.

Schooner Cruises

Capt. John C. Foss, Box 482, Rockland, Me. 04841.

Harvey Gamage, 39 Waterside Lane, Clinton, Conn. 06413.

Capt. Frederick B. Guild, Maine Coast Cruises, Box 368, Rockland, Me. 04841.

David A. Johnson, Box 482, Rockland, Me. 04841.

Capt. Douglas K. Lee, Box 482, Rockland, Me. 04841.

Capt. Orvil Young, Jr., Box 696, Camden, Me. 04843.

In addition to the lines listed, many shipping companies operate cargo-passenger vessels carrying twelve passengers on fairly regular schedules.

Some Leading Passenger Liners of the World

Source: Cruise Lines International Association.

Line	Ship and (flag)[1]	Length ft.	Tonnage	Crew	Knots	Passengers[2]
Baltic Shipping Co.	M/S Mikhail Lermontov (U)	580	19,860	340	21	700
	M/S Alexandr Pushkin (U)	580	19,860	340	21	700
Chandris, Inc.	S.S. Amerikanis (G)	576	19,377	250	18	650
	S.S. Australis (P)	723	34,449	600	20	2,258
	S.S. Britanis (G)	642	24,351	420	20	1,600
	S.S. Ellinis (G)	642	24,351	500	20	1,642
Costa Armatori, S.p.A.	Andrea C. (I)	467	8,600	180	15	400
	M/S Carla C: (I)	600	20,477	370	22	748
	Enrico C. (I)	579	16,000	300	20	700
	M/S Eugenio C. (I)	713	30,000	475	27	1,637
	S/S Federico C. (I)	606	20,416	350	21	800
Cunard Line Limited	Cunard Adventurer (B)	484	14,155	300	21.5	700
	Queen Elizabeth 2 (B)	963	66,000	1,000	28.5	1,815
Flagship Cruises Ltd.	Kungsholm (L)	660	26,678	350	21	612
Hellenic Mediterranean Lines	M/S Aquaris (G)	340	4,800	125	19.5	297
	M/S Castalia (G)	442	9,000	...	19	380
Holland America Cruises	M/S Prinsendam (N)	427	9,000	154	21	380
	S.S. Rotterdam (N)	748	38,000	560	21	1,050
	S.S. Statendam (N)	642	25,000	416	19	800
	S.S. Veedam (N)	617	23,500	300	21	650
Home Lines, Inc.	Doric (P)	629	25,300	...	21	675
	Oceanic (P)	774	39,241	...	23	1,035
Norwegian America Line	Sagafjord (N)	620	24,000	300	20	789
	Vistafjord (N)	628	25,000	370	20	600
Norwegian Caribbean Lines	M/S Skyward (N)	525	16,250	300	19	726
	M/S Southward (N)	536	17,000	302	19	732
	M/S Starward (N)	525	15,500	250	19	540
Orient Overseas Line	S.S. Oceanic Independence (P)	683	30,000	320	22	992
	S.S. Oriental Empress (P)	609	23,000	230	20	517
	M.V. Oriental Esmeralda (L)	609	22,000	200	17	352
	S.S. Universe Campus (L)	564	18,100	230	18	600
Pacific Far East Line	S.S. Mariposa (US)	563	20,600	276	20	336
	S.S. Monterey (US)	563	20,600	276	20	336
Pacquet Cruises Inc.	Massalia (F)	465	10,513	...	21.3	650
	Mermoz (F)	530	13,800	230	17	550
	Renaissance (F)	492	11,724	215	18.5	350
Polish Ocean Lines	TS/S Stefan Batory (Po)	503	15,024	340	15.5	779
Princess Cruises	Arcadia (B)	719	30,000	600	21	1,000
	Canberra (B)	820	45,000	1,000	27	1,500
	Island Princess (B)	550	20,000	330	20	622
	Oriana (B)	804	42,000	900	27	1,500
	Pacific Princess (B)	550	20,000	330	20	622
	Sun Princess (B)	535	17,000	320	20	700
Royal Caribbean Cruise Line	M/S Nordic Prince (N)	550	18,500	320	16	750
	M/S Song of Norway (N)	550	18,500	320	16	750
	M/S Sun Viking (N)	550	18,500	320	16	750
Royal Cruise Line	M/S Golden Odyssey (G)	427	10,500	200	22.5	460
Royal Viking Line	Viking Sea (N)	581	21,500	320	21.5	500
	Royal Viking Sky (N)	581	21,500	320	21.5	500
	Royal Viking Star (N)	581	21,500	320	21.5	485
Sitmar Cruises	T.S.S. Fairsea (L)	608	25,000	500	20–22	906
	T.S.S. Fairwind (L)	608	25,000	500	20–22	906
Sun Line Cruises	Stella Maris (G)	300	4,000	100	16	223
	Stella Oceanis (G)	350	6,000	140	17	369
	Stella Solaris (G)	550	18,000	310	20	650

[1] Country of Registry: (B)—British; (F)—France; (G)—Greece; (I)—Italy; (L)—Liberia; (N)—Netherlands; (P)—Panama; (Po)—Poland; (U)—Russia; (US)—United States.   [2] Figures given are for maximum capacity. On shorter cruises, capacity varies.

Mason and Dixon's Line

Mason and Dixon's Line (often called the Mason-Dixon Line) is the boundary between Pennsylvania and Maryland, running at a north latitude of 39°43′19.11″. The greater part of it was surveyed from 1763–67 by Charles Mason and Jeremiah Dixon, English astronomers who had been appointed to settle a dispute between the colonies. As the line was partly the boundary between the free and the slave states, it has come to signify the division between the North and the South.

Some Record Passages of Atlantic (Screw) Steamships since 1900

Source: U. S. Maritime Administration.

WESTWARD PASSAGES

Date	Ship and (flag*)	European port	Time D.	H.	M.	Speed knots	Nautical miles
1900,01	DEUTSCHLAND (G)	Southampton	5	11	54	23.15	3,044
1933	REX† (I)	Gibraltar	4	13	58	28.92	3,181
1935	NORMANDIE† (F)	Bishop's Rock	4	3	2	29.98	3,015
1938	QUEEN MARY† (B)	Bishop's Rock	3	21	48	30.99	2,907
1952	UNITED STATES† (US)	Bishop's Rock	3	12	12	34.51	2,906

EASTWARD PASSAGES

Date	Ship and (flag*)	European port	Time D.	H.	M.	Speed knots	Nautical miles
1900,01	DEUTSCHLAND† (G)	Eddystone Lt.	5	7	38	23.51	2,082
1937	NORMANDIE† (F)	Bishop's Rock	.4	..	6	30.99	2,978
1938	QUEEN MARY† (B)	Bishop's Rock	3	20	42	31.69	2,938
1952	UNITED STATES† (US)	Bishop's Rock	3	10	40	35.59	3,144

* (B)—British; (G)—German; (I)—Italian; (F)—French.   † Vessels which have held the Blue Riband.

TRANSATLANTIC AIRLINES, U. S.—EUROPE

(Many of these lines have offices in other principal cities of the United States)

Aer Lingus Irish Airlines, 564 Fifth Ave., New York City 10036.

Air Canada, 600 Madison Ave., New York City 10022.

Air France, 1350 Avenue of the Americas, New York City 10019.

Air India, 345 Park Ave., New York City 10022.

Alitalia, 666 Fifth Ave., New York City 10019. Attention: Tour Dept.

British Airways, 245 Park Ave., New York City 10017.

El Al Israel Airlines, 850 Third Ave., New York City 10022.

Iberia Air Lines of Spain, 97–77 Queens Blvd., Rego Park, N.Y. 11374.

Icelandic Airlines, 630 Fifth Ave., New York City 10022.

KLM-Royal Dutch Airlines, 609 Fifth Ave., New York City 10017.

Lufthansa German Airlines, Tour Department, Lufthansa Bldg., 1640 Hempstead Turnpike, East Meadow, N.Y. 11554.

Pakistan International Airlines, 545 Fifth Ave., New York City 10017.

Pan American World Airways, Pan Am Building, 200 Park Ave., New York City 10017.

Qantas Airways, 542 Fifth Ave., New York City 10036.

Sabena Belgian World Airlines, 125 Community Drive, Great Neck, N.Y. 11021.

Scandinavian Airlines System, 638 Fifth Ave., New York City 10020.

Swissair, 608 Fifth Ave., New York City 10020.

TAP, The Airline of Portugal, 1140 Avenue of the Americas, New York City 10036.

Trans World Airlines, 605 Third Ave., New York City 10016.

American Consuls for the Traveler Abroad

American consuls will advise or help you if you are in serious difficulty or distress. However, they cannot do the work of travel agencies, information bureaus, banks and the police; nor can they help you find work or get residence or driving permits; and it is not a part of their duties to act as travel couriers or interpreters, to search for missing luggage or to settle disputes with hotel managers.

Legal Aid—If you find yourself in a dispute which could lead to legal or police action, it is wise to consult the consul.

If Detained—If you are detained by the police or other authorities in a foreign country, you should ask at once to be allowed to communicate with the consul.

If Destitute—The consul may be able to assist you to make inquiries of your family, friends, bankers and employers, or anyone else you may designate, to see if there is any way of getting you out of your difficulties.

Finances—The American consul is not provided with funds to disburse to American citizens who find themselves in financial difficulties while abroad; nor can he cash or guarantee checks for you.

U.S. PASSPORT AND CUSTOMS INFORMATION

Source: Passport Office, Department of State, and U.S. Customs Service

Passports

With a few exceptions, a passport is required for all United States citizens to depart from and enter the United States and to enter most foreign countries. A United States citizen is not required by United States laws or regulations to have a valid passport for travel to or in North, South or Central America, except Cuba. It is, however, recommended that a passport be obtained for travel to Central and South America since many of the countries require that United States citizens be in possession of a valid passport. United States travelers should carry documentary evidence of their United States citizenship and identity to facilitate re-entry into the United States. Travelers should check passport and visa requirements with consular officials of the countries to be visited well in advance of their departure date.

United States passports are not valid for travel into or through Cambodia, Cuba, North Korea, North Vietnam or South Vietnam unless specifically validated for such travel by the Department of State.

Applications for passport may be made to any Passport Agent, a clerk of any Federal court, a clerk of any State court of record or a judge or clerk of any probate court, or at a Post Office designated by the Postmaster General. Passport agencies are located in Boston, Chicago, Honolulu, Los Angeles, Miami, New Orleans, New York, Philadelphia, San Francisco, Seattle and Washington, D.C.

A first passport must be applied for in person. Applicants must present evidence of citizenship (e.g., a birth certificate), personal identification (e.g., driver's license), two identical photographs taken within six months (2½×2½ inches, signed on the front along the left-hand side; vending machine photographs are not acceptable), and the application. A fee of $10 plus a $3 execution fee is charged.

You may apply by mail if: you have been the bearer of a passport issued within eight years prior to the date of a new application; are able to submit your most recent United States passport with your new application; your previous passport was not issued before your 18th birthday; you are not applying for an official, diplomatic or no-fee passport; you do not wish to include a member of your family. This procedure may be used only in the United States. If you are eligible to apply by mail, include your previous passport, completed and signed application for Passport by Mail, new signed photographs, and the $10 passport fee. The $3 execution fee is not required when applying by mail.

If you claim Citizenship by Naturalization, a Certificate of Naturalization is required.

Passports may be amended to show a married name or legal change of name, to correct descriptive data or to include or exclude your wife/husband, any minor children, brothers or sisters. You must personally present the amendment form and have it executed by an authorized person if the amendment is an inclusion.

Any alterations other than change of address and notification data appearing on the inside cover of the passport are forbidden.

Your passport is valid for five years from date of issue unless specifically limited by the Secretary of State to a shorter period of validity.

The passport is a traveler's principal means of identification abroad, and its loss is very serious. It should be reported immediately to the nearest United States embassy or consular office. Loss of a passport in the United States should be reported in writing to the Passport Office, Department of State, Washington, D.C. 20524.

Customs

The International Health Regulations adopted by the World Health Organization stipulate that vaccination against smallpox, cholera, and yellow fever may be required as a condition of entry to any country. For return to the United States, a Smallpox Certificate will be required only if, in the preceding 14 days, you visited a country reporting smallpox. Details concerning recommended and required immunizations and prophylaxis, for travel to all areas of the world, may be obtained from your local or State health department.

United States residents must declare all articles acquired abroad and in their possession at the time of their return. The wearing or use of an article acquired abroad does *not* exempt it from duty. Customs declaration forms are distributed on vessels and planes and should be prepared in advance of arrival for presentation to the immigration and customs inspectors.

If you have not exceeded the duty-free exemption allowed, you may make an oral declaration to the customs inspector. A written declaration is necessary when (1) total fair retail value of articles exceeds $100 (keep your sales slips), (2) over 1 quart of liquor or 100 cigars are included, (3) items are not intended for your personal or household use, or articles brought home for another person, and (4) when a customs duty or internal revenue tax is collectible on any article in your possession.

An exception to the above are regulations applicable to articles purchased in the Virgin Islands, American Samoa or Guam where you may receive a customs exemption of $200.

Other exemptions include in part: automobiles, boats, planes or other vehicles taken abroad for noncommercial use. Foreign-made personal articles (e.g., watches, cameras, etc.) taken abroad should be registered with Customs before departure. Gifts of not more than $10 can be shipped back to the United States tax and duty free ($20 if mailed from the Virgin Islands, American Samoa or Guam). Household effects and tools of trade which you take out of the United States are duty free at time of return.

Prohibited and restricted articles include in part: Absinthe, narcotics and dangerous drugs, obscene articles and publications, seditious and treasonable materials, hazardous articles (e.g., fireworks, dangerous toys, toxic and poisonous substances) and switchblade knives, biological materials of public health or veterinary importance, fruit, vegetables and plants, meats, poultry and products thereof; birds, monkeys and turtles. Merchandise originating in North Korea, Vietnam, Cambodia, Rhodesia and Cuba requires a Treasury license.

If you understate the value of an article you declare, or if you otherwise misrepresent an article in your declaration, the article may be liable to seizure and forfeiture. Duty must be paid even if the article is seized, and you may be liable for a personal penalty and in some cases criminal prosecution.

If you carry more than $5,000 into or out of the United States in currency (either United States or foreign money), negotiable instruments in bearer form, or travelers checks, a report must be filed with United States Customs at the time you arrive or depart with such amounts.

Patents

Source: Patent and Trademark Office.

A patent, in the most general sense, is a document issued by a government, conferring some special right or privilege. The term is now restricted mainly to patents for inventions; occasionally, land patents.

The grant of a patent for an invention gives the inventor the privilege, for a limited period of time, of excluding others from practicing a certain art or from making, using, or selling a certain article. However, it does not give him the right to make, use, or sell his own invention if it is an improvement on some unexpired patent whose claims are infringed thereby.

In the U. S., the law provides that a patent may be granted, for a term of 17 years, to any person who has invented or discovered any new and useful art, machine, manufacture, or composition of matter, as well as any new and useful improvements thereof. A patent may also be granted to a person who has invented or discovered and asexually reproduced a new and distinct variety of plant (other than a tuber-propagated one) or has invented a new, original and ornamental design for an article of manufacture.

A patent is granted only upon a regularly filed application, complete in all respects; upon payment of the fees; and upon determination that the disclosure is complete and that the invention is new, useful, and, in view of the prior art, unobvious to one skilled in the art. The disclosure must be of such nature as to enable others to reproduce the invention.

A complete application, which must be addressed to the Commissioner of Patents and Trademarks, Washington, D. C. 20231, consists of a petition, specification and claims, oath or declaration, drawing (whenever the nature of the case admits of it) and a basic filing fee of $65, plus certain additional charges for claims. The filing fee is not returned to the applicant if the patent is refused. If the patent is allowed, another fee of $100, plus additional printing charges, is required before the patent is issued. The fees for design patents vary.

Applications are considered in the order in which they are received. Patents are not granted for printed matter, for methods of doing business, or for devices for which claims contrary to natural laws are made. Applications for a perpetual-motion machine have been made from time to time, but until a working model is presented that actually fulfills the claim, no patent will be issued.

Trademarks

Source: Patent and Trademark Office.

A trademark may be defined as a word, letter, device, or symbol, as well as some combination of these, which is used in connection with merchandise and which points distinctly to the origin or ownership of it.

Certificates of registration of trademarks are issued under the seal of the Patent and Trademark Office and may be registered by the owner if he is engaged in interstate or foreign commerce, since any Federal jurisdiction over trademarks arises under the commerce clause of the Constitution. Trademarks may be registered by foreign owners who comply with our law, as well as by citizens of foreign countries with which the U. S. has treaties relating to trademarks. American citizens may register trademarks in foreign countries by complying with the laws of those countries. The right to registration and protection of trademarks in many foreign countries is guaranteed by treaties.

General jurisdiction in trademark cases involving Federal Registrations is given to Federal courts. Adverse decisions of examiners on applications for registration are appealable to the Trademark Trial and Appeal Board, whose affirmances and decisions in *inter partes* proceedings are subject to court review. Before adopting a trademark, a person should make a search of prior marks to avoid infringing unwittingly upon them.

The duration of a trademark registration is 20 years, but it may be renewed indefinitely for 20-year periods, provided the trademark is still in use at the time of expiration.

Copyrights

Source: Copyright Office.

A copyright is a statutory right obtained by writers, musicians, and artists, or their successors in interest, upon compliance with the provisions of the copyright law, to prevent the reproduction of their works without their consent.

Under the statute now in force, the copyright owner has the exclusive right to print, reprint, publish, copy, and vend the copyrighted work. Among the other rights possessed by the copyright owner are the exclusive rights to translate and dramatize literary works, to control public performance of dramas, and, in the case of nondramatic literary works and musical compositions, to control public performance for profit. Special provisions in regard to mechanical reproductions of musical compositions and in regard to sound recordings are included. Copyright protection extends to books, including bound volumes, pamphlets, and single pages containing text; periodicals and contributions to periodicals; lectures, sermons, and monologues; dramas and dramatico-musical compositions; musical compositions; maps; works of art and models or designs for works of art; reproductions of a work of art; drawings or sculptural works of a scientific or technical character; photographs; prints and pictorial illustrations; commercial prints and labels; motion pictures; and sound recordings.

As long as material remains unpublished and unregistered, it is protected by the common law against unauthorized use, without the necessity of any formality. Copyright lasts 28 years from the date of publication. In the case of material copyrighted by registration in the Copyright Office in unpublished form, the 28-year period is measured from the date of registration. However, only musical or dramatic works, lectures or similar works prepared for oral delivery, pictorial works, and films can be registered in the Copyright Office in unpublished form. Other materials, such as manuscripts of novels, stories, poems, and sound recordings, are not registrable until after they have been published with the copies bearing the prescribed notice of copyright; but they are protected by the common law prior to publication. The copyright may be renewed for an additional term; renewal must be made by registration in the Copyright Office during the last year of the original 28-year term or else the work falls into the public domain at the end of the first term. In general, works published before Sept. 19, 1906, are not under copyright protection in the U. S., so far as the original version is concerned.

The copyright of a book or similar publication is secured by publication of such work after printing on the title page, or the page immediately following, the required copyright notice. This notice consists of the word "Copyright," the abbreviation "Copr.," or the symbol ©, accompanied by the name of the copyright owner and the year date of publication. EXAMPLE: © *John Smith 1976*. In the case of sound recordings the notice consists of Ⓟ , the year of first publication of the sound recording, and the name of the copyright owner of the sound recording. EXAMPLE: Ⓟ *1976 Doe Records, Inc.* It is important to bear in mind that copyright comes into being at the time of first publication if this required notice appears on the work in one of the prescribed places. If publication occurs without this notice, the work falls into the public domain, and the Copyright Office cannot register the claim. In short, the Copyright Office does not grant copyrights; obtaining copyright protection depends on whether or not the claimant follows the statutory formalities.

It is important for U. S. authors and publishers desiring to obtain protection in foreign countries to use the symbol © in copyright notices. This will assure protection in all countries that belong to the Universal Copyright Convention.

The law requires that, promptly after the work has been published bearing notice of copyright, two copies must be deposited in the Copyright Office, along with the proper application form and the statutory fee of $6.00.

Further information may be obtained from the Copyright Office, Library of Congress, Washington, D. C. 20559. Free application forms may be obtained from the same source.

How a Bill Becomes a Law

When a Senator or a Representative introduces a bill, he sends it to the clerk of his house, who gives it a number and title. This is the *first reading,* and the bill is referred to the proper committee.

The committee may decide the bill is unwise or unnecessary and *table* it, thus killing it at once. Or it may decide the bill is worthwhile and hold hearings to listen to facts and opinions presented by experts and other interested persons. After members of the committee have debated the bill and perhaps offered amendments, a vote is taken; and if the vote is favorable, the bill is sent back to the floor of the house.

The clerk reads the bill sentence by sentence to the house, and this is known as the *second reading.* Members may then debate the bill and offer amendments. In the House of Representatives, the time for debate is limited by a *cloture rule,* but there is no such restriction in the Senate for cloture, where 60 votes are required. This makes possible a *filibuster,* in which one or more opponents hold the floor to defeat the bill.

The *third reading* is by title only, and the bill is put to a vote, which may be by voice or roll call, depending on the circumstances and parliamentary rules. Members who must be absent at the time but who wish to record their vote may be paired if each negative vote has a balancing affirmative one.

The bill then goes to the other house of Congress, where it may be defeated, or passed with or without amendments. If the bill is defeated, it dies. If it is passed with amendments, a joint Congressional committee must be appointed by both houses to iron out the differences.

After its final passage by both houses, the bill is sent to the President. If he approves, he signs it, and the bill becomes a law. However, if he disapproves, he *vetoes* the bill by refusing to sign it and sending it back to the house of origin with his reasons for the veto. The objections are read and debated, and a roll-call vote is taken. If the bill receives less than a two-thirds vote, it is defeated and goes no farther. But if it receives a two-thirds vote or greater, it is sent to the other house for a vote. If that house also passes it by a two-thirds vote, the President's veto is *overridden,* and the bill becomes a law.

Should the President desire neither to sign nor to veto the bill, he may retain it for ten days, Sundays excepted, after which time it automatically becomes a law without signature. However, if Congress has adjourned within those ten days, the bill is automatically killed, that process of indirect rejection being known as a *pocket veto.*

Motor Vehicle Laws as of 1976

(NOTE: A driver's license and Certificate of Title are required in every state.)

Source: American Automobile Association.

State	Date new license plates can be used	Minimum age of drivers[1]	Learner's permit required	State gasoline tax	% State tax[2]	Annual Inspection required
Alabama	Oct. 1	16	yes	$.07	1½	no[26]
Alaska	Jan. 1	18(16)[3]	no	.08	..	no[26]
Arizona	On issue	16[3]	yes	.08	4	no
Arkansas	On issue	18(14)[3]	yes	.085	3	yes
California	On issue	16[4]	yes	.07	6	no[26]
Colorado	Jan. 1	21(16)	yes	.07	3	yes
Connecticut	On issue	16[4]	no[5]	.10	7[6]	no[26]
Delaware	On issue	16[4]	yes	.09	(2[4])	yes
D. C.	On issue	16[3]	yes	.08	5	yes
Florida	July 1	16(15)[3,4]	yes	.08	4	yes
Georgia	Jan. 1	16	yes	.075	3	yes
Hawaii	On issue	15[3]	yes	(8)	(9)	yes[16]
Idaho	On issue	16(14)[10]	yes	.085	3	yes
Illinois	Dec. 1	18(16)[3,4]	yes	.075	4	no
Indiana	On issue	16[12]	yes	.08	4	yes
Iowa	Dec. 1	18[4]	yes	.07	3	(7)
Kansas	On issue	16(14)	yes	.07	3	no
Kentucky	Dec. 29	16[3]	yes	.09	5[13]	yes
Louisiana	Dec. 1	15	no	.08	3	yes
Maine	Feb. 1	17(15)[14]	yes	.09	5	6 mos.
Maryland	Mar. 1	18(16)[3,4]	yes	.09	4	yes
Massachusetts	On issue	18(16½)[3,4]	yes	.085	3	6 mos.
Michigan	Nov. 15	18(16)[10]	no	.09	4	no[26]
Minnesota	On issue	18(16)[4]	yes	.07	4	no[26]
Mississippi	Nov. 1	15	yes	.09	3	yes
Missouri	On issue	16[25]	no	.07	3	yes
Montana	On issue	16(14½)[3,10]	yes	.07	1½[18]	yes
Nebraska	On issue	16	yes	.085	2½	yes
Nevada	On issue	16[3]	yes	.06	2[19]	no
New Hampshire	On issue	18(16)[4]	no	.09	..	6 mos.
New Jersey	On issue	17(16)	no	.08	5	yes
New Mexico	Dec. 15	16(15)[10]	yes	.07	2	6 mos.
New York	On issue	18(16)[3,4]	no	.08	4	yes
North Carolina	Jan. 1	18(16)[3,4]	no[20]	.09	2[21]	yes
North Dakota	Feb. 15	16(14)	yes	.07	4	no[26]
Ohio	On issue	(16)	yes	.07	4	no[26]
Oklahoma	Dec. 11	16(15½)[10]	no	.065	2	yes
Oregon	On issue	16(14)	yes[22]	.07	..	no[26]
Pennsylvania	Mar. 15	18(16)[3]	yes	.09	6	6 mos.
Rhode Island	Mar. 1	16	yes	.10	5	yes
South Carolina	Sept. 30	16(15)	yes	.08	4	yes
South Dakota	Jan. 1	16(14)	yes	.08	3[23]	yes
Tennessee	Mar. 1	16(14)	yes	.07	3½	no
Texas	Feb. 1	18(16)[10]	yes	.05	4	yes
Utah	On issue	16[17]	yes	.07	4¾	yes
Vermont	Jan. 1	18(16)	yes	.09	4	6 mos.
Virginia	On issue	18(16)[3,4]	yes	.09	2	6 mos.
Washington	Jan. 2	16[4]	yes	.09	4½	no[26]
West Virginia	On issue	18(16)[3]	yes	.085	5	yes
Wisconsin	On issue	18(16)[4]	yes	.07	4	no
Wyoming	Jan. 1	16[11]	no	.07	3	yes

[1] Figures in parentheses indicate age at which applicant may obtain a provisional license or a restricted license or permit. [2] Applicable to car sales (local and county sales taxes extra where applicable). [3] If under 18, applicant must have written consent of parent or guardian. [4] If under 18, applicant must have completed driver education course. [5] Required for motorcycles only. [6] Sales or use tax on first registration of new or used cars. [7] Prior to first registration and transfers. [8] $.085 to $.11: varies by county. [9] 4% on cars purchased out of state only. [10] If under 16, applicant must have completed driver education course. [11] If under 19, applicant must have written consent of parent or guardian. [12] 16 years and 1 month if driver education test has been completed; otherwise 16½. [13] Use tax on 90% of original retail price. [14] If under 15, applicant must have completed driver education course. [15] At discretion of Secretary of State. [16] If car is 10 years or older, every 6 months. [17] If not previously licensed, applicant must have had completed driver education course. [18] Periodic reductions for cars purchased later in year. [19] Plus 1% school support tax. [20] However, new drivers cannot practice driving on highways without permit. [21] $120 maximum. [22] Unless applicant can already drive. [23] Tax on first registration. [24] Document fee of 2% of cost of car. [25] 15½ if applicant completed driver education course. [26] State troopers are authorized to inspect at their discretion.

NOTE: The national speed limit is 55 miles per hour.

Road Mileages Between U.S. Cities [1]

Cities	Birming-ham	Boston	Buffalo	Chicago	Cleveland	Dallas	Denver
Birmingham, Ala	....	1,194	947	657	734	653	1,318
Boston, Mass.	1,194	....	457	983	639	1,815	1,991
Buffalo, N.Y.	947	457	....	536	192	1,387	1,561
Chicago, Ill.	657	983	536	....	344	931	1,050
Cleveland, Ohio	734	639	192	344	....	1,205	1,369
Dallas, Tex.	653	1,815	1,387	931	1,205	....	801
Denver, Colo.	1,318	1,991	1,561	1,050	1,369	801	....
Detroit, Mich.	754	702	252	279	175	1,167	1,301
El Paso, Tex.	1,278	2,358	1,928	1,439	1,746	625	652
Houston, Tex.	692	1,886	1,532	1,092	1,358	242	1,032
Indianapolis, Ind.	492	940	510	189	318	877	1,051
Kansas City, Mo.	703	1,427	997	503	815	508	616
Los Angeles, Calif.	2,078	3,036	2,606	2,112	2,424	1,425	1,174
Louisville, Ky.	378	996	571	305	379	865	1,135
Memphis, Tenn.	249	1,345	965	546	773	470	1,069
Miami, Fla.	777	1,539	1,445	1,390	1,325	1,332	2,094
Minneapolis, Minn.	1,067	1,402	955	411	763	969	867
New Orleans, La.	347	1,541	1,294	947	1,102	504	1,305
New York, N.Y.	983	213	436	840	514	1,604	1,780
Omaha, Neb.	907	1,458	1,011	493	819	661	559
Philadelphia, Pa.	894	304	383	758	432	1,515	1,698
Phoenix, Ariz.	1,680	2,664	2,234	1,729	2,052	1,027	836
Pittsburgh, Pa.	792	597	219	457	131	1,237	1,411
St. Louis, Mo.	508	1,179	749	293	567	638	871
Salt Lake City, Utah	1,805	2,425	1,978	1,458	1,786	1,239	512
San Francisco, Calif.	2,385	3,179	2,732	2,212	2,540	1,765	1,266
Seattle, Wash.	2,612	3,043	2,596	2,052	2,404	2,122	1,373
Washington, D.C.	751	440	386	695	369	1,372	1,635

Cities	Detroit	El Paso	Houston	Indian-apolis	Kansas City	Los Angeles	Louisville
Birmingham, Ala.	754	1,278	692	492	703	2,078	378
Boston, Mass.	702	2,358	1,886	940	1,427	3,036	996
Buffalo, N.Y.	252	1,928	1,532	510	997	2,606	571
Chicago, Ill.	279	1,439	1,092	189	503	2,112	305
Cleveland, Ohio	175	1,746	1,358	318	815	2,424	379
Dallas, Tex.	1,167	625	242	877	508	1,425	865
Denver, Colo.	1,310	652	1,032	1,051	616	1,174	1,135
Detroit, Mich.	....	1,696	1,312	290	760	2,369	378
El Paso, Tex.	1,696	....	756	1,418	936	800	1,443
Houston, Tex.	1,312	756	....	1,022	750	1,556	981
Indianapolis, Ind.	290	1,418	1,022	....	487	2,096	114
Kansas City, Mo.	760	936	750	487	....	1,609	519
Los Angeles, Calif.	2,369	800	1,556	2,096	1,609	....	2,128
Louisville, Ky.	378	1,443	981	114	519	2,128	....
Memphis, Tenn.	756	1,095	586	466	454	1,847	396
Miami, Fla.	1,409	1,957	1,237	1,225	1,479	2,757	1,111
Minneapolis, Minn.	698	1,353	1,211	600	466	2,041	716
New Orleans, La.	1,101	1,121	365	839	839	1,921	725
New York, N.Y.	671	2,147	1,675	729	1,216	2,825	785
Omaha, Neb.	754	1,015	903	590	204	1,733	704
Philadelphia, Pa.	589	2,065	1,586	647	1,134	2,743	703
Phoenix, Ariz.	1,986	402	1,158	1,713	1,226	398	1,749
Pittsburgh, Pa.	288	1,778	1,395	360	847	2,456	416
St. Louis, Mo.	529	1,179	799	239	255	1,864	264
Salt Lake City, Utah	1,721	877	1,465	1,545	1,128	728	1,647
San Francisco, Calif.	2,475	1,202	1,958	2,299	1,882	403	2,401
Seattle, Wash.	2,339	1,760	2,348	2,241	1,909	1,150	2,355
Washington, D.C.	526	1,997	1,443	565	1,071	2,680	601

[1] These figures represent approximate estimates and are subject to change.

Road Mileages Between U.S. Cities

Cities	Memphis	Miami	Minne-apolis	New Orleans	New York	Omaha	Phila-delphia
Birmingham, Ala.	249	777	1,067	347	983	907	894
Boston, Mass.	1,345	1,539	1,402	1,541	213	1,458	304
Buffalo, N.Y.	965	1,445	955	1,294	436	1,011	383
Chicago, Ill.	546	1,390	411	947	840	493	758
Cleveland, Ohio	773	1,325	763	1,102	514	819	432
Dallas, Tex.	470	1,332	969	504	1,604	661	1,515
Denver, Colo.	1,069	2,094	867	1,305	1,780	559	1,698
Detroit, Mich.	756	1,409	698	1,101	671	754	589
El Paso, Tex.	1,095	1,957	1,353	1,121	2,147	1,015	2,065
Houston, Tex.	586	1,237	1,211	365	1,675	903	1,586
Indianapolis, Ind.	466	1,225	600	839	729	590	647
Kansas City, Mo.	454	1,479	466	839	1,216	204	1,134
Los Angeles, Calif.	1,847	2,757	2,041	1,921	2,825	1,733	2,743
Louisville, Ky.	396	1,111	716	725	785	704	703
Memphis, Tenn.	....	1,025	854	401	1,134	658	1,045
Miami, Fla.	1,025	....	1,801	892	1,328	1,683	1,239
Minneapolis, Minn.	854	1,801	....	1,255	1,259	373	1,177
New Orleans, La.	401	892	1,255	....	1,330	1,043	1,241
New York, N.Y.	1,134	1,328	1,259	1,330	....	1,315	93
Omaha, Neb.	658	1,683	373	1,043	1,315	....	1,233
Philadelphia, Pa.	1,045	1,239	1,177	1,241	93	1,233	....
Phoenix, Ariz.	1,464	2,359	1,644	1,523	2,442	1,305	2,360
Pittsburgh, Pa.	810	1,250	876	1,118	386	932	304
St. Louis, Mo.	295	1,241	559	696	968	459	886
Salt Lake City, Utah	1,556	2,571	1,243	1,743	2,282	967	2,200
San Francisco, Calif.	2,151	3,097	1,997	2,269	3,036	1,721	2,954
Seattle, Wash.	2,363	3,389	1,641	2,606	2,900	1,705	2,818
Washington, D.C.	902	1,101	1,114	1,098	229	1,170	140

Cities	Phoenix	Pitts-burgh	St. Louis	Salt Lake City	San Francisco	Seattle	Wash-ington
Birmingham, Ala.	1,680	792	508	1,805	2,385	2,612	751
Boston, Mass.	2,664	597	1,179	2,425	3,179	3,043	440
Buffalo, N.Y.	2,234	219	749	1,978	2,732	2,596	386
Chicago, Ill.	1,729	457	293	1,458	2,212	2,052	695
Cleveland, Ohio	2,052	131	567	1,786	2,540	2,404	369
Dallas, Tex.	1,027	1,237	638	1,239	1,765	2,122	1,372
Denver, Colo.	836	1,411	871	512	1,266	1,373	1,635
Detroit, Mich.	1,986	288	529	1,721	2,475	2,339	526
El Paso, Tex.	402	1,778	1,179	877	1,202	1,760	1,997
Houston, Tex.	1,158	1,395	799	1,465	1,958	2,348	1,443
Indianapolis, Ind.	1,713	360	239	1,545	2,299	2,241	565
Kansas City, Mo.	1,226	847	255	1,128	1,882	1,909	1,071
Los Angeles, Calif.	398	2,456	1,864	728	403	1,150	2,680
Louisville, Ky.	1,749	416	264	1,647	2,401	2,355	601
Memphis, Tenn.	1,464	810	295	1,556	2,151	2,363	902
Miami, Fla.	2,359	1,250	1,241	2,571	3,097	3,389	1,101
Minneapolis, Minn.	1,644	876	559	1,243	1,997	1,641	1,114
New Orleans, La.	1,523	1,118	696	1,743	2,269	2,626	1,098
New York, N.Y.	2,442	386	968	2,282	3,036	2,900	229
Omaha, Neb.	1,305	932	459	967	1,721	1,705	1,178
Philadelphia, Pa.	2,360	304	886	2,200	2,954	2,818	140
Phoenix, Ariz.	....	2,073	1,485	651	800	1,482	2,278
Pittsburgh, Pa.	2,073	....	599	1,899	2,653	2,517	241
St. Louis, Mo.	1,485	599	....	1,383	2,137	2,164	836
Salt Lake City, Utah	651	1,899	1,383	....	754	883	2,110
San Francisco, Calif.	800	2,653	2,137	754	....	817	2,864
Seattle, Wash.	1,482	2,517	2,164	883	817	....	2,755
Washington, D.C.	2,278	241	836	2,110	2,864	2,755	....

Air Distances Between U. S. Cities in Statute Miles
Source: National Geodetic Survey

Cities	Birming-ham	Boston	Buffalo	Chicago	Cleveland	Dallas	Denver
Birmingham, Ala.	....	1,052	776	578	618	581	1,095
Boston, Mass.	1,052	....	400	851	551	1,551	1,769
Buffalo, N. Y.	776	400	....	454	173	1,198	1,370
Chicago, Ill.	578	851	454	....	308	803	920
Cleveland, Ohio	618	551	173	308	....	1,025	1,227
Dallas, Tex.	581	1,551	1,198	803	1,025	....	663
Denver, Colo.	1,095	1,769	1,370	920	1,227	663	....
Detroit, Mich.	641	613	216	238	90	999	1,156
El Paso, Tex.	1,152	2,072	1,692	1,252	1,525	572	557
Houston, Tex.	567	1,605	1,286	940	1,114	225	879
Indianapolis, Ind.	433	807	435	165	263	763	1,000
Kansas City, Mo.	579	1,251	861	414	700	451	558
Los Angeles, Calif.	1,802	2,596	2,198	1,745	2,049	1,240	831
Louisville, Ky.	331	826	483	269	311	726	1,038
Memphis, Tenn.	217	1,137	803	482	630	420	879
Miami, Fla.	665	1,255	1,181	1,188	1,087	1,111	1,726
Minneapolis, Minn.	862	1,123	731	355	630	862	700
New Orleans, La.	312	1,359	1,086	833	924	443	1,082
New York, N. Y.	864	188	292	713	405	1,374	1,631
Omaha, Neb.	732	1,282	883	432	739	586	488
Philadelphia, Pa.	783	271	279	666	360	1,299	1,579
Phoenix, Ariz.	1,456	2,300	1,906	1,453	1,749	887	586
Pittsburgh, Pa.	608	483	178	410	115	1,070	1,320
St. Louis, Mo.	400	1,038	662	262	492	547	796
Salt Lake City, Utah	1,466	2,099	1,699	1,260	1,568	999	371
San Francisco, Calif.	2,013	2,699	2,300	1,858	2,166	1,483	949
Seattle, Wash.	2,082	2,493	2,117	1,737	2,026	1,681	1,021
Washington, D. C.	661	393	292	597	306	1,185	1,494

Cities	Detroit	El Paso	Houston	Indian-apolis	Kansas City	Los Angeles	Louisville
Birmingham, Ala.	641	1,152	567	433	579	1,802	331
Boston, Mass.	613	2,072	1,605	807	1,251	2,596	826
Buffalo, N. Y.	216	1,692	1,286	435	861	2,198	483
Chicago, Ill.	238	1,252	940	165	414	1,745	269
Cleveland, Ohio	90	1,525	1,114	263	700	2,049	311
Dallas, Tex.	999	572	225	763	451	1,240	726
Denver, Colo.	1,156	557	879	1,000	558	831	1,038
Detroit, Mich.	....	1,479	1,105	240	645	1,983	316
El Paso, Tex.	1,479	....	676	1,264	839	701	1,254
Houston, Tex.	1,105	676	....	865	644	1,374	803
Indianapolis, Ind.	240	1,264	865	....	453	1,809	107
Kansas City, Mo.	645	839	644	453	....	1,356	480
Los Angeles, Calif.	1,983	701	1,374	1,809	1,356	....	1,829
Louisville, Ky.	316	1,254	803	107	480	1,829	....
Memphis, Tenn.	623	976	484	384	369	1,603	320
Miami, Fla.	1,152	1,643	968	1,024	1,241	2,339	919
Minneapolis, Minn.	543	1,157	1,056	511	413	1,524	605
New Orleans, La.	939	983	318	712	680	1,673	623
New York, N. Y.	482	1,905	1,420	646	1,097	2,451	652
Omaha, Neb.	669	878	794	525	166	1,315	580
Philadelphia, Pa.	443	1,836	1,341	585	1,038	2,394	582
Phoenix, Ariz.	1,690	346	1,017	1,499	1,049	357	1,508
Pittsburgh, Pa.	205	1,590	1,137	330	781	2,136	344
St. Louis, Mo.	455	1,034	679	231	238	1,589	242
Salt Lake City, Utah	1,492	689	1,200	1,356	925	579	1,402
San Francisco, Calif.	2,091	995	1,645	1,949	1,506	347	1,986
Seattle, Wash.	1,938	1,376	1,891	1,872	1,506	959	1,943
Washington, D. C.	396	1,728	1,220	494	945	2,300	476

Air Distances Between U. S. Cities in Statute Miles

Source: **National Geodetic Survey**

Cities	Memphis	Miami	Minne-apolis	New Orleans	New York	Omaha	Phila-delphia
Birmingham, Ala.	217	665	862	312	864	732	783
Boston, Mass.	1,137	1,255	1,123	1,359	188	1,282	271
Buffalo, N. Y.	803	1,181	731	1,086	292	883	279
Chicago, Ill.	482	1,188	355	833	713	432	666
Cleveland, Ohio	630	1,087	630	924	405	739	360
Dallas, Tex.	420	1,111	862	443	1,374	586	1,299
Denver, Colo.	879	1,726	700	1,082	1,631	488	1,579
Detroit, Mich.	623	1,152	543	939	482	669	443
El Paso, Tex.	976	1,643	1,157	983	1,905	878	1,836
Houston, Tex.	484	968	1,056	318	1,420	794	1,341
Indianapolis, Ind.	384	1,024	511	712	646	525	585
Kansas City, Mo.	369	1,241	413	680	1,097	166	1,038
Los Angeles, Calif.	1,603	2,339	1,524	1,673	2,451	1,315	2,394
Louisville, Ky.	320	919	605	623	652	580	582
Memphis, Tenn.	. . .	872	699	358	957	529	881
Miami, Fla.	872		1,511	669	1,092	1,397	1,019
Minneapolis, Minn.	699	1,511	. . .	1,051	1,018	290	985
New Orleans, La.	358	669	1,051	. . .	1,171	847	1,089
New York, N. Y.	957	1,092	1,018	1,171	. . .	1,144	83
Omaha, Neb.	529	1,397	290	847	1,144	. . .	1,094
Philadelphia, Pa.	881	1,019	985	1,089	83	1,094	. . .
Phoenix, Ariz.	1,263	1,982	1,280	1,316	2,145	1,036	2,083
Pittsburgh, Pa.	660	1,010	743	919	317	836	259
St. Louis, Mo.	240	1,061	466	598	875	354	811
Salt Lake City, Utah	1,250	2,089	987	1,434	1,972	833	1,925
San Francisco, Calif.	1,802	2,594	1,584	1,926	2,571	1,429	2,523
Seattle, Wash.	1,867	2,734	1,395	2,101	2,408	1,369	2,380
Washington, D. C.	765	923	934	966	205	1,014	123

Cities	Phoenix	Pitts-burgh	St. Louis	Salt Lake City	San Francisco	Seattle	Wash-ington
Birmingham, Ala.	1,456	608	400	1,466	2,013	2,082	661
Boston, Mass.	2,300	483	1,038	2,099	2,699	2,493	393
Buffalo, N. Y.	1,906	178	662	1,699	2,300	2,117	292
Chicago, Ill.	1,453	410	262	1,260	1,858	1,737	597
Cleveland, Ohio	1,749	115	492	1,568	2,166	2,026	306
Dallas, Tex.	887	1,070	547	999	1,483	1,681	1,185
Denver, Colo.	586	1,320	796	371	949	1,021	1,494
Detroit, Mich.	1,690	205	455	1,492	2,091	1,938	396
El Paso, Tex.	346	1,590	1,034	689	995	1,376	1,728
Houston, Tex.	1,017	1,137	679	1,200	1,645	1,891	1,220
Indianapolis, Ind.	1,499	330	231	1,356	1,949	1,872	494
Kansas City, Mo.	1,049	781	238	925	1,506	1,506	945
Los Angeles, Calif.	357	2,136	1,589	579	347	959	2,300
Louisville, Ky.	1,508	344	242	1,402	1,986	1,943	476
Memphis, Tenn.	1,263	660	240	1,250	1,802	1,867	765
Miami, Fla.	1,982	1,010	1,061	2,089	2,594	2,734	923
Minneapolis, Minn.	1,280	743	466	987	1,584	1,395	934
New Orleans, La.	1,316	919	598	1,434	1,926	2,101	966
New York, N. Y.	2,145	317	875	1,972	2,571	2,408	205
Omaha, Neb.	1,036	836	354	833	1,429	1,369	1,014
Philadelphia, Pa.	2,083	259	811	1,925	2,523	2,380	123
Phoenix, Ariz.	. . .	1,828	1,272	504	653	1,114	1,983
Pittsburgh, Pa.	1,828	. . .	559	1,668	2,264	2,138	192
St. Louis, Mo.	1,272	559	. . .	1,162	1,744	1,724	712
Salt Lake City, Utah	504	1,668	1,162	. . .	600	701	1,848
San Francisco, Calif.	653	2,264	1,744	600	. . .	678	2,442
Seattle, Wash.	1,114	2,138	1,724	701	678	. . .	2,329
Washington, D. C.	1,983	192	712	1,848	2,442	2,329	. . .

Air Distances Between World Cities in Statute Miles

Source: Encyclopaedia Britannica.

Cities	Berlin	Buenos Aires	Cairo	Calcutta	Capetown	Caracas	Chicago
Berlin, Germany	....	7,402	1,795	4,368	5,981	5,247	4,405
Buenos Aires, Argentina	7,402	....	7,345	10,265	4,269	3,168	5,598
Cairo, Egypt	1,795	7,345	....	3,539	4,500	6,338	6,129
Calcutta, India	4,368	10,265	3,539	....	6,024	9,605	7,980
Capetown, South Africa	5,981	4,269	4,500	6,024	....	6,365	8,494
Caracas, Venezuela	5,247	3,168	6,338	9,605	6,365	....	2,501
Chicago, Ill., U. S.	4,405	5,598	6,129	7,980	8,494	2,501	....
Hong Kong (Victoria)	5,440	11,472	5,061	1,648	7,375	10,167	7,793
Honolulu, Hawaii, U. S.	7,309	7,561	8,838	7,047	11,534	6,013	4,250
Istanbul, Turkey	1,078	7,611	768	3,638	5,154	6,048	5,477
Lisbon, Portugal	1,436	5,956	2,363	5,638	5,325	4,041	3,990
London, England	579	6,916	2,181	4,947	6,012	4,660	3,950
Los Angeles, Calif., U. S.	5,724	6,170	7,520	8,090	9,992	3,632	1,745
Manila, Philippines	6,132	11,051	5,704	2,203	7,486	10,620	8,143
Mexico City, Mexico	6,047	4,592	7,688	9,492	8,517	2,232	1,691
Montreal, Canada	3,729	5,615	5,414	7,607	7,931	2,449	744
Moscow, U.S.S.R.	1,004	8,376	1,803	3,321	6,300	6,173	4,974
New York, N. Y., U. S.	3,965	5,297	5,602	7,918	7,764	2,132	713
Paris, France	545	6,870	1,995	4,883	5,807	4,736	4,134
Rio de Janeiro, Brazil	6,220	1,200	6,146	9,377	3,773	2,810	5,296
Rome, Italy	734	6,929	1,320	4,482	5,249	5,196	4,808
San Francisco, Calif., U. S.	5,661	6,467	7,364	7,814	10,247	3,904	1,858
Shanghai, China	5,218	12,201	5,183	2,117	8,061	9,501	7,061
Stockholm, Sweden	504	7,808	2,111	4,195	6,444	5,420	4,278
Sydney, Australia	10,006	7,330	8,952	5,685	6,843	9,513	9,272
Tokyo, Japan	5,540	11,408	5,935	3,194	9,156	8,799	6,299
Warsaw, Poland	320	7,662	1,630	4,048	5,958	5,517	4,667
Washington, D. C., U. S.	4,169	5,218	5,800	8,084	7,901	2,059	597

Cities	Hong Kong	Honolulu	Istanbul	Lisbon	London	Los Angeles	Manila
Berlin, Germany	5,440	7,309	1,078	1,436	579	5,724	6,132
Buenos Aires, Argentina	11,472	7,561	7,611	5,956	6,916	6,170	11,051
Cairo, Egypt	5,061	8,838	768	2,363	2,181	7,520	5,704
Calcutta, India	1,648	7,047	3,638	5,638	4,947	8,090	2,203
Capetown, South Africa	7,375	11,534	5,154	5,325	6,012	9,992	7,486
Caracas, Venezuela	10,167	6,013	6,048	4,041	4,660	3,632	10,620
Chicago, Ill., U. S.	7,793	4,250	5,477	3,990	3,950	1,745	8,143
Hong Kong (Victoria)	....	5,549	4,984	6,853	5,982	7,195	693
Honolulu, Hawaii, U. S.	5,549	....	8,109	7,820	7,228	2,574	5,299
Istanbul, Turkey	4,984	8,109	....	2,012	1,552	6,783	5,664
Lisbon, Portugal	6,853	7,820	2,012	....	985	5,621	7,546
London, England	5,982	7,228	1,552	985	....	5,382	6,672
Los Angeles, Calif., U. S.	7,195	2,574	6,783	5,621	5,382	....	7,261
Manila, Philippines	693	5,299	5,664	7,546	6,672	7,261	....
Mexico City, Mexico	8,782	3,779	7,110	5,390	5,550	1,589	8,835
Montreal, Canada	7,729	4,910	4,789	3,246	3,282	2,427	8,186
Moscow, U.S.S.R.	4,439	7,037	1,091	2,427	1,555	6,003	5,131
New York, N. Y., U. S.	8,054	4,964	4,975	3,364	3,458	2,451	8,498
Paris, France	5,985	7,438	1,400	904	213	5,588	6,677
Rio de Janeiro, Brazil	11,021	8,285	6,389	4,796	5,766	6,331	11,259
Rome, Italy	5,768	8,022	843	1,161	887	6,732	6,457
San Francisco, Calif., U. S.	6,897	2,393	6,703	5,666	5,357	347	6,967
Shanghai, China	764	4,941	4,962	6,654	5,715	6,438	1,150
Stockholm, Sweden	5,113	6,862	1,348	1,856	890	5,454	5,797
Sydney, Australia	4,584	4,943	9,294	11,302	10,564	7,530	3,944
Tokyo, Japan	1,794	3,853	5,560	6,915	5,940	5,433	1,866
Warsaw, Poland	5,144	7,355	863	1,715	899	5,922	5,837
Washington, D. C., U. S.	8,147	4,519	5,215	3,562	3,663	2,300	8,562

Air Distances Between World Cities in Statute Miles

Source: Encyclopaedia Britannica.

Cities	Mexico City	Montreal	Moscow	New York	Paris	Rio de Janeiro	Rome
Berlin, Germany	6,047	3,729	1,004	3,965	545	6,220	734
Buenos Aires, Argentina	4,592	5,615	8,376	5,297	6,870	1,200	6,929
Cairo, Egypt	7,688	5,414	1,803	5,602	1,995	6,146	1,320
Calcutta, India	9,492	7,607	3,321	7,918	4,883	9,377	4,482
Capetown, South Africa	8,517	7,931	6,300	7,764	5,807	3,773	5,249
Caracas, Venezuela	2,232	2,449	6,173	2,132	4,736	2,810	5,196
Chicago, Ill., U. S.	1,691	744	4,974	713	4,134	5,296	4,808
Hong Kong (Victoria)	8,782	7,729	4,439	8,054	5,985	11,021	5,768
Honolulu, Hawaii, U. S.	3,779	4,910	7,037	4,964	7,438	8,285	8,022
Istanbul, Turkey	7,110	4,789	1,091	4,975	1,400	6,389	843
Lisbon, Portugal	5,390	3,246	2,427	3,364	904	4,796	1,161
London, England	5,550	3,282	1,555	3,458	213	5,766	887
Los Angeles, Calif., U. S.	1,589	2,427	6,003	2,451	5,588	6,331	6,732
Manila, Philippines	8,835	8,186	5,131	8,498	6,677	11,259	6,457
Mexico City, Mexico	....	2,318	6,663	2,094	5,716	4,771	6,366
Montreal, Canada	2,318	....	4,386	320	3,422	5,097	4,080
Moscow, U.S.S.R.	6,663	4,386	....	4,665	1,544	7,175	1,474
New York, N. Y., U. S.	2,094	320	4,665	....	3,624	4,817	4,281
Paris, France	5,716	3,422	1,544	3,624	....	5,699	697
Rio de Janeiro, Brazil	4,771	5,097	7,175	4,817	5,699	....	5,684
Rome, Italy	6,366	4,080	1,474	4,281	697	5,684	....
San Francisco, Calif., U. S.	1,887	2,539	5,871	2,571	5,558	6,621	6,240
Shanghai, China	8,022	7,053	4,235	7,371	5,754	11,336	5,677
Stockholm, Sweden	5,959	3,667	762	3,924	958	6,651	1,234
Sydney, Australia	8,052	9,954	9,012	9,933	10,544	8,306	10,136
Tokyo, Japan	7,021	6,383	4,647	6,740	6,034	11,533	6,135
Warsaw, Poland	6,365	4,009	715	4,344	849	6,467	817
Washington, D. C., U. S.	1,887	488	4,858	205	3,829	4,796	4,434

Cities	San Francisco	Shanghai	Stockholm	Sydney	Tokyo	Warsaw	Washington
Berlin, Germany	5,661	5,218	504	10,006	5,540	320	4,169
Buenos Aires, Argentina	6,467	12,201	7,808	7,330	11,408	7,662	5,218
Cairo, Egypt	7,364	5,183	2,111	8,952	5,935	1,630	5,800
Calcutta, India	7,814	2,117	4,195	5,685	3,194	4,048	8,084
Capetown, South Africa	10,247	8,061	6,444	6,843	9,156	5,958	7,901
Caracas, Venezuela	3,904	9,501	5,420	9,513	8,799	5,517	2,059
Chicago, Ill., U. S.	1,858	7,061	4,278	9,272	6,299	4,667	597
Hong Kong (Victoria)	6,897	764	5,113	4,584	1,794	5,144	8,147
Honolulu, Hawaii, U. S.	2,393	4,941	6,862	4,943	3,853	7,355	4,519
Istanbul, Turkey	6,703	4,962	1,348	9,294	5,560	863	5,215
Lisbon, Portugal	5,666	6,654	1,856	11,302	6,915	1,715	3,562
London, England	5,357	5,715	890	10,564	5,940	899	3,663
Los Angeles, Calif., U. S.	347	6,438	5,454	7,530	5,433	5,922	2,300
Manila, Philippines	6,967	1,150	5,797	3,944	1,866	5,837	8,562
Mexico City, Mexico	1,887	8,022	5,959	8,052	7,021	6,365	1,887
Montreal, Canada	2,539	7,053	3,667	9,954	6,383	4,009	488
Moscow, U.S.S.R.	5,871	4,235	762	9,012	4,647	715	4,858
New York, N. Y., U. S.	2,571	7,371	3,924	9,933	6,740	4,344	205
Paris, France	5,558	5,754	958	10,544	6,034	849	3,829
Rio de Janeiro, Brazil	6,621	11,336	6,651	8,306	11,533	6,467	4,796
Rome, Italy	6,240	5,677	1,234	10,136	6,135	817	4,434
San Francisco, Calif., U. S.	....	6,140	5,361	7,416	5,135	5,841	2,442
Shanghai, China	6,140	....	4,825	4,899	1,097	4,951	7,448
Stockholm, Sweden	5,361	4,825	....	9,696	5,051	501	4,123
Sydney, Australia	7,416	4,899	9,696	....	4,866	9,696	9,758
Tokyo, Japan	5,135	1,097	5,051	4,866	....	5,249	6,772
Warsaw, Poland	5,841	4,951	501	9,696	5,249	....	4,457
Washington, D. C., U. S.	2,442	7,448	4,123	9,758	6,772	4,457	....

GEOGRAPHY
Miscellaneous Data for the United States
Source: U. S. Geological Survey.

Highest point: Mount McKinley, Alaska .... 20,320 ft.
Lowest point: Death Valley, Calif. .... 282 ft. below sea level
Approximate mean altitude .... 2,500 ft.
Points farthest apart (50 states): Log Point, Elliot Key, Fla., and Kure Island,
    Hawaii .... 5,852 mi.
Geographic center (50 states): In Butte County, S. D. (west of {   44° 58′ N. lat.
    Castle Rock) .... { 103° 46′ W. long.
Geographic center (48 conterminous states): In Smith County, Kan. }   39° 50′ N. lat.
    (near Lebanon)... { 98° 35′ W. long.
Boundaries: Between Alaska and Canada .... 1,538 mi.
    Between the 48 conterminous states and Canada (including Great Lakes) ... 3,987 mi.
    Between the United States and Mexico .... 1,933 mi.

Extreme Points of the United States (50 States)

Extreme point	Latitude	Longitude	Distance*
Northernmost point: Point Barrow, Alaska.........................	71° 23′ N.	156° 29′ W.	2,502 mi.
Easternmost point: West Quoddy Head, Me..........................	44° 49′ N.	66° 57′ W.	1,785 mi.
Southernmost point: Ka Lae (South Cape), Hawaii..................	18° 56′ N.	155° 41′ W.	3,456 mi.
Westernmost point: Cape Wrangell, Alaska (Attu Island)...........	52° 55′ N.	172° 27′ E.	3,620 mi.

* From geographic center of United States (incl. Alaska and Hawaii), west of Castle Rock, S.D., 44° 58′ N. lat., 103° 46′ W long.

Named Summits in the U. S. Over 14,000 Feet Above Sea Level
Source: U. S. Geological Survey.

Name	State	Height	Name	State	Height	Name	State	Height
Mt. McKinley	Alaska	20,320	Mt. Antero	Colo.	14,269	Windom Peak	Colo.	14,087
Mt. St. Elias	Alaska	18,008	Torreys Peak	Colo.	14,267	Mt. Russell	Calif.	14,086
Mt. Foraker	Alaska	17,400	Castle Peak	Colo.	14,265	Mt. Eolus	Colo.	14,084
Mt. Blackburn	Alaska	16,523	Quandary Peak	Colo.	14,265	Mt. Columbia	Colo.	14,073
Mt. Bona	Alaska	16,421	Mt. Evans	Colo.	14,264	Mt. Augusta	Alaska	14,070
Mt. Sanford	Alaska	16,237	Longs Peak	Colo.	14,255	Missouri Mtn.	Colo.	14,067
South Buttress	Alaska	15,885	Mt. Wilson	Colo.	14,246	Humboldt Peak	Colo.	14,064
Mt. Vancouver	Alaska	15,700	White Mtn.	Calif.	14,246	Mt. Bierstadt	Colo.	14,060
Mt. Churchill	Alaska	15,638	North Palisade	Calif.	14,242	Sunlight Peak	Colo.	14,059
Mt. Fairweather	Alaska	15,300	Shavano Peak	Colo.	14,229	Split Mtn.	Calif.	14,058
Mt. Hubbard	Alaska	15,015	Crestone Needle	Colo.	14,197	Handies Peak	Colo.	14,048
Mt. Bear	Alaska	14,831	Mt. Belford	Colo.	14,197	Culebra Peak	Colo.	14,047
East Buttress	Alaska	14,730	Mt. Princeton	Colo.	14,197	Mt. Lindsey	Colo.	14,042
Mt. Hunter	Alaska	14,573	Mt. Yale	Colo.	14,196	Middle Palisade	Calif.	14,040
Mt. Alverstone	Alaska	14,565	Mt. Bross	Colo.	14,172	Little Bear Peak	Colo.	14,037
Browne Tower	Alaska	14,530	Kit Carson Mtn.	Colo.	14,165	Mt. Sherman	Colo.	14,036
Mt. Whitney	Calif.	14,494	Mt. Wrangell	Alaska	14,163	Redcloud Peak	Colo.	14,034
Mt. Elbert	Colo.	14,433	Mt. Shasta	Calif.	14,162	Mt. Langley	Calif.	14,028
Mt. Massive	Colo.	14,421	Mt. Sill	Calif.	14,162	Mt. Tyndall	Calif.	14,018
Mt. Harvard	Colo.	14,420	El Diente Peak	Colo.	14,159	Pyramid Peak	Colo.	14,018
Mt. Rainier	Wash.	14,410	Maroon Peak	Colo.	14,156	Wilson Peak	Colo.	14,017
Mt. Williamson	Calif.	14,375	Tabeguache Mtn.	Colo.	14,155	Mt. Muir	Calif.	14,015
Blanca Peak	Colo.	14,345	Mt. Oxford	Colo.	14,153	Wetterhorn Peak	Colo.	14,015
La Plata Peak	Colo.	14,336	Mt. Sneffels	Colo.	14,150	No. Maroon Pk.	Colo.	14,014
Uncompahgre Pk.	Colo.	14,309	Mt. Democrat	Colo.	14,148	San Luis Peak	Colo.	14,014
Crestone Peak	Colo.	14,294	Capitol Peak	Colo.	14,130	Huron Peak	Colo.	14,005
Mt. Lincoln	Colo.	14,286	Pikes Peak	Colo.	14,110	Mt. of Holy Cross	Colo.	14,005
Grays Peak	Colo.	14,270	Snowmass Mtn.	Colo.	14,092	Sunshine Peak	Colo.	14,001

The Continental Divide

The Continental Divide is a ridge of high ground which runs irregularly north and south through the Rocky Mountains and separates eastward-flowing from westward-flowing streams. The waters which flow eastward empty into the Atlantic Ocean, chiefly by way of the Gulf of Mexico; those which flow westward empty into the Pacific.

Highest, Lowest, and Mean Altitudes in the United States

Source: U. S. Geological Survey.

State	Altitude, ft.[1]	Highest point	Altitude, ft.	Lowest point	Altitude, ft.
Alabama	500	Cheaha Mountain	2,407	Gulf of Mexico	Sea level
Alaska	1,900	Mount McKinley	20,320	Pacific Ocean	Sea level
Arizona	4,100	Humphreys Peak	12,633	Colorado River	70
Arkansas	650	Magazine Mountain	2,753	Ouachita River	55
California	2,900	Mount Whitney	14,494	Death Valley	282[2]
Colorado	6,800	Mount Elbert	14,433	Arkansas River	3,350
Connecticut	500	Mount Frissell, on south slope	2,380	Long Island Sound	Sea level
Delaware	60	On Ebright Road	442	Atlantic Ocean	Sea level
D. C.	150	Tenleytown, northwest part	410	Potomac River	1
Florida	100	Sec. 30, T6N, R20W[3]	345	Atlantic Ocean	Sea level
Georgia	600	Brasstown Bald	4,784	Atlantic Ocean	Sea level
Hawaii	3,030	Mauna Kea	13,796	Pacific Ocean	Sea level
Idaho	5,000	Borah Peak	12,662	Snake River	710
Illinois	600	Charles Mound	1,235	Mississippi River	279
Indiana	700	Franklin Township, Wayne County	1,257	Ohio River	320
Iowa	1,100	Sec. 29, T100N, R41W[4]	1,670	Mississippi River	480
Kansas	2,000	Mount Sunflower	4,039	Verdigris River	680
Kentucky	750	Black Mountain	4,145	Mississippi River	257
Louisiana	100	Driskill Mountain	535	New Orleans	5[2]
Maine	600	Mount Katahdin	5,268	Atlantic Ocean	Sea level
Maryland	350	Backbone Mountain	3,360	Atlantic Ocean	Sea level
Massachusetts	500	Mount Greylock	3,491	Atlantic Ocean	Sea level
Michigan	900	Mount Curwood	1,980	Lake Erie	572
Minnesota	1,200	Eagle Mountain	2,301	Lake Superior	602
Mississippi	300	Woodall Mountain	806	Gulf of Mexico	Sea level
Missouri	800	Taum Sauk Mountain	1,772	St. Francis River	230
Montana	3,400	Granite Peak	12,799	Kootenai River	1,800
Nebraska	2,600	Johnson Township, Kimball County	5,426	Southeast corner of state	840
Nevada	5,500	Boundary Peak	13,143	Colorado River	470
New Hampshire	1,000	Mount Washington	6,288	Atlantic Ocean	Sea level
New Jersey	250	High Point	1,803	Atlantic Ocean	Sea level
New Mexico	5,700	Wheeler Peak	13,161	Red Bluff Reservoir	2,817
New York	1,000	Mount Marcy	5,344	Atlantic Ocean	Sea level
North Carolina	700	Mount Mitchell	6,684	Atlantic Ocean	Sea level
North Dakota	1,900	White Butte	3,506	Red River	750
Ohio	850	Campbell Hill	1,550	Ohio River	433
Oklahoma	1,300	Black Mesa	4,973	Little River	287
Oregon	3,300	Mount Hood	11,235	Pacific Ocean	Sea level
Pennsylvania	1,100	Mount Davis	3,213	Delaware River	Sea level
Rhode Island	200	Jerimoth Hill	812	Atlantic Ocean	Sea level
South Carolina	350	Sassafras Mountain	3,560	Atlantic Ocean	Sea level
South Dakota	2,200	Harney Peak	7,242	Big Stone Lake	962
Tennessee	900	Clingmans Dome	6,643	Mississippi River	182
Texas	1,700	Guadalupe Peak	8,751	Gulf of Mexico	Sea level
Utah	6,100	Kings Peak	13,528	Beaverdam Creek	2,000
Vermont	1,000	Mount Mansfield	4,393	Lake Champlain	95
Virginia	950	Mount Rogers	5,729	Atlantic Ocean	Sea level
Washington	1,700	Mount Rainier	14,410	Pacific Ocean	Sea level
West Virginia	1,500	Spruce Knob	4,863	Potomac River	240
Wisconsin	1,050	Timms Hill	1,952	Lake Michigan	581
Wyoming	6,700	Gannett Peak	13,804	Belle Fourche River	3,100
United States	2,500	Mount McKinley (Alaska)	20,320	Death Valley (California)	282[2]

[1] Approximate mean altitude.   [2] Below sea level.   [3] Walton County.   [4] Osceola County.

Forest Resources of the United States

Source: U. S. Forest Service.

One third of the U. S. is forest land. Commercial areas include land capable of producing timber of commercial quantity and quality. Noncommercial areas include alpine, semidesert, and other forest types of low timber productivity. Also included in noncommercial areas are 19.9 million acres of land in public ownership suitable for growing timber, but withdrawn for such uses as state and national parks and wilderness areas, (17.2 million acres) or National Forest areas deferred while under study for possible inclusion in the wilderness system, (2.7 million acres).

U.S. Forest Land in Acres, 1970

Sawtimber stands	215,867,400
Pole timber stands	126,693,400
Seedling and sapling stands	131,368,000
Nonstocked and other areas	25,768,400
Total, commercial forest lands	499,697,200
Noncommercial forest	253,852,100
Total, all forest land	753,549,300

Rivers of the United States

(350 or more miles long)

ALABAMA (735 mi.; 1,242 km): From junction of Tallapoosa R. and Coosa R. in Alabama to Mobile R.

ALTAMAHA-OCMULGEE (392 mi.; 631 km): From junction of Yellow R. and South R., Newton Co. in Ga. to Atlantic Ocean.

APALACHICOLA-CHATTAHOOCHEE (524 mi.; 886 km): From Towns Co. in Ga. to Gulf of Mexico in Fla.

ARKANSAS (1,450 mi.; 2,333 km): From Lake Co. in Colorado to Mississippi R. in Arkansas.

BRAZOS (870 mi.; 1,400 km): From junction of Salt Fork and Double Mountain Fork in Texas to Gulf of Mexico.

CANADIAN (906 mi.; 1,458 km): From Las Animas Co. in Colorado to Arkansas R. in Oklahoma.

CIMARRON (600 mi.; 966 km): From Colfax Co. in New Mexico to Arkansas R. in Oklahoma.

CLARK FORK-PEND OREILLE (505 mi.; 813 km): From Silver Bow Co. in Mont. to Columbia R. in British Columbia.

COLORADO (1,450 mi.; 2,333 km): From Rocky Mountain National Park in Colorado to Gulf of California in Mexico.

COLORADO (840 mi.; 1,352 km): From Borden Co. in Texas to Matagorda Bay.

COLUMBIA (1,234 mi.; 2,086 km): From Columbia Lake in British Columbia to Pacific Ocean (entering between Oreg. and Wash.)

COLVILLE (350 mi.; 563 km): From Brooks Range in Alaska to Beaufort Sea.

CONNECTICUT (407 mi.; 655 km): From Third Connecticut Lake in New Hampshire to Long Island Sound in Connecticut.

CUMBERLAND (720 mi.; 1,159 km): From junction of Poor and Clover Forks in Harlan Co. in Kentucky to Ohio R.

DELAWARE (390 mi.; 659 km): From Schoharie County in New York to Liston Point, Delaware Bay.

GILA (630 mi.; 1,014 km): From Catron Co. in New Mexico to Colorado R. in Arizona.

GREEN (360 mi.; 579 km): From Lincoln Co. in Kentucky to Ohio R. in Kentucky.

GREEN (730 mi.; 1,175 km): From Sublette Co. in Wyoming to Colorado R. in Utah.

HUMBOLDT (390 mi.; 659 km): From Wells, Nev., to Humboldt Lake in Nevada.

ILLINOIS (420 mi.; 709 km): From St. Joseph Co. in Indiana to Mississippi R. at Grafton in Illinois.

JAMES (sometimes called DAKOTA) (710 mi.; 1,143 km): From Wells Co. in North Dakota to Missouri R. in South Dakota.

KANAWHA-NEW (352 mi.; 566 km): From junction of North and South Forks of New R. in North Carolina to Ohio R.

KOYUKUK (470 mi.; 756 km): From Brooks Range in Alaska to Yukon R.

KUSKOKWIM (680 mi.; 1,094 km): From Alaska Range in Alaska to Kuskokwim Bay.

LICKING (350 mi.; 591 km): From Magoffin Co. in Kentucky to Ohio R. at Cincinnati in Ohio.

LITTLE MISSOURI (560 mi.; 901 km): From Crook Co. in Wyoming to Missouri R. in North Dakota.

MILK (625 mi.; 1,006 km); From junction of forks in Alberta Province to Missouri R.

MISSISSIPPI (2,348 mi.; 3,779 km): From Lake Itasca in Minn. to mouth of Southwest Pass.

MISSISSIPPI-MISSOURI-RED ROCK (3,710 mi.; 6,271 km): From source of Red Rock R. in Montana to mouth of Southwest Pass in Louisiana.

MISSOURI (2,315 mi.; 3,726 km): From junction of Jefferson R., Gallatin R., and Madison R. in Montana to Mississippi R. near St. Louis.

MISSOURI-RED ROCK (2,533 mi.; 4,281 km): From source of Red Rock R. in Montana to Mississippi R. near St. Louis.

MOBILE-ALABAMA-COOSA (780 mi.; 1,255 km): From junction of Etowah R. and Oostanaula R. in Georgia to Mobile Bay.

NEOSHO (460 mi.; 740 km): From Morris Co. in Kansas to Arkansas R. in Oklahoma.

NIOBRARA (431 mi.; 694 km): From Niobrara Co. in Wyoming to Missouri R. in Nebraska.

NOATAK (350 mi.; 563 km): From Brooks Range in Alaska to Kotzebue Sound.

NORTH CANADIAN (760 mi.; 1,223 km): From Union Co. in New Mexico to Canadian R. in Oklahoma.

NORTH PLATTE (618 mi.; 995 km): From Jackson Co. in Colorado to junction with So. Platte R. in Nebraska to form Platte R.

OHIO (981 mi.; 1,579 km): From junction of Allegheny R. and Monongahela R. at Pittsburgh to Mississippi R. between Illinois and Kentucky.

OHIO-ALLEGHENY (1,306 mi.; 2,207 km): From Potter Co. in Pennsylvania to Mississippi R. at Cairo in Illinois.

OSAGE (500 mi.; 845 km): From east-central Kansas to Missouri R. near Jefferson City in Missouri.

OUACHITA (605 mi.; 974 km): From Polk Co. in Arkansas to Red R. in Louisiana.

PECOS (735 mi.; 1,183 km): From Mora Co. in New Mexico to Rio Grande in Texas.

PEARL (411 mi.; 694 km): From Neshoba County in Mississippi to Gulf of Mexico (Miss.-La.).

PEE DEE-YADKIN (435 mi.; 700 km): From Watauga Co. in North Carolina to Winyah Bay in South Carolina.

PEND OREILLE (490 mi.; 828 km): Near Butte in Montana to Columbia R. on Washington-Canada border.

PORCUPINE (460 mi.; 740 km): From Yukon Territory, Canada, to Yukon R. in Alaska.

POTOMAC (383 mi.; 647 km): From Garrett Co. in Maryland to Chesapeake Bay at Point Lookout in Maryland.

POWDER (375 mi.; 603 km): From junction of forks in Johnson Co. in Wyoming to Yellowstone R. in Montana.

RED (1,270 mi.; 2,044 km): From junction of forks in Harmon Co. in Oklahoma to Mississippi R. in Louisiana.

RED (officially called RED RIVER OF THE NORTH) (545 mi.; 877 km): From junction of

Otter Tail R. and Bois de Sioux R. in Minnesota to Lake Winnipeg in Manitoba.

REPUBLICAN (445 mi.; 716 km): From junction of North Fork and Arikaree R. in Nebraska to junction with Smoky Hill R. in Kansas to form Kansas R.

RIO GRANDE (1,885 mi.; 3,034 km): From San Juan Co. in Colorado to Gulf of Mexico.

ROANOKE (380 mi.; 612 km): From junction of forks in Montgomery Co. in Virginia to Albemarle Sound in North Carolina.

SABINE (380 mi.; 612 km): From junction of forks in Hunt Co. in Texas to Sabine Lake between Texas and Louisiana.

SACRAMENTO (377 mi.; 607 km): From Siskiyou Co. in California to Suisun Bay.

SAINT FRANCIS (425 mi.; 684 km): From Iron Co. in Missouri to Mississippi R. in Ark.

SALMON (420 mi.; 756 km): From Custer Co. in Idaho to Snake R.

SAN JOAQUIN (350 mi.; 563 km): From junction of forks in Madera Co. in California to Suisun Bay.

SAN JUAN (360 mi.; 579 km): From Archuleta Co. in Colorado to Colorado R. in Utah.

SANTEE-WATEREE-CATAWBA (538 mi.; 866 km): From McDowell Co. in North Carolina to Atlantic Ocean in South Carolina.

SMOKY HILL (540 mi.; 869 km): From Cheyenne Co. in Colorado to junction with Republican R. in Kansas to form Kansas R.

SNAKE (1,038 mi.; 1,670 km): From Ocean Plateau in Wyoming to Columbia R. in Wash.

SOUTH PLATTE (424 mi.; 682 km): From Park Co. in Colorado to junction with North Platte R. in Nebraska to form Platte R.

SUSQUEHANNA (444 mi.; 715 km): From Otsego Lake in New York to Chesapeake Bay in Maryland.

TANANA (620 mi.; 998 km): From Wrangell Mts. in Yukon Territory, Canada, to Yukon R. in Alaska.

TENNESSEE (652 mi.; 1,049 km): From junction of Holston R. and French Broad R. in Tennessee to Ohio R. in Kentucky.

TENNESSEE-FRENCH BROAD (900 mi.; 1,521 km): From Bland Co. in Virginia to Ohio R. at Paducah in Kentucky.

TOMBIGBEE (525 mi.; 845 km): From junction of forks in Itawamba Co. in Mississippi to Mobile R. in Alabama.

TRINITY (360 mi.; 579 km): From junction of forks in Dallas Co. in Texas to Galveston Bay.

WABASH (529 mi.; 894 km): From Darke Co. in Ohio to Ohio R. between Ill. and Ind.

WASHITA (500 mi.; 805 km): From Hemphill Co. in Texas to Red R. in Oklahoma.

WHITE (720 mi.; 1,159 km): From Madison Co. in Arkansas to Mississippi R.

WISCONSIN (430 mi.; 692 km): From Vilas Co. in Wisconsin to Mississippi R.

YELLOWSTONE (671 mi.; 1,080 km): From Park Co. in Wyoming to Missouri R. in N. Dak.

YUKON (1,770 mi.; 2,848 km): From junction of Lewes R. and Pelly R. in Yukon Territory, Canada, to Bering Sea in Alaska.

Coastline of the United States

Fourth (April 1, 1961) Edition

Source: National Oceanic and Atmospheric Administration, National Ocean Survey.

State	Lengths, statute miles		State	Lengths, statute miles	
	General coastline*	Tidal shoreline†		General coastline*	Tidal shoreline†
Atlantic Coast:			**Gulf Coast:**		
			Florida (Gulf)	770	5,095
Maine	228	3,478	Alabama	53	607
New Hampshire	13	131	Mississippi	44	359
Massachusetts	192	1,519	Louisiana	397	7,721
Rhode Island	40	384	Texas	367	3,359
Connecticut	...	618	Total Gulf coast	1,631	17,141
New York	127	1,850	**Pacific Coast:**		
New Jersey	130	1,792	California	840	3,427
Pennsylvania	...	89	Oregon	296	1,410
Delaware	28	381	Washington	157	3,026
Maryland	31	3,190	Hawaii	750	1,052
Virginia	112	3,315	Alaska (Pacific)	5,580	31,383
North Carolina	301	3,375	Total Pacific coast	7,623	40,298
South Carolina	187	2,876	**Arctic Coast:**		
Georgia	100	2,344	Alaska (Arctic)	1,060	2,521
Florida (Atlantic)	580	3,331	Total Arctic coast	1,060	2,521
Total Atlantic coast	2,069	28,673	STATES TOTAL	12,383	88,633

* Figures are lengths of general outline of seacoast. Measurements made with unit measure of 30 minutes of latitude on charts as near scale of 1:1,200,000 as possible. Coastline of bays and sounds is included to point where they narrow to width of unit measure, and distance across at such point is included.   † Figures obtained in 1939–40 with recording instrument on largest-scale maps and charts then available. Shoreline of outer coast, offshore islands, sounds, bays, rivers, and creeks is included to head of tidewater, or to point where tidal waters narrow to width of 100 feet.

WEATHER AND CLIMATE
Devastating North Atlantic Hurricanes of the 20th Century
Source: National Oceanic and Atmospheric Administration.

The following is a selected list of North Atlantic hurricanes based on casualties, damage and general public interest. Facts about each storm are taken from Weather records, although in some cases only estimates of wind speed are available. Data given in this list pertain only to U. S. land areas except where indicated otherwise.

Date	Areas hardest hit	Land stations with highest wind speed	Deaths (U. S. only)	Est. damage (millions)	Remarks
1900, Aug. 27–Sept. 15.	Galveston, Tex.	Galveston, Tex. (120* mph)	6,000	$ 30	Damage due to both winds and storm wave. Galveston Is. inundated.
1909, Sept. 10–21.....	Louisiana and Mississippi	New Orleans, La. (53 mph)	350	5	Winds 50–75 mi. W of New Orleans, where deaths occurred, were stronger than 68 mph.
1915, Aug. 5–23	East Texas and Louisiana	Galveston, Tex. (120 mph)	275	50	Water 5–6 ft. deep in Galveston business district. 90% of homes demolished. Warnings issued well ahead of time.
1915, Sept. 22–Oct. 1..	Mid-Gulf Coast	Burrwood, La. (140 mph)	275	13	Many casualties due to persons insisting on staying in low-lying areas despite warnings.
1919, Sept. 2–15......	Florida, Louisiana and Texas	Sand Key, Fla. (84* mph)	287	22	488 persons drowned at sea.
1926, Sept. 11–22.....	Florida and Alabama	Miami, Fla. (138 mph)	243	112	Most deaths were in Miami area. Said to have been one of most destructive storms of century.
1928, Sept. 6–20......	**Southern Florida**	Lake Okeechobee, Fla. (75* mph)	1,836	25	1,870 injured. Nearly all deaths were in Lake Okeechobee area. Winds estimated as high as 160 mph caused Lake to overflow into populated areas.
1935, Aug. 29–Sept. 10.	**Southern Florida**	Tampa, Fla. (86 mph)	408	6	Sustained winds over Florida Keys est. 150–200 mph. Remembered as "Labor Day Storm."
1938, Sept. 10–22.....	Long Island and Southern New England	Blue Hills Obs., Mass. (183 mph)	600	306	Unusually destructive. Storm center moved as fast as 56 mph at times. 1,754 injured.
1944, Sept. 9–16......	North Carolina to New England	Cape Henry, Va. (150* mph)	46	100	344 deaths at sea. Shipping lanes were crowded with war-time activity.
1944, Oct. 12–23......	Florida	Dry Tortugas Is. (120 mph)	18	100	About 300 were killed in Cuba area before storm reached U. S. Evacuation of thousands from threatened areas in Fla. prevented higher toll.
1947, Sept. 4–21......	Florida and Mid-Gulf Coast	Hillsboro Light, Fla. (155 mph)	51	110	Wind damage especially heavy along Gulf Coast and Florida east coast.
1954, Aug. 25–31......	North Carolina to New England	Block Island, R. I. (135 mph)	60	461	"CAROL"—more damage than any other single storm to this date. Water and high waves flooded low-lying areas; 1,000 injuries in Long Island–New England area.
1954, Sept. 2–14......	New Jersey to New England	Block Island, R.I. (87 mph)	21	40	"EDNA"—New England again heavily hit. Gusts of 120 mph at Martha's Vineyard, Mass.
1954, Oct. 5–18.......	South Carolina to New York	New York, N. Y. (113 mph) (See Remarks)	95	252	"HAZEL"—several N. C. localities had winds of 130–150 mph with unusually heavy wave damage resulting. Est. 400–1,000 casualties in Haiti. In Canada there were 78 deaths, mostly due to flooding.

Date	Areas hardest hit	Land stations with highest wind speed	Deaths (U. S. only)	Est. damage (millions)	Remarks
1955, Aug. 3–14......	North Carolina to New England	Ft. Macon, N. C. (100 mph)	25	46	"CONNIE"—center passed over Morehead City and Beaufort flooding these cities. 12.35 in. of rain in New York City.
1955, Aug. 7–21.......	North Carolina to New England	Wilmington, N. C. (83 mph)	184	832	"DIANE"—worst floods in history in Southern New England. 16 in. of rain in Hartford area.
1955, Sept. 10–23.....	North Carolina	Cherry Point, N. C. (107 mph)	7	88	"IONE"—center passed over Morehead City and Beaufort.
1957, June 25–28......	Texas to Alabama	Sabine Pass, Tex. (100 mph)	390	150	"AUDREY"—gave an early start to the hurricane season and wiped out Cameron, La. Two weeks later "BERTHA," a less destructive tropical storm, struck in the same area.
1960, Aug. 29–Sept. 13	Florida to New England	Ft. Myers, Fla. (92 mph) Block Island, R. I. (130 mph) (See Remarks)	50	500	"DONNA" — hurricane winds from a single storm swept the entire Atlantic seaboard from Florida to New England for the first time in a 75-year record. Winds estimated near 140 mph with gusts 175–180 mph on Central Keys and lower southwest Florida coast. 115 deaths in Antilles, most from flash floods in Puerto Rico.
1961, Sept. 3–15......	Texas coast	Port Lavaca, Tex. (145 mph)	46	408	"CARLA"—devastated Texas Gulf Coast Cities with 15-foot tides and 15-inch rains. Gusts to 175 mph at Port Lavaca.
1964, Aug. 20–Sept. 5 .	Southern Florida, Eastern Virginia	Miami, Fla. (110 mph)	3	129	"CLEO"—first hurricane in Miami area since 1950. Killed 214 in Caribbean Islands.
1964, Aug. 28–Sept. 16 ..	Northeastern Florida, Southern Georgia	St. Augustine, Fla. (125 mph)	5	250	"DORA"—first storm of full hurricane force on record to move inland from east over northeastern Florida.
1965, Aug. 27–Sept. 12	Southern Florida and Louisiana	Port Sulphur, La. (136 mph)	75	1,420	"BETSY"—damage in Louisiana, $1.2 billion. 27,000 homes destroyed, 17,500 injured or ill, 300,000 evacuated. Gusts est. at 165 mph at Pine Key, Fla.
1967, Sept. 5–22	Southern Texas	Brownsville, Texas (109 mph gust)	15	200	"BEULAH"—main damage was caused by torrential rains.
1969, Aug. 14–22......	Mississippi, Louisiana, Alabama, Virginia, W. Virginia	Oil drilling rig east of Boothville, La. (172 mph)	256	1,420	"CAMILLE"—68 additional persons missing. One of most destructive killer storms ever to hit U. S.
1970, July 23–Aug. 5 ..	Texas coast	Corpus Christi, Tex. (130 mph)	11	453.8	"CELIA"—Costliest storm in history to hit Texas coast. Gusts of 161 mph recorded.
1972, June 14–23	Florida to New York	Key West, Fla. (43 mph)	117	3,097	"AGNES"—Devastating floods with many record-breaking river crests. Pa. hardest hit, with 50 deaths.

* Wind-measuring equipment disabled at speed indicated. NOTE: Additional hurricanes may be listed in *News Chronology of 1976.*

Tropical Storms and Hurricanes, 1886–1975

	Jan.–Apr.	May	June	July	Aug.	Sept.	Oct.	Nov.	Dec.	Total
Number of tropical storms (incl. hurricanes)...	2	11	48	56	168	247	158	31	4	725
Number of tropical storms that reached hurricane intensity..........................	1	3	21	32	123	158	76	14	2	430

Groups of Tornadoes That Caused Outstanding Damage

Source: Data for 1884–1953, reprinted from *Tornadoes of the United States* by S. D. Flora.
Copyright, 1954, by University of Oklahoma Press. Used by permission. Also National Climatic Center.

Date	Number of tornadoes	Deaths	Property losses	States in which storms occurred
1884, Feb. 19	60	800	*	Mississippi, Alabama, North and South Carolina, Tennessee, Kentucky, Indiana
1917, May 26–27	*	249	$ 5,555,000	Illinois, Indiana, Arkansas, Kentucky, Tennessee, Alabama, Mississippi
1920, Apr. 20	6	220	3,525,000	Mississippi, Alabama, Tennessee
1924, Apr. 29–30	22	115	4,372,300	Oklahoma, Arkansas, Alabama, Georgia, Louisiana, North and South Carolina, Virginia
1924, June 28	4	96	13,050,000	Ohio and Pennsylvania
1925, Mar. 18	8	792	17,872,000	Missouri, Illinois, Indiana, Kentucky, Tennessee, Alabama
1927, May 8–9	36	227	7,877,000	Texas, Louisiana, Missouri, Nebraska, Indiana, Michigan
1932, Mar. 21	27	321	5,514,000	Alabama, Mississippi, Georgia, Tennessee
1936, Apr. 5–6	22	498	21,800,000	Arkansas, Alabama, Tennessee, Georgia, South Carolina
1944, June 23	4	153	5,160,000	Pennsylvania, West Virginia, Maryland
1947, Apr. 9–10	8	167	10,030,750	Texas, Oklahoma, Kansas
1952, Mar. 21–22	31	343	15,327,100	Arkansas, Tennessee, Missouri, Mississippi, Alabama, Kentucky
1953, June 7–9	12	234	93,230,840	Michigan, Ohio, and New England states.
1953, May 11	1	114	39,5000,000	Waco, Texas
1955, May 25	13	102	11,747,500	Oklahoma and Kansas.
1965, Apr. 11–12	47	257	200,000,000	Iowa, Illinois, Wisconsin, Michigan, Indiana, Ohio
1968, May 15	7	63	65,000,000	Arkansas, Iowa, Illinois
1970, May 11	1	26	135,000,000	Lubbock, Texas
1971, Feb. 21	*	117	17,000,000	Louisiana, Mississippi
1973, Mar. 31	2	9	115,000,000	Georgia, South Carolina
1973, May 26–28	96	22	*	18 states in South, Southwest, Midwest, East and Hawaii
1974, Apr. 3–4	144	307	500,000,000+	13 states in East, South and Midwest
1975, May 6	3	3	400,000,000+	Omaha, Neb.

* Not definitely known; believed to be large. NOTE: Additional storms may be listed in *News Chronology of 1976*.

CLIMATE OF SELECTED U.S. CITIES, 1975

Source: National Oceanic and Atmospheric Administration.

Asterisk (*) indicates less than one-half; T—indicates trace; n.a.—indicates not available.

Month	Temperature				Precipitation				Percentage relative humidity at noon
	Average maximum	Average minimum	Record high	Record low	Rainfall, inches	Snowfall, inches	Days with precipitation	Percentage possible sunshine	

BAKERSFIELD, CALIFORNIA (KERN COUNTY AIR TERMINAL) Lat 35° 25′ N, Long 119° 03′ W.   Elevation: 475 ft.

Month	Average maximum	Average minimum	Record high	Record low	Rainfall, inches	Snowfall, inches	Days with precipitation	Percentage possible sunshine	Percentage relative humidity at noon
January	57.5	36.0	71	26	0.06	0.0	1	n.a.	71
April	69.4	48.1	83	40	0.93	0.0	9	n.a.	52
July	97.5	71.1	110	56	0.00	0.0	0	n.a.	37
October	78.0	55.1	98	43	0.48	0.0	6	n.a.	53
Annual	77.7	54.1	110	26	4.10	0.0	37	n.a.	51

CARIBOU, MAINE (MUNICIPAL AIRPORT) Lat 46° 52′ N, Long 68° 01′ W.   Elevation: 624 ft.

Month	Average maximum	Average minimum	Record high	Record low	Rainfall, inches	Snowfall, inches	Days with precipitation	Percentage possible sunshine	Percentage relative humidity at noon
January	19.7	-.6	39	-29	2.71	31.2	18	n.a.	63
April	42.7	27.5	59	7	1.95	15.1	14	n.a.	53
July	78.8	58.4	88	45	4.28	0.0	15	n.a.	63
October	52.1	32.4	70	20	1.51	T	11	n.a.	58
Annual	48.8	29.1	95	-29	31.31	121.1	164	n.a.	59

CHARLESTON, SOUTH CAROLINA (MUNICIPAL AIRPORT) Lat 32° 54′ N, Long 80° 02′ W.   Elevation: 40 ft.

Month	Average maximum	Average minimum	Record high	Record low	Rainfall, inches	Snowfall, inches	Days with precipitation	Percentage possible sunshine	Percentage relative humidity at noon
January	63.9	43.6	81	26	4.92	0.0	13	56	64
April	73.4	51.1	88	34	3.74	0.0	9	76	52
July	87.2	71.2	92	62	9.34	0.0	19	72	67
October	79.5	58.4	86	40	1.97	0.0	4	68	57
Annual	76.5	56.3	96	21	56.19	0.0	134	68	59

Month	Temperature				Precipitation				Percentage relative humidity at noon
	Average maximum	Average minimum	Record high	Record low	Rainfall, inches	Snowfall, inches	Days with precipitation	Percentage possible sunshine	

CHICAGO, ILLINOIS (MIDWAY AIRPORT) Lat 41° 47′ N, Long 87° 45′ W.   Elevation: 607 ft.

Month	Average maximum	Average minimum	Record high	Record low	Rainfall, inches	Snowfall, inches	Days with precipitation	Percentage possible sunshine	Percentage relative humidity at noon
January	34.8	20.9	60	2	3.68	7.2	17	32	71
April	51.2	35.8	76	16	7.84	10.0	13	57	58
July	85.8	66.4	93	52	1.53	0.0	7	85	50
October	67.3	45.8	89	33	2.26	0.0	4	77	47
Annual	59.7	43.0	94	-6	42.05	53.3	145	59	60

DALLAS-FORT WORTH, TEXAS (REGIONAL AIRPORT) Lat 32° 54′ N, Long 97° 02′ W.   Elevation: 551 ft.

Month	Average maximum	Average minimum	Record high	Record low	Rainfall, inches	Snowfall, inches	Days with precipitation	Percentage possible sunshine	Percentage relative humidity at noon
January	59.0	38.9	81	17	3.34	T	9	n.a.	59
April	73.7	55.6	88	31	3.40	0.0	6	n.a.	59
July	93.5	73.6	100	65	5.06	0.0	6	n.a.	51
October	81.8	57.8	95	44	T	0.0	0	n.a.	47
Annual	76.2	55.0	100	17	29.10	4.1	75	n.a.	55

DENVER, COLORADO (STAPLETON INTERNATIONAL AIRPORT) Lat 39° 45′ N, Long 104° 52′ W.   Elevation: 5,283 ft.

Month	Average maximum	Average minimum	Record high	Record low	Rainfall, inches	Snowfall, inches	Days with precipitation	Percentage possible sunshine	Percentage relative humidity at noon
January	46.4	16.9	67	-9	0.23	3.6	5	64	40
April	58.2	30.0	82	-2	1.14	10.9	6	79	40
July	87.2	58.2	95	54	2.78	0.0	14	73	33
October	70.5	35.9	87	21	0.30	2.7	1	85	28
Annual	64.0	34.7	95	-11	15.51	64.1	91	70	38

DULUTH, MINNESOTA (INTERNATIONAL AIRPORT) Lat 46° 50′ N, Long 92° 11′ W.   Elevation: 1,428 ft.

Month	Average maximum	Average minimum	Record high	Record low	Rainfall, inches	Snowfall, inches	Days with precipitation	Percentage possible sunshine	Percentage relative humidity at noon
January	18.3	.8	33	-24	3.69	32.7	19	35	78
April	37.3	24.6	52	-5	2.21	0.4	10	46	70
July	79.1	58.3	93	42	2.26	0.0	9	80	61
October	54.7	38.6	78	18	1.20	0.1	7	53	58
Annual	46.4	29.1	93	-24	29.41	109.3	142	51	67

GREAT FALLS, MONTANA (INTERNATIONAL AIRPORT) Lat 47° 29′ N, Long 111° 22′ W.   Elevation: 3,662 ft.

Month	Average maximum	Average minimum	Record high	Record low	Rainfall, inches	Snowfall, inches	Days with precipitation	Percentage possible sunshine	Percentage relative humidity at noon
January	32.4	13.0	51	-16	1.14	13.2	10	34	65
April	39.9	21.9	60	-6	4.63	29.2	18	39	73
July	85.7	57.9	104	50	1.20	0.0	9	74	45
October	55.4	36.0	81	23	3.43	16.6	10	54	55
Annual	52.9	31.1	104	-24	25.24	99.6	137	57	57

KANSAS CITY, MISSOURI (INTERNATIONAL AIRPORT) Lat 39° 17′ N, Long 94 43′ W.   Elevation: 1,014 ft.

Month	Average maximum	Average minimum	Record high	Record low	Rainfall, inches	Snowfall, inches	Days with precipitation	Percentage possible sunshine	Percentage relative humidity at noon
January	38.7	21.0	55	0	2.14	5.4	7	58	67
April	62.8	42.8	85	12	6.61	2.3	12	56	57
July	93.2	68.5	100	54	0.25	0.0	4	87	44
October	70.2	47.5	89	30	0.35	0.0	3	78	51
Annual	64.0	44.5	103	-2	34.07	28.1	97	63	60

LOS ANGELES, CALIFORNIA (INTERNATIONAL AIRPORT) Lat 33° 56′ N, Long 118° 24′ W.   Elevation: 97 ft.

Month	Average maximum	Average minimum	Record high	Record low	Rainfall, inches	Snowfall, inches	Days with precipitation	Percentage possible sunshine	Percentage relative humidity at noon
January	67.3	46.4	87	37	0.01	0.0	1	n.a.	49
April	62.9	50.4	69	45	0.74	0.0	6	n.a.	68
July	74.8	62.9	81	58	T	0.0	0	n.a.	64
October	73.4	57.5	86	49	0.24	0.0	3	n.a.	59
Annual	69.2	54.4	104	37	7.32	0.0	29	n.a.	63

MIAMI, FLORIDA (INTERNATIONAL AIRPORT) Lat 25° 48′ N, Long 80° 16′ W.   Elevation: 7 ft.

Month	Average maximum	Average minimum	Record high	Record low	Rainfall, inches	Snowfall, inches	Days with precipitation	Percentage possible sunshine	Percentage relative humidity at noon
January	78.7	66.7	84	46	1.39	0.0	7	n.a.	62
April	84.3	70.7	93	52	0.53	0.0	3	n.a.	53
July	86.6	75.6	90	71	4.99	0.0	16	n.a.	69
October	84.5	73.8	88	67	6.25	0.0	17	n.a.	66
Annual	83.1	70.8	93	42	39.10	0.0	134	n.a.	62

Month	Temperature				Precipitation			Percentage possible sunshine	Percentage relative humidity at noon
	Average maximum	Average minimum	Record high	Record low	Rainfall, inches	Snowfall, inches	Days with precipitation		

NASHVILLE, TENNESSEE (METROPOLITAN AIRPORT) Lat 36° 07′ N, Long 86° 41′ W.   Elevation: 590 ft.

Month	Average maximum	Average minimum	Record high	Record low	Rainfall, inches	Snowfall, inches	Days with precipitation	Percentage possible sunshine	Percentage relative humidity at noon
January	53.3	33.5	76	15	4.67	4.2	12	42	69
April	69.3	47.7	84	32	3.55	T	8	60	51
July	88.5	68.4	93	57	2.96	0.0	8	72	59
October	72.6	52.1	85	37	5.86	0.0	9	54	65
Annual	69.9	50.5	94	11	60.58	4.2	119	46	63

NEW ORLEANS, LOUISIANA (INTERNATIONAL AIRPORT) Lat 29° 59′ N, Long 90° 15′ W.   Elevation: 4 ft.

Month	Average maximum	Average minimum	Record high	Record low	Rainfall, inches	Snowfall, inches	Days with precipitation	Percentage possible sunshine	Percentage relative humidity at noon
January	67.3	47.1	80	25	2.95	0.0	13	53	75
April	75.5	58.0	86	42	6.69	0.0	6	51	70
July	88.0	72.4	92	68	8.35	0.0	17	47	72
October	79.3	60.4	86	47	4.00	0.0	4	60	68
Annual	77.2	59.1	94	25	80.50	0.0	132	54	71

NEW YORK, NEW YORK (CENTRAL PARK) Lat 40° 47′ N, Long 73° 58′ W.   Elevation: 132 ft.

Month	Average maximum	Average minimum	Record high	Record low	Rainfall, inches	Snowfall, inches	Days with precipitation	Percentage possible sunshine	Percentage relative humidity at noon
January	43.3	31.3	63	15	4.76	2.0	14	37	65
April	56.6	39.1	74	27	3.04	T	7	61	41
July	83.4	68.2	93	58	11.77	0.0	14	53	61
October	67.0	51.4	83	31	3.70	0.0	9	67	60
Annual	62.3	47.5	98	15	61.21	15.2	130	55	n.a.

PHOENIX, ARIZONA (SKY HARBOR INTERNATIONAL AIRPORT) Lat 33° 26′ N, Long 112° 01′ W.   Elevation: 1,112 ft.

Month	Average maximum	Average minimum	Record high	Record low	Rainfall, inches	Snowfall, inches	Days with precipitation	Percentage possible sunshine	Percentage relative humidity at noon
January	66.4	38.1	81	27	0.02	0.0	1	78	37
April	76.6	48.5	91	41	0.43	0.0	3	89	27
July	106.1	82.4	113	72	0.38	0.0	2	87	29
October	87.3	58.5	100	43	0.23	0.0	2	97	28
Annual	84.9	57.0	116	27	4.51	0.0	24	89	29

SALT LAKE CITY, UTAH (INTERNATIONAL AIRPORT) Lat 40° 46′ N, Long 111° 58′ W.   Elevation: 4,220 ft.

Month	Average maximum	Average minimum	Record high	Record low	Rainfall, inches	Snowfall, inches	Days with precipitation	Percentage possible sunshine	Percentage relative humidity at noon
January	36.2	18.6	56	3	1.28	12.5	14	64	69
April	53.4	35.1	70	27	2.46	13.1	10	60	54
July	93.0	64.6	99	53	0.28	0.0	5	85	30
October	65.8	40.9	86	26	1.91	0.1	6	64	44
Annual	61.8	39.6	100	1	17.92	93.7	105	69	49

SAN FRANCISCO, CALIFORNIA (INTERNATIONAL AIRPORT) Lat 37° 37′ N, Long 122° 23′ W.   Elevation: 8 ft.

Month	Average maximum	Average minimum	Record high	Record low	Rainfall, inches	Snowfall, inches	Days with precipitation	Percentage possible sunshine	Percentage relative humidity at noon
January	55.9	38.8	64	30	2.60	T	8	n.a.	78
April	57.6	43.5	68	38	1.66	0.0	10	n.a.	66
July	70.4	53.2	88	50	0.13	0.0	1	n.a.	65
October	67.4	50.2	82	42	2.27	0.0	8	n.a.	67
Annual	63.7	47.1	94	30	17.25	T	65	n.a.	67

SEATTLE, WASHINGTON (SEATTLE-TACOMA AIRPORT) Lat 47° 27′ N, Long 122° 18′ W.   Elevation: 400 ft.

Month	Average maximum	Average minimum	Record high	Record low	Rainfall, inches	Snowfall, inches	Days with precipitation	Percentage possible sunshine	Percentage relative humidity at noon
January	43.1	34.4	53	25	6.01	1.3	25	17	81
April	53.6	38.0	67	29	2.49	0.2	13	56	71
July	78.0	57.0	90	50	0.27	0.0	4	64	61
October	57.0	45.8	81	35	7.75	0.0	19	39	82
Annual	58.7	43.8	90	22	44.48	5.7	164	52	71

WASHINGTON, D.C. (NATIONAL AIRPORT) Lat 38° 51′ N, Long 77° 02′ W.   Elevation: 10 ft.

Month	Average maximum	Average minimum	Record high	Record low	Rainfall, inches	Snowfall, inches	Days with precipitation	Percentage possible sunshine	Percentage relative humidity at noon
January	49.3	32.5	76	19	3.09	6.6	14	46	60
April	62.5	44.7	79	33	2.13	T	8	61	43
July	87.2	71.3	93	61	7.16	0.0	11	62	54
October	73.0	53.3	87	34	2.38	0.0	10	56	55
Annual	68.0	50.7	98	17	50.50	13.1	125	56	54

CROSSWORD PUZZLE GUIDE

Since most persons who can read and write occasionally or frequently indulge in the indoor pastime of working crossword puzzles, this section is offered as a handy help to solvers who may be stumped for a two-letter word meaning "three-toed sloth" or a three-letter word meaning "native of Mindanao."

We have those two words here, and plenty more. We have the Greek, Roman, Norse and Egyptian deities of myth and legend. And we have those "Greek letters" and "months of the Jewish year" so often needed to fill out little gaps.

The reader is warned that in mythology there are many confusing and even conflicting accounts of the identities and adventures of the various gods, goddesses and lesser figures. There is also considerable variation in the spelling of names, places and things. For instance, you may spell it ICON, IKON or EIKON, and similar options are plentiful all along the crossword line. If the reader will keep further possible variations in mind, it may help at a critical point.

Various other sections of our book will be found of use to the crossword puzzler—especially the section of world geography and statistics. See Geography in the index.

First Aid to Crossword Puzzlers

(We cannot, of course, begin to list all the odd words you will meet with in your daily and Sunday crossword puzzles, for such words run into many thousands. But we have tried to include those which turn up most frequently, as well as many others which should be of help to you when you are unable to go any further.

Also, we do not guarantee that the definitions in your puzzle will be exactly the same as ours, although we have checked every word with a standard dictionary and have followed its definition.

In nearly every case, we have used as the key word the principal noun of the definition, rather than any adjective, adjective phrase, or noun used as an adjective. And, to simplify your searching, we have grouped the words according to the number of spaces you have to fill.)

Words of Two Letters

Ambary, DA
And (French, Latin), ET
Article (Arabic), AL
    (French), LA, LE, UN
    (Spanish), EL, LA, UN
At the (French), AU
    (Spanish), AL
Behold, LO
Bird: Hawaiian, OO
Birthplace: Abraham's, UR
Bone, OS
Buddha, FO
Butterfly: Peacock, IO
Champagne, AY
Chaos, NU
Chief: Burmese, BO
Coin: Roman, AS
    Siamese, AT
Concerning, RE
Dialect: Chinese, WU
Double (Egy. relig.), KA
Drama: Japanese, NO
Egg (comb. form), OO
Esker, OS
Eye (Scotch), EE
Factor: Amplification, MU
Fifty (Greek), NU
Fish: Carplike, ID
Force, OD
Forty (Greek), MU
From (French, Latin, Spanish), DE
    (Latin prefix), AB

From the (French), DU
God: Babylonian, EA, ZU
    Egyptian sun, RA
    Hindu unknown, KA
    Semitic, EL
Goddess: Babylonian, AI
    Greek earth, GE
Gold (heraldry), OR
Gulf: Arctic, OB
Heart (Egy. relig.) AB
Indian: South American, GE
King: Of Bashan, OG
Language: Artificial, RO
    Assamese, AO
Lava: Hawaiian, AA
Letter: Greek, MU, NU, PI, XI
    Hebrew, HE, PE
Lily: Palm, TI
Measure: Annamese, LY
    Chinese, HO, HU, KO, LI, MU, PU, TO, TU
    Japanese, GO, JO, MO, RI, SE, TO
    Metric land, AR
    Netherlands, EL
    Portuguese, PE
    Siamese, WA
    Swedish, AM
    Type, EM, EN
Monk: Buddhist, BO

Month: Jewish, AB
Mouth, OS
Mulberry: Indian, AL
Native: Burmese, WA
Note: Of Scale, DO, FA, MI, LA, RE, TI
Of (French, Latin, Spanish), DE
Of the (French), DU
One (Scotch), AE
Pagoda: Chinese, TA
Plant: East Indian fiber, DA
Ridge: Sandy, AS, OS
River: Russian, OB
Sloth: Three-toed, AI
Soul (Egy. relig.), BA
Sound: Hindu mystic, OM
Suffix: Comparative, ER
The. See Article
To the: French, AU
    Spanish, AL
Tree: Buddhist sacred, BO
Tribe: Assamese, AO
Type: Jumbled, PI
Weight: Annamese, TA
    Chinese, LI
    Danish, ES
    Japanese, MO
    Roman, AS
Whirlwind: Faeroe Is., OE
Yes (German), JA
    (Italian, Spanish), SI
    (Russian), DA

Words of Three Letters

Adherent, IST
Again, BIS
Age, ERA
Antelope: African, GNU, KOB
Apricot: Japanese, UME
Article (German), DAS, DEM, DEN, DER, DES, DIE, EIN
(French), LES, UNE
(Spanish), LAS, LOS, UNA
Banana: Polynesian, FEI
Barge, HOY
Bass: African, IYO
Beak, NEB, NIB
Beard: Grain, AWN
Beetle: June, DOR
Being, ENS
Berry: Hawthorn, HAW
Beverage: Hawaiian, AVA
Bird: Australian, EMU
Crowlike, JAY
Extinct, MOA
Fabulous, ROC
Frigate, IWA
Parson, POE, TUE, TUI
Sea, AUK
Blackbird, ANI, ANO
Born, NEE
Bronze: Roman, AES
Bugle: Yellow, IVA
By way of, VIA
Canton: Swiss, URI
Cap: Turkish, FEZ
Catnip, NEP
Character: In "Faerie Queene," UNA
Coin: Afghan, PUL
Albanian, LEK
British Guiana, BIT
Bulgarian, LEV, LEW
French, ECU, SOU
Indian, PIE
Japanese, SEN, YEN
Korean, WON
Lithuanian, LIT
Macao, Timor, AVO
Palestinian, MIL
Persian, PUL
Peruvian, SOL
Rumanian, BAN, LEU, LEY
Scandinavian, ORE
Siamese, ATT
See also Money of account
Collection: Facts, ANA
Commune: Belgian, ANS, ATH
Netherlands, EDE, EPE
Community: Russian, MIR
Constellation: Southern, ARA
Contraction: Poetic, EEN, EER, OER
Covering: Apex of roof, EPI

Crab: Fiddler, UCA
Crag: Rocky, TOR
Cry: Crow, rook, raven, CAW
Cup: Wine, AMA
Cymbal: Oriental, TAL, ZEL
Disease: Silkworm, UJI
Division: Danish territorial, AMT
Geologic, EON
Doctrine, ISM
Dowry, DOT
Dry (French), SEC
Dynasty: Chinese, CHI, HAN, SUI, WEI, YIN
Eagle: Sea, ERN
Earth (comb. form), GEO
Egg: Louse, NIT
Eggs: Fish, ROE
Emmet, ANT
Enzyme, ASE
Equal (comb. form), ISO
Extension: building, ELL
Far (comb. form), TEL
Farewell, AVE
Fiber: Palm, TAL
Finial, EPI
Fish: Carplike, IDE
Pikelike, GAR
Flatfish, DAB
Fleur-de-lis, LIS, LYS
Food: Hawaiian, POI
Formerly, NEE
Friend (French), AMI
Game: Card, LOO
Garment: Camel-hair, ABA
Gateway, DAR
Gazelle: Tibetan, GOA
Genus: Ducks, AIX
Grasses, POA
Grasses (maize), ZEA
Herbs or shrubs, IVA
Lizards, UTA
Rodents (incl. house mice), MUS
Ruminants (incl. cattle), BOS
Swine, SUS
Gibbon: Malay, LAR
God: Assyrian, SIN
Babylonian, ABU, ANU, BEL, HEA, SIN, UTU
Irish sea, LER
Phrygian, MEN
Polynesian, ORO
Goddess: Babylonian, AYA
Etruscan, UNI
Hindu, SRI, UMA, VAC
Teutonic, RAN
Governor: Algerian, DEY
Turkish, BEY
Grampus, ORC
Grape, UVA
Grass: Meadow, POA
Gypsy, ROM
Hail, AVE
Hare: Female, DOE

Hawthorn, HAW
Hay: Spread for drying, TED
Herb: Japanese, UDO
Perennial, PIA
Used for blue dye, WAD
Herd: Whales, GAM, POD
Hero: Spanish, CID
High (music), ALT
Honey (pharm.), MEL
Humorist: American, ADE
I (Latin), EGO
I love (Latin), AMO
Indian: Algonquian, FOX, SAC, WEA
Chimakuan, HOH
Keresan, SIA
Mayan, MAM
Shoshonean, UTE
Siouan, KAW, OTO
South American, ITE, ONA, URO, URU, YAO
Tierra del Fuego, ONA
Wakashan, AHT
Ingot, PIG
Inlet: Narrow, RIA
Island: Cyclades, IOS
Dodecanese, COS, KOS
(French), ILE
River, AIT
Jackdaw, DAW
John (Gaelic), IAN
Keelbill, ANI, ANO
Kiln, OST
King: British legendary LUD
Kobold, NIS
Lace: To make, TAT
Lamprey, EEL
Language: Artificial, IDO
Bantu, ILA
Siamese, LAO, TAI
Leaf: Palm, OLA, OLE
Leaving, ORT
Left: Cause to turn, HAW
Letter: Greek, CHI, ETA, PHI, PSI, RHO, TAU
Hebrew, MEM, NUN, SIN, TAV, VAU
Lettuce, COS
Life (comb. form), BIO
Lily: Palm, TOI
Lizard, EFT
Louse: Young NIT
Love (Anglo-Irish), GRA
Lute: Oriental, TAR
Macaw: Brazilian, ARA
Marble, TAW
Match: Shooting (French), TIR
Meadow, LEA
Measure: Abyssinian, TAT
Algerian, PIK
Annamese, GON, MAU, NGU, VUO, SAO, TAO, TAT
Arabian, DEN, SAA

Belgian, VAT
Bulgarian, OKA, OKE
Chinese, FEN, TOU, YIN
Cloth, ELL
Cyprus, OKA, OKE, PIK
Czech, LAN, SAH
Danish, FOD, MIL, POT
Dominican Republic, ONA
Dutch, old, AAM
East Indian, KIT
Egyptian, APT, HEN, PIK, ROB
Electric, MHO, OHM
Energy, ERG
English, PIN
Estonian, TUN
French, POT
German, AAM
Greek, PIK
Hebrew, CAB, HIN, KOR, LOG
Hungarian, AKO
Icelandic, FET
Indian, GAZ, GUZ, JOW, KOS
Japanese, BOO, CHO, KEN, RIN, SHO, SUN, TAN
Malabar, ADY
Metric land, ARE
Netherlands, KAN, KOP, MUD, VAT, ZAK
Norwegian, FOT, POT
Persian, GAZ, GUZ, MOU, ZAR, ZER
Polish, CAL
Rangoon, DHA, LAN
Roman, PES, URN
Russian, FUT, LOF
Scotch, COP
Siamese, KEN, NIU, RAI, SAT, SEN, SOK, WAH, YOT
Somaliland, TOP
Spanish, PIE
Straits Settlements, PAU, TUN
Swedish, ALN, FOT, MIL, REF, TUM
Swiss, POT
Tunisian, SAA
Turkish, OKA, OKE, PIK
Wire, MIL
Württemberg, IMI
Yarn, LEA
Yugoslavian, OKA, RIF
Milk, LAC
Milkfish, AWA
Moccasin, PAC
Money: Yap stone, FEI
Money of Account: Anglo-Saxon, ORA, ORE
French, SOU
Indian, LAC
Japanese, RIN
Oman, GAJ
Virgin Islands, BIT
See also Coin

Monkey: Capuchin, SAI
Morsel, ORT
Mother: Peer Gynt's, ASE
Mountain: Asia Minor, IDA
Mulberry: Indian, AAL, ACH, AWL
Muttonbird: New Zealand, OII
Nahoor, SNA
Native: Mindanao, ATA
Neckpiece, BOA
Newt, EFT
No (Scotch), NAE
Note: Guido's highest, ELA
Of scale, SOL
Nursemaid: Oriental, AMA, IYA
Ocher: Yellow, SIL
One (Scotch), YIN
Ornament: Pagoda, TEE
Oven: Polynesian, UMU
Ox: Tibetan, YAK
Pagoda: Chinese, TAA
Parrot: Hawk, HIA
New Zealand, KEA
Part: Footlike, PES
Particle: Electrified, ION
Pasha, DEY
Pass: Mountain, COL
Paste: Rice, AME
Pea: Indian split, DAL
Peasant: Philippine, TAO
Penpoint, NEB, NIB
Piece out, EKE
Pigeon, NUN
Pine: Textile screw, ARA
Pistol (slang), GAT
Pit: Baking, IMU
Plant: Pepper, AVA
Play: By Capek, RUR
Poem: Old French, DIT
Porgy: Japanese, TAI
Priest: Biblical high, ELI
Prince Ethiopian, RAS
Pseudonym: Dickens', BOZ
Queen: Fairy, MAB
Quince: Bengal, BEL
Record: Ship's, LOG
Refuse: Flax (Scotch), PAB, POB
Resin, LAC
Resort, SPA
Revolver (slang), GAT
Right: Cause to turn, GEE
River: Scotch or English, DEE (Spanish), RIO
Swiss, AAR
Room: Harem, ODA
Rootstock: Fern, ROI
Rose (Persian), GUL
Ruff: Female, REE
Rule: Indian, RAJ
Sailor, GOB, TAR
Saint: Female (abbr.), STE
Mohammedan, PIR
Salt, SAL
Sash: Japanese, OBI
Scrap, ORT

Seed: Poppy, MAW
Small, PIP
Self, EGO
Serpent: Vedic sky, AHI
Sesame, TIL
Sheep: Female, EWE
Indian, SHA
Male, RAM
Sheepfold (Scotch), REE
Shelter, LEE
Shield, ECU
Shooting match (French), TIR
Shrew: European, ERD
Shrub: Evergreen, YEW
Silkworm, ERI
Snake, ASP, BOA
Soak, RET
Son-in-law: Mohammed's, ALI
Sorrel: Wood, OCA
Spade: Long, narrow, LOY
Spirit: Malignant, KER
Spot: Playing-card, PIP
Spread for drying, TED
Spring: Mineral, SPA
Sprite: Water, NIX
Statesman: Japanese, ITO
Stern: Toward, AFT
Stomach: Bird's, MAW
Street (French), RUE
Summer (French), ETE
Sun, SOL
Swamp, BOG, FEN
Swan: Male, COB
Tea: Chinese, CHA
Temple: Shinto, SHA
The. *See* Article
Thing (law), RES
Title: Etruscan, LAR
Monk's, FRA
Portuguese, DOM
Spanish, DON
Turkish, AGA, BEY
Tool: Cutting, ADZ, AXE
Mining, GAD
Piercing, AWL
Tree: Candlenut, AMA
Central American, EBO
East Indian, SAJ, SAL
Evergreen, YEW
Hawaiian, KOA, KOU
Indian, BEL, DAR
Linden, LIN
New Zealand, AKE
Philippine, DAO, TUA, TUI
Rubber, ULE
South American, APA
Tribe: New Zealand, ATI
Turmeric, REA
Twice, BIS
Twin: Siamese, ENG
Uncle (dialect), EAM, EME
Veil: Chalice, AER, AIR
Vessel: Wine, AMA
Vestment: Ecclesiastical, ALB

Vetch: Bitter, ERS
Victorfish, AKU
Vine: New Zealand, AKA
   Philippine, IYO
Wallaba, APA
Wapiti, ELK
Water (French), EAU
Waterfall, LIN
Watering place: Prussian,
   EMS
Weave: Designating plain,
   UNI
Weight: Annamese, CAN
   Bulgarian, OKA, OKE
   Burmese, MOO, VIS
   Chinese, FEN, HAO, KIN,
   SSU, TAN, YIN

Cyprus, OKA, OKE
Danish, LOD, ORT, VOG
East Indian, TJI
Egyptian, KAT, OKA, OKE
English, for wool, TOD
German, LOT
Greek, MNA, OKA, OKE
Indian, SER
Japanese, FUN, KIN, RIN,
   SHI
Korean, KON
Malacca, KIP
Mongolian, LAN
Netherlands, ONS
Norwegian, LOD
Polish, LUT
Rangoon, PAI
Roman, BES

Russian, LOT
Siamese, BAT, HAP, PAI
Swedish, ASS, ORT
Turkish, OKA, OKE
Yugoslavian, OKA, OKE
Whales: Herd, GAM, POD
Wildebeest, GNU
Wing, ALA
Witticism, MOT
Wolframite, CAL
Worm: African, LOA
Wreath: Hawaiian, LEI
Yale, ELI
Yam: Hawaiian, HOI
Yes (French), OUI
Young: Bring forth, EAN
Z (letter), ZED

Words of Four Letters

Aborigine: Borneo, DYAK
Agave, ALOE
Animal: Footless, APOD
Ant: White, ANAI, ANAY
Antelope: African, ASSE,
   BISA, GUIB, KOBA,
   KUDU, ORYX, POKU,
   PUKU, TOPI, TORA
Apoplexy: Plant, ESCA
Apple, POME
Apricot, ANSU
Ardor, ELAN
Armadillo, APAR, PEBA,
   PEVA, TATU
Ascetic: Mohammedan,
   SUFI
Association: Chinese, TONG
Astronomer: Persian, OMAR
Avatar: Of Vishnu, RAMA
Axillary, ALAR
Band: Horizontal (heral-
   dry), FESS
Barracuda, SPET
Bark: Mulberry, TAPA
Base: Column, DADO
Bearing (heraldry), ORLE
Beer: Russian, KVAS
Beige, ECRU
Being, ESSE
Beverage: Japanese rice,
   SAKE
Bird: Asian, MINA, MYNA
   Egyptian sacred, IBIS
   Extinct, DODO, MAMO
   Flightless, KIWI
   Gull-like, TERN
   Hawaiian, IIWI, MAMO
   Parson, KOKO
   Unfledged, EYAS
Birds: As class, AVES
Black, EBON
   (French), NOIR
Blackbird: European, MERL
Boat: Flat-bottomed, DORY
Bone: Forearm, ULNA
Bones, OSSA
Box: Japanese, INRO
Bravo (rare), EUGE

Buffalo: Indian wild, ARNA
Bull (Spanish), TORO
Burden, ONUS
Cabbage: Sliced, SLAW
Caliph: Mohammedan,
   OMAR
Canoe: Malay, PRAU, PROA
Cap: Military, KEPI
Cape, NESS
Capital: Ancient Irish,
   TARA
Case: Article, ETUI
Cat: Wild, BALU, EYRA
Chalcedony, SARD
Chamber: Indian ceremo-
   nial, KIVA
Channel: Brain, ITER
Cheese: Dutch, EDAM
Chest: Sepulchral stone,
   CIST
Chieftain: Arab, EMIR
Church: Part of, APSE,
   NAVE
   (Scotch), KIRK
Claim (law), LIEN
Cluster: Flower, CYME
Coin: Chinese, TAEL, YUAN
   German, MARK
   Indian, ANNA
   Iranian, RIAL
   Italian, LIRA
   Moroccan, OKIA
   Siamese, BAHT
   South American, PESO
   Spanish, DURO, PESO
   Turkish, PARA
Commune: Belgian, AATH
Composition: Musical,
   OPUS
Compound: Chemical, DIOL
Constellation: Southern,
   PAVO
Council: Russian, DUMA
Counsel, REDE
Covering: Seed, ARIL
Cross: Egyptian, ANKH
Cry: Bacchanalian, EVOE
Cup (Scotch), TASS

Cupbearer, SAKI
Dagger, DIRK
   Malay, KRIS
Dam: River, WEIR
Dash, ELAN
Date: Roman, IDES
Dawn: Pertaining to, EOAN
Dean: English, INGE
Decay: In fruit, BLET
Deer: Sambar, MAHA
Disease: Skin, ACNE
Disk: Solar, ATEN
Dog: Hunting, ALAN
Drink: Hindu intoxicating,
   SOMA
Duck, SMEE, SMEW, TEAL
Dynasty: Chinese. CHEN,
   CHIN, CHOU, CHOW,
   HSIA, MING, SUNG,
   TANG, TSIN
   Mongol, YUAN
Eagle: Biblical, GIER
   Sea, ERNE
Egyptian: Christian, COPT
Ear: Pertaining to, OTIC
Entrance: Mine, ADIT
Esau, EDOM
Escutcheon: Voided, ORLE
Eskers, OSAR
Evergreen: New Zealand,
   TAWA
Fairy: Persian, PERI
Family: Italian, ESTE
Far (comb. form), TELE
Farewell, VALE
Father (French), PERE
Fennel: Philippine, ANIS
Fever: Malarial, AGUE
Fiber: East Indian, JUTE
Firn, NEVE
Fish: Carplike, DACE
   Hawaiian, ULUA
   Herringlike, SHAD
   Mackerellike, CERO
   Marine, HAKE
   Sea, LING, MERO, OPAH
   Spiny-finned, GOBY
Food: Tropical, TARO

Foot: Metric, IAMB
Formerly, ERST
Founder: Of Carthage, DIDO
France: Southern, MIDI
Furze, ULEX
Gaelic, ERSE
Gaiter, SPAT
Game: Card, FARO, SKAT
Garlic: European wild, MOLY
Garment: Hindu, SARI
Roman, TOGA
Gazelle, CORA
Gem, JADE, ONYX, OPAL, RUBY
Genus: Amphibians (incl. frogs), RANA
Amphibians (incl. tree toads), HYLA
Antelopes, ORYX
Auks, ALCA, URIA
Bees, APIS
Birds (American ostriches), RHEA
Birds (cranes), GRUS
Birds (magpies), PICA
Birds (peacocks), PAVO
Cetaceans, INIA
Ducks (incl. mallards), ANAS
Fishes (burbots), LOTA
Fishes (incl. bowfins), AMIA
Geese (snow geese), CHEN
Gulls, XEMA
Herbs, ARUM, GEUM
Insects (water scorpions), NEPA
Lilies, ALOE
Mammals (mankind), HOMO
Orchids, DISA
Owls, ASIO, BUBO, OTUS
Palms, NIPA
Sea birds, SULA
Sheep, OVIS
Shrubs, Eurasian, ULEX
Shrubs (hollies), ILEX
Shrubs (incl. Virginia Willow), ITEA
Shrubs, tropical, EVEA
Snakes (sand snakes), ERYX
Swans, OLOR
Trees, chocolate, COLA
Trees (ebony family), MABA
Trees (incl. maples), ACER
Trees (olives), OLEA
Trees, tropical, EVEA
Turtles, EMYS
Goat: Wild, IBEX, KRAS, TAHR, TAIR, THAR
God: Assyrian, ASUR

Babylonian, ADAD, ADDU, ENKI, ENZU, IRRA, NABU, NEBO, UTUG
Celtic, LLEU, LLEW
Hindu, AGNI, CIVA, DEVA, DEWA, KAMA, RAMA, SIVA, VAYU
Phrygian, ATYS
Semitic, BAAL
Teutonic, HLER
Goddess: Babylonian, ERUA, GULA
Hawaiian, PELE
Hindu, DEVI, KALI, SHRI, VACH
Gooseberry: Hawaiian, POHA
Gourd, PEPO
Grafted (heraldry), ENTE
Grandfather (obsolete), AIEL
Grandparents: Pertaining to, AVAL
Grass: Hawaiian, HILO
Gray (French), GRIS
Green (heraldry), VERT
Groom: Indian, SYCE
Half (prefix), DEMI, HEMI, SEMI
Hamlet, DORP
Hammer-head: Part of, PEEN
Handle, ANSA
Harp: Japanese, KOTO
Hartebeest, ASSE, TORA
Hautboy, OBOE
Hawk: Taken from nest (falconry), EYAS
Hearing (law), OYER
Heater: For liquids, ETNA
Herb: Aromatic, ANET, DILL
Fabulous, MOLY
Perennial, GEUM, SEGO
Pot, WORT
Used for blue dye, WADE, WOAD
Hill: Flat-topped, MESA
Sand, DENE, DUNE
Hoarfrost, RIME
Hog: Immature female, GILT
Holly, ILEX
House: Cow, BYRE
(Spanish), CASA
Ice: Floating, FLOE
Image, ICON, IKON
Incarnation: Of Vishnu, RAMA
Indian: Algonquian, CREE, SAUK
Central American, MAYA
Iroquoian, ERIE
Mexican, CORA
Peruvian, CANA, INCA, MORO
Shoshonean, HOPI
Siouan, OTOE

Southwestern, HOPI, PIMA, YUMA, ZUNI
Insect: Immature, PUPA
Instrument: Stringed, LUTE, LYRE
Ireland, EIRE, ERIN
Jacket: English, ETON
Jail (British), GAOL
Jar, OLLA
Judge: Mohammedan, CADI
Juniper: European, CADE
Kiln, OAST, OVEN
King: British legendary, LUDD, NUDD
Kiss, BUSS
Knife: Philippine, BOLO
Koran: Section of, SURA
Laborer: Spanish American, PEON
Lake: Mountain, TARN
(Scotch), LOCH
Lamp: Miner's, DAVY
Landing place: Indian, GHAT
Language: Buddhist, PALI
Japanese, AINU
Latvian, LETT
Layer: Of iris, UVEA
Leaf: Palm, OLAY, OLLA
Legislature: Ukrainian, RADA
Lemur, LORI
Leopard, PARD
Let it stand, STET
Letter: Greek, BETA, IOTA, ZETA
Hebrew, AYIN, BETH, CAPH, KOPH, RESH, SHIN, TETH, YODH
Papal, BULL
Lily, ALOE
Literature: Hindu sacred, VEDA
Lizard, GILA
Monitor, URAN
Loquat, BIWA
Magistrate: Genoese or Venetian, DOGE
Man (Latin), HOMO
Mark: Omission, DELE
Marmoset: South American, MICO
Meadow: Fertile, VEGA
Measure: Electric, VOLT, WATT
Force, DYNE
Hebrew, OMER
Printing, PICA
Spanish or Portuguese, VARA
Swiss land, IMMI
Medley, OLIO
Merganser, SMEW
Milk (French), LAIT
Molding, GULA
Curved, OGEE
Mongoose: Crab-eating, URVA

Monk: Tibetan, LAMA
Monkey: African, MONA, WAAG
Ceylonese, MAHA
Cochin-China, DOUC
South American, SAKI, TITI
Monkshood, ATIS
Month: Jewish, ADAR, ELUL, IYAR
Mother (French), MERE
Mountain: Thessaly, OSSA
Mouse: Meadow, VOLE
Mythology: Norse, EDDA
Nail (French), CLOU
Native: Philippine, MORO
Nest: Of pheasants, NIDE
Network, RETE
No (German), NEIN
Noble: Mohammedan, AMIR
Notice: Death, OBIT
Novel: By Zola, NANA
Nursemaid: Oriental AMAH, AYAH, EYAH
Nut: Philippine, PILI
Oak: Holm, ILEX
Oil (comb. form), OLEO
Ostrich: American, RHEA
Oven, KILN, OAST
Owl: Barn, LULU
Ox: Celebes wild, ANOE
Extinct wild, URUS
Palm, ATAP, NIPA, SAGO
Parliament, DIET
Parrot: New Zealand, KAKA
Pass: Indian mountain, GHAT
Passage: Closing (music), CODA
Peach: Clingstone, PAVY
Peasant: Indian, RYOT
Old English, CARL
Pepper: Australasian, KAVA
Perfume, ATAR
Persia, IRAN
Person: Extraordinary, ONER
Pickerel or pike, ESOX
Pitcher, EWER
Plant: Aromatic, NARD
Century, ALOE
Indigo, ANIL
Pepper, KAVA
Platform: Raised, DAIS
Plum: Wild, SLOE
Pods: Vegetable, OKRA, OKRO
Poem: Epic, EPOS
Poet: Persian, OMAR
Roman, OVID
Poison, BANE
Arrow, INEE
Porkfish, SISI
Portico: Greek, STOA
Premium, AGIO
Priest: Mohammedan, IMAM
Prima donna, DIVA

Prong: Fork, TINE
Pseudonym: Lamb's, ELIA
Queen: Carthaginian, DIDO
Hindu, RANI
Rabbit, CONY
Race: Of Japan, AINU
Rail: Ducklike, COOT
North American, SORA
Redshank, CLEE
Refuse: After pressing, MARC
Regiment: Turkish, ALAI
Reliquary, ARCA
Resort: Italian, LIDO
Ridges: Sandy, ASAR, OSAR
River: German, ELBE, ODER
Italian, ADDA
Siberian, LENA
Road: Roman, ITER
Rockfish: California, RENA
Rodent: Mouselike, VOLE
South American, PACA
Rootstock, TARO
Salamander, NEWT
Salmon: Silver, COHO
Young, PARR
Same (Greek), HOMO
(Latin), IDEM
Sauce: Fish, ALEC
School: English, ETON
Seaweed, AGAR, ALGA, KELP
Secular, LAIC
Sediment, SILT
Seed: Dill, ANET
Of vetch, TARE
Serf, ILOT
Sesame, TEEL
Settlement: Eskimo, ETAH
Shark: Atlantic, GATA
European, TOPE
Sheep: Wild, UDAD
Sheltered, ALEE
Shield, EGIS
Ship: Jason's, ARGO
Left side of, PORT
Two-masted, BRIG
Shrine: Buddhist, TOPE
Shrub: New Zealand, TUTU
Sign: Magic, RUNE
Silkworm, ERIA
Skin: Beaver, PLEW
Skink: Egyptian, ADDA
Slave, ESNE
Sloth: Two-toed, UNAU
Smooth, LENE
Snow: Glacial, NEVE
Soapstone, TALC
Society: African secret, EGBO, PORO
Son: Of Seth, ENOS
Song (German), LIED
Unaccompanied, GLEE
Sound: Lung, RALE
Sour, ACID
Sow: Young, GILT
Spike: Brad-shaped, BROB

Spirit: Buddhist evil, MARA
Stake: Poker, ANTE
Star: Temporary, NOVA
Starch: East Indian, SAGO
Stone: Precious, OPAL
Strap: Bridle, REIN
Strewn (heraldry), SEME
Sweetsop, ATES, ATTA
Sword: Fencing, ÉPEE, FOIL
Tambourine: African, TAAR
Tapir: Brazilian, ANTA
Tax, CESS
Tea: South American, MATE
Therefore (Latin), ERGO
Thing: Extraordinary, ONER
Three (dice, cards, etc.), TREY
Thrush: Hawaiian, OMAO
Tide, NEAP
Tipster: Racing, TOUT
Tissue, TELA
Title: Etruscan, LARS
Hindu, BABU
Indian, RAJA
Mohammedan, EMIR, IMAM
Persian, BABA
Spanish, DONA
Turkish, AGHA, BABA
Toad: Largest known, AGUA
Tree, HYLA
Tool: Cutting, ADZE
Track: Deer, SLOT
Tract: Sandy, DENE
Tree: Apple, SORB
Central American, EBOE
East Indian, TEAK
Eucalyptus, YATE
Guiana and Trinidad, MORA
Javanese, UPAS
Linden, LIME, LINN, TEIL, TILL
Sandarac, ARAR
Sassafras, AGUE
Tamarisk salt, ATLE
Tribe: Moro, SULU
Trout, CHAR
Urchin: Street, ARAB
Vessel: Arab, DHOW
Vestment: Ecclesiastical, COPE
Vetch, TARE
Vine: East Indian, SOMA
Violinist: Famous, AUER
Vortex, EDDY
Wampum, PEAG
Wapiti, STAG
Waste: Allowance for, TRET
Watchman: Indian, MINA
Water (Spanish), AGUA
Waterfall, LINN
Wavy (heraldry), ONDE, UNDE
Wax, CERE
Chinese, PELA

Weed: Biblical, TARE
Weight: Ancient, MINA
    Danish (pl.), ESER
    East Asian, TAEL
    Greek, MINA
    Siamese, BAHT
Well done (rare), EUGE
Whale, CETE

Killer, ORCA
White, HUSE, HUSO
Whirlpool, EDDY
Wife: Of Geraint, ENID
Willow: Virginia, ITEA
Wine, PORT
Winged, ALAR
    (Heraldry), AILE

Wings, ALAE
Withered, SERE
Without (French), SANS
Wool: To comb, CARD
Work, OPUS
Wrong: Civil, TORT
Young: Bring forth, YEAN

Words of Five Letters

Abode of dead: Babylonian, ARALU
Aborigine: Borneo DAYAK
Aftersong, EPODE
Aloe, AGAVE
Animal: Footless, APODE
Ant, EMMET
Antelope: African, ADDAX, BEISA,
    CAAMA, ELAND, GUIBA, ORIBI,
    TIANG
    Goat, GORAL, SEROW
    Indian, SASIN
    Siberian, SAIGA
Arch: Pointed, OGIVE
Armadillo, APARA, POYOU, TATOU
Arrowroot, ARARU
Artery: Trunk, AORTA
Association: Russian, ARTEL
    Secret, CABAL
Author: English, READE
Automaton, GOLEM, ROBOT
Award: Motion-picture, OSCAR
Basket: Fishing, CREEL
Beer: Russian, KVASS
Bible: Mohammedan, KORAN
Bird: Asian, MINAH, MYNAH
    Indian, SHAMA
    Larklike, PIPIT
    Loonlike, GREBE
    Oscine, VIREO
    South American, AGAMI
    Swimming, GREBE
Black: (French), NOIRE
    (Heraldry), SABLE
Blackbird: European, MERLE, OUSEL,
    OUZEL
Block: Glacial, SERAC
Blue (heraldry), AZURE
Boat: Eskimo, BIDAR, UMIAK
Bobwhite, COLIN, QUAIL
Bone (comb. form), OSTEO
    Leg, TIBIA
    Thigh, FEMUR
Broom: Twig, BESOM
Brother (French), FRERE
    Moses', AARON
Canoe: Eskimo, BIDAR, KAYAK
Cape: Papal, FANON, ORALE
Caravansary, SERAI
Card: Old playing, TAROT
Caterpillar: New Zealand, AWETO
Catkin, AMENT
Cavity: Stone, GEODE
Cephalopod, SQUID
Cetacean, WHALE
Chariot, ESSED
Cheek: Pertaining to, MALAR
Chieftain: Arab, EMEER
Child (Scotch), BAIRN

Cigar, CLARO
Coating: Seed, TESTA
Cockatoo: Palm, ARARA
Coin: Costa Rican, COLON
    Danish, KRONE
    Ecuadorian, SUCRE
    English, GROAT, PENCE
    French, FRANC
    German, KRONE, TALER
    Hungarian, PENGO
    Icelandic, KRONA
    Indian, RUPEE
    Iraqi, DINAR
    Norwegian, KRONE
    Polish, ZLOTY
    Russian, COPEC, KOPEK, RUBLE
    Swedish, KRONA
    Turkish, ASPER
    Yugoslav, DINAR
Collar: Papal, FANON, ORALE
    Roman, RABAT
Commune: Italian, TREIA
Composition: Choral, MOTET
Compound: Chemical, ESTER
Conceal (law), ELOIN
Council: Ecclesiastical, SYNOD
Court: Anglo-Saxon, GEMOT
    Inner, PATIO
Crest: Mountain, ARETE
Crown: Papal, TIARA
Cuttlefish, SEPIA
Date: Roman, NONES
Decree: Mohammedan, IRADE
    Russian, UKASE
Deposit: Loam, LOESS
Desert: Gobi, SHAMO
Devilfish, MANTA
Disease: Cereals, ERGOT
Disk, PATEN
Dog: Wild, DHOLE, DINGO
Dormouse, LEROT
Drum, TABOR
Duck: Sea, EIDER
Dynasty: Chinese, CHING, LIANG, SHANG
Earthquake, SEISM
Eel, ELVER, MORAY
Ermine: European, STOAT
Ether: Crystalline, APIOL
Fabric: Velvetlike, PANNE
Fabulist, AESOP
Family: Italian, CENCI
Fiber: West Indian, SISAL
Fig: Smyrna, ELEME, ELEMI
Figure: Of speech, TROPE
Finch: European, SERIN
Fish: American small, KILLY
Flower: Garden, ASTER
Friend (Spanish), AMIGO

Fruit: Tropical, MANGO
Fungus: Rye, ERGOT
Furze, GORSE
Gateway, TORAN, TORII
Gem, AGATE, BERYL, PEARL, TOPAZ
Genus: Barnacles, LEPAS
  Bears, URSUS
  Birds (loons), GAVIA
  Birds (nuthatches), SITTA
  Cats, FELIS
  Dogs, CANIS
  Fishes (chiros), ELOPS
  Fishes (perch), PERCA
  Geese, ANSER
  Grasses, STIPA
  Grasses (incl. oats), AVENA
  Gulls, LARUS
  Hares, rabbits, LEPUS
  Hawks, BUTEO
  Herbs, old world, INULA
  Herbs, trailing or climbing, APIOS
  Herbs, tropical, TACCA, URENA
  Horses, EQUUS
  Insects (olive flies), DACUS
  Lice, plant, APHIS
  Lichens, USNEA
  Lizards, AGAMA
  Moles, TALPA
  Mollusks, OLIVA
  Monkeys, CEBUS
  Palms, ARECA
  Pigeons, GOURA
  Plants (amaryllis family), AGAVE
  Ruminants (goats), CAPRA
  Shrubs, Asiatic, SABIA
  Shrubs (heath), ERICA
  Shrubs (incl. raspberry), RUBUS
  Shrubs, tropical, IXORA, TREMA,
    URENA
  Ticks, ARGAS
  Trees (of elm family), TREMA, ULMUS
  Trees, tropical, IXORA, TREMA
Goat: Bezoar, PASAN
God: Assyrian, ASHIR, ASHUR, ASSUR
  Babylonian, DAGAN, SIRIS
  Gaelic, DAGDA
  Hindu, BHAGA, INDRA, SHIVA
  Japanese, EBISU
  Philistine, DAGON
  Phrygian, ATTIS
  Teutonic, AEGIR, GYMIR
  Welsh, DYLAN
Goddess: Babylonian, ISTAR, NANAI
  Hindu, DURGA, GAURI, SHREE
Group: Of six, HEXAD
Grove: Sacred to Diana, NEMUS
Growing out, ENATE
Guitar: Hindu, SITAR
Gull: PEWEE, PEWIT
Hartebeest, CAAMA
Headdress: Jewish or Persian, TIARA
  Liturgical, MITER, MITRE
Heath, ERICA
Herb: Grasslike marsh, SEDGE
Heron, EGRET
Hog: Young, SHOAT, SHOTE
Image, EIKON
Indian: Cariban, ARARA

Iroquoian, HURON
Mexican, AZTEC, OPATA, OTOMI
Muskhogean, CREEK
Siouan, OSAGE, TETON
Spanish American, ARARA, CARIB
Inflorescence: Racemose, AMENT
Insect: Immature, LARVA
Intrigue, CABAL
Iris: Yellow, SEDGE
Juniper, GORSE, RETEM
Kidneys: Pertaining to, RENAL
King: British legendary, LLUDD
Kite: European, GLEDE
Kobold, NISSE
Land: Cultivated, ARADA, ARADO
Landholder (Scotch), LAIRD, THANE
Language: Dravidian, TAMIL
Lariat, LASSO, REATA
Laughing, RIANT
Lawgiver: Athenian, DRACO, SOLON
Leaf: Calyx, SEPAL
  Fern, FROND
Lemur, LORIS
Letter: English, AITCH
  Greek, ALPHA, DELTA, GAMMA,
    KAPPA, OMEGA, SIGMA, THETA
  Hebrew, ALEPH, CHETH, GIMEL,
    SADHE, ZAYIN
Lichen, USNEA
Lighthouse, PHARE
Lizard: Old World, AGAMA
Loincloth, DHOTI
Louse: Plant, APHID
Macaw: Brazilian, ARARA
Mahogany: Philippine, ALMON
Mammal: Badgerlike, RATEL
  Civetlike, GENET
  Giraffelike, OKAPI
  Raccoonlike, COATI
Man (French), HOMME
Marble, AGATE
Mark: Insertion, CARET
Market place: Greek, AGORA
Marsupial: Australian, KOALA
Measure: Electric, FARAD, HENRY
  Energy, JOULE
  Metric, LITER, STERE
  Printing, AGATE
  Russian, VERST
Mixture: Smelting, MATTE
Mohicans: Last of, UNCAS
Molding: Convex, OVOLO, TORUS
Mole, TALPA
Monkey: African, PATAS
  Capuchin, SAJOU
  Howling, ARABA
Monkshood, ATEES
Month: Jewish, NISAN, SIVAN, TEBET
Museum (French), MUSEE
Musketeer, ATHOS
Native: Aleutian, ALEUT
  New Zealand, MAORI
Neckpiece: Ecclesiastical, AMICE
Nerve (comb. form), NEURO
Nest: Eagle's or hawk's, AERIE
  Insect's, NIDUS
Net: Fishing, SEINE
Newsstand, KIOSK

Nitrogen, AZOTE
Noble: Mohammedan, AMEER
Nodule: Stone, GEODE
Nostrils, NARES
Notched irregularly, EROSE
Nymph: Mohammedan, HOURI
Official: Roman, EDILE
Oleoresin, ELEMI
Opening: Mouthlike, STOMA
Oration: Funeral, ELOGE
Ostiole, STOMA
Page: Left-hand, VERSO
  Right-hand, RECTO
Palm, ARECA, BETEL
Park: Colorado, ESTES
Perfume, ATTAR
Philosopher: Greek, PLATO
Pillar: Stone, STELA, STELE
Pinnacle: Glacial, SERAC
Plain, LLANO
Plant: Century, AGAVE
  Climbing, LIANA
  Dwarf, CUMIN
  East Asian perennial, RAMIE
  Medicinal, SENNA
  Mustard family, CRESS
Plate: Communion, PATEN
Poem: Lyric, EPODE
Point: Lowest, NADIR
Poplar, ABELE, ALAMO, ASPEN
Porridge: Spanish American, ATOLE
Post: Stair, NEWEL
Priest: Mohammedan, IMAUM
Protozoan, AMEBA
Queen: (French), REINE
  Hindu, RANEE
Rabbit, CONEY
Rail, CRAKE
Red (heraldry), GULES
Religion: Moslem, ISLAM
Resin, ELEMI
Revoke (law), ADEEM
Rich man, MIDAS, NABOB
Ridge: Sandy, ESKAR, ESKER
River: French, LOIRE, SEINE
Rockfish: California, REINA
Rootstock: Fragrant, ORRIS
Ruff: Female, REEVE
Sack: Pack, KYACK
Salt: Ethereal, ESTER
Saltpeter, NITER, NITRE
Salutation: Eastern, SALAM
Sandpiper: Old World, TEREK
Scented, OLENT
School: Fish, SHOAL
  French public, LYCEE
Scriptures: Mohammedan, KORAN
Seaweeds, ALGAE
Seed: Aromatic, ANISE
Seraglio, HAREM, SERAI
Serf, HELOT
Sheep: Wild, AUDAD
Sheeplike, OVINE
Shield, AEGIS
Shoe: Wooden, SABOT
Shoots: Pickled bamboo, ACHAR
Shot: Billiard, CAROM, MASSE
Shrine: Buddhist, STUPA

Shrub: Burning bush, WAHOO
  Ornamental evergreen, TOYON
  Used in tanning, SUMAC
Silk: Watered, MOIRE
Sister (French), SOEUR
  (Latin), SOROR
Six: Group of, HEXAD
Skeleton: Marine, CORAL
Slave, HELOT
Snake, ABOMA, ADDER, COBRA, RACER
Soldier: French, POILU
  Indian, SEPOY
Sour, ACERB
Spirit: Air, ARIEL
Staff: Shepherd's, CROOK
Starwort, ASTER
Steel (German), STAHL
Stockade: Russian, ETAPE
Stop (nautical), AVAST
Storehouse, ETAPE
Subway: Parisian, METRO
Tapestry, ARRAS
Tea: Paraguayan, YERBA
Temple: Hawaiian, HEIAU
Terminal: Positive, ANODE
Theater: Greek, ODEON, ODEUM
Then (French), ALORS
Thread: Surgical, SETON
Thrush: Wilson's, VEERY
Title: Hindu, BABOO
  Indian, RAJAH, SAHEB, SAHIB
  Mohammedan, EMEER, IMAUM
Tree: Buddhist sacred, PIPAL
  East Indian cotton, SIMAL
  Hickory, PECAN
  Light-wooded, BALSA
  Malayan, TERAP
  Mediterranean, CAROB
  Mexican, ABETO
  Mexican pine, OCOTE
  New Zealand, MAIRE
  Philippine, ALMON
  Rain, SAMAN
  South American, UMBRA
  Tamarack, LARCH
  Tamarisk salt, ATLEE
  West Indian, ACANA
Trout, CHARR
Troy, ILION, ILIUM
Twin: Siamese, CHANG
Vestment: Ecclesiastical, STOLE
Violin: Famous, AMATI, STRAD
Volcano: Mud, SALSE
Wampum, PEAGE
War cry: Greek, ALALA
Wavy (heraldry), UNDEE
Weight: Jewish, GERAH
Wen, TALPA
Wheat, SPELT
Wheel: Persian water, NORIA
Whitefish, CISCO
Willow, OSIER
Window: Bay, ORIEL
Wine, MEDOC, RHINE, TINTA, TOKAY
Winged, ALATE
Woman (French), FEMME
Year: Excess of solar over lunar, EPACT
Zoroastrian, PARSI

Words of Six or More Letters

Agave, MAGUEY
Alkaloid: Crystalline, ESERIN, ESERINE
Alligator, CAYMAN
Amphibole, EDENITE, URALITE
Ant: White, TERMITE
Antelope: African, DIKDIK, DUIKER, GEMSBOK, IMPALA, KOODOO
   European, CHAMOIS
   Indian, NILGAI, NILGAU, NILGHAI, NILGHAU
Ape: Asian or East Indian, GIBBON
Appendage: Leaf, STIPEL, STIPULE
Armadillo, PELUDO, TATOUAY
Arrowroot, ARARAO
Ascetic: Jewish, ESSENE
Ass: Asian wild, ONAGER
Avatar: Of Vishnu, KRISHNA
Babylonian, ELAMITE
Badge: Shoulder, EPAULET
Baldness, ALOPECIA
Barracuda, SENNET
Bark: Aromatic, SINTOC
Bearlike, URSINE
Beetle, ELATER
Bible: Zoroastrian, AVESTA
Bird: Sea, PETREL
   South American, SERIEMA
   Wading, AVOCET, AVOSET
Bone: Leg, FIBULA
Branched, RAMATE
Brother (Latin), FRATER
Bunting: European, ORTOLAN
Call: Trumpet, SENNET
Canoe: Eskimo, BAIDAR, OOMIAK
Caravansary, IMARET
Cat: Asian or African, CHEETAH
   Leopardlike, OCELOT
Cenobite: Jewish, ESSENE
Centerpiece: Table, EPERGNE
Cetacean, DOLPHIN, PORPOISE
Chariot, ESSEDA, ESSEDE
Chief: Seminole, OSCEOLA
Claim: Release as (law), REMISE
Clock: Water, CLEPSYDRA
Cloud, CUMULUS, NIMBUS
Coach: French hackney, FIACRE
Coin: Czech, KORUNA
   Ethiopian, TALARI
   Finnish, MARKKA
   German, THALER
   Greek, DRACHMA
   Haitian, GOURDE
   Honduran, LEMPIRA
   Hungarian, FORINT
   Indo-Chinese, PIASTER
   Netherlands, GUILDER
   Panamanian, BALBOA
   Paraguayan, GUARANI
   Portuguese, ESCUDO
   Russian, COPECK, KOPECK, ROUBLE
   Spanish, PESETA
   Venezuelan, BOLIVAR
Communion: Last holy, VIATICUM
Conceal (law), ELOIGN
Confection, PRALINE
Construction: Sentence, SYNTAX
Convexity: Shaft of column, ENTASIS

Court: Anglo-Saxon, GEMOTE
Cow: Sea, DUGONG, MANATEE
Cylindrical, TERETE
Dagger, STILETTO
   Malay, CREESE, KREESE
Date: Roman, CALENDS, KALENDS
Deer, CARIBOU, WAPITI
Disease: Plant, ERINOSE
Doorkeeper, OSTIARY
Dragonflies: Order of, ODANATA
Drink: Of gods, NECTAR
Drum: TABOUR
   Moorish, ATABAL, ATTABAL
Duck: Fish-eating, MERGANSER
   Sea, SCOTER
Dynasty: Chinese, MANCHU
Eel, CONGER
Edit, REDACT
Envelope: Flower, PERIANTH
Eskimo, AMERIND
Ether: Crystalline, APIOLE
Excuse (law), ESSOIN
Eyespots, OCELLI
Fabric, ESTAMENE, ESTAMIN, ETAMINE
Falcon: European, KESTREL
Figure: Used as column, CARYATID, TELAMON
Fine: For punishment, AMERCE
Fish: Asian fresh-water, GOURAMI
   Pikelike, BARRACUDA
Five: Group of, PENTAD
Fly: African, TSETSE
Foot: Metric, ANAPEST, IAMBUS
Foxlike, VULPINE
Frying pan, SPIDER
Fur, KARAKUL
Galley: Greek or Roman, BIREME, TRIREME
Game: Card, ECARTE
Garment: Greek, CHLAMYS
Gateway, GOPURA, TORANA
Genus: Birds (ravens, crows), CORVUS
   Eels, CONGER
   Fishes, ANABAS
   Foxes, VULPES
   Herbs, ANEMONE
   Insects, CICADA
   Lemurs, GALAGO
   Mints (incl. catnip), NEPETA
   Mollusks, ANOMIA, ASTARTE, TEREDO
   Mollusks (incl. oysters), OSTREA
   Monkeys (spider monkeys), ATELES
   Thrushes (incl. robins), TURDUS
   Trees (of elm family), CELTIS
   Trees (incl. dogwood), CORNUS
   Trees, tropical American, SAPOTA
   Wrens, NANNUS
Gibbon, SIAMANG, WOUWOU
Gland: Salivary, RACEMOSE
Goat: Bezoar, PASANG
Goatlike, CAPRINE
God: Assyrian, ASHSHUR, ASSHUR
   Babylonian, BABBAR, MARDUK, MERODACH, NANNAR, NERGAL, SHAMASH
   Hindu, BRAHMA, KRISHNA, VISHNU
   Tahitian, TAAROA
Goddess: Babylonian, ISHTAR

Hindu, CHANDI, HAIMAVATI, LAKSHMI, PARVATI, SARASVATI, SARASWATI
Government, POLITY
Governor: Persian, SATRAP
Grandson (Scotch), NEPOTE
Group: Of five, PENTAD
Of nine, ENNEAD
Of seven, HEPTAD
Hare: In first year, LEVERET
Harpsichord, SPINET
Herb: Alpine, EDELWEISS
Chinese, GINSENG
South African, FREESIA
Hermit, EREMITE
Hero: Legendary, PALADIN
Heron, BITTERN
Horselike, EQUINE
Hound: Short-legged, BEAGLE
House (French), MAISON
Idiot, CRETIN
Implement: Stone, NEOLITH
Incarnation: Hindu, AVATAR
Indian, APACHE, COMANCHE, PAIUTE, SENECA
Inn: Turkish, IMARET
Insects: Order of, DIPTERA
Instrument: Japanese banjolike, SAMISEN
Musical, CLAVIER, SPINET
Interstice, AREOLA
Ironwood, COLIMA
Juniper: Old Testament, RAETAM
Kettledrum, ATABAL
King: Fairy, OBERON
Kneecap, PATELLA
Knife, MACHETE
Langur: Sumatran, SIMPAI
Legislature: Spanish, CORTES
Lemur: African, GALAGO
Madagascar, AYEAYE
Letter: Greek, EPSILON, LAMBDA, OMICRON, UPSILON
Hebrew, DALETH, LAMEDH, SAMEKH
Lighthouse, PHAROS
Lizard, IGUANA
Llama, ALPACA
Lockjaw, TETANUS
Locust, CICADA, CICALA
Macaw: Brazilian, MARACAN
Maid: Of Astolat, ELAINE
Mammal: Madagascar, TENDRAC, TENREC
Man (Spanish), HOMBRE
Marmoset: South American, TAMARIN
Marsupial, BANDICOOT, WOMBAT
Massacre, POGROM
Mayor: Spanish, ALCALDE
Measure: Electric, AMPERE, COULOMB, KILOWATT
Medicine: Quack, NOSTRUM
Member: Religious order, CENOBITE
Molasses, TREACLE
Monkey: African, GRIVET, NISNAS
Asian, LANGUR
Philippine, MACHIN
South American, PINCHE, SAIMIRI, SAMIRI, SAPAJOU
Monster, CHIMERA, GORGON

(Comb. form), TERATO
Cretan, MINOTAUR
Month: Jewish, HESHVAN, KISLEV, SHEBAT, TAMMUZ, TISHRI, VEADAR
Mountain: Asia Minor, ARARAT
Mulct, AMERCE
Musketeer, ARAMIS, PORTHOS
Nearsighted, MYOPIC
Net, TRAMMEL
New York City, GOTHAM
Nine: Group of, ENNEAD
Nobleman: Spanish, GRANDEE
Official: Roman, AEDILE
Onyx: Mexican, TECALI
Order: Dragonflies, ODANATA
Insects, DIPTERA
Organ: Plant, PISTIL
Ornament: Shoulder, EPAULET
Overcoat: Military, CAPOTE
Ox: Wild, BANTENG
Oxidation: Bronze or copper, PATINA
Paralysis: Incomplete, PARESIS
Pear: Alligator, AVOCADO
Persimmon: Mexican, CHAPOTE
Pipe: Peace, CALUMET
Plaid (Scotch), TARTAN
Plain, PAMPAS, STEPPE, TUNDRA
Plant: Buttercup family, ANEMONE
Century, MAGUEY
On rocks, LICHEN
Plowing: Fit for, ARABLE
Poem: Heroic, EPOPEE
Six-lined, SESTET
Point: Highest, ZENITH
Potion: Love, PHILTER, PHILTRE
Protozoan, AMOEBA
Punish, AMERCE
Purple (heraldry), PURPURE
Queen: Fairy, TITANIA
Race: Skiing, SLALOM
Rat, BANDICOOT, LEMMING
Retort, RIPOST, RIPOSTE
Ring: Harness, TERRET
Little, ANNULET
Rodent: Jumping, JERBOA
Spanish American, AGOUTI, AGOUTY
Sailor: East Indian, LASCAR
Salmon: Young, GRILSE
Salutation: Eastern, SALAAM
Sandpiper, PLOVER
Sandy, ARENOSE
Sapodilla, SAPOTA, SAPOTE
Saw: Surgical, TREPAN
Seven: Group of, HEPTAD
Sexes: Common to both, EPICENE
Shawl: Mexican, SERAPE
Sheathing: Flower, SPATHE
Sheep: Wild, AOUDAD, ARGALI
Shipworm, TEREDO
Shoes: Mercury's winged, TALARIA
Shortening: Syllable, SYSTOLE
Shrub, SPIRAEA
Sickle-shaped, FALCATE
Silver (heraldry), ARGENT
Snake, ANACONDA
Speech: Loss of, APHASIA
Spiral, HELICAL
Staff: Bishop's, CROSIER, CROZIER

Stalk: Plant, PETIOLE
State: Swiss, CANTON
Studio, ATELIER
Swan: Young, CYGNET
Swimming, NATANT
Sword-shaped, ENSATE
Terminal: Negative, CATHODE
Third (music), TIERCE
Thrust: Fencing, RIPOST, RIPOSTE
Tile: Pertaining to, TEGULAR
Tomb: Empty, CENOTAPH
Tooth (comb. form), ODONTO
Tower: Mohammedan, MINARET
Tree: African timber, BAOBAB
   Black gum, TUPELO
   East Indian, MARGOSA
   Locust, ACACIA
   Malayan, SINTOC
   Marmalade, SAPOTE
Urn: Tea, SAMOVAR
Vehicle, LANDAU, TROIKA

Verbose, PROLIX
Viceroy: Egyptian, KHEDIVE
Vulture: American, CONDOR

Warehouse (French), ENTREPOT
Whale: White, BELUGA
Whirlpool, VORTEX
Will: Addition to, CODICIL
   Having left, TESTATE
Wind, CHINOOK, MONSOON, SIMOOM, SIMOON, SIROCCO
Window: In roof, DORMER

Wine, BARBERA, BURGUNDY, CABERNET, CHABLIS, CHIANTI, CLARET, MUSCATEL, RIESLING, SAUTERNE, SHERRY, ZINFANDEL
Wolfish, LUPINE
Woman: Boisterous, TERMAGANT
Woolly, LANATE
Workshop, ATELIER
Zoroastrian, PARSEE

Old-Testament Names

(We do not pretend that this list is all-inclusive. We include only those names which in our opinion one meets most often in crossword puzzles.)

AARON: First high priest of Jews; son of Amram; brother of Miriam and Moses; father of Abihu, Eleazer, Ithamar, and Nadab.

ABEL: Son of Adam; slain by Cain.

ABIGAIL: Wife of Nabal; later, wife of David.

ABIHU: Son of Aaron.

ABIMELECH: King of Gerar.

ABNER: Commander of army of Saul and Ishbosheth; slain by Joab.

ABRAHAM (or ABRAM): Patriarch; forefather of the Jews; son of Terah; husband of Sarah; father of Isaac and Ishmael.

ABSALOM: Son of David and Maacah; revolted against David; slain by Joab.

ACHISH: King of Gath; gave refuge to David.

ACHSA (or ACHSAH): Daughter of Caleb; wife of Othniel.

ADAH: Wife of Lamech.

ADAM: First man; husband of Eve; father of Cain, Abel, and Seth.

ADONIJAH: Son of David and Haggith.

AGAG: King of Amalek; spared by Saul; slain by Samuel.

AHASUERUS: King of Persia; husband of Vashti and, later, Esther; sometimes identified with Xerxes the Great.

AHIJAH: Prophet; foretold accession of Jeroboam.

AHINOAM: Wife of David.

AMASA: Commander of army of David; slain by Joab.

AMNON: Son of David and Ahinoam; ravished Tamar; slain by Absalom.

AMRAM: Husband of Jochebed; father of Aaron, Miriam and Moses.

ASENATH: Wife of Joseph.

ASHER: Son of Jacob and Zilpah.

BALAAM: Prophet; rebuked by his donkey for cursing God.

BARAK: Jewish captain; associated with Deborah.

BARUCH: Secretary to Jeremiah.

BATHSHEBA: Wife of Uriah; later, wife of David.

BELSHAZZAR: Crown prince of Babylon.

BENAIAH: Warrior of David; proclaimed Solomon King.

BEN-HADAD: Name of several kings of Damascus.

BENJAMIN: Son of Jacob and Rachel.

BEZALEEL: Chief architect of tabernacle.

BILBAH: Servant of Rachel; mistress of Jacob.

BILDAD: Comforter of Job.

BOAZ: Husband of Ruth; father of Obed.

CAIN: Son of Adam and Eve; slayer of Abel; father of Enoch.

CAINAN: Son of Enos.

CALEB: Spy sent out by Moses to visit Canaan; father of Achsa.

CANAAN: Son of Ham.

CHILION: Son of Elimelech; husband of Orpah.

CUSH: Son of Ham; father of Nimrod.

DAN: Son of Jacob and Bilhah.

DANIEL: Prophet; saved from lions by God.

DEBORAH: Hebrew prophetess; helped Israelites conquer Canaanites.

DELILAH: Mistress and betrayer of Samson.

ELAM: Son of Shem.

ELEAZAR: Son of Aaron; succeeded him as high priest.

ELI: High priest and judge; teacher of Samuel; father of Hophni and Phinehas.

ELIAKIM: Chief minister of Hezekiah.

ELIEZER: Servant of Abraham.

ELIHU: Comforter of Job.

ELIJAH (or ELIAS): Prophet; went to heaven in chariot of fire.

ELIMELECH: Husband of Naomi; father of Chilion and Mahlon.

ELIPHAZ: Comforter of Job.

ELISHA (or ELISEUS): Prophet; successor of Elijah.

ELKANAH: Husband of Hannah; father of Samuel.

ENOCH: Son of Cain.

ENOCH: Father of Methuselah.

ENOS: Son of Seth; father of Cainan.

EPHRAIM: Son of Joseph.

ESAU: Son of Isaac and Rebecca; sold his birthright to his brother Jacob.

ESTHER: Jewish wife of Ahasuerus; saved Jews from Haman's plotting.

EVE: First woman; created from rib of Adam.

EZRA (or ESDRAS): Hebrew scribe and priest.

GAD: Son of Jacob and Zilpah.

GEHAZI: Servant of Elisha.

GIDEON: Israelite hero; defeated Midianites.

GOLIATH: Philistine giant; slain by David.

HAGAR: Handmaid of Sarah; concubine of Abraham; mother of Ishmael.

HAGGITH: Mother of Adonijah.

HAM: Son of Noah; father of Cush, Mizraim, Phut, and Canaan.

HAMAN: Chief minister of Ahasuerus; hanged on gallows prepared for Mordecai.

HANNAH: Wife of Elkanah; mother of Samuel.

HANUN: King of Ammonites.

HARAN: Brother of Abraham; father of Lot.

HAZAEL: King of Damascus.

HEPHZI-BAH: Wife of Hezekiah; mother of Mannaseh.

HIRAM: King of Tyre.

HOLOFERNES: General of Nebuchadnezzar; slain by Judith.

HOPHNI: Son of Eli.

ISAAC: Hebrew patriarch; son of Abraham and Sarah; half brother of Ishmael; husband of Rebecca; father of Esau and Jacob.

ISHMAEL: Son of Abraham and Hagar; half brother of Isaac.

ISSACHAR: Son of Jacob and Leah.

ITHAMAR: Son of Aaron.

JABAL: Son of Lamech and Adah.

JABIN: King of Hazor.

JACOB: Hebrew patriarch, founder of Israel; son of Isaac and Rebecca; husband of Leah and Rachel; father of Asher, Benjamin, Dan, Gad, Issachar, Joseph, Judah, Levi, Naphtali, Reuben, Simeon, and Zebulun.

JAEL: Slayer of Sisera.

JAPHETH: Son of Noah.

JEHOIADA: High priest; husband of Jehoshabeath; revolted against Athaliah and made Joash King of Judah.

JEHOSHABEATH (or JEHOSHEBA): Daughter of Jehoram of Judah; wife of Jehoiada.

JEPHTHAH: Judge in Israel; sacrificed his only daughter because of vow.

JESSE: Son of Obed; father of David.

JETHRO: Midianite priest; father of Zipporah.

JEZEBEL: Phoenician princess; wife of Ahab; mother of Ahaziah, Athaliah, and Jehoram.

JOAB: Commander in chief under David; slayer of Abner, Absalom, and Amasa.

JOB: Patriarch; underwent many afflictions; comforted by Bildad, Elihu, Eliphaz and Zophar.

JOCHEBED: Wife of Amram.

JONAH: Prophet; cast into sea and swallowed by great fish.

JONATHAN: Son of Saul; friend of David.

JOSEPH: Son of Jacob and Rachel; sold into slavery by his brothers; husband of Asenath; father of Ephraim and Manassah.

JOSHUA: Successor of Moses; son of Nun.

JUBAL: Son of Lamech and Adah.

JUDAH: Son of Jacob and Leah.

JUDITH: Slayer of Holofernes.

KISH: Father of Saul.

LABAN: Father of Leah and Rachel.

LAMECH: Son of Methuselah; father of Noah.

LAMECH: Husband of Adah and Zillah; father of Jabal, Jubal, and Tubal-Cain.

LEAH: Daughter of Laban; wife of Jacob.

LEVI: Son of Jacob and Leah.

LOT: Son of Haran; escaped destruction of Sodom.

MAACAH: Mother of Absalom and Tamar.

MAHLON: Son of Elimelech; first husband of Ruth.

MANASSEH: Son of Joseph.

MELCHIZEDEK: King of Salem.

METHUSELAH: Patriarch; son of Enoch; father of Lamech.

MICHAL: Daughter of Saul; wife of David.

MIRIAM: Prophetess; daughter of Amram; sister of Aaron and Moses.

MIZRAIM: Son of Ham.

MORDECAI: Uncle of Esther; with her aid, saved Jews from Haman's plotting.

MOSES: Prophet and lawgiver; son of Amram; brother of Aaron and Miriam; husband of Zipporah.

NAAMAN: Syrian captain; cured of leprosy by Elisha.

NABAL: Husband of Abigail.

NABOTH: Owner of vineyard; stoned to death because he would not sell it to Ahab.

NADAB: Son of Aaron.

NAHOR: Father of Terah.

NAOMI: Wife of Elimelech; mother-in-law of Ruth.

NAPHTALI: Son of Jacob and Bilhah.

NATHAN: Prophet; reproved David for causing Uriah's death.

NEBUCHADNEZZAR (or NEBUCHAD-REZZAR): King of Babylon; destroyer of Jerusalem.

NEHEMIAH: Jewish leader; empowered by Artaxerxes to rebuild Jerusalem.

NIMROD: Mighty hunter; son of Cush.

NOAH: Patriarch; Son of Lamech; escaped Deluge by building Ark; father of Ham, Japheth and Shem.

NUN (or NON): Father of Joshua.

OBED: Son of Boaz; father of Jesse.

OG: King of Bashan.

ORPAH: Wife of Chilion.

OTHNIEL: Kenezite; judge of Israel; husband of Achsa.

PHINEHAS: Son of Eleazer.

PHINEHAS: Son of Eli.

PHUT (or PUT): Son of Ham.

POTIPHAR: Egyptian official; bought Joseph.

RACHEL: Wife of Jacob.

REBECCA (or REBEKAH): Wife of Isaac.

REUBEN: Son of Jacob and Leah.

RUTH: Wife of Mahlon, later of Boaz; daughter-in-law of Naomi.

SAMSON: Judge of Israel; famed for strength; betrayed by Delilah.

SAMUEL: Hebrew judge and prophet; son of Elkanah.

SARAH (or SARA, SARAI): Wife of Abraham.

SENNACHERIB: King of Assyria.

SETH: Son of Adam; father of Enos.

SHEM: Son of Noah; father of Elam.

SIMEON: Son of Jacob and Leah.

SISERA: Canaanite captain; slain by Jael.

TAMAR: Daughter of David and Maachah; ravished by Amnon.

TERAH: Son of Nahor; father of Abraham.

TUBAL-CAIN: Son of Lamech and Zillah.

URIAH: Husband of Bathsheba; sent to death in battle by David.

VASHTI: Wife of Ahasuerus; set aside by him.

ZADOK: High priest during David's reign.

ZEBULUN (or ZABULON): Son of Jacob and Leah.

ZILLAH: Wife of Lamech.

ZILPAH: Servant of Leah; mistress of Jacob.

ZIPPORAH: Daughter of Jethro; wife of Moses.

ZOPHAR: Comforter of Job.

Kings of Judah and Israel

Kings Before Division of Kingdom

SAUL: First King of Israel; son of Kish; father of Ish-Bosheth, Jonathan and Michal.

ISH-BOSHETH (or ESHBAAL): King of Israel; son of Saul.

DAVID: King of Judah; later of Israel; son of Jesse; husband of Abigail, Ahinoam, Bathsheba, Michal, etc.; father of Absalom, Adonijah, Amnon, Solomon, Tamar, etc.

SOLOMON: King of Israel and Judah; son of David; father of Rehoboam.

RHEOBOAM: Son of Solomon; during his reign the kingdom was divided into Judah and Israel.

Kings of Judah (Southern Kingdom)

REHOBOAM: First King.

ABIJAH (or ABIJAM or ABIA): Son of Rehoboam.

ASA: Probably son of Abijah.

JEHOSHAPHAT: Son of Asa.

JEHORAM (or JORAM): Son of Jehoshaphat; husband of Athaliah.

AHAZIAH: Son of Jehoram and Athaliah.

ATHALIAH: Daughter of King Ahab of Israel and Jezebel; wife of Jehoram.

JOASH (or JEHOASH): Son of Ahaziah.

AMAZIAH: Son of Joash.

UZZIAH (or AZARIAH): Son of Amaziah.

JOTHAM: Regent, later King; son of Uzziah.

AHAZ: Son of Jotham.

HEZEKIAH: Son of Ahaz; husband of Hephzi-Bah.

MANASSEH: Son of Hezekiah and Hephzi-Bah.

AMON: Son of Manasseh.

JOSIAH (or JOSIAS): Son of Amon.

JEHOAHAZ (or JOAHAZ): Son of Josiah.

JEHOIACHIN: Son of Jehoiakim.

JEHOIAKIM: Son of Josiah.

ZEDEKIAH: Son of Josiah; kingdom overthrown by Babylonians under Nebuchadnezzar.

Kings of Israel (Northern Kingdom)

JEROBOAM I: Led secession of Israel.

NADAB: Son of Jeroboam I.

BAASHA: Overthrew Nadab.

ELAH: Son of Baasha.

ZIMRI: Overthrew Elah.

OMRI: Overthrew Zimri.

AHAB: Son of Omri; husband of Jezebel.

AHAZIAH: Son of Ahab.

JEHORAM (or JORAM): Son of Ahab.

JEHU: Overthrew Jehoram.

JEHOAHAZ (or JOAHAZ): Son of Jehu.

JEHOASH (or JOASH): Son of Jehoahaz.

JEROBOAM II: Son of Jehoash.
ZECHARIAH: Son of Jeroboam II.
SHALLUM: Overthrew Zechariah.
MENAHEM: Overthrew Shallum.

PEKAHIAH: Son of Menahem.
PEKAH: Overthrew Pekahiah.
HOSHEA: Overthrew Pekah; kingdom overthrown by Assyrians under Sargon II.

Prophets

Major

ISAIAH	JEREMIAH	EZEKIEL	DANIEL

Minor

HOSEA	OBADIAH	NAHUM	HAGGAI
JOEL	JONAH	HABAKKUK	ZECHARIAH
AMOS	MICAH	ZEPHANIAH	MALACHI

Foreign Phrases

(NOTE: The English meanings given are not necessarily literal translations.)

AB OVO: From the beginning.
ABSIT OMEN: Hope this is no bad luck.
AEQUO ANIMO: Undisturbed in mind.
AD VALOREM: According to its value.
ALEA JACTA EST: The die is cast.
ALMA MATER: One's college or school.
ALTER EGO: Other self.
AMICUS CURIAE: Friend of the court.
ANNO DOMINI: Year of our Lord.
BEL CANTO: A style of singing marked by virtuosity and beauty.
BETE NOIRE: Particular nemesis.
BONA FIDE: In good faith; genuine.
CARPE DIEM: Enjoy today.
CASUS BELLI: Cause of war.
CAVEAT EMPTOR: Buy at your own risk.
CORPUS DELICTI: Fundamental fact or facts necessary to commission of a crime.
CUI BONO: To whose advantage?
CUM GRANO SALIS: With a grain of salt.
DE FACTO: As a matter of fact; because of this fact.
DEO GRATIAS: Thanks be to God.
DEUS EX MACHINA: Artificially produced to bring a solution of some extreme difficulty.
ECCE HOMO: This is the man.
ERRARE HUMANUM (EST): To err is human.
FESTINA LENTE: Make haste slowly.
FIAT LUX: Let there be light.
FIDUS ACHATES: Faithful friend.
FLAGRANTE DELICTO: Caught in the act.
HABEAS CORPUS: Common-law writ to bring a person before a court or judge.
HIC JACET: Here lies. . . .
HOI POLLOI: The common people.
HONORIS CAUSA: For the sake of honor.

HORS D'OEUVRES: Appetizers.
IN VINO VERITAS: In wine there is truth.
IPSE DIXIT: An assertion made but not proved.
IPSO FACTO: By the very fact.
JEUNESSE DOREE: Gilded youth.
LABOR OMNIA VINCIT: Work overcomes all things.
LAISSEZ FAIRE: Noninterference.
MIRABILE DICTU: Wonderful to relate.
MULTUM IN PARVO: Much in little.
NIL ADMIRARI: To be astonished at nothing.
NOLENS, VOLENS: Willy-nilly.
O TEMPORA! O MORES!: What sad times and customs!
PERSONA GRATA: A favored person.
POST MORTEM: After death.
PRO BONO PUBLICO: For the public welfare.
PRO TEMPORE: For the time being.
RARA AVIS: Extraordinary person or thing.
REQUIESCAT IN PACE: Rest in peace.
SAVOIR FAIRE: Know-how; manners for all occasions.
SINE DIE: With no day set for the next meeting.
SINE QUA NON: Indispensable.
SPIRITUS FRUMENTI: Alcohol.
STATUS (IN) QUO: State in which anything is.
SUI GENERIS: In a class by itself.
SURSUM CORDA: Lift up your hearts.
TEMPUS FUGIT: Time flies.
ULTIMA THULE: The limit in an ideal way.
VAE VICTIS: Woe to the conquered.
VENI, VIDI, VICI: I came, I saw, I conquered.

Greek and Roman Mythology

(Most of the Greek deities were adopted by the Romans, although in many cases there was a change of name. In the list below, information is given under the Greek name; the name in parentheses is the Latin equivalent. However, all Latin names are listed with cross references to the Greek ones. In addition, there are several deities which were exclusively Roman.)

ACHERON: *See* Rivers.

ACHILLES: Greek warrior; slew Hector at Troy; slain by Paris, who wounded him in his vulnerable heel.

ACTAEON: Hunter; surprised Artemis bathing; changed by her to stag and killed by his dogs.

ADMETUS: King of Thessaly; his wife, Alcestis, offered to die in his place.

ADONIS: Beautiful youth loved by Aphrodite.

AEACUS: One of three judges of dead in Hades; son of Zeus.

AEËTES: King of Colchis; father of Medea; keeper of Golden Fleece.

AEGEUS: Father of Theseus; believing Theseus killed in Crete, he drowned himself, Aegean Sea named for him.

AEGISTHUS: Son of Thyestes; slew Atreus; with Clytemnestra, his paramour, slew Agamemnon; slain by Orestes.

AEGYPTUS: Brother of Danaüs; his sons, except Lynceus, slain by Danaïdes.

AENEAS: Trojan; son of Anchises and Aphrodite; after fall of Troy, led his followers eventually to Italy; loved and deserted Dido.

AEOLUS: *See* Winds.

AESCULAPIUS: *See* Asclepius.

AESON: King of Ioclus; father of Jason; overthrown by his brother Pelias; restored to youth by Medea.

AETHER: Personification of sky.

AETHRA: Mother of Theseus.

AGAMEMNON: King of Mycenae; son of Atreus; brother of Menelaus; leader of Greeks against Troy; slain on his return home by Clytemnestra and Aegisthus.

AGLAIA: *See* Graces.

AJAX: Greek warrior; killed himself at Troy because Achilles' armor was awarded to Odysseus.

ALCESTIS: Wife of Admetus; offered to die in his place but saved from death by Hercules.

ALCMENE: Wife of Amphitryon; mother by Zeus of Hercules.

ALCYONE: *See* Pleiades.

ALECTO: *See* Furies.

ALECTRYON: Youth changed by Ares into cock.

ALTHAEA: Wife of Oeneus; mother of Meleager.

AMAZONS: Female warriors in Asia Minor; supported Troy against Greeks.

AMOR: *See* Eros.

AMPHION: Musician; husband of Niobe; charmed stones to build fortifications for Thebes.

AMPHITRITE: Sea goddess; wife of Poseidon.

AMPHITRYON: Husband of Alcmene.

ANCHISES: Father of Aeneas.

ANCILE: Sacred shield that fell from heavens; palladium of Rome.

ANDRAEMON: Husband of Dryope.

ANDROMACHE: Wife of Hector.

ANDROMEDA: Daughter of Cepheus; chained to cliff for monster to devour; rescued by Perseus.

ANTEIA: Wife of Proetus; tried to induce Bellerophon to elope with her.

ANTEROS: God who avenged unrequited love.

ANTIGONE: Daughter of Oedipus; accompanied him to Colonus; performed burial rite for Polynices and was buried alive.

ANTINOÜS: Leader of suitors of Penelope; slain by Odysseus.

APHRODITE (VENUS): Goddess of love and beauty; daughter of Zeus; mother of Eros.

APOLLO: God of beauty, poetry, music; later identified with Helios as Phoebus Apollo; son of Zeus and Leto.

AQUILO: *See* Winds.

ARACHNE: Maiden who challenged Athena to weaving contest; changed to spider.

ARES (MARS): God of war; son of Zeus and Hera.

ARGO: Ship in which Jason and followers sailed to Colchis for Golden Fleece.

ARGUS: Monster with hundred eyes; slain by Hermes; his eyes placed by Hera into peacock's tail.

ARIADNE: Daughter of Minos; aided Theseus in slaying Minotaur; deserted by him on island of Naxos and married to Dionysus.

ARION: Musician; thrown overboard by pirates but saved by dolphin.

ARTEMIS (DIANA): Goddess of moon; huntress; twin sister of Apollo.

ASCLEPIUS (AESCULAPIUS): Mortal son of Apollo; slain by Zeus for raising dead; later deified as god of medicine. Also known as Asklepios.

ASTARTE: Phoenician goddess of love; variously identified with Aphrodite, Selene, and Artemis.

ASTRAEA: Goddess of Justice; daughter of Zeus and Themis.

ATALANTA: Princess who challenged her suitors to a foot race; Hippomenes won race and married her.

ATHENA (MINERVA): Goddess of wisdom; known poetically as Pallas Athene; sprang fully armed from head of Zeus.

ATLAS: Titan; held world on his shoulders as punishment for warring against Zeus; son of Iapetus.

ATREUS: King of Mycenae; father of Menelaus and Agamemnon; brother of Thyestes, three of whose sons he slew and served to him at banquet; slain by Aegisthus.

ATROPOS: *See* Fates.

AURORA: *See* Eos.

AUSTER: *See* Winds.

AVERNUS: Infernal regions; name derived from small vaporous lake near Vesuvius which was fabled to kill birds and vegetation.

BACCHUS: *See* Dionysus.

BELLEROPHON: Corinthian hero; killed Chimera with aid of Pegasus; tried to reach Olympus on Pegasus and was thrown to his death.

BELLONA: Roman goddess of war.

BOREAS: *See* Winds.

BRIAREUS: Monster of hundred hands; son of Uranus and Gaea.

BRISEIS: Captive maiden given to Achilles; taken by Agamemnon in exchange for loss of Chryseis, which caused Achilles to cease fighting, until death of Patroclus.

CADMUS: Brother of Europa; planter of dragon seeds from which first Thebans sprang.

CALLIOPE: *See* Muses.

CALYPSO: Sea nymph; kept Odysseus on her island Ogygia for seven years.

CASSANDRA: Daughter of Priam; prophetess who was never believed; slain with Agamemnon.

CASTOR: *See* Dioscuri.

CELAENO: *See* Pleiades.

CENTAURS: Beings half man and half horse; lived in mountains of Thessaly.

CEPHALUS: Hunter; accidentally killed his wife Procris with his spear.

CEPHEUS: King of Ethiopia; father of Andromeda.

CERBERUS: Three-headed dog guarding entrance to Hades.

CERES: *See* Demeter.

CHAOS: Formless void; personified as first of gods.

CHARON: Boatman on Styx who carried souls of dead to Hades; son of Erebus.

CHARYBDIS: Female monster; personification of whirlpool.

CHIMERA: Female monster with head of lion, body of goat, tail of serpent; killed by Bellerophon.

CHIRON: Most famous of centaurs.

CHRONOS: Personification of time.

CHRYSEIS: Captive maiden given to Agamemnon; his refusal to accept ransom from her father Chryses caused Apollo to send plague on Greeks besieging Troy.

CIRCE: Sorceress; daughter of Helios; changed Odysseus' men into swine.

CLIO: *See* Muses.

CLOTHO: *See* Fates.

CLYTEMNESTRA: Wife of Agamemnon, whom she slew with aid of her paramour, Aegisthus; slain by her son Orestes.

COCYTUS: *See* Rivers.

CREON: Father of Jocasta; forbade burial of Polynices; ordered burial alive of Antigone.

CREUSA: Princess of Corinth, for whom Jason deserted Medea; slain by Medea, who sent her poisoned robe; also known as Glauke.

CREUSA: Wife of Aeneas; died fleeing Troy.

CRONUS (SATURN): Titan; god of harvests; son of Uranus and Gaea; dethroned by his son Zeus.

CUPID: *See* Eros.

CYBELE: Anatolian nature goddess; adopted by Greeks and identified with Rhea.

CYCLOPES: Race of one-eyed giants (singular: Cyclops).

DAEDALUS: Athenian artificer; father of Icarus; builder of Labyrinth in Crete; devised wings attached with wax for him and Icarus to escape Crete.

DANAE: Princess of Argos; mother of Perseus by Zeus, who appeared to her in form of golden shower.

DANAIDES: Daughters of Danaüs; at his command, all except Hypermnestra slew their husbands, the sons of Aegyptus.

DANAÜS: Brother of Aegyptus; father of Danaïdes; slain by Lynceus.

DAPHNE: Nymph; pursued by Apollo; changed to laurel tree.

DECUMA: *See* Fates.

DEINO: *See* Graeae.

DEMETER (CERES): Goddess of agriculture; mother of Persephone.

DIANA: *See* Artemis.

DIDO: Founder and queen of Carthage; stabbed herself when deserted by Aeneas.

DIOMEDES: Greek hero; with Odysseus, entered Troy and carried off Palladium, sacred statue of Athena.

DIOMEDES: Owner of man-eating horses, which Hercules, as ninth labor, carried off.

DIONE: Titan goddess; mother by Zeus of Aphrodite.

DIONYSUS (BACCHUS): God of wine; son of Zeus and Semele.

DIOSCURI: Twins Castor and Pollux; sons of Leda by Zeus.

DIS: *See* Hades.

DRYADS: Wood nymphs.

DRYOPE: Maiden changed to Hamadryad.

ECHO: Nymph who fell hopelessly in love with Narcissus; faded away except for her voice.

ELECTRA: Daughter of Agamemnon and Clytemnestra; sister of Orestes; urged Orestes to slay Clytemnestra and Aegisthus.

ELECTRA: *See* Pleiades.

ELYSIUM: Abode of blessed dead.

ENDYMION: Mortal loved by Selene.

ENYO: *See* Graeae.

EOS (AURORA): Goddess of dawn.

EPIMETHEUS: Brother of Prometheus; husband of Pandora.

ERATO: *See* Muses.

EREBUS: Spirit of darkness; son of Chaos.

ERINYES: *See* Furies.

ERIS: Goddess of discord.

EROS (AMOR or CUPID): God of love; son of Aphrodite.

ETEOCLES: Son of Oedipus, whom he succeeded to rule alternately with Polynices; refused to give up throne at end of year; he and Polynices slew each other.

EUMENIDES: *See* Furies.

EUPHROSYNE: *See* Graces.

EUROPA: Mortal loved by Zeus, who, in form of white bull, carried her off to Crete.

EURUS: *See* Winds.

EURYALE: *See* Gorgons.

EURYDICE: Nymph; wife of Orpheus.

EURYSTHEUS: King of Argos; imposed twelve labors on Hercules.

EUTERPE: *See* Muses.

FATES: Goddesses of destiny: Clotho (Spinner of thread of life), Lachesis (Determiner of length), and Atropos (Cutter of thread); also called Moirae. Identified by Romans with their goddesses of fate; Nona, Decuma, and Morta; called Parcae.

FAUNS: Roman deities of woods and groves.

FAUNUS: *See* Pan.

FAVONIUS: *See* Winds.

FLORA: Roman goddess of flowers.

FORTUNA: Roman goddess of fortune.

FURIES: Avenging spirits: Alecto, Megaera, and Tisiphone; known also as Erinyes or Eumenides.

GAEA: Goddess of earth; daughter of Chaos; mother of Titans; known also as Ge, Gea, Gaia, etc.

GALATEA: Statue of maiden carved from ivory by Pygmalion; given life by Aphrodite.

GALATEA: Sea nymph; loved by Polyphemus.

GANYMEDE: Beautiful boy; successor to Hebe as cupbearer of gods.

GLAUCUS: Mortal who became sea divinity by eating magic grass.

GLAUKE: *See* Creüsa.

GOLDEN FLEECE: Fleece from ram that flew Phrixos to Colchis; Aeëtes placed it under guard of dragon; carried off by Jason.

GORGONS: Female monsters: Euryale, Medusa, and Stheno; had snakes for hair; their glances turned mortals to stone. *See* Medusa.

GRACES: Beautiful goddesses: Aglaia (Brilliance), Euphrosyne (Joy), and Thalia (Bloom); daughters of Zeus.

GRAEAE: Sentinels for Gorgons: Deino, Enyo, and Pephredo; had one eye among them, which passed from one to another.

HADES (DIS): Name sometimes given Pluto; also, abode of dead, ruled by Pluto.

HAEMON: Son of Creon; promised husband of Antigone; killed himself in her tomb.

HAMADRYADS: Tree nymphs; lived and died with trees they inhabited.

HARPIES: Monsters with heads of women and bodies of birds.

HEBE (JUVENTAS): Goddess of youth; cupbearer of gods before Ganymede; daughter of Zeus and Hera.

HECATE: Goddess of sorcery and witchcraft.

HECTOR: Son of Priam; slayer of Patroclus; slain by Achilles.

HECUBA: Wife of Priam.

HELEN: Fairest woman in world; daughter of Zeus and Leda; wife of Menelaus; carried to Troy by Paris, causing Trojan War.

HELIADES: Daughters of Helios; mourned for Phaëthon and were changed to poplar trees.

HELIOS (SOL): God of sun; later identified with Phoebus Apollo.

HELLE: Sister of Phrixos; fell from ram of Golden Fleece; water where she fell named Hellespont.

HEPHAESTUS (VULCAN): God of fire; celestial blacksmith; son of Zeus and Hera; husband of Aphrodite.

HERA (JUNO): Queen of heaven; wife of Zeus.

HERCULES: Hero and strong man; son of Zeus and Alcmene; performed twelve labors or deeds to be free from bondage under Eurystheus; after death, his mortal share was destroyed, and he became immortal. Also known as Herakles or Heracles. Labors: (1) killing Nemean lion; (2) killing Lernaean Hydra; (3) capturing Erymanthian boar; (4) capturing Cerynean hind; (5) killing man-eating Stymphalian birds; (6) procuring girdle of Hippolyte; (7) cleaning Augean stables; (8) capturing Cretan bull; (9) capturing man-eating horses of Diomedes; (10) capturing cattle of Geryon; (11) procuring golden apples of Hesperides; (12) bringing Cerberus up from Hades.

HERMES (MERCURY): God of physicians and thieves; messenger of gods; son of Zeus and Maia.

HERO: Priestess of Aphrodite; Leander swam Hellespont nightly to see her; drowned herself at his death.

HESPERUS: Evening star.

HESTIA (VESTA): Goddess of hearth; sister of Zeus.

HIPPOLYTE: Queen of Amazons; wife of Theseus.

HIPPOLYTUS: Son of Theseus and Hippolyte; falsely accused by Phaedra of trying to kidnap her; slain by Poseidon at request of Theseus.

HIPPOMENES: Husband of Atalanta, whom he beat in foot race by dropping golden apples, which she stopped to pick up.

HYACINTHUS: Beautiful youth accidentally killed by Apollo, who caused flower to spring up from his blood.

HYDRA: Nine-headed monster in marsh of Lerna; slain by Hercules.

HYGEIA: Personification of health.

HYMEN: God of marriage.

HYPERION: Titan; early sun god; father of Helios.

HYPERMNESTRA: Daughter of Danaüs; refused to kill her husband Lynceus.

HYPNOS (SOMNUS): God of sleep.

IAPETUS: Titan; father of Atlas, Epimetheus, and Prometheus.

ICARUS: Son of Daedalus; flew too near sun with wax-attached wings and fell into sea and was drowned.

IO: Mortal maiden loved by Zeus; changed by Hera into heifer.

IOBATES: King of Lycia; sent Bellerophon to slay Chimera.

IPHIGENIA: Daughter of Agamemnon; offered as sacrifice to Artemis at Aulis; carried by Artemis to Tauris where she became priestess; escaped from there with Orestes.

IRIS: Goddess of rainbow; messenger of Zeus and Hera.

ISMENE: Daughter of Oedipus; sister of Antigone.

IULUS: Son of Aeneas.

IXION: King of Lapithae; for making love to Hera he was bound to endlessly revolving wheel in Tartarus.

JANUS: Roman god of gates and doors; represented with two opposite faces.

JASON: Son of Aeson; to gain throne of Ioclus from Pelias, went to Colchis and brought back Golden Fleece; married Medea; deserted her for Creüsa.

JOCASTA: Wife of Laius; mother of Oedipus; unwittingly became wife of Oedipus; hanged herself when relationship was discovered.

JUNO: *See* Hera.

JUPITER: *See* Zeus.

JUVENTAS: *See* Hebe.

LACHESIS: *See* Fates.

LAIUS: Father of Oedipus, by whom he was slain.

LAOCOÖN: Priest of Apollo at Troy; warned against bringing wooden horse into Troy; destroyed with his two sons by serpents sent by Athena.

LARES: Roman ancestral spirits protecting descendants and homes.

LAVINIA: wife of Aeneas after defeat of Turnus.

LEANDER: Swam Hellespont nightly to see Hero; drowned in storm.

LEDA: Mortal loved by Zeus in form of Swan; mother of Helen, Clytemnestra, Dioscuri.

LETHE: *See* Rivers.

LETO (LATONA): Mother by Zeus of Artemis and Apollo.

LUCINA: Roman goddess of childbirth; identified with Juno.

LYNCEUS: Son of Aegyptus; husband of Hypermnestra; slew Danaüs.

MAIA: Daughter of Atlas; mother of Hermes.

MAIA: *See* Pleiades.

MANES: Souls of dead Romans, particularly of ancestors.

MARS: *See* Ares.

MARSYAS: Shepherd; challenged Apollo to music contest and lost; flayed alive by Apollo.

MEDEA: Sorceress; daughter of Aeëtes; helped Jason obtain Golden Fleece; when deserted by him for Creüsa, killed her children and Creüsa.

MEDUSA: Gorgon; slain by Perseus, who cut off her head.

MEGAERA: *See* Furies.

MELEAGER: Son of Althaea; his life would last as long as brand burning at his birth; Althaea quenched and saved it but destroyed it when Meleager slew his uncles.

MELPOMENE: *See* Muses.

MEMNON: Ethiopian king; made immortal by Zeus; son of Tithonus and Eos.

MENELAUS: King of Sparta; son of Atreus; brother of Agamemnon; husband of Helen.

MERCURY: *See* Hermes.

MEROPE: *See* Pleiades.

MEZENTIUS: Cruel Etruscan king; ally of Turnus against Aeneas; slain by Aeneas.

MIDAS: King of Phrygia; given gift of turning to gold all he touched.

MINERVA: *See* Athena.

MINOS: King of Crete; after death, one of three judges of dead in Hades; son of Zeus and Europa.

MINOTAUR: Monster, half man and half beast, kept in Labyrinth in Crete; slain by Theseus.

MNEMOSYNE: Goddess of memory; mother by Zeus of Muses.

MOIRAE: *See* Fates.

MOMUS: God of ridicule.

MORPHEUS: God of dreams.

MORS: *See* Thanatos.

MORTA: *See* Fates.

MUSES: Goddesses presiding over arts and sciences: Calliope (epic poetry), Clio (history), Erato (lyric and love poetry), Euterpe (music), Melpomene (tragedy), Polymnia or Polyhymnia (sacred poetry), Terpsichore (choral dance and song), Thalia (comedy and bucolic poetry), Urania (astronomy); daughters of Zeus and Mnemosyne.

NAIADS: Nymphs of waters, streams, and fountains.

NAPAEAE: Wood nymphs.

NARCISSUS: Beautiful youth loved by Echo; in punishment for not returning her love, he was made to fall in love with his image reflected in pool; pined away and became flower.

NEMESIS: Goddess of retribution.

NEOPTOLEMUS: Son of Achilles; slew Priam; also known as Pyrrhus.

NEPTUNE: *See* Poseidon.

NEREIDS: Sea nymphs; attendants on Poseidon.

NESTOR: King of Pylos; noted for wise counsel in expedition against Troy.

NIKE: Goddess of victory.

NIOBE: Daughter of Tantalus; wife of Amphion; her children slain by Apollo and Artemis; changed to stone but continued to weep her loss.

NONA: *See* Fates.

NOTUS: *See* Winds.

NOX: *See* Nyx.

NYMPHS: Beautiful maidens; inferior deities of nature.

NYX (NOX): Goddess of night.

OCEANIDS: Ocean nymphs; daughters of Oceanus.

OCEANUS: Eldest of Titans; god of waters.

ODYSSEUS (ULYSSES): King of Ithaca; husband of Penelope; wandered ten years after fall of Troy before arriving home.

OEDIPUS: King of Thebes; son of Laius and Jocasta; unwittingly murdered Laius and married Jocasta; tore his eyes out when relationship was discovered.

OENONE: Nymph of Mount Ida; wife of Paris, who abandoned her; refused to cure him when he was poisoned by arrow of Philoctetes at Troy.

OPS: *See* Rhea.

OREADS: Mountain nymphs.

ORESTES: Son of Agamemnon and Clytemnestra; brother of Electra; slew Clytemnestra and Aegisthus; pursued by Furies until his purification by Apollo.

ORION: Hunter; slain by Artemis and made heavenly constellation.

ORPHEUS: Famed musician; son of Apollo and Muse Calliope; husband of Eurydice.

PALES: Roman goddess of shepherds and herdsmen.

PALINURUS: Aeneas' pilot; fell overboard in his sleep and was drowned.

PAN (FAUNUS): God of woods and fields; part goat; son of Hermes.

PANDORA: Opener of box containing human ills; mortal wife of Epimetheus.

PARCAE: *See* Fates.

PARIS: Son of Priam; gave apple of discord to Aphrodite, for which she enabled him to carry off Helen; slew Achilles at Troy; slain by Philoctetes.

PATROCLUS: Great friend of Achilles; wore Achilles' armor and was slain by Hector.

PEGASUS: Winged horse that sprang from Medusa's body at her death; ridden by Bellerophon when he slew Chimera.

PELIAS: King of Ioclus; seized throne from his brother Aeson; sent Jason for Golden Fleece; slain unwittingly by his daughters at instigation of Medea.

PELOPS: Son of Tantalus; his father cooked and served him to gods; restored to life; Peloponnesus named for him.

PENATES: Roman household gods.

PENELOPE: Wife of Odysseus; waited faithfully for him for ten years while putting off numerous suitors.

PEPHREDO: *See* Graeae.

PERIPHETES: Giant; son of Hephaestus; slain by Theseus.

PERSEPHONE (PROSERPINE): Queen of infernal regions; daughter of Zeus and Demeter; wife of Pluto.

PERSEUS: Son of Zeus and Danaë; slew Medusa; rescued Andromeda from monster and married her.

PHAEDRA: Daughter of Minos; wife of Theseus; caused the death of her stepson, Hippolytus.

PHAËTHON: Son of Helios; drove his father's sun chariot and was struck down by Zeus before he set world on fire.

PHILOCTETES: Greek warrior who possessed Hercules' bow and arrows; slew Paris at Troy with poisoned arrow.

PHINEUS: Betrothed of Andromeda; tried to slay Perseus but turned to stone by Medusa's head.

PHLEGETHON: *See* Rivers.

PHOSPHOR: Morning star.

PHRIXOS: Brother of Helle; carried by ram of Golden Fleece to Colchis.

PIRITHOÜS: Son of Ixion; friend of Theseus; tried to carry off Persephone from Hades; bound to enchanted rock by Pluto.

PLEIADES: Alcyone, Celaeno, Electra, Maia, Merope, Sterope or Asterope, Taygeta; seven daughters of Atlas; transformed into heavenly constellation, of which six stars are visible (Merope is said to have hidden in shame for loving a mortal).

PLUTO (DIS): God of Hades; brother of Zeus.

PLUTUS: God of wealth.

POLLUX: *See* Dioscuri.

POLYMNIA: *See* Muses.

POLYNICES: Son of Oedipus; he and his brother Eteocles killed each other; burial rite, forbidden by Creon, performed by his sister Antigone.

POLYPHEMUS: Cyclops; devoured six of Odysseus' men; blinded by Odysseus.

POLYXENA: Daughter of Priam; betrothed to Achilles, whom Paris slew at their betrothal; sacrificed to shade of Achilles.

POMONA: Roman goddess of fruits.

PONTUS: Sea god; son of Gaea.

POSEIDON (NEPTUNE): God of sea; brother of Zeus.

PRIAM: King of Troy; husband of Hecuba; ransomed Hector's body from Achilles; slain by Neoptolemus.

PRIAPUS: God of regeneration.

PROCRIS: Wife of Cephalus, who accidentally slew her.

PROCRUSTES: Giant; stretched or cut off legs of victims to make them fit iron bed; slain by Theseus.

PROETUS: Husband of Anteia; sent Bellerophon to Iobates to be put to death.

PROMETHEUS: Titan; stole fire from heaven for man. Zeus punished him by chaining him to rock in Caucasus where vultures devoured his liver daily.

PROTEUS: Sea god; assumed various shapes when called on to prophesy.

PSYCHE: Beloved of Eros; punished by jealous Aphrodite; made immortal and united with Eros.

PYGMALION: King of Cyprus; carved ivory statue of maiden which Aphrodite gave life as Galatea.

PYRAMUS: Babylonian youth; made love to Thisbe through hole in wall; thinking Thisbe slain by lion, killed himself.

PYRRHUS: *See* Neoptolemus.

PYTHON: Serpent born from slime left by Deluge; slain by Apollo.

QUIRINUS: Roman war god.

REMUS: Brother of Romulus; slain by him.

RHADAMANTHUS: One of three judges of dead in Hades; son of Zeus and Europa.

RHEA (OPS): Daughter of Uranus and Gaea; wife of Cronus; mother of Zeus; identified with Cybele.

RIVERS OF UNDERWORLD: Acheron (woe), Cocytus (wailing), Lethe (forgetfulness), Phlegethon (fire), Styx (across which souls of dead were ferried by Charon).

ROMULUS: Founder of Rome; he and Remus suckled in infancy by she-wolf; slew Remus; deified by Romans.

SARPEDON: King of Lycia; son of Zeus and Europa; slain by Patroclus at Troy.

SATURN: *See* Cronus.

SATYRS: Hoofed demigods of woods and fields; companions of Dionysus.

SCIRON: Robber; forced strangers to wash his feet, then hurled them into sea where tortoise devoured them; slain by Theseus.

SCYLLA: Female monster inhabiting rock opposite Charybdis; menaced passing sailors.

SELENE: Goddess of moon.

SEMELE: Daughter of Cadmus; mother by Zeus of Dionysus; demanded Zeus appear before her in all his splendor and was destroyed by his lightnings.

SIBYLS: Various prophetesses; most famous, Cumaean sibyl, accompanied Aeneas into Hades.

SILENI: Minor woodland deities similar to satyrs (singular: silenus). Sometimes Silenus refers to eldest of satyrs, son of Hermes or of Pan.

SILVANUS: Roman god of woods and fields.

SINIS: Giant; bent pines, by which he hurled victims against side of mountain; slain by Theseus.

SIRENS: Minor deities who lured sailors to destruction with their singing.

SISYPHUS: King of Corinth; condemned in Tartarus to roll huge stone to top of hill; it always rolled back down again.

SOL: *See* Helios.

SOMNUS: *See* Hypnos.

SPHINX: Monster of Thebes; killed those who could not answer her riddle; slain by Oedipus. Name also refers to other monsters having body of lion, wings, and head and bust of woman.

STEROPE: *See* Pleiades.

STHENO: *See* Gorgons.

STYX: *See* Rivers.

SYMPLEGADES: Clashing rocks at entrance to Black Sea; Argo passed through, causing them to become forever fixed.

SYRINX: Nymph pursued by Pan; changed to reeds, from which he made his pipes.

TANTALUS: Cruel king; father of Pelops and Niobe; condemned in Tartarus to stand chin-deep in lake surrounded by fruit branches; as he tried to eat or drink, water or fruit always receded.

TARTARUS: Underworld below Hades; often refers to Hades.

TAYGETA: *See* Pleiades.

TELEMACHUS: Son of Odysseus; made unsuccessful journey to find his father.

TELLUS: Roman goddess of earth.

TERMINUS: Roman god of boundaries and landmarks.

TERPSICHORE: *See* Muses.

TERRA: Roman earth goddess.

THALIA: *See* Graces; Muses.

THANATOS (MORS): God of death.

THEMIS: Titan goddess of laws of physical phenomena; daughter of Uranus; mother of Prometheus.

THESEUS: Son of Aegeus; slew Minotaur; married and deserted Ariadne; later married Phaedra.

THISBE: Beloved of Pyramus; killed herself at his death.

THYESTES: Brother of Atreus; Atreus killed three of his sons and served them to him at banquet.

TIRESIAS: Blind soothsayer of Thebes.

TISIPHONE: *See* Furies.

TITANS: Early gods from which Olympian gods were derived; children of Uranus and Gaea.

TITHONUS: Mortal loved by Eos; changed into grasshopper.

TRITON: Demigod of sea; son of Poseidon.

TURNUS: King of Rutuli in Italy; betrothed to Lavinia; slain by Aeneas.

ULYSSES: *See* Odysseus.

URANIA: *See* Muses.

URANUS: Personification of Heaven; husband of Gaea; father of Titans; dethroned by his son Cronus.

VENUS: *See* Aphrodite.

VERTUMNUS: Roman god of fruits and vegetables; husband of Pomona.

VESTA: *See* Hestia.

VULCAN: *See* Hephaestus.

WINDS: Aeolus (keeper of winds), Boreas (Aquilo) (north wind), Eurus (east wind), Notus (Auster) (south wind), Zephyrus (Favonius) (west wind).

ZEPHYRUS: *See* Winds.

ZEUS (JUPITER): Chief of Olympian gods; son of Cronus and Rhea; husband of Hera.

Norse Mythology

AESIR: Chief gods of Asgard.

ANDVARI: Dwarf; robbed of gold and magic ring by Loki.

ANGERBOTHA (Angrbotha): Giantess; mother by Loki of Fenrir, Hel, and Midgard serpent.

ASGARD (Asgarth): Abode of gods.

ASK (Aske, Askr): First man; created by Odin, Hoenir, and Lothur.

ASYNJUR: Goddesses of Asgard.

ATLI: Second husband of Gudrun; invited Gunnar and Hogni to his court, where they were slain; slain by Gudrun.

AUDHUMLA (Audhumbla): Cow that nourished Ymir; created Buri by licking ice cliff.

BALDER (Baldr, Baldur): God of light, spring, peace, joy; son of Odin; slain by Hoth at instigation of Loki.

BIFROST: Rainbow bridge connecting Midgard and Asgard.

BRAGI (Brage): God of poetry; husband of Ithunn.

BRANSTOCK: Great oak in hall of Volsungs; into it, Odin thrust Gram, which only Sigmund could draw forth.

BRYNHILD: Valkyrie; wakened from magic sleep by Sigurd; married Gunnar; instigated death of Sigurd; killed herself and was burned on pyre beside Sigurd.

BUR (Bor): Son of Buri; father of Odin, Hoenir, and Lothur.

BURI (Bori): Progenitor of gods; father of Bur; created by Audhumla.

EMBLA: First woman; created by Odin, Hoenir, and Lothur.

FAFNIR: Son of Rodmar, whom he slew for gold in Otter's skin; in form of dragon, guarded gold; slain by Sigurd.

FENRIR: Wolf; offspring of Loki; swallows Odin at Ragnarok and is slain by Vitharr.

FORSETI: Son of Balder.

FREY (Freyr): God of fertility and crops; son of Njorth; originally one of Vanir.

FREYA (Freyja): Goddess of love and beauty; sister of Frey; originally one of Vanir.

FRIGG (Frigga): Goddess of sky; wife of Odin.

GARM: Watchdog of Hel; slays, and is slain by, Tyr at Ragnarok.

GIMLE: Home of blessed after Ragnarok.

GIUKI: King of Nibelungs; father of Gunnar, Hogni, Guttorm, and Gudrun.

GLATHSHEIM (Gladsheim): Hall of gods in Asgard.

GRAM (meaning "Angry"): Sigmund's sword; rewelded by Regin; used by Sigurd to slay Fafnir.

GREYFELL: Sigmund's horse; descended from Sleipnir.

GRIMHILD: Mother of Gudrun; administered magic potion to Sigurd which made him forget Brynhild.

GUDRUN: Daughter of Giuki; wife of Sigurd; later wife of Atli and Jonakr.

GUNNAR: Son of Giuki; in his semblance Sigurd won Brynhild for him; slain at hall of Atli.

GUTTORM: Son of Giuki; slew Sigurd at Brynhild's request.

HEIMDALL (Heimdallr): Guardian of Asgard.

HEL: Goddess of dead and queen of underworld; daughter of Loki.

HIORDIS: Wife of Sigmund; mother of Sigurd.

HOENIR: One of creators of Ask and Embla; son of Bur.

HOGNI: Son of Giuki; slain at hall of Atli.

HOTH (Hoder, Hodur): Blind god of night and darkness; slayer of Balder at instigation of Loki.

ITHUNN (Ithun, Iduna): Keeper of golden apples of youth; wife of Bragi.

JONAKR: Third husband of Gudrun.

JORMUNREK: Slayer of Swanhild; slain by sons of Gudrun.

JOTUNNHEIM (Jotunheim): Abode of giants.

LIF and LIFTHRASIR: First man and woman after Ragnarok.

LOKI: God of evil and mischief; instigator of Balder's death.

LOTHUR (Lodur): One of creators of Ask and Embla.

MIDGARD (Midgarth): Abode of mankind; the earth.

MIDGARD SERPENT: Sea monster; offspring of Loki; slays, and is slain by, Thor at Ragnarok.

MIMIR: Giant; guardian of well in Jotunnheim at root of Yggdrasill; knower of past and future.

MJOLLNIR: Magic hammer of Thor.

NAGLFAR: Ship to be used by giants in attacking Asgard at Ragnarok; built from nails of dead men.

NANNA: Wife of Balder.

NIBELUNGS: Dwellers in northern kingdom ruled by Giuki.

NIFLHEIM (Nifelheim): Outer region of cold and darkness; abode of Hel.

NJORTH: Father of Frey and Freya; originally one of Vanir.

NORNS: Demigoddesses of fate: Urth (Urdur) (Past), Verthandi (Verdandi) (Present), Skuld (Future).

ODIN (Othin): Head of Aesir; creator of world with Vili and Ve; equivalent to Woden (Wodan, Wotan) in Teutonic mythology.

OTTER: Son of Rodmar; slain by Loki; his skin filled with gold hoard of Andvari to appease Rodmar.

RAGNAROK: Final destruction of present world in battle between gods and giants; some minor gods will survive, and Lif and Lifthrasir will repeople world.

REGIN: Blacksmith; son of Rodmar; foster-father of Sigurd.

RERIR: King of Huns; son of Sigi.

RODMAR: Father of Regin, Otter, and Fafnir; demanded Otter's skin be filled with gold; slain by Fafnir, who stole gold.

SIF: Wife of Thor.

SIGGEIR: King of Goths; husband of Signy; he and his sons slew Volsung and his sons, except Sigmund; slain by Sigmund and Sinfiotli.

SIGI: King of Huns; son of Odin.

SIGMUND: Son of Volsung; brother of Signy, who bore him Sinfiotli; husband of Hiordis, who bore him Sigurd.

SIGNY: Daughter of Volsung; sister of Sigmund; wife of Siggeir; mother by Sigmund of Sinfiotli.

SIGURD: Son of Sigmund and Hiordis; wakened Brynhild from magic sleep; married Gudrun; slain by Guttorm at instigation of Brynhild.

SIGYN: Wife of Loki.

SINFIOTLI: Son of Sigmund and Signy.

SKULD: *See* Norns.

SLEIPNIR (Sleipner): Eight-legged horse of Odin.

SURT (Surtr): Fire demon; slays Frey at Ragnarok.

SVARTALFAHEIM: Abode of dwarfs.

SWANHILD: Daughter of Sigurd and Gudrun; slain by Jormunrek.

THOR: God of thunder; oldest son of Odin; equivalent to Germanic deity Donar.

TYR: God of war; son of Odin; equivalent to Tiu in Teutonic mythology.

ULL (Ullr): Son of Sif; stepson of Thor.

URTH: *See* Norns.

VALHALLA (Valhall): Great hall in Asgard where Odin received souls of heroes killed in battle.

VALI: Odin's son; Ragnarok survivor.

VALKYRIES: Virgins, messengers of Odin, who selected heroes to die in battle and took them to Valhalla; generally considered as nine in number.

VANIR: Early race of gods; three survivors, Njorth, Frey, and Freya, are associated with Aesir.

VE: Brother of Odin; one of creators of world.

VERTHANDI: *See* Norns.

VILI: Brother of Odin; one of creators of world.

VINGOLF: Abode of goddesses in Asgard.

VITHARR (Vithar): Son of Odin; survivor of Ragnarok.

VOLSUNG: Descendant of Odin, and father of Signy, Sigmund; his descendants were called Volsungs.

YGGDRASILL: Giant ash tree springing from body of Ymir and supporting universe; its roots extended to Asgard, Jotunnheim, and Nifiheim.

YMIR (Ymer): Primeval frost giant killed by Odin, Vili, and Ve; world created from his body; also, from his body sprang Yggdrasill.

Egyptian Mythology

AARU: Abode of the blessed dead.

AMEN (Amon, Ammon): One of chief Theban deities; united with sun god under form of Amen-Ra.

AMENTI: Region of dead where souls were judged by Osiris.

ANUBIS: Guide of souls to Amenti; son of Osiris; jackal-headed.

APIS: Sacred bull, an embodiment of Ptah; identified with Osiris as Osiris-Apis or Serapis.

GEB (Keb, Seb): Earth god; father of Osiris; represented with goose on head.

HATHOR (Athor): Goddess of love and mirth; cow-headed.

HORUS: God of day; son of Osiris and Isis; hawk-headed.

ISIS: Goddess of motherhood and fertility; sister and wife of Osiris.

KHEPERA: God of morning sun.

KHNEMU (Khnum, Chnuphis, Chnemu, Chnum): Ram-headed god.

KHONSU (Khensu, Khuns): Son of Amen and Mut.

MENTU (Ment): Solar deity, sometimes considered god of war; falcon-headed.

MIN (Khem, Chem): Principle of physical life.

MUT (Maut): Wife of Amen.

NEPHTHYS: Goddess of the dead; sister and wife of Set.

NU: Chaos from which world was created, personified as a god.

NUT: Goddess of heavens; consort of Geb.

OSIRIS: God of underworld and judge of dead; son of Geb and Nut.

PTAH (Phtha): Chief deity of Memphis.

RA: God of the Sun, the supreme god; son of Nut; Pharaohs claimed descent from him; represented as lion, cat, or falcon.

SERAPIS: God uniting attributes of Osiris and Apis.

SET (Seth): God of darkness or evil; brother and enemy of Osiris.

SHU: Solar deity; son of Ra and Hathor.

TEM (Atmu, Atum, Tum): Solar deity.

THOTH (Dhouti): God of wisdom and magic; scribe of gods; ibis-headed.

Rulers of England and Great Britain

Saxons[1]

Name	Born	Ruled[2]
Egbert[3]	c. 775	828– 839
Ethelwulf	?	839– 858
Ethelbald	?	858– 860
Ethelbert	?	860– 866
Ethelred I	?	866– 871
Alfred the Great	849	871– 899
Edward the Elder	c. 870	899– 924
Athelstan	895	924– 939
Edmund I the Deed-doer ..	921	939– 946
Edred	c. 925	946– 955
Edwy the Fair	c. 943	955– 959
Edgar the Peaceful	943	959– 975
Edward the Martyr	c. 962	975– 979
Ethelred II the Unready ..	968	979–1016
Edmund II Ironside	c. 993	1016–1016

Danes

Name	Born	Ruled[2]
Canute	995	1016–1035
Harold I Harefoot	c.1016	1035–1040
Hardecanute	c.1018	1040–1042

Saxons

Name	Born	Ruled[2]
Edward the Confessor	c.1004	1042–1066
Harold II	c.1020	1066–1066

House of Normandy

Name	Born	Ruled[2]
William I the Conqueror ..	1027	1066–1087
William II Rufus	c.1056	1087–1100
Henry I Beauclerc	1068	1100–1135
Stephen of Blois	c.1100	1135–1154

House of Plantagenet

Name	Born	Ruled[2]
Henry II	1133	1154–1189
Richard I Coeur de Lion ..	1157	1189–1199
John Lackland	1167	1199–1216
Henry III	1207	1216–1272
Edward I Longshanks	1239	1272–1307
Edward II	1284	1307–1327
Edward III	1312	1327–1377
Richard II	1367	1377–1399[4]

House of Lancaster

Name	Born	Ruled[2]
Henry IV Bolingbroke	1367	1399–1413
Henry V	1387	1413–1422
Henry VI	1421	1422–1461[5]

House of York

Name	Born	Ruled[2]
Edward IV	1442	1461–1483[5]
Edward V	1470	1483–1483
Richard III	1452	1483–1485

House of Tudor

Name	Born	Ruled[2]
Henry VII	1457	1485–1509
Henry VIII	1491	1509–1547
Edward VI	1537	1547–1553
Jane (Lady Jane Grey)[6]	1537	1553–1553
Mary I ("Bloody Mary")	1516	1553–1558
Elizabeth I	1533	1558–1603

House of Stuart

Name	Born	Ruled[2]
James I[7]	1566	1603–1625
Charles I	1600	1625–1649

Commonwealth

Name	Born	Ruled[2]
Council of State	....	1649–1653
Oliver Cromwell[8]	1599	1653–1658
Richard Cromwell[8]	1626	1658–1659[9]

Restoration of House of Stuart

Name	Born	Ruled[2]
Charles II	1630	1660–1685
James II	1633	1685–1688[10]

Restoration of House of Stuart (cont'd)

Name	Born	Ruled[2]
William III[11]	1650	1689–1702
Mary II[11]	1662	1689–1694
Anne	1665	1702–1714

House of Hanover

Name	Born	Ruled[2]
George I	1660	1714–1727
George II	1683	1727–1760
George III	1738	1760–1820
George IV	1762	1820–1830
William IV	1765	1830–1837
Victoria	1819	1837–1901

House of Saxe-Coburg[12]

Name	Born	Ruled[2]
Edward VII	1841	1901–1910

House of Windsor[12]

Name	Born	Ruled[2]
George V	1865	1910–1936
Edward VIII	1894	1936–1936[13]
George VI	1895	1936–1952
Elizabeth II	1926	1952–

[1] Dates for Saxon Kings are still subjects of controversy. [2] Year of end of rule is also that of death, unless otherwise indicated. [3] Became King of West Saxons in 802; considered (from 828) first King of all England. [4] Died 1400. [5] Henry VI reigned again briefly 1470–71. [6] Nominal Queen for 9 days; not counted as Queen by some authorities. She was beheaded in 1554. [7] Ruled in Scotland as James VI (1567–1625). [8] Lord Protector. [9] Died 1712. [10] Died 1701. [11] Joint rulers (1689–1694). [12] Name changed from Saxe-Coburg to Windsor in 1917. [13] Was known since his abdication as the Duke of Windsor; died 1972.

British Prime Ministers Since 1770

Name	Term
Lord North (Tory)	1770–1782
Marquis of Rockingham (Whig)	1782–1782
Earl of Shelburne (Whig)	1782–1783
Duke of Portland (Coalition)	1783–1783
William Pitt, the Younger (Tory)	1783–1801
Henry Addington (Tory)	1801–1804
William Pitt, the Younger (Tory)	1804–1806
Baron Grenville (Whig)	1806–1807
Duke of Portland (Tory)	1807–1809
Spencer Perceval (Tory)	1809–1812
Earl of Liverpool (Tory)	1812–1827
George Canning (Tory)	1827–1827
Viscount Goderich (Tory)	1827–1828
Duke of Wellington (Tory)	1828–1830
Earl Grey (Whig)	1830–1834
Viscount Melbourne (Whig)	1834–1834
Sir Robert Peel (Tory)	1834–1835
Viscount Melbourne (Whig)	1835–1841
Sir Robert Peel (Tory)	1841–1846
Earl Russell (Whig)	1846–1852
Earl of Derby (Tory)	1852–1852
Earl of Aberdeen (Coalition)	1852–1855
Viscount Palmerston (Liberal)	1855–1858
Earl of Derby (Conservative)	1858–1859
Viscount Palmerston (Liberal)	1859–1865
Earl Russell (Liberal)	1865–1866
Earl of Derby (Conservative)	1866–1868
Benjamin Disraeli (Conservative)	1868–1868
William E. Gladstone (Liberal)	1868–1874
Benjamin Disraeli (Conservative)	1874–1880
William E. Gladstone (Liberal)	1880–1885
Marquis of Salisbury (Conservative)	1885–1886
William E. Gladstone (Liberal)	1886–1886
Marquis of Salisbury (Conservative)	1886–1892
William E. Gladstone (Liberal)	1892–1894
Earl of Rosebery (Liberal)	1894–1895
Marquis of Salisbury (Conservative)	1895–1902
Earl Balfour (Conservative)	1902–1905
Sir H. Campbell-Bannerman (Liberal)	1905–1908
Herbert H. Asquith (Liberal)	1908–1915
Herbert H. Asquith (Coalition)	1915–1916
David Lloyd George (Coalition)	1916–1922
Andrew Bonar Law (Conservative)	1922–1923
Stanley Baldwin (Conservative)	1923–1924
James Ramsay MacDonald (Labour)	1924–1924
Stanley Baldwin (Conservative)	1924–1929
James Ramsay MacDonald (Labour)	1929–1931
James Ramsay MacDonald (Coalition)	1931–1935
Stanley Baldwin (Coalition)	1935–1937
Neville Chamberlain (Coalition)	1937–1940
Winston Churchill (Coalition)	1940–1945
Clement R. Attlee (Labour)	1945–1951
Sir Winston Churchill (Conserv.)	1951–1955
Sir Anthony Eden (Conservative)	1955–1957
Harold Macmillan (Conservative)	1957–1963
Sir Alec Frederick Douglas-Home (Conservative)	1963–1964
Harold Wilson (Labour)	1964–1970
Edward Heath (Conservative)	1970–1974
Harold Wilson (Labour)	1974–1976
James Callaghan (Labour)	1976–

"In God We Trust"

"In God We Trust" first appeared on U. S. coins after April 22, 1864, when Congress passed an act authorizing the coinage of a 2-cent piece bearing this motto. Thereafter, Congress extended its use to other coins. On July 30, 1956, it became the national motto.

Rulers of France

Carolingian Dynasty

Name	Born	Ruled[1]
Pepin the Short ....c.	714	751–768
Charlemagne[2]	742	768–814
Louis I the Debonair[3]	778	814–840
Charles I the Bald[4]	823	840–877
Louis II the Stammerer ...	846	877–879
Louis III[5] ....c.	863	879–882
Carloman[5]	?	879–884
Charles II the Fat[6]	839	884–887[7]
Eudes (Odo), Count of Paris	?	888–898
Charles III the Simple[8] ...	879	893–923[9]
Robert I[10] ....c.	865	922–923
Rudolf (Raoul), Duke of Burgundy	?	926–936
Louis IV d'Outremer ......c.	921	936–954
Lothair	941	954–986
Louis V the Sluggard .....c.	967	986–987

Capetian Dynasty

Name	Born	Ruled[1]
Hugh Capet ....c.	940	987–996
Robert II the Pious[11] ......c.	970	996–1031
Henry I	1008	1031–1060
Philip I	1052	1060–1108
Louis VI the Fat	1081	1108–1137
Louis VII the Young ......c.	1121	1137–1180
Philip II (Philip Augustus)	1165	1180–1223
Louis VIII the Lion	1187	1223–1226
Louis IX (St. Louis)	1214	1226–1270
Philip III the Bold	1245	1270–1285
Philip IV the Fair	1268	1285–1314
Louis X the Quarreler	1289	1314–1316
John I	1316	1316–1316
Philip V the Tall	1294	1316–1322
Charles IV the Fair	1294	1322–1328

House of Valois

Name	Born	Ruled[1]
Philip VI	1293	1328–1350
John II the Good	1319	1350–1364
Charles V the Wise	1337	1364–1380
Charles VI the Well-Beloved	1368	1380–1422
Charles VII	1403	1422–1461
Louis XI	1423	1461–1483
Charles VIII	1470	1483–1498
Louis XII the Father of the People	1462	1498–1515
Francis I	1494	1515–1547
Henry II	1519	1547–1559
Francis II	1544	1559–1560
Charles IX	1550	1560–1574
Henry III	1551	1574–1589

House of Bourbon

Name	Born	Ruled[1]
Henry IV of Navarre	1553	1589–1610
Louis XIII	1601	1610–1643
Louis XIV the Great	1638	1643–1715
Louis XV the Well-Beloved	1710	1715–1774

House of Bourbon (cont'd)

Name	Born	Ruled[1]
Louis XVI	1754	1774–1792[12]
Louis XVII (Louis Charles de France)[13]	1785	1793–1795

First Republic

Name	Born	Ruled[1]
National Convention		1792–1795
Directory (Directoire)		1795–1799

Consulate

Name	Born	Ruled[1]
Napoleon Bonaparte[14]	1769	1799–1804

First Empire

Name	Born	Ruled[1]
Napoleon I	1769	1804–1815[15]

Restoration of House of Bourbon

Name	Born	Ruled[1]
Louis XVIII le Désiré	1755	1814–1824
Charles X	1757	1824–1830[16]

Bourbon-Orleans line

Name	Born	Ruled[1]
Louis Philippe ("Citizen King")	1773	1830–1848[17]

Second Republic

Name	Born	Ruled[1]
Louis Napoleon[18]	1808	1848–1852

Second Empire

Name	Born	Ruled[1]
Napoleon III (Louis Napoleon)	1808	1852–1871[19]

Third Republic

Name	Born	Ruled[1]
Louis Adolphe Thiers[20]	1797	1871–1873[21]
Marie E. P. M. de MacMahon[20]	1808	1873–1879[22]
François P. J. Grévy[20]	1807	1879–1887[23]
Sadi Carnot[20]	1837	1887–1894
Jean Casimir-Périer[20]	1847	1894–1895[24]
François Félix Faure[20]	1841	1895–1899
Émile Loubet[20]	1838	1899–1906[25]
Clement Armand Fallières[20]	1841	1906–1913[26]
Raymond Poincaré[20]	1860	1913–1920[27]
Paul E. L. Deschanel[20]	1856	1920–1920[28]
Alexandre Millerand[20]	1859	1920–1924[29]
Gaston Doumergue[20]	1863	1924–1931[30]
Paul Doumer[20]	1857	1931–1932
Albert Lebrun[20]	1871	1932–1940[31]

Vichy Government

Name	Born	Ruled[1]
Henri Philippe Pétain[32] ...	1856	1940–1944[33]

Provisional Government

Name	Born	Ruled[1]
Charles de Gaulle[34]	1890	1944–1946[35]
Félix Gouin[34]	1884	1946–1946[36]
Georges Bidault[34]	1899	1946–1947[36]

Fourth Republic

Name	Born	Ruled[1]
Vincent Auriol[20]	1884	1947–1954[37]
René Coty[20]	1882	1954–1959[38]

Fifth Republic

Name	Born	Ruled[1]
Charles de Gaulle[20]	1890	1959–1969[35]
Georges Pompidou[20]	1911	1969–1974[1]
Valery Giscard d'Estaing[20].	1926	1974–

[1] Year of end of rule is also that of death, unless otherwise indicated. [2] Crowned Emperor of the West in 1800. [3] Holy Roman Emperor 814–840. [4] Holy Roman Emperor 875–877 as Charles II. [5] Ruled jointly 879–882. [6] Holy Roman Emperor 881–887 as Charles III. [7] Died 888. [8] King 893–898 in opposition to Eudes. [9] Died 929. [10] Not counted in regular line of Kings of France by some authorities. Elected by nobles but killed in Battle of Soissons. [11] Sometimes called Robert I. [12] Executed 1793. [13] Titular King only. He died in prison according to official reports, but many pretenders appeared during the Bourbon restoration. [14] As First Consul, Napoleon held the power of government. In 1804, he became Emperor. [15] Abdicated first time June 1814. Re-entered Paris Mar. 1815, after escape from Elba; Louis XVIII fled to Ghent. Abdicated second time June 1815. He named as his successor his son, Napoleon II, who was not acceptable to the Allies. He died 1821. [16] Died 1836. [17] Died 1850. [18] President; became Emperor in 1852. [19] Died 1873. [20] President. [21] Died 1877. [22] Died 1893. [23] Died 1891. [24] Died 1907. [25] Died 1929. [26] Died 1931. [27] Died 1934. [28] Died 1922. [29] Died 1942. [30] Died 1937. [31] Died 1950. [32] Chief of State. [33] Died 1951. [34] Interim President. [35] Died 1970. [36] Still alive. [37] Died 1966. [38] Died 1962.

Rulers of Germany and Prussia

Kings of Prussia

Name	Born	Ruled[1]
Frederick I[2]	1657	1701–1713
Frederick William I	1688	1713–1740
Frederick II the Great	1712	1740–1786
Frederick William II	1744	1786–1797
Frederick William III	1770	1797–1840
Frederick William IV	1795	1840–1861
William I	1797	1861–1871[3]

Emperors of Germany

Name	Born	Ruled[1]
William I	1797	1871–1888
Frederick III	1831	1888–1888
William II	1859	1888–1918[4]

Heads of the Reich

Name	Born	Ruled[1]
Friedrich Ebert[5]	1871	1919–1925
Paul von Hindenburg[5]	1847	1925–1934
Adolf Hitler[6,7]	1889	1934–1945
Karl Doenitz[6]	1891	1945–1945

German Federal Republic (Western)

Name	Born	Ruled[1]
Theodor Heuss[5]	1884	1949–1959[9]
Heinrich Luebke[5]	1895	1959–1969[8]
Gustav Heinemann[5,12]	1899	1969–1974
Walter Scheel[5]	1919	1974–

German Democratic Republic (Eastern)

Name	Born	Ruled[1]
Wilhelm Pieck[5]	1876	1949–1960
Walter Ulbricht[10]	1893	1960–1973
Willi Stoph[11]	1914	1973–

[1] Year of end of rule is also that of death, unless otherwise indicated. [2] Was Elector of Brandenburg (1688–1701) as Frederick III. [3] Became Emperor of Germany in 1871. [4] Died 1941. [5] President. [6] Führer. [7] Named Chancellor by President Hindenburg in 1933. [8] Died 1972. [9] Died 1963. [10] Chairman of Council of State. Died 1973. [11] Chairman Council of State. [12] Died 1976.

Rulers of Russia Since 1533

Name	Born	Ruled[1]
Ivan IV the Terrible	1530	1533–1584
Theodore I	1557	1584–1598
Boris Godunov	c.1551	1598–1605
Theodore II	1589	1605–1605
Demetrius I[2]	?	1605–1606
Basil IV Shuiski	?	1606–1610[3]
"Time of Troubles"	....	1610–1613
Michael Romanov	1596	1613–1645
Alexis I	1629	1645–1676
Theodore III	1656	1676–1682
Ivan V[4]	1666	1682–1689[5]
Peter I the Great[4]	1672	1682–1725
Catherine I	c.1684	1725–1727
Peter II	1715	1727–1730
Anna	1693	1730–1740
Ivan VI	1740	1740–1741[6]
Elizabeth	1709	1741–1762
Peter III	1728	1762–1762

Name	Born	Ruled[1]
Catherine II the Great	1729	1762–1796
Paul I	1754	1796–1801
Alexander I	1777	1801–1825
Nicholas I	1796	1825–1855
Alexander II	1818	1855–1881
Alexander III	1845	1881–1894
Nicholas II	1868	1894–1917[7]

Provisional Government

Name	Born	Ruled[1]
Prince Georgi Lvov[8]	1861	1917–1917[9]
Alexander Kerensky[8]	1881	1917–1917[10]

U.S.S.R.

Name	Born	Ruled[1]
N. Lenin[8]	1870	1917–1924
Joseph Stalin[11]	1879	1924–1953
Georgi M. Malenkov[8]	1902	1953–1955[12]
Nikolai A. Bulganin[8]	1895	1955–1958[12]
Nikita S. Khrushchev[8]	1894	1958–1964[13]
Aleksei N. Kosygin[8]	1904	1964–

[1] Year of end of rule is also that of death, unless otherwise indicated. [2] Also known as Pseudo-Demetrius. [3] Died 1612. [4] Ruled jointly until 1689, when Ivan was deposed. [5] Died 1696. [6] Died 1764. [7] Killed 1918. [8] Premier. [9] Died 1925. [10] Died 1970. [11] General Secretary of Communist party; Premier 1941–53. [12] Still alive. [13] Died 1971.

How Many Earth People Have There Been?

Several demographers, among them Professor Wilhelm Winkler of Austria, and Professor Nathan Keyfitz of the University of Chicago, have estimated how many people have lived on this planet since man evolved.

Professor Keyfitz's formula is a simple one. It says, as reported in *Demography* (3:2:581–2), that the number of people who have ever lived may be found algebraically from a single formula which may be applied to the successive intervals between guessed population numbers.

If at time t_1 the population was n_1 and at time t_2 ($t_2 > t_1$) the population was n_2, then the annual rate of growth r is

$$r = \frac{\ln n_2 - \ln n_1}{t_2 - t_1}$$

If, during the interval from time t_1 to t_2, the rate of increase was r, then at any given time the population was $n_1 e^{r(t-t_1)}$ and the total person-years lived was

$$\int_{t}^{t_2} n_1 e^{r(t-t_1)} dt = \frac{n_1}{r} \left[e^{r(t_2-t_1)} - 1 \right].$$

Substituting in the above, the value of r gives the following for the person-years lived:

$$\frac{n_2 - n_1}{r} = \frac{(n_2 - n_1)(t_2 - t_1)}{\ln n_2 - \ln n_1}.$$

This yields a set of data for the several intervals which add to 1.72×10^{12} person-years. Dividing by 25 as the average expectation of life gives 69 billion as the number of persons who have ever lived on the earth. Of this total the 3 billion earth people now living would be about 4%.

THE DECLARATION OF INDEPENDENCE

In CONGRESS, July 4, 1776

THE UNANIMOUS DECLARATION of the thirteen united STATES OF
AMERICA.

WHEN in the Course of human events it becomes necessary for one people to dissolve
the political bands which have connected them with another, and to assume among
the powers of the earth, the separate and equal station to which the Laws of Nature and of
Nature's God entitle them, a decent respect to the opinions of mankind requires that
they should declare the causes which impel them to the separation.

We hold these truths to be self-evident, that all men are created equal, that they are
endowed by their Creator with certain unalienable Rights, that among these are Life,
Liberty and the pursuit of Happiness.—That to secure these rights, Governments are
instituted among Men, deriving their just powers from the consent of the governed,—
That whenever any Form of Government becomes destructive of these ends, it is the
Right of the People to alter or to abolish it, and to institute new Government, laying
its foundation on such principles and organizing its powers in such form, as to them
shall seem most likely to effect their Safety and Happiness. Prudence, indeed, will dictate
that Governments long established should not be changed for light and transient causes;
and accordingly all experience hath shewn that mankind are more disposed to suffer,
while evils are sufferable, than to right themselves by abolishing the forms to which
they are accustomed. But when a long train of abuses and usurpations, pursuing invari-
ably the same Object evinces a design to reduce them under absolute Despotism, it is
their right, it is their duty, to throw off such Government, and to provide new Guards
for their future security.—Such has been the patient sufferance of these Colonies; and
such is now the necessity which constrains them to alter their former Systems of Government. The history of the present King of Great Britain is a history of repeated injuries
and usurpations, all having in direct object the establishment of an absolute Tyranny
over these States. To prove this, let Facts be submitted to a candid world.

He has refused his Assent to Laws, the most wholesome and necessary for the public
good.

He has forbidden his Governors to pass Laws of immediate and pressing importance,
unless suspended in their operation till his Assent should be obtained; and when so
suspended, he has utterly neglected to attend to them.

He has refused to pass other Laws for the accommodation of large districts of people,
unless those people would relinquish the right of Representation in the Legislature,
a right inestimable to them and formidable to tyrants only.

He has called together legislative bodies at places unusual, uncomfortable, and distant
from the depository of their Public Records, for the sole purpose of fatiguing them into
compliance with his measures.

He has dissolved Representative Houses repeatedly, for opposing with manly firmness
his invasions on the rights of the people.

He has refused for a long time, after such dissolutions, to cause others to be elected;
whereby the Legislative Powers, incapable of Annihilation, have returned to the People
at large for their exercise; the State remaining in the mean time exposed to all the dangers
of invasion from without, and convulsions within.

NOTE: On April 12, 1776, the legislature
of North Carolina authorized its delegates
to the Continental Congress to join with
others in a declaration of separation from
Great Britain; the first colony to instruct
its delegates to take the actual initiative
was Virginia on May 15. On June 7, 1776,
Richard Henry Lee of Virginia offered a
resolution to the Congress to the effect
"that these United Colonies are, and of
right ought to be, free and independent
States. . . ." A committee, consisting of
Thomas Jefferson, John Adams, Benjamin
Franklin, Robert R. Livingston, and Roger
Sherman was organized to "prepare a
declaration to the effect of the said first
resolution." The Declaration of Independence was adopted on July 4, 1776.

Most delegates signed the Declaration
August 2, but George Wythe (Va.) signed
August 27; Richard Henry Lee (Va.), Elbridge Gerry (Mass.), and Oliver Wolcott
(Conn.) in September; Matthew Thornton
(N. H.), not a delegate until September,
in November; and Thomas McKean (Del.),
although present on July 4, not until 1781
by special permission, having served in the
army in the interim.

He has endeavoured to prevent the population of these States; for that purpose obstructing the Laws for Naturalization of Foreigners; refusing to pass others to encourage their migrations hither, and raising the conditions of new Appropriations of Lands.

He has obstructed the Administration of Justice, by refusing his Assent to Laws for establishing Judiciary Powers.

He has made Judges dependent on his Will alone, for the tenure of their offices, and the amount and payment of their salaries.

He has erected a multitude of New Offices, and sent hither swarms of Officers to harass our people, and eat out their substance.

He has kept among us, in times of peace, Standing Armies without the Consent of our legislatures.

He has affected to render the Military independent of and superior to the Civil Power.

He has combined with others to subject us to a jurisidiction foreign to our constitution, and unacknowledged by our laws; giving his Assent to their Acts of pretended Legislation:

For quartering large bodies of armed troops among us:

For protecting them, by a mock Trial, from punishment for any Murders which they should commit on the Inhabitants of these States:

For cutting off our Trade with all parts of the world:

For imposing Taxes on us without our Consent:

For depriving us in many cases, of the benefits of Trial by Jury:

For transporting us beyond Seas to be tried for pretended offences:

For abolishing the free System of English Laws in a neighbouring Province, establishing therein an Arbitrary government, and enlarging its Boundaries so as to render it at once an example and fit instrument for introducing the same absolute rule into these Colonies:

For taking away our Charters, abolishing our most valuable Laws and altering fundamentally the Forms of our Governments:

For suspending our own Legislatures, and declaring themselves invested with power to legislate for us in all cases whatsoever.

He has abdicated Government here, by declaring us out of his Protection and waging War against us.

He has plundered our seas, ravaged our Coasts, burnt our towns, and destroyed the lives of our people.

He is at this time transporting large Armies of foreign Mercenaries to compleat the works of death, desolation and tyranny, already begun with circumstances of Cruelty & Perfidy scarcely paralleled in the most barbarous ages, and totally unworthy the Head of a civilized nation.

He has constrained our fellow Citizens taken Captive on the high Seas to bear Arms against their Country, to become the executioners of their friends and Brethren, or to fall themselves by their Hands.

He has excited domestic insurrections amongst us, and has endeavoured to bring on the inhabitants of our frontiers, the merciless Indian Savages, whose known rule of warfare, is an undistinguished destruction of all ages, sexes and conditions.

In every stage of these Oppressions We have Petitioned for Redress in the most humble terms: Our repeated Petitions have been answered only by repeated injury. A Prince, whose character is thus marked by every act which may define a Tyrant, is unfit to be the ruler of a free people.

Nor have We been wanting in attentions to our Brittish brethren. We have warned them from time to time of attempts by their legislature to extend an unwarrantable jurisdiction over us. We have reminded them of the circumstances of our emigration and settlement here. We have appealed to their native justice and magnanimity, and we have conjured them by the ties of our common kindred to disavow these usurpations, which would inevitably interrupt our connections and correspondence. They too have been deaf to the voice of justice and of consanguinity. We must, therefore, acquiesce in the necessity, which denounces our Separation, and hold them, as we hold the rest of mankind, Enemies in War, in Peace Friends.

WE, THEREFORE, the Representatives of the UNITED STATES OF AMERICA, in General Congress, Assembled, appealing to the Supreme Judge of the world for the rectitude of our intentions, do, in the Name, and by Authority of the good People of these Colonies, solemnly publish and declare, That these United Colonies are, and of Right ought to be

FREE AND INDEPENDENT STATES; that they are Absolved from all Allegiance to the British Crown, and that all political connection between them and the State of Great Britain, is and ought to be totally dissolved; and that as Free and Independent States, they have full Power to levy War, conclude Peace, contract Alliances, establish Commerce, and to do all other Acts and Things which Independent States may of right do.—And for the support of this Declaration, with a firm reliance on the protection of Divine Providence, we mutually pledge to each other our Lives, our Fortunes and our sacred Honor.

JOHN HANCOCK.

New Hampshire.
Josiah Bartlett,
Wm. Whipple,
Matthew Thornton.

Rhode Island.
Step. Hopkins,
William Ellery.

Connecticut.
Roger Sherman,
Sam'el Huntington,
Wm. Williams,
Oliver Wolcott.

New York.
Wm. Floyd,
Phil. Livingston,
Frans. Lewis,
Lewis Morris.

New Jersey.
Richd. Stockton,
Jno. Witherspoon,
Fras. Hopkinson,
John Hart,
Abra. Clark.

Pennsylvania.
Robt. Morris,
Benjamin Rush,
Benj. Franklin,
John Morton,
Geo. Clymer,
Jas. Smith,
Geo. Taylor,
James Wilson,
Geo. Ross.

Massachusetts-Bay.
Saml. Adams,
John Adams,
Robt. Treat Paine,
Elbridge Gerry.

Delaware.
Caesar Rodney,
Geo. Read,
Tho. M'Kean.

Maryland.
Samuel Chase,
Wm. Paca,
Thos. Stone,
Charles Carroll of Carrollton.

Virginia.
George Wythe,
Richard Henry Lee,
Th. Jefferson,
Benj. Harrison,
Ths. Nelson, Jr.,
Francis Lightfoot Lee,
Carter Braxton.

North Carolina.
Wm. Hooper,
Joseph Hewes,
John Penn.

South Carolina.
Edward Rutledge,
Thos. Heyward, Junr.,
Thomas Lynch, Junr.,
Arthur Middleton.

Georgia.
Button Gwinnett,
Lyman Hall,
Geo. Walton.

IN CONGRESS
JANUARY, 18, 1777.

Ordered:
That an authenticated copy of the Declaration of Independency, with the names of the Members of Congress subscribing the same, be sent to each of the United States, and that they be desired to have the same put on record.
By order of Congress.
Attest, CHAS. THOMSON, *Secy*. A true copy. JOHN HANCOCK, *Presidt*.

The Liberty Bell

The Liberty Bell was cast in England in 1752 for the Pennsylvania Statehouse (now named Independence Hall) in Philadelphia. It was recast in Philadelphia in 1753. It is inscribed with the words, "Proclaim liberty throughout all the land unto all the inhabitants thereof" (Lev. 25:10). The bell was rung on July 8, 1776, for the first public reading of the Declaration of Independence. Hidden in Allentown during the British occupation of Philadelphia, it was replaced in Independence Hall in 1778 where it remains today. The bell cracked on July 8, 1835, while tolling the death of Chief Justice John Marshall.

The Great Seal of the U. S.

On July 4, 1776, the Continental Congress appointed a committee consisting of Benjamin Franklin, John Adams, and Thomas Jefferson "to bring in a device for a seal of the United States of America." After many delays, a verbal description of a design by William Barton was finally approved by Congress on June 20, 1782. The seal shows an American bald eagle with a ribbon in its mouth bearing the device *E pluribus unum* (One out of many). In its talons are the arrows of war and an olive branch of peace.

CONSTITUTION
of the UNITED STATES OF AMERICA

(The bracketed words are designations for your convenience; they are not part of the Constitution.)

THE *oldest federal constitution in existence was framed by a convention of delegates from twelve of the thirteen original states in Philadelphia in May, 1787, Rhode Island failing to send a delegate. George Washington presided over the session, which lasted until September 17, 1787. The draft (originally a preamble and seven Articles) was submitted to all thirteen states and was to become effective when ratified by nine states. It went into effect on the first Wednesday in March, 1789, having been ratified by New Hampshire, the ninth state to approve, on June 21, 1788. The states ratified the Constitution in the following order:*

Delaware	December 7, 1787	South Carolina	May 23, 1788
Pennsylvania	December 12, 1787	New Hampshire	June 21, 1788
New Jersey	December 18, 1787	Virginia	June 25, 1788
Georgia	January 2, 1788	New York	July 26, 1788
Connecticut	January 9, 1788	North Carolina	November 21, 1789
Massachusetts	February 6, 1788	Rhode Island	May 29, 1790
Maryland	April 28, 1788		

[PREAMBLE]. WE THE PEOPLE of the United States, in Order to form a more perfect Union, establish Justice, insure domestic Tranquility, provide for the common defence, promote the general Welfare, and secure the Blessings of Liberty to ourselves and our Posterity, do ordain and establish this Constitution for the United States of America.

ARTICLE I

Section 1
[Legislative powers vested in Congress.] All legislative Powers herein granted shall be vested in a Congress of the United States, which shall consist of a Senate and House of Representatives.

Section 2
[Composition of the House of Representatives.—1.] The House of Representatives shall be composed of Members chosen every second Year by the People of the several States, and the Electors in each State shall have the Qualifications requisite for Electors of the most numerous Branch of the State Legislature.

[Qualifications of Representatives.—2.] No Person shall be a Representative who shall not have attained to the Age of twenty-five Years, and been seven Years a Citizen of the United States, and who shall not, when elected, be an Inhabitant of that State in which he shall be chosen.

[Apportionment of Representatives and direct taxes—census.*—3.] (Representatives and direct Taxes shall be apportioned among the several States which may be included within this Union, according to their respective Numbers, which shall be determined by adding to the whole Number of free Persons, including those bound to Service for a Term of Years, and ex-cluding Indians not taxed, three fifths of all other Persons.) The actual Enumeration shall be made within three Years after the first Meeting of the Congress of the United States, and within every subsequent Term of ten Years, in such Manner as they shall by Law direct. The Number of Representatives shall not exceed one for every thirty Thousand, but each State shall have at Least one Representative; and until such enumeration shall be made, the State of New Hampshire shall be entitled to chuse three, Massachusetts eight, Rhode-Island and Providence Plantations one, Connecticut five, New York six, New Jersey four, Pennsylvania eight, Delaware one, Maryland six, Virginia ten, North Carolina five, South Carolina five, and Georgia three.

[Filling of vacancies in representation.—4.] When vacancies happen in the Representation from any State, the Executive Authority thereof shall issue Writs of Election to fill such Vacancies.

[Selection of officers; power of impeachment.—5.] The House of Representatives shall chuse their Speaker and other Officers; and shall have the sole Power of Impeachment.

Section 3 †
[The Senate.—1.] The Senate of the United States shall be composed of two Senators from each State, chosen by the Legislature thereof, for six Years; and each Senator shall have one Vote.

[Classification of Senators; filling of vacancies.—2.] Immediately after they shall be assembled in Consequence of the first Election, they shall be divided as equally as may be into three Classes. The Seats of the Senators of the first Class shall be vacated at the Expiration of the second Year,

---

* The clause included in parentheses is amended by the 14th Amendment, Section 2.
† The 1st paragraph of this section and the part of the 2nd paragraph included in parentheses are amended by the 17th Amendment.

of the second Class at the Expiration of the fourth Year, and of the third Class at the Expiration of the sixth Year, so that one-third may be chosen every second Year; and if Vacancies happen by Resignation, or otherwise, during the Recess of the Legislature of any State, the Executive thereof may make temporary Appointments (until the next Meeting of the Legislature, which shall then fill such Vacancies).

[Qualification of Senators.—3.] No Person shall be a Senator who shall not have attained to the Age of thirty Years, and been nine Years a Citizen of the United States, and who shall not, when elected, be an Inhabitant of that State for which he shall be chosen.

[Vice President to be President of Senate. —4.] The Vice President of the United States shall be President of the Senate, but shall have no Vote, unless they be equally divided.

[Selection of Senate officers; President pro tempore.—5.] The Senate shall chuse their other Officers, and also a President pro tempore, in the Absence of the Vice President, or when he shall exercise the Office of President of the United States.

[Senate to try impeachments.—6.] The Senate shall have the sole Power to try all Impeachments. When sitting for that Purpose, they shall be on Oath or Affirmation. When the President of the United States is tried, the Chief Justice shall preside: And no Person shall be convicted without the Concurrence of two thirds of the Members present.

[Judgment in cases of impeachment.—7.] Judgment in Cases of Impeachment shall not extend further than to removal from Office, and disqualification to hold and enjoy any Office of honor, Trust, or Profit under the United States: but the Party convicted shall nevertheless be liable and subject to Indictment, Trial, Judgment and Punishment, according to Law.

Section 4

[Control of congressional elections.—1.] The Times, Places and Manner of holding Elections for Senators and Representatives, shall be prescribed in each State by the Legislature thereof; but the Congress may at any time by Law make or alter such Regulations, except as to the Places of chusing Senators.

[Time for assembling of Congress.*—2.] The Congress shall assemble at least once in every Year, and such Meeting shall be on the first Monday in December, unless they shall by Law appoint a different Day.

Section 5

[Each house to be the judge of the election and qualifications of its members; regulations as to quorum.—1.] Each House shall be the Judge of the Elections, Returns and Qualifications of its own Members, and a Majority of each shall constitute a Quorum to do Business; but a smaller Number may adjourn from day to day, and may be authorized to compel the Attendance of absent Members, in such Manner, and under such Penalties as each House may provide.

[Each house to determine its own rules. —2.] Each House may determine the Rules of its Proceedings, punish its Members for disorderly Behaviour, and, with the Concurrence of two thirds, expel a Member.

[Journals and yeas and nays.—3.] Each House shall keep a Journal of its Proceedings, and from time to time publish the same, excepting such Parts as may in their Judgment require Secrecy; and the Yeas and Nays of the Members of either House on any question shall, at the Desire of one fifth of those Present, be entered on the Journal.

[Adjournment.—4.] Neither House, during the Session of Congress, shall, without the Consent of the other, adjourn for more than three days, nor to any other Place than that in which the two Houses shall be sitting.

Section 6

[Compensation and privileges of members of Congress.—1.] The Senators and Representatives shall receive a Compensation for their Services, to be ascertained by Law, and paid out of the Treasury of the United States. They shall in all Cases, except Treason, Felony and Breach of the Peace, be privileged from Arrest during their Attendance at the Session of their respective Houses, and in going to and returning from the same; and for any Speech or Debate in either House, they shall not be questioned in any other Place.

[Incompatible offices; exclusions.—2.] No Senator or Representative shall, during the Time for which he was elected, be appointed to any civil Office under the Authority of the United States, which shall have been created, or the Emoluments whereof shall have been encreased during such time; and no Person holding any Office under the United States, shall be a Member of either House during his Continuance in Office.

Section 7

[Revenue bills to originate in House.—1.] All Bills for raising Revenue shall originate in the House of Representatives; but the Senate may propose or concur with Amendments as on other Bills.

[Manner of passing bills; veto power of President.—2.] Every Bill which shall have

---

* Amended by the 20th Amendment, Section 2.

passed the House of Representatives and the Senate, shall, before it becomes a Law, be presented to the President of the United States; If he approve he shall sign it, but if not he shall return it, with his Objections to that House in which it shall have originated, who shall enter the Objections at large on their Journal, and proceed to reconsider it. If after such Reconsideration two thirds of that House shall agree to pass the Bill, it shall be sent, together with the Objections, to the other House, by which it shall likewise be reconsidered, and if approved by two thirds of that House, it shall become a Law. But in all such Cases the Votes of both Houses shall be determined by Yeas and Nays, and the Names of the Persons voting for and against the Bill shall be entered on the Journal of each House respectively. If any Bill shall not be returned by the President within ten Days (Sundays excepted) after it shall have been presented to him, the Same shall be a Law, in like Manner as if he had signed it, unless the Congress by their Adjournment prevent its Return, in which Case it shall not be a Law.

[Concurrent orders or resolutions, to be passed by President.—3.] Every Order, Resolution, or Vote to which the Concurrence of the Senate and House of Representatives may be necessary (except on a question of adjournment) shall be presented to the President of the United States; and before the Same shall take Effect, shall be approved by him, or being disapproved by him, shall be repassed by two thirds of the Senate and House of Representatives, according to the Rules and Limitations prescribed in the Case of a Bill.

Section 8
[General powers of Congress.*]

[Taxes, duties, imposts, and excises.—1.] The Congress shall have Power To lay and collect Taxes, Duties, Imposts and Excises, to pay the Debts and provide for the common Defence and general Welfare of the United States; but all Duties, Imposts and Excises shall be uniform throughout the United States;

[Borrowing of money.—2.] To borrow Money on the credit of the United States;

[Regulation of commerce.—3.] To regulate Commerce with foreign Nations, and among the several States, and with the Indian Tribes;

[Naturalization and bankruptcy.—4.] To establish an uniform Rule of Naturalization, and uniform Laws on the subject of Bankruptcies throughout the United States;

[Money, weights and measures.—5.] To coin Money, regulate the Value thereof, and of foreign Coin, and fix the Standard of Weights and Measures;

[Counterfeiting.—6.] To provide for the Punishment of counterfeiting the Securities and current Coin of the United States;

[Post offices.—7.] To establish Post Offices and post Roads;

[Patents and copyrights.—8.] To promote the Progress of Science and useful Arts, by securing for limited Times to Authors and Inventors the exclusive Right to their respective Writings and Discoveries;

[Inferior courts.—9.] To constitute Tribunals inferior to the supreme Court;

[Piracies and felonies.—10.] To define and punish Piracies and Felonies committed on the high Seas, and Offences against the Law of Nations;

[War; marque and reprisal.—11.] To declare War, grant Letters of Marque and Reprisal, and make Rules concerning Captures on Land and Water;

[Armies.—12.] To raise and support Armies, but no Appropriation of Money to that Use shall be for a longer Term than two Years;

[Navy.—13.] To provide and maintain a Navy;

[Land and naval forces.—14.] To make Rules for the Government and Regulation of the land and naval Forces;

[Calling out militia.—15.] To provide for calling forth the Militia to execute the Laws of the Union, suppress Insurrections and repel Invasions;

[Organizing, arming and disciplining militia.—16.] To provide for organizing, arming, and disciplining, the Militia, and for governing such Part of them as may be employed in the Service of the United States, reserving to the States respectively, the Appointment of the Officers, and the Authority of training the Militia according to the discipline prescribed by Congress;

[Exclusive legislation over District of Columbia.—17.] To exercise exclusive Legislation in all Cases whatsoever, over such District (not exceeding ten Miles square) as may, by Cession of particular States, and the Acceptance of Congress, become the Seat of the Government of the United States, and to exercise like Authority over all Places purchased by the Consent of the Legislature of the State in which the Same shall be, for the Erection of Forts, Magazines, Arsenals, dock-Yards, and other needful Buildings;—And

[To enact laws necessary to enforce Constitution.—18.] To make all Laws which shall be necessary and proper for carrying into Execution the foregoing Powers, and all other Powers vested by this Constitu-

---

* By the 16th Amendment, Congress is given the power to lay and collect taxes on incomes.

tion in the Government of the United States, or in any Department or Officer thereof.

Section 9

[Migration or importation of certain persons not to be prohibited before 1808.—1.] The Migration or Importation of such Persons as any of the States now existing shall think proper to admit, shall not be prohibited by the Congress prior to the Year one thousand eight hundred and eight, but a Tax or duty may be imposed on such Importation, not exceeding ten dollars for each Person.

[Writ of habeas corpus not to be suspended; exception.—2.] The Privilege of the Writ of Habeas Corpus shall not be suspended, unless when in Cases of Rebellion or Invasion the public Safety may require it.

[Bills of attainder and ex post facto laws prohibited.—3.] No Bill of Attainder or ex post facto Law shall be passed.

[Capitation and other direct taxes.—4.] No Capitation, or other direct, Tax shall be laid, unless in Proportion to the Census or Enumeration herein before directed to be taken.*

[Exports not to be taxed.—5.] No Tax or Duty shall be laid on Articles exported from any State.

[No preference to be given to ports of any State; interstate shipping.—6.] No Preference shall be given by any Regulation of Commerce or Revenue to the Ports of one State over those of another: nor shall Vessels bound to, or from, one State, be obliged to enter, clear, or pay Duties in another.

[Money, how drawn from treasury; financial statements to be published.—7.] No Money shall be drawn from the Treasury, but in Consequence of Appropriations made by Law; and a regular Statement and Account of the Receipts and Expenditures of all public Money shall be published from time to time.

[Titles of nobility not to be granted; acceptance by government officers of favors from foreign powers.—8.] No Title of Nobility shall be granted by the United States: And no Person holding any Office of Profit or Trust under them, shall, without the Consent of the Congress, accept of any present, Emolument, Office, or Title, of any kind whatever, from any King, Prince, or foreign State.

Section 10

[Limitations of the powers of the several States.—1.] No State shall enter into any Treaty, Alliance, or Confederation; grant Letters of Marque and Reprisal; coin Money; emit Bills of Credit; make any Thing but gold and silver Coin a Tender in Payment of Debts; pass any Bill of Attainder, ex post facto Law, or Law impairing the Obligation of Contracts, or grant any Title of Nobility.

[State imposts and duties.—2.] No State shall, without the Consent of the Congress, lay any Imposts or Duties on Imports or Exports, except what may be absolutely necessary for executing its inspection Laws: and the net Produce of all Duties and Imposts, laid by any State on Imports or Exports, shall be for the Use of the Treasury of the United States; and all such Laws shall be subject to the Revision and Control of the Congress.

[Further restrictions on powers of States.—3.] No State shall, without the Consent of Congress, lay any Duty of Tonnage, keep Troops, or Ships of War in time of Peace, enter into any Agreement or Compact with another State, or with a foreign Power, or engage in War, unless actually invaded, or in such imminent Danger as will not admit of delay.

ARTICLE II

Section 1

[The President; the executive power.—1.] The executive Power shall be vested in a President of the United States of America. He shall hold his Office during the Term of four Years, and, together with the Vice President, chosen for the same Term, be elected, as follows

[Appointment and qualifications of presidential electors.—2.] Each State shall appoint, in such Manner as the Legislature thereof may direct, a Number of Electors, equal to the whole Number of Senators and Representatives to which the State may be entitled in the Congress: but no Senator or Representative, or Person holding an Office of Trust or Profit under the United States, shall be appointed an Elector.

[Original method of electing the President and Vice President.†] (The Electors shall meet in their respective States, and vote by Ballot for two Persons, of whom one at least shall not be an Inhabitant of the same State with themselves. And they shall make a List of all the Persons voted for, and of the Number of Votes for each; which List they shall sign and certify, and transmit sealed to the Seat of the Government of the United States, directed to the President of the Senate. The President of the Senate shall, in the Presence of the Senate and House of Representatives, open all the Certificates, and the Votes shall

---

* See the 16th Amendment.
† This clause has been superseded by the 12th Amendment.

then be counted. The Person having the greatest Number of Votes shall be the President, if such Number be a Majority of the whole Number of Electors appointed; and if there be more than one who have such Majority, and have an equal Number of Votes, then the House of Representatives shall immediately chuse by Ballot one of them for President; and if no person have a Majority, then from the five highest on the List the said House shall in like Manner chuse the President. But in chusing the President, the Votes shall be taken by States, the Representation from each State having one Vote; A quorum for this Purpose shall consist of a Member or Members from two thirds of the States, and a Majority of all the States shall be necessary to a Choice. In every Case, after the Choice of the President, the Person having the greatest Number of Votes of the Electors shall be the Vice President. But if there should remain two or more who have equal Votes, the Senate should chuse from them by Ballot the Vice President.)

[Congress may determine time of choosing electors and day for casting their votes.— 3.] The Congress may determine the Time of chusing the Electors, and the Day on which they shall give their Votes; which Day shall be the same throughout the United States.

[Qualifications for the office of President.*—4.] No Person except a natural born Citizen, or a Citizen of the United States, at the time of the Adoption of this Constitution, shall be eligible to the Office of President; neither shall any Person be eligible to that Office who shall not have attained to the Age of thirty five Years, and been fourteen Years a Resident within the United States.

[Filling vacancy in the office of President.†—5.] In Case of the Removal of the President from Office, or of his Death, Resignation, or Inability to discharge the Powers and Duties of the said Office, the same shall devolve on the Vice President, and the Congress may by Law provide for the Case of Removal, Death, Resignation or Inability, both of the President and Vice President, declaring what Officer shall then act as President, and such Officer shall act accordingly, until the Disability be removed, or a President shall be elected.

[Compensation of the President.—6.] The President shall, at stated Times, receive for his Services, a Compensation, which shall neither be encreased nor diminished during the Period for which he shall have been elected, and he shall not receive within that Period any other Emolument from the United States, or any of them.

[Oath to be taken by the President.—7.] Before he enter on the Execution of his Office, he shall take the following Oath or Affirmation:—"I do solemnly swear (or affirm) that I will faithfully execute the Office of President of the United States, and will to the best of my Ability, preserve, protect and defend the Constitution of the United States."

Section 2

[The President to be commander in chief of army and navy and head of executive departments; may grant reprieves and pardons.—1.] The President shall be Commander in Chief of the Army and Navy of the United States, and of the Militia of the several States, when called into the actual Service of the United States; he may require the Opinion, in writing, of the principal Officer in each of the executive Departments, upon any subject relating to the Duties of their respective Offices, and he shall have Power to grant Reprieves and Pardons for Offences against the United States, except in Cases of Impeachment.

[President may, with concurrence of Senate, make treaties, appoint ambassadors, etc.; appointment of inferior officers, authority of Congress over.—2.] He shall have Power, by and with the Advice and Consent of the Senate, to make Treaties, provided two thirds of the Senators present concur; and he shall nominate, and by and with the Advice and Consent of the Senate, shall appoint Ambassadors, other public Ministers and Consuls, Judges of the supreme Court, and all other Officers of the United States, whose Appointments are not herein otherwise provided for, and which shall be established by Law: but the Congress may by Law vest the Appointment of such inferior Officers, as they think proper, in the President alone, in the Courts of Law, or in the Heads of Departments.

[President may fill vacancies in office during recess of Senate.—3.] The President shall have Power to fill up all Vacancies that may happen during the Recess of the Senate, by granting Commissions which shall expire at the End of their next Session.

Section 3

[President to give advice to Congress; may convene or adjourn it on certain occasions; to receive ambassadors, etc.; have laws executed and commission all officers.] He shall from time to time give to the Congress Information of the State of the Union, and recommend to their Consideration such Measures as he shall judge necessary and expedient; he may, on extraordinary Occasions, convene both

---

* For qualifications of the Vice President, see 12th Amendment.

† Amended by the 20th Amendment, Sections 3 and 4.

Houses, or either of them, and in Case of Disagreement between them, with Respect to the Time of Adjournment, he may adjourn them to such Time as he shall think proper; he shall receive Ambassadors and other public Ministers; he shall take Care that the Laws be faithfully executed, and shall Commission all the Officers of the United States.

Section 4

[All civil officers removable by impeachment.] The President, Vice President and all civil Officers of the United States, shall be removed from Office on Impeachment for, and Conviction of, Treason, Bribery, or other high Crimes and Misdemeanors.

ARTICLE III
Section 1

[Judicial powers; how vested; term of office and compensation of judges.] The judicial Power of the United States, shall be vested in one supreme Court, and in such inferior Courts as the Congress may from time to time ordain and establish. The Judges, both of the supreme and inferior Courts, shall hold their Offices during good Behaviour, and shall, at stated Times, receive for their Services, a Compensation, which shall not be diminished during their Continuance in Office.

Section 2

[Jurisdiction of Federal courts.*—1.] The judicial Power shall extend to all Cases, in Law and Equity, arising under this Constitution, the Laws of the United States, and Treaties made, or which shall be made, under their Authority;—to all Cases affecting Ambassadors, other public Ministers and Consuls;—to all Cases of Admiralty and maritime Jurisdiction;—to Controversies to which the United States, shall be a Party;—to Controversies between two or more States;—between a State and Citizens of another State;—between Citizens of different States,—between Citizens of the same State claiming Lands under Grants of different States, and between a State, or the Citizens thereof, and foreign States, Citizens or Subjects.

[Original and appellate jurisdiction of Supreme Court.—2.] In all Cases affecting Ambassadors, other public Ministers and Consuls, and those in which a State shall be Party, the supreme Court shall have original Jurisdiction. In all the other Cases before mentioned, the supreme Court shall have appellate Jurisdiction, both as to Law and Fact, with such Exceptions, and under such Regulations as the Congress shall make.

[Trial of all crimes, except impeachment, to be by jury.—3.] The Trial of all Crimes, except in Cases of Impeachment, shall be by Jury; and such Trial shall be held in the State where the said Crimes shall have been committed; but when not committed within any State, the Trial shall be at such Place or Places as the Congress may by Law have directed.

Section 3

[Treason defined; conviction of.—1.] Treason against the United States, shall consist only in levying War against them, or, in adhering to their Enemies, giving them Aid and Comfort. No Person shall be convicted of Treason unless on the Testimony of two Witnesses to the same overt Act, or on Confession in open Court.

[Congress to declare punishment for treason; proviso.—2.] The Congress shall have power to declare the Punishment of Treason, but no Attainder of Treason shall work Corruption of Blood, or Forfeiture except during the Life of the Person attainted.

ARTICLE IV
Section 1

[Each State to give full faith and credit to the public acts and records of other States.] Full Faith and Credit shall be given in each State to the public Acts, Records, and judicial Proceedings of every other State. And the Congress may by general Laws prescribe the Manner in which such Acts, Records and Proceedings shall be proved, and the Effect thereof.

Section 2

[Privileges of citizens.—1.] The Citizens of each State shall be entitled to all Privileges and Immunities of Citizens in the several States.

[Extradition between the several States.—2.] A Person charged in any State with Treason, Felony, or other Crime, who shall flee from Justice, and be found in another State, shall on Demand of the executive Authority of the State from which he fled, be delivered up, to be removed to the State having Jurisdiction of the Crime.

[Persons held to labor or service in one State, fleeing to another, to be returned.†—3.] No Person held to Service or Labour in one State, under the Laws thereof, escaping into another, shall, in Consequence of any Law or Regulation therein, be discharged from such Service or Labour, but shall be delivered up on Claim of the Party to whom such Service or Labour may be due.

Section 3

[New States.—1.] New States may be admitted by the Congress into this Union;

---

* This section is abridged by the 11th Amendment.
† See the 13th Amendment.

but no new State shall be formed or erected within the Jurisdiction of any other State; nor any State be formed by the Junction of two or more States, or Parts of States, without the Consent of the Legislatures of the States concerned as well as of the Congress.

[Regulations concerning territory.—2.] The Congress shall have Power to dispose of and make all needful Rules and Regulations respecting the Territory or other Property belonging to the United States; and nothing in this Constitution shall be so construed as to Prejudice any Claims of the United States, or of any particular State.

Section 4

[Republican form of government and protection guaranteed the several States.] The United States shall guarantee to every State in this Union a Republican Form of Government, and shall protect each of them against Invasion; and on Application of the Legislature, or of the Executive (when the Legislature cannot be convened) against domestic Violence.

ARTICLE V

[Ways in which the Constitution can be amended.] The Congress, whenever two thirds of both Houses shall deem it necessary, shall propose Amendments to this Constitution, or, on the Application of the Legislatures of two thirds of the several States, shall call a Convention for proposing Amendments, which, in either Case, shall be valid to all Intents and Purposes, as Part of this Constitution, when ratified by the Legislatures of three fourths of the several States, or by Conventions in three fourths thereof, as the one or the other Mode of Ratification may be proposed by the Congress; Provided that no Amendment which may be made prior to the Year One thousand eight hundred and eight shall in any Manner affect the first and fourth Clauses in the Ninth Section of the first Article; and that no State, without its Consent, shall be deprived of its equal Suffrage in the Senate.

ARTICLE VI

[Debts contracted under the confederation secured.—1.] All Debts contracted and Engagements entered into, before the Adoption of this Constitution, shall be as valid against the United States under this Constitution, as under the Confederation.

[Constitution, laws and treaties of the United States to be supreme.—2.] This Constitution, and the Laws of the United States which shall be made in Pursuance thereof; and all Treaties made, or which shall be made, under the Authority of the United States, shall be the supreme Law of the Land; and the Judges in every State shall be bound thereby, any Thing in the Constitution or Laws of any State to the Contrary notwithstanding.

[Who shall take constitutional oath; no religious test as to official qualification.— 3.] The Senators and Representatives before mentioned, and the Members of the several State Legislatures, and all executive and judicial Officers, both of the United States and of the several States, shall be bound by Oath or Affirmation, to support this Constitution; but no religious Test shall ever be required as a Qualification to any Office or public Trust under the United States.

ARTICLE VII

[Constitution to be considered adopted when ratified by nine States.] The Ratification of the Conventions of nine States shall be sufficient for the Establishment of this Constitution between the States so ratifying the Same.

Done in Convention by the Unanimous Consent of the States present the Seventeenth Day of September in the Year of our Lord one thousand seven hundred and Eighty seven and of the Independence of the United States of America the Twelfth. In witness whereof We have hereunto subscribed our Names.

G⁰. WASHINGTON
Presidt and Deputy from Virginia

NEW HAMPSHIRE
John Langdon   Nicholas Gilman

MASSACHUSETTS
Nathaniel Gorham   Rufus King

CONNECTICUT
Wm Saml Johnson   Roger Sherman

NEW YORK
Alexander Hamilton

NEW JERSEY
Wil: Livingston   Wm Paterson
David Brearley   Jona: Dayton

PENNSYLVANIA
B Franklin   Thomas Mifflin
Robt Morris   Geo. Clymer
Thos FitzSimons   Jared Ingersoll
James Wilson   Gouv Morris

DELAWARE
Geo: Read   Gunning Bedford Jun
John Dickinson   Richard Bassett
Jaco: Broom

MARYLAND
James McHenry   Dan of St Thos Jenifer
Danl Carroll

VIRGINIA
John Blair —   James Madison Jr.

NORTH CAROLINA
Wm Blount   Richd Dobbs Spaight
Hu Williamson

SOUTH CAROLINA
J. Rutledge   Charles Cotesworth Pinckney
Charles Pinckney   Pierce Butler

GEORGIA
William Few   Abr Baldwin
Attest: William Jackson, Secretary.

AMENDMENTS TO THE CONSTITUTION OF THE UNITED STATES

(Amendments I to X inclusive, popularly known as the Bill of Rights, were proposed and sent to the states by the first session of the First Congress. They became effective Dec. 15, 1791.)

ARTICLE I

[Freedom of religion, speech, of the press, and right of petition.] Congress shall make no law respecting an establishment of religion, or prohibiting the free exercise thereof; or abridging the freedom of speech, or of the press; or the right of the people peaceably to assemble, and to petition the Government for a redress of grievances.

ARTICLE II

[Right of people to bear arms not to be infringed.] A well regulated Militia, being necessary to the security of a free State, the right of the people to keep and bear Arms, shall not be infringed.

ARTICLE III

[Quartering of troops.] No Soldier shall, in time of peace be quartered in any house, without the consent of the Owner, nor in time of war, but in a manner to be prescribed by law.

ARTICLE IV

[Persons and houses to be secure from unreasonable searches and seizures.] The right of the people to be secure in their persons, houses, papers, and effects, against unreasonable searches and seizures, shall not be violated, and no Warrants shall issue, but upon probable cause, supported by Oath or affirmation, and particularly describing the place to be searched, and the persons or things to be seized.

ARTICLE V

[Trials for crimes; just compensation for private property taken for public use.] No person shall be held to answer for a capital, or otherwise infamous crime, unless on a presentment or indictment of a Grand Jury, except in cases arising in the land or naval forces, or in the Militia, when in actual service in time of War or public danger; nor shall any person be subject for the same offence to be twice put in jeopardy of life or limb; nor shall be compelled in any criminal case to be a witness against himself, nor be deprived of life, liberty, or property, without due process of law: nor shall private property be taken for public use, without just compensation.

ARTICLE VI

[Civil rights in trials for crimes enumerated.] In all criminal prosecutions, the accused shall enjoy the right to a speedy and public trial, by an impartial jury of the State and district wherein the crime shall have been committed, which district shall have been previously ascertained by law, and to be informed of the nature and cause of the accusation; to be confronted with the witnesses against him; to have compulsory process for obtaining witnesses in his favor, and to have the Assistance of Counsel for his defence.

ARTICLE VII

[Civil rights in civil suits.] In Suits at common law, where the value in controversy shall exceed twenty dollars, the right of trial by jury shall be preserved, and no fact tried by a jury, shall be otherwise reexamined in any Court of the United States, than according to the rules of the common law.

ARTICLE VIII

[Excessive bail, fines and punishments prohibited.] Excessive bail shall not be required, nor excessive fines imposed, nor cruel and unusual punishments inflicted.

ARTICLE IX

[Reserved rights of people.] The enumeration in the Constitution, of certain rights, shall not be construed to deny or disparage others retained by the people.

ARTICLE X

[Powers not delegated, reserved to states and people respectively.] The powers not delegated to the United States by the Constitution, nor prohibited by it to the States, are reserved to the States respectively, or to the people.

ARTICLE XI

(The proposed amendment was sent to the states Mar. 5, 1794, by the Third Congress. It became effective Jan. 8, 1798.)

[Judicial power of United States not to extend to suits against a State.] The Judicial power of the United States shall not be construed to extend to any suit in law or equity, commenced or prosecuted against one of the United States by Citizens of another State, or by Citizens or Subjects of any Foreign State.

ARTICLE XII

(The proposed amendment was sent to the states Dec. 12, 1803, by the Eighth Congress. It became effective Sept. 25, 1804.)

[Present mode of electing President and Vice-President by electors.*] The Electors shall meet in their respective states, and vote by ballot for President and Vice-President, one of whom, at least, shall not be an inhabitant of the same state with themselves; they shall name in their ballots the person voted for as President, and in distinct ballots the person voted for as Vice-

---

* Amended by the 20th Amendment, Sections 3 and 4.

President, and they shall make distinct lists of all persons voted for as President, and of all persons voted for as Vice-President, and of the number of votes for each, which lists they shall sign and certify, and transmit sealed to the seat of the government of the United States, directed to the President of the Senate;—The President of the Senate shall, in the presence of the Senate and House of Representatives, open all the certificates and the votes shall then be counted;—The person having the greatest number of votes for President, shall be the President, if such number be a majority of the whole number of Electors appointed; and if no person have such majority, then from the persons having the highest numbers not exceeding three on the list of those voted for as President, the House of Representatives shall choose immediately, by ballot, the President. But in choosing the President, the votes shall be taken by states, the representation from each State having one vote; a quorum for this purpose shall consist of a member or members from two-thirds of the states, and a majority of all the states shall be necessary to a choice. And if the House of Representatives shall not choose a President whenever the right of choice shall devolve upon them, before the fourth day of March next following, then the Vice-President shall act as President, as in the case of the death or other constitutional disability of the President.—The person having the greatest number of votes as Vice-President, shall be the Vice-President, if such number be a majority of the whole number of Electors appointed, and if no person have a majority, then from the two highest numbers on the list, the Senate shall choose the Vice-President; a quorum for the purpose shall consist of two-thirds of the whole number of Senators, and a majority of the whole number shall be necessary to a choice. But no person constitutionally ineligible to the office of President shall be eligible to that of Vice-President of the United States.

ARTICLE XIII

(The proposed amendment was sent to the states Feb. 1, 1865, by the Thirty-eighth Congress. It became effective Dec. 18, 1865.)

Section 1

[Slavery prohibited.] Neither slavery nor involuntary servitude, except as a punishment for crime whereof the party shall have been duly convicted, shall exist within the United States, or any place subject to their jurisdiction.

Section 2

[Congress given power to enforce this article.] Congress shall have power to enforce this article by appropriate legislation.

ARTICLE XIV

(The proposed amendment was sent to the states June 16, 1866, by the Thirty-ninth Congress. It became effective July 28, 1868.)

Section 1

[Citizenship defined; privileges of citizens.] All persons born or naturalized in the United States, and subject to the jurisdiction thereof, are citizens of the United States and of the State wherein they reside. No State shall make or enforce any law which shall abridge the privileges or immunities of citizens of the United States; nor shall any State deprive any person of life, liberty, or property, without due process of law; nor deny to any person within its jurisdiction the equal protection of the laws.

Section 2

[Apportionment of Representatives.] Representatives shall be apportioned among the several States according to their respective numbers, counting the whole number of persons in each State, excluding Indians not taxed. But when the right to vote at any election for the choice of electors for President and Vice-President of the United States, Representatives in Congress, the Executive and Judicial officers of a State, or the members of the Legislature thereof, is denied to any of the male inhabitants of such State, being twenty-one years of age, and citizens of the United States, or in any way abridged, except for participation in rebellion, or other crime, the basis of representation therein shall be reduced in the proportion which the number of such male citizens shall bear to the whole number of male citizens twenty-one years of age in such State.

Section 3

[Disqualification for office; removal of disability.] No person shall be a Senator or Representative in Congress, or elector of President and Vice President, or hold any office, civil or military, under the United States, or under any State, who, having previously taken an oath, as a member of Congress, or as an officer of the United States, or as a member of any State legislature, or as an executive or judicial officer of any State, to support the Constitution of the United States, shall have engaged in insurrection or rebellion against the same, or given aid or comfort to the enemies thereof. But Congress may by a vote of two-thirds of each House, remove such disability.

Section 4

[Public debt not to be questioned; payment of debts and claims incurred in aid of rebellion forbidden.] The validity of the public debt of the United States, authorized by law, including debts incurred for payment of pensions and bounties for services in suppressing insurrection or rebellion, shall not be questioned. But neither the United States nor any State shall assume or pay any debt or obligation incurred in aid of insurrection or rebellion against the United States, or any claim for the loss or emancipation of any slave; but all such debts, obligations and claims shall be held illegal and void.

Section 5

[Congress given power to enforce this article.] The Congress shall have power to enforce, by appropriate legislation, the provisions of this article.

ARTICLE XV

(The proposed amendment was sent to the states Feb. 27, 1869, by the Fortieth Congress. It became effective Mar. 30, 1870.)

Section 1

[Right of certain citizens to vote established.] The right of citizens of the United States to vote shall not be denied or abridged by the United States or by any State on account of race, color, or previous condition of servitude.

Section 2

[Congress given power to enforce this article.] The Congress shall have power to enforce this article by appropriate legislation.

ARTICLE XVI

(The proposed amendment was sent to the states July 12, 1909, by the Sixty-first Congress. It became effective Feb. 25, 1913.)

[Taxes on income; Congress given power to lay and collect.] The Congress shall have power to lay and collect taxes on incomes, from whatever source derived, without apportionment among the several States, and without regard to any census or enumeration.

ARTICLE XVII

(The proposed amendment was sent to the states May 16, 1912, by the Sixty-second Congress. It became effective May 31, 1913.)

[Election of United States Senators; filling of vacancies; qualifications of electors.]

The Senate of the United States shall be composed of two Senators from each State, elected by the people thereof, for six years; and each Senator shall have one vote. The electors in each State shall have the qualifications requisite for electors of the most numerous branch of the State legislatures.

When vacancies happen in the representation of any State in the Senate, the executive authority of such State shall issue writs of election to fill such vacancies: *Provided,* That the legislature of any State may empower the executive thereof to make temporary appointment

until the people fill the vacancies by election as the legislature may direct.

This amendment shall not be so construed as to affect the election or term of any Senator chosen before it becomes valid as part of the Constitution.

ARTICLE XVIII *

(The proposed amendment was sent to the states Dec. 18, 1917, by the Sixty-fifth Congress. It was approved by three-quarters of the states by Jan. 16, 1919, and became effective Jan. 16, 1920.)

Section 1

[Manufacture, sale or transportation of intoxicating liquors, for beverage purposes, prohibited.] After one year from the ratification of this article the manufacture, sale, or transportation of intoxicating liquors within, the importation thereof into, or the exportation thereof from the United States and all territory subject to the jurisdiction thereof for beverage purposes is hereby prohibited.

Section 2

[Congress and the several States given concurrent power to pass appropriate legislation to enforce this article.] The Congress and the several States shall have concurrent power to enforce this article by appropriate legislation.

Section 3

[Provisions of article to become operative, when adopted by three-fourths of the States.] This article shall be inoperative unless it shall have been ratified as an amendment to the Constitution by the legislatures of the several States, as provided in the Constitution, within seven years from the date of the submission hereof to the States by Congress.

ARTICLE XIX

(The proposed amendment was sent to the states June 4, 1919, by the Sixty-sixth Congress. It became effective Aug. 26, 1920.)

[The right of citizens to vote shall not be denied because of sex.] The right of citizens of the United States to vote shall not be denied or abridged by the United States or by any State on account of sex.

[Congress given power to enforce this article.] Congress shall have power to enforce this article by appropriate legislation.

ARTICLE XX

(The proposed amendment, sometimes called the "Lame Duck Amendment," was sent to the states Mar. 3, 1932, by the Seventy-second Congress. It became effective Feb. 6, 1933; but, in accordance with Section 5, Sections 1 and 2 did not go into effect until Oct. 15, 1933.)

Section 1

[Terms of President, Vice-President, Senators and Representatives.] The terms of the President and Vice-President shall end at noon on the twentieth day of January, and the terms of Senators and Representa-

---

* Repealed by the 21st Amendment.

tives at noon on the third day of January, of the years in which such terms would have ended if this article had not been ratified; and the terms of their successors shall then begin.

Section 2

[Time of assembling Congress.] The Congress shall assemble at least once in every year, and such meeting shall begin at noon on the third day of January, unless they shall by law appoint a different day.

Section 3

[Filling vacancy in office of President.] If, at the time fixed for the beginning of the term of the President, the President-elect shall have died, the Vice-President-elect shall become President. If a President shall not have been chosen before the time fixed for the beginning of his term, or if the President-elect shall have failed to qualify, then the Vice-President-elect shall act as President until a President shall have qualified; and the Congress may by law provide for the case wherein neither a President-elect nor a Vice-President-elect shall have qualified, declaring who shall then act as President, or the manner in which one who is to act shall be selected, and such person shall act accordingly until a President or Vice-President shall have qualified.

Section 4

[Power of Congress in Presidential succession.] The Congress may by law provide for the case of the death of any of the persons from whom the House of Representatives may choose a President whenever the right of choice shall have devolved upon them, and for the case of the death of any of the persons from whom the Senate may choose a Vice-President whenever the right of choice shall have devolved upon them.

Section 5

[Time of taking effect.] Sections 1 and 2 shall take effect on the 15th day of October following the ratification of this article.

Section 6

[Ratification.] This article shall be inoperative unless it shall have been ratified as an amendment to the Constitution by the legislatures of three-fourths of the several States within seven years from the date of its submission.

ARTICLE XXI

(The proposed amendment was sent to the states Feb. 20, 1933, by the Seventy-second Congress. It became effective Dec. 5, 1933.)

Section 1

[Repeal of Prohibition Amendment.] The eighteenth article of amendment to the Constitution of the United States is hereby repealed.

Section 2

[Transportation of intoxicating liquors.] The transportation or importation into any State, Territory, or possession of the United States for delivery or use therein of intoxicating liquors, in violation of the laws thereof, is hereby prohibited.

Section 3

[Ratification.] This article shall be inoperative unless it shall have been ratified as an amendment to the Constitution by convention in the several States, as provided in the Constitution, within seven years from the date of the submission thereof to the States by the Congress.

ARTICLE XXII

(The proposed amendment was sent to the states Mar. 21, 1947, by the Eightieth Congress. It became effective Feb. 26, 1951.)

Section 1

[Limit to number of terms a President may serve.] No person shall be elected to the office of the President more than twice, and no person who has held the office of President, or acted as President, for more than two years of a term to which some other person was elected President shall be elected to the office of the President more than once. But this Article shall not apply to any person holding the office of President when this Article was proposed by the Congress, and shall not prevent any person who may be holding the office of President, or acting as President, during the term within which this Article becomes operative from holding the office of President or acting as President during the remainder of such term.

Section 2

[Ratification.] This article shall be inoperative unless it shall have been ratified as an amendment to the Constitution by the legislatures of three-fourths of the several States within seven years from the date of its submission to the States by the Congress.

ARTICLE XXIII

(The proposed amendment was sent to the states June 16, 1960, by the Eighty-sixth Congress. It became effective Mar. 29, 1961.)

Section 1

[Electors for the District of Columbia.] The District constituting the seat of Government of the United States shall appoint in such manner as the Congress may direct:

A number of electors of President and Vice President equal to the whole number of Senators and Representatives in Congress to which the District would be entitled if it were a State, but in no event more than the least populous State; they shall be in addition to those appointed by the States, but they shall be considered, for the purposes of the election of President and Vice President, to be electors appointed by a State; and they shall meet in the District and perform such duties as provided by the twelfth article of amendment.

Section 2

[Congress given power to enforce this article.] The Congress shall have the power to enforce this article by appropriate legislation.

ARTICLE XXIV

(The proposed amendment was sent to the states Aug. 27, 1962, by the Eighty-seventh Congress. It became effective Jan. 23, 1964.)

Section 1

[Payment of poll tax or other taxes not to be prerequisite for voting in federal elections.] The right of citizens of the United States to vote in any primary or other election for President or Vice-President, for electors for President or Vice-President, or for Senator or Representative in Congress, shall not be denied or abridged by the United States or any State by reasons of failure to pay any poll tax or other tax.

Section 2

[Congress given power to enforce this article.] The Congress shall have the power to enforce this article by appropriate legislation.

ARTICLE XXV

(The proposed amendment was sent to the states July 6, 1965, by the Eighty-ninth Congress. It became effective Feb. 10, 1967.)

Section 1

[Succession of Vice President to Presidency.] In case of the removal of the President from office or of his death or resignation, the Vice President shall become President.

Section 2

[Vacancy in office of Vice President.] Whenever there is a vacancy in the office of the Vice President, the President shall nominate a Vice President who shall take office upon confirmation by a majority vote of both Houses of Congress.

Section 3

[Vice President as Acting President.] Whenever the President transmits to the President pro tempore of the Senate and the Speaker of the House of Representatives his written declaration that he is unable to discharge the powers and duties of his office, and until he transmits to them a written declaration to the contrary, such powers and duties shall be discharged by the Vice President as Acting President.

Section 4

[Vice President as Acting President.] Whenever the Vice President and a majority of either the principal officers of the executive departments or of such other body as Congress may by law provide, transmit to the President pro tempore of the Senate and the Speaker of the House of Representatives their written declaration that the President is unable to discharge the powers and duties of his office, the Vice President shall immediately assume the powers and duties of the office as Acting President.

Thereafter, when the President transmits to the President pro tempore of the Senate and the Speaker of the House of Representatives his written declaration that no inability exists, he shall resume the powers and duties of his office unless the Vice President and a majority of either the principal officers of the executive department or of such other body as Congress may by law provide, transmit within four days to the President pro tempore of the Senate and the Speaker of the House of Representatives their written declaration that the President is unable to discharge the powers and duties of his office. Thereupon Congress shall decide the issue, assembling within forty-eight hours for that purpose if not in session. If the Congress, within twenty-one days after receipt of the latter written declaration, or, if Congress is not in session, within twenty-one days after Congress is required to assemble, determines by two-thirds vote of both Houses that the President is unable to discharge the powers and duties of his office, the Vice President shall continue to discharge the same as Acting President; otherwise, the President shall resume the powers and duties of his office.

ARTICLE XXVI

(The proposed amendment was sent to the states Mar. 23, 1971, by the Ninety-second Congress. It became effective July 1, 1971.)

Section 1

[Voting for 18-year-olds.] The right of citizens of the United States, who are 18 years of age or older, to vote shall not be denied or abridged by the United States or by any state on account of age.

Section 2

[Congress given power to enforce this article.] The Congress shall have power to enforce this article by appropriate legislation.

The Early Congresses

At the urging of Massachusetts and Virginia, the First Continental Congress met in Philadelphia on Sept. 5, 1774, and was attended by representatives of all the colonies except Georgia. Patrick Henry of Virginia declared: "The distinctions between Pennsylvanians, New Yorkers and New Englanders are no more. I am not a Virginian but an American." This Congress, which adjourned Oct. 26, 1774, passed intercolonial resolutions calling for extensive boycott by the colonies against British trade.

The following year, most of the delegates from the colonies were chosen by popular election to attend the Second Continental Congress, which assembled in Philadelphia on May 10. As war had already begun between the colonies and England, the chief problems before the Congress were the procuring of military supplies, the establishment of an army and proper defenses, the issuing of continental bills of credit, etc. On June 15, 1775, George Washington was elected to command the Continental army. Congress adjourned Dec. 12, 1776.

Other Continental Congresses were held in Baltimore (1776–77), Philadelphia (1777), Lancaster, Pa. (1777), York, Pa. (1777–78), and Philadelphia (1778–81).

In 1781, the Articles of Confederation, although establishing a league of the thirteen states rather than a strong central government, provided for the continuance of Congress. Known thereafter as the Congress of the Confederation, it held sessions in Philadelphia (1781–83), Princeton, N. J. (1783), Annapolis, Md. (1783–84), and Trenton, N. J. (1784). Five sessions were held in New York City between the years 1785 and 1789.

The Congress of the United States, established by the ratification of the Constitution, held its first meeting on Mar. 4, 1789, in New York City. Several sessions of Congress were held in Philadelphia, and the first meeting in Washington, D. C., was on Nov. 17, 1800.

Presidents of the Continental Congresses

Name	Elected	Born	Died
Peyton Randolph, Va.	Sept. 5, 1774	c.1721	1775
Henry Middleton, S. C.	Oct. 22, 1774	1717	1784
Peyton Randolph, Va.	May 10, 1775	c.1721	1775
John Hancock, Mass.	May 24, 1775	1737	1793
Henry Laurens, S. C.	Nov. 1, 1777	1724	1792
John Jay, N. Y.	Dec. 10, 1778	1745	1829
Samuel Huntington, Conn.	Sept. 28, 1779	1731	1796
Thomas McKean, Del.	July 10, 1781	1734	1817
John Hanson, Md.	Nov. 5, 1781	1715	1783
Elias Boudinot, N. J.	Nov. 4, 1782	1740	1821
Thomas Mifflin, Pa.	Nov. 3, 1783	1744	1800
Richard Henry Lee, Va.	Nov. 30, 1784	1732	1794
John Hancock, Mass.*	Nov. 23, 1785	1737	1793
Nathaniel Gorham, Mass.	June 6, 1786	1738	1796
Arthur St. Clair, Pa.	Feb. 2, 1787	1734	1818
Cyrus Griffin, Va.	Jan. 22, 1788	1748	1810

* Resigned May 29, 1786, never having served, because of continued illness.

The Monroe Doctrine

The Monroe Doctrine was announced in President James Monroe's message to Congress, during his second term on Dec. 2, 1823, in part as follows:

"In the discussions to which this interest has given rise, and in the arrangements by which they may terminate, the occasion has been deemed proper for asserting as a principle in which rights and interests of the United States are involved, that the American continents, by the free and independent condition which they have assumed and maintain, are henceforth not to be considered as subjects for future colonization by any European power. . . . We owe it, therefore, to candor and to the amicable relations existing between the United States and those powers to declare that we should consider any attempt on their part to extend their system to any portion of this hemisphere as dangerous to our peace and safety. With the existing colonies or dependencies of any European power we have not interfered and shall not interfere. But with the governments who have declared their independence and maintain it, and whose independence we have, on great consideration and on just principles, acknowledged, we could not view any interposition for the purpose of oppressing them or controlling in any other manner their destiny by any European power in any other light than as the manifestation of an unfriendly disposition toward the United States."

The Star-Spangled Banner
Francis Scott Key, 1814

O say, can you see, by the dawn's early light,
What so proudly we hail'd at the twilight's last gleaming?
Whose broad stripes and bright stars, thro' the perilous fight,
O'er the ramparts we watch'd, were so gallantly streaming?
And the rockets' red glare, the bombs bursting in air,
Gave proof thro' the night that our flag was still there.
O say, does that star-spangled banner yet wave
O'er the land of the free and the home of the brave?

On the shore dimly seen thro' the mists of the deep,
Where the foe's haughty host in dread silence reposes,
What is that which the breeze, o'er the towering steep,
As it fitfully blows, half conceals, half discloses?
Now it catches the gleam of the morning's first beam,
In full glory reflected, now shines on the stream:
'T is the star-spangled banner: O, long may it wave
O'er the land of the free and the home of the brave!

And where is that band who so vauntingly swore
That the havoc of war and the battle's confusion,
A home and a country should leave us no more?
Their blood has wash'd out their foul footsteps' pollution.
No refuge could save the hireling and slave
From the terror of flight or the gloom of the grave:
And the star-spangled banner in triumph doth wave
O'er the land of the free and the home of the brave.

O thus be it ever when free-men shall stand
Between their lov'd home and the war's desolation;
Blest with vict'ry and peace, may the heav'n-rescued land
Praise the Pow'r that hath made and preserv'd us a nation!
Then conquer we must, when our cause it is just,
And this be our motto: "In God is our trust!"
And the star-spangled banner in triumph shall wave
O'er the land of the free and the home of the brave!

On Sept. 13, 1814, Francis Scott Key visited the British fleet in Chesapeake Bay to secure the release of Dr. William Beanes, who had been captured after the burning of Washington, D. C. The release was secured, but Key was detained on ship overnight during the shelling of Fort McHenry, one of the forts defending Baltimore. In the morning, he was so delighted to see the American flag still flying over the fort that he began a poem to commemorate the occasion. Entitled "The Star-Spangled Banner," the poem soon attained wide popularity as sung to the tune "Anacreon in Heaven." The origin of this tune is obscure, but it may have been written by John Stafford Smith, a British composer born in 1750. "The Star-Spangled Banner" was officially made the National Anthem by Congress in 1931, although it had been already adopted as such by the Army and the Navy.

The White House
Source: National Park Service.

The White House, the official residence of the President, is at 1600 Pennsylvania Avenue in Washington, D. C. The site covering about 18 acres was selected by President Washington and Pierre Charles L'Enfant, and the architect was James Hoban. The design of the residence is said to have been suggested by the Duke of Leinster's house in Ireland. The cornerstone was laid Oct. 13, 1792, and the first residents were President and Mrs. John Adams in November, 1800. The building was fired by the British in 1814. The sandstone exterior was painted white during the course of the construction.

From December, 1948, to March, 1952, the interior of the White House was re-built, and the outer walls were strengthened.

The rooms for public functions are on the first floor; on the second and third are the President's apartments. The most celebrated public room is the East Room, where formal receptions take place. Other public rooms are the Red Room, the Green Room, and the Blue Room. The State Dining Room is used for formal dinners. There are 132 rooms.

The Emancipation Proclamation
January 1, 1863

By the President of the United States of America:

A Proclamation.

Whereas on the 22d day of September, A.D. 1862, a proclamation was issued by the President of the United States, containing, among other things, the following, to wit:

"That on the 1st day of January, A.D. 1863, all persons held as slaves within any State or designated part of a State the people whereof shall then be in rebellion against the United States shall be then, thenceforward, and forever free; and the executive government of the United States, including the military and naval authority thereof, will recognize and maintain the freedom of such persons and will do no act or acts to repress such persons, or any of them, in any efforts they may make for their actual freedom.

"That the executive will on the 1st day of January aforesaid, by proclamation, designate the States and parts of States, if any, in which the people thereof, respectively, shall then be in rebellion against the United States; and the fact that any State or the people thereof shall on that day be in good faith represented in the Congress of the United States by members chosen thereto at elections wherein a majority of the qualified voters of such States shall have participated shall, in the absence of strong countervailing testimony, be deemed conclusive evidence that such State and the people thereof are not then in rebellion against the United States."

Now, therefore, I, Abraham Lincoln, President of the United States, by virtue of the power in me vested as Commander-in-Chief of the Army and Navy of the United States in time of actual armed rebellion against the authority and government of the United States, and as a fit and necessary war measure for suppressing said rebellion, do, on this 1st day of January, A.D. 1863, and in accordance with my purpose so to do, publicly proclaimed for the full period of one hundred days from the first day above mentioned, order and designate as the States and parts of States wherein the people thereof, respectively, are this day in rebellion against the United States the following, to wit:

Arkansas, Texas, Louisiana (except the parishes of St. Bernard, Plaquemines, Jefferson, St. John, St. Charles, St. James, Ascension, Assumption, Terrebonne, Lafourche, St. Mary, St. Martin, and Orleans, including the city of New Orleans), Mississippi, Alabama, Florida, Georgia, South Carolina, North Carolina, and Virginia (except the forty-eight counties designated as West Virginia, and also the counties of Berkeley, Accomac, Northhampton, Elizabeth City, York, Princess Anne, and Norfolk, including the cities of Norfolk and Portsmouth), and which excepted parts are for the present left precisely as if this proclamation were not issued.

And by virtue of the power and for the purpose aforesaid, I do order and declare that all persons held as slaves within said designated States and parts of States are, and henceforward shall be, free; and that the Executive Government of the United States, including the military and naval authorities thereof, will recognize and maintain the freedom of said persons.

And I hereby enjoin upon the people so declared to be free to abstain from all violence, unless in necessary self-defense; and I recommend to them that, in all cases when allowed, they labor faithfully for reasonable wages.

And I further declare and make known that such persons of suitable condition will be received into the armed service of the United States to garrison forts, positions, stations, and other places, and to man vessels of all sorts in said service.

And upon this act, sincerely believed to be an act of justice, warranted by the Constitution upon military necessity, I invoke the considerate judgment of mankind and the gracious favor of Almighty God.

The Confederate States of America

State	Seceded from Union	Readmitted to Union*	State	Seceded from Union	Readmitted to Union*
1. South Carolina....	Dec. 20, 1860	July 9, 1868	7. Texas............	Mar. 2, 1861	Mar. 30, 1870
2. Mississippi.......	Jan. 9, 1861	Feb. 23, 1870	8. Virginia..........	Apr. 17, 1861	Jan. 26, 1870
3. Florida...........	Jan. 10, 1861	June 25, 1868	9. Arkansas.........	May 6, 1861	June 22, 1868
4. Alabama.........	Jan. 11, 1861	July 13, 1868	10. North Carolina....	May 20, 1861	July 4, 1868
5. Georgia..........	Jan. 19, 1861	July 15, 1870†	11. Tennessee........	June 8, 1861	July 24, 1866
6. Louisiana........	Jan. 26, 1861	July 9, 1868			

* Date of readmission to representation in U. S. House of Representatives.   † Second readmission date. First date was July 21, 1868, but the representatives were unseated Mar. 5, 1869.   NOTE: 4 other slave states—Delaware, Kentucky, Maryland, and Missouri—remained in the Union.

The Mayflower Compact

On Sept. 6, 1620, the *Mayflower,* a sailing vessel of about 180 tons, started her memorable voyage from Plymouth, England, with about 100* pilgrims aboard, bound for Virginia to establish a private permanent colony in North America. Arriving at what is now Provincetown, Mass., on Nov. 11 (Nov. 21, new style calendar), 41 of the passengers signed the famous "Mayflower Compact" as the boat lay at anchor in that Cape Cod harbor. A small detail of the pilgrims, led by William Bradford, assigned to select a place for permanent settlement landed at what is now Plymouth, Mass., on Dec. 21, N.S.

The text of the compact follows:

I N THE NAME OF GOD, Amen. We, whose names are underwritten, the Loyal Subjects of our dread Sovereign Lord, King *James,* by the Grace of God, of *Great Britain, France* and *Ireland,* King, *Defender of the Faith,* &,

Having undertaken for the Glory of God, and Advancement of the Christian Faith, and the Honour of our King and Country, a voyage to plant the first colony in the northern Parts of Virginia; do by these Presents, solemnly and mutually in the Presence of God and one of another, covenant and combine ourselves together into a civil Body Politick, for our better Ordering and Preservation, and Furtherance of the Ends aforesaid; And by Virtue hereof to enact, constitute, and frame, such just and equal Laws, Ordinances, Acts, Constitutions and Offices, from time to time, as shall be thought most meet and convenient for the General good of the Colony; unto which we promise all due Submission and Obedience.

In WITNESS whereof we have hereunto subscribed our names at *Cape Cod* the eleventh of *November,* in the Reign of our Sovereign Lord, King *James* of *England, France* and *Ireland,* the eighteenth, and of *Scotland* the fifty-fourth. *Anno Domini,* 1620

John Carver	William Mullins	Thomas Tinker	Edward Tilly
Digery Priest	Thomas English	Samuel Fuller	John Craxton
William Brewster	John Howland	Richard Clark	Thomas Rogers
Edmund Margesson	Stephen Hopkins	John Allerton	John Goodman
John Alden	Edward Winslow	Richard Warren	Edward Fuller
George Soule	Gilbert Winslow	Edward Liester	Richard Gardiner
James Chilton	Miles Standish	William Bradford	William White
Francis Cooke	Richard Bitteridge	Thomas Williams	Edward Doten
Moses Fletcher	Francis Eaton	Isaac Allerton	
John Ridgate	John Tilly	Peter Brown	
Christopher Martin	John Billington	John Turner	

* Historians differ as to whether 100, 101, or 102 passengers were aboard.

Lincoln's Gettysburg Address

The Battle of Gettysburg, one of the most noted battles of the Civil War, was fought on July 1, 2, and 3, 1863. On Nov. 19, 1863, the field was dedicated as a national cemetery by President Lincoln in a two-minute speech that was to become immortal. At the time of its delivery the speech was relegated to the inside pages of the papers, while a two-hour address by Edward Everett, the leading orator of the time, caught the headlines.

The following is the text of the address revised by President Lincoln from his own notes:

F OURSCORE and seven years ago our fathers brought forth on this continent a new nation conceived in liberty and dedicated to the proposition that all men are created equal. Now we are engaged in a great civil war testing whether that nation, or any nation so conceived and so dedicated, can long endure. We are met on a great battlefield of that war. We have come to dedicate a portion of that field as a final resting-place for those who here gave their lives that that nation might live. It is altogether fitting and proper that we should do this. But, in a larger sense, we cannot dedicate, we cannot consecrate, we cannot hallow this ground. The brave men, living and dead, who struggled here have consecrated it far above our poor power to add or detract. The world will little note nor long remember what we say here, but it can never forget what they did here. It is for us the living rather to be dedicated here to the unfinished work which they who fought here have thus far so nobly advanced. It is rather for us to be here dedicated to the great task remaining before us—that from these honored dead we take increased devotion to that cause for which they gave the last full measure of devotion—that we here highly resolve that these dead shall not have died in vain, that this nation under God shall have a new birth of freedom, and that government of the people, by the people, for the people shall not perish from the earth.

History of the Flag

Source: Encyclopaedia Britannica.

THE FIRST OFFICIAL AMERICAN flag, the Continental or Grand Union flag, was displayed on Prospect Hill, Jan. 1, 1776, in the American lines besieging Boston. It had 13 alternate red and white stripes, with the British Union Jack in the upper left corner.

On June 14, 1777, the Continental Congress adopted the design for a new flag, which actually was the Continental flag with the red cross of St. George and the white cross of St. Andrew replaced on the blue field by 13 stars, one for each state. No rule was made as to the arrangement of the stars, and while they were usually shown in a circle, there were various other designs. It is uncertain when the new flag was first flown, but its first official announcement is believed to have been on Sept. 3, 1777.

The first public assertion that Betsy Ross made the first Stars and Stripes appeared in a paper read before the Historical Society of Pennsylvania on March 14, 1870, by William J. Canby, a grandson. However, Mr. Canby on later investigation found no official documents of any action by Congress on the flag before June 14, 1777. Betsy Ross's own story, according to her daughter, was that Washington, Robert Morris, and George Ross, as representatives of Congress, visited her in Philadelphia in June, 1776, showing her a rough draft of the flag and asking her if she could make one. However, the only actual record of the manufacture of flags by Betsy Ross is a voucher in Harrisburg, Pa., for 14 pounds and some shillings for flags for the Pennsylvania navy.

On Jan. 13, 1794, Congress voted to add two stars and two stripes to the flag in recognition of the admission of Vermont and Kentucky to the Union. By 1818, there were 20 states in the Union, and as it was obvious that the flag would soon become unwieldly, Congress voted April 18 to return to the original 13 stripes and to indicate the admission of a new state simply by the addition of a star the following July 4. The 49th star, for Alaska, was added July 4, 1959; and the 50th star, for Hawaii, was added July 4, 1960.

The first Confederate flag, adopted in 1861 by the Confederate convention in Montgomery, Ala., was called the Stars and Bars; but because of its similarity in colors to the American flag, there was much confusion in the Battle of Bull Run. To remedy this situation, Gen. G. T. Beauregard suggested a battle flag, which was used by the Southern armies throughout the war. The flag consisted of a red field on which was placed a blue cross of St. Andrew separated from the field by a white fillet and adorned with 13* white stars for the Confederate states. In May, 1863, at Richmond, an official flag was adopted by the Confederate Congress. This flag was white and twice as long as wide; the union, two-thirds the width of the flag, contained the battle flag designed for Gen. Beauregard. A broad transverse stripe of red was added Feb. 4, 1865, so that the flag might not be mistaken for a signal of truce.

* 11 states formally seceded, and unofficial groups in Kentucky and Missouri adopted ordinances of secession. On this basis, these two states were admitted to the Confederacy, although the official state governments remained in the Union.

Flag Etiquette (Public Law 829—77th Congress)

JOINT RESOLUTION
Public Law 94-344, approved July 7, 1976: To amend the joint resolution entitled "Joint resolution to codify and emphasize existing rules and customs pertaining to the display and use of the flag of the United States of America."

Resolved by the Senate and House of Representatives of the United States of America in Congress Assembled, That Public Law Numbered 623, approved June 22, 1942, entitled "Joint resolution to codify and emphasize existing rules and customs pertaining to the display and use of the flag of the United States of America," be, and the same is hereby amended to read as follows:

That the following codification of existing rules and customs pertaining to the display and use of the flag of the United States of America be, and it is hereby, established for the use of such civilians or civilian groups or organizations as may not be required to conform with regulations promulgated by one or more executive departments of the Government of the United States. The flag of the United States for the purpose of this chapter shall be defined according to title 4, United States Code, chapter 1, section 1 and section 2 and Executive Order 10834 issued pursuant thereto.

NOTE: On July 5, 1968, a law was enacted making it a federal crime to desecrate the U.S. flag by knowingly casting contempt on it, by publicly mutilating or burning it, etc. The offense is punishable by a $1,000 fine and/or a year in prison.

Sec. 2. (a) It is the universal custom to display the flag only from sunrise to sunset on buildings and on stationary flagstaffs in the open. However, when a patriotic effect is desired, the flag may be displayed twenty-four hours a day if properly illuminated during the hours of darkness.

(b) The flag should be hoisted briskly and lowered ceremoniously.

(c) The flag should not be displayed on days when the weather is inclement, except when an all-weather flag is displayed.

(d) The flag should be displayed on all days, especially on New Year's Day, January 1; Inauguration Day, January 20; Lincoln's Birthday, February 12; Washington's Birthday, third Monday in February; Easter Sunday (variable); Mother's Day, second Sunday in May; Armed Forces Day, third Saturday in May; Memorial Day (half-staff until noon), the last Monday in May; Flag Day, June 14; Independence Day, July 4; Labor Day, first Monday in September; Constitution Day, September 17; Columbus Day, second Monday in October; Navy Day, October 27; Veterans Day, November 11; Thanksgiving Day, fourth Thursday in November; Christmas Day, December 25; and such other days as may be proclaimed by the President of the United States; the birthdays of States (date of admission); and on state holidays.

(e) The flag should be displayed daily on or near the main administration building of every public institution.

(f) The flag should be displayed in or near every polling place on election days.

(g) The flag should be displayed during school days in or near every schoolhouse.

Sec. 3. That the flag, when carried in a procession with another flag or flags, should be either on the marching right; that is, the flag's own right, or, if there is a line of other flags, in front of the center of that line.

(a) The flag should not be displayed on a float in a parade except from a staff, or as provided in subsection (i).

(b) The flag should not be draped over the hood, top, sides, or back of a vehicle or of a railroad train or a boat. When the flag is displayed on a motorcar, the staff shall be fixed firmly to the chassis or clamped to the right fender.

(c) No other flag or pennant should be placed above or, if on the same level, to the right of the flag of the United States of America, except during church services conducted by naval chaplains at sea, when the church pennant may be flown above the flag during church services for the personnel of the Navy. No person shall display the flag of the United Nations or any other national or international flag equal, above, or in a position of superior prominence or honor to, or in place of, the flag of the United States at any place within the United States or any Territory or possession thereof: *Provided,* That nothing in this section shall make unlawful the continuance of the practice heretofore followed of displaying the flag of the United Nations in a position of superior prominence or honor, and other national flags in positions of equal prominence or honor, with that of the flag of the United States at the headquarters of the United Nations.*

(d) The flag of the United States of America, when it is displayed with another flag against a wall from crossed staffs, should be on the right, the flag's own right, and its staff should be in front of the staff of the other flag.

(e) The flag of the United States of America should be at the center and at the highest point of the group when a number of flags of States or localities or pennants of societies are grouped and displayed from staffs.

(f) When flags of States, cities, or localities, or pennants of societies are flown on the same halyard with the flag of the United States, the latter should always be at the peak. When the flags are flown from adjacent staffs, the flag of the United States should be hoisted first and lowered last. No such flag or pennant may be placed above the flag of the United States or to the United States flag's right.

(g) When flags of two or more nations are displayed, they are to be flown from separate staffs of the same height. The flags should be of approximately equal size. International usage forbids the display of the flag of one nation above that of another nation in time of peace.

(h) When the flag of the United States is displayed from a staff projecting horizontally or at an angle from the window sill, balcony, or front of a building, the union of the flag should be placed at the peak of the staff unless the flag is at half-staff. When the flag is suspended over a sidewalk from a rope extending from a house to a pole at the edge of the sidewalk, the flag should be hoisted out, union first, from the building.

(i) When displayed either horizontally or vertically against a wall, the union should be uppermost and to the flag's own right, that is, to the observer's left. When displayed in a window, the flag should be displayed in the same way, with the union or blue field to the left of the observer in the street.

(j) When the flag is displayed over the middle of the street, it should be suspended vertically with the union to the north in an east and west street or to the east in a north and south street.

(k) When used on a speaker's platform,

---

* Section 3 (c) was amended by Public Law 107, approved July 9, 1953, to designate the position of the United Nations flag.

the flag, if displayed flat, should be displayed above and behind the speaker. When displayed from a staff in a church or public auditorium, the flag of the United States of America should hold the position of superior prominence, in advance of the audience, and in the position of honor at the clergyman's or speaker's right as he faces the audience. Any other flag so displayed should be placed on the left of the clergyman or speaker or to the right of the audience.

(*l*) The flag should form a distinctive feature of the ceremony of unveiling a statue or monument, but it should never be used as the covering for the statue or monument.

(*m*) The flag, when flown at half-staff, should be first hoisted to the peak for an instant and then lowered to the half-staff position. The flag should be again raised to the peak before it is lowered for the day. On Memorial Day, the flag should be displayed at half-staff until noon only, then raised to the top of the staff. By order of the President, the flag shall be flown at half-staff upon the death of principal figures of the United States Government and the Governor of a State, territory, or possession, as a mark of respect to their memory. In the event of the death of other officials or foreign dignitaries, the flag is to be displayed at half-staff according to Presidential instructions or orders, or in accordance with recognized customs or practices not inconsistent with law. In the event of the death of a present or former official of the government of any State, territory, or possession of the United States, the Governor of that State, territory, or possession may proclaim that the National flag shall be flown at half-staff. The flag shall be flown at half-staff thirty days from the death of the President or a former President; ten days from the day of the death of the Vice President, the Chief Justice or a retired Chief Justice of the United States, or the Speaker of the House of Representatives; from the day of death until interment of an Associate Justice of the Supreme Court, a Secretary of an executive or military department, a former Vice President, or the Governor of a State, territory, or possession; and on the day of death and the following day for a Member of Congress.

(*n*) When the flag is used to cover a casket, it should be so placed that the union is at the head and over the left shoulder. The flag should not be lowered into the grave or allowed to touch the ground.

(*o*) When the flag is suspended across a corridor or lobby in a building with only one main entrance, it should be suspended vertically with the union of the flag to the observer's left upon entering. If the building has more than one main entrance, the flag should be suspended vertically near the center of the corridor or lobby with the union to the north, when entrances are to the east and west

or to the east when entrances are to the north and south. If there are entrances in more than two directions, the union should be to the east.

SEC. 4. That no disrespect should be shown to the flag of the United States of America, the flag should not be dipped to any person or thing. Regimental colors, State flags, and organization or institutional flags are to be dipped as a mark of honor.

(*a*) The flag should never be displayed with the union down, except as a signal of dire distress in instances of extreme danger to life or property.

(*b*) The flag should never touch anything beneath it, such as the ground, the floor, water, or merchandise.

(*c*) The flag should never be carried flat or horizontally, but always aloft and free.

(*d*) The flag should never be used as wearing apparel, bedding or drapery. It should never be festooned, drawn back, nor up, in folds, but always allowed to fall free. Bunting of blue, white and red, always arranged with the blue above, the white in the middle and the red below, should be used for covering a speaker's desk, draping the front of the platform and for decoration in general.

(*e*) The flag should never be fastened, displayed, used or stored in such a manner as to permit it to be easily torn, soiled or damaged in any way.

(*f*) The flag should never be used as a covering for a ceiling.

(*g*) The flag should never have placed upon it, nor on any part of it, nor attached to it any mark, insignia, letter, word, figure, design, picture, or drawing of any nature.

(*h*) The flag should never be used as a receptacle for receiving, holding, carrying, or delivering anything.

(*i*) The flag should never be used for advertising purposes in any manner whatsoever. It should not be embroidered on such articles as cushions or handkerchiefs and the like, printed or otherwise impressed on paper napkins or boxes or anything that is designed for temporary use and discard. Advertising signs should not be fastened to a staff or halyard from which the flag is flown.

(*j*) No part of the flag should ever be used as a costume or athletic uniform. However, a flag patch may be affixed to the uniform of military personnel, firemen, policemen and members of patriotic organizations. The flag represents a living country and is itself considered a living thing. Therefore, the lapel flag pin, being a replica, should be worn on the left lapel near the heart.

(*k*) The flag, when it is in such condition that it is no longer a fitting emblem for display, should be destroyed in a dignified way, preferably by burning.

SEC. 5. During the ceremony of hoisting

or lowering the flag or when the flag is passing in a parade or in review, all persons present except those in uniform should face the flag and stand at attention with the right hand over the heart. Those present in uniform should render the military salute. When not in uniform, men should remove their headdress with their right hand and hold it at the left shoulder, the hand being over the heart. Aliens should stand at attention. The salute to the flag in a moving column should be rendered at the moment the flag passes.

Sec. 6. During rendition of the national anthem when the flag is displayed, all present except those in uniform should stand at attention facing the flag with the right hand over the heart. Men not in uniform should remove their headdress with their right hand and hold it at the left shoulder, the hand being over the heart. Persons in uniform should render the military salute at the first note of the anthem and retain this position until the last note. When the flag is not displayed, those present should face toward the music and act in the same manner they would if the flag were displayed there.

Sec. 7. The Pledge of Allegiance* to the Flag, "I pledge allegiance to the Flag of the United States of America, and to the Republic for which it stands, one Nation under God,† indivisible, with liberty and justice for all.", should be rendered by standing at attention facing the flag with the right hand over the heart. When not in uniform, men should remove their headdress with their right hand and hold it at the left shoulder, the hand being over the heart. Persons in uniform should remain silent, face the flag and render the military salute.

Sec. 8. Any rule or custom pertaining to the display of the flag of the United States of America, set forth herein, may be altered, modified or repealed, or additional rules with respect thereto may be prescribed by the Commander in Chief of the Armed Forces of the United States, whenever he deems it to be appropriate or desirable; and any such alteration or additional rule shall be set forth in a proclamation.

Approved, July 7, 1976.

---

* The idea originated in 1892 with James B. Upham, an editor of *Youth's Companion*. The claim that Upham was also the author is disputed by some who credit Francis Bellamy. † The phrase "under God" was added to the pledge on June 14, 1954.

The Statue of Liberty

The Statue of Liberty ("Liberty Enlightening the World") is a 225-ton, steel-reinforced copper female figure, 152 ft. in height, facing the ocean from Liberty* Island in New York Harbor. The right hand holds aloft a torch, and the left hand carries a tablet upon which is inscribed: "July IV MDCCLXXVI."

The statue was designed by Frédéric Auguste Bartholdi of Alsace as a gift to the United States from the people of France to memorialize the alliance of the two countries in the American Revolution and their abiding friendship. The French people contributed the $250,000 cost.

The 150-foot pedestal was designed by Richard M. Hunt and built by Gen. Charles P. Stone, both Americans. It contains steel underpinnings designed by Alexander Eiffel of France to support the statue. The $270,000 cost was borne by popular subscription in this country. President Grover Cleveland accepted the statue

* Called Bedloe's Island prior to 1956.

for the United States on October 28, 1886.

On September 26, 1972, President Richard M. Nixon dedicated the American Museum of Immigration, housed in structural additions to the base of the statue. Some 200 exhibits memorialize the flow of immigrants into the United States, including as many as 5,000 a day on nearby Ellis Island.

On a tablet inside the pedestal is engraved the following sonnet, written by Emma Lazarus (1849–1887):

The New Colossus

Not like the brazen giant of Greek fame,
With conquering limbs astride from land to land;
Here at our sea-washed, sunset gates shall stand
A mighty woman with a torch, whose flame
Is the imprisoned lightning, and her name
Mother of Exiles. From her beacon-hand
Glows world-wide welcome; her mild eyes command
The air-bridged harbor that twin cities frame.
"Keep, ancient lands, your storied pomp!" cries she
With silent lips. "Give me your tired, your poor,
Your huddled masses yearning to breathe free,
The wretched refuse of your teeming shore.
Send these, the homeless, tempest-tost to me,
I lift my lamp beside the golden door!"

BIOGRAPHIES OF THE PRESIDENTS

GEORGE WASHINGTON

was born February 22, 1732 (February 11, 1731/2, old style) in Westmoreland County, Virginia. He early trained as a surveyor; but in 1752 he was appointed adjutant in the Virginia militia, and for the next three years he took an active part in the wars against the French and Indians, serving as General Braddock's aide in the disastrous campaign against Fort Duquesne. In 1759 he resigned from the militia, married Martha Dandridge Custis, a widow, and settled down as a gentleman farmer at Mount Vernon.

As a militiaman, he had been exposed to the arrogance of the British officers, and his experience as a planter with British commercial restrictions increased his anti-British sentiment. He opposed the Stamp Act of 1765 and after 1770 became increasingly prominent in organizing resistance. A delegate to the Continental Congress, Washington was selected as commander in chief of the Continental Army and took command at Cambridge, Massachusetts, on July 3, 1775.

Inadequately supported and sometimes covertly sabotaged by the Congress, in charge of troops who were inexperienced, badly equipped, and impatient of discipline, Washington conducted the war on the policy of avoiding major engagements with the British and wearing them down by harassing tactics. His able generalship, along with the French alliance and the growing weariness within Britain, brought the war to a conclusion with the surrender of Cornwallis at Yorktown on October 19, 1781.

The chaotic years under the Articles of Confederation led Washington to return to public life in the hope of promoting the formation of a strong central government. He presided over the Constitutional Convention and yielded to the universal demand that he serve as first President. In office, he sought to unite the nation in the service of establishing the authority of the new government at home and abroad. Greatly distressed by the emergence of the Hamilton-Jefferson rivalry, he worked to maintain neutrality but actually sympathized more with Hamilton. Following his unanimous re-election in 1792, his second term was dominated by the Federalists. His Farewell Address rebuked party spirit and warned against foreign entanglements.

He died at Mt. Vernon on December 14, 1799. Tall, dignified and impressive, Washington gave a public impression of austerity, though he was capable of gaiety in private. His life was characterized by a strict sense of duty to his people.

JOHN ADAMS

was born on October 30 (October 19, old style), 1735, at Braintree (now Quincy), Massachusetts. A Harvard graduate, he considered teaching and the ministry but finally turned to law and was admitted to the bar in 1758. He opposed the Stamp Act, served as lawyer for patriots indicted by the British and, by the time of the Continental Congresses, was in the vanguard of the movement for independence. In 1778 he went to France as commissioner. Subsequently he helped negotiate the peace treaty with Britain, and in 1785 became the U. S. envoy to London. Resigning in 1788, he was elected Vice President under Washington, and was re-elected in 1792.

Though a Federalist, Adams did not get along with Hamilton, who sought to prevent his election to the presidency in 1796, and thereafter intrigued against his administration. Adams was chosen with 71 electoral votes to 68 for his closest competitor, Thomas Jefferson, who became Vice President. In 1798 Adams' independent policy averted a war with France but completed the break with Hamilton and the right-wing Federalists while, at the same time, the enactment of the Alien and Sedition Acts, directed against foreigners and against critics of the government, exasperated the Jeffersonian opposition. The split between Adams and Hamilton elected Jefferson in 1800. Adams retired to his home in Quincy, Massachusetts. He later corresponded with Jefferson and they died on the same day, July 4, 1826.

Stout, somewhat vain and irascible, Adams was honest, fearless and essentially fair-minded. His *Defence of the Constitutions of Government of the United States* (1787) contains original and striking if conservative political ideas. He married Abigail Smith in 1764, and their life together was long and happy.

THOMAS JEFFERSON

was born on April 13 (April 2, old style), 1743, at Shadwell in Goochland (now Albemarle) County, Virginia. A William and Mary graduate, he studied law but from the start showed an interest in science and philosophy. His literary skill and political clarity brought him to the forefront of the revolutionary movement in Virginia. As delegate to the Continental Congress, he drafted the Declaration of Independence. In 1776 he entered the Virginia House of Delegates and initiated a comprehensive reform program for the abolition of feudal survivals in land tenure and the separation of church and state.

In 1779 he became governor, but constitutional limitations on his power combined with his own lack of executive energy caused an unsatisfactory administration, culminating in Jefferson's virtual abdication when the British invaded Virginia in 1781. He now retired to his beautiful home at Monticello, to his wife, Martha Wayles Skelton, whom he had married in 1772 and who died in 1782, and to his children.

Jefferson's *Notes on Virginia* (1784–85) illustrate his many-faceted interests, his limitless intellectual curiosity, his deep faith in agrarian democracy. Sent to Congress in 1783, he helped lay down the decimal system and drafted basic reports on the organization of the western lands. In 1785 he was appointed minister to France, where the Anglo-Saxon liberalism he had drawn from Locke was stimulated by contact with the thought which would soon ferment in the French Revolution. In 1789 Washington appointed him Secretary of State. While favoring the Constitution and a strengthened central government, Jefferson came to believe that Hamilton contemplated the establishment of a monarchy. Growing differences resulted in Jefferson's resignation on Dec. 31, 1793.

Elected Vice President in 1796, Jefferson continued to serve as spiritual leader of the opposition to Federalism, particularly to the repressive Alien and Sedition Acts. He was elected President in 1801 by the House of Representatives as a result of Hamilton's decision to throw the Federalist votes to him rather than to Aaron Burr, who had tied him in electoral votes. The purchase of Louisiana from France in 1803, though in violation of his earlier constitutional scruples, was the most notable act of his administration. Re-elected in 1804 with 162 electoral votes to 14 for the Federalist Charles C. Pinckney, Jefferson tried desperately during his second term to keep the United States out of the Napoleonic Wars in Europe, employing to this end the unpopular embargo policy.

After his retirement to Monticello in 1809, he developed his interest in education, founding the University of Virginia and watching its development with never-flagging interest. He died at Monticello on July 4, 1826. Tall, loose-jointed, a poor speaker, Jefferson had an enormous variety of interests and skills, ranging from education and science to architecture and music. Economically his conception of democracy presupposed an essentially rural community of small freeholds; but his deep and abiding faith in the common man provides inspiration for future generations.

JAMES MADISON

was born in Port Conway, Virginia, on March 16, 1751 (March 5, 1750/1, old style). A Princeton graduate, he joined the struggle for independence on his return to Virginia in 1771. In the seventies and eighties he was active both in state politics, where he championed the Jefferson reform program, and in the Continental Congress. He was influential in the Constitutional Convention as leader of the group favoring a strong central government and as recorder of the debates; and he subsequently wrote, in collaboration with Alexander Hamilton and John Jay, the *Federalist* papers to aid the campaign for the adoption of the Constitution.

In the new Congress, Madison soon emerged as the leader in the House of the men who opposed Hamilton's financial program and his pro-British leanings in foreign policy. Retiring from Congress in 1797, he continued active in Virginia and drafted the Virginia Resolution protesting the Alien and Sedition Acts. His intimacy with Jefferson made him the natural choice for Secretary of State in 1801.

In 1809 Madison succeeded Jefferson as President, with 122 electoral votes to 47 for the Federalist, C. C. Pinckney, and 6 scattering. His attractive wife, Dolley Payne Todd, whom he married in 1794, brought a new social sparkle to the executive mansion. In the meantime, increasing tension with Britain culminated in the War of 1812—a war for which the United States was unprepared, and for which Madison lacked the executive talent to clear out incompetence and mobilize the nation's energies. Madison was re-elected in 1812, with 128 electoral votes to 89 for the Federalist, De Witt Clinton. In 1814 the British actually captured Washington and forced Madison to flee to Virginia.

In his domestic program, Madison capitulated to the Hamiltonian policies that he had resisted twenty years before, signing bills to establish a United States Bank and a higher tariff. Following his presidency, he remained in retirement in Virginia until his death on June 28, 1836. Small, wrinkled, unimpressive, Madison had an acute political intelligence but lacked executive force.

JAMES MONROE

was born on April 28, 1758, in Westmoreland County, Virginia. A William and Mary graduate, he served in the army during the first years of the Revolution and was wounded at Trenton. He then entered Virginia politics and later national politics under the sponsorship of Jefferson. In 1786 he married Elizabeth (Eliza) Kortright.

Fearing centralization, Monroe opposed the adoption of the Constitution and, as senator from Virginia, was highly critical of the Hamiltonian program. In 1794 he was appointed minister to France where his ardent sympathies with the Revolution exceeded the wishes of the State Department. A troubled diplomatic career ended with his recall in 1796. From 1799 to 1802 he was governor of Virginia. In 1803 Jefferson sent him to France to help negotiate the Louisiana Purchase and for the next few years he was active in various continental negotiations.

In 1808 Monroe flirted with the radical wing of the Republican party, which opposed Madison's candidacy; but the presidential boom came to naught and, after a brief term as governor of Virginia in 1811, Monroe accepted Madison's offer of the State Department. During the war he vainly sought a field command and served as Secretary of War from September, 1814, to March, 1815.

Elected President in 1816 with 183 electoral votes to 34 for the Federalist Rufus King, and re-elected without opposition in 1820, Monroe, the last of the Virginia dynasty, pursued the course of systematic tranquilization which won for his terms the name "the era of good feeling." He continued Madison's surrender to the Hamiltonian domestic program, signed the Missouri Compromise, acquired Florida and, with the able assistance of his Secretary of State, John Quincy Adams, promulgated the Monroe Doctrine in 1823, declaring against foreign colonization or intervention in the Americas. He died in New York City on July 4, 1831.

A sound man of medium abilities, Monroe possessed qualities of judgment rather than of leadership.

JOHN QUINCY ADAMS

was born on July 11, 1767, at Braintree (now Quincy), Massachusetts, the son of John Adams. He spent his early years in Europe with his father, graduated from Harvard, and entered law practice. His anti-Jeffersonian newspaper articles won him political attention. In 1794 he became minister to the Netherlands, the first of several diplomatic posts which occupied him until his return to Boston in 1801. In 1797 he married Louisa Catherine Johnson.

In 1803 he was elected to the Senate, nominally as a Federalist, but his repeated displays of independence on such issues as the Louisiana Purchase and the embargo caused his party to compel his resignation and ostracize him socially. In 1809 Madison rewarded him for his support of Jefferson by appointing him minister to St. Petersburg. He helped negotiate the Treaty of Ghent in 1814 and in 1815 became minister to London. In 1817 Monroe appointed him Secretary of State where he served with great distinction, gaining Florida from Spain without hostilities and playing an equal part with Monroe in formulating the Monroe Doctrine.

When no presidential candidate received a majority of electoral votes in 1824,

Adams, with the support of Henry Clay, was elected by the House in 1825 over Andrew Jackson, who had the original plurality. Adams had ambitious plans of government activity to foster internal improvements and promote the arts and sciences; but congressional obstructionism combined with his own unwillingness or inability to play the role of a politician meant that little was accomplished. Retiring to Quincy after his defeat in 1828, he was elected to the House of Representatives in 1831 where, though nominally a Whig, he pursued as ever an independent course. He led the fight to force Congress to receive anti-slavery petitions and fathered the Smithsonian Institution.

Stricken on the floor of the House, he died on February 23, 1848. Tactless, brusque, conscientious, a rough and savage debater, Adams spared neither himself nor his enemies. His long and detailed *Diary* gives a unique picture of the personalities and politics of the times.

ANDREW JACKSON

was born on March 15, 1767, in what is now generally agreed to be Waxhaw, South Carolina. After a turbulent boyhood as an orphan and a British prisoner, he moved west to Tennessee where he soon qualified for law practice but found time for such frontier pleasures as horse racing, cockfighting, and dueling. His marriage to Rachel Donelson Robards in 1791 was complicated by subsequent legal uncertainties about the status of her divorce. During the seventeen-nineties Jackson served in the Tennessee constitutional convention, the federal House of Representatives, the federal Senate, and the Tennessee supreme court.

After some years as a country gentleman, living at the Hermitage near Nashville, Jackson in 1812 was given command of Tennessee troops sent against the Creeks. He defeated the Indians at Horseshoe Bend in 1814; subsequently he became a major general and won the Battle of New Orleans over veteran British troops though after the treaty of peace had been signed at Ghent. In 1818 General Jackson invaded Florida, captured Pensacola and hanged two Englishmen named Arbuthnot and Ambrister, creating an international incident. A presidential boom began for him in 1821 and in its service he returned to the Senate (1823–25). Though he won a plurality of electoral votes in 1824, he lost in the House when Clay threw his strength to Adams; he won easily in 1828 by an electoral vote of 178 to 83.

As President, Jackson greatly expanded the power and prestige of the presidential office and carried through an unexampled program of domestic reform, vetoing the bill to extend the United States Bank, moving toward a hard-money currency policy, and checking the program of federal internal improvements. He also vindicated federal authority against South Carolina with its doctrine of nullification and against France on the question of debts. The support given his policies by the workingmen of the East as well as by the farmers of the East, West, and South resulted in his triumphant re-election in 1832 over Clay by an electoral vote of 219 to 49, with 18 scattering and 2 not cast.

After watching the inauguration of his hand-picked successor, Martin Van Buren, Jackson retired to the Hermitage, where he maintained a lively interest in national affairs until his death on June 8, 1845. A tall, dignified man with a drawn and wrinkled face, Jackson has been endowed by partisan historians with a violence and irascibility he appears not to have possessed. His great contribution was to adjust the presidential office and the democratic doctrines of Jefferson to the new situation created by the Industrial Revolution.

MARTIN VAN BUREN

was born on December 5, 1782, at Kinderhook, New York. After graduating from the village school, he became a law clerk, entered practice in 1803, and soon became active in state politics as state senator and attorney general. In 1821 he was elected to the United States Senate. He threw the support of his efficient political organization, known as the Albany Regency, to William H. Crawford in 1824 and to Jackson in 1828. After leading the opposition to Adams' administration in the Senate, he served briefly as governor of New York and resigned to become Jackson's Secretary of State. He soon became on close personal terms with Jackson and played an important part in turning the Jacksonian program from the lines intended by his original Western backers.

In 1832 Van Buren became Vice President; in 1836, President, with an electoral vote of 170 against 124 scattered among four opponents. The Panic of 1837 overshadowed his term. He attributed it to the overexpansion of the credit and favored the establishment of an independent treasury as repository for the federal funds. In 1840 he established a ten-hour day on public works. Defeated by Harrison in 1840, he was the leading contender for the Democratic nomination in 1844 until he publicly opposed immediate annexation of Texas and was subsequently beaten by the Southern delegations at the Baltimore convention. This incident increased his growing misgivings about the slave power.

After working behind the scenes among the antislavery Democrats, Van Buren joined in the movement which led to the Free-Soil party and became its candidate for President in 1848. He subsequently returned to the Democratic party while continuing to object to its pro-Southern policy. He died in Kinderhook on July 24, 1862. His *Autobiography* throws valuable sidelights on the political history of the times.

Small, erect, dapper, Van Buren had a reputation for slick politicking which won him such sobriquets as the Little Magician and the Red Fox of Kinderhook; but, as his later career showed, he was capable of taking firm and unpopular stands on public issues. His wife Hannah Hoes, whom he married in 1807, died in 1819.

WILLIAM HENRY HARRISON

was born in Charles City County, Virginia, on February 9, 1773. Joining the army in 1791, he was active in Indian fighting in the Northwest, became secretary of the Northwest Territory in 1798 and governor of Indiana in 1800. He married Anna Symmes in 1795. Growing discontent over white encroachments on Indian lands led to the formation of an Indian alliance under Tecumseh to resist further aggressions. In 1811 Harrison won a nominal victory over the Indians at Tippecanoe and in 1813 a more decisive one at the Battle of the Thames, where Tecumseh was killed.

After resigning from the army in 1814, Harrison had an obscure career in politics and diplomacy, ending up in twenty years as a county recorder in Ohio. Nominated for President in 1835 as a military hero whom the conservative politicians hoped to be able to control, he ran surprisingly well against Van Buren in 1836. Four years later he defeated Van Buren by an electoral vote of 234 to 60 but caught pneumonia and died in Washington a month after his inauguration, April 4, 1841. Harrison's qualities were those of a soldier rather than of a statesman or political leader.

JOHN TYLER

was born in Charles City County, Virginia, on March 29, 1790. A William and Mary graduate, he entered law practice and politics, serving in the House of Representatives (1816–21) and later as governor of Virginia (1825–27), and as senator. A thorough-going strict constructionist, he supported Crawford in 1824 and Jackson in 1828 but broke with Jackson over his Bank policy and became a member of the Southern state-rights group which cooperated with the Whigs. In 1836 he resigned from the Senate rather than follow instructions from the Virginia legislature to vote for a resolution expunging censure of Jackson from the Senate record.

Elected Vice President on the Whig ticket in 1840, Tyler succeeded to the presidency on Harrison's death. His strict-constructionist views soon caused a split with the Henry Clay wing of the Whig party and a stalemate on domestic questions. Tyler's more considerable achievements were his support of the Webster-Ashburton Treaty with Britain and his success in bringing about the annexation of Texas.

After his presidency he lived in retirement in Virginia until the outbreak of the Civil War, when he emerged briefly as chairman of a peace convention and then as delegate to the provisional Congress of the Confederacy. He died on January 18, 1862. He was married first to Letitia Christian in March 1813 and, two years after her death in 1842, to Julia Gardiner. Witty, amiable, courteous, Tyler was a Virginia gentleman whose presidency was hamstrung by the basic contradiction between his own ideas and those of the party which put him on the ticket as Vice President.

JAMES KNOX POLK

was born in Mecklenburg County, North Carolina, on November 2, 1795. A graduate of the University of North Carolina, he moved west to Tennessee, was admitted to the bar and soon became prominent in state politics. In 1825 he was elected to the House of Representatives where he opposed Adams and, after 1829, became Jackson's floor leader in the fight against the Bank. In 1835 he became Speaker of the House. In 1839 he was elected governor of Tennessee but was beaten in tries for re-election in 1841 and 1843.

The supporters of Van Buren for the Democratic nomination in 1844 counted on Polk as his running mate; but, when Van Buren's stand on Texas alienated Southern support, the convention swung to Polk on the ninth ballot. He was elected over Henry Clay, the Whig candidate, by an electoral vote of 170 to 105. Rapidly disillusioning those who thought that he would not run his own administration, Polk proceeded steadily and precisely to achieve four major objectives—the acquisition of California, the settlement of the Oregon question, the reduction of the tariff, and the establishment of the independent treasury. He also enlarged the Monroe Doctrine to exclude all non-American intervention in American affairs, whether forcible or not, and he forced Mexico into a war which he waged to a successful conclusion. His wife Sarah Childress, whom he married in 1824, was a woman of charm and ability. Polk died in Nashville, Tennessee, on June 15, 1849.

Serious, hardworking, lacking in color, Polk has long been underrated by his-

torians who mistakenly regarded him as a slaveholders' puppet; in fact, few Presidents have so thoroughly controlled their own administration or have so ably accomplished the purposes they set for themselves. Polk's *Diary* reflects the mood and problems of his presidency.

ZACHARY TAYLOR

was born at Montebello, Orange County, Virginia, on November 24, 1784. Embarking on a military career in 1808, Taylor fought in the War of 1812, the Black Hawk War, and the Seminole War, holding in between garrison jobs on the frontier or desk jobs in Washington. A brigadier general as a result of his victory over the Seminoles at Lake Okeechobee (1837), Taylor held a succession of Southwestern commands and in 1846 established a base on the Rio Grande, where his forces engaged in hostilities which precipitated the war with Mexico. He captured Monterrey in Sept., 1846, and, disregarding Polk's orders to stay on the defensive, defeated Santa Anna at Buena Vista in February, 1847, ending the war in the northern provinces.

Though Taylor had never cast a vote for President, his party affiliations were Whiggish, and his availability was increased by his difficulties with Polk. He was elected President over the Democrat Lewis Cass by an electoral vote of 163 to 127. During the revival of the slavery controversy, which was to result in the Compromise of 1850, Taylor began to take an increasingly firm stand against appeasing the South; but he died in Washington on July 9, 1850, in the midst of the fight over the Compromise. He married Margaret Mackall Smith in 1810. His bluff and simple soldierly qualities won him the name of Old Rough and Ready. During his brief term as President he displayed a growing insight into political questions.

MILLARD FILLMORE

was born at Locke, Cayuga County, New York, on January 7, 1800. A lawyer, he entered politics as an Antimason under the sponsorship of Thurlow Weed, editor and party boss, and subsequently followed Weed into the Whig party. He served in the House of Representatives (1833–35 and 1837–43) and played a leading role in writing the tariff of 1842. Defeated for governor of New York in 1844, he became comptroller in 1848, was put on the Whig ticket with Taylor as a concession to the Clay wing of the party and became President upon Taylor's death in 1850.

As President, Fillmore broke with Weed and William H. Seward and associated himself with the pro-Southern Whigs, supporting the Compromise of 1850. Defeated for the Whig nomination in 1852, he ran for President in 1856 as candidate of the American or Know-Nothing party, which sought to unite the country against foreigners in the alleged hope of diverting it from the explosive slavery issue. Fillmore opposed Lincoln during the Civil War. He died in Buffalo on March 8, 1874. He was married in 1826 to Abigail Powers, who died in 1853, and in 1858 to Caroline Carmichael McIntosh. Urbane, gracious, colorless, and weak, Fillmore was an undistinguished President.

FRANKLIN PIERCE

was born at Hillsboro, New Hampshire, on November 23, 1804. A Bowdoin graduate and lawyer, he won rapid political advancement in the Democratic party, in part because of the prestige of his father, Governor Benjamin Pierce. By 1831 he was Speaker of the New Hampshire House of Representatives; from 1833 to 1837 he served in the federal House and from 1837 to 1842 in the Senate. His wife, Jane Means Appleton, whom he had married in 1834, disliked Washington and the somewhat dissipated life led by Pierce; and in 1842 Pierce, resigning from the Senate, took up a successful law practice in Concord, New Hampshire.

During the Mexican War Pierce was a brigadier general. Thereafter he continued to oppose antislavery tendencies within the Democratic party. As a result, he was the Southern choice to break the deadlock at the Democratic convention of 1852 and was nominated on the 49th ballot. Pierce rolled up 254 electoral votes to 42 for Winfield Scott, the Whig candidate.

As President, Pierce followed a course of appeasing the South at home and of playing with schemes of territorial expansion abroad. The failure of both his foreign and domestic policies prevented his renomination; and he died in Concord, New Hampshire, on October 8, 1869, in relative obscurity. A kindly and courteous person, Pierce was weak, unstable, and lacking in presidential qualities.

JAMES BUCHANAN

was born near Mercersburg, Pennsylvania, on April 23, 1791. A Dickinson graduate and a lawyer, he entered Pennsylvania politics as a Federalist. With the disappearance of the Federalist party, he became a Jacksonian Democrat. He served with ability in the House (1821–31), as minister to St. Petersburg (1832–33) and in the Senate (1834–45), and in 1845 became Polk's Secretary of State. Disappointed in the presidential nomination in 1852, Buchanan became minister to Britain in 1853 where he participated with other American diplomats in Europe in drafting the expansionist Ostend Manifesto.

In 1856 Buchanan received the Democratic nomination and won the election, gaining 174 electoral votes to 114 for John C. Frémont, the Republican candidate, and 8 for Millard Fillmore, American party. The growing crisis over slavery presented Buchanan with problems he lacked the will to tackle. His appeasement of the South alienated the Stephen Douglas wing of the Democratic party without reducing Southern militancy on slavery issues. While denying the right of secession, Buchanan also denied that the federal government could do anything about it. He supported the administration during the Civil War and died in Lancaster, Pennsylvania, on June 1, 1868.

The only President to remain a bachelor throughout his term, Buchanan used his charming niece Harriet Lane as White House hostess. Legalistic, indecisive, and timorous as President, Buchanan filled his other public offices capably.

ABRAHAM LINCOLN

was born in Hardin (now Larue) County, Kentucky, on February 12, 1809. His family moved to Indiana and then to Illinois, and Lincoln gained what education he could along the way. While reading law, he worked in a store, managed a mill, surveyed, and split rails. In 1834 he went to the state legislature as a Whig and became the party's floor leader. For the next twenty years he remained in law practice in Springfield, except for a single term (1847–49) in Congress, where he denounced the Mexican War. In 1855 he was a candidate for senator and in 1856 he joined the new Republican party.

A leading but unsuccessful candidate for the vice-presidential nomination with Frémont, Lincoln gained national attention in 1858 when, as Republican candidate for senator from Illinois, he engaged in a series of debates with Stephen A. Douglas, the Democratic candidate. He lost the senatorial election, but continued to prepare the way for the 1860 Republican convention and was rewarded with the presidential nomination on the third ballot. He polled 180 electoral votes, as against the 123 of his three opponents, but had only a plurality of the popular vote.

From the start, Lincoln made clear that, unlike Buchanan, he believed the national government had the power to crush the rebellion. Not an abolitionist, he held the slavery issue subordinate to that of preserving the Union but soon perceived that the war could not be brought to a successful conclusion without freeing the slaves. His administration was hampered by the incompetence of many Union generals, the inexperience of the troops, and the harassing political tactics both of the

Republican Radicals, who favored a hard policy toward the South, and the Democratic Copperheads, who desired a negotiated peace. The Gettysburg Address of November 19, 1863, marks the high point in the record of American eloquence. His patient search for a winning combination finally brought Generals Ulysses S. Grant and William T. Sherman to the top; and their series of victories in 1864 dispelled the mutterings from both Radicals and Peace Democrats which at one time seemed to threaten Lincoln's re-election. He received 212 electoral votes to 21 for George B. McClellan, the Democratic candidate. His inaugural address urged leniency toward the South: "With malice toward none, with charity for all . . . let us strive on to finish the work we are in; to bind up the nation's wounds . . ." This policy aroused growing opposition on the part of the Republican Radicals, but Lincoln was shot by the actor John Wilkes Booth at Ford's Theater, Washington, on April 14, 1865, before the matter could be put to test. He died the following day.

Lincoln's marriage to Mary Todd in 1842 was often unhappy and turbulent, in part because of his wife's pronounced instability. By his remarkable literary artistry, his essential patience and devotion, his profound sense of the importance of government by, for and of the people, by the manner of his life and of his death, Lincoln has won a unique place in the hearts of Americans.

ANDREW JOHNSON

was born at Raleigh, North Carolina, on December 29, 1808. Self-educated, he became a tailor in Greeneville, Tennessee, but soon went into politics, where he rose steadily. From 1843 to 1853 he served in the House of Representatives, 1853–57 as governor of Tennessee, and in 1857 was elected Senator. Politically he was a Jacksonian Democrat, and his specialty was the fight for a more equitable land policy. Alone among the Southern Senators, he stood by the Union during the Civil War. In 1862 he became war governor of Tennessee and carried out a thankless and difficult job with great courage. Johnson became Lincoln's running mate in 1864 as result of an attempt to give the ticket a nonpartisan and nonsectional character. Succeeding to the presidency on Lincoln's death, Johnson sought to carry out his policy but without his political skill. The result was a hopeless conflict with the Radical Republicans who dominated Congress, passed measures over Johnson's vetoes, and attempted to limit the power of the executive concerning appointments and removals. The conflict culminated with Johnson's impeachment for attempting to remove his disloyal Secretary of War in defiance of the Tenure of Office Act which required senatorial concurrence for such dismissals. The opposition failed by one vote to get the two-thirds necessary for conviction.

After his presidency, Johnson maintained an interest in politics and in 1875 was elected to the Senate. He died near Carter Station, Tennessee, on July 31, 1875. He married Eliza McCardle in 1827. An honest, courageous, and intelligent man, Johnson lacked the tact, patience, and self-control to be an effective President.

ULYSSES SIMPSON GRANT

was born (as Hiram Ulysses Grant) at Point Pleasant, Ohio, on April 27, 1822. He finished West Point in 1843 and served without particular distinction in the Mexican War. In 1848 he married Julia Dent. He resigned from the army in 1854, following warnings from his commanding officer about his drinking habits, and for the next six years held a wide variety of jobs in the Middle West. With the outbreak of the Civil War, he sought a command and soon, to his surprise, was made a brigadier general. His continuing successes in the western theaters, culminating in the capture of Vicksburg in 1863, brought him national fame and soon the command of all the Union armies. His dogged, implacable policy of concentrating on dividing and destroying the Confederate armies brought the war to an end in 1865. In 1866 he was made full general.

Grant's relations with Johnson grew steadily worse; and in 1868, as the Republican candidate for President, Grant was elected with 214 electoral votes to 80 for the Democrat Horatio Seymour. From the start Grant showed his unfitness for the office. His cabinet was weak, his domestic policy was confused, many of his intimate associates were corrupt. The notable achievement in foreign affairs was the settlement of controversies with Great Britain in the Treaty of London (1871), negotiated by his able Secretary of State, Hamilton Fish.

Nominated for a second term, he defeated Horace Greeley, the Democratic and Liberal Republican candidate, 286 votes to 63. The Panic of 1873 created difficulties for his second term.

After retiring from office, Grant toured Europe for two years and returned in time to accede to a third-term boom, but was beaten in the convention of 1880. Illness and bad business judgment darkened his last years, but he worked steadily at the *Personal Memoirs* which were to be so successful when published after his death at Mount McGregor, near Saratoga, New York, on July 23, 1885. Inarticulate, taciturn, loyal to his friends, he was an able general who should never have accepted the presidency.

RUTHERFORD BIRCHARD HAYES

was born at Delaware, Ohio, on October 4, 1822. A graduate of Kenyon College and the Harvard Law School, he practiced law in Lower Sandusky (now Fremont) and then in Cincinnati, Ohio. In 1852 he married Lucy Webb. A Whig, he joined the Republican party in 1855. During the Civil War he rose to the rank of major general. He served in Congress from 1865 to 1867 and then confirmed a reputation for honesty and efficiency in two terms as governor of Ohio. His re-election as governor in 1875 made him the logical candidate for those Republicans who wished to stop James G. Blaine in 1876, and he was successfully nominated.

The result of the election was for some time in doubt and hinged upon disputed returns from South Carolina, Louisiana, Florida, and Oregon. Samuel J. Tilden, the Democratic candidate, had the larger popular vote but was adjudged by the strictly partisan decisions of the Electoral Commission to have one less electoral vote, 185 to 184. The national acceptance of this result was due in part to the general understanding that Hayes would pursue a conciliatory policy toward the South. He withdrew the troops from the South, took a conservative position on financial and labor issues, and urged civil service reform.

Hayes served only one term by his own wish and spent the rest of his life in various humanitarian endeavors. He died in Fremont, Ohio, on January 17, 1893. A hard-working, conscientious, sensible man, Hayes represented the best type of Republican of his day.

JAMES ABRAM GARFIELD,

the last President to be born in a log cabin, was born at Cuyahoga County, Ohio, on November 19, 1831. A Williams graduate, he taught school for a time and entered Republican politics in Ohio. In 1858 he married Lucretia Rudolph. During the Civil War he had a promising career, rising to the rank of major general of volunteers; but in 1863 he was elected to the House of Representatives, where he served until 1880. His oratorical and parliamentary abilities soon made him the leading Republican in the House, though his record was marred by his unorthodox acceptance of a fee in the DeGolyer paving contract case and by suspicions of his complicity in the Crédit Mobilier scandal.

In 1880 Garfield was elected to the Senate, but instead became the presidential candidate on the 36th ballot as a result of a deadlock in the Republican convention. He gained 214 electoral votes to 155 for General Winfield Scott Hancock, the Democratic candidate. Garfield's administration was barely under way when he was shot by Charles J. Guiteau, a disap-

pointed office seeker, in July. He died in Elberon, New Jersey, on September 19, 1881. An attractive and eloquent man, he was much beloved in his day.

CHESTER ALAN ARTHUR

was born at Fairfield, Vermont, on October 5, 1830. A graduate of Union College, he became a successful New York lawyer. In 1859 he married Ellen Herndon. During the Civil War he held administrative jobs in the Republican state administration and in 1871 was appointed collector of the Port of New York by Grant. This post gave him control over considerable patronage; and, though not personally corrupt, Arthur managed his power in the interests of the New York machine so openly that President Hayes in 1877 called for an investigation, and in 1878 Arthur was suspended from his responsibilities.

In 1880 Arthur was nominated for Vice President in the hope of conciliating the followers of Grant and the powerful New York machine. As President on Garfield's assassination, Arthur, stepping out of his familiar role as spoilsman, backed civil service reform, reorganized the cabinet and prosecuted political associates accused of post office graft. Losing machine support and failing to gain the reformers, he was not renominated. He died in New York City on November 18, 1886. A tall, handsome, dignified man with real administrative abilities, he was a better President than his previous record promised.

STEPHEN GROVER CLEVELAND

was born at Caldwell, New Jersey, on March 18, 1837. He was admitted to the bar in Buffalo, New York, in 1859 and lived there as a lawyer, with occasional incursions into Democratic politics, for more than twenty years. He did not participate in the Civil War. As mayor of Buffalo in 1881, he carried through a reform program so ably that the Democrats ran him successfully for governor in 1882. In 1884 he won the Democratic nomination for President. The campaign contrasted Cleveland's spotless public career with the uncertain record of James G. Blaine, the Republican candidate, and Cleveland received enough Mugwump (independent Republican) support to win by 219 to 182 electoral votes.

As President, Cleveland pushed civil service reform, opposed the pension grab and attacked the high tariff rates. While in the White House he married Frances Folsom (1886). Renominated in 1888, Cleveland was defeated by Benjamin Harrison, polling more popular but fewer electoral votes. In 1892 he was re-elected over Harrison, 277 to 145, with 22 votes for James B. Weaver, the Populist candidate. When the Panic of 1893 burst upon the country, Cleveland's attempts to solve it by sound-money measures alienated the free-silver wing of the party, while his tariff policy alienated the protectionists. In 1894 he sent troops to break the Pullman strike. In foreign affairs his firmness caused Great Britain to back down in the Venezuela border dispute.

In his last years Cleveland was an active and much respected public figure. He died in Princeton, New Jersey, on June 24, 1908. An honest, stubborn, high-principled man, Cleveland was an old-fashioned liberal in the nineteenth-century sense who was baffled by the new problems of industrial society.

BENJAMIN HARRISON

was born in North Bend, Ohio, on August 20, 1833, the grandson of William Henry Harrison. A graduate of Miami University, he took up the law in Indiana and became active in Republican politics. In 1853 he married Caroline Lavinia Scott. During the Civil War he rose to the rank of brigadier general. A sound-money Republican, he was elected senator from Indiana in 1880 and in 1888 received the Republican nomination for President on the 8th ballot. Though behind on the popular vote, he won over Grover Cleveland in the electoral college by 233 to 168.

As President, Benjamin Harrison failed to please either the bosses or the reform element in the party. In foreign affairs he backed Secretary of State Blaine, whose policy foreshadowed later American imperialism. In 1892 Harrison was renominated, but Cleveland beat him in the election. His wife died in the White House in 1892, and Harrison married her niece, Mary Scott (Lord) Dimmick, in 1896. After his presidency, he resumed law practice. He died in Indianapolis, Indiana, on March 13, 1901. Harrison was an honest man of very medium abilities.

WILLIAM McKINLEY

was born in Niles, Ohio, on January 29, 1843. He taught school, then served in the Civil War, rising from the ranks to become a major. Subsequently he opened a law office in Canton, Ohio, and in 1871 married Ida Saxton. Elected to Congress in 1876, he served there steadily till 1891, except for 1883–85. His faithful advocacy of business interests culminated in the passage of the highly protective McKinley Tariff of 1890. With the support of Mark Hanna, a shrewd Cleveland businessman interested in safeguarding tariff protection, McKinley became governor of Ohio in 1892 and Republican presidential candidate in 1896. The business community, alarmed by the progressivism of William Jennings Bryan, the Democratic candidate, spent considerable money to assure McKinley's victory, which was by the margin of 271 to 176 in the electoral college.

The chief event of McKinley's adminis-

tration was the war with Spain, which resulted in our acquisition of the Philippines and other islands. With imperialism as an issue, McKinley defeated Bryan again in the election of 1900 by 292 to 155. On September 6, 1901, he was shot at Buffalo by Leon F. Czolgosz, an anarchist, and he died there on September 14.

THEODORE ROOSEVELT

was born in New York City on October 27, 1858. A Harvard graduate, he was early interested in ranching, in politics, and in writing picturesque historical narratives. He was a Republican member of the New York Assembly in 1882–84, an unsuccessful candidate for mayor of New York in 1886, a U. S. Civil Service Commissioner under Harrison, Police Commissioner of New York City in 1895, and Assistant Secretary of the Navy under McKinley in 1897. He resigned in 1898 to help organize a volunteer regiment named the Rough Riders and take a more direct part in the war with Spain. He won the New York gubernatorial nomination in 1898 in spite of lack of enthusiasm on the part of the bosses.

Assuming the presidency of the assassinated McKinley in 1901, Roosevelt embarked on a wide-ranging program of government reform and conservation of natural resources. He ordered antitrust suits against several large corporations, threatened to intervene in the anthracite coal strike of 1902, which prompted the operators to accept arbitration, and, in general, championed the rights of the "little man" and fought the "malefactors of great wealth." He was also responsible for such progressive legislation as the Elkins Act of 1901, which outlawed freight rebates by railroads; the bill establishing the Department of Commerce and Labor; the Hepburn Act, which gave the I.C.C. greater control over the railroads; the Meat Inspection Act; and the Pure Food and Drug Act.

In foreign affairs he pursued a strong policy, permitting the instigation of a revolt in Panama to dispose of Colombian objections to the Panama Canal and helping to maintain the balance of power in the East by bringing the Russo-Japanese war to an end, for which he won the Nobel Peace Prize, the first American to achieve this award and the first American to achieve a Nobel prize in any category. In 1904 he decisively defeated Alton B. Parker, his conservative Democratic opponent, by an electoral margin of 336 to 140.

Roosevelt's increasing coldness toward Taft after he left the White House led him to overlook his earlier disclaimer of third-term ambitions and to re-enter politics. Defeated by the machine in the Republican convention of 1912, he organized the Progressive Party and polled more votes than Taft, though the split brought about the election of Wilson. From 1915 on, Roosevelt strongly favored intervention in the European war. He became deeply embittered at Wilson's refusal to allow him to raise a volunteer division. He died in Oyster Bay, New York, on January 6, 1919. He was married twice: in 1880 to Alice Hathaway Lee, who died in 1884; and in 1886 to Edith Kermit Carow.

An advocate of the strenuous life, and a man of spirit and vigor, Roosevelt captured the imagination of the American people.

WILLIAM HOWARD TAFT

was born in Cincinnati, Ohio, on September 15, 1857. A Yale graduate, he entered Ohio Republican politics in the eighteen eighties. In 1886 he married Helen Herron. From 1887 to 1890, he served on the Ohio superior court; 1890–92, as solicitor general of the United States; 1892–1900, on the federal circuit court. In 1900 McKinley appointed him president of the Philippine Commission and in 1901 governor general. Taft had great success in pacifying the Filipinos, solving the problem of the church lands, improving economic conditions and establishing limited self-government. His period as Secretary of War (1904–08) further demonstrated his capacity as administrator and conciliator; and he was Roosevelt's hand-picked successor in 1908. In the election he polled 321 electoral votes to 162 for William Jennings Bryan.

As President, though he carried on many of Roosevelt's policies, Taft got into increasing trouble with the progressive wing of the party and displayed mounting irritability and indecision. After his defeat in 1912, he became professor of constitutional law at Yale. In 1921 he was appointed Chief Justice of the United States. He died in Washington on March 8, 1930. Enormously large, deliberate, and good-humored, Taft excelled as an administrator and judge, not as a political leader.

THOMAS WOODROW WILSON

was born in Staunton, Virginia, on December 28, 1856. A Princeton graduate, he turned from law practice to post-graduate work in political science at Johns Hopkins University, receiving his Ph.D. in 1886. He taught at Bryn Mawr, Wesleyan, and Princeton, and in 1902 was made president of Princeton. After an unsuccessful attempt to democratize the social life of Princeton, he welcomed an invitation in 1910 to be the Democratic gubernatorial candidate in New Jersey. His success in fighting the machine and putting through a reform program attracted national attention.

In 1912, after a protracted contest at Baltimore, Wilson won the Democratic nomination on the 46th ballot. In the election he received 435 electoral votes to

88 for Roosevelt and 8 for Taft. During his first term Wilson proceeded under the standard of the New Freedom to enact a program of domestic reform, including the Federal Reserve Act, the Clayton Antitrust Act, the establishment of the Federal Trade Commission, and other measures designed to restore competition in the face of the great monopolies. In foreign affairs, while privately sympathetic with the Allies, he strove to maintain neutrality in the European war and warned both sides against encroachments on American interests.

Re-elected in 1916 as a peace candidate, he tried to mediate between the warring nations; but, when the Germans resumed unrestricted submarine warfare in 1917, Wilson brought the United States into what he now believed was a war to make the world safe for democracy. He supplied the classic formulations of Allied war aims; and the armistice of November, 1918, was negotiated on the basis of Wilson's Fourteen Points. In 1919 he strove at Versailles to lay the foundations for enduring peace. He accepted the imperfections of the Versailles Treaty in the expectation that they could be remedied by action within the League of Nations. He probably could have secured ratification of the treaty if he had adopted a more conciliatory attitude toward the mild reservationists; but his insistence on all or nothing eventually caused the diehard isolationists and diehard Wilsonites to unite in rejecting a compromise.

In September, 1919, Wilson suffered a paralytic stroke which limited his future activity. After the presidency he lived on in retirement in Washington, dying February 3, 1924. He was married twice—in 1885 to Ellen Louise Axson, who died in 1914, and in 1915 to Edith Bolling Galt. A man of high principle, inspiring eloquence, and great intellectual ability, Wilson was the first leader to fire the imagination of the masses of the world with the vision of world peace.

WARREN GAMALIEL HARDING

was born in Morrow County, Ohio, on November 2, 1865. After attending Ohio Central College, Harding became interested in journalism and in 1884 bought the *Marion* (Ohio) *Star*. In 1891 he married a wealthy widow, Florence Kling De Wolfe. As his paper prospered, he entered Republican politics, serving as state senator (1899–1903), and as lieutenant governor (1904–06). In 1910 he was defeated for governor but in 1914 was elected to the Senate. His reputation as orator made him keynoter in the 1916 convention.

When the 1920 Republican convention was deadlocked between Leonard Wood and Frank O. Lowden, Harding was made the dark-horse nominee on his solemn affirmation that there was no reason in his past that he should not be. Straddling the League question, Harding was elected easily, with 404 electoral votes to 127 for James M. Cox, his Democratic opponent. His Cabinet contained some able men, but also some manifestly unfit for public office. Harding's own intimates were mediocre when they were not corrupt. The impending disclosure of scandals in the Interior and Justice departments and in the Veterans' Bureau, as well as political setbacks, profoundly worried him. On his return from Alaska in 1923, he died suddenly at San Francisco on August 2. A handsome and genial man, undiscriminating in his associates, lacking in political ideas or fortitude, Harding was totally unfitted for the presidency.

JOHN CALVIN COOLIDGE

was born in Plymouth, Vermont, on July 4, 1872. An Amherst graduate, he went into law practice at Northampton, Massachusetts, in 1897. He married Grace Anna Goodhue in 1905. He entered Republican state politics, becoming successively mayor of Northampton, state senator, lieutenant governor and, in 1919, governor. His conduct in regard to the Boston police strike in 1919 won him a somewhat undeserved reputation for decisive action and brought him the Republican vice-presidential nomination in 1920. After Harding's death Coolidge handled the Washington scandals with care and finally managed to save the Republican party from public blame for the widespread corruption.

In 1924 Coolidge won re-election without difficulty, getting 382 electoral votes to 136 for the Democrat, John W. Davis, and 13 for Robert M. La Follette running on the Progressive ticket. His second term, like his first, was characterized by a general satisfaction with the existing economic order. He stated that he did not choose to run in 1928.

After his presidency, Coolidge lived quietly in Northampton, writing an unilluminating *Autobiography* and conducting a syndicated column. He died in Northampton, Massachusetts, on January 5, 1933. His dry, Yankee humor, his frugality and glumness made him a paradoxically popular President in the boom period.

HERBERT CLARK HOOVER

was born at West Branch, Iowa, on August 10, 1874. A Stanford graduate, he worked from 1895 to 1913 as a mining engineer and consultant in North America, Europe, Asia, Africa, and Australia. In 1899 he married Lou Henry. During the First World War he served with distinction as chairman of the American Relief Committee in London, as chairman of the Commission for Relief in Belgium and as United States Food Administrator. His political affilia-

tions were still sufficiently indeterminate for him to be mentioned as a possibility for both Republican and Democratic nominations in 1920; but after the election he served both Harding and Coolidge as Secretary of Commerce.

In the election of 1928 Hoover received 444 electoral votes to 87 for Alfred E. Smith, the Democratic candidate. He soon faced the worst depression in the nation's history; but his attacks upon it were hampered by his devotion to the theory that the forces which brought the crisis would soon bring the revival, and then by his belief that in too many areas the federal government had no power to act. In a succession of vetoes he struck down measures proposing a national employment system or national relief; he reduced income tax rates; and only at the end of his term did he yield to popular pressure and set up agencies such as the Reconstruction Finance Corporation to make emergency loans to assist business.

After his 1932 defeat, Hoover returned to private business. In 1946, President Truman charged him with various world food missions; and from 1947 to 1949 and again from 1953 to 1955, he was head of the Commission on Organization of the Executive Branch of the Government. He died in New York City on Oct. 20, 1964.

FRANKLIN DELANO ROOSEVELT

was born in Hyde Park, New York, on January 30, 1882. A Harvard graduate, he attended Columbia Law School and was admitted to the New York bar. In 1910 he was elected to the New York state senate as a Democrat. Re-elected in 1912, he was appointed Assistant Secretary of the Navy by Woodrow Wilson in 1913. In 1920 his radiant personality and his war services resulted in his nomination for Vice President as James M. Cox's running mate. After his defeat, he returned to law practice in New York. In August, 1921, Roosevelt was stricken with infantile paralysis while at Campobello, New Brunswick. After a long and gallant fight against the disease he recovered partial use of his legs. In 1924 and 1928 he led the fight at the Democratic national conventions for the nomination of Governor Alfred E. Smith of New York; and in 1928 Roosevelt was himself induced to run for governor of New York. He was elected and was re-elected in 1930.

In 1932 Roosevelt received the Democratic nomination for President and immediately launched a campaign which brought new spirit to a weary and discouraged nation. He won the election over Herbert Hoover by a margin of 472 to 59 in the electoral college. His first term was characterized by an unfolding of the New Deal program, with greater benefits for labor, the farmers, and the unemployed, and the progressive estrangement of most of the business community.

At an early stage Roosevelt became aware of the menace to world peace involved in the existence of totalitarian fascism, and from 1937 on he tried to focus public attention on the trend of events in Europe and Asia. As a result he was widely denounced as a warmonger. He was re-elected in 1936 over Alfred M. Landon by the overwhelming electoral margin of 523 to 8; and the gathering international crisis caused him to decide to run again in 1940. He defeated Wendell L. Willkie by a vote of 449 to 82.

Roosevelt's program to bring maximum aid to Britain and, after June, 1941, to Russia was opposed, until the Japanese attack on Pearl Harbor restored national unity. During the war Roosevelt shelved the New Deal in the interests of conciliating the business community, both in order to get full production during the war and to prepare the way for a united acceptance of the peace settlements after the war. A series of conferences with Winston Churchill and Joseph Stalin laid down the bases for the postwar world. In 1944 he was elected to a fourth term, running against Thomas E. Dewey.

On April 12, 1945, Roosevelt died at Warm Springs, Georgia, shortly after his return from the Yalta Conference. His wife, Anna Eleanor Roosevelt, whom he married in 1905, was a woman of great ability who made significant contributions to her husband's policies. No other President has been faced with so many staggering responsibilities, both at home and abroad.

HARRY S. TRUMAN

was born on a farm near Lamar, Missouri, on May 8, 1884. During the First World War he served in France with the 129th Field Artillery. He married Bess Wallace in 1919. After engaging briefly and unsuccessfully in the haberdashery business in Kansas City, Truman entered local politics. Under the sponsorship of Thomas Pendergast, Democratic boss of Missouri, he held a number of local offices, preserving his personal honesty in the midst of a notoriously corrupt political machine. In 1934 he was elected to the Senate and was re-elected in 1940. During his first term he was a loyal but quiet supporter of the New Deal; but in the course of his second term, an appointment as head of a Senate committee to investigate war production brought out his special qualities of honesty, common sense, and hard work, and he won widespread respect.

Elected Vice President in 1944, Truman became President upon Roosevelt's sudden death in April 1945, and was immediately faced with the problems of winding down the war against the Axis and preparing the nation for postwar adjustment. He at-tended the Potsdam conference in July and August, at which the Allies met to implement the Yalta agreements and to delegate among themselves authority over a demilitarized Germany.

The years 1947–48 were distinguished by civil rights proposals, the Truman Doctrine to contain the spread of Communism and the Marshall Plan to aid in the economic reconstruction of war-ravaged nations. Truman's general record, highlighted by a vigorous Fair Deal campaign, brought about his unexpected election in 1948 over the heavily favored Thomas E. Dewey.

Truman's second term was primarily concerned with the Cold War with the Soviet Union, the implementing of the North Atlantic Pact, the United Nations police action in Korea, and the vast rearmament program with its accompanying problems of economic stabilization.

On March 29, 1952, Truman announced that he would not run again for the presidency. After leaving the White House, he returned to his home in Independence, Mo., to write his memoirs. He further busied himself with the Harry S. Truman Library there. He died in Kansas City, Mo., on Dec. 26, 1972.

DWIGHT DAVID EISENHOWER

was born in Denison, Texas, on October 14, 1890. His ancestors lived in Germany, and emigrated to America, settling in Pennsylvania, early in the 18th century. His father, David, had a general store in Hope, Kansas, which failed. After a brief time in Texas, the family moved to Abilene, Kansas.

After graduating from Abilene High School in 1909, Dwight Eisenhower did odd jobs for almost two years. He won an appointment to the Naval Academy at Annapolis, but it turned out that he was too old for admittance. Then he received an appointment in 1910 to West Point. He was graduated a 2nd lieutenant in 1915.

He did not see service in World War I, having been assigned to the 19th Infantry at Fort Sam Houston, Texas. There he met Mamie Geneva Doud, whom he married in Denver on July 1, 1916, and by whom he had two sons: Doud Dwight (died in infancy) and John Sheldon Doud.

Eisenhower served in the Philippines from 1935 to 1939 with Gen. Douglas MacArthur. Afterwards, Gen. George C. Marshall brought him into the War Department's General Staff and, in 1942, put him in command of the invasion of North Africa. In 1944, he was made Supreme Allied Commander for the invasion of Europe.

After the war, Eisenhower served as Army Chief of Staff from November, 1945, until February, 1948, when he was appointed president of Columbia University. In December, 1950, President Truman recalled Eisenhower to active duty to command the North Atlantic Treaty Organization forces in Europe. He held this post until the end of May, 1952.

In the Republican Convention of July, 1952, in Chicago, Eisenhower won the Presidential nomination on the first ballot in a close race with Senator Robert A. Taft of Ohio. In November, he won the election, defeating Gov. Adlai E. Stevenson of Illinois by an electoral vote of 442 to 89.

Through two terms, Eisenhower hewed to moderate domestic policies. He quested for peace through Free World strength in an era of new nationalisms, nuclear rockets, and space exploration. He fostered alliances pledging the U.S. to resist Red aggression in Europe, Asia, and Latin America. The Eisenhower Doctrine of 1957 extended commitments to the Middle East. Arms budgets focused on nuclear "massive retaliation." Stepped-up space programs followed the Soviet Sputnik I (1957). Meetings with Soviet Premier Khrushchev in 1955 and 1959 saw some relaxation of tensions. But the 1960 Summit meeting died when Eisenhower rejected Khrushchev's demand for a U.S. apology for the U-2 "spy" flights over the U.S.S.R.

At home, the popular President lacked G.O.P. Congressional majorities after 1954, but he was re-elected in 1956 by 457 electoral votes to 73 for Adlai E. Stevenson.

While retaining most Fair Deal programs, he stressed "fiscal responsibility" in domestic affairs. A moderate in civil rights, he sent troops to Little Rock, Ark., to enforce court-ordered school integration.

With his wartime rank restored by Congress, Eisenhower returned to private life and the role of elder statesman with his vigor hardly impaired by a heart attack, ileitis operation and mild stroke suffered while in office. He died in Washington, D. C., on March 28, 1969.

JOHN FITZGERALD KENNEDY

was born in Brookline, Massachusetts, on May 29, 1917. His father, Joseph P. Kennedy, was U. S. Ambassador to Great Britain from 1937 to 1940.

Kennedy was graduated from Harvard University in 1940, and joined the Navy in 1941. He became skipper of a PT boat that was sunk in the Pacific by a Japanese destroyer. Although given up for lost, he swam to a safe island, towing an injured enlisted man.

After recovering from a war-aggravated spinal injury, Kennedy entered politics in 1946 and was elected to Congress. In 1952 he ran against Senator Henry Cabot Lodge, Jr., of Massachusetts, and won.

Kennedy was married on September 12, 1953, to Jacqueline Lee Bouvier, by whom he had three children: Caroline, John Fitzgerald, Jr., and Patrick Bouvier (died in infancy).

In 1957 Kennedy won the Pulitzer Prize for a book he had written earlier, *Profiles in Courage.*

After strenuous primary battles Kennedy won the Presidential Democratic nomination on the first ballot at the 1960 Los Angeles convention. With a plurality of only 118,574 votes, he carried the November election with an electoral vote of 303 to Vice President Richard M. Nixon's 219, becoming the first Roman Catholic President.

Kennedy brought to the White House the dynamic idea of a "New Frontier" approach in dealing with problems at home, abroad, and in the dimensions of space. Out of his leadership in his first few months in office came the 10-year Alliance for Progress to aid Latin America, the Peace Corps, and accelerated programs which brought the first Americans into orbit in the race in space.

Failure of the U. S.-supported Cuban invasion in April, 1961, led to the entrenchment of the Communist-backed Castro regime, only 90 miles from United States soil. When it became known that Soviet offensive missiles were being installed in Cuba in 1962, the President ordered a naval "quarantine" of the island and moved troops into position to eliminate this threat to U. S. security. The world seemed on the brink of a nuclear war until Khrushchev ordered the removal of the missiles.

A sudden "thaw," or the appearance of one, in the cold war, came with the agreement with the Soviet Union on a limited test-ban treaty signed in Moscow on August 6, 1963.

In his domestic policies Kennedy's proposals for medical care for the aged, expanded area redevelopment, and aid to education were defeated, but on minimum wage, trade legislation, and other measures he won important victories.

Widespread racial disorders and demonstrations led to Kennedy's proposing sweeping civil rights legislation. As his third year in office drew to a close, he also recommended an $11-billion tax cut to bolster the economy. Both measures were pending in Congress when Kennedy, looking forward to a second term, journeyed to Texas for a series of speeches.

While riding in a procession in Dallas on November 22, 1963, he was shot to death by an assassin firing from an upper floor of a building. The alleged assassin, Lee Harvey Oswald, was killed two days later in the Dallas city jail by Jack Ruby, owner of a strip-tease place.

At 46 years of age, Kennedy became the fourth President to be assassinated and the eighth to die in office.

LYNDON BAINES JOHNSON

was born in Stonewall, Texas, on August 27, 1908. On both sides of his family he had a political heritage mingled with a Baptist background of preachers and teachers. Both his father and his paternal grandfather served in the Texas House of Representatives.

After having been graduated from Southwest Texas State Teachers College, Johnson taught school for two years. He went to Washington in 1932 as secretary to Representative Richard M. Kleberg. During this time he married Claudia Alta Taylor, known as "Lady Bird." They had two children: Lynda Bird (Robb) and Luci Baines (Nugent).

In 1935, Johnson became Texas administrator for the National Youth Administration. Two years later he was elected to Congress as an all-out supporter of Franklin D. Roosevelt. He was the first member of Congress to enlist in the armed forces after the attack on Pearl Harbor. He served in the Navy in the Pacific and won a Silver Star.

Johnson lost his first bid for a Senate seat in 1941 but won in 1948 after he had captured the Democratic nomination by only 87 votes. He was 40 years old. He became the Senate Democratic leader in 1953. A heart attack in 1955 threatened the end of his active political career, but he recovered fully and resumed his duties.

At the height of his power as Senate leader, Johnson sought the Democratic nomination for President in 1960. When he lost to John F. Kennedy he surprised even some of his closest associates by accepting second place on the ticket.

Johnson was riding in another car in the motorcade when Kennedy was assassinated in Dallas, Tex., on November 22, 1963. He took the oath of office in the presidential jet on the Dallas airfield.

As John F. Kennedy had dispelled the idea that no Catholic could be elected President, Johnson sought to erase the feeling that no Southerner in these times could fill the office without regional prejudices. In his first address to Congress he called for a strong civil rights bill as a memorial to the slain President.

With Johnson's insistent backing, Congress finally adopted a far-reaching civil rights bill, a voting rights bill, a Medicare program for the aged and measures to improve education and conservation. Congress also began what Johnson described as "an all-out war" on poverty.

With a record-breaking majority of nearly 16 million votes, Johnson was elected President in his own right in 1964. His electoral vote was 486 to 52 for his Republican opponent, Barry M. Goldwater.

Johnson interpreted his victory at the polls as a popular mandate and proposed stepped-up social and economic programs which he called, "The Great Society." Before much progress could be made on such undertakings, a worsening situation in Southeast Asia brought a fateful decision by Johnson to step up American forces in Vietnam. In time, the number of these forces reached more than 500,000.

The double tragedy of a war in Asia and urban riots at home marked Johnson's last two years in office. Faced with disunity in the nation and challenges within his own party, Johnson surprised the country on Mar. 31, 1968, with the announcement that he would not be a candidate for reelection. He died of a heart attack on Jan. 22, 1973.

RICHARD MILHOUS NIXON

was born in Yorba Linda, California, on January 9, 1913, to Midwestern-bred parents, Francis A. and Hannah Milhous Nixon, who raised their five sons as Quakers.

Nixon was a high school debater and was undergraduate president at Whittier College in California, where he was graduated in 1934. As a scholarship student at Duke University Law School, in North Carolina, he graduated third in his class in 1937.

After five years as a lawyer, Nixon joined the Navy in August, 1942. He was an air transport officer in the South Pacific and a legal officer stateside before his discharge in 1946 as a lieutenant commander.

Nixon ran for Congress as a Republican in 1946 and defeated Rep. Jerry Voorhis (D-Calif.). On the House Un-American Activities Committee, he made a name as an investigator of Alger Hiss, who was later jailed for perjury. In 1950, Nixon defeated Rep. Helen Gahagan Douglas, a Democrat, for a vacant California Senate seat. He was criticized for portraying her as a Communist dupe.

Nixon's anti-Communism, his Western base and his youth figured in his selection in 1952 to run for Vice President on the ticket headed by Dwight D. Eisenhower. Demands for Nixon's withdrawal followed disclosure that California businessmen had paid some of his Senate office expenses. His televised rebuttal, known as "the Checkers speech" (named for a cocker spaniel given to the Nixons), brought him support from the public and from Eisenhower. The ticket won easily in 1952 and again in 1956.

Eisenhower gave Nixon substantive assignments, including missions to 56 foreign countries. In Moscow in 1959, Nixon won acclaim for his defense of U.S. interests in an impromptu "kitchen debate" with Soviet Premier Nikita S. Khrushchev.

Nixon won the 1960 GOP Presidential nomination, but lost the election to Democratic Senator John F. Kennedy by 118,-574 votes out of 68,838,219. The electoral vote was 303 to 219.

In 1962, Nixon failed in a bid for California's Governorship and seemed to be finished as a national candidate. He became a Wall Street lawyer, but kept his old party ties and developed new ones through constant travels to speak for Republicans.

Nixon won the 1968 GOP Presidential nomination after a shrewd primary campaign, then made Maryland Governor Spiro T. Agnew his surprise choice for Vice President. In the election, they edged out the Democratic ticket headed by Vice President Hubert H. Humphrey by 510,314 votes out of 73,212,065. The electoral vote was 301 to 191.

Committed to wind down the U.S. role in the Vietnam war, Nixon pursued "Vietnamization"—training and equipping South Vietnamese to do their own fighting. American ground combat forces in Vietnam fell steadily from 540,000 when Nixon took office to none in 1973, when the military draft was ended. But there was heavy continuing use of U.S. air power.

Before the costly war tapered off, it caused intense protest demonstrations, notably after Nixon's announcement late in April, 1970, of an "incursion" against Communist forces in officially neutral Cambodia. In an ensuing riot at Kent State University in Ohio, four students were killed by National Guardsmen's bullets.

Nixon improved relations with Moscow and reopened the long-closed door to mainland China with a good-will trip there in February, 1972. In May of that year, he visited Moscow and signed agreements on arms limitation and trade expansion and approved plans for a joint U.S.-Soviet space mission in 1975.

Inflation was a campaign issue for Nixon, but he failed to master it as President. On Aug. 15, 1971, with unemployment edging up, Nixon abruptly announced a new economic policy: A 90-day wage-price freeze, stimulative tax cuts, a temporary 10% tariff, spending cuts. A second phase, imposing guidelines on wage, price and rent boosts, was announced Oct. 7.

The economy responded in time for the 1972 campaign, in which Nixon played up his foreign policy achievements. Played down was the burglary on June 17, 1972, of Democratic national headquarters in Washington's Watergate apartment complex.

The Nixon-Agnew re-election campaign cost a record $60 million and it swamped the Democratic ticket headed by Senator George S. McGovern of South Dakota with a plurality of 17,999,528 out of 77,718,554 votes. Only Massachusetts, with 14 electoral votes, and the District of Columbia, with 3, went for McGovern.

In January, 1973, hints of a cover-up emerged at the trial of six men found guilty of the Watergate burglary. With a Senate investigation under way, Nixon announced on April 30 the resignations of his top aides, H. R. Haldeman and John D. Ehrlichman, and the dismissal of White House counsel John Dean III. Dean was the star witness at televised Senate hearings that exposed both a White House cover-up of Watergate and massive illegalities in GOP fund-raising in 1972.

The hearings also disclosed that Nixon had routinely tape-recorded his office meetings and telephone conversations. The last year of his administration was shadowed by a losing legal battle to retain White House control of the tapes. In October, 1973, a court order for selected tapes was obtained by Archibald Cox, special prosecutor named by Attorney General Elliot L. Richardson to probe the scandals. Cox was fired and Richardson resigned.

Cox's successor, Leon Jaworski, pressed prosecutions that led to convictions of 14 former White House assistants and campaign aides, three of them former Cabinet officers. The House Judiciary Committee began an impeachment study.

On Oct. 10, 1973, Agnew resigned as Vice President, then pleaded no contest to a negotiated Federal charge of evading income taxes on alleged bribes. Two days later, Nixon nominated the House minority leader, Rep. Gerald R. Ford of Michigan, as the new Vice President. Congress confirmed Ford Dec. 6, 1973.

In June, 1974, Nixon visited Israel and four Arab nations. In July, he met in Moscow with Soviet leader Leonid I. Brezhnev and reached preliminary nuclear arms limitation agreements.

In the month after his return, Watergate ended the Nixon regime. On July 24, the Supreme Court orded Nixon to surrender tapes subpoenaed by Jaworski. On July 30, the Judiciary Committee referred three impeachment articles to the House. On Aug. 5, Nixon bowed to the Supreme Court and released tapes showing he halted an FBI probe of the Watergate burglary six days after it occurred. It was in effect an admission of obstruction of justice, and impeachment appeared inevitable.

Nixon resigned Aug. 9, 1974, the first President ever to do so. A month later, President Ford issued an unconditional pardon for any offenses Nixon might have committed as President, thus forestalling possible prosecution.

A week after the pardon, Nixon entered a California hospital for treatment of phlebitis suffered initially during his Middle Eastern tour in June. The state of his health kept him hospitalized or in seclusion at his estate at San Clemente, California, for months after his resignation. In June, 1975, he submitted to 11 hours of secret questioning by special prosecutors and members of the Watergate grand jury at a hearing in offices adjoining his estate. The grand jury was investigating possible obstruction of justice in connection with obliteration of a portion of a key White House tape.

In 1940, Nixon married Thelma Catherine (Pat) Ryan. They had two daughters, Patricia (Tricia), born in 1946, the wife of New York lawyer Edward Finch Cox, and Julie, born in 1948, who married Dwight David Eisenhower II, grandson of the former President.

GERALD RUDOLPH FORD

was born in Omaha, Nebraska, on July 14, 1913, the only child of Leslie and Dorothy Gardner King. His parents were divorced in 1915. His mother moved to Grand Rapids, Mich., and married Gerald R. Ford. The boy was renamed for his stepfather.

Ford captained his high school football team in Grand Rapids, and a football scholarship took him to the University of Michigan, where he starred as varsity center before his graduation in 1935. A job as assistant football coach at Yale gave him an opportunity to attend Yale Law School, where he graduated in the top third of his class in 1941.

He returned to Grand Rapids to practice law, but entered the Navy in April, 1942. He saw wartime service in the Pacific on the light aircraft carrier Monterey and was a lieutenant commander when he returned to Grand Rapids early in 1946 to resume law practice and dabble in politics.

Ford got to Congress in 1948 by scoring a primary victory over Republican Rep. Bartel J. Jonkman, a conservative isolationist, and then winning the first of 13 elections to the House. He was soon assigned to the influential Appropriations Committee and rose to become the ranking Republican on the subcommittee on Defense Department appropriations and an expert in the field.

When a first-termer, Ford knew Richard Nixon as a House colleague, and their friendship continued through the years. He helped stifle a move to deprive Nixon of renomination for Vice President in 1956 and supported Nixon's nomination for President in 1960.

As a legislator, Ford described himself as "a moderate on domestic issues, a conservative in fiscal affairs and a dyed-in-the-wool internationalist." He carried the ball for Pentagon appropriations, was a hawk on Vietnam and kept a low profile on civil rights issues.

He was also dependable and hard-working and popular with his colleagues. In 1963, he was elected chairman of the House Republican Conference. He served in 1963–64 as a member of the Warren Commission that investigated the assassination of President John F. Kennedy. A revolt by dissatisfied younger Republicans in 1965 made him minority leader.

As minority leader, Ford worked for a decade to abet the election of a Republican majority, which would put him in line for the Speakership. But the GOP failed to win control of the House, even though Nixon was elected President in 1968 and 1972. Ford was permanent chairman of both GOP conventions that nominated Nixon.

Ford shelved his hopes for the Speakership on Oct. 12, 1973, when Nixon nominated him to fill the Vice Presidency left vacant by the resignation under fire of Spiro T. Agnew. It was the first use of the procedures for filling vacancies in the Vice Presidency laid down in the 25th Amendment of the Constitution, which Ford had helped enact.

Congress confirmed Ford as Vice President on Dec. 6, 1973. Once in office, he said in speeches he did not believe Nixon was involved in the Watergate scandals, but criticized the President's stubborn court battle against releasing tape-recordings of Watergate-related conversations for use as evidence.

The scandals led to Nixon's unprecedented resignation on Aug. 9, 1974, and Ford was sworn in immediately as the 38th President, the first to enter the White House without winning an election to national office.

Ford assured the nation when he took office that "our long national nightmare is over" and pledged "openness and candor" in all his actions. He won a warm response from the Democratic 93rd Congress when he said he wanted "a good marriage," rather than a honeymoon with his former colleagues. In December, 1974, Congressional majorities backed his choice of former New York Governor Nelson A. Rockefeller as his successor in the again-vacant Vice Presidency.

The cordiality was chilled by Ford's announcement on Sept. 8, 1974, that he had granted an unconditional pardon to Nixon for any crimes he might have committed as President. Although no formal charges were pending, Ford said he feared "ugly passions" would be aroused if Nixon were brought to trial. The pardon was widely criticized.

Ford inherited serious problems at home and abroad. The economy was superheated by inflation and racked by energy shortages. Overseas, American policy was threatened by war scares in the Middle East and by disastrous defeats of U.S.-backed regimes in Southeast Asia.

To fight inflation, the new President first proposed fiscal restraints and spending curbs and a 5% tax surcharge that got nowhere in Congress. But rising unemployment led him early in 1975 to propose a broad tax reduction program and energy conservation measures that were expected to produce a record peacetime budget deficit of at least $60 billion in fiscal year 1976. Congress was slow to respond.

Congress rebuffed Ford in the spring of 1975 when he appealed for emergency military aid to help the governments of South Vietnam and Cambodia resist massive Communist offensives. Both regimes capitulated in April. Ford ordered a massive air-sea rescue operation that brought evacuation of 6,000 Americans and 130,000 anti-Communist South Vietnamese and Cambodians. Over considerable domestic resistance, he opened the door for resettlement of the refugees in the United States.

Ford refused to participate in efforts to fix blame for the Southeast Asian disaster. He took pains to reassure other friendly nations that it would not affect his administration's determination to fulfill U.S. treaty commitments.

In November, 1974, Ford visited Japan, South Korea and the Soviet Union, where he and Soviet leader Leonid I. Brezhnev conferred in Vladivostok and reached a tentative agreement to limit the number of strategic offensive nuclear weapons. It was Ford's first meeting as President with Brezhnev, who planned a return visit to Washington in the fall of 1975.

Ford visited Western Europe May 28–June 3, 1975, primarily to attend a NATO summit meeting in Brussels, where he reassured U.S. allies of continued U.S. commitment despite the defeats in Indochina. He went on to Austria for talks on the Middle East with Egyptian President Anwar el-Sadat and also visited Spain and Italy.

Reports of illegal domestic spying by the Central Intelligence Agency led Ford to name Rockefeller as head of an eight-member investigating commission, which reported June 10, 1975, that the CIA had engaged in some "plainly unlawful" activities and recommended 30 corrective actions. Ford declined to make public a section of the report dealing with alleged CIA support of assassination plots against foreign heads of state, calling it "incomplete and extremely sensitive." He forwarded the material to the Justice Department and made it available to a special Senate committee probe of the CIA.

Politically, Ford's fortunes improved steadily in the first half of 1975. Badly divided Democrats in Congress were unable to muster votes to override his vetoes of spending bills that exceeded his budget. He faced some right-wing opposition in his own party, but moved to pre-empt it with an early announcement—on July 8, 1975—of his intention to be a candidate in 1976.

In 1948, Ford married Elizabeth Anne (Betty) Bloomer. They had four children, Michael Gerald, John Gardner, Steven Meigs and Susan Elizabeth.

(For Gerald Ford's Campaign *see* Special Section.)

Presidents of the United States

(For further information, see pages 533–49.)

Name and (party)[1]	Term	State of birth	Born	Died	Religion	Age at inaug.	Age at death
1. Washington (F)[2]	1789–1797	Va.	2/22/1732	12/14/1799	Episcopalian	57	67
2. J. Adams (F)	1797–1801	Mass.	10/30/1735	7/4/1826	Unitarian	61	90
3. Jefferson (DR)	1801–1809	Va.	4/13/1743	7/4/1826	Deist	57	83
4. Madison (DR)	1809–1817	Va.	3/16/1751	6/28/1836	Episcopalian	57	85
5. Monroe (DR)	1817–1825	Va.	4/28/1758	7/4/1831	Episcopalian	58	73
6. J. Q. Adams (DR)	1825–1829	Mass.	7/11/1767	2/23/1848	Unitarian	57	80
7. Jackson (D)	1829–1837	S. C.	3/15/1767	6/8/1845	Presbyterian	61	78
8. Van Buren (D)	1837–1841	N. Y.	12/5/1782	7/24/1862	Reformed Dutch	54	79
9. W. H. Harrison (W)[3]	1841	Va.	2/9/1773	4/4/1841	Episcopalian	68	68
10. Tyler (W)	1841–1845	Va.	3/29/1790	1/18/1862	Episcopalian	51	71
11. Polk (D)	1845–1849	N. C.	11/2/1795	6/15/1849	Methodist	49	53
12. Taylor (W)[3]	1849–1850	Va.	11/24/1784	7/9/1850	Episcopalian	64	65
13. Fillmore (W)	1850–1853	N. Y.	1/7/1800	3/8/1874	Unitarian	50	74
14. Pierce (D)	1853–1857	N. H.	11/23/1804	10/8/1869	Episcopalian	48	64
15. Buchanan (D)	1857–1861	Pa.	4/23/1791	6/1/1868*	Presbyterian	65	77
16. Lincoln (R)[4]	1861–1865	Ky.	2/12/1809	4/15/1865	Liberal	52	56
17. A. Johnson (U)[5]	1865–1869	N. C.	12/29/1808	7/31/1875	([6])	56	66
18. Grant (R)	1869–1877	Ohio	4/27/1822	7/23/1885	Methodist	46	63
19. Hayes (R)	1877–1881	Ohio	10/4/1822	1/17/1893	Methodist	54	70
20. Garfield (R)[4]	1881	Ohio	11/19/1831	9/19/1881	Disciples of Christ	49	49
21. Arthur (R)	1881–1885	Vt.	10/5/1830	11/18/1886	Episcopalian	50	56
22. Cleveland (D)	1885–1889	N. J.	3/18/1837	6/24/1908	Presbyterian	47	71
23. B. Harrison (R)	1889–1893	Ohio	8/20/1833	3/13/1901	Presbyterian	55	67
24. Cleveland (D)[7]	1893–1897	.....	....	....	....	..	..
25. McKinley (R)[4]	1897–1901	Ohio	1/29/1843	9/14/1901	Methodist	54	58
26. T. Roosevelt (R)	1901–1909	N. Y.	10/27/1858	1/6/1919	Reformed Dutch	42	60
27. Taft (R)	1909–1913	Ohio	9/15/1857	3/8/1930	Unitarian	51	72
28. Wilson (D)	1913–1921	Va.	12/28/1856	2/3/1924	Presbyterian	56	67
29. Harding (R)[3]	1921–1923	Ohio	11/2/1865	8/2/1923	Baptist	55	57
30. Coolidge (R)	1923–1929	Vt.	7/4/1872	1/5/1933	Congregationalist	51	60
31. Hoover (R)	1929–1933	Iowa	8/10/1874	10/20/1964	Quaker	54	90
32. F. D. Roosevelt (D)[3]	1933–1945	N. Y.	1/30/1882	4/12/1945	Episcopalian	51	63
33. Truman (D)	1945–1953	Mo.	5/8/1884	12/26/1972	Baptist	60	88
34. Eisenhower (R)	1953–1961	Tex.	10/14/1890	3/28/1969	Presbyterian	62	78

Presidents of the United States (continued)

Name and (party)	Term	State of birth	Born	Died	Religion	Age at inaug.	Age at death
35. Kennedy (D)[4]	1961–1963	Mass.	5/29/1917	11/22/1963	Roman Catholic	43	46
36. L. B. Johnson (D)	1963–1969	Tex.	8/27/1908	1/22/1973	Disciples of Christ	55	64
37. Nixon (R)[8]	1969–1974	Calif.	1/9/1913	....	Quaker	56	..
38. Ford (R)	1974–	Neb.	7/14/1913	....	Episcopalian	61	..

[1] F—Federalist; DR—Democratic–Republican; D—Democratic; W—Whig; R—Republican; U—Union. [2] No party for first election. The party system in the U.S. made its appearance during Washington's first term. [3] Died in office. [4] Assassinated in office. [5] The Republican National Convention of 1864 adopted the name Union Party. It renominated Lincoln for President; for Vice President it nominated Johnson, a War Democrat. Although frequently listed as a Republican Vice President and President, Johnson undoubtedly considered himself strictly a member of the Union Party. When that party broke apart after 1868, he returned to the Democratic Party. [6] Johnson was not a professed church member; however, he admired the Baptist principles of church government. [7] Second nonconsecutive term. [8] Resigned Aug. 9, 1974.

Vice Presidents of the United States

Name and (party)[1]	Term	State of birth	Birth and death dates	President served under
1. John Adams (F)[2]	1789–1797	Massachusetts	1735–1826	Washington
2. Thomas Jefferson (DR)	1797–1801	Virginia	1743–1826	J. Adams
3. Aaron Burr (DR)	1801–1805	New Jersey	1756–1836	Jefferson
4. George Clinton (DR)[3]	1805–1812	New York	1739–1812	Jefferson and Madison
5. Elbridge Gerry (DR)[3]	1813–1814	Massachusetts	1744–1814	Madison
6. Daniel D. Tompkins (DR)	1817–1825	New York	1774–1825	Monroe
7. John C. Calhoun[4]	1825–1832	South Carolina	1782–1850	J. Q. Adams and Jackson
8. Martin Van Buren (D)	1833–1837	New York	1782–1862	Jackson
9. Richard M. Johnson (D)	1837–1841	Kentucky	1780–1850	Van Buren
10. John Tyler (W)[5]	1841	Virginia	1790–1862	W. H. Harrison
11. George M. Dallas (D)	1845–1849	Pennsylvania	1792–1864	Polk
12. Millard Fillmore (W)[5]	1849–1850	New York	1800–1874	Taylor
13. William R. King (D)[3]	1853	North Carolina	1786–1853	Pierce
14. John C. Breckinridge (D)	1857–1861	Kentucky	1821–1875	Buchanan
15. Hannibal Hamlin (R)	1861–1865	Maine	1809–1891	Lincoln
16. Andrew Johnson (U)[5]	1865	North Carolina	1808–1875	Lincoln
17. Schuyler Colfax (R)	1869–1873	New York	1823–1885	Grant
18. Henry Wilson (R)[3]	1873–1875	New Hampshire	1812–1875	Grant
19. William A. Wheeler (R)	1877–1881	New York	1819–1887	Hayes
20. Chester A. Arthur (R)[5]	1881	Vermont	1830–1886	Garfield
21. Thomas A. Hendricks (D)[3]	1885	Ohio	1819–1885	Cleveland
22. Levi P. Morton (R)	1889–1893	Vermont	1824–1920	B. Harrison
23. Adlai E. Stevenson (D)	1893–1897	Kentucky	1835–1914	Cleveland
24. Garret A. Hobart (R)[3]	1897–1899	New Jersey	1844–1899	McKinley
25. Theodore Roosevelt (R)[5]	1901	New York	1858–1919	McKinley
26. Charles W. Fairbanks (R)	1905–1909	Ohio	1852–1918	T. Roosevelt
27. James S. Sherman (R)[3]	1909–1912	New York	1855–1912	Taft
28. Thomas R. Marshall (D)	1913–1921	Indiana	1854–1925	Wilson
29. Calvin Coolidge (R)[5]	1921–1923	Vermont	1872–1933	Harding
30. Charles G. Dawes (R)	1925–1929	Ohio	1865–1951	Coolidge
31. Charles Curtis (R)	1929–1933	Kansas	1860–1936	Hoover
32. John N. Garner (D)	1933–1941	Texas	1868–1967	F. D. Roosevelt
33. Henry A. Wallace (D)	1941–1945	Iowa	1888–1965	F. D. Roosevelt
34. Harry S. Truman (D)[5]	1945	Missouri	1884–1972	F. D. Roosevelt
35. Alben W. Barkley (D)	1949–1953	Kentucky	1877–1956	Truman
36. Richard M. Nixon (R)	1953–1961	California	1913–	Eisenhower
37. Lyndon B. Johnson (D)[5]	1961–1963	Texas	1908–1973	Kennedy
38. Hubert H. Humphrey (D)	1965–1969	South Dakota	1911–	Johnson
39. Spiro T. Agnew (R)[6]	1969–1973	Maryland	1918–	Nixon
40. Gerald R. Ford (R)[7]	1973–1974	Nebraska	1913–	Nixon
41. Nelson A. Rockefeller (R)[8]	1974–	Maine	1908–	Ford

[1] F—Federalist; DR—Democratic-Republican; D—Democratic; W—Whig; R—Republican; U—Union. [2] No party for first election. The party system in the U.S. made its appearance during Washington's first term as President. [3] Died in office. [4] Democratic-Republican with J. Q. Adams; Democratic with Jackson. Calhoun resigned in 1832 to become a U.S. Senator. [5] Succeeded to presidency on death of President. [6] Resigned Oct. 10, 1973, after pleading no contest to Federal income tax evasion charges. [7] Nominated by Nixon on Oct. 12, 1973, under provisions of 25th Amendment. Confirmed by Congress on Dec. 6, 1973, and was sworn in same day. He became President Aug. 9, 1974, upon Nixon's resignation. [8] Nominated by Ford Aug. 20, 1974; confirmed by Congress on Dec. 19, 1974, and was sworn in same day.

Wives and Children of the Presidents of the United States

President	Wife's name	Year and place of wife's birth	Married	Wife died	Children of President* Sons	Daughters
Washington...........	Mrs. Martha Dandridge Custis	1732, Va.	1759	1802	..	..
John Adams..........	Abigail Smith	1744, Mass.	1764	1818	3	2
Jefferson.............	Mrs. Martha Wayles Skelton	1748, Va.	1772	1782	1	5
Madison.............	Mrs. Dorothy "Dolley" Payne Todd	1768, N. C.	1794	1849	..	..
Monroe..............	Elizabeth "Eliza" Kortright	1768, N. Y.	1786	1830	..	2
J. Q. Adams.........	Louisa Catherine Johnson	1775, England	1797	1852	3	1
Jackson..............	Mrs. Rachel Donelson Robards	1767, Va.	1791	1828	..	..
Van Buren...........	Hannah Hoes	1788 N. Y.	1807	1819	4	..
W. H. Harrison.........	Anna Symmes	1775, N. J.	1795	1864	6	4
Tyler................	Letitia Christian	1790, Va.	1813	1842	3	4
	Julia Gardiner	1820, N. Y.	1844	1889	5	2
Polk.................	Sarah Childress	1803, Tenn.	1824	1891	..	..
Taylor...............	Margaret Smith	1788, Md.	1810	1852	1	5
Fillmore.............	Abigail Powers	1798, N. Y.	1826	1853	1	1
	Mrs. Caroline Carmichael McIntosh	1813, N. J.	1858	1881	..	..
Pierce...............	Jane Means Appleton	1806, N. H.	1834	1863	3	..
Buchanan............	(Unmarried)	....	....	....	..	..
Lincoln.............	Mary Todd	1818, Ky.	1842	1882	4	..
A. Johnson...........	Eliza McCardle	1810, Tenn.	1827	1876	3	2
Grant...............	Julia Dent	1826, Mo.	1848	1902	3	1
Hayes...............	Lucy Ware Webb	1831, Ohio	1852	1889	7	1
Garfield.............	Lucretia Rudolph	1832, Ohio	1858	1918	5	2
Arthur...............	Ellen Lewis Herndon	1837, Va.	1859	1880	2	1
Cleveland............	Frances Folsom	1864, N. Y.	1886	1947	2	3
B. Harrison...........	Caroline Lavinia Scott	1832, Ohio	1853	1892	1	1
	Mrs. Mary Scott Lord Dimmick	1858, Pa.	1896	1948	..	1
McKinley.............	Ida Saxton	1847, Ohio	1871	1907	..	2
T. Roosevelt.........	Alice Hathaway Lee	1861, Mass.	1880	1884	..	1
	Edith Kermit Carow	1861, Conn.	1886	1948	4	1
Taft.................	Helen Herron	1861, Ohio	1886	1943	2	1
Wilson...............	Ellen Louise Axson	1860, Ga.	1885	1914	..	3
	Mrs. Edith Bolling Galt	1872, Va.	1915	1961	..	..
Harding..............	Mrs. Florence Kling DeWolfe	1860, Ohio	1891	1924	..	..
Coolidge.............	Grace Anna Goodhue	1879, Vt.	1905	1957	2	..
Hoover..............	Lou Henry	1875, Iowa	1899	1944	2	..
F. D. Roosevelt.......	Anna Eleanor Roosevelt	1884, N. Y.	1905	1962	5	1
Truman..............	Bess Wallace	1885, Mo.	1919	....	..	1
Eisenhower..........	Mamie Geneva Doud	1896, Iowa	1916	....	2	..
Kennedy.............	Jacqueline Lee Bouvier	1929, N. Y.	1953	....	2*	1
L. B. Johnson........	Claudia Alta Taylor	1912, Tex.	1934	....	..	2
Nixon	Thelma Catherine "Patricia" Ryan	1912, Nev.	1940	....	..	2
Ford	Mrs. Elizabeth "Betty" Bloomer Warren	1918, Ill.	1948	....	3	1

*Includes children who died in infancy.

HOW A PRESIDENT IS NOMINATED AND ELECTED

THE NATIONAL CONVENTIONS of both major parties are held sometime during the summer of a presidential-election year. Earlier, each party selects delegates by primaries, conventions, committees, etc.

For their 1976 National Convention, the Republicans allowed each state a base of 6 delegates at large; the District of Columbia, 14; Puerto Rico, 8; Guam and the Virgin Islands, 4 each. In addition, each state received 3 district delegates for each of its Representatives in the House. This did not apply to the District of Columbia, Puerto Rico, Guam and the Virgin Islands.

Each state was awarded additional delegates at large on the basis of having supported or elected Republican candidates for President, Senator, Governor and U.S. Representative in the 1972 and 1974 elections.

The number of delegates at the 1976 convention, held in Kansas City, was 2,259. Following is the apportionment of delegates by state:

Ala.	37	Fla.	66	Ky.	37	Mont.	20	Ohio	97	Tex.	100
Alaska	19	Ga.	48	La.	41	Neb.	25	Okla.	36	Utah	20
Ariz.	29	Guam	4	Me.	20	Nev.	18	Ore.	30	Vt.	18
Ark.	27	Hawaii	19	Md.	43	N.H.	21	Pa.	103	Va.	51
Calif.	167	Idaho	21	Mass.	43	N.J.	67	P.R.	8	V.I.	4
Colo.	31	Ill.	101	Mich.	84	N.M.	21	R.I.	19	Wash.	38
Conn.	35	Ind.	54	Minn.	42	N.Y.	154	S.C.	36	W.Va.	28
Del.	17	Iowa	36	Miss.	30	N.C.	54	S.D.	20	Wis.	45
D.C.	14	Kan.	34	Mo.	49	N.D.	18	Tenn.	43	Wyo.	17

The Democrats also based the number of delegates on a state's showing in a recent election, taking into account party enrollment as of Jan. 1, 1976, and total population. Thus, there were 3,048 delegates casting 3,008[1] votes, at the convention which was held in New York City. Following is the apportionment of votes by states:

Ala.	35	D.C.	17	Kan.	34	Mo.	71	N.D.	13	Tenn.	46
Alaska	10	Fla.	81	Ky.	46	Mont.	17	Ohio	152	Tex.	130
Ariz.	25	Ga.	50	La.	41	Neb.	23	Okla.	37	Utah	18
Ark.	26	Guam	3	Me.	20	Nev.	11	Ore.	34	Vt.	12
Calif.	280	Hawaii	17	Md.	53	N.H.	17	Pa.	178	V.I.	3
Canal Zone	3	Idaho	16	Mass.	104	N.J.	108	P.R.	22	Va.	54
Colo.	35	Ill.	169	Mich.	133	N.M.	18	R.I.	22	Wash.	53
Conn.	51	Ind.	75	Minn.	65	N.Y.	274	S.C.	31	W.Va.	33
Del.	12	Iowa	47	Miss.	24	N.C.	61	S.D.	17	Wis.	68
										Wyo.	10

[1] Includes 3 votes for Democrats abroad.

The Conventions

At each convention a temporary chairman is chosen. After a credentials committee seats the delegates, a permanent chairman is elected. The convention then votes on a platform, drawn up by the platform committee.

By the third or fourth day, presidential nominations begin. The chairman calls the roll of states alphabetically. A state may place a candidate in nomination or yield to another state.

Voting, again alphabetically by voice vote, begins after all nominations have been made and seconded. A simple majority is required in each party, although this may require many ballots.

Finally, the vice-presidential candidate is selected. Although there is no law saying that the candidates *must* come from different states, it is practically necessary for this to be the case. Otherwise, according to the Constitution (*see* Amendment XII), electors from that state could vote for only one of the candidates and would have to cast their other vote for some person of another state. This could result in a presidential candidate's receiving a majority electoral vote and his running mate's failing to.

The Electoral College

The next step in the process is the nomination of electors in each state, according to its laws. These electors must not be Federal office holders. In the November election, the voters cast their votes for electors, not for President. In some states, the ballots include only the names of the presidential and vice-presidential candidates; in others, they include only names of the electors. Nowadays, it is rare for electors to be split between parties. The last such occurrence was in North Carolina in 1968;* the last before that,

in Tennessee in 1948. On three occasions (1824, 1876 and 1888), the presidential candidate with the largest popular vote failed to obtain an electoral-vote majority.

Each state has as many electors as it has Senators and Representatives. For the 1972 election, the total electors were 538, based on 100 Senators, 435 Representatives, plus 3 electoral votes from the District of Columbia as a result of the 23rd Amendment to the Constitution.

On the first Monday after the second Wednesday in December, the electors cast their votes in their respective state capitols. Constitutionally they may vote for someone other than the party candidate but usually they do not since they are pledged to one party and its candidate on the ballot. Should the presidential or vice-presidential candidate die between the November election and the December meetings, the electors pledged to vote for him could vote for whomever they pleased. However, it seems certain that the national committee would attempt to get an agreement among the state party leaders for a replacement candidate.

The votes of the electors, certified by the states, are sent to Congress, where the president of the Senate opens the certificates and has them counted in the presence of both Houses on January 6. The new President is inaugurated at noon on January 20.

Should no candidate receive a majority of the electoral vote for President, the House of Representatives chooses a President from among the three highest candidates, voting, not as individuals, but as states, with a majority (now 26) needed to elect. Should no vice-presidential candidate obtain the majority, the Senate, voting as individuals, chooses from the highest two.

* In 1956, 1 of Alabama's 11 electoral votes was cast for Walter B. Jones. In 1960, 6 of Alabama's 11 electoral votes and 1 of Oklahoma's 8 electoral votes were cast for Harry Flood Byrd. (Byrd also received all 8 of Mississippi's electoral votes.)

Facts About Elections

Candidate with highest popular vote: Nixon (1972), 47,169,911.

Candidate with highest electoral vote: F. D. Roosevelt (1936), 523.

Candidate carrying most states: Nixon (1972), 49.

Candidate running most times: Norman Thomas, 6 (1928, 1932, 1936, 1940, 1944, 1948).

Candidate elected, defeated, then reelected: Cleveland (1884, 1888, 1892).

Presidential Elections, 1789 to 1972

NOTE: For the original method of electing the President and the Vice President (elections of 1789, 1792, 1796, and 1800), see Article II, Section 1, of the Constitution. The election of 1804 was the first one in which the electors voted for President and Vice President on separate ballots. (See Amendment XII to the Constitution.)

Year	Presidential candidates	Party	Electoral vote	Year	Presidential candidates	Party	Electoral vote
1789[1]	George Washington	(no party)	69	1796	John Adams	Federalist	71
	John Adams	(no party)	34		Thomas Jefferson	Dem.-Rep.	68
	Scattering	(no party)	35		Thomas Pinckney	Federalist	59
	Votes not cast		8		Aaron Burr	Dem.-Rep.	30
1792	George Washington	Federalist	132		Scattering		48
	John Adams	Federalist	77	1800[2]	Thomas Jefferson	Dem.-Rep.	73
	George Clinton	Anti-Federalist	50		Aaron Burr	Dem.-Rep.	73
	Thomas Jefferson	Anti-Federalist	4		John Adams	Federalist	65
	Aaron Burr	Anti-Federalist	1		Charles C. Pinckney	Federalist	64
	Votes not cast		6		John Jay	Federalist	1

Year	Presidential candidates	Party	Electoral vote	Vice-presidential candidates	Party	Electoral vote
1804	Thomas Jefferson	Dem.-Rep.	162	George Clinton	Dem.-Rep.	162
	Charles C. Pinckney	Federalist	14	Rufus King	Federalist	14
1808	James Madison	Dem.-Rep.	122	George Clinton	Dem.-Rep.	113
	Charles C. Pinckney	Federalist	47	Rufus King	Federalist	47
	George Clinton	Dem.-Rep.	6	John Langdon	Ind. (no party)	9
	Votes not cast		1	James Madison	Dem.-Rep.	3
				James Monroe	Dem.-Rep.	3
				Votes not cast		1
1812	James Madison	Dem.-Rep.	128	Elbridge Gerry	Dem.-Rep.	131
	De Witt Clinton	Federalist	89	Jared Ingersoll	Federalist	86
	Votes not cast		1	Votes not cast		1
1816	James Monroe	Dem.-Rep.	183	Daniel D. Tompkins	Dem.-Rep.	183
	Rufus King	Federalist	34	John E. Howard	Federalist	22
	Votes not cast		4	James Ross	Ind. (no party)	5
				John Marshall	Federalist	4
				Robert G. Harper	Ind. (no party)	3
				Votes not cast		4
1820	James Monroe	Dem.-Rep.	231	Daniel D. Tompkins	Dem.-Rep.	218
	John Quincy Adams	Ind. (no party)	1	Richard Stockton	Ind. (no party)	8
	Votes not cast		3	Daniel Rodney	Ind. (no party)	4
				Richard Rush	Ind. (no party)	1
				Robert G. Harper	Ind. (no party)	1
				Votes not cast		3
1824[3]	John Quincy Adams	(no party)	84	John C. Calhoun	(no party)	182
	Andrew Jackson	(no party)	99	Nathan Sanford	(no party)	30
	William H. Crawford	(no party)	41	Nathaniel Macon	(no party)	24
	Henry Clay	(no party)	37	Andrew Jackson	(no party)	13
				Martin Van Buren	(no party)	9
				Henry Clay	(no party)	2
				Votes not cast		1
1828	Andrew Jackson	Democratic	178	John C. Calhoun	Democratic	171
	John Quincy Adams	Natl. Rep.	83	Richard Rush	Natl. Rep.	83
				William Smith	Democratic	7
1832	Andrew Jackson	Democratic	219	Martin Van Buren	Democratic	189
	Henry Clay	Natl. Rep.	49	John Sergeant	Natl. Rep.	49
	John Floyd	Ind. (no party)	11	Henry Lee	Ind. (no party)	11
	William Wirt	Antimasonic[4]	7	Amos Ellmaker	Antimasonic	7
	Votes not cast		2	William Wilkins	Ind. (no party)	30
				Votes not cast		2
1836	Martin Van Buren	Democratic	170	Richard M. Johnson[5]	Democratic	147
	William H. Harrison	Whig	73	Francis Granger	Whig	77
	Hugh L. White	Whig	26	John Tyler	Whig	47
	Daniel Webster	Whig	14	William Smith	Ind. (no party)	23
	W. P. Mangum	Ind. (no party)	11			

[1] Only 10 states participated in the election. The New York legislature chose no electors, and North Carolina and Rhode Island had not yet ratified the Constitution.   [2] As Jefferson and Burr were tied, the House of Representatives chose the President. In a vote by states, 10 votes were cast for Jefferson, 4 for Burr; 2 votes were not cast.   [3] As no candidate had an electoral-vote majority, the House of Representatives chose the President from the first three. In a vote by states, 13 votes were cast for Adams, 7 for Jackson, and 4 for Crawford.   [4] The Antimasonic party on Sept. 26, 1831, was the first party to hold a nominating convention to choose candidates for President and Vice President. [5] As Johnson did not have an electoral-vote majority, the Senate chose him 33–14 over Granger, the others being legally out of the race.

Year	Presidential candidates	Party	Electoral vote	Vice-presidential candidates	Party	Electoral vote
1840	William H. Harrison[1]	Whig	234	John Tyler	Whig	234
	Martin Van Buren	Democratic	60	Richard M. Johnson	Democratic	48
				L. W. Tazewell	Ind. (no party)	11
				James K. Polk	Democratic	1
1844	James K. Polk	Democratic	170	George M. Dallas	Democratic	170
	Henry Clay	Whig	105	Theo. Frelinghuysen	Whig	105
1848	Zachary Taylor[2]	Whig	163	Millard Fillmore	Whig	163
	Lewis Cass	Democratic	127	William O. Butler	Democratic	127
1852	Franklin Pierce	Democratic	254	William R. King	Democratic	254
	Winfield Scott	Whig	42	William A. Graham	Whig	42
1856	James Buchanan	Democratic	174	John C. Breckinridge	Democratic	174
	John C. Frémont	Republican	114	William L. Dayton	Republican	114
	Millard Fillmore	American[3]	8	A. J. Donelson	American[3]	8
1860	Abraham Lincoln	Republican	180	Hannibal Hamlin	Republican	180
	John C. Breckinridge	Democratic	72	Joseph Lane	Democratic	72
	John Bell	Const. Union	39	Edward Everett	Const. Union	39
	Stephen A. Douglas	Democratic	12	H. V. Johnson	Democratic	12
1864	Abraham Lincoln[4]	Union[5]	212	Andrew Johnson	Union[5]	212
	George B. McClellan	Democratic	21	G. H. Pendleton	Democratic	21
1868	Ulysses S. Grant	Republican	214	Schuyler Colfax	Republican	214
	Horatio Seymour	Democratic	80	Francis P. Blair, Jr.	Democratic	80
	Votes not counted[6]		23	Votes not counted[6]		23

Year	Presidential candidates	Party	Electoral vote	Popular vote	Vice-presidential candidates and party
1872	Ulysses S. Grant	Republican	286	3,597,132	Henry Wilson—R
	Horace Greeley	Dem., Liberal Rep.	(⁷)	2,834,125	B. Gratz Brown—D, LR—(47)
	Thomas A. Hendricks	Democratic	42		Scattering—(19)
	B. Gratz Brown	Dem., Liberal Rep.	18		Votes not counted—(14)
	Charles J. Jenkins	Democratic	2		
	David Davis	Democratic	1		
	Votes not counted		17		
1876[8]	Rutherford B. Hayes	Republican	185	4,033,768	William A. Wheeler—R
	Samuel J. Tilden	Democratic	184	4,285,992	Thomas A. Hendricks—D
	Peter Cooper	Greenback	0	81,737	Samuel F. Cary—G
1880	James A. Garfield[9]	Republican	214	4,449,053	Chester A. Arthur—R
	Winfield S. Hancock	Democratic	155	4,442,035	William H. English—D
	James B. Weaver	Greenback	0	308,578	B. J. Chambers—G
1884	Grover Cleveland	Democratic	219	4,911,017	Thomas A. Hendricks—D
	James G. Blaine	Republican	182	4,848,334	John A. Logan—R
	Benjamin F. Butler	Greenback	0	175,370	A. M. West—G
	John P. St. John	Prohibition	0	150,369	William Daniel—P
1888	Benjamin Harrison	Republican	233	5,440,216	Levi P. Morton—R
	Grover Cleveland	Democratic	168	5,538,233	A. G. Thurman—D
	Clinton B. Fisk	Prohibition	0	249,506	John A. Brooks—P
	Alson J. Streeter	Union Labor	0	146,935	Charles E. Cunningham—UL
1892	Grover Cleveland	Democratic	277	5,556,918	Adlai E. Stevenson—D
	Benjamin Harrison	Republican	145	5,176,108	Whitelaw Reid—R
	James B. Weaver	People's[10]	22	1,041,028	James G. Field—Peo
	John Bidwell	Prohibition	0	264,133	James B. Cranfill—P
1896	William McKinley	Republican	271	7,035,638	Garret A. Hobart—R
	William J. Bryan	Dem., People's[10]	176	6,467,946	Arthur Sewall—D—(149)
					Thomas E. Watson—Peo—(27)
	John M. Palmer	Natl. Dem.	0	133,148	Simon B. Buckner—ND
	Joshua Levering	Prohibition	0	132,007	Hale Johnson—P

[1] Harrison died Apr. 4, 1841, and Tyler succeeded him Apr. 6. [2] Taylor died July 9, 1850, and Fillmore succeeded him July 10. [3] Also known as the Know-Nothing party. [4] Lincoln died Apr. 15, 1865, and Johnson succeeded him the same day. [5] Name adopted by the Republican National Convention of 1864. Johnson was a War Democrat. [6] 23 Southern electoral votes were excluded. [7] See Election of 1872 in *Unusual Voting Results* under Elections, Presidential in Index. [8] See Election of 1876 in *Unusual Voting Results* under Elections, Presidential in Index. [9] Garfield died Sept. 19, 1881; Arthur succeeded him Sept. 20. [10] Members of People's party were called Populists.

Year	Presidential candidates	Party	Electoral vote	Popular vote	Vice-presidential candidates and party
1900	William McKinley[1]	Republican	292	7,219,530	Theodore Roosevelt—R
	William J. Bryan	Dem., People's[2]	155	6,358,071	Adlai E. Stevenson—D, Peo
	Eugene V. Debs	Social Democratic	0	94,768	Job Harriman—SD
1904	Theodore Roosevelt	Republican	336	7,628,834	Charles W. Fairbanks—R
	Alton B. Parker	Democratic	140	5,084,491	Henry G. Davis—D
	Eugene V. Debs	Socialist	0	402,400	Benjamin Hanford—S
1908	William H. Taft	Republican	321	7,679,006	James S. Sherman—R
	William J. Bryan	Democratic	162	6,409,106	John W. Kern—D
	Eugene V. Debs	Socialist	0	420,820	Benjamin Hanford—S
1912	Woodrow Wilson	Democratic	435	6,286,214	Thomas R. Marshall—D
	Theodore Roosevelt	Progressive	88	4,126,020	Hiram Johnson—Prog
	William H. Taft	Republican	8	3,483,922	Nicholas M. Butler—R[3]
	Eugene V. Debs	Socialist	0	897,011	Emil Seidel—S
1916	Woodrow Wilson	Democratic	277	9,129,606	Thomas R. Marshall—D
	Charles E. Hughes	Republican	254	8,538,221	Charles W. Fairbanks—R
	A. L. Benson	Socialist	0	585,113	G. R. Kirkpatrick—S
1920	Warren G. Harding[4]	Republican	404	16,152,200	Calvin Coolidge—R
	James M. Cox	Democratic	127	9,147,353	Franklin D. Roosevelt—D
	Eugene V. Debs	Socialist	0	917,799	Seymour Stedman—S
1924	Calvin Coolidge	Republican	382	15,725,016	Charles G. Dawes—R
	John W. Davis	Democratic	136	8,385,586	Charles W. Bryan—D
	Robert M. LaFollette	Progressive, Socialist	13	4,822,856	Burton K. Wheeler—Prog S
1928	Herbert Hoover	Republican	444	21,392,190	Charles Curtis—R
	Alfred E. Smith	Democratic	87	15,016,443	Joseph T. Robinson—D
	Norman Thomas	Socialist	0	267,420	James H. Maurer—S
1932	Franklin D. Roosevelt	Democratic	472	22,821,857	John N. Garner—D
	Herbert Hoover	Republican	59	15,761,841	Charles Curtis—R
	Norman Thomas	Socialist	0	884,781	James H. Maurer—S
1936	Franklin D. Roosevelt	Democratic	523	27,751,597	John N. Garner—D
	Alfred M. Landon	Republican	8	16,679,583	Frank Knox—R
	Norman Thomas	Socialist	0	187,720	George Nelson—S
1940	Franklin D. Roosevelt	Democratic	449	27,244,160	Henry A. Wallace—D
	Wendell L. Willkie	Republican	82	22,305,198	Charles L. McNary—R
	Norman Thomas	Socialist	0	99,557	Maynard C. Krueger—S
1944	Franklin D. Roosevelt[5]	Democratic	432	25,602,504	Harry S. Truman—D
	Thomas E. Dewey	Republican	99	22,006,285	John W. Bricker—R
	Norman Thomas	Socialist	0	80,518	Darlington Hoopes—S
1948	Harry S. Truman	Democratic	303	24,179,345	Alben W. Barkley—D
	Thomas E. Dewey	Republican	189	21,991,291	Earl Warren—R
	J. Strom Thurmond	States' Rights Dem.	39	1,176,125	Fielding L. Wright—SR
	Henry A. Wallace	Progressive	0	1,157,326	Glen Taylor—Prog
	Norman Thomas	Socialist	0	139,572	Tucker P. Smith—S
1952	Dwight D. Eisenhower	Republican	442	33,936,234	Richard M. Nixon—R
	Adlai E. Stevenson	Democratic	89	27,314,992	John J. Sparkman—D
1956[6]	Dwight D. Eisenhower	Republican	457	35,590,472	Richard M. Nixon—R
	Adlai E. Stevenson	Democratic	73	26,022,752	Estes Kefauver—D
1960[7]	John F. Kennedy[8]	Democratic	303	34,226,731	Lyndon B. Johnson—D
	Richard M. Nixon	Republican	219	34,108,157	Henry Cabot Lodge—R
1964	Lyndon B. Johnson	Democratic	486	43,129,484	Hubert H. Humphrey—D
	Barry M. Goldwater	Republican	52	27,178,188	William E. Miller—R
1968	Richard M. Nixon	Republican	301	31,785,480	Spiro T. Agnew—R
	Hubert H. Humphrey	Democratic	191	31,275,166	Edmund S. Muskie—D
	George C. Wallace	American Independent	46	9,906,473	Curtis F. LeMay—AI
1972	Richard M. Nixon[10]	Republican	520[9]	47,169,911	Spiro T. Agnew—R
	George McGovern	Democratic	17	29,170,383	Sargent Shriver—D
	John G. Schmitz	American	0	1,099,482	Thomas J. Anderson—A

[1] McKinley died Sept. 14, 1901, and Roosevelt succeeded him the same day. [2] The members of the People's party were known as Populists. [3] James S. Sherman, Republican candidate for Vice President, died Oct. 30, 1912, and the Republican Electoral votes were cast for Butler. [4] Harding died Aug. 2, 1923, and Coolidge succeeded him Aug. 3 [5] Roosevelt died Apr. 12, 1945, and Truman succeeded him the same day. [6] One electoral vote from Alabama was cast for Walter B. Jones. [7] Sen. Harry F. Byrd received 15 electoral votes. [8] Kennedy died Nov. 22, 1963, and Johnson succeeded him the same day. [9] One electoral vote from Virginia was cast for John Hospers, Libertarian Party. [10] Nixon resigned Aug. 9, 1974, and Gerald R. Ford succeeded him the same day.

Presidential Election of 1960

Source: America at the Polls, compiled and edited by Richard M. Scammon.

PRINCIPAL CANDIDATES FOR PRESIDENT AND VICE PRESIDENT

Democratic—John F. Kennedy; Lyndon B. Johnson.
Republican—Richard M. Nixon; Henry Cabot Lodge.

State	Total	Dem.	Rep.	Plur.	Electoral D	Electoral R	Byrd[1]	Votes at National Conventions Dem.	Votes at National Conventions Rep.
Alabama	570,225	324,050	237,981	86,069 D	5	..	6[2]	29	22
Alaska	60,762	29,809	30,953	1,144 R	..	3	..	9	6
Arizona	398,491	176,781	221,241	44,460 R	..	4	..	17	14
Arkansas	428,509	215,049	184,508	30,541 D	8	..	..	27	16
California	6,506,578	3,224,099	3,259,722	35,623 R	..	32	..	81	70
Colorado	736,236	330,629	402,242	71,613 R	..	6	..	21	18
Connecticut	1,222,883	657,055	565,813	91,242 D	8	..	..	21	22
Delaware	196,683	99,590	96,373	3,217 D	3	..	..	11	12
Florida	1,544,176	748,700	795,476	46,776 R	..	10	..	29	26
Georgia	733,349	458,638	274,472	184,166 D	12	..	..	33	24
Hawaii	184,705	92,410	92,295	115 D	3	..	..	9	12
Idaho	300,450	138,853	161,597	22,744 R	..	4	..	13	14
Illinois	4,757,409	2,377,846	2,368,988	8,858 D	27	..	..	69	60
Indiana	2,135,360	952,358	1,175,120	222,762 R	..	13	..	34	32
Iowa	1,273,810	550,565	722,381	171,816 R	..	10	..	26	26
Kansas	928,825	363,213	561,474	198,261 R	..	8	..	21	22
Kentucky	1,124,462	521,855	602,607	80,752 R	..	10	..	31	26
Louisiana	807,891	407,339	230,980	176,359 D	10	..	..	26	26
Maine	421,767	181,159	240,608	59,449 R	..	5	..	15	16
Maryland	1,055,349	565,808	489,538	76,270 D	9	..	..	24	24
Massachusetts	2,469,480	1,487,174	976,750	510,424 D	16	..	..	41	38
Michigan	3,318,097	1,687,269	1,620,428	66,841 D	20	..	..	51	46
Minnesota	1,541,887	779,933	757,915	22,018 D	11	..	..	31	28
Mississippi	298,171	108,362	73,561	7,886 U[3]	..	..	8[2]	23	12
Missouri	1,934,422	972,201	962,221	9,980 D	13	..	..	39	26
Montana	277,579	134,891	141,841	6,950 R	..	4	..	17	14
Nebraska	613,095	232,542	380,553	148,011 R	..	6	..	16	18
Nevada	107,267	54,880	52,387	2,493 D	3	..	..	15	12
New Hampshire	295,761	137,772	157,989	20,217 R	..	4	..	11	14
New Jersey	2,773,111	1,385,415	1,363,324	22,091 D	16	..	..	41	38
New Mexico	311,107	156,027	153,733	2,294 D	4	..	..	17	14
New York	7,291,079	3,830,085[4]	3,446,419	383,666 D	45	..	..	114	96
North Carolina	1,368,556	713,136	655,420	57,716 D	14	..	..	37	28
North Dakota	278,431	123,963	154,310	30,347 R	..	4	..	11	14
Ohio	4,161,859	1,944,248	2,217,611	273,363 R	..	25	..	64	56
Oklahoma	903,150	370,111	533,039	162,928 R	..	7	1	29	22
Oregon	776,421	367,402	408,060	40,658 R	..	6	..	17	18
Pennsylvania	5,006,541	2,556,282	2,439,956	116,326 D	32	..	..	81	70
Rhode Island	405,535	258,032	147,502	110,530 D	4	..	..	17	14
South Carolina	386,688	198,129	188,558	9,571 D	8	..	..	21	13
South Dakota	306,487	128,070	178,417	50,347 R	..	4	..	11	14
Tennessee	1,051,792	481,453	556,577	75,124 R	..	11	..	33	28
Texas	2,311,084	1,167,567	1,121,310	46,257 D	24	..	..	61	54
Utah	374,709	169,248	205,361	36,113 R	..	4	..	13	14
Vermont	167,324	69,186	98,131	28,945 R	..	3	..	9	12
Virginia	771,449	362,327	404,521	42,194 R	..	12	..	33	30
Washington	1,241,572	599,298	629,273	29,975 R	..	9	..	27	24
West Virginia	837,781	441,786	395,995	45,791 D	8	..	..	25	22
Wisconsin	1,729,082	830,805	895,175	64,370 R	..	12	..	31	30
Wyoming	140,782	63,331	77,451	14,120 R	..	3	..	15	12
TOTAL	68,838,219	34,226,731	34,108,157	118,574 D	303	219	15	1,521[5]	1,331[6]

[1] For Senator Harry Flood Byrd, who was not a candidate. [2] Unpledged electors. [3] An unpledged Democratic elector ticket (116,248 votes) carried the state. [4] Contains 3,423,909 Democratic and 406,176 Liberal votes. [5] Includes 24 votes allocated to District of Columbia and U. S. territories. [6] Includes 12 votes allocated to District of Columbia and U. S. territories.

OTHER CANDIDATES FOR PRESIDENT: Conservative Party, C. Benton Coiner; Conservative Party, J. Bracken Lee; Constitution Party, Merritt B. Curtis; Constitution Party, Charles L. Sullivan; Independent Afro-American Party, Clennon King; National States' Rights Party, Orval E. Faubus; Prohibition Party, Rutherford L. Decker; Socialist Labor Party, Eric Hass; Socialist Workers Party, Farrell Dobbs; Tax Cut Party, Lar Daly.

NATIONAL TOTALS OF OTHER VOTES: Socialist Labor, 47,522; Prohibition, 46,203; National States' Rights, 44,977; Socialist Workers, 40,165; Constitution, 19,563; Conservative, 12,912; Tax Cut, 1,767; Independent Afro-American, 1,485; others and scattered, 288,737.

Presidential Election of 1964

Source: America at the Polls, compiled and edited by Richard M. Scammon.

PRINCIPAL CANDIDATES FOR PRESIDENT AND VICE PRESIDENT

Democratic—Lyndon B. Johnson; Hubert H. Humphrey.
Republican—Barry M. Goldwater; William E. Miller.

State	Total	Dem.	Rep.	Plurality	Electoral D	Electoral R	Votes at National Conventions Dem.	Votes at National Conventions Rep.
Alabama..........	689,818	([1])	479,085	268,353 R[2]	..	10	38	20
Alaska...........	67,259	44,329	22,930	21,399 D	3	..	12	12
Arizona..........	480,770	237,753	242,535	4,782 R	..	5	19	16
Arkansas.........	560,246	314,197	243,264	70,933 D	6	..	32	12
California........	7,057,586	4,171,877	2,879,108	1,292,769 D	40	..	154	86
Colorado.........	776,986	476,024	296,767	179,257 D	6	..	23	18
Connecticut.......	1,218,578	826,269	390,996	435,273 D	8	..	43	16
Delaware.........	201,320	122,704	78,078	44,626 D	3	..	22	12
D. C.............	198,597	169,796	28,801	140,995 D	3	..	16	9
Florida...........	1,854,481	948,540	905,941	42,599 D	14	..	51	34
Georgia..........	1,139,335	522,556	616,584	94,028 R	..	12	53	24
Hawaii...........	207,271	163,249	44,022	119,227 D	4	..	25	8
Idaho............	292,477	148,920	143,557	5,363 D	4	..	15	14
Illinois...........	4,702,841	2,796,833	1,905,946	890,887 D	26	..	114	58
Indiana..........	2,091,606	1,170,848	911,118	259,730 D	13	..	51	32
Iowa.............	1,184,539	733,030	449,148	283,882 D	9	..	35	24
Kansas...........	857,901	464,028	386,579	77,449 D	7	..	27	20
Kentucky.........	1,046,105	669,659	372,977	296,682 D	9	..	34	24
Louisiana.........	896,293	387,068	509,225	122,157 R	..	10	46	20
Maine............	380,965	262,264	118,701	143,563 D	4	..	16	14
Maryland........	1,116,547	730,912	385,495	345,417 D	10	..	48	20
Massachusetts.....	2,344,798	1,786,422	549,727	1,236,695 D	14	..	69	34
Michigan.........	3,203,102	2,136,615	1,060,152	1,076,463 D	21	..	92	48
Minnesota........	1,554,462	991,117	559,624	431,493 D	10	..	50	26
Mississippi.......	409,146	52,618	356,528	303,910 R	..	7	24	13
Missouri.........	1,817,879	1,164,344	653,535	510,809 D	12	..	58	24
Montana.........	278,628	164,246	113,032	51,214 D	4	..	17	14
Nebraska.........	584,154	307,307	276,847	30,460 D	5	..	19	16
Nevada..........	135,433	79,339	56,094	23,245 D	3	..	22	6
New Hampshire....	288,093	184,064	104,029	80,035 D	4	..	15	14
New Jersey.......	2,847,663	1,868,231	964,174	904,057 D	17	..	77	40
New Mexico.......	328,645	194,015	132,838	61,177 D	4	..	26	14
New York........	7,166,275	4,913,102[3]	2,243,559	2,669,543 D	43	..	179	92
North Carolina....	1,424,983	800,139	624,844	175,295 D	13	..	58	26
North Dakota.....	258,389	149,784	108,207	41,577 D	4	..	15	14
Ohio.............	3,969,196	2,498,331	1,470,865	1,207,466 D	26	..	99	58
Oklahoma........	932,499	519,834	412,665	107,169 D	8	..	30	22
Oregon..........	786,305	501,017	282,779	218,238 D	6	..	24	18
Pennsylvania.....	4,822,690	3,130,954	1,673,657	1,457,297 D	29	..	125	64
Rhode Island......	390,091	315,463	74,615	240,848 D	4	..	27	14
South Carolina....	524,779	215,723	309,048	93,325 R	..	8	38	16
South Dakota.....	293,118	163,010	130,108	32,902 D	4	..	15	14
Tennessee........	1,144,046	635,047	508,965	126,082 D	11	..	40	28
Texas............	2,626,811	1,663,185	958,566	704,619 D	25	..	99	56
Utah.............	401,413	219,628	181,785	37,843 D	4	..	16	14
Vermont.........	163,809	108,127	54,942	53,185 D	3	..	12	12
Virginia..........	1,042,267	558,038	481,334	76,704 D	12	..	42	30
Washington.......	1,258,374	779,699	470,366	309,333 D	9	..	35	24
West Virginia.....	792,040	538,087	253,953	284,134 D	7	..	37	14
Wisconsin........	1,691,815	1,050,424	638,495	411,929 D	12	..	46	30
Wyoming.........	142,716	80,718	61,998	18,720 D	3	..	15	12
TOTAL...........	70,644,510	43,129,484	27,178,188	15,951,296 D	486	52	2,316[4]	1,308[5]

[1] The Alabama Democratic elector slate was unpledged; thus no specific Johnson vote was obtainable. [2] Plurality over 210,732 unpledged Democratic votes. [3] Contains 4,570,670 Democratic and 342,432 Liberal votes. [4] Includes 21 votes allocated to U. S. territories. [5] Includes 8 votes allocated to U. S. territories.

OTHER CANDIDATES FOR PRESIDENT: Constitution Party, Joseph B. Lightburn; National States' Rights Party, John Kasper; Prohibition Party, E. Harold Munn; Socialist Labor Party, Eric Hass; Socialist Workers Party, Clifton DeBerry; Universal Party, James Hensley.

NATIONAL TOTALS OF OTHER VOTES: Socialist Labor, 45,219; Socialist Workers, 32,720; Prohibition, 23,267; National States' Rights, 6,953; Constitution, 5,060; Universal, 19; unpledged Democratic elector ticket (Alabama), 210,732; scattered, 12,868.

Presidential Election of 1968

Source: America Votes, compiled and edited by Richard M. Scammon.

PRINCIPAL CANDIDATES FOR PRESIDENT AND VICE PRESIDENT

Republican—Richard M. Nixon; Spiro T. Agnew.
Democratic—Hubert H. Humphrey; Edmund S. Muskie.
American Independent Party—George C. Wallace; Curtis E. LeMay.

State	Total	Rep.	Dem.	Am. Ind.	Plurality	R	D	A	Dem.	Rep.
Alabama	1,049,922	146,923	196,579[1]	691,425[2]	494,846 A	..	..	10	32	26
Alaska	83,035	37,600	35,411	10,024	2,189 R	3	..	..	22	12
Arizona	486,936	266,721	170,514	46,573	96,207 R	5	..	..	19	16
Arkansas	619,969	190,759	188,228	240,982	50,223 A	..	..	6	33	18
California	7,251,587	3,467,664	3,244,318	487,270	223,346 R	40	..	..	174	86
Colorado	811,199	409,345	335,174	60,813	74,171 R	6	..	..	35	18
Connecticut	1,256,232	556,721	621,561	76,650	64,840 D	..	8	..	44	16
Delaware	214,367	96,714	89,194	28,459	7,520 R	3	..	..	22	12
D. C.	170,578	31,012	139,566	.....	108,554 D	..	3	..	23	9
Florida	2,187,805	886,804	676,794	624,207	210,010 R	14	..	..	63	34
Georgia	1,250,266	380,111	334,440	535,550	155,439 A	..	..	12	43	30
Hawaii	236,218	91,425	141,324	3,469	49,899 D	..	4	..	26	14
Idaho	291,183	165,369	89,273	36,541	76,096 R	4	..	..	25	14
Illinois	4,619,749	2,174,774	2,039,814	390,958	134,960 R	26	..	..	118	58
Indiana	2,123,597	1,067,885	806,659	243,108	261,226 R	13	..	..	63	26
Iowa	1,167,931	619,106	476,699	66,422	142,407 R	9	..	..	46	24
Kansas	872,783	478,674	302,996	88,921	175,678 R	7	..	..	38	20
Kentucky	1,055,893	462,411	397,541	193,098	64,870 R	9	..	..	46	24
Louisiana	1,097,450	257,535	309,615	530,300	220,685 A	..	..	10	36	26
Maine	392,936	169,254	217,312	6,370	48,058 D	..	4	..	27	14
Maryland	1,235,039	517,995	538,310	178,734	20,315 D	..	10	..	49	26
Massachusetts	2,331,752	766,844	1,469,218	87,088	702,374 D	..	14	..	72	34
Michigan	3,306,250	1,370,665	1,593,082	331,968	222,417 D	..	21	..	96	48
Minnesota	1,588,506	658,643	857,738	68,931	199,095 D	..	10	..	52	26
Mississippi	654,509	88,516	150,644	415,349	264,705 A	..	..	7	24	20
Missouri	1,809,502	811,932	791,444	206,126	20,488 R	12	..	..	60	24
Montana	274,404	138,835	114,117	20,015	24,718 R	4	..	..	26	14
Nebraska	536,851	321,163	170,784	44,904	150,379 R	5	..	..	30	16
Nevada	154,218	73,188	60,598	20,432	12,590 R	3	..	..	22	12
New Hampshire	297,298	154,903	130,589	11,173	24,314 R	4	..	..	26	8
New Jersey	2,875,395	1,325,467	1,264,206	262,187	61,261 R	17	..	..	82	40
New Mexico	327,350	169,692	130,081	25,737	39,611 R	4	..	..	26	14
New York	6,791,688	3,007,932	3,378,470[3]	358,864	370,538 D	..	43	..	190	92
North Carolina	1,587,493	627,192	464,113	496,188	131,004 R	12	..	1	59	26
North Dakota	247,882	138,669	94,769	14,244	43,900 R	4	..	..	25	8
Ohio	3,959,698	1,791,014	1,700,586	467,495	90,428 R	26	..	..	115	58
Oklahoma	943,086	449,697	301,658	191,731	148,039 R	8	..	..	41	22
Oregon	819,622	408,433	358,866	49,683	49,567 R	6	..	..	35	18
Pennsylvania	4,747,928	2,090,017	2,259,405	378,582	169,388 D	..	29	..	130	64
Rhode Island	385,000	122,359	246,518	15,678	124,159 D	..	4	..	27	14
South Carolina	666,978	254,062	197,486	215,430	38,632 R	8	..	..	28	22
South Dakota	281,264	149,841	118,023	13,400	31,818 R	4	..	..	26	14
Tennessee	1,248,617	472,592	351,233	424,792	47,800 R	11	..	..	51	28
Texas	3,079,406	1,227,844	1,266,804	584,269	38,960 D	..	25	..	104	56
Utah	422,568	238,728	156,665	26,906	82,063 R	4	..	..	26	8
Vermont	161,404	85,142	70,255	5,104	14,887 R	3	..	..	22	12
Virginia	1,361,491	590,319	442,387	321,833	147,932 R	12	..	..	54	24
Washington	1,304,281	588,510	616,037	96,990	27,527 D	..	9	..	47	24
West Virginia	754,206	307,555	374,091	72,560	66,536 D	..	7	..	38	14
Wisconsin	1,691,538	809,997	748,804	127,835	61,193 R	12	..	..	59	30
Wyoming	127,205	70,927	45,173	11,105	25,754 R	3	..	..	22	12
TOTAL	73,212,065	31,785,480	31,275,166	9,906,473	510,314 R	301	191	46	2,622[4]	1,333[5]

[1] This vote, cast for Humphrey, is a combination of National Democratic (54,144) and Independent Democratic (142,435). [2] This vote for Wallace was cast as Democratic in Alabama. [3] Contains 3,066,848 Democratic and 311,622 Liberal votes. [4] Includes 23 votes allocated to U.S. territories. [5] Includes 8 votes allocated to U.S. territories.

OTHER CANDIDATES FOR PRESIDENT: New Party, Dick Gregory; Peace and Freedom Party, Eldridge Cleaver; Prohibition Party, E. Harold Munn; Socialist Labor Party, Hennings Blomen; Socialist Workers Party, Fred Halstead.

NATIONAL TOTAL OF OTHER VOTES: 244,946, from 30 states.

Presidential Election of 1972

Source: America Votes 10, compiled and edited by Richard M. Scammon.

PRINCIPAL CANDIDATES FOR PRESIDENT AND VICE PRESIDENT

Republican—Richard M. Nixon; Spiro T. Agnew.

Democratic—George McGovern; Sargent Shriver.

American Party[1]—John G. Schmitz; Thomas J. Anderson.

State	Total	Nixon Republican	McGovern Democratic	Schmitz American	Plur.	Electoral vote R	D	A	Votes at 1972 Natl. Convs. Dem.	Rep.
Alabama	1,006,111	728,701	256,923	11,928	471,778 R	9			37	17
Alaska	95,219	55,349	32,967	6,903	22,382 R	3			10	12
Arizona	622,926	402,812	198,540	21,208	204,272 R	6			25	18
Arkansas	651,320	448,541	199,892	2,887	248,649 R	6			27	18
California	8,367,862	4,602,096	3,475,847	232,554	1,126,249 R	45			271	96
Colorado	953,884	597,189	329,980	17,269	267,209 R	7			36	20
Connecticut	1,384,277	810,763	555,498	17,239	255,265 R	8			51	22
Delaware	235,516	140,357	92,283	2,638	48,074 R	3			13	12
D. C.	163,421	35,226	127,627	. . . .	92,401 D		3		15	9
Florida	2,583,283	1,857,759	718,117	. . . .	1,139,642 R	17			81	40
Georgia	1,174,772	881,496	289,529	812	591,967 R	12			53	24
Hawaii	270,274	168,865	101,409	. . . .	67,456 R	4			17	14
Idaho	310,379	199,384	80,826	28,869	118,558 R	4			17	14
Illinois	4,723,236	2,788,179	1,913,472	2,471	874,707 R	26			170	58
Indiana	2,125,529	1,405,154	708,568	. . . .	696,586 R	13			76	32
Iowa	1,225,944	706,207	496,206	22,056	210,001 R	8			46	20
Kansas	916,095	619,812	270,287	21,808	349,525 R	7			35	24
Kentucky	1,067,499	676,446	371,159	17,627	305,287 R	9			47	20
Louisiana	1,051,491	686,852	298,142	52,099	388,710 R	10			44	8
Maine	417,042	256,458	160,584	. . . .	95,874 R	4			20	26
Maryland	1,353,812	829,305	505,781	18,726	323,524 R	10			53	34
Massachusetts	2,458,756	1,112,078	1,332,540	2,877	220,462 D		14		102	48
Michigan	3,489,727	1,961,721	1,459,435	63,321	502,286 R	21			132	26
Minnesota	1,741,652	898,269	802,346	31,407	95,923 R	10			64	26
Mississippi	645,963	505,125	126,782	11,598	378,343 R	7			25	13
Missouri	1,855,803	1,153,852	697,147	. . . .	456,705 R	12			73	30
Montana	317,603	183,976	120,197	13,430	63,779 R	4			17	14
Nebraska	576,289	406,298	169,991	. . . .	236,307 R	5			24	16
Nevada	181,766	115,750	66,016	. . . .	49,734 R	3			11	12
New Hampshire	334,055	213,724	116,435	3,386	97,289 R	4			18	14
New Jersey	2,997,229	1,845,502	1,102,211	34,378	743,291 R	17			109	40
New Mexico	386,241	235,606	141,084	8,767	94,522 R	4			18	14
New York	7,165,919	4,192,778	2,951,084	. . . .	1,241,694 R	41			278	88
North Carolina	1,518,612	1,054,889	438,705	25,018	616,184 R	13			64	32
North Dakota	280,514	174,109	100,384	5,646	73,725 R	3			14	12
Ohio	4,094,787	2,441,827	1,558,889	80,067	882,938 R	25			153	56
Oklahoma	1,029,900	759,025	247,147	23,728	511,878 R	8			39	22
Oregon	927,946	486,686	392,760	46,211	93,926 R	6			34	18
Pennsylvania	4,592,106	2,714,521	1,796,951	70,593	917,570 R	27			182	60
Rhode Island	415,808	220,383	194,645	25	25,738 R	4			22	8
South Carolina	673,960	477,044	186,824	10,075	290,220 R	8			32	22
South Dakota	307,415	166,476	139,945	. . . .	26,531 R	4			17	14
Tennessee	1,201,182	813,147	357,293	30,373	455,854 R	10			49	26
Texas	3,471,281	2,298,896	1,154,289	6,039	1,144,607 R	26			130	52
Utah	478,476	323,643	126,284	28,549	197,359 R	4			19	14
Vermont	186,947	117,149	68,174	. . . .	48,975 R	3			12	12
Virginia	1,457,019	988,493	438,887	19,721	549,606 R	11[2]			53	30
Washington	1,470,847	837,135	568,334	58,906	268,801 R	9			52	24
West Virginia	762,399	484,964	277,435	. . . .	207,529 R	6			35	18
Wisconsin	1,852,890	989,430	810,174	47,525	179,256 R	11			67	18
Wyoming	145,570	100,464	44,358	748	56,106 R	3			11	12
TOTAL	77,718,554	47,169,911	29,170,383	1,099,482	17,999,528 R	520	17	0	3,016[3]	1,346[4]

[1] Known as American Independent Party and by other names in some states. [2] One Virginia elector cast vote for Libertarian Party. [3] Includes 16 votes allocated to U.S. Territories. [4] Includes 11 votes allocated to U.S. Territories.
  OTHER CANDIDATES FOR PRESIDENT: Communist, Gus Hall; Libertarian Party, John Hospers; Peoples Party, Benjamin Spock; Prohibition Party, Earle H. Munn; Socialist Labor Party, Louis Fisher; Socialist Workers Party, Linda Jenness.
  NATIONAL TOTALS OF OTHER VOTES: People's, 78,756; Social Workers, 66,677; Socialist Labor, 53,814; Communist, 25,595; Prohibition, 13,505; others and scattered, 40,431.

Electoral Vote for President, 1920-1956

(For electoral votes by state from 1960 to 1972, see pages 556-59. For 1976, see Special Section.)

States	1920 Harding, Rep.	1920 Cox, Dem.	1924 Coolidge, Rep.	1924 Davis, Dem.	1924 LaFollette, Prog.	1928 Hoover, Rep.	1928 Smith, Dem.	1932 Roosevelt, Dem.	1932 Hoover, Rep.	1936 Roosevelt, Dem.	1936 Landon, Rep.	1940 Roosevelt, Dem.	1940 Willkie, Rep.	1944 Roosevelt, Dem.	1944 Dewey, Rep.	1948 Truman, Dem.	1948 Dewey, Rep.	1948 Thurmond, Sts.Rgts.	1952 Eisenhower, Rep.	1952 Stevenson, Dem.	1956 Eisenhower, Rep.	1956 Stevenson, Dem.
Alabama		12		12			12	11		11		11		11				11		11		10
Arizona	3		3			3		3		3		3		4		4			4		4	
Arkansas		9		9			9	9		9		9		9		9				8		8
California	13		13			13		22		22		22		25		25			32		32	
Colorado	6		6			6		6		6			6		6	6			6		6	
Connecticut	7		7			7			8	8		8		8			8		8		8	
Delaware	3		3			3			3	3		3		3			3		3		3	
Florida		6		6		6		7		7		7		8		8			10		10	
Georgia		14		14			14	12		12		12		12		12				12		12
Idaho	4		4			4		4		4		4		4		4			4		4	
Illinois	29		29			29		29		29		29		28		28			27		27	
Indiana	15		15			15		14		14			14		13		13		13		13	
Iowa	13		13			13		11		11			11		10	10			10		10	
Kansas	10		10			10		9		9			9		8		8		8		8	
Kentucky		13	13			13		11		11		11		11		11				10	10	
Louisiana		10		10			10	10		10		10		10				10		10	10	
Maine	6		6			6			5		5		5		5		5		5		5	
Maryland	8		8			8		8		8		8		8			8		9		9	
Massachusetts	18		18				18	17		17		17		16		16			16		16	
Michigan	15		15			15		19		19			19	19			19		20		20	
Minnesota	12		12			12		11		11		11		11		11			11		11	
Mississippi		10		10			10	9		9		9		9				9		8		8
Missouri	18		18			18		15		15		15		15		15			13			13
Montana	4		4			4		4		4		4		4		4			4		4	
Nebraska	8		8			8		7		7			7		6		6		6		6	
Nevada	3		3			3		3		3		3		3		3			3		3	
New Hampshire	4		4			4			4	4		4		4			4		4		4	
New Jersey	14		14			14		16		16		16		16			16		16		16	
New Mexico	3		3			3		3		3		3		4		4			4		4	
New York	45		45			45		47		47		47		47			47		45		45	
North Carolina		12		12		12		13		13		13		14		14				14		14
North Dakota	5		5			5		4		4			4		4		4		4		4	
Ohio	24		24			24		26		26		26			25	25			25		25	
Oklahoma	10			10		10		11		11		11		10		10			8		8	
Oregon	5		5			5		5		5		5		6			6		6		6	
Pennsylvania	38		38			38			36	36		36		35			35		32		32	
Rhode Island	5		5				5	4		4		4		4		4			4		4	
South Carolina		9		9			9	8		8		8		8				8		8		8
South Dakota	5		5			5		4		4			4		4		4		4		4	
Tennessee	12			12		12		11		11		11		12		11		1	11		11	
Texas		20		20		20		23		23		23		23		23			24		24	
Utah	4		4			4		4		4		4		4		4			4		4	
Vermont	4		4			4			3		3		3		3		3		3		3	
Virginia		12		12		12		11		11		11		11		11			12		12	
Washington	7		7			7		8		8		8		8		8			9		9	
West Virginia	8		8			8		8		8		8		8		8				8	8	
Wisconsin	13				13	13		12		12		12			12	12			12		12	
Wyoming	3		3			3		3		3		3			3	3			3		3	
TOTAL	404	127	382	136	13	444	87	472	59	523	8	449	82	432	99	303	189	39	442	89	457	73

Plurality and Majority

In order to win a plurality, a candidate must receive a greater number of votes than anyone running against him. If he receives 50 votes, for example, and two other candidates receive 49 and 2, he will have a plurality of one vote over his closest opponent.

However, a candidate does not have a majority unless he receives more than 50% of the total votes cast. In the example above, the candidate does not have a majority, because his 50 votes are less than 50% of the 101 votes cast.

Estimated Population of Voting Age, by Age and Race, 1974[1]

Source: Bureau of the Census.

(in thousands.)

State	Total 18 years Old and Over		18-24 Years		25-44 Years		45-64 Years		65 Years and Over	
	All races	Black	All races	Black	All races	Black	All races	Black	All races	Black
Alabama . . .	2,392	537	454	115	860	169	705	157	373	96
Alaska . . .	206	. . .	53	. . .	97	. . .	47	. . .	9	. . .
Arizona	1,442	35	276	8	532	14	422	9	212	4
Arkansas . . .	1,417	209	242	42	485	60	422	59	268	48
California . . .	14,509	973	2,728	222	5,528	411	4,256	254	1,997	86
Colorado . . .	1,719	51	370	15	678	22	465	10	206	4
Connecticut . .	2,124	116	341	25	784	55	683	28	316	8
Delaware . . .	391	49	77	12	151	19	115	13	48	5
Dist. of Columbia	526	369	102	78	208	156	144	102	72	33
Florida	5,799	699	924	152	1,837	271	1,756	195	1,282	81
Georgia . . .	3,227	743	639	177	1,266	269	903	198	419	99
Hawaii	571	. . .	125	. . .	228	. . .	164	. . .	54	. . .
Idaho	519	. . .	100	. . .	187	. . .	155	. . .	77	. . .
Illinois	7,646	913	1,371	203	2,792	389	2,337	232	1,146	89
Indiana	3,603	233	686	54	1,335	91	1,058	63	524	25
Iowa	2,002	. . .	357	. . .	683	. . .	600	. . .	362	. . .
Kansas	1,601	71	308	19	546	25	464	17	283	10
Kentucky . . .	2,296	154	438	36	820	49	674	44	364	25
Louisiana . . .	2,457	659	507	157	908	230	703	176	339	96
Maine	700	. . .	123	. . .	242	. . .	210	. . .	125	. . .
Maryland . . .	2,781	461	522	105	1,090	189	830	122	339	45
Massachusetts .	4,086	120	769	31	1,425	52	1,229	27	663	10
Michigan . . .	6,037	673	1,185	165	2,259	257	1,787	185	806	66
Minnesota . .	2,634	. . .	509	. . .	956	. . .	735	. . .	434	. . .
Mississippi . .	1,495	459	307	106	518	140	418	125	252	88
Missouri . . .	3,296	311	581	70	1,149	115	970	83	596	43
Montana . . .	484	. . .	92	. . .	172	. . .	148	. . .	72	. . .
Nebraska . . .	1,068	. . .	201	. . .	367	. . .	307	. . .	193	. . .
Nevada . . .	382	. . .	65	. . .	158	. . .	118	. . .	41	. . .
New Hampshire	550	. . .	97	. . .	206	. . .	160	. . .	87	. . .
New Jersey . .	5,099	510	818	111	1,843	222	1,682	130	756	47
New Mexico . .	731	. . .	154	. . .	283	. . .	207	. . .	87	. . .
New York . . .	12,700	1,487	2,110	302	4,583	670	3,995	390	2,012	125
North Carolina .	3,635	705	736	171	1,362	240	1,060	203	477	91
North Dakota .	431	. . .	89	. . .	143	. . .	128	. . .	71	. . .
Ohio	7,281	637	1,350	138	2,666	246	2,204	179	1,061	74
Oklahoma . . .	1,879	110	339	26	659	36	550	29	331	19
Oregon . . .	1,587	. . .	284	. . .	572	. . .	477	. . .	254	. . .
Pennsylvania .	8,336	683	1,400	138	2,817	258	2,767	201	1,352	86
Rhode Island .	691	. . .	131	. . .	231	. . .	217	. . .	112	. . .
South Carolina .	1,831	474	396	118	691	163	522	132	222	61
South Dakota .	464	. . .	90	. . .	149	. . .	141	. . .	84	. . .
Tennessee . .	2,881	399	531	89	1,071	134	851	113	428	63
Texas	8,050	928	1,614	218	3,046	346	2,262	239	1,128	125
Utah	746	. . .	175	. . .	287	. . .	196	. . .	88	. . .
Vermont . . .	316	. . .	62	. . .	116	. . .	87	. . .	51	. . .
Virginia . . .	3,331	548	672	119	1,275	193	970	164	414	72
Washington . .	2,377	48	453	14	885	19	683	12	356	3
West Virginia .	1,238	41	211	7	417	10	400	13	210	11
Wisconsin . . .	3,121	82	596	23	1,102	37	915	17	508	5
Wyoming . .	244	. . .	47	. . .	89	. . .	75	. . .	33	. . .
TOTAL . . .	144,928	14,646	26,807	3,308	52,754	5,626	43,374	3,955	21,994	1,756

[1] As of November. NOTE: Leaders indicate fewer than 50,000 black population in state; therefore state breakdown does not add to total.

U. S. Cabinet Members with Dates of Appointment

Although the Constitution made no provision for a President's advisory group, the heads of the three executive departments (State, Treasury, and War) and the Attorney General were organized by Washington into such a group; and by about 1793, the name "Cabinet" was applied to it. With the exception of the Attorney General up to 1870 and the Postmaster General from 1829 to 1872, Cabinet members have been heads of executive departments.

A Cabinet member is appointed by the President, subject to the confirmation of the Senate; and as his term is not fixed, he may be replaced at any time by the President. At a change in Administration, it is customary for him to tender his resignation, but he remains in office until a successor is appointed.

The table of Cabinet members lists only those members who actually served after being duly commissioned.

The dates shown are those of appointment. "Contd" indicates that the term continued from the previous Administration for a substantial amount of time.

With the creation of the Department of Transportation in 1966, the Cabinet consisted of 12 members. This figure was reduced to 11 when the Post Office Department became an independent agency in 1970.

WASHINGTON

Secretary of State
Thomas Jefferson...... 1789
Edmund Randolph..... 1794
Timothy Pickering..... 1795

Secretary of the Treasury
Alexander Hamilton.... 1789
Oliver Wolcott, Jr...... 1795

Secretary of War
Henry Knox........... 1789
Timothy Pickering..... 1795
James McHenry...... 1796

Attorney General
Edmund Randolph..... 1789
William Bradford...... 1794
Charles Lee.......... 1795

J. ADAMS

Secretary of State
Timothy Pickering.... Contd
John Marshall......... 1800

Secretary of the Treasury
Oliver Wolcott, Jr..... Contd
Samuel Dexter........ 1801

Secretary of War
James McHenry...... Contd
Samuel Dexter........ 1800

Attorney General
Charles Lee.......... Contd

Secretary of the Navy
Benjamin Stoddert.... 1798

JEFFERSON

Secretary of State
James Madison....... 1801

Secretary of the Treasury
Samuel Dexter....... Contd
Albert Gallatin........ 1801

Secretary of War
Henry Dearborn....... 1801

Attorney General
Levi Lincoln.......... 1801
Robert Smith......... 1805
John Breckinridge..... 1805

Caesar A. Rodney..... 1807

Secretary of the Navy
Benjamin Stoddert... Contd
Robert Smith......... 1801

MADISON

Secretary of State
Robert Smith......... 1809
James Monroe........ 1811

Secretary of the Treasury
Albert Gallatin....... Contd
George W. Campbell... 1814
Alexander J. Dallas.... 1814
William H. Crawford... 1816

Secretary of War
William Eustis......... 1809
John Armstrong....... 1813
James Monroe........ 1814
William H. Crawford... 1815

Attorney General
Caesar A. Rodney.... Contd
William Pinckney...... 1811
Richard Rush......... 1814

Secretary of the Navy
Paul Hamilton........ 1809
William Jones......... 1813
B. W. Crowninshield... 1814

MONROE

Secretary of State
John Quincy Adams.... 1817

Secretary of the Treasury
William H. Crawford.. Contd

Secretary of War
John C. Calhoun....... 1817

Attorney General
Richard Rush........ Contd
William Wirt.......... 1817

Secretary of the Navy
B. W. Crowninshield.. Contd
Smith Thompson...... 1818
Samuel L. Southard... 1823

J. Q. ADAMS

Secretary of State
Henry Clay........... 1825

Secretary of the Treasury
Richard Rush......... 1825

Secretary of War
James Barbour........ 1825
Peter B. Porter........ 1828

Attorney General
William Wirt......... Contd

Secretary of the Navy
Samuel L. Southard.. Contd

JACKSON

Secretary of State
Martin Van Buren..... 1829
Edward Livingston..... 1831
Louis McLane......... 1833
John Forsyth.......... 1834

Secretary of the Treasury
Samuel D. Ingham..... 1829
Louis McLane......... 1831
William J. Duane...... 1833
Roger B. Taney[3]...... 1833
Levi Woodbury....... 1834

Secretary of War
John H. Eaton......... 1829
Lewis Cass........... 1831

Attorney General
John M. Berrien....... 1829
Roger B. Taney........ 1831
Benjamin F. Butler.... 1833

Postmaster General[1]
William T. Barry...... 1829
Amos Kendall......... 1835

Secretary of the Navy
John Branch.......... 1829
Levi Woodbury........ 1831
Mahlon Dickerson..... 1834

VAN BUREN

Secretary of State
John Forsyth......... Contd

Secretary of the Treasury
Levi Woodbury....... Contd

Secretary of War
Joel R. Poinsett....... 1837

Attorney General
Benjamin F. Butler... Contd
Felix Grundy.......... 1838
Henry D. Gilpin....... 1840

Postmaster General
Amos Kendall........ Contd
John M. Niles........ 1840

Secretary of the Navy
Mahlon Dickerson.... Contd
James K. Paulding.... 1838

W. H. HARRISON

Secretary of State
Daniel Webster........ 1841

Secretary of the Treasury
Thomas Ewing........ 1841

Secretary of War
John Bell............. 1841

Attorney General
John J. Crittenden..... 1841

Postmaster General
Francis Granger....... 1841

Secretary of the Navy
George E. Badger...... 1841

TYLER

Secretary of State
Daniel Webster...... Contd
Abel P. Upshur....... 1843
John C. Calhoun....... 1844

Secretary of the Treasury
Thomas Ewing....... Contd
Walter Forward....... 1841
John C. Spencer[3]...... 1843
George M. Bibb....... 1844

Secretary of War
John Bell............. Contd
John C. Spencer....... 1841
James M. Porter[3]...... 1843
William Wilkins....... 1844

Attorney General
John J. Crittenden.... Contd
Hugh S. Legaré....... 1841

John Nelson.......... 1843

Postmaster General
Francis Granger...... Contd
Charles A. Wickliffe.... 1841

Secretary of the Navy
George E. Badger..... Contd
Abel P. Upshur....... 1841
David Henshaw*....... 1843
Thomas W. Gilmer..... 1844
John Y. Mason........ 1844

POLK

Secretary of State
James Buchanan....... 1845

Secretary of the Treasury
Robert J. Walker...... 1845

Secretary of War
William L. Marcy...... 1845

Attorney General
John Y. Mason........ 1845
Nathan Clifford....... 1846
Isaac Toucey......... 1848

Postmaster General
Cave Johnson......... 1845

Secretary of the Navy
George Bancroft....... 1845
John Y. Mason........ 1846

TAYLOR

Secretary of State
John M. Clayton....... 1849

Secretary of the Treasury
William M. Meredith... 1849

Secretary of War
George W. Crawford.... 1849

Attorney General
Reverdy Johnson...... 1849

Postmaster General
Jacob Collamer........ 1849

Secretary of the Navy
William B. Preston..... 1849

Secretary of the Interior
Thomas Ewing........ 1849

FILLMORE

Secretary of State
Daniel Webster........ 1850
Edward Everett........ 1852

Secretary of the Treasury
Thomas Corwin....... 1850

Secretary of War
Charles M. Conrad..... 1850

Attorney General
John J. Crittenden..... 1850

Postmaster General
Nathan K. Hall........ 1850
Samuel D. Hubbard.... 1852

Secretary of the Navy
William A. Graham.... 1850
John P. Kennedy....... 1852

Secretary of the Interior
Thos. M. T. McKennan. 1850
Alex. H. H. Stuart..... 1850

PIERCE

Secretary of State
William L. Marcy...... 1853

Secretary of the Treasury
James Guthrie........ 1853

Secretary of War
Jefferson Davis........ 1853

Attorney General
Caleb Cushing........ 1853

Postmaster General
James Campbell....... 1853

Secretary of the Navy
James C. Dobbin...... 1853

Secretary of the Interior
Robert McClelland..... 1853

BUCHANAN

Secretary of State
Lewis Cass........... 1857
Jeremiah S. Black..... 1860

Secretary of the Treasury
Howell Cobb.......... 1857
Philip F. Thomas...... 1860
John A. Dix........... 1861

Secretary of War
John B. Floyd......... 1857
Joseph Holt........... 1861

Attorney General
Jeremiah S. Black..... 1857
Edwin M. Stanton..... 1860

Postmaster General
Aaron V. Brown....... 1857
Joseph Holt........... 1859
Horatio King.......... 1861

Secretary of the Navy
Isaac Toucey......... 1857

Secretary of the Interior
Jacob Thompson...... 1857

LINCOLN

Secretary of State
William H. Seward..... 1861

Secretary of the Treasury
Salmon P. Chase...... 1861
William P. Fessenden.. 1864
Hugh McCulloch....... 1865

Secretary of War
Simon Cameron....... 1861
Edwin M. Stanton..... 1862

Attorney General
Edward Bates......... 1861
James Speed......... 1864

Postmaster General
Montgomery Blair..... 1861
William Dennison...... 1864

Secretary of the Navy
Gideon Welles........ 1861

Secretary of the Interior
Caleb B. Smith........ 1861
John P. Usher......... 1863

A. JOHNSON

Secretary of State
William H. Seward.... Contd

Secretary of the Treasury
Hugh McCulloch...... Contd

Secretary of War
Edwin M. Stanton.... Contd
John M. Schofield..... 1868

Attorney General
James Speed........ Contd
Henry Stanbery....... 1866
William M. Evarts..... 1868

Postmaster General
William Dennison..... Contd
Alexander W. Randall.. 1866

Secretary of the Navy
Gideon Welles........ Contd

Secretary of the Interior
John P. Usher........ Contd
James Harlan......... 1865
Orville H. Browning.... 1866

GRANT

Secretary of State
Elihu B. Washburne.... 1869
Hamilton Fish......... 1869

Secretary of the Treasury
George S. Boutwell.... 1869
William A. Richardson.. 1873
Benjamin H. Bristow... 1874
Lot M. Morrill......... 1876

Secretary of War
John A. Rawlins....... 1869
William W. Belknap.... 1869
Alphonso Taft......... 1876
James D. Cameron..... 1876

Attorney General
Ebenezer R. Hoar...... 1869
Amos T. Akerman..... 1870
George H. Williams.... 1871
Edwards Pierrepont.... 1875
Alphonso Taft......... 1876

Postmaster General
John A. J. Creswell.... 1869
Marshall Jewell....... 1874
James N. Tyner....... 1876

Secretary of the Navy
Adolph E. Borie....... 1869
George M. Robeson.... 1869

Secretary of the Interior
Jacob D. Cox......... 1869
Columbus Delano...... 1870
Zachariah Chandler.... 1875

HAYES

Secretary of State
William M. Evarts..... 1877

Secretary of the Treasury
John Sherman 1877

Secretary of War
George W. McCrary.... 1877
Alexander Ramsey..... 1879

Attorney General
Charles Devens........ 1877

Postmaster General
David M. Key......... 1877
Horace Maynard....... 1880

Secretary of the Navy
Richard W. Thompson.. 1877
Nathan Goff, Jr........ 1881

Secretary of the Interior
Carl Schurz........... 1877

GARFIELD

Secretary of State
James G. Blaine....... 1881

Secretary of the Treasury
William Windom....... 1881

Secretary of War
Robert T. Lincoln..... 1881

Attorney General
Wayne MacVeagh...... 1881

Postmaster General
Thomas L. James...... 1881

Secretary of the Navy
William H. Hunt....... 1881

Secretary of the Interior
Samuel J. Kirkwood... 1881

ARTHUR

Secretary of State
James G. Blaine....... Contd
F. T. Frelinghuysen.... 1881

Secretary of the Treasury
William Windom...... Contd
Charles J. Folger...... 1881
Walter Q. Gresham.... 1884
Hugh McCulloch....... 1884

Secretary of War
Robert T. Lincoln......Contd

Attorney General
Wayne MacVeagh......Contd
Benjamin H. Brewster. 1881

Postmaster General
Thomas L. James..... Contd
Timothy O. Howe...... 1881
Walter Q. Gresham.... 1883
Frank Hatton......... 1884

Secretary of the Navy
William H. Hunt...... Contd
William E. Chandler.... 1882

Secretary of the Interior
Samuel J. Kirkwood... Contd
Henry M. Teller...... 1882

CLEVELAND

Secretary of State
Thomas F. Bayard..... 1885

Secretary of the Treasury
Daniel Manning....... 1885
Charles S. Fairchild.... 1887

Secretary of War
William C. Endicott.... 1885

Attorney General
Augustus H. Garland... 1885

Postmaster General
William F. Vilas....... 1885
Don M. Dickinson..... 1888

Secretary of the Navy
William C. Whitney.... 1885

Secretary of the Interior
Lucius Q. C. Lamar.... 1885
William F. Vilas....... 1888

Secretary of Agriculture
Norman J. Colman..... 1889

B. HARRISON

Secretary of State
James G. Blaine....... 1889
John W. Foster........ 1892

Secretary of the Treasury
William Windom....... 1889
Charles Foster........ 1891

Secretary of War
Redfield Proctor....... 1889
Stephen B. Elkins..... 1891

Attorney General
William H. H. Miller.... 1889

Postmaster General
John Wanamaker...... 1889

Secretary of the Navy
Benjamin F. Tracy..... 1889

Secretary of the Interior
John W. Noble........ 1889

Secretary of Agriculture
Jeremiah M. Rusk..... 1889

CLEVELAND

Secretary of State
Walter Q. Gresham.... 1893

Richard Olney......... 1895

Secretary of the Treasury
John G. Carlisle....... 1893

Secretary of War
Daniel S. Lamont...... 1893

Attorney General
Richard Olney......... 1893
Judson Harmon....... 1895

Postmaster General
Wilson S. Bissell...... 1893
William L. Wilson...... 1895

Secretary of the Navy
Hilary A. Herbert...... 1893

Secretary of the Interior
Hoke Smith........... 1893
David R. Francis....... 1896

Secretary of Agriculture
Julius Sterling Morton. 1893

McKINLEY

Secretary of State
John Sherman........ 1897
William R. Day........ 1898
John Hay............. 1898

Secretary of the Treasury
Lyman J. Gage........ 1897

Secretary of War
Russell A. Alger....... 1897
Elihu Root............ 1899

Attorney General
Joseph McKenna...... 1897
John W. Griggs........ 1898
Philander C. Knox..... 1901

Postmaster General
James A. Gary........ 1897
Charles E. Smith...... 1898

Secretary of the Navy
John D. Long......... 1897

Secretary of the Interior
Cornelius N. Bliss..... 1897
Ethan A. Hitchcock.... 1898

Secretary of Agriculture
James Wilson......... 1897

T. ROOSEVELT

Secretary of State
John Hay............. Contd
Elihu Root............ 1905
Robert Bacon......... 1909

Secretary of the Treasury
Lyman J. Gage....... Contd
Leslie M. Shaw....... 1902
George B. Cortelyou... 1907

Secretary of War
Elihu Root........... Contd
William H. Taft........ 1904
Luke E. Wright........ 1908

Attorney General
Philander C. Knox.... Contd
William H. Moody..... 1904
Charles J. Bonaparte... 1906

Postmaster General
Charles E. Smith..... Contd
Henry C. Payne....... 1902
Robert J. Wynne 1904
George B. Cortelyou.... 1905
George von L. Meyer... 1907

Secretary of the Navy
John D. Long........ Contd
William H. Moody..... 1902
Paul Morton.......... 1904
Charles J. Bonaparte... 1905
Victor H. Metcalf...... 1906
Truman H. Newberry.. 1908

Secretary of the Interior
Ethan A. Hitchcock.... Contd
James R. Garfield..... 1907

Secretary of Agriculture
James Wilson........ Contd

Secretary of Commerce
and Labor
George B. Cortelyou... 1903
Victor H. Metcalf...... 1904
Oscar S. Straus....... 1906

TAFT

Secretary of State
Philander C. Knox.... 1909

Secretary of the Treasury
Franklin MacVeagh.... 1909

Secretary of War
Jacob M. Dickinson.... 1909
Henry L. Stimson...... 1911

Attorney General
George W. Wickersham. 1909

Postmaster General
Frank H. Hitchcock.... 1909

Secretary of the Navy
George von L. Meyer... 1909

Secretary of the Interior
Richard A. Ballinger... 1909
Walter L. Fisher....... 1911

Secretary of Agriculture
James Wilson........ Contd

Secretary of Commerce
and Labor
Charles Nagel........ 1909

WILSON

Secretary of State
William J. Bryan...... 1913
Robert Lansing........ 1915
Bainbridge Colby..... 1920

Secretary of the Treasury
William G. McAdoo.... 1913
Carter Glass.......... 1918
David F. Houston...... 1920

Secretary of War
Lindley M. Garrison.... 1913
Newton D. Baker...... 1916

Attorney General
James C. McReynolds.. 1913
Thomas W. Gregory.... 1914
A. Mitchell Palmer..... 1919

Postmaster General
Albert S. Burleson..... 1913

Secretary of the Navy
Josephus Daniels...... 1913

Secretary of the Interior
Franklin K. Lane...... 1913
John B. Payne........ 1920

Secretary of Agriculture
David F. Houston...... 1913
Edwin T. Meredith..... 1920

Secretary of Commerce
William C. Redfield.... 1913
Joshua W. Alexander... 1919

Secretary of Labor
William B. Wilson..... 1913

HARDING

Secretary of State
Charles E. Hughes....'.. 1921

Secretary of the Treasury
Andrew W. Mellon..... 1921

Secretary of War
John W. Weeks........ 1921

Attorney General
Harry M. Daugherty.... 1921

Postmaster General
Will H. Hays.......... 1921
Hubert Work.......... 1922
Harry S. New......... 1923

Secretary of the Navy
Edwin Denby......... 1921

Secretary of the Interior
Albert B. Fall......... 1921
Hubert Work.......... 1923

Secretary of Agriculture
Henry C. Wallace...... 1921

Secretary of Commerce
Herbert Hoover....... 1921

Secretary of Labor
James J. Davis........ 1921

COOLIDGE

Secretary of State
Charles E. Hughes.... Contd
Frank B. Kellogg...... 1925

Secretary of the Treasury
Andrew W. Mellon.... Contd

Secretary of War
John W. Weeks....... Contd
Dwight F. Davis....... 1925

Attorney General
Harry M. Daugherty... Contd
Harlan F. Stone....... 1924
John G. Sargent....... 1925

Postmaster General
Harry S. New........ Contd

Secretary of the Navy
Edwin Denby........ Contd
Curtis D. Wilbur....... 1924

Secretary of the Interior
Hubert Work....... Contd
Roy O. West.......... 1928

Secretary of Agriculture
Henry C. Wallace..... Contd
Howard M. Gore....... 1924
William M. Jardine.... 1925

Secretary of Commerce
Herbert Hoover....... Contd
William F. Whiting....: 1928

Secretary of Labor
James J. Davis....... Contd

HOOVER

Secretary of State
Frank B. Kellogg..... Contd
Henry L. Stimson...... 1929

Secretary of the Treasury
Andrew W. Mellon.... Contd
Ogden L. Mills........ 1932

Secretary of War
James W. Good........ 1929
Patrick J. Hurley...... 1929

Attorney General
William D. Mitchell.... 1929

Postmaster General
Walter F. Brown....... 1929

Secretary of the Navy
Charles F. Adams..... 1929

Secretary of the Interior
Ray Lyman Wilbur..... 1929

Secretary of Agriculture
Arthur M. Hyde....... 1929

Secretary of Commerce
Robert P. Lamont...... 1929
Roy D. Chapin........ 1932

Secretary of Labor
James J. Davis....... Contd
William N. Doak....... 1930

F. D. ROOSEVELT

Secretary of State
Cordell Hull.......... 1933
E. R. Stettinius, Jr..... 1944

Secretary of the Treasury
William H. Woodin..... 1933
Henry Morgenthau, Jr,. 1934

Secretary of War
George H. Dern........ 1933
Harry H. Woodring.... 1936
Henry L. Stimson...... 1940

Attorney General
Homer S. Cummings... 1933
Frank Murphy........ 1939
Robert H. Jackson.... 1940
Francis Biddle........ 1941

Postmaster General
James A. Farley....... 1933
Frank C. Walker....... 1940

Secretary of the Navy
Claude A. Swanson.... 1933
Charles Edison........ 1940
Frank Knox.......... 1940
James Forrestal....... 1944

Secretary of the Interior
Harold L. Ickes........ 1933

Secretary of Agriculture
Henry A. Wallace...... 1933
Claude R. Wickard..... 1940

Secretary of Commerce
Daniel C. Roper....... 1933
Harry L. Hopkins...... 1938
Jesse H. Jones........ 1940
Henry A. Wallace...... 1945

Secretary of Labor
Frances Perkins....... 1933

TRUMAN

Secretary of State
E. R. Stettinius, Jr.... Contd
James F. Byrnes...... 1945
George C. Marshall.... 1947
Dean Acheson........ 1949

Secretary of the Treasury
Henry Morgenthau, Jr. Contd
Frederick M. Vinson... 1945
John W. Snyder....... 1946

Secretary of Defense
James Forrestal....... 1947
Louis A. Johnson...... 1949
George C. Marshall.... 1950
Robert A. Lovett....... 1951

Attorney General
Francis Biddle........ Contd
Tom C. Clark.......... 1945
J. Howard McGrath.... 1949
James P. McGranery... 1952

Postmaster General
Frank C. Walker..... Contd
Robert E. Hannegan.... 1945
Jesse M. Donaldson.... 1947

Secretary of the Interior
Harold L. Ickes...... Contd
Julius A. Krug........ 1946
Oscar L. Chapman.... 1949

Secretary of Agriculture
Claude R. Wickard.... Contd
Clinton P. Anderson... 1945
Charles F. Brannan.... 1948

Secretary of Commerce
Henry A. Wallace..... Contd
W. Averell Harriman... 1946
Charles Sawyer...... 1948

Secretary of Labor
Frances Perkins...... Contd
Lewis B. Schwellenbach 1945
Maurice J. Tobin...... 1948

Secretary of War[2]
Henry L. Stimson..... Contd
Robert P. Patterson.... 1945
Kenneth C. Royall..... 1947

Secretary of the Navy[2]
James Forrestal...... Contd

EISENHOWER

Secretary of State
John Foster Dulles..... 1953
Christian A. Herter.... 1959

Secretary of the Treasury
George M. Humphrey.. 1953
Robert B. Anderson.... 1957

Secretary of Defense
Charles E. Wilson...... 1953
Neil H. McElroy...... 1957
Thomas S. Gates, Jr.... 1959

Attorney General
Herbert Brownell, Jr... 1953
William P. Rogers..... 1958

Postmaster General
Arthur E. Summerfield. 1953

Secretary of the Interior
Douglas McKay....... 1953
Frederick A. Seaton... 1956

Secretary of Agriculture
Ezra Taft Benson...... 1953

Secretary of Commerce
Sinclair Weeks........ 1953
Lewis L. Strauss[3]..... 1958
Frederick H. Mueller... 1959

Secretary of Labor
Martin P. Durkin...... 1953
James P. Mitchell..... 1953

Secretary of Health, Education, and Welfare
Oveta Culp Hobby..... 1953
Marion B. Folsom..... 1955
Arthur S. Flemming... 1958

KENNEDY

Secretary of State
Dean Rusk............ 1961

Secretary of the Treasury
C. Douglas Dillon...... 1961

Secretary of Defense
Robert S. McNamara... 1961

Attorney General
Robert F. Kennedy..... 1961

Postmaster General
J. Edward Day........ 1961
John A. Gronouski..... 1963

Secretary of the Interior
Stewart L. Udall....... 1961

Secretary of Agriculture
Orville L. Freeman..... 1961

Secretary of Commerce
Luther H. Hodges...... 1961

Secretary of Labor
Arthur J. Goldberg..... 1961
W. Willard Wirtz...... 1962

Secretary of Health, Education, and Welfare
Abraham A. Ribicoff... 1961
Anthony J. Celebrezze 1962

L. B. JOHNSON

Secretary of State
Dean Rusk.......... Contd

Secretary of the Treasury
C. Douglas Dillon..... Contd
Henry H. Fowler....... 1965
Joseph W. Barr[4]...... 1968

Secretary of Defense
Robert S. McNamara . Contd
Clark M. Clifford...... 1968

Attorney General
Robert F. Kennedy... Contd
N. de B. Katzenbach.. 1965
Ramsey Clark......... 1967

Postmaster General
John A. Gronouski.... Contd
Lawrence F. O'Brien.. 1965
W. Marvin Watson..... 1968

Secretary of the Interior
Stewart L. Udall...... Contd

Secretary of Agriculture
Orville L. Freeman ... Contd

Secretary of Commerce
Luther H. Hodges..... Contd
John T. Connor....... 1964
A. B. Trowbridge....... 1967
C. R. Smith........... 1968

Secretary of Labor
W. Willard Wirtz...... Contd

Secretary of Health, Education, and Welfare
Anthony J. Celebrezze Contd
John W. Gardner..... 1965
Wilbur J. Cohen...... 1968

Secretary of Housing and Urban Development
Robert C. Weaver..... 1966
Robert C. Wood[4]....... 1969

Secretary of Transportation
Alan S. Boyd 1966

NIXON

Secretary of State
William P. Rogers . . . 1969
Henry A. Kissinger . . . 1973

Secretary of the Treasury
David M. Kennedy . . . 1969
John B. Connally . . . 1970
George P. Shultz . . . 1972
William E. Simon . . . 1974

Secretary of Defense
Melvin R. Laird . . . 1969
Elliot L. Richardson . . 1973
James R. Schlesinger . . 1973

Attorney General
John N. Mitchell 1969
Richard G. Kleindienst . . 1972
Elliot L. Richardson . . . 1973
William B. Saxbe . . . 1974

Postmaster General[5]
William M. Blount . . . 1969

Secretary of the Interior
Walter J. Hickel 1969
Rogers C. B. Morton . . 1971

Secretary of Agriculture
Clifford M. Hardin . . . 1969
Earl L. Butz 1971

Secretary of Commerce
Maurice H. Stans . . . 1969
Peter G. Peterson . . . 1972
Frederick B. Dent . . . 1973

Secretary of Labor
George P. Shultz . . . 1969
James D. Hodgson . . . 1970
Peter J. Brennan . . . 1973

Secretary of Health, Education, and Welfare
Robert H. Finch 1969
Elliot L. Richardson . . . 1970
Caspar W. Weinberger . . 1973

Secretary of Housing and Urban Development
George Romney 1969
James T. Lynn 1973

Secretary of Transportation
John A. Volpe 1969
Claude S. Brinegar . . . 1973

FORD

Secretary of State
Henry A. Kissinger . . Contd

Secretary of the Treasury
William E. Simon . . . Contd

Secretary of Defense
James R. Schlesinger . Contd
Donald H. Rumsfeld . . . 1975

Attorney General
William B. Saxbe . . . Contd
Edward H. Levi 1975

Secretary of the Interior
Rogers C. B. Morton . . Contd
Stanley K. Hathaway . . 1975
Thomas S. Kleppe . . . 1975

Secretary of Agriculture
Earl L. Butz 1976

Secretary of Commerce
Frederick B. Dent . . Contd
Rogers C. B. Morton . . 1975
Elliot L. Richardson . . . 1976

Secretary of Labor
Peter J. Brennan . . . Contd
John T. Dunlop 1975
William J. Usery Jr. . . . 1976

Secretary of Health, Education and Welfare
Caspar W. Weinberger . Contd
F. David Mathews . . . 1975

Secretary of Housing and Urban Development
James T. Lynn . . . . Contd
Carla A. Hills 1975

Secretary of Transportation
Claude S. Brinegar . . Contd
William T. Coleman, Jr. . 1975

[1] The Postmaster General did not become a Cabinet member until 1829. Earlier Postmasters General were: Samuel Osgood (1789), Timothy Pickering (1791), Joseph Habersham (1795), Gideon Granger (1801), Return J. Meigs, Jr. (1814) and John McLean (1823). [2] On July 26, 1947, the Departments of War and of the Navy were incorporated into the Department of Defense. [3] Not confirmed by the Senate. [4] Recess appointment. [5] The Postmaster General is no longer a Cabinet member.

FEDERAL JUDICIARY

Supreme Court of the U.S.
(Washington, D. C. 20543)

Chief Justice: Warren E. Burger

Associate Justices:
William J. Brennan, Jr.
Potter Stewart
Byron R. White
Thurgood Marshall
Harry A. Blackmun
Lewis F. Powell, Jr.
William H. Rehnquist
John Paul Stevens

U.S. Courts of Appeals
(CJ indicates Chief Judge)

District of Columbia: David L. Bazelon, CJ, J. Skelly Wright, Carl McGowan, Edward Allen Tamm, Harold Leventhal, Spottswood W. Robinson III, Roger Robb, George E. MacKinnon, Malcolm R. Wilkey, all Washington, D.C.

First Circuit (Me., Mass., N.H., R.I., Puerto Rico): Frank M. Coffin, CJ, Portland, Me.; Edward M. McEntee, Providence, R.I.; Levin H. Campbell, Boston, Mass.

Second Circuit (Conn., N.Y., Vt.): Irving R. Kaufman, CJ, Wilfred Feinberg, Walter R. Mansfield, William H. Mulligan, Murray I. Gurfein, all New York City; Ellsworth A. Van Graafeiland, Rochester, N.Y.; James L. Oakes, Brattleboro, Vt.; William H. Timbers, Bridgeport, Conn.; Thomas J. Meskill, Hartford, Conn.

Third Circuit (Del., N.J., Pa., Virgin Is.): Collins J. Seitz, CJ, Wilmington, Del.; Francis L. Van Dusen, Arlin M. Adams, both Philadelphia; Ruggero J. Aldisert, Joseph F. Weis, Jr., both Pittsburgh; John J. Gibbons, Leonard I. Garth, both Newark, N.J.; Max Rosenn, Wilkes-Barre, Pa.; James Hunter, III, Camden, N.J.

Fourth Circuit (Md., N.C., S.C., Va., W.Va): Clement F. Haynsworth, Jr., CJ, Greenville, S.C.; J. Braxton Craven, Jr., Asheville, N.C.; Harrison L. Winter, Baltimore, Md.; John D. Butzner, Jr., Richmond, Va.; Donald Stuart Russell, Spartanburg, S.C.; H. Emory Widener, Jr., Abingdon, Va.

Fifth Circuit (Ala., Fla., Ga., La., Miss., Tex., Canal Zone): John R. Brown, CJ, Houston, Tex.; John Minor Wisdom, Robert A. Ainsworth, Jr., both New Orleans; Walter Pettus Gewin, Tuscaloosa, Ala.; Homer Thornberry, Thomas G. Gee, both Austin, Tex.; James P. Coleman, Ackerman, Miss.; Irving L. Goldberg, Dallas, Tex.; John C. Godbold. Montgomery, Ala.; David W. Dyer, Miami, Fla.; Lewis R. Morgan, Newnan, Ga.; Charles Clark, Jackson, Miss.; Paul H. Roney, St. Petersburg, Fla.; Gerald B. Tjoflat, Jacksonville, Fla.

Sixth Circuit (Ky., Mich., Ohio, Tenn.): Harry Phillips, CJ, Nashville, Tenn.; Paul C. Weick, Akron, Ohio; George Clifton Edwards, Jr., John W. Peck, both Cincinnati; Wade Hampton McCree, Jr., Detroit, Mich.; Anthony J. Celebrezze, Cleveland, Ohio; Albert J. Engel,

Grand Rapids, Mich.; Pierce Lively, Danville, Ky.

Seventh Circuit (Ill., Ind., Wis.): Thomas E. Fairchild, CJ, Luther M. Swygert, Walter J. Cummings, Wilbur F. Pell, Jr., Robert A. Sprecher, Philip W. Tone, William J. Bauer, Harlington Wood, Jr., all Chicago, Ill.

Eighth Circuit (Ark., Iowa, Minn., Mo., Neb., N.D., S.D.): Floyd R. Gibson, CJ, Kansas City, Mo.; Donald P. Lay, Donald R. Ross, both Omaha, Neb.; Gerald W. Heaney, Duluth, Minn.; Myron H. Bright, Fargo, N.D.; Roy L. Stephenson, Des Moines, Iowa; William H. Webster, St. Louis, Mo.; J. Smith Henley, Harrison, Ark.

Ninth Circuit (Ariz., Calif., Idaho, Mont., Nev., Ore., Wash., Alaska, Hawaii, Guam): Richard H. Chambers, CJ, Ben Cushing Duniway, James R. Browning, Joseph T. Sneed, all San Francisco; Walter Ely, Shirley M. Hufstedler, both Los Angeles; J. Clifford Wallace, San Diego, Calif.; Eugene A. Wright, Seattle, Wash.; Ozell M. Trask, Phoenix, Ariz.; Herbert Y. C. Choy, Honolulu, Hawaii; Alfred T. Goodwin, Portland, Ore.; Anthony M. Kennedy, Sacramento, Calif.

Tenth Circuit (Colo., Kan., N.M., Okla., Utah, Wyo.): David T. Lewis, CJ, Salt Lake City. Utah; Delmas C. Hill, Wichita, Kan.; Oliver Seth, Santa Fe, N.M.; William J. Holloway, Jr., Oklahoma City, Okla.; Robert H. McWilliams, William E. Doyle, both Denver, Colo.; James E. Barrett, Cheyenne, Wyo.

U.S. Court of Claims
(Washington, D. C. 20005)

Chief Judge: Wilson Cowen.
Associate Judges: Oscar H. Davis, Byron G. Skelton, Philip Nichols, Jr., Shiro Kashiwa, Robert L. Kunzig, Marion T. Bennett.

U.S. Court of Customs and Patent Appeals
(Washington, D. C. 20439)

Chief Judge: Howard T. Markey.
Associate Judges: Giles S. Rich, Phillip B. Baldwin, Donald E. Lane, Jack R. Miller.

U.S. Customs Court
(One Federal Plaza, New York, N. Y. 10007)

Chief Judge: Nils A. Boe.
Judges: Paul P. Rao, Morgan Ford, Scovel Richardson, Frederick Landis, James L. Watson, Herbert N. Maletz, Bernard Newman, Edward D. Re.

U.S. Tax Court
(Washington, D.C. 20217)

Chief Judge: Howard A. Dawson, Jr.
Judges: Arnold Raum, Bruce M. Forrester, William Miller Drennen, Irene Feagin Scott, William M. Fay, Theodore Tannenwald, Jr., Charles R. Simpson, C. Moxley Featherston, Leo H. Irwin, Samuel B. Sterrett, William H. Quealy, William A. Goffe, Cynthia Holcomb Hall, Darrell D. Wiles, Richard C. Wilbur, John Gregory Bruce, Norman O. Tietjens.

U.S. District Courts
(CJ indicates Chief Judge)

Alabama, Northern: Frank H. McFadden, CJ, James Hughes Hancock, J. Foy Guin, Jr., Sam C. Pointer, Jr., all Birmingham.

Alabama, Middle: Frank M. Johnson, Jr., CJ, Robert E. Varner, both Montgomery.

Alabama, Southern: Virgil Pittman, CJ, William Brevard Hand, both Mobile.

Alaska: James A. von der Heydt, CJ, James M. Fitzgerald, both Anchorage.

Arizona: Walter Early Craig, CJ, C. A. Muecke, William P. Copple, all Phoenix; James A. Walsh, William C. Frey, both Tucson.

Arkansas, Eastern: Garnett Thomas Eisele, CJ, Terry L. Shell, both Little Rock.

Arkansas, Western: Paul X. Williams, CJ, Ft. Smith; Terry L. Shell, Little Rock.

California, Northern: Robert F. Peckham, CJ, San Jose; Lloyd H. Burke, Stanley A. Weigel, Robert H. Schnacke, Samuel Conti, Charles B. Renfrew, William H. Orrick, Jr., all San Francisco; Spencer M. Williams, San Jose.

California, Eastern: Thomas J. MacBride, CJ, Philip C. Wilkins, both Sacramento; M. D. Crocker, Fresno.

California, Central: Albert Lee Stephens, Jr., CJ, Francis C. Whelan, Irving Hill, A. Andrew Hauk, William P. Gray, Warren J. Ferguson, Manuel L. Real, Harry Pregerson, David W. Williams, Robert J. Kelleher, William Matthew Byrne, Jr., Malcolm M. Lucas, Lawrence T. Lydick, Robert Firth, all Los Angeles.

California, Southern: Edward J. Schwartz, CJ, Howard B. Turrentine, Gordon Thompson, Jr., Leland C. Nielsen, William B. Enright, all San Diego.

Colorado: Alfred A. Arraj, CJ, Fred M. Winner, Sherman G. Finesilver, Richard P. Matsch, all Denver.

Connecticut: T. Emmet Clarie, CJ, M. Joseph Blumenfeld, Jon O. Newman, all Hartford; Robert C. Zampano, New Haven.

Delaware: James L. Latchum, CJ, Murray M. Schwartz, Walter K. Stapleton, all Wilmington.

District of Columbia: William B. Jones, CJ, George L. Hart, Jr., John J. Sirica, Howard F. Corcoran, Oliver Gasch, William H. Bryant, John Lewis Smith, Jr., Aubrey E. Robinson, Jr., Joseph C. Waddy, Gerhard A. Gesell, John H. Pratt, June L. Green, Barrington D. Parker, Charles R. Richey, Thomas A. Flannery, all Washington, D.C.

Florida, Northern: Winston E. Arnow, CJ, Pensacola; William H. Stafford, Jr., Tallahassee.

Florida, Middle: George C. Young, CJ, John A. Reed, Jr., both Orlando; Charles R. Scott, Jacksonville; Ben Krentzman, William Terrell Hodges, both Tampa.

Florida, Southern: Charles B. Fulton, CJ, West Palm Beach; C. Clyde Atkins, Joe Eaton, Peter T. Fay, James Lawrence King, all Miami; Norman C. Roettger, Jr., Ft. Lauderdale.

Georgia, Northern: Newell Edenfield, CJ, William C. O'Kelley, Richard C. Freeman, James C. Hill, Albert J. Henderson, Jr., Charles A. Moye, Jr., all Atlanta.

Georgia, Middle: J. Robert Elliott, CJ, Columbus; Wilbur D. Owens, Jr., Macon.

Georgia, Southern: Alexander A. Lawrence, CJ, Savannah; Anthony A. Alaimo, Augusta.

Hawaii: Samuel P. King, CJ, Dick Yin Wong, both Honolulu.

Idaho: Ray McNichols, CJ, J. Blaine Anderson, both Boise.

Illinois, Eastern: Henry S. Wise, CJ, Danville; James L. Foreman, East St. Louis.

Illinois, Northern: James B. Parsons, CJ, Hubert L. Will, Bernard M. Decker, William J. Lynch, Frank J. McGarr, Thomas R. McMillen, Prentice H. Marshall, Joel M. Flaum, Alfred Y. Kirkland, John F. Grady, George N. Leighton, all Chicago.

Illinois, Southern: Robert D. Morgan, CJ, Peoria.

Indiana, Northern: Jesse E. Eschbach, CJ, Ft. Wayne; Allen Sharp, Phil M. McNagny, Jr., both Hammond.

Indiana, Southern: William E. Steckler, CJ, Cale J. Holder, S. Hugh Dillin, James E. Noland, all Indianapolis.

Iowa, Northern: Edward J. McManus, CJ, Cedar Rapids; William C. Hanson, Ft. Dodge.

Iowa, Southern: William C. Hanson, CJ, Ft. Dodge; William C. Stuart, Des Moines.

Kansas: Wesley E. Brown, CJ, Frank G. Theis, both Wichita; Earl E. O'Connor, Kansas City; Richard Dean Rogers, Topeka.

Kentucky, Eastern: Bernard T. Moynahan, Jr., CJ, Eugene E. Siler, Jr., both Lexington; Howard David Hermansdorfer, Catlettsburg.

Kentucky, Western: Rhodes Bratcher, CJ, Charles M. Allen, both Louisville; Eugene E. Siler, Jr., Lexington.

Louisiana, Eastern: Frederick J. R. Heebe, CJ, Edward J. Boyle, Sr., Lansing L. Mitchell, Fred J. Cassibry, Alvin B. Rubin, R. Blake West, Jack M. Gordon, Morey L. Sear, all New Orleans.

Louisiana, Middle: E. Gordon West, Baton Rouge.

Louisiana, Western: Nauman S. Scott, CJ, Alexandria; Tom Stagg, Shreveport.

Maine: Edward Thaxter Gignoux, Portland.

Maryland: Edward S. Northrop, CJ, Frank A. Kaufman, Alexander Harvey, II, James R. Miller, Jr., Herbert F. Murray, C. Stanley Blair, Joseph H. Young, all Baltimore.

Massachusetts: Andrew A. Caffrey, CJ, W. Arthur Garrity, Jr., Frank J. Murray, Frank H. Freedman, Joseph L. Tauro, Walter Jay Skinner, all Boston.

Michigan, Eastern: Damon J. Keith, CJ, Lawrence Gubow, Cornelia G. Kennedy, John Feikens, Philip Pratt, Robert E. DeMascio, Charles W. Joiner, James P. Churchill, Ralph B. Guy, Jr., all Detroit; James Harvey, Bay City.

Michigan, Western: Noel P. Fox, CJ, Wendell A. Miles, both Grand Rapids.

Minnesota: Edward J. Devitt, CJ, Donald D. Alsop, both St. Paul; Earl R. Larson, Miles W. Lord, both Minneapolis.

Mississippi, Northern: William C. Keady, CJ, Greenville; Orma R. Smith, Aberdeen.

Mississippi, Southern: Dan M. Russell, Jr., CJ, Gulfport; Walter L. Nixon, Jr., Biloxi; William Harold Cox, Jackson.

Missouri, Eastern: James H. Meredith, CJ, John K. Regan, H. Kenneth Wangelin, John F. Nangle, all St. Louis; William R. Collinson, Kansas City.

Missouri, Western: William H. Becker, CJ, John W. Oliver, William R. Collinson, Elmo B. Hunter, all Kansas City; H. Kenneth Wangelin, St. Louis.

Montana: Russell E. Smith, CJ, Missoula; James F. Battin, Billings.

Nebraska: Warren K. Urbom, CJ, Lincoln; Robert V. Denney, Albert G. Schatz, both Omaha.

Nevada: Roger D. Foley, CJ, Las Vegas; Bruce R. Thompson, Reno.

New Hampshire: Hugh H. Bownes, Concord.

New Jersey: Lawrence A. Whipple, CJ, Frederick B. Lacey, Vincent P. Biunno, Herbert J. Stern, H. Curtis Meanor, all Newark; George H. Barlow, Clarkson S. Fisher, both Trenton; John F. Gerry, Stanley S. Brotman, both Camden.

New Mexico: H. Vearle Payne, CJ, Howard C. Bratton, Edwin L. Mechem, all Albuquerque.

New York, Eastern: Jacob Mishler, CJ, John F. Dooling, Jr., Jack B. Weinstein, Mark A. Costantino, Edward R. Neaher, Thomas C. Platt Jr., Henry Bramwell, George C. Pratt, all Brooklyn.

New York, Northern: James T. Foley, CJ, Albany.

New York, Southern: David N. Edelstein, CJ, Edward Weinfeld, Charles M. Metzner, Lloyd F. MacMahon, Dudley B. Bonsal, Inzer B. Wyatt, John M. Cannella, Charles H. Tenney, Marvin E. Frankel, Constance Baker Motley, Milton Pollack, Morris E. Lasker, Lawrence W. Pierce, Charles L. Brieant, Jr., Lee P. Gagliardi, Whitman H. Knapp, Charles E. Stewart, Jr., Thomas P. Griesa, Robert L. Carter, Robert J. Ward, Kevin Thomas Duffy, William C. Conner, Richard Owen, Henry F. Werker, Gerard L. Goettel, Charles S. Haight, Jr., all New York City.

New York, Western: John T. Curtin, CJ, John T. Elfvin, both Buffalo; Harold P. Burke, Rochester.

North Carolina, Eastern: John D. Larkins, Jr., CJ, Trenton; Algernon L. Butler, Clinton; Franklin T. Dupree, Jr., Raleigh.

North Carolina, Middle: Eugene A. Gordon, CJ, Greensboro; Hiram H. Ward, Winston-Salem.

North Carolina, Western: Woodrow Wilson Jones, CJ, Rutherfordton; James B. McMillan, Charlotte.

North Dakota: Paul Benson, CJ, Fargo; Bruce M. Van Sickle, Bismarck.

Ohio, Northern: Frank J. Battisti, CJ, William K. Thomas, Thomas D. Lambros, Robert B. Krupansky, John M. Manos, all Cleveland; Don J. Young, Nicholas J. Walinski, both Toledo; Leroy J. Contie, Jr., Akron.

Ohio, Southern: Timothy S. Hogan, CJ, David S. Porter, both Cincinnati; Joseph P. Kinneary, Robert M. Duncan, both Columbus; Carl B. Rubin, Dayton.

Oklahoma, Eastern: Joseph W. Morris, CJ, Muskogee; Frederick A. Daugherty, Oklahoma City; H. Dale Cook, Tulsa.

Oklahoma, Northern: Allen E. Barrow, CJ, H. Dale Cook, both Tulsa; Frederick A. Daugherty, Oklahoma City.

Oklahoma, Western: Frederick A. Daugherty, CJ, Luther B. Eubanks, Ralph G. Thompson, all Oklahoma City; H. Dale Cook, Tulsa.

Oregon: Robert C. Belloni, CJ, Otto R. Skopil, Jr., James M. Burns, all Portland.

Pennsylvania, Eastern: Joseph S. Lord, III, CJ, Alfred L. Luongo, A. Leon Higginbotham, Jr., John P. Fullam, Charles R. Weiner, John B. Hannum, Donald W. Van Artsdalen, J. William Ditter, Jr., Edward R. Becker, James H. Gorbey, Raymond J. Broderick, E. Mac Troutman, Daniel H. Huyett, III, Clarence C. Newcomer, Clifford S. Green, Louis Charles Bechtle, Herbert A. Fogel, Joseph L. McGlynn, Jr., Edward N. Cahn, all Philadelphia.

Pennsylvania, Middle: Michael H. Sheridan, CJ, Wilkes-Barre; William J. Nealon, Jr., Scranton; R. Dixon Herman, Harrisburg; Malcolm Muir, Williamsport.

Pennsylvania, Western: Herbert P. Sorg, CJ, Rabe Ferguson Marsh, Edward Dumbauld, Hubert I. Teitelbaum, Barron P. McCune, Daniel J. Snyder, Jr., Maurice B. Cohill, Jr., all Pittsburgh; Gerald J. Weber, William W. Knox, both Erie.

Puerto Rico: José V. Toledo, CJ., Herman G. Pesquera, Juan R. Torruella, all San Juan.

Rhode Island: Raymond J. Pettine, CJ, Providence.

South Carolina: J. Robert Martin, Jr., CJ, Greenville; Robert W. Hemphill, Columbia; Charles E. Simons, Jr., Aiken; Solomon Blatt, Jr., Charleston; Robert F. Chapman, Florence.

South Dakota: Fred J. Nichol, CJ, Sioux Falls; Andrew W. Bogue, Rapid City.

Tennessee, Eastern: Frank W. Wilson, CJ, Chattanooga; C. G. Neese, Greeneville; Robert L. Taylor, Knoxville.

Tennessee, Middle: Frank Gray, Jr., CJ, L. Clure Morton, both Nashville.

Tennessee, Western: Bailey Brown, CJ, Robert M. McRae, Jr., Harry W. Wellford, all Memphis.

Texas, Northern: William M. Taylor, Jr., CJ, Robert M. Hill, Robert W. Porter, Patrick E. Higginbotham, all Dallas; Halbert O. Woodward, Lubbock; Eldon B. Mahon, Fort Worth.

Texas, Southern: Reynaldo G. Garza, CJ, Brownsville; James Noel, Jr., John V. Singleton, Jr., Woodrow B. Seals, Carl O. Bue, all Houston; Owen D. Cox, Corpus Christi; Robert O'Conor, Jr., Laredo.

Texas, Eastern: Joe J. Fisher, CJ, William M. Steger, both Beaumont; William Wayne Justice, Tyler.

Texas, Western: Adrian A. Spears, CJ, Dorwin W. Suttle, John H. Wood, Jr., all San Antonio; William S. Sessions, El Paso; Jack Roberts, Austin.

Utah: Willis W. Ritter, CJ, Aldon J. Anderson, both Salt Lake City.

Vermont: James S. Holden, CJ, Rutland; Albert W. Coffrin, Burlington.

Virginia, Eastern: Richard B. Kellam, CJ, J. Calvitt Clarke, Jr., John A. MacKenzie, all Norfolk; Albert V. Bryan, Jr., Alexandria; D. Dortch Warriner, Robert R. Merhige, Jr., both Richmond.

Virginia, Western: James C. Turk, CJ, Ted Dalton, both Roanoke.

Washington, Eastern: Marshall A. Neill, CJ, Spokane.

Washington, Western: Walter T. McGovern, CJ, Morell E. Sharp, Donald S. Voorhees, all Seattle.

West Virginia, Northern: Robert Earl Maxwell, CJ, Elkins; Charles H. Haden II, Charleston.

West Virginia, Southern: Dennis Raymond Knapp, CJ, Kenneth K. Hall, Charles H. Haden II, all Charleston.

Wisconsin, Eastern: John W. Reynolds, CJ, Myron L. Gordon, Robert W. Warren, all Milwaukee.

Wisconsin, Western: James E. Doyle, Madison.

Wyoming: Clarence A. Brimmer, Cheyenne.

Territorial Courts

Canal Zone: Guthrie F. Crowe, Balboa Heights.

Guam: Cristobal C. Duenas, Agana.

Virgin Islands: Almeric L. Christian, CJ, St. Thomas; Warren H. Young, St. Croix.

Special Trial Judges of the Court

Chief Special Trial Judge: Randolph F. Caldwell, Jr. **Trial Judges:** James M. Gussis, Joseph N. Ingolia, Charles R. Johnston, John H. Sacks, Lehman C. Aarons, Murray H. Falk.

Members of the Supreme Court of the United States

Name	Birth Place	Birth Date	Religious affiliation (Source: Library of Congress)	Appointment From	Appointment President	Oath taken Date	Oath taken Age	Service terminated Date	Service terminated Cause	Service terminated Years served	Service terminated Age	Death Date	Death Age
CHIEF JUSTICES													
John Jay	N.Y.	1745	Episcopal	N.Y.	Washington	1789	44	1795	resigned	5	49	1829	83
John Rutledge	S.C.	1739	Church of England	S.C.	Washington	1795	55	1795	rejected	0	56	1800	60
Oliver Ellsworth	Conn.	1745	Congregational	Conn.	Washington	1796	50	1800	resigned	4	55	1807	62
John Marshall	Va.	1755	Episcopal	Va.	J. Adams	1801	45	1835	death	34	79	1835	79
Roger B. Taney	Md.	1777	Roman Catholic	Md.	Jackson	1836	59	1864	death	28	87	1864	87
Salmon P. Chase	N.H.	1808	Episcopal	Ohio	Lincoln	1864	56	1873	death	8	65	1873	65
Morrison R. Waite	Conn.	1816	Episcopal	Ohio	Grant	1874	57	1888	death	14	71	1888	71
Melville W. Fuller	Me.	1833	Episcopal	Ill.	Cleveland	1888	55	1910	death	21	77	1910	77
Edward D. White	La.	1845	Roman Catholic	La.	Taft	1910	65	1921	death	10	75	1921	75
William H. Taft	Ohio	1857	Unitarian	Conn.	Harding	1921	63	1930	retired	8	72	1930	72
Charles E. Hughes	N.Y.	1862	Baptist	N.Y.	Hoover	1930	67	1941	retired	11	79	1948	86
Harlan F. Stone	N.H.	1872	Episcopal	N.Y.	F. Roosevelt	1941	68	1946	death	4	73	1946	73
Frederick M. Vinson	Ky.	1890	Methodist	Ky.	Truman	1946	56	1953	death	7	63	1953	63
Earl Warren	Calif.	1891	Protestant	Calif.	Eisenhower	1953	62	1969	retired	15	78		83
Warren E. Burger	Minn.	1907	Presbyterian	Va.	Nixon	1969	61						
ASSOCIATE JUSTICES													
James Wilson	Scotland	1742	Episcopal	Pa.	Washington	1789	47	1798	death	8	55	1798	55
John Rutledge	S.C.	1739	Church of England	S.C.	Washington	1790	50	1791	resigned	1	51	1800	60
William Cushing	Mass.	1732	Unitarian	Mass.	Washington	1790	57	1810	death	20	78	1810	78
John Blair	Va.	1732	Presbyterian	Va.	Washington	1790	58	1796	resigned	5	64	1800	68
James Iredell	England	1751	Episcopal	N.C.	Washington	1790	38	1799	death	9	48	1799	48
Thomas Johnson	Md.	1732	Episcopal	Md.	Washington	1792	59	1793	resigned	0	60	1819	86
William Paterson	Ireland	1745	Protestant	N.J.	Washington	1793	47	1806	death	13	60	1806	60
Samuel Chase	Md.	1741	Episcopal	Md.	Washington	1796	54	1811	death	15	70	1811	70
Bushrod Washington	Va.	1762	Episcopal	Va.	J. Adams	1799	36	1829	death	30	67	1829	67
Alfred Moore	N.C.	1755	Episcopal	N.C.	J. Adams	1800	45	1804	resigned	3	48	1810	55
William Johnson	S.C.	1771	Presbyterian	S.C.	Jefferson	1804	32	1834	death	30	62	1834	62
Brockholst Livingston	N.Y.	1757	Presbyterian	N.Y.	Jefferson	1807	49	1823	death	16	65	1823	65
Thomas Todd	Va.	1765	Presbyterian	Ky.	Jefferson	1807	42	1826	death	18	61	1826	61
Gabriel Duval	Md.	1752	French Protestant	Md.	Madison	1811	58	1835	resigned	23	82	1844	91
Joseph Story	Mass.	1779	Unitarian	Mass.	Madison	1812	32	1845	death	33	65	1845	65
Smith Thompson	N.Y.	1768	Presbyterian	N.Y.	Monroe	1823	55	1843	death	20	75	1843	75
Robert Trimble	Va.	1777	Protestant	Ky.	J. Q. Adams	1826	49	1828	death	2	51	1828	51
John McLean	N.J.	1785	Methodist-Epis.	Ohio	Jackson	1830	44	1861	death	31	76	1861	76
Henry Baldwin	Conn.	1780	Trinity Church	Pa.	Jackson	1830	50	1844	death	14	64	1844	64
James M. Wayne	Ga.	1790	Protestant	Ga.	Jackson	1835	45	1867	death	32	77	1867	77

Name	Birth Place	Birth Date	Religious affiliation (Source: Library of Congress)	Appointment From	Appointment President	Oath taken Date	Oath taken Age	Service terminated Date	Service terminated Cause	Service terminated Years served	Service terminated Age	Death Date	Death Age
Philip P. Barbour	Va.	1783	Episcopal	Va.	Jackson	1836	52	1841	death	4	57	1841	57
John Catron	Pa.	1786	Presbyterian	Tenn.	Van Buren	1837	51	1865	death	28	79	1865	79
John McKinley	Va.	1780	Protestant	Ala.	Van Buren	1837	57	1852	death	14	72	1852	72
Peter V. Daniel	Va.	1784	Episcopal	Va.	Van Buren	1841	57	1860	death	18	76	1860	76
Samuel Nelson	N.Y.	1792	Protestant	N.Y.	Tyler	1845	52	1872	retired	27	80	1873	81
Levi Woodbury	N.H.	1789	Protestant	N.H.	Polk	1845	55	1851	death	5	61	1851	61
Robert C. Grier	Pa.	1794	Presbyterian	Pa.	Polk	1846	52	1870	retired	23	75	1870	76
Benjamin R. Curtis	Mass.	1809	(*)	Mass.	Fillmore	1851	41	1857	resigned	5	47	1874	64
John A. Campbell	Ga.	1811	Episcopal	Ala.	Pierce	1853	41	1861	resigned	8	49	1889	77
Nathan Clifford	N.H.	1803	(1)	Maine	Buchanan	1858	54	1881	death	23	77	1881	77
Noah H. Swayne	Va.	1804	Quaker	Ohio	Lincoln	1862	57	1881	retired	18	76	1884	79
Samuel F. Miller	Ky.	1816	Unitarian	Iowa	Lincoln	1862	46	1890	death	28	74	1890	74
David Davis	Md.	1815	(4)	Ill.	Lincoln	1862	47	1877	resigned	14	61	1886	71
Stephen J. Field	Conn.	1816	Episcopal	Calif.	Lincoln	1863	46	1897	retired	34	81	1899	82
William Strong	Conn.	1808	Presbyterian	Pa.	Grant	1870	61	1880	retired	10	72	1895	87
Joseph P. Bradley	N.Y.	1813	Presbyterian	N.J.	Grant	1870	57	1892	death	21	78	1892	78
Ward Hunt	N.Y.	1810	Episcopal	N.Y.	Grant	1872	62	1882	disabled	9	71	1886	75
John M. Harlan	Ky.	1833	Presbyterian	Ky.	Hayes	1877	44	1911	death	33	78	1911	78
William B. Woods	Ohio	1824	Protestant	Ga.	Hayes	1880	56	1887	death	6	62	1887	62
Stanley Matthews	Ohio	1824	Presbyterian	Ohio	Garfield	1881	56	1889	death	7	64	1889	64
Horace Gray	Mass.	1828	(5)	Mass.	Arthur	1882	53	1902	death	20	74	1902	74
Samuel Blatchford	N.Y.	1820	Presbyterian	N.Y.	Arthur	1882	62	1893	death	11	73	1893	73
Lucius Q. C. Lamar	Ga.	1825	Methodist	Miss.	Cleveland	1888	62	1893	death	5	67	1893	67
David J. Brewer	Asia Minor	1837	Protestant	Kans.	Harrison	1889	52	1910	death	20	72	1910	72
Henry B. Brown	Mass.	1836	Protestant	Mich.	Harrison	1890	54	1906	retired	15	70	1913	77
George Shiras, Jr.	Pa.	1832	Presbyterian	Pa.	Harrison	1892	60	1903	retired	10	71	1924	92
Howell E. Jackson	Tenn.	1832	Baptist	Tenn.	Harrison	1893	60	1895	death	2	63	1895	63
Edward D. White	La.	1845	Roman Catholic	La.	Cleveland	1894	48	1910	promoted	16	65	1921	75
Rufus W. Peckham	N.Y.	1838	Episcopal	N.Y.	Cleveland	1895	57	1909	death	13	70	1909	70
Joseph McKenna	Pa.	1843	Roman Catholic	Calif.	McKinley	1898	54	1925	retired	26	81	1926	83
Oliver W. Holmes	Mass.	1841	Unitarian	Mass.	T. Roosevelt	1902	61	1932	retired	29	90	1935	93
William R. Day	Ohio	1849	Protestant	Ohio	T. Roosevelt	1903	53	1922	retired	19	73	1923	74
William H. Moody	Mass.	1853	Episcopal	Mass.	T. Roosevelt	1906	52	1910	disabled	3	56	1917	63
Horace H. Lurton	Ky.	1844	Episcopal	Tenn.	Taft	1909	65	1914	death	4	70	1914	70
Charles E. Hughes	N.Y.	1862	Baptist	N.Y.	Taft	1910	48	1916	resigned	5	54	1948	86
Willis Van Devanter	Ind.	1859	Episcopal	Wyo.	Taft	1910	51	1937	retired	26	78	1941	81
Joseph R. Lamar	Ga.	1857	Ch. of Disciples	Ga.	Taft	1910	53	1916	death	4	58	1916	58
Mahlon Pitney	N.J.	1858	Presbyterian	N.J.	Taft	1912	54	1922	disabled	10	64	1924	66
James C. McReynolds	Tenn.	1862	Disciples of Christ	Tenn.	Wilson	1914	52	1941	retired	26	78	1946	84
Louis D. Brandeis	Ky.	1856	Hebrew	Mass.	Wilson	1916	59	1939	retired	22	82	1941	84
John H. Clarke	Ohio	1857	Protestant	Ohio	Wilson	1916	59	1922	resigned	5	65	1945	87
George Sutherland	England	1862	Episcopal	Utah	Harding	1922	60	1938	retired	15	75	1942	80

Pierce Butler	Minn.	1866	Roman Catholic	Harding	Minn.	1923	56	1939	death	16	73	1939	73
Edward T. Sanford	Tenn.	1865	Episcopal	Harding	Tenn.	1923	57	1930	death	7	64	1930	64
Harlan F. Stone	N. H.	1872	Episcopal	Coolidge	N. Y.	1925	52	1941	promoted	16	68	1946	73
Owen J. Roberts	Pa.	1875	Episcopal	Hoover	Pa.	1930	55	1945	resigned	15	70	1955	80
Benjamin N. Cardozo	N. Y.	1870	Hebrew	Hoover	N. Y.	1932	61	1938	death	6	68	1938	68
Hugo L. Black	Ala.	1886	Baptist	F. Roosevelt	Ala.	1937	51	1971	retired	34	85	1971	85
Stanley F. Reed	Ky.	1884	Protestant	F. Roosevelt	Ky.	1938	53	1957	retired	19	72		
Felix Frankfurter	Austria	1882	Hebrew	F. Roosevelt	Mass.	1939	56	1962	retired	23	79	1965	82
William O. Douglas	Minn.	1898	Presbyterian	F. Roosevelt	Conn.	1939	40	1975	retired	36	77		
Frank Murphy	Mich.	1890	Roman Catholic	F. Roosevelt	Mich.	1940	49	1949	death	9	59	1949	59
James F. Byrnes	S. C.	1879	Episcopal	F. Roosevelt	S. C.	1941	62	1942	resigned	1	63	1972	92
Robert H. Jackson	N. Y.	1892	Episcopal	F. Roosevelt	N. Y.	1941	49	1954	death	13	62	1954	62
Wiley B. Rutledge	Ky.	1894	Unitarian	F. Roosevelt	Iowa	1943	48	1949	death	6	55	1949	55
Harold H. Burton	Mass.	1888	Unitarian	Truman	Ohio	1945	57	1958	retired	13	70	1964	76
Tom C. Clark	Tex.	1899	Presbyterian	Truman	Tex.	1949	49	1967	retired	17	67		
Sherman Minton	Ind.	1890	Roman Catholic	Truman	Ind.	1949	58	1956	retired	7	65	1965	74
John M. Harlan	Ill.	1899	Presbyterian	Eisenhower	N. Y.	1955	55	1971	retired	16	72	1971	72
William J. Brennan, Jr.	N. J.	1906	Roman Catholic	Eisenhower	N. J.	1956	50						
Charles E. Whittaker	Kan.	1901	Methodist	Eisenhower	Mo.	1957	56	1962	disabled	5	61	1973	73
Potter Stewart	Mich.	1915	Episcopal	Eisenhower	Ohio	1958	43						
Byron R. White	Colo.	1917	Episcopal	Kennedy	Colo.	1962	44						
Arthur J. Goldberg	Ill.	1908	Hebrew	Kennedy	Ill.	1962	54	1965	resigned	2	56		
Abe Fortas	Tenn.	1910	Hebrew	Johnson	Tenn.	1965	55	1969	resigned	3	58		
Thurgood Marshall	Md.	1908	Episcopalian	Johnson	N. Y.	1967	59						
Harry A. Blackmun	Ill.	1908	Methodist	Nixon	Minn.	1970	61						
Lewis F. Powell, Jr.	Va.	1907	Presbyterian	Nixon	Va.	1972	64						
William H. Rehnquist	Minn.	1924	Lutheran	Nixon	Wisc.	1972	47						
John Paul Stevens	Ill.	1920	Protestant	Ford	Ill.	1975	55						

[1] Congregationalist; later Unitarian. [2] Unitarian; then Episcopal. [3] Unitarian or Congregational. [4] Not a member of any Church.

Impeachments of Federal Officials

Source: *Congressional Directory.*

(The procedure for the impeachment of Federal officials is detailed in Article I, Section 3, of the Constitution. It may be found on p. 514.)

The Senate has sat as a court of impeachment in the following cases:

WILLIAM BLOUNT, Senator from Tennessee; charges dismissed for want of jurisdiction, January 14, 1799.

JOHN PICKERING, Judge of the U. S. District Court for New Hampshire; removed from office March 12, 1804.

SAMUEL CHASE, Associate Justice of the Supreme Court; acquitted March 1, 1805.

JAMES H. PECK, Judge of the U. S. District Court for Missouri; acquitted Jan. 31, 1831.

WEST H. HUMPHREYS, Judge of the United States District Court for the middle, eastern, and western districts of Tennessee; removed from office June 26, 1862.

ANDREW JOHNSON, President of the United States; acquitted May 26, 1868.

WILLIAM W. BELKNAP, Secretary of War; acquitted Aug. 1, 1876.

CHARLES SWAYNE, Judge of the United States District Court for the northern district of Florida; acquitted Feb. 27, 1905.

ROBERT W. ARCHBALD, Associate Judge, U. S. Commerce Court; removed Jan. 13, 1913.

GEORGE W. ENGLISH, Judge of U. S. District Court for eastern district of Illinois; resigned Nov. 4, 1926; proceedings dismissed.

HAROLD LOUDERBACK, Judge of the U. S. District Court for the northern district of California; acquitted May 24, 1933.

HALSTED L. RITTER, Judge of the U. S. District Court for the southern district of Florida; removed from office April 17, 1936.

U. S. TREATIES SINCE 1947

Organization of American States (OAS) and the Rio Treaty

In Sept., 1947, eighteen Latin American countries (Nicaragua and Ecuador were excluded) and the United States signed at Rio de Janeiro the Rio Treaty under which all signatories agreed to protect against aggression every state in the Western Hemisphere. In Apr., 1948, all the American nations (twenty-one—Canada not included) joined in the Organization of American States (OAS) to implement the Rio Treaty and form a collective security system.

North Atlantic Treaty Organization (NATO)

(Formed: April 4, 1949)

Members: United States, Canada, Iceland, Norway, Great Britain, Netherlands, Denmark, Belgium, Luxemburg, Portugal, France, Italy, Greece, Turkey, West Germany

In 1948, the United States government began talks with the signers of the Brussels Pact and Canada concerning the formation of a regional defense treaty in the North Atlantic area. It represented the first important security pact with European nations since the French Alliance of 1778 and marked the first time in United States history that the United States pledged itself to go to war in support of allies before the actual outbreak of hostilities. The U. S. Senate ratified the treaty July 21, 1949.

The United States, acting under Article 3 of the Treaty, began a program of military assistance which at the end of the fiscal year 1959 amounted to over $10 billion. Roughly half of all United States military assistance has gone to members of NATO. However, approximately 85% of NATO's military preparation has come from the European countries themselves.

NATO now united most of the countries of the Atlantic community plus Greece, Turkey, and West Germany, which were added to the original membership. Its organization comprises the top foreign, economic, defense, and financial ministers of the member countries. The military responsibilities of NATO are divided into two major commands—SHAPE for Europe and SACLANT for the Atlantic Ocean area.

Following are key quotations from the North Atlantic Treaty text. (Complete text in 1960 Information Please Almanac.)

From Article 1: "The Parties undertake . . . to refrain in their international relations from the threat or use of force in any manner inconsistent with the purposes of the United Nations."

From Article 2: "The Parties . . . will seek to eliminate conflict in their international economic policies and will encourage economic collaboration between any or all of them."

From Article 5: "The Parties agree that an armed attack against one or more of them in Europe or North America shall be considered an attack against them all; and consequently they agree that, if such an armed attack occurs, each of them, in exercise of the right of individual or collective self-defense recognized by Article 51 of the Charter of the United Nations, will assist the Party or Parties so attacked by taking forthwith, individually and in concert with other Parties, such action as it deems necessary, including the use of armed force, to restore and maintain the security of the North Atlantic area."

From Article 9: "The Parties hereby establish a council, on which each of them shall be represented, to consider matters concerning the implementation of this Treaty."

Tripartite Security (Anzus) Treaty

(United States, Australia, New Zealand)

Major provisions of the Tripartite agreement signed on Sept. 1, 1951, at San Francisco:

1. The parties undertake to settle by peaceful means any international disputes in which they may be involved.

2. The parties will maintain and develop their individual and collective capacity to resist armed attack.

3. The parties will consult together whenever the territorial integrity, political independence or security of any of the parties is threatened in the Pacific.

4. Each party recognizes that an armed attack in the Pacific area on either of the other parties would be dangerous to its own peace and safety.

5. The parties hereby establish a council, consisting of their foreign ministers or their deputies, to consider matters concerning the implementation of this treaty.

6. This treaty shall remain in force indefinitely.

(A Defense Treaty similar in its provisions to the Tripartite Security Treaty was signed by the U. S. and the Philippines in Washington, D. C., Aug. 30, 1951.)

Japanese Peace Treaty

The Japanese Peace Treaty was signed at San Francisco on September 8, 1951, by 49 nations; the U.S.S.R., Poland, and Czechoslovakia were present but refused to sign. Among the major provisions of the treaty are the following:

Peace: The state of war between Japan and the Allies is terminated.

Sovereignty: Japan's full sovereignty is recognized as is its right to apply for U. N. membership.

Territory: Japan recognizes the independence of Korea; renounces all rights, titles, or claims to Formosa, the Pescadores, the Kuriles, Sakhalin, the Pacific islands formerly under mandate to Japan, the Antarctic area, Spratly Island, and the Paracels.

Japan agrees to U. N. trusteeship over the Ryukyu and Daito Islands, the Bonins, Rosario Island, the Volcano Islands, Parece Vela, and Marcus Island. Disposition of Japanese property on these islands is to be negotiated by Japan and the administering authorities.

Security: Japan agrees to settle its international disputes peaceably, to refrain from the threat of or the use of force and to abide by the principles of the U. N.

All occupation forces are to be withdrawn as soon as possible but not later than 90 days after a majority of the signatory countries have given notice of ratification of this treaty. Nothing in this provision shall, however, prevent the stationing or retention of foreign armed forces in Japanese territory by agreement with one or more of the Allies.

Political-Economic Clauses: Japan may enter into fisheries treaties; may negotiate most-favored-nation trade and maritime treaties with the Allies; renounces all special rights and interests in China.

Japan accepts the judgments of the International Military Tribunal and Allied War Crimes Courts.

Claims and Property: Japan recognizes its responsibility to pay reparations but the Allies recognize its limited economic capacity; therefore, Japan shall pay through goods to be manufactured in Japan from raw materials provided by the victimized nations and by services. The Allies may retain certain properties seized from Japan but require the latter to return their properties within 6 months. Japan recognizes Allied industrial, literary, and artistic property rights. It agrees to indemnify prisoners of war who suffered unduly but renounces similar claims against the Allies.

Settlement of Disputes: Any disagreements arising out of the interpretation of this treaty and not otherwise settled shall be submitted to the International Court of Justice.

Southeast Asia Treaty Organization (SEATO)
(Signed: Sept. 8, 1954)

Members: United States, Great Britain, France, Australia, New Zealand, Pakistan (withdrew in November 1972), Thailand, Philippines

Weaker than NATO, SEATO did not include rigid provisions for collective defense but stated that armed attack on any member would be regarded as a threat to safety of the others. SEATO represented the United States' desire to counterbalance the power of Communist China. SEATO was disbanded in February 1976.

Central Treaty Organization (CENTO)
(Formerly Baghdad Pact)

(Signed: by Turkey and Iraq, Feb. 24, 1955; by Great Britain, Apr. 14, 1955; by Pakistan, Sept. 23, 1955; by Iran, Nov. 3, 1955.)

Members: Turkey, Iran, Great Britain, Pakistan. (Iraq, withdrew in March, 1959). On July 28, 1958, the United States signed a declaration of collective security committing the U. S. to cooperate with the member nations.

The purpose of CENTO is to provide a defense shield on the northern tier of the Middle East against Soviet penetration. The headquarters were transferred in October, 1958, from Baghdad to Ankara, and the name was changed from Baghdad Pact to Central Treaty Organization in August, 1959.

U. S.–Japanese Treaty
(Signed: Jan. 19, 1960)

This treaty affirms the obligation of the parties to settle international differences in a manner consistent with the U.N. Charter, to strengthen economic and other ties between the two countries, and to resist armed attack individually and by mutual assistance.

Summary of Major Provisions

Article I: The Parties undertake to settle by peaceful means any international disputes in which they may be involved. They will endeavor to strengthen the United Nations so that its mission of peace may be discharged more effectively.

Article II: They will seek to eliminate conflict and encourage collaboration in their economic policies.

Article III: They will maintain and develop, subject to their constitutional provisions, their capacities to resist attack.

Article IV: They will consult together

whenever the security of Japan or the Far East is threatened.

Article V: Each Party recognizes that an armed attack against either in the territories under the administration of Japan would be dangerous to its own peace and declares that it would meet the common danger in accordance with its constitution.

Such measures shall be reported to the Security Council and be terminated when the Security Council has taken the measures necessary to restore international peace and security.

Article VI: For the security of Japan and the Far East, the United States is granted the use by its land, air, and naval forces of facilities and areas in Japan.

Article VII: This Treaty does not affect the rights and obligations of the Parties under the Charter of the United Nations or the responsibility of the United Nations for the maintenance of international peace and security.

Article X: After this Treaty has been in force for ten years, either Party may give notice to the other Party of its intention to terminate the Treaty, in which case it shall terminate one year later.

Treaty for a Partial Nuclear Test Ban
(United States, United Kingdom, U.S.S.R.)

Major provisions of the agreement signed on Aug. 5 1963, at Moscow. The treaty went into effect on Oct. 10, 1963. Over 100 other nations, with the notable exceptions of France and Communist China, have since joined the Big Three as signatories.

From Article I: "Each of the parties to this treaty undertakes to prohibit, to prevent, and not to carry out any nuclear weapon test explosion, or any other nuclear explosion at any place under its jurisdiction or control: (a) In the atmosphere, beyond its limits, including outer space, or underwater, including territorial waters or high seas; or (b) In any other environment if such explosion causes radioactive debris to be present outside the territorial limits of the state under whose jurisdiction or control such explosion is conducted . . ."

From Article III: "This treaty shall be open to all states for signature. . . ."

From Article IV: ". . . Each party shall in exercising its national sovereignty have the right to withdraw from the treaty if it decides that extraordinary events, related to the subject matter of this treaty, have jeopardized the supreme interests of its country. It shall give notice of such withdrawal to all other parties to the treaty three months in advance."

ALLIED POLICY DECISIONS OF WORLD WAR II

The Cairo Conference

Important provisions of the Conference, which was held Nov. 22-26, 1943:

The several military missions have agreed upon future military operations against Japan. The Three Great Allies expressed their resolve to bring unrelenting pressure against their brutal enemies by sea, land, and air. This pressure is already rising.

The Three Great Allies are fighting this war to restrain and punish the aggression of Japan. They covet no gain for themselves and have no thought of territorial expansion. It is their purpose that Japan shall be stripped of all the islands in the Pacific which she has seized or occupied since the beginning of the first World War in 1914, and that all the territories Japan has stolen from the Chinese, such as Manchuria, Formosa, and the Pescadores, shall be restored to the Republic of China. Japan will also be expelled from all other territories which she has taken by violence and greed. The aforesaid Three Great Powers, mindful of the enslavement of the people of Korea, are determined that in

due course Korea shall become free and independent.

With these objectives in view the three Allies, in harmony with those of the United Nations at war with Japan, will continue to persevere in the serious and prolonged operations necessary to procure the unconditional surrender of Japan.

The Teheran Conference

(Nov. 28–Dec. 1, 1943)

The President of the United States of America, the Premier of the Union of Soviet Socialist Republics, and the Prime Minister of the United Kingdom have consulted with each other and, with the Prime Minister of Iran, desire to declare the mutual agreement of their three Governments regarding relations with Iran.

The Governments of the United States of America, the Union of Soviet Socialist Republics, and the United Kingdom recognize the assistance which Iran has given in the prosecution of the war against the common enemy, particularly by facilitating transportation of supplies from overseas to the Soviet Union. The three Governments realize that the war has caused special economic difficulties for Iran and they are agreed that they will continue to make available to the Government of Iran such economic assistance as may be possible, having regard to the heavy demands made upon them by their worldwide military operations and to the worldwide shortage of transport, raw materials, and supplies for civilian consumption.

With respect to the post-war period, the Governments of the United States of America, the Union of Soviet Socialist Republics, and the United Kingdom are in accord with the Government of Iran that any economic problem confronting Iran at the close of hostilities should receive full consideration along with those of the other members of the United Nations by conferences or international agencies held or created to deal with international economic matters.

The Governments of the United States of America, the Union of Soviet Socialist Republics, and the United Kingdom are at one with the Government of Iran in their desire for the maintenance of the independence, sovereignty, and territorial integrity of Iran. They count upon the participation of Iran together with all other peace-loving nations in the establishment of international peace, security, and prosperity after the war in accordance with the principles of the Atlantic Charter, to which all four governments have continued to subscribe.

The Yalta Conference
Important provisions of the Conference, which was held Feb. 4-11, 1945:

The Occupation and Control of Germany

We have agreed on common policies and plans for enforcing the unconditional surrender terms which we shall impose together on Nazi Germany after German armed resistance has been finally crushed. These terms will not be made known until the final defeat of Germany has been accomplished. Under the agreed plan, the forces of the three powers will each occupy a separate zone of Germany. Coordinated administration and control has been provided for under the plan through a central Control Commission, consisting of the supreme commanders of the three powers, with headquarters in Berlin. It has been agreed that France should be invited by the three powers, if she should so desire, to take over a zone of occupation, and to participate as a fourth member of the Control Commission. The limits of the French zone will be agreed upon by the four Governments concerned through their representatives on the European Advisory Commission.

It is our inflexible purpose to destroy German militarism and nazism and to ensure that Germany will never again be able to disturb the peace of the world. We are determined to disarm and disband all German armed forces; break up for all time the German General Staff that has repeatedly contrived the resurgence of German militarism; remove or destroy all German military equipment; eliminate or control all German industry that could be used for military production; bring all war criminals to just and swift punishment and exact reparation in kind for the destruction wrought by the Germans; wipe out the Nazi Party, Nazi laws, organizations, and institutions, remove all Nazi and militarist influences from public office and from the cultural and economic life of the German people; and take in harmony such other measures in Germany as may be necessary to the future peace and safety of the world. It is not our purpose to destroy the people of Germany, but only when nazism and militarism have been extirpated will there be hope for a decent life for Germans, and a place for them in the comity of nations.

Terms Under Which Russia Entered the War Against Japan

The leaders of the Three Great Powers—the Soviet Union, the United States of America, and Great Britain—have agreed that in two or three months after Germany has surrendered and the war in Europe has terminated the Soviet Union shall enter into the war against Japan on the side of the Allies on condition that:

1. The status quo in Outer Mongolia (The Mongolian People's Republic) shall be preserved;

2. The former rights of Russia violated by the treacherous attack of Japan in 1904 shall be restored, viz.:

(a) the southern part of Sakhalin as well as all the islands adjacent to it shall be returned to the Soviet Union,

(b) the commercial port of Dairen shall be internationalized, the preeminent interests of the Soviet Union in this port being safeguarded and the lease of Port Arthur as a naval base of the U.S.S.R. restored,

(c) the Chinese-Eastern Railroad and the South-Manchurian Railroad which provides an outlet to Dairen shall be jointly operated by the establishment of a joint Soviet-Chinese Company, it being understood that the preeminent interests of the Soviet Union shall be safeguarded and that China shall retain full sovereignty in Manchuria;

3. The Kurile Islands shall be handed over to the Soviet Union.

It is understood that the agreement concerning Outer Mongolia and the ports and railroads referred to above will require concurrence of Generalissimo Chiang Kai-shek. The President will take measures in order to obtain this concurrence on advice from Marshal Stalin.

The Heads of the Three Great Powers have agreed that these claims of the Soviet Union shall be unquestionably fulfilled after Japan has been defeated.

For its part the Soviet Union expresses its readiness to conclude with the National Government of China a pact of friendship and alliance between the U.S.S.R. and China in order to render assistance to China with its armed forces for the purpose of liberating China from the Japanese yoke.

The Potsdam Declaration

Text of the declaration issued at Potsdam, Germany, July 26, 1945, outlining the terms under which Japan would be allowed to surrender:

1. We, the President of the United States, the President of the national government of the Republic of China, and the Prime Minister of Great Britain, representing the hundreds of millions of our countrymen, have conferred and agreed that Japan shall be given the opportunity to end this war.

2. The prodigious land, sea, and air forces of the United States, the British Empire, and China, many times reinforced by their armies and air fleets from the west, are poised to strike the final blow at Japan. This military power is sustained and inspired by the determination of all allied nations to prosecute the war against Japan until she ceases to resist.

3. The result of the futile and senseless German resistance to the might of the aroused free peoples of the world stands forth in awful clarity as an example to the people of Japan.

The might that now converges on Japan is immeasurably greater than that which, when applied to the resisting Nazis, necessarily laid waste to the land, the industry, and the method of life of the whole German people.

The full application of our military power, backed by our resolve, will mean the inevitable and complete destruction of the Japanese armed forces and just as inevitably the utter devastation of the Japanese homeland.

4. The time has come for Japan to decide whether she will continue to be controlled by these self-willed militaristic advisers whose unintelligent calculations have brought the empire of Japan to the threshold of annihilation, or whether she will follow the path of reason.

5. The following are our terms: we will not deviate from them; there are no alternatives; we shall brook no delay.

6. There must be eliminated for all time the authority and influence of those who have deceived and misled the people of Japan into embarking on world conquest, for we insist that a new order of peace, security, and justice will be impossible until irresponsible militarism is driven from the world.

7. Until such a new order is established and until there is convincing proof that Japan's war-making power is destroyed, points in Japanese territory to be designated by the Allies shall be occupied to secure the achievement of the basic objectives we are here setting forth.

8. The terms of the Cairo declaration shall be carried out and Japanese sovereignty shall be limited to the Islands of Honshu, Hokkaido, Kyushu, Shikoku, and such minor islands as we determine.

9. Japanese military forces after being completely disarmed shall be permitted to return to their homes with the opportunity to lead peaceful and productive lives.

10. We do not intend that the Japanese shall be enslaved as a race or destroyed as a nation, but stern justice shall be meted out to all war criminals, including those who have visited cruelties upon our prisoners.

The Japanese government shall remove all obstacles to the revival and strengthening of democratic tendencies among the Japanese people. Freedom of speech and religion and of thought, as well as respect for the fundamental human rights, shall be established.

11. Japan shall be permitted to maintain such industries as will sustain her economy and permit the payment of just reparation in kind, but not those industries which will enable her to rearm for war.

To this end, access to, as distinguished from control of, raw materials shall be permitted. Eventual Japanese participation in world trade relations shall be permitted.

12. The occupying forces of the Allies shall be withdrawn from Japan as soon as these objectives have been accomplished and there has been established in accordance with the freely expressed will of the Japanese people a peacefully inclined and responsible government.

13. We call upon the government of Japan to proclaim now the unconditional surrender of all Japanese armed forces, and to provide proper and adequate assurances of their good faith in such action. The alternative for Japan is prompt and utter destruction.

U. S. POLICY DECISIONS SINCE 1947

Truman Doctrine

President Truman took a decisive step in March, 1947, when he obtained from Congress authorization to spend $400 million to aid Greece and Turkey. His move followed directly on withdrawal of aid to those countries by Great Britain, whose resources were dwindling. Greece suffered from Communist guerrilla infiltration; Turkey lived under threat of Russia's constant pressures. Besides the appropriation, Congress authorized shipment of military equipment and dispatch of a military and technical mission. By 1950, the Red guerrillas had given up the struggle, and in Turkey results were much more immediately successful. The Truman Doctrine is regarded as the first significant experiment in the policy of "containment," although it preceded by four months the intellectual presentation of this policy by George Kennan.

The Marshall Plan

After World War II, recovery programs among the nations of Europe, as well as contributions from the United States, were un-coordinated. In June, 1947, Gen. George C. Marshall, then Secretary of State, asserted the need for integrated recovery efforts against "hunger, poverty, desperation, and chaos." Congress, in April, 1948, appropriated $5.4 billion. The United States established the Economic Cooperation Administration while European nations set up the Organization for European Economic Administration. Under a system of counterpart funds, each participating government set aside, in its own currency, amounts matching the aid it received. As the European Recovery Program, Marshall Plan aid was economic in its early stages but with the worsening international situation—particularly after Korea—emphasis was shifted to rearmament. When ERP ended in Dec., 1951, a year ahead of schedule, it had cost $11 billion, but substantial amounts had been committed to collateral military ventures.

Eisenhower Doctrine

On Jan. 5, 1957, President Eisenhower, noting the unsettled state of the Middle East, asked authority from Congress to co-operate with any nation in that area for economic development, to undertake programs of military assistance for such nations which desired it and to use U. S. armed forces to protect Mid-East countries "requesting such aid" against "overt armed aggression from any nation controlled by international communism." In March, Congress authorized expenditures up to $200 million for 1957. Anti-Communist declarations were immediately forthcoming from Lebanon and Libya; and, more important, King Hussein of Jordan took a strong stand against the leftist drift in his country. Arms also were shipped to the area to counter the build-up of Soviet military equipment in Syria.

Alliance for Progress Agreement

In the Declaration of Punta del Este, adopted Aug. 17, 1961, by the United States and 19 other American republics (Cuba abstained), the United States agreed to provide the major part of $20,000,000,000 needed over the next 10 years for economic development in Latin America, while the other nations pledged themselves to increase their own contributions to economic and social development and to make the reforms necessary so that all would share fully in the benefits under the Alliance for Progress.

The Atlantic Charter

(In a dramatic meeting off Newfoundland, August 9–10, 1941, President Roosevelt and Winston Churchill formulated this statement of common war aims, which was issued August 14.)

The President of the United States of America and the Prime Minister, Mr. Churchill, representing His Majesty's Government in the United Kingdom, being met together, deem it right to make known certain common principles in the national policies of their respective countries on which they base their hopes for a better future for the world.

FIRST, their countries seek no aggrandizement, territorial or other;

SECOND, they desire to see no territorial changes that do not accord with the freely expressed wishes of the peoples concerned;

THIRD, they respect the right of all peoples to choose the form of government under which they will live; and they wish to see sovereign rights and self-government restored to those who have been forcibly deprived of them;

FOURTH, they will endeavor, with due respect for their existing obligations, to further the enjoyment by all States, great or small, victor or vanquished, of access, on equal terms, to the trade and to the raw materials of the world which are needed for their economic prosperity;

FIFTH, they desire to bring about the fullest collaboration between all nations in the economic field with the object of securing, for all, improved labor standards, economic advancement and social security;

SIXTH, after the final destruction of Nazi tyranny, they hope to see established a peace which will afford to all nations the means of dwelling in safety within their own boundaries, and which will afford assurance that all men in all lands may live out their lives in freedom from fear and want;

SEVENTH, such a peace should enable all men to traverse the high seas and oceans without hindrance;

EIGHTH, they believe that all the nations of the world, for realistic as well as spiritual reasons, must come to the abandonment of the use of force. Since no future peace can be maintained if land, sea or air armaments continue to be employed by nations which threaten, or may threaten, aggression outside of their frontiers, they believe, pending the establishment of a wider and permanent system of general security, that the disarmament of such nations is essential. They will likewise aid and encourage all other practicable measures which will lighten for peace-loving peoples the crushing burden of armaments.

UNUSUAL VOTING RESULTS

Election of 1872

The presidential and vice-presidential candidates of the Liberal Republicans and the northern Democrats in 1872 were Horace Greeley and B. Gratz Brown. Greeley died Nov. 29, 1872, before his 66 electors voted. In the electoral balloting for President, 63 of Greeley's votes were scattered among four other men, including Brown.

Election of 1876

In the election of 1876 Samuel J. Tilden, the Democratic candidate, received a popular majority but lacked one undisputed electoral vote to carry a clear majority of the electoral college. The crux of the problem was in the 22 electoral votes which were in dispute because Florida, Louisiana, South Carolina, and Oregon each sent in 2 sets of election returns. In the 3 southern states Republican election boards threw out enough Democratic votes to certify the Republican candidate, Hayes. In Oregon, the Democratic governor disqualified a Republican elector, replacing him with a Democrat. Since the Senate was Republican and the House of Representatives Democratic, it seemed useless to refer the disputed returns to the two houses for solution. Instead Congress appointed an Electoral Commission with 5 representatives each from the Senate, the House, and the Supreme Court. All but one Justice was named, giving the Commission 7 Republican and 7 Democratic members. The naming of the fifth Justice was left to the other four. He was a Republican who first favored Tilden but, under pressure from his party, switched to Hayes, ensuring his election by the Commission voting 8 to 7 on party lines.

Minority Presidents

Fifteen candidates have become President of the United States with a popular vote less than 50% of the total vote cast. It should be noted, however, that in elections before 1872, presidential electors were not chosen by popular vote in all states. Adams' election in 1824 was by the House of Representatives, which chose him over Jackson, who had a plurality of both electoral and popular votes, but not a majority in the electoral college.

Besides Jackson in 1824, only two other candidates receiving the largest popular vote have failed to gain a majority in the electoral college—Samuel J. Tilden (D) in 1876 and Grover Cleveland (D) in 1888.

The "minority" Presidents follow:

Vote Received by Minority Presidents

Year	President	Electoral Pct.	Popular vote Pct.
1824	John Q. Adams...............	31.8	29.8
1844	James K. Polk (D)............	61.8	49.3
1848	Zachary Taylor (W)..........	56.2	47.3
1856	James Buchanan (D)	58.7	45.3
1860	Abraham Lincoln (R)........	59.4	39.9
1876	Rutherford B. Hayes (R)......	50.1	47.9
1880	James A. Garfield (R).........	57.9	48.3
1884	Grover Cleveland (D)........	54.6	48.8
1888	Benjamin Harrison (R).......	58.1	47.8
1892	Grover Cleveland (D)........	62.4	46.0
1912	Woodrow Wilson (D)........	81.9	41.8
1916	Woodrow Wilson (D).........	52.1	49.3
1948	Harry S. Truman (D)........	57.1	49.5
1960	John F. Kennedy (D).........	56.4	49.7
1968	Richard M. Nixon (R).........	56.1	43.4

Principal Bills and Treaties Since 1906

(Enactment Dates in Parentheses)

Agriculture

Farm Loan Act (July 17, 1916). Set up system of land banks to lend money to farmers.

Farm Mortgage Refinancing Act (Jan. 31, 1934). Created to assist farmers in mortgage payments.

Farm Bankruptcy Act (Frazier-Lemke Act). (June 28, 1934). Declared moratorium on farm mortgage foreclosures. (Declared unconstitutional in May 1935). On following Aug. 14, the Farm Mortgage Moratorium Act allowed three-year moratorium on foreclosures with court permission on payment of reasonable rental.

Soil Conservation and Domestic Allotment Act (Mar. 2, 1936). Granted payments to farmers who let land lie fallow or planted cover crops.

Agriculture Adjustment Act (Feb. 16, 1938). Continued soil conservation program; provided parity payments and commodity loans; established crop insurance corporations and "ever normal" granary plan.

Price Parity (Oct. 31, 1949). Supported prices for wheat, corn, cotton, rice, peanuts at 90% through 1950; 80-90% through 1951 and 75-90% on sliding scale thereafter.

Alaska Pipeline (Nov. 13, 1973). Bill authorized construction of trans-Alaska pipeline; oil promised by 1977.

Alien Registration (Smith Act) (June 28, 1940). Required fingerprinting of aliens; made it unlawful to advocate overthrow of U.S. Government or to belong to any group advocating such.

Antitrust

Clayton Act (Oct. 25, 1914). Prohibited monopolistic price discrimination, restrictive sales or leases, intercorporate stock holding, interlocking directorates of competing companies capitalized at $1 million or more. Exempted labor from antitrust laws and declared peaceful picketing legal.

Robinson-Patman Act (June 20, 1936). Forbade discrimination in prices to different purchasers where result would lessen competition.

Armed Neutrality Act (Mar. 4, 1917). Allowed U.S. vessels to be armed in World War I war zones.

Atomic Energy

Five-man commission created without military representation but with military liaison; permitted Army and Navy to make atomic weapons; forbade distribution of fissionable materials or atomic energy information (Aug. 1, 1946); A.E.C. replaced by Nuclear Regulatory Commission (Oct. 10, 1974).

Atom Data (Oct. 30, 1954). Authorization for exchange of certain non-weapon data with friendly nations.

Car Safety/Highway Safety Act (Aug. 9, 1966). Set safety standards for motor vehicles and tires.

Child Labor

Keating-Owens Act (Sept. 1, 1918). Forbade shipping in interstate commerce of goods produced by children. (Declared unconstitutional in 1918).

Civilian Conservation Corps (Mar. 31, 1933). Set up to ease unemployment and to provide work in reforestation, road building and flood control.

Civil Rights

Bill of May 6, 1960—Made obstruction of school integration a crime and set up federal referees in voter registration disputes.

Civil Rights Act (July 2, 1964). Opened all public places to everyone on equal basis.

Voting Rights Act (Aug. 2, 1965). Insured blacks right to register and vote.

Communist Control Act (Aug. 24, 1954). Outlawed Communist Party, though membership in party was not made crime.

Declarations of War

Against Japan (Dec. 8, 1941).

Against Germany (Dec. 14, 1941).

Education (July 31, 1974). Extended Elementary and Secondary Act of 1965, consolidating programs.

Eisenhower Doctrine (Mar. 8, 1957). Provided economic and military aid to Mideast nations.

Election Campaign Financing (Oct. 10, 1974). Provided for public financing for Presidential and Congressional campaigns.

Energy (May 2, 1974). Created the Federal Energy Administration.

Federal Deposit Insurance Corporation (F.D.I.C.) Created by Glass-Steagall Act (June 16, 1933) to insure deposits up to $5,000, now $40,000.

Federal Reserve (Dec. 13, 1913). Established under Glass-Owens Bill.

Federal Trade Commission (Sept. 26, 1914). Established to enforce antitrust laws.

Food Stamps (Authorized Aug. 31, 1964).

Football TV (Sept. 13, 1973). Ended TV blackout of National Football League games sold out 72 hours in advance.

Freedom of Information. Assures wider public access to public information. (Passed Nov. 21, 1974, over President's veto.)

Gold Reserve Act (Jan. 30, 1934). Gave President power to devalue gold and to impound for Treasury all gold in Federal system and to establish Exchange Stabilization Fund.

Greek-Turkey Aid Bill (June 14, 1947). Authorized $400 million to aid Greece and Turkey.

Gulf of Tonkin Resolution (Aug. 7, 1964). Backed President on steps to maintain peace in Southeast Asia.

Gun Control Bill (Oct. 10, 1968). Banned interstate mail order sale of guns and out-of-state sales, among other provisions.

Holidays (June 24, 1968). Approved four Monday holidays: Washington's Birthday, Memorial Day, Veteran's Day, Columbus Day.

Housing

H.O.L.C. (June 13, 1933). Established Home Owners Loan Corporation to take over mortgages to save families from losing homes.

F.H.A. (June 28, 1934). Created Federal Housing Administration under National Housing Act to provide loans for modernizing homes and new construction.

U.S. Housing Authority (Sept. 1, 1937). Set up to administer loans to communities and states for rural and urban construction.

Private Construction Loans (Aug. 10, 1945). Designed to stimulate building of low-cost homes and pre-fabs.

Expanded Housing Program (Apr. 20, 1950). Authorized $3.5 billion in Government loans and mortgage insurance.

Public Housing Bill (Aug. 2, 1954). Allowed 35,000 units a year, limited to cities where slum clearance displaced families.

Other Major Housing Bills: $6.1 billion (June 30, 1961); $7.8 billion (Aug. 10, 1965); $5.3 billion (July 26, 1968); $4.8 billion (Dec. 12, 1969); $2.9 billion (Feb. 19, 1970).

Open Housing (Apr. 11, 1968).

Demonstration Cities (Oct. 20, 1966). Provided 80% Federal financing to rebuild areas in 60 to 70 cities.

H.U.D. (Sept. 9, 1965). Established Department of Housing and Urban Development of Cabinet rank.

Immigration

McCarran–Walter Act. Ended racial bars on immigration and retained quota system based on national origin (veto of June 25, 1952 overridden June 27). Refugee Immigration Act of Aug. 7, 1953 admitted 214,000 refugees in next 3 years over quotas. (National Origins System eliminated Oct. 3, 1963).

Korea

G.I. Bill of Rights (July 16, 1952). Granted Korea veterans with 90 days' service as of June 27, 1950 rights and benefits similar to those of World War II veterans.

Labor

Adamson Act (Sept. 5, 1916). Limited working hours of rail employees to 8 a day on interstate lines.

Norris-LaGuardia Act (Mar. 23, 1932). Limited injunctions against labor; outlawed "yellow dog" contracts.

National Labor Relations Act (Wagner-Connery Act) (July 8, 1938). Created NLRB with power to determine appropriate collective bargaining unit subject to election.

Taft-Hartley (Labor–Management Relations Act of 1947). Prohibited closed shop, but allowed union shop by majority vote of employees; made unions subject to damage suits for unfair labor practices; required union financial reports; required union leaders to file statements they were not Communists. (Veto of June 20, 1947 overridden June 23.)

Taft-Hartley Law Amendment (Oct. 22, 1951). Permitted union shop contracts without first polling employees.

Marshall Plan (European Recovery Program) (April 3, 1948). Provided $5.3 billion for E.R.P. of total of $6 billion in foreign assistance. Many foreign aid bills have been passed (1945-72 total was $146.3 billion) and detailed reports are obtainable from the Department of Commerce.

Mass Transit (Sept. 9, 1974). Set capital grants and operating grants for mass transit systems.

Minimum Wage

Wages and Hours Act (June 25, 1938). Set hourly minimum wage of 25 cents, to rise to 40 cents after six years. Increases have been legislated in ensuing years, reaching the present $2 for most workers, rising to $2.10 Jan. 1, 1975 and $2.30 a year later.

National Industrial Recovery Act (Enacted June 16, 1933, declared unconstitutional in 1935). Created NRA; authorized trade associations; suspended antitrust laws; authorized codes of fair competition; guaranteed collective bargaining and required employers to accept maximum and minimum wage provisions.

National Security Act (July 26, 1947). Reorganized Armed Forces with Secretary of Defense, (Cabinet rank), and Secretaries of Army, Navy and Air Force.

NATO (July 21, 1949). See "North Atlantic Treaty Organization" under "U.S. Treaties" section.

Nuclear Testing

Nuclear Test Ban Treaty (Ratified Sept. 24, 1963).

Nuclear Non-Proliferation Treaty (Ratified Nov. 24, 1969).

Outer Space

Treaty on Outer Space (Ratified Apr. 25, 1967).

Peace Treaties

With Italy, Bulgaria, Hungary (June 14, 1947).

State of war with Germany ended (Oct. 19, 1951). With Japan (Mar. 20, 1952).

U.S.-Japanese Security Treaty (June 22, 1960).

Pensions (Aug. 22, 1974). Provided Federal regulation of private pensions with broader protection for workers.

Philippines

Tydings–McDuffie Act (Mar. 24, 1934). Provided for independence in 1946.

Poll Tax

24th Amendment to Constitution banning poll tax; sent to states Aug. 27, 1962 and went into effect Jan. 22, 1964.

Presidential Assassination (Aug. 20, 1966). Made it a Federal crime to kill or kidnap President.

Presidential Succession Act (July 18, 1947). Made Speaker of House and President of Senate pro tempore next in line after Vice President. A Constitutional amendment, submitted to the states July 6, 1965 and effective on Feb. 10, 1967, provided for Presidential disability and filling vacancy in Vice Presidency.

Prohibition

18th Amendment (Adopted by states Jan. 16, 1919; effective Jan. 16, 1920). Prohibited manufacture, sale or transportation of intoxicating liquors.

Volstead Act (Vetoed Oct. 27, 1919; veto overridden Oct. 27, 1919). Provided enforcement legislation prohibiting manufacture, sale and transportation of beverages containing more than .5% alcohol.

3.2 Liquor Law (Mar. 22, 1933). Legalized manufacture and sale of wines and beer with 3.2% alcoholic content.

21st Amendment (Approved by states Dec. 5, 1933; effective immediately). Repealed 18th Amendment and ended Volstead Act.

Puerto Rico (July 3, 1952). New island Constitution made it a Commonwealth with greater home rule.

Pure Food and Drug Act (June 30, 1906). Made shipments in interstate commerce of adulterated foods and drugs illegal.

Reconstruction Finance Corporation (Jan. 22, 1932). Established with funds of $500 million, with power to borrow more to release frozen assets in banks and mortgage companies and to aid bankrupt railroads.

St. Lawrence Seaway (Authorized May 13, 1954).

Selective Service (Sept. 16, 1940). Compulsory service in Armed Forces. (Extended Aug. 16, 1941.)

Social Security and Medicare

Social Security Act (Aug. 14, 1935). Set up old age benefits based on earnings before 65; unemployment insurance administered under state laws; grants to states to aid needy aged, blind, orphans, widows, etc. Old age tax of 1% on covered earnings levied on employers and workers; this has been increased at various times to present 5.85%, including 1% for hospital insurance under Medicare (enacted July 30, 1965) and benefits have been broadened. (For detailed information on present benefits see section under "Social Security.")

Soviet Consular Treaty (Mar. 31, 1967). Provided for Consulates in U.S. and Soviet.

Stocks and Bonds

Federal Securities Act (May 18, 1933). Required that all stocks and bonds be registered and approved.

Securities and Exchange Act (June 6, 1934). Established Securities and Exchange Commission; required licensing of stock exchanges; made certain speculative practices illegal; gave Federal Reserve power to fix margins; required full financial statements from registered companies.

Strategic Arms Limitation (Sept. 25, 1972). Known as SALT, agreements limited defensive and offensive missiles.

Tariff

Hawley-Smoot Act (June 17, 1939). Set very high protective tariff but gave President power to raise or lower rates.

Tidelands (May 22, 1953). Gave coastal states rights to all minerals in submerged lands within their historic boundaries. Federal control of rest of Continental Shelf retained.

Trade (Dec. 20, 1974). Granted favorable trade arrangements with many countries. (Soviet Union nullified 1972 trade agreement with U.S. because trade bill sought freer emigration policies.)

Transportation

Department of Transportation created (Oct. 15, 1966).

Treaty of Versailles (Defeated Nov. 19, 1919 and Mar. 19, 1920.)

Tennessee Valley Authority (T.V.A.) (May 18, 1933). Created to develop and sell electric power, serve as yardstick for electric rates, develop rural electrification, establish flood control and produce fertilizer.

Truth in Packaging (Oct. 3, 1966). Set Federal standards for packaging and labeling.

U.N. Charter. (Ratified July 28, 1945). For text of Charter see Index.

Voting Age (June 17, 1970). Lowered voting age to 18. Bill also reduced residency requirements and ended literacy tests.

War Debt Moratorium (Dec. 23, 1931). Provided for moratorium of interest and war debt installments.

War Powers Act (Nov. 7, 1973). Congress overrides Nixon veto of bill limiting President's power to wage war without Congress approval.

(Bills passed in 1976 will be found in 1976 News Chronology.)

CONGRESSIONAL BILLS VETOED: 1913 TO 1974

PERIOD	President	VETOED BILLS			Vetoes sustained	Bills passed over veto
		Total	Regular	Pocket		
1913–1921	Wilson	44	33	11	38	6
1921–1923	Harding	6	5	1	6	–
1923–1929	Coolidge	50	20	30	46	4
1929–1933	Hoover	37	21	16	34	3
1933–1945	F. Roosevelt	635	372	263	626	9
1945–1953	Truman	250	180	70	238	12
1953–1961	Eisenhower	181	73	108	179	2
1961–1963	Kennedy	21	12	9	21	–
1963–1969	Johnson	30	16	14	30	–
1969–1973	Nixon	41	23	18	36	5
1973–1974	Nixon-Ford [1]	35	22	13	31	4

— Represents zero. [1] Nixon resignation effective August 8, 1974. Source: U.S. Congress, Senate Library, *Presidential Vetoes . . . 1789–1968;* U.S. Congress, *Calendars of the U.S. House of Representatives and History of Legislation.*

Annual Salaries of Federal Officials

President of the U.S.	$200,000[1]	Secretaries of the Army, Navy, Air Force	44,625
Vice President of the U.S.	65,625[2]	Senators and Representatives	44,625
Cabinet members	63,000	President Pro Tempore of Senate	51,975
Under secretaries of executive departments	42,000	Speaker of the House	65,625
Deputy Secretaries of State, Defense, Treasury	44,625	Majority & Minority Leader of the Senate	51,975
Deputy Attorney General	44,625	Majority & Minority Leader of the House	51,975
Under Secretary of Transportation	44,625	Chief Justice of the United States	65,625
		Associate Justices of the Supreme Court	63,000

[1] Plus taxable $50,000 for expenses and a nontaxable sum (not to exceed $40,000 a year) for travel expenses. [2] Plus taxable $10,000 for expenses. NOTE: All salaries shown above are taxable.

Assassinations and Attempts in U. S. Since 1865

CERMAK, Anton J. (Mayor of Chicago): Shot Feb. 15, 1933, in Miami by Giuseppe Zangara, who attempted to assassinate Franklin D. Roosevelt; Cermak died Mar. 6.

FORD, Gerald R. (President of U.S.): Escaped assassination attempt Sept. 5, 1975, in Sacramento, Calif., by Lynette Alice (Squeaky) Fromm, who pointed but did not fire .45-caliber pistol.

FORD, Gerald R. (President of U.S.): Escaped assassination attempt in San Francisco, Calif., Sept. 22, 1975, by Sara Jane Moore, who fired one shot from a .38-caliber pistol that was deflected.

GARFIELD, James A. (President of U. S.): Shot July 2, 1881, in Washington, D. C., by Charles J. Guiteau; died Sept. 19.

KENNEDY, John F. (President of U. S.): Shot Nov. 22, 1963, in Dallas, Tex., allegedly by Lee Harvey Oswald; died same day. Injured was Gov. John B. Connally of Texas. Oswald was shot and killed two days later by Jack Ruby.

KENNEDY, Robert F. (U. S. Senator from New York): Shot June 5, 1968, in Los Angeles by Sirhan Bishara Sirhan; died June 6.

KING, Martin Luther, Jr. (civil rights leader): Shot Apr. 4, 1968, in Memphis by James Earl Ray; died same day.

LINCOLN, Abraham (President of U. S.): Shot Apr. 14, 1865, in Washington, D. C., by John Wilkes Booth; died Apr. 15.

LONG, Huey P. (U. S. Senator from Louisiana): Shot Sept. 8, 1935, in Baton Rouge by Dr. Carl A. Weiss; died Sept. 10.

McKINLEY, William (President of U. S.): Shot Sept. 6, 1901, in Buffalo by Leon Czolgosz; died Sept. 14.

ROOSEVELT, Franklin D. (President-elect of U. S.): Escaped assassination unhurt Feb. 15, 1933, in Miami. *See* Cermak.

ROOSEVELT, Theodore (ex-President of U. S.): Escaped assassination (though shot) Oct. 14, 1912, in Milwaukee while campaigning for President.

SEWARD, William H. (Secretary of State): Escaped assassination (though injured) Apr. 14, 1865, in Washington, D. C., by Lewis Powell (or Paine), accomplice of John Wilkes Booth.

TRUMAN, Harry S. (President of U. S.): Escaped assassination unhurt Nov. 1, 1950. in Washington, D. C., as 2 Puerto Rican nationalists attempted to shoot their way into Blair House.

WALLACE, George C. (Governor of Alabama): Shot and critically wounded in assassination attempt May 15. 1972, at Laurel, Md. by Arthur Herman Bremer.

Firsts in America

Other sources may differ with this list. Our selection is based on our editorial judgment.

Admiral in U. S. Navy: David Glasgow Farragut, 1866.

Air-mail route, first transcontinental: Between New York City and San Francisco, 1920.

Assembly, representative: House of Burgesses, founded in Virginia, 1619.

Bank established: Bank of North America, Philadelphia, 1781.

Birth in America of English parents: Virginia Dare, born Roanoke Island, N. C., 1587.

Botanic garden: Established by John Bartram in Philadelphia, 1728. (Oldest existing one was established in Cambridge, Mass., in 1807.)

Cartoon, colored: "The Yellow Kid," by Richard Outcault, in *New York World,* 1895.

College in America: Harvard, founded 1636.

College to confer degrees on women: Oberlin (Ohio) College, 1841.

College to establish coeducation: Oberlin (Ohio) College, 1833.

Electrocution of a criminal: William Kemmler in Auburn Prison, Auburn, N. Y., Aug. 6, 1890.

Five and Ten Cents Store: Founded by Frank Woolworth, Utica, N. Y., 1879 (moved to Lancaster, Pa., same year).

Fraternity: Phi Beta Kappa; founded Dec. 5, 1776, at College of William and Mary.

Law to be declared unconstitutional by U. S. Supreme Court: Judiciary Act of 1789. Case: *Marbury* v. *Madison,* 1803.

Library, circulating: Philadelphia, 1731.

Newspaper published for a continuous period: *The Boston News-Letter,* April, 1704.

Newspaper, illustrated daily: *New York Daily Graphic,* 1873.

Newspaper published daily: *Pennsylvania Packet and General Advertiser,* Philadelphia, September, 1784.

Newsreel: Pathé Frères of Paris, in 1910, circulated a weekly issue of their *Pathé Journal.*

Oil well, commercial: Titusville, Pa., 1859.

Panel quiz show on radio: *Information Please*, May 17, 1938.

Postage stamps issued: 1847.

Railroad, transcontinental: Central Pacific and Union Pacific railroads joined at Promontory, Utah, May 10, 1869.

Savings bank: The Provident Institute for Savings, Boston, 1816.

Science museum: Founded by Charleston (S. C.) Library Society, 1773.

Skyscraper: Home Insurance Co., Chicago, 1885 (10 floors, 2 added later).

Slaves brought into America: At Jamestown, Va., 1619, from a Dutch ship.

Sorority: Kappa Alpha Theta, at De Pauw University, 1870.

State to abolish capital punishment: Michigan, 1847.

State to enter Union after original 13: Vermont, 1791.

Steam-heated building: Eastern Hotel, Boston, 1845.

Steam railroad (carried passengers and freight): Baltimore & Ohio, 1830.

Strike on record by union: Journeymen Printers, New York City, 1776.

Subway: Opened in Boston, 1897.

"Tabloid" picture newspaper: *The Illustrated Daily News* (now *The Daily News*), New York City, 1919.

Vaudeville theater: Gaiety Museum, Boston, 1883.

Woman cabinet member: Frances Perkins, Secretary of Labor, 1933.

Woman candidate for President: Victoria Claflin Woodhull, nominated by National Woman's Suffrage Assn. on ticket of Nation Radical Reformers, 1872.

Woman doctor of medicine: Elizabeth Blackwell; M.D. from Geneva Medical College of Western New York, 1849.

Woman elected governor of a state: Mrs. Nellie Tayloe Ross, Wyoming, 1925.

Woman elected to U. S. Senate: Mrs. Hattie Caraway, Arkansas; elected Nov., 1932.

Woman graduate of law school: Mrs. Ada H. Kepley, Union College of Law, Chicago, 1870.

Woman member of U. S. House of Representatives: Jeannette Rankin; elected November, 1916.

Woman member of U. S. Senate: Mrs. Rebecca Latimer Felton of Georgia; appointed Oct. 3, 1922.

Woman suffrage granted: Wyoming Territory, 1869.

Written constitution: *Fundamental Orders of Connecticut*, 1639.

Qualifications for Voting in the United States

Source: Questionnaires from the States.

(The Supreme Court decision of March 21, 1972, declared lengthy requirements for voting in state and local elections unconstitutional and suggested that 30 days was an ample period. Most of the states have changed or eliminated their durational residency requirements to comply with the ruling, as shown in the table below.)

No durational residency requirement	30-day residency requirement	Other
Alabama, California, Connecticut, Delaware, District of Columbia,[2] Georgia,[2] Hawaii, Idaho, Indiana,[5] Iowa,[6] Louisiana, Maine, Maryland, Massachusetts,[8] Nebraska,[9] New Hampshire, New Mexico,[7] North Carolina, Oklahoma, South Dakota,[10] Tennessee, Texas, Virginia, West Virginia, Wisconsin,[11] Wyoming[2]	Alaska, Arizona,[12] Arkansas, Illinois, Kentucky[2] Mississippi, Montana, New Jersey, North Dakota,[3] Ohio, Oregon, Rhode Island, South Carolina, Utah, Washington.	Colorado,[1] Florida[13]; Kansas, Minnesota, 20 days; Michigan, 45 days; Missouri[4]; Nevada, 6 months; New York, Pennsylvania, 90 days; Vermont, 24 days.

[1] 29-day for Presidential elections, 32 for all other.   [2] 30-day registration requirement.   [3] 10-day for Presidential elections.   [4] 28 days in St. Louis County, 4th Wednesday prior to elections in rest of state.   [5] None for Presidential elections, 60 for state.   [6] 10-day registration requirement.   [7] 42-day registration requirement.   [8] 28-day registration requirement for state or primary elections.   [9] Registration requirement, 2nd Friday prior to elections.   [10] 15-day registration requirement.   [11] None for Presidential elections, 10 for state.   [12] 50-day for state.   [13] 45-day for Presidential elections, 30 for all other.

Order of Presidential Succession

1. The Vice President.
2. Speaker of the House.
3. President pro tempore of the Senate.
4. Secretary of State.
5. Secretary of the Treasury.
6. Secretary of Defense.
7. Attorney General.
8. Secretary of the Interior.
9. Secretary of Agriculture.
10. Secretary of Commerce.
11. Secretary of Labor.
12. Secretary of Health, Education, and Welfare.
13. Secretary of Housing and Urban Development.
14. Secretary of Transportation.

NOTE: An official cannot succeed to the Presidency unless he meets the Constitutional requirements.

Executive Departments and Agencies

Source: U. S. Government Organization Manual.

Unless otherwise indicated, addresses shown are in Washington, D.C.

Executive Office of the President

THE WHITE HOUSE OFFICE
1600 Pennsylvania Ave., NW. (20500).

Counsellors to President: Robert T. Hartmann, John O. Marsh, Jr.
Special Counsellors to President: David R. Gergen, Michael Raoul-Duval.
Counsel to President: Philip W. Buchen, William E. Casselman II, Roderick M. Hills. *Associate Counsel:* Kenneth A. Lazarus, Barbara G. Kilberg. *Deputy Counsel to President:* Edward C. Schmults.
Special Consultant to President: Robert A. Goldwin.
Assistants to President: Richard B. Cheney. *For Management and Budget:* James T. Lynn. *For Economic Affairs:* L. William Seidman. *For Domestic Affairs:* James M. Cannon. *For Public Liaison:* William J. Baroody, Jr. *For Legislative Affairs:* Max L. Friedersdorf. *For National Security Affairs:* Lt. Gen. Brent Scowcroft, USAF.
Deputy Assistants to President: For Domestic Affairs: Arthur F. Quern. *For Economic Affairs:* William F. Gorog. *For Legislative Affairs (Senate):* William T. Kendall; *(House):* Charles Leppert, Jr. *For National Security Affairs:* William G. Hyland. *For Urban Affairs:* Arthur A. Fletcher.
Special Assistants to President: Thomas Aranda, Jr., John C. Calhoun, Byron M. Caveney, Jr., Milton A. Friedman, Maj. Gen. Jeanne M. Holm, USAF, Joseph S. Jenckes, V, Jerry H. Jones, Virginia H. Knauer, Myron B. Kuropas, Thomas G. Loeffler, Robert Orben, James H. Cavanaugh, J. Patrick Rowland, Roger B. Porter, William F. Rhatican, Russell A. Ruorke, Douglas J. Smith, Robert K. Wolthuis.
Staff Secretary to President: James E. Connor. *Deputy Staff Secretary:* David C. Hoopes.
Press Secretary to President: Ron Nessen. *Deputy Press Secretary:* John G. Carlson. *Assistant Press Secretaries:* Margareta E. White, Larry M. Speakes, John W. Roberts, Margaret K. Earl.
Personal Secretary to President: Dorothy E. Downton.
Personal Assistant to President: Mildred V. Leonard.
Aide to President: Terrence O'Donnell.
Military Assistant to President: Capt. Leland S. Kollmorgen, USN.
Personal Photographer to President: David Hume Kennerly.
Secretary to Cabinet: James E. Connor.
Press Secretary to First Lady: Shelia Rabb Weidenfeld.
Physician to President: Rear Adm. William M. Lukash, USN.

Chief Executive Clerk: Robert D. Linder.
Chief Usher: Rex W. Scouten.

CENTRAL INTELLIGENCE AGENCY (CIA)
Washington, D.C. (20505).
Established: 1947.
Director: George Bush.
Activities: Coordinates intelligence activities of certain government departments and agencies by making recommendations to the National Security Council; correlates and evaluates intelligence and disseminates the results; performs certain additional services for existing intelligence agencies when the National Security Council determines that these can be more efficiently accomplished centrally.

COUNCIL OF ECONOMIC ADVISERS (CEA)
Executive Office Bldg. (20506).
Members: 3. *Established:* Feb. 20, 1946.
Chairman: Alan Greenspan.
Activities: Assists President in preparation of economic reports to Congress; studies economic trends; appraises government activities on nation's economy; recommends economic policies.

COUNCIL ON ENVIRONMENTAL QUALITY
722 Jackson Pl., NW (20006).
Members: 3. *Established:* 1969.
Chairman: Russell W. Peterson.
Activities: Develops and recommends to President national policies that promote environmental quality.

COUNCIL ON INTERNATIONAL ECONOMIC POLICY
Executive Office Bldg. (20500).
Members: 10. *Established:* Jan. 19, 1971.
Chairman: William E. Simon.
Executive Director: J. M. Dunn (acting).
Activities: Provides focus for international economic policy issues; aims to achieve consistency between domestic and foreign economic policy.

COUNCIL ON WAGE AND PRICE STABILITY
726 Jackson Place, NW. (20506).
Members: 8. *Established:* Aug. 24, 1974.
Chairman: William E. Simon.
Director: Michael H. Moskow.
Activities: Monitors wages and prices and provides guidance on broad terms to labor and management. The Council will expire Aug. 15, 1975, by law.

DOMESTIC COUNCIL

1600 Pennsylvania Ave., NW. (20500).
Members: 19. *Established:* July 1, 1970.
Chairman: President of U.S.
Executive Director: James Cannon.
Activities: Formulates and coordinates domestic policy recommendations to President. Endeavors to resolve federal-state-local problems.

ENERGY RESOURCES COUNCIL

Executive Office Building (20500).
Members: 23. *Established:* Oct. 11, 1974.
Chairman: Elliot L. Richardson.
Executive Director: Frank G. Zarb.
Activities: Coordinates energy policy at Presidential level. Develops over-all framework to provide for development and implementation of policy toward management of energy resources and initiatives.

FEDERAL PROPERTY COUNCIL

Executive Office Bldg. Annex (20504).
Members: 8. *Established:* June 25, 1973.
Chairman: (Vacant)
Activities: Encourages development of more effective policies regarding use of federal properties. Reviews all real-property policies and recommends necessary reforms or modifications.

NATIONAL SECURITY COUNCIL (NSC)

Executive Office Bldg. (20506).
Members: 4. *Established:* July 26, 1947.
Chairman: President of U.S.
Other members: Vice President; Secretary of State; Secretary of Defense.
Activities: Assesses and appraises objectives, commitments and risks of United States in relation to our actual and potential military power.

OFFICE OF DRUG ABUSE POLICY

Executive Office Building (20500).
Established: March 19, 1976.
Activities: Advises the President on objectives, policies, and priorities for Federal drug abuse functions. Coordinates the performance of those functions by Federal departments and agencies.

OFFICE OF MANAGEMENT AND BUDGET

Executive Office Bldg. (20503).
Established: July 1, 1970.
Director: James T. Lynn.
Activities: Assists President in preparing budget and formulating fiscal program; supervises administration of budget; coordinates advice on proposed legislation; plans improvements in statistical services; keeps President informed of progress of activities by government agencies so that Congressional appropriations are spent most economically.

OFFICE OF SCIENCE AND TECHNOLOGY POLICY

Executive Office Building (20500).
Established: June 8, 1962.
Director: H. Guyford Stever.
Activities: Advises the President on scientific, engineering and technological aspects of issues requiring his attention.

OFFICE OF THE SPECIAL REPRESENTATIVE FOR TRADE NEGOTIATIONS

1800 G St., NW. (20506).
Established: Jan. 15, 1963.
Special Representative: Frederick B. Dent.
Activities: Advises the President on the administration and carrying out of the trade agreements program and on non-tariff barriers to international trade and international commodity agreements; chairs the Trade Expansion Act Advisory Committee.

OFFICE OF TELECOMMUNICATIONS POLICY

1800 G St., NW. (20504).
Established: Apr. 20, 1970.
Director: Thomas J. Houser.
Activities: Coordinates telecommunications activities of government.

Executive Departments

DEPARTMENT OF STATE

2201 C St., NW. (20520).
Established: 1781 as Department of Foreign Affairs; reconstituted, 1789, following adoption of Constitution; name changed to Department of State Sept. 15, 1789.
Secretary: Henry A. Kissinger.
Deputy Secretary: Charles W. Robinson.
Activities: Determines government policy in relation to international problems; formulates measures for promoting friendship with other countries; develops policies and programs for U.S. participation in U.N. and other international organizations; conducts correspondence with our representatives abroad and accredited foreign representatives here; administers Peace Corps.

DEPARTMENT OF THE TREASURY

15th St. & Pennsylvania Ave., NW. (20220).
Established: Sept. 2, 1789.
Secretary: William E. Simon.
Deputy Secretary: George H. Dixon.
Treasurer of the U.S.: Mrs. Francine Irving Neff.
Comptroller of the Currency: James E. Smith.
Activities: Manages national finances; grants warrants for money drawn from Treasury pursuant to legal appropriations; handles collection of revenue; keeps and renders public accounts; prepares plans for improvement of revenue and for support of

public credit; controls coinage and printing of money; administers Secret Service, Customs Service, Internal Revenue Service, Bureau of Engraving and Printing, Bureau of the Mint, Bureau of Alcohol, Tobacco and Firearms.

DEPARTMENT OF DEFENSE

The Pentagon (20301).
Established: July 26, 1947, as National Department Establishment; name changed to Department of Defense on Aug. 10, 1949. Subordinate to Secretary of Defense are Secretaries of Army, Navy, Air Force.
Secretary: Donald H. Rumsfeld.
Deputy Secretary: William P. Clements, Jr.
Secretary of Army: Martin R. Hoffmann.
Secretary of Navy: J. William Middendorf II.
Secretary of Air Force: Thomas C. Reed.
Commandant of Marine Corps: Gen. Louis Wilson.
*Joint Chiefs of Staff:** Gen. George S. Brown, Chairman; Adm. James L. Holloway III, Navy; Gen. David C. Jones, Air Force; Gen. Frederick C. Weyand, Army; Gen. Louis H. Wilson, Marine Corps.
Activities: Provides for security of U.S. by establishing integrated policies and procedures; co-ordinates and directs the activities of three separately administered military departments (Army, Navy, and Air Force).

DEPARTMENT OF JUSTICE

Constitution Ave. & 10th St., NW. (20530).
Established: Office of Attorney General was created Sept. 24, 1789. Although he was one of original Cabinet members, he was not executive department head until June 22, 1870, when Department of Justice was established.
Attorney General: Edward H. Levi.
Deputy Attorney General: Harold R. Tyler, Jr.
Solicitor General: Robert H. Bork.
Director of FBI: Clarence M. Kelley.
Activities: Provides means for enforcing Federal laws; investigates and detects violations; represents U.S. in legal matters generally and gives advice and opinions when requested by President or heads of executive departments; directs FBI, Bureau of Prisons, Immigration and Naturalization Service, Drug Enforcement Administration, Law Enforcement Assistance Administration, Marshals Service.

DEPARTMENT OF THE INTERIOR

C St. between 18th & 19th Sts., NW. (20240).
Established: Mar. 3, 1849.
Secretary: Thomas S. Kleppe.
Under Secretary: D. Kent Frizzell.

Activities: Develops and conserves natural resources of U.S. and territories; supervises public business relating to such offices as Bureau of Land Management, Bureau of Reclamation, Geological Survey, Bureau of Indian Affairs, National Park Service, Bureau of Mines, Fish and Wildlife Service, Bureau of Outdoor Recreation.

DEPARTMENT OF AGRICULTURE

14th St. & Independence Ave., SW. (20250).
Established: May 15, 1862. Administered by Commissioner of Agriculture until 1889, when it was made executive department.
Secretary: John A. Knebel (acting).
Under Secretary: (vacant).
Activities: Conducts comprehensive research and educational program relating to agriculture; provides crop reports, commodity standards, meat inspection and other marketing services; administers national forests; aids in flood control; administers price-support and production-adjustment programs; makes loans to farmers.

DEPARTMENT OF COMMERCE

14th St. between Constitution Ave. & E St., NW. (20230).
Established: Department of Commerce and Labor was created Feb. 14, 1903. On Mar. 4, 1913, all labor activities were transferred out of Department of Commerce and Labor and it was renamed Department of Commerce.
Secretary: Elliot L. Richardson.
Under Secretary: James A. Baker, 3rd.
Activities: Fosters and develops foreign and domestic commerce of U.S.; maintains Bureau of the Census, Domestic and International Business Administration, Economic Development Administration, Office of Minority Business Enterprise, Patent and Trademark Office, National Oceanic and Atmospheric Administration (including National Weather Service), National Technical Information Service, Social and Economic Statistics Administration, Office of Telecommunications, Travel Service, National Fire Prevention and Control Administration.

DEPARTMENT OF LABOR

14th St. & Constitution Ave., NW. (20210).
Established: Bureau of Labor was created in 1884 under Department of the Interior; later became independent department without executive rank. Returned to bureau status in Department of Commerce and Labor, but on Mar. 4, 1913, became independent executive department under its present name.
Secretary: W. J. Usery, Jr.
Under Secretary: (Vacant)
Activities: Promotes welfare of wage earners of U.S., improving working conditions and advancing opportunities for profitable

---

* Consisting of chairman and chiefs of each service.

employment; directs collection and collation of statistics concerning labor conditions; promulgates and enforces certain maximum-hour, minimum-wage, child-labor, safety and health standards. Maintains Manpower Administration, Labor-Management Services Administration, Employment Standards Administration, Occupational Safety and Health Administration, Bureau of Labor Statistics.

DEPARTMENT OF HEALTH, EDUCATION, AND WELFARE

330 Independence Ave., SW. (20201).
Established: Apr. 11, 1953, replacing Federal Security Agency created in 1939.
Secretary: F. David Mathews.
Under Secretary: Marjorie Lynch.
Activities: Supervises and co-ordinates various organizations within the department. Organizations are: Food and Drug Administration, Office of Human Development, Office of Education, Social and Rehabilitation Service, Public Health Service, Social Security Administration, Alcohol, Drug Abuse and Mental Health Administration, National Institutes of Health, Center for Disease Control, Office of Child Development.

DEPARTMENT OF HOUSING AND URBAN DEVELOPMENT

451 7th St., SW., (20410).
Established: 1965, replacing Housing and Home Finance Agency created in 1947.
Secretary: Carla A. Hills.
Under Secretary: John B. Rhinelander.
Activities: Supervises and coordinates Community Development Corporation, Federal Disaster Assistance Administration, Federal Insurance Administration, Federal National Mortgage Association.

DEPARTMENT OF TRANSPORTATION

400 7th St., SW. (20590).
Established: Oct. 15, 1966, as result of Department of Transportation Act, which became effective Apr. 1, 1967.
Secretary: William T. Coleman, Jr.
Deputy Secretary: John W. Barnum.
Activities: Supervises and coordinates activities of Coast Guard, Federal Aviation Administration, Federal Highway Administration, Federal Railroad Administration, St. Lawrence Seaway Development Corporation, National Highway Traffic Safety Administration, Urban Mass Transportation Administration.

Independent Agencies
(Titles and addresses of independent agencies not described below follow on page 590.)

Executive Department

CIVIL AERONAUTICS BOARD (CAB)

1825 Connecticut Ave., NW (20428).
Members: 5. *Established:* June 30, 1940.

Chairman: John E. Robson.
Activities: Regulates economic aspects of U.S. air carrier operation; assists in development of international air transportation; promotes safety in civil aviation.

COMMUNITY SERVICES ADMINISTRATION

1200 19th St., NW (20506).
Established: 1974.
Director: Samuel Martinez.
Activities: Assists low-income individuals and persons of limited English-speaking ability to attain the skills, knowledge and opportunities to become self-sufficient.

ENERGY RESEARCH AND DEVELOPMENT ADMINISTRATION

Washington, D.C. (20545).
Established: Jan. 19, 1975.
Administrator: Dr. Robert C. Seamans, Jr.
Activities: ERDA seeks to assure coordinated development of all energy sources, increase productivity of the national economy, protect and enhance environmental quality and assure public health and safety.

ENVIRONMENTAL PROTECTION AGENCY (EPA)

401 M St., SW. (20460).
Established: Dec. 2, 1970.
Administrator: Russell E. Train.
Activities: Coordinates governmental action to assure protection of the environment by abating and controlling pollution.

FARM CREDIT ADMINISTRATION (FCA)

490 L'Enfant Plaza East, SW. (20578).
Established: July 17, 1916.
Members: 13.
Chairman of Federal Farm Credit Board: Earl S. Smittcamp.
Activities: Supervises and coordinates cooperative credit system for agriculture; provides long- and short-term credit to farmers and their cooperative marketing, purchasing, and business service organizations.

FEDERAL COMMUNICATIONS COMMISSION (FCC)

1919 M St., NW. (20554).
Members: 7. *Established:* 1934.
Chairman: Richard D. Lichwardt.
Activities: Regulates interstate and foreign communications by wire and radio, including amateur radio and TV; regulates operator's licenses; classifies radio stations and prescribes their services.

FEDERAL ELECTION COMMISSION (FEC)

1325 K St., NW (20463).
Members: 6. *Established:* 1975.
Chairman: Vernon O. Thomson.

Activities: Certifies distribution of public funding of federal elections; regulates compliance with Federal Election Campaign Act; makes available to the public copies of reports filed with the commission.

FEDERAL ENERGY ADMINISTRATION

New Post Office Building, 12th St. and Pennsylvania Ave., NW (20461).
Established: May 7, 1974.
Administrator: Frank G. Zarb.
Activities: Development of national energy policy and program for production, conservation, control and rationing of all forms of energy and promulgation and enforcement of appropriate rules and regulations.

FEDERAL MARITIME COMMISSION

1100 L St., NW (20573).
Members: 5. *Established:* Aug. 12, 1961.
Chairman: Karl E. Bakke.
Activities: Regulates waterborne shipping in foreign and domestic offshore commerce of U.S.

FEDERAL MEDIATION AND CONCILIATION SERVICE (FMCS)

2100 K St., NW (20427).
Established: 1947.
Director: James F. Scearce.
Activities: Assists in labor-management disputes in industries affecting interstate commerce to reach settlements by mediation or conciliation.

FEDERAL POWER COMMISSION (FPC)

825 N. Capitol St., NE. (20426).
Members: 5. *Established:* June 23, 1930.
Chairman: Richard L. Dunham.
Activities: Licenses hydroelectric projects on U.S. Government lands or navigable waters; has jurisdiction over interstate commerce involving sale of electric energy and natural gas and companies engaged therein; handles transmission of electric energy and natural gas between U.S. and foreign countries.

FEDERAL RESERVE SYSTEM (FRS), BOARD OF GOVERNORS OF

20th St. & Constitution Ave., NW. (20551).
Members: 7. *Established:* Dec. 23, 1913.
Chairman: Arthur F. Burns.
Activities: Supervises the 12 Federal Reserve banks, 24 branches and member commercial banks; determines country's monetary policy, including setting maximum interest paid by member banks, amount of credit extended for purchase of securities and discount rates charged by members; handles Government deposits and debt issues; regulates open-market operations; issues Federal Reserve notes.

FEDERAL TRADE COMMISSION (FTC)

Pennsylvania Ave. at 6th St., NW. (20580).
Members: 5. *Established:* Sept. 26, 1914.
Chairman: Calvin J. Collier.
Activities: Prevents unfair competition, deceptive practices, false advertising, price discrimination, monopolies.

GENERAL SERVICES ADMINISTRATION (GSA)

18th and F St., NW. (20405).
Established: July 1, 1949.
Administrator: Jack Eckerd.
Activities: Establishes policy and provides efficient system for management of the government's property and records, including construction and operation of buildings, procurement and distribution of supplies, stockpiling of strategic materials and utilization and disposal of property. Directs National Archives and Records Service, Federal Supply Service and Public Buildings Service.

INTERSTATE COMMERCE COMMISSION (ICC)

12th St. & Constitution Ave., NW. (20423).
Members: 11. *Established:* Feb. 4, 1887.
Chairman: George M. Stafford.
Activities: Regulates railroads, motor carriers, water carriers and freight forwarders as to rates, through-routes, services and bills of lading; authorizes mergers or consolidations; authorizes issue of securities by carriers.

NATIONAL AERONAUTICS AND SPACE ADMINISTRATION (NASA)

400 Maryland Ave., SW. (20546).
Established: 1958.
Administrator: James C. Fletcher.
Activities: Conducts research into problems of flight within and outside earth's atmosphere.

NATIONAL FOUNDATION ON THE ARTS AND THE HUMANITIES

806 15th St., NW. (20506).
Established: 1965.
Chairmen: National Endowment for the Arts, Nancy Hanks; National Endowment for the Humanities, Ronald S. Berman.
Activities: Encourages and supports national progress in the humanities and the arts. Also includes Federal Council on the Arts and the Humanities, which coordinates activities of the two endowments and related programs of other agencies.

NATIONAL LABOR RELATIONS BOARD (NLRB)

1717 Pennsylvania Ave., NW. (20570).
Members: 5. *Established:* July 5, 1935.

Chairman: Betty Southard Murphy.

Activities: Prevents unfair labor practices by employers or labor organizations; conducts secret ballots among employees to determine bargaining representatives.

NATIONAL SCIENCE FOUNDATION (NSF)

1800 G St., NW. (20550).
Established: 1950.
Chairman: Norman Hackerman.
Activities: Awards grants and contracts to support research in the sciences. Encourages research in areas that can lead to improvements in economic growth, productivity and environmental quality.

NATIONAL TRANSPORTATION SAFETY BOARD

800 Independence Ave., SW (20594).
Members: 5. *Established:* April 1, 1975.
Chairman: John H. Reed.
Activities: Conducts investigations into accidents, assesses techniques of accident investigation and recommends safety-improvement measures.

NUCLEAR REGULATORY COMMISSION (NRC)

1717 H. St., NW. (20555) and Bethesda, Md. (20014).
Members: 5. *Established:* Jan. 19, 1975.
Chairman: Marcus A. Rowden.
Activities: Regulates civilian nuclear facilities to assure protection of public health and safety and the environment, and safeguarding of nuclear materials and facilities.

SECURITIES AND EXCHANGE COMMISSION (SEC)

500 N. Capitol St., NW. (20549).
Members: 5. *Established:* June 6, 1934.
Chairman: Roderick M. Hills.
Activities: Registers and issues regulations for securities and exchanges; registers securities offered for public sale; penalizes violators of regulations subject to appeal to U.S. Court of Appeals.

SELECTIVE SERVICE SYSTEM (SSS)

1724 F St., NW. (20435).
Established: 1948.
Director: Byron V. Pepitone.
Activities: Handles registration, examination, classification and selection for induction into armed forces or other disposition of men required to register under Universal Military Training and Service Act.

SMALL BUSINESS ADMINISTRATION (SBA)

1441 L St., NW. (20416).
Established: July 30, 1953.
Administrator: Mitchell P. Kobelinski.

Activities: Aids and assists the interests of small business firms to insure a fair share of total government contracts; makes loans to small firms and victims of flood and disaster.

TENNESSEE VALLEY AUTHORITY (TVA)

Commercial Realty Management Bldg., Knoxville, Tenn. (37902). Washington office: Woodward Bldg., 15th & H Sts., NW. (20444).
Members of Board of Directors: 3. *Established:* May 18, 1933.
Chairman: Aubrey J. Wagner.
Activities: Provides navigable channel and flood control of Tennessee River and some of its larger tributaries; disposes of surplus electric power; improves, increases and cheapens fertilizer production.

U.S. CIVIL SERVICE COMMISSION (CSC)

1900 E St., NW. (20415).
Members: 3. *Established:* Jan. 16, 1883.
Chairman: Robert E. Hampton.
Activities: Provides examinations to test fitness of applicants for positions in competitive service; provides personnel in response to requests from appointing officers; investigates applicants for national security purposes; classifies positions; provides leadership to Federal agencies in personnel matters.

U.S. INFORMATION AGENCY (USIA)

1750 Pennsylvania Ave., NW. (20547).
Established: Aug. 1, 1953.
Director: James Keogh.
Activities: Directs information to foreign peoples, such as explanation of policies of U.S. Government and delineation of U.S. life and culture.

U.S. INTERNATIONAL TRADE COMMISSION

Tariff Commission Building, E St. between 7th & 8th Sts., NW. (20436).
Members: 6. *Established:* Sept. 8, 1916.
Chairman: Will E. Leonard.
Activities: Investigates customs laws, unfair competition and foreign and domestic manufacturing costs; advises the President on duty rates.

U.S. POSTAL SERVICE

475 L'Enfant Plaza West (20260).
Established: Office of Postmaster General and temporary post office system created in 1789. Act of Feb. 20, 1792, made detailed provisions for Post Office Department. Postmaster General became Cabinet member in 1829, and Department received executive status in 1872. In 1970 became independent agency headed by 11-member board of governors. Postmaster General, no longer Cabinet member, is chosen by nine governors, who, with Postmaster General, choose Deputy Postmaster General.

Postmaster General: Benjamin F. Bailar.
Deputy Postmaster General: William F. Bolger.
Activities: Maintains Postal system of U.S.

VETERANS ADMINISTRATION (VA)

Vermont Ave. between H & I Sts., NW. (20420).
Established: July 21, 1930.
Administrator: Richard L. Roudebush.
Activities: Administers laws authorizing benefits for veterans and dependents or beneficiaries. Included are hospitals, pensions, insurance, loans, education, etc.

Other Independent Agencies— Executive Department

Action—806 Connecticut Ave., NW (20525).
Administrative Conference of the United States —2120 L St., NW. (20037).
American Battle Monuments Commission— Forrestal Bldg. (20314).
Appalachian Regional Commission—1666 Connecticut Ave., NW. (20235).
Canal Zone Government—312 Pennsylvania Bldg. (20004).
Commission of Fine Arts—708 Jackson Place, NW. (20006).
Commission on Civil Rights—1121 Vermont Ave., NW. (20425).
Commodity Futures Trading Commission—2033 K St., NW (20581).
Consumer Product Safety Commission—1750 K St., NW. (20207).
District of Columbia—District Bldg., 1358 E St., NW. (20004).
Equal Employment Opportunity Commission—2401 E St., NW. (20506).
Export-Import Bank of the United States— 811 Vermont Ave., NW. (20571).
Federal Deposit Insurance Corporation— 550 17th St., NW. (20429).
Federal Home Loan Bank Board—320 First St., NW. (20552).
Foreign Claims Settlement Commission of the U.S.—1111 20th St., NW. (20579).
Indian Claims Commission—1730 K St., NW. (20006).
Inter-American Foundation—1515 Wilson Blvd., Rosslyn, Va. (22209).
National Credit Union Administration—2025 M St., NW. (20456).
National Mediation Board—1425 K St., NW. (20572).
Occupational Safety and Health Review Commission—1825 K St., NW. (20006).
Overseas Private Investment Corporation— 1129 20th St., NW. (20527).
Panama Canal Company—312 Pennsylvania Bldg. (20004).
Pension Benefit Guaranty Corporation—2020 K St., NW (20006).
Postal Rate Commission—2000 L St., NW. (20268).
Railroad Retirement Board (RRB)—844 Rush St., Chicago, Ill. (60611). Washington Liaison Office: Room 444, 425 13th St., NW. (20004).

Renegotiation Board—2000 M St., NW. (20446).
Selective Service System—National Headquarters, 1724 F St., NW (20435).
Smithsonian Institution—1000 Jefferson Dr., SW. (20560).
U.S. Arms Control and Disarmament Agency —Dept. of State Bldg. (20451).

Legislative Department

ARCHITECT OF THE CAPITOL

U.S. Capitol Building (20515).
Established: First Architect of the Capitol was appointed in 1793; office has been continuous since 1851.
Architect of Capitol: George M. White.
Activities: Architect of the Capitol has charge of structural and mechanical care of Capitol Building and various other government buildings in Washington.

COST ACCOUNTING STANDARDS BOARD

441 G St., NW. (20548).
Members: 5. *Established:* Aug. 15, 1970.
Chairman: Elmer B. Staats.
Activities: Establishes standards in cost accounting principles followed by contractors under federal contracts.

GENERAL ACCOUNTING OFFICE

441 G Street, NW. (20548).
Established: 1921.
Comptroller General: Elmer B. Staats.
Deputy Comptroller General: Robert F. Keller.
Activities: Assists Congress in providing legislative control over receipt, disbursement, and application of public funds.

GOVERNMENT PRINTING OFFICE (GPO)

North Capitol & H St., NW. (20401).
Established: June 23, 1860.
Public Printer: Thomas F. McCormick.
Superintendent of Documents: Wellington H. Lewis.
Activities: Executes printing and binding orders for Congress and Federal agencies; distributes government publications.

LIBRARY OF CONGRESS

10 First St., SE (20540).
Established: Apr. 24, 1800.
Librarian of Congress: Daniel J. Boorstin.
Activities: See listing in Index.

UNITED STATES BOTANIC GARDEN

Office of Director, 245 First St., SW. (20024).
Established: 1820.
Director: George M. White (acting).
Activities: Collects, cultivates, and grows various vegetable products for exhibition and study.

THE UNITED STATES ARMED SERVICES

U. S. MILITARY ACADEMY

Source: U. S. Military Academy.

Established in 1802 by an Act of Congress, the U. S. Military Academy is located on the west bank of the Hudson River some 50 miles north of New York City. To gain admission a candidate must first secure a nomination from an authorized source. These sources, and the number of cadetships allocated to each, are:

Congressional

Representatives	5 each
Senators	5 each
Other: Vice Presidential	5
District of Columbia	5
Puerto Rico	6
Am. Samoa, Canal Zone, Guam, Virgin Is.	1 each

Military–Service–Connected Nominations
(each class)

Presidential	100
Enlisted members of Army	85
Enlisted members of Army Reserve/ National Guard	85
Sons of deceased and disabled Veterans (approximately)	10
Honor military, naval schools and ROTC	20
Sons of persons awarded the Medal of Honor	(unlimited)

Others

Foreign cadets (Latin American Republics, 20; Philippines, 4)	24

Candidates may be nominated for vacancies during the year preceding the day of admission, which occurs in the first week of July. The best time to apply is during the junior year in high school.

Candidates must be citizens of the U. S., be of good moral character, be unmarried, be between the ages of 17 and 22, have a secondary-school education or its equivalent, and be able to meet the academic, medical, and physical aptitude requirements. Academic qualification is determined by an analysis of entire scholastic record, and performance on either the American College Testing (ACT) Assessment Program Test or the College Entrance Examination Board Scholastic Aptitude Test (SAT). Entrance requirements and procedures for appointment are described in the Admissions Bulletin, available without charge from Admissions, U. S. Military Academy, West Point, N. Y. 10996.

Cadets receive their entire education at Government expense and are paid over $3,600 a year. From this sum, they pay for their uniforms, textbooks, and incidental expenses. Upon successful completion of the 4-year course, the graduate receives the degree of Bachelor of Science and is commissioned a second lieutenant in the Regular Army with a requirement to serve as an officer for a minimum of five years.

U. S. NAVAL ACADEMY

Source: U. S. Naval Academy.

The Naval School, established in 1845 at Fort Severn, Annapolis, Md., was renamed the U. S. Naval Academy in 1850. A 4-year course was adopted a year later.

The Superintendent is an admiral. A civilian Academic Dean heads the academic program. A senior Navy captain heads the 4,200-man Brigade of Midshipmen and military, professional, and physical training. The faculty is half military and half civilian.

Graduates are awarded the Bachelor of Science or Bachelor of Science in Engineering and are commissioned as officers in the U. S. Navy or Marine Corps.

The primary avenues to selection for appointment as midshipmen follow:

Congressmen, the Vice President, the Mayor of Washington, D. C., and the Resident Commissioner of Puerto Rico may each have 5 midshipmen at Academy at any one time. Ten candidates may be nominated for each vacancy. Well over half of the more than 1,300 appointments as midshipmen made annually originate from these sources.

The President appoints the 65 best-qualified sons and daughters of deceased or disabled veterans, or sons and daughters of prisoners of war or servicemen missing in action, and the 100 best-qualified sons and daughters of officers and enlisted men in the regular Armed Services. He also appoints sons and daughters of Medal of Honor holders.

The Secretary of the Navy awards 170 (85 + 85) appointments to regular and reserve personnel of the Navy or Marine Corps; 150 to congressional alternate nominees, all on a competitive, best-qualified basis; and 20 outstanding graduates of NROTC or Honor Naval and Military Schools. He may also make additional appointments each year, to bring the Brigade up to authorized strength, from among qualified congressional and competitive nominees, again on a best-qualified basis. Three-fourths of these additional appointments must, by law, be congressional nominees.

There are also limited numbers of appointments available from the Philippines, Canal Zone, Virgin Islands, Guam, American Samoa, and the American republics.

To have basic eligibility for admission, candidates must be citizens of the U. S., of good moral character, at least 17 and not more than 22 years of age on July 1 of their entering year, in the top 40% of their high school class, and unmarried.

In order to be considered for admission, a candidate must obtain a nomination from one of the sources of appointments listed above. The Admissions Board at the Naval Academy examines the candidate's school record, College Board or ACT scores, recommendations from school officials, extracurricular activities, and evidence from other sources concerning his or her character, leadership potential, academic preparation, and physical fitness. Qualification for admission is based on all of the above factors.

Tuition, board, lodging, medical and dental care are provided. Midshipmen receive $317.10 a month for books, uniforms, and personal needs.

For a catalogue or answers to specific questions, write: Superintendent, U. S. Naval Academy, (Attention: Candidate Guidance), Annapolis, Md. 21402.

U. S. COAST GUARD ACADEMY
Source: U. S. Coast Guard Academy.

One of the four United States military service academies, the U.S. Coast Guard Academy, New London, Conn., was founded on July 31, 1876 to serve as the "School of Instruction" for the Revenue Cutter Service, predecessor to the Coast Guard.

The J.C. Dobbin, a converted schooner, housed the first Coast Guard Academy, and was succeeded in 1878 by the barque Chase, a ship built for cadet training. First winter quarters were in a sail loft at New Bedford, Mass. The school was moved in 1900 to Curtis Bay, Md., to provide a more technical education, and in 1910 was moved back to New England to Fort Trumbull, New London, Conn. In 1932 the Academy moved to its present location, in New London.

The Academy today offers a four-year curriculum for the professional and academic training of cadets which leads to a Bachelor of Science degree and a commission as ensign in the Coast Guard.

Cadets receive appointment through nationwide competition, which includes either the December administration of the College Entrance Examination Board tests, or the American College Testing (ACT) Program tests. Applications must be submitted to the Coast Guard not later than December 15 and to the College Entrance Examination Board, 30 days prior to the tests.

Women were admitted to the Coast Guard Academy for the first time during 1976 as members of the Class of 1980. Candidates must be between 17 and 22 years of age, physically sound, unmarried and at least 5'4" tall. They must agree to remain unmarried until graduation and to serve at least five years on active duty. Cadets receive $4,340.00 per year to cover their uniform and incidental expenses, and are furnished their rations and quarters. Applications may be made to Director of Admissions, U.S. Coast Guard Academy, New London, Conn. 06320.

U. S. MERCHANT MARINE ACADEMY
Source: U.S. Merchant Marine Academy.

The U. S. Merchant Marine Academy, situated at Kings Point, N. Y., on the south shore of Long Island Sound, was dedicated Sept. 30, 1943. It is maintained by the Department of Commerce under direction of the Maritime Administration.

The Academy has a complement of 1,000 men and women representing every state, D. C., the Canal Zone, Puerto Rico, Guam, American Samoa, and the Virgin Islands. It is also authorized to admit up to 12 candidates from Central and South America.

Competitive examinations are held annually among candidates nominated by Senators and members of the House of Representatives. Appointments to the Academy are governed by a state and territory quota system based on population and the results of the College Entrance Examination Board tests.

A candidate must be an unmarried citizen not less than 17 and not yet 22 years of age by July 1 of the year in which admission is sought. Fifteen high school credits, including 3 units in mathematics (from algebra, geometry and/or trigonometry), 1 unit in science (physics or chemistry) and 3 in English are required.

The course is 4 years and includes 1 year of practical training aboard a merchant ship. Study includes marine engineering including nuclear studies, navigation, satellite navigation and communications, electricity, ship construction, naval science and tactics, economics, business, languages, history, etc.

Upon completion of the course of study, a graduate receives a Bachelor of Science degree, a license as a merchant marine deck or engineering officer; and a commission as an ensign in the Naval Reserve.

U. S. AIR FORCE ACADEMY
Source: U. S. Air Force Academy.

The bill establishing the Air Force Academy was signed by President Eisenhower on Apr. 1, 1954. The first class of 306 cadets was sworn in on July 11, 1955, at Lowry Air Force Base, Denver, Colo., the Academy's temporary location. The Cadet Wing moved into the Academy's permanent home north of Colorado Springs in 1958.

Cadets receive 4 years of academic, military, and physical education to prepare them for leadership as officers in the Air Force. The Academy is authorized a total of 4,417 cadets. Each new class averages 1,500. This includes approximately 1,350 men and 150 women. The candidates for the Academy must be at least 17 but less than 22 on July 1 of the year for which they seek admission, must be a United States citizen, be single, and be able to meet the mental and physical requirements. A candidate is required to take the following examinations and tests: (1) the Service Academies' Qualifying Medical Examination; (2) either the American College Testing (ACT) Assessment Program test or the College Entrance Examination Board Scholastic Aptitude Test (SAT), and (3) a Physical Aptitude Examination.

Cadets receive their entire education at Government expense and, in addition, are paid one half the pay of a second lieutenant. From this sum, they pay for most of their uniforms, and textbooks. Upon completion of the 4-year course, leading to a Bachelor of Science degree, a cadet who meets the physical qualifications is commissioned a second lieutenant in the regular U. S. Air Force. Many go on to pilot or aerospace training. For details on admissions, write: Associate Director of Admissions, USAF Academy, Colo. 80840.

The National Guard
Source: National Guard Bureau.

The National Guard of the U.S. originated with the Old North Regiment of the Colonial Militia in Massachusetts in 1636. It is the oldest military force in the country. Guardsmen have served overseas in every major conflict in which the U. S. has participated.

As of March 31, 1976, the Army and Air National Guard totaled about 476,224 men and women, serving in 4,307 Army and Air units in more than 2,600 communities in all 50 states, Puerto Rico, the Virgin Islands and the District of Columbia.

By Act of Congress, the Guard is the primary backup force of the Army and Air Force. In peacetime, it is commanded by the state governors and serves in state emergencies, disasters, and civil disturbances.

The Army National Guard has Federal equipment and vehicles valued at $4.2 billion. The Army National Guard's budget request for fiscal year 1977 is approximately $1.465 billion. The Air National Guard has Federal equipment and aircraft valued at over $3.5 billion; its fiscal year 1977 budget request is approximately $1.023 billion. Additional money is appropriated directly for the National Guard by the states. Substantial support is also provided by state, county and municipal governments in land, police and fire protection, maintenance of roads, and the provision of direct county and municipal fiscal support to local units.

Army National Guard forces are an integral part of the nation's first line defenses. For example, the 29th Infantry Brigade in the Hawaii National Guard is a roundout brigade for the active Army 25th Infantry Division. Under the roundout concept, National Guard units work and train with the active Army unit to which they would be assigned upon mobilization. Under the total force policy, the program for improving readiness is continually being studied. National Guard units take part in Joint Chiefs of Staff and Army exercises with the active forces to further develop the readiness of both units and individuals.

The Air National Guard flying force consists of 91 flying squadrons, the majority of which will be gained by Tactical Air Command upon mobilization, and the remainder by Aerospace Defense Command and the Military Airlift Command. Within the TAC-gained force are fighter, reconnaissance, air refueling, tactical-electronic warfare, special operations, and tactical air support units. Within the air defense force there are fighter interceptors and defense evaluation units designed for testing defense systems. The Air Guard provides about two-thirds of the daily alert in support of the air defense of the United States.

The National Guard is administered by the National Guard Bureau, a joint Army-Air Force office in the Pentagon. Chief of the Bureau is Maj. Gen. LaVern E. Weber of Oklahoma.

If openings exist, young men between the ages of 17 and 35, without prior service, may enlist in the National Guard for a period of six years. Upon enlistment, they serve a minimum of twelve weeks on active duty, training with the U.S. Army or the U.S. Air Force, depending upon which branch of the National Guard they choose. The remainder of their six years is spent in part-time training with their Guard unit. During this period, they are subject to call to active duty with their unit at any time by the President, Congress, or the governor of their state. The National Guard has a recruiting and retention campaign designed to provide prior-service personnel with a one-year enlistment option. It also offers Army Guardsmen nearing the expiration of service the option of a one-year extension.

A woman between the ages of 17 and 35 who has no previous military experience may enlist in the National Guard for a period of three years. Women in the Army National Guard will receive basic training at either Fort McClellan, Alabama, or Fort Jackson, South Carolina; women in the Air National Guard at Lackland Air Force Base, Texas. Advanced individual training will be received at an appropriate training center. Pay, promotion and retirement benefits are the same as for men.

A Guardsman receives a full day's pay of his military rank for each unit assembly he attends. Additionally, he receives a day's pay of his military rank for each day of his 15 days of Annual Training, plus any other days on active duty for training at military schools or special assignments.

History of the Armed Services
Source: U. S. Department of Defense.

U. S. ARMY

On June 14, 1775, The Continental Congress "adopted" the New England Army—a mixed force of militia and volunteers besieging the British in Boston—by appointing a committee to draft "Rules and regulations for the government of the Army" and voting to raise 10 rifle companies as a reinforcement. The next day it appointed Washington commander-in-chief of the "Continental forces to be raised for the defense of liberty," and he took command at Boston on July 3, 1775. The Continental Army that fought the Revolution was our first national military organization and hence the Army is the senior service. After the war, the Continental Army was radically reduced but enough survived to form a small Regular Army of about 700 men under the Constitution in 1789, a nucleus for expansion in the 1970s to successfully meet threats from the Indians and from France. From these humble beginnings, the U.S. Army has developed, normally expanding rapidly by absorbing citizen soldiers in wartime and contracting just as rapidly after each war.

U. S. NAVY

The antecedents of the U. S. Navy go back to Sept. 1775, when Gen. Washington commissioned 7 schooners and brigantines to prey on British supply vessels bound for the colonies or Canada. In Oct. 1775, a motion in the Continental Congress called for the construction of 2 vessels for the purpose of intercepting enemy transports. With its passage a Naval Committee of 7 men was formed, and they rapidly obtained passage of legislation calling for construction of additional vessels. The Continental Navy was supplemented by privateers and ships operated as state navies, but soon after the British surrender it was disestablished.

In 1794, because of dissatisfaction with the payment of tribute to the Barbary pirates, Congress authorized construction of 6 frigates. The first, *United States*, was launched May 10, 1797, but the Navy still remained under the control of the Secretary of War until April 1798, when the Secretary of the Navy was given full Cabinet rank and the U. S. Navy came into its own.

U. S. AIR FORCE

Until creation of the National Military Establishment in September 1947, which united the services under one department, military aviation was a part of the U. S. Army. In the Army, aeronautical operations came under the Signal Corps from 1907 to 1918, when the U. S. Air Service was established. In 1926, the U. S. Air Corps came into being and remained until 1942, when the Army Air Forces succeeded it as the Army's air arm. In 1947, the U. S. Air Force was established as an independent military service under the National Military Establishment. At that time, the name "Army Air Forces" was abolished.

U. S. COAST GUARD

Our country's oldest continuous seagoing service, the U. S. Coast Guard traces its history back to 1790 when the First Congress authorized the construction of ten vessels for the collection of revenue. Known first as the Revenue Marine, and later as the Revenue Cutter Service, the Coast Guard received its present name in 1915 under an act of Congress combining the Revenue Cutter Service with the Life-Saving Service. In 1939, the Lighthouse Service was also consolidated with this unit. The Bureau of Marine Inspection and Navigation was transferred temporarily to the Coast Guard in 1942, permanently in 1946. Through its antecedents, the Coast Guard is one of the oldest organizations under the Federal Government and, until the Navy Department was established in 1798, served as the only U. S. armed force afloat. In time of peace it operates under the Department of Transportation, serving as the Nation's primary agency for promoting marine safety and enforcing Federal maritime laws. In time of war, or on direction of the President, it is attached to the Navy Department.

U. S. MARINE CORPS

Founded in 1775 and observing its official birthday on Nov. 10, the U. S. Marine Corps was developed to be able to serve to advantage on land, on sea, and in the air.

Marines have fought in every U. S. war. From an initial two battalions in the Revolution, the Corps reached a peak strength of six divisions and five aircraft wings in World War II. Its present strength is three active divisions and aircraft wings and a Reserve division/aircraft wing team. In 1947, the National Security Act set Marine Corps strength at not less than three divisions and three aircraft wings.

Women in the Armed Forces[1]
Source: Department of Defense.

Army (WAC). Director, Brigadier General M.E. Clarke. 45,872 members. Officers, 4,777; enlisted, 41,095.

Navy. 22,146 members. Officers, 3,583; enlisted, 18,437.

Air Force. Director, Colonel Bianca D. Trimeloni. 32,403 members. Officers, 5,086; enlisted, 27,317.

Marines. Director, Colonel Margaret Ann Brewer. 3,412 members. Officers, 358; enlisted 3,054.

Defense Advisory Committee on Women in the Services (DACOWITS). Established in 1951. Appointed by the Secretary of Defense for three years and selected on basis of their outstanding reputations in business, the professions, public service or civic leadership. Limited membership of 25.

[1]As of November, 1975.

Highest Ranking Officers in the Armed Forces

ARMY
General of the Army: Omar N. Bradley
Generals: Frederick C. Weyand, Chief of Staff; George S. Blanchard; John R. Deane; William E. DePuy; Alexander M. Haig, Jr.; John J. Hennessey; Walter T. Kerwin, Jr.; William A. Knowlton; Bernard W. Rogers; John W. Vessey, Jr.

AIR FORCE
Generals: George S. Brown, Chairman, Joint Chiefs of Staff; David C. Jones, Chief of Staff; Paul K. Carlton; Robert J. Dixon; Russell E. Dougherty; Richard H. Ellis; William J. Evans; Robert E. Huyser; Daniel James, Jr.; William V. McBride; Felix M. Rogers; Louis T. Seith; Louis L. Wilson, Jr.

NAVY
Admirals: James L. Holloway, III, Chief of Naval Operations; David H. Bagley; Noel A. M. Gayler; Isaac C. Kidd, Jr.; Frederick H. Michaelis; Harold E. Shear; Stansfield Turner; John P. Weinel; Maurice F. Weisner.

MARINE CORPS
Generals: Louis H. Wilson, Commandant of the Marine Corps; Samuel Jaskilka, Asst. Commandant.
Lieutenant Generals: Robert H. Barrow; Leslie E. Brown; Joseph C. Fegan, Jr.; John N. McLaughlin; Thomas H. Miller, Jr.; Robert L. Nichols; Lawrence F. Snowden.

COAST GUARD
Admiral: Owen Siler, Commandant.
Vice Admirals: Ellis Lee Perry, Assistant Commandant: William F. Rea; Austin C. Wagner.

Insignia and Ranks of the Armed Forces

| Army, Air Force, and Marines | | Navy and Coast Guard | | |
Insignia	Rank	Insignia	Rank	Stripes[1]
Five silver stars	General of the Army, AF	Five silver stars	Fleet Admiral	1—4—0
Four silver stars	General	Four silver stars	Admiral	1—3—0
Three silver stars	Lieutenant General	Three silver stars	Vice Admiral	1—2—0
Two silver stars	Major General	Two silver stars	Rear Admiral	1—1—0
One silver star	Brigadier General	One silver star	Commodore	1—0—0[2]
Silver eagle	Colonel	Silver eagle	Captain	0—4—0
Silver oak leaf	Lieutenant Colonel	Silver oak leaf	Commander	0—3—0
Gold oak leaf	Major	Gold oak leaf	Lt. Commander	0—2—1
Two silver bars	Captain	Two silver bars	Lieutenant	0—2—0
One silver bar	First Lieutenant	One silver bar	Lieutenant (jg)	0—1—1
One gold bar	Second Lieutenant	One gold bar	Ensign	0—1—0
Silver bar with 3 enamel bands[3]	Chief Warrant Officer (W-4)	Silver bar with 3 enamel bands[3]	Chief Warrant Officer (W-4)	0—1—0[4]
Silver bar with 2 enamel bands[3]	Chief Warrant Officer (W-3)	Silver bar with 2 enamel bands[3]	Chief Warrant Officer (W-3)	0—1—0[5]
Gold bar with 3 enamel bands[3]	Chief Warrant Officer (W-2)	Gold bar with 3 enamel bands[3]	Chief Warrant Officer (W-2)	0—1—0[6]
Gold bar with 2 enamel bands[3]	Warrant Officer (W-1)	Gold bar with 2 enamel bands[3]	Warrant Officer (W-1)	0—0—1[6]

[1] Of gold embroidery; first figure is number of 2-in. stripes, second is number of ½-inch stripes, third is number of ¼-in. stripes. [2] Wartime only. [3] Navy and Marine Corps use same size insignia as Army when worn on shoulder straps, but miniature size on shirt collars. Enamel bands are scarlet for Army and Marines, medium blue for Air Force, and blue for Navy and Coast Guard. [4] One break. [5] Two breaks. [6] Three breaks.

Pay Grades of Enlisted Personnel
Source: Department of Defense, Public Information Office.

Army ranks[1]	Air Force ranks	Marine ranks	Navy and Cst. Gd. ranks	Pay grades[2]
Command Sergeant Major and Staff Sergeant Major	Chief Master Sergeant	Sergeant Major and Master Gunnery Sergeant	Mast. Ch. Petty Officer	E-9
1st Sgt. and Master Sgt.	Sr. Master Sergeant	1st Sgt. and Master Sgt.	Sr. Ch. Petty Officer	E-8
Sergeant 1st Class	Master Sergeant	Gunnery Sergeant	Chief Petty Officer	E-7
Staff Sergeant	Technical Sergeant	Staff Sergeant	Petty Officer 1st Class	E-6
Sergeant	Staff Sergeant	Sergeant	Petty Officer 2nd Class	E-5
Corporal	Sergeant	Corporal	Petty Officer 3rd Class	E-4
Private 1st Class	Airman 1st Class	Lance Corporal	Seaman	E-3
Private	Airman	Private 1st Class	Seaman Apprentice	E-2
Private	Airman/Basic	Private	Seaman Recruit	E-1

[1] Army specialist pay grades correspond to numbers: Specialist 4 (E-4), etc. [2] See page 597.

Pay Grades of Commissioned Officers and Warrant Officers

Source: Department of Defense, Public Information Office.

Rank				Monthly allowances for quarters	
Army, Air Force, and Marine Corps	Navy, Coast Guard, and Environmental Science Serv. Adm.	Public Health Service	Pay grade	Without dependents	With dependents
General	Admiral[1]	....	O-10	$255.30	$319.20
Lieutenant General	Vice Admiral	....	O-9	255.30	319.20
Major General	Rear Admiral (upper half)	Surgeon General; Deputy Surgeon General; Assistant Surgeon General	O-8	255.30	319.20
Brigadier General	Rear Admiral (lower half) and Commodore	Assistant Surgeon General	O-7	255.30	319.20
Colonel	Captain	Director Grade	O-6	234.60	286.20
Lieutenant Colonel	Commander	Senior Grade	O-5	219.60	264.60
Major	Lieutenant Commander	Full Grade	O-4	198.00	238.80
Captain	Lieutenant	Senior Assistant Grade	O-3	175.50	216.60
First Lieutenant	Lieutenant (junior grade)	Assistant Grade	O-2	153.60	194.70
Second Lieutenant	Ensign	Junior Assistant Grade	O-1	120.60	156.90
Chief Warrant Officer	Chief Warrant Officer[1]	....	W-4	191.10	230.40
Chief Warrant Officer	Warrant Officer[1]	....	W-3	172.20	212.40
Chief Warrant Officer	Warrant Officer[1]	....	W-2	151.80	192.60
Warrant Officer	Warrant Officer[1]	....	W-1	137.40	178.20

[1] Not applicable to Environmental Science Services Administration.

Monthly Salaries of Officers and Warrant Officers by Years of Service

O-10[1]—Under 2 yrs service, $2,841.00; 2-8 yrs, $2,940.90; 8-12 yrs, $3,053.70; 12-16 yrs,[2] $3,287.70; 16-20 yrs,[2] $3,522.90; 20-26 yrs,[2] $3,758.40; 26 yrs and over,[2] $3,992.70.

O-9—Under 2 yrs, $2,517.90; 2 yrs, $2,584.20; 3-8 yrs, $2,639.10; 8-12 yrs, $2,706.00; 12-16 yrs, $2,818.20; 16-20 yrs, $3,053.70; 20-26 yrs,[2] $3,287.70; 26 yrs and over,[2] $3,522.90.

O-8—Under 2 yrs, $2,280.60; 2 yrs, $2,349.00; 3-8 yrs, $2,404.80; 8-12 yrs, $2,584.20; 12-16 yrs, $2,706.00; 16-18 yrs, $2,818.20; 18-20 yrs, $2,943.90; 20-22 yrs, $3,053.70; 22 yrs and over,[2] $3,176.10.

O-7—Under 2 yrs, $1,894.80; 2-6 yrs, $2,024.10; 6-10 yrs, $2,114.40; 10-14 yrs, $2,237.40; 14-16 yrs, $2,349.00; 16-18 yrs, $2,584.20; 18 yrs and over, $2,761.80.

O-6—Under 2 yrs, $1,404.60; 2 yrs, $1,543.50; 3-14 yrs, $1,644.00; 14-16 yrs, $1,699.80; 16-18 yrs, $1,968.90; 18-20 yrs, $2,069.70; 20-22 yrs, $2,114.40; 22-26 yrs, $2,237.40; 26 yrs and over, $2,426.10.

O-5—Under 2 yrs, $1,123.20; 2 yrs, $1,319.40; 3-10 yrs, $1,410.30; 10-12 yrs, $1,453.50; 12-14 yrs, $1,530.90; 14-16 yrs, $1,633.20; 16-18 yrs, $1,755.90; 18-20 yrs, $1,856.70; 20-22 yrs, $1,912.50; 22 yrs and over, $1,979.70.

O-4—Under 2 yrs, $947.10; 2 yrs, $1,152.60; 3-6 yrs, $1,230.30; 6-8 yrs, $1,252.50; 8-10 yrs, $1,308.30; 10-12 yrs, $1,397.10; 12-14 yrs, $1,476.00; 14-16 yrs, $1,543.50; 16-18 yrs, $1,610.70; 18 yrs and over, $1,655.40.

O-3[3]—Under 2 yrs, $880.20; 2 yrs, $983.70; 3 yrs, $1,051.50; 4-6 yrs, $1,163.70; 6-8 yrs, $1,219.20; 8-10 yrs, $1,263.30; 10-12 yrs, $1,330.80; 12-14 yrs, $1,397.10; 14 yrs and over, $1,431.30.

O-3[4]—4-6 yrs, $1,163.70; 6-8 yrs, $1,219.20; 8-10 yrs,

$1,263.30; 10-12 yrs, $1,330.80; 12-14 yrs, $1,397.10; 14 yrs and over, $1,453.50.

O-2[3]—Under 2 yrs, $767.10; 2 yrs, $838.20; 3 yrs, $1,006.80; 4-6 yrs, $1,040.40; 6 yrs and over, $1,062.30.

O-2[4]—4-6 yrs, $1,040.40; 6-8 yrs, $1,062.30; 8-10 yrs, $1,095.90; 10-12 yrs, $1,152.60; 12-14 yrs, $1,197.30; 14 yrs and over, $1,230.30.

O-1[3]—Under 2 yrs, $666.00; 2 yrs, $693.30; 3 yrs and over, $838.20.

O-1[4]—4-6 yrs, $838.20; 6-8 yrs, $894.90; 8-10 yrs, $928.20; 10-12 yrs, $961.80; 12-14 yrs, $995.40; 14 yrs and over, $1,040.40.

W-4—Under 2 yrs, $896.40; 2-4 yrs, $961.80; 4-6 yrs, $983.70; 6-8 yrs, $1,028.70; 8-10 yrs, $1,073.70; 10-12 yrs, $1,118.70; 12-14 yrs, $1,197.30; 14-16 yrs, $1,252.50; 16-18 yrs, $1,296.90; 18-20 yrs, $1,330.80; 20-22 yrs, $1,374.90; 22-26 yrs, $1,420.80; 26 yrs and over, $1,530.90.

W-3—Under 2 yrs, $815.10; 2-4 yrs, $884.10; 4-6 yrs, $894.90; 6-8 yrs, $905.70; 8-10 yrs, $972.00; 10-12 yrs, $1,028.70; 12-14 yrs, $1,062.30; 14-16 yrs, $1,095.90; 16-18 yrs, $1,128.60; 18-20 yrs, $1,163.70; 20-22 yrs, $1,208.40; 22-26 yrs, $1,252.50; 26 yrs and over, $1,296.90.

W-2—Under 2 yrs, $713.70; 2-4 yrs, $771.90; 4-6 yrs, $794.40; 6-8 yrs, $838.20; 8-10 yrs, $884.10; 10-12 yrs, $917.40; 12-14 yrs, $950.70; 14-16 yrs, $983.70; 16-18 yrs, $1,018.20; 18-20 yrs, $1,051.50; 20-22 yrs, $1,084.80; 22 yrs and over, $1,128.60.

W-1—Under 2 yrs, $594.60; 2-4 yrs, $681.90; 4-6 yrs, $738.60; 6-8 yrs, $771.90; 8-10 yrs, $805.50; 10-12 yrs, $838.20; 12-14 yrs, $872.70; 14-16 yrs, $905.70; 16-18 yrs, $939.30; 18-20 yrs, $972.00; 20 yrs and over, $1,006.80.

[1] While serving as Chairman of the Joint Chiefs of Staff, Chief of Staff of the Army, Chief of Naval Operations, Chief of Staff of the Air Force, or Commandant of the Marine Corps, basic pay for this grade is $4,405.50 regardless of cumulative years of service. [2] Limited under existing law to $3,150.00 by Level V of the Executive Schedule. [3] For commissioned officers who have not been credited with over 4 years' active service as an enlisted member. [4] For commissioned officers who have been credited with over 4 years' active service as an enlisted member.

MONTHLY ALLOWANCES FOR QUARTERS: 0-1—no dependents, $120.60; with dependents, $156.90. 0-2—no dependents, $153.60; with dependents, $194.70. 0-3—no dependents, $175.50; with dependents, $216.60. 0-4—no dependents, $198.00; with dependents, $238.80. 0-5—no dependents, $219.60; with dependents, $264.60. 0-6—no dependents, $234.60; with dependents, $286.20. 0-7 through 0-10—no dependents, $255.30; with dependents, $319.20. W-1—no dependents, $137.40; with dependents, $178.20. W-2—no dependents, $151.80; with dependents, $192.60. W-3—no dependents, $172.20; with dependents, $212.40. W-4—no dependents, $191.10; with dependents, $230.40.

Monthly Basic Pay Rates of Enlisted Personnel by Years of Service

E-9[1]—10-12 yrs, $1,018.50; 12-14 yrs, $1,041.60; 14-16 yrs, $1,065.30; 16-18 yrs, $1,089.90; 18-20 yrs, $1,113.90; 20-22 yrs, $1,135.80; 22-26 yrs, $1,195.80; 26 yrs and over, $1,311.60.

E-8—8-10 yrs, $854.70; 10-12 yrs, $878.40; 12-14 yrs, $901.80; 14-16 yrs, $925.50; 16-18 yrs, $949.50; 18-20 yrs, $971.70; 20-22 yrs, $995.70; 22-26 yrs, $1,053.90; 26 yrs and over $1,171.80.

E-7—Under 2 yrs, $596.70; 2 yrs, $643.80; 3 yrs, $667.80; 4-6 yrs, $691.20; 6-8 yrs, $715.20; 8-10 yrs, $737.40; 10-12 yrs, $760.80; 12-14 yrs, $784.80; 14-16 yrs, $820.20; 16-18 yrs, $843.30; 18-20 yrs, $867.00; 20-22 yrs, $878.40; 22-26 yrs, $937.50; 26 yrs and over, $1,053.90.

E-6—Under 2 yrs, $515.40; 2 yrs, $561.90; 3 yrs, $585.30; 4-6 yrs, $609.60; 6-8 yrs, $632.70; 8-10 yrs, $656.10; 10-12 yrs, $679.80; 12-14 yrs, $715.20; 14-16 yrs, $737.40; 16-18 yrs, $760.80; 18 yrs and over, $772.80.

E-5—Under 2 yrs, $452.40; 2 yrs, $492.60; 3 yrs, $516.30; 4-6 yrs, $538.80; 6-8 yrs, $573.90; 8-10 yrs, $597.30; 10-12 yrs, $621.30; 12-14 yrs, $643.80; 14 yrs and over, $656.10.

E-4—Under 2 yrs, $435.00; 2 yrs, $459.30; 3 yrs, $486.00; 4-6 yrs, $524.10; 6 yrs and over, $544.50.

E-3—Under 2 yrs, $418.20; 2 yrs, $441.30; 3 yrs, $459.00; 4 yrs and over, $477.00.

E-2—All service time, $402.60.

E-1—All service time, $361.20.

[1] While serving as Sergeant Major of the Army, Master Chief Petty Officer of the Navy, Chief Master Sergeant of the Air Force, or Sergeant Major of the Marine Corps, basic pay for this grade is $1,594.50 regardless of cumulative years of service.

MONTHLY ALLOWANCES FOR QUARTERS: E-1—no dependents, $66.60; with dependents, $116.10. E-2—no dependents, $70.80; with dependents, $116.10. E-3—no dependents, $80.10; with dependents, $116.10. E-4—no dependents, $90.30; with dependents, $134.40. E-5—no dependents, $102.60; with dependents, $153.60. E-6—no dependents, $106.20; with dependents, $166.20. E-7—no dependents, $115.80; with dependents, $178.80. E-8—no dependents, $135.00; with dependents, $190.80. E-9—no dependents, $144.90; with dependents, $204.00. Master Sergeant—no dependents, $144.90; with dependents, $204.00.

Special Pay

Medical, Dental, and Veterinary Officers

Monthly special pay for medical officers is based on cumulative service: 0-2 years, $100; 2 or more years, $350. For dental officers: 0-2 years, $100; 2-6 years, $150; 6-10 years, $250; 10 or more years, $350.

Monthly special pay for veterinary officers is $100 regardless of years of service.

Variable Incentive Pay for Physicians

Selected physicians who are serving in critical specialties and have completed at least 4 years of an initial active duty obligation may, if otherwise qualified and approved, agree in writing to remain on active duty for a specified number of years for which they may be paid not more than $13,-500 for each year of the agreement. This is in addition to other pays and allowances.

Diving Duty

The monthly pay is not more than $110 for periods during which diving duty is actually performed. It may not be paid in addition to incentive pay.

Sea Duty and Duty at Certain Places
(For pay grades, see page 596)

An enlisted member of a uniformed service is entitled to special pay while on sea duty to or while on duty at a designated place outside the contiguous 48 states and the District of Columbia.

The monthly rates are: E-9, E-8, and E-7, $22.50; E-6, $20; E-5, $16; E-4, $13; E-3, $9; E-2 and E-1, $8.

Proficiency Pay for Enlisted Members
(For pay grades, see pages 595, 597)

1. A qualified career member serving in a designated specialty may receive shortage specialty. This type of proficiency pay is paid to personnel in high training cost specialties in which there is a critical shortage of career members. Monthly rates are: P-3, $100 and $150; P-2, $75; P-1, $50.

2. A qualified member serving in a designated duty assignment may receive special duty assignment pay. This is paid to individuals on special duty assignments for which the number of volunteers is inadequate. Monthly rates are: P-1, $30 and $50. By a special waiver of criteria, recruiters are authorized $50, $100 and $150 per month depending on job tenure.

3. When employed, eligible members serving in a specialty not designated for receipt of another type of proficiency pay may compete for superior performance pay. Monthly rate is: P-1, $30 and $50. (Not being used in FY 1977).

Duty Subject to Hostile Fire

Except in time of war declared by Congress, and under regulations prescribed by the Secretary of Defense, special pay at the rate of $65 a month will be paid to a member of the uniformed services for any month during which he was subject to hostile fire.

Extra Pay for Service during Hostilities

Act of March 3, 1847, during the Mexican War, provided for $2 a month extra pay for "distinguished service." This continued beyond the war and applied in the Civil War.

In the Spanish-American War, there was a 20% increase in enlisted men's pay for war service.

In World War I, additional incentive pay was offered for all types of services. Among these items was pay for certificate of merit of $2 a month. By the law passed in 1920, the reasons for additional pay had expanded. Recipients of the Medal of Honor, Distinguished Service Cross, and Distinguished Service Medal received $2 a month extra, while each bar in lieu of these medals also added another $2 a month. Added to this was a foreign service bonus of 20%.

Act of June 30, 1944, authorized $5 a month to enlisted men qualified as expert infantrymen and $10 to those qualified as combat infantrymen. Amounts were payable for the duration of war and 6 months thereafter.

By the Act of July 6, 1945, for the duration of war and for 6 months thereafter, enlisted men entitled to wear Medical Badges received additional pay of $10 a month.

Act of July 10, 1952, authorized $45 a month for each month beginning after May 31, 1950, for which the member was entitled to receive basic pay and during which he was a member of a combat unit in Korea.

The Combat Duty Pay Act of 1952 was repealed by the Uniformed Services Pay Act of 1963, which authorized special pay for duty subject to hostile fire under certain conditions at the rate of $55 (now $65) a month.

Incentive Pay for Hazardous Duty

Members of the uniformed services are entitled to incentive pay for special kinds of hazardous duty. For the following kinds, an officer is entitled to $110 a month, and an enlisted man to $55 a month:

1. Frequent and regular participation in aerial flights *not* as a crew member.

2. Frequent and regular participation in glider flights.

3. Parachute jumping as an essential part of military duty.

4. Duty involving contact with lepers.

5. Demolition of explosives as primary duty (including training).

6. Duty inside a high- or low-pressure chamber.

7. Duty as a human acceleration or deceleration experimental subject.

8. Duty as a human test subject in thermal stress experiments.

9. Frequent and regular participation in flight operations on the flight deck of an aircraft carrier.

For duty as an enlisted crew member of an aircraft or a crew member of a submarine, the rates for incentive pay are as follows (for pay grades, see pages 595 and 597):

O-10—$165 regardless of yrs of service.
O-9—$165 regardless of yrs of service.
O-8—Under 3 yrs service, $155; over 3 yrs, $165.
O-7—Under 3 yrs service, $150; over 3 yrs, $160.
O-6—Under 3 yrs service, $200; 3–16 yrs, $215; 16–18 yrs, $220; over 18 yrs, $245.
O-5—Under 3 yrs service, $190; 3–12 yrs, $205; 12–14 yrs,

$210; 14–16 yrs, $225; 16–18 yrs, $230; over 18 yrs, $245.
O-4—Under 3 yrs service, $170; 3–8 yrs, $185; 8–10 yrs, $195; 10–12 yrs, $210; 12–14 yrs, $215; 14–16 yrs, $220; 16–18 yrs, $230; over 18 yrs, $240.
O-3—Under 3 yrs service, $145; 3–4 yrs, $155; 4–6 yrs, $165; 6–8 yrs, $180; 8–10 yrs, $185; 10–12 yrs, $190; 12–14 yrs, $200; over 14 yrs, $205.
O-2—Under 2 yrs service, $115; 2–3 yrs, $125; 3–6 yrs, $150; 6–8 yrs, $160; 8–10 yrs, $165; 10–12 yrs, $170; 12–14 yrs, $180; over 14 yrs, $185.
O-1—Under 2 yrs service, $100; 2–3 yrs, $105; 3–6 yrs, $135; 6–8 yrs, $140; 8–10 yrs, $145; 10–12 yrs, $155; 12–14 yrs, $160; over 14 yrs, $170.
W-4—Under 6 yrs service, $115; 6–8 yrs, $120; 8–10 yrs, $125; 10–12 yrs, $135; 12–14 yrs, $145; 14–16 yrs, $155; 16–18 yrs, $160; over 18 yrs, $165.
W-3—Under 2 yrs service, $110; 2–6 yrs, $115; 6–10 yrs, $120; 10–12 yrs, $125; 12–14 yrs, $135; over 14 yrs, $140.
W-2—Under 2 yrs service, $105; 2–6 yrs, $110; 6–8 yrs, $115; 8–10 yrs, $120; 10–12 yrs, $125; 12–14 yrs, $130; over 14 yrs, $135.
W-1—Under 2 yrs service, $100; 2–6 yrs, $105; 6–8 yrs, $110; 8–10 yrs, $120; 10–12 yrs, $125; over 12 yrs, $130.
E-9—$105 regardless of yrs of service.
E-8—$105 regardless of yrs of service.
E-7—Under 2 yrs service, $80; 2–6 yrs, $85; 6–8 yrs, $90; 8–10 yrs, $95; 10–12 yrs, $100; over 12 yrs, $105.
E-6—Under 2 yrs service, $70; 2–4 yrs, $75; 4–6 yrs, $80; 6–8 yrs, $85; 8–10 yrs, $90; 10–14 yrs, $95; over 14 yrs, $100.
E-5—Under 2 yrs service, $60; 2–4 yrs, $70; 4–8 yrs, $80; 8–10 yrs, $85; 10–12 yrs, $90; over 12 years, $95.
E-4—Under 2 yrs service, $55; 2–4 yrs, $65; 4–6 yrs, $70; 6–8 yrs, $75; over 8 yrs, $80.
E-3—Under 2 yrs service, $55; over 2 yrs, $60.
E-2—Under 2 yrs service, $50; over 2 yrs, $60.
E-1—Under 2 yrs service, $50; over 2 yrs, $55.

Family Separation Allowance

Military members with dependents in grades E-4 (over 4 years of service) and above are entitled to an allowance of $30 a month in addition to allowances or per diem when on a permanent change of station, with movement of dependents not authorized and dependents not residing near his station; or be on board ship or temporary duty for more than 30 days, with dependents not residing near the temporary duty station.

Allowances for Subsistence

Officers receive $53.05 per month. Enlisted personnel receive allowances for subsistence under the following provisions: (1) when rations in kind are not available, $2.85 per day; (2) when permission to mess separately is granted, $2.53 per day; leave, hospital, and field rations also paid at rate of $2.53 per day; (3) * when assigned to duty under emergency conditions where no government messing facilities are available, $3.79 per day.

* Applicable only within the U.S.

Aviation Career Incentive Pay System

The incentive system defines an aviation career as being 25 years of officer service for commissioned officers and as a full military career for warrant officers. It awards Aviation Career Incentive Pay on the basis of aviation service rather than total military service and pay grade. The purpose is to improve aviator retention through the concentration of the highest rates of pay in the most flight-intensive period of an aviator's career, and to treat the current aviation force as fair and equitably as possible during the transition into the Aviation Career Incentive Pay System. Rated officers, flight surgeons, and other designated medical officers in pay grade 0–7 may not be paid incentive pay at a rate greater than $160 per month. Those in pay grade 0–8 or above may not be paid incentive pay at a rate greater than $165 per month.

MONTHLY INCENTIVE PAY RATES		
Years of Aviation Service[1] (Monthly rate)		**Years of Service as an Officer** (Monthly rate)
$100 . . . . 2 or less	$225 . . . . Over 18	
$125 . . . . over 2	$205 . . . . over 20	
$150 . . . . over 3	$185 . . . . over 22	
$165 . . . . over 4	$165 . . . . over 24	
$245 . . . . over 6	$000 . . . . over 25	

Veterans' Benefits

Although benefits of various kinds date back to Colonial days, veterans of World War I were the first to receive disability compensation, allotments for dependents, life insurance, medical care, and vocational rehabilitation. In 1940, these benefits were slowly broadened.

The following benefits available to veterans of World War II, the Korean conflict, the post-Korean conflict, and the Vietnam conflict require certain minimum periods of active duty, except for servicemen, are applicable only to those whose discharge was not dishonorable.

Unemployment allowances: Every effort is being made to secure employment for returning Vietnam veterans. Unemployment benefits are administered by the U. S. Department of Labor.

Loans: GI loans are made for a variety of purposes, such as: to buy or build a home; to purchase a mobile home with or without a lot; and to refinance a home presently owned and occupied by the veteran. The VA will guarantee the lender against loss up to 60% of a home loan with a maximum of $17,500. On mobile-home loans, the amount of the guaranty is 30% of the loan. The interest rate may not exceed the maximum rate set by the VA and in effect when the loan is made.

Compensation and rehabilitation benefits: These are available to those having some service-connected illness or disability:

Disability compensation: The VA pays from $35 to $655 per month, and for specific conditions up to $1,628 per month, plus allowances for dependents, where the disability is rated 50% or more.

Vocational rehabilitation: Necessary training expenses, special equipment, etc., toward a definite job objective are paid for, plus a monthly allowance of up to $209, with increased amounts for dependents, in addition to compensation.

Medical and dental care: This includes care in VA, non-VA, or certain Federal hospitals. It also covers treatment (not requiring hospitalization) at a VA field station or by an approved private physician or dentist. Medicine, appliances, equipment, etc., are supplied. Full domiciliary care is also provided where necessary. Nursing home care may be provided at certain VA medical facilities or in approved community nursing homes. Hospital and other medical care may also be provided for the spouse and child dependents of a veteran who is permanently and totally disabled due to a service-connected disability or are survivors of a veteran who dies from a service-connected disability. These latter benefits are usually provided in non-federal facilities. Eligibility criteria for these benefits vary, and veterans and/or their dependents or survivors should always apply in advance. Contact the nearest VA station with medical facilities.

Dependents' Educational Assistance: $270 a month for up to 36 months of schooling may be paid to sons and daughters of veterans who died of service-connected causes or who were permanently and totally disabled from service-connected causes or while permanently and totally disabled or who are prisoners of war or are missing in action. Students must usually be between 18 and 26.

Spouses of veterans whose deaths are adjudged to be service-connected, and spouses of veterans who are permanently and totally disabled due to service-connected causes or who are prisoners of war or are missing in action are also eligible for this educational benefit.

Veterans' readjustment education: Veterans who served on active duty for at least 181 days after Jan. 31, 1955, may receive monthly educational assistance under the new GI Bill for post-

Korean conflict veterans, varying from $270 for single full-time students to $366 for veterans with two dependents, plus $22 for each additional dependent.

Pensions: The Veterans Pension Act of 1959, effective July 1, 1960, provides a sliding-scale formula for pension benefits for wartime veterans totally disabled from nonservice connected causes. These benefits are based on need. Widows and orphans of Mexican Border service, World War II,

Korea, and Vietnam veterans have the same eligibility status.

Insurance: The VA life insurance programs have 8.5 million policy holders with total coverage of $99.3 billion. Detailed information on Service-Disabled Veterans Insurance, conversion of Servicemen's Group Life Insurance and on Veterans Mortgage Life Insurance may be obtained at any VA office. Information regarding Veterans Group Life Insurance may be obtained from the Office of Servicemen's Group Life Insurance, 212 Washington St., Newark, N.J. 07102.

U. S. Military Actions Other Than Declared Wars

HAWAII (1893): U. S. Marines, ordered to land by U. S. Minister Stevens, aided the revolutionary Committee of Safety in overthrowing the native government. Stevens then proclaimed Hawaii a U. S. protectorate. Annexation, resisted by the Democratic regime in Washington, was not formally accomplished until 1898.

CHINA (1900): Boxers (a group of Chinese revolutionists) occupied Peking and laid siege to foreign legations. U. S. troops joined an international expedition which relieved the city.

PANAMÁ (1903): After Colombia had rejected a proposed agreement for relinquishing sovereignty over the Panama Canal Zone, revolution broke out, aided by promoters of the Panama Canal Co. Two U. S. warships were standing by to protect American privileges. The U. S. recognized the Republic of Panamá on Nov. 6.

DOMINICAN REPUBLIC (1904): When the Dominican Republic failed to meet debts owed to the U. S. and foreign creditors, Theodore Roosevelt declared the U. S. intention of exercising "international police power" in the Western Hemisphere whenever necessary. The U. S. accordingly administered customs and managed debt payments of the Dominican Republic from 1905–07.

NICARAGUA (1911): The possibility of foreign control over Nicaragua's canal route led to U. S. intervention and agreement. The U. S. landed Marines in Nicaragua (Aug. 14, 1912) to protect American interests there. A small detachment remained until 1933.

MEXICO (1914): Mexican Dictator Huerta, opposed by President Wilson, had the support of European governments. An incident involving unarmed U. S. sailors in Tampico led to the landing of U. S. forces on Mexican soil. Veracruz was bombarded by the Navy to prevent the landing of munitions from a German vessel. At the point of war, both powers agreed to mediation by Argentina, Brazil and Chile. Huerta abdicated, and Carranza succeeded to the presidency.

HAITI (1915): U.S. Marines imposed a military occupation. Haiti signed a treaty making it a virtual protectorate of the U.S. until troops were withdrawn in 1934.

MEXICO (1916): Raids by Pancho Villa cost American lives on both sides of the border. President Carranza consented to a

punitive expedition led by Gen. Pershing, but antagonism grew in Mexico. Wilson withdrew the U.S. force when war with Germany became imminent.

DOMINICAN REPUBLIC (1916): Renewed intervention in the Dominican Republic with internal administration by U.S. naval officers lasted until 1924.

KOREA (1950): In this undeclared war, which terminated with the July 27, 1953, truce at Panmunjom and the establishment of a neutral nations' supervisory commission, the U.S. and 15 member-nations of the U.N. came to the aid of the Republic of South Korea, whose 38th-parallel border was crossed by the invading Russian Communist-controlled North Koreans, who were later joined by the Chinese Communists.

LEBANON (1958): Fearful of the newly formed U.A.R. abetting the rebels of his politically and economically torn country, President Chamoun appealed to the American Government for military assistance. U.S. troops landed in Beirut in mid-July and left before the end of the year, after internal and external quiet was restored.

DOMINICAN REPUBLIC (1965): On Apr. 28, when a political coup-turned-civil war endangered the lives of American nationals, President Johnson rushed 400 marines into Santo Domingo, the beginning of an eventual U.S. peak-commitment of 30,000 troops, constituting the preponderant military strength of the OAS-created Inter-American Peace Force. 6,500 troops, including 5,000 Americans, remained until after the peaceful inauguration of President Joaquín Balaguer on July 1, 1966, and the entire force left the country on Sept. 20.

VIETNAM: This longest war in U.S. history began with economic and technical assistance after 1954 Geneva accords ending the Indochinese War. By 1964 it had escalated into a major conflict.

This involvement spanning the administrations of five Presidents led to domestic discontent in the late 1960's. By April, 1969, U.S. troop strength reached a peak of 543,400. Peace negotiations began in Paris in 1968 but proved fruitless. Finally, on Jan. 27, 1973, a peace accord was signed in Paris by the U.S., North and South Vietnam and the Vietcong. Within 60 days, U.S. POW's were returned and the U.S. withdrew all military forces from South Vietnam.

U. S. Casualties in Major Wars

Source: Department of Defense.

War	Branch of service	Numbers engaged	Battle deaths	Other deaths	Total deaths	Wounds not mortal	Total casualties[1]
Revolutionary War	Army	......	4,044	......	......	6,004	......
1775 to 1783	Navy	......	342	......	......	114	......
	Marines	......	49	......	......	70	......
	Total	......	4,435	......	......	6,188	......
War of 1812	Army	......	1,950	......	......	4,000	......
1812 to 1815	Navy	......	265	......	......	439	......
	Marines	......	45	......	......	66	......
	Total	286,730	2,260	......	......	4,505	......
Mexican War	Army	......	1,721	11,550	13,271	4,102	17,373
1846 to 1848	Navy	......	1	......	......	3	......
	Marines	......	11	......	......	47	......
	Total	78,718	1,733	......	......	4,152	......
Civil War[2]	Army	2,128,948	138,154	221,374	359,528	280,040	639,568
1861 to 1865	Navy	} 84,415	2,112	2,411	4,523	1,710	6,233
	Marines		148	312	460	131	591
	Total	2,213,363	140,414	224,097	364,511	281,881	646,392
Spanish-American War	Army	280,564	369	2,061	2,430	1,594	4,024
1898	Navy	22,875	10	0	10	47	57
	Marines	3,321	6	0	6	21	27
	Total	306,760	385	2,061	2,446	1,662	4,108
World War I	Army	4,057,101	50,510	55,868	106,378	193,663	300,041
1917 to 1918	Navy	599,051	431	6,856	7,287	819	8,106
	Marines	78,839	2,461	390	2,851	9,520	12,371
	Total	4,734,991	53,402	63,114	116,516	204,002	320,518
World War II	Army[3]	11,260,000	234,874	83,400	318,274	565,861	884,135
1941 to 1946	Navy	4,183,466	36,950	25,664	62,614	37,778	100,392
	Marines	669,100	19,733	4,778	24,511	67,207	91,718
	Total	16,112,566	291,557	113,842	405,399	670,846	1,076,245
Korean War	Army	2,834,000	27,704	9,429	37,133	77,596	114,729
1950 to 1953	Navy	1,177,000	458	4,043	4,501	1,576	6,077
	Marines	424,000	4,267	1,261	5,528	23,744	29,272
	Air Force	1,285,000	1,200	5,884	7,084	368	7,452
	Total	5,720,000	33,629	20,617	54,246	103,284	157,530
War in Southeast Asia[4]	Army	4,386,000	30,684	7,191	37,875	201,536	239,411
	Navy[5]	1,842,000	1,523	910	2,443	10,078	12,521
	Marines	794,000	13,009	1,684	14,693	88,633	104,326
	Air Force	1,740,000	1,282	603	1,885	3,457	5,342
	Total	8,744,000	46,498	10,388	56,886	303,704	361,600[6]

[1] Excludes captured or interned and missing in action who were subsequently returned to military control. [2] Union forces only. Totals should probably be somewhat larger as data on disposition of prisoners are far from complete. Final Confederate deaths, based on incomplete returns, were 133,821, to which should be added 26,000–31,000 personnel who died in Union prisons. [3] Army data include Air Force. [4] Casualty figures are for Jan. 1, 1961, through March 31, 1975. [5] Includes a small number of Coast Guard. [6] Includes casualties incurred in the Mayaquez Incident. In addition, 63 persons were missing as of Mar. 31, 1976. NOTE: All data are subject to revision. For wars before World War I, information represents best data from available records. However, due to incomplete records and possible difference in usage of terminology, reporting systems, etc., figures should be considered estimates. Leaders (....) indicate that information is not available.

The American's Creed

By William Tyler Page

"I believe in the United States of America as a government of the people, by the people, for the people; whose just powers are derived from the consent of the governed; a democracy in a republic; a sovereign Nation of many sovereign States; a perfect union, one and inseparable; established upon those principles of freedom, equality, justice, and humanity for which American patriots sacrificed their lives and fortunes.

"I therefore believe it is my duty to my country to love it; to support its Constitution; to obey its laws; to respect its flag, and to defend it against all enemies."

NOTE: William Tyler Page, Clerk of the U.S. House of Representatives, wrote "The American's Creed" in 1917. It was accepted by the House on behalf of the American people on April 3, 1918.

Casualties in World War I

(Additional U.S. figures are to be found on p. 601)

Country	Total mobilized forces	Killed or died[1]	Wounded	Prisoners or missing	Total casualties
Austria-Hungary.............	7,800,000	1,200,000	3,620,000	2,200,000	7,020,000
Belgium....................	267,000	13,716	44,686	34,659	93,061
British Empire[2].............	8,904,467	908,371	2,090,212	191,652	3,190,235
Bulgaria...................	1,200,000	87,500	152,390	27,029	266,919
France[2]....................	8,410,000	1,357,800	4,266,000	537,000	6,160,800
Germany...................	11,000,000	1,773,700	4,216,058	1,152,800	7,142,558
Greece....................	230,000	5,000	21,000	1,000	27,000
Italy......................	5,615,000	650,000	947,000	600,000	2,197,000
Japan.....................	800,000	300	907	3	1,210
Montenegro................	50,000	3,000	10,000	7,000	20,000
Portugal...................	100,000	7,222	13,751	12,318	33,291
Romania...................	750,000	335,706	120,000	80,000	535,706
Russia....................	12,000,000	1,700,000	4,950,000	2,500,000	9,150,000
Serbia....................	707,343	45,000	133,148	152,958	331,106
Turkey....................	2,850,000	325,000	400,000	250,000	975,000
United States..............	4,734,991	116,516	204,002	....	320,518

[1] Includes deaths from all causes.   [2] Official figures.

Casualties in World War II

(Additional U.S. figures are to be found on p. 601)

Country	Men in war	Battle deaths	Wounded
Australia...............................	1,000,000	26,976	180,864
Austria................................	800,000	280,000	350,117
Belgium...............................	625,000	8,460	55,513[1]
Brazil[2]................................	40,334	943	4,222
Bulgaria..............................	339,760	6,671	21,878
Canada...............................	1,041,080	32,412	53,145
China[3]................................	17,250,521	1,324,516	1,762,006
Czechoslovakia........................	....	6,683[4]	8,017
Denmark..............................	....	4,339	....
Finland...............................	500,000	79,047	50,000
France................................	....	201,568	400,000
Germany..............................	20,000,000	3,250,000[4]	7,250,000
Greece................................	....	17,024	47,290
Hungary..............................	....	147,435	89,313
India..................................	2,393,891	32,121	64,354
Italy..................................	3,100,000	149,496[4]	66,716
Japan................................	9,700,000	1,270,000	140,000
Netherlands...........................	280,000	6,500	2,860
New Zealand..........................	194,000	11,625[4]	17,000
Norway...............................	75,000	2,000	....
Poland................................	....	664,000	530,000
Romania..............................	650,000[5]	350,000[6]	....
South Africa, Union of	410,056	2,473	....
U.S.S.R...............................	....	6,115,000[4]	14,012,000
United Kingdom.......................	5,896,000	357,116[4]	369,267
Yugoslavia............................	3,741,000	305,000	425,000
United States.........................	16,112,566	291,557	670,846

[1] Civilians only.   [2] Army and navy figures.   [3] Figures cover period July 7, 1937–Sept. 2, 1945, and concern only Chinese regular troops. They do not include casualties suffered by guerrillas and local military corps.   [4] Deaths from all causes.   [5] Against Soviet Russia; 385,847 against Nazi Germany.   [6] Against Soviet Russia; 169,822 against Nazi Germany.   NOTE: The figures in this table are unofficial estimates obtained from various sources.

U. S. Armed Forces Personnel

Source: Department of Defense; U.S. Coast Guard.

Year	Army	Air Force[1]	Navy	Marines	Men[2]	Women	Coast Guard[3]
1940	269,023	....	160,997	28,345	456,984	1,381	13,621
1941	1,462,315	....	284,427	54,359	1,794,997	6,104	19,036
1942	3,075,608	....	640,570	142,613	3,844,538	14,253	58,998
1943	6,994,472	....	1,741,750	308,523	8,918,574	126,171	154,976
1944	7,994,750	....	2,981,365	475,604	11,241,173	210,542	169,264
1945	8,267,958	....	3,380,817	474,680	11,858,449	265,006	171,518
1946	1,891,011	....	983,398	155,679	2,972,081	58,007	29,736
1947	991,285	....	498,661	93,053	1,563,241	19,758	18,972
1950	593,167	411,277	381,538	74,279	1,438,192	22,069	23,190
1951	1,531,774	788,381	736,680	192,620	3,209,830	39,625	29,000
1955	1,109,296	959,946	660,695	205,170	2,899,916	35,191	28,500
1957	997,994	919,835	677,108	200,861	2,763,625	32,173	28,322
1959	861,964	840,435	626,340	175,571	2,472,456	31,718	29,984
1962	1,066,404	884,025	666,428	190,962	2,775,606	32,213	31,500
1966	1,199,784	887,353	745,205	261,716	3,061,469	32,589	34,767
1968	1,570,343	904,850	765,457	307,252	3,509,505	38,397	36,534
1969	1,512,169	862,353	775,869	309,771	3,420,656	39,506	38,331
1970	1,322,548	791,349	692,660	259,737	3,024,815	41,479	38,172
1971	1,123,810	755,300	623,248	212,369	2,671,952	42,775	38,029
1972	810,960	725,838	588,043	198,238	2,278,046	45,033	37,866
1973	800,812	688,414	566,953	193,602	2,249,781	n.a.	36,588
1974	779,642	646,624	542,737	187,200	2,151,203	69,229	36,407
1975	778,792	623,209	548,369	194,730	2,145,100	89,714	35,952[4]
1976	771,301	595,650	527,296	193,409	1,982,460	107,196	36,730

[1] Before July 26, 1947, when the National Military Establishment was established, the Air Force was a part of the Army. [2] Not including men in the Coast Guard. [3] In peacetime, Coast Guard operates under Dept. of Transportation; in time of war or at direction of President, it is attached to Navy Dept. [4] As of May 1.

U. S. Navy Combatant Vessels

Type	Number	Type	Number
Carriers	13	Mine warfare	3
Destroyers	73	Patrol ships	7
Cruisers	26	Amphibious warfare	62
Frigates	64	Auxiliaries	116
Submarines	116	Total	480

NOTE: As of 1976; exact figures are classified information.

Arlington National Cemetery

Arlington National Cemetery occupies 517.83 acres in Virginia on the Potomac River, directly opposite Washington. This land was part of the estate of John Parke Custis, Martha Washington's son, who built the mansion which later became the home of Robert E. Lee. In 1864, Arlington became a military cemetery. Over 160,000 persons, including many thousands of soldiers as well as hundreds of distinguished Americans, are buried there. Expansion of the cemetery began in fiscal year 1965, using a 180-acre tract of land directly east of the present site.

In 1921, an Unknown American Soldier of World War I was buried in a temporary crypt in the cemetery; the completed Tomb was opened to the public without ceremony in 1932. Two additional Unknowns, one from World War II and one from the Korean War, were buried May 30, 1958. The inscription carved on the side of the Tomb, formerly the Tomb of the Unknown Soldier and now called the Tomb of the Unknowns, reads:

HERE RESTS IN

HONORED GLORY

AN AMERICAN

SOLDIER

KNOWN BUT TO GOD

U. S. POSTAL REGULATIONS

FIRST CLASS:

Letters and written and sealed matter: 13¢ for the first oz. or fraction; 11¢ for each additional oz., up to 13 oz. Pieces over 13 oz. will be subject to priority mail (heavy pieces) rates, and shall be entitled to the most expeditious handling and transportation practicable.

Limit of weight: 70 lb.

Stamped government envelopes: 15¢; government postal cards: single, 9¢; double, 16¢. Private mailing or post cards: 9¢. Limit of size 3" x 4¼"; maximum 4¼" x 6". Business reply mail: cards, 14¢; other than cards, not over 2 oz., 13¢ for the first oz., plus 11¢ for the second oz., plus 5¢ per piece; 2 to 13 oz., applicable first-class rate plus 8¢ per piece; over 13 oz., priority mail (heavy pieces) rates apply plus 8¢ per piece.

PRIORITY MAIL (OVER 10 OZ. TO 70 LB.):

The zone rates shall apply to mailable matter over 10 oz. of any class carried by air. Such matter shall not exceed 100 in. in length and girth combined, including written and other matter of the first class, whether sealed or unsealed.

Parcels weighing less than 15 lb. and measuring more than 84 in., but not more than 100 in. in length and girth combined, shall be subject to the 15-lb. rate.

The 8th-zone rate shall be charged on air parcel post between the U. S. and its territories and possessions, except that air parcels mailed at New York City and addressed to Puerto Rico or the Virgin Islands are subject to the 7th-zone rate.

Air parcels addressed to military post offices overseas (Army, Air Force, and Fleet post offices, and Naval vessels) require postage at the airmail zone rate applicable between the mailing post office and the post office shown in the address. *For restrictions to certain military post offices overseas, consult local post office.*

Limit of size to most military post offices overseas: 100 in. length and girth; limit of weight, 70 lb. *For exceptions, consult local post office.*

AIRMAIL (LIMIT 10 OZ.):

17¢ for the first oz. or fraction; plus 15¢ for each additional oz. or fraction within the continental U. S., within any Territory or possession of the U. S., or between any of the foregoing. Over 10 oz. priority mail (heavy pieces) rates apply.

Air postal or post cards, 14¢. Business reply mail: cards, 19¢; other than cards, not over 2 oz., 17¢ for the first oz. or fraction, plus 15¢ for the second oz. or fraction, plus 5¢ per piece; over 2 oz., the appropriate air mail rate applies, plus 8¢

per piece; over 10 oz., priority mail (heavy pieces) rates apply plus 8¢ per piece.

SECOND CLASS (NO WEIGHT LIMIT):

Newspapers, magazines, and other periodicals with notice of second-class entry.

For rates for publications mailed by the publishers or registered news agents, consult local postmaster.

Transient rate for matter mailed by others than the publishers or registered news agents: 8¢ for the first 2 oz., 4¢ for each additional oz. or fraction, or the fourth class rate, whichever is lower.

THIRD CLASS (UNDER 16 OZ.):

Circulars, books, printed matter, and all other mailable matter not in first or second class. Regular rate:

0 to 2 oz. . . . . .14¢	over 8 oz. to 10 oz. . . . .61¢
over 2 oz. to 4 oz. . . . .28¢	over 10 oz. to 12 oz. . . .72¢
over 4 oz. to 6 oz. . . . .39¢	over 12 oz. to 14 oz. . . .83¢
over 6 oz. to 8 oz. . . . .50¢	over 14 oz. to 15.99 oz. . .94¢

Bulk rate: fee $40 a calendar year. Separately addressed identical pieces of third-class matter in quantities of not less than 50 lb. or of not less than 200 pieces are subject to the lb. rates of postage applicable to the entire bulk mailed at one time. The bulk rate for miscellaneous printed matter, etc., is 41¢ per lb., with a minimum charge of 7.7¢ per piece for the first 250,000 pieces, and 7.9¢ per piece thereafter. For books and catalogs of 24 pages or more, seeds, etc., the rate is 32¢ per lb. with a minimum charge of 7.7¢ per piece for the first 250,000 pieces, and 7.9¢ per piece thereafter.

FOURTH CLASS (PARCEL POST) (16 OZ. AND OVER):

Merchandise, books, printed matter, and all other mailable matter not in first, second, or third classes.

The zone rates shall apply to fourth-class matter, except certain books, library books, publications or records for the blind, and certain controlled circulation publications.

Limit of size between two first-class post offices: All zones, 84 in. in length and girth combined.

Limit of weight between two first-class post offices: 40 lb.

Note: The following five items have a size limit of 100 in. in length and girth combined, a weight limit of 70 lb.: (1) parcels sent to or from rural or star routes; (2) parcels sent to or from second-, third-, and fourth-class post offices; (3) parcels containing baby fowl, live plants, trees, shrubs, or agricultural commodities (not including manufactured products thereof); (4) parcels containing books or the other items listed in the next paragraph; (5) parcels mailed between the U. S. and any Army or Fleet post office (with certain exceptions) or between the U. S. and any U. S. Territory or possession; also Hawaii and Alaska.

SPECIAL FOURTH-CLASS RATES (LIMIT 70 LB.):

Books of 24 or more pages (at least 22 of which are printed) and containing no advertising matter other than incidental announcements of books, 16-mm. (or smaller) films and catalogs of such films, in final state for viewing, printed objective school test materials, printed music (in bound or sheet form), sound recordings, and manuscripts for books, periodicals and music, 21¢ first lb., 9¢ each additional lb. through 7 lbs., 8¢ each additional lb. or fraction over 7 lbs. (Rate applies for films and catalogs except when mailed to commercial theaters.) Must be endorsed "Special 4th-Class Rate: Books [or Sound Recordings, etc., whichever is applicable]."

LIBRARY RATE (LIMIT 70 LB.):

Books (containing no advertising), printed music (in bound or sheet form), bound volumes of academic theses, periodicals, sound recordings, other library materials, museum materials: 8¢ first lb. or fraction, 4¢ each additional lb. The rate also applies to 16-mm. films, slides, etc., scientific or mathematical kits, etc., when sent to and from schools, colleges, universities, public libraries, educational, scientific, agricultural, labor, veterans or nonprofit religious organizations. Must be endorsed "Library Rate."

CERTIFIED MAIL:

Certified mail service provides for a receipt to the sender and a record of delivery at the office of address. No record is kept at the office where mailed. It is handled in the ordinary mails and no insurance coverage is provided.

Any mail prepaid at the first-class rate having no intrinsic value will be accepted as certified mail. This does not exclude articles of a nonnegotiable character and other matter which would involve a cost of duplication if lost or destroyed. The mail may be sent by air on payment of the required postage. Return receipt service, requested at the time of mailing only, and special-delivery service are available.

Fee in addition to postage, 60¢; restricted delivery (additional fee), 60¢.

Return Receipts

Certified Mail–Numbered Insured–Registered

Requested at time of mailing:
Showing to whom and date delivered . . . . .25¢
Showing to whom, date, and address where delivered . . .45¢
Requested after mailing:
Showing to whom and date delivered . . . . .45¢

REGISTERED MAIL:

Value	Fees (in addition to postage)	
	Articles not covered by commercial or other insurance	Articles also covered by other insurances
$0.00 to $100	$2.10	$2.10
$100.01 to $200	2.30	2.30
$200.01 to $400	2.60	2.60
$400.01 to $600	2.90	2.90
$600.01 to $800	3.20	3.20
$800.01 to $1,000	3.50	3.50
$1,000.01 to $2,000	3.80	3.80
$2,000.01 to $3,000	4.10	3.50 plus handling charge of 25¢ per $1,000 or fraction over first $1,000
$3,000.01 to $4,000	4.40	
$4,000.01 to $5,000	4.70	
$5,000.01 to $6,000	5.00	
$6,000.01 to $7,000	5.30	
$7,000.01 to $8,000	5.60	
$8,000.01 to $9,000	5.90	
$9,000.01 to $10,000	6.20	
$10,000.01 to $1,000,000 .	$6.20 plus handling charge of 25¢ per $1,000 or fraction over first $10,000.	
$1,000,000.01 to $15,000,000	$253.70 plus handling charge of 20¢ per $1,000 or fraction over first $1,000,000.	$253.25 plus handling charge of 20¢ per $1,000 or fraction over first $1,000,000.
Over $15,000,000	Additional charges may be made based on consideration of weight, space, and value.	

Restricted Delivery (Additional fee) . . . . .60¢

INSURED MAIL:

Fees, in addition to postage, for coverage against loss or damage:

Liability	Fee
$5.01 to $15	$ .40
$15.01 to $50	.60
$50.01 to $100	.80
$100.01 to $150	1.00
$150.01 to $200*	1.20
Restricted delivery (Not available for mail insured for $15.00 or less) . . .	60¢

* Liability is limited to $200.

MONEY ORDERS:

Money orders for safe transmission of money. Amounts from 1¢ to $300 are issued. Fees:

Amount of money order	Domestic	International
$0.01 to $10.00...........	$.50	$ .65
$10.01 to $50.00.........	.70	.90
$50.01 to $300.00........	.90	1.15

SPECIAL DELIVERY AND HANDLING:

The prepayment of the special-delivery fee entitles mail to the most expeditious transportation and delivery.

Prepayment of the special-handling fee entitles 3rd- and 4th-class matter to the most expeditious handling and transportation, but not special delivery.

Fees (in addition to postage):

Weight	Special delivery First class*	Special delivery All other classes	Special handling (3rd and 4th class)
Up to 2 lb.	$1.25	$1.75	$ .50
Over 2 lb. to 10 lb.	1.50	1.85	.70
Over 10 lb.	1.75	2.15	1.00

* Including air and priority mail.

C.O.D. MAIL:

Fees, in addition to postage, for domestic unregistered C.O.D. mail (third- and fourth-class matter and sealed domestic-mail matter of any class bearing postage at the first-class rate). Consult Postmaster for conditions of mailing:

Amount to be collected*	Fee
$0.01 to $10.	$ .85
$10.01 to $25.	1.05
$25.01 to $50.	1.25
$50.01 to $100.	1.45
$100.01 to $200.	1.65
$200.01 to $300.	1.85
Restricted delivery	.60
Notice of nondelivery	.25
Alteration of charges or designation of new addressee	.50

* Or insurance coverage desired

SURFACE PARCEL POST:

Destination	1st 2 lbs.	Each add. lb. or fr.
Central America, Caribbean Islands, Bahamas, Bermuda, St. Pierre and Miquelon	$1.75	$.50
All other countries	$1.90	$.57

Adhesive Stamps Available

ORDINARY POSTAGE

Single or sheet: 1, 2, 3, 4, 5, 6, 7, 8, 9, 10, 11, 12, 13, 14, 15, 16, 18, 20, 21, 24, 25, 30, 40, and 50 cents; $1 and $5.

Books: combination ordinary air mail: 6 13-cent & 6 2-cent stamps: 90 cents.
23 13-cent stamps: $2.99.

Coil of 100: 10- and 13-cent stamps.[1]

Coils of 500 and 3,000: 1-, 2-, 3-, 5-, 6-, 8-, 10-, 13- and $1.00 stamps.

Coil of 3,000: 25-cent stamps.

AIRMAIL POSTAGE[2]

Single or sheet: 21, 25 and 31 cents.

[1] Dispenser to hold coils of 100 stamps may be purchased for 5¢ additional. [2] For use on airmail only.

MISCELLANEOUS:

Fees for effecting delivery of domestic registered, insured, and C.O.D. mail to addressee only or to addressee or order: 60¢.

Certificates of mailing for ordinary mail of any class: 6¢ for each article described thereon. Additional copies of original certificates for registered, insured, and C.O.D. mail: 2¢ for each article described thereon.

C.O.D. mail cannot be sent to Navy personnel on board ships or at overseas shore stations, or to APO's.

FOREIGN REGULAR MAIL:

Letter: To Canada and Mexico: 13¢ first oz., 11¢ each additional oz. through 13 oz. Consult postmaster for heavier weights. Printed matter and small packets, 13¢ first 2 oz., 11¢ each additional oz. or fraction through 16 oz. For heavier weights consult postmaster. Parcel post, $1.75 for first 2 lbs, 50¢ each additional lb. or fraction.

To other countries:

Weight	Fee
First oz.	$.18
Over 1 oz., but not over 2	.31
Over 2 oz., but not over 4	.41
Over 4 oz., but not over 8	.82
Over 8 oz., but not over 16	1.58
Over 1 lb., but not over 2	2.75
Over 2 lbs., but not over 4	4.46
Each additional 32 oz.	.72
Post cards, 12¢.	

FOREIGN AIRMAIL:

Destination	Letters, letter packages[1]	Post cards	Air letter sheets[2]
Canada and Mexico, Central America, South America, Caribbean Islands, Bahamas, Bermuda, St. Pierre and Miquelon	$.17 first oz. .25 per ½ oz.	$.09 .14	$.22 .22
All other countries	.31 per ½ oz.	.14	.22

[1] Weight limit: Canada, 60 lbs; all other countries, 4 lbs. [2] No enclosures permitted.

NOTE: For other international rates consult your local Postmaster.

United Nations Stamps

United Nations stamps in U.S. denominations are valid for postage only if mailed at the U.N. Post Office, U.N. Headquarters, New York, N.Y. Stamps in Swiss denominations are valid for postage only if mailed at the Palais des Nations, Geneva, Switzerland. They may be purchased over the counter, by mail or by opening a Customer Deposit Account. They are sold at face value subject to stock being available.

1976	Subject	Price
Mar. 12	Commemorative	13¢,26¢
Apr. 23	UNCTAD (Conference on Trade and Development)	13¢,31¢
May 28	Human Settlement	13¢,25¢
Oct. 8	25th Anniversary, U.N. Postal Administration	13¢,31¢

Fourth-Class (Parcel Post and Catalogue) Zone Rates

(NOTE: Zone rates are determined from an official zone chart, available free at local post offices.)

Weight— 1 pound and not exceeding 70 lbs.	Zones							
	Local	1 and 2 (Up to 150 mi.)	3 (150–300)	4 (300–600)	5 (600–1,000)	6 (1,000–1,400)	7 (1,400–1,800)	8 (over 1,800)
2	$0.77	$0.90	$0.93	$1.04	$1.15	$1.28	$1.40	$1.48
3	.82	.97	1.02	1.15	1.29	1.46	1.62	1.74
4	.86	1.04	1.10	1.25	1.42	1.63	1.84	2.00
5	.91	1.11	1.19	1.36	1.56	1.81	2.06	2.26
6	.95	1.18	1.27	1.46	1.69	1.98	2.28	2.52
7	1.00	1.25	1.36	1.57	1.83	2.16	2.50	2.78
8	1.04	1.32	1.44	1.67	1.96	2.33	2.72	3.04
9	1.09	1.39	1.53	1.78	2.10	2.51	2.94	3.30
10	1.13	1.46	1.61	1.88	2.23	2.68	3.16	3.56
11	1.18	1.53	1.70	1.99	2.37	2.86	3.38	3.82
12	1.22	1.60	1.78	2.09	2.50	3.03	3.60	4.08
13	1.27	1.67	1.87	2.20	2.64	3.21	3.82	4.34
14	1.31	1.74	1.95	2.30	2.77	3.38	4.04	4.60
15	1.36	1.81	2.04	2.41	2.91	3.56	4.26	4.86
16	1.40	1.88	2.12	2.51	3.04	3.73	4.48	5.12
17	1.45	1.95	2.21	2.62	3.18	3.91	4.70	5.38
18	1.49	2.02	2.29	2.72	3.31	4.08	4.92	5.64
19	1.54	2.09	2.38	2.83	3.45	4.26	5.14	5.90
20	1.58	2.16	2.46	2.93	3.58	4.43	5.36	6.16
21	1.63	2.23	2.55	3.04	3.72	4.61	5.58	6.42
22	1.67	2.30	2.63	3.14	3.85	4.78	5.80	6.68
23	1.72	2.37	2.72	3.25	3.99	4.96	6.02	6.94
24	1.76	2.44	2.80	3.35	4.12	5.13	6.24	7.20
25	1.81	2.51	2.89	3.46	4.26	5.31	6.46	7.46
26	1.85	2.58	2.97	3.56	4.39	5.48	6.68	7.72
27	1.90	2.65	3.06	3.67	4.53	5.66	6.90	7.98
28	1.94	2.72	3.14	3.77	4.66	5.83	7.12	8.24
29	1.99	2.79	3.23	3.88	4.80	6.01	7.34	8.50
30	2.03	2.86	3.31	3.98	4.93	6.18	7.56	8.76
31	2.08	2.93	3.40	4.09	5.07	6.36	7.78	9.02
32	2.12	3.00	3.48	4.19	5.20	6.53	8.00	9.28
33	2.17	3.07	3.57	4.30	5.34	6.71	8.22	9.54
34	2.21	3.14	3.65	4.40	5.47	6.88	8.44	9.80
35	2.26	3.21	3.74	4.51	5.61	7.06	8.66	10.06
36	2.30	3.28	3.82	4.61	5.74	7.23	8.88	10.32
37	2.35	3.35	3.91	4.72	5.88	7.41	9.10	10.58
38	2.39	3.42	3.99	4.82	6.01	7.58	9.32	10.84
39	2.44	3.49	4.08	4.93	6.15	7.76	9.54	11.10
40	2.48	3.56	4.16	5.03	6.28	7.93	9.76	11.36
41	2.53	3.63	4.25	5.14	6.42	8.11	9.98	11.62
42	2.57	3.70	4.33	5.24	6.55	8.28	10.20	11.88
43	2.62	3.77	4.42	5.35	6.69	8.46	10.42	12.14
44	2.66	3.84	4.50	5.45	6.82	8.63	10.64	12.40
45	2.71	3.91	4.59	5.56	6.96	8.81	10.86	12.66
46	2.75	3.98	4.67	5.66	7.09	8.98	11.08	12.92
47	2.80	4.05	4.76	5.77	7.23	9.16	11.30	13.18
48	2.84	4.12	4.84	5.87	7.36	9.33	11.52	13.44
49	2.89	4.19	4.93	5.98	7.50	9.51	11.74	13.70
50	2.93	4.26	5.01	6.08	7.63	9.68	11.96	13.96
51	2.98	4.33	5.10	6.19	7.77	9.86	12.18	14.22
52	3.02	4.40	5.18	6.29	7.90	10.03	12.40	14.48
53	3.07	4.47	5.27	6.40	8.04	10.21	12.62	14.74
54	3.11	4.54	5.35	6.50	8.17	10.38	12.84	15.00
55	3.16	4.61	5.44	6.61	8.31	10.56	13.06	15.26
56	3.20	4.68	5.52	6.71	8.44	10.73	13.28	15.52
57	3.25	4.75	5.61	6.82	8.58	10.91	13.50	15.78
58	3.29	4.82	5.69	6.92	8.71	11.08	13.72	16.04
59	3.34	4.89	5.78	7.03	8.85	11.26	13.94	16.30
60	3.38	4.96	5.86	7.13	8.98	11.43	14.16	16.56
65	3.61	5.31	6.29	7.66	9.66	12.31	15.26	17.86
70	3.83	5.66	6.71	8.18	10.33	13.18	16.36	19.16

EXCEPTIONS: Consult postmaster for exceptions and weight and size limits.

Priority Mail (Heavy Pieces)

Weight over 9 ounces and not exceeding 70 lbs.	Rate					
	Local zones 1, 2, and 3 (up to 300 mi.)	Zone 4 (300–600)	Zone 5 (600–1,000)	Zone 6 (1,000–1,400)	Zone 7 (1,400–1,800)	Zone 8 (over 1,800)
1	$1.56	$1.58	$1.60	$1.62	$1.64	$1.67
1.5	1.73	1.77	1.84	1.90	1.97	2.07
2	1.89	1.96	2.07	2.18	2.29	2.46
2.5	2.05	2.15	2.29	2.43	2.59	2.78
3	2.21	2.33	2.50	2.68	2.88	3.09
3.5	2.37	2.51	2.70	2.91	3.15	3.38
4	2.53	2.69	2.90	3.14	3.41	3.67
4.5	2.68	2.86	3.09	3.35	3.65	3.94
5	2.83	3.03	3.27	3.56	3.88	4.20
Each additional pound	.30	.34	.37	.42	.47	.52

Authorized 2-Letter State Abbreviations

When the Post Office instituted the ZIP Code for mail in 1963, it also drew up a list of two-letter abbreviations for the states which would gradually replace the traditional ones in use. Following is the official list, including the District of Columbia, Guam, Puerto Rico and the Virgin Islands (note that all capital letters are used):

Alabama	AL	Illinois	IL	Montana	MT	Puerto Rico	PR
Alaska	AK	Indiana	IN	Nebraska	NE	Rhode Island	RI
Arizona	AZ	Iowa	IA	Nevada	NV	South Carolina	SC
Arkansas	AR	Kansas	KS	New Hampshire	NH	South Dakota	SD
California	CA	Kentucky	KY	New Jersey	NJ	Tennessee	TN
Colorado	CO	Louisiana	LA	New Mexico	NM	Texas	TX
Connecticut	CT	Maine	ME	New York	NY	Utah	UT
Delaware	DE	Maryland	MD	North Carolina	NC	Vermont	VT
Dist. of Col.	DC	Massachusetts	MA	North Dakota	ND	Virginia	VA
Florida	FL	Michigan	MI	Ohio	OH	Virgin Islands	VI
Georgia	GA	Minnesota	MN	Oklahoma	OK	Washington	WA
Guam	GU	Mississippi	MS	Oregon	OR	West Virginia	WV
Hawaii	HI	Missouri	MO	Pennsylvania	PA	Wisconsin	WI
Idaho	ID					Wyoming	WY

America's Tallest Buildings

Source: Questionnaires to Cities

City	Building	Stories	Height, ft.	City	Building	Stories	Height, ft.
Chicago	Sears Tower	110	1,454	New York	Pan Am	59	808
New York	World Trade Center	110	1,350	New York	Woolworth	60	792
New York	Empire State	102	1,250[1]	Los Angeles	Security Pacific Bank	55	783
Chicago	Standard Oil (Indiana)	82	1,136	New York	One Penn Plaza	57	774
Chicago	John Hancock Center	100	1,107	Minneapolis	IDS Center	57	772
New York	Chrysler	77	1,046	San Francisco	Bank of America	52	770
New York	60 Wall Tower	67	950	New York	Exxon	54	750
New York	40 Wall Tower	71	900	Boston	Prudential Tower	52	745
Chicago	Water Tower Place	74	859	New York	One Liberty Plaza	54	743
Los Angeles	United California Bank	62	858	New York	City Bank–Farmers Trust	57	741
San Francisco	Transamerica Pyramid	48	853	San Antonio	Tower of the Americas	...	750
Chicago	First National Bank	60	850	New York	One Astor Plaza	54	730
New York	RCA	70	850	Detroit	Plaza Hotel	70	727
Pittsburgh	U.S. Steel Headquarters	64	841	New York	Marine Midland	52	724
New York	Chase Manhattan	60	813	Atlanta	Peachtree Plaza Hotel	70	723
Boston	John Hancock	60	812	Houston	One Shell Plaza	50	714

[1] With TV tower, 1,472 ft. NOTE: Does not include buildings under construction and not completed in 1976.

SOCIAL SECURITY

(For details of the Medicare program, see page 614.)

The original Social Security Act was passed in 1935 and amended in 1939, 1946, 1950, 1952, 1954, 1956, 1958, 1960, 1961, 1965, 1967, 1969, 1972 and 1974.

The act is administered by the Social Security Administration, part of the Department of Health, Education, and Welfare.

For purposes of clarity, the explanations given below will describe the provisions of the act as amended.

Who Is Covered?

Practically everyone who works fairly regularly is covered by social security. Many state and local government employees are covered under voluntary agreements between states and the Secretary of Health, Education, and Welfare. Workers not covered include most federal civilian employees, career railroad workers and a few other exceptions.

Cash tips count for social security if they amount to $20 or more in a month from employment with a single employer.

To qualify for benefits or make payments possible for your survivors you must be in work covered by the law for a certain number of "quarters of coverage." In general, a quarter of coverage is earned if a worker is paid $50 or more wages in a 3-month calendar quarter. A self-employed person gets 4 "quarters of coverage" for a year in which his net earnings are $400 or more. The number of quarters needed differs for different persons and depends on the date of your birth; in general, it is related to the number of years after 1950, or after the year you reach 21, if later, and up to the year before you reach 62, become disabled, or die. One "quarter of coverage" is required for each such year in order for you or your family to get benefits. No one will need more than 40 quarters. Your local social security office can tell you how long you need to work.

Who Pays for the Insurance?

Both workers and their employers pay for the workers' insurance. Self-employed persons pay their own social security contributions annually along with their income tax. The rates include the cost of Medicare hospital insurance. The contribution and benefit base is $15,300 for 1976, and will increase automatically in future years as earnings levels rise. The contribution rate schedules under present law are shown below:

The separate payroll contribution to finance hospital insurance is placed in a separate trust fund in the U.S. Treasury. In addition, the medical insurance premiums, currently $7.20 a month, and the government's shares go into another separate trust fund.

How to Apply for Benefits

You apply for benefits by filing a claim either in person, by mail, or by telephone at any social security office. You can get the address either from the post office or from the phone book under the listing, United States Government—Department of Health, Education, and Welfare—Social Security Administration. You will need certain kinds of proof, depending upon the type of benefit you are claiming. If it is a retirement benefit, you should provide a birth or

Contribution and Rate Schedule for Employees and Employers
(Percent of covered earnings)

Years	Retirement, Survivors, and Disability Insurance	Hospital Insurance	Total
1974–1977 . . .	4.95	.90	5.85
1978–1980 . . .	4.95	1.10	6.05
1981–1985 . . .	4.95	1.35	6.30
1986–2010 . . .	4.95	1.50	6.45
2011 & later . .	5.95	1.50	7.45

Contribution and Rate Schedule for Self-Employed People
(Percent of covered earnings)

Years	Retirement, Survivors, and Disability Insurance	Hospital Insurance	Total
1974–1977 . . .	7.0	.90	7.90
1978–1980 . . .	7.0	1.10	8.10
1981–1985 . . .	7.0	1.35	8.35
1986 & later . .	7.0	1.50	8.50

baptismal certificate. If you are unable to get these documents, other old documents showing your age or date of birth—such as census records, school records, early naturalization certificate, etc.—may be acceptable. A widow 60 or older who is claiming widow's benefits based on her husband's earnings should have both proof of age and a copy of the marriage certificate. If formal proof is not available, the social security office will tell you what kinds of information will be acceptable.

What Does Social Security Offer?

The social security contribution you pay gives you four different kinds of protection: (1) retirement benefits, (2) survivors' benefits, (3) disability benefits, and (4) Medicare health insurance benefits.

Retirement benefits. A worker becomes eligible for the full amount of his retirement benefit at age 65, if he has retired under the definition in the law. A worker may retire at 62 and get 80% of his full benefit. The closer he is to age 65 when he starts collecting his benefit, the larger is the fraction of his full benefit that he will get.

The amount of the retirement benefit you are entitled to at 65 is the key to all other benefits under the program. The retirement benefit is based on average monthly earnings, generally those after 1950. (See table above.)

A worker who doesn't get any benefits before 65 and who delays his retirement past age 65 will get a special credit that can mean a larger benefit. The credit adds to a worker's benefits 1% for each year (1/12 of 1% for each month) from age 65 to age 72 for which he did not get benefits.

Examples of Monthly Social Security Payments

(Effective as of June, 1976)

Benefits can be paid to a	$923 or less	$3,000	$4,000	$5,000	$6,000	$8,000[1]	$10,000[1]
Retired worker at 65	107.90	223.20	262.60	304.50	344.10	427.80	474.00
Under 65 and disabled................	107.90	223.20	262.60	304.50	344.10	427.80	474.00
Retired worker at 62..................	86.40	178.60	210.10	243.60	275.30	342.30	379.20
Wife or dependent husband at 65	54.00	111.60	131.30	152.30	172.10	213.90	237.00
Wife or dependent husband at 62	40.50	83.70	98.50	114.30	129.10	160.50	177.80
Wife under 65, 1 child	54.00	118.00	186.20	257.40	287.20	321.00	355.60
Widow or dependent widower at 65 (if worker never reduced .... benefits)	107.90	223.20	262.60	304.50	344.10	427.80	474.00
Widow or dependent widower at 60 (if sole survivor)	77.20	159.60	187.80	217.80	246.10	305.90	339.00
Widow or dependent widower at 50 and disabled (if sole survivor).......	56.80	111.70	131.40	152.40	172.20	214.00	237.10
Widow or widower, 1 child............	161.90	334.80	394.00	456.80	516.20	641.80	711.00
Maximum family payment	161.90	341.20	448.80	561.90	631.30	748.70	829.50

[1] Maximum earnings covered by social security were lower in past years and must be included in figuring your average earnings. This average determines your payment amount. Because of this, amounts shown in the last two columns generally won't be payable until future years. The maximum retirement benefit generally payable to a worker who is 65 in 1976 is $387.30.

The law provides a special minimum benefit at retirement for people who worked under social security more than 20 years. This provision will help people who had low incomes, but above a specific level, in their working years. The amount of the special minimum depends on the number of years of coverage. For a worker retiring at 65 with 25 years of coverage, the minimum would be $135.00 a month; with 30 or more years of coverage, the minimum would be $180. These benefits are reduced if a worker is under 65.

Using the table as a guide, you will see that average monthly earnings of $500 ($6,000 a year) would give you a benefit of $344.10 a month when you retire at 65.

If your wife is also 65, then she will get a wife's benefit that is equal to half your benefit. So if your benefit is $344.10, your wife gets $172.10.

If your wife is between ages 62 to 65, she can draw a reduced benefit; the amount depends on the number of months before 65 that she starts getting checks. If she draws her benefit when she is 62, she will get about ⅜ of your basic benefit, or $129.10. (She will get this amount for the rest of her life, unless you should die first; then she can start getting widow's benefit, described below.)

If your wife is entitled to a worker's retirement benefit on her own earnings, she can draw whichever—the worker's or the wife's—is larger.

If you have children under 18 or a child in school aged 18 up to 22 or a son or daughter who became totally disabled prior to reaching age 22, when you retire they will get a benefit equal to half your full retirement benefits (subject to maximum payments that can be made to a family). If your wife is caring for a child who is under 18 or who became disabled before 22 (and getting benefits too), she is eligible for benefits, even if she is under 62.

In general, the highest retirement check that can be paid to a worker who is 65 in 1976 is about $387.30 a month. Maximum payment to the family of a re-

tired worker is about $689.90. When your children reach age 18, their benefits will stop except for children in school aged 18 up to 22, and except for a benefit that is going to a son or daughter who became totally disabled before attaining age 22. Such a person can continue to get his benefits as long as his disability meets the definition in the law.

If you are a woman worker entitled to a retirement benefit and you have a dependent husband aged 62 or over, he may draw a benefit similar to a wife's benefit at 62.

Survivor benefits. This feature of the social security program gives your family valuable life insurance protection—in some cases benefits to a family could amount to $100,000 or more over a period of years. The amount of protection is again geared to what the worker would be entitled to at 65. If you can estimate from the table what your basic monthly benefit would be at 65, this is what your survivors would get:

1. A cash payment to help cover your burial expenses. This "lump-sum death payment" is $255.

2. A benefit for each child until he reaches 18, or 22 if the child is in school, or at any age if disabled before 22. Each eligible child receives 75% of the basic benefit (subject to reduction for the family maximum). (A disabled child can continue to collect benefits after age 22). If certain conditions are met, dependent grandchildren of insured workers can receive survivor or dependent benefits.

3. A benefit for your widow, or widower, if she has children under 18 or disabled in her care. Her benefit is also 75% of the basic benefit. She can collect this as long as she has a child under 18 or disabled in her care. Payments stop then (they will start again upon application when she is 60 at a slightly lower amount).

Total family survivor benefits can go to as high as $959.40 a month in 1976.

4. If there are no children either under 18 or disabled, your wife can get a widow's benefit starting at

age 60. This would come to 71½% of the basic amount at age 60. A widow who first becomes entitled at 65 or later may get 100% of her deceased husband's basic amount (provided neither he nor she ever drew reduced benefits).

5. Dependent parents can sometimes collect survivors' benefits. They are usually eligible if: (a) they were getting at least half their support from the deceased worker when he died, (b) they have reached 62, and (c) they are not eligible for a greater retirement benefit based on their own earnings. A single surviving parent can then get 82½% of the basic benefit. If two parents are eligible, each would get 75%.

A woman worker can provide survivors' benefits for any of these dependents: (1) her children under age 18, or for children in school up to age 22, (2) her disabled child after 18, if the child is unmarried and was disabled before 22, (3) her dependent widowed husband at age 60, if he hasn't remarried, or (4) her parents if they meet the tests in paragraph 5 above. Also, a widowed father can get benefits on the same basis as a widowed mother.

Here is an example of survivors' benefits in one family situation: John Jones dies, leaving a wife and two children aged one and three. His average monthly earnings were $450. Family survivors benefits would include: (1) a cash lump-sum death payment of $255.00; (2) a total monthly benefit of $597 for the family. When the children reach 18, their benefits stop unless they are attending school full-time, in which case payments continue up to age 22. When the older child no longer collects benefits, the widow and younger child continue to receive $479.80 a month until that child is 18. If he continues in school, he will get $239.90 a month, but Mrs. Jones' checks will stop. When Mrs. Jones becomes 60 (assuming she has not remarried), she will be paid $228.70 a month if she so chooses. If she waits until age 65, the monthly check will be $319.80.

Disability benefits. Disability benefits are paid to three groups of people:

1. An insured worker under age 65 with a severe disability can collect the same amount as if he were 65. Eligible dependents of disabled workers will receive the usual benefits. To be eligible for disability benefits, a person must: (a) have worked in employment (or self-employment) covered by social security long enough and recently enough (any social security office can tell you exactly); (b) be suffering from a physical or mental disability that is expected to last for at least 12 months; and (c) be so disabled that he can't work, or at least "engage in any substantial gainful activity." If he meets those tests, his benefits will start after a 5-month waiting period.

The applicant is referred to the state vocational rehabilitation agency and, if rehabilitation services are offered and the applicant refuses them without good cause, his disability benefit will be withheld.

2. The permanently disabled son or daughter of a worker who is receiving retirement or disability benefits, or who has died can collect benefits after age 18 (when children's benefits are ordinarily cut off). If the child is eligible, his mother can also get a benefit if the child is in her care. The child must be unmarried and have been disabled before age 22 (but he need not have been drawing benefits before 22). The child's benefit would be 50% of a retired or disabled parent's or 75% of a deceased parent's basic benefit and his mother would get the same amount.

The benefit for an adult disabled since childhood can actually be paid to adults, if the above tests are met. For example, an unmarried person, aged 40, who was born blind and is dependent on his father for support, can collect a benefit as soon as his father starts drawing a retirement or disability benefit or dies.

3. The disabled widow, dependent widower, or (under certain conditions) the surviving divorced wife of a worker who worked long enough under social security, may be able to get benefits as early as age 50 if he or she is disabled. The benefit is reduced (50% of the worker's benefit if the widow starts getting checks at 50). A widow (or widower or surviving divorced wife) needs no work credits of her own. She is considered disabled only if she has an impairment that is so severe that it would ordinarily prevent a person from working and that is expected to last at least 12 months. Vocational factors cannot be considered. In general, a widow cannot get these benefits unless her disability starts before her spouse's death or within seven years after his death. However, a widow who received benefits as a mother can be eligible if she becomes disabled before those payments end or within seven years after they end. There is a 5-month waiting period before benefits can start.

Medicare. Most people 65 and over and many under 65 who have been entitled to disability checks at least 2 years have Medicare protection. So do insured people and their dependents who need a kidney transplant or dialysis treatment because of permanent kidney failure.

The hospital insurance part of Medicare helps pay the cost of inpatient hospital care and certain kinds of follow-up care. The medical insurance part helps pay for the cost of doctors' services, and outpatient hospital services, and for certain other medical items and services.

A person who is eligible for monthly benefits at 65 gets hospital insurance automatically and does not have to pay a premium. He does pay a monthly premium for medical insurance, however, and this is currently $7.20 (in mid-1976).

You Can Earn Income Without Losing Benefits

If you are 72 or over, you can earn any amount and still get all your benefits. If you are under 72, you can earn $2,760 without losing any benefits. (Only earned income is counted, not pensions, dividends, etc.) If you earn more than $2,760 in a year, $1 of your benefits (or your family benefits) may be withheld for each $2 you earn over $2,760. Family benefits include all benefits payable to you and to any dependents receiving payments based on your social security record. But you will not lose your benefit for any month in which you did not work as an employee for $230 or more and did not perform substantial services in self-employment. For example, if you earned $4,000 in 3 months and were idle the rest of the year, you would lose no more than 3 months' benefits.

If a widow with young children loses her benefits by working, the children will continue to get theirs.

Anyone earning over $2,760 a year while receiving benefits (and under age 72) must report these earnings to the Social Security Administration. If you continue to work after you have applied for social security, your additional earnings may increase the amount of your monthly payment. This will be done automatically by the Social Security Administration. You need not ask for it.

Supplemental Security Income. A new supplemental security income program started January 1974. These federal payments assure a minimum level of income for aged, blind, and disabled people who have limited income and resources.

The new program is administered by the Social Security Administration, but it is financed from general revenues, not from social security contributions. Before 1974, payments to these people were made by state and local public assistance agencies.

Payments of up to $167.80 a month for an individual and up to $251.80 a couple can be made. Further information is available from any social security office.

How to Protect Your Social Security Record

Always show your social security card when you start a new job. In that way you will be sure that your earnings will be credited to *your* social security record and not someone else's. If you lose your social security card, apply for a new one at any social security office. When a woman marries, she should apply for a new card showing her married name (and the same number).

Public Assistance

The Federal government makes grants to the states to help them provide financial assistance, medical care, and social services to certain persons in need, including children dependent because of the death, absence from home, incapacity, or (in some states) unemployment of a parent. In addition, in all states some help is provided from only state and/or local funds to some other needy persons.

Under the Social Security Act, federal sharing in state assistance costs is based on each state's average monthly payment times the number of recipients in each program. The act fixes maximums on the amount of payment to be shared, and sets the ratio of federal contributions. Administrative costs in all the programs are shared equally by the federal and state governments.

Within these and other general patterns set by the requirements of the Social Security Act and their administrative interpretations, each state initiates and administers its own public assistance programs, including the determination of who is eligible to receive assistance, and how much can be granted and under what conditions. Assistance is in the form of cash payments made to recipients, except for payments for medical care. Other social services are provided, in some instances, to help assistance recipients increase their capacity for self-care and self-support or to strengthen family life.

In the medical assistance Medicaid program, federal funds pay 50% to 83% of the costs for medical care. If it is to a state's benefit, it may use the Medicaid formula for federal sharing for its money payment programs, ignoring the maximum on dollar amounts per recipient.

The federal government pays 75% of the cost for services that help recipients become personally and financially self-sufficient.

UNEMPLOYMENT INSURANCE

Unemployment insurance is managed jointly by the states and the federal government. Most states began paying benefits in 1938 and 1939.

Under What Conditions Can the Worker Collect?

The laws vary from state to state. In general, a waiting period of one week is required after a claim is filed before collecting unemployment insurance; the worker must be able to work, must not have quit without good cause or have been discharged for misconduct; he must not be involved in a labor dispute; above all, he must be ready and willing to work. He may be disqualified if he refuses, without good cause, to accept a job which is suitable for him in terms of his qualifications and experience, unless the wages, hours and working conditions offered are substantially less favorable than those prevailing for similar jobs in the community.

The unemployed worker must go to the local state employment security office and register for work. If that office has a suitable opening available, he must accept it or lose his unemployment payments, unless he has good cause for the refusal. If a worker moves out of his own state, he can still collect at his new residence; the state in which he is now located will act as agent for the other state, which will pay his benefits.

Benefits are paid only to unemployed workers who have had at least a certain amount of recent past employment or earnings in a job covered by the state law. The amount of employment or earnings, and the period used to measure them, vary from state to state, but the intent of the various laws is to limit benefits to workers whose recent records indicate that they are members of the labor force. The amount of benefits an unemployed worker may receive for any week is also determined by application to his past wages of a formula specified in the law. The general objective is to provide a weekly benefit which is about half the worker's customary weekly wages, up to a maximum set by the law (see table). In a majority of states, the total benefits a worker may receive in a 12-month period is limited to a fraction of his total wages in a prior 12-month period, as well as to a stated number of weeks. Thus, not all workers in a state are entitled to benefits for the number of weeks shown in the table.

Who Pays for the Insurance?

The total cost is borne by the employer in all but three states. Each state has a sliding scale of rates. The standard rate is set at 2.7% of taxable payroll in most states. But employers with records of less unemployment (that is, with fewer unemployment benefits paid to their former workers) are rewarded with rates lower than the standard 2.7%. The estimated average rate for employers in 1976 was 2.0%. As of July 5, 1976, taxes are payable on the first $4,200 of a worker's pay, except that the limit is $4,500: Mo.; $4,800: Ala., Mont., R.I.; $5,400: Mich., N.J.; $6,000: Conn., Ga., Iowa, Utah, Wis.; $6,100: Nev.; $6,200: Minn.; $7,000: Calif., Oreg.; $7,200: Wash.; $7,800: Hawaii, Idaho; and Alaska: $10,000. Employees as well as employers pay a tax in Alaska ranging from 0.3% to 0.8% in accordance with their employer's tax; in New Jersey, employees pay 0.5% for unemployment insurance. In Alabama, employees pay contributions of 0.5% only when the fund is below a specified amount.

Employers pay an additional unemployment tax to the federal government—0.5% of the first $4,200 paid to each employee. This money is used for the federal and state costs of administering the employment security program, including both unemployment insurance and the employment service. Any amount over these costs, up to the greater of $550 million or 0.125% of total wages subject to contributions under the state unemployment compensation laws for the calendar year, is put in a special fund on which the states draw when the benefit payment funds are low. Any remaining excess is distributed to the states in proportion to their taxable payrolls. These excess funds may be used for benefit payments, or may be used for administrative expenses if so appropriated by the state legislature.

Requirements vary from state to state, but all states cover firms having at least one employee for 20 weeks or a quarterly payroll of $1,500 in the current or preceding calendar year. In some states, firms with one employee at any time are covered. Certain classes of workers are specifically excluded under some or all state laws—employees of the state and its political subdivisions, farm workers, domestic workers, members of the employer's family, insurance agents on commission, student nurses, internes, and casual labor.

During periods of high unemployment on either a state or national level, federal-state extended benefits are available to workers who have exhausted their regular benefits. An unemployed worker may receive benefits equal to the weekly benefit he received under the state program for one half the weeks of his basic entitlement to benefits up to a maximum (including regular benefits) of 39 weeks and for up to 26 additional weeks under the Federal Supplemental Benefits program.

Federal Unemployment Insurance Programs

Amendments to the Social Security Act provided unemployment insurance for Federal civilian employees (1954) and for ex-servicemen (1958). Benefits under these programs are paid by state employment security agencies as agents of the federal government under agreements with the Secretary of Labor. Eligibility for benefits and the amount of benefits paid are determined according to the terms and conditions of the applicable state unemployment insurance law. Thus, federal civilian employees and ex-servicemen are subject to the same eligibility, disqualification, and benefit payment provisions as are claimants for benefits under the state unemployment insurance system.

RAILROAD WORKERS

These are covered by the federal Railroad Retirement Act which provides retirement and survivor annuities and lump-sum death benefits for aged or disabled employees and their families. Railroad workers are also covered by the Railroad Unemployment Insurance Act, which provides unemployment and sickness benefits as well as a placement service. Both acts are administered by the U.S. Railroad Retirement Board. Those covered by the railroad retirement system also participate in the health insurance program (Medicare) provided by the Social Security Act.

State Unemployment Compensation Maximums, July 5, 1976
Source: Department of Labor, Employment and Training Administration

State	Maximum weekly benefit amount[1]	Maximum duration, weeks	State	Maximum weekly benefit amount[1]	Maximum duration, weeks
Alabama	$90	26	Montana	$94	26
Alaska	90-120	28	Nebraska	80	26
Arizona	85	26	Nevada	94	26
Arkansas	100	26	New Hampshire	95	26
California	104	26	New Jersey	96	26
Colorado	114	26	New Mexico	78	30
Connecticut	110-165	26	New York	95	26
Delaware	125	26	North Carolina	97	26
D. C.	139	34	North Dakota	107	26
Florida	82	26	Ohio	95-150	26
Georgia	90	26	Oklahoma	93	26
Hawaii	112	26	Oregon	102	26
Idaho	99	26	Pennsylvania	125-133	30
Illinois	106-135	26	Puerto Rico	55	20
Indiana	69-115	26	Rhode Island	100-120	26
Iowa	116	39	South Carolina	103	26
Kansas	101	26	South Dakota	89	26
Kentucky	87	26	Tennessee	85	26
Louisiana	90	28	Texas	63	26
Maine	79-119	26	Utah	110	36
Maryland	89	26	Vermont	96	26
Massachusetts	101-152	30	Virginia	103	26
Michigan	97-136	26	Washington	102	30
Minnesota	113	26	West Virginia	128	26
Mississippi	80	26	Wisconsin	122	34
Missouri	85	26	Wyoming	95	26

[1] Maximum amounts. When two amounts are shown, higher includes dependents' allowances.

MEDICARE PROGRAM

The Medicare program is a federal health-insurance program for persons 65 and over. Most disabled people under 65 who have been entitled to social security disability benefits at least 24 consecutive months; and insured workers and their dependents who need dialysis treatment or a kidney transplant because of permanent kidney failure also have Medicare protection.

Medicare's official name is Title XVIII of the Social Security Amendments of 1965. These amendments also carried Title XIX, providing federal assistance to state medical-aid programs, which has come to be known as Medicaid.

Medicare

It will be helpful to your understanding of the Medicare program if you keep the following points in mind:

- The federal health-insurance program does not of itself offer medical services. It helps pay hospital, doctor and other medical bills. You choose your own doctor, who prescribes your treatment and place of treatment.
- There are two parts of the program:
  (1) The hospital insurance part for the payment of most of the cost of covered care provided by participating hospitals, skilled nursing facilities, and home health agencies.
  (2) The medical insurance part which helps pay doctors' bills and certain other expenses.
- Another important point to remember: While Medicare pays the major share of the costs of many illnesses requiring hospitalization, it does not offer adequate protection for long-term illness or mental illness.
- Therefore, it may be advisable not to cancel any private health insurance you now carry. You may wish to cancel a policy whose benefits are duplicated by the Federal program, and consider a new policy that will provide for the payment of costs not covered by the Federal program. Private insurance companies offer policies supplementing the protection offered by the federal program.

Do You Qualify for Hospital Insurance?

If you're entitled to monthly social security or railroad retirement checks (as a worker, dependent, or survivor), you have hospital insurance protection automatically when you're 65. Disabled people will have hospital insurance automatically after they have been entitled to social security disability benefits for 24 consecutive months. (Disabled people who get railroad annuities must meet special requirements.) People 65 or older who are not entitled to monthly benefits need credit for some work under social security to get hospital insurance without paying a monthly premium. If they do not have enough work, they can buy hospital insurance. The premium is $45 a month for the 12-month period starting July 1, 1976.

To be sure your protection will start the month you reach 65, apply for Medicare insurance 3 months before reaching 65, even if you don't plan to retire.

Do You Qualify for Voluntary Medical Insurance?

The voluntary medical insurance plan is a vital supplement to the hospital plan. It helps pay for doctors' and other medical services. Many people have not been able to obtain such insurance because they could not afford it or because of their medical histories.

One difference between the hospital insurance plan and the medical insurance plan is that you do not have to be under the social security or railroad retirement systems to enroll in the medical plan. Anyone who is 65 or older or who is eligible for hospital insurance can enroll in medical insurance.

People who get social security benefits or retirement benefits under the railroad retirement system and who live in one of the 50 States or the District of Columbia will be enrolled automatically for medical insurance—unless they say they don't want it—when they become entitled to hospital insurance. People who have medical insurance pay a monthly premium covering part of the cost of this protection. The other part is paid from general Federal revenues. The basic premium for enrollees is $7.20 a month for the 12-month period beginning July 1, 1976.

Is Other Insurance Necessary?

As already indicated, Medicare provides only partial reimbursement. Therefore, you should know how much medical costs you can bear and perhaps arrange for other insurance.

For the first 60 days of inpatient hospital care in each benefit period, hospital insurance pays for all covered services except for the first $104. For the 61st through 90th day of a covered inpatient hospital stay, hospital insurance pays for all covered services except for $26 a day. People who need to be in a hospital for more than 90 days in a benefit period can use their 60 inpatient hospital reserve days. Hospital insurance pays for all covered services except for $52 a day for each reserve day used. Hospital insurance also does not pay the full cost of an inpatient stay in a skilled nursing facility.

Under medical insurance, the patient must meet an annual deductible of $60. After the patient has $60 in reasonable charges for covered services each year, medical insurance generally pays 80 per cent of the reasonable charges for any additional covered services the patient receives during the rest of the year.

How You Obtain Coverage

If you are receiving social security or railroad retirement monthly benefits, you will receive from the government information concerning Medicare about 3 months before you become entitled to hospital insurance.

If you are not receiving benefits or are not covered under social security, contact any social security office to find out how you can get Medicare. People who have permanent kidney failure also should contact a social security office to apply for Medicare.

Medicaid Services by State

Source: Department of Health, Education, and Welfare.

BASIC REQUIRED MEDICAID SERVICES: Every Medicaid program must cover at least these services for persons receiving aid to families with dependent children and in most states those persons who receive Supplemental Security Income benefits*: inpatient hospital care; outpatient hospital services; other laboratory and X-ray services; skilled nursing facilities and home health services for individuals 21 and older; early and periodic screening, diagnosis and treatment for individuals under 21; family planning services; and physicians' services. Federal financial participation is also available to states electing to expand their Medicaid programs by covering additional services and/or by including people eligible for medical but not for financial assistance. For the latter group, states may offer the services required for financial assistance recipients or may substitute a combination of eight services.

Definitions and limitations of services vary from state to state. Details are available from local welfare offices and state Medicaid agencies.

* Effective January 1, 1974, states may restrict coverage of the aged, blind and disabled by using eligibility criteria more stringent than the criteria used under the Supplemental Security Income program.

State	Annual income level for medically needy As of May 1976			Selected additional services for which federal financial participation is available to the states as of May 1976					
	1 person	2 persons	Family of 4	Clinic services	Prescribed drugs	Dental services	Eye-glasses	Optometrists' services	Intermediate care facilities
Alabama	....	....	....	-	-	-	0	-	0
Alaska	....	....	....	-	-	-	0	0	0
Arizona	....	....	....	-	-	-	-	-	-
Arkansas	$2,000	$2,000	$2,400	X	X	X	-	-	0
California	2,400	3,400	5,100	X	X	X	X	X	X
Colorado	....	....	....	-	0	-	-	-	0
Connecticut	2,300	2,900	4,000	X	X	X	X	X	X
Delaware	....	....	....	0	0	-	-	-	0
D.C.	2,100	2,800	3,600	X	X	-	X	X	X
Florida	....	....	....	-	0	-	-	-	0
Georgia	....	....	....	0	0	-	-	-	0
Guam	1,500	2,500	3,000	X	X	X	X	X	-
Hawaii	2,500	3,500	4,500	X	X	X	X	X	X
Idaho	....	....	....	0	0	-	-	0	0
Illinois	1,800	2,400	3,600	X	X	X	X	X	X
Indiana	....	....	....	0	0	0	0	0	0
Iowa	....	....	....	-	0	0	0	0	0
Kansas	3,400	4,000	5,000	X	X	X	X	X	X
Kentucky	1,800	2,200	3,800	X	X	X	-	-	X
Louisiana	....	....	....	0	0	-	-	-	0
Maine	2,600	2,700	4,500	0	X	-	-	-	0
Maryland	1,700	2,300	3,200	X	X	-	X	X	X
Massachusetts	3,500	4,300	5,300	X	X	-	X	-	X
Michigan	2,600	3,400	4,900	X	X	-	-	-	X
Minnesota	2,600	3,300	4,500	X	X	X	X	X	X
Mississippi	....	....	....	-	0	0	-	-	0
Missouri	....	....	....	-	0	0	-	0	0
Montana	2,100	3,500	5,000	X	X	X	X	X	X
Nebraska	2,500	3,000	4,000	X	X	X	X	X	X
Nevada	....	....	....	0	0	0	0	0	0
New Hampshire	3,000	3,500	4,600	X	X	-	X	X	X
New Jersey	....	....	....	0	0	0	0	0	0
New Mexico	....	....	....	0	0	0	0	0	0
New York	2,500	3,400	5,000	X	X	X	X	X	X
North Carolina	1,700	2,200	2,800	X	X	X	X	X	X
North Dakota	1,800	2,400	3,600	X	X	X	X	X	X
Ohio	....	....	....	0	0	0	0	0	0
Oklahoma	1,600	2,400	3,700	0	0	X	-	-	X
Oregon	....	....	....	0	0	0	0	0	0
Pennsylvania	2,000	2,500	4,000	X	0	0	X	X	X
Puerto Rico	2,500	3,200	4,400	X	X	X	-	-	-
Rhode Island	3,000	4,000	4,800	-	X	X	X	X	X
South Carolina	....	....	....	0	0	0	0	0	0
South Dakota	....	....	....	0	0	-	-	0	0
Tennessee	1,400	1,600	2,200	X	X	-	-	-	X
Texas	....	....	....	-	0	0	0	0	0
Utah	1,600	2,200	3,400	X	X	X	X	X	X
Vermont	2,700	3,400	4,400	X	X	-	-	-	X
Virgin Islands	2,200	2,800	3,700	X	X	X	X	-	-
Virginia	1,900	2,500	3,300	X	X	-	X	X	X
Washington	2,400	3,400	4,500	X	X	X	X	X	X
West Virginia	1,500	2,000	2,200	X	X	X	X	X	X
Wisconsin	3,400	4,000	5,600	X	X	X	X	X	X
Wyoming	....	....	....	-	-	-	-	0	0

NOTE: O = Offered for people receiving federally supported financial assistance or for people who are considered categorically needy. X = Offered also for people who would, except for their income, be eligible for financial assistance. For complete information consult the Medicaid listing under your local government in the telephone directory, or a local social service agency.

FEDERAL AND STATE TAXES
FEDERAL INDIVIDUAL INCOME TAX
Prepared by Tax Foundation, Inc.

The Federal individual income tax is levied on the taxable income of both citizens and non-citizens who earn income from U.S. sources. Taxable income is defined as adjusted gross income less personal exemptions and deductions. Four tax rate schedules apply—to single persons, married persons filing separate returns, married persons filing joint returns, and heads of households. The tax rates are graduated, ranging from a minimum of 14% on the first $1,000 of taxable income to 70% on incomes above $200,000 (for joint returns). The maximum rate on earned income, however, is 50%.

Adjusted Gross Income—Adjusted gross income is determined by subtracting from gross income those business-type expenses considered necessary in earning income. Gross income consists of wages and salaries, tips and gratuities, interest, dividends, annuities, rents and royalties, and certain other types of income. Among the items excluded from adjusted gross income, and thus not subject to tax, are social security payments, unemployment and workmen's compensation benefits, public assistance benefits, interest on exempt securities (mostly state and local bonds), the first $100 of dividends received, and one half of net long-term capital gains.

Deductions—Taxpayers may itemize deductions or use one of two forms of the standard deduction. In itemizing deductions, the following are the major items which may be deducted (with limits in some instances): interest payments, state and local general sales, income, property, and gasoline taxes; medical expenses; charitable contributions; casualty losses; and child care expenses. For a taxpayer with adjusted gross income of $10,000 or over ($15,000 in 1975), a percentage standard deduction may be used. This deduction is 16% of adjusted gross income with a maximum of $2,600 for joint returns and $2,300 for single persons. In the absence of further action by Congress, the amount, after 1975, will revert to 15% of adjusted gross income, with a maximum of $2,000. The other type of standard deduction is the low-income allowance. Legislation in 1975 raised the low-income allowance for the year from the regular $1,300 to $1,900 for joint returns and $1,600 for single persons.

Personal Exemption—A personal exemption is available to the taxpayer, his spouse, and dependents. The amount is $750 for each individual. Additional exemptions of $750 each are granted for persons 65 and over and for the blind. A temporary provision of the law provides a $30 credit for each exemption.

A minimum tax is imposed on certain tax preference items which result from special deductions and deferrals of tax liability (e.g., the excluded portion of capital gains). The tax is imposed at 10% on preference items, reduced by a $30,000 exemption and by the regular income tax for the year.

Changes in Returns—In addition to other changes, the Tax Reduction Act of 1975 provides rebates of taxes, generally equal to 10% of tax liability up to a maximum of $200, aggregating $8.1 billion for all taxpayers. The Act also granted, for 1975 only, a refundable earned income credit for lower-income households with dependent children, with a maximum credit of $400 phased out as adjusted gross income rises from $4,000 to $8,000. Altogether the law provided for an estimated $18 billion in tax relief for individuals.

Note: On Oct. 4, 1976 President Ford signed a tax-revision bill extending, with

---

Federal Income Tax to Be Paid: Comparisons, 1963, 1969, 1971, and 1976[1]

Taxes given at selected income brackets, after standard deductions and, on joint return, 4 exemptions.

Income	Single Return				Joint Return			
	1963	1969[2]	1971	1976[2]	1963	1969[2]	1971	1976[3]
$ 3,000	$ 422	$ 362	$ 189	$ 62	$ 60	$ 0	$ 0	$−300[4]
5,000	818	738	552	404	420	290	178	−300[4]
10,000	2,096	1,916	1,596	1,476	1,372	1,225	1,000	709
15,000	3,787	3,469	2,739	2,560	2,486	2,268	1,897	1,612
20,000	5,900	5,410	4,077	3,817	3,800	3,476	2,935	2,590
25,000	8,324	7,680	5,639	5,295	5,318	4,853	4,114	3,700

[1] Per the extension of Tax Reduction Act of 1975. [2] A 10% surcharge was in effect. [3] Includes $30 tax credit per dependent and earned income credit for families with dependent children ($400 maximum) earning up to $8,000 gross income. [4] Refund.

some modifications, the reductions in effect in 1975. His action came too late to revise the data in this section.

Filing Time and Estimated Tax—For individuals on a calendar year basis, April 15 is the final date for filing income tax returns and for payment of any tax due.

The Government collects the great bulk of the income tax currently through withholding by employers. In cases where withholding does not apply or is insufficient to cover tax liability, individuals must file advance declarations of estimated tax, and pay the tax in installments on the 15th of April, June, September, and January.

FEDERAL ESTATE TAX
Source: Tax Foundation, Inc.

The Federal Government requires that a tax return be filed for any citizen or resident whose estate exceeds $60,000 at time of death, or if he is married and entitled to the marital deduction, the tax would apply, when the estate exceeds $120,000. A limit of 9 months is set for payment of the estate tax. In case of hardship, however, extensions may be granted. The tax is levied at rates ranging from 3% to 77% of the taxable estate. For a nonresident (not a citizen), a return must be filed if his gross estate in the U. S. exceeds $30,000; tax rates range from 5% to 25%.

Certain deductions are allowed on the estate tax: funeral expenditures, administrative costs, claims and bequests to religious, charitable, and fraternal organizations, or government welfare agencies; also some allowance is made for state death taxes.

The marital deduction will apply only if the surviving spouse has a right to the income from the estate for life. If the spouse controls only a part of the estate, the deduction is limited to that part—or at most, to the value of one half of the adjusted gross estate.

Life insurance payable to named beneficiaries is not included in the gross estate, provided that the insured did not retain any incidents of ownership in the policy. (An incident of ownership would be a reversionary interest exceeding 5% of the value of the policy.)

Estate Tax Rate
(The rates in the table have already allowed for deductions and exemptions as indicated in the copy above.)

If the taxable estate is:	The tax shall be:
Not over $5,000	3% of the taxable estate
Over $ 5,000 but not over $ 10,000	$ 150, plus 7% of excess over $ 5,000
Over $ 10,000 but not over $ 20,000	$ 500, plus 11% of excess over $ 10,000
Over $ 20,000 but not over $ 30,000	$ 1,600, plus 14% of excess over $ 20,000
Over $ 30,000 but not over $ 40,000	$ 3,000, plus 18% of excess over $ 30,000
Over $ 40,000 but not over $ 50,000	$ 4,800, plus 22% of excess over $ 40,000
Over $ 50,000 but not over $ 60,000	$ 7,000, plus 25% of excess over $ 50,000
Over $ 60,000 but not over $ 100,000	$ 9,500, plus 28% of excess over $ 60,000
Over $ 100,000 but not over $ 250,000	$ 20,700, plus 30% of excess over $ 100,000
Over $ 250,000 but not over $ 500,000	$ 65,700, plus 32% of excess over $ 250,000
Over $ 500,000 but not over $ 750,000	$ 145,700, plus 35% of excess over $ 500,000
Over $ 750,000 but not over $1,000,000	$ 233,200, plus 37% of excess over $ 750,000
Over $ 1,000,000 but not over $1,250,000	$ 325,700, plus 39% of excess over $ 1,000,000
Over $ 1,250,000 but not over $1,500,000	$ 423,200, plus 42% of excess over $ 1,250,000
Over $ 1,500,000 but not over $2,000,000	$ 528,200, plus 45% of excess over $ 1,500,000
Over $ 2,000,000 but not over $2,500,000	$ 753,200, plus 49% of excess over $ 2,000,000
Over $ 2,500,000 but not over $3,000,000	$ 998,200, plus 53% of excess over $ 2,500,000
Over $ 3,000,000 but not over $3,500,000	$1,263,200, plus 56% of excess over $ 3,000,000
Over $ 3,500,000 but not over $4,000,000	$1,543,200, plus 59% of excess over $ 3,500,000
Over $ 4,000,000 but not over $5,000,000	$1,838,200, plus 63% of excess over $ 4,000,000
Over $ 5,000,000 but not over $6,000,000	$2,468,200, plus 67% of excess over $ 5,000,000
Over $ 6,000,000 but not over $7,000,000	$3,138,200, plus 70% of excess over $ 6,000,000
Over $ 7,000,000 but not over $8,000,000	$3,838,200, plus 73% of excess over $ 7,000,000
Over $ 8,000,000 but not over $10,000,000	$4,568,200, plus 76% of excess over $ 8,000,000
Over $10,000,000	$6,088,200, plus 77% of excess over $10,000,000

FEDERAL GIFT TAX .

Any citizen or resident alien who gives away more than $3,000 to any one individual within a calendar year must file a gift-tax return. Since 1971, the tax has been levied quarterly on a return due 1 1/2 months after the end of a quarter. There is a lifetime exemption of $30,000 which may be taken all at once, or spread over several years. In the case of married couples, the spouse who makes the gift is entitled to an exemption of one half of the value of the gift. In addition, gifts given to a third party by either husband or wife may be considered as made, one half by each.

Gift Tax Rate

If the taxable gifts are: The tax will be:

Not over $5,000 .... 2¼ % of the taxable gifts

Over $ 5,000 but not over $ 10,000	$ 112.50, plus 5¼ % of excess over $	5,000
Over $ 10,000 but not over $ 20,000	$ 375, plus 8¼ % of excess over $	10,000
Over $ 20,000 but not over $ 30,000	$ 1,200, plus 10½ % of excess over $	20,000
Over $ 30,000 but not over $ 40,000	$ 2,250, plus 13½ % of excess over $	30,000
Over $ 40,000 but not over $ 50,000	$ 3,600, plus 16½ % of excess over $	40,000
Over $ 50,000 but not over $ 60,000	$ 5,250, plus 18¾ % of excess over $	50,000
Over $ 60,000 but not over $ 100,000	$ 7,125, plus 21% of excess over $	60,000
Over $ 100,000 but not over $ 250,000	$ 15,525, plus 22½ % of excess over $	100,000
Over $ 250,000 but not over $ 500,000	$ 49,275, plus 24% of excess over $	250,000
Over $ 500,000 but not over $ 750,000	$ 109,275, plus 26¼ % of excess over $	500,000
Over $ 750,000 but not over $ 1,000,000	$ 174,900, plus 27¾ % of excess over $	750,000
Over $ 1,000,000 but not over $ 1,250,000	$ 244,275, plus 29¼ % of excess over $	1,000,000
Over $ 1,250,000 but not over $ 1,500,000	$ 317,400, plus 31½ % of excess over $	1,250,000
Over $ 1,500,000 but not over $ 2,000,000	$ 396,150, plus 33¾ % of excess over $	1,500,000
Over $ 2,000,000 but not over $ 2,500,000	$ 564,900, plus 36¾ % of excess over $	2,000,000
Over $ 2,500,000 but not over $ 3,000,000	$ 748,650, plus 39¾ % of excess over $	2,500,000
Over $ 3,000,000 but not over $ 3,500,000	$ 947,400, plus 42% of excess over $	3,000,000
Over $ 3,500,000 but not over $ 4,000,000	$1,157,400, plus 44¼ % of excess over $	3,500,000
Over $ 4,000,000 but not over $ 5,000,000	$1,378,650, plus 47¼ % of excess over $	4,000,000
Over $ 5,000,000 but not over $ 6,000,000	$1,851,150, plus 50¼ % of excess over $	5,000,000
Over $ 6,000,000 but not over $ 7,000,000	$2,353,650, plus 52½ % of excess over $	6,000,000
Over $ 7,000,000 but not over $ 8,000,000	$2,878,650, plus 54¾ % of excess over $	7,000,000
Over $ 8,000,000 but not over $10,000,000	$3,426,150, plus 57% of excess over $	8,000,000
Over $10,000,000	$4,566,150, plus 57¾ % of excess over	$10,000,000

FEDERAL CORPORATION TAXES

For taxable years ending before and after 1975, the tax on net income of corporations is 22% on the first $25,000 and 26% on income above $25,000. The Tax Reduction Act of 1975 reduced the rate, for taxable years ending in 1975 only, to 20% on the first $25,000 of net income, 22% on the next $25,000, and 48% on net income above $50,-000. (As of September 1976, legislation was pending that would extend these rates on either a temporary or permanent basis.) Net operating losses may be applied against profits over an eight-year period; they may be carried back three years and forward five.

Among the major provisions of the corporate tax laws are the Asset Depreciation Range (ADR) system, introduced in 1971, which increases allowable depreciation expenses for current tax purposes, thus shortening the period over which invested capital can be recovered; a tax deferral system known as Domestic International Sales Corporation (DISC), under which 50% of the profits are not taxed on a current basis but deferred and taxed when the profits are distributed to shareholders; and an investment tax credit whereby taxpayers can receive a credit against tax liabilities equal to 10% of the purchase price of eligible property. The 10% rate applies during the period January 22, 1975, through December 31, 1976 only; before and after this period, the credit is 7% for most firms and 4% for certain public utilities. Also on a temporary basis, the 10% credit can be raised to 11% if the employer establishes an employee stock ownership plan meeting specified criteria.

In 1975, Congress enacted increases in taxes which affect mainly energy-producing firms. Large producers of oil and gas can no longer claim the 22% depletion allowance.

STATE PERSONAL INCOME TAX RATES

Source: Questionnaires to the states.

(The rates on individuals are applicable, unless otherwise indicated, to net income, less personal exemptions. The following states have no income taxes: Connecticut, Florida, Nevada, New Hampshire, South Dakota, Texas, Washington, and Wyoming. Nonresidents of several states receiving certain income from those states' sources are liable for the state tax applicable to that income—these provisions apply in: California, Hawaii, Massachusetts, Nebraska, New Hampshire, New Jersey, New Mexico, North Carolina and Wisconsin.)

Rates	Exemptions

ALABAMA

On 1st $1,000: 1.5%	Single: $1,500
On next $2,000: 3%	Married: $3,000
On next $2,000: 4.5%	Head of household:
On balance: 5%	$3,000
	Each dependent: $300

ALASKA

For single persons: Residents: $750
On 1st $2,000: 3% Part-year residents:
On next $2,000: 3.5% $750, prorated
On next $2,000: 4%
On next $2,000: 5%
On next $2,000: 5.5%
On next $2,000: 6%
On next $2,000: 7%

On next $2,000: 7.5%	On next $4,000: 5%
On next $2,000: 8%	On next $4,000: 5.5%
On next $2,000: 8.5%	On next $4,000: 6%
On next $2,000: 9%	On next $4,000: 7%
On next $4,000: 9.5%	On next $4,000: 7.5%
On next $6,000: 10%	On next $4,000: 8%
On next $6,000: 10.5%	On next $4,000: 8.5%
On next $6,000: 11%	On next $4,000: 9%
On next $6,000: 11.5%	On next $8,000: 9.5%
On next $10,000: 12%	On next $12,000: 10%
On next $10,000: 12.5%	On next $12,000: 10.5%
On next $10,000: 13%	On next $12,000: 11%
On next $10,000: 13.5%	On next $12,000: 11.5%
On next $60,000: 14%	On next $20,000: 12%
On balance: 14.5%	On next $20,000: 12.5%
For joint returns:	On next $20,000: 13%
On 1st $4,000: 3%	On next $20,000: 13.5%
On next $4,000: 3.5%	On next $120,000: 14%
On next $4,000: 4%	On balance: 14.5%

ARIZONA

For single persons:[1]

On 1st $1,000: 2.0%	Single: $1,000
On 2nd $1,000: 3.0%	Married: $2,000
On 3rd $1,000: 4.0%	Head of household:
On 4th $1,000: 5.0%	$2,000
On 5th $1,000: 6.0%	Each dependent: $600
On 6th $1,000: 7.0%	Blindness: $500 addl.
On balance: 8.0%	Over 65 years: $1,000
	addl.

For joint returns:[2]

On 1st $2,000: 2.0%	
On 2nd $2,000: 3.0%	On 5th $2,000: 6.0%
On 3rd $2,000: 4.0%	On 6th $2,000: 7.0%
On 4th $2,000: 5.0%	On balance: 8.0%

[1] Or separate return of a married person. [2] Or single person filing as head of household.

ARKANSAS[1]

On 1st $2,999: 1% *Credits against tax*
On next $3,000: 2.5% *(no exemptions):*
On next $3,000: 3.5% Single: $17.50

[1] Single persons with income of $3,000 or less; couples with no dependent children with income of $4,000 or less; couples with one child with income of $4,500 or less; and

ARKANSAS (Contd.)

On next $6,000: 4.5%	Married: $35
On next $10,000: 6%	Head of family: $35
On balance: 7%	Each dependent: $6
	Mentally retarded
	child kept at home:
	$50
	Blind: $17.50 if hus-
	band or wife; does
	not apply to depen-
	dents

CALIFORNIA

For single persons and married—separate returns:[1]

	Exemption credits:[3]
On 1st $2,000: 1%	Single persons or mar-
On next $1,500: 2%	ried persons filing
On next $1,500: 3%	separately: $25
On next $1,500: 4%	Married persons filing
On next $1,500: 5%	joint return, head of
On next $1,500: 6%	household or widow
On next $1,500: 7%	(er) with dependent
On next $1,500: 8%	child: $50
On next $1,500: 9%	Dependents: $8 each
On next $1,500: 10%	Blindness: $8 addl.
On balance: 11%	each

For joint returns:[2]

On 1st $4,000: 1%	On next $3,000: 7%
On next $3,000: 2%	On next $3,000: 8%
On next $3,000: 3%	On next $3,000: 9%
On next $3,000: 4%	On next $3,000: 10%
On next $3,000: 5%	On balance: 11%
On next $3,000: 6%	

[1] For head of household: 1% on 1st $4,000, 2% on next $2,000; otherwise same as single persons: 3% on next $1,500, etc. [2] Or widow(er) with dependent child. [3] Do not apply to nonresidents: nonresidents must prorate their exemption credits in same ratio as California income relates to total income.

COLORADO[1]

On 1st $1,000: 2.5%	Single: $750
On 2nd $1,000: 3%	Married: $1,500
On 3rd $1,000: 3.5%	Each dependent: $750
On 4th $1,000: 4%	Mentally retarded: $750
On 5th $1,000: 4.5%	addl.
On 6th $1,000: 5%	Blindness: $750 addl.
On 7th $1,000: 5.5%	Over 65 years: $750
On 8th $1,000: 6%	addl.
On 9th $1,000: 6.5%	
On 10th $1,000: 7.5%	
On balance: 8%	

[1] Add 2% surtax on intangible income from interest and dividends in excess of $5,000.
Optional tax table on adjusted gross income up to $10,000 may be used.

couples with two children with income of $5,000 or less are exempt from state tax. Tax on income above these limits is computed on either a special reduced-tax table or the regular tax rate schedule.

Rates	Exemptions

DELAWARE

On 1st $1,000: 1.6%	Single: $600
On 2nd $1,000: 2.2%	Married: $1,200
On 3rd $1,000: 3.3%	Each dependent: $600
On 4th $1,000: 4.4%	Blindness: $600 addl.
On 5th $1,000: 5.5%	Over 65 years: $600
On 6th $1,000: 6.6%	addl.
On next $2,000: 7.7%	
On next $12,000: 8.8%	
On next $5,000: 9.3%	
On next $5,000: 9.9%	
On next $10,000: 12.1%	
On next $10,000: 13.2%	
On next $25,000: 15.4%	
On next $25,000: 16.5%	
On balance: 19.8%	

DISTRICT OF COLUMBIA

On 1st $1,000: 2%	Single: $750
On 2nd $1,000: 3%	Married: $1,500
On 3rd $1,000: 4%	Head of family:
On 4th $1,000: 5%	$1,500
On 5th $1,000: 6%	Each dependent: $750
On next $5,000: 7%	Blindness: $750 addl.
On next $3,000: 8%	Over 65 years: $750
On next $4,000: 9%	addl.
On next $8,000: 10%	
On balance: 11%	

GEORGIA

For single persons:

On 1st $750: 1%	Single: $1,500
On next $1,500: 2%	Married: $3,000
On next $1,500: 3%	Head of household:
On next $1,500: 4%	$3,000
On next $1,750: 5%	Each dependent: $700[1]
On balance: 6%	Blindness: $700 addl.
	Over 65 years: $700
	addl.

For joint returns:

On 1st $1,000: 1%	
On next $2,000: 2%	On next $2,000: 4%
On next $2,000: 3%	On next $3,000: 5%
	On balance: 6%

[1] An additional $700 credit is allowed for each dependent college student; also for each dependent son, stepson, daughter, stepdaughter, or ward, under 21 years of age, who is physically handicapped or mentally retarded and is not a ward of the state but is eligible to be a ward of the state.

HAWAII

For single persons:[1]

Not over $500: 2.25%	For each exemption al-
On next $500: 3.25%	lowed on federal in-
On next $500: 4.5%	come tax: $750.
On next $500: 5%	Blind, deaf, totally dis-
On next $1,000: 6.5%	abled: $5,000 in lieu
On next $2,000: 7.5%	of all other exemp-
On next $5,000: 8.5%	tions
On next $4,000: 9.5%	
On next $6,000: 10%	
On next $10,000: 10.5%	
On balance: 11%	

For joint returns:[2]

Not over $1,000: 2.25%	On next $10,000: 8.5%
On next $1,000: 3.25%	On next $8,000: 9.5%
On next $1,000: 4.5%	On next $12,000: 10%
On next $1,000: 5%	On next $20,000: 10.5%
On next $2,000: 6.5%	On balance: 11%
On next $4,000: 7.5%	

[1] Or separate return of a married person. [2] And certain widows and widowers.

HAWAII (Contd.)

For head of household:

Not over $500: 2.25%	On next $5,000: 7.9%
On next $500: 2.75%	On next $10,000: 9.15%
On next $500: 3.9%	On next $10,000: 10.05%
On next $500: 4.1%	On next $10,000: 10.5%
On next $1,000: 5.5%	On next $20,000: 10.75%
On next $2,000: 6.6%	On balance: 11%

IDAHO

For single persons:[1]

On 1st $1,000: 2%	For each exemption al-
On 2nd $1,000: 4%	lowed on Federal in-
On 3rd $1,000: 4.5%	come tax: $750
On 4th $1,000: 5.5%	
On 5th $1,000: 6.5%	
On balance: 7.5%	

For joint returns:[2]

On 1st $2,000: 2%	On 4th $2,000: 5.5%
On 2nd $2,000: 4%	On 5th $2,000: 6.5%
On 3rd $2,000: 4.5%	On balance: 7.5%

[1] Or separate return of a married person. [2] Effective 1969, includes surviving spouse and head of household.

ILLINOIS

Flat 2.5% on adjusted gross income, following Federal income tax statute.[1] — For each exemption allowed on Federal income tax: $1,000[2]

[1] Exceptions: tax-exempt interest, 50% long-term capital gains and Federal dividend exclusion are not deductible; interest on U.S. government obligations, amounts received by reason of active duty in armed forces and compensation from employee benefit plans are. [2] Prorated by part-year residents and nonresidents where income earned both within and without Illinois.

INDIANA[1]

Income tax: 2%

On income tax:
Taxpayer: $1,000
Taxpayer and spouse: $500 to $1,000, depending on amount of income
Each dependent: $500
Blindness: $500 addl.
Over 65 years: $500 addl.

[1] Applied to adjusted gross income.

IOWA

On 1st $1,000: 0.50%	*Exemption credits:*
On 2nd $1,000: 1.25%	Single: $15 reduction
On 3rd $1,000: 2.75%	in tax
On 4th $1,000: 3.50%	Married, joint return:
On next $3,000: 5.00%	$30 reduction
On next $2,000: 6%	Head of household:
On next $6,000: 7%	$30 reduction
On next $5,000: 8%	Each dependent: $10
On next $5,000: 9%	reduction
On next $5,000: 10%	Over 65 years: $15 re-
On next $10,000: 11%	duction addl.
On next $35,000: 12%	Blindness: $15 reduc-
On balance: 13%	tion addl.

Rates	Exemptions	Rates	Exemptions

KANSAS

For single persons:[1]
  On 1st $2,000: 2%
  On next $1,000: 3.5%
  On next $2,000: 4%
  On next $2,000: 5%
  On balance: 6.5%

For joint returns:
  On 1st $4,000: 2%
  On next $2,000: 3.5%
  On next $4,000: 4%
  On next $4,000: 5%
  On balance: 6.5%

Single: $600
Married: $1,200
Each dependent: $600
Blindness: $600 addl.
Over 65 years: $600 addl.

[1] Or separate return of a married person.

KENTUCKY [1]

On 1st $3,000: 2%
On next $1,000: 3%
On next $1,000: 4%
On next $3,000: 5%
On balance: 6%

Exemption credits:
Single: $20 reduction in tax
Married, joint return: $40 reduction
Each dependent: $20 reduction
Blindness: $40 reduction addl.
65 or over: $40 reduction addl.

[1] Rates apply to net income after deduction of Federal income tax and standard deduction or itemized deductions.

LOUISIANA

On first $10,000: 2%
On next $40,000: 4%
On balance: 6%

Single: $2,500
Married $5,000
Each dependent: $400

MAINE

For single persons:[1]
  On 1st $2,000: 1%
  On next $2,000: 2%
  On next $1,000: 3%
  On next $1,000: 3.5%
  On next $2,000: 4.5%
  On next $2,000: 5%
  On next $5,000: 6%
  On next $10,000: 6.5%
  On next $25,000: 7.5%
  On balance: 8%

For each exemption allowed on Federal income tax: $1,000

On next $2,000: 3%
On next $2,000: 3.5%
On next $4,000: 4.5%
On next $4,000: 5%
On next $10,000: 6%
On next $20,000: 6.5%
On next $50,000: 7.5%
On balance: 8%

For joint returns:[2]
  On 1st $4,000: 1%
  On next $4,000: 2%

[1] Or separate return of a married person. [2] For married taxpayers and widows and widowers filing joint federal returns.

MARYLAND

On 1st $1,000: 2%
On 2nd $1,000: 3%
On 3rd $1,000: 4%
On balance: 5%

Single: $800
Married: $1,600
Each dependent: $800
Blindness: $800 addl.
Blind spouse: $800 addl.
Over 65 years: $800 addl.
Spouse or dependent over 65 years: $800 addl.

MASSACHUSETTS [1]

Interest, dividends, and gains from capital assets: 10%
All other income including Mass. savings deposit interest: 5%
Plus surtax of 7.5%

Single: $2,000
Married: Up to $4,000 if both spouses have earnings: $2,600 if not
Each dependent: $600
Blindness: $2,000 addl.
Combat zone: I.R.C. exclusion.
Over 65: $600 addl.

[1] For each taxpayer, a $4 tax credit for himself, $4 for his spouse, and $8 for each dependent, provided income of taxpayer and spouse does not exceed $5,000. No tax on income if total less than $3,000 (single), or $5,000 (joint).

MICHIGAN

Flat 4.6% on taxable income, following Federal income tax statute[1]

For each exemption allowed on Federal income tax: $1,500

[1] Credits for rents and certain taxes and contributions.

MINNESOTA

Normal tax:
  On 1st $500: 1.6%
  On 2nd $500: 2.2%
  On next $1,000: 3.5%
  On next $1,000: 5.8%
  On next $1,000: 7.3%
  On next $1,000: 8.8%
  On next $1,000: 10.2%
  On next $1,000: 10.2%
  On next $1,000: 11.5%
  On next $1,000: 11.5%
  On next $3,500: 12.8%
  On next $7,500: 14%
  Over $20,000: 15%

Single: $21 reduction in normal tax
Married: $42 reduction in normal tax
Each dependent: $21 addl. reduction in normal tax
Blindness: $21 addl. reduction in normal tax if single, $25 if married
Over 65 years: $21 addl. reduction in normal tax
Additional reductions allowed for senior citizens, renters, persons with low income, pollution-control equipment used in businesses, political contributions and agricultural electricity

MISSISSIPPI

On 1st $5,000: 3%
On balance: 4%

Single: $4,500
Married: $6,500
Head of family and one dependent: $6,500
Each dependent: $750
Over 65: $750 addl.
Blindness: $750 addl.

MISSOURI

On 1st $1,000: 1.5%
On 2nd $1,000: 2%
On 3rd $1,000: 2.5%
On 4th $1,000: 3%
On 5th $1,000: 3.5%
On 6th $1,000: 4%
On 7th $1,000: 4.5%
On 8th $1,000: 5%
On 9th $1,000: 5.5%
On balance: 6%

Single: $1,200
Married—joint return: $2,400
Married—separate return: $1,200
Head of household (same as Federal): $2,000
Each dependent (same as Federal): $400

Rates	Exemptions

MONTANA

On 1st $1,000: 2%
On next $1,000: 3%
On next $2,000: 4%
On next $2,000: 5%
On next $2,000: 6%
On next $2,000: 7%
On next $4,000: 8%
On next $6,000: 9%
On next $15,000: 10%
On balance: 11%
Plus surtax of 10%

Single: $650
Married: $1,300
Each dependent: $650
Blindness: $650 addl.
Over 65 years: $650 addl.

NEBRASKA[1]

15% of adjusted liability on Federal tax

Interest on U. S. Government obligations

[1] Nonresidents subject to tax at same rate on all income from Nebraska sources.

NEW JERSEY

Rates	Exemptions

On 1st $20,000: 2%
On balance: 2.5%

Taxpayer: $1,000
Spouse: $1,000
Over 65 years: $1,000 addl.
Blindness: $1,000 addl.
Dependent child: $1,000[1]

[1] Additional $1,000 exemption for children attending non-private elementary or secondary schools and for persons under 22 attending institution of higher education where taxpayer furnishes at least one-half of tuition and maintenance.

NEW MEXICO

For single persons:
On 1st $500: 0.9%
On next $500: 1.1%
On next $500: 1.3%
On next $500: 1.5%
On next $1,000: 1.6%
On next $1,000: 1.9%
On next $1,000: 2.3%
On next $1,000: 2.4%
On next $1,000: 3.0%
On next $1,000: 3.3%
On next $2,000: 3.6%
On next $2,000: 4.3%
On next $8,000: 6.1%
On next $30,000: 8.0%
On next $50,000: 8.5%
On balance: 9.0%

For each exemption allowed on Federal income tax: $750

For heads of household and married—joint returns:

On first $1,000: 0.9%	On next $2,000: 4.2%
On next $1,000: 1.3%	On next $2,000: 4.8%
On next $1,000: 1.3%	On next $4,000: 5.5%
On next $1,000: 1.7%	On next $4,000: 6.4%
On next $2,000: 2.1%	On next $16,000: 7.5%
On next $2,000: 2.6%	On next $60,000: 8.0%
On next $2,000: 3.1%	On next $100,000: 8.5%
On next $2,000: 3.6%	On balance: 9.0%

For married—separate returns:

On 1st $500: 0.9%	On next $1,000: 2.6%
On next $500: 1.3%	On next $1,000: 3.1%
On next $500: 1.3%	On next $1,000: 3.6%
On next $500: 1.7%	On next $1,000: 4.2%
On next $1,000: 2.1%	On next $1,000: 4.8%

Rates	Exemptions

NEW MEXICO (Contd.)

On next $2,000: 5.5%
On next $2,000: 6.4%
On next $8,000: 7.5%

On next $30,000: 8.0%
On next $50,000: 8.5%
On balance: 9.0%

NEW YORK

On 1st $1,000: 2%
On next $2,000: 3%
On next $2,000: 4%
On next $2,000: 5%
On next $2,000: 6%
On next $2,000: 7%
On next $2,000: 8%
On next $2,000: 9%
On next $2,000: 10%
On next $2,000: 11%
On next $2,000: 12%
On next $2,000: 13%
On next $2,000: 14%
On balance: 15%

Single: $650
Married, joint return: $1,300
Married, separate return: $650
Head of household: $650
Each dependent: $650
Blind: $650 addl.
Over 65 years: $650 addl.

NORTH CAROLINA

On 1st $2,000: 3%
On 2nd $2,000: 4%
On 3rd $2,000: 5%
On next $4,000: 6%
On balance: 7%

Single: $1,000
Married: $2,000
Head of household: $2,000
Each dependent: $600
Blindness: $1,000 addl.
Widow or widower with minor child: $2,000
Over 65 years: $1,000 addl.
Each student in inst. of higher learning: $600
Dependent with I.Q. under 40: $2,000 addl.
Hemophiliac: $1,000 addl.

NORTH DAKOTA

On 1st $1,000: 1%
On next $2,000: 2%
On next $2,000: 3%
On next $1,000: 5%
On next $2,000: 7½%
On balance: 10%

Rates apply to Federal taxable income after certain state adjustments, including federal tax deductions
Married, joint return: $300 addl.
Head of household: $300 addl.
Surviving spouse: $300 addl.

OHIO

On first $5,000: .5%
On next $5,000: 1%
On next $5,000: 2%
On next $5,000: 2½%
On next $20,000: 3%
On balance: 3½%

For taxpayer, his spouse and each dependent: $650

OKLAHOMA

For single persons and married individuals filing separately:
On 1st $1,000: .5%.
On next $1,500: 1%
On next $1,250: 2%
On next $1,250: 3%

Each person, $750

On next $1,250: 4%
On next $1,250: 5%
On balance: 6%

Rates	Exemptions

OREGON [1]

For single persons:
On 1st $500: 4%
On next $500: 5%
On next $1,000: 6%
On next $1,000: 7%
On next $1,000: 8%
On next $1,000: 9%
On balance: 10%

Same as for Federal: $750 each exemption

For joint returns:[2]

On 1st $1,000: 4%	On next $2,000: 8%
On 2nd $1,000: 5%	On next $2,000: 9%
On next $2,000: 6%	On balance: 10%
On next $2,000: 7%	

[1] Follows Federal Internal Revenue Code of 1954 on net income with specified adjustments. Federal income tax paid is deductible in computing taxable income up to $5,000. [2] Or for head of household.

PENNSYLVANIA

2% of taxable income for residents and non-residents.

RHODE ISLAND

Tax is 17% of the federal tax liability on residents and non-residents.

SOUTH CAROLINA

On 1st $2,000: 2%
On 2nd $2,000: 3%
On 3rd $2,000: 4%
On 4th $2,000: 5%
On 5th $2,000: 6%
On balance: 7%

Single: $800
Married: $1,600
Head of household: $1,600
Each dependent: $800
Blindness: $800 addl.
Over 65 years: $800 addl.

TENNESSEE

On income from stocks and bonds: 6%, if over $25.00 for single persons or over $50.00 for joint owners
On income from corporation stock, if 75% of corporation property is assessable in Tennessee: 4%

Income of the blind
Income from securities of pension trusts and profit-sharing trusts exempted from Federal income taxation
Income from general welfare corporations, if not going to individuals or corporations for profit
Income from Tennessee state bonds and from Federal securities exempt from taxation
Persons 65 or older with income of $4,800 or less.
Married persons with total income of $6,000 or less filing joint return and either spouse is 65.

UTAH

For single persons:
On 1st $750: 2.25%
On 2nd $750: 3.25%
On 3rd $750: 4.25%
On 4th $750: 5.25%
On 5th $750: 6.25%
On 6th $750: 7.25%
On balance: 7.75%

For each exemption allowed on Federal income tax: $750

For joint returns:

On 1st $1,500: 2.75%	On 4th $1,500: 5.75%
On 2nd $1,500: 3.75%	On 5th $1,500: 6.75%
On 3rd $1,500: 4.75%	On balance: 7.75%

VERMONT

27.25% of Federal tax[1]

[1] Before allowance for any credits other than allowance for retirement, investment, foreign tax, and covenant bond interest.

VIRGINIA

On 1st $3,000: 2%
On next $2,000: 3%
On next $7,000: 5%
On balance: 5¾%

Single: $600
Married: $1,200[1]
Each dependent: $600
Blindness: $600 addl.
Over 65 years: $1,000 addl.

[1] If spouse has no income, or if husband and wife file a joint return.

WEST VIRGINIA

For individuals and heads of households:
On 1st $2,000: 2.1%
On 2nd $2,000: 2.3%
On 3rd $2,000: 2.8%
On 4th $2,000: 3.2%
On 5th $2,000: 3.5%
On 6th $2,000: 4.0%
On 7th $2,000: 4.6%
On 8th $2,000: 4.9%
On 9th $2,000: 5.3%
On 10th $2,000: 5.4%
On 11th $2,000: 6.0%
On next $4,000: 6.1%
On next $6,000: 6.5%
On next $6,000: 6.8%

For each exemption allowed on Federal income tax: $600

On next $6,000: 7.2%
On next $6,000: 7.5%
On next $10,000: 7.9%
On next $10,000: 8.2%
On next $10,000: 8.6%
On next $10,000: 8.8%
On next $10,000: 9.1%
On next $50,000: 9.3%
On next $50,000: 9.5%
On balance: 9.6%

For joint return or surviving spouse:

On 1st $4,000: 2.1%
On 2nd $4,000: 2.3%
On 3rd $4,000: 2.8%
On 4th $4,000: 3.2%
On 5th $4,000: 3.5%
On 6th $4,000: 4.0%
On 7th $4,000: 4.6%
On 8th $4,000: 4.9%
On 9th $4,000: 5.3%
On 10th $4,000: 5.4%
On 11th $4,000: 6.0%
On next $8,000: 6.1%

On next $12,000: 6.5%
On next $12,000: 6.8%
On next $12,000: 7.2%
On next $12,000: 7.5%
On next $20,000: 7.9%
On next $20,000: 8.2%
On next $20,000: 8.6%
On next $20,000: 8.8%
On next $20,000: 9.1%
On next $100,000: 9.3%
On next $100,000: 9.5%
On balance: 9.6%

Rates	Exemptions	Rates	Exemptions
WISCONSIN		On 9th $1,000: 8.2%	Taxpayer and spouse,
On 1st $1,000: 3.1%	Single: $20 reduction in tax	On 10th $1,000: 8.8%	65 and over: $25 reduction in tax each
On 2nd $1,000: 3.4%		On 11th $1,000: 9.3%	
On 3rd $1,000: 3.6%	Married: $40 reduction in tax	On 12th $1,000: 9.9%	
On 4th $1,000: 4.8%		On 13th $1,000: 10.5%	
On 5th $1,000: 5.4%	Head of a family:[1] $20 reduction in tax	On 14th $1,000: 11.1%	
On 6th $1,000: 5.9%		On balance: 11.4%	
On 7th $1,000: 6.5%	Each dependent: $20 reduction in tax		
On 8th $1,000: 7.6%			

State General Sales and Use Taxes[1]

Source: Tax Foundation, Inc.

State	% Rate	State	% Rate	State	% Rate
Alabama	4	Kentucky	5	Ohio	4
Arizona	4	Louisiana	3	Oklahoma	2
Arkansas	3	Maine	5	Pennsylvania	6
California	4.75	Maryland	4	Rhode Island	6
Colorado	3	Massachusetts	5	South Carolina	4
Connecticut	7	Michigan	4	South Dakota	4
D.C.	5	Minnesota	4	Tennessee[2]	4.5
Florida	4	Mississippi	5	Texas	4
Georgia[1]	3	Missouri	3	Utah	4
Hawaii	4	Nebraska	2.5	Vermont	3
Idaho	3	Nevada	3	Virginia	4
Illinois	4	New Jersey	5	Washington[3]	4.6
Indiana	4	New Mexico	4	West Virginia	3
Iowa	3	New York	4	Wisconsin	4
Kansas	3	North Carolina	3	Wyoming	3
		North Dakota	4		

[1]Local and county taxes, if any, are additional. [2]3% effective July 1, 1977. [3]4.5% effective July 1, 1977. NOTE: Alaska, Delaware, Montana, New Hampshire and Oregon have no statewide sales and use taxes.

Sales Tax Rates in Selected Cities[1]

Source: Tax Foundation, Inc.

City	% Rate	City	% Rate	City	% Rate
Amarillo, Tex.	1	Ithaca, N.Y.[2]	3	Richmond, Va.	1
Anaheim, Calif.[2]	1.25	Jefferson City, Mo.	1	Roanoke, Va.	1
Austin, Tex.	1	Lincoln, Neb.	1	Sacramento, Calif.[2]	1.25
Baton Rouge, La.[3]	3	Los Angeles, Calif.[2]	1.25	St. Louis, Mo.	1
Berkeley, Calif.[2 4]	1.75	Lynchburg, Va.	1	San Antonio, Tex.	1
Birmingham, Ala.	1	Mobile, Ala.	2	San Diego, Calif.[2]	1.25
Boulder, Colo.	2	Montgomery, Ala.	2	San Francisco, Calif.[2 4]	1.75
Chicago, Ill.[2]	2	New Orleans, La.[3]	3	Seattle, Wash.[2]	0.925
Dallas, Tex.	1	New York, N.Y.	4	Shreveport, La.[3]	2
Denver, Colo.	3	Nome, Alaska	3	Spokane, Wash.[2]	0.925
Duluth, Minn.	1	Norfolk, Va.	1	Springfield, Ill.[2]	2
El Paso, Tex.	1	Oakland, Calif.[2 4]	1.75	Topeka, Kan.	0.5
Fort Worth, Tex.	1	Oklahoma City, Okla.	1	Troy, N.Y.[2]	3.5
Fresno, Calif.[2]	1.25	Omaha, Neb.	1	Tucson, Ariz.	2
Glendale, Calif.[2]	1.25	Pasadena, Calif.[2]	1.25	Tulsa, Okla.	2
Houston, Tex.	1	Phoenix, Ariz.	1	Washington, D.C.	5
Huntsville, Ala.	2	Rapid City, S.D.	1.5	Yonkers, N.Y.[2]	4

[1]Excludes state and county sales taxes unless otherwise indicated. [2]Combined city and county rate. [3]Includes Parish School Board tax. [4]Includes 0.5% imposed by San Francisco Bay Area Rapid Transit District.

City Income Taxes

(Population exceeding 50,000)

Source: Tax Foundation, Inc.

City	Rate %	Year begun	City	Rate %	Year begun
Akron, Ohio	1.5	1962	Kettering, Ohio	1	1968
Allentown, Pa.	1	1958	Lakewood, Ohio	1	1968
Altoona, Pa.	1	1948	Lancaster, Pa.	0.5	1959
Baltimore, Md.	(¹)	1966	Lansing, Mich.	1	1968
Bethlehem, Pa.	1	1957	Lexington, Ky.	2	1952
Birmingham, Ala.	1	1970	Lima, Ohio	1	1959
Canton, Ohio	1.5	1954	Lorain, Ohio	1	1967
Chester, Pa.	1	1956	Louisville, Ky.	2	1948
Cincinnati, Ohio	2	1954	Mansfield, Ohio	1	1966
Cleveland, Ohio	1	1967	New York, N. Y.	0.9-4.3	1966
Cleveland Heights, Ohio	1	1968	Owensboro, Ky.	1	1960
Columbus, Ohio	1.5	1947	Parma, Ohio	1	1967
Covington, Ky.	2.5	1956	Philadelphia, Pa.	3.3125	1939
Dayton, Ohio	1.75	1949	Pontiac, Mich.	1	1968
Detroit, Mich.	2	1965	Reading, Pa.	1	1969
District of Columbia	2-10	1947	Saginaw, Mich.	1	1965
Elyria, Ohio	1	1969	St. Louis, Mo.	1	1948
Erie, Pa.	1	1948	Scranton, Pa.	2	1948
Euclid, Ohio	1	1967	Springfield, Ohio	2	1948
Flint, Mich.	1	1965	Toledo, Ohio	1.5	1946
Gadsden, Ala.	2	1956	Warren, Ohio	1	1952
Grand Rapids, Mich.	1	1967	Wilkes-Barre, Pa.	1	1966
Hamilton, Ohio	1.5	1960	Wilmington, Del.	1.25	1970
Harrisburg, Pa.	1	1966	York, Pa.	1	1965
Kansas City, Mo.	1	1964	Youngstown, Ohio	1.5	1948

¹ Tax is 50% of state income tax. NOTE: Rates are for residents only, except in Kentucky, Ohio, and Pennsylvania cities, where non-resident rate is the same.

Major U.S. Symphony Orchestras and Their Conductors

Source: American Symphony Orchestra League.

Atlanta Symphony: Robert Shaw.

Baltimore Symphony: Sergiu Comissiona.

Boston Symphony: Seiji Ozawa.

Buffalo Philharmonic: Michael Tilson Thomas.

Chicago Symphony: Georg Solti.

Cincinnati Symphony: Thomas Schippers.

Cleveland Orchestra: Lorin Maazel.

Dallas Symphony: Louis Lane.

Denver Symphony: Brian Priestman.

Detroit Symphony: Aldo Ceccato.

Honolulu Symphony: Robert LaMarchina.

Houston Symphony: Lawrence Foster.

Indianapolis Symphony: Oleg Kovalenko.

Kansas City Philharmonic: Maurice Peress.

Los Angeles Philharmonic: Zubin Mehta.

Milwaukee Symphony: Kenneth Schermerhorn.

Minnesota Orchestra: Stanislaw Skrowaczewski.

National Symphony (Washington, D.C.): Antal Dorati.

New Jersey Symphony: Max Rudolf.

New Orleans Philharmonic Symphony: Werner Torkanowsky.

New York Philharmonic: Pierre Boulez.[1]

North Carolina Symphony: John Gosling.

Philadelphia Orchestra: Eugene Ormandy.

Pittsburgh Symphony: André Previn.

Rochester Philharmonic: David Zinman.

St. Louis Symphony: George Semkow.

San Antonio Symphony: Victor Alessandro.

San Francisco Symphony: Seiji Ozawa.[2]

Seattle Symphony: Rainer Miedel.

Syracuse Symphony: Christopher Keene.

Utah Symphony: Maurice Abravanel.

[1] Leaving at end of 1976–77 season. Zubin Mehta to become conductor starting with 1978–79 season. [2] To be succeeded by Edo de Waart starting with 1977–78 season.

THE UNITED STATES

STATES, TERRITORIES, AND CITIES

State flower, bird, etc., are official unless otherwise indicated; dates in parentheses are those of adoption. Largest cities include incorporated places only. Land areas for 1970 are revised figures. For secession and readmission dates of the former Confederate states, see Index. For list of Governors and Senators, including those elected in November 1976, see Index.

ALABAMA

Capital: Montgomery.
Governor: George C. Wallace, Dem. (to Jan. 1979).
Lieut. Governor: Jere Beasley (to Jan. 1979).
Secy. of State: Agnes Baggett (to Jan. 1979).
Controller: Fred E. Zeigler.
Atty. General: William J. Baxley (to Jan. 1979).
Organized as territory: Mar. 3, 1817.
Entered Union & (rank): Dec. 14, 1819 (22).
Present constitution adopted: 1901.
Motto: *Audemus jura nostra defendere* (We dare defend our rights).
State flower: Camellia (1959).
State bird: Yellowhammer (1927).
State song: "Alabama" (1931).
State tree: Southern pine (longleaf) (1949).
Nickname: Yellowhammer State.
Origin of name: May come from Choctaw meaning "thicket-clearers" or "vegetation-gatherers."
1970 population & (rank): 3,444,165 (21).
1975 est. population & (rank): 3,614,000 (21).
1970 land area & (rank): 50,708 sq mi. (131,334 sq km) (28).
Geographic center: In Chilton Co., 12 mi. SW of Clanton.
Number of counties: 67.
Largest cities (1973 est.): Birmingham (295,686); Mobile (188,531); Montgomery (153,013); Huntsville (137,750); (1970 census): Tuscaloosa (65,773).
State forests: 8 (14,248.58 ac.).
State parks: 39 (41,959.35 ac.).
Total tax receipts (1973–74): $1,031,368,531.
Total net receipts (1973–74): $2,306,186,392.
Total net disbursements (1973–74): $1,870,575,348.

Alabama is the leading heavy-industry state in the South. Textiles, iron, and steel lead its manufacturing, which centers around the "Pittsburgh of the South"—Birmingham. Industry is growing rapidly in other areas, including the Tennessee River Valley, with its great Muscle Shoals power plant. Manufactures include cement, feeds, fertilizer, chemicals, rubber, and aluminum products. The state ranks high in the output of poultry, cotton, cattle, hogs, corn, potatoes, peanuts, and fruit.

At Tuskegee Institute, founded by Booker T. Washington, Dr. George Washington Carver carried out his famed agricultural research. Redstone Arsenal at Huntsville is a major space research center.

The Confederacy was founded at Montgomery in February 1861, and for a time the city was the Confederate capital.

ALASKA

Capital: Juneau.
Governor: Jay S. Hammond, Rep. (to Dec. 1978).
Lieut. Governor: Lowell Thomas, Jr. (to Dec. 1978).
Commissioner of Administration: Andrew S. Warwick.
Atty. General: Avrum M. Gross (apptd. by Governor).
Organized as territory: 1912.
Entered Union & (rank): Jan. 3, 1959 (49).
Constitution ratified: April 24, 1956.
Motto: North to the Future.
State flower: Forget-me-not.
State tree: Sitka spruce.
State bird: Willow ptarmigan.
State fish: King salmon.
State song: "Alaska's Flag."
Nickname: The state is commonly called "The Last Frontier" or "Land of the Midnight Sun."
Origin of name: Corruption of Aleut word meaning "great land" or "that which the sea breaks against."
1970 population & (rank): 302,173 (50).
1975 est. population & (rank): 352,000 (50).
1970 land area & (rank): 566,432 sq mi. (1,467,059 sq km) (1).
Geographic center: 60 mi. NW of Mt. McKinley.
Number of boroughs: 12.
Largest cities (1970): Anchorage (48,029); Fairbanks (14,771); Ketchikan (6,994); Juneau (6,050); Kenai (3,533).
State forests: None.
State parks: 4; 59 waysides and areas (1.5 million ac.).
General funds (1975–76 est.): $576,000,000.
General Expenditure (1975–76 est.): $600,000,000.

Vitus Bering, a Dane working for the Russians, and Alexei Chirikov discovered the Alaskan mainland and the Aleutian Islands in 1741. The tremendous land mass of Alaska—equal to one fifth of the rest of the United States—was unexplored in 1867, when Secretary of State Seward arranged for its purchase from the Russians for $7,200,000. The transfer of the territory took place on Oct. 18, 1867. Despite a price of about two cents an acre, the purchase was widely ridiculed as "Seward's Folly." The first official census (1880) reported a total of 33,426 Alaskans, all but 430 being of aboriginal stock. The Gold Rush of 1898 resulted in a mass influx of more than 30,000 people. Since then, Alaska has returned billions of dollars' worth of products to the United States.

Petroleum, fisheries and timber are the state's largest revenue producers. Oil was discovered in 1957, and with the 1968 discovery of a large oil and gas reservoir near Prudhoe Bay on the Arctic Coast, Alaska leaped to second place among the states in crude oil reserves and third in natural gas reserves. The Prudhoe Bay reservoir, with an estimated recoverable 10 billion barrels of oil and 27 trillion cubic feet of gas, is twice as large as any oil field in North America.

During World War II, Japanese troops occupied Attu and Kiska islands in the Aleutians in June, 1942. This action spurred the development of the Alaska Highway from the United States to Alaska, thereby providing a land route for the development of the then territory. In May, 1943, U. S. troops invaded and retook Attu; Kiska was evacuated by the Japanese in August, 1943, after an intensive shelling and bombardment of the island by U. S. forces.

Alaska now serves as the eyes and ears of the nation's defense effort. The Alaskan DEW line and the BMEWS site are vital to the defense of the entire continent.

Since statehood, the volume of Alaska's foreign trade has grown more than fortyfold. Geographically the state is in a favored position for trading with the Pacific nations, and a large amount of the foreign trade is carried on with Japan.

ARIZONA

Capital: Phoenix.
Governor: Raul H. Castro, Dem. (to Jan. 1979).
Secy. of State: Wesley Bolin (to Jan. 1979).
Atty. General: Bruce Babbitt (to Jan. 1979).
State Treasurer: Bartlett S. Fleming (to Jan. 1979).
Organized as territory: Feb. 24, 1863.
Entered Union & (rank): Feb. 14, 1912 (48).
Present constitution adopted: 1911.
Motto: *Ditat Deus* (God enriches).
State flower: Flower of saguaro cactus (1931).
State bird: Cactus wren (1931).
State colors: Blue and old gold (1915).
State song: "Arizona," a march song (1919).
State tree: Paloverde (1957).
Nickname: Grand Canyon State.
Origin of name: From the Indian "Arizonac," meaning "little spring."
1970 population & (rank): 1,772,482 (33).
1975 est. population & (rank): 2,224,000 (32).
1970 land area & (rank): 113,417 sq mi. (293,750 sq km) (32).
Geographic center: In Yavapai Co., 55 mi. ESE of
Number of counties: 14.
Largest cities (1975 special census): Phoenix (669,005); Tucson (298,683); Mesa (100,763); Tempe (93,822); Scottsdale (78,065); Glendale (67,298).
State forests: None.
State parks: 10.
State revenue (1974): $1,339,553.
State expenditure (1974): $1,237,830.

Manufacturing now ranks first among Arizona's revenue-producing industries. Next in rank is the mining of copper, gold, vanadium, uranium, and silver. Arizona produces over half the country's total output of copper.

Agriculture is the third-largest industry and tourism is the fourth-largest. By means of irrigation, once arid acres produce alfalfa, cotton, wheat, sorghum, vegetables, citrus fruits, and dates. Income from livestock ranks high from both range and feeder cattle.

Phoenix and Tucson, health and winter resorts, are becoming electronic centers; Phoenix also ships cotton and vegetables; Douglas loads cattle and smelts copper; Yuma is an agricultural center.

With the Navajo, Papago, Hopi, and Apache tribes, Arizona has the largest U. S. Indian population, spread over seventeen reservations. It also has some of the country's most famous scenery. In the north is the Grand Canyon; in the east are the Petrified Forest and Painted Desert.

Marcos de Niza, a Franciscan friar, entered the area in 1539 in search of the mythical Seven Cities of Cibola, and was followed a year later by Coronado.

ARKANSAS

Capital: Little Rock.
Governor: David Pryor, Dem. (to Jan. 1977).
Lieut. Governor: Joe Purcell (to Jan. 1977).
Secy. of State: George O. Jernigan, Jr. (to Jan. 1977).
Atty. General: Jim Guy Tucker (to Jan. 1977).
Auditor of State: Jimmie "Red" Jones (to Jan. 1977).
Treasurer of State: Mrs. Nancy Hall (to Jan. 1977).
Land Commissioner: Sam Jones (to Jan. 1977).
Organized as territory: Mar. 2, 1819.
Entered Union & (rank): June 15, 1836 (25).
Present constitution adopted: 1874.
Motto: *Regnat populus* (The people rule).
State flower: Apple Blossom (1901).
State tree: Pine (1939).
State bird: Mockingbird (1929).
State insect: Honey bee.
State song: "Arkansas" (1963).
Nickname: Land of Opportunity.
Origin of name: From the Quapaw Indians.
1970 population & (rank): 1,923,295 (32).
1975 est. population & (rank): 2,116,000 (33).
1970 land area & (rank): 51,945 sq mi. (134,538 sq km) (27).
Geographic center: In Pulaski Co., 12 mi. NW of Little Rock.
Number of counties: 75.
Largest cities (1973 est.): Little Rock (142,065); **(1970 census):** Fort Smith (62,802); North Little Rock (60,040); Pine Bluff (57,389); Hot Springs (35,631).
State forests: None.
State parks: 30.
State tax receipts (1975): $671,736,615.
Taxes from all sources (1975): $1,302,824,816.
State general expenditure (1975): $1,287,304,774.

Arkansas produces 97% of the nation's high-grade domestic bauxite—the source of aluminum. It also has the only active diamond mine, located near Murfreesboro in Pike County. The mine is a tourist attraction and was purchased as a State Park.

The state is almost equally divided between mountains and delta areas and has more year-round fishable lakes and streams than any other state. There are three large national forests in the Ouachita, Ozark and St. Francis mountain ranges. Hot Springs entertains fifteen times its population in guests each year. Its 47 curative springs flow water at an average of 143°F the year round.

Arkansas is a leader in the production of cotton, rice and soybeans, and also produces large quantities of corn, wheat and other grains, fruit, vegetables, broilers, turkeys, and livestock. Lumber provides 51% of the state's industrial employment, and several of the country's largest wood and wood products processing plants are in Arkansas. The largest archery manufacturing plant in the nation is in Pine Bluff. The state also produces oil and natural gas.

CALIFORNIA

Capital: Sacramento.
Governor: Edmund G. Brown, Jr., Dem. (to Jan. 1979).
Lieut. Governor: Mervin M. Dymally (to Jan. 1979).
Secy. of State: March Fong Eu (to Jan. 1979).
Controller: Ken Cory (to Jan. 1979).
Atty. General: Evelle J. Younger (to Jan. 1979).
Treasurer: Jesse M. Unruh (to Jan. 1979).
Entered Union & (rank): Sept. 9, 1850 (31).
Present constitution adopted: 1879.
Motto: *Eureka* (I have found it).
State flower: Golden poppy (1903).
State tree: California redwoods *(Sequoia sempervirens & Sequoia gigantea)* (1937 & 1953).
State bird: California valley quail (1931).
State animal: California grizzly bear (1953).
State fish: California golden trout (1947).
State insect: California dog-face butterfly (unofficial).
State colors: Blue and gold (1951).
State song: "I Love You, California" (1951).
Nickname: Golden State.
Origin of name: From a book, *Las Sergas de Esplandián*, by García Ordóñez de Montalvo, c. 1500.
1970 population & (rank): 19,953,134 (1).
1975 est. population & (rank): 21,185,000 (1).
1970 land area & (rank): 156,361 sq mi. (404,975 sq km) (3).
Geographic center: In Madera Co., 35 mi. NE of Madera.
Number of counties: 58.
Largest cities (1973 est): Los Angeles (2,746,854); San Diego (757,148); San Francisco (687,450); San Jose (523,116); Long Beach (346,793).
State forests: 8 (70,283 ac.).
State parks and beaches: 180 (723,000 ac.).
State general revenue (1974–75): $8,408,870,000.
State general expenditure (1974–75): $8,263,598,000.

California earns more money from raising food and catching fish than any other state, and it stands high in oil production, lumbering, and manufacturing. It has more motor vehicles than any other state. Out-of-state tourist visitors and the travel and recreation expenditures of the state's residents continue to play an important part in the expansion of trade and employment opportunities. Irrigation makes possible the production of more than 200 commercial crops.

Nature is spectacular. Death Valley, in the southeast, is 282 feet below sea level, the lowest spot in the nation; Lassen Peak is the only active U. S. volcano outside of Alaska and Hawaii, although its last eruptions were recorded in the years from 1914 to 1917; the General Sherman Tree in Sequoia National Park is estimated to be about 3,500 years old; and a stand of bristlecone pine trees in the White Mountains is estimated to be over 4,000 years old. San Pedro is the world's largest man-made harbor, and the Bank of America National Trust and Savings Association, founded by the Giannini family, is the largest privately owned bank in the United States and ranks usually first or second in the world.

Gold, which was responsible for the state's settlement boom, is still found here, but the state's most important mineral products today are oil, natural gas and its liquids, cement, miscellaneous stones, borates, and mercury.

California is a leader in electrical energy, and its cities specialize in aircraft and parts, missiles, food processing, electrical and electronic equipment, machinery and fabricated metal products.

The San Francisco-Oakland and Golden Gate bridges are among the world's engineering marvels.

COLORADO

Capital: Denver.
Governor: Richard D. Lamm, Dem. (to Jan. 1979).
Lieut. Governor: George Brown (to Jan. 1979).
Secy. of State: Mary Estill Buchanan (to Jan. 1979).
Treasurer: Sam Brown.
Controller: Dan S. Whittemore.
Atty. General: J. D. MacFarlane (to Jan. 1979).
Organized as territory: Feb. 28, 1861.
Entered Union & (rank): Aug. 1, 1876 (38).
Present constitution adopted: 1876.
Motto: *Nil sine Numine* (Nothing without Providence).
State flower: Rocky Mountain columbine (1899).
State tree: Colorado blue spruce (1939).
State bird: Lark bunting (1931).
State animal: Rocky Mountain bighorn sheep.
State colors: Blue and white (1911).
State gemstone: Aquamarine (1971).
State song: "Where the Columbines Grow" (1915).
Nickname: Centennial State.
Origin of name: From the Spanish, meaning "ruddy" or "red."
1970 population & (rank): 2,207,259 (30).
1975 est. population & (rank): 2,534,000 (28).
1970 land area & (rank): 103,766 sq mi. (268,754 sq km) (8).
Geographic center: In Park Co., 30 mi. NW of Pikes Peak.
Number of counties: 63.
Largest cities (1973 est.): Denver (515,593); Colorado Springs (175,745); Lakewood (106,476); Pueblo (103,163); **(1970 census):** Aurora (74,974).
State forests: 1 (71,000 ac.).
Total State revenue (1975–76): $1,760,600,000.
Total state expenditure (1975–76): $1,782,930,000.

Colorado has the highest mean elevation of any state, with 54 of its peaks over 14,000 feet in height and more than 1,000 going beyond the 10,000-foot mark. It began as a miner of gold and silver. Manufacturing is more prominent now than agriculture. Wheat, hay, beans, sugar beets, corn, potatoes, barley, and truck vegetables head the crop list. Livestock raising is an important industry.

The state has a highly developed irrigation system to counteract its dry climate and promote farming.

Colorado is one of the nation's largest producers of molybdenum, uranium, and vanadium; also mined are gold, silver, lead, zinc, copper, coal, and several nonmetallics. The state is also a leading oil producer.

Denver has become a leader in electronics and space-age industry. Pueblo, the "Pittsburgh of the West," makes iron, steel, brick, tile, and foundry products. Colorado Springs, with the nearby U. S. Air Force Academy, is perhaps the most popular tourist center in the Rocky Mountain sector. Aspen and Vail are now major skiing resorts.

Mount Evans Highway is the highest continuous auto road in North America. The world's highest suspension bridge stretches 1,053 feet over the Royal Gorge of the Arkansas River.

Of archeological interest are the cliff dwellings in the southwestern part of the state.

CONNECTICUT

Capital: Hartford.
Governor: Ella T. Grasso, Dem. (to Jan. 1979).
Lieut. Governor: Robert K. Killian (to Jan. 1979).
Secy. of State: Gloria Schaffer (to Jan. 1979).
Comptroller: J. Edward Caldwell (to Jan. 1979).
Treasurer: Henry E. Parker (to Jan. 1979).
Atty. General: Carl R. Ajello, Jr. (to Jan. 1979).
Entered Union & (rank): Jan. 9, 1788 (5).
Present constitution adopted: Dec. 30, 1965.
Motto: *Qui transtulit sustinet* (He who transplanted still sustains).
State flower: Mountain laurel (1907).
State tree: White Oak (1947).
State animal: Sperm whale (1975).
State bird: American robin (1943).
State song: None.
Official designation: Constitution State (1959).
Nickname: Nutmeg State.
Origin of name: From an Indian word (Quinnehtukqut) meaning "beside the long tidal river."
1970 population & (rank): 3,032,217 (24)
1975 est. population & (rank): 3,095,000 (24).
1970 land area & (rank): 4,862 sq mi. (12,593 sq km) (48).
Geographic center: In Hartford Co., at East Berlin.
Number of counties: 8.
Largest cities (1973 est.): Hartford (148,526); Bridgeport (148,337); New Haven (131,262); Waterbury (110,698); Stamford (104,651).
State forests: 29 (134,028 ac.).
State parks: 86 (30,868 ac.).
State and local general revenue (1973-74): $3,054,800,000.
State and local general expenditure (1973-74): $2,947,600,000.

Connecticut earned its sobriquet, the "Arsenal of the Nation," by its ability to turn out firearms and ammunition in early days, and from this developed an ability to turn out precision instruments of all classes.

Connecticut's factories produce arms, sewing machines, aircraft engines, helicopters, counting devices, motors, hardware, cutlery, tools, clocks, locks, machinery, brass products, ball bearings, silverware, and submarines. Hartford, which has the oldest U. S. newspaper still being published—the *Courant,* established 1764—is the insurance capital of the nation.

Connecticut devotes its farmland mainly to dairying, fruit growing, and poultry raising. It stands high in tobacco growing and no crop in the nation receives as high a price per acre as her shade-grown tobacco.

The state is a popular resort area both for its beaches on Long Island Sound and for its inland lakes and forested hills. The southwest part of the state is a suburban area of New York City.

Connecticut was the first state to have a written constitution, the *Fundamental Orders,* adopted by three original towns of Colonial days in January, 1639.

DELAWARE

Capital: Dover.
Governor: Sherman W. Tribbitt, Dem. (to Jan. 1977).
Lieut. Governor: Eugene D. Bookhammer (to Jan. 1977).
Secy. of State: Robert H. Reed (to Jan. 1977).
State Treasurer: Mary D. Jornlin (to Jan. 1977).
Atty. General: Richard R. Wier, Jr. (to Jan. 1977).
Entered Union & (rank): Dec. 7, 1787 (1).
Present constitution adopted: 1897.
Motto: Liberty and independence.

State colors: Colonial blue and buff.
State flower: Peach blossom.
State tree: American holly.
State bird: Blue Hen chicken.
State song: "Our Delaware."
Nicknames: Diamond State; First State.
Origin of name: From Delaware River and Bay; named in turn for Sir Thomas West, Lord De La Warr.
1970 population & (rank): 548,104 (46).
1975 est. population & (rank): 579,000 (47).
1970 land area & (rank): 1,982 sq mi. (5,133 sq km) (49).
Geographic center: In Kent Co., 11 mi. S of Dover.
Number of counties: 3.
Largest cities (1970): Wilmington (80,386); Newark (20,757); Dover (17,488); Elsmere (8,415); Seaford (5,537).
State forests: 2 (6,200 ac.).
State parks: 9.
State total receipts (1975): $386,045,689.
State total disbursements (1975): $391,306,641.

Little Delaware, at the lowest mean elevation of any state, grows a great variety of fruits and vegetables and is a U. S. pioneer in the industry of food canning. Corn, soybeans, potatoes and hay are leading crops. Fishing is an important industry. Delaware's broiler farms are one of the great supply sources for the big markets of the East.

Manufactures in Delaware include chemicals, vulcanized fiber, glazed kid and morocco leathers, textiles, paper, dental supplies, metal products, machinery, machine tools, and automobiles. In 1844, the *Bangor,* the first iron sea-going propellor-type vessel constructed in the United States was launched at Wilmington.

Delaware was the first state to ratify the U. S. Constitution, on Dec. 7, 1787. During the Civil War, although a slave state, Delaware refused to secede from the Union. It is said to have supplied more men, per capita, to the Union army than any other state.

Henry Hudson discovered Delaware Bay in his exploration of 1609. First settlers in the state were Dutchmen, who arrived in 1631, but who were shortly afterward massacred by the Indians. Permanent settlement was made by Swedes in 1638.

DISTRICT OF COLUMBIA

(See listing at end of *50 Largest Cities of the United States,* page 660.)

FLORIDA

Capital: Tallahassee.
Governor: Reubin Askew, Dem. (to Jan. 1978).
Lieut. Governor: J. H. Williams (to Jan. 1978).
Secy. of State: Bruce Smathers (to Jan. 1978).
Comptroller: Gerald Lewis (to Jan. 1978).
Commissioner of Agriculture: Doyle Conner.
Atty. General: Robert L. Shevin (to Jan. 1978).
Organized as territory: Mar. 30, 1822.
Entered Union & (rank): Mar. 3, 1845 (27).
Present constitution adopted: 1969.
Motto: In God we trust (1868).
State flower: Orange blossom (1909).
State bird: Mockingbird (1927).
State song: "Suwannee River" (1935).
Nickname: Sunshine State (1970).
Origin of name: From the Spanish, meaning "feast of flowers" (Easter).

1970 population & (rank): 6,789,443 (9).
1975 est. population & (rank): 8,357,000 (8).
1970 land area & (rank): 54,090 sq mi. (140,093 sq km) (26).
Geographic center: In Hernando Co., 12 mi. NNW of Brooksville.
Number of counties: 67.
Largest cities (1973 est.): Jacksonville (548,007); Miami (353,984); Tampa (275,643); St. Petersburg (234,284); Fort Lauderdale (155,605).
State forests: 4 (306,881 ac.).
State parks: 77 (187,763 ac.).
State tax receipts (1974–75): $2,921,059,451.
Other state revenue (1974–75): $6,068,468,572.
State expenditures (1974–75): $9,210,118,756.

Florida's economy rests on a solid tripod of tourism, manufacturing, and agriculture. The state entertained more than 25 million visitors, who spent more than $5 billion, in 1973. There are now more visitors to Florida in the summer than in the winter.

Oranges and grapefruit lead Florida's crop list. Next are sugarcane, tomatoes, tobacco, beans, celery, potatoes, field corn, honey, watermelons, limes and mangoes. Forestry, truck gardening, commercial fishing, and cattle are leading industries. Deep-sea fishing for sport is a leading tourist industry.

Florida is expanding in all areas of industry, with the greatest development taking place in the research-oriented manufacturing of the Space Age. The state produces 80% of the nation's phosphate.

Florida's low elevation is dotted by some 30,000 small lakes and the Everglades National Park in the south. St. Augustine, founded in 1565, is the oldest town of European origin in the United States. Key West, island resort city, is connected to the mainland by the Overseas Highway.

In 1513, Ponce de León, seeking the mythical "Fountain of Youth," was possibly the first white man to see the state.

GEORGIA

Capital: Atlanta.
Governor: George Busbee, Dem. (to Jan. 1979).
Lieut. Governor: Zell Miller (to Jan. 1979).
Secy. of State: Ben Forston (to Jan. 1979).
Comptroller General: Johnnie Caldwell (to Jan. 1979).
Atty. General: Arthur K. Bolton (to Jan. 1979).
Entered Union & (rank): Jan. 2, 1788 (4).
Present constitution adopted: 1945.
Motto: Wisdom, justice and moderation.
State flower: Cherokee rose (1916).
State tree: Live oak (1937).
State bird: Brown thrasher (1935).
State song: "Georgia" (1922).
Nicknames: Peach State; Empire State of the South.
Origin of name: In honor of George II of England.
1970 population & (rank): 4,589,575 (15).
1975 est. population & (rank): 4,926,000 (14).
1970 land area & (rank): 58,073 sq mi. (150,409 sq km) (21).
Geographic center: In Twiggs Co., 18 mi. SE of Macon.
Number of counties: 159.
Largest cities (1973 est.): Atlanta (451,123); Columbus (161,209); Macon (121,714); Savannah (105,768); **(1970 census):** Albany (72,623).
State forests: 25,258,000 ac. (67% of total state area).
State parks: 53 (42,600 ac.).
State revenue receipts (1975): $1,690,551,114.
State revenue distribution (1975): $1,690,551,114.

Georgia is typical of the changing South. The value of its factory products has passed the value of its farm products, and industrialization is ever increasing. Atlanta, communications and transportation center for the Southeast, is also the area's chief distributor of goods. The state leads the nation in the production of paper and board, tufted textile products and processed chicken. Other major manufactured products are transportation equipment, food products, apparel and chemicals.

Important agricultural products are corn, peanuts, cotton, soybeans, tobacco, eggs and pimento peppers. From its vast stands of pine come more than half the world's resins and turpentine and 74.4% of the U.S. supply. Cattle grazing is extensive.

The state is a leader in the production of clay products. Its marble is world-renowned.

The "Little White House," used by Franklin D. Roosevelt at Warm Springs, and where he died Apr. 12, 1945, is a tourist attraction.

Hernando de Soto, a Spaniard, in 1540, looked over the red clay of Georgia, and General James Oglethorpe founded its first British colony Feb. 12, 1733, at Savannah.

HAWAII

Capital: Honolulu (on Oahu).
Governor: George R. Ariyoshi, Dem. (to Dec. 1978).
Lieut. Governor: Nelson K. Doi (to Dec. 1978).
Comptroller: Hideo Murakami (to Dec. 1978).
Atty. General: Ronald Y. Amemiya (to Dec. 1978).
Organized as territory: 1900.
Entered Union & (rank): Aug. 21, 1959 (50).
Motto: *Ua Mau Ke Ea O Ka Aina I Ka Pono* (The life of the land is perpetuated in righteousness).
State flower: Hibiscus.
State song: "Hawaii Ponoi."
State bird: Nene (Hawaiian goose).
Nickname: Aloha State.
Origin of name: Uncertain. The islands may have been named by Hawaii Loa, their traditional discoverer. Or they may have been named after Hawaii or Hawaiki, the traditional home of the Polynesians.
1970 population & (rank): 769,913 (40).
1975 est. population & (rank): 865,000 (40).
1970 land area & (rank): 6,425 sq mi. (16,641 sq km) (47).
Geographic center: In Hawaii Co., off Maui Island.
Number of counties: 4.
Largest cities (1970): Honolulu (324,871); Hilo (26,353).*
State parks and historic sites: 47.
Total state government revenues (1975): $1,032,196,371.
Total state government expenditures (1975): $1,071,-523,335.

Hawaii, 2,100 miles west-southwest of San Francisco, is a 1,600-mile chain of islets and eight main islands—Hawaii, Kahoolawe, Maui, Lanai, Molokai, Oahu, Kauai, and Niihau. Kure (Ocean) Island, an uninhabited islet in the Leeward Islands, is administratively part of Hawaii.

Hawaii's temperature is mild and the soil is fertile for tropical fruits and vegetables. Cane sugar and pineapple are its chief products, approximately 35% of the world's canned pineapple being produced in the islands. Hawaii also grows coffee, rice, bananas, nuts, and potatoes. The tourist business is one of Hawaii's largest sources of income.

Hawaii's highest peak is Mauna Kea (13,796 ft.). Mauna Loa (13,680 ft.) is the largest volcanic mountain in the world in cubic content.

* Honolulu and Hilo have legally established limits and are therefore treated as incorporated places. All other places are unincorporated.

Hawaii was discovered in 1778 by Captain James Cook, who named it the Sandwich Islands. It was ruled by native monarchs until 1893, thereafter as a republic until 1898, when it ceded itself to the United States.

IDAHO

Capital: Boise.
Governor: Cecil D. Andrus, Dem. (to Jan. 1979).
Lieut. Governor: John V. Evans (to Jan. 1979).
Secy. of State: Pete T. Cenarrusa (to Jan. 1979).
State Auditor: Joe R. Williams (to Jan. 1979).
Atty. General: Wayne Kidwell (to Jan. 1979).
Organized as territory: Mar. 3, 1863.
Entered Union & (rank): July 3, 1890 (43).
Present constitution adopted: 1890.
Motto: *Esto perpetua* (May you last forever).
State flower: Syringa (1931).
State tree: White pine (1935).
State bird: Mountain bluebird (1931).
State horse: Appaloosa.
State gem: Star garnet (1967).
State song: "Here We Have Idaho."
Nicknames: Gem State; Spud State; Panhandle State.
Origin of name: Means "Gem of the Mountains."
1970 population & (rank): 713,008 (42).
1975 est. population & (rank): 820,000 (41).
1970 land area & (rank): 82,677 sq mi. (214,133 sq km) (11).
Geographic center: In Custer Co., at Custer, SW of Challis.
Number of counties: 44, plus small part of Yellowstone National Park.
Largest cities (1970): Boise (74,990); Lewiston (26,068); Twin Falls (21,914); **(1975 special census):** Pocatello (42,565); Idaho Falls (37,126).
State forests: 981,200 ac.
State parks: 18 (21,838 ac.).
State revenue (1974–75): $977,643,437.
State expenditure (1974–75): $967,389,976.

Most of Idaho slopes to the west from high, central wilderness mountains and the continental divide peaks in the east.

Mining, lumbering, and irrigation farming have been important for years. Idaho produces more than one third of all the silver mined in the U. S. The state's most impressive growth began when World War II military needs made processing agricultural products a big industry. Crops include potatoes, wheat, apples, corn, barley, and hops. Manufacturing is steadily increasing.

With increase in winter sports, tourism now outranks mining in dollar revenue. Streams and lakes provide fishing, camping and boating sites. The nation's largest elk herds draw hunters from all over the world, and the famed Sun Valley resort attracts thousands of visitors each year to its swimming and skiing facilities.

ILLINOIS

Capital: Springfield.
Governor: Dan Walker. Dem. (to Jan. 1977).
Lieut. Governor: Neil Hartigan (to Jan. 1977).
Secy. of State: Michael Howlett (to Jan. 1977).
Comptroller: George W. Lindberg (to Jan. 1977).
Atty. General: William J. Scott (to Jan. 1977).
Treasurer: Alan J. Dixon (to Jan. 1979).
Organized as territory: Feb. 3, 1809.
Entered Union & (rank): Dec. 3, 1818 (21).

Present constitution adopted: 1970.
Motto: State sovereignty, national union.
State flower: Violet (1908).
State tree: White oak (1973).
State bird: Cardinal (1929).
State insect: Monarch butterfly.
State song: "Illinois" (1925).
State slogan: Land of Lincoln.
State mineral: Fluorite (1965).
Nickname: Prairie State.
Origin of name: From an Indian word and French suffix meaning "tribe of superior men."
1950 population & (rank): 8,712;176 (4).
1975 est. population & (rank): 11,145,000 (5).
1970 land area & (rank): 56,400 sq mi. (146,076 sq km) (24).
Geographic center: In St. Clair County near Mascoutah.
Number of counties: 102.
Largest cities (1973 est.): Chicago (3,172,929); Rockford (142,173); Peoria (127,898); **(1970 census):** Springfield (92,400); Decatur (91,000).
Public use areas: 187 (275,000 ac.), incl. state parks, memorials, forests and conservation areas.
State revenue (1975): $6,886,341.
State expenditure (1975): $7,290,304.

Illinois anchors the Midwest like a rich giant, versatile in every big wealth-making industry. It stands high in manufacturing, coal mining, farm cash income, oil production. The sprawling Chicago district (including a slice of Indiana) is a great iron and steel producer, meat packer, grain exchange, and railroad center. Chicago is also a busy long-flight airport city and Great Lakes port area.

In agriculture, Illinois is first in the nation in soybeans and the export of agricultural products, and second in hog production. It ranks high in corn, oats, wheat, barley, rye, truck vegetables, and nursery products. It is also an important dairying state.

Illinois manufactures almost everything. Railroad cars, clothing, furniture, tractors, liquor, watches, and farm implements are some of the items made in several of its cities. An important U. S. arsenal is located on a Mississippi island off Rock Island.

Central Illinois is noted for shrines and memorials associated with the life of Abraham Lincoln. In Springfield are the Lincoln Home, the Lincoln Tomb, and the restored Old State Capitol. About 25 miles northwest of Springfield is the restored Village of New Salem where Lincoln lived 1831–37.

INDIANA

Capital: Indianapolis.
Governor: Dr. Otis R. Bowen (to Jan. 1977).
Lieut. Governor: Robert D. Orr (to Jan. 1977).
Secy. of State: Larry A. Conrad (to Dec. 1978).
Treasurer: Jack L. New (to Feb. 1979).
Atty. General: Theodore L. Sendak (to Jan. 1977).
Organized as territory: May 7, 1800.
Entered Union & (rank): Dec. 11, 1816 (19).
Present constitution adopted: 1851.
Motto: The Crossroads of America.
State flower: Peony (1957).
State tree: Tulip tree (1931).
State bird: Cardinal (1933).
State song: "On the Banks of the Wabash, Far Away" (1913).
Nickname: Hoosier State.
Origin of name: Meaning "land of Indians."

1970 population & (rank): 5,193,669 (11).
1975 est. population & (rank): 5,311,000 (12).
1970 land area & (rank): 36,097 sq mi. (93,491 sq km) (38).
Geographic center: In Boone Co., 14 mi. NNW of Indianapolis.
Number of counties: 92.
Largest cities (1973 est.): Indianapolis (738,657); Fort Wayne (185,483); Gary (177,925); Evansville (136,165); South Bend (122,004).
State parks: 23 (54,425 ac.).
State memorials: 17 (922 ac.).
State general revenue (1973–74): $2,543,700,000.
State general expenditure (1973–74): $1,370,700,000.

Indiana's 41-mile Lake Michigan waterfront is one of the great industrial centers of the world, turning out iron and steel and oil products to make this state a leader in manufacturing. Its cities have some of the world's largest industrial plants and their great output is further swelled by the inland factories. The list of products includes automobile parts and accessories, mobile homes and recreational vehicles, truck and bus bodies, aircraft engines, farm machinery and fabricated structural steel. The state is a significant producer of phonograph records, wood office furniture and pharmaceuticals.

The state stands high in soybeans, corn, tobacco, onions, wheat, oats, rye, and tomatoes.

Wyandotte Cave, one of the largest in the United States, is located in Crawford County of Southern Indiana. West Baden and French Lick are well known for their mineral springs. Indiana was one of the early states to adopt the secret ballot based on the Australian system.

IOWA

Capital: Des Moines.
Governor: Robert D. Ray, Rep. (to Jan. 1979).
Lieut. Governor: Arthur A. Neu (to Jan. 1979).
Secy. of State: Melvin J. Synhorst (to Jan. 1979).
Treasurer: Maurice E. Baringer (to Jan. 1979).
Atty. General: Richard Turner (to Jan. 1979).
Organized as territory: June 12, 1838.
Entered Union & (rank): Dec. 28, 1846 (29).
Present constitution adopted: 1857.
Motto: Our liberties we prize and our rights we will maintain.
State flower: Wild rose (1897).
State bird: Eastern goldfinch (1933).
State colors: Red, white and blue (in state flag).
State song: "Song of Iowa."
Nickname: Hawkeye State.
Origin of name: Probably from an Indian word meaning "I-o-w-a, this is the place."
1970 population & (rank): 2,825,041 (25).
1975 est. population & (rank): 2,870,000 (25).
1970 land area & (rank): 55,941 sq mi. (144,887 sq km) (23).
Geographic center: In Story Co., 5 mi. NE of Ames.
Number of counties: 99.
Largest cities (1973 est.): Des Moines (199,145); **(1975 special census):** Cedar Rapids (108,987); Waterloo (73,064); Dubuque (61,728); **(1970 census):** Davenport (98,469); Sioux City (85,925).
State forests: 6 (23,500 ac.).
State parks: 95 (40,402 ac.).
Total receipts (fiscal 1974–75): $2,202,906,000.
Total expenditures (fiscal 1974–75): $1,977,383,000.

The value of Iowa's manufactured products is almost 2½ times that of its agricultural products. Major industries are food and kindred products, non-electrical machinery, electrical equipment, printing and publishing and fabricated metal products.

Iowa stands in a class by itself as an agricultural state. Its farms sell over $6.9 billion worth of crops and livestocks annually, of which $2.9 billion is from crops and $4 billion from livestock. Iowa leads the nation in all livestock and hog marketings, with about 22% of the pork supply and 13% of the grain-fed cattle.

The Hawkeye state's crop production in 1974 was $3.5 billion, of which $2 billion was from corn. The state ranks second in soybean production, with $1.4 billion.

West Branch is the birthplace of Herbert Hoover, who was the first U. S. President born west of the Mississippi.

KANSAS

Capital: Topeka.
Governor: Robert F. Bennett, Rep. (to Jan. 1979).
Lieut. Governor: Shelby Smith (to Jan. 1979).
Secy. of State: Elwill Shanahan (to Jan. 1977).
Treasurer: Joan Finney (to Jan. 1977).
Atty. General: Curt Schneider (to Jan. 1977).
Organized as territory: May 30, 1854.
Entered Union & (rank): Jan. 29, 1861 (34).
Present constitution adopted: 1859.
Motto: *Ad astra per aspera* (To the stars through difficulties).
State flower: Sunflower (1903).
State tree: Cottonwood (1937).
State bird: Western meadow lark (1937).
State animal: Buffalo (1955).
State song: "Home on the Range" (1947).
State march: "The Kansas March" (1935).
Nicknames: Sunflower State; Jayhawk State.
Origin of name: From a Siouan word meaning "people of the south wind."
1970 population & (rank): 2,249,071 (28).
1975 est. population & (rank): 2,267,000 (31).
1970 land area & (rank): 81,787 sq mi. (211,828 sq km) (13).
Geographic center: In Barton Co., 15 mi. NE of Great Bend.
Number of counties: 105.
Largest cities (1973 est.): Kansas City (172,994); Topeka (136,059); **(1970 census):** Overland Park (79,034); Lawrence (45,698).
State parks: 22 (14,394 ac.).
State operating revenue (1974–75): $1,234,503,000.
State operating expenditure (1974–75): $1,112,219,000.

Kansas finds its strength in wheat growing, flour milling, and a variety of manufacturing enterprises. Slaughtering and meat packing are also extensively pursued. In the western part of the state, where a replica of Dodge City's Front Street recalls the old West and the city's heyday as a famous cowtown, rich prairie land sprawls over a large area and gives an abundance of winter wheat and fine grazing.

Corn, sorghums, oats, barley, soy beans, and potatoes are other crops. Besides oil, Kansas mines zinc, coal, salt, and lead. Kansas is the nation's leading producer of helium.

Wichita is a leader in the production of military and civilian aircraft. Kansas City is an important transportation, milling, and meat-packing center.

Points of interest include: the Kansas State Historical Society Museum at Topeka; Eisenhower's boyhood home and the new Eisenhower Memorial Museum and Presidential Library at Abilene; John Brown's cabin at Osawatomie; recreated Front Street at Dodge City; Ft. Larned, once the most important military post on the Santa Fe Trail; and Ft. Leavenworth and Ft. Riley, both still active military posts.

KENTUCKY

Capital: Frankfort.
Governor: Julian M. Carroll, Dem. (to Dec. 1979).
Lieut. Governor: Thelma L. Stovall (to Jan. 1980).
Secy. of State: Drexell Davis (to Jan. 1980).
State Treasurer: Francis Jones Mills (to Jan. 1980).
State Auditor: George Atkins (to Jan. 1980).
Atty. General: Robert Stephens (to Jan. 1980).
Entered Union & (rank): June 1, 1792 (15).
Present constitution adopted: 1891.
Motto: United we stand, divided we fall.
State flower: Goldenrod.
State bird: Kentucky cardinal.
State song: "My Old Kentucky Home."
Nickname: Bluegrass State.
Origin of name: From an Iroquoian Indian word "Ken-tah-ten" meaning "land of tomorrow."
1970 population & (rank): 3,219,311 (23).
1975 est. population & (rank): 3,396,000 (23).
1970 land area & (rank): 39,650 sq mi. (102,694 sq km) (37).
Geographic center: In Marion Co., 3 mi. NNW of Lebanon.
Number of counties: 120.
Largest cities (1973 est.): Louisville (335,696); **(1970 census):** Lexington (108,137); Covington (52,535); Owensboro (50,329); Bowling Green (36,253).
State forests: 9 (44,173 ac.).
State parks: 43 (40,574 ac.).
Total state revenue (1974–75): $2,150,683,000.
Total state expenditure (1974–75): $2,116,562,000.

Kentucky prides itself on producing some of the nation's best tobacco, horses, and whisky. It stands high in the production of native asphalt, coal, corn, oil.

Among the manufactured items produced by its cities are furniture, aluminum ware, brooms, shoes, lumber products, machinery, textiles, and iron and steel products. Besides coal and oil, important minerals are natural gas and quarry products.

Louisville, the largest city, famed for the Kentucky Derby at Churchill Downs, has a large state university, distills whisky and is a great cigarette maker. The Bluegrass country is the home of some of the world's finest race horses. Lexington, standing in the center of this country, is a leading tobacco producer. Mammoth Cave, with its many miles of underground passages, is one tourist attraction. Another is Kentucky Lake, 184 miles long, one of the largest man-made bodies of water in the world.

Kentucky was credited with a star in the Confederate flag because a secessionist group in the southwest part of the state set up a short-lived government and joined the Confederacy. The legitimate government, however, remained in the Union throughout the Civil War.

Marquette and Joliet in 1673 saw Kentucky when it was the "Dark and Bloody Ground," fiercely contested by Indian tribes. Daniel Boone explored the country in 1767.

LOUISIANA

Capital: Baton Rouge.
Governor: Edwin W. Edwards, Dem. (to March 1980).
Lieut. Governor: James E. Fitzmorris, Jr. (to March 1980).
Secy. of State: Paul J. Hardy (to March 1980).
Comptroller: S. E. Vines, Jr. (to March 1980).
Atty. General: William J. Guste, Jr. (to March 1980).
Organized as territory: Mar. 26, 1804.
Entered Union & (rank): Apr. 30, 1812 (18).
Present constitution adopted: 1974.
Motto: Union, justice and confidence.
State flower: Magnolia (1900).
State bird: Pelican.
State song: "Give Me Louisiana."
Nicknames: Pelican State; Sportsman's Paradise; Creole State; Sugar State.
Origin of name: In honor of Louis XIV of France.
1970 population & (rank): 3,643,180 (20).
1975 est. population & (rank): 3,791,000 (20).
1970 land area & (rank): 44,930 sq mi. (116,369 sq km) (33).
Geographic center: In Avoyelles Parish, 3 mi. SE of Marksville.
Number of parishes (counties): 64.
Largest cities (1973 est.): New Orleans (573,479); Shreveport (184,030); **(1970 census):** Baton Rouge (165,921); Lake Charles (77,998); Lafayette (68,908).
State forests: 1 (8,000 ac.).
State parks: 31 (14,360 ac.).
State general revenue (1975–76): $2,207,275,654; Federal grants, $671,822,192.
State general expenditure (1975–76): $3,128,871,515.

Louisiana, which still calls its counties parishes after the Spanish religious divisions, is one of the leading states in fur trapping, with a rich annual bag of mink, muskrat, opossum, and raccoon pelts. Other important agricultural products are sugar cane, strawberries, sweet potatoes, rice, and cotton. The state is rapidly becoming industrialized, and is an important producer of petroleum and petrochemicals, pulp and paper, natural gas, sulfur, chemicals, and salt.

New Orleans, home of the Mardi Gras, avoids flooding only by an expensive levee and spillway system. Its industry is making increased use of raw materials from South and Central America. The Vieux Carré, in this Old World city, called by many the "Little Paris" of the New World, has some of the celebrated restaurants of the nation.

Louisiana has a great variety and abundance of game birds. Its state-owned wildlife sanctuaries are among the world's largest.

Hernando de Soto, in the year 1540, is usually considered the first white man to see the state, but claims are made for Narváez, who is reputed to have seen the state as early as 1528.

MAINE

Capital: Augusta.
Governor: James B. Longley, Ind. (to Jan. 1979).
Secy. of State: Markham L. Gartley (to Jan. 1979).
Controller: Richard A. Dieffenbach (term indefinite).
Atty. General: Joseph E. Brennan (to Jan. 1979).
Entered Union & (rank): Mar. 15, 1820 (23).
Present constitution adopted: 1820.
Motto: *Dirigo* (I direct).
State flower: White pine cone and tassel (1895).
State tree: White pine tree (1945).
State bird: Chickadee (1927).
State fish: Landlocked salmon (1969).

State mineral: Tourmaline (1971).
State song: "State of Maine Song" (1937).
Nickname: Pine Tree State.
Origin of name: First used to distinguish the *main*land from the offshore islands. It has been considered a compliment to Henrietta Maria, Queen of Charles I of England. She was said to have owned the province of Mayne in France.
1970 population & (rank): 993,663 (38).
1975 est. population & (rank): 1,059,000 (38).
1970 land area & (rank): 30,920 sq mi. (80,083 sq km) (39).
Geographic center: In Piscataquis Co., 18 mi. N of Dover-Foxcroft.
Number of counties: 16.
Largest cities (1970): Portland (65,116); Lewiston 41,779); Auburn (24,151); South Portland (23,267); **1975 special census:** Bangor (32,205).
State forests: 1 (21,000 ac.).
State parks: 26 (247,627 ac.).
State historic sites: 18 (403 ac.).
State general revenue (1975): $657,600,000.
State general expenditure (1975): $715,400,000.

Maine produces one out of every twelve potatoes raised in the United States, and 95% of the nation's low bush blueberries. The poultry industry has climbed from $300,000 after the last war to over $160 million today.

Maine is one of the world's largest pulp-paper producers. It ranks fifth in boot and shoe manufacturing. It has the largest forest area in the East, and planned cutting promises an unending wood supply for pulp-paper mills, lumber mills, and hardwood processing plants.

The state leads the world in the production of the familiar flat tins of sardines, producing 200 million of them normally. Lobstermen catch 80–90% of the nation's total of true lobsters.

The Appalachian range within the state is named the "Longfellow Mountains of Maine," in honor of Henry Wadsworth Longfellow, who was born in the state. Mt. Katahdin (5,267 ft.) is the highest peak.

MARYLAND

Capital: Annapolis.
Governor: Marvin Mandel, Dem. (to Jan. 1979).
Lieut. Governor: Blair Lee III.
Secy. of State: Fred L. Wineland (appointed by governor).
Comptroller of the Treasury: Louis L. Goldstein (to Jan. 1979).
Treasurer: William S. James (to Jan. 1979).
Atty. General: Francis B. Burch (to Dec. 1978).
Entered Union & (rank): Apr. 28, 1788 (7).
Present constitution adopted: 1867.
Motto: *Fatti maschii, parole femine* (Manly deeds, womanly words).
State flower: Black-eyed susan (1918).
State tree: White oak (1941).
State bird: Baltimore oriole (1882).
State dog: Chesapeake Bay retriever (1964).
State fish: Rockfish (1965).
State insect: Baltimore checkerspot butterfly (1973).
State sport: Jousting (1962).
State song: "Maryland! My Maryland!" (1939).
Nicknames: Free State; Old Line State.
Origin of name: In honor of Henrietta Maria (Queen of Charles I of England).
1970 population & (rank): 3,922,399 (18).
1975 est. population & (rank): 4,098,000 (18).
1970 land area & (rank): 9,891 sq mi. (25,618 sq km) (42).

Geographic center: In Prince Georges Co., 4½ mi. NW of Davidsonville.
Number of counties: 23, and 1 independent city.
Largest cities (1973 est.): Baltimore (877,838); **(1970 census):** Rockville (41,564); Hagerstown (35,862); Bowie (35,028); Cumberland (29,724).
State forests: 9 (118,362 ac.).
State parks: 34 (63,525 ac.).
State general revenue (1975): $9,942,059,114.
State general expenditure (1975): $9,935,660,361.

Maryland is cut almost in two by Chesapeake Bay, and the many estuaries and rivers create one of the longest water fronts of any state. The Bay produces more seafood—oysters, crabs, clams, fin fish—than any comparable body of water, and is a major crabbing center. Important agricultural products, in order of cash value, are broilers, dairy products, corn, cattle, tobacco and vegetables. Maryland is a leader in vegetable canning. Sand and gravel, lime and cement, stone, coal, and clay are the chief mineral products.

Manufactures, which center in Baltimore, include missiles, airplanes, steel, clothing, and chemicals. The port of Baltimore ranks second in the country in foreign trade tonnage. Baltimore is the home of The Johns Hopkins University and Hospital. In Annapolis, home of the U. S. Naval Academy, is one of the earliest state houses (1772–79) still in regular use by a State government.

The Charter of Maryland was granted in 1632 to Lord Baltimore, who died before it had passed the Great Seal; it was issued to his oldest son, Cecil. The first settlers landed at St. Mary's in 1634.

MASSACHUSETTS

Capital: Boston.
Governor: Michael S. Dukakis, Dem. (to Jan. 1979).
Lieut. Governor: Thomas P. O'Neill III (to Jan. 1979).
Secy. of the Commonwealth: Paul H. Guzzi (to Jan. 1979).
Atty. General: Francis X. Bellotti (to Jan. 1979).
Treasurer & Receiver-General: Robert Q. Crane (to Jan. 1979).
Auditor of the Commonwealth: Thaddeus Buczko (to Jan. 1979).
Entered Union & (rank): Feb. 6, 1788 (6).
Motto: *Ense petit placidam sub libertate quietem* (By the sword we seek peace, but peace only under liberty).
State flower: Mayflower (1918).
State tree: American elm (1941).
State bird: Chickadee (1941).
State colors: Blue and gold.
State song: "All Hail to Massachusetts" (1966).
State beverage: Cranberry juice (1970).
State horse: Morgan horse (1970).
State insect: Lady bug (1974).
Nicknames: Bay State; Old Colony State.
Origin of name: From two Indian words meaning "Great mountain place."
1970 population & (rank): 5,689,170 (10).
1975 est. population & (rank): 5,828,000 (10).
1970 land area & (rank): 7,826 sq mi. (20,269 sq km) (45).
Geographic center: In Worcester Co., in S part of city of Worcester.
Number of counties: 14.
Largest cities (1973 est.): Boston (618,275); Worcester (170,730); Springfield (160,358); **(1970 census):** New Bedford (101,777); Cambridge (100,361).

State forests and parks: 123 (232,000 ac.).*
State general revenue (1974-75): $3,958,814,919.
State general expenditure (1974-75): $4,214,257,589.

Although Massachusetts is noted historically as a leading shoe and textile state, these industries are now replaced in importance by activity in the electronics field. Logan International Airport in East Boston, with two runways of 10,000 feet each, ranks among the world's great airfields.

Agricultural output has been ranked in order of importance as milk, eggs, nursery and greenhouse products, vegetables and fruit.

The growth of factories brought to this state many immigrants, and today Boston has one of the largest Irish populations in the nation. Descendants of Italian immigrants are also prominent in the state.

The Pilgrims landed at Plymouth Rock in 1620 as the first large group to settle here but legend has it that Leif Erikson and his Norsemen saw the state in the year 1000.

Faneuil Hall in Boston was known as the "Cradle of Liberty." From the belfry of Christ Church (Old North Church), on Copp's Hill, Paul Revere received the lantern message that began his famous ride. Boston was also the site of the Battle of Bunker Hill. Massachusetts is the only state with its original Constitution, which is the oldest written Constitution in the world.

* The Metropolitan District Commission, an agency of the Commonwealth serving municipalities in the Boston area, has about 14,000 acres of parkways and reservations under its jurisdiction.

MICHIGAN

Capital: Lansing.
Governor: William G. Milliken, Rep. (to Jan. 1979).
Lieut. Governor: James J. Damman (to Jan. 1979).
Secy. of State: Richard H. Austin (to Jan. 1979).
Atty. General: Frank J. Kelley (to Jan. 1979).
Organized as territory: Jan. 11, 1805.
Entered Union & (rank): Jan. 26, 1837 (26).
Present constitution adopted: Apr. 1, 1963, (effective Jan. 1, 1964).
Motto: *Si quaeris peninsulam amoenam circumspice* (If you seek a pleasant peninsula, look around you).
State flower: Apple blossom (1897).
State bird: Robin.
State fish: Brook trout (1965).
State gem: Isle Royal Greenstone (Chlorastrolite) (1972).
State stone: Petoskey stone (1965).
Nickname: Wolverine State.
Origin of name: From two Indian words meaning "great lake."
1970 population & (rank): 8,875,083 (7).
1975 est. population & (rank): 9,157,000 (7).
1970 land area & (rank): 56,817 sq mi. (147,156 sq km) (22).
Geographic center: In Wexford Co., 5 mi. NNW of Cadillac.
Number of counties: 83.
Largest cities (1973 est.): Detroit (1,386,817); Grand Rapids (190,696); Flint (181,684); Warren (175,927); Lansing (129,186); Livonia (114,922).
State forests: 33 (3,762,184 ac.).
State parks and recreation areas: 92 (216,857 ac.).
State general revenue (1974): $3,964,879,000.
State general expenditure (1974): $5,242,198,000.

The headquarters of all the U. S. passenger-car companies are located within an 85-mile circle drawn around Detroit. Of these 13 companies, 12 have assembly plants within the same area. This industry, which sprang up about 60 years ago from the carriage-building business, is not the only activity of this state. Airplane parts, furniture, diesel engines, hoists, pumps, boilers are among its leading items of production. Most of the nation's refrigerators are made in Michigan and Michigan is the country's sole producer of iodine. On its farms are grown dry beans, grapes, peaches, potatoes, sugar beets, etc.

Michigan is split completely in two parts. The northern peninsula is mining and timber country. The southern part is agricultural and manufacturing country. Connecting Lakes Superior and Huron is one of the busiest canals in the world—the Sault Ste. Marie.

Michigan has the greatest area of inland water for fisheries in the world. The state is now introducing the coho salmon, and is managing steelhead trout to restore the Great Lakes fisheries for both sport and commercial fishing.

Michigan's 11,037 inland lakes, 36,000 miles of streams, and 2,242 miles of Great Lakes shoreline make the state an excellent vacationland.

MINNESOTA

Capital: St. Paul.
Governor: Wendell R. Anderson (to Jan. 1979).
Lieut. Governor: Dr. Rudy Perpich (to Jan. 1979).
Secy. of State: Joan Grow (to Jan. 1979).
State Auditor: Robert W. Mattson (to Jan. 1979).
Atty. General: Warren Spannus (to Jan. 1979).
State Treasurer: Jim Lord (to Jan. 1979).
Organized as territory: Mar. 3, 1849.
Entered Union & (rank): May 11, 1858 (32).
Present constitution adopted: 1858.
Motto: *L'Etoile du Nord* (The North Star).
State flower: Showy lady slipper (1902).
State tree: Red (or Norway) pine.
State bird: Common loon (also called Great Northern Diver).
State song: "Hail Minnesota."
Nicknames: North Star State; Gopher State; Land of 10,000 Lakes.
Origin of name: From a Dakota Indian word meaning "sky-tinted water."
1970 population & (rank): 3,805,069 (19).
1975 est. population & (rank): 3,926,000 (19).
1970 land area & (rank): 79,289 sq mi. (205,359 sq km) (14).
Geographic center: In Crow Wing Co., 10 mi. SW of Brainerd.
Number of counties: 87.
Largest cities (1973 est.): Minneapolis (382,423); St. Paul (287,305); (1975 special census): Bloomington (79,119); (1970 census): Duluth (100,578); Rochester (53,766).
State forests: 55 (2,984,000 ac.).
State parks: 92 (202,205 ac.).
Total revenue (fiscal 1975): $3,601,778,924.
Total expenditures (fiscal 1975): $3,389,554,666.

A few square miles of northern Minnesota, in the Mesabi, Cuyuna, and Vermilion ranges, produce about 60% of the nation's iron ore, and, with grain, keep the port of Duluth busy. Farm and factory are equally important in Minnesota. Its farms produce soybeans, oats, butter, eggs, milk, corn, wheat, potatoes, sweet corn, green peas, sugar beets, hay, barley, turkeys, hogs, etc. Its factory production includes non-electrical machinery, fabricated metals, flour-mill products, plastics, electronic computers, apparel, scientific instruments, and processed foods.

Minneapolis is the trade center of the Northwest. St. Paul is the nation's biggest publisher of calendars and law books. These twin cities are the nation's third-largest trucking center.

With over 15,291 lakes of 10 acres or more, the state is famous for its fishing and hunting. It has many well-known resort regions.

MISSISSIPPI

Capital: Jackson.
Governor: Charles C. (Cliff) Finch, Dem. (to Jan. 1980).
Lieut. Governor: Evelyn Gandy (to Jan. 1980).
Secy. of State: Heber A. Ladner (to Jan. 1980).
Treasurer: Edwin Lloyd Pittman (to Jan. 1980).
Atty. General: A. F. Summer (to Jan. 1980).
Organized as Territory: Apr. 7, 1798.
Entered Union & (rank): Dec. 10, 1817 (20).
Present constitution adopted: 1890.
Motto: *Virtute et armis* (By valor and arms).
State flower: Flower or bloom of the magnolia or evergreen magnolia (1952).
State tree: Magnolia (1938).
State bird: Mockingbird (1944).
State song: "Go, Mississippi" (1962).
Nickname: Magnolia State.
Origin of name: From an Indian word meaning "Father of Waters."
1970 population & (rank): 2,216,912 (29).
1975 est. population & (rank): 2,346,000 (29).
1970 land area & (rank): 47,296 sq mi. (122,497 sq km) (31).
Geographic center: In Leake Co., 9 mi. WNW of Carthage.
Number of counties: 82.
Largest cities (1973 est.): Jackson (163,924); **(1970 census):** Biloxi (48,486); Meridian (45,083); Gulfport (40,791); Greenville (39,648).
State forests: 1 (1,760 ac.).
State parks: 15 (16,220 ac.).
State general and special revenue (1975): $1,643,336,498.
State general and special expenditure (1975): $1,656,431,140.

Mississippi, the stronghold of the Old South, has until the past decade been one of the least industrialized states, with more than half its population making a living from the soil. A recent program of industrialization, however, has attracted numerous manufacturing concerns. Cotton, nevertheless, is still king. The world's largest cotton plantation (35,000 ac.) is located at Scott. Other crops are corn, peanuts, oats, pecans, soybeans, rice, tung nuts, sugar cane, and hay.

The state abounds in historical landmarks and is the home of the Vicksburg National Military Park commemorating Grant's victory in 1863.

Other National Park Service areas are Brices Cross Roads National Battlefield Site, Vicksburg National Cemetery, Tupelo National Battlefield, and part of Natchez Trace National Parkway.

MISSOURI

Capital: Jefferson City.
Governor: Christopher S. Bond, Rep. (to Jan. 1977).
Lieut. Governor: William C. Phelps (to Jan. 1977).
Secy. of State: James C. Kirkpatrick (to Jan. 1977).
Auditor: George H. Lehr (to Jan. 1979).
Treasurer: James I. Spainhower (to Jan. 1977).
Atty. General: John C. Danforth (to Jan. 1977).
Organized as territory: June 4, 1812.

Entered Union & (rank): Aug. 10, 1821 (24).
Present constitution adopted: 1945.
Motto: *Salus populi suprema lex esto* (The welfare of the people shall be the supreme law).
State flower: Hawthorn (1923).
State bird: Bluebird (1927).
State colors: Red, white and blue (1913).
State song: "Missouri Waltz" (1949).
State rock: Mozarkite (1967).
State mineral: Galena (1967).
Nickname: Show-me State.
Origin of name: Named after a tribe called Missouri Indians. Missouri means "town of the large canoes."
1970 population & (rank): 4,677,399 (13).
1975 est. population & (rank): 4,765,000 (15).
1970 land area & (rank): 68,995 sq mi. (178,697 sq km) (18).
Geographic center: In Miller Co., 20 mi. SW of Jefferson City.
Number of counties: 114, plus 1 independent city.
Largest cities (1973 est.): St. Louis (558,006); Kansas City (487,799); Springfield (128,310); Independence (114,272); **(1970 census):** St. Joseph (72,691).
State forests and Tower sites: 125 (210,000 ac.).
State parks: 57 (79,059 ac.).*
State cash receipts (1975): $2,053,945,730.
State general expenditure (1975): $2,096,103,557.

Missouri is composed of fertile farmlands in the north, flat lowlands in the southeast, rolling plains in the west, and the rugged Ozark Mountains which extend through the center of the state south into Arkansas. Once noted for its corncob pipes and Missouri mules, the state is now a popular vacationland. It has 11 major lakes and numerous fishing streams, springs, and caves. Bagnell Dam, across the Osage River in the Ozarks, completed in 1931, created one of the largest man-made lakes in the world, covering 65,000 acres of surface area.

Missouri is a leading producer of transportation equipment, shoes, lead, and beer. It also grows corn, soybeans, wheat, oats, barley, potatoes, tobacco, and cotton. Eads Bridge, spanning the Mississippi River at St. Louis, probably handles more freight cars than any other bridge in the world.

Historically, Missouri played a leading role as a gateway to the West, St. Joseph, Mo., being the eastern starting point of the Pony Express. During the Civil War Missourians' loyalties were divided between North and South, but the state itself remained in the Union.

The birthplaces of Harry S. Truman, Gen. John J. Pershing, and Mark Twain, as well as the Truman Library in Independence, are tourist attractions.

* Includes 19 historic sites and 1 archaeological site. † Includes all Federal grants.

MONTANA

Capital: Helena.
Governor: Thomas L. Judge, Dem. (to Jan. 1977).
Lieut. Governor: W. E. Christiansen (to Jan. 1977).
Secy. of State: Frank Murray (to Jan. 1977).
Auditor: E. V. "Sonny" Omholt (to Jan. 1977).
Atty. General: Robert L. Woodahl (to Jan. 1977).
Organized as territory: May 26, 1864.
Entered Union & (rank): Nov. 8, 1889 (41).
Present constitution adopted: 1972.
Motto: *Oro y plata* (Gold and silver).
State flower: Bitterroot (1895).
State tree: Ponderosa pine (1949).

State stones: Sapphire and agate (1969).
State bird: Western meadow lark (1931).
State song: "Montana" (1945).
Nickname: Treasure State.
Origin of name: Chosen from Latin dictionary by J. M. Ashley. It is a Latinized Spanish word.
1970 population & (rank): 694,409 (43).
1975 est. population & (rank): 748,000 (43).
1970 land area & (rank): 145,587 sq mi. (377,070 sq km) (4).
Geographic center: In Fergus Co., 12 mi. W of Lewistown.
Number of counties: 56, plus small part of Yellowstone National Park.
Largest cities (1970): Billings (61,581); Great Falls (60,091); Missoula (29,497); Butte (23,368); Helena (22,730).
State forests: 7 (214,000 ac.).
State parks and recreation areas: 68 (18,273 ac.).
State general revenue (1974–75): $156,641,727.
State general expenditure (1974–75): $146,247,584.

Montana's story is the old Western story—few settlers until a gold strike in 1862 brought an influx. Mining is its present occupation, and copper, lead, zinc, silver, coal, and oil are taken from its earth.

Butte, sitting on the "richest hill in the world," is the center of the area that once supplied half of the U. S. copper.

Livestock, wool, lumber, tourism, and dude ranching round out the state's interests. Agriculture is dependent on irrigation.

Glacier National Park is a popular tourist area with its rugged scenery and dude ranches. Montana's winter recreation development compares favorably with any other in the West.

NEBRASKA

Capital: Lincoln.
Governor: J. James Exon, Dem. (to Jan. 1979).
Lieut. Governor: Gerald T. Whelan (to Jan. 1979).
Secy. of State: Allen J. Beermann (to Jan. 1979).
Atty. General: Paul L. Douglas (to 1979).
Auditor: Ray A. C. Johnson (to Jan. 1979).
Treasurer: Frank Marsh (to Jan. 1979).
Organized as territory: May 30, 1854.
Entered Union & (rank): Mar. 1, 1867 (37).
Present constitution adopted: Nov. 1, 1875 (extensively amended 1919-20).
Motto: Equality before the law.
State flower: Goldenrod (1895).
State tree: Cottonwood (1972).
State bird: Western meadow lark (1929).
State insect: Honey bee.
State gem stone: Blue agate (1967).
State rock: Prairie agate (1967).
State fossil: Mammoth (1967).
State song: "Beautiful Nebraska" (1967).
Nicknames: Cornhusker State; Beef State; Tree Planters State.
Origin of name: From an Oto Indian word meaning "flat water."
1970 population & (rank): 1,483,791 (35).
1975 est. population & (rank): 1,546,000 (35).
1970 land area & (rank): 76,483 sq mi. (198,091 sq km) (15).
Geographic center: In Custer Co., 10 mi. NW of Broken Bow.
Number of counties: 93.
Largest cities (1973 est.): Omaha (377,292); Lincoln (163,440); (1970 census): Grand Island (31,269); Hastings (23,580); Fremont (22,962).

State forests: None.
State parks: 93 areas, 4 categories, 5 major areas.
State general revenue (1974–75): $277,568,216.
State general expenditure (1974–75): $300,220,578.

Nebraska lives by its expansive sea of grain, reflected in its bumper crops of rye, corn, and wheat. There are more varieties of grass growing in this state, valuable for forage, than in any other state in the nation. Its sizable cattle and hog industries help to make Omaha a great stockyard and meat-packing center. Nebraska produces farm machinery, clothing, mobile homes, fertilizers, and precision instruments. Oil was discovered in 1939, and natural gas in 1949.

In 1937, Nebraska became the only state in the Union to have a unicameral (one-house) legislature. Members are elected to it without party designation.

NEVADA

Capital: Carson City.
Governor: Mike O'Callaghan, Dem. (to Jan. 1979).
Lieut. Governor: Robert Rose (to Jan. 1979).
Secy. of State: William D. Swackhamer (to Jan. 1979).
State Treasurer: Michael Mirabelli (to Jan. 1979).
Controller: Wilson McGowan (to Jan. 1979).
Atty. General: Robert List (to Jan. 1979).
Organized as territory: Mar. 2, 1861.
Entered Union & (rank): Oct. 31, 1864 (36).
Present constitution adopted: 1864.
Motto: All for Our Country.
State flower: Sagebrush (1967).
State tree: Single-leaf pinon (1953).
State bird: Mountain bluebird (1967).
State animal: Desert bighorn sheep (1973).
State colors: Silver and blue (unofficial).
State song: "Home Means Nevada" (1933).
Nicknames: Sagebrush State; Silver State; Battle Born State.
Origin of name: Spanish: "snowcapped."
1970 population & (rank): 488,738 (47).
1975 est. population & (rank): 592,000 (46).
1970 land area & (rank): 109,889 sq mi. (284,613 sq km) (7).
Geographic center: In Lander Co., 26 mi. SE of Austin.
Number of counties: 16, plus 1 independent city.
Largest cities (1973 est.): Las Vegas (144,333); (1970 census): Reno (72,863); North Las Vegas (36,216); Sparks (24,187); Henderson (16,395).
State forests: None.
State parks: 13 (104,255 ac., including leased lands).
General fund revenue (1974–75): $160,912,451.
General fund expenditure (1974–75): $149,760,911.

Nevada was made famous by the discovery of the fabulous Comstock Lode in 1859, and its mines have produced large quantities of gold, silver, copper, lead, zinc, mercury, and tungsten. Oil was discovered in 1954. Copper now far exceeds all other minerals in value of production.

In 1931, the state created two industries, divorce and gambling. For many years, Reno and Las Vegas were the "divorce capitals of the nation." More liberal divorce laws in many states have ended this distinction. The state is something of a marriage capital, however, with over 100,000 performed in 1975. Nevada is the gambling and entertainment capital of the United States. State gambling taxes account for 43% of tax revenues. Although Nevada leads the nation in per capita gambling revenue, it ranks only third in total gambling revenue.

Near Las Vegas, on the Colorado River, stands

Hoover Dam, which impounds the waters of Lake Mead, one of the world's largest artificial lakes. The state's agricultural crop consists mainly of hay, alfalfa seed, barley, and wheat.

Nevada was the first state to use gas for capital punishment.

NEW HAMPSHIRE

Capital: Concord.
Governor: Meldrim Thomson, Jr., Rep. (to Jan. 1977).
Secy. of State: Robert L. Stark (to Jan. 1977).
Controller: Arthur H. Fowler.
Atty. General: David Souter.
Entered Union & (rank): June 21, 1788 (9).
Present constitution adopted: 1784.
Motto: Live free or die.
State flower: Purple lilac (1919).
State tree: White birch (1947).
State bird: Purple finch (1957).
State songs: "Old New Hampshire" (1949) and "New Hampshire, My New Hampshire" (1963).
Nickname: Granite State.
Origin of name: From the English county of Hampshire.
1970 population & (rank): 737,681 (41).
1975 est. population & (rank): 818,000 (42).
1970 land area & (rank): 9,027 sq mi. (23,380 sq km) (44).
Geographic center: In Belknap Co., 3 mi. E of Ashland.
Number of counties: 10.
Largest cities (1970): Manchester (87,754); Nashua (55,820); Concord (30,022); Portsmouth (25,717); Dover (20,850).
State forests & parks: 175 (96,975 ac.).
State revenue (1974): $327,042,883.
State expenditure (1974): $298,722,430.

New Hampshire is the only state that ever played host at the formal conclusion of a foreign war when, in 1905, Portsmouth was the scene of the treaty ending the Russo-Japanese War.

Principal agricultural pursuits include dairy and poultry farming and the growing of fruit, truck vegetables, corn, potatoes, and hay. The chief manufacturing is of electrical products, machinery, leather goods, textiles, pulp, and paper products.

New Hampshire was the first state to declare its independence from Great Britain and to adopt a constitution. Mt. Washington has recorded some of the world's strongest wind velocities, the last recording of record proportions being registered at 231 miles per hour. The state also has the largest legislative body; it may vary from 375 to 400.

With 1,300 lakes, the highest mountains in the Northeast, and good climate for both winter sports and summer vacations, the state is popular as a resort area.

NEW JERSEY

Capital: Trenton.
Governor: Brendan T. Byrne, Dem. (to Jan. 1978).
Secy. of State: J. Edward Crabiel (to Jan. 1978).
Treasurer: Richard C. Leone (to Jan. 1978).
Atty. General: William F. Hyland (to Jan. 1978).
Entered Union & (rank): Dec. 18, 1787 (3).
Present constitution adopted: 1947.
Motto: Liberty and prosperity.
State flower: Purple violet (1913).
State bird: Eastern goldfinch (1935).
State insect: Honeybee.
State tree: Red oak (1950).

State colors: Buff and blue.
State song: None.
Nickname: Garden State.
Origin of name: From the Channel Isle of Jersey.
1970 population & (rank): 7,168,164 (8).
1975 est. population & (rank): 7,316,000 (9).
1970 land area & (rank): 7,521 sq mi. (19,479 sq km) (46).
Geographic center: In Mercer Co., 5 mi. SE of Trenton.
Number of counties: 21.
Largest cities (1973 est.): Newark (367,683); Jersey City (255,030); Paterson (143,372); Elizabeth (110,303); Trenton (104,156).
State forests: 10 (176,679 ac.).
State parks: 40 (73,483 ac.).
State general revenue (1974): $4,085,342,011.
State appropriations (1974): $4,205,129,798.

New Jersey, situated in an area of wide industrial diversification between the major markets of Philadelphia and New York, is known as the crossroads of the East. Products from over 15,000 factories and shops can be delivered overnight to about 58 million people, representing 12 states and the District of Columbia. The greatest single industry is chemicals, and New Jersey is one of the foremost research centers of the world. Oil refining at Linden has some of the largest installations of this kind. Other important manufactures are apparel, instruments, and electrical goods.

Of the total land area, 43% is forested and about 24% is devoted to agriculture. The state rates high in practically all garden vegetables. Among its fruit crops are the famous cultivated blueberries, which originated in New Jersey. The poultry industry is one of the principal phases of the state's agriculture, and dairying occupies a prominent place.

The oldest U. S. highway of any length was built in Sussex County. The New Jersey Turnpike links New York, Pennsylvania, and Delaware. Its span at Florence over the Delaware River connects with the Pennsylvania Turnpike, giving motorists an uninterrupted road from New York to Chicago. A bridge between Bridgeport, N.J., and Chester, Pa., was opened in 1973, and one between Delair, N.J., and Philadelphia, the Betsy Ross Bridge, opened in 1976.

The Cape May-Lewes, Del., ferry (16.3 mi.) connects the Garden State Parkway (toll) from Cape May to the New York Thruway (173 mi.), while the Atlantic City Expressway links Philadelphia and Atlantic City (58 mi.).

New Jersey is a popular resort state with over 100 resort areas.

NEW MEXICO

Capital: Santa Fe.
Governor: Jerry Apodaca, Dem. (to Jan. 1979).
Lieut. Governor: Robert E. Ferguson (to Jan. 1979).
Secy. of State: Ernestine D. Evans (to Jan. 1979).
Atty. General: Toney Anaya (to Jan. 1979).
State Auditor: Max Sanchez (to Jan. 1979).
State Treasurer: Edward M. Murphy (to Jan. 1979).
Commissioner of Public Lands: Phil R. Lucero (to Jan. 1979).
Organized as territory: Sept. 9, 1850.
Entered Union & (rank): Jan. 6, 1912 (47).
Present constitution adopted: 1911.
Motto: *Crescit eundo* (It grows as it goes).
State flower: Yucca (1927).
State tree: Pinon (1949).
State animal: Black bear (1963).

State bird: Road runner (1949).
State fish: Cutthroat trout (1955).
State vegetables: Chile and frijol (1965).
State gem: Turquoise (1967).
State colors: Red and yellow of old Spain (1925).
State song: "O Fair New Mexico" (1917).
Spanish language state song: "Asi Es Nuevo Mejico" (1971).
Nicknames: Land of Enchantment; Sunshine State.
Origin of name: From the country of Mexico.
1970 population & (rank): 1,016,000 (37).
1975 est. population & (rank): 1,147,000 (37).
1970 land area & (rank): 121,412 sq mi. (314,457 sq km) (5).
Geographic center: In Torrance Co., 12 mi. SSW of Willard.
Number of counties: 32.
Largest cities (1973 est.): Albuquerque (273,902); (1970 census): Santa Fe (41,167); Las Cruces (37,857); Roswell (33,908); Clovis (28,495).
State-owned forested land: 933,000 ac.
State parks: 29 (105,012 ac.).
State general revenue (1974): $831,506,000.
State general expenditure (1974): $756,133,000.

New Mexico's chief industries are mining, agriculture, ranching tourism and scientific research.

The state is home to many Indian tribes, among them the Navajo, Apache, Zuni, Pueblo and Ute. Important reservations include the Navajo, in the northwest corner of the state and extending into Arizona; the Jicarilla Apache, at Horse Lake; the Mescalero Apache, northeast of Alamogordo; the Navajo, in San Juan and the McKinley counties; the Zuni, south of Gallup; and the Southern Ute, in the northern part of San Juan County. Carlsbad Caverns, the largest in the world, attract many visitors annually. The Rio Grande State Park, established in March, 1959, is over 80 miles long and contains the first federally designated and administered "wild river."

Santa Fe, the oldest seat of government in the United States, was founded by the Spaniards in 1609-10.

Los Alamos is the site of an atomic-energy laboratory. The first atomic explosion in history was at the Alamogordo air base. The state exceeds all others in the production and milling of uranium ore.

NEW YORK

Capital: Albany.
Governor: Hugh L. Carey, Dem. (to Jan. 1979).
Lieut. Governor: Mary Anne Krupsak (to Jan. 1979).
Secy. of State: Mario M. Cuomo (to Jan. 1979).
Comptroller: Arthur Levitt (to Jan. 1979).
Atty. General: Louis J. Lefkowitz (to Jan. 1979).
Entered Union & (rank): July 26, 1788 (11).
Present constitution adopted: 1777 (last revised 1938).
Motto: *Excelsior* (Ever upward).
State animal: Beaver (1975).
State fish: Brook trout (1975).
State gem: Garnet (1969).
State flower: Rose (1955).
State tree: Sugar maple (1956).
State bird: Bluebird.
State song: None.
Nickname: Empire State.
Origin of name: In honor of the English Duke of York.
1970 population & (rank): 18,241,266 (2).
1975 est. population & (rank): 18,120,000 (2).
1970 land area & (rank): 47,831 sq mi. (123,882 sq km) (30).

Geographic center: In Madison Co., 12 mi. S of Oneida and 26 mi. SW of Utica.
Number of counties: 62.
Largest cities (1973 est.): New York (7,646,818); Buffalo (425,101); Rochester (276,796); Yonkers (195,542); Syracuse (184,710); Albany (111,373).
State forest preserves: Adirondacks, 2,404,536 ac.; Catskills, 248,557 ac.
State parks: 139 (more than 220,000 ac.).
State general fund income (1975-76 est.): $10,209,000,000.
State general fund outgo (1975-76 est.): $10,658,000,000.

New York, with the great metropolis of New York City, is the spectacular nerve center of the nation. It leads in manufacturing, foreign trade, commercial and financial transactions, book and magazine publishing, theatrical production, etc.

New York City is not only a national but an international leader. It is a leading seaport of the world, and John F. Kennedy International Airport is one of the busiest airports in the world. The largest manufacturing center in the country, it had, in 1975, over 24,000 manufacturing establishments employing 757,300 persons and reported $11.6 billion of value added by manufacture. The apparel industry is the city's largest manufacturing employer, with printing and publishing second.

Nearly all the rest of the state's manufacturing is done on Long Island, along the Hudson River north to Albany and through the Mohawk Valley, Central New York, and Southern Tier regions to Buffalo. The St. Lawrence seaway and power projects have opened the North Country to industrial expansion. The seaway has given the state a second seacoast. In 1962, the Niagara power development was completed, giving the state the largest hydroelectric installation in the free world.

The state is the nation's manufacturing leader, with 1,679,300 employees and $30.4 billion in value added by manufacture in 1975. The principal industries are machinery, printing and publishing, instruments, apparel and food.

Dairying, truck gardening, and the raising of potatoes, onions, cabbage, fruits, and poultry keep the farmers prosperous. The state is a leading wine producer.

New York's extremely rapid commercial growth may be partly attributed to Governor De Witt Clinton, who pushed through the construction of the Erie Canal (Buffalo to Albany) which was opened in 1825. Today, the 559-mile Governor Thomas E. Dewey Thruway connects New York City with Buffalo and with Connecticut, Massachusetts, and Pennsylvania express highways. Two toll-free superhighways, the Adirondack Northway (linking Albany with the Canadian border) and the North-South-Expressway (crossing central New York from the Pennsylvania border to the Thousand Islands) have been opened.

The convention and tourist business is one of the state's most important sources of income.

For a short time, New York City was the U. S. capital, and George Washington was inaugurated there as the first President on Apr. 30, 1789.

NORTH CAROLINA

Capital: Raleigh.
Governor: James E. Holshouser, Jr., Rep. (to Jan. 1977).
Lieut. Governor: James B. Hunt, Jr. (to Jan. 1977).
Secy. of State: Thad Eure (to Jan. 1977.
Treasurer: Edwin Gill (to Jan. 1977.
Auditor: Henry L. Bridges (to Jan. 1977).

Atty. General: Rufus Edmisten (to Jan. 1977).
Entered Union & (rank): Nov. 21, 1789 (12).
Present constitution adopted: 1971.
Motto: *Esse quam videri* (To be rather than to seem)
State flower: Dogwood (1941).
State tree: Pine (1963).
State bird: Cardinal (1943).
State mammal: Gray squirrel (1969).
State insect: Honey bee (1973).
State gem stone: Emerald (1973).
State shell: Scotch bonnet (1965).
State song: "The Old North State" (1927).
State colors: Red and blue (1945).
Nickname: Tar Heel State.
Origin of name: In honor of Charles I of England.
1970 population & (rank): 5,082,059 (12).
1975 est. population & (rank): 5,451,000 (11).
1970 land area & (rank): 48,798 sq mi. (126,387 sq km) (29).
Geographic center: In Chatham Co., 10 mi. NW of Sanford.
Number of counties: 100.
Largest cities (1973 est.): Charlotte (284,738); Greensboro (155,514); Winston-Salem (139,711); Raleigh (133,050); Durham (102,328).
State forests: 1.
State parks: 23 (63,676 ac.).
State revenues (1975-76): $1,931,802,723.*
State expenditure (1975-76): $2,043,452,768.†

North Carolina is the nation's largest furniture, tobacco, brick, and textile producer. It holds second place in the Southeast in population and first place in the value of its industrial and agricultural production. This production is highly diversified, with metalworking, chemicals, and paper constituting enormous industries. Tobacco, corn, cotton, hay, peanuts, and truck and vegetable crops are of major importance. It is the country's leading producer of mica and lithium.

More than 30 state and national parks and forests, including the Great Smoky Mountains National Park, the Blue Ridge Parkway, and the Cape Hatteras and Cape Lookout national seashores. Mt. Mitchell (6,684 ft.) is the highest mountain in the eastern United States.

The largest military reservation in the nation (Fort Bragg) and the largest Marine amphibious training base (Camp Lejeune) are in North Carolina.

The first English colony in America was established on Roanoke Island in 1585. Virginia Dare, born there in 1587, was the first child of English parentage born in America.

* Excluding Federal funds other than shared Federal revenue. † State law prohibits deficit-spending; General Fund surplus and Highway Fund surplus at beginning of year accounts for discrepancy.

NORTH DAKOTA

Capital: Bismarck.
Governor: Arthur A. Link, Dem. (to Jan. 1977).
Lieut. Governor: Wayne Sanstead (to Jan. 1977).
Secy. of State: Ben Meier (to Jan. 1977).
Auditor: Robert W. Peterson (to Jan. 1977).
Atty. General: Allen I. Olson (to Jan. 1977).
Organized as territory: Mar. 2, 1861.
Entered Union & (rank): Nov. 2, 1889 (39).
Present constitution adopted: 1889.
Motto: Liberty and union, now and forever: one and inseparable.
State tree: American elm (1947).
State bird: Western meadow lark (1947).

State song: "North Dakota Hymn" (1947).
Nickname: Sioux State; Flickertail State.
Origin of name: From the Dakotah tribe, meaning "allies."
1970 population & (rank): 617,761 (45).
1975 est. population & (rank): 635,000 (45).
1970 land area & (rank): 69,273 sq mi. (179,417 sq km) (17).
Geographic center: In Sheridan Co., 5 mi. SW of McClusky.
Number of counties: 53.
Largest cities (1970): Fargo (53,365); Grand Forks (39,008); Bismarck (34,703); Jamestown (15,385); (1975 special census): Minot (32,823).
State forests: None.
State parks: 5 (2,981 ac.).
Total state collections (1975): $832,569,493.
Total state disbursements (1975): $768,839,026.

North Dakota, politically progressive, operates the only state-owned bank, flour mill, and grain elevator in the nation. The state owes its main activity to agriculture with over 87% of its acreage devoted to the growth of barley, wheat, rye, oats, and livestock. Most of its manufacturing consists of dairy products and some farm equipment.

The finest farming land is in the Red River Valley. Cattle raising is centered in the Missouri Slope.

The state is a leader in producing durum and hard red spring wheat. It also produces petroleum, natural gas, lignite, salt, clay, sand and gravel, light industrial goods, and dairy products.

The Garrison Dam on the Missouri River provides extensive irrigation and produces 400,000 kw. of electricity for use in the Missouri Basin areas.

OHIO

Capital: Columbus.
Governor: James A. Rhodes, Rep. (to Jan. 1979).
Lieut. Governor: Richard F. Celeste (to Jan. 1979).
Secy. of State: Ted W. Brown (to Jan. 1979).
Auditor: Thomas E. Ferguson (to Jan. 1979).
Treasurer: Gertrude W. Donahey (to Jan. 1979).
Atty. General: William J. Brown (to Jan. 1979).
Entered Union & (rank): Mar. 1, 1803 (17).
Present constitution adopted: 1851.
Motto: With God, all things are possible.
State flower: Scarlet carnation (1904).
State tree: Buckeye (1953).
State bird: Cardinal (1933).
State gem stone: Flint (1965).
State song: "Beautiful Ohio."
State drink: Tomato juice (1965).
Nickname: Buckeye State.
Origin of name: From an Iroquoian word meaning "great river."
1970 population & (rank): 10,652,017 (6).
1975 est. population & (rank): 10,795,000 (6).
1970 land area & (rank): 40,975 sq mi. (106,125 sq km) (35).
Geographic center: In Delaware Co., 25 mi. NNE of Columbus.
Number of counties: 88.
Largest cities (1973 est.): Cleveland (768,615); Columbus (540,933); Cincinnati (426,245); Toledo (377,423); Akron (261,520); Dayton (214,377).
State forests: 18 (163,972 ac.).
State parks: 63 (167,145 ac.).
State actual revenue (fiscal 1975): $5,280,447,649.
State actual expenditure (fiscal 1975): $5,502,981,736.

With vast coal and oil fields on the one hand, with Great Lakes iron ore close by on the other, Ohio automatically developed into one of the nations greatest industrial states. The vast and varied factory output of its cities runs from wire, nails, nuts, bolts, paper, radios, cash registers, golf clubs, refrigerators, to motors of all kinds and sizes. Cleveland is one of the world's largest handlers of iron ore. Toledo is the nation's largest shipper of coal. Akron makes most of the automobile tires used in the United States.

Ohio's thousands of factories almost overshadow its importance in two other basic industries—mining and agriculture. Its fertile soil produces soybeans, corn, wheat, grapes, and tobacco. Dairying and greenhouse products are important. Mining is centered in coal, oil, sand, gravel, and clay.

OKLAHOMA

Capital: Oklahoma City.
Governor: David L. Boren, Dem. (to Jan. 1979).
Lieut. Governor: Jerome W. Byrd (to Jan. 1979).
Secy. of State: John M. Rogers (to Jan. 1979).
Treasurer: Leo Winters (to Jan. 1979).
Atty. General: Larry Derryberry (to Jan. 1979).
Organized as territory: May 2, 1890.
Entered Union & (rank): Nov. 16, 1907 (46).
Present constitution adopted: 1907.
Motto: *Labor omnia vincit* (Labor conquers all things).
State flower: Mistletoe (1893).
State tree: Redbud (1937).
State bird: Scissor-tailed Flycatcher (1951)
State animal: Bison (1972).
State reptile: Mountain boomer lizard (1969).
State stone: Rose Rock (barite rose) (1968).
State colors: Green and white (1915).
State song: "Oklahoma" (1953).
Nickname: Sooner State.
Origin of name: From two Choctaw Indian words meaning "red people."
1970 population & (rank): 2,559,253 (27).
1975 est. population & (rank): 2,712,000 (27).
1970 land area & (rank): 68,782 sq mi. (178,145 sq km) (19).
Geographic center: In Oklahoma Co., 8 mi. N of Oklahoma City.
Number of counties: 77.
Largest cities (1973 est.): Oklahoma City (373,717); Tulsa (335,444); **(1970 census):** Lawton (74,470); Norman (52,117); Midwest City (48,114).
State forests: None.
State parks: 28 (88,959 ac.).
Total state revenue (1975): $1,845,060,343.
Total state expenditure (1975): $1,789,932,908.

Oil has made Oklahoma a rich state and Tulsa one of the world's wealthiest cities per capita. Oil refining, meat packing, management industries, and electronics are its chief factory industries. Wheat, broomcorn, corn, cotton, sorghum, and beef cattle are its agricultural crops of chief importance. Recreation is a growing industry.

In 1834, Oklahoma was set aside as Indian Territory. It remained so until Apr. 22, 1889, when the first opening to homestead settlement occurred. On that one day, 50,000 people swarmed in, and the term "sooners" was born to apply to those who had sneaked into the state sooner than the noon deadline. A series of land openings by "runs" and lotteries extended through 1901, and sales by sealed bid of remaining lands were held in 1906 and 1910.

OREGON

Capital: Salem.
Governor: Robert W. Straub, Dem. (to Jan. 1979).
Secy. of State: Clay Myers (to Jan. 1977).
Treasurer: James A. Redden (to Jan. 1977).
Atty. General: R. Lee Johnson (to Jan. 1977).
Organized as territory: Aug. 14, 1848.
Entered Union & (rank): Feb. 14, 1859 (33).
Present constitution adopted: 1859.
Motto: The Union (1957).
State flower: Oregon grape (1899).
State tree: Douglas fir (1939).
State animal: Beaver (1969).
State bird: Western meadow lark (1927).
State fish: Chinook salmon (1961).
State rock: Thunderegg (1965).
State colors: Navy blue and gold (1959).
State song: "Oregon, My Oregon" (1927).
Nickname: Beaver State.
Origin of name: Unknown. However, it is generally accepted that the name, first used by Jonathan Carver in 1778, was taken from the writings of Maj. Robert Rogers, an English army officer.
1970 population & (rank): 2,091,385 (31).
1975 est. population & (rank): 2,288,000 (30).
1970 land area & (rank): 96,184 sq mi. (249,117 sq km) (10).
Geographic center: In Crook Co., 25 mi. SSE of Prineville.
Number of counties: 36.
Largest cities (1973 est.): Portland (378,134); **(1970 census):** Eugene (78,389); Salem (68,856); Corvallis (35,153); Medford (28,454).
State forests: 785,062 ac.
State parks: 237 (95,800 ac.).
State general revenue (1975): $2,262,470,594.
State general expenditure (1975): $2,188,799,938.

Oregon, with the greatest U. S. reserve of standing timber, has a billion-dollar wood processing industry. Its salmon-fishing industry, centered at Astoria at the mouth of the Columbia, is one of the world's largest.

In agriculture, the state leads in growing peppermint, holly, lily bulbs, cranberries, filberts, Blue Lake beans, and cover seed crops, and also raises strawberries, hops, wheat and other grains, sugar beets, potatoes, green peas, fiber flax, dairy products, livestock and poultry, apples, pears, and cherries. Oregon is the source of all the nickel produced in the U. S.

With the low-cost electric power provided by Bonneville Dam, McNary Dam, and other dams in the Pacific Northwest, Oregon has developed steadily as a manufacturing state. Leading manufactures are lumber and plywood, metalwork, machinery, aluminum, chemicals, paper, food packing, and electronic equipment.

Crater Lake National Park, Mount Hood, and Bonneville Dam on the Columbia are major tourist attractions. Oregon Dunes National Recreation Area has been established near Florence.

PENNSYLVANIA

Capital: Harrisburg.
Governor: Milton J. Shapp, Dem. (to Jan. 1979).
Lieut. Governor: Ernest P. Kline (to Jan. 1979).
Secy. of the Commonwealth: C. De Lores Tucker (term indefinite).
Auditor General: Robert P. Casey (to Jan. 1976).
Atty. General: Robert Kane (to Jan. 1979).

Entered Union & (rank): Dec. 12, 1787 (2).
Present constitution adopted: 1874.
Motto: Virtue, liberty and independence.
State flower: Mountain laurel (1933).
State tree: Hemlock (1931).
State bird: Ruffed grouse (1931).
State insect: Firefly.
State dog: Great Dane (1965).
State colors: Blue and gold.
State song: None.
Nickname: Keystone State.
Origin of name: In honor of Adm. Sir William Penn, father of William Penn. It means "Penn's Woodland."
1970 population & (rank): 11,793,909 (3).
1975 est. population & (rank): 11,827,000 (4).
1970 land area & (rank): 44,966 sq mi. (116,462 sq km) (32).
Geographic center: In Centre Co., 2½ mi. SW of Bellefonte.
Number of counties: 67.
Largest cities (1973 est.): Philadelphia (1,861,719); Pittsburgh (479,276); Erie (130,084); Allentown (108,655); **(1970 census):** Scranton (103,564).
State forests: 1,915,906 ac.
State parks: 120 (297,438 ac.).
Total estimated revenue subject to general appropriations (fiscal 1976): $4,577,200.*
Total approved appropriations (fiscal 1976): $4,847,695.

Approximately 23% of all American pig iron steel is made in Pennsylvania. Other manufactures include electrical apparatus and machinery, storage batteries, motor vehicles and trailers, helicopters, computers, textiles, apparel, shoes, wire, plastics, and explosives. Pennsylvania produces all the anthracite (hard coal) and cobalt mined in the U.S.

The first radio broadcasting station, KDKA, was established at Pittsburgh in 1920, and the first electronic computer, the Eniac, was constructed at Philadelphia in 1945.

Agricultural products include apples, peaches, potatoes, corn, hay, barley, wheat, buckwheat, mushrooms, and tobacco.

Pennsylvania is rich in historical lore. Philadelphia was the seat of the Federal government almost continuously from 1776 until 1800, and there the Declaration of Independence was signed and the Constitution drawn up. Valley Forge, of the Revolution, and Gettysburg, the turning-point of the Civil War, are both in Pennsylvania. The Liberty Bell is located in Independence Hall in Philadelphia.

The Rockville Bridge, spanning the Susquehanna River between Marysville and Rockville, is recognized as the longest stone arch bridge in the world. This 4-track railroad bridge is 3,810 feet long and has 48 arches.

* Does not include surplus.

RHODE ISLAND

Capital: Providence.
Governor: Philip W. Noel, Dem. (to Jan. 1977).
Lieut. Governor: J. Joseph Garrahy (to Jan. 1977).
Secy. of State: Robert F. Burns (to Jan. 1977).
Controller: James A. Carter (civil service).
Atty. General: Julius C. Michaelson (to Jan. 1977).
Entered Union & (rank): May 29, 1790 (13).
Present constitution adopted: 1843.
Motto: Hope.
State flower: Violet (unofficial).
State tree: Red maple (official).

State bird: Rhode Island Red (official).
State colors: Blue, white and gold (in state flag).
State song: "Rhode Island" (1946).
Nickname: The Ocean State.
Origin of name: From the Greek island of Rhodes.
1970 population & (rank): 949,723 (39).
1975 est. population & (rank): 927,000 (39).
1970 land area & (rank): 1,049 sq mi. (2,717 sq km) (50).
Geographic center: In Kent Co., 1 mi. SSW of Crompton.
Number of counties: 5.
Largest cities (1973 est.): Providence (169,731); **(1970 census):** Warwick (83,694); Pawtucket (76,984); Cranston (74,287); East Providence (48,207).
State forests: 11 (20,900 ac.).
State parks: 17 (8,200 ac.).
State general revenue (1974–75): $560,150,987.
State general expenditure (1974–75): $576,506,072.

Rhode Island, with the greatest density of population barring the District of Columbia and New Jersey, boasts one of the highest proportions of industrial workers of all the states. Leading industry is jewelry and silverware, largely concentrated in Providence County, particularly the city of Providence. However, today the combined metal and machinery groups exceed both the jewelry and silverware industry, and textiles in importance.

With more than eight-tenths of the population living in urban areas, adjacent parts of the state are interested in dairying, poultry, and truck farming. Nursery and greenhouse products and stock, potatoes, corn, apples, oats, and hay lead the crop list. Of the state's land area, about one-tenth is farm cropland and open pasture; six-tenths is forested.

Newport is the site of the Naval War College and was long a show place for the luxurious summer homes built by some of New York's wealthiest people.

Roger Williams founded Providence, and subsequently Rhode Island, in 1636.

SOUTH CAROLINA

Capital: Columbia.
Governor: James B. Edwards, Rep. (to Jan. 1979).
Lieut. Governor: W. Brantley Harvey (to Jan. 1979).
Secy. of State: O. Frank Thornton (to Jan. 1979).
Comptroller General: John Henry Mills (to Jan. 1979).
Atty. General: Daniel R. McLeod (to Jan. 1979).
Entered Union & (rank): May 23, 1788 (8).
Present constitution adopted: 1895.
Mottoes: *Animis opibusque parati* (Prepared in mind and resources) and *Dum spiro spero* (While I breathe, I hope).
State flower: Carolina yellow jessamine (1924).
State tree: Palmetto tree (1939).
State bird: Carolina wren (1948).
State song: "Carolina" (1911).
Nickname: Palmetto State.
Origin of name: In honor of Charles I of England.
1970 population & (rank): 2,590,516 (26).
1975 est. population & (rank): 2,818,000 (26).
1970 land area & (rank): 30,225 sq mi. (78,283 sq km) (40).
Geographic center: In Richland Co., 13 mi. SE of Columbia.
Number of counties: 46.
Largest cities (1973 est.): Columbia (112,164); **(1970 census):** Charleston (66,945); Greenville (61,436); Spartanburg (44,546); Rock Hill (33,846).
State forests: 4 (124,052 ac.).
State parks: 49 (59,621 ac.).

State general fund revenue (1974-75): $873,330,008.*
State general expenditures (1974-75): $917,544,491.*

Once primarily agricultural, South Carolina has built so many big textile and other mills that today the state's factories produce eight times the output of its farms in cash value. Agriculture has not, however, been totally replaced, and today the chief products are livestock, cotton, tobacco, peaches, corn, hay, oats, soybeans, sweet potatoes, and peanuts, which are enhanced by the recent development of modern soil-conservation methods. Charleston makes asbestos, wood, pulp, and steel products.

The first European settlement in what is now the United States was probably made by the Spaniard Vasquez de Ayllon on the shore of Winyah Bay in 1526. Civil War hostilities were started in this state at Charleston, when, on Apr. 12, 1861, South Carolina men bombarded and captured Fort Sumter.

* Highway Department has separate funding and expenditures.

SOUTH DAKOTA

Capital: Pierre.
Governor: Richard F. Kneip, Dem. (to Jan. 1979).
Lieut. Governor: Harvey Wollman (to Jan. 1979).
Atty. General: William Janklow (to Jan. 1979).
Secy. of State: Lorna B. Herseth (to Jan. 1979).
State Auditor: Alice Kundert (to Jan. 1979).
State Treasurer: David L. Volk (to Jan. 1979).
Organized as territory: Mar. 2, 1861.
Entered Union & (rank): Nov. 2, 1889 (40).
Present constitution adopted: 1889.
Motto: Under God the people rule.
State flower: American pasqueflower (1903).
State grass: Western wheat grass (1970).
State tree: Black Hills spruce (1947).
State bird: Ring-necked pheasant (1943).
State animal: Coyote (1949).
State mineral stone: Rose quartz (1966).
State gem stone: Fairburn agate (1966).
State colors: Blue and gold (in state flag).
State song: "Hail! South Dakota" (1943).
Nicknames: Sunshine State; Coyote State.
Origin of name: Same as for North Dakota.
1970 population & (rank): 666,257 (44).
1975 est. population & (rank): 683,000 (44).
1970 land area & (rank): 75,955 sq mi. (196,723 sq km) (16).
Geographic center: In Hughes Co., 8 mi. NE of Pierre.
Number of counties: 67 (64 county governments).
Largest cities (1970): Sioux Falls (72,488); Rapid City (43,836); Aberdeen (26,476); Huron (14,299); Brookings (13,717).
State forests: None.*
State parks: 12 plus 31 recreational areas (87,269 ac.).†
State general revenue (1974-75): $416,852,271.†
State general expenditure (1974-75): $389,289,869.‡

South Dakota, a leading agricultural state, is rapidly diversifying, with only 25% of the people engaged in farming. Livestock leads farm output that includes wheat, corn, barley, rye, oats, and bluegrass. The richest gold mine, the Homestake, is at Lead and South Dakota is the nation's second leading producer of gold. Other minerals produced

in South Dakota include beryllium, bentonite and granite.

The Black Hills, a great tourist attraction, are the highest mountains east of the Rockies. Mt. Rushmore, in this group, is celebrated for the likenesses of Washington, Jefferson, Lincoln, and Theodore Roosevelt, which were carved in stone by Gutzon Borglum. The Badlands offer scenic masses of bare rock and clay unrelieved by any vegetation. It was in this state that the Sioux Indians, angered at the influx of the white men who were searching for gold, started the hostilities which ended in Custer's massacre, on June 25, 1876, at Little Big Horn in Montana.

TENNESSEE

Capital: Nashville.
Governor: Ray Blanton, Dem. (to Jan. 1979).
Lieut. Governor: John S. Wilder (to Jan. 1977).
Secy. of State: Joe C. Carr (to Jan. 1977).
Comptroller: William R. Snodgrass (to Jan. 1977).
Atty. General: R. A. Ashley, Jr. (to Sept. 1982).
Entered Union & (rank): June 1, 1796 (16).
Present constitution adopted: 1870; amended 1953, 1960, 1965 and 1973.
Motto: "Tennessee—America at its best" (1965).
State flower: Iris (1933).
State tree: Tulip poplar (1947).
State bird: Mockingbird (1933).
State horse: Tennessee walking horse.
State animal: Raccoon.
State wild flower: Passion flower.
State song: "Tennessee Waltz" (1965).
Nickname: Volunteer State.
Origin of name: Of Cherokee origin; the exact meaning is unknown.
1970 population & (rank): 3,924,164 (17).
1975 est. population & (rank): 4,188,000 (17).
1970 land area & (rank): 41,328 sq mi. (107,040 sq km) (34).
Geographic center: In Rutherford Co., 5 mi. NE of Murfreesboro.
Number of counties: 95.
Largest cities (1973 est.): Memphis (658,868); Nashville-Davidson (449,109); Knoxville (182,276); Chattanooga (137,957); (1970 census): Jackson (39,996).
State forests: 14 (155,752 ac.).
State parks: 21 (130,000 ac.).
State general revenue (1974): $1,836,566.
State general expenditure (1974): $1,910,115.

Tennessee is now predominantly industrial, and in 1970, 58.8% of its population was in urban areas.

The state has an industrial payroll of $1,560,-820,000. This includes the production of chemicals, food, virgin aluminum, shoes, textiles, and wood and metal products.

Tennessee, with 50 colleges and universities, is the academic center of the South. The University of Tennessee has the largest college of business administration in the South and the second-largest college of dentistry. It also has the third-largest college of medicine in the nation. A new multi-million-dollar Space Institute operates as part of the University in conjunction with the Arnold Engineering Development Center at Tullahoma.

Stone is Tennessee's leading mineral in dollar value. Cement ranks second and coal third in dollar value. The state ranks first in the production of ball clay, zinc, pyrite, and marble.

* No designated state forests; about 13,000 ac. of state land is forest land. † Acreage includes 31 recreation areas and 80 roadside parks, in addition to 12 state parks. ‡ Includes Federal funds.

TEXAS

Capital: Austin.
Governor: Dolph Briscoe, Dem. (to Jan. 1979).
Lieut. Governor: William P. Hobby (to Jan. 1979).
Secy. of State: Mark White (to Jan. 1979).
Comptroller: Bob Bullock (to Jan. 1979).
Atty. General: John Hill (to Jan. 1979).
Entered Union & (rank): Dec. 29, 1845 (28).
Present constitution adopted: 1876.
Motto: Friendship.
State flower: Bluebonnet (1901).
State tree: Pecan (1919).
State bird: Mockingbird (1927).
State song: "Texas, Our Texas" (1930).
Nickname: Lone Star State.
Origin of name: From an Indian word meaning "friends."
1970 population & (rank): 11,196,730 (4).
1975 est. population & (rank): 12,237,000 (3).
1970 land area & (rank): 262,134 sq mi. (678,927 sq km) (2).
Geographic center: In McCulloch Co., 15 mi. NE of Brady.
Number of counties: 254.
Largest cities (1973 est.): Houston (1,320,018); Dallas (815,866); San Antonio (756,226); Fort Worth (359,542); El Paso (353,226); Austin (291,214).
State forests: 4 (6,306 ac.).
State parks: 83 (64 developed)
State revenue receipts (1974–75): $5,693,910,357.
State government cost (1974–75): $5,433,446,598.

Texas is the richest political subdivision in the world, with the possible exception of the Soviet Ukraine, and is the only state that may, by Congressional statute, divide into five parts if it so desires. There is very little possibility of this ever being done because Texas and Texans live by its bigness. Texas is a natural leader in oil, natural gas, cotton, cattle, helium, sheep, wool, onions, and turkeys.

The distance from El Paso to Beaumont is a greater distance than from New York to Chicago. Over the Neches River, at Port Arthur, is the most elevated highway bridge over tidal waters in the world.

Cabeza de Vaca explored the state in 1528. Since 1685, it has been under the jurisdiction of six separate governments: those of France, Spain, Mexico, the Republic of Texas, the Confederacy, and the United States.

UTAH

Capital: Salt Lake City.
Governor: Calvin L. Rampton, Dem. (to Jan. 1977).
Secy. of State: Clyde L. Miller (to Jan. 1977).
Atty. General: Vernon B. Romney (to Jan. 1977).
Organized as territory: Sept. 9, 1850.
Entered Union & (rank): Jan. 4, 1896 (45).
Present constitution adopted: 1896.
Motto: Industry.
State flower: Sego lily (1911).
State tree: Blue spruce (1933).
State bird: Seagull (1955).
State emblem: Beehive.
State song: "Utah, We Love Thee."
Nickname: Beehive State.
Origin of name: From the Ute tribe, meaning "people of the mountains."
1970 population & (rank): 1,059,273 (36).
1975 est. population & (rank): 1,206,000 (36).

1970 land area & (rank): 82,096 sq mi. (212,629 sq km) (12).
Geographic center: In Sanpete Co., 3 mi. N of Manti.
Number of counties: 29
Largest cities (1970): Salt Lake City (175,885); Ogden (69,478); Provo (53,491); Bountiful (27,956); Orem (25,729).
State forests: None.
State parks: 35 (64,097 ac.).
Total state receipt (1974–75): $680,239,756.
Total state disbursements (1974–75): $702,050,021.
Cash balance (1974–75): $91,279,179.

Utah, rich in natural resources, has long been recognized for its copper, gold, silver, lead, and zinc. Also, it produces all the elements necessary for the manufacture of steel: iron, lime, dolomite, fluorspar, manganese, and coal for coking. The state is also developing an oil industry and in 1970 ranked 13th among the states in total production.

Utah's crops requiring extensive irrigation include sugar beets, potatoes, hay, onions, and wheat. Various garden crops, such as beans, peas, and tomatoes, and fruits, such as pears, peaches, apples, and apricots, make up an ever-growing industry. Eggs and commercial poultry are also among the products of Utah.

Brigham Young led the Mormons into the area in 1847.

Great Salt Lake, lying in the north central area, has long been a world wonder. It has no known outlet, and its salt content is about six times that of the ocean. Because of its natural beauty and pioneer culture, Utah is an ideal place for tourists to visit.

VERMONT

Capital: Montpelier.
Governor: Thomas P. Salmon, Dem. (to Jan. 1977).
Lieut. Governor: Brian D. Burns (to Jan. 1977).
Secy. of State: Richard C. Thomas (to Jan. 1977).
Treasurer: Stella B. Hackel (to Jan. 1977).
Auditor of Accounts: Alexander V. Acebo (to Jan. 1977).
Atty. General: M. Jerome Diamond (to Jan. 1977).
Entered Union & (rank): Mar. 4, 1791 (14).
Present constitution adopted: 1793.
Motto: Vermont, Freedom and Unity.
State flower: Red clover (1894).
State tree: Sugar maple (1949).
State bird: Hermit thrush (1941).
State animal: Morgan horse (1961).
State song: "Hail, Vermont!" (1938).
Nickname: Green Mountain State.
Origin of name: From the French "vert mont," meaning "green mountain."
1970 population & (rank): 444,732 (48).
1975 est. population & (rank): 471,000 (48).
1970 land area & (rank): 9,276 sq mi. (24,025 sq km) (48).
Geographic center: In Washington Co., 3 mi. E of Roxbury.
Number of counties: 14.
Largest cities (1970): Burlington (38,633); Rutland (19,293); Barre (10,209); South Burlington (10,032); Montpelier (8,609).
State forests: 34 (111,306 ac.).
State parks: 42 (30,906 ac.).
State receipts (fiscal 1975): $372,072,035.
State disbursements (fiscal 1975): $422,494,625.

Vermont, the only New England state without a seacoast (and the last to be settled because of this), leads the nation in production of monumental granite, marble, and maple syrup and ranks high in the production of granite and asbestos. In ratio to population it keeps more dairy cows than any other state. Vermont's soil is devoted to dairying, truck farming, and fruit growing, its rugged area precluding extensive farming. This same quality, however, along with a bracing dry climate, makes the state popular as a summer resort and also as a center of winter sports.

From 1777 to 1791, Vermont was an independent state of indefinite status with some national perquisites and then was the first state after the original 13 to join the Union. It was also the first state to forbid slavery and the first to adopt universal manhood suffrage (1777).

Vermont's first Democratic governor in 109 years was elected in 1962 and served until 1969.

VIRGINIA

Capital: Richmond.
Governor: Mills E. Godwin, Jr., Rep. (to Jan. 1978).
Lieut. Governor: John N. Dalton (to Jan. 1978).
Secy. of the Commonwealth: Mrs. Pat Perkinson. (apptd. by Governor).
Comptroller: Charles B. Walker (apptd. by Governor).
Atty. General: Andrew P. Miller (to Jan. 1978).
Entered Union & (rank): June 25, 1788 (10).
Present constitution adopted: 1970.
Motto: *Sic semper tyrannis* (Thus always to tyrants).
State flower: American dogwood (1918).
State bird: Cardinal (1950).
State dog: American foxhound (1966).
State shell: Oyster shell.
State song: "Carry Me Back to Old Virginia" (1940).
Nicknames: The Old Dominion; Mother of Presidents.
Origin of name: In honor of Elizabeth, "Virgin Queen" of England.
1970 population & (rank): 4,648,494 (14).
1975 est. population & (rank): 4,967,000 (13).
1970 land area & (rank): 39,780 sq mi. (103,030 sq km) (36).
Geographic center: In Buckingham Co., 5 mi. SW of Buckingham.
Number of counties: 95, plus 41 independent cities.
Largest cities (1973 est.): Norfolk (283,064); Richmond (238,087); Virginia Beach (199,613); Newport News (137,827); Hampton (128,119).
State forests: 8 (49,566 ac.).
State parks and recreational parks: 19, plus 7 in process of acquisition and/or development (42,722 ac.).*
State revenue (1974-75): $3,348,132,149.
State expenditure (1974-75): $3,339,574,102.

The history of America is closely tied to that of Virginia, particularly in the Colonial period. Jamestown, founded in 1607, was the first permanent English settlement in North America, and slavery was introduced there in 1619. The surrenders ending both the American Revolution and the Civil War occurred in Virginia. The state is called the "Mother of Presidents" because eight chief executives of the United States were born there.

Points of historic interest include Mount Vernon and other places associated with George Washington; Monticello, home of Thomas Jefferson; Strat-

ford, home of the Lees; Richmond, capital of the Confederacy and of Virginia; and Williamsburg, the restored Colonial capital.

Among Virginia's natural wonders are the famous Natural Bridge and the limestone caverns of the Shenandoah Valley. The most important natural resources are beds of bituminous coal, forest lands, oyster beds, and commercial fisheries.

Manufacturing includes chemicals, textiles, lumber and wood products, foods, transportation equipment (including shipbuilding), apparel, electrical equipment, and furniture. Agricultural products of Virginia include livestock, poultry, dairy goods, tobacco, apples, grains, and hay crops.

WASHINGTON

Capital: Olympia.
Governor: Daniel J. Evans, Rep. (to Jan. 1977).
Lieut. Governor: John A. Cherberg (to Jan. 1977).
Secy. of State: Bruce K. Chapman (to Jan. 1977).
State Treasurer: Robert S. O'Brien (to Jan. 1977).
Atty. General: Slade Gorton (to Jan. 1977).
Organized as territory: Mar. 2, 1853.
Entered Union & (rank): Nov. 11, 1889 (42).
Present constitution adopted: 1889.
Motto: *Al-Ki* (Indian word meaning By and by).
State flower: Rhododendron (1949).
State tree: Western hemlock (1947).
State bird: Willow goldfinch (1951).
State gem: Petrified wood (1975).
State colors: Green and gold (1925).
State song: "Washington, My Home" (1959).
Nicknames: Evergreen State; Chinook State.
Origin of name: In honor of George Washington.
1970 population & (rank): 3,409,169 (22).
1975 est. population & (rank): 3,544,000 (22).
1970 land area & (rank): 66,570 sq mi. (172,416 sq km) (20).
Geographic center: In Chelan Co., 10 mi. WSW of Wenatchee.
Number of counties: 39.
Largest cities (1973 est.): Seattle (503,073); Spokane (173,971); Tacoma (149,420); (1970 census): Bellevue (61,102); Everett (53,622).
State forest lands: 1,843,020 ac.
State parks: 173 (79,212 ac.).
State revenue (all funds, fiscal 1974): $3,622,000,000.
State expenditure (all funds, fiscal 1974): $3,621,000,000.

Washington is one of the leaders in lumber production. Its rugged surface is rich in stands of Douglas fir, hemlock, ponderosa and white pine, spruce, larch, and cedar. The state produces wheat and is a leader in apples. Food and lumber products, aircraft and missiles, and a wide variety of other goods flow from Washington factories.

The Columbia River contains one third of the potential water power of America. Largest dam is Grand Coulee, one of the greatest power producers in the world. Other mighty dams on the Columbia include Bonneville, McNary, The Dalles, and John Day, which are shared with Oregon, and Chief Joseph, Rock Island, Priest Rapids, Rocky Reach and Wanapum, which are not shared. There are 90 dams in Washington, built for various purposes including power, irrigation, flood control, water storage, etc. Washington's abundance of electrical power makes it the nation's largest producer of refined aluminum.

The Hanford atomic works at Richland is emerging as a world center for nuclear research.

---

* Does not include portion of Breaks Interstate Park (Va.-Ky., 1,200 ac.) which lies in Virginia.

WEST VIRGINIA

Capital: Charleston.
Governor: Arch A. Moore, Jr. Rep. (to Jan. 1977).
Secy. of State: James R. McCartney (to Jan. 1977).
State Auditor: John M. Gates, (to Jan. 1977).
Atty. General: Chauncey H. Browning, Jr. (to Jan. 1977).
Entered Union & (rank): June 20, 1863 (35).
Present constitution adopted: 1872.
Motto: *Montani semper liberi* (Mountaineers are always free).
State flower: Rhododendron (1903).
State tree: Sugar maple (1949).
State bird: Cardinal (1949).
State animal: Black bear.
State colors: Blue and gold (unofficial).
State songs: "West Virginia, My Home Sweet Home," "The West Virginia Hills," and "This Is My West Virginia" (adopted by Legislature in 1947, 1961 and 1963 as official state songs).
Nickname: Mountain State.
Origin of name: Same as for Virginia.
1970 population & (rank): 1,744,237 (34).
1975 est. population & (rank): 1,803,000 (34).
1970 land area & (rank): 24,070 sq mi. (62,341 sq km) (41).
Geographic center: In Braxton Co., 4 mi. E of Sutton.
Number of counties: 55.
Largest cities (1970): Huntington (74,315); Charleston (71,505); Wheeling (48,188); Parkersburg (44,208); Weirton (27,131).
State forests: 9 (77,000 ac.).
State parks: 34 (65,861 ac.).
Total state revenue (1974–75): $1,476,066,287.
Total state expenditure (1974–75): $1,392,100,507.

Mountainous West Virginia leads the nation in bituminous coal production. The state also ranks high in steel, glass, aluminum, and chemical manufacture, natural gas, oil, quarry products, and hardwood lumber. Cattle is the main agricultural product. Leading crops include wheat, corn, hay, tobacco, fruit, and potatoes.

West Virginia was created when its residents refused to secede from the Union and severed the state from Virginia during the Civil War era.

Like many mountain states, West Virginia has an equable climate without extremes. White Sulphur Springs, in Greenbrier County, is a famous health resort.

WISCONSIN

Capital: Madison.
Governor: Patrick J. Lucey, Dem. (to Jan. 1979).
Lieut. Governor: Martin J. Schreiber (to Jan. 1979).
Secy. of State: Douglas J. LaFollette (to Jan. 1979).
State Treasurer: Charles P. Smith (to Jan. 1979).
Atty. General: Bronson C. LaFollette (to Jan. 1979).
Organized as territory: July 4, 1836.
Entered Union & (rank): May 29, 1848 (30).
Present constitution adopted: 1848.
Motto: Forward.
State flower: Wood violet.
State tree: Sugar maple.
State bird: Robin.
State animal: Badger; "wild life" animal: white-tailed deer; "domestic" animal: dairy cow.
State fish: Musky (Muskellunge).
State song: "On Wisconsin."
State mineral: Galena (1971).
State rock: Red granite (1971).
Nickname: Badger State.

Origin of name: French corruption of an Indian word meaning "gathering of waters."
1970 population & (rank): 4,417,933 (16).
1975 est. population & (rank): 4,607,000 (16).
1970 land area & (rank): 54,464 sq mi. (141,062 sq km) (25).
Geographic center: In Wood Co., 9 mi. SE of Marshfield.
Number of counties: 72.
Largest cities (1973 est.): Milwaukee (690,685); Madison (169,749); (1970 census): Racine (95,162); Green Bay (87,809); Kenosha (78,805).
State forests: 10 (447,504 ac.).
State parks: 51 (49,177 ac.).
State total net revenue (all funds, 1974–75): $4,218,954,213.
State total net expenditure (all funds, 1974–75): $4,073,-423,281.

Wisconsin leads the nation in milk and cheese production. In 1972, the state ranked first in the number of milk cows (1,832,000), and produced 16% of the nation's total output of milk. Other important farm products are: peas, beets, corn, potatoes, cabbage, maple sugar, and cranberries.

The chief industrial products of the state are automobiles, machinery, furniture, paper, beer, and processed foods. Wisconsin ranks second among the 47 paper-producing states. Tourism also ranks among the major industries.

Wisconsin pioneered in social legislation, providing pensions for the blind (1907), aid to dependent children (1913), and old-age assistance (1925). In 1932, it was the first state to enact an unemployment compensation law. In labor legislation, the state has also pioneered in important laws, among them the first workmen's compensation law actually to take effect. Wisconsin had the first state-wide primary-election law and the first successful income-tax law.

In recent years, Wisconsin has been in the forefront in the enactment of legislation relating to seat belts, water pollution, and state government reorganization.

WYOMING

Capital: Cheyenne.
Governor: Ed Herschler, Dem. (to Jan. 1979).
Secy. of State: Thyra G. Thomson (to Jan. 1979).
Auditor: James B. Griffith (to Jan. 1979).
Treasurer: Edwin J. Witzenburger (to Jan. 1979).
Supt. of Public Instruction: Robert G. Schrader (to Jan. 1979).
Atty. General: V. Frank Mendicino (apptd. by Governor).
Organized as territory: May 19, 1869.
Entered Union & (rank): July 10, 1890 (44).
Present constitution adopted: 1890.
Motto: Equal rights (1955).
State flower: Indian paintbrush (1917).
State tree: Cottonwood (1947).
State bird: Meadow lark (1927).
State gemstone: Jade (1967).
State insignia: Bucking horse (unofficial).
State song: "Wyoming" (1955).
Nickname: Equality State.
Origin of name: From the Indian, meaning "mountains and valleys alternating"; named after the Wyoming Valley in Pennsylvania.
1970 population & (rank): 332,416 (49).
1975 est. population & (rank): 374,000 (49).
1970 land area & (rank): 97,203 sq mi. (251,756 sq km) (9).

Geographic center: In Fremont Co., 58 mi. ENE of Lander.

Number of counties: 23, plus Yellowstone National Park.

Largest cities (1970): Cheyenne (40,914); Casper (39,361); Laramie (23,143); Rock Springs (11,657); Sheridan (10,856).

State forests: None.

State parks: 9 (44,732 ac.).

Estimated income available (general fund, 1976–78): $288,272,267.

Estimated expenditure (general fund, 1976–78): $268,-457.619.

Wealthy in wool, cattle, oil, uranium, and coal, Wyoming was first in U. S. history to insure woman's place in politics. In 1869, it gave women the vote, and Mrs. Nellie Tayloe Ross, who held office in 1925–27, was the first woman Governor in the United States.

Second in mean elevation to Colorado, Wyoming has many attractions for the tourist trade, notably Yellowstone National Park. Cheyenne is famous for its annual "Frontier Days" celebration, which brings in visitors from everywhere. One of the world's largest subbituminous coal fields lies near Gillette. Big game hunting is good in many parts of the state.

COMMONWEALTH OF PUERTO RICO

Capital: San Juan.

Governor: Rafael Hernández Colón, Pop. Dem. (to Jan. 1977).

Song: "La Borinqueña."

1950 population: 2,210,703.

1960 population: 2,349,544.

1970 population: 2,712,033.

1970 land area: 3,421 sq mi. (8,860 sq km).

Largest cities (1970): San Juan (452,749); Ponce (128,233); Bayamón (147,552); Carolina (94,271); Mayagüez (68,872).

Puerto Rico is an island about 100 miles long and 35 miles wide at the northeastern end of the Caribbean Sea. It is a self-governing Commonwealth freely and voluntarily associated with the United States. Under its Constitution, a Governor and a Legislative Assembly are elected by direct vote for a four-year period. The judiciary is vested in a Supreme Court and lower courts established by law. The people elect a Resident Commissioner to the U. S. House of Representatives, where he has a voice but no vote. The island was formerly an unincorporated territory of the United States after being ceded by Spain as a result of the Spanish-American War.

The Commonwealth, established in 1952, has one of the highest standards of living in Latin America. Featuring Puerto Rican economic development is Operation Bootstrap. This program has established over 2,300 new factories and has greatly increased agricultural production, transportation and communications facilities, electric power, housing, and other industries.

The island's chief exports are chemicals, textiles, fish products and petroleum products.

Columbus discovered the island on his second voyage to America in 1493.

NON-SELF-GOVERNING U. S. TERRITORIES

AMERICAN SAMOA

Capital: Pago Pago (on Tutuila Island).

Governor: Earl B. Ruth.

Lieut. Governor: Frank E. Barnett.

1950 population: 18,937.

1960 population: 20,051.

1973 est. population: 30,000.

1970 land area: 76 sq mi. (197 sq km).

American Samoa, a group of five volcanic islands and two coral atolls located some 2,400 miles south of Hawaii in the South Pacific Ocean, is an unincorporated, unorganized territory of the United States, administered by the Department of the Interior.

By the Treaty of Berlin signed Dec. 2, 1899, and ratified Feb. 16, 1900, the United States was internationally acknowledged to have rights extending over all the islands of the Samoa group east of longitude 171° west of Greenwich. On Apr. 17, 1900, the chiefs of Tutuila and Aunu'u ceded those islands to the United States. In 1904, the King and chiefs of Manu'a ceded the islands of Ofu, Olosega and Tau (composing the Manu'a group) to the United States. Swains Island, some 200 miles north of Samoa, was included as part of the territory by Act of Congress Mar. 4, 1925; and on Feb. 20, 1929, Congress formally accepted sovereignty over the entire group and placed the responsibility for administration in the hands of the President. From 1900 to 1951, by Presidential direction, the Department of the Navy governed the territory. On July 1, 1951, administration was transferred to the Department of the Interior. The first Constitution for the territory was signed on Apr. 27, 1960, and became effective on Oct. 17, 1960. It was revised in 1967 and 1973.

The principal products are canned tuna, pet food, fish meal, mats, handicrafts and ginger.

BAKER, HOWLAND, AND JARVIS

These Pacific islands were not to play a role in the extraterritorial plans of the United States until May 13, 1936. President F. D. Roosevelt, at that time, placed them under the control of and jurisdiction by the Secretary of the Interior for administration purposes.

Baker Island is a saucer-shaped atoll with an area of approximately one square mile. It is about 1,650 miles from Hawaii.

Howland Island, 36 miles to the northeast, is approximately one and a half miles long and half a mile wide.

Jarvis Island is several hundred miles to the east and is approximately two miles long by one and an eighth miles wide.

Baker, Howland, and Jarvis have been uninhabited since 1942.

CANAL ZONE

Headquarters: Balboa Heights, C. Z.; 4400 Dauphine St., New Orleans, La. 70146; 425 Thirteenth St., N.W., Washington, D.C. 20004.
Governor-President: H. R. Parfitt.
1950 population: 52,822.
1960 population: 42,122.
1970 population: 44,198.
1970 land area: 553 sq mi. (1,432 sq km).

The Canal Zone is a 50-mile strip between the Atlantic and Pacific Oceans which was granted to the United States in perpetuity by the Republic of Panama by treaty in 1903 (ratified Feb. 26, 1904) for the purpose of building, maintaining, protecting, and operating a canal. The zone extends roughly five miles on either side of the center line of the Panama Canal.

The 1903 treaty empowered the United States to act as sovereign within the zone to the exclusion of the exercise of any such sovereign rights by the Republic.

In return for the perpetual sovereign grant, the United States guaranteed the independence of the Republic and agreed to pay $10,000,000 to Panama upon ratification of the treaty and $250,000 in gold annually, beginning nine years after ratification. The annual payments were increased to $430,000 after the United States went off the gold standard. The annuity was increased by the 1955 treaty and is currently $2,328,200.

The history of the Canal goes back to 1534, when King Charles V of Spain ordered a survey made. In 1876 a concession to construct a Panama Canal was granted by Colombia to an American citizen, Anthony de Gogorza. A revised concession was granted in 1878 to St. Lucien N. B. Wyse, who represented a French company. Construction of the waterway was formally inaugurated in January, 1880, by the French Canal Co. Twenty years later, the French gave up their efforts to build a canal and sold their canal rights and properties to the United States for $40,000,000, the transfer being made May 4, 1904, in Panama City. The construction of the canal was completed 10 years later.

The Canal is 40.27 miles from shore line to shore line and 50.72 miles from deep water in the Caribbean to deep water in the Pacific. The Panama Railroad, completed in 1855 by private U. S. enterprise, is owned by the Panama Canal Co. It roughly parallels the Canal channel, running 47.64 miles from Colon to Panama City and is the oldest transcontinental railroad in the Americas.

The Panama Canal Locks lift or lower ships 85 feet between sea level and Gatún Lake level in three steps on each side of the Isthmus. On the Atlantic side the three steps are at Gatún Locks. On the Pacific side there are two steps at Miraflores Locks and one step at the Pedro Miguel Locks. Each of the twin chambers in every flight of locks has a nominal length of 1,000 feet, a width of 110 feet, and a minimum depth of water of 40 feet.

The Canal Zone is, in effect, a U. S. government reservation, and in general no private enterprise is permitted except that relating directly to the operation of the waterway. The Governor, who is appointed by the U. S. President, administers the Canal Zone Government, which is responsible for such civil functions as health, sanitation, and protection of the Zone. The Governor is also exofficio President of the Panama Canal Company, which is a corporate agency of the United States charged with the operation of the Canal and its related activities.

In February 1974, the U.S. and the Republic of Panama agreed on an eight-point Joint Statement of Principles that would lead to a new treaty arrangement. The 1903 treaty would be abrogated; the concept of perpetuity would be eliminated and the Panamanian territory in which the canal is situated would be returned to the Republic of Panama. Other points dealt with administration, protection and the sharing of revenues.

CANTON AND ENDERBURY

Canton and Enderbury islands, the largest of the Phoenix group, are jointly administered by the United States and Great Britain after an agreement signed Apr. 6, 1939.

Canton is triangular in shape and the largest of the eight islands of this group. It lies about 1,600 miles southwest of Hawaii and was discovered at the turn of the 18th century by United States whalers. After World War II it served as an aviation support facility, and later as a missile tracking station. Since 1967, however, the island has been uninhabited.

Enderbury is rectangular in shape and is 3.5 miles long by 1.5 miles wide. It is unpopulated and lies about 32 miles southeast of Canton.

GUAM

Capital: Agaña.
Governor: Ricardo J. Bordallo.
1950 population: 59,498.
1960 population: 67,044.
1970 population: 84,996.
1970 land area: 212 sq mi. (549 sq km).

Guam, the largest of the Mariana Islands, is independent of the trusteeship assigned to the United States in 1947. It was acquired by the United States from Spain in 1898 (occupied 1899) and was placed under the Navy Department.

In World War II, Guam was seized by the Japanese on Dec. 11, 1941; but on July 21, 1944, it was once more in U. S. hands.

On Aug. 1, 1950, President Truman signed a bill which granted U.S. citizenship to the people of Guam and established self-government. However, the people do not vote in national elections. In 1972 Guam elected its first delegate to the U.S. Congress. The Executive Branch of the Guam government is under the general supervision of the U.S. Secretary of the Interior. In November 1970, Guam elected its first Governor, Carlos G. Camacho, and a 21-man legislature.

Military installations and tourism are important factors in Guam's economy.

JOHNSTON ATOLL

Johnston is a coral atoll about 700 miles southwest of Hawaii. It consists of four small islands—Johnston Island, Sand Island, Hikina Island, and Akau Island—which are surrounded by a reef about 12 miles in circumference.

The atoll was discovered by Capt. Charles James Johnston of *H.M.S. Cornwallis* in 1807. In 1858 it was claimed by Hawaii, and later became a U. S. possession.

KINGMAN REEF

Kingman Reef, located about 1,000 miles south of Hawaii, was discovered by Capt. E. Fanning in 1798, but named for Capt. W. E. Kingman, who rediscovered it in 1853. It is about 9.5 miles long and 5 miles wide within the 100-fathom curve. It dries at low water on its northeastern, eastern, and southeastern edges. A small islet, 3 feet high, lies on its eastern side.

MIDWAY

Midway, lying about 1,200 miles west-northwest of Hawaii, was discovered by Captain N. C. Brooks of the Hawaiian bark *Gambia* on July 5, 1859, in the name of the United States. It was formally declared a United States possession in 1867, and in 1903 Theodore Roosevelt made it a naval reservation.

Sand and Eastern Islands, with 850 acres and 328 acres respectively, are its largest individual islands. The circular atoll enclosing the islands is 6 miles in diameter.

The total group comprises an area of two square miles and has no native population. The Navy Department maintains an installation and has jurisdiction over the atoll.

SWAN ISLANDS

The Swan Islands are two small islands, Great Swan and Little Swan, in the Caribbean Sea, 98 miles north of Honduras. They were claimed by the United States in 1863, but Honduras also claimed them on the basis of their discovery by the Spanish. After years of dispute, the U.S. in 1971 signed a treaty recognizing Honduran sovereignty over the islands. The treaty was ratified by both countries on Sept. 1, 1972.

VIRGIN ISLANDS OF THE U. S.

Capital: Charlotte Amalie (on St. Thomas).
Governor: Cyril E. King.
1950 population: 26,665.

1960 population: 32,099.
1970 population: 62,468 (St. Thomas, 28,960; St. Croix, 31,779; St. John, 1,729).
1974 est. population: 100,000 (St. Thomas, 47,825; St. Croix, 49,666; St. John, 2,509).
1970 land area: 132 sq mi. (342 sq km) (St. Croix, 82 [212 sq km]; St. Thomas, 32 [83 sq km]; St. John, 20 [52 sq km]).

The Virgin Islands, consisting of nine main islands and some 75 islets, were discovered by Columbus in 1493. Since 1666, England has held six of the main islands; the other three (St. Croix, St. Thomas, and St. John), as well as about 50 of the islets, were eventually acquired by Denmark, which named them the Danish West Indies. In 1917, these islands were purchased by the United States from Denmark for $25 million.

Congress granted U. S. citizenship to Virgin Islanders in 1927; and, in 1931, administration was transferred from the Navy to the Department of the Interior. Universal suffrage was given in 1936 to all persons who could read and write the English language. The Governor was elected by popular vote for the first time in 1970; previously he had been appointed by the President of the U. S. A unicameral 15-man legislature serves the Virgin Islands, and recent Congressional legislation gave the islands a non-voting Representative in Congress.

About 80% of the population is black, and there is limited farming, fishing, and cattle raising. Industrial products include rum, watches, costume jewelry, clothing, alumina, pharmaceuticals, and petroleum products. Tourism is the principal industry.

The chief exports are sugar, rum, petroleum products, watches and jewelry, with over 90% going to the United States.

WAKE ISLAND

Wake Island, about halfway between Midway and Guam, is an atoll comprising the three islets of Wilkes, Peale, and Wake. They were discovered by the British in 1796 and annexed by the United States in 1898. The entire area comprises 3 square miles and has no native population. In 1938, Pan American Airways established a seaplane base and Wake Island has been used as a commercial base since then. On Dec. 8, 1941, it was attacked by the Japanese, who finally took possession on Dec. 23. It was surrendered by the Japanese on Sept. 4, 1945.

The Federal Aviation Administration maintained a station on Wake Island until June 1972, when civil administration of the island was taken over by the U.S. Air Force. In 1962, the area was placed under the jurisdiction of the Department of the Interior.

TRUST TERRITORY OF THE PACIFIC ISLANDS (MICRONESIA)

In 1885, Germany assumed a protectorate over the Marshall Islands; and, in 1899, she purchased the Northern Mariana and Caroline Islands from Spain. These islands were occupied by the Japanese in 1914 and were mandated to Japan by the League of Nations in 1919. On Apr. 2, 1947, the U. N. Security Council approved a trusteeship agreement proposed by the United States under which the Northern Mariana, Caroline, and Marshall Islands became a Strategic Trust Territory under the administration of the United States. The measure was approved by the President, with the agreement of Congress, on July 18, 1947. Administration was transferred from the Navy to the Department of the Interior on July 1, 1951. However, during 1953, administration of the islands of the Northern Marianas, except Rota, was transferred back to the Navy. The Department of the Interior again took over administration of these islands in July, 1962.

In February 1975 a covenant was signed by the United States and the Marianas Political Status Commission that would make the 17 islands in the Northern Marianas a commonwealth under American sovereignty. The covenant was overwhelmingly ratified by the people of the islands and was approved by President Ford on March 24, 1976.

The entire group comprises more than 2,000 islands, but the total land area is only 717 square miles, many of the islands being only tiny coral reefs. The Micronesians are the main ethnic group; however, the inhabitants of two outlying islands, Kapingamarangi and Nukuoro, are Polynesian. The population of the Trust Territory in 1974 was 114,973.

MARIANA ISLANDS

The Mariana Islands, east of the Philippines and south of Japan, include the islands of Guam, Rota, Saipan, Tinian, Pagan, Guguan, Agrihan, and Aguijan. Guam, the largest, is independent of the trusteeship, having been acquired by the United States from Spain in 1898. (For information on Guam, see pg. 648).

Chief crops are copra and fresh fruits and vegetables.

CAROLINE ISLANDS

The Caroline Islands, east of the Philippines and south of the Marianas, include the Yap, Truk, and the Palau groups and the islands of Ponape and Kusaie, as well as many coral atolls.

The islands are composed chiefly of volcanic rock, and their peaks rise 2,000 to 3,000 feet above sea level. Chief exports of the islands are copra, fish products, and handicrafts.

MARSHALL ISLANDS

The Marshall Islands, east of the Carolines, are divided into two chains: the western or Ralik group, including the atolls Jaluit, Kwajalein, Wotho, Bikini, and Eniwetok; and the eastern or Ratak group, including the atolls Mili, Majuro, Maloelap, Wotje, and Likiep.

The islands are of the coral-reef type and rise only a few feet above sea level. The chief crop is coconuts; exports include copra, tortoise shell, mother-of-pearl, etc.

Bikini and Eniwetok have been the scene of several atom-bomb tests. A rehabilitation program to allow the return of the former residents of Bikini is under way. Eniwetok was returned to Trust Territory administration effective January 1974, and rehabilitation of the atoll will begin preparatory to return of its original inhabitants.

TERRITORIES RECENTLY TRANSFERRED OUT OF U. S. ADMINISTRATION

Certain former Japanese islands in the Pacific —the Ryukyus, the Bonins, the Volcanos, Rosario Island, Parece Vela, and Marcus Island—were placed under U. S. military control at the end of World War II.

In 1952, Japan agreed to concur with any proposal of the United States to place these islands under U. N. trusteeship with the United States as the administering authority. Japan also agreed that the United States should administer the islands pending the trusteeship arrangement. However, no action was taken by the United States toward bringing about the trusteeship.

In 1967, the United States and Japan began consultations regarding arrangements for the early return of these islands to Japan. On Apr. 5, 1968, an agreement was signed by the two countries for the return to Japanese administration of the Bonins, the Volcanos (which include the historic island of Iwo Jima), Rosario Island, Parece Vela, and Marcus Island. The actual turnover of administration to Japan took place on June 26, 1968.

RYUKYU ISLANDS

The Ryukyus, consisting of some 73 islands, extend from southern Japan to Taiwan. They have a total area of 848 square miles, and had a population of 945,111 by the Japanese census of October, 1970. The largest island is Okinawa (454 sq. mi.), which had a population of 839,787 in October, 1970.

On May 15, 1972, the Ryukyu Islands were returned to Japanese administration under the terms of the Okinawa Reversion Treaty of June 17, 1971. Okinawa is now a prefecture of Japan.

CORN ISLANDS

The Corn Islands are two small islands in the Caribbean Sea, about 40 miles from Nicaragua. In 1914, the United States leased them from Nicaragua for 99 years. The United States terminated its lease of the Corn Islands from Nicaragua by a Convention that entered into force on April 25, 1971.

Warsaw Pact

(Signed: May 14, 1955)

Members: Albania, Bulgaria, Czechoslovakia, East Germany, Hungary, Poland, Romania, U.S.S.R.

The Warsaw Pact is the Communist equivalent of NATO. Article 4 contains the same provisions as Article 5 of NATO, stating that an attack on one shall be regarded as an attack on all. Article 5 provides for a unified military command.

50 LARGEST CITIES OF THE UNITED STATES IN 1970

Since we planned the INFORMATION PLEASE ALMANAC as a book of national scope and interest, we avoided emphasis on and identification with a single city or state, as has been characteristic of all almanacs heretofore. To obtain accurate and authoritative information, we have gone to the city officials. We appreciate their cooperation. The tabular material listed here is the latest provided by the sources. Source of population and land area: U. S. Census Bureau. Television households apply to county or counties in which a city is located, except for independent cities; source: A.C.Nielson Co. Telephones; source: American Telephone & Telegraph Co.

ATLANTA, GA.

Incorporated as city: 1847.
Mayor: Maynard Jackson (to Jan. 1978).
1960 population & (rank): 487,455 (24).
1970 population & (rank): 495,039 (27).
1960–70 population change: +1.6%.
1975 city land area: 136.0 sq. mi.
Altitude: Highest, 1,050 ft.; lowest, 940.
Location: In NW central part of state, near Chattahoochee River.
Counties: Fulton, De Kalb.
Churches (5-county area): 2,000.
City-owned parks and parkways: 164 (2,802 ac.).
Telephones (Jan. 1, 1975): 833,868.
Houses with radios (1975, 15-county area): 572,767 (98.6%).
Television households (Sept. 1974): 348,030 (98%).
Radio stations (15-county area): AM, 20; FM, 8; educational, 5.
Television stations (15-county area): 5 commercial; 2 educational.
Gross assessed valuation (City, 1975): $2,857,119,676.
City tax rate (1975): $48.79 per $1,000.
Total bonded debt (1975): $169,207,014.25; school.
Revenue (1975, incl. General Fund, Airport Revenue, Water/Sewer Fund): $157,656,179.70.
Expenditure (1975): $156,270,397.63.
Chamber of Commerce: Atlanta Chamber of Commerce, 1300 Commerce Building, Atlanta, Ga. 30303.

Information is gathered on 3 geographic areas: City of Atlanta, 5-county metro area, 15-county SMSA.

BALTIMORE, MD.

Incorporated as city: 1797.
Mayor: William D. Schaefer (to Dec. 1979).
1960 population & (rank): 939,024 (6).
1970 population & (rank): 905,787 (7).
1960–70 population change: –3.5%.
1970 land area: 78.3 sq. mi.
Altitude: Highest, 490 ft.; lowest, sea level.
Location: On Patapsco River, about 12 mi. from Chesapeake Bay.
County: Independent city.
Churches: Roman Catholic, 68; Jewish, 50; Protestant and others, 356.
City-owned parks: 347 park areas and tracts (5,970 ac.).
Telephones (Jan. 1, 1975): 1,203,137.
Television households (Sept. 1974): 496,080 (98%).
Radio stations: AM, 11; FM, 9.
Television stations: 5.
Assessed valuation (1975): $6,498,000,000.
City tax rate (1976–77): $58.80 per $1,000.
Net bonded debt (May 31, 1976): $624,500,122.
Current revenue (1975): $858,566,990.95.
Current expenditure (1975): $858,566,990.95.
Chamber of Commerce: Chamber of Commerce of Metropolitan Baltimore, 22 Light St., Baltimore, Md. 21202.

BIRMINGHAM, ALA.

Incorporated as city: 1871.
Mayor: David Vann (to Oct. 1979).
1960 population & (rank): 340,887 (36).
1970 population & (rank): 300,910 (48).
1960–70 population change: –11.7%.
1971 land area: 79.5 sq. mi.
Altitude: Highest, 1,260 ft.; lowest, 580.
Location: In north central part of state.
County: Seat of Jefferson Co.
Churches: over 1,000.
Telephones (Jan. 1, 1975): 390,363.
Television households (Sept. 1974): 215,140 (98%).
Radio stations: AM, 13; FM, 6.
Television stations: 3 commercial; 1 educational.
Assessed valuation (1975): $704,396,264.
City tax rate (1975): $51.00 per $1,000.
Net bonded debt (1975): $44,563,125.
Revenue (general fund, 1975): $49,996,379.
Expenditure (1975): $50,441,713.
Chamber of Commerce: Birmingham Area Chamber of Commerce, 1914 Sixth Ave. North, Birmingham, Ala. 35203.

BOSTON, MASS.

Incorporated as city: 1822.
Mayor: Kevin H. White (to Jan. 1980).
1960 population & (rank): 697,197 (13).
1970 population & (rank): 641,071 (16).
1960–70 population change: –8.1%.
1970 land area: 46.0 sq. mi.
Altitude: Highest, 330 ft.; lowest, sea level.
Location: On Massachusetts Bay, at mouths of Charles and Mystic Rivers.
County: Seat of Suffolk Co.
Churches: Protestant, 187; Roman Catholic, 73; Jewish, 28; others, 100.
City-owned parks, playgrounds, etc.: 2,276.36 ac.
Telephones (Jan. 1, 1975): 515,447.
Television households (Sept. 1974): 252,700 (96%).
Radio sets (Greater Boston Area): 3,311,000.
Radio stations: AM, 9; FM, 8.
Television stations: 7.
Assessed valuation (1975–76): $1,793,473,000.
City tax rate (1975–76): $196.70 per $1,000.
Net bonded debt (June 30, 1975): $376,370,080.
Revenue (1974–75): $651,283,410.
Expenditures (1974–75): $636,948,156.
Chamber of Commerce: Boston Chamber of Commerce, 125 High St., Boston, Mass. 02110.

New fiscal year now in effect, July 1 to June 30 from 1974.

BUFFALO, N. Y.

Incorporated as city: 1832.
Mayor: Stanley M. Makowski (to Dec. 1977).
1960 population & (rank): 532,759 (20).
1970 population & (rank): 462,768 (28).
1960–70 population change: –13.1%.
1970 land area: 41.3 sq. mi.
Altitude: Highest, 698 ft.; lowest, 571.
Location: At east end of Lake Erie, on Niagara River.
County: Seat of Erie Co.
Churches: 60 denominations, with over 400 churches.
City-owned parks: 10 public parks (3,000 ac.).
Telephones (Jan. 1, 1975): 432,469.
Television households (Sept. 1974): 359,260 (98%).
Radio sets: 223,400.

Radio stations: AM, 12; FM, 13.
Television stations: 5 (plus reception from 3 Canadian stations).
Assessed valuation (1974-75): $1,031,743,608.
City tax rate (1973-74): $82.93 per $1,000.
Net bonded debt (1970): $159,691,000.
Revenue (1973-74): $213,401,487.
Expenditure (1973-74): $245,780,640.
Chamber of Commerce: Buffalo Area Chamber of Commerce, 238 Main St., Buffalo, N.Y. 14202.

CHICAGO, ILL.

Incorporated as city: 1837.
Mayor: Richard J. Daley (to Apr. 1979).
1960 population & (rank): 3,550,404 (2).
1970 population & (rank): 3,369,357 (2).
1960-70 population change: -5.1%.
1975 land area: 128.124 sq. mi.
Altitude: Highest, 672 ft.; lowest, 581.
Location: On lower west shore of Lake Michigan.
County: Seat of Cook Co.
Churches: Protestant, 850; Roman Catholic, 280; Jewish, 59.
City-owned parks: 568.
Telephones (Jan. 1, 1975): 2,454,644.
Television households (Sept. 1974): 1,846,530 (97%).
Radio stations: AM, 17; FM, 20.
Television stations: 8.
Assessed valuation (1974): $12,297,365,927.
Total Chicago tax rate (1974): $85.57 per $1,000.
Total gross bonded debt (1974): $969,060,000.
Revenue (1976 est.): $1,169,364,607.
Expenditure (1976 est.): $1,154,510,865.
Chamber of Commerce: Chicago Association of Commerce & Industry, 130 S. Michigan Ave., Chicago, Ill. 60603.

CINCINNATI, OHIO

Incorporated as city: 1819.
Mayor: Ms. Bobbie Stern (to Dec. 1976).
City Manager: William V. Donaldson.
1960 population & (rank): 502,550 (21).
1970 population & (rank): 451,410 (30).
1960-70 population change: -10.1%.
1970 land area: 78.1 sq. mi.
Altitude: Highest, 960 ft.; lowest, 441.
Location: In SW corner of state on Ohio River.
County: Seat of Hamilton Co.
Churches: 850.
City-owned parks: 96 (3,879 ac.).
Telephones (Jan. 1, 1975): 689,894.
Homes with radios (est. Jan. 1, 1966): 269,250.
Television households (Sept. 1974): 309,120 (98%).
Radio stations: AM, 9; FM, 8 (Greater Cincinnati).
Television stations: 5.
Assessed valuation (1975): $1,858,955,180.
City tax rate (1975): $13.48 per $1,000.
Bonded debt (1975): $202,801,510.
Revenue (general fund, 1975): $89,876,830.
Expenditure (general fund, 1975): $94,801,953.
Chamber of Commerce: Cincinnati Chamber of Commerce, 309 Vine St., Cincinnati, Ohio 45202.

CLEVELAND, OHIO

Incorporated as city: 1836.
Mayor: Ralph J. Perk (to Dec. 1977).
1960 population & (rank): 876,050 (8).
1970 population & (rank): 750,879 (10).
1960-70 population change: -14.3%.
1970 land area: 75.9 sq. mi.
Altitude: Highest, 865 ft.; lowest, 573.
Location: On Lake Erie at mouth of Cuyahoga River.
County: Seat of Cuyahoga Co.

Churches:* Protestant, 717; Roman Catholic, 162; Jewish, 23; Eastern Orthodox, 18.
City-owned parks: 341 (2,130 ac.).
Telephones (Jan. 1, 1975): 892,052.
Television households (Sept. 1974): 561,270 (98%).
Radio homes (1967): 1,713,300.*
Radio stations: AM, 13; FM, 14.
Television stations: 7.
Assessed valuation (1976): $2,863,422.
City tax rate (1976): $71.10 per $1,000.
Bonded debt (1976): $384,079,000.
Revenue (1976): $324,827,319.
Expenditures (1976): $324,827,319.
Chamber of Commerce: Greater Cleveland Growth Association, 690 Union Commerce Building, Cleveland, Ohio 44115.
* 100-mile area.

COLUMBUS, OHIO

Incorporated as city: 1834.
Mayor: Tom Moody (to Jan. 1980).
1960 population & (rank): 471,316 (28).
1970 population & (rank): 540,025 (21).
1960-70 population change: +14.6%.
1970 land area: 143.9 sq. mi.
Altitude: Highest, 902 ft.; lowest, 702.
Location: In central part of state, on Scioto River.
County: Seat of Franklin Co.
Churches: Protestant, 412; Roman Catholic, 43; Jewish, 5.
City-owned parks: 111 (10,548.8 ac.).
Telephones (Jan. 1, 1975): 467,694.
Television households (Sept. 1974): 287,880 (99%).
Homes with radios (1969): 235,000.
Television sets (1969): 434,000.
Radio stations: AM, 8; FM, 6.
Television stations: 3 commercial, 2 educational.
Assessed valuation (1976): $3,053,390,310.
City tax rate (1976): $39.60 per $1,000.
Net bonded debt (Dec. 31, 1975): $292,017,214.26.
All revenue (1975)*: $745,190,431.14.
All expenditures (1975)*: $742,726,218.16.
Chamber of Commerce: Columbus Area Chamber of Commerce, P.O. Box 1527, Columbus, Ohio 43216.
* Detailed Financial Report is available from City Auditor.

DALLAS, TEX.

Incorporated as city: 1856.
Mayor: Bob Folsom (to May 1977).
City Manager: George Schrader (apptd. Dec. 1972).
1960 population & (rank): 679,684 (14).
1970 population & (rank): 844,401 (8).
1960-70 population change: +24.2%.
1970 land area: 265.6 sq. mi.
Altitude: Highest, 750 ft.; lowest, 375.
Location: In NE part of state, on Trinity River.
County: Seat of Dallas Co.
Churches: 1,200 (in Dallas Co.).
City-owned parks: 244 (20,555 ac.).
Telephones (Jan. 1, 1975): 742,724.
Radio sets (1970): 428,919.
Television households (Sept. 1974): 468,050 (97%).
Radio stations: AM, 12; FM, 9.
Television stations: 7
Assessed valuation (1974): $8,183,515,990.
City tax rate (1974-75): $13.95 per $1,000.
Net revenue bond debt (Sept. 30, 1975): $185,400,000.
Net tax supported debt (Sept. 30, 1975): $296,016,037.
Revenue (est. 1975-76): $274,001,728.
Expenditure (budget est. 1975-76): $273,187,215.
Chamber of Commerce: Dallas Chamber of Commerce, Fidelity Union Tower, Dallas, Tex. 75201.

DENVER, COLO.

Incorporated as city: 1861.
Mayor: William H. McNichols, Jr. (to July 1, 1979).
1960 population & (rank): 493,887 (23).
1970 population & (rank): 514,678 (25).
1960–70 population change: +4.2%.
1975 land area: 115.08 sq. mi.
Altitude: Highest, 5,470 ft.; lowest, 5,130.
Location: In NE central part of state, on South Platte River.
County: Coextensive with Denver Co.
Churches: Protestant, 815; Roman Catholic, 63; Jewish, 13.*
City-owned parks: 155 (3,600 ac.).
City-owned mountain parks: 40 (13,447.6 ac.).
Telephones (Jan. 1, 1975): 1,021,448.
Television households (Sept. 1974): 188,840 (96%).
Radio stations: AM, 18; FM, 13.*
Television stations: 5.
Assessed valuation (1975): $1,878,042,460.
City tax rate (1975): $27.64 per $1,000 (excl. school district, urban drainage and regional transportation district).
Bonded debt (1975): $386,700,000 (incl. all funds, except school district).
Revenue (1975): $537,417,566 (incl. all funds, except school district).
Expenditures (1975): $576,442,482 (incl. all funds, except school district).
Chamber of Commerce: Denver Chamber of Commerce, 1301 Welton, Denver, Colo. 80204.

* Metropolitan area.

DETROIT, MICH.

Incorporated as city: 1815.
Mayor: Coleman A. Young (to Jan. 1978).
1960 population & (rank): 1,670,144 (5).
1970 population & (rank): 1,514,063 (5).
1960–70 population change: −9.4%.
1970 land area: 143.3 sq. mi.
Altitude: Highest, 685 ft.; lowest, 574.
Location: In SE part of state, on Detroit River.
County: Seat of Wayne Co.
Churches:* Protestant, 2,000; Roman Catholic, 331; Jewish, 42.
City-owned parks: 394 sites (5,851.1 ac.).
Telephones (Jan. 1, 1975): 1,451,549.
Television households (Sept. 1974): 854,350 (98%).
Homes with radios: 1,544,700 (98.6%).*
Radio stations: AM, 18; FM, 32.*
Television stations: 8.*
Assessed valuation (1976): $5,046,446,260.
City tax rate (1975–76): $28.51 per $1,000.†
Net bonded debt (Feb. 1, 1975): General obligations $359,341,198, revenue and self-supporting debt, $380,886,900.
Revenue (1975–76): $808,684,264.
Expenditures (1975–76): $808,684,264.
Chamber of Commerce: Greater Detroit Chamber of Commerce, 150 Michigan Ave., Detroit, Mich. 48226.

* 6-County metropolitan area. † Excludes school system.

EL PASO, TEX.

Incorporated as city: 1873.
Mayor: Don Henderson (to April 1977).
1960 population & (rank): 276,687 (46).
1970 population & (rank): 322,261 (45).
1960–70 population change: +16.5%.
1975 land area: 106.7 sq. mi.
Altitude: 4,000 ft.
Location: In far west part of state, on Rio Grande.
County: Seat of El Paso Co.

Churches: Protestant, 212; Roman Catholic, 36; Jewish, 2; others, 13.
City-owned parks: 82 (1,419.8 ac.).
Telephones (Jan. 1, 1975): 230,044.
Radio sets (1972): 265,000.*
Television households (Sept. 1974): 107,160 (97%).
Radio stations: AM, 9; FM, 5.
Television stations: 3.
Assessed valuation (1975): $930,323,000.
City tax rate (1974): $17.70 per $1,000 (based on 65% of valuation).
Bonded debt (July 1975): $51,314,000.
Revenue (est. 1975–76): $40,658,500.**
Expenditure (est. 1975–76): $40,658,500.
Chamber of Commerce: El Paso Chamber of Commerce, 10 Civic Center Plaza, El Paso, Tex. 79944.

* Metropolitan area. ** Portion provided by revenue sharing.

FORT WORTH, TEX.

Incorporated as city: 1873.
Mayor: Clif Overcash (to Apr. 1977).
City Manager: R. N. Line (apptd. Apr., 1971).
1960 population & (rank): 356,268 (34).
1970 population & (rank): 393,476 (33).
1960–70 population change: +10.4%.
1976 land area: 238.1 sq. mi.
Altitude: Highest, 780 ft.; lowest, 520.
Location: In north central part of state, on Trinity River.
County: Seat of Tarrant Co.
Churches: Protestant, 392, Roman Catholic, 16; Jewish, 2.
City-owned parks: 119 (7,817 ac.; 3,500 ac. in Nature Center).
Telephones (Jan. 1, 1975): 309,255.
Radio sets (1970): 510,000.
Television households (Sept. 1974): 241,980 (98%).
Radio stations: AM, 7 (12 others providing coverage); FM, 6 (9 others providing coverage).
Television stations: 6 (2 local).
Assessed valuation (1975–76): $1,878,119,380.
City tax rate (1976): $16.90 per $1,000.
Bonded debt (Sept. 30, 1975): $170,953,501.
Revenue (1975–76): $87,222,559.
Expenditure (1975–76): $87,222,559.
Chamber of Commerce: Fort Worth Chamber of Commerce, 700 Throckmorton, Fort Worth, Tex. 76102.

HONOLULU, HAWAII

Incorporated as City and County: 1907.
Mayor: Frank F. Fasi (to Jan. 1977).
1960 population & (rank): 294,194 (43).
1970 population & (rank): 324,871 (44).
1960–70 population change: +10.4%.
1975 population of City & County: 690,200.
1974 land area of city: 604 sq. mi.
Altitude: Highest, 4,025 ft.; lowest, sea level.
Location: The City and County Government's jurisdiction includes the entire island of Oahu.
Churches: Roman Catholic, 33; Buddhist, 32; Jewish, 2; Protestant and others, 320.
City-owned parks: 4,556 ac.
Telephones (Jan. 1, 1975): 323,844.
Television households (Sept. 1973): 179,760 (96%).
Radio stations: AM, 18; FM, 5.
Television stations: 5.
Assessed valuation (June 1975): $6,372,730,603 (70% of market value.)
Bonded debt (June 1976): $204,828,037.
Net revenue (1974–75): $224,399,729.
Net expenditure (1974–75): $170,293,561; capital improvement budget, $52,812,000.
Chamber of Commerce: Chamber of Commerce of Hawaii, 735 Bishop St., Honolulu, Hawaii 96813.

HOUSTON, TEX.

Incorporated as city: 1839.
Mayor: Fred Hoffheinz (to Jan. 1978).
1960 population & (rank): 938,219 (7).
1970 population & (rank): 1,233,535 (6).
1960–70 population change: +31.5%.
1974 land area: 503.33 sq. mi.
Altitude: Highest, 54 ft.; lowest, sea level.
Location: In SE part of state, near Gulf of Mexico.
County: Seat of Harris Co.
Churches: Approximately 1,200.*
City-owned parks: 255 (5,712 ac., not including parkways).
Telephones (Jan. 1, 1975): 1,165,823.
Radio sets: 1,975,000.
Television households (Sept. 1974): 620,760 (97%).
Radio stations: AM, 12; FM, 16.
Television stations: 5.
Assessed valuation (1975): $8,556,661,830.
City tax rate (1975): $15.80 per $1,000.
Bonded debt (1975): $712,943,000.
Revenue (1975): $348,225,895.
Expenditure (1975): $327,501,490.
Chamber of Commerce: Houston Chamber of Commerce, P.O. Box 53600, Houston, Tex. 77052.

  * Metropolitan area (Harris County).

INDIANAPOLIS, IND.

Incorporated as city: 1847.
Mayor: William H. Hudnut III (to Jan. 1980).
1960 population & (rank): 476,258 (26).
1970 population & (rank): 742,925 (11).
1960–70 population change: +55.9%.
1970 land area: 379.4 sq. mi.
Altitude: Highest, 840 ft.; lowest, 700.
Location: In central part of state, on West Fork of White River.
County: Seat of Marion Co.
Churches: 580.*
City-owned parks: 130 (10,200+ ac.).
Telephones (Jan. 1, 1975): 624,813.
Families with radios: 264,000.
Television households (Sept. 1974): 266,980 (98%).
Radio stations: AM, 9; FM, 13.*
Television stations: 6.*
Assessed Valuation (1974): (consolidated city), $1,958,-300,754; (Marion county) $2,085,302,004.
City tax rate (Center Township, 1975): $125.84.
Gross debt (consolidated city, Dec. 31, 1974): $176,263,000.
Revenue (1974): $128,388,512.
Expenditure (1974): $128,355,945.
Chamber of Commerce: Indianapolis Chamber of Commerce, 320 N. Meridian St., Indianapolis, Ind. 46202.

  * Marion County.

JACKSONVILLE, FLA.

Incorporated as city: 1822.
Mayor: Hans G. Tanzler, Jr. (to July 1, 1979).
1960 population & (rank): 201,030.
1970 population & (rank): 528,865 (23).*
1960–1970 population change: +163.1%.*
1970 land area: 766.0 sq. mi.*
Altitude: Highest, 71 ft.; lowest, sea level.
Location: On St. Johns River, 20 miles from Atlantic Ocean.
County: Duval.
Churches: Protestant, 598; Roman Catholic, 17; Jewish, 3; others, 10.
City-owned parks and playgrounds: 136 (1,475 ac.).
Telephones (Jan. 1, 1975): 393,619.
Television households (Sept. 1974): 184,760 (98%).
Radio stations: AM, 14; FM, 7.

Television stations: 3 commercial, 1 educational.
Assessed valuation (1974–75): $4,022,506,845.
City tax rate (1974–75): $19.04 per $1,000 (old city area); $17.82 (old county area).
Bonded debt (1974–75): $49,301,628.
Revenue (1974–75): $563,646,719 (includes Federal aid).
Expenditure (1974–75): $563,646,719.
Chamber of Commerce: Jacksonville Area Chamber of Commerce, Jacksonville, Fla. 32202.

  * Result of consolidation of city and Duval County, Oct. 1, 1968.

KANSAS CITY, MO.

Incorporated as city: 1853.
Mayor: Dr. Charles B. Wheeler, Jr. (to Apr. 1979).
City Manager: Robert A. Kipp (apptd. Jan. 1974).
1960 population & (rank): 475,539 (27).
1970 population & (rank): 507,330 (26).
1960–70 population change: +6.7%.
1970 land area: 316.33 sq. mi.
Altitude: Highest, 1,014 ft.; lowest, 722.
Location: In western part of state, at conjunction of Missouri and Kansas Rivers.
County: Located in Jackson, Clay, and Platte Counties.
Churches: 1,100 churches of all denominations.
City-owned parks and playgrounds: 131 (8,784 ac.).
Telephones (Jan. 1, 1975): 337,057.
Television households (Sept. 1974): 305,110 (98%).
Radio stations: AM, 14; FM, 15.*
Television stations: 6.*
Assessed valuation (1975–76): $1,594,218,320.
City tax rate (1975–76): $15.20 per $1,000.
Bonded debt (1975): $96,935,000.†
Revenue (1974–75): $121,584,596.‡
Expenditure (1974–75): $114,286,417.
Budget (gross total, 1975–76): $169,434,976.
Chamber of Commerce: Chamber of Commerce of Greater Kansas City, 920 Main St., Kansas City, Mo. 64105.

  * Metropolitan area. † General obligation. ‡ Operating and debt.

LONG BEACH, CALIF.

Founded: 1881.
Mayor: Dr. Thomas J. Clark (to July 1978).
City Manager: John R. Mansell (apptd. Mar. 1961).
1960 population & (rank): 344,168 (35).
1970 population & (rank): 359,879 (40).
1960–70 population change: +4.3%.
1970 land area: 50 sq. mi.
Altitude: Highest, 170 ft.; lowest, sea level.
Location: On San Pedro Bay, south of Los Angeles.
County: In Los Angeles Co.
Churches: 236.
City-owned parks: 43 (1,620 ac.).
Telephones: (included in Los Angeles area).
Television households (included in Los Angeles area).
Radio stations: AM, 2; FM, 6.
Television stations: 1 (cable).
Assessed valuation (1975–76): $1,176,311,063.
City tax rate (1975–76): $20.845 per $1,000.
Bonded debt (June 1976): $8,050,000.
Revenue (1975–76): $176,598,054.*
Expenditure (1975–76): $217,714,221.
Chamber of Commerce: Long Beach Chamber of Commerce, 121 Linden Ave., Long Beach, Calif. 90802.

  * Does not include 1975–76 beginning surplus of $41,-116,167.

LOS ANGELES, CALIF.

Incorporated as city: 1850.
Mayor: Tom Bradley (to June 1977).
1960 population & (rank): 2,479,015 (3).
1970 population & (rank): 2,811,801 (3).

1960-70 population change: +13.4%.
1976 land area: 463.9 sq. mi.
Altitude: Highest, 5,081 ft.; lowest, sea level.
Location: In SW part of state, on Pacific Ocean.
County: Seat of Los Angeles Co.
Churches: 1,928 of all denominations.
City-owned parks: 273 (13,786 ac.).
Telephones (extended area, Jan. 1, 1975): 5,333,005.*
Radio sets (1970): 3,749,981.
Television households (Sept. 1974): 2,495,040 (96%).*
Radio stations: AM, 32; FM, 40.
Television stations: 18.
Assessed valuation (1975): $9,486,088,917.
City property tax rate (1975-76): $3.0813 per $100 of assessed value.
Gross debt (June 30, 1975): General obligation bonds, $167,925,000; revenue bonds, $1,773,403,000.
Revenue (est. 1975-76): $1,766,622,430.
Expenditures (est. 1975-76): $2,360,609,652.
Chamber of Commerce: Los Angeles Chamber of Commerce, 404 S. Bixel St., Los Angeles, Calif. 90054.

* Includes Long Beach, Calif.

LOUISVILLE, KY.

Incorporated as city: 1828.
Mayor: Harvey I. Sloane (to Dec. 1977).
1960 population & (rank): 390,639 (31).
1970 population & (rank): 361,706 (38).
1960-70 population change: −7.4%.
1970 land area: 65.2 sq. mi.
Altitude: Highest, 565 ft.; lowest, 477.
Location: In north central part of state, on Ohio River.
County: Seat of Jefferson Co.
Churches: 678.*
City-owned parks and playgrounds: 159 (over 7,000 ac.).
Telephones (Jan. 1, 1975): 504,354.*
Radio sets (1970): 160,324.*
Television households (Sept. 1974): 233,950 (98%).
Radio stations: 16.
Television stations: 5.
Assessed valuation (1975): $2,059,459,111.
City tax rate (1975-76): $0.566 per $100 (city purposes only; exclusive of schools).
Net bonded debt (Dec. 31, 1975): $48,979,000.
Revenue (1975-76): $68,990,531.
Expenditures (1975-76): $67,017,740.
Chamber of Commerce: Louisville Area Chamber of Commerce, 300 W. Liberty St., Louisville, Ky. 40202.

* Metropolitan area.

MEMPHIS, TENN.

Incorporated as city: 1826.
Mayor: Wyeth Chandler (to Jan. 1980).
1960 population & (rank): 497,524 (22).
1970 population & (rank): 623,530 (17).
1960-70 population change: +25.3%.
1970 land area: 280.89 sq. mi.
Altitude: Highest, 331 ft.
Location: In SW corner of state, on Mississippi River.
County: Seat of Shelby Co.
Churches: 800.
Parks and playgrounds: 117 (5,565 ac.).
Telephones (Jan. 1, 1975): 533,789.
Television households (Sept. 1974): 235,380 (97%).
Radio stations: AM, 12; FM, 9.
Television stations: 4.
Assessed valuation (1974): $1,873,327,089.
City tax rate (1975-76): $3.06 per $100.*
Bonded debt (1975): $349,402,000.
Revenue (1975-76): $160,278,539.
Expenditure (1975-76): $160,278,539.
Chamber of Commerce: Memphis Area Chamber of Commerce, P.O. Box 224, Memphis, Tenn. 38103.

* Includes school indebtedness.

MIAMI, FLA.

Incorporated as city: 1896.
Mayor: Maurice A. Ferre (to Nov. 1976).
City manager: Joseph R. Grassie (apptd. May 5, 1976.)
1960 population & (rank): 291,688 (44).
1970 population & (rank): 334,859 (42).
1960-70 population change: +14.8%.
1970 land area: 34.3 sq. mi.
Altitude: Average, 12 ft.
Location: In SE part of state, on Biscayne Bay.
County: Seat of Dade Co.
Churches: Protestant, 592; Roman Catholic, 53; Jewish, 48.
City-owned parks: 90.
Telephones (Jan. 1, 1975): 943,340.*
Radio sets (home & auto, 1970): over 2,100,000.
Television households (Sept. 1974): 512,570 (97%).
Radio stations: AM, 18; FM, 20; educational, 1.
Television stations: 5 commercial, 2 educational, 2 closed-circuit.
Assessed valuation (1974-75): $3,596,933,488.
City tax rate (1974-75): $10.93 per $1,000.
Bonded debt (1974-75): $103,595,000.
Revenue (1974-75): $55,201,878.
Expenditure (1975-76): $92,932,761.
Chamber of Commerce: Greater Miami Chamber of Commerce, 1200 Biscayne Blvd., Miami, Fla. 33132.

* Includes all of Dade County.

MILWAUKEE, WIS.

Incorporated as city: 1846.
Mayor: Henry W. Maier (to Apr. 1980).
1960 population & (rank): 741,324 (11).
1970 population & (rank): 717,372 (12).
1960-70 population change: −3.2%.
1970 land area: 95.0 sq. mi.
Altitude: 580.60 ft.
Location: In SE part of state, on Lake Michigan.
County: Seat of Milwaukee Co.
Churches: 769.
County-owned parks: 14,200 ac.
Telephones (Jan. 1, 1975): 791,978.
Families with radio sets (1970): 435,100.†
Television households (Sept. 1974): 360,540 (98%).
Radio stations: AM, 8; FM, 5.
Television stations: 8.
Assessed valuation (1975): $6,213,594,060.
City and school tax rate (1975): $38.26 per $1,000.
Gross debt (Dec. 1975): $145,868,550.
Total appropriations (1976): $632,754,222.
Chamber of Commerce: Metropolitan Milwaukee Association of Commerce, 828 N. Broadway, Milwaukee, Wis. 53202.

† Milwaukee County.

MINNEAPOLIS, MINN.

Incorporated as city: 1867.
Mayor: Charles S. Stenvig (to Jan. 1978).
1960 population & (rank): 482,872 (25).
1970 population & (rank): 434,400 (32).
1960-70 population change: −10.0%.
1970 land area: 55.1 sq. mi.
Altitude: Highest, 945 ft.; lowest, 695.
Location: In SE central part of state, on Mississippi River.
County: Seat of Hennepin Co.
Churches: 419.
City-owned parks: 153.
Telephones (incl. St. Paul, Jan. 1, 1975): 1,486,400.
Television households (Sept. 1974): 319,150 (98%).
Radio sets (1960): 432,000.
Radio stations: AM, 17; FM, 15 (metro area).
Television stations: 6 (metro area).

Assessed valuation (1974): $1,421,501,423.†
City tax rate (1975): $124.003 per $1,000 of assessed valuation.
Net debt (Dec. 1975): $182,704,000.
Revenue (1976): $147,849,377.
Expenditure (1976): $147,849,377.
Chamber of Commerce: Greater Minneapolis Chamber of Commerce, 15 S. Fifth Street, Minneapolis, Minn. 55402.

† Assessed valuations on majority of properties now range from 25% (homesteads) to 43% (commercial, industrial) of actual market value.

NASHVILLE-DAVIDSON, TENN.

Incorporated as city: 1806.
Mayor: Richard H. Fulton (to Sept. 1979).
1960 population & (rank): 170,874 (73).
1970 population & (rank): 447,877 (31).*
1960–70 population change: +162.1%.*
1970 land area: 507.8 sq. mi.
Altitude: Highest, 1,100 ft.; lowest, approx. 400 ft.
Location: North-central part of state, on Cumberland River.
County: Davidson.
Churches: Protestant, 702; Roman Catholic, 15; Jewish, 3.
City-owned parks: 47 (6,200 ac.).
Telephones (Jan. 1, 1975): 357,427.
Television households (Sept. 1974): 150,340 (98%).
Radio stations: AM, 14; FM, 11.
Television stations: 5.
Assessed valuation (1975): $1,660,778,348.
City tax rate (1974): $60 per $1,000.
Bonded debt (June 1975): $264,070,150.
Revenue (1975): $206,221,193.
Expenditure (1974): $190,076,361.
Chamber of Commerce: Nashville Area Chamber of Commerce, 161 Fourth Ave. North, Nashville, Tenn. 37219.

* Large increase is a reflection of inclusion of all of Davidson County in Metropolitan Nashville as of April, 1963. Actual 1960–70 population increase for county was 12%.

NEW ORLEANS, LA.

Incorporated as city: 1805.
Mayor: Moon Landrieu (to Apr. 1978).
1960 population & (rank): 627,525 (15).
1970 population & (rank): 593,471 (19).
1960–70 population change: −5.4%.
1970 land area: 197.1 sq. mi.
Altitude: Highest, 15 ft.; lowest, −4.
Location: In SE part of state, between Mississippi River and Lake Pontchartrain.
Parish: Seat of Orleans Parish.
Churches: 644.
City-owned parks: 69 (21,000 ac.).
Telephones (Jan. 1, 1975): 631,407.
Television households (Sept. 1974): 199,810 (97%).
Radio sets (1972): 1,200,400.
Radio stations: AM, 12; FM, 5.
Television stations: 5.
Assessed valuation (Jan. 1, 1975): $1,414,332,330.
City tax rate (1975): $38.2 per $1,000.
Bonded debt (1976): $159,976,000.
Revenue (operating budget, 1976): $186,614,337.
Expenditure (operating budget, 1976): $186,614,337.
Chamber of Commerce: Chamber of Commerce of the New Orleans Area, 301 Camp Street, New Orleans, La. 70130.

NEW YORK, N. Y.

Chartered as "Greater New York": 1898.
Mayor: Abraham D. Beame (to Dec. 31, 1977).
Borough Presidents: Bronx, Robert Abrams; Brooklyn,

Sebastian Leone; Manhattan, Percy E. Sutton; Queens, Donald R. Manes; Staten Island, Robert T. Connor.
1960 population & (rank): 7,781,984 (1).
1970 population & (rank): 7,895,563 (1).*
1960–70 population change: +1.1%.
1970 land area: 320.38 sq. mi. (Queens, 118.63; Brooklyn, 80.95; Staten Island, 57.00; Bronx, 41.44; Manhattan, 22.36).
Altitude: Highest, 410 ft.; lowest, sea level.
Location: At mouth of Hudson River; also known as the North river as it passes Manhattan.
Counties: Consists of 5 counties: Bronx, Kings (Brooklyn), New York (Manhattan), Queens, Staten Island.
Churches: Protestant, 1,766; Jewish, 1,256; Roman Catholic, 437; Orthodox, 66.
City-owned parks: 1,588 (37,369 ac.).
Telephones (Jan. 1, 1975): 5,913,942.
Television households (Sept. 1974): 2,821,040 (96%).
Housing units with radios: 2,509,677.
Radio stations: AM & FM, 7; AM only, 10; FM only, 12.
Television stations: 6.
Assessed valuation (1974–75): $39,404,009,742.†
City tax rate (1974–75): $7.349 per $100.‡
Net funded debt (June 30, 1974): $6,728,683,951.
Revenue (total income-expense budget, 1974–75): $12,017,867,876.
Expenditure (total expenditures-expense budget, 1974–75): $12,017,684,521.
Chamber of Commerce: New York Chamber of Commerce and Industry, 65 Liberty St., New York, N.Y. 10005.

* For population of boroughs, *see* Index. † Taxable property only. ‡ Manhattan.

NEWARK, N. J.

Incorporated as city: 1836.
Mayor: Kenneth A. Gibson (to July 1978).
1960 population & (rank): 405,220 (30).
1970 population & (rank): 381,930 (35).
1960–70 population change: −5.7%.
1970 land area: 23.5 sq. mi.
Altitude: Highest, 273.4 ft.; lowest, sea level.
Location: In NE part of state, on Passaic River and Newark Bay.
County: Seat of Essex Co.
Churches: Roman Catholic, 34; Jewish, 4; Protestant and others, 120.
City-owned parks: 40 (and 20 mini parks); (39.3 ac.).
County-governed parks in city: 7 (743.97 ac.).
Telephones (Jan. 1, 1975): 315,746.
Television households (Sept. 1974): 312,950 (97%).
Radio stations: AM, 3; FM, 4.
Television stations: UHF, 1; VHF, 1.
Assessed valuation (1976): $1,191,268,600.
City tax rate (1976): $100 per $1,000.
Net bonded debt (Dec. 1975): $148,247,000.
Revenue (1976): $246,324,775.
Expenditure (1976): $246,324,775.
Chamber of Commerce: Greater Newark Chamber of Commerce, 1180 Raymond Blvd., Newark, N.J. 07102.

NORFOLK, VA.

Incorporated as city: 1845.
Mayor: Irvine B. Hill (to Aug. 31, 1976).
1960 population & (rank): 304,869 (41).
1970 population & (rank): 307,951 (47).
1960–70 population change: +1.0%.
1970 land area: 52.6 sq. mi.
Location: In SE part of state, on Elizabeth River and Hampton Roads.
County: Independent City.
Churches: 236.

Telephones (Jan. 1, 1975): 409,463.*
Radio stations: AM, 12; FM, 9.
Television households (Sept. 1974): 147,110 (97%).
Television stations: 5.
Assessed valuation (Apr. 30, 1976): $1,098,332,793.
City tax rate (1975-76): Real, $2.70 per $100 at 60% of fair market value; personal $4 per $100; machinery $1.60 per $100.
Bonded debt (Apr. 30, 1976): $100,036,963.
Revenue (fiscal 1975-76): $158,686,001. Surplus used to balance budget, $4,581,569.
Expenditure (fiscal 1975-76): $163,267,570.
Chamber of Commerce: Norfolk Chamber of Commerce. 475 Saint Paul's Blvd., Norfolk, Va. 23510.

   * Metro area.

OAKLAND, CALIF.

Incorporated as city: 1854.
Mayor: John H. Reading (to June 30, 1977).
City Manager: Cecil S. Riley (took office Sept. 1972).
1960 population & (rank): 367,548 (33).
1970 population & (rank): 361,561 (39).
1960-70 population change: −1.6%.
1970 land area: 53.4 sq. mi.
Altitude: Highest, 1,700 ft.; lowest, sea level.
Location: In west central part of state, on east side of San Francisco Bay.
County: Seat of Alameda Co.
Churches: Protestant, 150; Roman Catholic, 23; Jewish, 3; others, 84.
City-owned parks: 2,196 ac.
Telephones (Jan. 1, 1975): 544,908.**
Homes with radios (1973): 1,720,000.*
Television households (Sept. 1974): 393,340 (95%).*
Radio Stations: AM, 4; FM, 10.
Television stations: 8* commercial; 3 educational.**
Assessed valuation (1975-76): $1,251,174,637.
City tax rate (1975-76): $29.586 per $1,000.
Bonded debt (est. June 1976): $7,920,000.
Revenue (all funds, 1975-76): $88,148,597.
Expenditure (all funds, 1975-76): $91,961,492.
Chamber of Commerce: Oakland Chamber of Commerce, 1939 Harrison St., Suite 400, Oakland, Calif. 94612.

   * Alameda County. ** Included in East Bay Exchange.

OKLAHOMA CITY, OKLA.

Incorporated as city: 1890.
Mayor: Mrs. Patience Latting (to April, 1979).
City Manager: James J. Cook (apptd. Apr. 3, 1976).
1960 population & (rank): 324,253 (37).
1970 population & (rank): 368,164 (37).
1960-70 population change: +13.5%.
1975 land area: 648.5 sq. mi.
Altitude: Highest, 1,320 ft.; lowest, 1,140.
Location: In central part of state, on North Canadian River.
County: Seat of Oklahoma Co.
Churches: Roman Catholic, 15; Jewish, 2; Protestant and others, 741.
City-owned parks: 130 (3,701 ac.).
Telephones (Jan. 1, 1975): 528,767.
Television households (Sept. 1974): 201,000 (98%).
Radio stations: AM, 10; FM, 14.
Assessed valuation (net, 1975-76): $710,875,996.
City tax rate (1974-75): $27.85 per $1,000.
New bonded indebtedness (June 30, 1976): $176,150,939.39.
Revenue (general fund, July 30, 1974): $54,495,800.
Expenditure (general fund, July 30, 1974): $54,495,800.
Chamber of Commerce: Oklahoma City Chamber of Commerce, 1 Santa Fe Plaza, Oklahoma City, Okla. 73102.

OMAHA, NEB.

Incorporated as city: 1857.
Mayor: Edward Zorinsky (to May, 1977).

1960 population & (rank): 301,598 (42).
1970 population & (rank): 354,389 (41).
1960-70 population change: +17.5%.
1970 land area: 76.6 sq. mi.
Altitude: Highest, 1,270 ft.
Location: In eastern part of state, on Missouri River.
County: Seat of Douglas Co.
Churches: Protestant, 246; Roman Catholic, 44; Jewish, 4.
City-owned parks: 99 (3,671.6 ac.).
Telephones (Jan. 1, 1975): 400,800.
Television households (Sept. 1974): 136,290 (97%).
Radio sets: 310,000.
Radio Stations: AM, 7; FM, 6.
Television stations: 4.
Assessed valuation (1975): $1,065,881,089.
City tax rate (Jan. 1, 1975): $25.60 per $1,000.
Bonded debt (Jan. 1, 1976): $64,600,500.
Revenue (1974): $89,014,466.
Expenditure (1974): $89,014,466.
Chamber of Commerce: Omaha Chamber of Commerce, 1620 Dodge St., Omaha, Neb. 68102.

PHILADELPHIA, PA.

First charter as city: 1701.
Mayor: Frank L. Rizzo (to Jan. 1980).
1960 population & (rank): 2,002,512 (4).
1970 population & (rank): 1,949,996 (4).
1960-70 population change: −2.6%.
1970 land area: 129.7 sq. mi.
Altitude: Highest, 440 ft.; lowest, sea level.
Location: In SE part of state, at junction of Schuylkill and Delaware Rivers.
County: Seat of Philadelphia Co. (conterminous).
Churches: Roman Catholic, 149; Jewish, 85; Protestant and others, 853.
City-owned parks: 134 (8,164 ac.).
Telephones (Jan. 1, 1975): 1,622,069.
Television households (Sept. 1974): 635,350 (97%).
Radio stations: AM, 20; FM, 22.
Television stations: 8.
Assessed valuation (Jan. 1975): $5,543,560,550 taxable.
City and school district tax rate (effective 1975): $47.75 per $1,000.
Net bonded debt (general obligation June 30, 1975): $1,151,223,000 (incl. Bond anticipation notes of $82,000,000); Revenue Bonds of $75,000,000 water and sewer, and $35,000,000 as work bonds.
Revenue (fiscal, 1975): $698,665,000.
Expenditure (fiscal, 1975): $729,478,000.
Chamber of Commerce: Greater Philadelphia Chamber of Commerce, 1528 Walnut St., Philadelphia, Pa. 19103.

PHOENIX, ARIZ.

Incorporated as city: 1881.
Mayor: Margaret T. Hance (to Jan. 1978).
City Manager: John B. Wentz (apptd. July 1970).
1960 population & (rank): 439,170 (29).
1970 population & (rank): 587,213 (20).
1960-70 population change: +33.7%.
1975 land area: 269.4 sq. mi.
Altitude: Highest, 2,740 ft.; lowest, 1,017.
Location: In center of state, on Salt River.
County: Seat of Maricopa Co.
City-owned parks: 132 major areas (25,124 ac.).
Telephones (Jan. 1, 1975): 790,738.*
Radio sets (est. 1973): 417,100.*
Television households (Sept. 1974): 387,410 (97%).
Radio stations: AM, 20; FM, 14.
Television stations: 5 commercial; 1 educational.
Assessed valuation (1975-76): $1,436,826,000.
City tax rate (1975-76): $18.80 per $1,000 assessed valuation.

   * Metropolitan Phoenix.

Bonded debt (est. Mar. 1975): $258,654,000.
Resources (est. 1975-76): operating $196,070,865; capital, $131,983,685.
Expenditures (est. 1975-76): operating $192,489,149; capital $78,842,592.
Chamber of Commerce: Phoenix Chamber of Commerce, 805 N. Second St., Phoenix, Ariz. 85004.

PITTSBURGH, PA.

Incorporated as city: 1816.
Mayor: Peter F. Flaherty (to Jan. 1978).
1960 population & (rank): 604,332 (16).
1970 population & (rank): 520,089 (24).
1960-70 population change: −13.9%.
1970 land area: 55 sq. mi.
Altitude: Highest, 1,240 ft.; lowest, 715.
Location: In SW part of state, at beginning of Ohio River.
County: Seat of Allegheny Co.
Churches: Protestant, 348; Roman Catholic, 86; Jewish, 28; Orthodox, 26.
City-owned parks and playgrounds: 88 (2,471 ac.).
Television households (Sept. 1974): 521,460 (98%).
Telephones (Jan. 1, 1975): 770,670.
Radio sets: 700,464.*
Radio stations: AM, 18; FM, 9.
Television stations: 4.
Assessed valuation (1975): Land, $394,631,006; buildings, $1,067,945,452.
City tax rate (1975): Land, $49.50 per $1,000; buildings, $24.75 per $1,000.
Net bonded debt (Mar. 31, 1975): $194,337,242.97.
Revenue (1974; excl. revenue sharing): $94,502,513.60.
Expenditure (1974): $92,843,921.12.
Chamber of Commerce: The Chamber of Commerce of Greater Pittsburgh, 411 Seventh Ave., Pittsburgh, Pa. 15222.

   * Pittsburgh Metro Market.

PORTLAND, ORE.

Incorporated as city: 1851.
Mayor: Neil Goldschmidt (to Jan. 1977).
1960 population & (rank): 372,676 (32).
1970 population & (rank): 379,967 (36).
1960-70 population change: +1.9%.
1970 land area: 89.1 sq. mi.
Altitude: Highest, 1,073 ft.; lowest, sea level.
Location: In NW part of state, on Willamette River.
County: Seat of Multnomah Co.
Churches: Protestant, 332; Roman Catholic, 27; Jewish, 4; Buddhist, 4; Vedanta Society, 1.
City-owned parks: 135 (7,233 ac.).
Telephones (Jan. 1, 1975): 451,082.
Television households (Sept. 1974): 206,100 (96%).
Radio stations: AM, 15· FM, 12.
Television stations: 5.
Assessed valuation (1975-76): $4,994,465 (at 100% of true cash value).
City tax rate (1975-76): $8.35 per $1,000 of assessed value.
Bonded debt (June 30, 1976): $26,528,000.
Revenue (budgeted 1975-76): $145,490,187.
Expenditure (budgeted 1975-76): $145,347,578.
Chamber of Commerce: Portland Chamber of Commerce, 824 SW Fifth Ave., Portland, Ore. 97204.

ROCHESTER, N. Y.

Incorporated as city: 1834.
Mayor: Thomas P. Ryan, Jr. (to Jan. 1978).
City Manager: Elisha C. Freedman.
1960 population & (rank): 318,611 (38).
1970 population & (rank): 295,011 (49).
1960-70 population change: −7.4%.
1970 land area: 36.4 sq. mi.

Altitude: Highest, 655 ft.; lowest, 246.
Location: In western part of state, on Genesee River and Lake Ontario.
County: Seat of Monroe Co.
Churches: Protestant, 128; Roman Catholic, 38; Jewish, 19; others, 22.
City-owned parks: 23 (9 county-operated).
Telephones (Jan. 1, 1975): 361,971.
Television households (Sept. 1974): 229,690 (98%).
Radio sets (1966): 211,700.
Radio stations: AM, 6; FM, 9.
Television stations: 4 (1 educational).
Assessed valuation (1974-75): $765,514,761.
City tax rate (1974-75): City, $49.37 per $1,000; schools, $58.66.
Bonded debt (1974-75): $45,375,000.*
Revenue (1974-75): $105,442,659.*
Expenditure (1974-75): City, $105,442,659; schools, $86,011,095.
Chamber of Commerce: Rochester Chamber of Commerce, 55 St. Paul St., Rochester, N.Y. 14604.

   * City and schools.

ST. LOUIS, MO.

Incorporated as city: 1822.
Mayor: John H. Poelker (to Apr. 1977).
1960 population & (rank): 750,026 (10).
1970 population & (rank): 622,236 (18).
1960-70 population change: −17.0%.
1970 land area: 61.2 sq. mi.
Altitude: Highest, 616 ft.; lowest, 413.
Location: On Mississippi River.
County: Independent city.
Churches: 1,600.*
City-owned parks: 83 (2,637 ac.).
Telephones (Jan. 1, 1975): 567,793.
Homes with radios (1975): 184,000.†
Television households (Sept. 1974): 490,590 (97%).
Radio stations: AM, 18; FM, 16.
Television stations: 5 commercial; 1 educational.
Assessed valuation (1974): $1,484,140,155.
City tax rate (1973): $56.30 per $1,000.
Bonded debt (general obligation, 1974): $93,162,700.
Revenue (1974-75): $157,930,617.
Expenditure (1974-75): $167,419,857.
Chamber of Commerce: St. Louis Regional Commerce and Growth Association, 10 Broadway, St. Louis, Mo. 63102.

   * Metropolitan area. † City of St. Louis and St. Louis County.

ST. PAUL, MINN.

Chartered as city: 1854.
New Charter: June 6, 1972.
Mayor: George Latimer (to June 1978).
1960 population & (rank): 313,411 (41).
1970 population & (rank): 309,866 (46).
1960-70 population change: −1.1%.
1970 land area: 55.44 sq. mi.
Altitude: Highest, 1,045 ft.; lowest, 683 ft.
Location: In SE central part of state, on Mississippi River.
County: Seat of Ramsey Co.
Churches: Protestant, 348; Roman Catholic, 65; Jewish 6; Orthodox, 8.
City-owned parks: 34 (1,650 ac.).
Telephones (incl. Minn., Jan. 1, 1975): 1,486,400.
Television households (Sept. 1974): 151,140 (98%).
Radio stations: 35.†
Television stations: 6, incl. 2 educational.
Assessed valuation (1975): $831,737,200.
Tax rate (collectible during 1975): 10.06 mills.
Bonded debt (Sept. 1974): $137,620,000.

   † Metropolitan area.

Revenue (est. 1975): $71,479,966.
Expenditure (est. 1975): $71,479,966.
Chamber of Commerce: Greater St. Paul Area Chamber of Commerce, Osborn Bldg., 370 Wabasha St., St. Paul, Minn. 55102.

SAN ANTONIO, TEX.

Incorporated as city: 1837.
Mayor: Mrs. Lila Cockrell (to May 1977).
City Manager: Sam Granata, Jr. (apptd. May 1973).
1960 population & (rank): 587,718 (17).
1970 population & (rank): 707,503 (14).
1960–70 population change: +20.3%.
1975 land area: 263.086 sq. mi.
Altitude: 717 ft.
Location: In south central part of state, on San Antonio River.
County: Seat of Bexar Co.
City-owned parks: Approximately 5,250 ac.
Telephones (Jan. 1, 1975): 381,555.
Television households (Sept. 1974): 263,150 (96%).
Radio stations: AM, 13; FM, 12.
Television stations: 5.
Assessed valuation (1975): $2,447,003,500.
City tax rate (1975): $16.50 per $1,000.
Net funded debt (1975): $88,434,610.
Revenue (1975-76): $124,233,795.
Expenditure (1975-76): $119,918,040.
Chamber of Commerce: Greater San Antonio Chamber of Commerce, P.O. Box 1628, 602 E. Commerce, San Antonio, Tex. 78296.

SAN DIEGO, CALIF.

Incorporated as city: 1850; again in 1872.
Mayor: Pete Wilson (to Dec. 1979).
City Manager: Hugh McKinley (apptd. Apr. 1975).
1960 population & (rank): 573,224 (18).
1970 population & (rank): 697,027 (15).
1960–70 population change: +21.6%.
1975 land area: 319.5 sq. mi.
Altitude: Highest, 1,591 ft.; lowest, sea level.
Location: In south part of state, on San Diego Bay.
County: Seat of San Diego Co.
Churches: Roman Catholic, 80; Jewish, 8; Protestant, 334; East. Orth., 7; other, 6.
City park & recreation facilities: 197 (9,460.22 ac.).
Telephones (Jan. 1, 1975): 919,547.*
Television households (Sept. 1974): 509,520 (97%).
Radio stations: AM, 10; FM, 11.
Television stations: 4.
Assessed valuation (1976): $2,797,033,137.
City tax rate (1976): $17.33 per $1,000.
Bonded debt (1976): $102,028,000.
Revenue (Combined Operating and Capital Improvements, 1976): $208,369,961.
Expenditure (Combined Operating and Capital Improvements, 1976): $177,507,356.
Chamber of Commerce: San Diego Chamber of Commerce, 233 A Street, San Diego, Calif. 92101.
   * Extended area.

SAN FRANCISCO, CALIF.

Incorporated as city: 1850.
Mayor: George R. Moscone (to Jan. 1980).
1960 population & (rank): 740,316 (12).
1970 population & (rank): 715,674 (13).
1960–70 population change: –3.3%.
1970 land area: 46.6 sq. mi.
Altitude: Highest, 925 ft.; lowest, sea level.
Location: Between Pacific Ocean and San Francisco Bay.
County: Coextensive with San Francisco City.
Churches: 493 of all denominations.

City-owned parks and squares: 133.
Telephones (Jan. 1, 1974): 744,519.
Homes with radios (1962): 268,180.
Television households (Sept. 1974): 270,200 (91%).
Radio stations: 22.
Television stations: 6.
Assessed valuation (1973–74): $2,540,316,860.
City and county tax rate (1973–74): $12.75 per $100.
Bonded debt (June 1973): $391,464,000.
General city revenue (1972–73): $663,186,120.
General city expenditure (1972–73): $676,629,889.
Chamber of Commerce: Greater San Francisco Chamber of Commerce, 400 Montgomery St., San Francisco, Calif. 94104.

SAN JOSE, CALIF.

Incorporated as city: 1897.
Mayor: Janet Gray Hayes (to Dec. 31, 1978).
1960 population & (rank): 204,196 (57).
1970 population & (rank): 459,913 (29).
1960–70 population change: +124.7%.
1975 land area: 150 sq. mi.
Altitude: 80 ft.
Location: On south San Francisco Bay, 50 miles from San Francisco.
County: Santa Clara.
Churches: Protestant, 151; Roman Catholic, 24; Jewish, 4; others, 28.
City-owned parks and playgrounds: 107 (2,087 ac.).
Telephones (Jan. 1, 1975): 506,315.
Television households (Sept. 1974): 367,730 (97%).
Radio stations: AM, 5; FM, 3.
Television stations: 2 commercial; 1 educational.
Assessed valuation (1975–76): $1,873,996,000.
City tax rate (1975–76): $17.05 per $1,000.
Bonded debt (June 1976): $65,179,000.
Revenue (all sources, 1975–76): $251,635,000.
Expenditure (all sources, 1975–76): $251,635,000.
Chamber of Commerce: San Jose Chamber of Commerce, San Jose, Calif. 95114.

SEATTLE, WASH.

Incorporated as city: 1869.
Mayor: Wes Uhlman (to Nov. 1976).
1960 population & (rank): 557,087 (19).
1970 population & (rank): 530,831 (22).
1975 population: 503,500.
1960–70 population change: –4.7%.
1970 land area: 83.6 sq. mi.
Altitude: Highest, 540 ft.; lowest, sea level.
Location: In west central part of state, on Puget Sound.
County: Seat of King Co.
Churches: Roman Catholic, 36; Jewish, 13; Protestant and others, 535.
City-owned parks, playgrounds, etc.: 278 (4,773.4 ac.).
Telephones (Jan. 1, 1975): 577,720.
Homes with radios (1973): 770,000.*
Television households (Sept. 1974): 394,650 (96%).
Radio stations: AM, 26; FM, 25; AM-FM, 10.
Television stations: 4 commercial; 1 educational.
Assessed valuation (1975): $7,284,128,000.
City tax rate (1976): $13.46 per $1,000.
Bonded debt (1976): $168,820,000.
Revenue (1975): $342,496,579.
Expenditure (1975): $396,624,000.
Chamber of Commerce: Seattle Chamber of Commerce, 215 Columbia Street, Seattle, Wash. 98104.
   * For radio-TV market area. In use.

TAMPA, FLA.

Incorporated as city: 1855.
Mayor: William F. Poe (to Sept. 30, 1979).
1960 population & (rank): 274,970 (48).
1970 population & (rank): 277,714 (50).
1960-70 population change: +1.0%.
1970 land area: 84.5 sq. mi.
Altitude: Highest, 84 ft.; lowest, sea level.
Location: In west central part of state, on Tampa Bay.
County: Seat of Hillsborough Co.
City-owned parks: 54 (25 major parks).
Telephones (Jan. 1, 1975): 356,990.
Households with radios: 168,555.
Television households (Sept. 1974): 195,130 (97%).
Radio stations: AM, 8; FM, 4.
Television stations: 7.
Assessed valuation (Sept. 1974): $1,743,345,515.
City tax rate (1974-75): $9.50 per $1,000.
Bonded debt (1974-75): $115,102,000.
Revenue (1974-75 budget): $90,522,379.
Expenditure (1974-75 budget): $90,522,379.
Chamber of Commerce: Greater Tampa Chamber of Commerce, 801 E. Kennedy Blvd., Tampa, Fla. 33601.

TOLEDO, OHIO

Incorporated as city: 1837.
Mayor: Harry Kessler (to Dec. 1977).
City Manager: James D. Daken (apptd. Feb. 1971).
1960 population & (rank): 318,003 (39).
1970 population & (rank): 383,062 (30).
1960-70 population change: +20.4%.
1976 land area: 82.28 sq. mi.
Altitude: 630 ft.
Location: In NW part of state, on Maumee River at Lake Erie.
County: Seat of Lucas Co.
Churches: Protestant, 297; Roman Catholic, 55; Jewish, 4; others, 98.
City-owned parks & playgrounds: 134 (2,650.90 ac.).
Telephones (Jan. 1, 1975): 293,409.
Television households (Feb. 1976): 165,100 (98.3%).
Radio sets (1976): 721,500.
Radio stations: AM, 8; FM, 8.
Television stations: 4.
Assessed valuation (1975): $1,489,525,380.
City tax rate (1976): $46.70 per $1,000.
Bonded debt (Jan. 1, 1976): $118,565,178.
Revenue (1975): $215,150,078.44.
Expenditure (1975): $195,226,183.49.
Chamber of Commerce: Toledo Area Chamber of Commerce, 218 Huron St., Toledo, Ohio 43604.

TULSA, OKLA.

Incorporated as city: 1898.
Mayor: Robert La Fortune (to May 1978).
1960 population & (rank): 261,685 (50).
1970 population & (rank): 330,350 (43).
1960-70 population change: +26.2%.
1975 land area: 181.14 sq. mi.
Altitude: 674 ft.
Location: In NE part of state, on Arkansas River.
County: Seat of Tulsa Co.
Churches: Protestant, 593; Roman Catholic, 32; Jewish, 2; others, 4.
City parks and playgrounds: 107 (4,811 ac.).
Telephones (Jan. 1, 1975): 350,879.
Television households (Sept. 1974): 146,660 (97%).
Radio stations: AM, 9; FM, 6.
Television stations: 3 commercial; 1 educational; 1 cable.
Assessed valuation (1975-76): $830,595,103.
City tax rate (1975-76): $86.11 per $1,000.
Bonded debt (June 1975): $137,704,000.

Revenue (1974-75): $72,766,355.
Expenditure (1974-75): $68,808,663.
Chamber of Commerce: Metropolitan Tulsa Chamber of Commerce, 616 S. Boston, Tulsa, Okla. 74119.

WASHINGTON, D.C.

Land ceded to Congress: 1788 by Maryland; 1789 by Virginia (retroceded to Virginia Sept. 7, 1846).
Seat of government transferred to D. C.: Dec. 1, 1800.
Created municipal corporation: Feb. 21, 1871.
Mayor: Walter E. Washington (to Jan. 1979).*
Motto: *Justitia omnibus* (Justice to all).
Flower: American beauty rose.
Tree: Scarlet oak.
Origin of name: in honor of Columbus.
1950 population & (rank as city): 802,178 (9).
1960 population & (rank as city): 763,956 (9).
1970 population & (rank): 756,668 (9).
1960-70 population change: -1.0%.
1970 land area: 68 sq. mi.
1970 land area: 68 sq. mi.
Geographic center: Near corner of Fourth and L Sts., NW.
Altitude: Highest, 420 ft.; lowest, sea level.
Location: Between Virginia and Maryland, on Potomac River.
Churches: Protestant, 446; Roman Catholic, 23; Jewish, 10; others, 23.
City parks: 753 (7,725 ac.).
Telephones (Jan. 1, 1975): 981,443.
Homes with radios (1970 census): 165,831.
Homes with television sets (Sept. 1974): 264,500 (96%).
Radio stations: AM, 15; FM, 16.
Television stations: 6 (including 2 UHF stations).
Assessed valuation (1974): $4,168,382,183.**
City tax rate (1973-74): $3.32 per $100.
Bonded debt: None.
Revenue (fiscal 1974): $1,718,888,120.**
Expenditures (fiscal 1974): $1,651,873,116.**

The District of Columbia—identical with the City of Washington—is the capital of the United States and the first carefully planned capital in the world.

D. C. history began in 1790 when Congress directed selection of a new capital site, 10 miles square, along the Potomac. When the site was determined, it included 30.75 square miles on the Virginia side of the river. In 1846, however, Congress returned that area to Virginia.

The city was planned and partly laid out by Major Pierre Charles L'Enfant, a French engineer. This work was perfected and completed by Major Andrew Ellicott. In 1814, during the War of 1812, a British force fired the capital, and it was from the white paint applied to cover fire damage that the President's home was called the White House.

Until November 3, 1967, the District of Columbia was administered by three commissioners appointed by the President. On that day, a government consisting of a mayor-commissioner and a nine member Council, all appointed by the President with the approval of the Senate, took office. On May 7, 1974, the citizens of the District of Columbia approved the Home Rule Charter, giving them their first form of elected government in over 100 years. The District also has one non-voting member in the House of Representatives.

(For additional information on Washington, D.C., *see* Travel Section, page 454.)

* Elected in November, 1974, took office January 2, 1975, becoming the Nation's Capital's first elected mayor in over a century. ** On taxable property only. More than 50% of all land in District of Columbia is owned by the Federal government and tax-exempt organizations, and therefore is nontaxable.

Tabulated Data on City Governments

Source: Questionnaires to the cities.

City	MAYOR Term, years	MAYOR Salary[1]	City manager's salary[2]	COUNCIL OR COMMISSION Name	Members	Term, years	Salary[3]
Atlanta, Ga.	4	$40,000	......	Council	19	4	$8,800
Baltimore, Md.	4	40,000	......	Council	19	4	16,000
Birmingham, Ala.	4	32,500	......	Council	9	(5)	6,900
Boston, Mass.	4	40,000	......	Council	9	2	20,000
Buffalo, N. Y.	4	35,000	......	Council	15	2[7]	18,500
Chicago, Ill.	4	60,000	......	Council	50	4	17,500
Cincinnati, Ohio	2	11,500	$49,220	Council	9	2	8,000
Cleveland, Ohio	2	35,000	......	Council	33	2	12,500
Columbus, Ohio	4	40,000	......	Council	7	4	8,000
Dallas, Tex.	2	50[8]	50,500	Council	11	2	50[8]
Denver, Colo.	4	40,000	......	Council	13	4	12,500
Detroit, Mich.	4	41,029	......	Council	9	4	24,800
El Paso, Tex.	2	9,600	......	Council	5[9]	2	4,800
Fort Worth, Tex.	2	10[10]	39,875	Council	9	2	10[10]
Honolulu, Hawaii	4	40,000	39,720	Council	9	4	17,500[11]
Houston, Tex.	2	20,000	......	Council	8	2	300[12]
Indianapolis, Ind.	4	32,000	......	Council	29	4	3,600[22]
Jacksonville, Fla.	4	30,000	......	Council	19	4	8,400
Kansas City, Mo.	4	25,000	39,500	Council	13[9]	4	4,800
Long Beach, Calif.	3	525[4]	54,646	Council	9[20]	3	525[4]
Los Angeles, Calif.	4	55,000	......	Council	15	4	33,000
Louisville, Ky.	4	26,000	......	Bd. of Aldermen	12	2	7,200
Memphis, Tenn.	4	35,000	28,620	Council	13	4	6,000
Miami, Fla.	2	5,000[6]	48,730	Commission	5[9]	4	5,000
Milwaukee, Wis.	4	36,351	......	Council	16	4	19,349
Minneapolis, Minn.	2	32,000	......	Council	13	2	21,976
Nashville, Tenn.	4	25,000	......	Council	41	4	3,600
New Orleans, La.	4	49,260	......	Council	7	4	15,000
New York, N. Y.	4	55,000	49,894[23]	Council	43	4	20,000
Newark, N. J.	4	35,000	35,000[14]	Council	9	4	15,000
Norfolk, Va.	2	7,200	43,500	Council	7	4	4,800
Oakland, Calif.	4	15,000	48,300	Council	9[9]	4	(15)
Oklahoma City, Okla.	4	2,000	36,500	Council	8	4	20[16]
Omaha, Neb.	4	27,500	......	Council	7	4	6,000
Philadelphia, Pa.	4	55,000	42,000[17]	Council	17	4	25,000
Phoenix, Ariz.	2	15,000	49,365	Council	7[9]	2	7,500
Pittsburgh, Pa.	4	35,000	......	Council	9	4	17,504
Portland, Ore.	4	35,527	......	Commission	4	4	27,897
Rochester, N. Y.	4	15,000	45,000	Council	9[20]	4	7,500
St. Louis, Mo.	4	25,000	......	Bd. of Aldermen	29	4	7,500
St. Paul, Minn.	2	32,237	38,870	Council	7	2	21,026
San Antonio, Tex.	2	3,000[18]	47,700	Council	9	2	20[21]
San Diego, Calif.	4	25,000	40,403	Council	8	4	17,000
San Francisco, Calif.	4	53,131	42,647	Bd. of Supervisors	11	4	9,600
San Jose, Calif.	4	7,200	49,980	Council	7	4	4,800
Seattle, Wash.	4	45,527	......	Council	9	4	(13)
Tampa, Fla.	4	35,000	......	Council	7	4	9,600
Toledo, Ohio	2	23,350	33,000	Council	9[20]	2	7,800
Tulsa, Okla.	2	30,000	......	Commission	4	2	22,500
Washington, D. C.	4	42,000	......	Council	13	4	25,200[24]

[1] Annual salary unless otherwise indicated. [2] Annual salary. City Manager's term is indefinite and at will of Council. [3] Annual salary unless otherwise indicated. In some cities, President of Council receives a higher salary. [4] Per month. [5] Staggered terms, 5 Councilmen being elected every 2 years, one to serve a 2-year term, the others 4-year terms. [6] Plus annual expense account of $2,500. [7] For 9 District Councilmen; 4 years for 5 Councilmen-at-Large. [8] Per Council meeting; not over $2,600 per year. [9] Including Mayor. [10] Per week and per Council meeting. [11] Managing Director appointed by Mayor; no Council approval required. [12] Per month part-time. [13] Staggered terms: old council $25,838, new council $28,422. [14] Business Administrator, appointed by Mayor and confirmed by Council. [15] Flat $500 per mo. or $6,000 annually. [16] Per Council meeting; not to exceed 5 meetings in a month. [17] Appointed by Mayor, with title of Managing Director. [18] Plus Council pay. [19] Chief Administrative Officer; appointed by Mayor for life. [20] Including Mayor and Vice-Mayor. [21] Per council meeting; not over $1,040 per year. [22] Plus $50 per meeting for two meetings a month. [23] At present, no city manager, salary is for 1st Deputy Mayor. [24] $10,000 additional for Chairman.

Tabulated Data on State Governments

Source: Questionnaires to the states.

State	GOVERNOR		LEGISLATURE[1]					HIGHEST COURT[2]		
	Term, years	Annual salary	Membership U[3]	L[4]	Term, yrs. U[3]	L[4]	Salaries of members[5]	Members	Term, years	Annual salary[6]
Alabama	4[10]	$25,000	35	106	4	4	3,600 per annum	9	6	$33,500
Alaska	4	50,000	20	40	4	2	14,720 per annum	5	(8)	52,992
Arizona	4	35,000	30	60	2	2	6,000 per annum	5	6	32,000
Arkansas	2	10,000	35	100	4	2	1,200 per annum	8	8	34,024
California	4	49,100	40	80	4	2	21,120 per annum	7	12	46,583
Colorado	4	40,000	35	65	4	2	7,600 per annum	7	10	35,000
Connecticut	4	42,000	36	151	2	2	6,500 per biennium[24]	6	8	36,000
Delaware	4[9]	35,000	21	41	4	2	9,000 per annum	3	12	42,000
Florida	4[10]	50,000	40	120	4	2	12,000 per annum	7	6	40,000
Georgia	4[7]	50,000	56	180	2	2	7,200 per annum	7	6	40,000
Hawaii	4	46,000	25	51	4	2	12,000 per session	5	10	41,400
Idaho	4	33,000	35	70	2	2	40 per diem	5	6	31,500
Illinois	4	50,000	59	177	4-2	2	20,000 per annum	7	10	50,000
Indiana	4[10]	36,000	50	100	4	2	6,000 per annum	5	6	38,100
Iowa	4	40,000	50	100	4	2	8,000 per annum	9	8	36,000[6]
Kansas	4	35,000	40	125	4	2	35 per diem	7	6	34,000
Kentucky	4[7]	39,500	38	100	4	2	50 per diem[25]	7	8	39,000
Louisiana	4	50,000	39	105	4	4	50 per diem[23]	7	10	37,500
Maine	4	35,000	33	151	2	2	5,000 per session[16]	6	7	26,000
Maryland	4[10]	25,000	47	141	4	4	12,500 per annum	7	15	44,100
Massachusetts	4	40,000	40	240	2	2	12,688 per annum	7	Life	40,788
Michigan	4	45,000	38	110	4	2	19,000 per annum	7	8	42,000
Minnesota	4	41,000	67	134	4	2	8,400 per annum	9	6	40,000
Mississippi	4[7]	43,000	52	122	4	4	8,100 per session	9	8	34,000
Missouri	4[10]	37,500	34	163	4	2	8,400 per annum[5]	7	12	31,500
Montana	4	30,000	50	100	4	2	26.34 per diem	5	6	27,000
Nebraska	4[10]	25,000	49[11]		4[11]		4,800 per annum	7	6	30,500[22]
Nevada	4	40,000	20	40	4	2	3,600 per biennium	5	6	35,000
New Hampshire	2	34,070	24	(12)	2	2	200 per biennium	5	(18)	33,800
New Jersey	4[10]	55,000	40	80	4[14]	2	10,000 per annum	7	7[15]	45,000
New Mexico	4[7]	35,000	42	70	4	2	40 per diem	5	8	33,500
New York	4	85,000	60	150	2	2	23,500 per annum	7	14	60,575
North Carolina	4[7]	38,500	50	120	2	2	4,800 per annum	7	8	38,000
North Dakota	4	40,000	51	102	4	2	60 per diem[26]	5	10	33,000
Ohio	4	50,000	33	99	4	2	17,500 per annum	7	6	40,000
Oklahoma	4	42,500	48	101	4	2	9,960 per annum	(19)	6	30,000
Oregon	4[10]	38,500	30	60	4	2	4,800 per annum	7	6	35,200
Pennsylvania	4	60,000	50	203	4	2	19,200 per annum	7	10	50,000
Rhode Island	2	42,500	50	100	2	2	5 per diem[17]	5	(18)	30,000
South Carolina	4[7]	39,000	46	124	4	2	7,000 per annum	5	10	37,762
South Dakota	4[10]	27,500	35	70	2	2	5,000 per biennium	5	8	28,000
Tennessee	4[7]	50,000	33	99	4	2	6,088.50 per annum	5	8	24,000
Texas	4[22]	65,000	31	150	4	2	7,200 per annum	(20)	6	45,600
Utah	4	35,000	29	75	4	2	25 per diem	5	10	30,000
Vermont	2	36,100	30	150	2	2	150 per week[21]	5	6	31,400
Virginia	4[7]	50,000	40	100	4	2	5,475 per annum	7	12	41,300
Washington	4	34,300	49	98	4	2	7,200 per annum	9	6	39,412
West Virginia	4	50,000	34	100	4	2	4,800 per annum	5	12	35,000
Wisconsin	4	44,292	33	99	4	2	17,843 per annum	7	10	42,462
Wyoming	4	45,000	30	62	4	2	51 per diem	5	8	32,500

[1]**General Assembly** in Ark., Colo., Conn., Del., Ga., Ind., Ky., Md., Mo., N. C., Ohio, Pa., R. I., S. C., Tenn., Vt., Va., **Legislative Assembly** in Mont., N. D., Ore.; **General Court** in Mass., N. H.; **Legislature** in other states. Meets **biennially** in Calif., Ky., Me., Mont., Nev., N. H., N. J., N. C., N. D., Ore., Penn., Texas, Wash. and Wyo.; meets **annually** in other states. [2]**Court of Appeals** in Ky., Md., N. Y., **Supreme Court of Virginia** in Va.; **Supreme Judicial Court** in Me., Mass.; **Supreme Court** in other states. [3]**Upper house: Senate** in all states. [4]**Lower house: Assembly** in Calif., Nev., N. Y., Wis.; **House of Delegates** in Md., Va.,

W. Va.; **General Assembly** in N. J.; **House of Representatives** in other states. [5]Does not include additional payments for expenses, mileage, special sessions, etc., or additional per diem payments beyond salary shown. [6]In some states, Chief Justice receives a higher salary. [7]Cannot succeed himself. [8]Appointed for 3 years; thereafter, elected popularly for 10-year term. [9]May serve only 2 terms, consecutive or otherwise. [10]May not serve 3rd consecutive term. [11]Unicameral legislature. [12]Constitutional - number: 375-400. [13]Until 70 years old. [14]When term begins in Jan. of 2nd year following U. S. census, term shall be 2 years. [15]2nd term

receive tenure, mandatory retirement at 70. [16]Senate Pres. and House Speaker to receive 50% above compensation; Majority, Minority leaders, 25%; and Assistant Majority, Minority leaders 12½%. [17]For 60 days only. [18]Term of good behavior. [19]9 members in Supreme Court, highest in civil cases; 3 in Court of Criminal Appeals. [20]9 members in Supreme Court, highest in civil cases; 5 in Court of Criminal Appeals. [21]To limit of $4,500 per biennium. [22]Length of term will be 4 years beginning 1975. [23]$500 per mo. when not in session. [24]$4,500 for 2nd year, plus $1,000 per year expenses, plus mileage. [25]As of 1978. [26]Plus $75 per month.

Museums of the United States[1]

Source: Questionnaires to Museums

NEW YORK CITY

American Academy of Arts and Letters: Audubon Terrace, Broadway bet. 155th and 156th Sts., NYC 10032. Open: Tues.–Sun. 1–4 during exhibitions (closed Mon. and natl. holidays). Free.

Annual exhibitions of work of members, recipients of awards and honors, Hassam Fund Purchases.

American Museum of Natural History: Central Park West at 79th St., NYC 10024. Open: wkdys. 10–4:45, Sun. & hldys. 11–5 (closed Thnks. Day, Xmas).

All branches of natural sciences with exhibits including astronomy at American Museum-Hayden Planetarium.

Brooklyn Museum, The: 188 Eastern Pkwy., Brooklyn, N.Y. 11238. Open: Wed.–Sat. 10–5, Sun. 12–5, hldys. 1–5 (closed NY Day and Xmas). Free.

Egyptian art, American paintings, decorative arts and period rooms, contemporary prints and drawings. Arts of primitive and New World cultures, Oriental, Middle Eastern and Islamic arts. Two reference libraries, sculpture garden.

Cloisters, The: Ft. Tryon Pk., NYC 10040. Open: wkdys. 10–4:45 (closed Mon.), Sun., hldys. 1–4:45. Discretionary admission fee.

Cloisters, chapel, chapter house, apse. The various cloisters are reconstituted from elements of 12–15th-century French cloisters. Apse has been relocated here in its entirety. Frescoes, polychromed statues, stained glass, tapestries. Medieval branch of The Metropolitan Museum of Art.

Cooper-Hewitt Museum, the Smithsonian Institution's National Museum of Design: 2 E. 91st St., NYC 10028. Open: Tues. 10–9, Wed.–Sat. 10–5, Sun. 12–5 (closed Mon., NY Day, July 4, Thnks. Day, Xmas). Adm. $1 (free on Tues.).

Over 100,000 decorative arts objects and related library.

Frick Collection: 1 E. 70th St., NYC 10021. Open: Sept.–May–Tues.–Sat. 10–6, Sun. & most hldys. 1–6 (closed Mon.; also NY Day, Thnks. Day, Dec. 24-25); June–Aug.—Sun. 1–6, Wed.–Sat. 10–6 (closed Mon. & Tues.; also July 4). Discretionary admission fee.

Paintings, prints, drawings of 14th to 19th centuries. Italian Renaissance and French sculpture and furniture. Chinese and French porcelain. Concerts, lectures.

Guggenheim Museum, The Solomon R.: 1071 Fifth Ave. at 88th St., NYC 10028. Open: Tues. 11–8; Wed.–Sun. and hldys. 11–5 (closed Mon., except hldys., and Xmas). Adm. $1 (children under 7, free). Tues. 5–8 free. College students with ID's and senior citizens, 50¢; school children in groups of 10 with a teacher, 25¢.

Works of leading 20th-century foreign and American painters and sculptors.

Hayden Planetarium. *See* American Museum of Natural History.

Hispanic Society of America, The (Museum and Library): Broadway between West 155th and 156th Sts., NYC 10032. Museum open: Tues.– Sat. 10–4:30, Sun. 1–4 (closed Mon.; also Jan. 1, Feb. 12, Feb. 22, Good Friday, Easter, May 30, July 4, Oct. 12, Thnks. Day, Dec. 24, 25, 31). Library open: Tues.–Fri. 1–4:30, Sat. 10–4:30 (closed Sun., Mon.; also hldys., Good Friday, month of Aug., Dec. 24–Jan. 1 incl.). Free.

Paintings, sculpture, decorative arts, manuscripts and incunabula, representative of Hispanic culture. Works on Hispanic art, history, literature.

Jewish Museum: Fifth Ave. at 92nd St., NYC 10028. Open: Mon.–Thurs., 12–5, Sun. 11–6 (closed Fri. & Sat., also Jewish holidays). Adm. $1.50 (children and students, 50¢). Members free, senior citizens pay-what-you-wish.

Former Warburg mansion and adjoining Albert A. List building house most extensive collection of Jewish ceremonial objects in U.S. Changing contemporary exhibits of sculpture, paintings, photography and architecture illuminate Jewish experience, culture and tradition. Also children's programs.

Metropolitan Museum of Art, The: Fifth Ave. at 82nd St., NYC 10028. Open: Tues. 10–8:45, Wed.–Sat. 10–4:45, Sun. & hldys. 11–4:45. Discretionary admission fee.

Comprehensive collection of European and American paintings, drawings, sculpture, decorative arts, prints. Egyptian, Greek, Roman, Near and Far Eastern art. Musical instruments, arms and armor. European and American period rooms. Costumes and textiles. *See also* Cloisters.

Museum of the American Indian, Heye Foundation: Broadway at 155th St., NYC 10032. Open: Tues.–Sun. 1–5 (closed Mon., also Dec. 31–Jan. 1, Feb. 22, Easter, Mem. Day, July 4, Thnks. Day, Dec. 24-25). Free.

Archeology, ethnology, primitive arts of North, Central, and South America, in completely remodeled galleries. This is the largest Indian museum in the world.

Museum of the City of New York: 1220 Fifth Ave. at 104th St., NYC 10029. Open: Tues.–Sat. 10–5, Sun. & hldys. 1–5 (closed Mon.; also Xmas). Free.

History and life of New York City. Period costumes, furniture, miniature scenes, portraits, paintings, prints, manuscripts, theater and music collection, silver, dolls and doll houses.

Museum of Modern Art: 11 W. 53rd St., NYC 10019. Open: Mon., Tues., Fri., Sat. & Sun. 11–6, Thurs. 11–9 (closed Wed. and Xmas). Adm. $2; full-time students with ID's, $1.25; children and senior citizens, 75¢; members, free; Tuesday, pay what you wish.

Founded 1929 to help people enjoy and understand the art of our times. Changing exhibitions of contemporary painting, sculpture, drawings, prints, photography, architecture, industrial and graphic design, films.

National Academy of Design: 1083 Fifth Ave.

---

[1] For leading world museums, see p. 296.

at 90th St., NYC 10028. Open: wkdys. & Sun. 1–5 (during exhibitions).

Special annual exhibitions by selected organizations Oct. through May.

New-York Historical Society: 170 Central Park West at 77th St., NYC 10024. Museum open: Tues.–Fri. & Sun. 1–5, Sat. 10–5 (closed Mon.). Library open to adults: Tues.–Sat. 10–5 (closed Sun. & Mon.). (Both closed NY Day, July 4, Thnks. Day, Xmas). Library adm. $1 to nonmembers; museum, free.

New York city and state historical exhibits. Early American paintings and portraits. Period rooms. Audubon watercolors. Gallery of American silver.

Pierpont Morgan Library: 29 E. 36th St. NYC 10016. Open: Tues.–Sat. 10:30–5, Sun. 1–5 (closed Mon.; also legal hldys. and month of August).

Medieval and Renaissance illuminated manuscripts, rare books, music and autograph manuscripts, old master drawings, bindings, early children's books, ancient written records.

Whitney Museum of American Art: 945 Madison Ave. at 75th St., NYC 10021. Open: Wed.–Sat. 11–6, Tues. 11–10 (free 6–10), Sun. & hldys. 12–6 (closed Xmas and Mon.) Adm. $1.50.

Sculpture, paintings, watercolors, drawings, and prints by 20th-century-American artists. Exhibitions of contemporary and historical American art. Daily film showings; occasional music programs in spring.

CHICAGO

Art Institute of Chicago: Michigan Ave. at Adams St., Chicago, Ill. 60603. Open: Mon.–Wed., Fri. & Sat. 10–5, Thurs. 10–8:30, Sun. & hldys. 12–5 (closed Xmas). Voluntary admission fee, $1.50.

Paintings, sculpture, prints, drawings, textiles, photography. Oriental arts; European, American decorative arts; primitive art. Thorne Miniature Rooms. Junior Museum. Goodman Theatre, School of Drama, School of Art.

Beverly Art Center: 2153 W. 111th St., Chicago, Ill. 60643. Open: daily 9 a.m. to 10 p.m. Art Gallery open Tues., Thurs. & Sun. 1–4.

Shows change monthly.

Chicago Academy of Sciences, Museum of Natural History: Lincoln Park—2001 North Clark St., Chicago, Ill. 60614. Open: daily 10–5 (closed Xmas). Free.

Exhibits of ecology of animal and plant life, minerals and fossils of Chicago region. Lectures, field trips, movies.

Chicago Historical Society: North Clark St. at North Ave., Chicago, Ill. 60614. Open: Mon.–Sat. 9:30–4:30, Sun. 12–5 (closed NY Day, Thnks. Day, Xmas). Adults, $1; children 6–17, 50¢; senior citizens, 25¢. Free admission Monday. Research library open Tues.–Sat. 9:30–4:30.

Exhibits and collections relating to Chicago and Illinois history, Illinois pioneer crafts, Lincoln, Civil War.

Field Museum of Natural History, The: Roosevelt Rd. at Lake Shore Dr., Chicago, Ill. 60605. Open: wkdys.–Nov.–Feb. 9-4 (weekends 9–5); May–Aug. 9–6 (Wed., Fri., Sat., Sun. from mid-June to Labor Day 9–9); Mar., Apr., Sept., Oct. 9–5; Fri., year round, 9–9 (closed Xmas & NY Day). Adm. families, $2.50; adults, $1; children (6–17), 35¢; students with ID's and senior citizens, 35¢. Free on Fri. (9–9).

Exhibits in anthropology, botany, geology, zoology. Restorations of prehistoric animals. Dioramas of Stone-Age Europe. Vast Egyptian collection.

Museum of Science and Industry: 57th St. and Lake Shore Dr., Chicago, Ill. 60637. Open: May 1– Labor Day 9:30–5:30; rest of year, Mon.–Fri. 9:30–4, Sat., Sun. & hldys. 9:30–5:30 (closed Xmas). Free (small fee to four exhibits).

Operating coal mine, captured German submarine, giant heart, Paul Bunyan house, Colleen Moore's Fairy Castle, The Farm, the Apollo 8 spacecraft, Sears' Cinema Circus, historic and advanced forms of planes, ships, trains, and cars.

Oriental Institute Museum of the University of Chicago: 1155 E. 58th St., Chicago, Ill. 60637. Open: Tues.–Sat. 10–4, Sun. 12–4 (closed Mon. & hldys.). Free. Ancient Near Eastern objects, including 40-ton human-headed winged bull from Khorsabad in Assyria, 16-ft. statue of Tutankhamen from Egypt, colossal bull's head from Persepolis; glyptic, bronze and ivory artifacts.

Vanderpoel (John H.) Memorial Art Gallery: 2135 W. 111th St., Chicago, Ill. 60643. Open: wkdys. & Sun. 9–5 (closed hldys.). Free.

Paintings, watercolors, etchings, sculpture contributed by the artists in tribute to Mr. Vanderpoel.

WASHINGTON, D.C.

Anacostia Neighborhood Museum, Smithsonian Institution: 2405 Martin Luther King, Jr. Ave. SE, Washington, D.C. 20020. Open: Mon.–Fri. 10–6, Sat. & Sun. 1–6 (closed Xmas). Free.

Exhibits on Afro-American history, urban problems, art. Programs for children.

Arts and Industries Building, Smithsonian Institution: 900 Jefferson Dr. SW, Washington, D.C. 20560. Open: daily 10–5:30; summer 10–9 (closed Xmas). Free.

Constructed to house exhibits from 1876 Centennial Exhibition, building has been restored as nearly as possible to original appearance.

Corcoran Gallery of Art: 17th St. at New York Ave. NW, Washington, D.C. 20006. Open: Tues.–Sun. 11–5 (closed Mon.; also NY Day, July 4, Thnks. Day, Xmas). Free Tues. & Wed.; $1.50 adm. Thurs.–Sun. (members free).

Possesses comprehensive collection of American paintings, sculpture, graphics. Choice selection of European art.

Freer Gallery of Art, Smithsonian Institution: Jefferson Dr. at 12th St. SW, Washington, D.C. 20560. Open: daily 10–5:30 (closed Xmas). Free.

Oriental paintings, sculpture, bronzes, pottery, metalwork, manuscripts. Largest extant Whistler collection.

Hirshhorn Museum and Sculpture Garden, Smithsonian Institution: Eighth St. at Independence Ave. SW, Washington, D.C. 20560. Open: daily, 10–5:30 (closed Xmas). Free.

Collection numbers 4,000 paintings and 2,000 sculptures, tracing development of modern art from 19th century to present. Rodin, Moore, Picasso, Calder, Miró and Matisse among those represented.

National Air and Space Museum, Smithsonian Institution: Independence Ave. bet. 5th & 7th Sts. SW, Washington, D.C. 20560. Open: daily 10–5:30, summer 10–9 (closed Xmas). Free.

Exhibits on aviation and space age; Wright Brothers' *Kitty Hawk Flyer,* Lindbergh's *Spirit of St. Louis.*

National Collection of Fine Arts, Smithsonian Institution: Eighth and G Sts. NW, Washington, D.C. 20560. Open: daily 10–5:30 (closed Xmas). Free.

Collections survey 300 years of American art. Paintings, sculpture, graphic art. Large selection of contemporary art.

National Gallery of Art: Constitution Ave. bet. 3rd & 7th Sts. NW, Washington, D.C. 20565. Open: Mon.–Sat. 10–5, Sun. 12–9* (closed NY Day, Xmas). Free.

Paintings, sculpture, drawings, prints, decorative arts given by Mellon, Kress, Widener, Rosenwald, Dale, Harriman, and others. Index of American Design.

National Museum of History and Technology, Smithsonian Institution: 12th St. and Constitution Ave. NW, Washington, D.C. 20560. Open: daily 10–5:30; summer, 10–9. (closed Xmas). Free.

Exhibits showing scientific, technological, and cultural development of U.S. Original Star-Spangled Banner. Costumes and furnishings. Gowns of First Ladies. Inventions. Stamps, coins, musical instruments, ceramics and crafts.

National Museum of Natural History and National Museum of Man. Smithsonian Institution: 10th St. and Constitution Ave. NW, Washington, D.C. 20560. Open: daily 10–5:30; summer, 10–9. (closed Xmas). Free.

Origin, development and physical characteristics of man. Dioramas of peoples and animals in natural settings. Land and sea mammals, birds, fish, reptiles and gems, minerals, meteorites, volcanoes, prehistoric animals.

National Portrait Gallery, Smithsonian Institution: Eighth and F Sts. NW, Washington, D.C. 20560. Open: daily 10–5:30 (closed Xmas). Free.

Only major museum in hemisphere devoted exclusively to portraiture. Exhibits likenesses of persons who have made significant contributions to U.S. history, development, and culture.

Renwick Gallery, Smithsonian Institution: 17th St. and Pennsylvania Ave. NW, Washington, D.C. 20560. Open: daily 10–5:30 (closed Xmas). Free.

American crafts, decorative arts and design, housed in a mid-19th-century building restored to its original appearance.

Smithsonian Institution Building: 1000 Jefferson Dr. SW, Washington, D.C. 20560. Open: daily 10–5:30 (closed Xmas). Free.

Information center and James Smithson's tomb are in original building. Institution maintains the museums and art galleries indicated above; also Cooper-Hewitt Museum of Decorative Arts and Design in New York City and National Zoological Park in Washington, D.C., and research facilities elsewhere.

* Summer hours (Apr. 1–Labor Day); Mon.–Sat. 10–9, Sun. 12–9.

PHILADELPHIA

Academy of Natural Sciences of Philadelphia: 19th St. and the Parkway, Philadelphia, Pa. 19103. Whole Earth Museum open: Mon.–Sat. 10–5, Sun. 1–5 (closed NY Day, Thnks. Day, Xmas). Adm. $1.25 (children, 75¢). Group rates available.

Exhibits on shells, extinct species. Animal habitat dioramas. Birds, gems. Live animal show daily.

Franklin Institute, The: 20th St. and the Parkway, Philadelphia, Pa. 19103. Open: daily 10–5 (closed NY Day, Thnks. Day, Dec. 24 & Xmas). Adm: $2.50 (senior citizens, $1.25; students 12-college, $2; children 5–11, $1.50; children under 5, 50¢). Planetarium 50¢ additional.

Nonprofit educational and research institution operating science museum, planetarium, library, and research laboratories.

Pennsylvania Academy of the Fine Arts: Broad and Cherry Sts., Philadelphia, Pa. 19102. Open: wkdys. 10–5, Sun. 1–5 (closed NY Day & Xmas). Adm. $1 (children under 12, 50¢).

Oldest art museum in U.S. Collection devoted to American art. Lectures, concerts.

Philadelphia Museum of Art: 26th St. and the Parkway, Philadelphia 19130. Open: daily 9–5 (closed major hldys.). Adm. $1.50 (children, 75¢). (free Sun. 9–1).

Paintings, drawings, prints, from old masters to present. Sculpture, decorative arts, period rooms. Oriental collections. New American Wing scheduled to open December 1976. Rodin Museum at Parkway and 22nd St. Colonial Houses in Fairmont Park. Samuel S. Fleisher Art Memorial, 715–19 Catharine St.

MUSEUMS IN OTHER CITIES

Addison Gallery of American Art: Phillips Academy, Andover, Mass. 01810. Open: Tues.–Sat. 10–5, Sun. 2:30–5 (closed Mon.). Free.

Art of 18th, 19th and 20th centuries. Changing exhibitions.

Alabama, University of, Museum of Natural History: Smith Hall, on campus of U. of Alabama, Tuscaloosa, Ala. 35486. Open: Mon.–Sat. 8–5, Sun. 1–5. Free.

All phases of natural history. *See also* Mound State Monument Museum.

Albright-Knox Art Gallery: 1285 Elmwood Ave., Buffalo, N.Y. 14222. Open: Tues.–Sat. 10–5; Sun. 12–5 (closed Mon., NY Day, Thnks. Day, Xmas). Voluntary admission fee.

Comprehensive collection of contemporary paintings; 18th–19th-century English, French and American paintings. Sculpture since 3000 B.C.

Atomic Energy, American Museum of: 300 South Tulane, Oak Ridge, Tenn. 37830. Open: Mon.–Sat. 9–5; Sun. 12:30–5 (closed NY Day, Thnks. Day, Xmas). Free.

Demonstrations, exhibits, motion pictures, models, etc., relating to atomic and other forms of energy. Traveling exhibits available free to qualified exhibitors in U.S.*

* Send inquiries to Museum Division, Oak Ridge Associated Universities, P.O. Box 117, Oak Ridge, Tenn. 37830.

Baltimore Museum of Art: Art Museum Dr., Baltimore, Md. 21218. Open: Tues.-Sat. 11–5, Thurs. evening 7–10 (except in summer). Sun. 1–5 (closed Mon.). Free.
Paintings, sculpture, graphics, 2nd–6th century mosaics from Antioch. Concerts, dance recitals, educational programs for all ages.
Downtown Gallery: Charles and Redwood Sts., Baltimore, Md. 21201. Open: Mon.-Fri. 10–4:30. Free.

Baseball Hall of Fame and Museum, National: Main St., Cooperstown, N.Y. 13326. Open: May–Oct. 9–9; Nov.–Apr. 9–5 (closed NY Day, Thnks. Day, Xmas). Adm. $2.25 (children 7–15, $1).
Relics, pictures, documents of baseball history. Bronze plaques of game's immortals. *See also* Hall of Fame in index.

Berkshire Museum: 39 South St., Pittsfield, Mass. 01201. Open: Tues.-Sat. 10–5, Sun. 2–5 (closed Mon.; also NY Day, July 4, Thnks. Day, Xmas). Open Mon. in July and Aug. Free.
Painting, sculpture, decorative arts—ancient to modern. Loan exhibits. Galleries on biology, birds, man, minerals, and American history. Live exhibits. Junior Department. Movies, lectures.

Birmingham Museum of Art: 2000 Eighth Ave. North, Birmingham, Ala. 35203. Open: Mon.-Wed. Fri. & Sat. 10–5, Thurs. 10–9; Sun. 2–6 (closed NY Day and Xmas). Free.
Kress Collection of Italian art; 17th-century Dutch, Flemish and English paintings; modern American painting; silver, porcelain.

(Boston) Museum of Fine Arts: Huntington Ave., Boston, Mass. 02115. Open: Wed.-Sun. 10–5; Tues. 10–9 (closed Mon.; NY Day, July 4, Labor Day, Thnks. Day, Xmas Eve. Xmas). Adm. $1.50 (Tues. 5–9 & Sun., 75¢; free to senior citizens on Fri.) (members and children under 16, free).
European and American paintings, sculpture, furniture, interiors, tapestries, textiles, silver, costumes, musical instruments. Prints, drawings, watercolors. Egyptian, Asiatic, contemporary collections.

Buffalo Museum of Science: Humboldt Park, Buffalo, N.Y. 14211. Open: Mon.-Sat. 10–5 (Fri. 10–10, except July and Aug., 10–5), Sun. & hldys. 1:30–5:30 (closed Xmas). Free.
Exhibits of astronomy, geology, zoology, botany, anthropology. Main exhibits are arranged to tell story of science in natural sequence. Kellogg Observatory, Children's Museum.

California Academy of Sciences: Golden Gate Park, San Francisco, Calif. 94118. Open: daily 10–5. Adm. 50¢ (children 12–18, 25¢; under 12 and over 65, free). Free adm. first day of month.
North American and African habitat groups. Astronomical exhibits, clocks, watches, lamps, minerals, fossils, plants. Steinhart Aquarium, Morrison Planetarium.

California Palace of the Legion of Honor: 34th Ave. and Clement St., Lincoln Park, San Francisco, Calif. 94121. Open: daily 10–5, incl. hldys. Adm. 75¢ (youths 12–18, 25¢; under 12 and senior citizens, free). Free adm. first day of month.
Devoted to arts of France: paintings, sculpture

and decorative arts; prints and drawings of all periods.

Carnegie Institute: 4400 Forbes Ave., Pittsburgh, Pa. 15213. Open: Tues.-Sat. 10–5; Sun. 1–6 (closed Mon. & major hldys.). Suggested contributions: Adults, $1; children and students, 50¢. Sat. free.
Museum of Art: European and American paintings, sculpture and decorative arts. Carnegie Museum of Natural History: exhibits in natural history and science.

Carriage and Harness Museum: Elk St., Cooperstown, N.Y. 13326. Open: daily 9–12, 1–5 (closed Sun. & Mon., Oct. 31–Apr. 30; NY Day, Thnks. Day, Xmas). Adm. $1.25 (children, 75¢).
Collection of horse-drawn sporting vehicles and accouterments. Operated by New York State Historical Association.

Cincinnati Art Museum: Eden Park, Cincinnati, Ohio 45202. Open: wkdys. 10–5, Sun. & hldys. 1–5 (closed Thnks. Day, Xmas). Adm. $1 (children 12–18, 50¢; 11 and under, free). Free to everyone on Sat.
European and American painting, prints, decorative arts, sculpture, costumes. Egyptian, Greco-Roman, Medieval, Near and Far Eastern arts. Ancient musical instruments. Temporary exhibits.

Clark (Sterling and Francine) Art Institute: Williamstown, Mass. 01267. Open: daily except Monday, 10–5 (closed NY Day, Thnks. Day, Xmas). Free.
Paintings from 14th to 19th centuries, including works by Corot, Renoir, Degas, Toulouse-Lautrec, Homer; sculpture, antique silver, prints and drawings.

Cleveland Museum of Art: 11150 East Boulevard, Cleveland, Ohio 44106. Open: Tues. 10–6, Wed. 10–10, Thurs. & Fri. 10–6, Sat. 9–5, Sun. 1–6 (closed Mon.; also NY Day, July 4, Thnks. Day, Xmas). Free.
Paintings, sculpture, graphic arts, furniture, silver, gold, arms, armor, textiles, ceramics from all cultures and periods.

Cleveland Museum of Natural History: Wade Oval, University Circle, Cleveland, Ohio 44106. Open: Mon.-Sat. 10–5, Sun. 1–5:30 (closed NY Day, Mem. Day, July 4, Labor Day, Thnks. Day, Xmas). Adm. $1.50 (children 6–18, 50¢). Free Tues. after 1.
Dinosaurs, area fossils, minerals, birds, mammals, insects, reptiles, plants. American Indian and Eskimo displays. Planetarium, observatory. Hall of Man's Ecology.

Colonial Williamsburg: Williamsburg, Va. 23185. Open: daily. Tickets for 8, 14 or 25 admissions, adults, $6–10; children 6–12, $3–5.
Restored 18th-century capital of Virginia colony; 173 acres of colonial city with more than 30 exhibition homes, craft shops and public buildings; 90 acres of gardens; outdoor events; colonial lodging and dining.

Colorado Springs Fine Arts Center: 30 W. Dale St., Colorado Springs, Colo. 80903. Open: Mon.-Sat. 10–5, Sun. 1:30–5 (closed NY Day, Thnks. Day, Xmas). Free.
Art produced within limits of U.S. from pre-

historic to contemporary, including decorative and fine arts. Survey of arts of world.

Columbus Gallery of Fine Arts: 480 E. Broad St., Columbus, Ohio 43215. Open: daily, 12–5. Free.

Renaissance, baroque and 19th- and 20th-century American and European paintings; lithographs and paintings of George Bellows. Decorative arts and prints.

Corning Glass Center: Centerway, Corning, N.Y. 14830. Open: daily 9:30–5 (closed Mon. from Nov. through May; also closed NY Day, Thnks. Day, Dec. 24, Xmas). July & Aug.–daily 8:30–5. Free. Parking $1.50 in summer.

Museum has most comprehensive collection of glass in world. All-new Hall of Science shows contemporary uses of glass. Tour of Steuben crystal-making factory.

Currier Gallery of Art: 192 Orange St., Manchester, N.H. 03104. Open: Tues.–Sat. 10–4, Sun. 2–5 (closed major hldys.). Free.

European and American paintings, 13th–20th century. American decorative arts, 18th–19th century, including New England furniture, silver, and early glass.

Davenport Museum: *See* Putnam Museum.

Delaware Art Museum, The: 2301 Kentmere Pkwy., Wilmington, Del. 19806. Open: Mon.–Sat. 10–5, Sun. 1–5. Adm.: $1 (youths 12–18 and students, 50¢; children under 12, members and senior citizens, free).

English pre-Raphaelite; 19th- and 20th-century American art; complete set of John Sloan's graphic work; complete first folio of Audubon's "Birds of America."

Denver Art Museum, The: 100 W. 14th Ave. Parkway, Denver, Colo. 80204. Open: Tues.–Sat. 9–5, Sun. 1–5; also Wed. 6–9 P.M.

Art from nearly every culture and period.

Denver Museum of Natural History: City Park, Denver, Colo. 80205. Open: Mon.–Sat. 9–4:30, Sun. & hldys. 12–4:30 (closed NY Day, Thnks. Day, Dec. 24, Xmas, Dec. 31). Free.

Sixty life-size ecological habitat dioramas. Animals from three continents, earth-science exhibits, dinosaurs, displays of fossil mammals and historic native Americans. Planetarium (small charge).

Des Moines Art Center: Greenwood Park, 45th St. and Grand Ave., Des Moines, Iowa 50312. Open: Tues.–Sat. 11–5, Sun. 12–5. Free.

Permanent collection includes Calder, Rodin, Arp, Goya, Bellows, Johns, David Smith and Morris Louis, among others.

Detroit Historical Museum: 5401 Woodward Ave., Detroit, Mich. 48202. Open: Wed.–Sun. 9–5 (closed Mon., Tues. & legal hldys.).

Detroit-related industrial, transportation, social history and ethnic exhibits. Detroit streets of 1840–50, 1870–80, 1895–1905. Urban history. Corridor of Costumes. Marine exhibits at Dossin Great Lakes Museum on Belle Isle; military history exhibits at Ft. Wayne, at the foot of Livernois.

Detroit Institute of Arts, The: 5200 Woodward Ave., Detroit, Mich. 48202. Open: Wed.–Sun. 9:30–5:30 (closed Mon. and Tues.; also national holidays). Voluntary admission fee.

Survey of history as expressed in arts. Paintings, sculpture, furniture, glass, gold work, ivory, graphic arts, textiles, armor. Murals by Diego Rivera. African art gallery.

Dickson Mounds Museum: off Route 97–78 near Lewistown, Ill. 61542. Open: Daily 8:30–5 (closed NY Day, Easter, Thnks. Day, Xmas). Free.

Museum of prehistoric Illinois Indians. Branch of Illinois State Museum.

Farmers' Museum: Lake Rd., Route 80, Cooperstown, N.Y. 13326. Open: summer season, Tues.–Sun. 9–5; winter season, Tues.–Sat. 9–5, Sun. 1–5 (closed Mon.; also NY Day, Thnks. Day, Xmas). Adm. $2.75† (children $1).

Re-created village crossroads. Early farm and handicraft tools. School house, country store, smithy, print shop, doctor's and lawyer's offices, pharmacy, tavern, church, farm unit. Cardiff Giant. Operated by New York State Historical Association.

Fenimore House: Lake Rd., Route 80, Cooperstown, N.Y. 13326. Open: summer season, daily, 9–5; winter season, Tues.–Sat. 9–5, Sun. 1–5 (closed Mon.; also NY Day, Thnks. Day, Xmas). Adm. $2.25† (children $1).

American portraits, genre paintings. Browere life masks of Founding Fathers. James Fenimore Cooper memorabilia. Folk art. Library. Operated by New York State Historical Association.

Florida State Museum, University of Florida: Museum Road, Gainesville, Fla. 32611. Open: Mon.–Fri. 9–4:30, Sat. 9–5, Sun. 1–5 (closed Xmas). Free.

State and University museum with research emphasis on natural and social history of Florida, southeastern United States, and Caribbean area.

Fogg Art Museum: Harvard University, 32 Quincy St., Cambridge, Mass. 02138. Open: Mon.–Sat. 9–5, Sun. 2–5 (closed weekends from July 1 to Labor day; also natl. holidays). Free.

Collections illustrate evolution of Eastern and Western art from ancient to modern times. Chinese sculpture and bronzes; Romanesque sculpture; Italian primitives; French 19th-century paintings; European drawings and prints.

Gardner (Isabella Stewart) Museum: 280 The Fenway, Boston, Mass. 02115. Open: Tues., 1–9:30, Wed.–Sun. 1–5:30. July–Aug., Tues.–Sun. 1–5:30 (closed natl. hldys., Sunday before Labor Day). Adm.: Tues.–Sat. free, Sun. $1.

Paintings, 14th–20th centuries, in building of Venetian palace style. Sculpture, tapestries, furniture. Flowering courtyard.

Getty (J. Paul) Museum, The: 17985 Pacific Coast Hgwy., Malibu, Calif. 90265. Open: Mon.–Fri. 10–5 (June–Sept.), Tues.–Sat. 10–5 (Oct–May); (closed NY Day, Feb. 22, Mem. Day, July 4, Labor Day, Thnks. Day, Xmas). Free. Reservations for free parking should be made a week in advance.

Recreation of Roman seaside villa destroyed by Vesuvius in 79 A.D. Greek and Roman antiquities, European paintings, French decorative arts, authentic Roman gardens. Research library.

Heard Museum: 22 East Monte Vista Rd., Phoenix, Ariz. 85004. Open: Mon.–Sat. 10–5,

† Combination rates are available for Farmers' Museum and Fenimore House.

Sun. 1-5 (closed hldys.). Adm.: suggested dona-
tion, $1 for adults (students, 50¢).

Anthropology and primitive arts, with emphasis on rich heritage of Southwest.

High Museum of Art: 1280 Peachtree St. NE,
Atlanta, Ga. 30309. Open: Mon.-Sat. 10-5, Sun.
12-5 (closed natl. holidays). Free.

Paintings and sculpture from 14th to 18th
century in Samuel H. Kress Collection. Ralph
K. Uhry Print Collection; decorative arts;
Richman Collection of African Art.

(Houston) Museum of Fine Arts, The: 1001
Bissonnet at Main, Houston, Tex. 77005. Open:
Tues.-Sat. 9:30-5, Sun. 12-6 (closed Mon., July 4,
Labor Day, Thnks. Day, Xmas). Free.
Day, Thnks. Day, Xmas). Free.

American and European art through 20th
century; Southwest American Indian art and
artifacts; early American furniture and decorative arts; pre-Columbian and Far Eastern
art; native arts from Africa, Australia, South
Pacific. Impressionist and post-Impressionist
paintings.

**Huntington Library, Art Gallery, and Bo-
tanical Gardens:** 1151 Oxford Rd., San Marino,
Calif. 91108. Open: Tues.-Sun. 1-4:30 (closed
Mon.; also month of Oct., NY Day, Easter,
Mem. Day, July 4, Labor Day, Thnks. Day.
Xmas). Free.

18th-century British paintings, including
Gainsborough's "Blue Boy" & Lawrence's
"Pinkie." Manuscript and rare-book exhibits
include Gutenberg Bible, Franklin's autobiography in his handwriting. Botanical gardens. Research library.

Illinois State Museum: Spring and Edwards
Sts., Springfield, Ill. 62706. Open: Mon.-Sat.
8:30-5, Sun. 1:30-5 (closed NY Day, Easter,
Thnks. Day, Xmas). Free.

Museum of natural science, anthropology,
and art.

Indianapolis Museum of Art: 1200 W. 38th
St., Indianapolis, Ind. 46208. Krannert and
Clowes Pavilions open: Tues.-Sun. & hldys.
11-5 (closed Mon., Xmas). Free. Lilly Pavilion
of Decorative Arts open Tues.-Sun. 1-4 (closed
Mon. & Xmas). Free.

Paintings, sculpture, graphics, textiles, ceramics, and silver spanning 4,000 years. Oriental art, 17th-century Dutch and Flemish, early
19th-century British, late 19th- and 20th-
century Impressionism.

Los Angeles County Museum of Art: 5905
Wilshire Blvd., Los Angeles, Calif. 90036. Open:
Tues.-Fri. 10-5, Sat. 10-6, Sun. 10-6 (closed
Mon.; also Thnks. Day, Xmas, NY Day). Free.

Ahmanson Gallery houses permanent collections covering entire range of history of art.
Special Exhibitions Gallery (free for members,
$1 for adult nonmembers, 50¢ for children to
18).

**(Los Angeles County) Natural History Mu-
seum:** 900 Exposition Blvd., Exposition Park,
Los Angeles, Calif. 90007. Open: Tues.-Sun. 10-
5 (closed Mon.; also Thnks. Day, Xmas). Free.

Exhibits in Pre-Columbian archeology, Pacific Islands and African ethnology, Southern
California botany, evolution of life, mineralogy. Dinosaur and Pleistocene fossil recon-
structions. North American and African animal

habitat groups. U.S., California and Western
History.

Rancho La Brea tar pits, a designated natural history landmark, are at 5801 Wilshire
Blvd., Hancock Park. Open: Tues.-Sun. 11-4.

Milwaukee Art Center: Milwaukee County
War Memorial Bldg., 750 North Lincoln Memorial
Dr., Milwaukee, Wis. 53202. Open: Tues.-Sun.
10-5 (closed Mon.). Adm. $1 (students, senior citi-
zens and children under 12 with adult, 50¢).

European and American painting of 20th century; sculpture, drawings, prints, American art
and decorative arts of all periods. Villa Terrace—
Branch Museum for Decorative Arts, 2220 North
Terrace Ave.; seasonal hours.

Mint Museum of Art: 501 Hempstead Pl.,
Charlotte, N.C. 28207. Open: Tues.-Fri. 10-5,
Sat.-Sun. 2-5 (closed Mon.; also national &
Charlotte hldys.). Free.

Paintings, sculpture, decorative arts, prints
(Renaissance-20th century), pre-Columbian
Collection. Delhom Gallery and Institute for
Study and Research in Ceramics. Coins and
artifacts from 19th-century Charlotte branch
of U.S. Mint.

**Mound State Monument Archaeological Mu-
seum:** Rte. 69, Moundville, Ala. 35474. Open:
wkdys. & Sun. 9-5 (closed Xmas). Adm. $1
(children, 50¢).

Indian artifacts, recreated temple and village of
Moundville Indians. Trailer and tent camp-
grounds. Operated by University of Alabama
Museums.

Mystic Seaport: Mystic, Conn. 06355. Open:
daily. Dec.-Mar. 10-4, Apr.-Nov. 9-5 (closed
Xmas). Adm: Dec.-Mar. $3.75 (children 6-15
$1.50); Apr.-Nov., $4.25 (children $1.75). Two-day
tickets and group rates available.

Maritime museum emphasizing Age of Sail.
Waterfront village. _Charles W. Morgan,_ last
of wooden whaleships. Smallcraft collection;
craft demonstrations. Working shipyard.
Planetarium.

Navaho Ceremonial Art, Museum of: 704
Camino Lejo (mailing address: P.O. Box 5153),
Santa Fe, N.M. 87501. Open: Tues.-Sat. 10-5,
Sun. 2-5 (closed Mon.; also NY Day, Thnks.
Day, Xmas). Free.

Sandpaintings, ceremonial objects, baskets,
textiles, pottery, jewelry. Contemporary Indian
painting.

**Nelson (William Rockhill) Gallery—Atkins
Museum of Fine Arts:** 4525 Oak St., Kansas
City, Mo. 64111. Open: Tues.-Sat. 10-5, Sun.
2-6 (closed Mon.; also NY Day, Mem. Day,
July 4, Thnks. Day, Xmas). Adm. 50¢ (children
6-12, 25¢). Free on Sun.

Egyptian, Oriental, classic, and European
art. American paintings and decorative arts;
five Early American rooms. Pre-Columbian
and Indian art. Children's Museum.

New Mexico, Museum of: Admin. bldg. at
113 Lincoln St., P.O. Box 2087, Santa Fe, N.M.
87501. Museum of Fine Arts, Museum of International Folk Art, Palace of the Governors. Open:
Mon.-Sat. 9-5, Sun. & hldys. 2-5 (closed Mon.
from Sept. 15 to May 15). Laboratory of Anthropology. Open: Mon.-Fri. 8-12, 1-5 (closed
Sat., Sun. & hldys.).

Exhibits of fine arts, folk arts; history of Southwest and of American Indian; archeology; ethnology.

New Orleans Museum of Art: Lelong Ave., City Park, New Orleans, La. 70179. Open: Tues.-Sat. 10-5; Sun. 1-6 (closed Mon.; also hldys., Mardi Gras, Good Friday). Free on Sat.

Old master paintings from 14th to 19th centuries, including Kress Collection of Italian Art; 20th-century European and American art; African, Oriental and pre-Columbian collections; Latin Colonial painting and sculpture; prints and photographs.

New York State Historical Association: Lake Rd., Rte. 80, Cooperstown, N.Y. 13326.

Administers Farmers' Museum, Fenimore House, Carriage and Harness Museum. *See* those entries. Also, Cooperstown Graduate Program in American Folk Culture, History Museum Training and Art Conservation.

Newark Museum: 49 Washington St., Newark, N.J. 07101. Open: Mon.-Sat. 12-5, Sun. & hldys. 1-5 (closed NY Day, July 4, Thnks. Day, Xmas). Free.

Collections: American painting, sculpture; Tibetan, Chinese, Japanese arts; decorative arts, ancient glass & ceramics; natural science, ethnology. Planetarium and observatory. Sculpture garden. Junior museum.

Norton Simon Museum of Art at Pasadena: Colorado Blvd. at Orange Grove, Pasadena, Calif. 91105. Open: Thurs.-Sun. 12-6. Adm. $1.50 (students, 50¢; children under 12, free).

Paintings by Old Masters and from Italian Renaissance; Dutch 17th-century school; paintings and sculpture by Impressionist and early 20th-century masters; Southeast Asian stone sculptures and bronzes.

Putnam Museum: 1717 W. 12th St., Davenport, Iowa 52804. Open: Tues.-Sat. 9-5, Sun. 1-5 (closed Mon., NY Day, Easter, Mem. Day, July 4, Labor Day, Thnks. Day, Xmas). Adm. 75¢ (children 25¢).

Art, history and natural history collections from the Orient, Africa, and North, Central and South America.

Ringling (John & Mable) Museums: P.O. Box 1838, Sarasota, Fla. 33578. Museum of Art, Asolo Theater, John Ringling Residence, Museum of the Circus open Mon.-Fri. 9 A.M-10 P.M., Sat. 9-5, Sun. 11-6. Adm.: $3 (children under 12, free).

Collection of old masters, especially Rubens. Only 18th-century Italian theater in America. Elaborate furnishings in Residence. Historical equipment and wagons in Circus Museum.

Rosicrucian Egyptian Museum and Art Gallery: Park and Naglee Aves., San Jose, Calif. 95191. Open: Tues.-Fri. 9-5, Sat.-Mon. 12-5 (closed NY Day, July 4, Aug. 2, Thnks. Day, Xmas). Free.

Egyptian and Oriental antiquities. Mummies, statuary, jewelry, utensils, clothing. Reproduction of Egyptian rock tomb. Babylonian collection. Art gallery.

St. Louis Art Museum: Forest Park, St. Louis, Mo. 63110. Open: Tues. 2:30-9:30, Wed.-Sun. 10-5 (closed Mon.; also Xmas, NY Day). Free.

American, European, and Asian painting, sculpture, and decorative arts. American and European period rooms.

San Diego, Fine Arts Gallery of: Balboa Park, San Diego, Calif. 92112. Open: Tues.-Sat. 10-5, Sun. 12:30-5 (closed Mon.; also NY Day, Thnks. Day, Xmas). Free.

European paintings of Renaissance and Baroque periods. American paintings; oriental and modern art.

San Diego Museum of Man: California Building, Balboa Park, San Diego, Calif. 92101. Open: daily 10-4:45 (closed NY Day, Thnks. Day, Xmas). Adm. 75¢ (children 6-16, 10¢; under 6, free). Free adm. on Wed.

Exhibits on Man of the Americas, early man and Indians' life style.

San Diego Society of Natural History—Natural History Museum: Balboa Park, San Diego, Calif. 92112. Open: wkdys. & Sun. 10-4:30 (closed Xmas, NY Day). Adm. $1 (children, free).

Mammals, birds, fossils, shells, plants, insects, minerals, marine biology. Emphasis on Southwestern U.S., Sonora, and Lower California.

San Francisco, The Fine Arts Museums of, M.H. de Young Memorial Museum: Kennedy Dr. and Eighth Ave., Golden Gate Park, San Francisco, Calif. 94118. Open: Daily 10-5. Adm. 75¢ (children 12-18, 25¢; under 12 and over 65, free). Free adm. first day of month.

Art of Europe, America, ancient Egypt and Rome; traditional arts of Africa, Oceania and the Americas. Paintings, sculpture and decorative arts. *See also* California Palace of the Legion of Honor.

San Francisco Museum of Modern Art: Van Ness at McAllister, San Francisco, Calif. 94102. Open: Tues.-Fri. 10-10, Sat. & Sun. 10-5 (closed Mon.; also NY Day, Mem. Day, July 4, Labor Day, Thnks. Day, Xmas). Free ($1 adm. for changing exhibitions).

Contemporary American and international paintings, sculpture, graphics, photography and ceramics.

Seattle Art Museum: Volunteer Park, Seattle, Wash. 98112. Open: Tues.-Sat. 10-5, Thurs. 7-10 P.M., Sun. 12-5 (closed Mon.; also NY Day, Thnks. Day, Xmas). Adm. $1; 50¢ for students and senior citizens; children under 12 with adult, free. Free on Thurs.

Asian art and jade; Greek and Roman art; 14th-20th century European paintings; tribal art. Samuel H. Kress Collection of 14th-18th-century European painting and sculpture.

Southwest Museum, Inc.: Marmion Way at Museum Dr., Highland Pk., Los Angeles, Calif. 90065. Open: Tues.-Sun. 1-4:45 (closed Aug. 15-Sept. 15, Mon., NY Day, July 4, Thnks. Day, Xmas). Free.

American Indian exhibits, ancient and modern. Research library. Casa de Adobe, reproduction of adobe hacienda, at 4605 N. Figueroa St.; open Wed., Sat. & Sun. 1-4:45 (closed Aug. 15-Sept. 15).

Toledo Museum of Art, The: 2445 Monroe St., Toledo, Ohio 43620. Open: wkdys. 9-5; Sun. Mon. & hldys 1-5 (closed legal hldys.). Free..

European and American paintings and decorative arts. Ancient and medieval art; books, manuscripts, prints, graphics. Ancient European and American glass.

Virginia Museum of Fine Arts: Boulevard at Grove Ave., Richmond, Va. 23221. Open: Tues.-Sat. 11–5, Sun. 1–5 (closed Mon.; also NY Day, July 4, Xmas). Adm. 50¢.

Wadsworth Atheneum: 600 Main St., Hartford, Conn. 06103. Open: Tues.-Sat. 11–4, Sun. 1–5 (closed Mon.; also NY Day, July 4, Thnks. Day, Xmas). Suggested contribution: adults, $1; teenagers, 50¢ (children free).
European and American paintings and drawings. Sculpture. Bronzes, silver, porcelain, American period furniture, firearms.

Walters Art Gallery: Charles and Centre Sts., Baltimore, Md. 21201. Open: Mon. 1–5, Tues.-Sat. 11–5 (July-Aug. Mon. 1–4, Tues.-Sat. 11–4), Sun. & hldys. 2–5 (closed NY Day, July 4, Thnks. Day, Xmas Eve, Xmas). Free.
Art from ancient empires through 19th-century Europe. Collections of paintings, sculpture, decorative arts, and manuscripts.

Worcester Art Museum: 55 Salisbury St., Worcester, Mass. 01608. Open: Tues.-Sat. 10–5, Sun. 2–6 (closed Mon.; also NY Day, July 4, Thnks. Day, Xmas). Free.
Art from Egyptian to modern times, including Far East.

Presidential Libraries and Museums

Presidential Libraries, including Museums, are administered by the National Archives and Records Service of the General Services Administration. They contain presidential and related papers, books, and audiovisual material for scholarly use, and exhibits and films for the general public. Children 15 and under and educational groups admitted free.

Herbert Hoover Presidential Library: Interstate 80, West Branch, Iowa 52358. Open: Labor Day-April 30—Mon.-Sat. 9–5, Sun. 2–5; May 1-Labor Day—Mon.-Sat. 9–6, Sun. 10–6. (closed NY Day, Thnks. Day, Xmas). Adm. 50¢ (children 15 and under free).
Exhibits portray Hoover as engineer, public servant, and humanitarian. Located in surrounding park are birthplace cottage, Quaker Meeting House, replica of Jesse Hoover's blacksmith shop, and graves of President and Mrs. Hoover.

Franklin D. Roosevelt Library: Albany Post Road, Hyde Park, N.Y. 12538. Open: daily 9–5 (closed Xmas). Adm. 50¢. Archives open Mon.-Fri. 9–5 (closed natl. hldys).
Exhibits feature lives and special interests of Franklin D. and Eleanor Roosevelt. Archives contain historic papers of President and Mrs. Roosevelt and of prominent figures in his Administration. Adjoining Library is Roosevelt family home, which is open to public, and graves of President and Mrs. Roosevelt.

Harry S. Truman Library and Museum: U.S. Highway 24 and Delaware St., Independence, Mo. 64050. Open: daily, 9–5 (closed NY Day, Thnks. Day, Xmas). Adm. 50¢ (children under 15 free).
Copy of Truman's White House office, United Nations Charter Table, state gifts and Japanese surrender documents. Film programs. Mural by Thomas Hart Benton decorates entrance hall. Truman gravesite in courtyard is open 9–5 daily.

Dwight D. Eisenhower Library: Kansas Highway 15, Abilene, Kan. 67410. Open: daily 9–4:45 (closed NY Day, Thnks. Day, Xmas). Adm. 50¢.
Exhibits of paintings and memorabilia relating to Eisenhower Administration are on display in Library and Museum. Place of Meditation, where Eisenhower is buried, and his boyhood home are nearby and are open to visitors.

John Fitzgerald Kennedy Library: Open for research and some other library activities in Federal Records Center, 380 Trapelo Road, Waltham, Mass. 02154, pending construction of permanent building.
When completed, Library will house papers and memorabilia of Kennedy and exhibits of his life and times.

Lyndon Baines Johnson Library: 2313 Red River, Austin, Tex. 78705. Open daily 9–5 (closed Xmas). Free.
Documents, photographs, art objects and memorabilia concerning the Presidency are exhibited. Audio tapes and film recreate four decades of U.S. history. Archives house 31 million documents. Replica of Oval Office during Johnson's Presidency is on view.

Homes of the Presidents

Source: American Automobile Association *Tour Books* and questionnaires to the homes.

GEORGE WASHINGTON

George Washington Birthplace National Monument: Washingtons Birthplace, Va. 22575. Open: daily 9–5 (closed NY Day, Xmas). Free admission.

Mount Vernon: on George Washington Memorial Parkway, Mount Vernon, Va. 22121 (16 mi. south of Washington, D.C.). Open: Mar. 1–Sept. 30—daily 9–5; Oct. 1-Feb. 28–daily 9–4. Adm. $1.50 (children 6–11, 75¢, under 6, free).
Washington's home.

JOHN ADAMS and JOHN QUINCY ADAMS

John Adams Birthplace: 133 Franklin St., Quincy, Mass. 02169. Open: Apr. 19–Sept. 30–daily except Monday 9–5. Adm. 75¢ (children under 16, 25¢).*
Farmhouse where John Adams was born in 1735.

John Quincy Adams Birthplace: 141 Franklin St., Quincy, Mass. 02169. Open: Apr. 19–Sept. 30–daily except Monday 9–5. Adm. 75¢ (children under 16, 25¢).*
Farmhouse home of John Adams and birthplace of John Quincy Adams in 1767.

Adams National Historic Site: 135 Adams St., Quincy, Mass. 02169. Open: Apr. 19–Nov. 10—daily 9–5. Adm. 50¢ (children under 16 free).
Home of Adams family from 1788 to 1927; built in 1731. Contains furnishings used by four Adams generations.

* The combined admission to both Adams birthplaces is $1; children 50¢.

THOMAS JEFFERSON

Monticello: on Route 53, 3 mi. southeast of Charlottesville, Va. 22902. Open: Mar. 1–Oct. 31–daily 8–5; Nov. 1–Feb. 28–daily. 9–4:30. Adm. $2 (children 6–11, 50¢).

Home of Jefferson; begun in 1769; finished in 1809. National shrine contains Jefferson mementos.

JAMES MADISON

Montpelier: on Route 20, 5 mi. west of Orange, Va. 22960. Estate not open to public, but graveyard may be visited.

Madison's home.

JAMES MONROE

Ash Lawn: off Route 53, 2½ mi. beyond Monticello, near Charlottesville, Va. 22901. Open: daily, Mar.–Oct. 9–6, Nov.–Feb. 9–5. Adm. $1 (children under 12, 50¢; under 6, free).

Monroe's home from 1799 to 1823; built in 1798 by Jefferson on his design.

ANDREW JACKSON

The Hermitage: near I-40 east on U.S. 70N, 13 mi. east of Nashville, Tenn. 37076. Open: June 1–Labor Day, daily 8–6; rest of year, daily 9–5 (closed Xmas). Adm. $2.50 (children 6–13, 75¢; under 6, free). Student rates available.

Jackson's home.

MARTIN VAN BUREN

Lindenwald: on Route 9H, 2½ mi. south of Kinderhook, N.Y. 12106.

Van Buren's home from 1840 to 1862. Designated a National Historic Site in 1974, the house is now undergoing restoration by the National Park Service.

WILLIAM HENRY HARRISON

Berkeley Plantation (Harrison's Landing): halfway between Richmond and Williamsburg, Va., on Virginia Route 5. Open daily 8–5. Adm. $2 (children 6–12, $1). Group rate $1.75.

Ancestral home of William Henry and Benjamin Harrison. Site of first official Thanksgiving in America, in 1619.

JOHN TYLER

Sherwood Forest: on Virginia Route 5, 20 mi. west of Colonial Williamsburg, Charles City, Va. 23030. Tyler's home; built circa 1730, it is believed to be the longest frame residence in America—300 feet in length.

FRANKLIN PIERCE

Franklin Pierce Homestead: near junction of Routes 9 and 31, northwest of Hillsboro, N.H. 03244. Open: mid-June–Labor Day, Tues.–Sun. Adm. 50¢ (visitors under 18 free).

Pierce's home.

JAMES BUCHANAN

Wheatland: Marietta Ave., Route 23, Lancaster, Pa. 17603. Open: Apr. 1–Nov. 30—Mon.–Sat. 10–5, Sun. 10–5. Last tour: 4:30. Adm. $1.50 (children under 12 50¢). Group rate 75¢ (children 50¢).

Home of the nation's only bachelor President; built in 1828.

ABRAHAM LINCOLN

Lincoln Home National Historic Site: 430 South 8th St., Springfield, Ill. 62701. Open: daily, 8–5 (closed NY Day & Xmas). Free admission.

House is only home owned by Lincoln.

ANDREW JOHNSON

Andrew Johnson National Historic Site: Greeneville, Tenn. 37743. Open: daily 9–5 (closed Xmas). Adm. (June 1–Sept. 15): 50¢ (children under 16 free).

Contains two houses where Johnson lived, tailor shop where he worked, and Andrew Johnson National Cemetery.

ULYSSES S. GRANT

U. S. Grant Home State Memorial: 511 Bouthillier, Galena, Ill. 61036. Open: daily 9–5 (closed NY Day, Thnks. Day, Xmas). Free admission.

RUTHERFORD B. HAYES

Rutherford B. Hayes Library and Museum State Memorial: 1337 Hayes Ave., Fremont, Ohio 43420. Museum open: Mon.–Sat. 9–5, Sun. & hldys. 1:30–5 (closed NY Day, Thnks. Day, Xmas); adm. $1 (children 50¢). Library open: Mon.–Fri. 9–5, Sat. 9–12 (closed Sun. & Hldys.); free. Hayes Home open: Wed–Sat. 9–5, Sun.–Tues. & hldys. 2–5; adm. $1 (children under 13, 50¢; with parents, free). Special rates for groups; advance reservation required for groups.

Estate is known as Spiegel Grove. It contains Hayes' home, his tomb, and White House gates.

JAMES A. GARFIELD

Lawnfield: 8095 Mentor Ave., Mentor, Ohio 44060. Open: May 1–Oct. 31—Tues.–Sat. 9–5, Sun and hldys. 1–5. Adm. $1.25 (children 12–18, 75¢; under 12 with adult, free). Group rates available.

Garfield's home and Lake County Historical Society Museum.

BENJAMIN HARRISON

Benjamin Harrison Memorial Home: 1230 North Delaware St., Indianapolis, Ind. 46202. Open: Mon.–Sat. 10–4, Sun. 12:30–4 (closed Thnks. Day, Dec. 25–Jan. 1). Adm. $1 (students, 50¢).

Harrison's home; completed in 1874.

THEODORE ROOSEVELT

Theodore Roosevelt Birthplace National Historic Site: 28 E. 20th St., New York, N.Y. 10003. Open: daily 9–4:30. Adm. 50¢. (children under 16 and persons 62 and over, free).

Sagamore Hill National Historic Site: 3 mi. east of Oyster Bay, L.I., N.Y. 11771, via E. Main St. Open: daily, 9:30–4:30. Adm. 50¢ (children under 16 and persons 62 and over, free).

Roosevelt's home; built in 1884.

WOODROW WILSON

Birthplace of Woodrow Wilson: Coalter and Frederick Sts., Staunton, Va. 24401. Open: daily 9–5 (closed Sun., Dec.–Feb.; NY Day, Thnks. Day, Xmas). Adm. $1.50 (students and children, $1).

Woodrow Wilson House: 2340 S St. NW., Washington, D.C. 20008. Open: daily 10–4 (closed Xmas). Adm. $1.25 (students and senior citizens, 60¢).

Wilson retired to this house after his second term and died here three years later in 1924.

WARREN G. HARDING

Warren G. Harding Home and Museum: 380 Mt. Vernon Ave., Marion, Ohio 43302. Open: Mar. 15–Nov. 15, Tues.–Sun. 1–5 (closed Mon.). Adm. $1 (children 6–18, 50¢).

CALVIN COOLIDGE

Calvin Coolidge Home: Route 100A, Plymouth, Vt. 05056. Open: mid-May to mid-Oct.–daily 9:30–5:30. Adm. $1 (children under 12 free).

HERBERT HOOVER

Herbert Hoover National Historic Site: ½ mi. north of I-80, exit 63, West Branch, Iowa 52358. Grounds open daily 8–5. (closed NY Day, Thnks. Day, Xmas). Free admission.

Restored two-room cottage where Hoover was born; replica of his father's blacksmith shop. Quaker meetinghouse, grave site.

FRANKLIN D. ROOSEVELT

Home of Franklin D. Roosevelt National Historic Site: on U.S. 9, south end of Hyde Park, N.Y. 12538. Open: daily 9–5 (closed NY Day, Xmas). Adm. 50¢ (children under 16 free). Adm. fee includes admission to Vanderbilt Mansion National Historic Site.

HARRY S. TRUMAN

Harry S. Truman Birthplace State Historic Site: Truman Ave. & 11th St., Lamar, Mo. 64759. Open: Mon.–Sat. 10–4; Sun. May–Labor Day, noon–6; rest of year, noon–5 (closed NY Day, Easter, Thnks. Day, Xmas). Free.

DWIGHT D. EISENHOWER

Eisenhower Birthplace State Historical Site: 208 E. Day St., Denison, Tex. 75020. Open: June 1–Aug. 31, daily 8–12 and 1–5; Sept. 1–May 31, daily, 10–12 and 1–5 (closed Xmas). Adm. 25¢ (children 6–12, 10¢; under 6 free).

JOHN F. KENNEDY

John F. Kennedy National Historic Site: 83 Beals St., Brookline, Mass. 02146. Open: daily 9–5 (closed NY Day, Xmas). Adm. 50¢ (children under 16 with adult, free).

Kennedy's birthplace.

LYNDON B. JOHNSON

Lyndon B. Johnson National Historic Site: P.O. Box 329, Johnson City, Tex. 78636. Open: daily 9–5 (closed Xmas). Free.

Site includes LBJ Ranch, birthplace and family cemetery at Stonewall (15 miles west of Johnson City) and his boyhood home and grandfather's old ranch in Johnson City.

The National Park System of the United States

Source: National Park Service.

The National Park System of the United States is administered by the National Park Service, a bureau of the Department of the Interior. Started with the establishment of Yellowstone National Park in 1872, the system includes not only the most extraordinary and spectacular scenic exhibits in the United States but also a large number of sites distinguished either for their historic or prehistoric importance or scientific interest, or for their superior recreational assets. The number and extent of the various types of areas which comprise the system are as follows:

Type of area	Number	Total acreage[1]	Type of area	Number	Total acreage[1]
National Parks	37	15,617,008.12	National Lakeshores	4	192,268.83
National Monuments	81	9,849,441.36	National Scenic Riverways	3	244,305.61
National Battlefield Parks	3	6,661.98	National Recreation Areas	16	3,412,801.38
National Battlefields	7	6,017.76	National Parkways	4	159,639.11
National Battlefield Sites	2	1,812.36	National Scenic Trail	1	52,034.25
National Cemeteries[2]		218.36	Parks (Other)[3]	9	31,896.48
National Military Parks	11	34,772.04	National Preserves	2	654,550.00
National Historical Parks	16	62,353.52	White House	1	18.07
National Historical Sites	51	13,554.59	National Mall	1	146.35
National Memorials	22	6,124.83	National Visitor Center	1	0.00
National Memorial Park	1	70,408.64	National Capital Parks[4]	1	6,452.06
National Seashores	10	604,241.22	Total National Park System	285	31,026,508.56

[1] Acreage as of December 31, 1975 for most areas. New areas and those subject to boundary changes authorized between June 30, 1974 and January 1, 1975 reflect data available at time of authorization. [2] 10 national cemeteries administered by the National Park Service are administered in conjunction with associated historical units and are not listed separately. [3] Parks without national designation. [4] Comprises 346 units within the District of Columbia, Maryland and Virginia.

National Parks

Name, location, and year established	Acreage	Outstanding characteristics
Acadia (Maine), 1919	37,722.21	Rugged seashore on Mt. Desert Island and adjacent mainland
Arches (Utah), 1971	73,378.98	Unusual stone arches, windows, pedestals caused by erosion
Big Bend (Texas), 1935	708,118.40	Mountains and desert bordering the Rio Grande
Bryce Canyon (Utah), 1924	37,277.10	Area of grotesque eroded rocks brilliantly colored
Canyonlands (Utah), 1964	377,570.43	Colorful wilderness with impressive red-rock canyons, spires, arches
Capitol Reef (Utah), 1971	241,865.48	Highly colored sedimentary rock formations in high, narrow gorges

Name, location, and year established	Acreage	Outstanding characteristics
Carlsbad Caverns (N. Mex.), 1930.....	46,755.33	The world's largest known caves.
Crater Lake (Oregon), 1902..........	160,290.33	Deep blue lake in heart of inactive volcano
Everglades (Florida), 1934	1,400,533.00	Subtropical area with abundant bird and animal life
Glacier (Montana), 1910...............	1,013,598.42	Rocky Mountain scenery with many glaciers and lakes
Grand Canyon (Arizona), 1919........	1,218,375.24	Mile-deep gorge, 4 to 18 miles wide, 217 miles long
Grand Teton (Wyoming), 1929........	310,417.98	Picturesque range of high mountain peaks
Great Smoky Mts. (N. C.-Tenn.), 1926 ..	517,014.22	Highest mountain range east of Black Hills; luxuriant plant life
Guadalupe Mountains (Texas), 1966...	76,398.31	Contains highest point in Texas: Guadalupe Peak (8,751 ft.)
Haleakala (Hawaii), 1960.............	27,823.74	World-famous 10,023-foot Haleakala volcano (dormant)
Hawaii Volcanoes (Hawaii), 1916.......	229,177.03	Spectacular volcanic area; luxuriant vegetation at lower levels
Hot Springs (Arkansas), 1921..........	5,800.69	47 mineral hot springs said to have therapeutic value
Isle Royale (Michigan), 1931..........	539,279.94	Largest wilderness island in Lake Superior; moose, wolves, lakes
Kings Canyon (California), 1940......	460,136.19	Huge canyons; high mountains; giant sequoias
Lassen Volcanic (California), 1916.....	106,372.22	Exhibits of impressive volcanic phenomena
Mammoth Cave (Kentucky), 1926......	52,128.92	Vast limestone labyrinth with underground river
Mesa Verde (Colorado), 1906.........	52,036.24	Best preserved prehistoric cliff dwellings in United States
Mount McKinley (Alaska), 1917......	1,939,492.80	Highest mountain in North America; spectacular wildlife
Mount Rainier (Washington), 1899.....	235,404.00	Single-peak glacial system; dense forests, flowered meadows
North Cascades (Washington), 1968...	504,785.33	Roadless Alpine landscape; jagged peaks; mountain lakes; glaciers
Olympic (Washington), 1938..........	897,909.04	Finest Pacific Northwest rain forest; scenic mountain park
Petrified Forest (Arizona), 1962.......	94,189.33	Extensive natural exhibit of petrified wood
Redwood (California), 1968............	62,147.14	Coastal redwood forests; contains world's tallest known tree (369.2 ft.)
Rocky Mountain (Colorado), 1915.....	263,792.99	Section of the Rocky Mountains; 107 named peaks over 10,000 feet
Sequoia (California), 1890.............	386,823.00	Giant sequoias; magnificent High Sierra scenery, including Mt. Whitney
Shenandoah (Virginia), 1926	190,532.05	Tree-covered mountains; scenic Skyline Drive
Virgin Islands (U. S. Virgin Is.), 1956..	14,470.38	Beaches; lush hills; prehistoric Carib Indian relics
Voyageurs (Minnesota), 1971.........	219,128.00	Wildlife, canoeing, fishing and hiking
Wind Cave (South Dakota), 1903......	28,060.03	Limestone caverns in Black Hills; buffalo herd
Yellowstone (Wyo.-Mont.-Ida.), 1872...	2,219,822.70	World's greatest geyser area; abundant falls, wildlife and canyons
Yosemite (California), 1890...........	760,916.25	Mountains; inspiring gorges and waterfalls; giant sequoias
Zion (Utah), 1919....................	146,552.71	Multicolored gorge in heart of southern Utah desert

National Historical Parks

Name and location	Total acreage
Appomattox Court House (Va.) ..	994.69
Boston (Mass.)	34.74
Chalmette (La.)	142.85
Chesapeake and Ohio Canal (Md., W.Va., D.C.)	20,239.00
City of Refuge (Hawaii)	181.80
Colonial (Va.)	9,833.83
Cumberland Gap (Ky.-Tenn.-Va.)	20,273.04
George Rogers Clark (Ind.)	24.30
Harpers Ferry (W.Va.-Md.)	1,909.47
Independence (Pa.)	21.46
Klondike Goldrush (Alaska)	13,271.00
Minute Man (Mass.)	745.37
Morristown (N.J.)	1,544.17
Nez Perce (Idaho)	2,113.78
San Juan Island (Wash.)	1,751.99
Saratoga (N.Y.)	2,432.41
Sitka (Alaska)	107.71
Valley Forge (Pa.)	2,300.00

National Monuments

Name and location	Total acreage
Agate Fossil Beds (Neb.)	3,054.43
Alibates Flint Quarries (Tex.)	92.56
Aztec Ruins (N.M.).	27.14
Badlands (S.D.)	243,302.33
Bandelier (N.M.)	29,661.20
Biscayne (Fla.)	103,701.23
Black Canyon (Colo.)	13,672.13
Booker T. Washington (Va.)	223.92
Buck Island Reef (Virgin Is.)	880.00
Cabrillo (Calif.)	143.94
Canyon de Chelly (Ariz.)	83,840.00

Name and location	Total acreage
Capulin Mountain (N.M.)	775.38
Casa Grande Ruins (Ariz.)	472.50
Castillo de San Marcos (Fla.)	20.49
Castle Clinton (N.Y.)	1.00
Cedar Breaks (Utah)	6,154.60
Chaco Canyon (N.M.)	21,510.32
Channel Islands (Calif.)	18,388.07
Chiricahua (Ariz.)	10,648.25
Colorado (Colo.)	17,668.52
Craters of the Moon (Idaho)	53,545.05
Custer Battlefield (Mont.)	765.34
Death Valley (Calif.-Nev.)	2,067,832.46
Devils Postpile (Calif.)	798.46
Devils Tower (Wyo.)	1,346.91
Dinosaur (Utah-Colo.)	211,050.65
Effigy Mounds (Iowa)	1,474.63
El Morro (N.M.)	1,278.72
Florissant Fossil Beds (Colo.)	5,992.32
Fort Frederica (Ga.)	214.52
Fort Jefferson (Fla.)	47,125.00
Fort McHenry (Md.)	43.26
Fort Matanzas (Fla.)	298.51
Fort Pulaski (Ga.)	5,615.50
Fort Stanwix (N.Y.)	15.52
Fort Sumter (S.C.)	64.27
Fort Union (N.M.)	720.60
Fossil Butte (Wyo.)	8,178.00
George Washington Birthplace (Va.).	455.98
George Washington Carver (Mo.)	210.00
Gila Cliff Dwellings (N.M.)	533.13
Glacier Bay (Alaska)	2,805,269.49
Gran Quivira (N.M.)	610.94
Grand Portage (Minn.)	709.97

Name and location	Total acreage
Great Sand Dunes (Colo.)	36,826.50
Hohokam-Pima (Ariz.)	1,555.40
Homestead (Neb.)	194.57
Hovenweep (Utah-Colo.)	785.43
Jewel Cave (S.D.)	1,274.56
John Day 'Fossil Beds (Oregon) . .	14,402.00
Joshua Tree (Calif.)	559,959.72
Katmai (Alaska)	2,792,137.00
Lava Beds (Calif.)	46,821.33
Lehman Caves (Nev.)	640.00
Montezuma Castle (Ariz.)	841.75
Mound City Group (Ohio)	67.50
Muir Woods (Calif.)	553.55
Natural Bridges (Utah)	7,779.14
Navajo (Ariz.)	360.00
Ocmulgee (Ga.)	683.48
Oregon Caves (Ore.)	465.80
Organ Pipe Cactus (Ariz.)	330,690.00
Pecos (N.M.)	341.30
Pinnacles (Calif.)	14,497.77
Pipe Spring (Ariz.)	40.00
Pipestone (Minn.)	281.78
Rainbow Bridge (Utah)	160.00
Russell Cave (Ala.)	310.45
Saguaro (Ariz.)	78,977.96
Saint Croix Island (Me.)	35.39
Scotts Bluff (Neb.)	2,987.97
Statue of Liberty (N.Y.-N.J.) . .	58.38
Sunset Crater (Ariz.)	3,040.00
Timpanogos Cave (Utah)	250.00
Tonto (Ariz.)	1,120.00
Tumacacori (Ariz.)	10.15
Tuzigoot (Ariz.)	57.78
Walnut Canyon (Ariz.)	2,249.46
White Sands (N.M.)	145,334.76
Wupatki (Ariz.)	32,253.24
Yucca House (Colo.)	10.00

National Preserves

Name and location	Total acreage
Big Cypress (Fla.)	570,000.00
Big Thicket (Tex.)	84,550.00

National Military Parks

Name and location	Total acreage
Chickamauga and Chattanooga (Ga.-Tenn.)	8,092.85
Fort Donelson (Tenn.)	544.64
Fredericksburg and Spotsylvania (Va.)	6,019.26
Gettysburg (Pa.)	3,863.93
Guilford Courthouse (N.C.)	220.44
Horseshoe Bend (Ala.)	2,040.00
Kings Mountain (S.C.)	3,945.29
Moores Creek (N.C.)	77.25
Pea Ridge (Ark.)	4,300.31
Shiloh (Tenn.)	3,753.00
Vicksburg (Miss.)	1,740.78

National Memorial Park

Name and location	Total acreage
Theodore Roosevelt (N.D.)	70,408.64

National Battlefields

Name and location	Total acreage
Big Hole (Mont.)	655.61
Cowpens (S.C.)	825.28
Fort Necessity (Pa.)	910.84
Petersburg (Va.)	1,514.85
Stones River (Tenn.)	330.86
Tupelo (Miss.)	1.00
Wilson's Creek (Mo.)	1,749.91

National Battlefield Parks

Name and location	Total acreage
Kennesaw Mountain (Ga.)	2,884.38
Manassas (Va.)	3,031.67
Richmond (Va.)	745.93

National Battlefield Sites

Name and location	Total acreage
Antietam (Md.)	1,800.00
Brices Cross Roads (Miss.)	1.00

National Historic Sites

Name and location	Total acreage
Abraham Lincoln Birthplace (Ky.) .	116.50
Adams (Mass.)	8.45
Allegheny Portage Railroad (Pa.) .	760.21
Andersonville (Ga.)	488.15
Andrew Johnson (Tenn.)	16.68
Bent's Old Fort (Colo.)	178.00
Carl Sandburg Home (N.C.) . . .	247.37
Christiansted (Virgin Is.)	27.15
Clara Barton (Md.)	1.09
Edison (N.J.)	19.96
Eisenhower (Pa.)	492.54
Ford's Theatre (Lincoln Museum) (D.C.)	0.25
Fort Bowie (Ariz.)	1,000.00
Fort Davis (Tex.)	460.00
Fort Laramie (Wyo.)	571.36
Fort Larned (Kan.)	718.39
Fort Point (Calif.)	29.00
Fort Raleigh (N.C.)	158.60
Fort Smith (Ark.)	18.58
Fort Union Trading Post (N.D. Mont.)	398.45
Fort Vancouver (Wash.)	212.22
Golden Spike (Utah)	2,203.20
Grant-Kohrs Ranch (Mont.)	1,527.69
Hampton (Md.)	45.42
Herbert Hoover (Iowa)	186.80
Home of F. D. Roosevelt (N.Y.) . .	187.69
Hopewell Village (Pa.)	848.06
Hubbell Trading Post (Ariz.)	160.09
Jefferson National Expansion Memorial (Mo.)	90.96
John F. Kennedy (Mass.)	0.09
John Muir (Calif.)	8.90
Kniff River Indian Villages (N.D.) .	1,303.64
Lincoln Home (Ill.)	12.28
Longfellow (Mass.)	1.98
Lyndon B. Johnson (Tex.)	240.81
Mar-a-Lago (Fla.)	17.17
Martin Van Buren (N.Y.)	42.00
Puukohola Heiau (Hawaii)	76.57
Sagamore Hill (N.Y.)	85.00
Saint-Gaudens (N.H.)	86.00
Salem Maritime (Mass.)	8.80
San Juan (Puerto Rico)	53.20
Saugus Iron Works (Mass.)	8.51
Sewall-Belmont House (D.C.) . . .	0.35
Springfield Armory (Mass.)	55.00
Theodore Roosevelt Birthplace (N.Y.)	0.11
Theodore Roosevelt Inaugural (N.Y.)	1.03
Tuskegee Institute (Ala.)	69.66
Vanderbilt Mansion (N.Y.)	211.65
Whitman Mission (Wash.)	98.15
William Howard Taft (Ohio)	0.83

Name and location	Total acreage

National Memorials

Arkansas Post (Ark.)	385.11
Chamizal (Tex.)	54.90
Coronado (Ariz.)	2,834.16
DeSoto (Fla.)	30.00
Federal Hall (N.Y.)	0.45
Fort Caroline (Fla.)	128.88
Fort Clatsop (Ore.)	124.97
Frederick Douglass Home (D.C.)	8.08
General Grant (N.Y.)	0.76
Hamilton Grange (N.Y.)	0.71
John F. Kennedy Center for Performing Arts (D.C.)	17.50
Johnstown Flood (Pa.)	109.80
Lincoln Boyhood (Ind.)	200.00
Lincoln Memorial (D.C.)	163.63
Lyndon Baines Johnson Memorial Grove on the Potomac (D.C.)	121.00
Mount Rushmore (S.D.)	1,278.45
Perry's Victory and International Peace (Ohio)	25.64
Roger Williams (R.I.)	4.58
Thaddeus Kosciuszko (Pa.)	0.02
Theodore Roosevelt Island (D.C.)	88.50
Thomas Jefferson (D.C.)	18.36
Washington Monument (D.C.)	106.01
Wright Brothers (N.C.)	431.40

National Cemeteries[1]

Antietam (Md.)	11.36
Battleground (D.C.)	1.03
Fort Donelson (Tenn.)	15.34
Fredericksburg (Va.)	12.00
Gettysburg (Pa.)	20.58
Poplar Grove (Va.)	8.72
Shiloh (Tenn.)	10.05
Stones River (Tenn.)	20.09
Vicksburg (Miss.)	116.28
Yorktown (Va.)	2.91

National Seashores

Assateague Island (Md.-Va.)	39,630.92
Cape Cod (Mass.)	44,600.00
Canaveral (Fla.)	67,500.00
Cape Hatteras (N.C.)	30,326.24
Cape Lookout (N.C.)	24,732.00
Cumberland Island (Ga.)	36,876.51
Fire Island (N.Y.)	19,356.55
Gulf Islands (Fla., Miss.)	142,009.05
Padre Island (Tex.)	133,918.72
Point Reyes (Calif.)	65,291.23

National Parkways

Blue Ridge (Va.-N.C.-Ga.)	81,784.02
George Washington Memorial (Va.-Md.)	7,141.63
Natchez Trace (Miss.-Tenn.-Ala.)	46,936.24
John D. Rockefeller, Jr., Memorial (Wyo.)	23,777.22

[1] The National Cemeteries are not independent areas of the National Park System; each is part of the military park, battlefield, etc., with which it is related. Their acreage is kept separately. Arlington National Cemetery is under the Department of the Army. *See* page 603.

Name and location	Total acreage

National Lakeshores

Apostle Islands (Wis.)	42,011.82
Indiana Dunes (Ind.)	8,329.81
Pictured Rocks (Mich.)	70,822.20
Sleeping Bear Dunes (Mich.)	71,105.00

National Rivers

Buffalo (Ark.)	94,146.00
Lower St. Croix (Minn.-Wis.)	7,845.00

National Scenic Riverways & Rivers

Ozark (Mo.)	79,587.00
Saint Croix (Minn.-Wis.)	67,727.61

National Capital Parks

National Capital Parks (D.C.-Va.-Md.)	6,451.03

White House

White House (D.C.)	18.07

Parks (Other)

Arlington House, the Robert E. Lee Memorial (Va.)	27.91
Catoctin Mountain (Md.)	5,768.90
Fort Washington Park (Md.)	341.00
Greenbelt Park (Md.)	1,077.86
Piscataway (Md.)	4,216.53
Prince William Forest (Va.)	18,571.55
Rock Creek Park (D.C.)	1,754.37
Wolf Trap Farm Park for the Performing Arts (Va.)	130.28

National Recreation Areas

Amistad (Tex.)	62,451.74
Bighorn Canyon (Wyo.-Mont.)	140,434.20
Chickasaw (Okla.)	9,294.17
Coulee Dam (Wash.)	10,000.59
Curecanti (Colo.)	41,571.66
Cuyahoga Valley (Ohio)	29,112.19
Delaware Water Gap (Pa.-N.J.)	47,676.38
Gateway (N.Y.-N.J.)	26,172.00
Glen Canyon (Ariz.-Utah)	1,235,080.00
Golden Gate (Calif.)	34,938.29
Lake Chelan (Wash.)	61,889.84
Lake Mead (Ariz.-Nev.)	1,492,794.87
Lake Meredith (Tex.)	45,964.30
Ross Lake (Wash.)	117,574.09
Shadow Mountain (Colo.)	19,003.58
Whiskeytown-Shasta-Trinity (Calif.)	42,497.45

National Scenic Trail

Appalachian (Me., N.H. Vt., Mass., Conn., N.Y., N.J., Pa., Md., W.Va., Va., N.C., Tenn., Ga.)	52,034.25

National Mall

National Mall (D.C.)	146.35

National Visitor Center

National Visitor Center (D.C.)	0.00

Name and location	Total acreage	Name and location	Total acreage
Affiliated Areas		Ice Age (Wis.)[2]	32,500.00
(National Historic Sites unless otherwise noted.)		Jamestown (Va.)	20.63
		McLoughlin House (Ore.)	0.63
Benjamin Franklin (Pa.)[1]	0.00	Pennsylvania Avenue (D.C.)	0.00
Chicago Portage (Ill.)	91.20	Roosevelt–Campobello International	
Chimney Rock (Neb.)	83.36	Park (Canada)	2,721.50
Dorchester Heights (Mass.)	5.43	St. Paul's Church (N.Y.)	6.09
Fort Scott (Kan.)	6.69	St. Thomas (V.I.)	1.66
Gloria Dei Church (Pa.)	3.73	San Jose Mission (Tex.)	4.13
		Tuoro Synagogue (R.I.)	0.23

[1] National Memorial.   [2] National Scientific Reserve.

Notable American Zoos

Source: Questionnaires to the zoos.

Atlanta Zoological Park: 800 Cherokee Ave., Atlanta, Ga. 30315

Audubon Park Zoo and Odenheimer Aquarium: St. Charles Ave. between Walnut and Exposition Blvd., New Orleans, La. 70118.

Baltimore Zoo: Druid Hill Park, Baltimore, Md. 21217.

Belle Isle Aquarium & Children's Zoo: Detroit, Mich. Mailing address: Royal Oak, Mich. 48068.

Bronx Zoo. *See* New York Zoological Park.

Buffalo Zoological Gardens: Delaware Park, Buffalo, N.Y. 14214.

Burnet Park Zoo: Coleridge and Wilbur Ave., Syracuse, N.Y. 13204.

Central Park Zoo: 830 Fifth Ave. at 64th St., New York, N.Y. 10021.

Cheyenne Mountain Zoological Park: Cheyenne Mountain Hgwy., P.O. Box 158, Colorado Springs, Colo. 80901.

Chicago Zoological Park (Brookfield Zoo): First Ave. and 31st St., Brookfield, Ill. 60513.

Cincinnati, Zoological Society of: 3400 Vine St., Cincinnati, Ohio 45220.

Cleveland Metroparks Zoo: Brookside Park, Cleveland, Ohio 44109.

Columbus Zoo: 9990 Riverside Drive, Powell, Ohio 43065.

Dallas Zoo: 621 East Clarendon Drive, Dallas, Tex. 75203.

Denver Zoological Gardens: City Park, Denver, Colo 80205.

Detroit Zoological Park: Woodward and Ten Mile Road, Royal Oak, Mich. 48068.

El Paso Zoological Park: Evergreen and Paisano, El Paso, Tex. 79905.

Fort Worth Zoological Park: 2727 Zoological Park Drive, Fort Worth, Tex. 76110.

Franklin Park Zoo & Children's Zoo: Blue Hill Ave. and Columbia Rd., Boston, Mass. 02121.

Hogle Zoological Gardens: 2600 East Sunnyside Ave., Salt Lake City, Utah 84108.

Houston Zoological Gardens: Hermann Park, P.O. Box 1562, Houston, Tex. 77001.

Jacksonville Zoological Park: 8605 Zoo Road, Jacksonville, Fla. 32218.

Kansas City Zoo: Swope Park, Kansas City, Mo. 64132.

Lincoln Municipal Zoo: 1300 South 27th St., Lincoln, Neb. 68502.

Lincoln Park Zoological Gardens: 100 Webster Street, Chicago, Ill. 60614.

Los Angeles Zoo: 5333 Zoo Drive, Los Angeles, Calif. 90027.

Mesker Park Zoo: Bement Ave., Evansville, Ind. 47712.

Milwaukee County Zoo: 10001 West Bluemound, Milwaukee, Wis. 53226.

National Zoological Park: 3000 block of Connecticut Ave., N.W. Washington, D.C. 20009.

New York Zoological Park (Bronx Zoo): Southern Blvd. and 185th St., Bronx, N.Y. 10460.

Oakland Zoo: Knowland Park, Oakland, Calif. 94605.

Oklahoma City Zoo: N.E. 50th and N. Eastern Ave., Oklahoma City, Okla. 73111.

Overton Park Zoo and Aquarium: Memphis, Tenn. 38112.

Pittsburgh Zoo: Highland Park, Pittsburgh, Pa. 15206.

Portland Zoological Gardens: 4001 S.W. Canyon Rd., Portland, Ore. 97221.

Rio Grande Zoological Park: 903 Tenth St., S.W., Albuquerque, N.M. 87102.

St. Louis Zoological Park: Forest Park, St. Louis, Mo. 63110.

St. Paul's Como Park Zoo: Hamline and Midway Pkwy., St. Paul, Minn. 55103.

San Diego Zoological Garden: Park Blvd. and Zoo Place, San Diego, Calif. 92112.

San Francisco Zoological Gardens: Zoo Rd. and Skyline Blvd., San Francisco, Calif., 94132.

Seneca Park Zoo: 2222 St. Paul St., Rochester, N.Y. 14621.

Staten Island Zoo: Barrett Park, W. Brighton, Staten Island, New York 10310.

Toledo Zoological Gardens: 2700 Broadway, Toledo, Ohio 43609.

Woodland Park Zoological Gardens: 5500 Phinney Ave. N., Seattle, Wash. 98103.

Some Leading U.S. Foundations

Source: Questionnaires to foundations.

CARNEGIE CORPORATION OF NEW YORK, 437 Madison Ave., New York, N.Y. 10022: Founded 1911 by Andrew Carnegie to advance knowledge and understanding in U.S. and certain British Commonwealth countries. Grants made to universities and organizations primarily for research or projects in education and public affairs. Total assets (1976): $280,000,000.

CARNEGIE ENDOWMENT FOR INTERNATIONAL PEACE, 345 E. 46th St., New York, N.Y. 10017; 11 Dupont Circle, N.W., Washington, D.C. 20036: Founded 1910 by Andrew Carnegie, to seek practical paths to peace. Assets (June 30, 1975): $37,963,542.

COMMONWEALTH FUND, 1 E. 75th St., New York, N.Y. 10021: Founded 1918 by Mrs. Stephen V. Harkness. Focuses on education for medicine within the university, with particular attention to the interface between a university's college of liberal arts and its medical school. Endowment (1975): $122,729,941.

DANFORTH FOUNDATION, 222 S. Central Ave., St. Louis, Mo. 63105: Founded 1927 by Mr. and Mrs. William H. Danforth to give aid and encouragement to persons and educational institutions, to emphasize the humane values coming from a democratic heritage, and to strengthening the essential quality of education through fellowships and grants. Total assets (May 31, 1975): $98,948,826.

DUKE ENDOWMENT, THE, 30 Rockefeller Plaza, New York, N.Y. 10020: Founded 1924 by James Buchanan Duke. Purpose is to assist specified beneficiaries in North and South Carolina, including colleges, universities, hospitals, orphanages, rural Methodist churches, and retired Methodist ministers. Income available for distribution and allocation (Dec. 31, 1975): $19,712,472.

FIELD FOUNDATION INC., 100 E. 85th St., New York, N.Y. 10028: Founded 1940 by Marshall Field. Present grants are mainly for programs of race relations, child welfare and poverty. Assets (1975): $17,000,000.

FLEISCHMANN (MAX C.) FOUNDATION, 1 E. Liberty St., Reno, Nev. 89505: Established in 1952, with grants going to organizations in education, law, medical and scientific research, youth work and conservation. Capital assets (June 30, 1974) $94,941,158.

FORD FOUNDATION, 320 E. 43rd St., New York, N.Y. 10017. Founded 1936 by Henry and Edsel Ford to advance human welfare by identifying problems of national and international importance and granting funds toward their solution, primarily through educational means. Total assets (1975): $2,070,728,000.

GUGGENHEIM (JOHN SIMON) MEMORIAL FOUNDATION, 90 Park Ave., New York N.Y. 10016: Founded 1925 to offer fellowships to advanced workers in all fields. Endowment (1976): $90,000,000.

HARTFORD (JOHN A.) FOUNDATION, 405 Lexington Ave., New York, N.Y. 10017: Founded 1929. Grants made for biomedical research projects in U.S. and Canadian medical schools and hospitals. Principal fund (1975): $171,500,000.

HOUSTON ENDOWMENT INC., P.O. Box 52338, Houston, Tex. 77052: Founded 1937 by Mr. and Mrs. Jesse H. Jones for the support of any charitable, educational or religious undertaking. Total assets (1975): $209,551,042.

JOHNSON (THE ROBERT WOOD) FOUNDATION, Forrestal Center, P.O. Box 2316, Princeton, N.J. 08540: Founded 1936. Devotes its resources almost exclusively to advancement of health care delivery in U.S. Priority is given to programs that are of broad national and regional significance. Market value of assets (1975): $1,058,047,886.

KELLOGG (W. K.) FOUNDATION, 400 North Ave., Battle Creek, Mich. 49016: Founded 1930 by W. K. Kellogg. Operates by making grants supporting experimental programs in health, agricultural and educational fields. Assets (Aug. 31, 1975): $70,804,398 (book value), $747,012,414 (market value).

KRESGE FOUNDATION, 2401 W. Big Beaver Rd., Troy, Mich. 48084: Established in 1924 by Sebastian S. Kresge. Makes construction grants principally in the fields of higher education, health care, conservation, music and the arts, and care of the young or old. Assets (Dec. 31, 1975): $623,638,421, market value.

LILLY ENDOWMENT, INC., 2801 N. Meridian St., Indianapolis, Ind. 46208: Founded in 1937 by the Lilly family for support of religious, educational and charitable purposes. Assets (Dec. 1975): $761,962,535.

LONGWOOD FOUNDATION, INC., 2024 Du Pont Bldg., Wilmington, Del. 19898: Established in 1937 by Pierre S. du Pont. Grants funds primarily for capital purposes to educational institutions, hospitals, conservation-related organizations and other community projects in Wilmington area. Assets (Sept. 30, 1975): $102,245,852.

MELLON (ANDREW W.) FOUNDATION, 140 E. 62nd St., New York, N.Y. 10021: Established in 1969, with particular emphasis on support for higher educational institutions. Also assists cultural organizations. Assets (Dec. 1975): $652,399,240.

RICHARD KING MELLON FOUNDATION. 525 William Penn Plaza, Pittsburgh, Pa. 15219: Founded 1947 by Lt. Gen. Richard King Mellon as a general-purpose foundation principally interested in the quality of life in Pittsburgh and Western Pennsylvania. Total assets (as of Dec. 31, 1975): $231,365,510.

MOODY FOUNDATION, Galveston, Tex. 77550: Founded in 1942 by William L. Moody, Jr., and his wife, Libbie Shearn Moody. Supports activities that are directed toward general well-being of the people of Texas. Net worth (1975): $117,000,000.

MOTT (CHARLES STEWART) FOUNDATION, 500 Mott Foundation Bldg., Flint, Mich. 48502: Founded in 1926 to support community programs in health, education, recreation, social services and for the general welfare. Assets (1975): $377,043,407.

PEW MEMORIAL TRUST, THE, c/o Glenmede Trust Co., 1529 Walnut St., Philadelphia, Pa. 19102: Founded in 1948 in memory of Joseph N. Pew and Mary Anderson Pew. Awards grants to tax-exempt organizations principally in fields of education, charity, medicine and religion. Grants distributed in 1975: $28,380,000.

ROCKEFELLER BROTHERS FUND, 30 Rockefeller Plaza, New York, N.Y. 10020: A general-purpose foundation organized in 1940. Interests include environmental concerns, equal opportunity, quality of life, education, international development assistance programs and improvement of international relations. Grants are made to philanthropic organizations. Assets (Dec. 1975): $185,755,103.

ROCKEFELLER FOUNDATION, 1133 Avenue of the Americas, New York, N.Y. 10036. Founded 1913. Devotes its resources toward world-wide conquest of hunger, population stabilization, university development and resolution of conflict in international relations; in U.S. toward equal opportunity for all, quality of the environment and cultural development. Principal fund (1975): $703,175,132.

RUSSELL SAGE FOUNDATION, 230 Park Ave., New York, N.Y. 10017: Founded in 1907 by Mrs. Russell Sage to improve social and living conditions in U.S. Program emphasizes utilization of social sciences research. Assets (Sept. 1975): $36,000,000.

SARAH SCAIFE FOUNDATION, 1114 Oliver Bldg., Pittsburgh, Pa. 15222: Founded 1941 by Mrs. Sarah Mellon Scaife for medical research and public, religious, charitable, scientific, literary and educational purposes for the furtherance of the public welfare and the benefit of mankind in general. Total assets (1975): $71,899,345 (market value).

SLOAN (ALFRED P.) FOUNDATION, 630 Fifth Ave., New York, N.Y. 10020: Founded 1934 by Alfred P. Sloan, Jr. Supports research and instruction in science, engineering, management and related problems of society. Assets, at market value (December 1975): $256,662,156.

TWENTIETH CENTURY FUND, 41 E. 70th St., New York, N.Y. 10021: Founded in 1919 and endowed by Edward A. Filene. A research foundation that undertakes timely, critical and analytical studies of major economic, political and social institutions and issues. Assets (1975): $21,981,762.

U.S. Societies and Associations

Source: Questionnaires to the organizations.

Names are listed alphabetically according to key word in title; figure in parentheses is year of founding; other figure is membership.

Abortion, Association for the Study of (1965): 120 W. 57th St., New York, N.Y. 10019. 27,000; Jimmye Kimmey, Executive Director.

African-American Institute, The (1953): 833 United Nations Plaza, New York, N.Y. 10017. Robert Denerstein, Director of Publications and General Information.

Air Pollution Control Association (1907): 4400 Fifth Ave., Pittsburgh, Pa. 15213. 6,500; Lewis H. Rogers, Executive Vice President.

Alcoholics Anonymous (1935): P.O. Box 459, Grand Central Station, New York, N.Y. 10017. 1,000,000; Address communications to Secretary.

American Academy of Arts and Letters (1904): 633 W. 155th St., New York, N.Y. 10032. 50; Margaret M. Mills, Executive Director.

American Alliance for Health, Physical Education and Recreation (1885): 1201 16th St., N.W., Washington, D.C. 20036. 50,000; George F. Anderson, Executive Director.

American Anti-Vivisection Society, The (1883): 1903 Chestnut St., Philadelphia, Pa. 19103. 15,000; Owen B. Hunt, President.

American Arbitration Association (1926): 140 W. 51st St., New York, N.Y. 10020. 3,527; E. W. Dippold, Corporate Secretary.

American Association for the Advancement of Science (1848): 1515 Massachusetts Ave., N.W., Washington, D.C. 20005. 120,000; Carol L. Rogers, Public Information.

American Association of Museums (1906): 2233 Wisconsin Ave., N.W., Washington, D.C. 20007. 5,970; Richard McLanathan, Executive Officer.

American Association of Retired Persons (1958): 1909 K St., N.W., Washington, D.C. 20049. 8,700,000; Harriet Miller, Executive Director.

American Association of University Women (1882): 2401 Virginia Ave., N.W., Washington, D.C. 20037. 190,000; Helen B. Wolfe, General Director.

American Astronomical Society (1899): Leander-McCormick Observatory, Box 3818, University Station, Charlottesville, Va. 22903. 3,028; Laurence W. Frederick, Secretary.

American Automobile Association (1902): 8111 Gatehouse Rd., Falls Church, Va. 22042. 18,000,000; J. B. Creal, Executive Vice President.

American Bible Society (1816): 1865 Broadway, New York, N.Y. 10023. 275,000; Charles W. Baas, Laton E. Holmgren, Warner A. Hutchinson, General Officers.

American Camping Association, The (1910): Bradford Woods, Martinsville, Ind. 46151. 7,500; Armand Ball, Executive Vice President.

American Cancer Society (1913): 777 Third Ave., New York, N.Y. 10017. 2,300,000; Lane W. Adams, Executive Vice President.

American Chemical Society (1876): 1155 16th St., N.W., Washington, D.C. 20036. 107,000; Robert W. Cairns, Executive Director.

American Civil Liberties Union (1920): 22 E. 40th St., New York, N.Y. 10016. 275,000; Alan Reitman, Associate Director.

American Contract Bridge League (1927): 2200 Democrat Rd., Memphis, Tenn. 38116. 200,000; Richard L. Goldberg, Executive Secretary.

American Council for Judaism (1943): 309 Fifth Ave., New York, N.Y. 10016. 10,000; Clarence L. Coleman, Jr., President.

American Dental Association (1859): 211 E. Chicago Ave., Chicago, Ill. 60611. 124,511; C. Gordon Watson, Executive Director.

American Diabetes Association (1940): 1 W. 48th St., New York, N.Y. 10020. Ernest M. Frost, Executive Vice President.

American Farm Bureau Federation (1919): 225 Touhy Ave., Park Ridge, Ill. 60068. 2,393,731 member families; Creston Foster, Director of Information.

American Federation of Labor and Congress of Industrial Organizations (1955): 815 16th St., N.W., Washington, D.C. 20006. 14,300,000; Albert J. Zack, Director of Public Relations.

American Federation of Teachers (1916): 11 Dupont Circle, N.W., Washington, D.C. 20036. 400,000; Albert Shanker, President.

American Friends of the Middle East (1951): 1717 Massachusetts Ave., N.W., Washington, D.C. 20036. 500; Virgil C. Crippin, President.

American Friends Service Committee (1917): 1501 Cherry St., Philadelphia, Pa. 19102. Marjorie Seeley, Information Associate.

American Geriatrics Society (1942): 10 Columbus Circle, New York, N.Y. 10019. 9,000; Kathryn S. Henderson, Executive Director.

American Heart Association, Inc. (1948): 7320 Greenville Ave., Dallas, Tex. 75231. 105,000; William W. Moore, Executive Vice President.

American Home Economics Association (1909): 2010 Massachusetts Ave., N.W., Washington, D.C. 20036. 52,000; Kinsey Green, Executive Director.

American Horticultural Society (1922): Mt. Vernon, Va. 22121. 30,000; Keister Evans, Executive Director.

American Hospital Association (1898): 840 N.

Lake Shore Dr., Chicago, Ill. 60611. 6,590 institutions; Dwight Geduldig, Director of Public Affairs.

American Humane Association (1877): P.O. Box 1266, Denver, Colo. 80201. Milton C. Searle, Executive Director.

American Institute of Aeronautics and Astronautics (1932): 1290 Avenue of the Americas, New York, N.Y. 10019. 25,700; James J. Harford, Executive Secretary.

American Jewish Committee (1906): 165 E. 56th St., New York, N.Y. 10022. 40,000; Morton Yarmon, Director of Public Relations.

American Kennel Club (1884): 51 Madison Ave., New York, N.Y. 10010. 402 member clubs; Mark T. Mooty, Secretary.

American Legion (1919): P.O. Box 1055, Indianapolis, Ind. 46206. 2,500,000; William F. Hauck, National Adjutant.

American Legion Auxiliary (1919): 777 N. Meridian St., Indianapolis, Ind. 46204. 940,000; Doris Anderson, National Secretary.

American Library Association (1876): 50 E. Huron St., Chicago, Ill. 60611. 31,627; Robert Wedgeworth, Executive Director.

American Management Associations (1923): 135 W. 50th St., New York, N.Y. 10020. 55,000; Joseph P. Keyes, Director of Public Relations.

American Medical Association (1847): 535 N. Dearborn St., Chicago, Ill. 60610.

American National Red Cross (1881): 17th and D Sts., N.W., Washington, D.C. 20006. 30,945,344; George M. Elsey, President.

American Newspaper Publishers Association (1887): P.O. Box 17407, Dulles International Airport, Washington, D.C. 20041. 11,000; Jo Kirks, Librarian.

American Nurses' Association (1896): 2420 Pershing Rd., Kansas City, Mo. 64108. 200,000.

American Philatelic Society (1886): P.O. Box 800, State College, Pa. 16801. 38,000; James DeVoss, Executive Secretary.

American Philosophical Society (1743): 104 S. 5th St., Philadelphia, Pa. 19106. 600; George W. Corner, Executive Officer.

American Physical Society (1899): 335 E. 45th St., New York, N.Y. 10017. 29,000; W. W. Havens, Jr., Executive Secretary.

American Psychiatric Association (1844): 1700 18th St., N.W., Washington, D.C. 20009. 21,000; Robert Gibson, M.D., President.

American Public Health Association (1872): 1015 18th St., N.W., Washington, D.C. 20036. 24,000; William H. McBeath, M.D., Executive Director.

American Society for the Prevention of Cruelty to Animals (1866): 441 E. 92nd St., New York, N.Y. 10028. 3,000; Albert E. Hart, Jr., Chairman.

American Society of Composers, Authors and Publishers (ASCAP) (1914): One Lincoln Plaza, New York, N.Y. 10023. 24,896 composers, lyricists and music publishers; Stanley Adams, President.

American Society of Travel Agents, Inc. (ASTA) (1931): 711 Fifth Ave., New York, N.Y. 10022. 14,500; Richard P. Ramaglia, Executive Vice President.

American Speech and Hearing Association (1925): 9030 Old Georgetown Rd., Washington, D.C. 20014. 20,500; Kenneth Johnson, Executive Secretary.

American Veterans Committee (AVC) (1944): 1333 Connecticut Ave., N.W., Washington, D.C. 20036. 25,000; June A. Willenz, Executive Director.

American Veterinary Medical Association (1863): 930 N. Meacham Rd., Schaumburg, Ill. 60196. 25,000; Dr. D. A. Price, Executive Vice President.

American Youth Hostels, Inc. (1934): National Campus, Delaplane, Va. 22025. 80,000.

Americans for Democratic Action (1947): 1424 16th St., N.W., Washington, D.C. 20036. 75,000; Leon Shull, National Director.

Ancient Accepted Scottish Rite, Northern Masonic Jurisdiction, Supreme Council, 33° (1813): 33 Marrett Rd., Lexington, Mass. 02173. 512,992; Winthrop L. Hall, Executive Secretary.

Ancient and Accepted Scottish Rite, Southern Jurisdiction, Supreme Council (1801): 1733 16th St., N.W., Washington, D.C. 20009. 638,000; C. Fred Kleinknecht, Grand Secretary General.

Anti-Defamation League of B'nai B'rith (1913): 315 Lexington Ave., New York, N.Y. 10016. Benjamin R. Epstein, National Director.

Arthritis Foundation (1948): 475 Riverside Dr., New York, N.Y. 10027. 73 local chapters; Clifford M. Clarke, Executive Director.

Athletic Union of the U.S., Amateur (1888): 3400 W. 86th St., Indianapolis, Ind. 46268. 330,000; Ollan Cassell, Executive Director.

Authors League of America (1912): 234 W. 44th St., New York, N.Y. 10036. 6,500.

Big Brothers of America (1946): 220 Suburban Station Bldg., Philadelphia, Pa. 19103. D. Theodore Brownworth, Director of Information Services.

Blue Shield Plans, National Association of (1946): 211 E. Chicago Ave., Chicago, Ill. 60611. 71 affiliates; Tom K. Mura, Vice President, Communications.

B'nai B'rith (1843): 1640 Rhode Island Ave., N.W., Washington, D.C. 20036. 500,000; Bernard Simon, Director of Public Relations.

Boy Scouts of America, National Council (1910): North Brunswick, N.J. 08902. 5,803,885.

Boys' Clubs of America (1906): 771 First Ave., New York, N.Y. 10017. 1,000,000; E. J. Stapleton, Director of National Communications and Special Events.

Brookings Institution (1927): 1775 Massachusetts Ave., N.W., Washington, D.C. 20036. James D. Farrell, Information Editor.

Camp Fire Girls (1910): 1740 Broadway, New York, N.Y. 10019. 500,000; Dr. Hester Turner, National Executive Director.

CARE (Cooperative for American Relief Everywhere) (1945): 660 First Ave., New York, N.Y. 10016. 25 agencies; Frank Goffio, Executive Director.

Catholic Bishops, National Conference of (1966): 1312 Massachusetts Ave., N.W., Washington, D.C. 20005. 306; Most Rev. Joseph L. Bernardin, President.

Catholic Charities, National Conference of (1910): 1346 Connecticut Ave., N.W., Washington, D.C. 20036. 3,000; Rev. Msgr. Lawrence Corcoran, Executive Director.

Catholic Conference, United States (1966): 1312 Massachusetts Ave., N.W., Washington, D.C. 20005. Bishop James Rausch, General Secretary.

Catholic Daughters of America (1903): 10 W. 71st St., New York, N.Y. 10023. 185,000; Lorraine McMahon, Executive Secretary.

Catholic War Veterans of the U.S.A. (1935): 2 Massachusetts Ave., N.W., Washington, D.C. 20001. 75,000; Francis X. McBarron, Office Administrator.

Chamber of Commerce of the U.S. (1912): 1615 H St., N.W., Washington, D.C. 20062. 59,000; Richard L. Lesher, President.

Child Study Association of America/Wel Met, Inc. (1900): 50 Madison Ave., New York, N.Y. 10010. Harriet Dronska, Executive Director.

Common Cause (1970): 2030 M St., N.W., Washington, D.C. 20036. 300,000; John W. Gardner, Chairman.

Congress of Racial Equality (CORE) (1942): 200 W. 135th St., New York, N.Y. 10030. Nationwide network of chapters; Roy Innis, National Director.

Conscientious Objectors, Central Committee for (1948): 2016 Walnut St., Philadelphia, Pa. 19103. Stephen M. Gulick, Associate Secretary.

Cooperative League of the U.S.A. (1916): 1828 L St., N.W., Washington, D.C. 20036. 23,000,000; Stanley Dreyer, President.

Council on Foreign Relations, Inc. (1921): 58 E. 68th St., New York, N.Y. 10021. 1,705; Bayless Manning, President.

Country Music Association (1958): 7 Music Circle North, Nashville, Tenn. 37203. 5,000; Jo Walker, Executive Director.

Daughters of the American Revolution, National Society (1890): 1776 D St., N.W., Washington, D.C. 20006. 200,000; Mrs. Wakelee Rawson Smith, President General.

Disabled American Veterans (1922): P.O. Box 14301, Cincinnati, Ohio 45214. 510,000; Richard M. Wilson, Assistant National Adjutant for Public Relations.

Eagles, Fraternal Order of (1898): 2401 W. Wisconsin Ave., Milwaukee, Wis. 53233. 850,000; Art Ehrmann, Publications Editor.

Easter Seal Society for Crippled Children and Adults, The National (1921): 2023 W. Ogden Ave., Chicago, Ill. 60612. 52 affiliated state societies; Jayne Shover, Executive Director.

Eastern Star, Order of the, General Grand Chapter (1876): 1618 New Hampshire Ave., N.W., Washington, D.C. 20009. 3,000,000; Marguerite Kennerdell, Most Worthy Grand Matron.

Elks of the U.S.A., Benevolent & Protective Order of the (1868): 2750 Lake View Ave., Chicago, Ill. 60614. 1,582,735; Homer Huhn, Jr., Grand Secretary.

English-Speaking Union of the United States (1920): 16 E. 69th St., New York, N.Y. 10021. 32,000; Charles P. Dennison, Executive Director.

Family Service Association of America (1911): 44 E. 23rd St., New York, N.Y. 10010. 320 member agencies; W. Keith Daugherty, General Director.

Foreign Policy Association (1918): 345 E. 46th St., New York, N.Y. 10017. Thetis Reavis, Director of Publishing and Information.

Foster Parents Plan International (1937): Box 400, Warwick, R.I. 02886. 63,000; George W. Ross, Jr., Executive Director.

4-H Program (early 1900's): Extension Service, U.S. Department of Agriculture, Washington, D.C. 20250. 5,500,000; E. Dean Vaughan, Director.

Geophysicists, Society of Exploration (1930): P.O. Box 3098, Tulsa, Okla. 74101. 9,400; H. R. Breck, Executive Secretary.

Gideons International, The (1899): 2900 Lebanon Rd., Nashville, Tenn. 37214. 43,500; M. A. Henderson, Executive Director.

Girl Scouts of the U.S.A., Inc. (1912): 830 Third Avenue, New York, N.Y. 10022. 3,234,000; Richard G. Knox, Director Public Relations.

Girls Clubs of America (1945): 133 E. 62nd St., New York, N.Y. 10021. 151,000; Edith B. Phelps, National Executive Director.

Hadassah, The Women's Zionist Organization of America (1912): 50 W. 58th St., New York, N.Y. 10019. 335,000; Aline Kaplan, Executive Director.

Imperial Council of Ancient Arabic Order of Nobles of the Mystic Shrine (1872): 323 N. Michigan Ave., Chicago, Ill. 60601. 919,082; George M. Saunders, Imperial Recorder.

Indian Rights Association (1882): 1505 Race St., Philadelphia, Pa. 19102. 2,000; Theodore B. Hetzel, General Secretary.

Intercollegiate (Big Ten) Conference (1896): 1111 Plaza Dr., Schaumburg, Ill. 60172. 10; Jeff Elliott, Service Bureau Director.

Jewish Community Centers, World Federation of (1946): 15 E. 26th St., New York, N.Y. 10010. Herbert Millman, Executive Director.

Jewish War Veterans of the U.S.A. (1896): 1712 New Hampshire Ave., N.W., Washington, D.C. 20009.

John Birch Society (1958): 395 Concord Ave., Belmont, Mass. 02178. 100,000; Ellen Sproul, Clerk of Corporation.

Junior Achievement, Inc. (1919): 550 Summer St., Stamford, Conn. 06901. 190,000; Diana Jacobs, National Public Relations Director.

Junior Leagues, Inc., Association of (1921): 825 Third Ave., New York, N.Y. 10022. 116,000.

Kiwanis International (1915): 101 E. Erie, Chicago, Ill. 60611. 282,000; R. P. Merridew, Secretary.

Knights of Columbus (1882): One Columbus Plaza, New Haven, Conn. 06507. 1,200,000; Virgil Dechant, Supreme Secretary.

Knights of Pythias, Supreme Lodge (1864): 47 N. Grant St., Stockton, Calif. 95202. 165,756; Jule O. Pritchard, Supreme Secretary.

Knights Templar, Grand Encampment of (1816): 14 E. Jackson Blvd., Suite 1700, Chicago, Ill. 60604. 380,000; Paul C. Rodenhauser, Grand Recorder.

League of Women Voters of the U.S. (1920): 1730 M St., N.W., Washington, D.C. 20036. 136,000; Peggy Lampl, Executive Director.

Lions Clubs, The International Association of (1917): York and Cermak Rds., Oak Brook, Ill. 60521. 1,140,604; Gene H. Samuelsen, Manager of Public Relations and Communications.

Marine Corps League (1923): 933 N. Kenmore St., Arlington, Va. 22201. 20,000; F. B. Starr, National Adjutant Paymaster.

Mayflower Descendants, General Society of (1897): 4 Winslow St., P.O. Box 297, Plymouth, Mass. 02360. 15,795; Mrs. Lester A. Hall, Historian General.

Modern Language Association of America (1883): 62 Fifth Ave., New York, N.Y. 10011. 30,000; Jeffrey Howitt, Promotion and Production Manager.

Moose, Loyal Order of (1888): Mooseheart, Ill. 60539. 1,492,502; Carl A. Weis, Supreme Secretary.

National Aeronautic Association (1922): 806 15th St., N.W., Washington, D.C. 20005. 100,000; Brooke E. Allen, Executive Director.

National Association for Hearing and Speech Action (1919): 814 Thayer Ave., Silver Spring, Md. 20910. 153 agencies.

National Association for Mental Health (1909): 1800 N. Kent St., Arlington, Va. 22209. 1,000,000; William Perry, Jr., Director of Communications.

National Association for Retarded Citizens (1950): 2709 Avenue E East, Arlington, Tex. 76011. 1,800 units; Philip Roos, Executive Director.

National Association for the Advancement of Colored People (1909): 1790 Broadway, New York, N.Y. 10019. 406,000; Roy Wilkins, Executive Director.

National Association of Colored Women's Clubs (1896): 5808 16th St., N.W., Washington, D.C. 20011. 100,000; Mrs. Juanita White Brown, National President.

National Association of Intercollegiate Athletics (1940): 1205 Baltimore St., Kansas City, Mo. 64105. 560; Harry Fritz, Executive Secretary.

National Association of Manufacturers (1895): 610 Fifth Ave., New York, N.Y. 10020. 12,500; John McGraw, Secretary.

National Association of Social Workers, Inc. (1955): 1425 H St., N.W., Washington, D.C. 20005. 70,000; Chauncey A. Alexander, Executive Director.

National Audubon Society (1905): 950 Third Ave., New York, N.Y. 10022. 325,000; Robert C. Boardman, Public Information Officer.

National Conference of Christians and Jews (1928): 43 W. 57th St., New York, N.Y. 10019. 200,000; David Hyatt, President.

National Conference on Social Welfare (1873): 22 W. Gay St., Columbus, Ohio 43215. 8,500; Margaret E. Berry, Executive Director.

National Congress of Parents and Teachers (1897); 700 N. Rush St., Chicago, Ill. 60611. 6,621,000; Robert M. Crum, Managing Director.

National Council of Churches (1950): 475 Riverside Drive, New York, N.Y. 10027. 30 Christian communions; Claire Randall, General Secretary.

National Council of Jewish Women (1893): 15 E. 26th St., New York, N.Y. 10010. Esther R. Landa, National President.

National Council on Crime and Delinquency (1907): Continental Plaza, Hackensack, N.J. 07601. 60,000; Milton Rector, President.

National Democratic Club (1834): Chemists Club, 52 E. 41st St., New York, N.Y. 10017. 500; James Driscoll, Secretary.

National Education Association (1857): 1201 16th St., N.W., Washington, D.C. 20036. 1,870,000. Terry Herndon, Executive Secretary.

National Federation of the Blind (1940): 218 Randolph Hotel Bldg., Des Moines, Iowa 50309. 50,000; Kenneth Jernigan, President.

National Foundation—March of Dimes (1938): 1275 Mamaroneck Ave., White Plains, N.Y. 10605. 2,100 chapters; George Voss, Vice President.

National Geographic Society (1888): 17th & M Sts., N.W., Washington, D.C. 20036. 9,000,000; Gilbert M. Grosvenor, Editor.

National Grange, The (1867): 1616 H St., N.W., Washington, D.C. 20006. 600,000; John Scott, Master.

National Interfraternity Conference (1909): P.O. Box 40368, Indianapolis, Ind. 46240. 47; Jack L. Anson, Executive Director.

National Multiple Sclerosis Society (1946): 205 E. 42nd St., New York, N.Y. 10017. Sylvia Lawry, Executive Director.

National Parks and Conservation Association (1919): 1701 18th St., N.W., Washington, D.C. 20009. 45,000; Anthony Wayne Smith, President.

National Rifle Association of America (1871): 1600 Rhode Island Ave., N.W., Washington, D.C. 20036. 1,035,000; Maxwell E. Rich, Executive Vice President.

National Safety Council (1913): 425 N. Michigan Ave., Chicago, Ill. 60611. George V. Budrean, Director Public Information.

National Society for the Prevention of Blindness (1908): 79 Madison Ave., New York, N.Y. 10016. 304; Virginia Boyce, Executive Director.

National Society of the Sons of the American Revolution (1889): 2412 Massachusetts Ave., N.W., Washington, D.C. 20008. 20,000; Warren S. Woodward, Executive Secretary.

National Urban League (1910): 500 E. 62nd St., New York, N.Y. 10021. 103; James D. Williams, Director of Communications.

Odd Fellows, Independent Order of (1819): 16 W. Chase St., Baltimore, Md. 21201. 1,200,000; A. Ford Winters, Sovereign Grand Secretary.

Olympic Committee, United States (1921): 57 Park Ave., New York, N.Y. 10016. 222; Bob Paul, Director of Communications.

Organization of American States (1890): 17th St. and Constitution Ave., N.W., Washington, D.C. 20006. 24 member nations.

Photographic Society of America (1933): 2005 Walnut St., Philadelphia, Pa. 19103. 17,300; Charles E. Morris, Executive Secretary.

Planned Parenthood Federation of America (1916): 810 Seventh Ave., New York, N.Y. 10019. 189 affiliates; Robin Elliott, Information and Education Director.

Political Science, Academy of (1880): 2852 Broadway, New York, N.Y. 10025. 11,000; William V. Farr, Business Manager.

Rotary International (1905): 1600 Ridge Ave., Evanston, Ill. 60201. 791,500; Harry Stewart, General Secretary.

Salvation Army (1865): 120 W. 14th St., New York, N.Y. 10011. 366,471; Col. George Nelting, National Chief Secretary.

Screen Actors Guild (1933): 7750 Sunset Blvd., Hollywood, Calif. 90046. 32,000; Judith Rheiner, Information Director.

Seeing Eye (1929): Morristown, N.J. 07960. 25,000; Stuart Grout, Executive Vice President.

Sierra Club (1892): 530 Bush St., San Francisco, Calif. 94108. 158,000; Michael McCloskey, Executive Director.

Sons of Italy in America, Order (1905): 1520 Locust St., Philadelphia, Pa. 19102. 2,300 lodges; John G. Spattuza, Supreme Venerable.

Soroptimist International of the Americas (1921): 1616 Walnut St., Philadelphia, Pa. 19103. 31,000; Valerie F. Levitan, Executive Director.

Southern Christian Leadership Conference (1957): 334 Auburn Ave., N.E., Atlanta, Ga. 30303. 1,000,000; 350 chapters, 260 affiliated organizations; Rev. Ralph D. Abernathy, President.

Sports Car Club of America (1944): 1562 S. Parker Rd., Denver, Colo. 80231. 23,000; Del Owens, Director Public Relations.

Travelers Aid Society of New York (1905): 204 E. 39th St., New York, N.Y. 10016. 3,002; Elizabeth P. Anderson, General Director.

United Cerebral Palsy Associations, Inc. (1949): 66 E. 34th St., New York, N.Y. 10016. 300 affiliates; Earl H. Cunerd, Executive Director.

United Daughters of the Confederacy (1894): 328 N. Boulevard, Richmond, Va. 23220. 35,000; Mrs. Charlotte P. Crippen, Executive Secretary.

United Jewish Appeal Inc. (1939): 1290 Avenue of the Americas, New York, N.Y. 10019. Irving Bernstein, Executive Vice Chairman.

United Negro College Fund, Inc. (1944): 500 E. 62nd St., New York, N.Y. 10021. 41 colleges; Christopher F. Edley, Executive Director.

Veterans of Foreign Wars of the U.S. (1899): V.F.W. Bldg., 34th and Bway., Kansas City, Mo. 64111. V.F.W. and Auxiliary, 2,300,000; Julian Dickenson, Adjutant General.

Women's American ORT (1927): 1250 Broadway, New York, N.Y. 10001. 125,000; Nathan Gould, National Executive Director.

Women's Clubs, General Federation of (1890): 1734 N St., N.W., Washington, D.C. 20036. 700,-000; Mrs. John T. Crippen, Executive Secretary.

Young Men's Christian Associations, National Council of (1844): 291 Broadway, New York, N.Y. 10007. 8,741,903; Robert W. Harlan, Executive Director.

Young Women's Christian Association of the U.S.A. (1858 in U.S.A., 1855 in England): 600 Lexington Ave., New York, N.Y. 10022. 2,367,000; Ida Sloan Snyder, Director of Communications.

Zionist Organization of America (1897): ZOA House, 4 E. 34th St., New York, N.Y. 10016. 120,000; Leon Ilutovich, National Executive Director.

Forms of Address[1]

Reprinted by permission. From Webster's New Collegiate Dictionary, copyright © 1976 by G. & C. Merriam Co., Publishers of the Merriam-Webster Dictionaries.

Abbot. *Address:* The Right Reverend _____, O.S.B. (*or* other initials of the order), Abbot of _____. *Begin:* Right Reverend and dear Father.

Alderman. *Address:* The Honorable _____. *Begin:* Dear Mr. _____.

Ambassador (American). *Address:* The Honorable _____, American Ambassador. *Begin:* Sir; *or* Dear Mr. Ambassador.

Ambassador (to U.S.). *Address:* His Excellency _____, Ambassador of _____ (country). *Begin:* Sir; *or* Dear Mr. Ambassador.

Archbishop. *Address:* The Most Reverend Archbishop of _____; *or* The Most Reverend _____, Archbishop of _____. *Begin:* Your Excellency; *or* Dear Archbishop _____.

Archdeacon. *Address:* The Venerable the Archdeacon of _____. *Begin:* Venerable Sir.

Assemblyman. *Address:* The Honorable _____, State Assembly, State Capitol. *Begin:* Dear Mr. _____.

Associate Justice. *Address:* Mr. Justice _____, The Supreme Court of the United States. *Begin:* Dear Mr. Justice.

Attorney. *Address:* Mr. _____ _____, Attorney-at-Law; *or* _____ _____, Esq. *Begin:* Dear Mr. _____.

Attorney General (of U.S.). *Address:* The Honorable _____, Attorney General of the United States. *Begin:* Dear Sir.

Baron. *Address:* The Right Honourable Lord _____; *or* The Lord _____. *Begin:* My Lord.

Baroness. *Address:* The Right Honourable the Baroness _____; *or* The Lady _____. *Begin:* Madam.

Baronet. *Address:* Sir John _____, Bt. *or* Bart. *Begin:* Sir.

Baronet's wife. See *Lady*.

Baron's wife. = *Baroness.*

Bishop (Episcopal). *Address:* The Right Reverend _____, Bishop of _____. *Begin:* Right Reverend Sir; *or* Dear Bishop _____.

Bishop (Roman Catholic). *Address:* The Most Reverend _____ _____, Bishop of _____. *Begin:* Your Excellency; *or* Dear Bishop _____.

Bishop (other denominations). *Address:* The Reverend _____ _____. *Begin:* Reverend Sir; *or* Dear Bishop _____.

Brother of a Religious Order. *Address:* Brother _____, (followed by initials of the order). *Begin:* Dear Brother _____.

Cabinet Officers (U.S.) *Address:* The Honorable _____, Secretary of State (*or* Labor, etc.). *Begin:* Dear Sir.

Cardinal. *Address:* His Eminence _____ Cardinal _____. *Begin:* Your Eminence; *or* Dear Cardinal _____.

Chargé d'Affaires (American). *Address:* _____, Esq., American Chargé d'Affaires. *Begin:* Dear Sir.

Chief Justice of the U.S. *Address:* The Chief Justice of the United States. *Begin:* Dear Mr. Chief Justice.

Clergyman (Protestant). *Address:* The Reverend _____; *or* The Reverend Dr. _____ (if a Doctor of Divinity). *Begin:* Dear Sir; *or* Dear Mr. _____; *or* Dear Dr. _____.

Commissioner. *Address:* The Honorable _____. *Begin:* Dear Mr. _____.

Congressman (U.S.) *Address:* The Honorable _____, The United States House of Representatives. *Begin:* Dear Mr. _____.

Consul. *Address:* _____ _____, Esq., American Consul. *Begin:* Dear Sir.

Countess. *Address:* To the Right Honourable The Countess of _____. *Begin:* Madam.

Dame. *Address:* Dame _____. *Begin:* Madam.

Deacon. *Address:* The Reverend Deacon _____. *Begin:* Reverend Sir.

Dean (of a cathedral). *Address:* The Very Reverend _____; *or* Dean _____. *Begin:* Very Reverend Sir; *or* Dear Dean _____.

Dean (of a college). *Address:* Dean _____. *Begin:* Dear Dean _____.

Dentist. *Address:* _____ _____, D.D.S. (office address); *or* Dr. _____ _____ (home Address). *Begin:* Dear Dr. _____.

Divorced woman. *Address:* Ordinarily use *Mrs.* with her maiden name as prename. Some divorced women prefer to resume the *Miss.*

Doctor of Divinity. *Address:* _____ _____, D.D.; *or* Rev. Dr. _____. *Begin:* Dear Sir; *or* Dear Dr. _____.

Doctor of Philosophy, Laws, Medicine, etc. *Address:* _____ _____, Ph.D. (LL.D.) (M.D.); *or* Dr. _____ _____. *Begin:* Dear Sir; *or* Dear Dr. _____.

Dowager. See *Widow.*

Duchess. *Address:* Her Grace the Duchess of _____; *or* The Most Noble the Duchess of _____. *Begin:* Madam; *or* Your Grace.

Duchess of the Blood Royal. *Address:* Her Royal Highness The Duchess of _____. *Begin:* Madam; *or* May it please your Royal Highness.

Duke. *Address:* His Grace the Duke of _____; *or* The Most Noble the Duke of _____. *Begin:* My Lord Duke; *or* Your Grace.

Duke of the Blood Royal. *Address.* His Royal Highness The Duke of _____. *Begin:* Sir; *or* May it please your Royal Highness.

Earl. *Address:* The Right Honourable The Earl of _____; *or* The Earl of _____. *Begin:* My Lord.

Earl's wife. = *Countess.*

Envoy. Same as Minister (Diplomatic).

---

[1] When two salutations are given, the formal one precedes the informal. In salutations where the addressee is a woman, the formal address Madam is to be substituted for Sir and, in informal address, Mrs., Miss or Ms. may be substituted for Mr.

Esquire. *Address:* _____ _____, Esq. *Begin:* Sir; *or* Dear Mr. _____. (*Esq.* is never used if the person is addressed by any other title, even *Mr.*).

Governor. *Address:* The Honorable _____ _____, Governor of _____. *Begin:* Dear Governor _____.

Governor-General of Canada. *Address:* His Excellency The Right Honourable _____ _____ (plus personal rank or title, if any). *Begin:* My Lord; *or* Sir.

Governor-General's wife. *Address:* Her Excellency _____ _____ (plus personal rank or title, if any). *Begin:* Madam.

Judge (state or local). *Address:* The Honorable _____ _____, Chief Judge of the Court of Appeals. *Begin:* Dear Judge _____.

Judge (of a U.S. Court). *Address:* The Honorable _____ _____, United States District Judge. *Begin:* Dear Judge _____.

King. *Address:* The King's Most Excellent Majesty; *or* His Most Gracious Majesty, King _____. *Begin:* Sir; *or* May it please your Majesty.

King's Counsel. *Address:* To _____ _____, Esq., K.C. *Begin:* Sir; *or* Dear Sir.

Knight. *Address:* Sir _____ _____ (initials of his order, if any, as K.C.B.). *Begin:* Sir.

Knight's wife. See *Lady.*

Lady. *Address:* Lady _____; *or* (if daughter of a baron or viscount) Hon. Lady _____; *or* (if the daughter of an earl, marquess or duke) Lady Florence _____. *Begin:* Madam; *or* My Lady; *or* Your Ladyship.

Lieutenant Governor. *Address:* The Honorable _____ _____, Lieutenant Governor of _____. *Begin:* Dear Mr. _____.

Marchioness. *Address:* The Most Honourable the Marchioness of _____. *Begin:* Madam.

Marquess. *Address:* The Most Honourable the Marquess of _____; *or* The Marquess of _____. *Begin:* My Lord Marquess.

Mayor (in Canadian cities and towns, and English boroughs and cities). *Address:* The Right Worshipful the Mayor of _____ (English cities only); His Worship, The Mayor of _____ (other). *Begin:* Sir.

Mayor (in the U.S.). *Address:* The Honorable _____ _____, Mayor of _____. *Begin:* Dear Mayor _____.

Member of Parliament (or of a Provincial Legislative Council or Legislature, etc.). The ordinary form of address followed by M.P. (*or* M.P.P.; *or* M.L.A., etc.). *Begin:* Sir.

Military officers. *Address:* (Full Rank) _____ _____, (abbreviation of branch of service— U.S.A. *or* U.S.N. *or* U.S.M.C., etc.). *Begin:* Sir (for Generals and Admirals only); *or* Dear (Rank) _____ (for all ranks). Use Mr. in salutation for Navy petty officers (*or* Chief for chief petty officers) and Army warrant officers.

Minister (Diplomatic). *Address:* The Honorable _____ _____, Minister of _____. *Begin:* Sir; *or* Dear Mr. Minister.

Minister of Religion. See *Clergyman, Priest, Rabbi.*

Monsignor. *Address:* The Right Reverend Monsignor _____. *Begin:* Dear Monsignor _____.

Mother Superior of a Sisterhood. *Address:* The Reverend Mother Superior, Convent of _____; *or* Reverend Mother _____, O.S.D. (or other initials of the order). *Begin:* Reverend Mother; *or* Dear Reverend Mother.

Nun. See *Sister of a Religious Order.*

Papal Nuncio or Internuncio or Apostolic Delegate. *Address:* His Excellency, The Papal Nuncio (*or* Internuncio *or* Apostolic Delegate) to _____. *Begin:* Your Excellency.

Patriarch (Eastern Church). *Address:* His Beatitude the Patriarch of _____. *Begin:* Most Reverend Lord.

Physician. *Address:* _____ _____, M.D. (office address); *or* Dr. _____ _____ (home address). *Begin:* Dear Dr. _____.

Pope. *Address:* His Holiness Pope _____; *or* His Holiness the Pope. *Begin:* Your Holiness; *or* Most Holy Father.

President of a College or University. *Address:* President _____ _____. *Begin:* Dear President _____.

President of a Theological Seminary. *Address:* The Reverend President _____ _____. *Begin:* Dear Sir; *or* Dear President _____.

President of State Senate. *Address:* The Honorable _____ _____, President of the Senate of _____. *Begin:* Sir.

President of the Senate of the U.S. *Address:* The Honorable, The President of the Senate of the United States; *or* The Honorable _____ _____, President of the Senate. *Begin:* Sir.

President of the U.S. *Address:* The President. *Begin:* Dear Mr. President.

Priest (Catholic). *Address:* The Reverend Father _____; *or* The Reverend _____ _____. *Begin:* Dear Father _____: *or* Dear Father.

Prime Minister of Canada. *Address:* The Right Honourable _____ _____. P.C., Prime Minister of Canada. *Begin:* Sir.

Prime Minister of the United Kingdom. *Address:* The Right Honourable _____ _____, P.C., M.P., Prime Minister. *Begin:* Sir.

Prince of the Blood Royal. *Address:* His Royal Highness Prince _____ (given name). *Begin:* Sir.

Prince of Wales. *Address:* His Royal Highness The Prince of Wales. *Begin:* Sir; *or* May it please your Royal Highness.

Princess of the Blood Royal. *Address:* Her Royal Highness the Princess _____ (given name). *Begin:* Madam.

Privy Councillor (British Imperial). *Address:* To the Right Honourable _____ _____, P.C. *Begin:* Sir. (If other titles are used, they should come after *The Right Honourable;* as, The Right Honourable Sir John _____.)

Privy Councillor (of Canada). *Address:* The Honourable _____ _____. *Begin:* Sir.

Professor at a College or University. *Address:* Professor _____ _____. *Begin:* Dear Professor _____.

Queen. *Address:* The Queen's Most Excellent Majesty; *or* Her Gracious Majesty, The Queen. *Begin:* Madam; *or* May it please your Majesty.

Queen Mother. *Address:* Her Gracious Majesty Queen _____. *Begin:* Madam; *or* May it please your Majesty.

Rabbi. *Address:* Rabbi _____; *or* Rabbi _____, D.D. (if having a doctor's degree). *Address:* Dear Rabbi _____; *or* Dear Dr. _____.

Rector of a Religious House or of a Seminary. *Address:* The Very Reverend _____ _____, O.S.B. (*or* other initials of the order), Rector, Brothers of St. Francis. *Begin:* Very Reverend and dear Father.

Representative (State): See *Assemblyman.*

Representative (U.S.). See *Congressman.*

Secretary-General of the U.N. *Address:* His Excellency _____ _____, Secretary-General of the United Nations. *Begin:* Excellency; *or* Dear Mr. Secretary-General; *or* Dear Mr. _____.

Senator (State). *Address:* The Honorable _____ _____, The State Senate, State Capitol. *Begin:* Dear Senator _____.

Senator (U.S.). *Address:* The Honorable _____ _____, United States Senate. *Begin:* Dear Senator _____.

Sister of a Religious Order. *Address:* Sister _____ _____, (followed by initials of the order). *Begin:* Dear Sister _____ _____; *or* Dear Sister.

Speaker of the House of Commons (Canada). *Address:* The Honourable _____ _____, The Speaker of the House of Commons. *Begin:* Dear Mr. Speaker.

Speaker of the House of Representatives (U.S.). *Address:* The Honorable _____ _____. Speaker of the House of Representatives. *Begin:* Dear Mr. Speaker.

Superior of a Brotherhood (Catholic). *Address:* Brother _____ (followed by initials of the order), _____ Superior. *Begin:* Dear Brother _____.

Superior of a Sisterhood (Catholic). *Address:* The Reverend Mother Superior, (followed by initials of the order). *Begin:* Reverend Mother; *or* Dear Reverend Mother.

Under Secretary of State (U.S.). *Address:* The Under Secretary of State; *or* The Honorable _____ _____, Under Secretary of State. *Begin:* Sir; *or* Dear Mr. _____.

United Nations Representative (Foreign Ambassador). *Address:* His Excellency _____ _____, Representative of _____ to the United Nations. *Begin:* Excellency; *or* Sir; *or* My dear Mr. Ambassador.

United Nations Representative (U.S.). *Address:* The Honorable _____ _____, United States Representative to the United Nations. *Begin:* Sir; *or* My dear Mr. _____.

Veterinarian. *Address:* _____ _____, D.V.M. (office address); *or* Dr. _____ _____ (home address). *Begin:* Dear Dr. _____.

Vice President. *Address:* The Vice President, United States Senate. *Begin:* Dear Mr. Vice President.

Viscount. *Address:* The Right Honourable the Viscount _____; *or* The Viscount _____. *Begin:* My Lord.

Viscountess. *Address:* The Right Honourable the Viscountess _____; *or* The Viscountess _____. *Begin:* Madam.

Widow. Ordinarily addressed by her former title; as, Mrs. John Doe, not Mrs. Jane Doe, unless the latter form is preferred by the person herself.

Note: Forms of Address for foreign dignitaries may be obtained from their United Nations mission in New York City.

CONSUMER COMPLAINTS GUIDE

With the growth of the consumer movement over the last ten years, more consumers are reporting their complaints. Never before have there been so many government- or industry-sponsored groups to help consumers. If the consumer has a complaint about merchandise purchased, both the manufacturer and retailer—if they are reputable—appreciate these comments as it helps to improve their products and their consumer relations.

The first place to register a complaint is at the store where the merchandise was purchased. If this does not bring about a satisfactory answer after a reasonable period of time, write to the manufacturer. If you do not have the address it can be obtained from your local Better Business Bureau.

In 40 of the states, consumer protection is the responsibility of the State Attorney General. In the remaining states, consumer protection agencies have been set up within the governor's office or within a designated state department, such as, agriculture, commerce or labor. Many large corporations have set up toll-free (800) phone numbers for the use of the consumer.

In New York, radio station **WMCA** has a service **Call for Action.** To register a complaint, telephone between 11 A.M. and 1 P.M., Monday through Thursday. The staff is volunteer and covers every range of complaints (212–586–6666). On television, **WABC (Channel 7)** has a service called **Eyewitness Help Center.** Complaints must be in writing. Write to **Eyewitness Help Center,** Box 777, N.Y., N.Y. 10023; **WNBC (Channel 4)** has a similar service called **Action 4** with Betty Furness. Complaints must be in writing. Write to **Action 4,** Box 4000, N.Y., N.Y. 10019. Include your telephone number and enclose a stamped, self-addressed envelope; also copies (*not* originals) of any pertinent documents.

Below are guidelines of federal, state, local, industry, corporate, and private offices where the consumer may write or call to register a complaint or to get action on the complaint.

AIRLINES—Office of Consumer Affairs, CAB, 1825 Connecticut Ave. N.W., Washington, D.C. 20506. The main office address of all major airlines can be obtained from your local branch.

AUTOMOTIVE—National Highway Traffic Safety Administration, Department of Transportation, Washington, D.C. 20690; National Automobile Dealers Association, 8400 Westpark Dr., McLean, Va. 22101; AutoCAPS (for data on local and state pilot automobile consumer-action panels); American Motors (800) 521-7500; Chrysler Corp., P.O. Box 1086, Consumer Affairs, Detroit, Mich. 48321; Ford Motor Co., The American Road, Dearborn, Mich. 48121; General Motors Corp., General Motors Building, Detroit, Mich. 48202.

CREDIT CARDS—Board of Governors of the Federal Reserve System, Washington, D.C. 20551. Telephone or write all major credit card companies.

DEPARTMENT STORES/MAIL ORDER HOUSES—Marshall Field & Co., 111 North State, Chicago, Ill. 60690; Kresge Co., 3100 W. Big Beaver, Troy, Mich. 48084; Montgomery Ward & Co., Montgomery Ward Plaza, Chicago, Ill. 60671; J.C. Penney Co., Inc., 1301 Avenue of the Americas, New York, N.Y. 10019; R.H. Macy & Co., Inc., 151 W. 34th St., New York, N.Y. 10001; Sears Roebuck & Co., Dept. 731A, Sears Tower, Chicago, Ill. 60684; Spiegel, Inc., 2511 West 23rd, Chicago, Ill. 60608; F. W. Woolworth's Co., 233 Broadway, New York, N.Y. 10007.

EMPLOYMENT AGENCIES—National Employment Association, 200 K St. N.W., Washington, D.C. 20006.

FOOD PRODUCTS—U.S. Department of Agriculture, Office of Communication, Washington, D.C. 20250; Food and Drug Administration (FDA), 5600 Fishers Lane, Rockville, Md. 20852; General Foods Corp., 250 North St., White Plains, N.Y. 10625; General Mills, Inc., Consumer Response, P.O. Box 1113, Minneapolis, Minn. 55440; Kellogg Co., Battle Creek, Mich. 49016.

FURNITURE AND CARPETING—Furniture Industry Consumer Advisory Panel (FICAP), Box 951, High Point, N.C. 27261; National Association of Furniture Manufacturers, 8401 Connecticut Ave., Suite 911, Washington, D.C. 20015; Drexel Enterprises, Drexel, N.C. 28619; Ethan Allen, Inc., Ethan Allen Drive, Danbury, Conn. 06810; Carpet and Rug Institute, Box 2048, Dalton, Ga. 30720; Armstrong Cork Co., Liberty & Charlotte Sts., Lancaster, Pa. 17604; Lees Carpets, Div. of Burlington Ind., Valley Forge Corp. Center, King of Prussia, Pa. 19406.

HOUSEHOLD APPLIANCES—Major Appliance Consumer Action Panel (MACAP), 20 N. Wacker Drive, Chicago, Ill. 60606; Consumer Electronics Group, Electronics Industries Association, 2001 Eye St., N.W., Washington, D.C. 20006; General Electric Corp., Manager of Customer Relations, 570

Lexington Ave., New York, N.Y. 10022; RCA Corp., Consumer Relations, 30 Rockefeller Plaza, New York, N.Y. 10020; Westinghouse Corp., (800) 245-0600; Whirlpool Corp., (800) 253-1301.

MEDICAL—Fee complaints should be referred to your local County Medical Society.

NURSING HOMES—Joint Commission on Accreditation of Hospitals, 875 N. Michigan Ave., Chicago, Ill. 60611; American Association of Homes for the Aging, 1050 17th St., N.W., Washington, D.C. 20036; American Health Care Association, 1200 Fifteenth St., N.W., Washington, D.C. 20005.

PHOTOGRAPHIC EQUIPMENT—Eastman Kodak Co., Consumer Photo Information Department, 343 State St., Rochester, N.Y. 14650; Nikon, Inc., 623 Steward Ave., Garden City, L.I., N.Y. 11530; Photo Marketing Association, 603 Lansing Ave., Jackson, Mich. 40202; Polaroid Corp., 549 Technology Square, Cambridge, Mass. 02139.

SERVICE STATIONS/GASOLINE AND OIL—Atlantic Richfield Co., Marketing Manager, P.O. Box 2679 T.A., Los Angeles, Calif. 96051; Exxon, Marketing Department, Box 2180, Houston, Texas 77001; Gulf Oil Corp., P.O. Box 2100, Houston, Tex. 77002; Texaco Inc., Retail Sales Office, 135 E. 42nd St., New York, N.Y. 10017.

TIRES—Firestone Tire & Rubber Co., Consumer Affairs, Director, 1200 Firestone Parkway, Akron, Ohio 44317; Goodyear Tire & Rubber Co., Director of Consumer Relations, 1144 East Market St., Akron, Ohio 44316.

TOYS—Creative Playthings, Princeton, N.J. 08540; Fisher-Price Toys, 606 Girard Ave., East Aurora, N.Y. 14052; Mattel, Inc., 5150 Rosecrans Ave., Hawthorne, Calif. 90251; Playskool, Inc., 4501 W. Augusta Blvd., Chicago, Ill. 60651.

TV & RADIO—Admiral Group, Rockwell International, 1701 E. Woodfield Rd., Schaumburg, Ill. 60172. Motorola, Inc., 9401 W. Grand Ave., Franklin Park, Ill. 60131; Sony Corp. of America, 9 W. 57th St., New York, N.Y. 10019; Zenith Radio Corp., 1900 N. Austin Ave., Chicago, Ill. 60639.

OTHER GOVERNMENT AGENCIES—Virginia Knauer, Special Assistant to the President for Consumer Affairs and Director, Office of Consumer Affairs, Department of Health, Education and Welfare, Washington, D.C. 20201; U.S. Bureau of Consumer Protection, Federal Trade Commission, Washington, D.C. 20580; U.S. Consumer Product Safety Commission (CPSC), 5401 Westbard Ave., Washington, D.C. 20207 (800) 638-2666. In Maryland (800) 492-2937; U.S. Postal Inspection Service, Washington, D.C. 20260; Council of Better Business Bureaus, 1150 17th St., Washington, D.C. 20036.

Portraits and Designs of U.S. Paper Currency[1]

Currency	Portrait	Design on back	Currency	Portrait	Design on back
$1	Washington	ONE between obverse and reverse of Great Seal of U. S.	$50	Grant	U. S. Capitol.
			$100	Franklin	Independence Hall.
$2[2]	Jefferson	Monticello.	$500	McKinley	Ornate FIVE HUNDRED
$2[3]	Jefferson	"The Signing of the Declaration of Independence"	$1,000	Cleveland	Ornate ONE THOUSAND
			$5,000	Madison	Ornate FIVE THOUSAND
$5	Lincoln	Lincoln Memorial.	$10,000	Chase	Ornate TEN THOUSAND
$10	Hamilton	U. S. Treasury Building.	$100,000[4]	Wilson	Ornate ONE HUNDRED THOUSAND
$20	Jackson	White House.			

[1] Denominations of $500 and higher were discontinued in 1969. [2] Discontinued in 1966. [3] New issue, April 13, 1976. [4] For use only in transactions between Federal Research System and Treasury Department.

English Language Daily and Sunday U. S. Newspapers
(number of newspapers as of Feb. 1, 1975; circulation reported for Sept. 30, 1975).

Source: Editor & Publisher.

State	Morning papers & circulation		Evening papers & circulation		Total M & E & circulation		Sunday papers & circulation	
Alabama	7	206,124	17	530,871	24	736,995	17	666,398
Alaska	1	14,012	6	73,028	7	87,040	1	39,458
Arizona	2	261,199	12	253,249	14	514,448	4	429,572
Arkansas[1]	5	173,402	30	285,304	34	458,706	13	388,838
California[1]	22	2,597,472	101	3,090,177	122	5,687,649	41	4,894,314
Colorado	3	280,937	24	452,433	27	733,370	10	749,756
Connecticut	6	310,928	22	601,833	28	912,761	8	673,903
Delaware	1	45,574	2	112,033	3	157,607	2	151,228
District of Columbia	1	534,400	1	353,168	2	887,568	2	1,072,614
Florida	16	1,355,817	36	841,268	51	2,197,085	34	2,156,057
Georgia	6	403,343	31	606,220	37	1,009,563	15	985,700
Hawaii	1	17,937	3	138,931	4	210,868	2	196,347
Idaho	4	86,566	12	122,399	16	208,965	5	151,361
Illinois[1]	20	1,672,184	71	1,850,529	88	3,522,713	20	2,542,523
Indiana[1]	8	451,500	72	1,211,771	80	1,663,271	17	1,126,735
Iowa[1]	5	337,340	38	599,832	42	937,172	9	788,436
Kansas[1]	5	223,185	48	428,665	52	651,850	14	448,799
Kentucky	5	316,820	22	451,911	27	768,731	12	586,456
Louisiana	5	399,817	21	423,948	26	823,765	14	751,254
Maine	5	204,344	4	65,639	9	269,983	1	108,694
Maryland	5	234,278	8	498,112	13	732,390	4	676,009
Massachusetts	5	928,973	41	1,131,597	46	2,060,570	8	1,450,280
Michigan	1	623,846	53	1,835,959	54	2,459,805	14	2,262,862
Minnesota[1]	6	399,102	26	686,231	31	1,085,333	9	1,001,994
Mississippi	5	122,017	18	256,256	23	378,273	10	282,414
Missouri	10	738,400	47	985,391	57	1,723,791	17	1,404,017
Montana	4	145,680	7	44,930	11	190,610	8	189,792
Nebraska	3	171,333	16	318,385	19	489,718	4	362,370
Nevada	3	74,224	6	105,240	9	179,464	4	154,532
New Hampshire[1]	1	31,244	9	149,472	9	180,716	2	69,745
New Jersey	7	616,356	22	1,084,972	29	1,701,328	13	1,363,065
New Mexico	1	75,576	19	166,835	20	242,411	12	212,609
New York[1]	19	4,130,336	59	2,878,920	77	7,009,256	24	6,647,900
North Carolina	10	577,379	42	714,000	52	1,291,379	22	1,015,583
North Dakota[1]	2	36,985	9	156,539	10	193,524	2	102,145
Ohio	7	837,985	88	2,510,379	95	3,348,364	23	2,338,383
Oklahoma	9	412,506	44	430,527	53	843,033	42	843,771
Oregon	3	272,012	19	366,579	22	638,591	5	533,228
Pennsylvania[1]	31	1,225,303	79	2,642,091	105	3,867,394	12	2,976,364
Rhode Island	1	66,741	6	244,194	7	310,935	2	217,024
South Carolina	8	379,385	11	182,512	19	561,897	7	446,973
South Dakota	1	3,306	12	173,525	13	176,831	4	121,656
Tennessee	9	472,740	25	629,400	34	1,102,140	14	961,842
Texas[1]	24	1,517,623	90	1,712,866	114	3,230,489	87	3,309,308
Utah	1	70,990	4	180,763	5	251,753	4	250,382
Vermont	2	68,633	6	44,754	8	113,387	1	6,742
Virginia	10	454,809	23	559,808	33	1,014,617	13	699,041
Washington[1]	4	317,279	19	724,438	22	1,041,717	13	1,001,201
West Virginia	9	220,610	20	262,683	29	483,293	9	395,100
Wisconsin[1]	4	258,054	32	971,663	35	1,229,717	6	835,275
Wyoming	6	59,580	3	23,015	9	82,595	6	56,273
Total U.S., Sept. 30, 1975	339	25,490,186	1,436	35,165,245	1,756	60,655,431	639	51,096,323
Total U.S., Sept. 30, 1974	340	26,144,966	1,449	35,732,231	1,768	61,877,197	641	51,678,726
Total U.S., Sept. 30, 1973	343	26,524,140	1,451	36,623,140	1,774	63,147,280	634	51,717,465
Total U.S., Sept. 30, 1972	337	26,078,386	1,441	36,431,856	1,761	62,510,242	605	50,000,669
Total U.S., Sept. 30, 1971	339	26,116,131	1,425	36,115,127	1,749	62,231,258	590	49,664,643
Total U.S., Sept. 30, 1970	334	25,933,783	1,429	36,173,744	1,748	62,107,527	586	49,216,602
Total U.S., Sept. 30, 1965	320	24,106,776	1,444	36,250,787	1,751	60,357,563	562	48,600,090

[1] "All-day" newspapers are listed in morning and evening columns, and their circulations are divided between morning and evening figures. Adjustments have been made in state and U. S. total figures.

U. S. Daily Newspapers

Source: Audit Bureau of Circulations: Publishers' Statements for 6-month period ending March 31, 1976.

| | Net Paid Circulation | | |
City and newspaper	Morning[1]	Evening[1]	Sunday
Akron (Ohio): BEACON JOURNAL	.....	168,278	216,078
Albany (N.Y.): TIMES-UNION (M & S); KNICKERBOCKER NEWS-UNION STAR (E)	76,186	62,069	134,006
Albuquerque (N.M.): JOURNAL (M & S); TRIBUNE (E)	76,083[5]	37,554[5]	110,686[5]
Allentown (Pa.): CALL (M); CHRONICLE (E); CALL-CHRONICLE (S)	100,588	21,698	151,335
Asbury Park (N.J.): PRESS	.....	90,367	120,836
Atlanta: CONSTITUTION (M); JOURNAL (E); JOURNAL AND CONSTITUTION (S)	204,623	225,948	522,915
Austin (Tex): AMERICAN (M)[3]; STATESMAN (E)[3]; AMERICAN-STATESMAN (S)	69,304	34,761	109,604
Baltimore: SUN	173,571[4]	177,088[4]	348,812
NEWS-AMERICAN		181,525[4]	263,084
Baton Rouge (La.): ADVOCATE (M & S); STATE-TIMES (E)	66,459	45,578	104,039
Bergen County (N.J.): RECORD (E)[3]; SUNDAY RECORD (Hackensack, N.J.)	.....	154,063[3]	198,238[5]
Birmingham (Ala.): POST-HERALD (M); NEWS (E & S)	73,899[4]	184,776[4]	222,821
Boston: GLOBE	276,116[4]	172,930[4]	598,637
HERALD AMERICAN (M); HERALD ADVERTISER (S)	313,703[4]		456,009
CHRISTIAN SCIENCE MONITOR	172,786[4]		
Buffalo (N.Y.): COURIER-EXPRESS (M & S); NEWS (E)	122,060	279,298[4]	270,806
Camden (N.J.): COURIER-POST	.....	122,179[5]	.....
Charleston (W. Va.): GAZETTE (M); DAILY MAIL (E); GAZETTE-MAIL (S)	55,667	55,671	102,348
Charlotte (N.C.): OBSERVER (M & S); NEWS (E)	167,508	57,107	226,021
Chicago: TRIBUNE	747,715[3,6]	.....	1,110,865
SUN-TIMES	560,124[4]	.....	687,356
DAILY NEWS	.....	374,406[4]	.....
WALL STREET JOURNAL (Midwest edition)[3]	450,487		
Cincinnati: ENQUIRER (M & S); POST (E)	185,061	207,596	284,653
Cleveland: PLAIN DEALER (M & S); PRESS (E)	375,100	327,359	450,657
Columbia (S.C.): STATE (M & S); RECORD (E)	101,027	31,897	118,409
Columbus (Ohio): DISPATCH (E & S); CITIZEN-JOURNAL (M)	108,771	197,704	325,124
Dallas: NEWS	257,565		315,987
TIMES-HERALD	.....	223,524[4]	314,881
WALL STREET JOURNAL (Southwest edition)[3]	157,590	.....	
Dayton (Ohio): NEWS (E & S); JOURNAL (M)	103,216	151,240	222,070
Denver: POST	.....	246,146[4]	333,585
ROCKY MOUNTAIN NEWS	224,053	.....	246,679
Des Moines (Iowa): REGISTER (M & S); TRIBUNE (E)	229,047	93,383	433,865
Detroit: NEWS	.....	627,461[4]	824,776
FREE PRESS	622,339[4]		734,738
Evansville (Ind.): COURIER (M); PRESS (E); COURIER & PRESS (S)	64,399	45,826	118,961
Flint (Mich.): JOURNAL	.....	106,658	107,229
Fort Lauderdale (Fla.): NEWS & SUN-SENTINEL (S); NEWS (E)	.....	106,077[4]	159,363
Fort Wayne (Ind.): JOURNAL-GAZETTE (M & S); NEWS-SENTINEL (E)	61,433[5]	72,341[5]	101,405[5]
Fort Worth (Tex.): STAR-TELEGRAM	85,706	138,946	228,430
Fresno (Calif.): BEE	.....	112,689	133,737
Grand Rapids (Mich,): PRESS	.....	124,939	136,198
Greensboro (N.C.): NEWS (M & S); RECORD (E)	75,892	32,030	104,234
Harrisburg (Pa.): PATRIOT (M); EVENING NEWS (E)[3]; SUNDAY PATRIOT-NEWS	47,419[4]	67,513	164,411
Hartford (Conn.): COURANT	183,188	.....	247,957
Honolulu: ADVERTISER (M); STAR-BULLETIN (E); STAR-BULLETIN & ADVERTISER (S)	75,755	116,769	187,342
Houston: CHRONICLE	.....	303,459[4]	378,272
POST	292,008[4]	.....	353,537
Indianapolis: STAR (M & S); NEWS (E)	218,954[5]	159,895[5]	354,965[5]
Jackson (Miss.): CLARION-LEDGER (M); DAILY NEWS (E); CLARION LEDGER-DAILY NEWS (S)	61,781	43,400	113,648
Jacksonville (Fla.): FLORIDA TIMES-UNION (M & S); JOURNAL (E)	147,010	54,230	179,971
Kansas City (Mo.): STAR (E & S); TIMES (M)	324,617	300,619	395,950
Knoxville (Tenn.): NEWS-SENTINEL (E & S); JOURNAL (M)	60,215	104,927	161,513
Lancaster (Pa.): INTELLIGENCER (M); NEW ERA (E); NEWS (S)	38,964[5]	58,418[5]	130,693[5]
Little Rock (Ark.): ARKANSAS GAZETTE	123,024[4]	.....	147,095
ARKANSAS DEMOCRAT	.....	61,924[4]	111,850
Long Beach (Calif.): INDEPENDENT (M); PRESS-TELEGRAM (E); INDEPENDENT PRESS-TELEGRAM (S)	62,116[4]	87,355[4]	137,259
Los Angeles: TIMES	1,004,718[4]		1,271,018
HERALD-EXAMINER	.....	352,459[4]	356,454
Louisville (Ky.): COURIER-JOURNAL (M); TIMES (E); COURIER-JOURNAL & TIMES (S)	210,171	161,272	343,668
Madison (Wis.): STATE JOURNAL (M & S); CAPITAL TIMES (E)	74,082	40,903	118,492
Memphis (Tenn.): COMMERCIAL APPEAL (M & S); PRESS SCIMITAR (E)	204,747	111,957	285,457

City and newspaper	Net Paid Circulation		
	Morning[1]	Evening[1]	Sunday
Miami (Fla.): HERALD (M & S); NEWS (E)	424,280	78,246	521,087
Milwaukee: JOURNAL (E & S); SENTINEL (M)	166,533	343,420	529,089
Minneapolis: TRIBUNE (M & S); STAR (E)	225,957	240,594	604,763
Nashville: TENNESSEAN (M & S); BANNER (E) . . .	128,058	86,006	217,416
Nassau County (N.Y.): NEWSDAY (Garden City, N.Y.)	. . . . .	463,376	430,524
New Haven (Conn.): REGISTER (E & S); JOURNAL-COURIER (M)	30,555	101,595	131,079
New Orleans: TIMES-PICAYUNE (M & S); STATES-ITEM (E)	207,925[5]	117,675[4,5]	311,696[5]
New York City: NEWS	1,902,717[4]	. . . . .	2,818,281
TIMES	841,476	. . . . .	1,475,430
POST	. . . . .	505,757	334,082[7]
WALL STREET JOURNAL (Eastern edition)[3]	583,603	. . . . .	. . . . .
LONG ISLAND PRESS (Jamaica, N.Y.) . . .	. . . . .	280,702[5]	270,020[5]
Newark (N.J.): STAR-LEDGER	393,095[4,5]	. . . . .	584,162[5]
Norfolk-Portsmouth-Virginia Beach-Chesapeake (Va.):			
VIRGINIA-PILOT (M & S); LEDGER-STAR (E) . .	124,474[5]	93,287[5]	184,320[5]
Oakland (Calif.): TRIBUNE	. . . . .	173,414[4]	202,936
Oklahoma City: DAILY OKLAHOMAN (M); TIMES (E); SUNDAY OKLAHOMAN	171,918[4]	87,512[4]	287,494
Omaha (Neb.): WORLD-HERALD	124,340[4]	111,490[4]	278,826
Orange County (Calif.): REGISTER (Santa Ana, Calif.) . .	85,114[4]	116,893[4]	230,842
Orlando (Fla.): SENTINEL STAR	184,612[4,6]	. . . . .	209,763
Palo Alto (Calif.): WALL STREET JOURNAL (Pacific Coast edition)[3]	273,953	. . . . .	. . . . .
Peoria (Ill.): JOURNAL-STAR	105,125[3,6]	. . . . .	119,197
Philadelphia: INQUIRER	410,254[4]	. . . . .	847,442
BULLETIN	. . . . .	554,381[4]	652,024
DAILY NEWS	. . . . .	238,951[4]	. . . . .
Phoenix (Ariz.): REPUBLIC (M & S); GAZETTE (E) . .	229,445[5]	111,553[5]	339,874[5]
Pittsburgh: PRESS (E & S); POST-GAZETTE, SUN-TELEGRAPH (M)	188,886[4]	265,114[4]	667,297
Portland (Me.): PRESS-HERALD (M); EXPRESS (E); MAIN SUNDAY TELEGRAM	53,219	30,434	108,301
Portland (Ore.): OREGONIAN (M & S); OREGON JOURNAL (E)	226,235	106,528[4]	400,848
Providence (R.I.): JOURNAL (M & S); BULLETIN (E) .	66,260[4]	142,892[4]	209,426
Raleigh (N.C.): NEWS & OBSERVER (M); TIMES (E) .	125,534[5]	32,294[5]	155,129[5]
Richmond (Va.): TIMES-DISPATCH (M & S); NEWS-LEADER (E)	131,677	112,259	199,633
Roanoke (Va.): TIMES (M & S); WORLD-NEWS (E) . .	63,313	50,816	113,189
Rochester (N.Y.): DEMOCRAT & CHRONICLE (M & S); TIMES-UNION (E)	127,619	130,416	222,126
Sacramento (Calif.): BEE	. . . . .	172,603[4]	204,531
St. Louis: POST-DISPATCH	. . . . .	286,031[4]	468,220
GLOBE-DEMOCRAT	274,917	. . . . .	275,019[2]
St. Paul (Minn.): PIONEER PRESS (M & S); DISPATCH (E)	102,288	118,704	240,179
St. Petersburg (Fla.): TIMES (M & S); INDEPENDENT (E)	203,070	35,586	253,935
Salt Lake City: TRIBUNE (M & S); DESERET NEWS (E)	100,788	72,088	171,463
San Antonio (Tex.): EXPRESS (M); NEWS (E); EXPRESS AND NEWS (S)	80,092[4]	76,243[4]	160,080
LIGHT	. . . . .	126,032[4]	174,394
San Diego (Calif.): UNION (M & S); TRIBUNE (E) . .	181,907[5]	126,363[5]	297,687[5]
San Francisco: CHRONICLE (M); EXAMINER (E); EXAMINER & CHRONICLE (S)	443,097[4]	150,698[4]	637,201
San Jose (Calif.): MERCURY (M); NEWS (E); MERCURY-NEWS (S)	135,264[4]	66,885[4]	230,584
Seattle: TIMES	. . . . .	223,478[4]	310,203
POST-INTELLIGENCER	185,009[4]	. . . . .	249,010
Shreveport (La.): TIMES (M & S); JOURNAL (E) . .	89,399[5]	40,755[5]	122,566[5]
South Bend-Mishawaka (Ind.): TRIBUNE	. . . . .	111,495	121,326
Spokane (Wash.): SPOKESMAN (M); CHRONICLE (E); SPOKESMAN-REVIEW (S)	74,290	61,841	123,480
Springfield (Mass.): UNION (M); NEWS (E); REPUBLICAN (S)	74,472	80,615	140,715
Syracuse (N.Y.): POST-STANDARD (M); HERALD-JOURNAL (E);			
HERALD-AMERICAN (S)	83,670[4]	123,773	244,840
Tacoma (Wash.): NEWS TRIBUNE (E); NEWS-TRIBUNE AND LEDGER	. . . . .	97,294	101,122
Tampa (Fla.): TRIBUNE (M & S); TIMES (E)	172,126	22,516	203,650
Toledo (Ohio): BLADE	. . . . .	173,144	207,503
Tucson (Ariz.): DAILY STAR (M & S); CITIZEN (E) . .	65,374[5]	63,961[5]	118,372[5]
Tulsa (Okla.): WORLD (M & S); TRIBUNE (E) . . .	117,282[5]	78,488[5]	204,431[5]
Washington (D.C.): POST	514,849[4]	. . . . .	718,806
STAR	. . . . .	390,414[4]	382,025
West Palm Beach (Fla.): POST (M); TIMES (E); POST-TIMES (S)	74,660[4]	29,319[4]	110,557
Wichita (Kan.): EAGLE (M); BEACON (E); EAGLE AND BEACON (S)	121,102	47,049	178,489
Worcester (Mass.): TELEGRAM (M & S); GAZETTE (E) .	53,995[5]	88,776[5]	107,364[5]
Youngstown (Ohio): VINDICATOR	. . . . .	99,584[5]	155,196[5]

[1] Unless otherwise indicated, figure is average of Monday through Saturday circulation.   [2] Week-end edition.   [3] Except Saturday.   [4] Average Monday through Friday circulation.   [5] Three-month average ending March 31, 1976.   [6] All-day edition.   [7] Saturday edition.

Leading Magazines: United States and Canada

Source: Audit Bureau of Circulations: Publishers' Statements for six-month period ending June 30, 1976.

Magazine	Circulation[1]
A.D.	386,068[3]
American Girl	678,508[2]
American Home	2,500,813
American Journal of Nursing	301,830
American Legion Magazine	2,672,858
Apartment Life	717,527
Argosy	603,618
Atlantic Monthly	342,764
Better Homes & Gardens	8,093,646
Boys' Life	1,859,196
Bride's	314,152
Business Week	768,203
Business Week/Industrial	305,947
Camping Journal	280,843
Capper's Weekly	424,783
Car Craft	316,797
Car & Driver	730,624
Carte Blanche	481,786[2]
Catholic Digest	530,119[2]
Chatelaine	1,017,296
Chatelaine (French Language Edition)	275,531
Club	651,457
Co-ed	905,796[2]
Cosmopolitan	2,214,655
Cue	265,585
Cycle	424,488
Daytime TV	323,479
Decorating & Craft Ideas Made Easy	672,353
Ebony	1,288,149
Elks Magazine	1,602,373
Esquire	1,079,253
Essence	500,035
Exploring	384,533
Family Circle	8,479,519
Family Handyman Mag. (incl. Home Garden)	711,595[2]
Family Health	880,015
Family Weekly	10,800,000
Farm Journal	1,554,199
Farmer-Stockman, The	327,968
Field & Stream	2,000,073
Flower & Garden Magazine	552,885
Flying	422,406
Forbes	646,965
Fortune	624,428
Genesis	387,826
Gentlemen's Quarterly	261,498
Glamour	1,855,835
Golf (incl. Golfing)	608,973
Golf Digest	834,208
Good Housekeeping	5,312,449
Gourmet	616,347
Grit	1,287,755
Guns & Ammo (incl. Guns & Hunting)	379,551
Harper's Bazaar	540,339
Harper's Magazine	288,199
Harvest Farm Unit	436,719
High Times	405,412
Hoard's Dairyman	262,423
High Fidelity	306,129
Holiday	387,488
Hot Rod Magazine (incl. Rod & Custom)	858,691
House Beautiful	840,629
House & Garden	1,159,197
Hustler	1,476,569
Instructor	265,053
Jet	623,933
Junior Scholastic	1,024,837[2]
Kiwanis Magazine, The	270,368
Ladies' Home Journal	6,080,058
Lady's Circle	351,173

Magazine	Circulation[1]
Legion Magazine	405,247
Lion Magazine, The	697,753
Lutheran, The	547,633[3]
Maclean's Magazine	677,790
Mademoiselle	873,686
McCall's	6,511,891
Mechanix Illustrated	1,586,331
Midnight	1,133,834
Modern Bride	332,011
Modern Photography	537,912
Modern Romances	569,935
Modern Screen	579,429
Money	666,019
Motor Trend (incl. Car Life, Sports Graphic & Wheels Afield)	721,019
Ms. Magazine	380,733[2]
National Enquirer	4,502,730
National Future Farmer	486,136
National Geographic, The	9,211,957
National Lampoon	763,935
National Observer, The	465,163
Nation's Business	1,030,596
Natural History	396,696
New Times	268,967
New Woman	330,751
New York Magazine	365,268
New Yorker, The	491,684
Newsweek	3,012,945
Nursing '76	405,688
OUI	1,258,249
Our Sunday Visitor	345,609
Outdoor Life	1,782,773
Parade	19,537,044[4]
Parents' Magazine & Better Homemaking	1,506,103
Penthouse	4,365,679
Penthouse Forum	556,885
People	1,776,953
Photoplay	960,332[2]
Playboy	5,405,443
Playgirl	1,006,755
Popular Electronics	398,796
Popular Hot Rodding	321,940
Popular Mechanics	1,671,216
Popular Photography	750,085
Popular Science	1,822,736
Prairie Farmer	275,054
Progressive Farmer	936,162
Psychology Today	1,108,822
Reader's Digest	18,164,833
Reader's Digest (Canadian-English & Canadian-French Editions)	1,970,744
Redbook Magazine	4,574,495
Road & Track	457,977
Rolling Stone	452,773
Rona Barrett's Gossip	275,183
Rona Barrett's Hollywood	296,056
Rotarian, The	463,088
Saturday Evening Post, The	456,999
Saturday Review	493,028
Scholastic Magazines	3,925,208[2]
Scientific American	642,282
Scouting	1,177,124
Selection du Reader's Digest	274,529
Senior Scholastic Unit	2,900,371[2]
Seventeen	1,450,105
Signature	718,410
Ski (incl. Ski Life)	420,138
Skiing Magazine	442,921
Smithsonian	1,264,182
Southern Living	1,279,645

Magazine	Circulation[1]	Magazine	Circulation[1]
Sphere Magazine	655,968[2]	True	585,890
Sport	1,373,952	True Confessions	312,200[2]
Sporting News, The	330,210	True Story	1,702,962[2]
Sports Afield (combined with Rod & Gun)	1,110,464	TV Guide	20,249,384
Sports Illustrated	2,310,879	TV Radio Mirror	593,795[2]
Stereo Review	422,336	United Church Observer, The	311,629[3]
Successful Farming	764,322	U.S. News & World Report	2,056,991
Sunset, The Magazine of Western Living	1,366,043	V.F.W. Magazine	1,629,934
'Teen	908,016	Vogue (incorp. Vanity Fair)	770,954
Tiger Beat	272,823	Vogue Patterns	384,644
Time, The Weekly Newsmagazine	4,522,776	Weight Watchers Magazine	792,648
Time Worldwide	5,881,344	Westways	441,374
Time Atlantic	469,024	Woman's Day	8,164,817
Time in Canada	432,591	Workbasket, The	1,796,688
Time Pacific	332,550	Workbench	447,112
Today's Education	1,791,878		

[1] Average total paid circulation for the six-month period ending June 30, 1976. The table lists magazines of over 260,000 circulation. [2] 1975 figures, 1976 statement not filed by press time. [3] Religious publication using congregation-wide subscription plan. [4] As of Sept. 1, 1976.

Radio and Television Stations and Networks

Source: National Association of Broadcasters.

Major networks	Radio broadcast stations (June 1, 1976)			TV stations (June 1, 1976)	
	Owned and operated FM	AM	Affiliated	Owned and operated	Affiliated
ABC—American Broadcasting Companies, Inc.	6	6	1,455	5	185
CBS—CBS Inc.	7	7	266	5	205
MBS—Mutual Broadcasting System, Inc.	..	..	690	..	...
NBC—National Broadcasting Company, Inc.	4	4	232	5	213

Number of stations [1] (May 31, 1976)	Radio		Television	
	AM	FM	VHF	UHF
Commercial	4,476	2,813	513	195
Educational	.....	842	98	155
Total	4,476	3,655	611	350

[1] *Source:* Federal Communications Commission, and individual networks. [2] Primary stations only.

Television Statistics for the United States, 1975

Source: Electronic Industries Association.

Type of equipment	Number	Type of equipment	Number
TV sets in use	125,300,000	Monochrome	4,418,000
Color	59,300,000	TV sets sold[1]	11,606,000
Monochrome	66,000,000	Color	6,651,000
TV sets manufactured[1]	10,637,000	Monochrome	4,955,000
Color	6,219,000		

[1] Includes imports.

Radio and Audio Statistics for the United States, 1975

Source: Electronic Industries Association.

Type of equipment	Number	Type of equipment	Number
Radios in use	413,000,000	Portable	16,382,000
Auto radios	104,000,000	Automobile	9,239,000
Others	309,000,000	Radios sold	25,545,000
Radios manufactured[1]	34,515,000	Phonographs in use	13,100,000
Table	2,253,000	Phonographs manufactured	3,164,000
Clock	6,641,000	Phonographs sold	5,265,000

[1] Includes imports.

UNITED STATES STATISTICS
POPULATION
Population Growth of the United States
Source: Bureau of the Census.
Colonial Estimates (round numbers)

Year	Population	Year	Population	Year	Population	Year	Population
1610........	350	1660......	75,100	1710......	331,700	1760......	1,593,600
1620........	2,300	1670......	111,900	1720......	466,200	1770......	2,148,100
1630........	4,600	1680......	151,500	1730......	629,400	1780......	2,780,400
1640........	26,600	1690......	210,400	1740......	905,600		
1650........	50,400	1700......	250,900	1750......	1,170,800		

National Censuses[1]

Year	Resident population[2]	Land area, sq. mi.	Pop. per sq. mi.	Year	Resident population[2]	Land area, sq. mi.	Pop. per sq. mi.
1790........	3,929,214	864,746	4.5	1890.......	62,947,714	2,969,640	21.2
1800........	5,308,483	864,746	6.1	1900.......	75,994,575	2,969,834	25.6
1810........	7,239,881	1,681,828	4.3	1910.......	91,972,266	2,969,565	31.0
1820........	9,638,453	1,749,462	5.5	1920.......	105,710,620	2,969,451	35.6
1830........	12,866,020	1,749,462	7.4	1930.......	122,775,046	2,977,128	41.2
1840........	17,069,453	1,749,462	9.8	1940.......	131,669,275	2,977,128	44.2
1850........	23,191,876	2,940,042	7.9	1950.......	150,697,361	2,974,726	50.7
1860........	31,443,321	2,969,640	10.6	1960.......	179,323,175	3,540,911	50.6
1870........	39,818,449	2,969,640	13.4	1970.......	203,235,298	3,536,855	57.5
1880........	50,155,783	2,969,640	16.9				

[1] Beginning with 1960, figures include Alaska and Hawaii. [2] Excludes armed forces overseas.

Population Projections, 1980-2000[1]

Race, sex and age	1980	1985	1990	1995	2000
MALE, WHITE	93,880,000	97,921,000	101,874,000	105,140,000	107,761,000
Up to 19 years . . .	30,460,000	30,339,000	31,575,000	32,976,000	33,402,000
20 to 39 years . . .	30,765,000	33,258,000	33,132,000	31,646,000	30,154,000
40 to 59 years . . .	19,605,000	20,326,000	22,595,000	25,877,000	29,458,000
60 to 79 years . . .	11,617,000	12,480,000	12,866,000	12,765,000	12,714,000
80 years and over . . .	1,435,000	1,517,000	1,706,000	1,875,000	2,031,000
FEMALE, WHITE	98,283,000	102,627,000	106,812,000	110,256,000	113,024,000
Up to 19 years	29,113,000	28,919,000	30,031,000	31,341,000	31,751,000
20 to 39 years . . .	30,539,000	32,979,000	32,871,000	31,410,000	29,875,000
40 to 59 years . . .	20,671,000	21,249,000	23,424,000	26,712,000	30,337,000
60 to 79 years . . .	15,001,000	16,228,000	16,751,000	16,632,000	16,512,000
80 years and over . . .	2,959,000	3,253,000	3,734,000	4,162,000	4,550,000
TOTAL WHITE	192,162,000	200,548,000	208,686,000	215,396,000	220,785,000
MALE, BLACK	12,579,000	13,494,000	14,369,000	15,155,000	15,879,000
Up to 19 years . . .	5,358,000	5,410,000	5,567,000	5,678,000	5,678,000
20 to 39 years . . .	3,872,000	4,449,000	4,743,000	4,833,000	4,842,000
40 to 59 years . . .	2,113,000	2,270,000	2,569,000	3,060,000	3,687,000
60 to 79 years . . .	1,109,000	1,229,000	1,330,000	1,404,000	1,480,000
80 years and over . . .	130,000	136,000	159,000	178,000	193,000
FEMALE, BLACK	13,792,000	14,810,000	15,779,000	16,649,000	17,446,000
Up to 19 years . . .	5,276,000	5,288,000	5,400,000	4,221,000	5,468,000
20 to 39 years . . .	4,380,000	5,014,000	5,340,000	5,428,000	5,403,000
40 to 59 years . . .	2,460,000	2,639,000	2,982,000	3,543,000	4,236,000
60 to 79 years . . .	1,441,000	1,616,000	1,752,000	1,845,000	1,956,000
80 years and over . . .	236,000	253,000	306,000	356,000	393,000
TOTAL BLACK	26,371,000	28,304,000	30,148,000	31,804,000	33,325,000
TOTAL UNITED STATES[2] . .	222,769,000	234,068,000	245,075,000	254,495,000	262,494,000
Median age	29.9	31.1	32.3	33.6	34.8

[1] Based on average of 2.1 lifetime births per woman. [2] Includes all races.

United States Population by State, 1790-1970

Source: Bureau of the Census.

NOTE: For estimated 1974 population, and rank, *see* the individual states beginning Page 626.

State	1790	1900	1950	1960	1970	% change, 1960-70	Pop. per sq. mi., 1970	Pop. rank, 1970
Alabama.............	....	1,828,697	3,061,743	3,266,740	3,444,165	5.4	67.9	21
Alaska.............	....	63,592	128,643	226,167	302,173	33.6	0.5	50
Arizona.............	....	122,931	749,587	1,302,161	1,772,482	36.1	15.6	33
Arkansas.............	....	1,311,564	1,909,511	1,786,272	1,923,295	7.7	37.0	32
California.............	....	1,485,053	10,586,223	15,717,204	19,953,134	27.0	127.6	1
Colorado.............	....	539,700	1,325,089	1,753,947	2,207,259	25.8	21.3	30
Connecticut..........	237,946	908,420	2,007,280	2,535,234	3,032,217	19.6	623.7	24
Delaware.............	59,096	184,735	318,085	446,292	548,104	22.8	276.5	46
D. C.............	....	278,718	802,178	763,956	756,510	−1.0	12,401.8	....
Florida.............	....	528,542	2,771,305	4,951,560	6,789,443	37.1	125.5	9
Georgia.............	82,548	2,216,331	3,444,578	3,943,116	4,589,575	16.4	79.0	15
Hawaii.............	....	154,001	499,794	632,772	769,913	21.7	119.8	40
Idaho.............	....	161,772	588,637	667,191	713,008	6.9	8.6	42
Illinois.............	....	4,821,550	8,712,176	10,081,158	11,113,976	10.2	199.4	5
Indiana.............	....	2,516,462	3,934,224	4,662,498	5,193,669	11.4	143.9	11
Iowa.............	....	2,231,853	2,621,073	2,757,537	2,825,041	2.4	50.5	25
Kansas.............	....	1,470,495	1,905,299	2,178,611	2,249,071	3.2	27.5	28
Kentucky.............	73,677	2,147,174	2,944,806	3,038,156	3,219,311	6.0	81.2	23
Louisiana.............	....	1,381,625	2,683,516	3,257,022	3,643,180	11.9	81.1	20
Maine.............	96,540	694,466	913,774	969,265	993,663	2.5	32.1	38
Maryland.............	319,728	1,188,044	2,343,001	3,100,689	3,922,399	26.5	396.6	18
Massachusetts........	378,787	2,805,346	4,690,514	5,148,578	5,689,170	10.5	727.0	10
Michigan.............	....	2,420,982	6,371,766	7,823,194	8,875,083	13.4	156.2	7
Minnesota.............	....	1,751,394	2,982,483	3,413,864	3,805,069	11.5	48.0	19
Mississippi.............	....	1,551,270	2,178,914	2,178,141	2,216,912	1.8	46.9	29
Missouri.............	....	3,106,665	3,954,653	4,319,813	4,677,399	8.3	67.8	13
Montana.............	....	243,329	591,024	674,767	694,409	2.9	4.8	43
Nebraska.............	....	1,066,300	1,325,510	1,411,330	1,483,791	5.1	19.4	35
Nevada.............	....	42,335	160,083	285,278	488,738	71.3	4.4	47
New Hampshire.......	141,885	411,588	533,242	606,921	737,681	21.5	81.7	41
New Jersey.............	184,139	1,883,669	4,835,329	6,066,782	7,168,164	18.2	953.1	8
New Mexico.............	....	195,310	681,187	951,023	1,016,000	6.8	8.4	37
New York.............	340,120	7,268,894	14,830,192	16,782,304	18,241,266	8.4	381.3	2
North Carolina........	393,751	1,893,810	4,061,929	4,556,155	5,082,059	11.5	104.1	12
North Dakota.........	....	319,146	619,636	632,446	617,761	−2.3	8.9	45
Ohio.............	....	4,157,545	7,946,627	9,706,397	10,652,017	9.7	260.0	6
Oklahoma.............	....	790,391[1]	2,233,351	2,328,284	2,559,253	9.9	37.2	27
Oregon.............	....	413,536	1,521,341	1,768,687	2,091,385	18.2	21.7	31
Pennsylvania.........	434,373	6,302,115	10,498,012	11,319,366	11,793,909	4.2	262.3	3
Rhode Island.........	68,825	428,556	791,896	859,488	949,723	10.5	905.4	39
South Carolina.........	249,073	1,340,316	2,117,027	2,382,594	2,590,516	8.7	85.7	26
South Dakota.........	....	401,570	652,740	680,514	666,257	−2.2	8.8	44
Tennessee.............	35,691	2,020,616	3,291,718	3,567,089	3,924,164	10.0	95.0	17
Texas.............	....	3,048,710	7,711,194	9,579,677	11,196,730	16.9	42.7	4
Utah.............	....	276,749	688,862	890,627	1,059,273	18.9	12.9	36
Vermont	85,425	343,641	377,747	389,881	444,732	14.1	48.0	48
Virginia.............	747,610	1,854,184	3,318,680	3,966,949	4,648,494	17.2	116.9	14
Washington.............	....	518,103	2,378,963	2,853,214	3,409,169	19.5	51.2	22
West Virginia.........	....	958,800	2,005,552	1,860,421	1,744,237	−6.2	72.5	34
Wisconsin.............	....	2,069,042	3,434,575	3,951,777	4,417,933	11.8	81.1	16
Wyoming.............	....	92,531	290,529	330,066	332,416	0.7	3.4	49
Total.............	3,929,214	76,212,168	151,325,798	179,323,175	203,235,298	13.3	57.4	..

[1] Includes population of Indian Territory: 1900, 392,960. NOTE: In April 1973, the Census Bureau reported that it had overlooked 5,300,000 people in the 1970 Census. However, by law, the total figure listed above is official.

Population Gain for 1975-1976 Falls Off

The estimated population of the United States on July 1, 1976 was 215,118,000, representing an increase of 1,578,000 over the figure for July 1975. This reverses the upward trend in gains that prevailed since 1972. The increase was the lowest since 1945–46 and only slightly over the peak of 3,058,000 recorded in 1956–57. The population estimate for 1976 indicates that the United States has grown by 10,783,000 people since the census of April 1, 1970, the date on which current estimates are based.

LARGE METROPOLITAN AREAS—POPULATION, 1960, 1970, AND 1973

In thousands, except as indicated. Covers 138 large SMSA's with estimated population of 250,000 or more as of July 1, 1973, as defined in *Standard Metropolitan Statistical Areas, 1967* (as amended up to April 16, 1975) as issued by the Executive Office of the President, Office of Management and Budget. Figures for 1970 include corrections through May 1975. Change measured from April 1, 1960, to April 1, 1970, and from April 1, 1970, to July 1, 1973; minus sign (−) indicates decrease. Rank based on unrounded figures.

STANDARD METROPOLITAN STATISTICAL AREA	POPULATION				POPULATION CHANGE					
	Apr. 1, 1960	Apr. 1, 1970	July 1, 1973		1960–1970			1970–1973		
			Total	Rank	Number	Percent	Net migration	Number	Percent	Net migration
Akron, Ohio	605	679	677	54	74	12.2	2	−2	−0.3	−20
Albany-Schenectady-Troy, N.Y	715	778	800	43	63	8.8	9	22	2.9	11
Albuquerque, N. Mex.	276	333	376	92	57	20.6	17	43	12.9	29
Allentown-Bethlehem-Easton, Pa.-N.J.	545	594	611	59	49	9.0	15	16	2.8	10
Anaheim-Santa Ana-Garden Grove, Calif.	704	1,421	1,597	19	717	101.9	552	176	12.4	126
Appleton-Oshkosh, Wis.	232	277	281	122	45	19.4	9	4	1.6	−3
Atlanta, Ga.	1,169	1,596	1,748	18	426	36.5	229	152	9.6	90
Augusta, Ga.-S.C	230	276	269	129	46	19.9	9	−7	−2.4	−17
Austin, Tex.	232	323	375	93	91	39.3	51	52	16.1	38
Bakersfield, Calif.	292	330	336	106	38	13.1	−6	5	1.6	−6
Baltimore, Md.	1,804	2,071	2,128	14	267	14.8	53	57	2.8	17
Baton Rouge, La.	300	376	402	85	76	25.3	20	26	6.9	10
Beaumont, Port Arthur-Orange, Tex.	331	348	346	102	17	5.1	−26	−2	−0.5	−11
Binghamton, N.Y.-Pa.	284	303	302	112	6	6.7	−13	(z)	−0.1	−6
Birmingham, Ala.	747	767	787	44	21	2.8	−50	20	2.6	4
Boston, Mass.	2,688	2,899	2,898	8	211	7.9	(NA)	−1	(z)	−50
Bridgeport, Conn.	350	402	397	86	52	14.7	(NA)	−5	−1.2	−18
Buffalo, N.Y.	1,307	1,349	1,345	26	42	3.2	−84	−4	−0.3	−25
Canton, Ohio	361	394	406	84	33	9.0	−3	12	3.0	3
Charleston-North Charleston, S.C	279	336	352	97	57	20.5	−1	16	4.8	1
Charleston, W. Va.	276	257	256	136	−19	−7.0	−46	−2	−0.6	−6
Charlotte-Gastonia, N.C	444	558	588	62	114	25.7	42	30	5.5	10
Chattanooga-Tenn.-Ga.	340	371	389	90	31	9.1	−8	18	4.8	7
Chicago, Ill.	6,221	6,978	7,002	2	757	12.2	8	25	0.4	−156
Cincinnati, Ohio-Ky.-Ind.	1,268	1,385	1,383	23	117	9.2	−36	−2	−0.2	−36
Cleveland, Ohio	1,909	2,064	2,006	16	154	8.1	−45	−57	−2.8	−99
Colorado Springs, Colo.	146	239	289	119	93	63.6	72	49	20.7	36
Columbia, S.C.	261	323	349	100	62	23.8	23	26	8.0	14
Columbus, Ohio	845	1,018	1,057	35	173	20.4	52	39	3.9	6
Corpus Christi, Tex.	267	285	298	116	18	6.8	−35	13	4.6	−2
Dallas-Ft. Worth, Tex.	1,738	2,378	2,464	10	640	36.8	362	86	3.6	−2
Davenport-Rock Island-Moline, Iowa-Ill.	319	363	365	96	43	13.5	5	2	0.5	−7
Dayton, Ohio	727	853	848	42	125	17.2	27	−4	−0.5	−50
Denver-Boulder, Colo.	935	1,239	1,377	24	305	32.6	163	138	11.1	98
Des Moines, Iowa	287	314	325	108	26	9.2	−7	12	3.7	3
Detroit, Mich.	3,950	4,435	4,446	5	485	12.3	−23	11	0.2	−116
Duluth-Superior, Minn.-Wis.	277	265	264	131	−11	−4.1	−30	−1	−0.5	−4
El Paso, Tex.	314	359	390	88	45	14.4	−30	31	8.6	8
Erie, Pa.	251	264	273	126	13	5.2	−13	9	3.4	2
Evansville, Ind.-Ky.	272	285	290	118	13	4.7	−10	5	1.7	(z)
Flint, Mich.	428	509	517	70	81	18.9	4	8	1.6	−12
Fort Lauderdale-Hollywood, Fla.	334	620	756	47	286	85.7	256	136	21.9	131
Fort Wayne, Ind.	306	362	372	95	56	18.2	12	10	2.7	−3
Fresno, Calif.	366	413	435	77	47	12.9	−7	22	5.3	9
Gary-Hammond-East Chicago, Ind.	574	633	641	57	60	10.4	−26	7	1.2	−14
Grand Rapids, Mich.	462	539	553	66	77	16.7	11	14	2.5	−2
Greensboro-Winston-Salem-High Point, N.C.	622	724	757	46	102	16.4	19	32	4.5	12
Greenville-Spartanburg, S.C.	413	473	509	72	61	14.7	6	36	7.6	21
Harrisburg, Pa.	372	411	425	79	39	10.5	7	15	3.6	8
Hartford, Conn.	588	721	733	51	132	22.5	(NA)	12	1.7	−4
Honolulu, Hawaii	500	631	686	53	130	26.0	18	56	8.8	24
Houston, Tex.	1,430	1,999	2,168	13	569	39.8	311	169	8.5	82
Huntington-Ashland, W. Va-Ky. Ohio	284	287	291	117	3	1.0	5	4	1.3	−2
Huntsville, Ala.	202	282	287	120	81	39.9	38	4	1.4	−6
Indianapolis, Ind.	944	1,111	1,137	31	167	17.7	37	25	2.3	−10
Jackson, Miss.	221	259	275	125	38	17.0	1	16	6.2	6
Jacksonville, Fla.	530	622	661	55	92	17.4	11	39	6.2	18
Jersey City, N.J.	611	608	598	60	−3	−0.5	−47	−10	−1.6	−18
Johnstown, Pa.	281	263	266	130	−18	−6.4	−33	3	1.2	(z)
Kalamazoo-Portage, Mich.	218	258	261	134	40	18.2	12	3	1.3	−4
Kansas City, Mo.-Kans.	1,109	1,274	1,299	27	165	14.9	30	25	2.0	−10
Knoxville, Tenn.	377	409	427	78	33	8.7	−8	17	4.2	8
Lakeland-Winter Haven, Fla.	195	229	255	138	33	17.4	11	26	11.4	20
Lancaster, Pa.	278	320	335	107	42	15.0	11	15	4.7	7
Lansing-East Lansing, Mich.	342	424	438	76	82	24.0	28	14	3.3	−2
Las Vegas, Nev.	127	273	308	110	146	115.2	109	34	12.5	23
Lawrence-Haverhill, Mass.-N.H.	218	259	271	127	40	18.4	(NA)	13	5.0	8
Lexington, Ky.	212	267	282	121	55	25.8	25	16	5.9	7
Little Rock-North Little Rock, Ark.	272	323	350	99	51	18.9	12	26	8.2	14

See footnotes at end of table.

Large Metropolitan Areas—Population, 1960, 1970, and 1973—Continued
In thousands, except as indicated.

STANDARD METROPOLITAN STATISTICAL AREA	POPULATION				NET INCREASE					
	Apr. 1, 1960	Apr. 1, 1970	July 1, 1973		1960–1970			1970–1973		
			Total	Rank	Number	Percent	Net migration	Number	Percent	Net migration
Long Branch-Asbury Park, N.J	334	462	480	73	127	38.1	89	18	3.9	9
Lorain-Elyria, Ohio	218	257	263	132	39	18.1	6	6	2.5	−3
Los Angeles-Long Beach, Calif	6,039	7,042	6,924	3	1,003	16.6	263	−118	−1.7	−291
Louisville, Ky.-Ind	754	867	886	39	113	15.0	22	18	2.1	−5
Madison, Wis	222	290	301	113	68	30.7	29	11	3.8	2
Memphis, Tenn.-Ark.-Miss	727	834	863	41	107	14.7	−7	29	3.5	1
Miami, Fla	935	1,268	1,370	25	333	35.6	254	102	8.1	86
Milwaukee, Wis	1,279	1,404	1,417	21	125	9.8	−38	13	0.9	−19
Minneapolis-St. Paul, Minn.-Wis	1,598	1,965	2,000	17	368	23.0	119	34	1.7	−24
Mobile, Ala	363	377	389	89	13	3.7	42	13	3.4	(Z)
Nashville-Davidson, Tenn	597	699	732	52	102	17.2	30	33	4.7	14
Nassau-Suffolk, N.Y	1,967	2,556	2,630	9	589	29.9	359	74	2.9	29
New Brunswick-Perth Amboy-Sayreville, N.J	434	584	594	61	150	34.6	86	11	1.8	−4
New Haven-West Haven, Conn	361	414	415	82	53	14.7	(NA)	2	0.4	−6
New Orleans, La	907	1,046	1,083	33	139	15.4	8	36	3.5	4
New York, N.Y.-N.J	9,540	9,974	9,739	1	434	4.5	−329	−235	−2.4	−372
Newark, N.J	1,833	2,057	2,053	15	224	12.2	47	−5	−0.2	−40
Newport News-Hampton, Va	255	333	347	101	78	30.7	30	14	4.3	1
Norfolk-Va. Beach-Portsmouth, Va.-N.C	629	733	745	50	104	16.5	−2	12	1.7	−14
Northeast, Pa	621	622	629	58	1	0.1	−13	8	1.2	8
Oklahoma City, Okla	566	699	750	49	133	23.5	55	51	7.3	27
Omaha, Nebr.-Iowa	458	543	575	63	85	18.5	7	33	6.0	14
Orlando, Fla	338	453	549	67	116	34.3	69	96	21.2	83
Oxnard-Simi Valley-Ventura, Calif	199	378	420	80	179	90.1	134	41	10.9	27
Paterson-Clifton-Passaic, N.J	407	461	461	74	54	13.3	13	1	0.1	−10
Pensacola, Fla	203	243	259	135	40	19.5	−1	16	6.4	5
Peoria, Ill	313	342	351	98	29	9.1	−9	9	2.7	(Z)
Philadelphia, Pa.-N.J	4,343	4,824	4,806	4	481	11.1	51	−18	−0.4	−100
Phoenix, Ariz	664	969	1,127	32	306	46.1	190	157	16.2	121
Pittsburgh, Pa	2,405	2,401	2,365	12	−4	−0.2	−167	−37	−1.5	−58
Portland, Oreg.-Wash	822	1,007	1,062	34	185	22.5	117	55	5.5	37
Providence-Warwick-Pawtucket, R.I.-Mass	821	909	926	38	88	10.7	(NA)	17	1.8	2
Raleigh-Durham, N.C	324	419	458	75	95	29.4	50	39	9.3	27
Reading, Pa	275	296	304	111	21	7.6	6	8	2.6	5
Richmond, Va	457	542	563	65	85	18.5	34	21	3.9	10
Riverside-San Bernardino-Ontario, Calif	810	1,141	1,197	29	332	40.9	216	55	4.9	26
Rochester, N.Y	801	962	972	36	161	20.1	69	10	1.0	−13
Rockford, Ill	230	272	271	128	42	18.2	8	−1	−0.3	−10
Sacramento, Calif	626	804	864	40	178	28.5	88	61	7.5	41
St. Louis, Mo.-Ill	2,144	2,411	2,391	11	266	12.4	20	−19	−0.8	−73
Salinas-Seaside-Monterey, Calif	198	247	255	137	49	24.8	16	8	3.2	−2
Salt Lake City, Utah	576	705	753	48	129	22.4	7	48	6.8	7
San Antonio, Tex	736	888	960	37	152	20.7	15	72	8.1	29
San Diego, Calif	1,033	1,358	1,470	20	325	31.4	169	112	8.2	72
San Francisco-Oakland, Calif	2,649	3,107	3,143	6	460	17.4	182	36	1.2	−18
San Jose, Calif	642	1,065	1,157	30	423	65.9	284	91	8.6	55
Santa Barbara-Santa Maria-Lompoc, Calif	169	264	277	124	95	56.4	65	12	4.7	6
Seattle-Everett, Wash	1,107	1,425	1,383	22	317	28.7	187	−42	−2.9	−70
Shreveport, La	321	334	343	103	13	3.9	−32	10	2.9	−2
South Bend, Ind	271	280	281	123	9	3.3	−18	1	0.3	−5
Spokane, Wash	278	287	301	114	9	3.3	−14	14	4.7	7
Springfield-Chicopee-Holyoke, Mass.-Conn	504	542	546	68	38	7.5	(NA)	5	0.8	−5
Stockton, Calif	250	291	299	115	41	16.4	16	7	2.6	1
Syracuse, N.Y	564	637	643	56	73	12.9	2	6	1.0	−9
Tacoma, Wash	322	412	392	87	91	28.2	46	−20	−4.8	−31
Tampa-St. Petersburg, Fla	809	1,089	1,276	28	279	34.5	253	187	17.2	187
Toledo, Ohio-Mich	695	763	782	45	67	9.7	−9	20	2.6	−2
Trenton, N.J	266	304	315	109	38	14.2	12	11	3.7	6
Tucson, Ariz	266	352	416	81	86	32.3	47	64	18.2	52
Tulsa, Okla	475	549	572	64	74	15.5	24	23	4.2	9
Utica-Rome, N.Y	331	341	341	105	10	3.0	−21	(Z)	(Z)	−6
Vallejo-Fairfield-Napa, Calif	200	251	263	133	51	25.3	20	12	4.7	4
Washington, D.C.-Md.-Va	[1] 2,097	2,910	3,020	7	801	38.0	423	109	3.8	13
West Palm Beach-Boca Raton, Fla	228	349	412	83	121	53.0	100	63	18.1	60
Wichita, Kans	382	389	375	94	8	2.0	−47	−15	−3.8	−26
Wilmington, Del.-N.J.-Md	415	499	515	71	85	20.5	28	16	3.3	3
Worcester, Mass	354	372	377	91	18	5.1	(NA)	4	1.2	−5
York, Pa	290	330	343	104	39	13.5	10	14	4.2	6
Youngstown-Warren, Ohio	509	537	543	69	28	5.5	−18	6	1.2	−5

NA Not available.   Z Less than 500 or 0.05 percent.   [1] Adjusted to exclude 12,520 double count of Ft. Belvoir, Fairfax County, Va. Source: U.S. Bureau of the Census, 1970 Census of Population and Housing, PHC (2), *General Demographic Trends for Metropolitan Areas, 1960 to 1970, Characteristics of the Population,* Part 1, *United States Summary;* and *Current Population Reports,* series P-25 Nos. 546-595.

Population of U.S. Cities Over 45,000, 1920–1970

Source: U. S. Bureau of the Census.

Asterisk denotes more than one Zip code for a city and refers to general delivery. To find the Zip code for a particular address, consult the Zip code directory available in every post office. NOTE: U = unincorporated area; T = town.

City and Major Zip Code	1920 Census	1940 Census	1960 Census	1970 Census	1970 Rank	% Change 1960-70
Abilene, Tex. (79604*)	10,274	26,612	90,368	89,653	181	—0.8
Akron, Ohio (44309*)	208,435	244,791	290,351	275,425	52	—5.1
Alameda, Calif. (94501)	28,806	36,256	63,855	70,968	260	11.1
Albany, Ga. (31706*)	11,555	19,055	55,890	72,263	249	29.9
Albany, N.Y. (12201*)	113,344	130,577	129,726	115,781	127	—10.8
Albuquerque, N.M. (87101*)	15,157	35,449	201,189	243,751	59	21.2
Alexandria, Va. (22313*)	18,060	33,523	91,023	110,927	134	21.9
Alhambra, Calif. (91802*)	9,096	38,935	54,807	62,125	310	13.4
Allentown, Pa. (18105*)	73,502	96,904	108,347	109,871	139	1.4
Altoona, Pa. (16603*)	60,331	80,214	69,407	63,115	305	—9.1
Amarillo, Tex. (79105*)	15,494	51,686	137,969	127,010	116	—7.9
Anaheim, Calif. (92803*)	5,526	11,031	104,184	166,408	82	59.7
Anchorage, Alaska (99510*)	1,856	3,495	44,237	48,081	405	8.7
Anderson, Ind. (46011*)	29,767	41,572	49,061	70,787	261	44.3
Ann Arbor, Mich. (48106*)	19,516	29,815	67,340	100,035	157	48.5
Appleton, Wis. (54911)	19,561	28,436	48,411	57,143	342	18.0
Arden-Arcade, Calif. (U) (95825)	....	....	73,352	82,492	209	12.5
Arlington, Tex. (76010*)	3,031	4,240	44,775	90,032	180	101.0
Arlington, Va. (U) (22210*)	....	26,615	163,401	174,284	78	6.9
Arlington Heights, Ill. (60004*)	2,250	5,668	27,878	64,884	294	132.7
Arvada, Colo. (80001*)	915	1,482	19,242	46,814	418	143.3
Asheville, N.C. (28801*)	28,504	51,310	60,192	57,681	336	—4.2
Atlanta, Ga. (30301*)	200,616	302,288	487,455	495,039	27	1.6
Atlantic City, N.J. (08401*)	50,707	64,094	59,544	47,859	407	—19.6
Augusta, Ga. (30903*)	52,548	65,919	70,626	59,864	344	—15.2
Aurora, Colo. (80010*)	983	3,437	48,548	74,974	237	54.5
Aurora, Ill. (60507*)	36,397	47,710	63,715	74,182	241	16.4
Austin, Tex. (78767*)	34,876	87,930	186,545	251,808	57	35.0
Bakersfield, Calif. (93302*)	18,638	29,252	56,848	69,515	268	22.3
Baldwin Park, Calif. (91706)	....	....	33,951	47,285	410	39.3
Baltimore, Md. (21233*)	733,826	859,100	939,024	905,787	7	—3.5
Baton Rouge, La. (70821*)	21,782	34,719	152,419	165,921	83	8.9
Bay City, Mich. (48706)	47,554	47,956	53,604	49,449	393	—7.8
Bayonne, N.J. (07002)	76,754	79,198	74,215	72,743	245	—2.0
Beaumont, Tex. (77704*)	40,422	59,061	119,175	117,548	125	—1.4
Bellevue, Wash. (98009*)	....	....	12,809	61,102	317	377.0
Bellflower, Calif. (90706)	....	....	45,909	51,454	380	12.1
Berkeley, Calif. (94701*)	56,036	85,547	111,268	114,091	128	2.5
Berwyn, Ill. (60402)	14,150	48,451	54,224	52,502	376	—3.2
Bethesda, Md. (U) (20014)	....	....	56,527	71,621	255	26.7
Bethlehem, Pa. (18015*)	50,358	58,490	75,408	72,686	247	—3.6
Billings, Mont. (59101*)	15,100	23,261	52,851	61,581	314	16.5
Biloxi, Miss. (39530*)	10,937	17,475	44,053	48,486	400	10.1
Binghamton, N.Y. (13902*)	66,800	78,309	75,941	64,123	297	—15.6
Birmingham, Ala. (35203*)	178,806	267,583	340,887	300,910	48	—11.7
Bloomington, Minn. (55420)	....	....	50,498	81,970	211	62.3
Boise, Idaho (83701*)	21,393	26,130	34,481	74,990	236	117.5
Boston, Mass. (02109*)	748,060	770,816	697,197	641,071	16	—8.1
Boulder, Colo. (80302*)	11,006	12,958	37,718	66,870	287	77.3
Bridgeport, Conn. (06601*)	143,555	147,121	156,748	156,542	88	—0.1
Bristol, Conn. (06010)	20,620	30,167	45,499	55,487	355	22.0
Brockton, Mass. (02403)	66,254	62,343	72,813	89,040	184	22.3
Brownsville, Tex. (78520)	11,791	22,083	48,040	52,522	375	9.3
Buena Park, Calif. (90622*)	....	....	46,401	63,646	301	37.2
Buffalo, N.Y. (14240*)	506,775	575,901	532,759	462,768	28	—13.1
Burbank, Calif. (91505*)	2,913	34,337	90,155	88.871	185	—1.4
Cambridge, Mass. (02138*)	109,694	110,879	107,716	100,361	155	—6.8
Camden, N.J. (08101*)	116,309	117,536	117,159	102,551	150	—12.5
Canton, Ohio (44711*)	87,091	108,401	113,631	110,053	137	—3.1
Carson, Calif. (90745*)	....	....	38,059	71,150	259	86.9
Cedar Rapids, Iowa (52401*)	45,566	62,120	92,035	110,642	135	20.2
Champaign, Ill. (61820)	15,873	23,302	49,583	56,532	346	14.0
Charleston, S.C. (29401*)	67,957	71,275	65,925	66,945	284	1.5
Charleston, W.Va. (25301*)	39,608	67,914	85,796	71,505	257	—16.7
Charlotte, N.C. (28202*)	46,338	100,899	201,564	274,640	53	36.2

City and Major Zip Code	1920 Census	1940 Census	1960 Census	1970 Census	1970 Rank	% Change 1960–70
Chattanooga, Tenn. (37401*)	57,895	128,163	130,009	141,904	97	9.1
Chesapeake, Va. (23320*)	....	....	....	89,580	182	....
Chester, Pa. (19013*)	58,030	59,285	63,658	56,331	348	—11.5
Chicago, Ill. (60607*)	2,701,705	3,396,808	3,550,404	3,369,359	2	—5.1
Chicopee, Mass. (01021*)	36,214	41,664	61,553	66,676	288	8.3
Chula Vista, Calif. (92010*)	1,718	5,138	42,034	67,901	280	61.5
Cicero, Ill. (60650)	44,995	64,712	69,130	67,058	283	—3.0
Cincinnati, Ohio (45202*)	401,247	455,610	502,550	451,410	30	—10.1
Clearwater, Fla. (33515*)	2,427	10,136	34,653	52,074	379	50.3
Cleveland, Ohio (44101*)	796,841	878,336	876,050	750,879	10	—14.3
Cleveland Heights, Ohio (44118)	15,236	54,992	61,813	60,767	318	—1.7
Clifton, N.J. (07015*)	26,470	48,827	82,084	82,437	210	0.4
Colorado Springs, Colo. (80901*)	30,105	36,789	70,194	135,060	107	92.4
Columbia, Mo. (65201)	10,392	18,399	36,650	58,804	330	60.4
Columbia, S.C. (29201*)	37,524	62,396	97,433	113,542	129	16.5
Columbus, Ga. (31902*)	31,125	53,280	116,779	155,028	90	32.7
Columbus, Ohio (43216*)	237,031	306,087	471,316	540,025	21	14.6
Compton, Calif. (90220*)	1,478	16,198	71,812	78,611	223	9.5
Concord, Calif. (94520)	912	1,373	36,000	85,164	205	136.5
Corpus Christi, Tex. (78408*)	10,522	57,301	167,690	204,525	62	22.0
Costa Mesa, Calif. (92626*)	....	....	37,550	72,660	248	93.5
Council Bluffs, Iowa (51501)	36,162	41,439	55,641	60,348	320	8.5
Covington, Ky. (41011*)	57,121	62,018	60,376	52,535	374	—13.0
Cranston, R.I. (02910)	29,407	47,085	66,766	74,287	240	11.3
Cuyahoga Falls, Ohio (44222*)	10,200	20,546	47,922	49,678	392	3.7
Dallas, Tex. (75221*)	158,976	294,734	679,684	844,401	8	24.2
Daly City, Calif. (94015*)	3,779	9,625	44,791	66,922	285	49.4
Danbury, Conn. (06810)	18,943	22,339	22,928	50,781	384	121.5
Danville, Va. (24541)	21,539	32,749	46,577	46,391	421	—0.4
Davenport, Iowa (52802*)	56,727	66,039	88,981	98,469	160	10.7
Dayton, Ohio (45401*)	152,559	210,718	262,332	242,917	60	—7.4
Daytona Beach, Fla. (32015*)	825	22,584	37,395	45,327	432	21.2
Dearborn, Mich. (48120*)	2,470	63,584	112,007	104,199	148	—7.0
Dearborn Heights, Mich. (48127)	....	....	....	80,069	215	....
Decatur, Ill. (62521*)	43,818	59,305	78,004	90,397	177	15.9
Denver, Colo. (80201*)	256,491	322,412	493,887	514,678	25	4.2
Des Moines, Iowa (50318*)	126,468	159,819	208,982	201,404	64	—3.9
Des Plaines, Ill. (60016*)	3,451	9,518	34,886	57,239	341	64.1
Detroit, Mich. (48226*)	993,678	1,623,452	1,670,144	1,514,063	5	—9.4
Downey, Calif. (90241*)	....	....	82,505	88,445	187	7.2
Duluth, Minn. (55806*)	98,917	101,065	106,884	100,578	154	—5.9
Dundalk, Md. (U) (21222)	....	....	82,428	85,377	203	3.6
Durham, N.C. (27701*)	21,719	60,195	78,302	95,438	165	21.9
East Chicago, Ind. (46312)	35,967	54,637	57,669	46,982	414	—18.5
East Detroit, Mich. (48021)	....	8,584	45,756	45,920	426	0.4
East Lansing, Mich. (48823)	1,889	5,839	30,198	47,540	408	57.4
East Los Angeles, Calif. (U) (90022)	....	....	104,270	105,033	146	0.7
East Orange, N.J. (07019*)	50,710	68,945	77,259	75,471	234	—2.3
East Providence, R.I. (02914)	....	....	41,955	48,207	403	14.9
East St. Louis, Ill. (62201*)	66,767	75,609	81,712	69,996	266	—14.3
El Cajon, Calif. (92020*)	469	1,471	37,618	52,273	377	39.0
El Monte, Calif. (91734*)	1,283	4,746	13,163	69,852	267	430.7
El Paso, Tex. (79940*)	77,560	96,810	276,687	322,261	45	16.5
Elgin, Ill. (60120)	27,454	38,333	49,447	55,691	353	12.6
Elizabeth, N.J. (07207*)	95,783	109,912	107,698	112,654	131	4.6
Elmhurst, Ill. (60126)	4,594	15,458	36,991	48,887	397	32.1
Elyria, Ohio (44035*)	20,474	25,120	43,782	53,427	367	22.0
Erie, Pa. (16501*)	93,372	116,955	138,440	129,231	114	—6.7
Euclid, Ohio (44117)	3,363	17,866	62,998	71,552	256	13.6
Eugene, Ore. (97401*)	10,593	20,838	50,977	78,389	224	53.8
Evanston, Ill. (60204*)	37,234	65,389	79,283	79,808	216	0.7
Evansville, Ind. (47708*)	85,264	97,062	141,543	138,764	103	—2.0
Everett, Wash. (98201*)	27,644	30,224	40,304	53,622	365	33.0
Fall River, Mass. (02722*)	120,485	115,428	99,942	96,898	162	—3.0
Fargo, N.D. (58102)	21,961	32,580	46,662	53,365	368	14.4
Fayetteville, N.C. (28302*)	8,877	17,428	47,106	53,510	366	13.6
Flint, Mich. (48502*)	91,599	151,543	196,940	193,317	67	—1.8
Florissant, Mo. (63033*)	682	1,369	38,166	65,908	290	72.7
Fort Lauderdale, Fla. (33310*)	2,065	17,996	83,648	139,590	101	66.9
Fort Smith, Ark. (72901)	28,870	36,584	52,991	62,802	308	18.5
Fort Wayne, Ind. (46802*)	86,549	118,410	161,776	178,021	74	10.0

City and Major Zip Code	1920 Census	1940 Census	1960 Census	1970 Census	1970 Rank	% Change 1960-70
Fort Worth, Tex. (76101*)	106,482	177,662	356,268	393,476	33	10.4
Framingham, Mass. (T) (01701)	17,033	23,214	44,526	64,048	299	43.8
Fremont, Calif. (94538*)	....	....	43,790	100,869	153	130.3
Fresno, Calif. (93706*)	45,086	60,685	133,929	165,655	84	23.6
Fullerton, Calif. (92631*)	4,415	10,442	56,180	85,987	199	53.1
Gadsden, Ala. (35901*)	14,737	36,975	58,088	53,928	362	—7.2
Gainesville, Fla. (32601)	6,860	13,757	29,701	64,510	295	117.2
Galveston, Tex. (77550*)	44,255	60,862	67,175	61,809	311	—8.0
Garden Grove, Calif. (92640*)	....	....	84,238	121,155	121	43.8
Garland, Tex. (75040*)	1,421	2,233	38,501	81,437	213	111.5
Gary, Ind. (46401*)	55,378	111,719	178,320	188,398	69	5.6
Gastonia, N.C. (28052)	12,871	21,313	37,276	47,142	413	26.5
Glendale, Calif. (91209*)	13,536	82,582	119,442	132,664	111	11.1
Grand Prairie, Tex. (75050)	1,595	14,595	30,386	50,904	382	67.5
Grand Rapids, Mich. (49501*)	137,634	164,292	177,313	197,649	65	11.5
Great Falls, Mont. (59401*)	24,121	29,928	55,244	60,091	321	8.8
Green Bay, Wis. (54305*)	31,017	46,235	62,888	87,809	191	39.6
Greensboro, N.C. (27420*)	19,861	59,319	119,574	144,076	96	20.5
Greenville, S.C. (29602*)	23,127	34,734	66,188	61,436	315	—7.2
Hamilton, Ohio (45012*)	39,675	50,592	72,354	67,865	281	—6.2
Hammond, Ind. (46320*)	36,004	70,184	111,698	107,983	143	—3.3
Hampton, Va. (23369*)	6,138	5,898	89,258	120,779	122	35.3
Harrisburg, Pa. (17105*)	75,917	83,893	79,697	68,061	277	—14.6
Hartford, Conn. (06101*)	138,036	166,267	162,178	158,017	87	—2.6
Haverhill, Mass. (01830)	53,884	46,752	46,346	46,120	425	—0.5
Hawthorne, Calif. (90250)	....	8,263	33,035	53,304	369	61.4
Hayward, Calif. (94544*)	3,487	6,736	72,700	93,058	169	28.0
Hialeah, Fla. (33010*)	....	3,958	66,972	102,452	151	52.9
High Point, N.C. (27260*)	14,302	38,495	62,063	63,259	304	4.2
Hoboken, N.J. (07030)	68,166	50,115	48,441	45,380	431	—6.3
Hollywood, Fla. (33022*)	....	6,239	35,237	106,873	144	203.3
Holyoke, Mass. (01040)	60,203	53,750	52,689	50,112	390	—4.9
Honolulu, Hawaii (96819*)	83,327	179,326	294,194	324,871	44	10.4
Houston, Tex. (77052*)	138,276	384,514	938,219	1,233,535	6	31.5
Huntington, W. Va. (25701*)	50,177	78,836	83,627	74,315	239	—11.1
Huntington Beach, Calif. (92647*)	1,687	3,738	11,492	115,960	126	909.0
Huntsville, Ala. (35804*)	8,018	13,050	72,365	139,282	102	90.9
Independence, Mo. (64050*)	11,686	16,066	62,328	111,630	132	79.2
Indianapolis, Ind. (46204*)	314,194	386,972	476,258	742,925	11	55.9
Inglewood, Calif. (90306*)	3,286	30,114	63,390	89,985	179	42.0
Iowa City, Iowa (52240)	11,267	17,182	33,443	46,850	416	40.1
Irving, Tex. (75061*)	357	1,089	45,985	98,961	159	115.2
Jackson, Mich. (49201*)	48,374	49,656	50,720	45,484	430	—10.3
Jackson, Miss. (39205*)	22,817	62,107	144,422	162,380	86	12.4
Jacksonville, Fla. (32201*)	91,558	173,065	201,030	528,865	23	163.1
Janesville, Wis. (53545)	18,293	22,992	35,164	46,426	420	32.0
Jersey City, N.J. (07303*)	298,103	301,173	276,101	260,350	55	—5.7
Joliet, Ill. (60431*)	38,442	42,365	66,780	78,887	221	18.0
Kalamazoo, Mich. (49003*)	48,487	54,097	82,089	85,555	202	4.2
Kansas City, Kan. (66110*)	101,177	121,458	121,901	178,561	73	46.4
Kansas City, Mo. (64108*)	324,410	399,178	475,539	507,330	26	6.7
Kenosha, Wis. (53140)	40,472	48,765	67,899	78,805	222	16.1
Kettering, Ohio (45429)	....	....	54,462	71,864	252	32.0
Knoxville, Tenn. (37901*)	77,818	111,580	111,827	174,587	77	56.1
La Crosse, Wis. (54601)	30,421	42,707	47,575	51,153	381	7.5
Lafayette, La. (70501)	7,855	19,210	40,400	68,908	273	70.6
Lake Charles, La. (70601)	13,088	21,207	63,392	77,998	228	23.0
Lakewood, Calif. (90714*)	....	....	67,126	82,973	208	23.6
Lakewood, Colo. (80215)	....	....	19,338	92,743	170	379.8
Lakewood, Ohio (44107)	41,732	69,160	66,154	70,173	264	6.1
Lancaster, Pa. (17604*)	53,150	61,345	61,055	57,690	335	—5.5
Lansing, Mich. (48924*)	57,327	78,753	107,807	131,403	113	21.8
Laredo, Tex. (78040)	22,710	39,274	60,678	69,024	272	13.8
Las Vegas, Nev. (89114*)	2,304	8,422	64,405	125,787	118	95.3
Lawrence, Kan. (66044)	12,456	13,390	32,858	45,698	427	39.1
Lawrence, Mass. (01842*)	94,270	84,323	70,933	66,915	286	—5.7
Lawton, Okla. (73501*)	8,930	18,055	61,697	74,470	238	20.7
Lexington, Ky. (40507*)	41,534	49,304	62,810	108,137	141	72.2
Lima, Ohio (45801*)	41,326	44,711	51,037	53,734	364	5.3
Lincoln, Neb. (68501*)	54,948	81,984	128,521	149,518	92	16.3
Lincoln Park, Mich. (48146)	....	15,236	53,933	52,984	372	—1.8

City and Major Zip Code	1920 Census	1940 Census	1960 Census	1970 Census	1970 Rank	% Change 1960-70
Little Rock, Ark. (72201*)	65,142	88,039	107,813	132,483	112	22.9
Livonia, Mich. (48150*)	....	8,728	66,702	110,109	136	65.1
Long Beach, Calif. (90801*)	55,593	164,271	344,168	358,879	40	4.3
Longview, Tex. (75601)	5,713	13,758	40,050	45,547	429	13.7
Lorain, Ohio (44052*)	37,295	44,125	68,932	78,185	226	13.4
Los Angeles, Calif. (90053*)	576,673	1,504,277	2,479,015	2,811,801	3	13.4
Louisville, Ky. (40202*)	234,891	319,077	390,639	361,706	38	—7.4
Lowell, Mass. (01853*)	112,759	101,389	92,107	94,239	168	2.3
Lubbock, Tex. (79408*)	4,051	31,853	128,691	149,101	93	15.9
Lynchburg, Va. (24505*)	30,070	44,541	54,790	54,083	361	—1.3
Lynn, Mass. (01901*)	99,148	98,123	94,478	90,294	178	—4.4
Macon, Ga. (31201)	52,995	57,865	69,764	122,423	120	75.5
Madison, Wis. (53703)	38,378	67,447	126,706	171,809	80	35.6
Malden, Mass. (02148)	49,103	58,010	57,676	56,127	350	—2.7
Manchester, N.H. (03101*)	78,384	77,685	88,282	87,754	192	—0.6
Mansfield, Ohio (44901*)	27,824	37,154	47,325	55,047	358	16.3
Medford, Mass. (02155)	39,038	63,083	64,971	64,397	296	—0.9
Memphis, Tenn. (38101*)	162,351	292,942	497,524	623,530	17	25.3
Meriden, Conn. (06450)	29,867	39,494	51,850	55,959	351	7.9
Meridian, Miss. (39301)	23,399	35,481	49,374	45,083	434	—8.7
Mesa, Ariz. (85201*)	3,036	7,222	33,772	62,853	307	86.1
Mesquite, Tex. (75149)	674	1,045	27,526	55,131	356	100.3
Metairie, La. (U) (70001*)	....	....	....	136,477	106	....
Miami, Fla. (33101*)	29,571	172,172	291,688	334,859	42	14.8
Miami Beach, Fla. (33139)	644	28,012	63,145	87,072	196	37.9
Middletown, Ohio (45042)	23,594	31,220	42,115	48,767	398	15.8
Midland, Tex. (79701)	1,795	9,352	62,625	59,463	327	—5.0
Midwest City, Okla. (73110)	....	....	36,058	48,212	402	33.7
Milford, Conn. (06460)	....	....	41,662	50,858	383	22.1
Milwaukee, Wis. (53201*)	457,147	587,472	741,324	717,372	12	—3.2
Minneapolis, Minn. (55401*)	380,582	492,370	482,872	434,400	32	—10.0
Mobile, Ala. (36601*)	60,777	78,720	194,856	190,026	68	—2.5
Modesto, Calif. (95350*)	9,241	16,379	36,585	61,712	312	68.7
Moline, Ill. (61265)	30,734	34,608	42,705	46,237	423	8.3
Monroe, La. (71201)	12,675	28,309	52,219	56,374	347	8.0
Monterey Park, Calif. (91754)	4,108	8,531	37,821	49,166	395	30.0
Montgomery, Ala. (36104*)	43,464	78,084	134,393	140,102	99	4.2
Mount Vernon, N.Y. (10551*)	42,726	67,632	76,010	72,778	244	—4.3
Mountain View, Calif. (94042*)	1,888	3,946	30,889	54,206	359	75.5
Muncie, Ind. (47302*)	36,524	49,720	68,603	69,082	271	0.7
Nashua, N.H. (03060)	23,379	32,927	39,096	55,820	352	42.8
Nashville-Davidson, Tenn. (37202*)	118,342	167,402	170,874	447,877	31	162.1
New Bedford, Mass. (02741*)	121,217	110,341	102,477	101,777	152	—0.7
New Britain, Conn. (06050*)	59,316	68,685	82,201	83,441	207	1.5
New Haven, Conn. (06510*)	162,537	160,605	152,048	137,707	105	—9.4
New Orleans, La. (70140*)	387,219	494,537	627,525	593,471	19	—5.4
New Rochelle, N.Y. (10802*)	36,213	58,408	76,812	75,385	235	—1.9
New York, N.Y.	5,620,048	7,454,995	7,781,984	7,895,563	1	1.1
Bronx borough (10451*)	732,016	1,394,711	1,424,815	1,471,701	....	3.3
Brooklyn borough (11201*)	2,018,356	2,698,285	2,627,319	2,602,012	....	—1.0
Manhattan borough (10001*)	2,284,103	1,889,924	1,698,281	1,539,233	....	—10.2
Queens borough[1]	469,042	1,297,634	1,809,578	1,987,174	....	9.1
Staten Island borough (10314)	116,531	174,441	221,991	295,443	....	33.1
Newark, N.J. (07101)*	414,524	429,760	405,220	381,930	35	—5.7
Newport Beach, Calif. (92660*)	894	4,438	26,564	49,422	394	86.0
Newport News, Va. (23607*)	35,596	37,067	113,662	138,177	104	21.6
Newton, Mass. (02158)	46,054	69,873	92,384	91,263	176	—1.2
Niagara Falls, N.Y. (14302*)	50,760	78,029	102,394	85,615	201	—16.4
Norfolk, Va. (23501*)	115,777	144,332	304,869	307,951	47	1.0
Norman, Okla. (73069)	5,004	11,429	33,412	52,117	378	56.0
North Chicago, Ill. (60064)	5,839	8,465	22,938	47,275	411	106.1
North Little Rock, Ark. (72114*)	14,048	21,137	58,032	60,040	322	3.5
Norwalk, Calif. (90650)	....	....	88,739	91,827	173	3.5
Norwalk, Conn. (06856*)	27,743	39,849	67,775	79,113	217	16.7
Oak Park, Ill. (60303*)	39,858	66,015	61,093	62,511	309	2.3
Oakland, Calif. (94617*)	216,261	302,163	367,548	361,561	39	—1.6
Odessa, Tex. (79760*)	....	9,573	80,338	78,380	225	—2.4
Ogden, Utah (84401*)	32,804	43,688	70,197	69,478	269	—1.0
Oklahoma City, Okla. (73125*)	91,295	204,424	324,253	368,164	37	13.5
Omaha, Neb. (68108*)	191,601	223,844	301,598	354,389	41	17.5
Ontario, Calif. (91761*)	7,280	14,197	46,617	64,118	298	37.5

City and Major Zip Code	1920 Census	1940 Census	1960 Census	1970 Census	1970 Rank	% Change 1960-70
Orange, Calif. (92667*)	4,884	7,901	26,444	77,365	231	192.6
Orlando, Fla. (32802*)	9,282	36,736	88,135	99,006	158	12.3
Oshkosh, Wis. (54901)	33,162	39,089	45,110	53,221	370	18.0
Overland Park, Kan. (66204)	....	....	21,110	79,034	219	274.4
Owensboro, Ky. (42301)	17,424	30,245	42,471	50,329	387	18.5
Oxnard, Calif. (93030)	4,417	8,519	40,265	71,225	258	76.9
Palo Alto, Calif. (94302*)	5,900	16,774	52,287	56,181	349	7.4
Parma, Ohio (44129)	....	16,365	82,845	100,216	156	21.0
Pasadena, Calif. (91109*)	45,354	81,864	116,407	112,951	130	—2.9
Pasadena, Tex. (77501*)	....	3,436	58,737	89,277	183	52.0
Passaic, N.J. (07055*)	63,841	61,394	53,963	55,124	357	2.2
Paterson, N.J. (07510*)	135,875	139,656	143,663	144,824	95	0.8
Pawtucket, R.I. (02860*)	64,248	75,797	81,001	76,984	232	—5.0
Peabody, Mass. (01960)	19,552	21,711	32,202	48,080	406	49.3
Pensacola, Fla. (32502*)	31,035	37,449	56,752	59,507	326	4.9
Peoria, Ill. (61601*)	76,121	105,087	103,162	126,963	117	23.1
Philadelphia, Pa. (19104*)	1,823,779	1,931,334	2,002,512	1,949,996	4	—2.6
Phoenix, Ariz. (85026*)	29,053	65,414	439,170	587,213	20	33.7
Pico Rivera, Calif. (90660)	....	....	49,150	54,170	360	10.2
Pine Bluff, Ark. (71601)	19,280	21,290	44,037	57,389	338	30.3
Pittsburgh, Pa. (15230*)	588,343	671,659	604,332	520,089	24	—13.9
Pittsfield, Mass. (01201)	41,763	49,684	57,879	57,020	343	—1.5
Plainfield, N.J. (07061*)	27,700	37,469	45,330	46,862	415	3.4
Pomona, Calif. (91766*)	13,505	23,539	67,157	87,384	195	30.1
Pontiac, Mich. (48056*)	34,273	66,626	82,233	85,279	204	3.7
Port Arthur, Tex. (77640)	22,251	46,140	66,676	57,371	340	—14.0
Portland, Me. (04101*)	69,272	73,643	72,566	65,116	293	—10.3
Portland, Ore. (97208*)	258,288	305,394	372,676	379,967	36	1.9
Portsmouth, Va. (23705*)	54,387	50,745	114,773	110,963	133	—3.3
Providence, R.I. (02940*)	237,595	253,504	207,498	179,116	72	—13.6
Provo, Utah (84601)	10,303	18,071	36,047	53,131	371	47.4
Pueblo, Colo. (81002*)	43,050	52,162	91,181	97,774	160	7.2
Quincy, Ill. (62301*)	35,978	40,469	43,793	45,288	433	3.4
Quincy, Mass. (02169)	47,876	75,810	87,409	87,966	190	0.6
Racine, Wis. (53401*)	58,593	67,195	89,144	95,162	167	6.8
Raleigh, N.C. (27611*)	24,418	46,897	93,931	123,793	119	31.7
Reading, Pa. (19603*)	107,784	110,568	98,177	87,643	194	—10.7
Redondo Beach, Calif. (90277*)	4,913	13,092	46,986	57,425	337	22.2
Redwood City, Calif. (94063*)	4,020	12,453	46,290	55,686	354	20.3
Reno, Nev. (89501*)	12,016	21,317	51,470	72,863	242	41.6
Richardson, Tex. (75080)	....	720	16,810	48,582	399	189.0
Richfield, Minn. (55423)	2,411	6,750	42,523	47,231	412	11.1
Richmond, Calif. (94802*)	16,843	23,642	71,854	79,043	218	10.0
Richmond, Va. (23232*)	171,667	193,042	219,958	249,431	58	13.4
Riverside, Calif. (92502*)	19,341	34,696	84,332	140,089	100	66.1
Roanoke, Va. (24001*)	50,842	69,287	97,110	92,115	171	—5.1
Rochester, Minn. (55901*)	13,722	26,312	40,663	53,766	363	32.2
Rochester, N.Y. (14603*)	295,750	324,975	318,611	295,011	49	—7.4
Rock Island, Ill. (61201)	35,177	42,775	51,863	50,166	388	—3.3
Rockford, Ill. (61125*)	65,651	84,637	126,706	147,370	94	16.3
Rome, N.Y. (13440)	26,341	34,214	51,646	50,148	389	—2.9
Roseville, Mich. (48066)	....	9,023	50,195	60,529	319	20.6
Royal Oak, Mich. (48067*)	6,007	25,087	80,612	86,238	198	7.0
Sacramento, Calif. (95814*)	65,908	105,958	191,667	257,105	56	34.1
Saginaw, Mich. (48605*)	61,903	82,794	98,265	91,849	172	—6.5
St. Clair Shores, Mich. (48083*)	....	10,405	-76,657	88,093	189	14.9
St. Joseph, Mo. (64501*)	77,939	75,711	79,673	72,691	246	—8.8
St. Louis, Mo. (63166*)	772,897	816,048	750,026	622,236	18	—17.0
St. Louis Park, Minn. (55426)	2,281	7,737	43,310	48,922	396	13.0
St. Paul, Minn. (55101*)	234,698	287,736	313,411	309,866	46	—1.1
St. Petersburg, Fla. (33733*)	14,237	60,812	181,298	216,159	61	19.3
Salem, Ore. (97301*)	17,679	30,908	49,142	68,856	274	40.1
Salinas, Calif. (93901)	4,308	11,586	28,957	58,896	328	103.4
Salt Lake City, Utah (84101*)	118,110	149,934	189,454	175,885	76	—7.2
San Angelo, Tex. (76901)	10,050	25,802	58,815	63,884	300	8.6
San Antonio, Tex. (78291*)	161,379	253,854	587,718	707,503	14	20.3
San Bernardino, Calif. (92403*)	18,721	43,646	91,922	106,869	145	16.2
San Diego, Calif. (92101*)	74,361	203,341	573,224	697,027	15	21.6
San Francisco, Calif. (94101*)	506,676	634,536	740,316	715,674	13	—3.3
San Jose, Calif. (95113*)	39,642	68,457	204,196	459,913	29	124.7
San Leandro, Calif. (94577*)	5,703	14,601	65,962	68,698	275	4.1

City and Major Zip Code	1920 Census	1940 Census	1960 Census	1970 Census	1970 Rank	% Change 1960-70
San Mateo, Calif. (94402*)	5,979	19,403	69,870	78,991	220	13.1
Santa Ana, Calif. (92711*)	15,485	31,921	100,350	155,710	89	55.1
Santa Barbara, Calif. (93102*)	19,441	34,958	58,768	70,215	263	19.5
Santa Clara, Calif. (95050*)	5,220	6,650	58,880	87,717	193	49.0
Santa Monica, Calif. (90406*)	15,252	53,500	83,249	88,289	188	6.1
Santa Rosa, Calif. (95402*)	8,758	12,605	31,027	50,006	391	61.2
Savannah, Ga. (31402*)	83,252	95,996	149,245	118,349	124	—20.7
Schenectady, N.Y. (12305*)	88,723	87,549	81,682	77,958	229	—4.6
Scottsdale, Ariz. (85251*)	....	....	10,026	67,823	282	576.5
Scranton, Pa. (18501*)	137,783	140,404	111,443	103,564	149	—7.1
Seattle, Wash. (98101*)	315,312	368,302	557,087	530,831	22	—4.7
Sheboygan, Wis. (53081)	30,955	40,638	45,747	48,484	401	6.0
Shreveport, La. (71101*)	43,874	98,167	164,372	182,064	70	10.8
Silver Spring, Md. (U) (20907*)	....	....	66,348	77,496	230	16.8
Simi Valley, Calif. (93065)	....	....	....	59,832	325	...
Sioux City, Iowa (51101*)	71,227	82,364	89,159	85,925	200	—3.6
Sioux Falls, S.D. (57101*)	25,202	40,832	65,466	72,488	251	10.7
Skokie, Ill. (60076)	763	7,172	59,364	68,627	276	15.6
Somerville, Mass. (02143)	93,091	102,177	94,697	88,779	186	—6.2
South Bend, Ind. (46624*)	70,983	101,268	132,445	127,328	115	—3.8
South Gate, Calif. (90280)	....	26,945	53,831	56,909	344	5.7
South San Francisco, Calif. (94080)	4,411	6,629	39,418	46,646	419	18.3
Southfield, Mich. (48075)	....	....	31,501	69,285	270	119.9
Spokane, Wash. (99210*)	104,437	122,001	181,608	170,516	81	—6.1
Springfield, Ill. (62708*)	59,183	75,503	83,271	91,753	174	10.2
Springfield, Mass. (01101*)	129,614	149,554	174,463	163,905	85	—6.1
Springfield, Mo. (65801*)	39,631	61,238	95,865	120,096	123	25.3
Springfield, Ohio (45501*)	60,840	70,662	82,723	81,941	212	—1.0
Stamford, Conn. (06904*)	35,096	47,938	92,713	108,798	140	17.3
Sterling Heights, Mich. (48077*)	....	....	....	61,365	316	...
Stockton, Calif. (95202*)	40,296	54,714	86,321	109,963	138	27.4
Sunnyvale, Calif. (94088*)	1,675	4,373	52,898	95,976	164	81.4
Syracuse, N.Y. (13201*)	171,717	205,967	216,038	197,297	66	—8.7
Tacoma, Wash. (98402*)	96,965	109,408	147,979	154,407	91	4.3
Tallahassee, Fla. (32301*)	5,637	16,240	48,174	72,586	250	50.1
Tampa, Fla. (33602*)	51,608	108,391	274,970	277,714	50	1.0
Taylor, Mich. (48180)	....	....	....	70,020	265	...
Tempe, Ariz. (85282*)	1,963	2,906	24,897	63,550	302	155.3
Terre Haute, Ind. (47808*)	66,083	62,693	72,500	70,335	262	—3.1
Toledo, Ohio (43601*)	243,164	282,349	318,003	383,062	34	20.4
Topeka, Kan. (66601*)	50,022	67,833	119,484	132,952	110	11.2
Torrance, Calif. (90510*)	....	9,950	100,991	134,968	108	33.3
Towson, Md. (U) (21204*)	....	....	19,090	77,999	227	307.6
Trenton, N.J. (08608*)	119,289	124,697	114,167	104,786	147	—8.2
Troy, N.Y. (12180*)	71,996	70,304	67,492	62,918	306	—6.8
Tucson, Ariz. (85702*)	20,292	35,752	212,892	265,799	54	24.8
Tulsa, Okla. (74101*)	72,075	142,157	261,685	330,350	43	26.2
Tuscaloosa, Ala. (35401)	11,996	27,493	63,370	65,773	291	3.8
Tyler, Tex. (75701)	12,085	28,279	51,230	57,770	334	12.8
Union City, N.J. (07087)	20,651	56,173	52,180	58,537	332	12.2
University City, Mo. (63130)	6,792	33,023	51,249	46,309	422	—9.6
Utica, N.Y. (13503*)	94,156	100,518	100,410	91,611	175	—8.8
Vallejo, Calif. (94590*)	21,107	20,072	60,877	71,710	253	17.8
Ventura, Calif. (93001*)	....	....	29,114	57,964	333	99.0
Vineland, N.J. (08360)	6,432	9,914	37,685	47,399	409	25.8
Virginia Beach, Va. (23458*)	846	2,600	8,091	172,106	79	1,000+
Waco, Tex. (76703*)	38,500	55,982	97,808	95,326	166	—2.5
Waltham, Mass. (02154)	30,915	40,020	55,413	61,582	313	11.1
Warren, Mich. (48089*)	....	582	89,246	179,260	71	100.9
Warren, Ohio (44482*)	27,500	42,837	59,648	63,494	303	6.4
Warwick, R.I. (02887*)	13,481	28,757	68,504	83,694	206	22.2
Washington, D.C. (20013*)	437,571	663,091	763,956	756,668	9	—1.0
Waterbury, Conn. (06720*)	91,715	99,314	107,130	108,033	142	0.8
Waterloo, Iowa (50701*)	36,230	51,743	71,755	75,533	233	5.3
Waukegan, Ill. (60085*)	19,226	34,241	55,719	65,269	292	17.1
Wauwatosa, Wis. (53213)	5,818	27,769	56,923	58,676	331	3.1
West Allis, Wis. (53214)	13,745	36,364	68,157	71,649	254	5.1
West Covina, Calif. (91793*)	....	1,072	50,645	68,034	278	34.3
West Hartford, Conn. (T) (06107)	8,854	33,776	62,382	68,031	279	9.1
West Haven, Conn. (06516)	....	....	....	52,851	373	...
West Palm Beach, Fla. (33401*)	8,659	33,693	56,208	57,375	339	2.1

City and Major Zip Code	1920 Census	1940 Census	1960 Census	1970 Census	1970 Rank	% Change 1960-70
Westland, Mich. (48185)	....	....	....	86,749	197	...
Westminster, Calif. (92683)	....	....	25,750	59,874	323	132.5
Wheaton, Md. (U) (20902)	....	....	54,635	66,247	289	21.3
Wheeling, W. Va. (26003)	56,208	61,099	53,400	48,188	404	—9.8
White Plains, N.Y. (10602*)	21,031	40,327	50,485	50,346	385	—0.3
Whittier, Calif. (90605*)	7,995	16,115	33,663	72,863	243	116.4
Wichita, Kan. (67202*)	72,217	114,966	254,698	276,554	51	8.6
Wichita Falls, Tex. (76307*)	40,079	45,112	101,724	96,265	163	—5.3
Wilkes-Barre, Pa. (18703)*	73,833	86,236	63,551	58,856	329	—7.4
Wilmington, N.C. (28401*)	33,372	33,407	44,013	46,169	424	4.9
Wilmington, Del. (19899*)	110,168	112,504	95,827	80,386	214	—16.1
Winston-Salem, N.C. (27102*)	48,395	79,815	111,135	133,683	109	21.2
Woonsocket, R.I. (02895)	43,496	49,303	47,080	46,820	417	—0.6
Worcester, Mass. (01613*)	179,754	193,694	186,587	176,572	75	—5.4
Wyoming, Mich. (49509)	....	....	45,829	56,560	345	23.4
Yakima, Wash. (98901*)	18,539	27,221	43,284	45,588	428	5.3
Yonkers, N.Y. (10701*)	100,176	142,598	190,634	204,297	63	7.2
York, Pa. (17405*)	47,512	56,712	54,504	50,335	386	—7.6
Youngstown, Ohio (44501*)	132,358	167,720	166,689	140.909	98	—15.5

[1] Queens has four major Zip codes: 11690*–Far Rockaway; 11352*–Flushing; 11431*–Jamaica; 11101*–Long Island City.

Indian Population Residing on Largest Federal Reservations, 1973[1]

Source: Field estimates, Bureau of Indian Affairs.

Navajo (Ariz., N.M., Utah)	136,686
Cherokee (Okla.)[2]	21,414
Creek (Okla.)[2]	15,480
Pine Ridge (S.D.)	11,478
Choctaw (Okla.)[2]	11,066
Gila River (Ariz.)	8,331
Rosebud (S.D.)	7,538
Yakima (Wash.)	6,300
Turtle Mountain (N.D.)	7,385
Papago (Ariz.)	7,703
Fort Apache (Ariz.)	7,200
Hopi (Ariz.)	6,567
Blackfeet (Mont.)	6,216
Northern Pueblos (N.M.)	6,202
Fort Peck (Mont.)	6,050
Zuni (N.M.)	5,428
Chickasaw (Okla.)[2]	4,946
Cherokee (N.C.)	4,940

[1] March. [2] Indians residing on trust land within boundaries of former reservation areas in Oklahoma. NOTE: The Bureau of Indian Affairs lists 542,900 Indians residing on or near Federal reservations. Figures are latest available.

Territorial Expansion of U. S.

Source: Bureau of the Census.

Accession	Date	Area[1]
United States	....	3,615,122
Territory in 1790	....	888,685
Louisiana Purchase	1803	827,192
Florida	1819	58,560
By treaty with Spain	1819	13,443
Texas	1845	390,143
Oregon	1846	285,580
Mexican Cession	1848	529,017
Gadsden Purchase	1853	29,640
Alaska	1867	586,412
Hawaii	1898	6,450
Other territory	....	12,944
Philippines	1898	115,600[2]
Puerto Rico	1899	3,435
Guam	1899	212
American Samoa	1900	76
Canal Zone	1904	553
Corn Islands[3]	1914	4
Virgin Islands of U.S.	1917	133
Trust Territory of Pacific Islands	1947	8,489
All other	....	42
Total, 1970	....	3,628,066

[1] Total land and water area in square miles. [2] Became independent in 1946; area not included in total. [3] Leased from Nicaragua for 99 years in 1914, but returned April 25, 1971; area included in total.

Total U. S. Population

Source: Bureau of the Census.

Area	1940	1960	1970
50 states of U.S.	......	179,323,175	203,235,298
48 coterminous	131,669,275	178,464,236	202,163,212
Alaska	72,524	226,167	302,173
Hawaii	422,770	632,772	769,913
American Samoa	12,908	20,051	27,159
Canal Zone	51,827	42,122	44,198
Canton Island	40	320	......
Corn Islands	1,523	1,872	(4)
Guam	22,290	67,044	84,996
Johnston Island	69	156	1,007
Midway	437	2,356	2,220
Philippines	16,356,000	......	......
Puerto Rico	1,869,255	2,349,544	2,712,033
Swan Islands	(1)	28	22
Trust Ter. of Pac. Is.	......	70,724	90,940
Virgin Is. of U.S.	24,889	32,099	62,468
Wake Island	(1)	1,097	1,647
Population abroad	118,933	1,374,421	1,737,836
Armed forces	(2)	609,720	1,057,776
Other[3]	14	......	......
Total	150,622,754	183,285,009	207,999,824

[1] Not enumerated. [2] Not available. [3] Includes Baker Island (3), Enderbury Island (4), Howland Island (4), and Jarvis Island (3); uninhabited in 1950 and 1960. [4] Returned to Nicaragua April 25, 1971.

Distribution of U. S. Population According to Size of Place, 1790–1970 Censuses

Source: Bureau of the Census.

| Census year | Total population | Total urban | Population distribution (Total for year = 100%) | | | | Number of places of 2,500 or more | | |
| | | | Places of 2,500 or more | | | Total rural | | | |
			1,000,000 or more	100,000 to 1,000,000	Under 100,000		1,000,000 or more	100,000 to 1,000,000	Under 100,000
1790........	3,929,214	5.1	—	—	5.1	94.9	—	—	24
1800........	5,308,483	6.1	—	—	6.1	93.9	—	—	33
1810........	7,239,881	7.3	—	—	7.3	92.7	—	—	46
1820........	9,638,453	7.2	—	1.3	5.9	92.8	—	1	60
1830........	12,866,020	8.8	—	1.6	7.2	91.2	—	1	89
1840........	17,069,453	10.8	—	3.0	7.8	89.2	—	3	128
1850........	23,191,876	15.3	—	5.1	10.2	84.7	—	6	230
1860........	31,443,321	19.8	—	8.4	11.4	80.2	—	9	383
1870........	39,818,449	25.7	—	10.7	15.0	74.3	—	14	649
1880........	50,155,783	28.2	2.4	10.0	15.8	71.8	1	19	919
1890........	62,947,714	35.1	5.8	9.6	19.7	64.9	3	25	1,320
1900........	75,994,575	39.7	8.5	10.2	21.0	60.3	3	35	1,699
1910........	91,972,266	45.7	9.2	12.9	23.6	54.3	3	47	2,212
1920........	105,710,620	51.2	9.6	16.3	25.3	48.8	3	65	2,654
1930........	122,775,046	56.2	12.3	17.3	26.6	43.8	5	88	3,072
1940........	131,669,275	56.5	12.1	16.8	27.6	43.5	5	87	3,372
1950[1]......	150,697,361	59.0	11.5	18.0	29.5	41.0	5	102	3,916
1950[2]......	150,697,361	64.0	11.5	17.9	34.6	36.0	5	101	4,635
1960[2,3]....	179,323,175	69.9	9.8	18.7	41.4	30.1	5	127	5,909
1970[2,3]....	203,235,298	73.5	9.2	18.5	45.8	26.5	6	150	6,279

[1] Old urban definition.   [2] New urban definition.   [3] Includes Alaska and Hawaii.

U.S. Population by Age, Sex, and Race, 1975

Source: Bureau of the Census.

| Age | White | | Black | | All persons[1] | |
	Male	Female	Male	Female	Male	Female
Under 5 years	6,729,000	6,413,000	1,209,000	1,186,000	8,119,000	7,777,000
Under 1 year...........	1,310,000	1,248,000	229,000	223,000	1,575,000	1,506,000
1 to 4 years	5,418,000	5,165,000	980,000	962,000	6,544,000	6,271,000
5 to 9 years	7,403,000	7,076,000	1,263,000	1,256,000	8,836,000	8,499,000
10 to 14 years	8,783,000	8,401,000	1,459,000	1,443,000	10,410,000	10,008,000
15 to 19 years	9,081,000	8,767,000	1,405,000	1,416,000	10,674,000	10,354,000
20 to 24 years	8,379,000	8,165,000	1,132,000	1,214,000	9,683,000	9,559,000
25 to 29 years	7,446,000	7,361,000	839,000	958,000	8,436,000	8,505,000
30 to 34 years	6,095,000	6,114,000	683,000	806,000	6,919,000	7,075,000
35 to 39 years	5,015,000	5,151,000	571,000	692,000	5,677,000	5,953,000
40 to 44 years	4,839,000	4,958,000	547,000	651,000	5,476,000	5,718,000
45 to 49 years	5,102,000	5,339,000	544,000	624,000	5,728,000	6,062,000
50 to 54 years	5,181,000	5,551,000	510,000	588,000	5,763,000	6,218,000
55 to 59 years	4,553,000	4,969,000	419,000	489,000	5,024,000	5,512,000
60 to 64 years	3,908,000	4,439,000	368,000	445,000	4,321,000	4,923,000
65 to 69 years	3,220,000	4,050,000	329,000	436,000	3,584,000	4,515,000
70 to 74 years	2,224,000	3,072,000	187,000	233,000	2,443,000	3,332,000
75 to 79 years	1,434,000	2,248,000	116,000	157,000	1,572,000	2,429,000
80 to 84 years	874,000	1,558,000	76,000	118,000	960,000	1,688,000
85 years and over	548,000	1,155,000	53,000	99,000	613,000	1,265,000
All ages	90,813,000	94,788,000	11,722,000	12,813,000	104,239,000	109,393,000
14 years and over	69,752,000	74,673,000	8,093,000	9,227,000	79,063,000	85,216,000
18 years and over	62,436,000	67,655,000	6,917,000	8,064,000	70,434,000	76,902,000
21 years and over	57,010,000	62,387,000	6,111,000	7,240,000	64,092,000	70,706,000
65 years and over	8,299,000	12,082,000	760,000	1,043,000	9,172,000	13,228,000
Median age, years	28.4	31.0	22.3	24.6	27.6	30.0

[1] Includes other races. NOTE: Figures represent resident population of the 50 states and armed forces overseas.

United States Population Distribution by Age, Race, Nativity, and Sex, 1860-1975

Sources: Mortimer Spiegelman, *Introduction to Demography;* and Bureau of the Census.

Year	Total	Age					Race and nativity			
		Under 5	5–19	20–44	45–64	65 and over	White			Nonwhite
							Total	Native born	Foreign born	
				Per cent distribution						
1860[1]	100.0	15.4	35.8	35.7	10.4	2.7	85.6	72.6	13.0	14.4
1870[1]	100.0	14.3	35.4	35.4	11.9	3.0	87.1	72.9	14.2	12.9
1880[1]	100.0	13.8	34.3	35.9	12.6	3.4	86.5	73.4	13.1	13.5
1890[2]	100.0	12.2	33.9	36.9	13.1	3.9	87.5	73.0	14.5	12.5
1900	100.0	12.1	32.3	37.8	13.7	4.1	87.9	74.5	13.4	12.1
1910	100.0	11.6	30.4	39.1	14.6	4.3	88.9	74.4	14.5	11.1
1920	100.0	11.0	29.8	38.4	16.1	4.7	89.7	76.7	13.0	10.3
1930	100.0	9.3	29.5	38.3	17.5	5.4	89.8	78.4	11.4	10.2
1940	100.0	8.0	26.4	38.9	19.8	6.9	89.8	81.1	8.7	10.2
1950[3]	100.0	10.7	23.2	37.7	20.3	8.1	89.5	82.8	6.7	10.5
1960[3]	100.0	11.3	27.1	32.4	20.0	9.2	88.6	83.4	5.2	11.4
1970[3]	100.0	8.4	29.4	31.7	20.6	9.9	87.7	83.4	4.3	12.3
1975[3]	100.0	7.4	27.5	34.2	20.4	10.5	86.9	(4)	(4)	13.1
				Males per 100 females						
1860[1]	104.7	102.4	101.2	107.9	111.5	98.3	105.3	103.7	115.1	101.2
1870[1]	102.2	102.9	101.2	99.2	114.5	100.5	102.8	100.6	115.3	98.4
1880[1]	103.6	103.0	101.3	104.0	110.2	101.4	104.0	102.1	115.9	100.7
1890[2]	105.0	103.6	101.4	107.3	108.3	104.2	105.4	102.9	118.7	102.2
1900	104.4	102.1	100.9	105.8	110.7	102.0	104.9	102.8	117.4	101.0
1910	106.0	102.5	101.3	108.1	114.4	101.1	106.6	102.7	129.2	101.3
1920	104.0	102.5	100.8	102.8	115.2	101.3	104.4	101.7	121.7	100.9
1930	102.5	103.0	101.4	100.5	109.1	100.5	102.9	101.1	115.8	99.1
1940	100.7	103.2	102.0	98.1	105.2	95.5	101.2	100.1	111.1	96.7
1950[3]	99.0	103.9	102.9	97.0	100.2	89.6	99.4	99.0	103.9	96.2
1960[3]	97.1	103.4	103.0	96.9	95.8	82.9	97.9	97.5	94.2	95.1
1970[3]	94.8	104.0	103.3	95.1	91.4	72.2	95.7	95.9	83.8	(4)
1975[3]	95.3	104.4	103.7	98.3	91.7	69.3	95.8	(4)	(4)	91.9

[1] Excludes Indians in Indian Territory and on Indian reservations. [2] The age figures exclude all persons residing on Indian reservations, whether white or nonwhite; these persons are included in the race and nativity distributions. [3] Data by age and race include, and data by nativity exclude, armed forces overseas and other persons abroad. [4] Not available. NOTE: For 1860, the data in the census reports at ages 40–49 and 60–69 are published in 10-year age groupings; these were subdivided into 5-year age groupings by the author.

Distribution of U. S. Population by Race, 1850-1970

Source: Bureau of the Census.

Year[1]	White	Black	Indian	Japanese	Chinese	All other	Total nonwhite
1850	19,553,068	3,638,808	....	....	....	......	3,638,808
1860	26,922,537	4,441,830	44,021	....	34,933	......	4,520,784
1870	33,589,377	4,880,009	25,731	55	63,199	......	4,968,994
1880	43,402,970	6,580,793	66,407	148	105,465	......	6,752,813
1890	55,101,258	7,488,676	248,253	2,039	107,488	......	7,846,456
1900	66,809,196	8,833,994	237,196	24,326	89,863	......	9,185,379
1910	81,731,957	9,827,763	265,683	72,157	71,531	3,175	10,240,309
1920	94,820,915	10,463,131	244,437	111,010	61,639	9,488	10,889,705
1930	110,286,740	11,891,143	332,397	138,834	74,954	50,978	12,488,306
1940	118,214,870	12,865,518	333,969	126,947	77,504	50,467	13,454,405
1950	134,942,028	15,042,286	343,410	141,768	117,629	110,240	15,755,333
1960	158,831,732	18,871,831	523,591	464,332	237,292	394,397	20,491,443
1970	177,748,975	22,580,289	792,730	591,290	435,062	1,063,580	25,462,951
Urban	128,773,240	18,367,318	355,738	523,651	418,779	886,204	20,551,690
Rural	48,975,735	4,212,971	436,992	67,639	16,283	177,376	4,911,261

[1] Beginning with 1960, data include Alaska and Hawaii.

White and Black Population by State, 1970 Census

Source: Bureau of the Census.

State	White	Black	Other	State	White	Black	Other
Alabama	2,533,831	903,467	6,867	Montana	663,043	1,995	29,371
Alaska	236,767	8,911	54,704	Nebraska	1,432,867	39,911	10,715
Arizona	1,604,948	53,344	112,608	Nevada	448,177	27,762	12,799
Arkansas	1,565,915	352,445	4,935	New Hampshire	733,106	2,505	2,070
California	17,761,032	1,400,143	791,959	New Jersey	6,349,908	770,292	47,964
Colorado	2,112,352	66,411	28,496	New Mexico	915,815	19,555	80,630
Connecticut	2,835,458	181,177	15,074	New York	15,834,090	2,168,949	233,928
Delaware	466,459	78,276	3,369	North Carolina	3,901,767	1,126,478	53,814
D. C.[1]	209,272	537,712	9,526	North Dakota	599,485	2,494	15,782
Florida	5,719,343	1,041,651	28,449	Ohio	9,646,997	970,477	34,543
Georgia	3,391,242	1,187,149	11,184	Oklahoma	2,280,362	171,892	106,975
Hawaii	298,160	7,573	462,828	Oregon	2,032,079	26,308	32,998
Idaho	698,802	2,130	11,635	Pennsylvania	10,737,732	1,016,514	39,663
Illinois	9,600,381	1,425,674	87,921	Rhode Island	914,757	25,338	6,630
Indiana	4,820,324	357,464	15,881	South Carolina	1,794,430	789,041	7,045
Iowa	2,782,762	32,596	9,018	South Dakota	630,333	1,627	33,547
Kansas	2,122,068	106,977	17,533	Tennessee	3,293,930	621,261	8,496
Kentucky	2,981,766	230,793	6,147	Texas	9,717,128	1,399,005	80,597
Louisiana	2,541,498	1,086,832	12,976	Utah	1,031,926	6,617	20,730
Maine	985,276	2,800	3,972	Vermont	442,553	761	1,016
Maryland	3,194,888	699,479	28,032	Virginia	3,761,514	861,368	25,612
Massachusetts	5,477,624	175,817	35,729	Washington	3,251,055	71,308	86,806
Michigan	7,833,474	991,066	50,543	West Virginia	1,673,480	67,342	3,415
Minnesota	3,736,038	34,868	34,065	Wisconsin	4,258,959	128,224	30,548
Mississippi	1,393,283	815,770	7,859	Wyoming	323,024	2,568	6,824
Missouri	4,177,495	480,172	18,834	TOTAL, U. S	177,748,975	22,580,289	2,882,662

[1] For census purposes, the District of Columbia is counted as a state.

BLACK POPULATION, BY REGION AND RESIDENCE: 1940 TO 1973

Prior to 1960, excludes Alaska and Hawaii.

REGION	1940	1950	1960	1970	1973	RESIDENCE [1]	1960	1970	1973[2]
Percent distribution	100	100	100	100	100	Population........millions	18.9	22.6	23.2
North	22	28	34	39	40	Metropolitan areas	12.8	16.8	17.6
Northeast	11	13	16	19	19	Central cities	9.9	13.1	13.9
North Central	11	15	18	20	21	Outside central cities	2.8	3.6	3.8
South	77	68	60	53	52	Nonmetropolitan areas	6.1	5.8	5.6
West	1	4	6	8	8				
Percent of all classes	10	10	11	11	11	Percent distribution	100	100	100
North	4	5	7	8	8	Metropolitan areas	68	74	76
Northeast	4	5	7	9	9	Central cities	53	58	60
North Central	4	5	7	8	9	Outside central cities	15	16	16
South	24	22	21	19	19	Nonmetropolitan areas	32	26	24
West	1	3	4	5	5				

[1] Refers to 243 SMSA's as defined in 1970 census publications; see text, section 34. [2] Based on five-quarter average centered on Apr. 1973. Source: U.S. Bureau of the Census, *U.S. Census of Population: 1970*, vol. I, part B, and *Current Population Reports*, series P-23, No. 48.

Income of Households by Age of Head, 1974

Source: Bureau of the Census.

Age of head	Under $4,000	$4,000 to $6,999	$7,000 to $9,999	$10,000 to $14,999	$15,000 to $24,999	$25,000 and over	Total
TOTAL	100%	100%	100%	100%	100%	100%	100%
14 to 24 years	10.3	12.1	13.5	8.9	3.7	0.7	8.2
25 to 34 years	10.8	15.9	23.3	28.2	26.1	13.7	21.0
35 to 44 years	6.9	10.6	13.7	18.5	24.4	23.6	16.7
45 to 54 years	9.4	10.9	14.3	17.5	24.5	35.5	18.2
55 to 64 years	14.7	15.6	15.3	16.2	15.2	20.3	15.9
65 years and over	47.9	34.9	20.0	10.8	6.1	6.2	20.1

Immigration by Country of Origin, 1820-1975

Source: Immigration and Naturalization Service.

(Figures are totals, not annual averages, and were tabulated as follows: 1820-67, alien passengers arrived; 1868-91 and 1895-97, immigrant aliens arrived; 1892-94 and 1898 to present, immigrant aliens admitted. Data before 1906 relate to country whence alien came; since 1906, to country of last permanent residence.)

Countries	1975	1820-1975	1961-70	1951-60	1941-50	1931-40	1921-30	1820-1920
Europe: Albania[1]	12	2,438	98	59	85	2,040	....	....
Austria[2]	507	4,312,252	20,621	67,106	24,860	3,563	32,868	3,626,110
Belgium	437	200,575	9,192	18,575	12,189	4,817	15,846	137,542
Bulgaria[3]	83	67,464	619	104	375	938	2,945	61,973
Czechoslovakia[1]	267	135,995	3,273	918	8,347	14,393	102,194	3,426
Denmark	342	362,833	9,201	10,984	5,393	2,559	32,430	300,036
Estonia[1]	8	1,111	163	185	212	506	....	....
Finland[1]	215	32,626	4,192	4,925	2,503	2,146	16,691	756
France	1,816	742,442	45,237	51,121	38,809	12,623	49,610	532,765
Germany[2]	5,861	6,954,160	190,796	477,765	226,578	114,058	412,202	5,495,691
Great Britain: England	10,662	3,136,572	174,452	156,171	112,252	21,756	157,420	2,462,015
Scotland	1,015	817,018	29,849	32,854	16,131	6,887	159,781	567,106
Wales	134	94,709	2,052	2,589	3,209	735	13,012	72,647
Not specified[4]	433	803,507	3,675	3,884	....	....	....	793,741
Greece	9,799	629,349	85,969	47,608	8,973	9,119	51,084	370,405
Hungary[2]	554	....	5,401	36,637	3,469	7,861	30,680	442,693
Ireland	1,069	4,720,427	37,461	57,332	26,967	13,167	220,591	4,358,350
Italy	10,966	5,269,992	214,111	185,491	57,661	68,028	455,315	4,195,880
Latvia[1]	5	2,505	510	352	361	1,192	....	....
Lithuania[1]	11	3,782	562	242	683	2,201	....	....
Luxembourg[1]	21	2,789	556	684	820	565	....	....
Netherlands	755	356,282	30,606	52,277	14,860	7,150	26,948	219,661
Norway[5]	372	855,337	15,484	22,935	10,100	4,740	68,531	731,584
Poland[6]	3,482	502,658	53,539	9,985	7,571	17,026	227,734	169,995
Portugal	11,291	411,136	76,065	19,588	7,423	3,329	29,994	222,721
Romania[7]	825	165,747	2,531	1,039	1,076	3,871	67,646	85,428
Spain	2,573	246,334	44,659	7,894	2,898	3,258	28,958	137,907
Sweden[5]	507	1,269,969	17,116	21,697	10,665	3,960	97,249	1,116,239
Switzerland	673	346,468	18,453	17,675	10,547	5,512	29.676	260,492
U.S.S.R.[8]	4,713	3,354,026	2,336	584	548	1,356	61,742	3,280,249
Yugoslavia[3]	2,942	106,108	20,381	8,225	1,576	5,835	49,064	1,888
Other Europe	424	54,472	4,203	8,155	3,983	2,361	22,983	10,716
Total Europe	72,774	35,961,083	1,123,363	1,325,640	621,124	347,552	2,463,194	29,658,016
Asia: China[9]	9,201	487,803	34,764	9,657	16,709	4,928	29,907	347,338
India	14,336	107,446	27,189	1,973	1,761	496	1,886	7,491
Japan[10]	4,807	391,389	39,988	46,250	1,555	1,948	33,462	242.181
Turkey	1,071	382,324	10,142	3,519	798	1,065	33,824	326,347
Other Asia	99,781	905,910	315,688	88,707	11,537	7,644	12,980	22,915
Total Asia[11]	129,196	2,274,872	427,771	150,106	32,360	16,081	112,059	946,272
America: Canada & Newfoundland[12]	11,215	4,048,329	413,310	377,952	171,718	108,527	924,515	1,972,686
Central America	62,552	1,911,951	101,330	44,751	21,665	5,861	15,769	27,524
Mexico[13]	66,975	1,408,027	453,937	299,811	60,589	22,319	459,287	296,649
South America	9,800	262,533	257,954	91,628	21,831	7,803	42,215	71,284
West Indies	24,183	607,356	470,213	123,091	49,725	15,502	74,899	356,570
Other America[13]	7	109,419	19,630	59,711	29,276	25	31	....
Total America	174,732	8,347,615	1,716,374	996,944	354,804	160,037	1,516,716	2,724,713
Africa	5,868	104,421	28,954	14,092	7,367	1,750	6,286	18,024
Australia & New Zealand	1,804	110,560	19,562	11,506	13,805	2,231	8,299	44,002
Pacific Islands[14]	198	23,984	1,769	4,698	5,437	780	427	9,938
Countries not specified[15]	1,622	276,384	3,884	12,493	142	....	228	253,838
Total all countries	386,194	47,098,919	3,321,677	2,515,479	1,135,039	528,431	4,107,209	33,654,803

[1] Countries established since beginning of World War I are theretofore included with countries to which they belonged. [2] Data for Austria-Hungary not reported until 1861. Austria and Hungary recorded separately after 1905, Austria included with Germany 1938-45. [3] Bulgaria, Serbia, Montenegro first reported in 1899. Bulgaria reported separately since 1920. In 1920, separate enumeration for Kingdom of Serbs, Croats, Slovenes; since 1922, recorded as Yugoslavia. [4] United Kingdom not specified; for 1901-51, included in "Other Europe." [5] Norway included with Sweden 1820-68. [6] Included with Austria-Hungary, Germany, and Russia 1899-1919. [7] No record of immigration until 1880. [8] From 1931-63, the U.S.S.R. was broken down into European U.S.S.R. and Asian U.S.S.R. Since 1964, total U.S.S.R. has been reported in Europe. [9] Beginning in 1957, China includes Taiwan. [10] No record of immigration until 1861. [11] From 1952, Asia included Philippines. From 1934-51, Philippines were included in Pacific Islands; before 1934, recorded in separate tables as insular travel. [12] Includes all British North American possessions, 1820-98. [13] No record of immigration, 1886-93. [14] Included with "Countries not specified" prior to 1925. [15] Includes 32,897 persons returning in 1906 to their homes in U.S.

Immigrant and Nonimmigrant Aliens Admitted to U.S., 1901-1975

Source: Immigration and Naturalization Service.

Period[1]	Immigrants	Non-immigrants	Total	Period[1]	Immigrants	Non-immigrants	Total
1901-10	8,795,386	1,007,909	9,803,295	1956-60	1,427,841	4,458,562	5,886,403
1911-20	5,735,811	1,376,271	7,112,082	1961-65	1,450,312	7,879,564	9,329,876
1921-30	4,107,209	1,774,896	5,882,090	1966-70	1,871,365	16,227,660	18,099,025
1931-35	220,209	729,694	949,903	1971	370,478	4,403,761	4,774,239
1936-40	308,222	844,377	1,152,599	1972	384,685	5,171,460	5,556,145
1941-45	170,952	541,470	712,422	1973	400,063	5,977,324	6,377,387
1946-50	864,087	1,919,889	2,783,976	1974	394,861	6,908,708	7,303,569
1951-55	1,087,638	2,654,461	3,742,009	1975	386,194	7,083,937	7,470,131

[1] Fiscal years ending June 30.

Persons Naturalized in the United States Since 1907

Source: Immigration and Naturalization Service.

Period[1]	Civilian	Military	Total	Period[1]	Civilian	Military	Total
1907-30	2,713,389	300,506	3,013,895	1972	107,740	8,475	116,215
1931-40	1,498,573	19,891	1,518,464	1973	112,944	7,796	120,740
1941-50	1,837,229	149,799	1,987,028	1974	124,807	6,848	131,655
1951-60	1,148,241	41,705	1,189,946	1975	135,323	6,214	141,537
1961-70	1,084,195	36,068	1,120,263	1907-75	8,861,299	586,851	9,448,150
1971	98.858	9,549	108,407				

MARRIAGE AND DIVORCE

(New statutory enactments and recent judicial decisions or interpretation may affect the following summary; therefore, Government officials or an attorney should be consulted for advice.)

Marriages and Divorces in the United States, 1900-1975

Source: National Center for Health Statistics, Department of Health, Education, and Welfare.

Year	Marriage Number	Marriage Rate[1]	Divorce[2] Number	Divorce[2] Rate[1]	Year	Marriage Number	Marriage Rate[1]	Divorce[2] Number	Divorce[2] Rate[1]
1900..........	709,000	9.3	55,751	.7	1953.........	1,546,000	9.8	390,000	2.5
1905..........	842,000	10.0	67,976	.8	1954.........	1,490,000	9.2	379,000	2.4
1910..........	948,166	10.3	83,045	.9	1955.........	1,531,000	9.3	377,000	2.3
1915..........	1,007,595	10.0	104,298	1.0	1956.........	1,585,000	9.5	382,000	2.3
1920..........	1,274,476	12.0	170,505	1.6	1957.........	1,518,000	8.9	381,000	2.2
1925..........	1,188,334	10.3	175,449	1.5	1958.........	1,451,000	8.4	368,000	2.1
1929..........	1,232,559	10.1	205,876	1.7	1959.........	1,494,000	8.5	395,000	2.2
1931..........	1,060,914	8.6	188,003	1.5	1960.........	1,523,000	8.5	393,000	2.2
1933..........	1,098,000	8.7	165,000	1.3	1961.........	1,548,000	8.5	414,000	2.3
1935..........	1,327,000	10.4	218,000	1.7	1962.........	1,577,000	8.5	413,000	2.2
1937..........	1,451,296	11.3	249,000	1.9	1963.........	1,654,000	8.8	428,000	2.3
1939..........	1,403,633	10.7	251,000	1.9	1964.........	1,725,000	9.0	450,000	2.4
1941..........	1,695,999	12.7	293,000	2.2	1965.........	1,800,000	9.3	479,000	2.5
1943..........	1,577,050	11.7	359,000	2.6	1966.........	1,857,000	9.5	499,000	2.5
1944..........	1,452,394	10.9	400,000	2.9	1967.........	1,927,000	9.7	523,000	2.6
1945..........	1,612,992	12.2	485,000	3.5	1968.........	2,069,258	10.4	584,000	2.9
1946..........	2,291,045	16.4	610,000	4.3	1969.........	2,145,438	10.6	639,000	3.2
1947..........	1,991,878	13.9	483,000	3.4	1970	2,158,802	10.6	708,000	3.5
1948..........	1,811,155	12.4	408,000	2.8	1971	2,190,481	10.6	773,000	3.7
1949..........	1,579,798	10.6	397,000	2.7	1972	2,282,154	11.0	845,000	4.1
1950..........	1,667,231	11.1	385,144	2.6	1973	2,284,108	10.9	915,000	4.4
1951..........	1,594,694	10.4	381,000	2.5	1974[3]	2,229,667	10.5	977,000	4.6
1952..........	1,539,318	9.9	392,000	2.5	1975[3]	2,126,000	10.0	1,026,000	4.8

[1] Per 1,000 population. Divorce rates for 1941-46 are based on population including armed forces overseas. Marriage rates are based on population excluding armed forces overseas. [2] Includes annulments. [3] Provisional. NOTE: Marriage and divorce figures for most years include some estimated data. Alaska is included beginning 1959, Hawaii beginning 1960.

Marriage Information, by State

Sources: Legal information, *Information Please Almanac* questionnaires to states; Marriage statistics, National Center for Health Statistics, Department of Health, Education, and Welfare.

State	Legal minimum marriage age				Blood test required	Waiting period[1]		Marriages[2]	
	With parental consent[3]		Without parental consent			Before license	After license	1975	1974[4]
	M	F	M	F					
Alabama	17	14	21	18	yes	none	none	44,734	46,811
Alaska	16	16	18	18	yes	3 da.	none	4,789	3,949
Arizona	18	18	18	18	yes	none	none	27,963	27,038
Arkansas	18	16	18	18	yes	3 da.	none	23,069	24,735
California	18	16	18	18	yes	none	none	159,698	160,887
Colorado	16[21]	16[21]	18	18	yes[18]	none	none	27,220	25,999
Connecticut	16	16	18	18	yes	4 da.	none	22,887	24,462
Delaware	18	18	18	18	yes[11]	none	24 hr.[5]	3,947	4,143
D. C.	18	16	21	18	yes[22]	5 da.[6]	none	5,033	5,271
Florida	18	16	18	18	yes	3 da.	none	86,152	90,337
Georgia	18	16	18	18	yes	3 da.[7]	none	60,116	66,656
Hawaii	16	16	18	18	yes	none	none	9,686	9,649
Idaho	18	16	21	18	yes	3 da.	none	12,794	12,489
Illinois	16	16	18	18	yes	none	none	111,372	116,419
Indiana	17	17[12,17]	18	18	yes	3 da.	none	55,844	60,524
Iowa	18	16	18	18	yes	3 da.	none	25,620	27,209
Kansas	18	16	21	18	yes	3 da.	none	23,887	24,491
Kentucky	(19)	(19)	18	18	yes	3 da.	none	33,788	32,800
Louisiana	18	16	18	16	yes	none	72 hr.	36,789	38,185
Maine	16	16	18	18	no	5 da.	none	11,189	11,546
Maryland	18	16	21	18	no	48 hr.	none	44,667	47,013
Massachusetts	14-17[12]	12-15[12]	18	18	yes	3 da.	none	42,085	44,243
Michigan	18	16[8]	18	18	yes	3 da.	none	81,356	88,023
Minnesota	18	16	21	18	no	5 da.	none	30,457	33,547
Mississippi	17	15	21	21	yes	3 da.	none	26,451	27,613
Missouri	15[12]	15[12]	18	18	yes	3 da.	none	45,618	51,434
Montana	18	18	18	18	yes	5 da.	none	7,318	7,741
Nebraska	18	16	19	19	yes	2 da.	none	13,153	13,873
Nevada	16	16	18	18	no	none	none	98,469	103,287
New Hampshire	14[12,15]	13[12,15]	18	18	yes[11]	5 da.	none	8,529	9,239
New Jersey	18	16	18	18	yes	72 hr.	none	50,345	56,449
New Mexico	16	16	18	18	yes	none	none	13,505	15,886
New York	16	14[9]	21	18	yes	none	(10)	141,973	148,012
North Carolina	16	16	18	18	yes	none	none	42,514	45,015
North Dakota	18	15	18	18	yes	none	none	6,055	5,905
Ohio	18	16	21	21	yes	5 da.	none	101,380	102,458
Oklahoma	16[17]	16[17]	18	18	yes	none[14]	none	39,001	40,160
Oregon	18	15	21	18	yes	7 da.	none	18,682	20,002
Pennsylvania	16	16	18	18	yes	3 da.	none	89,313	96,663
Rhode Island	18	16[9]	18	18	yes	none	none	6,697	7,255
South Carolina	16	14	18	18	no	24 hr.	none	49,944	52,996
South Dakota	16	16	18	18	yes	none	none	11,075	11,928
Tennessee	16	16	18	18	yes	none[14]	none	51,673	54,606
Texas	16[18]	16[13]	18	18	yes	none	none	153,826	153,002
Utah	16	14	18	18	yes	none	none	13,899	15,166
Vermont	16	16	18	18	yes	none	5 da.[16]	4,351	4,652
Virginia	16	16	18	18	yes	none	none	55,666	56,617
Washington	17	17	18	18	no	3 da.	none	43,361	41,577
West Virginia	18	16	18	18	yes	3 da.	none	17,002	17,409
Wisconsin	18	16	18	18	yes	5 da.	none	35,862	38,248
Wyoming	18[20]	16[20]	18[20]	18[20]	yes	none	none	5,705	6,048

[1] In some states, waiting period may be waived or reduced by court order. [2] By place of occurrence. [3] In most states, persons younger than the age shown may be married by court permission. [4] Provisional figures; data represent marriages reported, marriage intentions filed, or marriage licenses issued. [5] 96 hours if nonresidents. [6] Day of application and day of pickup are included in 5-day waiting period. [7] If applicants are under 21 but over 19 and female is not pregnant. [8] Consent of one parent or guardian necessary for female only. [9] Females 14 to 16 years old must also have consent of judge of Family Court. [10] Marriage may not be solemnized within 10 days from date on which specimen was taken for serological test, and not until 24 hours after issuance of marriage license. Waiting period may be waived by court order. [11] Blood test may be waived by court order. [12] Need court order. [13] Parent must appear in person or provide doctor's affidavit of his or her illness. [14] 3 days if either party is under legal age. [15] If pregnant. [16] After date on which marriage application has been filed with town clerk, excluding date of filing. [17] Males under 18 and females under 15 only if female is pregnant. [18] Blood test for rubella and RH type not required of females over 45 years or found by physician to be incapable of bearing children. [19] No age limit. [20] If under 18 or 16 need court order. [21] Males and females under age of 16 may obtain a license with judicial approval. [22] No exceptions granted under this age.

Divorce Information, by State

Sources: Legal information, *Information Please Almanac* questionnaires to states; Divorce statistics, National Center for Health Statistics, Department of Health, Education, and Welfare.

State	Residence for divorce	Period before parties may remarry		Divorces[1]	
		Plaintiff	Defendant	1975[2]	1974
Alabama	1 yr.	60 da.	60 da.	22,260	21,123
Alaska	1 yr.	none	none	2,890	2,450
Arizona	90 da.	none	none	([3])	([3])
Arkansas	90 da.	none	none	15,562	15,840
California	6 mo.	none	none	129,144	121,714
Colorado	90 da.[20]	none	none	15,613	15,082
Connecticut	1 yr.	none	none	11,957	10,846
Delaware	6 mo.[20]	none[12]	none[12]	2,745	2,354
D.C.	1 yr.	60 da.	60 da.	2,508	3,176
Florida	6 mo.	none	none	63,267	59,611
Georgia	6 mo.	none	none	28,187	26,918
Hawaii	1 yr.	none	none	4,264	4,111
Idaho	6 wk.	none	none	5,223	4,808
Illinois	1 yr.	none	none	51,899	48,361
Indiana	6 mo.	none	none	([3])	([3])
Iowa	1 yr.[11]	1 yr.	1 yr.	10,387	9,480
Kansas	1 yr.	30 da.	30 da.	12,565	11,484
Kentucky	6 mo.[4,24]	none	none	15,118	13,791
Louisiana	1 yr.	none[8]	none[8]	([3])	([3])
Maine	6 mo.	none	none	5,447	4,876
Maryland	1 yr.	none	none	14,909	15,070
Massachusetts	1 yr.	([23])	none[23]	16,164	16,116
Michigan	1 yr.	none	none	41,249	41,850
Minnesota	1 yr.	6 mo.	6 mo.	12,473	12,237
Mississippi	1 yr.	([10])	([10])	12,671	11,866
Missouri	90 da.	none	none	25,455	22,088
Montana	1 yr.	none	none	4,307	3,940
Nebraska	1 yr.[5]	none	none	5,573	5,193
Nevada	6 wk.	none	none	9,906	10,045
New Hampshire	1 yr.	none	none	4,507	4,051
New Jersey	1 yr.	none	none	18,768	19,870
New Mexico	6 mo.[13]	none	none	7,223	7,863
New York	([14])	none	none	55,502	54,015
North Carolina	6 mo.	none	none	22,182	20,049
North Dakota	1 yr.	([9])	([9])	1,737	1,588
Ohio	6 mo.[6]	none	none	51,367	49,239
Oklahoma	6 mo.[22]	6 mo.[21]	6 mo.[21]	20,104	22,521
Oregon	6 mo.	60 da.	60 da.	15,453	13,538
Pennsylvania	1 yr.	none	none[15]	32,384	32,572
Rhode Island	2 yr.	none	none	2,657	2,522
South Carolina	1 yr.	none	none	9,158	8,816
South Dakota	([7])	none	none	2,233	2,016
Tennessee	1 yr.	none	none[16]	24,507	23,725
Texas	30 da.	30 da.[16]	30 da.[16]	77,438	69,762
Utah	3 mo.	3 mo.[12]	3 mo.[12]	6,160	5,670
Vermont	6 mo.[19]	none	none	1,866	1,623
Virginia	6 mo.	none	none	19,412	16,704
Washington	none[20]	none	none	25,065	23,909
West Virginia	1 yr.[17]	([18])	([18])	8,427	7,176
Wisconsin	6 mo.	6 mo.	6 mo.	14,840	12,350
Wyoming	60 da.	none	none	2,809	2,523

[1]By place of occurrence, including reported annulments. [2]Provisional. [3]Data not available. [4]Only one party must have resided in the state for 180 days. [5]Decree not final until 6 months after trial and decision. [6]6-month residence in state; 90-day residence in county. [7]Physical presence plus intent to make state the place of residence. [8]In case of adultery, guilty party cannot marry correspondent. [9]At discretion of court. [10]Until court that grants the divorce is adjourned. [11]No time required if both parties are residents of state and intend to make state their place of residence. [12]3 months between first and final judgment. [13]Servicemen acquire residence by being continuously stationed at military base in state for 6 months. [14]Action for divorce may be maintained only where (1) parties were married in the state and either has been a resident for one year preceding the action; (2) parties have resided in the state as husband and wife and either has been a resident for one year preceding the action; (3) cause for divorce occurred in the state and either party has been a resident for one year preceding the action; (4) cause for divorce occurred in the state and both parties are residents at time of the action; (5) either party is a resident for at least 2 years preceding the action. [15]Party guilty of adultery may not marry the corespondent during lifetime of former spouse. [16]Parties may remarry each other at any time. [17]2 years if residence is acquired after cause of divorce action arose. [18]Court can lengthen waiting period if desired. [19]Court must find resumption of marital relations not reasonably probable. [20]Must be domiciled in state. [21]30 days from date of judgment of appeal. [22]5 years if on grounds of insanity and insane spouse is in institution. [23]6-month wait between date decree is granted, and decree becomes final. [24]No decree shall be entered until parties have lived apart for 60 days.

Grounds for Divorce

Source: Information Please Almanac questionnaires to the states.

State	Adultery	Cruelty	Desertion	Alcoholism	Impotence	Felony conviction	Neglect to provide	Insanity	Pregnancy at marriage[1]	Bigamy	Separation	Indignities	Drug addiction	Violence	Fraudulent contract	Others
Alabama	yes	yes	yes[2]	yes	yes	yes[16]	yes[3]	yes[6]	yes		yes[5]		yes	yes		(27.29.34)
Alaska	yes	yes	yes[2]	yes	yes	yes	yes	yes[9]				yes	yes	yes		
Arizona																(29)
Arkansas	yes	yes	yes[2]	yes	yes	yes	yes	yes		yes	yes[4]	yes		yes	yes	(12.31.48)
California																(28)
Colorado																(29.52)
Connecticut	yes	yes	yes[2]	yes		yes[20]		yes[6]			yes		yes	yes	yes	(9.23.28.30.34.42.46)
Delaware																(29.50)
D.C.	yes	yes[53]	yes[2]			yes[15]					yes[2]					
Florida																(29.44.49.52)
Georgia	yes	yes	yes[2]	yes	yes	yes[15]	yes	yes	yes	yes	yes	yes	yes	yes	yes	(29.31.48.49)
Hawaii											yes[3]					(29)
Idaho	yes	yes	yes			yes		yes[4]		yes						(26.28.42)
Illinois	yes	yes	yes[2]	yes[3]	yes	yes				yes			yes[3]	yes		(32.37.56)
Indiana				yes				yes[3]								(29.33.52)
Iowa																(49)
Kansas	yes	yes	yes[2]	yes		yes		yes[6]							yes	(31.48)
Kentucky																(49)
Louisiana	yes	yes	yes	yes		yes				yes	yes[3]		yes	yes		(37.58)
Maine	yes	yes	yes	yes	yes	yes[20]							yes			(28)
Maryland	yes	yes	yes[9]		yes[45]	yes[18]		yes[4]			yes[9]					(35)
Massachusetts	yes	yes	yes[2]	yes	yes	yes[19]					yes					(29.35.49)
Michigan																(29)
Minnesota	yes		yes[2]	yes[2]		yes		yes[4]			yes[3]					(36.49)
Mississippi	yes	yes	yes	yes	yes	yes[22]		yes[47]	yes	yes	yes[2]		yes	yes		(10.31)
Missouri	yes	yes	yes	yes	yes	yes			yes	yes		yes				(10.30.32)
Montana																(29)
Nebraska																(49)
Nevada								yes[3]			yes[2]					(27)
New Hampshire	yes	yes	yes[3]	yes[3]	yes	yes[14]	yes[3]							yes		(25.28.40.57.60)
New Jersey	yes	yes	yes[2]	yes[2]	yes[51]	yes[9]		yes[3]		yes[51]	yes[9]			yes[2]	yes[51]	(49)
New Mexico	yes	yes	yes													(27)
New York	yes	yes	yes[2]			yes[17]					yes[2]					
North Carolina	yes				yes			yes[6]			yes[2]					(34)
North Dakota	yes		yes[2]	yes[2]		yes	yes[2]	yes[6]								(28)
Ohio	yes	yes	yes	yes[4]	yes	yes	yes	yes[5]		yes	yes[2]				yes	(12.41.55.24)
Oklahoma	yes	yes	yes[2]	yes	yes	yes[21]	yes	yes[6]	yes	yes					yes	(27.41.55)
Oregon																(49)
Pennsylvania	yes	yes	yes[3]		yes[45]	yes[15]		yes		yes		yes		yes	yes	(31)
Rhode Island	yes	yes	yes[6]	yes		yes[7]	yes[2]	yes[48]			yes[3]		yes	yes	yes	(13.38)
South Carolina	yes	yes[39]	yes[2]	yes							yes[4]		yes			(50)
South Dakota	yes	yes	yes[2]	yes[2]		yes	yes[2]	yes[6]		yes[61]					yes[61]	
Tennessee	yes	yes	yes[2]	yes[43]	yes	yes		yes	yes	yes	yes		yes			(32.37.59)
Texas	yes	yes	yes[2]			yes[54]		yes[4]			yes[4]	yes		yes		
Utah	yes	yes	yes[2]					yes[4]			yes[4]					
Vermont	yes	yes	yes[7]			yes[17]	yes	yes[6]			yes[8]					(29)
Virginia	yes	yes	yes[2]			yes					yes[2]					
Washington																(29)
West Virginia	yes	yes	yes[2]	yes		yes		yes			yes[3]		yes			
Wisconsin	yes	yes	yes[2]	yes[2]		yes[17]	yes				yes					(11.46)
Wyoming	yes	yes	yes[2]	yes	yes	yes	yes[2]	yes[3]	yes		yes[3]	yes				(11.25)

[1]If unknown to husband. [2]1 year. [3]2 years. [4]3 years. [5]4 years. [6]5 years. [7]7 years. [8]6 months. [9]18 months. [10]Absence of 1 year. [11]Absence of 1 year voluntarily, or under legal separation judgment. [12]Absence of 3 years. [13]Absence of one spouse; presumption of death. [14]With imprisonment of 1 year. [15]With imprisonment of 2 years. [16]With imprisonment of 2 years, sentence being for 7 years or more. [17]With imprisonment of 3 years. [18]With imprisonment of three years, eighteen months of which have been served. [19]With imprisonment of 5 years. [20]With imprisonment for life. [21]Imprisonment of other party in state or Federal penal institution under sentence thereto for commission of felony at time the petition is filed. [22]Unless pardoned before sentencing. [23]Noncohabitation for 18 months. [24]Court of Common Pleas may grant a dissolution of marriage—6 months residency required. [25]Noncohabitation for 2 years. [26]Noncohabitation for 5 years. [27]Incompatibility. [28]Irreconcilable differences. [29]Irretrievable breakdown of marriage relationship. [30]Irretrievably broken upon proof, decree of dissolution. [31]Relationship within prohibited degree. [32]Infamous crime. [33]Infamous crime subsequent to marriage. [34]Crime against nature. [35]Exclusively vicious conduct; any cause which, by laws of state, renders marriage null and void at its inception. [36]A course of

(Footnotes continued on next page)

Per Cent of Population Ever Married: U.S., 1900–1975

Source for tables on this page: Bureau of the Census.

Age group, years	1900	1910	1920	1930	1940	1950	1960	1970	1975
Males: 14–19	0.9	1.0	1.8	1.5	1.5	2.9	3.3	2.6	2.7
20–24	22.2	24.7	29.1	29.0	27.8	41.0	46.9	45.3	40.1
25–29	54.1	57.1	60.5	63.2	64.0	76.2	79.2	80.9	77.7
30–34	72.3	73.9	75.8	78.8	79.3	86.8	88.1	90.6	88.9
35–44	83.0	83.3	83.8	85.7	86.0	90.4	91.9	93.3	92.1
45–54	89.7	88.8	88.0	88.6	88.9	91.5	92.6	92.5	93.7
Females: 14–19	9.4	9.8	10.8	10.9	10.0	14.4	13.5	9.7	9.3
20–24	48.4	51.5	54.4	53.9	52.8	67.7	71.6	64.2	59.7
25–29	72.4	75.0	76.9	78.3	77.2	86.7	89.5	89.5	86.2
30–34	83.4	83.8	85.1	86.8	85.3	90.7	93.1	93.8	92.5
35–44	88.9	88.6	88.6	90.0	89.6	91.7	93.9	94.8	95.1
45–54	92.2	91.4	90.4	90.9	91.3	92.2	93.0	95.1	95.4

Marriage Prospects of Single Men and Women

Age	Per cent of population single[1] Male	Female	Per cent who ever marry[2] Male	Female	Age	Per cent of population single[1] Male	Female	Per cent who ever marry[2] Male	Female
15	99.4	97.6	95.8	97.4	33	10.9	6.3	63.5	49.7
16	99.0	94.3	95.9	97.4	34	10.3	6.4	60.2	46.0
17	98.1	87.9	96.0	97.3	35	9.9	6.4	57.2	42.9
18	94.6	75.5	96.0	97.0	36	9.0	6.1	54.1	40.0
19	87.3	59.6	95.9	96.4	37	8.7	6.0	51.0	37.3
20	75.8	45.8	95.6	95.5	38	8.1	5.7	48.0	34.7
21	63.3	35.1	95.0	94.2	39	8.1	6.2	45.1	32.2
22	51.4	25.8	94.1	92.2	40	7.6	6.1	42.3	29.9
23	40.5	19.4	92.8	89.4	41	7.5	6.0	39.7	27.6
24	33.5	15.6	91.1	86.1	42	6.9	5.9	37.2	25.5
25	27.8	13.1	89.1	82.5	43	7.1	6.0	34.8	23.6
26	23.9	11.5	86.6	78.4	44	7.4	6.5	32.7	21.7
27	19.6	9.9	83.6	74.2	45	7.1	6.1	30.6	20.0
28	17.3	9.3	80.3	70.3	50	7.6	7.4	21.6	12.8
29	15.9	8.7	77.3	65.7	55	7.9	7.9	13.9	7.7
30	14.2	7.9	73.8	61.2	60	8.0	7.8	8.2	4.4
31	12.9	7.2	70.4	57.3	65 and over	7.7	8.5	...	...
32	11.7	6.6	67.1	53.3					

[1] Per cent single within specified year of age in 1960, in 5% sample of population (latest available data). [2] Per cent of white persons single at beginning of year of age who marry during that year and all later years, based on data for 1958–60. NOTE: "Single" excludes widowed and divorced.

Median Age at First Marriage in the U.S., 1890–1975

Year	Males	Females	Year	Males	Females	Year	Males	Females	Year	Males	Females
1890	26.1	22.0	1920	24.6	21.2	1950	22.8	20.3	1972	23.3	20.9
1900	25.9	21.9	1930	24.3	21.3	1960	22.8	20.3	1974	23.1	21.1
1910	25.1	21.6	1940	24.3	21.5	1970	23.1	20.8	1975	23.5	21.1

Footnotes for Grounds for Divorce (contd.)

conduct detrimental to the marriage relationship of the party seeking the divorce. [37]Attempt by one party on life of other. [38]Any other gross misbehavior or wickedness. [39]Physical cruelty only. [40]Treatment such as to injure health or endanger reason. [41]Gross neglect of duty. [42]Habitual intemperance. [43]Habitual drunkenness contracted after marriage. [44]Mental incompetence. [45]If at time of marriage and incurable. [46]Involuntary commitment to mental institution for 1 year subsequent to marriage. [47]Incurable, regardless when it occurs. [48]Insanity at time of marriage. [49]No fault divorce. [50]No fault divorce after 3 years' separation. [51]Grounds for nullity. [52]The term divorce is no longer used. The term now used is Dissolution of Marriage. [53]Limited divorce; may be enlarged into absolute divorce after separation of 1 year. [54]Suit for divorce cannot be sustained until 12 months after final judgment of conviction. Divorce cannot be obtained if plaintiff's testimony contributed toward conviction. [55]Defendant obtained divorce from plaintiff in any other state or country. [56]Infected other party with communicable venereal disease. [57]Joining a religious cult disbelieving in marriage. [58]Public defamation. [59]Wife's refusal to remove with husband to this state and willfully absenting herself for 2 years. [60]Wife gone to reside outside state and absent 10 years. [61]Annulment.

Marital Status of the Population, 1970

Source: Bureau of the Census.

State	Males Population 14 yrs. old & over	% distribution[1] Single	Married	Widowed or divorced	Females Population 14 yrs. old & over	% distribution[1] Single	Married	Widowed or divorced
Alabama	1,180,777	27.5	67.1	5.4	1,318,246	20.9	61.6	17.5
Alaska	113,657	33.8	60.7	5.4	89,907	20.6	71.4	8.0
Arizona	616,883	27.6	66.5	5.8	359,801	23.4	62.6	14.0
Arkansas	677,205	25.1	68.5	6.3	744,748	18.4	63.3	18.2
California	7,200,777	29.2	64.0	6.8	7,612,951	25.7	63.0	11.3
Colorado	784,269	29.3	65.0	5.6	824,381	22.5	62.3	15.1
Connecticut	1,066,148	28.7	66.3	4.9	1,171,577	24.1	61.1	14.7
Delaware	188,807	27.9	67.0	5.2	205,376	22.8	62.6	14.5
D. C.	263,148	38.0	54.2	7.8	317,659	33.9	46.8	19.3
Florida	2,448,895	24.4	68.9	6.7	2,718,123	18.0	63.1	18.9
Georgia	1,580,841	28.3	66.4	5.3	1,731,422	20.9	62.1	17.0
Hawaii	289,176	36.2	58.8	5.0	264,612	25.7	63.0	11.3
Idaho	253,439	27.4	66.9	5.7	258,988	20.0	66.0	14.0
Illinois	3,890,046	28.7	65.4	6.0	4,273,777	22.9	60.5	16.6
Indiana	1,805,978	26.4	67.7	5.9	1,964,067	20.9	63.0	16.2
Iowa	990,235	27.4	67.2	5.4	1,085,637	22.0	61.9	14.1
Kansas	811,073	27.5	66.9	5.6	865,667	20.5	63.0	16.5
Kentucky	1,141,799	27.9	66.3	5.7	1,221,486	20.5	62.5	16.9
Louisiana	1,225,885	30.3	64.7	5.0	1,340,100	23.2	60.6	16.1
Maine	346,929	28.0	65.5	6.5	379,054	22.2	60.5	17.3
Maryland	1,366,887	28.7	66.3	5.0	1,475,767	22.8	62.7	14.4
Massachusetts	1,974,450	31.5	63.0	5.5	2,255,547	27.5	56.2	16.3
Michigan	3,066,393	28.5	65.9	5.7	3,293,574	22.9	62.3	14.8
Minnesota	1,317,587	30.6	64.5	4.9	1,418,152	25.3	60.4	14.3
Mississippi	744,715	29.9	64.5	5.6	823,336	22.5	60.0	17.5
Missouri	1,645,308	26.5	67.3	6.2	1,833,614	20.8	61.2	18.1
Montana	249,067	30.0	63.7	6.3	252,855	21.4	63.2	15.4
Nebraska	525,680	28.7	66.0	5.3	567,722	22.5	61.7	15.9
Nevada	179,430	25.6	65.2	9.2	174,714	17.2	67.0	15.9
New Hampshire	258,217	28.4	65.9	5.7	279,376	22.7	61.6	15.6
New Jersey	2,521,425	28.1	67.0	4.8	2,792,336	22.9	61.8	15.3
New Mexico	341,352	30.0	64.7	5.3	359,801	23.4	62.6	14.0
New York	6,397,876	30.1	64.7	5.2	7,297,798	25.1	58.7	16.1
North Carolina	1,801,631	29.2	66.4	4.3	1,932,810	21.8	63.2	15.0
North Dakota	223,926	34.4	61.3	4.3	222,124	24.5	62.1	13.4
Ohio	3,690,880	27.2	66.8	6.0	4,074,270	22.5	61.4	16.1
Oklahoma	920,467	25.3	68.1	6.6	1,001,092	17.7	63.3	19.0
Oregon	754,947	26.1	67.2	6.7	809,409	20.6	63.6	15.8
Pennsylvania	4,163,587	28.5	65.7	5.7	4,683,918	24.1	59.6	16.3
Rhode Island	345,459	31.5	63.1	5.4	368,509	25.0	58.8	16.2
South Carolina	901,191	31.6	64.2	4.3	958,508	23.1	61.5	15.4
South Dakota	237,278	32.1	63.0	5.0	245,994	23.8	61.3	14.9
Tennessee	1,378,997	26.6	67.8	5.6	1,527,547	20.3	62.5	17.2
Texas	3,906,008	27.3	67.0	5.7	4,195,817	20.4	63.2	16.4
Utah	355,852	30.0	65.6	4.4	375,329	24.5	62.9	12.7
Vermont	154,288	30.8	63.8	5.4	167,774	24.8	59.4	15.8
Virginia	1,671,230	29.7	65.6	4.7	1,747,387	22.1	63.2	14.8
Washington	1,239,721	28.2	65.3	6.4	1,280,861	20.6	63.6	15.8
West Virginia	620,693	27.5	66.6	5.9	685,531	21.3	61.3	17.4
Wisconsin	1,541,822	30.4	64.3	5.4	1,650,691	24.9	60.6	14.6
Wyoming	120,033	27.6	66.3	6.1	120,911	19.6	66.1	14.2
TOTAL, U. S.	71,492,364	28.6	65.8	5.6	77,914,869	22.4	61.3	16.3

[1] Total for ages 14 and over = 100%. NOTE: Data are latest available.

1976 Marriage Rate Stabilizes as Divorces Continue Rise

The marriage rate for the first half of 1976 remained at 9.3 per 1,000 population, the figure for the comparable period in 1975. Some 987,000 marriages were reported, up 7,000 over Jan.–June 1975. Indications are that the downward trend that began in 1973 is ending. Divorces, on the other hand, continued to rise steadily, going from 498,000 in the first half of 1975 to 538,000 in Jan.–June 1976. The rate rose to 5 per 1,000 from 4.7 in the previous year.

BIRTHS

Registered Live Births and Birth Rates, 1970–1975

Source: National Center for Health Statistics, Department of Health, Education and Welfare.

State	1975 Number	1975 Rate	1974 Number	1974 Rate	1970[1] Number	1970[1] Rate
Alabama	58,182	16.1	58,926	16.5	67,235	19.5
Alaska	7,350	20.9	7,014	20.8	7,406	24.5
Arizona	39,465	17.7	39,846	18.5	37,290	21.0
Arkansas	33,852	16.0	33,856	16.4	34,633	18.0
California	314,311	14.8	312,034	14.9	364,007	18.2
Colorado	40,270	15.9	39,815	16.0	42,758	19.4
Connecticut	35,166	11.4	36,382	11.8	49,862	16.4
Delaware	8,416	14.5	8,438	14.7	10,234	18.7
D.C.	19,438	27.1	19,866	27.5	24,846	32.8
Florida	106,031	12.7	109,780	13.6	113,831	16.8
Georgia	81,161	16.5	84,696	17.3	96,069	20.9
Hawaii	15,838	18.3	15,514	18.3	16,591	21.5
Idaho	15,743	19.2	15,160	19.0	13,891	19.5
Illinois	167,341	15.0	166,532	15.0	203,309	18.3
Indiana	83,837	15.8	83,432	15.7	97,129	18.7
Iowa	41,514	14.5	40,562	14.2	49,131	17.4
Kansas	32,386	14.3	31,295	13.8	36,277	16.1
Kentucky	56,188	16.5	54,388	16.2	61,015	19.0
Louisiana	67,394	17.8	65,988	17.5	72,348	19.9
Maine	14,408	13.6	14,753	14.1	17,528	17.6
Maryland	45,501	11.1	46,724	11.4	60,759	15.5
Massachusetts	68,907	11.8	71,900	12.4	95,978	16.9
Michigan	132,754	14.5	136,422	15.0	169,798	19.1
Minnesota	56,983	14.5	55,856	14.3	68,529	18.0
Mississippi	42,846	18.3	43,568	18.7	47,678	21.5
Missouri	71,701	15.1	71,915	15.1	84,285	18.0
Montana	11,781	15.8	12,084	16.4	12,431	17.9
Nebraska	23,767	15.4	23,962	15.5	26,222	17.7
Nevada	8,673	14.7	8,782	15.3	9,018	18.5
New Hampshire	10,918	13.3	11,428	14.1	12,750	17.3
New Jersey	88,025	12.0	91,866	12.5	116,322	16.2
New Mexico	20,413	17.8	21,112	18.8	21,874	21.5
New York	237,116	13.1	241,016	13.3	318,891	17.5
North Carolina	80,868	14.8	84,294	15.7	98,755	19.4
North Dakota	11,275	17.8	10,716	16.8	11,528	18.7
Ohio	161,191	15.0	160,848	15.0	202,823	19.0
Oklahoma	41,441	15.3	40,954	15.1	43,411	17.0
Oregon	34,271	15.0	33,438	14.8	36,167	17.3
Pennsylvania	150,058	12.7	152,572	12.9	193,004	16.4
Rhode Island	10,698	11.8	11,696	12.5	16,196	17.1
South Carolina	45,247	16.1	47,005	16.9	50,861	19.6
South Dakota	11,126	16.3	10,962	16.1	11,584	17.4
Tennessee	67,035	16.0	67,988	16.5	75,673	19.3
Texas	222,988	18.2	221,264	18.4	227,126	20.3
Utah	32,641	27.1	30,648	26.1	27,438	25.9
Vermont	5,999	12.7	6,550	13.9	8,080	18.2
Virginia	68,122	13.7	67,974	13.8	81,564	17.5
Washington	50,132	14.1	49,672	14.3	60,990	17.9
West Virginia	27,686	15.4	27,726	15.5	29,449	16.9
Wisconsin	64,634	14.0	65,114	14.3	77,125	17.5
Wyoming	6,453	17.3	6,298	17.5	6,336	19.1
United States	3,149,811	14.8	3,159,958	14.9	3,731,386	18.2

[1] By place of occurrence. NOTE: Rates are per 1,000 population in each area, estimated as of December.

Live Births in the United States, 1910-1975

Source: National Center for Health Statistics, Department of Health, Education, and Welfare.

Year	Births[1]	Rate[2]	Year	Births[1]	Rate[2]	Year	Births[1]	Rate[2]
1910	2,777,000	30.1	1944	2,939,000	21.2	1960[3]	4,257,850	23.7
1915	2,965,000	29.5	1945	2,858,000	20.4	1961[3]	4,268,326	23.3
1920	2,950,000	27.7	1946	3,411,000	24.1	1962[3]	4,167,362	22.4
1925	2,909,000	25.1	1947	3,817,000	26.6	1963[3]	4,098,020	21.7
1928	2,674,000	22.2	1948	3,637,000	24.9	1964[3]	4,027,490	21.0
1930	2,618,000	21.3	1949	3,649,000	24.5	1965[3]	3,760,358	19.4
1932	2,440,000	19.5	1950	3,632,000	24.1	1966[3]	3,606,274	18.4
1934	2,396,000	19.0	1951[3]	3,823,000	24.9	1967[4]	3,520,959	17.8
1936	2,355,000	18.4	1952[3]	3,913,000	25.1	1968	3,501,564	17.5
1937	2,413,000	18.7	1953[3]	3,965,000	25.1	1969	3,600,206	17.8
1938	2,496,000	19.2	1954[3]	4,078,000	25.3	1970	3,731,386	18.4
1939	2,466,000	18.8	1955	4,104,000	25.0	1971	3,555,970	17.2
1940	2,559,000	19.4	1956[3]	4,218,000	25.2	1972	3,258,411	15.6
1941	2,703,000	20.3	1957[3]	4,308,000	25.3	1973	3,136,965	14.9
1942	2,989,000	22.2	1958[3]	4,255,000	24.5	1974	3,159,958	14.9
1943	3,104,000	22.7	1959[3]	4,295,000	24.3	1975[5]	3,149,000	14.8

[1] Figures through 1959 include adjustment for underregistration; beginning 1960, figures represent number registered. For comparison, the 1959 registered count was 4,245,000. [2] Rates are per 1,000 population estimated as of July 1 for each year except 1940, 1950, and 1960, which are as of April 1, the census date; for 1941–46 based on population including armed forces overseas. [3] Based on 50% sample of births. [4] Based on 20–50% sample of births. [5] Provisional. NOTE: Alaska is included beginning 1959, Hawaii beginning 1960.

Live Births by Order of Birth, 1940-1974

Source: National Center for Health Statistics, Department of Health, Education, and Welfare.

Year & race[1]	Total	Birth Order						
		1st	2nd	3rd	4th	5th	6th & 7th	8th & over
1940	2,558,647	940,116	639,236	349,941	205,443	131,099	154,138	138,674
1945	2,858,449	961,456	763,494	445,705	248,607	148,251	159,100	131,836
1950	3,631,512	1,140,398	1,096,716	630,102	314,067	165,808	162,039	133,382
1958[2]	4,255,005	1,140,328	1,085,413	826,025	511,090	285,603	257,392	149,154
1959 (adj.)[2]	4,294,829	1,133,011	1,076,384	830,962	526,308	297,710	272,655	157,799
1959 (reg.)[2]	4,244,796	1,125,396	1,086,305	823,330	519,269	291,814	265,171	151,511
1960[2]	4,247,850	1,122,691	1,054,308	823,402	526,631	300,176	273,902	156,740
1962[2]	4,167,362	1,117,422	1,004,835	783,961	513,040	304,082	280,281	163,741
1964[2]	4,027,490	1,166,928	964,867	720,538	470,318	280,744	265,547	158,548
1966[2]	3,606,274	1,225,469	888,448	585,116	362,876	215,159	204,521	124,685
1968[2]	3,501,564	1,312,354	918,549	539,504	307,837	171,138	158,225	93,957
1970[2]	3,731,386	1,430,680	1,013,394	573,016	301,610	159,634	135,174	75,048
1974[2]	3,159,958	1,314,194	980,875	435,645	189,716	87,426	69,076	35,677
White	2,575,792	1,074,068	822,898	355,383	149,287	66,347	49,038	22,325
Black	507,162	208,151	133,944	69,763	35,964	18,889	18,126	12,247
				Birth Rate				
1940	79.9	29.3	20.0	10.9	6.4	4.1	4.8	4.3
1945	85.9	28.9	22.9	13.4	7.5	4.5	4.8	4.0
1950	106.2	33.3	32.1	18.4	9.2	4.8	4.7	3.6
1958[2]	120.2	32.2	30.6	23.3	14.4	8.1	7.3	4.2
1959 (adj.)[2]	120.2	31.7	30.1	23.2	14.7	8.3	7.6	4.4
1959 (reg.)[2]	118.8	31.5	29.9	23.0	14.5	8.2	7.4	4.2
1960[2]	118.0	31.1	29.2	22.8	14.6	8.3	7.6	4.3
1962[2]	112.1	30.1	27.0	21.1	13.8	8.2	7.5	4.4
1964[2]	104.8	30.4	25.1	18.8	12.2	7.3	6.9	4.1
1966[2]	91.3	31.0	22.5	14.8	9.2	5.4	5.2	3.2
1968[2]	85.7	32.1	22.5	13.2	7.5	4.2	3.9	2.3
1970[2]	87.9	34.2	24.2	13.6	7.2	3.8	3.2	1.8
1974[2]	68.4	28.9	21.5	9.6	4.2	1.9	1.5	0.8
White	64.7	27.4	21.0	9.0	3.8	1.7	1.2	0.6
Black	90.8	38.1	24.4	12.7	6.5	3.4	3.3	2.2

[1] Data for 1940–58 are adjusted for underregistration; 1959 data show both registered and adjusted births; beginning 1960, registered births only are shown. Alaska is included beginning 1959, Hawaii beginning 1960. [2] Based on birth data from a 50% sample.
NOTE: Birth order refers to number of children born alive to mother. Figures are shown to the last digit as computed for convenience in summation. They are not assumed to be accurate to the last digit. Figures for births of order not stated are distributed, including births that occurred in Massachusetts, which did not require the reporting of birth order. Rates are live births per 1,000 female population aged 15–44 years in each specified group. Population enumerated as of April 1 for 1940, 1950, and 1960, and estimated as of July 1 for all other years.

Live Births by Sex and Sex Ratio, 1960-1974

Source: National Center for Health Statistics, Department of Health, Education and Welfare.

Year	Total			White			Black		
	Male	Female	Males per 1,000 females	Male	Female	Males per 1,000 females	Male	Female	Males per 1,000 females
1960[1] . . .	2,179,708	2,078,142	1,049	1,848,192	1,752,552	1,055	303,566	298,698	1,016
1965[1] . . .	1,927,054	1,833,304	1,051	1,604,422	1,519,438	1,056	294,272	286,854	1,026
1970[1,2] . .	1,915,378	1,816,008	1,055	1,590,140	1,501,124	1,059	290,508	281,854	1,031
1971[1,2] . .	1,822,910	1,733,060	1,052	1,499,958	1,419,788	1,056	286,430	278,530	1,028
1972[1,3] . .	1,669,927	1,588,484	1,051	1,364,578	1,290,980	1,057	268,842	262,487	1,024
1973[1,3] . .	1,608,326	1,528,639	1,052	1,311,032	1,239,998	1,057	259,877	252,720	1,028
1974[1,2] . .	1,622,114	1,537,844	1,055	1,325,019	1,250,773	1,059	257,277	249,885	1,030

[1] Based on 50% sample of births.   [2] Excludes births to nonresidents of U.S.   [3] Based on 100% of births in selected states and 50% sample in all others.

Live Births in the United States by Age of Mother, 1940-1974

Source: National Center for Health Statistics, Department of Health, Education, and Welfare.

Year[1] and race	Total[2]	Age of mother							
		Under 15 yrs.[3]	15–19 yrs.	20–24 yrs.	25–29 yrs.	30–34 yrs.	35–39 yrs.	40–44 yrs.	45 yrs. and over[4]
1940	2,558,647	3,865	332,667	799,537	693,268	431,468	222,015	68,269	7,558
1945	2,858,449	4,028	298,868	832,746	785,299	554,906	296,852	78,853	6,897
1950	3,631,512	5,413	432,911	1,155,167	1,041,360	610,816	302,780	77,743	5,322
1955[5] . . .	4,014,112	6,181	493,770	1,290,939	1,133,155	732,540	352,320	89,777	5,430
1960[5] . . .	4,257,850	6,780	586,966	1,426,912	1,092,816	687,722	359,908	91,564	5,182
1962[5] . . .	4,167,362	7,340	600,298	1,444,978	1,045,086	638,382	334,708	91,490	5,080
1964[5] . . .	4,027,490	7,816	585,701	1,439,486	1,007,362	585,006	309,814	87,626	4,670
1966[5] . . .	3,606,274	8,128	621,426	1,297,990	872,786	474,542	252,526	74,440	4,436
1968[5] . . .	3,501,564	9,504	591,312	1,306,872	903,890	419,696	206,062	60,438	3,790
1970[5] . . .	3,731,386	11,752	644,708	1,418,874	994,904	427,806	180,244	49,952	3,146
1972[5] . . .	3,258,411	12,082	616,280	1,174,183	900,392	375,001	141,328	36,861	2,284
1974[5] . . .	3,159,958	12,529	595,449	1,108,051	923,318	372,907	118,115	27,878	1,711
White	2,575,792	5,053	420,152	911,453	803,169	317,017	95,575	22,046	1,327
Black	507,162	7,291	164,430	173,860	95,138	42,900	18,250	4,953	340

		Birth rate							
1940.	79.9	0.7	54.1	135.6	122.8	83.4	46.3	15.6	1.9
1945.	85.9	0.8	51.1	138.9	132.2	100.2	56.9	16.6	1.6
1950.	106.2	1.0	81.6	196.6	166.1	103.7	52.9	15.1	1.2
1955[5]	118.0	0.9	89.7	240.4	190.8	115.8	59.5	15.7	1.1
1960[5]	118.0	0.8	89.1	258.1	197.4	112.7	56.2	15.5	0.9
1962[5]	112.1	0.8	81.3	243.8	191.3	108.7	52.6	14.8	0.9
1964[5]	104.8	0.9	72.9	219.8	178.8	103.5	49.9	13.8	0.8
1966[5]	91.3	0.9	70.6	185.9	149.4	85.9	42.2	11.7	0.7
1968[5]	85.7	1.0	66.1	167.4	140.3	74.9	35.6	9.6	0.6
1970[5]	87.9	1.2	68.3	167.8	145.1	73.3	31.7	8.1	0.5
1972[5]	73.4	1.2	62.0	131.0	118.7	60.2	24.8	6.2	0.4
1974[5]	68.4	1.2	58.1	119.0	113.3	54.4	20.2	4.8	0.3
White	64.7	0.6	48.3	114.2	113.5	53.5	18.9	4.4	0.2
Black	90.8	5.0	118.3	148.7	104.8	54.8	26.8	7.5	0.6

[1] Data for 1940–50 are adjusted for underregistration; beginning 1960, registered births only are shown. Alaska and Hawaii are included beginning 1960.   [2] Rates computed by relating total births, regardless of age of mother, to female population aged 15–44 years.   [3] Rates computed by relating births to mothers under 15 years, to female population aged 10–14.   [4] Rates computed by relating births to mothers 45 years and over, to female population aged 45–49 years.   [5] Based on birth data from a 50% sample; figures by color for 1962 exclude New Jersey because this state did not require reporting of this item.

NOTE: Data refer only to births occurring within the U.S. Figures are shown to the last digit as computed for convenience in summation. They are not assumed to be accurate to the last digit. Figures for age of mother not stated are distributed. Rates are live births per 1,000 female population in each specified group, enumerated as of Apr. 1 for 1940, 1950, and 1960, and estimated as of July 1 for all other years.

Live Births and Birth Rates by Race

Source: National Center for Health Statistics, Department of Health, Education, and Welfare.

Rates per 1,000 population in each specified group. Rates for 1940 and 1950 based on births adjusted for under-registration; data for 1974, registered births.

Race	Births 1974[1]	Rates 1974	Rates 1950	Rates 1940	Race	Births 1974[1]	Rates 1974	Rates 1950	Rates 1940
White............	2,575,792	14.0	23.0	18.6	Chinese........	8,001	n.a.	43.9	14.5
Black	507,162	21.0	33.1	26.5	Other..........	34,609	n.a.	19.1	22.0
Indian...........	26,631	n.a.	45.8	42.0	All races.......	3,159,958	14.9	24.1	19.4
Japanese........	7,763	n.a.	24.5	15.0					

[1] Based on a 50% sample of births. 1974 figures include Alaska and Hawaii. NOTE: n.a. = not available.

Births and Birth and Fertility Rates

Source: National Center for Health Statistics, Department of Health, Education, and Welfare.

Year	White Births[2]	White Birth Rate[3]	White Fertility Rate[4]	All Other[1] Births[2]	All Other[1] Birth Rate[3]	All Other[1] Fertility Rate[4]	Black Births[1]	Black Birth Rate[2]	Black Rate[3]
1950	3,108,000	23.0	102.3	524,000	33.3	137.3	466,718	31.0	126.9
1955	3,485,000	23.8	113.7	613,000	34.5	154.3	558,251	. . .	. . . .
1960	3,600,744	22.7	113.2	657,106	32.1	153.6	602,264	31.9	153.5
1965	3,123,860	18.3	91.4	636,498	27.6	133.9	581,126	27.5	133.9
1970[5]	3,091,264	17.4	84.1	640,122	25.1	113.0	572,362	25.3	115.4
1974[5]	2,575,792	14.0	64.7	584,166	21.4	91.0	507,162	21.0	90.8

[1] Includes Black. [2] Based on 50% sample of births. [3] Per 1,000 population in specified group. [4] Per 1,000 women aged 15–44 years in specified group. [5] Excludes births to nonresidents of U.S.

Crude Birth Rate for Selected Countries, 1938–1975

Source: Statistical Office of the United Nations.

Country	Rate[1] 1975	1964	1953	1938	Country	Rate[1] 1975	1964	1953	1938
North America					**Europe (cont.)**				
Canada............	15.4[2]	23.4	28.1	20.7	Hungary..........	18.4	13.1	21.5	19.9
Costa Rica.........	29.5[2]	43.0	49.2	45.0	Ireland...........	22.3[2]	22.4	21.2	19.4
El Salvador........	40.1	47.1	47.9	43.7	Italy..............	14.8	19.9	17.7	23.8
Mexico............	43.4[2]	44.8	44.7	43.5	Luxembourg.......	11.2	16.0	15.2	14.9
Nicaragua.........	39.4[5]	42.8	42.3	40.8	Netherlands.......	13.0	20.7	21.7	20.5
Panama[3].........	31.7	33.9	37.9	45.5	Norway...........	14.0	17.7	18.7	15.4
Puerto Rico........	23.3[5]	30.6	35.3	38.6	Portugal..........	19.6[2]	23.8	23.4	26.6
United States.......	14.8	21.0	24.7	17.6[4]	Romania..........	19.7	15.2	23.8	29.5
South America					Spain[10].........	18.2	22.2	20.6	20.1
Chile..............	27.6[7]	34.1	34.6	36.1	Sweden...........	12.6	16.0	15.4	14.9
Peru[6]...........	27.8[8]	38.9	36.0	. . . .	Switzerland.......	12.4	19.2	17.0	15.2
Venezuela[6]........	26.8[8]	43.4	46.1	33.7	United Kingdom...	12.4	18.8	15.9	15.5
Europe					**Asia**				
Austria............	12.3	18.5	14.8	13.9	India	42.8[11]	. . .	24.8	33.3
Belgium...........	12.3	17.2	16.6	16.0	Israel............	28.3	25.7	32.1[13]	26.3[12]
Bulgaria...........	17.2[2]	16.1	20.9	22.8	Japan[14]	17.2	17.8	21.5[15]	27.1[15]
Czechoslovakia.....	19.5	17.2	21.2	16.7	Sri Lanka.........	29.5[8]	33.2	38.7	35.8
Denmark..........	14.2[2]	17.7	17.9	18.1	**Other**				
Finland...........	14.2	17.6	21.9	21.0[9]	Australia[16]	17.2	20.6	22.9	17.4
France............	15.2[2]	18.2	18.9	15.0	New Zealand	18.4	24.2	25.4	19.3
Germany, West.....	9.7	18.5	15.8	19.7	South Africa[17]...	23.1[7]	23.7	25.2	25.0

[1] Number of births per 1,000 population. [2] 1974 figure. [3] Excluding tribal Indians. Figure for 1953 includes Indians in Bocas del Toro and Dairen Provinces. [4] Excluding Alaska and Hawaii. [5] 1973 figure. [6] Excluding Indian jungle population. [7] 1971 figure. [8] 1972 figure. [9] Finnish nationals in Finland only. [10] Includes Spanish North Africa. [11] 1970 figure. [12] Jewish population only. [13] Excluding Bedouin population in the Negev. [14] Japanese nationals in Japan only. [15] Excluding Amami Islands. Also excluding Tokara Archipelago in 1938. [16] Excluding full-blooded aborigines. [17] White population only (about 20% of total) through 1964.

Families in the U. S., 1950-1970

Sources: Statistical Bureau of the Metropolitan Life Insurance Company and reports by the Bureau of the Census.

	Families					Percentage of families with own children— under age 18	
	Number in thousands			Percent increase[1]			
State	1950	1960	1970	1950-60	1960-70	1960	1970
Alabama	731	791	870	8.2	10.0	59	55
Alaska	24[2]	47	66	96.9	41.1	69	67
Arizona	182	312	439	71.1	40.6	62	56
Arkansas	472	452	502	−4.1	11.0	55	51
California	2,803	3,992	4,988	42.4	25.0	58	55
Colorado	337	439	545	30.2	24.3	60	58
Connecticut	519	654	767	26.0	17.3	57	55
Delaware	81	112	136	38.4	21.6	59	58
D. C.	196	174	163	−11.5	6.4	46	51
Florida	721	1,297	1,806	79.9	39.3	52	47
Georgia	831	949	1,144	14.2	20.5	59	57
Hawaii	96	131	170	35.7	30.2	70	62
Idaho	148	166	179	12.1	7.9	63	57
Illinois	2,291	2,592	2,784	13.2	7.4	55	55
Indiana	1,057	1,198	1,318	13.4	10.0	57	56
Iowa	686	712	713	3.7	.2	56	54
Kansas	512	569	579	11.0	1.8	56	53
Kentucky	715	753	821	5.3	9.1	56	54
Louisiana	650	771	868	18.7	12.5	59	58
Maine	224	240	246	7.4	2.2	57	54
Maryland	590	763	972	29.5	27.3	59	57
Massachusetts	1,176	1,292	1,388	9.9	7.4	55	54
Michigan	1,657	1,944	2,182	17.3	12.2	59	58
Minnesota	751	837	917	11.4	9.5	59	57
Mississippi	509	501	530	−1.6	5.9	57	55
Missouri	1,051	1,133	1,200	7.8	5.9	52	52
Montana	146	166	170	13.7	2.6	61	57
Nebraska	347	366	372	5.3	1.8	56	54
Nevada	41	72	124	75.3	70.9	58	56
New Hampshire	137	153	183	11.8	19.3	56	55
New Jersey	1,267	1,581	1,833	24.8	16.0	56	55
New Mexico	159	222	242	39.3	9.0	67	62
New York	3,883	4,336	4,585	11.7	5.7	54	53
North Carolina	944	1,092	1,286	15.6	17.8	60	56
North Dakota	148	150	147	1.4	1.8	62	57
Ohio	2,108	2,465	2,683	16.9	8.8	57	56
Oklahoma	582	613	677	5.3	10.4	55	52
Oregon	410	460	542	12.0	17.8	57	53
Pennsylvania	2,660	2,903	2,999	9.1	3.3	55	53
Rhode Island	205	220	235	7.1	7.0	55	53
South Carolina	482	541	624	12.2	15.3	61	58
South Dakota	161	167	160	3.7	4.0	60	56
Tennessee	809	894	1,020	10.5	14.2	56	54
Texas	1,973	2,393	2,810	21.3	17.4	59	56
Utah	170	209	249	23.3	19.0	67	63
Vermont	92	94	106	2.9	12.7	57	56
Virginia	784	955	1,159	21.8	21.4	59	56
Washington	622	725	862	16.4	18.9	59	56
West Virginia	483	462	452	−4.4	2.2	57	52
Wisconsin	879	987	1,072	12.3	8.7	57	56
Wyoming	72	84	84	16.5	0.8	63	57
United States	38,574	45,128	50,969	17.0	12.9	57	55

[1] Minus sign (—) denotes decrease.   [2] Estimated.   NOTE: Figures are latest available.

Characteristics of Households With Female Heads

(numbers in thousands)

Source: Bureau of the Census.

Characteristics	1975	Characteristics	1975
All households	71,120	Household income:	
Female head	16,777	Under $2,000	2,349
Per cent of all households	23.6	$2,000 to $3,999	4,618
Persons per household	2.0	$4,000 to $5,999	2,707
Under 18 years	10,369	$6,000 to $7,999	2,125
Percentage under 18 years	30.7	$8,000 to $9,999	1,523
18 years and over	23,408	$10,000 to $14,999	2,102
Percentage 18 years and over	69.3	$15,000 to $24,999	1,111
Marital status of female head:		$25,000 to $49,000	216
Married, husband absent	2,213	$50,000 and over	26
Widowed	8,232	Median income	$5,051
Divorced	3,271		
Single	3,062		

Illegitimate Live Births in the U.S., 1940–1974

(in thousands, except as indicated)

Source: National Center for Health Statistics, Department of Health, Education, and Welfare.

Age and race	1974	1970	1965	1960	1955	1950	1945	1940
By age:								
Under 15 years	10.6	9.5	6.1	4.6	3.9	3.2	2.5	2.1
15–19 years	210.8	190.4	123.1	87.1	68.9	56.0	49.2	40.5
20–24 years	122.7	126.7	90.7	68.0	55.7	43.1	39.3	27.2
25–29 years	44.9	40.6	36.8	32.1	28.0	20.9	14.1	10.5
30–34 years	18.6	19.1	19.6	18.9	16.1	10.8	7.1	5.2
35–39 years	8.2	9.4	11.4	10.6	8.3	6.0	4.0	3.0
40 years and over	2.3	3.0	3.7	3.0	2.4	1.7	1.2	1.0
By race:								
White	168.5	175.1	123.7	82.5	64.2	53.5	56.4	40.3
Black and other	249.6	223.6	167.5	141.8	119.2	88.1	60.9	49.2
Total illegitimate births	418.1	398.7	291.2	224.3	183.4	141.6	117.3	89.5
Per cent of all births[1]	13.2	10.7	7.7	5.3	4.5	3.9	4.1	3.5
Rate[2]	24.1	26.4	23.4	21.8	19.3	14.1	10.1	7.1

[1] Through 1955, based on data adjusted for underregistration; thereafter, registered births. [2] Rate per 1,000 unmarried (never married, widowed, and divorced) women, 15–44 years old. NOTE: Figures are estimates based on 50% sample of births in 39 states and District of Columbia.

MORTALITY

Mortality from Motor Vehicle Accidents, 1974

Source: National Highway Traffic Safety Administration.

Country	Motor vehicles[1]	Death rate[2]	Death rate[3]	Country	Motor Vehicles[1]	Death rate[2]	Death rate[3]
United States	640	21	31	United Kingdom	310	13	41
France	440	26	58	Italy	360	18	51
Denmark	390	15	39	Ireland	190	19	100
Netherlands	410	20	49	Spain	170	15	85
Australia	470	27	57	Sweden	360	15	41
Norway	290	13	45	Switzerland	420	21	51
West Germany[4]	330	24	72	Yugoslavia	80	20	260
Austria	370	33	89	Japan	320	12	38
Finland	280	18	65	Belgium	360	27	74

[1] Per 1,000 population. [2] Deaths per 100,000 population. [3] Deaths per 100,000 registered motor vehicles. [4] Including West Berlin. NOTE: Accuracy of data does not warrant a finer breakdown beyond two significant figures. Information is latest available.

Deaths and Death Rates, 1974-1975

Source: National Center for Health Statistics, Department of Health, Education, and Welfare.

State	1975[1] Total deaths Number	Rate	Infant mortality Number	Rate	1974 Total deaths Number	Rate	Infant mortality Number	Rate
Alabama	34,041	9.4	1,171	20.1	41,822	10.1	1,251	18.4
Alaska	1,587	4.5	99	13.5	1,491	4.4	120	17.1
Arizona	17,543	7.9	566	14.3	17,396	8.1	598	15.0
Arkansas	21,681	10.2	571	16.9	21,915	10.6	537	15.9
California	171,121	8.1	4,222	13.4	170,672	8.2	4,276	13.7
Colorado	17,634	7.0	641	15.9	18,449	7.4	662	16.6
Connecticut	25,921	8.4	530	15.1	26,194	8.5	351	15.1
Delaware	4,904	8.5	100	11.9	5,191	9.1	126	14.9
D. C.	9,522	13.3	490	25.2	9,759	13.5	456	23.0
Florida	88,859	10.6	1,868	17.6	89,495	11.1	1,902	17.3
Georgia	43,084	8.7	1,419	17.5	43,550	8.9	1,527	18.0
Hawaii	4,579	5.3	218	13.8	4,599	5.4	254	16.4
Idaho	6,219	7.6	167	10.6	6,239	7.8	193	12.7
Illinois	100,816	9.0	2,957	17.7	105,542	9.5	3,158	19.0
Indiana	47,107	8.9	1,134	13.5	48,256	9.1	1,345	16.1
Iowa	28,936	10.0	554	13.3	28,615	10.2	580	14.3
Kansas	21,176	9.3	405	12.5	21,686	9.6	459	14.7
Kentucky	33,197	9.8	806	14.3	33,238	9.9	884	16.3
Louisiana	33,597	8.9	1,198	17.8	33,895	9.0	1,230	18.6
Maine	10,275	9.7	170	11.8	10,711	10.2	236	16.0
Maryland	31,203	7.6	573	12.6	32,129	7.8	730	15.6
Massachusetts	55,791	9.6	925	13.4	56,388	9.7	1,023	14.2
Michigan	73,668	8.0	2,173	16.4	75,364	8.3	2,384	17.5
Minnesota	33,701	8.6	800	14.0	34,154	8.7	841	15.1
Mississippi	25,103	10.7	843	19.7	22,728	9.8	988	22.7
Missouri	50,558	10.6	1,255	17.5	51,672	10.8	1,287	17.9
Montana	6,493	8.7	173	14.7	6,500	8.8	196	16.2
Nebraska	14,705	9.5	318	13.4	15,107	9.8	385	16.1
Nevada	4,743	8.0	138	15.9	4,656	8.1	175	19.9
New Hampshire	7,070	8.6	127	11.6	7,673	9.5	134	11.7
New Jersey	64,630	8.8	1,187	13.5	65,786	9.0	1,318	14.3
New Mexico	7,877	6.9	334	16.4	8,029	7.2	376	17.8
New York	169,274	9.3	3,970	16.7	176,007	9.7	3,987	16.5
North Carolina	46,069	8.5	1,560	19.3	19,652	11.0	524	18.9
North Dakota	5,673	8.9	172	15.3	5,928	9.3	179	16.7
Ohio	96,834	9.0	2,602	16.1	98,964	9.2	2,604	16.2
Oklahoma	26,729	9.9	655	15.8	26,440	9.8	720	17.6
Oregon	20,253	8.9	519	15.1	20,363	9.0	501	15.0
Pennsylvania	120,323	10.2	2,454	16.4	122,793	10.4	2,714	17.8
Rhode Island	9,029	9.7	185	16.9	9,155	9.8	188	16.1
South Carolina	23,142	8.2	860	19.0	23,776	8.5	1,001	21.3
South Dakota	6,327	9.3	180	16.2	6,525	9.6	211	19.2
Tennessee	41,757	10.0	1,215	18.1	41,822	10.1	1,251	18.4
Texas	100,324	8.2	3,655	16.4	100,981	8.4	3,852	17.4
Utah	7,871	6.5	467	14.3	7,705	6.6	422	13.8
Vermont	4,080	8.7	77	12.8	4,427	9.4	84	12.8
Virginia	39,677	8.0	1,169	17.2	39,725	8.1	1,140	16.8
Washington	30,256	8.5	798	15.9	30,051	8.6	764	15.4
West Virginia	19,746	11.0	503	18.2	19,652	11.0	524	18.9
Wisconsin	39,931	8.7	870	13.5	41,027	9.0	889	13.7
Wyoming	3,017	8.1	98	15.2	3,090	8.6	79	12.5
United States	1,907,666	9.0	50,141	16.1	1,936,476	9.2	52,882	16.7

[1] By place of occurrence. NOTE: Data exclude fetal deaths. Rates for total deaths are per 1,000 population in each area, estimated as of December for each year. Infant mortality rates are deaths under 1 year per 1,000 live births in each area.

Number of U.S. Families Up 8.9% Since 1970

The number of families in the United States increased by 8.9% since 1970 and now stands at 56,076,000. Of these, 47,297,000 are headed by a husband and wife, 7,335,000 by a female and 1,424,000 by a male. The number of families with a female head jumped 33.4% in the six-year period; those with a male head rose 16%, while those with a husband and wife were up only 5.7%.

Death Rates in the United States, 1900–1975

Source: National Center for Health Statistics, Department of Health, Education, and Welfare.

Year	Rate	Year	Rate	Year	Deaths	Rate
1900	17.2	1930	11.3	1953	1,517,541	9.6
1902	15.5	1931	11.1	1954	1,481,091	9.2
1904	16.4	1932	10.9	1955	1,528,717	9.3
1906	15.7	1933	10.7	1956	1,564,476	9.4
1908	14.7	1934	11.1	1957	1,633,128	9.6
1910	14.7	1935	10.9	1958	1,647,886	9.5
1912	13.6	1936	11.6	1959	1,656,814	9.4
1914	13.3	1937	11.3	1960	1,711,982	9.5
1915	13.2	1938	10.6	1961	1,701,522	9.3
1916	13.8	1939	10.6	1962	1,756,720	9.5
1917	14.0	1940	10.8	1963	1,813,549	9.6
1918	18.1	1941	10.5	1964	1,798,051	9.4
1919	12.9	1942	10.3	1965	1,828,136	9.4
1920	13.0	1943	10.9	1966	1,863,149	9.5
1921	11.5	1944	10.6	1967	1,851,323	9.4
1922	11.7	1945	10.6	1968	1,930,082	9.7
1923	12.1	1946	10.0	1969	1,921,990	9.5
1924	11.6	1947	10.1	1970[1]	1,921,031	9.5
1925	11.7	1948	9.9	1971[1]	1,927,542	9.3
1926	12.1	1949	9.7	1972[1]	1,963,944	9.4
1927	11.3	1950	9.6	1973[1]	1,973,003	9.4
1928	12.0	1951	9.7	1974[1]	1,934,388	9.2
1929	11.9	1952	9.6	1975[2]	1,910,000	9.0

[1] Excludes deaths of nonresidents. [2] Provisional. NOTE: Includes only deaths occurring within the registration area. Beginning with 1933, area includes entire U.S.; with 1959 includes Alaska, and with 1960 includes Hawaii. Excludes fetal deaths. Rates per 1,000 population residing in area, as of April 1 for 1940, 1950, and 1960, and estimated as of July 1 for all other years.

Death Rates by Age, Color, and Sex; U.S., 1900–1975

Source: National Center for Health Statistics, Department of Health, Education, and Welfare.

Age[1]	1975[2]	1970	1960	1940	1920	1900	1975[2]		1960	1940	1920	1900
	White Males						White Females					
Under 1	15.9	21.1	26.9	56.7	98.1	175.9	12.5	16.1	20.1	43.6	76.1	142.6
1–4	0.7	0.8	1.0	2.8	9.8	20.2	0.6	0.7	0.9	2.4	9.0	18.7
5–14	0.4	0.5	0.5	1.1	2.7	3.8	0.3	0.3	0.3	0.8	2.3	3.8
15–24	1.7	1.7	1.4	2.0	4.2	5.8	0.5	0.6	0.5	1.4	4.3	5.6
25–34	1.7	1.8	1.6	2.8	5.9	8.1	0.7	0.8	0.9	2.2	6.5	8.1
35–44	3.0	3.4	3.3	5.1	7.7	10.6	1.7	1.9	1.9	3.7	7.3	9.6
45–54	7.8	8.8	9.3	11.4	12.0	15.5	4.1	4.6	4.6	7.5	10.9	14.0
55–64	20.0	22.0	22.3	25.2	24.2	28.5	9.6	10.1	10.8	16.8	21.7	25.5
65–74	45.7	48.1	48.5	54.0	54.2	59.1	22.6	24.7	27.8	41.5	49.9	53.4
75–84	101.8	101.0	103.0	122.0	122.5	128.2	63.7	67.0	77.0	104.8	116.4	118.9
85 and over	184.2	185.5	217.5	251.4	253.6	269.2	146.4	159.8	194.8	235.0	247.0	256.7
	All Other Males						All Other Females					
Under 1	29.7	40.2	51.9	101.2	167.7	369.3	25.1	31.7	40.7	77.4	131.1	299.5
1–4	1.1	1.4	2.1	5.3	15.0	43.4	0.8	1.2	1.7	4.4	14.2	43.5
5–14	0.6	0.6	0.8	1.6	3.7	7.8	0.3	0.4	0.5	1.4	3.9	10.1
15–24	2.5	3.0	2.1	5.0	9.9	11.8	0.8	1.1	1.1	5.0	10.8	11.2
25–34	4.6	5.0	3.9	8.5	12.2	12.5	1.7	2.2	2.6	7.4	13.5	11.7
35–44	7.5	8.7	7.3	13.2	14.4	14.2	3.5	4.9	5.5	11.7	16.0	15.6
45–54	14.0	16.5	15.5	24.5	20.1	24.7	7.4	9.8	11.4	21.1	23.4	23.9
55–64	28.9	30.5	31.5	37.1[3]	31.1	42.1	16.6	18.9	24.1	33.2[3]	35.8	42.1
65–74	53.2	54.7	56.6	62.8[3]	60.2	71.6	35.3	36.8	39.8	52.3[3]	60.4	66.4
75–84	89.1	89.8	86.6	108.8	116.0	131.4	62.8	63.9	67.1	84.1	106.4	113.2
85 and over	116.5	114.1	152.4	199.7	247.1	249.3	88.8	102.9	128.7	159.7	221.2	195.8

[1] In years. [2] Estimated from a 10% sample of death certificates. [3] Based on enumerated population adjusted for age bias in nonwhite population at ages 55–69 years. NOTE: For 1900–20, data refer only to deaths occurring within the registration area; for 1940–62 they include the entire U. S. Alaska and Hawaii are included beginning 1960. Excludes fetal deaths. Rates are per 1,000 population in each group, enumerated as of April 1 for 1940, 1950, and 1960, and estimated as of July 1 for all other years.

Average of Annual Death Rates for Selected Causes; U.S., 1900-1975

Source: National Center for Health Statistics, Department of Health, Education, and Welfare.

| | Death rates per 100,000 | | | | | | |
| | 8th Revision | | 6th Revision | 5th Revision | | | |
Cause of death	1975[1]	1974	1950	1945–49	1940–44	1920–24	1900–04
Typhoid fever.................	([3])	0.0	0.1	0.2	0.6	7.3	26.7
Communicable diseases of childhood.......................	0.0	0.0	1.3	2.3	4.6	33.8	65.2
Measles.....................	0.0	0.0	0.3	0.6	1.1	7.3	10.0
Scarlet fever.................	([3])	0.0	0.2	0.1	0.4	4.0	11.8
Whooping cough.............	0.0	0.0	0.7	1.0	2.2	8.9	10.7
Diphtheria..................	([3])	0.0	0.3	0.7	1.0	13.7	32.7
Gastritis, duodenitis, enteritis, and colitis....................	([3])	0.0	5.1	6.5	9.8	42.8	115.3
Pneumonia and influenza.......	26.3	25.9	31.3	41.3	63.7	140.3	184.3
Influenza....................	2.2	1.0	4.4	5.0	13.0	34.8	22.8
Pneumonia...................	24.1	24.9	26.9	37.2	50.7	105.5	161.5
Tuberculosis.................	1.5	1.7	22.5	33.3	43.4	96.7	184.7
Cancer......................	174.4	170.5	139.8	134.0	123.1	86.9	67.7
Diabetes mellitus.............	16.8	17.7	16.2	24.1	26.2	17.1	12.2
Cardiovascular-renal diseases....	458.3	478.2	510.8	493.1	490.4	369.9	359.5
Diseases of the heart.........	338.6	349.2	356.8	325.1	303.2	169.8	153.0
Cerebral hemorrhage.........	12.6	14.4	104.0	93.8	91.7	93.5	106.3
Chronic nephritis.............	3.1	3.1	16.4	48.4	72.1	81.5	84.3
Syphilis.....................	0.2	0.1	5.0	8.4	12.7	17.6	12.9
Appendicitis.................	0.4	0.4	2.0	3.5	7.2	14.0	9.4
Accidents, all forms..........	46.9	49.5	60.6	67.6	73.0	70.8	79.2
Motor vehicle accidents........	20.9	22.0	23.1	22.3	22.7	12.9	([3])
Infant mortality[2].............	16.1	16.7	29.2	33.3	42.4	76.7	([3])
Neonatal mortality[2]...........	11.8	12.3	20.5	22.9	26.2	39.7	([3])
Fetal mortality[2].............	([3])	11.5	22.9	24.3	28.5	39.2[4]	([3])
Maternal mortality[2]...........	0.2	0.1	0.8	1.4	2.8	6.9	([3])
All causes...................	896.3	915.1	963.8	1,003.3	1,062.0	1,196.6	1,621.6

[1] Estimated from a 10 per cent sample of death certificates.   [2] Rates per 1,000 live births.   [3] Not available.   [4] 1922-24.
NOTE: Includes only deaths occurring within the registration area. Beginning with 1933, area includes the entire United States; beginning with 1960, it includes Alaska and Hawaii. Rates per 100,000 population residing in area, enumerated as of April 1 for 1940 and 1950 and estimated as of July 1 for all other years. Average rates computed from 5-year totals of deaths occurring in area and corresponding population. Due to major changes between the Fifth and Sixth Revisions of the International Lists of Causes of Death, the death rates are not strictly comparable.

Households, Families, and Married Couples in the United States, 1890-1976

Source: Bureau of the Census.

| | Households | | Families | | Married couples |
Date	Number	Average population per household	Number	Average population per family	Number
June 1890..............	12,690,000	4.93	....	...	....
April 1930..............	29,905,000	4.11	....	...	25,174,000
April 1940..............	34,949,000	3.67	32,166,000	3.76	28,517,000
March 1950.............	43,554,000	3.37	39,303,000	3.54	36,091,000
March 1960[1]............	52,799,000	3.33	45,111,000	3.67	40,200,000
March 1970[1]............	63,401,000	3.14	51,586,000	3.58	45,373,000
March 1976[1]	72,867,000	2.89	56,245,000	3.39	47,866,000

[1] Figures for 1960 and later include Alaska and Hawaii.

Accidental Death Rates, 1970

(Rates per 100,000 population by place of residence)

Source: Statistical Bureau of the Metropolitan Life Insurance Co.

Area	Total accidents	Motor vehicle Total	Motor vehicle Pedestrian	Falls	Fires and flames	Drownings[1]	Firearms	All others
UNITED STATES...	56.4	26.9	4.4	8.3	3.3	3.1	1.2	13.6
New England	44.6	17.9	4.1	10.7	2.9	2.5	0.5	10.1
Maine	56.7	24.0	4.0	9.4	4.4	3.2	(2)	15.7
New Hampshire..	54.1	27.0	3.8	9.5	4.6	(2)	(2)	13.0
Vermont	49.5	21.1	(2)	9.7	(2)	(2)	(2)	18.7
Massachusetts...	46.3	17.2	4.5	13.1	2.9	2.6	0.4	10.1
Rhode Island....	36.6	13.7	4.7	10.0	2.1	(2)	(2)	10.8
Connecticut	37.1	15.8	3.3	7.2	2.2	2.4	(2)	9.5
Middle Atlantic	41.7	18.8	5.0	8.2	2.5	1.7	0.4	10.1
New York	38.3	17.9	5.6	7.8	2.0	1.6	0.3	8.7
New Jersey	41.8	18.3	4.4	8.5	2.7	1.8	0.4	10.1
Pennsylvania	46.9	20.4	4.3	8.8	3.1	1.7	0.6	12.3
East North Central..	51.2	24.8	3.8	8.6	2.9	2.5	0.9	11.5
Ohio	51.8	24.5	3.8	10.9	2.8	2.3	0.7	10.6
Indiana	56.4	29.9	4.0	8.5	3.0	2.5	1.1	11.4
Illinois	48.4	21.9	3.7	7.3	3.3	2.5	1.0	12.4
Michigan	50.1	25.7	4.2	7.6	2.5	2.6	0.9	10.8
Wisconsin	52.8	24.7	3.3	8.8	2.8	2.9	1.1	12.5
West North Central.	61.6	30.3	3.2	10.3	2.8	2.8	1.2	14.2
Minnesota	55.8	27.2	4.3	9.1	2.4	2.6	0.7	13.8
Iowa	61.1	32.8	2.3	9.3	2.3	2.7	(2)	14.0
Missouri	64.2	30.6	3.8	11.8	3.5	2.6	1.5	14.2
North Dakota....	62.8	29.5	(2)	9.1	(2)	3.6	(2)	20.6
South Dakota....	71.4	36.9	(2)	9.8	(2)	3.8	(2)	20.9
Nebraska	65.4	30.1	2.7	11.9	2.8	3.0	1.7	15.9
Kansas	61.0	30.1	2.0	10.0	2.7	3.3	1.2	13.6
South Atlantic	64.1	30.9	5.4	7.5	4.5	4.5	1.6	15.1
Delaware	56.6	28.8	4.9	8.4	(2)	(2)	(2)	19.4
Maryland	47.9	20.8	4.6	8.2	3.7	3.2	0.7	11.3
D.C.	69.3	22.6	8.5	11.8	7.5	(2)	(2)	27.4
Virginia	56.8	26.0	4.4	8.6	3.8	3.5	1.2	13.7
West Virginia....	71.1	30.8	4.2	9.3	4.4	3.3	1.9	21.4
North Carolina...	66.2	33.9	6.3	6.2	4.8	4.0	1.7	15.6
South Carolina...	73.0	37.9	7.3	5.9	6.6	5.2	2.0	15.4
Georgia	73.7	38.5	4.9	6.5	5.6	4.2	2.7	16.2
Florida	65.1	31.1	5.5	7.7	3.3	6.8	1.6	14.6
East South Central..	71.9	36.8	4.6	7.6	5.1	3.7	2.5	16.2
Kentucky	68.5	32.5	4.8	10.5	3.6	3.0	1.7	17.2
Tennessee	66.7	35.8	4.4	7.2	4.7	3.3	1.9	13.8
Alabama	74.8	38.8	4.7	6.8	5.8	4.0	3.2	16.2
Mississippi	81.6	41.5	4.7	5.5	7.2	5.1	3.9	18.4
West South Central.	65.3	31.9	4.0	6.9	4.2	4.4	2.1	15.8
Arkansas	69.4	31.1	4.2	7.1	6.2	4.8	2.3	17.9
Louisiana	68.0	32.2	4.2	6.4	4.7	5.7	2.4	16.6
Oklahoma	67.8	30.9	3.0	7.8	4.7	3.6	2.5	18.3
Texas	63.1	32.1	4.2	6.8	3.5	4.2	1.8	14.7
Mountain	72.5	37.8	5.0	7.5	2.7	4.0	2.1	18.4
Montana	81.1	42.6	(2)	11.2	(2)	4.5	(2)	22.8
Idaho	82.9	43.9	4.6	7.2	(2)	5.0	2.8	24.0
Wyoming	100.2	51.1	(2)	9.0	(2)	(2)	(2)	40.1
Colorado	58.3	29.4	3.0	9.4	2.1	2.5	1.3	13.6
New Mexico../..	89.1	46.9	8.4	7.7	5.8	4.5	2.9	21.3
Arizona	75.9	40.0	6.5	4.1	3.9	4.8	2.5	20.6
Utah	58.2	30.5	5.1	7.7	(2)	3.8	(2)	16.2
Nevada	74.7	40.5	7.2	4.9	(2)	5.9	(2)	23.4
Pacific	59.2	26.9	4.3	8.3	2.9	3.6	0.9	16.6
Washington	60.0	27.0	3.6	9.3	3.6	3.9	0.7	15.5
Oregon	66.4	34.8	4.4	8.0	3.3	4.4	1.0	14.9
California	58.3	26.3	4.5	8.4	2.7	3.4	0.9	16.6
Alaska	117.2	34.7	(2)	(2)	10.3	8.6	(2)	63.6
Hawaii	35.8	17.7	4.0	2.9	(2)	3.6	(2)	11.6

[1] Exclusive of deaths in water transportation. [2] Fewer than 20 deaths; rate not computed. NOTE: Data are latest available.

Crude Death Rate for Selected Countries, 1938–1975

Source: Statistical Office of the United Nations.

Country	Rate[1] 1975	1964	1953	1938	Country	Rate[1] 1975	1964	1953	1938
North America					**Europe (contd.)**				
Canada............	7.4[2]	7.5	8.6	9.7	Hungary..........	12.4	10.0	11.7	14.3
Costa Rica.........	5.0[2]	8.5	11.7	17.7	Ireland...........	11.2[2]	11.4	11.7	13.6
El Salvador........	8.0	10.4	14.7	19.1	Italy.............	9.9	9.6	10.0	14.1
Mexico............	7.2[2]	9.9	15.8	22.9	Luxembourg.......	12.2	11.8	12.5	12.7
Nicaragua..........	6.6[5]	7.3	10.2	14.5	Netherlands.......	8.3	7.7	7.7	8.5
Panama[3].........	5.3[2]	7.3[4]	9.2	14.2	Norway...........	9.9	9.5	8.5	9.9
Puerto Rico........	6.5[5]	7.2	8.2	18.7	Portugal..........	11.0[2]	10.6	11.3	15.4
United States......	9.0	9.4	9.6	10.6[6]	Romania..........	9.1[2]	8.1	11.6	19.1
South America					Spain.............	8.1	8.7	9.7	19.3
Chile.............	8.4[7]	11.1	12.4	23.1	Sweden...........	10.8	10.0	9.7	11.5
Peru[8]............	8.3[9]	10.1	12.2	16.2	Switzerland.......	8.8	9.1	10.2	11.6
Venezuela[8]	6.8[5]	7.1	9.9	18.3	United Kingdom...	11.8	11.3	11.4	11.8
Europe					**Asia**				
Austria...........	12.7	12.3	12.0	14.0	India	16.7[17]	...	14.5	23.7
Belgium...........	12.0	11.7	12.1	13.2	Israel	7.2	6.3	6.7[12]	8.1[11]
Bulgaria..........	9.8[2]	8.2[2]	9.3	13.7	Japan[13]	6.4	6.9	8.9[14]	17.7[14]
Czechoslovakia.....	11.5	9.6	10.5	13.2	Sri Lanka	7.7[9]	8.8	10.7	21.0
Denmark..........	10.2[2]	9.9	9.0	10.3	**Other**				
Finland...........	9.4	9.3	9.6	12.8[10]	Australia[15]	8.1	9.0	9.1	9.6
France............	10.4[2]	10.8	13.1	15.8	New Zealand	8.1	8.8	9.0	10.5
Germany, West.....	12.1	10.8	11.2	11.4	South Africa[16].....	8.5[7]	7.7[4]	8.6	9.5

[1] Number of deaths per 1,000 population. [2] 1974 figure. [3] Excluding tribal Indians. Figure for 1953 includes Indians in Bocas del Toro and Dairen Provinces. [4] 1965 figure. [5] 1973 figure. [6] Excluding Alaska and Hawaii. [7] 1971 figure. [8] Excluding Indian jungle population. [9] 1972 figure. [10] Finnish nationals in Finland only. [11] Jewish population only. [12] Excluding Bedouin population in the Negev. [13] Japanese nationals in Japan only. [14] Excluding Amami Islands. Also excluding Tokara Archipelago in 1938. [15] Excludes full-blooded aborigines. [16] White population only (about 20% of total) through 1964. [17] 1969-70 average.

Transportation-Accident Death Rates, 1973–1975

Source: National Safety Council.

Kind of transportation	1975 Passenger miles	Passenger deaths	Death rate[1]	1973–75 average death rate[1]
Passenger automobiles and taxis[2]	1,940,000,000,000	27,200	1.40	1.50
Passenger automobiles on turnpikes[2]	47,000,000,000	320	0.70	0.80
Buses	73,000,000,000	110	0.15	0.20
Intercity buses	18,100,000,000	3	0.02	0.08
Railroad passenger trains	9,600,000,000	8	0.08	0.07
Scheduled air transport planes (domestic)	131,000,000,000	113	0.09	0.10

[1] Per 1,000,000 passenger miles. [2] Drivers of passenger automobiles are considered passengers.

Twelve Accidental Deaths Every Hour

Source: National Safety Council.

The nation's 1975 accident totals can be figured at the following approximate rates:

Class of accident		One every		Class of accident		One every	
All accidents	Deaths	5	minutes	Workers off-job	Deaths	14	minutes
	Injuries	3	seconds		Injuries	10	seconds
Motor-vehicle	Deaths	11	minutes	Home	Deaths	21	minutes
	Injuries	18	seconds		Injuries	8	seconds
Work	Deaths	42	minutes	Public non-motor-vehicle	Deaths	23	minutes
	Injuries	14	seconds		Injuries	11	seconds

Motor-Vehicle Deaths by Type of Accident, 1937-1975

Source: National Safety Council.

Year	Total deaths[1]	Pedes-trians	Other motor vehicles	Railroad trains	Street cars	Bicycles	Animal-drawn vehicle or animal	Fixed objects	Deaths from non-collision accidents
					Deaths from collisions with—				
1937..........	39,643	15,500	10,320	1,810	264	700	200	1,160	9,690
1939..........	32,386	12,400	8,700	1,330	150	710	200	1,000	7,900
1941..........	39,969	13,550	12,500	1,840	118	910	250	1,350	9,450
1943..........	23,823	9,900	5,300	1,448	171	450	160	700	5,690
1945..........	28,076	11,000	7,150	1,703	163	500	130	800	6,600
1947..........	32,697	10,450	9,900	1,736	102	550	150	1,000	8,800
1949..........	31,701	8,800	10,500	1,452	56	550	140	1,100	9,100
1951..........	36,996	9,150	13,100	1,573	46	390	100	1,400	11,200
1953..........	37,955	8,750	13,400	1,506	26	420	120	1,500	12,200
1955..........	38,426	8,200	14,500	1,490	15	410	90	1,600	12,100
1957..........	38,702	7,850	15,400	1,376	13	460	80	1,700	11,800
1959..........	37,910	7,850	14,900	1,202	6	480	70	1,600	11,800
1961..........	38,091	7,650	14,700	1,267	5	490	80	1,700	12,200
1963..........	43,564	8,200	17,600	1,385	10	580	80	1,900	13,800
1964..........	47,700	9,000	19,600	1,580	5	710	100	2,100	14,600
1966..........	53,041	9,400	22,200	1,800	2	740	100	2,500	16,300
1968..........	54,862	9,900	22,400	1,570	4	790	100	2,700	17,400
1969..........	55,791	10,100	23,700	1,495	2	800	100	3,900	15,700
1970..........	54,633	9,900	23,200	1,459	3	780	100	3,800	15,400
1971..........	54,381	9,900	23,100	1,378	2	800	100	3,800	15,300
1972..........	56,278	10,300	23,900	1,260	2	1,000	100	3,900	15,800
1973..........	55,511	10,200	23,600	1,194	2	1,000	100	3,800	15,600
1974..........	46,402	8,500	19,700	1,209	1	1,000	100	3,100	12,800
1975..........	46,000	8,600	20,300	1,000	([2])	1,000	100	3,100	11,900

[1] Yearly totals do not quite equal sums of various types because totals for most types are estimated, and these have been made only to nearest 10 deaths for some types and to nearest 50 deaths for others. [2] Not available.

Motor-Vehicle Traffic Deaths by States, 1974-1975

Source: National Safety Council.

State	1974	Rate[1]	1975	Rate[1]	State	1974	Rate[1]	1975	Rate[1]
Alabama..............	976	4.1	975	3.9	Montana...............	299	5.1	298	5.2
Alaska...............	85	4.1	114	4.5	Nebraska.............	388	3.5	376.	3.4
Arizona..............	748	4.8	676	4.2	Nevada..............	216	5.1	220	4.9
Arkansas.............	527	3.9	566	4.1	New Hampshire.......	166	3.3	151	2.9
California.............	4,019	3.1	4,189	3.2	New Jersey..........	1,112	2.4	1,080	2.2
Colorado.............	615	3.8	591	3.6	New Mexico..........	568	5.7	548	5.7
Connecticut...........	398	2.2	395	2.2	New York............	2,633	4.0	2,459	3.8
Delaware.............	113	3.3	125	3.4	North Carolina........	1,585	4.5	1,518	4.2
District of Columbia....	78	2.6	74	2.4	North Dakota........	162	3.7	169	3.8
Florida..............	2,270	3.7	2,040	3.2	Ohio................	1,900	3.0	1,809	2.8
Georgia..............	1,557	4.4	1,387	3.5	Oklahoma............	751	3.5	762	3.4
Hawaii...............	129	3.3	146	3.5	Oregon.............	672	4.4	571	3.6
Idaho................	327	6.0	283	4.9	Pennsylvania........	2,155	3.2	2,082	3.3
Illinois...............	2,007	3.4	2,084	3.4	Rhode Island.........	98	1.8	111	1.9
Indiana..............	1,244	3.4	1,133	3.0	South Carolina.......	873	4.4	821	4.0
Iowa.................	685	3.6	674	3.4	South Dakota........	229	4.5	198	3.9
Kansas..............	519	3.4	517	3.3	Tennessee...........	1,274	4.1	1,145	3.5
Kentucky.............	795	3.3	882	3.6	Texas...............	3,046	3.9	3,429	4.1
Louisiana............	864	4.4	940	4.6	Utah................	229	3.1	275	3.5
Maine................	217	3.3	226	3.3	Vermont.............	127	4.2	143	4.3
Maryland.............	737	3.1	691	2.7	Virginia.............	1,050	3.1	1,030	3.0
Massachusetts.........	961	3.4	883	3.0	Washington..........	761	3.4	771	3.2
Michigan.............	1,875	3.4	1,812	3.1	West Virginia........	449	4.4	486	4.6
Minnesota............	852	3.5	777	3.0	Wisconsin...........	912	3.3	940	3.3
Mississippi...........	643	4.7	612	4.3	Wyoming............	195	5.6	213	5.8
Missouri.............	1,046	3.5	1,073	3.5	TOTAL U. S.........	....	3.6	46,000	3.5

[1] Number of deaths per 100,000,000 vehicle-miles. NOTE: Source, state traffic authorities, by place of accident.

LAW ENFORCEMENT AND CRIME

Full-Time Police Department Employees, Oct. 31, 1974[1]

Source: Federal Bureau of Investigation.

City	Police officers	Civilians	Total	City	Police officers	Civilians	Total
Atlanta, Ga.	1,586	308	1,894	Minneapolis, Minn.	830	109	939
Baltimore, Md.	3,527	623	4,150	Nashville, Tenn.	862	175	1,037
Birmingham, Ala.	652	125	777	New Orleans, La.	1,383	454	1,837
Boston, Mass.	2,498	379	2,877	New York, N. Y.	31,033	4,620	35,653
Buffalo, N. Y.	1,327	203	1,530	Newark, N. J.	1,603	183	1,786
Chicago, Ill.	13,266	1,669	14,935	Norfolk, Va.	537	115	652
Cincinnati, Ohio	1,148	146	1,294	Oakland, Calif.	682	253	935
Cleveland, Ohio	2,345	293	2,638	Oklahoma City, Okla.	629	97	726
Columbus, Ohio	1,145	225	1,370	Omaha, Neb.	588	122	710
Dallas, Tex.	1,939	605	2,544	Philadelphia, Pa.	8,245	1,002	9,247
Denver, Colo.	1,362	306	1,668	Phoenix, Ariz.	1,342	254	1,596
Detroit, Mich.	5,371	735	6,106	Pittsburgh, Pa.	1,465	23	1,488
El Paso, Tex.	572	87	659	Portland, Ore.	733	192	925
Fort Worth, Tex.	683	122	805	Rochester, N. Y.	628	111	739
Honolulu, Hawaii	1,366	375	1,741	St. Louis, Mo.	2,217	605	2,822
Houston, Tex.	2,332	460	2,792	St. Paul, Minn.	517	123	640
Indianapolis, Ind.	1,097	195	1,292	San Antonio, Tex.	1,099	241	1,340
Jacksonville, Fla.	914	403	1,317	San Diego, Calif.	1,110	279	1,389
Kansas City, Mo.	1,280	379	1,659	San Francisco, Calif.	1,958	495	2,453
Long Beach, Calif.	661	207	868	San Jose, Calif.	687	166	853
Los Angeles, Calif.	7,389	2,748	10,137	Seattle, Wash.	1,086	276	1,362
Louisville, Ky.	780	200	980	Tampa, Fla.	647	159	806
Memphis, Tenn.	1,277	331	1,608	Toledo, Ohio	732	78	810
Miami, Fla.	778	241	1,019	Tulsa, Okla.	568	100	668
Milwaukee, Wis.	2,124	188	2,312	Washington, D. C.	4,597	961	5,558

[1] At press time, latest figures available.

AVERAGE ANNUAL SALARY SCALES OF POLICEMEN AND FIREFIGHTERS, BY CITY SIZE-GROUPS: 1965 TO 1974

In dollars. Based on a study covering cities with a population of 100,000 or more.

EMPLOYEE GROUP AND YEAR	MINIMUM ANNUAL SCALES					MAXIMUM ANNUAL SCALES				
	Total	City population size-group				Total	City population size-group			
		100,000–249,999	250,000–499,999	500,000–999,999	1,000,000 or more		100,000–249,999	250,000–499,999	500,000–999,999	1,000,000 or more
POLICEMEN										
1965	5,763	5,134	5,404	5,603	6,193	6,919	6,007	6,390	6,659	7,550
1970	8,448	7,357	7,926	7,888	9,300	10,017	8,648	9,385	9,616	10,927
1971	8,874	7,939	8,414	8,291	9,675	10,576	9,408	9,960	10,109	11,452
1972	9,446	8,342	8,747	8,749	10,465	11,298	9,988	10,423	10,667	12,417
1973	9,928	8,842	9,251	9,364	10,870	12,278	10,640	11,065	11,684	13,626
1974 (prel.)	10,539	9,401	9,890	9,790	11,595	13,041	11,323	11,885	12,239	14,524
FIREFIGHTERS										
1965	5,633	5,046	5,310	5,646	6,293	6,689	5,892	6,297	6,607	7,630
1970	8,041	7,103	7,685	7,786	9,253	9,482	8,349	9,089	9,293	10,828
1971	8,490	7,672	8,179	8,215	9,596	10,060	9,080	9,649	9,839	11,327
1972	9,022	8,098	8,480	8,743	10,410	10,725	9,642	10,080	10,485	12,284
1973	9,507	8,596	9,053	9,211	10,832	11,589	10,242	10,788	11,240	13,564
1974 (prel.)	10,055	9,097	9,743	9,561	11,541	12,308	10,889	11,657	11,808	14,450

Source: U.S. Bureau of Labor Statistics, *Current Wage Developments*, March 1975. Based on data from International City Management Assoc., Fraternal Order of Police, and International Assoc. of Firefighters.

POLICE OFFICERS KILLED, BY GEOGRAPHIC DIVISIONS: 1960 TO 1973

Covers law enforcement officers killed in line of duty.

ITEM	1960	1964	1965	1967	1968	1969	1970	1971	1972	1973
Total killed	48	88	83	123	123	125	146	178	153	169
By felons	(NA)	57	53	76	64	86	100	126	112	127
In accidents	(NA)	31	30	47	59	39	46	52	41	42
New England	3	4	3	4	3	3	2	5	2	7
Middle Atlantic	7	12	10	15	10	15	29	31	21	21
East North Central	9	12	10	29	19	31	38	32	23	21
West North Central	3	5	3	8	12	10	6	13	11	6
South Atlantic	13	25	15	20	34	15	23	28	38	35
East South Central	2	5	9	9	9	9	5	13	12	13
West South Central	6	13	14	14	15	19	15	23	27	30
Mountain	–	2	7	6	4	6	4	11	7	16
Pacific	5	10	12	18	17	17	24	22	12	20

— Represents zero. NA Not available. Source: U.S. Federal Bureau of Investigation, *Uniform Crime Reports for the United States,* annual.

HOMICIDE VICTIMS AND SUICIDES, BY RACE AND SEX: 1930 TO 1973

YEAR	HOMICIDE VICTIMS					SUICIDES				
	Total	White		Black and other		Total	White		Black and other	
		Male	Female	Male	Female		Male	Female	Male	Female
NUMBER										
1930	[1] 10,331	[1] 4,605	[1] 1,236	[1] 3,628	[1] 862	18,323	13,877	3,863	442	141
1935	[1] 10,396	[1] 4,200	[1] 1,116	[1] 4,167	[1] 913	18,214	13,465	4,094	477	178
1940	8,329	2,977	796	3,670	886	18,907	13,990	4,294	476	147
1945	7,547	2,759	791	3,210	787	14,782	10,374	3,920	380	108
1950	7,942	2,586	952	3,503	901	17,145	12,755	3,713	542	135
1955	7,418	2,439	922	3,191	866	16,760	12,430	3,662	531	137
1960	8,464	2,832	1,154	3,437	1,041	19,041	13,825	4,296	714	206
1965	10,712	3,660	1,379	4,488	1,185	21,507	14,624	5,718	866	299
1968	14,686	5,106	1,700	6,417	1,463	21,372	14,520	5,692	859	301
1969	15,477	5,215	1,801	6,951	1,510	22,364	14,886	6,152	971	355
1970 [2]	16,848	5,865	1,938	7,413	1,632	23,480	15,591	6,468	1,038	383
1971 [2]	18,787	6,455	2,106	8,357	1,869	24,092	15,802	6,775	1,058	457
1972 [2]	19,638	6,820	2,156	8,822	1,840	25,004	16,476	6,788	1,292	448
1973 [2]	20,465	7,411	2,575	8,429	2,050	25,118	16,823	6,589	1,285	421
RATE [3]										
1930	[1] 12.4	[1] 12.1	[1] 3.3	[1] 92.6	[1] 21.8	22.1	36.4	10.4	11.3	3.6
1935	[1] 11.2	[1] 9.9	[1] 2.7	[1] 94.4	[1] 20.2	19.6	31.8	9.8	10.8	3.9
1940	8.4	6.7	1.8	79.9	18.5	19.2	31.3	9.6	10.4	3.1
1945	7.7	6.8	1.7	71.4	15.2	15.1	25.6	8.2	8.5	2.1
1950	7.2	5.3	1.9	67.4	16.2	15.6	26.0	7.4	10.4	2.4
1955	6.4	4.8	1.7	57.8	14.4	14.5	24.5	6.9	9.6	2.3
1960	6.9	5.3	2.0	56.2	15.6	15.4	25.7	7.6	11.7	3.1
1965	8.0	6.3	2.2	66.6	15.9	16.1	25.3	9.2	12.9	4.0
1968	10.5	8.5	2.6	90.0	18.2	15.2	24.2	8.8	12.1	3.8
1969	10.9	8.6	2.7	95.1	18.3	15.7	24.4	9.3	13.3	4.3
1970 [2]	11.6	9.5	2.9	95.9	18.5	16.2	25.3	9.6	13.4	4.3
1971 [2]	12.6	10.2	3.1	105.9	20.7	16.2	25.0	9.9	13.4	4.8
1972 [2]	13.0	10.6	3.1	108.3	19.7	16.5	25.6	9.7	15.9	4.8
1973 [2]	13.3	11.3	3.6	100.7	21.4	16.3	25.7	9.3	15.4	4.4

[1] Excludes legal executions. [2] Excludes non-resident deaths. [3] Per 100,000 resident population 15 years old and over; enumerated as of April 1 for 1930, 1940, 1950, 1960, and 1970; estimated as of July 1 for all other years. Source: U.S. National Center for Health Statistics, *Vital Statistics of the United States,* annual.

MURDER VICTIMS, BY WEAPONS USED: 1965 TO 1973

YEAR	Murder victims, total	WEAPONS USED OR CAUSE OF DEATH						
		Guns	Percent	Cutting or stabbing	Blunt object [1]	Strangulations, beatings	Drownings, arson, etc.	All other [2]
1965	8,773	5,015	57.2	2,021	505	894	226	112
1966	9,552	5,660	59.3	2,134	516	896	203	143
1967	11,114	6,998	63.0	2,200	789	957	211	159
1968	12,503	8,105	64.8	2,317	713	936	294	138
1969	13,575	8,876	65.4	2,534	613	1,039	322	191
1970	13,649	9,039	66.2	2,424	604	1,031	353	198
1971	16,183	10,712	66.2	3,017	645	1,295	314	200
1972	15,832	10,379	65.6	2,974	672	1,291	331	185
1973	17,123	11,249	65.7	2,985	848	1,445	[3] 173	423

[1] Refers to club, hammer, etc.   [2] Includes poison, explosives, unknown, and not stated; for 1973 includes drowning.   [3] Arson only.

FIREARMS—DOMESTIC PRODUCTION AND IMPORTS: 1960 TO 1974

In thousands. Includes firearms sold under civilian marksmanship program of Department of Defense.

ITEM	1960	1965	1966	1967	1968	1969	1970	1971 [1]	1972 [1]	1973 [1]	1974 [1]
Total	2,163	3,121	3,522	4,087	5,266	6,180	(NA)	(NA)	(NA)	6,018	6,935
Domestic production	1,508	2,355	2,526	2,879	[2]3,515	5,290	(NA)	(NA)	(NA)	4,844	5,639
Handguns	475	666	700	926	[2]1,259	2,840	(NA)	(NA)	(NA)	1,734	1,715
Rifles	469	790	850	909	[2]1,100	} 2,450	} (NA)	(NA)	(NA)	1,830	2,099
Shotguns	564	899	976	1,044	[2]1,155			(NA)	(NA)	1,280	1,825
Imports for consumption	655	766	996	1,208	1,751	890	826	951	1,200	1,174	1,296
Handguns	128	347	513	747	1,155	349	227	301	468	559	652
Rifles	402	245	291	239	277	207	237	243	197	195	188
Shotguns	125	174	192	222	318	334	363	406	535	420	456

NA Not available.   [1] Fiscal-year data.   [2] Estimated. Source: 1960–1970, U.S. Bureau of the Census, *U.S. Imports, General and Consumption, Schedule A Commodity and Country,* FT 135, and National Commission on the Causes and Prevention of Violence, Task Force report, *Firearms and Violence in American Life.* Beginning 1971, U.S. Bureau of Alcohol, Tobacco, and Firearms, *Alcohol, Tobacco and Firearms, Summary Statistics,* Publication ATF P. 1323.1.

Federal Prisoners Sentenced by Courts, 1945–1975

Fiscal years ending June 30

Source: Bureau of Prisons.

Offense	1975[1]	1974[1]	1970[1]	1965	1961	1954	1950	1945
Counterfeiting	297	258	341	212	180	88	260	47
Drug laws: Marihuana	0[2]	0[2]	486	238	191	509	878	454
Narcotics	2,302	2,155	764	1,119	1,196	1,366	1,151	680
Non-narcotics	1,182	1,205	....	....	....	....	....	....
Controlled substances	512	388	....	....	....	....	....	....
Embezzlement and fraud	657	510	440	509	645	445	609	340
Forgery	672	560	675	1,193	1,737	1,484	1,274	626
Immigration laws	2,310	2,028	1,109	1,626	1,478	7,277	3,463	3,996
Income tax	219	178	97	184	170	203	164	15
Juvenile delinquency	216	251	339	677	881	829	658	911
Kidnaping	97	59	46	26	30	41	41	20
Liquor laws	149	279	640	1,819	1,958	2,143	2,304	2,988
Robbery	1,379	1,012	802	592	270	193	92	45
Theft from interstate commerce	277	214	280	375	349	320	270	475
Transportation, etc., of stolen motor vehicle	929	1,025	2,157	3,245	3,607	2,838	2,486	1,072
White-slave traffic	41	37	38	69	143	242	185	209
Govt. reservation, D. C., high seas and terr. cases	650	369	336	735	671	1,487	1,145	986
Other	3,350	4,494	2,073	2,135	2,280	1,851	2,104	1,748
National security offenses:								
Selective Service Acts	29	135	368	186	142	342	136	2,613
Other national-defense and security laws	6	2	13	46	39	167	130	2,150
Military court-martial cases: Army	13	18	36	1	21	639	606	1,793
Navy	4	4	20	3	4	33	107	32
TOTAL ALL OFFENSES	15,291	15,181	11,060	14,990	15,992	22,497	18,063	21,200

[1] Excludes Federal prisoners committed to non-Federal institutions.   [2] New classification for drug offenses became effective in 1973.

Total Arrests, Distribution by Sex, 1974[1]

Source: Federal Bureau of Investigation.

(Data in this table are from reports furnished the FBI by 5,298 agencies. This represents a total population of 134,082,000).

Offense charged	Males	Per cent	Females	Per cent	Total	Per cent
Criminal homicide						
Murder and nonnegligent manslaughter..............	11,800	85.4	2,018	14.6	13,818	0.2
Manslaughter by negligence.......................	1,950	87.6	276	12.4	2,226	(2)
Forcible rape..	17,804	100.0	....	....	17,804	0.3
Robbery..	101,098	93.2	7,383	6.8	108,481	1.8
Aggravated assault.................................	133,779	86.6	20,735	13.4	154,514	2.5
Burglary—breaking or entering.....................	322,214	94.6	18,483	5.4	340,697	5.5
Larceny—theft.......................................	505,701	69.3	223,960	30.7	729,661	11.8
Motor vehicle theft	100,270	93.5	6,956	6.5	107,226	1.7
Other assaults......................................	232,088	86.1	37,555	13.9	269,643	4.4
Arson...	9,630	89.5	1,126	10.5	10,756	0.2
Forgery and counterfeiting.........................	28,359	71.4	11,382	28.6	39,741	0.6
Fraud...	61,437	67.4	29,739	32.6	91,176	1.5
Embezzlement......................................	4,344	73.7	1,547	26.3	5,891	0.1
Stolen property; buying, receiving, possessing.........	69,155	89.9	7,788	10.1	76,943	1.2
Vandalism...	134,760	92.1	11,501	7.9	146,261	2.4
Weapons; carrying, possessing, etc....................	109,433	91.8	9,756	8.2	119,189	1.9
Prostitution and commercialized vice.................	13,026	24.4	40,283	75.6	53,309	0.9
Sex offenses (except forcible rape and prostitution).....	40,894	92.2	3,481	7.8	44,375	0.7
Narcotic drug laws..................................	390,231	85.8	64,717	14.2	454,948	7.4
Gambling...	41,958	91.4	3,942	8.6	45,900	0.7
Offenses against family and children.................	30,739	88.1	4,163	11.9	34,902	0.6
Driving under the influence.........................	567,193	92.0	49,356	8.0	616,549	10.0
Liquor laws...	162,350	84.9	28,863	15.1	191,213	3.1
Drunkenness...	846,167	92.8	65,670	7.2	911,837	14.8
Disorderly conduct..................................	432,933	79.5	111,388	20.5	544,321	8.8
Vagrancy..	28,691	87.5	4,111	12.5	32,802	0.5
All other offenses (except traffic)...................	637,715	84.2	119,325	15.8	757,040	12.2
Suspicion...	28,705	86.0	4,658	14.0	33,363	0.5
Curfew and loitering law violations..................	53,794	76.7	16,373	23.3	70,167	1.1
Runaways..	66,892	43.3	87,761	56.7	154,653	2.5
TOTAL..	5,185,110	83.9	994,296	16.1	6,179,406	100.0

[1] At press time, latest figures available.   [2] Less than .1%. NOTE: Because of rounding, the sum of the individual classifications may not add to precisely 100.0 per cent.

Total Arrests, by Age Groups, 1974[1]

Source: Federal Bureau of Investigation.

Age	Arrests	Age	Arrests	Age	Arrests	Age	Arrests	Age	Arrests
Under 15.....	606,548	18..........	364,268	22..:......	235,840	30–34......	453,238	50–54........	222,481
15..........	325,482	19..........	319,882	23..........	217,693	35–39......	349,228	55 & over.....	298,538
16..........	377,420	20..........	286,134	24..........	202,155	40–44......	314,705	Not known....	7,978
17..........	373,623	21..........	259,692	25–29......	686,747	45–49......	277,754	TOTAL......	6,179,406

[1] At press time, latest figures available. NOTE: Data are from same sources as table above.

National Crime Rate, 1966–1974[1]

Source: Federal Bureau of Investigation.

Offense	1974	% rise over 1973	1972	1970	1968	1966
Murder.....................................	9.7	4.3	8.9	7.8	6.8	5.6
Forcible rape	26.1	7.0	22.3	18.3	15.5	12.9
Robbery....................................	208.8	14.3	179.9	171.5	131.0	80.3
Aggravated assault.........................	214.2	7.7	186.6	162.4	141.3	118.4
Burglary...................................	1,429.0	17.6	1,126.1	1,067.7	915.1	708.3
Larceny ($50 and over).....................	2,473.0	20.2	882.6	859.4	636.0	456.8
Motor vehicle theft........................	460.6	4.4	423.1	453.5	389.1	284.4
TOTAL	4,821.4	16.7	2,829.5	2,740.5	2,234.8	1,666.6

[1] At press time, latest figures available.   NOTE: Rate per 100,000 inhabitants in the year shown.

Suicide Rates Around the World

(Deaths per 100,000 population, 1973)

Source: United Nations Demographic Yearbook, 1974.

Country	Rate	Country	Rate	Country	Rate
Angola	1.0	Guatemala[2]	3.6	Poland	11.7
Australia	11.6	Hong Kong	12.1	Portugal	8.6
Austria[2]	21.9	Hungary	36.9	Puerto Rico	9.1
Barbados[1]	1.7	Iceland	13.2	Singapore	11.0
Belgium[2]	15.4	Ireland[1]	3.0	South Africa[2]	
Bulgaria	11.6	Israel	5.6	Black	7.3
Canada	12.5	Italy[1]	5.8	White	14.5
Chile[2]	5.2	Jamaica[2]	1.0	Spain[1]	4.4
Colombia[3]	2.7	Japan	17.5	Sweden[1]	20.3
Costa Rica	2.6	Jordan[1]	0.1	Switzerland[1]	19.2
Cuba[3]	11.9	Luxembourg	13.4	Trinidad & Tobago[1]	9.7
Czechoslovakia[1]	24.7	Malta	0.6	Turkey[2]	1.9
Denmark[1]	23.8	Mauritius	6.2	United Kingdom:	
Ecuador[1]	3.2	Mexico	0.7	England and Wales	7.8
El Salvador[2]	8.7	Netherlands[1]	8.2	Northern Ireland	4.5
Finland[1]	24.0	New Zealand[1]	9.0	Scotland	8.4
France[3]	15.4	Norway[1]	9.0	United States	11.9
Germany, East[3]	30.5	Panama	2.6	Uruguay[1]	11.1
Germany, West[1]	19.9	Paraguay[2]	1.5	Venezuela	5.5
Greece	3.0	Philippines[3]	0.6		

[1] 1972.   [2] 1971.   [3] 1970.

Methods of Execution in the United States[1]

Source: Information Please Almanac questionnaires to the states.

State	Method	State	Method
Alabama[2]	Electrocution	New Hampshire[2]	Hanging
Alaska	No death penalty	New Jersey	Electrocution
Arizona[2]	Lethal gas	New Mexico[2]	Lethal gas
Arkansas[2]	Electrocution	New York[2]	Electrocution
California[2]	Lethal gas	North Carolina[2]	Lethal gas
Colorado[2]	Lethal gas	North Dakota	No death penalty
Connecticut[2]	Electrocution	Ohio[2]	Electrocution
Delaware[2]	Hanging	Oklahoma[2]	Electrocution
D.C.	No death penalty	Oregon	No death penalty
Florida[2]	Electrocution	Pennsylvania[2]	Electrocution
Georgia[2]	Electrocution	Rhode Island[2]	No death penalty[3]
Hawaii	No death penalty	South Carolina[2]	Electrocution
Idaho[2]	Hanging	South Dakota	Electrocution
Illinois[2]	Electrocution	Tennessee[2]	Electrocution
Indiana[2]	Electrocution	Texas[2]	Electrocution
Iowa	No death penalty	Utah[2]	Hanging or shooting
Kansas	Hanging		
Kentucky[2]	Electrocution	Vermont	No death penalty
Louisiana[2]	Electrocution	Virginia[2]	Electrocution
Maine	No death penalty	Washington[2]	Hanging
Maryland[2]	Lethal gas	West Virginia	No death penalty
Massachusetts	No death penalty	Wisconsin	No death penalty
Michigan	No death penalty	Wyoming[2]	Lethal gas
Minnesota	No death penalty	U.S. (Fed. Gov't.)	[4]
Mississippi[2]	Lethal gas	American Samoa	Hanging
Missouri[2]	Lethal gas	Canal Zone	Hanging
Montana[2]	Hanging	Guam	Hanging
Nebraska[2]	Electrocution	Puerto Rico	No death penalty
Nevada[2]	Lethal gas	Virgin Islands	No death penalty

[1] On July 1, 1976, by a 7–2 decision, the U.S. Supreme Court upheld the death penalty as not being "cruel or unusual." However, in another ruling the same day, the Court, by a 5–4 vote, stated that states may not impose "mandatory" capital punishment on every person convicted of murder. These decisions left uncertain the fate of 611 condemned persons throughout the U.S. There have been no executions in this country since 1967. [2] Voted to restore death penalty after June 29, 1972, Supreme Court decision ruling capital punishment unconstitutional. [3] Person shall be executed by gas if he commits murder while serving a prison term. [4] Method shall be that used by state in which sentence is imposed. If state does not have death penalty, Federal Judge shall prescribe method for carrying out sentence. NOTE: On Oct. 4, the Court refused to reconsider its July ruling, which will allow some states to proceed with executions of condemned prisoners.

Narcotics Abuse in the United States, 1960-1975

Source for narcotics tables: Drug Enforcement Administration.

	1975	1970	1968	1960	% Change 1960-75
New addicts reported[1]	9,308	12,201	7,219	7,479	+24.5
By age: Under 21 years	1,674	2,923	1,458	1,090	+53.6
21–30 years	5,777	6,874	4,411	4,149	+39.2
31–40 years	1,423	1,720	1,069	1,675	-15.4
41 and over	434	684	281	565	-23.2
By race: White	4,620	6,813	3,785	3,582	+29.0
Black	4,658	5,345	3,425	3,808	+22.3
Other	30	43	9	89	-66.3
By sex: Male	7,788	10,343	6,137	6,067	+28.4
Female	1,520	1,858	1,083	1,412	+ 7.6
Total active addicts	89,788[2]	68,864	64,011	44,906	+99.9
Rate per 100,000 population	40[3]	34.4	31.6	25.0	+60.0

[1] Statistics are compiled from reports voluntarily submitted by state and local authorities. There is no method of gathering information on abusers who never come to the attention of any authority. Estimates of the actual number of abusers in the U.S. range from 500,000 to 700,000. [2] Includes 8,841 abusers previously reported who are still active. Principal narcotics used include heroin and methadone (by 96% of new abusers in 1975). [3] Rate per 100,000 based upon U.S. Commerce Department July 1975 estimated population of 213,631,000.

Reported Active Narcotics Abusers in Selected Cities

City	1960	1975	% Change 1960-75	City	1960	1975	% Change 1960-75
Baltimore, Md.	300	1,117	+272.3	New York, N.Y.	20,187	42,805	+112.0
Buffalo, N.Y.	255	1,050	+311.8	Norfolk, Va.	44	723	+1,543.2
Chicago, Ill.	6,482	4,581	- 29.3	Paterson, N.J.	110	1,282	+1,065.5
Detroit, Mich.	2,112	7,379	+249.4	Philadelphia, Pa.	392	1,348	+243.9
Indianapolis, Ind.	207	824	+298.0	Phoenix, Ariz.	122	839	+587.7
Newark, N.J.	598	1,112	+ 86.0	San Francisco, Calif.	820	1,729	+110.9
New Orleans, La.	336	720	+114.3	Washington, D.C.	596	1,950	+227.2

Minimum Legal Age for Purchase of Liquor, Wine and Beer

Source: Distilled Spirits Council of the U.S.

State	Liquor	Wine	Beer	State	Liquor	Wine	Beer
Alabama	19	19	19	Montana	18	18	18
Alaska	19	19	19	Nebraska	19	19	19
Arizona	19	19	19	Nevada	21	21	21
Arkansas	21	21	21	New Hampshire	18	18	18
California	21	21	21	New Jersey	18	18	18
Colorado	21	21	21[1]	New Mexico	21	21	21
Connecticut	18	18	18	New York	18	18	18
Delaware	20	20	20	North Carolina	21	21[2]	18
D.C.	21	21[2]	18	North Dakota	21	21	21
Florida	18	18	18	Ohio	21	21	21[1]
Georgia	18	18	18	Oklahoma	21	21	21[3]
Hawaii	18	18	18	Oregon	21	21	21
Idaho	19	19	19	Pennsylvania	21	21	21
Illinois	21	19	19	Rhode Island	18	18	18
Indiana	21	21	21	South Carolina	21	18	18
Iowa	18	18	18	South Dakota	21	21	21[1]
Kansas	21	21	21[1]	Tennessee	18	18	18
Kentucky	21	21	21	Texas	18	18	18
Louisiana	18	18	18	Utah	21	21	21
Maine	18	18	18	Vermont	18	18	18
Maryland	21	18	18	Virginia	21	21	21[1]
Massachusetts	18	18	18	Washington	21	21	21
Michigan	18	18	18	West Virginia	18	18	18
Minnesota	19	18	18	Wisconsin	18	18	18
Mississippi	21	21	18	Wyoming	19	19	19
Missouri	21	21	21				

[1] 3.2 beer: 18.   [2] Light wine: 18.   [3] 3.2 beer (female): 18.

Hospital Facilities in the U.S., 1974

Source: American Hospital Association.

State	Total—all hospitals[1]			State	Total—all hospitals[1]		
	No. of hospitals	No. of beds	Admissions during year		No. of hospitals	No. of beds	Admissions during year
Alabama	150	26,534	661,954	Montana	66	4,406	141,244
Alaska	26	1,601	53,005	Nebraska	105	11,209	296,431
Arizona	80	10,901	351,155	Nevada	24	3,118	98,511
Arkansas	96	11,577	389,555	New Hampshire	35	6,275	131,372
California	650	123,951	3,298,005	New Jersey	145	49,908	1,035,580
Colorado	98	14,812	452,638	New Mexico	55	6,428	176,772
Connecticut	68	20,263	450,312	New York	415	168,471	2,775,812
Delaware	14	4,710	76,896	North Carolina	160	34,375	866,503
D. C.	20	11,512	219,777	North Dakota	61	5,908	135,894
Florida	228	53,504	1,394,254	Ohio	244	74,359	1,779,336
Georgia	183	33,385	867,934	Oklahoma	147	17,436	494,750
Hawaii	30	4,989	107,878	Oregon	88	11,959	358,343
Idaho	52	3,746	126,736	Pennsylvania	321	101,614	1,892,669
Illinois	293	81,162	1,983,646	Rhode Island	21	7,830	145,185
Indiana	139	36,195	852,031	South Carolina	89	19,412	447,535
Iowa	147	21,689	546,038	South Dakota	63	6,059	138,229
Kansas	164	19,028	440,222	Tennessee	157	32,376	819,296
Kentucky	127	19,942	600,882	Texas	577	79,282	2,237,582
Louisiana	157	26,820	703,911	Utah	40	4,844	187,981
Maine	56	7,826	179,251	Vermont	21	4,050	77,921
Maryland	81	29,666	514,354	Virginia	128	35,724	752,126
Massachusetts	198	52,223	960,011	Washington	127	16,750	569,166
Michigan	255	55,317	1,415,407	West Virginia	87	16,214	382,317
Minnesota	192	33,179	716,590	Wisconsin	182	33,486	785,126
Mississippi	113	17,194	434,485	Wyoming	31	2,733	66,927
Missouri	168	36,737	916,655	TOTAL	7,174	1,512,689	35,506,190

[1] All registered hospitals; data estimated for nonreporting hospitals. NOTE: Data are latest available.

EXPECTATION OF LIFE
Expectation of Life and Mortality Rates, 1974

Sources: National Center for Health Statistics and Metropolitan Life Insurance Co.

Age, years	Expectation of life in years					Mortality rate per 1,000				
	Total persons	White		All Other		Total persons	White		All Other	
		Male	Female	Male	Female		Male	Female	Male	Female
0	71.9	68.9	76.6	62.9	71.2	16.75	16.82	12.86	27.28	22.41
1	72.2	69.1	76.6	63.7	71.8	1.00	1.05	0.78	1.51	1.30
2	71.2	68.2	75.6	62.8	70.9	0.79	0.80	0.63	1.25	1.07
3	70.3	67.3	74.7	61.8	70.0	0.64	0.63	0.51	1.05	0.86
4	69.3	66.3	73.7	60.9	69.1	0.53	0.54	0.42	0.89	0.69
5	68.4	65.3	72.7	60.0	68.1	0.46	0.49	0.36	0.76	0.55
6	67.4	64.4	71.8	59.0	67.2	0.41	0.46	0.31	0.67	0.45
7	66.4	63.4	70.8	58.0	66.2	0.37	0.43	0.28	0.58	0.37
8	65.5	62.4	69.8	57.1	65.2	0.34	0.39	0.25	0.51	0.31
9	64.5	61.4	68.8	56.1	64.2	0.30	0.34	0.23	0.45	0.28
10	63.5	60.5	67.8	55.1	63.2	0.27	0.30	0.22	0.41	0.27
11	62.5	59.5	66.9	54.2	62.3	0.28	0.30	0.23	0.42	0.28
12	61.5	58.5	65.9	53.2	61.3	0.33	0.38	0.25	0.50	0.31
13	60.6	57.5	64.9	52.2	60.3	0.45	0.56	0.30	0.67	0.36
14	59.6	56.6	63.9	51.2	59.3	0.60	0.81	0.36	0.91	0.42
15	58.6	55.6	62.9	50.3	58.3	0.78	1.10	0.44	1.17	0.50
16	57.7	54.7	62.0	49.3	57.4	0.95	1.35	0.51	1.44	0.58
17	56.7	53.7	61.0	48.4	56.4	1.10	1.57	0.57	1.76	.068
18	55.8	52.8	60.0	47.5	55.4	1.20	1.70	0.59	2.13	0.79
19	54.8	51.9	59.1	46.6	54.5	1.26	1.78	0.59	2.53	0.90
20	53.9	51.0	58.1	45.7	53.5	1.32	1.85	0.58	2.96	1.02
21	53.0	50.1	57.1	44.9	52.6	1.34	1.92	0.58	3.37	1.14

Expectation of Life and Mortality Rates (Continued)

Age, years	Expectation of life in years					Mortality rate per 1,000				
	Total persons	White		All Other		Total persons	White		All Other	
		Male	Female	Male	Female		Male	Female	Male	Female
22	52.1	49.2	56.2	44.0	51.7	1.43	1.94	0.58	3.70	1.24
23	51.1	48.3	55.2	43.2	50.7	1.43	1.92	0.59	3.90	1.32
24	50.2	47.4	54.2	42.3	49.8	1.41	1.85	0.61	4.02	1.37
25	49.3	46.5	53.3	41.5	48.8	1.38	1.77	0.62	4.11	1.43
26	48.3	45.5	52.3	40.7	47.9	1.36	1.69	0.64	4.22	1.49
27	47.4	44.6	51.3	39.8	47.0	1.35	1.64	0.66	4.33	1.57
28	46.5	43.7	50.4	39.0	46.1	1.37	1.62	0.69	4.44	1.65
29	45.5	42.8	49.4	38.2	45.1	1.40	1.62	0.72	4.58	1.75
30	44.6	41.8	48.4	37.4	44.2	1.45	1.65	0.75	4.71	1.87
31	43.7	40.9	47.5	36.5	43.3	1.50	1.68	0.80	4.85	1.99
32	42.7	40.0	46.5	35.7	42.4	1.56	1.73	0.85	5.03	2.13
33	41.8	39.0	45.5	34.9	41.5	1.64	1.80	0.92	5.25	2.28
34	40.7	38.1	44.6	34.1	40.6	1.74	1.90	0.99	5.52	2.46
35	39.9	37.2	43.6	33.2	39.7	1.86	2.02	1.07	5.82	2.64
36	39.0	36.2	42.7	32.4	38.8	1.99	2.17	1.17	6.15	2.85
37	38.1	35.3	41.7	31.6	37.9	2.16	2.34	1.28	6.50	3.10
38	37.2	34.4	40.8	30.8	37.0	2.34	2.54	1.42	6.87	3.41
39	36.2	33.5	39.8	30.1	36.1	2.55	2.76	1.57	7.28	3.76
40	35.3	32.6	38.9	29.3	35.3	2.79	3.00	1.74	7.72	4.14
41	34.4	31.7	38.0	28.5	34.4	3.05	3.29	1.92	8.20	4.54
42	33.5	30.8	37.0	27.7	33.6	3.35	3.65	2.12	8.75	4.93
43	32.6	29.9	36.1	27.0	32.7	3.69	4.10	2.34	9.37	5.30
44	31.8	29.0	35.2	26.2	31.9	4.07	4.62	2.58	10.06	5.67
45	30.9	28.1	34.3	25.5	31.1	4.50	5.21	2.85	10.82	6.05
46	30.0	27.3	33.4	24.7	30.3	4.95	5.83	3.13	11.62	6.47
47	29.2	26.5	32.5	24.0	29.4	5.40	6.45	3.41	12.45	6.94
48	28.3	25.6	31.6	23.3	28.6	5.85	7.03	3.70	13.31	7.48
49	27.5	24.8	30.7	22.6	27.9	6.31	7.62	3.98	14.21	8.08
50	26.7	24.0	29.8	22.0	27.1	6.79	8.23	4.29	15.13	8.72
51	25.8	23.2	29.0	21.3	26.3	7.33	8.94	4.63	16.12	9.40
52	25.0	22.4	28.1	20.6	25.6	7.96	9.77	5.02	17.30	10.08
53	24.2	21.6	27.2	20.0	24.8	8.69	10.76	5.48	18.70	10.78
54	23.4	20.8	26.4	19.4	24.1	9.51	11.90	5.99	20.30	11.49
55	22.7	20.1	25.5	18.7	23.4	10.39	13.12	6.55	22.02	12.20
56	21.9	19.3	24.7	18.2	22.6	11.32	14.42	7.14	23.76	12.97
57	21.1	18.6	23.9	17.6	21.9	12.34	15.84	7.78	25.45	13.89
58	20.4	17.9	23.1	17.0	21.2	13.46	17.39	8.46	27.00	15.03
59	19.7	17.2	22.2	16.5	20.5	14.66	19.07	9.20	28.46	16.32
60	19.0	16.5	21.4	16.0	19.9	15.98	20.88	10.02	30.01	17.88
61	18.3	15.9	20.7	15.4	19.2	17.38	22.80	10.91	31.68	19.47
62	17.6	15.2	19.9	14.9	18.6	18.77	24.80	11.79	33.28	20.69
63	16.9	14.6	19.1	14.4	18.0	20.11	26.89	12.65	34.74	21.34
64	16.2	14.0	18.3	13.9	17.4	21.46	29.08	13.54	36.15	21.64
65	15.6	13.4	17.6	13.4	16.7	22.85	31.39	14.49	37.36	21.50
70	12.5	10.6	14.0	11.1	13.7	34.41	46.51	23.04	55.93	39.10
75	9.8	8.3	10.7	9.6	11.8	53.23	70.10	40.11	76.40	53.65
80	7.6	6.4	8.1	8.3	9.9	79.48	103.33	65.96	89.85	62.27
85 and over .	5.7	4.9	6.0	6.7	7.8	. . . .	. . . .	. . . .	. . . .	. . . .

NOTE: Data are latest available.

Americans Spent Record $10.1 Billion for Travel in 1975

United States residents spent a record $10.1 billion in 1975 for travel abroad. Of this figure, $6.4 billion covered expenses in foreign countries and the remainder went for air and sea fare. The chief beneficiaries of 6.4 million Americans on the move were Mexico, where $1.6 billion was spent, and Canada, which was the recipient of $1.3 billion. The combined figure represents 46% of the year's total travel expenses. Of the $3.5 billion spent over-seas, $1.9 billion, or 55%, went to Europe and the Mediterranean area. However, the number of travelers to Europe, 3.2 million, was 15% less than in 1974.

Some 3.7 million foreign visitors to the U.S. in 1975 spent $4.9 billion, a 21% rise over the previous year. Most of this increase resulted from higher spending by Canadians and Mexicans.

Expectation of Life in the United States, 1850-1974

Source: Statistical Bureau of Metropolitan Life Insurance Company; Division of Vital Statistics, National Center for Health Statistics; and Bureau of the Census.

Calendar period	Age								
	0	10	20	30	40	50	60	70	80
White Males									
1850[1]	38.3	48.0	40.1	34.0	27.9	21.6	15.6	10.2	5.9
1890[1]	42.50	48.45	40.66	34.05	27.37	20.72	14.73	9.35	5.40
1900-1902[2]	48.23	50.59	42.19	34.88	27.74	20.76	14.35	9.03	5.10
1909-1911[2]	50.23	51.32	42.71	34.87	27.43	20.39	13.98	8.83	5.09
1919-1921[3]	56.34	54.15	45.60	37.65	29.86	22.22	15.25	9.51	5.47
1929-1931	59.12	54.96	46.02	37.54	29.22	21.51	14.72	9.20	5.26
1930-1939	60.62	55.86	46.77	38.06	29.57	21.71	14.86	9.29	5.30
1939-1941	62.81	57.03	47.76	38.80	30.03	21.96	15.05	9.42	5.38
1949-1951	66.31	58.98	49.52	40.29	31.17	22.83	15.76	10.07	5.88
1959-1961	67.55	59.78	50.25	40.98	31.73	23.22	16.01	10.29	5.89
1969-71	67.94	59.69	50.22	41.07	31.87	23.34	16.07	10.38	6.18
1974	68.9	60.5	51.0	41.8	32.6	24.0	16.5	10.6	6.4
White Females									
1850[1]	40.5	47.2	40.2	35.4	29.8	23.5	17.0	11.3	6.4
1890[1]	44.46	49.62	42.03	35.36	28.76	22.09	15.70	10.15	5.75
1900-1902[2]	51.08	52.15	43.77	36.42	29.17	21.89	15.23	9.59	5.50
1909-1911[2]	53.62	53.57	44.88	36.96	29.26	21.74	14.92	9.38	5.35
1919-1921[3]	58.53	55.17	46.46	38.72	30.94	23.12	15.93	9.94	5.70
1929-1931	62.67	57.65	48.52	39.99	31.52	23.41	16.05	9.98	5.63
1930-1939	64.52	58.98	49.71	40.90	32.24	23.96	16.44	10.19	5.76
1939-1941	67.29	60.85	51.38	42.21	33.25	24.72	17.00	10.50	5.88
1949-1951	72.03	64.26	54.56	45.00	35.64	26.76	18.64	11.68	6.59
1959-1961	74.19	66.05	56.29	46.63	37.13	28.08	19.69	12.38	6.67
1969-71	75.49	66.97	57.24	47.60	38.12	29.11	20.79	13.37	7.59
1974	76.6	67.8	58.1	48.4	38.9	29.8	21.4	14.0	8.1
All Other Males [1]									
1900-1902[2]	32.54	41.90	35.11	29.25	23.12	17.34	12.62	8.33	5.12
1909-1911[2]	34.05	40.65	33.46	27.33	21.57	16.21	11.67	8.00	5.53
1919-1921[3]	47.14	45.99	38.36	32.51	26.53	20.47	14.74	9.58	5.83
1929-1931	47.55	44.27	35.95	29.45	23.36	17.92	13.15	8.78	5.42
1930-1939	50.06	46.56	38.05	31.11	24.65	18.98	14.13	9.53	6.01
1939-1941	52.26	48.34	39.52	32.05	25.06	19.06	14.37	10.11	6.58
1949-1951	58.91	52.96	43.73	35.31	27.29	20.25	14.91	10.74	7.07
1959-1961	61.48	55.19	45.78	37.05	28.72	21.28	15.29	10.81	6.87
1969-71	60.98	53.67	44.37	36.20	28.29	21.24	15.35	10.68	7.57
1974	62.9	55.1	45.7	37.4	29.3	22.0	16.0	11.1	8.3
All Other Females [1]									
1900-1902[2]	35.04	43.02	36.89	30.70	24.37	18.67	13.60	9.62	6.48
1909-1911[2]	37.67	42.84	36.14	29.61	23.34	17.65	12.78	9.22	6.05
1919-1921[3]	46.92	44.54	37.15	31.48	25.60	19.76	14.69	10.25	6.58
1929-1931	49.51	45.33	37.22	30.67	24.30	18.60	14.22	10.38	6.90
1930-1939	52.62	48.29	39.90	32.88	26.11	20.09	15.28	10.88	7.18
1939-1941	55.56	50.75	42.04	34.40	27.19	20.95	16.10	11.82	8.02
1949-1951	62.70	56.17	46.77	38.02	29.82	22.67	16.95	12.29	8.15
1959-1961	66.47	59.72	50.07	40.83	32.16	24.31	17.83	12.46	7.66
1969-71	69.05	61.49	51.85	42.61	33.87	25.97	19.02	13.30	9.01
1974	71.2	63.2	53.5	44.2	35.3	27.1	19.9	13.7	9.9

[1] Massachusetts only; white and nonwhite combined, the latter being about one percent of the total. [2] Original Death Registration States. [3] Death Registration States of 1920. [4] Data for periods 1900-1902 to 1929-1931 and 1939-1941 relate to blacks only. NOTE: Data are latest available.

Expectation of Life by Age and Sex for Selected Countries

Source: United Nations, *Demographic Yearbook, 1974.*

Country	Period	Males						Females					
		0	1	10	20	40	60	0	1	10	20	40	60
North America													
United States [1] . . .	1972	67.4	67.8	59.2	49.8	31.7	16.1	75.2	75.4	66.7	57.0	38.1	20.9
Canada	1970–72	69.3	69.8	61.2	51.7	33.2	17.0	76.4	76.6	67.9	58.2	39.0	21.4
Mexico	1970	59.4	63.1	57.0	47.9	31.4	17.1	63.4	66.6	60.8	51.5	34.1	18.5
Puerto Rico	1971–73	68.9	70.1	61.4	51.9	34.2	18.6	76.1	76.9	68.2	58.0	39.0	21.5
South America													
Argentina	1965–70	64.1	....	....	....	....	....	70.2	....	....	....	....	....
Bolivia	1949–51	49.7	56.1	54.8	46.9	33.4	20.4	49.7	55.9	54.8	47.2	32.9	19.2
Brazil[4]	1960–70	57.6	....	56.2	47.0	30.0	15.0	61.1	....	58.9	49.7	32.5	16.6
Chile	1969–70	60.5	64.9	56.7	47.3	29.9	15.5	66.0	70.0	62.2	52.7	34.5	18.0
Colombia	1950–52	44.2	50.4	48.2	39.6	24.8	11.8	45.9	51.1	49.4	40.9	26.6	12.8
Venezuela[4]	1961	66.4	68.8	61.8	52.4	34.6	18.9	....	....	....	....	....	....
Europe													
Austria	1973	67.4	....	59.7	50.3	32.0	15.7	74.7	....	66.5.	56.8	37.5	19.8
Belgium	1968–72	67.8	68.4	59.9	50.3	31.6	15.2	74.2	74.5	65.9	56.1	36.9	19.2
Czechoslovakia . . .	1970	66.2	67.0	58.4	49.9	30.6	14.6	72.9	72.6	64.9	55.2	35.9	18.3
Denmark[2]	1971–72	70.7	70.9	62.3	52.7	33.8	17.0	76.1	76.0	67.3	57.5	38.2	20.7
England and Wales .	1970–72	68.9	69.3	60.6	52.0	31.9	15.3	75.1	75.3	66.6	56.8	37.4	19.9
Finland	1971	65.9	65.9	61.3	51.6	29.3	14.3	74.2	74.0	65.3	55.5	36.2	18.3
France	1972	68.6	68.6	60.0	51.0	32.2	16.3	76.4	76.3	67.6	57.9	38.7	21.1
Germany (West)[6] . .	1970–72	67.4	68.2	59.7	50.2	31.8	15.3	73.8	74.3	65.7	56.0	36.8	19.1
Germany (East)[6] . .	1969–70	68.9	69.3	60.8	51.2	32.7	16.1	74.2	74.4	65.8	56.1	36.9	19.3
Greece	1960–62	67.5	70.5	62.5	52.9	34.0	17.0	70.7	73.5	65.5	55.8	36.7	18.9
Hungary	1972	66.9	68.4	59.8	50.1	31.8	15.6	72.6	73.8	65.1	55.3	36.1	18.6
Iceland	1966–70	70.7	70.9	62.4	48.4	34.6	18.0	76.3	76.0	67.3	57.5	38.2	20.5
Ireland	1965–67	68.6	69.5	60.8	51.2	32.2	15.6	72.9	73.4	64.8	54.9	35.7	18.4
Italy	1970–72	69.0	70.1	61.6	52.0	33.2	16.7	74.9	75.8	67.1	57.3	38.1	20.2
Netherlands	1973	71.2	71.2	62.6	53.0	34.0	17.0	77.2	77.0	68.2	58.4	39.1	21.1
Norway	1971–72	71.2	71.3	62.7	53.1	34.3	17.4	77.4	77.2	68.5	58.7	39.2	21.0
Poland	1970–72	66.8	68.0	59.4	49.8	31.6	15.5	73.8	74.6	66.0	56.2	37.0	19.3
Portugal[4]	1973	68.0	70.2	62.2	52.7	34.1	17.2	....	....	....	....	....	....
Sri Lanka	1967	64.8	67.4	60.5	51.2	33.2	17.0	66.9	68.9	62.4	53.0	35.0	17.8
Syria	1970	54.5	60.7	56.4	47.4	30.5	15.2	58.7	64.1	59.5	50.5	33.3	17.3
Scotland	1971–73	67.2	67.8	59.2	49.8	31.3	15.0	73.6	74.1.	65.4	55.6	36.3	18.9
Spain[1]	1970	69.7	. . .	62.0	52.4	33.7	17.0	75.0	....	66.9	57.1	38.0	20.1
Sweden	1973	72.1.	71.9	63.2	53.5	34.7	17.6	77.7	77.4	68.6	58.8	39.4	21.3
Switzerland	1969–72	70.2	70.4	61.9	52.3	33.6	16.7	76.2	76.2	67.5	57.7	38.4	20.4
U.S.S.R.	1971–72	64.0	....	....	....	....	....	74.0	....	....	....	....	....
Asia													
Burma	1954	40.8	49.8	45.5	36.8	21.1	10.6	43.8	51.6	47.0	38.3	23.7	12.4
India	1951–60	41.9	48.4	45.2	36.9	22.1	11.8	40.6	46.0	43.8	35.6	22.4	12.9
Israel	1973	70.2	71.1	62.5	52.9	33.9	17.1	73.2	73.8	65.2	55.4	36.1	18.4
Japan[3]	1972	70.5	70.4	61.9	52.3	33.7	16.8	75.9	75.7	67.1	57.3	38.1	20.2
Jordan	1959–63	52.6	58.2	52.7	44.1	28.6	14.4	52.0	58.2	54.4	46.0	30.7	15.7
Korea	1970	63.0	66.0	58.0	49.0	31.0	16.0	67.0	69.0	61.0	52.0	34.0	17.0
Africa													
Egypt	1960	51.6	56.2	56.6	47.7	30.5	15.1	53.8	59.9	62.0	52.9	35.0	18.0
Kenya	1969	46.9	52.6	51.0	43.0	28.3	14.5	51.2	56.6	54.1	45.7	30.3	15.7
South Africa													
(white population) .	1959–61	64.7	65.9	57.5	48.0	30.2	15.0	71.7	72.5	64.1	54.4	35.5	18.6
Oceania													
Australia[5]	1965–67	67.6	68.1	59.5	50.0	31.4	15.8	74.2	74.4	65.8	56.0	36.9	19.5
New Zealand . . .	1960–62	68.4	69.2	60.7	51.2	32.5	16.0	73.8	74.2	65.6	55.9	36.7	19.3

[1] Provisional. [2] Excluding data for Faeroe Islands and Greenland. [3] Japanese nationals in Japan only. [4] Figures for male and female together. [5] Excludes full-blooded aborigines. [6] Includes relevant data relating to Berlin. No separate data has been supplied.

EDUCATION

Elementary and Secondary Public School Statistics, 1974-75[1]

Source: National Center for Education Statistics.

Region and state	No. schools elementary and secondary[2]	Pupils enrolled[4]		Classroom teachers[4]	Pupil/ teacher ratio	Annual expenditure (thousands)	Annual expenditure per pupil	Average annual salary of classroom teachers
		Elementary Kindergarten through Grade 8	Secondary Grades 9-12 and postgraduate					
NORTH ATLANTIC								
Connecticut	1,031	452,000	203,000	35,620	18.4	$ 979,000	$1,596	$12,051
Delaware	189	86,000	43,000	6,380	20.2	205,260	1,723	12,110
Maine	850	171,000	77,000	12,070	20.5	264,540	1,130	13,202
Maryland	1,302	611,000	276,000	42,980	20.6	1,409,534	1,771	13,282
Massachusetts	2,512	822,000	378,000	67,500	17.8	1,630,500	1,504	12,468
New Hampshire	445	118,000	53,000	9,400	18.2	186,926	1,173	10,016
New Jersey	2,477[3]	1,004,000	454,000	79,610	18.3	2,420,234	1,713	n.a.
New York	4,244	2,282,000	1,129,000	189,740	18.0	7,006,500	2,241	15,000
Pennsylvania	4,131	1,484,000	777,000	110,760	20.4	3,547,927	1,587	12,200
Rhode Island	388	122,000	55,000	9,370	18.9	280,609	1,665	12,885
Vermont	398	73,000	31,000	6,250	16.6	126,937	1,267	9,206
D. C.	189	96,000	34,000	6,960	18.7	241,277	1,957	14,716
GREAT LAKES & PLAINS								
Illinois	4,508	1,545,000	733,000	113,220	20.1	3,425,224	1,637	13,469
Indiana	1,995	799,000	378,000	49,510	23.8	1,405,418	1,298	11,358
Iowa	1,989	410,000	206,000	32,850	18.8	804,820	1,400	10,598
Kansas	1,654	293,000	153,000	25,680	17.4	674,764	1,607	9,770
Michigan	4,018	1,423,000	698,000	90,860	23.3	3,449,978	1,770	14,224
Minnesota	1,812	577,000	307,000	44,000	20.1	1,482,076	1,635	12,852
Missouri	2,259	669,000	325,000	47,590	20.9	1,101,704	1,203	10,257
Nebraska	1,876	211,000	105,000	17,440	18.1	412,903	1,378	9,715
North Dakota	794	84,000	48,000	7,610	17.3	156,971	1,199	9,176
Ohio	4,168	1,559,000	755,000	104,950	22.0	2,749,000	1,270	11,100
South Dakota	900	101,000	52,000	8,150	18.8	157,070	1,062	8,860
Wisconsin	2,312	630,000	338,000	48,740	19.9	1,333,962	1,452	13,046
SOUTHEAST								
Alabama	803	518,000	239,000	35,530	21.3	674,458	933	9,503
Arkansas	1,192	312,000	139,000	20,760	21.7	455,785	1,087	9,021
Florida	1,886	1,059,000	485,000	71,140	21.7	1,963,447	1,392	10,780
Georgia	1,456	755,000	317,000	46,640	23.0	1,082,054	1,087	10,641
Kentucky	1,481	477,000	218,000	31,890	21.8	625,300	960	9,240
Louisiana	1,227	580,000	253,000	42,310	19.7	882,400	1,637	9,800
Mississippi	1,083	355,000	154,000	23,680	21.5	477,269	921	8,338
North Carolina	1,909	805,000	364,000	51,430	22.7	1,443,489	1,151	11,275
South Carolina	1,158	439,000	183,000	27,920	22.3	648,470	1,125	9,770
Tennessee	1,690	607,000	258,000	39,440	21.9	834,564	997	9,878
Virginia	1,710	743,000	341,000	53,500	20.3	1,270,647	1,231	11,279
West Virginia	1,298	278,000	123,000	19,070	21.0	383,660	1,020	9,124
WEST & SOUTHWEST								
Arizona	791	341,000	142,000	21,290	22.7	713,694	1,546	11,168
California	7,037	2,969,000	1,425,000	203,760	21.6	6,934,627	1,373	14,915
Colorado	1,226	381,000	182,000	27,340	20.6	758,520	1,423	11,554
Idaho	543	123,000	63,000	8,600	21.6	214,281	1,232	9,573
Montana	839	113,000	58,000	9,050	18.9	221,600	1,392	10,160
Nevada	255	94,000	42,000	5,640	24.1	167,300	1,308	12,854
New Mexico	642	185,000	95,000	12,700	22.0	356,140	1,282	10,200
Oklahoma	1,880	404,000	187,000	29,110	20.3	634,200	1,131	9,208
Oregon	1,279	316,000	157,000	22,390	21.1	717,425	1,642	10,958
Texas	5,303	1,955,000	807,000	134,320	20.6	2,698,413	1,073	10,136
Utah	540	207,000	97,000	12,570	24.2	369,992	1,265	10,150
Washington	1,670	524,000	255,000	33,720	23.1	1,085,480	1,339	12,538
Wyoming	379	58,000	27,000	5,010	17.0	115,793	1,404	10,350
Alaska	304	60,000	26,000	4,110	20.9	184,335	2,228	16,906
Hawaii	211	120,000	55,000	7,840	22.3	262,523	1,600	13,665
TOTALS	86,334	30,931,000	14,125,000	2,168,000	20.8[5]	61,629,000[5]	1,431[5]	12,070[5]

[1] Estimated. [2] 1973-74 figures. [3] 1972-73 figures. [4] 1975 figures. [5] Average.

State Compulsory School Attendance Laws

Source: National Center for Education Statistics.

State	Enactment[1]	Age limits	State	Enactment[1]	Age limits
Alabama	1915	7–16	Montana	1883	7–16
Alaska	1929	7–16	Nebraska	1887	7–16
Arizona	1899	8–16	Nevada	1873	7–17
Arkansas	1909	7–16	New Hampshire	1871	6–16
California	1874	8–16	New Jersey	1875	6–16
Colorado	1889	7–16	New Mexico	1891	6–17
Connecticut	1872	7–16	New York	1874	6–16
Delaware	1907	6–16	North Carolina	1907	7–16
D. C.	1864	7–16	North Dakota	1883	7–16
Florida	1915	7–16	Ohio	1877	6–18
Georgia	1916	7–16	Oklahoma	1907	7–18
Hawaii	1896	6–18	Oregon	1889	7–18
Idaho	1887	7–16	Pennsylvania	1895	8–17
Illinois	1883	7–16	Rhode Island	1883	7–16
Indiana	1897	7–16	South Carolina	1915	7–16
Iowa	1902	7–16	South Dakota	1883	7–16
Kansas	1874	7–16	Tennessee	1905	7–17
Kentucky	1896	7–16	Texas	1915[3]	7–17
Louisiana	1910	7–16	Utah	1890	6–18
Maine	1875	7–16	Vermont	1867	7–16
Maryland	1902	7–16	Virginia	1908	6–17
Massachusetts	1852	7–16	Washington	1871	8–16
Michigan	1871	6–16	West Virginia	1897	7–16
Minnesota	1885	7–16	Wisconsin	1879	7–18
Mississippi	1918	(2)	Wyoming	1876	7–17
Missouri	1905	7–16			

[1] Date of enactment of 1st compulsory attendance law. [2] Mississippi repealed its compulsory attendance law in 1956. [3] A compulsory school attendance law was contained in a law of 1873 establishing free public schools. However, the provision was omitted in superseding legislation passed in 1876.

High School and College Graduates, 1900–1975

(Public and private schools; beginning in 1959-60, Alaska and Hawaii are included.)

Source: National Center for Education Statistics.

Year of graduation	HIGH SCHOOL			COLLEGE[1]		
	Men	Women	Total	Men	Women	Total
1900	38,075	56,808	94,883	22,173	5,237	27,410
1910	63,676	92,753	156,429	28,762	8,437	37,199
1920	123,684	187,582	311,266	31,980	16,642	48,622
1929–30	300,376	366,528	666,904	73,615	48,869	122,484
1939–40	578,718	642,757	1,221,475	109,546	76,954	186,500
1949–50	570,700	629,000	1,199,700	328.841	103,217	432,058
1957–58	725,500	780,400	1,505,900	241,560	121,942	363,502
1959–60	898,000	966,000	1,864,000	254,063	138,377	392,440
1960–61	958,000	1,013,000	1,971,000	254,215	144,495	398,710
1961–62	941,000	984,000	1,925,000	260,531	157,315	417,846
1962–63	959,000	991,000	1,950,000	273,169	174,453	447,622
1963–64	1,123,000	1,167,000	2,290,000	296,676	197,477	494,153
1964–65	1,314,000	1,351,000	2,665,000	316,286	213,717	530,003
1965–66	1,308,000	1,325,000	2,632,000	328,863	222,194	551,047
1966–67	1,332,000	1,348,000	2,679,000	353,349	237,198	590,547
1967–68	1,341,000	1,361,000	2,702,000	390,507	276,203	666,710
1968–69	1,402,000	1,427,000	2,829,000	444,380	319,805	764,185
1969–70	1,433,000	1,463,000	2,896,000	484,174	343,060	827,234
1970–71	1,456,000	1,487,000	2,943,000	511,138	366,538	877,676
1971–72	1,490,000	1,516,000	3,006,000	541,313	389,371	930,684
1972–73	1,501,000	1,536,000	3,037,000	564,680	407,700	972,380
1973–74	1,512,000	1,557,000	3,069,000	575,843	423,749	999,592
1974–75	n.a.	n.a.	n.a.	553,797	425,052	978,849

[1] Includes Bachelors' and First-professional degrees. NOTE: Because of rounding, details may not add to totals.

Statistics of State School Systems, 1963-1976

Source: National Center for Education Statistics.

	Enrollment			High-school graduates[1]				Current expenditure per pupil in average daily attendance
Years	Total	Preprimary through Grade 8	Grades 9 through 12 and postgraduate	Total	Boys	Girls	Total expenditures (in thousands)	
1963-64	41,025,000	29,907,000	11,118,000	2,008,371	984,967	1,023,404	$21,324,993	$460
1965-66	42,835,000	31,177,000	11,658,000	2,326,811	1,160,727	1,166,084	26,248,026	537
1967-68	43,891,000	31,642,000	12,249,000	2,394,535	1,193,425	1,201,110	32,977,182	658
1969-70	45,619,000	32,597,000	13,022,000	2,589,025	1,286,087	1,302,938	40,683,429	816
1971-72	46,081,000	32,265,000	13,816,000	2,708,000	1,347,000	1,361,000	48,050,283	990
1973-74[2]	45,429,000	31,353,000	14,077,000	2,762,000[3]	1,364,000	1,398,000	56,031,041	1,116
1974-75[2]	45,056,000	30,931,000	14,125,000	2,832,000[3]	1,389,353	1,433,670	61,629,000	1,255
1975-76[2]	44,838,490	30,544,746	14,293,744	2,818,000[3]	1,390,000[3]	1,428,000[3]	67,102,569	1,388

[1] Regular day school programs. [2] Data from *Fall Statistics of Public Day Schools.* Expenditure figures are estimated. [3] Estimated.

Federal Grants and Loans for Education, Fiscal Year 1976

Source: National Center for Education Statistics.

Type of support, level, and program area	Amount in millions[1]	Type of support, level, and program area	Amount in millions[1]
Grants, total..............................	$16,211.9	Basic research.........................	$1,412.0
Elementary-secondary education............	4,873.8	Research facilities.....................	199.0
School assistance in federally affected areas	364.4	Training grants, fellowships	
Economic opportunity programs..........	879.2	and traineeships	1,000.2
National Defense Education Act...........	28.5	Facilities and equipment................	122.0
Supporting services.....................	411.7	Other institutional support..............	419.7
Assistance for educationally deprived		Other student assistance................	4,119.0
children.............................	2,088.2	Vocational-technical and continuing education	3,606.6
Teacher Corps.........................	36.4	Vocational-technical & work training	2,675.5
Vocational education....................	264.0	Veterans' education....................	773.5
Dependents' schools abroad..............	233.9	General continuing education.............	145.7
Public lands revenue for schools..........	157.0	Training state and local personnel.........	11.9
Assistance in special areas..............	124.1	Loans, total (higher education).............	459.5
Veterans' education.....................	79.8	Student loan program, National Defense	
Emergency school assistance	152.8	Education Act.....................	486.9
Other................................	53.9	College facilities loans..................	−27.4
Higher education...........................	7,271.9	TOTAL GRANTS AND LOANS...............	$17,130.9

[1] Estimated outlay for fiscal year 1976. NOTE: The table lists the federal funds that support education in educational institutions. Excluded are certain other federal funds for education and related activities.

Exceptional Children in Special Educational Programs, 1963 & 1973-74

Source: Office of Education.

Area of exceptionality[2]	Enrollment, February 1963			Enrollment, 1973-74[1]		
	Total enrollment	Local public schools	Public and private residential schools	Total enrollment	Local public schools	Public and private residential schools
Visually handicapped.................	21,531	13,962	7,569	24,000	15,000	9,000
Deaf and hard of hearing..............	45,594	28,551	17,043	78,000	58,000	20,000
Speech impaired.....................	802,197	802,197	(3)	1,237,000	1,237,000	(3)
Crippled and special health problems...	64,842	64,842	(3)	269,000	269,000	(3)
Emotionally and socially maladjusted...	99,873	51,157	48,716[4]	100,000	42,000	58,000
Mentally retarded....................	431,890	393,237	38,653	830,000	784,000	46,000
Other handicapping conditions........	1,753	1,753	(3)	126,000	126,000	(3)
Gifted..............................	214,671	214,671	(3)	481,000	481,000	(3)
TOTAL..............................	1,682,351	1,570,370	111,981	3,158,000	3,025,000	133,000

[1] Estimated. [2] Pupils are reported according to the major type of exceptionality for which they are receiving special education. [3] Not included in survey of residential schools. [4] Includes education programs in public hospitals for the mentally ill.

INSTITUTIONS OF HIGHER EDUCATION—ENROLLMENT, BY CHARACTERISTICS, 1960 TO 1973, AND PROJECTIONS TO 1983

In thousands, except percent. As of fall opening.

CHARACTERISTIC	1960	1965	1968	1969	1970	1971	1972	1973	1980	1983
Total	3,789	5,921	7,513	8,005	8,581	8,949	9,215	9,602	10,756	10,577
Degree credit	3,583	5,526	6,928	7,484	7,920	8,116	8,265	8,520	9,210	8,940
Undergraduate	3,227	4,829	6,043	6,529	6,889	7,104	7,199	7,397	7,920	7,660
Percent of persons, 18–21 years	33.2	39.1	41.8	45.1	46.7	47.2	46.9	47.1	47.2	48.0
Male	2,004	2,910	3,561	3,829	4,005	4,102	4,074	4,125	4,319	4,155
Female	1,223	1,919	2,482	2,700	2,884	3,002	3,125	3,271	3,601	3,505
4-year	2,776	3,988	4,754	5,000	5,259	5,379	5,407	5,475	5,746	5,547
Full time	2,077	3,159	3,861	4,041	4,234	4,358	4,350	4,351	4,266	3,967
Part time	699	829	893	959	1,025	1,021	1,057	1,124	1,480	1,580
2-year	451	841	1,289	1,528	1,630	1,725	1,792	1,922	2,174	2,113
Public	1,929	3,184	4,308	4,749	5,076	5,302	5,401	5,589	6,094	5,897
Private	1,298	1,645	1,735	1,780	1,813	1,802	1,799	1,807	1,826	1,763
1st time enrolled	923	1,442	1,640	1,749	1,780	1,766	1,740	1,757	1,751	1,583
Graduate, resident only[1]	356	697	885	955	1,031	1,012	1,066	1,123	1,290	1,280
Nondegree credit	206	395	585	521	661	833	950	1,082	1,546	1,637

[1] Beginning 1972, includes resident and extension. Source: U.S. National Center for Education Statistics, *Projections of Educational Statistics to 1983–84.*

School Enrollment, 3 to 34 Years Old, October 1975

Source: Bureau of the Census.

Age	White		Black		Spanish origin[1]	
	Number enrolled	% enrolled	Number enrolled	% enrolled	Number enrolled	% enrolled
3 and 4 years	1,697,000	30.8	344,000	34.2	120,000	27.3
5 and 6 years	5,494,000	94.8	972,000	94.4	467,000	92.1
7 to 13 years	21,892,000	99.3	3,759,000	99.2	1,718,000	99.4
14 to 17 years	13,312,000	93.8	2,138,000	92.2	913,000	90.8
18 and 19 years	3,185,000	46.5	485,000	47.1	215,000	44.0
20 to 24 years	3,603,000	22.7	435,000	19.9	190,000	19.9
25 to 29 years	1,459,000	10.0	163,000	9.4	74,000	8.3
30 to 34 years	788,000	6.6	103,000	7.1	44,000	5.5
TOTAL	51,430,000	53.1	8,400,000	57.8	3,741,000	54.8

[1] Persons of Spanish origin may be of any race. NOTE: Figures include children enrolled in nursery school, kindergarten, elementary school, high school, and college.

School Enrollment by Grade Level, Type of Control and Race, Fall 1974 and Fall 1975

Source: Bureau of the Census.

Grade level and Type of control	White		Black		All races	
	Fall 1974	Fall 1975	Fall 1974	Fall 1975	Fall 1974	Fall 1975
Nursery school: Public	293,000	392,000	121,000	171,000	423,000	574,000
Private	1,048,000	1,040,000	106,000	105,000	1,184,000	1,174,000
Kindergarten: Public	2,268,000	2,363,000	416,000	426,000	2,726,000	2,851,000
Private	477,000	483,000	47,000	42,000	526,000	542,000
Grades 1–8: Public	23,063,000	22,351,000	4,455,000	4,344,000	27,956,000	27,166,000
Private	2,990,000	3,059,000	131,000	165,000	3,169,000	3,279,000
Grades 9–12: Public	11,966,000	12,112,000	2,072,000	2,140,000	14,275,000	14,503,000
Private	1,107,000	1,112,000	54,000	59,000	1,172,000	1,180,000
College: Public	6,049,000	6,724,000	659,000	782,000	6,905,000	7,704,000
Private	1,732,000	1,792,000	155,000	166,000	1,922,000	1,994,000
Total enrollment	50,992,000	51,430,000	8,215,000	8,400,000	60,259,000	60,969,000

Enrollment in Educational Institutions, 1919-1975

Source: National Center for Education Statistics.

Level of instruction, by type of school	1974-75	1959-60	1949-1950	1939-1940	1929-1930	1919-1920
Kindergarten: Public[1]	(6)	1,922,712	1,034,203	594,647	723,443	481,266
Nonpublic[1]	(6)	354,000	133,000	57,341	54,456	29,683
Residential schools for exceptional children..	(6)	4,800	4,459[4]	5,777	5,164[3]	(2)
Other[5]	(6)	11,980	3,650	3,144	3,400	(2)
Total kindergarten	(6)	2,293,492	1,175,312	660,909	786,463	510,949
Grades 1–8 inclusive: Public[1]	30,700,000[11]	25,679,190	18,352,603	18,237,451	20,555,150	18,897,661
Nonpublic[1]	3,500,000[11]	4,285,696	2,574,777	2,095,938	2,255,430	1,455,878
Residential schools for exceptional children..	(2)	59,400	48,894[4]	55,954	124,153[3]	99,234[7]
Other[5]	200,000[11]	94,488	55,655	76,769	18,644	(2)
Total grades 1–8	......	30,118,774	21,031,929	20,466,112	22,953,377	20,452,773
Total kindergarten through grade 8	34,400,000	32,412,266	22,207,241	21,127,021	23,739,840	20,963,722
Grades 9–12[9]: Public high schools[1]	14,300,000	8,484,869	5,724,621	6,601,444	4,399,422	2,200,389
Nonpublic high schools[1]	1,200,000	1,035,274	672,362	457,768	341,158	213,920
Residential schools for exceptional children..	(2)	23,800	9,784[4]	9,727	4,388[3]	4,500[7]
Other[5]	110,000	55,894	46,242	61,040	66,832	81,367
Total grades 9–12[8]	15,610,000	9,599,810	6,453,009	7,129,979	4,811,800	2,500,176
Total kindergarten through grade 12[8]	50,010,000	42,012,076	28,660,250	28,257,000	28,551,640	23,463,898
Higher education: Publicly controlled	6,700,000	1,831,782	1,354,902	796,531	532,647	315,382
Privately controlled	2,200,000	1,383,762	1,304,119	697,672	568,090	282,498
Total higher education	8,900,000	3,215,544	2,659,021	1,494,203	1,100,737	597,880
Total all levels[9]	58,910,000	45,227,620	31,319,271	29,751,203	29,652,377	24,061,778

[1] Does not include subcollegiate departments of institutions of higher education, residential schools for exceptional children or Federal schools. [2] Not available. [3] 1926-27. [4] 1945-46. [5] Subcollegiate departments of institutions of higher education and Federal schools for Indians and others. Complete data not available before 1959. [6] Included in Grades 1–8. [7] 1917-18. [8] And postgraduate. [9] Does not include schools of nursing not affiliated with institutions of higher learning. [10] Data for fall 1974. [11] Includes kindergarten.

Enrollment in Federally Aided Vocational Education Classes, 1974

Source: U.S. Office of Education.

Program	Secondary classes	Post secondary classes	Adult classes	All classes
Agriculture	659.316	47,458	269,545	976,319
Distributive	353,339	133,214	346,352	832,905
Health	103,780	228,180	172,953	504,913
Home economics	2,877,069	71,590	754,025	3,702,684
Office	1,765,691	426,346	565,427	2,757,464
Technical	40,736	231,387	120,764	392,887
Trades and industry	1,218,461	412,669	1,193,187	2,824,317
Other	1,610,025	46,098	146,900	1,803,023
Total	8,628,417	1,596,942	3,569,153	13,794,512

NOTE: Some enrolees counted in more than one program.

Percent of High School Dropouts Among Persons 14-19 Years of Age

Source: Bureau of the Census.

Age	1974				1970			
	Black		White		Black		White	
	Male	Female	Male	Female	Male	Female	Male	Female
14 years old	2.5	1.8	1.2	1.7	0.9	2.9	1.4	1.1
15 years old	5.2	2.4	2.4	2.1	3.3	2.7	2.0	2.4
16 years old	5.9	9.4	6.2	6.4	10.9	11.1	5.0	6.7
17 years old	11.3	15.4	12.7	11.8	16.0	13.7	7.6	10.2
18 years old	24.5	16.7	16.5	14.3	29.8	27.8	13.6	14.1
19 years old	30.6	24.0	18.4	13.4	44.1	25.8	12.9	15.7
TOTAL	12.1	11.3	9.2	8.3	15.9	13.3	6.7	8.1

NOTE: Dropouts are persons who are not enrolled in school and who are not high school graduates.

Education of U. S. Adults[1]

Source: Bureau of the Census.

Age and race	Total population (thousands)	Less than 4 years high school	High school, 4 years	College, 1 year or more	Median years of school completed
WHITE					
20 and 21 years old	6,635	1,035	2,997	2,604	12.8
22 to 24 years old	9,248	1,190	3,875	4,184	12.9
25 to 29 years old	14,385	2,242	5,981	6,163	12.8
30 to 34 years old	11,988	2,436	5,046	4,504	12.4
35 to 44 years old	19,818	5,167	8,625	6,024	12.5
45 to 54 years old	21,045	7,021	8,852	5,172	12.4
55 to 64 years old	17,623	7,994	6,315	3,315	12.1
65 to 74 years old	12,161	7,162	2,813	2,185	10.3
75 years old and over	7,045	4,884	1,175	986	8.7
BLACK AND OTHER RACES					
20 and 21 years old	1,053	285	465	305	12.5
22 to 24 years old	1,424	385	600	440	12.5
25 to 29 years old	2,007	526	825	656	12.6
30 to 34 years old	1,711	498	693	521	12.5
35 to 44 years old	2,789	1,277	906	607	12.1
45 to 54 years old	2,540	1,538	628	374	10.7
55 to 64 years old	1,863	1,394	308	161	8.7
65 to 74 years old	1,263	1,078	123	62	7.0
75 years old and over	658	566	63	30	5.5

[1] Years of school completed for persons 20 years old and over, by age and race, March 1975.

College and University Endowments, 1974-75

(in millions of dollars)

Source: Council for Financial Aid to Education.

Institution	Endowment (market value)	Voluntary support[1]	Expen- ditures[2]	Institution	Endowment (market value)	Voluntary support[1]	Expen- ditures[2]
Harvard U	1,322	52.4	n.a.	Rensselaer PI	78.2	3.4	27.0
Yale U	517.7	27.4	158.4	Oberlin C	77.6	2.0	15.6
Princeton U	403.4	19.2	69.3	Amherst C	77.0	3.5	11.0
Massachusetts IT	399.8	21.7	152.4	Case Western Reserve U	70.1	18.4	74.0
Stanford U	363.8	45.1	n.a.	Berea C	69.3	7.0	6.5
U of Rochester	347.5	7.1	88.3	Vassar C	63.9	3.6	11.3
U of California	341.0	40.2	1,198.6	U of So. California	63.2	19.2	137.8
Cornell U	286.2	26.1	208.1	Rochester IT	63.1	8.6	33.9
Columbia U	257.5	21.4	199.5	U of Cincinnati	62.7	15.6	97.8
Northwestern U	235.8	16.6	107.7	Williams C	62.3	5.2	10.9
Rice U	187.1	8.3	28.0	U of Kansas	60.2	4.8	125.5
Washington U (St. Louis)	161.3	19.1	99.0	Swarthmore	58.5	1.7	8.0
Dartmouth C	160.4	10.7	45.7	U of Wisconsin	56.8	19.6	240.1
Johns Hopkins U	157.1	15.7	121.4	U of Richmond	55.5	3.1	10.5
Rockefeller U	153.0	5.6	26.9	Lehigh U	53.2	6.5	25.6
Emory U	150.9	7.0	56.5	Trinity U	52.7	1.7	12.2
Vanderbilt U	148.8	13.6	86.3	Ohio State U	52.3	10.2	218.8
California IT	142.1	10.6	46.6	Syracuse U	48.3	4.7	70.5
U of Pennsylvania	129.7	34.0	240.0	Stevens IT	46.0	1.0	12.9
New York University	120.1	19.7	244.4	Southern Methodist U	45.2	13.1	137.8
Wesleyan U	109.7	1.0	18.9	Brandeis U	44.8	10.4	23.4
U of Virginia	108.3	11.3	119.8	Wabash C	44.8	2.5	5.4
Duke U	105.8	16.1	91.0	Tulane U	44.5	10.1	47.5
U of Michigan	103.6	22.2	267.8	Wake Forest U	42.0	6.3	34.0
Carnegie-Mellon U	103.4	4.0	38.3	Mount Holyoke C	41.4	2.7	9.1
Wellesley C	101.0	5.2	13.2	Lafayette C	40.3	2.1	9.6
Brown U	95.5	10.3	n.a.	Bowdoin C	39.1	4.2	8.2
U. of Notre Dame	92.7	7.1	38.5	Buffalo State U	38.8	1.6	107.4
Smith C	81.8	7.7	17.5	Agnes Scott C	38.2	8.9	3.1
U of Pittsburgh	84.4	6.3	146.0	Baylor U	38.2	6.6	17.0

[1] Gifts from business, alumni, religious denominations, and others. [2] Figure represents about 80% of typical operating budget. Does not include auxiliary enterprises and capital outlays. NOTE: C—College; U—University; IT—Institute of Technology; PI—Polytechnic Institute. The designation n.a. means not available.

Degrees Conferred by Institutions of Higher Education, 1972-73

Source: National Center for Education Statistics.

Field of study	Bachelor's and first professional[1]		Second level (master's)		Doctorate	
	Men	Women	Men	Women	Men	Women
Agriculture and natural resources	13,661	1,095	2,588	219	1,031	28
Architecture, environmental design . . .	6,042	920	1,943	364	54	4
Biological sciences	29,636	12,597	4,354	1,909	2,926	710
Business and management	113,445	13,385	29,638	1,528	879	53
Communications	9,074	5,243	1,546	860	114	25
Computer and information sciences . . .	3,664	640	1,888	225	181	15
Education	51,433	142,777	44,022	61,220	5,501	1,813
Engineering	50,652	613	16,341	278	3,438	54
Fine and applied arts	14,267	21,750	4,005	3,249	449	167
Foreign languages	4,608	14,356	1,536	2,753	592	399
Health professions	7,754	25,810	3,567	4,795	485	161
Nursing	460	14,947	109	1,970	4	13
Pharmacy	3,771	1,193	131	36	221	75
Speech pathology and audiology . . .	315	2,259	237	1,167	46	23
Home economics	503	13,030	156	1,523	40	125
Law	434	40	977	71	36	1
Letters	29,233	41,727	5,301	7,048	1,925	829
Library sciences	87	1,072	1,676	6,020	60	42
Mathematics	13,796	9,271	3,525	1,503	966	102
Military sciences	253	...	...	...	...	...
Physical sciences	17,626	3,070	5,414	843	3,738	268
Chemistry	8,188	1,911	1,679	451	1,533	153
Physics	3,827	296	1,628	107	1,256	47
Psychology	2,463	379	688	83	258	12
Public affairs and services	24,976	22,719	3,495	2,336	1,484	605
Social sciences	9,520	8,323	5,883	5,107	177	42
Economics	99,909	56,452	12,545	4,773	3,569	661
Geology	12,735	2,035	1,945	280	793	52
History	26,987	13,956	3,447	1,583	977	163
Political science, government . . .	24,219	5,881	1,918	480	652	95
Sociology	15,580	19,856	1,146	777	429	154
Theology	2,621	913	2,036	742	644	22
Interdisciplinary studies	13,533	6,759	1,384	1,162	165	34
TOTAL	615,272	465,275	166,712	115,462	34,623	6947

[1] Includes Bachelor of Arts, Bachelor of Science and such first professional degrees as M.D., LL.B., D.D.S., B.D. NOTE: Data are latest available.

Median Salaries of Staffs at 4-Year Colleges and Universities

Position	1973-74	1971-72	1969-70	1967-68	1965-66	1963-64	1959-60
Instructional staff							
All ranks	$14,373	$12,932	$11,745	$10,235	$ 9,081	$ 8,163	$ 6,711
Professors	19,897	18,091	16,799	14,713	12,953	11,312	9,107
Associate professors	15,331	13,958	12,985	11,393	10,058	8,969	7,332
Assistant professors	12,644	11,511	10,698	9,472	8,417	7,539	6,231
Instructors and lecturers . .	10,211	9,347	8,416	7,496	6,761	6,114	5,095
Administrative officers							
President	31,342	29,750	25,979	22,303	19,638	17,330	13,827
Vice president	27,667	26,313	23,250	21,458	19,012	17,130	14,154
Dean of the college	22,000	19,975	19,125	16,141	15,703	13,644	10,723
Dean of students	19,117	17,830	16,050	14,086	12,027	10,694	8,796
Dean of admissions	15,773	14,280	12,983	11,446	10,364	9,572	7,680
Registrar	14,443	13,108	11,743	10,366	9,123	8,142	6,340
Chief librarian	16,417	14,891	13,439	11,817	10,225	8,883	7,078
Director of athletics	17,515	15,821	14,311	12,470	11,125	9,871	8,104
Head football coach . . .	16,159	14,591	13,395	11,488	10,716	9,321	7,824
Head basketball coach . . .	14,700	13,208	11,779	10,485	9,383	8,542	6,888

NOTE: Salaries of instructional staff are for 9 months of full-time teaching; salaries of administrative officers are usually for 11 or 12 months. From: "Economic Status of the Teaching Profession, 1960-70" and "Salaries Paid and Salary-Related Practices in Higher Education, 1971-72." Copyright © 1972 by the National Education Association. All rights reserved.

CATHOLIC ELEMENTARY AND SECONDARY SCHOOLS: 1950 TO 1973
As of October 1. Regular sessions only.

ITEM	1950	1960	1965	1968	1969	1970	1971	1972	1973
Elementary schools.....number..	8,589	10,501	10,879	10,113	9,695	9,362	8,982	8,761	8,550
Pupils enrolled...........1,000..	2,561	4,373	4,492	3,860	3,607	3,355	3,076	2,871	2,711
Teachers, total............1,000..	67	108	120	[1] 126	110	112	106	105	103
Religious..............1,000..	62	79	76	68	56	52	47	44	41
Lay....................1,000..	5	29	44	58	54	60	59	61	62
Secondary schools.......number..	2,189	2,392	2,413	2,192	2,076	1,981	1,857	1,773	1,719
Pupils enrolled...........1,000..	506	880	1,082	1,081	1,051	1,008	959	919	903
Teachers, total............1,000..	28	44	57	53	53	54	53	51	51
Religious..............1,000..	23	33	38	33	29	28	26	24	22
Lay....................1,000..	5	11	19	23	23	26	27	27	29

[1] Includes part-time teachers. Source: National Catholic Educational Association, Washington, D.C., *A Statistical Report on Catholic Elementary and Secondary Schools for the Year 1967–68 to 1969–70* and *U.S. Catholic Schools, 1973–74,* and subsequent annual issues. (Copyright.)

SCHOOL EXPENDITURES—PUBLIC AND PRIVATE, BY SOURCE OF FUNDS: 1960 TO 1975
Estimates for school years ending in year shown. Actual school expenditure data for private and secondary schools are not available. Consequently, amounts for this sector, or including this sector, are estimated.

ITEM	TOTAL (bil. dol.)							PERCENT						
	1960	1966	1970	1972	1973 est.	1974 est.	1975 est.	1960	1966	1970	1972	1973 est.	1974 est.	1975 est.
Total........	24.7	45.2	70.0	84.7	89.1	98.8	110.4	100.0	100.0	100.0	100.0	100.0	100.0	100.0
Federal............	1.7	5.1	7.7	9.4	9.7	11.1	12.1	6.9	11.3	11.0	11.1	10.9	11.2	11.0
State..............	7.2	13.1	22.5	26.9	29.3	32.8	36.9	29.1	29.0	32.1	31.8	32.9	33.2	33.4
Local..............	9.7	15.0	21.9	27.3	27.9	30.0	33.6	39.3	33.2	31.3	32.2	31.3	30.4	30.4
All other..........	6.1	12.0	17.9	21.1	22.2	24.9	27.8	24.7	26.5	25.6	24.9	24.9	25.2	25.2
Public.............	19.7	35.3	56.6	68.9	72.6	80.5	90.1	100.0	100.0	100.0	100.0	100.0	100.0	100.0
Federal..........	1.2	3.7	6.0	7.5	7.7	8.9	9.8	6.1	10.5	10.6	10.9	10.6	11.1	10.9
State............	7.2	13.0	22.4	26.7	29.1	32.5	36.6	36.6	36.8	39.6	38.7	40.1	40.4	40.6
Local............	9.7	15.0	21.8	27.2	27.8	29.9	33.5	49.2	42.5	38.5	39.5	38.3	37.1	37.2
All other........	1.6	3.6	6.4	7.5	8.0	9.2	10.2	8.1	10.2	11.3	10.9	11.0	11.4	11.3
Private............	5.0	9.9	13.4	15.8	16.5	18.3	20.3	100.0	100.0	100.0	100.0	100.0	100.0	100.0
Federal..........	.5	1.4	1.7	1.9	2.0	2.2	2.3	10.0	14.1	12.7	12.0	12.0	12.0	11.3
State............	(Z)	.1	.1	.2	.2	.3	.3	(Z)	1.0	0.7	1.3	1.2	1.6	1.5
Local............	(Z)	(Z)	.1	.1	.1	.1	.1	(Z)	(Z)	0.7	0.6	0.6	0.6	0.5
All other........	4.5	8.4	11.5	13.6	14.2	15.7	17.6	90.0	84.9	85.9	86.1	86.2	85.8	86.7
Elementary and														
secondary [1].....	18.0	30.0	45.3	55.5	57.7	63.4	70.9	100.0	100.0	100.0	100.0	100.0	100.0	100.0
Federal............	.7	2.2	3.6	4.6	4.6	5.4	5.9	3.9	7.3	7.9	8.3	8.0	8.5	8.3
State..............	5.6	9.6	16.1	19.0	20.7	23.0	25.9	31.1	32.0	35.5	34.2	35.9	36.3	36.5
Local..............	9.5	14.6	21.0	26.1	26.6	28.6	32.1	52.8	48.7	46.4	47.0	46.1	45.1	45.3
All other..........	2.2	3.6	4.6	5.8	5.8	6.4	7.0	12.2	12.0	10.2	10.5	10.0	10.1	9.9
Public.............	15.9	26.5	40.8	49.8	52.0	57.1	64.0	100.0	100.0	100.0	100.0	100.0	100.0	100.0
Federal..........	.7	2.2	3.6	4.6	4.7	5.4	5.9	4.6	8.3	8.8	9.3	8.8	9.5	9.2
State............	5.6	9.6	16.1	19.0	20.7	23.0	25.9	35.4	36.2	39.5	38.1	39.8	40.2	40.5
Local............	9.5	14.6	21.0	26.1	26.6	28.6	32.1	59.6	55.1	51.5	52.4	51.2	50.1	50.1
All other........	.1	.1	.1	.1	.1	.1	.1	0.4	0.4	0.2	0.2	0.2	0.2	0.2
Private, all other..	2.1	3.5	4.5	5.7	5.7	6.3	6.9	100.0	100.0	100.0	100.0	100.0	100.0	100.0
Institutions of														
higher education.	6.7	15.2	24.7	29.2	31.4	35.4	39.5	100.0	100.0	100.0	100.0	100.0	100.0	100.0
Federal............	1.0	2.9	4.1	4.8	5.1	5.7	6.2	14.9	19.1	16.6	16.4	16.3	16.1	15.7
State..............	1.6	3.5	6.4	7.9	8.6	9.8	11.0	23.9	23.0	25.9	27.1	27.4	27.7	27.9
Local..............	.2	.4	.9	1.2	1.3	1.4	1.5	3.0	2.6	3.6	4.1	4.1	4.0	3.8
All other..........	3.9	8.4	13.3	15.3	16.4	18.5	20.8	58.2	55.3	53.9	52.4	52.2	52.2	52.6
Public.............	3.8	8.8	15.8	19.1	20.6	23.4	26.1	100.0	100.0	100.0	100.0	100.0	100.0	100.0
Federal..........	.5	1.5	2.4	2.9	3.1	3.5	3.9	14.9	17.6	15.0	15.0	15.0	15.0	15.0
State............	1.6	3.4	6.3	7.7	8.4	9.5	10.7	41.4	38.4	40.0	40.8	40.8	40.8	40.8
Local............	.2	.4	.8	1.1	1.2	1.3	1.4	4.6	4.1	5.1	5.5	5.5	5.5	5.5
All other........	1.5	3.5	6.3	7.4	7.9	9.1	10.1	39.1	39.9	39.9	38.7	38.7	38.7	38.7
Private............	2.9	6.4	8.9	10.1	10.8	12.0	13.4	100.0	100.0	100.0	100.0	100.0	100.0	100.0
Federal..........	.5	1.4	1.7	1.9	2.0	2.2	2.3	17.0	22.1	18.8	18.6	18.6	18.6	18.6
State............	(Z)	.1	.1	.2	.2	.3	.3	1.5	1.5	1.6	2.0	2.1	2.2	2.2
Local............	(Z)	(Z)	.1	.1	.1	.1	.1	0.2	0.1	0.7	0.5	0.7	0.8	0.8
All other........	2.4	4.9	7.0	7.9	8.5	9.4	10.7	81.3	76.3	78.9	78.9	78.6	78.4	78.4

Z Less than $50 million or less than 0.05 percent.   [1] Includes residential schools for exceptional children, Federal schools for Indians, and federally operated elementary and secondary schools on military posts.

Source: U.S. National Center for Education Statistics (see text, p. 107), *Projections of Educational Statistics to 1983–84.*

Selected Degree Abbreviations

Source: This material has been taken from *American Universities and Colleges*, 10th and 11th editions, published by the American Council on Education.

A.B. Bachelor of Arts
Ae.E. Aeronautical Engineer
A.M. Master of Arts
A.M.T. Master of Arts in Teaching
B.A. Bachelor of Arts
B.A.E. Bachelor of Arts in Education, or Bachelor of Art Education, Aeronautical Engineering, Agricultural Engineering, or Architectural Engineering
B.Ag. Bachelor of Agriculture
B.Arch. Bachelor of Architecture
B.B.A. Bachelor of Business Administration
B.C.E. Bachelor of Civil Engineering or Bachelor of Christian Education
B.Ch.E. Bachelor of Chemical Engineering
B.D. Bachelor of Divinity
B.E. Bachelor of Education or Bachelor of Engineering
B.E.E. Bachelor of Electrical Engineering
B.F. Bachelor of Forestry
B.F.A. Bachelor of Fine Arts
B.J. Bachelor of Journalism
B.L.S. Bachelor of Liberal Studies or Bachelor of Library Science
B.Litt. Bachelor of Literature
B.M. Bachelor of Medicine or Bachelor of Music
B.Mus. Bachelor of Music
B.N. Bachelor of Nursing
B.Pharm. Bachelor of Pharmacy
B.R.E. Bachelor of Religious Education
B.S. Bachelor of Science
B.S.Ed. Bachelor of Science in Education
C.E. Civil Engineer
Chem.E. Chemical Engineer
D.B.A. Doctor of Business Administration
D.D. Doctor of Divinity[1]
D.D.S. Doctor of Dental Surgery or Doctor of Dental Science
D.L.S. Doctor of Library Science
D.M.D. Doctor of Dental Medicine
D.O. Doctor of Osteopathy
D.M.S. Doctor of Medical Science
D.P.A. Doctor of Public Administration[2]
D.P.H. Doctor of Public Health
D.R.E. Doctor of Religious Education
D.S.W. Doctor of Social Welfare or Doctor of Social Work
D.Sc. Doctor of Science[3]
D.V.M. Doctor of Veterinary Medicine
Ed.D. Doctor of Education[2]
Ed.S. Education Specialist

E.E. Electrical Engineer
E.M. Engineer of Mines or Mining Engineer
E.Met. Engineer of Metallurgy
I.E. Industrial Engineer
J.D. Doctor of Jurisprudence[2]
J.S.D. Doctor of the Science of Law
L.H.D. Doctor of Humane Letters[3]
Litt.M. Master of Letters[4]
LL.B. Bachelor of Laws
LL.D. Doctor of Laws[3]
LL.M. Master of Laws
M.A. Master of Arts
M.Aero.E. Master of Aeronautical Engineering
M.B.A. Master of Business Administration
M.C.E. Master of Christian Education or Master of Civil Engineering
M.C.S. Master of Commercial Science or Master of Computer Science
M.D. Doctor of Medicine
M.Div. Master of Divinity
M.E. Master of Engineering
M.Ed. Master of Education
M.Eng. Master of Engineering
M.F. Master of Forestry
M.F.A. Master of Fine Arts
M.L.S. Master of Library Science
M.M. Master of Music
M.M.E. Master of Mechanical Engineering or Master of Music Education
M.Mus. Master of Music
M.Nurs. Master of Nursing
M.R.E. Master of Religious Education
M.S. Master of Science
M.S.W. Master of Social Work
M.Th. Master of Theology
Nuc.E. Nuclear Engineer
O.D. Doctor of Optometry
Pharm.D. Doctor of Pharmacy[2]
Ph.B. Bachelor of Philosophy
Ph.D. Doctor of Philosophy
S.B. Bachelor of Science
Sc.D. Doctor of Science[3]
S.J.D. Doctor of Juridical Science or Doctor of the Science of Law
S.Sc.D. Doctor of Social Science
S.T.B. Bachelor of Sacred Theology
S.T.D. Doctor of Sacred Theology[3]
S.T.M. Master of Sacred Theology
Th.B. Bachelor of Theology
Th.D. Doctor of Theology
Th.M. Master of Theology

[1] Honorary. [2] Earned and honorary. [3] Usually honorary. [4] Sometimes honorary.

Academic Costume: Colors Associated with Fields

Agriculture	Maize	Music	Pink
Arts, Letters, Humanities	White	Nursing	Apricot
Commerce, Accountancy, Business	Drab	Oratory (Speech)	Silver gray
		Pharmacy	Olive green
Dentistry	Lilac	Philosophy	Dark blue
Economics	Copper	Physical Education	Sage green
Education	Light Blue	Public Admin. including Foreign Service	Peacock blue
Engineering	Orange		
Fine Arts, Architecture	Brown	Public Health	Salmon pink
Forestry	Russet	Science	Golden yellow
Journalism	Crimson	Social Work	Citron
Law	Purple	Theology	Scarlet
Library Science	Lemon	Veterinary Science	Gray
Medicine	Green		

U.S. Community, Junior and Technical Colleges

Source: Community, Junior and Technical College Directory, 1976. Published by the American Association of Community and Junior Colleges.

Institution	Location	Institution	Location
ALABAMA		Eastern Arizona College	Thatcher
Publicly controlled		*Maricopa County Community College District, Phoenix:*	
Alabama Aviation & Tech. Coll.	Ozark	Glendale Community College	Glendale
Alabama Technical College	East Gadsden	Maricopa Technical Community Coll.	Phoenix
Alexander City State Junior College	Alexander City	Mesa Community College	Mesa
Brewer State Junior College	Fayette	Phoenix College	Phoenix
Chattahoochee Valley Comm. College	Phenix City	Scottsdale Community College	Scottsdale
Ed E. Reid State Tech. Coll.	Evergreen	Mohave Community College	Kingman
Enterprise State Junior College	Enterprise	Navajo Community College	Chinle
Gadsden State Junior College	East Gadsden	Northland Pioneer College	Holbrook
George C. Wallace State Comm. Coll.	Dothan	Pima Community College	Tucson
Harry M. Ayers State Tech. Coll.	Anniston	*Pinal County Community College District, Coolidge:*	
Hobson State Technical College	Thomasville	Arizona College of Technology	Winkelman
James H. Faulkner State Junior College	Bay Minette	Central Arizona College	Coolidge
Jefferson Davis State Junior College	Brewton	Yavapai College	Prescott
Jefferson State Junior College	Birmingham	Privately controlled	
John C. Calhoun State Comm. Coll.	Decatur	College of Ganado	Ganado
John M. Patterson State Tech. Coll.	Montgomery		
Lawson State Community College	Birmingham		
Lurleen B. Wallace State Junior Coll.	Andalusia		
Northeast Alabama State Junior College	Rainsville	**ARKANSAS**	
Northwest Alabama State Junior College	Phil Campbell	Publicly controlled	
Northwest Alabama State Tech. Coll.	Hamilton	Arkansas State Univ.-Beebe Branch	Beebe
Patrick Henry State Junior College	Monroeville	East Arkansas Comm. College	Forrest City
S. D. Bishop State Junior College	Mobile	Garland County Comm. Coll	Hot Springs
Shelton State Tech. Coll.	Tuscaloosa	Mississippi County Comm. Coll.	Blytheville
Snead State Junior College	Boaz	North Arkansas Comm. Coll.	Harrison
Southern Union State Junior College	Wadley	Phillips County Community College	Helena
Southwest State Tech. Coll.	Mobile	Southern State College	Magnolia
Trenholm State Tech. Coll.	Montgomery	El Dorado Branch	El Dorado
Wallace State Comm. Coll.	Selma	Southwest Technical Institute	East Camden
		Westark Community College	Fort Smith
Privately controlled			
Alabama Christian College	Montgomery	Privately controlled	
Alabama Lutheran Jr. Coll.-Acad.	Selma	Central Baptist College	Conway
Cullman College	Cullman	Crowley's Ridge College	Paragould
Marion Institute	Marion	Shorter College	North Little Rock
Selma University	Selma	Southern Baptist College	Walnut Ridge
Walker College	Jasper		
		CALIFORNIA	
ALASKA		Publicly controlled	
Publicly controlled		Allan Hancock College	Santa Maria
Univ. of Alaska Community Colleges:		Antelope Valley College	Lancaster
Anchorage Community College	Anchorage	Barstow College	Barstow
Juneau-Douglas Community College	Auke Bay	Butte College	Oroville
Kenai Peninsula Community College	Soldotna	Cabrillo College	Aptos
Ketchikan Community College	Ketchikan	Canyons, College of the	Valencia
Kodiak Community College	Kodiak	Cerritos College	Norwalk
Kuskokwim Community College	Bethel	Chabot College	Hayward
Matanuska Susitna Community Coll.	Palmer	Chaffey College	Alta Loma
Northwest Community College	Nome	Citrus College	Azusa
Sitka Community College	Sitka	*Coast Community College District, Costa Mesa:*	
Tanana Valley Community College	Fairbanks	Golden West College	Huntington Beach
Privately controlled		Orange Coast College	Costa Mesa
Sheldon Jackson College	Sitka	Compton Community College	Compton
		Contra Costa Community College District, Martinez:	
AMERICAN SAMOA		Contra Costa College	San Pablo
Publicly controlled		Diablo Valley College	Pleasant Hill
American Samoa Comm. Coll.	Pago Pago	Los Medanos College	Pittsburg
		Cuesta College	San Luis Obispo
		Desert, College of the	Palm Desert
ARIZONA		El Camino College	Via Torrance
Publicly controlled		*Foothill Community College District, Los Altos Hills:*	
Arizona Western College	Yuma	De Anza College	Cupertino
Cochise College	Douglas	Foothill College	Los Altos Hills

Institution	Location
Gavilan College	Gilroy
Glendale College	Glendale
Grossmont Community College District, El Cajon:	
Grossmont College	El Cajon
Hartnell College	Salinas
Imperial Valley College	Imperial
Kern Community College District, Bakersfield:	
Bakersfield College	Bakersfield
Cerro Coso Community College	Ridgecrest
Porterville College	Porterville
Lake Tahoe Community Coll.	South Lake Tahoe
Lassen College	Susanville
Long Beach City College	Long Beach
Los Angeles Community College District:	
East Los Angeles College	Los Angeles
Los Angeles City College	Los Angeles
Los Angeles Harbor College	Wilmington
Los Angeles Mission College	San Fernando
Los Angeles Pierce College	Woodland Hills
Los Angeles Southwest College	Los Angeles
Los Angeles Trade-Technical College	Los Angeles
Los Angeles Valley College	Van Nuys
West Los Angeles College	Culver City
Los Rios Community College District, Sacramento:	
American River College	Sacramento
Cosumnes River College	Sacramento
Sacramento City College	Sacramento
Marin County Community College District, Kentfield:	
Indian Valley Colleges	Novato
Marin, College of	Kentfield
Mendocino College	Ukiah
Merced College	Merced
Mira Costa College	Oceanside
Monterey Peninsula College	Monterey
Mt. San Antonio College	Walnut
Mt. San Jacinto College	San Jacinto
Nairobi College	East Palo Alto
Napa Community College	Napa
North Orange Community College District, Fullerton:	
Cypress College	Cypress
Fullerton College	Fullerton
Ohlone College	Fremont
Palo Verde College	Blythe
Palomar College	San Marcos
Pasadena City College	Pasadena
Peralta Community College District, Oakland:	
Alameda, College of	Alameda
Feather River College	Quincy
Laney College	Oakland
Merritt College	Oakland
Peralta Coll. for Non-Traditional Study	Berkeley
Redwoods, College of the	Eureka
Rio Hondo College	Whittier
Riverside City College	Riverside
Saddleback College	Mission Viejo
San Bernardino Community College Dist., San Bernardino:	
Crafton Hills College	Yucaipa
San Bernardino Valley College	San Bernardino
San Diego Community College District, San Diego:	
San Diego City College	San Diego
San Diego Evening College	San Diego
San Diego Mesa College	San Diego
San Diego Miramar College	San Diego
San Francisco, City College of	San Francisco
San Joaquin Delta College	Stockton
San Jose Community College District, San Jose:	
Evergreen Valley College	San Jose
San Jose City College	San Jose
San Mateo Community College District, San Mateo:	
Canada College	Redwood City
College of San Mateo	San Mateo
Skyline College	San Bruno

Institution	Location
Santa Ana College	Santa Ana
Santa Barbara City College	Santa Barbara
Santa Monica College	Santa Monica
Santa Rosa Junior College	Santa Rosa
Sequoias, College of the	Visalia
Shasta College	Redding
Sierra College	Rocklin
Siskiyous, College of	Weed
Solano Community College	Suisun City
Southwestern College	Chula Vista
State Center Community College District, Fresno:	
Fresno City College	Fresno
Reedley College	Reedley
Taft College	Taft
Ventura County Community College District, Ventura:	
Moorpark College	Moorpark
Oxnard College	Oxnard
Ventura College	Ventura
Victor Valley College	Victorville
West Hills College	Coalinga
West Valley College	Saratoga
Yosemite Junior College District, Modesto:	
Columbia Junior College	Columbia
Modesto Junior College	Modesto
Yuba College	Marysville

Privately controlled

Deep Springs College	Via Dyer, Nevada
Don Bosco Tech. Inst.	Rosemead
Humphreys College	Stockton
Marymount Palos Verdes College	Palos Verdes
Menlo College	Menlo Park

CANAL ZONE

Publicly controlled

Canal Zone College	Balboa

COLORADO

Publicly controlled

Aims College	Greeley
Arapahoe Community College	Littleton
Colorado Mountain Coll., Glenwood Spgs.:	
East Campus	Leadville
West Campus	Glenwood Spgs.
Colorado Northwestern Comm. Coll.	Rangely
Denver, Community College of:	
Auraria Campus	Denver
North Campus	Denver
Red Rocks Campus	Golden
El Paso Community College	Colorado Spgs.
Lamar Community College	Lamar
Morgan Community College	Fort Morgan
Northeastern Junior College	Sterling
Otero Junior College	La Junta
Trinidad State Junior College	Trinidad
University of Southern Colorado	Pueblo
Coll. for Comm. Svcs. and Career Ed.	Pueblo

CONNECTICUT

Publicly controlled

Asnuntuck Community College	Enfield
Greater Hartford Community College	Hartford
Hartford State Technical College	Hartford
Housatonic Community College	Bridgeport
Manchester Community College	Manchester
Mattatuck Community College	Waterbury

Institution	Location
Middlesex Community College	Middletown
Mohegan Community College	Norwich
Northwestern Connecticut Comm. College	Winsted
Norwalk Community College	Norwalk
Norwalk State Technical College	Norwalk
Quinebaug Valley Community College	Danielson
South Central Community College	New Haven
Thames Valley State Technical College	Norwich
Tunxis Community College	Farmington
Waterbury State Technical College	Waterbury

Privately controlled

Hartford College for Women	Hartford
Mitchell College	New London
Mount Sacred Heart College	Hamden
Post College	Waterbury
Saint Thomas Seminary	Bloomfield
University of Bridgeport	Bridgeport
Junior College Division	Bridgeport

DELAWARE

Publicly controlled

Delaware Technical & Community Coll., Dover:

Kent Campus	Dover
Southern Campus	Georgetown
Stanton Campus	Newark
Wilmington Campus	Wilmington

Privately controlled

Brandywine College	Wilmington
Goldey Beacom College	Wilmington
Wesley College	Dover

DISTRICT OF COLUMBIA

Publicly controlled

Washington Technical Institute	Washington

Privately controlled

Immaculata College of Washington	Washington
Mount Vernon College	Washington
Southeastern University-Jr. Coll. Div.	Washington

FLORIDA

Publicly controlled

Boca Raton, College of	Boca Raton
Brevard Community College	Cocoa
Broward Community College	Ft. Lauderdale
Central Florida Community College	Ocala
Chipola Junior College	Marianna
Daytona Beach Community College	Daytona Beach
Edison Community College	Fort Myers
Florida Jr. Coll. at Jacksonville	Jacksonville
Florida Keys Community College	Key West
Gulf Coast Community College	Panama City
Hillsborough Community College	Tampa
Indian River Community College	Ft. Pierce
Lake City Community College	Lake City
Lake-Sumter Community College	Leesburg
Manatee Junior College	Bradenton
Miami-Dade Community College, Miami:	
Downtown Campus	Miami
Medical Center, The	Miami
North Campus	Miami
South Campus	Miami
North Florida Junior College	Madison
Okaloosa-Walton Junior College	Niceville

Institution	Location
Palm Beach Junior College	Lake Worth
Pasco-Hernando Comm. College	Dade City
Pensacola Junior College	Pensacola
Polk Community College	Winter Haven
St. Johns River Junior College	Palatka
St. Petersburg Junior College	St. Petersburg
Santa Fe Community College	Gainesville
Seminole Junior College	Sanford
South Florida Junior College	Avon Park
Tallahassee Community College	Tallahassee
Valencia Community College	Orlando

Privately controlled

Florida College	Temple Terrace
St. John Vianney Jr. College	Miami
Webber College	Babson Park

GEORGIA

Publicly controlled

Abraham Baldwin Agricultural College	Tifton
Albany Junior College	Albany
Atlanta Junior College	Atlanta
Bainbridge Junior College	Bainbridge
Brunswick Junior College	Brunswick
Clayton Junior College	Morrow
Dalton Junior College	Dalton
DeKalb Community College	Clarkston
Emmanuel County Junior College	Swainsboro
Floyd Junior College	Rome
Gainesville Junior College	Gainesville
Georgia Military College	Milledgeville
Gordon Junior College	Barnesville
Kennesaw Junior College	Marietta
Macon Junior College	Macon
Middle Georgia College	Cochran
South Georgia College	Douglas

Privately controlled

Andrew College	Cuthbert
Brewton Parker College	Mt. Vernon
Emmanuel College	Franklin Springs
Oxford College of Emory University	Oxford
Reinhardt College	Waleska
Truett McConnell College	Cleveland
Young Harris College	Young Harris

HAWAII

Publicly controlled

Univ. of Hawaii Community College System:

Hawaii Community College	Hilo
Honolulu Community College	Honolulu
Kapiolani Community College	Honolulu
Kauai Community College	Lihue
Leeward Community College	Pearl City
Maui Community College	Kahului
Windward Community College	Kaneohe

IDAHO

Publicly controlled

North Idaho College	Coeur d'Alene
Southern Idaho, College of	Twin Falls

Privately controlled

Ricks College	Rexburg
St. Gertrude, College of	Cottonwood

Institution	Location	Institution	Location

ILLINOIS

Publicly controlled

Belleville Area College	Belleville
Black Hawk College	Moline
East Campus	Kewanee
Quad Cities Campus	Moline
Carl Sandburg College	Galesburg

Chicago, City Colleges of:

Kennedy-King College	Chicago
Loop College, The	Chicago
Malcolm X College	Chicago
Mayfair College	Chicago
Olive Harvey College	Chicago
Southwest College	Chicago
Wilbur Wright College	Chicago
Danville Junior College	Danville
DuPage, College of	Glen Ellyn
Elgin Community College	Elgin
Highland Community College	Freeport
Illinois Central College	East Peoria

Illinois Eastern Community Colleges, Olney:

Lincoln Trail College	Robinson
Olney Central College	Olney
Wabash Valley College	Mt. Carmel
Illinois Valley Community College	Oglesby
John A. Logan College	Carterville
John Wood Community College	Quincy
Joliet Junior College	Joliet
Kankakee Community College	Kankakee
Kaskaskia College	Centralia
Kishwaukee College	Malta
Lake County, College of	Grayslake
Lake Land College	Mattoon
Lewis and Clark Community College	Godfrey
Lincoln Land Community College	Springfield
McHenry County College	Crystal Lake
Moraine Valley Community College	Palos Hills
Morton College	Cicero
Oakton Community College	Morton Grove
Parkland College	Champaign
Prairie State College	Chicago Heights
Rend Lake College	Ina
Richland Community College	Decatur
Rock Valley College	Rockford
Sauk Valley College	Dixon
Shawnee Community College	Ullin
Southeastern Illinois College	Harrisburg
Spoon River College	Canton
State Comm. Coll. of East St. Louis	East St. Louis
Thornton Community College	South Holland
Triton College	River Grove
Waubonsee Community College	Sugar Grove
William Rainey Harper College	Palatine

Privately controlled

Central YMCA Community College	Chicago
Felician College	Chicago
Kendall College	Evanston
Lincoln University	Lincoln
MacCormac College	Chicago
Mallinckrodt College	Wilmette
Springfield College in Illinois	Springfield

INDIANA

Publicly controlled

Indiana Vocational Tech. Coll., Indianapolis:

Columbus Campus	Columbus
Evansville Campus	Evansville
Fort Wayne Campus	Fort Wayne
Gary Campus	Gary
Indianapolis Campus	Indianapolis
Jeffersonville Campus	Jeffersonville
Kokomo Campus	Kokomo
Lafayette Campus	Lafayette
Madison Campus	Madison
Muncie Campus	Muncie
Richmond Campus	Richmond
South Bend Campus	South Bend
Terre Haute Campus	Terre Haute
Vincennes University	Vincennes

Privately controlled

Ancilla College	Donaldson
Holy Cross Junior College	Notre Dame

IOWA

Publicly controlled

Des Moines Area Community College, Ankeny:

Ankeny Campus	Ankeny
Boone Campus	Boone

Eastern Iowa Comm. Coll. District, Davenport:

Clinton Community College	Clinton
Muscatine Community College	Muscatine
Scott Community College	Bettendorf
Hawkeye Institute of Technology	Waterloo
Indian Hills Community College	Ottumwa
Centerville Campus	Centerville
Ottumwa Campus	Ottumwa
Iowa Central Community College	Fort Dodge
Eagle Grove Center	Eagle Grove
Fort Dodge Center	Fort Dodge
Webster City Center	Webster City
Iowa Lakes Community College	Estherville
North Attendance Center	Estherville
South Attendance Center	Emmetsburg

Iowa Valley Comm. Coll. Dist., Marshalltown:

Ellsworth Community College	Iowa Falls
Marshalltown Community College	Marshalltown

Iowa Western Community College, Council Bluffs:

Clarinda Campus	Clarinda
Council Bluffs Campus	Council Bluffs
Kirkwood Community College	Cedar Rapids
North Iowa Area Community College	Mason City
Northeast Iowa Area Voc.-Tech. Sch.	Calmar
North Center	Calmar
South Center	Dubuque
Northwest Iowa Technical College	Sheldon

Southeastern Community College, West Burlington:

North Campus	West Burlington
South Campus	Keokuk
Southwestern Community College	Creston
Western Iowa Tech. Comm. Coll.	Sioux City

Privately controlled

Mount St. Clare College	Clinton
Ottumwa Heights College	Ottumwa
Palmer Junior College	Davenport
Sioux Empire College	Hawarden
Waldorf College	Forest City

KANSAS

Publicly controlled

Allen County Community Junior College	Iola
Barton County Community Jr. College	Great Bend
Butler County Community Junior College	El Dorado

Institution	Location
Cloud County Community Junior College	Concordia
Coffeyville Community Junior College	Coffeyville
Colby Community College	Colby
Cowley County Community College	Arkansas City
Dodge City Community College	Dodge City
Fort Scott Community College	Fort Scott
Garden City Community Junior College	Garden City
Haskell Indian Junior College	Lawrence
Highland Community Junior College	Highland
Hutchinson Community Junior College	Hutchinson
Independence Community Junior College	Independence
Johnson County Community Jr. College	Overland Park
Kansas City Kans. Community Jr. College	Kansas City
Kansas Technical Institute	Salina
Labette Community Junior College	Parsons
Neosho County Community Junior College	Chanute
Pratt Community Junior College	Pratt
Seward County Community Jr. College	Liberal

Privately controlled

Central College	McPherson
Donnelly College	Kansas City
Hesston College	Hesston
St. John's College	Winfield

KENTUCKY

Publicly controlled

Bowling Green Community College	Bowling Green
Richmond Community College	Richmond

Univ. of Kentucky Community Colleges, Lexington:

Ashland Community College	Ashland
Elizabethtown Community College	Elizabethtown
Hazard Community College	Hazard
Henderson Community College	Henderson
Hopkinsville Community College	Hopkinsville
Jefferson Community College	Louisville
Lexington Technical Institute	Lexington
Madisonville Community College	Madisonville
Maysville Community College	Maysville
Paducah Community College	Paducah
Prestonburg Community College	Prestonburg
Somerset Community College	Somerset
Southeast Community College	Cumberland

Privately controlled

Alice Lloyd College	Pippa Passes
Lees Junior College	Jackson
Lindsey Wilson College	Columbia
Midway College	Midway
St. Catharine College	St. Catharine
Southeastern Christian College	Winchester
Sue Bennett College	London

LOUISIANA

Publicly controlled

Bossier Parish Comm. College	Bossier City
Delgado Junior College	New Orleans

Louisiana State Univ., Baton Rouge:

Alexandria Campus	Alexandria
Eunice Campus	Eunice
St. Bernard Parish Community College	Chalmette

Southern University, Baton Rouge:

Shreveport-Bossier City Campus	Shreveport

Privately controlled

John Curtis Junior College	New Orleans

MAINE

Publicly controlled

Central Maine Vocational Tech. Inst.	Auburn
Eastern Maine Vocational Tech. Inst.	Bangor
Kennebec Valley Vocational Tech. Inst.	Waterville
Northern Maine Vocational Tech. Inst.	Presque Isle
Southern Maine Voc. Technical Institute	South Portland
University of Maine	Bangor
Augusta Branch	Augusta
Bangor Community College	Bangor
Washington County Voc. Tech. Inst	Calais

Privately controlled

Westbrook College	Portland

MARYLAND

Publicly controlled

Allegany Community College	Cumberland
Anne Arundel Community College	Arnold
Baltimore, Community College of	Baltimore
Catonsville Community College	Baltimore
Cecil Community College	North East
Charles County Community College	La Plata
Chesapeake College	Wye Mills
Dundalk Community College	Baltimore
Essex Community College	Baltimore Cnty.
Frederick Community College	Frederick
Garrett Community College	McHenry
Hagerstown Junior College	Hagerstown
Harford Junior College	Bel Air
Howard Community College	Columbia

Montgomery College, Rockville:

Germantown Campus	Germantown
Rockville Campus	Rockville
Takoma Park Campus	Takoma Park
Prince George's Community College	Largo

Privately controlled

Bay College of Maryland	Baltimore
Villa Julie College	Stevenson

MASSACHUSETTS

Publicly controlled

Berkshire Community College	Pittsfield
Blue Hills Regional Tech. Inst.	Canton
Bristol Community College	Fall River
Bunker Hill Community College	Charlestown
Cape Cod Community College	W. Barnstable
Franklin Institute of Boston	Boston
Greenfield Community College	Greenfield
Holyoke Community College	Holyoke
Massachusetts Bay Community College	Watertown
Massasoit Community College	Brockton
Middlesex Community College	Bedford
Mount Wachusett Community College	Gardner
Newton Junior College	Newtonville
North Shore Community College	Beverly
Northern Essex Community College	Haverhill
Quincy Junior College	Quincy
Quinsigamond Community College	Worcester
Roxbury Community College	Roxbury
Springfield Technical Community Coll.	Springfield

Privately controlled

Aquinas Junior College	Milton

Institution	Location	Institution	Location
Bay Path Junior College	Longmeadow	Brainerd Community College	Brainerd
Becker Junior College	Worcester	Fergus Falls Community College	Fergus Falls
Chamberlayne Junior College	Boston	Hibbing Community College	Hibbing
Dean Junior College	Franklin	Inver Hills Community College	Inver Grove Heights
Endicott College	Beverly	Itasca Community College	Grand Rapids
Fisher Junior College	Boston	Lakewood Community College	White Bear Lake
Garland Junior College	Boston	Mesabi Community College	Virginia
Grahm Junior College	Boston	Metropolitan Community College	Minneapolis
Laboure Junior College	Boston	*Minnesota, U. of, Technical College, Minneapolis:*	
Lasell Junior College	Newton	Crookston Campus	Crookston
Leicester Junior College	Leicester	Waseca Campus	Waseca
Mount Ida Junior College	Newton Centre	Normandale Community College	Bloomington
Newbury Junior College	Boston	North Hennepin Community College	Brooklyn Park
Pine Manor Junior College	Chestnut Hill	Northland Community College	Thief River Falls
Simon's Rock	Gt. Barrington	Rainy River Community College	International Falls
Wentworth Institute	Boston	Rochester Community College	Rochester
Worcester Junior College	Worcester	Vermilion Community College	Ely
		Willmar Community College	Willmar
		Worthington Community College	Worthington

Privately controlled

Institution	Location
Bethany Lutheran College	Mankato
Crosier Seminary Junior College	Onamia
Golden Valley Lutheran College	Minneapolis
St. Mary's Junior College	Minneapolis

MICHIGAN

Publicly controlled

Institution	Location
Alpena Community College	Alpena
Bay de Noc Community College	Escanaba
Charles Stewart Mott Comm. Coll.	Flint
Delta College	University Center
Glen Oaks Community College	Centreville
Gogebic Community College	Ironwood
Grand Rapids Junior College	Grand Rapids
Henry Ford Community College	Dearborn
Highland Park Community College	Highland Park
Jackson Community College	Jackson
Kalamazoo Valley Community College	Kalamazoo
Kellogg Community College	Battle Creek
Kirtland Community College	Roscommon
Lake Michigan College	Benton Harbor
Lansing Community College	Lansing
Macomb County Community College, Warren:	
Center Campus	Mt. Clemens
South Campus	Warren
Mid Michigan Community College	Harrison
Monroe County Community College	Monroe
Montcalm Community College	Sidney
Muskegon Community College	Muskegon
North Central Michigan College	Petoskey
Northwestern Michigan College	Traverse City
Oakland Community College, Bloomfield Hills:	
Auburn Hills Campus	Auburn Heights
Highland Lakes Campus	Union Lake
Orchard Ridge Campus	Farmington
Southeast Campus	Oak Park
St. Clair County Community College	Port Huron
Schoolcraft College	Livonia
Southwestern Michigan College	Dowagiac
Washtenaw Community College	Ann Arbor
Wayne County Community College	Detroit
West Shore Community College	Scottville

Privately controlled

Institution	Location
Concordia Lutheran Junior College	Ann Arbor
Davenport College of Business	Grand Rapids
Michigan Christian Junior College	Rochester
Suomi College	Hancock

MINNESOTA

Publicly controlled

Institution	Location
Anoka-Ramsey Community College	Coon Rapids
Austin Community College	Austin

MISSISSIPPI

Publicly controlled

Institution	Location
Coahoma Junior College	Clarksdale
Copiah-Lincoln Junior College	Wesson
East Central Junior College	Decatur
East Mississippi Junior College	Scooba
Hinds Junior College	Raymond
Holmes Junior College	Goodman
Itawamba Junior College	Fulton
Jones County Junior College	Ellisville
Meridian Junior College	Meridian
Mississippi Delta Junior College	Moorhead
Mississippi Gulf Coast Junior College, Perkinston:	
Jackson County Campus	Gautier
Jefferson Davis Campus	Gulfport
Perkinston Campus	Perkinston
Northeast Mississippi Junior College	Booneville
Northwest Mississippi Junior College	Senatobia
Pearl River Junior College	Poplarville
Southwest Mississippi Junior College	Summit
Utica Junior College	Utica

Privately controlled

Institution	Location
Clarke College	Newton
Mary Holmes College	West Point
Southeastern Baptist College	Laurel
Westminster College	Florence
Wood Junior College	Mathiston

MISSOURI

Publicly controlled

Institution	Location
Crowder College	Neosho
East Central Junior College	Union
Jefferson College	Hillsboro
Metropolitan Community Colleges, The, Kansas City:	
Longview Community College	Lee's Summit
Maple Woods Community College	Kansas City
Penn Valley Community College	Kansas City
Mineral Area College	Flat River
Moberly Area Junior College	Moberly

Institution	Location	Institution	Location

St. Louis County Junior College District, St. Louis:
Florissant Valley Community College . . St. Louis
Forest Park Community College . . . St. Louis
Meramec Community College . . . . St. Louis
State Fair Community College . . . . Sedalia
Three Rivers Community College . . . Poplar Bluff
Trenton Junior College . . . . Trenton

Privately controlled

Cottey College . . . . Nevada
Hannibal LaGrange College . . . . . Hannibal
Kemper Military School & College . . Boonville
St. Mary's College of O'Fallon . . . . O'Fallon
St. Paul's College . . . . Concordia
Wentworth Military Academy . . . . . Lexington

MONTANA

Publicly controlled

Dawson College . . . . Glendive
Flathead Valley Community College . . Kalispell
Miles Community College . . . . . Miles City

NEBRASKA

Publicly controlled

Central Nebraska Tech. Comm. College Area, Grand Island:
Central Technical Community College . Hastings
Platte Technical Community College . . Columbus
Metropolitan Technical Community Coll. . Omaha
Mid-Plains Technical Comm. Coll. Area, North Platte:
McCook Community College . . . . McCook
Mid-Plains Community College . . . North Platte
Northeast Tech. Comm. Coll. . . . . . Norfolk
Southeast Community College, Lincoln:
Fairbury Campus . . . . Fairbury
Lincoln Campus . . . . Lincoln
Milford Campus . . . . Milford
Univ. of Nebraska Sch. of Tech. Agr. . . Curtis
Western Nebraska Tech. Comm. Coll. Area, Scottsbluff:
Nebraska Western College . . . . Scottsbluff
Western Nebraska Technical College . Sidney

Privately controlled

York College . . . . York

NEVADA

Publicly controlled

Nevada Community Coll. System, University of, Reno:
Clark County Community College . . . North Las Vegas
Northern Nevada Community College . . Elko
Western Nevada Community College . Carson City

NEW HAMPSHIRE

Publicly controlled

New Hampshire Technical Institute . . . Concord
New Hampshire Vocational Technical College:
Berlin Campus . . . . Berlin
Claremont Campus . . . . Claremont
Laconia Campus . . . . Laconia
Manchester Campus . . . . Manchester
Nashua Campus . . . . Nashua
Portsmouth Campus . . . . Portsmouth

Privately controlled

Colby Sawyer College-New Hampshire . New London
New England Aeronautical Institute . . Nashua
White Pines College . . . . Chester

NEW JERSEY

Publicly controlled

Atlantic Community College . . . . . . Mays Landing
Bergen Community College . . . . . Paramus
Brookdale Community College . . . . Lincroft
Burlington County College . . . . . . Pemberton
Camden County College . . . . Blackwood
Cumberland County College . . . . . Vineland
Essex County College . . . . Newark
Gloucester County College . . . . . Sewell
Hudson County Comm. Coll. Commission . Jersey City
Mercer County Community College . . Trenton
Middlesex County College . . . . . . Edison
Morris, County College of . . . . . . Dover
Ocean County College . . . . Toms River
Passaic County Community College . . Paterson
Salem Community College . . . . . . Penns Grove
Somerset County College . . . . . . Somerville

Privately controlled

Centenary College for Women . . . . Hackettstown
Edward Williams College . . . . . . Hackensack
Luther Coll. of Bible & Liberal Arts . . Teaneck
Union College . . . . Cranford

NEW MEXICO

Publicly controlled

Eastern New Mexico University, Portales:
Clovis Campus . . . . Clovis
Roswell Campus . . . . Roswell
Luna Vocational Technical Institute . . Las Vegas
New Mexico Junior College . . . . . Hobbs
New Mexico Military Institute . . . . Roswell
New Mexico State University, Las Cruces:
Alamogordo Campus . . . . Alamogordo
Carlsbad Campus . . . . Carlsbad
Dona Ana Cnty. Occupational Ed. Branch Las Cruces
Grants Campus . . . . Grants
San Juan Campus . . . . Farmington
University of New Mexico, Albuquerque:
Albuquerque Tech.-Voc. Institute . . . Albuquerque
Gallup Campus . . . . Gallup
Northern Campus . . . . Espanola

NEW YORK

Publicly controlled

Adirondack Community College . . . . Glens Falls
Bennett College . . . . Millbrook
Broome Community College . . . . . Binghamton
Cayuga County Community College . . Auburn
Clinton Community College . . . . . Plattsburgh
Columbia-Greene Community College . . Hudson
Corning Community College . . . . . Corning
Dutchess Community College . . . . . Poughkeepsie
Erie Community College, Buffalo:
City Campus . . . . Buffalo
North Campus . . . . Williamsville
South Campus . . . . Orchard Park
Fashion Institute of Technology . . . . New York
Finger Lakes, Community College of the . Canandaigua
Five Towns College . . . . Merrick
Fulton-Montgomery Community College . Johnstown
Genesee Community College . . . . . Batavia
Herkimer County Community College . Herkimer
Hudson Valley Community College . . Troy
Jamestown Community College . . . . Jamestown
Jefferson Community College . . . . Watertown
Mohawk Valley Community College . . Utica
Monroe Community College . . . . . Rochester

Institution	Location
Nassau Community College	Garden City
New York, City Univ. of:	
Borough of Manhattan Community Coll.	New York
Bronx Community College	New York
Hostos Community College	Bronx
Kingsborough Community College	Brooklyn
La Guardia Community College	Long Island City
New York City Community College	Brooklyn
Queensborough Community College	Bayside
Staten Island Community College	Staten Island
New York, State University of, Agr. & Tech. Colleges:	
Alfred Campus	Alfred
Canton Campus	Canton
Cobleskill	Cobleskill
Delhi Campus	Delhi
Farmingdale Campus	Farmingdale
Morrisville Campus	Morrisville
Niagara County Community College	Sanborn
North Country Community College	Saranac Lake
Onondaga Community College	Syracuse
Orange County Community College	Middletown
Rockland Community College	Suffern
Schenectady County Community College	Schenectady
Suffolk County Community College	Seldon
Sullivan County Community College	Loch Sheldrake
Tompkins-Cortland Community College	Dryden
Trocaire College	Buffalo
Ulster County Community College	Stone Ridge
Westchester Community College	Valhalla

Privately controlled

Aeronautics, Academy of	Flushing
Albany, Junior College of	Albany
Cazenovia College	Cazenovia
College for Human Services	New York
Elizabeth Seton College	Yonkers
Harriman College	Harriman
Hilbert College	Hamburg
Maria College	Albany
Maria Regina College	Syracuse
Mater Dei College	Ogdensburg
Paul Smith's College of Arts & Sciences	Paul Smiths
Villa Maria College of Buffalo	Buffalo

NORTH CAROLINA

Publicly controlled

Alamance, Technical Institute of	Burlington
Albemarle, College of the	Elizabeth City
Anson Technical Institute	Ansonville
Asheville-Buncombe Technical Institute	Asheville
Beaufort County Technical Institute	Washington
Bladen Technical Institute	Dublin
Caldwell Comm. Coll. and Tech. Inst.	Lenoir
Cape Fear Technical Institute	Wilmington
Carteret Technical Institute	Morehead City
Catawba Valley Technical Institute	Hickory
Central Carolina Technical Institute	Sanford
Central Piedmont Community College	Charlotte
Cleveland County Technical Institute	Shelby
Coastal Carolina Community College	Jacksonville
Craven Community College	New Bern
Davidson County Community College	Lexington
Durham Technical Institute	Durham
Edgecombe Technical Institute	Tarboro
Fayetteville Technical Institute	Fayetteville
Forsyth Technical Institute	Winston-Salem
Gaston College	Dallas
Guilford Technical Institute	Jamestown
Halifax County Technical Institute	Weldon
Haywood Technical Institute	Clyde

Institution	Location
Isothermal Community College	Spindale
James Sprunt Institute	Kenansville
Johnston Technical Institute	Smithfield
Lenoir Community College	Kinston
Martin Technical Institute	Williamston
Mayland Technical Institute	Spruce Pine
McDowell Technical Institute	Marion
Mitchell Community College	Statesville
Montgomery Technical Institute	Troy
Nash Technical Institute	Rocky Mount
Pamlico Technical Institute	Alliance
Piedmont Technical Institute	Roxboro
Pitt Technical Institute	Greenville
Randolph Technical Institute	Asheboro
Richmond Technical Institute	Hamlet
Roanoke-Chowan Technical Institute	Ahoskie
Robeson Technical Institute	Saint Pauls
Rockingham Community College	Wentworth
Rowan Technical Institute	Salisbury
Sampson Technical Institute	Clinton
Sandhills Community College	Southern Pines
Southeastern Community College	Whiteville
Southwestern Technical Institute	Sylva
Stanly Technical Institute	Albermarle
Surry Community College	Dobson
Tri-County Technical Institute	Murphy
Vance-Granville Technical Institute	Henderson
Wake Technical Institute	Raleigh
Wayne Community College	Goldsboro
Western Piedmont Community College	Morganton
Wilkes Community College	Wilkesboro
Wilson County Technical Institute	Wilson

Privately controlled

Blue Ridge Technical Institute	Flat Rock
Brevard College	Brevard
Chowan College	Murfreesboro
Lees-McRae College	Banner Elk
Louisburg College	Louisburg
Montreat-Anderson College	Montreat
Mount Olive College	Mount Olive
Peace College	Raleigh
St. Mary's College	Raleigh
Wingate College	Wingate

NORTH DAKOTA

Publicly controlled

Bismarck Junior College	Bismarck
Lake Region Junior College	Devils Lake
North Dakota University of, Grand Forks:	
Williston Center	Williston
North Dakota State School of Science	Wahpeton
NDSU-Bottineau	Bottineau

OHIO

Publicly controlled

Akron, Univ. Comm. & Tech. Coll. of	Akron
Belmont Technical College	St. Clairsville
Central Ohio Technical College	Newark
Cincinnati Technical College	Cincinnati
Cincinnati, University of, Cincinnati:	
Clermont General & Tech. Coll.	Batavia
Ohio College of Applied Science	Cincinnati
Raymond Walters Gen. & Tech. College	Cincinnati
Tri-County Academic Center	Sardinia
University College	Cincinnati
Clark Technical College	Springfield
Columbus Technical Institute	Columbus

Institution	Location
Cuyahoga Community College, Cleveland:	
Eastern Campus	Warrensville Twnsp.
Metropolitan Campus	Cleveland
Western Campus	Parma
Edison State General & Tech. Coll.	Piqua
Hocking Technical College	Nelsonville
Jefferson County Technical Institute	Steubenville
Kent State University, Kent:	
Ashtabula Campus	Ashtabula
Salem Regional Campus	Salem
Tuscarawas Campus	New Philadelphia
Lakeland Community College	Mentor
Lima Technical College	Lima
Lorain County Community College	Elyria
Marion Technical College	Marion
Miami University, Oxford:	
Hamilton Campus	Hamilton
Middletown Campus	Middletown
Michael J. Owens Technical College	Toledo
Muskingum Area Technical Institute	Zanesville
North Central Technical College	Mansfield
Northwest Technical College	Archbold
Ohio State University, Columbus:	
Agricultural Technical Institute	Wooster
Lima Campus	Lima
Mansfield Campus	Mansfield
Marion Campus	Marion
Newark Campus	Newark
Ohio University, Athens:	
Belmont County Campus	St. Clairsville
Chillicothe Campus	Chillicothe
Lancaster Campus	Lancaster
Zanesville Campus	Zanesville
Shawnee State General & Tech. Coll.	Portsmouth
Sinclair Community College	Dayton
Stark Technical College	Canton
Terra Technical College	Fremont
Toledo, U. of, Comm. & Tech. College	Toledo
Washington Technical College	Marietta
Wright State University, Dayton	
Western Ohio Branch Campus	Celina
Youngstown St. U. Tech. & Comm. Coll.	Youngstown

Privately controlled

Chatfield	Saint Martin
Kettering College of Medical Arts	Kettering
Lourdes College	Sylvania
Rio Grande Community College	Rio Grande

OKLAHOMA

Publicly controlled

Carl Albert Junior College	Poteau
Claremore Junior College	Claremore
Connors State College	Warner
Eastern Oklahoma State College	Wilburton
El Reno Junior College	El Reno
Murray State College	Tishomingo
Northeastern Oklahoma A & M College	Miami
Northern Oklahoma College	Tonkawa
Oklahoma State U. Tech. Inst.	Oklahoma City
Oscar Rose Junior College	Midwest City
Sayre Junior College	Sayre
Seminole Junior College	Seminole
South Oklahoma City Junior College	Oklahoma City
Tulsa Junior College	Tulsa
Western Oklahoma State Coll.	Altus

Privately controlled

Bacone College	Bacone
Hillsdale Free Will Baptist College	Moore

Institution	Location
St. Gregory's College	Shawnee
Southwestern College	Oklahoma City

OREGON

Publicly controlled

Blue Mountain Community College	Pendleton
Central Oregon Community College	Bend
Chemeketa Community College	Salem
Clackamas Community College	Oregon City
Clatsop Community College	Astoria
Lane Community College	Eugene
Linn-Benton Community College	Albany
Mt. Hood Community College	Gresham
Oregon Inst. of Technology	Klamath Falls
Portland Community College	Portland
Rogue Community College	Grants Pass
Southwestern Oregon Community College	Coos Bay
Treasure Valley Community College	Ontario
Umpqua Community College	Roseburg

Privately controlled

Concordia College	Portland
Judson Baptist College	Portland

PENNSYLVANIA

Publicly controlled

Allegheny County, Community College of, Pittsburgh:	
Allegheny Campus	Pittsburgh
Boyce Campus	Monroeville
College Center-North	Pittsburgh
South Campus	West Mifflin
Beaver County, Community Coll. of	Monaca
Bucks County Community College	Newtown
Butler County Community College	Butler
Delaware County Community College of	Media
Harrisburg Area Community College	Harrisburg
Lehigh County Community College	Schenecksville
Luzerne County Community College	Nanticoke
Montgomery County Community College	Blue Bell
Northampton County Area Comm. Coll	Bethlehem
Philadelphia, Community Coll. of	Philadelphia
Reading Area Community College	Reading
Westmoreland County Community Coll.	Youngwood
Williamsport Area Community College	Williamsport

Privately controlled

Cushing Junior College	Bryn Mawr
Harcum Junior College	Bryn Mawr
Keystone Junior College	La Plume
Lackawanna Junior College	Scranton
Manor Junior College	Jenkintown
Mount Aloysius Junior College	Cresson
Northeastern Christian Junior College	Villanova
Peirce Junior College	Philadelphia
Pennsylvania Junior Coll. of Medical Arts	Harrisburg
Pinebrook Junior College	East Stroudsburg
Robert Morris College	Coraopolis
Spring Garden College	Philadelphia
United Wesleyan College	Allentown
Valley Forge Military Junior College	Wayne

PUERTO RICO

Publicly controlled

Puerto Rico, University of:	
Aguadilla Regional College	Aguadilla
Arecibo Regional College	Arecibo

Location

Bayamon Regional College	Bayamon
Carolina Regional College	Carolina
Humacao Regional College	Humacao
Ponce Regional College.	Ponce

Privately controlled

Catholic University of Puerto Rico, Ponce:

Aguadilla Center.	Aguadilla
Arecibo Center	Arecibo
Guayama Regional College	Guayama
Ponce Center	Ponce
College of the Sacred Heart–Jr. Coll.	Santurce

Inter-American University of Puerto Rico, San German:

Aguadilla Regional College	Aguadilla
Arecibo Regional College	Arecibo
Barranquitas Regional College	Barranquitas
Bayamon Regional College	Bayamon
Fajardo Regional College	Fajardo
Guayama Regional College	Guayama
Ponce Regional College.	Ponce
Puerto Rico Junior College	Rio Piedras

RHODE ISLAND

Publicly controlled

Rhode Island Junior College	Warwick

Privately controlled

Johnson & Wales College	Providence

SOUTH CAROLINA

Publicly controlled

State System of Technical Colleges, Columbia:

Aiken Tech. Ed. Ctr.	Aiken
Beaufort Tech. Ed. Ctr.	Beaufort
Chesterfield-Marlboro Tech. Coll.	Cheraw
Denmark Tech. Ed. Ctr.	Denmark
Florence-Darlington Tech. Coll.	Florence
Greenville Technical College	Greenville
Horry-Georgetown Tech. Ed. Ctr.	Conway

Midlands Technical College, Columbia:

Airport Campus	West Columbia
Beltline Campus	Columbia
Orangeburg-Calhoun Tech. Coll.	Orangeburg
Piedmont Technical College	Greenwood

South Carolina, Univ. of, Columbia:

Beaufort Regional Campus	Beaufort
Lancaster Regional Campus	Lancaster
Salkehatchie Regional Campus	Allendale
Sumter Regional Campus	Sumter
Union Regional Campus	Union
Spartanburg Technical College	Spartanburg
Sumter Area Technical College	Sumter
Tri-County Technical College	Pendleton

Trident Technical College, No. Charleston:

North Campus	No. Charleston
Palmer Campus	Charleston
Williamsburg Tech. Ed. Ctr.	Kingstree
York Technical College	Rock Hill

Privately controlled

Anderson College	Anderson
Clinton Junior College	Rock Hill
Friendship Junior College	Rock Hill
North Greenville Junior College	Tigerville
Spartanburg Methodist College	Spartanburg

SOUTH DAKOTA

Publicly controlled

Black Hills State College, Spearfish:

Junior College Division	Spearfish
Oglala Sioux Community College	Pine Ridge

Privately controlled

Freeman Junior College	Freeman
Presentation College	Aberdeen
Sinte Gleska College Center	Rosebud

TENNESSEE

Publicly controlled

Chattanooga State Tech. Comm. Coll.	Chattanooga
Cleveland State Community College	Cleveland
Columbia State Community College	Columbia
Dyersburg State Community College	Dyersburg
Jackson State Community College	Jackson
Motlow State Community College.	Tullahoma
Nashville State Technical Institute	Nashville
Roane State Community College	Harriman
Shelby State Community College	
State Technical Institute at Knoxville	
State Technical Institute at Memphis	
Volunteer State Community College	Gallatin
Walters State Community College	Morristown

Privately controlled

Aquinas Junior College	Nashville
Cumberland College of Tennessee	Lebanon
Hiwassee College	Madisonville
John A. Gupton College	Nashville
Martin College	Pulaski
Morristown College.	Morristown
Tomlinson College	Cleveland

TEXAS

Publicly controlled

Air Force, Community College of the	Randolph AFB
Alvin Community College	Alvin
Amarillo College	Amarillo
Angelina College	Lufkin
Austin Community College	Austin
Bee County College	Beeville
Blinn College	Brenham
Brazosport College	Lake Jackson
Central Texas College	Killeen
Cisco Junior College	Cisco
Clarendon College	Clarendon
College of the Mainland	Texas City
Cooke County College	Gainesville

Dallas County Community College District, Dallas:

Eastfield College	Mesquite
El Centro College	Dallas
Mountain View College	Dallas
Richland College	Dallas
Del Mar College	Corpus Christi
El Paso Community College	El Paso
Frank Phillips College	Borger
Galveston College	Galveston
Grayson County College	Denison
Henderson County Junior College	Athens
Hill Junior College	Hillsboro
Houston Community College	Houston
Howard College at Big Spring	Big Spring
Kilgore College	Kilgore

Institution	Location
Lamar University, Beaumont	
Orange County Branch	Orange
Port Arthur Branch	Port Arthur
Laredo Junior College	Laredo
Lee College	Baytown
McLennan Community College	Waco
Midland College	Midland
Navarro College	Corsicana
North Harris County College	Houston
Odessa College	Odessa
Panola Junior College	Carthage
Paris Junior College	Paris
Ranger Junior College	Ranger
San Antonio Union Junior College District, San Antonio:	
St. Philip's College	San Antonio
San Antonio College	San Antonio
San Jacinto College, Pasadena:	
North Campus	Houston
South Campus	Pasadena
South Plains College	Levelland
Southwest Texas Junior College	Uvalde
Tarrant County Junior College District, Ft. Worth:	
Northeast Campus	Hurst
Northwest Campus	Fort Worth
South Campus	Ft. Worth
Temple Junior College	Temple
Texarkana Community College	Texarkana
Texas Southmost College	Brownsville
Texas State Tech. Institute, Waco:	
James Connally Campus	Waco
Mid-Continent Campus	Amarillo
Rio Grande Campus	Harlingen
Rolling Plains Campus	Sweetwater
Tyler Junior College	Tyler
Vernon Regional Junior College	Vernon
Victoria College	Victoria
Weatherford College	Weatherford
Western Texas College	Snyder
Wharton County Junior College	Wharton

Privately controlled

Concordia Lutheran College	Austin
Jacksonville College	Jacksonville
Lon Morris College:	Jacksonville
Schreiner College	Kerrville
Southern Bible College	Houston
Southwestern Christian College	Terrell
Southwestern Junior College	Waxahachie

UTAH

Publicly controlled

Dixie College	St. George
Eastern Utah, College of	Price
Snow College	Ephraim
Utah Technical College at Provo	Provo
Utah Technical College at Salt Lake	Salt Lake City

VERMONT

Publicly controlled

Vermont, Community College of	Montpelier
Vermont Technical College	Randolph Center

Privately controlled

Champlain College	Burlington
Ethan Allen Community College	Manchester Ctr.
Green Mountain College	Poultney
Vermont College of Norwich Univ.	Montpelier
Vermont Inst. of Community Involvement	So. Burlington

Institution	Location
VIRGINIA	
Publicly controlled	
Blue Ridge Community College	Weyers Cave
Central Virginia Community College	Lynchburg
Dabney S. Lancaster Community College	Clifton Forge
Danville Community College	Danville
Eastern Shore Community College	Melfa
Germanna Community College	Locust Grove
J. Sargeant Reynolds Comm. College, Richmond	
Downtown Campus	Richmond
Parham Road Campus	Richmond
John Tyler Community College	Chester
Lord Fairfax Community College	Middletown
Mountain Empire Community College	Big Stone Gap
New River Community College	Dublin
Northern Virginia Community College, Annandale:	
Alexandria Campus	Alexandria
Annandale Campus	Annandale
Loudoun Campus	Sterling
Manassas Campus	Manassas
Woodbridge Campus	Woodbridge
Patrick Henry Community College	Martinsville
Paul D. Camp Community College	Franklin
Piedmont Virginia Comm. College	Charlottesville
Rappahannock Community College, Glenns:	
North Campus	Warsaw
South Campus	Glenns
Richard Bland College	Petersburg
Southside Virginia Comm. Coll., Alberta:	
Christanna Campus	Alberta
John H. Daniel Campus	Keysville
Southwest Virginia Community College	Richlands
Thomas Nelson Community College	Hampton
Tidewater Community College, Portsmouth:	
Chesapeake Campus	Chesapeake
Frederick Campus	Portsmouth
Virginia Beach Campus	Virginia Beach
Virginia Highlands Community College	Abingdon
Virginia Western Community College	Roanoke
Wytheville Community College	Wytheville

Privately controlled

Bluefield Junior College	Bluefield
Ferrum College	Ferrum
Marymount College of Virginia	Arlington
Southern Seminary Junior College	Buena Vista
Sullins College	Bristol

WASHINGTON

Publicly controlled

Bellevue Community College	Bellevue
Big Bend Community College	Moses Lake
Centralia Community College	Centralia
Clark Community College	Vancouver
Columbia Basin College	Pasco
Community College District V, Everett:	
Edmonds Community College	Lynnwood
Everett Community College	Everett
Community College District VI, Seattle:	
North Seattle Community College	Seattle
Seattle Central Community College	Seattle
South Seattle Community College	Seattle
Community College District XVII, Spokane:	
Spokane Community College	Spokane
Spokane Falls Community College	Spokane
Fort Steilacoom Community College	Tacoma
Grays Harbor College	Aberdeen
Green River Community College	Auburn

Institution	Location
Highline Community College	Midway
Lower Columbia College	Longview
Olympia Vocational Tech. Institute	Olympia
Olympic College	Bremerton
Peninsula College	Port Angeles
Shoreline Community College	Seattle
Skagit Valley College	Mt. Vernon
Tacoma Community College	Tacoma
Walla Walla Community College	Walla Walla
Wenatchee Valley College	Wenatchee
Whatcom Community College	Bellingham
Yakima Valley College	Yakima

WEST VIRGINIA

Publicly controlled

Fairmont Community College	Fairmont
Marshall Univ. Community College	Huntington
Parkersburg Community College	Parkersburg
Shepherd College-Comm. Coll. Component	Shepherdstown
Southern West Virginia Comm. Coll., Logan:	
Logan Campus	Logan
Williamson Campus	Williamson
West Virginia Inst. of Tech., Montgomery:	
Community and Tech. Coll.	Montgomery
West Virginia Northern Comm. Coll., Wheeling:	
Weirton Campus	Weirton
Wheeling Campus	Wheeling
West Virginia University, Morgantown:	
Potomac State College	Keyser

Privately controlled

Beckley College	Beckley
Ohio Valley College	Parkersburg

WISCONSIN

Publicly controlled

University Center System, Madison:	
Baraboo-Sauk County Campus	Baraboo
Barron County Campus	Rice Lake
Fond Du Lac Campus	Fond Du Lac
Fox Valley Campus	Menasha
Marathon County Campus	Wausau
Marshfield Wood County Campus	Marshfield
Medford Campus	Medford
Richland Center Campus	Richland Center
Rock County Campus	Janesville
Sheboygan Campus	Sheboygan
Washington County Campus	West Bend
Waukesha County Campus	Waukesha
Vocational, Tech. and Adult Education System, Madison:	
Blackhawk VTAE District:	*Janesville*
Blackhawk Technical Institute	Janesville
Beloit Campus	Beloit
District One Tech. Inst.	*Eau Claire*
VTAE District Four:	*Madison*
Fort Atkinson Voc.-Tech. School	
Madison Area Tech. Coll.	Madison
Watertown Center	Watertown
Fox Valley VTAE District:	*Appleton*
Fox Valley Technical Institute	Appleton
Appleton Campus	Appleton
Oshkosh Campus	Oshkosh

Institution	Location
Gateway VTAE District:	*Kenosha*
Gateway Technical Institute	Kenosha
Elkhorn Campus	Elkhorn
Kenosha Campus	Kenosha
Racine Campus	Racine
Lakeshore VTAE District:	*Cleveland*
Lakeshore Technical Institute	Cleveland
Mid-State VTAE District:	*Wisconsin Rapids*
Mid-State Technical Institute	Wisconsin Rapids
Marshfield Campus	Marshfield
Stevens Point Campus	Stevens Point
Wisconsin Rapids Campus	Wisconsin Rapids
Milwaukee Area VTAE District:	*Milwaukee*
Milwaukee Area Tech. College	Milwaukee
Cudahy Campus	Cudahy
Port Washington Campus	Port Washington
South Milwaukee Campus	South Milwaukee
West Allis Campus	West Allis
Moraine Park VTAE District:	*Fond Du Lac*
Moraine Park Tech. Institute	Fond Du Lac
Beaver Dam Campus	Beaver Dam
Fond Du Lac Campus	Fond Du Lac
West Bend Campus	West Bend
Nicolet VTAE District:	*Rhinelander*
Nicolet Coll. and Tech. Inst.	Rhinelander
North Central VTAE District:	*Wausau*
North Central Tech. Inst.	Wausau
Antigo Campus	Antigo
Wausau Campus	Wausau
Northeast Wisconsin VTAE District:	*Green Bay*
Northeast Wisconsin Tech. Inst.	Green Bay
Green Bay Campus	Green Bay
Marinette Campus	Marinette
Sturgeon Bay Campus	Sturgeon Bay
Southwest Wisconsin VTAE District:	*Fennimore*
Southwest Wisconsin Tech. Inst.	Fennimore
Waukesha County Area VTAE District:	*Pewaukee*
Waukesha County Tech. Inst.	Pewaukee
Western Wisconsin VTAE District:	*LaCrosse*
Western Wisconsin Tech. Inst.	LaCrosse
Wisconsin Indianhead VTAE District:	*Shell Lake*
Indianhead Technical Institute	Shell Lake
Ashland Campus	Ashland
Grantsburg Campus	Grantsburg
New Richmond Campus	New Richmond
Rice Lake Campus	Rice Lake
Superior Campus	Superior

Privately controlled

Concordia College	Milwaukee
Milwaukee School of Engineering	Milwaukee

WYOMING

Publicly controlled

Casper College	Casper
Central Wyoming College	Riverton
Eastern Wyoming College	Torrington
Laramie County Community College	Cheyenne
Northern Wyoming Community College	Sheridan
Northwest Community College	Powell
Western Wyoming Community College	Rock Springs

# # #

Accredited U.S. Senior Colleges and Universities, Spring 1976

Only schools fully accredited by one of the institutional and professional accrediting associations recognized by the Council on Postsecondary Accreditation are listed. The number of students is for matriculated undergraduate and graduate students who are working for a degree.

Tuition, room and board listed are average annual figures and are subject to fluctuation. Tuition costs vary from school to school, depending on type, location and control. For State- or Public-controlled schools, tuition given is average figure for residents; nonresidents pay tuition that ranges from one to thirteen times higher.

Abbreviations used for controls:

AC	Advent Christian	End	Endowed	P	Private
AG	Assembly of God	F	Federal	Pres	Presbyterian
AL	American Lutheran	FM	Free Methodist	Pub	Public
AME	African Meth. Episcopal	GO	Greek Orthodox	PUS	Presbyterian, U.S.
B	Baptist	ID	Interdenominational	RC	Roman Catholic
CB	Church of Brethren	Ind	Independent	RCA	Reformed Church in America
CC	Church of Christ	J	Jewish	RP	Reformed Presbyterian
CG	Church of God	L	Lutheran	S	State
CMA	Christian & Mis. Alliance	LCA	Lutheran Church of America	SB	Southern Baptist
CME	Christian Methodist Epis.	LDS	Latter Day Saints	SDA	Seventh Day Adventist
Co	County	LMS	Lutheran–Missouri Synod	SOF	Society of Friends
CP	Cumberland Presbyterian	M	Methodist	Sw	Swedenborgian
CR	Christian Reformed	MB	Mennonite Brethren	UCC	United Church of Christ
DC	Disciples of Christ	MC	Missionary Church	UM	United Methodist
E	Episcopalian	Men	Mennonite	UP	United Presbyterian
EC	Evangelical Covenant	Mun	Municipal	W	Wesleyan
		Naz	Nazarene		

Institution and location	Chief executive	Tuition	Rm/Bd	Students[*]	Control
Abilene Christian University; Abilene, Tex. 79601	John C. Stevens	1580	1070	3,603 C	P
Academy of Art College; San Francisco, Calif. 94102	Richard A. Stephens	n.a.	n.a.	690 C[1]	P
Adams State College; Alamosa, Colo. 81101	John A. Marvel	405	1093+	2,805 C	S
Adelphi University; Garden City, N.Y. 11530	Timothy W. Costello	2990	2120	9,678 C	P
Adrian College; Adrian, Mich. 49221	John H. Dawson	2450	1406	1,010 C	P
Agnes Scott College; Decatur, Ga. 30030	Marvin Banks Perry, Jr.	2700	1400	594 F	P
Akron, The University of; Akron, Ohio 44325	D. J. Guzzetta	780	1476	21,757 C[2]	S
Alabama, The University of; University, Ala. 35486	Richard Thigpen	617	1134	15,774 C	S
Alabama, The Univ. of, in Birmingham; Birmingham, Ala. 35294	Joseph F. Volker	(3)	n.a.	11,019 C	S
Alabama, The Univ. of, in Huntsville; Huntsville, Ala. 35807	Benjamin B. Graves	792	2160	3,421 C	S
Alabama A&M University; Normal, Ala. 35762	Richard David Morrison	n.a.	n.a.	4,470 C	S
Alabama State University; Montgomery, Ala. 36101	Levi Watkins	465	990	3,523 C	S
Alaska, University of; Fairbanks, Alas. 99701	Robert W. Hiatt	472	1778	2,321 C	S
Northern Region; Fairbanks, Alas. 99701	Earl Beistline	n.a.	n.a.	4,645 C[1]	S
South Central Region; Anchorage, Alas. 99504	Lewis E. Haines	n.a.	n.a.	7,281 C[1]	S
Alaska Methodist University; Anchorage, Alas. 99504	Robert K. Dellenbach	n.a.	n.a.	878 C[1]	P/UM
Albany State College; Albany, Ga. 31705	Charles L. Hayes	549	939	1,958 C	S
Albertus Magnus College; New Haven, Conn. 06511	Sister F. de Sales Heffernan	2500	1650	438 F	P/RC
Albion College; Albion, Mich. 49224	Bernard T. Lomas	2976	1564	1,731 C	P/UM
Albright College; Reading, Pa. 19604	Arthur L. Schultz	2850	1400	1,396 C	P/UM
Albuquerque, University of; Albuquerque, N.M. 87140	Gil Cordova	1500	1200	3,083 C	P/RC
Alcorn State University; Lorman, Miss. 39096	Walter Washington	444	759	2,719 C	S
Alderson–Broaddus College; Philippi, W. Va. 26416	Richard E. Shearer	2050	1104	822 C	P
Alfred University; Alfred, N.Y. 14802	M. Richard Rose	3300	1575	2,088 C	P
Allegheny College; Meadville, Pa. 16335	Lawrence L. Pelletier	2850	1180	1,837 C	P
Allentown College of St. Francis de Sales; Center Valley, Pa. 18034	V. Rev. J. Stuart Dooling	2500	1500	650 C	P/RC
Alliance College; Cambridge Springs, Pa. 16403	Herman A. Szymanski	2204	1100	240 C	P
Alma College; Alma, Mich. 48801	Robert D. Swanson	2650	1600	1,081 C	P
Alvernia College; Reading, Pa. 19607	Sister Mary Victorine	1500	1300	553 C[2]	P/RC
Alverno College; Milwaukee, Wis. 53215	Sister Joel Read	1950	1000	813 F	P
American Baptist College; Nashville, Tenn. 37207	Charles E. Boddie	290	680	147 C	P/B
American College in Paris; Paris, France	Damon B. Smith	2500	2700	610 C	P
American Conservatory of Music; Chicago, Ill. 60603	Leo E. Heim	1900	n.a.	474 C	P
American Grad. School of Int. Mgt.; Glendale, Ariz. 85306	William Voris	4110	1845	784 C	P
American International College; Springfield, Mass. 01109	Harry J. Courniotes	2070	1334	1,150 C	P
American University, The; Washington, D.C. 20016	Joseph J. Sisco	3064	1598	12,275 C	P/M
Americas, University of the; Puebla, Mexico	Fernando Macias Rendon	1275	390[7]	850 C	P
Amherst College; Amherst, Mass. 01002	John William Ward	3800	1357	1,289 C	P
Ana G. Méndez Educational Foundation; Rio Piedras, P.R. 00928	Ana G. Méndez	n.a.	n.a.	5,937 C[1]	P
Turabo University College; Caguas, P.R. 00625	Jorge E. Berríos	1200[4]	2500[4]	3,000 C[4]	P
Anderson College; Anderson, Ind. 46011	Robert H. Reardon	2200	1000	1,702 C	P/CG

756

Institution and location	Chief executive	Tuition	Rm/Bd	Students*Control	
Andrews University; Berrien Springs, Mich. 49104	Richard Hammill	2592	1368	2,415 C	P/SDA
Angelo State University; San Angelo, Tex. 76901	Lloyd D. Vincent	369	935	4,495 C	S
Anna Maria College; Paxton, Mass. 01612	Sister Caroline Finn	1950	1650	964 C	P/RC
Annhurst College; Woodstock, Conn. 06281	Sister Marie Janelle	2200	1700	339 C	P/RC
Antioch College; Yellow Springs, Ohio 45387	William M. Birenbaum	n.a.	n.a.	5,009 C[2]	P
Appalachian Bible Institute; Bradley, W. Va. 25818	Lester E. Pipkin	750	1125	278 C[5]	P
Appalachian State Univ. See Univ. System of North Carolina.					
Aquinas College; Grand Rapids, Mich. 49506	Norbert J. Hruby	2440	1310	1,641 C	P/RC
Arizona, University of; Tucson, Ariz. 85721	John Paul Schaefer	450	1175	28,971 C	S
Arizona State University; Tempe, Ariz. 85281	John W. Schwada	450	1200	33,346 C	S
Arkansas, University of; Fayetteville, Ark. 72701	Charles E. Bishop	400	1100	12,250 C	S
Univ. of Arkansas at Little Rock; Little Rock, Ark. 72204	G. Robert Ross	400	n.a.	8,500 C[2]	S
Univ. of Arkansas at Monticello; Monticello, Ark. 71655	Claude H. Babin	400	950	1,624 C	S
Univ. of Arkansas at Pine Bluff; Pine Bluff, Ark. 71601	Herman B. Smith, Jr.	400	1197	2,556 C	S
Arkansas College; Batesville, Ark. 72501	Dan C. West	1500	1200	462 C	P/PUS
Arkansas Polytechnic College; Russellville, Ark. 72801	Kenneth Kersh	430	970	2,142 C	S
Arkansas State University; State University, Ark. 72467	Ross J. Pritchard	580	1200	6,541 C	S
Armstrong College; Berkeley, Calif. 94704	John E. Armstrong	1503	n.a.	600 C	P
Armstrong State College; Savannah, Ga. 31406	Henry L. Ashmore	495	n.a.	3,500 C	S
Art Center College of Design; Pasadena, Calif. 91103	Don Kubly	2500	n.a.	882 C	P
Asbury College; Wilmore, Ky. 40390	Dennis F. Kinlaw	2025	1125	1,179 C	P
Ashland College; Ashland, Ohio 44805	Glenn L. Clayton	3002	1260	1,770 C	P
Assumption College; Worcester, Mass. 01609	Pasquale Di Pasquale	2400	1475	1,730 C	P/RC
Athens State College; Athens, Ala. 35611	Sidney E. Sandridge	(6)	1026+	1,000 C	S
Atlanta Christian College; East Point, Ga. 30344	James C. Redmon	800	940	306 C	P/CC
Atlanta College of Art; Atlanta, Ga. 30309	William J. Voos	2000	n.a.	300 C	P
Atlanta University; Atlanta, Ga. 30314	Thomas D. Jarrett	1600	550[7]	1,092 C	P
Atlantic Christian College; Wilson, N.C. 27893	Arthur D. Wenger	3410	985	1,581 C	P/DC
Atlantic Union College; South Lancaster, Mass. 01561	Dale McCune	2800	1200	700 C	P/SDA
Auburn University; Auburn, Ala. 36830	Harry M. Philpott	549	1275	5,332 C	S
Auburn University at Montgomery; Montgomery, Ala. 36109	H. H. Funderburk, Jr.	525	n.a.	3,800 C	S
Augsburg College; Minneapolis, Minn. 55454	Oscar A. Anderson	2550	1300	1,604 C	P/AL
Augusta College; Augusta, Ga. 30904	George A. Christenberry	435	n.a.	3,440 C	S
Augustana College; Rock Island, Ill. 61201	J. Thomas Tredway	2460[8]	1323[8]	2,170 C	P
Augustana College; Sioux Falls, S.D. 57102	Charles L. Balcer	2250[8]	1095	2,158 C	P/L
Aurora College; Aurora, Ill. 60507	Lloyd M. Richardson	2400	1500	901 C	P
Austin College; Sherman, Tex. 75090	John D. Moseley	2400	1200	1,157 C	P/PUS
Austin Peay State University; Clarksville, Tenn. 37040	Robert Riggs	442	775	4,143 C[5]	S
Averett College; Danville, Va. 24541	Conwell A. Anderson	3200[9]		1,975 C[2]	P
Avila College; Kansas City, Mo. 64145	Sister Olive Louise Dallavis	1800	1200	1,703 C	P/RC
Azusa Pacific College; Azusa, Calif. 91702	Malcolm R. Robertson	2268	1400	1,130 C	P/ID
Babson College; Babson Park, Mass. 02157	Ralph Z. Sorenson	3100	1490	2,563 C[2]	P
Baker University; Baldwin City, Kan. 66006	Jerald C. Walker	1870	1150	742 C	P/M
Baldwin-Wallace College; Berea, Ohio 44130	Alfred B. Bonds, Jr.	2679	1290	2,869 C	P/UM
Ball State University; Muncie, Ind. 47306	John J. Pruis	720	1152	15,884 C[5]	S
Baltimore, University of; Baltimore, Md. 21201	H. Mebane Turner	700	n.a.	5,800 C	S
Baltimore Hebrew College; Baltimore, Md. 21215	Rabbi Leivy Smolar	568	n.a.	223 C	P
Bank Street College of Education; New York, N.Y. 10025	Francis J. Roberts	5200	n.a.	1,416 C[2]	P
Baptist College at Charleston; Charleston, S.C. 29411	John A. Hamrick	2253	1480	1,279 C	P
Barat College; Lake Forest, Ill. 60045	Sister Judith Cagney	2300	1640	852 F[2]	P
Barber-Scotia College; Concord, N.C. 28025	Mable P. McLean	1082	954	480 C[2]	P/UP
Bard College; Annandale-on-Hudson, N.Y. 12504	Leon Botstein	4010	1680	648 C	P
Barnard College. See Columbia University.					
Barrington College; Barrington, R.I. 02806	Harold F. Fickett, Jr.	2185	1325	538 C	P
Barry College; Miami, Fla. 33161	Sister M. Trinita Flood	2200	1200	1,425 C	P/RC
Bates College; Lewiston, Me. 04240	Thomas Hedley Reynolds	3650	1300	1,263 C	P
Bayamón Central University; Bayamón, P.R. 00619	Rev. Vincent A. M. van Rooij	1100	n.a.	1,568 C	P/RC
Baylor College of Medicine; Houston, Tex. 77025	Joseph Merrill	300[10]	n.a.	701 C[1]	P
Baylor University; Waco, Tex. 76703	Abner V. McCall	1350	1200	8,247 C	B
Beaver College; Glenside, Pa. 19038	Edward D. Gates	2800	1600	1,421 C	P
Belhaven College; Jackson, Miss. 39202	Howard J. Cleland	1550	1000	724 C	Pres
Bellarmine College; Louisville, Ky. 40205	Eugene V. Petrik	1850	1150	1,550 C	P/RC
Belmont Abbey College; Belmont, N.C. 28012	Rev. John P. Bradley	1830	1140	725 C	P/RC
Belmont College; Nashville, Tenn. 37203	Herbert C. Gabhart	1500	1000	1,045 C	P/B
Beloit College; Beloit, Wis. 53511	Martha Peterson	3600[8]	1400[8]	1,504 C	P
Bemidji State College. See Minnesota State College System.					
Benedict College; Columbia, S.C. 29204	Henry Ponder	1500	920	1,667 C	P
Benedictine College; Atchison, Kan. 66002	Rev. Gerard Senecal	1900	1195	928 C	P/RC
Bennett College; Greensboro, N.C. 27420	Isaac H. Miller, Jr.	1565	935	563 F	P
Bennington College; Bennington, Vt. 05201	Joseph S. Murphy	5250	1300	591 C	P
Bentley College; Waltham, Mass. 02154	Gregory H. Adamian	2800[8]	2072	4,512 C	P
Berea College; Berea, Ky. 40403	Willis D. Weatherford	3900[11]	1175	1,355 C	P

Institution and location	Chief executive	Tuition	Rm/Bd	Students*	Control
Berklee College of Music; Boston, Mass. 02215	Lawrence Berk	2250	1475	2,185 C	P
Berkshire Christian College; Lenox, Mass. 01240	Vincent E. Taber	1470	1520	158 C	P/AC
Bernard M. Baruch College. See New York, City University of.					
Berry College; Mount Berry, Ga. 30149	John R. Bertrand	1695	1335	1,569 C	P
Bethany Bible College; Santa Cruz, Calif. 95066	C. Morse Ward	1330	1221	529 C	P/AG
Bethany College; Bethany, W. Va. 26032	Orville Wake	2650	1230	1,108 C²	P
Bethany College; Lindsborg, Kan. 67456	Arvin W. Hahn	1757	1160	725 C	P/LCA
Bethany Nazarene College; Bethany, Okla. 73008	Stephen W. Nease	1300	1100	1,208 C²	Naz
Bethel College; McKenzie, Tenn. 38201	William L. Odom	1365	1062	291 C	P/CP
Bethel College; Mishawaka, Ind. 46544	Albert J. Beutler	1923	1080	425	P/MC
Bethel College; North Newton, Kan. 67117	Harold J. Schultz	1898	1160	615 C	P/Men
Bethel College; St. Paul, Minn. 55112	Carl H. Lundquist	2520	1100	1,565 C	P/B
Bethune–Cookman College; Daytona Beach, Fla. 32015	Oswald P. Bronson	1506	1028	1,411 C²	P
Biola College; La Mirada, Calif. 90639	J. Richard Chase	2400	1425	2,066 C	P/ID
Birmingham–Southern College; Birmingham, Ala. 35204	Neal R. Berte	2000	1100	840 C	P/M
Biscayne College; Miami, Fla. 33054	Rev. John J. Farrell	2150	1500	1,788 C	P/RC
Bishop College; Dallas, Tex. 75241	Milton K. Curry, Jr.	1500⁴	960⁴	1,843 C⁴	P
Black Hills State College; Spearfish, S.D. 57783	Maurice Fitzgerald	504	875	1,848 C	S
Blackburn College; Carlinville, Ill. 62626	John R. Alberti	2000	350¹²	628 C²	P
Bloomfield College; Bloomfield, N.J. 07003	Merle F. Allshouse	2350	1480	1,590 C	P
Bloomsburg State College; Bloomsburg, Pa. 17815	James H. McCormick	820	900	5,711 C	S
Blue Mountain College; Blue Mountain, Miss. 38610	E. Harold Fisher	960	1000	301 F	P/B
Bluefield State College; Bluefield, W. Va. 24701	J. Wade Gilley	306	n.a.	1,525 C	S
Bluffton College; Bluffton, Ohio 45817	Benjamin E. Sprunger	2574⁸	1136⁸	638 C	P/Men
Boise State University; Boise, Idaho 83725	John B. Barnes	362	1199	11,500 C	S
Borromeo College of Ohio; Wickliffe, Ohio 44092	Msgr. Lawrence P. Cahill	2270	1200	116 Co	P/RC
Boston, The Art Institute of; Boston, Mass. 02215	William H. Willis, Jr.	1470	1600	407 C	P
Boston College; Chestnut Hill, Mass. 02167	Rev. J. Donald Monan	3175+	774+	13,545 C	P
Boston Conservatory of Music; Boston, Mass. 02215	George A. Brambilla	2500	1600	471 C	P
Boston State College; Boston, Mass. 02115	Kermit C. Morrissey	250	n.a.	5,530 C	S
Boston University; Boston, Mass. 02215	John R. Silber	3580	1875	15,866 C	P
Bowdoin College; Brunswick, Me. 04011	Roger Howell, Jr.	3800	1650	1,422 C	P
Bowie State College; Bowie, Md. 20715	Samuel L. Myers	200	1320	3,098 C²	S
Bowling Green State University; Bowling Green, Ohio 43403	Hollis A. Moore	858	1353	16,412 C	S
Bradford College; Bradford, Mass. 01830	Jack L. Armstrong	3175	1625	306 C	P/Ind
Bradley University; Peoria, Ill. 61625	Martin G. Abegg	2550	640	4,537 C	P
Brandeis University; Waltham, Mass. 02154	Marver H. Bernstein	3875	1900	3,420 C	P
Brenau College; Gainesville, Ga. 30501	James T. Rogers	2004	1496	662 C	P
Brescia College; Owensboro, Ky. 42301	Sister George Ann Cecil	1280	1100	900 C	P/RC
Briar Cliff College; Sioux City, Iowa 51104	Kasper C. Marking	1920	1005	764 C	P/RC
Briarcliff College; Briarcliff Manor, N.Y. 10510	Josiah Bunting III	3100	2150	350 F	P
Bridgeport, University of; Bridgeport, Conn. 06602	Leland Miles	3100	1750	6,841 C	P
Bridgewater College; Bridgewater, Va. 22812	Wayne F. Geisert	2350	1250	804 C¹³	P
Bridgewater State College; Bridgewater, Mass. 02324	Adrian Rondileau	500	615	4,535 C²	S
Brigham Young University; Provo, Utah 84602	Dallin H. Oaks	720¹⁴	1080	25,337 C	P/LDS
Hawaii Campus; Laie, Hawaii 96762	Dan W. Anderson	500¹⁵	1000	1,024 C	P/LDS
Brooklyn College. See New York, City University of.					
Brooklyn Law School; Brooklyn, N.Y. 11201	Raymond E. Lisle	1066	n.a.	1,026 C²	P
Brooks Institute; Santa Barbara, Calif. 93108	Ernest H. Brooks II	2430	n.a.	731 C²	P
Brown University; Providence, R.I. 02912	Donald F. Hornig	4300	2075	6,511 C	P
Bryan College; Dayton, Tenn. 37321	Theodore C. Mercer	1600	1450	538 C	P
Bryant College; Smithfield, R.I. 02917	Nelson J. Gulski	2300	1525	2,600 C	P
Bryn Mawr College; Bryn Mawr, Pa. 19010	Harris L. Wofford, Jr.	4225⁸	1790⁸	1,605 F²	P
Bucknell University; Lewisburg, Pa. 17837	(Vacant)	3575	1400	3,181 C²	P
Buena Vista College; Storm Lake, Iowa 50588	Keith G. Briscoe	2200	1050	864 C	P/Pres
Butler University; Indianapolis, Ind. 46208	Alexander E. Jones	1025	1100	4,156 C	P
Cabrini College; Radnor, Pa. 19087	Sister Mary Louise Sullivan	2180	1640	494 C	P/RC
Caldwell College; Caldwell, N.J. 07006	Sister M. A. J. O'Loughlin	1900⁴	1100⁴	805 Co¹	RC
California, San Francisco, Univ. of; San Francisco, Calif. 94122	P. R. Lee	n.a.	n.a.	n.a.	S
California, University of; Berkeley, Calif. 94720	David S. Saxon				S
UC, Berkeley, Berkeley, Calif. 94720	Albert H. Bowker	637+	1600	28,298 C	S
UC, Davis; Davis, Calif. 95616	James H. Meyer	637	2400	16,950 C⁵	S
UC, Irvine; Irvine, Calif. 92717	Daniel G. Aldrich, Jr.	627	1600	8,622 C	S
UC, Los Angeles; Los Angeles, Calif. 90024	Charles E. Young	630	1500	31,735 C²	S
UC, Riverside; Riverside, Calif. 92502	Ivan B. Hinderaker	1500¹⁰	1185¹⁰	5,129 C¹	S
UC, San Diego; La Jolla, Calif. 92093	William D. McElroy	636	1825	9,428 C⁵	S
UC, Santa Barbara; Santa Barbara, Calif. 93106	Vernon I. Cheadle	600⁸	1642⁸	14,178 C⁵	S
UC, Santa Cruz; Santa Cruz, Calif. 95064	Angus E. Taylor	695⁸	1550⁸	6,105 C²	S
California Baptist College; Riverside, Calif. 92504	James R. Staples	1400	1010	814 C	P
California Coll. of Arts and Crafts; Oakland, Calif. 94618	Harry X. Ford	2400	800¹⁶	1,024 C	P
California Coll. of Podiatric Medicine; San Francisco, Calif. 94115	Harold D. Bailey	4600	n.a.	338 C	P
California Inst. of Technology; Pasadena, Calif. 91125	Harold Brown	3375	1224	1,516 C²	P

Institution and location	Chief executive	Tuition	Rm/Bd	Students*	Control
California Institute of the Arts; Valencia, Calif. 91355	Robert Fitzpatrick	3450	680+[7]	583 C	P
California Lutheran College; Thousand Oaks, Calif. 91360	Mark A. Mathews	2500	1380	2,493 C	P
California Polytech. St. Univ.; San Luis Obispo, Calif. 93407	Robert E. Kennedy	200	1600	14,508 C	S
California State College; Bakersfield, Calif. 93309	Jacob P. Frankel	([17])	1340	3,000 C	S
California State College; California, Pa. 15419	John P. Watkins	800	852	5,075 C	S
California State College; Dominguez Hills, Calif. 90747	Leo F. Cain	191	n.a.	6,600 C	S
California State College; San Bernardino, Calif. 92407	John M. Pfau	n.a.	1300	4,000 C	S
California State Coll., Sonoma; Rohnert Park, Calif. 94928	Marjorie Downing Wagner	n.a.	n.a.	5,900 C	S
California State Coll., Stanislaus; Turlock, Calif. 95380	Walter Olson	190[18]	1755	3,126 C	S
California State Polytechnic Univ.; Pomona, Calif. 91768	Robert C. Kramer	190[18]	1500	12,651 C[2]	S
California State Univ., Chico; Chico, Calif. 95926	Stanford Cazier	105[18]	1145	12,920 C	S
California State Univ., Fresno; Fresno, Calif. 93740	Norman A. Baxter	200[18]	1500	15,300 C	S
California State Univ., Fullerton; Fullerton, Calif. 92634	L. Donald Shields	190[18]	1400	21,700 C	S
California State Univ., Hayward; Hayward, Calif. 94542	Ellis E. McCune	168	n.a.	11,205 C[5]	S
California State Univ., Long Beach; Long Beach, Calif. 90840	Stephen Horn	190	1500	31,700 C	S
California State Univ., Los Angeles; Los Angeles, Calif. 90032	John A. Greenlee	200	n.a.	25,500 C	S
California State Univ., Northridge; Northridge, Calif. 91330	James W. Cleary	190	n.a.	27,778 C[2]	S
California State Univ., Sacramento; Sacramento, Calif. 95819	James G. Bond	190	1300	20,808 C	S
Calumet College; East Chicago, Ind. 46312	Rev. James McCabe	1070	n.a.	1,526 C[2]	P/RC
Calvary Bible College; Kansas City, Mo. 64111	Rev. Leslie Madison	1152	870	293 C	P
Calvin College; Grand Rapids, Mich. 49506	Anthony J. Diekema	2060	1130	3,506 C	P/CR
Cameron University; Lawton, Okla. 73501	Don Owen	396	1062	6,000 C	S
Campbell College; Buie's Creek, N.C. 27506	Norman A. Wiggins	1250	1200	1,720 C[2]	P/SB
Campbellsville College; Campbellsville, Ky. 42718	W. R. Davenport	1420	1170	711 C[2]	P/SB
Canisius College; Buffalo, N.Y. 14208	Rev. James M. Demske	2500	1250	4,274 C[2]	P
Capital University; Columbus, Ohio 43209	Thomas H. Langevin	2960	1330	2,523 C	P/AL
Cardinal Stritch College; Milwaukee, Wis. 53217	Sister M. Camille Kliebhan	1700	1095	1,300 C[2]	P/RC
Caribbean Center for Advanced Studies; Carolina, P.R. 00630	William P. Haugaard	n.a.	n.a.	121 C[1]	Ind
Carleton College; Northfield, Minn. 55057	Howard R. Swearer	3475	1475	1,607 C	P
Carlow College; Pittsburgh, Pa. 15213	Sister Jane Scully	2550	1450	1,000 F	P/RC
Carnegie-Mellon University; Pittsburgh, Pa. 15213	Richard M. Cyert	5500	1800	4,332 C	P
Carroll College; Helena, Mont. 59601	Francis J. Kerins	1520	1150	1,397 C[2]	P/RC
Carroll College; Waukesha, Wis. 53186	Robert V. Cramer	3088	1190	1,136 C	P
Carson-Newman College; Jefferson City, Tenn. 37760	John Albert Fincher	1300	970	1,559 C[2]	B
Carthage College; Kenosha, Wis. 53140	Harold H. Lentz	2500	1080	1,371 C	P/L
Case Western Reserve University; Cleveland, Ohio 44124	Louis Adelbert Toepfer	3300	1750	8,600 C	P
Castleton State College; Castleton, Vt. 05735	Dorothy M. Burns	620	1320	1,328 C	S
Catawba College; Salisbury, N.C. 28144	Martin L. Shotzberger	2183	1064	1,000 C	P/UCC
Cathedral Coll. of the Immac. Concep.; Douglaston, N.Y. 11362	Msgr. Thomas J. Gradilone	2000	2000	213 M	RC
Catholic University of America, The; Washington, D.C. 20064	Clarence C. Walton	3000	950	7,300 C[2]	P/RC
Catholic University of Puerto Rico; Ponce, P.R. 00731	Francisco J. Carreras	1000[4]	1000[4]	8,247 C[4]	P/RC
Cedar Crest College; Allentown, Pa. 18104	Pauline Tompkins	3050	1400	663 F	P
Cedarville College; Cedarville, Ohio 45314	James T. Jeremiah	1845	1335	1,076 C	P/B
Centenary College of Louisiana; Shreveport, La. 71104	John H. Allen	1400	1100	802 C	P/M
Central Arkansas, University of; Conway, Ark. 72032	Jefferson D. Farris, Jr.	400	1000	4,736 C	S
Central Bible College; Springfield, Mo. 65802	Philip Crouch	1100	1100	1,109 C	P/AG
Central College; Pella, Iowa 50219	Kenneth J. Weller	2400	1000	1,252 C	P/RCA
Central Connecticut State College; New Britain, Conn. 06050	F. Don James	601	1100	8,027 C[2]	S
Central Methodist College, Fayette, Mo. 65248	Harold P. Hamilton	1700	850	658 C	P/M
Central Michigan University; Mt. Pleasant, Mich. 48859	Harold Abel	625[19]	1350[19]	14,836 C[5]	S
Central Missouri State University; Warrensburg, Mo. 64093	Warren C. Lovinger	315[18]	960	9,678 C[2]	S
Central State University; Edmond, Okla. 73034	William Lillard	340	752	11,250 C	S
Central State University; Wilberforce, Ohio 45384	Lionel H. Newsom	771	1359	2,086 C	S
Central Washington State College; Ellensburg, Wash. 98926	James Brooks	507	1500	8,000 C	S
Central Wesleyan College; Central, S.C. 29630	Claude R. Rickman	2000	900	386 C	P/W
Centre College of Kentucky; Danville, Ky. 40422	Thomas A. Spragens	2975	1425	749 C	P
Chadron State College; Chadron, Neb. 69337	Edwin C. Nelson	465	1020	2,023 C	S
Chaminade College of Honolulu; Honolulu, Hawaii 96816	Rev. Charles J. Lees	1410	1600	2,434 C	P/RC
Chapman College; Orange, Calif. 92666	Davis Chamberlin	2530	1588	1,800 C	P
Charleston, College of; Charleston, S.C. 29401	Theodore S. Stern	500	1400	5,397 C[2]	S
Chatham College; Pittsburgh, Pa. 15232	Edward D. Eddy	3200	1640	642 F	P
Chestnut Hill College; Philadelphia, Pa. 19118	Sister Mary Xavier Kirby	2000	1300-	500 F	P/RC
Cheyney State College; Cheyney, Pa. 19319	Wade Wilson	1834	1000	2,750 C	S
Chicago, The University of; Chicago, Ill. 60637	John T. Wilson	3420	1850	9,008 C	P
Chicago, School of the Art Institute of; Chicago, Ill. 60603	Donald J. Irving	2100[8]	n.a.	1,517 C	P
Chicago Coll. of Osteopathic Medicine; Chicago, Ill. 60615	Thaddeus P. Kawalek	3300	3250	384 C	P
Chicago Conservatory College; Chicago, Ill. 60605	Francois d'Albert	n.a.	n.a.	175 C	P
Chicago State University; Chicago, Ill. 60628	Benjamin H. Alexander	484	n.a.	6,633 C[5]	S
Christian Brothers College; Memphis, Tenn. 38104	Brother Bernard LoCoco	1800	1350	872 C[2]	P/RC
Christopher Newport College; Newport News, Va. 23606	James C. Windsor	690	n.a.	3,069 C	S
Cincinnati, Art Academy of; Cincinnati, Ohio 45202	Gerald L. McDowell	1200	n.a.	150 C	P
Cincinnati, University of; Cincinnati, Ohio 45221	Warren Bennis	795	1452	32,000 C	Mun/S

Institution and location	Chief executive	Tuition	Rm/Bd	Students*Control	
Cincinnati Bible Seminary, The; Cincinnati, Ohio 45204	Harvey C. Bream, Jr.	1250[18]	1010	699 C	P/CC
Citadel, The; Charleston, S.C. 29409	Lt. Gen. G. M. Seignious II	1239	1181	1,922 M	S
City College (NYC). See New York, City University of.					
Claflin College; Orangeburg, S.C. 29115	H. V. Manning	1300	891	903 C	P
Claremont Colleges:					
Claremont Graduate School; Claremont, Calif. 91711	Barnaby C. Keeney	2600	500[7]	1,260 C	P
Claremont Men's College; Claremont, Calif. 91711	Jack Lee Stark	3750	1740	800 C	P
Harvey Mudd College; Claremont, Calif. 91711	D. K. Baker	3500	1675	450 C	P
Pitzer College; Claremont, Calif. 91773	Robert H. Atwell	3310	1425	789 C	P
Pomona College; Claremont, Calif. 91711	J. David Alexander	3300[19]	1750[19]	1,300 C	P
Scripps College; Claremont, Calif. 91711	John H. Chandler	3630	1870	548 F	P
Clarion State College; Clarion, Pa. 16214	James Gemmell	820	882	4,321 C	S
Clark College; Atlanta, Ga. 30314	Charles L. Knight	1600	1165	1,625 C	P/UM
Clark University; Worcester, Mass. 01610	H. Mortimer Appley	3625	1650	2,268 C	P
Clarke College; Dubuque, Iowa 52001	Robert J. Giroux	2250	1300	620 F	P/RC
Clarkson College of Technology; Potsdam, N.Y. 13676	Robert A. Plane	3350	1700	2,832 C	P
Cleary College; Ypsilanti, Mich. 48197	Lynn D. Brenneman	1550	900	506 C	P
Clemson University; Clemson, S.C. 29631	Robert C. Edwards	660	1080	10,970 C	S
Cleveland Institute of Art; Cleveland, Ohio 44106	Joseph McCullough	2125[8]	1680[8]	476 C	P
Cleveland State University, The; Cleveland, Ohio 44115	Walter B. Waetjen	795	1500	16,974 C	S
Clinch Valley College. See University of Virginia.					
Coe College; Cedar Rapids, Iowa 52402	Leo L. Nussbaum	2710	1000	1,150 C	P/UP
Coker College; Hartsville, S.C. 29550	Hilburn C. Womble	1899	1215	466 C	P
Colby College; Waterville, Me. 04901	Robert E. L. Strider II	3300	1415	1,607 C	P
Colby-Sawyer College; New London, N.H. 03257	Louis C. Vaccaro	2950	1375	700 F	P
Colgate University; Hamilton, N.Y. 13346	Thomas A. Bartlett	3825	1630	2,500 C	P
College Misericordia; Dallas, Pa. 18612	Sister Ann Miriam Gallagher	1800	1400	943 F	P/RC
Colorado, University of; Boulder, Colo. 80302	Frederick P. Thieme	576[10]	1256[10]	22,420 C[1]	S
U. of Colo. at Colo. Springs; Colorado Springs, Colo. 80907	Lawrence Silverman	400	n.a.	3,344 C	S
U. of Colorado at Denver; Denver, Colo. 80202	Harold H. Haak	364	n.a.	8,097 C[2]	S
Colorado College, The; Colorado Springs, Colo. 80903	Lloyd E. Worner	3100	1200	1,925 C	P
Colorado School of Mines; Golden, Colo. 80401	Guy T. McBride, Jr.	532	985	2,204 C[2]	S
Colorado State University; Fort Collins, Colo. 80523	Adrian R. Chamberlain	476	1310	15,867 C	S
Colorado Women's College; Denver, Colo. 80220	Marjorie Bell Chambers	2800	1700	650 F	P
Columbia Bible College; Columbia, S.C. 29203	J. Robertson McQuilkin	1350	1080	713 C	P
Columbia College; Chicago, Ill. 60606	Mirron Alexandroff	1975	n.a.	1,625 C	P
Columbia College; Columbia, Mo. 65201	W. Merle Hill	2200	1340	1,076 C	P
Columbia College; Columbia, S.C. 29203	R. Wright Spears	1800[8]	1500[8]	890 F[2]	P/M
Columbia Union College; Takoma Park, Md. 20012	Colin D. Standish	2352	1320	924 C	SDA
Columbia University; New York, N.Y. 10027	William J. McGill	4100	2018	15,976 C[2]	P
Barnard College; New York, N.Y. 10027	Jacquelyn A. Mattfeld	3770	1555	1,926 F[2]	P
Teachers College; New York, N.Y. 10027	Lawrence A. Cremin	([20])	n.a.	5,804 C	P
Columbus College; Columbus, Ga. 31907	Thomas Y. Whitley	435	n.a.	5,497 C[5]	S
Concord College; Athens, W. Va. 24712	Meredith N. Freeman	318	1372	1,640 C	S
Concordia College; Moorhead, Minn. 56560	Paul J. Dovre	2500	960	2,446 C	P/L
Concordia College; St. Paul, Minn. 55104	Gerhardt W. Hyatt	1920	1050	632 C	P/L
Concordia Senior College; Fort Wayne, Ind. 46825	Herbert G. Bredemeier	1266	1165	366 C	LMS
Concordia Teachers College; River Forest, Ill. 60305	Rev. Paul A. Zimmerman	1680	1209	1,204 C	P/L
Concordia Teachers College; Seward, Neb. 68434	Rev. W. Theophil Janzow	1830	1110	1,154 C[2]	P/L
Connecticut, The University of; Storrs, Conn. 06268	Glenn W. Ferguson	940	1330	22,025 C	S
Connecticut College; New London, Conn. 06320	Oakes Ames	3990	1460	2,033 C[2]	P
Conservatory of Music; San Juan, P.R. 00936	Elías López Sobá	150	n.a.	293 C[1]	S
Converse College; Spartanburg, S.C. 29301	Robert T. Coleman, Jr.	3000	1200	826 F	P
Cooper Union; New York, N.Y. 10003	John F. White	n.a.	n.a.	915 C[2]	P
Coppin State College; Baltimore, Md. 21216	Calvin W. Burnett	550	n.a.	2,359 C[2]	S
Cornell College; Mt. Vernon, Iowa 52314	Philip B. Secor	3100	1250	858 C	P
Cornell University; Ithaca, N.Y. 14853	Dale R. Corson	1650	1800	16,044 C	P/End
Covenant College; Lookout Mountain, Tenn. 37350	Marion D. Barnes	2060	1270	543 C	P/Pres
Cranbrook Academy of Art; Bloomfield Hills, Mich. 48013	Wallace Mitchell	2400	1700	145 C	P
Creighton University, The; Omaha, Neb. 68178	Rev. Joseph J. Labaj	2490	1275	4,513 C	P/RC
Culver-Stockton College; Canton, Mo. 63425	Harold C. Doster	1980	1300	548 C	P/DC
Cumberland College; Williamsburg, Ky. 40769	J. M. Boswell	1200	800	1,750 C[2]	P/B
Curry College; Milton, Mass. 02186	John S. Hafer	2800	1700	980 C	P
Dakota State College; Madison, S.D. 57042	Clyde K. Brashier	632	1060	820 C	S
Dakota Wesleyan University; Mitchell, S.D. 57301	Donald E. Messer	1625	1080	517 C[5]	P/UM
Dallas, University of; Irving, Tex. 75061	Donald A. Cowan	1900	1200	1,708 C[13]	RC
Dallas Baptist College; Dallas, Tex. 75211	William E. Thorn	1200[4]	1200[4]	1,215 C[4]	P
Dallas Bible College; Dallas, Tex. 75228	Rev. V. A. Doiron	1280	1060	302 C[5]	Ind
Dallas Theological Seminary; Dallas, Tex. 75204	John F. Walvoord	1500	1200	870 M[2]	P
Dana College; Blair, Neb. 68008	Earl R. Mezoff	2270[8]	1070[8]	580 C[2]	P/AL
Dartmouth College; Hanover, N.H. 03755	John M. Kemeny	4230[8]	1900[8]	3,220 C	P
David Lipscomb College; Nashville, Tenn. 37203	Athens Clay Pullias	1440	1200	1,970 C	P/CC

Institution and location	Chief executive	Tuition	Rm/Bd	Students	*Control
Davidson College; Davidson, N.C. 28036	Samuel R. Spencer, Jr.	4320[9]		1,279 C	P/PUS
Davis and Elkins College; Elkins, W. Va. 26241	Gordon E. Hermanson	2850	1300	818 C	P/Pres
Dayton, University of; Dayton, Ohio 45469	Rev. Raymond A. Roesch	2000	1300	8,370 C[2]	P/RC
Defiance College, The; Defiance, Ohio 43512	Marvin J. Ludwig	2710	1180	742 C	P/UCC
Delaware, University of; Newark, Del. 19711	E. Arthur Trabant	795	1600	12,600 C	P/S
Delaware State College; Dover, Del. 19901	Luna I. Mishoe	575	1050	2,150 C	S
Delaware Valley Coll. of Sci. & Agri.; Doylestown, Pa. 18901	Joshua Feldstein	1929	1090	1,393 C	P
Delta State University; Cleveland, Miss. 38732	Kent Wyatt	498	784	3,060 C	S
Denison University; Granville, Ohio 43023	Robert C. Good	3375	1440	2,200 C	P
Denver, University of; Denver, Colo. 80210	Maurice B. Mitchell	3375	1470	6,791 C	P
DePaul University; Chicago, Ill. 60604	V. Rev. John R. Cortelyou	2130[4]	1380[4]	10,010 C[1]	P
DePauw University; Greencastle, Ind. 46135	Thomas Wyard Binford	3350	1500	2,310 C[2]	P/UM
Detroit, University of; Detroit, Mich. 48221	Rev. Malcolm Carron	2450	1500	7,911 C	P/RC
Detroit Bible College; Detroit, Mich. 48235	Wendell G. Johnston	527	1220	280 C	P
Detroit College of Business; Dearborn, Mich. 48126	Frank Paone	1475	n.a.	3,115 C	P
Detroit College of Law; Detroit, Mich. 48201	John S. Abbott	2000	n.a.	980 C	P
Detroit Institute of Technology, The; Detroit, Mich. 48201	Dewey F. Barich	1400	n.a.	1,712 C	P
DeVry Institute of Technology; Chicago, Ill. 60618	Samuel R. Edmonds	2300	n.a.	2,793 C	P
DeVry Institute of Technology; Dallas, Tex. 75235	D. A. Kerr	2450[21]	n.a.	921 C[2]	P
DeVry Institute of Technology; Phoenix, Ariz. 85016	F. Roger Hess	n.a.	n.a.	2,355 C[1]	P
Dickinson College; Carlisle, Pa. 17013	Samuel A. Banks	3280	1560	1,641 C	P
Dickinson School of Law; Carlisle, Pa. 17013	Dale F. Shughart	1850	500[7]	446 C	P
Dickinson State College; Dickinson, N.D. 58601	R. C. Gillund	477	891	980 C	S
Dillard University; New Orleans, La. 70122	Samuel DuBois Cook	1800	1000	1,212 C	P
District of Columbia Teachers Coll.; Washington, D.C. 20009	Wendell P. Russell	105	n.a.	1,576 C	Mun
Divine Word College; Epworth, Iowa 52045	Rev. Louis J. Luzbetak	2000	1000	105 M[5]	P/RC
Doane College; Crete, Neb. 68333	Philip R. Heckman	2150	1000	581 C	P
Dominican College of Blauvelt; Blauvelt, N.Y. 10913	Sister Natalie Casey	1300	n.a.	1,113 C	P/RC
Dominican College of San Rafael; San Rafael, Calif. 94901	Sister Mary Samuel Conlan	1950	1400	734 C	Ind/RC
Dordt College; Sioux Center, Iowa 51250	Rev. B. J. Haan	2000	840	950 C	P/CR
Douglass College. See Rutgers University.					
Dowling College; Oakdale, N.Y. 11769	Allyn P. Robinson	2500	1400	1,965 C	P
Drake University; Des Moines, Iowa 50311	Wilbur C. Miller	2930[8]	1580	6,881 C[2]	P
Drew University; Madison, N.J. 07940	Paul Hardin	3180[8]	1550[8]	2,038 C[2]	P/UM
Drexel University; Philadelphia, Pa. 19104	W. W. Hagerty	2748	900	9,400 C	P
Dropsie University, The; Philadelphia, Pa. 19132	Abraham I. Katsh	2900	n.a.	85 C	P
Drury College; Springfield, Mo. 65802	William E. Everheart	2238	1195	2,400 C	P
Dubuque, University of; Dubuque, Iowa 52001	Walter F. Peterson	2000	1100	790 C	P
Duke University; Durham, N.C. 27706	Terry Sanford	3230	1613	8,956 C	P
Duns Scotus College; Southfield, Mich. 48075	Rev. James Van Vurst	1500	1000	45 M	P/RC
Duquesne University; Pittsburgh, Pa. 15219	Rev. Henry J. McAnulty	2314	1405	7,221 C	P/RC
D'Youville College; Buffalo, N.Y. 14201	Sister Mary C. Barton	2300	1300	1,143 C	P
Earlham College; Richmond, Ind. 47374	Franklin W. Wallin	3360	1445	1,110 C	P/SOF
East Carolina Univ. See Univ. System of North Carolina.					
East Central Oklahoma State University; Ada, Okla. 74820	Stanley P. Wagner	375	900	3,000 C	S
East Stroudsburg State College; East Stroudsburg, Pa. 18301	Darrell Holmes	800	864	3,853 C	S
East Tennessee State University; Johnson City, Tenn. 37601	Delos P. Culp	426	950	9,244 C	S
East Texas Baptist College; Marshall, Tex. 75670	Jerry F. Dawson	1050	900	788 C[2]	P/SB
East Texas State University; Commerce, Tex. 75428	F. H. McDowell	340	1200	8,982 C[2]	S
Eastern College; St. Davids, Pa. 19087	Harold C. Howard	2520	1250	618 C	P/B
Eastern Connecticut State College; Willimantic, Conn. 06226	Charles R. Webb, Jr.	300	1090	2,089 C	S
Eastern Illinois University; Charleston, Ill. 61920	Gilbert C. Fite	600	1180	8,994 C[2]	S
Eastern Kentucky University; Richmond, Ky. 40475	Robert R. Martin	420	900	13,430 C[2]	S
Eastern Mennonite College; Harrisonburg, Va. 22801	Myron S. Augsburger	2250	975	986 C	P/Men
Eastern Michigan University; Ypsilanti, Mich. 48197	James H. Brickley	625	1384	17,704 C[5]	S
Eastern Montana College; Billings, Mont. 59101	Stanley J. Heywood	474	1021	3,351 C[5]	S
Eastern Nazarene College; Quincy, Mass. 02170	Rev. Donald Irwin	1800	1200	815 C[2]	P/Naz
Eastern New Mexico University; Portales, N.M. 88130	Warren B. Armstrong	478	1150	3,730 C	S
Eastern Oregon State College; La Grande, Ore. 97850	Rodney A. Briggs	645	1350	1,414 C	S
Eastern Washington State College; Cheney, Wash. 99004	Emerson Shuck	507	1300	6,305 C	S
Eckerd College; St. Petersburg, Fla. 33733	Billy O. Wireman	4100	1255	852 C	P
Edgecliff College; Cincinnati, Ohio 45206	Sister Margaret A. Molitor	1600[10]	1275[10]	826 C[1]	P/RC
Edgewood College; Madison, Wis. 53711	Sister Cecilia Carey	1950	1200	524 C	P/RC
Edinboro State College; Edinboro, Pa. 16444	Chester T. McNerney	840	888	7,041 C	S
Eisenhower College; Seneca Falls, N.Y. 13148	Joseph D. Coffee, Jr.	2800	1500	446 C	P
Elizabeth City State Univ. See Univ. System of North Carolina.					
Elizabethtown College; Elizabethtown, Pa. 17022	Morley J. Mays	2440	570	1,284 C	P
Elmhurst College; Elmhurst, Ill. 60126	Ivan E. Frick	2770	1520	1,486 C	P/UCC
Elmira College; Elmira, N.Y. 14901	J. Ralph Murray	3300	1425	3,320 C	P
Elon College; Elon College, N.C. 27244	J. Fred Young	1625	982	2,059 C	P
Embry-Riddle Aeronautical Univ.; Daytona Beach, Fla. 32015	Jack R. Hunt	1900	1400	1,862 C	P/Ind
Emerson College; Boston, Mass. 02116	Gus Turbeville	3215	2020	1,358 C	P
Emmanuel College; Boston, Mass. 02115	Sister Mary Frances McCarthy	2560	1275	1,248 F[2]	P/RC

Institution and location	Chief executive	Tuition	Rm/Bd	Students*	Control
Emory and Henry College; Emory, Va. 24327	Thomas F. Chilcote	1695	975	757 C	UM
Emory University; Atlanta, Ga. 30322	Sanford S. Atwood	3150	1550	6,580 C	P/M
Emporia Kansas State College; Emporia, Kan. 66801	John E. Visser	405	1100	5,888 C	S
Erskine College; Due West, S.C. 29639	Melvin Stanyarne Bell	1900	2280	731 C[2]	P
Eureka College; Eureka, Ill. 61530	Ira W. Langston	2350	1410	370 C	P
Evangel College; Springfield, Mo. 65802	Robert H. Spence	1470	1320	1,091 C	P/AG
Evansville, University of; Evansville, Ind. 47702	Wallace B. Graves	2130	1299	5,169 C[2]	P/UM
Evergreen State College, The; Olympia, Wash. 98505	Charles McCann	507	1335	2,500 C[2]	S
Fairfield University; Fairfield, Conn. 06430	Rev. Thomas R. Fitzgerald	2700	1600	5,107 C[2]	P/RC
Fairleigh Dickinson University; Rutherford, N.J. 07070	Jerome M. Pollack	....	....	17,312 C	P
Florham-Madison Campus; Madison, N.J. 07940	Jerome M. Pollack	2560	1625	4,472 C	P
Rutherford Campus, Rutherford, N.J. 07070	Jerome M. Pollack	2560	1625	4,739 C	P
Teaneck-Hackensack Campus; Teaneck, N.J. 07666	Jerome M. Pollack	2560	1625	8,101 C	P
Fairmont State College; Fairmont, W. Va. 26554	Wendell G. Hardway	309	1435	5,078 C	S
Faith Baptist Bible College; Ankeny, Iowa 50021	David Nettleton	1200	1200	599 C	P/B
Federal City College; Washington, D.C. 20005	Wendell P. Russell	105	n.a.	7,774 C	F
Felician College; Lodi, N.J. 07644	Sister Justitia M. Lawniczak	1700	n.a.	729 F	P/RC
Ferris State College; Big Rapids, Mich. 49307	Robert L. Ewigleben	564	1488	8,608 C	S
Findlay College; Findlay, Ohio 45840	Glen R. Rasmussen	2385	1104	940 C[5]	P/CG
Fisk University; Nashville, Tenn. 37203	Rutherford H. Adkins	2200	1385	1,330 C	P
Fitchburg State College; Fitchburg, Mass. 01420	Vincent Mara	500	1272	3,433 C[2]	S
Flagler College; St. Augustine, Fla. 32084	William L. Proctor	1600	1150	611 C	P
Florida, University of; Gainesville, Fla. 32611	Robert Q. Marston	1700	1800	28,189 C[2]	S
Florida A. & M. University; Tallahassee, Fla. 32307	Benjamin L. Perry, Jr.	630	1200	5,600 C[5]	S
Florida Atlantic University; Boca Raton, Fla. 33421	Glenwood L. Creech	675	1100	6,846 C	S
Florida Institute of Technology; Melbourne, Fla. 32901	Jerome P. Keuper	2256	1440	2,750 C	P
Florida International University; Miami, Fla. 33199	Harold Crosby	750	n.a.	11,000 C	S
Florida Memorial College; Miami, Fla. 33054	Lester B. Brown	1922	563	650 C	P/B
Florida Southern College; Lakeland, Fla. 33802	Robert A. Davis	1900	1530	1,435 C[2]	P/M
Florida State University; Tallahassee, Fla. 32306	J. Stanley Marshall	2800[9]		19,128 C	S
Florida Technological University; Orlando, Fla. 32816	Charles N. Millican	675	1300	10,641 C[2]	S
Fontbonne College; St. Louis, Mo. 63105	Sister Jane Hassett	2200	1550	1,588 C	P/RC
Fordham University; Bronx, N.Y. 10458	Rev. James C. Finlay	2700	800[7]	14,274 C	P
Fort Hays Kansas State College; Hays, Kan. 67601	Gerald W. Tomanek	510	1244	4,532 C	S
Fort Lewis College; Durango, Colo. 81301	Rexer Berndt	1399	972	2,724 C	S
Fort Valley State College, The; Fort Valley, Ga. 31030	Cleveland W. Pettigrew	531	975	1,862 C	S
Fort Wayne Bible College; Fort Wayne, Ind. 46807	Timothy M. Warner	1454	1280	490 C	P/MC
Fort Wright College; Spokane, Wash. 99204	Sister Helen C. Volkomener	1920	1400	435 C	P/RC
Framingham State College; Framingham, Mass. 01701	D. Justin McCarthy	500	1243	2,925 C	S
Francis Marion College; Florence, S.C. 29501	Walter Douglas Smith	410	n.a.	2,681 C[2]	S
Franconia College; Franconia, N.H. 03580	I. Ira Goldenberg	3945	1270	339 C	P
Franklin and Marshall College; Lancaster, Pa. 17604	Keith Spalding	3435	1345	1,933 C	P
Franklin College of Indiana; Franklin, Ind. 46131	Edwin A. Penn	2670	1240	690 C	P/B
Franklin Pierce College; Rindge, N.H. 03461	Walter R. Peterson	2750	1550	861 C	P
Franklin University; Columbus, Ohio 43215	Joseph F. Frasch	1200	n.a.	3,686 C	P
Friends University; Wichita, Kan. 67213	Harold C. Cope	1650	1070	850 C	P
Frostburg State College; Frostburg, Md. 21532	Nelson P. Guild	200	1250	3,385 C	S
Furman University; Greenville, S.C. 29613	Gordon Williams Blackwell	2392	1590	2,732 C[2]	P/SB
Gallaudet College; Washington, D.C. 20002	Edward C. Merrill, Jr.	594	1625	1,114 C	P
Gannon College; Erie, Pa. 16501	Msgr. Wilfrid J. Nash	1975	1160	2,715 C[2]	P/RC
Gardner-Webb College; Boiling Springs, N.C. 28017	Thomas J. McGraw	1940	1130	1,341 C	SB
General Motors Institute; Flint, Mich. 48502	Harold P. Rodes	800	728	2,297 C	P
Geneva College; Beaver Falls, Pa. 15010	Edwin C. Clarke	2350	1245	1,379 C	P/RP
George Fox College; Newberg, Ore. 97132	David C. Le Shana	2256	1230	525 C	P/SOF
George Mason University; Fairfax, Va. 22030	Vergil H. Dykstra	768	n.a.	7,843 C	S
George Peabody College for Teachers; Nashville, Tenn. 37203	John Dunworth	1950	1050+	1,900 C	P
George Washington University, The; Washington, D.C. 20052	Lloyd Hartman Elliott	2500	1789	22,120 C[2]	P
George Williams College; Downers Grove, Ill. 60515	Richard E. Hamlin	2526	1395	1,587 C	P
Georgetown College; Georgetown, Ky. 40324	Robert Lee Mills	1950	1195	976 C	P/B
Georgetown University; Washington, D.C. 20057	Rev. Timothy S. Healy	3250	1700	10,682 C	P/RC
Georgia, Medical College of; Augusta, Ga. 30902	William H. Moretz	1480	440	2,281 C	S
Georgia, University of; Athens, Ga. 30602	Fred C. Davison	666	1146	21,442 C[2]	S
Georgia College; Milledgeville, Ga. 31061	J. Whitney Bunting	435	945	3,770 C	S
Georgia Institute of Technology; Atlanta, Ga. 30332	Joseph Mayo Pettit	675	1421+	7,815 C	S
Southern Technical Institute; Marietta, Ga. 30060	Walter O. Carlson	490	1100	2,078 C[2]	S
Georgia Southern College; Statesboro, Ga. 30458	Pope A. Duncan	435	950	5,400 C	S
Georgia Southwestern College; Americus, Ga. 31709	William B. King	516	1020	2,559 C	S
Georgia State University; Atlanta, Ga. 30303	Noah Langdale, Jr.	550	n.a.	21,075 C	S
Georgian Court College; Lakewood, N.J. 08701	Sister Maria Cordis Richey	1900	1150	752 F	P/RC
Gettysburg College; Gettysburg, Pa. 17325	Carl Arnold Hanson	3300	1180	1,881 C	P
Glassboro State College; Glassboro, N.J. 08028	Mark M. Chamberlain	535	1240	11,674 C	S
Glenville State College; Glenville, W. Va. 26351	D. Banks Wilburn	296	1200	1,500 C[5]	S

Institution and location	Chief executive	Tuition	Rm/Bd	Students*	Control
Goddard College; Plainfield, Vt. 05667	Richard Graham	2937	875	465 C	P
Golden Gate University; San Francisco, Calif. 94105	Otto W. Butz	1100	n.a.	9,300 C	P
Gonzaga University; Spokane, Wash. 99218	Rev. Bernard J. Coughlin	2380	1360	2,870 C	P/RC
Gordon College; Wenham, Mass. 01984	Richard F. Gross	3450	1365	917 C	P
Goshen College; Goshen, Ind. 46526	J. Lawrence Burkholder	2335	1110	1,230 C[5]	P/Men
Goucher College; Towson, Baltimore, Md. 21204	Rhoda M. Dorsey	3430	2000	872 F	P
Governors State University; Park Forest South, Ill. 60466	W. E. Engbretson	636	n.a.	4,583 C[5]	S
Grace Bible College; Grand Rapids, Mich. 49509	Jack T. Dean	750	1100	139 C	P/Ind
Grace College of the Bible; Omaha, Neb. 68108	Robert W. Benton	1152	1340	551 C	P/Men
Graceland College; Lamoni, Iowa 50140	Gerald L. Knutson	2340[8]	1120[8]	1,355 C	P
Grambling State University; Grambling, La. 71245	Ralph W. E. Jones	438	969	3,749 C	S
Grand Canyon College; Phoenix, Ariz. 85017	William R. Hintze	1588	1261	1,211 C	P/SB
Grand Valley State Colleges; Allendale, Mich. 49401	Arend D. Lubbers	675	1338	6,803 C	S
Gratz College; Philadelphia, Pa. 19141	Daniel Isaacman	235	n.a.	146 C	P
Great Falls, College of; Great Falls, Mont. 59405	Msgr. Anthony M. Brown	1650	1060	1,223 C	P
Greensboro College; Greensboro, N.C. 27420	Howard C. Wilkinson	1470	1185	539 C	P/UM
Greenville College; Greenville, Ill. 62246	Orley R. Herron	2090	1300	815 C	P/FM
Grinnell College; Grinnell, Iowa 50112	A. Richard Turner	3575	1145	1,145 C	P
Grove City College; Grove City, Pa. 16127	Charles S. MacKenzie	1680	1140	2,125 C	P
Guam, University of; Agana, Guam 96910	Forrest G. Rogers	300	1200	3,300 C	S
Guilford College; Greensboro, N.C. 27410	Grimsley T. Hobbs	2449	1200	956 C	SOF
Gulf-Coast Bible College; Houston, Tex. 77008	John W. Conley	1150	541	337 C	P/CG
Gustavus Adolphus College; St. Peter, Minn. 56082	Edward Lindell	2500	1500	2,098 C	P/LCA
Gwynedd-Mercy College; Gwynedd Valley, Pa. 19437	Sister Isabelle Keiss	2000	1400	920 C	P/RC
Hamilton College; Clinton, N.Y. 13323	J. Martin Carovano	3300	1600	965 M	P
Hamline University; St. Paul, Minn. 55104	Jerry E. Hudson	2900	1150	1,119 C	P/M
Hampden–Sydney College; Hampden–Sydney, Va. 23943	Rev. Walter Taylor Reveley	2425	1100	746 M	P/Pres
Hampshire College; Amherst, Mass. 01002	Charles R. Longsworth	4090	880	1,219 C	P
Hampton Institute; Hampton, Va. 23668	Roy D. Hudson	2065	1035	2,867 C[2]	P
Hanover College; Hanover, Ind. 47243	John E. Horner	2215	1130	930 C	P/UP
Hardin–Simmons University; Abilene, Tex. 79601	Elwin L. Skiles	1260	995	1,660 C	P/B
Harding College; Searcy, Ark. 72143	Clifton L. Ganus, Jr.	1700	1100	2,430 C	P
Harris Teachers College; St. Louis, Mo. 63103	Richard A. Stumpe	250	n.a.	1,011 C	Mun/S
Hartford, University of; West Hartford, Conn. 06117	Archibald M. Woodruff	2650	1894	8,929 C	P
Hartford Graduate Center. See Rensselaer Polytechnic Institute.					
Hartwick College; Oneonta, N.Y. 13820	Earl E. Deubler	3850	1700	1,734 C	P
Harvard University; Cambridge, Mass. 02138	Derek C. Bok	4100	2330	4,400 M	P
Radcliffe College, Cambridge, Mass. 02138	Matina S. Horner	4100	2330	1,800 F	P
Harvey Mudd College. See Claremont Colleges.					
Hastings College; Hastings, Neb. 68901	Clyde B. Matters	2250	1200	694 C	P
Haverford College; Haverford, Pa. 19041	John R. Coleman	2880	1950	870 M	P
Hawaii, University of, at Manoa[22]; Honolulu, Hawaii 96822	Douglas Yamamura	478	944	20,397 C	S
Hawaii Loa College; Kaneohe, Hawaii 96744	Chandler W. Rowe	1600	1850	217 C	P
Hawaii Pacific College; Honolulu, Hawaii 96813	George A. Warmer	1550	n.a.	1,351 C	P
Hebrew College; Brookline, Mass. 02146	Eli Grad	500	n.a.	116 C	P
Heidelberg College; Tiffin, Ohio 44883	Leslie H. Fishel, Jr.	3120	1210	1,062 C	P
Hellenic College; Brookline, Mass. 02146	Bishop Iakovos	1500	1500	160 C	GO
Henderson State University; Arkadelphia, Ark. 71923	Martin B. Garrison	420	1100	3,350 C	S
Hendrix College; Conway, Ark. 72032	Roy B. Shilling, Jr.	1650	1005	1,028 C[2]	UM
Herbert H. Lehman College. See New York, City University of.					
High Point College; High Point, N.C. 27262	Wendell M. Patton	1450	950	1,132 C	P/M
Hillsdale College; Hillsdale, Mich. 49242	George C. Roche III	2890	1425	1,000 C	P
Hilo College, Univ. of Hawaii at Hilo[22]; Hilo, Hawaii 96720	Erwin Mookini	300	2210	3,815 C	S
Hiram College; Hiram, Ohio 44234	Elmer Jagow	2910	1020	1,151 C[5]	Ind
Hobart and William Smith Colleges:					
Hobart College; Geneva, N.Y. 14456	Allan A. Kuusisto	3570	1630	1,073 M	P
William Smith College; Geneva, N.Y. 14456	Allan A. Kuusisto	3570	1630	666 F	P
Hofstra University; Hempstead, N.Y. 11550	James M. Shuart	3188	1700	10,073 C	P
Hollins College; Hollins College, Va. 24020	Carroll W. Brewster	3600	1375	1,023 F	P
Holy Cross, College of the; Worcester, Mass. 01610	Rev. John E. Brooks	3450	1550	2,522 C	P/RC
Holy Family College; Mission San Jose, Calif. 94538	Sister M. Jeanette Kelly	n.a.	n.a.	125 F[1]	P/RC
Holy Family College; Philadelphia, Pa. 19114	Sister Mary Lillian	1750	n.a.	945 C	P/RC
Holy Names College; Oakland, Calif. 94619	Sister M. Irene Woodward	2100	1566	675 C	P
Hood College; Frederick, Md. 21701	Martha E. Church	2670	1400	1,343 F	P
Hope College; Holland, Mich. 49423	Gordon J. Van Wylen	2370	3575	2,275 C[2]	P/RCA
Houghton College; Houghton, N.Y. 14744	Wilber T. Dayton	2108	1215	1,182 C	P/W
Houston, University of; Houston, Tex. 77004	Philip G. Hoffman	328	1260	28,714 C	S
Houston Baptist University; Houston, Tex. 77074	W. H. Hinton	1500	1100	1,351 C	P/SB
Howard Payne University; Brownwood, Tex. 76801	Roger L. Brooks	1300	1040	1,394 C	SB
Howard University; Washington, D.C. 20059	James E. Cheek	1350[19]	1530[19]	9,046 C	P
Humboldt State University; Arcata, Calif. 95521	Alistair W. McCrone	190	1500	7,706 C[2]	S
Hunter College. See New York, City University of.					

Institution and location	Chief executive	Tuition	Rm/Bd	Students*Control	
Huntingdon College; Montgomery, Ala. 36106	Allen K. Jackson	1650	1430	541 C	UM
Huntington College; Huntington, Ind. 46750	E. DeWitt Baker	2250	1360	576 C	P/RC
Huron College; Huron, S.D. 57350	Richard E. Hill	1800	1050	350 C²	P/Pres
Husson College; Bangor, Me. 04401	Franklin A. Peters	2000	1350	1,047 C⁵	P
Huston-Tillotson College; Austin, Tex. 78702	John T. King	950	1150	725 C⁵	P/UM
Idaho, The College of; Caldwell, Idaho 83605	William C. Cassell	2650	1265	718 C²	P
Idaho, University of; Moscow, Idaho 83843	Ernest W. Hartung	400	900+	8,134 C	S
Idaho State University; Pocatello, Idaho 83201	Charles H. Kegel	410	1270+	9,412 C	S
Illinois, University of; Urbana, Ill. 61801	John E. Corbally	....	....	56,752 C	S
Univ. of Illinois at Chicago Circle; Chicago, Ill. 60680	Donald H. Riddle	666	n.a.	19,519 C⁵	S
Univ. of Illinois at the Medical Center; Chicago, Ill. 60680	Joseph S. Begando	777+	1328+	4,410 C⁵	S
Univ. of Illinois at Urbana-Champaign; Urbana, Ill. 61801	Jack W. Peltason	710	1426	32,823 C	S
Illinois Benedictine College; Lisle, Ill. 60532	Richard Becker	2300	1450	1,213 C	P/RC
Illinois College; Jacksonville, Ill. 62650	Donald C. Mundinger	1875	1115	800 C	P
Illinois College of Optometry; Chicago, Ill. 60616	Alfred A. Rosenbloom, Jr.	3120	1800	566 C	P
Illinois College of Podiatric Medicine; Chicago, Ill. 60610	Philip R. Brachman	n.a.	n.a.	491 C¹	P
Illinois Institute of Technology; Chicago, Ill. 60616	Thomas L. Martin, Jr.	2900	1400	6,459 C	P
Illinois State University; Normal, Ill. 61761	Genet A. Budig	603	1374	19,000 C²	S
Illinois Wesleyan University; Bloomington, Ill. 61701	Robert S. Eckley	3250	1430	1,644 C²	P/M
Immaculata College; Immaculata, Pa. 19345	Sister Marie Antoine	2000	1400	650 F	P/RC
Immaculate Heart College; Los Angeles, Calif. 90027	Helen Kelley	2320	n.a.	622 C	P
Incarnate Word College; San Antonio, Tex. 78209	Sister Margaret P. Slattery	1560	1220	1,440 C	P/RC
Indiana Central College; Indianapolis, Ind. 46227	Gene E. Sease	2230⁸	1270	2,887 C²	P/UM
Indiana Institute of Technology; Fort Wayne, Ind. 46803	Charles W. Terrell	2160	1445	350 C⁵	P
Indiana State University; Terre Haute, Ind. 47809	Richard G. Landini	744	1139	10,531 C	S
Evansville Campus; Evansville, Ind. 47712	David L. Rice	620	n.a.	2,748 C	P
Indiana University; Bloomington, Ind. 47401	John W. Ryan	....	....	78,115 C	S
Indiana Univ. at Bloomington; Bloomington, Ind. 47401	Robert O'Neil	722	1070+	32,651 C²	S
Indiana Univ. at Kokomo; Kokomo, Ind. 46901	Victor M. Bogle	640	n.a.	2,562 C	S
I.U.-Purdue U. at Fort Wayne; Fort Wayne, Ind. 46805	Donald Schwartz	700	n.a.	8,418 C	S
I.U.-Purdue U. at Indianapolis; Indianapolis, Ind. 46202	Glenn W. Irwin, Jr.	650	1230	20,131 C	S
Indiana Univ. at South Bend; South Bend, Ind. 46616	Lester M. Wolfson	850	n.a.	5,771 C	S
Indiana University Northwest; Gary, Ind. 46408	Danilo Orescanin	630	n.a.	4,900 C	S
Indiana University Southeast; New Albany, Ind. 47150	Edwin W. Crooks	528	n.a.	3,682 C⁵	S
Indiana University of Pennsylvania; Indiana, Pa. 15701	Robert C. Wilburn	750	822	10,873 C	S
Instituto Tecnológico; Monterrey, Mexico	Fernando Garcia Roel	1600	1200	16,500 C	P
Insurance, The College of; New York, N.Y. 10038	A. Leslie Leonard	2850	4000	1,835 C	P
International Training, School for; Brattleboro, Vt. 05301	Alfredo J. Perez	3000	1000	120 C	P
Iona College; New Rochelle, N.Y. 10801	Rev. Br. John G. Driscoll	2380	1400	4,975 C²	P
Iowa, University of; Iowa City, Iowa 52240	Willard L. Boyd	682	1304	21,134 C	S
Iowa State University; Ames, Iowa 50011	Robert W. Parks	660	1095	21,205 C²	S
Iowa Wesleyan College; Mount Pleasant, Iowa 52641	Louis A. Haselmayer	2435	1100	631 C²	P/M
Ithaca College; Ithaca, N.Y. 14850	James J. Whalen	3676	1656	4,000 C	P
Jackson College for Women. See Tufts University.					
Jackson State University; Jackson, Miss. 39217	John A. Peoples, Jr.	432	848	7,718 C	S
Jacksonville State University; Jacksonville, Ala. 36265	Ernest Stone	500	1600	6,400 C	S
Jacksonville University; Jacksonville, Fla. 32211	Robert Harry Spiro	1980	1360	2,308 C	P
Jamestown College; Jamestown, N.D. 58401	J. N. Anderson	2030	1250	497 C	P/Pres
Jarvis Christian College; Hawkins, Tex. 75765	John P. Jones	1140	925	450 C	P/DC
Jersey City State College; Jersey City, N.J. 07305	William J. Maxwell	700	1300	11,603 C	S
Jewish Theol. Sem. of America, The; New York, N.Y. 10027	Rabbi Gerson D. Cohen	3000	1000⁷	524 C	P/J
John Brown University; Siloam Springs, Ark. 72761	John E. Brown, Jr.	1400	1100	558 C	P/ID
John Carroll University; Cleveland, Ohio 44118	Rev. Henry F. Birkenhauer	2180	1100	3,709 C²	P/RC
John F. Kennedy University; Orinda, Calif. 94563	Robert M. Fisher	1800	n.a.	543 C	P
John Jay Coll. of Criminal Justice. See New York, City Univ. of.					
John Marshall Law School, The; Chicago, Ill. 60604	Fred F. Herzog	2380	n.a.	1,515 C	P
Johns Hopkins University, The; Baltimore, Md. 21218	Steven Muller	3500⁸	2075⁸	9,685 C	P
Johnson and Wales College; Providence, R.I. 02903	Morris J. W. Gaebe	1905	1425	1,700 C	P
Johnson Bible College; Knoxville, Tenn. 37920	David L. Eubanks	650	960	430 C	P/CC
Johnson C. Smith University; Charlotte, N.C. 28216	Wilbert Greenfield	1400	1000	1,375 C	P/Pres
Johnson State College; Johnson, Vt. 05656	Edward M. Elmendorf	670	1400	1,189 C	S
Johnston College, Univ. of Redlands; Redlands, Calif. 92373	William Thomas	3150	1500	315 C	P
Jones College; Jacksonville, Fla. 32211	Delores C. Jones	1200	720⁷	1,834 C⁵	P
Jones College; Orlando, Fla. 32803	Delores C. Jones	1200	n.a.	1,902 C⁵	P
Judson College; Elgin, Ill. 60120	Harm A. Weber	1770	1270	390 C²	P/B
Judson College; Marion, Ala. 36756	N. H. McCrummen	1200⁴	1400⁴	406 F⁴	P/B
Juilliard School, The; New York, N.Y. 10023	Peter Mennin	2600	2400²³	898 C	P
Juniata College; Huntingdon, Pa. 16652	Frederick M. Binder	2920⁸	1370⁸	1,015 C	P
Kalamazoo College; Kalamazoo, Mich. 49007	George N. Rainsford	2991⁸	1416⁸	1,497 C²	P/B
Kansas, University of; Lawrence, Kan. 66045	Archie R. Dykes	576	1200	23,541 C²	S
Kansas City Art Institute; Kansas City, Mo. 64111	John W. Lottes	2700	1050⁷	598 C²	P
Kansas City Coll. of Osteopathic Med.; Kansas City, Mo. 64124	Rudolph S. Bremen	5000	n.a.	577 C	P

Institution and location	Chief executive	Tuition	Rm/Bd	Students*Control	
Kansas Newman College; Wichita, Kan. 67213	Rev. Roman S. Galiardi	1860	1140	624 C	P/RC
Kansas State College of Pittsburg, Pittsburg, Kan. 66762	George F. Budd	390	1300	5,688 C²	S
Kansas State University; Manhattan, Kan. 66506	Duane Acker	558	1219	17,901 C	S
Kansas Wesleyan; Salina, Kan. 67401	Daniel L. Bratton	1810	1075	429 C	P/UM
Kean College of New Jersey; Union, N.J. 07083	Nathan Weiss	535	810⁷	13,600 C	S
Kearney State College; Kearney, Neb. 68847	Brendan J. McDonald	496	920	5,234 C	S
Keene State College; Keene, N.H. 03431	Leo F. Redfern	617⁴	1175⁴	3,032 C¹	S
Kent State University; Kent, Ohio 44242	Glenn A. Olds	855	1200	26,800 C²	S
Kentucky, University of; Lexington, Ky. 40502	Otis A. Singletary	480	1400	18,845 C	S
Kentucky Christian College; Grayson, Ky. 41143	J. Lowell Lusby	512	1000	424 C	P/CC
Kentucky State University; Frankfort, Ky. 40601	William A. Butts	440	992	2,246 C²	S
Kentucky Wesleyan College; Owensboro, Ky. 42301	William James	1424	1230	700 C	P/M
Kenyon College; Gambier, Ohio 43022	Philip H. Jordan, Jr.	3420	1663	1,403 C²	P
Keuka College; Keuka Park, N.Y. 14478	William L. Boyle, Jr.	3400	1230	553 F	P
King College; Bristol, Tenn. 37620	Powell A. Fraser	2000	1150	293 C	Pres
King's College; Wilkes-Barre, Pa. 18711	Rev. Charles D. Sherrer	2300	1280	2,292 C²	P/RC
King's College, The; Briarcliff Manor, N.Y. 10510	Robert A. Cook	2325	1275	735 C⁵	P
Kirkland College; Clinton, N.Y. 13323	Samuel F. Babbitt	3850	1600	630 F	P
Kirksville Coll. of Osteopathic Med.; Kirksville, Mo. 63501	H. Charles Moore	5250	2600	487 C	P
Knox College; Galesburg, Ill. 61401	E. Inman Fox	3530	1280	1,150 C	P
Knoxville College; Knoxville, Tenn. 37921	Robert H. Harvey	1420	1080	885 C	P/UP
Kutztown State College; Kutztown, Pa. 19530	Lawrence M. Stratton	800	884	5,143 C	S
Ladycliff College; Highland Falls, N.Y. 10928	Rt. Rev. F. J. Breidenbach	2200	1350	484 C	P
Lafayette College; Easton, Pa. 18042	K. Roald Bergethon	3500	1500	1,970 C	P
LaGrange College; LaGrange, Ga. 30240	Waights G. Henry, Jr.	1530	975	675 C	P/M
Lake Erie College; Painesville, Ohio 44077	Paul Weaver	4500⁹		581 F	P
Lake Forest College; Lake Forest, Ill. 60045	Eugene Hotchkiss III	3650	1520	1,017 C	P
Lake Superior State College; Sault Ste. Marie, Mich. 49783	Kenneth J. Shouldice	591	1385	2,115 C	S
Lakeland College; Sheboygan, Wis. 53081	Rev. Ralph T. Mirse	2180	1445	435 C	P/UCC
Lamar University; Beaumont, Tex. 77710	John E. Gray	350	1530	12,156 C	S
Lambuth College; Jackson, Tenn. 38301	James S. Wilder, Jr.	1850	1100	870 C	P/UM
Lancaster Bible College; Lancaster, Pa. 17601	Stuart E. Lease	1400	1325	376 C	P/ID
Lander College; Greenwood, S.C. 29646	Larry A. Jackson	500	1200	1,570 C	S
Lane College; Jackson, Tenn. 38301	Herman Stone, Jr.	1050	1060	660 C	P/CME
Langston University; Langston, Okla. 73050	Thomas E. English	390	960	1,159 C	S
La Roche College; Pittsburgh, Pa. 15237	Sister Mary Joan Coultas	1850	725+	729 C	P/RC
La Salle College; Philadelphia, Pa. 19141	Brother Daniel W. Burke	2400	1250	3,361 C	P/RC
La Verne College; La Verne, Calif. 91750	Armen Sarafian	2700	1370	706 C	P
Lawrence Institute of Technology; Southfield, Mich. 48075	Wayne H. Buell	1200	2000	4,400 C²	P
Lawrence University; Appleton, Wis. 54911	Thomas S. Smith	3754	1236	1,353 C	P
Institute of Paper Chemistry, The; Appleton, Wis. 54911	Harry A. Posner, Jr.	3000	1300	80 C	P
Lebanon Valley College; Annville, Pa. 17003	Frederick P. Sample	2803⁸	1400⁸	1,011 C	P/UM
Lee College; Cleveland, Tenn. 37311	Charles W. Conn	1120	1100	1,065 C	P/CG
Lehigh University; Bethlehem, Pa. 18015	W. Deming Lewis	3550	1505	6,025 C	P
Le Moyne College; Syracuse, N.Y. 13214	Rev. William J. O'Halloran	1200	1400	1,859 C	P
LeMoyne-Owen College; Memphis, Tenn. 38106	Walter L. Walker	1350	n.a.	1,103 C	P/B
Lenoir Rhyne College; Hickory, N.C. 28601	Raymond Morris Bost	1950	900	1,285 C	P/LCA
Lesley College; Cambridge, Mass. 02138	Don A. Orton	3090	1840	2,222 F²	P
LeTourneau College; Longview, Tex. 75601	Richard Le Tourneau	1920	1245	700 C	P
Lewis and Clark College; Portland, Ore. 97219	John R. Howard	3100	1300	2,913 C	P
Lewis-Clark State College; Lewiston, Idaho 83501	Jerold O. Dugger	155	915+	1,495 C	S
Lewis University; Lockport, Ill. 60441	Lester Carr	2240	1450	3,318 C²	P/RC
Limestone College; Gaffney, S.C. 29340	Jack Jones Early	1825	1175	690 C	P
Lincoln Christian College; Lincoln, Ill. 62656	Robert E. Phillips	1500	900	769 C	P/CC
Lincoln Memorial University; Harrogate, Tenn. 37752	Frank W. Welch	(²⁴)	1050	840 C²	P
Lincoln University; Jefferson City, Mo. 65101	James Frank	360	830	2,485 C²	S
Lincoln University; Lincoln University, Pa. 19363	Herman R. Branson	1030	1350	1,150 C	S
Lindenwood Colleges, The; St. Charles, Mo. 63301	William C. Spencer	2400	1500	1,572 Co	P
Linfield College; McMinnville, Ore. 97128	Charles U. Walker	2440⁸	1400⁸	1,092 C²	P/B
Livingston University; Livingston, Ala. 35470	Asa N. Green	550	945	1,236 C	S
Livingstone College, Salisbury, N.C. 28144	F. George Shipman	1000	900	857 C	P/AME
Lock Haven State College; Lock Haven, Pa. 17745	Francis N. Hamblin	800	936+	2,268 C	S
Loma Linda Univ., La Sierra Campus; Riverside, Calif. 92505	V. Norskov Olsen	2700	3930	4,396 Co²⁵	SDA
Loma Linda Univ., Loma Linda Campus; Loma Linda, Calif. 92354	V. Norskov Olsen	2700	3930	4,396 Co²⁵	SDA
Lone Mountain College; San Francisco, Calif. 94118	Sister Gertrude Patch	2250	1500	900 C	P
Long Island University System; Greenvale, N.Y. 11548	Albert Bush-Brown			18,581 C	P
Brooklyn Center; Brooklyn, N.Y. 11201	Edward A. Clark	1920	1086⁷	6,616 C⁵	P
Brooklyn Center of Pharmacy; Brooklyn, N.Y. 11216	Arthur G. Zupko	2686	2000	850 C	P
C. W. Post Center; Brookville, N.Y. 11548	Edward J. Cook	2750	1800	9,950 C	P
Southampton College; Southampton, N.Y. 11968	Harry A. Marmion	2800	1990	1,165 C	P
Longwood College; Farmville, Va. 23901	Henry I. Willett, Jr.	585	1465	2,266 C	S
Loras College; Dubuque, Iowa 52001	Msgr. Francis P. Friedl	2000	1200	1,462 C	P/RC

Institution and location	Chief executive	Tuition	Rm/Bd	Students*	Control
Loretto Heights College; Denver, Colo. 80236	F. Adele Phelan	2950[8]	1650	720 C	P
Los Angeles Baptist College; Newhall, Calif. 91322	John R. Dunkin	1800	1200	303 C	P/B
Louisiana College; Pineville, La. 71360	Robert L. Lynn	780	950	1,170 C	P/B
Louisiana State Univ. System; Baton Rouge, La. 70803	Martin D. Woodin	....	....	42,841 C	S
LSU—Baton Rouge; Baton Rouge, La. 70803	Paul W. Murrill	330	1016	22,693 C	S
LSU in Shreveport; Shreveport, La. 71105	Donald E. Shipp, Jr.	280	n.a.	2,932 C	S
LSU Medical Center; New Orleans, La. 70112	Allen A. Copping	465	360[7]	2,071 C	S
Louisiana Tech University; Ruston, La. 71270	F. Jay Taylor	358	1050	8,174 C	S
Louisville, University of; Louisville, Ky. 40208	James Grier Miller	780	460[7]	15,781 C	S
Lowell, University of; Lowell, Mass. 01854	John B. Duff	345	1445	8,000 C	S
Loyola College; Baltimore, Md. 21210	Rev. Joseph A. Sellinger	1950	1400	1,685 C	P/RC
Loyola Marymount University; Los Angeles, Calif. 90045	Rev. Donald P. Merrifield	2800	1505	3,180 C	P/RC
Loyola University, New Orleans; New Orleans, La. 70118	Rev. James C. Carter	2100	701	4,462 C[2]	P/RC
Loyola University of Chicago; Chicago, Ill. 60611	Rev. Raymond C. Baumhart	2370	1507	12,354 C[5]	P
Lubbock Christian College; Lubbock, Tex. 79407	W. Joe Hacker	1472	730	1,004 C	P/CC
Luther College; Decorah, Iowa 52101	Elwin D. Farwell	2750	900	1,825 C	P
Lycoming College; Williamsport, Pa. 17701	Harold H. Hutson	3800	600	1,295 C	P/M
Lynchburg College; Lynchburg, Va. 24501	Carey Brewer	2450[8]	1350[8]	1,450 C	P
Lyndon State College; Lyndonville, Vt. 05851	Dr. Edward Stevens	720[4]	1280[4]	840 C	S
Macalester College; St. Paul, Minn. 55105	John B. Davis	3000	1250	1,586 C	P
MacMurray College; Jacksonville, Ill. 62650	John J. Wittich	2800	1250	749 C	P/UM
Madison College; Harrisonburg, Va. 22801	Ronald E. Carrier	672	1172	7,071 C	S
Madonna College; Livonia, Mich. 48150	Sister Mary Danatha	1120	1470	2,022 C[5]	P
Maine, University of:	Stanley L. Freeman	....	....	22,226 C	S
U. of Maine at Farmington; Farmington, Me. 04938	Einar A. Olsen	550	1395	2,032 C	S
U. of Maine at Fort Kent; Fort Kent, Me. 04743	Richard J. Spath	1100	1395	707 C	S
U. of Maine at Machias; Machias, Me. 04654	Arthur S. Buswell	550	1395	760 C[2]	S
U. of Maine at Orono; Orono, Me. 04473	Howard R. Neville	675	1505	10,513 C	S
U. of Maine at Portland-Gorham; Portland, Me. 04103	N. Edd Miller	600	1395	6,800 C	S
U. of Maine at Presque Isle; Presque Isle, Me. 04769	Stanley F. Salwak	550	1410	1,414 C[2]	S
Maine Maritime Academy; Castine, Me. 04421	Rr. Adm. E. A. Rodgers	700	1600	622 C[2]	S
Malone College; Canton, Ohio 44709	Lon D. Randall	1953	1084	842 C	P/SOF
Manchester College; North Manchester, Ind. 46962	A. Blair Helman	2200	1140	1,121 C	P/CB
Manhattan Christian College; Manhattan, Kan. 66502	W. F. Lown	1040	1050	275 C	P/CC
Manhattan College; Riverdale, Bronx, N.Y. 10471	Brother Stephen J. Sullivan	2600	1600+	4,283 C	P
Manhattan School of Music; New York, N.Y. 10027	George Schick	2650	n.a.	850 C[2]	P
Manhattanville College; Purchase, N.Y. 10577	Barbara Knowles Debs	3300	1800	2,498 C	P
Mannes College of Music; New York, N.Y. 10021	Rise Stevens	n.a.	n.a.	304 C[1]	P
Mansfield State College; Mansfield, Pa. 16933	Lawrence Park	800	925	3,000 C	S
Marian College; Indianapolis, Ind. 46222	Louis C. Gatto	1820	1120	801 C	P/RC
Marian College of Fond du Lac; Fond du Lac, Wis. 54935	James M. Hanlon	1550	1150	511 C	P/RC
Marietta College; Marietta, Ohio 45750	Sherrill Cleland	2700	1200	1,491 C	P
Marion College; Marion, Ind. 46952	Robert Luckey	1996	1220	840 C[2]	P/M
Marist College; Poughkeepsie, N.Y. 12601	Linus Richard Foy	2310	1380	1,867 C	P
Marlboro College; Marlboro, Vt. 05344	Thomas B. Ragle	3470	1570	196 C	P
Marquette University; Milwaukee, Wis. 53233	Rev. John P. Raynor	2650	1350	12,001 C[2]	P/RC
Mars Hill College; Mars Hill, N.C. 28754	Fred Blake Bentley	2050	850	1,605 C	P/SB
Marshall University; Huntington, W. Va. 25701	Robert B. Hayes	336	1500	10,367 C	S
Mary Baldwin College; Staunton, Va. 24401	Patricia H. Menk	3150	1300	577 F	P/Pres
Mary College; Bismarck, N.D. 58501	Harold J. Miller	1360	1050	853 C[2]	P/RC
Mary Hardin-Baylor College; Belton, Tex. 76513	Bobby E. Parker	1370	1060	1,091 C	P/B
Mary Washington College; Fredericksburg, Va. 22401	Prince B. Woodard	410	640	2,064 C	S
Marycrest College; Davenport, Iowa 52804	Ron Van Ryswyk	2250	1320	875 C	P/RC
Marygrove College; Detroit, Mich. 48221	Raymond A. Fleck	2000	1090	835 C	P
Maryland, University of (System); College Park, Md. 20742	Wilson H. Elkins	....	....		S
UM at Baltimore (UMAB); Baltimore, Md. 21201	Albin O. Kuhn	550[10]	475[7,10]	5,527 C[1]	S
UM, Baltimore County (UMBC); Catonsville, Md. 21228	Calvin B. T. Lee	758	2100	5,600 C	S
UM at College Park (UMCP); College Park, Md. 20742	Robert Gluckstern	1067	1808	33,803 C	S
UM Eastern Shore (UMES); Princess Anne, Md. 21853	William P. Hytche	1000	1300	1,034 C	S
UM University College (UMUC); College Park, Md. 20742	Stanley J. Drazek	(26)	n.a.	12,455 C	S
Maryland Institute, College of Art; Baltimore, Md. 21218	William Finn	2700	2100	950 C	P
Marymount College; Salina, Kan. 67401	Sister Mary Buser	1600	1190	705 C	P/RC
Marymount College; Tarrytown, N.Y. 10591	Robert E. Christin	2725[4]	1825[4]	872 F[1]	P
Marymount Manhattan College; New York, N.Y. 10021	Sister Colette Mahoney	2150	1750[7]	1,761 F	P
Maryville College; Maryville, Tenn. 37801	Joseph J. Copeland	1800	1025	607 C	P
Maryville College; St. Louis, Mo. 63141	Sister Harriet Kern Switzer	2350	1400	1,162 C	P
Marywood College; Scranton, Pa. 18509	Sister M. Coleman Nee	1700	1400	2,637 F	P/RC
Massachusetts at Amherst, Univ. of; Amherst, Mass. 01002	Randolph W. Bromery	345	1491	24,772 C	S
Massachusetts at Boston, Univ. of; Boston, Mass. 02125	Carlo L. Golino	300[4]	n.a.	7,380 C[1]	S
Massachusetts College of Art; Boston, Mass. 02215	John F. Nolan	500	n.a.	1,601 C[5]	S
Massachusetts Coll. of Optometry. See New England Coll. of Optometry.					

Institution and location	Chief executive	Tuition	Rm/Bd	Students*	Control
Massachusetts College of Pharmacy; Boston, Mass. 02115	Raymond A. Gosselin	2425	2100	1,200 C	P
Massachusetts Institute of Tech.; Cambridge, Mass. 01902	Jerome B. Wiesner	4000	2368	8,482 C[2]	P
Massachusetts Maritime Academy; Buzzards Bay, Mass. 02532	Lee Harrington	500	1600	745 M	S
Mayville State College; Mayville, N.D. 58257	James A. Schobel	472	885	675 C[2]	S
McKendree College; Lebanon, Ill. 62254	Julian Murphy	2304	1300	711 C[13]	M
McMurry College; Abilene, Tex. 79605	Thomas K. Kim	1470	1050	1,308 C	P/M
McNeese State University; Lake Charles, La. 70601	Thomas S. Leary	364	1080	5,720 C	S
McPherson College; McPherson, Kan. 67460	Paul W. Hoffman	1730	1060	485 C	CB
Medaille College; Buffalo, N.Y. 14214	Robert R. Hesse	1600	n.a.	683 C	P/Ind
Meharry Medical College; Nashville, Tenn. 37208	Lloyd C. Elam	2500	(27)	790 C[2]	P
Memphis Academy of Arts, The; Memphis, Tenn. 38112	Jameson M. Jones	1250	1500	220 C	P
Memphis State University; Memphis, Tenn. 38152	Billy Mac Jones	840[28]	1300	21,305 C	S
Menlo College Sch. of Bus. Admin.; Menlo Park, Calif. 94025	Richard F. O'Brien	2980	1680	540 C	P
Mercer University; Macon, Ga. 31207	Rufus Carrollton Harris	2514	1221	3,611 C[2]	P/SB
Mercer University in Atlanta; Atlanta, Ga. 30341	Jean Hendricks	1821	n.a.	1,004 C[5]	P/B
Mercer U. Southern School of Pharmacy; Atlanta, Ga. 30312	Oliver M. Littlejohn	2250	n.a.	345 C	P/B
Mercy College; Dobbs Ferry, N.Y. 10522	Donald Grunewald	1700	n.a.	4,681 C	P
Mercy College of Detroit; Detroit, Mich. 48219	Sister Agnes Mary Mansour	1800	1300	2,150 C	P/RC
Mercyhurst College; Erie, Pa. 16504	Marion L. Shane	2200	1155	1,484 C[2]	P/RC
Meredith College; Raleigh, N.C. 27611	John E. Weems	1900	1050	1,219 F	P/B
Merrimack College; North Andover, Mass. 01845	Rev. John A. Coughlan	2519	1650	1,800 C	P
Mesa College; Grand Junction, Colo. 81501	John U. Tomlinson	516	1060	4,093 C	S
Messiah College; Grantham, Pa. 17027	D. Ray Hostetter	2330	1260	997 C	P
Methodist College; Fayetteville, N.C. 28301	Richard W. Pearce	1380	1220	625 C	P/M
Metropolitan State College; Denver, Colo. 80204	James D. Palmer	348	n.a.	12,500 C[5]	S
Metropolitan State University; St. Paul, Minn. 55101	David E. Sweet	495	n.a.	1,730 C	S
Miami, University of; Coral Gables, Fla. 33124	Henry King Stanford	3463	1638	16,769 C	P
Miami University; Oxford, Ohio 45056	Phillip R. Shriver	870[19]	1440[19]	14,390 C[5]	S
Michigan, The University of; Ann Arbor, Mich. 48104	Robben W. Fleming	848[19]	1550[19]	37,505 C[2]	S
U. of Michigan—Dearborn; Dearborn, Mich. 48128	Leonard E. Goodall	640	n.a.	4,858 C[2]	S
U. of Michigan—Flint; Flint, Mich. 48503	William E. Moran	614	n.a.	3,474 C[2]	S
Michigan State University; East Lansing, Mich. 48824	Clifton R. Wharton	877	1342	40,808 C	S
Michigan Technological University; Houghton, Mich. 49931	Raymond L. Smith	645	1361	5,481 C	S
Mid-America Nazarene College; Olathe, Kan. 66061	R. Curtis Smith	n.a.	n.a.	975 C[1]	P/Naz
Mid-South Bible College; Memphis, Tenn. 38112	James B. Crichton	1274	1240	131 C	P
Middle Tennessee State Univ.; Murfreesboro, Tenn. 37132	M. G. Scarlett	406	799	9,701 C	S
Middlebury College; Middlebury, Vt. 05753	Olin C. Robison	5300[8,9]		1,832 C	P
Midland Lutheran College; Fremont, Neb. 68025	L. Dale Lund	2175	1060	685 C	P/LCA
Midwestern State University; Wichita Falls, Tex. 76308	John G. Barker	345	1110	4,540 C	S
Miles College; Birmingham, Ala. 35208	W. Clyde Williams	1164	1008	1,400 C	P/E
Millersville State College; Millersville, Pa. 17551	William H. Duncan	800	1000	6,179 C	S
Milligan College; Milligan College, Tenn. 37682	Jess W. Johnson	1630	1354	762 C	P/CC
Millikin University; Decatur, Ill. 62521	J. Roger Miller	2950	1200	1,500 C	P/UP
Mills College; Oakland, Calif. 94613	Barbara M. White	3025	1925	927 F	P
Millsaps College; Jackson, Miss. 39210	Edward M. Collins, Jr.	1886	940	915 C	P/M
Milton College; Milton, Wis. 53563	Joseph W. Kipper	2250	1250	477 C	P
Milwaukee School of Engineering; Milwaukee, Wis. 53201	Karl O. Werwath	2400	1260	2,200 C	P
Minneapolis Coll. of Art & Design; Minneapolis, Minn. 55404	Jerome Hausman	2200	1500	650 C	P
Minnesota, The University of; Minneapolis–St. Paul, Minn. 55455	C. Peter Magrath	630	1500	70,000 C[5]	S
U. of Minnesota, Duluth; Duluth, Minn. 55812	Raymond W. Darland	748	1380	5,500 C	S
U. of Minnesota, Morris; Morris, Minn. 56267	John Q. Imholte	630	1100	1,574 C[5]	S
Minnesota Bible College; Rochester, Minn. 55901	Bruce E. Miller	870	1200	137 C	P/CC
Minnesota Metropolitan State College; St. Paul, Minn. 55101	David E. Sweet	n.a.	n.a.	962 C[1]	S
Minnesota State College System; St. Paul, Minn. 55101	G. Theodore Mitau			39,929 C	S
Bemidji State University; Bemidji, Minn. 56601	Robert D. Decker	564	1115	4,208 C[2]	S
Mankato State University; Mankato, Minn. 56001	Douglas R. Moore	558	1145	13,616 C[2]	S
Moorhead State University; Moorhead, Minn. 56560	Roland Dille	432	1135	6,374 C[2]	S
St. Cloud State University; St. Cloud, Minn. 56301	Charles J. Graham	396	935+	10,118 C	S
Southwest Minnesota State University; Marshall, Minn. 56258	Catherine Tisinger	375	1100	1,600 C	S
Winona State University; Winona, Minn. 55987	R. A. DuFresne	558	1182	4,013 C[2]	S
Minot State College; Minot, N.D. 58701	Gordon B. Olson	459	900	2,210 C	S
Mississippi, The University of; University, Miss. 38677	Porter L. Fortune, Jr.	603	1000	8,500 C	S
Mississippi College; Clinton, Miss. 39058	Lewis Nobles	1200	890	2,889 C	B
Mississippi State University; Starkville, Miss. 39762	William L. Giles	561	1300	11,709 C[2]	S
Mississippi University for Women; Columbus, Miss. 39701	Charles P. Hogarth	480	1094	2,696 F	S
Mississippi Valley State University; Itta Bena, Miss. 38941	Ernest A. Boykins	432	748	2,752 C	S
Missouri, University of; Columbia, Mo. 65201	C. Brice Ratchford			51,000 C	S
Univ. of Missouri—Columbia; Columbia, Mo. 65201	Herbert W. Schooling	540	1220	23,400 C[2]	S
Univ. of Missouri—Kansas City; Kansas City, Mo. 64110	James C. Olson	540	1250	11,400 C[2]	S
Univ. of Missouri—Rolla; Rolla, Mo. 65401	Raymond Bisplinghoff	540	1250	4,350 C	S
Univ. of Missouri—St. Louis; St. Louis, Mo. 63121	Arnold B. Grobman	540	n.a.	11,850 C	S
Missouri Institute of Technology; Kansas City, Mo. 64108	C. R. LeValley	n.a.	n.a.	635 C[1]	P

Institution and location	Chief executive	Tuition	Rm/Bd	Students*	Control
Missouri Southern State College; Joplin, Mo. 64801	Leon C. Billingsly	310	900	3,711 C	S
Missouri Valley College; Marshall, Mo. 65340	Donald F. Ziemke	1844	1256	469 C	P
Missouri Western State College; St. Joseph, Mo. 64507	Marvin O. Looney	392	900	3,642 C	S
Mobile College; Mobile, Ala. 36613	William K. Weaver, Jr.	1300	1200	856 C	P/B
Molloy College; Rockville Centre, N.Y. 11570	Sister Janet A. Fitzgerald	2200	n.a.	1,225 F²	P/RC
Monmouth College; Monmouth, Ill. 61462	DeBow Freed	2780	1350	635 C	P/Pres
Monmouth College; West Long Branch, N.J. 07764	Richard J. Stonesifer	2730	1400	3,775 C	P
Montana, University of; Missoula, Mont. 59801	Richard C. Bowers	541	1497	8,693 C⁵	S
Montana College of Mineral Science & Technology; Butte, Mont. 59701	Fred W. DeMoney	425	1127	933 C	S
Montana State University; Bozeman, Mont. 59715	Carl W. McIntosh	510	1179	8,002 C	S
Montclair State College; Upper Montclair, N.J. 07043	David W. D. Dickson	680	608	15,107 C	S
Monterey Inst. of Foreign Studies; Monterey, Calif. 93940	Stuart H. McIntyre	2500	2430	390 C	P
Montevallo, University of; Montevallo, Ala. 35115	Kermit A. Johnson	400	900	4,000 C	S
Moody Bible Institute; Chicago, Ill. 60610	George Sweeting	n.a.	835	1,300 C	P/ID
Moore College of Art; Philadelphia, Pa. 19103	Mellicent B. Allen	3050	1450	685 F	P
Moorhead State Univ. See Minnesota State College System.					
Moravian College; Bethlehem, Pa. 18018	Herman E. Collier, Jr.	3060	1220	1,165 C	P
Morehead State University; Morehead, Ky. 40351	Adron Doran	450	1200	7,318 C	S
Morehouse College; Atlanta, Ga. 30313	Hugh M. Gloster	1900	1380	1,307 M	P
Morgan State University; Baltimore, Md. 21239	Andrew Billingsley	737	1440	4,583 C	*S
Morningside College; Sioux City, Iowa 51106	Thomas S. Thompson	2444	956	1,453 C	P/M
Morris Brown College; Atlanta, Ga. 30314	Robert Threatt	1600	2785	1,600 C	P/AME
Morris Harvey College; Charleston, W. Va. 25304	Robert Bliss	960	1050	2,134 C²	P
Mount Holyoke College; South Hadley, Mass. 01075	David Bicknell Truman	3350	1950	1,850 F	P
Mount Marty College; Yankton, S.D. 57078	Bruce E. Weier	1920	1130	564 C	P/RC
Mount Mary College; Milwaukee, Wis. 53222	Sister Mary Nora Barber	1750	1220	1,027 F	P
Mount Mercy College; Cedar Rapids, Iowa 52402	Sister Mary A. Hennessey	2205⁸	1089	900 C²	P/RC
Mount St. Joseph on the Ohio, College of; Mt. St. Joseph, Ohio 45051	Robert E. Wolverton	2000	1380	836 F²	P/RC
Mount Saint Mary College; Hooksett, N.H. 03106	Sister Amy Hoey	2000	1500	205 F	P/RC
Mount Saint Mary College; Newburgh, N.Y. 12550	William T. O'Hara	2220	1440	892 C²	P
Mount Saint Mary's College; Emmitsburg, Md. 21727	John J. Dillon	2170	1548	1,250 C	P/RC
Mount St. Mary's College; Los Angeles, Calif. 90049	Sister Cecilia Louise Moore	2000	1400	1,049 F	P/RC
Mount Saint Vincent, College of; Riverdale, N.Y. 10471	Sister Doris Smith	2300	1650	1,135 C²	P
Mount Senario College; Ladysmith, Wis. 54848	Robert E. Lovett	2150	1200	259 C¹³	P
Mount Sinai School of Medicine; New York, N.Y. 10029	Thomas C. Chalmers	4700	2500	333 C	P
Mount Union College; Alliance, Ohio 44601	Ronald G. Weber	2790	1245	1,012 C	P
Mount Vernon College; Washington, D.C. 20007	Peter D. Pelham	2900	2000	431 F	P
Mount Vernon Nazarene College; Mount Vernon, Ohio 43050	Rev. L. Guy Nees	1550	1100	801 C	P/Naz
Muhlenberg College; Allentown, Pa. 18104	John H. Morey	3125	1300	1,595 C²	P/L
Mundelein College; Chicago, Ill. 60660	Sister Susan Rink	2265	1425	1,300 F	P/RC
Murray State University; Murray, Ky. 42071	Constantine W. Curris	965	950	8,232 C²	S
Museum Art School; Portland, Ore. 97205	Warren A. Wolf	1430	n.a.	181 C	P
Museum of Fine Arts, School of the; Boston, Mass. 02115	William A. Bagnall	n.a.	n.a.	543 C¹	P
Muskingum College; New Concord, Ohio 43762	John Anthony Brown	2700	1180	1,033 C²	P
Nasson College; Springvale, Me. 04083	William Graham Cole	2940	1500	592 C	P
Nathaniel Hawthorne College; Antrim, N.H. 03440	Kenneth F. McLaughlin	2150	1100	500 C	P
National College of Business; Rapid City, S.D. 57701	John W. Hauer	1575	1200	4,304 C	P
National College of Education; Evanston, Ill. 60201	Calvin E. Gross	3000	1761	4,941 C	P
Naval Postgraduate School; Monterey, Calif. 93940	R. Adm. Isham Linder	n.a.	n.a.	987 C	F
Nazareth College at Kalamazoo; Nazareth, Mich. 49074	John Lore	2400	620	485 C⁵	RC
Nazareth College of Rochester; Rochester, N.Y. 14610	Robert A. Kidera	2500	1550	2,500 C	P
Nebraska, University of; Lincoln, Neb. 68508	D. B. Varner	555	1095	20,892 C	S
Nebraska at Omaha, University of; Omaha, Neb. 68101	Ronald W. Roskens	540	n.a.	14,294 C	S
Nebraska Wesleyan University; Lincoln, Neb. 68504	Vance D. Rogers	2100	1180	1,169 C²	P
Nevada, University of; Reno, Nev. 89507	Neil D. Humphrey			16,607 C	S
University of Nevada, Las Vegas; Las Vegas, Nev. 89154	Donald H. Baepler	450	1432	8,382 C	S
University of Nevada, Reno; Reno, Nev. 89507	Max Milam	2000	1200	8,225 C	S
New College of the U. of South Florida; Sarasota, Fla. 33580	George W. Mayer	1700	1350	440 C²	S
New England College; Henniker, N.H. 03242	J. Kenneth Cummiskey	3100	1500	1,280 C	P
New England College of Optometry²⁹; Boston, Mass. 02115	William R. Baldwin	3300	2700	300 C	P
New England Conservatory of Music; Boston, Mass. 02115	Gunther Schuller	3500	1992	759 C	P
New England School of Law; Boston, Mass. 02116	Colin W. Gillis	2300	n.a.	887 C	P
New Hampshire, University of; Durham, N.H. 03824	Eugene S. Mills	900	1400	9,800 C	S
New Hampshire College; Manchester, N.H. 03104	Edward M. Shapiro	2700	1616	844 C	P
New Haven, University of; West Haven, Conn. 06516	Phillip S. Kaplan	2150	1450	6,500 C	P
New Jersey Inst. of Technology; Newark, N.J. 07102	Paul H. Newell, Jr.	585	n.a.	4,835 C	S
New Mexico, The University of; Albuquerque, N.M. 87131	William Davis	520	1080	20,032 Co	S
New Mexico Highlands University; Las Vegas, N.M. 87701	John Arágon	349	960	2,099 C²	S
New Mexico Inst. of Mining & Tech.; Socorro, N.M. 87801	Kenneth W. Ford	264	1500	873 C	S
New Mexico State University; Las Cruces, N.M. 88001	Gerald W. Thomas	552	1070	10,092 C	S

Institution and location	Chief executive	Tuition	Rm/Bd	Students	*Control
New Orleans, University of; New Orleans, La. 70122	Homer L. Hitt	324	1168	13,031 C	S
New Orleans Baptist Theol. Sem.; New Orleans, La. 70126	Landrum P. Leavell II	210	1400	1,011 C	P/SB
New Rochelle, College of; New Rochelle, N.Y. 10801	Sister Dorothy Ann Kelly	2400	1600	2,897 C	P
New School for Social Research; New York, N.Y. 10011	John R. Everett	(30)	n.a.	16,000 C	P
New York, City University of; New York, N.Y. 10021	Robert J. Kibbee	....	....	225,425 C	Mun
Bernard M. Baruch College; New York, N.Y. 10010	Clyde J. Wingfield	775[13]	n.a.	16,220 C	Mun
Brooklyn College; Brooklyn, N.Y. 11210	John W. Kneller	775[13]	n.a.	36,972 C[2]	Mun
City College; New York, N.Y. 10031	Robert E. Marshak	775[13]	n.a.	18,690 C	Mun
Graduate School & Univ. Center; New York, N.Y. 10036	Harold M. Proshansky	1500	n.a.	2,680 C	Mun/S
Herbert H. Lehman College; Bronx, N.Y. 10468	Leonard Lief	775[13]	n.a.	12,782 C	Mun
Hunter College, New York, N.Y. 10021	Jacqueline G. Wexler	775[13]	n.a.	21,400 C	Mun
John Jay Coll. of Criminal Justice; New York, N.Y. 10019	Donald H. Riddle	775[13]	n.a.	9,729 C[1]	Mun
Queens College; Flushing, N.Y. 11367	(Vacant)	775[13]	n.a.	25,009 C	Mun
Richmond College; Staten Island, N.Y. 10301	Edmond L. Volpe	775[13]	n.a.	3,600 C	Mun
York College; Jamaica, N.Y. 11451	Milton G. Bassin	775[13]	n.a.	5,202 C[4]	Mun
New York, State University of; Albany, N.Y. 12210	Ernest L. Boyer	....	....	....	S
SUNY at Albany; Albany, N.Y. 12222	Emmett B. Fields	650+	1380	14,750 C	S
SUNY at Binghamton; Binghamton, N.Y. 13901	Clifford D. Clark	750+	1550	9,695 C[2]	S
SUNY at Buffalo; Buffalo, N.Y. 14214	Robert L. Ketter	750+	1590	24,971 C	S
SUNY at Stony Brook; Stony Brook, N.Y. 11794	John S. Toll	750+	1500	15,713 C	S
SUNY Coll. at Brockport; Brockport, N.Y. 14420	Albert W. Brown	725	1340	11,103 C	S
SUNY Coll. at Buffalo; Buffalo, N.Y. 14222	E. K. Fretwell, Jr.	650	1400	12,081 C	S
SUNY Coll. at Cortland, Cortland, N.Y. 13045	Richard C. Jones	750+	1459+	5,665 C	S
SUNY Coll. at Fredonia, Fredonia, N.Y. 14063	Dallas K. Beal	1450	2620	4,937 C	S
SUNY Coll. at Geneseo, Geneseo, N.Y. 14454	Robert W. MacVittie	883	1300	6,031 C	S
SUNY Coll. at New Paltz; New Paltz, N.Y. 12561	Stanley K. Coffman, Jr.	750+	1550[13]	8,892 C[2]	S
SUNY Coll. at Oneonta; Oneonta, N.Y. 13820	Clifford J. Craven	650+	1275	6,253 C[2]	S
SUNY Coll. at Oswego; Oswego, N.Y. 13126	James E. Perdue	800[4]	1355[4]	9,143 C[1]	S
SUNY Coll. at Plattsburgh; Plattsburgh, N.Y. 12901	Joseph C. Burke	883+	700	6,181 C	S
SUNY Coll. at Potsdam; Potsdam, N.Y. 13676	Thomas M. Barrington	650+	1400	4,047 C	S
SUNY Empire State College; Saratoga Springs, N.Y. 12866	James W. Hall	650+	n.a.	4,000 C	S
Coll. of Environmental Sci. & Forestry; Syracuse, N.Y. 13210	Edward E. Palmer	650[4]	1500[4]	2,062 C[4]	S
Downstate Medical Center; Brooklyn, N.Y. 11203	Calvin H. Plimpton	2200	n.a.	1,486 C[13]	S
Maritime College; Fort Schuyler, Bronx, N.Y. 10465	Rr. Adm. Sheldon H. Kinney	750+	1900	834 C[2]	S
Upstate Medical Center; Syracuse, N.Y. 13210	Richard P. Schmidt	725[4]	1492[4]	973 C[4]	S
New York Coll. of Podiatric Medicine; New York, N.Y. 10035	Murray Edelstein	3500	n.a.	351 C	P
New York Inst. of Technology; Old Westbury, N.Y. 11568	Alexander Schure	2200	2000	19,685 C[2]	P
New York Law School; New York, N.Y. 10013	E. Donald Shapiro	n.a.	n.a.	1,030 C	P
New York Medical College; New York, N.Y. 10029	Lawrence B. Slobody	n.a.	n.a.	705 C[1]	P
New York University; New York, N.Y. 10003	John C. Sawhill	3400	2000	29,698 C	P
Newberry College; Newberry, S.C. 29108	Glenn E. Whiteside	2225	1175	827 C	LCA
Newcomb College. See Tulane University.					
Niagara University; Niagara Falls, N.Y. 14109	Rev. Gerard Mahoney	1125	1350	4,123 C	P/RC
Nicholls State University; Thibodaux, La. 70301	Vernon F. Galliano	350	960	6,066 C	S
Nichols College; Dudley, Mass. 01570	Darcy C. Coyle	2250	3800	583 C	P
Norfolk State College; Norfolk, Va. 23504	Harrison B. Wilson	481	1144	6,827 C	S
North Adams State College; North Adams, Mass. 01247	James T. Amsler	500	1315	2,075 C	S
North Alabama, University of; Florence, Ala. 35630	Robert M. Guillot	520	980	4,624 C	S
North Carolina, University System of; Chapel Hill, N.C. 27514	William C. Friday	....	....	102,699 C	S
Appalachian State University; Boone, N.C. 28608	Herbert W. Wey	544	1055	9,945 C	S
East Carolina University; Greenville, N.C. 27834	Leo W. Jenkins	483	1110	11,015 C	S
Elizabeth City State University; Elizabeth City, N.C. 27909	Marion D. Thorpe	641	970	1,605 C	S
Fayetteville State University; Fayetteville, N.C. 28301	Charles A. Lyons, Jr.	246	1031+	2,002 C	S
North Carolina Agri. & Tech. St. U.; Greensboro, N.C. 274	Lewis C. Dowdy	276	960	5,209 C	S
North Carolina Central University; Durham, N.C. 27707	Albert N. Whiting	282	1065	4,729 C	S
North Carolina Sch. of the Arts; Winston-Salem, N.C. 27107	Robert Suderburg	516	1385	561 C	S
N.C. State Univ. at Raleigh; Raleigh, N.C. 27607	Joab L. Thomas	524	1350	16,542 C	S
Pembroke State University; Pembroke, N.C. 28372	English E. Jones	220	870	2,033 C	S
Univ. of N.C. at Asheville; Asheville, N.C. 28804	William E. Highsmith	246	840	1,841 C	S
Univ. of N.C. at Chapel Hill; Chapel Hill, N.C. 27514	N. Ferebee Taylor	330	1350	19,370 C	S
Univ. of N.C. at Charlotte; Charlotte, N.C. 28223	D. W. Colvard	240	1025	7,252 C	S
Univ. of N.C. at Greensboro; Greensboro, N.C. 27412	James S. Ferguson	330	1080	9,155 C	S
Univ. of N.C. at Wilmington; Wilmington, N.C. 28401	William H. Wagoner	362	1150	3,033 C	S
Western Carolina University; Cullowhee, N.C. 28723	Harold Frank Robinson	282	915	6,084 C[5]	S
Winston-Salem State Univ.; Winston-Salem, N.C. 27102	Kenneth R. Williams	560	1208	2,323 C	S
North Carolina Wesleyan College; Rocky Mount, N.C. 27801	S. Bruce Petteway	1720	1060	481 C	P/M
North Central Bible College; Minneapolis, Minn. 55404	Rev. E. M. Clark	1152	1008	530 C	P
North Central College; Naperville, Ill. 60540	Gael D. Swing	2715	1290	882 C	P/M
North Dakota, University of; Grand Forks, N.D. 58202	Thomas J. Clifford	456	950	8,632 C[2]	S
North Dakota State University; Fargo, N.D. 58102	L. D. Loftsgard	504	1100	6,957 C[2]	S
North Florida, University of; Jacksonville, Fla. 32216	Thomas G. Carpenter	900	1870[23]	3,994 C	Mun

Institution and location	Chief executive	Tuition	Rm/Bd	Students*	Control
North Georgia College; Dahlonega, Ga. 30533	John H. Owen	543	1080	1,765 C	S
North Park College; Chicago, Ill. 60625	Lloyd H. Ahlem	2595	1365	1,041 C	P/EC
North Texas State University; Denton, Tex. 76203	C. C. Nolen	190	1200	15,607 C	S
Northeast Louisiana University; Monroe, La. 71201	Delbert D. Vines	342	1080	9,040 C	S
Northeast Missouri State University; Kirksville, Mo. 63501	Charles J. McClain	310	980	5,500 C	S
Northeastern Bible College; Essex Fells, N.J. 07021	Charles W. Anderson	1600	1280	413 C	P
Northeastern Illinois University; Chicago, Ill. 60625	(Vacant)	420	n.a.	9,492 C[5]	S
Northeastern Oklahoma State Univ.; Tahlequah, Okla. 74464	Robert E. Collier	360	1100	5,763 C	S
Northeastern University; Boston, Mass. 02115	Kenneth G. Ryder	2370	1700	14,600 C	P
Northern Arizona University; Flagstaff, Ariz. 86001	J. Lawrence Walkup	400	1000+	10,956 C	S
Northern Colorado, University of; Greeley, Colo. 80639	Richard R. Bond	525	1170	9,655 C	S
Northern Illinois University; DeKalb, Ill. 60115	Richard J. Nelson	619	1300+	20,117 C	S
Northern Iowa, University of; Cedar Falls, Iowa 50613	John J. Kamerick	630	1100	8,676 C	S
Northern Kentucky University; Highland Heights, Ky. 41076	A. D. Albright	420	n.a.	5,618 C	S
Northern Michigan University; Marquette, Mich. 49855	John X. Jamrich	666	1376	8,800 C	S
Northern Montana College; Havre, Mont. 59501	Duane M. Leach	435	1040	1,160 C	S
Northern State College; Aberdeen, S.D. 57401	Norbert K. Baumgart	504	938	2,369 C[2]	S
Northland College; Ashland, Wis. 54806	Malcolm McLean	2360	1380	710 C	P
Northrop University; Inglewood, Calif. 90306	B. J. Shell	2250	1485	1,500 C	P
Northwest Bible College; Minot, N.D. 58701	Laud O. Vaught	(31)	1050	145 C	P/CG
Northwest Christian College; Eugene, Ore. 97401	Barton A. Dowdy	1125	1065	453 C	P/CC
Northwest College; Kirkland, Wash. 98033	D. V. Hurst	1185	1069	540 C	P/AG
Northwest Missouri State University; Maryville, Mo. 64468	Robert P. Foster	330	980	4,503 C	S
Northwest Nazarene College; Nampa, Idaho 83651	Kenneth H. Pearsall	2785	1200	1,112 C[2]	P/Naz
Northwestern College; Orange City, Iowa 51041	Virgil Rowenhorst	1875	913	755 C[2]	P/RCA
Northwestern Oklahoma State University; Alva, Okla. 73717	Joe J. Struckle	352	960	1,819 C	S
Northwestern State University of La.; Natchitoches, La. 71457	Arnold R. Kilpatrick	315	990	6,685 C	S
Northwestern University; Evanston, Ill. 60201	Robert H. Strotz	4280[8]	1700[8]	10,100 C[5]	P
Northwood Institute; Midland, Mich. 48640	Arthur E. Turner	2010	1180	1,200 C	P
Norwich University; Northfield, Vt. 05663	Loring E. Hart	4590	n.a.	1,099 C	P
Notre Dame, College of; Belmont, Calif. 94002	Sister C. J. Cunningham	2000	1450	1,000 C	RC
Notre Dame, University of; Notre Dame, Ind. 46556	Rev. Theodore M. Hesburgh	3180	1360	8,600 C	P/RC
Notre Dame College; Cleveland, Ohio 44121	Sister Mary Marthe Reinhard	1650	1230	605 F	P/RC
Notre Dame College; Manchester, N.H. 03104	Sister Jeannette Vezeau	1800	400	400 F	P/RC
Notre Dame College; St. Louis, Mo. 63125	Sister Barbara Brumleve	1250	n.a.	381 C	P/RC
Notre Dame of Maryland, College of; Baltimore, Md. 21210	Sister Kathleen Feeley	2100	1400+	802 F	P/RC
Nova University; Ft. Lauderdale, Fla. 33314	Abraham S. Fischler	2000	3500	3,886 C	P
Nyack College; Nyack, N.Y. 10960	Thomas P. Bailey	2040	1210	639 C	P/CMA
Oakland University; Rochester, Mich. 48063	Donald D. O'Dowd	725	1418	9,976 C[5]	S
Oakwood College; Huntsville, Ala. 35806	Calvin B. Rock	2982	1005	980 C	P/SDA
Oberlin College; Oberlin, Ohio 44074	Emil C. Danenberg	3775[8]	1560	2,750 C	P
Occidental College; Los Angeles, Calif. 90041	Richard C. Gilman	3552	1740	1,671 C	P
Oglethorpe University; Atlanta, Ga. 30319	Manning Pattillo	2386	1200	830 C	P
Ohio at Toledo, Medical College of; Toledo, Ohio 43614	Marion C. Anderson	1200	n.a.	246 C	S
Ohio College of Podiatric Medicine; Cleveland, Ohio 44106	Abe Rubin	3500	n.a.	487 C	P
Ohio Dominican College; Columbus, Ohio 43219	Sister Suzanne Uhrhane	2200	1360	1,010 C[2]	P/RC
Ohio Institute of Technology; Columbus, Ohio 43209	R. A. Czerniak	1880	1292	3,162 C[2]	P
Ohio Northern University; Ada, Ohio 45810	Samuel L. Meyer	2511	1245	2,571 C	P/UM
Ohio State University, The; Columbus, Ohio 43210	Harold L. Enarson	....	....	50,425 C	S
Columbus, Ohio 43210	Harold L. Enarson	810	1473	46,817 C	S
Lima Campus; Lima, Ohio 45804	James S. Biddle	765	n.a.	811 C	S
Mansfield Campus; Mansfield, Ohio 44906	James B. Heck	765	n.a.	905 C	S
Marion Campus; Marion, Ohio 43302	C. Eugene Maynard	765	n.a.	607 C	S
Newark Campus; Newark, Ohio 43055	Robert A. Barnes	765	n.a.	656 C	S
Ohio University; Athens, Ohio 45701	Charles J. Ping	825	1545	15,140 C	S
Ohio Wesleyan University; Delaware, Ohio 43015	Thomas E. Wenzlau	3375	1400	2,115 C	P
Oklahoma, University of; Norman, Okla. 73019	Paul F. Sharp	448	1054	19,799 C	S
Oklahoma, Univ. of Science and Arts of; Chickasha, Okla. 73018	Roy Troutt	350	1000	1,400 C	S
Oklahoma Baptist University; Shawnee, Okla. 74801	William G. Tanner	1050	920	1,644 C	P/B
Oklahoma Christian College; Oklahoma City, Okla. 73111	J. Terry Johnson	1300	1040	1,450 C[2]	P/CC
Oklahoma City University; Oklahoma City, Okla. 73106	Dolphus Whitten, Jr.	1500	980	3,000 C	P
Oklahoma Coll. of Osteopathic Med.& Surgery; Tulsa, Okla. 74119	John Barson	1725	n.a.	168 C	S
Oklahoma Panhandle State University; Goodwell, Okla. 73939	Thomas L. Palmer	325	940	963 C	S
Oklahoma State University; Stillwater, Okla. 74074	Robert B. Kamm	474[4]	900[4]	18,009 C[4]	S
Old Dominion University; Norfolk, Va. 23508	Alfred B. Rollins, Jr.	620	1350	13,160 C[2]	S
Olivet College; Olivet, Mich. 49076	Ray B. Loeschner	2450	1380	792 C	P
Olivet Nazarene College; Kankakee, Ill. 60901	Leslie Parrott	1600	1080	1,693 C	P/E
Oral Roberts University; Tulsa, Okla. 74102	Oral Roberts	1400	1300	3,500 C	P
Oregon, University of; Eugene, Ore. 97403	William Beatty Boyd	650	1357	15,488 C	S
Oregon College of Education; Monmouth, Ore. 97361	Leonard W. Rice	680	1260	3,400 C	S
Oregon Graduate Center; Beaverton, Ore. 97005	Ira C. Keller	(32)	n.a.	26 C	P
Oregon Institute of Technology; Klamath Falls, Ore. 97601	Winston D. Purvine	700	1400	1,855 C	S

Institution and location	Chief executive	Tuition	Rm/Bd	Students*	Control
Oregon State University; Corvallis, Ore. 97331	Robert W. MacVicar	639	1215	16,188 C[5]	S
Osteopathic Med. & Surgery, Coll. of; Des Moines, Iowa 50312	J. Leonard Azneer	5500	n.a.	522 C	P
Otis Art Inst. of Los Angeles County; Los Angeles, Calif. 90057	Gurdon Woods	1010	n.a.	190 C	Co
Ottawa University; Ottawa, Kan. 66067	Peter H. Armacost	2160	1170	608 C	P
Otterbein College; Westerville, Ohio 43081	Thomas Jefferson Kerr IV	3215	1105	1,260 C	P/UM
Ouachita Baptist University; Arkadelphia, Ark. 71923	Daniel R. Grant	1360	1240	1,594 C	P/B
Our Lady of Angels College; Aston, Pa. 19014	Sister M. M. Cunningham	1700	n.a.	516 F	P/RC
Our Lady of Holy Cross College; New Orleans, La. 70114	Sister Enda Eileen Byrne	1300	n.a.	934 C	P/RC
Our Lady of the Elms, College of; Chicopee, Mass. 01013	Edward R. D'Alessio	1900	1200	410 F	P/RC
Our Lady of the Lake Coll. See Our Lady of the Lake Univ. of San Antonio.					
Our Lady of the Lake University of San Antonio; San Antonio, Tex. 78285	Gerald P. Burns	1740	1535	1,978 C	RC
Ozarks, The College of the; Clarksville, Ark. 72830	R. L. Qualls	810	950	450 C	P/Pres
Ozarks, The School of the; Point Lookout, Mo. 65726	M. Graham Clark	(33)		1,114 C	P
Pace University; New York; N.Y. 10038	Edward J. Mortola	2300	1100	6,366 C	P
Pacific, University of the; Stockton, Calif. 95211	Stanley E. McCaffrey	3766	1806	4,289 C	P
Pacific Christian College; Fullerton, Calif. 92631	Medford H. Jones	1350[8]	1386[8]	466 C	P/CC
Pacific College of Fresno; Fresno, Calif. 93702	Edmund Janzen	1800	1500	465 C[2]	P/MB
Pacific Lutheran University; Tacoma, Wash. 98447	William O. Rieke	2688	1300	3,314 C	P
Pacific Oaks College; Pasadena, Calif. 91105	Karen Fite	2160	n.a.	313 C	P
Pacific Union College; Angwin, Calif. 94508	John W. Cassell, Jr.	2655	1320	2,089 C	P/SDA
Pacific University; Forest Grove, Ore. 97116	James V. Miller	2660	1328	1,062 C	P/UCC
Paine College; Augusta, Ga. 30901	Julius S. Scott, Jr.	1250	1000	835 C	P/M
Palm Beach Atlantic College; West Palm Beach, Fla. 33403	Warner Earle Fusselle	1550	1170	458 C	P/B
Pan American University; Edinburg, Tex. 78539	Ralph F. Schilling	290	1000	8,249 C	S
Paper Chemistry, The Institute of. See Lawrence University.					
Park College; Parkville, Mo. 64152	Gerald Knutson	2320	1250	884 C[2]	P
Parks College of St. Louis University; Cahokia, Ill. 62206	Leon Z. Seltzer	1750	1215	710 C	P/RC
Paul Quinn College; Waco, Tex. 76704	Stanley E. Rutland	840	1100	462 C	P/AME
Peabody Conservatory of Music; Baltimore, Md. 21202	Richard Franko Goldman	2700[4]	1050[4]	473 C[4]	P
Pembroke State Univ. See Univ. System of North Carolina.					
Pennsylvania, Baptist Bible Coll. of; Clarks Summit, Pa. 18411	Ernest D. Pickering	1552	1335	811 C	P/B
Pennsylvania, Medical Coll. of; Philadelphia, Pa. 19129	Jeanne Brugger	5000[8]	n.a.	389 C	P
Pennsylvania, University of; Philadelphia, Pa. 19174	Martin Meyerson	4125	2100	19,260 C	P
Pennsylvania College of Optometry; Philadelphia, Pa. 19141	Norman E. Wallis	3125	2000	545 C	P
Pennsylvania Coll. of Podiatric Med.; Philadelphia, Pa. 19107	James E. Bates	3600	5330	454 C	P
Pennsylvania State University, The; University Park, Pa. 16802	John W. Oswald	1095	1389	70,767 C	S
Pepperdine University; Malibu, Calif. 90265	William S. Banowsky	3400	1600	9,200 C	P
Peru State College; Peru, Neb. 68421	Douglas W. Pearson	496	990	820 C[2]	S
Pfeiffer College; Misenheimer, N.C. 28109	Douglas Reid Sasser	1600	1150	969 C	P/M
Philadelphia College of Art; Philadelphia, Pa. 19102	Thomas F. Schutte	3465	1500	1,030 C	P
Philadelphia College of Bible; Philadelphia, Pa. 19103	Rev. Douglas B. MacCorkle	1600	1176	673 C	P/ID
Philadelphia Coll. of Osteopathic Med.; Philadelphia, Pa. 19131	Thomas M. Rowland, Jr.	2100	n.a.	798 C	P
Philadelphia Coll. of Pharmacy & Sci.; Philadelphia, Pa. 19104	John V. Bergen	2425	725[7]	1,047 C	P
Philadelphia Coll. of Textiles & Sci.; Philadelphia, Pa. 19144	Lawson A. Pendleton	2100[19]	1375[19]	1,097 C	P
Philadelphia Musical Academy; Philadelphia, Pa. 19107	Joseph Castaldo	2600	n.a.	265 C	P
Philander Smith College; Little Rock, Ark. 72203	Walter R. Hazzard	650	775	775 C	P/UM
Phillips University; Enid, Okla. 73701	Thomas Edward Broce	1200	1000	1,384 C	P
Piedmont Bible College; Winston-Salem, N.C. 27101	Donald K. Drake	1300	1010	469 C	P/B
Piedmont College; Demorest, Ga. 30535	James E. Walter	1175	1200	455 C	P/Ind
Pikeville College; Pikeville, Ky. 41501	Jackson O. Hall	1100	990+	618 C	P
Pittsburgh, University of; Pittsburgh, Pa. 15260	Wesley W. Posvar	1140	1400	35,120 C[2]	P&S
Pitzer College. See Claremont Colleges.					
Plymouth State College; Plymouth, N.H. 03264	Harold E. Hyde	700	1220	3,014 C[2]	S
Point Loma College; San Diego, Calif. 92106	W. Shelburne Brown	2400	1095	1,638 C	P/Naz
Point Park College; Pittsburgh, Pa. 15222	John V. Hopkins	1945	1380	991 C	P
Polytechnic Institute of New York; Brooklyn, N.Y. 11201	George Bugliarello	1650	1400[19]	4,366 C	P
Pomona College. See Claremont Colleges.					
Portland, University of; Portland, Ore. 97203	Rev. Paul E. Waldschmidt	2450	750	2,222 C	P
Portland State University; Portland, Ore. 97207	Joseph C. Blumel	648	n.a.	13,500 C	S
Prairie View A&M University[34]; Prairie View, Tex. 77445	Alvin I. Thomas	136	769	5,236 C	S
Pratt Institute; Brooklyn, N.Y. 11205	Richardson Pratt, Jr.	3162	1500[7]	4,345 C	P
Presbyterian College; Clinton, S.C. 29325	Marc C. Weersing	2180	1120	833 C	P
Princeton University; Princeton, N.J. 08540	William G. Bowen	4300[8]	1975	5,964 C	P
Principia College; Elsah, Ill. 62028	David K. Andrews	3375	1800	850 C	P
Providence College; Providence, R.I. 02918	V. Rev. Thomas R. Peterson	2425	1450	3,250 C	P
Puerto Rico, Inter American U. of; San Germán, P.R. 00753	Sol Luis Descartes	840	1116	23,279 C[2]	P/Ind
Puerto Rico, University of; Rio Piedras, P.R. 00931	Arturo Morales Carrión	180	n.a.	25,719 C[2]	S
Cayey University College; Cayey, P.R. 00633	Fernando Torres	n.a.	n.a.	2,573 C[1]	Pub
Mayaguez Campus; Mayaguez, P.R. 00708	Rafael Pietre Oms	90	300	9,334 C	S
Medical Sciences Center; San Juan, P.R. 00936	Jorge Fernandez	640	n.a.	2,086 C	S

Institution and location	Chief executive	Tuition	Rm/Bd	Students*	Control
Rio Piedras Campus; Rio Piedras, P.R. 00931	Ismael Rodriguez Bou	n.a.	n.a.	26,042 C[1]	Pub
Puget Sound, University of; Tacoma, Wash. 98416	Philip M. Phibbs	2899	1400	3,012 C	P
Purdue University; West Lafayette, Ind. 47907	Arthur G. Hansen	750	1390	27,768 C	S
Calumet Campus; Hammond, Ind. 46323	R. J. Combs	900	n.a.	6,478 C	S
Fort Wayne Campus. See Indiana University.					
Indiana U.-Purdue U. at Indianapolis. See Indiana U.					
Queens College; Charlotte, N.C. 28274	Alfred O. Canon	2160	1240	571 F[2]	P
Quincy College; Quincy, Ill. 62301	Rev. Titus Ludes	1980	1290	1,137 C	P
Quinnipiac College; Hamden, Conn. 06518	Leonard J. Kent	2200	1450	3,173 C	P
Radcliffe College. See Harvard University.					
Radford College; Radford, Va. 24142	Donald Newton Dedmon	702	1386	4,500 C	S
Randolph-Macon College; Ashland, Va. 23005	Luther W. White III	2840	1050	763 C	P
Randolph-Macon Woman's College; Lynchburg, Va. 24503	William Fletcher Quillian, Jr.	3050	1725	686 F	P
Redlands, University of; Redlands, Calif. 92373	Eugene E. Dawson	3425	1425	2,598 C[2]	P
Reed College; Portland, Ore. 97202	Paul E. Bragdon	3880	1550	1,180 C[2]	P
Reformed Bible College; Grand Rapids, Mich. 49506	Dick L. Van Halsema	1100	1000	198 C	P
Regis College; Denver, Colo. 80221	Rev. David M. Clarke	1360	1486	1,017 C	P
Regis College; Weston, Mass. 02193	Sister Thérèse Higgins	2300	1450+	753 F	P/RC
Rensselaer Polytechnic Institute; Troy, N.Y. 12181	George Low	3700	1675	4,882 C	P
Rensselaer Hartford Graduate Center; Hartford, Conn. 06120	Homer D. Babbidge, Jr.	([35])	n.a.	710 C	P
Rhode Island, University of; Kingston, R.I. 02881	Frank Newman	n.a.	1620	10,968 C	S
Rhode Island College; Providence, R.I. 02908	Charles B. Willard	625	1410	8,714 C	S
Rhode Island School of Design; Providence, R.I. 02903	Lee Hall	3500	1550	1,441 C	P
Rice University; Houston, Tex. 77001	Norman Hackerman	2300	1697	3,598 C	P
Richmond, University of; Richmond, Va. 23173	E. Bruce Heilman	2600	1375	2,900 C	P/B
Richmond College (NYC). See New York, City University of.					
Ricker College; Houlton, Me. 04730	William D. Abbott	2500	1250	827 C	P
Rider College; Lawrenceville, N.J. 08602	Frank N. Elliott	2400	1300	5,785 C	P
Rio Grande College; Rio Grande, Ohio 45674	Paul D. Hines	650+	1275	950 C[2]	P
Ripon College; Ripon, Wis. 54971	Bernard S. Adams	2950	1140	898 C	P
Rivier College; Nashua, N.H. 03060	Sister Doris Benoit	1700	1300	1,016 F	P/RC
Roanoke College; Salem, Va. 24153	Norman D. Fintel	2525[8]	1345	1,252 C[2]	P
Robert Morris College; Coraopolis, Pa. 15108	Charles L. Sewall	1750	1200	3,575 C	P
Roberts Wesleyan College; Rochester, N.Y. 14624	Paul L. Adams	2214	1350	632 C[5]	P/FM
Rochester, The University of; Rochester, N.Y. 14627	Robert L. Sproull	3775	1883	7,958 C	P
Rochester Institute of Technology; Rochester, N.Y. 14623	Paul A. Miller	2898	1593	12,671 C[2]	P
Rockford College; Rockford, Ill. 61101	John A. Howard	2400	1280	1,375 C	P
Rockhurst College; Kansas City, Mo. 64110	Rev. Maurice E. Van Ackeren	2050	1290	3,401 C	P/RC
Rocky Mountain College; Billings, Mont. 59102	Bruce T. Alton	1650	1050	450 C	P[36]
Roger Williams College; Bristol, R.I. 02809	William Rizzini	2096	1590	1,563 C	P
Rollins College; Winter Park, Fla. 32789	Jack B. Critchfield	2850	1450	1,250 C	P
Roosevelt University; Chicago, Ill. 60605	Rolf A. Weil	2327	1697	7,447 C	P
Rosary College; River Forest, Ill. 60305	Sister Candida Lund	2300	1560	1,257 C	P/RC
Rosary Hill College; Snyder, N.Y. 14226	Robert S. Marshall	2450	1350	1,375 C	P
Rose-Hulman Inst. of Technology; Terre Haute, Ind. 47803	Samuel F. Hulbert	2700	1275	1,000 M	P
Rosemont College; Rosemont, Pa. 19010	Sister Ann Marie Durst	2650[8]	1700[8]	694 F	P/RC
Rush University; Chicago, Ill. 60612	James A. Campbell	2850	1500	600 C	P
Russell Sage College; Troy, N.Y. 12180	William Kahl	2600	1700	1,214 F	P
Rust College; Holly Springs, Miss. 38635	William A. McMillan	2220	995	832 C	P/UM
Rutgers University; New Brunswick, N.J. 08903	Edward J. Bloustein	585	1275	46,305 C[2]	S
Douglass College; New Brunswick, N.J. 08903	Jewel P. Cobb	750	1650	3,473 F	S
Sacred Heart, College of the; Santurce, P.R. 00914	Pedro González-Ramos	1200	1425[16]	3,351 C[2]	P/RC
Sacred Heart College; Belmont, N.C. 28012	Sister Mary Michel Boulus	1200	1225	315 F	P/RC
Sacred Heart University; Bridgeport, Conn. 06605	(Vacant)	2100	n.a.	2,382 C	P
Saginaw Valley State College; University Center, Mich. 48710	Jack M. Ryder	680	1400	3,046 C[5]	S
St. Ambrose College; Davenport, Iowa 52803	William J. Bakrow	2160	1266	1,426 C	P/RC
St. Andrews Presbyterian College; Laurinburg, N.C. 28352	Alvin P. Perkinson, Jr.	1940	1055	526 C	P/Pres
St. Anselm's College; Manchester, N.H. 03102	Rev. Brendan P. Donnelly	2430	1420	1,801 C[2]	P/RC
St. Augustine's College; Raleigh, N.C. 27611	Prezell R. Robinson	1150[4]	950[4]	1,515 C[1]	P/RC
St. Benedict, College of; St. Joseph, Minn. 56374	Beverly W. Miller	2210	1250	1,607 F	P/RC
St. Bernard College. See Southern Benedictine College.					
St. Bonaventure University; St. Bonaventure, N.Y. 14778	V. Rev. Mathias Doyle	2550	1465	2,546 C[2]	Pub
St. Catherine, The College of; St. Paul, Minn. 55105	Sister Alberta Huber	2300	1240	1,750 F	P/RC
St. Cloud State Univ. See Minnesota State College System.					
St. Edward's University; Austin, Tex. 78704	Brother Stephen Walsh	1850	1250	1,655 C	P/RC
St. Elizabeth, College of; Convent Station, N.J. 07961	Sister Elizabeth Ann Maloney	2250	1500	632 F[2]	P/RC
St. Fidelis College; Herman, Pa. 16044	Rev. Robert McCreary	1200	700+	43 M	P/RC
St. Francis, College of; Joliet, Ill. 60435	John C. Orr	1990	1260	2,040 C	P/RC
St. Francis College; Biddeford, Me. 04005	Jack S. Ketchum	2490	1530	328 C	P
St. Francis College; Brooklyn, N.Y. 11201	Brother Donald Sullivan	2200	n.a.	3,453 C	P
St. Francis College; Fort Wayne, Ind. 46808	Sister M. JoEllen Scheetz	1440	1300	1,181 C[5]	P/RC
St. Francis College; Loretto, Pa. 15940	Rev. Sean M. Sullivan	2300	1250	1,573 C[5]	P/RC

Institution and location	Chief executive	Tuition	Rm/Bd	Students*	Control
St. Francis de Sales College; Milwaukee, Wis. 53207	Rev. John E. Twomey	850	750	85 M	P/RC
St. John Fisher College; Rochester, N.Y. 14618	Rev. Charles J. Lavery	2525	1425	1,656 C	P
St. John's College; Annapolis, Md. 21404	Richard Daniel Weigle	3700	1400	378 C	P
St. John's College; Santa Fe, N.M. 87501	Richard Daniel Weigle	3625	1335	285 C	P
St. John's College; Camarillo, Calif. 93010	Rev. James Galvin	1540[4,9]		207 M[4]	RC
St. John's University; Jamaica, N.Y. 11439	V. Rev. Joseph T. Cahill	2330	n.a.	14,759 C	P/RC
St. Joseph College; West Hartford, Conn. 06117	Sister Mary C. O'Connor	2450	1600	925 F	P/RC
St. Joseph the Provider, College of; Rutland, Vt. 05701	Sister Mary A. Polworth	1740	1375	325 C	P
St. Joseph's College; Brooklyn, N.Y. 11205	Sister George A. O'Connor	2000	n.a.	1,264 C[2]	P/RC
St. Joseph's College; North Windham, Me. 04062	Bernard P. Currier	1825	1300	470 C	P/RC
St. Joseph's College; Philadelphia, Pa. 19131	Rev. Terrence Toland	2250+	1526+	2,085 C	P/RC
St. Joseph's College; Rensselaer, Ind. 47978	Rev. Charles H. Banet	2050	1200	1,091 C[2]	RC
St. Lawrence University; Canton, N.Y. 13617	Frank Peter Piskor	3395	1540	2,250 C	P
St. Leo College; St. Leo, Fla. 33574	Thomas B. Southard	2190	1200	900 C	P/RC
St. Louis College of Pharmacy; St. Louis, Mo. 63110	Charles C. Rabe	1870	1530	694 C	P
St. Louis Conservatory of Music; St. Louis, Mo. 63130	Stephen Jay	2350	n.a.	30 C	P
St. Louis University; St. Louis, Mo. 63103	Rev. Daniel C. O'Connell	2400	1500	10,406 C[2]	P/RC
St. Martin's College; Olympia, Wash. 98503	V. Rev. Matthew Naumes	1980[4]	1330[4]	1,000 C[4]	RC
St. Mary, College of; Omaha, Neb. 68124	Sister Mary Angelica Costello	(37)	1150	517 F	P/RC
St. Mary College; Leavenworth, Kan. 66048	Sister Mary Janet McGilley	1275	1075	672 F	P/RC
St. Mary of the Plains College; Dodge City, Kan. 67801	William V. Tucker	1600[4]	1050[4]	425 C[4]	RC
St. Mary-of-the-Woods College; St. Mary-of-the-Woods, Ind. 47876	Sister Jeanne Knoerle	1980	1300	572 F	RC
St. Mary's College; Notre Dame, Ind. 46556	John M. Duggan	2700	1570	1,669 Co	P/RC
St. Mary's College; Winona, Minn. 55987	Brother Peter Clifford	2400	1350	1,130 C[13]	P/RC
St. Mary's College of California; Moraga, Calif. 94575	Brother T. Mel Anderson	2660	1500	1,104 C	P/RC
St. Mary's College of Maryland; St. Mary's City, Md. 20686	J. Renwick Jackson, Jr.	600	1135	1,053 C	S
St. Mary's Dominican College; New Orleans, La. 70118	Sister Mary E. Cazayoux	1700	1300	905 F	P/RC
St. Mary's University; San Antonio, Tex. 78284	Rev. James A. Young	1700	1190	3,196 C	P/RC
St. Michael's College; Winooski, Vt. 05404	Edward L. Henry	2530	1300	1,550 C	P/RC
St. Norbert College; De Pere, Wis. 54115	Neil J. Webb	2300	930	1,461 C[2]	P/RC
St. Olaf College; Northfield, Minn. 55057	Sidney A. Rand	2600	1300	2,731 C	P/L
St. Paul's College; Lawrenceville, Va. 23868	James A. Russell, Jr.	1734	1050	542 C	P/E
St. Peter's College; Jersey City, N.J. 07306	V. Rev. Victor R. Yanitelli	2080	n.a.	4,400 C	P/RC
St. Rose, The College of; Albany, N.Y. 12203	Thomas A. Manion	1900	1225	2,083 C[2]	P
St. Scholastica, College of; Duluth, Minn. 55811	Bruce Stender	2200	2000	1,192 C[2]	P/RC
St. Teresa, College of; Winona, Minn. 55987	Sister Joyce Rowland	2200	1125	1,070 F	P/RC
St. Thomas, College of; St. Paul, Minn. 55105	Msgr. Terrence J. Murphy	2280	1175	3,184 M	P/RC
St. Thomas, University of; Houston, Tex. 77006	Rev. Patrick O. Braden	1500	1200	1,585 C	RC
St. Thomas Aquinas College; Sparkill, N.Y. 10976	Donald T. McNelis	1700	1250	962 C	P
St. Thomas Seminary College; Denver, Colo. 80210	V. Rev. Francis H. Agnew	1050	1200	194 M	P/RC
St. Vincent College; Latrobe, Pa. 15650	Rev. Cecil G. Diethrich	2070	1340	974 M	P/RC
St. Xavier College; Chicago, Ill. 60655	Sister M. Irenaeus Chekouras	2280	1450	1,450 C	P/RC
Salem College; Salem, W. Va. 26426	Dallas B. Bailey	2100	1400	1,090 C	P
Salem College; Winston-Salem, N.C. 27108	Merrimon Cuninggim	2650	1550	700 F	P
Salem State College; Salem, Mass. 01970	Edward M. Penson	300	984	4,729 C	S
Salisbury State College; Salisbury, Md. 21801	Norman C. Crawford, Jr.	200	1110	3,723 C	S
Salve Regina College; Newport, R.I. 02840	Sister Lucille McKillop	2240	1400	1,747 C	P/RC
Sam Houston State University; Huntsville, Tex. 77340	Elliott T. Bowers	280	1000	9,864 C	S
Samford University; Birmingham, Ala. 35209	Leslie S. Wright	1600	1350	3,676 C	P/SB
San Diego, University of; San Diego, Calif. 92110	Author E. Hughes	2550	1500	3,108 C[2]	P/RC
San Diego State University; San Diego, Calif. 92182	Brage Golding	188[18]	1375	30,121 C	S
San Francisco, University of; San Francisco, Calif. 94117	Rev. William C. McInnes	2635	1550	6,750 C	P
San Francisco Art Institute; San Francisco, Calif. 94133	Roy Ascott	2360	n.a.	895 C	P
San Francisco Conserv. of Music; San Francisco, Calif. 94122	Milton Salkind	2700	1500	177 C[2]	P
San Francisco State University; San Francisco, Calif. 94132	Paul F. Romberg	191[18]	1200	25,000 C	S
San Jose Bible College; San Jose, Calif. 95108	E. Woodrow Phillips	1008	870	286 C	P/CC
San Jose State University; San Jose, Calif. 95192	John H. Bunzel	192[18]	1260	27,000 C	S
Sangamon State University; Springfield, Ill. 62708	Robert C. Spencer	404	1500	3,977 C	S
Santa Clara, University of; Santa Clara, Calif. 95053	Rev. Thomas D. Terry	2718	1626	7,010 C[2]	P/RC
Santa Fe, College of; Santa Fe, N.M. 87501	Brother Cyprian Luke Roney	1600	1300	1,273 C	P/RC
Sarah Lawrence College; Bronxville, N.Y. 10708	Charles R. DeCarlo	4450	2200	841 C	P
Savannah State College; Savannah, Ga. 31404	Prince A. Jackson, Jr.	540	945	2,504 C	S
Scranton, University of; Scranton, Pa. 18510	Rev. William J. Byron	1850	1120	4,122 C	P/RC
Scripps College. See Claremont Colleges.					
Seattle Pacific College; Seattle, Wash. 98119	David L. McKenna	2367	1323	2,047 C	P/FM
Seattle University; Seattle, Wash. 98122	Rev. William Sullivan	2340	1260	3,550 C	RC
Seton Hall University; South Orange, N.J. 07079	Rev. Msgr. Thomas G. Fahy	2400	1200	9,900 C[2]	RC
Seton Hill College; Greensburg, Pa. 15601	Sister Mary T. Schmidt	2250	1225	839 F	P/RC
Shaw University; Raleigh, N.C. 27602	J. Archie Hargraves	1620	870	1,555 C	P/B
Shepherd College, Shepherdstown, W. Va. 25443	James A. Butcher	728	2600	2,190 C	S
Sherwood Music School; Chicago, Ill. 60605	Walter A. Erley	1700	1500	30 C	P

Institution and location	Chief executive	Tuition	Rm/Bd	Students*	Control
Shimer Collège; Mt. Carroll, Ill. 61053	Ralph W. Conant	2700	1400	190 C	P
Shippensburg State College; Shippensburg, Pa. 17257	Gilmore B. Seavers	800	1005	5,506 C[2]	S
Shorter College; Rome, Ga. 30161	Randall Hunter Minor	1575	2650	729 C	P/B
Siena College; Loudonville, N.Y. 12211	Rev. Matthew T. Conlin	2300	1585	2,238 C	P
Siena Heights College; Adrian, Mich. 49221	Hugh L. Thompson	1380+	1302	1,063 C	P
Silver Lake College of the Holy Family; Manitowoc, Wis. 54220	Sister Anne Kennedy	1500	n.a.	400 C[2]	P
Simmons College; Boston, Mass. 02115	William J. Holmes	3488	1856	2,625 F[2]	P
Simpson College; Indianola, Iowa 50125	Richard B. Lancaster	2540	1110	875 C	P/M
Simpson College; San Francisco, Calif. 94134	Mark W. Lee	1500	1220	633 C	P/ID
Sioux Falls College; Sioux Falls, S.D. 57101	Owen P. Halleen	1850	1154	715 C	P
Skidmore College; Saratoga Springs, N.Y. 12866	Joseph C. Palamountain, Jr.	3975	1890	2,434 C[2]	P
Slippery Rock State College; Slippery Rock, Pa. 16057	Albert A. Watrel	800	932	5,815 C	S
Smith College; Northampton, Mass. 01060	Jill Ker Conway	3700	1700	2,518 F[4]	P
South, The University of the; Sewanee, Tenn. 37375	James Jefferson Bennett	2700	1110	978 C	P/E
South Alabama, University of; Mobile, Ala. 36688	Frederick P. Whiddon	597	1272	6,067 C	S
South Carolina, Medical Univ. of; Charleston, S.C. 29401	William H. Knisely	1200	1125	2,216 C	S
South Carolina, University of; Columbia, S.C. 29208	William H. Patterson	584[4]	900[4]	29,378 C[4]	S
South Carolina State College; Orangeburg, S.C. 29117	M. Maceo Nance, Jr.	500	1080	3,589 C	S
South Dakota, University of; Vermillion, S.D. 57069	Richard L. Bowen	660	1115	5,450 C	S
U. of South Dakota at Springfield; Springfield, S.D. 57062	Carrol Krause	500	1000	763 C	S
South Dakota Schl. of Mines & Tech.; Rapid City, S.D. 57701	R. A. Schleuseur	700	900	1,625 C	S
South Dakota State University; Brookings, S.D. 57006	Sherwood O. Berg	600	950	6,412 C[2]	S
South Texas College of Law; Houston, Tex. 77002	Garland R. Walker	n.a.	n.a.	885 C[1]	Pub
South-Eastern Bible College; Lakeland, Fla. 33801	Cyril E. Homer	880	780	1,070 C	P/AG
South Florida, University of; Tampa, Fla. 33620	M. Cecil Mackey	660	1350	21,196 C	S
Southeast Missouri State Univ.; Cape Girardeau, Mo. 63701	Robert E. Leestamper	250	990	7,550 C	S
Southeastern Bible College; Birmingham, Ala. 35205	Alden A. Gannett	1100	1300	260 C	P
Southeastern Louisiana University; Hammond, La. 70401	Clea E. Parker	360	1200	6,700 C	S
Southeastern Massachusetts U.; No. Dartmouth, Mass. 02747	Donald E. Walker	350	2171	4,679 C	S
Southeastern Oklahoma State Univ.; Durant, Okla. 74701	Leon Hibbs	370	1030	4,162 C	S
Southern Baptist Theological Sem.; Louisville, Ky. 40206	Duke K. McCall	250[18]	n.a.	1,670 C	SB
Southern Benedictine College[38]; St. Bernard, Ala. 35138	(Vacant)	1145	1250	372 C	P/RC
Southern Bible College; Houston, Tex. 77078	Worden McDonald	700	990	185 C	P
Southern California, University of; Los Angeles, Calif. 90007	John R. Hubbard	3400[4]	1500[4]	21,000 C[4]	P
Southern California College; Costa Mesa, Calif. 92626	Wayne Kraiss	1350	1260	591 C	P/AG
Southern Calif. Coll. of Optometry; Fullerton, Calif. 92631	Richard L. Hopping	3355	n.a.	372 C	P
Southern College of Optometry; Memphis, Tenn. 38104	Spurgeon B. Eure	6000	2013	592 C	P
Southern Colorado, University of; Pueblo, Colo. 81001	Harry P. Bowes	561	1220	6,000 C	S
Southern Colorado State Coll. See Univ. of Southern Colorado.					
Southern Connecticut State Coll.; New Haven, Conn. 06515	Manson Van B. Jennings	540	1200	12,497 C	S
Southern Illinois University; Carbondale, Ill. 62901	Warren W. Brandt	428	1400	21,214 C[2]	S
Southern Illinois Univ.—Carbondale; Carbondale, Ill. 62901	Warren Brandt	600	1400	21,000 C	S
So. Illinois Univ.—Edwardsville; Edwardsville, Ill. 62025	Andrew Kochman	600	1100	12,212 C	S
Southern Methodist University; Dallas, Tex. 75275	Willis M. Tate	2864	1517	10,722 C	P
Southern Missionary College; Collegedale, Tenn. 37315	Frank Knittel	2430	1080	1,611 C	P/SDA
Southern Mississippi, Univ. of; Hattiesburg, Miss. 39401	Aubrey K. Lucas	558	795	11,404 C[2]	S
Southern Oregon State College; Ashland, Ore. 97520	James K. Sours	660	1250[4]	4,537 C[5]	S
Southern State College; Magnolia, Ark. 71753	Harold T. Brinson	550	1121	1,867 C	S
Southern University A&M College; Baton Rouge, La. 70813	Jesse N. Stone, Jr.	324	1145	8,351 C	S
Southern Univ. in New Orleans; New Orleans, La. 70126	Emmett W. Bashful	290	n.a.	3,546 C	S
Southern Utah State College; Cedar City, Utah 84720	Royden C. Braithwaite	429	1050	1,644 C	S
Southwest Baptist College; Bolivar, Mo. 65613	James L. Sells	1320	1110	1,355 C	P/B
Southwest Minnesota State Univ. See Minnesota State Coll. System.					
Southwest Missouri State University; Springfield, Mo. 65802	Duane G. Meyer	360	890	11,000 C	S
Southwest Texas State University; San Marcos, Tex. 78666	Lee H. Smith	354	1012	13,011 C	S
Southwestern Assemblies of God College; Waxahachie, Tex. 75165	Blake L. Farmer	945	1368	644 C	P/AG
Southwestern at Memphis; Memphis, Tenn. 38112	James H. Daughdrill, Jr.	2500	1261	1,082 C[2]	P/Pres
Southwestern Baptist Theological Seminary; Ft. Worth, Tex. 76122	Robert E. Naylor	n.a.	n.a.	2,813 C	SB
Southwestern College; Winfield, Kan. 67156	Donald B. Ruthenberg	1650	1180	695 C	P/M
Southwestern Louisiana, Univ. of; Lafayette, La. 70501	Ray P. Authement	368	808	12,329 C	S
Southwestern Medical School; Dallas, Tex. 75222	Frederick J. Bonte	n.a.	n.a.	527 C[40]	S
Southwestern Oklahoma State Univ.; Weatherford, Okla. 73096	Leonard Campbell	352	800	4,961 C[2]	S
Southwestern Union College; Keene, Tex. 76059	Don McAdams	2400	1280	705 C	P/SDA
Southwestern University; Georgetown, Tex. 78626	Durwood Fleming	2100	1025	858 C	M
Southwestern U. School of Law; Los Angeles, Calif. 90005	Paul W. Wildman	2200	n.a.	1,534 C	P
Spalding College; Louisville, Ky. 40203	Sister Eileen M. Egan	1500	1100	1,072 C	P
Spelman College; Atlanta, Ga. 30314	Donald Stewart	1700[8]	1500[8]	1,200 F[2]	P
Spertus College of Judaica; Chicago, Ill. 60605	David Weinstein	920	n.a.	638 C	P
Spring Arbor College; Spring Arbor, Mich. 49283	Ellwood A. Voller	2300	1150	833 C	P/FM
Spring Garden College; Philadelphia, Pa. 19118	Robert H. Thompson	1100	n.a.	936 C	P
Spring Hill College; Mobile, Ala. 36608	V. Rev. Paul S. Tipton	2100	795	815 C	P/RC

Institution and location	Chief executive	Tuition	Rm/Bd	Students*	Control
Springfield College; Springfield, Mass. 01109	Wilbert E. Locklin	2600	1350	2,400 C	P
Stanford University; Stanford, Calif. 94305	Richard W. Lyman	4275[8]	1850[8]	12,641 C[2]	P
Steed College; Johnson City, Tenn. 37601	Howard S. Steed	1237	n.a.	2,167 C[2]	P
Stephen F. Austin State Univ.; Nacogdoches, Tex. 75961	William R. Johnson	300	1000	10,225 C	S
Stephens College; Columbia, Mo. 65201	Arland Christ-Janer	4475[8,9]		1,802 F	P
Sterling College; Sterling, Kan. 67579	Charles Schoenherr	1950	1100	525 C[2]	P
Stetson University; DeLand, Fla. 32720	John E. Johns	2300	1265	1,789 C	P
Stetson College of Law; St. Petersburg, Fla. 33707	Richard T. Dillon	2400[4]	400[4]	462 C	P
Steubenville, The College of; Steubenville, Ohio 43952	Rev. Michael Scanlan	1950	1250	890 C	P/RC
Stevens Institute of Technology; Hoboken, N.J. 07030	Kenneth C. Rogers	3300	1540	2,050 C	P
Stillman College; Tuscaloosa, Ala. 35401	Harold Nathaniel Stinson	1400	1200	785 C[2]	P/PUS
Stonehill College; North Easton, Mass. 02356	Rev. Ernest J. Bartell	2575	1570	2,201 C	P
Strayer College; Washington, D.C. 20005	Murray T. Donoho, III	1680	1575	1,609 C	P
Suffolk University; Boston, Mass. 02114	Thomas A. Fulham	1850	n.a.	4,672 C	P
Sul Ross State University; Alpine, Tex. 79830	Hugh E. Meredith	250	980	2,714 C	S
Susquehanna University; Selinsgrove, Pa. 17870	Gustave W. Weber	2740	1246	1,388 C	P/LCA
Swarthmore College; Swarthmore, Pa. 19081	Theodore W. Friend	3500[8]	1700[8]	1,240 C[2]	P
Sweet Briar College; Sweet Briar, Va. 24595	Harold B. Whiteman, Jr.	3550	1350	656 F	P
Syracuse University; Syracuse, N.Y. 13210	Melvin A. Eggers	3340	1750	22,642 C	P
Tabor College; Hillsboro, Kan. 67063	Roy Just	2000	1130	489 C	MB
Talladega College; Talladega, Ala. 35160	Herman H. Long	1240	1175	549 C	P
Tampa, The University of; Tampa, Fla. 33606	B. D. Owens	2600	1450	1,907 C	P
Tampa College; Tampa, Fla. 33609	Delores C. Jones	1200	n.a.	1,642 C	P
Tarkio College; Tarkio, Mo. 64491	Eldon E. Breazier	2240	1160	417 C[5]	P/PUS
Tarleton State College[34]; Stephenville, Tex. 76402	W. O. Trogden	128	1110	2,855 C	S
Taylor University; Upland, Ind. 46989	Robert C. Baptista	2520	1380	1,382 C	P
Temple University; Philadelphia, Pa. 19122	Marvin Wachman	1300	1750	34,950 C[2]	P&S
Tennessee State University; Nashville, Tenn. 37203	Frederick Humphries	936	552	5,128 C	S
Tennessee System, University of:	Edward J. Boling	....	....	49,082 C[2]	S
U. of Tennessee at Chattanooga; Chattanooga, Tenn. 37401	James E. Drinnon, Jr.	468	1270	5,808 C[2]	S
U. of Tennessee at Knoxville; Knoxville, Tenn. 37916	Jack E. Reese	453	1186	29,999 C[2]	S
U. of Tennessee at Martin; Martin, Tenn. 38238	Larry T. McGehee	498	960	5,188 C[2]	S
Univ. Center for the Health Sciences; Memphis, Tenn. 38163	T. Albert Farmer	n.a.	1250	2,594 C[2]	S
U. of Tennessee at Nashville; Nashville, Tenn. 37203	Charles E. Smith	408	n.a.	5,493 C[2]	S
Tennessee Technological University; Cookeville, Tenn. 38501	Arliss L. Roaden	411[18]	915	7,120 C[2]	S
Tennessee Wesleyan College; Athens, Tenn. 37303	George E. Naff, Jr.	1440	990	450 C	P
Texas A&I University in Kingsville; Kingsville, Tex. 78363	Gerald B. Robins	626	995	7,441 C	S
Texas A&I University at Laredo; Laredo, Tex. 78040	Billy F. Cowart	160	1600	884 C	S
Texas A&M University; College Station, Tex. 77843	Jack K. Williams	120	1300	24,293 C	S
Texas Christian University; Fort Worth, Tex. 76129	James M. Moudy	2368	1280	5,803 C	P/DC
Texas College; Tyler, Tex. 75701	Allen C. Hancock	1350	1150	590 C	M
Texas Coll. of Osteopathic Medicine; Fort Worth, Tex. 76107	Marion E. Coy	400	n.a.	234 C	S
Texas Eastern University; Tyler, Tex. 75701	James H. Stewart, Jr.	345	n.a.	1,229 C	S
Texas Health Sci. Ctr. at Dallas, U. of; Dallas, Tex. 75235	Charles C. Sprague	300	n.a.	1,000 C	S
Texas Health Sci. Ctr. at Houston, U. of; Houston, Tex. 77025	Charles Berry	300[4]	n.a.	170 C[4]	S
Texas Health Sci. Ctr. at San Antonio, U. of; San Antonio, Tex. 78284	Frank Harrison	400	n.a.	795 C	S
Texas Medical Branch, U. of; Galveston, Tex. 77550	William C. Levin	400	2800	1,108 C[2]	S
Texas Lutheran College; Seguin, Tex. 78155	Charles H. Oestreich	1890	1050	977 C	P
Texas Southern University; Houston, Tex. 77004	Granville M. Sawyer	400	1250	8,531 C	S
Texas System, University of; Austin, Tex. 78701	Charles A. LeMaistre	....	....	78,427 C	S
Univ. of Texas at Arlington; Arlington, Tex. 76019	Wendell H. Nedderman	160	1500	16,000 C	S
Univ. of Texas at Austin; Austin, Tex. 78712	Lorene Rogers	2800	1600	42,598 C	S
Univ. of Texas at Dallas; Dallas, Tex. 75080	Bryce Jordan	100+	n.a.	3,586 C	S
Univ. of Texas at El Paso; El Paso, Tex. 79968	Arleigh B. Templeton	374	1100	13,600 C	S
Univ. of Texas at San Antonio; San Antonio, Tex. 78225	Peter T. Flawn	120	n.a.	4,643 C	S
Texas Tech University; Lubbock, Tex. 79409	Grover E. Murray	400	1084	20,820 C	S
Texas Wesleyan College; Fort Worth, Tex. 76105	W. M. Pearce	1350	1380	1,782 C	P/M
Texas Woman's University; Denton, Tex. 76204	Mary Evelyn Huey	100	1150	8,086 F	S
Thiel College; Greenville, Pa. 16125	Frank H. Bretz	2550	1260	1,097 C	P/L
Thomas College; Waterville, Me. 04901	John L. Thomas, Jr.	2450	1500	415 C	P
Thomas M. Cooley Law School; Lansing, Mich. 48933	Thomas E. Brennan	1710	n.a.	720 C	P
Thomas More College; Fort Mitchell, Ky. 41017	Richard A. DeGraff	1600	1230[4]	1,350 C	P/RC
Tiffin University; Tiffin, Ohio 44883	Richard C. Pfeiffer	1620	880	1,026 C	P
Tift College; Forsyth, Ga. 31029	Robert W. Jackson	1200	990	610 F	P
Toccoa Falls College; Toccoa Falls, Ga. 30577	Kenneth W. Opperman	1590	1200	429 C	P/Ind
Toledo, The University of; Toledo, Ohio 43606	Glen R. Driscoll	795	1545	14,953 C	S
Tougaloo College; Tougaloo, Miss. 39174	George A. Owens	1150	900	812 C	P
Towson State College; Towson, Md. 21204	James L. Fisher	200	1027	13,838 C	S
Transylvania University; Lexington, Ky. 40508	William Kelly	2340	1230	646 C	P
Trenton State College; Trenton, N.J. 08625	Clayton R. Brower	535	1375	7,000 C	S
Trevecca Nazarene College; Nashville, Tenn. 37210	Mark R. Moore	1770	1050	782 C	P/Naz

Institution and location	Chief executive	Tuition	Rm/Bd	Students*	Control
Trinity College; Burlington, Vt. 05401	Sister Elizabeth Candon	2240	1235	493 C	P/RC
Trinity College; Deerfield, Ill. 60015	Harry L. Evans	2380	1310	839 C	P
Trinity College; Hartford, Conn. 06106	Theodore D. Lockwood	3600	1620	1,705 C	P
Trinity College; Washington, D.C. 20017	Sister Rose Ann Fleming	2600	1500	496 F[2]	P/RC
Trinity University; San Antonio, Tex. 78284	Duncan Wimpress	2250	1426	3,529 C	P
Tri-State College; Angola, Ind. 46703	Carl H. Elliott	2025	1350	1,129 C	P
Troy State University; Troy, Ala. 36081	Ralph W. Adams	495	1035	10,136 C	S
Tufts University; Medford, Mass. 02155	Jean Mayer	3800[13]	2160[13]	6,232 C[2]	P
Tulane University; New Orleans, La. 70118	F. Sheldon Hackney	3300	1595	8,796 C	P
Newcomb College; New Orleans, La. 70118	James F. Davidson	3040	1640+	1,544 F	P
Tulsa, The University of; Tulsa, Okla. 74104	J. Paschal Twyman	1550	1130	6,540 C[2]	P
Turabo University Coll. See Ana G. Méndez Educational Foundation.					
Tusculum College; Greeneville, Tenn. 37743	Thomas G. Voss	1800	1335+	361 C	P/PUS
Tuskegee Institute; Tuskegee Institute, Ala. 36088	Luther H. Foster	1500	1090	3,437 C	P
Union College; Barbourville, Ky. 40906	Mahlon A. Miller	1680	920	1,045 C	P/UM
Union College; Lincoln, Neb. 68506	Myrl O. Manley	2575	1150	882 C[2]	P/SDA
Union College; Schenectady, N.Y. 12308	Thomas N. Bonner	3750	1600	2,013 C[2]	P
Union Theological Seminary; New York, N.Y. 10027	Donald W. Shriver, Jr.	2300	700[7]	407 C[2]	P/ID
Union University; Jackson, Tenn. 38301	Robert E. Craig	1670	994	922 C	P/B
U.S. Air Force Academy; USAF Academy, Colo. 80840	Lt. Gen. James R. Allen	n.a.	n.a.	4,000 C	F
U.S. Coast Guard Academy; New London, Conn. 06320	R. Adm. W. A. Jenkins	n.a.	n.a.	1,107 M[41]	F
U.S. International University; San Diego, Calif. 92131	William C. Rust	2550	1770	2,772 C	P
U.S. Merchant Marine Academy; Kings Point, N.Y. 11024	R. Adm. Arthur B. Engel	n.a.	n.a.	1,028 C	F
U.S. Military Academy; West Point, N.Y. 10996	Lt. Gen. Sidney Berry	n.a.	n.a.	4,400 C	Pub
U.S. Naval Academy; Annapolis, Md. 21402	R. Adm. Kinnaird R. McKee	n.a.	n.a.	4,300 C	F
United Wesleyan College; Allentown, Pa. 18103	Earle L. Wilson	1370	1100	163 C	P/W
Unity College; Unity, Me. 04988	Alan B. Karstetter	2160	1100	360 C[5]	P
Upper Iowa University; Fayette, Iowa 52142	Aldrich K. Paul	2380	1070	3,311 C	P
Upsala College; East Orange, N.J. 07019	(Vacant)	2500	1540	1,589 C	P/L
Urbana College; Urbana, Ohio 43078	Roland D. Patzer	2010	1500	411 C	P/Sw
Ursinus College; Collegeville, Pa. 19426	William S. Pettit	2730	1270	1,100 C	P
Ursuline College; Cleveland, Ohio 44124	Sister Mary Kenan Dulzer	1970	1350	800 F	P/RC
Utah, University of; Salt Lake City, Utah 84112	David P. Gardner	525	1316	23,500 C	S
Utah State University; Logan, Utah 84322	Glen L. Taggart	496	1200	8,926 Co[5]	S
Valdosta State College; Valdosta, Ga. 31601	S. Walter Martin	522	990	5,012 C[5]	S
Valley City State College; Valley City, N.D. 58072	Ted D. DeVries	363	966	766 C	S
Valparaiso University; Valparaiso, Ind. 46383	Rev. Albert G. Huegli	2490	1416	3,827 C	P/LMS
Vanderbilt University; Nashville, Tenn. 37240	Alexander Heard	3400	1800	6,731 C	P
VanderCook College of Music; Chicago, Ill. 60616	Richard E. Brittain	1790	1400	125 C	P
Vassar College; Poughkeepsie, N.Y. 12601	Alan Simpson	3600	1675	2,250 C	P
Vennard College; University Park, Iowa 52595	Merne A. Harris	1128	1064	270 C	P/ID
Vermont, University of; Burlington, Vt. 05482	Lattie F. Coor	1200	1492	8,287 C	S
Vermont College. See Norwich University.					
Vermont Law School; South Royalton, Vt. 05068	Thomas M. Debevoise	3000	n.a.	333[2]	P
Villa Maria College; Erie, Pa. 16505	Sister Lawreace Antoun	2200	1400	531 F	P/RC
Villanova University; Villanova, Pa. 19085	Rev. John M. Driscoll	5400	3400	9,130 C	P/RC
Virgin Islands, College of the; St. Thomas, V.I. 00801	Lawrence C. Wanlass	314	1083	1,893 C	S
Virginia, University of; Charlottesville, Va. 22903	Frank L. Hereford, Jr.	455	1480	14,933 C	S
Clinch Valley College; Wise, Va. 24293	Joseph C. Smiddy	520	1200	1,000 C	S
Virginia Commonwealth University; Richmond, Va. 23284	T. Edward Temple	650	1340	17,988 C[2]	S
Virginia Intermont College; Bristol, Va. 24201	Floyd V. Turner	1950	1410	532 F	P/B
Virginia Military Institute; Lexington, Va. 24450	Lt. Gen. Richard L. Irby	520	970	1,137 M	S
Virginia Polytech. Inst. & State Univ.; Blacksburg, Va. 24060	William E. Lavery	570	1000	18,477 C	S
Virginia State College; Petersburg, Va. 23803	Thomas M. Law	762	873	4,327 C	S
Virginia Union University; Richmond, Va. 23220	Allix B. James	1600[4]	1015[4]	1,356 C[1]	P
Virginia Wesleyan College; Norfolk, Va. 23502	Lambuth M. Clarke	2400	1200	611 C	P/UM
Viterbo College; La Crosse, Wis. 54601	Rev. J. Thomas Finucan	1990	1100+	876 C	P
Voorhees College; Denmark, S.C. 29042	Harry P. Graham	1500	1165	950 C	P/E
Wabash College; Crawfordsville, Ind. 47933	Thaddeus Seymour	3000[8]	1400	821 M	P
Wagner College; Staten Island, N.Y. 10301	John Satterfield	3100	1650	2,609 C	P/L
Wake Forest University; Winston-Salem, N.C. 27109	James Ralph Scales	2500	840+	4,225 C	P/B
Walla Walla College; College Place, Wash. 99324	N. Clifford Sorenson	2685	1200	1,767 C	P/SDA
Walsh College; Canton, Ohio 44720	Brother R. A. Francoeur	2000	1200	704 C	P/RC
Walsh Coll. of Accountancy & Business Admin.; Troy, Mich. 48084	Jeffrey W. Barry	1130	n.a.	854 C	P
Warner Pacific College; Portland, Ore. 97215	E. Joe Gilliam	2025	1175	400 C	P/CG
Warren Wilson College; Swannanoa, N.C. 28778	Reuben A. Holden	2000	960[42]	445 C	P/UP
Wartburg College; Waverly, Iowa 50677	William W. Jellema	2478	1050	1,202 C[2]	P/AL
Washburn University of Topeka; Topeka, Kan. 66621	John W. Henderson	750	1300	5,477 C	Mun
Washington, University of; Seattle, Wash. 98195	John R. Hogness	564	1500	35,434 C[2]	S
Washington and Jefferson College; Washington, Pa. 15301	Howard J. Burnett	3150+[8]	1350[8]	972 C	P
Washington and Lee University; Lexington, Va. 24450	Robert E. R. Huntley	2900	1305	1,592 M	P

Institution and location	Chief executive	Tuition	Rm/Bd	Students*Control	
Washington Bible College; Lanham, Md. 20801	George A. Miles	1300	1310	510 C	P
Washington College; Chestertown, Md. 21620	Joseph H. McLain	2300	1150	931 C	P&S
Washington State University; Pullman, Wash. 99163	Glenn Terrell	564	1430	15,637 C	S
Washington University; St. Louis, Mo. 63130	William H. Danforth	3650	1725	10,615 C	P
Wayland Baptist College; Plainview, Tex. 79072	Roy C. McClung	1050	1006	1,070 C	B
Wayne State College; Wayne, Neb. 68787	Lyle E. Seymour	496	1032	1,825 C[2]	S
Wayne State University; Detroit, Mich. 48202	George E. Gullen, Jr.	855	n.a.	34,323 C	S
Waynesburg College; Waynesburg, Pa. 15370	Joseph F. Marsh	2400	1200	746 C	P/UP
Webb Institute of Naval Architecture; Glen Cove, N.Y. 11542	Adm. Charles N. Payne	n.a.	1600	78 C	P
Weber State College; Ogden, Utah 84408	Joseph L. Bishop	486	1030	9,458 C	S
Webster College; St. Louis, Mo. 63119	Leigh Gerdine	2650	2000	4,200 C	P
Wellesley College; Wellesley, Mass. 02181	Barbara W. Newell	3600[8]	1900[8]	2,045 F[2]	P
Wells College; Aurora, N.Y. 13026	Frances Farenthold	3200	1600	500 F	P
Wesleyan College; Macon, Ga. 31201	W. Earl Strickland	2400	1210	578 F[2]	P/UM
Wesleyan University; Middletown, Conn. 06457	Colin G. Campbell	3900	1750	2,570 C	P
West Chester State College; West Chester, Pa. 19380	Charles G. Mayo	750	725	6,000 C	S
West Coast University; Los Angeles, Calif. 90020	Victor Elconin	1400	n.a.	1,192 C	P
Orange County Center; Orange, Calif. 92668	Willard G. Huggins	n.a.	n.a.	398 C[1]	P
West Florida, The University of; Pensacola, Fla. 32504	James A. Robinson	697	1291	5,231 C[5]	S
West Georgia College; Carrollton, Ga. 30117	Maurice K. Townsend	534	960	5,464 C	S
West Liberty State College; West Liberty, W. Va. 26074	James L. Chapman	300	1250	2,680 C[2]	S
West Texas State University; Canyon, Tex. 79016	Lloyd I. Watkins	128	800	6,701 C[2]	S
West Virginia College of Grad. Studies; Institute, W. Va. 25112	Roy E. McTarnaghan	252[4]	900[4]	2,500 C[4]	S
West Virginia Inst. of Technology; Montgomery, W. Va. 25136	Leonard C. Nelson	350	1340	2,656 C	S
West Virginia State College; Institute, W. Va. 25112	Harold M. McNeill	300	1314	3,955 C	S
West Virginia University; Morgantown, W. Va. 26506	James G. Harlow	318[4]	1350[4]	16,500 C[4]	S
West Virginia Wesleyan College; Buckhannon, W. Va. 26201	Ronald E. Sleeth	2090	1467	1,800 C[2]	P/UM
Westbrook College; Portland, Me. 04103	James F. Dickinson	2500	1570+	813 C	P
Western Baptist Bible College; Salem, Ore. 97302	W. Thomas Younger	1569	1071	430 C	P/B
Western Bible Institute; Morrison, Colo. 80465	Adrian L. House	1024	1070	194 C	P
Western Carolina Univ. See Univ. System of North Carolina.					
Western Connecticut State College; Danbury, Conn. 06810	Robert M. Bersi	450	1070	4,981 C	S
Western Illinois University; Macomb, Ill. 61455	Leslie F. Malpass	420	1278	14,000 C	S
Western Kentucky University; Bowling Green, Ky. 42101	Dero G. Downing	423	850	13,040 C[2]	S
Western Maryland College; Westminster, Md. 21157	Ralph Candler John	2650	1275	2,330 C[2]	P
Western Michigan University; Kalamazoo, Mich. 49008	John T. Bernhard	775	1440	19,914 C[5]	S
Western Montana College; Dillon, Mont. 59725	(Vacant)	468	1045	759 C[2]	S
Western New England College; Springfield, Mass. 01119	Beaumont A. Herman	2040	1305	1,480 C	P
Western New Mexico University; Silver City, N.M. 88061	John H. Snedeker	333[19]	960	1,830 C[2]	S
Western State College; Gunnison, Colo. 81230	John P. Mellon	510	1200	2,965 C	S
Western Washington State College; Bellingham, Wash. 98225	Paul Olscamp	507	1260	8,840 C	S
Westfield State College; Westfield, Mass. 01085	Robert L. Randolph	600	1062	2,563 C	S
Westmar College; LeMars, Iowa 51031	Laurence C. Smith	1955	1025	664 C	P/UM
Westminster Choir College; Princeton, N.J. 08540	Ray E. Robinson	2845	1330	414 C	P
Westminster College; Fulton, Mo. 65251	William Stucker	2600	1100	700 M	P
Westminster College; New Wilmington, Pa. 16142	Earland I. Carlson	2430	1200	1,843 C	P
Westminster College; Salt Lake City, Utah 84105	Helmut Hofmann	1560	1086	1,260 C	P
Westmont College; Santa Barbara, Calif. 93108	David Winter	2800	1100	894 C	P
Wheaton College; Norton, Mass. 02766	Alice F. Emerson	4270	1525	1,229 F	P
Wheaton College; Wheaton, Ill. 60187	Hudson T. Armerding	2610	1470	2,195 C[5]	P
Wheeling College; Wheeling, W. Va. 26003	Rev. Charles L. Currie	2090	1462	771 C[2]	P
Wheelock College; Boston, Mass. 02215	Gordon L. Marshall	3050	1600	770 C	P
White Plains, College of, of Pace Univ., White Plains, N.Y. 10603	Edward B. Kenny	2300	1700	700 C	P
Whitman College; Walla Walla, Wash. 99362	Robert A. Skotheim	2770	1250	1,055 C[2]	P
Whittier College; Whittier, Calif. 90608	W. Roy Newsom	2950	1434	1,350 C	P
Whitworth College; Spokane, Wash. 99251	Edward B. Lindaman	2700	1350	1,350 C	P/Pres
Wichita State University; Wichita, Kan. 67208	Clark D. Ahlberg	487	1150	14,231 C	S
Widener College; Chester, Pa. 19013	Clarence R. Moll	2970	1450	1,350 C	P
Wilberforce University; Wilberforce, Ohio 45384	Rembert E. Stokes	1890[8]	1110	1,054 C	P/AME
Wiley College; Marshall, Tex. 75670	Rev. Robert E. Hayes, Sr.	1500	1370	612 C	P/UM
Wilkes College; Wilkes-Barre, Pa. 18703	Robert S. Capin	2300	1300	2,624 C	P
Willamette University; Salem, Ore. 97301	Robert P. Lisensky	2700	1356	1,633 C	P
William and Mary in Virginia, Coll. of; Williamsburg, Va. 23185	Thomas A. Graves, Jr.	944	1336	5,947 C	S
William Carey College; Hattiesburg, Miss. 39401	J. Ralph Noonkester	1350	950	1,749 C[2]	P/SB
William Jewell College; Liberty, Mo. 64068	Thomas S. Field	1725	1025	1,612 C[2]	P
William Mitchell College of Law; St. Paul, Minn. 55105	Bruce Burton	1500	n.a.	1,000 C	P
William Paterson College of New Jersey; Wayne, N.J. 07470	William J. McKeefrey	535	865[7]	13,204 C	S
William Penn College; Oskaloosa, Iowa 52577	Duane Moon	2515	1270	700 C	P
William Smith College. See Hobart & William Smith Colleges.					
William Woods College; Fulton, Mo. 65251	Randall B. Cutlip	2645[13]	1325[13]	910 F[5]	P
Williams College; Williamstown, Mass. 01267	John W. Chandler	3750	1780	1,850 C	P
Wilmington College; New Castle, Del. 19720	Donald E. Ross	950	950	800 C	P

Institution and location	Chief executive	Tuition	Rm/Bd	Students*	Control
Wilmington College; Wilmington, Ohio 45177	Robert E. Lucas	2160	1245	560 C	P/SOF
Wilson College; Chambersburg, Pa. 17201	Margaret A. Waggoner	2700	1500	362 F	P/Pres
Windham College; Putney, Vt. 05346	John L. Stones	3925[19]	1230[19]	550 C	P
Winona State University. See Minnesota State College System.					
Winston-Salem State U. See U. System of North Carolina.					
Winthrop College; Rock Hill, S.C. 29733	Charles B. Vail	690	1042	3,501 C	S
Wisconsin, The Medical College of; Milwaukee, Wis. 53233	Gerald A. Kerrigan	2750[4]	n.a.	553 C[2]	P
Wisconsin, University of; Madison, Wis. 53706	John C. Weaver	....	....		S
U. of Wisconsin—Eau Claire; Eau Claire, Wis. 54701	Leonard Haas	658	1084	9,359 C	S
U. of Wisconsin—Green Bay; Green Bay, Wis. 54302	Edward W. Weidner	655	1395	3,600 C	S
U. of Wisconsin—La Crosse; La Crosse, Wis. 54601	Kenneth E. Lindner	670	1077	7,163 C	S
U. of Wisconsin—Madison; Madison, Wis. 53706	H. Edwin Young	671	1295	38,545 C[2]	S
U. of Wisconsin—Milwaukee; Milwaukee, Wis. 53211	Werner A. Baum	638	1600	23,596 C	S
U. of Wisconsin—Oshkosh; Oshkosh, Wis. 54901	Robert Birnbaum	600[4]	1190[4]	10,600 C[4]	S
U. of Wisconsin—Parkside; Kenosha, Wis. 53140	Allen E. Guskin	650	1530[4]	5,400 C[2]	S
U. of Wisconsin—Platteville; Platteville, Wis. 53818	Bjarne R. Ullsvik	600[4]	1060+[4]	3,941 C[4]	S
U. of Wisconsin—River Falls; River Falls, Wis. 54022	George R. Field	600	1200	4,032 C	S
U. of Wisconsin—Stevens Point; Stevens Point, Wis. 54481	Lee Sherman Dreyfus	710	1260	8,220 C[2]	S
U. of Wisconsin—Stout; Menomonie, Wis. 54751	Robert S. Swanson	700	1250	5,600 C	S
U. of Wisconsin—Superior; Superior, Wis. 54880	Karl W. Meyer	674	1140	2,610 C	S
U. of Wisconsin—Whitewater; Whitewater, Wis. 53190	James R. Connor	675	1300	8,200 C	S
Wittenberg University; Springfield, Ohio 45501	William A. Kinnison	3072	1462	2,333 C[13]	P/LCA
Wofford College; Spartanburg, S.C. 29301	Joab M. Lesesne, Jr.	2540	1425	965 C	M
Woodbury University; Los Angeles, Calif. 90017	Dora E. Kirby	1890	707[7]	1,419 C[2]	P
Wooster, The College of; Wooster, Ohio 44691	J. Garber Drushal	4830[9]		1,854 C	P
Worcester Art Museum, School of the; Worcester, Mass. 01608	Sante Graziani	1500	n.a.	115 C	P
Worcester Polytechnic Institute; Worcester, Mass. 01609	George W. Hazzard	3450	1400	2,785 C	P
Worcester State College; Worcester, Mass. 01602	Joseph J. Orze	500	1250	3,140 C	S
Wright State University; Dayton, Ohio 45431	Robert J. Kegerreis	810	1515	12,500 C	S
Wyoming, University of; Laramie, Wyo. 82071	William D. Carlson	434	1221	8,078 C	S
Xavier University; Cincinnati, Ohio 45207	Rev. Robert W. Mulligan	1940	1415	6,265 C	P
Xavier University of Louisiana; New Orleans, La. 70125	Norman C. Francis	1700	1260	1,800 C[2]	P/RC
Yale University; New Haven, Conn. 06520	Kingman Brewster, Jr.	4050	1870	9,910 C	P
Yankton College; Yankton, S.D. 57078	Alfred M. Gibbens	2250	1250	305 C	P/UCC
Yeshiva University; New York, N.Y. 10033	Norman Lamm	2750	1620	6,094 Co	P
York College (NYC). See New York, City University of.					
York College of Pennsylvania; York, Pa. 17405	Robert V. Iosue	868	608	2,954 C	P
Youngstown State University; Youngstown, Ohio 44555	John J. Coffelt	678	1075	14,264 C	S

*M—All or predominantly male; F—all or predominantly female; C—coeducational; Co—coordinate, i.e., separate schools for men and women. In schools marked M or F, members of the opposite sex are in many cases admitted for special courses or graduate work. [1]Fall 1974. [2]Fall 1975. [3]$28 per semester hour. [4]Spring 1975. [5]Winter 1976. [6]$15 per semester hour. [7]Room only. [8]1976–77. [9]Comprehensive fee covering tuition, room and board. [10]Spring 1974. [11]Each student receives $3,900 cost-of-education scholarship. [12]Plus 15 hours' work per week. [13]Fall 1976. [14]Member LDS church, 1976–77. [15]Member LDS (Pac.) church. [16]Women only. [17]Resident fee, 12 or more units: $48. [18]Fees. [19]1975–76. [20]$117 per point. [21]For 1st year, 4 quarters; subsequent years, $2280. [22]Member University of Hawaii System. [23]Off campus estimate. [24]$32 per quarter hour. [25]Two campuses combined, Fall 1975. [26]$34 per credit. [27]$150–$175 per month. [28]Only out-of-state students. [29]Formerly Massachusetts College of Optometry. [30]$85 per credit point. [31]$32.50 per hour. [32]Tuition remission. [33]960 hours' work per year. [34]Member Texas A&M System. [35]$405 per course. [36]Church related: UCC/M/PUS. [37]$68 per credit hour. [38]Formerly St. Bernard College. [39]Formerly Southern Colorado State College. [40]1973. [41]Female students admitted as of Fall 1976 semester. [42]Worked out in Work Program.

Purposes of Institutional Accreditation

Institutional accreditation of the postsecondary level is a means used by the accrediting commissions for the purposes of: fostering excellence in postsecondary education through the development of criteria and guidelines for assessing educational effectiveness; encouraging institutional improvement of educational endeavors through continuous self-study and evaluation; assuring the educational community, the general public, and other agencies or organizations that an institution has clearly defined and appropriate objectives, has established conditions under which their achievement can reasonably be expected, appears in fact to be accomplishing them substantially, and is so organized, staffed and supported that it can be expected to continue to do so; providing counsel and assistance to established and developing institutions; protecting institutions against encroachments which might jeopardize their educational effectiveness or academic freedom.

Accreditation is attained through a process of evaluation and periodic review of total institutions conducted by the commission in accord with policies and procedures approved by the Council on Postsecondary Accreditation.

AWARDS

★
NOBEL PRIZES

The Nobel prizes are awarded under the will of Alfred Bernhard Nobel, Swedish chemist and engineer, who died in 1896. The interest of the fund is divided annually among the persons who have made the most outstanding contributions in the field of physics, chemistry, and physiology or medicine, who have produced the most distinguished literary work of an idealist tendency, and who have contributed most toward world peace.

In 1968, a Nobel Prize for economic sciences was established by Riksbank, the Swedish bank, in celebration of its 300th anniversary. The prize was awarded for the first time in 1969.

The prizes for physics and chemistry are awarded by the Swedish Academy of Science in Stockholm, the one for physiology or medicine by the Caroline Medical Institute in Stockholm, that for literature by the academy in Stockholm, and that for peace by a committee of five elected by the Norwegian Storting. The distribution of prizes was begun on December 10, 1901, the anniversary of Nobel's death. The amount of each prize varies with the income from the fund and currently is about $143,000. No Nobel prizes were awarded for 1940, 1941, and 1942; prizes for Literature were not awarded for 1914, 1918, and 1943.

Year	Literature	Peace
1901	René F. A. Sully Prudhomme (France)	Henri Dunant (Switz.); Frederick Passy (Fr.)
1902	Theodor Mommsen (Germany)	Elie Ducommun and Albert Gobat (Switz.)
1903	Björnstjerne Björnson (Norway)	Sir William R. Cremer (England)
1904	Frédéric Mistral (France) and José Echegaray (Spain)	Institut de Droit International (Belgium)
1905	Henryk Sienkiewicz (Poland)	Bertha von Suttner (Austria)
1906	Giosuè Carducci (Italy)	Theodore Roosevelt (U. S.)
1907	Rudyard Kipling (England)	Ernesto T. Moneta (Italy) and Louis Renault (France)
1908	Rudolf Eucken (Germany)	Klas P. Arnoldson (Sweden) and Frederik Bajer (Denmark)
1909	Selma Lagerlöf (Sweden)	Auguste M. F. Beernaert (Belgium) and Baron Paul H. B. B. d'Estournelles de Constant de Rebecque (France)
1910	Paul von Heyse (Germany)	Bureau International Permanent de la Paix (Switzerland)
1911	Maurice Maeterlinck (Belgium)	Tobias M. C. Asser (Holland) and Alfred H. Fried (Austria)
1912	Gerhart Hauptmann (Germany)	Elihu Root (U. S.)
1913	Rabindranath Tagore (India)	Henri La Fontaine (Belgium)
1915	Romain Rolland (France)	No award
1916	Verner von Heidenstam (Sweden)	No award
1917	Karl Gjellerup (Denmark) and Henrik Pontoppidan (Denmark)	International Red Cross
1919	Carl Spitteler (Switzerland)	Woodrow Wilson (U. S.)
1920	Knut Hamsun (Norway)	Léon Bourgeois (France)
1921	Anatole France (France)	Karl H. Branting (Sweden) and Christian L. Lange (Norway)
1922	Jacinto Benavente (Spain)	Fridtjof Nansen (Norway)
1923	William B. Yeats (Ireland)	No award
1924	Wladyslaw Reymont (Poland)	No award
1925	George Bernard Shaw (England)	Sir Austen Chamberlain (England) and Charles G. Dawes (U. S.)
1926	Grazia Deledda (Italy)	Aristide Briand (France) and Gustav Stresemann (Germany)
1927	Henri Bergson (France)	Ferdinand Buisson (France) and Ludwig Quidde (Germany)
1928	Sigrid Undset (Norway)	No award
1929	Thomas Mann (Germany)	Frank B. Kellogg (U. S.)
1930	Sinclair Lewis (U. S.)	Lars O. J. Söderblom (Sweden)
1931	Erik A. Karlfeldt (Sweden)	Jane Addams and Nicholas M. Butler (U. S.)
1932	John Galsworthy (England)	No award
1933	Ivan G. Bunin (Russia)	Sir Norman Angell (England)
1934	Luigi Pirandello (Italy)	Arthur Henderson (England)
1935	No award	Karl von Ossietzky (Germany)
1936	Eugene O'Neill (U. S.)	Carlos de S. Lamas (Argentina)
1937	Roger Martin du Gard (France)	Lord Cecil of Chelwood (England)
1938	Pearl S. Buck (U. S.)	Office International Nansen pour les Réfugiés (Switzerland)
1939	Frans Eemil Sillanpää (Finland)	No award
1944	Johannes V. Jensen (Denmark)	International Red Cross
1945	Gabriela Mistral (Chile)	Cordell Hull (U. S.)

Year	Literature	Peace
1946	Hermann Hesse (Switzerland)	Emily G. Balch and John R. Mott (U. S.)
1947	André Gide (France)	Am. Friends Service Com. (U. S.), Brit. Soc. of Friends' Service Council (England)
1948	Thomas Stearns Eliot (England)	No award
1949	William Faulkner (U. S.)	Lord John Boyd Orr (Scotland)
1950	Bertrand Russell (England)	Ralph J. Bunche (U. S.)
1951	Pär Lagerkvist (Sweden)	Léon Jouhaux (France)
1952	François Mauriac (France)	Albert Schweitzer (French Equatorial Africa)
1953	Sir Winston Churchill (England)	George C. Marshall (U. S.)
1954	Ernest Hemingway (U. S.)	Office of U.N. High Commissioner for Refugees
1955	Halldór Kiljan Laxness (Iceland)	No award
1956	Juan Ramón Jiménez (Spain)	No award
1957	Albert Camus (France)	Lester B. Pearson (Canada)
1958	Boris Pasternak (U.S.S.R.) (declined)	Rev. Dominique Georges Henri Pire (Belgium)
1959	Salvatore Quasimodo (Italy)	Philip John Noel-Baker (England)
1960	St.-John Perse (Alexis St.-Léger Léger) (France)	Albert John Luthuli (South Africa)
1961	Ivo Andric (Yugoslavia)	Dag Hammarskjöld (Sweden)
1962	John Steinbeck (U. S.)	Linus Pauling (U. S.)
1963	Giorgios Seferis (Seferiades) (Greece)	Intl. Comm. of Red Cross; League of Red Cross Societies (both Geneva, Switz.)
1964	Jean-Paul Sartre (France) (declined)	Rev. Dr. Martin Luther King, Jr. (U.S.)
1965	Mikhail Sholokhov (U.S.S.R.)	UNICEF (United Nations Children's Fund)
1966	Shmuel Yosef Agnon (Israel) and Nelly Sachs (Sweden)	No award
1967	Miguel Angel Asturias (Guatemala)	No award
1968	Yasunari Kawabata (Japan)	René Cassin (France)
1969	Samuel Beckett (France)	International Labour Organisation
1970	Aleksandr Solzhenitsyn (U.S.S.R.)	Norman E. Borlaug (U.S.)
1971	Pablo Neruda (Chile)	Willy Brandt (West Germany)
1972	Heinrich Boll (Germany)	No award
1973	Patrick White (Australia)	Henry A. Kissinger (U.S.); Le Duc Tho (North Vietnam) *
1974	Eyvind Johnson and Harry Martinson (both Sweden)	Eisaku Sato (Japan); Sean MacBride (Ireland)
1975	Eugenio Montale (Italy)	Andrei D. Sakharov (U.S.S.R.)

* Le Duc Tho refused prize charging that peace had not yet been really established in South Vietnam.

Year	Physics	Chemistry	Physiology or Medicine
1901	Wilhelm K. Roentgen (Germany), for discovery of Roentgen rays.	Jacobus H. van't Hoff (Netherlands), for laws of chemical dynamics and osmotic pressure in solutions.	Emil A. von Behring (Germany), for work on serum therapy against diphtheria.
1902	Hendrik A. Lorentz and Pieter Zeeman (Netherlands), for work on influence of magnetism upon radiation.	Emil Fischer (Germany), for experiments in sugar and purin groups of substances.	Sir Ronald Ross (England), for work on malaria.
1903	A. Henri Becquerel (France), for work on spontaneous radioactivity; and Pierre and Marie Curie (France), for study of radiation.	Svante A. Arrhenius (Sweden), for his electrolytic theory of dissociation.	Niels R. Finsen (Denmark), for his treatment of lupus vulgaris with concentrated light rays.
1904	John Strutt (Lord Rayleigh) (England), for discovery of argon in investigating gas density.	Sir William Ramsay (England), for discovery and determination of place of inert gaseous elements in air.	Ivan P. Pavlov (U.S.S.R.), for work on the physiology of digestion.
1905	Philipp Lenard (Germany), for work with cathode rays.	Adolf von Baeyer (Germany), for work on organic dyes and hydroaromatic combinations.	Robert Koch (Germany), for work on tuberculosis.
1906	Sir Joseph Thomson (England), for investigations on passage of electricity through gases.	Henri Moissan (France), for isolation of fluorine, and introduction of electric furnace.	Camillo Golgi (Italy) and Santiago Ramón y Cajal (Spain), for work on structure of the nervous system.

Year	Physics	Chemistry	Physiology or Medicine
1907	Albert A. Michelson (U.S.), for spectroscopic and metrologic investigations.	Eduard Buchner (Germany), discovery of cellless fermentation and investigations in biological chemistry.	Charles L. A. Laveran (France), for work with protozoa in the generation of disease.
1908	Gabriel Lippmann (France), for method of reproducing colors by photography.	Sir Ernest Rutherford (England), for investigations into disintegration of elements.	Paul Ehrlich (Germany), and Elie Metchnikoff (U.S.S.R.), for work on immunity.
1909	Guglielmo Marconi (Italy) and Ferdinand Braun (Germany), for development of wireless.	Wilhelm Ostwald (Germany), for work on catalysis and investigations into chemical equilibrium and reaction rates.	Theodor Kocher (Switzerland), for work on the thyroid gland.
1910	Johannes D. van der Waals (Netherlands), for work with the equation of state for gases and liquids.	Otto Wallach (Germany), for work in the field of alicyclic compounds.	Albrecht Kossel (Germany), for achievements in the chemistry of the cell.
1911	Wilhelm Wien (Germany), for his laws governing the radiation of heat.	Marie Curie (France), for discovery of elements radium and polonium.	Allvar Gullstrand (Sweden), for work on the dioptrics of the eye.
1912	Gustaf Dalén (Sweden), for discovery of automatic regulators used in lighting lighthouses and light buoys.	Victor Grignard (France), for reagent discovered by him; and Paul Sabatier (France), for methods of hydrogenating organic compounds.	Alexis Carrel (France), for work on vascular ligature and grafting of blood vessels and organs.
1913	Heike Kamerlingh-Onnes (Netherlands), for work leading to production of liquid helium.	Alfred Werner (Switzerland), for linking up atoms within the molecule.	Charles Richet (France), for work on anaphylaxy.
1914	Max von Laue (Germany), for discovery of diffraction of Roentgen rays passing through crystals.	Theodore W. Richards (U.S.), for determining atomic weight of many chemical elements.	Robert Bárány (Austria), for work on physiology and pathology of the vestibular system.
1915	Sir William Bragg and William L. Bragg (England), for analysis of crystal structure by X rays.	Richard Willstätter (Germany), for research into coloring matter of plants, especially chlorophyll.	No award.
1917	Charles G. Barkla (England), for discovery of Roentgen radiation of the elements.	No award.	No award.
1918	Max Planck (Germany), discoveries in connection with quantum theory.	Fritz Haber (Germany), for synthetic production of ammonia.	No award.
1919	Johannes Stark (Germany), discovery of Doppler effect in Canal rays and decomposition of spectrum lines by electric fields.	No award.	Jules Bordet (Belgium), for discoveries in connection with immunity.
1920	Charles E. Guillaume (Switzerland), for discoveries of anomalies in nickel steel alloys.	Walther Nernst (Germany), for work in thermochemistry.	August Krogh (Denmark), for discovery of regulation of capillaries' motor mechanism.
1921	Albert Einstein (Germany), for discovery of the law of the photoelectric effect.	Frederick Soddy (England), for investigations into origin and nature of isotopes.	No award.
1922	Niels Bohr (Denmark), for investigation of structure of atoms and radiations emanating from them.	Francis W. Aston (England), for discovery of isotopes in nonradioactive elements and for discovery of the whole number rule.	In 1923, the 1922 prize was shared by Archibald V. Hill (England), for discovery relating to heat-production in muscles; and Otto Meyerhof (Germany), for correlation between consumption of

Year	Physics	Chemistry	Physiology or Medicine
			oxygen and production of lactic acid in muscles.
1923	Robert A. Millikan (U.S.), for work on elementary charge of electricity and photoelectric phenomena.	Fritz Pregl (Austria), for method of microanalysis of organic substances discovered by him.	Sir Frederick Banting (Canada) and John J. R. Macleod (Scotland), for discovery of insulin.
1924	Karl M. G. Siegbahn (Sweden), for investigations in X-ray spectroscopy.	No award.	Willem Einthoven (Netherlands), for discovery of the mechanism of the electrocardiogram.
1925	James Franck and Gustav Hertz (Germany), for discovery of laws governing impact of electrons upon atoms.	In 1926, the 1925 prize was awarded to Richard Zsigmondy (Germany), for work on the heterogeneous nature of colloid solutions.	No award.
1926	Jean B. Perrin (France), for work on discontinuous structure of matter and discovery of the equilibrium of sedimentation.	Theodor Svedberg (Sweden), for work on disperse systems.	Johannes Fibiger (Denmark), for discovery of the Spiroptera carcinoma.
1927	Arthur H. Compton (U.S.), for discovery of Compton phenomenon; and Charles T. R. Wilson (England), for method of perceiving paths taken by electrically charged particles.	In 1928 the 1927 prize was awarded to Heinrich Wieland (Germany), for investigations of bile acids and kindred substances.	Julius Wagner-Jauregg (Austria), for use of malaria inoculation in treatment of dementia paralytica.
1928	In 1929, the 1928 prize was awarded to Sir Owen Richardson (England), for work on the phenomenon of thermionics and discovery of the Richardson Law.	Adolf Windaus (Germany), for investigations on constitution of the sterols and their connection with vitamins.	Charles Nicolle (France), for work on typhus exanthematicus.
1929	Prince Louis Victor de Broglie (France), for discovery of the wave character of electrons.	Sir Arthur Harden (England) and Hans K. A. S. von Euler-Chelpin (Sweden), for research of fermentation of sugars.	Christiaan Eijkman (Netherlands), for discovery of the antineuritic vitamins; and Sir Frederick Hopkins (England), for discovery of growth-promoting vitamins.
1930	Sir Chandrasekhara Raman (India), for work on diffusion of light and discovery of the Raman effect.	Hans Fischer (Germany), for work on coloring matter of blood and leaves and for his synthesis of hemin.	Karl Landsteiner (U. S.), for discovery of human blood groups.
1931	No award.	Karl Bosch and Friedrich Bergius (Germany), for invention and development of chemical high-pressure methods.	Otto H. Warburg (Germany), for discovery of the character and mode of action of the respiratory ferment.
1932	In 1933, the prize for 1932 was awarded to Werner Heisenberg (Germany), for creation of the quantum mechanics.	Irving Langmuir (U. S.), for work in realm of surface chemistry.	Sir Charles Sherrington (England) and Edgar D. Adrian (U. S.), for discoveries of the function of the neuron.
1933	Erwin Schrödinger (Austria) and Paul A. M. Dirac (England), for discovery of new fertile forms of the atomic theory.	No award.	Thomas H. Morgan (U. S.), for discoveries on hereditary function of the chromosomes.
1934	No award.	Harold C. Urey (U. S.), for discovery of heavy hydrogen.	George H. Whipple, George R. Minot, and William P. Murphy (U. S.), for

Year	Physics	Chemistry	Physiology or Medicine
			discovery of liver therapy against anemias.
1935	James Chadwick (England), for discovery of the neutron.	Frédéric and Irène Joliot-Curie (France), for synthesis of new radioactive elements.	Hans Spemann (Germany), for discovery of the organizer-effect in embryonic development.
1936	Victor F. Hess (Austria), for discovery of cosmic radiation; and Carl D. Anderson (U. S.), for discovery of the positron.	Peter J. W. Debye (Netherlands), for investigations on dipole moments and diffraction of X rays and electrons in gases.	Sir Henry Dale (England) and Otto Loewi (Germany), for discoveries on chemical transmission of nerve impulses.
1937	Clinton J. Davisson (U. S.) and George P. Thomson (England), for discovery of diffraction of electrons by crystals.	Walter N. Haworth (England), for research on carbohydrates and Vitamin C; and Paul Karrer (Switzerland), for work on carotenoids, flavins and Vitamins A and B.	Albert Szent-Györgyi von Nagyrapolt (Hungary), for discoveries on biological combustion.
1938	Enrico Fermi (Italy), for identification of new radioactivity elements and discovery of nuclear reactions effected by slow neutrons.	Richard Kuhn (Germany), for carotinoid study and vitamin research (declined the prize).	Corneille Heymans (Belgium), for determining importance of sinus and aorta mechanisms in the regulation of respiration.
1939	Ernest Orlando Lawrence (U. S.), for development of the cyclotron.	Adolf Butenandt (Germany), for work on sexual hormones (declined the prize); and Leopold Růžička (Switzerland), for work with polymethylenes.	Gerhard Domagk (Germany), for antibacterial effect of prontocilate.
1943	Otto Stern (U. S.), for detection of magnetic momentum of protons.	Georg Hevesy De Heves (Hungary), for work on use of isotopes as indicators.	Henrik Dam (Denmark) and Edward A. Doisy (U. S.), for analysis of Vitamin K.
1944	Isidor Isaac Rabi (U. S.), for work on magnetic movements of atomic particles.	Otto Hahn (Germany), for work on atomic fission.	Joseph Erlanger and Herbert Spencer Gasser (U. S.), for work on functions of the nerve threads.
1945	Wolfgang Pauli (Austria), for work on atomic fissions.	Artturi Ilmari Virtanen (Finland), for research in the field of conservation of fodder.	Sir Alexander Fleming, Ernst Boris Chain, and Sir Howard Florey (England), for discovery of penicillin.
1946	Percy Williams Bridgman (U. S.), for studies and inventions in high-pressure physics.	James B. Sumner (U. S.), for crystallizing enzymes; John H. Northrop and Wendell M. Stanley (U. S.), for preparing enzymes and virus proteins in pure form.	Herman J. Muller (U. S.), for hereditary effects of X rays on genes.
1947	Sir Edward Appleton (England), for discovery of layer which reflects radio short waves in the ionosphere.	Sir Robert Robinson (England), for research in plant substances.	Carl F. and Gerty T. Cori (U. S.), for work on animal starch metabolism; Bernardo A. Houssay (Argentina), for study of pituitary.
1948	Patrick M. S. Blackett (England), for improvement on Wilson chamber and discoveries in cosmic radiation.	Arne Tiselius (Sweden), for biochemical discoveries and isolation of mouse paralysis virus.	Paul Mueller (Switzerland), for discovery of insect-killing properties of DDT.

Year	Physics	Chemistry	Physiology or Medicine
1949	Hideki Yukawa (Japan), for mathematical prediction, in 1935, of the meson.	William Francis Giauque (U. S.), for research in thermodynamics, especially effects of low temperature.	Walter Rudolf Hess (Switzerland), for research on brain control of body; and Antonio Caetano de Abreu Freire Egas Moniz (Portugal), for development of brain operation.
1950	Cecil Frank Powell (England), for method of photographic study of atom nucleus, and for discoveries about mesons.	Otto Diels and Kurt Alder (Germany), for discovery of diene synthesis enabling scientists to study structure of organic matter.	Philip S. Hench, Edward C. Kendall (both U. S.), and Tadeus Reichstein (Switzerland), for discoveries about hormones of adrenal cortex.
1951	Sir John Douglas Cockcroft (England) and Ernest T. S. Walton (Ireland), for work in 1932 on transmutation of atomic nuclei.	Glenn T. Seaborg and Edwin H. McMillan (U. S.), for discovery of plutonium.	Max Theiler (South Africa), for development of anti-yellow-fever vaccine.
1952	Edward Mills Purcell and Felix Bloch (U. S.), for work in measurement of magnetic fields in atomic nuclei.	Archer John Porter Martin and Richard Laurence Millington Synge (England), for development of partition chromatography.	Selman A. Waksman (U. S.), for co-discovery of streptomycin.
1953	Fritz Zernike (Netherlands), for development of "phase contrast" microscope.	Hermann Staudinger (Germany), for research in giant molecules.	Fritz A. Lipmann (Germany-U. S.) and Hans Adolph Krebs (Germany-England), for studies of living cells.
1954	Max Born (England), for work in quantum mechanics; and Walther Bothe (Germany), for work in cosmic radiation.	Linus C. Pauling (U. S.), for study of forces holding together protein and other molecules.	John F. Enders, Thomas H. Weller, and Frederick C. Robbins (U. S.), for work with cultivation of polio virus.
1955	Polykarp Kusch and Willis E. Lamb, Jr. (U. S.), for atomic measurements.	Vincent du Vigneaud (U. S.), for work on pituitary hormones.	Hugo Theorell (Sweden), for work on oxidation enzymes.
1956	William Shockley, Walter H. Brattain, and John Bardeen (U. S.), for developing electronic transistor.	Sir Cyril Hinshelwood (England) and Nikolai N. Semenov (U.S.S.R.), for parallel research on chemical reaction kinetics.	Dickinson W. Richards, Jr., André F. Cournand (both U. S.), and Werner Forssmann (Germany), for new techniques in treating heart disease.
1957	Tsung Dao Lee and Chen Ning Yang (China), for disproving principle of conservation of parity.	Sir Alexander Todd (England), for research with chemical compounds that are factors in heredity.	Daniel Bovet (Italy), for development of drugs to relieve allergies and relax muscles during surgery.
1958	Pavel A. Cherenkov, Ilya M. Frank, and Igor E. Tamm (U.S.S.R.), for work resulting in development of cosmic-ray counter.	Frederick Sanger (England), for determining molecular structure of insulin.	Joshua Lederberg (U. S.), for work with genetic mechanisms; George W. Beadle and Edward L. Tatum (U. S.), for discovering how genes transmit hereditary characteristics.
1959	Emilio Segre and Owen Chamberlain (U. S.), for demonstrating the existence of the anti-proton.	Jaroslav Heyrovsky (Czechoslovakia), for development of polarography, an electrochemical method of analysis.	Severo Ochoa and Arthur Kornberg (U. S.), for discoveries related to compounds within chromosomes, which play a vital role in heredity.
1960	Donald A. Glaser (U. S.), for invention of "bubble chamber" to study subatomic particles.	Willard F. Libby (U. S.), for "atomic time clock" to measure age of objects by measuring their radioactivity.	Sir Macfarlane Burnet (Australia) and Peter Brian Medawar (England), for discovery of acquired immunological tolerance.

Year	Physics	Chemistry	Physiology or Medicine
1961	Robert Hofstadter (U. S.), for determination of shape and size of atomic nucleus; Rudolf Mössbauer (Germany), for method of producing and measuring recoil-free gamma rays.	Melvin Calvin (U. S.), for establishing chemical steps during photosynthesis.	Georg von Bekesy (U. S.), for discoveries about physical mechanisms of stimulation within cochlea.
1962	Lev D. Landau (U.S.S.R.), for his theories about condensed matter.	Max F. Perutz and John C. Kendrew (England), for mapping protein molecules with X rays.	James D. Watson (U. S.) Maurice H. F. Wilkins, and Francis H. C. Crick (England), for determining structure of deoxyribonucleic acid (DNA).
1963	Eugene Paul Wigner, Maria Goeppert Mayer (both U. S.), and J. Hans D. Jensen (Germany), for research on structure of atom and its nucleus.	Carl Ziegler (Germany) and Giulio Natta (Italy), for work in uniting simple hydrocarbons into large molecule substances.	Alan Lloyd Hodgkin, Andrew Fielding Huxley (both England), and Sir John Carew Eccles (Australia), for research on nerve cells.
1964	Charles Hard Townes (U. S.), Nikolai G. Basov, and Aleksandr M. Prochorov (both U.S.S.R.), for developing maser and laser principle of producing high-intensity radiation.	Dorothy Mary Crowfoot Hodgkin (England), for determining structure of compounds needed in combating pernicious anemia.	Konrad E. Bloch (U. S.) and Feodor Lynen (Germany), for research on mechanism and regulation of cholesterol and fatty acid metabolism.
1965	Richard P. Feynman, Julian S. Schwinger (both U. S.) and Shinichero Tomonaga (Japan), for research in quantum electrodynamics.	Robert B. Woodward (U. S.), for work in synthesizing complicated organic compounds.	François Jacob, André Lwolff, and Jacques Monod (France), for study of regulatory activities in body cells.
1966	Alfred Kastler (France), for work on energy levels inside atom.	Robert Sanderson Mulliken (U. S.), for research on bond holding atoms together in molecule.	Charles Brenton Huggins (U. S.), for studies in hormone treatment of cancer of prostate; Francis Peyton Rous (U. S.), for discovery of tumor-producing viruses.
1967	Hans A. Bethe (U. S.), for work on energy production of stars.	Manfred Eigen (Germany), Ronald G. W. Norrish, and George Porter (both England), for work in high-speed chemical reactions.	Haldan K. Hartline, George Wald, and Ragnar Granit (U. S.), for work on human eye.
1968	Luis Walter Alvarez (U. S.), for study of subatomic particles.	Lars Onsager (U. S.), for development of system of equations in thermodynamics.	Robert W. Holley, Har Gobind Khorana, and Marshall W. Nirenberg (U. S.), for studies of genetic code.
1969	Murray Gell-Mann (U. S.), for study of subatomic particles.	Derek H. R. Barton (England) and Odd Hassel (Norway), for study of organic molecules.	Max Delbruck, Alfred D. Hershey, and Salvador E. Luria (U. S.), for study of mechanism of virus infection in living cells.
1970	Hannes Alfvén (Sweden), for theories in plasma physics; and Louis Néel (France), for discoveries in antiferromagnetism and ferrimagnetism.	Luis F. Leloir (Argentina), for discovery of sugar nucleotides and their role in biosynthesis of carbohydrates.	Julius Axelrod (U. S.), Ulf S. von Euler (Sweden), and Sir Bernard Katz (England), for studies of how nerve impulses are transmitted within the body.

Year	Physics	Chemistry	Physiology or Medicine
1971	Dennis Gabor (England), for invention of holographic method of three-dimensional imagery.	Gerhard Herzberg (Canada), for contributions to knowledge of electronic structure and geometry of molecules, particularly free radicals.	Earl W. Sutherland, Jr., (U. S.), for research on how hormones work.
1972	John Bardeen, Leon N. Cooper, John Robert Schrieffer (all U.S.), for theory of superconductivity, where electrical resistance in certain metals vanishes above absolute zero temperature.	Christian Boehmer Anfinsen, Stanford Moore, William Howard Stein (all U.S.), for pioneering studies in enzymes.	Gerald M. Edelman (U.S.), and Rodney R. Porter (U.K.), for research on the chemical structure and nature of antibodies.
1973	Ivar Giaever (U.S.), Leo Esaki (Japan) and Brian D. Josephson (U.K.), for theories that have advanced and expanded the field of miniature electronics.	Ernst Otto Fischer (W. Germany) and Geoffrey Wilkinson (U.K.), for work that could solve problem of automobile exhaust pollution.	Karl von Frisch and Konrad Lorenz (Austria), and Nikolaas Tinbergen (Netherlands), for their studies of individual and social behavior patterns.
1974	Antony Hewish (England), for discovery of pulsars; Martin Ryle (England), for using radiotelescopes to probe outer space with high degree of precision.	Paul J. Flory (U.S.), for developing analytic methods to study properties and molecular structure of long-chain molecules.	George E. Palade and Christian de Duve (both U.S.) and Albert Claude (Belgium), for contributions to understanding inner workings of living cells.
1975	James Rainwater (U.S.) and Ben Mottelson and Aage N. Bohr (both Denmark), for showing that the atomic nucleus is asymmetrical.	John W. Cornforth (Australia) and Vladimir Prelog (Switzerland), for research on structure of biological molecules such as antibiotics and cholesterol.	David Baltimore, Howard M. Temin and Renato Dulbecco (all U.S.), for work in interaction between tumor viruses and genetic material of the cell.

Year	Economics
1969	Ragnar Frisch (Norway) and Jan Tinbergen (Netherlands), for work in econometrics (application of mathematics and statistical methods to economic theories and problems).
1970	Paul A. Samuelson (U. S.), for efforts to raise the level of scientific analysis in economic theory.
1971	Simon Kuznets (U. S.), for developing concept of using a country's gross national product to determine its economic growth.
1972	Kenneth J. Arrow (U.S.) and Sir John R. Hicks (U.K.), for theories that help to assess business risk and government economic and welfare policies.
1973	Wassily Leontief (U.S.), for devising the input–output technique to determine how different sectors of an economy interact.
1974	Gunnar Myrdal (Sweden) and Friedrich A. von Hayek (Austria), for pioneering analysis of the interdependence of economic, social and institutional phenomena.
1975	Leonid V. Kantorovich (U.S.S.R.) and Tjalling C. Koopmans (U.S.), for work on the theory of optimum allocation of resources.

Winners of Bollingen Prize in Poetry, 1949–76

($5,000 award is currently given biennially)

1949—Ezra Pound
1950—Wallace Stevens
1951—John Crowe Ransom
1952—Marianne Moore
1953—Archibald MacLeish and
    William Carlos Williams
1954—W. H. Auden
1955—Léonie Adams and
    Louise Bogan

1956—Conrad Aiken
1957—Allen Tate
1958—E.E. Cummings
1959—Theodore Roethke
1960—Delmore Schwartz
1961—Yvor Winters
1962—John Hall Wheelock and
    Richard Eberhart
1963—Robert Frost

1965—Horace Gregory
1967—Robert Penn Warren
1969—John Berryman and
    Karl Shapiro
1971—Richard Wilbur and
    Mona Van Duyn
1973—James Merrill
1975—Archie Randolph Ammons

Pulitzer Prize Awards

Source: Columbia University.
(For years not listed, no award was made.)

Pulitzer Prizes in Journalism

MERITORIOUS PUBLIC SERVICE

1918 *New York Times;* also special award to MINNA LEWINSON and HENRY BEETLE HOUGH

1919 *Milwaukee Journal*

1921 *Boston Post*

1922 *New York World*

1923 *Memphis Commercial Appeal*

1924 *New York World*

1926 *Columbus (Ga.) Enquirer Sun*

1927 *Canton (Ohio) Daily News*

1928 *Indianapolis Times*

1929 *New York Evening World*

1931 *Atlanta Constitution*

1932 *Indianapolis News*

1933 *New York World-Telegram*

1934 *Medford (Ore.) Mail Tribune*

1935 *Sacramento Bee*

1936 *Cedar Rapids (Iowa) Gazette*

1937 *St. Louis Post-Dispatch*

1938 *Bismarck (N. D.) Tribune*

1939 *Miami Daily News*

1940 *Waterbury (Conn.) Republican & American*

1941 *St. Louis Post-Dispatch*

1942 *Los Angeles Times*

1943 *Omaha World-Herald*

1944 *New York Times*

1945 *Detroit Free Press*

1946 *Scranton (Pa.) Times*

1947 *Baltimore Sun*

1948 *St. Louis Post-Dispatch*

1949 *(Lincoln) Nebraska State Journal*

1950 *Chicago Daily News; St. Louis Post-Dispatch*

1951 *Miami Herald; Brooklyn Eagle*

1952 *St. Louis Post-Dispatch*

1953 *Whiteville (N. C.) News Reporter; Tabor City (N. C.) Tribune*

1954 *Newsday (Garden City, L. I.)*

1955 *Columbus (Ga.) Ledger & Sunday Ledger-Enquirer*

1956 *Watsonville (Calif.) Register-Pajaronian*

1957 *Chicago Daily News*

1958 *(Little Rock) Arkansas Gazette*

1959 *Utica (N. Y.) Observer Dispatch* and the *Utica Daily Press*

1960 *Los Angeles Times*

1961 *Amarillo (Tex.) Globe-Times*

1962 *Panama City (Fla.) News-Herald*

1963 *Chicago Daily News*

1964 *St. Petersburg (Fla.) Times*

1965 *Hutchinson (Kan.) News*

1966 *Boston Globe*

1967 *Louisville Courier-Journal; Milwaukee Journal*

1968 *Riverside (Calif.) Press-Enterprise*

1969 *Los Angeles Times*

1970 *Newsday (Garden City, L. I.)*

1971 *Winston-Salem (N. C.) Journal and Sentinel*

1972 *New York Times*

1973 *Washington Post*

1974 *Newsday (Garden City, L.I.)*

1975 *Boston Globe*

1976 *Anchorage (Alaska) Daily News*

EDITORIAL

1917 *New York Tribune*

1918 *Louisville Courier-Journal*

1920 HARVEY E. NEWBRANCH (*Omaha Evening World-Herald*)

1922 FRANK M. O'BRIEN (*New York Herald*)

1923 WILLIAM ALLEN WHITE (*Emporia [Kan.] Gazette*)

1924 *Boston Herald* (FRANK BUXTON); special prize: FRANK I. COBB (*New York World*)

1925 *Charleston (S. C.) News and Courier*

1926 *New York Times* (EDWARD M. KINGSBURY)

1927 *Boston Herald* (F. LAURISTON BULLARD)

1928 GROVER CLEVELAND HALL (*Montgomery [Ala.] Advertiser*)

1929 LOUIS ISAAC JAFFE (*Norfolk Virginian-Pilot*)

1931 CHARLES S. RYCKMAN (*Fremont [Neb.] Tribune*)

1933 *Kansas City (Mo.) Star*

1934 E. P. CHASE (*Atlantic [Iowa] News Telegraph*)

1936 FELIX MORLEY (*Washington [D.C.] Post*); GEORGE B. PARKER (Scripps-Howard Newspapers)

1937 JOHN W. OWENS (*Baltimore Sun*)

1938 W. W. WAYMACK (*Des Moines Register & Tribune*)

1939 RONALD G. CALLVERT (*Portland Oregonian*)

1940 BART HOWARD (*St. Louis Post-Dispatch*)

1941 REUBEN MAURY (*New York Daily News*)

1942 GEOFFREY PARSONS (*New York Herald Tribune*)

1943 FORREST W. SEYMOUR (*Des Moines Register & Tribune*)

1944 *Kansas City (Mo.) Star* (HENRY J. HASKELL)

1945 GEORGE W. POTTER (*Providence [R. I.] Journal-Bulletin*)

1946 HODDING CARTER ([Greenville, Miss.] *Delta Democrat-Times*)

1947 WILLIAM H. GRIMES (*Wall Street Journal*)

1948 VIRGINIUS DABNEY (*Richmond Times-Dispatch*)

1949 JOHN H. CRIDER (*Boston Herald*); HERBERT ELLISTON (*Washington [D.C.] Post*)

1950 CARL M. SAUNDERS (*Jackson [Mich.] Citizen Patriot*)

1951 WILLIAM H. FITZPATRICK (*New Orleans States*)

1952 LOUIS LaCOSS (*St. Louis Globe-Democrat*)

1953 VERMONT C. ROYSTER (*Wall Street Journal*)

1954 *Boston Herald* (DON MURRAY)

1955 *Detroit Free Press* (ROYCE HOWES)

1956 LAUREN K. SOTH (*Des Moines Register & Tribune*)

1957 BUFORD BOONE (*Tuscaloosa [Ala.] News*)

1958 HARRY S. ASHMORE (*Arkansas Gazette*)

1959 RALPH McGILL (*Atlanta Constitution*)

1960 LENOIR CHAMBERS (*Virginian-Pilot*)

1961 WILLIAM J. DORVILLIER (*San Juan* [P.R.] *Star*)
1962 THOMAS M. STORKE (*Santa Barbara* [Calif.] *News-Press*)
1963 IRA B. HARKEY, JR. (*Pascagoula* [Miss.] *Chronicle*)
1964 HAZEL BRANNON SMITH (*Lexington* [Miss.] *Advertiser*)
1965 JOHN R. HARRISON (*Gainesville* [Fla.] *Daily Sun*)
1966 ROBERT LASCH (*St. Louis Post-Dispatch*)
1967 EUGENE PATTERSON (*Atlanta Constitution*)
1968 JOHN S. KNIGHT (Knight Newspapers)
1969 PAUL GREENBERG (*Pine Bluff* [Ark.] *Commercial*)
1970 PHILIP L. GEYELIN (*Washington Post*)
1971 HORANCE G. DAVIS, JR. (*Gainesville* [Fla.] *Sun*)
1972 JOHN STROHMEYER (*Bethlehem* [Pa.] *Globe Times*)
1973 ROGER BOURNE LINSCOTT (*Berkshire Eagle*)
1974 F. GILMAN SPENCER (*Trenton* [N.J.] *Trentonian*)
1975 JOHN DANIELL MAURICE (*Charleston* [W. Va.] *Daily Mail*)
1976 PHILIP P. KERBY (*Los Angeles Times*)

CORRESPONDENCE

1929 PAUL SCOTT MOWRER (*Chicago Daily News*)
1930 LELAND STOWE (*New York Herald Tribune*)
1931 H. R. KNICKERBOCKER (*Philadelphia Public Ledger* and *New York Evening Post*)
1932 WALTER DURANTY (*New York Times*); CHARLES G. ROSS (*St. Louis Post-Dispatch*)
1933 EDGAR ANSEL MOWRER (*Chicago Daily News*)
1934 FREDERICK T. BIRCHALL (*New York Times*)
1935 ARTHUR KROCK (*New York Times*)
1936 WILFRED C. BARBER (*Chicago Tribune*)
1937 ANNE O'HARE McCORMICK (*New York Times*)
1938 ARTHUR KROCK (*New York Times*)
1939 LOUIS P. LOCHNER (Associated Press)
1940 OTTO D. TOLISCHUS (*New York Times*)

1941 Group award*
1942 CARLOS P. ROMULO (*Philippines Herald*)
1943 HANSON W. BALDWIN (*New York Times*)
1944 ERNIE PYLE (Scripps-Howard Newspaper Alliance)
1945 HAROLD V. (HAL) BOYLE (Associated Press)
1946 ARNALDO CORTESI (*New York Times*)
1947 BROOKS ATKINSON (*New York Times*)
1948 Discontinued

CARTOON

1922 ROLLIN KIRBY (*New York World*)
1924 JAY NORWOOD DARLING (*New York Tribune*)
1925 ROLLIN KIRBY (*New York World*)
1926 D. R. FITZPATRICK (*St. Louis Post-Dispatch*)
1927 NELSON HARDING (*Brooklyn Eagle*)
1928 NELSON HARDING (*Brooklyn Eagle*)
1929 ROLLIN KIRBY (*New York World*)
1930 CHARLES R. MACAULEY (*Brooklyn Eagle*)
1931 EDMUND DUFFY (*Baltimore Sun*)
1932 JOHN T. McCUTCHEON (*Chicago Tribune*)
1933 H. M. TALBURT (*Washington* [D.C.] *Daily News*)
1934 EDMUND DUFFY (*Baltimore Sun*)
1935 ROSS A. LEWIS (*Milwaukee Journal*)
1937 C. D. BATCHELOR (*New York Daily News*)
1938 VAUGHN SHOEMAKER (*Chicago Daily News*)
1939 CHARLES G. WERNER (*Daily Oklahoman* [Oklahoma City])
1940 EDMUND DUFFY (*Baltimore Sun*)
1941 JACOB BURCK (*Chicago Times*)
1942 HERBERT L. BLOCK (NEA Service)
1943 JAY NORWOOD DARLING (*New York Herald Tribune*)
1944 CLIFFORD K. BERRYMAN (*Washington* [D. C.] *Evening Star*)
1945 BILL MAULDIN (United Features Syndicate)
1946 BRUCE ALEXANDER RUSSELL (*Los Angeles Times*)

* For the public services and the individual achievements of American news reporters in the war zones.

1947 VAUGHN SHOEMAKER (*Chicago Daily News*)
1948 REUBEN L. GOLDBERG (*New York Sun*)
1949 LUTE PEASE (*Newark Evening News*)
1950 JAMES T. BERRYMAN (*Washington* [D. C.] *Evening Star*)
1951 REG (REGINALD W.) MANNING (*Arizona Republic* [Phoenix])
1952 FRED L. PACKER (*New York Mirror*)
1953 EDWARD D. KUEKES (*Cleveland Plain Dealer*)
1954 HERBERT L. BLOCK (*Washington* [D. C.] *Post & Times-Herald*)
1955 DANIEL R. FITZPATRICK (*St. Louis Post-Dispatch*)
1956 ROBERT YORK (*Louisville Times*)
1957 TOM LITTLE (*Nashville Tennessean*)
1958 BRUCE M. SHANKS (*Buffalo Evening News*)
1959 BILL MAULDIN (*St. Louis Post-Dispatch*)
1961 CAREY ORR (*Chicago Tribune*)
1962 EDMUND S. VALTMAN (*Hartford Times*)
1963 FRANK MILLER (*Des Moines Register*)
1964 PAUL CONRAD (formerly of *Denver Post*, later on *Los Angeles Times*)
1966 DON WRIGHT (*Miami News*)
1967 PATRICK B. OLIPHANT (*Denver Post*)
1968 EUGENE GRAY PAYNE (*Charlotte* [N. C.] *Observer*)
1969 JOHN FISCHETTI (*Chicago Daily News*)
1970 THOMAS F. DARCY (*Newsday* [Garden City, L. I.)]
1971 PAUL CONRAD (*Los Angeles Times*)
1972 JEFFREY K. MacNELLY (*Richmond* [Va.] *News Leader*)
1974 PAUL SZEP (*Boston Globe*)
1975 GARRY TRUDEAU (Universal Press Syndicate)
1976 TONY AUTH (*Philadelphia Inquirer*)

NEWS PHOTOGRAPHY

1942 MILTON BROOKS (*Detroit News*)
1943 FRANK NOEL (Associated Press)
1944 FRANK FILAN (Associated Press); EARLE L. BUNKER (*Omaha World-Herald*)

1945 JOE ROSENTHAL (Associated Press)
1947 ARNOLD HARDY
1948 FRANK CUSHING (*Boston Traveler*)
1949 NAT FEIN (*New York Herald Tribune*)
1950 BILL CROUCH (*Oakland Tribune*)
1951 MAX DESFOR (Associated Press)
1952 JOHN ROBINSON & DON ULTANG (*Des Moines Register & Tribune*)
1953 WILLIAM M. GALLAGHER (*Flint* [Mich.] *Journal*)
1954 MRS. WALTER M. SCHAU
1955 JOHN L. GAUNT, JR. (*Los Angeles Times*)
1956 *New York Daily News*
1957 HARRY A. TRASK (*Boston Traveler*)
1958 WILLIAM C. BEALL (*Washington* [D. C.] *Daily News*)
1959 WILLIAM SEAMAN (*Minneapolis Star*)
1960 ANDREW LOPEZ (United Press International)
1961 YASUSHI NAGAO (Mainichi Newspapers, Tokyo)
1962 PAUL VATHIS: (Harrisburg [Pa.] bureau of Associated Press)
1963 HECTOR RONDON (*La Republica*, Caracas, Venezuela)
1964 ROBERT H. JACKSON (*Dallas Times Herald*)
1965 HORST FAAS (Associated Press)
1966 KYOICHI SAWADA (United Press International)
1967 JACK R. THORNELL (Associated Press)
1968 News: ROCCO MORABITO (*Jacksonville* [Fla.] *Journal*); features: TOSHIO SAKAI (United Press International)
1969 Spot news: EDWARD T. ADAMS (Associated Press); features: MONETA SLEET, JR.
1970 Spot news: STEVE STARR (Associated Press); features: DALLAS KINNEY (*Palm Beach Post*)
1971 Spot news: JOHN PAUL FILO (*Valley Daily News and Daily Dispatch* [Tarentum and New Kensington, Pa.]): features: Jack Dykinga (*Chicago Sun-Times*)
1972 Spot news: HORST FAAS and MICHEL LAURENT (Associated Press): features: DAVE KENNERLY (United Press International)
1973 Spot News: HUYNH CONG UT (*Associated Press*);

features: BRIAN LANKER (*Topeka Capital-Journal*)
1974 Spot news: ANTHONY K. ROBERTS (Associated Press); features: SLAVA VEDER (Associated Press)
1975 Spot news: GERALD H. GAY (*Seattle Times*); features: MATTHEW LEWIS (*Washington Post*)
1976 Spot news: STANLEY J. FORMAN (*Boston Herald-American*); features: photographic staff of *Louisville Courier-Journal and Times*)

NATIONAL TELEGRAPHIC REPORTING

1942 LOUIS STARK (*New York Times*)
1944 DEWEY L. FLEMING (*Baltimore Sun*)
1945 JAMES RESTON (*New York Times*)
1946 EDWARD A. HARRIS (*St. Louis Post-Dispatch*)
1947 EDWARD T. FOLLIARD (*Washington* [D. C.] *Post*)

NATIONAL REPORTING

1948 BERT ANDREWS (*New York Herald Tribune*); NAT S. FINNEY (*Minneapolis Tribune*)
1949 C. P. TRUSSELL (*New York Times*)
1950 EDWIN O. GUTHMAN (*Seattle Times*)
1952 ANTHONY LEVIERO (*New York Times*)
1953 DON WHITEHEAD (Associated Press)
1954 RICHARD WILSON (Cowles Newspapers)
1955 ANTHONY LEWIS (*Washington* [D. C.] *Daily News*)
1956 CHARLES L. BARTLETT (*Chattanooga Times*)
1957 JAMES RESTON (*New York Times*)
1958 RELMAN MORIN (Associated Press) and CLARK MOLLENHOFF (*Des Moines Register & Tribune*)
1959 HOWARD VAN SMITH (*Miami News*)
1960 VANCE TRIMBLE (Scripps-Howard Newspaper Alliance)
1961 EDWARD R. CONY (*Wall Street Journal*)

1962 NATHAN G. CALDWELL and GENE S. GRAHAM (*Nashville Tennessean*)
1963 ANTHONY LEWIS (*New York Times*)
1964 MERRIMAN SMITH (United Press International)
1965 LOUIS M. KOHLMEIER (*Wall Street Journal*)
1966 HAYNES JOHNSON (*Washington* [D. C.] *Evening Star*)
1967 STANLEY PENN and MONROE KARMIN (*Wall Street Journal*)
1968 HOWARD JAMES (*Christian Science Monitor*); NATHAN K. (NICK) KOTZ (*Des Moines Register and Minneapolis Tribune*)
1969 ROBERT CAHN (*Christian Science Monitor*)
1970 WILLIAM J. EATON (*Chicago Daily News*)
1971 LUCINDA FRANKS and THOMAS POWERS (United Press International)
1972 JACK ANDERSON (*United Feature Syndicate*)
1973 ROBERT BOYD and CLARK HOYT (*Knight Newspapers*)
1974 JACK WHITE (*Providence* [R.I.] *Journal-Bulletin*); and JAMES R. POLK (*Washington Star-News*)
1975 DONALD L. BARLETT and JAMES B. STEELE (*Philadelphia Inquirer*)
1976 JAMES RISSER (*Des Moines Register*)

INTERNATIONAL TELEGRAPHIC REPORTING

1942 LAURENCE EDMUND ALLEN (Associated Press)
1943 IRA WOLFERT (North American Newspaper Alliance, Inc.)
1944 DANIEL DE LUCE (Associated Press)
1945 MARK S. WATSON (*Baltimore Sun*)
1946 HOMER W. BIGART (*New York Herald Tribune*)
1947 EDDY GILMORE (Associated Press)

INTERNATIONAL REPORTING

1948 PAUL W. WARD (*Baltimore Sun*)
1949 PRICE DAY (*Baltimore Sun*)
1950 EDMUND STEVENS (*Christian Science Monitor*)

1951 KEYES BEECH & FRED
SPARKS (*Chicago Daily
News*); HOMER BIGART
& MARGUERITE HIGGINS
(*New York Herald Trib-
une*); RELMAN MORIN &
DON WHITEHEAD (Asso-
ciated Press)

1952 JOHN M. HIGHTOWER (Associated Press)

1953 AUSTIN C. WEHRWEIN
(*Milwaukee Journal*)

1954 JIM G. LUCAS (Scripps-
Howard Newspapers)

1955 HARRISON E. SALISBURY
(*New York Times*)

1956 WILLIAM RANDOLPH HEARST,
JR., & FRANK CONNIFF
(Hearst newspapers) &
KINGSBURY SMITH (INS)

1957 RUSSELL JONES (United
Press)

1958 *New York Times*

1959 JOSEPH MARTIN & PHILIP
SANTORA (*New York
Daily News*)

1960 A. M. ROSENTHAL (*New
York Times*)

1961 LYNN HEINZERLING (Associated Press)

1962 WALTER LIPPMANN (New
York Herald Tribune
Syndicate)

1963 HAL HENDRIX (*Miami
News*)

1964 MALCOLM W. BROWNE (As-
sociated Press) and
DAVID HALBERSTAM (*New
York Times*)

1965 J. A. LIVINGSTON (*Philadelphia Bulletin*)

1966 PETER ARNETT (Associated
Press)

1967 R. JOHN HUGHES (*Christian Science Monitor*)

1968 ALFRED FRIENDLY (*Washington* [D.C.] *Post*)

1969 WILLIAM TUOHY (*Los
Angeles Times*)

1970 SEYMOUR M. HERSH (Dispatch News Service)

1971 JIMMIE LEE HOAGLAND
(*Washington* [D. C.]
Post)

1972 PETER R. KANN (*Wall
Street Journal*)

1973 MAX FRANKEL (*New York
Times*)

1974 HEDRICK SMITH (*New York
Times*)

1975 WILLIAM MULLEN and
OVIE CARTER (*Chicago
Tribune*)

1976 SYDNEY H. SCHANBERG
(*New York Times*)

REPORTING

1917 HERBERT B. SWOPE (*New
York World*)

1918 HAROLD A. LITTLEDALE
(*New York Evening
Post*)

1920 JOHN J. LEARY, JR. (*New
York World*)

1921 LOUIS SEIBOLD (*New York
World*)

1922 KIRKE L. SIMPSON (Associated Press)

1923 ALVA JOHNSTON (*New
York Times*)

1924 MAGNER WHITE (*San
Diego Sun*)

1925 JAMES W. MULROY &
ALVIN H. GOLDSTEIN
(*Chicago Daily News*)

1926 WILLIAM BURKE MILLER
(*Louisville Courier-
Journal*)

1927 JOHN T. ROGERS (*St.
Louis Post-Dispatch*)

1929 PAUL Y. ANDERSON (*St.
Louis Post-Dispatch*)

1930 RUSSELL D. OWEN (*New
York Times*); special
award: W. O. DAPPING
(*Auburn* [N. Y.] *Citi-
zen*)

1931 A. B. MACDONALD (*Kansas City* [Mo.] *Star*)

1932 W. C. RICHARDS, D. D.
MARTIN, J. S. POOLER,
F. D. WEBB, J. N. W.
SLOAN (all of *Detroit
Free Press*)

1933 FRANCIS A. JAMIESON (Associated Press)

1934 ROYCE BRIER (*San Francisco Chronicle*)

1935 WILLIAM H. TAYLOR (*New
York Herald Tribune*)

1936 LAUREN D. LYMAN (*New
York Times*)

1937 JOHN J. O'NEILL (*New
York Herald Tribune*),
WILLIAM LEONARD LAU-
RENCE (*New York
Times*), HOWARD W.
BLAKESLEE (Associated
Press), GOBIND BEHARI
LAL (Universal Serv-
ice), DAVID DIETZ
(Scripps-Howard News-
papers)

1938 RAYMOND SPRIGLE (*Pittsburgh Post-Gazette*)

1939 THOMAS L. STOKES (*New
York World-Telegram*)

1940 S. BURTON HEATH (*New
York World-Telegram*)

1941 WESTBROOK PEGLER (*New
York World-Telegram*)

1942 STANTON DELAPLANE (*San
Francisco Chronicle*)

1943 GEORGE WELLER (*Chicago
Daily News*)

1944 PAUL SCHOENSTEIN & associates (*New York
Journal-American*)

1945 JACK S. McDOWELL (*San
Francisco Call-Bulle-
tin*)

1946 WILLIAM LEONARD LAU-
RENCE (*New York
Times*)

1947 FREDERICK WOLTMAN (*New
York World-Telegram*)

1948 GEORGE E. GOODWIN (*Atlanta Journal*)

1949 MALCOLM JOHNSON (*New
York Sun*)

1950 MEYER BERGER (*New York
Times*)

1951 EDWARD S. MONTGOMERY
(*San Francisco Exam-
iner*)

1952 GEORGE DE CARVALHO (*San
Francisco Chronicle*)

1953 Editorial staff (*Providence Journal & Eve-
ning Bulletin*);* ED-
WARD J. MOWERY (*New
York World-Telegram
and Sun*)†

1954 *Vicksburg* (Miss.) *Sunday Post-Herald*;* AL-
VIN SCOTT McCOY (*Kan-
sas City* [Mo.] *Star*)†

1955 MRS. CARO BROWN (*Alice
[Tex.] Daily Echo*);*
ROLAND KENNETH TOW-
ERY (*Cuero* [Tex.] *Rec-
ord*)†

1956 LEE HILLS (*Detroit Free
Press*);* ARTHUR DALEY
(*New York Times*)†

1957 *Salt Lake Tribune*;* WAL-
LACE TURNER and WIL-
LIAM LAMBERT (*Portland
Oregonian*)†

1958 *Fargo* [N. D.] *Forum*;*
GEORGE BEVERIDGE
(*Washington* [D. C.]
Evening Star)†

1959 MARY LOU WERNER (*Wash-
ington* [D. C.] *Evening
Star*);* JOHN HAROLD
BRISLIN *Scranton* [Pa.]
*Tribune & Scranton-
ian*)†

1960 JACK NELSON (*Atlanta
Constitution*);* MIRIAM
OTTENBERG (*Washington*
[D. C.] *Evening Star*)†

1961 SANCHE DE GRAMONT (*New
York Herald Tribune*);*
EDGAR MAY (*Buffalo
Evening News*)†

1962 ROBERT D. MULLINS (*Des-
eret News*, Salt Lake
City);* GEORGE BLISS
(*Chicago Tribune*) †

1963 SYLVAN FOX, ANTHONY
SHANNON, and WILLIAM
LONGGOOD (*New York
World-Telegram and
Sun*);* OSCAR GRIFFIN,
JR. (former editor of
Pecos [Tex.] *Independ-

* Reporting under pressure of edition deadlines. † Reporting not under pressure of edition deadlines.

ent and Enterprise,
now on staff of *Houston
Chronicle*)†

GENERAL LOCAL REPORTING

1964 NORMAN C. MILLER (*Wall
Street Journal*)
1965 MELVIN H. RUDER (*Hungry
Horse News*, Columbia
Falls, Mont.)
1966 Staff of *Los Angeles
Times*
1967 ROBERT V. COX (*Cham-
bersburg* [Pa.] *Public
Opinion*)
1968 Staff of *Detroit Free
Press*
1969 JOHN FETTERMAN (*Louisville Times & Courier-
Journal*)
1970 THOMAS FITZPATRICK (*Chicago Sun-Times*)
1971 Staff of *Akron* (Ohio)
Beacon
1972 RICHARD COOPER and JOHN
MACHACEK (*Rochester
[N. Y.] Times-Union*)
1973 *Chicago Tribune*
1974 ARTHUR M. PETACQUE and
HUGH F. HOUGH (*Chi-
cago Sun-Times*)
1975 *Xenia* (Ohio) *Daily Gazette*
1976 GENE MILLER (*Miami
Herald*)

SPECIAL LOCAL REPORTING

1964 JAMES V. MAGEE, ALBERT
V. GAUDIOSI, and FRED-
ERICK A. MEYER (*Phila-
delphia Bulletin*)
1965 GENE GOLTZ (*Houston
Post*)
1966 JOHN A. FRASCA (*Tampa
Tribune*)
1967 GENE MILLER (*Miami
Herald*)
1968 J. ANTHONY LUKAS (*New
York Times*)
1969 ALBERT L. DELUGACH and
DENNY WALSH (*St.
Louis Globe-Democrat*)
1970 HAROLD EUGENE MARTIN
(*Montgomery Adver-
tiser*)
1971 WILLIAM HUGH JONES
(*Chicago Tribune*)
1972 TIMOTHY LELAND, GERARD
N. O'NEILL, STEPHEN A.
KURKJIAN, and ANN
DESANTIS (*Boston
Globe*)
1973 Sun Newspapers of Omaha, Neb.
1974 WILLIAM SHERMAN (*New
York Daily News*)
1975 *Indianapolis Star*
1976 *Chicago Tribune*

† Reporting not under pressure of
edition deadlines.

COMMENTARY

1970 MARQUIS W. CHILDS (*St.
Louis Post-Dispatch*)
1971 WILLIAM A. CALDWELL
(*Record* [Hackensack,
N. J.])
1972 MIKE ROYKO (*Chicago
Daily News*)
1973 DAVID S. BRODER (*Washington Post*)
1974 EDWIN A. ROBERTS, JR.
(*National Observer*)
1975 MARY MCGRORY (*Wash-
ington Star*)
1976 WALTER W. (RED) SMITH
(*New York Times*)

CRITICISM

1970 ADA LOUISE HUXTABLE
(*New York Times*)
1971 HAROLD C. SCHONBERG
(*New York Times*)
1972 FRANK PETERS, JR. (*St.
Louis Post-Dispatch*)
1973 RONALD POWERS (*Chicago
Sun-Times*)
1974 EMILY GENAUER (Newsday
Syndicate)
1975 ROGER EBERT (*Chicago
Sun-Times*)
1976 ALAN M. KRIEGSMAN
(*Washington Post*)

SPECIAL CITATIONS

1938 *Edmonton* (Alberta)
Journal, special bronze
plaque for editorial
leadership in defense
of freedom of press in
Province of Alberta.
1941 *New York Times* for
the public educational
value of its foreign
news report.
1944 BYRON PRICE, Director of
the Office of Censor-
ship, for the creation
and administration of
the newspaper and ra-
dio codes. MRS. WIL-
LIAM ALLEN WHITE, for
her husband's interest
and services during the
past seven years as a
member of the Advisory
Board of the Graduate
School of Journalism,
Columbia University.
RICHARD RODGERS and
OSCAR HAMMERSTEIN II
for their musical *Okla-
homa!*
1945 The cartographers of the
American press for
their war maps.

1947 (Pulitzer centennial
year.) Columbia Uni-
versity and the Gradu-
ate School of Journal-
ism, for their efforts to
maintain and advance
the high standards
governing the Pulitzer
Prize awards. The *St.
Louis Post-Dispatch*,
for its unswerving ad-
herence to the public
and professional ideals
of its founder and its
leadership in American
journalism.
1948 DR. FRANK D. FACKEN-
THAL, for his interest
and service.
1951 CYRUS L. SULZBERGER (*New
York Times*) for his ex-
clusive interview with
Archbishop Stepinac in
a Yugoslav prison.
1952 *Kansas City Star* for coverage of 1951 floods;
MAX KASE (*New York
Journal-American*) for
exposures of bribery in
college basketball.
1953 *New York Times* for its
17-year publication of
"News of the Week in
Review"; and LESTER
MARKEL, its founder.
1957 KENNETH ROBERTS for his
historical novels.
1958 WALTER LIPPMANN (*New
York Herald Tribune*)
for his "wisdom, per-
ception and high sense
of responsibility" in
his commentary on na-
tional and interna-
tional affairs.
1960 GARRETT MATTINGLY, for
The Armada.
1961 *American Heritage Picture History of the
Civil War*, as distin-
guished example of
American book publish-
ing.
1964 Gannett Newspapers, Rochester, N. Y.
1973 JAMES THOMAS FLEXNER
for his biography
George Washington.
1974 ROGER SESSIONS, for his
"life's work in music."
1976 JOHN HOHENBERG for
"services for 22 years
as administrator of the
Pulitzer Prizes."
SCOTT JOPLIN for his con-
tributions to American
music.

Pulitzer Prizes in Letters

FICTION*

1918 *His Family.* By ERNEST POOLE

1919 *The Magnificent Ambersons.* By BOOTH TARKINGTON

1921 *The Age of Innocence.* By EDITH WHARTON

1922 *Alice Adams.* By BOOTH TARKINGTON

1923 *One of Ours.* By WILLA CATHER

1924 *The Able McLaughlins.* By MARGARET WILSON

1925 *So Big.* By EDNA FERBER

1926 *Arrowsmith.* By SINCLAIR LEWIS

1927 *Early Autumn.* By LOUIS BROMFIELD

1928 *The Bridge of San Luis Rey.* By THORNTON WILDER

1929 *Scarlet Sister Mary.* By JULIA PETERKIN

1930 *Laughing Boy.* By OLIVER LA FARGE

1931 *Years of Grace.* By MARGARET AYER BARNES

1932 *The Good Earth.* By PEARL S. BUCK

1933 *The Store.* By T. S. STRIBLING

1934 *Lamb in His Bosom.* By CAROLINE MILLER

1935 *Now in November.* By JOSEPHINE WINSLOW JOHNSON

1936 *Honey in the Horn.* By HAROLD L. DAVIS

1937 *Gone with the Wind.* By MARGARET MITCHELL

1938 *The Late George Apley.* By JOHN PHILLIPS MARQUAND

1939 *The Yearling.* By MARJORIE KINNAN RAWLINGS

1940 *The Grapes of Wrath.* By JOHN STEINBECK

1942 *In This Our Life.* By ELLEN GLASGOW

1943 *Dragon's Teeth.* By UPTON SINCLAIR

1944 *Journey in the Dark.* By MARTIN FLAVIN

1945 *A Bell for Adano.* By JOHN HERSEY

1947 *All the King's Men.* By ROBERT PENN WARREN

1948 *Tales of the South Pacific.* By JAMES A. MICHENER

1949 *Guard of Honor.* By JAMES GOULD COZZENS

1950 *The Way West.* By A. B. GUTHRIE, JR.

1951 *The Town.* By CONRAD RICHTER

* Before 1948, award was for novels only.

1952 *The Caine Mutiny.* By HERMAN WOUK

1953 *The Old Man and the Sea.* By ERNEST HEMINGWAY

1955 *A Fable.* By WILLIAM FAULKNER

1956 *Andersonville.* By MacKINLAY KANTOR

1958 *A Death in the Family.* By JAMES AGEE

1959 *The Travels of Jaimie McPheeters.* By ROBERT LEWIS TAYLOR

1960 *Advise and Consent.* By ALLEN DRURY

1961 *To Kill a Mockingbird.* By HARPER LEE

1962 *The Edge of Sadness.* By EDWIN O'CONNOR

1963 *The Reivers.* By WILLIAM FAULKNER

1965 *The Keepers of the House.* By SHIRLEY ANN GRAU

1966 *Collected Stories of Katherine Anne Porter.* By KATHERINE ANNE PORTER

1967 *The Fixer.* By BERNARD MALAMUD

1968 *The Confessions of Nat Turner.* By WILLIAM STYRON

1969 *House Made of Dawn.* By N. SCOTT MOMADAY

1970 *Collected Stories.* By JEAN STAFFORD

1972 *Angle of Repose.* By WALLACE STEGNER

1973 *The Optimist's Daughter.* By EUDORA WELTY

1975 *The Killer Angels.* By MICHAEL SHAARA

1976 *Humboldt's Gift.* By SAUL BELLOW

DRAMA

1918 *Why Marry?* By JESSE LYNCH WILLIAMS

1920 *Beyond the Horizon.* By EUGENE O'NEILL

1921 *Miss Lulu Bett.* By ZONA GALE

1922 *Anna Christie.* By EUGENE O'NEILL

1923 *Icebound.* By OWEN DAVIS

1924 *Hell-Bent Fer Heaven.* By HATCHER HUGHES

1925 *They Knew What They Wanted.* By SIDNEY HOWARD

1926 *Craig's Wife.* By GEORGE KELLY

1927 *In Abraham's Bosom.* By PAUL GREEN

1928 *Strange Interlude.* By EUGENE O'NEILL

1929 *Street Scene.* By ELMER L. RICE

1930 *The Green Pastures.* By MARC CONNELLY

1931 *Alison's House.* By SUSAN GLASPELL

1932 *Of Thee I Sing.* By GEORGE S. KAUFMAN, MORRIE RYSKIND, and IRA GERSHWIN

1933 *Both Your Houses.* By MAXWELL ANDERSON

1934 *Men in White.* By SIDNEY KINGSLEY

1935 *The Old Maid.* By ZOË AKINS

1936 *Idiot's Delight.* By ROBERT E. SHERWOOD

1937 *You Can't Take It with You.* By MOSS HART and GEORGE S. KAUFMAN

1938 *Our Town.* By THORNTON WILDER

1939 *Abe Lincoln in Illinois.* By ROBERT E. SHERWOOD

1940 *The Time of Your Life.* By WILLIAM SAROYAN

1941 *There Shall Be No Night.* By ROBERT E. SHERWOOD

1943 *The Skin of Our Teeth.* By THORNTON WILDER

1945 *Harvey.* By MARY CHASE

1946 *State of the Union.* By RUSSEL CROUSE and HOWARD LINDSAY

1948 *A Streetcar Named Desire.* By TENNESSEE WILLIAMS

1949 *Death of a Salesman.* By ARTHUR MILLER

1950 *South Pacific.* By RICHARD RODGERS, OSCAR HAMMERSTEIN II, and JOSHUA LOGAN

1952 *The Shrike.* By JOSEPH KRAMM

1953 *Picnic.* By WILLIAM INGE

1954 *The Teahouse of the August Moon.* By JOHN PATRICK

1955 *Cat on a Hot Tin Roof.* By TENNESSEE WILLIAMS

1956 *The Diary of Anne Frank.* By FRANCES GOODRICH and ALBERT HACKETT

1957 *Long Day's Journey Into Night.* By EUGENE O'NEILL

1958 *Look Homeward, Angel.* By KETTI FRINGS

1959 *J.B.* By ARCHIBALD MacLEISH

1960 *Fiorello!* By GEORGE ABBOTT, JEROME WEIDMAN, JERRY BOCK, and SHELDON HARNICK

1961 *All the Way Home.* By TAD MOSEL

1962 *How to Succeed Without Really Trying.* By FRANK LOESSER and ABE BURROWS

1965 *The Subject Was Roses.* By FRANK D. GILROY

1967 *A Delicate Balance.* By EDWARD ALBEE

1969 *The Great White Hope.* By HOWARD SACKLER

1970 *No Place to Be Somebody.* By CHARLES GORDONE

1971 *The Effect of Gamma Rays on Man-in-the-Moon Marigolds.* By PAUL ZINDEL

1973 *That Championship Season.* By JASON MILLER

1975 *Seascape.* By EDWARD ALBEE

1976 *A Chorus Line.* Conceived by MICHAEL BENNETT

HISTORY OF UNITED STATES

1917 *With Americans of Past and Present Days.* By J. J. JUSSERAND, Ambassador of France to United States

1918 *A History of the Civil War, 1861–1865.* By JAMES FORD RHODES

1920 *The War with Mexico.* By JUSTIN H. SMITH

1921 *The Victory at Sea.* By WILLIAM SOWDEN SIMS in collaboration with BURTON J. HENDRICK

1922 *The Founding of New England.* By JAMES TRUSLOW ADAMS

1923 *The Supreme Court in United States History.* By CHARLES WARREN

1924 *The American Revolution—A Constitutional Interpretation.* By CHARLES HOWARD McILWAIN

1925 *A History of the American Frontier.* By FREDERIC L. PAXSON

1926 *The History of the United States.* By EDWARD CHANNING

1927 *Pinckney's Treaty.* By SAMUEL FLAGG BEMIS

1928 *Main Currents in American Thought.* By VERNON LOUIS PARRINGTON

1929 *The Organization and Administration of the Union Army, 1861–1865.* By FRED ALBERT SHANNON

1930 *The War of Independence.* By CLAUDE H. VAN TYNE

1931 *The Coming of the War: 1914.* By BERNADOTTE E. SCHMITT

1932 *My Experiences in the World War.* By JOHN J. PERSHING

1933 *The Significance of Sections in American History.* By FREDERICK J. TURNER

1934 *The People's Choice.* By HERBERT AGAR

1935 *The Colonial Period of American History.* By CHARLES McLEAN ANDREWS

1936 *The Constitutional History of the United States.* By ANDREW C. McLAUGHLIN

1937 *The Flowering of New England.* By VAN WYCK BROOKS

1938 *The Road to Reunion, 1865–1900.* By PAUL HERMAN BUCK

1939 *A History of American Magazines.* By FRANK LUTHER MOTT

1940 *Abraham Lincoln: The War Years.* By CARL SANDBURG

1941 *The Atlantic Migration, 1607–1860.* By MARCUS LEE HANSEN

1942 *Reveille in Washington.* By MARGARET LEECH

1943 *Paul Revere and the World He Lived In.* By ESTHER FORBES

1944 *The Growth of American Thought.* By MERLE CURTI

1945 *Unfinished Business.* By STEPHEN BONSAL

1946 *The Age of Jackson.* By ARTHUR M. SCHLESINGER, JR.

1947 *Scientists Against Time.* By JAMES PHINNEY BAXTER, 3RD

1948 *Across the Wide Missouri.* By BERNARD DE VOTO

1949 *The Disruption of American Democracy.* By ROY FRANKLIN NICHOLS

1950 *Art and Life in America.* By OLIVER W. LARKIN

1951 *The Old Northwest, Pioneer Period 1815–1840.* By R. CARLYLE BULEY

1952 *The Uprooted.* By OSCAR HANDLIN

1953 *The Era of Good Feelings.* By GEORGE DANGERFIELD

1954 *A Stillness at Appomattox.* By BRUCE CATTON

1955 *Great River: The Rio Grande in North American History.* By PAUL HORGAN

1956 *The Age of Reform.* By RICHARD HOFSTADTER

1957 *Russia Leaves the War: Soviet-American Relations, 1917–1920.* By GEORGE F. KENNAN

1958 *Banks and Politics in America: From the Revolution to the Civil War.* By BRAY HAMMOND

1959 *The Republican Era: 1869–1901.* By LEONARD D. WHITE, assisted by JEAN SCHNEIDER

1960 *In the Days of McKinley.* By MARGARET LEECH

1961 *Between War and Peace: The Potsdam Conference.* By HERBERT FEIS

1962 *The Triumphant Empire, Thunder-Clouds Gather in the West.* By LAWRENCE H. GIPSON

1963 *Washington, Village and Capital, 1800–1878.* By CONSTANCE McLAUGHLIN GREEN

1964 *Puritan Village: The Formation of a New England Town.* By SUMNER CHILTON POWELL

1965 *The Greenback Era.* By IRWIN UNGER

1966 *Life of the Mind in America.* By PERRY MILLER

1967 *Exploration and Empire: The Explorer and Scientist in the Winning of the American West.* By WILLIAM H. GOETZMANN

1968 *The Ideological Origins of the American Revolution.* By BERNARD BAILYN

1969 *Origins of the Fifth Amendment.* By LEONARD W. LEVY

1970 *Present at the Creation: My Years in the State Department.* By DEAN ACHESON

1971 *Roosevelt: The Soldier of Freedom.* By JAMES McGREGOR BURNS

1972 *Neither Black Nor White. Slavery and Race Relations in Brazil and the United States.* By CARL N. DEGLER

1973 *People of Paradox: An Inquiry Concerning the Origin of American Civilization.* By MICHAEL KAMMEN

1974 *The Americans: The Democratic Experience,* Vol. 3. By DANIEL J. BOORSTIN

1975 *Jefferson and His Time.* By DUMAS MALONE

1976 *Lamy of Santa Fe.* By PAUL HORGAN

BIOGRAPHY OR AUTOBIOGRAPHY

1917 *Julia Ward Howe.* By LAURA E. RICHARDS and MAUDE HOWE ELLIOTT, assisted by FLORENCE HOWE HALL

1918 *Benjamin Franklin, Self-Revealed.* By WILLIAM CABELL BRUCE

1919 *The Education of Henry Adams.* By HENRY ADAMS

1920 *The Life of John Marshall.* By ALBERT J. BEVERIDGE

1921 *The Americanization of Edward Bok.* By ED-WARD BOK

1922 *A Daughter of the Middle Border.* By HAMLIN GARLAND

1923 *The Life and Letters of Walter H. Page.* By BURTON J. HENDRICK

1924 *From Immigrant to Inventor.* By MICHAEL ID-VORSKY PUPIN

1925 *Barrett Wendell and His Letters.* By M. A. DE-WOLFE HOWE

1926 *The Life of Sir William Osler.* By HARVEY CUSH-ING

1927 *Whitman.* By EMORY HOLLOWAY

1928 *The American Orchestra and Theodore Thomas.* By CHARLES EDWARD RUSSELL

1929 *The Training of an American. The Earlier Life and Letters of Walter H. Page.* By BURTON J. HENDRICK

1930 *The Raven.* By MARQUIS JAMES

1931 *Charles W. Eliot.* By HENRY JAMES

1932 *Theodore Roosevelt.* By HENRY F. PRINGLE

1933 *Grover Cleveland.* By ALLAN NEVINS

1934 *John Hay.* By TYLER DEN-NETT

1935 *R. E. Lee.* By DOUGLAS S. FREEMAN

1936 *The Thought and Character of William James.* By RALPH BARTON PERRY

1937 *Hamilton Fish.* By ALLAN NEVINS

1938 *Pedlar's Progress.* By ODELL SHEPARD. *Andrew Jackson.* By MARQUIS JAMES

1939 *Benjamin Franklin.* By CARL VAN DOREN

1940 *Woodrow Wilson. Life and Letters,* Vols. VII

and VIII. By RAY STANNARD BAKER

1941 *Jonathan Edwards.* By OLA E. WINSLOW

1942 *Crusader in Crinoline.* By FORREST WILSON

1943 *Admiral of the Ocean Sea.* By SAMUEL ELIOT MORISON

1944 *The American Leonardo: The Life of Samuel F. B. Morse.* By CARLE-TON MABEE

1945 *George Bancroft: Brahmin Rebel.* By RUSSEL BLAINE NYE

1946 *Son of the Wilderness.* By LINNIE MARSH WOLFE

1947 *The Autobiography of William Allen White*

1948 *Forgotten First Citizen: John Bigelow.* By MAR-GARET CLAPP

1949 *Roosevelt and Hopkins.* By ROBERT E. SHERWOOD

1950 *John Quincy Adams and the Foundations of American Foreign Policy.* By SAMUEL FLAGG BEMIS

1951 *John C. Calhoun: American Portrait.* By MAR-GARET LOUISE COIT

1952 *Charles Evans Hughes.* By MERLO J. PUSEY

1953 *Edmund Pendleton 1721–1803.* By DAVID J. MAYS

1954 *The Spirit of St. Louis.* By CHARLES A. LIND-BERGH

1955 *The Taft Story.* By WIL-LIAM S. WHITE

1956 *Benjamin Henry Latrobe.* By TALBOT F. HAMLIN

1957 *Profiles in Courage.* By JOHN F. KENNEDY

1958 *George Washington.* By DOUGLAS SOUTHALL FREE-MAN (Vols. 1–6) and JOHN ALEXANDER CAR-ROLL and MARY WELLS ASHWORTH (Vol. 7)

1959 *Woodrow Wilson, American Prophet.* By ARTHUR WALWORTH

1960 *John Paul Jones* By SAMUEL ELIOT MORISON

1961 *Charles Sumner and the Coming of the Civil War.* By DAVID DONALD

1963 *Henry James: Vol. II, The Conquest of London, 1870–1881; Vol. III, The Middle Years, 1881–1895.* By LEON EDEL

1964 *John Keats.* By WALTER JACKSON BATE

1965 *Henry Adams* (3 vols.). By ERNEST SAMUELS

1966 *A Thousand Days.* By AR-THUR M. SCHLESINGER, JR.

1967 *Mr. Clemens and Mark Twain.* By JUSTIN KAP-LAN

1968 *Memoirs, 1925–1950.* By GEORGE F. KENNAN

1969 *The Man from New York.* By B. L. REID

1970 *Huey Long.* By T. HARRY WILLIAMS

1971 *Robert Frost: The Years of Triumph, 1915–1938.* By LAWRANCE R. THOMP-SON

1972 *Eleanor and Franklin: The Story of Their Relationship Based on Eleanor Roosevelt's Private Papers.* By JOSEPH P. LASH

1973 *Luce and His Empire.* By W. A. SWANBERG

1974 *O'Neill, Son and Artist.* By LOUIS SHEAFFER.

1975 *The Power Broker: Robert Moses and the Fall of New York.* By RO-BERT A. CARO

1976 *Edith Wharton: A Biography.* By RICHARD W. B. LEWIS

POETRY*

1918 *Love Songs.* By SARA TEASDALE

1919 *Old Road to Paradise.* By MARGARET WIDDEMER; *Corn Huskers.* By CARL SANDBURG

1922 *Collected Poems.* By ED-WIN ARLINGTON ROBIN-SON

1923 *The Ballad of the Harp-Weaver; A Few Figs from Thistles; eight sonnets in American Poetry, 1922, A Miscellany.* By EDNA ST. VIN-CENT MILLAY

1924 *New Hampshire: A Poem with Notes and Grace Notes.* By ROBERT FROST

1925 *The Man Who Died Twice.* By EDWIN AR-LINGTON ROBINSON

1926 *What's O'Clock.* By AMY LOWELL

1927 *Fiddler's Farewell.* By LEONORA SPEYER

1928 *Tristram.* By EDWIN AR-LINGTON ROBINSON

1929 *John Brown's Body.* By STEPHEN VINCENT BENÉT

1930 *Selected Poems,* By CON-RAD AIKEN

* This prize was established in 1922. The 1918 and 1919 awards were made from gifts provided by the Poetry Society.

1931 *Collected Poems.* By Robert Frost

1932 *The Flowering Stone.* By George Dillon

1933 *Conquistador.* By Archibald MacLeish

1934 *Collected Verse.* By Robert Hillyer

1935 *Bright Ambush.* By Audrey Wurdemann

1936 *Strange Holiness.* By Robert P. T. Coffin

1937 *A Further Range.* By Robert Frost

1938 *Cold Morning Sky.* By Marya Zaturenska

1939 *Selected Poems.* By John Gould Fletcher

1940 *Collected Poems.* By Mark Van Doren

1941 *Sunderland Capture.* By Leonard Bacon

1942 *The Dust Which Is God.* By William Rose Benét

1943 *A Witness Tree.* By Robert Frost

1944 *Western Star.* By Stephen Vincent Benét

1945 *V-Letter and Other Poems.* By Karl Shapiro

1947 *Lord Weary's Castle.* By Robert Lowell

1948 *The Age of Anxiety.* By W. H. Auden

1949 *Terror and Decorum.* By Peter Viereck

1950 *Annie Allen.* By Gwendolyn Brooks

1951 *Complete Poems.* By Carl Sandburg

1952 *Collected Poems.* By Marianne Moore

1953 *Collected Poems 1917–1952.* By Archibald MacLeish

1954 *The Waking.* By Theodore Roethke

1955 *Collected Poems.* By Wallace Stevens

1956 *Poems—North & South.* By Elizabeth Bishop

1957 *Things of This World.* By Richard Wilbur

1958 *Promises: Poems 1954–1956.* By Robert Penn Warren

1959 *Selected Poems, 1928–1958.* By Stanley Kunitz

1960 *Heart's Needle.* By William Snodgrass

1961 *Times Three: Selected Verse from Three Decades.* By Phyllis McGinley

1962 *Poems.* By Alan Dugan

1963 *Pictures from Breughel.* By William Carlos Williams

1964 *At the End of the Open Road.* By Louis Simpson

1965 *77 Dream Songs.* By John Berryman

1966 *Selected Poems.* By Richard Eberhart

1967 *Live or Die.* By Anne Sexton

1968 *The Hard Hours.* By Anthony Hecht

1969 *Of Being Numerous.* By George Oppen

1970 *Untitled Subjects.* By Richard Howard

1971 *The Carrier of Ladders.* By William S. Merwin

1972 *Collected Poems.* James Wright

1973 *Up Country.* By Maxine Winokur Kumin

1974 *The Dolphin.* By Robert Lowell.

1975 *Turtle Island.* By Gary Snyder

1976 *Self-Portrait in a Convex Mirror.* By John Ashbery

GENERAL NONFICTION

1962 *The Making of the President 1960.* By Theodore H. White

1963 *The Guns of August.* By Barbara W. Tuchman

1964 *Anti-intellectualism in American Life.* By Richard Hofstadter

1965 *O Strange New World.* By Howard Mumford Jones

1966 *Wandering Through Winter.* By Edwin Way Teale

1967 *The Problem of Slavery in Western Culture.* By David Brion Davis

1968 *Rousseau and Revolution.* By Will and Ariel Durant

1969 *So Human an Animal.* By Rene Jules Dubos
The Armies of the Night. By Norman Mailer

1970 *Gandhi's Truth.* By Erik H. Erikson

1971 *The Rising Sun.* By John Toland

1972 *Stilwell and the American Experience in China, 1911-1945.* By Barbara W. Tuchman.

1973 *Fire in the Lake: The Vietnamese and the Americans in Vietnam.* By Frances FitzGerald; and *Children of Crisis* (Vols. 1 and 2). By Robert M. Coles

1974 *The Denial of Death.* By Ernest Becker

1975 *Pilgrim at Tinker Creek.* By Annie Dillard

1976 *Why Survive? Being Old in America.* By Robert N. Butler

Pulitzer Prizes in Music

1943 *Secular Cantata No. 2, A Free Song.* By William Schuman

1944 *Symphony No. 4* (Op. 34). By Howard Hanson

1945 *Appalachian Spring.* By Aaron Copland

1946 *The Canticle of the Sun.* By Leo Sowerby

1947 *Symphony No. 3.* By Charles Ives

1948 *Symphony No. 3.* By Walter Piston

1949 *Louisiana Story* music. By Virgil Thomson

1950 *The Consul.* By Gian-Carlo Menotti

1951 Music for opera *Giants in the Earth.* By Douglas Stuart Moore

1952 *Symphony Concertante.* By Gail Kubik

1954 *Concerto for Two Pianos and Orchestra.* By Quincy Porter

1955 *The Saint of Bleecker Street.* By Gian-Carlo Menotti

1956 *Symphony No. 3.* By Ernst Toch

1957 *Meditations on Ecclesiastes.* By Norman Dello Joio

1958 *Vanessa.* By Samuel Barber

1959 *Concerto for Piano & Orchestra.* By John La Montaine

1960 *Second String Quartet.* By Elliott Carter

1961 *Symphony No. 7.* By Walter Piston

1962 *The Crucible.* By Robert Ward

1963 *Piano Concerto No. 1.* By Samuel Barber

1966 *Variations for Orchestra.* By Leslie Bassett

1967 *Quartet No. 3.* By LEON KIRCHNER

1968 *Echoes of Time and the River.* By GEORGE CRUMB

1969 *String Quartet No. 3.* By KAREL HUSA

1970 *Time's Encomium.* By CHARLES WUORINEN

1971 *Synchronisms No. 6 for Piano and Electronic Sound.* By MARIO DAVIDOWSKY

1972 *Windows.* JACOB DRUCKMAN

1973 *String Quartet No. 3.* By ELLIOTT CARTER

1974 *Notturno.* By DONALD MARTINO.

1975 *From the Diary of Virginia Woolf.* By DOMINICK ARGENTO

1976 *Air Music.* By NED ROREM

Poets Laureate of England

Source: Encyclopaedia Britannica.

Poet	Term	Poet	Term
Edmund Spenser	1591–1599	William Whitehead	1757–1785
Samuel Daniel	1599–1619	Thomas Warton	1785–1790
Ben Jonson	1619–1637	Henry James Pye	1790–1813
William Davenant	1638–1668	Robert Southey	1813–1843
John Dryden[1]	1670–1689	William Wordsworth	1843–1850
Thomas Shadwell	1689–1692	Alfred Lord Tennyson	1850–1892
Nahum Tate	1692–1715	Alfred Austin	1896–1913
Nicholas Rowe	1715–1718	Robert Bridges	1913–1930
Laurence Eusden	1718–1730	John Masefield	1930–1967
Colley Cibber	1730–1757	C. Day Lewis	1967–1972
[1] First to bear the title officially.		John Betjeman	1972–

American Academy of Arts and Letters

(633 W. 155th St., New York, N.Y. 10032)

The American Academy of Arts and Letters was created as a section of the National Institute of Arts and Letters in 1904, and was incorporated by an Act of Congress signed by the President on Apr. 17, 1916. Its membership is limited to 50 persons chosen from the membership of the Institute.

Members of the Academy

Ivan L. Albright
Samuel Barber
Saul Bellow
Isabel Bishop
Peter Blume
Kenneth Burke
Alexander Calder
Elliott C. Carter
Bruce Catton
John Cheever
Marchette Chute
Gilmore D. Clarke

Henry Steele Commager
Aaron Copland
Malcolm Cowley
José de Creeft
Babette Deutsch
Edwin Dickinson
Leon Edel
Ralph Ellison
Naum Gabo
Lillian Hellman
John Hersey
Philip Johnson

George F. Kennan
Stanley Kunitz
Jack Levine
Robert Lowell
Archibald MacLeish
Arthur Miller
Isamu Noguchi
Georgia O'Keeffe
I. M. Pei
Walter Piston
Katherine Anne Porter
William Schuman

Roger Sessions
Raphael Soyer
Allen Tate
Virgil Thomson
Barbara W. Tuchman
Robert Penn Warren
Eudora Welty
Glenway Wescott
John Hall Wheelock
E. B. White
Richard Wilbur[1]
Andrew Wyeth

[1] President.

Honorary Members of the Academy-Institute

Alvar Henrik Aalto
Rafael Alberti
Louis Aragon
Germán Arciniegas
Giorgio Bassani
Sir Isaiah Beriin
Sir John Betjeman
Heinrich Böll
José Luis Borges
Pierre Boulez
Benjamin Britten
Italo Calvino
Marc Chagall
Sir Charles Chaplin
Carlos Chávez
Lord Clark of Saltwood

Carlos Drummond de Andrade
William Empson
Max Frisch
Rómulo Gallegos
Gabriel Gárcia Marquez
Alberto Ginastera
Richard Hughes
Marcel Jouhandeau
Arthur Koestler
Oskar Kokoschka
Doris Lessing
Witold Lutoslawski
Gian Francesco Malipiero
André Malraux
Giacomo Manzù
Marino Marini

Gian Carlo Menotti
Olivier Messiaen
Joan Miró
Henry Moore
Alberto Moravia
Iris Murdoch
Pier Luigi Nervi
Oscar Niemeyer
Octavio Paz
V. S. Pritchett
Ivor Armstrong Richards
Henri Sauguet
Karl Schmidt-Rottluff
Léopold Sédar Senghor
Ravi Shankar
Ignazio Silone

Georges Simenon
Lord Snow
Aleksandr I. Solzhenitsyn
Stephen Spender
Graham Sutherland
Rufino Tamayo
Kenzo Tange
Sir Michael Tippett
Andrei A. Voznesensky
Sylvia Townsend Warner
Dame Veronica Wedgwood
Dame Rebecca West
Iannis Xenakis
José Luis Zorilla de San Martín

National Institute of Arts and Letters

(633 W. 155th St., New York, N. Y. 10032)

The National Institute of Arts and Letters was founded in 1898 by the American Social Science Association and was incorporated by an Act of Congress signed by the President on Feb. 4, 1913, for the furtherance of literature and the fine arts in the U. S. Its membership is limited to 250 native or naturalized citizens qualified by notable achievements in art, literature, or music. It confers certain awards and honors for work of distinction; and, together with its affiliate, the American Academy of Arts and Letters, it elects as honorary members many distinguished artists, writers, and composers from other countries.

Members of the Institute

Department of Literature

Léonie Adams
Edward Albee
Louis S. Auchincloss
James Baldwin
Djuna Barnes
John Barth
Jacques Barzun
Saul Bellow
Elizabeth Bishop
Kay Boyle
Cleanth Brooks
Gwendolyn Brooks
Kenneth Burke
Erskine Caldwell
Joseph Campbell
Truman Capote
Bruce Catton
Stuart Chase
John Cheever
Marchette Chute
John Ciardi
Eleanor Clark
Henry Steele Commager
Marc Connelly
Malcolm Cowley
James Gould Cozzens
Edward Dahlberg
Babette Deutsch
Peter De Vries
James Dickey
Will Durant
Richard Eberhart
Leon Edel
Loren Eiseley
Ralph Ellison
Richard Ellmann
James T. Farrell
Francis Fergusson
Robert Fitzgerald
Janet Flanner
James Thomas Flexner
John Kenneth Galbraith
Allen Ginsberg
Julian Green
Paul Eliot Green
Horace Gregory
Anthony Hecht
Lillian Hellman
John Hersey
Paul Horgan
Christopher Isherwood
Edgar Johnson
Matthew Josephson
Alfred Kazin
George F. Kennan
Louis Kronenberger
Stanley Kunitz
Richmond Lattimore
Harry Levin
Robert Lowell
Dwight Macdonald
Archibald MacLeish

Norman Mailer
Bernard Malamud
Peter Matthiessen
William Maxwell
Mary McCarthy
Phyllis McGinley
Margaret Mead
William Meredith
James Merrill
Arthur Miller
Henry Miller
Joseph Mitchell
Wright Morris
Howard Moss
Lewis Mumford
Robert Nathan
Howard Nemerov
Anaïs Nin
Walker Percy
S. J. Perelman
Katherine Anne Porter
J. F. Powers
Kenneth Rexroth
Philip Roth
Muriel Rukeyser
Harrison E. Salisbury[1]
William Saroyan
Meyer Schapiro
Arthur M. Schlesinger, Jr.
Mark Schorer
Karl Shapiro
Isaac Bashevis Singer
William Jay Smith
W. D. Snodgrass
Jean Stafford
Francis Steegmuller
Wallace Stegner
William Styron
May Swenson
Allen Tate
Peter Taylor
Barbara W. Tuchman
Louis Untermeyer
John Updike
Kurt Vonnegut, Jr.
Austin Warren
Robert Penn Warren
Eudora Welty
Glenway Wescott
John Hall Wheelock
Elwyn Brooks White
Richard Wilbur
Tennessee Williams
C. Vann Woodward
James Wright

[1] President.

Department of Art

Ivan Albright
Edmond Amateis
Peggy Bacon

Leonard Baskin
Romare Bearden
Pietro Belluschi
Isabel Bishop
Hyman Bloom
Peter Blume
Marcel Breuer
Alexander Brook
James Brooks
Gorden Bunshaft
Paul Cadmus
Alexander Calder
Gilmore D. Clarke
Gardner Cox
José de Creeft
Willem de Kooning
Donald De Lue
Jean de Marco
José de Rivera
Sidney E. Dickenson
Edwin Dickinson
Richard Diebenkorn
Helen Frankenthaler
R. Buckminster Fuller
Naum Gabo
Morris Graves
Dorothea Greenbaum
Balcomb Greene
William Gropper
Chaim Gross
Philip Guston
Charles Gwathmey
Robert Gwathmey
Walker Hancock
Wallace K. Harrison
John Heliker
Joseph Hirsch
C. Paul Jennewein
Jasper Johns
Philip Johnson
Ellsworth Kelly
Gyorgy Kepes
John Koch
Armin Landeck
Gertrude Lathrop
Jacob Lawrence
Clare Leighton
Julian Levi
Jack Levine
Richard Lindner
Richard Lippold
Seymour Lipton
Loren MacIver
Conrad Marca-Relli
Bruce Moore
Robert Motherwell
Reuben Nakian
Alice Neel
Louise Nevelson
Costantino Nivola
Isamu Noguchi
Georgia O'Keeffe
Claes Oldenberg
I. M. Pei

Abraham Rattner
George Rickey
Kevin Roche
Theodore J. Roszak
Paul Rudolph
Eugene F. Savage
José Luis Sert
Raphael Soyer
Francis Speight
Saul Steinberg
Edward Durell Stone
William Thon
Stuyvesant Van Veen
Katharine Lane Weems
Stow Wengenroth
Andrew Wyeth

Department of Music

Milton Babbitt
Samuel Barber
Jack Beeson
Arthur Berger
William Bergsma
Leonard Bernstein
John Cage
Elliott C. Carter
Aaron Copland
George Crumb
Norman Dello Joio
David Diamond
Ross Lee Finney
Lukas Foss
Miriam Gideon
Howard Hanson
Roy Harris
Lou Harrison
Andrew W. Imbrie
Leon Kirchner
Ernst Krenek
Otto Luening
Peter Mennin
Nicolas Nabokov
Vincent Persichetti
Walter Piston
Richard Rodgers
Gunther Schuller
William Schuman
Roger Sessions
Louise Talma
Alexander Tcherepnin
Randall Thompson
Virgil Thomson
Vladimir Ussachevsky
Robert Ward
Ben Weber
Hugo Weisgall

New York Film Critics Circle Awards

(1—best motion picture; 2—best male performance; 3—best feminine performance; 4—best direction; 5—best foreign-language film (discontinued in 1969); 6—special award; 7—screenplay writing; 8—best supporting actor; 9—best supporting actress.)

1935 1. *The Informer*, RKO
2. Charles Laughton, *Mutiny on the Bounty* and *Ruggles of Red Gap*
3. Greta Garbo, *Anna Karenina*
4. John Ford, *The Informer*

1936 1. *Mr. Deeds Goes to Town*, Columbia
2. Walter Huston, *Dodsworth*
3. Luise Rainer, *The Great Ziegfeld*
4. Rouben Mamoulian, *The Gay Desperado*
5. *La Kermesse Héroique* (French)

1937 1. *The Life of Emile Zola*, Warner Bros.
2. Paul Muni, *The Life of Emile Zola*
3. Greta Garbo, *Camille*
4. Gregory La Cava, *Stage Door*
5. *Mayerling* (French)

1938 1. *The Citadel*, M-G-M
2. James Cagney, *Angels with Dirty Faces*
3. Margaret Sullavan *Three Comrades*
4. Alfred Hitchcock, *The Lady Vanishes*
5. *Grande Illusion* (Fr.)
6. *Snow White and the Seven Dwarfs*, Disney-RKO

1939 1. *Wuthering Heights*, Goldwyn-UA
2. James Stewart, *Mr. Smith Goes to Washington*
3. Vivien Leigh, *Gone with the Wind*
4. John Ford, *Stagecoach*
5. *Harvest* (French)

1940 1. *The Grapes of Wrath*, 20th Century-Fox
2. Charles Chaplin, *The Great Dictator* (refused award)
3. Katharine Hepburn, *The Philadelphia Story*
4. John Ford, *The Grapes of Wrath; The Long Voyage Home*
5. *The Baker's Wife* (French)
6. Walt Disney, *Fantasia*

1941 1. *Citizen Kane*, RKO-Mercury

2. Gary Cooper, *Sergeant York*
3. Joan Fontaine, *Suspicion*
4. John Ford, *How Green Was My Valley*

1942 1. *In Which We Serve*, UA-Noel Coward
2. James Cagney, *Yankee Doodle Dandy*
3. Agnes Moorehead, *The Magnificent Ambersons*
4. John Farrow, *Wake Island*

1943 1. *Watch on the Rhine*, Warner Bros.
2. Paul Lukas, *Watch on the Rhine*
3. Ida Lupino, *The Hard Way*
4. George Stevens, *The More the Merrier*

1944 1. *Going My Way*, Paramount
2. Barry Fitzgerald, *Going My Way*
3. Tallulah Bankhead, *Lifeboat*
4. Leo McCarey, *Going My Way*

1945 1. *The Lost Weekend*, Paramount
2. Ray Milland, *The Lost Weekend*
3. Ingrid Bergman, *Spellbound* and *The Bells of St. Mary's*
4. Billy Wilder, *The Lost Weekend*
5. (None)
6. *The True Glory* and *The Fighting Lady*

1946 1. *The Best Years of Our Lives*, Goldwyn-RKO Radio
2. Laurence Olivier, *Henry V*
3. Celia Johnson, *Brief Encounter*
4. William Wyler, *The Best Years of Our Lives*
5. *Open City* (Italian)

1947 1. *Gentleman's Agreement*, 20th Century-Fox
2. William Powell, *Life with Father*
3. Deborah Kerr, *The Adventuress* and *Black Narcissus*

4. Elia Kazan, *Gentleman's Agreement* and *Boomerang*
5. *To Live in Peace* (Italian)

1948 1. *Treasure of Sierra Madre*, Warner Bros.
2. Sir Laurence Olivier, *Hamlet*
3. Olivia de Havilland, *The Snake Pit*
4. John Huston, *Treasure of Sierra Madre*
5. *Paisan* (Italian)

1949 1. *All the King's Men*, Rossen-Columbia
2. Broderick Crawford, *All the King's Men*
3. Olivia de Havilland, *The Heiress*
4. Carol Reed, *The Fallen Idol*
5. *The Bicycle Thief* (Italian)

1950 1. *All About Eve*, 20th Century-Fox
2. Gregory Peck, *Twelve O'Clock High*
3. Bette Davis, *All About Eve*
4. Joseph L. Mankiewicz, *All About Eve*
5. *Ways of Love* (Franco-Italian)

1951 1. *A Streetcar Named Desire*, Warner Bros.
2. Arthur Kennedy, *Bright Victory*
3. Vivien Leigh, *A Streetcar Named Desire*
4. Elia Kazan, *A Streetcar Named Desire*
5. *Miracle in Milan* (Italian)

1952 1. *High Noon*, United Artists
2. Ralph Richardson, *Breaking the Sound Barrier*
3. Shirley Booth, *Come Back, Little Sheba*
4. Fred Zinnemann, *High Noon*
5. *Forbidden Games* (French)

1953 1. *From Here to Eternity*, Columbia
2. Burt Lancaster, *From Here to Eternity*
3. Audrey Hepburn, *Roman Holiday*
4. Fred Zinnemann, *From*

Here to Eternity
5. *Justice Is Done* (French)
6. *A Queen Is Crowned* (JARO) and *The Conquest of Everest* (JARO)

1954 1. *On the Waterfront,* Columbia
2. Marlon Brando, *On the Waterfront*
3. Grace Kelly, *The Country Girl, Rear Window, Dial M for Murder*
4. Elia Kazan, *On the Waterfront*
5. *Gate of Hell* (Japanese)

1955 1. *Marty,* United Artists
2. Ernest Borgnine, *Marty*
3. Anna Magnani, *The Rose Tattoo*
4. David Lean, *Summertime*
5. *Diabolique* (French) and *Umberto D.* (Italian)

1956 1. *Around the World in 80 Days.* The Michael Todd Co., Inc., UA
2. Kirk Douglas, *Lust for Life*
3. Ingrid Bergman, *Anastasia*
4. John Huston, *Moby Dick*
5. *La Strada* (Italian)

1957 1. *The Bridge on the River Kwai,* Columbia
2. Alec Guinness, *The Bridge on the River Kwai*
3. Deborah Kerr, *Heaven Knows, Mr. Allison*
4. David Lean, *The Bridge on the River Kwai*
5. *Gervaise* (French)

1958 1. *The Defiant Ones,* United Artists
2. David Niven, *Separate Tables*
3. Susan Hayward, *I Want to Live!*
4. Stanley Kramer, *The Defiant Ones*
5. *Mon Oncle* (French)
6. (None)
7. Nathan E. Douglas & Harold J. Smith, *The Defiant Ones*

1959 1. *Ben-Hur,* M-G-M
2. James Stewart, *Anatomy of a Murder*
3. Audrey Hepburn, *The Nun's Story*
4. Fred Zinnemann, *The Nun's Story*
5. *The 400 Blows* (French)

6. (None)
7. Wendell Mayes, *Anatomy of a Murder*

1960 1. *The Apartment,* United Artists; *Sons and Lovers,* 20th Century-Fox
2. Burt Lancaster, *Elmer Gantry*
3. Deborah Kerr, *The Sundowners*
4. Billy Wilder, *The Apartment;* Jack Cardiff, *Sons and Lovers*
5. *Hiroshima, Mon Amour* (French)
6. (None)
7. Billy Wilder & I. A. L. Diamond, *The Apartment*

1961 1. *West Side Story,* Mirisch Pictures, Inc.
2. Maximilian Schell, *Judgment at Nuremberg*
3. Sophia Loren, *Two Women*
4. Robert Rossen, *The Hustler*
5. *La Dolce Vita* (Italian)
6. (None)
7. Abby Mann, *Judgment at Nuremberg*

1962 (No awards given)

1963 1. *Tom Jones,* Woodfall Productions, Ltd.
2. Albert Finney, *Tom Jones*
3. Patricia Neal, *Hud*
4. Tony Richardson, *Tom Jones*
5. *8½* (Italian)
6. (None)
7. Irving Ravetch and Harriet Frank, Jr., *Hud*

1964 1. *My Fair Lady,* Warner Bros.
2. Rex Harrison, *My Fair Lady*
3. Kim Stanley, *Seance on a Wet Afternoon*
4. Stanley Kubrick, *Dr. Strangelove*
5. *That Man from Rio* (French)
6. *To Be Alive,* shown by Johnson's Wax Co. at the New York World's Fair
7. Harold Pinter, *The Servant*

1965 1. *Darling,* Embassy Pictures
2. Oskar Werner, *Ship of Fools*
3. Julie Christie, *Darling*
4. John Schlesinger, *Darling*
5. *Juliet of the Spirits* (Italian)

6. (None)
7. (None)

1966 1. *A Man for All Seasons,* Columbia
2. Paul Scofield, *A Man for All Seasons*
3. Elizabeth Taylor, *Who's Afraid of Virginia Woolf?*; Lynn Redgrave, *Georgy Girl*
4. Fred Zinnemann, *A Man for All Seasons*
5. *The Shop on Main Street* (Czechoslovakian)
6. (None)
7. *A Man for All Seasons*

1967 1. *In the Heat of the Night,* Mirisch Corp.
2. Rod Steiger, *In the Heat of the Night*
3. Dame Edith Evans, *The Whisperers*
4. Mike Nichols, *The Graduate*
5. *La Guerre est Finie* (French)
6. (None)
7. David Newman and Robert Benton, *Bonnie and Clyde*

1968 1. *The Lion in Winter,* Avco Embassy Pictures
2. Alan Arkin, *The Heart Is a Lonely Hunter*
3. Joanne Woodward, *Rachel, Rachel*
4. Paul Newman, *Rachel, Rachel*
5. *War and Peace* (Russian)
6. (None)
7. Lorenzo Semple, Jr., *Pretty Poison*

1969 1. *Z,* Cinema V Distributing
2. Jon Voigt, *Midnight Cowboy*
3. Jane Fonda, *They Shoot Horses, Don't They?*
4. Costa-Gavras, *Z*
6. (None)
7. Paul Mazursky and Larry Tucker, *Bob & Carol & Ted & Alice*
8. Jack Nicholson, *Easy Rider*
9. Dyan Cannon, *Bob & Carol & Ted & Alice*

1970 1. *Five Easy Pieces,* Columbia
2. George C. Scott, *Patton*
3. Glenda Jackson, *Women in Love*

4. Bob Rafelson, *Five Easy Pieces*
6. (None)
7. Eric Rohmer, *Ma Nuit Chez Maud*
8. Chief Dan George, *Little Big Man*
9. Karen Black, *Five Easy Pieces*

1971 1. *A Clockwork Orange,* Warner Bros.
2. Gene Hackman, *The French Connection*
3. Jane Fonda, *Klute*
4. Stanley Kubrick, *A Clockwork Orange*
6. (None)
7. Penelope Gilliat, *Sunday Bloody Sunday;* Larry McMurtry and Peter Bogdanovich, *The Last Picture Show*
8. Ben Johnson, *The Last Picture Show*
9. Ellen Burstyn, *The Last Picture Show*

1972 1. *Cries and Whispers,* New World
2. Laurence Olivier, *Sleuth*
3. Liv Ullmann, *Cries and Whispers*
4. Ingmar Bergman, *Cries and Whispers*
6. *The Sorrow and the Pity,* French documentary
7. Ingmar Bergman, *Cries and Whispers*
8. Robert Duvall, *The Godfather*
9. Jeannie Berlin, *The Heartbreak Kid*

1973 1. *Day for Night,* Warner Bros.
2. Marlon Brando, *Last Tango in Paris*
3. Joanne Woodward, *Summer Wishes, Winter Dreams*
4. François Truffaut, *Day for Night*
6. (None)
7. George Lucas, Gloria Katz, Willard Huyck, *American Graffiti*
8. Robert De Niro, *Mean Streets*
9. Valentina Cortese, *Day for Night*

1974 1. *Amarcord,* Roger Corman/New World Films

2. Jack Nicholson, *The Last Detail* and *Chinatown*
3. Liv Ullmann, *Scenes From a Marriage*
4. Federico Fellini, *Amarcord*
6. (None)
7. Ingmar Bergman, *Scenes From a Marriage*
8. Charles Boyer, *Stavisky*
9. Valerie Perrine, *Lenny*

1975 1. *Nashville,* ABC Entertainment
2. Jack Nicholson, *One Flew Over the Cuckoo's Nest*
3. Isabelle Adjani, *The Story of Adele H.*
4. Robert Altman, *Nashville*
6. (None)
7. François Truffaut, Jean Gruault, Suzanne Schiffman, *The Story of Adele H.*
8. Alan Arkin, *Hearts of the West*
9. Lily Tomlin, *Nashville*

New York Drama Critics' Circle Awards

1935–36 *Winterset,* by Maxwell Anderson
1936–37 *High Tor,* by Maxwell Anderson
1937–38 *Of Mice and Men,* by John Steinbeck
Shadow and Substance, by Paul Vincent Carroll [1]
1938–39 (No award)
The White Steed, by Paul Vincent Carroll [1]
1939–40 *The Time of Your Life,* by William Saroyan
1940–41 *Watch on the Rhine,* by Lillian Hellman
The Corn Is Green, by Emlyn Williams [1]
1941–42 (No award)
Blithe Spirit, by Noel Coward [1]
1942–43 *The Patriots,* by Sidney Kingsley
1943–44 (No award)
Jacobowsky and the Colonel, by Franz Werfel–S. N. Behrman [1]
1944–45 *The Glass Menagerie,* by Tennessee Williams

1945–46 (No award)
Carousel, by Richard Rodgers & Oscar Hammerstein II [2]
1946–47 *All My Sons,* by Arthur Miller
No Exit, by Jean-Paul Sartre [1]
Brigadoon, by Alan Jay Lerner and Frederick Loewe [2]
1947–48 *A Streetcar Named Desire,* by Tennessee Williams
The Winslow Boy, by Terence Rattigan [1]
1948–49 *Death of a Salesman,* by Arthur Miller
The Madwoman of Chaillot, by Jean Giraudoux – Maurice Valency [1]
South Pacific, by Richard Rodgers, Oscar Hammerstein II & Joshua Logan [2]
1949–50 *The Member of the Wedding,* by Carson McCullers
The Cocktail Party, by T. S. Eliot [1]

The Consul, by Gian-Carlo Menotti [2]
1950–51 *Darkness at Noon,* by Sidney Kingsley [3]
The Lady's Not for Burning, by Christopher Fry [1]
Guys and Dolls, by Abe Burrows, Jo Swerling & Frank Loesser [2]
1951–52 *I Am a Camera,* by John Van Druten [4]
Venus Observed, by Christopher Fry [1]
Pal Joey, by Richard Rodgers, Lorenz Hart & John O'Hara [2]
Don Juan in Hell, by George B. Shaw [5]
1952–53 *Picnic,* by William Inge
The Love of Four Colonels, by Peter Ustinov [1]
Wonderful Town, by Joseph Fields, Jerome Chodorov, Betty Comden, Adolph Green & Leonard Bernstein [2]
1953–54 *The Teahouse of the*

August Moon, by John Patrick
Ondine, by Jean Giraudoux[1]
The Golden Apple, by John Latouche & Jerome Moross[2]

1954–55 *Cat on a Hot Tin Roof*, by Tennessee Williams
Witness for the Prosecution, by Agatha Christie[1]
The Saint of Bleecker Street, by Gian-Carlo Menotti [2]

1955–56 *The Diary of Anne Frank*, by Frances Goodrich & Albert Hackett
Tiger at the Gates, by Jean Giraudoux–Christopher Fry[1]
My Fair Lady, by Frederick Loewe & Alan Jay Lerner[2]

1956–57 *Long Day's Journey Into Night*, by Eugene O'Neill
Waltz of the Toreadors, by Jean Anouilh[1]
The Most Happy Fella, by Frank Loesser[2,6]

1957–58 *Look Homeward, Angel*, by Ketti Frings[7]
Look Back in Anger, by John Osborne[1]
The Music Man, by Meredith Willson[2]

1958–59 *A Raisin in the Sun*, by Lorraine Hansberry
The Visit, by Friedrich Duerrenmatt–Maurice Valency[1]
La Plume de ma Tante, by Robert Dhery & Gerard Calvi[2]

1959–60 *Toys in the Attic*, by Lillian Hellman
Five Finger Exercise, by Peter Shaffer[1]
Fiorello!, by Jerome Weidman, George Abbott, Jerry Bock, Sheldon Harnick[2]

1960–61 *All the Way Home*, by Tad Mosel [8]
A Taste of Honey, by Shelagh Delaney[1]

Carnival, by Michael Stewart[2]

1961–62 *The Night of the Iguana*, by Tennessee Williams
A Man for All Seasons, by Robert Bolt[1]
How to Succeed in Business Without Really Trying, by Abe Burrows, Jack Weinstock, Willie Gilbert & Frank Loesser[2,9]

1962–63 *Who's Afraid of Virginia Woolf?*, by Edward Albee
Beyond the Fringe, by Alan Bennett, Peter Cook, Jonathan Miller, and Dudley Moore[10]

1963–64 *Luther*, by John Osborne
Hello, Dolly! by Michael Stewart and Jerry Herman[2,11]
The Trojan Women, by Euripides[10,12]

1964–65 *The Subject Was Roses*, by Frank D. Gilroy
Fiddler on the Roof, by Joseph Stein, Jerry Bock, and Sheldon Harnick[2,13]

1965–66 *The Persecution and Assassination of Marat as Performed by the Inmates of the Asylum of Charenton under the Direction of the Marquis de Sade*, by Peter Weiss
The Man of La Mancha, by Dale Wasserman, Mitch Leigh & Joe Darion

1966–67 *The Homecoming*, by Harold Pinter
Cabaret, by Joe Masteroff, John Kander, and Fred Ebb[2,14]

1967–68 *Rosencrantz and Guildenstern Are Dead*, by Tom Stoppard
Your Own Thing, by Donald Driver, Hal Hester, and Danny Apolinar[2]

1968–69 *The Great White Hope*, by Howard Sackler
1776, by Sherman Edwards and Peter Stone[2]

1969–70 *Borstal Boy*, by Frank McMahon[15]
The Effect of Gamma Rays on Man-in-the-Moon Marigolds, by Paul Zindel [16]
Company, by George Furth and Stephen Sondheim[2]

1970–71 *Home*, by David Storey
The House of Blue Leaves, by John Guare[16]
Follies, by James Goldman and Stephen Sondheim[2]

1971–72 *That Championship Season*, by Jason Miller
Two Gentlemen of Verona, adapted by John Guare and Mel Shapiro[2]
The Screens, by Jean Genet [1]

1972–73 *The Changing Room*, by David Storey
The Hot l Baltimore, by Lanford Wilson[16]
A Little Night Music, by Hugh Wheeler and Stephen Sondheim[2]

1973–74 *The Contractors*, by David Storey
Short Eyes, by Miguel Piñero[16]
Candide, by Leonard Bernstein, Hugh Wheeler, Richard Wilbur[2]

1974–75 *Equus*, by Peter Shaffer
The Taking of Miss Janie, by Ed Bullins[16]
A Chorus Line, by James Kirkwood and Nicholas Dante[2]

1975–76 *Travesties*, by Tom Stoppard
Streamers, by David Rabe[16]
Pacific Overtures, by Stephen Sondheim, John Weidman, Hugh Wheeler[2]

---

[1] Citation for best foreign play. [2] Citation for best musical. [3] Based on a novel by Arthur Koestler. [4] Based on Christopher Isherwood's *Berlin Stories*. [5] For "distinguished and original contribution to the theater." [6] Based on Sidney Howard's *They Knew What They Wanted*. [7] Based on a novel by Thomas Wolfe. [8] Based on James Agee's *A Death in the Family*. [9] Based on a book by Shepherd Mead. [10] Special citation. [11] Based on Thornton Wilder's *The Matchmaker*. [12] Translated by Edith Hamilton. [13] Based on Sholem Aleichem's Tevye stories, translated by Arnold Perl. [14] Based on John Van Druten's *I Am a Camera*, which won the award for the best play in 1951–52. [15] Based on Brendan Behan's autobiography. [16] Citation for best American play.

Motion Picture Academy Awards (Oscars)

BEST PICTURE	DIRECTING
1928 *Wings,* Paramount	Frank Borzage, *Seventh Heaven;* Lewis Milestone, *Two Arabian Nights*
1929 *The Broadway Melody,* M-G-M	Frank Lloyd, *The Divine Lady*
1930 *All Quiet on the Western Front,* Universal	Lewis Milestone, *All Quiet on the Western Front*
1931 *Cimarron,* RKO Radio	Norman Taurog, *Skippy*
1932 *Grand Hotel,* M-G-M	Frank Borzage, *Bad Girl*
1933 *Cavalcade,* Fox	Frank Lloyd, *Cavalcade*
1934 *It Happened One Night,* Columbia	Frank Capra, *It Happened One Night*
1935 *Mutiny on the Bounty,* M-G-M	John Ford, *The Informer*
1936 *The Great Ziegfeld,* M-G-M	Frank Capra, *Mr. Deeds Goes to Town*
1937 *The Life of Emile Zola,* Warner Bros.	Leo McCarey, *The Awful Truth*
1938 *You Can't Take It with You,* Columbia	Frank Capra, *You Can't Take It with You*
1939 *Gone with the Wind,* Selznick-M-G-M	Victor Fleming, *Gone with the Wind*
1940 *Rebecca,* Selznick-UA	John Ford, *The Grapes of Wrath*
1941 *How Green Was My Valley,* 20th Century-Fox	John Ford, *How Green Was My Valley*
1942 *Mrs. Miniver,* M-G-M	William Wyler, *Mrs. Miniver*
1943 *Casablanca,* Warner Bros.	Michael Curtiz, *Casablanca*
1944 *Going My Way,* Paramount	Leo McCarey, *Going My Way*
1945 *The Lost Weekend,* Paramount	Billy Wilder, *The Lost Weekend*
1946 *The Best Years of Our Lives,* Goldwyn-RKO Radio	William Wyler, *The Best Years of Our Lives*
1947 *Gentleman's Agreement,* 20th Century-Fox	Elia Kazan, *Gentleman's Agreement*
1948 *Hamlet,* Rank-Two Cities-U-I	John Huston, *Treasure of Sierra Madre*
1949 *All the King's Men,* Rossen-Columbia	Joseph L. Mankiewicz, *A Letter to Three Wives*
1950 *All About Eve,* 20th Century-Fox	Joseph L. Mankiewicz, *All About Eve*
1951 *An American in Paris,* M-G-M	George Stevens, *A Place in the Sun*
1952 *The Greatest Show on Earth,* DeMille-Paramount	John Ford, *The Quiet Man*
1953 *From Here to Eternity,* Columbia	Fred Zinnemann, *From Here to Eternity*
1954 *On the Waterfront,* Horizon-American Corp., Columbia	Elia Kazan, *On the Waterfront*
1955 *Marty,* Hecht and Lancaster, United Artists	Delbert Mann, *Marty*
1956 *Around the World in 80 Days,* the Michael Todd Co., Inc.-UA	George Stevens, *Giant*
1957 *The Bridge on the River Kwai,* Horizon Picture, Columbia	David Lean, *The Bridge on the River Kwai*
1958 *Gigi,* Arthur Freed Productions, Inc., M-G-M	Vincente Minnelli, *Gigi*
1959 *Ben-Hur,* M-G-M	William Wyler, *Ben-Hur*
1960 *The Apartment,* Mirisch Co., Inc., United Artists	Billy Wilder, *The Apartment*
1961 *West Side Story,* Mirisch Pictures, Inc., and B and P Enterprises, Inc., United Artists	Robert Wise and Jerome Robbins, *West Side Story*
1962 *Lawrence of Arabia,* Horizon Pictures, Ltd.-Columbia	David Lean, *Lawrence of Arabia*
1963 *Tom Jones,* A Woodfall Production, UA-Lopert Pictures	Tony Richardson, *Tom Jones*
1964 *My Fair Lady,* Warner Bros.	George Cukor, *My Fair Lady*
1965 *The Sound of Music,* Argyle Enterprises Production, 20th Century-Fox	Robert Wise, *The Sound of Music*
1966 *A Man for All Seasons,* Highland Films, Ltd., Production, Columbia	Fred Zinnemann, *A Man for All Seasons*
1967 *In the Heat of the Night,* Mirisch Corp. Production, United Artists	Mike Nichols, *The Graduate*
1968 *Oliver!,* Columbia Pictures	Sir Carol Reed, *Oliver!*
1969 *Midnight Cowboy,* Jerome Hellman-John Schlesinger Production, United Artists	John Schlesinger, *Midnight Cowboy*
1970 *Patton,* Frank McCarthy-Franklin J. Schaffner Production, 20th Century-Fox	Franklin J. Schaffner, *Patton*
1971 *The French Connection,* D'Antoni Productions, 20th Century Fox	William Friedkin, *The French Connection*

1972	*The Godfather*, Albert S. Ruddy production, Paramount
1973	*The Sting*, Universal–Bill–Phillips–George Roy Hill production, Universal
1974	*The Godfather, Part II*, Coppola Co. production, Paramount
1975	*One Flew Over the Cuckoo's Nest*, Fantasy Films Production, United Artists

Bob Fosse, *Cabaret*

George Roy Hill, *The Sting*

Francis Ford Coppola, *The Godfather, Part II*

Milos Forman, *One Flew Over the Cuckoo's Nest*

ACTRESS

1928 Janet Gaynor, *Seventh Heaven, Street Angel, Sunrise*
1929 Mary Pickford, *Coquette*
1930 Norma Shearer, *The Divorcee*
1931 Marie Dressler, *Min and Bill*
1932 Helen Hayes, *The Sin of Madelon Claudet*
1933 Katharine Hepburn, *Morning Glory*
1934 Claudette Colbert, *It Happened One Night*
1935 Bette Davis, *Dangerous*
1936 Luise Rainer, *The Great Ziegfeld*
1937 Luise Rainer, *The Good Earth*
1938 Bette Davis, *Jezebel*
1939 Vivien Leigh, *Gone with the Wind*
1940 Ginger Rogers, *Kitty Foyle*
1941 Joan Fontaine, *Suspicion*
1942 Greer Garson, *Mrs. Miniver*
1943 Jennifer Jones, *The Song of Bernadette*
1944 Ingrid Bergman, *Gaslight*
1945 Joan Crawford, *Mildred Pierce*
1946 Olivia de Havilland, *To Each His Own*
1947 Loretta Young, *The Farmer's Daughter*
1948 Jane Wyman, *Johnny Belinda*
1949 Olivia de Havilland, *The Heiress*
1950 Judy Holliday, *Born Yesterday*
1951 Vivien Leigh, *A Streetcar Named Desire*
1952 Shirley Booth, *Come Back, Little Sheba*
1953 Audrey Hepburn, *Roman Holiday*
1954 Grace Kelly, *The Country Girl*
1955 Anna Magnani, *The Rose Tattoo*
1956 Ingrid Bergman, *Anastasia*
1957 Joanne Woodward, *The Three Faces of Eve*
1958 Susan Hayward, *I Want to Live!*
1959 Simone Signoret, *Room at the Top*
1960 Elizabeth Taylor, *Butterfield 8*
1961 Sophia Loren, *Two Women*
1962 Anne Bancroft, *The Miracle Worker*
1963 Patricia Neal, *Hud*
1964 Julie Andrews, *Mary Poppins*
1965 Julie Christie, *Darling*
1966 Elizabeth Taylor, *Who's Afraid of Virginia Woolf?*
1967 Katharine Hepburn, *Guess Who's Coming to Dinner*
1968 Katharine Hepburn, *The Lion in Winter*, and Barbra Streisand, *Funny Girl*
1969 Maggie Smith, *The Prime of Miss Jean Brodie*
1970 Glenda Jackson, *Women in Love*
1971 Jane Fonda, *Klute*
1972 Liza Minnelli, *Cabaret*
1973 Glenda Jackson, *A Touch of Class*
1974 Ellen Burstyn, *Alice Doesn't Live Here Anymore*
1975 Louise Fletcher, *One Flew Over the Cuckoo's Nest*

ACTOR

Emil Jannings, *The Way of All Flesh, The Last Command*
Warner Baxter, *In Old Arizona*
George Arliss, *Disraeli*
Lionel Barrymore, *A Free Soul*
Fredric March, *Dr. Jekyll and Mr. Hyde*, and Wallace Beery, *The Champ*
Charles Laughton, *The Private Life of Henry VIII*
Clark Gable, *It Happened One Night*

Victor McLaglen, *The Informer*
Paul Muni, *The Story of Louis Pasteur*
Spencer Tracy, *Captains Courageous*
Spencer Tracy, *Boys Town*
Robert Donat, *Goodbye, Mr. Chips*
James Stewart, *The Philadelphia Story*
Gary Cooper, *Sergeant York*
James Cagney, *Yankee Doodle Dandy*
Paul Lukas, *Watch on the Rhine*

Bing Crosby, *Going My Way*
Ray Milland, *The Lost Weekend*
Fredric March, *The Best Years of Our Lives*
Ronald Colman, *A Double Life*
Laurence Olivier, *Hamlet*
Broderick Crawford, *All the King's Men*
José Ferrer, *Cyrano de Bergerac*
Humphrey Bogart, *The African Queen*

Gary Cooper, *High Noon*
William Holden, *Stalag 17*
Marlon Brando, *On the Waterfront*
Ernest Borgnine, *Marty*
Yul Brynner, *The King and I*
Alec Guinness, *The Bridge on the River Kwai*

David Niven, *Separate Tables*
Charlton Heston, *Ben-Hur*
Burt Lancaster, *Elmer Gantry*
Maximilian Schell, *Judgment at Nuremberg*
Gregory Peck, *To Kill a Mockingbird*
Sidney Poitier, *Lilies of the Field*
Rex Harrison, *My Fair Lady*
Lee Marvin, *Cat Ballou*
Paul Scofield, *A Man for All Seasons*

Rod Steiger, *In the Heat of the Night*

Cliff Robertson, *Charly*

John Wayne, *True Grit*

George C. Scott, *Patton*
Gene Hackman, *The French Connection*
Marlon Brando, *The Godfather*
Jack Lemmon, *Save the Tiger*
Art Carney, *Harry and Tonto*

Jack Nicholson, *One Flew Over the Cuckoo's Nest*

ACTRESS (SUPPORTING ROLE)	ACTOR (SUPPORTING ROLE)

1936 Gale Sondergaard, *Anthony Adverse*   Walter Brennan, *Come and Get It*
1937 Alice Brady, *In Old Chicago*   Joseph Schildkraut, *The Life of Emile Zola*
1938 Fay Bainter, *Jezebel*   Walter Brennan, *Kentucky*
1939 Hattie McDaniel, *Gone with the Wind*   Thomas Mitchell, *Stagecoach*
1940 Jane Darwell, *The Grapes of Wrath*   Walter Brennan, *The Westerner*
1941 Mary Astor, *The Great Lie*   Donald Crisp, *How Green Was My Valley*
1942 Teresa Wright, *Mrs. Miniver*   Van Heflin, *Johnny Eager*
1943 Katina Paxinou, *For Whom the Bell Tolls*   Charles Coburn, *The More the Merrier*
1944 Ethel Barrymore, *None But the Lonely Heart*   Barry Fitzgerald, *Going My Way*
1945 Anne Revere, *National Velvet*   James Dunn, *A Tree Grows in Brooklyn*
1946 Anne Baxter, *The Razor's Edge*   Harold Russell, *The Best Years of Our Lives*
1947 Celeste Holm, *Gentleman's Agreement*   Edmund Gwenn, *Miracle on 34th Street*
1948 Claire Trevor, *Key Largo*   Walter Huston, *Treasure of Sierra Madre*
1949 Mercedes McCambridge, *All the King's Men*   Dean Jagger, *Twelve O'Clock High*
1950 Josephine Hull, *Harvey*   George Sanders, *All About Eve*
1951 Kim Hunter, *A Streetcar Named Desire*   Karl Malden, *A Streetcar Named Desire*
1952 Gloria Grahame, *The Bad and the Beautiful*   Anthony Quinn, *Viva Zapata!*
1953 Donna Reed, *From Here to Eternity*   Frank Sinatra, *From Here to Eternity*
1954 Eva Marie Saint, *On the Waterfront*   Edmond O'Brien, *The Barefoot Contessa*
1955 Jo Van Fleet, *East of Eden*   Jack Lemmon, *Mister Roberts*
1956 Dorothy Malone, *Written on the Wind*   Anthony Quinn, *Lust for Life*
1957 Miyoshi Umeki, *Sayonara*   Red Buttons, *Sayonara*
1958 Wendy Hiller, *Separate Tables*   Burl Ives, *The Big Country*
1959 Shelley Winters, *The Diary of Anne Frank*   Hugh Griffith, *Ben-Hur*
1960 Shirley Jones, *Elmer Gantry*   Peter Ustinov, *Spartacus*
1961 Rita Moreno, *West Side Story*   George Chakiris, *West Side Story*
1962 Patty Duke, *The Miracle Worker*   Ed Begley, *Sweet Bird of Youth*
1963 Margaret Rutherford, *The V.I.P.s*   Melvyn Douglas, *Hud*
1964 Lila Kedrova, *Zorba the Greek*   Peter Ustinov, *Topkapi*
1965 Shelley Winters, *A Patch of Blue*   Martin Balsam, *A Thousand Clowns*
1966 Sandy Dennis, *Who's Afraid of Virginia Woolf?*   Walter Matthau, *The Fortune Cookie*
1967 Estelle Parsons, *Bonnie and Clyde*   George Kennedy, *Cool Hand Luke*
1968 Ruth Gordon, *Rosemary's Baby*   Jack Albertson, *The Subject Was Roses*
1969 Goldie Hawn, *Cactus Flower*   Gig Young, *They Shoot Horses, Don't They?*
1970 Helen Hayes, *Airport*   John Mills, *Ryan's Daughter*
1971 Cloris Leachman, *The Last Picture Show*   Ben Johnson, *The Last Picture Show*
1972 Eileen Heckart, *Butterflies Are Free*   Joel Grey, *Cabaret*
1973 Tatum O'Neal, *Paper Moon*   John Houseman, *The Paper Chase*
1974 Ingrid Bergman, *Murder on the Orient Express*   Robert De Niro, *The Godfather, Part II*
1975 Lee Grant, *Shampoo*   George Burns, *The Sunshine Boys*

Some Other Academy Awards for 1975

Art direction: *Barry Lyndon*, Ken Adam and Roy Walker. **Set decoration:** Vernon Dixon.
Cinematography: John Alcott, *Barry Lyndon*.
Costume design: Ulla-Britt Soderlund and Milena Canonero, *Barry Lyndon*.
Documentary (feature): *The Man Who Skied Down Everest*.
Documentary (short subject): *The End of the Game*.
Editing: Verna Fields, *Jaws*.
Foreign-language film: *Dersu Uzala* (U.S.S.R.).
Irving G. Thalberg Memorial Award: Mervin Leroy.
Jean Hersholt Humanitarian Award: Jules Stein.
Music (original dramatic score): John Williams, *Jaws*.

Scoring (adaptation): Leonard Rosenman, *Barry Lyndon*.
Screenplay (original): Frank Pierson, *Dog Day Afternoon*.
Screenplay (adaptation): Lawrence Hauben and Bo Goldman, *One Flew Over the Cuckoo's Nest*.
Short subject (animated): *Great*.
Short subject (live): *Angel and Big Joe*.
Song: "I'm Easy," by Keith Carradine, from *Nashville*.
Sound: Robert L. Hoyt, Roger Heman, Earl Madery and John Carter, *Jaws*.
Special award: Mary Pickford.

Major TV Emmy Awards, 1976

Actor (drama series): Peter Falk, *Columbo*, NBC.

Actress (drama series): Michael Learned, *The Waltons*, CBS.

Actor (comedy series): Jack Albertson, *Chico and the Man*, NBC.

Actress (comedy series): Mary Tyler Moore, *The Mary Tyler Moore Show*, CBS.

Actor (special program): Anthony Hopkins, *The Lindbergh Kidnapping Case*, NBC.

Actress (special program): Susan Clark, *Babe*, CBS.

Actor (single appearance in a series): Edward Asner, *Rich Man, Poor Man*, ABC.

Actress (single appearance in a series): Kathryn Walker, *The Adams Chronicles*, PBS.

Actor (limited series): Hal Holbrook, *Sandburg's Lincoln*, NBC.

Actress (limited series): Rosemary Harris, *Notorious Woman*, PBS.

Supporting actor (drama series): Anthony Zerbe, *Harry O*, ABC.

Supporting actress (drama series): Ellen Corby, *The Waltons*, CBS.

Supporting actor (special program): Ed Flanders, *A Moon for the Misbegotten*, ABC.

Supporting actress (special program): Rosemary Murphy, *Eleanor and Franklin*, ABC.

Supporting actor (comedy series): Ted Knight, *The Mary Tyler Moore Show*, CBS.

Supporting actress (comedy series): Betty White, *The Mary Tyler Moore Show*, CBS.

Supporting actor (variety or music): Chevy Chase, *Saturday Night*, NBC.

Supporting actress (variety or music): Vickie Lawrence, *The Carol Burnett Show*, CBS.

Supporting actor (single appearance, limited series): Gordon Jackson, *Upstairs, Downstairs*, PBS.

Supporting actress (single appearance, limited series): Fionnuala Flannagan, *Rich Man, Poor Man*, ABC.

Drama series: *Police Story*, NBC.

Comedy series: *The Mary Tyler Moore Show*, CBS.

Comedy-variety or music series: *Saturday Night*, NBC.

Limited series: *Upstairs, Downstairs*, PBS.

Special (drama or comedy): *Eleanor and Franklin*, ABC.

Special (comedy-variety or music): *Gypsy in My Soul* with Shirley MacLaine, CBS.

Classical music: *Bernstein and the New York Philharmonic*, PBS.

Children's special: *You're a Good Sport Charlie Brown*, CBS, and *Huckleberry Finn*, ABC.

Sports event: *1975 World Series*, NBC.

Sports series: *NFL Monday Night Football*, ABC.

Sports personality: Jim McKay, *ABC's Wide World of Sports*, ABC.

Total prime-time awards: ABC, 17; CBS, 15; NBC, 11; PBS, 6.

Antoinette Perry (Tony) Awards for 1976

Dramatic play: *Travesties*, by Tom Stoppard.

Musical: *A Chorus Line*, by Michael Bennett.

Actress (play): Irene Worth, *Sweet Bird of Youth*.

Actor (play): John Wood, *Travesties*.

Actress (musical): Donna McKechnie, *A Chorus Line*.

Actor (musical): George Rose, *My Fair Lady*.

Actress, featured (play): Shirley Knight, *Kennedy's Children*.

Actor, featured (play): Edward Herrmann, *Mrs. Warren's Profession*.

Actress, featured (musical): Kelly Bishop, *A Chorus Line*.

Actor, featured (musical): Sammy Williams, *A Chorus Line*.

Director (play): Ellis Rabb, *The Royal Family*.

Director (musical): Michael Bennett, *A Chorus Line*.

Score: Marvin Hamlisch (music) and Edward Kleban (lyrics), *A Chorus Line*.

Book: James Kirkwood and Nicholas Dante, *A Chorus Line*.

Scenic design: Boris Aronson, *Pacific Overtures*.

Costume design: Florence Klotz, *Pacific Overtures*.

Lighting design: Tharon Musser, *A Chorus Line*.

Choreography: Bob Avian and Michael Bennett, *A Chorus Line*.

Special awards: George Abbott, Mathilde Pincus, Thomas H. Fitzgerald (posthumous), Arena Stage and Circle in the Square.

Major Grammy Awards for Recording, 1975

Album: Paul Simon ("Still Crazy After All These Years").

Record: The Captain and Tennille ("Love Will Keep Us Together").

Song of the Year: "Send in the Clowns" (Stephen Sondheim).

Pop Vocalists: Janis Ian ("At Seventeen"); Paul Simon ("Still Crazy After All These Years").

Pop Group: The Eagles ("Lyin' Eyes").

Pop Instrumental: Van McCoy ("The Hustle").

Rhythm and Blues Vocalists: Ray Charles ("Living for the City"); Natalie Cole ("This Will Be").

Rhythm and Blues Group: Earth, Wind and Fire ("Shining Star").

Rhythm and Blues Instrumental: Silver Convention ("Fly, Robin, Fly").

Rhythm and Blues Song: "Where is the Love" (H. W. Casey, Richard Finch, Willie Clarke, Betty Wright).

New Artist: Natalie Cole.

Country Vocalists: Linda Ronstadt ("I Can't Help It if I'm Still in Love With You"); Willie Nelson ("Blue Eyes Crying in the Rain").

Country Group: Kris Kristofferson and Rita Coolidge ("Lover Please").

Country Instrumental: Chet Atkins ("The Entertainer").

Country Song: "(Hey Won't You Play) Another Somebody Done Somebody Wrong Song" (Chips Moman and Larry Butler).

Big Band: Phil Woods with Michel Legrand ("Images").

Jazz Soloist: Dizzy Gillespie ("Oscar Peterson and Dizzy Gillespie").

Jazz Group: Chick Corea and Return Forever ("No Mystery").

Soul Gospel Performance: Andrae Crouch and the Disciples ("Take Me Back").

Latin Recording: Eddie Palmieri ("Sun of Latin Music").

Classical Album: "Beethoven: Symphonies Complete" (Chicago Symphony, Georg Solti conductor).

Orchestra Performance: "Ravel: Daphnis et Chloe" (New York Philharmonic, Pierre Boulez conductor).

Instrumental Soloist (without orchestra): Nathan Milstein ("Bach: Sonatas and Partitas for Violin").

Vocal Soloist: Janet Baker ("Mahler: Kindertotenlieder").

Motion Picture or TV Score: John Williams ("Jaws").

Overseas Press Club of America Awards, 1976

Bob Considine Memorial Award for best reporting from abroad requiring exceptional courage and initiative: Sydney H. Schanberg *(New York Times)*.

Robert Capa Gold Medal for still photography from abroad, requiring exceptional courage and enterprise: Dirck Halstead *(Time)*.

Daily newspaper or wire service reporting from abroad: Sydney H. Schanberg *(New York Times)*.

Daily newspaper or wire service interpretation of foreign events: Joseph C. Harsch *(Christian Science Monitor)*.

Photographic reporting from abroad: K. Kenneth Paik *(Kansas City Times)*.

Business news reporting from abroad: J. A. Livingston *(Philadelphia Inquirer)*.

Cartoon on foreign affairs: Tony Auth *(Philadelphia Inquirer)*.

Book on foreign affairs: *The First Casualty*, by Phillip Knightley.

Magazine reporting from abroad: John J. Putman *(National Geographic)*.

Magazine interpretation of foreign affairs: Arnaud de Borchgrave *(Newsweek)*.

TV spot news reporting from abroad: Bruce Dunning, "Back From Danang" (CBS News).

TV interpretation or documentary on foreign affairs: Howard K. Smith and Bill Seamans, "Rabin: Action Biography" (ABC News).

Radio spot news reporting from abroad: CBS News for coverage of fall of South Vietnam and Cambodia.

Radio interpretation of foreign affairs: "Scenes From a War" (ABC News) and "America in Vietnam" (CBS News).

Madeline Dane Ross Award for Reporting that Demonstrates a Concern for Humanity: Mayo Mohs *(Time)*.

National Book Awards, 1976

Arts and Letters: *The Great War and Modern Memory,* by Paul Fussell (Oxford University Press).

Children's Books: *Bert Breen's Barn,* by Walter D. Edmonds (Little, Brown).

Contemporary Affairs: *Passage to Ararat,* by Michael J. Arlen (Farrar, Straus & Giroux).

Fiction: *J R,* by William Gaddis (Knopf).

History and Biography: *The Problem of Slavery in the Age of Revolution: 1770–1823,* by David Briôn Davis (Cornell University Press).

Poetry: *Self-Portrait in a Convex Mirror,* by John Ashbery (Viking Press).

American Library Association Awards for Children's Books

Newbery Medal for best book: *Grey King,* by Susan Cooper.

Caldecott Medal for best illustration: *Why Mosquitoes Buzz in People's Ears,* by Leo and Diane Dillon.

Significant Books Published in 1976

Selected by the Staff of the Information Please Almanac on the basis of significance and/or popularity as determined by frequency of citation on best-seller lists. Books are listed alphabetically.

Fiction

1. **Bloodshed,** Cynthia Ozick
2. **Agent in Place,** Helen McInnes
3. **Details of a Sunset,** Vladimir Nabokov
4. **Dolores,** Jacqueline Susann
5. **1876,** Gore Vidal
6. **Foreign Affairs and Other Stories,** Sean O'Faolain
7. **Guerrillas,** V. A. Naipaul
8. **Humboldt's Gift,** Saul Bellow
9. **I Hear America Swinging,** Peter De Vries
10. **Kinflicks,** Lisa Alther
11. **Memoirs,** Tennessee Williams
12. **Miss Herbert (The Suburban Wife),** Christina Steas
13. **The Boys From Brazil,** Ira Levin
14. **The Deep,** Peter Benchley
15. **The Franchiser,** Stanley Elkin
16. **The Family Arsenal,** Paul Theroux
17. **The Lonely Lady,** Harold Robbins
18. **The Spectator Bird,** Wallace Stegner
19. **The Stranger in the Mirror,** Sidney Sheldon
20. **Trinity,** Leon Uris

Nonfiction

1. **A Complete Guide to Therapy From Psycho-analysis to Behavior Modification,** Joel Kovel
2. **Andre Malraux,** Jean Lacouture
3. **Autobiography,** Margot Fonteyn
4. **Diplomacy for a Crowded World: An American Foreign Policy,** George W. Ball
5. **Economists at Bay,** Robert Lekachman
6. **Giai Phong! The Fall and Liberation of Saigon,** Tiziano Terzani
7. **It Changed My Life: Writings on the Women's Movement,** Betty Friedan
8. **Josh,** Joshua Logan
9. **Life on the Run,** Bill Bradley
10. **Lindbergh,** Leonard Mosley
11. **Lyndon Johnson and the American Dream,** Doris Kearns
12. **Power Shift,** Kirkpatrick Sale
13. **Scoundrel Time,** Lillian Hellman
14. **Singularities,** John Simon
15. **Sports in America,** James Michener
16. **The Children of the Sun,** Martin Green
17. **The Devil Finds Work,** James Baldwin
18. **The Dying of the Light,** Arnold Rogow
19. **The Final Days,** Bob Woodward and Carl Bernstein
20. **The Lardners: My Family Remembered,** Ring Lardner, Jr.
21. **The Life of Bertrand Russell,** Ronald W. Clark
22. **The Next 200 Years,** Herman Kahn
23. **The Rockefellers,** Peter Collier and David Horowitz
24. **The Silent Clowns,** Walter Kerr
25. **The Time of Illusion,** Jonathan Schell
26. **Unequal Justice,** Jerold S. Auerbach
27. **World of our Fathers,** Irving Howe

Plays and Movies

Longest Broadway Runs[1]		Top Money-Making Films[2]	
1. Fiddler on the Roof (M) (1964–72)	3,242	1. Jaws (1975)	$102,650,000
2. Life With Father (1939–47)	3,224	2. The Godfather (1972)	85,747,184
3. Tobacco Road (1933–41)	3,182	3. The Sound of Music (1965)	78,400,000
4. Hello, Dolly! (M) (1964–71)	2,844	4. Gone With the Wind (1939)	74,236,000
5. My Fair Lady (M) (1956–62)	2,717	5. The Sting (1973)	72,100,000
6. Man of La Mancha (M) (1965–71)	2,329	6. The Exorcist (1973)	71,715,000
7. Abie's Irish Rose (1922–27)	2,327	7. Towering Inferno (1975)	55,000,000
8. Oklahoma! (M) (1943–48)	2,212	8. Love Story (1970)	50,000,000
9. Harvey (1944–49)	1,775	9. The Graduate (1968)	49,978,000
10. Hair (M) (1968–72)	1,742[3]	10. Doctor Zhivago (1965)	46,232,000
11. South Pacific (M) (1949–54)	1,694	11. Airport (1970)	45,300,000
12. Born Yesterday (1946–49)	1,642	12. American Graffiti (1973)	45,000,000
13. Mary, Mary (1961–64)	1,572	13. Butch Cassidy and the Sundance Kid (1969)	44,300,000
14. Voice of the Turtle (1943–48)	1,557	14. The Ten Commandments	43,000,000
15. Barefoot in the Park (1963–67)	1,532	15. The Poseidon Adventure (1972)	42,500,000
16. Mame (M) (1966–70)	1,508	16. Mary Poppins (1964)	42,250,000
17. Arsenic and Old Lace (1941–44)	1,444	17. M*A*S*H (1970)	40,850,000
18. Sound of Music (M) (1959–63)	1,443	18. Ben-Hur (1959)	36,550,000
19. How to Succeed in Business Without Really Trying (M) (1961–65)	1,417	19. Fiddler on the Roof (1971)	35,550,000
20. Hellzapoppin' (M) (1938–41)	1,404	20. Earthquake (1974)	32,000,000
21. Music Man (M) (1957–61)	1,375	21. Billy Jack (1971)	31,000,000
22. Funny Girl (M) (1964–67)	1,348	22. Benji (1974)	30,800,000
23. Oh! Calcutta! (M) (1969–72)	1,316[4]	23. Young Frankenstein (1975)	30,000,000
24. Angel Street (1941–44)	1,295	24. The Godfather, Part II	28,900,000
24. Lightnin' (1918–21)	1,291	25. Thunderball (1970)	28,300,000

[1] M indicates musical. Years are those of opening and closing. [2] Figures are rentals collected by film distributors in U.S. and Canada as of Jan. 1, 1976. [3] Does not include 94 non-Broadway performances given December 1967–January 1968. [4] Includes 710 off-Broadway performances. Source of tables: *Variety.*

Birthstones

Source: Jewelry Industry Council.

January	Garnet	July	Ruby or Star Ruby
February	Amethyst	August	Peridot or Sardonyx
March	Aquamarine or Bloodstone	September	Sapphire or Star Sapphire
April	Diamond	October	Opal or Tourmaline
May	Emerald	November	Topaz
June	Pearl, Alexandrite or Moonstone	December	Turquoise or Zircon

Presidential Medal of Freedom

The nation's highest civilian award, the Presidential Medal of Freedom, was instituted by President John F. Kennedy to honor those "who contribute significantly to the quality of American life." It was awarded for the first time on July 4, 1963.

1963 Awards (By President Kennedy)

Marian Anderson (contralto)
Ralph J. Bunche (U. N. undersecretary)
Ellsworth Bunker (diplomat)
Pablo Casals (cellist)
Genevieve Caulfield (educator)
James B. Conant (educator)
John F. Enders (bacteriologist)
Felix Frankfurter (jurist)
Karl Holton (youth authority)
John XXIII (Pope) *
John F. Kennedy (President of U. S.) *
Robert J. Kiphuth (athletic director)
Edwin H. Land (inventor)
Herbert H. Lehman (statesman)
Robert A. Lovett (statesman)
J. Clifford MacDonald (educator)
John J. McCloy (banker and statesman)
George Meany (labor leader)
Alexander Meiklejohn (philosopher)
Ludwig Mies van der Rohe (architect)
Jean Monnet (European statesman)
Luis Muñoz-Marín (Governor, Puerto Rico)
Clarence B. Randall (industrialist)
Rudolf Serkin (pianist)
Edward Steichen (photographer)
George W. Taylor (educator)
Alan T. Waterman (scientist)
Mark S. Watson (journalist)
Annie D. Wauneka (public health worker)
E. B. White (author)
Thornton Wilder (author)
Edmund Wilson (author and critic)
Andrew N. Wyeth (artist)

1964 Awards (By President Johnson)

Dean Acheson (statesman)
Detlev W. Bronk (neurophysiologist)
Aaron Copland (composer)
Willem de Kooning (painter)
Walt Disney (animated cartoonist)
J. Frank Dobie (author)
Lena F. Edwards (physician, humanitarian)
Thomas Stearns Eliot (poet)
Lynn Fontanne (actress)
John W. Gardner (educator)
Rev. Theodore M. Hesburgh (educator)
Clarence L. Johnson (aircraft engineer)
Frederick R. Kappel (telephone executive)
Helen A. Keller (educator)
John L. Lewis (labor leader)
Walter Lippmann (journalist)
Alfred Lunt (actor)
Ralph Emerson McGill (journalist)
Samuel Eliot Morison (historian)
Lewis Mumford (urban planner and critic)
Edward R. Murrow (radio-TV commentator)
Reinhold Niebuhr (theologian)
Leontyne Price (soprano)
A. Philip Randolph (labor leader)
Carl Sandburg (poet, biographer)
John Steinbeck (author)
Helen B. Taussig (pediatrician)
Carl Vinson (legislator)
Thomas J. Watson, Jr. (industrialist)
Paul Dudley White (physician)

1967 Awards (By President Johnson)

Ellsworth Bunker (diplomat)
Eugene M. Locke (diplomat)
Robert W. Komer (government worker)

1968 Awards (By President Johnson)

Robert S. McNamara (government official)
James Webb (NASA administrator)

1969 Awards (By President Johnson)

Eugene R. Black (banker)
McGeorge Bundy (government official)
Clark M. Clifford (statesman)
Michael E. DeBakey (surgeon)
David Dubinsky (labor leader)
Henry Ford II (industrialist)
Ralph Ellison (author)
W. Averell Harriman (statesman)
Bop Hope (comedian)
Edgar Kaiser (industrialist)
Mary Lasker (philanthropist)
John W. Macy, Jr. (government official)
Gregory Peck (actor)
Laurance S. Rockefeller (conservationist)
Walt W. Rostow (government official)
Dean Rusk (statesman)
Merriman Smith (journalist)
Cyrus R. Vance (government official)
William S. White (journalist)
Roy Wilkins (social welfare executive)
Whitney M. Young (social welfare executive)

1969 Awards (By President Nixon)

Col. Edwin E. Aldrin, Jr. (astronaut)
Neil A. Armstrong (astronaut)
Lt. Col. Michael Collins (astronaut)
Duke Ellington (musician)

1970 Awards (By President Nixon)

Apollo 13 Mission Operations Team
Earl Charles Behrens (journalist)
Edward T. Folliard (journalist)
Fred Wallace Haise, Jr. (astronaut)
William M. Henry (journalist) *
Arthur Krock (journalist)
David Lawrence (journalist)
George Gould Lincoln (journalist)
James A. Lovell, Jr. (astronaut)
Raymond Moley (journalist)
Eugene Ormandy (conductor)
Adela Rogers St. Johns (journalist)
John Leonard Swigert, Jr. (astronaut)

1971 Awards (By President Nixon)

Sam Goldwyn (film producer)
Manlio Brosio (NATO secretary general)
William J. Hopkins (White House executive clerk)

1972 Awards (By President Nixon)

Lila and DeWitt Wallace (founders of Reader's Digest)
John Paul Vann (adviser in Vietnam war) *

1973 Awards (By President Nixon)

John Ford (film director)
William P. Rogers (diplomat)

1974 Awards (By President Nixon)

Melvin R. Laird (government official)
Dr. Charles L. Lowman (orthopedist)
Paul G. Hoffman (statesman)

---

* Awarded posthumously by President Johnson.   * Awarded posthumously.

The Hall of Fame for Great Americans

Source: Hall of Fame

The Hall of Fame for Great Americans, established in 1900 on what was then the Bronx campus of New York University, is an open-air colonnade with busts and tablets for the 99 persons so far honored for national achievements. New names are voted on every three years* by a College of Electors of about 100 eminent men and women from all the states. To be elected to the Hall of Fame, an individual must have been dead more than 25 years† and must have been a citizen of the U.S. Nominations may be made by any citizen.

Names	Elected	Names	Elected
John Adams (statesman)	1900	Sidney Lanier (poet)	1945
Jane Addams (social worker)	1965	Robert E. Lee (military officer)	1900
John Quincy Adams (statesman)	1905	Abraham Lincoln (statesman)	1900
Louis Agassiz (naturalist)	1915	Henry W. Longfellow (poet)	1900
Susan B. Anthony (reformer)	1950	James Russell Lowell (poet)	1905
John James Audubon (naturalist)	1900	Mary Lyon (educator)	1905
George Bancroft (historian)	1910	Edward Alexander MacDowell (composer)	1960
Henry Ward Beecher (clergyman)	1900	James Madison (statesman)	1905
Alexander Graham Bell (inventor)	1950	Horace Mann (educator)	1900
Daniel Boone (explorer)	1915	John Marshall (jurist)	1900
Edwin Booth (actor)	1925	Matthew F. Maury (oceanographer)	1930
Louis D. Brandeis (jurist)	1973	Albert Abraham Michelson (physicist)	1970
Phillips Brooks (clergyman)	1910	Maria Mitchell (astronomer)	1905
William Cullen Bryant (poet)	1910	James Monroe (statesman)	1930
George Washington Carver (chemist)	1973	Samuel F. B. Morse (inventor)	1900
William Ellery Channing (clergyman)	1900	William T. G. Morton (dentist)	1920
Rufus Choate (lawyer)	1915	John Lothrop Motley (historian)	1910
Henry Clay (statesman)	1900	Simon Newcomb (astronomer)	1935
Samuel L. Clemens (Mark Twain) (author)	1920	Thomas Paine (author)	1945
Grover Cleveland (statesman)	1935	Alice Freeman Palmer (educator)	1920
James Fenimore Cooper (author)	1910	Francis Parkman (historian)	1915
Peter Cooper (philanthropist)	1900	George Peabody (philanthropist)	1900
Charlotte S. Cushman (actress)	1915	William Penn (colonizer)	1935
James Buchanan Eads (engineer)	1920	Edgar Allan Poe (author)	1910
Thomas A. Edison (inventor)	1960	Walter Reed (surgeon)	1945
Jonathan Edwards (clergyman)	1900	Franklin Delano Roosevelt (statesman)	1973
Ralph Waldo Emerson (author)	1900	Theodore Roosevelt (statesman)	1950
David G. Farragut (naval officer)	1900	Augustus Saint-Gaudens (sculptor)	1920
Stephen C. Foster (song composer)	1940	William T. Sherman (army officer)	1905
Benjamin Franklin (statesman)	1900	John Philip Sousa (composer)	1973
Robert Fulton (inventor)	1900	Joseph Story (jurist)	1900
Josiah Willard Gibbs (physicist)	1950	Harriet Beecher Stowe (author)	1910
William Crawford Gorgas (physician)	1950	Gilbert Charles Stuart (painter)	1900
Ulysses S. Grant (statesman)	1900	Sylvanus Thayer (educator)	1965
Asa Gray (botanist)	1900	Henry David Thoreau (author)	1960
Alexander Hamilton (statesman)	1915	Lillian D. Wald (nurse, social worker)	1970
Nathaniel Hawthorne (author)	1900	Booker T. Washington (educator)	1945
Joseph Henry (physicist)	1915	George Washington (statesman)	1900
Patrick Henry (statesman)	1920	Daniel Webster (statesman)	1900
Oliver Wendell Holmes (author)	1910	George Westinghouse (inventor)	1955
Oliver Wendell Holmes, Jr. (jurist)	1965	J. A. McNeill Whistler (painter)	1930
Mark Hopkins (educator)	1915	Walt Whitman (poet)	1930
Elias Howe (inventor)	1915	Eli Whitney (inventor)	1900
Washington Irving (author)	1900	John Greenleaf Whittier (poet)	1905
Andrew Jackson (statesman)	1910	Emma Willard (educator)	1905
Thomas ("Stonewall") Jackson (military officer)	1955	Frances Elizabeth Willard (reformer)	1910
		Roger Williams (clergyman)	1920
Thomas Jefferson (statesman)	1900	Woodrow Wilson (statesman)	1950
John Paul Jones (naval officer)	1925	Orville Wright‡ (inventor)	1965
James Kent (jurist)	1900	Wilbur Wright (inventor)	1955

* Elections were held every five years before 1970. † Stipulation was ten years before 1922. ‡ Rule that individual must have been dead for 25 years was waived for Orville Wright, who died in 1948.

Distinguished Painters, Sculptors and Architects

The following list of artists and representative works covers only a small field of the distinguished artists throughout the world. We hope the list selected will prove interesting and helpful to the reader.

Aalto, Alvar (1898-1976). Finnish architect: *Baker House*, M.I.T. (1947-49); Cambridge, Mass.

Albers, Josef (1888-1976). German-American painter: *Homage to the Square: Apparition* (1959), oil on board; Guggenheim Mus., N.Y.C.

Archipenko, Alexandre (1887-1964). Russian-American sculptor: *Medrano* (1915), painted tin, glass, wood and oilcloth; Guggenheim Mus., N.Y.C.

Arp, Jean Hans (1887-1966). Alsatian born sculptor and painter: *Mountain Table Anchors Navel* (1925), oil on board with cut-outs; Mus. of Modern Art, N.Y.C.

Audubon, John J. (1785-1851). American ornithologist and painter: *The Birds of America;* New York Hist. Soc., N.Y.C.

Beardsley, Aubrey Vincent (1872-98). English illustrator: *Salome with the Head of John the Baptist* (1893), india ink and watercolor; Princeton U. Lib., Princeton, N.J.

Bellows, George (1882-1925). American Realist painter: *Dempsey and Firpo* (1924); Whitney Mus., N.Y.C.

Benton, Thomas Hart (1889-1975). American Regionalist painter: *Homestead* (1934), oil; Mus. of Modern Art, N.Y.C.

Bernini, Gian Lorenzo (1598-1680). Italian Baroque sculptor and architect: *Agony of St. Theresa* (1645-52); Cornaro Chapel, Rome.

Bingham, George Caleb (1811-79). American Genre painter: *Fur Traders Descending the Missouri* (1845); Metropolitan Mus., N.Y.C.

Bonnard, Pierre (1867-1947). French painter: *The Window* (1925); Tate Gallery, London.

Bosch, Hieronymus (c.1450-1516). Flemish painter of fantasies: *The Garden of Delights* (c.1500), triptych panel; Prado Mus., Madrid.

Botticelli, Sandro (c.1444-1510?). Florentine painter: *The Birth of Venus* (c.1480), canvas; Uffizi Gallery, Florence.

Brancusi, Constantin (1876-1957). Rumanian sculptor: *Bird in Space* (1919), bronze; Mus. of Modern Art, N.Y.C.

Braque, Georges (1882-1963). French painter, evolved Cubism with Picasso: *Le Courrier* (1913), collage; Philadelphia Mus. of Art.

Breuer, Marcel (1902-   ). Hungarian-born architect and designer: *Whitney Museum of American Art* (1966); N.Y.C.

Bruegel, Pieter (elder) (c.1525-69). Flemish painter: *Peasant Wedding* (c.1565); panel; Kunsthistorisches Mus., Vienna.

Calder, Alexander (1898-   ). American sculptor and graphic artist: *Lobster Trap and Fish Tail* (1939), mobile: steel wire and sheet aluminum; Mus. of Modern Art, N.Y.C.

Caravaggio, Michelangelo Merisi da (1573-1610). Italian Baroque painter: *The Calling of St. Matthew* (c.1597-98), canvas; Contrelli Chapel, S. Luigi dei Francesi, Rome.

Cassatt, Mary (1844-1926). American Impressionist painter: *The Bath* (c.1891); Art Inst. of Chicago.

Cellini, Benvenuto (1500-71). Italian sculptor and metalsmith: *Perseus* (1545-54), bronze; Loggia dei Lanzi, Florence.

Cezanne, Paul (1839-1906). French post-Impressionist painter: *Basket of Apples* (1890-94); Art Inst. of Chicago.

Chagall, Marc (1887-   ). Russian painter: *Calvary* (1912); Mus. of Modern Art, N.Y.C.

Cole, Thomas (1801-48). English born American painter, leader of the Hudson River School: *The Oxbow* (1846); Metropolitan Mus., N.Y.C.

Constable, John (1776-1837). English landscape painter: *Hampstead-Evening* (1822), oil on paper; Victoria and Albert Mus., London.

Copley, John Singleton (1738-1815). American portrait painter: *Watson and the Shark* (1778); Boston Mus. of Fine Arts.

Corot, Jean Baptiste (1796-1875). French landscape painter associated with the Barbizon School: *The Church of Marissel* (1866); Louvre, Paris.

Courbet, Gustave (1819-77). French Realist painter: *Burial at Ornans* (1850); Louvre, Paris.

Dali, Salvador (1904-   ). Spanish Surrealist painter: *Persistence of Memory* (1931); Mus. of Modern Art, N.Y.C.

Daumier, Honoré (1808-79). French Realist painter, sculptor, lithographer: *Crispin and Scapin* (1858-60); Louvre, Paris.

David, Jacques Louis (1748-1825). French Neoclassicist painter: *The Death of Marat* (1793); Royal Mus. of Fine Arts, Brussels.

Degas, Edgar (1834-1917). French Impressionist painter: *Absinthe Drinkers* (1876); Louvre, Paris.

de Kooning, Willem (1904-   ). Dutch-born American Abstract Expressionist painter: *Woman I* (1950-52); Mus. of Modern Art, N.Y.C.

Delacroix, Eugene (1798-1863). Major exponent of French Romantic painting: *Abduction of Rebecca* (1846); Metropolitan Mus., N.Y.C.

di Chirico, Giorgio (1888-   ). Italian Surrealist-influenced painter: *The Disquieting Muses* (1917); Mattioli Coll., Milan.

Donatello (c.1386-1466). Early Renaissance Florentine sculptor: *St. Mark* (1411-13), marble; Or S. Michele, Florence.

Duchamp, Marcel (1887-1968). French painter and theorist associated with Dada and Surrealism: *Nude Descending a Staircase* (1911); Mus. of Modern Art, N.Y.C.

Dufy, Raoul (1877-1953). French painter briefly associated with Fauvism: *Posters at Trouville* (1906); Natl. Mus. of Modern Art, Paris.

Dürer, Albrecht (1471-1528). German Renaissance painter, printmaker and draughtsman: *Adam and Eve* (1504), engraving; Mus. of Fine Arts, Boston.

Eakins, Thomas (1844-1916). American Naturalist painter: *Max Schmitt in a Single Scull* (1871); Metropolitan Mus., N.Y.C.

El Greco (c.1542-1614). Cretan-born Spanish Religious painter noted for quasi-Mannerism: *View of Toledo* (c.1610); Metropolitan Mus., N.Y.C.

Epstein, Sir Jacob (1880-1959). American-born English sculptor: *Joseph Conrad* (1924), bronze; Birmingham City Mus. and Art Gallery, Ala.

Ernst, Max (1891-1976). German painter, activator of Dada, associated with Surrealism: *Woman, Old Man and Flower* (1923-24); Mus. of Modern Art, N.Y.C.

Eyck, Jan Van (c.1390-1441). Leading painter of the Netherlandish School: *Madonna with Chancellor Rolin* (c.1435); Louvre, Paris.

Fra Angelico (c.1387-1455). Italian painter: *The Annunciation* (c.1440-50), fresco; S. Marco, Florence.

Fragonard, Jean-Honoré (1732-1806). French Rococo painter: *Love Letter* (c.1771-72); Metropolitan Mus., N.Y.C.

Gainsborough, Thomas (1727-88). English portrait and landscape painter: *Robert Andrews and his Wife* (c.1748-50); National Gallery, London.

Gauguin, Paul (1848-1903). French post-Impressionist painter: *Yellow Christ* (1889); Fine Arts Academy, Buffalo, N.Y.

Ghiberti, Lorenzo (c.1378-1455). Florentine sculptor in bronze and gold; his masterpiece is the eastern portal of the Baptistry in Florence which Michelangelo called *The Gates of Paradise.*

Giacometti, Alberto (1901-66). Swiss sculptor, important member of the Surrealist group (1931-34): *Man Pointing* (1947), bronze; Tate Gallery, London.

Giotto (c.1266-1337). Italian painter, "Father" of the Italian Renaissance: *Arena Chapel Fresco Cycle* (1305-06); Padua, Italy.

Gorky, Arshile (1904-48). Armenian-born Abstract Expressionist painter: *Agony* (1947); Mus. of Modern Art, N.Y.C.

Goya, Francisco de (1746-1828). Spanish painter: *The Third of May, 1808* (1814-15); Prado Mus., Madrid.

Gris, Juan (1887-1927). Spanish cubist painter: *Composition, 1914* (1914); Mus. of Modern Art, N.Y.C.

Gropius, Walter (1883-1969). German-American architect, originator of the International Style, Bauhaus chief and noted professor in America: *The Graduate Center* (1949-50); Harvard U., Cambridge, Mass.

Grosz, George (1893-1959). German-American painter and caricaturist: *Night Cafe* (1916), india ink; Staatsgalerie, Stuttgart.

Hals, Frans (1580-1666). Dutch painter: *Laughing Cavalier* (1624); Wallace Coll., London.

Hofmann, Hans (1880-1966). German-American Abstract Expressionist painter: *Magenta and Blue* (1950); Whitney Mus., N.Y.C.

Hogarth, William (1697-1764). English painter and engraver with satirical leanings: *Marriage à la Mode: Shortly After the Marriage* (1744); National Gallery, London.

Holbein, Hans (younger) (c.1497-1543). German Renaissance painter: *Sir Thomas More* (1527); Frick Coll., N.Y.C.

Homer, Winslow (1836-1910). American painter and illustrator: *Gulf Stream* (1899); Metropolitan Mus., N.Y.C.

Ingres, Jean Auguste Dominique (1780-1867). French history and portrait painter associated with Neoclassicism: *La Baigneuse de Valpincon* (1808); Louvre, Paris.

Johns, Jasper (1930-   ). American Pop artist: *Flag* (1954), encaustic, collage, canvas; Philip Johnson Coll., N.Y.C.

Johnson, Philip C. (1906-   ). American architect: *New York State Theatre, Lincoln Center* (1962-64); N.Y.C.

Jones, Inigo (1573-1652). English Renaissance architect, stage designer and painter: *Banqueting House* (1619-22); Whitehall Palace, London.

Kandinsky, Wassily (1866-1944). Russian abstract painter: *Tension in Red* (1926); Guggenheim Mus., N.Y.C.

Klee, Paul (1879-1940). Swiss painter: *Twittering Machine* (1922); Mus. of Modern Art, N.Y.C.

Le Corbusier (Charles Edouard Jeanneret) (1887-1965). Swiss-born French architect: *Unité d'Habitation* (Apartment House) (1947-52); Marseilles.

Lichtenstein, Roy (1923-   ). American Pop artist: *Whaam!* (1963), acrylic; Tate Gallery, London.

Lipchitz, Jacques (1891-1973). Lithuanian-born American sculptor: *Sailor with a Guitar* (1914), bronze; Albright-Knox Art Gallery, Buffalo, N.Y.

Magritte, René (1898-1967). Belgian Surrealist painter: *The Menaced Assassin* (1926); Mus. of Modern Art, N.Y.C.

Maillol, Aristide (1861-1944). French sculptor: *Mediterranée* (1902-1905), bronze; Boymans van Beuningen Mus., Rotterdam.

Marisol (1930-   ). Venezuelan-born American sculptress: *Women and Dog* (1964), mixed media; Whitney Mus., N.Y.C.

Matisse, Henri (1869-1954). French Fauvist painter: *The Blue Window* (1911); Mus. of Modern Art, N.Y.C.

Michelangelo Buonarroti (1475-1564). High Renaissance Italian sculptor, painter, architect: *Pietà* (1498-99), marble; *Last Judgment* (1535-41), fresco; Sistine Chapel, Vatican, Rome.

Mies van der Rohe, Ludwig (1886-1969). German-born American architect and designer: *Seagram Building* (1956-59); N.Y.C.

Millet, Jean-Francois (1814-75). French painter associated with Barbizon group: *Going to Work* (c.1850); Glasgow Art Gall. and Mus., Glasgow.

Modigliani, Amedeo (1884-1920). Italian Expressionist painter: *Anna de Zborowska* (1917); Mus. of Modern Art, N.Y.C.

Mondrian, Piet (1872-1944). Dutch Neo-Plasticist painter: *Composition 1921* (1921); Kunstmuseum, Basle.

Monet, Claude (1840-1926). French Impressionist painter: *La Grenouillère* (1869); Metropolitan Mus., N.Y.C.

Moore, Henry (1898-   ). English Abstract sculptor: *Recumbent Figure* (1938); Tate Gallery, London.

Moses, Grandma (Anna Mary R.) (1860-1961). American Primitive painter: *Sugaring Off* (1938); Mr. and Mrs. Albert D. Lasker Coll., N.Y.C.

Munch, Edvard (1863-1944). Norwegian Expressionist painter and printmaker: *Dance of Life* (1899-1900); National Gallery, Oslo.

Nevelson, Louise (1900-   ). Russian-born American sculptress: *Young Shadows* (1959-60), wood; Whitney Mus., N.Y.C.

O'Keeffe, Georgia (1887-   ). American Regionalist painter: *Black Iris* (1926); Metropolitan Mus., N.Y.C.

Oldenburg, Claes (1929-   ). Swedish-born American Pop artist: *Ice Bag-Scale C* (1971); Whitney Mus., N.Y.C.

Orozco, Jose C. (1883-1949). Mexican Muralist painter: *Prometheus* (1930); Frary Hall, Pomona College, Claremont, Calif.

Pei, I. M. (1917-   ). Chinese-born American architect: *Everson Museum of Art* (1965-68); Syracuse, N.Y.

Perrault, Claude (1613-88). French architect: *East Front of the Louvre* (1667-70); Paris.

Picasso, Pablo (1881-1973). Spanish-born French painter and sculptor: *Guernica* (1937); Mus. of Modern Art, N.Y.C.

Pissarro, Camille Jacob (1830-1903). French Impressionist painter: *Boulevard Montmarte* (1897); National Gall. of Art, Washington, D.C.

Pollock, Jackson (1912-56). American Abstract Expressionist, developer of Action Painting: *Ocean Greyness* (1953); Guggenheim Mus., N.Y.C.

Praxiteles (c.370-c.330 B.C.). Athenian sculptor of the later Attic School: *Hermes*, marble; Olympia Mus., Greece.

Raphael (Raffaello Sanzio) (1483-1520). Italian Renaissance painter and architect: *Madonna of the Goldfinch* (c.1505); Uffizi Gall., Florence.

Rauschenberg, Robert (1925-   ). American Pop artist: *Estate* (1963); Philadelphia Mus. of Art.

Rembrandt (Harmensz van Rijn) (1606-69). Dutch Baroque painter, etcher and draughtsman: *The Night Watch* (1642); Rijksmuseum, Amsterdam.

Renoir, Pierre Auguste (1841-1919). French Impressionist painter: *Luncheon at the Boating Party* (1881); Phillips Gall., Washington, D.C.

Reynolds, Sir Joshua (1723-92). English portrait painter: *Lord Heathfield* (1788); National Gallery, London.

Rivera, Diego (1886-1957). Mexican mural painter: *Frescoes on the Mexican Revolution*, Ministry of Education, Mexico City.

Rivers, Larry (1923-   ). American Abstract Expressionist painter and Pop artist: *The Dutchmasters and Cigars* (1963); Whitney Mus., N.Y.C.

Rodin, Auguste (1840-1917). French sculptor: *The Thinker* (1880-1900), bronze; Rodin Mus., Paris.

Rothko, Mark (1903-70). Russian-born American Abstract Expressionist painter: *Number 10, 1950* (1950); Metropolitan Mus., N.Y.C.

Rouault, Georges (1871-1958). French Expressionist painter also associated with Fauvism: *Christ Mocked By Soldiers* (c.1932); Mus. of Modern Art, N.Y.C.

Rousseau, Henri (1844-1910). French Primitive painter: *The Sleeping Gypsy* (1897); Mus. of Modern Art, N.Y.C.

Rubens, Sir Peter Paul (1577-1640). Flemish Baroque painter: *The Garden of Love* (c.1632-34); Prado Mus., Madrid.

Saarinen, Eero (1910-61). Finnish-born American architect: *TWA Terminal* (1962); Kennedy Airport, N.Y.C.

Sargent, John Singer (1865-1925). American Portrait painter: *Asher Wertheimer* (1898); Tate Gallery, London.

Seurat, Georges (1859-91). French painter, chief exponent of Pointillism; *Sunday Afternoon on the Island of La Grande Jatte* (1884-86); Art Inst. of Chicago.

Shahn, Ben (1898-1969). American Realist painter: *Passion of Sacco and Vanzetti* (1931-32); Whitney Mus., N.Y.C.

Sisley, Alfred (1839-99). French Impressionist painter: *Flood at Port Marly* (1876); Louvre, Paris.

Smith, David (1906-1965). American sculptor: *Cubi XIX* (1964), metal; Tate Gallery, London.

Stuart, Gilbert (1755-1828). American Portrait painter: *Mrs. Richard Yates* (1793-94); National Gall., Washington, D.C., Andrew Mellon Coll.

Sullivan, Louis Henry (1856-1924). American architect, mentor of Frank Lloyd Wright: *Carson, Pirie & Scott Building*, Chicago.

Tintoretto, Jacopo (c.1518-94). Venetian Mannerist painter: *The Last Supper* (1592-94); S. Giorgio Maggiore, Venice.

Titian (Tiziano Vecelli) (c.1477-1576). Venetian High Renaissance painter noted for bravura brushwork and use of chiaroscuro: *Rape of Europa* (c.1562); Isabella Stewart Gardner Mus., Boston.

Toulouse-Lautrec, Henri de (1864-1901). French post-Impressionist painter and lithographer: *At the Moulin Rouge* (1892); Art Inst. of Chicago.

Turner, Joseph M. W. (1775-1851). English Romantic landscape painter: *Calais Pier* (1803); National Gallery, London.

Utrillo, Maurice (1883-1955). French post-Impressionist painter: *L'Impasse Cottin* (c.1910); Musée National d'Art Moderne, Paris.

Van Dyck, Sir Anthony (1599-1641). Flemish painter, one-time assistant to Rubens: *Charles I of England* (c.1635); Louvre, Paris.

van Gogh, Vincent (1853-90). Dutch-born French Impressionist-influenced painter: *Cypresses and Two Figures* (1890); Kroller Muller Mus., Amsterdam.

Velázquez, Diego (1599-1660). Spanish Portrait painter: *The Maids of Honor* (1656); Prado Mus., Madrid.

Vermeer, Jan (1632-75). Dutch Genre painter: *View of Delft* (c.1658); Isabella Stewart Gardner Mus., Boston.

Vinci, Leonardo da (1452-1519). Italian Renaissance painter, sculptor, architect: *Mona Lisa* (1503); Louvre, Paris.

Vlaminck, Maurice de (1876-1958). French Fauvist painter: *House at Chanton* (1903); Art Inst. of Chicago.

Warhol, Andy (1928-   ). American Pop artist and film maker: *Marilyn Six-Pak* (1962); silkscreen; Carter Burden Coll., N.Y.C.

Watteau, Jean-Antoine (1684-1721). French painter of "fetes galantes" and exponent of the Rococo idiom: *Embarkation to Cythera* (c.1717); Louvre, Paris.

Whistler, James Abbott McNeil (1834-1903). American painter influenced by Impressionism and Japanese prints: *Nocturne—Black and Gold, The Fire Wheel* (c.1870); Tate Gallery, London.

Wood, Grant (1891-1942). American Regionalist scene painter: *Dinner for Threshers* (1933); Whitney Mus., N.Y.C.

Wren, Sir Christopher (1632-1723). English architect: *St. Paul's Cathedral;* (1675-1710); London.

Wright, Frank Lloyd (1867-1959). Innovative American architect: *Robie House* (1909); Chicago.

Wyeth, Andrew N. (1917-   ). American Realist painter: *Christina's World* (1948); Mus. of Modern Art, N.Y.C.

Glossary of Art Movements

ABSTRACT EXPRESSIONISM: American art movement of the 1940s which emphasized form and color within a nonrepresentational framework. Jackson Pollock initiated the revolutionary technique of splattering the paint directly on canvas to achieve the subconscious interpretation of the artist's inner vision of reality.

ART DECO: A 1920s style characterized by setbacks, zigzag forms and the use of chrome and plastic ornamentation. New York's Chrysler Building is an architectural example of the style.

ART NOUVEAU: An 1890s style in architecture, graphic arts and interior decoration characterized by writhing forms, curving lines and asymmetrical organization. Some critics regard the style as the first stage of modern architecture.

ASHCAN SCHOOL: A group of New York realist artists, formed in 1908, who abandoned decorous subject matter and portrayed the more common as well as the sordid aspects of city life.

ASSEMBLAGE (COLLAGE): Forms of modern sculpture and painting utilizing readymades, found objects and pasted fragments to form an abstract composition. Louise Nevelson's boxlike enclosures, each with its own composition of assembled objects, illustrates the style in sculpture. Picasso developed the technique of cutting and pasting natural or manufactured materials to a painted or unpainted surface.

BARBIZON SCHOOL (LANDSCAPE PAINTING): A group of mid-nineteenth century painters who reacted against classical landscape and advocated a direct study of nature. They were influenced by English and Dutch landscape masters. Theodore Rousseau, one of the principal figures of the group, led the fight for outdoor painting. In this respect, the school was a forerunner of Impressionism.

BAROQUE: European art and architecture of the 17th and 18th centuries. Bernini, a major exponent of the style, believed in the union of the arts of architecture, painting and sculpture to overwhelm the spectator with ornate and highly dramatized themes. Although the style originated in Rome as the instrument of the Church, it spread throughout Europe in such monumental creations as the Palace of Versailles.

BEAUX ARTS: Elaborate and formal architectural style characterized by symmetry and an abundance of sculptured ornamentation. New York's old Custom House at Bowling Green is an example of the style.

BLACK OR AFRO-AMERICAN ART: The work of American artists of African descent produced in various styles characterized by a mood of protest and a search for identity and historical roots.

CLASSICISM: A form of art derived from the study of Greek and Roman styles characterized by harmony, balance and serenity. In contrast, the Romantic Movement gave free rein to the artist's imagination and to the love of the exotic.

CONSTRUCTIVISM: A form of sculpture using wood, metal, glass and modern industrial materials expressing the technological society. The mobiles of Alexander Calder are examples of the movement.

CUBISM: Early 20th century French movement marked by a revolutionary departure from representational art. Picasso and Bracque penetrated the surface of objects stressing basic abstract geometric forms that presented the object from many angles simultaneously.

DADA: A product of the turbulent and cynical post-World War I period, this anti-art movement extolled the irrational, the absurd, the nihilistic and the nonsensical. The reproduction of Mona Lisa adorned with a mustache is a famous example. The movement is regarded as a precursor of Surrealism. Some critics regard HAPPENINGS as a recent development of Dada. This movement incorporates environment and spectators as active and important ingredients in the production of random events.

EXPRESSIONISM: A 20th century European art movement which stresses the expression of emotion and the inner vision of the artist rather than the exact representation of nature. Distorted lines, shapes and exaggerated colors are used for emotional impact. Van Gogh is regarded as the precursor of this movement.

FAUVISM: The name "wild beasts" was given to this group of early 20th century French painters because their work was characterized by distortion and violent colors. Matisse and Rouault were leaders of this group.

FUTURISM: This early 20th century movement originating in Italy glorified the machine age and attempted to represent machines and figures in motion. The aesthetics of Futurism affirmed the beauty of technological society.

GENRE: This French word meaning "type" now refers to paintings that depict scenes of everyday life without any attempt at idealization. Genre paintings can be found in all ages, but the Dutch productions of peasant and tavern scenes are typical.

IMPRESSIONISM: Late 19th century French school dedicated to defining transitory visual impressions painted directly from nature, with light and color of primary importance. If the atmosphere changed, a totally different picture would emerge. It was not the object or event that counted but the visual impression as caught at a certain time of day under a certain light. Monet and Pissarro were leaders of the movement.

MANNERISM: A 17th century movement, Italian in origin, although El Greco was a major practitioner of the style. The human figure, distorted and elongated, was the most frequent subject.

NEOCLASSICISM: An 18th century reaction to the excesses of Baroque and Rococo, this European art movement tried to recreate the art of Greece and Rome by imitating the ancient classics both in style and subject matter.

OP ART: The 1960s movement known as Optical Painting is characterized by geometrical forms which create an optical illusion in which the eye is required to blend the colors at a certain distance.

POP ART: In this return to representational art, the artist returns to the world of tangible objects in a reaction against abstraction. Materials are drawn from the everyday world of popular culture—comic strips, canned goods and science fiction.

ROCOCO: A French style of interior decoration developed during the reign of Louis XV consisting mainly of asymmetrical arrangements of curves in paneling, porcelain, gold and silver objects. The characteristics of ornate curves, prettiness and gaiety can also be found in the painting and sculpture of the period.

SURREALISM: A further development of Collage, Cubism and Dada, this 20th century movement stresses the weird, the fantastic and the dreamworld of the subconscious. Dali's distorted timepiece in the desert is typical.

★ CELEBRATED PERSONS ★

Locations and dates are those of birth. The date of birth listed gives the month, day, and year, in that order. Boldface years in parentheses are year of birth and death in that order. A name in parentheses is the original name or form of the name of the individual.

The listings in this section have been gathered from various sources, including the subjects thereof, but the *Information Please Almanac* cannot guarantee the accuracy of each individual item. We have learned to accept the date and place of birth that any lady or gentleman claims for herself or himself and not argue about it. Where we have not been able to learn the date and place of birth, we have not attempted to invent the items.

Many public figures who do not appear in this list may be found in other sections of the *Information Please Almanac*. For your convenience, a brief table of references follows.

For a selected list of architects, painters and sculptors, see pages 810–12.

Aaron, Hank (Henry) (baseball); Mobile, Ala., 2/5/1934.

Abbott, Bud (William) (comedian); b. Asbury Park, N.J. **(1898–1974).**

Abbott, George (stage producer); Forestville, N.Y., 6/25/1889.

Abdul–Jabbar, Kareem (Lewis Ferdinand Alcindor, Jr.) (basketball); New York City, 4/16/1947.

Abel, Sid (hockey); Melville, Saskatchewan, Canada, 2/22/1918.

Abel, Walter (actor); St. Paul, Minn., 6/6/1898.

Abernathy, Ralph (civil rights leader); Linden, Ala., 3/11/1926.

Acheson, Dean (statesman); b. Middletown, Conn. **(1893–1971).**

Acuff, Eddie (actor); b. Caruthersville, Mo. **(1908–1956).**

Acuff, Roy (musician); Maynardsville, Tenn. 9/15/1903.

Adams, Charles Francis (diplomat); b. Boston, Mass. **(1807–1886).**

Adams, Don (actor); New York City, 4/9/1927.

Adams, Edie (actress); Kingston, Pa., 4/16/1929.

Adams, Franklin Pierce (columnist, author); b. Chicago, Ill. **(1881–1960).**

Adams, Henry Brooks (historian); b. Boston, Mass. **(1838–1918).**

Adams, Joey (comedian); New York City, 1/6/1911.

Adams, Maude (Maude Kiskadden) (actress); b. Salt Lake City, Utah **(1872–1953).**

Adams, Samuel (American Revolutionary patriot); b. Boston, Mass **(1722–1803).**

Adamson, Joy (naturalist); Troppau, Silesia, 1/20/1910.

Addams, Charles (cartoonist); Westfield, N.J., 1/7/1912.

Addams, Jane (social worker); b. Cedarville, Ill. **(1860–1935).**

Adderley, Julian "Cannonball" (jazz saxophonist); b. Tampa, Fla. **(1928–1975).**

Ade, George (humorist); b. Kentland, Ind. **(1866–1944).**

Adenauer, Konrad (statesman); b. Cologne, Germany **(1876–1967)**

Adler, Alfred (psychoanalyst); b. Vienna, Austria **(1870–1937).**

Adler, Larry (musician); Baltimore, Md., 2/10/1914.

Adler, Richard (songwriter); New York City, 8/3/1921.

Adoree, Renée (Renée La Fonte) (actress); b. Lille, France **(1898–1933).**

Aeschylus (dramatist); b. Eleusis, Attica **(525–456 B.C.).**

Aesop (fabulist); birthplace unknown **(lived c. 600 B.C.).**

Aherne, Brian (actor); King's Norton, Worcestershire, England, 5/2/1902.

Aiken, Conrad (poet); b. Savannah, Ga. **(1889–1973).**

Ailey, Alvin (choreographer); Rogers, Tex., 1/5/1931.

Aimee, Anouk (actress); Paris, France, 4/27/1934.

Albanese, Licia (soprano); Bari, Italy, 7/22/1913.

Albee, Edward (playwright); Washington, D.C., 3/12/1928.

Alberghetti, Anna Maria (singer); Pesaro, Italy, 5/15/1936.

Albert, Eddie (Edward Albert Heimberger) (actor); Rock Island, Ill., 4/22/1908.

Albertson, Jack (actor); Malden, Mass., 6/16/1910(?).

Albright, Lola (actress); Akron, Ohio, 7/20/1925.

Alcindor, Lew. *See* Abdul-Jabbar.

Alcott, Louisa May (novelist); b. Germantown, Pa. **(1832–1888).**

Alda, Alan (actor); New York City, 1/28/1936.

Alda, Robert (actor); New York City, 2/26/1914.

Alden, John (American Pilgrim); b. England **(1599–1687).**

Aldrin, Edwin E., Jr. (astronaut); Montclair, N.J., 1/20/1930.

Alexander the Great (monarch & conqueror); b. Pella, Macedonia **(356–323 B.C.).**

Alger, Horatio (author); b. Revere, Mass. **(1834–1899).**

Algren, Nelson (novelist); Detroit, Mich., 3/28/1909.

Ali, Muhammad (Cassius Clay) (boxing); Louisville, Ky., 1/18/1942.

Alioto, Joseph L. (ex-Mayor of San Francisco); San Francisco, Calif., 2/12/1916.

Allen, Dick (Richard Anthony) (baseball); Wampum, Pa., 3/8/1942.

Allen, Ethan (American Revolutionary soldier); b. Litchfield, Conn. **(1738–1789).**

Allen, Fred (John Florence Sullivan) (comedian); b. Cambridge, Mass. **(1894–1956).**

Allen, Gracie (Grace Ethel Cecile Rosalie Allen) (comedienne); b. San Francisco, Calif. **(1906–1964).**

Allen, Mel (sportscaster); Birmingham, Ala., 2/14/1913.

Allen, Steve (TV entertainer); New York City, 12/26/1921.

Allen, Woody (Heywood Allen) (comedian); Brooklyn, N.Y., 12/1/1935.

Allgood, Sara (actress); b. Dublin, Ireland **(1883–1950).**

Allison, Bobby (Robert Arthur) (hockey); Hueytown, Ala., 12/3/1937.

Allison, Fran (actress); LaPorte City, Iowa, 1924(?).

Allyson, June (Jan Allyson) (actress); New York City, 10/7/1923.

Alpert, Herb (band leader); Los Angeles, Calif., 3/31/1935(?).

Alsop, Joseph W., Jr. (journalist); Avon, Conn., 10/11/1910.

Alsop, Stewart (journalist); b. Avon, Conn. **(1914–1974).**

Alston, Walter (baseball); Butler County, Ohio, 12/1/1911.

Altman, Robert (director); Kansas City, Mo., 2/20/1925.

Alworth, Lance (football); Houston, Tex., 8/3/1940.

Ambler, Eric (suspense writer); London, England, 6/28/1909.

Ameche, Don (Dominic) (actor); Kenosha, Wis., 5/31/1908.

Amis, Kingsley (novelist); London, England, 4/16/1922.

Amory, Cleveland (writer and conservationist); Nahant, Mass., 9/2/1917.

Amos (Freeman F. Gosden) (radio comedian); Richmond, Va., 5/5/1899.

Amsterdam, Morey (actor); Chicago, Ill., 12/14/1914.

Anders, William A. (astronaut); Hong Kong, 10/17/1933.

Andersen, Hans Christian (author of fairy tales); b. Odense, Denmark **(1805–1875).**

Anderson, Dame Judith (actress); Adelaide, Australia, 2/10/1898.

Anderson, Dick (Richard P.) (football); Midland, Mich., 2/10/1946.

Anderson, Eddie. *See* Rochester.

Anderson, Jack (journalist); Long Beach, Calif., 10/19/1922.

Anderson, Lindsay (Gordon) (director); Bangalore, India, 4/17/1923.

Anderson, Lynn (country music artist); Grand Forks, N.D., 9/26/1947.

Anderson, Marian (contralto); Philadelphia, Pa., 2/17/1902.

Anderson, Maxwell (dramatist); b. Atlantic, Pa. **(1888–1959).**

Anderson, Robert (playwright); New York City, 4/28/1917.

Anderson, Sparky (George) (baseball); Bridgewater, S.D., 2/22/1934.

Andersson, Bibi (actress); Stockholm, Sweden, 11/11/1935.

Andreadis, Christina. *See* Onassis, Christina.
Andress, Ursula (actress); Switzerland, 3/19/1938.
Andretti, Mario (auto racing); Montona, Trieste, Italy, 2/28/1940.
Andrews, Dana (actor); Collins, Miss., 1/1/1909.
Andrews, Julie (Julia Wells) (actress, singer); Walton-on-Thames, England, 10/1/1935.
Andrews, La Verne (singer); b. Minneapolis, Minn. **(1916–1967)**
Andrews, Maxene (singer); Minneapolis, Minn., 1918.
Andrews, Patti (singer); Minneapolis, Minn., 1920.
Andy (Charles J. Correll) (radio comedian); b. Peoria, Ill. **(1890–1972).**
Angel, Heather (actress); Oxford, England, 2/9/1909.
Angeles, Victoria de los (Victoria Gamez Cima) (soprano); Barcelona, Spain, 11/1/1924.
Angeli, Piēr (Anna Maria Pierangeli) (actress); b. Sardinia, Italy **(1932–1971).**
Anka, Paul (singer); Ottawa, Ont., Canada, 7/30/1941.
Ann-Margret (actress); Stockholm, Sweden, 4/28/1941.
Annabella (actress); Paris, France, 1912.
Anouilh, Jean (playwright); Bordeaux, France, 6/23/1910.
Anthony, Susan Brownell (woman suffragist); b. Adams, Mass. **(1820–1906)**
Antonioni, Michelangelo (director); Ferrara, Italy, 9/29/1912.
Antony, Mark (Marcus Antonius) (statesman); b. Rome **(83?–30** B.C.).
Anuszkiewicz, Richard (painter); Erie, Pa., 5/23/1930.
Aquinas, St. Thomas (philosopher); b. near Aquino, Italy **(1225?–1274).**
Arbuckle, Roscoe "Fatty" (actor-director); b. San Jose, Calif. **(1887–1933).**
Arcaro, Eddie (George Edward) (jockey); Cincinnati, Ohio, 2/19/1916.
Archer, George (golf); San Francisco, Calif. 10/1/1939.
Archimedes (physicist & mathematician); b. Syracuse, Sicily **(287?–212** B.C.).
Arden, Eve (actress); Mill Valley, Calif., 4/30/1912.
Arendt, Hannah (historian); b. Hannover, Germany **(1906–1975).**
Arfons, Arthur Eugene (auto racing); Akron, Ohio, 2/3/1926.
Aristophanes (dramatist); b. Athens **(448?–380** B.C.).
Aristotle (philosopher); b. Stagira **(384–322** B.C.).
Arkin, Alan (actor, director); New York City, 3/26/1934.
Arlen, Harold (Hyman Arluck) (composer); Buffalo, N.Y., 2/15/1905.
Arlen, Richard (actor); b. Charlottesville, Va. **(1900–1976).**
Arliss, George (actor); b. London, England **(1868–1946).**
Armstrong, Louis (musician); b. New Orleans, La. **(1900–1971).**
Armstrong, Neil A. (astronaut); Wapakoneta, Ohio, 8/5/1930.
Armstrong-Jones, Anthony, Earl of Snowden (ex-husband of Princess Margaret); London, England, 3/7/1930.
Arnaz, Desi (Desiderio) (actor and producer); Santiago, Cuba, 3/2/1917.
Arnaz, Desi, Jr. (actor); Los Angeles, Calif., 1953.
Arness, James (James Aurness) (TV actor); Minneapolis, Minn., 5/26/1923.
Arno, Peter (cartoonist); b. New York City **(1904–1968).**
Arnold, Benedict (American Revolutionary War General, convicted of treason); b. Norwich, Conn. **(1741–1801).**
Arnold, Eddy (singer); Henderson, Tenn., 5/15/1918.
Arnold, Matthew (poet & critic); b. Laleham, Middlesex, England **(1822–1888).**
Arquette, Cliff ("Charley Weaver") (actor); b. Toledo, Ohio **(1905–1974).**
Arrau, Claudio (pianist); Chillán, Chile, 2/6/1903.
Arthur, Bea (Bernice Frankel) (actress); New York City, 5/13/1926(?).
Arthur, Jean (Gladys Greene) (actress); New York City, 10/17/1908.
Asch, Sholem (novelist); b. Kutno, Poland **(1880–1957).**
Ashe, Arthur (tennis); Richmond, Va., 7/10/1943.
Ashkenazy, Vladimir (concert pianist); Gorki, U.S.S.R., 7/6/1937.
Asimov, Isaac (author); Petrovichi, Russia, 1/2/1920
Asner, Edward (actor); Kansas City, Kan., 11/15/1929.
Astaire, Fred (Frederick Austerlitz) (dancer, actor); Omaha, Neb., 5/10/1899.
Astor, John Jacob (financier); b. Waldorf, Germany **(1763–1848).**
Astor, Mary (Lucile Langhanke) (actress); Quincy, Ill., 5/3/1906.
Atkins, Chet (guitarist); nr. Luttrell, Tenn., 6/20/1924.
Atkinson, Brooks (drama critic); Melrose, Mass., 11/28/1894.
Attenborough, Richard (actor); Cambridge, England, 8/29/1923.
Attila (King of Huns, called "Scourge of God"); **(406?–453).**
Attlee, Clement Richard (statesman); b. London, England **(1883–1967).**
Auden, W. H. (poet); b. York, England **(1907–1973).**
Auer, Leopold (violinist & teacher); b. Veszprém, Hungary **(1845–1930).**
Auer, Mischa (actor); b. St. Petersburg, Russia **(1905–1967).**
Augustine, Saint (Aurelius Augustinus) (philosopher); b. Numidia **(354–430).**
Augustus (Gaius Octavius) (Roman emperor); b. Rome **(63** B.C.–A.D. **14).**
Aumont, Jean-Pierre (actor); Paris, France, 1/5/1913.
Austen, Jane (novelist); b. Steventon, Hampshire, England **(1775–1817).**
Autry, Gene (singer, actor); Tioga, Tex., 9/29/1907.
Avalon, Frankie (singer); Philadelphia, Pa., 9/18/1940.

Avedon, Richard (photographer); New York City, 5/15/1923.
Avery, Earle (harness racing); Knowlesville, N.Y., 2/24/1894.
Avery, Milton (painter); b. Altmar, N.Y. **(1893–1965).**
Axelrod, Albert (fencing); New York City, 2/21/1921.
Axelrod, George (playwright); New York City, 6/9/1922.
Ayres, Lew (actor); Minneapolis, Minn., 12/28/1908.
Aznavour, Charles (Varenagh Aznavourian) (singer, actor); Paris, France, 5/22/1924.
Babashoff, Shirley (swimming); Whittier, Calif., 1/31/1957.
Bacall, Lauren (Betty Joan Perske) (actress); New York City, 9/16/1924.
Bach, Johann Sebastian (composer); b. Eisenach, Germany **(1685–1750).**
Bacharach, Burt (composer); Kansas City, Mo., 5/12/1929.
Backus, Jim (actor); Cleveland, Ohio, 2/25/1913.
Bacon, Francis (painter); Dublin, Ireland, 1910.
Bacon, Francis (philosopher & essayist); b. London, England **(1561–1626).**
Bacon, Roger (philosopher & scientist); b. Ilchester, Somerset, England **(1214?–1294).**
Baedeker, Karl (travel-guidebook publisher); b. Essen, Germany **(1801–1859).**
Baer, Max (boxer); b. Omaha, Neb. **(1909–1959).**
Baez, Joan (folk singer); Staten Island, N.Y., 1/9/1941.
Bagnold, Enid (Lady Jones) (novelist); Rochester, Kent, England, 10/27/1889.
Bailey, F. Lee (lawyer); Waltham, Mass., 6/10/1933.
Bailey, Pearl (singer); Newport News, Va., 3/29/1918.
Bainter, Fay (actress); b. Los Angeles, Calif. **(1891–1968).**
Baird, Bil (William B.) (puppeteer); Grand Island, Neb., 8/15/1904.
Baker, Belle (actress); b. New York City **(1895–1957).**
Baker, Carroll (actress); Johnstown, Pa., 5/28/1935.
Baker, Josephine (singer, dancer); b. St. Louis, Mo. **(1906–1975).**
Baker, Kenny (singer, actor); Monrovia, Calif., 9/30/1912.
Bakken, Jim (James Leroy) (football); Madison, Wis., 11/2/1940.
Balanchine, George (choreographer); St. Petersburg, Russia, 1/9/1904.
Balboa, Vasco Nuñez de (explorer); b. Jerez do los Caballeros, Spain **(1475–1517).**
Baldwin, Faith (writer); New Rochelle, N.Y., 10/1/1893.
Baldwin, James (novelist); New York City, 8/2/1924.
Balenciaga, Cristóbal (fashion designer); b. Guetaria, Spain **(1896–1972).**
Ball, Catherine (Catie) (swimming); Jacksonville, Fla., 9/30/1951.
Ball, Lucille (comedienne); Jamestown, N.Y., 8/6/1911.
Ballard, Kaye (Catherine Gloria Balotta) (actress); Cleveland, Ohio, 11/20/1926.
Balmain, Pierre (fashion designer); St.-Jean-de-Maurienne, France, 5/18/1914.
Balsam, Martin (actor); New York City, 11/4/1919.
Balzac, Honoré de (novelist); b. Tours, France **(1799–1850).**
Bancroft, Anne (Annamarie Italiano) (actress); New York City, 9/17/1931.
Bancroft, George (actor); b. Philadelphia, Pa. **(1882–1956).**
Bankhead, Tallulah (actress); b. Huntsville, Ala. **(1903–1968).**
Banks, Ernie (baseball); Dallas, Tex., 1/31/1931.
Bannister, Roger (runner); Harrow, England, 3/24/1929.
Bara, Theda (Theodosia Goodman) (actress); b. Cincinnati, Ohio **(1890–1955).**
Barber, Red (Walter Lanier) (sports announcer); Columbus, Miss., 2/17/1908.
Barber, Samuel (composer); West Chester, Pa., 3/9/1910.
Bardot, Brigitte (actress); Paris, France, 1935.
Barenboim, Daniel (pianist, conductor); Buenos Aires, Argentina, 11/15/1942.
Barkley, Alben William (statesman); b. Graves County, Ky. **(1877–1956).**
Barnard, Christiaan N. (heart surgeon); Beauford West, South Africa, 1923.
Barnum, Phineas Taylor (showman); b. Bethel, Conn. **(1810–1891).**
Barrie, Sir James Matthew (author); b. Kirriemuir, Forfarshire, Scotland **(1860–1937).**
Barry, Gene (actor); New York City, 6/4/1922.
Barry, Rick (Richard) (basketball); Elizabeth, N.J., 3/28/1944.
Barrymore, Diana (actress); b. New York City **(1921–1960).**
Barrymore, Ethel (actress); b. Philadelphia, Pa. **(1879–1959).**
Barrymore, John (actor); b. Philadelphia, Pa. **(1882–1942).**
Barrymore, Lionel (actor); b. Philadelphia, Pa. **(1878–1954).**
Barthelmess, Richard (actor); b. New York City **(1897–1963).**
Bartholomew, Freddie (actor); London, England, 3/28/1924.
Bartok, Béla (composer); b. Nagyszentmiklos, Transylvania, Hungary **(1881–1945).**
Baruch, Bernard Mannes (statesman); b. Camden, S.C. **(1870–1965).**
Baryshnikov, Mikhail Nikolayevich (ballet dancer); Riga, Latvia, 1/27/1948.
Basehart, Richard (actor); Zanesville, Ohio, 8/31/1919.
Basie, Count (William) (band leader); Red Bank, N.J., 8/21/1904.
Basserman, Albert (actor); b. Mannheim, Germany **(1865–1952).**
Bassey, Shirley (singer); Cardiff, Wales, 1937.
Batchelor, Clarence Daniel (political cartoonist); Osage City, Kan.
Bates, Alan (actor); Allestree, England, 2/17/1934.
Bates, Blanche (actress); b. Portland, Ore. **(1873–1941).**

Baudelaire, Charles Pierre (poet); b. Paris, France **(1821–1867).**
Baudouin (King); Palace of Laeken, Belgium, 9/7/1930.
Bauer, Hank (Henry) (baseball); East St. Louis, Ill., 7/31/1922.
Baugh, Sammy (football); Temple, Tex., 3/17/1914.
Baxter, Anne (actress); Michigan City, Ind., 5/7/1923.
Baxter, Warner (actor); b. Columbus, Ohio **(1891–1951).**
Bayi, Filbert (runner); Karratu, Tanganyika, 6/23/1953.
Baylor, Elgin (basketball); Washington, D.C., 9/16/1934.
Beamon, Bob (long jumper); New York City, 8/2/1946.
Bean, Alan (astronaut); Wheeler, Tex., 3/15/1932.
Bean, Orson (Dallas Frederick Burrows) (actor); Burlington, Vt., 7/22/1928.
Beard, Frank (golf); Dallas, Tex., 5/1/1939.
Beaton, Cecil (photographer and designer); London, England, 1/14/1904.
Beatty, Warren, (actor, producer); Richmond, Va., 3/30/1937.
Becket, Thomas à (Archbishop of Canterbury); b. London, England (1118?–1170).
Beckett, Samuel (playwright); Dublin, Ireland, 4/13/1906.
Beckmann, Max (painter); b. Leipzig, Germany **(1884–1950).**
Bede, Saint ("The Venerable Bede") (scholar); b. Monkwearmouth, England **(673–735).**
Beecham, Sir Thomas (orchestra conductor); b. St. Helens, England **(1879–1961).**
Beecher, Henry Ward (clergyman); b. Litchfield, Conn. **(1813–1887).**
Beerbohm, Sir Max (author); b. London, England **(1872–1956).**
Beery, Noah, Jr. (actor); New York City, 8/10/1916.
Beery, Wallace (actor); b. Kansas City, Mo. **(1886–1949).**
Beethoven, Ludwig van (composer); b. Bonn, Germany **(1770–1827).**
Begley, Ed (actor); b. Hartford, Conn. **(1901–1970).**
Belafonte, Harry (singer, actor); New York City, 3/1/1927.
Belasco, David (dramatist & producer); b. San Francisco, Calif. **(1854–1931).**
Beliveau, Jean (hockey); Three Rivers, Quebec, Canada, 8/31/1931.
Bell, Alexander, Graham (inventor); b. Edinburgh, Scotland, **(1847–1922).**
Bellamy, Edward (author); b. Chicopee Falls, Mass. **(1850–1898).**
Bellamy, Ralph (actor); Chicago, Ill., 6/17/1904.
Bellini, Giovanni (painter); b. Venice, Italy **(c. 1430–1516).**
Bellow, Saul (novelist); Lachine, Quebec, Canada, 7/10/1915.
Belmondo, Jean-Paul (actor); Neuilly-sur-Seine, France, 4/9/1933.
Beman, Deane (golf); Washington, D.C., 4/22/1938.
Ben-Gurion, David (David Green) (statesman); b. Plónsk, Poland **(1886–1973).**
Bench, Johnny (Johnny Lee) (baseball); Oklahoma City, Okla., 12/7/1947.
Benchley, Peter Bradford (novelist); New York City, 5/8/1940.
Benchley, Robert Charles (humorist); b. Worcester, Mass. **(1889–1945).**
Bendix, William (actor); b. New York City **(1906–1964).**
Benes, Eduard (statesman); b. Kozlany, Bohemia **(1884–1948).**
Benét, Stephen Vincent (poet & story writer); b. Bethlehem, Pa. **(1898–1943).**
Benét, William Rose (poet & novelist); b. Ft. Hamilton, Brooklyn, N.Y. **(1886–1950).**
Benjamin, Richard (actor); New York City, 5/22/1938.
Bennett, Constance (actress); b. New York City **(1905–1965).**
Bennett, Enoch Arnold (novelist & dramatist); b. Hanley, Staffordshire, England **(1867–1931).**
Bennett, James Gordon (editor); b. Keith, Banffshire, Scotland **(1795–1872).**
Bennett, Joan (actress); Palisades, N.J., 2/27/1910.
Bennett, Robert Russell (composer); Kansas City, Mo., 6/15/1894.
Bennett, Tony (singer); Astoria, Queens, N.Y., 8/3/1926.
Benny, Jack (Benjamin Kubelsky) (comedian); B. Chicago, Ill. **(1894–1974).**
Benzell, Mimi (Miriam) (soprano); Bridgeport, Conn. **(1924–1970).**
Berg, Gertrude (writer, actress); b. New York City **(1899–1966).**
Berg, Patty (Patricia Jane) (golf); Minneapolis, Minn., 2/13/1918.
Bergen, Candice (actress); Beverly Hills, Calif., 5/9/1946.
Bergen, Edgar (ventriloquist); Chicago, Ill., 2/16/1903.
Bergen, Polly (actress, singer); Knoxville, Tenn., 7/14/1930.
Berger, Senta (actress); Vienna, Austria, 1941.
Bergerac, Jacques (actor); Biarritz, France, 5/26/1927.
Bergman, Ingmar (director); Uppsala, Sweden, 7/14/1918.
Bergman, Ingrid (actress); Stockholm, Sweden, 8/29/1917.
Berle, Milton (Milton Berlinger) (comedian); New York City, 7/12/1908.
Berlin, Irving (Israel Baline) (composer); Temum, Russia, 5/11/1888.
Berlioz, Louis Hector (composer); b. La Côte-St.-André, France **(1803–1869).**
Berman, Shelley (Sheldon) (comedian); Chicago, Ill., 2/3/1926.
Bernardi, Herschel (actor); New York City, 1923.
Bernhardt, Sarah (Rosine Bernard) (actress); b. Paris, France **(1844–1923).**
Berning, Susie Maxwell (golf); Pasadena, Calif., 7/22/1941.
Bernstein, Leonard (conductor); Lawrence, Mass., 8/25/1918.
Berra, Yogi (Lawrence) (baseball); St. Louis, Mo., 5/12/1925.
Betjeman, Sir John (Poet Laureate); London, Eng., 8/28/1906.
Bickford, Charles (actor); b. Cambridge, Mass. **(1889–1967).**

Bierce, Ambrose Gwinnett (journalist); b. Meigs County, Ohio **(1842–1914?).**
Bikel, Theodore (actor, singer); Vienna, Austria, 5/2/1924.
Biletnikoff, Frederick (football); Erie, Pa., 2/23/1943.
Bing, Sir Rudolf (opera manager); Vienna, Austria, 1/9/1902.
Bishop, Joey (Joseph Gottlieb) (comedian); New York City, 2/3/1919.
Bismarck-Schönhausen, Prince Otto Eduard Leopold von (statesman); b. Schönhausen, Prussia **(1815–1898).**
Bisset, Jacqueline (actress); Weybridge, England, 9/13/1944.
Bixby, Bill (actor); San Francisco, Calif., 1/22/1934.
Bizet, Georges (Alexandre César Léopold Bizet) (composer); b. Paris, France **(1838–1875).**
Black, Hugo La Fayette (jurist); b. Harlan, Ala. **(1886–1971).**
Black, Karen (actress); Park Ridge, Ill., 7/1/1942.
Black, Shirley Temple (former actress; United States Chief of Protocol); Santa Monica, Calif., 4/23/1928.
Blackman, Honor (actress); London, England, 8/22/1929.
Blackmer, Sidney (actor); b. Salisbury, N.C. **(1898–1973).**
Blackstone, Sir William (jurist); b. London, England **(1723–1780).**
Blaik, Earl H. (football); Detroit, Mich., 2/15/1897.
Blaine, Vivian (actress, singer); Newark, N.J., 11/21/1924.
Blair, Janet (actress); Altoona, Pa., 4/23/1921.
Blake, Amanda (Beverly Louise Neill) (actress); Buffalo, N.Y., 1931.
Blake, Eubie (James Hubert) (pianist); Baltimore, Md., 2/7/1883.
Blake, Robert (Michael Gubitosi) (actor); Nutley, N.J., 9/18/1933.
Blake, William (poet & artist); b. London, England **(1757–1827).**
Blanc, Melvin Jerome (actor; voice specialist); San Francisco, Calif., 5/30/1908.
Blanda, George Frederick (football); Youngwood, Pa., 9/17/1927.
Blass, Bill (fashion designer); Fort Wayne, Ind., 6/22/1922.
Bliss, Anthony A. (Executive Director, Metropolitan Opera); New York City, 4/19/1913.
Bloch, Ernest (composer); b. Geneva, Switzerland **(1880–1959).**
Blondell, Joan (actress); New York City, 8/30/1912.
Bloom, Claire (actress); London, England, 2/15/1931.
Bloomgarden, Kermit (producer); b. Brooklyn, N.Y. **(1904–1976).**
Blue, Monte (actor); b. Indianapolis, Ind. **(1890–1963).**
Blue, Vida (baseball); Mansfield, La., 7/28/1949.
Blyth, Ann (actress); New York City, 8/16/1928.
Boccaccio, Giovanni (author); b. Paris, France **(1313–1375).**
Boccioni, Umberto (painter and sculptor); b. Reggio di Calabria, Italy **(1882–1916).**
Bogarde, Dirk (Derek Van den Bogaerde) (actor); Hampstead, London, England, 3/28/1921.
Bogart, Humphrey DeForest (actor); b. New York City **(1899–1957).**
Bogdanovich, Peter (producer-director); Kingston, N.Y., 7/30/1939.
Bohlen, Charles E. (diplomat); b. Clayton, N.Y. **(1904–1974).**
Bohr, Neils (physicist); b. Copenhagen, Denmark **(1885–1962).**
Boland, Mary (actress); b. Philadelphia, Pa. **(1880–1965).**
Bolger, Ray (dancer, actor); Dorchester, Mass., 1/10/1904.
Bolivar, Simón (South American liberator); b. Caracas, Venezuela **(1783–1830).**
Bologna, Giovanni da (sculptor); b. Douai, Belgium **(1529–1608).**
Bond, Julian (Georgia legislator); Nashville, Tenn., 1/14/1940.
Bono, Sonny (Salvatore) (singer); Detroit, Mich., 2/16/1935.
Boone, Daniel (frontiersman); b. near Reading, Pa. **(1734–1820).**
Boone, Pat (Charles) (singer); Jacksonville, Fla., 6/1/1934.
Boone, Richard (actor); Los Angeles, Calif., 6/18/1917.
Booth, Edwin Thomas (actor); b. Bel Air, Md. **(1833–1893).**
Booth, Evangeline Cory (religious leader); b. London, England **(1865–1950).**
Booth, John Wilkes (actor, assassin of Lincoln); b. Hartford County, Md. **(1838–1865).**
Booth, Shirley (Thelma Booth Ford) (actress); New York City, 8/30/1909.
Boozer, Emerson (football); Augusta, Ga., 7/4/1943.
Bordoni, Irene (actress); b. Ajaccio, Corsica **(1895–1953).**
Borg, Björn (tennis); Stockholm, Sweden, 6/6/1956.
Borge, Victor (pianist, comedian); Copenhagen, Denmark, 1/3/1909.
Borgia, Cesare (nobleman & soldier); b. Rome **(1475?–1507).**
Borgia, Lucrezia (Duches of Ferrara); b. Rome **(1480–1519).**
Borgnine, Ernest (actor); Hamden, Conn., 1/24/1917.
Borman, Frank (astronaut); Gary, Ind., 3/14/1928.
Boros, Julius (golf); Fairfield, Conn., 3/3/1920.
Borromini, Francesco (architect); b. Bissone, Italy **(1599–1667).**
Borzage, Frank (director); b. Salt Lake City, Utah **(1893–1962).**
Bosley, Tom (actor); Chicago, Ill., 10/1/1927.
Boston, Ralph (long jumper); Laurel, Miss., 5/9/1939.
Boswell, Connee (singer); b. New Orleans, La. **(1907–1976).**
Boswell, James (diarist & biographer); b. Edinburgh, Scotland **(1740–1795).**
Boulez, Pierre (conductor); Montbrison, France, 3/26/1925.
Bouton, Jim (James Alan) (baseball, TV announcer); Newark, N.J., 3/8/1939.
Bow, Clara (actress); b. Brooklyn, N.Y. **(1905–1965).**
Bowen, Catherine Drinker (biographer); b. Haverford, Pa. **(1897–1973).**
Bowie, James (soldier); b. Burke County, Ga. **(1799–1836).**
Bowles, Chester (diplomat); Springfield, Mass., 4/5/1901.
Bowman, Lee (actor); Cincinnati, Ohio, 12/28/1914.
Boyd, Bill (William) ("Hopalong Cassidy") (actor); b. Cambridge, Ohio **(1898–1972).**

Boyd, Stephen (actor); Belfast, Ireland, 7/4/1928.
Boyer, Charles (actor); Figeac, France, 8/28/1899.
Bracken, Eddie (actor); Astoria, N.Y., 2/7/1920.
Bradbury, Ray Douglas (science-fiction writer); Waukegan, Ill., 8/22/1920.
Bradlee, Benjamin C. (editor); Boston, Mass., 8/26/1921.
Bradley, Bill (William Warren) (basketball); Crystal City, Mo., 7/28/1943.
Bradley, Omar N. (5-star general); Clark, Mo., 2/12/1893.
Bradley, Thomas (Mayor of Los Angeles); Calvert, Tex., 12/29/1917.
Bradshaw, Terry (football); Shreveport, La., 9/2/1948.
Brady, Scott (actor); Brooklyn, N.Y., 9/13/1924.
Brahms, Johannes (composer); b. Hamburg, Germany **(1833–1897)**.
Braille, Louis (teacher of blind); b. Coupvray, France **(1809–1862)**.
Brailowsky, Alexander (pianist); b. Kiev, Russia **(1896–1976)**.
Bramante, Donato D'Agnolo (architect); b. Monte Asdrualdo (now Fermignano), Italy **(1444–1514)**.
Brandeis, Louis Dembitz (jurist); b. Louisville, Ky. **(1856–1941)**.
Brando, Marlon (actor); Omaha, Neb., 4/3/1924.
Brandt, Willy (Herbert Frahm) (ex-Chancellor); Lübeck, Germany, 12/18/1913.
Brasselle, Keefe (actor); Elyria, Ohio, 2/7/1923.
Braun, Wernher von (rocket scientist); Wirsitz, Germany, 3/23/1912.
Brazzi, Rossano (actor); Bologna, Italy, 9/18/1916.
Brecht, Bertold (dramatist and poet); b. Augsburg, Bavaria **(1898–1956)**.
Breedlove, Craig (Norman) (speed driving); Los Angeles, Calif., 3/23/1938.
Brel, Jacques (singer-composer); Brussels, Belgium, 4/8/1929.
Brennan, Walter (actor); b. Lynn, Mass. **(1894–1974)**.
Brent, George (actor); Dublin, Ireland, 3/15/1904.
Breslin, Jimmy (journalist); New York City, 10/17/1930.
Brewer, Teresa (singer); Toledo, Ohio, 5/7/1931.
Brewster, Kingman (president of Yale); Longmeadow, Mass., 6/17/1919.
Brezhnev, Leonid I. (Communist Party Secretary); Dneprodzerzhinsk, Ukraine, 12/19/1906.
Brice, Fanny (Fannie Borach) (comedienne); b. New York City **(1892–1951)**.
Bridges, Beau (actor); Los Angeles, Calif., 12/9/1941.
Bridges, Lloyd (actor); San Leandro, Calif., 1/15/1913.
Brinkley, David (newscaster); Wilmington, N.C., 7/10/1920.
Britt, May (actress); Sweden, 3/22/1936.
Britten, Benjamin (composer); Lowestoft, Suffolk, England, 11/22/1913.
Britton, Barbara (actress); Long Beach, Calif., 1923.
Bromfield, Louis (novelist); b. Mansfield, Ohio **(1896–1956)**.
Bronson, Charles (Charles Buchinsky) (actor); Ehrenfield, Pa., 11/3/1922(?)
Bronte, Charlotte (novelist); b. Thornton, Yorkshire, England **(1816–1855)**.
Bronte, Emily Jane (novelist); b. Thornton, Yorkshire, England **(1818–1848)**.
Bronzino, Agnolo (painter); b. Monticelli, Italy **(1503–1572)**.
Brook, Peter (director); London, England, 3/21/1925.
Brooke, Rupert (poet); b. Rugby, War., England **(1887–1915)**.
Brooks, Geraldine (Geraldine Stroock) (actress); New York City, 10/29/1925.
Brooks, Gwendolyn (poet); Topeka, Kan., 6/7/1917.
Brooks, Mel (Melvin Kaminsky) (writer, director); Brooklyn, N.Y., 1926(?).
Broun, Matthew Heywood Campbell (journalist); b. Brooklyn, N.Y. **(1888–1939)**.
Brown, Doris (runner); Tacoma, Wash., 9/17/1942.
Brown, Helen Gurley (author); Green Forest, Ark., 2/18/1922.
Brown, James (singer); Augusta, Ga., 5/3/1934.
Brown, Jimmy (football); St. Simon Island, Ga., 2/17/1936.
Brown, Joe E. (comedian); b. Holgate, Ohio **(1892–1973)**.
Brown, John (abolitionist); b. Torrington, Conn. **(1800–1859)**.
Brown, John Mason (critic); b. Louisville, Ky. **(1900–1969)**.
Brown, Larry (football); Clairton, Pa., 9/19/1947.
Brown, Les (band leader); Reinerton, Pa. 1912.
Brown, Pamela (actress); b. London, England, **(1918–1975)**.
Brown, Vanessa (Smylla Brind) (actress); Vienna, Austria, 3/24/1928.
Browning, Elizabeth Barrett (poet); b. Coxhoe Hall, Durham, England **(1806–1861)**.
Browning, Robert (poet); b. London, England **(1812–1889)**.
Brubeck, Dave (musician); Concord, Calif., 12/6/1920.
Bruhn, Erik (Belton Evers) (ballet dancer); Copenhagen, Denmark, 10/3/1928.
Brumel, Valeri (high jumper); Tolbuzino, Siberia, 4/14/1942.
Brundage, Avery (Olympics executive); b. Detroit, Mich. **(1887–1975)**.
Brunelleschi, Filippo (architect); b. Florence, Italy **(1377–1446)**.
Brutus, Marcus Junius (Roman politician) **(85?–42 B.C.)**.
Bryan, William Jennings (orator & politician); b. Salem, Ill. **(1860–1925)**.
Bryant, Anita (entertainer); Barnsdall, Okla., 3/25/1940.
Bryant, William Cullen (poet & editor); b. Cummington, Mass. **(1794–1878)**.

Brynner, Yul (actor); Sakhalin (an island off Japan), 7/11/1920.
Buber, Martin (philosopher-theologian); b. Vienna, Austria **(1878–1965)**.
Buchanan, Edgar (actor); Humansville, Mo., 1903.
Buchholz, Horst (actor); Berlin, Germany, 12/4/1933.
Buchwald, Art (Arthur) (columnist); Mount Vernon, N.Y., 10/20/1925.
Buck, Pearl S(ydenstricker) (author); b. Hillsboro, W. Va. **(1892–1973)**.
Buckley, William F., Jr. (journalist); New York City, 11/24/1925.
Buddha. *See* Gautama Buddha.
Buffalo Bill (William Frederick Cody) (scout); b. Scott County, Iowa **(1846–1917)**.
Bujold, Genevieve (actress); Montreal, Canada, 7/1/1942.
Bujones, Fernando (ballet dancer); Miami, Fla., 3/9/1955.
Bumbry, Grace (mezzo-soprano); St. Louis, Mo., 1/4/1937.
Bunche, Ralph J. (statesman); b. Detroit, Mich. **(1904–1971)**.
Bundy, McGeorge (Ford Foundation president); Boston, Mass., 3/30/1919.
Bundy, William Putnam (editor); Washington, D.C., 9/24/1917.
Buñuel, Luis (director); Calanda, Spain, 2/22/1900.
Bunyan, John (preacher & author); b. Elstow, England **(1628–1688)**.
Burbank, Luther (horticulturist); b. Lancaster, Mass. **(1849–1926)**.
Burke, Adm. Arleigh A. (ex-Chief of Naval Operations); Boulder, Colo., 10/19/1901.
Burke, Billie (comedienne); b. Washington, D.C. **(1885–1970)**.
Burke, Edmund (statesman); b. Dublin, Ireland **(1729–1797)**.
Burne-Jones, Edward Coley (painter); b. Birmingham, England **(1833–1898)**.
Burnett, Carol (comedienne); San Antonio, Tex., 4/26/1936.
Burns, George (Nathan Birnbaum) (comedian); New York City, 1/20/1896.
Burns, Robert (poet); b. Alloway, Scotland **(1759–1796)**.
Burr, Aaron (U.S. political leader); b. Newark, N.J. **(1756–1836)**.
Burr, Raymond (William Stacey Burr) (actor); New Westminster, British Columbia, Canada, 5/21/1917.
Burrows, Abe (playwright, director); New York City, 12/18/1910.
Burstyn, Ellen (actress); Detroit, Mich., 12/7/1932.
Burton, Michael (swimming); Des Moines, Iowa, 7/3/1947.
Burton, Richard (Richard Jenkins) (actor); Pontrhydfen, Wales, 11/10/1925.
Busch, Mae (actress); b. Melbourne, Australia **(1891–1946)**.
Bush, Vannevar (scientist); b. Everett, Mass. **(1890–1974)**.
Bushman, Francis X. (actor); b. Baltimore, Md. **(1883–1966)**.
Butkus, Dick (Richard Marvin) (football); Chicago, Ill., 12/9/1942.
Butler, Samuel (author); b. Langar, Notts, England **(1835–1902)**.
Buttons, Red (Aaron Chwatt) (actor); New York City, 5/5/1919.
Buzzi, Ruth (comedienne); Wequetequock, Conn., 7/24/1936.
Byrd, Richard Evelyn (polar explorer); b. Winchester, Va. **(1888–1957)**.
Byron, George Gordon (6th Baron Byron) (poet); b. London, England **(1788–1824)**.
Caan, James (actor); New York City, 3/26/1939.
Cabot, John (Giovanni Caboto) (navigator); b. Genoa **(1450–1498)**.
Cabot, Sebastian (navigator); b. Venice **(1476?–1557)**.
Cadmus, Paul (painter, etcher); New York City, 12/17/1904.
Caesar, Gaius Julius (statesman); b. Rome **(100?–44 B.C.)**.
Caesar, Sid (comedian); Yonkers, N.Y., 9/8/1922.
Cagney, James (actor); New York City, 7/17/1900.
Cahn, Sammy (song writer); New York City, 6/18/1913.
Caine, Michael (Maurice J. Micklewhite) (actor); London, England, 3/14/1933.
Caldwell, Erskine (novelist); White Oak, Ga., 12/17/1903.
Caldwell, Sarah (opera director, conductor); Maryville, Mo., 1928.
Caldwell, Taylor (novelist); Preswich, England, 9/7/1900.
Caldwell, Zoe (actress); Hawthorne, Australia, 9/14/1933.
Calhern, Louis (Carl Henry Vogt) (actor); b. Brooklyn, N.Y. **(1895–1956)**.
Calhoun, John Caldwell (statesman); b. near Calhoun Mills, S.C. **(1782–1850)**.
Calisher, Hortense (novelist); New York City, 12/20/1911.
Callas, Maria (Maria Calogeropoulos) (dramatic soprano); New York City, 12/4/1923.
Calloway, Cab (Cabell) (band leader); Rochester, N.Y., 12/25/1907.
Calvet, Corinne (actress); Paris, France, 4/30/1926.
Calvin, John (Jean Chauvin) (religious reformer); b. Noyon, Picardy **(1509–1564)**.
Cambridge, Godfrey (comedian); New York City, 2/26/1933.
Cameron, Rod (actor); Calgary, Alberta, Canada, 12/7/1912.
Campanella, Roy (baseball); Homestead, Pa., 11/19/1921.
Campbell, Glen (singer); nr. Delight, Ark., 4/22/1938.
Camus, Albert (author); Mondovi, Algeria **(1913–1960)**.
Caniff, Milton (cartoonist); Hillsboro, Ohio, 2/28/1907.
Cannon, Dyan (actress); Tacoma, Wash., 1/4/1937.
Canova, Judy (actress); Jacksonville, Fla., 11/20/1916.
Cantinflas (Mario Moreno) (comedian); Mexico City, Mexico, 8/12/1911.
Cantor, Eddie (Edward Iskowitz) (actor); b. New York City **(1892–1964)**.
Cantrell, Lana (singer); Sydney, Australia, 1944.
Caponi, Donna Maria (golf); Detroit, 1/29/1945.
Capote, Truman (novelist); New Orleans, La., 9/30/1924.

Capp, Al (Alfred Gerald Caplin) (cartoonist); New Haven, Conn., 9/28/1909.
Cappelletti, Gino (football); Keewatin, Minn., 3/26/1934.
Capra, Frank (producer-director); Palermo, Sicily, 5/8/1897.
Cardin, Pierre (fashion designer); nr. Venice, Italy, 7/7/1922.
Cardinale, Claudia (actress); Tunis, Tunisia, 1939.
Cardozo, Benjamin Nathan (jurist); b. New York City **(1870–1938).**
Carew, Rod (Rodney Cline) (baseball); Gatun, Panama, 10/1/1945.
Carey, Harry (actor); b. New York City **(1878–1947).**
Carey, Macdonald (actor); Sioux City, Iowa, 3/15/1913.
Carlisle, Kitty (singer, actress); New Orleans, La., 9/3/1915.
Carlos, John (sprinter); New York City, 6/5/1945.
Carlson, Richard (actor); Albert Lea, Minn., 4/29/1912.
Carlyle, Thomas (essayist & historian); b. Ecclefechan, Dumfries-shire, Scotland **(1795–1881).**
Carmichael, Hoagy (song writer); Bloomington, Ind., 11/22/1899.
Carne, Judy (singer); Northampton, England, 1939.
Carnegie, Andrew (industrialist); b. Dunfermline, Scotland **(1835–1919).**
Carner, Joanne Gunderson (Mrs. Don) (golf); Kirkland, Wash., 3/4/1939.
Carney, Art (actor); Mt. Vernon, N.Y., 11/4/1918.
Carnovsky, Morris (actor); St. Louis, Mo., 9/5/1897.
Caron, Leslie (actress); Paris, France, 7/1/1931.
Carpenter, Malcolm Scott (astronaut); Boulder, Colo., 5/1/1925.
Carr, Catherine (swimming); Albuquerque, N.M., 5/27/1954.
Carr, Vikki (singer); El Paso, Tex., 7/19/1942.
Carracci, Annibale (painter); b. Bologna, Italy **(1560–1609).**
Carracci, Lodovico (painter); b. Bologna, Italy **(1555–1619).**
Carradine, David (actor); Hollywood, Calif., 12/8/1936.
Carradine, John (actor); New York City, 2/5/1906.
Carrillo, Leo (actor); b. Los Angeles, Calif. **(1881–1961).**
Carroll, Diahann (Carol Diahann Johnson) (singer, actress); Bronx, N.Y., 7/17/1935.
Carroll, Leo G. (actor); b. Weedon, England **(1892–1972).**
Carroll, Lewis (Charles Lutwidge Dodgson) (author & mathematician); b. Daresbury, Cheshire, England **(1832–1898).**
Carroll, Madeleine (actress); West Bromwich, England, 2/26/1909.
Carroll, Pat (comedienne); Shreveport, La., 5/5/1927.
Carson, Johnny (TV entertainer); Corning, Iowa, 10/23/1925.
Carson, Kit (Christopher) (scout); b. Madison Co., Ky. **(1809–1868).**
Carson, Rachel (biologist & author); b. Springdale, Pa. **(1907–1964).**
Carter, Jack (comedian); New York City, 1923.
Caruso, Enrico (Errico) (tenor); b. Naples, Italy **(1873–1921).**
Carver, George Washington (botanist); b. Missouri **(1864–1943).**
Cary, Arthur Joyce Lunel (novelist); b. Londonderry, Ireland **(1888–1957).**
Casals, Pablo (cellist); b. Vendrell, Spain **(1876–1973).**
Casals, Rosemary (tennis); San Francisco, Calif., 9/16/1948.
Casanova de Seingalt, Giovanni Jacopo (adventurer); b. Venice, Italy **(1725–1798).**
Cash, Johnny (singer); nr. Kingsland, Ark., 2/26/1932.
Casper, Billy (golf); San Diego, Calif., 6/24/1931.
Cass, Peggy (comedienne); Boston, Mass., 5/21/1926.
Cassavetes, John (actor, director); New York City, 12/9/1929.
Cassidy, David (singer); New York City, 4/12/1950.
Cassidy, Jack (actor); Richmond Hill, Queens, N.Y., 3/5/1927.
Cassini, Oleg (Oleg Lolewski-Cassini) (fashion designer); Paris, France, 4/11/1913.
Castagno, Andrea del (painter); b. San Martino a Corella, Italy (c. 1421–1457).
Castellano, Richard (actor); New York City, 9/2/1934.
Castle, Irene (Irene Foote) (actress, dancer); b. New Rochelle, N.Y. **(1893–1969).**
Castro Ruz, Fidel (Premier); Mayari, Oriente, Cuba, 8/13/1926.
Cather, Willa Sibert (novelist); b. Winchester, Va. **(1876–1947).**
Cato, Marcus Porcius (called Cato the Elder) (statesman); b. Tusculum **(234–149 B.C.).**
Catt, Carrie Chapman (née Lane) (woman suffragist); b. Ripon, Wis. **(1859–1947).**
Catton, Bruce (historian); Petoskey, Mich., 10/9/1899.
Cavallaro, Carmen (band leader); New York City, 1913.
Cavett, Dick (Richard) (TV entertainer); Gibbon, Neb., 11/19/1936.
Cernan, Eugene Andrew (astronaut); Chicago, Ill., 3/14/1934.
Cervantes Saavedra, Miguel de (novelist); b. Alcalà de Henares, Spain **(1547–1616).**
Chaliapin, Feodor Ivanovitch (basso); b. Kazan, Russia **(1873–1938).**
Chamberlain, Arthur Neville (statesman); b. Edgbaston, England **(1869–1940).**
Chamberlain, Richard (actor); Los Angeles, Calif., 3/31/1935(?).
Chamberlain, Wilt (Wilton) (basketball); Philadelphia, Pa., 8/21/1936.
Champion, Gower (choreographer); Geneva, Ill., 6/22/1921.
Champion, Marge (actress, dancer); Los Angeles, Calif., 9/2/1923.
Champlain, Samuel de (explorer); b. nr. Rochefort, France **(1567?–1635).**
Chancellor, John (TV commentator); Chicago, Ill., 7/14/1927.
Chanel, "Coco" (Gabriel Bonheur) (fashion designer); b. Issoire, France **(1883–1971).**

Chaney, Lon (actor); b. Colorado Springs, Colo. **(1883–1930).**
Channing, Carol (actress); Seattle, Wash., 1/31/1923.
Chaplin, Geraldine (actress); Santa Monica, Calif., 1944.
Chaplin, Sir Charles (actor); London England, 4/16/1889.
Chaplin, Sydney (actor); b. Cape Town, South Africa **(1885–1956).**
Chaplin, Sydney (actor); Los Angeles, Calif., 3/31/1926.
Chapot, Frank (equestrian); Camden, N.J., 2/24/1934.
Charisse, Cyd (Tula Finklea) (dancer, actress); Amarillo, Tex., 3/8/1923.
Charlemagne (Holy Roman Emperor); birthplace unknown **(742–814).**
Charles, Ray (Ray Charles Robinson) (singer); Albany, Ga., 9/23/1932.
Chase, Ilka (author, actress); New York City, 4/8/1905.
Chase, Lucia (ballet company manager); Waterbury, Conn., 3/24/1907.
Chatterton, Ruth (actress); b. New York City **(1893–1961).**
Chaucer, Geoffrey (poet); b. London, England **(1340?–1400).**
Chavez, Carlos (composer); nr. Mexico City, Mexico, 6/13/1899.
Chavez, César (labor leader); nr. Yuma, Ariz., 3/31/1927.
Chayefsky, Paddy (Sidney) (playwright); New York City, 1/29/1923.
Cheever, John (writer); Quincy, Mass., 5/27/1912.
Chekhov, Anton Pavlovich (author); b. Taganrog, Russia **(1860–1904).**
Cher (Cherilyn LaPiere) (singer); El Centro, Calif., 5/20/1946.
Chesterton, Gilbert Keith (author); b. Kensington, England **(1874–1936).**
Chevalier, Maurice (entertainer); b. Paris, France **(1888–1972).**
Chiang Ch'ing (political leader); Chucheng, Shantung Province, China, 1913(?).
Chiang Kai-shek (Chief of State); b. Feng-hwa, China **(1887–1975).**
Child, Julia (food expert); Pasadena, Calif., 8/15/1912.
Chippendale, Thomas (cabinet-maker); b. Otley, England **(1718?–1779).**
Chopin, Frédéric François (composer); b. nr. Warsaw, Poland **(1810–1849).**
Chou En-lai (Premier); Hualyin, China **(1898–1976).**
Christian, Linda (Blanca Rosa Welter) (actress); Tampico, Mexico, 11/13/1924.
Christians, Mady (actress); b. Vienna, Austria **(1900–1951).**
Christie, Agatha (mystery writer); b. Torquay, England **(1890–1976).**
Christie, Julie (actress); Chukua, Assam, India, 4/14/1941.
Christopher, Jordon (actor, musician); Youngstown, Ohio, 1941.
Christy, June (singer); Springfield, Ill., 1925.
Churchill, Sarah (actress); London, England, 10/7/1914.
Churchill, Sir Winston Leonard Spencer (statesman); b. Blenheim Palace, Oxfordshire, England **(1874–1965).**
Cicero, Marcus Tullius (orator & statesman); b. Arpinum, Italy **(106–43 B.C.).**
Cilento, Diane (actress); Queensland, Australia, 10/5/1933.
Cimabue, Giovanni (painter); b. Florence, Italy **(c. 1240–c. 1302).**
Clair, René (René Chomette) (director); Paris, France, 11/11/1898.
Claire, Ina (Ina Fagan) (actress); Washington, D.C., 10/15/1895.
Clark, Dane (actor); New York City, 2/18/1915.
Clark, Dick (TV personality); Mt. Vernon, N.Y., 11/30/1929.
Clark, Petula (singer); Epsom, England, 11/15/1934.
Clark, Roy (country music artist); 4/15/1933.
Clark, William (explorer); b. Caroline County, Va. **(1770–1838).**
Claude Lorrain (painter); b. Champagne, Lorraine **(1600–1682).**
Clay, Cassius. See Muhammad Ali.
Clay, Henry (statesman); b. Hanover County, Va. **(1777–1852).**
Clay, Lucius D. (banker, ex-general); Marietta, Ga., 4/23/1897.
Clarke, Bobby (Robert Earle) (hockey); Flin Flon, Manitoba, Canada, 8/13/1949.
Clemenceau, Georges (statesman); b. Mouilleron-en-Pareds, Vendée, France **(1841–1929).**
Clemens, Samuel L. See Mark Twain.
Cleopatra (Queen of Egypt); b. Alexandria, Egypt **(69–30 B.C.).**
Cliburn, Van (Harvey Lavan Cliburn, Jr.) (pianist); Shreveport, La., 7/12/1934.
Clifford, Clark M. (ex-Secretary of Defense); Ft. Scott, Kan., 12/25/1906.
Clift, Montgomery (actor); b. Omaha, Neb. **(1920–1966).**
Clooney, Rosemary (singer); Maysville, Ky., 5/23/1928.
Clurman, Harold (producer); New York City, 9/18/1901.
Cobb, Irvin Shrewsbury (humorist); b. Paducah, Ky. **(1876–1944).**
Cobb, Lee J. (actor); b. New York City **(1911–1976).**
Cobb, Tyrus Raymond (Ty) (baseball player); b. Banks County, Ga. **(1886–1961).**
Coburn, Charles Douville (actor); b. Savannah, Ga. **(1877–1961).**
Coburn, James (actor); Laurel, Neb., 8/31/1928.
Coca, Imogene (comedienne); Philadelphia, Pa., 1914(?).
Cochran, Barbara Ann (skiing); Claremont, N.H., 1/4/1951.
Cochran, Marilyn (skiing); Burlington, Vt., 2/7/1950.
Cochran, Robert (skiing); Claremont, N.H., 12/11/1951.
Coco, James (actor); New York City, 3/21/1929.
Cocteau, Jean (author); b. Maison-Lafitte, France **(1891–1963).**
Cody, Lew (actor); b. Waterville, Me. **(1887–1934).**
Cody, W. F. See Buffalo Bill.
Cohan, George Michael (actor & dramatist); b. Providence, R.I. **(1878–1942).**

Colavito, Rocky (Rocco Domenico) (baseball); New York City, 8/10/1933.
Colbert, Claudette (Lily Chauchoin) (actress); Paris, France, 9/13/1905.
Colby, William E. (Ex-Director C.I.A.); St. Paul, Minn., 1/4/1920.
Cole, Nat "King" (singer); b. Montgomery, Ala. **(1919–1965).**
Coleridge, Samuel Taylor (poet); b. Ottery St. Mary, Devonshire, England **(1772–1834).**
Colette (Sidonie-Gabrielle Colette) (novelist); b. St.-Sauveur, France **(c. 1873–1954).**
Collingwood, Charles (TV commentator); Three Rivers, Mich., 6/4/1917.
Collins, Dorothy (Marjorie Chandler) (singer); Windsor, Ontario, Canada, 11/18/1926.
Collins, Judy (singer); Seattle, Wash., 5/1/1939.
Collins, Michael (museum director, former astronaut); Rome, Italy, 10/31/1930.
Colman, Ronald (actor); b. Richmond, Surrey, Eng. **(1891–1958).**
Colonna, Jerry (comedian); Boston, Mass., 1905.
Columbus, Christopher (Cristoforo Colombo) (discoverer of America); b. Genoa. Italy **(1451–1506).**
Comaneci, Nadia (gymnast); Onesti, Romania, 11/12/1961.
Comden, Betty (writer); New York City, 5/3/1919.
Commager, Henry Steele (historian); Pittsburgh, Pa., 10/25/1902.
Como, Perry (Pierino) (singer); Canonsburg, Pa., 5/18/1913.
Compton, Karl Taylor (physicist); b. Wooster, Ohio **(1887–1954).**
Conant, James B. (educator, statesman); Dorchester, Mass., 3/26/1893.
Condon, Eddie (jazzman); b. Goodland, Ind. **(1905–1973).**
Confucius (K'ung Fu-tzu) (philosopher); b. Shantung province, China **(c. 551–479 B.C.).**
Congreve, William (dramatist); b. nr. Leeds, England **(1670–1729).**
Connelly, Marc (playwright); McKeesport, Pa., 12/13/1890.
Connery, Sean (actor); Edinburgh, Scotland, 8/25/1930.
Conniff, Ray (band leader); Attleboro, Mass., 1916.
Connors, Chuck (actor); Brooklyn, N.Y., 4/10/1921.
Connors, Jimmy (James Scott) (tennis); East St. Louis, Ill., 9/2/1952.
Connors, Mike (Krekor Ohanian) (actor); Fresno, Calif., 8/15/1925.
Conrad, Charles, Jr. (Pete) (astronaut); Philadelphia, Pa., 6/2/1930.
Conrad, Joseph (Teodor Jozef Konrad Korzeniowski) (novelist); b. Berdichev, Ukraine **(1857–1924).**
Conrad, William (actor); Louisville, Ky., 9/27/1920.
Conried, Hans (actor); Baltimore, Md., 1917.
Constantine II (ex-King); Athens, Greece, 6/2/1940.
Conte, Richard (actor); b. New York City **(1916–1975).**
Coogan, Jackie (actor); Los Angeles, Calif., 10/26/1914.
Cooke, Alistair (Alfred Alistair); (TV narrator, journalist); Manchester, England, 11/20/1908.
Cooley, Denton A(rthur) (heart surgeon); Houston, Tex., 8/22/1920.
Cooper, Alice (Vincent Furnier) (rock musician); Detroit, Mich., 2/4/1948.
Cooper, Gary (Frank James Cooper) (actor); b. Helena, Mont. **(1901–1961).**
Cooper, Jackie (actor); Los Angeles, Calif., 9/15/1922.
Cooper, James Fenimore (novelist); b. Burlington, N.J. **(1789–1851).**
Cooper, Leroy Gordon, Jr. (astronaut); Shawnee, Okla., 3/6/1927.
Cooper, Peter (industrialist & philanthropist); b. New York City **(1791–1883).**
Copernicus, Nicolaus (Mikolaj Kopernik) (astronomer); b. Thorn, Poland **(1473–1543).**
Copland, Aaron (composer); Brooklyn, N.Y., 11/14/1900.
Cordero, Angel (jockey); Santurce, Puerto Rico, 5/8/1942.
Corelli, Franco (tenor); Ancona, Italy, 4/8/1923.
Corneille, Pierre (dramatist); b. Rouen, France **(1606–1684).**
Cornell, Katharine (actress); b. Berlin, Germany **(1893–1974).**
Correggio, Antonio Allegri da (painter); b. Correggio, Italy **(c. 1494–c. 1534).**
Corsaro, Frank (opera director); New York harbor, 12/22/1924.
Cortés (or Cortez), Hernando (explorer); b. Medellín, Spain **(1485–1547).**
Cosby, Bill (actor); Philadelphia, Pa., 7/12/1937.
Cosell, Howard (Cohen) (sportscaster); Winston-Salem, N.C., 3/25/1929.
Costa-Gavras, (Henri) (Kostantinos Gavras) (film director); Athens, Greece, 1933.
Costello, Lou (comedian); b. Paterson, N.J. **(1906–1959).**
Cotten, Joseph (actor); Petersburg, Va., 5/15/1905.
Cournover, Yvan Serge (hockey); Drummondville, Quebec, Canada, 11/22/1943.
Courrèges, André (fashion designer); Pau, France, 3/9/1923.
Court, Margaret Smith (tennis); Albury, New South Wales, Australia, 7/16/1942.
Courtenay, Tom (actor); Hull, Yorkshire, England, 2/25/1937.
Cousins, Norman (publisher); Union Hill, N.J., 6/24/1915.
Cousteau, Jacques Ives (marine explorer); St. André-de-Cubzac, France, 6/11/1910.
Cousy, Bob (basketball); New York City, 8/9/1928.
Coward, Sir Noel (playwright, actor); b. Teddington, England **(1899–1973).**
Cowles, Gardner (newspaper publisher); Algona, Iowa, 1/31/1903.
Cowper, William (poet); b. Great Berkhamstead, Hertfordshire, England **(1731–1800).**

Cozzens, James Gould (novelist); Chicago, Ill., 8/19/1903.
Crabbe, Buster (Clarence) (actor); Oakland, Calif., 2/7/1908.
Crain, Jeanne (actress); Barstow, Calif., 5/25/1925.
Cranach, Lucas, the elder (painter); b. Kronach, Germany **(1472–1553).**
Crane, Bob (actor); Waterbury, Conn., 1928.
Crane, Stephen (novelist & poet); b. Newark, N.J. **(1871–1900).**
Crawford, Broderick (actor); Philadelphia, Pa., 12/9/1911.
Crawford, Cheryl (producer); Akron, Ohio, 9/24/1902.
Crawford, Joan (Lucille LeSueur) (actress, business executive); San Antonio, Tex., 3/23/1908.
Crenna, Richard (actor); Los Angeles, Calif., 11/30/1927.
Crichton, Michael (novelist); Chicago, Ill., 10/23/1942.
Croce, Benedetto (philosopher); b. Pescasseroli, Aquila, Italy **(1866–1952).**
Crockett, Davy (David) (frontiersman); b. Greene County, Tenn. **(1786–1836).**
Cromwell, Oliver (statesman); b. Huntington, England **(1599–1658).**
Cronin, A. J. (Archibald J. Cronin) (novelist); Cardross, Scotland, 7/19/1896.
Cronin, Joe (baseball exec.); San Francisco, Calif., 10/12/1906.
Cronkite, Walter (newscaster); St. Joseph, Mo., 11/4/1916.
Cronyn, Hume (actor); London, Ontario, Canada, 7/18/1911.
Crosby, Bing (Harry Lillis) (singer, actor); Tacoma, Wash., 5/2/1904(?).
Crosby, Bob (musician); Spokane, Wash., 8/23/1913.
Cross, Milton (opera commentator); b. New York City **(1897–1975).**
Crouse, Russel (dramatist); b. Findlay, Ohio **(1893–1966).**
Cugat, Xavier (band leader); Barcelona, Spain, 1/1/1900.
Cukor, George (director); New York City, 7/7/1899.
Cullen, Bill (William Lawrence Cullen) (radio & TV entertainer); Pittsburgh, Pa., 2/18/1920.
Culp, Robert (actor); Berkeley, Calif., 8/16/1931.
Cummings, E. E. (Edward Estlin Cummings) (poet); b. Cambridge, Mass. **(1894–1962).**
Cummings, Robert (actor); Joplin, Mo., 6/9/1910.
Cunningham, R. Walter (astronaut); Creston, Iowa, 3/16/1932.
Curie, Marie (Marja Sklodowska) (physical chemist); b. Warsaw, Poland **(1867–1934).**
Curtin, Phyllis (soprano); Clarksburgh, W. Va., 12/3/1927.
Curtis, Tony (Bernard Schwartz) (actor); New York City, 6/3/1925.
Curzon, Clifford (pianist); London, England, 5/18/1907.
Custer, George Armstrong (army officer); b. New Rumley, Ohio **(1839–1876).**
Czonka, Larry (Lawrence Richard) (football); Stow, Ohio, 12/25/1946.
Daché, Lilly (fashion designer); Bèigles, France.
Dahl, Arlene (actress); Minneapolis, Minn., 8/11/1928.
Dailey, Dan (actor, dancer); New York City, 12/14/1917.
Daley, Richard J. (Mayor of Chicago); Chicago, Ill., 5/15/1902.
Daly, James (actor); Wisconsin Rapids, Wis., 10/23/1918.
Daly, John (radio & TV news analyst); Johannesburg, South Africa, 2/20/1914.
d'Amboise, Jacques (ballet dancer); Bedham, Mass., 7/28/1934.
Damone, Vic (Vito Farinola) (singer); Brooklyn, N.Y., 6/12/1928.
Damrosch, Walter Johannes (orchestra conductor); b. Breslau, Germany **(1862–1950).**
Dana, Charles Anderson (editor); b. Hinsdale, N.H. **(1819–1897).**
Dancer, Stanley (harness racing); New Egypt, N.J., 7/25/1927.
Dandridge, Dorothy (actress); b. Cleveland, Ohio **(1923–1965).**
Dangerfield, Rodney (comedian); Babylon, L.I., N.Y., 1921.
Daniels, Bebe (Virginia Daniels) (actress); b. Dallas, Tex. **(1901–1971).**
Danilova, Alexandra (ballerina); Peterhof, Russia, 1/20/1904.
D'Annunzio, Gabriele (soldier & author); b. Francaville al Mare, Pescara, Italy **(1863–1938).**
Dante (or Durante) Alighieri (poet); b. Florence **(1265–1321).**
Danton, Georges Jacques (French Revolutionary leader); b. Arcissur-Aube, France **(1759–1794).**
Darcel, Denise (Denise Billecard) (actress); Paris, France, 9/8/1925.
Darin, Bobby (Walden Robert Cassotto) (entertainer); b. New York City **(1936–1973).**
Dark, Alvin (baseball); Comanche, Okla., 1/7/1922.
Darnell, Linda (actress); b. Dallas, Tex. **(1921–1965).**
Darren, James (actor); Philadelphia, Pa., 6/8/1936.
Darrieux, Danielle (actress); Bordeaux, France, 5/1/1917.
Darrow, Clarence Seward (lawyer); b. Kinsman, Ohio **(1857–1938).**
Darwin, Charles Robert (naturalist); b. Shrewsbury, Shropshire, England **(1809–1882).**
daSilva, Howard (actor); Cleveland, Ohio. 5/4/1909.
Dassin, Jules (director); Middletown, Conn., 12/18/1911.
Dauphin, Claude (actor); Corbeil, France, 8/19/1903.
Davenport, Willie (hurdler); Troy, Ala., 6/8/1943.
David (King of Israel & Judah) **(died c. 973 B.C.).**
Davies, Marion (Marion Douras) (actress); b. New York City **(1898?–1961).**
Davis, Bette (actress); Lowell, Mass., 4/5/1908.
Davis, Elmer Holmes (radio commentator); b. Aurora, Ind. **(1890–1958).**
Davis, Jefferson (Pres. of Confederacy); b. Christian (now Todd) County, Ky. **(1808–1889).**

Davis, Miles (trumpeter); Alton, Ill., 5/25/1926.
Davis, Ossie (actor, writer); Cogdell, Ga., 12/18/1917.
Davis, Sammy, Jr. (actor); New York City, 12/8/1925.
Davis, Stuart (painter); b. Philadelphia, Pa. **(1894–1964).**
Davis, Tommy (baseball); Brooklyn, N.Y., 3/21/1939.
Dawson, Leonard Ray (football); Alliance, Ohio, 6/20/1935.
Day, Dennis (singer); New York City, 5/21/1917.
Day, Doris (Doris von Kappelhoff) (singer, actress); Cincinnati, Ohio, 4/3/1924.
Day, Laraine (actress); Roosevelt, Utah, 10/13/1920.
Dayan, Moshe (ex-Defense Minister of Israel); Degania A., Palestine, 5/20/1915.
Dean, Dizzy (Jay Hanna) (baseball player); b. Lucas, Ark. **(1911–1974).**
Dean, James (actor); b. Marion, Ind. **(1931–1955).**
Dean, Jimmy (singer); near Plainview, Tex., 8/10/1928.
De Bakey, Michael E. (heart surgeon); Lake Charles, La., 9/7/1908.
de Beauvoir, Simone (novelist and philosopher); Paris, France, 1/9/1908.
Debs, Eugene Victor (Socialist leader); b. Terre Haute, Ind. **(1855–1926).**
DeBusschere, Dave (basketball); Detroit, Mich., 10/16/1940.
Debussy, Claude Achille (composer); b. St. Germain-en-Laye, France **(1862–1918).**
De Carlo, Yvonne (actress); Vancouver, B.C., Canada, 9/1/1924.
Dee, Ruby (Ruby Ann Wallace) (actress); Cleveland, Ohio, 10/27/1924.
Dee, Sandra (actress); Bayonne, N.J., 4/23/1942.
Defoe, Daniel (novelist); b. London, England **(1659?–1731).**
DeFore, Don (J.) (actor); Cedar Rapids, Iowa, 8/25/1917.
De Gaulle, Charles André Joseph Marie (soldier-statesman); b. Lille, France **(1890–1970).**
De Havilland, Olivia (actress); Tokyo, Japan, 7/1/1916.
Dekker, Albert (actor); b. Brooklyn, N.Y. **(1904–1968).**
de La Renta, Oscar (fashion designer); Santo Domingo, Dominican Republic, 7/22/1932.
De Laurentiis, Dino (producer); Torre Annunziata, Bay of Naples, Italy, 8/8/1919.
DeHaven, Gloria (actress); Los Angeles, Calif., 7/23/1925.
Dulaunay, Robert (painter); b. Paris, France **(1885–1941).**
Delon, Alain (actor); Sceaux, France, 11/8/1935.
Del Rio, Dolores (actress); Durango, Mexico, 8/3/1905.
DeLuise, Dom (comedian); Brooklyn, N.Y., 1933.
Delvecchio, Alex Peter (hockey); Fort William, Ontario, Canada, 12/4/1931.
Demarest, William (actor); St. Paul, Minn., 2/27/1892.
Demaret, Jim (golf); Houston, Tex., 5/10/1910.
de Mille, Agnes (choreographer); New York City.
De Mille, Cecil Blount (movie director); b. Ashfield, Mass. **(1881–1959).**
Demosthenes (orator); b. Athens **(385?–322** B.C.)
Dempsey, Jack (William H.) (boxing); Manassa, Colo., 6/24/1895.
Deneuve, Catherine (actress); Paris, France, 10/22/1943.
Dennis, Sandy (actress); Hastings, Neb., 4/27/1937.
Denver, John (Henry John Deutschendorf, Jr.) (singer); Roswell, N. Mex., 12/31/1943.
Derain, Andre (painter); b. Chatou, Seine-et-Oise, France **(1880–1954).**
Descartes, René (philosopher & mathematician); b. La Haye, France **(1596–1650).**
De Seversky, Alexander P. (aviator); b. Tifflis, Russia **(1894–1974).**
De Sica, Vittorio (film director); b. Sora, Italy **(1901–1974).**
Desmond, Johnny (composer); Detroit, Mich., 11/14/1921.
Desmond, William (actor); b. Dublin, Ireland **(1878–1949).**
De Soto, Hernando (explorer); b. Barcarrota, Spain **(1500?–1542).**
De Valera, Eamon (ex-President of Ireland); b. New York City **(1882–1975).**
DeVicenzo, Roberto (golf); Buenos Aires, Arg., 4/14/1923.
Devine, Andy (actor); Flagstaff, Ariz., 10/7/1905.
De Vries, Peter (novelist); Chicago, Ill., 2/27/1910.
Dewey, George (admiral); b. Montpelier, Vt. **(1837–1917).**
Dewey, John (philosopher & educator); b. Burlington, Vt. **(1859–1952).**
Dewey, Thomas E. (politician); b. Owosso, Mich. **(1902–1971).**
Dewhurst, Colleen (actress); Montreal, Canada, 1926(?).
Dexter, John (Director of Production, Metropolitan Opera); Derby, England, 8/2/1925.
Dickens, Charles John Huffam (novelist); b. Portsea, England **(1812–1870).**
Dickey, James (poet); Atlanta, Ga., 2/2/1923.
Dickinson, Angie (Angeline Brown) (actress); Kulm, N.D., 9/30/1931.
Dickinson, Emily Elizabeth (poet); b. Amherst, Mass. **(1830–1886).**
Diefenbaker, John G. (ex-Prime Minister); Grey County, Ontario, Canada, 9/18/1895.
Dietrich, Marlene (Maria Magdalene von Losch) (actress); Berlin, Germany, 2/27/1904.
Dietz, James W. (rowing); New York, N.Y., 1/12/1949.
Diggs, Dudley (actor); b. Dublin, Ireland **(1879–1947).**
Diller, Phyllis (Phyllis Driver) (comedienne); Lima, Ohio, 7/17/1917.
Dillman, Bradford (actor); San Francisco, Calif., 4/14/1930.
DiMaggio, Joe (baseball); Martinez, Calif., 11/25/1914. ·

Dine, Jim (painter); Cincinnati, Ohio, 6/16/1935.
Diogenes (philosopher); b. Sinope, Asia Minor **(412?–323** B.C.).
Dior, Christian (fashion designer); b. Granville, France **(1905–1957).**
Disney, Walt(er) Elias (film animator-producer); b. Chicago, Ill. **(1901–1966).**
Disraeli, Benjamin (Earl of Beaconsfield) (statesman); b. London, England **(1804–1881).**
Dix, Richard (Ernest Carlton Brimmer) (actor); b. St. Paul, Minn. **(1894–1949).**
Dixon, Jeane (Jeane Pinckert) (seer); Medford, Wis., 1918.
Dodgson, C. L. *See* Lewis Carroll.
Dolin, Anton (dancer); Slinfold, Sussex, England, 7/27/1904.
Dominguín, Luis Miguel (matador); Madrid, Spain, 12/9/1926.
Domino, Fats (Antoine) (musician); New Orleans, La., 2/26/1928.
Donahue, Troy (actor); New York City, 1/27/1938.
Donne, John (poet); b. London, England **(1573–1631).**
Doolittle, James H. (ex-Air Force general); Alameda, Calif., 12/14/1896.
Dorati, Antal (conductor); Budapest, Hungary, 4/9/1906.
Dors, Diana (actress); Swindon, Wiltshire, England, 10/23/1931.
Dos Passos, John (author); b. Chicago, Ill. **(1896–1970).**
Dostoevski, Fyodor Mikhailovich (novelist); b. Moscow, Russia **(1821–1881).**
Douglas, Helen Gahagan (ex-Representative); Boonton, N.J., 11/25/1900.
Douglas, Kirk (Issur Danielovitch) (actor); Amsterdam, N.Y., 12/9/1916.
Douglas, Melvyn (Melvyn Hesselberg) (actor); Macon, Ga., 4/5/1901.
Douglas, Mike (Michael D. Dowd, Jr.) (TV personality); Chicago, Ill. 8/11/1925(?).
Douglas, Stephen Arnold (politician); b. Brandon, Vt. **(1813–1861).**
Douglass, Bobby (football); Manhattan, Kan., 6/22/1947.
Dowling, Eddie (Edward Goucher) (actor, producer); b. Woonsocket, R.I. **(1894–1976).**
Downs, Hugh (TV entertainer); Akron, Ohio, 2/14/1921.
Doyle, Sir Arthur Conan (novelist & spiritualist); b. Edinburgh, Scotland **(1859–1930).**
Drake, Alfred (singer, actor); New York City, 10/7/1914.
Drake, Sir Francis (navigator); b. Tavistock, Devonshire, England **(1545–1596).**
Dressler, Marie (Leila Koeber) (actress); b. Cobourg, Ontario, Canada **(1869–1934).**
Dreyfus, Alfred (French army officer); b. Alsace **(1859–1935).**
Dreyfuss, Richard (actor); Brooklyn, N.Y., 10/29/1947.
Drummond, Roscoe (columnist); Theresa, N.Y.
Drury, Allen (novelist); Houston, Tex., 9/2/1918.
Dryden, John (poet); b. Northamptonshire, England **(1631–1700).**
Drysdale, Don (baseball); Van Nuys, Calif., 7/23/1936.
Dubček, Alexander (ex-President of Czechoslovakia); Uhroved, Slovakia, 11/27/1921.
Dubinsky, David (David Dobnievski) (labor leader); Brest-Litovsk, Poland, 2/22/1892.
Duchin, Peter (pianist); New York City, 7/28/1937.
Duke, Patty (Anna Marie Duke) (actress); New York City, 12/14/1946.
Dullea, Keir (actor); Cleveland, Ohio, 5/30/1936(?).
Dulles, Allen Welsh (former C.I.A. director); b. Watertown, N.Y. **(1893–1969).**
Dulles, John Foster (statesman); b. Washington, D.C. **(1888–1959).**
Dumas, Alexandre (called Dumas père) (novelist); b. Villers-Cotterets, France **(1802–1870).**
Dumas, Alexandre (called Dumas fils) (novelist); b. Paris, France **(1824–1895).**
Du Maurier, Daphne (novelist); London, England, 5/13/1907.
Du Maurier, George Louis Palmella Busson (novelist); b. Paris, France **(1834–1896).**
Dumont, Margaret (actress) **(1889–1965).**
Dunaway, Faye (actress); Bascom, Fla., 1/14/1941.
Duncan, Isadora (dancer); b. San Francisco, Calif. **(1878–1927).**
Dunn, James (actor); b. Santa Monica, Calif. **(1905–1967).**
Dunne, Irene (actress); Louisville, Ky., 12/20/1904.
Dunnock, Mildred (actress); Baltimore, Md., 1/25/(?).
Durante, Jimmy (comedian); New York City, 2/10/1893.
Durbin, Deanna (actress); Winnipeg, Canada, 12/4/1922.
Durocher, Leo (baseball); West Springfield, Mass., 7/27/1906.
Durr, Francois (tennis); Algiers, Algeria, 12/25/1942.
Durrell, Lawrence George (novelist); Julundur, India, 2/27/1912.
Duse, Eleonora (actress); b. Chioggia, Italy **(1859–1924).**
Duvalier, Jean-Claude (President; son of "Papa Doc"); Port-au-Prince, Haiti, 7/3/1951.
Dvorak, Antonin (composer); b. Mühlhausen, Bohemia **(1841–1904).**
Dylan, Bob (Robert Zimmerman) (singer); Duluth, Minn., 5/24/1941.
Eagels, Jeanne (actress); b. Kansas City, Mo. **(1894–1929).**
Earhart, Amelia (aviator); b. Atchison, Kan. **(1898–1937).**
Eastman, George (inventor); b. Waterville, N.Y. **(1854–1932).**
Eastwood, Clint (actor); San Francisco, Calif., 5/31/1931(?).
Ebsen, Buddy (Christian Ebsen, Jr.) (actor); Belleville, Ill., 4/2/1908.
Eckstine, Billy (singer); Pittsburgh, Pa., 7/8/1914.
Eddy, Mary Baker (religious leader); b. Bow, N.H. **(1821–1910).**

Eden, Barbara (actress); Tucson, Ariz., 1934.
Eddy, Nelson (baritone); b. Providence, R.I., **(1901–1967)**.
Eden, Sir Anthony (Earl of Avon) (ex-Prime Minister); Durham, England, 6/12/1897.
Edison, Thomas Alva (inventor); b. Milan, Ohio **(1847–1931)**.
Edwards, Ralph (TV & radio producer); Merino, Colo., 1913.
Edwards, Vincent (actor); Brooklyn, N.Y., 7/7/1928.
Egan, Richard (actor); San Francisco, Calif., 7/29/1923.
Eggar, Samantha (actress); Hampstead, London, England, 5/3/1939.
Eglevsky, André (ballet dancer); Moscow, Russia, 12/21/1917.
Ehrlich, Paul (bacteriologist); b. Silesia prov., Prussia **(1854–1915)**.
Einstein, Albert (physicist); b. Ulm, Germany **(1879–1955)**.
Eisele, Donn F. (astronaut); Columbus, Ohio, 6/23/1930.
Eisenhower, Mamie Doud (President's widow); Boone, Iowa, 11/14/1896.
Eisenhower, Milton S. (educator); Abilene, Kan., 9/15/1899.
Eisenstaedt, Alfred (photographer, photojournalist); Dirschau, Germany, 12/6/1898.
Ekberg, Anita (actress); Malmo, Sweden, 9/29/1931.
El Cordobés (Manuel Benítez Pérez) (matador); Palma del Río, Córdoba, Spain, 5/4/1936(?).
Elder, Lee (golf); Dallas, Tex., 7/14/1934.
Eldridge, Florence (Florence McKechnie) (actress); Brooklyn, N.Y., 9/5/1901.
Elgar, Sir Edward (composer); b. Worcester, England **(1857–1934)**.
Elgart, Larry (band leader); New London, Conn., 3/20/1922.
Eliot, George (Mary Ann Evans) (novelist); b. Chilvers Coton, Warwickshire, England **(1819–1880)**.
Eliot, Thomas Stearns (poet); b. St. Louis, Mo. **(1888–1965)**.
Ellington, Duke (Edward Kennedy) (jazz musician); b. Washington, D.C. **(1899–1974)**.
Elliot, "Mama" Cass (Ellen Naomi Cohen) (pop singer); b. Baltimore, Md. **(1941–1974)**.
Elliott, Michael (skiing); Durango, Colo., 4/3/1942.
Ellis, Jimmy (equestrian); Louisville, Ky., 2/24/1940.
Elman, Mischa (violinist); b. Stalnoye, Ukraine **(1891–1967)**.
Emerson, Ralph Waldo (philosopher & poet); b. Boston, Mass. **(1803–1882)**.
Emerson, Roy (tennis); Kingsway, Australia, 11/3/1936.
Ender, Kornelia (swimming); Plauen, East Germany, 10/25/1958.
Enesco, Georges (composer); b. Dorohoi, Romania **(1881–1955)**.
Engels, Friedrich (Socialist writer); b. Barman, Germany **(1820–1895)**.
Epicurus (philosopher); b. Samos **(341–270 B.C.)**.
Erasmus, Desiderius (Gerhard Gerhards) (scholar); b. Rotterdam **(1466?–1536)**.
Erhard, Ludwig (ex-Chancellor); Furth, Bavaria, Germany, 2/4/1897.
Erickson, Leif (actor); Alameda, Calif., 10/27/1911.
Ericson, Leif (navigator) **(c. 10th century A.D.)**.
Erikson, Erik H. (psychoanalyst); Frankfurt, Germany, 6/15/1902.
Ervin, Frank (harness racing); Pekin, Ill., 8/12/1904.
Erving, Julius (Dr. J) (basketball); Hempstead, N.Y., 2/22/1950.
Esposito, Phil (Philip Anthony) (hockey); Sault Ste. Marie, Ontario, Canada, 2/20/1942.
Euclid (mathematician) **(c. 300 B.C.)**.
Euripides (dramatist); b. Salamis **(c. 484–407 B.C.)**.
Evans, Dale (actress, singer); Uvalde, Tex., 10/31/1912.
Evans, Dame Edith (actress); London, England, 2/8/1888.
Evans, Lee (runner); Mandena, Calif., 2/25/1947.
Evans, Maurice (actor); Dorchester, England, 6/3/1901.
Evers, Charles (civil rights leader); Decatur, Miss., 9/14/1923.
Evert, Chris (Christine Marie) (tennis); Fort Lauderdale, Fla., 12/21/1954.
Ewbank, Weeb (football); Richmond, Ind., 5/6/1907.
Ewell, Tom (Yewell Tompkins) (actor); Owensboro, Ky., 4/29/1909.
Fabian (Fabian Anthony Forte) (singer); Philadelphia, Pa., 2/6/1943.
Fabray, Nanette (Nanette Fabarés) (actress); San Diego, Calif., 10/27/1922.
Fadiman, Clifton (literary critic); Brooklyn, N.Y., 5/15/1904.
Fairbanks, Douglas (actor); b. Denver, Colo. **(1883–1939)**.
Fairbanks, Douglas, Jr. (actor); New York City, 12/9/1909.
Faith, Percy (musician); b. Toronto, Ont., Canada **(1908–1976)**.
Falk, Peter (actor); New York City, 9/16/1927.
Falla, Manuel de (composer); b. Cadiz, Spain **(1876–1946)**.
Faraday, Michael (physicist); b. Newington, Surrey, England **(1791–1867)**.
Farentino, James (actor); Brooklyn, N.Y., 2/24/1938.
Farmer, James (civil rights leader); Marshall, Tex., 1/12/1920.
Farnum, William (actor); b. Boston, Mass. **(1876–1953)**.
Farrell, Charles (actor); Onset Bay, Mass., 1901.
Farrell, Eileen (soprano); Willimantic, Conn., 2/13/1920.
Farrell, Glenda (actress); b. Enid, Okla. **(1904–1971)**.
Farrell, James T. (novelist); Chicago, Ill., 2/27/1904.
Farrell, Suzanne (ballerina); Cincinnati, Ohio, 8/16/1945.
Farrow, Mia (actress); Los Angeles, Calif., 2/9/1946.
Fasanella, Ralph (painter); New York City, 9/2/1914.
Fast, Howard (novelist); New York City, 11/11/1914.
Faulkner, William (novelist); b. New Albany, Miss. **(1897–1962)**.
Fay, Frank (actor); b. San Francisco, Calif. **(1894–1961)**.
Faye, Alice (Ann Leppert) (actress); New York City, 5/5/1915.
Fazenda, Louise (actress); b. Lafayette, Ind. **(1889–1962)**.

Feiffer, Jules (cartoonist); New York City, 1/26/1929.
Feininger, Lyonel (painter); b. New York City **(1871–1956)**.
Felker, Clay S. (editor, publisher); St. Louis, Mo., 10/2/1925(?).
Feldon, Barbara (actress); Pittsburgh, Pa., 3/12/1941.
Feliciano, José (singer); Larez, Puerto Rico, 9/10/1945.
Fellini, Federico (director); Rimini, Italy, 1/20/1920.
Ferber, Edna (author); b. Kalamazoo, Mich. **(1885–1968)**.
Fermi, Enrico (physicist); b. Rome, Italy **(1901–1954)**.
Fernandel (Fernand Joseph Desire Contandin) (actor); b. Marseilles, France **(1903–1971)**.
Ferrell, Barbara (sprinter); Hattiesburg, Miss., 7/28/1947.
Ferrer, José (actor, director); Santurce, Puerto Rico, 1/8/1912.
Ferrer, Mel (actor); Elberon, N.J., 8/25/1917.
Fetchit, Stepin (comedian); Key West, Fla., 1902.
Fiedler, Arthur (conductor); Boston, Mass., 12/17/1894.
Field, Betty (actress); b. Boston, Mass. **(1918–1973)**.
Field, Eugene (poet); b. St. Louis, Mo. **(1850–1895)**.
Field, Sally (actress); Pasadena, Calif., 11/6/1946.
Fielding, Henry (novelist); b. nr. Glastonbury, Somerset, England **(1707–1754)**.
Fields, Gracie (comedienne); Rochdale, England, 1/9/1898.
Fields, Totie (comedienne); Hartford, Conn., 1931.
Fields, W. C. (Claude William Dukenfield) (actor); b. Philadelphia, Pa. **(1880–1946)**.
Finch, Peter (actor); Kensington, England, 9/28/1916.
Finley, Charles O. (sportsman); Ensley, Ala., 2/22/1918.
Finney, Albert (actor); Salford, Lancashire, England, 5/9/1936.
Firkusny, Rudolf (pianist); Napajedia, Czechoslavakia, 2/11/1912.
Fischer, Bobby (chess); Chicago, Ill., 3/9/1943.
Fischer-Dieskau, Dietrich (baritone); Berlin, Germany, 5/28/1925.
Fisher, Eddie (Edwin) (singer); Philadelphia, Pa., 8/10/1928.
Fiske, Minnie Maddern (née Davey) (actress); b. New Orleans, La. **(1865–1932)**.
Fittipaldi, Emerson (auto racer); São Paolo, Brazil, 12/12/1946.
Fitzgerald, Barry (William Joseph Shields) (actor); b. Dublin, Ireland **(1888–1961)**.
Fitzgerald, Ella (singer); Newport News, Va., 4/25/1918.
Fitzgerald, Geraldine (actress); Dublin, Ireland, 11/24/1914.
Fitzgerald, F. Scott (Francis Scott Key) (novelist); b. St. Paul, Minn. **(1896–1940)**.
Fitzsimmons, Bob (Robert Prometheus) (boxer); b. Cornwall, England **(1862–1917)**.
Flack, Roberta (singer); Black Mountain, N.C., 2/10/1940.
Flagstad, Kirsten (Wagnerian soprano); b. Hamar, nr. Oslo, Norway **(1895–1962)**.
Flaubert, Gustave (novelist); b. Rouen, France **(1821–1880)**.
Fleming, Peggy Gale (ice skating); San Jose, Calif., 7/27/1948.
Fleming, Rhonda (Marilyn Louis) (actress); Los Angeles, Calif., 8/10/1923.
Fleming, Sir Alexander (bacteriologist); b. Lochfield, Scotland **(1881–1955)**.
Flynn, Errol (actor); b. Hobart, Tasmania **(1909–1959)**.
Foch, Nina (actress); Leyden, Netherlands, 4/20/1924.
Fodor, Eugene (violinist); Turkey Creek, Colo., 3/5/1950.
Fonda, Henry (actor); Grand Island, Neb., 5/16/1905.
Fonda, Jane (actress); New York City, 12/21/1937.
Fonda, Peter (actor); New York City, 2/23/1939.
Fontaine, Frank (singer, comedian); Cambridge, Mass., 1920.
Fontaine, Joan (actress); Tokyo, Japan, 10/22/1917.
Fontanne, Lynn (actress); London, England, 12/6/1887(?).
Fonteyn, Dame Margot (Margaret Hookham) (ballerina); Reigate, England, 5/18/1919.
Forbes, Malcolm S(tevenson) (publisher, sportsman); Brooklyn, N.Y., 8/19/1919.
Ford, Glenn (Gwyllyn Ford) (actor); Quebec, Canada, 5/1/1916.
Ford, Henry (industrialist); b. Greenfield, Mich. **(1863–1947)**.
Ford, Henry, II (auto maker); Detroit, Mich., 9/4/1917.
Ford, John (director); b. Cape Elizabeth, Me. **(1895–1973)**.
Ford, Paul (actor); b. Baltimore, Md. **(1901–1976)**.
Ford, Tennessee Ernie (singer); Bristol, Tenn., 2/13/1919.
Ford, Whitey (Edward) (baseball); New York City, 10/28/1928.
Foreman, George (boxing); Marshall, Tex., 1/10/1949.
Forsythe, John (actor); Carney's Point, N.J., 1/29/1918.
Fosbury, Richard (high jumper); Portland, Ore., 3/6/1947.
Fosdick, Harry Emerson (clergyman); b. Buffalo, N.Y. **(1878–1968)**.
Fosse, Bob (Robert Louis) (choreographer); Chicago, Ill., 6/23/1927.
Foster, Stephen Collins (composer); b. nr. Pittsburgh, Pa. **(1826–1864)**.
Fox, Nellie (Jacob Nelson) (baseball); b. St. Thomas, Pa. **(1927–1975)**.
Foxx, Redd (John Elroy Sanford) (actor, comedian); St. Louis, Mo., 12/9/1922.
Foy, Eddie, Jr. (dancer, actor); New Rochelle, N.Y., 2/4/1905.
Foyt, A. J. (auto racing); Houston, Tex., 1/16/1935.
Fracci, Carla (ballerina); Milan, Italy, 8/20/1936.
France, Anatole (Jacques Anatole François Thibault) (author); b. Paris, France **(1844–1924)**.
Francescatti, Zino (violinist); Marseilles, France, 8/9/1905.
Franciosa, Anthony (Anthony Papaleo) (actor); New York City, 10/25/1928.
Francis, Arlene (Arlene Francis Kazanjian) (actress); Boston, Mass. 1908.

Francis, Connie (Concetta Franconero) (singer); Newark, N.J., 12/12/1938.
Francis, Emile (hockey); North Battleford, Sask., 9/13/1926.
Francis, Kay (Katherine Edwina Gibbs) (actress); b. Oklahoma City, Okla. (1903–1968).
Franciscus, James (actor); Clayton, Mo., 1/31/1934.
Franck, César Auguste (composer); b. Liège, Belgium (1822–1890).
Franco Bahamonde, Francisco (Chief of State); b. El Ferrol, Spain (1892–1975).
Franklin, Aretha (singer); Memphis, Tenn., 3/25/1942.
Franklin, Benjamin (statesman & scientist); b. Boston, Mass. (1706–1790).
Frazer, Sir James George (anthropologist); b. Glasgow, Scotland (1854–1941).
Frazier, Joe (boxing); Beauford, S.C., 1/17/1944.
Frazier, Walt (basketball); Atlanta, Ga., 3/29/1945.
Freud, Sigmund (psychoanalyst); b. Freiberg, Moravia (1856–1939).
Frick, Ford C. (baseball); Wawaka, Ind., 12/19/1894.
Friedan, Betty (Betty Naomi Goldstein) (feminist); Peoria, Ill., 2/4/1921.
Fromm, Erich (psychoanalyst); Frankfurt-am-Main, Germany, 3/23/1900.
Frost, David (TV entertainer); Tenterden, Kent, England, 4/7/1939.
Frost, Robert Lee (poet); b. San Francisco, Calif. (1874–1963).
Fry, Christopher (playwright); Bristol, England, 12/18/1907.
Frye, David (impressionist); Brooklyn, N.Y., 1934.
Fuller, R(ichard) Buckminster (Jr.) (architect, educator); Milton, Mass., 7/12/1895.
Fulton, Robert (inventor); b. Lancaster County, Pa. (1765–1815).
Funston, George Keith (business executive); Waterloo, Iowa, 10/12/1910.
Funt, Allen (TV Producer); Brooklyn, N.Y., 9/16/1914.
Furness, Betty (Elizabeth) (actress, consumer advocate); New York City, 1/3/1916.
Gabel, Martin (actor, producer); Philadelphia, Pa., 1912.
Gabin, Jean (actor); Paris, France, 5/17/1904.
Gable, Dan (wrestling); Waterloo, Iowa, 10/25/1945.
Gable, (William) Clark (actor); b. Cadiz, Ohio (1901–1960).
Gabo, Naum (sculptor); Briansk, Russia, 8/5/1890.
Gabor, Eva (actress); Budapest, Hungary, 2/11/1926(?).
Gabor, Zsa Zsa (Sari) (actress); Budapest, Hungary, 2/6/1923.
Gabriel, Roman (football); Wilmington, N.C., 8/5/1940.
Galbraith, John Kenneth (economist); Iona Station, Ontario, Canada, 10/15/1908.
Galilei, Galileo (astronomer & physicist); b. Pisa, Italy (1564–1642).
Gallagher, Michael Donald (skiing); Yonkers, N.Y., 10/3/1941.
Gallico, Paul (novelist); b. New York City, (1897–1976).
Gallup, George H. (poll taker); Jefferson, Iowa, 11/18/1901.
Galsworthy, John (novelist & dramatist); b. Coombe, Surrey, England (1867–1933).
Gam, Rita (actress); Pittsburgh, Pa., 4/2/1928.
Gandhi, Indira (Indira Nehru) (Prime Minister); Alahabad, India, 11/19/1917.
Gandhi, Mohandas Karamchand (called Mahatma Gandhi) (Hindu leader); b. Porbandar, India (1869–1948).
Garbo, Greta (Greta Gustafsson) (actress); Stockholm, Sweden, 9/18/1905.
Gardner, Ava (actress); Smithfield, N.C., 12/24/1922.
Gardner, Erle Stanley (author); b. Malden, Mass. (1889–1970).
Garfield, John (Jules Garfinkle) (actor); b. New York City (1913–1952).
Garfunkel, Art (Arthur) (singer); New York City, 10/1942.
Gargan, William (actor); Brooklyn, N.Y., 7/17/1905.
Garibaldi, Giuseppe (Italian nationalist leader); b. Nice, France (1807–1882).
Garland, Judy (Frances Gumm) (actress, singer); b. Grand Rapids, Minn. (1922–1969).
Garner, Erroll (jazz pianist); Pittsburgh, Pa., 5/15/1921.
Garner, James (James Bumgarner) (actor); Norman, Okla., 4/7/1928.
Garner, Peggy Ann (actress); Canton, Ohio, 2/3/1932.
Garrick, David (actor); b. Hereford, Herefordshire, England (1717–1779).
Garrison, William Lloyd (abolitionist); b. Newburyport, Mass. (1805–1879).
Garroway, Dave (TV host); Schenectady, N.Y., 7/13/1913.
Garson, Greer (actress); County Down, Northern Ireland, 9/29/1912(?).
Gary, John (singer); Watertown, N.Y., 11/29/1932.
Gassman, Vittorio (actor); Genoa, Italy, 9/1/1922.
Gaudi, Antonio (architect); b. Reus, Tarragona, Spain (1852–1926).
Gautama Buddha (Prince Siddhartha) (philosopher); b. Kapilavastu, India (563?–483 B.C.).
Gavin, John (actor); Los Angeles, Calif., 4/8/1935.
Gaynor, Janet (actress); Philadelphia, Pa., 10/6/1906.
Gaynor, Mitzi (Francesca Mitzi Marlene de Czanyi von Gerber) (actress); Chicago, Ill., 9/4/1931.
Gazzara, Ben (Biago Anthony Gazzara) (actor); New York City, 8/28/1930.
Geddes, Barbara Bel (actress); New York City, 10/31/1922.

Gehrig, Lou (Henry Louis Gehrig) (baseball); b. New York City (1903–1941).
Gehringer, Charlie (baseball); Fowlerville, Mich., 5/11/1903.
Genet, Jean (playwright); Paris, France, 12/19/1910.
Geneviève (Ginette Marguerite Auger) (entertainer); Paris, France, 4/17/1930.
Genghis Khan (Temujin) (conqueror); b. nr. Lake Baikal in Asia (1162–1227).
Genn, Leo (actor); London, England, 8/9/1905.
Gentry, Bobbie (singer); Chickasaw Co., Miss., 1944.
Geoffrion, Bernie (Boom Boom) (hockey); Montreal, Canada, 2/14/1931.
Gericault, Jean Louis (painter); b. Rouen, France (1791–1824).
Gernreich, Rudi (fashion designer); Vienna, Austria, 8/8/1922.
Geronimo (Goyathlay) (Apache chieftain); b. Arizona (1829–1909).
Gershwin, George (composer); b. Brooklyn, N.Y. (1898–1937).
Gershwin, Ira (lyricist); New York City, 12/6/1896.
Getty, J. Paul (oil executive); b. Minneapolis, Minn. (1892–1976).
Getz, Stan (saxophonist); Philadelphia, Pa., 2/2/1927.
Giacomin, Ed (hockey); Sudbury, Ontario, Canada, 6/6/1939.
Gibbon, Edward (historian); b. Putney, England (1737–1794).
Gibson, Bob (baseball); Omaha, Neb., 11/9/1935.
Gibson, Charles Dana (illustrator); b. Roxbury, Mass. (1867–1944).
Gibson, Hoot (Edward) (actor); b. Tememah, Neb. (1892–1962).
Gide, André (author); b. Paris, France (1869–1951).
Gielgud, Sir John (actor); London, England, 4/14/1904.
Gifford, Frank (football; TV broadcaster); Santa Monica, Calif., 8/16/1930.
Gilbert, John (movie actor); b. Logan, Utah (1897–1936).
Gilbert, Rod (Rodrique) (hockey); Montreal, Canada, 7/1/1941.
Gilbert, Sir William Schwenck (librettist); b. London, England (1836–1911).
Gilels, Emil (pianist); Odessa, Ukraine, 1916.
Giles, Warren (baseball); Tiskilwa, Ill., 5/28/1896.
Gillespie, Dizzy (John Birks Gillespie) (trumpeter); Cheraw, S.C., 10/21/1917.
Gilmore, Artis (basketball); Chiplia, Fla., 9/21/1949.
Gingold, Hermione (actress); London, England, 12/9/1897.
Ginsberg, Allen (poet); Newark, N.J., 6/3/1926.
Giorgione (painter); b. Castelfranco, Italy (c. 1477–1510).
Giovanni, Nikki (poet); Knoxville, Tenn., 6/7/1943.
Giroud, Françoise (French government official); Geneva, Switzerland, 9/21/1916.
Gish, Dorothy (actress); Massillon, Ohio (1898–1968).
Gish, Lillian (actress); Springfield, Ohio, 10/14/1896.
Givenchy, Hubert (fashion designer); Beauvais, France, 2/21/1927.
Gladstone, William Ewart (statesman); b. Liverpool, England (1809–1898).
Gleason, Jackie (actor); Brooklyn, N.Y., 2/26/1916.
Glenn, John Herschel, Jr. (astronaut, Senator); Cambridge, Ohio, 7/18/1921.
Gluck, Christoph Willibald (composer); b. Erasbach, Bavaria (1714–1787).
Godard, Jean Luc (film director); Paris, France, 12/3/1930.
Goddard, Paulette (actress); Great Neck, N.Y., 6/3/1911.
Godfrey, Arthur (entertainer); New York City, 8/31/1903.
Goebbels, Joseph Paul (Nazi leader); b. Rheydt, Germany (1897–1945).
Goering, Hermann (Nazi leader); b. Rosenheim, Bavaria (1893–1946).
Goethals, George Washington (engineer); b. Brooklyn, N.Y. (1858–1928).
Goethe, Johann Wolfgang von (poet); b. Frankfurt am Main, Germany (1749–1832).
Gogol, Nikolai Vasilievich (novelist); b. nr. Mirgorod, Poltava, Ukraine (1809–1852).
Golden, Harry (Harry Goldhurst) (author); New York City, 5/6/1902.
Goldsmith, Oliver (dramatist & poet); b. County Longford, Ireland (1728–1774).
Goldwyn, Samuel (Samuel Goldfish) (movie producer); b. Warsaw, Poland (1882–1974).
Golenpaul, Dan (creator of Information Please quiz show and editor of almanac of same name); b. New York City (1900–1974).
Gompers, Samuel (labor leader); b. London, England (1850–1924).
Gonzalez, Pancho (tennis); Los Angeles, Calif., 5/9/1928.
Goodall, Jane. See van-Lawick-Goodall.
Goodman, Benny (clarinetist); Chicago, Ill., 5/30/1909.
Goodyear, Charles (inventor); b. New Haven, Conn. (1800–1860).
Goolagong, Evonne (tennis); Griffith, Australia, 7/31/1951.
Gordon, Max (producer); New York City, 1892.
Gordon, Richard Francis, Jr. (astronaut); Seattle, Wash., 10/5/1929.
Gordon, Ruth (actress); Wollaston, Mass., 10/30/1896.
Gore, Albert A. (ex-Senator); Granville, Tenn., 12/26/1907.
Gore, Lesley (singer); Tenafly, N.J., 1946.
Goren, Charles H. (bridge expert); Philadelphia, Pa., 3/4/1901.
Gorki, Maxim (Alexei Maximovich Peshkov) (author); b. Nizhni Novgorod, Russia (1868–1936).
Gorman, Tom (Thomas Warner) (tennis); Seattle, Wash., 1/19/1946.
Gormé, Eydie (singer); New York City, 8/16/1932.
Gorshin, Frank (actor); Pittsburg, Pa., 4/5/1934.

Gosden, Freeman F. *See* Amos.

Gould, Chester (cartoonist); Pawnee, Okla., 11/20/1900.

Gould, Elliott (actor); Brooklyn, N.Y., 8/29/1938.

Gould, Glenn (pianist); Toronto, Canada, 9/25/1932.

Gould, Morton (composer); Richmond Hill, N.Y., 12/10/1913.

Goulet, Robert (singer); Lawrence, Mass., 11/26/1933.

Gounod, Charles François (composer); b. Paris, France (1818–1893).

Grable, Betty (actress); b. St. Louis, Mo. (1916–1973).

Graebner, Clark Edward (tennis); Cleveland, Ohio, 11/4/1943.

Graham, Billy (William F.) (evangelist); Charlotte, N.C., 11/7/1918.

Graham, Katharine Meyer (newspaper publisher); New York City, 6/16/1917.

Graham, Martha (choreographer); Pittsburgh, Pa., 5/11/1894(?).

Graham, Otto Everett (football); Waukegan, Ill., 12/6/1921.

Grahame, Gloria (actress); Los Angeles, Calif., 11/28/1929.

Gramm, Donald (bass-baritone); Milwaukee, Wis., 2/26/1927.

Grange, Red (Harold) (football); Forskville, Pa., 6/13/1904.

Granger, Farley (actor); San Jose, Calif., 7/1/1925.

Granger, Stewart (James Stewart) (actor); London, England, 5/6/1913.

Grant, Cary (Alexander Archibald Leach) (actor); Bristol, England, 1/18/1904.

Grant, Lee (Lyova Haskell Rosenthal) (actress); New York City, 10/31/1929(?).

Granville, Bonita (actress and producer); New York City, 1923.

Grass, Günter (novelist); Danzig, Poland, 10/16/1927.

Grauer, Ben (radio and television announcer); New York City, 6/2/1908.

Graves, Peter (actor); Minneapolis, Minn., 3/18/1926.

Graves, Robert (poet); London, England, 7/26/1895.

Gray, Barry (Bernard Yaroslaw) (radio interviewer); Atlantic City, N.J., 7/2/1916.

Gray, Dolores (singer, actress); Chicago, Ill., 6/7/1930.

Gray, Thomas (poet); b. London, England (1716–1771).

Grayson, Kathryn (Zelma Hednick) (singer, actress); Winston-Salem, N.C., 2/9/1923.

Greco, Buddy (singer); Philadelphia, Pa., 8/14/1926.

Greco, José (dancer); Montorio nei Frentani, Italy, 12/23/1918.

Greeley, Horace (journalist & politican); b. Amherst, N.H., (1811–1872).

Green, Adolph (actor, lyricist); New York City, 12/2/1915.

Green, Paul (playwright); Lillington, N.C., 3/17/1894.

Greene, Charles E. (sprinter); Pine Bluff, Ark., 3/21/1945.

Greene, Graham (novelist); Berkhamsted, England, 10/2/1904.

Greene, Lorne (actor); Ottawa, Ont., Canada, 2/12/1915.

Greene, Martyn (actor); b. London, England (1899–1975).

Greenstreet, Sydney (actor); b. Sandwich, Kent, England (1879–1954).

Greenwood, Joan (actress, director); London, England, 3/4/1921.

Greer, Germaine (feminist); Melbourne, Australia, 1/29/1939.

Gregory, Dick (comedian); St. Louis, Mo., 1932.

Greuze, Jean-Baptiste (painter); b. Tournus, France (1725–1805).

Grey, Joel (Joel Katz) (actor); Cleveland, Ohio, 4/11/1932.

Grey, Zane (author); b. Zanesville, Ohio (1875–1939).

Grieg, Edvard Hagerup (composer); b. Bergen, Norway (1843–1907).

Grier, Roosevelt (entertainer; former athlete); Cuthbert, Ga., 7/14/1932.

Griese, Bob (Robert Allen) (football); Evansville, Ind., 2/3/1945.

Griffin, Merv (TV entertainer); San Mateo, Calif., 7/6/1925.

Griffith, Andy (actor); Mount Airy, N.C., 6/1/1926.

Griffith, David Lewelyn Wark (movie producer); b. La Grange, Ky. (1875–1948).

Grigorovich, Yuri (choreographer); Leningrad, U.S.S.R., 1/1/1927.

Grimes, Tammy (actress); Lynn, Mass., 1/30/1934.

Grimm, Jacob (author of fairy tales); b. Hanau, Germany (1785–1863).

Grimm, Wilhelm (author of fairy tales); b. Hanau, Germany (1786–1859).

Grizzard, George (actor); Roanoke Rapids, N.C., 4/1/1928.

Gromyko, Andrei A. (diplomat); Starye Gromyki, Russia, 7/5/1909.

Gropper, William (painter, illustrator); New York City, 12/3/1897.

Grove, Lefty (Robert Moses) (baseball); b. Lonaconing, Md. (1900–1975).

Groza, Lou (football); Martins Ferry, Ohio, 1/25/1924.

Guardino, Harry (actor); New York City, 12/23/1925.

Guinness, Sir Alec (actor); Marylebone, London, England, 4/2/1914.

Guitry, Sacha (Alexandre) (actor & movie director); b. St. Petersburg, Russia (1895–1957).

Gunter, Nancy Richey (tennis); San Angelo, Tex., 8/23/1942.

Gunther, John (author); b. Chicago, Ill. (1901–1970).

Gutenberg, Johann (printer); b. Mainz, Germany (1400?–1468?).

Guthrie, Arlo (singer); New York City, 7/10/1947.

Guthrie, Woody (folk-singer, composer); Okemah, Okla. (1912–1967).

Hackett, Bobby (trumpeter); b. Providence, R.I., (1915–1976).

Hackett, Buddy (Leonard Hacker) (comedian, actor); Brooklyn, N.Y., 8/31/1924.

Hackman, Gene (actor); San Bernardino, Calif., 1/30/1931.

Hadl, John Willard (football); Lawrence, Kan., 2/15/1940.

Hagan, Uta (actress); Göttingen, Germany, 6/12/1919.

Haggard, Merle (songwriter); Bakersfield, Calif., 4/6/1937.

Haig, Alexander Meigs, Jr. (general); Bala-Cynwyd, Pa., 12/2/1924.

Haile Selassie (Ras Tafari Makonnen) (ex-Emperor); b. Ethiopia (1892–1975).

Hailey, Arthur (novelist); Luton, England, 4/5/1920.

Haise, Fred W., Jr. (astronaut); Biloxi, Miss., 11/14/1933.

Halas, George (football); Chicago, Ill., 2/2/1895.

Halberstam, David (journalist); New York City, 4/10/1934.

Hale, Nathan (American Revolutionary officer); b. Coventry, Conn. (1755–1776).

Hall, Albert W. (weight thrower); Manchester, N.H., 8/2/1934.

Hall, Gary (swimming); Fayetteville, N.C., 8/7/1951.

Halsey, William Frederick Jr. (naval officer); b. Elizabeth, N.J. (1882–1959).

Hamill, Dorothy (figure skater); Riverside, Greenwich, Conn., 1956(?).

Hamill, Pete (journalist); Brooklyn, N.Y., 6/24/1935.

Hamilton, Alexander (statesman); b. Leeward Is. (1757?–1804).

Hamilton, George (actor); Memphis, Tenn., 8/12/1939.

Hamlisch, Marvin (composer, pianist); New York City, 6/2/1944.

Hammarskjold, Dag (U.N. statesman); b. Jönköping, Sweden (1905–1961).

Hammerstein, Oscar, II (librettist, producer); b. New York City (1895–1960).

Hammond, Kathy (runner); Sacramento, Calif., 11/2/1951.

Hampden, Walter (Walter Hampden Dougherty) (actor); b. Brooklyn, N.Y. (1879–1955).

Hampton, James (actor); Oklahoma City, Okla., 7/9/1936.

Hampton, Lionel (vibraharpist, band leader); Birmingham, Ala., 4/20/1914.

Hancock, John (statesman); b. Braintree, Mass. (1737–1793).

Hand, Learned (jurist); b. Albany, N.Y. (1872–1961).

Handel, George Frederick (Georg Friedrich Händel) (composer); b. Halle, Germany (1685–1759).

Handy, William Christopher (blues composer); b. Florence, Ala. (1873–1958).

Hannibal (Carthaginian general) (247–183 B.C.).

Hanson, Howard (conductor); Wahoo, Neb., 10/28/1896.

Harburg, E. Y. "Yip" (lyricist); New York City, 4/8/1898.

Harding, Ann (actress); San Antonio, Tex. 8/7/1902.

Hardwicke, Sir Cedric (actor); b. Stourbridge, Worcestershire, England (1893–1964).

Hardy, Oliver (comedian); b. Atlanta, Ga. (1892–1957).

Hardy, Thomas (novelist); b. Dorsetshire, England (1840–1928).

Harlow, Jean (Harlean Carpentier) (actress); b. Kansas City, Mo. (1911–1937).

Harnick, Sheldon (songwriter); Chicago, Ill., 4/30/1924.

Harper, Valerie (actress); Suffern, N.Y., Aug. 22, 1940(?).

Harriman, W. (William) Averell (ex-Governor of New York); New York City, 11/15/1891.

Harris, Barbara (actress); Evanston, Ill., 1935.

Harris, Jed (producer); Vienna, Austria, 2/25/1900.

Harris, Julie (actress); Grosse Pointe Park, Mich., 12/2/1925.

Harris, Phil (actor); Linton, Ind., 6/24/1906.

Harris, Richard (actor); Limerick, Ireland, 10/1/1933.

Harris, Rosemary (actress); Ashby, Suffolk, England, 9/19/1930.

Harris, Roy (composer); Lincoln County, Okla., 2/12/1898.

Harrison, George (singer); Liverpool, England, 2/25/1943.

Harrison, Noel (actor); London, England, 1/29/1936.

Harrison, Rex (actor); Huyton, England, 3/5/1908.

Hart, Moss (dramatist); b. New York City (1904–1961).

Hart, William S. (actor); b. Newburgh, N.Y. (1862–1946).

Hartack, William, Jr. (jockey); Colver, Pa., 12/9/1932.

Harte, Bret (Francis Brett Harte) (author); b. Albany, N.Y. (1836–1902).

Hartford, Huntington (George Huntington Hartford II) (A. & P. heir); New York City, 4/18/1911.

Hartman, Elizabeth (actress); Youngstown, Ohio, 12/23/1941.

Harvey, Doug (hockey); South Gate, Calif., 3/13/1930.

Harvey, Laurence (actor); b. Joniskis, Lithuania (1928–1973).

Harvey, William (physician); b. Folkestone, Kent, England (1578–1657).

Hasso, Signe (actress); Stockholm, Sweden, 8/15/1915.

Haughton, William (harness racing); Gloversville, N.Y., 11/2/1923.

Haver, June (actress); Rock Island, Ill., 6/10/1926.

Havlicek, John (basketball); Martins Ferry, Ohio, 4/8/1940.

Havoc, June (June Hovick) (actress); Seattle, Wash.

Hawkins, Jack (actor); b. London, England (1910–1973).

Hawn, Goldie (actress); Washington, D.C., 11/21/1945.

Haworth, Jill (actress); Sussex, England, 1945.

Hawthorne, Nathaniel (novelist); b. Salem, Mass. (1804–1864).

Hay, John Milton (statesman); b. Salem, Ind. (1838–1905).

Hayakawa, Sessue (actor); b. Honshu, Japan (1890–1973).

Hayden, Melissa (ballerina); Toronto, Canada, 4/25/1928.

Haydn, Franz Joseph (composer); b. Rohrau, Austria (1732–1809).

Hayes, Helen (Helen Hayes Brown) (actress); Washington, D.C., 10/10/1900.

Hayes, Isaac (composer); Covington, Tenn., 8/20/1942.

Haynie, Sandra (golf); Fort Worth, Tex., 6/4/1943.

Hayward, Susan (Edythe Marrener) (actress); b. Brooklyn, N.Y. (1919–1975).

Hayworth, Rita (Margarita Cansino) (actress); New York City, 10/17/1918.

Head, Edith (costume designer); Los Angeles, Calif., 10/28/1907.

Hearst, William Randolph (publisher); b. San Francisco, Calif. (1863–1951).

Hearst, William Randolph, Jr. (publisher); New York City, 1/27/1908.

Heath, Edward (ex-Prime Minister); Broadstairs, England, 7/9/1916.

Heatherton, Joey (actress); Rockville Centre, N.Y., 9/14/1944.

Hecht, Ben (author); b. New York City **(1894–1964)**.

Heckart, Eileen (actress); Columbus, Ohio, 3/29/1919.

Heflin, Van (Emmet Evan Heflin) (actor); b. Walters, Okla. **(1910–1971)**.

Hefner, Hugh (publisher); Chicago, Ill., 4/9/1926.

Hegel, Georg Wilhelm Friedrich (philosopher); b. Stuttgart, Germany **(1770–1831)**.

Heifetz, Jascha (violinist); Vilna, Russia, 2/2/1901.

Heine, Heinrich (Harry) (poet); b. Düsseldorf, Germany **(1797–1856)**.

Heinemann, Gustav (ex-President of Germany); b. Schweim, Westphalia **(1899–1976)**.

Heller, Joseph (novelist); Brooklyn, N.Y., 5/1/1923.

Hellman, Lillian (playwright); New Orleans, La., 6/20/1905.

Hemingway, Ernest Miller (author); b. Oak Park, Ill. **(1899–1961)**.

Hencken, John (swimming); Culver City, Calif., 5/29/1954.

Henderson, Florence (actress); Dale, Ind., 2/14/1934.

Henderson, Skitch (Lyle Russell Cedric) (conductor, pianist); Birmingham, England(?), 1/27/1918.

Henie, Sonja (ice skater); b. Oslo, Norway **(1912–1969)**.

Henreid, Paul (actor); Trieste, 1/10/1908.

Henri, Robert (painter); b. Cincinnati, Ohio **(1865–1926)**.

Henry, O. (William Sydney Porter) (story writer); b. Greensboro, N.C. **(1862–1910)**.

Henry, Patrick (statesman); b. Hanover Co., Va. **(1736–1799)**.

Hepburn, Audrey (actress); Brussels, Belgium, 5/4/1929.

Hepburn, Katharine (actress); Hartford, Conn., 11/8/1909.

Hepplewhite, George (furniture designer); b. England **(?–1786)**.

Hepworth, Barbara (sculptor); b. Wakefield, England **(1903–1975)**.

Herbert, Hugh (comedian); b. Binghamton, N.Y. **(1887–1952)**.

Herbert, Victor (composer); b. Dublin, Ireland **(1859–1924)**.

Herblock (Herbert L. Block) (political cartoonist); Chicago, Ill., 10/13/1909.

Herman, Woody (Woodrow Charles) (band leader); Milwaukee, Wis., 5/16/1913.

Herod (Herodes) (called Herod the Great) (King of Judea) **(73?–4 B.C.)**.

Herodotus (historian); b. Halicarnassus, Asia Minor **(c. 484–425 B.C.)**.

Hershfield, Harry (humorist and raconteur); b. Cedar Rapids, Iowa **(1885–1974)**.

Hersholt, Jean (actor); b. Copenhagen, Denmark **(1886–1956)**.

Heston, Charlton (actor); Evanston, Ill., 10/4/1924.

Heyerdahl, Thor (ethnologist, explorer); Larvik, Norway, 10/6/1914.

Hickcox, Charles (swimming); Phoenix, Ariz., 2/6/1947.

Hildegarde (Hildegarde Loretta Sell) (singer); Adell, Wis., 2/1/1906.

Hillary, Sir Edmund (mountain climber); New Zealand, 7/20/1919.

Hiller, Wendy (actress); Bramhall, England, 8/15/1912.

Hilliard, Harriet. *See* Nelson, Harriet.

Hindemith, Paul (composer); b. Hanau, Germany **(1895–1963)**.

Hindenburg, Paul von (statesman); b. Posen, Prussia **(1847–1934)**.

Hines, Earl "Fatha" (pianist); Duquesne, Pa., 12/28/1905.

Hines, James (sprinter); Dumas, Ark., 9/10/1946.

Hines, Jerome (Jerome Heinz) (basso); Los Angeles, Calif., 11/8/1921.

Hines, Mimi (actress and singer); Vancouver, B.C., Canada, 1933.

Hingle, Pat (actor); Denver, Colo., 7/19/1924.

Hippocrates (physician); b. Kos, Dodecanese **(406?–377 B.C.)**.

Hirohito (Emperor); Tokyo, Japan, 4/29/1901.

Hirschfeld, Al (Albert) (cartoonist); St. Louis, Mo., 6/21/1903.

Hirschhorn, Joseph Herman (financier, speculator, art collector); Mitau, Latvia, 8/11/1899.

Hirt, Al (trumpeter); New Orleans, La., 11/7/1922.

Hitchcock, Alfred J. (director); London, England, 8/13/1899.

Hitler, Adolf (Schicklgruber) (German dictator); b. Braunau, Austria **(1899–1945)**.

Hobson, Laura Z. (Laura K. Zametkin) (novelist); New York City.

Hodges, Eddie (actor); Hattiesburg, Miss., 3/5/1947.

Hodges, Gil (baseball); b. Princeton, Ind. **(1924–1972)**.

Hoffa, James R(iddle) (labor leader); Brazil, Ind., 2/14/1913.

Hoffman, Dustin (actor, director); Los Angeles, Calif., 8/8/1937.

Hogan, Ben (golf); Dublin, Tex., 8/13/1912.

Holbein, Hans (the Elder) (painter); b. Augsburg, Bavaria **(1465?–1524)**.

Holbein, Hans (the Younger) (painter); b. Augsburg, Bavaria **(1497?–1543)**.

Holbrook, Hal (actor); Cleveland, Ohio, 2/17/1925.

Holden, William (William Franklin Beedle, Jr.) (actor); O'Fallon, Ill., 4/17/1918.

Holder, Geoffrey (dancer); Port-of-Spain, Trinidad, W.I., 8/1/1930.

Holliday, Judy (Judith Tuvim) (actress); b. New York City **(1922–1965)**.

Holloway, Stanley (actor); London, England, 10/1/1890.

Holloway, Sterling (actor); Cedartown, Ga.

Holm, Celeste (actress); New York City, 4/29/1919.

Holmes, Oliver Wendell (author); b. Cambridge, Mass. **(1809–1894)**.

Holmes, Oliver Wendell (jurist); b. Boston, Mass. **(1841–1935)**.

Holt, Jack (actor); b. Winchester, Va. **(1888–1951)**.

Holtz, Lou (comedian); San Francisco, Calif., 4/11/1898.

Home, Lord (Alexander Frederick Douglas-Home) (diplomat); London, England, 7/2/1903.

Homer (Greek poet) **(c. 850 B.C.?)**.

Homolka, Oscar (actor); Vienna, Austria, 1898.

Honegger, Arthur (composer); b. Le Havre, France **(1892–1955)**.

Hook, Sidney (philosopher); New York City, 12/20/1902.

Hoover, J. Edgar (FBI director); b. Washington, D.C. **(1895–1972)**.

Hope, Bob (Leslie Townes Hope) (comedian); London, England, 5/29/1903.

Hopper, Dennis (actor); Dodge City, Kan., 5/17/1936.

Horace (Quintus Horatius Flaccus) (poet); b. Venosa, Lucania **(65–8 B.C.)**.

Horne, Lena (singer); Brooklyn, N.Y., 6/30/1917.

Horne, Marilyn (soprano); Bradford, Pa., 1/16/1934.

Hornsby, Rogers (baseball coach); b. Winters, Tex. **(1896–1963)**.

Hornung, Paul (football); Louisville, Ky., 12/23/1935.

Horowitz, Vladimir (pianist); Kiev, Russia, 10/1/1904.

Horton, Edward Everett (comedian); b. Brooklyn, N.Y. **(1887–1970)**.

Houdini, Harry (Ehrich Weiss) (magician); b. Appleton, Wis. **(1874–1926)**.

Hough, Lawrence A. (rowing); Janesville, Wis., 4/4/1944.

Houk, Ralph (baseball); Lawrence, Kan., 8/9/1919.

Houseman, John (John Haussmann) (producer-director); Bucharest, Romania, 9/22/1902.

Housman, Alfred Edward (poet); b. Fockburg, Worcestershire, England **(1859–1936)**.

Houston, Samuel (political leader); b. Rockbridge Co., Va. **(1793–1863)**.

Howard, Elston (baseball); St. Louis, Mo., 2/23/1930.

Howard, Frank (baseball); Columbus, Ohio, 8/8/1936.

Howard, Leslie (Leslie Stainer) (actor); b. London, England **(1893–1943)**.

Howard, Trevor (actor); Kent, England, 9/29/1916.

Howe, Elias (inventor); b. Spencer, Mass. **(1819–1867)**.

Howe, Gordon (hockey); Floral, Sask., Canada, 3/31/1928.

Howell, Jim Lee (football); Lonoke, Ark., 9/27/1914.

Howes, Sally Ann (actress); London, England, 7/20/1934.

Hubbell, Carl (baseball); Carthage, Mo., 6/22/1903.

Hudson, Henry (English navigator) **(?–1611)**.

Hudson, Rock (born Roy Scherer, Jr.; took Roy Fitzgerald as legal name) (actor); Winnetka, Ill., 11/17/1925.

Huff, Sam (Robert Lee) (football); Morgantown, W. Va., 10/4/1934.

Hughes, Charles Evans (jurist); b. Glens Falls, N.Y. **(1862–1948)**.

Hughes, Howard (industrialist, film producer); b. Houston, Tex., **(1905–1976)**.

Hugo, Victor Marie (author); b. Besançon, France **(1802–1885)**.

Hull, Bobby (hockey); Point Anne, Ontario, Canada, 1/3/1939.

Hume, David (philosopher); b. Edinburgh, Scotland **(1711–1776)**.

Humperdinck, Engelbert (composer); b. Siegburg, Germany **(1854–1921)**.

Humperdinck, Engelbert (Arnold Dorsey) (singer); Madras, India, 5/2/1936.

Hunt, Marsha (actress); Chicago, Ill., 10/17/1917.

Hunter, Jim (Catfish) (baseball); Hertford, N.C., 4/8/1946.

Hunter, Kim (Janet Cole) (actress); Detroit, Mich., 11/12/1922.

Hunter, Tab (Arthur Andrew Gelien) (actor); New York City, 7/11/1931.

Huntley, Chet (TV newscaster); b. Cardwell, Mont. **(1911–1974)**.

Hurok, Sol (impresario); b. Pogar, Russia **(1888–1974)**.

Hurst, Fannie (author); b. Hamilton, Ohio **(1889–1968)**.

Hussein I (King); Jordan, 5/2/1935.

Huston, John (film director, writer); Nevada, Mo., 8/5/1906.

Huston, Walter (Walter Houghston) (actor); b. Toronto, Ontario, Canada **(1884–1950)**.

Hutchins, Robert M. (educator); Brooklyn, N.Y., 1/17/1899.

Hutson, Donald (football); Pine Bluff, Ark., 1/31/1913.

Hutton, Barbara (Woolworth heiress); New York City, 11/14/1912.

Hutton, Betty (Betty Thornberg) (actress); Battle Creek, Mich., 2/26/1921.

Huxley, Aldous (author); b. Godalming, England **(1894–1963)**.

Huxley, Sir Julian S. (biologist, author); b. London, England **(1887–1975)**.

Huxley, Thomas Henry (biologist); b. Ealing, England **(1825–1895)**.

Ibsen, Henrik (dramatist); b. Skien, Norway **(1828–1906)**.

Inness, George (painter); b. nr. Newburgh, N.Y. **(1825–1894)**.

Insko, Del (harness racing); Amboy, Minn., 7/10/1931.

Ionesco, Eugène (playwright); Slatina, Romania, 11/26/1912.

Ireland, John (actor); Vancouver, B.C., Canada, 1/30/1915.

Irving, Washington (author); b. New York City **(1783–1859)**.

Irwin, Hale (golf); Joplin, Mo., 6/3/1945.

Isherwood, Christopher (novelist, playwright); nr. Dilsey and High Lane, Cheshire, England, 8/26/1904.

Iturbi, José (pianist); Valencia, Spain, 11/28/1895.

Ives, Burl (Icle Ivanhoe) (singer); Hunt, Ill., 6/14/1909.

Ives, Charles E(dward) (composer); b. Danbury, Conn. **(1874–1954)**.

Jackson, Anne (actress); Allegheny, Pa., 9/3/1926.

Jackson, Glenda (actress); Hoylake, England, 1937(?).

Jackson, Mahalia (gospel singer); b. New Orleans, La. **(1912–1972)**.

Jackson, Reggie (baseball); Wyncote, Pa., 5/18/1946.
Jackson, Rev. Jesse (civil rights leader); Greenville, N.C., 10/8/1941.
Jackson, Thomas Jonathan ("Stonewall") (general); b. Clarksburg, Va. (now W. Va.) **(1824–1863)**.
Jacobi, Lou (actor); Toronto, Ontario, Canada, 12/28/1913.
Jaffe, Sam (actor); New York City, 3/8/1898.
Jagger, Dean (actor); Lima, Ohio, 11/7/1903.
Jagger, Mick (Michael Philip) (singer); Dartford, England, 7/26/1944.
James, Harry (trumpeter); Albany, Ga., 3/15/1916.
James, Henry (novelist); b. New York City **(1843–1916)**.
James, Jesse Woodson (outlaw); b. Clay County Mo. **(1847–1882)**.
James, William (psychologist); b. New York City **(1842–1910)**.
Jameson, (Margaret) Storm (novelist); Whitby, England, 1897.
Janis, Byron (pianist); McKeesport, Pa., 3/24/1928.
Jannings, Emil (actor); b. Brooklyn, N.Y. **(1886–1950)**.
Janssen, David (actor); Naponee, Neb., 3/27/1930.
Jay, John (statesman & jurist); b. New York City **(1745–1829)**.
Jeanmaire, Renée (dancer); Paris, France, 4/29/1924.
Jeffries, James J. (boxer); b. Carroll, Ohio **(1875–1953)**.
Jenkins, Ferguson Arthur (baseball); Chatham, Ontario, Canada, 12/13/1943.
Jenner, Edward (physician); b. Berkeley, Glocestershire, England **(1749–1823)**.
Jenner, (W.) Bruce (track); Mt. Kisco, N.Y., 10/28/1949.
Jeritza, Maria (soprano); Brno, Moravia, 1888.
Jessel, George (entertainer); New York City, 4/3/1898.
Jessup, Philip C. (jurist); New York City, 1/5/1897.
Joan of Arc (Jeanne d'Arc) (saint & patriot); b. Domremy-la-Pucelle, France **(1412–1431)**.
Job, Brian (swimming); Warren, Ohio, 11/29/1951.
Joffrey, Robert (Abdullah Jaffa Bey Khan) (choreographer); Seattle, Wash., 12/24/1930.
John, Elton (Reginald Kenneth Dwight) (singer-pianist); Pinner, Middlesex, England, 3/25/1947.
Johns, Glynis (actress); Pretoria, South Africa, 10/5/1923.
Johnson, Anthony (rowing); Washington, D.C., 11/16/1940.
Johnson, Jack (John Arthur Johnson) (boxer); b. Galveston, Tex. **(1876–1946)**.
Johnson, Rafer (decathlon); Hillsboro, Tex., 8/18/1935.
Johnson, Samuel (lexicographer & author); b. Lichfield, Staffordshire, England **(1709–1784)**.
Johnson, Van (actor); Newport, R.I., 8/20/1916.
Joliot-Curie, Frédéric (physicist); b. Paris, France **(1900–1958)**.
Joliot-Curie, Irène (Irène Curie) (physicist); b. France **(1897–1956)**.
Jolliet (or Joliet), Louis (explorer); b. Beaupré, Canada **(1645–1700)**.
Jolson, Al (Asa Yoelson) (actor & singer); b. St. Petersburg, Russia **(1886–1950)**.
Jones, Carolyn (singer, actress); Amarillo, Tex., 4/28/1933.
Jones, Cleon (baseball); Plateau, Ala., 8/4/1942.
Jones, Deacon (David) (football); Eatonville, Fla., 12/9/1938.
Jones, Dean (actor); Morgan Co., Ala., 1/25/1935.
Jones, James (novelist); Robinson, Ill., 11/6/1921.
Jones, James Earl (actor); Arkabutla, Miss., 1/17/1931.
Jones, Jennifer (Phyllis Isley) (actress); Tulsa, Okla., 3/2/1919.
Jones, John Paul (John Paul) (naval officer); b. Scotland **(1747–1792)**.
Jones, Shirley (singer, actress); Smithtown, Pa., 3/31/1934.
Jones, Tom (Thomas Jones Woodward) (singer); Pontypridd, Wales, 6/7/1940.
Jong, Erica (writer); New York City, 3/26/1942.
Jonson, Ben (Benjamin) (poet & dramatist); b. Westminster, England **(1572–1637)**.
Jooss, Kurt (choreographer); Wasseralfingen, Würtemberg, Germany, 1/12/1901.
Joplin, Janis (singer); b. Port Arthur, Tex. **(1943–1970)**.
Jordan, James. See Fibber McGee.
Jory, Victor (actor); Dawson City, Yukon, Canada, 11/23/1903.
Jourdan, Louis (Louis Gendre) (actor); Marseilles, France, 6/19/1920.
Joyce, James (novelist); b. Dublin, Ireland **(1882–1941)**.
Juantoreno, Alberto (track); Santiago, Cuba, 12/3/1951.
Juárez, Benito Pablo (statesman); b. Guelatao, Oaxaca, Mexico **(1806–1872)**.
Juliana (Queen); The Hague, Netherlands, 4/30/1909.
Jung, Carl Gustav (psychoanalyst); b. Basel, Switz. **(1875–1961)**.
Jurado, Katy (actress); Guadalajara, Mexico, 1927.
Jurgensen, Sonny (football); Wilmington, N.C., 8/23/1934.
Kabalevsky, Dmitri (composer); St. Petersburg, Russia, 12/30/1904.
Kádár, János (Communist Party leader); Hungary, 1912.
Kaline, Al (Albert) (baseball); Baltimore, Md., 12/19/1934.
Kaminska, Ida (actress); Odessa, Russia, 9/4/1899.
Kanin, Garson (playwright); Rochester, N.Y., 11/24/1912.
Kant, Immanuel (philosopher); b. Königsberg, Prussia **(1724–1804)**.
Kantor, MacKinlay (novelist); Webster City, Iowa, 2/4/1904.
Karajan, Herbert von (conductor); Salzburg, Austria, 4/5/1908.
Karloff, Boris (William Henry Pratt) (actor); b. London, England **(1887–1969)**.
Kaufman, George S. (dramatist); b. Pittsburgh, Pa. **(1889–1961)**.

Kaye, Danny (David Daniel Kominski) (comedian); Brooklyn, N.Y., 1/18/1913.
Kaye, Nora (Nora Koreff) (ballerina); New York City, 1920.
Kaye, Sammy (band leader); Cleveland, Ohio, 3/13/1910.
Kazan, Elia (director); Constantinople, Turkey, 9/7/1909.
Kazan, Lanie (singer); New York City, 1940.
Keach, Stacy (actor); Savannah, Ga., 6/2/1941.
Keaton, Buster (Joseph Frank Keaton) (comedian); b. Piqua, Kan. **(1896–1966)**.
Keaton, Diane (actress); Santa Ana, Calif., 1946.
Keats, John (poet); b. London, England **(1795–1821)**.
Keel, Howard (singer, actor); Gillespie, Ill., 4/13/1919.
Keeler, Ruby (Lehy Keeler) (actress, dancer); Halifax, Nova Scotia, Canada, 8/25/1910.
Kefauver, Estes (legislator); b. Madisonville, Tenn. **(1903–1963)**.
Keino, Kipchoge (runner); Kapchemoiymo, Kenya, 1/1940.
Keith, Brian (actor); Bayonne, N.J., 11/14/1921.
Keller, Helen Adams (author & educator); b. Tuscumbia, Ala. **(1880–1968)**.
Kellerman, Sally (actress); Long Beach, Calif., 6/2/1938.
Kelly, Emmett (clown); Sedan, Kan., 12/9/1898.
Kelly, Gene (dancer, actor); Pittsburgh, Pa., 8/23/1912.
Kelly, Grace (Princess Grace of Monaco) (former actress); Philadelphia, Pa., 11/12/1929.
Kelly, Leroy (football); Philadelphia, Pa., 5/20/1942.
Kelly, Patsy (actress); Brooklyn, N.Y., 1/12/1910.
Kelly, Red (Leonard Patrick) (hockey); Simcoe, Ontario, Canada, 7/9/1927.
Kelly, Walt (cartoonist); b. Philadelphia, Pa. **(1913–1973)**.
Kemal Ataturk (Mustafa Kemal) (statesman); b. Salonika, Turkey **(1881–1938)**.
Kennan, George F. (diplomat); Milwaukee, Wis., 2/16/1904.
Kennedy, Arthur (actor); Worcester, Mass., 2/17/1914.
Kennedy, George (actor); New York City, 2/18/1925.
Kennedy, Jacqueline. See Jacqueline Onassis.
Kennedy, James Walter (basketball); Stamford, Conn., 6/8/1912.
Kennedy, Robert Francis (legislator); b. Brookline, Mass. **(1925–1968)**.
Kennedy, Rose Fitzgerald (President's mother); Boston, Mass., 7/22/1890.
Kent, Rockwell (painter); b. Tarrytown Heights, N.Y. **(1882–1971)**.
Kenton, Stan (musician); Wichita, Kan., 2/19/1912.
Kepler, Johannes (astronomer); b. Weil, Württemberg, Germany **(1571–1630)**.
Kerensky, Alexander Fedorovich (statesman); b. Simbirks, Russia **(1881–1970)**.
Kern, Jerome David (composer); b. New York City **(1885–1945)**.
Kerr, Deborah (actress); Helensburgh, Scotland, 9/30/1921.
Key, Francis Scott (lawyer); b. Frederick (now Carroll) County. Md. **(1779–1843)**.
Keyes, Frances Parkinson (novelist); Charlottesville, Va., 7/21/1885.
Keynes (1st Baron of Tilton) (John Maynard Keynes) (economist); b. Cambridge, England **(1883–1946)**.
Khachaturian, Aram (composer); Tiflis, Russia, 6/6/1903.
Khrushchev, Nikita S. (Soviet leader); Kalinovka, nr. Kursk, the Ukraine **(1894–1971)**.
Kibbee, Guy (actor); b. El Paso, Tex. **(1886–1956)**.
Kidd, Michael (choreographer); Brooklyn, N.Y., 1917.
Kidd, William (called Capt. Kidd) (pirate); b. Greenock, Scotland **(1645?–1701)**.
Kiepura, Jan (tenor); b. Sosnowiec, Poland **(1904?–1966)**.
Kieran, John (sports columnist); New York City, 8/2/1892.
Kiesinger, Kurt Georg (diplomat); Ebingen, Germany, 4/6/1904.
Kiley, Richard (actor, singer); Chicago, Ill., 3/31/1922.
Killebrew, Harmon (baseball); Payette, Idaho, 6/29/1936.
Killy, Jean Claude (skiing); Saint-Cloud, France, 8/30/1943.
Kilmer, Alfred Joyce (poet); b. New Brunswick, N.J. **(1886–1918)**.
Kilmer, Bill (William Orland) (football); Topeka, Kan., 9/5/1939.
King, Alan (entertainer); Brooklyn, N.Y., 12/26/1927.
King, Billie Jean (Billie Jean Moffitt) (tennis); Long Beach, Calif., 11/22/1943.
King, Carole (singer); Brooklyn, N.Y., 2/9/1941.
King, Coretta Scott (civil rights leader); Marion, Ala., 4/27/1927.
King, Harriet (fencing); New York City, 9/22/1935.
King, Martin Luther, Jr. (civil rights leader); b. Atlanta, Ga. **(1929–1968)**.
King, Micki (diving); Pontiac, Mich., 7/26/1944.
Kingsley, Sidney (Sidney Kirschner) (playwright); New York City, 10/18/1906.
Kinsella, John (swimming); Oak Park, Ill., 8/26/1952.
Kipling, Rudyard (author); b. Bombay, India **(1865–1936)**.
Kipnis, Alexander (basso); Ukraine, 2/1/1891.
Kirk, Grayson (educator); Jeffersonville, Ohio, 10/12/1903.
Kirk, Lisa (actress, singer); Charleroi, Pa., 1925.
Kirk, Phyllis (actress); Plainfield, N.J., 9/18/1930.
Kirkland, Gelsey (ballerina); Bethlehem, Pa., 12/29/1952.
Kirkpatrick, Ralph (harpsichordist); Leominster, Mass., 6/10/1911.
Kirkwood, James (actor); b. Grand Rapids, Mich. **(1883–1963)**.
Kirsten, Dorothy (soprano); Montclair, N.J., 7/6/1919.
Kissinger, Henry (Heinz Alfred Kissinger) (Secretary of State); Furth, Germany, 5/27/1923.
Kitt, Eartha (singer); North, S.C., 1/26/1928.
Klemperer, Werner (actor); Cologne, Germany, 3/22/1920.
Klugman, Jack (actor); Philadelphia, Pa., 1922.

Knievel, Evel (Robert Craig) (daredevil motorcyclist); Butte, Mont., 10/17/1938.
Knight, Gladys (singer); Atlanta, Ga., 5/28/1944.
Knight, John S. (publisher); Bluefield, W.Va., 10/26/1894.
Knopf, Alfred A. (publisher); New York City, 9/12/1892.
Knotts, Don (actor); Morgantown, W.Va., 7/21/1924.
Knox, John (religious reformer); b. Haddington, East Lothian, Scotland **(1505–1572).**
Koch, Robert (physician); b. Klausthal, Hanover **(1843–1910).**
Kodes, Jan (tennis); Prague, Czechoslovakia, 3/1/1946.
Koestler, Arthur (novelist); Budapest, Hungary, 9/5/1905.
Kokoschka, Oskar (painter); Póchlarn, Austria, 3/1/1886.
Kolb, Claudia (swimming); Hayward, Calif., 12/19/1949.
Koosman, Jerry Martin (baseball); Appleton, Minn., 12/23/1942.
Korbut, Olga (gymnast); Grodno, Byelorussia, U.S.S.R., 1956.
Korman, Harvey (actor); Chicago, Ill., 2/15/1927.
Kosciusko, Thaddeus (Tadeusz Andrzej Bonawentura Kosciuszko) (military officer); b. Lithuania, Poland **(1746–1817).**
Kostelanetz, André (orchestra conductor); St. Petersburg, Russia, 12/22/1901.
Kosygin, Aleksei N. (Premier); St. Petersburg, Russia, 2/20/1904.
Koufax, Sandy (Sanford) (baseball); Brooklyn, N.Y., 12/30/1935.
Koussevitzky, Serge (Sergei) Alexandrovitch (orchestra conductor); b. Vishni Volochek, Tver, Russia **(1874–1951).**
Kovacs, Ernie (comedian); b. Trenton, N.J. **(1919–1962).**
Kramer, Jack (tennis); Las Vegas, Nev., 8/1/1921.
Kramer, Jerry (football); Jordan, Mont., 1/23/1936.
Kramer, Stanley E. (film producer-director); New York City, 9/29/1913.
Kraus, Lili (pianist); Budapest, Hungary, 3/4/1905(?).
Kreisler, Fritz (violinist & composer); b. Vienna, Austria **(1875– 1962).**
Krips, Josef (conductor); b. Vienna, Austria **(1902–1974).**
Kristofferson, Kris (singer); Brownsville, Tex., 6/22/1936.
Krock, Arthur (journalist); b. Glasgow, Ky. **(1886–1974).**
Kruger, Otto (actor); b. Toledo, Ohio **(1885–1974).**
Krupa, Gene (drummer); b. Chicago, Ill. **(1909–1973).**
Kubelik, Rafael (conductor); Bychory, Bohemia, 6/29/1914.
Kublai Khan (Mongol conqueror); **(1216–1294).**
Kubrick, Stanley (producer-director); New York City, 7/26/1928.
Kuhn, Bowie Kent (baseball); Takoma Park, Md., 10/28/1926.
Kurosawa, Akira (director); Tokyo, Japan, 3/23/1910.
Kurtz, Efrem (conductor); St. Petersburg, Russia, 11/7/1900.
Kwalik, Ted (Thaddeus John) (football); McKees Rocks, Pa., 4/15/1947.
Ky, Nguyen Cao (ex-Vice President of South Vietnam); Son Tay, French Indochina, 9/8/1930.
Ladd, Alan (actor); b. Hot Springs, Ark. **(1913–1964).**
Lafayette, Marquis de (Marie Joseph Paul Yves Roch Gilbert du Motier) (military officer); b. Auvergne, France **(1757–1834).**
La Follette, Robert Marin (politician); b. Primrose, Wis. **(1855– 1925).**
La Guardia, Fiorello Henry (Mayor of New York); b. New York City **(1882–1947).**
Lahr, Bert (comedian); b. New York City **(1895–1967).**
Laine, Frankie (Frank Paul LoVecchio) (singer); Chicago, Ill., 3/30/1913.
Laird, Melvin R. (ex-Sec. of Defense); Omaha, Neb., 9/1/1922.
Laird, Ronald (walker); Louisville, Ky., 5/31/1935.
Lamarck, Chevalier de (Jean Baptiste Pierre Antoine de Monet) (naturalist); b. Bazantin, Picardy **(1744–1829).**
Lamarr, Hedy (actress); Vienna, Austria, 1915.
Lamas, Fernando (actor); Buenos Aires, Argentina, 1/9/1915.
Lamb, Charles (essayist); b. London, England **(1775–1834).**
Lamonica, Daryle (football); Fresno, Calif., 7/17/1941.
Lamour, Dorothy (actress); New Orleans, La., 10/10/1914.
Lancaster, Burt (actor); New York City, 11/2/1913.
Lanchester, Elsa (Elsa Sullivan) (actress); London, England, 10/28/1902.
Landau, Martin (actor); Brooklyn, N.Y. 1925(?).
Landers, Ann (columnist); Sioux City, Iowa, 7/14/1918.
Landi, Elissa (actress); b. Venice, Italy **(1904–1948).**
Landis, Kenesaw Mountain (1st baseball commissioner); b. Millville, Ohio **(1866–1944).**
Landon, Michael (actor); Forest Hills, Queens, N.Y., 1936.
Landry, Tom (football); Mission, Tex., 9/11/1924.
Landy, John (runner); Australia, 4/4/1930.
Lane, Abbe (singer); New York City, 1933.
Lang, Fritz (director); b. Vienna, Austria **(1890–1976).**
Lang, Paul Henry (music critic); Budapest, Hungary, 8/28/1901.
Lange, Hope (actress); Redding Ridge, Conn., 11/28/1933.
Langford, Frances (singer); Lakeland, Fla., 4/4/1913.
Langtry, Lily (née Emily Le Breton) (actress); b. island of Jersey **(1852–1929).**
Lansbury, Angela (actress); London, England, 10/16/1925.
Lansing, Robert (actor); San Diego, Calif., 6/5/1929.
Lanza, Mario (Alfred Arnold Cocozza) (singer, actor); b. Philadelphia, Pa. **(1925–1959).**
Lao-Tzu (or **Lao-Tse)** (Li Erh) (philosopher); b. Honan province, China **(c. 604–531 b.c.).**
Lardner, Ring (Ringgold Wilmer Lardner) (story writer); b. Niles, Mich. **(1885–1933).**
Larrieu, Francie. *See* Francie Larrieu Lutz.

La Salle, Sieur de (Robert Cavelier) (explorer); b. Rouen, France **(1643–1687).**
Lauder, Sir Harry (Harry MacLennan) (singer); b. Portobello, Scotland **(1870–1950).**
Laughton, Charles (actor); b. Scarborough, England **(1899–1962).**
Laurel, Stan (comedian); b. Ulverston, England **(1890–1965).**
Laurents, Arthur (playwright); New York City, 7/14/1918.
Laurie, Piper (actress); Detroit, Mich., 1/22/1932.
Laver, Rod (tennis); Rockhampton, Australia, 8/9/1938.
Lavoisier, Antoine Laurent (chemist); b. Paris, France **(1743– 1794).**
Lawford, Peter (actor); London, England, 9/7/1923.
Lawrence, Carol (Carol Maria Laraia) (dancer, actress); Melrose Park, Ill., 9/5/1932.
Lawrence, David Herbert (novelist); b. Nottingham, England **(1885–1930).**
Lawrence, Gertrude (Gertrud Klasen) (actress); b. London, England **(1900–1952).**
Lawrence, Marjorie (singer); Deans Marsh, Australia, 2/17/1909.
Lawrence, Steve (Sidney Leibowitz) (singer); Brooklyn, N.Y., 7/8/1935.
Lawrence of Arabia (Thomas Edward Lawrence; later changed name to Shaw) (author & soldier); b. Tremadoc, Wales **(1888– 1935).**
Leachman, Cloris (actress); Des Moines, Iowa, 4/30/1926(?).
Lean, David (director); Croydon, England, 3/25/1908.
Lear, Edward (nonsense poet); b. London, England **(1812–1888).**
Le Carré, John (David John Moore Cornwell) (novelist); Poole, England, 10/19/1931.
Lederer, Francis (actor); Prague, Czechoslovakia, 11/6/1906.
Lee, Christopher (actor); London, England, 5/27/1922.
Lee, Gypsy Rose (Rose Hovick) (entertainer); b. Seattle, Wash. **(1919–1970).**
Lee, Peggy (Norma Engstrom) (singer); Jamestown, N.D., 5/26/1920.
Lee, Robert Edward (Confederate general); b. Stratford Estate, Va. **(1807–1870).**
Leek, Sybil (Sybil Falk) (astrologer); Staffordshire, England, 1923.
Le Gallienne, Eva (actress); London, England, 1/11/1899.
Lehar, Franz (composer); b. Komàrom, Hungary **(1870–1948).**
Lehman, Herbert H. (Governor-Senator); b. New York City **(1878–1963).**
Lehmann, Lotte (soprano); b. Perleberg, Prussia **(1888–1976).**
Leigh, Janet (Jeanette Morrison) (actress); Merced, Calif., 7/6/1927.
Leigh, Vivien (Vivien Mary Hartley) (actress); b. Darjeeling, India **(1913–1967).**
Leighton, Margaret (actress); b. nr. Birmingham, England, **(1922– 1976).**
Leinsdorf, Erich (conductor); Vienna, Austria, 2/4/1912.
Lemmon, Jack (actor); Boston, Mass., 2/8/1925.
Lenin, Nicolai (Vladimir Ilich Ulyanov) (Soviet leader); b. Simbirsk, Russia **(1870–1924).**
Lennon, Dianne (singer); Los Angeles, Calif., 1939.
Lennon, Janet (singer); Culver City, Calif. 1946.
Lennon, John (singer); Liverpool, England, 10/9/1940.
Lennon, Kathy (singer); Santa Monica, Calif., 1934.
Lennon, Peggy (singer); Los Angeles, Calif., 1941.
Lenya, Lotte (Karoline Balmauer) (singer, actress); Hitzing, Austria, 1905.
Leonard, Benny (Benjamin Leiner) (boxer); b. New York City **(1896–1947).**
Leonard, Sheldon (actor, director); New York City, 2/22/1907.
Lerner, Alan Jay (lyricist); New York City, 8/31/1918.
Lerner, Max (columnist); Minsk, Russia, 12/20/1902.
Le Roy, Mervyn (producer); San Francisco, Calif., 10/15/1900.
Leslie, Joan (actress); Detroit, Mich. 1/26/1925.
Lessing, Doris (novelist); Kermanshan, Persia, 10/22/1919.
Levant, Oscar (pianist); b. Pittsburgh, Pa. **(1906–1972).**
Levene, Sam (actor); Russia, 8/28/1905.
Levenson, Sam (humorist); New York City, 12/28/1911.
Levi, Carlo (novelist); b. Turin, Italy **(1902–1975).**
Levine, James (Music Director, Metropolitan Opera); Cincinnati, Ohio, 6/23/1943.
Lewis, Jerry (Joseph Levitch) (comedian, film director); Newark, N.J., 3/16/1926.
Lewis, Jerry Lee (singer); Ferriday, La., 1935.
Lewis, John Llewellyn (labor leader); b. Lucas, Iowa **(1880–1969).**
Lewis, Meriwether (explorer); b. Albemarle Co., Va. **(1774–1809).**
Lewis, Shari (Shari Hurwitz) (puppeteer); New York City, 1/17/1934.
Lewis, Sinclair (novelist); b. Sauk Centre, Minn. **(1885–1951).**
Lewis, Ted (entertainer); Circleville, Ohio **(1891–1971).**
Ley, Willy (science writer); b. Berlin, Germany **(1906–1969).**
Liberace (Wladziu Liberace) (pianist); West Allis, Wis., 5/16/1919.
Lichtenstein, Roy (painter); New York City, 10/27/1923.
Lie, Trygve Halvdan (1st U.N. Secretary-General; b. Oslo, Norway **(1896–1968).**
Lillie, Beatrice (lady Peel) (actress, comedienne); Toronto, Ontario, Canada, 5/29/1898.
Lilly, Robert (football); Olney, Tex., 7/26/1939.
Lin Yutang (author); b. Changchow, China, **(1895–1976).**
Lind, Jenny (Johanna Maria Lind) (soprano); b. Stockholm, Sweden **(1820–1887).**
Lindbergh, Anne Morrow (author); Englewood, N.J., 6/22/1906.

Lindbergh, Charles A. (aviator); b. Detroit, Mich. **(1902–1974).**
Linden, Hal (actor); New York City, 3/20/1931.
Lindfors, Viveca (actress); Uppsala, Sweden, 12/29/1920.
Lindsay, Howard (dramatist); b. Waterford, N.Y. **(1889–1968).**
Lindsay, John Vliet (ex-Mayor of New York City); New York City, 11/24/1921.
Lindstrom, Pia (TV newscaster); Stockholm, Sweden, 11/?/1938.
Linkletter, Art (radio-TV personality); Moose Jaw, Saskatchewan, Canada, 7/17/1912.
Lippmann, Walter (columnist, author and political analyst); b. New York City **(1889–1974).**
Liquori, Marty (runner); Montclair, N.J., 9/11/1949.
Lisi, Verna (actress); Italy, 1937.
Lister, (1st Baron of Lyme Regis) (Joseph Lister) (surgeon); b. Upton, Essex, England **(1827–1912).**
Liszt, Franz (composer & pianist); b. Raiding, Hungary **(1811–1886).**
Little, Cleavon (actor & comedian); Chicasha, Okla. 6/1/1939.
Little, Floyd Douglas (football); New Haven, Conn., 7/4/1942.
Little, Lou (football); Leominster, Mass., 12/6/1893.
Little, Rich (impressionist); Ottawa, Canada, 11/26/1938.
Littler, Gene (golf); San Diego, Calif., 11/16/1920.
Livesey, Roger (actor); b. Barry, Wales **(1906–1976).**
Livingstone, David (missionary & explorer); b. Lanarkshire, Scotland **(1813–1873).**
Livingstone, Mary (comedienne); Seattle, Wash., 1909.
Llewellyn, Richard (novelist); St. David's, Wales.
Lloyd, Harold (comedian); b. Burchard, Neb. **(1894–1971).**
Lloyd George, David (Earl of Dwyfor) (statesman); b. Manchester, England **(1863–1945).**
Locke, John (philosopher); b. Somersetshire, England **(1632–1704).**
Lockhart, Gene (actor); b. London, Ont., Canada **(1891–1957).**
Lockhart, June (actress); New York City, 6/25/1925.
Lockwood, Margaret (actress); Karachi, India, 9/15/1916.
Lodge, Henry Cabot (legislator); b. Boston, Mass. **(1850–1924).**
Lodge, Henry Cabot, Jr. (diplomat); Nahant, Mass., 7/5/1902.
Loesser, Frank (composer); b. New York City **(1910–1969).**
Loewe, Frederick (composer); Vienna, Austria, 6/10/1904.
Logan, Joshua (director-producer); Texarkana, Tex., 10/5/1908.
Lollobrigida, Gina (actress); Subiaco, Italy, 1928.
Lombard, Carole (Carol Jane Peters) (actress); b. Ft. Wayne, Ind. **(1908–1942).**
Lombardi, Vince (football); b. Brooklyn, N.Y. **(1913–1970).**
Lombardo, Guy (band leader); London, Ont., Canada, 6/19/1902.
London, George (baritone); Montreal, Canada, 5/30/1920.
London, Jack (John Griffith London) (novelist); b. San Francisco, Calif. **(1876–1916).**
London, Julie (Julie Peck) (singer, actress); Santa Rosa, Calif., 9/26/1926.
Long, Huey Pierce (politician); b. Winnfield, La. **(1893–1935).**
Longden, Johnny (horse racing); Wakefield, England, 2/14/1907.
Longfellow, Henry Wadsworth (poet); b. Portland, Me. **(1807–1882).**
Longworth, Alice Roosevelt (social figure); New York City, 2/12/1884.
Loos, Anita (novelist); Sissons, Calif., 4/26/1893.
Lopez, Al (baseball); Tampa, Fla., 8/20/ 1908.
Lopez, Trini (Trinidad Lopez III) (singer); Dallas, Tex., 5/15/1937.
Lopez, Vincent (band leader); b. Brooklyn, N.Y. **(1895–1975).**
Lord, Jack (actor); New York City, 12/30/1930.
Loren, Sophia (Sofia Scicolone) (actress); Rome, Italy, 9/20/1934.
Lorre, Peter (actor); b. Rosenberg, Hungary **(1904–1964).**
Louise, Tina (actress); New York City, 2/11/1937.
Louis, Joe (Joe Louis Barrow) (Boxing); Lexington, Ala., 5/13/1914.
Lovell, James A., Jr. (astronaut); Cleveland, Ohio, 3/25/1928.
Lowell, Amy (poet); b. Brookline, Mass. **(1874–1925).**
Lowell, James Russell (poet); b. Cambridge, Mass. **(1819–1891).**
Lowell, Robert (poet); Boston, Mass, 3/1/1917.
Loy, Myrna (Myrna Williams) (actress); near Helena, Mont., 8/2/1905.
Loyola, St. Ignatius of (Iñigo de Oñez y Loyola) (founder of Jesuits); b. Gúipuzcoa province, Spain **(1491–1556).**
Lubitsch, Ernst (movie director); b. Berlin, Germany **(1892–1947).**
Luce, Clare Boothe (playwright, ex-Ambassador); New York City, 4/10/1903.
Luce, Henry Robinson (editor and publisher); b. Tengchow, China **(1898–1967).**
Lugosi, Bela (Bela Lugosi Blasko) (actor); b. Logos, Hungary **(1888–1956).**
Lukas, Paul (actor); b. Budapest, Hungary **(1895–1971).**
Lumet, Sidney (director); Philadelphia, Pa., 6/25/1924.
Lundigan, William (actor); Syracuse, N.Y., 1914.
Lunt, Alfred (actor); Milwaukee, Wis., 8/19/1892.
Lupino, Ida (actress, director); London, England, 2/4/1918.
Luther, Martin (religious reformer); b. Eisleben, Germany **(1483–1546).**
Lutz, Francie Larrieu (runner); Palo Alto, Calif., 11/23/1952
Lutz, Robert Charles (tennis); Lancaster, Pa., 8/29/1947.
Lynde, Paul (comedian); Mt. Vernon, Ohio, 6/13/1926.
Lynley, Carol (actress); New York City, 2/13/1942.
Lynn, Janet (figure skating); Rockford, Ill., 4/6/1953.
Lynn, Jeffrey (actor); Auburn, Mass., 1909.
Lynn, Loretta (singer); Butcher Hollow, Ky., 4/14/1932(?).

Lyon, Ben (actor); Atlanta, Ga., 1901.
Maazel, Lorin (conductor); Neuilly, France, 3/5/1930.
MacArthur, Douglas (five-star general); b. Little Rock Barracks, Ark. **(1880–1964).**
MacArthur, James (actor); Los Angeles, Calif., 12/8/1937.
Macaulay, Thomas Babington (author); b. Rothley Temple, Leicestershire, England **(1800–1959).**
MacDermot, Galt (composer); Montreal, Canada, 12/19/1928.
MacDonald, James Ramsey (statesman); b. Lossiemouth, Scotland **(1886–1937).**
MacDonald, Jeanette (soprano); b. Philadelphia, Pa. **(1907–1965).**
MacDowell, Edward Alexander (composer); b. New York City, **(1861–1908).**
Macfadden, Bernarr (physical culturist); b. nr. Mill Spring, Mo. **(1868–1955).**
MacGraw, Ali (actress); New York City, 4/1/1939.
Machiavelli, Niccolò (political philosopher); b. Florence, Italy **(1469–1527).**
Mack, Connie (Cornelius Alexander McGillicuddy) (baseball executive); b. East Brookfield, Mass. **(1862–1956).**
Mack, Ted (TV personality); b. Greeley, Colo. **(1904–1976).**
MacKenzie, Gisele (Marie Marguerite Louise Gisele LaFleche) (singer, actress); Winnipeg, Manitoba, Canada, 1/10/1927.
Mackey, John (football); New York City, 9/24/1941.
MacLaine, Shirley (actress); Richmond Va., 4/24/1934.
MacLeish, Archibald (poet); Glencoe, Ill., 5/7/1892.
MacMahon, Ed (TV personality); Detroit, Mich., 3/6/1923.
Macmillan, Harold (ex-Prime Minister); London, England, 2/10/1894.
MacMurray, Fred (actor); Kankakee, Ill., 8/30/1908.
MacNeil, Cornell (baritone); Minneapolis, Minn., 1925.
MacRae, Gordon (singer); East Orange, N.J., 3/12/1921.
MacRae, Sheila (comedienne); London, England, 9/24/1924.
Madison, Guy (Robert Moseley) (actor); Bakersfield, Calif., 1/19/1922.
Maeterlinck, Count Maurice (author); b. Ghent, Belgium **(1862–1949).**
Magellan, Ferdinand (Fernando de Magalhaes) (navigator); b. Sabrosa, Portugal **(1480?–1521).**
Magnani, Anna (actress); b. Rome, Italy **(1908–1973).**
Magsaysay, Ramón (statesman); b. Iba, Luzon, Philippines **(1907–1957).**
Mahan, Alfred Thayer (naval historian); b. West Point, N.Y. **(1840–1914).**
Mahler, Gustav (composer & conductor); b. Kalischt, Bohemia **(1860–1911).**
Mahovlich, Frank (Francis William) (hockey); Timmins, Ontario, Canada, 1/10/1938.
Mailer, Norman (novelist); Long Branch, N.J., 1/31/1923.
Main, Marjorie (Mary Tomlinson Krebs) (actress); b. Acton, Ind. **(1890–1975).**
Mainbocher (Main Bocher) (fashion designer); Chicago, Ill., 10/24/1890.
Makarova, Natalia (ballerina); Leningrad, U.S.S.R., 11/21/1940.
Makeba, Miriam (singer); Prospect Township, Johannesburg, South Africa, 3/4/1932.
Malamud, Bernard (novelist); New York City, 4/26/1914.
Malden, Karl (Mladen Sekulovich) (actor); Chicago, Ill. 3/22/1914.
Malone, Dorothy (actress); Chicago, Ill., 1/30/1925.
Malraux, André (author); Paris, France, 11/3/1901.
Manchester, William (writer); Attleboro, Mass., 4/1/1922.
Mancini, Henry (composer, conductor); Cleveland, Ohio, 4/16/1924.
Manet, Edouard (painter); b. Paris, France **(1832–1883).**
Mangano, Silvana (actress); Rome, Italy, 4/21/1930.
Mankiewicz, Frank F. (columnist); New York City, 5/16/1924.
Mankiewicz, Joseph L. (writer, director); Wilkes-Barre, Pa., 2/11/1909.
Mann, Carol (golf); Buffalo, N.Y., 2/3/1941.
Mann, Horace (educator); b. Franklin, Mass. **(1796–1859).**
Mann, Thomas (novelist); b. Lübeck, Germany **(1875–1955).**
Mannes, Marya (author); New York City, 11/14/1904.
Manning, Madeline (runner); Cleveland, Ohio, 1/11/1948.
Mansfield, Jayne (Jayne Palmer) (actress); b. Bryn Mawr, Pa. **(1932–1967).**
Mansfield, Katherine (story writer); b. Wellington, New Zealand **(1888–1923).**
Mantle, Mickey Charles (baseball); Spavinaw, Okla., 10/20/1931.
Mantovani, Annunzio (conductor); Venice, Italy, 1905.
Mao Tse-tung (Chinese leader); b. Shao Shan, China **(1893–1976).**
Marat, Jean Paul (French revolutionist); b. Boudry, Neuchâtel, Switzerland **(1743–1793).**
Marceau, Marcel (mime); Strasbourg, France, 3/22/1923.
March, Fredric (Frederick Bickel) (actor); b. Racine, Wis. **(1897–1975).**
Marconi, Guglielmo (inventor); b. Bologna, Italy **(1874–1937).**
Marcus Aurelius (Marcus Annius Verus) (Roman emperor); b. Rome **(121–180).**
Marcuse, Herbert (philosopher); Berlin, Germany, 7/19/1898.
Margaret Rose (Princess); Glamis Castle, Angus, Scotland, 8/21/1930.
Margrethe II (Queen); Copenhagen, Denmark, 4/16/1940.
Marichal, Juan (baseball); Laguna Verde, Montecristi, Dominican Republic, 10/20/1937.

Marie Antoinette (Josèphe Jeanne Marie Antoinette) (Queen of France); b. Vienna, Austria **(1755–1793)**.
Maris, Roger (baseball); Hibbing, Minn., 9/10/1934.
Markova, Dame Alicia (ballerina); London, England, 12/1/1910.
Marlowe, Julia (Sarah Frances Frost) (actress); b. Cumberlandshire, England **(1866–1950)**.
Marquand, John Phillips (novelist); b. Wilmington, Del. **(1893–1960)**.
Marquette, Jacques (missionary & explorer); b. Laon, France **(1637–1675)**.
Marshall, E. G. (actor); Owatonna, Minn., 6/18/1910.
Marshall, George Catlett (general); b. Uniontown, Pa. **(1880–1958)**.
Marshall, Herbert (actor); b. London, England **(1890–1968)**.
Marshall, John (jurist); b. nr. Germantown, Va. **(1755–1835)**.
Martin, Billy (Alfred Manuel) (baseball); Berkeley, Calif., 5/16/1928.
Martin, Dean (Dino Crocetti) (singer, actor); Steubenville, Ohio, 6/17/1917.
Martin, Dick (actor, comedian); Mich., 1/30/1922.
Martin, Mary (singer, actress); Weatherford, Tex., 12/1/1914.
Martin, Tony (singer); San Francisco, Calif., 12/25/1914.
Martin, William McChesney, Jr. (ex-chairman of Federal Reserve Board); St. Louis, Mo., 12/17/1906.
Martinelli, Giovanni (tenor); b. Montagnana, nr. Padua, Italy **(1885–1969)**.
Marvin, Lee (actor); New York City, 2/19/1924.
Marx, Chico (Leonard) (comedian); b. New York City **(1891–1961)**.
Marx, Groucho (Julius) (comedian); New York City, 10/2/1890.
Marx, Harpo (Arthur) (comedian); b. New York City **(1893–1964)**.
Marx, Karl (Socialist writer); b. Treves, Prussia **(1818–1883)**.
Marx, Zeppo (Herbert) (comedian); New York City, 2/25/1901.
Mary Stuart (Queen of Scotland); b. Linlithgow, Scotland **(1542–1587)**.
Masaryk, Jan Garrigue (statesman); b. Prague, Bohemia **(1886–1948)**.
Masaryk, Thomas Garrigue (statesman); b. Hodonin, Moravia **(1850–1937)**.
Masefield, John (poet); b. Ledbury, Herefordshire, England **(1878–1967)**.
Mason, James (actor); Huddersfield, England, 5/15/1909.
Massenet, Jules Emile Frédéric (composer); b. Montaud, France **(1842–1912)**.
Massey, Raymond (actor); Toronto, Ontario, Canada, 8/30/1896.
Massine, Léonide (choreographer); Moscow, Russia, 8/9/1896.
Masters, Edgar Lee (poet); b. Garnett, Kan. **(1869–1950)**.
Mastroianni, Marcello (actor); Fontana Liri, Italy, 9/28/1924.
Mathews, Ed (Edwin) (baseball); Texarkana, Tex., 10/13/1931.
Mathis, Johnny (singer); San Francisco, Calif., 9/30/1935.
Matson, Randy (shot putter); Kilgore, Tex., 3/5/1945.
Matthau, Walter (Walter Matuschanskayasky) (actor); New York City, 10/1/1920.
Mature, Victor (actor); Louisville, Ky., 1/19/1916.
Maugham, (William) Somerset (author); b. Paris, France **(1874–1965)**.
Mauldin, Bill (political cartoonist); Mountain Park, N.M., 10/29/1921.
Maupassant, Henri René Albert Guy de (story writer); b. Normandy, France **(1850–1893)**.
Maurois, André (Emile Herzog) (author); b. Elbeuf, France **(1885–1967)**.
Maximilian (Ferdinand Maximilian Joseph) (Emperor of Mexico); b. Vienna, Austria **(1832–1867)**.
Maxwell, James Clerk (physicist); b. Edinburgh, Scotland **(1831–1879)**.
May, Elaine (entertainer); Philadelphia, Pa., 1932.
May, Rollo (psychologist); Ada, Ohio, 4/21/1909.
Maynard, Don (football); Crosbyton, Tex., 1/25/1937.
Maynor, Dorothy (soprano); Norfolk, Va., 9/3/1910.
Mayo, Virginia (actress); St. Louis, Mo., 1920.
Mays, Willie (baseball); Westfield, Ala., 5/6/1931.
McBride, Mary Margaret (radio personality); b. Paris, Mo., **(1899–1976)**.
McBride, Patricia (ballerina); Teaneck, N.J., 8/23/1942.
McCallum, David (actor); Glasgow, Scotland, 9/19/1933.
McCambridge, Mercedes (actress); Joliet, Ill., 3/17/1918.
McCarthy, Eugene J. (ex-Senator); Watkins, Minn., 3/29/1916.
McCarthy, Joe (Joseph Vincent) (baseball); Philadelphia, Pa. 4/21/1887.
McCarthy, Joseph Raymond (legislator); b. Grand Chute, Wis. **(1908–1957)**.
McCarthy, Kevin (actor); Seattle, Wash., 1915.
McCarthy, Mary (novelist); Seattle, Wash., 6/21/1912.
McCartney, Paul (singer); Liverpool, England, 6/18/1942.
McClellan, George Brinton (general); b. Philadelphia, Pa. **(1826–1885)**.
McCloy, John J. (lawyer, banker); Philadelphia, Pa., 3/31/1895.
McClure, Doug (actor); Glendale, Calif., 5/11/1938.
McCormack, John (tenor); b. Athlone, Ireland **(1884–1945)**.
McCormack, John W. (ex-Speaker of House); Boston, Mass., 12/21/1891.
McCormack, Patty (actress); New York City, 8/21/1945.

McCormick, Cyrus Hall (inventor); b. Rockbridge County, Va. **(1809–1884)**.
McCovey, Willie Lee (baseball); Mobile, Ala., 1/10/1938.
McCoy, Tim (actor); Saginaw, Mich., 4/10/1891.
McCracken, James (dramatic tenor); Gary, Ind., 12/16/1926.
McCrea, Joel (actor); Los Angeles, Calif., 11/5/1906.
McCullers, Carson (author); b. Columbus, Ga. **(1917–1967)**.
McDivitt, James Alton (astronaut); Chicago, Ill., 6/10/1929.
McDowall, Roddy (actor); London, England, 9/17/1928.
McDowell, Malcolm (actor); Leeds, England, 6/19/1943.
McGavin, Darren (actor); San Joaquin, Calif., 5/7/1922.
McGee, Fibber (James Jordan) (radio personality); Peoria, Ill., 11/16/1896.
McGinley, Phyllis (poet); Ontario, Ore., 3/21/1905.
McGoohan, Patrick (actor); Astoria, Queens, N.Y., 1928.
McGraw, John Joseph (baseball manager); b. Truxton, N.Y. **(1873–1934)**.
McGuire, Dorothy (actress); Omaha, Neb., 6/14/1919.
McHugh, Frank (actor); Homestead, Pa., 5/23/1898.
McKenna, Siobhan (actress); Belfast, No. Ireland, 5/24/1923.
McKuen, Rod (singer, composer); Oakland, Calif., 4/29/1933.
McLaglen, Victor (actor); b. Tunbridge Wells, Kent, England **(1886–1959)**.
McLain, Dennis (baseball); Chicago, Ill., 3/24/1944.
McLean, Don (singer); New Rochelle, N.Y., 10/2/1945.
McLuhan, Marshall (Herbert Marshall) (communications writer); Edmonton, Alberta, Canada, 7/21/1911.
McNamara, Robert S. (president of World Bank); San Francisco, Calif., 6/9/1916.
McQueen, Steve (Terence Stephen McQueen) (actor); Indianapolis, Ind., 3/24/1930(?).
Mead, Margaret (anthropologist); Philadelphia, Pa., 12/16/1901.
Meadows, Audrey (actress); Wuchang, China, 1922(?)
Meadows, Jayne (actress); Wuchang, China, 9/27/1926.
Meany, George (labor leader); New York City, 8/16/1894.
Medici, Lorenzo de' (called Lorenzo the Magnificant) (Florentine ruler); b. Florence **(1449–1492)**.
Medina, Harold R. (jurist); Brooklyn, N.Y., 2/16/1888.
Meeker, Ralph (Ralph Rathgeber) (actor); Minneapolis, Minn., 11/21/1920.
Mehta, Zubin (conductor); Bombay, India, 4/29/1936.
Meir, Golda (Golda Myerson, nee Mabovitz) (ex-Premier of Israel); Kiev, Russia, 5/3/1898.
Melba, Dame Nellie (Helen Porter Mitchell) (soprano); b. nr. Melbourne, Australia **(1861–1931)**.
Melchior, Lauritz (Lebrecht Hommel) (heroic tenor); b. Copenhagen, Denmark **(1890–1973)**.
Mellon, Andrew William (financier); b. Pittsburgh, Pa. **(1855–1937)**.
Melville, Herman (novelist); b. New York City **(1819–1891)**.
Mencken, Henry Louis (author); b. Baltimore, Md. **(1880–1956)**.
Mendel, Gregor Johann (botanist); b. Heinzendorf, Silesia **(1822–1884)**.
Mendeleyev, Dmitri Ivanovich (chemist); b. Tobolsk, Siberia **(1834–1907)**.
Mendelssohn-Bartholdy, Jakob Ludwig Felix (composer); b. Hamburg, Germany **(1809–1847)**.
Mendès-France, Pierre (ex-Premier); Paris, France, 1/11/1905.
Menjou, Adolphe (actor); b. Pittsburgh, Pa. **(1890–1963)**.
Mennin, Peter (Peter Mennini) (composer); Erie, Pa., 5/17/1923.
Menotti, Gian Carlo (composer); Cadegliano, Italy, 7/7/1911.
Menuhin, Yehudi (violinist, conductor); New York City, 4/22/1916.
Menzies, Robert Gordon (ex-Prime Minister); Jeparit, Australia, 12/20/1894.
Mercer, Johnny (song writer); b. Savannah, Ga., **(1909–1976)**.
Mercer, Mabel (singer); Burton-on-Trent, England, 1/1900.
Mercouri, Melina (actress); Athens, Greece, 10/18/1925.
Meredith, Burgess (actor); Cleveland, Ohio, 11/16/1908.
Merkel, Una (actress); Covington, Ky., 12/10/1903.
Merman, Ethel (Ethel Zimmerman) (singer, actress); Astoria, Queens, N.Y., 1/16/1909.
Merrick, David (David Margulois) (producer); St. Louis, Mo., 11/27/1912.
Merrill, Dina (actress); New York City, 12/9/1925.
Merrill, Gary (actor); Hartford, Conn., 8/2/1914.
Merrill, Robert (baritone); Brooklyn, N.Y., 6/4/1919.
Mesmer, Franz Anton (physician); b. Itzmang, nr. Constance, Baden **(1733–1815)**.
Mesta, Perle (social figure); b. Sturgis, Mich. **(1889–1975)**.
Metreveli, Alexander (tennis); Tblisi, Georgia, U.S.S.R., 11/2/1944.
Metternich, Prince Klemens Wenzel Nepomuk Lothar von (statesman); b. Coblenz, Austria **(1773–1859)**.
Meyer, Deborah (swimming); Haddonfield, N.J., 8/14/1952.
Michener, James A. (novelist); New York City, 2/3/1907.
Middlecoff, Cary (golf); Halls, Tenn., 1/6/1921.
Midler, Bette (singer); Honolulu, Hawaii, 1945(?)
Mielziner, Jo (stage designer); b. Paris, France **(1901–1976)**.
Mikita, Stan (hockey); Sokolce, Czechoslovakia, 5/20/1940.
Mikoyan, Anastas I. (diplomat); Sanain, Armenia, 11/25/1895.
Milanov, Zinka (soprano); Zagreb, Yugoslavia, 5/17/1908.
Milburn, Rodney, Jr. (hurdler); Opelousas, La., 5/18/1950.
Miles, Sarah (actress); Essex, England, 12/31/1943.
Miles, Sylvia (actress); New York City, 9/9/1932.
Miles, Vera (actress); nr. Boise City, Okla., 8/23/1929.

Milhaud, Darius (composer); b. Aix-en-Provence, France **(1892–1974)**.
Mill, John Stuart (philosopher); b. London, England **(1806–1873)**.
Milland, Ray (actor); Neath, Wales, 1/3/1907.
Millay, Edna St. Vincent (poet); b. Rockland, Me. **(1892–1950)**.
Miller, Ann (Lucy Ann Collier) (dancer, actress); Chirno, Tex., 4/12/1919.
Miller, Arthur (playwright); New York City, 10/17/1915.
Miller, Glenn (band leader); b. Clarinda, Iowa **(1909?–1944)**.
Miller, Henry (novelist); New York City, 12/26/1891.
Miller, Jason (John Miller) (playwright); New York City, 1939(?).
Miller, Johnny (golf); San Francisco, Calif., 4/29/1947.
Miller, Mitch (Mitchell) (musician); Rochester, N.Y., 7/4/1911.
Millett, Kate (feminist); St. Paul, Minn., 9/14/1934.
Mills, Hayley (actress); London, England, 4/18/1946.
Mills, John (actor); Felixstowe, England, 2/22/1908.
Milne, Alan Alexander (author); b. London, Eng. **(1882–1956)**.
Milstein, Nathan (violinist); Odessa, Russia, 12/31/1904.
Milton, John (poet); b. London, England **(1608–1674)**.
Mimieux, Yvette (actress); Hollywood, Calif., 1/8/1941.
Mineo, Sal (actor); b. New York City **(1939–1976)**.
Minnelli, Liza (singer, actress); Hollywood, Calif., 3/12/1946.
Minnelli, Vincente (film director); Chicago, Ill., 2/28/1913.
Minuit, Peter (Governor of New Amsterdam); b. Wesel, Rhenish Prussia **(1580–1638)**.
Miranda, Carmen (Maria do Carmo da Cunha) (singer); b. Lisbon, Portugal **(1913–1955)**.
Miró, Joan (painter); Barcelona, Spain, 4/20/1893.
Mitchell, Cameron (actor); Dallastown, Pa., 4/11/1918.
Mitchell, Guy (actor); Detroit, Mich., 2/27/1927.
Mitchell, John N. (former Attorney General); Detroit, Mich., 9/15/1913.
Mitchell, Joni (singer); Ft. MacCleod, Alberta, Canada, 11/7/1943.
Mitchell, Margaret (novelist); b. Atlanta, Ga. **(1900–1949)**.
Mitchell, Thomas (actor); b. Elizabeth, N.J. **(1895–1962)**.
Mitchum, Robert (actor); Bridgeport, Conn., 8/6/1917.
Mitropoulos, Dimitri (orchestra conductor); b. Athens, Greece **(1896–1960)**.
Mix, Tom (actor); b. El Paso, Tex. **(1880–1940)**.
Moffo, Anna (soprano); Wayne, Pa., 6/27/1934.
Mohammed (prophet); b. Mecca, Arabia **(570–632)**.
Molière (Jean Baptiste Poquelin) (dramatist); b. Paris, France **(1622–1673)**.
Mollet, Guy (ex-Premier); b. Flers, Orne, France **(1905–1975)**.
Molnar, Ferenc (dramatist); b. Budapest, Hungary **(1878–1952)**.
Molotov, Vyacheslav M. (V. M. Skryabin) (diplomat); Kukarka, Russia, 3/9/1890.
Moms Mabley (comedienne); b. Brevard, N.C. **(1894?–1975)**.
Monk, Thelonious (pianist); Rocky Mount, N.C., 10/10/1918.
Monroe, Marilyn (Norma Jean Mortenson or Baker) (actress); b. Los Angeles, Calif. **(1926–1962)**.
Monroe, Vaughn (Wilton) (band leader); b. Akron, Ohio **(1912–1973)**.
Monsarrat, Nicholas (novelist); Liverpool, England, 3/22/1910.
Montaigne, Michel Eyquem de (essayist); b. nr. Bordeaux, France **(1533–1592)**.
Montalban, Ricardo (actor); Mexico City, Mexico, 11/25/1920.
Montand, Yves (Yves Montand Livi) (actor, singer); Mansummano, Tuscany, Italy, 10/13/1921.
Montez, Maria (actress); b. Dominican Republic **(1918–1951)**.
Montezuma II (Aztec emperor); b. Mexico **(1480?–1520)**.
Montgomery, Elizabeth (actress); Hollywood, Calif., 4/15/1933.
Montgomery, George (actor); Brady, Mont., 1929.
Montgomery, Jim (swimming); Madison, Wis., 1/24/1955.
Montgomery, Robert (Henry, Jr.) (actor); Beacon, N.Y., 5/21/1904.
Montgomery of Alamein, 1st Viscount of Hindhead (Sir Bernard Law Montgomery) (military leader); b. London, England **(1887–1976)**.
Montoya, Carlos (guitarist); Madrid, Spain, 12/13/1903.
Moore, Archie (boxing); Benoit, Miss., 12/13/1916.
Moore, Clement Clarke (author); b. New York City **(1779–1863)**.
Moore, Garry (Thomas Garrison Morfit) (TV personality); Baltimore, Md., 1/31/1915.
Moore, Grace (soprano); b. Jellico, Tenn. **(1901–1947)**.
Moore, Marianne (poet); b. Kirkwood, Mo. **(1887–1972)**.
Moore, Mary Tyler (actress); Brooklyn, N.Y., 12/29/1937.
Moore, Melba (Beatrice) (singer, actress); New York City, 10/27/1945.
Moore, Roger (actor); London, England, 10/14/1927(?).
Moore, Thomas (poet); b. Dublin, Ireland **(1779–1852)**.
Moore, Victor (actor); b. Hammonton, N.J. **(1876–1962)**.
Moorehead, Agnes (actress); b. Clinton, Mass. **(1906–1974)**.
More, Sir Thomas (statesman & author); b. London, England **(1478–1535)**.
Moreau, Jeanne (actress); Paris, France, 1/23/1928.
Moreno, Rita (Rosita Dolores Alverio) (actress); Humacao, Puerto Rico, 12/11/1931.
Morgan, Dennis (actor); Prentice, Wis., 12/10/1920.
Morgan, Helen (singer); b. Danville, Ohio **(1900?–1941)**.
Morgan, Henry (comedian); New York City, 3/31/1915.
Morgan, Jane (singer); Boston, Mass, 1920.
Morgan, John Pierpont (financier); b. Hartford, Conn. **(1837–1913)**.
Moriarty, Michael (actor); Detroit, Mich., 4/5/1941.

Morini, Erica (violinist); Vienna, Austria, 1/5/1910.
Morison, Samuel Eliot (historian); b. Boston, Mass. **(1887–1976)**.
Morley, Christopher Darlington (novelist); b. Haverford, Pa. **(1890–1957)**.
Morley, Robert (actor); Semley, Wiltshire, England, 5/26/1908.
Morrall, Earl (football); Muskegon, Mich., 5/17/1934.
Morris, Mercury (Eugene) (football); Pittsburgh, Pa., 1/5/1947.
Morse, Robert (actor); Newton, Mass., 5/18/1931.
Morse, Samuel Finley Breese (painter & inventor); b. Charlestown, Mass. **(1791–1872)**.
Morse, Wayne L. (legislator); b. Madison, Wis. **(1900–1974)**.
Morton, Craig L. (football); Flint, Mich., 2/5/1943.
Mosconi, Willie (pocket billiards); Philadelphia, Pa., 6/27/1913.
Moses, Robert (urban planner); New Haven, Conn., 12/18/1888.
Mostel, Zero (Samuel Joel Mostel) (actor); Brooklyn, N.Y., 2/28/1915.
Moussorgsky, Modest Petrovich (composer); b. Karev, Russia **(1839–1881)**.
Moyers, Bill D. (Billy Don) (journalist); Hugo, Okla., 6/5/1934.
Moynihan, Daniel Patrick (educator; former U.S. Ambassador to U.N.); Tulsa, Okla., 3/16/1927.
Mozart, Wolfgang Amadeus (Johannes Chrysostomus Wolfgangus Theophilus Mozart) (composer); b. Salzburg, Austria **(1756–1791)**.
Mudd, Roger (news broadcaster); Washington, D.C., 2/9/1928.
Muggeridge, Malcolm (Thomas) (writer); Croydon, Surrey, England, 3/24/1904.
Muhammad, Elijah (Elijah Poole) (religious leader); Sandersville, Ga. **(1897–1975)**.
Mulhare, Edward (actor); Ireland, 1923.
Mumford, Lewis (city planner); Flushing, N.Y., 10/19/1895.
Muni, Paul (Muni Weisenfreund) (actor); b. Lemburg, Austria **(1895–1967)**.
Munsel, Patrice (soprano); Spokane, Wash., 5/14/1925.
Murillo, Bartolomé Esteban (painter); b. Seville, Spain **(1617–1682)**.
Murphy, Audie (actor, war hero); b. Kingston, Tex. **(1924–1971)**.
Murphy, George (actor, dancer, ex-Senator); New Haven, Conn., 7/4/1902.
Murray, Arthur (dance teacher); New York City, 4/4/1895.
Murray, Kathryn (dance teacher); Jersey City, N.J., 1906.
Murray, Ken (Don Court) (producer); New York City, 7/14/1903.
Murray, Mae (Marie Adrienne Koenig) (actress); b. Portsmouth, Va. **(1890–1965)**.
Murrow, Edward R. (commentator-government official); b. Greensboro, N.C. **(1908–1965)**.
Musial, Stan (baseball); Donora, Pa., 11/21/1920.
Mussolini, Benito (Italian dictator); b. Dovia, Forli, Italy **(1883–1945)**.
Myerson, Bess (consumer advocate); Bronx, N.Y., 1924.
Myrdal, Gunnar (sociologist, economist); Gustaf Parish, Sweden, 12/6/1898.
Naber, John (swimming); Evanston, Ill., 1/20/1956.
Nabokov, Vladimir (novelist); St. Petersburg, Russia, 4/23/1899.
Nabors, Jim (actor, singer); Sylacauga, Ala., 6/12/1933.
Nader, Ralph (consumer advocate); Winsted, Conn., 2/27/1934.
Nagel, Conrad (actor); b. Keokuk, Iowa **(1897–1970)**.
Naish, J. Carrol (actor); b. New York City **(1900–1973)**.
Naldi, Nita (Anita Donna Dooley); b. New York City **(1899–1961)**.
Namath, Joe (Joseph William) (football); Beaver Falls, Pa., 5/31/1943.
Napoleon Bonaparte (Emperor of the French); b. Ajaccio, Corsica **(1769–1821)**.
Nash, Ogden (poet); b. Rye, N.Y. **(1902–1971)**.
Nasser, Gamal Abdel (statesman); b. Beni Mor, Egypt **(1918–1970)**.
Nast, Thomas (cartoonist); b. Landau, Germany **(1840–1902)**.
Nastase, Ilie (tennis); Bucharest, Romania, 7/19/1946.
Nation, Carry Amelia (temperance leader); b. Garrard County, Ky. **(1846–1911)**.
Natwick, Mildred (actress); Baltimore, Md., 6/19/1908.
Navratilova, Martina (tennis); Revnice, Czechoslovakia, 2/18/1956(?).
Nazimova, Alla (actress); b. Yalta, Crimea, Russia **(1879–1945)**.
Neagle, Anna (Marjorie Robertson) (actress); London, England, 10/20/1908.
Neal, Patricia (actress); Packard, Ky., 1/20/1926.
Neff, Hildegarde (actress); Ulm, Germany, 12/28/1925.
Negri, Pola (actress); Bromberg, Poland, about 1897.
Nehru, Jawaharlal (First Prime Minister of India); b. Allahabad, India **(1889–1964)**.
Nelson, Barry (actor); San Francisco, Calif., 1920.
Nelson, David (actor); New York City, 10/24/1936.
Nelson, Harriet Hilliard (Peggy Lou Snyder) (actress); Des Moines, Iowa.
Nelson, Ozzie (Oswald) (actor); b. Jersey City, N.J. **(1907–1975)**.
Nelson, Ricky (Eric) (singer, actor); Teaneck, N.J., 5/8/1940.
Nelson, Viscount Horatio (naval officer); b. Burnham Thorpe, Norfolk, England **(1758–1805)**.
Nenni, Pietro (Socialist leader); Faenza, Italy, 2/9/1891.
Nero (Nero Claudius Caesar Drusus Germanicus) (Roman emperor); b. Antium, Latium, Italy **(A.D. 37–68)**.
Nero, Peter (pianist); New York City, 5/22/1934.
Nesbit, Cathleen (actress); Cheshire, England, 1889.

Newcombe, John (tennis); Sydney, Australia, 5/23/1943.
Newhart, Bob (entertainer); Chicago, Ill., 9/5/1929.
Newhouse, Samuel I. (publisher); New York City, 5/24/1895.
Newley, Anthony (actor, song writer); Hackney, London, England, 9/24/1931.
Newman, Edwin (news commentator); New York City, 1/25/1919.
Newman, Paul (actor, director); Cleveland, Ohio, 1/26/1925.
Newton, Huey (black activist); New Orleans, La., 2/17/1942.
Newton, Sir Isaac (mathematician & scientist); b. nr. Grantham, Lincolnshire, England (1642–1727).
Newton, Wayne (singer); Norfolk, Va., 4/3/1942.
Nichols, Mike (director); Berlin, Germany, 11/6/1931.
Nicholson, Jack (actor); Neptune, N.J., 4/22/1937.
Nicklaus, Jack (golf); Columbus, Ohio, 1/21/1940.
Nietzsche, Friedrich Wilhelm (philosopher); b. nr. Lützen, Saxony (1844–1900).
Nightingale, Florence (nurse); b. Florence, Italy (1820–1910).
Nijinsky, Waslaw (dancer); b. Warsaw, Poland (1890–1950).
Nilsson, Birgit (soprano); West Karup, Sweden, 5/17/1923.
Nimitz, Chester W. (naval officer); b. Fredericksburg, Tex. (1885–1966).
Nimoy, Leonard (actor); Boston, Mass., 3/26/31.
Nin, Anaïs (author, diarist); Neuilly, France, 2/21/1903.
Niven, David (actor); Kirriemuir, Scotland, 3/1/1910.
Nizer, Louis (lawyer, author); London, England, 2/6/1902.
Nobel, Alfred Bernhard (industrialist); b. Stockholm, Sweden (1833–1896).
Noguchi, Isamu (sculptor); Los Angeles, Calif., 11/7/1904.
Nolan, Lloyd (actor); San Francisco, Calif., 8/11/1902.
Norell, Norman (Norman Levinson) (fashion designer); b. Nobles-ville, Ind. (1900–1972).
Norstad, Gen. Lauris (ex-commander of NATO forces); Minneapo-lis, Minn., 3/24/1907.
North, John Ringling (circus director); Baraboo, Wis., 8/14/1903.
North, Lowell (yachting); Springfield, Mo., 12/2/1929.
North, Sheree (actress); Los Angeles, Calif., 1/17/1933.
Nostradamus (Michel de Notredame) (astrologer); b. St. Rémy, France (1503–1566).
Novaes, Guiomar (pianist); São João de Boa Vista, Brazil, 2/28/1895.
Novak, Kim (Marilyn Novak) (actress); Chicago, Ill., 2/13/1933.
Novarro, Ramon (Ramon Samaniegoes) (actor); b. Durango, Mex-ico (1899–1968).
Nugent, Elliott (actor, director); Dover, Ohio, 9/20/1899.
Nureyev, Rudolf (ballet dancer); U.S.S.R., 3/17/1938.
Nuyen, France (actress); Marseilles, France, 7/31/1939.
Oakie, Jack (actor); Sedalia, Mo., 11/12/1903.
Oates, Joyce Carol (novelist); Lockport, N.Y., 6/16/1938.
Oberon, Merle (Estelle Merle O'Brien Thompson) (actress); Tas-mania, 2/19/1911.
O'Brian, Hugh (Hugh J. Krampe) (actor); Rochester, N.Y., 4/19/1930.
O'Brien, Edmond (actor); New York City, 9/10/1915.
O'Brien, Lawrence F. (commissioner of National Basketball Associ-ation); Springfield, Mass., 7/7/1917.
O'Brien, Margaret (Angela Maxine O'Brien) (actress); San Diego, Calif., 1/15/1937.
O'Brien, Pat (William Joseph O'Brien, Jr.) (actor); Milwaukee, Wis., 11/11/1899.
O'Casey, Sean (dramatist); b. Dublin, Ireland (1881–1964).
Ochs, Adolph Simon (publisher); b. Cincinnati, Ohio (1858–1935).
O'Connor, Carroll (actor); New York City, 8/2/1924.
O'Connor, Donald (actor); Chicago, Ill., 8/28/1925.
Odets, Clifford (playwright); b. Philadelphia, Pa. (1906–1963).
Odetta (Odetta Holmes) (folk singer, actress); Birmingham, Ala., 12/31/1930.
Oerter, Al (discus thrower); New York City, 9/19/1936.
Offenbach, Jacques (composer); b. Cologne, Germany (1819–1880).
O'Hara, John (author); b. Pottsville, Pa. (1905–1970).
O'Hara, Maureen (Maureen FitzSimons) (actress); Dublin, Ireland, 8/17/1921.
Oistrakh, David (violinist); b. Odessa, Russia (1908–1974).
Okker, Tom (tennis); Amsterdam, Netherlands, 2/22/1944.
Oland, Warner (actor); b. Umea, Sweden (1880–1938).
Olav V (King of Norway); Sandringham, England, 7/2/1903.
Oldfield, Barney (racing driver); b. Fulton County, Ohio (1878–1946).
Oliva, Tony (Pedro) (baseball); Pinar Del Rio, Cuba, 7/20/1940.
Oliver, Edna Mae (actress); b. Malden, Mass., (1883–1942).
Olivier, Lord (Laurence) (actor); Dorking, England, 5/22/1907.
Olsen, Merlin Jay (football); Logan, Utah, 9/15/1940.
Olsen, Ole (John Sigvard Olsen) (comedian); b. Peru, Ind. (1892–1963).
O'Malley, Walter (baseball); New York City, 10/9/1903.
Omar Khayyam (poet & astronomer); b. Nishapur, Khurasan, Persia (died c. 1123).
Onassis, Aristotle (shipping executive); b. Smyrna, Turkey (1906–1975).
Onassis, Christina (shipping executive); New York City, 12/11/1950.
Onassis, Jaqueline Kennedy (Jacqueline Bouvier) (President's widow); Southampton, N.Y., 7/28/1929.
O'Neal, Ryan (Patrick) (actor); Los Angeles, Calif., 4/20/1941.

O'Neill, Eugene Gladstone (dramatist); b. New York City (1888–1953).
O'Neill, Jennifer (actress); Rio de Janeiro, Brazil, 2/20/1949.
Oppenheimer, J. Robert (nuclear physicist); b. New York City (1904–1967).
Ormandy, Eugene (conductor); Budapest, Hungary, 11/18/1899.
Orr, Bobby (hockey); Parry Sound, Ont., Canada, 3/20/1948.
Osborn, Paul (playwright); Evansville, Ind., 9/4/1901.
Osborn, John (playwright); London, England, 12/12/1929.
Osler, Sir William (physician); b. Bondhead, Ontario, Canada (1849–1919).
O'Sullivan, Maureen (actress); County Roscommon, Ireland, 5/17/1911.
O'Toole, Peter (actor); Connemara, Ireland, 8/2/1933.
Ovid (Publius Ovidius Naso) (poet); b. Sulmona, Italy (43 B.C.–?A.D. 17).
Owens, Buck (country music artist); Sherman, Tex., 1929.
Owens, Jesse (sprinter); Decatur, Ala., 9/12/1918.
Paar, Jack (TV performer); Canton, Ohio, 5/1/1918.
Pacino, Al (Alfred) (actor); New York City, 4/25/1940.
Packard, Vance (author); Granville Summit, Pa., 5/22/1914.
Paderewski, Ignace Jan (pianist & statesman); b. Podolia province, Poland (1860–1941).
Paganini, Nicolò (violinist); b. Genoa, Italy (1782–1840).
Page, Geraldine (actress); Kirksville, Mo., 11/22/1924.
Page, Patti (Clara Ann Fowler) (singer, entertainer); Claremore, Okla., 11/8/1927.
Paige, Janis (actress); Tacoma, Wash., 9/16/1922.
Paige, Satchel (Leroy) (baseball); Mobile, Ala., 7/7/1906.
Paine, Thomas (political philosopher); b. Thetford, England (1737–1809).
Palance, Jack (actor); Lattimer, Pa., 2/18/1920.
Paley, William S. (broadcasting executive); Chicago, Ill., 9/28/1901.
Palmer, Arnold (golf); Latrobe, Pa., 9/10/1929.
Palmer, Betsy (actress); East Chicago, Ind. 1929.
Palmer, Lilli (actress); Posen, Germany, 5/24/1914.
Palmerston, Henry John Temple (3rd Viscount) (statesman); b. Broadlands, Hampshire, England (1784–1865).
Papas, Irene (actress); Chiliomodion, Greece, 1929.
Papp, Joseph (Joseph Papirofsky) (producer, director); Brooklyn, N.Y., 6/22/1921.
Parent, Bernard Marcel (hockey); Montreal, Canada, 4/3/1945.
Park, Chung Hee (President of South Korea); Sangmo-ri, Korea, 9/30/1917.
Parker, Dorothy (Dorothy Rothschild) (author); b. West End, N.J. (1893–1967).
Parker, Eleanor (actress); Cedarville, Ohio, 6/26/1922.
Parker, Fess (actor); Fort Worth, Tex., 1925.
Parker, Suzy (model, actress); San Antonio, Tex., 10/28/1933.
Parkinson, C. (Cyril) Northcote (historian); Durham, England, 7/30/1909.
Parks, Bert (Jacobson) (entertainer); Atlanta, Ga., 12/30/1914.
Parks, Gordon (film director); Ft. Scott, Kan., 11/30/1912.
Parnell, Charles Steward (statesman); b. Avondale, Wicklow, Ire-land (1846–1891).
Parnis, Mollie (Mollie Parnis Livingston) (fashion designer); New York City, 3/18/1905.
Parseghian, Ara (football); Akron, Ohio, 5/21/1923.
Parsons, Estelle (actress); Marblehead, Mass., 11/20/1927.
Parton, Dolly (singer); Sevierville, Tenn., 1/19/1946.
Pasarell, Charles (tennis); San Juan, Puerto Rico, 2/12/1944.
Pascal, Blaise (philosopher); b. Clermont, France (1623–1662).
Pasternak, Boris Leonidovich (author); b. Moscow, Russia (1890–1960).
Pasternak, Joseph (film producer); Silagy-Somlyo, Romania, 9/19/1901.
Pasteur, Louis (chemist); b. Dôle, Jura, France (1822–1895).
Patterson, Floyd (boxing); Waco, N.C., 1/4/1935.
Patton, George Smith, Jr. (general); b. San Gabriel, Calif. (1885–1945).
Paul VI (Giovanni Battista Montini) (Pope); Concesio, nr. Brescia, Italy, 9/26/1897.
Pauling, Linus Carl (chemist); Portland, Ore., 2/28/1901.
Paulsen, Pat (comedian); South Bend, Wash.
Pavan, Marisa (actress); Cagliari, Italy, 6/19/1932.
Pavarotti, Luciano (tenor); Modena, Italy, 10/12/1935.
Pavlov, Ivan Petrovich (physiologist); b. Ryazan district, Russia (1849–1936).
Pavlova, Anna (ballerina); b. St. Petersburg, Russia (1885–1931).
Payne, John (actor); Roanoke, Va., 1912.
Peale, Norman Vincent (clergyman); Bowersville, Ohio, 5/31/1898.
Pearl, Minnie (Sarah Ophelia Colley Cannon) (comedienne, singer); Centerville, Tenn., 10/25/1912.
Pears, Peter (tenor); Farnham, Surrey, England, 6/22/1910.
Pearson, David Gene (auto racing); 12/22/1934.
Pearson, Drew (Andrew Russel Pearson) (columnist); b. Evanston, Ill. (1897–1969).
Pearson, Lester B. (statesman); b. Toronto, Ontario, Canada (1897–1972).
Peary, Robert Edwin (explorer); b. Cresson, Pa. (1856–1920).
Peckinpah, Sam (director); Fresno, Calif., 2/21/1925.
Peck, Gregory (actor); La Jolla, Calif., 4/5/1916.
Peerce, Jan (tenor); New York City, 1904.

Pegler, (James) Westbrook (columnist); b. Minneapolis, Minn. **(1894–1969).**

Pelé (Edson Arantes do Nascimento) (soccer); Tres Coracoes, Brazil, 10/23/1940.

Penn, Arthur (director); Philadelphia, Pa., 9/27/1922.

Penn, William (American colonist); b. London, England **(1644–1718).**

Pennel, John (pole vaulter); Memphis, Tenn., 7/25/1940.

Peppard, George (actor); Detroit, Mich., 10/1/1933.

Pepys, Samuel (diarist); b. Bampton, England **(1633–1703).**

Perelman, S. J. (Sidney J.) (humorist); Brooklyn. N.Y., 2/1/1904.

Pericles (statesman); b. Athens **(died 429** B.C.**).**

Perkins, Osgood (actor); b. West Newton, Mass. **(1892–1937).**

Perkins, Tony (Anthony) (actor); New York City, 4/14/1932.

Perlman, Itzhak (violinist); Tel Aviv, 8/31/1945.

Perón, Isabel (Mariá Estela Martínez Cartas) (former chief of state) La Rioja, Argentina, 2/4/1931.

Perón, Juan D. (statesman); b. nr. Lobos, Argentina **(1895–1974).**

Perón, Maria Eva Duarte de (political leader); b. Los Toldos, Argentina **(1919–1952).**

Perrine, Valerie (actress, dancer); Galveston, Tex., 9/3/1943.

Perry, Gaylord (baseball); Williamston, N.C., 9/13/1938.

Pershing, John Joseph (general); b. Linn County, Mo. **(1860–1948).**

Peters, Jean (actress); Canton, Ohio, 10/15/1926.

Peters, Roberta (Roberta Peterman) (soprano); New York City, 5/4/1930.

Petrarch (Francesco Petrarca) (poet); b. Arezzo, Italy **(1304–1374).**

Pettit, Bob (basketball); Baton Rouge, La., 12/12/1932.

Petty, Richard Lee (auto racing); Randleman, N.C., 7/2/1937.

Philip (Philip Mountbatten) (Duke of Edinburgh); Corfu, 6/10/1921.

Piaf, Edith (Edith Gassion) (chanteuse); b. Paris, France **(1916–1963).**

Piatigorsky, Gregor (cellist); b. Ekaterinoslav, Russia, **(1903–1976).**

Piazza, Ben (actor); Little Rock, Ark., 7/30/1934.

Piazza, Marguerite (soprano); New Orleans, La., 5/6/1926.

Pickford, Jack (Jack Smith) (actor); b. Toronto, Ontario, Canada **(1896–1933).**

Pickford, Mary (Gladys Mary Smith) (actress); Toronto, Ontario, Canada, 4/8/1893.

Picon, Molly (actress); New York City, 6/1/1898.

Pidgeon, Walter (actor); East St. John, New Brunswick, Canada, 9/23/1898.

Pinter, Harold (playwright); London, England, 10/10/1930.

Pinza, Ezio (basso); b. Rome, Italy **(1892–1957).**

Pirandello, Luigi (dramatist & novelist); b. nr. Girgenti, Sicily **(1867–1936).**

Piston, Walter (composer); Rockland, Me., 1/20/1894.

Pitt, William ("Younger Pitt") (statesman); b. near Bromley, England **(1759–1806).**

Pitts, ZaSu (actress); b. Parsons, Kan. **(1898–1963).**

Pius XII (Eugenio Pacelli) (Pope); b. Rome, Italy **(1876–1958).**

Pizarro, Francisco (explorer); b. Trujillo, Spain **(1470?–1541).**

Plante, Jacques (hockey); Shawinigan Falls, Quebec, Canada, 1/17/1929.

Plato (Aristocles) (philosopher); b. Athens (?) **(427?–347** B.C.**).**

Player, Gary (golf); Johannesburg, South Africa, 11/1/1935.

Pleasence, Donald (actor); Worksop, England, 10/5/1919.

Pleshette, Suzanne (actress); New York City, 1/31/1937.

Plimpton, George (author); New York City, 3/18/1927.

Plisetskaya, Maya (ballerina); Moscow, U.S.S.R., 11/20/1925.

Plowright, Joan (actress); Brigg, Lincolnshire, England, 10/28/1929.

Plummer, Christopher (actor); Toronto, Canada, 12/13/1929.

Plunkett, Jim (football); San Jose, Calif., 12/5/1947.

Plutarch (biographer); b. Chaeronea, Boeotia (A.D. **46?–?120).**

Pocahontas (Matoaka) (American Indian princess); b. Virginia (?) **(1595?–1617).**

Podhoretz, Norman (author); Brooklyn, N.Y., 1/16/1930.

Podres, Johnny (baseball); Witherbee, N.Y., 9/30/1932.

Poe, Edgar Allan (poet & story writer); b. Boston, Mass. **(1809–1849).**

Poitier, Sidney (actor); Miami, Fla., 2/20/1924.

Polanski, Roman (director); Paris, France, 8/18/1933.

Pollard, Michael J. (actor); Passaic, N.J., 5/30/1939.

Polo, Marco (traveler); b. Venice **(1254?–?1324).**

Pompey (Gnaeus Pompeius Magnus) (general); b. Rome (?) (106–48 B.C.**).**

Ponce de León, Juan (explorer); b. Servas, Spain **(1460?–1521).**

Pons, Lily (coloratura soprano); b. Cannes, France **(1904–1976).**

Pope, Alexander (poet); b. London, England **(1688–1744).**

Porter, Cole (songwriter); b. Peru, Ind. **(1892–1964).**

Porter, Katherine Anne (novelist); Indian Creek, Tex., 5/15/1890.

Post, Wiley (aviator); b. Grand Plain, Tex. **(1900–1935).**

Poston, Tom (actor); Columbus, Ohio, 10/17/1927.

Potok, Chaim (author); New York City, 2/17/1929.

Potter, Cynthia (diving); Houston, Tex., 8/27/1950.

Pound, Ezra (poet); b. Hailey, Idaho **(1885–1972).**

Powell, Boog (John) (baseball); Lakeland, Fla., 8/17/1941.

Powell, Dick (actor); b. Mt. View, Ark. **(1904–1963).**

Powell, Eleanor (actress); Springfield, Mass., 11/21/1912.

Powell, Jane (Suzanne Burce) (actress, singer); Portland, Ore., 4/1/1929.

Powell, William (actor); Pittsburgh, Pa., 7/29/1892.

Powers, Stephanie (actress); Hollywood, Calif., 7/29/1942.

Prefontaine, Steve Roland (runner); b. Coos Bay, Ore. **(1951–1975).**

Preminger, Otto (film director-producer); Vienna, Austria, 12/5/1906.

Prentiss, Paula (actress); San Antonio, Tex., 1939.

Presley, Elvis (singer, actor); Tupelo, Miss., 1/8/1935.

Preston, Robert (Robert Preston Meservey) (actor); Newton Highlands, Mass., 6/8/1918.

Previn, André (conductor); Berlin, Germany, 4/6/1929.

Previn, Dory (singer); Rahway, N.J., 10/22/1929(?).

Prevost, Marie (Marie Bickford Gunn) (actress); b. Sarnia, Ontario, Canada **(1898–1937).**

Prey, Hermann (lyric baritone); Berlin, Germany, 7/11/1929.

Price, Leontyne (Mary) (soprano); Laurel, Miss., 2/10/1927.

Price, Ray (country music artist); Perryville, Tex., 1/12/1926.

Price, Vincent (actor); St. Louis, Mo., 5/27/1911.

Pride, Charley (singer); Sledge, Miss., 3/18/1938(?).

Priestley, J. B. (John B.) (author); Bradford, England, 9/13/1894.

Priestley, Joseph (chemist); b. nr. Leeds, England **(1733–1804).**

Primrose, William (violist); Glasgow, Scotland, 8/23/1904.

Prince, Harold (producer); New York City, 1/30/1928.

Prinze, Freddie (actor); New York City, 6/22/1954.

Pritchett, V. S. (Victor Sawdon) (literary critic); Ipswich, England, 12/16/1900.

Proell, Annemarie Moser (Alpine skier); Kleinarl, Austria, 3/27/1953.

Prokofieff, Sergei Sergeevich (composer); b. St. Petersburg, Russia **(1891–1953).**

Proust, Marcel (novelist); b. Paris, France **(1871–1922).**

Provine, Dorothy (actress); Deadwood, S. Dak., 1/20/1937.

Prowse, Juliet (actress); Bombay, India, 9/25/1936.

Ptolemy (Claudius Ptolemaeus) (astronomer and geographer); b. Ptolemais Hermii **(2nd century** A.D.**).**

Pucci, Emilio (Marchese di Barsento) (fashion designer); Naples, Italy, 11/20/1914.

Puccini, Giacomo (composer); b. Lucca, Italy **(1858–1924).**

Pulitzer, Joseph (publisher); b. Makó, Hungary **(1847–1911).**

Pullman, George (inventor); b. Brockton, N.Y. **(1831–1897).**

Purviance, Edna (actress); b. Reno, Nev. **(1894–1958).**

Pusey, Nathan M. (educator); Council Bluffs, Iowa, 4/4/1907.

Pushkin, Alexander Sergeevich (poet & dramatist); b. Moscow, Russia **(1799–1837).**

Puzo, Mario (novelist); New York City, 10/15/1921.

Pyle, Ernest Taylor (journalist); b. Dana, Ind. **(1900–1945).**

Pythagoras (mathematician and philosopher); b. Samos **(6th century** B.C.**).**

Quayle, Anthony (actor); Ainsdale, Lancashire, England, 9/7/1913.

Quinn, Anthony (actor); Chihuahua, Mexico, 4/21/1916.

Rabe, David (playwright); Dubuque, Iowa, 3/10/1940.

Rabelais, François (satirist); b. nr. Chinon, France **(1494?–1553).**

Rabi, I. I. (Isidor Isaac) (physicist); Rymanow, Austria, 7/29/1898.

Rachmaninoff, Sergei Wassilievitch (pianist & composer); b. Oneg Estate, Novgorod, Russia **(1873–1943).**

Racine, Jean Baptiste (dramatist); b. La Ferté-Milon, France **(1639–1699).**

Raft, George (actor); New York City, 9/27/1896.

Raines, Ella (actress); Snoqualmie Falls, Wash., 1921.

Rainer, Luise (actress); Vienna, Austria, 1912.

Rainier III (Prince); Monaco, 5/31/1923.

Rains, Claude (actor); b. London, England **(1889–1967).**

Raleigh, Sir Walter (courtier & navigator); b. London, England **(1552?–1618).**

Rallins, Mamie (hurdler); Chicago, Ill., 7/8/1941.

Ralston, Dennis (tennis); Bakersfield, Calif., 7/27/1942.

Randall, Tony (actor); Tulsa, Okla., 2/26/1924.

Randolph, Asa Philip (labor leader); Crescent City, Fla., 4/15/1889.

Rasputin, Grigori Efimovich (monk); b. Tobolsk province, Siberia **(1871?–1916).**

Rathbone, Basil (actor); b. Johannesburg, South Africa **(1892–1967).**

Rather, Dan (TV newscaster); Wharton, Tex., 10/31/1931.

Ratoff, Gregory (movie director); b. St. Petersburg, Russia **(1897–1960).**

Rattigan, Terence (playwright); London, England, 6/10/1911.

Ravel, Maurice Joseph (composer); b. Ciboure, France **(1875–1937).**

Rawls, Betsy (Elizabeth Earle) (swimming); Spartanburg, S.C., 5/4/1928.

Ray, Man (painter); Philadelphia, Pa., 8/27/1890.

Ray, Satyajat (producer); Calcutta, India, 5/2/1922.

Rayburn, Gene (TV personality); Christopher, Ill., 12/22/1917.

Raye, Martha (Margie Yvonne Reed) (comedienne, actress); Butte, Mont., 8/27/1916.

Raymond, Gene (actor); New York City, 8/13/1908.

Reagan, Ronald (former actor, ex-Gov. California); Tampico, Ill., 2/6/1911.

Reasoner, Harry (TV news commentator); Dakota City, Iowa, 4/17/1923.

Reddy, Helen (singer); Melbourne, Australia, 10/25/1941.

Redford, Robert (Charles Robert Redford, Jr.) (actor); Santa Monica, Calif., 8/18/1937.

Redgrave, Lynn (actress); London, England, 3/8/1943.

Redgrave, Sir Michael (actor); Bristol, England, 3/20/1908.
Redgrave, Vanessa (actress); London, England, 1/30/1937.
Reed, Donna (actress); Denison, Iowa, 1/27/1921.
Reed, Rex (critic); Ft. Worth, Tex., 10/2/1940.
Reed, Walter (army surgeon); b. Belroi, Va. **(1851–1902).**
Reed, Willis (basketball); Hico, La., 6/25/1942.
Reese, Della (Deloreese Patricia Early) (singer); Detroit, Mich., 7/6/1932.
Reese, Pee Wee (Harold) (baseball); Ekron, Ky., 7/23/1919.
Reid, Wallace (actor); b. St. Louis, Mo. **(1891–1923).**
Reiner, Carl (actor); New York City, 3/20/1922.
Reiner, Robert (actor); Bronx, N.Y., 1945.
Reinhardt, Max (Max Goldman) (theater producer); b. nr. Vienna, Austria **(1873–1943).**
Remarque, Erich Maria (author); b. Osnabruk, Germany **(1898–1970).**
Remick, Lee (Ann) (actress); Boston, Mass., 12/14/1935.
Rennert, Günther (opera director & producer); Essen, Germany, 4/1/1911.
Rennie, Michael (actor); b. Bradford, Yorkshire, England **(1909–1971).**
Renoir, Jean (director, writer); Paris, France, 9/15/1894.
Resnais, Alain (director); Vannes, France, 6/3/1922.
Resnik, Regina (mezzo-soprano); New York City, 8/30/1922.
Respighi, Ottorino (composer); b. Bologna, Italy **(1879–1936).**
Reston, James (journalist); Clydebank, Scotland, 11/3/1909.
Reuther, Walter (labor leader); b. Wheeling, W. Va. **(1907–1970).**
Revere, Paul (silversmith and hero of famous ride); b. Boston, Mass. **(1735–1818).**
Reynolds, Burt (actor); Waycross, Ga., 2/11/1936.
Reynolds, Debbie (Marie Frances Reynolds) (actress); El Paso, Tex., 4/1/1932.
Rhodes, Cecil John (South African statesman); b. Bishop Stortford, Hertfordshire, England **(1853–1902).**
Rice, Elmer (playwright); b. New York City **(1892–1967).**
Rice, Grantland (sports writer); b. Murfreesboro, Tenn. **(1880–1954).**
Rich, Buddy (Bernard) (drummer); Brooklyn, N.Y., 6/30/1917.
Richard, Maurice (hockey); Montreal, Canada, 8/14/1924.
Richards, Paul (baseball); Waxahachie, Tex., 11/21/1908.
Richardson, Elliot L. (diplomat); Boston, Mass., 7/20/1920.
Richardson, Sir Ralph (actor); Cheltenham, Gloucestershire, England, 12/19/1902.
Richardson, Tony (director); Shipley, Yorks., England, 6/5/1928.
Richelieu, Duc de (Armand Jean du Plessis) (cardinal); b. Paris, France **(1585–1642).**
Richey, Cliff (George Clifford, Jr.) (tennis); San Angelo, Tex., 12/31/1946.
Richter, Charles Francis (seismologist); Hamilton, Ontario, Canada, 4/26/1900.
Richter, Sviatoslav (pianist); Zhitomir, Ukraine, 3/20/1914.
Rickenbacker, Edward V. (aviator); b. Columbia, Ohio **(1890–1973).**
Rickles, Don (comedian); New York City, 5/8/1926.
Rickover, Vice Admiral Hyman G. (atomic energy expert); Russia, 1/27/1900.
Riddle, Nelson (composer); Hackensack, N.J., 6/1/1921.
Ridgway, General Matthew B. (ex-Army Chief of staff); Ft. Monroe, Va., 3/3/1895.
Riessen, Martin (tennis); Hinsdale, Ill., 12/4/1941.
Rigg, Diana (actress); Doncaster, England, 7/20/1938.
Rigney, William (baseball); Alameda, Calif., 1/29/1918.
Riley, James Whitcomb (poet); b. Greenfield, Ind. **(1849–1916).**
Rimsky-Korsakov, Nikolai Andreevich (composer); b. Tikhvin, Russia **(1844–1908).**
Rinehart, Mary (née Roberts) (novelist); b. Pittsburgh, Pa. **(1876–1958).**
Ritchard, Cyril (actor, director); Sydney, Australia, 12/1/1898.
Ritz, Al (Al Joachim) (comedian); b. Newark, N.J., **(1901–1965).**
Rivera, Geraldo (Miguel) (newscaster); New York City, 7/3/1943.
Rivers, Joan (comedienne); Brooklyn, N.Y., 1935(?).
Rizzuto, Phil (baseball, TV announcer); New York City, 9/25/1918.
Roark, Helen Wills Moody (tennis); Centerville, Calif., 10/6/1922.
Robards, Jason, Jr. (actor); Chicago, Ill., 7/26/1922.
Robards, Jason, Sr. (actor); b. Hillsdale, Mich. **(1892–1963).**
Robbins, Harold (novelist); New York City, 5/21/1916.
Robbins, Jerome (Jerome Rabinowitz) (choreographer); New York City, 10/11/1918.
Roberts, (Granville) Oral, Rev. (evangelist, publisher); nr. Ada, Okla., 1/24/1918.
Robertson, Cliff (actor); La Jolla, Calif., 9/9/1925.
Robertson, Dale (actor); Oklahoma City, Okla., 1923.
Robertson, Oscar (basketball); Charlotte, Tenn., 11/24/1938.
Robeson, Paul (singer, actor); b. Princeton, N.J. **(1898–1976).**
Robespierre, Maximilien François Marie Isidore de (French Revolutionist); b. Arras, France **(1758–1794).**
Robinson, Bill "Bojangles" (Luther) (dancer); b. Richmond, Va., **(1878–1949).**
Robinson, Brooks (baseball); Little Rock, Ark., 5/18/1937.
Robinson, Edward G. (Emmanuel Goldberg) (actor); b. Bucharest, Romania **(1893–1973).**
Robinson, Edwin Arlington (poet); b. Head Tide, Me. **(1869–1935).**
Robinson, Frank (baseball); Beaumont, Tex., 8/31/1935.

Robinson, Jackie (baseball player); b. Cairo, Ga. **(1919–1972).**
Robinson, Ray (boxing); Detroit, Mich., 5/30/1920.
Robson, Dame Flora (actress); South Shields, Durham, England, 3/28/1902.
Robson, May (actress); b. Melbourne, Australia **(1858–1942).**
Rochester (Eddie Anderson) (actor); Oakland, Calif., 9/18/1905.
Rockefeller, David (banker); New York City, 6/12/1915.
Rockefeller, John Davison (capitalist); b. Richford, N.Y. **(1839–1937).**
Rockefeller, John Davison, Jr. (industrialist); b. Cleveland, Ohio **(1874–1960).**
Rockefeller, John D., 3rd (philanthropist); New York City, 3/21/1906.
Rockefeller, Laurance S. (conservationist); New York City, 5/26/1910.
Rockne, Knute Kenneth (football coach); b. Voss, Norway **(1888–1931).**
Rockwell, Martha (skiing); Providence, R.I., 4/26/1944.
Rockwell, Norman (painter, illustrator); New York City, 2/3/1894.
Rodgers, Richard (composer); New York City, 6/28/1902.
Roentgen, Wilhelm Konrad (physicist); b. Lennep, Prussia **(1845–1923).**
Rogers, Buddy (Charles) (actor); Olathe, Kan., 8/13/1904.
Rogers, Ginger (Virginia McMath) (dancer, actress); Independence, Mo., 7/16/1911.
Rogers, Roy (Leonard Slye) (actor); Cincinnati, Ohio, 11/5/1912.
Rogers, Will (William Penn Adair Rogers) (humorist); b. Oologah, Okla. **(1879–1935).**
Rogers, Will, Jr. (actor); New York City, 10/20/1911.
Rogers, William P. (ex-Sec. of State); Norfolk, N.Y., 6/23/1913.
Roland, Gilbert (actor); Juarez, Mexico, 12/11/1905.
Rolland, Romain (author); b. Clamecy, France **(1866–1944).**
Rollins, Sonny (saxophonist); New York City, 9/7/1930.
Romberg, Sigmund (composer); b. Szeged, Hungary **(1887–1951).**
Rome, Harold (composer); Hartford, Conn., 5/27/1908.
Romero, Cesar (actor); New York City, 2/15/1907.
Romney, George W. (ex-Secretary of HUD); Chihuahua, Mexico, 7/8/1907.
Romulo, Carlos P. (diplomat, educator); Manila, Philippines, 1/14/1899.
Rooney, Mickey (Joe Yule, Jr.) (actor); Brooklyn, N.Y., 9/23/1920.
Roosevelt, Anna Eleanor (reformer, humanitarian); New York City **(1884–1962).**
Rose, Billy (showman); New York City **(1899–1966).**
Rose, Pete (Peter Edward) (baseball); Cincinnati, Ohio, 4/14/1942.
Rosenbloom, Maxie (boxing); b. New York City **(1904–1976).**
Rosenstock, Joseph (conductor); Krakow, Poland, 1/27/1895.
Rosewall, Ken (tennis); Sydney, Australia, 11/2/1934.
Ross, Diana (singer); Detroit, Mich., 3/26/1944.
Ross, Katharine (actress); Hollywood, Calif., 1/29/1943.
Rossellini, Roberto (film director); Rome, Italy, 5/8/1906.
Rossetti, Dante Gabriel (painter & poet); b. London, England **(1828–1882).**
Rossini, Gioacchino Antonio (composer); b. Pesaro, Italy **(1792–1868).**
Rostand, Edmond (dramatist); b. Marseilles, France **(1868–1918).**
Rostow, Walt Whitman (economist); New York City, 10/7/1916.
Rostropovich, Mstislav (violin cellist); Baku, Azerbaijan, S.S.R., 8/12/1927.
Rote, Kyle (football, TV announcer); San Antonio, Tex., 10/27/1928.
Roth, Lillian (singer); Boston, Mass., 12/13/1910.
Roth, Philip (novelist); Newark, N.J., 3/19/1933.
Rothhammer, Keena (swimming); Little Rock, Ark., 2/26/1957.
Roundtree, Richard (actor); New Rochelle, N.Y., 9/7/1942.
Rousseau, Jean Jacques (philosopher); b. Geneva, Switzerland **(1712–1778).**
Rowan, Dan (comedian); Beggs, Okla., 7/2/1922.
Rowlands, Gena (actress); Cambria, Wis., 6/19/1936(?).
Rozelle, Pete (Alvin Ray) (commissioner of National Football League); South Gate, Calif., 3/1/1926.
Rubinstein, Artur (pianist); Lódz, Poland, 1/28/1887.
Rudel, Julius (conductor); Vienna, Austria, 3/6/1921.
Rudolph, Wilma Glodean (sprinter); St. Bethlehem, Tenn., 6/23/1940.
Ruggles, Charles (actor); b. Los Angeles, Calif. **(1892–1970).**
Rule, Janice (actress); Norwood, Ohio, 8/15/1931.
Runyon, Alfred Damon (journalist); b. Manhattan, Kan. **(1884–1946).**
Rusk, Dean (ex-Sec. of State); Cherokee County, Ga., 2/9/1909.
Ruskin, John (art critic); b. London, England **(1819–1900).**
Russell, Bill (basketball); Monroe, La., 2/12/1934.
Russell, Jane (actress); Bemidji, Minn., 6/21/1921.
Russell, Lillian (Helen Louise Leonard) (soprano); b. Clinton, Iowa **(1861–1922).**
Russell, Lord (Bertrand Arthur William) (mathematician-philosopher); b. Trelleck, Wales **(1872–1970).**
Russell, Nipsy (comedian); Atlanta, Ga. 1924(?).
Russell, Rosalind (actress); Waterbury, Conn., 6/4/1912.
Ruth, Babe (George Herman Ruth) (baseball player); b. Baltimore, Md. **(1895–1948).**
Rutherford, Dame Margaret (actress); b. Balham, England **(1892–1972).**

Rutherford, Johnny (auto racing); 2/12/1938.
Ryan, Nolan (Lynn Nolan, Jr.) (baseball); Refugio, Tex., 1/31/1947.
Ryan, Robert (actor); b. Chicago, Ill. (1909–1973).
Rydell, Bobby (singer); Philadelphia, Pa., 1942.
Rysanek, Leonie (dramatic soprano); Vienna, Austria, 11/14/1928.
Ryun, Jim (runner); Wichita, Kan., 4/29/1947.
Sabin, Albert B. (polio researcher); Bialystok, Poland, 8/26/1906.
Sadat, Anwar (President); Egypt, 12/25/1918.
Sagan, Françoise (novelist); Cajarc, France, 6/21/1935.
Sahl, Mort (Morton Lyon Sahl) (comedian); Montreal, Canada, 5/11/1927.
Saint, Eva Marie (actress); Newark, N.J., 7/4/1924.
Saint-Gaudens, Augustus (sculptor); b. Dublin, Ireland (1848–1907).
St. John, Jill (actress); Los Angeles, Calif., 8/19/1940.
Saint-Laurent, Yves (Henri Donat Mathieu) (fashion designer); Oran, Algeria, 8/1/1936.
Saint-Saens, Charles Camille (composer); b. Paris, France (1835–1921).
Sainte-Marie, Buffy (Beverly) (folk singer); Craven, Saskatchewan, Canada, 2/20/1942(?).
Salinger, J. D. (Jerome David) (novelist); New York City, 1/1/1919.
Salisbury, Harrison E. (journalist); Minneapolis, Minn., 11/14/1908.
Salk, Jonas (polio researcher); New York City, 10/28/1914.
Sand, George (Amandine Lucille Aurore Dudevant, née Dupin) (novelist); b. Paris, France (1804–1876).
Sandburg, Carl (poet & biographer); b. Galesburg, Ill. (1878–1967).
Sanders, George (actor); b. St. Petersburg, Russia (1906–1972).
Sanderson, Derek (hockey); Niagara Falls, Ontario, Canada, 6/16/1946.
Sands, Tommy (singer); Chicago, Ill., 8/27/1937.
Sanger, Margaret (birth control leader); b. Corning, N.Y. (1883–1966).
Santana, Manuel (Manuel Santana Martínez) (tennis); Chamartin, Spain, 5/10/1938.
Santayana, George (philosopher); b. Madrid, Spain (1863–1952).
Sappho (poet); b. Lesbos (lived c. 600 B.C.).
Saroyan, William (novelist); Fresno, Calif., 8/31/1908.
Sarrazin, Michael (actor); Quebec City, Canada, 5/22/1940.
Sarto, Andrea del (Andrea Domenico d'Agnolo di Francesco) (painter); b. Florence, Italy (1486–1531).
Sartre, Jean-Paul (existentialist writer); Paris, France, 6/21/1905.
Sassoon, Vidal (hair stylist); London, England, 1/?/1928.
Saul (King of Israel) (11th century B.C.).
Savalas, Telly (Aristoteles) (actor); Garden City, Long Island, N.Y., 1/21/1924(?).
Sayao, Bidú (soprano); Rio de Janeiro, Brazil, 5/11/1906.
Sayers, Gale (football); Wichita, Kan., 5/30/1943.
Scaasi, Arnold (Arnold Isaacs) (fashion designer); Montreal, Quebec, Canada.
Schary, Dore (producer, writer); Newark, N.J., 8/31/1905.
Schell, Maria (actress); Vienna, Austria, 1/15/1926.
Schell, Maximilian (actor); Vienna, Austria, 12/8/1930.
Schiaparelli, Elsa (fashion designer); b. Rome, Italy (1890?–1973).
Schiff, Dorothy (newspaper publisher); New York City, 3/11/1903.
Schildkraut, Joseph (actor); b. Vienna, Austria (1896–1964).
Schiller, Johann Christoph Friedrich von (dramatist & poet); b. Marbach, Württemberg, Germany (1759–1805).
Schippers, Thomas (conductor); Kalamazoo, Mich., 3/9/1930.
Schirra, Walter Marty, Jr. (astronaut); Hackensack, N.J., 3/12/1923.
Schisgal, Murray (playwright); Brooklyn, N.Y., 11/25/1926.
Schlesinger, Arthur M., Jr. (historian); Columbus, Ohio, 10/15/1917.
Schneider, Romy (actress); Vienna, Austria, 9/23/1938.
Schoendienst, Al (Albert) (baseball); Germantown, Ill., 2/2/1923.
Schollander, Donald (swimming); Charlotte, N.C., 4/30/1946.
Schönberg, Arnold (composer); b. Vienna, Austria (1874–1951).
Schopenhauer, Arthur (philosopher); b. Danzig (1788–1860).
Schubert, Franz Peter (composer); b. Vienna, Austria (1797–1828).
Schulberg, Budd (novelist); New York City, 3/27/1914.
Schulz, Charles M. (cartoonist); Minneapolis, Minn., 11/26/1922.
Schuman, Robert (statesman); b. Luxembourg (1886–1963).
Schuman, William (composer); New York City, 8/4/1910.
Schumann, Robert Alexander (composer); b. Zwickau, Saxony, Germany (1810–1856).
Schumann-Heink, Ernestine (née Roessler) (contralto); b. nr. Prague, Bohemia (1861–1936).
Schwartz, Maurice (actor); b. Russia (1891–1960).
Schwarzkopf, Elisabeth (soprano); Jarotschin, Poznan, Poland, 12/9/1915.
Schweikart, Russell Louis (astronaut); Neptune, N.J., 10/25/1935.
Schweitzer, Albert (humanitarian); b. Kaysersburg, Upper Alsace (1875–1965).
Scofield, Paul (actor); Hurstpierpoint, Sussex, England, 1/21/1922.
Scott, David Randolph (astronaut); San Antonio, Tex., 6/6/1932.
Scott, George C. (actor); Wise, Va., 10/18/1927.
Scott, Lizabeth (actress); Scranton, Pa., 1923.
Scott, Martha (actress); Jamesport, Mo., 9/22/1914.
Scott, Randolph (actor); Orange County, Va., 1/23/1903.
Scott, Robert Falcon (explorer); b. Devonport, England (1868–1912).

Scott, Sir Walter (novelist); b. Edinburgh, Scotland (1771–1832).
Scott, Zachary (actor); b. Austin, Tex. (1914–1965).
Seagren, Bob (Robert Lloyd) (pole vaulter); Pomona, Calif., 10/17/1946.
Seaver, Tom (baseball); Fresno, Calif., 11/17/1944.
Sebastian, John (composer); New York City, 3/17/1944.
Seberg, Jean (actress); Marshalltown, Iowa, 11/13/1938.
Seeger, Pete (folk singer); New York City, 5/3/1919.
Segal, Erich (novelist); Brooklyn, N.Y., 6/16/1937.
Segal, George (actor); New York City, 2/13/1936.
Segovia, Andrés (guitarist); Linares, Spain, 2/18/1894.
Sellers, Peter (actor); Southsea, England, 9/8/1925.
Selznick, David O. (producer); b. Pittsburgh, Pa. (1902–1965).
Sennett, Mack (Michael Sinnott) (producer); b. Richmond, Quebec, Canada (1880–1960).
Serkin, Rudolf (pianist); Eger, Bohemia, 3/28/1903.
Serling, Rod (author); b. Syracuse, N.Y. (1924–1975).
Sessions, Roger (composer); Brooklyn, N.Y., 12/28/1896.
Seurat, Georges (painter); b. Paris, France (1851–1891).
Seuss, Dr. (Theodor Seuss Geisel) (author, illustrator); Springfield, Mass., 3/2/1904.
Sevareid, Eric (TV commentator); Velva, N.D., 11/26/1912.
Shakespeare, William (dramatist); b. Stratford on Avon, England (1564–1616).
Shankar, Ravi (sitar player); Benares, India, 4/7/1920.
Shanker, Albert (labor leader); New York City, 9/14/1928.
Shapley, Harlow (astronomer); b. Nashville, Mo. (1885–1972).
Sharif, Omar (Shalhoub) (actor); Alexandria, Egypt, 4/10/1932.
Shatner, William (actor); Montreal, Quebec, Canada, 3/22/1931.
Shaw, Artie (band leader); New York City, 5/23/1910.
Shaw, George Bernard (dramatist); b. Dublin, Ireland (1856–1950).
Shaw, Irwin (novelist); Brooklyn, N.Y., 2/27/1913.
Shaw, Robert (actor); Lancashire, England, 8/9/1927.
Shaw, Robert (conductor); Red Bluff, Calif., 4/30/1916.
Shearer, Moira (ballerina); Dunfermline, Fifes., Scotland, 1/17/1926.
Shearer, Norma (actress); Montreal, Canada, 1904.
Shearing, George (pianist); London, England, 8/13/1920.
Sheean, Vincent (James Vincent Sheean) (author, foreign correspondent); b. Pana, Ill. (1899–1975).
Sheen, Fulton J. (Roman Catholic bishop); El Paso, Ill., 5/8/1895.
Shelley, Percy Bysshe (poet); nr. Horsham, Sussex, England (1792–1822).
Shepard, Alan B., Jr. (astronaut); East Derry, N.H., 11/18/1923.
Sheraton, Thomas (furniture designer); b. Stockton-on-Tees, England (1751–1806).
Sheridan, Ann (actress); b. Denton, Tex. (1915–1967).
Sheridan, Philip (army officer); b. Albany, N.Y. (1831–1888).
Sheridan, Richard Brinsley (dramatist); b. Dublin, Ireland (1751–1816).
Sherman, Allie (football); Brooklyn, N.Y., 2/10/1923.
Sherman, William Tecumseh (army officer); b. Lancaster, Ohio (1820–1891).
Sherriff, Robert (playwright); b. Kingston-on-Thames, England (1896–1975).
Sherwood, Robert Emmet (dramatist); b. New Rochelle, N.Y. (1896–1955).
Shirer, William L. (journalist, historian); Chicago, Ill., 2/23/1904.
Shoemaker, Willie (jockey); Fabens, Tex., 8/19/1931.
Sholokhov, Mikhail (novelist); Veshenskaya, Russia, 5/24/1905.
Shore, Dinah (Frances Rose Shore) (singer); Winchester, Tenn., 3/1/1917(?).
Short, Bobby (Robert Waltrip Short) (singer, pianist); Danville, Ill., 9/15/1924.
Shorter, Frank (runner); Munich, Germany, 10/31/1947.
Shostakovich, Dmitri (composer); b. St. Petersburg, Russia (1906–1975).
Shriver, Sargent (Robert Sargent Shriver, Jr.)(business executive); Westminster, Md., 11/9/1915.
Shula, Don (Donald Francis) (football); Grand River, Ohio, 1/4/1930.
Shulman, Max (novelist); St. Paul, Minn., 3/14/1919.
Shumlin, Herman (stage producer); Atwood, Colo., 12/6/1898.
Sibelius, Jean (Johann Julius Christian Sibelius) (composer); b. Tavastehus, Finland (1865–1957).
Sidney, Sylvia (actress); New York City, 8/8/1910.
Siepi, Cesare (basso); Milan, Italy, 2/14/1923.
Signoret, Simone (Simone Kaminker) (actress); Wiesbaden, Germany, 3/25/1921.
Sikorsky, Igor I. (inventor); b. Kiev, Russia (1889–1972).
Sills, Beverly (Belle Silverman) (soprano); Brooklyn, N.Y., 5/25/1929.
Silone, Ignazio (Secondo Tranquilli) (novelist); Pescina del Marsi, Italy, 5/1/1900.
Silvers, Phil (Philip Silversmith) (comedian); Brooklyn, N.Y., 5/11/1912.
Silvester, Jay (discus thrower); Tremonton, Utah, 2/27/1937.
Sim, Alastair (actor); b. Edinburgh, Scotland (1900–1976).
Simenon, Georges (Georges Sim) (mystery writer); Liège, Belgium, 2/13/1903.
Simmons, Jean (actress); Crouch Hill, London, England, 1/31/1929.
Simon, Neil (playwright); Bronx, N.Y., 7/4/1927.
Simon, Norton (business executive); Portland, Ore., 2/5/1907.

Simon, Paul (singer); Newark, N.J., 11/5/1942.
Simon, Simone (actress); Marseilles, France, 4/23/1914.
Simone, Nina (Eunice Kathleen Waymon) (singer, pianist); Tryon, N.C., 2/21/1933.
Simpson, Adele (Adele Smithline) (fashion designer); New York City, 12/8/1903.
Simpson, O. J. (Orenthan James) (football); San Francisco, 7/9/1947.
Sinatra, Frank (singer, actor); Hoboken, N.J., 12/12/1915.
Sinatra, Nancy (singer); Jersey City, N.J., 6/8/1940.
Sinclair, Upton Beall (author); b. Baltimore, Md. **(1878–1968)**.
Singer, Isaac Bashevis (novelist); Radzymin, Poland, 7/14/1904.
Siqueiros, David (painter);ᵇb. Chihuahua, Mexico **(1896–1974)**.
Sitting Bull (Prairie Sioux Indian Chief); b. on Grand River, S.D. **(c. 1835–1890)**.
Skelton, Red (Richard) (comedian); Vincennes, Ind., 7/18/1913.
Skinner, B. F. (Burrhus Frederic) (psychologist); Susquehanna, Pa., 3/20/1904.
Skinner, Cornelia Otis (writer, actress); Chicago, Ill., 5/30/1901.
Skinner, Otis (actor); b. Cambridge, Mass. **(1858–1942)**.
Slayton, Donald K. "Deke" (astronaut); Sparta, Wis., 3/1/1924.
Slezak, Walter (actor); Vienna, Austria, 5/3/1902.
Sloan, John (painter); b. Lock Haven, Pa. **(1871–1951)**.
Smetana, Bedrich (composer); b. Litomysl, Bohemia **(1824–1884)**.
Smith, Adam (economist); b. Kirkaldy, Fife, Scotland **(1723–1790)**.
Smith, Alexis (actress); Penticon, B.C., Canada, 6/8/1921.
Smith, Alfred Emanuel (politician); b. New York City **(1873–1944)**.
Smith, Bubba (Charles Aaron) (football); Orange, Tex., 2/28/1945.
Smith, H. Allen (humorist); b. McLeansboro, Ill. **(1907–1976)**.
Smith, Howard K. (TV commentator); Ferriday, La., 5/12/1914.
Smith, John (American colonist); b. Willoughby, Lincolnshire, England **(1580–1631)**.
Smith, Joseph (religious leader); b. Sharon, Vt. **(1805–1844)**.
Smith, Kate (Kathryn) (singer); Greenville, Va., 5/1/1909.
Smith, Maggie (actress); Ilford, England, 12/28/1934.
Smith, Red (Walter) (sports columnist); Green Bay, Wis., 9/25/1905.
Smith, Ronnie Ray (sprinter); Los Angeles, Calif., 3/28/1949.
Smith, Stanley Roger (tennis); Pasadena, Calif., 12/14/1946.
Smith, Tommie (sprinter); Clarksville, Tex., 6/5/1944.
Smith, Tracy (runner); Altadena, Calif., 3/15/1945.
Smoke, Marcia Jones (canoeing); Oklahoma City, 7/18/1941.
Smothers, Dick (Richard) (comedian); Governors Island, New York City, 11/20/1939.
Smothers, Tom (Thomas) (comedian); Governors Island, New York City, 2/2/1937.
Snead, Sam (golf); Hot Springs, Va., 5/27/1912.
Snell, Matt (football); Garfield, Ga., 8/18/1941.
Snider, Duke (Edwin) (baseball); Los Angeles, Calif., 9/19/1926.
Snow, Lord (Charles Percy) (author); Leicester, England, 10/15/1905.
Socrates (philosopher); b. Athens **(469–399 B.C.)**.
Solomon (King of Israel); b. Jerusalem (?) **(died c. 933 B.C.)**.
Solon (lawgiver); b. Salamis, Greece **(638?–?559 B.C.)**.
Solti, Georg (conductor); Budapest, Hungary, 10/21/1912.
Solzhenitsyn, Aleksandr (novelist); Kislovodsk, Russia, 12/11/1918.
Sommer, Elke (actress); Berlin, Germany, 11/5/1942.
Sondheim, Stephen (composer); New York City, 3/22/1930.
Sontag, Susan (author); New York City, 1/28/1933.
Sophocles (dramatist); b. nr. Athens **(496?–406 B.C.)**.
Sothern, Ann (Harriette Lake) (actress); Valley City, N.D., 1/22/1911.
Sousa, John Philip (composer); b. Washington, D.C. **(1854–1932)**.
Soyer, Raphael (painter); Borisoglebsk, Russia, 12/25/1899.
Spaak, Paul-Henri (statesman); b. Brussels, Belgium **(1899–1972)**.
Spahn, Warren (baseball); Buffalo, N.Y., 4/23/1921.
Spark, Muriel (novelist); Edinburgh, Scotland, 2/1/1918.
Spassky, Boris (chess); Leningrad, U.S.S.R., 1/30/1937.
Spellman, Francis Joseph (Cardinal); b. Whitman, Mass. **(1889–1967)**.
Spencer, Herbert (philosopher); b. Derby, England **(1820–1903)**.
Spender, Stephen (poet); nr. London, England, 2/28/1909.
Spengler, Oswald (philosopher); b. Blankenburg, Germany **(1880–1936)**.
Spenser, Edmund (poet); b. London, England **(1552?–1599)**.
Spewack, Bella (playwright); Hungary, 1899.
Spiegel, Sam (producer); Jaroslaw, Poland, 11/11/1901.
Spillane, Mickey (Frank Spillane) (mystery writer); Brooklyn, N.Y., 3/9/1918.
Spinoza, Baruch (philosopher); b. Amsterdam, Holland **(1632–1677)**.
Spitz, Mark (swimming); Modesto, Calif., 2/10/1950.
Spivak, Lawrence (TV producer); Brooklyn, N.Y., 1900.
Spock, Benjamin (pediatrician); New Haven, Conn., 5/2/1903.
Sproul, Robert G. (educator); b. San Francisco, Calif. **(1891–1975)**.
Stack, Robert (actor); Los Angeles, Calif., 1/13/1919.
Stafford, Jo (singer); Coalinga, Calif., 1918.
Stafford, Thomas Patton (astronaut); Weatherford, Okla., 9/17/1930.
Stagg, Amos Alonzo (football); b. West Orange, N.J. **(1862–1965)**.
Stalin, Joseph Vissarionovich (Iosif V. Dzhugashvili) (Soviet leader); b. nr. Tiflis, Georgia, Russia **(1879–1953)**.

Stalina, Svetlana Alliluyeva (Stalin's daughter); Moscow, U.S.S.R., 2/28/1926.
Stamp, Terrence (actor); London, England, 1940.
Stang, Arnold (comedian); Chelsea, Mass., 1925.
Stanislavski (Konstantin Sergeevich Alekseev) (stage producer); b. Moscow, Russia **(1863–1938)**.
Stanely, Kim (Patricia Reid) (actress); Tularosa, N.M., 2/11/1925.
Stanely, Sir Henry Morton (John Rowlands) (explorer); b. Denbigh, Wales **(1841–1904)**.
Stans, Maurice H. (ex-Secretary of Commerce); Shakope, Minn., 3/22/1908.
Stanton, Frank (broadcasting executive); Muskegon, Mich., 3/20/1908.
Stanwyck, Barbara (Rúby Stevens) (actress); Brooklyn, N.Y., 7/16/1907.
Stapleton, Jean (Jeanne Murray) (actress); New York City, 1/19/1923.
Stapleton, Maureen (actress); Troy, N.Y., 6/21/1925.
Stapleton, Pat (hockey); Sarnia, Ontario, Canada, 7/4/1940.
Stargell, Willie (Wilver Dornell) (baseball); Earlsboro, Okla., 3/6/1941.
Starker, János (cellist); Budapest, Hungary, 7/5/1926.
Starr, Bart (football); Montgomery, Ala., 1/9/1934.
Starr, Kay (Starks) (singer); Dougherty, Okla., 7/21/1922.
Starr, Ringo (Richard Starkey) (singer); Dingle, Liverpool, England, 7/7/1940.
Stassen, Harold E. (ex-government official); West St. Paul, Minn., 4/13/1907.
Staubach, Roger (football); Cincinnati, Ohio, 2/5/1942.
Steber, Eleanor (soprano); Wheeling, W. Va., 7/17/1916.
Stecher, Renate (track); Suptitz, East Germany, 5/12/1950.
Steegmuller, Francis (biographer); New Haven, Conn., 7/3/1906.
Steele, Tommy (singer); London, England, 12/17/1936.
Steiger, Rod (Rodney) (actor); Westhampton, N.Y., 4/14/1925.
Stein, Gertrude (author); b. Allegheny, Pa. **(1874–1946)**.
Steinbeck, John Ernst (author); b. Salinas, Calif. **(1902–1968)**.
Steinberg, William (conductor); Cologne, Germany, 8/1/1899.
Steinem, Gloria (feminist); Toledo, Ohio, 3/25/1935(?).
Steinkraus, William C. (equestrian); Cleveland, Ohio, 10/12/1925.
Stendhal (Marie Henri Beyle) (novelist); b. Grenoble, France **(1783–1842)**.
Stenerud, Jan (football); Fetsund, Norway, 11/26/1942.
Stengel, Casey (Charles Dillon) (baseball); b. Kansas City, Mo. **(1891–1975)**.
Stenmark, Ingemar (Alpine skier); Tarnaby, Sweden, 3/18/1956.
Sterling, Jan (actress); New York City, 1923.
Stern, Isaac (violinist); Kreminiecz, Russia, 7/21/1920.
Sterne, Laurence (novelist); b. Clonmel, Ireland **(1713–1768)**.
Stevens, Connie (singer); Brooklyn, N.Y., 8/8/1938.
Stevens, George (director); b. Oakland, Calif. **(1905–1975)**.
Stevens, Risë (mezzo-soprano); New York City, 6/11/1913.
Stevens, Roger L. (producer); Detroit, Mich., 3/12/1910.
Stevens, Stella (actress); Yazoo City, Miss., 10/1/1936.
Stevenson, Adlai Ewing (statesman); b. Los Angeles, Calif. **(1900–1965)**.
Stevenson, Robert Louis Balfour (novelist & poet); b. Edinburgh, Scotland **(1850–1894)**.
Stewart, James (actor); Indiana, Pa., 5/20/1908.
Stickney, Dorothy (actress); Dickinson, N. Dak., 6/21/1903.
Stokes, Carl (TV newscaster); Cleveland, Ohio, 6/21/1927.
Stokowski, Leopold (conductor); London, England, 4/18/1882.
Stone, Edward Durrell (architect); Fayetteville, Ark., 3/9/1902.
Stone, Ezra (actor, producer); New Bedford, Mass., 12/2/1917.
Stone, Fred (actor); b. Denver, Colo. **(1873–1959)**.
Stone, I. F. (Isidor Feinstein Stone) (journalist); Philadelphia, Pa., 12/24/1907.
Stone, Irving (Irving Tennenbaum) (novelist); San Francisco, Calif., 7/14/1903.
Stone, Lewis (actor); b. Worcester, Mass. **(1879–1953)**.
Stone, Lucy (woman suffragist); b. nr. West Brookfield, Mass. **(1818–1893)**.
Stone, Sly (Sylvester) (musician); 1944.
Stones, Dwight Edwin (track); Los Angeles, Calif., 12/6/1953.
Storm, Gale (actress); Bloomington, Tex., 1922.
Stout, Rex (mystery writer); b. Noblesville, Ind. **(1886–1975)**.
Stowe, Harriet Elizabeth (nee Beecher) (novelist); b. Litchfield, Conn. **(1811–1896)**.
Stradivari. Antonio (violinmaker); b. Cremona, Italy **(1644–1737)**.
Stanahan, Frank R. (golf); Toledo, Ohio, 8/5/1922.
Strasberg, Lee (director); Budanov, Austria, 11/17/1901.
Strasberg, Susan (actress); New York City, 5/22/1938.
Straus, Oskar (composer); b. Vienna, Austria **(1870–1954)**.
Strauss, Johann (composer); b. Vienna, Austria **(1825–1899)**.
Strauss, Lewis L. (Naval officer & scientist); b. Charleston, W. Va. **(1896–1974)**.
Strauss, Richard (composer); b. Munich, Germany **(1864–1949)**.
Stravinsky, Igor (composer); b. Orienbaum, Russia **(1882–1971)**.
Streisand, Barbra (singer, actress); Brooklyn, N.Y., 4/24/1942.
Stritch, Elaine (actress); Detroit, Mich., 2/2/1928.
Struthers, Sally Ann (actress); Portland, Ore., 7/28/1948.
Stuart, James Ewell Brown (known as Jeb) (Confederate army officer); b. Patrick County, Va. **(1833–1864)**.
Stuyvesant, Peter (Governor of New Amsterdam); b. West Fries-

land, Netherlands **(1592–1672)**.

Styron, William (William Clark Styron, Jr.) (novelist); Newport News, Va., 6/11/1925.

Sullavan, Margaret Brooke (actress); b. Norfolk, Va. **(1911–1960)**.

Sullivan, Barry (Patrick Barry) (actor); New York City, 8/29/1912.

Sullivan, Ed (columnist & TV personality); b. New York City **(1901–1974)**.

Sullivan, Francis Loftus (actor); b. London, England **(1903–1956)**.

Sullivan, Frank (Francis John) (humorist); b. Saratoga Springs, N.Y., **(1892–1976)**.

Sullivan, John Lawrence (boxer); b. Boston, Mass. **(1858–1918)**.

Sullivan, Sir Arthur Seymour (composer); b. London, England **(1842–1900)**.

Sulzberger, Arthur Ochs (newspaper publisher); New York City, 2/5/1926.

Sumac, Yma (singer); Ichocan, Peru, 9/10/1927.

Sun Yat-sen (statesman); b. nr. Macao, China **(1866–1925)**.

Susskind, David (TV producer); New York City, 12/19/1920.

Sutherland, Joan (soprano); Sydney, Australia, 11/7/1926.

Suzman, Janet (actress); Johannesburg, South Africa, 2/9/1939.

Suzuki, Pat (actress); Cressey, Calif., 1931.

Swanson, Gloria (Josephine Swenson) (actress); Chicago, Ill., 3/27/1899.

Swarthout, Gladys (soprano); b. Deepwater, Mo. **(1904–1969)**.

Swayze, John Cameron (news commentator); Wichita, Kan., 4/4/1906.

Swift, Jonathan (satirist); b. Dublin, Ireland **(1667–1745)**.

Swigert, John L., Jr. (astronaut); Denver, Colo., 8/30/1931.

Swinburne, Algernon Charles (poet); b. London, England **(1837–1909)**.

Swope, Herbert Bayard (journalist); b. St. Louis, Mo. **(1882–1958)**.

Sydow, Max von (Carl Adolf von Sydow) (actor); Lund, Sweden, 4/10/1929.

Synge, John Millington (dramatist); b. nr. Dublin, Ireland **(1871–1909)**.

Taft, Robert Alphonso (legislator); b. Cincinnati, Ohio **(1889–1953)**.

Tagore, Sir Rabindranath (poet); b. Calcutta, India **(1861–1941)**.

Tallchief, Maria (ballerina); Fairfax, Okla., 1/24/1925.

Talleyrand-Périgord, Charles Maurice de (statesman); b. Paris, France **(1754–1838)**.

Talmadge, Norma (actress); b. Niagara Falls, N.Y. **(1897–1957)**.

Tamerlane (Timur) (Mongol conqueror); b. near Samarkand, Siberia **(1336?–1405)**.

Tandy, Jessica (actress); London, England, 6/7/1909.

Tarkenton, Fran (Francis) (football); Richmond, Va., 2/3/1940.

Tarkington, Newton Booth (novelist); b. Indianapolis, Ind. **(1869–1946)**.

Tate, Allen (John Orley) (poet-critic); Winchester, Ky., 11/19/1899.

Tate, Sharon (actress); b. Dallas, Tex. **(1943–1969)**.

Tati, Jacques (Jacques Tatischeff) (actor); Pecq, France, 10/9/1908.

Taylor, Elizabeth (actress); London, England, 2/27/1932.

Taylor, Estelle (actress); b. Wilmington, Del. **(1899–1958)**.

Taylor, Harold (educator); Toronto, Ont., Canada, 9/28/1914.

Taylor, James (singer); Boston, Mass., 3/12/1948.

Taylor, (Joseph) Deems (composer); b. New York City **(1885–1966)**.

Taylor, Laurette (Laurette Cooney) (actress); b. New York City **(1884–1946)**.

Taylor, Gen. Maxwell D. (former Army Chief of Staff); Keytesville, Mo., 8/26/1901.

Taylor, Robert (Spangler Arlington Brugh) (actor); b. Filley, Neb. **(1911–1969)**.

Taylor, Rod (actor); Sydney, Australia, 1/11/1930.

Tchaikovsky, Peter (Petr) Ilich (composer); b. Ural region, Russia **(1840–1893)**.

Tebaldi, Renata (lyric soprano); Pesaro, Italy, 1/2/1922.

Tebbetts, Birdie (George R.) (baseball); Nashua, N.J., 11/10/1914.

Tecumseh (Shawnee Indian chief); b. nr. Springfield, Ohio **(1768?–1813)**.

Teller, Edward (atomic physicist); Budapest, Hungary, 1/15/1908.

Temple, Shirley, *See* Shirley Temple Black.

Tennyson, Alfred (1st Baron Tennyson) (poet); b. Somersby, Lincolnshire, England **(1809–1892)**.

Tereshkova, Valentina V. (cosmonaut); Maslennikovo, U.S.S.R., 3/6/1937.

Terry, Ellen Alicia (actress); b. Coventry, England **(1848–1928)**.

Terry-Thomas (Thomas Terry Hoar Stevens) (actor); London, England, 7/14/1911.

Thackeray, William Makepeace (novelist); b. Calcutta, India **(1811–1863)**.

Thant, U (U.N. statesman); b. Pantanaw, Burma **(1909–1974)**.

Tharp, Twyla (dancer, choreographer); Portland, Ind., 7/1/1941(?).

Thatcher, Margaret (political leader); Grantham, Lincolnshire, England, 10/13/1925.

Thaxter, Phyllis (actress); Portland, Me., 1921.

Thebom, Blanche (mezzo-soprano); Monessen, Pa., 9/19/1919.

Thieu, Nguyen Van (ex-President of South Vietnam); Trithuy, Annam, 4/5/1923.

Thoeni, Gustavo (Alpine skier); Trafoi, Italy, 2/28/1951.

Thomas, Danny (Amos Jacobs) (entertainer, TV producer); Deerfield, Mich., 1/6/1914.

Thomas, Dylan Marlais (poet); b. Carmarthenshire, Wales **(1914–1953)**.

Thomas, Lowell (explorer, commentator); Woodington, Ohio, 4/6/1892.

Thomas, Marlo (actress); Detroit, Mich., 11/21/1943.

Thomas, Michael Tilson (conductor); Hollywood, Calif., 12/21/1944.

Thomas, Norman Mattoon (Socialist leader); b. Marion, Ohio **(1884–1968)**.

Thomas, Richard (actor); New York City, 6/13/1951.

Thompson, Dorothy (writer); Lancaster, N.Y. **(1894–1961)**.

Thoreau, Henry David (naturalist & author); b. Concord, Mass. **(1817–1862)**.

Thorndike, Dame Sybil (actress); b. Gainsborough, Lincolnshire, England, **(1882–1976)**.

Thorpe, Jim (James Francis Thorpe) (athlete); b. nr. Prague, Okla. **(1888–1953)**.

Thurber, James Grover (author & cartoonist); b. Columbus, Ohio **(1894–1961)**.

Tibbett, Lawrence (baritone); b. Bakersfield, Calif. **(1896–1960)**.

Tierney, Gene (actress); Brooklyn, N.Y., 11/20/1920.

Tiffin, Pamela (actress); Oklahoma City, Okla., 10/13/1942.

Tilden, William Tatem, II (tennis player); b. Philadelphia, Pa. **(1893–1953)**.

Tillstrom, Burr (puppeteer); Chicago, Ill., 10/13/1917.

Tiny Tim (Herbert Khaury) (entertainer); New York City, 1923(?).

Tiomkin, Dmitri (composer); Russia, 5/10/1899.

Tito (Josip Broz or Brozovich) (President of Yugoslavia); Croatia, 5/25/1892.

Titov, Gerhman S. (cosmonaut); Verkhneye Zhilino, Siberia, 9/11/1935.

Tittle, Y. A. (Yelberton Abraham) (football); Marshall, Tex., 10/24/1926.

Tocqueville, Alexis de (writer); b. Verneuil, France **(1805–1859)**.

Todd, Thelma (actress); b. Lawrence, Mass. **(1905–1935)**.

Tolstoi, Count Leo (Lev) Nikolaevich (novelist); b. Tula province, Russia **(1828–1910)**.

Tomlin, Lily (comedienne); Detroit, Mich., 1939(?).

Tone, Franchot (actor); b. Niagara Falls, N.Y. **(1905–1968)**.

Toomey, William (decathlon); Philadelphia, Pa., 1/10/1939.

Tormé, Mel (Melvin) (singer); Chicago, Ill., 9/13/1925.

Toscanini, Arturo (orchestra conductor); b. Parma, Italy **(1867–1957)**.

Tourel, Jennie (mezzo-soprano); b. Montreal, Canada **(1910–1973)**.

Toynbee, Arnold J. (historian); b. London, England **(1889–1975)**.

Tracy, Lee (actor); b. Atlanta, Ga. **(1898–1968)**.

Tracy, Spencer (actor); b. Milwaukee, Wis. **(1900–1967)**.

Traubel, Helen (Wagnerian soprano); b. St. Louis, Mo. **(1903–1972)**.

Treacher, Arthur (actor); b. Brighton, England **(1894–1975)**.

Trevino, Lee (golf); Dallas, Tex., 12/1/1939.

Trevor, Claire (actress); New York City, 1909.

Trigere, Pauline (fashion designer); Paris, France, 11/4/1912.

Trilling, Lionel (author, educator); b. New York City **(1905–1975)**.

Trotsky, Leon (Lev Davidovich Bronstein) (statesman); b. Elisavetgrad, Russia **(1879–1940)**.

Trudeau, Pierre Elliott (Prime Minister); Montreal, Canada, 10/18/1919.

Truffaut, François (film director); Paris, France, 2/6/1932.

Trujillo y Molina, Rafael Leonidas (Dominican Republic dictator); b. San Cristóbal, Dominican Republic **(1891–1961)**.

Truman, Margaret (Mrs. Clifton Daniel) (author); Independence, Mo., 2/17/1924.

Tryon, Thomas (actor, novelist); Hartford, Conn., 1/14/1926.

Tucker, Forrest (actor); Plainfield, Ind., 2/12/1919.

Tucker, Richard (tenor); b. New York City **(1914–1975)**.

Tucker, Sophie (Sophie Abuza) (singer); b. Boston, Mass. **(1884?–1966)**.

Tudor, Antony (choreographer); London, England, 4/4/1909.

Tuero, Linda (tennis); Metairie, La., 10/21/1954.

Tunney, Gene (James J.) (boxing); New York City, 5/25/1898.

Turgenev, Ivan Sergeevich (novelist); b. Orel, Russia **(1818–1883)**.

Turner, Ike (singer); Clarksdale, Miss., 11/?/1931.

Turner, Lana (Julia Jean Turner) (actress); Wallace, Idaho, 2/8/1920.

Turner, Tina (Annie Mae Mullock) (signer); Brownsville, Tex., 1939.

Turpin, Ben (comedian); b. New Orleans, La. **(1874–1940)**.

Tushingham, Rita (actress); Liverpool, England, 3/14/1942.

Twain, Mark (Samuel Langhorne Clemens) (author); b. Florida, Mo. **(1835–1910)**.

Tweed, William Marcy (politician); b. New York City **(1823–1878)**.

Twiggy (Leslie Hornby) (model); London, England, 9/19/1949.

Twining, Gen. Nathan F. (former Air Force Chief of Staff); Monroe, Wis., 10/11/1897.

Tyson, Cicely (actress); New York City, 12/19/1939(?).

Tyus, Wyomia (runner); Griffin, Ga., 8/29/1945.

Udall, Stewart L. (ex-Sec. of Interior); St. Johns, Ariz., 1/31/1920.

Uggams, Leslie (singer, actress); New York City, 5/25/1943.

Ulanova, Galina (ballerina); St. Petersburg, Russia, 1/10/1910.

Ullmann, Liv (actress); Tokyo, Japan, 12/16/1939.

Ulric, Lenore (actress); b. New Ulm, Minn. **(1894–1970)**.

Unitas, John (football); Pittsburgh, Pa., 5/7/1933.

Unser, Al (auto racing); Albuquerque, N. Mex., 5/29/1939.

Unser, Bobby (auto racing); Albuquerque, N. Mex., 2/20/1934.
Untermeyer, Louis (anthologist); New York City, 10/1/1885.
Updike, John (novelist); Shillington, Pa., 3/18/1932.
Urey, Harold C. (physicist); Walkerton, Ind., 4/29/1893.
Uris, Leon (novelist); Baltimore, Md., 8/3/1924.
Ustinov, Peter (actor, producer); London, England, 4/16/1921.
Vaccaro, Brenda (actress); Brooklyn, N.Y., 11/18/1939.
Valentine, Karen (actress); Santa Rosa, Calif., 1947.
Valentino (Valentino Garavani) (fashion designer); nr. Milan, Italy, 5/11/1932.
Valentino, Rudolph (Rodolpho d'Antonguolla) (actor); b. Castellaneta, Italy **(1895–1926)**.
Vallee, Rudy (Hubert Vallée) (band leader, singer); Island Pond, Vt., 7/28/1901.
Van Allen, James Alfred (space physicist); Mt. Pleasant, Iowa, 9/7/1914.
Van Brocklin, Norm (football); Eagle Butte, S. Dak., 3/15/1926.
Van Buren, Abigail (Mrs. Morton Phillips) (columnist); Sioux City, Iowa, 7/14/1918.
Van Doren, Mamie (actress); Rowena, S.D., 1933.
van-Lawick-Goodall, (Baroness) Jane (ethologist); London, England, 4/3/1934.
Vance, Vivian (actress); Cherryvale, Kan., 1912.
Vandenberg, Arthur Hendrick (legislator); b. Grand Rapids, Mich. **(1884–1951)**.
Vanderbilt, Alfred G. (sportsman); London, England, 9/22/1912.
Vanderbilt, Cornelius (financier); b. Port Richmond, N.Y. **(1794–1877)**.
Vanderbilt, Gloria (artist, heiress); New York City, 2/20/1924.
Van Dyke, Dick (actor); West Plains, Mo., 12/13/1925.
Van Heusen, Jimmy (Edward Chester Babcock) (songwriter); Syracuse, N.Y., 1/26/1913.
Van Peebles, Melvin (playwright); Chicago, Ill., 9/21/1932.
Vaughn, Robert (actor); New York City, 11/22/1932.
Vaughan, Sarah (singer); Newark, N.J., 3/27/1924.
Vaughan Williams, Ralph (composer); b. Down Ampney, England **(1872–1958)**.
Veidt, Conrad (actor); b. Berlin, Germany **(1893–1943)**.
Velez, Lupe (Guadelupe Velez de Villalobos) (actress); b. San Luis Potosi, Mexico **(1908–1944)**.
Venturi, Robert (Charles) (architect); Philadelphia, Pa., 6/25/1925.
Verdi, Giuseppe (composer); b. Roncole, Parma, Italy **(1813–1901)**.
Verdon, Gwen (actress); Culver City, Calif., 1/13/1926.
Vereen, Ben (actor, singer); Miami, Fla., 10/10/1946.
Verne, Jules (author); b. Nantes, France **(1828–1905)**.
Verrazano, Giovanni da (navigator); b. Florence, Italy **(1485?–1528)**.
Verrett, Shirley (mezzo-soprano); New Orleans, La., 5/31/1933.
Vespucci, Amerigo (navigator); b. Florence, Italy **(1454–1512)**.
Vickers, Jon (tenor); Prince Albert, Sask., Canada, 10/29/1926.
Vidal, Gore (novelist); West Point, N.Y., 10/3/1925.
Vidor, King (director-producer); Galveston, Tex., 2/8/1895.
Villa, Pancho (Doroteo Arango) (bandit); b. Rio Grande, Mexico **(1877–1923)**.
Villella, Edward (ballet dancer); Bayside, Queens, N.Y., 10/1/1936.
Villon, François de Montcorbier) (poet); b. Paris, France **(1431–1463)**.
Vinton, Bobby (singer); Canonsburg, Pa., 1935.
Viren, Lasse (track); Myrskyla, Finland, 7/12/1949.
Virgil (or Vergil) (Publius Vergilius Maro) (poet); b. Mantua, Gaul **(70–19 B.C.)**.
Vishnevskaya, Galina (soprano); Leningrad, U.S.S.R., 10/25/1926.
Voight, Jon (actor); Yonkers, N.Y., 12/29/1938.
Voltaire (François Marie Arouet) (author); b. Paris, France **(1694–1778)**.
Von Braun. *See* Braun.
von Furstenberg, Betsy (actress); Neiheim-Heusen, Germany, 8/16/1935.
Vonnegut, Kurt Jr. (novelist); Indianapolis, Ind., 11/11/1922.
Von Stroheim, Erich Oswald Hans Carl Maria von Nordenwall (actor, director); b. Vienna, Austria **(1885–1957)**.
von Sydow, Max. *See* Sydow.
Vorster, Balthazar Johannes (Prime Minister); Jamestown, Cape Province, South Africa, 12/13/1915.
Wade, Virginia (tennis); Bournemouth, England, 7/10/1945.
Wagner, Honus (John Wagner) (baseball player); b. Mansfield, Pa. **(1874–1955)**.
Wagner, Robert (actor); Detroit, Mich., 2/10/1930.
Wagner, Robert F. (ex-Mayor of New York City); New York City, 4/20/1910.
Wagner, Wilhelm Richard (composer); b. Leipzig, Germany **(1813–1883)**.
Walcott, Jersey Joe (Arnold Cream) (boxing); Merchantville, N.J., 1/31/1914.
Waldheim, Kurt (U.N. Secretary-General); St. Andrae-Wörden, Austria, 12/21/1918.
Walker, Clint (actor); Hartford, Ill., 5/30/1927.
Walker, Mickey (boxing); Elizabeth, N.J., 7/13/1901.
Walker, Nancy (Ann Myrtle Swoyer) (actress, comedienne); Philadelphia, Pa., 5/10/1922.
Wallace, DeWitt (publisher); St. Paul, Minn., 11/12/1889.
Wallace, George C. (Governor); Clio, Ala., 8/25/1919.

Wallace, Henry Agard (statesman); b. Adair County, Iowa **(1888–1965)**.
Wallace, Irving (novelist); Chicago, Ill., 3/19/1916.
Wallace, Mike (Myron Wallace) (TV interviewer & commentator); Brookline, Mass., 5/9/1918.
Wallach, Eli (actor); Brooklyn, N.Y., 12/7/1915.
Waller, Thomas "Fats" (pianist); b. New York City **(1904–1943)**.
Wallis, Hal (producer); Chicago, Ill., 9/14/1899.
Waltari, Mika (novelist); Helsinki, Finland, 9/19/1908.
Walter, Bruno (Bruno Walter Schlesinger) (orchestra conductor); b. Berlin, Germany **(1876–1962)**.
Walters, Barbara (TV broadcaster); Boston, Mass., 9/25/1931.
Walthall, Henry B. (actor); b. Shelby City, Ala. **(1878–1936)**.
Walton, Izaak (author); b. Stafford, England **(1593–1683)**.
Ward, Barbara (economist); York, England, 5/23/1914.
Waring, Fred (band leader); Tyrone, Pa., 6/9/1900.
Warner, H. B. (Henry Bryan Warner Lickford) (actor); b. London, England **(1876–1958)**.
Warren, Earl (U.S. Chief Justice); b. Los Angeles, Calif. **(1891–1974)**.
Warren, Robert Penn (novelist); Guthrie, Ky., 4/24/1905.
Warwicke, Dionne (singer); East Orange, N.J., 1941.
Washington, Booker Taliaferro (educator); b. Franklin County, Va. **(1856–1915)**.
Waters, Ethel (actress, singer); Chester, Pa., 10/31/1900.
Watson, Thomas John (industrialist); b. Campbell, N.Y. **(1874–1956)**.
Watt, James (inventor); b. Greenock, Scotland **(1736–1819)**.
Watts, André (pianist); Nuremberg, Germany, 6/20/1946.
Waugh, Alex (Alexander Raban Waugh) (novelist); London, England, 7/8/1898.
Wayne, Anthony (military officer); b. Waynesboro, Pa. **(1745–1796)**.
Wayne, David (David McMeakan) (actor); Traverse City, Mich., 1/30/1914.
Wayne, John (Marion Michael Morrison) (actor); Winterset, Iowa, 5/26/1907.
Weaver, Dennis (actor); Joplin, Mo., 6/14/1925.
Weaver, Earl (baseball); St. Louis, Mo., 8/14/1930.
Weaver, Fritz (actor); Pittsburgh, Pa., 1/19/1926.
Webb, Clifton (Webb Parmelee Hollenbeck) (actor); b. Indianapolis, Ind. **(1893–1966)**.
Webb, Jack (actor, producer); Santa Monica, Calif., 4/2/1920.
Weber, Karl Maria Friedrich Ernst von (composer); b. nr. Lübeck, Germany **(1786–1826)**.
Webster, Alex (football); Kearny, N.J., 4/19/1931.
Webster, Daniel (statesman); b. Salisbury, N.H. **(1782–1852)**.
Webster, Noah (lexicographer); b. West Hartford, Conn. **(1758–1843)**.
Weill, Kurt (composer); b. Dessau, Germany **(1900–1950)**.
Weiskopf, Tom (golf); Massillon, Ohio, 11/9/1942.
Weiss, George (baseball executive); b. New Haven, Conn. **(1895–1972)**.
Weissmuller, Johnny (swimmer, actor); Windber, Pa., 6/2/1904.
Weizmann, Chaim (Israeli statesman); b. Grodno province, Russia **(1874–1952)**.
Welch, Raquel (Raquel Tejada) (actress); Chicago, Ill., 9/5/1942.
Weld, Tuesday (Susan) (actress); New York City, 8/27/1943.
Welk, Lawrence (band leader); Strasburg, N.D., 3/11/1903.
Welles, Orson (actor, producer); Kenosha, Wis., 5/6/1915.
Wellington, Duke of (Arthur Wellesley) (statesman); b. Ireland **(1769–1852)**.
Wells, Herbert George (author); b. Bromley, Kent, England **(1866–1946)**.
Welty, Eudora (novelist); Jackson, Miss., 4/13/1909.
Werfel, Franz (novelist); b. Prague, Bohemia **(1890–1945)**.
Werner, Oskar (actor, director); Vienna, Austria, 11/13/1922.
Wesley, John (religious leader); b. Epworth Rectory, Lincolnshire, England **(1703–1791)**.
West, Dame Rebecca (Cicily Fairfield) (novelist); County Kerry, Ireland, 12/25/1892.
West, Jerry (basketball); Cheylan, W. Va., 5/28/1938.
West, Mae (actress); Brooklyn, N.Y., 8/17/1893.
Westinghouse, George (inventor); b. Central Bridge, N.Y. **(1846–1914)**.
Westmoreland, William Childs (ex-Army Chief of Staff); Saxon, S.C., 3/26/1914.
Wharton, Edith Newbold (née Jones) (novelist); b. New York City **(1862–1937)**.
Wheeler, Bert (Albert Jerome Wheeler) (comedian); b. Paterson, N.J. **(1895–1968)**.
White, E. B. (Elwyn Brooks White) (author); Mt. Vernon, N.Y., 7/11/1899.
White, Paul Dudley (heart specialist); b. Roxbury, Mass. **(1886–1973)**.
White, Theodore H. (historian); Boston, Mass., 5/6/1915.
White, William Allen (journalist); b. Emporia, Kan. **(1868–1944)**.
White, Willye B. (long jumper); Money, Miss., 1/1/1936.
Whitehead, Alfred North (mathematician-philosopher); b. Isle of Thanet, England **(1861–1947)**.
Whiteman, Paul (musician); b. Denver, Colo. **(1891–1967)**.
Whitman, Walt (Walter) (poet); b. West Hills, N.Y. **(1819–1892)**.
Whitmore, James (actor); White Plains, N.Y., 10/1/1921.

Whitney, Cornelius Vanderbilt (sportsman); New York City, 2/20/1899.
Whitney, Eli (inventor); b. Westboro, Mass. **(1765–1825)**.
Whitney, John Hay (publisher); Ellsworth, Me., 8/17/1904.
Whittier, John Greenleaf (poet); b. Haverhill, Mass. **(1807–1892)**.
Whitworth, Kathy (golf); Monahans, Tex., 9/27/1939.
Widmark, Richard (actor); Sunrise, Minn., 12/26/1914.
Wiesel, Elie (Eliezer) (author); Sighet, Romania, 9/30/1928.
Wilbur, Doreen (archery); Jefferson, Iowa, 1/8/1930.
Wilbur, Richard (poet); New York City, 3/1/1921.
Wilde, Cornel (actor, producer); New York City, 10/13/1918.
Wilde, Oscar Fingal O'Flahertie Wills (author); b. Dublin, Ireland **(1854–1900)**.
Wilder, Billy (producer-director); Vienna, Austria, 6/22/1906.
Wilder, Gene (actor); Milwaukee, Wis., 6/11/1935.
Wilder, Thornton, (author); b. Madison, Wis. **(1897–1975)**.
Wilding, Michael (actor); Westcliff, Essex, England, 7/23/1912.
Wilkins, Lennie (basketball); 11/25/1937.
Wilkins, Roy (civil rights leader); St. Louis, Mo., 8/30/1901.
Wilkins, Sir George Hubert (explorer); b. Mt. Bryan East, Australia **(1888–1958)**.
Wilkinson, Bud (football); Minneapolis, Minn., 4/23/1916.
Williams, Andy (singer); Wall Lake, Iowa, 12/3/1930.
Williams, Dick (baseball); St. Louis, Mo., 5/7/1929.
Williams, Edward Bennett (lawyer); Hartford, Conn., 5/31/1920.
Williams, Emlyn (actor); Mostyn, Wales, 11/26/1905.
Williams, Esther (actress); Los Angeles, Calif., 8/8/1923.
Williams, Gluyas (cartoonist); San Francisco, Calif., 7/23/1888.
Williams, Roger (clergyman); b. London, England **(1603?–1683)**.
Williams, Ted (baseball); San Diego, Calif., 8/30/1918.
Williams, Tennessee (Thomas L. Williams) (playwright); Columbus, Miss., 3/26/1911.
Willkie, Wendell Lewis (lawyer); b. Elwood, Ind. **(1892–1944)**.
Wills, Maury (baseball); Washington, D.C., 10/2/1932.
Willson, Meredith (composer); Mason City, Iowa, 5/18/1902.
Wilson, Don (radio & TV announcer); Lincoln, Neb., 1924.
Wilson, Flip (Clerow) (comedian); Jersey City, N.J., 12/8/1933.
Wilson, Harold (ex-Prime Minister); Huddersfield, Yorkshire, England, 3/11/1916.
Wilson, Nancy (singer); Chillicothe, Ohio, 2/20/1937.
Wilson, Sloan (novelist); Norwalk, Conn., 5/8/1920.
Winchell, Walter (columnist); b. New York City **(1897–1972)**.
Windsor, Duchess of (Bessie Wallis Warfield); Blue Ridge Summit, Pa., 6/19/1896.
Windsor, Duke of (formerly King Edward VIII of England); b. Richmond Park, England **(1894–1972)**.
Winters, Jonathan (comedian); Dayton, Ohio, 11/11/1925.
Winters, Shelley (Shirley Schrift) (actress); East St. Louis, Ill., 8/18/1922.
Winthrop, John (first Governor Massachusetts Bay Colony); b. Suffolk, England **(1588–1649)**.
Wise, Stephen Samuel (rabbi); b. Budapest, Hungary **(1874–1949)**.
Withers, Jane (actress); Atlanta, Ga., 1927.
Wodehouse, P. G. (Pelham Grenville) (novelist); b. Guildford, England **(1881–1975)**.
Wohlhuter, Richard C. (runner); Geneva, Ill., 12/23/1945.
Wolfe, Thomas Clayton (novelist); b. Asheville, N.C. **(1900–1938)**.
Wolfe, Tom (journalist); Richmond, Va., 3/2/1931.
Wolheim, Louis (actor); b. New York City **(1880–1931)**.
Wolsey, Thomas (prelate & statesman); b. Ipswich, England **(1475?–1530)**.
Wonder, Stevie (Steveland Judkins, later Steveland Morris) (singer); Saginaw, Mich., 5/13/1950.
Wong, Anna May (Lu Tsong Wong) (actress); b. Los Angeles, Calif. **(1907–1961)**.

Wood, Natalie (Natasha Gurdin) (actress); San Francisco, Calif., 7/20/1938.
Woodward, Joanne (actress); Thomasville, Ga., 2/27/1930.
Woolf, Adeline Virginia (née Stephens) (novelist); b. London, England **(1882–1941)**.
Woollcott, Alexander (author); b. Phalanx, N.J. **(1887–1943)**.
Woolley, Monty (Edgar Montillion Woolley) (actor); b. New York City **(1888–1963)**.
Wordsworth, William (poet); b. Cockermouth, Cumberland, England **(1770–1850)**.
Worley, Jo Anne (actress); Lowell, Ind., 9/6/1937.
Wottle, David James (runner); Canton, Ohio, 8/7/1950.
Wouk, Herman (novelist); New York City, 5/27/1915.
Wray, Fay (actress); Alberta, Canada, 1907.
Wright, Mickey (Mary Kathryn) (golf); San Diego, Calif., 2/14/1935.
Wright, Orville (inventor); b. Dayton, Ohio **(1871–1948)**.
Wright, Richard (novelist); b. nr. Natchez, Miss. **(1908–1960)**.
Wright, Teresa (actress); New York City, 10/27/1918.
Wright, Wilbur (inventor); b. Millville, Ind. **(1867–1912)**.
Wyatt, Jane (actress); Campgaw, N.J., 8/12/1912.
Wycherly, Margaret (actress); b. London, England **(1881–1956)**.
Wyler, William (director); Mulhouse, France, 7/1/1902.
Wyman, Jane (Sarah Jane Fulks) (actress); St. Joseph, Mo., 1/4/1914.
Wynette, Tammy (singer); Red Bay, Ala., 1942.
Wynn, Ed (Isaiah Edwin Leopold) (comedian); b. Philadelphia, Pa. **(1886–1966)**.
Wynn, Keenan (actor); New York City, 7/27/1916.
Wynter, Dana (actress); London, England, 6/8/1930.
Yarborough, Cale (William Caleb) (auto racing); Timmonsville, S.C., 3/27/1939.
Yastrzemski, Carl (baseball); Southampton, N.Y., 8/22/1939.
Yeats, William Butler (poet); b. nr. Dublin, Ireland **(1865–1939)**.
Yevtushenko, Yevgeny (poet); Zima, U.S.S.R., 7/18/1933.
York, Michael (actor); Fulmer, England, 3/27/1942.
York, Susannah (Fletcher) (actress); London, England, 1/9/1942.
Yorty, Samuel W. (ex-Mayor of Los Angeles); Lincoln, Neb., 10/1/1909.
Young, Alan (actor); North Shield, England, 11/19/1919.
Young, Brigham (religious leader); b. Whitingham, Vt. **(1801–1877)**.
Young, Clara Kimball (actress); b. Chicago, Ill. **(1890–1960)**.
Young, Cy (Denton True Young) (baseball); b. Gilmore, Ohio **(1867–1955)**.
Young, Gig (Byron Barr) (actor); St. Cloud, Minn., 11/4/1917.
Young, John Watts (astronaut); San Francisco, Calif., 9/24/1930.
Young, Loretta (Gretchen Young) (actress); Salt Lake City, Utah, 1/6/1913.
Young, Robert (actor); Chicago, Ill., 2/22/1907.
Young, Sheila (speed skater, bicycle racer) Detroit, Mich., 10/14/1950.
Youngman, Henny (comedian); England, 1906.
Ysaÿe, Eugène (violinist); b. Liege, Belgium **(1858-1931)**.
Zanuck, Darryl F. (movie producer); Wahoo, Nab., 9/5/1902.
Zeffirelli, Franco (director); Florence, Italy, 2/12/1923.
Ziegfeld, Florenz (theatrical producer); b. Chicago, Ill. **(1869–1932)**.
Zimbalist, Efrem (violinist); Rostov-on-Don, Russia, 4/9/1889.
Zimbalist, Efrem, Jr. (actor); New York City, 11/30/1923.
Zola, Emile (novelist); b. Paris, France **(1840–1902)**.
Zoroaster (religious leader); b. Persia **(lived about the 6th century B.C.)**.
Zweig, Arnold (author); b. Gross Glogau, Germany **(1887–1968)**.
Zweig, Stefan (author); b. Vienna, Austria **(1881–1942)**.

Modern Wedding Anniversary Gift List
Source: Jewelry Industry Council.

1st anniversary: Clocks.	11th anniversary: Fashion jewelry and accessories.	25th anniversary: Sterling Silver Jubilee.
2nd anniversary: China.	12th anniversary: Pearls or colored gems.	30th anniversary: Diamond.
3rd anniversary: Crystal, glass.	13th anniversary: Textiles, furs.	35th anniversary: Jade
4th anniversary: Electrical appliances.	14th anniversary: Gold jewelry.	40th anniversary: Ruby.
5th anniversary: Silverware.	15th anniversary: Watches.	45th anniversary: Sapphire.
6th anniversary: Wood.	16th anniversary: Silver hollowware.	50th anniversary: Golden Jubilee.
7th anniversary: Desk sets—pen and pencil sets.	17th anniversary: Furniture.	55th anniversary: Emerald.
8th anniversary: Linens, laces.	18th anniversary: Porcelain.	60th anniversary: Diamond Jubilee.
9th anniversary: Leather.	19th anniversary: Bronze.	
10th anniversary: Diamond jewelry.	20th anniversary: Platinum.	

SPORTS

> **For 1976 sports champions and records, see special section beginning on Page 922.**

THE OLYMPIC GAMES

(W)—Site of Winter Games. (S)—Site of Summer Games.

1896—Athens	1928—Amsterdam (S)	1956—Cortina d'Am-	1968—Mexico City
1900—Paris	1932—Lake Placid (W)	pezzo, Italy (W)	(S)
1904—St. Louis	1932—Los Angeles (S)	1956—Melbourne (S)	1972—Sapporo, Ja-
1906—Athens	1936—Garmisch-Parten-	1960—Squaw Valley,	pan (W)
1908—London	kirchen (W)	Calif. (W)	1972—Munich (S)
1912—Stockholm	1936—Berlin (S)	1960—Rome (S)	1976—Innsbruck,
1920—Antwerp	1948—St. Moritz (W)	1964—Innsbruck,	Austria (W)
1924—Chamonix (W)	1948—London (S)	Austria (W)	1976—Montreal (S)
1924—Paris (S)	1952—Oslo (W)	1964—Tokyo (S)	1980—Lake Placid (W)
1928—St. Moritz (W)	1952—Helsinki (S)	1968—Grenoble,	1980—Moscow (S)
		France (W)	

THE first Olympic Games of which there is record occurred in 776 B.C. and consisted of one event, a great foot race of about 200 yards held on a plain by the River Alpheus (now the Ruphia) just outside the little town of Olympia in Greece. It was from that date that the Greeks began to keep their calendar by "Olympiads," the four-year spans between the celebrations of the famous games.

The modern Olympic Games, which started in Athens in 1896, are the result of the devotion of a French educator, Baron Pierre de Coubertin, to the idea that, since boys and athletics have gone together down the ages, education and athletics might well go hand-in-hand toward a better international understanding.

OLYMPIC GAMES CHAMPIONS, 1896-1972

TRACK AND FIELD

100-Meter Run

1896	Thomas Burke, United States	12s.
1900	F. W. Jarvis, United States	10.8s
1904	Archie Hahn, United States	11s.
1906	Archie Hahn, United States	11.2s.
1908	Reginald Walker, South Africa	10.8s.
1912	Ralph Craig, United States	10.8s.
1920	Charles Paddock, United States	10.8s.
1924	Harold Abrahams, Great Britain	10.6s.
1928	Percy Williams, Canada	10.8s.
1932	Eddie Tolan, United States	10.3s.
1936	Jesse Owens, United States	10.3s.*
1948	Harrison Dillard, United States	10.3s.
1952	Lindy Remigino, United States	10.4s.
1956	Bobby Morrow, United States	10.5s.
1960	Armin Hary, Germany	10.2s.
1964	Robert Hayes, United States	10s.
1968	James Hines, United States	9.9s.
1972	Valery Borzov. U.S.S.R.	10.14s.

* Wind assisted.

200-Meter Run

1900	John Tewksbury, United States	22.2s.
1904	Archie Hahn, United States	21.6s.

1908	Robert Kerr, Canada	22.6s.
1912	Ralph Craig, United States	21.7s.
1920	Allan Woodring, United States	22s.
1924	Jackson Scholz, United States	21.6s.
1928	Percy Williams, Canada	21.8s.
1932	Eddie Tolan, United States	21.2s.
1936	Jesse Owens, United States	20.7s.
1948	Melvin E. Patton, United States	21.1s.
1952	Andrew Stanfield, United States	20.7s.
1956	Bobby Morrow, United States	20.6s.
1960	Livio Berruti, Italy	20.5s.
1964	Henry Carr, United States	20.3s.
1968	Tommie Smith, United States	19.8s.
1972	Valery Borzov, U.S.S.R.	20s.

400-Meter Run

1896	Thomas Burke, United States	54.2.
1900	Maxey Long, United States	49.4.
1904	Harry Hillman, United States	49.2.
1906	Paul Pilgrim, United States	53.2.
1908	Wyndham Halswelle, Great Britain (walkover)	50s.
1912	Charles Reidpath, United States	48.2s.
1920	Bevil Rudd, South Africa	49.6s.
1924	Eric Liddell, Great Britain	47.6s.

838

1928	Ray Barbuti, United States..................	47.8s.	
1932	William Carr, United States.................	46.2s.	
1936	Archie Williams, United States.............	46.5s.	
1948	Arthur Wint, Jamaica, B.W.I...............	46.2s.	
1952	George Rhoden, Jamaica, B. W. I...........	45.9s.	
1956	Charles Jenkins, United States.............	46.7s.	
1960	Otis Davis, United States....	44.9s.	
1964	Mike Larrabee, United States...............	45.1s.	
1968	Lee Evans, United States...................	43.8s.	
1972	Vincent Matthews, United States	44.66s.	

800-Meter Run

1896	Edwin Flack, Great Britain................	2m.11s.
1900	Alfred Tysoe, Great Britain...............	2m.1.4s.
1904	James Lightbody, United States...........	1m.56s.
1906	Paul Pilgrim, United States...............	2m.1.2s.
1908	Mel Sheppard United States.............	1m.52.8s.
1912	Ted Meredith, United States..............	1m.51.9s.
1920	Albert Hill, Great Britain................	1m.53.4s.
1924	Douglas Lowe, Great Britain..............	1m.52.4s.
1928	Douglas Lowe, Great Britain..............	1m.51.8s.
1932	Thomas Hampson, Great Britain...........	1m.49.9s.
1936	John Woodruff, United States.............	1m.52.9s.
1948	Malvin Whitfield, United States...........	1m.49.2s.
1952	Malvin Whitfield, United States...........	1m.49.2s.
1956	Tom Courtney, United States..............	1m.47.7s.
1960	Peter Snell, New Zealand.................	1m.46.3s.
1964	Peter Snell, New Zealand.................	1m.45.1s.
1968	Ralph Doubell, Australia.................	1m.44.3s.
1972	David Wottle, United States	1m.45.9s.

1,500-Meter Run

1896	Edwin Flack, Great Britain................	4m.33.2s.
1900	Charles Bennett, Great Britain............	4m.6s.
1904	James Lightbody, United States...........	4m.5.4s.
1906	James Lightbody, United States...........	4m.12s.
1908	Mel Sheppard, United States.............	4m.3.4s.
1912	Arnold Jackson, Great Britain.............	3m.56.8s.
1920	Albert Hill, Great Britain................	4m.1.8s.
1924	Paavo Nurmi, Finland....................	3m.53.6s.
1928	Harry Larva, Finland....................	3m.53.2s.
1932	Luigi Beccali, Italy.....................	3m.51.2s.
1936	Jack Lovelock, New Zealand..............	3m.47.8s.
1948	Henri Eriksson, Sweden..................	3m.49.8s.
1952	Joseph Barthel, Luxemburg..............	3m.45.2s.
1956	Ron Delany, Ireland....................	3m.41.2s.
1960	Herb Elliott, Australia...................	3m.35.6s.
1964	Peter Snell, New Zealand................	3m.38.1s.
1968	Kipchoge Keino, Kenya..................	3m.34.9s.
1972	Pekka Vasala, Finland...................	3m.36.3s.

5,000-Meter Run

1912	Hannes Kolehmainen, Finland...........	14m.36.6s.
1920	Joseph Guillemot, France...............	14m.55.6s.
1924	Paavo Nurmi, Finland...................	14m.31.2s.
1928	Willie Ritola, Finland...................	14m.38s.
1932	Lauri Lehtinen, Finland.................	14m.30s.
1936	Gunnar Hockert, Finland................	14m.22.2s.
1948	Gaston Reiff, Belgium...................	14m.17.6s.
1952	Emil Zatopek Czechoslovakia............	14m.6.6s.
1956	Vladimir Kuts, U.S.S.R.................	13m.39.6s.
1960	Murray Halberg, New Zealand...........	13m.43.4s.
1964	Bob Schul, United States................	13m.48.8s.
1968	Mohamed Gammoudi, Tunisia............	14m.05s.
1972	Lasse Viren. Finland....................	13m.26.4s.

5-Mile Run

1906	H. Hawtrey, Great Britain................	26m.26.2s.
1908	Emil Voigt, Great Britain	25m.11.2s.

10,000-Meter Run

1912	Hannes Kolehmainen, Finland...........	31m.20.8s.
1920	Paavo Nurmi, Finland...................	31m.45.8s.

1924	Willie Ritola, Finland...................	30m.23.2s.
1928	Paavo Nurmi, Finland...................	30m.18.8s.
1932	Janusz Kusocinski, Poland...............	30m.11.4s.
1936	Ilmari Salminen, Finland................	30m.15.4s.
1948	Emil Zatopek, Czechoslovakia............	29m.59.6s.
1952	Emil Zatopek, Czechoslovakia............	29m.17s.
1956	Vladimir Kuts, U.S.S.R.................	28m.45.6s.
1960	Peter Bolotnikov, U.S.S.R...............	28m.32.2s.
1964	Billy Mills, United States...............	28m.24.4s.
1968	Naftali Temu, Kenya	29m.27.4s.
1972	Lasse Viren, Finland	27m.38.4s.

Marathon

1896	Spiridon Loues, Greece................	2h.58m.50s.
1900	Michel Teato, France...................	2h.59m.45s.
1904	Thomas Hicks, United States..........	3h.28m.53s.
1906	W. J. Sherring, Canada................	2h.51m.236s.
1908	John J. Hayes, United States..........	2h.55m.18.4s.
1912	Kenneth McArthur, South Africa.......	2h.36m.54.8s.
1920	Hannes Kolehmainen, Finland.........	2h.32m.35.8s.
1924	Albin Stenroos, Finland...............	2h.41m.22.6s.
1928	A. B. El Ouafi, France.................	2h.32m.57s.
1932	Juan Zabala, Argentina................	2h.31m.36s.
1936	Kitei Son, Japan......................	2h.29m.19.2s.
1948	Delfo Cabrera, Argentina..............	2h.34m.51.6s.
1952	Emil Zatopek, Czechoslovakia..........	2h.23m.3.2s.
1956	Alain Mimoun, France.................	2h.25m.
1960	Abebe Bikila, Ethiopia.................	2h.15m.16.2s.
1964	Abebe Bikila, Ethiopia.................	2h.12m.11.2s.
1968	Mamo Wold, Ethiopia	2h.20m.26.4s.
1972	Frank Shorter, United States...........	2h.12m.19.8s.

110-Meter Hurdles

1896	Thomas Curtis, United States............	17.6s.
1900	Alvin Kraenzlein, United States..........	15.4s.
1904	Frederick Schule, United States..........	16s.
1906	R. G. Leavitt, United States.............	16.2s.
1908	Forrest Smithson, United States.........	15s.
1912	Frederick Kelly, United States...........	15.1s.
1920	Earl Thomson, Canada...:.............	14.8s.
1924	Daniel Kinsey, United States............	15s.
1928	Sydney Atkinson, South Africa..........	14.8s.
1932	George Saling, United States............	14.6s.
1936	Forrest Towns, United States............	14.2s.
1948	William Porter, United States...........	13.9s·
1952	Harrison Dillard, United States..........	13.7s.
1956	Lee Calhoun, United States.............	13.5s.
1960	Lee Calhoun, United States.............	13.8s.
1964	Hayes Jones, United States.............	13.6s.
1968	Willie Davenport, United States.........	13.3s.
1972	Rodney Milburn, United States..........	13.24s.

200-Meter Hurdles

1900	Alvin Kraenzlein, United States..........	25.4s.
1904	Harry Hillman, United States............	24.6s.

400-Meter Hurdles

1900	John Tewksbury, United States..........	57.6s.
1904	Harry Hillman, United States............	53s.
1908	Charles Bacon, United States............	55s.
1920	Frank Loomis, United States............	54s.
1924	F. Morgan Taylor, United States.........	52.6s.
1928	Lord David Burghley, Great Britain.......	53.4s.
1932	Robert Tisdall, Ireland.................	51.8s.*
1936	Glenn Hardin, United States............	52.4s.
1948	Roy Cochran, United States.............	51.1s.
1952	Charles Moore, United States...........	50.8s.
1956	Glenn Davis, United States.............	50.1s.
1960	Glenn Davis, United States.............	49.3s.
1964	Rex Cawley, United States..............	49.6s.
1968	David Hemery, Great Britain	48.1s.
1972	John Akii-Bua, Uganda.................	48.52s.

* Record not allowed.

2,500-Meter Steeplechase

1900	George Orton, United States	7m.34s.
1904	James Lightbody, United States	7m.39.6s.

3,000-Meter Steeplechase

1920	Percy Hodge, Great Britain	10m.0.4s.
1924	Willie Ritola, Finland	9m.33.6s.
1928	Toivo Loukola, Finland	9m.21.8s.
1932	Volmari Iso-Hollo, Finland	10m.33.4s.*
1936	Volmari Iso-Hollo, Finland	9m.3.8s.
1948	Thure Sjoestrand, Sweden	9m.4.6s.
1952	Horace Ashenfelter, United States	8m.45.4s.
1956	Chris Brasher, Great Britain	8m.41.2s.
1960	Zdzislaw Krzyskowiak, Poland	8m.34.2s.
1964	Gaston Roelants, Belgium	8m.30.8s.
1968	Amos Biwott, Kenya	8m.51s.
1972	Kipchoge Keino, Kenya	8m.23.6s.

* About 3,450 meters—extra lap by error.

Cross-Country

1912	Hannes Kolehmainen, Finland (8,000 meters)	45m.11.6s.
1920	Paavo Nurmi, Finland (10,000 meters)	27m.15s.
1924	Paavo Nurmi, Finland (10,000 meters)	32m.54.8s.

Cross-Country Team Races

		Pts.
1912	Sweden (8,000 meters)	10
1920	Finland (10,000 meters)	10
1924	Finland (10,000 meters)	11

1,500-Meter Walk

1906	George V. Bonhag, United States	7m.12.6s.

3,000-Meter Walk

1920	Ugo Frigerio, Italy	13m.14.2s.

10,000-Meter Walk

1912	George Goulding, Canada	46m.28.4s.
1920	Ugo Frigerio, Italy	48m.6.2s.
1924	Ugo Frigerio, Italy	47m.49s.
1948	John Mikaelsson, Sweden	45m.13.2s.
1952	John Mikaelsson, Sweden	45m.2.8s.

20,000-Meter Walk

1956	Leonid Spirin, U.S.S.R.	1h.31m.27.4s.
1960	Vladimir Golubnichy, U.S.S.R.	1h.34m.7.2s.
1964	Ken Mathews, Great Britain	1h.29m.34s.
1968	Vladimir Golubnichy, U.S.S.R.	1h.33m.58.4s.
1972	Peter Frenkel, East Germany	1h.26m.42.4s.

50,000-Meter Walk

1932	Thomas W. Green, Great Britain	4h.50m.10s.
1936	Harold Whitlock, Great Britain	4h.30m.41.1s.
1948	John Ljunggren, Sweden	4h.41m.52s.
1952	Giuseppe Dordoni, Italy	4h.28m.7.8s.
1956	Norman Read, New Zealand	4h.30m.42.8s.
1960	Donald Thompson, Great Britain	4h.25m.30s.
1964	Abdon Pamich, Italy	4h.11m.12.4s.
1968	Christoph Hohne, East Germany	4h.20m.13.6s.
1972	Bern Kannernberg, West Germany	3h.56m.11.6s.

400-Meter Relay (4 x 100)

1912	Great Britain	42.4s.
1920	United States	42.2s.
1924	United States	41s.
1928	United States	41s.
1932	United States	40s.
1936	United States	39.8s.
1948	United States	40.6s.
1952	United States	40.1s.
1956	United States	39.5s.
1960	Germany	39.5s.
1964	United States	39s.
1968	United States	38.2s.
1972	United States	38.19s.

1,600 Meter Relay (200-200-400-800)

1908	United States	3m.27.2s.

1,600-Meter Relay (4 x 400)

1912	United States	3m.16.6s.
1920	Great Britain	3m.22.2s.
1924	United States	3m.16s.
1928	United States	3m.14.2s.
1932	United States	3m.8.2s.
1936	Great Britain	3m.9s.
1948	United States	3m10.4s.
1952	Jamaica, B. W. I.	3m.3.9s.
1956	United States	3m.4.8s.
1960	United States	3m.2.2s.
1964	United States	3m.0.7s.
1968	United States	2m.56.1s.
1972	Kenya	2m.59.8s.

Team Race

		Pts.
1900	Great Britain (5,000 meters)	26
1904	United States (4 miles)	27
1908	Great Britain (3 miles)	6
1912	United States (3,000 meters)	9
1920	United States (3,000 meters)	10
1924	Finland (3,000 meters)	9

Standing High Jump

1900	Ray Ewry, United States	5 ft. 5 in.
1904	Ray Ewry, United States	4 ft. 11 in.
1906	Ray Ewry, United States	5 ft. 1⅝ in.
1908	Ray Ewry, United States	5 ft. 2 in.
1912	Platt Adams, United States	5 ft. 4⅛ in.

Running High Jump

1896	Ellery Clark, United States	5 ft. 11¼ in.
1900	Irving Baxter, United States	6 ft. 2¾ in.
1904	Samuel Jones, United States	5 ft. 11 in.
1906	Con Leahy, Ireland	5 ft. 9⅞ in.
1908	Harry Porter, United States	6 ft. 3 in.
1912	Alma Richards, United States	6 ft. 4 in.
1920	Richard Landon, United States	6 ft. 4¼ in.
1924	Harold Osborn, United States	6 ft. 5 15/16 in.
1928	Robert W. King, United States	6 ft. 4⅜ in.
1932	Duncan McNaughton, Canada	6 ft. 5⅝ in.
1936	Cornelius Johnson, United States	6 ft. 7 15/16 in.
1948	John Winter, Australia	6 ft. 6 in.
1952	Walter Davis, United States	6 ft. 8 5/16 in.
1956	Charles Dumas, United States	6 ft. 11¼ in.
1960	Robert Shavlakadze, U.S.S.R.	7 ft. 1 in.
1964	Valeri Brumel, U.S.S.R.	7 ft. 1¾ in.
1968	Dick Fosbury, United States	7 ft. 4¼ in.
1972	Yuri Tarmak, U.S.S.R.	7 ft. 3¾ in.

Standing Long Jump

1900	Ray Ewry, United States	10 ft. 6⅖ in.
1904	Ray Ewry, United States	11 ft. 4⅞ in.
1906	Ray Ewry, United States	10 ft. 10 in.
1908	Ray Ewry, United States	10 ft. 11¼ in.
1912	Constantin Tsicilitiras, Greece	11 ft. ¼ in.

Long Jump

1896	Ellery Clark, United States	20 ft. 9¾ in.
1900	Alvin Kraenzlein, United States	23 ft. 6⅞ in.
1904	Myer Prinstein, United States	24 ft. 1⅜ in.
1906	Myer Prinstein, United States	23 ft. 7½ in.
1908	Frank Irons, United States	24 ft. 6½ in.
1912	Albert Gutterson, United States	24 ft. 11¼ in.
1920	Wm. Pettersson, Sweden	23 ft. 5½ in.
1924	DeHart Hubbard, United States	24 ft. 5⅛ in.
1928	Edward B. Hamm, United States	25 ft. 4¾ in.
1932	Edward Gordon, United States	25 ft. ¾ in.
1936	Jesse Owens, United States	26 ft. 5⁵⁄₁₆ in.
1948	Willie Steele, United States	25 ft. 8 in.
1952	Jerome Biffle, United States	24 ft. 10 in.
1956	Gregory Bell, United States	25 ft. 8¼ in.
1960	Ralph Boston, United States	26 ft. 7¾ in.
1964	Lynn Davies, Great Britain	26 ft. 5¾ in.
1968	Bob Beamon, United States	29 ft. 2½ in.
1972	Randy Williams, United States	27 ft. ½ in.

Standing Triple Jump

1900	Ray Ewry, United States	34 ft. 8½ in.
1904	Ray Ewry, United States	34 ft. 7¼ in.

Triple Jump

1896	James B. Connolly, United States	45 ft.
1900	Myer Prinstein, United States	47 ft. 4¼ in.
1904	Myer Prinstein, United States	47 ft.
1906	P. G. O'Connor, Ireland	46 ft. 2 in.
1908	Timothy Ahearne, Great Britain	48 ft. 11¼ in.
1912	Gustaf Lindblom, Sweden	48 ft. 5⅛ in.
1920	Vilho Tuulos, Finland	47 ft. 6⅞ in.
1924	Archie Winter, Australia	50 ft. 11⅛ in.
1928	Mikio Oda, Japan	49 ft. 10¹³⁄₁₆ in.
1932	Chuhei Nambu, Japan	51 ft. 7 in.
1936	Naoto Tajima, Japan	52 ft. 5⅞ in.
1948	Arne Ahman, Sweden	50 ft. 6¼ in.
1952	Adhemar da Silva, Brazil	53 ft. 2½ in.
1956	Adhemar da Silva, Brazil	53 ft. 7½ in.
1960	Jozef Schmidt, Poland	55 ft. 1¾ in.
1964	Jozef Schmidt, Poland	55 ft. 3¼ in.
1968	Viktor Saneyev, U.S.S.R.	57 ft. 0¾ in.
1972	Viktor Saneyev, U.S.S.R.	56 ft. 11 in.

Pole Vault

1896	William Hoyt, United States	10 ft. 9¾ in.
1900	Irving Baxter, United States	10 ft. 9⅞ in.
1904	Charles Dvorak, United States	11 ft. 6 in.
1906	Fernand Gouder, France	11 ft. 6 in.
1908	A. C. Gilbert, United States, and Edward Cook, United States (tie)	12 ft. 2 in.
1912	Harry Babcock, United States	12 ft. 11½ in.
1920	Frank Foss, United States	13 ft. 5 in.
1924	Lee Barnes, United States	12 ft. 11½ in.
1928	Sabin W. Carr, United States	13 ft. 9⅜ in.
1932	William Miller, United States	14 ft. 1⅞ in.
1936	Earle Meadows, United States	14 ft. 3¼ in.
1948	Guinn Smith, United States	14 ft. 1¼ in.
1952	Robert Richards, United States	14 ft. 11⅛ in.
1956	Robert Richards, United States	14 ft. 11½ in.
1960	Don Bragg, United States	15 ft. 5⅛ in.
1964	Fred Hansen, United States	16 ft. 8¾ in.
1968	Bob Seagren, United States	17 ft. 8½ in.
1972	Wolfgang Nordwig, East Germany	18 ft. ½ in.

16-Lb Shot-Put

1896	Robert Garrett, United States	36 ft. 9¾ in.
1900	Richard Sheldon, United States	46 ft. 3⅛ in.
1904	Ralph Rose, United States	48 ft. 7 in.
1906	Martin Sheridan, United States	40 ft. 4⅘ in.
1908	Ralph Rose, United States	46 ft. 7½ in.
1912	Pat McDonald, United States	50 ft. 4 in.
1920	Ville Porhola, Finland	48 ft. 7⅛ in.
1924	Clarence Houser, United States	49 ft. 2½ in.
1928	John Kuck, United States	52 ft. ¹¹⁄₁₆ in.
1932	Leo Sexton, United States	52 ft. 6³⁄₁₆ in.
1936	Hans Woellke, Germany	53 ft. 1¾ in.
1948	Wilbur Thompson, United States	56 ft. 2 in.
1952	Parry O'Brien, United States	57 ft. 1⁷⁄₁₆ in.
1956	Parry O'Brien, United States	60 ft. 11 in.
1960	Bill Nieder, United States	64 ft. 6¾ in.
1964	Dallas Long, United States	66 ft. 8¼ in.
1968	Randy Matson, United States	67 ft. 4¾ in.
1972	Wladyslaw Konar, Poland	69 ft. 6 in.

16-Lb Shot-Put (Both Hands)

1912	Ralph Rose, United States	90 ft. 5⅜ in.

Discus Throw

1896	Robert Garrett, United States	95 ft. 7½ in.
1900	Rudolf Bauer, Hungary	118 ft. 2⅞ in.
1904	Martin Sheridan, United States	128 ft. 10½ in.
1906	Martin Sheridan, United States	136 ft. ⅓ in.
1908	Martin Sheridan, United States	134 ft. 2 in.
1912	Armas Taipale, Finland	148 ft. 3.9 in.
1920	Elmer Niklander, Finland	146 ft. 7 in.
1924	Clarence Houser, United States	151 ft. 5¼ in.
1928	Clarence Houser, United States	155 ft. 2⅘ in.
1932	John Anderson, United States	162 ft. 4⅞ in.
1936	Ken Carpenter, United States	165 ft. 7⅜ in.
1948	Adolfo Consolini, Italy	173 ft. 2 in.
1952	Simeon Iness, United States	180 ft. 6½ in.
1956	Al Oerter, United States	184 ft. 10½ in.
1960	Al Oerter, United States	194 ft. 2 in.
1964	Al Oerter, United States	200 ft. 1½ in.
1968	Al Oerter, United States	212 ft. 6½ in.
1972	Ludvik Danek, Czechoslovakia	211 ft. 3½ in.

Discus Throw—Greek Style

1906	Werner Jaervinen, Finland	115 ft. 4 in.
1908	Martin Sheridan, United States	124 ft. 8 in.

Discus Throw (Both Hands)

1912	Armas Taipale, Finland	271 ft. 10⅛ in.

Javelin Throw

1906	Eric Lemming, Sweden	175 ft. 6 in.
1908	Eric Lemming, Sweden	179 ft. 10½ in.
1912	Eric Lemming, Sweden	198 ft. 11¼ in.
1920	Jonni Myyra, Finland	215 ft. 9¾ in.
1924	Jonni Myyra, Finland	206 ft. 6¾ in.
1928	Eric Lundquist, Sweden	218 ft. 6⅛ in.
1932	Matti Jarvinen, Finland	238 ft. 7 in.
1936	Gerhard Stoeck, Germany	235 ft. 8⁵⁄₁₆ in.
1948	Kaj Rautavaara, Finland	228 ft. 10½ in.
1952	Cy Young, United States	242 ft. ¾ in.
1956	Egil Danielsen, Norway	281 ft. 2¼ in.
1960	Viktor Tsibulenko, U.S.S.R.	277 ft. 8⅜ in.
1964	Pauli Nevala, Finland	271 ft. 2¼ in.
1968	Janis Lusis, U.S.S.R.	295 ft. 7 in.
1972	Klaus Wolfermann, West Germany	296 ft. 10 in.

Javelin Throw—Free Style

1908	Eric Lemming, Sweden	178 ft. 7½ in.

Javelin Throw (Both Hands)

1912	Julius Saaristo, Finland	358 ft. 11½ in.

16-Lb Hammer Throw

1900	John Flanagan, United States	167 ft. 4 in.
1904	John Flanagan, United States	168 ft. 1 in.
1908	John Flanagan, United States	170 ft. 4¼ in.

1912	Matt McGrath, United States	179 ft. 7⅛ in.
1920	Pat Ryan, United States	173 ft. 5⅝ in.
1924	Fred Tootell, United States	174 ft. 10¼ in.
1928	Patrick O'Callaghan, Ireland	168 ft. 7½ in.
1932	Patrick O'Callaghan, Ireland	176 ft. 11⅛ in.
1936	Karl Hein, Germany	185 ft. 4 in.
1948	Imre Nemeth, Hungary	183 ft. 11½ in.
1952	Jozsef Csermak, Hungary	197 ft. 11⁹⁄₁₆ in.
1956	Harold Connolly, United States	207 ft. 2¾ in.
1960	Vasily Rudenkov, U.S.S.R.	220 ft. 1⅝ in.
1964	Romuald Klim, U.S.S.R.	228 ft. 9½ in.
1968	Gyula Zsivotzky, Hungary	240 ft. 8 in.
1972	Anatoly Bondarchuk, U.S.S.R.	247 ft. 8½ in.

Throwing the Stone (14 lbs.)

1906	Nicolas Georgantas, Greece	65 ft. 4⅛ in.

56-Lb Weight Throw

1904	Etienne Desmarteau, Canada	34 ft. 4 in.
1920	Pat McDonald, United States	36 ft. 11⅝ in.

All-Around

1904	Thomas Kiely, Great Britain	6,036 pts.

Pentathlon

1906	H. Mellander, Sweden	24 pts.
1912	Ferdinand Bie, Norway	21 pts.
1920	Eero Lehtonen, Finland	14 pts.
1924	Eero Lehtonen, Finland	16 pts.

Decathlon

1912	Hugo Wieslander, Sweden	7,724.495 pts.
1920	Helge Lovland, Norway	6,804.35 pts.
1924	Harold Osborn, United States	7,710.775 pts.
1928	Paavo Yrjola, Finland	8,053.29 pts.
1932	James Bausch, United States	8,462.23 pts.
1936	Glenn Morris, United States	7,900 pts.*
1948	Robert B. Mathias, United States	7,139 pts.
1952	Robert B. Mathias, United States	7,887 pts.
1956	Milton Campbell, United States	7,937 pts.
1960	Rafer Johnson, United States	8,392 pts.
1964	Willi Holdorf, Germany	7,887 pts.*
1968	Bill Toomey, United States	8,193 pts.
1972	Nikolai Avilov, U.S.S.R.	8,454 pts.

* Point system revised.

Tug of War

1904	United States	1912 Sweden
1906	Germany	1920 Great Britain
1908	Great Britain	

TRACK AND FIELD—WOMEN
100-Meter Run

1928	Elizabeth Robinson, United States	12.2s.
1932	Stella Walsh, Poland	11.9s.
1936	Helen Stephens, United States	11.5s.
1948	Fanny Blankers-Koen, Netherlands	11.9s.
1952	Marjorie Jackson, Australia	11.5s.
1956	Betty Cuthbert, Australia	11.5s.
1960	Wilma Rudolph, United States	11s.
1964	Wyomia Tyus, United States	11.4s.
1968	Wyomia Tyus, United States	11s.
1972	Renate Stecher, East Germany	11.07s.

200-Meter Run

1948	Fanny Blankers-Koen, Netherlands	24.4s.
1952	Marjorie Jackson, Australia	23.7s.
1956	Betty Cuthbert, Australia	23:4s.
1960	Wilma Rudolph, United States	24s.
1964	Edith McGuire, United States	23s.
1968	Irena Szewinska, Poland	22.5s.
1972	Renate Stecher, East Germany	22.4s.

400-Meter Run

1964	Betty Cuthbert, Australia	52s.
1968	Colette Besson, France	52s.
1972	Monika Zehrt, East Germany	51.08s.

800-Meter Run

1928	Lina Radke, Germany	2m.16.8s.
1960	Ljudmila Shevcova, U.S.S.R.	2m.4.3s.
1964	Ann Packer, Great Britain	2m.1.1s.
1968	Madeline Manning, United States	2m.0.9s.
1972	Hildegard Falck, West Germany	1m.58.6s.

1,500-Meter Run

1972	Ludmila Bragina, U.S.S.R.	4m.01.4s.

80-Meter Hurdles

1932	Mildred Didrikson, United States	11.7s.
1936	Trebisonda Valla, Italy	11.7s.
1948	Fanny Blankers-Koen, Netherlands	11.2s.
1952	Shirley S. de la Hunty, Australia	10.9s.
1956	Shirley S. de la Hunty, Australia	10.7s.
1960	Irina Press, U.S.S.R.	10.8s.
1964	Karin Balzer, Germany	10.5s.*
1968	Maureen Caird, Australia	10.3s.

* Wind assisted.

100-Meter Hurdles

1972	Annelie Ehrhardt, East Germany	12.59s.

400-Meter Relay

1928	Canada	48.4s.
1932	United States	47s.
1936	United States	46.9s.
1948	Netherlands	47.5s.
1952	United States	45.9s.
1956	Australia	44.5s.
1960	United States	44.5s.
1964	Poland	43.6s.
1968	United States	42.8s.
1972	West Germany	42.81s.

1,600-Meter Relay

1972	East Germany	3m.23s.

Running High Jump

1928	Ethel Catherwood, Canada	5 ft. 3 in.
1932	Jean Shiley, United States	5 ft. 5¼ in.
1936	Ibolya Csak, Hungary	5 ft. 3 in.
1948	Alice Coachman, United States	5 ft. 6⅛ in.
1952	Ester Brand, South Africa	5 ft. 5¾ in.
1956	Mildred McDaniel, United States	5 ft. 9¼ in.
1960	Iolanda Balas, Romania	6 ft. ¾ in.
1964	Iolanda Balas, U.S.S.R.	6 ft. 2¾ in.
1968	Miloslava Rezkova, Czechoslovakia	5 ft. 11¾ in.
1972	Urike Meyfarth, West Germany	6 ft. 3¼ in.

Long Jump

1948	Olga Gyarmati, Hungary	18 ft. 8¼ in.
1952	Yvette Williams, New Zealand	20 ft. 5¹¹⁄₁₆ in.
1956	Elzbieta Krzesinska, Poland	20 ft. 10 in.
1960	Vera Krepkina, U.S.S.R.	20 ft. 10¾ in.
1964	Mary Rand, Great Britain	22 ft. 2 in.
1968	Viorica Viscopoleanu, Romania	22 ft. 4½ in.
1972	Heidemarie Rosendahl, West Germany	22 ft. 3 in.

Shot-Put

1948	Micheline Ostermeyer, France	45 ft. 1½ in.
1952	Galina Zybina, U.S.S.R.	50 ft. 2½ in.
1956	Tamara Tishkyevich, U.S.S.R.	54 ft. 5 in.
1960	Tamara Press, U.S.S.R.	56 ft. 9⅞ in.

1964 Tamara Press, U.S.S.R. .... 59 ft. 6 in.
1968 Margita Gummel, East Germany....... 64 ft. 4 in.
1972 Nadezhda Chizhova, U.S.S.R............ 69 ft.

Discus Throw

1928 Helena Konopacka, Poland.......... 129 ft. 11⅞ in.
1932 Lillian Copeland, United States....... 133 ft. 2 in.
1936 Gisela Mauermayer, Germany........ 156 ft. 3 3/16 in.
1948 Micheline Ostermeyer, France........ 137 ft. 6½ in.
1952 Nina Romaschkova, U.S.S.R.......... 168 ft. 8 7/16 in.
1956 Olga Fikotova, Czechoslovakia....... 176 ft. 1½ in.
1960 Nina Ponomareva, U.S.S.R............ 180 ft. 8¼ in.
1964 Tamara Press, U.S.S.R............... 187 ft. 10¾ in.
1968 Lia Manoliu, Romania .... 191 ft. 2½ in.
1972 Faina Melnik, U.S.S.R................ 218 ft. 7 in.

Javelin Throw

1932 Mildred Didrikson, United States..... 143 ft. 4 in.
1936 Tilly Fleischer, Germany............ 148 ft. 2¾ in.
1948 Herma Bauma, Austria.............. 149 ft. 6 in.
1952 Dana Zatopek, Czechoslovakia....... 165 ft. 7 in.
1956 Inessa Janzeme, U.S.S.R............. 176 ft. 8½ in.
1960 Elvira Ozolina, U.S.S.R.............. 183 ft. 8 in.
1964 Mihaela Penes, Romania............ 198 ft. 7½ in.
1968 Angela Nemeth, Hungary............. 198 ft. 0½ in.
1972 Ruth Fuchs, East Germany .... 209 ft. 7 in.

Pentathlon

1964 Irina Press, U.S.S.R.................. 5,246 pts.
1968 Ingrid Becker, West Germany.......... 5,098 pts.
1972 Mary Peters, Britain .... 4,801 pts.

SWIMMING

Freestyle

50 Yards

1904 Zoltan de Halmay, Hungary.................... 28s.

100 Meters

1896 Alfred Hajos, Hungary.................. 1m.22.2s.
1904 Zoltan de Halmay, Hungary............... 1m.2.8s.*
1906 Charles Daniels, United States........... 1m.13s.
1908 Charles Daniels, United States........... 1m.5.6s.
1912 Duke P. Kahanamoku, United States...... 1m.3.4s.
1920 Duke P. Kahanamoku, United States...... 1m.1.4s.
1924 John Weissmuller, United States.......... 59s.
1928 John Weissmuller, United States.......... 58.6s.
1932 Yasuji Miyazaki, Japan .... 58.2s.
1936 Ferenc Csik, Hungary.................... 57.6s.
1948 Walter Ris, United States................ 57.3s.
1952 Clarke Scholes, United States............ 57.4s.
1956 Jon Henricks, Australia.................. 55.4s.
1960 John Devitt, Australia................... 55.2s.
1964 Don Schollander, United States........... 53.4s.
1968 Michael Wenden, Australia............... 52m.2s.
1972 Mark Spitz, United States................ 51.22s.

* 100 yards.

200 Meters

1900 Frederick Lane, Australia............... 2m.25.2s.
1904 Charles Daniels, United States........... 2m.44.2s.*
1968 Michael Wenden, Australia.............. 1m.55.2s.
1972 Mark Spitz, United States .... 1m.52.78s.

* 220 yards.

400 Meters

1896 Paul Neumann, Austria................ 8m.12.6s.*
1904 Charles Daniels, United States........... 6m.16.2s.†
1906 Otto Sheff, Austria..................... 6m.23.8s.
1908 Henry Taylor, Great Britain.............. 5m.36.8s.
1912 George Hodgson, Canada................ 5m.24.4s.
1920 Norman Ross, United States............ 5m.26.8s.
1924 John Weissmuller, United States......... 5m.4.2s.
1928 Albert Zorilla, Argentina................ 5m.1.6s.
1932 Clarence Crabbe, United States.......... 4m.48.4s.
1936 Jack Medica, United States............. 4m.44.5s.
1948 William Smith, United States........... 4m.41s.
1952 Jean Boiteux, France................... 4m.30.7s.
1956 Murray Rose, Australia.................. 4m.27.3s.
1960 Murray Rose, Australia.................. 4m.18.3s.
1964 Don Schollander, United States.......... 4m.12.2s.
1968 Mike Burton, United States............. 4m.9s.
1972 ‡ Bradford Cooper, Australia.............. 4m.00.27s.

* 500 meters. † 440 yards. ‡ Rick DeMont, United States, won but was disqualified following day for medical reasons.

1,200 Meters

1896 Alfred Hajos, Hungary................ 18m.22.2s.

1,500 Meters

1904 Emil Rausch, Germany................. 27m.18.2s.*
1906 Henry Taylor, Great Britain............. 28m.28s.†
1908 Henry Taylor, Great Britain............. 22m.48.4s.
1912 George Hodgson, Canada............... 22m.
1920 Norman Ross, United States............ 22m.23.2s.
1924 Andrew Charlton, Australia............. 20m.6.6s.
1928 Arne Borg, Sweden.................... 19m.51.8s.
1932 Kusuo Kitamura, Japan................ 19m.12.4s.
1936 Noboru Terada, Japan................. 19m.13.7s.
1948 James McLane, United States........... 19m.18.5s.
1952 Ford Konno, United States............. 18m.30s.
1956 Murray Rose, Australia................ 17m.58.9s.
1960 Jon Konrads, Australia................ 17m.19.6s.
1964 Robert Windle, Australia.............. 17m.1.7s.
1968 Michael Burton, United States........... 16m.38.9s.
1972 Mike Burton, United States .... 15m.52.58s.

One mile. † 1,600 meters.

4,000 Meters

1900 John Jarvis, Great Britain.............. 58m.24s.

100-Meter Backstroke

1900 Ernst Hoppenberg, Germany............ 2m.47s.*
1904 Walter Brack, Germany................ 1m.16.8s.†
1908 Arno Bieberstein, Germany............. 1m.24.6s.
1912 Harry Hebner, United States........... 1m.21.2s.
1920 Warren Kealoha, United States.......... 1m.15.2s.
1924 Warren Kealoha, United States.......... 1m.13.2s.
1928 George Kojac, United States............ 1m.8.2s.
1932 Masaji Kiyokawa, Japan................ 1m.8.6s.
1936 Adolph Kiefer, United States........... 1m.5.9s.
1948 Allen Stack, United States............. 1m.6.4s.
1952 Yoshinobu Oyakawa, United States....... 1m.5.4s.
1956 David Thiele, Australia................ 1m.2.2s.
1960 David Thiele, Australia................ 1m.1.9s.
1968 Roland Matthes, East Germany .... 58.7s.
1972 Roland Matthes, East Germany .... 56.58s.

* 200 meters. † 100 yards.

200-Meter Backstroke

1964 Jed Graef, United States............... 2m.10.3s.
1968 Roland Matthes, East Germany............ 2m.9.6s.
1972 Roland Matthes, East Germany............ 2m.2.82s.

100-Meter Breast Stroke

1968 Donald McKenzie, United States......... 1m.7.7s.
1972 Nobutaka Taguchi, Japan .... 1m.4.94s.

200-Meter Breast Stroke

1908 Frederick Holman, Great Britain......... 3m.9.2s.
1912 Walter Bathe, Germany................. 3m.1.8s.
1920 Haken Malmroth, Sweden............... 3m.4.4s.

1924	Robert Skelton, United States	2m.56.6s.
1928	Yoshiyuki Tsuruta, Japan	2m.48.8s.
1932	Yoshiyuki Tsuruta, Japan	2m.45.4s.
1936	Tetsuo Hamuro, Japan	2m.42.5s.
1948	Joseph Verdeur, United States	2m.39.3s.
1952	John Davies, Australia	2m.34.4s.
1956	Masura Furukawa, Japan	2m.34.7s.
1960	Bill Mulliken, United States	2m.37.4s.
1964	Ian O'Brien, Australia	2m.27.8s.
1968	Felipe Munoz, Mexico	2m.28.7s.
1972	John Hencken, United States	2m.21.55s.

400-Meter Breast Stroke

1904	Georg Zacharias, Germany	7m.23.6s.*
1912	Walter Bathe, Germany	6m.29.6s.
1920	Haken Malmroth, Sweden	6m.31.8s.

* 440 yards.

100-Meter Butterfly

| 1968 | Douglas Russell, United States | 55.9s. |
| 1972 | Mark Spitz, United States | 54.27s. |

200-Meter Butterfly

1956	Bill Yorzyk, United States	2m.19.3s.
1960	Mike Troy, United States	2m.12.8s.
1964	Kevin Berry, Australia	2m.6.6s.
1968	Carl Robie, United States	2m.8.7s.
1972	Mark Spitz, United States	2m.00.7s.

200-Meter Medley

| 1968 | Charles Hickcox, United States | 2m.12s. |
| 1972 | Gunnar Larsson, Sweden | 2m.7.17s. |

400-Meter Medley

1964	Dick Roth, United States	4m.45.4s.
1968	Charles Hickcox, United States	4m.48.4s.
1972	Gunnar Larsson, Sweden	4m.31.98s.

60-Meter Underwater

| 1900 | de Vaudeville, France | 1m.53.4s. |

200-Meter Obstacle

| 1900 | Frederick Lane, Australia | 2m.38.4s. |

Relays

1900	Germany (200 meters, 5 men)	32 pts.
1904	United States (200 yards)	2m.4.6s.
1906	Hungary (1,000 meters)	16m.52.4s.

400-Meter Freestyle Relay

1964	United States	3m.33.2s.
1968	United States	3m.31.7s.
1972	United States	3m.26.42s.

800-Meter Freestyle Relay

1908	Great Britain	10m.55.6s.
1912	Australia	10m.11.2s.
1920	United States	10m.4.4s.
1924	United States	9m.53.4s.
1928	United States	9m.36.2s.
1932	Japan	8m.58.4s.
1936	Japan	8m.51.5s.
1948	United States	8m.46s.
1952	United States	8m.31.1s.
1956	Australia	8m.23.6s.
1960	United States	8m.10.2s.
1964	United States	7m.52.1s.
1968	United States	7m.52.3s.
1972	United States	7m.35.78s.

400-Meter Medley Relay

1960	United States	4m.5.4s.
1964	United States	3m.58.4s.
1968	United States	3m.54.9s.
1972	United States	3m.48.16s.

Springboard Dive

		Points
1908	Albert Zuerner, Germany	85.5
1912	Paul Guenther, Germany	79.23
1920	Louis Kuehn, United States	10
1924	Albert White, United States	696.4
1928	Pete Desjardins, United States	185.04
1932	Michael Galitzen, United States	161.38
1936	Richard Degener, United States	163.57
1948	Bruce Harlan, United States	163.64
1952	David Browning, United States	205.59
1956	Robert Clotworthy, United States	159.56
1960	Gary Tobian, United States	170.00
1964	Ken Sitzberger, United States	159.90
1968	Bernard Wrightson, United States	170.15
1972	Vladimir Vasin, U.S.S.R.	594.09

High Dive

		Points
1904	G. E. Sheldon, United States	12.75
1906	Gottlob Walz, Germany	156
1908	Hialmar Johansson, Sweden	83.75
1912	Erik Adlerz, Sweden	73.94
1920	Clarence Pinkston, United States	7
1924	Albert White, United States	487.3
1928	Pete Desjardins, United States	98.74
1932	Harold Smith, United States	124.80
1936	Marshall Wayne, United States	113.58
1948	Samuel Lee, United States	130.05
1952	Samuel Lee, United States	156.28
1956	Joaquin Capilla, Mexico	152.44
1960	Bob Webster, United States	~165.56
1964	Bob Webster, United States	148.58
1968	Klaus Dibiasi, Italy	164.18
1972	Klaus Dibiasi, Italy	504.12

Plain High Dive

		Points
1912	Erik Adlerz, Sweden	40
1920	Arvid Wallman, Sweden	7
1924	Richard Eve, Australia	160

Plunge for Distance

| 1904 | W. E. Dickey, United States | 62 ft. 6 in. |

SWIMMING—WOMEN
100 Meters

1912	Fanny Durack, Australia	1m.22.2s.
1920	Ethelda Bleibtrey, United States	1m.13.6s.
1924	Ethel Lackie, United States	1m.12.4s.
1928	Albina Osipowich, United States	1m.11s.
1932	Helene Madison, United States	1m.6.8s.
1936	Hendrika Mastenbroek, Netherlands	1m.5.9s.
1948	Greta Andersen, Denmark	1m.6.3s.
1952	Katalin Szoke, Hungary	1m.6.8s.
1956	Dawn Fraser, Australia	1m.2s.
1960	Dawn Fraser, Australia	1m.1.2s.
1964	Dawn Fraser, Australia	59.5s.
1968	Jan Henne, United States	1m.
1972	Sandra Neilson, United States	58.59s.

200 Meters

| 1968 | Debbie Meyer, United States | 2m.10.5s. |
| 1972 | Shane Gould, Australia | 2m.3.56s. |

400 Meters

1920	Ethelda Bleibtrey, United States	4m.34s.*
1924	Martha Norelius, United States	6m.2.2s.
1928	Martha Norelius, United States	5m.42.8s.
1932	Helene Madison, United States	5m.28.5s.
1936	Hendrika Mastenbroek, Netherlands	5m.26.4s.
1948	Ann Curtis, United States	5m.17.8s.
1952	Valerie Gyenge, Hungary	5m.12.1s.
1956	Lorraine Crapp, Australia	4m.54.6s.
1960	Chris von Saltza, United States	4m.50.6s.
1964	Ginny Duenkel, United States	4m.43.3s.
1968	Debbie Meyer, United States	4m.31.8s.
1972	Shane Gould, Australia	4m.19.04s.

* 300 meters.

800 Meters

1968	Debbie Meyer, United States	9m.24s.
1972	Keena Rothhammer, United States	8m.53.68s.

100-Meter Backstroke

1924	Sybil Bauer, United States	1m.23.2s.
1928	Marie Braun, Netherlands	1m.22s.
1932	Eleanor Holm, United States	1m.19.4s.
1936	Dina Senff, Netherlands	1m.18.9s.
1948	Karen Harup, Denmark	1m.14.4s.
1952	Joan Harrison, South Africa	1m.14.3s.
1956	Judy Grinham, Great Britain	1m.12.9s.
1960	Lynn Burke, United States	1m.9.3s.
1964	Cathy Ferguson, United States	1m.7.7s.
1968	Kaye Hall, United States	1m.6.2s.
1972	Melissa Belote, United States	1m.5.78s.

200-Meter Backstroke

1968	Pokey Watson, United States	2m.24.8s.
1972	Melissa Belote, United States	2m.19.19s.

100-Meter Breast Stroke

1968	Djurdjica Bjedov, Yugoslavia	1m.15.8s.
1972	Catherine Carr, United States	1m.13.58s.

200-Meter Breast Stroke

1924	Lucy Morton, Great Britain	3m.33.2s.
1928	Hilde Schrader, Germany	3m.12.6s.
1932	Clare Dennis, Australia	3m.6.3s.
1936	Hideko Maehata, Japan	3m.6.s.
1948	Nel van Vliet, Netherlands	2m.57.2s.
1952	Eva Szekely, Hungary	2m.51.7s.
1956	Ursala Happe, Germany	2m.53.1s.
1960	Anita Lonsbrough, Great Britain	2m.49.5s.
1964	Galina Prozumenschikova, U.S.S.R.	2m.46.4s.
1968	Sharon Wichman, United States	2m.44.4s.
1972	Beverly Whitfield, Australia	2m.41.71s.

100-Meter Butterfly

1956	Shelley Mann, United States	1m.11s.
1960	Carolyn Schuler, United States	1m.9.5s.
1964	Sharon Stouder, United States	1m.4.7s.
1968	Lynn McClements, Australia	1m.5.5s.
1972	Mayumi Aoki, Japan	1m.3.34s.

200-Meter Butterfly

1968	Ada Kok, Netherlands	2m.24.7s.
1972	Karen Moe, United States	2m.15.57s.

200-Meter Medley

1968	Claudia Kolb, United States	2m.24.7s.
1972	Shane Gould, Australia	2m.23.07s.

400-Meter Medley

1964	Donna de Varona, United States	5m.18.7s.
1968	Claudia Kolb, United States	5m.8.5s.
1972	Gail Neall, Australia	5m.2.97s.

400-Meter Freestyle Relay

1912	Great Britain	5m.52.8s.
1920	United States	5m.11.6s.
1924	United States	4m.58.8s.
1928	United States	4m.47.6s.
1932	United States	4m.38s.
1936	Netherlands	4m.36s.
1948	United States	4m.29.2s.
1952	Hungary	4m.24.4s.
1956	Australia	4m.17.1s.
1960	United States	4m.8.9s.
1964	United States	4m.3.8s.
1968	United States	4m.2.5s.
1972	United States	3m.55.19s.

400-Meter Medley Relay

1960	United States	4m.41.1s.
1964	United States	4m.33.9s.
1968	United States	4m.28.3s.
1972	United States	4m.20.75s.

Springboard Dive

Year	Name	Points
1920	Aileen Riggin, United States	9
1924	Elizabeth Becker, United States	474.5
1928	Helen Meany, United States	78.62
1932	Georgia Coleman, United States	87.52
1936	Marjorie Gestring, United States	89.27
1948	Victoria M. Draves, United States	108.74
1952	Patricia McCormick, United States	147.30
1956	Patricia McCormick, United States	142.36
1960	Ingrid Kramer, Germany	155.81
1964	Ingrid Kramer Engel, Germany	145.00
1968	Sue Gossick, United States	150.77
1972	Micki King, United States	450.03

High Dive

Year	Name	Points
1912	Greta Johansson, Sweden	39.9
1920	Stefani Fryland, Denmark	6
1924	Caroline Smith, United States	166
1928	Elizabeth B. Pinkston, United States	31.60
1932	Dorothy Poynton, United States	40.26
1936	Dorothy Poynton Hill, United States	33.92
1948	Victoria M. Draves, United States	68.87
1952	Patricia McCormick, United States	79.37
1956	Patricia McCormick, United States	84.85
1960	Ingrid Kramer, Germany	91.28
1964	Lesley Bush, United States	99.80
1968	Milena Duchkova, Czechoslovakia	109.59
1972	Ulrika Knape, Sweden	390.00

BOXING

(U. S. Winners Only)

Flyweight

1904	George V. Finnegan, United States
1920	Frank De Genaro, United States
1924	Fidel La Barba, United States
1952	Nate Brooks, United States

Bantamweight

1904	O. L. Kirk, United States

Featherweight

1904	O. L. Kirk, United States
1924	Jackie Fields, United States

Lightweight

1904	H. J. Spanger, United States
1920	Samuel Mosberg, United States
1968	Ronnie Harris, United States

Light Welterweight

1952 Charles Adkins, United States
1972 Ray Seales, United States

Welterweight

1904 Al Young, United States
1932 Edward Flynn, United States

Light Middleweight

1960 Wilbert McClure, United States

Middleweight

1904 Charles Mayer, United States
1932 Carmen Barth, United States
1952 Floyd Patterson, United States
1960 Eddie Crook, United States

Light Heavyweight

1920 Edward Eagan, United States
1952 Norvel Lee, United States
1956 James Boyd, United States
1960 Cassius Clay, United States

Heavyweight

1904 Sam Berger, United States
1952 Edward Sanders, United States
1956 Peter Rademacher, United States
1964 Joe Frazier, United States
1968 George Foreman, United States

SKIING, ALPINE
Downhill

1948 Henry Oreiller, France.................... 2:55.0
1952 Zeno Colo, Italy......................... 2:30.8
1956 Anton Sailer, Austria.................... 2:52.2
1960 Jean Vuarnet, France.................... 2:06.2
1964 Egon Zimmermann, Austria.............. 2:18.16
1968 Jean-Claude Killy, France 1:59.85
1972 Bernhard Russi, Switzerland 1:51.43

Slalom

1948 Edi Reinalter, Switzerland............... 2:10.3
1952 Othmar Schneider, Austria............... 2:00.0
1956 Anton Sailer, Austria.................... 194.7 pts.
1960 Ernst Hinterseer, Austria................ 2:08.9
1968 Jean-Claude Killy, France................ 1:39.73
1972 Francisco Fernandez Ochoa, Spain.......... 1:49.27

Giant Slalom

1952 Stein Eriksen, Norway................... 2:25.0
1956 Anton Sailer, Austria.................... 3:00.1
1960 Roger Staub, Switzerland................ 1:48.3
1964 Francois Bonlieu, France................ 1:46.71
1968 Jean-Claude Killy, France 3:29.28
1972 Gustavo Thoeni, Italy................... 3:09.52

Women's Downhill

1948 Hedi Schlunegger, Switzerland............ 2:28.3
1952 Trude Jochum-Beiser, Austria............ 1:47.1
1956 Madeleine Berthod, Switzerland.......... 1:40.7
1960 Heidi Biebl, Germany.................... 1:37.6
1964 Christl Haas, Austria................... 1:55.39
1968 Olga Pall, Austria...................... 1:40.87
1972 Marie-Therese Nadig, Switzerland 1:36.68

Women's Slalom

1948 Gretchen Fraser, United States........... 1:57.2
1952 Andrea M. Lawrence, United States....... 2:10.6
1956 Renee Colliard, Switzerland .... 112.3 pts.
1960 Anne Heggtveigt, Canada................ 1:49.6
1964 Christine Goitschel, France.............. 1:29.86
1968 Marielle Goitschel, France................ 1:25.86
1972 Barbara Cochran, United States........... 1:31.24

Women's Giant Slalom

1952 Andrea M. Lawrence, United States....... 2:06.8
1956 Ossi Reichert, Germany.................. 1:56.5
1960 Yvonne Ruegg, Switzerland.............. 1:39.9
1964 Marielle Goitschel, France............... 1:52.24
1968 Nancy Greene, Canada.................. 1:51.97
1972 Marie-Therese Nadig, Switzerland 1:29.90

SULLIVAN AWARD WINNERS
(Amateur Athlete of the Year)

1930	Robert T. Jones, Jr.................	Golf
1931	Bernard E. Berlinger...	Track and field
1932	James A. Bausch.................	Track and field
1933	Glenn Cunningham................	Track and field
1934	William R. Bonthron...............	Track and field
1935	W. Lawson Little, Jr...............	Golf
1936	Glenn Morris.....................	Track and field
1937	J. Donald Budge.................	Tennis
1938	Donald R. Lash..................	Track and field
1939	Joseph W. Burk..................	Rowing
1940	J. Gregory Rice..................	Track and field
1941	Leslie MacMitchell.................	Track and field
1942	Cornelius Warmerdam.............	Track and field
1943	Gilbert L. Dodds.................	Track and field
1944	Ann Curtis.....................	Swimming
1945	Felix (Doc) Blanchard.............	Football
1946	Y. Arnold Tucker................	Football
1947	John B. Kelly, Jr.................	Rowing
1948	Robert B. Mathias................	Track and field
1949	Richard T. Button................	Figure skating
1950	Fred Wilt......................	Track and field
1951	Robert E. Richards................	Track and field
1952	Horace Ashenfelter..............	Track and field
1953	Major Sammy Lee................	Diving
1954	Malvin Whitfield.................	Track and field
1955	Harrison Dillard.................	Track and field
1956	Patricia McCormick..............	Diving
1957	Bobby Morrow...................	Track and field
1958	Glenn Davis.....................	Track and field
1959	Parry O'Brien...................	Track and field
1960	Rafer Johnson..................	Track and field
1961	Wilma Rudolph Ward.............	Track and field
1962	Jim Beatty.....................	Track and field
1963	John Pennel....................	Track and field
1964	Don Schollander.................	Swimming
1965	Bill Bradley....................	Basketball
1966	Jim Ryun.....................	Track and field
1967	Randy Matson...................	Track and field
1968	Debbie Meyer...................	Swimming
1969	Bill Toomey....................	Decathlon
1970	John Kinsella....................	Swimming
1971	Mark Spitz	Swimming
1972	Frank Shorter	Marathon
1973	Bill Walton	Basketball
1974	Rick Wohlhuter	Track
1975	Tim Shaw	Swimming

ROWING

Rowing goes back so far in history that there is no possibility of tracing it to any particular aboriginal source. The oldest rowing race still on the calendar is the "Doggett's Coat and Badge" contest among professional watermen of the Thames (England) that began in 1715. The first Oxford-Cambridge race was held at Henley in 1829. Competitive rowing in the United States began with matches between boats rowed by professional oarsmen of the New York water front. They were oarsmen who rowed the small boats that plied as ferries from Manhattan Island to Brooklyn and return, or who rowed salesmen down the harbor to meet ships arriving from Europe. Since the first salesman to meet an incoming ship had some advantage over his rivals, there was keen competition in the bidding for fast boats and the best oarsmen. This gave rise to match races for a purse or a side bet on many occasions. The first of such races was held in June, 1811, in four-oared gigs.

Amateur boat clubs sprang up in the United States between 1820 and 1830 and seven students of Yale joined together to purchase a four-oared lap-streak gig in 1843. The first Harvard-Yale race was held Aug. 3, 1852, on Lake Winnepesaukee, N. H. The first time an American college crew went abroad was in 1869 when Harvard challenged Oxford and was defeated on the Thames. There were early college rowing races on Lake Quinsigamond, near Worcester, Mass., and on Saratoga Lake, N. Y., but the Intercollegiate Rowing Association, in 1895, settled on the Hudson, at Poughkeepsie, as the setting for the annual "Poughkeepsie Regatta." In 1950 the I.R.A. shifted its classic to Marietta, Ohio, and in 1952 it was moved to Syracuse, N. Y. The National Association of Amateur Oarsmen, organized in 1872, has conducted annual championship regattas since that time. The first rowing races were held with lap-streak gigs but shells came into general favor about a century ago.

INTERCOLLEGIATE ROWING ASSOCIATION REGATTA
(Varsity Eight-Oared Shells)

Rowed at 4 miles, Poughkeepsie, N.Y., 1895–97, 1899–1916, 1925–32, 1934–41. Rowed at 3 miles, Saratoga, N.Y., 1898; Poughkeepsie, 1921–24, 1947–49; Syracuse, N.Y., 1952–1963, 1965–67. Rowed at 2,000 meters, Syracuse, N.Y., 1964 and from 1968 on. Rowed at 2 miles, Ithaca, N.Y., 1920; Marietta, Ohio, 1950–51. Suspended 1917–19, 1933, 1942–46.

Year	Time	First	Second	Year	Time	First	Second
1895	21:25	Columbia	Cornell	1935	18:52	California	Cornell
1896	19:59	Cornell	Harvard	1936	19:09 3/5	Washington	California
1897	20:47 4/5	Cornell	Columbia	1937	18:33 3/5	Washington	Navy
1898	15:51 1/2	Pennsylvania	Cornell	1938	18:19	Navy	California
1899	20:04	Pennsylvania	Wisconsin	1939	18:12 3/5	California	Washington
1900	19:44 3/5	Pennsylvania	Wisconsin	1940	22:42	Washington	Cornell
1901	18:53 1/5	Cornell	Columbia	1941	18:53 3/10	Washington	California
1902	19:05 3/5	Cornell	Wisconsin	1947	13:59 1/5	Navy	Cornell
1903	18:57	Cornell	Georgetown	1948	14:06 2/5	Washington	California
1904	20:22 3/5	Syracuse	Cornell	1949	14:42 3/5	California	Washington
1905	20:29	Cornell	Syracuse	1950	8:07.5	Washington	California
1906	19:36 4/5	Cornell	Pennsylvania	1951	7:50.5	Wisconsin	Washington
1907	20:02 2/5	Cornell	Columbia	1952	15:08.1	Navy	Princeton
1908	19:24 1/5	Syracuse	Columbia	1953	15:29.6	Navy	Cornell
1909	19:02	Cornell	Columbia	1954	16:04.4	*Navy	Cornell
1910	20:42 1/5	Cornell	Pennsylvania	1955	15:49.9	Cornell	Pennsylvania
1911	20:10 4/5	Cornell	Columbia	1956	16:22.4	Cornell	Navy
1912	19:31 2/5	Cornell	Wisconsin	1957	15:26.6	Cornell	Pennsylvania
1913	19:28 3/5	Syracuse	Cornell	1958	17:12.1	Cornell	Navy
1914	19:37 4/5	Columbia	Pennsylvania	1959	18:01.7	Wisconsin	Syracuse
1915	19:36 3/5	Cornell	Stanford	1960	15:57	California	Navy
1916	20:15 2/5	Syracuse	Cornell	1961	16:49.2	California	Cornell
1920	11:02 3/5	Syracuse	Cornell	1962	17:02.9	Cornell	Washington
1921	14:07	Navy	California	1963	17:24	Cornell	Navy
1922	13:33 3/5	Navy	Washington	1964	6:31.1	California	Washington
1923	14:03 1/5	Washington	Navy	1965	16:51.3	Navy	Cornell
1924	15:02	Washington	Wisconsin	1966	16:03.4	Wisconsin	Navy
1925	19:24 4/5	Navy	Washington	1967	16:13.9	Pennsylvania	Wisconsin
1926	19:28 3/5	Washington	Navy	1968	6:15.6	Pennsylvania	Washington
1927	20:57	Columbia	Washington	1969	6:30.4	Pennsylvania	Dartmouth
1928	18:35 4/5	California	Columbia	1970	6:39.3	Washington	Wisconsin
1929	22:58	Columbia	Washington	1971	6:06	Cornell	Washington
1930	21:42	Cornell	Syracuse	1972	6:22.6	Pennsylvania	Brown
1931	18:54 1/5	Navy	Cornell	1973	6:21	Wisconsin	Brown
1932	19:55	California	Cornell	1974	6:33	Wisconsin	Mass. Inst. of Technology
1934	19:44	California	Washington	1975	6:08.2	Wisconsin	M.I.T.

* Disqualified.

Standard Measurements in Sports

BASEBALL

Home plate to pitcher's box—60 feet 6 inches.

Plate to second base—127 feet 3⅜ inches.

Distance from base to base (home plate included)—90 feet.

Size of bases—15 inches by 15 inches.

Pitcher's plate—24 inches by 6 inches.

Batter's box—6 feet by 4 feet.

Home plate—17 inches by 17 inches, cut to a point at rear.

Home plate to backstop—Not less than 60 feet (recommended).

Weight of ball—Not less than 5 ounces nor more than 5¼ ounces.

Circumference of ball—Not less than 9 inches nor more than 9¼ inches.

Bat—Must be round, not over 2¾ inches in diameter at thickest part, nor more than 42 inches in length, and of solid wood in one piece or laminated.

FOOTBALL

Length of field—120 yards.*

Width of field—53⅓ yards (160 feet).

Height of goal posts—At least 20 feet.

Height of crossbar—10 feet.

Width of goal posts (above crossbar)—23 feet 4 inches, inside to inside, and not more than 24 feet, outside to outside.

Length of ball—11 to 11.25 inches (long axis).

Circumference of ball—21.25 to 21.50 inches (middle); 28 to 28.5 inches (long axis).

* Includes 10 yards of end zone at either end.

LAWN TENNIS

Size of court—Rectangle 78 feet long and 27 feet wide (singles); 78 feet long and 36 feet wide (doubles).

Height of net—3 feet in center, gradually rising to reach 3-foot 6-inch posts at a point 3 feet outside each side of court.

Ball—Shall be more than 2½ inches and less than 2⅝ inches in diameter and weigh more than 2 ounces and less than 2 1/16 ounces.

Service line—21 feet from net.

ICE HOCKEY

Size of rink—200 feet long by 85 feet wide surrounded by a wooden wall not less than 40 inches and not more than 48 inches above level of ice.

Size of goal—6 feet wide by 4 feet in height.

Puck—1 inch thick and 3 inches in diameter; made of vulcanized rubber; weight—between 5½ to 6 ounces.

Length of stick—Not more than 55 inches from heel to end of shaft nor 12½ inches from heel to end of blade. Blade should not be more than 3 inches in width but not less than 2 inches, except goalkeeper's stick, which shall not exceed 3½ inches in width except at the heel, where it must not exceed 4½ inches.

BOWLING

Lane dimensions—Overall length 62 feet 10 3/16 inches, measuring from foul line to pit (not including tail plank), with ½ inch tolerance permitted. Foul line to center of No. 1 pinspot 60 feet, with ½ inch tolerance permitted. Lane width, 41½ inches with a tolerance of ½ inch permitted. Approach, not less than 15 feet. Gutters, 9 5/16 inches wide with 3/16 plus or 5/16 minus tolerances permitted.

Ball—Circumference, not more than 27 inches. Weight, 16 pounds maximum.

GOLF

Weight of ball—Not greater than 1.620 ounces avoirdupois.

Size of ball—Not less than 1.680 inches in diameter.

Velocity of ball—Not greater than 250 feet per second when tested on U.S.G.A. apparatus, with 2 per cent tolerance.

Hole—Shall be 4¼ inches in diameter and at least 4 inches deep.

Clubs—14 is the maximum number permitted.

BASKETBALL

(National Collegiate A. A. Rules)

Playing court—College: 94 feet long by 50 feet wide. High School: 84 feet long by 50 feet wide (maximum inside dimensions).

Baskets—Rings 18 inches in inside diameter, with white cord 12-mesh nets, 15 to 18 inches in length. Each ring is made of metal, is not more than ⅝ of an inch in diameter and is bright orange in color.

Height of basket ring—10 feet (upper edge).

Weight of ball—Not less than 20 ounces nor more than 22.

Circumference of ball—No greater than 30 inches and not less than 29½.

Free-throw line—15 feet from the face of the backboard.

BOXING

Size of ring—Professional matches take place in an area not less than 18 nor more than 24 feet square including apron. It is enclosed by four covered ropes, each not less than one inch in diameter. The floor has a 2-inch padding with Ensolite padding base underneath ring cover for professional boxing shows, that extends at least 6 inches beyond the roped area in the case of elevated rings. For A.A.U. boxing, not less than 16 nor more than 24 feet square. The ring posts shall not be nearer to the ring ropes than 18 inches and must be properly padded.

Gloves—In professional fights, not less than 8-ounce gloves generally are used. A.A.U., not less than 10 ounces for all divisions.

YACHTING

JASON sailed in search of the Golden Fleece. Cleopatra (according to Shakespeare) had a royal barge with purple sails. Columbus had three sailing ships when he crossed the Atlantic westward in 1492. But who the first sailor was and where he launched his primitive craft nobody ever will know. The word "yacht" is of Dutch origin and the first "yacht race" of record in the English language was a sailing contest from Greenwich to Gravesend and return in 1662 between a Dutch yacht and an English yacht designed and, at some part of the race, sailed by Charles II of England. The royal yacht won.

The first yacht club was organized at Cork, Ireland, in 1720 under the name of the Cork Harbour Water Club, later changed to the Royal Cork Yacht Club.

The Royal Yacht Squadron was organized at Cowes in 1812 and the name changed to the Royal Yacht Club in 1820. The New York Yacht Club was organized aboard the Stevens schooner "Gimcrack" on July 30, 1844, and a clubhouse erected at Elysian Fields, Hoboken, N. J., the following year.

From that time until the Civil War races were held over courses starting from the water off the yacht club promontory.

In 1850 the celebrated "America" was built by a group of New York yachtsmen and sent abroad to compete at Cowes. In a race around the Isle of Wight, with a special cup as a prize, the "America" defeated fourteen English boats and brought back the trophy that has been raced for as "The America's Cup" in many international yacht races since that time.

AMERICA'S CUP RECORD

First race in 1851 around Isle of Wight, Cowes, England. First defense and all others through 1920 held 30 miles off New York Bay. Races since 1930 held 30 miles off Newport, R. I.

Conducted as one race only in 1851 and 1870; best four-of-seven basis, 1871; best two-of-three, 1876–1887; best three-of-five, 1893–1901; best four-of-seven, since 1930. Figures in parentheses indicate number of races won.

Year	Winner and owner	Loser and owner
1851	AMERICA (1), John C. Stevens, U. S.	*AURORA, T. Le Marchant, England
1870	MAGIC (1), Franklin Osgood, U. S.	†CAMBRIA, James Ashbury, England
1871	‡COLUMBIA (2), Franklin Osgood, U. S.	LIVONIA (1), James Ashbury, England
	SAPPHO (2), William P. Douglas, U. S.	
1876	MADELEINE (2), John S. Dickerson, U. S.	COUNTESS OF DUFFERIN, Chas. Gifford, Canada
1881	MISCHIEF (2), J. R. Busk, U. S.	ATALANTA, Alexander Cuthbert, Canada
1885	PURITAN (2), J. M. Forbes-Gen. Charles Paine, U. S.	GENESTA, Sir Richard Sutton, England
1886	MAYFLOWER (2), Gen. Charles Paine, U. S.	GALATEA, Lt. William Henn, England
1887	VOLUNTEER (2), Gen. Charles Paine, U. S.	THISTLE, James Bell et al, Scotland
1893	VIGILANT (3), C. Oliver Iselin et al, U. S.	VALKYRIE II, Lord Dunraven, England
1895	DEFENDER (3), C. O. Iselin-W. K. Vanderbilt-E. D. Morgan, U. S.	VALKYRIE III, Lord Dunraven-Lord Lonsdale-Lord Wolverton, England
1899	COLUMBIA (3), J. P. Morgan-C. O. Iselin, U. S.	SHAMROCK I, Sir Thomas Lipton, Ireland
1901	COLUMBIA (3), Edwin D. Morgan, U. S.	SHAMROCK II, Sir Thomas Lipton, Ireland
1903	RELIANCE (3), Cornelius Vanderbilt et al, U. S.	SHAMROCK III, Sir Thomas Lipton, Ireland
1920	RESOLUTE (3), Henry Walters et al, U. S.	SHAMROCK IV (2), Sir Thomas Lipton, Ireland
1930	ENTERPRISE (4), Harold S. Vanderbilt et al, U. S.	SHAMROCK V, Sir Thomas Lipton, Ireland
1934	RAINBOW (4), Harold S. Vanderbilt, U. S.	ENDEAVOUR (2), T. O. M. Sopwith, England
1937	RANGER (4), Harold S. Vanderbilt, U. S.	ENDEAVOUR II, T. O. M. Sopwith, England
1958	COLUMBIA (4), Henry Sears et al, U. S.	SCEPTRE, Hugh Goodson et al, England
1962	WEATHERLY (4), Henry D. Mercer et al, U. S.	GRETEL (1), Sir Frank Packer et al, Australia
1964	CONSTELLATION (4), New York Y. C. Syndicate, U. S.	SOVEREIGN (0), J. Anthony Bowden, England
1967	INTREPID (4), New York Y. C. Syndicate, U. S.	DAME PATTIE (0), Sydney (Aust.) Syndicate
1970	INTREPID (4), New York Y. C. Syndicate, U. S.	GRETEL II (1), Sydney (Aust.) Syndicate
1974	COURAGEOUS (4), New York Y. C. Syndicate, U. S.	SOUTHERN CROSS (0), Sydney (Aust.) Syndicate

* Fourteen British yachts started against America; Aurora finished second. † Cambria sailed against 23 U. S. yachts and finished tenth. ‡ Columbia was disabled in the third race, after winning the first two; Sappho substituted and won the fourth and fifth.

BOBSLEDDING
National Records

Made at Mt. Hoevenberg slide, Lake Placid, N. Y., the only bobsled run in America.

Mile Course	Half-Mile Course

2-man (single heat)—Wolfgang Zimmerer-Peter Utzschneider, West Germany (Feb. 10, 1973) 1:06.45

2-man (4 heats)—Wolfgang Zimmerer-Peter Utzschneider, West Germany (Feb. 11, 1973) 4:28.77

4-man (single heat)—Rene Stadler, driver; Werner Carmichael, Erich Scharer, Peter Scharer, brake, Switzerland (Feb. 18, 1973) 1:04.37

4-man (4 heats)—Wolfgang Zimmerer, driver, Stephen Geisreiter, Walter Steinbauer, Peter Utzschneider, brake, West Germany (Feb. 23, 1969)........... 4:20.75

2-man (single heat)—Gil Jones-James Compton, Saranac Lake (N. Y.) B. C. (Jan. 31, 1965)........ 0:37.83

2-man (4 heats)—Gil Jones-James Compton, Saranac Lake (N. Y.) B. C. (Jan. 31, 1965).............. 2:32.41

4-man (single heat)—Bill Hickey, driver; Bill Dundon; Reg Benham; Charles Pandolph, brake, Lake Placid (N. Y.) B. C. (Jan. 12, 1964)...................... 0:36.95

4-man (4 heats)—James Bickford, driver; Pat Buckley; Lucien Miron; William Dupree, brake, Saranac Lake (N. Y.) B. C. (Jan. 27, 1946)............... 2:29.07

WORLD ALL-TACKLE FISHING RECORDS

Caught with Rod and Reel in Fresh Water

Source: Mary Ball, *Field & Stream.*

Bass, Redeye	7–8	23″	18″	Lazer Creek. Ga.	1975	Jimmy L. Rogers
Bass, Rock	3	13½″	10¾″	York River, Ontario	1974	Peter Guigin
Bass, Spotted	8–10½	23½″	19⅞″	Smith Lake, Ala.	1972	Billy Henderson
Bass, White	5–5	19½″	17″	Ferguson Lake, Calif.	1972	Norman W. Mize
Bass, Yellow	2–2	14″	13″	Lake Monona, Wis.	1972	James Thrun
Black Bass, Largemouth	22–4	32½″	28½″	Montgomery Lake, Ga.	1932	George W. Perry
Black Bass, Smallmouth	11–15	27″	21⅔″	Dale Hollow Lake, Ky.	1955	David L. Hayes
Bluegill	4–12	15″	18¼″	Ketona Lake, Ala.	1950	T. S. Hudson
Bowfin	19–12	39″	....	Lake Marion, S.C.	1972	M. R. Webster
Buffalo, Bigmouth	47-2	43″	30″	Tippecanoe Lake, Ind.	1975	David F. Hulley
Buffalo, Smallmouth	26-10	34½″	28¼″	Lake Wylie, N.C.	1976	J. Gary Hill
Bullhead, Black	8	24″	17¾″	Lake Waccabuc, N.Y.	1951	Kani Evans
Carp	55–5	42″	31″	Clearwater Lake, Minn.	1952	Frank J. Ledwein
Catfish, Blue	97	57″	37″	Missouri River, S.D.	1959	Edward B. Elliott
Catfish, Channel	58	47¼″	29⅛″	Santee-Cooper Res., S.C.	1964	W. B. Whaley
Catfish, Flathead	79–8	44″	27″	White River, Indiana	1966	Glenn T. Simpson
Char, Arctic	29–11	39¾″	26″	Arctic River, N.W.T.	1968	Jeanne P. Branson
Crappie, Black	5	19¼″	18⅝″	Santee-Cooper Res., S.C.	1957	Paul E. Foust
Crappie, White	5–3	21″	19″	Enid Dam, Miss.	1957	Fred L. Bright
Dolly Varden	32	40½″	29¾″	Lake Pend Oreille, Idaho	1949	N. L. Higgins
Drum, Freshwater	54–8	31½″	29″	Nickajack Lake, Tenn.	1972	Benny E. Hull
Gar, Alligator	279	93″	....	Rio Grande River, Tex.	1951	Bill Valverde
Gar, Longnose	50–5	72¼″	22½″	Trinity River, Tex.	1954	Townsend Miller
Grayling, American	5–15	29⅞″	15⅛″	Katseyedie River, N.W.T.	1967	Jeanne P. Branson
Kokanee	6-9¾	24½″	14½″	Priest Lake, Idaho	1975	Jerry Verge
Muskellunge	69–15	64½″	31¾″	St. Lawrence River, N.Y.	1957	Arthur Lawton
Perch, White	4–12	19½″	13″	Messalonskee Lake, Maine	1949	Mrs. Earl Small
Perch, Yellow	4–3½	....	....	Bordentown, N.J.	1865	Dr. C. C. Abbot
Pickerel, Eastern chain	9–6	31″	14″	Homerville, Ga.	1961	Baxley McQuaig, Jr.
Pike, Northern	46–2	52½″	25″	Sacandaga Reservoir, N.Y.	1940	Peter Dubuc
Salmon, Atlantic	79–2	....	....	Tana River, Norway	1928	Henrik Henriksen
Salmon, Chinook	92	58½″	36″	Skeena River, B.C.	1959	Heinz Wichmann
Salmon, Chum	24–4	40½″	22⅞″	Margarita Bay, Alaska	1974	Richard Coleman
Salmon Landlocked	22–8	36″	....	Sebago Lake, Maine	1907	Edward Blakely
Salmon, Silver	31	....	....	Cowichan Bay, B.C.	1947	Mrs. Lee Hallberg
Sauger	8–12	28″	15″	Lake Sakakawea, N.D.	1971	Mike Fischer
Shad, American	9–2	25″	17½″	Enfield, Conn.	1973	Edward P. Nelson
Sturgeon, White	360	111″	86″	Snake River, Idaho	1956	Willard Cravens
Sunfish, Green	2–2	14¾″	14″	Stockton Lake, Mo.	1971	Paul M. Dilley
Sunfish, Redear	4–8	16¼″	17¾″	Chase City, Va.	1970	Maurice E. Ball
Trout, Brook	14–8	31½″	11½″	Nipigon River, Ontario	1916	Dr. W. J. Cook
Trout, Brown	39–8	....	....	Loch Awe, Scotland	1866	W. Muir
Trout, Cutthroat	41	39″	....	Pyramid Lake, Nev.	1925	John Skimmerhorn
Trout, Golden	11	28″	16″	Cook's Lake, Wyo.	1948	Charles S. Reed
Trout, Lake	65	52″	38″	Great Bear Lake, N.W.T.	1970	Larry Daunis
Trout, Rainbow or Steelhead	42–2	43″	23½″	Bell Island, Alaska	1970	David R. White
Trout, Sunapee	11–8	33″	17¼″	Lake Sunapee, N.H.	1954	Ernest Theoharis
Trout, Tiger	10	27″	16¾″	Deerskin River, Wis.	1974	Charles J. Mattek
Walleye	25	41″	29″	Old Hickory Lake, Tenn.	1960	Mabry Harper
Warmouth	2	12″	12½″	Sylvania, Ga.	1974	Carlton Robbins
Whitefish, Lake	13	32¼″	19″	Great Bear Lake, N.W.T.	1974	Robert L. Stintsman
Whitefish, Mountain	5	19″	14″	Athabasca River, Alberta, Can.	1963	Orville Welch

Caught with Rod and Reel in Salt Water

Source: International Game Fish Association.

Species	Lb.; oz.	Length	Girth	Where caught	Year	Angler
Albacore	74–13	....	....	Arguineguin, Canary Isl.	1973	Olaf Idegren
Amberjack	149	71″	41¾″	Bermuda	1964	Peter Simons
Barracuda	83	72¼″	29″	Lagos, Nigeria	1952	K. J. W. Hackett
*Barracuda	103–4	66″	31¼″	West End, Bahamas	1932	C. E. Benet
Bass, Black Sea	8	22″	19″	Nantucket Sound, Mass.	1951	H. R. Rider
Bass, Giant Sea	563–8	89″	72″	Anacapa Is., Calif.	1968	J. D. McAdam, Jr.
*Bass, Striped	73	60″	30½″	Vineyard Sound, Mass.	1913	C. B. Church
Bass, Striped	72	54½″	31″	Cuttyhunk, Mass.	1969	Edward J. Kirker
Blackfish (Tautog)	21–6	31½″	23½″	Cape May, N.J.	1954	R. N. Sheafer
Bluefish	31–12	47″	23″	North Carolina	1972	James M. Hussey
Bonefish	19	39⅝″	17″	Zululand, So. Africa	1962	Brian Batchelor
Cobia	110–5	63″	34″	Mambasa, Kenya	1964	Eric Titworth

Fish	Weight			Location	Year	Angler
Cod	98–12	63″	41″	Isle of Shoals, Mass.	1969	Alphonse Bielevich
Drum, Black	113–1	....	....	Lewes, Del.	1975	Gerald M. Townsend
Drum, Red	90	55½″	38¼″	Rodanthe, N.C.	1973	Elvin Hooper
Dolphin	85	69″	37½″	Spanish Wells, Bahamas	1968	Richard Seymour
Flounder	30–12	38½″	30½″	Chile	1971	Augusto Nunez Moreno
Jewfish	680	85½″	66″	Fernandina Beach, Fla.	1961	Lynn Joiner
Mackerel, King	90	....	....	Key West, Florida	1976	Norton I. Thornton
Marlin, Black	1560	174″	81″	Cabo Blanco, Peru	1953	A. C. Glassel, Jr.
Marlin, Atlantic Blue	1142	166″	80″	Nags Head, N.C.	1974	Jack Herrington
Marlin, Pacific Blue	1153	176″	73″	Ritidian Point, Guam	1969	Greg G. Perez
Marlin, Striped	415	132″	52″	Cape Brett. N.Z.	1964	B. C. Bain
Marlin, White	174–3	....	....	Vitoria, Brazil	1975	O. C. Reboucas
Permit	50–8	44¾″	33¼″	Key West, Fla.	1971	Marshal E. Earnest
Pollock	46–7	50½″	30″	Brielle, N.J.	1975	John T. Holton
Roosterfish	114	64″	33″	La Paz, Mexico	1960	Abe Sackheim
Runner, Rainbow	33–10	....	....	Clarion Is., Mexico	1976	R. A. Mikkelson
Sailfish, Atlantic	128–1	106¼″	34¼″	Luanda, Angola, Africa	1974	Harm Steyn
Sailfish, Pacific	221	129″	....	Santa Cruz Is., Galapagos Is.	1947	C. W. Stewart
Seabass, White	83–12	65½″	34″	San Felipe, Mexico	1953	L. C. Baumgardner
Sea Trout	15–3	34½″	20½″	Fort Pierce, Fla.	1949	C. W. Hubbard
	15–6	33″	23¼″	St. Lucie River, Fla.	1969	M. J. Foremny
Shark, Blue	{ 410	138″	52″	Rockport, Mass.	1960	Richard C. Webster
	{ 410	134″	52½″	Rockport, Mass.	1967	Martha C. Webster
Shark, Hammerhead	703	172″	63″	Jacksonville, Fla.	1975	H. B. Reasor
Shark, Mako	1061	146″	79½″	Mayor Island, N.Z.	1970	J. B. Penwarden
Shark, Porbeagle	430	96″	63″	Channel Islands, Eng.	1969	Desmond Bougourd
Shark, Thresher	739	106″	68″	Tutukaka, N.Z.	1975	Brian Galvin
Shark, Tiger	1780	166½″	103″	Cherry Grove, S.C.	1964	Walter Maxwell
Shark, White	2664	202″	114″	South Australia	1959	Alfred Dean
Snook (Robalo)	52–6	49½″	26″	La Paz, Mexico	1963	Jane Haywood
Swordfish	1182	179¼″	78″	Iquique, Chile	1953	L. E. Marron
Tanguigue	81	71½″	29¼″	Karachi, Pakistan	1960	George E. Rusinak
Tarpon	283	85 3/5″	....	Lake Maracaibo, Venezuela	1956	M. Salazar
Tautog (*See* Blackfish)						
Tuna, Alison (Yellowfin)	308	84″	57″	San Benedicto Is., Mex.	1973	Harold J. Tolson
Tuna, Atlantic Bigeye	335–1	100¾″	60¼″	Canary Islands	1975	Wilhelm Rapp
Tuna, Blackfin	{ 38	39½″	28¾″	Bermuda	1970	Archie L. Dickens
	{ 38	41″	28″	Islamorada, Fla.	1973	Elizabeth Jean Wade
Tuna, Bluefin	1120	....	....	North Lake, P.E.I., Can.	1973	Lee Coffin
Tuna, Dog-tooth	153–8	....	....	Cooktown, Australia	1975	William E. Chapman
Tuna, Pacific Big-Eyed	435	93″	63½″	Cabo Blanco, Peru	1957	R. V. A. Lee
Tuna, Skipjack	{ 39–15	39″	28″	Walker City, Bahamas	1952	R. Drawley
	{ 40	38¾″	27½″	Baie du Tambeau, Mauritius	1971	Joseph R. Cabache
Tunny, Little	27	....	....	Key Largo, Fla.	1976	Wm. F. Allison
Wahoo	149	79¾″	37½″	Cat Cay, Bahamas	1962	John Pirovano
Weakfish	19–8	37″	23¾″	Trinidad, W.I.	1962	Dennis B. Hall
Yellowtail	111	62″	38″	Bay of Islands, N.Z.	1961	A. F. Plim

* Lines not tested.

CHESS

World Champions		**United States Champions**	
1894–1921	Emanuel Lasker, Germany	1909–36	Frank J. Marshall, New York
1921–27	Jose R. Capablanca, Cuba	1936–44	Samuel Reshevsky, New York*
1927–35	Alexander A. Alekhine, U.S.S.R.	1944–46	Arnold S. Denker, New York
1935–37	Dr. Max Euwe, Netherlands	1946	Samuel Reshevsky, Boston
1937–46	Alexander A. Alekhine, U.S.S.R.*	1948	Herman Steiner, Los Angeles
1948–57	Mikhail Botvinnik, U.S.S.R.	1951	Larry Evans, New York
1957–58	Vassily Smyslov, U.S.S.R.	1954–57	Arthur Bisguier, New York
1958–60	Mikhail Botvinnik, U.S.S.R.	1958–61	Bobby Fischer, Brooklyn, N. Y.
1960–61	Mikhail Tal, U.S.S.R.	1962	Larry Evans, New York
1961–63	Mikhail Botvinnik, U.S.S.R.	1963–67	Bobby Fischer, New York
1963–68	Tigran Petrosian, U.S.S.R.	1968	Larry Evans, New York
1969–71	Boris Spassky, U.S.S.R.	1969–71	Samuel Reshevsky, Spring Valley, N. Y.
1972–74	Bobby Fischer, Los Angeles.	1972	Robert Byrne, Ossining N.Y.; Lubomir Kavelek, Washington; Samuel Reshevsky, Spring Valley, N.Y.
1975	Bobby Fischer;† Anatoly Karpov, U.S.S.R.	1973	Lubomir Kavelek-John Grefe, San Francisco
		1974–75	Walter Browne, Berkeley, Calif.

* Alekhine, a French citizen, died while champion.   † Relinquished title.

* In 1942, Isaac I. Kashdan of New York was co-champion for a while because of a tie with Reshevsky in that year's tournament. Reshevsky won the play-off.

HORSE RACING

ANCIENT DRAWINGS on stone and bone prove that horse racing is at least 3000 years old, but Thoroughbred Racing is a modern development. Practically every thoroughbred in training today traces its registered ancestry back to one or more of three sires that arrived in England about 1728 from the Near East and became known, from the names of their owners, as the Byerly Turk, the Darley Arabian and the Godolphin Arabian. The Jockey Club (English) was founded at Newmarket in 1750 or 1751 and became the custodian of the Stud Book as well as the court of last resort in deciding turf affairs.

There was horse racing in this country before the Revolution, but the great lift to the breeding industry came with the importation in 1798, by Col. John Hoomes of Virginia, of Diomed, winner of the Epsom Derby of 1780. Diomed's lineal descendants included such famous stars of the American turf as American Eclipse and Lexington. From 1800 to the time of the Civil War there were race courses and breeding establishments plentifully scattered through Virginia, North Carolina, South Carolina, Tennessee, Kentucky, and Louisiana.

The oldest stake event in North America is the Queen's Plate, a Canadian fixture that was first run in the Province of Quebec in 1836. The oldest stake event in the United States is The Travers, which was first run at Saratoga in 1864. The gambling that goes with horse racing and trickery by jockeys, trainers, owners, and track officials caused attacks on the sport by reformers and a demand among horse racing enthusiasts for an honest and effective control of some kind, but nothing of lasting value to racing came of this until the formation in 1894 of The Jockey Club.

HISTORY OF THE AMERICAN TRIPLE CROWN

Statistics relative to thoroughbred racing in this publication are reproduced from the *American Racing Manual*, by special permission of the copyright owners, TRIANGLE PUBLICATIONS, INC. Reproduction prohibited.

"TRIPLE CROWN" WINNERS IN THE UNITED STATES
(Kentucky Derby, Preakness and Belmont Stakes)

Year	Horse	Owner	Year	Horse	Owner
1919	Sir Barton	J. K. L. Ross	1943	Count Fleet	Mrs. John Hertz
1930	Gallant Fox	William Woodward	1946	Assault	Robert J. Kleberg
1935	Omaha	William Woodward	1948	Citation	Warren Wright
1937	War Admiral	Samuel D. Riddle	1973	Secretariat	Meadow Stable
1941	Whirlaway	Warren Wright			

KENTUCKY DERBY
Churchill Downs; 3-year-olds; 1¼ miles.

Year	Winner	Jockey	Wt.	Win val.	Year	Winner	Jockey	Wt.	Win val.
1875	Aristides	O. Lewis	100	$2,850	1906	Sir Huon	R. Troxler	117	4,850
1876	Vagrant	R. Swim	97	2,950	1907	Pink Star	A. Minder	117	4,850
1877	Baden Baden	W. Walker	100	3,300	1908	Stone Street	A. Pickens	117	4,850
1878	Day Star	J. Carter	100	4,050	1909	Wintergreen	V. Powers	117	4,850
1879	Lord Murphy	C. Schauer	100	3,550	1910	Donau	F. Herbert	117	4,850
1880	Fonso	G. Lewis	105	3,800	1911	Meridian	G. Archibald	117	4,850
1881	Hindoo	J. McLaughlin	105	4,410	1912	Worth	C. H. Shilling	117	4,850
1882	Apollo	B. Hurd	102	4,560	1913	Donerail	R. Goose	117	5,475
1883	Leonatus	W. Donohue	105	3,760	1914	Old Rosebud	J. McCabe	114	9,125
1884	Buchanan	I. Murphy	110	3,990	1915	Regret	J. Notter	112	11,450
1885	Joe Cotton	E. Henderson	110	4,630	1916	George Smith	J. Loftus	117	9,750
1886	Ben Ali	P. Duffy	118	4,890	1917	Omar Khayyam	C. Borel	117	16,600
1887	Montrose	I. Lewis	118	4,200	1918	Exterminator	W. Knapp	114	14,700
1888	Macbeth II	G. Covington	115	4,740	1919	Sir Barton	J. Loftus	112½	20,825
1889	Spokane	T. Kiley	118	4,970	1920	Paul Jones	T. Rice	126	30,375
1890	Riley	I. Murphy	118	5,460	1921	Behave Yourself	C. Thompson	126	38,450
1891	Kingman	I. Murphy	122	4,680	1922	Morvich	A. Johnson	126	46,775
1892	Azra	A. Clayton	122	4,230	1923	Zev	E. Sande	126	53,600
1893	Lookout	E. Kunze	122	4,090	1924	Black Gold	J. D. Mooney	126	52,775
1894	Chant	F. Goodale	122	4,020	1925	Flying Ebony	E. Sande	126	52,950
1895	Halma	J. Perkins	122	2,970	1926	Bubbling Over	A. Johnson	126	50,075
1896	Ben Brush	W. Simms	117	4,850	1927	Whiskery	L. McAtee	126	51,000
1897	Typhoon II	F. Garner	117	4,850	1928	Reigh Count	C. Lang	126	55,375
1898	Plaudit	W. Simms	117	4,850	1929	Clyde Van Dusen	L. McAtee	126	53,950
1899	Manuel	F. Taral	117	4,850	1930	Gallant Fox	E. Sande	126	50,725
1900	Lieut. Gibson	J. Boland	117	4,850	1931	Twenty Grand	C. Kurtsinger	126	48,725
1901	His Eminence	J. Winkfield	117	4,850	1932	Burgoo King	E. James	126	52,350
1902	Alan-a-Dale	J. Winkfield	117	4,850	1933	Brokers Tip	D. Meade	126	48,925
1903	Judge Himes	H. Booker	117	4,850	1934	Cavalcade	M. Garner	126	28,175
1904	Elwood	F. Prior	117	4,850	1935	Omaha	W. Saunders	126	39,525
1905	Agile	J. Martin	122	4,850	1936	Bold Venture	I. Hanford	126	37,725

KENTUCKY DERBY (Continued)

Year	Winner	Jockey	Wt.	Win val.	Year	Winner	Jockey	Wt.	Win val.
1937	War Admiral	C. Kurtsinger	126	52,050	1957	Iron Liege	W. Hartack	126	107,950
1938	Lawrin	E. Arcaro	126	47,050	1958	Tim Tam	I. Valenzuela	126	116,400
1939	Johnstown	J. Stout	126	46,350	1959	Tomy Lee	W. Shoemaker	126	119,650
1940	Gallahadion	C. Bierman	126	60,150	1960	Venetian Way	W. Hartack	126	114,850
1941	Whirlaway	E. Arcaro	126	61,275	1961	Carry Back	J. Sellers	126	120,500
1942	Shut Out	W. D. Wright	126	64,225	1962	Decidedly	W. Hartack	126	119,650
1943	Count Fleet	J. Longden	126	60,725	1963	Chateaugay	B. Baeza	126	108,900
1944	Pensive	C. McCreary	126	64,675	1964	Northern Dancer	W. Hartack	126	114,300
1945	Hoop Jr.	E. Arcaro	126	64,850	1965	Lucky Debonair	W. Shoemaker	126	112,000
1946	Assault	W. Mehrtens	126	96,400	1966	Kauai King	D. Brumfield	126	120,500
1947	Jet Pilot	E. Guerin	126	92,160	1967	Proud Clarion	R. Ussery	126	119,700
1948	Citation	E. Arcaro	126	83,400	1968	*Forward Pass	I. Valenzuela	126	122,600
1949	Ponder	S. Brooks	126	91,600					
1950	Middleground	W. Boland	126	92,650	1969	Majestic Prince	W. Hartack	126	113,200
1951	Count Turf	C. McCreary	126	98,050	1970	Dust Commander	M. Manganello	126	127,800
1952	Hill Gail	E. Arcaro	126	96,300	1971	Canonero II	G. Avila	126	145,500
1953	Dark Star	H. Moreno	126	90,050	1972	Riva Ridge	R. Turcotte	126	140,300
1954	Determine	R. York	126	102,050	1973	Secretariat	R. Turcotte	126	155,050
1955	Swaps	W. Shoemaker	126	108,400	1974	Cannonade	A. Cordero, Jr.	126	274,000
1956	Needles	D. Erb	126	123,450	1975	Foolish Pleasure	J. Vasquez	126	209,600

* Dancer's Image finished first, was disqualified after traces of drug were found in system.

PREAKNESS STAKES

Pimlico; 3-year-olds; 1 3/16 miles; first race 1873.

Year	Winner	Jockey	Wt.	Win val.	Year	Winner	Jockey	Wt.	Win val.
1919	Sir Barton	J. Loftus	126	24,500	1958	Tim Tam	I. Valenzuela	126	97,900
1930	Gallant Fox	E. Sande	126	51,925	1959	Royal Orbit	W. Harmatz	126	136,200
1935	Omaha	W. Saunders	126	25,325	1960	Bally Ache	R. Ussery	126	121,000
1936	Bold Venture	G. Woolf	126	27,325	1961	Carry Back	J. Sellers	126	126,200
1937	War Admiral	C. Kurtsinger	126	45,600	1962	Greek Money	J. Rotz	126	135,800
1941	Whirlaway	E. Arcaro	126	49,365	1963	Candy Spots	W. Shoemaker	126	127,500
1943	Count Fleet	J. Longden	126	43,190	1964	Northern Dancer	W. Hartack	126	124,200
1946	Assault	W. Mehrtens	126	96,620	1965	Tom Rolfe	R. Turcotte	126	128,100
1948	Citation	E. Arcaro	126	91,870	1966	Kauai King	D. Brumfield	126	129,000
1950	Hill Prince	E. Arcaro	126	56,115	1967	Damascus	W. Shoemaker	126	141,500
1951	Bold	E. Arcaro	126	83,110	1968	Forward Pass	I. Valenzuela	126	142,700
1952	Blue Man	C. McCreary	126	86,135	1969	Majestic Prince	W. Hartack	126	129,500
1953	Native Dancer	E. Guerin	126	65,200	1970	Personality	E. Belmonte	126	151,300
1954	Hasty Road	J. Adams	126	91,600	1971	Canonero II	G. Avila	126	137,400
1955	Nashua	E. Arcaro	126	67,550	1972	Bee Bee Bee	E. Nelson	126	135,300
1956	Fabius	W. Hartack	126	84,250	1973	Secretariat	R. Turcotte	126	129,900
1957	Bold Ruler	E. Arcaro	126	65,250	1974	Little Current	M. Rivera	126	156,000
					1975	Master Derby	D. McHargue	126	158,100

BELMONT STAKES

Belmont Park; 3-year-olds; 1½ miles.

Run at Jerome Park 1867 to 1890; at Morris Park 1890–94; at Belmont Park 1905–62; at Aqueduct 1963–67. Distance 1⅝ miles prior to 1874; reduced to 1½ miles, 1874; reduced to 1¼ miles, 1890; changed to 1⅛ miles, 1893; increased to 1¼ miles, 1895; increased to 1⅜ miles, 1896; changed to 1¼ miles in 1904 and 1905; increased to 1½ miles, 1926.

Year	Winner	Jockey	Wt.	Win val.	Year	Winner	Jockey	Wt.	Win val.
1919	Sir Barton	J. Loftus	126	11,950	1959	Sword Dancer	W. Shoemaker	126	93,525
1930	Gallant Fox	E. Sande	126	66,040	1960	Celtic Ash	W. Hartack	126	96,785
1935	Omaha	W. Saunders	126	35,480	1961	Sherluck	B. Baeza	126	104,900
1937	War Admiral	C. Kurtsinger	126	38,020	1962	Jaipur	W. Shoemaker	126	109,550
1941	Whirlaway	E. Arcaro	126	39,770	1963	Chateaugay	B. Baeza	126	101,700
1943	Count Fleet	J. Longden	126	35,340	1964	Quadrangle	M. Ycaza	126	110,850
1946	Assault	W. Mehrtens	126	75,400	1965	Hail to All	J. Sellers	126	104,150
1948	Citation	E. Arcaro	126	77,700	1966	Amberoid	W. Boland	126	117,700
1950	Middleground	W. Boland	126	61,350	1967	Damascus	W. Shoemaker	126	104,950
1951	Counterpoint	D. Gorman	126	82,000	1968	Stage Door Johnny	H. Gustines	126	117,700
1952	One Count	E. Arcaro	126	82,400	1969	Arts and Letters	B. Baeza	126	104,050
1953	Native Dancer	E. Guerin	126	82,500	1970	High Echelon	J. Rotz	126	115,000
1954	High Gun	E. Guerin	126	89,000	1971	Pass Catcher	R. Blum	126	97,710
1955	Nashua	E. Arcaro	126	83,700	1972	Riva Ridge	R. Turcotte	126	93,540
1956	Needles	D. Erb	126	83,600	1973	Secretariat	R. Turcotte	126	90,120
1957	Gallant Man	W. Shoemaker	126	77,300	1974	Little Current	M. Rivera	126	101,970
1958	Cavan	P. Anderson	126	73,440	1975	Avatar	W. Shoemaker	126	116,160

RECENT WINNERS OF OTHER TRADITIONAL STAKES
AMERICAN DERBY

(First running in 1900 was won by Sidney Lucas. Winners since 1950 are listed below.)

Year	Winner	Year	Winner	Year	Winner	Year	Winner
1950	Hill Prince	1957	Round Table	1964	Roman Brother	1970	The Pruner
1951	Hall of Fame	1958	Nadir	1965	Tom Rolfe	1971	Bold Reason
1952	Mark-Ye-Well	1959	Dunce	1966	Buckpasser	1972	Dubassoff
1953	Native Dancer	1960	T. V. Lark	1967	Damascus	1973	Bemo
1954	Errard King	1961	Beau Prince	1968	Forward Pass	1974	Determined King
1955	Swaps	1962	Black Sheep	1969	Fast Hilarious	1975	Honey Mark
1956	Swoon's Son	1963	Candy Spots				

EPSOM DERBY
Epsom Downs, England; 3-year-olds; 1 mile, 885 yards.

(First running in 1780 was won by Diomed. Winners since 1930 are listed below.)

Year	Winner	Year	Winner	Year	Winner	Year	Winner
1930	Blenheim	1942	Watling Street	1953	Pinza	1964	Santa Claus
1931	Cameronian	1943	Straight Lead	1954	Never Say Die*	1965	Sea Bird II
1932	April the Fifth	1944	Ocean Swell	1955	Phil Drake	1966	Charlottown
1933	Hyperion	1945	Dante	1956	Lavadin	1967	Royal Palace
1934	Windsor Lad	1946	Airborne	1957	Crepello	1968	Sir Ivor*
1935	Bahram	1947	Pearl Diver	1958	Hard Ridden	1969	Blakeney
1936	Mahmoud	1948	My Love	1959	Parthia	1970	Nijinsky
1937	Mid-Day Sun	1949	Nimbus	1960	St. Paddy	1971	Mill Reef*
1938	Bois Roussel	1950	Galcador	1961	Psidium	1972	Roberto*
1939	Blue Peter	1951	Arctic Prince	1962	Larkspur	1973	Morston
1940	Pont l'Eveque	1952	Tulyar	1963	Relko	1974	Snow Knight
1941	Owen Tudor					1975	Grundy

* American bred or owned.

GRAND NATIONAL STEEPLECHASE
Liverpool, England; 6-year-olds and over; 4 miles, 856 yards (Aintree Course).

(First running in 1839 was won by Lottery. Winners since 1946 are listed below.)

Year	Winner	Year	Winner	Year	Winner	Year	Winner
1946	Lovely Cottage	1953	Early Mist	1960	Merryman II	1967	Foinavon
1947	Caughoo	1954	Royal Tan	1961	Nicolaus Silver	1968	Red Alligator
1948	Sheila's Cottage	1955	Quare Times	1962	Kilmore	1969*	Highland Wedding
1949	Russian Hero	1956	E. S. B.	1963	Ayala	1970	Gay Trip
1950	Freebooter	1957	Sundew	1964	Team Spirit	1971	Specify
1951	Nickel Coin	1958	Mr. What	1965	Jay Trump	1972	Well to Do
1952	Teal	1959	Oxo	1966	Anglo	1973-74	Red Rum
						1975	L'Escargot

*American bred or owned.

HOLLYWOOD GOLD CUP
Hollywood Park; 3-year-olds and over; 1¼ miles.

Year	Winner, age	Year	Winner, age	Year	Winner, age	Year	Winner, age
1950	Noor (5)	1957	Round Table (3)	1963	Cadiz (7)	1969	Figonero (4)
1951	Citation (6)	1958	Gallant Man (4)	1964	Colorado King (5)	1970	Pleasure Seeker (4)
1952	Two Lea (6)	1959	Hillsdale (4)	1965	Native Diver (6)	1971	Ack Ack (4)
1953	Royal Serenade (5)	1960	Dotted Swiss (4)	1966	Native Diver (7)	1972	Quack (3)
1954	Correspondent (4)	1961	Prince Blessed (4)	1967	Native Diver (8)	1973	Kennedy Road (5)
1955	Rejected (5)	1962	Prove It (5)	1968	Princessnesian (4)	1974	Tree of Knowledge (4)
1956	Swaps (4)					1975	Ancient Title (5)

SANTA ANITA HANDICAP
Santa Anita Park; 3-year-olds and over; 1¼ miles.

Year	Winner, age	Year	Winner, age	Year	Winner, age	Year	Winner, age
1945	Thumbs Up (6)	1953	Mark-Ye-Well (4)	1961	Prove It (4)	1969	NoDouble (4)
1946	War Knight (6)	1954	Rejected (4)	1962	Physician (5)	1970	Quicken Tree (7)
1947	Olhaverry (8)	1955	Poona II (4)	1963	Crozier (4)	1971	Ack Ack (4)
1948	Talon (6)	1956	Bobby Brocato (5)	1964	Mr. Consistency (6)	1972	Triple Bend (4)
1949	Vulcan's Forge (4)	1957	Corn Husker (4)	1965	Hill Rise (4)	1973	Cougar II (7)
1950	Noor (5)	1958	Round Table (4)	1966	Lucky Debonair (4)	1974	Prince Dantan
1951	Moonrush (5)	1959	Terrang (6)	1967	Pretense (4)	1975	Stardust Mel (4)
1952	Miche (7)	1960	Linmold (4)	1968	Mr. Right (5)		

ANNUAL TURF LEADERS
(Since 1950)

Year	HORSES (Money Winners) Horse and age	Starts	1st	Earnings	JOCKEYS (No. of Winners) Jockey	Mts.	1st	TRAINERS (Winners Saddled) Trainer	1st	Earnings
1950	Noor, 5	12	7	346,940	{Joe Culmone / Wm. Shoemaker	1,676 / 1,640	388 / 388	R. H. McDaniel	156	441,590
1951	Counterpoint, 3	15	7	250,525	Charley Burr	1,319	310	R. H. McDaniel	164	539,204
1952	Crafty Admiral, 4	16	9	277,225	Tony DeSpirito	1,482	390	R. H. McDaniel	168	573,837
1953	Native Dancer, 3	10	9	513,425	Wm. Shoemaker	1,683	485	R. H. McDaniel	211	751,957
1954	Determine, 3	15	10	328,700	Wm. Shoemaker	1,251	380	R. H. McDaniel	206	834,390
1955	Nashua, 3	12	10	752,550	Bill Hartack	1,702	417	F. H. Merrill, Jr.	154	298,794
1956	Needles, 3	8	4	440,850	Bill Hartack	1,387	347	V. R. Wright	177	532,344
1957	Round Table, 3	22	15	600,383	Bill Hartack	1,238	341	V. R. Wright	192	527,271
1958	Round Table, 4	20	14	662,780	Wm. Shoemaker	1,133	300	F. H. Merrill, Jr.	171	320,827
1959	Sword Dancer, 3	13	8	537,004	Wm. Shoemaker	1,285	347	V. R. Wright	172	534,319
1960	Bally Ache, 3	15	10	455,045	Bill Hartack	1,402	307	F. H. Merrill, Jr.	143	344,459
1961	Carry Back, 3	16	9	565,349	John Sellers	1,394	328	V. R. Wright	178	442,650
1962	Never Bend, 2	10	7	402,969	Ronald Ferraro	1,755	352	W. H. Bishop	162	544,261
1963	Candy Spots, 3	12	7	604,481	Walter Blum	1,704	360	Howard Jacobson	140	730,418
1964	Gun Bow, 4	16	8	580,100	Walter Blum	1,577	324	Howard Jacobson	169	801,869
1965	Buckpasser, 2	11	9	568,096	Jesse Davidson	1,582	319	Howard Jacobson	200	863,721
1966	Buckpasser, 3	14	13	669,078	Avelino Gomez	996	318	Louis Cavalaris, Jr.	175	763,201
1967	Damascus, 3	16	12	817,941	Jorge Velasquez	1,939	438	Everett Hammond	200	325,905
1968	Forward Pass, 3	13	7	546,674	Angel Cordero	1,662	345	Jack Van Berg	256	776,330
1969	Arts and Letters, 3	14	8	555,604	Larry Snyder	1,645	352	Jack Van Berg	239	952,207
1970	Personality, 3	18	8	444,049	Sandy Hawley	1,908	452	Jack Van Berg	282	974,818
1971	Riva Ridge, 2	9	7	503,263	Laffit Pincay, Jr.	1,627	380	Dale Baird	245	290,553
1972	Droll Role, 4	19	7	471,633	Sandy Hawley	1,381	367	Jack Van Berg	286	1,381,067
1973	Secretariat, 3	12	9	860,404	Sandy Hawley	1,925	515	Dale Baird	305	416,592
1974	Chris Evert, 3	8	5	551,063	Chris McCarron	2,199	546	Jack Van Berg	329	1,567,418
1975	Foolish Pleasure, 3	11	5	716,278	Chris McCarron	2,194	468	Dick Dutrow	352	1,840,041

KELSO BIGGEST MONEY-EARNER

A victory in the 1964 Jockey Club Gold Cup at Aqueduct brought the lifetime earnings of Mrs. Richard C. duPont's Kelso to $1,803,362, surpassing the all-time record of $1,749,869 held by Round Table. The gelding was retired in 1966 after an ankle injury with total winnings of $1,977,896. Forego, the horse of the year in 1974 and 1975, moved into fourth place in 1976 with a victory in the Woodward. The leader through October 10, 1976.

	Starts	1st	2nd	3rd	Earning
Riva Ridge	30	17	3	1	$1,111,497
Fort Marcy	75	21	18	14	1,109,791
Citation	45	32	10	2	1,085,760
Native Diver	81	37	7	12	1,026,500
Royal Glint	52	21	9	4	1,004,815
Dr. Fager	22	18	2	1	1,002,642
Swoon's Son	51	30	10	3	970,605
Ancient Title	41	18	10	6	956,666
Roman Brother	42	16	10	5	943,473
Stymie	131	35	33	28	918,485
T.V. Lark	72	19	13	6	902,194
Rheingold	17	9	4	1	901,099
†Shuvee	44	16	10	6	890,445
Swaps	25	19	2	2	848,900
Nodouble	42	13	11	5	846,749
Sword Dancer	39	15	7	4	829,610
Candy Spots	22	12	5	1	824,718
Mongo	46	22	10	4	820,766
Armed	81	41	20	10	817,475
Find	110	22	27	27	803,615

	Starts	1st	2nd	3rd	Earning
Kelso	63	39	12	2	$1,977,896
Round Table	66	43	8	5	1,749,869
*Forego	47	29	7	7	1,655,017
†*Dahlia	44	15	3	7	1,540,639
†Allez France	21	13	3	1	1,380,565
Secretariat	21	16	3	1	1,316,808
Nashua	30	22	4	1	1,288,565
†Susan's Girl	63	29	14	11	1,251,668
Carry Back	62	21	11	11	1,241,165
*Foolish Pleasure	26	16	4	*5	1,216,705
Damascus	32	21	7	3	1,176,781
Cougar II	50	20	7	17	1,162,725

* Still active. † Filly.

LEADING MONEY-WINNING JOCKEYS

Laffit Pincay, Jr., in 1973, became the first jockey whose mounts won $4-million or more in a year. Bill Hartack had been the first to pass the $2-million mark in 1956 and $3-million the following year. The list of annual leaders beginning with Hartack:

Year	Jockey	Mts.	1st	Amt. won
1956	Bill Hartack	1,387	347	$2,343,955
1957	Bill Hartack	1,238	341	3,060,501
1958	Willie Shoemaker	1,133	300	2,961,693
1959	Willie Shoemaker	1,285	347	2,843,133
1960	Willie Shoemaker	1,227	274	2,123.961
1961	Willie Shoemaker	1,256	304	2,690,819
1962	Willie Shoemaker	1,126	311	$2,916,844
1963	Willie Shoemaker	1,203	271	2,526,925
1964	Willie Shoemaker	1,056	246	2,649,553
1965	Braulio Baeza	1,245	270	2,582,702
1966	Braulio Baeza	1,341	298	2,951,022
1967	Braulio Baeza	1,064	256	3,088,888
1968	Braulio Baeza	1,089	201	2,835,108
1969	Jorge Velasquez	1,442	258	2,542,305
1970	Laffit Pincay, Jr.	1.328	269	2,626,526
1971	Laffit Pincay, Jr.	1,627	380	3,784,377
1972	Laffit Pincay, Jr.	1,388	289	3,225,827
1973	Laffit Pincay, Jr.	1,444	350	4,093,492
1974	Laffit Pincay, Jr.	1,278	341	4,251,060
1975	Braulio Baeza	1,191	197	3,695,198

WORLD RECORDS

Distance	Horse, age, weight, track and location	Date	Time
¼	**Big Racket, 4, 114, Hipodromo de las Americas, Mexico City, Mexico**	**February 5, 1945**	**:20⅘**
2½ f.	**Tie Score, 5, 115, Hipodromo de las Americas, Mexico City, Mexico**	**February 5, 1946**	**:26⅘**
⅜	**Atoka, 6, 105, Butte, Mont.**	**September 7, 1906**	**:33½**
3½ f.	Joe Blair, 5, 115, Juarez, Mexico	February 5, 1916	:39
	Deep Sun, 7, 120, Shenandoah Downs, Charles Town, W. Va.	July 11, 1959	:39
	Crying for More, 7, 128 Shenandoah Downs, Charles Town, W. Va.	March 18, 1972	:39
½	Tamran's Jet, 2, 118, Sunland Park, N. M.	March 22, 1968	:44⅘
	Argus Ruler, 5, Cahokia Downs, Cahokia, Ill.	April 25, 1973	:44⅘
	Mighty Mr. A., 3, 116, Sportsman's Park, Cicero, Ill.	November 1, 1971	:44⅘
	Thief of Bagdad, 5, 114, Sportsman's Park, Cicero, Ill.	November 5. 1971	:44⅘
4½ f.	**Kathryn's Doll, 2, 111, Turf Paradise, Phoenix, Ariz.**	**April 9, 1967**	**:50⅗**
	Dear Ethel, 2, 114, Miles Park, Louisville, Ky.	**July 4, 1967**	**:50⅗**
	Bold Liz, 2, 118, Sunland Park, Sunland, N.M.	March 19, 1972	:50⅖
⅝	**Zip Pocket, 3, 122, Turf Paradise, Phoenix, Ariz.**	**April 22, 1967**	**:55⅖**
5½ f.	**Zip Pocket, 3, 129, Turf Paradise, Phoenix, Ariz.**	**November 19, 1967**	**1:01⅗**
5¾ f.	Last Freeby, 4, 116, Timonium, Timonium, Md.	July 20, 1974	1:07⅕
¾	*Gelding by Blink-Broken Tendril, 3,123, Brighton, England	August 6, 1929	1:06⅕
	Grey Papa, 6, 116, Longacres, Seattle	September 4, 1972	1:07⅕
6½ f.	Best Hitter, Longacres, Seattle	August 24, 1973	1:13⅘
⅞	Triple Bend, 4, 123, Hollywood Park, Inglewood, Calif.	May 6, 1972	1:19⅘
1 mi.	Dr. Fager, 4, 134, Arlington Park, Arlington Heights, Ill.	August 24, 1968	1:32⅕
1 mi. 70 yd.	Drill Site, 5, 115, Garden State, Cherry Hill, N.J.	October 12, 1964	1:38⅘
	Pass the Brandy, 7, 114, Arlington Park, Arlington Heights, Ill.	July 25, 1970	1:38⅘
1 1/16	**Swaps, 4, 130, Hollywood Park, Inglewood, Calif.**	**June 23, 1956**	**1:39**
1⅛ (turf)	Tentam, 4, 118, Saratoga Springs, N.Y.	August 10, 1973	1:45⅖
1⅛ (dirt)	Secretariat, 3, 124, Belmont Park, N.Y.	September 15, 1973	1:45⅖
1 3/16	Toonerville, 3, 120, Hialeah, Hialeah, Fla.	February 7, 1976	1:51⅖
1¼	Quilche, 6, 115, Santa Anita Park, Arcadia, Calif.	February 23, 1970	1:58
1⅜ (turf)	Cougar II, 6, 126, Hollywood Park, Inglewood, Calif.	April 29, 1972	2:11
1½	Fiddle Isle, 5, 124, Santa Anita Park, Arcadia, Calif.	March 21, 1970	2:23
1 9/16	Lone Wolf, 5, 115, Keeneland, Louisville, Ky.	October 13, 1961	2:37⅗
1⅝ (turf)	Red Reality, 6, 113, Saratoga, Saratoga Springs, N.Y.	August 23, 1972	2:37⅘
(turf)	Malwak, 5, 110, Saratoga, Saratoga Springs, N.Y.	August 22, 1973	2:37⅘
1 mi. 5½ f.	**Distribute, 9, 109, River Downs, Cincinnati, Ohio**	**September 7, 1940**	**2:51⅗**
1¾	**Swartz Pete, 6, Alexandra Park, Auckland, New Zealand**	**January 1, 1966**	**2:50⅘**
2	**Polazel, 3, 142, Salisbury, England**	**July 8, 1924**	**3:15**
2 mi. 40 yd.	**Winning Mark. 4. 107. Thistle Down Park, Cleveland, Ohio**	**July 20, 1940**	**3:29⅗**
2 mi. 70 yd.	Iberis, 4, 122, Hawthorne, Cicero. Ill.	**October 15, 1969**	**3:30⅗**
	Sun n Shine, 4, 113, Hawthorne, Cicero, Ill.	October 19, 1974	3:30⅖
2¼	Dakota, 4, 116, Lingfield, England	May 27, 1927	3:37⅗
2½	Miss Grillo, 6, 118, Pimlico, Baltimore, Md.	November 12, 1948	4:14⅗
2¾	Shot Put, 4, 126, Washington Park, Homewood, Ill.	August 14, 1940	4:48⅘
2⅞	**Bosh, 5, 100, Tijuana, Mexico**	**March 8, 1925**	**5:23**
3	**Farragut, 5, 113, Agua Caliente, Mexico**	**March 9, 1941**	**5:15**
3⅛	**Winning Mark, 4, 104, Washington Park, Homewood, Ill.**	**August 21, 1940**	**6:13**
4	**Sotemia, 5, 119, Churchill Downs, Louisville, Ky.**	**October 7, 1912**	**7:10⅘**

* 3/4 mile course at Brighton is started on a hill and is down grade to within one-third of a mile of the finish.

Man o' War's Racing Record

1919	Race	Fin.	Earnings
June 6	Purse	1	$ 500
June 9	Keene Memorial Stakes	1	4,200
June 21	Youthful Stakes	1	3,850
June 23	Hudson Stakes	1	2,825
July 5	Tremont Stakes	1	4,800
Aug. 2	United States Hotel Stakes	1	7,600
Aug. 13	Sanford Memorial Stakes	2	700
Aug. 23	Grand Union Hotel Stakes	1	7,600
Aug. 30	Hopeful Stakes	1	24,600
Sept. 13	Belmont Futurity	1	26,650

1920	Race	Fin.	Earnings
May 18	Preakness Stakes	1	23,000
May 29	Withers Stakes	1	4,825
June 12	Belmont Stakes	1	7,950
June 22	Stuyvesant Handicap	1	3,850
July 10	Dwyer Stakes	1	4,850
Aug. 7	Miller Stakes	1	4,700
Aug. 21	Travers Stakes	1	9,275
Sept. 4	Lawrence Realization Stakes	1	15,040
Sept. 11	Jockey Club Stakes	1	5,850
Sept. 18	Potomac Handicap	1	6,800
Oct. 12	Kenilworth Park Gold Cup	1	80,000

Recapitulation

Year	Age	Races	1st	2nd	Unp.	Earnings
1919	2	10	9	1	0	$ 83,325
1920	3	11	11	0	0	166,140
Totals		21	20	1	0	$249,465

HARNESS RACING

Oliver Wendell Holmes, the famous Autocrat of the Breakfast Table, wrote that the running horse was a gambling toy but the trotting horse was useful and, furthermore, "horse-racing is not a republican institution; horse-trotting is." Oliver Wendell Holmes was a born and bred New Englander and New England was the nursery of the harness racing sport in America. Pacers and trotters were matters of local pride and prejudice in Colonial New England and, shortly after the Revolution, the Messenger and Justin Morgan strains produced many winners in harness racing "matches" along the turnpikes of New York, Connecticut, Rhode Island, Massachusetts, Vermont, and New Hampshire.

There was English thoroughbred blood in Messenger and Justin Morgan and, many years later, it was blended in Rysdyk's Hambletonian, foaled in 1849. Hambletonian was not particularly fast under harness but his descendants have had almost a monopoly of prizes, titles, and records in the harness racing game. Hambletonian was purchased as a foal with its dam for a total of $124 by William Rysdyk of Goshen, N. Y., and made a modest fortune for the purchaser.

Trotters and pacers often were raced under saddle in the old days and, in fact, the custom still survives in some places in Europe. Dexter, the great trotter that lowered the mile record from 2:19¾ to 2:17¼ in 1867, was said to handle just as well under saddle as when pulling a sulky. But as sulkies were lightened in weight and improved in design, trotting under saddle became less common and finally faded out in this country.

WORLD RECORDS

Established in a Race or Against Time at One Mile

Source: Larry Evans, Publicity Director, United States Trotting Association.

TROTTING ON MILE TRACK

	Record	Holder	Driver	Where Made	Year
All Age	1:54 4/5	Nevele Pride	Stanley Dancer	Indianapolis	1969
2-year-old	1:58 2/5(r)	Nevele Pride	Stanley Dancer	Lexington, Ky.	1967
3-year-old	1:56 2/5(r)	Super Bowl	Stanley Dancer	DuQuoin, Ill.	1972
	1:56 2/5(r)	Steve Lobell	Billy Haughton	DuQuoin, Ill.	1976
4-year-old	1:54 4/5	Nevele Pride	Stanley Dancer	Indianapolis	1969

TROTTING ON HALF-MILE TRACK

	Record	Holder	Driver	Where Made	Year
All Age	1:56 4/5(r)	Nevele Pride	Stanley Dancer	Saratoga Springs, N. Y.	1969
2-year-old	2:00 1/5(r)	Ayres	John Simpson, Sr.	Delaware, Ohio	1963
3-year-old	1:58 3/5(r)	Songcan	George Sholty	Delaware, Ohio	1972
4-year-old	1:56 4/5(r)	Nevele Pride	Stanley Dancer	Saratoga Springs, N. Y.	1969

PACING ON MILE TRACK

	Record	Holder	Driver	Where Made	Year
All Age	1:52	Steady Star	Joe O'Brien	Lexington, Ky.	1971
2-year-old	1:55 4/5(r)	Alert Brett	Glen Garnsey	Lexington, Ky.	1974
	1:55 4/5(r)	Racy Goods	Joe O'Brien	DuQuoin, Ill.	1976
3-year-old	1:54	Steady Star	Joe O'Brien	Lexington, Ky.	1970
4-year-old	1:52	Steady Star	Joe O'Brien	Lexington, Ky.	1971

PACING ON HALF-MILE TRACK

	Record	Holder	Driver	Where Made	Year
All Age	1:55 3/5	Adios Butler	Edward Cobb	Delaware, Ohio	1963
	1:55 3/5(r)	Albatross	Stanley Dancer	Delaware, Ohio	1972
2-year-old	1:58 4/5(r)	Columbia George	Roland Beaulieu	Yonkers, N. Y.	1969
	1:58 4/5(r)	J. R. Skipper	Greg Wright	Delaware, Ohio	1972
	1:58 4/5(r)	Armbro Ranger	Joe O'Brien	Delaware, Ohio	1975
3-year-old	1:56 3/5	Strike Out	Keith Waples	Delaware, Ohio	1972
4-year-old	1:55 3/5(r)	Albatross	Stanley Dancer	Delaware, Ohio	1972

(r) Record made in race.

HARNESS RACING RECORDS FOR THE MILE

TROTTERS			PACERS		
Time	Trotter, age, driver	Year	Time	Pacer, age, driver	Year
2:00	Lou Dillon, 5, Millard Sanders	1903	2:00½	John R. Gentry, 7, W. J. Andrews	1896
1:58½	Lou Dillon, 5, Millard Sanders	1903	1:59¼	Star Pointer, 8, D. McClary	1897
1:58	Uhlan, 8, Charles Tanner	1912	1:59	Dan Patch, 7, M. E. McHenry	1903
1:58	Peter Manning, 5, T. W. Murphy	1921	1:56¼	Dan Patch, 7, M. E. McHenry	1903
1:57¾	Peter Manning, 5, T. W. Murphy	1921	1:56	Dan Patch, 8, H. C. Hersey	1904
1:57	Peter Manning, 6, T. W. Murphy	1922	1:55	Billy Direct, 4, Vic Fleming	1938
1:56¾	Peter Manning, 6, T. W. Murphy	1922	1:55	Adios Harry, 4, Luther Lyons	1955
1:56¾	Greyhound, 5, Sep Palin	1937	1:54⅗	Adios Butler, 4, Paige West	1960
1:56	Greyhound, 5, Sep Palin	1937	1:54	Bret Hanover, 4, Frank Ervin	1966
1:55¼	Greyhound, 6, Sep Palin	1938	1:53⅗	Bret Hanover, 4, Frank Ervin	1966
1:54⅘	Nevele Pride, 4, Stanley Dancer	1969	1:52	Steady Star, 4, Joe O'Brien	1971

HISTORY OF TRADITIONAL HARNESS RACING STAKES
The Hambletonian

Three-year-old trotters. One mile. Guy McKinney won first race in Syracuse in 1926; held at Goshen, N.Y., 1930-1942, 1944-1956; at Yonkers, N.Y., 1943; at Du Quoin, Ill., since 1957.

Year	Winner	Driver	Best time	Total purse
1950	Lusty Song	Del Miller	2:02	75,209.12
1951	Mainliner	Guy Crippen	2:02 3/5	95,263.93
1952	Sharp Note	Bi Shively	2:02 3/5	87,637.55
1953	Helicopter	Harry Harvey	(c)2:01 3/5	117,117.98
1954	Newport Dream	Del Cameron	2:02 4/5	106,830.62
1955	Scott Frost	Joe O'Brien	2:00 3/5	86,863.38
1956	The Intruder	Ned Bower	2:01 2/5	100,603.99
1957	Hickory Smoke	John Simpson, Sr.	2:01	111,126.25
1958	Emily's Pride	Flick Nipe	1:59 4/5	106,719.24
1959	Diller Hanover	Frank Ervin	2:01 1/5	125,283.98
1960	Blaze Hanover	Joe O'Brien	(d)1:59 3/5	144,590.14
1961	Harlan Dean	Jimmy Arthur	1:58 2/5	131,573.01
1962	A. C.'s Viking	Sanders Russell	1:59 3/5	116,612.78
1963	Speedy Scot	Ralph Baldwin	(e)1:57 3/5	115,549.28
1964	Ayres	John Simpson, Sr.	1:56 4/5	115,281.40
1965	Egyptian Candor	Del Cameron	(f)2:03 4/5	122,245.76
1966	Kerry Way	Frank Ervin	1:58 4/5	122,540.00
1967	Speedy Streak	Del Cameron	2:00	122,650.00
1968	Nevele Pride	Stanley Dancer	1:59 2/5	116,190.00
1969	Lindy's Pride	Howard Beissinger	1:57 3/5	124,910.00
1970	Timothy T.	John Simpson, Jr.	(g)1:58 2/5	143,630.00
1971	Speedy Crown	Howard Beissinger	1:57 2/5	129,770.00
1972	Super Bowl	Stanley Dancer	1:56 2/5	119,090.000
1973	Flirth	Ralph Baldwin	1:57 1/5	144,710.00
1974	Christopher T	Billy Haughton	1:58 3/5	160,150.00
1975	Bonefish	Stanley Dancer	(h)1:59	232,192.00

(a) By Hollyrood Dennis. (b) By Worthy Boy and by Volo Song. (c) By Morse Hanover. (d) By Quick Song and by Hoot Frost. (e) By Florlis. (f) By Ambro Flight. (g) By Formal Notice. (h) By Yankee Bambino.

Little Brown Jug

Three-year-old pacers. One Mile. Raced at Delaware County Fair Grounds, Delaware, Ohio.

Year	Winner	Driver	Best time	Total purse
1955	Quick Chief	Bill Haughton	(d)2:00	66,608.83
1956	Noble Adios	John Simpson, Sr.	2:00 4/5	52,666.05
1957	Torpid	John Simpson, Sr.	2:00 4/5	73,528.15
1958	Shadow Wave	Joe O'Brien	2:01	65,252.94
1959	Adios Butler	Clint Hodgins	1:59 2/5	76,582.00
1960	Bullet Hanover	John Simpson, Sr.	(e)1:58 3/5	66,510.89
1961	Henry T. Adios	Stanley Dancer	1:58 4/5	70,069.14
1962	Lehigh Hanover	Stanley Dancer	1:58 4/5	75,038.80
1963	Overtrick	John Patterson	1:57 1/5	68,294.90
1964	Vicar Hanover	Bill Haughton	(f)2:00 4/5	66,590.79
1965	Bret Hanover	Frank Ervin	1:57	70,000.00
1966	Romeo Hanover	George Sholty	1:59 3/5	74,616.69
1967	Best of All	Jim Hackett	(g)1:59	84,778.00
1968	Rum Customer	William Haughton	1:59 3/5	104,226.38
1969	Laverne Hanover	William Haughton	2:00 2/5	109,731.00
1970	Most Happy Fella	Stanley Dancer	1:57 1/5	100,110.04
1971	Nansemond	Herve Filion	1:57 2/5	102,994.72
1972	Strike Out	Keith Waples	1:56 3/5	104,916.00
1973	Melvin's Wo	Joe O'Brien	1:57 3/5	120,000.00
1974	Ambro Omaha	Billy Haughton	1:57	132,630.00
1975	Seatrain	Ben Webster	1:57	147,813.00

(a) By Royal Chief. (b) By Newport Chief. (c) By Phantom Lady. (d) By Dottie's Pick. (e) By Bullet Hanover and Muncy Hanover. (f) By Combat Time. (g) By Nardin's Byrd.

HARNESS HORSE OF THE YEAR

Chosen in poll conducted by United States Trotting Association in conjunction with the U.S. Harness Writers Assn.

1955	Scott Frost, Trotter	1962	Su Mac Lad, Trotter	1969	Nevele Pride, Trotter
1956	Scott Frost, Trotter	1963	Speedy Scot, Trotter	1970	Fresh Yankee, Trotter
1957	Torpid, Pacer	1964	Bret Hanover, Pacer	1971	Albatross, Pacer
1958	Emily's Pride, Trotter	1965	Bret Hanover, Pacer	1972	Albatross, Pacer
1959	Bye Bye Byrd, Pacer	1966	Bret Hanover, Pacer	1973	Sir Dalrae, Pacer
1960	Adios Butler, Pacer	1967	Nevele Pride, Trotter	1974	Delmonica Hanover, Trotter
1961	Adios Butler, Pacer	1968	Nevele Pride, Trotter	1975	Savoir, Trotter

BOWLING

AMERICAN BOWLING CONGRESS CHAMPIONS

Year	Singles	All-Events	Year	Singles	All-Events
1955	Eddie Gerzine	Fred Bujack	1965	Ken Roeth	Tom Hathaway
1956	George Wade	Bill Lillard	1966	Don Chapman	John Wilcox
1957	Bob Allen	Jim Spalding	1967	Frank Perry	Gary Lewis
1958	Ed Shay	Al Faragalli	1968	Wayne Kowalski	Vince Mazzanti
1959	Ed Lubanski	Ed Lubanski	1969	Greg Campbell	Eddie Jackson
1960	Paul Kulbaga	Vince Lucci	1970	Jake Yoder	Mike Berlin
1961	Lyle Spooner	Luke Karen	1971	Al Cohn	Al Cohn
1962	Andy Renaldo	Billy Young	1972	Bill Pointer	Mac Lowry
1963	Fred Delello	Bus Owalt	1973	Ed Thompson	Ron Woolet
1964	Jim Stefanich	Les Zikes, Jr.	1974	Gene Krause	Bob Hart
			1975	Jim Setser	Bobby Meadows

WOMEN'S INTERNATIONAL BOWLING CONGRESS CHAMPIONS

Year	Singles	All-Events	Year	Singles	All-Events
1955	Nellie Vella	Marion Ladewig	1965	Doris Rudell	Donna Zimmerman
1956	Lucille Noe	Doris Knechtges	1966	Gloria Bouvia	Kate Helbig
1957	Eleanor Towles	Anita Cantaline	1967	Gloria Paeth	Carol Miller
1958	Ruth Hertel	Mae Ploegman	1968	Norma Parks	Susie Reichley
1959	Mae Ploegman	Pat McBride	1969	Joan Bender	Helen Duval
1960	Marge McDaniels	Judy Roberts	1970	Dorothy Fothergill	Dorothy Fothergill
1961	Elaine Newton	Evelyn Teal	1971	Ginny Younginer	Lorrie Koch
1962	Martha Hoffman	Flossie Argent	1972	D. D. Jacobson	Millie Martorella
1963	Dot Wilkinson	Helen Shablis	1973	Bobby Buffaloe	Toni Calvery
1964	Jean Havlish	Jean Havlish	1974	Shirley Garms	Judy C. Soutar
			1975	Barbara Leicht	Virginia Park

HANDBALL

U.S.H.A. National Four-Wall Champions

SINGLES

1960	Jimmy Jacobs
1961	John Sloan
1962-63	Oscar Obert
1964-65	Jimmy Jacobs
1966-67	Paul Haber
1968	Simon (Stuffy) Singer
1969-71	Paul Haber
1972	Fred Lewis

1973	Terry Muck
1974	Fred Lewis
1975	Jay Bilyeu

DOUBLES

1960	Jimmy Jacobs-Dick Weisman
1961	John Sloan-Vic Hershkowitz
1962-63	Jimmy Jacobs-Marty Decatur
1964	John Sloan-Phil Elbert

1965	Jimmy Jacobs-Marty Decatur
1966	Pete Tyson-Bob Lindsay
1967-68	Jimmy Jacobs-Marty Decatur
1969	Lou Kramberg-Lou Russo
1970	Karl and Ruby Obert
1971	Ray Neveau-Simie Fein
1972	Kent Fusselman-Al Drews
1973-74	Ray Neveau-Simie Fein
1975	Marty Decatur-Steve Lott

LACROSSE

National Intercollegiate Champions

1946	Navy	1955-56	Maryland	1967	Johns Hopkins, Maryland, Navy
1947-48	Johns Hopkins	1957	Johns Hopkins	1968	Johns Hopkins
1949	Johns Hopkins, Navy	1958	Army	1969	Army, Johns Hopkins
1950	Johns Hopkins	1959	Army, Johns Hopkins,	1970	Johns Hopkins, Navy, Virginia
1951	Army, Princeton		Maryland	*1971	Cornell
1952	Virginia, R.P.I.	1960	Navy	1972	Virginia
1953	Princeton	1961	Army, Navy	1973	Maryland
1954	Navy	1962-66	Navy	1974	Johns Hopkins
				1975	Maryland

* First year of N.C.A.A. Championship Tournaments.

SQUASH RACQUETS

National Champions

1946-47	Charles W. Brinton	1954	G. Diehl Mateer, Jr.	1961	Henri Salaun	1967	Sam Howe
1948	Stanley W. Pearson, Jr.	1955	Henri Salaun	1962	Sam Howe	1968	Colin Adair
1949	Hunter H. Lott, Jr.	1956	G. Diehl Mateer, Jr.	1963	Ben Heckscher	1969-70	Anil Nayar, Bombay
1950-51	Edward Hahn	1957-58	Henri Salaun	1964	Ralph Howe	1971	Colin Adair
1952	Harry Conlon	1959	Ben Heckscher	1965	Stephen Vehslage	1972-75	Victor Niederhoffer
1953	Ernie Howard	1960	G. Diehl Mateer, Jr.	1966	Victor Niederhoffer		

AUTO RACING

THE FIRST automobiles on the road were erratic in action and driving them or even riding in them was considered a trifle risky, hence it became the sporting thing to do. Experimental excursions in crude cars gave rise to rivalry in speed over the rough roads of the Gay Nineties and this eventually led to formal contests, the first of which was a road race from Paris to Rouen in 1894, with 26 cars showing up at the starting line. Formal competition in the United States started with a road race in the Chicago district on Thanksgiving Day, 1895, and the winner, J. F. Duryea, covered the road distance of 54.36 miles at the astonishing average of 7.5 miles per hour!

Around 1900 Paris became the hub of road racing in Europe and each year there were raucous, dusty and dangerous races from Paris to Berlin, to Vienna, to Madrid and other cities on the Continent. Accidents were so numerous to drivers and spectators that, after a gory group of mishaps in the forepart of the Paris–Madrid race of 1903, the contest was halted at Bordeaux by public authorities and all road racing was brought under control. Other kinds of auto racing were exposed to view. Some contests, including 24-hour races for stock models, were held on circular or oval tracks originally built for horse racing. Finally came the special racing strips for autos, including such famous autodromes as Brooklands in England and the Indianapolis Speedway in the United States.

As a test of engine and chassis under severe conditions and great strain, auto racing rendered invaluable assistance in the development of the motor car of today.

National Champions
Source: United States Auto Club.

1910	Ray Harroun	1925	Peter DePaolo	1939	Wilbur Shaw	1960-61	A. J. Foyt
1911	Ralph Mulford	1926	Harry Hartz	1940-41	Rex Mays	1962	Rodger Ward
1912	Ralph DePalma	1927	Peter DePaolo	1946-48	Ted Horn	1963-64	A. J. Foyt
1913	Earl Cooper	1928-29	Louis Meyer	1949	Johnnie Parsons	1965-66	Mario Andretti
1914	Ralph DePalma	1930	Billy Arnold	1950	Henry Banks	1967	A. J. Foyt
1915	Earl Cooper	1931	Louis Schneider	1951	Tony Bettenhausen	1968	Bobby Unser
1916	Dario Resta	1932	Bob Carey	1952	Chuck Stevenson	1969	Mario Andretti
1917	Earl Cooper	1933	Louis Meyer	1953	Sam Hanks	1970	Al Unser
1918	Ralph Mulford	1934	Bill Cummings	1954	Jimmy Bryan	1971-72	Joe Leonard
1919	Howard Wilcox	1935	Kelly Petillo	1955	Bob Sweikert	1973	Roger McCluskey
1920-21	Thomas Milton	1936	Mauri Rose	1956-57	Jimmy Bryan	1974	Bobby Unser
1922	James Murphy	1937	Wilbur Shaw	1958	Tony Bettenhausen	1975	A. J. Foyt
1923	Eddie Hearne	1938	Floyd Roberts	1959	Rodger Ward		
1924	James Murphy						

NATIONAL ASSOCIATION FOR STOCK CAR AUTO RACING (NASCAR)
Grand National Champions

1948-49	Red Byron	1954	Lee Petty	1961	Ned Jarrett	1967	Richard Petty
1950	Bill Rexford	1955	Tim Flock	1962-63	Joe Weatherly	1968-69	David Pearson
1951	Herb Thomas	1956-57	Buck Baker	1964	Richard Petty	1970	Bobby Isaac
1952	Tim Flock	1958-59	Lee Petty	1965	Ned Jarrett	1971-72	Richard Petty
1953	Herb Thomas	1960	Rex White	1966	David Pearson	1973	Benny Parsons
						1974-75	Richard Petty

The One-Mile Speed Mark

The first recorded effort for one mile was made on Jan. 12, 1904, by Henry Ford, driving a Ford "999." He established a record of 39.40 sec. or 91.370 m.p.h. All prior records were established over the flying kilometer. The first man to travel better than 100 m.p.h. was Rigolly, on July 2, 1904, at 103.56 m.p.h. The first over 200 m.p.h. was Major H. O. D. Segrave, who drove a Sunbeam at 203.79 on Mar. 29, 1927, at Daytona, Fla.

In 1947 John Cobb of London became the first person to travel more than 400 m.p.h. on land. The Englishman accomplished the feat on Sept. 16 at Bonneville, Utah, while raising the world mile record to 394.2 m.p.h. and the world kilometer (.62137 of a mile) mark to 393.8 m.p.h. His car was a Railton-Mobil Special. Cobb's average speed was 9.1325 seconds.

Craig Breedlove of Los Angeles, driving "Spirit of America," a three-wheeled jet-powered car, at Bonneville on Aug. 5, 1963, attained a speed of 8.8355 seconds per mile or 407.45 m.p.h. The U. S. Auto Club created a new category for the record—jet unlimited class. The record was broken a number of times in 1964, Breedlove lifting it above 500 m.p.h. to 526.277 on Oct. 15. Again, in 1965, the mark was topped frequently—Breedlove and Art Arfons of Akron, Ohio, beating one another's records; finally, on Nov. 15, Breedlove surpassed 600 m.p.h., achieving a standard of 600.601 at Bonneville. Gary Gabelich, driving the Blue Flame, raised the record to 622.407 m.p.h., Oct. 23, 1970, at Bonneville. The rocket car, powered by a mixture of peroxide and natural gas, hit 617.602 on the first run and 627.287 on the second.

The record held by Cobb was surpassed by Britain's Donald Campbell at Lake Eyre in Australia on July 17, 1964. He drove his 30-foot, 4,250-horsepower Bluebird to two runs of 403.1 m.p.h. each. This was beaten by Bob Summers of Ontario, Calif., who drove his 32-foot four-engined Goldenrod to a speed of 409.227 m.p.h. at Bonneville on Nov. 12, 1965.

Indianapolis "500" Winners

Year	Winner	Car	Second	Time	m.p.h.
1911	Ray Harroun	Marmon	Mulford	6:42:08	74.59
1912	Joe Dawson	National	Tetzloff	6:21:06	78.72
1913	Jules Goux	Peugeot	Wishart	6:35:05	75.93
1914	Rene Thomas	Delage	Duray	6:03:45	82.47
1915	Ralph DePalma	Mercedes	Resta	5:33:55	89.84
1916*	Dario Resta	Peugeot	De Aleve	3:34:17	84.00
1919	Howard Wilcox	Peugeot	Hearne	5:40:42	88.05
1920	Gaston Chevrolet	Monroe	Thomas	5:38:32	88.62
1921	Tommy Milton	Frontenac	Sarles	5:34:44	89.62
1922	Jimmy Murphy	Murphy Special	Hartz	5:17:30	94.48
1923	Tommy Milton	H. C. S. Special	Hartz	5:29:50	90.95
1924	L. L. Corum–Joe Boyer	Dusenberg Special	Cooper	5:05:23	98.23
1925	Peter DePaolo	Dusenberg Special	Lewis	4:56:39	101.13
1926†	Frank Lockhart	Miller Special	Hartz	4:10:14	95.904
1927	George Souders	Dusenberg Special	Devore	5:07:33	97.54
1928	Louis Meyer	Miller Special	Moore	5:01:33	99.48
1929	Ray Keech	Simplex Special	Meyer	5:07:25	97.58
1930	Billy Arnold	Miller-Hartz Special	Cantlon	4:58:39	100.448
1931	Louis Schneider	Bowes Special	Frame	5:10:28	96.629
1932	Fred Frame	Miller-Hartz Special	Wilcox	4:48:03.79	104.144
1933	Louis Meyer	Tydol Special	Shaw	4:48:00.75	104.162
1934	Bill Cummings	Boyle Products Special	Rose	4:46:05.20	104.863
1935	Kelly Petillo	Gilmore Special	Shaw	4:42:22.71	106.240
1936	Louis Meyer	Ring Free Special	Horn	4:35:03.39	109.069
1937	Wilbur Shaw	Shaw-Gilmore Special	Hepburn	4:24:07.80	113.580
1938	Floyd Roberts	Burd Piston Ring Special	Shaw	4:15:58.40	117.200
1939	Wilbur Shaw	Boyle Special	Snyder	4:20:47.39	115.035
1940	Wilbur Shaw	Boyle Special	Mays	4:22:31.17	114.277
1941	Floyd Davis–Mauri Rose	Noc-Out Hose Clamp Special	Mays	4:20:36.24	115.117
1946	George Robson	Thorne Eng. Special	Jackson	4:21:26.71	114.820
1947	Mauri Rose	Blue Crown Special	Holland	4:17:52.17	116.338
1948	Mauri Rose	Blue Crown Special	Holland	4:10:23.33	119.814
1949	Bill Holland	Blue Crown Special	Parsons	4:07:15.97	121.327
1950‡	Johnnie Parsons	Wynn's Friction Proof Spl.	Holland	2:46:55.97	124.002
1951	Lee Wallard	Belanger Special	Nazaruk	3:57:38.05	126.244
1952	Troy Ruttman	Agajanian Special	Rathmann	3:52:41.88	128.922
1953	Bill Vukovich	Fuel Injection Spl.	Cross	3:53:01.69	128.740
1954	Bill Vukovich	Fuel Injection Spl.	Bryan	3:49:17.27	130.840
1955	Bob Sweikert	John Zink Special	Bettenhausen	3:53:59.53	128.209
1956	Pat Flaherty	John Zink Special	Hanks	3:53:28.84	128.490
1957	Sam Hanks	Belond Exhaust Special	Rathmann	3:41:14.25	135.601
1958	Jimmy Bryan	Belond A-P Special	Amick	3:44:13.80	133.791
1959	Rodger Ward	Leader Card 500 Rdstr.	Rathmann	3:40:49.20	135.857
1960	Jim Rathmann	Ken-Paul Special	Ward	3:36:11.36	138.767
1961	A. J. Foyt	Bowes Special	Sachs	3:35:37.49	139.130
1962	Rodger Ward	Leader Card Special	Sutton	3:33:50.38	140.292
1963	Parnelli Jones	Agajanian Special	Clark	3:29:35.40	143.137
1964	A. J. Foyt	Offenhauser Special	Ward	3:23:35.83	147.650
1965	Jim Clark	Lotus-Ford	Jones	3:19:05.34	150.686
1966	Graham Hill	Lola-Ford	Clark	3:27:52.53	144.317
1967§	A. J. Foyt	Coyote-Ford	Al Unser	3:18:24.44	151.207
1968	Bobby Unser	Eagle-Offenhauser	Dan Gurney	3:16:13.76	152.882
1969	Mario Andretti	STP Hawk-Ford	Dan Gurney	3:11:14.71	156.867
1970	Al Unser	P. J. Colt-Ford	Mark Donohue	3:12:37.04	155.749
1971	Al Unser	P. J. Colt-Ford	Peter Revson	3:10:11.56	157.735
1972	Mark Donohue	McLaren–Offenhauser	Al Unser	3:04:05.54	162.962
1973**	Gordon Johncock	Eagle-Offenhauser	Billy Vukovich	2:05:26.59	159.036
1974	Johnny Rutherford	McLaren–Offenhauser	Bobby Unser	3:09:10.06	158.589
1975††	Bobby Unser	Eagle-Offenhauser	Johnny Rutherford	2:54:55.08	149.213

* 300 miles. † Race ended at 400 miles because of heavy rain. ‡ Race ended at 345 miles because of rain. § Race, postponed after 18 laps because of rain on May 30, was finished on May 31. ** Race postponed May 28 and 29 was cut to 332.5 miles because of rain, May 30. †† Race ended at 435 miles because of rain.

Winners of USAC California 500 and Pocono 500-mile Races

CALIFORNIA 500

(Ontario, Calif., Motor Speedway)

1971 Joe Leonard, Parnelli-Offy; 152.354 m.p.h.
1972 Roger McCluskey, McLaren-Offy; 151.540 m.p.h.
1973 Wally Dallenbach, Eagle-Offy; 157.66 m.p.h.
1974 Bobby Unser, Eagle-Offy, 157.01 m.p.h.
1975 A. J. Foyt, Coyote-Ford, 154.344 m.p.h.

SCHAEFER (POCONO) 500

(Pocono International Speedway, Long Pond, Pa.)

1971 Mark Donohoe, McLaren-Offy; 138.648 m.p.h.
1972 Joe Leonard, Parnelli-Offy; 154.781 m.p.h.
1973 A. J. Foyt, Coyote-Ford; 144.944 m.p.h.
1974 Johnny Rutherford, McLaren-Offy; 156.701 m.p.h.
1975 A. J. Foyt, Coyote-Ford, 140.712 m.p.h.

World Grand Prix Driver Champions

1950 Giuseppe Farina, Italy, Alfa Romeo	1965 Jim Clark, Scotland, Lotus-Ford
1951 Juan M. Fangio, Argentina, Alfa Romeo	1966 Jack Brabham, Australia, Brabham-Repco
1952-53 Alberto Ascari, Italy, Ferrari	1967 Denis Hulme, New Zealand, Brabham-Repco
1955 Juan M. Fangio, Argentina, Maserati, Mercedes-Benz	1968 Graham Hill, England, Lotus-Ford
1955-56-57 Fangio, Mercedes-Benz (55);	1969 Jackie Stewart, Scotland, Matra-Ford
Lancia-Ferrari (56); Maserati (57)	1970 Jochen Rindt, Austria, Lotus-Ford
1958 Mike Hawthorn, England, Ferrari	1971 Jackie Stewart, Scotland, Tyrrell-Ford
1959-60. Jack Brabham, Australia, Cooper	1972 Emerson Fittipaldi, Brazil, Lotus-Ford
1961 Phil Hill, United States, Ferrari	1973 Jackie Stewart, Scotland, Tyrrell-Ford
1962 Graham Hill, England, BRM	1974 Emerson Fittipaldi, Brazil, McLaren-Ford
1963 Jim Clark, Scotland, Lotus-Ford	1975 Niki Lauda, Austria, Ferrari
1964 John Surtees, England, Ferrari	

MOTORCYCLING
Grand National Champions

1954	Joe Leonard	1962	Bart Markel	1967-68 Gary Nixon	1972 Mark Brelsford
1955	Brad Andres	1963	Dick Mann	1969 Mert Lawwill	1973-74 Ken Roberts
1956-57	Joe Leonard	1964	Roger Reiman	1970 Gene Romero	1975 Gary Scott
1958-61	Carroll Resweber	1966	Bart Markel	1971 Dick Mann	

ICE (FIGURE) SKATING
World Champions

1948-52 Richard Button, United States	1969-70 Tim Wood, United States	1954 Gundi Busch, Germany
1953-56 Hayes Jenkins, United States	1971-73 Ondrej Nepela, Czechoslovakia	1955 Tenley Albright, United States
1957-59 David Jenkins, United States	1974 Jan Hoffman, East Germany	1956-60 Carol Heiss, United States
1960 Alain Giletti, France	1975 Sergei Yolkov, U.S.S.R.	1961 No competition
1961 No competition		1962-64 Sjoukje Dijkstra, Netherlands
1962 Donald Jackson, Canada	**WOMEN**	1965 Petra Burka, Canada
1963 Don McPherson, Canada		1966-68 Peggy Fleming, United States
1964 Manfred Schnelldorfer,	1947-48 Barbara Ann Scott, Canada	1969-70 Gabriele Seyfert, E. Germany
Germany	1949-50 Aja Vrzanova, Czechoslovakia	1971-72 Beatrix Schuba, Austria
1965 Alain Calmat, France	1951 Jeannette Altwegg, England	1973 Karen Magnussen, Canada
1966-68 Emmerich Danzer, Austria	1952 Jacqueline du Bief, France	1974 Christine Errath, East Germany
	1953 Tenley Albright, United States	1975 Dianne de Leeuw, Netherlands

National Champions

1946-52 Richard Button	1967 Gary Visconti	1951 Sonya Klopfer
1953-56 Hayes Jenkins	1968-70 Tim Wood	1952-56 Tenley Albright
1957-60 David Jenkins	1971 John M. Petkevich	1957-60 Carol Heiss
1961 Bradley Lord	1972 Ken Shelley	1961 Laurence Owen
1962 Monty Hoyt	1973-75 Gordon McKellen	1962 Barbara Roles Pursley
1963 Tommy Litz		1963 Lorraine Hanlon
1964 Scott Allen	**WOMEN**	1964-68 Peggy Fleming
1965 Gary Visconti	1943-48 Gretchen Merrill	1969-73 Janet Lynn
1966 Scott Allen	1949-50 Yvonne Sherman	1974-75 Dorothy Hamill

---

ICE (SPEED) SKATING
National Outdoor Champions

1946 Robert Fitzgerald	1971 Jack Walters	1958-59 Jean Omelenchuk
1947 Ken Bartholomew	1972 Barth Levy	1960 Mary Novak
1948 George Fisher	1973 Mike Woods	1961 Jean Ashworth
1949 Ray Blum	1974 Leigh Barczewski, Mike	1962 Jean Omelenchuk
1950-56 Ken Bartholomew	Passarella	1963 Jean Ashworth
1957 Ken Bartholomew, Bobby	1975 Rich Wurster	1964 Diane White
Snyder		1965 Jean Omelenchuk
1958 Gene Sandvig	**WOMEN**	1966 Diane White
1959-60 Ken Bartholomew	1946 Elaine Gordon	1967 Jean Ashworth
1961 Ed Rudolph	1947 Geraldine Scott	1968 Helen Lutsch
1962 Floyd Bedbury	1948-49 Lorraine Sabbe	1969 Sally Blatchford
1963 Tom Gray	1950 Janet Christopherson	1970-71 Sheila Young
1964 Neil Blatchford	1951 Barbara DeSchepper,	1972 Ruth Moore and Nancy Thorne
1965-66 Richard Wurster	Gwendolyn DuBois	1973 Nancy Class
1967 Mike Passarella	1952 Barbara DeSchepper	1974 Kris Garbe
1968-70 Peter Cefalu	1953-56 Pat Gibson	1975 Nancy Swider
	1957 Mary Mayland	

BASKETBALL

BASKETBALL may be unique in sports. It is one game concerning which it is safe to state when, where and how it originated. In the winter of 1891–92, Dr. James Naismith, an instructor in the Y.M.C.A. Training College (now Springfield College) at Springfield, Mass., deliberately invented the game of basketball in order to provide indoor exercise and competition for the students between the closing of the football season and the opening of the baseball season. He affixed peach baskets overhead on the walls at opposite ends of the gymnasium and, with an association (soccer) football, organized teams to play his new game in which the purpose was to toss the ball into one basket and prevent,

as far as possible, the opponents from tossing the ball into the other basket. Fundamentally, the game is the same today, though there have been improvements in equipment and changes in rules.

Because Dr. Naismith had eighteen available players when he invented the game, the first rule was: "There shall be nine players on each side." Later the number of players became optional, depending upon the size of the available court, but the five-player standard was adopted when the game spread over the country. United States' soldiers introduced the game in Europe in World War I and, being taking up by foreign nations, it soon became a world-wide sport.

National Collegiate A. A. Champions

1939 Oregon	1947 Holy Cross	1955 San Francisco	1963 Loyola (Chicago)
1940 Indiana	1948 Kentucky	1956 San Francisco	1964 U.C.L.A.
1941 Wisconsin	1949 Kentucky	1957 North Carolina	1965 U.C.L.A.
1942 Stanford	1950 C.C.N.Y.	1958 Kentucky	1966 Texas Western
1943 Wyoming	1951 Kentucky	1959 California	1967–73 U.C.L.A.
1944 Utah	1952 Kansas	1960 Ohio State	1974 No. Carolina State
1945 Oklahoma A & M	1953 Indiana	1961 Cincinnati	1975 U.C.L.A.
1946 Oklahoma A & M	1954 La Salle	1962 Cincinnati	

National Invitation Tournament Champions (NIT)

1939 Long Island U.	1949 San Francisco	1958 Xavier (Cincinnati)	1967 So. Illinois
1940 Colorado	1950 C.C.N.Y.	1959 St. John's (Bklyn.)	1968 Dayton
1941 Long Island U.	1951 Brigham Young	1960 Bradley	1969 Temple
1942 West Virginia	1952 La Salle	1961 Providence	1970 Marquette
1943–44 St. John's (Bklyn.)	1953 Seton Hall	1962 Dayton	1971 North Carolina
1945 DePaul	1954 Holy Cross	1963 Providence	1972 Maryland
1946 Kentucky	1955 Duquesne	1964 Bradley	1973 Virginia Tech
1947 Utah	1956 Louisville	1965 St. John's (Bklyn.)	1974 Purdue
1948 St. Louis	1957 Bradley	1966 Brigham Young	1975 Princeton

---

N.C.A.A. Major College Individual Scoring Records
Single Season Averages

Player, Team	Year	G	FG	FT	Pts.	Avg.
Pete Maravich, Louisiana State	1969–70	31	*522	337	*1381	*44.5
Maravich	1968–69	26	433	282	1148	44.2
Maravich	1967–68	26	432	274	1138	43.8
Frank Selvy, Furman	1953–54	29	427	*355	1209	41.7
Johnny Neumann, Mississippi	1970–71	23	366	191	923	40.1
Billy McGill, Utah	1961–62	26	394	221	1009	38.8
Calvin Murphy, Niagara	1967–68	24	337	242	916	38.2
Austin Carr, Notre Dame	1969–70	29	444	218	1106	38.1

N.C.A.A. Career Scoring Totals
UNIVERSITY DIVISION

Player, Team	Last year	G	FG	FT	Pts.	Avg.
Pete Maravich, Louisiana State	1970	83	*1387	893	*3667	*44.2
Austin Carr, Notre Dame	1971	74	1017	526	2560	34.6
Oscar Robertson, Cincinnati	1960	88	1052	869	2973	33.8
Calvin Murphy, Niagara	1970	77	947	654	2548	33.1
† Dwight Lanar	1973	57	768	326	1862	32.7
Frank Selvy, Furman	1954	78	922	694	2538	32.5
Rick Mount, Purdue	1970	72	910	503	2323	32.3
Darrell Floyd, Furman	1956	71	868	545	2281	32.1
Dick Werkman, Seton Hall	1964	71	812	649	2273	32.0

* Record. † Also played two seasons in college division.

COLLEGE INDIVIDUAL SCORING (Continued)
COLLEGE DIVISION

	Last year	G	FG	FT	Pts.	Avg.
Travis Grant, Kentucky State	1972	121	*1760	525	*4045	*33.4
John Rinka, Kenyon	1970	99	1261	729	3251	32.8
Florindo Vieira, Quinnipiac	1957	69	671	741	2263	32.8
Willie Shaw, Lane	1964	76	960	459	2379	31.3
Mike Davis, Virginia Union	1969	89	1014	730	2758	31.0
Willie Scott, Alabama State	1969	103	1277	601	3155	30.6
Gregg Northington, Alabama State	1972	75	894	403	2191	29.2
Bob Hopkins, Grambling	1956	126	1403	953	3759	29.8

* Record.

Top Single-Game Scoring Marks

Player, Team (Opponent)	Yr	Pts.	Player, Team (Opponent)	Yr	Pts.
Selvy, Furman (Newberry)	1954	*100	Floyd, Furman (Morehead)	1955	67
Mikvy, Temple (Wilkes)	1951	73	Maravich, LSU (Tulane)	1969	66
Maravich, LSU (Alabama)	1970	69	Handlan, W & L (Furman)	1951	66
Murphy, Niagara (Syracuse)	1969	68			

* Record.

GLOSSARY OF BASKETBALL TERMS

Sources: National Collegiate Athletic Association and National Basketball Association.

All-Court Press—Close guarding by defense at all points, trying to force errors.

Back Court—Area between center line and basket which offensive team leaves as it moves toward own basket.

Ball Control—Prolonged possession of ball on attack, seeking good scoring chance.

Basket—The hoop through which ball is thrown; a team's basket is one it aims at, not one it defends; also, name for field goal counting 2 points.

Blocking—Impeding progress of opponent who does not have ball.

Boards—Backboards.

Bonus Free Throw—Second throw allowed, if first is made, on foul committed when team has six or more fouls in half.

Control of Boards—Indicates one team is retrieving most of rebounds.

Conversion—Sinking of free-throw attempt.

Cripple—An easy, unopposed field-goal attempt.

Double Team—Method of defense by which two defenders converge on one player, usually top scorer.

Dribble—Bouncing of ball on floor by player, usually while in motion, with either hand, not both; **double-dribble:** starting to dribble again after grasping ball with both hands, a violation.

Dunking—Reaching above rim and thrusting ball into basket; illegal in college and high school play.

Fast Break—Attempt to get into scoring position before defensive team can regain back court posts.

Foul—Illegal contact with opponent, usually player with ball, is called personal foul; non-contact foul is a technical; penalty is one or more free throws.

Free Throw—Unhindered shot allowed player from line in front of basket after he has been fouled.

Front Court—Area from center line to offensive team's basket where most of play occurs; area must be reached within 10 seconds after gaining possession of ball and play cannot go to back court unless ball is touched by opponent.

Give and Go—Player passes to teammate and races for basket anticipating return pass.

Goal Tending—Touching or knocking ball back from basket when ball is above or in opponent's basket.

Held Ball—Each of opponents has firm hold on ball, with neither in control.

High Post—Position near outer circle of free-throw line.

Jump Ball—Ball put into play by tossing up between two players in one of three circles marked on floor; usually after held ball.

Jump Shot—Field-goal attempt by player with both feet off floor, shooting over a guard.

Lay-Up—An easy shot, usually banked off backboard from side of basket, which is pushed rather than thrown.

Low Post—Position at side of basket outside free-throw lane.

Man-to-Man Defense—Player guards only the man he is assigned.

Overtime—Game in which extra periods are played to dissolve tie existing at end of regular time.

Pick—Block of defender by player that sets up teammate for field-goal attempt.

Rebound—Carom of ball off basket after field-goal attempt.

Running—See Traveling.

Screen—Legal action by player to delay opponent from reaching desired position.

Set Shot—Field-goal attempt, taken with deliberation, by player well out with both feet on floor.

Steps—See Traveling.

Stuffing—See Dunking.

3-Point Goal—Field goal from 25 feet out in American Basketball Association which counts 3 points instead of 2.

3-Point Play—Maximum score by player fouled in action of shooting field goal who converts the free throw.

Throw In—Method of putting ball into play after field goal or out of bounds; player must throw to teammate on court within five seconds.

Tipoff—Jump ball which starts game and second half.

10-Second Rule—See Front Court.

3-Second Rule—See Free-Throw Lane.

Traveling—Extra steps taken by player with ball, who is allowed one full step after receiving ball.

Turnover—Loss of ball by team before field-goal attempt.

Violations—Rule infractions, such as double-dribble, traveling, for which there is no free-throw penalty.

Zone Defense—Method by which player guards an area instead of one man; it is barred in National Basketball Association.

Professional Basketball
National Basketball Association Champions

The National Basketball Association was originally the Basketball Association of America. It took its current name in 1949 when it merged with the National Basketball League.

Season	Eastern Division (W–L)	Western Division (W–L)	Playoff Champions*
1946–47	Washington Capitols (49–11)	Chicago Stags (39–22)	Philadelphia Warriors
1947–48	Philadelphia Warriors (27–21)	St. Louis Bombers (29–19)	Baltimore Bullets
1948–49	Washington Capitols (38–22)	Rochester Royals (45–15)	Minneapolis Lakers
1949–50	Syracuse Nationals (51–13)	Indianapolis Olympians (39–25)†	Minneapolis Lakers
1950–51	Philadelphia Warriors (40–26)	Minneapolis Lakers (44–24)	Rochester Royals
1951–52	Syracuse Nationals (40–26)	Rochester Royals (41–25)	Minneapolis Lakers
1952–53	New York Knickerbockers (47–23)	Minneapolis Lakers (48–22)	Minneapolis Lakers
1953–54	New York Knickerbockers (44–28)	Minneapolis Lakers (46–26)	Minneapolis Lakers
1954–55	Syracuse Nationals (43–29)	Ft. Wayne Pistons (43–29)	Syracuse Nationals
1955–56	Philadelphia Warriors (45–27)	Ft. Wayne Pistons (37–35)	Philadelphia Warriors
1956–57	Boston Celtics (44–28)	St. Louis Hawks (34–38)	Boston Celtics
1957–58	Boston Celtics (48–23)	St. Louis Hawks (41–31)	St. Louis Hawks
1958–59	Boston Celtics (52–20)	St. Louis Hawks (49–23)	Boston Celtics
1959–60	Boston Celtics (59–16)	St. Louis Hawks (46–29)	Boston Celtics
1960–61	Boston Celtics (57–22)	St. Louis Hawks (51–28)	Boston Celtics
1961–62	Boston Celtics (60–20)	Los Angeles Lakers (54–26)	Boston Celtics
1962–63	Boston Celtics (58–22)	Los Angeles Lakers (53–27)	Boston Celtics
1963–64	Boston Celtics (59–21)	San Francisco Warriors (48–32)	Boston Celtics
1964–65	Boston Celtics (62–18)	Los Angeles Lakers (49–31)	Boston Celtics
1965–66	Philadelphia 76ers (55–25)	Los Angeles Lakers (45–35)	Boston Celtics
1966–67	Philadelphia 76ers (68–13)	San Francisco Warriors (44–37)	Philadelphia 76ers
1967–68	Philadelphia 76ers (62–20)	St. Louis Hawks (56–26)	Boston Celtics
1968–69	Baltimore Bullets (57–25)	Los Angeles Lakers (55–27)	Boston Celtics
1969–70	New York Knickerbockers (60–22)	Atlanta Hawks (48–34)	New York Knicks
1970–71	Baltimore Bullets (42–40)**	Milwaukee Bucks (66–16)‡	Milwaukee Bucks
1971–72	New York Knickerbockers (48–34)	Los Angeles Lakers (69–13)	Los Angeles Lakers
1972–73	††New York Knickerbockers (57–25)	Los Angeles Lakers (69–22)	New York Knicks
1973–74	Boston Celtics (56–26)	Milwaukee Bucks (59–23)	Boston Celtics
1974–75	Washington Bullets (60–22)	Golden State Warriors (48–34)	Golden State Warriors

* Playoffs involve teams other than division winners. ** Beat New York Knicks (52–30) in Playoffs. † Central Division: Minneapolis Lakers (51–17). ‡ Beat Los Angeles (48–34) in playoffs. †† Beat Boston (68–14) in playoffs.

Individual N.B.A. Scoring Champions

Season	Player, Team	G	FG	FT	Pts.	Avg.
1953–54	Neil Johnston, Philadelphia Warriors	72	591	577	1759	24.4
1954–55	Neil Johnston, Philadelphia Warriors	72	521	589	1631	22.7
1955–56	Bob Pettit, St. Louis Hawks	72	646	557	1849	25.7
1956–57	Paul Arizin, Philadelphia Warriors	71	613	591	1817	25.6
1957–58	George Yardley, Detroit Pistons	72	673	655	2001	27.8
1958–59	Bob Pettit, St. Louis Hawks	72	719	667	2105	29.2
1959–60	Wilt Chamberlain, Philadelphia Warriors	72	1065	577	2707	37.6
1960–61	Wilt Chamberlain, Philadelphia Warriors	79	1251	531	3033	38.4
1961–62	Wilt Chamberlain, Philadelphia Warriors	80	1597	835	4029	50.4
1962–63	Wilt Chamberlain, San Francisco Warriors	80	1463	660	3586	44.8
1963–64	Wilt Chamberlain, San Francisco Warriors	80	1204	540	2948	36.9
1964–65	Wilt Chamberlain, San Fran. Warriors–Phila. 76ers	73	1063	408	2534	34.7
1965–66	Wilt Chamberlain, Philadelphia 76ers	79	1074	501	2649	33.5
1966–67	Rick Barry, San Francisco Warriors	78	1011	753	2775	35.6
1967–68	Dave Bing, Detroit Pistons	79	835	472	2142	27.1
1968–69	Elvin Hayes, San Diego Rockets	82	930	467	2327	28.4
1969–70	Jerry West, Los Angeles Lakers	74	831	647	2309	31.2
1970–71	*Lew Alcindor, Milwaukee Bucks	82	1063	470	2596	31.7
1971–72	Kareem Abdul-Jabbar, Milwaukee Bucks	81	1159	504	2822	34.8
1972–73	Nate Archibald, Kansas City–Omaha	80	1028	663	2719	34.0
1973–74	Bob McAdoo, Buffalo	74	901	459	2261	30.8
1974–75	Bob McAdoo, Buffalo	82	1,095	641	2831	34.5

* (Kareem Abdul-Jabbar).

N.B.A. Most Valuable Players

1956—Bob Pettit	1961–63—Bill Russell	1970—Willis Reed
1957—Bob Cousy	1964—Oscar Robertson	1971–72—Lew Alcindor
1958—Bill Russell	1965—Bill Russell	(Kareem Abdul-Jabbar)
1959—Bob Pettit	1966–68—Wilt Chamberlain	1973—Dave Cowens
1960—Wilt Chamberlain	1969—Wes Unseld	1974—Kareem Abdul-Jabbar
		1975—Bob McAdoo, Buffalo

American Basketball Association Champions

Season	Eastern Division (W–L)	Western Division (W–L)	Playoff Champions
1967–68	Pittsburgh Pipers (54–24)	New Orleans Buccaneers (48–30)	Pittsburgh Pipers
1968–69	Indiana Pacers (44–34)	Oakland Oaks (60–18)	Oakland Oaks
1969–70	Indiana Pacers (59–25)	Denver Rockets (51–33)	Indiana Pacers
1970–71	Virginia Squires (55–29)	Indiana Pacers (58–26)	Utah Stars
1971–72	*New York Nets (44–40)	*Indiana Pacers (47–37)	Indiana Pacers
1972–73	*Kentucky Colonels (56–28)	*Indiana Pacers (51–33)	Indiana Pacers
1973–74	*New York Nets (55–29)	*Utah Stars (51–33)	New York Nets
1974–75	Kentucky Colonels (58–26)	*Indiana Pacers (45–39)	Kentucky Colonels
†Regular Season Winner		Playoff Finalist	Playoff Winner
1975–76	Denver Nuggest (60–24)**	New York Nets	New York Nets

* Won division playoffs; † League reduced to one division; ** Won final playoff berth.

Individual A.B.A. Scoring Champions

			Field Goals				
Season	Player, Team	G	2 pt.	3 pt.	FT	Pts.	Avg
1967–68	Connie Hawkins, Pittsburgh Pipers	70	633	2	603	1875	26.8
1968–69	Rick Barry, Oakland Oaks	36	389	3	403	1190	34.0
1969–70	Spencer Haywood, Denver Rockets	84	986	0	547	2519	29.99
1970–71	Dan Issel, Kentucky Colonels	83	938	0	604	2480	29.9
1971–72	Charlie Scott, Virginia Squires	73	927	29	525	2,524	34.5
1972–73	Julius Erving, Virginia	71	889	3	475	2,262	31.9
1973–74	Julius Erving, New York Nets	84	897	7	484	2,299	27.4
1975–76	Julius Erving, New York Nets	84	915	34	530	2,462	29.31
1974–75	George McGinnis, Indiana Pacers	79	811	62	545	2,353	29.78

National Basketball Association Lifetime Leaders
(Through June 1976)

SCORING

	Yrs	FG	FT	Pts
Wilt Chamberlain	14	12,681	6,057	31,419
Oscar Robertson	14	9,508	7,694	26,710
Jerry West	14	9,016	7,160	25,192
*John Havlicek	14	9,387	4,904	23,678
Elgin Baylor	14	8,693	5,763	23,149
Hal Greer	15	8,504	4,578	21,586
Walt Bellamy	14	7,914	5,113	20,941
Bob Pettit	11	7,349	6,182	20,880
Dolph Schayes	16	6,135	6,979	19,249
Chet Walker	13	6,876	5,079	18,831

SCORING AVERAGES

	Games	Points	Pct
Wilt Chamberlain	1,045	31,419	30.07
*Kareem Abdul-Jabbar	549	16,486	39.03
Elgin Baylor	846	23,149	27.4
Jerry West	932	25,192	27.0
*Rick Barry	481	12,826	26.7
Bob Pettit	792	20,880	26.4
Oscar Robertson	1,040	26,710	25.7
*Nate Archibald	433	10,894	25.2
*Elvin Hayes	652	15,920	24.4
Paul Arizin	713	16,266	22.8

FIELD GOAL PERCENTAGE

	Att	FG	Pct
*Kareem Abdul-Jabbar	12,515	6,816	.544
Wilt Chamberlain	23,497	12,681	.540
Walt Bellamy	15,340	7,914	.516
Terry Dischinger	6,836	3,457	.506
*Rudy Tomjanovich	6,815	3,427	.503
Bob McAdoo	6,996	3,515	.502
*Wes Unseld	5,878	2,944	.501
Jerry Lucas	11,441	5,709	.499

FREE THROW PERCENTAGE

	Att	FT	Pct
*Rick Barry	3,120	2,778	.890
Bill Sharman	3,557	3,143	.884
*Calvin Murphy	2,248	1,967	.875
Larry Siegfried	1,945	1,662	.854
Flynn Robinson	1,881	1,597	.849
Dolph Schayes	8,273	6,979	.844
*Jack Marin	2,813	2,374	.844
Larry Costello	2,891	2,432	.841

REBOUNDS

Wilt Chamberlain	23,924
Bill Russell	21,620
Walt Bellamy	14,241
Nate Thurmond	13,675
Jerry Lucas	12,942
Bob Pettit	12,849

PERSONAL FOULS

Hal Greer	3,855
Dolph Schayes	3,664
Walt Bellamy	3,536
Bailey Howell	3,498
Bill Bridges	3,375
Len Wilkens	3,285

ASSISTS

Oscar Robertson	9,887
Len Wilkens	7,211
Bob Cousy	6,959
Guy Rodgers	6,917
Jerry West	6,238
*John Havlicek	5,386

* Active.

NATIONAL BASKETBALL ASSOCIATION GOVERNMENT

Commissioner's Office: Lawrence F. O'Brien, Commissioner; Simon P. Gourdine, Deputy Commissioner; John P. Nucatola, Supervisor of Officials; Don Molinelli, Director of Communications; Matt Winick, Director of Media Information.

BOXING

WHETHER it be called pugilism, prize fighting or boxing, there is no tracing "the Sweet Science" to any definite source. Tales of rivals exchanging blows for fun, fame or money go back to earliest recorded history and classical legend. There was a mixture of boxing and wrestling called the "pancratium" in the ancient Olympic Games and in such contests the rivals belabored one another with hands fortified with heavy leather wrappings that were sometimes studded with metal. More than one Olympic competitor lost his life at this brutal exercise.

There was little law or order in pugilism until Jack Broughton, one of the early champions of England, drew up a set of rules for the game in 1743. Broughton, called "the father of English boxing," also

is credited with having invented boxing gloves. However, these gloves—or "mufflers" as they were called—were used only in teaching "the manly art of self-defense" or in training bouts. All professional championship fights were contested with "bare knuckles" until 1892, when John L. Sullivan lost the heavyweight championship of the world to James J. Corbett in New Orleans in a bout in which both contestants wore regulation gloves.

The Broughton rules were superseded by the London Prize Ring Rules of 1838. The 8th Marquis of Queensberry, with the help of John G. Chambers, put forward the "Queensberry Rules" in 1866, a code that called for gloved contests. Amateurs took quickly to the Queensberry Rules, the professionals slowly.

HISTORY OF WORLD HEAVYWEIGHT CHAMPIONSHIP FIGHTS
(Bouts in which a new champion was crowned)

Date	Where held	Winner, weight, age	Loser, weight, age	Rounds	Referee
Sept. 7, 1892	New Orleans, La. ...	James J. Corbett, 178 (26) ...	John L. Sullivan, 212 (33) ..	21	Prof. John Duffy
Mar. 17, 1897	Carson City, Nev. ...	Bob Fitzsimmons, 167 (34) ...	James J. Corbett, 183 (30) .	KO 14	George Siler
June 9, 1899	Coney Island, N. Y. .	(a)James J. Jeffries, 206 (24) ..	Bob Fitzsimmons, 167 (37).	KO 11	George Siler
Feb. 23, 1906	Los Angeles	(b)Tommy Burns, 180 (24) ...	Marvin Hart, 188 (29)	20	James J. Jeffries
Dec. 26, 1908	Sydney, N. S. W.....	Jack Johnson, 196 (30)	Tommy Burns, 176 (27)....	KO 14	Hugh McIntosh
April 5, 1915	Havana, Cuba	Jess Willard, 230 (33)	Jack Johnson, 205½ (37) .	KO 26	Jack Welch
July 4, 1919	Toledo, Ohio	Jack Dempsey, 187 (24)	Jess Willard, 245 (24)	KO 3	Ollie Pecord
Sept. 23, 1926	Philadelphia	(c)Gene Tunney, 189 (28)	Jack Dempsey, 190 (31)....	10	Pop Reilly
June 12, 1930	New York...........	Max Schmeling, 188 (24)....	Jack Sharkey, 197 (27)....	WF 4	Jim Crowley
June 21, 1932	Long Island City....	Jack Sharkey, 205 (29).....	Max Schmeling, 188 (26)...	15	Gunboat Smith
June 29, 1933	Long Island City....	Primo Carnera, 260½ (26)...	Jack Sharkey, 201 (30).....	KO 6	Arthur Donovan
June 14, 1934	Long Island City....	Max Baer, 209½ (25).......	Primo Carnera, 263¼ (27).	KO 11	Arthur Donovan
June 13, 1935	Long Island City....	Jim Braddock, 193¾ (29) ...	Max Baer, 209½ (26)	15	Jack McAvoy
June 22, 1937	Chicago...........	Joe Louis, 197¼ (23).......	Jim Braddock, 197 (31)....	KO 8	Tommy Thomas
June 22, 1949	Chicago...........	(d)Ezzard Charles, 181¾ (27)..	Joe Walcott, 195½ (35)....	15	Davey Miller
Sept. 27, 1950	New York...........	(e)Ezzard Charles, 184½ (29)..	Joe Louis, 218 (36)........	15	Mark Conn
July 18, 1951	Pittsburgh	Joe Walcott, 194 (37).......	Ezzard Charles, 182 (30)...	KO 7	Buck McTiernan
Sept. 23, 1952	Philadelphia	(f)Rocky Marciano, 184 (29) ...	Joe Walcott, 196 (38).....	KO 13	Charley Daggett
Nov. 30, 1956	Chicago...........	Floyd Patterson, 182¼ (21)..	Archie Moore, 187¾ (42) ..	KO 5	Frank Sikora
June 26, 1959	New York...........	Ingemar Johansson, 196 (26)	Floyd Patterson, 182 (24)...	KO 3	Ruby Goldstein
June 20, 1960	New York...........	Floyd Patterson, 190 (25)....	Ingemar Johansson, 194¾ (27)	KO 5	Arthur Mercante
Sept. 25, 1962	Chicago...........	Sonny Liston, 214 (28)......	Floyd Patterson, 189 (27)..	KO 1	Frank Sikora
Feb. 25, 1964	Miami Beach, Fla....	(g)Cassius Clay, 210 (22)......	Sonny Liston, 218 (30).....	KO 7	Barney Felix
Mar. 4, 1968	New York...........	(h)Joe Frazier, 204½ (24).....	Buster Mathis, 243½ (23)..	KO 11	Arthur Mercante
April 27, 1968	Oakland, Calif.......	(i)Jimmy Ellis, 197 (28).......	Jerry Quarry, 195 (22).....	15	Elmer Costa
Feb. 16, 1970	New York...........	(j)Joe Frazier, 205 (26).......	Jimmy Ellis, 201 (29)......	KO 5	Tony Perez
Jan. 22, 1973	Kingston, Jamaica ..	George Foreman, 217½ (24)..	Joe Frazier, 214 (29)......	KO 2	Arthur Mercante
Oct. 30, 1974	Kinshasa, Zaire	Muhammad Ali, 216½ (32)..	George Foreman, 220 (26)..	KO 8	Zack Clayton

(a) Jeffries retired as champion in March 1905. He named Marvin Hart and Jack Root as leading contenders and agreed to referee their fight in Reno, Nev., on July 3, 1905, with the stipulation that he would term the winner the champion. Hart, 190 (28), knocked out Root, 171 (29), in the 12th round. (b) Burns claimed the title after defeating Hart. (c) Tunney retired as champion after defeating Tom Heeney on July 26, 1928. (d) After Louis announced his retirement as champion on March 1, 1949, Charles won recognition from the National Boxing Association as champion by defeating Walcott. (e) Charles gained undisputed recognition as champion by defeating Louis, who came out of retirement. (f) Retired as champion April 27, 1956. (g) The World Boxing Association later withdrew its recognition of Clay as champion and declared the winner of a bout between Ernie Terrell and Eddie Machen would gain its version of the title. Terrell, 199 (25), won a 15-round decision from Machen, 192 (32), in Chicago on March 5, 1965. Clay, 212¼ (25) and Terrell, 212½ (27) met in Houston on Feb. 6, 1967, Clay winning a 15-round decision. (h) Winner recognized by New York, Massachusetts, Maine, Illinois, Texas and Pennsylvania in fight vacated title when Clay was stripped of championship for failing to accept U. S. Induction. (i) Bout was final of eight-man tournament to fill Clay's place and is recognized by World Boxing Association. (j) Bout settled controversy over title.

BARE KNUCKLE HEAVYWEIGHT CHAMPIONS, 1719–1892

1719—Jim Figg	1740—Jack Broughton	1760—Bill Stevens	1765—Bill Darts
1734—George Taylor	1750—Jack Slack	1761—George Meggs	1777—Harry Sellers

1780—Jack Harris
1785—Tom (Jackling) Johnson
1790—Big Ben Brain
1792—Daniel Mendoza
1795—John Jackson (retired)
1802—Jem Belcher
1805—Henry Pearce (Game Chicken)
1808—John Gully (declined title)
1809—Tom Cribb received belt, not transferable, and cup
1824—Tom Spring received four cups; resigned title.
1825—Jem Ward received belt, not transferable.
1838—James (Deaf) Burke claimed title.
1839—William Thompson (Bendigo) beat Burke; claimed championship; received belt from Jem Ward.
1841—Nick Ward (Jem's brother) beat Ben Caunt, Feb. 2. In return match Caunt beat Nick Ward and received belt by subscription. It was transferable.
1845—Thompson beat Caunt and got belt.
1850—Bill Perry (The Tipton Slasher), after fight with Paddock, claimed title.
1851—Harry Broome won title from Perry.
1853—Perry claimed title when Broome forfeited £200 to him in a match; retired from ring on Aug. 13.
1857—Tom Sayers beat Perry for £200 a side and new belt.
1860—Sayers retired after 42-round draw with John C. Heenan (The Benicia Boy), leaving old belt open for competition.
1860—Sam Hurst (The Stalybridge Infant) beat Paddock and received belt.
1861—Jem Mace beat Hurst.
1862—Mace beat Tom King for £200 a side and the belt.

1862—King beat Mace and claimed belt. Subsequently gave it up. Declined to meet Mace again. Mace claimed belt.
1863—King beat Heenan for £1,000 a side.
1865—Joe Wormald beat Andrew Marsden for £200 a side and belt, which had been claimed by both. Belt was given to Wormald, who forfeited £120 to Mace.
1866—Mace and Joe Goss fought draw with £200 a side and belt at stake.
1867—Wormald received £200 forfeit from Ned O'Baldwin and claimed belt when O'Baldwin failed to appear at starting place.
1867—Mace and O'Baldwin drew; £200 a side; title and belt in abeyance.
1869—Mike McCoole defeated Tom Allen and claimed American championship.
1870—Mace claimed world title by knocking out Allen in 10 rounds.
1873—Mace retired and Allen claimed title of world champion by defeating McCoole.
1876—Allen fought Joe Goss, ranked next to Mace in England. Allen was disqualified in the 27th round for fouling and Goss was recognized as world champion under London Prize Ring Rules.
1880—Paddy Ryan knocked out Goss in the 87th round on May 30, near Colliers Station, W. Va., and became the first American to hold the undisputed world's bare knuckle championship.
1882—John L. Sullivan knocked out Ryan in the 9th round at Mississippi City, Miss., on Feb. 7 and became the last bare knuckle champion.
1889—Sullivan defeated Jake Kilrain in the last bare knuckle championship fight. The bout, on July 8 at Richburg, Miss., went 75 rounds.

Boxing Statistics

Source: Nat Fleischer's Ring Boxing Encyclopedia and Record Book, published and copyrighted by The Ring Book Shop, Inc., 120 West 31st St., New York, N. Y. 10001.

Boxing's Biggest Gates

Date	Winner; weight Loser; weight	Rounds	Site	Receipts	Attendance
Sept. 22, 1927	Tunney (189½)-Dempsey (192½) (2d)..	10	Soldier Field, Chicago.	$2,658,660	104,943
June 19, 1946	Louis (207)-Conn (187) (2d).	KO 8	Yankee Stadium, New York.	1,925,564	45,266
Sept. 23, 1926	Tunney (189½)-Dempsey (190) (1st). . . .	10	Sesquicentennial Stdm., Phila. . . .	1,895,733	120,757
July 2, 1921	Dempsey (188)-Carpentier (172).	KO 4	Boyle's 30 Acres, Jersey City. . . .	1,789,238	80,183
March 8, 1971	Joe Frazier (205½)-Muhammad Ali (215).	15	New Madison Sq. Garden, N. Y. . . .	1,352,951	20,455
Sept. 14, 1923	Dempsey (192½)-Firpo (216½).	KO 2	Polo Grounds, New York.	1,188,603	82,000
July 21, 1927	Dempsey (194½)-Sharkey (196)	KO 7	Yankee Stadium, New York	1,083,530	75,000
Jan. 28, 1974	Ali (212) Frazier (209) (2d)	12	New Madison Square Garden, N.Y.	1,053,688	20,748
June 22, 1938	Louis (198¾)-Schmeling (193) (2d).	KO 1	Yankee Stadium, New York	1,015,012	70,043
Sept. 24, 1935	Louis (199¼)-Max Baer (210½).	KO 4	Yankee Stadium, New York.	1,000,832	88,150
Sept. 21, 1955	Marciano (188¼)-Moore (188).	KO 9	Yankee Stadium, New York.	948,117	61,574
June 25, 1948	Louis (213½)-Walcott (194¾) (2d).	KO 11	Yankee Stadium, New York.	841,739	42,667
June 20, 1960	Patterson (190)-Johansson (194¾) (2d).	KO 5	Polo Grounds, New York.	824,814	31,892
Sept. 12, 1951	Robinson (157½)-Turpin (159) (2d).	KO 10	Polo Grounds, New York.	767,626	61,370
June 12, 1930	Schmeling (188)-Sharkey (197) (1st). . . .	WF 4	Yankee Stadium, New York.	749,935	79,222
June 22, 1937	Louis (197¼)-Braddock (197).	KO 8	Comiskey Park, Chicago.	715,470	45,500
July 26, 1928	Tunney (192)-Heeney (203½).	KO 11	Yankee Stadium, New York.	691,014	45,890
Sept. 25, 1962	Liston (214)-Patterson (189) (1st).	KO 1	Comiskey Park, Chicago.	665,420	18,894
March 4, 1968	{Frazier (206)-Mathis. . . . . {Benvenuti (160)-Griffith (154½).	KO 11 15}	New Madison Sq. Garden, N. Y. . . .	658,503	18,096
Feb. 16, 1970	Joe Frazier (205)-Jimmy Ellis (201)	KO 5	New Madison Sq. Garden, N. Y. . . .	647,997	18,079
Sept. 29, 1941	Louis (202¼)-Nova (202½).	KO 6	Polo Grounds, New York.	583,711	56,549
Sept. 23, 1957	Basilio (153½)-Robinson (160) (1st). . . .	15	Yankee Stadium, New York.	556,467	38,072
June 19, 1936	Schmeling (192)-Louis (198) (1st).	KO 12	Yankee Stadium, New York.	547,541	42,088
June 17, 1954	Marciano (187½)-Charles (185½) (1st)..	15	Yankee Stadium, New York.	543,092	47,585
Sept. 11, 1924	Wills (217)-Firpo (224½)	ND 12	Boyle's 30 Acres, Jersey City	509,135	70,000
Sept. 23, 1952	Marciano (184)-Walcott (196) (1st).	KO 13	Municipal Stdm., Phila.	504,645	40,379
June 23, 1969	Joe Frazier (203½)-Jerry Quarry (198½).	KO 7	New Madison Sq. Garden, N. Y. . . .	502,518	16,570
Mar. 13, 1961	Patterson (194¾)-Johansson (206½) (3d)	KO 6	Convention Hall, Miami Beach, Fla.	502,000	13,984
June 17, 1972	Monzon (159½)-Bouttier (159¼).	KO 12	Olympic Stadium, Paris	500,000	25,000
Nov. 14, 1966	Clay (212¾)-Williams (210½).	KO 3	Astrodome, Houston	491,290	35,460
June 26, 1959	Johansson (196)-Patterson (182) (1st). . .	KO 3	Yankee Stadium, New York	470,717	18,215
July 16, 1926	Delaney (166½)-Berlenbach (174¼) (3d)	15	Ebbets Field, Brooklyn.	461,789	49,186

NOTE: KO—won by knockout; WF—won on foul; ND—no decision; 1st—first bout; 2d—second bout; 3d—third bout.

OTHER WORLD BOXING TITLEHOLDERS

LIGHT HEAVYWEIGHT

1903	—Jack Root, George Gardner
1903–05	—Bob Fitzsimmons
1905–12	—Philadelphia Jack O'Brien (r)
1912–16	—Jack Dillon
1916–20	—Battling Levinsky
1920–22	—Georges Carpentier
1923	—Battling Siki
1923–25	—Mike McTigue
1925–26	—Paul Berlenbach
1926–27	—Jack Delaney (a)
1927	—Mike McTigue
1927–29	—Tommy Loughran (a)
1930	—Jimmy Slattery
1930–34	—Maxie Rosenbloom
1934–35	—Bob Olin
1935–39	—John Henry Lewis (a)
1939	—Melio Bettina
1939–41	—Billy Conn (a)
1941	—Anton Christoforidis (NBA)
1941–48	—Gus Lesnevich
1948–50	—Freddie Mills
1950–52	—Joey Maxim
1952	—Archie Moore (x)
1961–63	—Harold Johnson
1963–65	—Willie Pastrano
1965–66	—Jose Torres
1966–67	—Dick Tiger
1968	—Dick Tiger, Bob Foster
1969–70	—Bob Foster
1971	—Bob Foster (y); Vicente Rondon (z)
1972–73	—Bob Foster (y, z)
1974	Bob Foster (§, z, r); John Conteh (y)
1975	—Victor Galindez (x); John Conteh (y)

(a)Abandoned title. (r)Retired. (x)NBA withdrew recognition in 1961, New York in 1962; recognized thereafter only by California and Europe. (y)—WBC.(z)—WBA.§—WBC withdrew recognition.

MIDDLEWEIGHT

1867–72	—Tom Chandler
1872–81	—George Rooke
1881–82	—Mike Donovan (r)
1884–91	—Jack (Nonpareil) Dempsey
1891–97	—Bob Fitzsimmons (a)
1908	—Stanley Ketchel, Billy Papke
1908–10	—Stanley Ketchel (d)
1913	—Frank Klaus
1913–14	—George Chip
1914–17	—Al McCoy
1917–20	—Mike O'Dowd
1920–23	—Johnny Wilson
1923–26	—Harry Greb
1926	—Tiger Flowers
1926–31	—Mickey Walker (a)
1931–41	—The National Boxing Association and New York State differed on titleholders. The following were regarded as champions by one or the other: Gorilla Jones, Ben Jeby, Marcel Thil, Lou Brouillard, Vince Dundee, Teddy Yarosz, Babe Risko, Freddy Steele, Al Hostak, Solly Krieger, Fred Apostoli, Ceferino Garcia, Ken Overlin, Billy Soose, Tony Zale.
1941–47	—Tony Zale
1947–48	—Rocky Graziano
1948	—Tony Zale
1948–49	—Marcel Cerdan
1949–51	—Jake La Motta
1951	—Ray Robinson, Randy Turpin
1951–52	—Ray Robinson (r)
1953–55	—Carl Olson
1955–57	—Ray Robinson
1957	—Gene Fullmer, Ray Robinson
1957–58	—Carmen Basilio
1958–60	—Ray Robinson (x)
1960–61	—Paul Pender (y)
1959–62	—Gene Fullmer (NBA)
1961–62	—Terry Downes (y)
1962	—Paul Pender (y)
1962–63	—Dick Tiger
1963–65	—Joey Giardello
1965–66	—Dick Tiger
1966	—Emile Griffith
1967	—Nino Benvenuti, Emile Griffith
1968	—Emile Griffith, Nino Benvenuti
1969	—Nino Benvenuti
1970	—Nino Benvenuti–Carlos Monzon
1971–73	—Carlos Monzon
1974–75	—Carlos Monzon (§), Rodrigo Valdez (z)

(a)Abandoned title. (d)Died. (r)Retired. (x)NBA withdrew recognition in 1959; recognized thereafter only by New York and Massachusetts. (y)Recognized by New York, Massachusetts and Europe. (z)—WBC. §—WBC withdrew recognition

WELTERWEIGHT

1892–94	—Mysterious Billy Smith
1894–96	—Tommy Ryan
1896	—Kid McCoy (a)
1896–1900	—Mysterious Billy Smith
1900	—Rube Ferns
1900–01	—Matty Matthews
1901	—Rube Ferns
1901–04	—Joe Walcott
1904	—Dixie Kid (a)
1904–06	—Joe Walcott
1906–07	—Honey Mellody
1907	—Mike (Twin) Sullivan (a)
1915–19	—Ted Lewis
1919–22	—Jack Britton
1922–26	—Mickey Walker
1926–27	—Pete Latzo
1927–29	—Joe Dundee
1929–30	—Jackie Fields
1930	—Young Jack Thompson
1930–31	—Tommy Freeman
1931	—Young Jack Thompson
1931–32	—Lou Brouillard
1932–33	—Jackie Fields
1933	—Young Corbett 3d
1933–34	—Jimmy McLarnin, Barney Ross
1934–35	—Jimmy McLarnin
1935–38	—Barney Ross
1938–40	—Henry Armstrong
1940–41	—Fritzie Zivic
1941–46	—Freddie Cochrane
1946	—Marty Servo (r)
1946–51	—Ray Robinson (a)
1951	—Johnny Bratton (NBA)
1951–54	—Kid Gavilan
1954–55	—Johnny Saxton
1955	—Tony DeMarco
1955–56	—Carmen Basilio
1956	—Johnny Saxton
1956–57	—Carmen Basilio (a)
1958	—Virgil Akins
1958–60	—Don Jordan
1960–61	—Benny (Kid) Paret
1961	—Emile Griffith
1961–62	—Benny (Kid) Paret
1962–63	—Emile Griffith, Luis Rodriguez
1963–66	—Emile Griffith (a)
1966–68	—Curtis Cokes
1969	—Curtis Cokes, José Napoles
1970	—Jose Napoles–Billy Backus
1971	—Billy Backus–Jose Napoles
1972–73	—Jose Napoles
1974	Jose Napoles
1975	—Jose Napoles (x, y, z); John Stracey (x); Angel Espada (y)

(a)Abandoned title. (r)Retired. (x)W.B.A.; (y)W.B.C.; (z)W.B.A. Withdrew recognition.

LIGHTWEIGHT

1896–99	—Kid Lavigne
1899–02	—Frank Erne
1902–08	—Joe Gans
1908–10	—Battling Nelson
1910–12	—Ad Wolgast
1912–14	—Willie Ritchie
1914–17	—Freddy Welsh
1917–25	—Benny Leonard (r)
1925	—Jimmy Goodrich
1925–26	—Rocky Kansas
1926–30	—Sammy Mandell
1930	—Al Singer
1930–33	—Tony Canzoneri
1933–35	—Barney Ross (a)
1935–36	—Tony Canzoneri
1936–38	—Lou Ambers
1938–39	—Henry Armstrong
1939–40	—Lou Ambers
1940–41	—Lew Jenkins
1941–42	—Sammy Angott (r)
1943–47	—New York champions were Beau Jack and Bob Montgomery; NBA: Sammy Angott, Juan Zurita and Ike Williams. Williams defeated Montgomery in 1947.
1947–51	—Ike Williams
1951–52	—James Carter
1952	—Lauro Salas
1952–54	—James Carter
1954	—Paddy DeMarco
1954–55	—James Carter
1955–56	—Wallace Smith
1956–62	—Joe Brown
1962–65	—Carlos Ortiz
1965	—Ismael Laguna
1965–68	—Carlos Ortiz
1968	—Teo Cruz
1969	—Teo Cruz, Mando Ramos
1970	—Mando Ramos, Ismael Laguna, Ken Buchanan
1971	—Ken Buchanan (y); Mando Ramos-Pedro Carrasco (z)
1972	—Ken Buchanan, Roberto Duran (y); Pedro Carrasco, Mando Ramos, Chango Carmona (z); Rodolfo Gonzalez (z)
1973	—Roberto Duran (y); Rodolfo Gonzalez (z)
1974	—Roberto Duran (y); Rodolfo Gonzalez (z), Guts Ishimatsu (z)
1975	—Roberto Duran (y); Guts Ishimatsu (z)

(a) Abandoned title. (r) Retired. (y) WBA. (z) WBC.

OTHER WORLD BOXING TITLEHOLDERS (Continued)

FEATHERWEIGHT

1889 —Dal Hawkins (a)
1890 —Billy Murphy
1892–1900—George Dixon
1900–01—Terry McGovern
1901 —Young Corbett (a)
1901–12—Abe Attell
1912–23—Johnny Kilbane
1923 —Eugene Criqui
1923–25—Johnny Dundee (a)
1925–27—Louis (Kid) Kaplan (a)
1927–28—Benny Bass
1928 —Tony Canzoneri
1928–29—Andre Routis
1929–32—Battling Battalino (a)
1932 —Tommy Paul (NBA); Kid Chocolate (N.Y. Comm.).
1933–36—Freddie Miller
1936–37—Petey Sarron
1937–38—Henry Armstrong (a)
1938–40—Joey Archibald
1940–41—Harry Jeffra, Joey Archibald
1941–42—Chalky Wright
1942–48—Willie Pep
1948–49—Sandy Saddler
1949–50—Willie Pep
1950–57—Sandy Saddler (r)
1957–59—Kid Bassey
1959–63—Davey Moore
1963–64—Sugar Ramos
1964–67—Vicente Saldivar (r)
1968 —Howard Winstone–Jose Legra (x)
1968 —Raul Rojas (y)–Sho Saijo (y)
1969 —Sho Saijo (y)–Johnny Famechon (x)
1970 —Sho Saijo (y), Johnny Famechon, Vicente Saldivar, Kuniaki Shibata.
1971 —Sho Saijo (y)–Antonio Gomez (y)–Kuniaki Shibata (z).
1972 —Antonio Gomez, Ernesto Marcel (y); Kuniaki Shibata, Clemente Sanchez, Jose Legra (z)
1973 —Ernesto Marcel (y); Jose Legra (x); Eder Jofre (x)
1974 —Ernesto Marcel (y, r); Ruben Olivares (y); Alexis Arguello (y); Eder Jofre (z), Bobby Chacon (z)
1975 —Alexis Arguello (y); Bobby Chacon (z); Ruben Olivares (z); David Kotey (z)

(a)Abandoned title. (r)Retired. (x)Recognized in Europe, Mexico, Orient. (y) Recognized by W.B.A. (z)Recognized by W.B.C.

BANTAMWEIGHT

1890–92—George Dixon (a)
1894–99—Jimmy Barry (r)
1899–1900—Terry McGovern (a)
1901 —Harry Harris (a)
1902–03—Harry Forbes
1903–04—Frankie Neil
1904 —Joe Bowker (a)
1905–07—Jimmy Walsh (a)
1910–14—Johnny Coulon
1914–17—Kid Williams
1917–20—Pete Herman
1920–21—Joe Lynch; 1921—Pete Herman
1921–22—Johnny Buff
1922–24—Joe Lynch; 1924—Abe Goldstein
1924–25—Eddie (Cannonball) Martin
1925 —Charlie (Phil) Rosenberg (d)
1927–28—Bud Taylor (NBA) (a)
1929–35—Al Brown
1935–36—Baltazar Sangchili; 1936—Tony Marino
1936–37—Sixto Escobar
1937–38—Harry Jeffra
1938–40—Sixto Escobar (r)
1940–42—Lou Salica
1942–47—Manuel Ortiz; 1947—Harold Dade
1947–50—Manuel Ortiz
1950–52—Vic Toweel
1952–54—Jimmy Carruthers (r)
1954–56—Robert Cohen
1956–57—Mario D'Agata
1956 —Raul Macias (NBA)
1957–59—Alphonse Halimi
1959–60—Jose Becerra (r)
1960–61—Alphonse Halimi (x)
1961–62—Johnny Caldwell (x)
1961–65—Eder Jofre
1965–68—Masahika (Fighting) Harada
1968 —Lionel Rose
1969 —Ruben Olivares
1970 —Ruben Olivares–Chucho Castillo
1971 —Ruben Olivares
1972 —Ruben Olivares, Rafael Herrera, Enrique Pinder
1973 —Enrique Pinder (y); Romeo Anaya (y); Arnold Taylor (z); Rodolfo Martinez (z); Rafael Herrera (z)
1974 —Arnold Taylor (y); Soo Hwan Hong (y); Rodolfo Martinez (z)
1975 —Soo Hwan Hong (y); Alfonso Zamora (y); Rodolfo Martinez (z)

(a)Abandoned title. (d)Deprived of title when unable to make weight

for championship bout. (r)Retired. (x) Recognized by Europe as champion. (y) W.B.A (z) W.B.C.

FLYWEIGHT

1916–23—Jimmy Wilde
1923–25—Pancho Villa (d)
1925 —Frankie Genaro
1925–27—Fidel La Barba (r)
1927–31—NBA and New York claimants were: Corporal Izzy Schwartz, Frankie Genaro, Emile (Spider) Pladner, Midget Wolgast and Young Perez.
1932–35—Jackie Brown
1935–38—Benny Lynch (a)
1939 —Peter Kane (a)
1943–47—Jackie Paterson (d)
1947–50—Rinty Monaghan (r)
1950 —Terry Allen
1950–52—Dado Marino
1952–54—Yoshio Shirai
1954–60—Pascual Perez
1960–62—Pone Kingpetch
1962–63—Masahika (Fighting) Harada
1963 —Pone Kingpetch
1963–64—Hiroyuki Ebihara
1964–65—Pone Kingpetch
1965–66—Salvatore Burrini
1966 —Horacio Accavallo (x)
1966 —Walter McGowan, Chartchai Chionoi
1966–68—Chartchai Chionoi
1969 —Bernabe Villacampa (x)–Efran Torres
1970 —Bernabe–Villachampa, Berkrerk Chartvanchai (x), Masao Ohba (x), Chartchai Chionoi, Erbito Salavarina
1971 —Masao Ohba (x)–Erbito Salavaria (y)
1972 —Masao Ohba (x); Erbito Salavaria; Betulio Gonzalez, Venice Borkorsor (y)
1973 —Masao Ohba (x) (d); Chartchai Chionoi (x); Venice Borkorsor (y); Betulio Gonzales (y)
1974 —Chartchai Chionoi (x); Susumu Hanagata (x); Betulio Gonzalez (y); Shoji Ogumo (y)
1975 —Susumu Hanagata (x); Erbito Salavaria (x); Shoji Oguma (y); Miguel Canto (y)

(a)Abandoned title. (d)Died. (r)Retired. (x) W.B.A. (y) W.B.C.

Joe Louis' Title Fights

June 22, 1937*	Jim Braddock, Chicago	KO 8	Feb. 17, 1941	Gus Dorazio, Philadelphia	KO 2
Aug. 30, 1937	Tommy Farr, Yankee Stad.	W 15	Mar. 21, 1941	Abe Simon, Detroit	KO 13
Feb. 23, 1938	Nathan Mann, Mad. Sq. Garden	KO 3	Apr. 8, 1941	Tony Musto, St. Louis	KO 9
Apr. 1, 1938	Harry Thomas, Chicago	KO 5	May 23, 1941	Buddy Baer, Washington, D.C.	W disq. 7
June 22, 1938	Max Schmeling, Yankee Stad.	KO 1	June 18, 1941	Billy Conn, Polo Grounds	KO 13
Jan. 25, 1939	John Henry Lewis, Mad. Sq. Garden	KO 1	Sept. 29, 1941	Lou Nova, Polo Grounds	KO 6
Apr. 17, 1939	Jack Roper, Los Angeles	KO 1	Jan. 9, 1942	Buddy Baer, Mad. Sq. Garden	KO 1
June 28, 1939	Tony Galento, Yankee Stad.	KO 4	Mar. 27, 1942	Abe Simon, Mad. Sq. Garden	KO 6
Sept. 20, 1939	Bob Pastor, Detroit	KO 11	June 19, 1946	Billy Conn, Yankee Stad.	KO 8
Feb. 9, 1940	Arturo Godoy, Mad. Sq. Garden	W 15	Sept. 18, 1946	Tami-Mauriello, Yankee Stad.	KO 1
Mar. 29, 1940	Johnny Paychek, Mad. Sq. Garden	KO 2	Dec. 5, 1947	Joe Walcott, Mad. Sq. Garden	W 15
June 20, 1940	Arturo Godoy, Yankee Stad.	KO 8	June 25, 1948	Joe Walcott, Yankee Stad.	KO 11
Dec. 16, 1940	Al McCoy, Boston	KO 6	Sept. 27, 1950†	Ezzard Charles, Yankee Stad.	L 15
Jan. 31, 1941	Red Burman, Mad. Sq. Garden	KO 5			

* Won title. † After announcing retirement as champion on Mar. 1, 1949, Louis returned to boxing and sought to regain title in bout with Charles.

FIGHTER OF THE YEAR
Selected by *The Ring* Magazine.

1928	Gene Tunney	1939	Joe Louis	1951	Ray Robinson	1963	Cassius Clay
1929	Tommy Loughran	1940	Billy Conn	1952	Rocky Marciano	1964	Emile Griffith
1930	Max Schmeling	1941	Joe Louis	1953	Bobo Olson	1965	Dick Tiger
1931	Tommy Loughran	1942	Ray Robinson	1954	Rocky Marciano	1966	No award
1932	Jack Sharkey	1943	Fred Apostoli	1955	Rocky Marciano	1967	Joe Frazier
1933	No award	1944	Beau Jack	1956	Floyd Patterson	1968	Nino Benvenuti
1934	Barney Ross and	1945	Willie Pep	1957	Carmen Basilio	1969	Jose Napoles
	Tony Canzoneri	1946	Tony Zale	1958	Ingemar Johansson	1970-71	Joe Frazier
1935	Barney Ross	1947	Gus Lesnevich	1959	Ingemar Johansson	1972	Carlos Monzon and
1936	Joe Louis	1948	Ike Williams	1960	Floyd Patterson		Muhammad Ali
1937	Henry Armstrong	1949	Ezzard Charles	1961	Joe Brown	1973	George Foreman
1938	Joe Louis	1950	Ezzard Charles	1962	Dick Tiger	1974-75	Muhammad Ali

Marciano Was Unbeaten as a Pro

Rocky Marciano, heavyweight boxing champion of the world and winner of each of his 49 fights as a professional, announced his retirement from the ring on Apr. 27, 1956. He was the only heavyweight champion ever to retire without losing a professional fight.

Marciano won the title on Sept. 23, 1952, in Philadelphia, by knocking out Joe Walcott in the 13th round.

Marciano, born in Brockton, Mass., on Sept. 1, 1924, was killed in a plane crash, Aug. 31, 1969. These were Marciano's championship fights:

Sept. 23, 1952*	Joe Walcott, Philadelphia	KO 13
May 15, 1953	Joe Walcott, Chicago	KO 1
Sept. 24, 1953	Roland LaStarza, Polo Grounds	KO 11
June 17, 1954	Ezzard Charles, Yankee Stad.	W 15
Sept. 17, 1954	Ezzard Charles, Yankee Stad.	KO 8
May 16, 1955	Don Cockell, San Francisco	KO 9
Sept. 21, 1955	Archie Moore, Yankee Stad.	KO 9

* Won title.

Title Bouts of Muhammad Ali (Cassius Clay)

Feb. 25, 1964*	Sonny Liston, Miami Beach	KO 7

(Liston failed to come out for seventh round)

May 25, 1965	Sonny Liston, Lewiston, Me.	KO 1
Nov. 22, 1965	Floyd Patterson, Las Vegas	KO 12
March 29, 1966	George Chuvalo, Toronto	W 15
May 21, 1966	Henry Cooper, London	KO 6
Aug. 6, 1966	Brian London, London	KO 3
Sept. 10, 1966	Karl Mildenberger, Frankfurt, Ger.	KO 12
Nov. 14, 1966	Cleveland Williams, Houston	KO 3
Feb. 6, 1967	Ernie Terrell, Houston	W 15
March 22, 1967	Zora Folley, New York	KO 7
March 8, 1971†	Joe Frazier, New York	L 15
Oct. 30, 1974*	George Foreman, Zaire	KO 8
March 24, 1975	Chuck Wepner, Richfield, Ohio	KO 15
May 16, 1975	Ron Lyle, Las Vegas, Nev.	KO 11
July 1, 1975	Joe Bugner, Kuala Lumpur	W 15
Sept. 30, 1975	Joe Frazier, Manila	KO 14
Feb. 20, 1976	Jean-Pierre Coopman, San Juan	KO 5
April 30, 1976	Jimmy Young, Landover, Md.	W 15
May 24, 1976	Richard Dunn, Munich	KO 5
Sept. 28, 1976	Ken Norton, New York	W 15

* Won world heavyweight championship. † Lost title officially. When Ali (Clay) refused induction into the United States armed services, April 18, 1967, the New York State Athletic Commission stripped him of his title and other official groups followed suit. He was convicted of draft evasion June 20, 1967, by a Federal Court and was inactive awaiting results of appeal. Ali regained license to fight in autumn of 1970, after resigning as titleholder. After losing to Frazier, United States Supreme Court reversed Federal court decision on technicalities in Justice Department's presentation of case, June 28, 1971.

Joe Frazier's Championship Boxing Bouts

Feb. 16, 1970*	Jimmy Ellis, New York	KO 5
Nov. 18, 1970	Bob Foster, Detroit	KO 2
March 8, 1971†	Muhammad Ali (Cassius Clay)	
	New York	W 15
Jan. 15, 1972	Terry Daniels, New Orleans	KO 4
May 25, 1972	Ron Stander, Omaha	KO 5
Jan. 22, 1973‡	George Foreman, Hayward, Calif.	KO by 2
Sept. 30, 1975	Muhammad Ali, Manila	KO by 14

* Bout ended dispute over title. Ellis held one version as survivor of elimination tournament after Muhammad Ali had been stripped of title by various commissions. Frazier was recognized in New York and five other states after beating Jerry Quarry at opening of new Madison Square Garden in New York. † Bout ended Ali's right to title. ‡ Referee stopped fight at 1:35 of 2d after Frazier was floored 6 times.

PROFESSIONAL WEIGHT LIMITS

Flyweight	112	Welterweight	147
Bantamweight	118	Middleweight	160
Featherweight	126	Light heavyweight	175
Lightweight	135	Heavyweight	over 175

CYCLING
NATIONAL AMATEUR CHAMPIONS

1951	Gus Gatto	1959-63	James Rossi	1967	Jack Simes, 3d	1971-72	Gary Campbell
1952	Steve Hromjak	1964	Jack Simes, 3d	1968	Jack Disney	1973	Roger Young
1953	Ronald Rhoads	1965*	Jack Simes, 3d	1969	Tim Mountford	1974-75	Steve Woznick
1954-58	Jack Disney	1966	Jack Disney	1970	Harry Cutting		

* Since 1965, sprint champion.

FOOTBALL

THE PASTIME of kicking a ball around goes back beyond the limits of recorded history. Ancient savage tribes played football of a primitive kind. There was a ball-kicking game played by Athenians and Spartans and Corinthians 2500 years ago and the Greeks had a name for it: *Episkuros.* The Romans had a somewhat similar game called *Harpastum* and are supposed to have carried the game with them when they invaded the British Isles in the First Century, B.C.

Undoubtedly the game known in the United States as Football traces directly to the English game of Rugby, though the modifications have been many. There was informal football on our college lawns well over a century ago and an annual Freshman-Sophomore series of "scrimmages" began at Yale in 1840. But the first formal intercollegiate football game was the Princeton-Rutgers contest at New Brunswick, N.J., on Nov. 6, 1869, with Rutgers winning by 6 goals to 4.

In those days games were played with 25, 20, 15,

or 11 men on a side. In 1880 there was a convention at which Walter Camp of Yale persuaded the delegates to agree to a rule calling for 11 players on a side. However, the game grew so rough that it was attacked as brutal, and some colleges abandoned the sport. Conditions were so bad in 1906 that President Theodore Roosevelt called a meeting of Yale, Harvard, and Princeton representatives at the White House in the hope of reforming and improving the game. The outcome was that the game, with the forward pass introduced and some other modifications of the rules inserted, became faster and cleaner.

The first professional game was played in 1895 at Latrobe, Pa. The National Football League was founded in 1921. The All-American Conference went into action in 1946. At the end of the 1949 season the two circuits merged, retaining the name of the older league. In 1960, the American Football League began operations. In 1970 the leagues merged. In 1974, the World Football League opened as a rival to the N.F.L.

Heisman Memorial Trophy Winners

The Heisman Memorial Trophy is presented annually by the Downtown Athletic Club of New York City to the nation's outstanding college football player, as determined by a poll of sportswriters and sportscasters.

1935	Jay Berwanger, Chicago	1949	Leon Hart, Notre Dame	1962	Terry Baker, Oregon State
1936	Larry Kelley, Yale	1950	Vic Janowicz, Ohio State	1963	Roger Staubach, Navy
1937	Clinton Frank, Yale	1951	Dick Kazmaier, Princeton	1964	John Huarte, Notre Dame
1938	Davey O'Brien, Texas Christian	1952	Billy Vessels, Oklahoma	1965	Mike Garrett, Southern California
1939	Nile Kinnick, Iowa	1953	Johnny Lattner, Notre Dame	1966	Steve Spurrier, Florida
1940	Tom Harmon, Michigan	1954	Alan Ameche, Wisconsin	1967	Gary Beban, U.C.L.A.
1941	Bruce Smith, Minnesota	1955	Howard Cassady, Ohio State	1968	O. J. Simpson, Southern California
1942	Frank Sinkwich, Georgia	1956	Paul Hornung, Notre Dame	1969	Steve Owens, Oklahoma
1943	Angelo Bertelli, Notre Dame	1957	John Crow, Texas A & M	1970	Jim Plunkett, Stanford
1944	Leslie Horvath, Ohio State	1958	Pete Dawkins, Army	1971	Pat Sullivan, Auburn
1945	Felix Blanchard, Army	1959	Billy Cannon, Louisiana State	1972	Johnny Rodgers, Nebraska
1946	Glenn Davis, Army	1960	Joe Bellino, Navy	1973	John Cappelletti, Penn State
1947	Johnny Lujack, Notre Dame	1961	Ernie Davis, Syracuse	1974-75	Archie Griffin, Ohio State
1948	Doak Walker, So. Methodist				

Army-Navy Series Record Since 1961

1961	Navy 13, Army 7	1966	Army 20, Navy 7	1971	Army 24, Navy 23
1962	Navy 34, Army 14	1967	Navy 19, Army 14	1972	Army 23, Navy 15
1963	Navy 21, Army 15	1968	Army 21, Navy 14	1973	Navy 51, Army 0
1964	Army 11, Navy 8	1969	Army 27, Navy 0	1974	Navy 19, Army 0
1965	Army 7, Navy 7	1970	Navy 11, Army 7	1975	Navy 30, Army 6

RECORD OF ANNUAL MAJOR BOWL COLLEGE FOOTBALL GAMES

ROSE BOWL

(At Pasadena, Calif.)

1902	Michigan 49, Stanford 0	1934	Columbia 7, Stanford 0	1955	Ohio State 20, So. California 7
1916	Washington State 14, Brown 0	1935	Alabama 29, Stanford 13	1956	Michigan State 17, U. C. L. A. 14
1917	Oregon 14, Pennsylvania 0	1936	Stanford 7, So. Methodist 0	1957	Iowa 35, Oregon State 19
1918	Mare Island Marines 19, Camp Lewis 7	1937	Pittsburgh 21, Washington 0	1958	Ohio State 10, Oregon 7
		1938	California 13, Alabama 0	1959	Iowa 38, California 12
1919	Great Lakes 17, Mare Island Marines 0	1939	So. California 7, Duke 3	1960	Washington 44, Wisconsin 8
		1940	So. California 14, Tennessee 0	1961	Washington 17, Minnesota 7
1920	Harvard 7, Oregon 6	1941	Stanford 21, Nebraska 13	1962	Minnesota 21, U. C. L. A. 3
1921	California 28, Ohio State 0	1942	Oregon State 20, Duke 16*	1963	So. California 42, Wisconsin 37
1922	Washington and Jefferson 0, California 0	1943	Georgia 9, U. C. L. A. 0	1964	Illinois 17, Washington 7
		1944	So. California 29, Washington 0	1965	Michigan 34, Oregon State 7
1923	So. California 14, Penn State 3	1945	So. California 25, Tennessee 0	1966	U. C. L. A. 14, Michigan State 12
1924	Navy 14, Washington 14	1946	Alabama 34, So. California 14	1967	Purdue 14, So. California 13
1925	Notre Dame 27, Stanford 10	1947	Illinois 45, U. C. L. A. 14	1968	So. California 14, Indiana 3
1926	Alabama 20, Washington 19	1948	Michigan 49, So. California 0	1969	Ohio State 27, So. California 16
1927	Alabama 7, Stanford 7	1949	Northwestern 20, California 14	1970	So. California 10, Michigan 3
1928	Stanford 7, Pittsburgh 6	1950	Ohio State 17, California 14	1971	Stanford 27, Ohio State 17
1929	Georgia Tech 8, California 7	1951	Michigan 14, California 6	1972	Stanford 13, Michigan 12
1930	So. California 47, Pittsburgh 14	1952	Illinois 40, Stanford 7	1973	So. California 42, Ohio State 17
1931	Alabama 24, Washington State 0	1953	So. California 7, Wisconsin 0	1974	Ohio State 42, So. California 21
1932	So. California 21, Tulane 12	1954	Michigan State 28, U. C. L. A. 20	1975	So. California 18, Ohio State 17
1933	So. California 35, Pittsburgh 0	* Played at Durham, N. C.	1976	U.C.L.A. 23, Ohio State 10

Orange Bowl (At Miami)	Sugar Bowl (At New Orleans)	Cotton Bowl (At Dallas)
1933 Miami (Fla.) 7, Manhattan 0	1935 Tulane 20, Temple 14	1937 Texas Christian 16, Marquette 6
1934 Duquesne 33, Miami (Fla.) 7	1936 Texas Christian 3, Louisiana	1938 Rice 28, Colorado 14
1935 Bucknell 26, Miami (Fla.) 0	State 2	1939 St. Mary's (Calif.) 20, Texas
1936 Catholic 20, Mississippi 19	1937 Santa Clara 21, Louisiana State 14	Tech. 13
1937 Duquesne 13, Mississippi State 12	1938 Santa Clara 6, Louisiana State 0	1940 Clemson 6, Boston College 3
1938 Auburn 6, Michigan State 0	1939 Texas Christian 15, Carnegie Tech 7	1941 Texas A & M 13, Fordham 12
1939 Tennessee 17, Oklahoma 0	1940 Texas A & M 14, Tulane 13	1942 Alabama 29, Texas A & M 21
1940 Georgia Tech 21, Missouri 7	1941 Boston College 19, Tennessee 13	1943 Texas 14, Georgia Tech 7
1941 Mississippi State 14, Georgetown 7	1942 Fordham 2, Missouri 0	1944 Randolph Field 7, Texas 7
1942 Georgia 40, Texas Christian 26	1943 Tennessee 14, Tulsa 7	1945 Oklahoma A & M 34, Texas
1943 Alabama 37, Boston College 21	1944 Georgia Tech 20, Tulsa 18	Christian 0
1944 Louisiana State 19, Texas A&M 14	1945 Duke 29, Alabama 26	1946 Texas 40, Missouri 27
1945 Tulsa 26, Georgia Tech 12	1946 Oklahoma A & M 33, St. Mary's	1947 Louisiana State 0, Arkansas 0
1946 Miami (Fla.) 13, Holy Cross 6	(Calif.) 13	1948 So. Methodist 13, Penn State 13
1947 Rice 8, Tennessee 0	1947 Georgia 20, North Carolina 10	1949 So. Methodist 21, Oregon 13
1948 Georgia Tech 20, Kansas 14	1948 Texas 27, Alabama 7	1950 Rice 27, North Carolina 13
1949 Texas 41, Georgia 28	1949 Oklahoma 14, North Carolina 6	1951 Tennessee 20, Texas 14
1950 Santa Clara 21, Kentucky 13	1950 Oklahoma 35, Louisiana State 0	1952 Kentucky 20, Texas Christian 7
1951 Clemson 15, Miami (Fla.) 14	1951 Kentucky 13, Oklahoma 7	1953 Texas 16, Tennessee 0
1952 Georgia Tech 17, Baylor 14	1952 Maryland 28, Tennessee 13	1954 Rice 28, Alabama 6
1953 Alabama 61, Syracuse 6	1953 Georgia Tech 24, Mississippi 7	1955 Georgia Tech 14, Arkansas 6
1954 Oklahoma 7, Maryland 0	1954 Georgia Tech 42, West Virginia 19	1956 Mississippi 14, Texas Christian 13
1955 Duke 34, Nebraska 7	1955 Navy 21, Mississippi 0	1957 Texas Christian 28, Syracuse 27
1956 Oklahoma 20, Maryland 6	1956 Georgia Tech 7, Pittsburgh 0	1958 Navy 20, Rice 7
1957 Colorado 27, Clemson 21	1957 Baylor 13, Tennessee 7	1959 Air Force 0, Texas Christian 0
1958 Oklahoma 48, Duke 21	1958 Mississippi 39, Texas 7	1960 Syracuse 23, Texas 14
1959 Oklahoma 21, Syracuse 6	1959 Louisiana State 7, Clemson 0	1961 Duke 7, Arkansas 6
1960 Georgia 14, Missouri 0	1960 Mississippi 21, Louisiana State 0	1962 Texas 12, Mississippi 7
1961 Missouri 21, Navy 14	1961 Mississippi 14, Rice 6	1963 Louisiana State 13, Texas 0
1962 Louisiana State 25, Colorado 7	1962 Alabama 10, Arkansas 3	1964 Texas 28, Navy 6
1963 Alabama 17, Oklahoma 0	1963 Mississippi 17, Arkansas 13	1965 Arkansas 10, Nebraska 7
1964 Nebraska 13, Auburn 7	1964 Alabama 12, Mississippi 7	1966 Louisiana State 14, Arkansas 7
1965 Texas 21, Alabama 17	1965 Louisiana State 13, Syracuse 10	1967 Georgia 24, So. Methodist 9
1966 Alabama 39, Nebraska 28	1966 Missouri 20, Florida 18	1968 Texas A & M 20, Alabama 16
1967 Florida 27, Georgia Tech 12	1967 Alabama 34, Nebraska 7	1969 Texas 36, Tennessee 13
1968 Oklahoma 26, Tennessee 24	1968 Louisiana State 20, Wyoming 13	1970 Texas 21, Notre Dame 17
1969 Penn State 15, Kansas 14	1969 Arkansas 16, Georgia 2	1971 Notre Dame 24, Texas 11
1970 Penn State 10, Missouri 3	1970 Mississippi 27, Arkansas 22	1972 Penn State 30, Texas 6
1971 Nebraska 17, Louisiana State 12	1971 Tennessee 34, Air Force	1973 Texas 17, Alabama 13
1972 Nebraska 38, Alabama 6	Academy 13	1974 Nebraska 19, Texas 3
1973 Nebraska 40, Notre Dame 6	1972 Oklahoma 40, Auburn 22	1975 Penn State 41, Baylor 20
1974 Penn State 16, Louisiana State 9	1973 Oklahoma 14, Penn State 0	1976 Arkansas 31, Georgia 10
1975 Notre Dame 13, Alabama 11	1974 Notre Dame 24, Alabama 23	
1976 Oklahoma 14, Michigan 6	1975 Nebraska 13, Florida 10	
	1976 Alabama 13, Penn State 6	

Gator Bowl

(At Jacksonville, Fla. Played on Saturday nearest New Year's Day of year indicated)

1953 Florida 14, Tulsa 13	1961 Florida 13, Baylor 12	1969 Missouri 35, Alabama 10
1954 Texas Tech 35, Auburn 13	1962 Penn State 30, Georgia Tech 15	1970 Florida 14, Tennessee 13
1955 Auburn 33, Baylor 13	1963 Florida 17, Penn State 7	1971 Auburn 35, Mississippi 28
1956 Vanderbilt 25, Auburn 13	1964 No. Carolina 35, Air Force 0	1972 Georgia 7, North Carolina 3
1957 Georgia Tech 21, Pittsburgh 14	1965 Florida State 36, Oklahoma 19	1973 Auburn 24, Colorado 3
1958 Tennessee 3, Texas A & M 0	1966 Georgia Tech 31, Texas Tech 21	1974 Texas Tech 28, Tennessee 19
1959 Mississippi 7, Florida 3	1967 Tennessee 18, Syracuse 12	1975 Auburn 27, Texas 3
1960 Arkansas 14, Georgia Tech 7	1968 Penn State 17, Florida State 17	1976 Maryland 13, Florida 0

NATIONAL COLLEGE FOOTBALL CHAMPIONS

The "National Collegiate A. A. Football Guide" recognizes as unofficial national champion the team selected each year by press association polls. Where The Associated Press poll (of writers) does not agree with the United Press International poll (of coaches), the guide lists both teams selected.

1937 Pittsburgh	1944 Army	1951 Tennessee	1957 Auburn and	1963 Texas	1969 Texas
1938 Texas Christian	1945 Army	1952 Michigan State	Ohio State	1964 Alabama	1970 Texas, Nebraska
1939 Texas A & M	1946 Notre Dame	1953 Maryland	1958 Louisiana State	1965 Alabama and	1971 Nebraska
1940 Minnesota	1947 Notre Dame	1954 Ohio State and	1959 Syracuse	Michigan State	1972 So. California
1941 Minnesota	1948 Michigan	U.C.L.A.	1960 Minnesota	1966 Notre Dame	1973 Notre Dame
1942 Ohio State	1949 Notre Dame	1955 Oklahoma	1961 Alabama	1967 So. California	1974 Oklahoma and
1943 Notre Dame	1950 Oklahoma	1956 Oklahoma	1962 So. California	1968 Ohio State	So. California
					1975 Oklahoma

MAJOR COLLEGE FOOTBALL RECORDS (1940-1975)

Source: National Collegiate Sports Services, compiled by Steve Boda, Jr.

LONGEST PLAYS

Rushing

	Yards
Ralph Thompson, W. Tex. State (Wichita State) 1970	99
Max Anderson, Arizona State (Wyoming) 1967	99
Gale Sayers, Kansas (Nebraska) 1963	99
Granville Amos, Virginia M. I. (Wm. & Mary) 1964	98
Jim Thacker, Davidson (George Washington) 1952	98
Bill Powell, California (Oregon State) 1951	98
Al Yannelli, Bucknell (Delaware) 1946	98
Meredith Warner, Iowa State (Iowa Pre-Flight) 1943	98
Art Malone, Arizona State (Utah) 1968	97
Dorsey Gibson, Oklahoma State (Houston) 1953	97
Walter Gruber, Detroit (Villanova) 1948	97
Blondy Black, Miss. State (Duquesne) 1942	97

Passing

Terry Peel-Robert Ford, Houston (San Diego St.) 1972	99
Terry Peel-Robert Ford, Houston (Syracuse) 1972	99
Colin Clapton-Eddie Jenkins, Holy Cross (Boston U.) 1970	99
Bo Burris-Warren McVea, Houston (Wash. St.) 1966	99
Fred Owens-Jack Ford, Portland (St. Mary's) 1947	99
Bruce Shaw-Pat Kenny, N.C. State (Penn State) 1972	98
Jerry Rhome-Jeff Jordan, Tulsa (Wichita State) 1963	98
Bob Dean-Norman Dawson, Cornell (Navy) 1947	98

Punt Returns

Jimmy Campagna, Georgia (Vanderbilt) 1952	100
Hugh McElhenny, Washington (So. Cal.) 1951	100
Frank Brady, Navy (Maryland) 1951	100
Bert Rechichar, Tennessee (Wash. & Lee) 1950	100
Eddie Macon, Pacific (Boston U.) 1950	100
Richie Luzzi, Clemson (Georgia) 1968	*100
Don Guest, California (Washington State) 1966	*100

* Returns of field goal attempts.

Punts

Pat Brady, Nevada (Loyola, L. A.) 1950	99
George O'Brien, Wisconsin (Iowa) 1952	96
John Hadl, Kansas (Oklahoma) 1959	94
Carl Knox, Texas Christian (Oklahoma State) 1947	94
Preston Johnson, SMU (Pittsburgh) 1940	94

Field Goals

Clark Kemble, Colorado State (Arizona) 1975	63
Dave Lawson, Air Force Acad. (Iowa State) 1975	62
Ray Guy, So. Mississippi (Utah State) 1972	61
Wayne Latimer, Virginia Tech (Florida State) 1975	61
Dave Lawson, Air Force (Colorado) 1974	60
Tony Di Rienzo, Oklahoma (Kansas) 1973	60
Bill McClard, Arkansas (SMU) 1970	60
Bubba Hicks, Baylor (Rice) 1975	60
Clark Kemble, Colorado State (Brigham Young) 1974	59
Don Bockhorn, Baylor (SMU) 1974	59
Rod Garcia, Stanford (So. California) 1973	59
Dave Strock, Virginia Tech (So. Mississippi) 1972	59
Marv Bateman, Utah (Utah State) 1971	59
Cloyce Hinton, Mississippi (Georgia) 1969	59
Tom Skadany, Ohio State (Illinois) 1975	59
Tony Franklin, Texas A&M (Rice) 1975	59

Kickoff Returns

96 players have returned kickoffs 100 yards or more since 1941. The most recent:

Rich Mauti, Penn State (Temple) 1975	100
Mel Jacobs, San Diego State (North Texas) 1975	100
Tim Morgan, Miami, Fla. (Houston) 1975	100
Duriel Harris, New Mexico State (Tulsa) 1975	100
Edvins Kreilis, Richmond (V.M.I.) 1975	100
Billy Waddy, Colorado (Kansas State) 1975	100
Jon Sutton, New Mexico State (New Mexico) 1975	100

BEST SINGLE-GAME PERFORMANCES

Most yards, rushing—350, Eric Allen, Michigan State (Purdue) 1971

Most yards, total offense—599, Virgil Carter, Brigham Young (Texas-El Paso) 1966

Most yards, passing—561, Tony Adams, Utah State (Utah) 1972

Most yards, pass receiving—349, Chuck Hughes, Texas-El Paso (North Texas State) 1965

Most points scored—43, Jim Brown, Syracuse (Colgate) 1956

Most passes attempted—69, Chuck Hixson, Southern Methodist (Ohio State) 1968

Most passes completed—42, Bill Anderson, Tulsa (Southern Illinois) 1965

Most passes caught—22, Jay Miller, Brigham Young (New Mexico) 1973

CAREER LEADERS

Rushing

	years	plays	yds	avg
Archie Griffin, Ohio State	1972-75	845	*5,177	6.13
Ed Marinaro, Cornell	1969-71	*918	4,715	5.14
Tony Dorsett, Pittsburgh	**1973-75	736	4,134	5.62
Ron Po James, New Mex. St.	1968-71	818	3,884	4.75
Steve Owens, Oklahoma	1967-69	905	3,867	4.27
Woody Green, Arizona State	1971-73	601	3,754	6.25
Mark Kellar, No. Illinois	1971-73	743	3,745	5.04
Anthony Davis, So. California	1972-74	728	3,426	4.71

* Record; ** Still active.

Passing

	years	cmp	pct	yds	td
Chuck Hixson, So. Methodist	1968-70	*642	.576	7,179	40
John Reaves, Florida	1969-71	603	.535	*7,549	54
Gene Swick, Toledo	1972-75	556	.593	7,267	44
Jim Plunkett, Stanford	1968-70	530	.551	7,544	52
Lynn Dickey, Kansas State	1968-70	501	.504	6,208	29
Steve Ramsey, North Texas St.	1967-69	491	.484	7,076	*69

Total Offense

	years	plays	yds	tdr†
Gene Swick, Toledo	1972-75	*1,579	*8,074	5.11
Jim Plunkett, Stanford	1968-70	1,174	7,887	6.72
John Reaves, Florida	1969-71	1,258	7,283	5.79
Chuck Hixson, So. Methodist	1968-70	1,358	6,884	5.07
Pat Sullivan, Auburn	1969-71	968	6,844	71
Tony Adams, Utah State	1970-72	1,132	6,587	62
Steve Ramsey, N.Tex. State	1967-69	1,132	6,568	71
Danny White, Arizona State	1971-73	813	6,453	*73

* Record.

† Touchdowns responsible for—scored or passed for.

Pass Receiving

	years	no	yds	td
Howard Twilley, Tulsa	1963-65	*261	3,343	32
Ron Sellers, Florida State	1966-68	212	*3,598	23
Phil Odle, Brig. Young	1965-67	181	2,548	25
Tim Delaney, San Diego St.	1968-70	180	2,535	22

Scoring

	years	td	x-pt	fg	pts
Glenn Davis, Army	1943-46	*59	0	0	*354
Art Luppino, Arizona	1953-56	48	49	0	337
Steve Owens, Oklahoma	1967-69	56	0	0	336
Wilford White, Arizona St.	1947-50	48	27	4	327
Ed Marinaro, Cornell	1969-71	52	6	0	318
Eddie Talboom, Wyoming	1948-50	34	99	0	303
Anthony Davis, So. California	1972-74	50	2	0	302

* Record.

N.C.A.A. DIVISION II AND III FOOTBALL RECORDS (1942-1975)

LONGEST PLAYS
Rushing

	yds
Croom, U. San Diego (Azusa Pacific), 1972	99
Stenger, Swarthmore (PMC Colleges), 1970	99
Knuttila, Hamline (St. Thomas), 1968	99
Lanoha, Colorado College (Tex. Lutheran), 1967	99
Pabst, UC Riverside (Cal Tech), 1965	99
Phillips, Concord (Davis & Elkins), 1961	99
White, Connecticut (Rhode Is.), 1960	99
Williams, St. Augustine's (Morris), 1960	99
Phelps, Cornell College (Monmouth), 1959	99
Lydon, Tufts (Bowdoin), 1958	99
Wells, Tufts (Williams), 1956	99
Moskal, Adelbert (Case Tech), 1956	99
Mariano, Kent State (Adelbert), 1954	99
Temple, Chico State (So. Oregon), 1953	99
Horton, Eureka (Rose Poly), 1952	99
Abbruzzi, Rhode Island (New Hampshire), 1951	99

Passing

Shope-Rudolph, Juniata (Moravian), 1973	99
Dusenberg-King, North Park (Illinois Wes.), 1970	99
Janesko-Stankiewicz, Emporia (Pittsburg St.), 1969	99
Williams-Carter, N.M. Highlands (Colo. St. Col.), 1964	99
Myers-Sayers, Neb.-Omaha (Drake), 1963	99
Wicinski-Lipford, John Carroll (Allegheny) 1975	99
Berry-West, Wash & Lee (Hampden-Sydney) 1975	99

Field Goals

Duren, Arkansas State (McNeese), 1974	63
Flater, Colo. Mines (Colo. Western), 1973	62
Shear, Cortland State (Hobart), 1966	61
Butler, Tex.-Arlington (E. Texas), 1968	60
Schoreder, Pacific, Calif. (Colo. St. U.), 1968	59
Petrone, Idaho State (Portland State), 1968	59
Stenerud, Montana State (Montana), 1965	59

Punts

Hurst, Emporia State (Cent. Mo. State), 1964	97
Frens, Hope (Olivet), 1966	96
Jarrett, North Dakota (South Dakota), 1957	96
Mills, Carlton (Monmouth), 1970	93
Fitins, Taylor (Georgetown, Ky.), 1966	93
Sweeney, Pomona (UC Riverside), 1960	93

CAREER LEADERS
Rushing

	years	plays	yds	avg
Jerry Linton, Panhandle State	1959-62	648	*4,839	7.47
Rich Kowalski, Hobart	1972-75	907	*4,631	5.11
Don Aleksiewicz, Hobart	1969-72	819	4,525	5.53
Dale Mills, NE Missouri	1957-60	751	4,502	5.99
Leo Lewis, Lincoln (Mo.)	1951-54	623	4,458	7.16
Bernie Peeters, Luther	1968-71	1,072	4,435	4.14
Larry Schreiber, Tenn. Tech.	1966-69	878	4,421	5.04
Brad Rowland, McMurry	1947-50	683	4,347	6.36
Bill Rhodes, Colorado Western	1953-56	506	4,294	*8.49
Lem Harkey, Col. of Emporia	1951-54	502	4,232	8.43

Scoring

	years	td	x-pts	fg	pts
Walter Payton, Jackson State	1971-74	*66	53	5	*464
Dale Mills, NE Missouri	1957-60	64	23	0	407
Garney Henley, Huron	1956-59	63	16	0	394
Leo Lewis, Lincoln (Mo.)	1951-54	*64	0	0	384
Billy Johnson, Widener	1971-73	62	0	0	372
Tank Younger, Grambling	1945-48	60	9	0	369
Bill Cooper, Muskingum	1957-60	54	37	1	364
Ole Gunderson, St. Olaf	1969-71	60	2	0	362

1975 CHAMPIONSHIP PLAYOFFS
DIVISION II
First Round

New Hampshire 35, Lehigh 21
Western Kentucky 14, Northern Iowa 12
Livingston 34, North Dakota 14
Northern Michigan 24, Boise State 21

Semifinals

Grantland Rice Bowl—Western Kentucky 14, New Hampshire 3
Pioneer Bowl—Northern Michigan 28, Livingston 26

Final

Camellia Bowl—Northern Michigan 16, Western Kentucky 14

DIVISION III
First Round

Ithaca 41, Fort Valley State 12
Wittenberg 17, Indiana Central 13
Widener 14, Albright 6
Millsaps 28, Mississippi College 21

Semifinals

Ithaca 23, Widener 14
Wittenberg 55, Millsaps 22

Final

Alonzo Stagg Bowl—Wittenberg 28, Ithaca 0

Passing

	years	cmp	pct	yds	td
Jim Lindsey, Abilene Chr.	1967-70	*642	.519	*8,521	61
Bob Caress, Bradley	1962-65	610	.528	7,115	64
Dan Miles, So. Oregon	1964-67	577	*.662	6,531	52
George Bork, N. Illinois	1960-63	577	.640	6,782	60
Kim McQuilken, Lehigh	1971-73	516	.558	6,996	37
Tim Von Dulm, Portland St.	1969-70	500	.541	5,967	51
Jerry Bishop, Austin	1962-65	464	.551	5,992	44

Pass Receiving

	years	no.	yards	td
Chris Myers, Kenyon	1967-70	*253	3,897	33
Bruce Cerone, Yankton-Emporia St.	1966-67; 68-69	241	*4,354	*49
Harold Roberts, Austin Peay	1967-70	232	3,005	31
Jerry Hendren, Idaho	1967-69	230	3,435	27
Terry Fredenberg, Wis.-Milwaukee	1965-68	206	2,789	24
Bil Wick, Carroll (Wis.)	1966-69	190	2,967	20
Don Hutt, Boise State	1971-73	187	2,716	30

* Record.

Total Offense

	years	plays	yds
Jim Lindsey, Abilene Christian	1967-70	*1,510	*8,385
Donald Smith, Langston	1958-61	998	7,376
Bruce Upstill, Coll. Emporia	1960-63	922	7,122
Kim McQuilken, Lehigh	1971-73	991	6,878
Bob Caress, Bradley	1962-65	1,361	6,757
Ken Anderson, Augustana (Ill.)	1967-70	1,135	6,682
Terry Bradshaw, La. Tech.	1966-69	1,028	6,664

MOST POINTS IN SEASON

	yr.	tds	pat	fg	pts
Terry Metcalf, Long Beach St.	1971	*29	4	0	*178
Jim Switzer, Coll. Emporia	1963	28	0	0	168
Carl Herakovich, Rose Poly	1958	25	18	0	168
Ted Scown, Sul Ross State	1948	28	0	0	168
Eddie McGovern, Rose Poly	1942	23	27	0	165
Leon Burns, Long Beach State	1969	27	2	0	164

* Record.

COLLEGE FOOTBALL HALL OF FAME
National Football Foundation, New York, N.Y.
(Date given is player's last year of competition)

Abell, Earl—Colgate, 1915
Agase, Alex—Purdue/Illinois, 1946
Agganis, Harry—Boston Univ., 1952
Albert, Frank—Stanford, 1941
Aldrich, Chas. (Ki)—T.C.U. 1938
Aldrich, Malcolm—Yale, 1921
Alexander, John—Syracuse, 1920
Ameche, Alan (Horse)—Wisconsin, 1954
Anderson, H. (Hunk)—Notre Dame, 1921
Bacon, C. Everett—Wesleyan, 1912
Baker, Hobart (Hobey)—Princeton, 1913
Ballin, Harold—Princeton, 1914
Barnes, Stanley—S. California, 1921
Barrett, Charles—Cornell, 1915
Baston, Bert—Minnesota, 1916
Battles, Cliff—W. Va. Wesleyan, 1931
Baugh, Sammy—Texas Christian U., 1936
Bausch, James—Kansas, 1930
Beckett, John—Oregon, 1913
Bednarik, Chuck—Pennsylvania, 1948
Benbrook, A.—Michigan, 1911
Bertelli, A.—Notre Dame, 1943
Berwanger, John (Jay)—Chicago, 1935
Bettencourt, Larry—St. Mary's, 1927
Blanchard, Felix (Doc)—Army, 1946
Bock, Ed—Iowa State, 1938
Bomar, Lynn—Vanderbilt, 1924
Bomeisler, Doug (Bo)—Yale, 1913
Booth, Albie—Yale, 1931
Borries, Fred—Navy, 1934
Boynton, Ben—Williams, 1920
Brewer, Charles—Harvard, 1895
Brooke, George—Pennsylvania, 1895
Brown, Gordon—Yale, 1900
Brown, John, Jr.—Navy, 1913
Brown, Johnny Mack—Alabama, 1925
Bunker, Paul—Army, 1902
Butler, Robert—Wisconsin, 1912
Cafego, George—Tennessee, 1939
Cagle, Chris—SW La./Army, 1929
Cain, John—Alabama, 1932
Cameron, Eddie—Wash. & Lee, 1924
Campbell, David C.—Harvard, 1901
Cannon, Jack—Notre Dame, 1929
Carideo, Frank—Notre Dame, 1930
Carney, Charles—Illinois, 1921
Carpenter, C. Hunter—VPI, 1905
Carroll, Charles—Washington, 1928
Casey, Edward L.—Harvard, 1919
Chamberlain, Guy—Nebraska, 1915
Christman, Paul—Missouri, 1940
Clark, Earl (Dutch)—Colo. College, 1929
Clevenger, Zora—Indiana, 1903
Cochran, Gary—Princeton, 1895
Cody, Josh—Vanderbilt, 1920
Coleman, Don—Mich. State, 1951
Conerly, Chuck—Mississippi, 1947
Connor, George—Notre Dame, 1947
Corbin, W.—Yale, 1888
Corbus, William—Stanford, 1933
Cowan, Hector—Princeton, 1889
Coy, Edward H. (Tad)—Yale, 1909
Crawford, Fred—Duke, 1933
Crow, John D.—Texas A&M, 1957
Crowley, James—Notre Dame, 1924
Cutter, Slade—Navy, 1934
Dalrymple, Gerald—Tulane, 1931
Dawkins, Peter—Army, 1958

Dalton, John—Navy, 1912
Daly, Charles—Harvard/Army, 1902
Daniell, Averell—Pittsburgh, 1936
Davies, Tom—Pittsburgh, 1921
Davis, Glenn—Army, 1946
DesJardien, Paul—Chicago, 1914
Devine, Aubrey—Iowa, 1921
DeWitt, John—Princeton, 1903
Dodd, Bobby—Tennessee, 1930
Dougherty, Nathan—Tennessee, 1909
Driscoll, Paddy—Northwestern, 1917
Drury, Morley—So. California, 1927
Dudley, William (Bill)—Virginia, 1941
Eckersall, Walter—Chicago, 1906
Edwards, Turk—Washington State, 1931
Edwards, William—Princeton, 1900
Eichenlaub, R.—Notre Dame, 1913
Evans, Ray—Kansas, 1947
Exendine, Albert—Carlisle, 1908
Falaschi, Nello—Santa Clara, 1937
Fears, Tom—Santa Clara/UCLA, 1947
Feathers, Beattie—Tennessee, 1933
Fenimore, Robert—Oklahoma State, 1947
Fenton, G.E. (Doc)—La. State U., 1910
Ferraro, John—So. California, 1944
Fesler, Wesley—Ohio State, 1930
Fincher, Bill—Georgia Tech, 1920
Fish, Hamilton—Harvard, 1909
Fisher, Robert—Harvard, 1911
Flowers, Abe—Georgia Tech, 1920
Frank, Clint—Yale, 1937
Friedman, Benny—Michigan, 1926
Garbisch, Edgar—Army, 1924
Gelbert, Charles—Pennsylvania, 1896
Geyer, Forest—Oklahoma, 1915
Giel, Paul—Minnesota, 1953
Gifford, Frank—So. California, 1951
Gilbert, Walter—Auburn, 1936
Gipp, George—Notre Dame, 1920
Gladchuk, Chet—Boston College, 1940
Goldberg, Marshall—Pittsburgh, 1938
Gordon, Walter—California, 1918
Graham, Otto—Northwestern, 1943
Grange, Harold (Red)—Illinois, 1925
Grayson, Robert—Stanford, 1935
Gulick, Merle—Hobart, 1929
Guyon, Joe—Georgia Tech, 1919
Hale, Edwin—Mississippi Col., 1921
Hamilton, Robert (Bones)—Stanford, 1935
Hamilton, Tom—Navy, 1925
Hanson, Vic—Syracuse, 1926
Hardwick, H. (Tack)—Harvard, 1914
Hare, T. Truxton—Pennsylvania, 1900
Harley, Chick—Ohio State, 1919
Harmon, Tom—Michigan, 1940
Harpster, Howard—Carnegie Tech, 1928
Hart, Edward J.—Princeton, 1911
Hart, Leon—Notre Dame, 1949
Hazel, Homer—Rutgers, 1924
Healey, Ed—Dartmouth, 1916
Heffelfinger, W. (Pudge)—Yale, 1891
Hein, Mel—Washington State, 1930
Henry, Wilber—Wash. & Jefferson, 1919
Herschberger, Clarence—Chicago, 1899
Herwig, Robert—California, 1937
Heston, Willie—Michigan, 1904
Hickman, Herman—Tennessee, 1931
Hickok, William—Yale, 1895

Hill, Dan—Duke, 1938
Hillebrand, A.R. (Doc)—Princeton, 1900
Hinkey, Frank—Yale, 1894
Hinkle, Carl—Vanderbilt, 1937
Hinkle, Clark—Bucknell, 1932
Hirsch, Elroy—Wis./Mich., 1943
Hitchcock, James—Auburn, 1932
Hogan, James J.—Yale, 1904
Holland, Jerome (Brud)—Cornell, 1938
Hollenbeck, William—Penn., 1908
Horrell, Edwin—California, 1924
Horvath, Les—Ohio State, 1944
Howe, Arthur—Yale, 1911
Howell, Millard (Dixie)—Alabama, 1934
Hubbard, Cal—Centenary, 1926
Hubbard, John—Amherst, 1906
Hubert, Allison—Alabama, 1925
Humble, Weldon G.—Rice, 1946
Hunt, Joel—Texas A&M, 1927
Huntington, Ellery—Colgate, 1914
Hutson, Don—Alabama, 1934
Ingram, James—Navy, 1906
Isbell, Cecil—Purdue, 1937
Janowicz, Vic—Ohio State, 1951
Jenkins, Darold—Missouri, 1941
Joesting, Herbert—Minnesota, 1927
Johnson, James—Carlisle, 1903
Juhan, Frank—Univ. of South, 1910
Justice, Charlie—North Carolina, 1949
Kaer, Mort—So. California, 1926
Kavanaugh, Kenneth—La. State U., 1939
Kaw, Edgar—Cornell, 1922
Kazmaier, Richard—Princeton, 1951
Keck, James—Princeton, 1921
Kelley, Larry—Yale, 1936
Kelly, William—Montana, 1926
Ketcham, Henry—Yale, 1913
Killinger, William—Penn State, 1922
Kirkpatrick, John Reed—Yale, 1910
Kimbrough, John—Texas A&M, 1940
Kinard, Frank—Mississippi, 1937
King, Phillip—Princeton, 1893
Kinnick, Nile—Iowa, 1939
Kipke, Harry—Michigan, 1923
Kitzmiller, John—Oregon, 1929
Koch, Barton—Baylor, 1931
Kitner, Malcolm—Texas, 1942
Lane, Myles—Dartmouth, 1927
Lautenschlaeger—Tulane, 1925
Layden, Elmer—Notre Dame, 1924
Layne, Bobby—Texas, 1947
Lea, Langdon—Princeton, 1895
Leech, James—Va. Mil. Inst., 1920
Locke, Gordon—Iowa, 1922
Lourie, Don—Princeton, 1921
Luckman, Sid—Columbia, 1938
Lujack, John—Notre Dame, 1947
Lund, J.L. (Pug)—Minnesota, 1934
Macomber, Bart—Illinois, 1915
Mahan, Edward W.—Harvard, 1915
Mallory, William—Yale, 1893
Mann, Gerald—So. Methodist, 1927
Markov, Vic—Washington, 1937
Marshall, Robert—Minnesota, 1907
Matson, Ollie—San Fran. U., 1952
Matthews, Ray—Texas Christ. U., 1928
Maulbetsch, John—Michigan, 1914
Mauthe, J.L. (Pete)—Penn State, 1912

College Football Hall of Fame (continued)

Maxwell, Robert—Chi./Swarthmore, 1906
McAfee, George—Duke, 1939
McColl, William F.—Stanford, 1951
McCormick, James B.—Princeton, 1907
McDowall, Jack—No. Car. State, 1927
McEver, Gene—Tennessee, 1931
McEwan, John—Minn./Army, 1916
McFadden, J.B.—Clemson, 1939
McClung, Thomas L.—Yale, 1891
McGovern, J.—Minnesota, 1910
McLaren, George—Pittsburgh, 1918
McMillan, Dan—U.S.C./Calif., 1922
McMillan, Bo—Centre, 1921
McWhorter, Robert—Georgia, 1913
Mercer, Leroy—Pennsylvania, 1912
Mickal, Abe—La. State U., 1935
Miller, Creighton—Notre Dame, 1943
Miller, Don—Notre Dame, 1925
Miller, Edgar (Rip)—Notre Dame, 1924
Miller, Eugene—Penn State, 1913
Minds, John—Pennsylvania, 1897
Moffatt, Alex—Princeton, 1884
Montgomery, Cliff—Columbia, 1933
Moomaw, Donn—U.C.L.A., 1952
Morley, William—Columbia, 1903
Morton, William—Dartmouth, 1931
Muller, Harold (Brick)—Calif., 1922
Nagurski, Bronko—Minnesota, 1929
Nevers, Ernie—Stanford, 1925
Newell, Marshall—Harvard, 1893
Newman, Harry—Michigan, 1932
Oberlander, Andrew—Dartmouth, 1925
O'Brien, Davey—Texas Christ. U., 1938
O'Dea, Pat—Wisconsin, 1899
O'Hearn, J.—Cornell, 1915
Oliphant, Elmer—Purdue/Army, 1917
Oosterbaan, Ben—Michigan, 1927
O'Rourke, Charles—Boston College, 1940
Osgood, W.D.—Cornell/Penn, 1895
Osmanski, William—Holy Cross, 1938
Parker, Clarence (Ace)—Duke, 1936
Parker, Jackie—Miss. State, 1953
Parker, James—Ohio State, 1956
Pazzetti, V.J.—Wes./Lehigh, 1912
Peabody, Endicott—Harvard, 1941
Peck, Robert—Pittsburgh, 1916
Pennock, Stanley B.—Harvard, 1914
Pfann, George—Cornell, 1923
Phillips, H.D.—U. of South, 1904
Pingel, John—Michigan State, 1938
Pihos, Pete—Indiana, 1945
Pinckert, Ernie—So. California, 1931
Poe, Arthur—Princeton, 1899

Pollard, Fritz—Brown, 1916
Poole, Barney—Miss./Army, 1947
Pund, Henry—Georgia Tech, 1928
Reeds, Claude—Oklahoma, 1913
Reid, William—Harvard, 1900
Reynolds, Robert—Stanford, 1935
Rinehart, Charles—Lafayette, 1897
Rodgers, Ira—West Virginia, 1919
Rogers, Edward L.—Minnesota, 1903
Rosenberg, Aaron—So. California, 1934
Rote, Kyle—So. Methodist, 1950
Routt, Joe—Texas A&M., 1937
Salmon, Louis—Notre Dame, 1904
Sauer, George—Nebraska, 1933
Scarlett, Hunter—Pennsylvania, 1909
Schoonover, Wear—Arkansas, 1929
Schreiner, Dave—Wisconsin, 1942
Schultz, Adolf (Germany)—Mich., 1908
Schwab, Frank—Lafayette, 1922
Schwartz, Marchmont—Notre Dame, 1931
Schwegler, Paul—Washington, 1931
Scott, Clyde—Arkansas, 1949
Seibels, Henry—Sewanee, 1899
Shelton, Murray—Cornell, 1915
Shevlin, Tom—Yale, 1905
Simons, Claude—Tulane, 1934
Sington, Fred—Alabama, 1930
Sinkwich, Frank—Georgia, 1942
Skladany, Joe—Pittsburgh, 1933
Slater, F.F. (Duke)—Iowa, 1921
Smith, Bruce—Minnesota, 1941
Smith, Ernie—So. California, 1932
Smith, Harry—So. California, 1939
Smith, John (Clipper)—Notre Dame, 1927
Snow, Neil—Michigan, 1901
Spears, Clarence W.—Dartmouth, 1915
Spears, W.D.—Vanderbilt, 1927
Sprackling, William—Brown, 1911
Sprague, M. (Bud)—Texas/Army, 1928
Stafford, Harrison—Texas, 1932
Stagg, Amos Alonzo—Yale, 1889
Steffen, Walter—Chicago, 1908
Stein, Herbert—Pittsburgh, 1921
Steuber, Robert—Missouri, 1943
Stevens, Mal—Yale, 1923
Stinchcomb, Gaylord—Ohio State, 1920
Stevenson, Vincent—Pennsylvania, 1905
Strong, Ken—New York Univ., 1928
Strupper, George—Georgia Tech, 1917
Stuhldreher, Harry—Notre Dame, 1924
Stydahar, Joe—West Virginia, 1935
Suffridge, Robert—Tennessee, 1940
Swanson, Clarence—Nebraska, 1921

Swiacki, Bill—Holy Cross/Colombia, 1947
Thompson, Joe—Pittsburgh, 1907
Thorne, Samuel B.—Yale, 1906
Thorpe, Jim—Carlisle, 1912
Ticknor, Ben—Harvard, 1930
Tigert, John—Vanderbilt, 1904
Tinsley, Gaynell—La. State U., 1936
Tipton, Eric—Duke, 1938
Torrey, Robert—Pennsylvania, 1906
Travis, Ed Tarkio—Missouri, 1920
Trippi, Charles—Georgia, 1946
Tryon, J. Edward—Colgate, 1925
Utay, Joe—Texas A&M, 1907
Van Brocklin, Norm—Oregon, 1948
Van Sickel, Dale—Florida, 1929
Van Surdam, Henderson—Wesleyan, 1905
Very, Dexter—Penn State, 1912
Vessels, Billy—Oklahoma, 1931
Wagner, Huber—Pittsburgh, 1913
Walker, Doak—So. Methodist, 1949
Walsh, Adam—Notre Dame, 1924
Warburton, I. (Cotton)—So. Calif., 1934
Warner, William—Cornell, 1903
Washington, Ken—U.C.L.A., 1939
Weekes, Harold—Columbia, 1902
Weir, Ed—Nebraska, 1925
Welch, Gus—Carlisle, 1914
Weller, John—Princeton, 1935
Wendell, Percy—Harvard, 1913
West, D. Belford—Colgate, 1919
Weyand, Alex—Army, 1915
Wharton, Charles—Pennsylvania, 1896
Wheeler, Arthur—Princeton, 1894
White, Byron (Whizzer)—Colorado, 1937
Whitmire, Don—Alabama/Navy, 1944
Wickhorst, Frank—Navy, 1926
Widseth, Ed—Minnesota, 1936
Wildung, Richard—Minnesota, 1942
Williams, James—Rice, 1949
Willis, William—Ohio State, 1945
Wilson, George—Washington, 1925
Wilson, Harry—Penn State/Army, 1923
Wistert, Albert A.—Michigan, 1942
Wistert, Frank (Whitey)—Mich., 1933
Wojciechowicz, Alex—Fordham, 1936
Wyant, Andrew—Bucknell/Chicago, 1894
Wyatt, Bowden—Tennessee, 1938
Wyckoff, Clint—Cornell, 1896
Young, Claude (Buddy)—Illinois, 1946
Young, Harry—Wash. & Lee, 1916
Zarnas, Gus—Ohio State, 1937

Coaches

Bill Alexander
Dr. Ed Anderson
Ike Armstrong
Matty Bell
Hugo Bezdek
Dana X. Bible
Bernie Bierman
Earl (Red) Blaik
Charles W. Caldwell
Walter Camp
Frank Cavanaugh
Fritz Crisler
Gil Dobie
Michael Donohue
Gus Dorais

Charles (Rip) Engle
Don Faurot
Jake Gaither
Ernest Godfrey
Edward K. Hall
Richard Harlow
Jesse Harper
Percy Haughton
John W. Heisman
R. A. (Bob) Higgins
William Ingram
Morley Jennings
Howard Jones
L. (Biff) Jones
Thomas (Tad) Jones

Andy Kerr
Frank Leahy
George E. Little
Lou Little
El (Slip) Madigan
Herbert McCracken
Daniel McGugin
DeOrmond (Tuss) Mclaughry
L. R. (Dutch) Meyer
Bernie Moore
Ray Morrison
George A. Munger
Clarence Munn
William Murray
Ed (Hooks) Mylin

Earle (Greasy) Neale
Jess Neely
Robert Neyland
Homer Norton
Frank (Buck) O'Neill
Bennie Owen
James Phalea
E. N. Robinson
Knute Rockne
E. L. (Dick) Romney
William W. Roper
George F. Sanford
Francis A. Schmidt
Clark Shaughnessy
Buck Shaw

Andrew L. Smith
Carl Snavely
Amos A. Stagg
Jock Sutherland
Frank W. Thomas
Wallace Wade
Lynn Waldorf
Glenn (Pop) Warner
E. E. (Tad) Wieman
John W. Wilce
Bud Wilkinson
Henry L. Williams
George W. Woodruff
Fielding H. Yost
Robert Zuppke

PROFESSIONAL FOOTBALL STANDING AND RECORDS
NATIONAL FOOTBALL LEAGUE FINAL STANDING 1975

AMERICAN CONFERENCE

Eastern Division

	W	L	T	Pct	Pts	OP
Baltimore	10	4	0	.714	395	269
Miami	10	4	0	.714	357	222
Buffalo	8	6	0	.571	420	355
New England	3	11	0	.214	258	358
New York Jets	3	11	0	.214	258	433

Central Division

Pittsburgh	12	2	0	.857	373	162
*Cincinnati	11	3	0	.786	340	246
Houston	10	4	0	.714	293	226
Cleveland	3	11	0	.214	218	372

Western Division

Oakland	11	3	0	.786	375	255
Denver	6	8	0	.429	254	307
Kansas City	5	9	0	.357	282	341
San Diego	2	12	0	.143	189	345

*Fourth qualifier for playoffs.

Playoffs—Pittsburgh 28, Baltimore 10; Oakland 31, Cincinnati 28.
Conference championship—Pittsburgh 16, Oakland 10.

NATIONAL CONFERENCE

Eastern Division

	W	L	T	Pct	Pts	OP
St. Louis	11	3	0	.786	356	276
*Dallas	10	4	0	.714	350	268
Washington	8	6	0	.571	325	276
New York Giants	5	9	0	.357	216	306
Philadelphia	4	10	0	.286	225	302

Central Division

Minnesota	12	2	0	.857	377	180
Detroit	7	7	0	.500	245	262
Chicago	4	10	0	.286	191	379
Green Bay	4	10	0	.286	226	285

Western Division

Los Angeles	12	2	0	.857	312	135
San Francisco	5	9	0	.357	255	286
Atlanta	4	10	0	.286	240	289
New Orleans	2	12	0	.143	165	360

*Fourth qualifier for playoffs.

Playoffs—Los Angeles defeated St. Louis, 35–23; Dallas defeated Minnesota, 17–14.
Conference championship—Dallas defeated Los Angeles, 37–7.

League Championship (Super Bowl X, at Miami, Jan. 18, 1976)

Dallas Cowboys	7	3	0	7	–17
Pittsburgh Steelers	7	0	0	14	–21

Scoring: Dallas: Touchdowns: D. Pearson, 29-yard pass from Staubach; Howard 34-yard pass from Staubach; Field goal: Fritsch, 36; conversions: Fritsch 2 (kicks). Pittsburgh: Touchdowns: Grossman, 7-yard pass from Bradshaw; Swann, 64-yard pass from Bradshaw. Field goals: Gerela (2) 36, 18; Conversion: Gerala (kick); Safety: Harrison blocked punt through end zone. Attendance—80,187 at Orange Bowl.

TEAM NICKNAMES AND HOME FIELD STADIUM CAPACITIES

AMERICAN CONFERENCE

Eastern Division

Baltimore Colts	Memorial Stadium (G)	60,020
Buffalo Bills	Rich Stadium (AT)	80,020
Miami Dolphins	Orange Bowl (G)	80,045
New England Patriots	*Schaefer Stadium (P-T)	61,279
New York Jets	Shea Stadium (G)	60,000

*At Foxboro, Mass.

Central Division

Cincinnati Bengals	Riverfront Stadium (AT)	56,200
Cleveland Browns	Cleveland Stadium (G)	80,165
Houston Oilers	Astrodome (AT)	50,000
Pittsburgh Steelers	Three Rivers Stadium (TT)	50,350

Western Division

Denver Broncos	Mile High Stadium (G)	63,500
Kansas City Chiefs	Arrowhead Stadium (TT)	78,000
Oakland Raiders	County Coliseum (G)	54,037
San Diego Chargers	San Diego Stadium (G)	52,568
Tampa Bay Buccaneers	Tampa Stadium (G)	71,000

Stadium playing surfaces (in parentheses): AT = Astro-Turf; G = grass; TT = TartanTurf; P-T = Poly-Turf.

NATIONAL CONFERENCE

Eastern Division

Dallas Cowboys	Texas Stadium (TT)	65,101
New York Giants	†Giants Stadium (A-T)	76,000
Philadelphia Eagles	Veterans Stadium (A-T)	66,052
St. Louis Cardinals	Busch Mem. Stadium (AT)	51,392
Washington Redskins	R. F. Kennedy Stadium (G)	55,004

† At East Rutherford, N.J.

Central Division

Chicago Bears	Soldier Field (AT)	55,753
Detroit Lions	Pontiac Met. Stadium (AT)	80,683
Green Bay Packers	{ Lambeau Field (G)	56,267
	Milwaukee Stadium (G)	55,896
Minnesota Vikings	Metropolitan Stadium (G)	48,446

Western Division

Atlanta Falcons	Atlanta-Fulton Stadium (G)	60,489
Los Angeles Rams	Memorial Coliseum (G)	91,038
New Orleans Saints	Louisiana Superdome (AT)	72,000
San Francisco 49ers	Candlestick Park (AT)	61,000
Seattle Seahawks	Kingdome (AT)	65,000

NATIONAL FOOTBALL LEAGUE GOVERNMENT

Commissioner's Office: Pete Rozelle, commissioner; Jim Kensil, executive director; Jan Van Duser, director of personnel; Don Weiss, director of public relations.

American Conference: Lamar Hunt, president; Val Pinchbeck Jr., assistant to the president; Joe Browne, director of information.

National Conference: George Halas, president; Ernie Accorsi, assistant to the president; Jim Heffernan, director of information.

N.F.L. Championship (Super Bowl)
National Conference Champion vs. American Conference Champion

Year	Site	Date	Attendance	Winner	Loser
1970	Orange Bowl, Miami	Jan. 17, 1971	79,204	Baltimore Colts., A.C., 16	Dallas Cowboys, N.C., 13
1971	Tulane Stadium, New Orleans	Jan. 16, 1972	80,591	Dallas Cowboys, N.C., 24	Miami Dolphins, A.C., 3
1972	Memorial Coliseum, Los Angeles	Jan. 14, 1973	90,182	Miami Dolphins A.C., 14	Washington Redskins, N.C., 7
1973	Rice Stadium, Houston	Jan. 13, 1974	68.142	Miami Dolphins A.C., 24	Minnesota Vikings, N.C., 7
1974	Tulane Stadium, New Orleans	Jan. 12, 1975	80,997	Pittsburgh Steelers, 16	Minnesota Vikings, 6
1975	Orange Bowl, Miami	Jan. 18, 1976	80,187	Pittsburgh Steelers, 21	Dallas Cowboys, 17

Inter-League Championship (Super Bowl)
National League Champion vs. American League Champion

1966	Memorial Coliseum, Los Angeles	Jan. 15, 1967	63,036	Green Bay Packers, N.L., 35	Kansas City Chiefs, A.L., 10
1967	Orange Bowl, Miami	Jan. 14, 1968	75,546	Green Bay Packers, N.L., 33	Oakland Raiders, A.L., 14
1968	Orange Bowl, Miami	Jan. 12, 1969	75,377	New York Jets, A.L. 16	Baltimore Colts, N.L. 7
1969	Tulane Stadium, New Orleans	Jan. 11, 1970	80,562	Kansas City Chiefs, A.L. 23	Minnesota Vikings, N.L. 7

National League Champions

Year	Champion (W–L–T)	Year	Champion (W–L–T)	Year	Champion (W–L–T)
1921	Chicago Bears (Staley's) (10-1-1)	1925	Chicago Cardinals (11-2-1)	1929	Green Bay Packers (12-0-1)
1922	Canton Bulldogs (10-0-2)	1926	Frankford Yellow Jackets (14-1-1)	1930	Green Bay Packers (10-3-1)
1923	Canton Bulldogs (11-0-1)	1927	New York Giants (11-1-1)	1931	Green Bay Packers (12-2-0)
1924	Cleveland Indians (7-1-1)	1928	Providence Steamrollers (8-1-2)	1932	Chicago Bears (7-1-6)

Year	Eastern Conference Winners (W–L–T)	Western Conference Winners (W–L–T)	League champion, playoff results
1933	New York Giants (11-3-0)	Chicago Bears (10-2-1)	Chicago Bears 23, New York 21
1934	New York Giants (8-5-0)	Chicago Bears (13-0-0)	New York 30, Chicago Bears 13
1935	New York Giants (9-3-0)	Detroit Lions (7-3-2)	Detroit 26, New York 7
1936	Boston Redskins (7-5-0)	Green Bay Packers (10-1-1)	Green Bay 21, Boston 6
1937	Washington Redskins (8-3-0)	Chicago Bears (9-1-1)	Washington 28, Chicago Bears 21
1938	New York Giants (8-2-1)	Green Bay Packers (8-3-0)	New York 23, Green Bay 17
1939	New York Giants (9-1-1)	Green Bay Packers (9-2-0)	Green Bay 27, New York 0
1940	Washington Redskins (9-2-0)	Chicago Bears (8-3-0)	Chicago Bears 73, Washington 0
1941	New York Giants (8-3-0)	Chicago Bears (10-1-1)†	Chicago Bears 37, New York 9
1942	Washington Redskins (10-1-1)	Chicago Bears (11-0-0)	Washington 14, Chicago Bears 6
1943	Washington Redskins (6-3-1)†	Chicago Bears (8-1-1)	Chicago Bears 41, Washington 21
1944	New York Giants (8-1-1)	Green Bay Packers (8-2-0)	Green Bay 14, New York 7
1945	Washington Redskins (8-2-0)	Cleveland Rams (9-1-0)	Cleveland 15, Washington 14
1946	New York Giants (7-3-1)	Chicago Bears (8-2-1)	Chicago Bears 24, New York 14
1947	Philadelphia Eagles (8-4-0)†	Chicago Cardinals (9-3-0)	Chicago Cardinals 28, Philadelphia 21
1948	Philadelphia Eagles (9-2-1)	Chicago Cardinals (11-1-0)	Philadelphia 7, Chicago Cardinals 0
1949	Philadelphia Eagles (11-1-0)	Los Angeles Rams (8-2-2)	Philadelphia 14, Los Angeles 0
1950*	Cleveland Browns (10-2-0)†	Los Angeles Rams (9-3-0)†	Cleveland 30, Los Angeles 28
1951*	Cleveland Browns (11-1-0)	Los Angeles Rams (8-4-0)	Los Angeles 24, Cleveland 17
1952*	Cleveland Browns (8-4-0)	Detroit Lions (9-3-0)†	Detroit 17, Cleveland 7
1953	Cleveland Browns (11-1-0)	Detroit Lions (10-2-0)	Detroit 17, Cleveland 16
1954	Cleveland Browns (9-3-0)	Detroit Lions (9-2-1)	Cleveland 56, Detroit 10
1955	Cleveland Browns (9-2-1)	Los Angeles Rams (8-3-1)	Cleveland 38, Los Angeles 14
1956	New York Giants (8-3-1)	Chicago Bears (9-2-1)	New York 47, Chicago Bears 7
1957	Cleveland Browns (9-2-1)	Detroit Lions (8-4-0)†	Detroit 59, Cleveland 14
1958	New York Giants (9-3-0)†	Baltimore Colts (9-3-0)	Baltimore 23, New York 17‡
1959	New York Giants (10-2-0)	Baltimore Colts (9-3-0)	Baltimore 31, New York 16
1960	Philadelphia Eagles (10-2-0)	Green Bay Packers (8-4-0)	Philadelphia 17, Green Bay 13
1961	New York Giants (10-3-1)	Green Bay Packers (11-3-0)	Green Bay 37, New York 0
1962	New York Giants (12-2-0)	Green Bay Packers (13-1-0)	Green Bay 16, New York 7
1963	New York Giants (11-3-0)	Chicago Bears (11-1-2)	Chicago 14, New York 10
1964	Cleveland Browns (10-3-1)	Baltimore Colts (12-2-0)	Cleveland 27, Baltimore 0
1965	Cleveland Browns (11-3-0)	Green Bay Packers (11-3-1)†	Green Bay 23, Cleveland 12
1966	Dallas Cowboys (10-3-1)	Green Bay Packers (12-2-0)	Green Bay 34, Dallas 27
1967	Dallas Cowboys (9-5-0)†	Green Bay Packers (9-4-1)†	Green Bay 21, Dallas 17
1968	Cleveland Browns (10-4-0)†	Baltimore Colts (13-1-0)†	Baltimore 34, Cleveland 0
1969	Cleveland Browns (10-3-1)†	Minnesota Vikings (12-2-0)†	Minnesota 27, Cleveland 7

* League was divided into American and National Conferences, 1950–52 and again in 1970, when leagues merged. † Won divisional playoff. ‡ Won at 8:15 of sudden death overtime period.

National Conference Champions

Year	Eastern Division Winners	Central Division	Western Division	Champion
1970	Dallas Cowboys (10-4-0)	Minnesota Vikings (12-2-0)	San Francisco 49ers (10-3-1)	Dallas
1971	Dallas Cowboys (11-3-0)	Minnesota Vikings (11-3-0)	San Francisco 49ers (9-5-0)	Dallas
1972	Washington Redskins (11-3-0)	Green Bay Packers (10-4-0)	San Francisco 49ers (8-5-1)	Washington
1973	Dallas Cowboys (10-4-0)	Minnesota Vikings (12-2-0)	Los Angeles Rams (12-2-0)	Minnesota
1974	St. Louis Cardinals (10-4-0)	Minnesota Vikings (10-4-0)	Los Angeles Rams (10-4-0)	Minnesota
1975	St. Louis Cardinals (11-3-0)	Minnesota Vikings (12-2-0)	Los Angeles Rams (10-4-0)	Dallas

American Conference Champions

Year	Eastern Division Winners	Central Division	Western Division	Champion
1970	Baltimore Colts (11-2-1)	Cincinnati Bengals (8-6-0)	Oakland Raiders (8-4-2)	Baltimore
1971	Miami Dolphins (10-3-1)	Cleveland Browns (9-5-0)	Kansas City Chiefs (10-3-1)	Miami
1972	Miami Dolphins (14-0-0)	Pittsburgh Steelers (11-3-0)	Oakland Raiders (10-3-1)	Miami
1973	Miami Dolphins (12-2-0)	Cincinnati Bengals (10-4-0)	Oakland Raiders (9-4-1)	Miami
1974	Miami Dolphins (11-3-0)	Pittsburgh Steelers (10-3-1)	Oakland Raiders (12-2-0)	Pittsburgh
1975	Baltimore Colts (10-4-0)	Pittsburgh Steelers (12-2-0)	Oakland Raiders (12-2-0)	Pittsburgh

American League Champions

Year	Eastern Division Winners (W–L–T)	Western Division Winners (W–L–T)	League champion, playoffs results
1960	Houston Oilers (10-4-0)	Los Angeles Chargers (10-4-0)	Houston 24, Los Angeles 16
1961	Houston Oilers (10-3-1)	San Diego Chargers (12-2-0)	Houston 10, San Diego 3
1962	Houston Oilers (11-3-0)	Dallas Texans (11-3-0)	Dallas 20, Houston 17*
1963	Boston Patriots (8-6-1)†	San Diego Chargers (11-3-0)	San Diego 51, Boston 10
1964	Buffalo Bills (12-2-0)	San Diego Chargers (8-5-1)	Buffalo 20, San Diego 7
1965	Buffalo Bills (10-3-1)	San Diego Chargers (9-2-3)	Buffalo 23, San Diego 0
1966	Buffalo Bills (9-4-1)	Kansas City Chiefs (11-2-1)	Kansas City 31, Buffalo 7
1967	Houston Oilers (9-4-1)	Oakland Raiders (13-1-0)	Oakland 40, Houston 7
1968	New York Jets (11-3-0)	Oakland Raiders (12-2-0)†	New York 27, Oakland 23
1969	New York Jets (10-4-0)	Oakland Raiders (12-1-1)	‡Kansas City 17, Oakland 7

* Won at 2:45 of second sudden death overtime period. † Won divisional playoff. ‡ Kansas City defeated New York, 13–6, and Oakland defeated Houston, 56–7, in interdivisional playoffs.

GLOSSARY OF FOOTBALL TERMS

Sources: National Collegiate Athletic Association and National Football League

Audible—Quarterback's vocal signals at scrimmage line, changing play called in huddle.

Balanced Line—Offensive line-up with guard, tackle, and end on each side of center.

Blind Side—Side opposite direction in which player is looking.

Blitz—Concentrated charge, usually on passer, by linebackers and defense backs.

Bomb—Long pass to receiver speeding deep toward goal line, intended for quick score.

Bootleg—Quarterback's run to side opposite to direction blockers have moved.

Buttonhook Pass—Receiver goes downfield and U-turns sharply to catch ball.

Check Off—See Audible.

Clipping—Throwing body across back of legs of non-ball-carrying opponent.

Down—A play by team in possession of ball; team has four downs to gain 10 yards, called first, second, etc.

Draw—Quarterback fakes as if to pass but hands off to another back for running play.

Fair Catch—Signal, with upraised arm, by kick receiver for chance to make catch unmolested; he cannot advance ball and a tackler is penalized.

Flanker—Back stationed wide right or left as pass receiver.

Flare—Pass to receiver swinging wide or flaring out of backfield.

Fly Pattern—See Bomb.

Front Four—Tackles and ends of defensive line.

Illegal Procedure—Usually applies to backfield man illegally in motion before ball is snapped.

Lateral—Pass tossed parallel with goal line or back toward player's goal.

Look-In Pass—Receiver breaks quickly downfield and turns at once to look over shoulder for pass.

Onside Kick—Short, usually angled kickoff, which kicking team hopes to recover after it travels required 10 yards.

Offside—Movement of player over line of scrimmage or kicking line before ball is put into play.

Option—Choice of ball carrier to run or pass or hand off ball.

Pass Rush—Charge of linemen against passer.

Pattern—Manner in which receiver runs and maneuvers to gain position.

Pocket—Small area amid blockers where passer stands while looking for receivers.

Possession—Player's holding of ball long enough to perform an act common to game.

Prevent Defense—Stratagem of lessening front-line strength for deep defense; allowing short yardage but cutting off long gain.

Punt—Ball dropped from hands by player and kicked before it hits ground.

Red Dog—See Blitz.

Reverse—Running play in which ball is carried in direction opposite to that in which play started.

Roll-Out—Quarterback runs laterally behind blockers, keeping or passing.

Safety—Occurrence in which ball becomes dead behind goal line of player in possession when impetus came from his team.

Screen Pass—Pass to receiver stationed behind wall of blockers as defenders harass passer.

Setbacks—Other backs placed to side or rear of quarterback.

Slot Back—Player placed at least one yard behind line of scrimmage between wide receiver and interior linemen.

Strong Side—Overbalance of linemen to one side of center.

Swing Pass—See Flare.

Touchback—Occurrence in which ball becomes dead behind goal line of team in possession when impetus came from other team.

Touchdown—Carrying of ball into, or catching pass or having possession of live ball in opponent's end zone.

Trap—Maneuver permitting defender into backfield to be blocked from side by another player.

Turnover—Loss of ball by misplay without scoring.

Weak Side—Opposite strong side.

Wide Receiver—Split end or flanker set wide of scrimmage line.

N.F.L. INDIVIDUAL LIFETIME, SEASON AND GAME RECORDS

(Through 1975, American Football League marks were incorporated in N.F.L. records after merger in 1970)

Scoring

Most points scored, lifetime—2,002, George Blanda, Chicago Bears, 1949-58; Baltimore, 1950; Houston, 1960-66; Oakland, 1967-75 (9tds, 943 pat, 335 fgs).

Most points, season—176, Paul Hornung, Green Bay, 1960 (15 td, 41 pat, 15 fg).

Most points, game—40, Ernie Nevers, Chicago Cards, 1929 (6 td, 4 pat).

Most points, one quarter—29, Don Hutson, Green Bay, 1945 (4 td, 5 pat).

Most touchdowns, lifetime—126, Jim Brown, Cleveland, 1957-65.

Most touchdowns, season—23, O. J. Simpson, Buffalo, 1975.

Most touchdowns, game—6, Ernie Nevers, Chicago Cards; William Jones, Cleveland, 1929; Gale Sayers, Chicago Bears, 1965.

Most points after touchdown, lifetime—943, George Blanda, Chicago Bears, 1949-58; Baltimore, 1950; Houston, 1960-66; Oakland, 1967-75.

Most points after touchdown, game—9, Pat Harder, Chicago Cards, 1948; Bob Waterfield, Los Angeles, 1950; Charlie Gogolak, Washington, 1966.

Most consecutive points after touchdown—234, Tommy Davis, San Francisco, 1959-65.

Most field goals, lifetime—335, George Blanda, Chicago Bears, 1949-58; Baltimore, 1950; Houston, 1960-66; Oakland, 1967-75.

Most field goals, season—34, Jim Turner, New York Jets, 1968.

Most field goals, game—7, Jim Bakken, St. Louis, 1967.

Longest field goal—63 yards, Tom Dempsey, New Orleans, 1970.

Rushing

Most yards gained, lifetime—12,312, Jim Brown, Cleveland, 1957-65.

Most yards gained, season—2,003, O. J. Simpson, Buffalo, 1973.

Most yards gained, game—250, O. J. Simpson, Buffalo, 1973.

Most touchdowns, lifetime—106, Jim Brown, Cleveland, 1957-65.

Most touchdowns, season—19, Jim Taylor, Green Bay, 1962.

Most touchdowns, game—6, Ernie Nevers, Chicago Cards, 1929.

Longest run from scrimmage—97 yards, Andy Uram, Green Bay, 1939; Bob Gage, Pittsburgh, 1949 (both for touchdowns).

Passing

Most passes completed, lifetime—2,931, Fran Tarkenton, Minnesota, 1961-66, 72-75; N.Y. Giants, 1967-71.

Most passes completed, season—288, Sonny Jurgensen, Washington, 1967.

Most passes completed, game—37, George Blanda, Houston, 1964 (68 attempts).

Most consecutive passes completed—17, Bert Jones, Baltimore, 1974.

Most yards gained, lifetime—40,239, John Unitas, Baltimore, 1956-72; San Diego, 1973.

Most yards gained, season—4,007, Joe Namath, New York Jets, 1967.

Most yards gained, game—554, Norm Van Brocklin, Los Angeles, 1951.

Most touchdown passes, lifetime—291, Fran Tarkenton, Minnesota, 1961-66, 72-75; N.Y. Giants, 1967-71.

Most touchdown passes, season—36, George Blanda, Houston, 1961; Y. A. Tittle, New York Giants, 1963.

Most touchdown passes, game—7, Sid Luckman, Chicago Bears, 1943; Adrian Burk, Philadelphia, 1954; George Blanda, Houston, 1961; Y. A. Tittle, New York Giants, 1963; Joe Kapp, Minnesota, 1969.

All-Time Leading Scorers

	yrs	tds	pat	fg	pts
George Blanda	26	9	943	335	2,002
Lou Groza	17	1	641	234	1,349
Fred Cox	13	0	462	255	1,227
Jim Bakken	14	0	439	244	1,171
Jim Turner	12	0	391	252	1,147
Gino Cappelletti	11	42	350	176	1,130*
Bruce Gossett	11	0	374	219	1,031

*Includes four 2-point plays.

All-time Leading Rushers

	yrs	yds	attps
Jim Brown	9	12,312	2,369
Jim Taylor	10	8,597	1,941
Joe Perry	14	8,378	1,737
Leroy Kelly	10	7,274	1,727
O. J. Simpson	7	8,123	1,707
John Henry Johnson	13	6,803	1,571
Floyd Little	9	6,323	1,641
Don Perkins	8	6,217	1,500
Ken Willard	10	6,105	1,622
Larry Csonka	7	5,900	1,286

All-time Leading Passers

	comp	comp%	yds	tds	int%	rating
Sonny Jurgensen	2,433	57.1	32,224	255	4.4	82.8
Len Dawson	2,136	57.1	28,711	239	4.9	82.6
Fran Tarkenton	2,931	56.1	38,840	291	4.1	81.4
Bart Starr	1,808	57.4	24,718	152	4.4	80.3
John Unitas	2,830	54.6	40,239	290	4.9	78.2
Otto Graham	872	55.7	13,499	88	6.0	78.1
Frank Ryan	1,090	51.1	16,042	149	5.2	77.7
Norm Van Brocklin	1,553	53.6	23,611	173	6.1	75.3
Sid Luckman	904	51.8	14,686	137	7.6	75.0
Bob Griese	1,199	54.4	16,002	128	5.3	74.9

(Rating points, awarded in inverse order, on completed pass percentage, touchdowns, interception percentage and average gain.)

All-time Leading Receivers

	yrs	no.	yds
Charley Taylor	12	635	8,952
Don Maynard	15	633	11,834
Raymond Berry	13	631	9,275
Lionel Taylor	10	567	7,195
Lance Alworth	11	542	10,266
Bobby Mitchell	11	521	7,954
Billy Howton	12	503	8,459
Tommy McDonald	12	495	8,410
Fred Biletnikoff	11	493	7,692
Don Hutson	11	488	7,991

All-time Leading Touchdown Scorers

	yrs	rush	rec	ret	tds
Jim Brown	9	106	20	0	126
Lenny Moore	12	63	48	2	113
Don Hutson	11	3	99	3	105
Jim Taylor	10	83	10	0	93
Bobby Mitchell	11	18	65	8	91
Leroy Kelly	10	74	13	3	90
Charley Taylor	12	11	79	0	90

Most consecutive games, touchdown passes—47, John Unitas, Baltimore.

Most consecutive passes attempted, none intercepted—294, Bart Starr, Green Bay, 1964-65.

Longest pass completion—99 yards, Frank Filchock (to Andy Farkas), Washington, 1939; George Izo (to Bob Mitchell), Washington, 1963; Karl Sweetan (to Pat Studstill), Detroit, 1966; Sonny Jurgensen (to Gerry Allen), Washington, 1968, (all for touchdowns).

Professional Football Individual Records (Continued)

Most pass receptions, lifetime—635, Washington, 1964–75.

Most pass receptions, season—101, Charley Hennigan, Houston, 1964.

Most pass receptions, game—18, Tom Fears, Los Angeles, 1950.

Most consecutive games, pass receptions—105, Dan Abramowicz. New Orleans, 1967–73; San Francisco. 1973–74.

Most yards gained, pass receptions, lifetime—11,834, Don Maynard, New York Giants, 1958; New York Jets, 1960–72; St. Louis, 1973.

Most yards gained receptions, season—1,746, Charley Hennigan, Houston, 1961.

Most yards gained receptions, game—303, Jim Benton, Cleveland Rams, 1945.

Most touchdown pass receptions, lifetime—99, Don Hutson, Green Bay, 1935–45.

Most touchdown pass receptions, season—17, Don Hutson, Green Bay, 1942; Elroy Hirsch, Los Angeles, 1951; Bill Groman, Houston, 1961.

Most touchdown pass receptions, game—5, Bob Shaw, Chicago Cards, 1950.

Most consecutive games, touchdown pass receptions—11, Elroy Hirsch, Los Angeles, 1950–51; Buddy Dial, Pittsburgh, 1959–60.

Most pass interceptions, lifetime—79, Emlen Tunnell, New York Giants, 1948–58 (74); Green Bay, 1959–61 (5).

Most pass interceptions, season—14, Richard (Night Train) Lane, Los Angeles, 1952.

Most pass interceptions, game—4, by 14 players.

Longest pass interception return—102 yards, Bob Smith, Chicago Bears, 1949; Erich Barnes, New York Giants, 1961.

Kicking

Longest punt—98 yards, Steve O'Neal, New York Jets, 1969.

Highest average punting, lifetime—45.10 yards, Sammy Baugh, Washington, 1937–52.

Longest punt return—98 yards, Gil LeFebvre, Cincinnati Reds, 1933; Charlie West, Minnesota, 1968; Dennis Morgan, Dallas, 1974.

Longest kick-off return—106 yards, Al Carmichael, Green Bay, 1956; Noland Smith, Kansas City, 1967.

PRO FOOTBALL HALL OF FAME

(National Football Museum, Canton, Ohio)

Team named is one with which player is best identified; figures in parentheses indicate number of playing seasons.

Battles, Cliff, back, Redskins (6)	1932–37
Baugh, Sammy, quarterback, Redskins (16)	1937–52
Bednarik, Chuck, center-lineback, Eagles (14)	1949–62
Bell, Bert, N.F.L. founder, owner Eagles and Steelers, N.F.L. Commissioner (13)	1946–59
Berry, Raymond, end, Colts (13)	1955–67
Bidwell, Charles W., owner Chi. Cardinals	1933–47
Brown, Jim, fullback, Browns (9)	1957–65
Brown, Paul E., coach, Browns (1946–62), Bengals (1968—)	1946–19–
Brown, Roosevelt, tackle, Giants (13)	1953–65
Canadeo, Tony, back, Packers (11)	1941–52
Carr, Joe, president N.F.L. (18)	1921–39
Chamberlin, Guy, end, 4 teams (9)	1919–27
Christiansen, Jack, def. back, Lions (8)	1951–58
Clark, Earl (Dutch), Qback, Spartans, Lions (7)	1931–38
Connor, George, tackle, linebacker, Bears (8)	1948–55
Conzelman, Jimmy, Qback 5 teams (10), owner	1921–48
Donovan, Art, def. tackle, Colts (12)	1950–61
Driscoll, John (Paddy), Qback, Cards, Bears (11)	1919–29
Dudley, Bill, back, Steelers, Lions, Skins (9)	1942–53
Edwards, Albert (Turk), tackle, Redskins (9)	1932–40
Fears, Tom, end, Rams (9)	1948–56
Flaherty, Ray, end 3 teams; coach, Redskins, N.Y. Yankees ( )	1928–49
Ford, Len, end, def. end, Browns ( )	1948–57
Fortmann, Daniel J., guard, Bears (8)	1936–43
George, Bill, linebacker, Bears, Rams (15)	1952–65
Graham, Otto, quarterback, Browns (10)	1946–55
Grange, Harold (Red), back, Bears, Yankees (9)	1925–34
Groza, Lou, place-kicker, tackle, Browns (21)	1946–67
Guyon, Joe, back, 6 teams (8)	1919–27
Halas, George, N.F.L. founder, owner and coach Staleys and Bears, end (11)	1919–19–
Healey, Ed, tackle, Bears (8)	1920–27
Hein, Mel, center, Giants (15)	1931–45
Henry, Wilbur (Pete), tackle, Bulldogs (8)	1920–28
Herber, Arnie, Qback, Packers, Giants (13)	1930–45
Hewitt, Bill, end, Bears, Eagles (9)	1932–43
Hinkle, Clarke, fullback, Packers (10)	1932–41
Hirsch, Elroy (Crazy Legs), back, end, Rams (12)	1946–57
Hubbard, R. (Cal), tackle, Giants, Packers (9)	1927–36
Hunt, Lamar, Founder A.F.L., owner Texans, Chiefs	1959–19–
Hutson, Don, end, Packers (11)	1935–45
Kiesling, Walt, guard, 6 teams (13)	1926–38
Kinard, Frank (Bruiser), tackle, Dodgers (9)	1938–47
Lambeau, Earl (Curly), N.F.L. founder, coach, end, back,	

Packers (11)	1919–53
Lane, Richard (Night Train), def. back, Cards, Lions, Steelers (14)	1948–62
Lavelli, Dante, end, Browns (11)	1946–56
Layne, Bobby, Qback, Lions, Steelers (15)	1948–62
Lombardi, Vince, coach, Packers, Redskins	1959–70
Luckman, Sid, quarterback, Bears (12)	1939–50
Lyman, William (Link), tackle, Bulldogs (11)	1922–34
Mara, Tim, N.F.L. founder, owner Giants	1925–59
Marchetti, Gino, defensive end, Colts (14)	1952–66
Marshall, George P., N.F.L. founder, owner Redskins	1932–65
Matson, Ollie, back, Chi. Cards, Rams (14)	1952–66
McAfee, George, back, Bears (8)	1940–50
McElhenny, Hugh, back, 49ers (13)	1952–64
McNally, John (Blood), back, 7 teams (15)	1925–39
Michalske, August, guard, Yankees, Packers (11)	1926–37
Millner, Wayne, end, Redskins (7)	1936–45
Moore, Lenny, back, Colts (13)	1956–67
Motley, Marion, fullback, Browns (9)	1946–55
Nagurski, Bronko, fullback, Bears (9)	1930–37
Neale, Earle (Greasy), coach, Eagles	1941–50
Nevers, Ernie, fullback, Chi. Cards (5)	1926–31
Nomellini, Leo, defensive tackle, 49ers (14)	1950–63
Owen, Steve, tackle Giants (9), coach Giants	1931–53
Parker, Clarence (Ace) Qback, Dodgers (7)	1937–46
Parker, Jim, guard, tackle, Colts (11)	1957–67
Perry, Joe, fullback, 49ers (16)	1948–62
Pihos, Pete, end, Eagles (9)	1947–55
Ray, Hugh, Shorty, N.F.L. advisor	1938–52
Reeves, Dan, owner Rams	1941–71
Robustelli, Andy, def. end, Rams, Giants (14)	1951–64
Rooney, Art, N.F.L. founder, owner Steelers	1933–19–
Schmidt, Joe, linebacker, Lions (13)	1953–65
Stautner, Ernie, def. tackle, Steelers (14)	1950–63
Strong, Ken, back, Giants, (14)	1929–47
Stydahar, Joe, tackle, Bears (9)	1936–42
Taylor, Jim, fullback, Packers (10)	1958–67
Thorpe, Jim, back, 7 teams (12)	1919–28
Tittle, Y.A., Qback, Colts, 49ers, Giants (17)	1948–64
Trafton, George, center, Bears (13)	1920–32
Trippi, Charley, back, Chi. Cards (9)	1947–55
Tunnell, Emlen, def. back, Giants, Packers (14)	1948–61
Turner, Clyde (Bulldog), center, Bears (13)	1940–52
Van Brocklin, Norm, Qback, Rams, Eagles (12)	1949–57
Van Buren, Steve, back, Eagles (8)	1944–51
Waterfield, Bob, quarterback, Rams (8)	1945–52
Wojciechowicz, Alex, center, Lions, Eagles (13)	1938–50

GOLF

IT MAY BE that golf originated in Holland—historians believe it did—but certainly Scotland fostered the game and is famous for it. In fact, in 1457 the Scottish Parliament, disturbed because football and golf had lured young Scots from the more soldierly exercise of archery, passed an ordinance that "futeball and golf be utterly cryit doun and nocht usit." James I and Charles I of the royal line of Stuarts were golf enthusiasts, whereby the game came to be known as "the royal and ancient game of golf."

The golf balls used in the early games were leather-covered and stuffed with feathers. Clubs of all kinds were fashioned by hand to suit individual players. The great step in spreading the game came with the change from the feather ball to the gutta-percha ball about 1850, and in 1860 formal competition began with the establishment of an annual tournament for the British Open championship. There are records of "golf clubs" in the United

States as far back as colonial days but no proof of actual play before John Reid and some friends laid out six holes on the Reid lawn in Yonkers, N.Y., in 1888 and played there with the golf balls and clubs brought over from Scotland by Robert Lockhart. This group then formed the St. Andrews Golf Club of Yonkers, and golf was established in this country.

However, it remained a rather sedate and almost aristocratic pastime until a 20-year-old ex-caddy, Francis Ouimet of Boston, defeated two great British professionals, Harry Vardon and Ted Ray, in the United States Open championship at Brookline, Mass., in 1913. This feat put the game and Francis Ouimet on the front pages of the newspapers and stirred a wave of enthusiasm for the sport. The greatest feat so far in golf history was that of Robert Tyre Jones, Jr., of Atlanta, Ga., in winning the British Open, the British Amateur, the U.S. Open and the U.S. Amateur titles in one year, 1930.

UNITED STATES OPEN CHAMPIONS

Year	Winner	Score	Where played	Year	Winner	Score	Where played
1895	Horace Rawlins	173	Newport	1935	Sam Parks, Jr.	299	Oakmont
1896	James Foulis	152	Shinnecock Hills	1936	Tony Manero	282	Baltusrol
1897	Joe Lloyd	162	Chicago	1937	Ralph Guldahl	281	Oakland Hills
1898*	Fred Herd	328	Myopia	1938	Ralph Guldahl	284	Cherry Hills
1899	Willie Smith	315	Baltimore	1939	Byron Nelson (a)	284	Philadelphia
1900	Harry Vardon	313	Chicago	1940	Lawson Little (a)	287	Canterbury
1901	Willie Anderson (a)	331	Myopia	1941	Craig Wood	284	Colonial
1902	Laurie Auchterlonie	307	Garden City	1942–45	No tournaments‡		
1903	Willie Anderson (a)	307	Baltusrol	1946	Lloyd Mangrum (a)	284	Canterbury
1904	Willie Anderson	303	Glen View	1947	Lew Worsham (a)	282	St. Louis
1905	Willie Anderson	314	Myopia	1948	Ben Hogan	276	Riviera
1906	Alex Smith	295	Onwentsia	1949	Cary Middlecoff	286	Medinah
1907	Alex Ross	302	Philadelphia	1950	Ben Hogan (a)	287	Merion
1908	Fred McLeod (a)	322	Myopia	1951	Ben Hogan	287	Oakland Hills
1909	George Sargent	290	Englewood	1952	Julius Boros	281	Northwood
1910	Alex Smith (a)	298	Philadelphia	1953	Ben Hogan	283	Oakmont
1911	John McDermott (a)	307	Chicago	1954	Ed Furgol	284	Baltusrol
1912	John McDermott	294	Buffalo	1955	Jack Fleck (a)	287	Olympic
1913	Francis Ouimet (a,b)	304	Brookline	1956	Cary Middlecoff	281	Oak Hill
1914	Walter Hagen	290	Midlothian	1957	Dick Mayer (a)	298	Inverness
1915	Jerome D. Travers (b)	297	Baltusrol	1958	Tommy Bolt	283	Southern Hills
1916	Charles Evans, Jr.(b)	286	Minikahda	1959	Bill Casper, Jr.	282	Winged Foot
1917–18	No tournaments †			1960	Arnold Palmer	280	Cherry Hills
1919	Walter Hagen (a)	301	Brae Burn	1961	Gene Littler	281	Oakland Hills
1920	Edward Ray	295	Inverness	1962	Jack Nicklaus (a)	283	Oakmont
1921	Jim Barnes	289	Columbia	1963	Julius Boros (a)	293	Country Club
1922	Gene Sarazen	288	Skokie	1964	Ken Venturi	278	Congressional
1923	R. T. Jones, Jr.(a,b)	296	Inwood	1965	Gary Player (a)	282	Bellerive
1924	Cyril Walker	297	Oakland Hills	1966	Bill Casper (a)	278	Olympic
1925	Willie Macfarlane (a)	291	Worcester	1967	Jack Nicklaus	275	Baltusrol
1926	R. T. Jones, Jr.(b)	293	Scioto	1968	Lee Trevino	275	Oak Hill
1927	Tommy Armour (a)	301	Oakmont	1969	Orville Moody	281	Champions G. C.
1928	Johnny Farrell (a)	294	Olympia Fields	1970	Tony Jacklin	281	Hazeltine
1929	R. T. Jones, Jr.(a,b)	294	Winged Foot	1971	Lee Trevino (a)	280	Merion
1930	R. T. Jones, Jr.(b)	287	Interlachen	1972	Jack Nicklaus	290	Pebble Beach
1931	Billy Burke (a)	292	Inverness	1973	Johnny Miller	279	Oakmont
1932	Gene Sarazen	286	Fresh Meadow	1974	Hale Irwin	287	Winged Foot
1933	John Goodman (b)	287	North Shore	1975	Lou Graham (a)	287	Medinah
1934	Olin Dutra	293	Merion				

(a) Winner in playoff.   (b) Amateur.   * In 1898 competition was extended to 72 holes.   † In 1917, Jock Hutchison, with a 292, won an Open Patriotic Tournament for the benefit of the American Red Cross at Whitemarsh Valley Country Club.   ‡ In 1942, Ben Hogan, with a 271 won a Hale American National Open Tournament for the benefit of the Navy Relief Society and USO at Ridgemoor Country Club.

UNITED STATES AMATEUR CHAMPIONS

1895	Charles B. Macdonald	1919	S. D. Herron	1939	Marvin H. Ward
1896–97	H. J. Whigham	1920	Charles Evans, Jr.	1940	R. D. Chapman
1898	Findlay S. Douglas	1921	Jesse P. Guilford	1941	Marvin H. Ward
1899	H. M. Harriman	1922	Jess W. Sweetser	1946	Ted Bishop
1900–01	Walter J. Travis	1923	Max R. Marston	1947	Robert Riegel
1902	Louis N. James	1924–25	R. T. Jones Jr.	1948	Willie Turnesa
1903	Walter J. Travis	1926	George Von Elm	1949	Charles Coe
1904–05	H. Chandler Egan	1927–28	R. T. Jones Jr.	1950	Sam Urzetta
1906	Eben M. Byers	1929	H. R. Johnston	1951	Billy Maxwell
1907–08	Jerome D. Travers	1930	R. T. Jones, Jr.	1952	Jack Westland
1909	Robert A. Gardner	1931	Francis Ouimet	1953	Gene Littler
1910	W. C. Fownes, Jr.	1932	Ross Somerville	1954	Arnold Palmer
1911	Harold H. Hilton	1933	G. T. Dunlap, Jr.	1955–56	Harvie Ward
1912–13	Jerome D. Travers	1934–35	Lawson Little	1957	Hillman Robbins
1914	Francis Ouimet	1936	John W. Fischer	1958	Charles Coe
1915	Robert A. Gardner	1937	John Goodman	1959	Jack Nicklaus
1916	Charles Evans, Jr.	1938	Willie Turnesa	1960	Deane Beman

1961	Jack Nicklaus
1962	Labron Harris, Jr.
1963	Deane Beman
1964	Bill Campbell
1965*	Robert Murphy, Jr.
1966	Gary Cowan (a)
1967	Bob Dickson
1968	Bruce Fleisher
1969	Steven Melnyk
1970	Lanny Wadkins
1971	Gary Cowan
1972	Vinny Giles 3d
1973†	Craig Stadler
1974	Jerry Pate
1975	Fred Ridley

* Tourney switched to medal play through 1972; † Return to match play (a) winner in playoff.

UNITED STATES P. G. A. CHAMPIONS

1916	Jim Barnes	1936–37	Denny Shute
1919	Jim Barnes	1938	Paul Runyan
1920	Jock Hutchison	1939	Henry Picard
1921	Walter Hagen	1940	Byron Nelson
1922–23	Gene Sarazen	1941	Victor Ghezzi
1924–27	Walter Hagen	1942	Sam Snead
1928–29	Leo Diegel	1944	Bob Hamilton
1930	Tommy Armour	1945	Byron Nelson
1931	Tom Creavy	1946	Ben Hogan
1932	Olin Dutra	1947	Jim Ferrier
1933	Gene Sarazen	1948	Ben Hogan
1934	Paul Runyan	1949	Sam Snead
1935	Johnny Revolta	1950	Chandler Harper

1951	Sam Snead	1964	Bobby Nichols
1952	Jim Turnesa	1965	Dave Marr
1953	Walter Burkemo	1966	Al Geiberger
1954	Chick Harbert	1967	Don January (a)
1955	Doug Ford	1968	Julius Boros
1956	Jack Burke, Jr.	1969	Ray Floyd
1957	Lionel Hebert	1970	Dave Stockton
1958*	Dow Finsterwald	1971	Jack Nicklaus
1959	Bob Rosburg	1972	Gary Player
1960	Jay Hebert	1973	Jack Nicklaus
1961	Jerry Barber (a)	1974	Lee Trevino
1962	Gary Player	1975	Jack Nicklaus
1963	Jack Nicklaus		

* Match play prior to 1958. (a) Winner in playoff.

THE MASTERS TOURNAMENT WINNERS
Augusta National Golf Club, Augusta, Ga.

1934	Horton Smith	284	1949	Sam Snead	282	1962	Arnold Palmer (a)	280
1935	Gene Sarazen (a)	282	1950	Jimmy Demaret	283	1963	Jack Nicklaus	286
1936	Horton Smith	285	1951	Ben Hogan	280	1964	Arnold Palmer	276
1937	Byron Nelson	283	1952	Sam Snead	286	1965	Jack Nicklaus	271
1938	Henry Picard	285	1953	Ben Hogan	274	1966	Jack Nicklaus (a)	288
1939	Ralph Guldahl	279	1954	Sam Snead (a)	289	1967	Gay Brewer, Jr.	280
1940	Jimmy Demaret	280	1955	Cary Middlecoff	279	1968	Bob Goalby	277
1941	Craig Wood	280	1956	Jack Burke	289	1969	George Archer	281
1942	Byron Nelson (a)	280	1957	Doug Ford	283	1970	Billy Casper (a)	279
1943–45	No Tournaments		1958	Arnold Palmer	284	1971	Charles Coody	279
1946	Herman Keiser	282	1959	Art Wall, Jr.	284	1972	Jack Nicklaus	286
1947	Jimmy Demaret	281	1960	Arnold Palmer	282	1973	Tommy Aaron	283
1948	Claude Harmon	279	1961	Gary Player	280	1974	Gary Player	278
						1975	Jack Nicklaus	276

(a) Winner in playoff.

UNITED STATES WOMEN'S AMATEUR CHAMPIONS

1895	Mrs. C. S. Brown	1916	Alexa Stirling
1896–98	Beatrix Hoyt	1919–20	Alexa Stirling
1899	Ruth Underhill	1921	Marion Hollins
1900	Frances C. Griscom	1922	Glenna Collett
1901–02	Genevieve Hecker	1923	Edith Cummings
1903	Bessie Anthony	1924	Dorothy Campbell Hurd
1904	Georgiana Bishop	1925	Glenna Collett
1905	Pauline Mackay	1926	Helen Stetson
1906	Harriot S. Curtis	1927	Mrs. M. B. Horn
1907	Margaret Curtis	1928–30	Glenna Collett
1908	Kate Harley	1931	Helen Hicks
1909–10	Dorothy Campbell	1932–34	Virginia Van Wie
1911–12	Margaret Curtis	1935	Glenna Collett Vare
1913	Gladys Ravenscroft	1936	Pamela Barton
1914	Mrs. Arnold Jackson	1937	Mrs. J. A. Page, Jr.
1915	Mrs. C. H. Vanderbeck	1938	Patty Berg

1939–40	Betty Jameson	1960	JoAnne Gunderson
1941	Mrs. Frank Newell	1961	Anne Quast Decker
1946	Mrs. M. D. Zaharias	1962	JoAnne Gunderson
1947	Louise Suggs	1963	Anne Quast Welts
1948	Grace Lenczyk	1964	Barbara McIntire
1949	Mrs. D. G. Porter	1965	Jean Ashley
1950	Beverly Hanson	1966	JoAnne Gunderson
1951	Dorothy Kirby		Carner
1952	Mrs. Jacqueline Pung	1967	Lou Dill
1953	Mary Lena Faulk	1968	JoAnne G. Carner
1954	Barbara Romack	1969	Catherine Lacoste
1955	Patricia Lesser	1970	Martha Wilkinson
1956	Marlene Stewart	1971	Laura Baugh
1957	JoAnne Gunderson	1972	Mary Ann Budke
1958	Anne Quast	1973	Carol Semple
1959	Barbara McIntire	1974	Cynthia Hill
		1975	Beth Daniel

UNITED STATES WOMEN'S OPEN CHAMPIONS

1946	Patty Berg (match play)	—	1956	Mrs. Katherine Cornelius (a)	302	1966	Sandra Spuzich	297
1947	Betty Jameson	295	1957	Betsy Rawls	299	1967	Catherine LaCoste (b)	294
1948	Mrs. Mildred D. Zaharias	300	1958	Mickey Wright	290	1968	Susie Berning	289
1949	Louise Suggs	291	1959	Mickey Wright	287	1969	Donna Caponi	294
1950	Mrs. Mildred D. Zaharias	291	1960	Betsy Rawls	291	1970	Donna Caponi	287
1951	Betsy Rawls	293	1961	Mickey Wright	293	1971	JoAnne Carner	288
1952	Louise Suggs	284	1962	Murle Lindstrom	301	1972	Susie Berning	299
1953	Betsy Rawls (a)	302	1963	Mary Mills	289	1973	Susie Berning	290
1954	Mrs. Mildred D. Zaharias	291	1964	Mickey Wright(a)	290	1974	Sandra Haynie	295
1955	Fay Crocker	299	1965	Carol Mann	290	1975	Sandra Palmer	295

(a) Winner in playoff. (b) Amateur.

BRITISH OPEN CHAMPIONS

(First tournament, held in 1860, was won by Willie Park, Sr.)

Year	Winner	Score	Year	Winner	Score	Year	Winner	Score
1920	George Duncan	303	1936	A. H. Padgham	287	1959	Gary Player	284
1921	Jock Hutchison (a)	296	1937	Henry Cotton	290	1960	Kel Nagle	278
1922	Walter Hagen	300	1938	R. A. Whitcombe	295	1961	Arnold Palmer	284
1923	A. G. Havers	295	1939	R. Burton	290	1962	Arnold Palmer	276
1924	Walter Hagen	301	1946	Sam Snead	290	1963	Bob Charles (a)	277
1925	Jim Barnes	300	1947	Fred Daly	294	1964	Tony Lema	279
1926	R. T. Jones, Jr.	291	1948	Henry Cotton	283	1965	Peter Thomson	285
1927	R. T. Jones, Jr.	285	1949	Bobby Locke (a)	283	1966	Jack Nicklaus	282
1928	Walter Hagen	292	1950	Bobby Locke	279	1967	Roberto de Vicenzo	278
1929	Walter Hagen	292	1951	Max Faulkner	285	1968	Gary Player	289
1930	R. T. Jones, Jr.	291	1952	Bobby Locke	287	1969	Tony Jacklin	280
1931	Tommy Armour	296	1953	Ben Hogan	282	1970	Jack Nicklaus (a)	283
1932	Gene Sarazen	283	1954	Peter Thomson	283	1971	Lee Trevino	278
1933	Denny Shute (a)	292	1955	Peter Thomson	281	1972	Lee Trevino	278
1934	Henry Cotton	283	1956	Peter Thomson	286	1973	Tom Weiskopf	276
1935	A. Perry	283	1957	Bobby Locke	279	1974	Gary Player	282
			1958	Peter Thomson (a)	278	1975	Tom Watson (a)	279

(a) Winner in playoff.

BRITISH AMATEUR CHAMPIONS

(Since 1920)

1930	R. T. Jones, Jr.	1947	Willie Turnesa	1956	John Beharrell	1965	Michael Bonallack
1931	E. Martin Smith	1948	Frank Stranahan	1957	Reid Jack	1966	Bobby Cole
1932	J. De Forest	1949	Max McCready	1958	Joe Carr	1967	Bob Dickson
1933	Michael Scott	1950	Frank Stranahan	1959	Dean Beman	1968–70	Michael Bonallack
1934–35	Lawson Little	1951	Richard D. Chapman	1960	Joe Carr	1971	Steve Melnyk
1936	H. Thomson	1952	Harvie Ward	1961	Michael Bonallack	1972	Trevor Homer
1937	Robert Sweeny, Jr.	1953	Joe Carr	1962	Richard Davis	1973	Dick Siderowf
1938	C. R. Yates	1954	Doug Bachli	1963	Michael Lunt	1974	Trevor Homer
1939	Alex Kyle	1955	Lt. Joe Conrad	1964	Gordon Clark	1975	Vinny Giles
1946	James Bruen						

INTERNATIONAL TEAM MATCHES

WALKER CUP

Men (amateur)

1922	U.S. 8, Britain 4
1923	U.S. 6, Britain 5
1924	U.S. 9, Britain 3
1926	U.S. 6, Britain 5
1928	U.S. 11, Britain 1
1930	U.S. 10, Britain 2
1932	U.S. 8, Britain 1
1934	U.S. 9, Britain 2
1936	U.S. 9, Britain 0
1938	Britain 7, U.S. 4
1947	U.S. 8, Britain 4
1949	U.S. 10, Britain 2
1951	U.S. 6, Britain 3
1953	U.S. 9, Britain 3
1955	U.S. 10, Britain 2
1957	U.S. 8, Britain 3
1959	U.S. 9, Britain 3
1961	U.S. 11, Britain 1
1963	U.S. 12, Britain 8
1965	U.S. 11, Britain 11 (tie)
1967	U.S. 13, Britain 7

1969	U.S. 10, Britain 8
1971	Britain 13, U.S. 11
1973	U.S. 14, Britain 10
1975	U.S. 15½, Britain 8½

RYDER CUP

Men (professional)

1927	U.S. 9½, Britain 2½
1929	Britain 7, U.S. 5
1931	U.S. 9, Britain 3
1933	Britain 6½, U.S. 5½
1935	U.S. 9, Britain 3
1937	U.S. 8, Britain 4
1947	U.S. 11, Britain 1
1949	U.S. 7, Britain 5
1951	U.S. 9½, Britain 2½
1953	U.S. 6½, Britain 5½
1955	U.S. 8, Britain 4
1957	Britain 7, U.S. 4
1959	U.S. 8½, Britain 3½
1961	U.S. 14½, Britain 9½
1963	U.S. 23, Britain 9
1965	U.S. 19½, Britain 12½

1967	U.S. 23½, Britain 8½
1969	U.S. 16, Britain 16
1971	U.S. 18½, Britain 13½
1973	U.S. 19, Britain 11
1975	U.S. 21, Britain 11

CURTIS CUP

Women (amateur)

1932	U.S. 5½, Britain 3½
1934	U.S. 6½, Britain 2½
1936	U.S. 4½, Britain 4½
1938	U.S. 5½, Britain 3½
1948	U.S. 6½, Britain 2½
1950	U.S. 7½, Britain 1½
1952	Britain 5, U.S. 4
1954	U.S. 6, Britain 3
1956	Britain 5, U.S. 4
1958	Britain 4½, U.S. 4½
1960	U.S. 6½, Britain 2½
1962	U.S. 8, Britain 1
1964	U.S. 10½, Britain 7½
1966	U.S. 13, Britain 5
1968	U.S. 10½, Britain 7½
1970	U.S. 11½, Britain 6½

1972	U.S. 10, Britain 8
1974	U.S. 13, Britain 5

WORLD AMATEUR CHAMPIONSHIP

Men

1958	Australia* (918)
1960	U.S. (834)
1962	U.S. (854)
1964	Britain (895)
1966	Australia (877)
1968	U.S. (868)
1970	U.S. (857)
1972	U.S. (865)
1974	U.S. (888)

Women

1964	France (588)
1966	U.S. (580)
1968	U.S. (616)
1970	U.S. (598)
1972	U.S. (583)
1974	U.S. (620)

* Winner in playoff.

ICE HOCKEY

ICE HOCKEY, by birth and upbringing a Canadian game, is an offshoot of field hockey. Some historians state that the first ice hockey game was played in Montreal in December, 1879, between two teams composed almost exclusively of McGill University students, but others assert that Kingston, Ont., or Halifax, N. S., were scenes of earlier hockey games. In the Montreal game of 1879 there were fifteen players on a side and they used an assortment of crude sticks to keep the puck in motion. Early rules allowed nine men on a side but the number was reduced to seven in 1886 and finally reduced to six.

The first governing body of the sport was the Amateur Hockey Association of Canada, organized in 1887. In the winter of 1894–5 a group of college students from the United States visited Canada, saw hockey played, became enthused over the game and introduced it as a winter sport when they returned home. The first professional league was the International Hockey League that operated in northern Michigan in 1904–06.

Until 1910, professionals and amateurs were allowed to play together on "mixed teams," but this arrangement ended with the formation of the first "big league," the National Hockey Association, in eastern Canada in 1910. The Pacific Coast League, to provide professional hockey in the West, was organized in 1911 with Seattle (and later other American cities) included in the circuit. The National Hockey League replaced the National Hockey Association in 1917. Boston, in 1924, was the first American city to join that circuit. The league expanded to include western cities in 1967. The Stanley Cup was competed for by "mixed teams" from 1894 to 1910, thereafter by professionals. It was awarded to the winner of the N.H.L. playoffs from 1926–67, and now to the league champion. The World Hockey Association began play in October 1972 in opposition to the N.H.L.

STANLEY CUP WINNERS
Emblematic of World Professional Championship; N.H.L. Championship After 1967

1894	Montreal A. A. A.	1912–13	Quebec Bulldogs	1930–31	Montreal Canadiens	1950	Detroit Red Wings
1895	Montreal Victorias	1914	Toronto	1932	Toronto Maple Leafs	1951	Toronto Maple Leafs
1896	Winnipeg Victorias	1915	Vancouver Millionaires	1933	N. Y. Rangers	1952	Detroit Red Wings
1897–99	Montreal Victorias	1916	Montreal Canadiens	1934	Chicago Black Hawks	1953	Montreal Canadiens
1900	Montreal Shamrocks	1917	Seattle Metropolitans	1935	Montreal Maroons	1954–55	Detroit Red Wings
1901	Winnipeg Victorias	1918	Toronto Arenas	1936–37	Detroit Red Wings	1956–60	Montreal Canadiens
1902	Montreal A. A. A.	1919	No champion	1938	Chicago Black Hawks	1961	Chicago Black Hawks
1903–05	Ottawa Silver Seven	1920–21	Ottawa Senators	1939	Boston Bruins	1962–64	Toronto Maple Leafs
1906	Montreal Wanderers	1922	Toronto St. Patricks	1940	N. Y. Rangers	1965–66	Montreal Canadiens
1907	Kenora Thistles*	1923	Ottawa Senators	1941	Boston Bruins	1967	Toronto Maple Leafs
1907	Mont. Wanderers†	1924	Montreal Canadiens	1942	Toronto Maple Leafs	1968–69	Montreal Canadiens
1908	Montreal Wanderers	1925	Victoria Cougars	1943	Detroit Red Wings	1970	Boston Bruins
1909	Ottawa Senators	1926	Montreal Maroons	1944	Montreal Canadiens	1971	Montreal Canadiens
1910	Montreal Wanderers	1927	Ottawa Senators	1945	Toronto Maple Leafs	1972	Boston Bruins
1911	Ottawa Senators	1928	N. Y. Rangers	1946	Montreal Canadiens	1973	Montreal Canadiens
		1929	Boston Bruins	1947–49	Toronto Maple Leafs	1974–75	Philadelphia Flyers

* January. † March.

NATIONAL HOCKEY LEAGUE YEARLY LEADERS
MOST VALUABLE PLAYER (The Hart Trophy)

1924	Frank Nighbor, Ottawa	1949	Sid Abel, Detroit
1925	Billy Burch, Hamilton	1950	Chuck Rayner, New York Rangers
1926	Nels Stewart, Montreal Maroons	1951	Milt Schmidt, Boston
1927	Herb Gardiner, Montreal Canadiens	1952–53	Gordon Howe, Detroit
1928	Howie Morenz, Montreal Canadiens	1954	Al Rollins, Chicago
1929	Roy Worters, New York Americans	1955	Ted Kennedy, Toronto
1930	Nels Stewart, Montreal Maroons	1956	Jean Beliveau, Montreal Canadiens
1931–32	Howie Morenz, Montreal Canadiens	1957–58	Gordon Howe, Detroit
1933	Eddie Shore, Boston	1959	Andy Bathgate, New York Rangers
1934	Aurel Joliat, Montreal Canadiens	1960	Gordon Howe, Detroit
1935–36	Eddie Shore, Boston	1961	Bernie Geoffrion, Montreal Canadiens
1937	Babe Siebert, Montreal Canadiens	1962	Jacques Plante, Montreal Canadiens
1938	Eddie Shore, Boston	1963	Gordon Howe, Detroit
1939	Toe Blake, Montreal Canadiens	1964	Jean Beliveau, Montreal Canadiens
1940	Ebbie Goodfellow, Detroit	1965–66	Bobby Hull, Chicago
1941	Bill Cowley, Boston	1967–68	Stan Mikita, Chicago
1942	Tom Anderson, New York Americans	1969	Phil Esposito, Boston
1943	Bill Cowley, Boston	1970–72	Bobby Orr, Boston
1944	Babe Pratt, Toronto	1973	Bobby Clarke, Philadelphia
1945	Elmer Lach, Montreal Canadiens	1974	Phil Esposito, Boston
1946	Max Bentley, Chicago	1975	Bobby Clarke, Philadelphia
1947	Maurice Richard, Montreal Canadiens		
1948	Buddy O'Connor, New York Rangers		

OTHER N.H.L. TROPHY WINNERS

Calder Trophy
(Rookie)

1953	Lorne Worsley, New York
1954	Camille Henry, New York
1955	Ed Litzenberger, Chicago
1956	Glenn Hall, Detroit
1957	Larry Regan, Boston
1958	Frank Mahovlich, Toronto
1959	Ralph Backstrom, Montreal
1960	Billy Hay, Chicago
1961	Dave Keon, Toronto
1962	Bobby Rousseau, Montreal
1963	Kent Douglas, Toronto
1964	Jacques Laperriere, Montreal
1965	Roger Crozier, Detroit
1966	Brit Selby, Toronto
1967	Bobby Orr, Boston
1968	Derek Sanderson, Boston
1969	Danny Grant, Minnesota
1970	Tony Esposito, Chicago
1971	Gilbert Perreault, Buffalo
1972	Ken Dryden, Montreal
1973	Steve Vickers, New York Rangers
1974	Denis Potvin, N.Y. Islanders
1975	Eric Vail, Atlanta

N.H.L. CAREER SCORING LEADERS
(Listed in order of total points scored)

	Yrs	Games	G	A	Pts
Gordie Howe (1)	25	1,687	786	1,023	1,809
*John Bucyk (6)	21	1,438	531	777	1,308
*Stan Mikita (9)	17	1,178	483	814	1,297
Alex Delvecchio (10)	23	1,549	456	825	1,281
*Phil Esposito (3)	13	922	582	691	1,253
Norm Ullman (8)	20	1,410	490	739	1,229
Jean Beliveau (7)	18	1,125	507	712	1,219
Bobby Hull (2)	15	1,036	604	549	1,153
Frank Mahovlich (5)	17	1,181	533	570	1,103
Henri Richard (17)	20	1,256	358	688	1,046
Andy Bathgate (18)	16	1,069	349	624	973
Maurice Richard (4)	18	978	544	421	965
*Rod Gilbert (14)	14	969	377	560	937
*Jean Ratelle (15)	14	929	367	540	907
*Bobby Orr (20)	10	631	264	624	888
Dean Prentice (12)	22	1,378	391	469	860
Dave Keon (16)	15	1,062	365	493	858
Ted Lindsay (13)	17	1,068	379	472	851
Red Kelly (19)	20	1,316	281	542	823
Bernie Geoffrion (11)	16	883	393	429	822

* Still active in N.H.L. (Figures in parentheses indicate ranking in goals scored.)

VEZINA TROPHY
(Leading Goalkeepers)

1952–53	Terry Sawchuk, Detroit
1954	Harry Lumley, Toronto
1955	Terry Sawchuk, Detroit
1956–60	Jacques Plante, Montreal
1961	Johnny Bower, Toronto
1962	Jacques Plante, Montreal
1963	Glenn Hall, Chicago
1964	Charlie Hodge, Montreal
1965	Sawchuk–Bower, Toronto
1966	Lorne Worsley–Hodge, Montreal
1967	Hall–Denis DeJordy, Chicago
1968	Worsley–Rogatien Vachon, Montreal
1969	Hall–Plante, St. Louis
1970	Tony Esposito, Chicago
1971	Ed Giacomin–Gilles Villemure, New York
1972	Tony Esposito–Gary Smith, Chicago
1973	Ken Dryden, Montreal
1974	Bernie Parent, Philadelphia, and Tony Esposito, Chicago
1975	Bernie Parent, Philadelphia

N.H.L. CHAMPIONS
Prince of Wales Trophy

1939	Boston	1956	Montreal
1940	Boston	1957	Detroit
1941	Boston	1958–62	Montreal
1942	New York	1963	Toronto
1943	Detroit	1964	Montreal
1944–47	Montreal	1965	Detroit
1948	Toronto	1966	Montreal
1948–55	Detroit	1967	Chicago

Eastern Division

1968–69	Montreal	1972	Boston
1970	Chicago	1973	Montreal
1971	Boston	1974	Boston

CAMPBELL BOWL
Western Division

1968	Philadelphia	1971–73	Chicago
1969	St. Louis	1974	Philadelphia
1970	St. Louis		

Art Ross Trophy
(Leading scorer)

1951–54	Gordie Howe, Detroit
1955	Bernie Geoffrion, Montreal
1956	Jean Beliveau, Montreal
1957	Gordie Howe, Detroit
1958–59	Dickie Moore, Montreal
1960	Bobby Hull, Chicago
1961	Bernie Geoffrion, Montreal
1962	Bobby Hull, Chicago
1963	Gordie Howe, Detroit
1964–65	Stan Mikita, Chicago
1966	Bobby Hull, Chicago
1967–68	Stan Mikita, Chicago
1969	Phil Esposito, Boston
1970	Bobby Orr, Boston
1971–74	Phil Esposito, Boston
1975	Bobby Orr, Boston

James Norris Trophy
(Defenseman)

1954	Red Kelly, Detroit
1955–58	Doug Harvey, Montreal
1959	Tom Johnson, Montreal
1960–62	Doug Harvey, Montreal, New York (62)
1963–65	Pierre Pilote, Chicago
1966	Jacques Laperriere, Montreal
1967	Harry Howell, New York
1968–75	Bobby Orr, Boston

Lady Byng Trophy
(Sportsmanship)

1960	Don McKenney, Boston
1961	Red Kelly, Detroit
1962–63	Dave Keon, Toronto
1964	Ken Wharram, Chicago
1965	Bobby Hull, Chicago
1966	Alex Delvecchio, Detroit
1967–68	Stan Mikita, Chicago
1969	Alex Delvecchio, Detroit
1970	Phil Goyette, St. Louis
1971	John Bucyk, Boston
1972	Jean Ratelle, New York
1973	Gil Perreault, Buffalo
1974	John Buyck, Boston
1975	Marcel Dionne, Detroit

WORLD HOCKEY ASSOCIATION YEARLY LEADERS

Most Valuable Player
1973 Bobby Hull, Winnipeg
1974 Gordie Howe, Houston
1975 Bobby Hull, Winnipeg

Best Defenseman
1973 J.C. Tremblay, Quebec
1974 Pat Stapleton, Chi.
1975 J.C. Tremblay, Quebec

Rookie of Year
1973 Terry Caffery, N.Eng.
1974 Mark Howe, Houston
1975 Anders Hedberg, Minn.

Scoring Champion
1973 Andre Lacroix, Phila.
1974 Mike Walton, Minn.
1975 Andre Lacroix, S. Diego

Best Goaltender
1973 Gerry Cheevers, Cleve.
1974 Don McLeod, Houston
1975 Ron Grahame, Houston

Most Gentlemanly
1973 Ted Hampson, Minn.
1974 Ralph Backstrom, Chi.
1975 Mike Rogers, Edmon.

W.H.L. CAREER SCORING LEADERS
(Listed in order of total points scored)

	Yrs	Games	G	A	Pts
Andre Lacroix	4	314	151	332	483
Bobby Hull	4	296	234	229	463
Danny Lawson	4	314	188	178	366
Chris Bordeleau	4	298	133	216	349
Larry Lund	4	303	111	222	333
Ron Ward	4	274	146	177	323
Tom Webster	4	262	169	152	321
Wayne Carleton	4	286	131	180	311
Serge Bernier	3	220	125	185	310
Marc Tardif	3	232	161	146	307
J.C. Tremblay	4	292	51	252	303
Gordie Howe	3	223	97	204	301

GLOSSARY OF HOCKEY TERMS

A (worn on shirt)—Alternate captain of team; has right to discuss issues with referee, as spokesman for coach, when captain is off ice.

Back Check—Delaying or stopping opponent with puck in your own defensive zone.

Blue Line—One of two lines dividing each team's zone from center zone; point at which puck must precede offensive player into zone.

Board Check—Illegal knocking or riding of opponent into dash board.

Body Check—Blocking or hitting opponent with body; legal when opponent has puck or has just released it.

Center Ice—Area between two defensive zones, where puck is faced off to start game and after offside call.

Charging—Hard-checking of opponent after taking more than three strides toward him; subject to penalty.

Cross-Checking—Hitting of opponent with both hands on stick and no part of stick on ice; subject to penalty.

Defense Zone—Area around own goal, up to blue line.

Elbowing—Striking of opponent with elbow; subject to penalty.

Face-Off—Dropping of puck between two opponents to start play in center ice, or in face-off circles on each side and forward of each goal after certain stoppages of play.

Fighting—Use of fists; subject to major penalty.

Fore Check—Stopping or delaying of opponent with puck in his own zone.

Forwards—Three players on front line, two wings and center.

Freezing—Pinning the puck against boards with feet or stick to force face-off.

Goalie—Guardian of the goal.

Goal Crease—Area in front of goal cage, outlined by lines, which can be occupied only by goalie.

Hat Trick—Scoring of three goals in game by one player.

High-Sticking—Carrying of stick above shoulder level, sometimes for whacking opponent. It is always illegal and is subject to penalty.

Holding—Use of hands to delay opponent; subject to penalty.

Hooking—Holding or delaying opponent with blade of stick; subject to penalty.

Icing—Shooting of puck from behind red line, or length of ice, into opponent's zone; illegal and play is restarted in zone where puck was hit; not illegal if team is short-handed.

Interference—Impeding an opponent who does not have puck; subject to penalty.

Major Penalty—Five-minute penalty, usually assessed for fighting, or drawing blood in rough play that normally would be minor penalty.

Match Penalty—Banning of player from remainder of game usually for unkind words to an official.

Minor Penalty—Two-minute penalty; most frequent penalty.

Misconduct Penalty—10 minute penalty to player but team can use a substitute; usually assessed for arguing with official too heatedly. Game misconduct is same as match penalty.

Off-Side—Illegal procedure of player with puck or teammate preceding puck across opponent's blue line; calls for face-off.

Penalty-Killer—Player adept at defensive play, who is used when team is man short.

Penalty Shot—Shot awarded a player when checked illegally while going in alone on opposing goalie, he has only goalie to beat on penalty shot.

Power Play—Offensive maneuver in effort to score when opponent has man in penalty box; usually four forwards and good defenseman shooter are used.

Poke Check—Poking of puck away from opponent with stick.

Roughing—Scuffling or show of fists; subject to penalty.

Slashing—Swinging of stick at opponent; subject to penalty.

Spearing—Using butt-end of stick to jab opponent; subject to penalty.

Sweep Check—Swinging of stick, low along ice, to dislodge puck from stick or to intercept pass.

Stick-Handling—Moving of puck around the ice.

LAWN TENNIS

LAWN TENNIS is a comparatively modern modification of the ancient game of court tennis. Major Walter Clopton Wingfield thought that something like court tennis might be played outdoors on lawns and in December, 1873, at Nantclwyd, Wales, he introduced his new game under the name of *Sphairistike* at a lawn party. The game was a success and spread rapidly, but the name was a total failure and almost immediately disappeared when all the players and spectators began to refer to the new game as "lawn tennis." In the early part of 1874 a young lady named Mary Ewing Outerbridge returned from Bermuda to New York, bringing with her the implements and necessary equipment of the new game that she had obtained from a British Army supply store in Bermuda. Miss Outerbridge and friends played the first game of lawn tennis in the United States on the grounds of the Staten Island Cricket and Baseball Club in the spring of 1874.

For a few years the new game went along in haphazard fashion until about 1880 when standard measurements for the court and standard equipment within definite limits became the rule. In 1881 the United States Lawn Tennis Association was formed and conducted the first national championship at Newport, R. I. The international matches for the Davis Cup began with a series between the British and United States players on the courts of the Longwood Cricket Club, Chestnut Hill, Mass., in 1900, with the home players winning.

Professional tennis, which got its start in 1926 when the French star Suzanne Lenglen was paid $50,000 for a tour, received its greatest recognition in 1968. Staid old Wimbledon, the London home of what are considered the world championships, let the pros compete. This decision ended a long controversy over open tennis and changed the format of the competition. The United States championships at Forest Hills switched, too. Pro tours for men and women became worldwide in play that continued throughout the year.

DAVIS CUP CHALLENGE ROUND
No matches in 1901, 1910, 1915-18, and 1940-45.

Year	Result	Year	Result	Year	Result
1900	United States 5, British Isles 0	1927	France 3, United States 2	1955	Australia 5, United States 0
1902	United States 3, British Isles 2	1928	France 4, United States 1	1956	Australia 5, United States 0
1903	British Isles 4, United States 1	1929	France 3, United States 2	1957	Australia 3, United States 2
1904	British Isles 5, Belgium 0	1930	France 4, United States 1	1958	United States 3, Australia 2
1905	British Isles 5, United States 0	1931	France 3, Great Britain 2	1959	Australia 3, United States 2
1906	British Isles 5, United States 0	1932	France 3, United States 2	1960	Australia 4, Italy 1
1907	Australia 3, British Isles 2	1933	Great Britain 3, France 2	1961	Australia 5, Italy 0
1908	Australasia 3, United States 2	1934	Great Britain 4, United States 1	1962	Australia 5, Mexico 0
1909	Australasia 5, United States 0	1935	Great Britain 5, United States 0	1963	United States 3, Australia 2
1911	Australasia 5, United States 0	1936	Great Britain 3, Australia 2	1964	Australia 3, United States 2
1912	British Isles 3, Australasia 2	1937	United States 4, Great Britain 1	1965	Australia 4, Spain 1
1913	United States 3, British Isles 2	1938	United States 3, Australia 2	1966	Australia 4, India 1
1914	Australasia 3, United States 2	1939	Australia 3, United States 2	1967	Australia 4, Spain 1
1919	Australasia 4, British Isles 1	1946	United States 5, Australia 0	1968	United States 4, Australia 1
1920	United States 5, Australasia 0	1947	United States 4, Australia 1	1969	United States 5, Romania 0
1921	United States 5, Japan 0	1948	United States 5, Australia 0	1970	United States 5, West Germany 0
1922	United States 4, Australasia 1	1949	United States 4, Australia 1	1971	United States 3, Romania 2
1923	United States 4, Australasia 1	1950	Australia 4, United States 1	1972	United States 3, Romania 2
1924	United States 5, Australasia 0	1951	Australia 3, United States 2	1973	Australia 5, United States 0
1925	United States 5, France 0	1952	Australia 4, United States 1	1974	South Africa (Default by India)
1926	United States 4, France 1	1953	Australia 3, United States 2	1975	Sweden 3, Czechoslovakia 2
		1954	United States 3, Australia 2		

UNITED STATES CHAMPIONS
Open—At Forest Hills, N. Y.

Men's Singles	Women's Singles	Women's Doubles
1968—Arthur Ashe	1968—Virginia Wade	1968—Maria Bueno-Margaret Court
1969—Rod Laver	1969-70—Margaret Court	1969—Darlene Hard-Francoise Durr
1970—Ken Rosewall	1971-72—Billie Jean King	1970—Margaret Court-Judy Dalton
1971—Stan Smith	1973—Margaret Court	1971—Rosemary Casals-Judy Dalton
1972—Ilie Nastase	1974—Billie Jean King	1972—Francoise Durr-Betty Stove
1973—John Newcombe	1975—Chris Evert	1973—Margaret Court-Virginia Wade
1974—Jimmy Connors		1974—Billie Jean King-Rosemary Casals
1975—Manuel Orantes		1975—Margaret Court-Virginia Wade

Men's Doubles

1968—Stan Smith-Bob Lutz	1972—Cliff Drysdale-Roger Taylor
1969—Fred Stolle-Ken Rosewall	1973—John Newcombe-Owen Davidson
1970—Nikki Pilic-Fred Barthes	1974—Bob Lutz-Stan Smith
1971—John Newcombe-Roger Taylor	1975—Jimmy Connors-Ilie Nastase

UNITED STATES CHAMPIONS (Continued)
National Singles

1881–87	Richard D. Sears	1914	R. N. Williams II	1936	Fred J. Perry	1954	Vic Seixas
1888–89	Henry Slocum, Jr.	1915	William Johnston	1937–38	Don Budge	1955	Tony Trabert
1890–92	Oliver S. Campbell	1916	R. N. Williams II	1939	Robert L. Riggs	1956	Ken Rosewall
1893–94	Robert D. Wrenn	1917–18	R. Lindley Murray†	1940	Donald McNeill	1957	Mal Anderson
1895	Fred H. Hovey	1919	William Johnston	1941	Robert L. Riggs	1958	Ashley Cooper
1896–97	Robert D. Wrenn	1920–25	Bill Tilden	1942	Fred Schroeder	1959–60	Neale Fraser
1898–1900	Malcolm Whitman	1926–27	Jean Rene Lacoste	1943	Joseph Hunt	1961	Roy Emerson
1901–02	William A. Larned	1928	Henri Cochet	1944–45	Frank Parker	1962	Rod Laver
1903	Hugh L. Doherty	1929	Bill Tilden	1946–47	Jack Kramer	1963	Rafael Osuna
1904	Holcombe Ward	1930	John H. Doeg	1948–49	Richard Gonzales	1964	Roy Emerson
1905	Beals C. Wright	1931–32	Ellsworth Vines	1950	Arthur Larsen	1965	Manuel Santana
1906	William J. Clothier	1933–34	Fred J. Perry	1951–52	Frank Sedgman	1966	Fred Stolle
1907–11	William A. Larned	1935	Wilmer L. Allison	1953	Tony Trabert	1967	John Newcombe
1912–13	Maurice					1968	Arthur Ashe‡
	McLoughlin*					1969	Stan Smith‡

* Challenge round abandoned in 1912. † Patriotic tournament in 1917.

National Doubles

1920	William Johnston–C. J. Griffin	1939	A. K. Quist–J. E. Bromwich	1953	Mervyn Rose–Rex Hartwig
1921–22	Bill Tilden–Vincent Richards	1940–41	Jack Kramer–F. R. Schroeder	1954	Vic Seixas–Tony Trabert
1923	Bill Tilden–B. I. C. Norton	1942	Gardnar Mulloy–Bill Talbert	1955	Kosei Kamo–Atsushi Miyagi
1924	H. O. Kinsey–R. G. Kinsey	1943	Jack Kramer–F. A. Parker	1956	Lewis Hoad–Ken Rosewall
1925–26	Vincent Richards–R. N. Williams II	1944	Don McNeill–Robert Falkenburg	1957	Ashley Cooper–Neale Fraser
				1958	Ham Richardson–Alex Olmedo
1927	Bill Tilden–Frank Hunter	1945	Gardnar Mulloy–Bill Talbert	1959–60	Neale Fraser–Roy Emerson
1928	G. M. Lott, Jr.–V. F. Hennessey	1946	Gardnar Mulloy–Bill Talbert	1961	Chuck McKinley–Dennis Ralston
1929–30	G. M. Lott, Jr.–J. H. Doeg	1947	Jack Kramer–Fred Schroeder		
1931	W. L. Allison–John Van Ryn	1948	Gardnar Mulloy–Bill Talbert	1962	Rafael Osuna–Antonio Palafox
1932	E. H. Vines, Jr.–Keith Gledhill	1949	John Bromwich–William Sidwell	1963–64	Chuck McKinley–Dennis Ralston
1933–34	G. M. Lott, Jr.–L. R. Stoefen				
1935	W. L. Allison–John Van Ryn	1950	John Bromwich–Frank Sedgman	1965–66	Fred Stolle–Roy Emerson
1936	Don Budge–C. G. Mako			1967	John Newcombe–Tony Roche
1937	Baron G. von Cramm–H. Henkel	1951	Frank Sedgman–Ken McGregor	1968	Stan Smith–Bob Lutz‡
1938	Don Budge–C. G. Mako	1952	Vic Seixas–Mervyn Rose	1969	Richard Crealy–Allan Stone‡

Women's National Singles

1887	Ellen F. Hansell	1904	May Sutton	1926	Molla B. Mallory	1948–50	Margaret Osborne duPont
1888–89	Bertha Townsend	1905	Elisabeth H. Moore	1927–29	Helen N. Wills		
1890	Ellen C. Roosevelt	1906	Helen Homans	1930	Betty Nuthall	1951–53	Maureen Connolly
1891–92	Mabel E. Cahill	1907	Evelyn Sears	1931	Helen Wills Moody	1954–55	Doris Hart
1893	Aline M. Terry	1908	Maud Bargar-Wallach	1932–35	Helen Jacobs	1956	Shirley Fry
1894	Helen R. Helwig			1936	Alice Marble	1957–58	Althea Gibson
1895	Juliette P. Atkinson	1909–11	Hazel V. Hotchkiss	1937	Anita Lizana	1959	Maria Bueno
1896	Elisabeth H. Moore	1912–14	Mary K. Browne	1938–40	Alice Marble	1960–61	Darlene Hard
1897–98	Juliette P. Atkinson	1915–18	Molla Bjurstedt	1941	Sarah Palfrey Cooke	1962	Margaret Smith
1899	Marion Jones	1919	Hazel Hotchkiss Wightman			1963–64	Maria Bueno
1900	Myrtle McAteer			1942–44	Pauline Betz	1965	Margaret Smith
1901	Elisabeth H. Moore	1920–22	Molla Bjurstedt Mallory	1945	Sarah Palfrey Cooke	1966	Maria Bueno
1902	Marion Jones			1946	Pauline Betz	1967	Billie Jean King
1903	Elisabeth H. Moore	1923–25	Helen N. Wills	1947	A. Louise Brough	1968–69	Margaret Smith Court‡

Women's National Doubles

1924	Mrs. G. W. Wightman–Helen Wills	1934	Helen Jacobs–Sarah Palfrey	1958–59	Darlene Hard–Jeanne Arth
		1935	Helen Jacobs–Mrs. Sarah Palfrey Fabyan	1960	Darlene Hard–Maria Bueno
1925	Mary K. Browne–Helen Wills			1961	Darlene Hard–Lesley Turner
1926	Elizabeth Ryan–Eleanor Goss	1936	Marjorie G. Van Ryn–Carolin Babcock	1962	Darlene Hard–Maria Bueno
1927	Mrs. L. A. Godfree–Ermyntrude Harvey	1937–40	Sarah Palfrey Fabyan–Alice Marble	1963	Margaret Smith–Robyn Ebbern
1928	Hazel Hotchkiss Wightman–Helen Wills	1941	Sarah Palfrey Cooke–Margaret Osborne	1964	Karen Hantze Susman–Billie Jean Moffitt
1929	Mrs. Phoebe Watson–Mrs. L. R. C. Michell	1942–47	A. Louise Brough–Margaret Osborne	1965	Nancy Richey–Carole Caldwell Graebner
1930	Betty Nuthall–Sarah Palfrey	1948–50	A. Louise Brough–Margaret O. duPont	1966	Nancy Richey–Maria Bueno
1931	Betty Nuthall–Mrs. E. B. Wittingstall			1967	Billie Jean King–Rosemary Casals
		1951–54	Doris Hart–Shirley Fry		
1932	Helen Jacobs–Sarah Palfrey	1955–57	A. Louise Brough–Margaret O. duPont	1968	Margaret Court–Maria Bueno‡
1933	Betty Nuthall–Freda James			1969	Margaret Court–Virginia Wade‡

‡ With the inaugural of the Open Tournament in 1968, the United States Lawn Tennis Association held a national championship at Longwood, Chestnut Hill, Mass. which barred contract professionals in 1968 and 1969.

UNITED STATES TENNIS CHAMPIONS (Cont.)
Indoor Champions

Men's Singles		Women's Singles	
1964—Charles McKinley	1970—Ilie Nastase	1964—Mary Ann Eisel	1970—Mrs. Mary Ann Curtis
1965—Erik Lundquist	1971—Clark Graebner	1965—Nancy Richey	1971—Mrs. Billie Jean King
1966—Charles Pasarell	1972—Stan Smith	1966—Mrs. Billie Jean King	1972—Andrea Voikos
1967—Charles Pasarell	1973—Jimmy Connors	1967—Mrs. Billie Jean King	1973—Evonne Goolagong
1968—Cliff Richey	1974—Jimmy Connors	1968—Mrs. Billie Jean King	1974—Mrs. Billie Jean King
1969—Stan Smith	1975—Jimmy Connors	1969—Mary Ann Eisel	1975—Martina Navratilova

Men's Doubles	Women's Doubles
1964—Manuel Santana-Jose Arilla	1964—Mary Ann Eisel-Kay Hubbell
1965—Charles McKinley-Dennis Ralston	1965—Mrs. Carol Aucamp-Mary Ann Eisel
1966—Bob Lutz-Stan Smith	1966—Rosemary Casals-Mrs. Billie King
1967—Arthur Ashe-Charles Pasarell	1967—Mrs. Carol Aucamp-Mary Ann Eisel
1968—Thomas Koch-Tom Okker	1968—Rosemary Casals-Mrs. Billie King
1969—Stan Smith-Bob Lutz	1969—Mary Ann Eisel-Valerie Ziegenfuss
1970—Arthur Ashe-Stan Smith	1970—Peaches Bartkowicz-Nancy Richey
1971—Manuel Orantes-Juan Gisbert	1971—Mrs. Billie Jean King-Rosemary Casals
1972—Manuel Orantes-Andres Gimeno	1972—Andrea Voikos-Darlene Rose
1973—Juan Gisbert-Jurgen Fassbender	1973—Olga Morozova-Marina Kroshina
1974—Jimmy Connors-Frew McMillan	1974—Not played
	1975—Billie Jean King-Rosemary Casals

BRITISH (WIMBLEDON) CHAMPIONS
(Amateur from inception in 1877 through 1967)

Singles

1908-09	Arthur Gore	1928	Rene Lacoste	1948	R. Falkenburg	1960	Neale Fraser
1910-13	A. F. Wilding	1929	Jean Cochet	1949	Fred Schroeder	1961-62	Rod Laver
1914	N. E. Brookes	1930	Bill Tilden	1950	Budge Patty	1963	Chuck McKinley
1919	G. L. Patterson	1931	S. B. Wood	1951	Richard Savitt	1964-65	Roy Emerson
1920-21	Bill Tilden	1932	Ellsworth Vines	1952	Frank Sedgman	1966	Manuel Santana
1922	G. L. Patterson	1933	J. H. Crawford	1953	Vic Seixas	1967	John Newcombe
1923	William Johnston	1934-36	Fred Perry	1954	Jaroslav Drobny	1968-69	Rod Laver
1924	Jean Borotra	1937-38	Don Budge	1955	Tony Trabert	1970-71	John Newcombe
1925	Rene Lacoste	1939	Robert L. Riggs	1956-57	Lewis Hoad	1972	Stan Smith
1926	Jean Borotra	1946	Yvon Petra	1958	Ashley Cooper	1973	Jan Kodes
1927	Henri Cochet	1947	Jack Kramer	1959	Alex Olmedo	1974	Jimmy Connors
						1975	Arthur Ashe

Doubles

1953	K. Rosewall-L. Hoad	1960	Dennis Ralston-Rafael Osuna	1966	John Newcombe-Ken Fletcher
1954	R. Hartwig-M. Rose	1961	Roy Emerson-Neale Fraser	1967	Bob Hewitt-Frew McMillan
1955	R. Hartwig-L. Hoad	1962	Fred Stolle-Bob Hewitt	1968-70	John Newcombe-Tony Roche
1956	L. Hoad-K. Rosewall	1963	Rafael Osuna-Antonio Palafox	1971	Rod Laver-Roy Emerson
1957	Gardner Mulloy-Budge Patty	1964	Fred Stolle-Bob Hewitt	1972	Bob Hewitt-Frew McMillan
1958	Sven Davidson-Ulf Schmidt	1965	John Newcombe-Anthony	1973	Jimmy Connors-Ilie Nastase
1959	Roy Emerson-Neale Fraser		Roche	1974	John Newcombe-Tony Roche
				1975	Vitas Gerulaitis-Sandy Mayer

Women's Singles

1919-23	Mlle. Lenglen	1935	Helen Wills Moody	1952-54	Maureen Connolly	1965	Margaret Smith
1924	Kathleen McKane	1936	Helen Jacobs	1955	A. Louise Brough	1966-67	Billie Jean King
1925	Mlle. Lenglen	1937	D. E. Round	1956	Shirley Fry	1968	Billie Jean King
1926	Mrs. Godfree	1938	Helen Wills Moody	1957-58	Althea Gibson	1969	Mrs. Ann Jones
1927-29	Helen Wills	1939	Alice Marble	1959-60	Maria Bueno	1970	Mrs. Margaret
1930	Helen Wills Moody	1946	Pauline M. Betz	1961	Angela Mortimer		Court
1931	Frl. C. Aussen	1947	Margaret Osborne	1962	Karen Susman	1971	Evonne Goolagong
1932-33	Helen Wills Moody	1948-50	A. Louise Brough	1963	Margaret Smith	1972-73	Billie Jean King
1934	D. E. Round	1951	Doris Hart	1964	Maria Bueno	1974	Chris Evert
						1975	Billie Jean King

Women's Doubles

1956	Althea Gibson-Angela Buxton		Jean Moffitt	1970-71	Billie Jean King-Rosemary
1957	Althea Gibson-Darlene Hard	1963	Darlene Hard-Maria Bueno		Casals
1958	Althea Gibson-Maria Bueno	1964	Margaret Smith-Les Turnerley	1972	Billie Jean King-Betty Stowe
1959	Darlene Hard-Jeanne Arth	1965	Billie Jean Moffitt-Maria Bueno	1973	Billie Jean King-Rosemary
1960	Darlene Hard-Maria Bueno	1966	Nancy Richey-Maria Bueno		Casals
1961	Karen Hantze-Billie Jean	1967-68	Billie Jean King-Rosemary	1974	Evonne Goolagong-Peggy Michel
	Moffitt		Casals	1975	Ann Kiyomura-Kazuko Sawamatsu
1962	Karen Hantze Susman-Billie	1969	Margaret Court-Judy Tegart		

1975 PAN-AMERICAN GAMES CHAMPIONS

(Mexico City, Mexico, October 12-26, 1975)

Track and Field

100 m—Silvio Leonard, Cuba	.0:10.15
200 m—James Gilkes, Guyana	.0:20.43
400 m—Ronnie Ray, Durham, N.C.	.0:44.45
800 m—Luis Medina, Cuba	.1:47.98
1,500 m—Tony Waldrop, Columbus, N.C.	.3:45.09
5,000 m—Domingo Tibaduiza, Colombia	14:02
10,000 m—Luis Hernandez, Mexico	29:19.28
110-m hurdles—Alejandro Casanas, Cuba	.0:13.44
400-m hurdles—Jim King, San Diego, Calif.	0:49.8
3,000-m steeplechase—Mike Manley, Eugene, Ore.	.9:04.29
20,000-m walk—Daniel Bautista, Mexico	1:33:5.87
Marathon—Rigoberto Mendoza, Cuba	2:25:2.81
400-m relay—United States (Clancy Edwards, Larry Brown, Donald Merrick, Bill Collins)	.0:38.31
1,600-m relay—United States (Herman Frazier, Robert Taylor, Maurice Peoples, Ronnie Ray)	.3:00.76
High jump—Tom Woods, Corvallis, Ore.	7 ft 4⅝ in.
Triple Jump—Joao de Oliveira, Brazil	58 ft 8¼ in. W
Long jump—Joao de Oliveira, Brazil	26 ft 10½ in.
Pole vault—Earl Bell, Jonesboro, Ark.	17 ft 8½ in.
Hammer—Larry Hart, Long Beach, Calif.	218 ft 4 in.
Discus—John Powell, Cupertino, Calif.	204 ft 7 in.
Shotput—Bruce Pirnie, Canada	63 ft 3 in.
Javelin—Sam Colson, Clemson, S.C.	275 ft
Decathlon—Bruce Jenner, San Jose, Calif.	8,045 pts

W—World record.

DISTRIBUTION OF MEDALS

	Gold	Silver	Bronze	Total
United States	118	85	45.	248
Cuba	56	45	32	133
Canada	19	34	38	91
Mexico	8	15	38	61
Brazil	7	14	22	43
Argentina	3	5	7	15
Venezuela	0	0	1	12
Colombia	2	4	4	10
Puerto Rico	0	2	8	10
Dominican Republic	0	1	7	8
Panama	0	2	3	5
Jamaica	0	1	3	4
Ecuador	1	1	1	3
Guyana	1	1	0	2
Peru	1	1	0	2
Bahamas	0	1	1	2
Chile	0	0	2	2
Uruguay	0	0	2	2
Trinidad-Tobago	0	1	0	1
Netherlands Antilles	0	1	0	1
Guatemala	0	0	1	1
Barbados	0	0	1	1
El Salvador	0	0	1	1
Nicaragua	0	0	1	1

WOMEN

100 m—Pamela Jiles, New Orleans	.0:11.38
200 m—Chandra Cheeseborough, Jacksonville, Fla.	.0:22.77
400 m—Joyce Yakubowich, Victoria, B.C.	.0:51.62
800 m—Kathy Weston, Reno, Nev.	.2:04.93
1,500 m—Jan Merrill, Waterford, Conn.	.4:18.32
100-m hurdles—Edith Noeding, Peru	.0:13.56
400-m relay—United States (Martha Watson, Brenda Morehead, Chandra Cheeseborough, Pamela Jiles)	0:42.9
1,600-m relay—Canada (Margaret MacGowan, Joanne McTaggart, Rachelle Campbell, Joyce Yakubowich)	.3:30.36
High jump—Joni Huntley, Sheridan, Ore.	6 ft 2½ in.
Long jump—Ana Alexander, Cuba	21 ft 9 in.
Shotput—Maria Sarria, Cuba	59 ft 1¾ in.
Discus—Carmen Romero, Cuba	197 ft 4 in.
Javelin—Sherry Calvert, Los Alamitos, Calif.	179 ft 5 in.
Pentathlon—Diane Jones, Saskatoon, Sask.	4,673 pts

Swimming and Diving

100-m freestyle—Richard Abbott, Cerrito, Calif.	.0:51.96
200-m freestyle—Jorge Delgado, Ecuador	1:55.45
400-m freestyle—Doug Northway, Tucson, Ariz.	4:00.51
1,500-m freestyle—Bobby Hackett, Yonkers, N.Y.	15:53.10
100-m backstroke—Peter Rocca, Orinda, Calif.	.0:58.31
200-m backstroke—Dan Harrigan, Mishawaka, Ind.	.2:06.69
100-m breaststroke—Rick Colella, Seattle	1:06.28
200-m breaststroke—Rick Colella	2:26
100-m butterfly—Michael Currington, Birmingham, Ala.	.0:56.09
200-m butterfly—Greg Jagenburg, West Chester, Pa.	.2:03.48
100-m ind. medley—Steve Furniss, Santa Ana, Calif.	2:09.77
400-m ind. medley—Steve Furniss	4:40.38
400-m freestyle relay—United States (Jack Babashoff, Art Ruble, Michael Grattan, Richard Abbott)	3:27.67
400-m medley relay—United States (Peter Rocca, Rick Colella, Michael Currington, Jack Babashoff)	.3:53.81
800-m freestyle relay—United States (Rick DeMont, Rex Favero, Brad Horner, Michael Currington)	.7:50.96
Springboard dive—Tim Moore, Cincinnati	579.75 pts
Platform dive—Carlos Giron, Mexico	532.95 pts

WOMEN

100-m freestyle—Kim Peyton, Portland, Ore.	.0:58.24
200-m freestyle—Kim Peyton	.2:04.57
400-m freestyle—Kathy Heddy, Summit, N.J.	4:23
800-m freestyle—Wendy Weinberg, Baltimore	.9:05.47
100-m backstroke—Lynn Chenard, Quebec	.1:06.59
200-m backstroke—Donna Wennerstrom, Northridge, Calif.	.2:19.93
100-m breaststroke—Lauri Siering, Modesto, Calif.	.1:15.17
200-m breaststroke—Lauri Siering	.2:42.35
100-m butterfly—Camille Wright, New Albany, Ind.	.1:02.71
200-m butterfly—Camille Wright	.2:18.57
200-m ind. medley—Kathy Heddy, Summit, N.J.	.2:22.22
400-m ind. medley—Kathy Heddy	.5:06.05
400-m freestyle relay—United States (Kathy Heddy, Bonnie Brown, Lisa Sterkel, Kim Peyton)	3:53.31
400-m medley relay—United States (Rosemary Boone, Marcia Morey, Camille Wright, Kim Peyton)	.4:22.34
Springboard dive—Jennifer Chandler, Lincoln, Ala.	427.62 pts
Platform dive—Janet Nutter, Winnipeg, Alberta	365.01 pts

Boxing

Light Flyweight—Jorge Hernandez, Cuba
Flyweight—Ramon Duvalon, Cuba
Bantamweight—Orlando Martinez, Cuba
Featherweight—David Armstrong, Puyallup, Wash.
Lightweight—Chris Clarke, Canada
Light Welterweight—Ray Leonard, Palmer Park, Md.
Welterweight—Clinton Jackson, Nashville, Tenn.
Light Middleweight—Rolando Garbey, Cuba
Middleweight—Alejandro Montoya, Cuba
Light Heavyweight—Orestes Pedrozo, Cuba
Heavyweight—Teofilo Stevenson, Cuba

Cycling

Sprint—Steven Woznick, Ridgefield Park, N.J.	
Road Race (110 miles)—Aldo Arencibia, Cuba	4:13:52.76
Pursuit—Balbino Jarmillo, Colombia	4:49.63
Time trial—Jocelyn Lovell, Canada	1:05.30
Team time trial—Mexico	2:09:28.08
Team pursuit—United States (Nelson Saldana, Paul Therrio, Roger Young, Paul Deem)	4:29.08

(Pan American Games Results, Continued)

Equestrian Events

Dressage—Christolot Boyden, Canada
Dressage, team—United States (John Winnett, Dorothy Morkis, Hilda Gurney)
3–Day—Tad Coffin, Strafford, Vt.
3-day, team—United States (Coffin, Beth Perkins, Bruce Davidson)
Jumping—Fernando Senderos, Mexico
Jumping, team—United States (Buddy Brown, Michael Matz, Dennis Murphy, Joe Fargis)

Fencing

Foil—Martin Lang, New York: team; Cuba
Epee—Mark Vergara, Argentina: team; United States (Scott Bozek, Brooke Makler, Paul Pesthy, William Reith)
Sabre—Manuel Ortiz, Cuba: team; Cuba
Women's foil—Margarita Rodriguez, Cuba: team; Cuba

Gymnastics

All-around—Jorge Cuervo, Cuba
Team—United States
Floor exercise—Peter Kormann, New Haven, Conn.
Parallel bars—R. Leon, Cuba
Pommel horse—Leon
Horizontal bar—Cuervo
Rings—Cuervo

WOMEN

All-around—Ann Carr, Philadelphia
Team—United States
Uneven parallel bars—Ann Carr-Roxanne Pierce, Kensington, Ind.
Vault—Colleen Casey, St. Paul
Floor exercise—Ann Carr
Balance Beam—Ann Carr

Judo

Featherweight—Brad Farrow, Canada
Lightweight—Wayne Erdman, Canada
Middleweight—Rainer Fisher, Canada
Light heavyweight—Campos, Brazil
Heavyweight—Allan Coage, East Orange, N.J.
Open—Jose Ibanez, Cuba

Rowing

Singles—Ricardo Ibarra, Argentina
Pairs with coxswain—United States (John Mathews, Darrell Vreugdenhil, Ken Dreyfuss, coxswain)
Pairs without coxswain—Brazil
Doubles—Brazil
Quadruples—Cuba
Fours without coxswain—United States
Fours with coxswain—Canada
Eights—United States

Shooting

Pistol, rapid fire—Melvin Makin, Salem, Ore.: team; United States
Pistol, center fire—Marvin Black, Columbus, Ga.: team; United States
Pistol, free—Hershel Anderson, Columbus, Ga.: team; United States
Air pistol—Hershel Anderson: team; Cuba
English match—David Ross, Houston, Tex.: team; United States
Rifle, small bore—Margaret Murdock, Topeka, Kan.: team; United States
Air rifle—Olecano Vazquez, Mexico: team; United States
Trapshooting—Dan Carlisle, Columbus, Ga.: team; United States
Clay pigeon—Athos Pisoni, Brazil: team; Cuba

TEAM SPORTS

Baseball—1, Cuba; 2, United States; 3, Venezuela
Basketball, men—1, United States; 2, Brazil; 3, Puerto Rico
Basketball, women—1, United States; 2, Mexico; 3, Cuba
Field hockey—1, Argentina; 2, Canada; 3, Mexico
Soccer—1, tie between Brazil and Mexico; 3, Argentina
Volleyball, men—1, Cuba; 2, Brazil; 3, Mexico
Volleyball, women—1, Cuba; 2, Peru; 3, Mexico
Water polo—1, Mexico; 2, United States; 3, Cuba

Synchronized Swimming

Singles—Gail Johnson Buzonas, Santa Clara, Calif.
Duet—Amanda Norrish-Robin Curren, San Jose, Calif.
Team—United States

Tennis

Singles—Butch Walts, Atherton, Calif.
Women's singles—Lele Forood, Fort Lauderdale, Fla.
Doubles—Walts-Bruce Manson, Los Angeles
Women's doubles—Sandy Stap, Deerfield, Ill.-Stefanie Tolleson, Phoenix, Ariz.
Mixed doubles—Lele Forood-Hank Pfister, Bakersfield, Calif.

Weight Lifting

Flyweight—F. Casameyor, Cuba	496
Bantamweight—Carlos Lastre, Cuba	524
Featherweight—R. Chang, Cuba	562
Lightweight—Roberto Urrutia, Canada	662
Middleweight—Ignacio Guanache, Cuba	667.5
Light heavyweight—Lee James, Clarksville, Tenn.	672
Middle heavyweight—Philip Grippaldi, Belleville, N.J.	755
Heavyweight—Russ Prior, Canada	805
Super heavyweight—Gerardo Fernandez, Cuba	838

Wrestling, Freestyle

106 lbs—J. Frias, Mexico
115 lbs—E. Abreu, Cuba
126 lbs—J. Ramus, Cuba
137 lbs—E. Beiler, Canada
150 lbs—Lt. Lloyd Keaser, U.S. Marines
163 lbs—P. Lesequer, Cuba
181 lbs—Gregory Hicks, Santa Ana, Calif.
198 lbs—Ben Peterson, Comstock, Wis.
229 lbs—Russ Hellickson, Oregon, Wis.
Over 229 lbs—Mike McCready, Dubuque, Iowa

Wrestling, Greco-Roman

106 lbs—S. Valdez, Cuba
115 lbs—Bruce Thompson, Prior Lake, Minn.
126 lbs—Daniel Mello, Bakersfield, Calif.
137 lbs—H. Stopp, Laval, Quebec
150 lbs—Patrick Marcy, Minneapolis
163 lbs—I. Barban, Cuba
181 lbs—Dan Chandler, Minneapolis
198 lbs—Willie Williams, Harvey, Ill.
220 lbs—Brad Rheingans, Appleton, Minn.
Over 220 lbs—Bill Van Worth, Bakersfield, Calif.

Yachting

Finn Class—Bill Allen, Welworth, Minn.
Snipe Class—Jeff Lenhart, San Diego, and David Ullman
Flying Dutchman Class—Brazil
Lightning Class—Bruce Goldsmith, Chicago

RODEO

Rodeo Cowboys' Association, All-Around Cowboy

1953	Bill Linderman	1960	Harry Tompkins	1963-65	Dean Oliver	1973	Larry Mahan
1954	Buck Rutherford	1961	Benny Reynolds	1966-70	Larry Mahan	1974	Tom Ferguson
1955	Casey Tibbs	1962	Tom Nesmith	1971-72	Phil Lyne	1975	Leo Camarillo and
1956-59	Jim Shoulders						Tom Ferguson

SWIMMING
WORLD RECORDS
Approved July 1975 by International Amateur Swimming Federation (F.I.N.A.)
(F.I.N.A. discontinued acceptance of records in yards in 1968)

FREESTYLE

Distance	Record	Holder	Country	Where Made	Date
100 Meters	0:49.99	Jim Montgomery	United States	Montreal	July 25, 1976
*100 Meters	0:49.44	Jonty Skinner	South Africa	Philadelphia	Aug. 14, 1976
200 Meters	1:50.29	Bruce Furniss	United States	Montreal	July 19, 1976
400 Meters	3:51.93	Brian Goodell	United States	Montreal	July 22, 1976
800 Meters	8:01.54	Bobby Hackett	United States	Long Beach, Calif.	June 21, 1976
1,500 Meters	15:02.40	Brian Goodell	United States	Montreal	July 20, 1976

BACKSTROKE

100 Meters	0:55.49	John Naber	United States	Montreal	July 19, 1976
200 Meters	1:59.19	John Naber	United States	Montreal	July 24, 1976

BREASTSTROKE

100 Meters	1:03.11	John Hencken	United States	Montreal	July 20, 1976
200 Meters	2:15.11	David Wilkie	Britain	Montreal	July 24, 1976

BUTTERFLY

100 Meters	0:54.27	Mark Spitz	United States	Munich	Aug. 31, 1972
200 Meters	1:59.23	Mike Bruner	United States	Montreal	July 18, 1976

INDIVIDUAL MEDLEY

200 Meters	2:06.08	Bruce Furniss	United States	Kansas City	Aug. 22, 1975
400 Meters	4:23.68	Rod Strachan	United States	Montreal	July 25, 1976

FREESTYLE RELAYS

400 Meters	3:24.85	National Team	United States	Cali, Colombia	July 23, 1975

(Bruce Furniss, Jim Montgomery, Andy Coan, John Murphy)

800 Meters	7:23.22	National Team	United States	Montreal	July 21, 1976

(Mike Bruner, Bruce Furniss, John Naber, Jim Montgomery)

MEDLEY RELAY
(Backstroke, Breaststroke, Butterfly, Freestyle)

400 Meters	3:42.22	National Team	United States	Montreal	July 22, 1976

(John Naber, John Hencken, Matt Vogel, Jim Montgomery)

WOMEN
FREESTYLE

100 Meters	0:55.65	Kornelia Ender	E. Germany	Montreal	July 19, 1976
200 Meters	1:59.26	Kornelia Ender	E. Germany	Montreal	July 22, 1976
400 Meters	4:09.89	Petra Thumer	E. Germany	Montreal	July 20, 1976
800 Meters	8:37.14	Petra Thumer	E. Germany	Montreal	July 25, 1976
1,500 Meters	16:33.94	Jenny Turrall	Australia	Concord, Calif.	Aug. 25, 1974

BACKSTROKE

100 Meters	1:01.51	Ulrike Richter	E. Germany	East Berlin	June 5, 1976
200 Meters	2:12.47	Birgit Treiber	E. Germany	East Berlin	June 4, 1976

BREASTSTROKE

100 Meters	1:10.86	Hannelore Anke	E. Germany	Montreal	July 22, 1976
200 Meters	2:33.35	Marina Koshevaia	U.S.S.R.	Montreal	July 21, 1976

BUTTERFLY

100 Meters	1:00.13	Kornelia Ender	E. Germany	Montreal	July 22, 1976
200 Meters	2:11.22	Rosemarie Gabriel	E. Germany	East Berlin	June 5, 1976

INDIVIDUAL MEDLEY

200 Meters	2:17.64	Kornelia Ender	E. Germany	East Berlin	June 5, 1976
400 Meters	4:42.72	Ulrike Tauber	E. Germany	Montreal	July 24, 1976

FREESTYLE RELAY

400 Meters	3:44.82	National Team	United States	Montreal	July 25, 1976

(Kim Peyton, Wendy Boglioli, Jill Sterkel, Shirley Babashoff)

MEDLEY RELAY

400 Meters	4:07.95	National Team	E. Germany	Montreal	July 18, 1976

(Ulrike Richter, Hannelore Anke, Andrea Pollack, Kornelia Ender)

* Betters listed world record.

UNITED STATES SHORT-COURSE SWIMMING RECORDS
(Listed by Amateur Athletic Union, January 1, 1975)

MEN

Freestyle

50 yards	0:20.06	John Trembley, 1974
100 yards	0:43.99	Andy Coan, 1975
†100 yards	0:43.92	Jonty Skinner, 1975
200 yards	1:38.04	George McDonnell, 1975
*200 yards	1:36.53	Jim Montgomery, 1976
*200 yards	1:36.91	Bruce Furniss, 1976
*200 yards	1:37.65	Jim Montgomery, 1975
500 yards	4:20.45	John Naber, 1975
*500 yards	4:19.05	Tim Shaw, 1976
1,650 yards	15:09.51	John Naber, 1975
*1,650 yards	15:06.76	Tim Shaw, 1976

Backstroke

100 yards	0:49.85	John Naber, 1975
200 yards	1:46.82	John Naber, 1975

Breaststroke

100 yards	0:55.50	John Hencken, 1974
200 yards	2:00.83	John Hencken, 1975
*†200 yards	2:00.74	David Wilkie, 1976

Butterfly

100 yards	0:47.98	Mark Spitz, 1972
200 yards	1:46.89	Mark Spitz, 1972

Individual Medley

200 yards	1:50.268	Fred Tyler, 1975
*200 yards	1:49.42	Lee Engstrand, 1976
400 yards	3:55.16	Steve Furniss, 1973
†400 yards	3:54.91	Andras Hargatay, 1975

Relays

400-yard freestyle	2:57.54	So. California, 1
400-yard freestyle	2:58.42	Indiana, 1975
*400-yard freestyle	2:57.54	So. California, 1976
400-yard medley	3:19.22	So. California, 1975
800-yard freestyle	6:35.61	So. California, 1975
*800-yard freestyle	6:33.13	So. California, 1976

WOMEN

Freestyle

100 yards	0:50.89	Kathy Heddy, 1974
200 yards	1:48.79	Shirley Babashoff, 1974
500 yards	4:47.34	Shirley Babashoff, 1974
1,650 yards	16:27.11	Jo Harshbarger, 1975

Backstroke

100 yards	0:57.30	Linda Stimpson, 1974
200 yards	2:04.01	Susie Atwood, 1972
*200 yards	2:03.7	Ellen Mangels, 1976
†200 yards	2:02.84	Nancy Garapick, 1975

Breaststroke

100 yards	1:05.25	Kim Dunson, 1975
*100 yards	1:04.56	Christine Jarvis, 1976
200 yards	2:18.77	Marcia Morey, 1975

Butterfly

100 yards	0:55.70	Deena Deardurff, 1975
*100 yards	0:55.60	Wendy Boglioli, 1976
200 yards	2:00.70	Valerie Lee, 1975

Individual Medley

100 yards	2:04.74	Jenni Franks, 1975
200 yards	4:24.51	Jenni Franks, 1975

Relays

200-yard freestyle	1:38.55	Arizona State U., 1975
200-yard medley	1:49.76	Miami (Fla.) U., 1975
400-yard freestyle	3:27.24	Mission Viejo S.C., 1975
400-yard medley	3:53.70	Santa Clara S.C., 1975
800-yard freestyle	7:28.77	Mission Viejo S.C., 1975

* Betters listed record by American citizens; recognition pending; † open American record, for non-U.S. citizens.

SOCCER

World Cup

1930	Uruguay	1942	No competition	1954	West Germany	1966	England
1934	Italy	1946	No competition	1958	Brazil	1970	Brazil
1938	Italy	1950	Uruguay	1962	Brazil	1974	West Germany

National Challenge Cup

1960-61	Ukrainian Nationals, Phila.	1965	New York Ukrainians	1971	Hota, New York
1962	Hungaria, New York	1966	Phila. Nationals	1972	Elizabeth, New Jersey
1963	Ukrainian Nationals, Phila.	1967-69	N.Y. Greek-Americans	1973	Maccabi, Los Angeles
1964	Kickers-Victoria, Los Angeles	1970	Elizabeth, N.J.	1974	N.Y. Greek-Americans
				1975	Maccabee, Los Angeles

National Amateur Challenge Cup

1956-61	Kutis, St. Louis	1966	Chicago Kickers	1970	Chicago Kickers
1962	Carpathia Kickers, Detroit	1967	Italian Americans, Hartford, Conn.	1971	Kutis, St. Louis
1963	Italian Americans, Rochester, N.Y.	1968	Chicago Kickers	1972	Busch, St. Louis
1964	Chicago Schwaben	1969	British Lions, Wash.	1973-74	Inter, Philadelphia
1965	United German-Hungarians, Phila.			1975	Chicago Kickers

COLLEGE COLORS AND NICKNAMES

Abilene Christian—Purple-White; Wildcats
Air Force—Silver-Blue; Falcons
Akron—Blue-Gold; Zips
Alabama—Crimson-White; Crimson Tide
Alfred—Purple-Gold; Saxons
Amherst—Purple-White; Lord Jeffs
Arizona—Red-Navy Blue; Wildcats
Arizona State—Maroon-Gold; Sun Devils
Arkansas—Cardinal-White; Razorbacks
Army—Black-Gold-Gray; Cadets
Auburn—Orange-Navy Blue; Tigers
Bates—Garnet; Bobcats
Baylor—Green-Gold; Bears
Boston Coll.—Maroon-Gold; Eagles
Boston U.—Scarlet-White; Terriers
Bowdoin—White; Polar Bears
Bowling Green—Brown-Orange; Falcons
Bradley—Cardinal-White; Braves
Brigham Young—Blue-White; Cougars
Brooklyn—Maroon-Gold; Kingsmen
Brown—Brown-White; Bruins
Bucknell—Orange-Blue; Bisons
Buffalo—Blue-White; Bulls
Butler—Blue-White; Bulldogs
California—Blue-Gold; Golden Bears
Canisius—Blue-Gold; Griffins
Carnegie-Mellon—Tartan Plaid; Tartans
Catholic—Red-Black; Cardinals
Centre—Gold-White; Colonels
Chicago—Maroon; Maroons
Cincinnati—Red-Black; Bearcats
Citadel—Blue-White; Bulldogs
City Coll. of N. Y.—Lavender; Beavers
Clemson—Purple-Orange; Tigers
Coast Guard—Blue-White; Cadets
Colgate—Maroon; Red Raiders
Colorado—Silver-Gold; Buffaloes
Colorado State—Green-Gold; Rams
Columbia—Blue-White; Lions
Connecticut—Blue-White; Huskies
Cornell—Carnelian-White; Big Red
Creighton—White-Blue; Blue Jays
Dartmouth—Green; Big Green
Davidson—Red-Black; Wildcats
Dayton—Red-Blue; Flyers
Delaware—Blue-Gold; Blue Hens
Denver—Red-Gold; Pioneers
DePaul—Scarlet-Blue; Blue Demons
Detroit—Cardinal-White; Titans
Drake—White-Blue; Bulldogs
Duke—Blue-White; Blue Devils
Duquesne—Red-Blue; Dukes
East Carolina—Purple-Gold; Pirates
Eastern Kentucky—Maroon-White; Maroons
Florida—Orange-Blue; Gators
Florida State—Garnet-Gold; Seminoles
Fordham—Maroon; Rams
Franklin & Marshall—Blue-White; Diplomats
Fresno State—Cardinal-Blue; Bulldogs
Furman—Purple-White; Paladines
Georgetown—Blue-Gray; Hoyas
George Washington—Buff-Blue; Colonials
Georgia—Red-Black; Bulldogs
Georgia Tech—White-Gold;Yellow Jackets
Gonzaga—Blue-White; Bulldogs
Hamilton—Buff-Blue; Continentals
Hampden-Sydney—Garnet-Gray; Tigers
Hardin-Simmons—Purple-Gold; Cowboys

Harvard—Crimson; The Crimson
Hobart—Orange-Purple; Statesmen
Holy Cross—Purple; Crusaders
Houston—Scarlet-White; Cougars
Howard—Blue-White; Bisons
Idaho—Silver-Gold; Vandals
Illinois—Orange-Blue; Illini
Indiana—Cream-Crimson; Hoosiers
Iowa—Gold-Black; Hawkeyes
Iowa State—Cardinal-Gold; Cyclones
Johns Hopkins—Blue-Black; Blue Jays
Kansas—Crimson-Blue; Jayhawkers
Kansas State—Purple-White; Wildcats
Kent State—Blue-Gold; Golden Flashes
Kentucky—Blue-White; Wildcats
Lafayette—Maroon-White; Leopards
La Salle—Blue-Gold; Explorers
Lehigh—Brown-White; Engineers
Louisiana State—Purple-Gold; Tigers
Louisville—Cardinal-Black; Cardinals
Loyola (Ill.)—Maroon-Gold; Ramblers
Maine—Blue-White; Black Bears
Manhattan—Green-White; Jaspers
Marquette—Blue-Gold; Warriors
Maryland—Red-White; Terrapins
Massachusetts—Maroon-White; Redmen
Merchant Marine—Blue-Gray; Mariners
Miami (Fla.)—Orange-Green-White; Hurricanes
Miami (Ohio)—Red-White; Redskins
Michigan—Maize-Blue; Wolverines
Michigan State—Green-White; Spartans
Middlebury—Blue-White; Panthers
Minnesota—Maroon-Gold; Gophers
Mississippi—Red-Blue; Rebels
Mississippi State—Maroon-White; Maroons
Missouri—Black-Gold; Tigers
M.I.T.—Cardinal-Gray; Beavers
Montana—Copper-Silver-Gold; Grizzlies
Navy—Blue-Gold; Midshipmen
Nebraska—Scarlet-Cream; Cornhuskers
Nevada—Silver-Blue; Wolfpack
New Hampshire—Blue-White; Wildcats
New Mexico—Cherry-Silver; Lobos
New York U.—Violet; Violets
Niagara—Purple-White; Purple Eagles
North Carolina—Blue-White; Tar Heels
North Carolina State—Scarlet-White; Wolfpack
North Dakota—Green-White; Sioux
North Texas State—Green-White; Eagles
Northeastern—Red-Black; Huskies
Northwestern—Purple-White; Wildcats
Notre Dame—Blue-Gold; Fighting Irish
Occidental—Orange-Black; Bengals
Ohio State—Scarlet-Gray; Buckeyes
Ohio U.—Green-White; Bobcats
Oklahoma—Red-White; Sooners
Okla. State—Orange-Black; Cowboys
Omaha—Red-Black; Indians
Oregon—Yellow-Green; Webfoots
Oregon State—Orange-Black; Beavers
Penn State—Blue-White; Nittany Lions
Pennsylvania—Red-Blue; Quakers
Pittsburgh—Blue-Gold; Panthers
Princeton—Orange-Black; Tigers
Providence—Black-White; Friars
Purdue—Gold-Black; Boilermakers
Rhode Island—Blue-White; Rams
Rice—Blue-Gray; Owls
Richmond—Red-Blue; Spiders

Rochester—Yellow; Yellowjackets
Rollins—Blue-Gold; Tars
R.P.I.—Cherry-White; Engineers
Rutgers—Scarlet; The Scarlet
St. Bonaventure—Brown-White; Bonnies
St. Francis (N. Y.)—Red-Blue; Terriers
St. John's (N. Y.)—Red-White; Redmen
St. Joseph's (Pa.)—Crimson-Gray; Hawks
St. Lawrence—Scarlet-Brown; Larries
St. Louis—Blue-White; Billikens
St. Mary's (Calif.)—Red-Blue; Gaels
San Diego State—Red-Black; Aztecs
San Francisco—Green-Gold; Dons
San Jose State—Gold-White; Spartans
Santa Clara—Cardinal-White; Broncos
Seattle—Maroon-White; Chieftains
Seton Hall—Blue-White; Pirates
Sewanee—Purple-Gold; Tigers
So. Carolina—Garnet-Black; Gamecocks
South Dakota—Scarlet-White; Coyotes
So. California—Cardinal-Gold; Trojans
So. Illinois—Maroon-White; Salukis
So. Methodist—Red-Blue; Mustangs
Springfield—Maroon-White; Maroons
Stanford—Cardinal-White; Cardinals
Swarthmore—Garnet; Little Quakers
Syracuse—Orange; Orangemen
Temple—Cherry-White; Owls
Tennessee—Orange-White; Vols
Tennessee A. & I.—Blue-White; Tigers
Texas—Orange-White; Longhorns
Texas A. & M.—Maroon-White; Aggies
Texas Christian—Purple-White; Horned Frogs
Texas, El Paso—Orange-White; Miners
Texas Tech—Scarlet-Black; Red Raiders
Toledo—Blue-Gold; Rockets
Trinity (Conn.)—Blue-Gold; Bantams
Tufts—Blue-Brown; Jumbos
Tulane—Green-Blue; Green Wave
Tulsa—Crimson-Blue-Gold; Golden Hurricane
Tuskegee—Gold-Crimson; Golden Tigers
U.C.L.A.—Blue-Gold; Bruins
Utah—Crimson-White; Utes
Utah State—Blue-White; Aggies
Vanderbilt—Gold-Black; Commodores
Vermont—Green-Gold; Catamounts
Villanova—Blue-White; Wildcats
Virginia—Blue-Orange; Cavaliers
V.M.I.—Red-White-Yellow; Keydets
V.P.I.—Orange-Maroon; Gobblers
Wake Forest—Gold-Black; Deacons
Washington & Lee—Blue-White; Generals
Washington (Mo.)—Myrtle-Maroon; Bears
Washington (Wash.)—Purple-Gold; Huskies
Washington State—Crimson-Gray; Cougars
Wesleyan—Cardinal-Black; Cardinals
Western Kentucky—Red-White; Hilltoppers
W. Virginia—Gold-Blue; Mountaineers
Wichita—Black-Gold; Wheatshockers
William & Mary—Green-Gold-Silver; Indians
Williams—Royal Purple; Ephmen
Wisconsin—Cardinal; Badgers
Wyoming—Brown-Yellow; Cowboys
Yale—Blue; Bulldogs, Elis

BASEBALL

THE POPULAR TRADITION that baseball was invented by Abner Doubleday at Cooperstown, N. Y., in 1839, has been enshrined in the Hall of Fame and National Museum of Baseball erected in that town, but research has proved that a game called "Base Ball" was played in this country and England before 1839. However, the first team baseball as we know it was played at the Elysian Fields, Hoboken, N. J., on June 19, 1846, between the Knickerbockers and the New York Nine. There was a gradual growth of baseball and an improvement of equipment and playing skill in the next fifty years.

Historians have it that the first pitcher to throw a curve was William A. (Candy) Cummings in 1867. The Cincinnati Red Stockings were the first all-professional team and in 1869 they played 64 games without a loss. The standard ball of the same size and weight, still the rule, was adopted in 1872. The first catcher's mask was worn in 1875. The National League was organized in 1876. The first chest protector was donned in 1885. The three-strike rule was put on the books in 1887 and the four-ball ticket to first base came in 1889. The pitching distance, formerly shorter, was lengthened to 60 feet 6 inches in 1893 and the rules have been only slightly modified since that time.

The American League, under the vigorous leadership of B. B. Johnson, blossomed forth as a major league in 1901. Judge Kenesaw Mountain Landis, by action of the two major leagues, became Commissioner of Baseball in 1921 and, upon his death (1944), Albert B. Chandler, former United States Senator from Kentucky, was elected to that office (1945). Chandler failed to obtain a new contract, and he was succeeded by Ford C. Frick (1951), the National League president. Frick retired after the 1965 season and William D. Eckert, a retired Air Force lieutenant general, was named to succeed him. Eckert resigned under pressure in December, 1968. Bowie Kuhn, a New York attorney, became interim commissioner for one year in February. His appointment was made permanent with a seven-year contract in August, 1969.

PROFESSIONAL BASEBALL GOVERNMENT
NATIONAL LEAGUE—AMERICAN LEAGUE—NATIONAL ASSOCIATION
Bowie Kuhn, Commissioner
Alexander Hadden, Secretary-Treasurer
Joseph L. Reichler, Special Assistant to Commissioner
John Johnson, Administrator
Bob Wirz, Director of Information
75 Rockefeller Plaza, New York, N. Y. 10019

NATIONAL LEAGUE	AMERICAN LEAGUE
Charles S. Feeney	Leland S. MacPhail, President
President	280 Park Avenue
220 Montgomery St.	New York, N. Y. 10017
San Francisco, Calif. 94104	Robert Holbrook, Secretary
John J. McHale	Robert O. Fishel
Vice President	Assistant to President
Fred G. Fleig	Rick White
Secretary-Treasurer	Public Relations Assistant

NATIONAL ASSOCIATION
Robert R. Bragan President-Treasurer
225 Fourth Street South. P. O. Box A, St. Petersburg, Fla. 33731

LONGEST GAMES IN THE MAJORS

A 26-inning tie between the Brooklyn Dodgers and the Boston Braves on May 1, 1920, was the longest game in major league history. Played at Braves Field, Boston, the game was called because of darkness with the score 1–1. Both starting pitchers, Leon Cadore of Brooklyn and Joe Oeschger, were still in the game at the end, 3 hours and 50 minutes after it had begun. The longest game in point of time, 7 hours and 23 minutes, was played by the New York Mets and the San Francisco Giants on May 31, 1964, in New York. The Giants won in 23 innings, 8–6. In the longest night game, the St. Louis Cards defeated the Mets at New York, 4–3, in 25 innings, Sept. 11, 1974. This game, played in 7 hours, 4 minutes, was longest in time at night.

Record of World Series Games

Source: *The Book of Baseball Records,* published by Seymour Siwoff, New York City.

Figures in parentheses for winning pitchers (WP) and losing pitchers (LP) indicate the game number in the series

1903—Boston A. L. 5 (Jimmy Collins); Pittsburgh 3 (Fred Clarke). WP—Bos.: Dinneen (2, 6, 8), Young (5, 7); Pitts.: Phillippe (1, 3, 4). LP—Bos.: Young (1), Hughes (2), Dinneen (4); Pitts.: Leever (2, 6), Kennedy (5), Phillippe (7, 8).

1904—No series.

1905—New York N. L. 4 (John J. McGraw); Philadelphia A. L. 1 (Connie Mack). WP—N. Y.: Mathewson (1, 3, 5); McGinnity (4); Phila.: Bender (2). LP—N. Y.: McGinnity (2); Phila.: Plank (1, 4), Coakley (3), Bender (5).

1906—Chicago A. L. 4 (Fielder Jones); Chicago N. L. 2 (Frank Chance). WP—Chi. A. L.: Altrock (1), Walsh (3, 5), White (6); Chi. N. L.: Reulbach (2), Brown (4). LP—Chi. A. L.: White (2), Altrock (4); Chi. N. L.: Brown (1, 6), Pfeister (2, 4).

1907—Chicago N. L. 4 (Frank Chance); Detroit A. L. 0 (Hugh Jennings). First game tied 3-3, 12 innings. WP—Pfeister (2), Reulbach (3), Overall (4), Brown (5). LP—Mullin (2, 5), Siever (3), Donovan (4).

1908—Chicago N. L. 4 (Frank Chance); Detroit A. L. 1 (Hugh Jennings). WP—Chi.: Brown (1, 4), Overall (2, 5); Det.: Mullin (3). LP—Chi.: Pfeister (3); Det.: Summers (1, 4), Donovan (2, 5).

1909—Pittsburgh N. L. 4 (Fred Clarke); Detroit A. L. 3 (Hugh Jennings). WP—Pitts.: Adams (1, 5, 7), Maddox (3); Det.: Donovan (2), Mullin (4, 6). LP—Pitts.: Camnitz (2), Leifield (4), Willis (6); Det.: Mullin (1), Summers (3, 5), Donovan (7).

1910—Philadelphia A. L. 4 (Connie Mack); Chicago N. L. 1 (Frank Chance). WP—Phila.: Bender (1), Coombs (2, 3, 5); Chi.: Brown (4). LP—Phila.: Bender (4); Chi.: Overall (1), Brown (2, 5), McIntyre (3).

1911—Philadelphia A. L. 4 (Connie Mack); New York N. L. 2 (John J. McGraw). WP—Phila.: Plank (2), Coombs (3), Bender (4, 6); N. Y.: Mathewson (1), Crandall (5). LP—Phila.: Bender (1), Plank (5); N. Y.: Marquard (2), Mathewson (3, 4), Ames (6).

1912—Boston A. L. 4 (J. Garland Stahl); New York N. L. 3 (John J. McGraw). Second game tied, 6-6, 11 innings. WP—Bos.: Wood (1, 4, 8), Bedient (5); N. Y.: Marquard (3, 6), Tesreau (7). LP—Bos.: O'Brien (3, 6), Wood (7); N. Y.: Tesreau (1, 4), Mathewson (5, 8).

1913—Philadelphia A. L. 4 (Connie Mack); New York N. L. 1 (John J. McGraw). WP—Phila.: Bender (1, 4), Bush (3), Plank (5); N. Y.: Mathewson (2); LP—Phila.: Plank (2); N. Y.: Marquard (1), Tesreau (3), Demaree (4), Mathewson (5).

1914—Boston N. L. 4 (George Stallings); Philadelphia A. L. 0 (Connie Mack). WP—Rudolph (1, 4), James (2, 3). LP—Bender (1), Plank (2), Bush (3), Shawkey (4).

1915—Boston A. L. 4 (Bill Carrigan); Philadelphia N. L. 1 (Pat Moran). WP—Bos.: Foster (2, 5), Leonard (3), Shore (4); Phila.: Alexander (1). LP—Bos.: Shore (1); Phila.: Mayer (2), Alexander (3), Chalmers (4), Rixey (5).

1916—Boston A. L. 4 (Bill Carrigan); Brooklyn N. L. 1 (Wilbert Robinson). WP—Bos.: Shore (1, 5), Ruth (2), Leonard (4); Bklyn.: Coombs (3). LP—Bos.: Mays (3); Bklyn.: Marquard (1, 4), Smith (2), Pfeffer (5).

1917—Chicago A. L. 4 (Clarence Rowland); New York N. L. 2 (John J. McGraw). WP—Chi.: Cicotte (1), Faber (2, 5, 6); N. Y.: Benton (3), Schupp (4). LP—Chi.: Cicotte (4), Faber (4); N. Y.: Sallee (1, 5), Anderson (2), Benton (6).

1918—Boston A. L. 4 (Ed Barrow); Chicago N. L. 2 (Fred Mitchell). WP—Bos.: Ruth (1, 4), Mays (3, 6); Chi.: Tyler (2), Vaughn (5). LP—Bos.: Bush (2), Jones (5); Chi.: Vaughn (1, 3), Douglas (4), Tyler (6).

1919—Cincinnati N. L. 5 (Pat Moran); Chicago A. L. 3 (William Gleason). WP—Cin.: Ruether (1), Sallee (2), Ring (4), Eller (5, 8); Chi.: Kerr (3, 6), Cicotte (7). LP—Cin.: Fisher (3), Ring (6), Sallee (7); Chi.: Cicotte (1, 4), Williams (2, 5, 8).

1920—Cleveland A. L. 5 (Tris Speaker); Brooklyn N. L. 2 (Wilbert Robinson). WP—Cleve.: Coveleski (1, 4, 7), Bagby (5), Mails (6); Bklyn.: Grimes (2), Smith (3). LP—Cleve.: Bagby (2), Caldwell (3). Bklyn.: Marquard (1), Cadore (4), Grimes (5, 7), Smith (6).

1921—New York N. L. 5 (John J. McGraw); New York A. L. 3 (Miller Huggins). WP—N. Y. N. L.: Barnes (3, 6), Douglas (4, 7), Nehf (8); N. Y. A. L.: Mays (1), Hoyt (2, 5). LP—N. Y. N. L.: Nehf (1, 5), Douglas (2). N. Y. A. L.: Quinn (3), Mays (4, 7), Shawkey (6), Hoyt (8).

1922—New York N. L. 4 (John J. McGraw); New York A. L. 0 (Miller Huggins). Second game tied 3-3, 10 innings. WP—Ryan (1), Scott (3), McQuillan (4), Nehf (5); LP—Bush (1, 5), Hoyt (3), Mays (4).

1923—New York A. L. 4 (Miller Huggins); New York N. L. 2 (John J. McGraw). WP—N. Y. A. L.: Pennock (2, 6), Shawkey (4), Bush (5); N. Y. N. L.: Ryan (1), Nehf (3). LP—N. Y. A. L.: Bush (1), Jones (3); N. Y. N. L.: McQuillan (2), Scott (4), Bentley (5), Nehf (6).

1924—Washington A. L. 4 (Bucky Harris); New York N. L. 3 (John J. McGraw). WP—Wash.: Zachary (2, 6), Mogridge (4), Johnson (9); N. Y.: Nehf (1), McQuillan (3), Bentley (5). LP—Wash.: Johnson (1, 5), Marberry (3); N. Y.: Bentley (2, 7), Barnes (4), Nehf (6).

1925—Pittsburgh N. L. 4 (Bill McKechnie); Washington A. L. 3 (Bucky Harris). WP—Pitts.: Aldridge (2, 5), Kremer (6, 7); Wash.: Johnson (1, 4), Ferguson (3). LP—Pitts.: Meadows (1), Kremer (3), Yde (4); Wash.: Coveleski (2, 5), Ferguson (6), Johnson (7).

1926—St. Louis N. L. 4 (Rogers Hornsby); New York A. L. 3 (Miller Huggins). WP—St. L.: Alexander (2, 6), Haines (3, 7); N. Y.: Pennock (1, 5), Hoyt (4). LP—St. L.: Sherdel (1, 5), Reinhart (4); N. Y.: Shocker (2), Ruether (3), Shawkey (6), Hoyt (7).

1927—New York A. L. 4 (Miller Huggins); Pittsburgh N. L. 0 (Donie Bush). WP—Hoyt (1), Pipgras (2), Pennock (3), Moore (4). LP—Kremer (1), Aldridge (2), Meadows (3), Miljus (4).

1928—New York A. L. 4 (Miller Huggins); St. Louis N. L. 0 (Bill McKechnie). WP—Hoyt (1, 4), Pipgras (2), Zachary (3). LP—Sherdel (1, 4), Alexander (2), Haines (3).

1929—Philadelphia A. L. 4 (Connie Mack); Chicago N. L. 1 (Joe McCarthy). WP—Phila.: Ehmke (1), Earnshaw (2), Rommel (4), Walberg (5); Chi.: Bush (3). LP—Phila.: Earnshaw (3); Chi.: Root (1), Malone (2, 5), Blake (4).

1930—Philadelphia A. L. 4 (Connie Mack); St. Louis N. L. 2 (Gabby Street). WP—Phila.: Grove (1, 5), Earnshaw (2, 6); St. L.: Hallahan (3), Haines (4). LP—Phila.: Walberg (3), Grove (4); St. L.: Grimes (1, 5), Rhem (2), Hallahan (6).

1931—St. Louis 4 (Gabby Street); Philadelphia A. L. 3 (Connie Mack). WP—St. L.: Hallahan (2, 5), Grimes (3, 7); Phila.: Grove (1, 6), Earnshaw (4). LP—St. L.: Derringer (1, 6), Johnson (4); Phila.: Earnshaw (2, 7), Grove (3), Hoyt (5).

1932—New York A. L. (Joe McCarthy); Chicago N. L. 0 (Charles Grimm). WP—Ruffing (1), Gomez (2), Pipgras (3), Moore (4); LP—Bush (1), Warneke (2), Root (3), May (4).

1933—New York N. L. 4 (Bill Terry); Washington A. L. 1 (Joe Cronin). WP—N. Y.: Hubbell (1, 4), Schumacher (2), Luque (5); Wash.: Whitehill (3). LP—N. Y.: Fitzsimmons (3); Wash.: Stewart (1) Crowder (2) Weaver (4), Russell (5).

1934—St. Louis N. L. 4 (Frank Frisch); Detroit A. L. 3 (Mickey Cochrane). WP—St. L.: J. Dean (1, 7), P. Dean (3, 6); Det.: Rowe (2), Auker (4), Bridges (5). LP—St. L.: W. Walker (2, 4), J. Dean (5); Det.: Crowder (1), Bridges (3), Rowe (6), Auker (7).

1935—Detroit A. L. 4 (Mickey Cochrane); Chicago N. L. 2 (Charles Grimm). WP—Det.: Bridges (2, 6), Rowe (3), Crowder (4); Chi.: Warneke (1, 5); LP—Det.: Rowe (1, 5); Chi.: Root (2), French (3, 6), Carleton (4).

1936—New York A. L. 4 (Joe McCarthy); New York N. L. 2 (Bill Terry). WP—N. Y. A. L.: Gomez (2, 6), Hadley (3), Pearson (4); N. Y. N. L.: Hubbell (1), Schumacher (5); LP—N. Y. A. L.: Ruffing (1), Malone (5); N. Y. N. L.: Schumacher (2), Fitzsimmons (3, 6), Hubbell (4).

1937—New York A. L. 4 (Joe McCarthy); New York N. L. 1 (Bill Terry). WP—N. Y. A. L.: Gomez (1, 5), Ruffing (2), Pearson (3); N. Y. N. L.: Hubbell (4). LP—N. Y. A. L.: Hadley (4); N. Y. N. L.: Hubbell (1), Melton (2, 5), Schumacher (3).

1938—New York A. L. 4 (Joe McCarthy); Chicago N. L. 0 (Gabby Hartnett). WP—Ruffing (1, 4), Gomez (2), Pearson (3). LP—Lee (1, 4), Dean (2), Bryant (3).

1939—New York A. L. 4 (Joe McCarthy); Cincinnati N. L. 0 (Bill McKechnie). WP—Ruffing (1), Pearson (2), Hadley (3), Murphy (4). LP—Derringer (1), Walters (2, 4), Thompson (3).

1940—Cincinnati N. L. 4 (Bill McKechnie); Detroit A. L. 3 (Del Baker). WP—Cin.: Walters (2, 6), Derringer (4, 7); Det.: Newsom (1, 5), Bridges (3). LP—Cin.: Derringer (1), Turner (3), Thompson (5); Det.: Rowe (2, 6), Trout (4), Newsom (7).

1941—New York A. L. 4 (Joe McCarthy); Brooklyn N. L. 1 (Leo Durocher). WP—N. Y.: Ruffing (1), Russo (3), Murphy (4), Bonham (5); Bklyn: Wyatt (2). LP—N. Y.: Chandler (2); Bklyn: Davis (1), Casey (3, 4), Wyatt (5).

1942—St. Louis N. L. 4 (Billy Southworth); New York A. L. 1 (Joe McCarthy). WP—St. L.: Beazley (2, 5), White (3), Lanier (4); N. Y.: Ruffing (1). LP—St. L.: Cooper (1); N. Y.: Bonham (2), Chandler (3), Donald (4), Ruffing (5).

1943—New York A. L. 4 (Joe McCarthy); St. Louis N. L. 1 (Billy Southworth). WP—N. Y.: Chandler (1, 5), Borowy (3), Russo (4); St. L.: Cooper (2). LP—N. Y.: Bonham (2); St. L.: Lanier (1), Brazle (3), Brecheen (4), Cooper (5).

1944—St. Louis N. L. 4 (Billy Southworth); St. Louis A. L. 2 (Luke Sewell). WP—St. L. N. L.: Donnelly (2), Brecheen (4), Cooper (5), Lanier (6); St. L. A. L.: Galehouse (1), Kramer (3). LP—St. L. N. L.: Cooper (1), Wilks (3); St. L. A. L.: Muncrief (2), Jakucki (4), Galehouse (5), Potter (6).

1945—Detroit A. L. 4 (Steve O'Neill); Chicago N. L. 3 (Charles Grimm). WP—Det.: Trucks (2), Trout (4), Newhouser (5, 7); Chi.: Borowy (1, 6), Passeau (3). LP—Det.: Newhouser (1), Overmire (3), Trout (6); Chi.: Wyse (2), Prim (4), Borowy (5, 7).

1946—St. Louis N. L. 4 (Eddie Dyer); Boston A. L. 3 (Joe Cronin). WP—St. L.: Brecheen (2, 6, 7), Munger (4); Bos.: Johnson (1), Ferriss (3), Dobson (5). LP—St. L.: Pollet (1), Dickson (3), Brazle (5); Bos.: Harris (2, 6), Hughson (4), Klinger (7).

1947—New York A. L. 4 (Bucky Harris); Brooklyn N. L. 3 (Burt Shotton). WP—N. Y.: Shea (1, 5), Reynolds (2), Page (7); Bklyn.: Casey (3, 4), Branca (6). LP—N. Y.: Newsom (3), Bevens (4), Page (6); Bklyn.: Branca (1), Lombardi (2), Barney (5), Gregg (7).

1948—Cleveland A. L. 4 (Lou Boudreau); Boston N. L. 2 (Billy Southworth). WP—Cleve.: Lemon (2, 6), Bearden (3), Gromek (4); Bos.: Sain (1), Spahn (5). LP—Cleve.: Feller (1, 5); Bos.: Spahn (2) Bickford (3) Sain (4) Voiselle (6).

1949—New York A. L. 4 (Casey Stengel); Brooklyn N. L. 1 (Burt Shotton). WP—N. Y.: Reynolds (1), Page (3), Lopat (4), Raschi (5); Bklyn.: Roe (2). LP—N. Y.: Raschi (1); Bklyn.: Newcombe (1, 4), Branca (3), Barney (5).

1950—New York A. L. 4 (Casey Stengel); Philadelphia N. L. 0 (Eddie Sawyer). WP—Raschi (1), Reynolds (2), Ferrick (3), Ford (4). LP—Konstanty (1), Roberts (2), Meyer (3), Miller (4).

1951—New York A. L. 4 (Casey Stengel); New York N. L. 2 (Leo Durocher). WP—N. Y. A. L.: Lopat (2, 5), Reynolds (4), Raschi (6); N. Y. N. L.: Koslo (1), Hearn (3). LP—N. Y. A. L.: Reynolds (1), Raschi (3); N. Y. N. L.: Jansen (2, 5), Maglie (4), Koslo (6).

1952—New York A. L. 4 (Casey Stengel); Brooklyn N. L. 3 (Chuck Dressen). WP—N. Y.: Raschi (2, 6), Reynolds (4, 7); Bklyn.: Black (1), Roe (3), Erskine (5). LP—N. Y.: Reynolds (1), Lopat (3), Sain (5); Bklyn.: Erskine (3), Black (4, 7), Loes (6).

1953—New York A. L. 4 (Casey Stengel); Brooklyn N. L. 2 (Chuck Dressen). WP—N. Y.: Sain (1), Lopat (2), McDonald (5), Reynolds (6); Bklyn.: Erskine (3), Loes (4). LP—N. Y.: Raschi (3), Ford (4); Bklyn.: Labine (1, 6), Roe (2), Podres (5).

1954—New York N. L. 4 (Leo Durocher); Cleveland A. L. 0 (Al Lopez). WP—Grissom (1), Antonelli (2), Gomez (3), Liddle (4). LP—Lemon (1, 4), Wynn (2), Garcia (3).

1955—Brooklyn N. L. 4 (Walter Alston); New York A. L. 3 (Casey Stengel). WP—Bklyn.: Podres (3, 7), Labine (4), Craig (5); N. Y.: Ford (1, 6), Bynre (2). LP—Bklyn.: Newcombe (1), Loes (2), Spooner (6); N. Y.: Turley (3), Larsen (4), Grim (5), Byrne (7).

1956—New York A. L. 4 (Casey Stengel); Brooklyn N. L. 3 (Walter Alston). WP—N. Y.: Ford (3), Sturdivant (4), Larsen (5), Kucks (7); Bklyn.: Maglie (1), Bessent (2), Labine (6). LP—N. Y.: Ford (1), Morgan (2), Turley (6); Bklyn.: Craig (3), Erskine (4), Maglie (5), Newcombe (7).

1957—Milwaukee N. L. 4 (Fred Haney); New York A. L. 3 (Casey Stengel). WP—Mil.: Burdette (2, 5, 7), Spahn (4); N. Y.: Ford (1), Larsen (3), Turley (6). LP—Mil.: Spahn (1), Buhl (3), Johnson (6); N. Y.: Shantz (2), Grim (4), Ford (5), Larsen (7).

1958—New York A. L. 4 (Casey Stengel); Milwaukee N. L. 3 (Fred Haney). WP—N. Y.: Larsen (3), Turley (5, 7), Duren (6); Mil.: Spahn (1, 4), Burdette (2). LP—N. Y.: Duren (1), Turley (2), Ford (4); Mil.: Rush (3), Burdette (5, 7), Spahn (6).

1959—Los Angeles N. L. 4 (Walter Alston); Chicago A. L. 2 (Al Lopez). WP—L. A.: Podres (2), Drysdale (3), Sherry (4, 6); Chi.: Wynn (1), Shaw (5). LP—L. A.: Craig (1), Koufax (5); Chi.: Shaw (2), Donovan (3), Staley (4), Wynn (6).

1960—Pittsburgh N. L. 4 (Danny Murtaugh); New York A. L. 3 (Casey Stengel). WP—Pitts.: Law (1, 4), Haddix (5, 7); N. Y.: Turley (2), Ford (3, 6). LP—Pitts.: Friend (2, 6), Mizell (3); N. Y.: Ditmar (1, 5), Terry (4, 7).

1961—New York A. L. 4 (Ralph Houk); Cincinnati N. L. 1 (Fred Hutchinson). WP—N. Y.: Ford (1, 4), Arroyo (3), Daley (5); Cin.: Jay (2). LP—N. Y.: Terry (2); Cin.: O'Toole (1, 4), Purkey (3), Jay (5).

1962—New York A. L. 4 (Ralph Houk); San Francisco N. L. 3 (Al Dark). WP—N. Y.: Ford (1), Stafford (3), Terry (5, 7); S. F.: Sanford (2), Larsen (4), Pierce (6). LP—N. Y.: Terry (2), Coates (4), Ford (6); S. F.: O'Dell (1), Pierce (3), Sanford (5, 7).

1963—Los Angeles N. L. 4 (Walter Alston); New York A. L. 0 (Ralph Houk). WP—Koufax (1, 4), Podres (2), Drysdale (3). LP—Ford (1, 4), Downing (2), Bouton (3).

1964—St. Louis N. L. 4 (Johnny Keane); New York A. L. 3 (Yogi Berra). WP—St. L.: Sadecki (1), Craig (4), Gibson (5, 7); N. Y.: Stottlemyre (2), Bouton (3, 6). LP—St. L.: Gibson (2), Schultz (3), Simmons (6); N. Y.: Ford (1), Downing (4), Mikkelsen (5), Stottlemyre (7).

1965—Los Angeles N. L. 4 (Walter Alston); Minnesota A. L. 3 (Sam Mele). WP—L. A.: Osteen (3), Drysdale (4), Koufax (5, 7); Minn.: Grant (1, 6), Kaat (2). LP—L. A.: Drysdale (1),

Koufax (2), Osteen (6); Minn.: Pascual (3), Grant (4), Kaat (5, 7).

1966—Baltimore A. L. 4 (Hank Bauer); Los Angeles N. L. 0 (Walter Alston). WP—Drabowsky (1), Palmer (2), Bunker (3), McNally (4). LP—Drysdale (1, 4), Koufax (2), Osteen (3).

1967—St. Louis N. L. 4 (Red Schoendienst); Boston A. L. 3 (Dick Williams). WP—St. L.: Gibson (1, 4, 7), Briles (3); Bos.: Lonborg (2, 5); Wyatt (6). LP—St. L.: Hughes (2), Carlton (5), Lamabe (6); Bos.: Santiago (1, 4), Bell (3), Lonborg (7).

1968—Detroit A. L. 4 (Mayo Smith); St. Louis N. L. 3 (Red Schoendienst). WP—Det.: Lolich (2, 5, 7), McLain (6); St. L.: Gibson (1, 4), Washburn (3), LP—Det.: McLain (1, 4), Wilson (3); St. L.: Briles (2), Hoerner (5), Washburn (6), Gibson (7).

1969—New York N. L. 4 (Gil Hodges); Baltimore A. L. 1 (Earl Weaver). WP—N. Y.: Koosman (2, 5), Gentry (3), Seaver (4); Balt.: Cuellar (1). LP—N. Y.: Seaver (1); Balt.: McNally (2), Palmer (3), Hall (4), Watt (5).

1970—Baltimore A. L. 4 (Earl Weaver); Cincinnati N. L. 1 (George Anderson) 1. WP—Balt.: Palmer (1), Phoebus (2), McNally (3), Cuellar (5); Cin.: Carroll (4). LP—Balt.: Nolan (1), Wilcox (2), Cloninger (3), Merritt (5); Balt.: Watt (4).

1971—Pittsburgh N. L. 4 (Danny Murtaugh); Baltimore A. L. 3 (Earl Weaver). WP—Pitts.: Blass (3, 7), Kison (4), Briles (5); Balt.: McNally (1, 6), Palmer (2). LP—Pitts.: Ellis (1), R. Johnson (2), Miller (6); Balt.: Cuellar (3, 7), Watt (4) McNally (5).

1972—Oakland A.L. 4 (Dick Williams); Cincinnati N.L. (George Anderson) 3. WP—Oakland: Holtzman (1), Hunter (2, 7), Fingers (4); Cincinnati: Billingham (3), Grimsley (5, 6). LP—Oakland: Odom (3), Fingers (5), Blue (6); Cincinnati: Nolan (1), Grimsley (2), Carroll (4), Bordon (7).

1973—Oakland A.L. 4 (Dick Williams): New York N.L. 3 (Yogi Berra). WP—Oakland: Holtzman (1, 7), Lindblad (3), Hunter (4). New York: McGraw (2), Matlack (4), Koosman (5). LP—Oakland: Fingers (2), Holtzman (4), Blue (5). New York: Matlack (1, 7) Parker (3), Seaver (6).

1974—Oakland A.L. 4 (Al Dark); Los Angeles N.L. 1 (Walter Alston). WP—Oakland: Fingers (1), Hunter (3), Holtzman (4), Odom (5). Los Angeles: Sutton (2). LP—Oakland: Blue (2), Los Angeles: Messersmith (1-4), Downing (3), Marshall (5).

1975—Cincinnati N.L. 4 (George Anderson); Boston A.L. 3 (Darrell Johnson).WP—Cincinnati: Eastwick(2-3), Gullett(5), Carroll(7); Boston: Tiant (1-4), Wise (6). LP—Cincinnati: Gullett (1), Norman (4), Darcy (6); Boston: Drago (2), Willoughby (3), Cleveland (5), Burton (7).

World Series Club Standing (Through 1975)

	Series	Won	Lost	Pct.		Series	Won	Lost	Pct.
Oakland (A)	3	3	0	1.000	Detroit (A)	8	3	5	.375
New York (A)	29	20	9	.690	N. York (N–Giants)	14	5	9	.357
St. Louis (N)	12	8	4	.667	Washington (A)	3	1	2	.333
Pittsburgh (N)	6	4	2	.667	Chicago (N)	10	2	8	.200
Cleveland (A)	3	2	1	.667	Brooklyn (N)	9	1	8	.111
Boston (A)	8	5	3	.625	St. Louis (A)	1	0	1	.000
Philadelphia (A)	8	5	3	.625	San Francisco (N)	1	0	1	.000
Los Angeles (N)	5	3	2	.600	Minnesota (A)	1	0	1	.000
Baltimore (A)	4	2	2	.500	Philadelphia (N)	2	0	2	.000
N. York (N-Mets)	2	1	1	.500					
Milwaukee (N)	2	1	1	.500					
Boston (N)	2	1	1	.500					
Chicago (A)	4	2	2	.500					
Cincinnati (A)	7	3	4	.429					

RECAPITULATION

	Won
American League	43
National League	29

SINGLE GAME AND SINGLE SERIES RECORDS

Most hits game—4, held by many players

Most hits inning—2, held by many players

Most hits series—13 (7 games) Bobby Richardson, New York A.L., 1964; Lou Brock, St. Louis, N.L., 1968; 12 (6 games) Billy Martin, New York A.L., 1953; 12 (8 games) Buck Herzog, New York N.L., 1912; Joe Jackson, Chicago A.L., 1919; 10 (4 games) Babe Ruth, New York A.L., 1928; 9 (5 games) held by 8 players

Most home runs, series—4 (7 games) Babe Ruth, New York A.L., 1926; Duke Snider, Brooklyn, N.L., 1952, 1955; Hank Bauer, New York A.L., 1958; Gene Tenace, Oakland, A.L., 1972; 4 (4 games) Lou Gehrig, New York A.L., 1928; 3 (6 games) Babe Ruth, New York A.L., 1923; Ted Kluszewski, Chicago A.L., 1959; 3 (5 games) Donn Clendenon, New York Mets N.L., 1969; 2 (8 games) Patrick Dougherty, Boston A.L., 1903.

Most home runs, game—3, Babe Ruth, New York A.L., 1926 and 1928

Most strikeouts, series—11 (7 games) Ed Mathews, Milwaukee N.L., 1958; Wayne Garrett, New York N.L., 1973; 10 (8 games) George Kelly, New York N.L., 1921; 9 (6 games) Jim Bottomley, St. Louis N.L., 1930; 8 (5 games) Rogers Hornsby, Chicago

N.L., 1929; Duke Snider, Brooklyn N.L., 1949; 7 (4 games) Bob Meusel, New York A.L., 1927

Most stolen bases, game—3, Honus Wagner, Pittsburgh N.L., 1909; Willie Davis, Los Angeles N.L., 1965; Lou Brock, St. Louis N.L., 1967 and 1968

Most strikeouts by pitcher: game—17, Bob Gibson, St. Louis N.L., 1968

Most strikeouts by pitcher in succession—6, Horace Eller, Cincinnati N.L., 1919; Moe Drabowsky, Baltimore A.L., 1966

Most strikeouts by pitcher, series—35 (7 games) Bob Gibson, St. Louis N.L., 1968; 28 (8 games) Bill Dinneen, Boston A.L., 1903; 23 (4 games) Sandy Koufax, Los Angeles, 1963; 20 (6 games) Chief Bender, Philadelphia A.L., 1911; 18 (5 games) Christy Mathewson, New York N.L., 1905

Most bases on balls, series—11 (7 games) Babe Ruth, New York A.L., 1926; Gene Tenace, Oakland, A.L., 1973; 8 (6 games) Babe Ruth, New York A.L., 1923; 7 (5 games) James Sheckard, Chicago N.L., 1910; Mickey Cochrane, Phila., A.L., 1929; Joe Gordon, New York, A.L. 1941.

LIFETIME WORLD SERIES RECORDS

Most hits—71, Yogi Berra, New York A. L., 1947, 1949-53, 1955-58, 1960-63.

Most runs—42, Mickey Mantle, New York A. L., 1951-53, 1955-58, 1960-64.

Most runs batted in—40, Mickey Mantle, New York A. L., 1951-53, 1955-58, 1960-64.

Most home runs—18, Mickey Mantle, New York A. L., 1951-53, 1955-58, 1960-64.

Most bases on balls—43, Mickey Mantle, New York A. L., 1951-53, 1955-58, 1960-64.

Most strikeouts—54, Mickey Mantle, New York A. L., 1951-53, 1955-58, 1960-64.

Most victories, pitcher—10, Whitey Ford, New York A. L.,

1950, 1953, 1955-58, 1960-64.

Most times member of winning team—10, Yogi Berra, New York A. L., 1947, 1949-53, 1956, 1958, 1961-62.

Most victories, no defeats—6, Vernon Gomez, New York A. L., 1932, 1936(2), 1937(2), 1938.

Most shutouts—4, Christy Mathewson, New York N. L., 1905 (3), 1913.

Most innings pitched—146, Whitey Ford, New York A. L., 1950, 1953, 1955-58, 1960, 1964.

Most consecutive scoreless innings—33⅔, Whitey Ford, New York A. L., 1960 (18), 1961 (14), 1962 (1⅓).

Most strikeouts by pitcher—94, Whitey Ford, New York A. L., 1950, 1953, 1955-58, 1960-64.

American League Home Run Champions

Year		No.	Year		No.	Year		No.
1901	Nap Lajoie, Phila.	13	1926	Babe Ruth, N. Y.	47	1952	Larry Doby, Cleve.	32
1902	Ralph Seybold, Phila.	16	1927	Babe Ruth, N. Y.	60	1953	Al Rosen, Cleve.	43
1903	Buck Freeman, Bost.	13	1928	Babe Ruth, N. Y.	54	1954	Larry Doby, Cleve.	32
1904	Harry Davis, Phila.	10	1929	Babe Ruth, N. Y.	46	1955	Mickey Mantle, N. Y.	37
1905	Harry Davis, Phila.	8	1930	Babe Ruth, N. Y.	49	1956	Mickey Mantle, N. Y.	52
1906	Harry Davis, Phila.	12	1931	Ruth and Gehrig.	46	1957	Roy Sievers, Wash.	42
1907	Harry Davis, Phila.	8	1932	Jimmy Foxx, Phila.	58	1958	Mickey Mantle, N. Y.	42
1908	Sam Crawford, Det.	7	1933	Jimmy Foxx, Phila.	48	1959	Rocky Colavito, Cleve. and	
1909	Ty Cobb, Det.	9	1934	Lou Gehrig, N. Y.	49		Harmon Killebrew, Wash.	42
1910	J. Garland Stahl, Bost.	10	1935	Jimmy Foxx, Phila. and		1960	Mickey Mantle, N. Y.	40
1911	Franklin Baker, Phila.	9		Hank Greenberg, Det.	36	1961	Roger Maris, N. Y.	61
1912	Franklin Baker, Phila.	10	1936	Lou Gehrig, N. Y.	49	1962	Harmon Killebrew, Minn.	48
1913	Franklin Baker, Phila.	12	1937	Joe DiMaggio, N. Y.	46	1963	Harmon Killebrew, Minn.	45
1914	Franklin Baker, Phila., and		1938	Hank Greenberg, Det.	58	1964	Harmon Killebrew, Minn.	49
	Sam Crawford, Det.	8	1939	Jimmy Foxx, Bost.	35	1965	Tony Conigliaro, Bost.	32
1915	Robert Roth, Chi.-Cleve.	7	1940	Hank Greenberg, Det.	41	1966	Frank Robinson, Balt.	49
1916	Wally Pipp, N. Y.	12	1941	Ted Williams, Bost.	37	1967	Carl Yastrzemski, Bost., and	
1917	Wally Pipp, N. Y.	9	1942	Ted Williams, Bost.	36		Harmon Killebrew, Minn	44
1918	Babe Ruth, Bost., and		1943	Rudy York, Det.	34	1968	Frank Howard, Wash.	44
	Clarence Walker, Phila.	11	1944	Nick Etten, N. Y.	22	1969	Harmon Killebrew, Minn.	49
1919	Babe Ruth, Bost.	29	1945	Vern Stephens, St. L.	24	1970	Frank Howard, Wash.	44
1920	Babe Ruth, N. Y.	54	1946	Hank Greenberg, Det.	44	1971	Bill Melton, Chicago.	33
1921	Babe Ruth, N. Y.	59	1947	Ted Williams, Bost.	32	1972	Dick Allen, Chicago	37
1922	Ken Williams, St. L.	39	1948	Joe DiMaggio, N. Y.	39	1973	Reggie Jackson, Oak.	32
1923	Babe Ruth, N. Y.	41	1949	Ted Williams, Bost.	43	1974	Dick Allen, Chicago	32
1924	Babe Ruth, N. Y.	46	1950	Al Rosen, Cleve.	37	1975	Reggie Jackson, Oak. and	
1925	Bob Meusel, N. Y.	33	1951	Gus Zernial, Chi.-Phila.	33		George Scott, Mil.	36

American League Batting Champions

Year		Avg.	Year		Avg.	Year		Avg.
1901	Nap Lajoie, Phila.	.422	1926	Heinie Manush, Det.	.378	1951	Ferris Fain, Phila.	.344
1902	Ed Delahanty, Wash.	.376	1927	Harry Heilmann, Det.	.398	1952	Ferris Fain, Phila.	.327
1903	Nap Lajoie, Cleve.	.355	1928	Goose Goslin, Wash.	.379	1953	Mickey Vernon, Wash.	.337
1904	Nap Lajoie, Cleve.	.381	1929	Lew Fonseca, Cleve.	.369	1954	Bobby Avila, Cleve.	.341
1905	Elmer Flick, Cleve.	.306	1930	Al Simmons, Phila.	.381	1955	Al Kaline, Det.	.340
1906	George Stone, St. L.	.358	1931	Al Simmons, Phila.	.390	1956	Mickey Mantle, N. Y.	.353
1907	Ty Cobb, Det.	.350	1932	Dale Alexander, Det.-Bost.	.367	1957	Ted Wiliams, Bost.	.388
1908	Ty Cobb, Det.	.324	1933	Jimmy Foxx, Phila.	.356	1958	Ted Williams, Bost.	.328
1909	Ty Cobb, Det.	.377	1934	Lou Gehrig, N. Y.	.363	1959	Harvey Kuenn, Det.	.353
1910	Ty Cobb, Det.	.385	1935	Buddy Myer, Wash.	.349	1960	Pete Runnels, Bost.	.320
1911	Ty Cobb, Det.	.420	1936	Luke Appling, Chi.	.388	1961	Norman Cash, Det.	.361
1912	Ty Cobb, Det.	.410	1937	Charles Gehringer, Det.	.371	1962	Pete Runnels, Bost.	.326
1913	Ty Cobb, Det.	.390	1938	Jimmy Foxx, Bost.	.349	1963	Carl Yastrzemski, Bost.	.321
1914	Ty Cobb, Det.	.368	1939	Joe DiMaggio, N. Y.	.381	1964	Tony Oliva, Minn.	.323
1915	Ty Cobb, Det.	.369	1940	Joe DiMaggio, N. Y.	.352	1965	Tony Oliva, Minn.	.321
1916	Tris Speaker, Cleve.	.386	1941	Ted Williams, Bost.	.406	1966	Frank Robinson, Balt.	.316
1917	Ty Cobb, Det.	.383	1942	Ted Williams, Bost.	.356	1967	Carl Yastrzemski, Bost.	.326
1918	Ty Cobb, Det.	.382	1943	Luke Appling, Chi.	.328	1968	Carl Yastrzemski, Bost.	.301
1919	Ty Cobb, Det.	.384	1944	Lou Boudreau, Cleve.	.327	1969	Rod Carew, Minn.	.332
1920	George Sisler, St. L.	.407	1945	George Sternweiss, N. Y.	.309	1970	Alex Johnson, Calif.	.329
1921	Harry Heilmann, Det.	.394	1946	Mickey Vernon, Wash.	.353	1971	Tony Oliva, Minn.	.337
1922	George Sisler, St. L.	.420	1947	Ted Williams, Bost.	.343	1972	Rod Carew, Minn.	.318
1923	Harry Heilmann, Det.	.403	1948	Ted Williams, Bost.	.369	1973	Rod Carew, Minn.	.350
1924	Babe Ruth, N. Y.	.378	1949	George Kell, Det.	.343	1974	Rod Carew, Minn.	.364
1925	Harry Heilmann, Det.	.393	1950	Billy Goodman, Bost.	.354	1975	Rod Carew, Minn.	.359

American League Pennant Winners

Year	Club	Manager	Won	Lost	Pct.
1901	Chicago	Clark C. Griffith	83	53	.610
1902	Philadelphia	Connie Mack	83	53	.610
1903*	Boston	Jimmy Collins	91	47	.659
1904†	Boston	Jimmy Collins	95	59	.617
1905	Philadelphia	Connie Mack	92	56	.622
1906*	Chicago	Fielder A. Jones	93	58	.616
1907	Detroit	Hugh A. Jennings	92	58	.613
1908	Detroit	Hugh A. Jennings	90	63	.588
1909	Detroit	Hugh A. Jennings	98	54	.645
1910*	Philadelphia	Connie Mack	102	48	.680
1911*	Philadelphia	Connie Mack	101	50	.669
1912*	Boston	J. Garland Stahl	105	47	.691
1913*	Philadelphia	Connie Mack	96	57	.627
1914	Philadelphia	Connie Mack	99	53	.651
1915*	Boston	William F. Carrigan	101	50	.669
1916*	Boston	William F. Carrigan	91	63	.591
1917*	Chicago	Clarence H. Rowland	100	54	.649
1918*	Boston	Ed Barrow	75	51	.595
1919	Chicago	William Gleason	88	52	.629
1920*	Cleveland	Tris E. Speaker	98	56	.636
1921	New York	Miller J. Huggins	98	55	.641
1922	New York	Miller J. Huggins	94	60	.610
1923*	New York	Miller J. Huggins	98	54	.645
1924*	Washington	Stanley R. Harris	92	62	.597
1925	Washington	Stanley R. Harris	96	55	.636
1926	New York	Miller J. Huggins	91	63	.591
1927*	New York	Miller J. Huggins	110	44	.714
1928*	New York	Miller J. Huggins	101	53	.656
1929*	Philadelphia	Connie Mack	104	46	.693
1930*	Philadelphia	Connie Mack	102	52	.662
1931	Philadelphia	Connie Mack	107	45	.704
1932*	New York	Joseph V. McCarthy	107	47	.695
1933	Washington	Joseph E. Cronin	99	53	.651
1934	Detroit	Mickey Cochrane	101	53	.656
1935*	Detroit	Mickey Cochrane	93	58	.616
1936*	New York	Joseph V. McCarthy	102	51	.667
1937*	New York	Joseph V. McCarthy	102	52	.662
1938*	New York	Joseph V. McCarthy	99	53	.651
1939*	New York	Joseph V. McCarthy	106	45	.702
1940	Detroit	Delmar D. Baker	90	64	.584
1941*	New York	Joseph V. McCarthy	101	53	.656
1942	New York	Joseph V. McCarthy	103	51	.669
1943*	New York	Joseph V. McCarthy	98	56	.636
1944	St. Louis	Luke Sewell	89	65	.578
1945*	Detroit	Steve O'Neill	88	65	.575
1946	Boston	Joseph E. Cronin	104	50	.675
1947*	New York	Stanley R. Harris	97	57	.630
1948*	Cleveland	Lou Boudreau	97	58	.626
1949*	New York	Casey Stengel	97	57	.630
1950*	New York	Casey Stengel	98	56	.636
1951*	New York	Casey Stengel	98	56	.636
1952*	New York	Casey Stengel	95	59	.617
1953*	New York	Casey Stengel	99	52	.656
1954	Cleveland	Al Lopez	111	43	.721
1955	New York	Casey Stengel	96	58	.623
1956*	New York	Casey Stengel	97	57	.630
1957	New York	Casey Stengel	98	56	.636
1958*	New York	Casey Stengel	92	62	.597
1959	Chicago	Al Lopez	94	60	.610
1960	New York	Casey Stengel	97	57	.630
1961*	New York	Ralph Houk	109	53	.673
1962*	New York	Ralph Houk	96	66	.593
1963	New York	Ralph Houk	104	57	.646
1964	New York	Yogi Berra	99	63	.611
1965	Minnesota	Sam Mele	102	60	.630
1966*	Baltimore	Hank Bauer	97	63	.606
1967	Boston	Dick Williams	92	70	.568
1968*	Detroit	Mayo Smith	103	59	.636
1969	Baltimore‡	Earl Weaver	109	53	.673
1970*	Baltimore‡	Earl Weaver	108	54	.667
1971	Baltimore‡	Earl Weaver	101	57	.639
1972	Oakland**	Dick Williams	93	62	.600
1973	Oakland*††	Dick Williams	94	68	.580
1974	Oakland*††	Alvin Dark	90	72	.556
1975	Boston§	Darrell Johnson	95	65	.594

* World Series winner.   † No World Series.   ‡ Defeated Minnesota, Western Division winner, in playoff.   § Defeated Oakland, Western Division leader, in playoff.   ** Defeated Detroit, Eastern Division winner, in playoff.   †† Defeated Baltimore, Eastern Division winner, in playoff.

BASEBALL'S PERFECTLY PITCHED GAMES
(No opposing runner reached base)

John Richmond—Worcester vs. Cleveland (NL) June 12, 1880	1–0
John M. Ward—Providence vs. Buffalo (NL) June 17, 1880	5–0
Cy Young—Boston vs. Philadelphia (AL) May 5, 1904	3–0
Addie Joss—Cleveland vs. Chicago (AL) Oct. 2, 1908	1–0
Ernest Shore—Boston vs. Washington (AL) June 23, 1917	4–0

(Shore, relief pitcher for Babe Ruth who walked first batter before being ejected by umpire, retired 26 batters who faced him and baserunner was out stealing)

Charles Robertson—Chicago vs. Detroit (AL) April 30, 1922	2–0
*Don Larsen—New York (AL) vs. Brooklyn (NL) Oct. 8, 1956	2–0
Jim Bunning—Philadelphia vs. New York (NL) June 21, 1964	6–0
Sandy Koufax—Los Angeles vs. Chicago (NL) Sept. 9, 1965	1–0
Jim Hunter—Oakland vs. Minnesota (AL) May 8, 1968	4–0

* World Series

Harvey Haddix, of Pittsburgh, pitched 12 perfect innings against Milwaukee (NL), May 26, 1959 but lost game in 13th on error and hit.

Larsen's Perfect Game in '56 World Series

Don Larsen of the New York Yankees pitched the only no-run no-hit game in World Series history in 1956 and hurled a perfect game in so doing. Facing the Brooklyn Dodgers at the Yankee Stadium in the fifth game before 64,519 on Oct. 8, Larsen retired 27 batters in a row. The Yankees won, 2 to 0.

Consecutive No-Hitters by Vander Meer

Johnny Vander Meer, a 23-year-old left-hander with the Cincinnati Reds, pitched consecutive no-hitters in June 1938, setting a mark of 18 innings of no-hit hurling. On June 11, in Cincinnati, he set down Boston without a hit as the Reds won, 3-0. Four days later, June 15, in the first night game in Brooklyn, he again held the opposition hitless as the Reds triumphed, 6-0. He was nicknamed Johnny (Double No-Hitter) Vander Meer.

National League Pennant Winners

Year	Club	Manager	Won	Lost	Pct.	Year	Club	Manager	Won	Lost	Pct.
1876	Chicago	Albert G. Spalding	52	14	.788	1924	New York	John J. McGraw	93	60	.608
1877	Boston	Harry Wright	31	17	.646	1925*	Pittsburgh	William B. McKechnie	95	58	.621
1878	Boston	Harry Wright	41	19	.683	1926*	St. Louis	Rogers Hornsby	89	65	.578
1879	Providence	George Wright	55	23	.705	1927	Pittsburgh	Donie Bush	94	60	.610
1880	Chicago	Adrian C. Anson	67	17	.798	1928	St. Louis	William B. McKechnie	95	59	.617
1881	Chicago	Adrian C. Anson	56	28	.667	1929	Chicago	Joseph V. McCarthy	98	54	.647
1882	Chicago	Adrian C. Anson	55	29	.655	1930	St. Louis	Gabby Street	92	62	.595
1883	Boston	John F. Morrill	63	35	.643	1931*	St. Louis	Gabby Street	101	53	.656
1884	Providence	Frank C. Bancroft	84	28	.750	1932	Chicago	Charles J. Grimm	90	64	.584
1885	Chicago	Adrian C. Anson	87	25	.777	1933*	New York	William H. Terry	91	61	.599
1886	Chicago	Adrian C. Anson	90	34	.726	1934*	St. Louis	Frank F. Frisch	95	58	.621
1887	Detroit	W. H. Watkins	79	45	.637	1935	Chicago	Charles J. Grimm	100	54	.649
1888	New York	James J. Mutrie	84	47	.641	1936	New York	William H. Terry	92	62	.597
1889	New York	James J. Mutrie	83	43	.659	1937	New York	William H. Terry	95	57	.625
1890	Brooklyn	William H. McGunnigle	86	43	.667	1938	Chicago	Gabby Hartnett	89	63	.586
1891	Boston	Frank G. Selee	87	51	.630	1939	Cincinnati	William B. McKechnie	97	57	.630
1892	Boston	Frank G. Selee	102	48	.680	1940*	Cincinnati	William B. McKechnie	100	53	.654
1893	Boston	Frank G. Selee	86	43	.667	1941	Brooklyn	Leo E. Durocher	100	54	.649
1894	Baltimore	Edward H. Hanlon	89	39	.695	1942*	St. Louis	William H. Southworth	106	48	.688
1895	Baltimore	Edward H. Hanlon	87	43	.669	1943	St. Louis	William H. Southworth	105	49	.682
1896	Baltimore	Edward H. Hanlon	90	39	.698	1944*	St. Louis	William H. Southworth	105	49	.682
1897	Boston	Frank G. Selee	93	39	.705	1945	Chicago	Charles J. Grimm	98	56	.636
1898	Boston	Frank G. Selee	102	47	.685	1946*	St. Louis	Edwin H. Dyer	98	58	.628
1899	Brooklyn	Edward H. Hanlon	88	42	.677	1947	Brooklyn	Burton E. Shotton	94	60	.610
1900	Brooklyn	Edward H. Hanlon	82	54	.603	1948	Boston	William H. Southworth	91	62	.595
1901	Pittsburgh	Fred C. Clarke	90	49	.647	1949	Brooklyn	Burton E. Shotton	97	57	.630
1902	Pittsburgh	Fred C. Clarke	103	36	.741	1950	Philadelphia	Edwin M. Sawyer	91	63	.591
1903	Pittsburgh	Fred C. Clarke	91	49	.650	1951	New York	Leo E. Durocher	98	59	.624
1904†	New York	John J. McGraw	106	47	.693	1952	Brooklyn	Charles W. Dressen	96	57	.627
1905*	New York	John J. McGraw	105	48	.686	1953	Brooklyn	Charles W. Dressen	105	49	.682
1906	Chicago	Frank L. Chance	116	36	.763	1954*	New York	Leo E. Durocher	97	57	.630
1907*	Chicago	Frank L. Chance	107	45	.704	1955*	Brooklyn	Walter Alston	98	55	.641
1908*	Chicago	Frank L. Chance	99	55	.643	1956	Brooklyn	Walter Alston	93	61	.604
1909*	Pittsburgh	Fred C. Clarke	110	42	.724	1957*	Milwaukee	Fred Haney	95	59	.617
1910	Chicago	Frank L. Chance	104	50	.675	1958	Milwaukee	Fred Haney	92	62	.597
1911	New York	John J. McGraw	99	54	.647	1959*	Los Angeles	Walter Alston	88	68	.564
1912	New York	John J. McGraw	103	48	.682	1960*	Pittsburgh	Danny Murtaugh	95	59	.617
1913	New York	John J. McGraw	101	51	.664	1961	Cincinnati	Fred Hutchinson	93	61	.604
1914*	Boston	George T. Stallings	94	59	.614	1962	San Francisco	Alvin Dark	103	62	.624
1915	Philadelphia	Patrick J. Moran	90	62	.592	1963*	Los Angeles	Walter Alston	99	63	.611
1916	Brooklyn	Wilbert Robinson	94	60	.610	1964*	St. Louis	Johnny Keane	93	69	.574
1917	New York	John J. McGraw	98	56	.636	1965*	Los Angeles	Walter Alston	97	65	.599
1918	Chicago	Fred L. Mitchell	84	45	.651	1966	Los Angeles	Walter Alston	95	67	.586
1919*	Cincinnati	Patrick J. Moran	96	44	.686	1967*	St. Louis	Red Schoendienst	101	60	.627
1920	Brooklyn	Wilbert Robinson	93	61	.604	1968	St. Louis	Red Schoendienst	97	65	.599
1921*	New York	John J. McGraw	94	59	.614	1969*	New York‡	Gil Hodges	100	62	.617
1922*	New York	John J. McGraw	93	61	.604	1970	Cincinnati§	Sparky Anderson	102	60	.630
1923	New York	John J. McGraw	95	58	.621	1971*	Pittsburgh**	Danny Murtaugh	97	65	.599
						1972	Cincinnati	Sparky Anderson	95	59	.617
						1973	New York††	Yogi Berra	82	79	.509
						1974	Los Angeles	Walter Alston	102	60	.630
						1975*	Cincinnati§	Sparky Anderson	108	54	.667

* World Series Winner. † No World Series. ‡ Defeated Atlanta, Western Division winner, in playoff. § Defeated Pittsburgh, Eastern Division winner, in playoff. ** Defeated San Francisco, Western Division winner in playoff. †† Defeated Cincinnati, Western Division winner in playoff.

Ted Williams' Major League Batting Record

(All games with Boston Red Sox)

	g	r	h	hr	rbi	avg		g	r	h	hr	rbi	avg		g	r	h	hr	rbi	avg
1939..	149	131	185	31	145*	.327	1948..	137	124	188	25	127	.369*	1956..	136	71	138	24	82	.345
1940..	144	134*	193	23	113	.344	1949..	155	150*	194	43*	159†	.343	1957..	132	96	163	38	87	.388*
1941..	143	135*	185	37*	120	.406*	1950..	89	82	106	28	97	.317	1958..	129	81	135	26	85	.328*
1942..	150	141*	186	36*	137*	.356*	1951..	148	109	169	30	126	.318	1959..	103	32	69	10	43	.254
1943–45..	In military service						1952..	6	2	4	1	3	.400	1960..	113	56	98	29	72	.316
1946..	150	142*	176	38	123	.342	1953..	37	17	37	13	34	.407							
1947..	156	125*	181	32*	114*	.343*	1954..	117	93	133	29	89	.345	Totals	2292	1798	2654	521	1839	.344
							1955..	98	77	114	28	83	.356							

* Led league.
† Tied for league lead.

National League Batting Champions

Year		Avg.	Year		Avg.	Year		Avg.
1876	Roscoe Barnes, Chi	.404	1909	Honus Wagner, Pitts	.339	1943	Stan Musial, St. L	.357
1877	Jim White, Bost	.385	1910	Sherwood Magee, Phila	.331	1944	Dixie Walker, Bklyn	.357
1878	Abner Dalrymple, Mil	.356	1911	Honus Wagner, Pitts	.334	1945	Phil Cavarretta, Chi	.355
1879	Cap Anson, Chi	.407	1912	Henry Zimmerman, Chi	.372	1946	Stan Musial, St. L	.365
1880	George Gore, Chi	.365	1913	Jake Daubert, Bklyn	.350	1947	Harry Walker, St. L.-Phila.	.363
1881	Cap Anson, Chi	.399	1914	Jake Daubert, Bklyn	.329	1948	Stan Musial, St. L	.376
1882	Dan Brouthers, Buff	.367	1915	Larry Doyle, N. Y	.320	1949	Jackie Robinson, Bklyn	.342
1883	Dan Brouthers, Buff	.371	1916	Hal Chase, Cin	.339	1950	Stan Musial, St. L	.346
1884	James O'Rourke, Buff	.350	1917	Edd Roush, Cin	.341	1951	Stan Musial, St. L	.355
1885	Roger Connor, N. Y	.371	1918	Zach Wheat, Bklyn	.335	1952	Stan Musial, St. L	.336
1886	King Kelly, Chi	.388	1919	Edd Roush, Cin	.321	1953	Carl Furillo, Bklyn	.344
1887	Cap Anson, Chi	.421	1920	Rogers Hornsby, St. L	.370	1954	Willie Mays, N. Y	.345
1888	Cap Anson, Chi	.343	1921	Rogers Hornsby, St. L	.397	1955	Richie Ashburn, Phila	.338
1889	Dan Brouthers, Bost	.373	1922	Rogers Hornsby, St. L	.401	1956	Henry Aaron, Mil	.328
1890	John Glasscock, N. Y	.336	1923	Rogers Hornsby, St. L	.384	1957	Stan Musial, St. L	.351
1891	Wm. Hamilton, Phila	.338	1924	Rogers Hornsby, St. L	.424	1958	Richie Ashburn, Phila	.350
1892	Dan Brouthers, Bklyn., and Clarence Childs, Cleve	.335	1925	Rogers Hornsby, St. L	.403	1959	Henry Aaron, Mil	.355
1893	Hugh Duffy, Bost	.378	1926	Gene Hargrave, Cin	.353	1960	Dick Groat, Pitts	.325
1894	Hugh Duffy, Bost	.438	1927	Paul Waner, Pitts	.380	1961	Roberto Clemente, Pitts	.351
1895	Jesse Burkett, Cleve	.423	1928	Rogers Hornsby, Bost	.387	1962	Tommy Davis, L. A	.346
1896	Jesse Burkett, Cleve	.410	1929	Lefty O'Doul, Phila	.398	1963	Tommy Davis, L. A	.326
1897	Willie Keeler, Balt	.432	1930	Bill Terry, N. Y	.401	1964	Roberto Clemente, Pitts	.339
1898	Willie Keeler, Balt	.379	1931	Chick Hafey, St. L	.349	1965	Roberto Clemente, Pitts	.329
1899	Ed Delahanty, Phila	.408	1932	Lefty O'Doul, Bklyn	.368	1966	Matty Alou, Pitts	.342
1900	Honus Wagner, Pitts	.381	1933	Chuck Klein, Phila	.368	1967	Roberto Clemente, Pitts	.357
1901	Jesse Burkett, St. L	.382	1934	Paul Waner, Pitts	.362	1968	Pete Rose, Cin	.335
1902	Clarence Beaumont, Pitts	.357	1935	Arky Vaughan, Pitts	.385	1969	Pete Rose, Cin	.348
1903	Honus Wagner, Pitts	.355	1936	Paul Waner, Pitts	.373	1970	Rico Carty, Atlanta	.366
1904	Honus Wagner, Pitts	.349	1937	Joe Medwick, St. L	.374	1971	Joe Torre, St. L	.363
1905	Cy Seymour, Cin	.377	1938	Ernie Lombardi, Cin	.342	1972	Billy Williams, Chi.	.333
1906	Honus Wagner, Pitts	.339	1939	John Mize, St. L	.349	1973	Pete Rose, Cin	.338
1907	Honus Wagner, Pitts	.350	1940	Debs Garms, Pitts	.355	1974	Ralph Garr, Atlanta	.353
1908	Honus Wagner, Pitts	.354	1941	Pete Reiser, Bklyn	.343	1975	Bill Madlock, Chicago	.354
			1942	Ernie Lombardi, Bost	.330			

Mickey Mantle's Major League Batting Record

(All games with New York Yankees)

	g	r	h	hr	rbi	avg		g	r	h	hr	rbi	avg		g	r	h	hr	rbi	avg
1951...	96	61	91	13	65	.267	1958...	150	*127	158	*42	97	.304	1965...	122	44	92	19	46	.255
1952...	142	94	171	23	87	.311	1959...	144	104	154	31	75	.285	1966...	108	40	96	23	56	.288
1953...	127	105	136	21	92	.295	1960...	153	*119	145	*40	94	.275	1967...	144	63	108	22	55	.245
1954...	146	*129	163	27	102	.300	1961...	153	*132	163	54	128	.317	1968...	144	57	103	18	54	.237
1955...	147	121	158	*37	99	.306	1962...	123	96	121	30	89	.321							
1956...	150	*132	188	*52	*130	*.353	1963...	65	40	54	15	35	.314	Totals..	2401	1677	2415	536	1509	.298
1957...	144	*121	173	34	94	.365	1964...	143	92	141	35	111	.303	* Led league.						

World Series Record

	g	r	h	hr	rbi	avg		g	r	h	hr	rbi	avg		g	r	h	hr	rbi	avg
1951.....	2	1	0	0	0	.200	1957...	6	3	5	1	2	.263	1963...	4	1	2	1	1	.133
1952.....	7	5	10	2	3	.345	1958...	7	4	6	2	3	.250	1964...	7	8	8	3	8	.333
1953.....	6	3	5	2	7	.208	1960...	7	8	10	3	11	.400							
1955.....	3	1	2	1	1	.200	1961...	2	0	1	0	0	.167	Totals...	65	†42	59	†18	†40	.257
1956.....	7	6	6	3	4	.250	1962...	7	2	3	0	0	.120	† Series record.						

Mantle also holds World Series records for most long hits (26), most total bases (123), most strikeouts (54), most bases on balls (43), and most games played by an outfielder (63).

Baseball's Triple Crown Winners

(Players leading league for season in batting, runs batted in and home runs)

Two-Time Winners

Rogers Hornsby, St. Louis (N. L.)—1922, 1925
Ted Williams, Boston (A. L.)—1942, 1947

Others

Ty Cobb, Detroit (A. L.)—1909
Heinie Zimmerman, Chicago (N. L.)—1912
Jimmy Foxx, Philadelphia (A. L.)—1933

Others (Cont.)

Chuck Klein, Philadelphia (N. L.)—1933
Lou Gehrig, New York (A. L.)—1934
Joe Medwick, St. Louis (N. L.)—1937
Mickey Mantle, New York (A. L.)—1956
Frank Robinson, Baltimore (A. L.)—1966
Carl Yastrzemski, Boston (A.L.)—1967

NATIONAL BASEBALL HALL OF FAME
Cooperstown, N. Y.

Member	Elected	Member	Elected	Member	Elected
Alexander, Grover Cleveland	1938	Flick, Elmer H.	1963	McCarthy, Thomas F.	1946
Anson, Adrian (Cap)	1939	Ford, Edward C. (Whitey)	1974	McGinnity, Joseph Jerome	1946
Appling, Lucius Benjamin	1964	Foxx, James Emory	1951	McGraw, John Joseph	1937
Averill, H. Earl	1975	Frick, Ford C.	1970	McKechnie, William B.	1962
Baker, J. Franklin (Home Run)	1955	Frisch, Frank F.	1947	Medwick, Joseph Michael (Ducky)	1968
Bancroft, David James (Beauty)	1971	Galvin, James F. (Pud)	1965	Musial, Stanley Frank	1969
Barrow, Edward Grant	1953	Gehrig, Henry Louis	1939	Nichols, Charles A. (Kid)	1949
Beckley, Jacob Peter	1971	Gehringer, Charles L.	1949	O'Rourke, James H.	1945
Bell, James (Cool Papa)	1974	Gibson, Josh	1972	Ott, Melvin Thomas	1951
Bender, Charles Albert (Chief)	1953	Gomez, Vernon L. (Lefty)	1972	Paige, Leroy Robert (Satchel)	1971
Berra, Lawrence Peter (Yogi)	1972	Goslin, Leon Allen (Goose)	1968	Pennock, Herbert J.	1948
Bottomley, James L. (Sunny Jim)	1974	Greenberg, Henry Benjamin	1956	Plank, Edward S.	1946
Boudreau, Louis	1970	Griffith, Clark C.	1946	Radbourn, Charles	1939
Bresnahan, Roger Philip	1945	Grimes, Burleigh Arland	1964	Rice, Edgar C. (Sam)	1963
Brouthers, Dennis (Dan)	1945	Grove, Robert Moses (Lefty)	1947	Rickey, Wesley Branch	1967
Brown, Mordecai (Three-Finger)	1949	Hafey, Charles James (Chick)	1971	Rixey, Eppa	1963
Bulkeley, Morgan G.	1937	Haines, Jesse Joseph	1970	Roberts, Robert E. (Robin)	1975
Burkett, Jesse C.	1946	Hamilton, William Robert	1961	Robinson, Jack R.	1962
Campanella, Roy	1969	Harridge, Will	1972	Robinson, Wilbert	1945
Carey, Max George	1961	Hartnett, Charles Leo (Gabby)	1955	Roush, Edd J.	1962
Cartwright, Alexander Joy	1938	Heilmann, Harry E.	1952	Ruffing, Charles Herbert (Red)	1967
Chadwick, Henry	1938	Herman, William J. B. (Billy)	1975	Ruth, George Herman (Babe)	1936
Chance, Frank LeRoy	1946	Hooper, Harry Bartholomew	1971	Schalk, Raymond	1955
Charleston, Oscar	1975	Hornsby, Rogers	1942	Simmons, Aloysius Harry	1953
Chesbro, John Dwight	1946	Hoyt, Waite Charles	1969	Sisler, George Harold	1939
Clarke, Fred C.	1945	Hubbell, Carl Owen	1947	Spahn, Warren Edward	1973
Clarkson, John G.	1963	Huggins, Miller James	1964	Spalding, Albert Goodwill	1939
Clemente, Roberto Walker	1973	Irvin, Monford (Monte)	1973	Speaker, Tristram E.	1937
Cobb, Tyrus Raymond	1936	Jennings, Hughie	1945	Stengel, Charles Dillon (Casey)	1966
Cochrane, Gordon (Mickey)	1947	Johnson, Byron Bancroft	1937	Terry, William Harold	1954
Collins, Edward Trowbridge	1939	Johnson, Walter Perry	1936	Thompson, Sam	1974
Collins, James L.	1945	Johnson, William (Judy)	1975	Tinker, Joseph B.	1946
Combs, Earle Bryan	1970	Keefe, Timothy J.	1964	Traynor, Harold J. (Pie)	1948
Comiskey, Charles Albert	1939	Keeler, Willie	1939	Vance, C. Arthur (Dazzy)	1955
Conlan, John B. (Jocko)	1974	Kelley, Joseph James	1971	Waddell, George E. (Rube)	1946
Connolly, Thomas H.	1953	Kelly, George Lange	1973	Wagner, John P. (Honus)	1936
Connor, Roger	1975	Kelly, Michael J. (King)	1945	Wallace, Roderick John	1953
Coveleski, Stanley	1969	Kiner, Ralph McPherran	1975	Walsh, Edward A.	1946
Crawford, Samuel E.	1957	Klem, William Joseph	1953	Waner, Lloyd James	1967
Cronin, Joseph Edward	1956	Koufax, Sanford (Sandy)	1972	Waner, Paul Glee	1952
Cummings, William Arthur (Candy)	1939	Lajoie, Napoleon	1937	Ward, John Montgomery	1964
Cuyler, Hazen S. (Kiki)	1968	Landis, Kenesaw Mountain	1944	Weiss, George Martin	1971
Dean, Jay Hanna (Dizzy)	1953	Lemon, Robert Granville	1975	Welch, Michael F. (Mickey)	1973
Delahanty, Edward J.	1945	Leonard, Walter F. (Buck)	1972	Wheat, Zachary Davis	1959
Dickey, William Malcolm	1954	Lindstrom, Fred Charles	1975	Williams, Theodore Samuel	1966
DiMaggio, Joseph Paul	1955	Lyons, Theodore Amar	1955	Wright, George	1937
Duffy, Hugh	1945	Mack, Connie	1937	Wright, William Henry (Harry)	1953
Evans, William G. (Billy)	1973	Mantle, Mickey Charles	1974	Wynn, Early	1972
Evers, John Joseph	1946	Manush, Henry Emmett (Heinie)	1964	Young, Denton T. (Cy)	1937
Ewing, William B. (Buck)	1939	Maranville, Walter J. (Rabbit)	1954	Youngs, Ross (Pep)	1972
Faber, Urban Charles (Red)	1964	Marquard, Richard William (Rube)	1971		
Feller, Robert W. A.	1962	Mathewson, Christopher	1936		
		McCarthy, Joseph V.	1957		

Stan Musial's Major League Batting Record
(All games with St. Louis Cardinals)

	g	r	h	hr	rbi	avg		g	r	h	hr	rbi	avg		g	r	h	hr	rbi	avg
1941...	12	8	20	1	7	.426	1950...	146	105	192	28	109	*.346	1959...	115	37	87	14	44	.255
1942...	140	87	147	10	72	.315	1951...	152	†124	205	32	108	*.355	1960...	116	49	91	17	63	.275
1943...	†157	108	*220	13	87	*.357	1952...	†154	*105	*194	21	91	*.336	1961...	123	46	107	15	70	.288
1944...	146	112	†197	12	94	.347	1953...	157	127	200	30	113	.337	1962...	135	57	143	19	82	.330
1945...	In military service						1954...	153	†120	195	35	126	.330	1963...	124	34	86	12	58	.255
1946...	†156	*124	*228	16	103	*.365	1955...	†154	97	179	33	108	.319							
1947...	149	113	183	19	95	.312	1956...	156	87	184	27	*109	.310	Totals.	.3026	1949	3630	475	1951	.331
1948...	155	*135	*230	39	*131	*.376	1957...	134	82	176	29	102	*.351	* Led league.						
1949...	*157	128	*207	36	123	.338	1958...	135	64	159	17	62	.337	† Tied for league lead.						

MOST VALUABLE PLAYERS
(Baseball Writers Association selections)

American League

1931	Lefty Grove, Philadelphia
1932-33	Jimmy Foxx, Philadelphia
1934	Mickey Cochrane, Detroit
1935	Hank Greenberg, Detroit
1936	Lou Gehrig, New York
1937	Charley Gehringer, Detroit
1938	Jimmy Foxx, Boston
1939	Joe DiMaggio, New York
1940	Hank Greenberg, Detroit
1941	Joe DiMaggio, New York
1942	Joe Gordon, New York
1943	Spurgeon Chandler, New York
1944-45	Hal Newhouser, Detroit
1946	Ted Williams, Boston
1947	Joe DiMaggio, New York
1948	Lou Boudreau, Cleveland
1949	Ted Williams, Boston
1950	Phil Rizzuto, New York
1951	Yogi Berra, New York
1952	Bobby Shantz, Philadelphia
1953	Al Rosen, Cleveland
1954-55	Yogi Berra, New York
1956-57	Mickey Mantle, New York
1958	Jackie Jensen, Boston
1959	Nellie Fox, Chicago
1960-61	Roger Maris, New York
1962	Mickey Mantle, New York
1963	Elston Howard, New York
1964	Brooks Robinson, Baltimore
1965	Zoilo Versalles, Minnesota
1966	Frank Robinson, Baltimore
1967	Carl Yastrzemski, Boston
1968	Dennis McLain, Detroit
1969	Harmon Killebrew, Minnesota
1970	John (Boog) Powell, Baltimore
1971	Vida Blue, Oakland
1972	Dick Allen, Chicago
1973	Reggie Jackson, Oakland
1974	Jeff Burroughs, Texas
1975	Fred Lynn, Boston

National League

1931	Frank Frisch, St. Louis
1932	Chuck Klein, Philadelphia
1933	Carl Hubbell, New York
1934	Dizzy Dean, St. Louis
1935	Gabby Hartnett, Chicago
1936	Carl Hubbell, New York
1937	Joe Medwick, St. Louis
1938	Ernie Lombardi, Cincinnati
1939	Bucky Walters, Cincinnati
1940	Frank McCormick, Cincinnati
1941	Dolph Camilli, Brooklyn
1942	Mort Cooper, St. Louis
1943	Stan Musial, St. Louis
1944	Marty Marion, St. Louis
1945	Phil Cavarretta, Chicago
1946	Stan Musial, St. Louis
1947	Bob Elliott, Boston
1948	Stan Musial, St. Louis
1949	Jackie Robinson, Brooklyn
1950	Jim Konstanty, Philadelphia
1951	Roy Campanella, Brooklyn
1952	Hank Sauer, Chicago
1953	Roy Campanella, Brooklyn
1954	Willie Mays, New York
1955	Roy Campanella, Brooklyn
1956	Don Newcombe, Brooklyn
1957	Henry Aaron, Milwaukee
1958-59	Ernie Banks, Chicago
1960	Dick Groat, Pittsburgh
1961	Frank Robinson, Cincinnati
1962	Maury Wills, Los Angeles
1963	Sandy Koufax, Los Angeles
1964	Ken Boyer, St. Louis
1965	Willie Mays, San Francisco
1966	Roberto Clemente, Pittsburgh
1967	Orlando Cepeda, St. Louis
1968	Bob Gibson, St. Louis
1969	Willie McCovey, San Francisco
1970	Johnny Bench, Cincinnati
1971	Joe Torre, St. Louis
1972	Johnny Bench, Cincinnati
1973	Pete Rose, Cincinnati
1974	Steve Garvey, Los Angeles
1975	Joe Morgan, Cincinnati

CY YOUNG AWARD

1956	Don Newcombe, Brooklyn N. L.
1957	Warren Spahn, Milwaukee N. L.
1958	Bob Turley, New York A. L.
1959	Early Wynn, Chicago A. L.
1960	Vernon Law, Pittsburgh N. L.
1961	Whitey Ford, New York A. L.
1962	Don Drysdale, Los Angeles N. L.
1963	Sandy Koufax, Los Angeles N. L.
1964	Dean Chance, Los Angeles A. L.
1965	Sandy Koufax, Los Angeles N. L.
1966	Sandy Koufax, Los Angeles N. L.
1967	Jim Lonborg, Boston A. L. and Mike McCormick, San Francisco N. L.
1968	Dennis McLain, Detroit A. L. and Bob Gibson, St. Louis N. L.
1969	Mike Cuellar, Baltimore, and Dennis McLain, Detroit, tied in A. L.; Tom Seaver, N. Y. N. L.
1970	Jim Perry, Minnesota A. L.; Bob Gibson, St. Louis N. L.
1971	Vida Blue. Oakland A. L.; Ferguson Jenkins, Chi. N. L.
1972	Gaylord Perry, Cleveland A.L. Steve Carlton, Phila. N.L.
1973	Jim Palmer, Baltimore A.L. Tom Seaver, New York N.L
1974	Catfish Hunter, Oakland A.L. Mike Marshall, Los Angeles N.L.
1975	Jim Palmer, Baltimore A.L. Tom Seaver, New York N.L.

ROOKIE OF THE YEAR
(Baseball Writers Association selections)

American League

1949	Roy Sievers, St. Louis
1950	Walt Dropo, Boston
1951	Gil McDougald, New York
1952	Harry Byrd, Philadelphia
1953	Harvey Kuenn, Detroit
1954	Bob Grim, New York
1955	Herb Score, Cleveland
1956	Luis Aparicio, Chicago
1957	Tony Kubek, New York
1958	Albie Pearson, Washington
1959	William Allison, Washington
1960	Ron Hansen, Baltimore
1961	Don Schwall, Boston
1962	Tom Tresh, New York
1963	Gary Peters, Chicago
1964	Tony Oliva, Minnesota
1965	Curt Blefary, Baltimore
1966	Tommy Agee, Chicago
1967	Rod Carew, Minnesota
1968	Stan Bahnsen, New York
1969	Lou Piniella, Kansas City
1970	Thurman Munson, New York
1971	Chris Chambliss, Cleveland
1972	Carlton Fisk, Boston
1973	Alonzo Bumbry, Baltimore
1974	Mike Hargrove, Texas
1975	Fred Lynn, Boston

National League

1949	Don Newcombe, Brooklyn
1950	Sam Jethroe, Boston
1951	Willie Mays, New York
1952	Joe Black, Brooklyn
1953	Jim Gilliam, Brooklyn
1954	Wally Moon, St. Louis
1955	Bill Virdon, St. Louis
1956	Frank Robinson, Cincinnati
1957	Jack Sanford, Philadelphia
1958	Orlando Cepeda, San Francisco
1959	Willie McCovey, San Francisco
1960	Frank Howard, Los Angeles
1961	Billy Williams, Chicago
1962	Ken Hubbs, Chicago
1963	Pete Rose, Cincinnati
1964	Richie Allen, Philadelphia
1965	Jim Lefebvre, Los Angeles
1966	Tommy Helms, Cincinnati
1967	Tom Seaver, New York
1968	John Bench, Cincinnati
1969	Ted Sizemore, Los Angeles
1970	Carl Morton, Montreal
1971	Earl Williams, Atlanta
1972	Jon Matlack, New York
1973	Gary Matthews, San Francisco
1974	Bake McBride, St. Louis
1975	John Montefusco, San Francisco

MAJOR LEAGUE ALL-STAR GAME

Year	Date	Winning league and manager	Runs	Losing league and manager	Runs	Winning pitcher	Losing pitcher	Site	Paid attendance
1933	July 6	A.L. (Mack)	4	N.L. (McGraw)	2	Gomez	Hallahan	Chicago A.L.	47,595
1934	July 10	A.L. (Cronin)	9	N.L. (Terry)	7	Harder	Mungo	New York N.L.	48,363
1935	July 8	A.L. (Cochrane)	4	N.L. (Frisch)	1	Gomez	Walker	Cleveland A.L.	69,831
1936	July 7	N.L. (Grimm)	4	A.L. (McCarthy)	3	J. Dean	Grove	Boston N.L.	25,556
1937	July 7	A.L. (McCarthy)	8	N.L. (Terry)	3	Gomez	J. Dean	Washington A.L.	31,391
1938	July 6	N.L. (Terry)	4	A.L. (McCarthy)	1	Vander Meer	Gomez	Cincinnati N.L.	27,067
1939	July 11	A.L. (McCarthy)	3	N.L. (Hartnett)	1	Bridges	Lee	New York A.L.	62,892
1940	July 9	N.L. (McKechnie)	4	A.L. (Cronin)	0	Derringer	Ruffing	St. Louis N.L.	32,373
1941	July 8	A.L. (Baker)	7	N.L. (McKechnie)	5	E. Smith	Passeau	Detroit A.L.	54,674
1942	July 6	A.L. (McCarthy)	3	N.L. (Durocher)	1	Chandler	Cooper	New York N.L.	34,178
1943	July 13*	A.L. (McCarthy)	5	N.L. (Southworth)	3	Leonard	Cooper	Philadelphia A.L.	31,938
1944	July 11*	N.L. (Southworth)	7	A.L. (McCarthy)	1	Raffensberger	Hughson	Pittsburgh N.L.	29,589
1946	July 9	A.L. (O'Neill)	12	N.L. (Grimm)	0	Feller	Passeau	Boston A.L.	34,906
1947	July 8	A.L. (Cronin)	2	N.L. (Dyer)	1	Shea	Sain	Chicago N.L.	41,123
1948	July 13	A.L. (Harris)	5	N.L. (Durocher)	2	Raschi	Schmitz	St. Louis A.L.	34,009
1949	July 12	A.L. (Boudreau)	11	N.L. (Southworth)	7	Trucks	Newcombe	Brooklyn N.L.	32,577
1950	July 11	N.L. (Shotton)	4	A.L. (Stengel)	3a	Blackwell	Gray	Chicago A.L.	46,127
1951	July 10	N.L. (Sawyer)	8	A.L. (Stengel)	3	Maglie	Lopat	Detroit A.L.	52,075
1952	July 8	N.L. (Durocher)	3	A.L. (Stengel)	2b	Rush	Lemon	Philadelphia N.L.	32,785
1953	July 14	N.L. (Dressen)	5	A.L. (Stengel)	1	Spahn	Reynolds	Cincinnati N.L.	30,846
1954	July 13	A.L. (Stengel)	11	N.L. (Alston)	9	Stone	Conley	Cleveland A.L.	68,751
1955	July 12	N.L. (Durocher)	6	A.L. (Lopez)	5c	Conley	Sullivan	Milwaukee N.L.	45,643
1956	July 10	N.L. (Alston)	7	A.L. (Stengel)	3	Friend	Pierce	Washington A.L.	28,843
1957	July 9	A.L. (Stengel)	6	N.L. (Alston)	5	Bunning	Simmons	St. Louis N.L.	30,693
1958	July 8	A.L. (Stengel)	4	N.L. (Haney)	3	Wynn	Friend	Baltimore A.L.	48,829
1959†	July 7	N.L. (Haney)	5	A.L. (Stengel)	4	Antonelli	Ford	Pittsburgh N.L.	35,277
	Aug. 3	A.L. (Stengel)	5	N.L. (Haney)	3	Walker	Drysdale	Los Angeles N.L.	55,105
1960†	July 11	N.L. (Alston)	5	A.L. (Lopez)	3	Friend	Monbouquette	Kansas City A.L.	30,619
	July 13	N.L. (Alston)	6	A.L. (Lopez)	0	Law	Ford	New York A.L.	38,362
1961†	July 11	N.L. (Murtaugh)	5	A.L. (Richards)	4d	Miller	Wilhelm	San Francisco N.L.	44,115
	July 31	N.L. (Murtaugh)	1	A.L. (Richards)	1e	—	—	Boston A.L.	31,851
1962†	July 10	N.L. (Hutchinson)	3	A.L. (Houk)	1	Marichal	Pascual	Washington A.L.	45,480
	July 30	A.L. (Houk)	9	N.L. (Hutchinson)	4	Herbert	Mahaffey	Chicago N.L.	38,359
1963	July 9	N.L. (Dark)	5	A.L. (Houk)	3	Jackson	Bunning	Cleveland A.L.	44,160
1964	July 7	N.L. (Alston)	7	A.L. (Lopez)	4	Marichal	Radatz	New York N.L.	50,850
1965	July 13	N.L. (Mauch)	6	A.L. (Lopez)	5	Koufax	McDowell	Minnesota A.L.	46,706
1966	July 12	N.L. (Alston)	2	A.L. (Mele)	1d	Perry	Richert	St. Louis N.L.	49,926
1967	July 11	N.L. (Alston)	2	A.L. (Bauer)	1f	Drysdale	Hunter	Anaheim A.L.	46,309
1968	July 9	N.L. (Schoendienst)	1	A.L. (Williams)	0	Drysdale	Tiant	Houston N.L.	48,321
1969	July 23	N.L. (Schoendienst)	9	A.L. (M. Smith)	3	Carlton	Stottlemyre	Washington A.L.	45,259
1970	July 14	N.L. (Hodges)	5	A.L. (Weaver)	4g	Osteen	Wright	Cincinnati N.L.	51,838
1971	July 13	A.L. (Weaver)	6	N.L. (Anderson)	4	Blue	Ellis	Detroit A.L.	53,559
1972	July 25	N.L. (Murtaugh)	4	A.L. (Weaver)	3d	McGraw	McNally	Atlanta N.L.	53,107
1973	July 24*	N.L. (Anderson)	7	A.L. (Williams)	1	Wise	Blyleven	Kansas City A.L.	40,849
1974	July 23*	N.L. (Berra)	7	A.L. (Williams)	2	Brett	Tiant	Pittsburgh A.L.	50,706
1975	July 15*	N.L. (Dark)	6	A.L. (Alston)	3	Matlack	Hunter	Milwaukee A.L.	51,540

* Night game. † Two games. aFourteen innings. bFive innings, rain. cTwelve innings. dTen innings. eCalled because of rain after nine innings. fFifteen innings. gTwelve innings. Note—No game in 1945.

Sandy Koufax's Major League Pitching Record
(1955–57, with Brooklyn Dodgers; 1958–66, with Los Angeles Dodgers)

	g	ip	h	bb	so	w	l	era
1955	12	42	33	28	30	2	2	3.00
1956	16	59	66	29	30	2	4	4.88
1957	34	104	83	51	122	5	4	3.89
1958	40	159	132	105	131	11	11	4.47
1959	35	153	136	92	173	8	6	4.06
1960	37	175	133	100	197	8	13	3.91
1961	42	256	212	96	*269	18	13	3.52
1962	28	184	134	57	216	14	7	*2.54
1963	40	311	214	58	*306	†25	5	*1.88
1964	29	223	154	58	223	19	5	*1.74
1965	43	*336	216	71	*382	*26	8	*2.04
1966	41	*323	241	77	*317	*27	9	*1.73
Totals	397	2,325	1,754	817	2,396	165	87	2.76

* Led league. † Tied for league lead.

World Series Record

	g	ip	h	bb	so	w	l	era
1959	2	9	5	1	7	0	1	1.00
1963	2	18	12	3	23	2	0	1.50
1965	3	24	13	5	29	2	1	0.38
1966	1	6	6	2	2	0	1	1.50
Totals	8	57	36	11	61	4	3	0.95

Note: Koufax pitched four no-hit games, more than any other man. They came in consecutive years—1962, 1963, 1964, and 1965. The 1965 no-hitter, against the Chicago Cubs, was a perfect game. Koufax won the Cy Young Award three times—more than any other pitcher.

MAJOR LEAGUE LIFETIME RECORDS

Source: The Book of Baseball Records, published and copyrighted by Seymour Siwoff, New York, N.Y. 10036.

LEADING BATTERS
(Over 2,000 Hits)

	Years	At Bat	Hits	Avg.
Ty Cobb	24	11429	4191	.367
Rogers Hornsby	23	8173	2930	.358
Ed Delehanty	16	7493	2593	.346
Dan Brouthers	19	6737	2347	.348
Willie Keeler	19	8564	2955	.345
Ted Williams	19	7706	2654	.344
Tris Speaker	22	10208	3515	.344
Billy Hamilton	14	6262	2157	.344
Harry Heilmann	17	7787	2660	.342
Babe Ruth	22	8399	2873	.342
Jesse Burkett	16	8389	2872	.342
Bill Terry	14	6428	2193	.341
Lou Gehrig	17	8001	2721	.340
George Sisler	16	8267	2812	.340
Nap Lajoie	21	9589	3251	.339
Cap Anson	22	9084	3081	.339
Sam Thompson	15	6005	2016	.336
Al Simmons	20	8761	2927	.334
Eddie Collins	25	9952	3313	.333
Paul Waner	20	9459	3152	.333
Stan Musial	22	10972	3630	.331
Heinie Manush	17	7653	2524	.330
Hugh Duffy	17	6999	2307	.330
Honus Wagner	21	10427	3430	.329
Joe Dimaggio	13	6821	2214	.325
Jimmy Foxx	20	8134	2646	.325
Roger Connor	18	7807	2535	.325

LEADING PITCHERS
(Over 250 Victories)

	Years	W	L	Pct.
Cy Young	22	511	315	.619
Walter Johnson	21	416	279	.599
Grover Alexander	20	373	208	.642
Christy Mathewson	17	373	188	.665
James Galvin	15	365	309	.542
Warren Spahn	21	363	245	.597
Charles Nichols	15	360	202	.641
Tim Keefe	14	346	225	.606
John Clarkson	12	328	175	.652
Eddie Plank	17	325	190	.631
Mickey Welch	13	316	214	.596
Hoss Radbourne	11	308	191	.617
Bob Grove	20	300	141	.680
Early Wynn	23	300	244	.551
Robin Roberts	19	286	245	.539
Tony Mullane	14	282	221	.561
Red Ruffing	22	273	225	.548
Burleigh Grimes	19	270	212	.560
Bob Feller	18	266	162	.621
Eppa Rixey	21	266	251	.515
Gus Weyhing	14	265	236	.529
Jim McCormick	10	264	217	.549
Ted Lyons	21	260	230	.531
Carl Hubbell	16	253	154	.622
Red Faber	20	254	212	.545
Amos Rusie	10	251	173	.592
Bob Gibson	17	251	174	.591

Other Lifetime Batting, Pitching, and Base-Running Records

Source: Baseball Record Book, published and copyrighted by *The Sporting News*, St. Louis, Mo. 63166.

HITS

Ty Cobb	4191
Henry Aaron	3771
Stan Musial	3630
Tris Speaker	3515
Honus Wagner	3430
Eddie Collins	3311
Willie Mays	3283
Nap Lajoie	3251
Paul Waner	3152
Cap Anson	3081
Al Kaline	3007
Roberto Clemente	3000
Edgar Rice	2987
Sam Crawford	2964
Willie Keeler	2955
Frank Robinson	2943
Jacob Beckley	2930
Rogers Hornsby	2930
Al Simmons	2927
Zach Wheat	2884
Frank Frisch	2880
Mel Ott	2876
Babe Ruth	2873

RUNS

Ty Cobb	2244
Babe Ruth	2174
Henry Aaron	2174
Willie Mays	2062
Stan Musial	1949
Lou Gehrig	1888
Tris Speaker	1881
Mel Ott	1859
Frank Robinson	1829
Eddie Collins	1818
Ted Williams	1798
Charlie Gehringer	1773
Jimmy Foxx	1751
Honus Wagner	1740
Willie Keeler	1720
Cap Anson	1712
Jesse Burkett	1708
Billy Hamilton	1690
Mickey Mantle	1677
John McPhee	1674
George Van Haltren	1650
James Ryan	1640

HOME RUNS

Henry Aaron	755
Babe Ruth	714
Willie Mays	660
Frank Robinson	586
Harmon Killebrew	573
Mickey Mantle	536
Jimmy Foxx	534
Ted Williams	521
Ernie Banks	512
Ed Mathews	512
Mel Ott	511
Lou Gehrig	493
Stan Musial	475
Willie McCovey	465
*Billy Williams	426
Duke Snider	407
Al Kaline	399
*Willie Stargell	388
Frank Howard	382
Orlando Cepeda	379
Norm Cash	377
Rocky Colavito	374

STRIKEOUTS

Mickey Mantle	1710
Harmon Killebrew	1699
*Willie Stargell	1598
*Lou Brock	1584
Frank Robinson	1532
Willie Mays	1526
Dick Allen	1520
Ed Mathews	1487
Frank Howard	1460

BASES ON BALLS

Babe Ruth	2056
Ted Williams	2018
Mickey Mantle	1734
Mel Ott	1708
Eddie Yost	1614
Stan Musial	1599
Harmon Killebrew	1559
Lou Gehrig	1510
Willie Mays	1464
Jimmy Foxx	1452
Ed Mathews	1444

EARNED RUN AVERAGE†

Walter Johnson	2.37
Grover Alexander	2.56
Whitey Ford	2.74
Stanley Coveleski	2.88
*Gaylord Perry	2.88
Juan Marichal	2.89
Wilbur Cooper	2.89
Robert Gibson	2.91
Carl Mays	2.92
Don Drysdale	2.95

STRIKEOUTS

Walter Johnson	3508
Robert Gibson	3117
Jim Bunning	2853
Cy Young	2819
*Mickey Lolich	2799
Warren Spahn	2583
Bob Feller	2581
Tim Keefe	2542
Mickey Lolich	2540
*Gaylord Perry	2670
Christy Mathewson	2505

SHUTOUTS

Walter Johnson	113
Grover Alexander	90
Christy Mathewson	83
Cy Young	77
Eddie Plank	64
Warren Spahn	63
Ed Walsh	58
James Galvin	57
Robert Gibson	56
Juan Marichal	52

STOLEN BASES

Billy Hamilton	937
Ty Cobb	892
*Lou Brock	865
Walter Latham	791
Harry Stovey	744
Eddie Collins	743
Max Carey	738
Honus Wagner	720
Tom Brown	697
George Davis	632

* Active player. †National League from 1912; American League from 1913.

Major League Individual All-Time Records

Highest Batting Average—.438, Hugh Duffy, Boston N. L., 1894. (Since 1900—.424, Rogers Hornsby, St. Louis N. L., 1924).

Most Times at Bat—12,364, Henry Aaron, Milwaukee N. L., 1954–65; Atlanta N. L., 1966–74; Milwaukee A. L., 1975–77.

Most Years Batted .300 or Better—23, Ty Cobb, Detroit A. L., 1906–26, Philadelphia A. L., 1927–28.

Most hits—4,191, Ty Cobb, Detroit A. L., 1905–26, Philadelphia, 1927–28.

Most Hits, Season—257, George Sisler, St. Louis A. L., 1920.

Most Hits, Game (9 innings)—7, Wilbert Robinson, Baltimore N. L., 6 singles, 1 double, 1892. Rennie Stennett, Pittsburgh N. L., 4 singles, 2 doubles, 1 triple, 1975.

Most Hits, Game (extra innings)—9, John Burnett, Cleveland A. L., 18 innings, 7 singles, 2 doubles, 1932.

Most Hits in Succession—12, Mike Higgins, Boston A. L., in four games, 1938; Walt Dropo, Detroit A. L., in three games, 1952.

Most Consecutive Games Batted Safely—56, Joe DiMaggio, New York A. L., 1941.

Most Runs—2,244, Ty Cobb, Detroit A. L., 1905–26, Philadelphia A. L., 1927–28.

Most Runs, Season—196, William Hamilton, Philadelphia N. L., 1894. (Since 1900—177, Babe Ruth, New York A. L., 1921.)

Most Runs, Game—7, Guy Hecker, Louisville A. A., 1886. (Since 1900—6, by Mel Ott, New York N. L., 1934, 1944; Johnny Pesky, Boston A. L., 1946; Frank Torre, Milwaukee N. L., 1957.)

Most Runs Batted In—2,297, Henry Aaron, Milwaukee N. L., 1954–1965; Atlanta N. L., 1966–74; Milwaukee A. L., 1975–77.

Most Runs Batted in, Season—190, Hack Wilson, Chicago N. L., 1930.

Most Runs Batted In, Game—12, Jim Bottomley, St. Louis N. L., 1924.

Most Home Runs—755, Henry Aaron, Milwaukee N. L., 1954–1965; Atlanta N. L., 1966–74; Milwaukee A. L., 1975–77.

Most Home Runs, Season—61, Roger Maris, New York A. L., 1961 (162-game season); 60, Babe Ruth, New York A. L., 1927 (154-game season).

Most Home Runs, Game—4, (See table on following page.)

Most Home Runs with Bases Filled—23, Lou Gehrig, New York A. L., 1927–38.

Most 2-Base Hits—793, Tris Speaker, Boston A. L., 1907–15, Cleveland A. L., 1916–26, Washington A. L., 1927, Philadelphia A. L., 1928.

Most 2-Base Hits, Season—67, Earl Webb, Boston A. L., 1931.

Most 2-Base Hits, Game—4, by many.

Most 3-Base Hits—312, Sam Crawford, Cincinnati N. L., 1899–1902, Detroit A. L., 1903–17.

Most 3-Base Hits, Season—36, Owen Wilson, Pittsburgh N. L., 1912.

Most 3-Base Hits, Game—4, George Strief, Philadelphia A. A., 1885; William Joyce, New York N. L., 1897. (Since 1900—3, by many.)

Most Games Played—3,218, Henry Aaron, Milwaukee N.L., 1954–1965; Atlanta, N. L., 1966–74; Milwaukee A. L., 1975–76.

Most Consecutive Games Played—2,130, Lou Gehrig, New York A. L., 1925–39.

Most Bases on Balls—2,056, Babe Ruth, Boston A. L., 1915–19; New York A. L., 1920–34, Boston N. L., 1935.

Most Bases on Balls, Season—170, Babe Ruth, New York A. L., 1923.

Most Bases on Balls, Game—6, Walter Wilmot, Chicago N. L., 1891; Jimmy Foxx, Boston A. L., 1938.

Most Strikeouts—1,710, Mickey Mantle, New York A. L., 1951–68.

Most Strikeouts, Season—189, Bobby Bonds, San Francisco N. L., 1970.

Most Strikeouts, Game (9 innings)—5, by many.

Most Strikeouts, Game (extra innings)—6, Carl Weilman, St. Louis A. L., 15 innings, 1913; Don Hoak, Chicago N. L., 17 innings, 1956; Fred Reichardt, California A. L., 17, innings, 1966; Billy Cowan, California A. L., 20, 1971; Cecil Cooper, Boston A. L., 15, 1974.

Most pinch-hits, lifetime—144, Forrest Burgess, Chi.–Mil.–Cin.–Pitt., N.L., 1949, 51–64; Chi., A.L., 1964–67.

Most Pinch-hits, season—25, Jose Morales, Montreal, N. L., 1976.

Most consecutive pinch-hits—9, Dave Philley, Phil. N.L., 1958 (8), 1959 (1).

Most pinch-hit home runs, lifetime—18, Gerald Lynch, Pitt.–Cin. N.L., 1957-66.

Most pinch-hit home runs, season—6, Johnny Frederick, Brooklyn, N.L., 1932.

Most stolen bases, lifetime (since 1900)—892, Ty Cobb, Detroit A.L., 1905-26, Philadelphia A.L., 1927–28.

Most stolen bases, season—156, Harry Stovey, Philadelphia, American Assn., 1888. Since 1900: 96, Ty Cobb, Detroit A.L. (156 games 1915); 118, Lou Brock, St. Louis, N.L. (154 games, 1974).

Most stolen bases, game—7, George Gore, Chicago N.L. 1881; William Hamilton, Philadelphia N.L. 1894. Since 1900: 6, Eddie Collins, Philadelphia A.L., 1912.

Most times stealing home, lifetime—35, Ty Cobb, Detroit–Phil. A.L., 1905-28.

PITCHING

Most Games Won—511, Cy Young, Cleveland N. L., 1890–98, St. Louis N. L., 1899–1900, Boston A. L., 1901–08, Cleveland A. L., 1909–11, Boston N. L., 1911.

Most Games Won, Season—60, Charles Radbourne, Providence N. L., 1884. (Since 1900—41, Jack Chesbro, New York A. L., 1904.)

Most Consecutive Games Won—24, Carl Hubbell, New York N. L., 1936 (16) and 1937 (8).

Most Consecutive Games Won, Season—19, Timothy Keefe, New York N. L., 1888; Rube Marquard, New York N. L., 1912.

Most Years Won 20 or More Games—16, Cy Young, Cleveland N. L., 1891–98, St. Louis N. L., 1899–1900, Boston A. L., 1901–04, 1907–08.

Most Shutouts—113, Walter Johnson, Wash. A. L., 1907–27.

Most Shutouts, Season—16, Grover Alexander, Philadelphia N. L., 1916.

Most Consecutive Shutouts—6, Don Drysdale, Los Angeles, N. L., 1968.

Most Consecutive Scoreless Innings—58, Don Drysdale, Los Angeles, N. L., 1968.

Most Strikeouts—3,508, Walter Johnson, Washington A. L., 1907–27.

Most Strikeouts, Season—505, Matthew Kilroy, Baltimore A. A., 1886. (Since 1900—383, Nolan Ryan, California, A. L., 1973.)

Most Strikeouts, Game—21, Tom Cheney, Washington A. L., 1962, 16 innings. Nine innings: 19, Charles McSweeney, Providence N. L., 1884; Hugh Dailey, Chicago U. A., 1884. (Since 1900—19, Steve Carlton, St. Louis N. L. vs. New York, Sept. 15, 1969; Tom Seaver, New York N. L. vs. San Diego, April 22, 1970; Nolan Ryan, California A.L. vs. Boston, Aug. 12, 1974.

Most Consecutive Strikeouts—10, Tom Seaver, New York N. L. vs. San Diego, April 22, 1970.

Most Games, Season—106, Mike Marshall, Los Angeles, N. L., 1974.

Most Complete Games, Season—74, William White, Cincinnati N. L., 1879. (Since 1900—48, Jack Chesbro, New York A. L., 1904.)

National League Home Run Champions

Year		No.	Year		No.	Year		No.
1876	George Hall, Phila. Athletics	5	1908	Tim Jordan, Bklyn.	12	1939	John Mize, St. L.	28
1877	George Shaffer, Louisville	3	1909	John Murray, N. Y.	7	1940	John Mize, St. L.	43
1878	Paul Hines, Providence	4	1910	Fred Beck, Bost., and		1941	Dolph Camilli, Bklyn.	34
1879	Charles Jones, Bost.	9		Frank Schulte, Chi.	10	1942	Mel Ott, N. Y.	30
1880	James O'Rourke, Bost. and		1911	Frank Schulte, Chi.	21	1943	Bill Nicholson, Chi.	29
	Harry Stovey, Worcester	6	1912	Henry Zimmerman, Chi.	14	1944	Bill Nicholson, Chi.	33
1881	Dan Brouthers, Buffalo	8	1913	Cliff Cravath, Phila.	19	1945	Tommy Holmes, Bost.	28
1882	George Wood, Det.	7	1914	Cliff Cravath, Phila.	19	1946	Ralph Kiner, Pitts.	23
1883	William Ewing, N. Y.	10	1915	Cliff Cravath, Phila.	24	1947	Kiner and John Mize, N. Y.	51
1884	Ed Williamson, Chi.	27	1916	Davis Robertson, N. Y., and		1948	Kiner and Mize	40
1885	Abner Dalrymple, Chi.	11		Fred Williams, Chi.	12	1949	Ralph Kiner, Pitts.	54
1886	Arthur Richardson, Det.	11	1917	Davis Cravath, N. Y., and		1950	Ralph Kiner, Pitts.	47
1887	Roger Connor, N. Y., and			Cliff Cravath, Phila.	12	1951	Ralph Kiner, Pitts.	42
	Wm. O'Brien, Wash.	17	1918	Cliff Cravath, Phila.	8	1952	Ralph Kiner, Pitts., and	
1888	Roger Connor, N. Y.	14	1919	Cliff Cravath, Phila.	12		Hank Sauer, Chi.	37
1889	Sam Thompson, Phila.	20	1920	Cy Williams, Phila.	15	1953	Ed Mathews, Mil.	47
1890	Tom Burns, Bklyn., and		1921	George Kelly, N. Y.	23	1954	Ted Kluszewski, Cin.	49
	Mike Tiernan, N. Y.	13	1922	Rogers Hornsby, St. L.	42	1955	Willie Mays, N. Y.	51
1891	Harry Stovey, Bost., and		1923	Cy Williams, Phila.	41	1956	Duke Snider, Bklyn.	43
	Mike Tiernan, N. Y.	16	1924	Jacques Fournier, Bklyn.	27	1957	Henry Aaron, Mil.	44
1892	Jim Holliday, Cin.	13	1925	Rogers Hornsby, St. L.	39	1958	Ernie Banks, Chi.	47
1893	Ed Delahanty, Phila.	19	1926	Hack Wilson, Chi.	21	1959	Ed Mathews, Mil.	46
1894	Hugh Duffy, Bost., and		1927	Hack Wilson, Chi., and		1960	Ernie Banks, Chi.	41
	Robert Lowe, Bost.	18		Cy Williams, Phila.	30	1961	Orlando Cepeda, San Fran.	46
1895	Bill Joyce, Wash.	17	1928	Hack Wilson, Chi., and		1962	Willie Mays, San Fran.	49
1896	Ed Delahanty, Phila., and			Jim Bottomley, St. L.	31	1963	Henry Aaron, Mil., and	
	Sam Thompson, Phila.	13	1929	Chuck Klein, Phila.	43		Willie McCovey, San Fran.	44
1897	Nap Lajoie, Phila.	10	1930	Hack Wilson, Chi.	56	1964	Willie Mays, San Fran.	47
1898	James Collins, Bost.	14	1931	Chuck Klein, Phila.	31	1965	Willie Mays, San Fran	52
1899	John Freeman, Wash.	25	1932	Chuck Klein, Phila., and		1966	Henry Aaron, Atlanta	44
1900	Herman Long, Bost.	12		Mel Ott, N. Y.	38	1967	Henry Aaron, Atlanta	39
1901	Sam Crawford, Cin.	16	1933	Chuck Klein, Phila.	28	1968	Willie McCovey, San Fran.	36
1902	Tom Leach, Pitts.	6	1934	Mel Ott, N. Y., and		1969	Willie McCovey, San Fran	45
1903	James Sheckard, Bklyn.	9		Rip Collins, St. L.	35	1970	Johnny Bench, Cin.	45
1904	Harry Lumley, Bklyn.	9	1935	Wally Berger, Bost.	34	1971	Willie Stargell, Pitts.	48
1905	Fred Odwell, Cin.	9	1936	Mel Ott, N. Y.	33	1972	Johnny Bench, Cin.	40
1906	Tim Jordan, Bklyn.	12	1937	Ott and Joe Medwick, St. L.	31	1973	Willie Stargell, Pitts.	44
1907	David Brain, Bost.	10	1938	Mel Ott, N. Y.	36	1974	Michael Schmidt, Phila.	36
						1975	Michael Schmidt, Phila.	38

MOST HOME RUNS IN ONE SEASON

61	Roger Maris, New York (A)	1961
60	Babe Ruth, New York (A)	1927
59	Babe Ruth, New York (A)	1921
58	Jimmy Foxx, Philadelphia (A)	1932
58	Hank Greenberg, Detroit (A)	1938
56	Hack Wilson, Chicago (N)	1930
54	Babe Ruth, New York (A)	1920
54	Babe Ruth, New York (A)	1928
54	Ralph Kiner, Pittsburgh (N)	1949
54	Mickey Mantle, New York (A)	1961
52	Mickey Mantle, New York (A)	1956
52	Willie Mays, San Francisco (N)	1965
51	Ralph Kiner, Pittsburgh (N)	1947
51	John Mize, New York (N)	1947
51	Willie Mays, New York (N)	1955
50	Jimmy Foxx, Boston (A)	1938
49	Babe Ruth, New York (A)	1930
49	Lou Gehrig, New York (A)	1934
49	Lou Gehrig, New York (A)	1936
49	Ted Kluszewski, Cincinnati (N)	1954
49	Willie Mays, San Francisco (N)	1962
49	Harmon Killebrew, Minnesota (A)	1964
49	Frank Robinson, Baltimore (A)	1966
49	Harmon Killebrew, Minnesota (A)	1969

Four Home Runs in One Game

Robert L. Lowe, Boston N.L., consecutive (3d (2), 5th, 6th) May 30, 1894

Edward J. Delahanty, Phila. N.L. (1st, 5th, 7th, 9th) July 13, 1896

Lou Gehrig, New York A.L., consecutive (1st, 4th, 5th, 7th) June 3, 1932

Chuck Klein, Phila. N.L. (1st, 5th, 7th, 10th) July 10, 1936

Pat Seerey, Chicago A.L. (4th, 5th, 6th, 11th) July 18, 1948

Gil Hodges, Brooklyn N.L. (2d, 3d, 6th, 8th) Aug. 31, 1950

Joe Adcock, Milwaukee N.L. (2d, 5th, 7th, 9th) July 31, 1954

Rocky Colavito, Cleveland A.L., consecutive (3d, 5th, 6th, 9th) June 10, 1959

Willie Mays, San Francisco N.L. (1st, 3d, 6th, 8th) April 30, 1961

Michael Schmidt, Philadelphia N.L. (5th, 7th, 8th, 10th) April 17, 1976

Others Hitting 4 Home Runs in Succession, 2 Games

Jimmy Foxx, Phila A L.	1933
Hank Greenberg, Detroit A.L.	1938
Ralph Kiner, Pittsburgh N.L.	1949
Ted Williams, Boston A.L.	1957
Charley Maxwell, Detroit A.L.	1959
John Blanchard, New York A.L.	1961
Willie Kirkland, Cleveland A.L.	1961
Mickey Mantle, New York A.	1962
Art Shamsky, Cincinnati N.	1966
Bobby Murcer New York A.	1970
Mike Epstein, Oakland A.L.	1971
Deron Johnson, Philadelphia N.	1971
Don Baylor, Baltimore A.	1975

MAJOR LEAGUE FRANCHISE SHIFTS AND ADDITIONS

1953—Boston Braves (N. L.) became Milwaukee Braves. Home attendance, last season in Boston (1952), 281,278; first season in Milwaukee (1953), 1,826,397.

1954—St. Louis Browns (A. L.) became Baltimore Orioles. Home attendance, last season in St. Louis (1953), 297,238; first season in Baltimore (1954), 1,060,910.

1955—Philadelphia Athletics (A. L.) became Kansas City Athletics. Home attendance, last season in Phila. (1954), 627,100; first season in K.C. (1955), 1,393,054.

1958—New York Giants (N. L.) became San Francisco Giants. Home attendance, last season in New York (1957), 653,923; first season in San Francisco (1958), 1,272,625.

1958—Brooklyn Dodgers (N. L.) became Los Angeles Dodgers. Home attendance, last season in Brooklyn (1957), 1,028,258; first season in Los Angeles (1958), 1,845,556.

1961—Washington Senators (A. L.) became Minnesota Twins. Home attendance, last season in Washington (1960), 743,404; first season in Minneapolis–St. Paul (1961), 1,256,722.

1961—Los Angeles Angels (later renamed the California Angels) enfranchised by the American League. Home attendance, first season (1961), 603,510.

1961—Washington Senators enfranchised by the American League (a new team, replacing the former Washington club, whose franchise was moved to Minneapolis–St. Paul).

Home attendance, first season, 597,287.

1962—Houston Colt .45's (later renamed the Houston Astros) enfranchised by the National League. Home attendance, first season (1962), 924,456.

1962—New York Mets enfranchised by the National League. Home attendance, first season (1962), 922,530.

1966—Milwaukee Braves (N. L.) became Atlanta Braves. Home attendance, last season in Milwaukee (1965), 555,584; first season in Atlanta (1966), 1,539,801.

1968—Kansas City Athletics (A.L.) became Oakland Athletics. Home attendance, last season in Kansas City (1967), 652,246; first season in Oakland (1968), 838,501.

1969—Two major leagues each added two teams for totals of 12 and split into two divisions. American League additions: Kansas City Royals and Seattle Pilots; National League additions: Montreal Expos and San Diego Padres. The Division leaders met for the league championship and the two league winners met in the World Series.

1970—Seattle franchise was shifted to Milwaukee, with final court approval coming on March 31. Club was renamed Milwaukee Brewers. Attendance for first season was 934,820.

1971—Washington franchise shifted at end of season to Dallas–Fort Worth Texas Rangers with field at Arlington, Tex.

1976—American League awarded franchises to Seattle and Toronto to play in 1977.

MAJOR LEAGUE STATISTICS

If—Left-field foul line; cf—center field; rf—right-field foul line. (2)—Indicates double-header.

American League

Club, nickname and grounds	Distance, feet lf	cf	rf	Seating capacity	Record attendance*	Visiting club	Date
Baltimore Orioles—Memorial Stadium	309	405	309	52,137	51,195	Kansas City (night)	May 8, 1976
Boston Red Sox—Fenway Park	315	420	302	33,524	41,766	New York (2)	Aug. 12, 1934
California Angels—Anaheim Stadium	333	404	333	43,204	44,631	Oakland	July 4, 1971
Chicago White Sox—Comiskey Park	352	400	352	46,550	55,555	Minnesota (2)	May 2, 1973
Cleveland Indians—Municipal Stadium	320	400	320	76,997	84,587	New York (2)	Sept. 12, 1954
Detroit Tigers—Tiger Stadium	340	440	325	54,220	58,369	New York (2)	July 20, 1947
Kansas City Royals—Royals Stadium	330	410	330	40,762	40,435	New York (night)	Aug. 9, 1976
Milwaukee Brewers—County Stadium	320	402	315	46,000	48,160	Cleveland	April 11, 1975
Minnesota Twins—Metropolitan Stadium	330	410	330	45,921	45,890	Kansas City (night)	July 4, 1973
New York Yankees—Yankee Stadium (old)	301	461	296	65,010	81,841	Boston (2)	May 30, 1938
New York Yankees—Yankee Stadium (new)	312	430	310	54,208	53,160	Chicago (day)	July 11, 1976
New York Yankees—Shea Stadium	341	410	330	55,300	53,631	Boston (2)	July 27, 1975
(Yankees played in New York National League Shea Stadium in 1974–75 while Yankee Stadium was being rebuilt)							
Oakland Athletics—Oakland Coliseum	330	400	330	50,000	50,182	Baltimore (night)	June 12, 1972
Seattle Mariners—Kingdome	315	410	315	57,247	(begins play in 1977)		
Texas Rangers—Arlington Stadium	330	400	330	35,698	40,854	California (night)	May 21, 1976
Toronto Blue Jays—Exhibition Stadium	330	400	330	35,000	(begins play in 1977)		

National League

	lf	cf	rf	capacity	attendance*	Visiting club	Date
Atlanta Braves—Atlanta Stadium	330	400	330	52,744	53,775	Los Angeles (night)	April 8, 1974
Chicago Cubs—Wrigley Field	355	400	353	37,741	46,965	Pittsburgh (2)	May 31, 1948
Cincinnati Reds—Riverfront Stadium	330	404	330	51,786	53,390	Houston (day)	April 11, 1976
Houston Astros—Astrodome	330	400	330	45,000	50,908	Los Angeles (night)	June 22, 1966
Los Angeles Dodgers—Dodger Stadium	330	395	330	56,000	55,110	San Diego (night)	June 26, 1970
Montreal Expos—Jarry Park (old)	340	420	340	28,000	34,331	Philadelphia	Sept. 13, 1973
Montreal Expos—1977 Olympic Stadium (new)	330	408	330	55,000e			
New York Mets—Shea Stadium	341	410	341	55,300	57,175	Los Angeles (2)	June 13, 1965
Philadelphia Phillies—Veterans Stadium	330	408	330	56,581	60,942	Los Angeles (day)	July 5, 1976
Pittsburgh Pirates—Three Rivers Stadium	335	400	335	50,230	51,726	San Diego (day)	June 6, 1976
St. Louis Cardinals—Busch Mem'l. Stadium	330	404	330	50,101	49,743	Atlanta	June 23, 1968
San Diego Padres—San Diego Stadium	330	410	330	48,460	50,569	St. Louis (night)	April 24, 1976
San Francisco Giants—Candlestick Park	335	410	335	58,000	44,256	Atlanta	Sept. 1, 1973

* Regular season in listed park. e—estimate.

MAJOR LEAGUE ATTENDANCE RECORDS

Single game—78,672, San Francisco at Los Angeles (N. L.), Apr. 18, 1958. (At Memorial Coliseum.)

Doubleheader—84,587, New York at Cleveland (A. L.), Sept. 12, 1954.

Night—78,382, Chicago at Cleveland (A. L.), Aug. 20, 1948.

Season, home—2,755,184, Los Angeles (N. L.), 1962.

Season, road—2,216,159, New York (A. L.), 1962.

Season, league—17,324,857, National League, 1971.

Season, both leagues—31,320,592, 1976.

World Series, single game—92,706, Chicago (A. L.) at Los Angeles (N. L.), Oct. 6, 1959.

World Series, all games (6)—420,784, Chicago (A. L.) and Los Angeles (N. L.), 1959.

HOME RUN RECORDS OF HENRY AARON AND BABE RUTH

Henry Aaron broke Babe Ruth's career home run record, April 8, 1974, by hitting the ball over the left-center field fence at Atlanta for his 715th homer. He had tied Ruth's mark, April 4, at Cincinnati. Aaron, of the Atlanta Braves, hit 20 homers during the 1974 season, raising the mark to 733. Playing for Milwaukee, he added 22 in the next two seasons for a 755 total. He made 3,771 hits and scored 2,174 runs.

HENRY AARON'S RECORD
REGULAR SEASON

Year	Club	No.	Year	Club	No.
1954	Milwaukee (NL)	13	1968	Atlanta (NL)	29
1955	Milwaukee (NL)	27	1969	Atlanta (NL)	44
1956	Milwaukee (NL)	26	1970	Atlanta (NL)	38
1957	Milwaukee (NL)	44	1971	Atlanta (NL)	47
1958	Milwaukee (NL)	30	1972	Atlanta (NL)	34
1959	Milwaukee (NL)	39	1973	Atlanta (NL)	40
1960	Milwaukee (NL)	40	1974	Atlanta (NL)	20
1961	Milwaukee (NL)	34	1975	Milwaukee (AL)	12
1962	Milwaukee (NL)	45	1976	Milwaukee (AL)	10
1963	Milwaukee (NL)	44			
1964	Milwaukee (NL)	24		Totals	
1965	Milwaukee (NL)	32		Regular Season	755
1966	Atlanta (NL)	44		World Series	2
1967	Atlanta (NL)	39		Playoff Games	3
				All-Star Games	2
					762

Aaron also set numerous other major league records as well as National League marks. They include:

MAJOR LEAGUE RECORDS

Most games	3,298
Most times at bat	12,364
Most runs batted in	2,297
Total bases	6,856
Most extra-base hits	1,475–

NATIONAL LEAGUE RECORDS

Most runs	2,107

BABE RUTH'S RECORD

Year	Club	No.			
1914	Boston (A)	0	1933	New York (A)	34
1915	Boston (A)	4	1934	New York (A)	22
1916	Boston (A)	3	1935	Boston (N)	6
1917	Boston (A)	2			
1918	Boston (A)	11		**World Series**	
1919	Boston (A)	29	Year	Club	No.
1920	New York (A)	54	1915	Boston (A)	0
1921	New York (A)	59	1916	Boston (A)	0
1922	New York (A)	35	1918	Boston (A)	0
1923	New York (A)	41	1921	New York (A)	1
1924	New York (A)	46	1922	New York (A)	0
1925	New York (A)	25	1923	New York (A)	3
1926	New York (A)	47	1926	New York (A)	4
1927	New York (A)	60	1927	New York (A)	2
1928	New York (A)	54	1928	New York (A)	3
1929	New York (A)	46	1932	New York (A)	2
1930	New York (A)	49		**Totals**	
1931	New York (A)	46		Regular season	714
1932	New York (A)	41		World Series	15
				All-Star	1

Games played	2,503
Times at bat	8,399

(Ruth was a pitcher mainly until 1918, when he also played outfield. That was the first year he appeared at bat over 150 times. He became regular outfielder in 1919.)

LITTLE LEAGUE WORLD SERIES

1947	Williamsport, Pa.	1957	Monterrey, Mexico	1967	West Tokyo, Japan
1948	Lock Haven, Pa.	1958	Monterrey, Mexico	1968	Wakayama, Japan
1949	Hammonton, N. J.	1959	Hamtramck, Mich.	1969	Taiwan (Nationalist China)
1950	Houston, Tex.	1960	Levittown, Pa.	1970	Wayne, N. J.
1951	Stamford, Conn.	1961	El Cajon, Calif.	1971	Taiwan (Nationalist China)
1952	Norwalk, Conn.	1962	San Jose, Calif.	1972	Taiwan (Nationalist China)
1953	Birmingham, Ala.	1963	Granada Hills, Calif.	1973	Taiwan (Nationalist China)
1954	Schenectady, N. Y.	1964	Staten Island, N. Y.	1974	Taiwan (Nationalist China)
1955	Morrisville, Pa.	1965	Windsor Locks, Conn.	1975	Lakewood Township, N.J.
1956	Roswell, N. M.	1966	Houston, Tex.		

SOFTBALL

Source: Amateur Softball Association.

Amateur Champions

1959	Aurora (Ill.) Sealmasters	1966	Clearwater (Fla.) Bombers	1972	Raybestos Cardinals, Stratford, Conn.
1960	Clearwater (Fla.) Bombers	1967	Aurora (Ill.) Sealmasters	1973	Clearwater (Fla.) Bombers
1961	Aurora (Ill.) Sealmasters	1968	Clearwater (Fla.) Bombers	1974	Santa Rosa (Calif.)
1962-63	Clearwater (Fla.) Bombers	1969	Raybestos Cardinals, Stratford, Conn.	1975	Rising Sun Hotel, Reading, Pa.
1964	Burch Gage & Tool, Detroit				
1965	Aurora (Ill.) Sealmasters	1971	Welty Way, Cedar Rapids, Iowa		

WORLD AND UNITED STATES WATER SKI JUMPING RECORDS

Men's world record—Wayne Grimditch, Hillsboro Beach, Fla.	180 ft
Women's world record—Liz Allan Shetter, Groveland, Fla.	127 ft
U.S. men's record—Grimditch	180 ft
*U.S. women's record—Linda Giddens, Eastman, Ga.	128 ft

    * Awaiting world ratification.

TRACK AND FIELD

RUNNING, jumping, hurdling and throwing weights—track and field sports, in other words—are as natural to boys and young men as eating, drinking and breathing. Unorganized competition in this form of sport goes back beyond the Cave Man era. Organized competition begins with the first recorded Olympic Games in Greece, 776 B. C., when Coroebus of Elis won the only event on the program, a race of approximately 200 yards. The Olympic Games, with an ever-widening program of events, continued until "the glory that was Greece" had faded and "the grandeur that was Rome" was tarnished, and finally were abolished by decree of Emperor Theodosius I of Rome in A. D. 394. The Tailteann Games of Ireland are supposed to have antedated the first Olympic Games by some centuries, but we have no records of the specific events and winners thereof.

Professional contests of speed and strength were popular at all times and in many lands, but the widespread competition of amateur athletes in track and field sports is a comparatively modern development. The first organized amateur athletic meet of record was sponsored by the Royal Military Academy at Woolwich, England, in 1849. Oxford and Cambridge track and field rivalry began in 1864 and the English amateur championships were established in 1866. In the United States such organizations as the New York Athletic Club and the Olympic Club of San Francisco conducted track and field meets in the 1870's, and a few colleges joined to sponsor a meet in 1874. The success of the college meet led to the formation of the Intercollegiate Association of Amateur Athletes of America and the holding of an annual set of championship games beginning in 1876. The Amateur Athletic Union, organized in 1888, has been the ruling body in American amateur athletics since that time.

MEN'S WORLD RECORDS
Recognized by the International Amateur Athletic Federation in July 1976
(The I.A.A.F. began in 1975 to recognize two sets of world marks, one hand-timed and one automatically, or electrically timed. Electrically timed records in these lists are marked E.)

RUNNING

Event	Record	Holder	Home country	Where made	Date
100 yards	0:09.0	Ivory Crockett	United States	Knoxville, Tenn.	May 11, 1974
		Houston McTear	United States	Winter Park, Fla.	May 9, 1975
220 yards (no turn)	0:19.5	Tommie Smith	United States	San Jose, Calif.	May 7, 1966
220 yards (turn)	0:20.0	Tommie Smith	United States	Sacramento, Calif.	June 11, 1966
440 yards	0:44.5	John Smith	United States	Eugene, Ore.	June 26, 1971
880 yards	1:44.1	Rick Wohlhuter	United States	Eugene, Ore.	June 8, 1974
1 mile	3:49.4	John Walker	Australia	Goteborg, Sweden	Aug. 12, 1975
2 miles	8:13.8	Brendan Foster	Britain	London	Aug. 27, 1973
3 miles	12:47.8	Emiel Puttemans	Belgium	Brussels	Sept. 20, 1972
6 miles	26:47.0	Ron Clarke	Australia	Oslo	July 14, 1965
10 miles	45:54.2	Jos Hermens	Netherlands	Papendal, Neth.	Sept. 14, 1975

RUNNING—METRIC DISTANCES

Event	Record	Holder	Home country	Where made	Date
100 meters	0:09.9	Charlie Greene	United States	Sacramento, Calif.	June 20, 1968
		Jim Hines	United States	Sacramento, Calif.	June 20, 1968
		Ronnie Ray Smith	United States	Sacramento, Calif.	June 20, 1968
		Eddie Hart	United States	Eugene, Ore.	July 1, 1972
		Reynaud Robinson	United States	Eugene, Ore.	July 1, 1972
		Steve Williams	United States	Los Angeles	June 21, 1974
		Silvio Leonard	Cuba	Ostrava, Czechoslovakia	June 5, 1975
		Harvey Glance	United States	Columbia, S.C.	April 3, 1976
		Don Quarrie	Jamaica	Modesto, Calif.	May 22, 1976
100 meters	0:09.95E	Jim Hines	United States	Mexico City	Oct. 14, 1968
200 meters (no turn)	0:19.5	Tommie Smith	United States	San Jose, Calif.	May 7, 1966
200 meters (turn)	0:19.8	Tommie Smith	United States	Mexico City	Oct. 16, 1968
		Don Quarrie	Jamaica	Cali, Colombia	Aug. 3, 1971
200 meters	0:19.81E	Don Quarrie,	Jamaica	Cali, Colombia	Mar. 8, 1971
400 meters	0:43.8	Lee Evans	United States	Mexico City	Oct. 18, 1968
400 meters	0:43.86E	Lee Evans	United States	Mexico City	Oct. 18, 1968
800 meters	1:43.5	Alberto Juantoreno	Cuba	Montreal	July 25, 1976
1,000 meters	2:13.9	Rick Wohlhuter	United States	Oslo, Norway	July 30, 1974

* Betters listed record, recognition pending.

Men's World Track Records (Continued)

Event	Record	Holder	Home country	Where made	Date
1,500 meters	3:32.2	Filbert Bayi	Tanzania	Christchurch, N.Z.	Feb. 2, 1974
2,000 meters	4:51.4	John Walker	New Zealand	Oslo	June 30, 1976
3,000 meters	7:35.2	Brendan Foster	Britain	Gateshead, Eng.	Aug. 3, 1974
5,000 meters	13:13	Emiel Puttemans	Belgium	Haysel, Belgium	Sept. 20, 1972
10,000 meters	27:30.8	David Bedford	Britain	London	Aug. 27, 1973
20,000 meters	57:24.2	Jos Hermens	Netherlands	Papendal	May 1, 1976
25,000 meters	1:14:55.6	Seppo Nikkari	Finland	Jyvaskyla, Fin.	Oct. 14, 1973
30,000 meters	1:31.30	Jim Alder	Great Britain	London	Sept. 5, 1970
3,000–m. steeplechase	8:08.02	Anders Garderud	Sweden	Montreal	July 28, 1976
One hour	13 miles, 10 yds.	Jos Hermens	Netherlands	Papendal	May 1, 1976

WALKING

Event	Record	Holder	Home country	Where made	Date
20 miles	2:30:38.6	Gerhard Weidner	West Germany	Hamburg, W. Ger.	May 24, 1974
30 miles	3:51:48.6	Gerhard Weidner	West Germany	Hamburg, W. Ger.	April 8, 1973
1 hour	8 mi. 1,485 yds.	Bernd Kannenberg	West Germany	Hamburg, W. Ger.	May 25, 1974
2 hours	16 mi. 1,517 yds.	Bernd Kannenberg	West Germany	Kassel, W. Ger.	May 11, 1974

WALKING—METRIC DISTANCES

Event	Record	Holder	Home country	Where made	Date
20,000 meters	1:24:45	Bernd Kannenberg	West Germany	Hamburg, W. Ger.	May 25, 1974
30,000 meters	2:12:58	Bernd Kannenberg	West Germany	Kassel, W. Ger.	May 11, 1974
50,000 meters	3:56.52	Berndt Kannenberg	West Germany	Milan	Nov. 16, 1976

HURDLES (10 hurdles)

Event	Record	Holder	Home country	Where made	Date
120 yards	0:13.0	Rod Milburn	United States	Eugene, Ore.	June 25, 1971
220 yards	0:21.9	Don Styron	United States	Baton Rouge, La.	April 2, 1960
440 yards	0:48.7	Jim Bolding	United States	Turin, Italy	July 24, 1974

HURDLES—METRIC DISTANCES

Event	Record	Holder	Home country	Where made	Date
110 meters	0:13.1	Rod Milburn	United States	Zurich	July 6, 1973
110 meters	0:13.24E	Rod Milburn	United States	Munich, W. Ger.	Sept. 7, 1972
400 meters	0:47.64	Edwin Moses	United States	Montreal	July 25, 1976

RELAY RACES

Event	Record	Holder	Home country	Where made	Date
440 yd. (4×110– 2 turns)	0:38.6	U. of So. Calif.	United States	Provo, Utah	June 17, 1967
		(Earl McCullouch, Fred Kuller, O. J. Simpson, Lennox Miller)			
880 yd. (4×220)	1:21.7	Texas A & M	United States	Des Moines	April 24, 1970
		(Don Rogers, Rockie Woods, Marvin and Curtis Mills)			
		Tennessee	United States	Knoxville	April 10, 1976
		(Lamar Preyor, Ronnie Harris, Jerome Morgan, Reggie Jones)			
1 mi. (4×440 yd.)	3:02.8	National Team	Trinidad-Tobago	Kingston, Jamaica	Aug. 13, 1967
		(Lennox Yearwood, Kent Bernard, Edwin Roberts, Wendell Mottley)			
*1 mi. (4×440 yds.)	3:02.4	National Team	United States	Durham, N.C.	July 19, 1975
		(Ronnie Ray, Robert Taylor, Maurice Peoples, Stan Vinson)			
2 mi. (4×880 yds.)	7:10.4	U. of Chicago T.C.	United States	Durham, N.C.	June 12, 1973
		(Tom Bach, Ken Sparks, Lowell Paul, Rick Wohlhuter)			
4 mi. (4×1 mi.)	16:02.8	National Team	New Zealand	Auckland	Feb. 3, 1972
		(K. Ross, A. Polhill, R. Taylor, R. Quax)			

RELAY RACES—METRIC DISTANCES

Event	Record	Holder	Home country	Where made	Date
400 m. (4×100)	0:38.2	National Team	United States	Mexico City	Oct. 19, 1968
		(Charlie Greene, Mel Pender, Ronnie Ray Smith, Jim Hines)			
800 m. (4×200)	1:21.5	National Team	Italy	Barletta, Italy	July 21, 1972
		(F. Ossola, P. Abeti, L. Benedetti, P. Mennea)			
		Tennessee	United States	Philadelphia	April 24, 1976
		(Lamar Preyor, Ronnie Harris, Jerome Morgan, Reggie Jones)			
1,600 m. (4×100)	2:56.1	National Team	United States	Mexico City	Oct. 20, 1968
		(Vince Matthews, Ron Freeman, Larry James, Lee Evans)			

FIELD EVENTS

Event	Record	Holder	Home country	Where made	Date
High jump	7 ft. 7 in.	Dwight Stones	United States	Philadelphia	June 5, 1976
*High jump	7 ft. 7¼ in.	Dwight Stones	United States	Philadelphia	Aug. 4, 1976
Long jump	29 ft. 2½ in.	Robert Beamon	United States	Mexico City	Oct. 18, 1968
Triple jump	58 ft. 8½ in.	Joao de Oliveira	Brazil	Mexico City	Oct. 15, 1975

* betters listed record, recognition pending.

Men's World Track Records (Continued)

Pole Vault	18 ft. 8¼ in.	Dave Roberts	United States	Eugene, Ore.	June 22, 1976
Shotput	71 ft. 8½ in.	Terry Albritton	United States	Honolulu	Feb. 21, 1976
*Shotput	72 ft. 2¼ in.	Alex. Barishnikov	U.S.S.R.	Paris	July 10, 1976
Discus	232 ft. 6 in.	Mac Wilkins	United States	San Jose, Cal.	May 1, 1976
Javelin	310 ft. 4 in.	Miklos Nemeth	Hungary	Montreal	July 26, 1976
Hammer	260 ft. 2 in.	Walter Schmidt	West Germany	Frankfurt	Aug. 17, 1975

DECATHLON

8,618 pts	Bruce Jenner	United States	Montreal	July 29-30, 1976

WOMEN'S WORLD RECORDS
RUNNING

100 yards	0:10.0	Chi Cheng	Taiwan	Portland, Ore.	June 13, 1970
220 yards	0:22.6	Chi Cheng	Taiwan	Los Angeles	July 3, 1970
		Monika Zehrt	East Germany	Paris	July 4, 1972
440 yards	0:52.2	Kathy Hammond	United States	Champaign, Ill.	Aug. 12, 1972
		Debra Sapenter	United States	Bakersfield, Cal.	June 29, 1974
*440 yards	0:51.71	Irena Szewinska	Poland	Edinburgh	Aug. 6, 1976
880 yards	2:02.0	Dixie Willis	Australia	Perth	Mar. 3, 1962
		Judy Pollock	Australia	Stockholm	July 5, 1968
1 mile	4:29.5	Paola Cacchi-Pigni	Italy	Viareggio	Aug. 8, 1973
3 miles	15.41.8	Peg Neppal	United States	Manhattan, Kan.	May 14, 1976
100 meters	0:10.8	Renate Stecher	East Germany	Dresden	July 20, 1973
100 meters	0:11.01E	Annegret Richter	West Germany	Montreal	July 25, 1976
200 meters	0:22.0	Irena Szewinska	Poland	Potsdam, E. Ger.	June 13, 1974
200 meters	0:22.21E	Irena Szewinska	Poland	Potsdam, E. Ger.	June 13, 1974
400 meters	0:49.9	Irena Szewinska	Poland	Warsaw	June 22, 1974
400 meters	0:49.29	Irena Szewinska	Poland	Montreal	July 29, 1976
800 meters	1:54.94	Tatyana Kazankina	U.S.S.R.	Montreal	July 26, 1976
1,000 meters	2:33.8	Nikolina Shtereva	U.S.S.R.	Belkemen, Bulgaria	July 4, 1976
1,500 meters	3:56	Tatyana Kazankina	U.S.S.R.	Moscow	June 28, 1976
3,000 meters	8:46.6	Greta Anderson	Norway	Oslo	June 24, 1975
*3,000 meters	8:45.5.	Greta A. Waitz	Norway	Oslo	June 3, 1976
*3,000 meters	8:27.1.	Ludmilla Bragina	U.S.S.R.	College Park, Md.	Aug. 7, 1976

RELAY RACES

440 yds (4×110)	0:44.07	National Team	West Germany	Durham, N.C.	July 19, 1975
		(Inge Helten, Birgit Wilkes, Annegret Kroniger, Maren Gang)			
880 yds (4×220)	1:35.8	Inter-State Team	Australia	Brisbane	Nov. 9, 1969
		(Marion Hoffman, Raelene Boyle, Pam Kilborn, Jenny Lamy)			
Mile (4×440)	3.33.9	National Team	United States	Urbana, Ill.	Aug. 12, 1972
		(Kathy Hammond, Mable Fergerson, Madelaine M. Jackson, Debbie Edward)			
*Mile (4×440)	3:30.25	National Team	West Germany	Durham, N.C.	July 19, 1975
		(Christine Krau, Dagman Fost, Erika Weinstein, Elke Barth)			
400 meters (4×100)	0:42.50	National Team	East Germany	East Berlin	May 29, 1976
		(Marlies Oelsner, Renate Stecher, Carla Bodendorf, Martina Blos)			
800 Meters (4×200)	1:32.6	Interstate Team	Australia	Brisbane	Jan. 26, 1976
		(Denise Robertson, Babara Wilson, Sue Jowett, Raelene Boyle)			
*800 meters (4×200)	1:32.4	National Team	East Germany	Jena	Aug. 13, 1976
		(Helga Behrend, Marlies Oelsner, Baerbel Eckert, Renate Stecher)			
1,600 meters	3:19.23	National Team	East Germany	Montreal	July 31, 1976
		(Doris Maletzki, Brigitte Rohde, Ellen Streidt, Christine Brehmer)			

HURDLES

100 meters	0:12.3	Annelie Ehrhardt	E. Germany	Dresden	July 22, 1973
200 meters	0:25.7	Pamela K. Ryan	Australia	Melbourne	Nov. 25, 1971
400 meters	0:56.5E	Krystyna Kasperczik	Poland	Augsburg, W. Ger.	July 13, 1974
400 meters	0:56.7	Danuta Piecyk	Poland	Warsaw	Aug. 11, 1973

FIELD EVENTS

High jump	6 ft. 5¼ in.	Rosemarie Ackermann	E. Germany	Dresden	May 8, 1976
Long jump	22 ft. 11¼ in.	Sigrun Siegl	East Germany	Dresden	May 19, 1976
Discus	231 ft. 3 in.	Faina Melnik	U.S.S.R.	Sochi, U.S.S.R.	April 24, 1976
Javelin	226 ft. 9 in.	Ruth Fuchs	East Germany	East Berlin	July 10, 1976
Shotput	71 ft. 9¾ in.	Ivanka Khristova	Bulgaria	Sofia	July 4, 1976
*Shotput	72 ft. 1¾ in.	Helena Fibingerova	Czechoslovakia	Prague	Sept. 26, 1976

* betters listed record, recognition pending.

HISTORY OF THE RECORD FOR THE MILE RUN

Time	Athlete	Country	Year	Where Made
4:36.5	Richard Webster	England	1865	England
4:29.0	William Chinnery	England	1868	England
4:28.8	Walter Gibbs	England	1868	England
4:26.0	Walter Slade	England	1874	England
4:24.5	Walter Slade	England	1875	London
4:23.2	Walter George	England	1880	London
4:21.4	Walter George	England	1882	London
4:18.4	Walter George	England	1884	Birmingham, England
4:18.2	Fred Bacon	Scotland	1894	Edinburgh
4:17.0	Fred Bacon	Scotland	1895	London
4:15.6	Thomas Conneff	United States	1895	Travers Island, N.Y.
4:15.4	John Paul Jones	United States	1911	Cambridge, Mass.
4:14.4	John Paul Jones	United States	1913	Cambridge, Mass.
4:12.6	Norman Taber	United States	1915	Cambridge, Mass.
4:10.4	Paavo Nurmi	Finland	1923	Stockholm
4:09.2	Jules Ladoumegue	France	1931	Paris
4:07.6	Jack Lovelock	New Zealand	1933	Princeton, N.J.
4:06.8	Glenn Cunningham	United States	1934	Princeton, N.J.
4:06.4	Sydney Wooderson	England	1937	London
4:06.2	Gundar Hägg	Sweden	1942	Göteborg, Sweden
4:06.2	Arne Andersson	Sweden	1942	Stockholm
4:04.6	Gunder Hägg	Sweden	1942	Stockholm
4:02.6	Arne Andersson	Sweden	1943	Göteborg, Sweden
4:01.6	Arne Andersson	Sweden	1944	Malmö, Sweden
4:01.4	Gunder Hägg	Sweden	1945	Malmö, Sweden
3:59.4	Roger Bannister	England	1954	Oxford, England
3:58.0	John Landy	Australia	1954	Turku, Finland
3:57.2	Derek Ibbotson	England	1957	London
3:54.5	Herb Elliott	Australia	1958	Dublin
3:54.4	Peter Snell	New Zealand	1962	Wanganui, N.Z.
3:54.1	Peter Snell	New Zealand	1964	Auckland, N.Z.
3:53.6	Michel Jazy	France	1965	Rennes, France
3:51.3	Jim Ryun	United States	1966	Berkeley, Calif.
3:51.1	Jim Ryun	United States	1967	Bakersfield, Calif.
3:51.0	Filbert Bayi	Tanzania	May 17, 1975	Kingston, Jamaica
3:49.4	John Walker	New Zealand	Aug. 12, 1975	Goteborg, Sweden

WORLD'S FASTEST MILES

3:49.4	John Walker	New Zealand	Aug. 12, 1975	Goteborg, Sweden
3:51.0	Filbert Bayi	Tanzania	May 17, 1975	Kingston, Jamaica
3:51.1	Jim Ryun	United States	June 23, 1967	Bakersfield, Calif.
3:51.3	Jim Ryun	United States	July 17, 1966	Berkeley, Calif.
3:52.0	Ben Jipcho	Kenya	July 2, 1973	Stockholm
3:52.2	John Walker	New Zealand	1975	Stockholm
3:52.2a	Marty Liquori	United States	May 17, 1975	Kingston, Jamaica
3:52.3	Tony Waldrop	United States	April 27, 1974	Philadelphia
3:52.6a	Filbert Bayi	Tanzania	July 2, 1973	Stockholm
3:52.8	Jim Ryun	United States	July 29, 1972	Toronto, Ont.
3:53.1	Kipchoge Keino	Kenya	Sept. 10, 1967	Kisumu
3:53.2	Jim Ryun	United States	June 2, 1967	Los Angeles, Calif.
3:53.3	Dave Wottle	United States	June 20, 1973	Eugene, Ore.
3:53.3b	Eamonn Coghlan	Ireland	May 17, 1975	Kingston, Jamaica
3:53.4	Kipchoge Keino	Kenya	Aug. 20, 1966	London
3:53.4a	Marty Liquori	United States	1975	Stockholm
3:53.6	Michel Jazy	France	June 9, 1965	Rennes, France
3:53.6b	Rod Dixon	New Zealand	1975	Stockholm
3:53.7	Jim Ryun	United States	June 4, 1966	Los Angeles
3:53.8	Jurgen May	East Germany	Dec. 11, 1965	Wanganui, N.Z.
3:53.8	Bodo Tummler	W. Germany	Aug. 22, 1968	Karlskrona, Sweden
3:53.8c	Rick Wohlhuter	United States	May 17, 1975	Kingston, Jamaica
3:54.1	Peter Snell	New Zealand	Nov. 17, 1964	Auckland, N.Z.
3:54.1	Jurgen May	East Germany	Dec. 15, 1965	Auckland, N.Z.
3:54.1c	Thomas Wesinghagl	West Germany	1975	Stockholm

INDOORS

3:55.0	Tony Waldrop	United States	Feb. 17, 1974	San Diego
3:55.8	Marty Liquori	United States	Feb. 7, 1975	Phila. Spectrum
3:56.1	Filbert Bayi	Tanzania	Feb. 27, 1976	New York
3:56.2	Ben Jipcho, pro	Kenya	Mar. 22, 1975	Los Angeles
3:56.4	Tom O'Hara	United States	Mar. 6, 1964	Chicago
3:56.4	Jim Ryun	United States	Feb. 19, 1971	San Diego
3:56.6	Tom O'Hara	United States	Feb. 13, 1964	New York

a Finished second; b Finished third; c Finished fourth; pro marks not accepted.

World's Fastest Miles—Indoor (continued)

3:56.6	Tom O'Hara	United States	Feb. 13, 1964	New York
3:56.8	Rod Dixon	New Zealand	Feb. 21, 1976	San Diego
3:57.0	Wilson Waigwa	Kenya	Feb. 15, 1975	Oklahoma City
3:57.2	Marty Liquori	United States	Feb. 13, 1971	Houston
3:57.2a	Wilson Waigwa	Kenya	Feb. 17, 1974	San Diego
3:57.5	Jim Ryun	United States	Feb. 9, 1968	New York
3:57.5a	Filbert Bayi	Tanzania	Feb. 21, 1976	San Diego
3:57.6	Paul Cummings	United States	Jan. 30, 1976	New York
3:57.7b	Paul Cummings	United States	Feb. 21, 1976	San Diego
3:57.7	Marty Liquori	United States	Jan. 10, 1975	College Park, Md.
3:57.7	Rick Wohlhuter	United States	Jan. 25, 1975	Bloomington, Ind.
3:57.9	Tom Von Ruden	United States	Feb. 4, 1972	Fort Worth, Tex.
3:58.0a	John Mason	United States	Feb. 19, 1971	San Diego
3:58.1b	Chuck LeBenz	United States	Feb. 19, 1971	San Diego

a Finished second; b Finished third.

HISTORY OF THE POLE VAULT

(Some of early dates are the winning heights of A.A.U. champion for that year, used to show progression from one foot level to the next. Figures from A.A.U. records and *Track & Field News*.)

		Feet	Inches			Feet	Inches			Feet	Inches
1877	G. McNichol	9	7					1966	Pennel	17	6¼
1879	W. J. Van Houten	10	4¾		**Fiberglas Poles**			1967	Seagren	17	7
1883	Hugh Baxter	11	0½	1961	George Davies	15	10¼	1967	Paul Wilson	17	7¾
				1962	John Uelses	16	0¾	1968	Seagren	17	9
	Bamboo Poles			1962	Dave Tork	16	2	1969	Pennel	17	10¼
1904	Norman Dole	12	1³⁄₁₀	1962	Pentti Nikula	16	2½	1970	Wolfgang Norwig	17	10½
1912	Robert Gardner	13	1	1963	John Pennel	16	4	1970	Chris Papanicolaou	18	0¼
1927	Sabin Carr	14	0	1963	Brian Sternberg	16	5	1972	Kjell Isaksson	18	1
1940	Cornelius Warmerdam	15	1	1963	Pennel	16	6¾	1972	Isaksson	18	2
1942	Warmerdam	15	7¾	1963	Sternberg	16	8	1972	Isaksson and Seagren	18	4¼
				1963	Pennel	16	10	1972	Seagren	18	5¾
	Metal Poles			1963	Pennel	17	0¾	1975	Dave Roberts	18	6½
1957	Bob Gutowski	15	8¼	1964	Fred Hansen	17	4	1976	Earl Bell	18	7¼
1960	Don Bragg	15	9¼	1966	Bob Seagren	17	5½	1976	Roberts	18	8¼

CROSS COUNTRY RACE CHAMPIONS

Amateur Athletic Union
(10,000 Meters)

Individual	Team
1968—John Mason, Fort Hays; Villanova
1969—Jack Bachelor, Gainesville, Fla.; Pacific Coast Club
1970—Frank Shorter, Gainesville, Fla.; Pacific Coast Club
1971—Frank Shorter, Gainesville, Fla.; Florida T.C.
1972—Frank Shorter, Gainesville, Fla.; Florida T.C.
1973—Frank Shorter, Gainesville, Fla.; Florida T.C.
1974—John Ngeno, Kenya; Colorado T.C.
1975—Greg Fredericks, Phila.; Colorado T.C.

N.C.A.A. (University)
(6 Miles)

1969—Gerry Lindgren, Washington State; Texas-El Paso
1970—Steve Prefontaine, Oregon; Villanova
1971—Steve Prefontaine; Oregon
1972—Neil Cusack, East Tennessee; Tennessee
1973—Steve Prefontaine, Oregon; Oregon
1974—Nick Rose, Western Kentucky; Oregon
1975—Craig Virgin, Illinois; Texas-El Paso

N.C.A.A. (College)
(5 Miles; 4 miles prior to 1968)

1969—Ron Stonitsch, C.W. Post; Eastern Illinois
1970—Mark Covert, Cal State, Fullerton; Eastern Michigan
1971—Mike Slack, North Dakota State; Cal State, Fullerton
1972—Mike Slack, North Dakota State; N. Dakota State
1973—Div. II: Gary Bentley, S. Dakota St.; S. Dak. State
    Div. III: Steve Foster, Ashland; Ashland
1974—Div. II: Garry Bentley, S. Dak. State; S.W. Missouri
    Div. III: David Maller, Rochester; Mount Union
1975—Div. II: Ralph Serna, Cal.-Irvine; Cal-Irvine
    Div. III: Vin Fleming, Lowell; N. Cent. Illinois

N.A.I.A.
(5 Miles)

1969—Ralph Foote, Taylor (Ind.); Fort Hays State
1970—Rex Maddaford, Eastern New Mexico; Eastern Michigan
1971—Dave Antognali, Edinboro State; Adams State
1972—Mike Nixon, Pittsburg State; Malone
1973—Tony Brien, Marymount; E. New Mexico
1974—Mike Boit, E. New Mexico; Eastern New Mexico
1975—Mike Boit, E. New Mexico; Edinboro State

UNITED STATES MARATHON CHAMPIONS
(26 miles, 385 Yards)

BOSTON

1968—Ambrose Burfoot, Wesleyan Col.	2:22:17
1969—Yoshiaki Unetani, Japan	2:13:44
1970—Ron Hill, England	2:10:30
1971—Alvaro Meija, Colombia	2:18:45
1972—Olavi Suomalainen, Finland	2:15:39
1973—Jon Anderson, Eugene, Ore.	2:16:03
1974—Neil Cusack, Ireland	2:13:39
1975—William H. Rodgers, Boston	2:09:55

AMATEUR ATHLETIC UNION

1968—George Young, Casa Grande, Ariz.	2:30:48
1969—Tom Heinonen, So. Calif.	2:24:43
1970—Bob Fitts, Wisconsin	2:24:11
1971—Ken Moore, Portland, Ore.	2:16:49
1972—Edmund Norris, Brockton, Mass.	2:24:42.8
1973—Doug Schmenk	2:15:48
1974—Ron Wayne, Eugene, Ore.	2:18:52
1975—Gary Tuttle, Beverly Hills Strider	2:17:27

World and American Best Performances in Indoor Track

(The International Amateur Athletic Federation does not recognize indoor records. The following best performances, often called world records, are from lists provided by The Amateur Athletic Union of the United States and *Track & Field News* published in Los Altos, Calif.; Bert Nelson, editor and publisher.)

Men's Track Events

50 yds—Kirk Clayton, San Jose, 1970	0:05.0
Herb Washington at Toronto, 1972	0:05.0
Manfred Ommer, Leverkusen, W.G., 1975	0:05.0
60 yds—Herb Washington E. Lansing, Mich., 1972	0:05.8
70 yds—Mike McFarland, Louisville, Ky.	0:06.7
100 yds—Don Quarrie, Pocatello, Idaho, 1971	0:09.3
Carl Lawson, Pocatello, 1971	0:09.3
Cliff Branch, Pocatello, 1972	0:09.3
300 yds—Marshall Dill, E. Lansing, Mich., 1974	0:29.3
440 yds—Tommie Smith, Louisville, 1967	0:46.2
500 yds—Lee Evans, College Park, Md., 1971	0:54.4
Pro—Larry James, Salt Lake City, 1973	0:53.9
600 yds—Martin McGrady, New York, 1970	1:07.6
880 yds—Ralph Doubell, Albuquerque, 1969	1:47.9
Tom Von Ruden (Am.), College Park, Md., 1971	1:48.5
1,000 yds—Mark Winzenried, Louisville, 1972	2:05.1
Mile—Tony Waldrop, San Diego, 1974	3:55.0
2 miles—Emiel Puttemans, Berlin, 1973	8:13.2
Terry O'Brien (Am.), San Diego, 1971	8:15.2
Steve Prefontaine (Am.), San Diego, 1974	8:20.4
3 miles—Emiel Puttemans, Vittel, France, 1974	13:05.2
Tracy Smith (Am.), New York, 1973	13:07.2

Men's Track Events—Metric Distances

50 m—Bill Gaines (Am.), at Highland Park, N.J., 1968	0:05.4
Manfred Kokot, E. Germany, 1971	0:05.4
60 m—Fydor Pankratov, U.S.S.R., 1967	0:06.4
Clifford Outlin (Am.), Moscow, 1974	0:06.4
(Mark equalled by 10 other European runners)	
70 m—Helmut Kornig, Germany, 1932	0:07.5
Ira Murchison (Am.), U.S.	0:07.5
Pro—John Carlos, Pocatello, 1974	0:07.3
(Mark equaled by 6 other European runners)	
100 m—Eugen Ray, East Berlin, 1976	0:10.16
Pro—Warren Edmonson, Pocatello, 1973	0:10.2
300 m—Marcello Fiasconaro, Italy, 1972	0:33.4
400 m—Fons Brydenbach, Sofia, 1974	0:45.9
500 m—Stan Vinson, Ypsilanti, Mich., 1974	1:02.4
Pro—Lee Evans, Pocatello, 1973	1:02.0
600 m—Martin Bilham, England, 1969	1:17.7
Pro—Lee Evans, Pocatello, 1973	1:16.7
800 m—Dieter Fromm, E. Germany, 1969	1:46.6
1,000 m—Paul-Heinz Wellmann, Dortmund, 1976	2:19.1
Tom Van Ruden (Am), New York, 1971	2:20.4
Pro—Chris Fisher, Daly City, Calif., 1973	2:19.7
1,500 m—Harald Norpoth, Berlin, 1971	3:37.8
Tony Waldrop (Am.), San Diego, 1974	3:39.8
2,000 m—Emiel Puttemans, Berlin, 1973	5:00.0
3,000 m—Emiel Puttemans, Berlin, 1973	7:39.2
Steve Prefontaine, San Diego, 1974	7:50.0
5,000 m—Emiel Puttemans, Paris, 1976	13:20.8
Miruts Yifter (Am.), Louisville, 1974	13:34.2
Jim Johnson (Am.), Moscow, 1974	13:56.4

HURDLES

50 yds—Willie Davenport, at Toronto, 1969	0:05.8
Rod Milburn, Toronto, 1973	0:05.8
Tom Hill, Toronto, 1973	0:05.8
Danny Smith, Toronto, 1975	0:05.8
Marcus Walker, Colorado, 1970	0:05.8
60 yds—Hayes Jones, Baltimore, 1964	0:06.8
Earl McCullouch, Oakland, 1968	0:06.8
Willie Davenport, Inglewood, Calif., 1969	0:06.8
Rod Milburn, College Park, 1974	0:06.8
Charles Foster, Richmond, 1975	0:06.8

WALKING

Mile—Don DeNoon, at Los Angeles, 1966	6:10.2
2 miles—Larry Walker, New York, 1974	13:24.0
3 miles—Vladimir Golubnichiy, Richmond, 1975	19:46.2

RELAYS

Mile—Pacific Coast Club, at Pocatello, 1971	3:09.4
2 miles—Univ. of Chicago T.C., Louisville, 1974	7:20.8
11-lap track—Kansas, Detroit, 1970	7:25.8
4 miles—Indiana Univ., Bloomington, 1974	16:34.8
4 miles-Villanova, Hanover, N.H., 1976	16:19
Sprint medley—Michigan, East Lansing, 1976	3:23.6
Distance medley—Villanova, Louisville, 1976	9:38.4

Men's Field Events

High jump—Dwight Stones, San Diego, 1976	7-6½
Pro—John Radetich, Salt Lake City, 1976	7-6
Long jump—Bob Beamon, Detroit, 1968	27-2¾
Triple jump—Viktor Saneyev, Moscow, 1976	56-3½
Tommy Haynes (Am), New York, 1976	55-5½
Pole Vault—Dan Ripley, New York, 1976	18-3¾
Pro—Steve Smith, New York, 1975	18-5
Shot put—George Woods, Englewood, Calif., 1974	72-2¾
Pro—Brian Oldfield, El Paso, Tex., 1975	75-0
35-lb weight—George Frenn, Boston, 1969	73-3½

Women's Track

50 yds—Iris Davis, at Toronto, 1973	0:05.5
Alice Annum, Pittsburgh, 1975	0:05.5
60 yds—Wyomia Tyus, Albuquerque, 1966	0:06.5
Mattline Render, Champaign, Ill., 1972	0:06.5
Angel Doyle, Philadelphia, 1975	0:06.5
100 yds—Renate Stecher, Berlin, 1974	0:10.5
Wilma Rudolph, U.S., 1960	0:10.7
Kathy Lawson, Pocatello, 1974	0:10.7
220 yds—Rosalyn Bryant, New York, 1975	0:23.6
300 yds—Rosalyn Bryant, Detroit, 1975	0:34.6
440 yds—Charlotte Cooke. Albuquerque. 1966	0:54.2
500 yds—Kathy Hammond, Oakland, 1972	1:04.2
600 yds—Yvonne Saunders, Toronto, 1974	1:18.4
Robin Campbell (Am.), Toronto, 1974	1:19.3
880 yds—Mary Decker, San Diego, 1974	2:02.4
1,000 yds—Mary Decker, Los Angeles, 1974	2:26.7
Mile—Francie Larrieu, Richmond, 1975	4:28.5
2 miles—Francie Larrieu, San Diego, 1974	9:39.4

Women's Track—Metric Distances

50 m—Barbara Ferrell, at Los Angeles, 1968	0:06.0
Renate Stecher, Berlin, 1971	0:06.0
60 m—Linda Haglund, Turku, Finland, 1976	0:07.0
Martha Watson (Am.), Moscow, 1974	0:07.1
Theresa Montgomery (Am.), Moscow, 1974	0:07.1
100 m—Sybille Priebsch, East Berlin, 1976	0:11.4
200 m—Rita Wilden, Stuttgart, 1975	0:23.4
Edith McGuire, (Am.), 1966	0:24.1
300 m—Rita Wilden, Stuttgart, 1975	0:37.4
400 m—Doris Maletski, East Berlin, 1976	0:51.9
500 m—Brenda Walsh, Canada, 1972	1:12.1
Wendy Knudson, Boulder, Colo., 1975	1:13.5
600 m—Verona Elder, Britain	1:29
Robin Campbell (Am) Moscow, 1974	1:30.1
800 m—Nikolina Shtereva, Sofia, 1976	2:01.1
Mary Decker (Am), San Diego, 1974	2:01.8
1,000 m—Francie Larrieu, Los Angeles, 1975	2:40.2
1,500 m—Francie Larrieu, Richmond, 1975	4:09.8
3,000 m—Francie Larrieu, San Diego, 1974	9:02.4

(Continued on next page)

WOMEN'S TRACK (Continued)

HURDLES

50 yds—Annelie Ehrhardt, at Toronto, 1975		0:06.2
Patty Johnson (Am.), Toronto, 1972		0:06.4
Mamie Rollins (Am.), Toronto, 1973		0:06.4
Lacey O'Neal (Am.), Toronto, 1973		0:06.4
Debby LaPlante, Louisville, 1976		0:08.8
60 yds—Karin Balzer, East Berlin, 1970		0:07.4
Patty J. VanWolvelaere, Toronto, 1972		0:07.4
70 yds—Mamie Rallins, Chicago, 1970		0:08.8
Deby LaPlante, Louisville, 1976		0:08.8
50 m—Annelie Ehrhardt, Berlin, 1972		0:06.6
60 m—Valerie Bufanu, Rumania, 1973		0:07.9
Patty Johnson (Am.), Los Angeles, 1974		0:08.4
100 m—Patty Johnson, Pocatello, 1974		0:013.2
Annelie Ehrhardt, Berlin, 1972		0:13.2

WALKING

Mile—Sue Brodock, New York, 1975 . . . . 7:22.5

RELAYS

640 yds—Atoms T.C., at College Park, Md.		1:10.4
Mile—Florida U., College Park, Md., 1976		3:44.2
880-yd medley—United States, 1968		1:45.1
Los Angeles Mercurettes, 1968		1:45.1
2 mile—Soviet Union, 1972		8:41.6

Women's Field Events

Long jump—Angela Voigt, East Berlin, 1976		22–2¼
Martha Watson (Am.), 1973		21–4¾
High jump—Rosemarie Ackerman, East Berlin, 1975		6–4½
Joni Huntley (Am.), Inglewood, Calif., 1975		6–2¼
Shotput—Helen Fibingerova, Jablonec, 1975		69–4
Maren Seidler (Am.), Oakland, 1975		56–11

(Professional records, usually achieved in meets run by the International Track Association are not recognized as best performances by amateur groups.)

TABLE TENNIS
National Champions

1945–49	Richard Miles
1950	John Leach
1951	Richard Miles
1952	Louis Pagliaro
1953–55	Richard Miles
1956	Erwin Klein
1957	Bernard Bukiet
1958	Martin Reisman
1959	Bob Gusikoff
1960	Martin Reisman
1961	Erwin Klein
1962	Dick Miles
1963	Bernard Bukiet
1964–65	Erwin Klein
1966	Bernard Bukiet

1967	Manji Fukushima
1968–73	Dal Joon Lee
1974–75	Kjell Johasson

WOMEN

1946	Bernice Charney
1947	Leah Thall
1948	Peggy McLean
1949	Leah Thall Neuberger
1950	Reba Kirson Monness
1951–53	Leah Thall Neuberger
1954	Mildred Shahian
1955–57	Leah Thall Neuberger
1958–59	Susie Hoshi
1960	Sharon Acton

1961	Leah Thall Neuberger
1962	Mildred Shahian
1963	Bernice Chotras
1964	Valleri Bellini
1965	Patty Martinez
1966	Violetta Nesukaitis
1967	Patti Martinez
1968	Violetta Nesukaitis
1969	Patti Martinez
1970	Violetta Nesukaitis
1971	Connie Sweeris
1972	Wendy Hicks
1973	Violetta Nesukaitis
1974	Yukei Ohzeki
1975	Chung Hyun Sook

DOG SHOWS
Westminster Kennel Club Exhibition

Year	Best in show	Breed	Owner
1950	Ch. Walsing Winning Trick of Edgerstoune	Scottish terrier	Mrs. John G. Winant
1951	Ch. Bang Away of Sirrah Crest	Boxer	Dr. and Mrs. R. C. Harris
1952–53	Ch. Rancho Dobe's Storm	Doberman pinscher	Mr. and Mrs. Len Carey
1954	Ch. Carmor's Rise and Shine	Cocker spaniel	Mrs. Carl E. Morgan
1955	Ch. Kippax Fearnought	Bulldog	Dr. John A. Saylor
1956	Ch. Wilber White Swan	Toy poodle	Bertha Smith
1957	Ch. Shirkhan of Grandeur	Afghan	Sunny Shay-Dorothy Chenade
1958	Ch. Puttencove Promise	Standard poodle	Mr. and Mrs. George Putnam
1959	Ch. Fontclair Festoon	Miniature poodle	Clarence Dillon
1960	Ch. Chik T'Sun of Caversham	Pekingese	Mr. and Mrs. C. C. Venable
1961	Ch. Cappoquin Little Sister	Toy poodle	Florence Michelson
1962	Ch. Elfinbrook Simon	West Highland terrier	Mrs. Florence Worcester
1963	Ch. Wakefield's Black Knight	English springer spaniel	Mrs. W. J. S. Borie
1964	Ch. Courtenay Fleetfoot of Pennyworth	Whippet	Mrs. Charles B. Newcombe
1965	Ch. Carmichael's Fanfare	Scottish terrier	Mr. and Mrs. Charles C. Stalter
1966	Ch. Zeloy Mooremaides Magic	Fox terrier, wire	Mrs. Marion G. Bunker
1967	Ch. Bardene Bingo	Scottish terrier	E. H. Stuart
1968	Ch. Stingray of Derryabah	Lakeland terrier	Mr. and Mrs. James A. Farrell
1969	Ch. Glamour Good News	Skye terrier	Walter and Mrs. Adele Goodman
1970	Ch. Arriba's Prima Donna	Boxer	Dr. and Mrs. P. J. Pagano and Dr. Theodore S. Fickes
1971–72	Ch. Chinoe's Adamant James	English springer spaniel	Dr. Milton E. Prickett
1973	Ch. Acadia Command Performance	Standard poodle	Mrs. Jo Ann Sering and Edward B. Jenner
1974	Ch. Gretchenhof Columbia River	German short-haired pointer	Richard P. Smith
1975	Ch. Sir Lancelot of Barvan	Old English sheepdog	Mr. and Mrs. Ronald Vanword

SPORTS ORGANIZATIONS AND INFORMATION BUREAUS

AMATEUR ATHLETIC UNION OF THE U. S. 3400 West 86th St., Indianapolis, Indiana 46862

AMATEUR BICYCLE LEAGUE OF AMERICA. See United States Cycling Federation

AMATEUR FENCERS LEAGUE OF AMERICA. 33 62d St., West New York, N. J. 07093

AMATEUR HOCKEY ASSN. OF THE U. S. 10 Lake Circle, Colorado Springs, Colo. 80906

AMATEUR SKATING UNION OF THE U. S. 4423 West Deming Place, Chicago, Ill. 60639

AMATEUR SOFTBALL ASSOCIATION. 2801 N. E. 50th St. P. O. Box 11437, Oklahoma City, Okla. 73111

AMATEUR TRAPSHOOTING ASSN. OF AMERICA. Vandalia, Ohio 45377

AMERICAN AMATEUR BASEBALL CONGRESS. Box 44, Battle Creek, Mich. 49016

AMERICAN ASSOCIATION (baseball). P.O. Box 382, Wichita, Kan. 67201

AMERICAN BADMINTON ASSOCIATION. 380 South Euclid Avenue, Pasadena, Calif. 91101

AMERICAN BASKETBALL ASSOCIATION, 1700 Broadway, New York, N. Y. 10019

AMERICAN BOWLING CONGRESS. 5301 South 76th St., Greendale, Wis. 53129

AMERICAN CANOE ASSOCIATION. 4260 East Evans Avenue, Denver, Colo. 80222

AMERICAN CASTING ASSN. P.O. Box 158, Jackson, Ky. 41339

AMERICAN HOCKEY LEAGUE. P.O. Box 100, West Springfield, Mass. 01089

AMERICAN HORSE SHOWS ASSN. 527 Madison Ave., New York, N. Y. 10022

AMERICAN KENNEL CLUB. 51 Madison Ave., New York, N. Y. 10010

AMERICAN LAWN BOWLING ASSN. 10337 Cheryl Drive, Sun City, Ari., 85351

AMERICAN LEAGUE (baseball). 280 Park Ave., New York, N.Y. 10017

AMERICAN MOTORCYCLE ASSN. P.O. Box 141, Westerville, Ohio 43081

AMERICAN POWER BOAT ASSN. 415 Burns Drive, Detroit, Mich. 48214

AMERICAN WATER SKI ASSN. 7th St. & Ave. G, S.W., Winter Haven, Fla. 33881

BASEBALL COMMISSIONER, 75 Rockefeller Plaza, New York, N.Y., 10019

BOWLING PROPRIETORS' ASSN. OF AMERICA. P.O. Box 5802, Arlington, Texas 76011

CENTRAL HOCKEY LEAGUE. 5740 Oakland Ave., St. Louis, Mo. 63110

EASTERN COLLEGE ATHLETIC CONFERENCE. P.O. Box 3, Centerville, Mass. 02632

ELIAS SPORTS BUREAU. 500 Fifth Ave., New York, N.Y. 10036

FISH AND WILDLIFE SERVICE. Dept. of the Interior, Washington, D. C. 20240

INTERNATIONAL AMATEUR ATHLETIC FEDERATION. Halton House, 23 Holborn, London, E. C. 1, England

INTERNATIONAL GAME FISH ASSN. 3000 East Las Olas Blvd., Fort Lauderdale, Fla. 33316

INTERNATIONAL LEAGUE (Baseball). Times Square Bldg., Rochester, N. Y. 14604

INTERNATIONAL MOTOR SPORTS ASSN. P.O. Box 805, Fairfield, Conn. 06430

INTERNATIONAL OLYMPIC COMMITTEE. Chateau de Vidy, Lausanne, Switzerland

THE JOCKEY CLUB. 300 Park Ave., New York, N. Y. 10022.

LADIES PROFESSIONAL GOLF ASSOCIATION., 919 Third Ave., New York, N. Y. 10022.

LITTLE LEAGUE BASEBALL. Williamsport, Pa. 17701.

NATL. ARCHERY ASSN. 1951 Geraldson Drive, Lancaster, Pa. 17601.

NATL. ASSN. OF AMATEUR OARSMEN. 4 Boathouse Row, Philadelphia, Pa. 19130

NATL. ASSN. OF INTERCOLLEGIATE ATHLETICS. 1205 Baltimore Avenue, Kansas City, Mo. 64105

NATL. ASSN. OF PROFESSIONAL BASEBALL LEAGUES (minors). P.O. Box A, St. Petersburg, Fla. 33731

NATIONAL ASSN. FOR STOCK CAR AUTO RACING. P.O. Box K, Daytona Beach, Fla. 32015

NATL. BASEBALL CONGRESS. Wichita, Kan. 67201

NATL. BASKETBALL ASSN. 2 Pennsylvania Plaza, New York, N. Y. 10001

NATL. COLLEGIATE ATHLETIC ASSN. P.O. Box 1906, Shawnee Mission, Kan. 66222

NATL. DUCK PIN BOWLING CONGRESS. 711-14th St. N.W., Washington, D.C. 20005

NATL. FIELD ARCHERY ASSN. Rt. 2, Box 514, Redlands, Calif. 92373

NATL. FOOTBALL LEAGUE. 410 Park Avenue, New York, N. Y. 10022

NATL. HOCKEY LEAGUE. 922 Sun Life Bldg., Montreal, Que., Canada

NATIONAL HORSESHOE PITCHERS ASSN., Route 5, Lucasville, Ohio, 45648

NATIONAL HOT ROD ASSOCIATION, 10639 Riverside Drive, North Hollywood, Calif., 91602

NATIONAL JUNIOR COLLEGE ATHLETIC ASSN. Hilton Inn, Hutchinson, Kan. 67501

NATIONAL LAWN TENNIS HALL OF FAME, Newport Casino, Newport, R.I., 02840

NATIONAL LEAGUE (baseball). 220 Montgomery St., San Francisco, Calif. 94104

NATL. RIFLE ASSN. OF AMERICA. 1600 Rhode Island Ave., N.W., Washington, D. C. 20036

NATL. SKEET SHOOTING ASSN. P.O. Box 28188, San Antonio, Tex. 78228

NEW YORK RACING ASSN. P.O. Box 90, Jamaica, N. Y. 11417

NEW YORK STATE ATHLETIC COMMISSION (boxing) 226 W. 47th St., New York, N. Y. 10036

NATIONAL SHUFFLEBOARD ASSOCIATION, 6815 Lake Ave., West Palm Beach, Fla. 33405

NORTH AMERICAN YACHT RACING UNION. See United States Yacht Racing Union

PROFESSIONAL GOLFERS' ASSN. OF AMERICA. Box 12458, Lake Park, Fla. 33403

RODEO COWBOYS ASSN. 2929 W. 19th Ave., Denver, Colo. 80204

ROLLER SKATING RINK OPERATORS. *See* United States of America Roller Skating Confederation.

SPORTS CAR CLUB OF AMERICA. P.O. Box 22476, Denver, Colo. 80222

TENNIS HALL OF FAME. See National Lawn Tennis Hall of Fame

THOROUGHBRED RACING ASSNS. OF THE U.S. 522 Fifth Ave., New York, N.Y. 10036.

UNITED STATES OF AMERICA ROLLER SKATING CONFEDERATION. 7700 'A' Street, Lincoln, Neb. 68510

U.S. AUTO CLUB, 49 W. 16th St., Speedway, Ind. 46202

U.S. CHESS FEDERATION, 479 Broadway, Newburgh, N.Y., 12550

U.S. CYCLING FEDERATION, Box 669, Wall Street Station, New York, N.Y. 10005

U. S. FIGURE SKATING ASSN. 575 Boylston St., Boston, Mass. 02116

U. S. GOLF ASSN. Far Hills, N. J., 07931

Sports Organizations and Information Bureaus (Continued)

U. S. HANDBALL ASSN. 4101 Dempster St., Skokie, III. 60077

U.S. TENNIS ASSN. 51 E. 42nd St., New York, N. Y., 10017

U.S. MEN'S CURLING ASSN., 1634 Lincoln Ave., Utica, N.Y. 13502

U. S. OLYMPIC COMMITTEE. Olympic House, 57 Park Ave., New York, N. Y. 10016

U. S. PARACHUTE ASSN., 806 Fifteenth St., N.W., Washington, D.C., 20005

U. S. POLO ASSN. 1301 W. 22d St., Oak Brook, III. 60521.

U. S. SKI ASSN. 1726 Champa St., Denver, Colorado 80202

U. S. SOCCER FOOTBALL ASSN. 350 Fifth Ave., New York, N. Y. 10001

U. S. SQUASH RACQUETS ASSN. 470 N. Latches Lane, Merion, Pa. 19066

U. S. TABLE TENNIS ASSN. 1500 N. Broom St., Wilmington, Del. 19806

U. S. TROTTING ASSN. 750 Michigan Ave., Columbus, Ohio 43215

U. S. VOLLEYBALL ASSN. 557 Fourth Street, San Francisco, Calif. 94107

U. S. YACHT RACING UNION. P.O. Box 209, Goat Island, Newport, R.I. 02840

WOMEN'S INTERNATIONAL BOWLING CONGRESS. 5301 South 76th St., Greendale, Wis. 53129

WORLD HOCKEY ASSN. 415 Yonge Street, Toronto, Ontario, M5B 2E7, Canada

YOUTH TENNIS LEAGUE, INC. 1701 Vandalia, Collinsville, III. 62234

CURLING
National Champions

1965 Superior, Wis. (Bud Somerville; skip; Bill Strum, Al Gagne, Thomas Wright)

1966 Fargo, N. D. (Joe Zbacnik, skip; Bruce Roberts, Mike O'Leary, Gerald Toutant)

1967 Seattle (Bruce Roberts, skip; Doug Walker, Tom Fitzpatrick, John Wright)

1968–69 Superior, Wis. (Bud Somerville, skip; Bill Strum, Al Gagne, Thomas Wright)

1970 Grafton, N. D. (Art Tallackson, skip; Trueman Thompson, Raymond Holt, Glenn Gilleshammer)

1971 Edmore, N. D. (Dal Dalziel, skip; Rodney Melland, Dennis Melland, Clark Sampson)

1972 Grafton, N. D. (Robert L. LaBonte, skip; Frank L. Aasand, John O. Aasand, Ray Morgan)

1973 Winchester, Mass. (Charles Reeves, Jr., skip; Barry Blanchard, Henry Shean, Douglas Carlson)

*1974 Superior, Wis. (Bud Somerville, skip; Tom Locken, Bill Strum, Bob Nichols)

1975 Seattle Granite Club (Ed Risling, skip; Chuck Lundgren, Gary Schnee, Dave Tellvik)

* Won World Championship.

FENCING
National Champions
FOIL

1950–51	Silvio Giolito	1958	Albert Axelrod	1965	Robert Russell	1972	Bert Freeman
1952–53	Daniel Bukantz	1959	Joseph Paletta	1966	Max Geuter	1973	Ed Ballinger
1954	Joseph Levis	1960	Albert Axelrod	1967–68	Heizaburo Okawa	1974	Heik Hambarzumian
1955	Albert Axelrod	1961	Lawrence Anastasi	1969	Carl Borack	1975	Ed Ballinger
1956	Sewall Shurtz	1962–63	Edwin Richards	1970	Albert Axelrod		
1957	Daniel Bukantz	1964	Herb Cohen	1971	Uriah Jones		

EPEE

1948–50	Norman Lewis	1957–58	Richard Berry	1964	Paul Pesthy	1973	Scott Bozer
1951	Jose de Capriles	1959	Henry Kolowrat	1965	Joseph Elliott	1974	Dan Cantillon
1952	Abelardo Memendez	1960	David Micahnik	1966–68	Paul Pesthy	1975	Scott Bozek
1953	Donald Thompson	1961	Robert Beck	1969	Steve Netburn		
1954	Sewall Shurtz	1962	Gil Eisner	1970	Joseph Elliott		
1955–56	Abram Cohen	1963	Lawrence Anastasi	1971–72	James Melcher		

SABER

1950–53	Tibor Nyilas	1959	Tomas Orley	1964	Attila Keresztes	1969–72	Alex Orban
1954	George Worth	1960	Eugene Hamori	1965	Alex Orban	1973	Paul Apostle
1955	Richard Dyer	1961	Daniel Magay	1966–67	Al Morales	1974–75	Peter Westbrook
1956	Tibor Nyilas	1962	Mike Dasaro	1968	Jack Keane		
1957–58	Daniel Magay	1963	Eugene Hamori				

WOMEN'S FOIL

1950–51	Janice Lee York	1958	Maxine Mitchell	1963	Harriet King	1970–71	Harriet King
1952	Maxine Mitchell	1959	Maria del Pilar	1964–66	Janice Lee Romary	1972	Ruth White
1953	Paula Sweeney		Roldan	1967	Harriet King	1973	Tatanya Adamovich
1954–55	Maxine Mitchell	1960–61	Janice Lee Romary	1968	Janice Lee Romary	1974	Gaye Jacobsen
1956–57	Janice Lee Romary	1962	Yoshie Takiuchie	1969	Ruth White	1975	Nikki Tomlinson

1976 CHAMPIONS AND RECORDS
1976 OLYMPIC GAMES CHAMPIONS
(Games of XXI Olympiad at Montreal, Quebec, Canada, July 17–Aug. 1)

(Champions receive gold medals, second-place finishers silver and third-place bronze; Olympic records are recognized only in archery, shooting, swimming, track and field and weight lifting.)

TRACK AND FIELD

TRACK EVENTS
100-Meter Dash
1—Hasely Crawford, Trinidad 0:10.06
2—Don Quarrie, Jamaica 0:10.08
3—Valery Borzov, U.S.S.R. 0:10.14

200-Meter Dash
1—Don Quarrie, Jamaica 0:20.23
2—Millard Hampton, San Jose, Calif. 0:20.29
3—Dwayne Evans, Phoenix, Ariz. 0:20.43

400-Meter Dash
1—Alberto Juantorena, Cuba 0:44.26
2—Fred Newhouse, Baton Rouge, La. 0:44.40
3—Herman Frazier, Philadelphia 0:44.95

800-Meter Run
1—Alberto Juantorena, Cuba 1:43.5W
2—Ivo Vandamme, Belgium 1:43.86
3—Rick Wohlhuter, Chicago 1:44.12

1,500-Meter Run
1—John Walker, New Zealand 3:39.17
2—Ivo Vandamme, Belgium 3:39.27
3—Paul Wellman, West Germany 3:39.33

5,000-Meter Run
1—Lasse Viren, Finland 13:24.76
2—Dick Quax, New Zealand 13:25.16
3—Klaus Hildenbrand, West Germany 13:25.38

10,000-Meter Run
1—Lasse Viren, Finland 27:40.38
2—Carlos Sousa Lopes, Portugal 27:45.17
3—Brendan Foster, Britain 27:54.92

3,000-Meter Steeplechase
1—Anders Garderud, Sweden 8:08.02W
2—Bronisla Malinowski, Poland 8:09.11
3—Frank Baumgartl, East Germany 8:10.36

20,000-Meter Walk
1—Daniel Bautista, Mexico 1:24:40.6
2—Hans Reimann, East Germany 1:25:13.8
3—Peter Frenkel, East Germany 1:25:29.4

Marathon
1—Waldemar Cierpinski, East Germany 2:09:55
2—Frank Shorter, Boulder, Colo 2:10:45.8
3—Karel Lismont, Belgium 2:11:12.6

110-Meter Hurdles
1—Guy Drut, France 0:13.30
2—Alejandro Casanas, Cuba 0:13.33
3—Willie Davenport, Baton Rouge, La. 0:13.38

400-Meter Hurdles
1—Edwin Moses, Dayton, Ohio 0:47.64W
2—Michael Shine, Youngsville, Pa. 0:48.69
3—Evgeny Gavrilenko, U.S.S.R. 0:49.45

400-Meter Relay
1—United States 0:38.33
(Harvey Glance, Phenix City, Ala.; John Jones, Lampasas, Tex.; Millard Hampton, San Jose, Calif.; Steve Riddick, Philadelphia)
2—East Germany 0:38.66
3—U.S.S.R. 0:38.78

1,600-Meter Relay
1—United States 2:58.65
(Herman Frazier, Philadelphia; Benjamin Brown, Milpitas, Calif.; Fred Newhouse, Baton Rouge, La.; Maxie Parks, Los Angeles)
2—Poland 3:01.43
3—West Germany 3:01.98

FIELD EVENTS
High Jump
(Figures in parentheses are meters; others are feet and inches.)

High Jump
1—Jacek Wszola, Poland . . . . (2.25) 7-4½*
2—Greg Joy, Canada . . . . (2.23) 7-3¾
3—Dwight Stones, Huntington Beach, Calif. . . . (2.21) 7-3

Long Jump
1—Arnie Robinson, San Diego, Calif. . . . . . . (8.35) 27-4¾
2—Randy Williams, Fresno, Calif. . . . . (8.11) 26-7¼
3—Frank Wartenberg, East Germany . . . . . . (8.02) 26-3¾

Triple Jump
1—Victor Saneyev, U.S.S.R. . . . . (17.29) 56-8¾
2—James Butts, Los Angeles . . . . (17.18) 56-4½
3—Joao de Oliviero, Brazil . . . . (16.9) 55-5½

Pole Vault
1—Tadeusz Slusarski, Poland . . . . (5.50) 18-0½**
2—Antti Kalliomaki, Finland . . . . (5.50) 18-0½**
3—Dave Roberts, Gainesville, Fla. . . . . (5.50) 18-0½**

Shotput
1—Udo Beyer, East Germany . . . . (21.05) 69-0¾
2—Evgeny Mironov, U.S.S.R. . . . . (21.03) 69-0
3—Alexander Barisnikov, U.S.S.R. . . . . (21.0) 68-10¾

Discus
1—Mac Wilkins, Portland, Ore. . . . . (67.5) 221-5
2—Wolfgang Schmidt, East Germany . . . . . . (66.22) 217-3
3—John Powell, Cupertino, Calif. . . . . (65.7) 215-6

Javelin
1—Miklos Nemeth, Hungary . . . . (94.58) 310-4W
2—Hannu Siitonen, Finland . . . . (87.92) 288-5
3—Gheorghe Megelea, Romania . . . . (87.16) 285-11

Hammer Throw
1—Yuri Sedyh, U.S.S.R. . . . . (77.52) 254-4*
2—Aleksei Spiridonov, U.S.S.R. . . . . (76.08) 249-7
3—Anatoly Bondarchuk, U.S.S.R. . . . . (75.48) 247-7½

Decathlon
1—Bruce Jenner, San Jose, Calif. . . . . 8,618 pts W
2—Guido Kratschmer, West Germany 8,411
3—Nikolai Avilov, U.S.S.R. 8,369
W—world record; *—Olympic record; **—equals Olympic record.

WOMEN
100-Meter Dash
1—Annegret Richter, West Germany 0:11.08
(Miss Richter set world record of 11.01 seconds in semifinals
2—Renate Stecher, East Germany 0:11.13
3—Inge Helten, West Germany 0:11.17

(1976 Olympic Games Results, Continued)

200-Meter Dash
1—Baerbel Eckert, East Germany 0:22.37*
2—Annegret Richter, West Germany 0:22.39
3—Renate Stecher, East Germany 0:22.47

400-Meter Dash
1—Irena Szewinska, Poland 0:49.29W
2—Christina Brehmer, East Germany 0:50.51
3—Ellen Streidt, East Germany 0:50.55

800-Meter Run
1—Tatiana Kazankina, U.S.S.R. 1:54.94W
2—Nikolina Chtereva, Bulgaria 1:55.42
3—Elfi Zinn, East Germany 1:55.60

1,500-Meter Run
1—Tatiana Kazankina, U.S.S.R. 4:05.48
2—Gunhild Hoffmeister, East Germany 4:06.02
3—Ulrike Klapezynski, East Germany 4:06.09

100-Meter Hurdles
1—Johanna Schaller, East Germany 0:12.77
2—Tatiana Anisimova, U.S.S.R. 0:12.78
3—Natalia Lebedeva, U.S.S.R. 0:12.80

400-Meter Relay
1—East Germany 0:42.55*
(Marlis Oelsner, Renate Stecher, Carla Bodendorf, Baerbel Eckert)
2—West Germany 0:42.59
3—U.S.S.R. 0:43.09

1,600-Meter Relay
1—East Germany . . . . 3:19.23 W
(Doris Maletzki, Brigitte Rohde, Ellen Streidt, Christina Brehmer)
2—United States 3:22.81
(Debra Sapenter, Prairie View, Tex.; Sheila Ingram, Washington; Pam Jiles, New Orleans; Rosalyn Bryant, Chicago)
3—U.S.S.R. 3:24.24

High Jump
1—Rosemarie Ackermann, East Germany . . . . (1.93) 6-4*
2—Sara Simeoni, Italy . . . . (1.91) 6-3¼
3—Yordanka Blagoeva, Bulgaria . . . . (1.91) 6-3¼

Long Jump
1—Angela Voigt, East Germany . . . . (6.72) 22-0½
2—Kathy McMillan, Raeford, N.C. . . . . . . (6.66) 21-10¼
3—Lidiya Alfeyeva, U.S.S.R. . . . . (6.60) 21-7¾

Shotput
1—Ivanka Christova, Bulgaria . . . . (21.16) 69-5*
2—Nadejda Chijova, U.S.S.R. . . . . (20.96) 68-9
3—Helena Fibingerova, Czechoslovakia . . . . . (20.67) 67-9½

Discus
1—Evelin Schlaak, East Germany . . . . (69.0) 226-4*
2—Maria Vergova, Bulgaria . . . . (67.3) 220-9½
3—Gabriele Hinzmann, East Germany . . . . . (66.84) 219-3¼

Javelin
1—Ruth Fuchs, East Germany . . . . (65.94) 216-4*
2—Marion Becker, West Germany . . . . . . (64.7) 212-3
3—Kathy Schmidt, Pacific Palisades, Calif. . . . (63.96) 209-10

Pentathlon
1—Siegrun Siegl, East Germany . . . . 4,745 pts
2—Christine Laser, East Germany . . . . 4,745 pts
(Miss Siegl awarded title for finishing ahead of Miss Laser in 3 of the 5 events)
3—Burglinde Pollak, East Germany . . . . 4,740 pts

W—World record; *—Olympic record; **—Equals Olympic record.

ARCHERY
Men—1, Darrell Pace, Cincinnati (2,571 points, Olympic record); 2, Hiroshi Michinaga, Japan (2,502); 3, Carlo Ferrari, Italy (2,495)
Women—1, Luann Ryon, Riverside, Calif. (2,499 points, Olympic record); 2, Valentina Kolpan, U.S.S.R. (2,460); 3, Zebinoso Rustamova, U.S.S.R. (2,407)

BASKETBALL
Men—1, United States; 2, Yugoslavia; 3, U.S.S.R.
(United States defeated Yugoslavia, 95–74, in final)
Women—1, U.S.S.R.; 2, United States; 3, Bulgaria
(U.S.S.R. undefeated in six-team round-robin)

BOXING
106 lbs—1, Jorge Hernandez, Cuba; 2, Byong Uk Li, North Korea; 3, Payao Pooltarat, Thailand, and Orlando Malfonado, Puerto Rico
112 lbs—1, Leo Randolph, Tacoma, Wash.; 2, Ramon Duvalon, Cuba; 3, David Torosyan, U.S.S.R., and Leszek Bazynski, Poland
119 lbs—1, Yong Jo Gu, North Korea; 2, Charles Mooney, Fayetteville, N.C.; 3, Patrick Cowdsell, Britain, and Victor Rybakov, U.S.S.R.
126 lbs—1, Angel Herrera, Cuba; 2, Richard Nowakowski, East Germany; 3, Peszik Kusedowski, Poland, and Juan Parades, Mexico
132 lbs—1, Howard Davis, Glen Cove, N.Y.; 2, Simion Cutov, Romania; 3, Vayile Solomin, U.S.S.R., and Ace Rusevski, Yugoslavia
140 lbs—1, Ray Leonard, Palmer Park, Md.; 2, Andres Aldama, Cuba; 3, Vladimir Kolev, Bulgaria, and Kazimier Szczerbc, Poland
147 lbs—1, Jochen Bachfeld, East Germany; 2, Pedro Gamarro, Venezuela; 3, Rheinharf Skricek, West Germany, and Victor Zilbermann, Romania
156 lbs—1, Jerzy Rybicki, Poland; 2, Tadijar Kacar, Yugoslavia; 3, Victor Sazchenko, U.S.S.R., and Roland Garhbey, Cuba
165 lbs—1, Mike Spinks, St. Louis; 2, Rufat Riskiev, U.S.S.R.; 3, Alex Nastec, Romania, and Luis Martinez, Cuba
178 lbs—1, Leon Spinks, Camp Lejeune, N.C.; 2, Sixto Soria, Cuba; 3, Costiea Dafinoiu, Romania, and Janusz Gortat, Poland
Heavyweight—1, Teofilo Stevenson, Cuba; 2, Mircea Simon, Romania; 3, John Tate, Knoxville, Tenn., and Clarence Hill, Bermuda

CANOEING
KAYAK
MEN
Singles, 500 meters—1, Vasile Diba, Romania; 2, Zoltan Sztanity, Hungary; 3, Rudiger Helm, East Germany
Singles, 1,000 meters—1, Rudiger Helm, East Germany; 2, Geza Csapo, Hungary; 3, Vasile Diba, Romania
Pairs, 500 meters—1, Joachim Mattern–Bernd Olbricht, East Germany; 2, U.S.S.R.; 3, Romania
Pairs, 1,000 meters—1, Sergei Nagorny–Vladimir Romanovsky, U.S.S.R.; 2, East Germany; 3, Hungary
Fours, 1,000 meters—1, U.S.S.R.; 2, Spain; 3, East Germany

WOMEN
Singles, 500 meters—1, Carola Zirzow, East Germany; 2, Tatiana Korshunova, U.S.S.R.; 3, Klara Rajnai, Hungary.
Pairs, 500 meters—1, Nina Gopova-Galina Kreft, U.S.S.R.; 2, Hungary; 3, East Germany

CANADIAN
Singles, 500 meters—1, Aleksandr Rogov, U.S.S.R.; 2, John Wood, Canada; 3, Matija Ljubek, Yugoslavia

(1976 Olympic Games Results, Continued)

Singles, 1,000 meters—1, Matija Ljubek, Yugoslavia; 2, Vasily Urchenko, U.S.S.R.; 3, Tamas Wichmann, Hungary
Pairs, 500 meters—1, Sergei Petrenko-Aleksandr Vinogradov, U.S.S.R.; 2, Poland; 3, Hungary
Pairs, 1,000 meters—1, Sergei Petrenko-Aleksandr Vinogradov, U.S.S.R.; 2, Romania; 3, Hungary

CYCLING

1,000 Meters—1, Klaus-Jurgen Grunke, East Germany; 2, Michel Vaarten, Belgium; 3, Niels Fredborg, Denmark
Sprint—1, Anton Tkac, Czechoslovakia; 2, Daniel Morelon, France; 3, Hanse-Jurven Gescheke, East Germany
4,000-Meter Pursuit, Individual—1, Gregor Braun, West Germany; 2, Herman Ponsteen, Netherlands; 3, Thomas Huschke, East Germany
Pursuit Team—1, West Germany; 2, U.S.S.R.; 3, Britain
Road Race, Individual (109 miles)—1, Bernt Johansson, Sweden—4:46:52; 2, Giuseppi Martinelli, Italy; 3, Mieczyslaw Nowicki, Poland
Road Race, Team, 100-kilometer road—1, U.S.S.R.; 2, Poland; 3, Denmark

EQUESTRIAN EVENTS

Dressage

Individual—1, Christine Stueckelberger, Switzerland; 2, Harry Boldt, West Germany; 3, Dr. Reiner Klimke, West Germany
Team—1, West Germany; 2, Switzerland; 3, United States (Hilda Gurney, Woodland Hills, Calif; Edith Master, New York; Dorothy Morkis, Raynham, Mass; John Winnett, Tuxedo Park, N.Y.)

Jumping

Individual—Alwin Schockemoehle, West Germany; 2, Michel Viallancourt, Canada; 3, Francis Mathy, Belgium
Team—1, France; 2, West Germany; 3, Belgium

3-Day Event

Individual—1, Tad Coffin, Strafford, Vt.; 2, Mike Plumb, Chesapeake, Md.; 3, Karl Schultz, West Germany.
Team—1, United States (Tad Coffin, Mike Plumb, Mary Ann Tauskey, New Vernon, N.Y.; Bruce Davidson, Unionville, Pa.); 2, West Germany; 3, Australia

FENCING

MEN

Foil, Individual—1, Fabio Dal Zotto, Italy; 2, Alexandr Romankov, U.S.S.R.; 3, Bernard Talvard, France
Foil, Team—1, West Germany; 2, Italy; 3, France
Epee, Individual—1, Alexander Pusch, West Germay; 2, Juergen Huhn, West Germany; 3, Gyozo Kulcsar, Hungary
Epee, Team—1, Sweden; 2, West Germany; 3, Switzerland
Saber, Individual—1, Victor Krovopovskov, U.S.S.R.; 2, Vladimir Nazlymov, U.S.S.R.; 3, Victor Sidiac, U.S.S.R.
Saber, Team—1, U.S.S.R.; 2, Italy; 3, Romania.

WOMEN

Foil, Individual—1, Ildiko Schwarczenberger, Hungary; 2, Marie Consolata Collino, Italy; 3, Elena Belova, U.S.S.R.
Foil, Team—1, U.S.S.R.; 2, France; 3, Hungary

FIELD HOCKEY

1, New Zealand; 2, Australia; 3, Pakistan (New Zealand defeated Australia, 1-0, in final) (Pakistan defeated Netherlands, 3-2, for third place)

HANDBALL (TEAM)

Women—1, U.S.S.R.; 2, East Germany; 3, Hungary
Men—1, U.S.S.R.; 2, Romania; 3, Poland

GYMNASTICS

MEN

All-Around—1, Nikolai Andrianov, U.S.S.R.; 2, Sawao Kato, Japan; 3, Mitsuo Tsukahara, Japan
Floor Exercises—1, Nikolai Andrianov, U.S.S.R.; 2, Valdimir Marchenko, U.S.S.R.; 3, Peter Kormann, New Haven, Conn.
Horizontal Bar—1, Mitsuo Tsukahara, Japan; 2, Eizo Kemmotsu, Japan; 3, tie between Henri Boerio, France, and Eberhard Gienger, West Germany
Long Horse—1, Nikolai Andrianov, U.S.S.R.; 2, Mitsuo Tsukahara, Japan; 3, Hiroshi Kajoyama, Japan
Parallel Bars—1, Sawao Kato, Japan; 2, Nikolai Andrianov, U.S.S.R.; 3, Mitsuo Tsukahara, Japan
Rings—1, Nikolai Andrianov, U.S.S.R.; 2, Alexandr Ditiatin, U.S.S.R.; 3, Danut Grecu, Romania
Side Horse—1, Zoltan Magyar, Hungary; 2, Eizo Kemmotsu, Japan; 3, tie between Nikolai Andrianov, U.S.S.R., and Michael Nikolay, East Germany
Team All-Around—1, Japan; 2, East Germany; 3, U.S.S.R.

WOMEN

All-Around—1, Nadia Comaneci, Romania; 2, Nelli Kim, U.S.S.R.; 3, Ludmila Tourischeva, U.S.S.R.
Balance Beam—1, Nadia Comaneci, Romania; 2, Olga Korbut, U.S.S.R.; 3, Marta Evervari, Hungary
Floor Exercises—1, Nelli Kim, U.S.S.R.; 2, Ludmila Tourischeva, U.S.S.R.; 3, Nadia Comaneci, Romania
Uneven Bars—1, Nadia Comaneci, Romania; 2, Teodora Ungureanu, Romania; 3, Marta Egervari, Hungary
Vault—1, Nelli Kim, U.S.S.R.; 2, tie between Ludmila Tourischeva, U.S.S.R., and Karola Dombeck, East Germany
Team All-Around—1, U.S.S.R.; 2, Romania; 3, East Germany

JUDO

Middleweight—1, Isamu Sonada, Japan; 2, Valeriy Dvoinikov, U.S.S.R.; 3, tie between Slavko Obadov, Yugoslavia, and Youngchul Park, South Korea
Light Heavyweight—1, Kazuhiro Ninomiya, Japan; 2, Ramaz Harshiladze, U.S.S.R.; 3, tie between Dave Starbrook, Britain, and Juerg Roethlisberger, Switzerland
Heavyweight—1, Sergei Novikov, U.S.S.R.; 2, Guenther Heureuther, West Germany; 3, tie between Allen Coage, Plainfield, N.J., and Sumio Endo, Japan

MODERN PENTATHLON

Team—1, Britain; 2, Czechoslovakia; 3, Hungary
Individual—1, Janucz Pyciak-Peciak, Poland; 2, Pvael Lednev, U.S.S.R.; 3, Jan Bartu, Czechoslovakia

ROWING

MEN

Single Sculls—1, Pertti Karppinen, Finland; 2, Peter Kolbe, West Germany; 3, Joachim Driefke, East Germany
Double Sculls—1, Norway (Frank and Alf Hansen); Britain; 3, East Germany
Pairs with coxswains—1, East Germany. (Harald Jahrling, Friedrich Ulrich, Georg Spohr); 2, U.S.S.R.; 3, Czechoslovakia
Pairs—1, East Germany (Jorg and Bernd Landvoigt); 2, United States (Calvin Coffey, Jewett City, Conn.-Michael Staines, Philadelphia); 3, West Germany
Fours with coxswains—1, U.S.S.R.; 2, East Germany; 3, West Germany
Fours—1, East Germany; 2, Norway; 3, U.S.S.R.
Quadruple Sculls—1, East Germany; 2, U.S.S.R.; 3, Czechoslovakia
Eights—1, East Germany; 2, Britain; 3, Finland

WOMEN

Single Sculls—1, Christine Scheiblich, East Germany; 2, Joan Lind, Long Beach, Calif.; 3, Elena Antonova, U.S.S.R.

(Olympics, Continued)

Double Sculls—1, Bulgaria; 2, East Germany; 3, U.S.S.R.
Quadruple Sculls—1, East Germany; 2, U.S.S.R.; 3, Romania
Pairs—1, Bulgaria; 2, East Germany; 3, U.S.S.R.
Fours with coxswains—1, East Germany; 2, Bulgaria, 3, U.S.S.R.
Eights—1, East Germany; 2, U.S.S.R.; 3, United States (Carol Brown, Lake Forest, Ill.; Anita DeFrantz, Indianapolis; Carie Graves, Spring Green, Wis.; Peggy Ann McCarthy, Madison, Wis.; Jacqueline Zoch, Madison, Wis.; Gail Ricketson, Plattsburgh, N.Y.; Anne Warner, Lexington, Mass.; Marion Grieg, Red Hook, N.Y.; Lynn Silliman, San Diego)

SHOOTING

Pistol, Free—1, Uwe Potteck, East Germany (573 points; world record); 2, Harald Vollmar, East Germany; 3, Rudolf Dollinger, Austria
Pistol, Rapid Fire—1, Norbert Klaar, East Germany; 2, Jurgen Wiefel, East Germany; 3, Roberto Ferraris, Italy
Small-bore Rifle, Prone—1, Karlheinz Smieszek, West Germany; 2, Ulrich Lind, West Germany; 3, Gennady Lushchikov, U.S.S.R.
Small-bore Rifle, 3 Positions—1, Lanny Bassham, Bedford, Tex.; 2, Margaret Murdock, Topeka, Kan.; 3, Werner Seibald, West Germany
Rifle, Running Game Target—1, Alexandr Gazov, U.S.S.R. (579 points, world record); U.S.S.R.; 3, Jerzy Grezkiewicz, Poland
Shotgun, Trap—1, Don Haldeman, Souderton, Pa.; 2, Armando Silva Marques, Portugal; 3, Ubaldeso Baldi, Italy
Shotgun, Skeet—1, Josef Panacek, Czechoslovakia; 2, Eric Swinkels, Netherlands; 3, Wiesla Gawlikowski, Poland

VOLLEYBALL

Women—1, Japan; 2, U.S.S.R.; 3, South Korea
Men—1, Poland; 2, U.S.S.R.; 3, Cuba

WEIGHT LIFTING

Featherweight—1, Nikolai Kolesnikov, U.S.S.R.; 2, Georgi Todorov, Bulgaria; 3, Kazumasa Hirai, Japan
Flyweight—1, Alexander Voronin, U.S.S.R.; 2, Gyorgy Kozegi, Hungary; 3, Mohammad Nassiri, Iran
Bantamweight—1, Norair Nurikian, Bulgaria; 2, Grzegorz Cziura, Poland; 3, Kenkichi Ando, Japan
Lightweight—1, †Zbigniew Kaezmarek, Poland; 2, Pytor Karol, U.S.S.R.; 3, Daniel Senet, France
Middleweight—1, Yordan Mitkov, Bulgaria; 2, Vartan Militosian, U.S.S.R.; 3, Peter Wenzel, East Germany
Light Heavyweight—1, Valery Shary, U.S.S.R.; 2, †Blagoi Blagoev, Bulgaria; 3, Trendafil Stoichev, Bulgaria
Middle Heavyweight—1, David Rigert, U.S.S.R.; 2, Lee James, Manchester, Pa.; 3, Atanas Chopov, Bulgaria
Heavyweight—1, †Valentin Khristov, Bulgaria; 2, Yuri Zaitsev, U.S.S.R.; 3, Krastio Scmerdjiev, Bulgaria
Super Heavyweight—1, Vasily Alexeyev, U.S.S.R.; 2, Gerd Bonk, East Germany; 3, Helmut Losch, East Germany

† Disqualified by I.O.C. in October for use of banned steroids and medals withdrawn; no change in placings.

WRESTLING, FREESTYLE

Paperweight (105.6 lbs)—1, Khassan Issaev, Bulgaria; 2, Roman Dmitriev, U.S.S.R.; 3, Akira Kudo, Japan
Flyweight (114.4 lbs)—1, Yuji Takata, Japan; 2, Alexandr Ivanov, U.S.S.R.; 3, Hae-Sup Jeon, South Korea
Bantamweight (125.4 lbs)—1, Vladimir Umin, U.S.S.R.; 2, Hans–Bieter Bruchert, East Germany; 3, Masao Ari, Japan
Featherweight (136 lbs)—1, Jung–Mo Jang, South Korea; 2, Oidov Zeveg, Mongolia; 3, Gene Davis, Lakewood, Calif.
Lightweight (149.6 lbs)—1, Pavel Pinigin, U.S.S.R.; 2, Lloyd Keaser, Baltimore; 3, Yasaburo Sugawara, Japan
Welterweight (162.8 lbs)—1, Date Jiichiro, Japan; 2, Mansour Barzegar, Iran; 3, Stan Dziedzik, Allentown, Pa.
Middleweight (180.4 lbs)—1, John Peterson, Comstock, Wis; 2, Viktor Novojilov, U.S.S.R.; 3, Adolf Seger, West Germany
Light Heavyweight (198 lbs)—1, Levan Tediashvili, U.S.S.R.; 2, Ben Peterson, Comstock, Wis; 3, Syelica Morcov, Romania

DISTRIBUTION OF MEDALS
SUMMER GAMES

	Gold	Silver	Bronze	Total
Soviet Union	47	43	35	125
East Germany	40	25	25	90
United States	34	35	25	94
West Germany	10	12	17	39
Japan	9	6	10	25
Poland	8	6	11	25
Bulgaria	7	8	9	24
Cuba	6	4	3	13
Romania	4	9	14	27
Hungary	4	5	12	21
Finland	4	2	0	6
Sweden	4	1	0	5
Britain	3	5	5	13
Italy	2	7	4	13
France	2	2	5	9
Yugoslavia	2	3	3	8
Czechoslovakia	2	2	4	8
New Zealand	2	1	1	4
South Korea	1	1	4	6
Switzerland	1	1	2	4
Jamaica	1	1	0	2
North Korea	1	1	0	2
Norway	1	1	0	2
Denmark	1	0	2	3
Mexico	1	0	1	2
Trinidad	1	0	0	1
Canada	0	5	6	11
Belgium	0	3	3	6
Netherlands	0	2	3	5
Portugal	0	2	0	2
Spain	0	2	0	2
Australia	0	1	4	5
Iran	0	1	1	2
Mongolia	0	1	0	1
Venezuela	0	1	0	1
Brazil	0	0	2	2
Austria	0	0	1	1
Bermuda	0	0	1	1
Pakistan	0	0	1	1
Puerto Rico	0	0	1	1
Thailand	0	0	1	1

(all weight-lifting medals included)

Heavyweight (220 lbs)—1, Ivan Yarygin, U.S.S.R.; 2, Russ Hellickson, Oregon, Wis.; 3, Dimo Kostov, Bulgaria
Unlimited—1, Soslan Andiev, U.S.S.R.; 2, Jozsef Balla, Hungary; 3, Ladislav Simon, Romania

WRESTLING, GRECO-ROMAN

Paperweight—1, Alexei Schumakov, U.S.S.R.; 2, Gheorghe Bereanu, Romania; 3, Stefan Anghelov, Bulgaria
Flyweight—1, Vitaly Konstantinov, U.S.S.R; 2, Nicu Ginga, Romania; 3, Kiochiro Hirayama, Japan
Bantamweight—1, Pertti Ukkola, Finland; 2, Ivan Frgic, Yugoslavia; 3, Farhat Mustfin, U.S.S.R.
Featherweight—1, Kazimier Lipien, Poland; 2, Nelson Davidian, U.S.S.R.; 3, Laszlo Reczi, Hungary
Lightweight—1, Suren Nalbandy, U.S.S.R.; 2, Stefan Rusu, Romania; 3, Heinz–Helmut Wehling, East Germany
Welterweight—1, Anatoly Bykov, U.S.S.R.; 2, Vitezslav Macha, Czechoslovakia; 3, Karlheinz Helbing, West Germany
Middleweight—1, Momir Petkovic, Yugoslavia; 2, Vladimir Ceboksarov, U.S.S.R.; 3, Ivan Kolev, Bulgaria
Light heavyweight—1, Valery Kezantsev, U.S.S.R.; 2, Stoyan Ivanov, Bulgaria; 3, Czeslaw Kweicinski, Poland
Heavyweight—1, Nikolai Bolboshin, U.S.S.R.; 2, Kamen Goranov, Bulgaria; 3, Andrzej Skrzylewski, Poland
Super Heavyweight—1, Alexandr Kolchinski, U.S.S.R.; 2, Alexandr Tomov, Bulgaria; 3, Roman Codreanu, Romania

(1976 Olympic Games Results, Continued)

SWIMMING

100-Meter Freestyle
1—Jim Montgomery, Madison, Wis.   0:49.99 W
2—Jack Babashoff, Fountain Valley, Calif.   0:50.81
3—Peter Nocke, West Germany   0:51.31

200-Meter Freestyle
1—Bruce Furniss, Long Beach, Calif.   1:50.29 W
2—John Naber, Menlo Park, Calif.   1:50.50
3—Jim Montgomery, Madison, Wis.   1:50.58

400-Meter Freestyle
1—Brian Goodell, Mission Viejo, Calif.   3:51.93 W
2—Tim Shaw, Long Beach, Calif.   3:52.54
3—Vladimir Raskatov, U.S.S.R.   3:55.76

1,500-Meter Freestyle
1—Brian Goodell, Mission Viejo, Calif.   15:02.40 W
2—Bobby Hackett, Yonkers, N.Y.   15:03.91
3—Stephen Holland, Australia   15:04.66

100-Meter Backstroke
1—John Naber, Menlo Park, Calif.   0:55.49 W
2—Peter Rocca, Orinda, Calif.   0:56.34
3—Roland Matthes, East Germany   0:57.22

200-Meter Backstroke
1—John Naber, Menlo Park, Calif.   1:59.19 W
2—Peter Rocca, Orinda, Calif.   2:00.55
3—Dan Harrigan, Mishawaka, Ind.   2:01.35

100-Meter Breaststroke
1—John Hencken, Santa Barbara, Calif.   1:03.11 W
2—David Wilkie, Britain   1:03.43
3—Arvidas Ivozaytis, U.S.S.R.   1:04.23

200-Meter Breaststroke
1—David Wilkie, Britain   2:15.11 W
2—John Hencken, Santa Barbara, Calif.   2:17.26
3—Rick Colella, Seattle, Wash.   2:19.20

100-Meter Butterfly
1—Matt Vogel, Fort Wayne, Ind.   0:54.35
2—Joe Bottom, Santa Clara, Calif.   0:54.50
3—Gary Hall, Cincinnati   0:54.65

200-Meter Butterfly
1—Mike Bruner, Stockton, Calif.   1:59.23 W
2—Steven Gregg, Wilmington, Del.   1:59.54
3—Bill Forrester, Birmingham, Ala.   1:59.96

400-Meter Individual Medley
1—Rod Strachan, Santa Ana, Calif.   4:23.68 W
2—Tim McKee, Newton Square, Pa.   4:24.62
3—Andrei Smirnov, U.S.S.R.   4:26.90

400-Meter Medley Relay
1—United States   3:42.22 W
   (John Naber, John Hencken, Matt Vogel, Jim Montgomery)
2—Canada   3:45.94
3—West Germany   3:47.29

800-Meter Freestyle Relay
1—United States   7:23.22 W
   (Mike Bruner, Bruce Furniss, John Naber, Jim Montgomery)
2—U.S.S.R.   7:27.97
3—Britain   7:32.11

WOMEN
100-Meter Freestyle
1—Kornelia Ender, East Germany   0:55.65 W
2—Petra Priemer, East Germany   0:56.49
3—Enith Brigitha, Netherlands   0:56.65

200-Meter Freestyle
1—Kornelia Ender, East Germany   1:59.26 W
2—Shirley Babashoff, Fountain Valley, Calif.   2:01.22
3—Enith Brigitha, Netherlands   2:01.40

400-Meter Freestyle
1—Petra Thumer, East Germany   4:09.89 W
2—Shirley Babashoff, Fountain Valley, Calif.   4:10.46
3—Shannon Smith, Canada   4:14.60

800-Meter Freestyle
1—Petra Thumer, East Germany   8:37.14 W
2—Shirley Babashoff, Fountain Valley, Calif.   8:37.59
3—Wendy Weinberg, Baltimore   8:42.60

100-Meter Backstroke
1—Ulrike Richter, East Germany   1:01.83*
2—Birgit Treiber, East Germany   1:03.41
3—Nancy Garapick, Canada   1:03.71

200-Meter Backstroke
1—Ulrike Richter, East Germany   2:13.43*
2—Birgit Treiber, East Germany   2:14.97
3—Nancy Garapick, Canada   2:15.60

100-Meter Breaststroke
1—Hannelore Anke, East Germany   1:11.16
2—Liubov Rusanova, U.S.S.R.   1:13.04
3—Marina Koshevaia, U.S.S.R.   1:13.30

200-Meter Breaststroke
1—Marina Koshevaia, U.S.S.R.   2:33.35 W
2—Marina Iurchenia, U.S.S.R.   2:36.08
3—Liubov Rusanova, U.S.S.R.   2:36.22

100-Meter Butterfly
1—Kornelia Ender, East Germany   1:00.13 W
2—Andrea Pollack, East Germany   1:00.98
3—Wendy Boglioli, Ocean City, N.J.   1:01.17

200-Meter Butterfly
1—Andrea Pollack, East Germany   2:11.41*
2—Ulrike Tauber, East Germany   2:12.50
3—Rosemarie Gabriel, East Germany   2:12.86

400-Meter Individual Medley
1—Ulrike Tauber, East Germany   4:42.77 W
2—Cheryl Gibson, Canada   4:48.10
3—Becky Smith, Canada   4:50.48

400-Meter Medley Relay
1—East Germany   4:07.95 W
   (Ulrike Richter, Hannelore Anke, Andrea Pollack, Kornelia Ender)
2—United States   4:14.55
   (Linda Jezek, Los Altos, Calif.; Lauri Siering, Modesto, Calif.; Camille Wright, New Albany, Ind.; Shirley Babashoff, Fountain Valley, Calif.)
3—Canada   4:15.22

400-Meter Freestyle Relay
1—United States   3:44.82 W
   (Kim Peyton, Portland, Ore.; Wendy Boglioli, Ocean City, N.J.; Jill Sterkel, Hacienda Heights, Calif.; Shirley Babashoff, Fountain Valley, Calif.)
2—East Germany   3:54.50
3—Canada   3:48.81
W—World record; *—Olympic Record.

WATER POLO
Team—1, Hungary; 2, Italy; 3, Netherlands

(1976 Olympic Games Results, Continued)

DIVING

WOMEN

Springboard—1, Jennifer Chandler, Lincoln, Ala.; 2, Christa Kohler, East Germany; 3, Cynthia McIngvale, Dallas
Platform—1, Elena Daytsekhovskaia, U.S.S.R.; 2, Ulrika Knape, Sweden; 3, Deborah Wilson, Columbus, Ohio

MEN

Springboard—1, Phil Boggs, Akron, Ohio; 2, Franco Cagnotto, Italy; 3, Aleksandr Kosenkov, U.S.S.R.
Platform—1, Klaus Dibiasi, Italy; 2, Greg Louganis, El Cajon, Calif.; 3, Vladimir Aleynik, U.S.S.R.

YACHTING

Finn—1, Jocken Schumann, East Germany; 2, Andrei Balashov, U.S.S.R.; 3, John Bertrand, Australia
Flying Dutchman—1, West Germany; 2, Britain; 3, Brazil
470 Class—1, West Germany; 2, Spain; 3, Australia
Soling—1, Denmark; 2, United States (John Kolius, LaPorte, Tex.; Walter Glasgow, Houston, Tex.; Richard Hoepfner, Houston); 3, East Germany
Tempest—1, Sweden; 2, U.S.S.R.; 3, United States (Dennis Conner, San Diego; Conn Findlay, Belmont, Calif.)
Tornado—1, Britain; 2, United States (David McFaull, Honolulu; Michael Rothwell, Honolulu); 3, West Germany

OLYMPIC WINTER GAMES

(Innsbruck, Austria, February 4–15)

BIATHLON

(20 Kilometers)
Individual

1—Nikolai Kruglov, U.S.S.R.	1:14:12.26
2—Heikki Ikola, Finland	1:15:54.10
3—Aleksandr Elizarov, U.S.S.R.	1:16:05.57

Relay

1—U.S.S.R.	1:57:55.64
2—Finland	2:01:45.58
3—East Germany	2:04:08.61

BOBSLEDDING

2-Man

1—East Germany (Meinhard Nehmer–Bernard Germeshausen)	3:44.42
2—West Germany (Wolfgang Zimmerer–Manfred Schumann)	3:44.99
3—Switzerland (Erich Schaerer–Josef Benz)	3:45.70

4-Man

1—East Germany (Meinhard Nehmer, driver)	3:40.43
2—Switzerland	3:40.89
3—West Germany	3:41.37

ICE SKATING, FIGURE

Singles, Men—1. John Curry, Britain; 2. Vladimir Kovalev, U.S.S.R.; 3. Toller Cranston, Canada
Singles, Women—1. Dorothy Hamill, Riverside, Conn.; 2. Dianne de Leeuw, Netherlands; 3. Christine Errath, East Germany
Pairs—1. Irina Rodnina-Aleksandr Zaitsev, U.S.S.R.; 2. Romy Kermer-Rolf Oesterreich, East Germany; 3. Manuela Gross-Uwe Kagelmann, East Germany.
Ice Dancing—1. Ludmila Pakhomova-Alexsandr Gorschkov, U.S.S.R.; 2. Irina Moiseeva-Andrei Minenkov, U.S.S.R.; 3. Colleen O'Connor-John Millns, Colorado Springs.

ICE SKATING, SPEED

MEN

500 Meters

1—Evgeni Kulikov, U.S.S.R.	39.17
2—Valery Muratov, U.S.S.R.	39.25
3—Dan Immerfall, Madison, Wis.	39.54

1,000 Meters

1—Peter Mueller, Mequon, Wis.	1:19.32
2—Jorn Didriksen, Norway	1:20.45
3—Valery Muratov, U.S.S.R.	1:20.57

1,500 Meters

1—Jan Egil Storhold, Norway	1:59.38
2—Yuri Kondakov, U.S.S.R.	1:59.97
3—Hans Van Helden, Netherlands	2:00.87

DISTRIBUTION OF MEDALS
WINTER GAMES

	Gold	Silver	Bronze	Total
U.S.S.R.	13	6	8	27
East Germany	7	5	7	19
United States	3	3	4	10
Norway	3	3	1	7
West Germany	2	5	3	10
Finland	2	4	1	7
Austria	2	2	2	6
Switzerland	1	3	1	5
Netherlands	1	2	3	6
Italy	1	2	1	4
Canada	1	1	1	3
Britain	1	0	0	0
Czechoslovakia	0	1	0	1
Liechtenstein	0	0	2	2
Sweden	0	0	2	2
France	0	1	1	1

Total countries competing: 26.
Total athletes: 1,036 (788 men, 248 women).

5,000 Meters

1—Sten Stensen, Norway	7:24.48
2—Piet Kleine, Netherlands	7:26.47
3—Hans Van Helden, Netherlands	7:26.54

10,000 Meters

1—Piet Kleine, Netherlands	14:50.59
2—Sten Stensen, Norway	14:53.30
3—Hans Van Helden, Netherlands	15:02.02

WOMEN
500 Meters

1—Sheila Young, Detroit	42.76
2—Cathy Priestner, Canada	43.12
3—Tatiana Averina, U.S.S.R.	43.17

1,000 Meters

1—Tatiana Averina, U.S.S.R.	1:28.43
2—Leah Poulos, Northbrook, Ill.	1:28.57
3—Sheila Young, Detroit	1:29.14

1,500 Meters

1—Galina Stepanskaya, U.S.S.R.	2:16.58
2—Sheila Young, Detroit	2:17.06
3—Tatiana Averina, U.S.S.R.	2:17.97

3,000 Meters

1—Tatiana Averina, U.S.S.R.	4:45.19
2—Andrea Mitscherlick, East Germany	4:45.23
3—Lisbeth Korsmo, Norway	4:45.24

(1976 Olympic Games Results, Continued)

ICE HOCKEY

	W	L	T	Pts		W	L	T	Pts
U.S.S.R.	5	0	0	10	Finland	2	3	0	4
*Czechoslovakia	3	2	0	6	United States	2	3	0	4
West Germany	2	3	0	4	*Poland	0	5	0	0

* Czechoslovakia forfeited game to Poland on drug charge. Poland not credited with victory. Czechoslovakia had won, 7-1.

LUGE
Men's Singles
1—Detlef Guenther, East Germany	3:27.688
2—Josef Fendt, West Germany	3:28.196
3—Hans Rinn, East Germany	3:28.574

Men's Doubles
1—Hans Rinn–Norbert Hahn, E. Germany	1:25.604
2—Hans Bradner–Balthasar Schwarm, W. Germany	1:25.889
3—Rudolf Schmid–Franz Schachner, Austria	1:25.919

Women's Singles
1—Margit Schumann, East Germany	2:50.621
2—Ute Ruehrold, East Germany	2:50.846
3—Elisabeth Demleitner, West Germany	2:51.056

SKIING
MEN
Downhill
1—Franz Klammer, Austria	1:45.73
2—Bernhard Russi, Switzerland	1:46.06
3—Herbert Plank, Italy	1:46.59

Slalom
1—Piero Gros, Italy	2:03.29
2—Gustavo Thoeni, Italy	2:03.73
3—Willy Frommelt, Liechtenstein	2:04.28

Giant Slalom
1—Heini Hemmi, Switzerland	3:26.97
2—Ernst Good, Switzerland	3:27.17
3—Ingemar Stenmark, Sweden	3:27.41

WOMEN
Downhill
1—Rosi Mittermaier, West Germany	1:46.16
2—Brigitte Totschnig, Austria	1:46.68
3—Cindy Nelson, Lutsen, Minn.	1:47.50

Slalom
1—Rosi Mittermaier, West Germany	1:30.54
2—Claudia Giordani, Italy	1:30.87
3—Hanni Wenzel, Liechtenstein	1:32.20

Giant Slalom
1—Kathy Kreiner, Canada	1:29.13
2—Rosi Mittermaier, West Germany	1:29.25
3—Daniele Debernard, France	1:29.95

SKIING, NORDIC
JUMPING
70 Meters
1—Hans-Georg Aschenbach, East Germany	252
(Jumps were 276 and 269 feet)	
2—Jochen Danneberg, East Germany	246.2
3—Karl Schnabl, Austria	242

90 Meters
1—Karl Schnabl, Austria	234.8
(Jumps were 320 and 318 feet)	
2—Toni Innauer, Austria	232.9
3—Henry Glass, East Germany	221.7

COMBINED
(70-meter jump and 15-kilometer cross-country)
1—Ulrich Wehling, East Germany	423.39
(first in jumping, 13th in cross-country)	
2—Urban Hettich, West Germany	418.90
(first in cross-country, 11th in jumping)	
3—Konrad Winkler, East Germany	417.47
(fourth in jumping, seventh in cross-country)	

MEN'S CROSS-COUNTRY
15-Kilometers
1—Nikola Bajukov, U.S.S.R.	43:58.47
2—Evgeny Beliaev, U.S.S.R.	44:01.10
3—Arto Koivisto, Finland	44:19.25

30 Kilometers
1—Sergei Saveliev, U.S.S.R.	1:30:29.38
2—Bill Koch, Guilford, Vt.	1:30:57.84
3—Ivan Garanin, U.S.S.R.	1:31:09.29

50 Kilometers
1—Ivar Formo, Norway	2:37:30.5
2—Gert-Dieter Klause, East Germany	2:38:13.21
3—Ben Soedergren, Sweden	2:39:29.21

40-kilometer Relay
1—Finland	2:07:59.72
2—Norway	2:09:58.36
3—U.S.S.R.	2:10:51.46

WOMEN'S CROSS-COUNTRY
5 Kilometers
1—Helena Takalo, Finland	15:48.69
2—Raisa Smetanina, U.S.S.R.	15:49.73
3—Nina Baldicheva, U.S.S.R.	16:12.82

10 Kilometers
1—Raisa Smetanina, U.S.S.R.	30:13.41
2—Helena Takalo, Finland	30:14.28
3—Galina Kulakova, U.S.S.R.	30:38.61

20-kilometer Relay
1—U.S.S.R.	1:07:49.75
2—Finland	1:08:36.57
3—East Germany	1:09:57.95

SQUASH RACQUETS

U.S. Squash Racquets Assn. Champions

Singles—Peter Briggs, New York
Veterans Singles (40-49 years)—Richard Radloff, Seattle
Senior Singles (50 and over)—Bob Stuckert, Milwaukee
Team—Mexico (defeated Ontario, 3-2, in final)
Doubles—Ralph Howe-Peter Briggs, New York
Veterans Doubles—Charles Wright, Toronto-Don Leggat, Hamilton, Ont.
Senior Doubles—Gordon Guyett-Eric Wiffen, Toronto

Intercollegiate Champions
Singles—Phil Mohtadi, Western Ontario

Team—Princeton (29 pts)

Other Championships
North American Open—Sharif Khan, Toronto
Lapham Cup (singles)—United States 11, Canada 4
Grant Trophy (doubles)—Canada 4, United States 3

Women
Singles—Mrs. Gretchen Spruance, Wilmington, Del.
Collegiate—Nancy Gengler, Princeton

HOCKEY
National Hockey League
Source: John Halligan, Publicity Director, New York Rangers
FINAL STANDING OF THE CLUBS

CLARENCE CAMPBELL CONFERENCE
Lester Patrick Division

	W	L	T	GF	GA	Pts
Philadelphia Flyers	51	13	16	348	209	118
New York Islanders	42	21	17	297	190	101
Atlanta Flames	35	33	12	262	237	82
New York Rangers	29	42	9	262	333	67

Connie Smythe Division

	W	L	T	GF	GA	Pts
Chicago Black Hawks	32	30	18	254	261	82
Vancouver Canucks	33	32	15	271	272	81
St. Louis Blues	29	37	14	249	290	72
Minnesota North Stars	20	53	7	195	303	47
Kansas City Scouts	12	56	12	190	351	36

PRINCE OF WALES CONFERENCE
James Norris Division

	W	L	T	GF	GA	Pts
Montreal Canadiens	58	11	11	337	174	127
Los Angeles Kings	38	33	9	263	265	85
Pittsburgh Penguins	35	33	12	339	305	82
Detroit Red Wings	26	44	10	226	300	62
Washington Capitals	11	59	10	224	394	32

Charles F. Adams Division

	W	L	T	GF	GA	Pts
Boston Bruins	48	15	17	313	237	113
Buffalo Sabres	46	21	13	339	240	105
Toronto Maple Leafs	34	31	15	294	276	83
California Golden Seals	27	42	11	250	279	65

Stanley Cup Playoffs
First Round

Buffalo defeated St. Louis, 2 games to 1
New York Islanders defeated Vancouver, 2 games to 0
Los Angeles defeated Atlanta, 2 games to 0
Toronto defeated Pittsburgh, 2 games to 1

Quarterfinals

Montreal defeated Chicago, 4 games to 0
Philadelphia defeated Toronto, 4 games to 3
Boston defeated Los Angeles, 4 games to 3
New York Islanders defeated Buffalo, 4 games to 2

Semifinals

Montreal defeated New York Islanders, 4 games to 1
  April 27—Montreal 3, Islanders 2
  April 29—Montreal 4, Islanders 3
  *May 1—Montreal 3, Islanders 2
  *May 4—Islanders 5, Montreal 2
  May 6—Montreal 5, Islanders 2

  * At Uniondale, N.Y.

Philadelphia defeated Boston, 4 games to 1
  April 27—Boston 4, Philadelphia 2
  April 29—Philadelphia 2, Boston 1 (overtime)
  *May 2—Philadelphia 5, Boston 2
  *May 4—Philadelphia 4, Boston 2
  May 6—Philadelphia 6, Boston 3

  * At Boston.

Championship

Montreal defeated Philadelphia, 4 games to 0
  May 9—Montreal 4, Philadelphia 3
  May 11—Montreal 2, Philadelphia 1
  *May 13—Montreal 3, Philadelphia 2
  *May 16—Montreal 5, Philadelphia 3
  * At Philadelphia.

N.H.L. ALL-STAR TEAMS

First Team	Pos.	Second Team
Ken Dryden, Montreal	Goal	Glenn Resch, N.Y. Islanders
Denis Potvin, N.Y. Islanders	Defense	Guy Lapointe, Montreal
Brad Park, Boston	Defense	Borje Salming, Toronto
Bobby Clarke, Philadelphia	Center	Gil Perreault, Buffalo
Guy Lafleur, Montreal	Right Wing	Reggie Leach, Philadelphia
Bill Barber, Philadelphia	Left Wing	Richard Martin, Buffalo

N.H.L. Leading Scorers

	GP	G	A	Pts
Guy Lafleur, Montreal	80	56	69	125
Bobby Clarke, Philadelphia	76	30	89	119
Gil Perreault, Buffalo	80	44	69	113
Bill Barber, Philadelphia	80	50	62	112
Pierre Larouche, Pittsburgh	76	53	58	111
Jean Ratelle, Boston	80	36	69	105
Pete Mahovlich, Montreal	80	34	71	105
Jean Pronovost, Pittsburgh	80	52	52	104
Darryl Sittler, Toronto	79	41	59	100
Syl Apps, Pittsburgh	80	32	67	99
Denis Potvin, Islanders	78	31	67	98
Bryan Trottier, Islanders	80	32	63	95
Marcel Dionne, Los Angeles	80	40	54	94
Lanny McDonald, Toronto	75	37	56	93
Reggie Leach, Philadelphia	80	61	30	91
Rene Robert, Buffalo	72	35	52	87
Rick Martin, Buffalo	80	49	37	86
Rod Gilbert, Rangers	70	36	50	86
Chuck Lefley, St. Louis	75	43	42	85

N.H.L. Leading Goaltenders

	GP	Mins	GA	Avg.
Ken Dryden, Montreal	62	3,580	121	2.03
Glenn Resch, Islanders	44	2,546	88	2.07
Wayne Stephenson, Philadelphia	66	3,819	164	2.58
Billy Smith, Islanders	39	2,254	98	2.61
Dan Bouchard, Atlanta	47	2,671	113	2.54
Gilles Gilbert, Boston	55	3,123	151	2.90
Gerry Desjardins, Buffalo	55	3,280	161	2.95
Tony Esposito, Chicago	68	4,003	198	2.97

TOP TEAM RECORDS
Montreal

	GP	Mins	GA	Avg.
Ken Dryden	62	3,580	121	2.03
Michel Larocque	22	1,220	50	2.56
Team	80	4,800	174	2.18

Islanders

	GP	Mins	GA	Avg.
Glenn Resch	44	2,546	88	2.07
Billy Smith	39	2,254	98	2.61
Team	80	4,800	190	2.39

N.H.L. TROPHY WINNERS

Hart (most valuable)—Bobby Clarke, Philadelphia
Ross (leading scorer)—Guy Lafleur, Montreal
Norris (defenseman)—Denis Potvin, N.Y. Islanders
Lady Byng (sportsmanship)—Jean Ratelle, Boston
Calder (rookie)—Bryan Trottier, N.Y. Islanders
Vezina (goalie)—Ken Dryden, Montreal
Conn Smythe (most valuable in playoffs)—Reggie Leach, Philadelphia
Masterson (courage)—Rod Gilbert, N.Y. Rangers

World Hockey Association

FINAL STANDING OF THE CLUBS

Canadian Division

	W	L	T	GF	GA	Pts
Winnipeg Jets	52	27	2	345	254	106
Quebec Nordiques	50	27	4	371	316	104
Calgary Cowboys	41	35	4	307	282	86
Edmonton Oilers	27	49	5	268	345	59
Toronto Toros	24	52	5	335	398	53
*Ottawa Civics	14	26	1	134	172	29

*Took over Denver franchise Jan. 2; disbanded Jan 17.

East Division

Indianapolis Pacers	35	39	6	245	247	76
Cleveland Crusaders	35	40	5	273	279	75
New England Whalers	33	40	7	255	290	73
Cincinnati Stingers	35	44	1	285	340	71

West Division

Houston Aeros	53	27	0	1341	263	106
Phoenix Roadrunners	39	35	6	302	287	84
San Diego Mariners	36	*38	6	303	290	78
**Minnesota Fighting Saints	30	25	4	211	212	64
†Denver Spurs	13	20	1	110	142	27

**Disbanded Feb. 28. †Franchise moved to Ottawa Jan. 2.

W.H.A. Leading Scorers

	GP	G	A	Pts
Marc Tardif, Quebec	81	71	77	148
Bobby Hull, Winnipeg	80	53	70	123
Real Cloutier, Quebec	80	60	54	114
Ulf Nilsson, Winnipeg	79	38	76	114
Robbie Ftorek, Phoenix	80	41	72	113
Chris Bordeleau, Quebec	74	37	72	109
Anders Hedberg, Winnipeg	76	50	55	105
Rejean Houle, Quebec	81	51	52	103
Serge Bernier, Quebec	70	34	68	102
Gordie Howe, Houston	78	32	70	102
Andre Lacroix, San Diego	80	29	72	101
Vaclav Nedomansky, Toronto	81	56	42	98
Danny Lawson, Calgary	80	44	52	96
Mark Napier, Toronto	78	43	50	93
Del Hall, Phoenix	80	47	44	91
Ray Adduono, San Diego	80	23	67	90

W.H.A. Leading Goaltenders

	GP	Mins	GA	Avg
Michel Dion, Indianapolis	31	1,860	85	2.74
Joe Daley, Winnipeg	61	3,552	168	2.84
Jack Norris, Phoenix	41	2,412	128	3.18
Ron Grahame, Houston	56	3,283	177	3.23
Ernie Wakely, San Diego	66	3,756	206	3.29
John Garrett, Toronto	61	3,730	210	3.38
Christer Abrahamsson, New England	41	2,385	136	3.42
Don McLeod, Calgary	61	3,464	199	3.45
Bruce Landon, New England	38	2,181	126	3.47
Bob Johnson, Cleveland	42	2,388	144	3.62

W.H.A. ALL-STAR TEAMS

First Team	Pos.	Second Team
Joe Daley, Winnipeg	Goal	Ron Grahame, Houston
J.C. Tremblay, Quebec	Defense	Kevin Morrison, San Diego
Paul Shmayr, Cleveland	Defense	Pat Stapleton, Indianapolis
Ulf Nilsson, Winnipeg	Center	Robbie Ftorek, Phoenix
Anders Hedberg, Winnipeg	Right Wing	Real Cloutier, Quebec
Marc Tardif, Quebec	Left Wing	Bobby Hull, Winnipeg

Avco World Trophy Playoffs

Canadian Division

Winnipeg defeated Edmonton, 4 games to 0
Calgary defeated Quebec, 4 games to 1

East Division

New England defeated Cleveland, 3 games to 0
New England defeated Indianapolis, 4 games to 3

West Division

San Diego defeated Phoenix, 3 games to 1
Houston defeated San Diego, 4 games to 2

Semifinals

Winnipeg defeated Calgary, 4 games to 1
*April 23—Winnipeg 6, Calgary 1
*April 25—Winnipeg 3, Calgary 2
April 28—Winnipeg 6, Calgary 3
April 30—Calgary 7, Winnipeg 3
*May 2—Winnipeg 4, Calgary 0

*At Winnipeg.

Houston defeated New England, 4 games to 3
May 5—New England 4, Houston 2
May 7—Houston 5, New England 2
*May 9—New England 4, Houston 1
*May 11—Houston 4, New England 3
May 13—Houston 4, New England 2
*May 15—New England 6, Houston 1
May 16—Houston 2, New England 0

*At Hartford, Conn.

Championship

Winnipeg defeated Houston, 4 games to 0
*May 20—Winnipeg 4, Houston 3
*May 23—Winnipeg 5, Houston 4
May 25—Winnipeg 6, Houston 3
May 27—Winnipeg 9, Houston 1

*At Houston.

W.H.A. AWARDS

Most valuable player—Marc Tardiff, Quebec
Scoring—Tardif
Rookie of the year—Mark Napier, Toronto
Best defenseman—Paul Shmyr, Cleveland
Goalie—Michel Dion, Indianapolis
Most Gentlemanly—Vaclav Nedomansky, Toronto
Most valuable in playoffs—Ulf Nilsson, Winnipeg, center

Amateur Champions

World—Czechoslovakia
N.C.A.A. (at Denver, March 25-27)—Minnesota (defeated Michigan Tech, 6-4, in final); third place: Brown (defeated Boston University, 8-7); semifinal scores: Minnesota 4, Boston University 2; Michigan Tech 7, Brown 6 (2 overtime periods)
E.C.A.C.—Division I: Regular season: Boston Univ. (24-2); playoffs: Boston Univ. (defeated Brown, 9-2, in final). Division II: Bowdoin (defeated Merrimack, 6-5, in final). Division III; Amherst (defeated Worcester State, 3-2 in overtime, in final). Players of year: Division I: Pete Brown, Boston Univ. defense; Division II: Cam McGregor, Norwich, forward; Division III: Rich Gallogly, Wesleyan, forward
W.C.H.A.—Regular season: Michigan Tech (25-7). Playoffs (for two places in N.C.A.A. semifinals): Michigan Tech (defeated Michigan, 10-7), total score 2 games; Minnesota (defeated Michigan State, 9-8, total for 2 games)
Central Collegiate—Regular season: Bowling Green (11-4). Playoffs; St. Louis University (defeated Western Michigan, 15-4, total in 2 games)
N.A.I.A.—Wisconsin-Superior (defeated St. Scholastica, 8-5 in final)
Canada—University of Toronto (defeated Guelph, 7-2, in final)

Minor League Hockey Champions
AMERICAN LEAGUE
North Division

	W	L	T	GF	GA	Pts
Nova Scotia Voyageurs	48	20	8	326	209	104
Rochester Americans	42	25	9	304	243	93
Providence Reds	34	34	8	294	300	76
Springfield Indians	33	39	4	267	321	70

South Division

	W	L	T	GF	GA	Pts
Hershey Bears	39	31	6	304	275	84
*Richmond Robins	29	39	8	262	297	66
New Haven Nighthawks	29	39	8	261	295	66
Baltimore Clippers	21	48	7	238	316	49

* Richmond awarded second place for playoffs.

CHAMPIONSHIP PLAYOFFS
Quarterfinals
Rochester defeated Providence, 3 games to 0
Richmond defeated New Haven, 3 games to 0

Semifinals
Nova Scotia defeated Rochester, 4 games to 0
Hershey defeated Richmond, 4 games to 1

Final
Nova Scotia defeated Hershey, 4 games to 1

CENTRAL LEAGUE

	W	L	T	GF	GA	Pts
Tulsa Oilers	45	21	10	301	228	100
Dallas Black Hawks	41	24	11	282	211	93
Salt Lake Golden Eagles	37	35	4	300	299	78
Oklahoma City Blazers	32	34	10	256	263	74
Fort Worth Texans	29	31	16	287	271	74
Tucson Mavericks	14	53	9	242	396	37

CHAMPIONSHIP PLAYOFFS
Semifinals
Tulsa defeated Oklahoma City, 4 games to 0
Dallas defeated Fort Worth, 4 games to 1

Final
Tulsa defeated Dallas, 4 games to 1

AMATEUR LEAGUES
International League—Regular season: North Division; Saginaw, South: Dayton. Playoffs: Dayton defeated Port Huron, 4 games to 0

North American League—Regular season: East Division; Beauce, West: Johnstown. Playoffs: Philadelphia defeated Beauce, 4 games to 2

Southern League—Regular season: Charlotte. Playoffs: Charlotte defeated Hampton, 4 games to 1

United States League—Regular season: Northern Division; Green Bay, Southern: Sioux City. Playoffs: Milwaukee defeated Green Bay, 3 games to 0

AMATEUR HOCKEY ASSN. OF THE U.S.
National Champions

Pee Wee—Chicago	Junior B—Springfield, Mass.
Bantam—Ecorse, Mich.	Junior A—Austin, Minn.
Midget—Bloomfield, Mich.	

Canada Captures Canada Cup
Team—Canada defeated Czechoslovakia, 2 games to 0, in the playoffs of the Canada Cup hockey series held Sept. 13-15. Other teams in preliminary six-team round robin at various rinks, starting Sept. 2, were Soviet Union, Sweden, United States and Finland.

GYMNASTICS
National Collegiate A.A.
DIVISION I
(Philadelphia, April 1–3)

All-around—Peter Kormann, So. Connecticut		108.95
Rings—Doug Wood, Iowa State		18.875
Floor exercise—Bob Robbins, Colorado State		18.90
Horizontal bar—Tom Beach, California		19.150
Pommel horse—Ted Marcy, Stanford		19.325
Parallel bars—Gene Whelan, Penn State		18.625
Vault—Sam Shaw, Cal State-Fullerton		18.90
Team—Penn State		432.075

A.A.U. National Championships
(Philadelphia, April 30–May 2)

	Pts
All-around—Coje Saito, Mobile, Ala.	106.45
Horizontal bar—Saito	18.75
Floor exercise—Ron Galimore, Tallahassee, Fla.	18.6
Parallel bars—Saito	18.25
Vault—Mike Carter, Louisiana State	18.525
Pommel horse—Ed Paul, Penn State	18.625
Rings—Tie between Vic Randozzo, New York A.C. and Todd Kuoni, Baton Rouge, La.	18.40

Women

All-around—Roxanne Pierce, Philadelphia	74.60
Balance beam—Roxanne Pierce	18.725
Uneven parallel bars—Ann Carr, Philadelphia	19.05
Vault—Ann Woods, Red Bank, N.J.	19.0
Floor exercise—Janice Baker, Syracuse, N.Y.	18.950

Other National Championships
A.I.A.W.

All-around—Connie Jo Israel, Clarion State	37.05
Team—Clarion State	107.95

U.S. Gymnastics Federation
Women

All-around—Robin Heubner, Dickinson, N.D.	37.95

TRAMPOLINE
(Memphis, Tenn., April 30–May 1)

Men—Stuart Ransom, Memphis, Tenn.
Men's synchronized—Chris Eilertsen-Jim Cartledge, Memphis, Tenn.
Women's synchronized—Leigh Hennessey, Lafayette, La.-Anne Thompson, Memphis, Tenn.
Men's double mini—Ronnie Merriott, Lafayette, La.
Women's double mini—Diane Goldsworthy, Rockford, Ill.

TUMBLING
(Memphis, Tenn., April 30–May 1)

Men—Eddie Goodman, Toledo, Ohio
Women—Nancy Quattrochi, Chicago

WEIGHT LIFTING
National A.A.U. Championships
(Philadelphia, June 18–20)

	Snatch	C&J*	Total
114 lbs—Joel Widdell, Dewar, Iowa	193	231¼	424¼
123 lbs—John Yamauchi, Honolulu	215	264½	479½
132 lbs—Dane Hussey, St. Louis	237	297½	534½
148 lbs—Dan Cantore, Pacifica, Calif.	281	285	628
165 lbs—Fred Lowe, East Lansing, Mich.	297½	374¾	672¼
181 lbs—Sam Bigler, Lancaster, Pa.	398½	396¾	705¼
198 lbs—Lee James, Manchester, Pa.	352½	430	782½
242 lbs—Mark Cameron, Middletown, R.I.	369¼	479½	848¾
Super heavyweight—Bruce Wilhelm, Los Altos, Calif.	374¾	474	848¾

*Clean and jerk.

PROFESSIONAL BASKETBALL
National Basketball Association
FINAL STANDING OF THE CLUBS

EASTERN CONFERENCE
Atlantic Division

	W	L	Pct	Scoring For	Agst
Boston Celtics	54	28	.659	106.2	103.9
Buffalo Braves	46	36	.561	107.3	106.4
Philadelphia 76ers	46	36	.561	106.5	106.3
New York Knicks	38	44	.463	102.7	103.9

Central Division

	W	L	Pct	For	Agst
Cleveland Cavaliers	49	33	.598	101.7	99.2
Washington Bullets	48	34	.585	102.8	100.4
Houston Rockets	40	42	.488	106.2	107.0
New Orleans Jazz	38	44	.463	104.1	105.0
Atlanta Hawks	29	53	.354	102.6	105.5

WESTERN CONFERENCE
Midwest Division

	W	L	Pct	Scoring For	Agst
Milwaukee Bucks	38	44	.463	101.8	103.3
Detroit Pistons	36	46	.439	104.9	106.0
Kansas City Kings	31	51	.378	103.3	106.2
Chicago Bulls	24	58	.293	95.9	98.8

Pacific Division

	W	L	Pct	For	Agst
Golden State Warriors	59	23	.720	109.8	103.1
Seattle SuperSonics	43	39	.524	106.4	106.7
Phoenix Suns	42	40	.512	105.1	104.5
Los Angeles Lakers	40	42	.488	106.9	106.8
Portland Trail Blazers	37	45	.451	104.1	105.3

Playoffs

EASTERN CONFERENCE
Qualifying Round
Buffalo defeated Philadelphia, 2 games to 1

Semifinals
Boston defeated Buffalo, 4 games to 2
Cleveland defeated Washington, 4 games to 3

Conference Final
Boston defeated Cleveland, 4 games to 2
May 6—Boston 111, Cleveland 99
May 9—Boston 94, Cleveland 89
*May 11—Cleveland 83, Boston 78
*May 14—Cleveland 106, Boston 87
May 16—Boston 99, Cleveland 94
*May 18—Boston 94, Cleveland 87

  *At Richfield, Ohio.

WESTERN CONFERENCE
Qualifying Round
Detroit defeated Milwaukee, 2 games to 1
Semifinals
Golden State defeated Detroit, 4 games to 2
Phoenix defeated Seattle, 4 games to 2

Conference Final
Phoenix defeated Golden State, 4 games to 3
*May 2—Golden State 128, Phoenix 103
*May 5—Phoenix 108, Golden State 101
May 7—Golden State 99, Phoenix 91
May 9—Phoenix 133, Golden State 129 (2 overtimes)
*May 12—Golden State 111, Phoenix 95
May 14—Phoenix 105, Golden State 104
*May 16—Phoenix 94, Golden State 86

  *At Oakland, Calif.

LEAGUE CHAMPIONSHIP
Boston defeated Phoenix, 4 games to 2
May 23—Boston 98, Phoenix 87
May 27—Boston 105, Phoenix 90
*May 30—Phoenix 105, Boston 98
*June 2—Phoenix 109, Boston 107
June 4—Boston 128, Phoenix 126 (3 overtimes)
*June 6—Boston 87, Phoenix 80

  *At Phoenix.

Leading Scorers

	G	FG	FT	Pts	Avg
Bob McAdoo, Buffalo	78	934	559	2,427	31.1
Kareem Abdul-Jabbar, Mil.	82	914	447	2,275	27.7
Pete Maravich, New Orleans	62	604	396	1,604	25.9
Nate Archibald, Kansas City	78	717	501	1,935	24.8
Fred Brown, Seattle	76	742	273	1,757	23.1
George McGinnis, Phila.	77	647	475	1,769	23.0
Randy Smith, Buffalo	82	702	383	1,787	21.8
John Drew, Atlanta	77	586	488	1,660	21.6
Bob Dandridge, Milwaukee	73	650	271	1,571	21.5
Rick Barry, Golden State	81	707	287	1,701	21.0
Calvin Murphy, Houston	82	675	372	1,722	21.0
Doug Collins, Philadelphia	77	614	372	1,600	20.8
Earl Monroe, New York	76	647	280	1,574	20.7
Paul Westphal, Phoenix	82	657	365	1,679	20.5
Phil Smith, Golden State	82	659	323	1,641	20.0

All-Star Team

First Team	Pos.	Second Team
Rick Barry, Golden State	F	Elvin Hayes, Washington
George McGinnis, Philadelphia 76ers	F	John Havlicek, Boston
Kareem Abdul-Jabbar, Los Angeles	C	Dave Cowens, Boston
Nate Archibald, Kansas City	G	Phil Smith, Golden State
Pete Maravich, New Orleans	G	Randy Smith, Buffalo

Other Awards
Most valuable player—Kareem Abdul-Jabbar, Los Angeles
Rookie of the Year—Alvan Adams, Phoenix
Most valuable player in playoffs—Jo Jo White, Boston

Assists Leaders

	G	No.	Avg
Don Watts, Seattle	82	661	8.1
Nate Archibald, Kansas City	78	615	7.9
Calvin Murphy, Houston	82	596	7.3
Norm Van Lier, Chicago	76	500	6.6
Rick Barry, Golden State	81	496	6.1
Dave Bing, Washington	82	492	6.0

Rebounding Leaders

	Off	Def	Total	Avg
Kareem Abdul-Jabbar, Mil.	272	1,111	1,383	16.9
Dave Cowens, Boston	335	911	1,246	16.0
Wes Unseld, Washington	271	765	1,036	13.3
Paul Silas, Boston	365	660	1,025	12.7
Sam Lacey, Kansas City	218	806	1,024	12.6
George McGinnis, Philadelphia	260	707	967	12.6

American Basketball Association

Final Standing

	W	L	Pct	Scoring For	Agst
Denver Nuggets	60	24	.714	121.87	115.88
New York Nets	55	29	.655	111.79	108.83
San Antonio Spurs	50	34	.595	115.56	111.45
Kentucky Colonels	46	38	.548	111.02	110.15
Indiana Pacers	39	45	.464	112.62	112.86
St. Louis Spirits	35	49	.417	108.88	112.10
*Virginia Squires	15	68	.181	106.90	116.55
†Utah Stars	11	4			
**San Diego Sails	2	8			

* Franchise abandoned at end of season; † franchise abandoned December 3, 1975; ** franchise abandoned November 10, 1975.

(St. Louis franchise moved to Utah at end of season)

Playoffs
First Round
Kentucky defeated Indiana, 2 games to 1
Semifinals
New York defeated San Antonio, 4 games to 3
*April 9—New York 116, San Antonio 101
*April 11—San Antonio 105, New York 79
April 14—San Antonio 111, New York 103
April 18—New York 110, San Antonio 108
*April 19—New York 110, San Antonio 108
April 21—San Antonio 106, New York 105
*April 24—New York 121, San Antonio 114
’ At Uniondale, N.Y.

Denver defeated Kentucky, 4 games to 3
April 15—Denver 110, Kentucky 107
April—Kentucky 138, Denver 119
*April 19—Kentucky 126, Denver 114
*April 21—Denver 108, Kentucky 106
April 22—Denver 127, Kentucky 117
*April 25—Kentucky 119, Denver 115
April 28—Denver 135, Kentucky 110
* At Louisville, Kentucky.

League Championship
New York defeated Denver, 4 games to 2
May 1—New York 120, Denver 118
May 4—Denver 127, New York 118
*May 6—New York 117, Denver 111
*May 8—New York 121, Denver 112
May 11—Denver 118, New York 110
*May 13—New York 112, Denver 106

*At Uniondale, N.Y.

Leading Scorers

	FG 2-pt.	3-pt.	FT	Pts	Avg
Julius Erving, New York .	915	34	530	2,462	29.31
Billy Knight, Indiana . . .	768	6	415	1,969	28.13
David Thompson, Denver .	804	3	541	2,158	26.00
Artis Gilmore, Kentucky .	773	0	521	2,067	24.61
Marvin Barnes, St. Louis	678	3	251	1,616	24.12
James Silas, San Antonio	718	0	564	2,000	23.81
Dan Issel, Denver	751	1	425	1,930	22.98
Ron Boone, St. Louis . .	697	16	277	1,719	22.04
George Gervin, San Antonio	692	14	342	1,768	21.83
Tickey Burden, Virginia .	553	8	283	1,413	19.90
Larry Kenon, San Antonio	647	0	221	1,515	18.70
Ralph Simpson, Denver .	615	4	273	1,515	18.70
Bird Averitt, Kentucky . .	506	40	266	1,398	17.92
Mike Green, Virginia . .	385	0	154	924	17.11
Maurice Lucas, Kentucky	617	3	217	1,460	16.98
Brian Taylor, New York .	322	32	164	904	16.74
Billy Paultz, San Antonio	566	0	238	1,370	16.51
John Williamson, New York	511	8	187	1,233	16.22

Pro Basketball Leagues are Merged

The National Basketball Association agreed to accept four American Basketball Association franchises as members on June 17 effecting a merger of the leagues. The N.B.A. absorbed the Denver Nuggets, Indianapolis Pacers, New York Nets and San Antonio Spurs. The 22-team N.B.A. was then divided into these four divisions:

Eastern Conference: Atlantic Division: Boston, Buffalo, New York Knicks, New York Nets and Philadelphia. Central Division: Atlanta, Cleveland, Houston, New Orleans, San Antonio and Washington.

Western Conference—Midwest Division: Chicago, Detroit, Denver, Indiana, Kansas City and Milwaukee. Pacific Division: Golden State, Los Angeles, Phoenix, Portland and Seattle.

ALL-STAR TEAM

First Team	Pos.	Second Team
Julius Erving, New York	F	David Thompson, Denver
Billy Knight, Indiana	F	Bobby Jones, Denver
Artis Gilmore, Kentucky	C	Dan Issel, Denver
James Silas, San Antonio	G	Don Buse, Indiana
Ralph Simpson, Denver	G	George Gervin, San Antonio

Other Awards

Most valuable player—Julius Erving (Dr. J.), New York Nets
Rookie of the Year—David Thompson, Denver Nuggets
Most valuable player in playoffs—Erving

ALL-STAR GAME
(At Denver, Jan. 27)
Denver Nuggets 144, All-Stars 138

2-Point Field Goals

	FG	Att	Pct
Bobby Jones, Denver	510	878	.581
Artis Gilmore, Kentucky	773	1,401	.552
Kim Hughes, New York	300	566	.530
James Silas, San Antonio	718	1,382	.520
David Thompson, Denver	804	1,548	.519
Byron Beck, Denver	329	635	.518
Ralph Simpson, Denver	615	1,187	.518

3-Point Goals

	FG	Att	Pct
Brian Taylor, New York	32	76	.421
Ron Boone, St. Louis	16	43	.372
Louie Dampier, Kentucky	32	87	.368
Bill Keller, Indiana	123	349	.352
Don Buse, Indiana	72	208	.346
Johnny Neumann, Kentucky . . .	71	208	.341
Julius Erving, New York	34	103	.330

Free Throw Leaders

	Att	FT	Pct
Bill Keller, Indiana	164	183	.896
Jim Eakins, New York	198	223	.888
Mack Calvin, Virginia	253	285	.888
James Silas, San Antonio	564	647	.872
Ron Boone, St. Louis	277	318	.871
George Gervin, San Antonio . . .	342	399	.857
Dave Robisch, Indiana	324	381	.850

Rebound Leaders

	Off	Def	Total	Pct
Artis Gilmore, Kentucky	402	901	1,303	15.51
Maurice Lucas, Kentucky	297	673	970	11.28
Caldwell Jones, St. Louis	246	607	853	11.22
Larry Kenon, San Antonio . . .	287	610	897	11.07
Julius Erving, New York	337	588	925	11.01
Dan Issel, Denver	303	620	923	10.99

COLLEGE BASKETBALL

National Collegiate A.A.
DIVISION I
Championship
(Philadelphia, March 29)

Indiana 86, Michigan 68

Third Place

U.C.L.A. 106, Rutgers 92

First Round
East

Rutgers 54, Princeton 53
Connecticut 80, Hofstra 78, overtime
DePaul 69, Virginia 60
Virginia Military 81, Tennessee 75

Mideast

Alabama 70, North Carolina 64
Marquette 79, Western Kentucky 60
Western Michigan 77, Virginia Tech 67
Indiana 90, St. John's 70

Midwest

Missouri 69, Washington 67
Michigan 74, Wichita State 73
Texas Tech 69, Syracuse 56
Notre Dame 79, Cincinnati 78

West

Nevada-Las Vegas 103, Boise State 78
U.C.L.A. 74, San Diego State 64
Arizona 83, Georgetown 76
Pepperdine 87, Memphis State 77

Second Round

Rutgers 93, Connecticut 79
Virginia Military 71, DePaul 66, overtime
Indiana 74, Alabama 69
Marquette 62, Western Michigan 57
Missouri 86, Texas Tech 78
Michigan 80, Notre Dame 76
Arizona 114, Nevada-Las Vegas 109, overtime
U.C.L.A. 70, Pepperdine 61

Regional Championships

Rutgers 91, Virginia Military 75
Indiana 65, Marquette 56
Michigan 95, Missouri 88
U.C.L.A. 82, Arizona 66

Semifinals
(Philadelphia, March 27)

Michigan 86, Rutgers 70
Indiana 65, U.C.L.A. 51

N.C.A.A. DIVISION II
Quarterfinals

Tennessee-Chattanooga 107, Nichols State 78
Eastern Illinois 81, Bridgeport 66
Old Dominion 90, Cheyney State 85
Puget Sound 80, North Dakota 77

Semifinals

Puget Sound 83, Old Dominion 78
Tennessee-Chattanooga 93, Eastern Illinois 84

Championship

Puget Sound 83, Tennessee-Chattanooga 74

Third Place

Eastern Illinois 78, Old Dominion 74

N.C.A.A. DIVISION III
Quarterfinals

Plattsburgh State 91, Rhode Island College 80
Wittenberg 101, Miles 75
Scranton 94, Sheppard 78
Augustana (Ill.) drew bye

Semifinals

Wittenberg 71, Plattsburgh State 58
Scranton 76, Augustana (Ill.) 65

Final

Scranton 60, Wittenberg 57 (overtime)

Third Place

Augustana (Ill.) 73, Plattsburgh State 69

National Association
of Intercollegiate Athletics
(Kansas City, March 8-13)
Quarterfinals

Coppin State (Md.) 88, Texas Southern 77
Henderson State 78, Lake Superior 61
Lincoln Memorial 75, Newberry 64
Marymount (Kan.) 78, Alabama-Huntsville 76

Semifinals

Coppin State 82, Marymount 81
Henderson State 80, Lincoln Memorial 79, 2 overtimes

Championship

Coppin State 96, Henderson State 91

Third Place

Marymount 78, Lincoln Memorial 75

All-America Selections
ASSOCIATED PRESS

First Team	Second Team
Adrian Dantley, Notre Dame	Richard Washington, U.C.L.A.
Scott May, Indiana	Mitch Kupchak, North Carolina
Kent Benson, Indiana	Robert Parish, Centenary
John Lucas, Maryland	Phil Ford, North Carolina
Phil Sellers, Rutgers	Ron Lee, Oregon

UNITED PRESS INTERNATIONAL

First Team	Second Team
Scott May, Indiana	Phil Sellers, Rutgers
Adrian Dantley, Notre Dame	Phil Ford, North Carolina
John Lucas, Maryland	Bernard King, Tennessee
Richard Washington, U.C.L.A.	Mitch Kupchak, North Carolina
Kent Benson, Indiana	Earl Tatum, Marquette

N.A.I.A. All-America Teams

First Team	Second Team
Archie Talley, Salem	Robert Reid, St. Mary's (Tex.)
David Everett, Grand Canyon	Ronald Barrow, Southern U.
Gerald Cunningham, Kentucky State	David Moore, Fairmount State
	Butch Gardner, Harding
Gary Cole, Wisconsin-Parkside	Lewis Lindner, Kentucky State
Clyde Agnew, Newberry	Gary Fors, Lake Superior
Purvis Short, Jackson State	Calvin Hunter, Georgia Southwestern
Jim Hearns, Marymount	
Bayard Forrest, Grand Canyon	John McGill, Alcorn State
Joe Pace, Coppin State	Alonzo Bradley, Texas Southern
Jack Sikma, Illinois Wesleyan	Jessie Campbell, Mercyhurst

(Basketball, Continued)

Association for Intercollegiate Athletics for Women (A.I.A.W.)
(University Park, Pa., March 23–27)

Quarterfinals
Immaculata (Pa.) 103, Montclair State 82
Delta State 97, Baylor 55
California State-Fullerton 64, William Penn 61
Wayland Baptist 75, Mississippi College 59

Semifinals
Immaculata 74, William Penn 52
Delta State 61, Wayland Baptist 60

Championship
Delta State 69, Immaculata 64

Third Place
Wayland Baptist 74, William Penn 54

National Invitation Tournament
(Madison Square Garden, New York, March 13–21)

Quarterfinals
North Carolina State 78, Holy Cross 68
North Carolina-Charlotte 79, Oregon 72
Kentucky 81, Kansas State 78
Providence 73, Louisville 67

Semifinals
Kentucky 79, Providence 78
North Carolina-Charlotte 80, North Carolina State 79

Final
Kentucky 71, North Carolina-Charlotte 67

Third Place
North Carolina State 74, Providence 69

A.A.U. Basketball
(Baton Rouge, La., April 1–4)

Quarterfinals
Armed Forces All-Stars 106, Topeka, Kan. 84
Athletes in Action, Tustin, Calif. 88, Merced, Calif. 79
California Junior College All-Stars, 108, Tulsa, Okla. 95
Ranco Raiders, Baton Rouge 114, Lexington, Ky. 86

Semifinals
Athletes in Action 79, California Juco Stars 78
Armed Forces All Stars 118, Ranco Raiders 101

Championship
Athletes in Action 79, Armed Forces All-Stars 80

Third Place
Ranco Raiders, Baton Rouge 91, California Juco Stars 83
Tourney's most valuable player—Irv Kiffin, Athletes in Action.

Women's A.A.U. Basketball
(Gallup, N.M., March 30–April 3)

Quarterfinals
Wayland Baptist 82, Detroit 47
Fullerton, Calif. 73, East Troy, Wis. 60
N.Y. City Planters Peanuts 68, Seattle 63
Darlington, S.C. 78, Ankeny, Iowa 71

Semifinals
Fullerton, Calif. 70, N.Y. City Planters Peanuts 62
Wayland Baptist 69, Darlington, S.C. 48

Championship
Fullerton, Calif. 67, Wayland Baptist 66

Third Place
Darlington, S.C. 74, N.Y. City Planters Peanuts 59

HANDBALL
United States Handball Association Champions
Four Wall
(Las Vegas, Nev., June 6–13)

Singles—Vern Roberts, Jr., Lake Forest, Ill.
Doubles—Gary Rohrer, Minneapolis-Dan O'Connor, St. Paul
Masters singles—Jack Scrivens, Portland, Ore.
Masters doubles—Arnold Aguilar-Gabe Enriquez, Los Angeles
Golden Masters singles—Murray Marcus, Miami, Fla.
Golden Masters doubles—Rudy Stadlberger-Tom Kelly, San Francisco
Super masters doubles—Ted Bystock, Miami, Fla.-Jack Weitz, Larchmont, N.Y.

Collegiate
(Memphis State University, March 5–7)

Singles—Ken Genty, Manhattan
B Singles—Pete Cristaudo, Memphis State
Doubles—Jack Roberts-Mickey Guzman, Lake Forest
Team—Lake Forest

Masters
(Norfolk, Va., Feb. 20–22)

Singles—Dr. Claude Benham, Norfolk, Va.
Golden singles—Fred DeNuccio, Norfolk, Va.
Super singles—Steve Subak, Minneapolis

Masters Doubles
(Schaumburg, Ill., Jan. 14–16)

Doubles—Jerry Cronin-Tom Schoendorf, Milwaukee
Golden doubles—Ken Schneider-Gus Lewis, Chicago
Super doubles—Ted Bystock, Miami, Fla.-Jack Weitz, Larchmont, N.Y.

Amateur Athletic Union
One Wall
(Brooklyn, N.Y., June–July)

Singles—Ruben Gonzalez, New York
Doubles—Artie Reyer-Al Torres, Brooklyn
Masters doubles—Ron Berkowitz-Morty Katz, Brooklyn

RACQUETBALL
National Championships
(San Diego, Calif., June 13–18)
Professional
Men—Charles Brumfield, San Diego
Women—Peggy Steding, Odessa, Tex.

Amateur
Men's singles—Ben Koltun, St. Louis
Women's singles—Sarah Green, Memphis, Tenn.
Seniors—Joe Gibbs, St. Louis
Masters—Bob McNamara, Minneapolis
Golden Masters—Stan Berney, San Diego
Doubles—D.C. Charlson, San Diego-Roger Souders, San Diego
Women's doubles—Jennifer Harding, Portland, Ore.-Camille McCarthy, Indianapolis
Senior doubles—Jim Austin, Houston-Dr. Chuck Hanna, San Diego
Masters doubles—Carl Loveday-George Brown, San Diego
Golden Masters doubles—Berney-Stan Murphy, San Diego

COURT TENNIS
World Open—Howard Angus, Britain
U.S. Singles—Gene Scott, New York
Doubles—William Shettle-Peter Clement, Philadelphia

DARTS
World Championship—Tony Money, Medina, Ohio

SWIMMING

A.A.U. National Championships
Indoor
(Long Beach, Calif., April 1-4)

100-m freestyle—Jim Montgomery, Bloomington,
Ind. 0:50.77
200-m free—Montgomery 1:51.41
400-m free—Doug Northway, Tucson, Ariz. 3:56.48
1,500-m free—Casey Converse, Mission Viejo
Nadadores 15:40.04
100-m back—John Naber, So. Calif. 0:56.99
200-yd back—Naber 2:03.25
100-m breaststroke—David Wilkie, Miami (Fla.) . . 1:04.46
200-m breaststroke—Wilkie 2:18.48
100-m butterfly—Steve Gregg, No. Car. State . . . 0:55.49
200-m butterfly—Mike Bruner, DeAnza S.C.,
Stockton, Calif. 2:02.49
200-m ind. medley—Wilkie 2:06.25
400-m ind. medley—Zoltan Verraszto, Hungary . . 4:26 W
400-m freestyle relay—Tennessee (Bob Sells,
Lee Engstrand, John Ebuna, John Newton) . . . 3:26.97
400-m medley relay—Gatorade S.C., Bloomington,
Ind. (John Murphy, Rick Hofstetter, Bob Alsfelder,
Tom Hickcox) 3:52.19
800-m freestyle relay—U. of Southern California
(Steve Furniss, Mark Greenwood, John Naber,
Bruce Furniss) 7:30.85
Team—University of Southern California . . . . . 483 pts

Women
100-m free—Kim Peyton, David Douglas S.C.,
Portland, Ore. 0:57.53
200-m free—Shirley Babashoff, Mission Viejo
Nadadores 2:02.54
400-m free—Shirley Babashoff 4:15.82
800-m free—Shannon Smith, Vancouver, B.C. . . . 8:46.39
100-m back—Linda Jezek, Santa Clara (Calif.)
S.C. 1:04.45
200-m back—Cheryl Gibson, Edmonton, Alberta . . 2:18.11
100-m breaststroke—Christine Jarvis, Tuscaloosa,
Ala. 1:14.70
200-m breaststroke—Noel Moran, Santa Clara,
Calif. 2:39.39
100-m butterfly—Wendy Boglioli, Central Jersey
A.A. 1:02.14
200-m butterfly—Nicole Kramer, Mission Viejo
Nadadores 2:19.01
200-m ind. medley—Kathy Heddy, Cent. Jersey A.A. . 2:23.02
400-m ind. medley—Cheryl Gibson 4:57.20
400-m freestyle relay—El Monte (Calif.) A.C. (Val
Seyfert, Diane Johnson, Sue Hinderaker, Jill
Sterkel) 3:57.90
400-m medley relay—Santa Clara (Calif.) S.C.
(Linda Jezek, Noel Moran, Sandy Thompson,
Kelly Rowell) 4:24.09
800-m freestyle relay—Central Jersey Aquatic Assn.
(Kathy Heddy, Ellen Wallace, Kathy Miller,
Wendy Boglioli) 8:22.98
Team—Mission Viejo (Calif.) Nadadores . . . . . 308 pts
Combined team—University of Southern California . 551 pts
W—World record.

Outdoor
(Philadelphia, Aug. 11-14)

100-m free—Jonty Skinner, Central Jersey A.C. . . 0:49.44 W
200-m free—Mark Greenwood, Fresno (Calif.) S.C. . 1:52.21
400-m free—Casey Convers, Mission Viejo (Calif.)
S.C. 3:54.65
1,500-m free—Converse 15:21.03
100-m back—John Naber, Ladera Oaks, Calif. . . . 0:56.48
200-m back—Naber 2:03.73

100-m breast—John Hencken, Santa Clara (Calif.)
S.C. 1:04.36
200-m breast—Hencken 2:21.17
100-m butterfly—Greg Janenberg, Suburban S.C.,
Newton Square, Pa. 0:55.72
200-m butterfly—Bill Forrester, Jacksonville, Fla. . . 2:00.03
200-m ind. medley—Steve Furniss, Long Beach,
Calif. 2:07.36
400-m ind. medley—Jesse Vassallo, Mission Viejo . . 4:28.34
400-m medley relay—Santa Clara S.C. (Mike Bottom,
John Hencken, Don Palestra, Dan Stephenson) . . 3:51.34
400-m freestyle relay—Central Jersey A.C. (Jonty
Skinner, Mike Reock, Ken Keim, Bill Kiss) 3:27.91
800-m freestyle relay—Mission Viejo (Calif.)
Nadadores (Taylor Howe, Art Ruble, Brian Goodell,
Casey Converse) 7:34.48
Team—Mission Viejo (Calif.) Nadadores . . . . . 297 pts

Women
100-m free—Jill Sterkel, El Monte (Calif.) S.C. . . . 0:57.20
200 m free—Kim Peyton, Douglas S.C., Portland,
Ore. 2:03.01
400-m free—Rebecca Perrott, New Zealand 4:17.60
1,500-m free—Evie Kosenkranius, Lake Wash. S.C.,
Seattle 16:41.77
100-m back—Linda Jezek, Santa Clara S.C. 1:04.49
200-m back—Linda Jezek 2:17.33
100-m breast—Dawn Rodighiero, Mission Viejo,
Calif. 1:14.64
200-m breast—Dawn Rodighiero 2:39.40
100-m butterfly—Wendy Boglioli, Central Jersey . . 1:01.76
200-m butterfly—Alice Browne, Mission Viejo, Calif. . 2:15.57
200-m ind. medley—Kathy Heddy, Central Jersey . . 2:21.54
400-m ind. medley—Donnalee Wennerstrom, West
Valley (Calif.) S.T. 4:57.74
400-m medley relay—Central Jersey A.C. (Ellen
Wallace, Dana Morton, Wendy Boglioli, Kathy
Heddy) 4:22.99
400-m freestyle relay—El Monte (Calif.) A.C. (Valerie
Seyfert, Diane Johnson, Sue Hinderaker, Jill
Sterkel) 3:53.76
800-m freestyle relay—Central Jersey A.C. (Kathy
Heddy, Ellen Wallace, Kathi Miller, Wendy Boglioli) . 8:21.40
Team—Mission Viejo Nadadores . . . . 376 pts
Combined team—Mission Viejo Nadadores . . . . 673 pts

National Collegiate A.A.
DIVISION I
Indoor
(Providence, R.I., March 24-27)

50-yd free—Joe Bottom, So. Calif. 0:20.081
100-yd free—Jim Montgomery, Indiana 0:44.40
200-yd free—Montgomery . . . . 1:36.53 A
500-yd free—Tim Shaw, Long Beach State . . . . . 4:19.053 A
1,650-yd free—Shaw . . . . 15:06.76 A
100-yd backstroke—John Naber, S. Calif. 0:49.94
200-yd backstroke—Naber 1:46.96
100-yd breaststroke—John Hencken, Stanford 0:56.04
200-yd breaststroke—David Wilkie, Miami (Fla.) . . . 2:00.74 A
100-yd butterfly—Matt Vogel, Tennessee 0:48.95
200-yd butterfly—Steve Gregg, No. Car. State 1:47
200-yd ind. medley—Lee Engstrand, Tennessee . . . 1:50.129
400-yd ind. medley—Rod Strachan, So. Calif. 3:55.64
400-yd freestyle relay—So. California (Joe Bottom,
Bruce Furniss, John Naber, Scott Findorff) . . . . 2:57.54 A
400-yd medley relay—So. California (John Naber,
Bob Shearin, Mike Bottom, Joe Bottom) 3:20.02
800-yd freestyle relay—So. California (John Naber,
Dick Hannula, Scott Findorff, Bruce Furniss . . . 6:33.13 A
1-m dive—Jim Kennedy, Tennessee . . . . 514.29 pts
3-m dive—Brian Bungum, Indiana . . . . 542.19 pts
Team—University of Southern California . . . . . . 398 pts
A—American record.

(Swimming, Continued)

National Association of Intercollegiate Athletics

(Marshall, Minn., March 4–6)

50-yd free—Gary MacDonald, Simon Fraser 0:21.24
100-yd free—MacDonald 0:46.89
200-yd free—Jon Stewart, Southwest (Minn.) 1:43.08
500-yd free—Stewart 4:36.34
1,650-yd free—Stewart 15:51.76
100-yd back—John Van Buren, Simon Fraser 0:52.46
200-yd back—Anders Sandberg, Simon Fraser 1:58.50
100-yd breaststroke—Rick Cleland, So. Oregon . . .0:50.28
200-yd breaststroke—David Heinbuch, Simon Fraser .2:01.73
100-yd butterfly—William Morrow, Claremont-Mudd .0:51.83
200-yd butterfly—Van Buren 1:52.20
200-yd ind. medley—Van Buren 1:54.34
400-yd ind. medley—Larry Steele, Simon Fraser . . .4:08.67
400-yd freestyle relay—Simon Fraser (MacDonald,
  John Trotter, Heinbuch, Van Buren) 3:06.28
400-yd medley relay—Simon Fraser (Van Buren,
  Heinbuch, MacDonald, Trotter) 3:29.52
800-yd freestyle relay—Simon Fraser (MacDonald,
  Trotter, Heinbuch, Van Buren) 6:54.10
1-m dive—Tony Perriello, Clarion State . . . . .473.13 pts
3-m dive—Mike Zucca, Clarion State . . . . . .332.97 pts
Team—Simon Fraser, Burnaby, British Columbia . . .412 pts

Association of Intercollegiate Athletics for Women

(Fort Lauderdale, Fla., March 18–20)

50-yd free—Vicky Stanley, Alabama 0:24.17
100-yd free—Wendy Boglioli, Monmouth 0:52.12
200-yd free—Ann Marshall, North Carolina 1:50.29
500-yd free—Kim Peters, So. California 4:52.48
50-yd back—Bonnie Broyles, Florida 0:27.73
100-yd back—Melissa Belote, Arizona State 0:59.04
200-yd back—Ann Marshall 2:04.93
50-yd breaststroke—Christine Jarvis, Alabama 0:30.05
100-yd breaststroke—Christine Jarvis . . . . . .1:04.56 AO
200-yd breaststroke—Christine Jarvis 2:18.79
50-yd butterfly—Wendy Boglioli 0:25.23
100-yd butterfly—Wendy Boglioli . . . . .0:55.60 A
200-yd butterfly—Karen Moe, U.C.L.A. 2:02.88
100-yd ind. medley—Lynn Vidali, San Jose State . .1:00.19
200-yd ind. medley—Robin Brannman, Miami (Fla.) . .2:07.11
1-m dive—Carrie Irish, Ohio State . . . . .433 pts
3-m dive—Peggy Anderson, Wisconsin 447.90
200-yd medley relay—Miami (Fla.) . . . . .1:47.82 A
400-yd freestyle relay—So. California 3:31.31
200-yd freestyle relay—Monmouth (N.J.) . . . . .1:37.37 A
400-yd medley relay—Alabama . . . . .1:37.53 A
Team—Miami (Florida) . . . . .445½ pts

A—American record; AO—American Open record.

A.A.U. Diving

Indoor

(Cleveland, March 31–April 3)

1 m—Tim Moore, Cincinnati 543.51
3 m—Moore 604.59
Platform—Moore 527.01

Women

1 m—Cynthia McIngvale, Dallas, Tex. 459.66
3 m—Jennifer Chandler, Lincoln, Ala. 504.06
Platform—Melissa Briley, Bothwell, Wash. 367.89

Outdoor

(Decatur, Ala., Aug. 17–21)

3-meter—Jim Kennedy, Finlay, Ohio
Platform—Kent Vosler, Eaton, Ohio

Women

1-meter—Cynthia McIngvale, Dallas, Tex.
Platform—Barbara Weinstein, Cincinnati

WRESTLING

A.A.U. National Champions

Freestyle

(Cleveland, May 1–3)

105.5 lbs—Bill Rosado, Arizona W.C.
114.5 lbs—Jim Haines, Wisconsin W.C., Madison
125.5 lbs—Jan Gitcho, Hawkeye W.C.
136.5 lbs—Kiyoshi Abe, New York A.C.
149.5 lbs—Lt. Lloyd Keaser, U.S. Marines
163 lbs—Stan Dziedzic, New York A.C.
180.5 lbs—Brady Hall, Los Angeles
198 lbs—Ben Peterson, Iowa W.C.
220 lbs—Russ Hellickson, Wisconsin W.C., Madison
Heavyweight—Mike McCready, Hawkeye W.C.
Outstanding wrestler—Keaser

Greco-Roman

(Cleveland, May 4–5)

105.5 lbs—Karoly Kanscar, San Francisco Peninsula Grapplers
114.5 lbs—Chris Sones, Hawkeye W.C.
125.5 lbs—Bruce Thompson, Minnesota W.C.
136.5 lbs—Hachiro Oishi, New York A.C.
149.5 lbs—Larry Morgan, Hawkeye W.C.
163.1 lbs—John Matthews, Michigan W.C.
180.5 lbs—Dan Chandler, Minnesota W.C.
198.1 lbs—Willie Williams, Mayor Daley Y.F., Chicago
220.1 lbs—Brad Rheingans, Minnesota W.C.
Unlimited—Mike McCready, Hawkeye W.C.
Outstanding wrestler—Bruce Thompson

National Collegiate A.A.

Division I

(Tucson, Ariz., March 11–13)

118 lbs—Mark DiGiralamo, Cal Poly-San Luis Obispo
126 lbs—Jack Reinwand, Wisconsin
134 lbs—Mike Frick, Lehigh
142 lbs—Brad Smith, Iowa
150 lbs—Chuck Yagla, Iowa
158 lbs—Lee Kemp, Wisconsin
167 lbs—Pat Christenson, Wisconsin
177 lbs—Chris Campbell, Iowa
190 lbs—Evan Johnson, Minnesota
Heavyweight—Jimmy Jackson, Oklahoma State
Outstanding wrestler—Yagla
Team—University of Iowa (123¼ pts)

Division II

Team—Cal State-Bakersfield (92½ pts)
Outstanding wrestler—Rick Jensen, South Dakota State (126 lbs)

Division III

Team—Montclair State (143 pts)
Outstanding wrestler—Vince Tundo, Montclair State (126 lbs)

N.A.I.A.

Team—Adams State of Colorado (83½ pts)
Outstanding wrestler—Glenn Guerin, Taylor of Indiana (126 lbs)

Synchronized Swimming

Outdoor

(Houston, Tex., July 5–11)

Solo—Sue Baross, Santa Clara (Calif.) Aquamaids
Duet—Robin Curren-Amanda Norrish, Santa Clara Aquamaids
Team—Santa Clara Aquamaids

SKIING

United States Champions

Alpine

(Copper Mountain, Colo., Feb. 26-28)

Downhill—Greg Jones, S. Tahoe City, Calif. 1:56.56
Slalom—Cary Adgate, Boyne City, Mich. 1:11.37
Giant slalom—Geoff Bruce, Corning, N.Y. 2:29.40
Combined—Adgate . . . . 13.50 pts

Women

Downhill—Susie Patterson, Sun Valley, Idaho 1:46.17
Slalom—Cindy Nelson, Lutsen, Minn. 1:48.94
Giant slalom—Lindy Cochran, Richmond, Vt. 1:18.87
Combined—Viki Fleckenstein, Syracuse, N.Y. . . . . 33.88 pts

NORDIC

Jumping

(Squaw Valley, Calif., Jan. 11)

Senior—Jim Denney, Duluth, Minn. 222.5
Junior—John Broman, Duluth, Minn. 187.5
Veteran—Earl Murphy, Brattleboro, Vt. 96.3

Cross-Country

(Big Sky, Mont., March 8-14)

15 kilometers—Devin Swigert, Sun Valley, Idaho . . 47:13.30
30 kilometers—Swigert 1:24:16.83
50 kilometers—Stan Dunklee, Brattleboro, Vt. . 2:48:21.92
Junior 15 kilometers—Tim Kelley, Middlebury, Vt. . . 43:13.32
40-km relay—Eastern (Tim Kelley, Don Nielson,
   Randy Kerr, Stan Dunklee) 2:18:37.70
Veterans 15 km—Ole Kristensen, Alaska 51:54.98

Women

5 kilometers—Jana Hlavaty, Chicago 18:13.91
10 kilometers—Jana Hlavaty 36:02.40
20 kilometers—Jana Hlavaty 1:21:53.46
20-km relay—Alaska (Margie Mahoney, Pam Richter,
   Alison Spencer, Lynne Von der Heide) 1:21:24.11

National Collegiate A.A.

(Lewiston, Me., March 3-6)

Giant slalom—Dave Cleveland, Dartmouth 2:56.96
Giant slalom, team—Colorado . . . . 42 pts
Slalom—Mike Meleski, Wyoming 1:34.74
Slalom, team—Wyoming . . . . 43 pts
Alpine combined—Meleski 347.7
Cross-country—Stan Dunklee, Vermont 42:11.7
Cross-country, team—Vermont . . . . 34 pts
Jumping—Kip Sundgaard, Utah 215.9
Jumping, team—Utah . . . . 41 pts
Nordic combined—Jack Turner, Colorado 365.9
Team championship—Tie between Colorado and Dartmouth . 112

Canadian-American Trophy Series

Men

	Pts
Overall—Eric Wilson, Montpelier, Vt.	142
Downhill—Wilson	70
Slalom—John Teague, Moretown, Vt.	65
Giant slalom—Ron Fuller, S. Lake Tahoe, Calif. . . .	65
Peter Dodge, St. Johnsbury, Vt.	65
(Fuller given title for best 4 finishes)	

Women

	Pts
Overall—Viki Fleckenstein, Syracuse, N.Y.	155
Downhill—Jeanette Zanier, Canada	75
Slalom—Christin Cooper, Sun Valley, Idaho	75
Giant slalom—Viki Fleckenstein	75
Jamie Kurlander, McAfee, N.J.	75

World Cup

Overall

Ingemar Stenmark, Sweden 249
Piero Gros, Italy 205
Gustavo Thoeni, Italy 190

Women

Rosi Mittermaier, West Germany 281
Lise—Marie Morerod, Switzerland 214
Monika Kaserer, Austria 171

Men's Event Leaders

Downhill—Franz Klammer, Austria 125
Slalom—Stenmark 125
Giant slalom—Stenmark 88

Women's Event Leaders

Downhill—Brigitte Totschnig, Austria 106
Slalom—Rosi Mittermaier 110
Giant slalom—Lise-Marie Morerod 120

Nations Cup

	Pts
Overall—Austria	1,123
Men—Italy	691
Women—Austria	600

Women's National Collegiate

(Boyne Falls, Mich., March 5-7)

Slalom—Toril Forland, Utah 1:15.24
Slalom, team—Utah . . . . .97.67 pts
Giant slalom—Toril Forland . . . . 103.96 pts
Giant slalom, team—Utah . . . . .99.85 pts
7.5-km cross-country—Mitzi Cain, Middlebury . . . 34:47.66
Cross-country, team—Middlebury . . . . .97.79 pts
Team championship—Middlebury . . . . 291.46 pts

BADMINTON

National Championships

(Philadelphia, April 12-14)

Singles—Chris Kinard, Pasadena, Calif.
Women's singles—Pam Bristol, Flint, Mich.
Doubles—Don Paup, Vienna, Va.-Bruce Pontow, Chicago
Women's doubles—Pam Bristol-Rosine Lemon, New York
Mixed doubles—Mike Walker, Manhattan Beach, Calif.-Judianne
   Kelly, Norwalk, Calif.
Senior singles—Jim Poole, Westminster, Calif.
Senior doubles—Poole-Tom Heden, Millwood, N.Y.
Senior women's doubles—Ethel Marshall-Bea Massman, Buffalo,
   N.Y.
Senior mixed doubles—Poole-Helen Tibbetts, Torrance, Calif.
Masters singles—Ed Phillips, Warwick, R.I.
Masters doubles—Charles Thomas, Natchitoches, La.-Richard
   Witte, St. Louis
Masters mixed doubles—Scott Garman, Lititz, Pa.-Ethel Marshall

National Open Championships

(Philadelphia, April 15-17)

Singles—Paul Whetnall, England
Women's singles—Gillian Gilks, England
Doubles—Roland Maywald-Willie Braun, West Germany
Women's doubles—Sue Whetnall, England-Gillian Gilks
Mixed doubles—David Eddy, England-Sue Whetnall

Racquets

National Champions

Singles—Bill Surtees, Chicago
Doubles—Surtees-Richard Lightfine, Chicago

SOCCER

North American Soccer League
FINAL STANDING OF THE TEAMS
Northern Division

	W	L	For	Agst.	BP*	Pts
Chicago Sting	15	9	52	32	42	132
Toronto Metros	15	9	38	30	33	123
Rochester Lancers	13	11	36	32	36	114
Hartford Bicentennials	12	12	37	56	35	107
Boston Minutemen	7	17	35	64	32	74

Eastern Division

	W	L	For	Agst.	BP*	Pts
Tampa Bay Rowdies	18	6	58	30	46	154
New York Cosmos	16	8	65	34	52	148
Washington Diplomats	14	10	46	38	42	126
Philadelphia Atoms	8	16	32	49	32	80
Miami Toros	6	18	29	58	27	63

Western Division

	W	L	For	Agst.	BP*	Pts
Minnesota Kicks	15	9	54	33	48	138
Seattle Sounders	14	10	40	31	39	123
Vancouver Whitecaps	14	10	38	30	36	120
Portland Timbers	8	16	23	40	23	71
St. Louis Stars	5	19	28	57	28	58

Southern Division

	W	L	For	Agst.	BP*	Pts
San Jose Earthquakes	14	10	47	30	39	123
Dallas Tornado	13	11	44	45	39	117
Los Angeles Aztecs	12	12	43	44	36	108
San Antonio Thunder	12	12	38	32	35	107
San Diego Jaws	9	15	29	47	28	82

* BP—Bonus Points awarded for each goal to a maximum of three per team per game; teams receive 6 points for victory, none for loss.

PLAYOFFS
First Round
New York 2, Washington 0
Seattle 1, Vancouver 0
Dallas 2, Los Angeles 0
Toronto 2, Rochester 1

Second Round
Tampa Bay 3, New York 1
Toronto 3, Chicago 2
San Jose 2, Dallas 0
Minnesota 3, Seattle 0

Semifinals
Minnesota 3, San Jose 1
Toronto 2, Tampa Bay 0

Championship
(At Seattle, Aug. 28)
Toronto 3, Minnesota 0

League Awards
Most valuable player—Pele, New York Cosmos
Leading scorer—George Chinaglia, New York Cosmos
Leading goalie—Tony Chursky, Seattle Sounders
Rookie of the Year—Steve Pecher, Dallas Tornado

United States Champions
Challenge Cup—San Francisco A.C. (defeated Inter-Guiliana, New York, 1-0, in final)
Amateur Cup—Bavarian Blue Ribbon, Milwaukee
Junior Cup—Annandale (Va.) Cavaliers
Bicentennial Cup—Brazil

College Champions
(November, December 1975)
N.C.A.A. Division I—Final: University of San Francisco (defeated Southern Illinois, Edwardsville, 4-0). Semifinals: San Francisco defeated Brown, 2-1; So. Illinois defeated Howard, 3-1

N.C.A.A. Division II—Baltimore (defeated Seattle Pacific, 3-1, in final)
N.C.A.A. Division III—Babson (defeated Brockport, 1-0, in final)
N.A.I.A.—Quincy (defeated Simon Fraser, 1-0, in final)

British Champions
English Association Cup—Southampton (defeated Manchester United, 1-0, in final)
English League Cup—Manchester City
Scottish Association Cup—Glasgow Rangers (defeated Hearts, 3-1, in final)
Scottish League Cup—Glasgow Rangers
English League, First Division—Liverpool
Scottish League, Premier Division—Glasgow Rangers

Other European Winners
European Federation Cup—Liverpool
European Nations Cup—Czechoslovakia
European Cup of Cups—Anderlecht, Belgium
European Supercup—Anderlecht, Belgium

LACROSSE
National Collegiate A.A.
DIVISION I
Final
(Providence, R.I., May 29)
Cornell 16, Maryland 13 (overtime)

Semifinals
Maryland 22, Navy 11
Cornell 13, Johns Hopkins 5

Quarterfinals
Maryland 17, Brown 8
Navy 13, North Carolina 9
Cornell 14, Washington and Lee 0
Johns Hopkins 11, Massachusetts 9

DIVISION II
Final
(Baltimore, May 22)
Hobart 18, Adelphi 9

Semifinals
Adelphi 13, Washington of Maryland 10
Hobart 14, Ohio Wesleyan 5

Quarterfinals
Adelphi 7, Baltimore 2
Washington of Maryland 17, Roanoke 15
Ohio Wesleyan 12, Cortland State 11
Hobart 10, Towson State 6

Other Championships
North 22, South 17
U.S. Club—Mount Washington Lacrosse Club, Baltimore

BILLIARDS
POCKET BILLIARDS
World Open
(Professional Pool Players Assn., Asbury Park, N.J. Aug. 11-16)
Men—Larry Lisciotti, Manchester, Conn.

United States Open
(Billiard Congress of America, Chicago, Aug. 10-15)
Men—Tom Jennings, Edison, N.J.
Women—Jean Balukas, Brooklyn, N.Y.

BOWLING
American Bowling Congress Tournament
(Oklahoma City, March 21–May 2)
Regular Division

Singles—Mike Putzer, Oshkosh, Wis. 758
Doubles—Fred Willen, Sr.-Gary Voss, St. Louis 1,356
All events—Jim Lindquist, Minneapolis 2,071
Team—Andy's Pro Shop, Tucson, Ariz. 3,187

Classic Division

Singles—Jim Schroeder, Buffalo, N.Y. 750
Doubles—Don Johnson, Las Vegas, Nev.-Paul Colwell,
   Tucson, Ariz. 1,442
All events—Gary Fust, Des Moines, Iowa 2,050
Team—Munsingwear No. 2, Minneapolis 3,281

Booster Division

Team—T's Truckers, League City, Tex. 2,806

Masters

Champion—Nelson Burton Jr., Minneapolis (won 7 matches,
   lost 0)

Collegiate
Association of College Unions-International

All events—Mark Schwabe, Wisconsin-Milwaukee . . . 2,116
Singles—Schwabe 731
Doubles—Tom Porwell, Florida State-Ellis Mitchell,
   Alabama 1,159

National Association of Intercollegiate Athletics
(Kansas City, April 19–21)

All Events—Sam Ferrell, Glenville State 3,050
Doubles—Doug Tuskey-Bernard Lilley, West Liberty . . 1,235
Team—Glenville State 16,313

Women's International Bowling Congress
(Denver, April 8–June 8)
Open Division

Singles—Bev Shonk, Canton, Ohio 686
Doubles—Eloise Vacco-Debbie Rainone, Cleveland
   Heights, Ohio 1,232
   (tie) Georgene Cordes-Shirley Sjostrom,
   Bloomington, Minn. 1,232
All events—Betty Morris, Stockton, Calif. 1,866
Team—PWBA No. 1, Oklahoma City 2,839

Division I

Singles—Vanda Philson, Sidney, Neb. 666
Doubles—Barbara Siemrzuch-Shirley Mansfield,
   Northglenn, Colo. 1,198
All events—Ethel Coverdell, Orlando, Fla. 1,748
Team—Famous Brand Shoes, St. Louis 2,753

Division II

Singles—Pat Wahner, Stanfield, Ore. 647
Doubles—Kay Larison-Margaret Bolyard, Hansen, Idaho 1,098
All events—Beverly Morgan, Long Beach, Calif. 1,678
Team—Partain Mech. Contractor, Texarkana, Ark. . . . 2,532

Bowling Proprietors Assn. of America
Open Champions

Men—Paul Moser, Medford, Ore. (defeated Jim Frazier, Spokane,
   Wash., 226-195, in final at Grand Prairie, Tex., March 20)
Women—Patty Costello, Scranton, Pa. (defeated Betty Morris,
   Stockton, Calif., 235-233, in final at Tulsa, Okla., June 5)

BOWLING, DUCKPINS
National Duckpin Bowling Congress
(Newington, Conn., March 27–May 9)

Singles—Bob Atlkins, Baltimore 501
Doubles—Tony Adams-Mike Piersanti, East Haven, Conn. . 923
All events—Mike Piersanti, New Haven, Conn. 1,426
Team—Conn. Frozen Food, Hamden, Conn. 2,125
Booster teams—Ansmor AA, Seymour, Conn. 2,088

WOMEN

Singles—Doris Shortt, Baltimore 467
Doubles—Lorraine Watts-Kathy Cahoon, Willimantic,
   Conn. 810
All events—Susan Slattery, Baltimore 1,244
Team—Overlea Exxon, Baltimore 1,926
Booster teams—Cappi Girls, Stamford, Conn. 1,830
Mixed teams—Tin Can Cuties, Glastonvury, Conn. . . . 1,914
Mixed booster teams—Fireballs, Kings Mountain, N.C. . 1,984

ROLLER SKATING
World Championships
(Rome, Sept. 23–26)

Singles—Thomas Nieder, West Germany
Women's singles—Natalie Dunn, Bakersfield, Calif.
Pairs—Ron Sabo-Darlene Waters, Columbus, Ohio
Dancing—Kerry Cavazzi-Jane Puracchio, East Meadow, N.Y.

National Championships
(Fort Worth, Tex., Aug. 8–18)

Singles—Paul Jones, Flint, Mich.
Women's singles—Lisa Bergin, Fort Worth, Tex.
Figures—William Combs, Columbus, Ohio
Women's figures—Donna Kiker, Decatur, Ga.
Figures, free skating—Kurt Anselmi, Pontiac, Mich.
Women's figures, free skating—Debbie Palm, East Meadow, N.Y.
Esquire figures—George Haver, Dayton, Ohio
Women's esquire figures—Elinor Saldi, Waltham, Mass.
International dance—Kerry Cavazzi-Jane Puracchio, East Meadow,
   N.Y.
American dance—John La Briola-Debra Coyne, Fountain Valley,
   Calif.
American esquire dance—Fred and Nancy Doyle, Norwood, Mass.
American free dance—Mark Howard-Cindy Smith, Richmond, Va.
Senior pairs—Ron Sabo-Darlene Waters, Columbus, Ohio
Speed—Tim Small, Loveland, Ohio
Women's speed—Marcia Yager, Loveland, Ohio
4-man relay—Tim and Tom Small-Peter Deibele-Greg Phillips,
   Loveland, Ohio
4-woman relay—Marcia Yager-Sandy Hoier-Brenda Haggard-
   Danna Capozzi, Loveland, Ohio
2-man relay—Tim and Tom Small, Loveland, Ohio
2-woman relay—Marcia Yager-Brenda Haggard, Loveland, Ohio
Mixed relay—Marcia Yager-Brenda Haggard-Tim and Tom Small,
   Loveland, Ohio

JUDO
(Baltimore, April 23–24)

139 lbs—George Cozzi, Chicago
154 lbs—Pat Burris, Anaheim, Calif.
176 lbs—Teimoc Jonstonono, New York
205 lbs—Irwin Cohen, Chicago
Heavyweight—Dean Sedgwick, River Forest, Ill.
Open—James Wooley, Houston, Tex.
Grand champion—Burris

Women

110 lbs—Lynn Lewis, Revere, Mass.
120 lbs—Diane Pierce, Minneapolis
130 lbs—Becky Tushek, Fort Lee, N.J.
142 lbs—Delores Brodie. Barstow, Calif.
154 lbs—Amy Kublin, Arlington, Mass.
Over 166 lbs—Debbie Fisher, Concord, Calif.
166 lbs—Frances Watkins, New York City
Open—Maureen Braziel, Brooklyn, N.Y.
Grand champion—Maureen Braziel

ICE (FIGURE) SKATING
World Championships
(Goteborg, Sweden, March 2–6)

Men—John Curry, Britain
Women—Dorothy Hamill, Riverside, Conn.
Pairs—Irina Rodnina-Alexsandr Zaitsev
Dance—Ludmila Pakhomova-Alexsandr Gorshkov

United States Champions
(Colorado Springs, Jan. 7–10)

Men—Terry Kubicka, Cypress, Calif.
Women—Dorothy Hamill, Riverside, Calif.
Pairs—Tai Babilonia-Randy Gardner, Los Angeles
Dance—Colleen O'Connor-Jim Millns, Colorado Springs
Junior men—Scott Hamilton, Bowling Green, Ohio
Junior women—Carrie Rugh, Los Angeles
Junior pairs—Tracy and Scott Prussack, Los Angeles
Junior dance—Bonnie and William Burton, Boston

ICE (SPEED) SKATING
World Championships
(Heerenveen, Netherlands, Feb. 28–29)

Champion—Piet Kleine, Netherlands	170.255 pts
500 m—Eric Heiden, Madison, Wis.	0:39.11
1,500 m—Kleine	2:02.33
5,000 m—Hans Van Helden, Netherlands	7:08.72
10,000 m—Kleine	15:12.25

WOMEN
(Gjovik, Norway, Feb. 21–22)

Champion—Sylvia Burka, Canada	184.84 pts
500 m—Sheila Young, Detroit	0:44.09
1,500 m—Sheila Young	1:28.69
5,000 m—Sylvia Burka	2:18.60
3,000 m—Karin Kessow, East Germany	4:51.01

SPRINTS
(Berlin, March 6–7)

Champion—Johann Granath, Sweden	160.845 pts
500 m (1st race)—Dan Immerfall, Madison, Wis.	0:39.73
500 m (2d race)—Immerfall	0:39.69
1,000 m (1st race)—Hans Van Helden, Netherlands	1:20.06
1,000 m (2d race)—Van Helden	1:19.93

WOMEN

Champion—Sheila Young, Detroit	173.95 pts
500 m (1st race)—Sheila Young	0:42.87
500 m (2d race)—Sheila Young	0:42.60
1,000 m (1st race)—Sheila Young	1:28.56
1,000 m (2d race)—Sheila Young	1:28.40

United States Championships
National Outdoor
(St. Paul, Jan. 31–Feb. 1)

Champion—John Wurster, Ballston Spa, N.Y.	21 pts
300 m—Jim Gulczynski, West Allis, Wis.	0:25.35
500 m—Gulczynski	0:39.76
800 m—John Wurster	1:20.88
1,000 m—Rich Wurster, Milwaukee	1:32.54
1,500 m—Mike Passarella, Chicago	2:31.03
3,000 m—John Wurster	6:21.83
5,000 m—John Wurster	9:04.72

WOMEN

Champion—Connie Carpenter, Madison, Wis.	21 pts
300 m—Celeste Chlapaty, Skokie, Ill.	0:29.97
500 m—Celeste Chlapaty	0:45.23
800 m—Connie Carpenter	1:19.12
1,000 m—Connie Carpenter	1:43.05
1,500 m—Connie Carpenter	2:27.30

National Indoor
(Lakewood, Ohio, March 13–14)

Champion—Alan Rattray, Los Angeles	16 pts
Women's champions—tie between Celeste Chlapaty, Skokie, Ill., and Peggy Hartrick, St. Louis	13 pts

BICYCLE RACING
World Championships
(Monteroni and Ostuni, Italy, Sept. 4–10)

Men's pro (178.9 miles)—Freddy Maertens, Belgium
Women's sprint—Sheila Young Ochowicz, Detroit
Women's road (38½ miles)—Kornelia Van Oosten-Hage, Netherlands
Men's pro pursuit—Francesco Moser, Italy
Men's pro sprint—John Nicholson, Australia

Other Foreign

Tour de France—Lucien Van Impe, Belgium (2,500 miles in riding time of 4 days, 20 hours, 22 minutes, 23 seconds)

National Championships
UNITED STATES CYCLING FEDERATION
Track Racing
(Northbrook, Ill., Aug. 4–7)

Sprint—Leigh Barszewski, West Allis, Wis.	
Women's sprint—Connie Carpenter, Madison, Wis.	
Kilometer—Bob Vehe, Mount Prospect, Ill.	1:09.83
10 mile—Ron Skarin, Van Nuys, Calif.	20:15.15
4,000-m pursuit—Leonard Nitz, Sacramento, Calif.	5:09.40
3,000-m women's pursuit—Connie Carpenter	4:23.05
Team pursuit—Southern California (Ron Skarin, Steve Lutz, Paul Deem, Paul Murray)	4:45.48
Junior—Chris Springer, San Jose, Calif.	17 pts
Junior women—Jane Brennan, Detroit	17 pts

Team Trials
(Carrollton, Ky., Aug. 11–12)

Men—John Howard, Houston, Tex.	55:36.6
Women—Lyn Lemaire, Wellesley, Mass.	1:00:06.7
Veterans—Nikola Farac-Ban, San Francisco	58:40.2
Junior—Andy Weaver, Florida	57:09.9

Road Racing
(Louisville, Ky., Aug. 14–15)

Men (114 miles)—Wayne Stetina, Indianapolis	4:35:52.22
Women (37 miles)—Connie Carpenter, Madison, Wis.	1:36:03
Veterans (41 miles)—Jim Meyers, Costa Mesa, Calif.	1:43.9
Junior (49 miles)—Larry Shields, Santa Barbara, Calif.	
Junior women (29 miles)—Francesca Saveri, San Francisco.	

VOLLEYBALL
United States Volleyball Association Champions

Men's open—Maccabi Union, Los Angeles
Women's open—Pasadena, Texas Volleyball Club
Senior—Olyrollers, Long Beach, Calif.
Collegiate—Penn State

Collegiate

N.C.A.A.—University of California, Los Angeles
N.A.I.A.—Graceland College
Junior College—Kellogg, Battle Creek, Mich.
A.I.A.W.—University of California, Los Angeles
A.I.A.W. small school—Texas Lutheran
A.I.A.W. junior college—Mesa (Ariz.) Community

Other Champions

A.A.U. men—Outrigger Canoe Club, Honolulu
A.A.U. women—Nick's Fish Market, Santa Monica, Calif.-Honolulu
Y.M.C.A. men—Columbus, Ohio Y
Y.M.C.A. women—Stonestown, San Francisco Y
Armed Forces—Air Force

ROWING

College

Intercollegiate Rowing Assn.

(Lake Onondaga, Syracuse, N.Y., June 3–5)

Eights—California, 6 minutes, 31 seconds; 2, Princeton, 6:34.5; 3, Wisconsin, 6:34.9; 4, Pennsylvania, 6:36.8; 5, Massachusetts Institute of Technology, 6:38.1; 6, Syracuse, 6:39.9.

Second varsity eights—Pennsylvania 6:31.4
Freshmen eights—Syracuse 6:13.4
Pairs with coxswains—Navy 8:08.6
Pairs without coxswains—Rutgers 7:41.5
Fours with coxswains—Navy 7:30.2
Fours without coxswains—Wisconsin 6:48
Freshmen fours—Boston Univ. 7:11.5
Team (Jim Ten Eyck Trophy)—Pennsylvania . . . . 259.8 pts

Other Regattas

Dad Vail Trophy (Philadelphia, May 7–8)—Varsity eights and trophy: Coast Guard Academy, 6:09.3; junior varsity (Bayer Trophy): Marietta, 6:21.4; Freshmen: Marietta, 6:19.7; women (Evelyn Bergman Trophy): Ithaca, 7:23.4. Lightweights: varsity eights: Coast Guard Academy, 6:21.5; junior varsity: Ithaca, 6:24.5; freshmen: Trinity (Hartford, Conn.), 6:37.4

Eastern Sprints (Lake Carnegie, Princeton, N.J., May 14–15)— Heavyweights: varsity: Harvard, 6:07.4; second varsity: Pennsylvania, 6:23.1; freshmen: Harvard, 6:20.7. Lightweights: varsity: Pennsylvania, 6:25.5; second varsity: Harvard, 6:39.1; freshmen: Yale, 6:43.3. Team—Rowe Cup (heavyweights): Harvard, 36 points; Jope Cup (lightweights): Harvard, 33 pts

Grimaldi Cup (New York, April 3)—Fordham 7:06.8

Hughes Cup (New York, April 10)—New York A.C. 16:57.8

Midwest championships (Madison, Wis., May 1)—Varsity: Wisconsin; junior varsity: Wisconsin; women's varsity: Wisconsin; women's lightweight: Purdue; singles: Neil Helein, Wisconsin.

Sulger Trophy (New York Met. championships, May 1)—Eights: New York State Maritime College: 7:46; junior varsity: Fordham 8:03.8; freshmen: New York Merchant Marine Academy 7:08; singles: Larry Kletcatsky, N.Y.A.C. 7:20.8. Team (Sulger Trophy): N.Y. State Maritime College (83 pts).

Western Sprints (Orinda, Calif., May 15)—varsity: Washington 6:03.2; junior varsity: California 6:02; freshmen: Washington 6:09.2; women: U.C.L.A. 3:15.5; lightweight varsity: Washington 6:36.3; lightweight women: Washington 3:54.2.

Dual Regattas

Harvard-Yale (Thames River, New London, Conn., 4 miles, May 22)—Harvard by 16 lengths in 23:43.9.

Oxford-Cambridge (Thames, London, 4½ miles, March 20)—Oxford by 6 lengths in record 16:58.

Washington-California (Oakland, Calif., 2,000 meters, April 24)— Washington by four-tenths of a second.

Women's Eastern Sprints (Lake Quinsigamond, Worcester, Mass.)— varsity: Wisconsin 5:39.2; lightweight varsity: Boston University: 6:11.8.

Henley Regatta

(Henley-on-Thames, England, June 28–July 4)

Diamond Sculls—E. O. Hale, Australia
Silver Goblets (pairs)—I. A. Luxford-C. D. Shinners, Australia
Stewards Cup (fours)—British Columbia University
Wyfold Cup (fours)—London R.C.
Visitors Cup (fours)—London University
Prince Philip Cup (fours with coxswains)—Thames Tradesmen
Thames Cup (eights)—Harvard
Ladies Plate (eights)—Trinity College, Hartford, Conn.
Princess Elizabeth Cup (schoolboy eights)—Holy Spirit High School, Absecon, N.J.
Grand Challenge Cup (eights)—Thames Tradesmen

United States Championships

(Philadelphia, Aug. 21–22)

Elite Division

Single sculls—Sean Drea, Ireland
Quarter-mile singles—Jim Dietz, New York A.C.
Double sculls—Dietz-Dr. Larry Klecatsky, New York A.C.
Pairs with coxswains—John Matthews-Mark Norelius-Ken Dreyfuss, coxswain, Vesper B.C., Philadelphia
Lightweight pairs—John Sonberg-Joe Caminiti, New York A.C.
Fours—Vesper B.C.
Lightweight Fours—New York A.C.
Quadruple sculls—New York A.C.
Eights—Vesper B.C.

CANOE RACING

Source: Marcia Smoke, Buchanan, Mich.

United States Championships

(Lake Sebago, N.Y., Aug. 12–15)

Kayak

500 m—Steve Kelly, Bronx, N.Y. 1:50
1,000 m—Kelly 3:44.99
10,000 m—Brent Turner, St. Charles, Ill. 46:00
500-m tandem—Kelly-Turner 1:42.01
1,000-m tandem—Kelly-Turner 3:27.06
10,000-m tandem—Bruce and Greg Barton, Horton, Mich. 42:04
1,000-m fours—Kelly-Turner-Bruce Barton-Pete Deyo, Niles, Mich. 3:12:11
10,000-m fours—Kelly-Turner-Paul Lowenwirth, Yonkers, N.Y.-Don Endrizzi, Brooklyn, N.Y. . . . . no time

WOMEN

500 m—Ann Turner, St. Charles, Ill. 2:05.73
5,000 m—Ann Turner 23:01
500-m tandem—Ann Turner-Linda Dragan, Oxon Hill, Md. 1:54.58
5,000-m tandem—Linda Dragan-Jackie Scribner, Alexandria, Va. 21:07
500-m fours—Marcia Smoke, Buchanan, Mich.-Julie Gannatal, Ventura, Calif.-Lynn Rapant, Schenectady, N.Y.-Ilana Effinger, Bronx, N.Y. 1:47.39
5,000-m fours—Linda Dragan-Jackie Scribner-Teresa Dimarino, Washington-Nancy Leahy, Baltimore . . 19:54.94

Canadian (Canoe)

500 m—Andy Weigand, Arlington, Va. 2:03.10
1,000 m—Andy Weigand 4:10.31
10,000 m—Andy Weigand 52:13.61
500-m tandem—Weigand-Roland Muhlen, Cincinnati . 1:54.83
1,000-m tandem—Weigand-Muhlen 3:53.25
10,000-m tandem—Weigand-Muhlen . . . . .No time
1,000-m fours—John, Robert and Richard Diebold, Glen Ellyn, Ill.-Muhlen 3:53.03

POLO

National Championships

Open—Willow Bend, Dallas (William S. Farish 3d, Charles Smith, Roy Berry Jr., Norman Brinker) defeated Tulsa, 10-5, in final
America Cup (16 goal)—Boca Raton, Fla.
Continental Cup (14 goal)—Jay Farm, Milwaukee
Gold Cup (18-22 goal)—Willow Bend, Dallas
Butler Handicap—Tulsa
Copper Cup (10 goal)—Village Farm

TRACK AND FIELD
National A.A.U. Championships

Indoor

(Madison Square Garden, New York, Feb. 27)

60 yds—Steve Williams, Florida T.C., Gainesville	0:06
60-yd hurdles—Guy Drut, France	0:07
600 yds—Fred Sowerby DC Striders, Washington	1:09.8
1,000 yds—Rick Wohlhuter, U. of Chicago T.C.	2:09.3
Mile—Filbert Bayi, Tanzania	3:56.1
3 miles—Suleiman Nyambui, Tanzania	13:15
2-mile walk—Ron Laird, New York A.C.	13:37
1,180-yd sprint medley relay—Maccabi Union T.C., Glendale, Calif. (Maxie Parks, James King, Mike Singletary, Benny Brown)	2:03.2
Mile relay—Philadelphia Pioneer Club (Alfred Daley, Bruce Collins, Robert Taylor, Charles Joseph)	3:16.2
2-mile relay—U. of Chicago T.C. (Tom Bach, Tom Bryan, Ken Sparks, Lowell Paul)	7:31.8
High jump—Robert Forget, Canada	7 ft 3 in.
Long jump—Larry Myricks, Mississippi College	26 ft ½ in.
Triple jump—Tommy Haynes, U.S. Army	55 ft 5½ in. A
Pole vault—Roland Carter, Gulf Coast T.C., Houston	18 ft ½ in.
Shotput—Terry Albritton, U. of Hawaii	65 ft 6 in.
35-lb weight—Larry Hart, New York A.C.	67 ft 9½ in.
Team—New York A.C.	17 pts

(Philadelphia Pioneer Club also had 17 points, but New York A.C. was awarded title for more first-place finishes.)

A—American record.

WOMEN

60 yds—Lisa Hopkins, Chicago Murcherettes	0:06.7
60-yd hurdles—Debra LaPlante, Belleville, Miss.	0:07.7
220 yds—Pamela Jiles, New Orleans Superdames	0:24
440 yds—Lorna Forde, Atoms T.C., Brooklyn, N.Y.	0:54.6
880 yds—Johanna Forman, Falmouth T.C.	2:07.9
Mile—Jan Merrill, Age Group A.A., Waterford, Conn.	4:38.5
2-mile run—Jan Merrill	9:59.6
Mile walk—Susan Brodcock Rialto (Calif.) Road Runners	7:12.7
640-yd relay—Atoms T.C., Brooklyn (Michele McMillan, Pat Collins El, Linda Cordy, Carmen Brown)	1:09.7
880-yd medley relay—Atoms T.C. (Cheryl Toussaint, Pat Collins El, Linda Cordy, Lorna Forde	1:46.2
Mile relay—Atoms T.C. (Robin Blaines, Cheryl Toussaint, Karol Jones, Michele McMillan)	3:50.6
High jump—Julie White, Canada	6 ft 1 in.
Long jump—Martha Watson, Lakewood (Calif.) Inter	20 ft 9½ in.
Shotput—Ann Turbyne, Waterville, Me.	51 ft 5¼ in.
Team—Atoms T.C., Brooklyn, N.Y.	23 pts

Outdoor

100 m—Chris Garpenborg, Maccabi T.C., Los Angeles	0:10.41
100 m—Millard Hampton, San Jose C.C.	0:20.89
400 m—Maxie Parks, Maccabi T.C.	0:44.82
800 m—James Robinson, California	1:46.6
1,500 m—Eamonn Coghlan, Villanova	3:42.4
3,000-m steeplechase—Randy Smith, Striders	8:26.8
5,000 m—Dick Buerkle, New York A.C.	13:31.2
10,000 m—Ed Leddy, Knoxville T.C.	28:46
110-m hurdles—Thomas Hill, U.S. Army	0:13.64
400-m hurdles—Tom Andrews, So. California	0:48.55
5,000-m walk—Ron Laird, New York A.C.	21:09
Pole vault—Earl Bell, Arkansas State	17 ft 10¼ in.
High jump—Dwight Stones, Long Beach State	7 ft 4¼ in.
Long jump—Arnie Robinson, Maccabi T.C.	27 ft 3½ in.
Triple jump—Tommy Haynes, U.S. Army	55 ft 9¾ in.
Hammer—Larry Hart, New York A.C.	225 ft 10 in.
Javelin—Fred Luke, Club Northwest, Seattle	280 ft 8 in.
Discus—Mac Wilkins, Pacific Coast Club, Long Beach	230 ft
Shotput—Terry Albritton, Hawaii Univ.	69 ft 4¾ in.

Women

100 m—Chandra Cheeseborough, Tennessee State	0:11.34
200 m—Brenda Morehead, Tennessee State	0:22.94
400 m—Lorna Forde, Atoms T.C., Brooklyn, N.Y.	0:52.30
800 m—Madeline Jackson, Cleveland T.C.	2:01
1,500 m—Francie Larrieu, Pacific Coast Club	4:09.9
3,000 m—Jan Merrill, Age Group A.A., Waterford, Conn.	8:57.2 A
5,000-m walk—Sue Brodock, Rialto (Calif.) R.R.	25:28.8
100-m hurdles—Jane Frederick, Los Angeles T.C.	0:13.29
400-m hurdles—Arthurine Gainer, Prairie View	0:57.24 A
440-yd relay—Tennessee State	0:44.99
880-yd medley relay—Los Angeles Mercurettes	1:38.7
Mile relay—Prairie View A&M	3:33.9 A
2-mile relay—Los Angeles T.C.	8:34.4 A
Javelin—Kathy Schmidt, Los Angeles T.C.	218 ft 3 in. A
Shotput—Maren Seidler, Mayor Daley Y.F., Chicago	54 ft 4 in.
Discus—Lynne Winbigler, Oregon T.C., Eugene	174 ft 1 in.
Long jump—Kathy McMillan, Raeford, N.C.	22 ft 3 in. A
High jump—Joni Huntley, Oregon T.C.	6 ft 2 in.

A—Betters listed American record.

United States Track and Field Federation Championships
Outdoor

(Wichita, Kan., May 28–29)

100 m—Larry Jackson, Kansas	0:10.10
200 m—Ed Preston, Arkansas State	0:20.2
400 m—Mark Collins, Baylor	0:46.59
800 m—Gerald Masterson, Ouchita Baptist	1:47.8
1,500 m—Jeff Jirele, Illinois	3:40.7
Mile—Rick Wohlhuter, U. of Chicago T.C.	3:56.8
5,000 m—Frank Shorter, Florida T.C.	13:42.2
10,000 m—Rick Rojas, unattached	29:31.6
3,000-m steeplechase—Don Timm, Athletes in Action	8:36.44
110-m hurdles—Vance Rowland, unattached	0:13.57
400-m hurdles—Jim Bolding, Pacific Coast Club	0:49.22
440-yd relay—Texas Christian U.	0:39.76
Mile Relay—Pacific Coast Club, Long Beach	3:05.2
Discus—Mac Wilkins, Pacific Coast Club	218 ft 7½ in.
Pole Vault—Earl Bell, Arkansas State	18 ft 7¼ in. W
Hammer—Andy Bessette, Backus T.C.	206 ft
Javelin—Sam Colson, Columbia, S.C.	257 ft 10½ in.
Shotput—George Woods, Pacific Coast Club	70 ft 3 in.
High jump—Dwight Stones, Long Beach State	7 ft 3 in.
Long jump—Dan Seay, Pacific Coast Club	26 ft 4¼ in.
Triple jump—John Craft, U. of Chicago T.C.	54 ft 2½ in.
Team—Pacific Coast Club, Long Beach, Calif.	84 pts

Women

100 m—Lori Green, Topeka A.C.	0:11.57
200 m—Beverly Day, Prairie View	0:24.05
400 m—Shirley Williams, Prairie View	0:52.16
800 m—Francie Larrieu, Pacific Coast Club	2:07.43
1,500 m—Francie Larrieu	4:16.86
3,000 m—Cindy Bremser, Wisconsin T.C.	9:27.47
100-m hurdles—Deby LaPlante, Ann Arbor, Mich.	0:13.2
400-m hurdles—Debbie Esser, Iowa State	0:57.94
440-yd relay—Prairie View A & M	0:44.99
Mile relay—Prairie View	3:36.7
Shotput—Kathy Devine, Emporia State	50 ft 5¼ in.
Long jump—Shelia Pettit, Prairie State	19 ft 11½ in.
High jump—Audrey Reid, Texas Women's U.T.C.	6 ft
Discus—Linda Montgomery, Texas Women's T.C.	156 ft 7 in.
Javelin—Susie Norton, Kansas State	133 ft 11¼ in.
Team—Prairie View A&M	80 pts

W—Betters listed World record.

Track and Field Championships (Continued)

National Collegiate A.A.
Indoor
(Cobo Hall, Detroit, March 12–13)

60 yds—Harvey Glance, Auburn	0:06.21
60-yd hurdles—Allen Misher, Louisiana State	0:07.29
440 yds—Evis Jennings, Mississippi State	0:48.42
600 yds—Charles Dramiga, New Mexico	1:10.58
880 yds—Bob Prince, Kansas State	1:53.03
1,000 yds—Mark Belger, Villanova	2:07.29
Mile—Eamonn Coghlan, Villanova	4:01.48
2 miles—Nick Rose, Western Kentucky	8:30.91
3 miles—John Ngeno, Washington State	13:20.34
Mile relay—Tennessee (Lamar Preyor, Mike Barlow, Ron Harris, Jerome Morgan)	3:16.03
2-mile relay—Wisconsin (Mark Randall, Steve Lacy, Mark Sang, Dick Moss)	7:26.79
Distance medley relay—Texas, El Paso (Joseph Gichongeri, Paul Njoroge, Joseph Munyala, Wilson Waigwa)	9:43.16
Long jump—Charlton Ehizuelen, Illinois	25 ft
Triple jump—Arnold Grimes, Texas, El Paso	53 ft 5½ in.
High jump—Dwight Stones, Long Beach State	7 ft 3 in.
Pole vault—Earl Bell, Arkansas State	18 ft ¼ in.
Shotput—Terry Albritton, Hawaii	67 ft 6½ in.
35-lb weight—Emmitt Berry, Texas, El Paso	65 ft 8 in.
Team—Texas at El Paso	23 pts

Outdoor
(Philadelphia, June 3–5)

100 m—Harvey Glance, Auburn	0:10.16
200 m—Glance	0:20.74
400 m—Ken Randle, So. California	0:45.2
800 m—Tom McLean, Bucknell	1:47.36
1,500 m—Eamonn Coghlan, Villanova	3:37.1
5,000 m—Josh Kimeta, Washington State	13:47.87
10,000 m—John Ngeno, Washington State	28:22.66
3,000-m steeplechase—James Munyala, Texas-El Paso	8:24.86
110-m hurdles—Dedy Cooper, San Jose State	0:13.89
400-m hurdles—Quentin Wheeler, San Diego State	0:48.55
400-m relay—Tennessee (Jon Young, Ricci Gardner, Jerome Morgan, Reggie Jones)	0:39.16
1,600-m relay—Arizona State (Clifton McKenzie, Richard Walker, Carl McCullough, Herman Frazier)	3:03.49
High jump—Dwight Stones, Long Beach State	7 ft 7 in. W
Triple jump—Phil Robins, So. Illinois	54 ft 8¼ in.
Long jump—Larry Myricks, Miss. College	26 ft 1½ in.
Hammer—Scott Neilson, Washington	216 ft 8 in.
Shotput—Dana Leduc, Texas	65 ft 5½ in.
Javelin—Phil Olsen, Tennessee	273 ft 2 in.
Discus—Borys Chambul, Washington	202 ft 3 in.
Pole Vault—Earl Bell, Arkansas State	18 ft 1¼ in.
Team—University of Southern California	64 pts

W—World Record.

Association of Intercollegiate Athletics for Women (AIAW)
(Manhattan, Kan., May 14–15)

100 m—Rosalyn Bryant, Cal State-Los Angeles	0:11.53
200 m—Rosalyn Bryant	0:23.70
400 m—Shirley Williams, Prairie View	0:53.21
800 m—Wendy Knudson, Colorado State	2:01.54
1,500 m—Wendy Knudson	4:24.09
2 miles—Peg Neppel, Iowa State	10:22.53
3 miles—Peg Neppel	15:41.69 W
100-m hurdles—Carol Thomas, Delaware	0:13.88
400-m hurdles—Debbie Esser, Iowa State	0:59.29
440-yd relay—Prairie View	0:46.09
Mile relay—Prairie View (Arthurene Gainer, Beverly Day, Shirley Williams, Mary Ayers)	3:50.77

2-mile relay—Kansas State (Jane Wittmyer, Teri Anderson, Renee Urish, Joyce Urish)	9:17.85
Javelin—Karin Smith, U.C.L.A.	161 ft 6 in.
Shotput—Kathy Devine, Emporia State	53 ft 1 in.
Discus—Lorna Griffin, Flathead Valley	154 ft 7¾ in.
Long jump—Sharon Walker, Seattle Pacific	19 ft 10½ in.
High jump—Audrey Reid, Texas Women's U.	5 ft 10 in.
Pentathlon—Heidi Hertz, Florida	3,805 pts
Team—Prairie View College	60 pts

W—betters listed world record.

Marathons

Boston (1,898 starters, April 19)—Jack Fultz, Arlington, Va.	2:20:19
First woman to finish—Kim Merritt, Kenosha, Wis.	2:47:10
U.S.T.F.F. (Drake Relays)—Greg Carlberg, Omaha	2:22:25
N.A.I.A.—Dave Elgre, Wisconsin-Stevens Point	2:28:07
Penn Relays—Marty Sudzina	2:28:19

Decathlons

U.S.T.F.F. (Drake Relays)—Bruce Jenner, San Jose, Calif.	8,250
I.C.4-A.—Al Hamlin, Maryland	7,204
N.A.I.A.—Bruce Kupersmith, Pacific Univ.	7,179
Penn Relays—Fred Samara, New York A.C.	7,669
U.S.T.F.F. (meet)—Jeff Bennett	7,766

Pentathlons

A.A.U. Women—Jane Frederick, Los Angeles, T.C.	4,676
A.A.U. Men—Mike Conti, Florida T.C.	2,988

TRAPSHOOTING
Grand American Tournament
(Vandalia, Ohio, Aug. 14–21)
Grand American Handicap

Men—Frank Crevatin, Tecumseh, Ontario (22½ yds.)	*99

Crevatin defeated Frank Little, Mechanicsburg, Pa. (27 yds.) and Merle Yohn, Sykesville, Md., (21½ yds.) in 25-target shoot-off. Crevatin hit 23, Little 21, Yohn 16.

Women—Judith Whittenberger, Fort Wayne, Ind. (18½ yds.)	97
Veterans—Ronald Cornwell, Washington Court House, Ohio (23 yds.)	97
Senior—Kenneth Kummer, Columbus, Ohio (19 yds.)	97
Subjunior—Robert Mathisen, Duluth, Minn. (22 yds.)	95
Industry—Arthur Wheaton, Edina, Minn. (24 yds.)	95

Doubles

Men—Larry McKinley, Rich Hill, Mo.	99
Women—Nyla Johnson, Chattaroy, Wash.	95
Junior—Eugene Leoni, Ambler, Pa.	97

* Won shootoff.

DOG SHOWS
(Best in Show)

WESTMINSTER (New York, Feb. 9–10)—Ch. Jo-Ni's Red Baron of Crofton, Lakeland terrier, owned by Virginia Dickson, La Habra, Calif. (3,098 dogs).

INTERNATIONAL (Chicago, 27–28)—Ch. Marinebull's All the Way, bulldog, owned by Karl and Joyce Dingman, Richfield, Minn. (3,206 dogs).

SANTA BARBARA, Calif. (July 25)—Ch. Dersade Bobby's Girl, Sealyham terrier, owned by Mrs. Dorothy Wimer, Churchtown, Pa. (3,995 dogs).

ARCHERY
World Championships
(Mondal, Sweden, Sept. 4–5)
Field Archery

Freestyle—Tommy Persson, Sweden 1,053
Women's freestyle—Anne-Marie Lehmann, West Germany . 914
Barbow—Jukka Virtanen, Finland 877
Women's Barebow—Shirley Sandiford, Britain 661

National Field Archery Association Championships
(Aurora, Ill., July 21–25)
Freestyle

Open—Kenneth Cranbeeg, Dallas City, Ill. 2,796
Open, limited—Terry Frazier, Houston, Tex. 2,769
Amateur—Barry Velarde, Fort Knox, Ky. 2,800
(Won shootoff from Phillip Schmidt, Tacoma, Wash., who also scored perfect 2,800)
Amateur, limited—Edwin Eliason, Seattle 2,751
Young adult—Donnie Turner, Houston, Tex. 2,760
Young adult, limited—Michael Andrews, Milwaukee . . .2,693
Professional—Ronald Lauhon, Huntington, W. Va. 2,783
Professional, limited—Jerry Podratz, Shakopee, N.M. . .2,721

Women's Freestyle

Open—Janet Boatman, Alden, N.Y. 2,767
Open, limited—Millie Foster, Kansas City, Mo. 2,609
Amateur—Michelle Sanderson, Hastings, Minn. 2,756
Amateur, limited—Valerie Gramzow, Creswell, Ore. . . .2,606
Young adult—Nancy Jacobs, Arlington Heights, Ill. 2,720
Young adult, limited—Tammy Wells, Bettendorf, Iowa . .2,039
Professional—Liz Colombo, Los Angeles 2,758

Bowhunter

Open—Hugh McConnell, Hiltons, Va. 2,600
Amateur—John Saporiti, Rockford, Ill. 2,251
Women—June Hardy, Houston, Tex. 1,820
Professional—Gilbert Smith, Pasadena, Calif. 2,426

Barebow

Open—David Hughes, Irving, Tex. 2,744
Amateur—Donald Morehead, Wheaton, Ill. 2,573
Young adult—Jim Moschetz, Milwaukee 2,537
Women's open—Frozine Greene, Liberal, Kan. 2,382
Women's amateur—Patricia Kramer, Fort Lauderdale, Fla. .2,320
Women's young adult—Mary Jane Jones, O'Fallon, Mo. . .1,460

National Archery Association
Target
(Valley Forge, Pa., Aug. 4–7)

Amateur—Darrell Pace, Cincinnati 2,576
Professional—John Williams, Rialto, Calif. 2,454
Crossbow—George Hall, Somerville, N.J. 3,089
Intermediate—Timothy Weaver, York, Pa. 2,315

WOMEN

Amateur—Luann Ryon, Riverside, Calif. 2,497
Professional—Marion Rhodes, Phoenix, Ariz. 2,260
Crossbow—Carol Pelosi, Greenbelt, Md. 2,890
Intermediate—Patti Iske, Phoenix, Ariz. 2,307

Field
(Oxford, Ohio, June 26–27)

Freestyle—Darrell Pace, Cincinnati 1,100
Barebow—Franklin Ditzler, Lebanon, Pa. 892
Intermediate—Glenn Meyers, Fremont, Miss. 907

WOMEN

Freestyle—Luann Ryon, Riverside, Calif. 1,020
Barebow—Eunice Anderson, Tijeras, N.M. 664
Intermediate—Cathy Meyers, Fremont, Miss. 672

WATER SKIING
National Championships
(Miami, Fla., Aug. 18–22)

Open overall—Chris Redmond, Canton, Ohio . . . .2,652 pts
Open slalom—Bob LaPoint, Castro Valley, Calif. . . .56½ buoys
Open tricks—Tony Krupa, Jackson, Mich. . . . . .5,710 pts
Open jumping—Bob LaPoint . . . . 171 ft

Women

Open overall—Cindy Todd, Pierson, Fla. . . . . . .2,876 pts
Open slalom—Cindy Todd . . . . .56 buoys
Open tricks—Cindy Todd . . . . .4,060 pts
Open jumping—Linda Giddens, Eastman, Ga. . . . . 129 ft

Senior Men

Overall—Dr. J. D. Morgan, Norfolk, Va. . . . . . .3,578 pts
Slalom—Morgan . . . . .49 buoys
Tricks—Jerry Hosner, Fenton, Mich. . . . . 190 pts
Jumping—Morgan . . . . 132 ft

Senior Women

Overall—Thelma Salmas, Canyon Lake, Calif. . . . .3,455 pts
Slalom—Barbara Cleveland, Hawthorne, Fla. . . . .51½ buoys
Tricks—Artis Price, Libertyville, Ill. . . . . . . .3,030 pts
Jumping—Barbara Cleveland . . . . 101 ft

Other Champions

Men Division I—Frankie Dees, Lakeland, Fla. . . . .2,320 pts
Men Division II—Paul Merrill, Winter Haven, Fla. . .2,933 pts
Women—Lisa Nock, Englewood, Colo. 2,606
Boys—Sammy Duvall, Greenville, S.C. . . . . . .3,044 pts
Girls—Camille Duvall, Greenville, S.C. . . . . . .3,470 pts

SKEET SHOOTING
National Skeet Shooting Association
(San Antonio, Tex., July 25–30)
All-Around Champions

Men—Charles Parks, Alliance, Ohio 550
(Parks' perfect score of 550x550 set world record)
Women—Valerie Johnson, San Antonio, Tex. 539
Junior—Alan Clark, Delmar, Calif. 540
Junior women—Kathryn Drennan, Ada, Okla. 515
Collegiate—Tito Killian, Trinity (Texas) 547
Senior—Tom Hanzel, San Antonio, Tex. 534
Sub-senior—Decatur Holcombe, Houston, Tex. 543
Veteran—Tom Sanfilipo, Fairfield, Calif. 532
Industry—Jimmy Prall, Tulsa, Okla. 547
Military—Al Mullins, Marines 544

Individual Gun

28 Gauge—Ricky Pope, San Antonio, Tex. *100
Women's 28 gauge—Cathy Kaufman, San Antonio . . . 99
20 Gauge—Tito Killian, San Antonio *100
Women's 20 gauge—Cathy Kaufman *100
12 gauge—Martin Wood, Dallas, Tex. *250
Women's 12 gauge—Karla Roberts, Bridgeton, Mo. . . *248
.410 gauge—Charles Parks, Alliance, Ohio *100
Women's .410—Ila Hill, Troy, Mich. *96

* Won shootoff

SPORTS PARACHUTING
National Championships

Overall—Jack Brake, U.S. Army, Fort Bragg, N.C.
Accuracy—Frank Paynter, Warrenton, Va.
Style—Jack Brake
10-man team—Captain Hook and His Sky Pirates, Elsinore, Calif.
WOMEN
Overall—Cheryl Stearns, Scottsdale, Ariz.
Accuracy—Debbie Schmidt, Joliet, Ill.
Style—Marie Ledbetter, Mesa, Ariz.
4-member team—Rainbow Flyers, Flint, Mich.

BOXING
CHAMPIONSHIP BOUTS

Mini-Flyweight
(108-pound limit)

Luis (Lumumbo) Estaba, of Venezuela, outpointed Juan Alvarez, of Mexico, at Caracas, May 2, and retained World Boxing Council title. It was his third defense.

Estaba defeated Rodolfo Rodriguez, Argentina, at Caracas, Sept. 25, and retained title.

Yoko Gushiken, Japan, knocked out Juan Guzman, Dominican Republic, in 7th round at Kofu, Japan, Oct. 10 and won World Boxing Association title.

Flyweight
(112-pound limit)

Alfonso Lopez, Panama, knocked out Erbito Salavarria, Philippines, at 33 seconds of 15th round and won World Boxing Association title at Manila, Feb. 27. Lopez weighed 111¼ and Salavarria 110, in second defense of title won in April 1974.

Lopez outpointed Shoji Oguma, Japan, at Tokyo, April 21, and remained unbeaten in 24 bouts.

Miguel Canto, Mexico, outpointed Susumo Hanagata, Japan, in his fourth defense of World Boxing Council championship at Merida, Mexico, May 15.

Guty Espadas, Mexico, stopped Lopez in 13th round and won W.B.A. title at Los Angeles, Oct. 2. Lopez, who was undefeated in 25 fights, was leading in points but Espadas knocked him down twice in the 12th round and three times in the 13th before referee stopped bout. Lopez weighed 109 and Espadas 109½.

Bantamweight
(118-pound limit)

Rodolfo Martinez, Mexico, won split decision from Venice Borkorsor, of Thailand, at Bangkok, Jan. 30, and retained World Boxing Council crown. Martinez was knocked down in second round. It was his third defense since taking title in December 1974.

Alfonso Zamora, Mexico, knocked out Eusebio Pedroza, Panama, at 1:03 of second round at Mexicali, Mexico, April 4, and retained World Boxing Association championship.

Carlos Zarate, Mexico City, knocked out Martinez at 1:51 of ninth round at Inglewood, Calif., May 8, and won W.B.C. title. Zarate weighed 116¼, Martinez 115½.

Zamora knocked out Gilberto Illueca, of Panama, in third round at Juarez, Mexico, July 10. It was his 27th knockout in 27 pro fights.

Zarate stopped Paul Ferreri, Australia, in 12th round and kept W.B.C. title at Inglewood, Calif., Aug. 28. Referee stopped fight at 2:44 of round because of bad cut over Ferreri's left eye.

Zamora, 117¾, stopped Hong Soo-Hwan, Korea, in 12th round at Inchon, Korea, Oct. 16 and retained W.B.A. title.

Junior Featherweight
(122 pound limit)

Rigoberto Riasco, Panama, stopped Waruinge Nakayama, Japan, in 8th round and won newly created World Boxing Council title at Tokyo.

Royal Kobayshi, Japan, knocked out Riasco, Oct. 9 at Tokyo and took W.B.C. crown.

Featherweight
(125-pound limit)

David (Poison) Kotey, Ghana, retained World Boxing Council title by stopping Harigu Uehara, Japan, in 12th round at Accra, Ghana, March 6.

Kotey knocked out Shige Fukuyama, Japan, at 21 seconds of third round at Tokyo, July 16.

Junior Lightweight
(130-pound limit)

Ben Villaflor, Philippines, knocked out Morito Kashiwaba, Japan, in 13th round at Tokyo, Jan. 12, and retained World Boxing Association title. It was his fourth defense of crown won in 1973. Referee stopped bout at 1:29 of round.

Alfredo Escalera, Puerto Rico, retained World Boxing Council championship by stopping Jose Fernandez, Dominican Republic, in 13th round at San Juan, P.R., Feb. 20. Referee stopped bout at 1:47 of round because of bad cut under Fernandez' left eye.

Bout between Escalera and Buzzsaw Yamabe, Japan, in Nara, Japan, April 1, was ruled no contest by Japanese boxing officials. Referee stopped fight in sixth round to save Yamabe from further punishment and near riot ensued.

Escalera won decision over Yamabe at Nara, July 1.

Villaflor fought to draw with Samuel Serrano, Puerto Rico, at Honolulu. Referee called fight even and one judge voted for each fighter.

Escalera stopped Ray Lunny 3d, Palo Alto, Calif., at San Juan, Puerto Rico, Sept. 19. Lunny did not come out for 13th round. It was Escalera's sixth defense of title.

Serrano outpointed Villaflor in rematch at San Juan, Puerto Rico, Oct. 16, and took W.B.A. title.

Lightweight
(135-pound limit)

Esteban de Jesus, Puerto Rico, won unanimous decision over Guts Ishimatsu, Japan, and took World Boxing Council title, May 8, at Bayamon, P.R. Each weighed 135 pounds.

Roberto Duran, Panama, knocked out Lou Dizzarro, Erie, Pa., in 14th round at Erie, Pa., May 23, in 8th defense of World Boxing Association title. His 44th knockout victory came at 2:59 of round. Duran weighed 133¼, Bizzaro 134. Duran won $125,000.

Duran knocked out Alvaro Rojas in first round at Hollywood, Fla., Oct. 15.

Junior Welterweight
(140-pound limit)

Saensak Muangsurin, Thailand, retained World Boxing Council title on unanimous decision over Tetsuc (Lion) Furuyama of Japan in Tokyo, Jan. 25. Champion weighed 139½ in his first title defense of title won in July 1975. Furuyama weighed 140.

Wilfredo Benitez, Puerto Rico, won split decision over Antonio (Kid Pambelo) Cervantes and took World Boxing Association title at San Juan, P.R., March 6. Benitez at 17 called youngest to hold a world boxing championship. He was unbeaten in 25 bouts.

Miguel Velasquez, Spain, was awarded W.B.C. title when Muangsurin was disqualified for low blow in 4th round at Madrid, June 30.

Benitez outpointed Emiliano Villa, in first defense of title at San Juan, P.R., May 31.

Benitez stopped Tony Petronelli, East Bridgewater, Mass., in 3d round at San Juan, Puerto Rico, Oct. 16, and retained title.

Welterweight
(147-pound limit)

John Stracey, Britain, stopped Hedgemon Lewis, Los Angeles, at 1:25 of 10th round at Wembley, England, March 20, and retained World Boxing Council title. It was first defense after taking title from Jose Napoles in December 1975.

Carlos Palomino, Westminster, Calif., stopped Stracey at 1:35 of 12th round in London, June 22, and won W.B.C. crown. Referee stopped fight after two knockdowns in round. Palomino, 25, was student at Long Beach State College.

Jose (Pipino) Cuevas, Mexico, stopped Angel Espada, Puerto Rico, in 2d round and won World Boxing Association title, July 17 at Mexicali, Mexico. Fight stopped after third knockdown.

(Boxing Championship Bouts, Continued)

Junior Middleweight
(154-pound limit)

Koichi Wajima, Japan, knocked out Yuh Jae-Do, South Korea, at 1:47 of 15th round and regained World Boxing Association title at Tokyo, Feb. 17. Wajima weighed 153, Yuh 154.

Elisha O'Bed, Bahamas, outpointed Sea Robinson, Ivory Coast, and kept World Boxing Council title at Abijan, April 24. O'Bed had gained crown by knocking out Miguel de Oliveira in 10th round in Paris, Nov. 13, 1975.

Jose Duran, Spain, knocked out Wajima in 14th round at Tokyo May 18 for W.B.A. title.

Eckard Dagge, West Germany, knocked out O'Bed in 10th round at West Berlin, June 18, for W.B.C. title.

Dagge defeated Emile Griffith, New York, Sept. 18 in West Berlin.

Middleweight
(160 pound limit)

Rodrigo Valdes, Colombia, kept World Boxing Council title at Paris, March 28, when his opponent, Max Cohen, France, quit in 4th round.

Carlos Monzon, Argentina, the World Boxing Association champion, outpointed Valdes in 15 rounds at Monte Carlo, Monaco, June 26, and became undisputed champion of class. It was 61st straight victory for 33-year-old Monzon. Valdes, who went down for count of 8 in 14th round, suffered first loss in 6 years.

Light Heavyweight
(175-pound limit)

Victor Galindez, Argentina, retained World Boxing Association title by knocking out Harald Skog, Norway, in 3d round at Oslo, March 28.

Galindez knocked out Richie Kates, Trenton, N.J., in 15th round at Johannesburg, South Africa, May 22. Kates was counted out one second before final bell.

Galindez outpointed Kosie Smith, South Africa, at Johannesburg, Oct. 5 and retained W.B.A. title.

Conteh, outpointed Alvaro Lopes, Stockton, Calif., at Copenhagen, Oct. 9 and retained W.B.C. title.

Heavyweight

Muhammad Ali knocked out Jean-Pierre Coopman, of Belgium, at 2:46 of 5th round at San Juan, Puerto Rico, Feb. 20, in fifth title defense of second reign (14th defense overall). 10,000 fans at Roberto Clemente Coliseum watched fight shown live in U.S. Ali weighed 226, Coopman 206. Champion received $1 million, Coopman $100,000.

Ali won decision over Jimmy Young, April 30, at Landover, Md., before 12,472. Referee Tom Kelly voted 72-65 for Ali, one judge scored bout 70-68 Ali and the others 71-64 for Ali. The champion weighed 230, Young 209.

Ali stopped Richard Dunn, of England, in 5th at Munich, West Germany, May 25. Dunn was knocked down three times in fourth round and twice in fifth before referee called halt at 2:05 of round. Ali weighed 220, Dunn 206½.

Ali won decision over Ken Norton, Sept. 28, at Yankee Stadium, winning by narrow margin on all three official score cards. Referee Arthur Mercante scored bout 8-6 in favor of champion with one round even. The judges, Barney Smith and Harold Lederman, each voted 8-7 Ali. Many in crowd of 30,298 booed decision, believing Norton had won. An official protest by Norton's manager was dismissed by New York State boxing board. There were no knockdowns. First Ali appearance in New York in five years failed to bring predicted record gate. It drew about $2.4 million. Ali was guaranteed $6 million and Norton $1.1 million from world-wide TV promotion.

Ali announced, in Turkey, Oct. 1, that he was retiring. The announcement was not considered definite.

Non-Title Bouts
(Heavyweights)

Ken Norton, 220, stopped Pedro Lovell, Argentina, 205, at 1:40 of 5th round at Las Vegas, Nev., Jan. 10, in scheduled 12-round bout.

George Foreman, 226, knocked out Ron Lyle, 220, at 2:28 of 5th round at Las Vegas, Nev., Jan. 24. Foreman was knocked down twice in 4th round. Lyle was floored once in same round. Foreman received $250,000 and Lyle $150,000.

Norton, 224, stopped Ron Stander, 229, in 5th round at Landover, Md., April 30.

Norton, 210, stopped Larry Middleton, 207½, in 10th round July 10 at San Diego, in tuneup for Ali bout.

Foreman defeated Joe Frazier in five rounds at Nassau Coliseum, Uniondale, N.Y., June 15. Frazier's manager told referee to stop bout after Frazier went down twice and was suffering from eye cuts. Crowd of 10,341 paid $512,075 to see fight. Each fighter weighed 224½ and each received $1 million. Frazier, 32, retired.

Foreman knocked out Scott LeDoux, of Minneapolis, in third round at Utica, N.Y., 14.

Foreman stopped Dino Dennis, North Attleboro, Mass., in fourth round at Hollywood, Fla., Oct. 16. Referee stopped bout at 2:25 of round.

AMATEUR BOXING
A.A.U. Champions
(Las Vegas, Nev., May 12–15)

106 lbs—Brett Summers, Marysville, Wash.
112 lbs—Leo Randolph, Tacoma, Wash.
119 lbs—Bernard Taylor, Charlotte, N.C.
125 lbs—Davey Armstrong, Puyallup, Wash.
132 lbs—Howard Davis, Glen Cove, N.Y.
139 lbs—Pete Seward, Columbus, Ohio
147 lbs—Clinton Jackson, Nashville, Tenn.
156 lbs—J. B. Williamson, Honolulu
165 lbs—Keith Broom, Charlotte, N.C.
178 lbs—Leon Spinks, St. Louis
Heavyweight—Marvin Stinson, Philadelphia
Team—Pacific Northwest

HORSESHOE PITCHING
World Championships
(Bristol, Pa., Aug. 2–9)

	W	L	Ringers No.	Pct.
*Carl Steinfeldt, Rochester, N.Y.	33	2	2,389	82.6
Curt Day, Frankfort, Ind.	33	2	2,309	94.3
Mark Seibold, Huntington, Ind.	31	4	2,475	84.9
Elmer Hohl, Wellesley, Ontario	29	6	2,511	83.3
Glen Henton, Maquoketa, Iowa	29	6	2,577	82.3

* Steinfeldt won playoff 2 games to 1 for championship.

WOMEN

	W	L	Pct.
*Ruth Hangen, Getzville, N.Y.	6	1	75.6
Lorraine Thomas, Lockport, New York	6	1	72.9

* Ruth Hangen won playoff, 2 games to 1, for championship.

Other champions

Junior—Jeff Williams, Auburn, Calif. (defeated his brother, Walter, Jr., in playoff)
Junior girls—Tari Carpenter, Armstrong, Ill.
Senior—Frank Stinson, Minneapolis
Intermediate—Paul Focht, Dayton, Ohio (won three-way playoff with Andy Paglariana, Hibbing, Minn., and Harvey Kohlenberger, Illinois.

HORSE RACING

THE TRIPLE CROWN
(Jockeys in parentheses)

KENTUCKY DERBY, Churchill Downs, Louisville, Ky., May 1, $217,700: 3-year olds, 126 pounds, 1¼ miles—1, Bold Forbes (Cordero); 2, Honest Pleasure (Baeza); 3, Elocutionist (Lively); 4, Amano (Melancon); 5, On the Sly (G. McCarron); 6, Cojak (C.J. McCarron); 7, Inca Roca (Nemeit); 8, Play the Red (Velasquez); 9, Bidson (MacBeth).

Time—2:01 3/5. Mutuels—1, Bold Forbes, owned by E. R. Tizol, $8.00, 2.40, 2.60; 2, Honest Pleasure, owned by B. R. Firestone, $2.40, 2.20; 3, Elocutionist, owned by E. C. Cashman, $2.60. Winner's purse $165,200. Margin of victory: 1 length. Attendance: 115,387.

PREAKNESS STAKES, Pimlico, Baltimore, Md., May 15, $182,200: 3 year olds, 126 pounds, 1 3/16 miles—1, Elocutionist (Lively); 2, Play the Red (Cruguet); 3, a-Bold Forbes (Cordero); 4. Cojak (Agnello); 5, Honest Pleasure (Baeza); 6, a-Life's Hope (Hawley). a-entry.

Time—1:55. Mutuels—1, Elocutionist, owned by E. C. Cashman, $22.20, 8.20, 3.60; 2, Play the Red, owned by Elmendorf Farm, $20.20, 6.00; 3, Bold Forbes, owned by E. R. Tizol, $2.80. Winner's purse: $129,700. Margin of victory: 3½ lengths. Attendance: 62,256.

BELMONT STAKES, Belmont Park, Elmont, L.I., June 5, $195,000: 3 year olds, 126 pounds, 1½ miles—1, Bold Forbes (Cordero); 2, Mackenzie Bridge (McHargue); 3, Great Contractor (Vasquez); 4, Majestic Light (Velasquez); 5, Aeronaut (Turcotte); 6, Play the Red (Cruguet); 7, Mullineaux (Rivera); 8, Best Laid Plans (Day); 9, Close to Noon (Venezia); 10, Quick Card (Solomone).

Time—2:29. Mutuels—1, Bold Forbes, owned by E. R. Tizol, $3.80, 3.40, 2.60; 2, Mackenzie Bridge, owned by Mrs. D. Carver, $5.00, 3.80; 3, Great Contractor, owned by H. P. Wilson, $3.30. Winner's purse: $117,000. Margin of victory: Neck. Attendance: 57,519.

Other Major U.S. Stakes Winners
(Gross purses over $100,000)

Race (track)	Winner (jockey)	Winners' purse
American Derby (Arlington)—Fifth Marine (R. L. Turcotte)		$93,400
Amory L. Haskell Handicap (Monmouth)—Hatchet Man (Braccialo)		71,793
Arkansas Derby (Oaklawn)—Elocutionist (Lively)		81,480
Arlington Handicap—Victorian Prince (Platts)		90,000
Arlington-Washington Park Futurity—Run Dusty Run (McHargue)		120,465
Arlington-Washington Lassie—Special Warmth (S. Maple)		68,700
Beldame (Belmont)—Proud Delta (Velasquez)		64,920
Brooklyn Handicap (Aqueduct)—Forego (Gustines)		67,860
California Derby (Golden Gate)—Telly's Pop (Mena)		85,000
Californian (Hollywood)—Ancient Title (Hawley)		65,300
Century (Hollywood)—Winds of Thought (Vergara)		66,500
Cinema (Hollywood)—Majestic Light (Hawley)		67,200
Coaching Club American Oaks (Belmont)—Revidere (Vasquez)		68,640
Cornhusker (Ak-Sar-Ben)—Dragset (S. Maple)		60,500
Delaware Handicap—Optimistic Gal (E. Maple)		65,040
Del Mar Futurity—Visible (Pincay)		74,435
Fantasy Stakes (Oaklawn)—T.V. Vixen (Walt)		73,170
Flamingo (Hialeah)—Honest Pleasure (Baeza)		85,605
Florida Derby (Gulfstream)—Honest Pleasure (Baeza)		91,440
Frizette (Belmont)—Sensational (Velasquez)		64,740
Futurity (Belmont)—For the Moment (E. Maple)		67,353
Golden Invitational (Arlington)—Foolish Pleasure (Fires)		75,000
Gulfstream Handicap—Hail the Pirates (Baeza)		73,560
Hawthorne Derby—Wardlaw (Tejeira)		82,200
Hollywood Derby—Crystal Water (Shoemaker)		152,750
Hollywood Gold Cup—Pay Tribute (Castenedas)		150,000
Hollywood Juvenile—Fleet Dragon (Olivares)		103,250
Hollywood Turf Handicap—Dahlia (Shoemaker)		120,000
Jerome Handicap (Belmont)—Dance Spell (Hernandez)		64,800
Jersey Derby (Garden State)—Life's Hope (M. Rivera)		86,905
Louisiana Derby (Fair Grounds)—Johnny Appleseed (Castenedas)		61,000
Marlboro Cup (Belmont)—Forego (Shoemaker)		170,220
Massachusetts Handicap (Suffolk)—Dancing Champ (McCarron)		60,000
Metropolitan Handicap (Belmont)—Forego (Gustines)		66,660
Michigan 1⅛ Mile—Sharp Gary (S. Maple)		65,000
Monmouth Invitational—Majestic Light (Hawley)		65,000
New Orleans Handicap (Fair Grounds)—Master Derby (McHargue)		61,000
Ohio Derby (Thistledown)—Return of the Native (Patterson)		75,000
Omaha Gold Cup (Ak-Sar-Ben)—Joachim (S. Maple)		62,150
Pan-American Turf Handicap (Gulfstream)—Improviser (Cruguet)		86,081
Santa Anita Derby—An Act (Pincay)		97,700
Santa Anita Handicap—Royal Glint (Tejeira)		155,900
San Luis Rey (Santa Anita)—Avatar (Pincay)		64,300
San Juan Capistrano (Santa Anita)—One on the Aisle (Hawley)		75,000
Secretariat Stakes (Arlington)—Joachim (S. Maple)		88,400
Sorority (Monmouth)—Squander (Cordero)		73,740
Strub (Santa Anita)—George Navoned (Toro)		76,900
Suburban (Aqueduct)—Foolish Pleasure (E. Maple)		65,280
Sunset (Hollywood)—Caucasus (Toro)		81,350
Swaps Stakes (Hollywood)—Majestic Light (Hawley)		98,200
Travers (Saratoga)—Honest Pleasure (Perret)		65,040
Trenton Handicap (Garden State)—Royal Glint (Tejeira)		72,182
United Nations Handicap (Atlantic City)—Intrepid Hero (Hawley)		65,000
Vanity (Hollywood)—Miss Toshiba (Toro)		67,200
Washington Park Handicap—Double Edge Sword (Bracciale)		70,400
Widener (Hialeah)—Hatchet Man (Gustines)		78,975
Wood Memorial (Aqueduct)—Bold Native (Cordero)		67,560
Woodward Stakes (Belmont)—Forego (Shoemaker)		104,820

Quarter Horses
(Ruidoso Downs, N.M., 440 yards)

All-American Derby (Aug. 29)—Mito Wise Dancer (owned by Carl Dodd, Gary Pogue and Jerry Rheudasil, Lewisville, Tex., and ridden by J. C. Wiley), 21.56 seconds. Total purse, $566,042; Winner's purse $188,491
Rainbow Futurity (Aug. 1)—Real Wind Owned by J. D. and Elsie Kitchens, Fort Sumner, N.M., and ridden by Jeff Fair) $121,140

Foreign Races

Canadian Derby—(Northlands)—Laissez-Paisser (Rog. Turcotte)		$30,000
Epsom Derby (England)—Empery (Piggott)		192,340
Epsom Oaks—Pawneese (Saint-Martin)		100,234
Grand National Steeplechase (England)—Rag Trade (J. Burke)		74,840
Grand Prix de Paris—Exceller (Saint-Martin)		100,000
Irish Sweeps Derby (Dublin)—Malacate (Paquet)		124,000
King George VI and Queen Elizabeth (England)—Pawneese (Saint-Martin)		145,800
1,000 Guineas (England)—Flying Water (Saint-Martin)		78,900
2,000 Guineas (England)—Wollow (Dettori)		99,160
Prix de l'Arc de Triomphe (France)—Ivanjica (Head)		240,000
Queens Plate (Canada)—Norcliffe (Fell)		89,716
St. Leger (England)—Crow (Saint-Martin)		85,820

PADDLE BALL
Collegiate Champions

Men—Howard Solomon, Brooklyn College
Women—Francine Davis, Brooklyn College

HARNESS RACING
MAJOR STAKES
Trotting

Hambletonian (Du Quoin, Ill., Sept. 4)—Steve Lobell, driven by Billy Haughton, won second and fourth one-mile heats. First heat won by Zoot Suit (Vernon Dancer) in 1:58 1-5; Steve Lobell's time of 1:56 2-5 in second heat equaled world record for 3-year-olds on one-mile track; third heat won by Armbro Regina (Joe O'Brien) in 1:56 3-5; Steve Lobell's time in fourth heat was 2:02 3-5. Final placings: 1, Steve Lobell 14-1-4-1, $131,762; 2, Zoot Suit 1-6-2-2, $65,881; 3, Armbro Regina, 17-2-1-3, $31,623.

Colonial (Liberty Bell, Sept. 19)—Armbro Regina (Joe O'Brien), 2:00 4-5 . . . . $62,382
Dexter (Roosevelt Raceway, July 16)—Soothsayer (Del Miller) 2:02 4-5 . . . . $60,000
Empire Trot (Syracuse, Aug. 21)—Tropical Storm (Ralph Baldwin), 1:57 3-5 . . . . $73,500
American-National Maturity (Sportsman's Park)—Songflori (Banks), 2:01 . . . . $36,200
Monticello-N.Y. City OTB Classic (June 25)—Oil Burner (Webster) $59,063
Roosevelt International (July 10, 1¼ miles)—Equileo (France, Bernard Froger, driver), 2:33 3-5 . . . . $100,000
Yonkers Trot (July 31)—Steve Lobell (Billy Haughton), 2:01 4-5 . . . . $100,000

Pacing

Little Brown Jug (Delaware, Ohio, Sept. 23)—Keystone Ore (Stanley Dancer). Armbro Ranger (O'Brien) won first heat in 1:56 4-5; Keystone Ore won second and third heats in 1:57 and 1:57 2/5 . . . . $56,903
Adios (Meadow Lands, Pa., Aug. 14)—Armbro Ranger (O'Brien) 1:56 . . . . $62,070
Cane (Yonkers, Aug. 21)—Keystone Ore (Stanley Dancer) 1:57 1-5 . . . . $100,000

Foreign Races

Prix d'Amerique Trot (Paris, 1 5/8 miles, Jan. 25)—Bellino II (Jean-Pierre Gougeon), 3:25.6 . . . $110,000
Prix d'Ete Pace (Blue Bonnets, Montreal, Aug. 29)—Precious Fella (Gary Cameron) $163,700

SHUFFLEBOARD
Summer
(Lakeside, Ohio, July 19–21)

Open—Dave Karaska, Detroit
Closed—Howard Hawkins, Springfield, Ohio
Women's open—Dorcas Donelson, Carey, Ohio
Women's closed—Elsie Hodges, Indiana
Doubles—Clarence Goodman, Toledo, Ohio.-Bailie Stepp, Hendersonville, N.C.
Women's doubles—Adele Pearson, Orlando, Fla.-Elnora Rhoades, Edgewater, Fla.

Winter
(St. Petersburg, Fla., March 8–10)

Open—Merritt Gordon, Millington, Md.
Closed—Ed Travis, Mount Holly, N.J.
Women's open—Mary Eldridge, Lake George, N.Y.
Women's closed—Wilma Krieg, Nebraska
Doubles—Austin Sutton, St. Ignace, Mich.-Bob Pearson, Winter Park, Fla.
Women's doubles—Wilma Krieg-Terese Charbonneau, St. Petersburg, Fla.

SQUASH TENNIS
National Champions

Singles—Pedro Baccallao, New York
Veterans Singles—Bill Lordi, New York

FRISBEE
World Championships

Men—Peter Bloeme, New York
Women—Monika Lou, Berkeley, Calif.

FENCING
National Champions
Fencing League of America
(Cherry Hill, N.J., June 25–July 2)

Foil—Lt. Ed Donofrio, U.S. Marines
Epee—George Masin, New York A.C.
Saber—Thomas Losonczy, New York A.C.
Women's foil—Ann O'Donnell, Salle Santelli, New York

Team

Foil—Wauwautosa (Wis) F.C. (Pedro Barcelo, Jack Biebel, John Tank, Jim Herring)
Epee—New York A.C. (David Lynn, Paul Pesthy, George Masin, Al Peterson)
Saber—Fencers Club, New York (Stephen Kaplan, Paul Apostol, Robert Dow, Peter Westerbrooke)
Women's foil—Salle D'Asaro, San Jose, Calif. (Miss Vincent Hurley, Stacey Johnson, Gay D'Asaro)

Under 19

Foil—Michael Marx, Portland, Ore.
Epee—Peter Schifrin, San Francisco
Saber—Stephen Renshaw, New York A.C.
Women's foil—Joy Ellingson, Los Angeles A.C.

National Collegiate A.A.
(Philadelphia, March 17–18)

Foil—Greg Benko, Wayne State
Saber—Brian Smith, Columbia
Epee—Randy Eggleton, Pennsylvania U.
Team—New York University

Women's Intercollegiate F.A.

Individual Champion—Stacey Johnson, Cal State-San Jose
Team—California State-San Jose

Softball
Amateur Softball Association Champions

Fast pitch—Raybestos Cardinals, Stratford, Conn.
Slow pitch—Warren Motors, Jacksonville, Fla.
16-inch slow pitch—Republic Bank Bobcats, Chicago
Industrial slow pitch—Armco Triangles, Middletown, Ohio
Industrial Class A slow pitch—New York Telephone, Long Island, N.Y.
Class A slow pitch—Reed's Nuts, Macon, Ga.
Class A fast pitch—Millersville, Pa.
National Church—Hickory Hammock Baptist, Milton, Fla.
Modified fast pitch—Clinica, Miami, Fla.
Boys 16-18 fast pitch—Rockford, Ill. Redwings
Boys 16-18 slow pitch—Chicago Bruins
Boys 13-15 fast pitch—Hyman Freightways, Sioux Falls, S.D.
Boys 13-15 slow pitch—Maysville, Ky.

WOMEN

Fast pitch—Raybestos Brakettes, Stratford, Conn.
Slow pitch—Sorrento's Pizza, Cincinnati
Class A fast pitch—Warminster, Pa.
Class A slow pitch—Rustic Bar, Duluth, Minn.
Girls 16-18 fast pitch—Sepulveda, Calif. Raiders
Girls 16-18 slow pitch—McKeesport, Pa.
Girls 13-15 fast pitch—Topeka 7-Up Ladybugs
Girls 13-15 slow pitch—Tifton, Ga., Tomboys

RECORD FIELD GOAL OF 69 YARDS

Ove Johansson, of Abilene Christian, kicked a 69-yard field goal—the longest in the history of football—Oct. 16 against East Texas State. A few minutes before his kick, Tony Franklin, of Texas A & M, had bettered the mark with a 64-yarder against Baylor. His record lasted 20 minutes. Later he kicked a 65-yarder. The previous collegiate record and professional record was 63 yards. Franklin's 65-yarder is, however, a National Collegiate A.A. record

TENNIS

United States Championships
Open
(Forest Hills, N.Y., September 1–12)

Singles—Jimmy Connors, Belleville, Ill., defeated Bjorn Borg, Sweden, 6–4, 3–6, 7–6, 6–4, in final; semifinals: Connors defeated Guillermo Vilas, Argentina, 6–4, 6–2, 6–1; Borg defeated Ilie Nastase, Romania, 6–3, 6–3, 6–4.

Women's singles—Chris Evert, Fort Lauderdale, Fla., defeated Evonne Goolagong, Australia, 6–3, 6–0, in final; semifinals: Miss Evert defeated Mima Jausovec, Yugoslavia, 6–3, 6–1; Miss Goolagong defeated Dianne Fromholtz, Australia, 7–6, 6–1.

Doubles—Marty Riessen, Amelia Island, Fla.–Tom Okker, Netherlands, defeated Paul Kronk–Cliff Letcher, Australia, 6–4, 6–4, in final.

Women's doubles—Linky Boshoff–Ilana Kloss, South Africa, defeated Olga Morozova, U.S.S.R., and Virginia Wade, England, 6–1, 6–4, in final.

Mixed doubles—Billie Jean King, New York–Phil Dent, Australia, defeated Betty Stove, Netherlands–Frew McMillan, South Africa, 3–6, 6–2, 7–5, in final.

Junior singles—Ricardo, Icaza, Ecuador, defeated Jose Luis Clerc, Argentina, 6–4, 5–7, 6–0, in final.

Junior women—Marise Kruger, South Africa, defeated Lucia Romanov, Romania, 6–3, 7–5, in final.

Over 45 doubles—Ham Richardson, New York–Bob Hewitt, South Africa, defeated Gardnar Mulloy, Miami Beach, Fla.–Fred Stolle, Australia, 6–2, 2–6, 6–3, in final.

National Indoor
(Salisbury, Md., Feb. 17–22)

Singles—Ilie Nastase, Romania (defeated Jimmy Connors, Belleville, Ill., 6–2, 6–3, 7–6, in final)

Doubles—Sherwood Stewart, Goose Creek, Tex.–Fred McNair, Chevy Chase, Md.

Women's National Indoor
(Atlanta, Ga., Sept. 17–19)

Singles—Virginia Wade, Britain (defeated Betty Stove, Netherlands, 5–7, 7–5, 7–5, in final)

Doubles—Rosemary Casals, Sausalito, Calif.–Francoise Durr, France

National Clay Court
(Indianapolis, Aug. 9–16)

Singles—Jimmy Connors, Belleville, Ill. (defeated Wojtek Fibak, Poland, 6–2, 6–4, in final)

Women's singles—Kathy May, Beverly Hills, Calif. (defeated Brigitte Cuypers, South Africa, 6–4, 4–6, 6–2, in final)

Doubles—Raul Ramirez, Mexico–Brian Gottfried, Fort Lauderdale, Fla.

Women's doubles—Linky Boshoff–Ilana Kloss, South Africa

National Amateur Clay Court
(Pittsburgh, June 21–27)

Women's singles—Candy Reynolds, Knoxville, Tenn. (defeated Diane Desfor, Long Beach, Calif., 6–3, 4–6, 6–4, in final)

Women's doubles—Candy Reynolds–Nancy Yeargin, Greenville, S.C.

Singles—Francisco Gonzalez, (defeated Hank Pfister, 1–6, 6–3, 6–3, in final)

Doubles—Bill Maze, Palo Alto, Calif.–Eric Friedler

National Amateur Grass Court
(Newport, R.I., July 12–18)

Singles—Chris Lewis, Los Angeles (defeated Bill Maze, Palo Alto, Calif., 6–3, 6–4, in final)

Women's singles—Diane Desfor, Long Beach, Calif. (defeated Paula Smith, Los Angeles, 7–5, 6–1, in final)

Doubles—Tim Garcia, Albuquerque, N.M.–Colon Nunez, Houston, Tex.

Women's doubles—Barbara Hallquist, Arcadia, Calif.–Barbara Jordan, King of Prussia, Pa.

Mixed doubles—Cindy Thomas, Los Angeles–Chris Lewis

U.S. TENNIS ASSN. LEADING 1976 EARNINGS
(Through Oct. 3)

	Tournament	Total
Jimmy Connors	$267,743	$526,743
Bjorn Borg	195,065	321,065
Ilie Nastase	155,085	317,085
Arthur Ashe	153,840	306,590
Raul Ramirez	179,082	201,582
Guillermo Vilas	158,473	167,473
Harold Solomon	137,587	142,837
Eddie Dibbs	131,329	139,579
Wojtek Fibak	119,337	122,337
Brian Gottfried	109,751	120,251
WOMEN		
Chris Evert	202,465	252,465
Evonne Goolagong	158,785	165,452
Virginia Wade	92,980	96,313
Rosemary Casals	68,085	90,585
Martina Navratilova	72,060	72,060
Betty Stove	63,950	67,283
Billie Jean King	31,870	59,370
Sue Barker	53,035	56,368
Mima Jausovec	42,755	42,755
Olga Morozova	42,560	42,560

Other U.S. Champions

N.C.A.A. Division I—Bill Scanlon, Trinity (Texas); doubles: Peter Fleming–Fredi Taygan, U.C.L.A.

N.C.A.A. Division II—Tim Monroe, California–Davis; doubles: Roger De Santis Guedes–Bruce Farnsworth, Hampton Institute

N.C.A.A. Division III—John Blomberg, Claremont; doubles: Larry Davidson–John Irwin, Swarthmore

N.A.I.A.—Kari Personen, Mercyhurst, Erie, Pa.; doubles: Reijo Tuomola–Marty Sturges, Mercyhurst

Women's Intercollegiate—Barbara Hallquist, So. California; doubles: Susie Hagey–Diane Morrison, Stanford

Junior college women—Mary Sawyer, Midland J.C.

Boys 18—Larry Gottfried, Lauderhill, Fla.; doubles Gottfried–John McEnroe, Douglas Manor, N.Y.

Girls 18—Lynn Epstein, Miami, Fla.; doubles: Sherry Acker, Kalamazoo, Mich.–Ann Smith, Dallas, Tex.

Boys 18, clay court—John McEnroe, Douglas Manor, N.Y.; doubles: McEnroe–Larry Gottfried, Lauderhill, Fla.

Girls 18, clay court—Lea Antonoplis, Glendora, Calif.; doubles: Ann Smith, Dallas, Tex.–Sherry Acker, Kalamazoo, Mich.

Other Championships
Wimbledon Open (England)
(June 18–July 3)

Singles—Bjorn Borg, Sweden (defeated Ilie Nastase, Romania, 6–4, 6–2, 9–7, in final). Semifinals: Borg defeated Roscoe Tanner, 6–4, 9–8, 6–4; Nastase defeated Raul Ramirez, 6–2, 9–7, 6–3

Women's Singles—Chris Evert, Fort Lauderdale, Fla. (defeated Evonne Goolagong, Australia, 6–3, 4–6, 8–6, in final). Semifinals: Miss Evert defeated Martina Navratilova, 6–3, 4–6, 6–4; Miss Goolagong defeated Virginia Wade, 6–1, 6–2

Doubles—Brian Gottfried, Fort Lauderdale, Fla.–Raul Ramirez, Mexico

Women's doubles—Chris Evert–Martina Navratilova

Mixed doubles—Francois Durr, France–Tony Roche, Australia

Junior singles—Heinz Guenthhardt, Switzerland

Junior girls singles—Natasha Chymreva, U.S.S.R.

Veterans doubles—Lennart Bergelin, Sweden–Budge Patty, U.S.

French Open
(Paris, June 4–13)

Singles—Adriano Panatta, Italy (defeated Harold Solomon, Silver Spring, Md., 6–1, 6–4, 4–6, 7–6, in final)

Women's singles—Sue Barker, England, (defeated Renata Tomanova, Czechoslovakia, 6–3, 1–6, 6–2, in final)

(Continued)

TENNIS (Continued)

Doubles—Fred McNair, Chevy Chase, Md.-Sherwood Stewart, Goose Creek, Tex.

Women's doubles—Fiorella Bonicelli, Uruguay-Gail Lovera, France

Mixed doubles—Ilana Kloss, South Africa-Kim Warwick, Australia

Australian Open
(Dec. 26, 1975–Jan. 4)

Singles—Mark Edmondson, Australia (defeated John Newcombe, Australia, 6–7, 6–3, 7–6, 6–1, in final)

Women's singles—Evonne Goolagong, Australia (defeated Renata Tomanova, Czechoslovakia, 6–2, 6–2, in final)

Doubles—Newcombe-Tony Roche, Australia

Women's doubles—Evonne Goolagong-Helen Gourlay, Australia

Davis Cup
Zone Competition
(Eliminations began in 1975)

American Zone—South Section: Peru defeated Uruguay, 3–2; Brazil defeated Peru, 5–0; Argentina defeated Ecuador, 5–0; Argentina defeated Brazil; Chile defeated Argentina, 3–2. North Section: Canada defeated Colombia, 5–0; Mexico defeated Caribbean, 5–0; Mexico defeated Canada, 5–0; United States defeated Venezuela, 5–0; Mexico defeated United States, 3–2; South Africa won from Mexico by default. Zone final: Chile defeated South Africa, 3–2.

Eastern Zone—India defeated Thailand, 5–0; Pakistan defeated Malaysia, 5–0; Indonesia defeated Korea, 3–2; Pakistan defeated Sri Lanka; India defeated Japan; Philippines defeated Taiwan; India defeated Philippines, 3–0; Indonesia defeated Pakistan, 4–1; New Zealand defeated India, 3–2; Australia defeated Indonesia, 5–0. Zone final: Australia defeated New Zealand, 4–1.

European Zone A—Belgium defeated Netherlands, 4–1; Denmark defeated Finland, 4–1; Monaco defeated Israel, 4–1; Egypt defeated Ireland; Hungary defeated Belgium, 5–0; West Germany defeated Denmark; U.S.S.R. defeated Monaco, 5–0; Hungary defeated Egypt, 5–0; U.S.S.R. defeated West Germany, 4–1; Hungary defeated Czechoslovakia, 4–1; U.S.S.R. defeated Spain, 4–1; Zone final: U.S.S.R., defeated Hungary, 4–1.

European Zone B—Portugal defeated Luxembourg, 5–0; Switzerland defeated Iran, 3–2; Austria defeated Bulgaria, 4–1; Poland defeated Norway, 5–0; Greece defeated Portugal, 4–1; Britain defeated Switzerland, 4–1; Romania defeated Austria, 4–1; Italy defeated Poland, 5–0; Yugoslavia defeated Greece, 5–0; Britain defeated Romania, 5–0; Italy defeated Yugoslavia, 5–0; Britain defeated France, 4–1; Italy defeated Sweden, 4-1. Zone final: Italy defeated Britain, 4–1.

Interzone—Semifinal Round

U.S.S.R. (European Zone A) defaulted to Chile (American Zone) for political reasons; Italy (European Zone B) defeated Australia (Eastern Zone), 3–2.

Federation Cup
(Philadelphia, Aug. 22–29)

Semifinals—Australia defeated Britain, 3–0; United States defeated Netherlands, 3–0

Final—United States defeated Australia, 2–1 (singles: Kerry Reid, Australia, defeated Rosemary Casals, 1–6, 6–3, 7–5; Billie Jean King, United States defeated Evonne Goolagong, 7–6, 6–4; doubles: Mrs. King and Miss Casals won, 7–5, 6–3)

Professional

World Championship Tennis tour final (Dallas, May 4–9)—Bjorn Borg, Sweden (defeated Guillermo Vilas, Argentina, 1–6, 6–1, 7–5, 6–1); doubles: (Kansas City, final May 2): Wojtek Fibak, Poland-Karl Meiler, West Germany (defeated Stan Smith-Bob Lutz, 6–3, 2–6, 3–6, 6–3, 6–4, in final)

Virginia Slims Championship (Los Angeles, April 9–17)—Evonne Goolagong, Australia (defeated Chris Evert, 6–3, 5–7, 6–3, in final)

United States Pro Championship (Brookline, Mass., Aug. 22–31)—Bjorn Borg, Sweden (defeated Harold Solomon, Silver Spring, Md. 6–7, 6–4, 6–1, 6–2, in final); doubles: Ray Ruffels-Alan Stone, Australia

World Team Tennis—New York Sets defeated San Francisco Golden Gaters, 3 matches to 0, for championship

---

CHESS
Source: Martin E. Morrison, United States Chess Federation

United States Champions

Open—Tie between Anatoly Lein, New York and Leonid Shamkovich, New York

Women's open—Diane Savareide, Culver City, Calif.

Women—Diane Savareide

Amateur—Laszlo Ficsor, Minneapolis

Women's amateur—Gwen Ratte, Norwood, Mass.

Junior Open—Steven Odendahl, Chevy Chase, Md.

Junior—Tie between Mark Diesen, Potomac, Md., and Michael Rohde, South Orange, N.J.

High school—Richard Kaner, Two Rivers, Wis.

Team—Garden State Chess Assn. Four, Woodridge, N.J.

Armed Forces—Russell Garber, Army; team Army

National Open—Tie between Edward Formanek, Chicago, and Anthony Miles, England

American open (Nov. 1975)—Tie between Kim Commons, West Los Angeles, Calif. and David Strauss, Riverside, Calif.

TABLE TENNIS
Source: Ping Neuberger, Historian United States Table Tennis Association
National Championships
(Philadelphia, June 10–13)

Singles, open—Dragutin Surbak, Yugoslavia

Singles, closed—Ray Guillen, Los Angeles

Women's open singles—Kim Soon Ok, South Korea

Women's closed singles—In Sock Bhusan, Columbus, Ohio

Mixed doubles—Desmond Douglas-Jill Hammersley, England

Women's doubles—Kim Soon Ok-Son Hye Soon, South Korea

Doubles—Surbak-Milivoj Karakasevic, Yugoslavia

Senior singles—Houshang Bozorgzadeh, Independence, Iowa

Senior women's singles—Leah Neuberger, New York

Senior doubles—George Rocker-Bill Sharpe, Philadelphia

Esquire singles (over 50)—Frank Dwelly, Natick, Mass.

Esquire singles (over 60)—Jim Verta, Kensington, Md.

Veterans (over 70)—Oliver Nicholas, Apache Junction, Ariz.

Junior singles (under 17)—Dean Galardi, Torrance, Calif.

Girls (under 17)—Biruta Plucas, Toronto

Junior doubles—Galardi-Dennis Barrish, Northridge, Calif.

Girls' doubles—Biruta Plucas-Gloria Nesukaitis, Toronto

PLATFORM TENNIS
World Champions

Doubles—Doug Russell, New York-Gordon Gray, Greenwich, Conn.

National Champions

Doubles—Steve and Chip Baird, Short Hills, N.J.

Mixed Doubles—Mrs. Ronald DeBree, Fair Haven, N.J.-Herb Fitz-Gibbon, New York

---

PADDLE TENNIS
National Open

Men's doubles—Sol Hauptman-Jeff Fleitman, Brooklyn, N.Y.

Women's doubles—Hilary Hilton-Christine Burton, Pacific Palisades, Calif.

MAJOR LEAGUE BASEBALL

NATIONAL LEAGUE
Eastern Division

	W	L	Pct.	GB
Philadelphia Phillies	101	61	.623	--
Pittsburgh Pirates	92	70	.568	9
New York Mets	86	76	.531	15
Chicago Cubs	75	87	.463	26
St. Louis Cardinals	72	90	.444	29
Montreal Expos	55	107	.340	46

Western Division

	W	L	Pct.	GB
Cincinnati Reds	102	60	.630	--
Los Angeles Dodgers	92	70	.568	10
Houston Astros	80	82	.494	22
San Francisco Giants	74	88	.457	28
San Diego Padres	73	89	.451	29
Atlanta Braves	70	92	.432	32

National League Playoffs
1st Game at Philadelphia, Oct. 9

```
Cincinnati    . . . . . . . . . 001 002 030-6  10  0
Philadelphia  . . . . . . . . . 100 000 002-3   6  1
```
Gullett, Eastwick (9) and Bench; Carlton, McGraw (8) and McCarver, Boone (8). Winner: Gullett. Loser: Carlton. Home Run: Cincinnati: Foster. A—62,640.

2d Game at Philadelphia, Oct. 10

```
Cincinnati    . . . . . . . . . 000 004 200-6   6  0
Philadelphia  . . . . . . . . . 010 010 000-2  10  1
```
Zachry, Borbon (6) and Bench; Lonborg, Garber (6), McGraw (7), Reed (7) and Boone. Winner: Zachry. Loser: Lonborg. Home Run: Philadelphia: Luzinski. A—62,651.

3d Game at Philadelphia, Oct. 12

```
Philadelphia  . . . . . . . . . 000 100 221-6  11  0
Cincinnati    . . . . . . . . . 000 000 403-7   9  2
```
Kaat, Reed (7), Garber (9), Underwood (9) and Boone, Oates (8); Nolan, Sarmiento (6), Borbon (7), Eastwick (8) and Bench. Winner: Eastwick. Loser: Garber. Home Runs: Cincinnati: Foster, Bench. A—55,047.

NATIONAL LEAGUE LEADERS

Batting—Bill Madlock, Chicago	339
Runs—Pete Rose, Cincinnati	130
Hits—Pete Rose, Cincinnati	215
Runs batted in—George Foster, Cincinnati	121
Doubles—Pete Rose, Cincinnati	42
Triples—Dave Cash, Philadelphia	12
Home Runs—Mike Schmidt, Philadelphia	38
Stolen Bases—Dave Lopes, Los Angeles	63

Pitching

Victories—Randy Jones, San Diego	22
Earned Run Average—John Denny, St. Louis	2.52
Strikeouts—Tom Seaver, New York	235
Shutouts—Jon Matlack, New York	6
John Montefusco, San Francisco	6
Innings Pitched—Randy Jones, San Diego	315

Four No-Hitters in 1976

Three pitchers in the National League hurled no-hit games and two in the American League. However, the two in the A.L. combined in the same game. They were John (Blue Moon) Odom and Francisco Barrios of the A's. The no-hitters:

Date	Pitcher	Teams	BB	So	Score
July 9	Larry Dierker	Houst. vs. Mont.	4	8	6-0
July 28	*2 Pitchers	Oak vs. Chicago	11	5	2-1
Aug. 9	J. Candelaria	Pitts. vs. L.A.	1	7	2-0
Sept. 29	J. Montefusco	S.F. at Atlanta	1	4	9-0

* John (Blue Moon) Odom pitched 5 innings; Francisco Barrios 4.

AMERICAN LEAGUE
Eastern Division

	W	L	Pct.	GB
New York Yankees	97	62	.610	--
Baltimore Orioles	88	74	.543	10½
Boston Red Sox	83	79	.512	15½
Cleveland Indians	81	78	.509	16
Detroit Tigers	74	87	.460	24
Milwaukee Brewers	66	95	.410	32

Western Division

	W	L	Pct.	GB
Kansas City Royals	90	72	.556	--
Oakland A's	87	74	.540	2½
Minnesota Twins	85	77	.525	5
California Angels	76	86	.469	14
Texas Rangers	76	86	.469	14
Chicago White Sox	64	97	.398	25½

American League Playoffs
1st Game at Kansas City, Oct. 9

```
New York    . . . . . . . . . 200 000 002-4  12  0
Kansas City . . . . . . . . . 000 000 010-1   5  2
```
Hunter and Munson; Gura, Littell (9) and Martinez, Wathan (9). Winner: Hunter. Loser: Gura. A—41,077.

2d Game at Kansas City, Oct. 10

```
New York    . . . . . . . . . 012 000 000-3  12  5
Kansas City . . . . . . . . . 200 002 03x-7   9  0
```
Figueroa, Tidrow (6) and Munson; Leonard, Splittorff (3). Mingori (9) and Martinez. Winner: Splittorff. Loser: Figueroa. A—41,091.

3d Game at New York, Oct. 12

```
Kansas City . . . . . . . . . 300 000 000-3   6  0
New York    . . . . . . . . . 000 203 00x-5   9  0
```
Hassler, Pattin (6), Hall (6), Mingori (6), Littell (6) and Martinez, Stinson (8); Ellis, Lyle (9) and Munson. Winner: Ellis. Loser: Hassler. Home Run: New York: Chambliss. A—56,808.

4th Game at New York, Oct. 13

```
Kansas City . . . . . . . . . 030 201 010-7   9  1
New York    . . . . . . . . . 020 000 101-4  11  0
```
Gura, Bird (3), Mingori (7) and Martinez; Hunter, Tidrow (4), Jackson (7) and Munson. Winner: Bird. Loser: Hunter. Home Runs: New York: Nettles 2. A—56,355.

5th Game at New York, Oct. 14

```
Kansas City . . . . . . . . . 210 000 030-6  11  1
New York    . . . . . . . . . 202 002 001-7  11  1
```
Leonard, Splittorff (1), Pattin (4), Hassler (5), Littell (7) and Martinez; Figueroa, Jackson (8), Tidrow (9) and Munson. Winner: Tidrow. Loser: Littell. Home Runs: Kansas City: Mayberry, Brett; New York: Chambliss. A—56,821.

AMERICAN LEAGUE LEADERS

Batting—George Brett, Kansas City	333
Runs—Roy White, New York	104
Hits—George Brett, Kansas City	215
Runs batted in—Lee May, Baltimore	109
Doubles—Amos Otis, Kansas City	41
Triples—George Brett, Kansas City	14
Home Runs—Graig Nettles, New York	32
Stolen Bases—Andy North, Oakland	75

Pitching

Victories—Jim Palmer, Baltimore	22
Earned run average—Mark Fidrych, Detroit	2.34
Strikeouts—Nolan Ryan, California	327
Shutouts—Nolan Ryan, California	7
Innings Pitched—Jim Palmer, Baltimore	315

AMERICAN LEAGUE AVERAGES
Unofficial

BATTING—CLUB

	AB	R	H	HR	RBI	AVG.		AB	R	H	HR	RBI	AVG
Minnesota	5574	743	1526	81	691	.274	Grieve, Texas	546	57	139	20	81	.255
New York	5555	730	1496	120	681	.269	Beniquez, Texas	478	49	122	0	33	.255
Kansas City	5540	713	1490	65	656	.269	Kelly, Chicago	311	42	79	5	33	.255
Boston	5512	716	1448	134	664	.263	Nettles, N.Y.	583	88	148	32	93	.254
Cleveland	5412	615	1423	85	567	.263	Spencer, Chicago	518	53	131	14	71	.253
Detroit	5441	609	1401	101	566	.257	Howell, Texas	491	55	124	8	53	.253
Chicago	5532	586	1410	73	538	.255	Yount, Mil.	638	59	161	2	54	.252
Texas	5555	616	1390	80	574	.250	Bumbry, Balt.	450	71	113	9	36	.251
Milwaukee	5396	570	1326	88	536	.246	Doyle, Boston	432	51	108	0	26	.250
Oakland	5353	686	1319	113	625	.246	Brohamer, Chicago	354	33	89	7	39	.251
Baltimore	5457	619	1326	119	576	.243	Tenace, Oakland	417	64	104	22	67	.249
California	5385	550	1265	63	511	.235	Dent, Chicago	562	44	138	2	52	.246
							Lemon, Chicago	451	46	111	4	39	.246

BATTING—INDIVIDUAL
(300 or more times at bat)

	AB	R	H	HR	RBI	AVG		AB	R	H	HR	RBI	AVG
							Evans, Boston	501	61	121	17	62	.242
							Patek, Kan. City	432	58	104	1	43	.241
							Bando, Oakland	550	75	132	27	84	.240
Brett, Kan. City	645	94	215	7	66	.333	Rodriguez, Det.	480	40	115	8	50	.240
McRae, Kan. City	527	75	175	8	73	.332	Burroughs, Texas	604	71	143	18	86	.237
Carew, Minn.	605	97	200	9	90	.331	DeCinces, Balt.	440	36	103	11	42	.234
Bostock, Minn.	474	75	153	4	60	.323	Spikes, Cleve.	334	36	78	3	31	.234
Leflore, Det.	544	93	172	4	39	.316	Mayberry, Kan. City	594	75	138	13	95	.232
Lynn, Boston	507	76	159	10	65	.314	Gamble, N.Y.	340	43	79	17	57	.232
Rivers, N.Y.	590	95	184	8	67	.312	White, Kan. City	446	40	102	2	46	.229
Carty, Cleve.	552	67	171	13	83	.310	Sundberg, Texas	448	33	102	3	34	.228
Munson, N.Y.	616	79	186	17	105	.302	R. Jackson, Calif.	410	44	93	8	40	.227
Poquette, Kan. City	344	43	104	2	34	.302	Muser, Balt.	326	25	74	1	30	.227
Staub, Det.	589	73	176	15	96	.300	Thompson, Texas	319	21	72	1	19	.226
Garr, Chicago	526	63	158	4	36	.300	Randle, Texas	539	53	121	1	51	.224
Chambliss, N.Y.	641	79	188	17	96	.293	Thompson, Det.	412	45	90	17	54	.218
Manning, Cleve.	552	73	161	6	43	.292	Chalk, Calif.	438	39	95	0	33	.217
Burleson, Boston	540	75	157	7	42	.291							
Braun, Minn.	417	73	120	3	60	.288							
Hargrove, Texas	541	80	155	7	58	.287							
White, N.Y.	626	104	179	14	65	.286			**PITCHING**					
Lezcano, Mil.	513	53	146	7	56	.285			(20 or more decisions)					
Oglivie, Det.	305	36	87	15	49	.285	Pitcher & Club	IP	H	BB	SO	W	L E.R.A.
Piniella, N.Y.	327	37	93	3	38	.284	Fidrych, Det.	250	217	53	97	19	9 2.34
Bell, Cleve.	604	75	171	7	60	.283	Hiller, Det.	121	93	67	117	12	8 2.38
Rice, Boston	581	75	164	25	85	.282	Blue, Oak.	298	268	63	166	18	13 2.38
Cooper, Boston	451	66	127	15	78	.282	Tanana, Calif.	288	212	73	261	19	10 2.43
Blanks, Cleve.	328	45	92	5	41	.280	Pattin, K.C.	141	114	38	65	8	14 2.49
Otis, Kan. City	592	93	165	18	85	.279	Torrez, Oak.	266	231	87	115	16	12 2.50
Singleton, Balt.	544	62	151	13	70	.278	Palmer, Balt.	315	255	84	159	22	13 2.51
Jackson, Balt.	498	84	138	27	91	.277	Fingers, Oak.	135	118	40	113	13	11 2.54
North, Oakland	590	91	163	2	31	.276	Garland, Balt.	232	224	64	113	20	7 2.67
Clines, Texas	446	52	123	0	38	.276	Travers, Mil.	240	211	95	120	15	16 2.81
Orta, Chicago	635	74	174	14	72	.274	Blyleven, Texas	298	283	81	219	13	16 2.87
Scott, Mil.	606	73	166	18	77	.274	Ross, Calif.	225	224	58	100	8	16 3.00
Hisle, Minn.	581	81	158	14	96	.272	Campbell, Minn.	168	145	63	115	17	5 3.01
Belanger, Balt.	522	66	141	1	40	.270	Figueroa, N.Y.	257	237	94	119	19	10 3.02
Rudi, Oakland	500	54	135	13	94	.270	Fitzmorris, K.C.	220	227	56	80	15	11 3.06
Stein, Chicago	390	32	105	4	35	.269	Tiant, Boston	279	274	64	131	21	12 3.06
Johnson, Det.	429	41	115	6	45	.268	Ellis, N.Y.	212	195	76	65	17	8 3.15
Yastrzemski, Boston	546	71	146	21	102	.267	Umbarger, Texas	197	208	54	105	10	12 3.15
Ford, Minn.	514	87	137	20	86	.267	Bibby, Cleve.	163	162	56	84	13	7 3.20
Randall, Minn.	475	55	127	1	34	.267	Perry, Cleve.	250	232	52	143	15	14 3.24
Money, Mil.	439	51	117	12	62	.267	Briles, Texas	210	224	47	98	11	9 3.26
Randolph, N.Y.	430	59	115	1	40	.267	Jenkins, Boston	209	201	43	142	12	11 3.27
Joshua, Mil.	423	44	113	5	28	.267	Augustine, Mil.	172	167	56	59	9	12 3.30
Bonds, Calif.	378	48	101	10	54	.267	Brett, Chi.	203	173	76	92	10	12 3.28
Grich, Balt.	518	93	138	13	54	.266	Ryan, Calif.	284	193	183	327	17	18 3.36
Cowens, Kan. City	581	69	154	3	59	.265	Goltz, Minn.	249	239	91	133	14	14 3.36
Hendrick, Cleve.	551	72	146	25	81	.265	Alexander, N.Y.	201	172	63	58	13	9 3.36
Collins, Calif.	365	45	96	4	29	.264	Bird, Kan. City	198	191	31	107	12	10 3.37
Kuiper, Cleve.	506	47	133	0	37	.263	Slaton, Mil.	293	287	94	138	14	15 3.44
Remy, Calif.	502	64	132	0	28	.263	Eckersley, Cleve.	199	155	78	200	13	12 3.43
Horton, Det.	401	40	105	14	56	.262	Dobson, Cleve.	217	226	66	117	16	12 3.48
Garner, Oakland	555	54	145	8	74	.261	Leonard, Kan. City	259	247	70	148	17	10 3.51
Harrah, Texas	584	64	152	15	67	.260	Hunter, N.Y.	299	268	68	173	17	15 3.53
Wynegar, Minn.	534	58	139	10	69	.260	Wise, Boston	224	218	48	93	14	11 3.53
Smalley, Minn.	513	61	133	3	43	.259	Holtzman, N.Y.	247	265	70	66	14	11 3.65
Bochte, Calif.	466	61	133	3	49	.259	Singer, Minn.	237	233	96	97	13	10 3.69
Campaneris, Oak.	531	67	137	1	52	.258	Colborn, Mil.	226	232	54	101	9	15 3.71
L. May, Balt.	530	61	137	25	109	.258	R. May, Balt.	220	205	70	109	15	10 3.72
Cubbage, Minn.	374	42	96	3	48	.257	Ruhle, Det.	200	227	59	88	9	12 3.92
C. May, N.Y.	351	45	91	3	43	.256	Gossage, Chi.	224	214	90	135	9	17 3.94
Downing, Chicago	317	38	81	3	30	.256	Splittorff, K.C.	159	169	59	59	11	8 3.97
Washington, Oak.	490	65	126	5	53	.255	Roberts, Det.	252	254	63	79	16	17 4.00
Fisk, Boston	487	76	124	17	58	.255	Brown, Cleve.	180	193	55	104	9	11 4.25
							B. Johnson, Chi.	211	231	62	91	9	16 4.73
							Hughes, Minn.	177	190	73	87	9	14 4.98

NATIONAL LEAGUE AVERAGES

(Unofficial)

BATTING—CLUB

	AB	R	H	HR	RBI	AVG
Cincinnati	5702	857	1599	141	802	.280
Philadelphia	5528	770	1505	110	701	.272
Pittsburgh	5604	708	1499	110	660	.267
St. Louis	5516	629	1432	63	584	.260
Houston	5464	625	1401	66	571	.256
Chicago	5519	611	1386	105	559	.251
Los Angeles	5472	608	1371	91	561	.251
San Diego	5369	570	1327	64	528	.247
New York	5415	615	1334	102	560	.246
San Francisco	5452	595	1340	85	552	.246
Atlanta	5346	620	1309	82	586	.245
Montreal	5428	531	1275	94	507	.235

BATTING—INDIVIDUAL

(300 or more times at bat)

	AB	R	H	HR	RBI	AVG
Madlock, Chi.	514	68	174	15	84	.339
Griffey, Cin.	562	111	189	6	74	.336
Maddox, Phila.	531	75	175	6	68	.330
Rose, Cin.	665	130	215	10	63	.323
Oliver, Pitts.	443	62	143	12	61	.323
Morgan, Cin.	472	113	151	27	111	.320
Johnstone, Phila.	440	62	140	5	53	.318
Garvey, L.A.	631	85	200	13	80	.317
Montanez, Atl.	650	74	206	11	84	.317
Parker, Pitts.	537	82	168	13	90	.313
Watson, Hous.	585	76	183	16	102	.313
Geronimo, Cin.	486	59	149	2	49	.307
Torre, N.Y.	310	36	95	5	31	.306
Foster, Cin.	562	86	172	29	121	.306
Luzinski, Phila.	533	74	162	21	95	.304
Crawford, St. L.	392	49	119	9	50	.304
Cruz, Hous.	439	49	133	4	61	.303
Robinson, Pitts.	393	55	119	21	64	.303
Brock, St. L.	498	73	150	4	67	.301
Buckner, L.A.	642	76	193	7	60	.301
Cardenal, Chi.	521	64	156	8	47	.299
Cedeno, Hous.	575	89	171	18	83	.297
Kranepool, N.Y.	415	47	121	10	49	.292
Ivie, San Diego	405	51	118	7	70	.291
Simmons, St. L.	546	60	159	5	75	.291
Sanguillen, Pitts.	389	52	113	2	36	.290
Paciorek, Atl.	324	39	94	4	36	.290
Zisk, Pitts.	581	91	168	21	89	.289
Hernandez, St. L.	374	54	108	7	46	.289
Herndon, San Fran.	337	42	97	2	23	.288
Boisclair, N.Y.	286	42	82	2	13	.287
Gross, Hous.	426	52	122	0	27	.286
Grubb, San Diego	384	54	109	5	27	.284
Cash, Phila.	666	92	189	1	56	.284
Winfield, San Diego	492	81	139	13	69	.283
Millan, N.Y.	531	55	150	1	35	.282
Office, Atl.	359	51	101	4	34	.281
Concepcion, Cin.	576	74	162	9	69	.281
Matthews, San Fran.	587	79	164	20	84	.279
Valentine, Mont.	305	36	85	7	39	.279
Cey, L.A.	502	69	139	23	80	.277
Russell, L.A.	554	53	152	5	65	.274
Morales, Chi.	537	66	147	16	67	.274
Cabell, Hous.	586	85	160	2	43	.273
Grote, N.Y.	323	30	88	4	28	.272
Monday, Chi.	534	107	145	32	77	.272
Boone, Phila.	361	40	98	4	54	.271
Milner, N.Y.	443	56	120	15	78	.271
Lacy, L.A.	338	42	91	3	34	.269
Allen, Phila.	298	54	80	15	49	.269
W. Davis, San Diego	493	61	132	5	46	.268
Reitz, San Fran.	577	40	154	5	66	.267
Turner, San Diego	282	40	75	5	37	.266
Fuentes, San Diego	520	48	137	2	36	.263
Rader, San Fran.	255	25	67	1	22	.263
Henderson, Atl.	435	52	114	13	61	.262
Schmidt, Phila.	584	112	153	38	107	.262
Foli, Mont.	546	41	143	6	54	.262
Tolan, Phila.	272	32	71	5	35	.261
Perez, Cin.	527	77	137	19	91	.260
Thomasson, San Fran.	328	45	85	8	38	.259
Murcer, San Fran.	533	73	138	23	90	.259
Taveras, Pitts.	519	76	134	0	24	.258
Mumphrey, St. L.	384	51	99	1	26	.258
Perez, San Fran.	428	49	110	3	32	.257
Stargell, Pitts.	428	54	110	20	65	.257
Rader, San Diego	471	45	121	9	55	.257
Stennett, Pitts.	654	59	168	2	60	.257
Andrews, Hous.	410	42	105	0	23	.256
Hernandez, San Diego	340	31	87	1	24	.256
Phillips, N.Y.	262	30	67	4	29	.256
Wallis, Chicago	338	51	86	5	21	.254
Jorgensen, Mont.	343	36	87	6	23	.254
Smith, L.A.	395	55	100	18	49	.253
Chaney, Atl.	496	42	125	1	50	.252
Gilbreath, Atl.	383	57	96	1	32	.251
Hebner, Pitts.	434	60	108	8	51	.249
Bowa, Phila.	624	71	155	0	49	.248
Royster, Atl.	534	65	132	5	45	.247
Kendall, San Diego	455	30	112	2	39	.246
Baker, L.A.	384	36	93	4	39	.242
Lopes, L.A.	427	72	103	4	20	.241
Kessinger, St. L.	502	55	120	1	40	.239
Trillo, Chi.	582	42	139	4	59	.239
Kingman, N.Y.	474	70	113	37	86	.238
Mangual, N.Y.	317	49	75	4	25	.237
Swisher, Chi.	377	25	89	5	42	.236
Bench, Cin.	465	62	109	16	74	.234
Foote, Mont.	350	32	82	7	27	.234
Harrelson, N.Y.	359	34	84	1	26	.234
Parrish, Mont.	543	54	126	11	61	.232
Garrett, Mont.	428	51	99	6	37	.231
Kelleher, Chi.	337	28	77	0	22	.228
Cruz, St. L.	526	54	120	13	71	.228
Unser, Mont.	496	57	113	12	40	.228
C. Johnson, Hous.	318	36	72	10	49	.226
Speier, San Fran.	495	51	112	3	40	.226

PITCHING

(20 or more decisions)

	IP	H	BB	SO	W	L	E.R.A.
Hough, L.A.	143	102	77	81	12	8	2.20
Denny, St. L.	207	189	74	74	11	9	2.25
Rau, L.A.	231	221	69	98	16	12	2.57
Seaver, N.Y.	271	211	77	235	14	11	2.59
Koosman, N.Y.	247	205	66	200	21	10	2.70
R. Jones, S. Diego	315	274	50	93	22	14	2.74
Zachry, Cin.	204	170	83	143	14	7	2.74
Richard, Hous.	291	221	151	214	20	15	2.75
Montefusco, S.F.	253	224	74	172	16	14	2.85
Barr, San Fran.	252	260	60	75	15	12	2.89
Matlack, N.Y.	262	236	57	153	17	10	2.95
Messersmith, L.A.	207	166	74	135	11	11	3.04
Sutton, L.A.	268	231	82	161	21	10	3.06
Kison, Pitts.	193	180	52	98	14	9	3.08
Lonborg, Phila.	222	210	50	118	18	10	3.08
John, L.A.	207	207	61	91	10	10	3.09
Burris, Chi.	249	251	70	112	15	13	3.11
Carlton, Phila.	253	224	72	195	20	7	3.13
Candelaria, Pitts.	220	173	60	138	16	7	3.15
Rogers, Mont.	230	212	69	150	7	17	3.21
Lolich, N.Y.	193	184	52	120	8	13	3.22
Falcone, St. L.	212	173	93	138	12	16	3.23
Hooton, L.A.	227	203	60	116	11	15	3.26
Strom, San Diego	211	188	73	103	12	16	3.28
P. Niekro, Atlanta	271	249	101	173	17	11	3.29
Rooker, Pitts.	199	201	72	92	15	8	3.35
Fryman, Mont.	216	218	76	123	13	13	3.38
G. Nolan, Cin.	239	232	27	113	15	9	3.46
Freisleben, S.D.	172	163	66	81	10	13	3.51
Reuschel, Chi.	260	260	64	146	14	12	3.46
Kaat, Phila.	209	214	52	114	14	9	3.53
Reuss, Pitts.	228	241	32	83	12	14	3.47
Halicki, San Fran.	186	171	61	130	12	14	3.67
Christenson, Phila.	169	199	42	54	13	8	3.67
Dierker, Hous.	188	171	72	112	13	14	3.69
Stanhouse, Mont.	184	182	92	79	9	12	3.77
McGlothen, St. L.	205	209	68	106	13	15	3.91
Renko, Chi.	176	179	46	116	8	12	3.99
Ruthven, Atlanta	240	255	90	142	14	17	4.20
Bonham, Cin.	196	215	96	110	9	13	4.27
Billingham, Cin.	177	190	62	76	12	10	4.32

WORLD SERIES

Cincinnati Reds (N.L.) defeated New York Yankees (A.L.), 4 games to 0

1st Game—At Cincinnati, Oct. 16

NEW YORK (A)	ab	r	h	bi	CINCINNATI (N)	ab	r	h	bi
Rivers, cf	4	0	0	0	Rose, 3b	2	0	0	1
White, lf	4	0	1	0	Griffey, rf	4	1	0	0
Munson, c	4	0	1	0	Morgan, 2b	4	1	1	1
Piniella, dh	3	1	1	0	Perez, 1b	4	0	3	1
May, dh	1	0	0	0	Driessen, dh	4	0	0	0
Chambliss, 1b	3	0	0	0	Foster, lf	3	1	2	0
Nettles, 3b	3	0	1	0	Bench, c	3	1	2	0
Maddox, rf	2	0	1	0	Geronimo, cf	3	0	1	0
Gamble, ph	1	0	0	0	Concepcion, ss	3	1	1	0
Randolph, 2b	2	0	0	0	Gullett, p	0	0	0	0
Stanley, ss	1	0	0	0	Borbon, p	0	0	0	0
Velez, ph	1	0	0	0	**Total**	**30**	**5**	**10**	**4**
Mason, ss	0	0	0	0					
Alexander, p	0	0	0	0					
Lyle, p	0	0	0	0					
Total	**29**	**1**	**5**	**1**					

New York Yankees . . . . 0 1 0 0 0 0 0 0 0—1
Cincinnati Reds . . . . . . 1 0 1 0 0 1 2 0 x—5

Errors—Geronimo, Chambliss. Double plays—Yankees 2, Cincinnati 2. Left on base—Yankees 6, Cincinnati 4. Two base hits—Piniella, Perez, Geronimo. Three base hits—Concepcion, Maddox, Bench. Home run—Morgan (1). Stolen base—Griffey. Sacrifice fly—Nettles, Rose.

	ip	h	r	er	bb	so
Alexander (L, 0-1)	6	9	5	5	2	1
Lyle	2	1	0	0	0	3
Gullett (W, 1-0)	7⅓	5	1	1	3	4
Borbon	1⅔	0	0	0	0	0

Hit by pitch—by Gullett (Chambliss). Wild Pitch—Lyle. Time of game—2:10. Attendance—54,826.

UMPIRES—Lee Weyer (N), plate; Lou DiMuro (A), first base; Billy Williams (N), second base; Bill Deegan (A), third base; Bruce Froemming (N), left field; Dave Phillips (A), right field. The umpires rotate after each game, the first base arbiter going to the plate, second base to first, etc. The plate umpire goes to right field for the following game.

2d Game—At Cincinnati, Oct. 17

NEW YORK (A)	ab	r	h	bi	CINCINNATI (N)	ab	r	h	bi
Rivers, cf	5	0	0	0	Rose, 3b	4	0	0	0
White, lf	3	0	1	0	Griffey, rf	4	1	0	1
Munson, c	4	1	1	1	Morgan, 2b	4	0	2	0
Piniella, rf	4	0	2	0	Perez, 1b	5	0	2	1
Chambliss, 1b	4	0	0	0	Driessen, dh	4	1	2	0
Nettles, 3b	4	0	1	1	Foster, lf	4	0	1	0
Maddox, dh	3	0	0	0	Bench, c	4	1	2	0
May, dh	1	0	0	0	Geronimo, cf	2	1	0	0
Randolph, 2b	4	1	1	0	Concepcion, ss	4	0	1	1
Stanley, ss	3	1	1	1	Norman, p	0	0	0	0
Hunter, p	0	0	0	0	Billingham, p	0	0	0	0
Total	**35**	**3**	**9**	**3**	**Total**	**35**	**4**	**10**	**4**

Two outs when winning run was scored.

New York Yankees . . . . 0 0 0 1 0 0 2 0 0—3
Cincinnati Reds . . . . . . 0 3 0 0 0 0 0 0 1—4

Errors—Stanley. Double plays—Cincinnati 1. Left on base—Yankees 7, Cincinnati 10. Two-base hits—Driessen, Bench, Stanley. Three-base hits—Morgan. Stolen bases—Morgan, Concepcion. Sacrifice fly—Griffey.

	ip	h	r	er	bb	so
Hunter (L, 0-1)	8⅔	10	4	3	4	5
Norman	6⅓	9	3	3	2	2
Billingham (W, 1-0)	2⅔	0	0	0	0	0

Time of Game—2:33. Attendance—54,816.

3d Game—New York, Tues., Oct. 19

CINCINNATI (N)	ab	r	h	bi	NEW YORK (A)	ab	r	h	bi
Rose, 3b	5	1	2	0	Rivers, cf	4	0	2	0
Griffey, rf	4	0	1	0	White, lf	3	0	0	0
Morgan, 2b	4	1	1	1	Munson, c	5	0	3	0
Perez, 1b	4	0	0	0	Chambliss, 1b	5	1	1	0
Driessen, dh	3	2	3	1	May, dh	4	0	0	0
Foster, lf	4	1	2	2	Nettles, 3b	2	0	0	0
Bench, c	4	0	2	0	Gamble, rf	3	0	1	1
Geronimo, cf	4	1	1	1	Piniella, rf	1	0	0	0
Concepcion, ss	4	0	1	1	Randolph, 2b	4	0	0	0
Zachry, p	0	0	0	0	Stanley, ss	1	0	0	0
McEnaney, p	0	0	0	0	Hendricks, ph	1	0	0	0
Total	**36**	**6**	**13**	**6**	Mason, ss	1	1	1	1
					Velez, ph	1	0	0	0
					Ellis, p	0	0	0	0
					Jackson, p	0	0	0	0
					Tidrow, p	0	0	0	0
					Total	**35**	**2**	**8**	**2**

Cincinnati Reds . . . . . . 0 3 0 1 0 0 0 2 0—6
New York Yankees . . . . 0 0 0 1 0 0 1 0 0—2

Errors—Perez, Concepcion. Double plays—Cincinnati 1, Yankees 3. Left on base—Cincinnati 4, Yankees 11. Two-base hits—Foster, Driessen, Morgan. Home runs—Driessen (1), Mason (1). Stolen base—Driessen, Geronimo.

	ip	h	r	er	bb	so
Zachry (W)	6⅔	6	2	2	5	6
McEnaney	2⅓	2	0	0	0	1
Ellis (L)	3⅓	7	4	4	0	1
Jackson	3⅔	4	2	2	0	3
Tidrow	2	2	0	0	1	1

Save—McEnaney (1). Time of game—2:42. Attendance—56,667.

4th Game—New York, Oct. 20

CINCINNATI (N)	ab	r	h	bi	NEW YORK (A)	ab	r	h	bi
Rose, 3b	5	0	1	0	Rivers, cf	5	1	1	0
Griffey, rf	5	0	0	0	White, lf	5	0	0	0
Morgan, 2b	3	1	1	0	Munson, c	4	1	4	1
Perez, 1b	3	1	0	0	Chambliss, 1b	4	0	1	1
Driessen, dh	3	1	1	0	May, dh	3	0	0	0
Foster, lf	3	1	1	1	Piniella, dh	1	0	0	0
Bench, c	4	2	2	5	Nettles, 3b	3	0	2	0
Geronimo, cf	4	1	1	0	Gamble, rf	4	0	0	0
Concepcion, ss	3	0	2	1	Randolph, 2b	4	0	0	0
Nolan, p	0	0	0	0	Stanley, ss	1	0	0	0
McEnaney, p	0	0	0	0	Hendricks, ph	1	0	0	0
Total	**33**	**7**	**9**	**7**	Mason, ss	0	0	0	0
					Velez, ph	1	0	0	0
					Figueroa, p	0	0	0	0
					Tidrow, p	0	0	0	0
					Lyle, p	0	0	0	0
					Total	**36**	**2**	**8**	**2**

Cincinnati Reds . . . . . . 0 0 0 3 0 0 0 0 4—7
New York Yankees . . . . 1 0 0 0 1 0 0 0 0—2

Errors—Morgan, Concepcion. Double plays—Yankees 1. Left on base—Cincinnati 4, Yankees 9. Two base hits—Rose, Chambliss, Geronimo, Concepcion. Home runs—Bench 2 (3). Stolen bases—Geronimo, Morgan, Rivers.

	ip	h	r	er	bb	so
Nolan (W, 1-0)	6⅔	8	2	2	1	1
McEnaney	2⅓	0	0	0	1	1
Figueroa (L, 0-1)	8	6	5	5	2	2
Tidrow	⅓	3	2	2	0	0
Lyle	⅔	0	0	0	0	0

Save—McEnaney (2). Wild pitch—Figueroa. Time of game—2:36. Attendance—56,700.

NATIONAL ALL-STARS WIN AGAIN

(At Philadelphia, July 13; attendance, 63,974)

American League 000 100 000 1 5 0
National League 202 000 00X 7 10 0

Fidrych, Hunter (3), Tiant (5), Tanana (7) and Munson, Fisk (5); Jones, Seaver (4), Montefusco (6), Rhoden (8), Forsch (9) and Bench, Boone (5). Winner: Jones; loser: Fidrych; Home runs: American: Lynn; National: Foster, Cedeno.

1976 World Series Composite Averages

BATTING (REGULARS)

CINCINNATI	g	ab	r	h	2b	3b	hr	rbi	so	bb	bat avg
Rose, 3b	4	16	1	3	1	0	0	1	2	2	.188
Griffey, rf	4	17	2	1	0	0	0	1	1	0	.059
Morgan, 2b	4	15	3	5	1	1	1	2	2	2	.333
Perez, 1b	4	16	1	5	1	0	0	2	2	1	.313
Driessen, dh	4	14	4	5	2	0	1	1	0	2	.357
Foster, lf	4	14	3	6	1	0	0	4	3	2	.429
Bench, c	4	15	4	8	1	1	2	6	1	0	.533
Geronimo, cf	4	13	3	4	2	0	1	2	2	2	.308
Concepcion, ss	4	14	1	5	1	1	0	3	3	1	.357

NEW YORK	g	ab	r	h	2b	3b	hr	rbi	so	bb	bat avg
Rivers, cf	4	18	1	3	0	0	0	0	2	1	.167
White, lf	4	15	0	2	0	0	0	0	0	3	.133
Munson, c	4	17	2	9	0	0	0	2	1	0	.529
Piniela, dh-rf	4	9	1	3	1	0	0	0	0	0	.333
May, dh	4	9	0	0	0	0	0	0	1	0	.000
Chambliss, 1b	4	16	1	5	1	0	0	1	2	0	.313
Nettles, 3b	4	12	0	3	0	0	2	1	3		.250
Gamble, ph-rf	3	8	0	1	0	0	1	0	0		.125
Randolph, 2b	4	14	1	1	0	0	0	3	1		.071
Stanley, ss	4	6	1	1	0	0	1	1	3		.167

PITCHING

CINCINNATI	g	ip	h	r	bb	so	w	l	pct	er	era
Gullett	1	7 1/3	5	1	3	4	1	0	1.000	1	1.29
Borbon	1	1 2/3	0	0	0	0	0		.000	0	0.00
Norman	1	6 1/3	9	3	2	2	0	0	.000	3	4.50
Billingham	1	2 2/3	0	0	0	1	1	0	1.000	0	0.00
Zachry	1	6 2/3	6	2	5	6	1	0	1.000	2	2.57
McEnaney	2	4 2/3	2	0	1	2	0	0	.000	0	0.00
Nolan	1	6 2/3	8	2	1	1	1	0	1.000	2	2.57
Total	4	36	30	8	12	16	4	0	1.000	8	2.00

NEW YORK	g	ip	h	r	bb	so	w	l	pct	er	era
Alexander	1	6	9	5	2	1	0	1	.000	5	7.50
Lyle	2	2 1/3	1	0	0	3	0	0	.000	0	0.00
Hunter	1	8 1/3	10	4	4	5	0	1	.000	3	3.00
Ellis	1	3 1/3	7	4	0	1	0	1	.000	4	12.00
Jackson	1	3 2/3	4	2	0	3	0	0	.000	2	4.50
Tidrow	2	2 1/3	5	2	1	1	0	0	.000	2	9.00
Figueroa	1	8	6	5	5	2	0	1	.000	5	5.63
Total	4	34 1/3	42	22	12	16	0	4	.000	21	5.40

MINOR LEAGUE BASEBALL

Class AAA

AMERICAN ASSOCIATION

East Division	W	L	Pct.	West Division	W	L	Pct.
Omaha	78	58	.584	Denver	86	50	.632
Iowa	68	68	.500	Oklahoma City	72	63	.533
Indianapolis	62	73	.459	Tulsa	65	70	.481
Evansville	55	81	.404	Wichita	56	79	.415

Playoff

Championship—Denver defeated Omaha, 4 games to 2

INTERNATIONAL LEAGUE

	W	L	Pct.		W	L	Pct.
Rochester	88	50	.638	Rhode Island	68	70	.4927
Syracuse	82	57	.590	Charleston	62	73	.59
Memphis	69	69	.500	Tidewater	60	78	.435
Richmond	69	21	.4928	Toledo	55	85	.393

Governors Cup Playoffs

Semifinals

Syracuse defeated Memphis, 3 games to 0
Richmond defeated Rochester, 3 games to 1

Final

Syracuse defeated Richmond, 3 games to 1

PACIFIC COAST LEAGUE

East Division	W	L	Pct.	West Division	W	L	Pct
Salt Lake City	90	54	.625	*Hawaii	77	68	.531
Phoenix	75	67	.528	Tacoma	76	69	.524
Albuquerque	66	78	.458	Sacramento	71	72	.497
Tucson	54	88	.380	Spokane	65	78	.455

* Hawaii defeated Tacoma, 3-1, in one-game playoff for division title

Playoff

Championship—Hawaii defeated Salt Lake City, 3 games to 2

MEXICAN LEAGUE

Championship

Mexico City Reds defeated Union Laguna, 4 games to 2

Class AA

Eastern League—Southern division and championship: West Haven; Northern Division: Three Rivers
Southern League—Eastern Division: Orlando; Western Division: first half: Chattanooga; second half and champion: Montgomery
Texas League—Eastern Division: Shreveport; Western Division and champion: Amarillo

Class A

California League—First half: Salinas; second half and champion: Reno
Carolina League—Winston-Salem won both halves and championship
Florida State League—Northern Division: Tampa; Southern Division: Miami; championship: Lakeland (defeated Miami, 2 games to 0, in semifinals and Tampa, 2 games to 0, in final)
Gulf States League—Western Division and champion: Corpus Christi; Eastern Division: Seguin (defeated Beeville in playoff)
Midwest League—Northern Division: Waterloo (won both halves) and championship; Southern Division: Quad Cities (defeated Cedar Rapids in playoff for second half and defeated Cedar Rapids, first-half winner, for division title.
New York-Penn League—Elmira won both halves and championship
Northwest League—Southern Division and champion: Walla Walla; Northern Division: Portland
Western Carolinas League—First half: Asheville; second half and champion: Greenwood

ROOKIE LEAGUES

Appalachian League—Southern Division: Johnson City (awarded league championship on best winning percentage); Northern Division: Bluefield
Pioneer League—Great Falls
Gulf Coast League—Rangers

AMATEUR BASEBALL

N.C.A.A. Division I—University of Arizona, defeated Eastern Michigan, 7-1, in final
N.C.A.A. Division II—Cal Poly-Pomona
N.C.A.A. Division III—California State-Stanislaus
N.A.I.A.—Lewis University (Illinois)
American Legion—Santa Monica, Calif.
Babe Ruth League—Manchester, N.H.
Big League Little League—Taiwan
Bronco League—Miami (Fla.) Cubans
Colt League—Tampa, Fla.
Connie Mack League—Corpus Christi (Tex.) Boys' Club
Little League—Japan (Tokyo) defeated Campbell, Calif., 10-3, in final
Little League Senior—Pin Tung, Taiwan
Mickey Mantle League—Cincinnati Midland Guardian Bank Cardinals
National Baseball Congress—Fairbanks, Alaska, defeated Anchorage, Alaska, 2-0, in final
Pee Wee Reese League—College Park (Ga.) Old National Braves
Pony League—Tampa, Fla.
Sandy Koufax League—Guaynabo, Puerto Rico
Stan Musial League—Ferry Cap and Screw Co, Cleveland, Ohio
Thorobred League—San Jose, Calif.
Willie Mays League—College Park (Ga.) Old National Red Sox

GOLF

U.S. Open Championship

(Atlanta, Ga., Athletic Club, June 17-20)

Jerry Pate, Pensacola, Fla.	71	69	69	68–277
Tom Weiskopf, Columbus, Ohio	73	70	68	68–279
Al Geiberger, Santa Barbara, Calif.	70	69	71	69–279
John Mahaffey, Houston, Tex.	70	68	69	73–280
Butch Baird, Miami	71	71	71	67–280
Hubert Green, Bay Point, Fla.	72	70	71	69–282
Tom Watson, Kansas City, Mo.	74	72	68	70–284
Lyn Lott, Douglas, Ga.	71	71	70	73–285
Ben Crenshaw, Austin, Tex.	72	68	72	73–285
Johnny Miller, Napa, Calif.	74	72	69	71–286

Prizes—Pate $42,000; Weiskopf and Geiberger $18,000; Mahaffey and Baird $11,250; Green $9,500; Watson $8,500; Lott and Crenshaw $7,000; Miller $5,500.

Masters Tournament

(National Golf Club, Augusta, Ga., April 8-11)

Ray Floyd	65	66	70	70–271	$40,000
Ben Crenshaw	70	70	72	67–279	25,000
Jack Nicklaus	67	69	73	73–282	16,250
Larry Ziegler	67	71	72	72–282	16,250
Charles Coody	72	69	70	74–285	11,166
Hale Irwin	71	77	67	70–285	11,166
Tom Kite	73	67	72	73–285	11,166
Billy Casper	71	76	71	69–287	8,000

British Open

(Royal Birkdale G.C., Southport, England, July 7-10)

Johnny Miller	72	68	73	66–279
Severiano Ballesteros	69	69	73	74–285
Jack Nicklaus	74	70	72	69–285
Ray Floyd	76	67	73	70–286
Christy O'Connor	69	73	75	71–288
Tom Kite	70	74	73	71–288
Tommy Horton	74	69	72	73–288
Mark James	76	72	74	66–288
Hubert Green	72	70	78	68–288

Professional Golfers' Association Championship

(Congressional Country Club, Bethesda, Md., Aug. 12-16)

Dave Stockton	70	72	69	70–281	$45,000
Ray Floyd	72	68	71	71–282	20,000
Don January	70	69	71	72–282	20,000
Jerry Pate	69	73	72	69–283	9,750
John Schlee	72	71	70	70–283	9,750
Jack Nicklaus	71	69	69	74–283	9,750
David Graham	70	71	70	72–283	9,750

Other Leading Tournaments

Canadian Open—Jerry Pate (267)	40,000
French Open—Vincent Tshabalala, South Africa (272)	
P.G.A. senior—Pete Cooper, Branford, Fla. (283)	
Tournament of Champions—Don January (277)	45,000
World Series of Golf—Jack Nicklaus (275)	100,000

Other P.G.A. Circuit Winners

Tucson Open—Johnny Miller (274)	$40,000
Phoenix Open—Bob Gilder (268)	40,000
Crosby Pro-Am—Ben Crenshaw (281)	37,000
Hawaiian Open—Ben Crenshaw (270)	46,000
Bob Hope Desert Classic—Johnny Miller (344)	36,000
San Diego Open—J.C. Snead (272)	36,000
Los Angeles Open—Hale Irwin (272)	37,000
Citrus Open—*Hale Irwin (270)	40,000
Doral-Eastern—Hubert Green (270)	40,000
Jacksonville Open—Hubert Green (276)	35,000
Heritage Classic—Hubert Green (274)	43,000

Greensboro Open—Al Geiberger (268)	46,000
Tallahassee Open—Gary Koch (277)	16,000
New Orleans Open—Larry Ziegler (274)	35,000
Houston Open—Lee Elder (278)	40,000
Byron Nelson Classic—Mark Hayes (273)	40,000
Colonial National—Lee Trevino (273)	40,000
Memphis Classic—Gibby Gilbert (273)	40,000
Memorial—*Roger Maltbie (288)	40,000
Philadelphia Classic—*Tom Kite (277)	40,000
Kemper Open—Joe Inman (277)	50,000
Western Open—Al Geiberger (288)	40,000
Milwaukee Open—Dave Hill (270)	26,000
Quad Cities—John Lister (268)	20,000
Westchester Classic—David Graham (272)	60,000
Pleasant Valley—Brian Allin (277)	40,000
B.C. Open—Bob Wynn (271)	40,000
Hartford Open—Rik Massengale (266)	42,000
American Classic—David Graham (274)	40,000
World Open—*Ray Floyd (274)	40,000
Ohio King's Island—Ben Crenshaw (271)	30,000
Kaiser International—J. C. Snead (274)	35,000
Sahara Invitation—George Archer (271)	27,000

* Won playoff.

LEADING 1976 P.G.A. EARNINGS

(Through Oct. 20)

Jack Nicklaus	$266,438	Don January	$163,622
Ben Crenshaw	256,834	Jerry Pate	150,727
Hale Irwin	252,718	Tom Watson	138,202
Hubert Green	211,406	Lee Trevino	136,679
Al Geiberger	194,821	Johnny Miller	135,887
J. C. Snead	192,645	Tom Weiskopf	129,706
Ray Floyd	178,318	Mark Hayes	126,699
David Graham	176,174	Rik Massengale	124,984

P.G.A. CAREER EARNINGS

(Through Oct. 20)

Jack Nicklaus	$2,808,211	Gary Player	$1,216,821
Arnold Palmer	1,740,131	Johnny Miller	1,083,039
Billy Casper	1,629,537	Miller Barber	1,080,877
Lee Trevino	1,533,638	Dave Hill	1,033,388
Bruce Crampton	1,373,494	Hale Irwin	1,012,774
Tom Weiskopf	1,354,561	Julius Boros	996,852
Gene Littler	1,264,013	Al Geiberger	984,590

AMATEUR

United States Championship

(Bel-Air C.C., Los Angeles, Sept. 2-5)

Final (36 holes)—Bill Sander, Kenmore, Wash., defeated Parker Moore, Laurens, S.C., 8 and 6

Quarterfinals—Stan Souza, Honolulu, defeated Mark Tinder, Monterey, Calif., 4 and 2; Moore defeated Mike Reid, Seattle, 1 up; Jim Mason, Kirkwood, Mo., defeated John Fought, Tualatin, Ore., 1 up; Sander defeated Skeeter Heath, Hampton, Va., 2 up

Semifinals—Moore defeated Souza, 19 holes; Sander defeated Mason, 8 and 7

Other Leading Tournaments

British Amateur—Dick Siderowf, Westport, Conn., defeated John Davies, England, 37 holes, in final

Canadian amateur—Jim Nelford, Burnaby, B.C.

U.S. Public Links—Eddie Mudd, Morehead, Ky., defeated Archie Dadian, Milwaukee, 37 holes, in final

U.S. Junior—Madden Hatcher, Columbus, Ga., defeated Doug Clarke, La Jolla, Calif., 3 and 2, in final

N.C.A.A. Division I—Scott Simpson, So. California	283
N.C.A.A. Division II—Mike Nicollette, Rollins	286
N.C.A.A. Division III—Dan Lisle, Cal State-Stanislaus	298
N.A.I.A.—Will Brewer, David Lipscomb	289
Junior College—Butch Girard, Brevard, J.C.	285

GOLF (Continued)

U.S.G.A. Senior—Lou Oehmig, Lookout Mountain, Tenn., defeated
   John Richardson, Laguna Niguel, Calif., 4 and 3, in final
U.S. Senior G.A.—*Dale Morey, High Point, N.C. 147
Amputee—Frank Cothran, Selma, Ala. 292
Eastern—Vance Heafner, Cary, N.C. 284
Porter Cup—Scott Simpson, San Diego 278
New England—Dave Lane, Chelmsford, Mass. 287
Pacific Coast—Mike Reid, Kirkland, Wash. 281
Southern—Tim Simpson, Atlanta, Ga. 284
World Junior—Chip Larson, Scottsdale, Ariz. 287
PGA Junior National—Larry Field, Oklahoma City 297
   * Won playoff.

TEAM

World (Penina, Portugal, Oct. 13-16)—Britain-Ireland . . 892
PGA Cup (Leeds, England, Oct. 13-15, pros)—U.S. 9½, Britain 6½
N.C.A.A. Division I—Oklahoma State 1,166
N.C.A.A. Division II—Troy State 1,181
N.C.A.A. Division III—Cal State-Stanislaus 1,221
N.A.I.A.—Gardner-Webb 1,193
Junior College—Brevard, Cocoa, Fla. 1,157

WOMEN

U.S. Open Championship

(Rolling Green G.C., Springfield, Pa., July 8-12)

*JoAnne Carner, Lake Worth, Fla. . .	71	71	77	73—292
Sandra Palmer, Palm Springs, Calif. .	70	74	73	75—292
Jane Blalock, Highland Beach, Fla. .	75	72	73	76—296
Susie McAllister, Beaumont, Tex. .	76	78	70	73—297
Amy Alcott, Santa Monica, Calif. .	72	75	78	74—299
Sharon Miller, Fort Worth, Tex. . .	75	75	77	72—299

   * Mrs. Carner won 18-hole playoff, 76–78.

   Prizes—Mrs. Carner $9,000; Miss Palmer $5,500; Miss Blalock
$3,454; Miss McAllister $2,654; Miss Alcott and Miss Miller
$2,329.

L.P.G.A. Championship

(Pine Ridge G.C., Baltimore, May 27-30)

Betty Burfeindt	71	72	73	71—287	$8,000
Judy Rankin	72	75	70	71—288	5,650
Carole Jo Skala	71	74	73	72—290	4,300
Jane Blalock	75	74	71	71—291	2,650
Donna Young	74	73	72	72—291	2,650
Jan Stephenson	71	75	72	73—291	2,650

Other L.P.G.A. Circuit Winners

Burdine's Invitation—Judy Rankin (213) $5,700
Sarah Coventry-Naples—Jan Stephenson (218) 8,500
Orange Blossom—*JoAnne Carner (209) 6,400
Bent Tree Classic—Kathy Whitworth (209) 8,500
Colgate Winners Circle—Judy Rankin (285) 32,000
Karsten-Ping Open—Judy Rankin (205) 14,000
Birmingham Classic—Jan Stephenson (203) 5,700
Lady Tara—JoAnne Carner (209) 7,000
International—Sally Little (281) 10,000
American Defender—Sue Roberts (211) 6,400
'76 LPGA Classic—Amy Alcott (209) 14,000
Girl Talk Classic—*Pat Bradley (217) 14,000
Peter Jackson Classic—*Donna Young (212) 12,000
Hoosier Classic—JoAnne Carner (210) 7,000
Zaharias Invitation—Judy Rankin (287) 15,000
Bloomington Bicentennial—Sandra Palmer (209) 7,000
Borden's Classic—Judy Rankin (205) 10,000
Lady Keystone—Susie Berning (215) 7,000
Colgate-European Open—Chako Higuchi (284) 15,000
Wheeling Classic—*Jane Blalock (217) 7,000
Patty Berg Classic—Kathy Whitworth (212) 8,000
Jewish Hospital Open—Sandra Palmer (206) 7,000
Jerry Lewis Classic—*Sandra Palmer (213) 15,000
   * Won Playoff.

L.P.G.A. LEADING EARNINGS

(Through October 1)

Judy Rankin . . .	$138,734	Jan Stephenson . .	$61,928
Jane Blalock . . .	90,127	Kathy Whitworth . .	57,614
JoAnne Carner . . .	86,908	Betty Burfeindt . .	57,213
Sandra Palmer . .	86,195	Amy Alcott . . .	52,773
Donna C. Young . .	79,806	Sandra Post . . .	47,197
Patricia Bradley . .	78,516	Sandra Haynie . . .	38,510

United States Championship

(Del Pasco C.C., Sacramento, Calif., Aug. 18-21)

Final—Donna Horton, Jacksonville, Fla., defeated Marianne Bret-
   ton, San Diego, Calif., 2 and 1, in final
Quarterfinals—Donna Horton defeated Debbie Massey, Bethlehem,
   Pa., 19 holes; Marianne Bretton defeated Nancy Lopez, Ros-
   well, N.M., 1 up; Rise Alexander, Gresham, Ore., defeated
   Margaret Brady, Gautier, Mass., 19 holes; Pat Cornett, Salinas,
   Calif., defeated Mrs. Jerry Keil, Sylvania, Ohio, 6 and 4
Semifinals—Marianne Bretton defeated Rise Alexander, 7 and 6;
   Donna Horton defeated Pat Cornett, 1 up

Other Leading Tournaments

U.S.G.A. Girls—Pilar Dorado, Hayward, Calif., defeated Kellii
   Doherty, Buena Park, Calif., 3 and 2, in final
U.S. Senior G.A.—Dot Porter, Cinnaminson, N.J. 233
U.S.G.A. senior—Mrs. Ceil MacLaurin, Savannah, Ga. . . . 230
Collegiate (A.I.A.W.)—Nancy Lopez, Tulsa 302

TEAM

Curtis Cup—United States 11½, Britain 8½
World (Vilamoura, Portugal, Oct. 6-9)—United States . . . 605
   (Individual: Nancy Lopez, Roswell, N.M., 297)
Collegiate (A.I.A.W.)—Furman 1,251

CASTING

Source: William B. Burke, American Casting Association

INLAND

(Lexington, Ky., August 9-14)

All around—Steve Rajeff, San Francisco
All distance (6 events)—Rajeff . . . . 5,141 ft
Distance plugs—Terry Schneider, New Albany, Ind. . 3,682 ft
Distance flies—Rajeff . . . . 1,681 ft
All accuracy (6 events)—Rajeff . . . . 591 pts

WOMEN

All accuracy (6 events)—Mollie Light, New Albany, Ind. . 296 pts
Accuracy plugs (3 events)—Mollie Light . . . . . . 268 pts
Accuracy flies (3 events)—Tie between Mollie Light and
   Pauline Cathcart, La Canada, Calif. . . . . 273 pts

Intermediates

All accuracy (6 events)—Bruce Rogers, St. Louis . . 535 pts
Accuracy plugs (3 events)—Baker Burke, Jackson, Ky. . 281 pts
Accuracy flies (3 events)—Bruce Rogers . . . . . . 269 pts

WORLD CHAMPIONSHIPS

(St. Louis, Sept. 24-Oct. 2)

Inland all around—Steve Rajeff, San Francisco
Surf all around—J. Engelbrecht, South Africa
Aggregate all around—J. DeKock, South Africa

CURLING

World (Duluth, Minn., March 22-28)—United States (Bruce
   Roberts, skip) defeated Scotland (Bill Muirhead, skip), 6-5.
United States Men (Wausau, Wis., March 1-8)—Hibbing, Minn.
   (Bruce Roberts, skip; Jerry Scott, Gary Kleffman, Joe Roberts)
   defeated Superior, Wis. (Bud Somerville, skip), 9-1, in playoff.
United States Women—Highland Park, Ill. (Jackie Warner, skip;
   Ann Brown, Cynthia Willis, Jean Nickoley) defeated St. Paul
   (Marsha Hulstrand, skip) in final.

WATER POLO

Men's A.A.U.—Concord (Calif.) P.C.
College (November 1975)—California

AUTO RACING

United States Auto Club

TRIPLE CROWN RACES

Indianapolis 500 (May 30, Indianapolis Motor Speedway, cut to 102 laps, 255 miles by rain)—1, Johnny Rutherford, Fort Worth, Tex., McLaren-Offenhauser; 102 laps; 1 hour, 42 minutes, 52.48 seconds for an average speed of 148.725 miles per hour; $256,121. 2, A. J. Foyt, Houston, Tex., Coyote-Foyt; 102 laps; $103,296. 3, Gordon Johncock, Phoenix, Ariz., Wildcat-DGS; 102 laps; $67,676. 4, Wally Dallenbach, Basalt, Colo., Wildcat-DGS; 101 laps; $38,049. 5, Pancho Carter, Brownsburg, Ind., Eagle-Offy; 101 laps; $33,777.

Schaefer 500 (June 27, Pocono International Raceway, Long Pond, Pa.)—1, Al Unser, Albuquerque, N.M., Parnelli-Cosworth; 200 laps; 3 hours, 28 minutes, 52.88 seconds for average speed of 143.622 m.p.h.; $84,300. 2, Mike Mosley, Fallbrick, Calif., Eagle-Offy; 200 laps; $2,350. 3, Wally Dallenbach, Wildcat-DGS; 200 laps; $26,900. 4, Johnny Rutherford, McLaren-Offy; 200 laps; $16,725.

California 500 (Ontario Motor Speedway, 500 miles, Sept. 5)—1, Bobby Unser, Albuquerque, N.M., Cobra-Offenhauser; 200 laps; 3:29:25.76; 143.246 m.p.h.; $82,986. 2, Johnny Rutherford, McLaren-Offy; 200; $37,736. 3, Gordon Johncock; Wildcat-Bignotti; 198; $30,311.

OTHER RACES

Bryan 150 (Phoenix, Ariz., March 14)—Bobby Unser, Eagle-Offy; 1:23:23.81; 107.918 m.p.h. $10,905.

Trentonian 200 (Trenton, N.J., May 2)—Johnny Rutherford, McLaren-Offy; 1:21:45.79; 147.499 m.p.h.; $13,290.

Rex Mays 150 (Milwaukee, June 13)—Mike Mosley, Eagle-Offy; 1:14:02.35; 121.557 m.p.h.; $17,457.

Norton 200 (Brooklyn, Mich., July 18)—Gordon Johncock; Wildcat-Offy; 1:12:42.76; 165.033 m.p.h.; $15,829.

Texas 150 (College Station, Tex., Aug. 1)—A. J. Foyt; Coyote-Ford; 52:03.46; 172.855 m.p.h.; $10,429.

Trenton Times 200 (Trenton, N.J., Aug. 15; cut to 175.5 miles by rain)—Johncock; 1:17:28; 135.929 m.p.h.; $11,803.

Bettenhausen 200 (Milwaukee, Aug. 22)—Al Unser; Parnelli-Cosworth; 1:38:26.13; 121.907 m.p.h.; $14,847.

Michigan Grand Prix (Brooklyn, Mich., Sept. 19)—Foyt; 54:51.32; 164.068; $13,466.

Championship Trail Point Leaders
(October 30)

1, Johnny Rutherford, 3,820; 2, Gordon Johncock, 3,680.

USAC SEASON CHAMPIONS

Dirt Track—Johnny Parsons, Indianapolis.
Midget—Ron (Sleepy) Tripp, Costa Mesa, Calif.
Sprint—Duane (Pancho) Carter, Brownsburg, Ind.

National Association for Stock Car Auto Racing (NASCAR)

Winston Western 500 (Riverside, Calif., Jan. 18)—David Pearson, Spartansburg, S.C.; Mercury; 5 hours, 2 minutes, 44 seconds; average speed: 99.189 miles per hour. First price: $17,295.

Daytona 500 (Daytona Beach, Fla., Feb. 15)—Pearson; 3:17:08; 152.181 m.p.h.; $46,800.

Carolina 500 (Rockingham, N.C., Feb. 29)—Richard Petty, Randleman, N.C.; Dodge; 4:24:08; 113.665 m.p.h.; $19,915.

Atlanta 500 (Atlanta, Ga., March 21)—Pearson; 3:52:16; 128.904 m.p.h.; $11,700.

Rebel 500 (Darlington, S.C., April 11)—Pearson; 4:04:36; 129.73 m.p.h.; $11,670.

Winston 500 (Talladega, Ala., May 2)—Buddy Baker, Charlotte, N.C.; Ford; 2:56:37; 169.887 m.p.h.; $25,285.

Mason Dixon 500 (Dover, Del., May 16)—Benny Parsons, Ellerbe, N.C.; Chevrolet; 4:19:53; 115.436 m.p.h.; $14,015.

World 600 (Charlotte, N.C., May 30)—Pearson; 4:22:06; 137.352 m.p.h.; $42,390.

Motor Oil 400 (Brooklyn, Mich., June 20)—Pearson; 2:50:02; 141.148 m.p.h.; $11,295.

Firecracker 400 (Daytona Beach, Fla., July 4)—Cale Yarborough, Timmonsville, S.C.; Chevrolet; 2:29:06; 160.966 m.p.h. $14,715.

Purolator 500 (Pocono, Long Pond, Pa., Aug. 1)—Petty; 4:18:54; 115.875 m.p.h.; $15,290.

Talladega 500 (Talladega, Ala., Aug. 8)—Dave Marcis, Wausau, Wis.; Dodge; 3:10:27; 157.547 m.p.h.; $21,310.

Champion Spark Plug 400 (Brooklyn, Mich., Aug. 22)—Pearson; 2:51:20; 140.078 m.p.h.; $11,950.

Southern 500 (Darlington, S.C., Sept. 6)—Pearson; 4:09:33; 120.534 m.p.h.; $16,155.

Delaware 500 (Dover, Sept. 20)—Yarborough; 4:15:06; 117.74; $10,710.

GRAND PRIX RACES
(Formula One Competition)

Brazil (Sao Paulo, 197.18 miles, Jan. 25)—Niki Lauda, Austria; Ferrari; time: 1 hour, 45 minutes, 26.78 seconds; average speed: 113 miles per hour

South Africa (Johannesburg, 198.94 miles, March 6)—Lauda; 1:42:18.4; 116 m.p.h.

United States West (Long Beach, Calif., 161.6 miles, March 28)—Clay Regazzoni, Switzerland; Ferrari; 1:53:18.471; 85.57 m.p.h.

Spain (Madrid, 158.6 miles, May 2)—James Hunt, Britain; McLaren-Ford; 1:42:20.43; 88.1 m.p.h. (Shortly after race, Hunt was disqualified because of over-length aerofoil and victory was awarded to Lauda. Decision was reversed by International Auto Federation, July 5, and first-place returned to Hunt.)

Belgium (Zolder, 182.275 miles, May 16)—Lauda; 1:42:53.23; 108.1 m.p.h.

Monaco (Monte Carlo, 160.6 miles, May 30)—Lauda; 1:59:51.47; 80.37 m.p.h.

Sweden (Anderstorp, 180 miles, June 13)—Jody Scheckter, South Africa; Tyrrell-Ford; 1:46:50; 100.9 m.p.h.

France (Le Castellet, 196 miles, July 4)—Hunt; 1:40:58.60; 115.84 m.p.h.

Great Britain (Brands Hatch, 200 miles, July 18)—Hunt won in 1:03:27.61 at 115.19 m.p.h. but International Auto Body disqualified him, Sept. 24, for illegal restart after car was damaged in accident. First place was awarded to Lauda.

Germany (Nuerburgring, 199.8 miles, Aug. 1)—Hunt; 1:41:20; 118 m.p.h. (Lauda crashed on third lap and was seriously burned.)

Austria (Zeltweg, 198.3 miles, Aug. 15)—John Watson, Ireland; Penske; 1:30:07.86; 132.770 m.p.h.

Netherlands (Zandvoort, 197 miles, Aug. 29)—Hunt; 1:44:52.09; 112.6 m.p.h.

Italy (Monza, 187 miles, Sept. 12)—Ronnie Peterson, Sweden; March; 1:30:35.6; 124 m.p.h. (Lauda returned to competition and finished third.)

Canada (Mosport, 196 miles, Oct. 3)—Hunt; 117.843 m.p.h.

United States (Watkins Glen, N.Y., 200 miles, Oct. 10)—1, Hunt; 1:42:40.74; 116.43 m.p.h.; 2, Scheckter, 1:42:48.771; 3, Lauda; 1:43:43.065.

Japan (Gotemba, 200 miles, Oct. 24)—Mario Andretti, Nazareth, Pa.; Lotus; 1:43:58.86; 114 m.p.h. (Hunt finished third, Lauda retired after first lap, fog.)

Final Driver Leaders

1, Hunt, 69 pts.; Lauda, 68; Scheckter, 49; Depailler, 39.

INTERNATIONAL MOTOR SPORTS ASSOCIATION
Camel GT Series

24 Hours of Daytona (Daytona Beach, Fla., Jan. 31-Feb. 1)—Peter Gregg, Jacksonville, Fla.-Brian Redman, England-John Fitzpatrick, England; BMW; 2,092.8 miles; average 104.04
(Continued)

Auto Racing (Contd.)

miles per hour (race halted for 3 hours and 55 minutes to clear water from fuel of nine cars; total running time 20 hours, 7 minutes

12 Hours of Sebring (Sebring, Fla., March 19-20)—Al Holbert, Warrington, Pa.-Mike Keyser, Towson, Md.; Porsche Carrera; 1,196 miles; 99.66 m.p.h.

IMSA CHAMPIONS

Camel GT Series—Al Holbert, Warrington, Pa.; Monza
Goodrich Radial—Carson Baird, Laurel, Md.; Dodge Colt
Formula Atlantic—Gill Villenueve, Wickham, Quebec; March

Other Sports Car Races

6 Hours of Watkins Glen (Watkins Glen, N.Y., July 10)—Rolf Stommelen-Manfred Schurti, West Germany, Porsche; 587.6 miles; 97.8 m.p.h. average

24 Hours of LeMans (LeMans, France, June 12-13)—Jacky Ickx, Belgium-Gijs Van Lennep, Netherlands; Porsche; 2,956.78 miles; 123.5 m.p.h.

SPORTS CAR CLUB OF AMERICA CHAMPIONS

Bosch Gold Cup for Super Vees (9 races)—Tom Bagley, State College, Pa.; Zink; 115 pts
Scirocco-Bilstein Cup (6 races)—Paul Hacker, East Greenbush, N.Y.; 150 pts
Trans-American (8 races)—Overall and Category II: George Follmer, Huntington Beach, Calif.; Porsche Carrera; 110 pts.; Category I: Jocko Maggiacomo, Poughkeepsie, N.Y.; Javelin; Manufacturers: Porsche

Formula 5000 in conjunction with USAC

Champion—Brian Redman, Skipton, England; Lola-Chevrolet; 132 pts

INTERNATIONAL RACE OF CHAMPIONS

1975-76 Series—Fourth Race (Daytona Beach, Fla., Feb. 13)—Benny Parsons, Ellerbe, N.C.; 100 miles, 168.146 m.p.h.
1975-76 Overall—A.J. Foyt, Houston, Tex.; 42 pts; $50,000

National Hot Rod Association

Drag Racing Championships

Nationals

(Indianapolis, Sept. 6)

Class	Driver	Time ¼ mile	Speed
Top Fuel—Richard Tharp, Dallas, Tex.		6.114	240.00
Funny Car—Gary Burgin, Stanton, Calif.		6.258	237.46
Pro stock—Wally Booth, Berkley, Mich.		8.68	155.17
Pro competition—Dave Settles, Fuless, Tex.		7.14	170.77
Competition—Don Carlton, Lenoir, N.C.		8.34	163.04
Modified—Donald Coonce, Cayuga, Ind.		11.39	101.69
Super stock—Dave Boertman, Muskegon, Mich.		10.94	122.28
Stock—Tom Reider, Trenton, Mich.		15.62	84.26
Fuel bike—T.C. Christensen, Kenosha, Wis.		8.30	164.53

MOTORCYCLE RACING
American Motorcycle Association Champions
Grand National Championship

	Pts
Camel Pro Series—Jay Springsteen, Flint, Mich.; Harley-Davidson	301

Motocross Champions

125 cc—Bob Hannah, Whittier, Calif.; Yamaha	347
250 cc—Tony DiStefano, Morrisville, Pa.; Suzuki	291
500 cc—Kent Howerton, San Antonio, Tex.; Husqvarna	286

Supercross

Overall—Jim Weinert, Laguna Beach, Calif.; Kawasaki	327

National Hill Climb

Class A—Earl Bowlby, Logan, Ohio; BSA	5,294
Class B—David Mosley, Allen, Ky.; Triumph	6,126

YACHTING
UNITED STATES YACHT RACING UNION CHAMPIONS

Mallory Cup—David Crockett, Alamitos Bay, Y.C., Long Beach, Calif.

Sears Cup (juniors)—Potomac River S.A., Washington

Smythe Trophy (junior single-handed)—Scott Young, White Rock B.C., Dallas, Tex.

Bemis Trophy—Chris Lloyd-Mark Perkins, Shrewsbury Y.C., Fair Haven, N.J.

Adams Trophy (women)—Galveston Bay Cruising Assn., Galveston, Tex. (Ellen Gerloff, skipper)

Mertz Trophy (women's single-handed)—Kiki Saltmarsh, Little Compton, R.I.

Women's double-handed—Diane Greene-Jennifer Lawson, Annapolis, Md.

O'Day Trophy (men's single-handed)—Buzz Reynolds, Notre Dame University

Prince of Wales Bowl (club)—Coronado (Calif.) Y.C. (Edward Trevelyan, Rod Davis, Jaime MacArthur)

National Sea Exploring Championship—Brian Kfoury-Wesley Stillwell, Newport Beach, Calif.

U.S. Youth Championships

Single-handed—Stewart Neff, Oyster Bay, N.Y.
Double-handed—Pete Melvin-Dave Woolsey, Lighthouse Point, Fla.

OCEAN AND DISTANCE RACING

Trans-Atlantic, Single-handed (Plymouth, England to Newport, R.I., 3,000 miles; start June 5)—Pen Duick VI, Eric Tabarly, France; 23 days, 20 hours, 12 minutes

Newport-Bermuda (635 miles, 161 boats; start June 18)—Running Tide (Class A); Al Van Metre, Alexandria, Va.; 72:14:00. First to finish: Tempest, Eric Ridder, Oyster Bay, N.Y., 3:15:19

COLLEGE CHAMPIONSHIPS

Fowle Trophy (overall)—Tufts
Foster Trophy (single-handed)—James McCreary, Tufts
Morss Bowl (double-handed)—Tufts (Neal Fowler Jr.-Sam Altrueter)
Shields Trophy (sloops)—University of California-Santa Cruz
Women—Princeton (Nina Nielsen, Ann Preston, Nonnie Cooney)

POWERBOAT RACING
Unlimited Hydroplanes

Champion Spark Plugs Regatta (Miami, 30 miles, May 23)—Atlas Van Lines; Bill Muncey, driver and owner; 99.931 miles per hour.

President's Cup (Washington, 37½ miles, May 30)—Olympia Beer; Billy Schumacher; 107.2 m.p.h.

Gold Cup (Detroit, June 27)—Miss U.S.; Tom d'Eath; 108.021 m.p.h.

Governor's (Indiana) Cup (Madison, Ind., July 4)—Atlas Van Lines; 109.462 m.p.h.

Governor's (Kentucky) Cup (Owensboro, July 11)—Atlas Van Lines; 104.387 m.p.h.

Columbia Cup (Tri Cities, Wash., Aug. 1)—Atlas Van Lines; 116.249 m.p.h.

Seafair (Seattle, Aug. 8)—Miss Budweiser, Mickey Remund; 114.090.

San Diego (Sept. 19)—Olympia Beer; 107.862.

Champion—Atlas Van Lines, Bill Muncey, driver; 9,750 pts.

Off Shore Races

Swift Hurricane Classic (St. Petersburg, Fla.; 186.3 miles, April 11)—Joel Halpern, Bronxville, N.Y.; 59.7 m.p.h.

Bacardi Trophy (Miami, 168 miles; May 8)—Preston Henn, Fort Lauderdale, Fla.; 64.4 m.p.h.

Benihana Grand Prix (Point Pleasant, N.J., 200 miles, July 21)—Roger Penske, Reading, Pa.-Bob Magoon, Miami; 2:33; 56.72 m.p.h.

Production Class (119 miles)—Bob Solovei, North Miami, Fla.

Marina Del Rey (Calif.) Classic (188 miles, Aug. 30)—Halpern.

San Francisco (181 miles, Sept. 18)—Henn; 69.6 m.p.h.

Bahamas 500 (275 miles, June 4)—Rocky Aoki, Englewood Cliffs, N.J., 74 m.p.h.

INDEX

We have endeavored to prepare the INDEX for easy use by professional researchers and the average Mr. and Mrs. Public. This goal presents many difficulties and we modestly hope we have succeeded. Where we have failed we would appreciate your help. If you cannot find anything quickly and you think it's our fault, kindly send suggestions and criticisms to:

THE INFORMATION PLEASE ALMANAC
502 Park Avenue
New York, N.Y. 10022

—— B ——

Legislation, 581
Foreign trade (world):
Each country's, 110, 118–266
Exports-imports table, 267
Forests:
Resources of countries, 118–266
State forests, 626–60
U.S. resources, 475
Forgery, 727, 728
Formosa. *See* Taiwan
Forms of address, 683–85
Formulas, math & physics, 400–01
Fort Sumter, Battle of, 643
Fort Worth, Tex., 644, 653
See also Cities (U.S.)
Foundations & societies, 677–82
Fountain pen, 408
Four Noble Truths, 414–15
Fourteen Points, 323
Fourth of July, 435, 436
Fractions & decimals, 401
France, 159–64
Famous structures, 299
NATO, 161
Nuclear weapons tests, 410
Rulers, 508
Universities, 293–94
See also Countries
Franciscan Order, 320
Franco, Francisco, 232–33, 822
Franco-Prussian War, 160, 320
Frankfurt am Main, Ger., 166
See also Cities (world)
Franklin Institute, 665
Fraternity, first, 582
Freedom of the press, 320, 520
Freedoms, Constitutional, 520
Freetown, Sierra Leone, 229
Freezing point of water, 398
Freight ton (measure), 406
Freight traffic, 83
French and Indian War, 320
French Guiana, 160, 162
French Polynesia, 160, 162
French Republic, 160
French Revolution, 160, 320
French Somaliland. *See* French Terr. of Afars and Issas
French Southern & Antarctic Lands, 160, 163–64
French Sudan. *See* Mali
French Territory of Afars and Issas, 160, 162
Freud, Sigmund, 409, 822
Frick Collection, 663
Friendly Islands, 241
Friends (Quakers), 420, 421–22
Fruit:
Calories & vitamins, 112–14
Econ. statistics, 68, 82, 93
Fuel, 66, 100, 108–09
See also specific fuels
Fujiyama, 300
Fundamental churches, 101, 102
"Fundamental Orders," 629
Fur, 93
Furies (mythology), 500
Furniture:
Economic statistics, 66, 71, 78, 93
Industry, hours & wages, 71
Stores, 78
Fusion bombs, 410
Futurity Stakes, 948

— G —

Gabon, 164
See also Countries
Gadsden Purchase, 702
Gagarin, Yuri A., 247, 328, 388
Galápagos Islands, 153, 292
Galaxy, 357
Galilee, Sea of, 187
Gambia, 164–65, 251
See also Countries
Gambia River, 291
Gambier Island, 162
Gambling, arrests for, 728
Gandhi, Indira, 178, 822
Gandhi, M.K., 177, 822
Ganges River, 126, 179, 307
Garfield, James A., 540, 582
See also Presidents (U.S.)
Garrison Dam, 640
Gas, natural & manufactured, 100, 109
Gases, laws governing, 409
Gasoline service stations, 78
Gasoline taxes, 467
Gator Bowl, 873
Gaza Strip, 185
Gemini flights, 386
General Accounting Office, 590
General Agreement on Tariffs and Trade, 346
General Assembly, U.N., 344
General Services Admn., 588
General Sherman Tree, 628
Generals (U.S.), 595, 596
Geneva, Lake, 238
Geneva Conference (1954), 327
Geographic centers:
Of states, 626–60
Of United States, 474
Geography:
Caves and caverns, 306
Coastline of U.S., 477
Continental Divide, 474
Continents, 304, 318
Deserts, 314
Distances between cities, 468–73
Elevations, 318
Explorations and discoveries, 291–92
Geysers, 302–03
Islands, 315
Lakes, 308, 309
Map section, 271–86
Mountain peaks, 313–14
National Parks, 672
Oceans & seas, 304
Of countries, 118–266
Rivers, 307–08
United States, 474–77
Volcanoes, 300–01
Waterfalls, 309–10
World, 291–318
Geological periods, 305–06
Geological Survey, 586
Geology, lunar, 392
Geometric formulas, 400
Georgia, 630
See also States (U.S.)
Georgia, U.S.S.R., 246
German measles, 407
Germany:
History, 165–68
Libraries, 295

Museums, 296–97
Nazi regime, 167, 324–26
Rulers, 509
Universities, 294
World War I, 323–24
World War II, 325–26
Zoos, 302
See also Germany (East); Germany (West)
Germany (East), 165–66
See also Countries
Germany (West), 166–68
Peace resolution, 580
See also Countries
Gestation periods, animals, 104
Gettysburg, Battle of, 319, 528
Gettysburg Address, 528
Geysers, 302–03
Ghana, 168–69, 251
See also Countries
Ghent, Treaty of, 323
GI Bill of Rights, 580
Gibraltar, 251, 256
Gift taxes, federal, 90, 618
Gila River, 476
Gilbert Islands, 211, 251, 256–57
Girl Scouts of U.S.A., 681
Giscard d'Estaing, Valéry, 508
Glacier National Park, 637, 673
Glasgow, Scotland, 249
Glass:
Economic statistics, 66, 93
Glass Center, Corning, 667
Glenn, John H., Jr., 328, 388
Glossaries:
Art, 813
Basketball, 864
Football terms, 880
Hockey terms, 888
Political, 21
Wall Street & economic terms, 96
Gobi Desert, 143, 314
Gods & goddesses, 498–506
Godwin Austen, Mt., 313
Gold:
As element, 403, 404
Embargo (1933), 324
Measure of purity, 406
World production, 108
Gold Coast. *See* Ghana
Gold Reserve Act, 579
Gold Rush:
Alaska, 626
California, 320
Golden Gate Bridge, 316, 628
Golf, 883–85, 957–58
History, 883
Standard measurements, 848
U.S. Amateur Champions, 884, 885, 957–58
U.S. Open Champions, 883, 885, 957–58
U.S. P.G.A. Champions, 884, 957
Gonorrhea, 407
Good Friday, 434, 438
Good Hope, Cape of, 232, 291
Gorki, U.S.S.R., 245
Gothic architecture, 299
Gotland, 237
Government, U.S. *See* United States Government
Government employment, 75